KOMPASS
Industrial Trade names | Register

KOMPASS PUBLISHERS
St. James House
150 London Road
East Grinstead
West Sussex
RH19 1ES
England

Telephone: (0800) 0185 882
Fax: (01342) 327940
       Marketing: (01342) 778560

e-mail: kompasseditorial@kompass.co.uk
Internet: www.kompass.co.uk

**The 22nd Edition of Kompass
Industrial Trade Names**

Supported by

The Chartered
Institute of Marketing

Chartered Institute of
Library and Information
Professionals

ISSN 1353-1093
ISBN (this volume) 978-0-86268-530-0
ISBN (set) 978-0-86268-531-7

Kompass (UK) Limited. Registered in England Number 7819067. Registered Office: 1 Swan Wood Park, Gun Hill, Horam, East Sussex TN21 0LL
Printed in the UK by CPI William Clowes Ltd, Beccles, NR34 7TL

Preface

Welcome to this, the 21st edition of **INDUSTRIAL TRADE NAMES**, part of the Kompass Register Series, which for over thirty years has been recognised as **"The Authority on British Industry"**.

For ease of use this volume comprises three sections. The first lists over 42,000 different trade names and their users. The second section lists over 9,000 companies, giving full contact details and a comprehensive list of their trade names listed in section 1. Finally, section 3 lists overseas companies and their UK agents or distributors.

In compiling this directory, it was necessary to impose two limitations:

(1) Trade names and marks which have lapsed, or are not in current use, have been excluded from Section 1. Only "active" names in use in the United Kingdom have been included.

(2) There are no entries for industries engaged in the preparation of food, drink, tobacco and pharmaceuticals.

The industrial classes which are included in the publication are listed below and the sources from which the information was collected are the Patent Office file and the companies themselves. It is inevitable however that some trade names will have been omitted and we would be pleased to receive the details of any such names in order that they may be included in the next edition of this publication. Readers are also requested to notify us of any changes of address, new trade names or other alterations. It should be stressed that the entries indicate users and do not necessarily imply ownership of the trade name.

The publication should not be confused with the Register of Trade Marks kept by the Patent Office under the 1994 Trade Marks Act. All trade marks registered at the Patent Office are included in the Official Register of Trade Marks. Companies wishing to use a trade name or trade mark must not assume that its inclusion in INDUSTRIAL TRADE NAMES is an indication that it has been registered at the Patent Office, nor that its omission indicates that the name or design is free and can be used. The publishers would like to thank all the many thousands of companies who have co-operated in the preparation of this book. The greatest care has been taken to ensure accuracy but the publisher can accept no responsibility for errors or omissions nor for any liability occasioned by relying on its content.

Registration Classifications used in compiling this Publication:

Class	Description
1.	Chemical Products used in Industry.
2.	Paints, Varnishes, Lacquers and Preservatives.
3.	Bleaching Preparations and Cleaning Substances.
4.	Industrial Oils and Greases.
6.	Unwrought and Partly Wrought Common Metals.
7.	Machines and Machine Tools.
9.	Scientific, Nautical, Surveying and Electrical Apparatus and Instruments.
11.	Installations for Lighting, Heating, Water Supply and Sanitation.
12.	Vehicles: Land, Air or Water.
14.	Precious Metals and Alloys.
16.	Paper, Cardboard and Associated Industries.
17.	Rubber and Plastic Materials for use in Manufacturing.
19.	Building Materials, Natural and Artificial.
22.	Ropes, Fabrics and Associated Goods.
23.	Yarns, Threads.
24.	Textile Articles.
25.	Clothing including Footwear and Headgear.
27.	Carpets, Rugs, Mats and Matting.
35.	Advertising and Business.
36.	Insurance and Finance.
37.	Construction and Repair.
38.	Communication.
39.	Transportation and Storage.
40.	Material Treatment.

INDUSTRIAL TRADE NAMES

For ease of reference this volume is clearly divided into 3 sections.

- TRADE NAMES
- COMPANY INFORMATION
- AGENCIES

- **Section 1: TRADE NAMES**
- Trade Names Listed Alphabetically
- Brief Description of Trade Name
- User of Trade Name

> **Flexin** – Interlocking tubing – A.B. Smith & Co.
> **Flexin** – reinforced polythene – Polypro Ltd.
> *Flexin (U.S.A.)** – Interlocking fencing – Interlock Ltd.
> **Flexipig** – multisized pig launching equipment – Pipescan Ltd.
> **Flexir** – infared scanners – Infscan Ltd.
> **Flexisure** – inter-changeable shelving systems – Flexure Ltd.

- **Section 2: COMPANY INFORMATION**

This section lists companies alphabetically, with full contact details.
- Companies Listed Alphabetically
- Full Contact Details of Company
- Summary of Trade Names,
    Listed in Section 1, used by this Company

> **Smith A.B. & Co.,** 7 Sandy Lane, Coventry CV2 0XB
> *Tel:* (01203) 463714 *Fax:* (01203) 463747 *Flexin – Flexion – Gromlin – Hytol*

Trade Names marked in Sections 1 & 2 by an asterisk (*) indicates an imported item

- **Section 3: AGENCIES**
- Foreign companies listed alphabetically, identifying their country of origin, product and U.K. Agent/Distributor

OVERSEAS COMPANY	COUNTRY OF ORIGIN	PRODUCT	UK COMPANY
Papst	Germany	Cooling Fans	Micromech Ltd
Parker Hannifin	USA	Fluid Connectors	Hydrasun Ltd
Pas by	Holland	Modular Filing System	Glimex International plc
Pasche & Schon	West Germany	Aluminium Extrusions	Indalex Ltd

About the Trade Marks register

The major source of information for this publication is the Register of Trade marks held at the Patent Office. The register is maintained by the Comptroller-General of Patents, Designs and Trade Marks ("The Registrar") under the Trade Marks Act 1994 ("The Act").

The Act defines the manner in which the register is maintained and the authority for requesting and making changes to it. With regard to this publication the particular areas of interest are:

(i)   the trade marks themselves;

(ii)   the identity of the proprietor; and

(iii)   the address of the proprietor.

Whilst there are obvious benefits in maintaining the register as up to date as possible proprietors are under no obligation to inform the Registrar of any changes to their name or address, nor to request the amendment of the register to reflect name and address changes. Indeed, should the Registrar be aware that a proprietor's name or address has changed, the Act does not give him the authority to amend the register unless the proprietor specifically requests him to make those changes. Although this may restrict the Registrar's ability to maintain an up to date register there are issues relating to the naming of companies of which the Registrar would not be aware. For example, "name swapping" where different companies have the same name but at different times can lead to erroneous assumptions being made that the two companies are one and the same.

The existence of a mark on the register does not give any indication of the use, if any, to which the mark is being put. However, the non use of a mark exposes it to the possibility of revocation proceedings by an aggrieved party, this being the main means by which third parties can have marks removed from the register. The fact that a proprietor decides to cease using a mark is not immediately reflected in the register unless he requests its surrender. That mark will remain on the register until it fails to be renewed or is removed by revocation proceedings. As the registration period is for ten years and may be renewed for further periods of ten years marks which are no longer of interest to the proprietor can remain on the register for up to ten years.

In the event that a trade mark proprietor ceases to trade any trade marks recorded in the name of that proprietor will remain on the register. However, the marks can be assigned, either by the proprietor or by the liquidator (or receiver), and the assignment to a new proprietor recorded on the register.

In addition to the large number of registered trade marks there is widespread use of unregistered trade marks which whilst not protected by the Act are protected under other legislation. Marks may remain unregistered because their proprietors choose not to apply for registration, or have had an application rejected on the grounds that it does not comply with the requirements of the Act.

The register of Trade Marks is open to public inspection at the Patent Office (London, Newport and Manchester) at prescribed times.

BY COURTESY OF THE PATENT OFFICE.

TRADE NAMES

Imported items are marked with an asterix and wherever possible
indicate the country of origin.
For addresses to the following entries, please refer to the company
information section.

0

0 S D 569 – oil spill dispersant – Agma Ltd
007 – insertion sample probes for refined liquid hydrocarbon products – Jiskoot Ltd
0844 – Non Geographical Numbers – Intelesis Ltd

1

1/2 Hour Fire Resisting Roller Shutter – fire door – Bolton Gate Co. Ltd
1.4mb Disk Drive Floppy Ide Int Laptop Teac Teac – Tekdata Distribution Ltd
*1 Stop – Cattle Information Services
@-10-u-8 – Tiflex Ltd
100 Series – industrial diesel engines – Perkins Engines Group Ltd
1000 Series – industrial diesel engines – Perkins Engines Group Ltd
1000 System Resin – building products – Addagrip Surface Treatments Ltd
1001 – carpet cleaner – P Z Cussons International Ltd
1001 – Jones & Shipman Grinding Ltd
101 PC Games – magazine – Future Publishing Ltd
1066 Blocks – blue or yellow blocks packed in buckets – Evans Vanodine International plc
110700 Commodore Black – versatile black ink for all press types with good drying and varnishability – Shackell Edwards & Co
118140 Commodore Hi-tone Black – higher toned version of commodore Black – Shackell Edwards & Co
118185 Intense I.R. Black – extremely dense, premium quality 'blue shade' black ink – Shackell Edwards & Co
1200 – mullion drained vertical & slope glaze curtain wall – Kawneer UK Ltd
1200 – zone drained vertical curtain wall system – Kawneer UK Ltd
1200 – structural silicone glazing – Kawneer UK Ltd
121 – the kit will allow the user to record calls whilst they are on the move by recording from mobiles and cordless phones - complete kit, also available as micro-cassette based kit – Retell
121 – water based lubricant – Bodywise Ltd
124 Facilities Ltd – Channel Four Television Co. Ltd
1300 – Jones & Shipman Grinding Ltd
*1300 Series (U.S.A.) – industrial diesel engines – Perkins Engines Group Ltd
13000 Series – tube puller – B S A Tube Runner
1300x – Jones & Shipman Grinding Ltd
1305 – Jones & Shipman Grinding Ltd
1310 – Jones & Shipman Grinding Ltd
1400 – Jones & Shipman Grinding Ltd
1400e – Jones & Shipman Grinding Ltd
1400x – Jones & Shipman Grinding Ltd
1415 – Jones & Shipman Grinding Ltd
15 SBi – System Boiler – Worcester Bosch Group Ltd
15000 Series – tube puller – B S A Tube Runner
151 – this small modular handset connector can be inserted between a headset or handset to record calls, ideal for call centre agents – Retell
151 Brand – car products – Shonn Bros Manchester Ltd
1548 A.M. Capital Gold – Global Radio
160 – this clever connector will allow the user to record from any mobile or cordless phone; it can also be used to record from landlines. can be purchased as part of a kit or as an accessory – Retell
1600 – curtain wall system – Kawneer UK Ltd
1700 Series – kitchen knives – Amefa
1745 Trading Company – Scottish Quest
1800 Helpmates – griddle scrapers, turners – Amefa
18000 series – tube puller – B S A Tube Runner
1823 – rugby balls – Gray Nicolls

2

1880 Cider – H Weston & Sons Ltd
1890's – period bathroom water fittings – Barber Wilson & Company Ltd
190, 350, 1040 – commercial doors – Kawneer UK Ltd

2-2-7 – single and two-storey educational play system for the younger child, incorporating activity panels, steps, slides etc – S M P Playgrounds
2 Brush Mascara – traditional and waterproof mascaras – Elizabeth Arden
2-N-Heptyl Cyclopentanone – perfume speciality – Quest International UK Ltd
'2 Ton' Epoxy – extremely strong, non sagging and water resistant adhesive – I T W Devcon
20/20 Interlock Clay Plain Tile – clay – Sandtoft Holdings Ltd
20 Plus – Cogne UK Ltd
20 Plus HS – Cogne UK Ltd
200 Series – fully hinged system – Brockhouse Modernfold Ltd
2000 – Jones & Shipman Grinding Ltd
2000 – Cox Building Products Ltd
2000 ES Diamond – cremators – J G Shelton & Co. Ltd
2000 Series – industrial diesel engines – Perkins Engines Group Ltd
21 Series – battery chargers – Chloride Motive Power C M P Batteries Ltd
210 – insertion sample probes and full bore cell samplers for crude oil and liquids – Jiskoot Ltd
2100 Series – propeller fans – Flakt Woods Ltd
2200 – ventilator – Space Labs Healthcare
22o Celsius Blinds – made to measure – Hallis Hudson Group Ltd
22o Celsius Fabrifix – blind roller kits and material stiffening solution – Hallis Hudson Group Ltd
2370 Titan – full range 16 items s/s table cutlery – Amefa
240 Magnum – air pistol – B S A Guns UK Ltd
2440 Diva Eicon – Tekdata Distribution Ltd
24CDi – gas boilers – Worcester Bosch Group Ltd
24i – gas boilers – Worcester Bosch Group Ltd
24Seven-Nero – Geerings Of Ashford Ltd
24Seven-Spa – Geerings Of Ashford Ltd
25 Beautiful Homes – I P C Media Ltd
25 SBi – System Boiler – Worcester Bosch Group Ltd
260 – curved stairs – Stannah Management Services Ltd
26CDi Xtra – Condensing Boiler – Worcester Bosch Group Ltd
*280 Hollow Bar (Sweden) – Ovako Ltd
2800 Laser – business papers – Howard Smith Paper Ltd
28CDi – gas boilers – Worcester Bosch Group Ltd

3

3 – Premier Mobiles
3.5 Disk Drive Floppy – Tekdata Distribution Ltd
3.5in Disk Drive FDD Floppy OEM OEM – Tekdata Distribution Ltd
3.M. (United Kingdom) – adhesives and sealants & tapes – R D Taylor & Co. Ltd
3 M – S J Wharton Ltd
3 Step Mat – contamination control mats – Dycem Ltd
30-45 – staples – Office Depot UK
300 – straight stairs – Stannah Management Services Ltd
3000 Series – industrial diesel engines – Perkins Engines Group Ltd
306 coater – AESpump
306 coater – Technical Vacuum Services Ltd
30li Unitainer – 30li, 150mm screw top lid – Fibrestar Drums Ltd
35CDi – gas boilers – Worcester Bosch Group Ltd
3Com (U.S.A.) – Kingston Communications
3D Graphics – advertising photography – W.G. Photo

3D Perception – Lamphouse Ltd
3D Sports Ltd (India) – football and cricket clothing and equipment – 3D Sports
3D World – magazine – Future Publishing Ltd
3E – 3E UK Ltd
3G – Anritsu Ltd
3G, Blue Tooth. – Anritsu Ltd
3G Breaded Scampi – 3g Foodservice Ltd
3G Desserts – 3g Foodservice Ltd
3G Food Service – 3g Foodservice Ltd
3G Individual Entrees – 3g Foodservice Ltd
3G Prawns – 3g Foodservice Ltd
3G Ready Meals – 3g Foodservice Ltd
3G Sausages – 3g Foodservice Ltd
3G Seafood Solutions – 3g Foodservice Ltd
3G Select – 3g Foodservice Ltd
3G Select Premium Desserts – 3g Foodservice Ltd
3L – UK Office Direct
3M – Lamphouse Ltd
3M – Review Display Systems Ltd
3M – Austen Tapes Ltd
3M – Tri Pack Supplies Ltd
3M – Lusso Interiors
3M – B D K Industrial Products Ltd
3M – R W Greeff
3M – UK Office Direct
3M – Letchford Supplies Ltd
3M – Shand Higson & Co. Ltd
3M – General Fabrications Ltd
3M – capacitive and resistive touch sensors, desktop and industrial chassis monitors, CRT or LCD. – Display Solutions Ltd
3M – Quality pens – Connect Two Promotions Ltd
3M (United Kingdom) – speciality self adhesive tape – Stokvis Tapes UK Ltd
3M – respirator masks – Engelbert Strauss
3M – abrasive materials – Finishing Aids & Tools Ltd
3M – adhesive tapes – North British Tapes Ltd
3M – Helman Workwear
3M – Cyclops Electronics Ltd
3M Glass Bubbles – spherical glass extenders – Lawrence Industries Ltd
3M Health Care – pharmaceutical & health care products – 3 M Healthcare Ltd
3M Safety Products – Wessex Welding & Industrial Supplies Ltd
3M, Stera-tape, Lohman, Advance, Tesa, Rotunda, Evode, Jiffy, Velcro, Mima films.. – Austen Tapes Ltd
3R Plus – 400ml great value maintenance spray for home, garden and car – F M C G Ltd
3rd Dimension – greetings card – Second Nature Ltd
3rd Harmonic Filter – harmonic filtration – S D C Industries Ltd
3V Cogeim – filter dryers/filters nutsche – A J G Waters Equipment Ltd
3V Mabo – thin film evaporators – A J G Waters Equipment Ltd

4

4 Mation – computer software – 4mation Educational Software Ltd
4 Mation Educational Resources – 4mation Educational Software Ltd
4 N 1 Cleaner – carpet cleaning liquids – Clantex Ltd
4 ply 100g – Sirdar Spinning Ltd
4 PLY 50g – Sirdar Spinning Ltd
4 Star – carpets – Cormar Carpets
4 X 4 – I P C Media Ltd
40-30 Cryogenic Cryogenics – AESpump
400 – framing system – Kawneer UK Ltd

4000 Series – industrial diesel engines – Perkins Engines Group Ltd

420 Plus – Cogne UK Ltd

428 Trackpactor – track mounted primary impact crushing plant – Terex

4400 – programmer controller – West Instruments

451 – non thermal framing system – Kawneer UK Ltd

451T – thermally framing system – Kawneer UK Ltd

491 – turnstiles – Clarke Instruments Ltd

4B (U.S.A.) – Braime Elevator Components Ltd

4CC Art – Digital Products - Toner Sheet Fed - Coated – Howard Smith Paper Ltd

4CC Reels – Digital Products - Xeikon - Coated – Howard Smith Paper Ltd

4CC Silk – Digital Products - Toner Sheet Fed - Coated – Howard Smith Paper Ltd

4Living Furniture – The Winnen Furnishing Company

5

5-Language Guide to London – map & guide – Francis Chichester Ltd

'5 Minute' Epoxy – extremely strong, non sagging and water resistant adhesive – I T W Devcon

5 Star – carpets – Cormar Carpets

5 Star – UK Office Direct

5 Star – excavators – Neuson Ltd

50-60 – staples – Office Depot UK

500 Series – aluminium framed operable wall – Brockhouse Modernfold Ltd

501 – casement window – Kawneer UK Ltd

502 – pivot window – Kawneer UK Ltd

503 – tilturn window – Kawneer UK Ltd

504 – top swing window – Kawneer UK Ltd

524 – Jones & Shipman Grinding Ltd

532 Naturelle – Interface Europe Ltd

536 Perspectives – Interface Europe Ltd

537 Perspectives Prints – Interface Europe Ltd

540 – Jones & Shipman Grinding Ltd

540e – Jones & Shipman Grinding Ltd

540x – Jones & Shipman Grinding Ltd

55 Series – broadcast console – A M S Neve Ltd

5s – Transcend Group Ltd

5V 50 – Forward Chemicals Ltd

6

6 S – pheromones – Bodywise Ltd

6% Moly (Uns31254) – S & N Stainless Pipeline Products Ltd

60 Minute Money – Transformation 4 Life

600 Series – 50mm thick aluminium partitioning system – Komfort Workspace plc

600 Series – steel framed acoustic operable wall – Brockhouse Modernfold Ltd

6000 Series – process controllers – West Instruments

620 System – in process measuring module – P G T Ceewrite Ltd

6200 – ventilator – Space Labs Healthcare

6240 – prismatic lens – Holophane Europe Ltd

65 – golf balls – Dunlop Slazenger International Ltd

661 – automatic vehicle control barrier – Clarke Instruments Ltd

6X – natural fertiliser in pellets and fibrous slug and snail killer – Organic Concentrates Ltd

6X Energy Drink – grass growth enhancer – Organic Concentrates Ltd

7

700 Series – industrial diesel engines – Perkins Engines Group Ltd

701 – telephone recorder designed to be used at home or at least two meters from office equipment, also available as micro-cassette based kit – Retell

704 – telephone conversation recorder for business use, designed to work too all office equipment - complete kit with a standard sized recorder also available as micro-cassette based kit – Retell

710 – insertion sample probes and full bore cell samplers for crude oil and liquids – Jiskoot Ltd

7110 – wrap-around lens – Holophane Europe Ltd

720 Moresque – Interface Europe Ltd

7200 Series – UPS power supply – Emerson Network Power Ltd

725 Phoenix – Interface Europe Ltd

737 – pnuematic demount equipment-7.5 Tonne CHS – Abel Demountable Systems Ltd

7400 Series – UPS power supply – Emerson Network Power Ltd

752 – this award winning telephone recording connector that just clips onto the curly cable is feature in the 704, 705 & 904 kits can also be purchased as an accessory – Retell

771 – solenoid locks – Clarke Instruments Ltd

8

*80/20 (U.S.A.) – extruded aluminium assembly system – The West Group Ltd

800 Series – Call System – C-Tec Security Ltd

8000 Series – controllers – West Instruments

8010 – indicator – West Instruments

8200s – ventilator – Space Labs Healthcare

8224 – refractive grid lens – Holophane Europe Ltd

8888 – structural primer for metal – Craig & Rose Ltd

9

*9 Bar – Wholebake Ltd

9-Decenal – perfume speciality – Quest International UK Ltd

900 Series – industrial diesel engines – Perkins Engines Group Ltd

9000 Series – UPS power supply – Emerson Network Power Ltd

9000 System – price ticket computer system – Masson Seeley & Co. Ltd

902 – this 60 minutes pocket sized digital recorder will allow the user to record mobile phone calls, as well as being used as a note-taking machine. This kit is available in two other version with additional telephone recording connectors – Retell

913,903,966 – electric release for mortice latches – Clarke Instruments Ltd

918, 919 – electric release for sash locks – Clarke Instruments Ltd

919 – Thermo Electrical

929 – Thermo Electrical

939 – Thermo Electrical

939QZ – Thermo Electrical

9400 – Thermo Electrical

9406 – Mid Blue International Ltd

942, 957, 984 – electric release for dead locks – Clarke Instruments Ltd

95.8 Capital F.M. – Global Radio

953 – this standalone telephone answering machines has the ability to record upto 900 hours and also acts as a meeting recording unit, telephone conversation recorder and voice response unit – Retell

955 – the Soft Call Recorder is a PC based recording unit, which will allow the use to record upto 240 hours per gigabyte, all calls are date & time stamped and can be played back through the computers soundcard – Retell

969 – Thermo Electrical

969Z – Thermo Electrical

988 – process pumps to latest API 670 edition – Weir Group Senior Executives Pension Trust Ltd

989 – Thermo Electrical

989QZ – Thermo Electrical

A

A. 100 – valves – David Auld Valves Ltd

A.2000 (Germany) – pressure plumber – Mer Products Ltd

A.260 Milling Cartridge System – Ceratizit UK Ltd

A & A Foods Ltd – Spanish Food Importers – A & A Wines Ltd

A.A.H. Pharmaceuticals – pharmaceutical wholesalers – A A H Pharmaceuticals

A&A Lifting and Safety – Suppliers of leading brand lifting and height safety equipment. – A&A Lifting and Safety Ltd

A-A-Tishoo – property maintenance – J E Roberts & Son

A & A Wines Ltd – Wine Importer – A & A Wines Ltd

A Access garage doors – garage doors – Access Garage Doors Ltd

A Access Garage Doors & Gates Ltd – garage doors and gates – Access Garage Doors Ltd

A.B.A. – Hose Clips – Springmasters Ltd

*A.B.B. (Germany) – electric motors – Power Plant & Drives

A.B.C. – English wax prints african textiles – Cosmopolitan Textile Company Ltd

A.B.C. – ligament and tendon repair system – Surgicraft Ltd

A.B. Cork (Portugal) – unsealed domestic density cork floor tiles – Siesta Cork Tile Co.

A B N – cubic boron nitride abrasives – Diamond Detectors

A.B.S. – rachet-lashings – Spanset Ltd

A.B.S. – rigid plastic sheet – V T S Royalite

A.B.S. – PVC sheet – V T S Royalite

A.B.S. (Italy) – slip resistant, safety & occupational footwear – L H Safety Ltd

A B S – Hydraulic & Offshore Supplies Ltd

A.C. 2000 – nebuliser systems for the treatment of respiratory diseases – Clement Clarke International Ltd

A.C. Delco – Harrier Fluid Power Ltd

A.C.H. – hydraulic equipment and systems – A C Hydraulics Ltd

A.C.N. – access communication node – Nortel Networks UK Ltd

A.C. & R – air conditioning and refrigeration components – Henry Technologies Ltd

A.C.S. – mortars and coatings – Calderys UK Ltd

A.C.S. – anatomic cushioned sole – Bunzl S W S

A.C.T. – AC current transformer – Telcon Ltd

A.C.T. – acid cleaner for toilets – Selden Research Ltd

A-code – clothing for active lifestyles – Pioner Fristads

a-code – Wenaas Ltd

A.D. – anglian developments – Anglian Developments Ltd

A.D. 4000 Hi-Swivel – high discharge-power swivel dumper – Thwaites Ltd

A.D.R. – training courses for drivers – Friendberry Ltd

A.D.T. Fire and Security – intruder alarm systems, closed circuit television, fire detectionn systems and access control systems – ADT

A.D.U. – data logging equipment – Ele International

A.E.B.-L. – stainless knife steel – Uddeholm Steel Stockholders

A.E.G. – equipment & spares – Bearwood Engineering Supplies

A.E.G. – power tools – Brilec Power Tools Ltd

A.E.S. – DIY brushes – A E Southgate Ltd

A.F.3 Autoflash – flashpoint tester – Sanyo Gallenkamp plc

A. Forester – textiles – Maurice Phillips

A.G. Gear Oils – high grade straight mineral gear lubricants – Morris Lubricants

A.G.S. – anti-grafitti product – Tensid UK Ltd

A.G.T. Tools & Materials – watch straps, bands and jewellery – A G Thomas Bradford Ltd

A.H. Presses – Rhodes - HME presses – Joseph Rhodes Ltd

A. & I. – industrial silencers – A & I (Peco) Acoustics Ltd

A.I.C. – alginate impression compounds – Prima Dental Group Ltd

A.I. Welders – welding machines – Bearwood Engineering Supplies

A K D – engineers-general, steel fabricators, machining and assembly – A K D Engineering Ltd

A.K. Industries – precision injection and injection blow mouldings in a range of materials, work includes welding, assembly printing and design – A K Industries Ltd

A.K. Kardan – Bailey Morris Ltd

A.K.M. – chemical blending, predispersions and packaging – Safic Alcan UK Ltd

A.L.Z. – Cogne UK Ltd

*A la Perruche – Ivory & Ledoux Ltd

A Laverton – woollen and worsted piece goods – Bower Roebuck & Co. Ltd

A. Lewis & Sons – A Lewis & Sons Willenhall Ltd

A-LOU – Hydraulic & Offshore Supplies Ltd

A.M.F. Alloys – precious metal and non ferrous reclamation, plastic granulations, reclamation, washing and drying – A M F Polymers Ltd

A.M.F. Polymers – precious metal and non ferrous reclamation, plastic granulations, reclamations, washing and drying – A M F Polymers Ltd

A.M.I. – international cargo wholesalers – John Menzies plc

A.M. System (UK) – shop design and fitting – A M System UK Ltd

A.N.C. Express – express delivery service – Wyvern Cargo Distribution Ltd

A.N.O. 1000F/1200S – sliding folding insulated acoustic doors – Kaba Door Systems

A.N.O. Acmex – collapsible gates – Kaba Door Systems

A.O.F. – 2 ply rubber coated fabrics – Ferguson Polycom Ltd

A.P. – scrubbers and plastic fabrications – APMG Ltd

A.P.F.C. – air portable fuel containers – G K N Aerospace Ltd

A P L I – labels – Pelltech Ltd

A.P.M. – pressed parts and assemblies for the automotive industry – T K A Body Stampings Ltd

A.P.M. – Harrier Fluid Power Ltd

A.P.N.S.S. – network signalling systems – Nortel Networks UK Ltd

A.P.O. – Piller UPS systems – Piller UK Ltd

A.P. Precision – Harrier Fluid Power Ltd

A.P. Valve – automatic breathing valve for divers lifejackets – A P Valves

A. & R. – diaphragm pumps – Hypro Eu Ltd

*A.R.B. (U.S.A.) – roller bearings – R A Rodriguez UK Ltd

A.R.C. – York Archaeological Trust For Excavation & Research Ltd

A.R.C.S. – satellite access units – Nortel Networks UK Ltd

A R Davies & Co. – chartered patent agents – Mark's & Clerk LLP

A R Harley & Sons Ltd – sale of parts and accessories for harley-davidson motorcycles – A R Harley & Sons

A R O – Hydraulic & Offshore Supplies Ltd

A & R - pumps; Eezifit - range of nozzle holders; Lo-Drift drift reducing spray nozzles; Twin Cap - nozzle holders; DriftBETA - drift reducing spray nozzles - Berthoud Knapsacks. – Hypro Eu Ltd

A Rail – Berry Systems

A Range Actuator – Electric Multi-turn valve actuator – Rotork plc

*A.S.K. Linear Bearings (Japan) – linear bearings, ball bushings and shaft – Hepco Motion

A.S.P. – tungsten carbide products – Artisan Sintered Products Ltd
A.S.P. – clays – Lawrence Industries Ltd
***A/S Ruko (Denmark)** – security cylinders – Assa Abloy Security Solutions
A.S. Trailers – agricultural trailers – Marston Agricultural Services Ltd
A. Series – self-priming centrifugal pumps – Calpeda Ltd
A Shade Above (United Kingdom) – handmade handfinished lampshades for the interior design & lighting markets – A Shade Above
A.T.A. – pneumatic tools abrasives and rotary cutters – A T A Grinding Processes Ltd
A T D – Acketts Group Ltd
A T I – tools – Tatem Industrial Automation Ltd
A.T.P. – automotive transmissiion remanufacturing specialists – A T P Automatic Transmission Parts UK Ltd
A.T.S. Technirent – renting of computer systems – Hire It Limited
A.V.A. – anti vibration mountings & rubber bonded-to-metal products – A V A Ltd
***A.V.K. Industrial Products (U.S.A.)** – blind threaded inserts and studs – B A S Components Ltd
A.V.O. – testing equipment – Bearwood Engineering Supplies
A/V Sync – audio visual synchroniser unit – A M S Neve Ltd
A. & W. – manufacturing jewellers – Alabaster & Wilson Ltd
A.W.D. – comprehensive workflow management solution – D S T Global Solutions
A.W.G – water and sewerage services – Awg plc
A.W. Hainsworth & Sons – woollens and worsted – Hainsworth Industrial Textiles
A.W.I. – microwave oven components distributors – AWI Ltd
A-Z – Geographers A Z Map Co. Ltd
A1 Service (pan) – bus and coach service – Stagecoach Ltd
A2000 – Spiral Bevel Gearboxes – Francis and Francis Ltd
A2Z – distributors of confectionary – Thornycroft Ltd
A50 – digital readout – Newall Measurement Systems Ltd
AA – UK Office Direct
AA Buses – bus & coach service – Stagecoach Ltd
AA Rouge – Osborn Unipol Ltd
AAACO – Harrier Fluid Power Ltd
Aaeon – embedded and industrial computers, panel PCs, sunlight readable LCDs – Display Solutions Ltd
Aaeon – Review Display Systems Ltd
AAF – Hydraulic & Offshore Supplies Ltd
Aardvark – mine clearing – Aardvark Clear Mine Ltd
Aavid Thermalloy – Cyclops Electronics Ltd
Aavid Thermalloy – heatsinks – Anglia
AB – industrial air curtain – Airbloc
AB Connectors – Connectors – Dax International Ltd
Abac – Trafalgar Tools
ABAC – Hydraulic & Offshore Supplies Ltd
ABAC – Harrier Fluid Power Ltd
Abacus – The Little Brown Book Group
Abacus (United Kingdom) – alarm control panel – Bosch Security Systems
Abacus – steel lighting columns, steel raising and lowering lighting columns, shelters and covered walkways, steel fencing, illuminated and non-illuminated bollards, outdoor lighting design, street furniture, flood lights, luminears and amenity lighting – Abacus Lighting Ltd
Abacus II – data collection system – Northern Design Ltd
Abadi – typeface – Monotype Imaging Ltd
Abak – Capex Office Interiors
Abal – CV truck and trailer spares – Abal Engineering UK
Abalyn – methyl abietate resin – Hercules Holding Ii Ltd
ABB – Electric Motors – Sprint Engineering & Lubricant
ABB – Hydraulic & Offshore Supplies Ltd
ABB – Proplas International Ltd
ABB – motor service partner – E M R Slivertorn Ltd
ABB – European Drives & Motor Repairs
ABB ACS 150 – Proplas International Ltd
ABB ACS 350 – Proplas International Ltd
ABB ACS 550 – Proplas International Ltd
ABB Drives – Proplas International Ltd
ABB/entrelec – E Preston Electrical Ltd
ABB Industrial Systems – AC inverter drives – Disco Drive Kings Lynn Ltd
ABB Preciflex – European Technical Sales Ltd
Abbesyn – matt and silk vinyl finishes – T & R Williamson Ltd
Abbey – single skinned GRP up and over garage door – P C Henderson Ltd
Abbey – cleaning products industrial and domestic textiles – Robert Scott & Sons
Abbey Bits – Abbey England Ltd
Abbey Cross – containers, cabinets and buildings for the safe storage and handling of highly flammable liquids, chemicals, pesticides and acids – Safety Unlimited
ABBEY EXTRUSTIONS LTD – Hydraulic & Offshore Supplies Ltd
Abbey National – Abbey Current Accounts
Abbey Pynford – under pinning – Abbey Pynford plc
Abbey Thermosets – pigments – Abbey Masterbatch Ltd
AbbeyFlex – claycoated corrugated fibreboard for flex printing – Abbey Board
AbbeyLite – microflute corrugated fibreboard – Abbey Board
AbbeyScreen – claycoated corrugated fibreboard for screen printing – Abbey Board
Abbeyview – Magazine for Abbey National Staff – John Brown Publishing
Abbicoil – springs, wire forms, needles, coat hangers and hooks – Abbicoil Springs
Abbotsford Collection – carpets - axminster – Brintons Carpets Ltd
ABC Glass Box – plastic storage and carry box for glasses – A B C Catering & Party Equipment Hire Ltd
ABC Selfstore – A B C Selfstore
Abcare – health and beauty products – Rand Rocket Ltd
Abcite – thermoplastic powder coating – Mallatite Ltd
Abco – power transmission products – Airport Bearing Co. Ltd
Abdoscan – G E Healthcare
ABEKO – Chaintec Ltd
Abel – reg name mark – Knight Scientific Ltd
Abel bodies – all types of vehicle bodywork – Abel Demountable Systems Ltd
Abelmatic – guide rail demount equipment – Abel Demountable Systems Ltd
Abercrombie – distilling equipment – R G Abercrombie
Aberdare – Prima Care
Abex – Pop Up, Portable and Modular Displays – Ace Exhibitions Displays & Installation
Abex-Denison – hydraulic equipment, pumps, motors and valves – Parker Hannisin plc
ABEX DENISON – Hydraulic & Offshore Supplies Ltd
ABEX MEAD – Hydraulic & Offshore Supplies Ltd
ABG Professional Information – Institute Of Chartered Accountants
Abgel Hand Cleanser – beaded hand cleanser gel – Morris Lubricants
Abington – canned bitter – Wells & Young's Brewing Co.
Abitol – hydroabietyl alcohol – Hercules Holding Ii Ltd
ABL Heatsinks – A B L Aluminium Components Ltd
Able – labels, towels, name tapes and wove – Able Direct Centre Ltd
Able Internet Payroll Ltd – Able Internet Payroll Ltd
Ablespacer – Medication holding chamber for the treatment of respiratory disorders – Clement Clarke International Ltd
Ablex – audio cassettes, floppy disks and compact discs – Docdata Ltd
ABLI Fire retardant coatings – Trowell Plant Sales Ltd
Abloy – locks – J L M Security
***ABLOY (Finland)** – locks – Abloy UK
ABLOY Disklock Pro – patented cylinder locks – Abloy UK
ABLOY Exec – Patented cylinder locks – Abloy UK
Abloy - locks, Chubb - locks, Yale - locks – J L M Security
ABMAGS – electro magnetic locks – Abloy UK
***Abnox (Switzerland)** – grease guns and air operated drum pumps – Lumatic Ga Ltd
ABOT – Automatic box opening machines – T M Robotics (Europe) Ltd
Abracadabra – starch oxident – Roquette UK Ltd
Abracap – abrasive caps and sleeves on rubber holders – Kemet International Ltd
Abracarb – liquid animal feeds – Roquette UK Ltd
Abradisc – self adhesive abrasive grinding discs and rubber holders – Kemet International Ltd
Abrafloc – coagulents – Roquette UK Ltd
Abragel – Gresolvent Ltd
Abramix – rotor stator mixers – Silverson Machines Ltd
Abrapro – liquid animal feed – Roquette UK Ltd
Abraret – retention aids – Roquette UK Ltd
Abrasoft – water softeners – Roquette UK Ltd
Abrasol – Gresolvent Ltd
Abrasorb – super aborbers – Roquette UK Ltd
Abrastarch – native wheat starch – Roquette UK Ltd
Abrilflo – amides – Abril Industrial Waxes Ltd
Abrilube – amide waxes – Abril Industrial Waxes Ltd
Abriwax – amide waxes – Abril Industrial Waxes Ltd
Abroclamp – handrail brackets – Gabriel & Co. Ltd
Abrotube – handrail tubing – Gabriel & Co. Ltd
ABS – Pumps – Wendage Pollution Control Ltd
ABS – Flow Mech Products Ltd
ABS – Naylor Specialists Plastics
Absolta – sintered wire cloth – G Bopp & Co. Ltd
Absolute – air filters – Waterloo Air Products
Absolute – porcelain wall & floor tiles – Johnson Tiles Ltd
Absolute – Encoders UK
Absolute Search – Executive research services for executive search, headhunters – Absolute Search Ltd
Abstract – paper – Fenner Paper Co. Ltd
ABT Products Ltd – cab manufacturers to the forklift truck and mechanical handling industry – A B T Products Ltd
Abur (United Kingdom) – hairnets – Aburnet Ltd
Abus – Gem Tool Hire & Sales Ltd
ABUS – crane manufrs – ABUS Crane Systems Ltd
***Abus (Germany)** – home security, padlocks, security items – Carl Kammerling International Ltd
Abwood – grinding machines, machine vices – Abwood Machine Tools Ltd
Abwood – Red House Industrial Services Ltd
AC – Harrier Fluid Power Ltd
AC – commercial air curtain – Airbloc
AC bedrooms – Sliding wardrobes – A C Bedrooms
AC/DC Lighting Systems – low voltage cold cathode/fluorescent lighting, emergency lighting, covelite – A C D C Led Ltd
AC & DC Motors – AC induction motors, DC brushless and brushed motors – AMETEK Airscrew Limited
Academy – 300MM scale rules – Blundell Harling Ltd
Academy – jigsaw puzzles and calendars – J Salmon Ltd
ACADEMY – taps and mixers – Ideal Standard Ltd
Academy Class – Computer Training in London – Academy Class Ltd
ACC Electrolux – hermetic compressors and condensing units from cubigel – Thermofrost Cryo plc
Accelar – access switch – Nortel Networks UK Ltd
Accelerated Learning Systems – language courses, maths and art courses, training and development programme and learning to learn and child development programme – Accelerated Learning Systems Ltd
Accelerometers – scientific instruments – Sandhurst Instruments Ltd
Accent – luxury washbasins, bidets and closets – Ideal Standard Ltd
Access – vertical lift controller – P G Drive Technology
Access – Kitchens for disabled use – Anson Concise Ltd
Access – 19" racking system – Cooper B Line Ltd
Access All Areas – Accesscaff International Ltd
Access Brands Towers – Accesscaff International Ltd
Access Control – marine and recovery equipment – Zap Controls Ltd
Access Direct – Accesscaff International Ltd
Access Floor Fire Stops – floors, voids – Rockwool Rockpanel B V
Access Garden Products – garden frames and minigreenhouses – Access Irrigation Ltd
Access Irrigation – irrigation systems for horticulture – Access Irrigation Ltd
Access Mate Towers – Accesscaff International Ltd
Access Platforms – Accesscaff International Ltd
Access Pod Towers – Accesscaff International Ltd
Access Rental Platforms – Accesscaff International Ltd
Access Systems – Accesscaff International Ltd
Accessories – horticultural plant support products – Nutscene
Accia-Feed – caterpiller machine for plastic and rubber extrusion – Peter Gillard Company Ltd
Acclaim – modern concept cistern – Thomas Dudley Ltd
Acclaim – polyol – I M C D UK Ltd
Acclaim Powder Coaters – powder coaters – Batchglow Ltd
Accodata – UK Office Direct
Accolade – loudspeaker enclosure – Lowther Loudspeaker Systems Ltd
Accolade – electric instantaneous shower – Heatrae Sadia
Accolade – seating – Audience Systems Ltd
Accolado – wine – Rodney Densem Wines Ltd
Accommodation 2 (United Kingdom) – broadloom – Checkmate Industries Ltd
Accommodator – Churchtown Buildings Ltd
Accord – Foremost Electronics Ltd
Accord Compact – steel panel and convector radiator with factory fitted grilles and end panels – Stelrad Group Ltd
***Accorroni (Italy)** – small gas heaters – William May Ltd
Accountancy Magazine – Institute Of Chartered Accountants
Accounting and Business Research – Institute Of Chartered Accountants
Accounting Software Package – Topaz Computer Systems Ltd
Accrafill – automatic sack filling & weighing equipment – A T Sack Fillers
Accu-tone – broadcasting studios – I A C Company Ltd
***Accu Trak (U.S.A.)** – hubodometers – O E M Group Ltd
Accu-trak – Precision Tools
AccuBird – Gesipa Blind Riveting Systems Ltd
Accudos – metered dose spray applicator for spot applications of herbicides, fungicides & insecticides. – Micron Sprayers Ltd
Accudos 2/25P – metered dose spray applicator for spot applications of herbicides, fungicides & insecticides – Micron Sprayers Ltd
***Acculok (Germany)** – self tightening milling cutter chuck – Macinnes Tooling Ltd
Accupaque – G E Healthcare
Accuramatic – liquid dispensing equipment – Accuramatic Laboratory Equipment
Accuratus (Taiwan) – full range of own brand keyboards – Ceratech Electronics Ltd
Accuride – Specialty Fasteners & Components Ltd
Accurist – watches – Accurist Watches

ACCUSPRAY – Hydraulic & Offshore Supplies Ltd
*Accutemp – M C S Technical Products Ltd
Accuwriter – handwriting pen – Office Depot UK
ACDOCO – various concentrated vegetable oil based soap powders and detergents, stain removers, colour run removers and household cleaners – ACDOCO Ltd
ACE – Hydraulic & Offshore Supplies Ltd
Ace – buttons – Jason Buttons Ltd
Ace – Display and Exhibition products and Installation Services – Ace Exhibitions Displays & Installation
Ace – Clamps – Isla Components Ltd
Ace – record label – Ace Records Ltd
Ace – Tyco
Ace – Lever locks – Walsall Locks Ltd
Ace Coat – Sumitomo Electric Hardmetal Ltd
Ace Package – waste water solids conditioning & dewatering – The Haigh Group Ltd
Ace Shock Absorbers – European Technical Sales Ltd
Ace Signs Group Ltd – Ace Signs Group
Ace System – waste water solids removal & dewatering – The Haigh Group Ltd
Aceframe – diy re-usable modular construction system – B C G Creative FX
ACER – Quintech Computer Systems Ltd
*Acer (Germany and Holland) – stand alone PC's, notebooks, file server, monitors and printers – Acer UK Ltd
Acer – Lamphouse Ltd
Acer – Apex Computer Services Wales Ltd
Acer Acros – stand alone PC's specifically for the mass merchandising channel – Acer UK Ltd
*Acer Altos (U.S.A.) – multi-user unix computer systems – Acer UK Ltd
*Acesa (Spain) – hand tools, spanners, sockets and accessories – Electro Group Ltd
Acetylcedrene FLC – perfume speciality – Quest International UK Ltd
Acfil – automotive battery fillers – Gordon Equipments Ltd
Achiever – educational stationery and drawing instruments – Helix Trading Ltd
Acid Brite – acid cleaner – Evans Vanodine International plc
Acidgen – Cleansorb Ltd
Acidgen FG – Cleansorb Ltd
Acidgen HA – Cleansorb Ltd
Aciduma – acid resisting cement – Vitcas Ltd
Aciera – European Technical Sales Ltd
Ackworthie – drilling and tapping multiheads – Herbert Tooling Ltd
Acme – transformers – Bearwood Engineering Supplies
Acme – metal and plastic whistles – J Hudson & Co Whistles Ltd
Acme Brand – carding machine accessories – Arthur Heaton & Co Ltd
Acme Thunderer – metal and plastic whistles – J Hudson & Co Whistles Ltd
ACORN – geodemographic consumer classification – C A C I
Acorn – tools, brushes and decorating sundries – Hamilton Acorn Ltd
Acorn – wood carving tools – Henry Taylor Tools Ltd
Acorn – UK Office Direct
Acoustack – jet engine silencer – I A C Company Ltd
Acoustalay – pe foam cross linked flooring underlay – Functional Foam Beacons Products Ltd
Acoustic Barrier – impact attenuating acoustic flooring – Tiflex Ltd
Acoustic Partition Slab – partitions, floors – Rockwool Rockpanel B V
Acoustic Party Wall DPC – minimised flanking sound transmission at party walls – Rockwool Rockpanel B V
Acoustic Partywall DPC – insulated DPC minimises cold bridge in wall construction – Rockwool Rockpanel B V
Acousticurtain – flexible noise barrier – Acousticabs Industrial Noise Control Ltd
Acoustifoam – Acousticabs Industrial Noise Control Ltd
Acoustilouvre – acoustic louvre – Acousticabs Industrial Noise Control Ltd
Acoustilux – British Vita plc
Acoustimass – virtually invisible speaker systems – Bose Ltd
Acoustislab – acoustic panel – Acousticabs Industrial Noise Control Ltd
Acoustitag – G E Healthcare
Acoustone – ceiling systems (suspended) – U S G UK Ltd
Acoustray – acoustic & fire stop cavity tray – Timloc Building Products
ACPA – Selectronix Ltd
Acquisitions – fireplaces – Acquisitions Victorian Edwardian Fireplaces
ACR – aircraft crash recovery systems – R F D Beaufort Ltd
ACR – commercial air curtain – Airbloc
Acramil – Kennametal UK Ltd
Acriflow – organic dispersing/scale prevention agent – Witton Chemical Co. Ltd
Acrogrip – Hydrafeed Ltd
Acroil – artboard – Oasis Art & Craft Products Ltd

Acrokool – refrigerated drinking water coolers, industrial coolers and bespoke chillers – Acrokool Ltd
Acroloop – Motor Technology Ltd
Acrotone – Wright Dental Group
Acrow Props – Accesscaff International Ltd
Acrulite – casting resin and metrology replica material – Rubert & Co. Ltd
Acrylacote – acrylic primer – Dacrylate Paints Ltd
Acrylene – modified basic dye stuffs – Town End Leeds plc
Acrylite – artificial teeth – WHW Plastics Ltd
Acrythane – paint – H M G Paints Ltd
ACS Whittaker – distributor of catering disposables, vending ingredients, hygiene and cleaning products – Bunzl Catering Supplies Ltd
Acsellerate (United Kingdom) – ECi Software Solutions Limited
Act – fault code reader – Crypton Ltd
ACT – commercial air curtain – Airbloc
ACT – I T Works
ACT – Access Control Systems – Access Controlled Solutions Ltd
ACT 2000 – I T Works
ACT Professional – I T Works
ACT Professional for workgroups – I T Works
*Acta (Denmark/Norway) – Norba wood and waste crushers – Pulp & Paper Machinery Ltd
Actane – dry acid salts – Cookson Electronics Ltd
Actane 70 – added to acids to assist pickling – Cookson Electronics Ltd
Actane 73 – activation of alloys – Cookson Electronics Ltd
Actane 85 – oxide removal and activation – Cookson Electronics Ltd
Actane 97 – pickle for copper – Cookson Electronics Ltd
Actane Inhibitor – pickling additive – Cookson Electronics Ltd
Actane L 59 – pickling, cleaning – Cookson Electronics Ltd
Actaris – Stream Measurement Ltd
Actek – H T S Direct Ltd
Actel – Cyclops Electronics Ltd
Actellic – insecticide – Sorex Ltd
Acticarbone – activated carbon – Atosina UK Ltd
Actifresh – bacteriostatic and fungistatic chemicals for the hygienic protection of textiles, plastics, rubber products footwear etcagainst bacteria, associated odour formation, fungi and moulds – British Sanitized Ltd
Actimatic – grease converter – Wade International Ltd
*Actini (France) – tubular heat exchangers – Engelmann & Buckham Ltd
Action (United Kingdom) – cam locking q/q couplers & crwofoot couplings – Hydrasun Ltd
Action Can – blue crystal glass cleaner and range of industrial products in aerosol – Action Can Ltd
Action Can – S J Wharton Ltd
Action Can AC-90 – instant maintenance spray (industrial/automotive lubricant) – Action Can Ltd
Action Can Amaze – dash and bumper cleaner – Action Can Ltd
Action Can AS-90 – welding anti spatter – Action Can Ltd
Action Can CT-90 – cutting and tapping lubricant (industrial lubricant) – Action Can Ltd
*Action Discs – cutting & grinding of abrasive discs – J R Webster & Co Ltd
Action Force – toys – P M S International Group plc
Action Handling Equipment – materials handling equipment – Action Handling Equipment Ltd
Action Knives – pocket knives – Egginton Bros Ltd
Action Pack – steel framed, timber or polyethylene clad, multi-functional, multi-level play structures that incorporate sliding, climbing, swinging crawling etc – S M P Playgrounds
Action Research – medical research registered charity – Action Medical Research
ACTION-SEALTITE – Hydraulic & Offshore Supplies Ltd
Action Sockets – Yokota UK
Action Transfers – childrens transfers – Acorn Marketing Ltd
Actionair – Ruskin Air Management Ltd
Actipron – crop protection products – B P plc
activ – self cleaning glass – Pilkington Group Ltd
Activ – continence & cleansing range – Robinson Healthcare Ltd
Activ-8 – chlorine dioxide treatment for microbiological control in potablewater systems – Feedwater Ltd
Activ-Ox – chlorine dioxide treatment for microbiological control in potable water systems – Feedwater Ltd
Activ-Ox – chlorine dioxide on-line disinfection system for potable and stored water – Feedwater Ltd
Activ-V – high efficiency active carbon filter units – Emcel Filters Ltd
Activ Web Design – Activ Web Design
Activated Carbon Cells – Replacement Carbon Filter cells and panels of any size to suit any existing filter installation – Emcel Filters Ltd
*Active – Mower – Active Grounds Maintenance Ltd
Active – anti bacterial handwashes in six great fragrances – F M C G Ltd
Active – spring supports – Maineport Ltd

Active-Guard – gas barrier systems – Timloc Building Products
ACTIVECM – I B M UK Ltd
Activox C50.C80 – ultra high surface area zinc oxide for catalyst and cosmetic industry – Rockwood Pigments
Activox R50/R90 – ultra high surface area zinc oxide for rubber compounding – Rockwood Pigments
Actona – The Winnen Furnishing Company
Actona Furniture – The Winnen Furnishing Company
Actreg (Spain) – Pneumatic activator manufacture – Trimline Valves
Actrilawn 10 – herbicide for the control of broad-leaved weeds in newly sown grass at or beyond the two leaf stage – Bayer Crop Science
ACTU – pressure switches and gauges – Black Teknigas & Electro Controls Ltd
ACU-RITE – HEIDENHAIN GB LTD
Acu-rite – Encoders UK
Acugrip – Precision hydraulic & mechanical work holding equipment – Acugrip Ltd
Acuity (U.S.A.) – Laser distance sensors – Schmitt Europe Ltd
Acuma – fishing tackle – Drennan International Ltd
Acumedic Centre – acupuncture and Chinese medicine, clinics, health books and products and medicinal equipment – Acumedic Centre Ltd
Acumet – instruments – Canongate Technology Ltd
Acupad – medical electrotherapy products-pain relief and physiotherapy – Nidd Valley Medical Ltd
Acupaque – G E Healthcare
Acute – USB Instrumentation – StanTronic Instruments
Acvoke – cable spiking guns, vices, machine and production – Accles & Shelvoke Ltd
ACWa – air, water, sewage, industrial effluent treatment – A C W A Services Ltd
Acxiom Directors At Home Database – consumer marketing database of all British registered directors – Acxiom Ltd
Acxiom Directors At Home Database – Acxiom Ltd
AD/Advantage – application development system – Cincom Systems UK Ltd
Ad Bikes – promotional bicycles and tricycles – Pashley Cycles Ltd
Ad-Hyde – Nederman Ltd
Ad Lib – footwear, fashion accessories – Mitex Ltd
AD2000 – Funke
Adamant – gauge glasses and rods – J B Treasure & Co. Ltd
*Adamas (U.S.A.) – roundback guitars – John Hornby Skewes & Co. Ltd
Adams – earthenware tableware and giftware – Wedgewood Travel Ltd
Adams – lubrication equipment – Adams Lubetech Ltd
Adams Lubtech – B L Pneumatics Ltd
Adamsez – baths – Adamsez NI Ltd
ADAN – Hydraulic & Offshore Supplies Ltd
ADAP-KOOL – refrigeration control (electronic) – Danfoss Ltd
ADAPT/2000 – software – Transoft Ltd
Adaptafile – expanding document wallets – Logax Ltd
Adaptainer – container sales and hire onsite storage – Adaptainer Ltd
Adaptalok – nylon 6 conduit system with kwik-fit adaptor – Adaptaflex Ltd
Adaptaring – nylon & conduit systems with IP40 fittings – Adaptaflex Ltd
Adaptaseal – nylon 6 conduit system with IP67 fittings – Adaptaflex Ltd
Adaptasteel – range of steel based conduit and fittings systems – Adaptaflex Ltd
Adaptoplast – first aid dressing – Cuxson Gerrard & Company Ltd
Adast Dominant – P P S Rotaprint Ltd
Adastra – audio, electronic and public address accessories and equipment – Skytronic Ltd
Adatab – preparation of antibiotic containing culture plates for break-point and M.I.C. susceptibility testing – The Mast Group Ltd
Adatest – software verification toolset for Ada – I P L Information Processing Ltd
AdBlue – Fuel Proof Ltd
ADC – Clean Machine UK Ltd
Adco – industrial lubricants – B P plc
Adcock & Shipley – Red House Industrial Services Ltd
Adcut – industrial lubricants – B P plc
Add-Infinitum – tables – E F G Matthews Office Furniture Ltd
Addaclenz Floor Cleaner – cleaners/misc items – Addagrip Surface Treatments Ltd
Addacrete – chemical resistant floor screed – Addagrip Surface Treatments Ltd
Addaflex – building products – Addagrip Surface Treatments Ltd
Addaflor – coloured top coats – Addagrip Surface Treatments Ltd
ADDAGRIP – Resin Bonded Surfacing
Addagrip Heavy Duty Mortar – mortars – Addagrip Surface Treatments Ltd

Addalevel – self levelling systems – Addagrip Surface Treatments Ltd
Addamortar – mortars – Addagrip Surface Treatments Ltd
Addamortar Colour Pack – mortars – Addagrip Surface Treatments Ltd
Addapatch – mortars – Addagrip Surface Treatments Ltd
Addaprime – cold applied epoxy compounds – Addagrip Surface Treatments Ltd
Addaseal 20 (clear) – Polyurethane coatings – Addagrip Surface Treatments Ltd
Addaseal 50 (clear) – polyurethane coatings – Addagrip Surface Treatments Ltd
Addaseal Colour Pack – polyurethane coatings – Addagrip Surface Treatments Ltd
ADDASET – Resin Bonded Surfacing
Addasol Primer – cold applied epoxy compounds – Addagrip Surface Treatments Ltd
Addasol Top Coat – coloured top coats – Addagrip Surface Treatments Ltd
ADDASTONE – Resin Bonded Surfacing
Addastone – Thornbury Surfacing Chippenham Ltd
Addastone Adhesive – forecourt systems – Addagrip Surface Treatments Ltd
Addastone Primer – forecourt systems – Addagrip Surface Treatments Ltd
Addastone Sealer – forecourt systems – Addagrip Surface Treatments Ltd
Addawall (Wall Coating) – coloured top coats – Addagrip Surface Treatments Ltd
Addeco Alfred Marks – employment agency – Adecco UK Ltd
Addis – UK Office Direct
Addison machines – Phil Geesin Machinery Ltd
Additive A – clay conditioner – Borregaard UK
Additive A/Traffaid – clay conditioners – Borregaard UK
AddSorb – adsorption of inorganic gas – Jacobi Carbons
Addstone – Type of cast stone / reconstructed stone – Addstone Cast Stone
Adel Rootstein – manufacture display mannequins – Adel Rootstein
Adept Doors Ltd – Industrial Doors and Garage Doors – adeptdoors Ltd
Adesco – adhesive – Anixter Industrial Ltd
Adesco – adhesives, mastics and sealants – Anixter Ltd
***Adesso (Italy and UK)** – ladies and mens shoes and handbags – Kurt Geiger Ltd
Adflex – metallic hose – Dixon Group Europe Ltd
Adform – industrial lubricants – B P plc
Adformal – industrial lubricants – B P plc
Adformax – industrial lubricants – B P plc
Adglow – point of sale services – Adglow Ltd
Adgrips – poster gripper – Alplus
Adheart – soil ameliorant – Melcourt Industries
Adhesive suppliers – Techsil Ltd
Adhoc (Italy) – premium self adhesive papers – Davies Harvey & Murrell
ADI – Lamphouse Ltd
ADI METALPARTS – stamped steel components of Spain – Mapra Technik Co.
***Adidas (Austria)** – eye protection and spectacle frames – Silhouette UK Ltd
Adidas – toiletries & fragrance – Coty UK Ltd
ADIGE – B L M Group UK Ltd
Adine – brominated fire retardants – Atosina UK Ltd
Adinmix – Food Ingredient Blends – Synergy Food Ingredients Ltd
Adixen – vacuum – AESpump
Adizem XL – hypertension and angina – Napp Pharmaceutical Group Ltd
***Adjustabed (Netherlands)** – adjustable posture and variable height beds – Golden Plan Ltd
Adjustagrip Hard Jaws – chuck jaws – Thame Engineering Co. Ltd
Adkemet – industrial lubricants – B P plc
Adkriss – industrial lubricants – B P plc
Adline – advertising gifts, personalised merchandise, corporate promotions/presentations and awards, product sourcing, scottish products – Adline Personalised Products
Adlite – open architecture light box for display colour transparencies or printed graphics – T P S Visual Communications Ltd
Adlock – high and low pressure industrial hose couplings – Dixon Group Europe Ltd
ADM Computing – IT value added reseller – A D M Computing
Adman – Logo Bugs Plus Ltd
AdMark audio – German Designed Line Array passive flying PA System – Turnaround 360
Admax – industrial lubricants – B P plc
Admiral – steel bath – Armitage Shanks Ltd
Admiral – Stainless Steel Bollard – Alto Bollards UK Ltd
Admiral – stainless steel bars and forgings – Abbey Forged Products Ltd
Admiral (United Kingdom) – cotton rich satin fabric – Carrington Career & Work Wear
Admiral – building and civil engineering contractors – Admiral
Admiral Skates & Accessories – M V Sport & Leisure Ltd
Admix – wall mounted mixers – Sheardown Engineering Ltd
Admoist – stems conditioning – Garbuiodickinson
Adobe – UK Office Direct
Adormo – British Vita plc
Adour – aero engine – Rolls-Royce plc
ADP (U.S.A.) – payroll and related services – A D P Ltd
ADP – polarimeter – Bellingham & Stanley Ltd
Adpol – silicone rubber and flurocarbon elastomer specialists – Advanced Polymers Ltd
ADR Auto – concrete compression machine – Ele International
AdRail – rail station advertising service mark – J C Decaux UK Ltd
Adrecool – V E S Ltd
Adriatic – brass foundry for bathrooms and kitchens in chrome and gold – F W Hipkin Ltd
Adroit – UK Office Direct
Adron – textile warp treatments – S T R UK Ltd
Ads for Free – newspaper publishers – Independent News & Media (NI) Ltd
Adshead Ratcliffe – County Construction Chemicals Ltd
Adshel – advertising hoardings – Clear Channel International Ltd
Adsim – software products for process engineer – Aspentech Ltd
Adsit – cash drawers – M A Lloyd & Son Ltd
Adsit - V.J. Green. – M A Lloyd & Son Ltd
ADSL Balancing Load – Tekdata Distribution Ltd
AdStorm – Advertising Agency – Adstorm
Adsum Life & Career Coaching – One-to-one personal coaching – Adsum Auxilium Limited
ADT – Eagle Security Solutions Ltd
Adtac – hydrocarbon resin – Hercules Holding Ii Ltd
Aduvex – ultraviolet light absorbers – Pentagon Fine Chemicals Ltd
Advance – adhesive tapes – Advance Tapes Group Ltd
Advance – Shand Higson & Co. Ltd
Advance (United Kingdom) – Austen Tapes Ltd
Advance 2 – Display Wizard Ltd
Advance Agro – UK Office Direct
Advance Copystands – Kauser International Trading Ltd
Advance Galatrek (United Kingdom) – ups systems power line conditioners – Powersense Technology
Advance Machine – Harrier Fluid Power Ltd
Advance Tapes – B D K Industrial Products Ltd
Advance Tooling – Sarginsons Industries
Advanced – Kuwait Petroleum International Lubricants UK Ltd
Advanced Counters and Services – Manitowoc Food Service UK
Advanced Films – B P I Films Ltd
Advanced Hi-Fill (United Kingdom) – ionized sputter chamber – Aviza Technology UK Ltd
Advanced Materials (U.S.A.) – Fuel cell bipolar plates and fuel reformation materials – Porvair plc
Advanced TCA – Harting Ltd
Advanced Technology Machines Ltd – CNC lathes & machining centres – Advanced Technology Machines Ltd
Advancer Crystar – high temperature refractories – Saint Gobain Industrial Ceramics Ltd
Advantage – assembly service – Schneider
Advantage – wheat flakes – Weetabix Ltd
Advantage – range of water powered chemical injection – Access Irrigation Ltd
Advantage – boiler water chemicals – Ashland UK
Advantage - Altistart - Altivar - Axiom SP&N - Canalis - CIDS - Clearstart - Compact NS - Domae - Easergy - Evolis - Factorylink - Fast trans - FIPIO - Form3Fast - Genie - GDV2 - GM set - GM6 - Harmony - IHC - I-Line - Integral - Interpact - Isobar 4c - Isobar 4 SP&N - Isobar 4 TP&N - LoadCentre KQ2 - Magelis - Masterbloc - Masterpact - MC set - MDS - Merlin Gerin - Micro - Micrologic - Minipact - Modbus - Modbus Plus - Modicon - Modicon TSX - Momentum - Multi-Form - Nano - NS Feeder pillar - Nu-Lec - Opus - Osiris - Panelmate - Power 2 rack - Power Pact 4 - Power-Style 3 - Power-Style 4 - PowerLogic - Premium - Prisma Evolution - Prisma G - Prisma GK - Prisma GX - Prisma P - Prisma PH - Profibus - Quadbreak - Quantum - Qwikline II - Rectiphase - Rectivar - Reactivar - Ringmaster C - Ringmaster compact - RM6 - Safepact 2 - SAIF feeder pillars - Sarel - Sepam - Shielded feeder pillars - Sinewave - SM6 - Square D - Standard Plus - Startpact - Tego Dial - Tego Power - Telemecanique - Tesys - Transparent building - Transparent factory - Transparent infrastructure - Transparent Ready - Tricast - Trihal - Twinbreak - Twido - Twineline/Lexium - Varlogic - Varplus - Vijeo Look - VIP 300 - YSF6 - Zelio. – Schneider
Advantra – high performance melt adhesives – H B Fuller
Advent – Vidlink International Ltd
Advent – Advanced Computer Controller – AMET (Europe) Ltd
Adventure – rigid inflatable boats – Avon Inflatables Ltd
Adventure Bark – lias playground surface – Melcourt Industries
Adventure Lights – Thomas Jacks Ltd
Adverc (United Kingdom) – automotive & marine battery management systems, electronic alternator voltage regulators, converters, inverters, marine chargers, digital circuit monitors, alternators and low voltage protection – Adverc B M Ltd
Advert – Lamphouse Ltd
Advertiser Series – newspaper – Mail News Media
Advertiser Series, The – weekly free newspapers – The Bournemouth Daily Echo
AEA – flonge alignment system – Hytorc Unex Ltd
Aebi – Embankment Tractors – Loxston Garden Machinery
AEG – E M R Sliverthorn Ltd
***AEG (Spain)** – electric motors – Micro Clutch Developments Ltd
AEG – Gem Tool Hire & Sales Ltd
AEG Electric Tools – power tools for craftsmen – Atlas Copco Tools Ltd
Aegis – anti-counterfeit encrypted graphic imaging system – Opsec Security Ltd
Aegis Security Enclosures – Kemco Fabrications Ltd
AEL – AEL Heating Solutions Ltd
AEL Heating Solutions – AEL Heating Solutions Ltd
AELtherm – AEL Heating Solutions Ltd
Aemoti Operated Vehicles – explosive equipment – A B Precision Poole Ltd
Aeolus – pheromones – Bodywise Ltd
Aerco – heat exchangers, automatic thermostatically operated valves, heat reclamation equipment and systems – B S S Pipe Fitting Stockholders Head Office
Aerco Ltd – electrical and electronic components – Aerco Ltd
Aeresta – textiles – Maurice Phillips
Aergo – rucsac back system – Karrimor Ltd
Aerial Platforms – Accesscaff International Ltd
Aerial Runway – single direction cableway – S M P Playgrounds
Aero – Knighton Tool Supplies
Aero – Bushboard Ltd
Aero-Cord – sash line – Ibex Marina Ropes
Aero Electric – Connectors – Dax International Ltd
Aero-motive – Gustair Materials Handling Equipment Ltd
***Aero-Pro (Germany)** – airbrushing equipment – Technical Sales Ltd
Aero Pure – carbon filters – Norit UK Ltd
Aeroboost – body/trailer streamlining kits – Aerodyne Equipment
Aerocin – air heater, recouperator and thermal oxidiser – The Aerogen Co. Ltd
Aerocoater – fluidbed coating – Aeromatic Fielder Ltd
Aeroflow – tap – Worldwide Dispensers
Aerogen – gas, oil and dual fuel burners – The Aerogen Co. Ltd
Aerographic – paper – Fenner Paper Co. Ltd
Aerogrip – bushes for sheet metal and aircraft industries – Talbot Tool Co. Ltd
Aerokleen – cleaner for aircraft maintenance – Dasic International Ltd
Aerolite – aerospace liferafts – R F D Beaufort Ltd
Aerolor – carbon and carbon composites – Mersen UK
Aeron Seating – Capex Office Interiors
Aeropeltor – headsets – Hayward & Green Aviation Ltd
Aeroplane – I P C Media Ltd
AEROQUIP – Hydraulic & Offshore Supplies Ltd
Aeroquip – Fairway Hydraulics Ltd
Aerosil – fumed silica – Lawrence Industries Ltd
Aerospace – lifejackets – R F D Beaufort Ltd
Aerospace Europe – United Business Media Ltd
aerospace metrology & electromechanical calibratio – Gloss – Amecal
Aerosplit – British Rema Process Equipment Ltd
Aerosplit – powder classifier – British Rema Manufacturing Co. Ltd
Aerostrip 323 – unique patented water based paint remover for aviation industry – Dasic International Ltd
***Aerotop (Japan)** – electric folding fabric sunroof – Webasto Products UK Ltd
AerOver – body/trailer streamlining kits – Aerodyne Equipment
Aerovox – Cyclops Electronics Ltd
Aerovox – breathers & spares – Bearwood Engineering Supplies
Aerowrap – wrapping & packaging film – B P plc
Aerox – industrial ceramic filters – Fairey Industrial Ceramics
AES – Mobile phone intercoms – Seamless Aluminium International Ltd
AES – paper machine showers, felt cleaning equipment, drainage, filtratation and cleaning and conditioning equipment – Kadant UK Ltd
***Aesculup (Germany)** – electric hair clippers and veterinary equipment – Diamond Edge Ltd

AETC – precision cast and machined gas turbine OEM engine airfoil components. Airfoil repair and overhaul to approved repair schemes – AETC Ltd
Aetel – Timing system electric – Castle Dataware Ltd
Aethra – Videonations Ltd
AF – UK Office Direct
Afco of London Sundries – Double Gee Hair Fashions Ltd
Afco-Wigs – hair treatments, curl activators and moisturisers, shampoo and ornaments for the hair and gro-aid products – Double Gee Hair Fashions Ltd
Affco – cosmetics – Double Gee Hair Fashions Ltd
Affinity – Resinex UK Ltd
Affinity – disposable respirators – M S A Britain Ltd
Afghan – carpets – Bond Worth
Aflas (Japan) – fluoroelastomer – AGC Chemicals Ltd
AFLEX PTFE HOSE & FITTINGS – Hydraulic & Offshore Supplies Ltd
Aflon (Japan) – etfe, lm-etfe,pfa, ultra pure pfa, ptfe – AGC Chemicals Ltd
AFM – Kennametal Extrude Hone Ltd
AFM – Bystronic UK Ltd
AFON – Hydraulic & Offshore Supplies Ltd
Afos – automatic smoking kilns, ventilated work stations for hospital laboratories – Afos Ltd
AFP – Analogue addressable fire panel – C-Tec Security Ltd
Afrazine Spray – nasal spray – M S D Animal Health
AFTON CHEMICAL LTD – Hydraulic & Offshore Supplies Ltd
AG – calibration materials – Bellingham & Stanley Ltd
AG Fluoropolymers (U.S.A.) – AGC Chemicals Ltd
Aga – Submarine Manufacturing & Products Ltd
Aga C – solid fuel domestic cooking appliance – AGA Rayburn
Aga CB – solid fuel domestic cooking appliance and hot water – AGA Rayburn
Aga E – solid fuel domestic cooking appliance – AGA Rayburn
Aga EC – electric domestic cooking appliance – AGA Rayburn
Aga ECM – electric domestic cooking appliance – AGA Rayburn
Aga EE – electric domestic cooking appliance – AGA Rayburn
Aga GC – gas-fired domestic cooking appliance (balanced, conventional and power flue options) – AGA Rayburn
Aga GCB – gas-fired domestic cooking appliance and water heater (balanced, conventional and power flue options) – AGA Rayburn
Aga GCBM – gas-fired domestic cooking appliance and water heater (balanced, conventional and power flue options) – AGA Rayburn
Aga GCM – gas-fired domestic cooking appliance (balanced, conventional and power flue options) – AGA Rayburn
Aga GE – gas-fired domestic cooking appliance (balanced, conventional and power flue options) – AGA Rayburn
Aga GEB – gas-fired domestic cooking appliance and water heater (balanced, conventional and power flue options) – AGA Rayburn
Aga GEBM – gas-fired domestic cooking appliance and water heater (balanced and conventional flue options – AGA Rayburn
Aga GEM – gas-fired domestic cooking appliance (balanced, conventional and power flue options) – AGA Rayburn
Aga OC – oil-fired domestic cooking appliance – AGA Rayburn
Aga OCB 135 – oil-fired domestic cooking appliance and water heater – AGA Rayburn
Aga OCB 90 – oil-fired domestic cooking appliance and water heater – AGA Rayburn
Aga OCBM 135 – oil-fired domestic cooking appliance and water heater – AGA Rayburn
Aga OCBM 90 – oil-foired domestic cooking appliance and water heater – AGA Rayburn
Aga OCM – oil-fired domestic cooking appliance and water heater – AGA Rayburn
Aga OE – oil-fired domestic cooking appliance – AGA Rayburn
Aga OEB – oil-fired domestic cooking appliance and water heater – AGA Rayburn
Aga OEBM – oil-fired domestic cooking appliance and water heater – AGA Rayburn
Aga OEM – oil-fired domestic cooking appliance – AGA Rayburn
Agabekov – interior lighting – Crescent Lighting Ltd
Agar Scientific – medical laboratory equipment, electron microscopy accessories – Agar Scientific
Agatex – high tensile steel woven mesh – Screen Systems Wire Workers Ltd
Agathon – Red House Industrial Services Ltd
AGCO – Anderson Greenwood – Anderson Greenwood Instrumentation
AGCO - Anderson Greenwood – Anderson Greenwood Instrumentation
AGEMA – Harrier Fluid Power Ltd
AGET Language Services – translators and interpreters – A S K Group
***AGFA. (Belgium)** – microfilm, motion picture film, x-ray equipment, graphic systems, colour film and paper – Agfa Gevaert
***Agfacolor (Germany)** – colour print and slide film and colour paper – Agfa Gevaert
Agglio – conglomerate stone tiles – A Elder Reed & Co. Ltd
Agglomaster – Hosokawa Micron Ltd
***Agglosimplex (Italy)** – conglomerate marble tiles and slabs – MFS Stone Surfaces Ltd
Agie – Agie Charmilles Ltd
Agiflite – hand held aerial camera for oblique photography – Meggitt Avionics
Agilent – Cyclops Electronics Ltd
***Agio (Cuba)** – cigars – Hunters & Frankau Ltd
Agio Furniture – Capex Office Interiors
Agitan – defoamers – Lawrence Industries Ltd
Aglite – lightweight building blocks – Plasmor Ltd
Agma – caustic calcined magnesite – Chance & Hunt Ltd
Agmacote – temporary transparent hard coating for machines metal surfaces – Agma Ltd
Agmapak – hard surface cleaner – Agma Ltd
Agmasol – range of solvent based cleaners – Agma Ltd
Agproshield – paint coatings – Hubdean Contracting Ltd
***Agralan Envirofleece** – Agralan Ltd
***Agralan Enviromesh** – Agralan Ltd
***Agralan Revive** – Agralan Ltd
***Agribudget** – F C G Software Solutions Ltd
Agricon – insect attractants – International Pheromone Systems Ltd
Agricultural parts suppliers – Kramp UK Ltd
Agripa – patented flexible advertisng solution for vehcles, banners, billboards – Agripa Solutions
Agripa Fleet Media – Suppliers of the globally patented Agripa system – Agripa Solutions
Agripa Holdings – Owners and inventors of the globally patented Agripa system – Agripa Solutions
Agriseal – vermin protection and energy conservation in food and agricultural industry – Kleeneze Sealtech Ltd
Agritape – adhesive tapes for agricultural use – Advance Tapes Group Ltd
Agro – cable glands – Ses Sterling Ltd
Agro Textiles – Capatex Ltd
Agroband – agricultural machinery – Horstine Farmery
AHBB – direct fired gas fired unit heaters – Nordair Niche
AHBB – direct fired gas fired unit heater – Nordair Niche
AIAG – Harrier Fluid Power Ltd
AICHI – Harrier Fluid Power Ltd
AICHI – Chaintec Ltd
Aichi Platforms – Accesscaff International Ltd
Aid Blankets – J Bradbury & Co. Ltd
***Aignep (Italy)** – pneumatic fittings – The West Group Ltd
AIGNEP – Hydraulic & Offshore Supplies Ltd
Aiki – carpets – Interface Europe Ltd
AIM – computer systems and software house – Iris Group
AIM (Automated INFOS Migration) – software – Transoft Ltd
Aimer – lab and industrial glassblowers – Aimer Products Ltd
Aimont – Melitzer Safety Equipment
Aintex – hide palm leather gloves – Bennett Safetywear
Aintree – loose boxes – Browns of Wem Ltd
AIR – advanced infrared gas detection system – Flametec Ltd
Air-Aware – software products – Symbol Technologies Ltd
***Air Blast Cooler (Sweden)** – Fawcett Christie Hydraulics Ltd
Air BP – B P plc
Air Comp – Trafalgar Tools
Air Flow – Alpha Electronics Southern Ltd
Air Force – warm air dryers – Vectair Systems Ltd
Air Freight – AZ gateway / Web – AMG Forwarding Ltd
Air Freshener – general purpose air freshener – Premiere Products Ltd
Air-Go – bubble design rubber anti-fatigue standing mats – Jaymart Roberts & Plastics Ltd
Air-Lift – an appliance for lifting downer cows – Henshaw Inflatables Ltd
Air Line – warm air dryers – Vectair Systems Ltd
***Air Logic (U.S.A.)** – pneumatic accessories – The West Group Ltd
AIR LOGIC – Hydraulic & Offshore Supplies Ltd
Air Logic & Cylinders – Gustair Materials Handling Equipment Ltd
Air Maze – Harrier Fluid Power Ltd
Air-Maze – breathers – Bearwood Engineering Supplies
Air-o-leaf – balancing dampers – Senior Hargreaves Ltd
Air-o-seal – access panels – Senior Hargreaves Ltd
Air-o-strip – supporting band – Senior Hargreaves Ltd
Air-o-tite – insulated access doors – Senior Hargreaves Ltd
Air-o-turn – turning vanes and mounting track – Senior Hargreaves Ltd
AIR-PAK FIFTY – Self contained breathing apparatus – Scott International Ltd
AIR PINCH – Hydraulic & Offshore Supplies Ltd
Air Pressure Whisk – Morton Mixers & Blenders Ltd
Air PRO – Trafalgar Tools
Air Products – S J Wharton Ltd
Air Purity Analyser (H) – Factair Ltd
Air Receivers – Abbott & Co Newark Ltd
Air Sanitiser – sanitiser and deodoriser – Premiere Products Ltd
Air Sea – supply transport containers for dangerous goods – Air Sea Containers
Air Sentry – advanced fume cupboard – S & B UK Ltd
Air Studios – music recording studio – Air Studios Lyndhurst Hall
Air Treatment Products – Amcor Ltd
Air Turn – non contact roll for paper webs – Spooner Industries Ltd
AIR-VAC – Hydraulic & Offshore Supplies Ltd
***Air-Vac (U.S.A.)** – vacuum control equipment – The West Group Ltd
Air Zone – Peak Expiratory Flow Meter for Measuring Pulmonary Function – Clement Clarke International Ltd
Airberth – Floating Boat Lift – Wave Seven Marine Ltd
Aircap – coated bubblefilm – A Latter & Co. Ltd
Aircell – air diffusser – Waterloo Air Products
Airchamp – industrial power transmissions – Matrix International Ltd
Airclaims – aviation loss adjusters, aviation information services and aviation consultants – Airclaims Group Ltd
Airco (United Kingdom) – air conditioning (AC) service products – Primalec
AIRCO-LUBE – Airconditioning lubricants – Primalec
Airco-Seal Pro – air conditioning leak repair – Primalec
AircoFlush (United Kingdom) – air conditioner flushing system – Primalec
Aircol – mineral and synthetic based air compressor lubricants – Castrol UK Ltd
Aircomp – Southern Valve & Fitting Co. Ltd
Aircool – oil coolers – Kenlowe Accessories & Co. Ltd
Airdale Cleanroom – Airedale Environmental Services Ltd
Airdor – door curtains – S & P Coil Products Ltd
Airdri – warm air-hand and face dryers – Airdri Ltd
Airdromatic – intensifiers – Minni-Die Ltd
Airedale – springs, wire forms, pressings – Airedale Springs
Airedale Clean Room – Airedale Environmental Services Ltd
AIRFIT – Hydraulic & Offshore Supplies Ltd
***Airflex** – pinch valves – A J G Waters Equipment Ltd
Airflow – fans – Beatson Fans & Motors Ltd
Airflow – fans and instruments – Airflow Developments Ltd
Airfoil – clothing – Berghaus Ltd
Airforce Compressor Lubricants Range – oils – Morris Lubricants
Airform – laboratory fume cupboards – APMG Ltd
Airframe – Display Wizard Ltd
Airfresh – air and fabric aerosol freshener and cfc free apple perfume – Evans Vanodine International plc
Airgard – volume control damper for HVAC ductwork – Gilberts Blackpool Ltd
Airglide – Air Supported belt conveyor – Geo Robson & Co Conveyors Ltd
Airgonomics – airfilm equipment M7ES07 – Airgonomics Ltd
Airgonomics - Airfilm equipment M7ES07 – Airgonomics Ltd
Airguard – air filters – Airguard Filters Ltd
Airheart (U.S.A.) – hydraulic & mechanical disc brakes – Robert Cupitt Ltd
Airjet – variable air volume terminals for air conditioning systems – Gilberts Blackpool Ltd
Airjustor – overload clutches, detent and pneumanic – British Autogard Ltd
Airking – air conditioners – Tev Ltd
Airlay – carpet underlay – William S Graham & Sons Dewsbury Ltd
Airline – V E S Ltd
AIRLINES PNEUMATICS – Hydraulic & Offshore Supplies Ltd
Airlink – air compressors – Motivair Compressors Ltd
Airlite – disposable cutlery – Plastico Ltd
Airlite – lightweight demount equipment-3/4 tonne CHS – Abel Demountable Systems Ltd
Airlite - Clarity - Elite - Flexy-Glass - Hilite - Rollor - Shatterproof - Spork - Starlite - Superjet – Plastico Ltd
Airmachines – Gustair Materials Handling Equipment Ltd
Airmaster – Red House Industrial Services Ltd
Airmaster – air pollution control, dust filtration and dust extraction equipment – Dantherm Filtration Ltd
Airmaster – breathing regulators for divers – A P Valves
Airmaster 500 – submersible pressure gauges – A P Valves
Airmaster Auto M – dust control units – Dantherm Filtration Ltd
Airmaster M J C – filter and dust control units – Dantherm Filtration Ltd
Airmaster M J X – filter and dust control units – Dantherm Filtration Ltd
Airmat – air expanding shafts/chucks – Airmat Machinery Ltd
***Airmate (Italy)** – air compressors – S I P Industrial Products Ltd
Airmec (United Kingdom) – facilities services business – Sembcorp Bournemouth Water Ltd
Airmover – B L Pneumatics Ltd
Airnesco – self feeding compressed air operated cleaning and clearing tools – Airnesco Group Ltd

Airodek – light-weight soffit support systems – RMD Kwikform Limited
Airoduct – spirally wound ductwork – Senior Hargreaves Ltd
AiroGen – vehicle mounted compressors and generators – Factair Ltd
Airoll – semi-automatic truck loading system – Joloda Hydraroll Ltd
Airone – fume cupboards – E X X Projects
Airone – fume cupboards – Safelab Systems Ltd
Aironet – wireless products – Symbol Technologies Ltd
Airpax – Cyclops Electronics Ltd
***AirPinch (U.S.A.)** – pinch valves – The West Group Ltd
AirRide 2000 – Househam Sprayers Ltd
AirRide 2500 – Househam Sprayers Ltd
AirRide 3000 – Househam Sprayers Ltd
AirRide 3600 – Househam Sprayers Ltd
AirRide Trailed 3000 – Househam Sprayers Ltd
AirRide Trailed 4000 – Househam Sprayers Ltd
Airscrew – AMETEK Airscrew Limited
Airscrew 1000 – electronic cooling fans – AMETEK Airscrew Limited
Airscrew 2000 – fans air movement systems – AMETEK Airscrew Limited
Airscrew 3000 – fans axial (cooling) – AMETEK Airscrew Limited
Airscrew 4000 – specialist flexible design axial fans – AMETEK Airscrew Limited
Airsep – air extractor for central heating system – T F C Group
Airspa – Ideal Standard Ltd
Airsprung – spring interior and divan – Airsprung Furniture Group plc
Airsprung Beds and Airsprung & Reclining Figure Device – Airsprung Furniture Group plc
Airsprung Beds Relax Logo – Airsprung Furniture Group plc
Airsprung Super Coil – spring interior and divan – Airsprung Furniture Group plc
Airstep – High quality mens shoes – UK Distributors Footwear Ltd
***Airstream (Italy)** – air compressors – S I P Industrial Products Ltd
Airstrip – linear glazed in ventilator – R W Simon Ltd
Airtec – twin fluid nozzle for cropspraying – Cleanacres Machinery Ltd
Airtec Quality Controller – sprayer controller – Cleanacres Machinery Ltd
Airtowel – hotel bathroom hairdryer – Vectair Systems Ltd
***Airtrol (U.S.A.)** – regulators & switches – The West Group Ltd
Airturbo – compressed air operated safety lamps – Wolf Safety Lamp Company Ltd
Airvert – wheel balance weights, tyre repair materials, skin care products – Airvert
Airwash – bag top cleaner – Fischbein-Saxon
Airwave – warm air dryers – Vectair Systems Ltd
Airwhite – minerals – Viaton Industries Ltd
Aish – electrical contracting – Aish Electro-Mechanical Services
Aisle-master – Stacatruc
AIX – scythe blade – Burgon & Ball Ltd
Ajanta – current – Harlequin
Ajax – chisels – Universal Air Tool Company Ltd
Ajax – Peter Rushton Ltd
Ajax – elevators and conveyors – Ajax Equipment Ltd
Ajax – riot control gloves – Bennett Safetywear
Ajett Anaeorobics – thread locking, returning and sealing – C G P Chemicals Ltd
AJett Cyanoacrylates – engineering & instant adhesives – C G P Chemicals Ltd
Ajover (Darnelwrap) – clingfilm – A B L Perpack 1985 Ltd
AK20 Nobel Aerospace Coatings (United Kingdom) – Aerospace coatings – R D Taylor & Co. Ltd
***Akapp (Netherlands)** – enclosed conductor system – Metreel Ltd
Akcrostab – Akcros Chemicals Ltd
Akemat – machining for grinding saws – Vollmer UK Ltd
Akerman – Harrier Fluid Power Ltd
Akernat – machining for grinding saws – Vollmer UK Ltd
Akhter – computer manufacture – Akhter Computers Ltd
AKO – oils and fats – Aarhuskarlshamn Hull Ltd
***Akron** – Storage silos and fan units – B D C Systems
Akura – UK Office Direct
Akylux – plastic corrugated extruded board, light hygienic containers and packaging solutions. – D S Smith Correx
Akyplen – solid polypropylene board for graphic, display & stationary products. – D S Smith Correx
Akyver – structured polycarbonate for glazing display units, signs and architectural structures. – D S Smith Correx
AL-KO – T M Machinery Sales Ltd
AL-KO – AL-KO Kober Ltd
AL-KO Kober – trailer axles and chassis – AL-KO Kober Ltd
AL'S Feet – Alan James Raddon
Al Verde – wine – Rodney Densem Wines Ltd
AL50 – S G System Products Ltd
AL6000 – Brathalyzer Direct
AL7000 – Brathalyzer Direct
Alag – aggregate – Kerneos Ltd
Alamatic – industrial disc brakes – Alanco Alamatic Ltd
Alan Browne – gauge block-slip gauge calibration – Alan Browne Gauges Ltd
Alan Dale Pumps – water pump and system specialists – Alan Dale Pumps Ltd
Alan James Raddon – designer, shoemaker, reflexologist – Alan James Raddon
Alanco – industrial disc brakes – Alanco Alamatic Ltd
Alasdair Lowe – Lambourne Agricultural Consultants Ltd
Alaska – winter oilseed rape variety – Limagrain UK Ltd
Alba – UK Office Direct
Alba (United Kingdom) – polyester cotton shirt fabric – Carrington Career & Work Wear
Albacom – travelling wave tubes, and amplifiers, high voltage & low voltage power supplies, resonant power supplies, connection systems – Albacom
Albacrete – dense concrete masonary blocks – Brand & Rae
Albalite – ultra lightweight building block – Brand & Rae
Albalite – setting new standards in tableware – Steelite International plc
Albany – rotary gear and centrifugal pumps – Albany Pumps
Albany – Gear Pumps – Robert Craig & Sons Ltd
Albany – blinds – Hillarys Blinds Northern Ltd
Albany plus – brass & chrome wiring accessories – M K Electric Ltd
Albatherm – lightweight building block – Brand & Rae
Albatrose Sea-Air Service – Cromac Smith Ltd
ALBE – tungsten carbide – Albe England Ltd
Albeam – aluminium formwork systems – RMD Kwikform Limited
Albemet – Materion Brush Ltd
***Albenil** – Worming drench, cattle & sheep – Virbac Ltd
Alber – E P C
***Albert Otto (Germany)** – tube milling tools – Brandone Machine Tool Ltd
Alberto Balsam – balsam shampoo and conditioner – Alberto-Culver Co. (UK) Ltd
Albin S.L.P. – stainless steel rotary lobe pumps – Wrightflow Technologies Ltd
Albion – Seating – Bucon Ltd
Albion – paint brushes – Whitaker & Sawyer Brushes Ltd
Albion – sporting goods – Phillips Tuftex Ltd
Albion Chairs – Office Chairs – Stanwell Office Furniture
Albis – plastic compounders – Albis UK Ltd
Albrecht Baumer – foam converting machines – Apropa Machinery Ltd
Albright – DC contactors – Albright International Ltd
ALBROCO – Hydraulic & Offshore Supplies Ltd
***Alcad (Sweden and France)** – industrial nickel cadmium batteries – Alcad
Alcad – Industrial Batteries UK Ltd
Alcantara – marine plywood – Plaut International
Alcatel – high vacuum pumps and plant – AESpump
Alcatel – Direct Voice & Data Ltd
Alchemie – Epoxy, polyurethane and other chemical compounds – Alchemie Ltd
Alchemix – Epoxy, Polyurethane and other chemical compounds – Alchemie Ltd
***Alchemy Fine China** – Churchill China UK Ltd
Alchromate – protective coating for aluminium – P M D UK Ltd
Alco – one fingered mitts – Bennett Safetywear
Alco – ball and needle valves, manifolds, double block twin blok-high performance double block and bleed valves rhino valves-severe service valves, bleed valves, sub sea valves, high pressure valves – Alco Valves
***Alco (Germany)** – refrigeration flow and pressure controls and air conditioning – Emerson Climate Technologies Ltd
Alco – Harrier Fluid Power Ltd
Alcoa Fastening Systems – Specialty Fasteners & Components Ltd
Alcoform – solutions of formaldehyde in alcohols – Synthite Ltd
Alcohawk – Brathalyzer Direct
Alcohols – pure alcohols – Alcohols Ltd
***Alcoluge** – Icework Ltd
Alcomax – Adcutech Ltd
Alcon – Arun Pumps Ltd
Alcontrol – laboratory facilities and chemical-analytical research – Kelda Group
Alcosa – forges – Vaughans Hope Works Ltd
Alcosa – B O B Stevenson Ltd
Alcoseal – foam compound – Angus Fire
Alcosol – Solvents – Alcohols Ltd
***Alcosorb** – B A S F
Alcoswitch – switches – Anglia
Alcryn – Resinex UK Ltd
Alcuma – Vitcas Ltd
Alder – cleaners sink – Armitage Shanks Ltd
Alderley – vertical sliding window – Kawneer UK Ltd
Aldershot Courier Series – Times Review Series Of Newspapers
Aldershot Mail Series – Times Review Series Of Newspapers
Aldershot News Series – Times Review Series Of Newspapers
Aldi – Supply Chain Solution Ltd
Aldona Seals Ltd – seals, rubber to metal bondings, special plastic mouldings – Aldona Seals
ALDONA SEALS LTD – Hydraulic & Offshore Supplies Ltd
Aldrex – mail order catalogue – J D Williams Mail Order Group
Aldridge – milling cutters – Burcas Ltd
Aldridge Print Group – Aldridge Print Group
Aldridge Print Group - APG. – Aldridge Print Group
Aldrissi – interior designers and furniture sales – Albrissi Interiors
Alembicol D – oils – Alembic Foods Ltd
ALENCO – Hydraulic & Offshore Supplies Ltd
***Alenti (Sweden)** – bathing hoist which transports patients from a bed or chair to be toileted or bathed – Arjo Med AB Ltd
Alenya – wine – Rodney Densem Wines Ltd
Aleph – Switches – Aleph Europe Ltd
Alero – 16 seat low access bus – Optare Group Ltd
Alert – Electronic Hearing Protection – Scott International Ltd
Alertmaster – emergency telephone alert system – Storacall Engineering Ltd
Alerton – gas odourant – Atosina UK Ltd
***Alesa (Switzerland)** – HSS-saw blades and cutters – Brunner Machine Tools Ltd
Alex – equipment mounting racks – Nortel Networks UK Ltd
Alex Borlands – glaziers – Hurry Bros Ltd
Alexa – 12v flourescent lighting – Lab Craft Ltd
Alexander Collection, The – internet watch selling company – Identilabel Ltd
Alexander of Scotland – wool fabricators – Smiths Of Peter Head
Alexander Ramage Associates – trade mark attorneys – Alexander Ramage Associates LLP
***Alexanderwerk (Germany)** – compaction and granulating machinery – Orthos Engineering Ltd
Alexandra – concrete kerbs, slabs, paving blocks, decorative paving and traffic calming units – The Alexandra Stone Co.
Alexika (United Kingdom) – translation services – Alexika Ltd
Alexoy – acid resisting bronze and castings – Westley Of Cardiff
***Alfa (Italy)** – garage equipment – Lumatic Ga Ltd
Alfa – L M C Hadrian Ltd
Alfa-A – horse feed – Dengie Crops Ltd
Alfa Acid Clean – dairy chemicals – Delaval
Alfa Blue Plus – dairy chemicals – Delaval
ALFA GOMMA – Hydraulic & Offshore Supplies Ltd
Alfa Laval – pumps – Alfa Laval Eastbourne Ltd
Alfa Laval Agri – agricultural machinery – Delaval
Alfa Laval Saunders – spares & equipment – Bearwood Engineering Supplies
Alfa Plast – farm maintenance – Delaval
Alfa Red – teat dip – Delaval
Alfa Sept Mint – ointment – Delaval
Alfabloc – Poundfield Products Ltd
Alfabloc Walling Systems – Poundfield Products Ltd
Alfafeed – out of parlour feeding system-microchip – Delaval
Alfagamma – Hampshire Hose Services Ltd
Alfaklor – dairy chemicals – Delaval
Alfer – Baxi Group
***Alfi** – Insulated flasks – W M F UK Ltd
Alfinance – financial services – Delaval
Alfing – European Technical Sales Ltd
Alfix – C E S Hire Ltd
Alfoil – PVDC coated PVC for pharm use – Klockner Pentaplast Ltd
Alform – aluminium formwork system – RMD Kwikform Limited
Alfrax – high temperature refractories – Saint Gobain Industrial Ceramics Ltd
Alfred Herbert – CNC lathes and capstans – B S A Machine Tools
Alfred Herbert – Red House Industrial Services Ltd
Alfred Herbert – drilling and tapping machines and spares – Herbert Tooling Ltd
Alfred Herbert Rebuilding Services – CNC re-build experts – Marrill Engineering Co. Ltd
***Algas (Norway)** – filters and thickeners – Pulp & Paper Machinery Ltd
ALGAS SDI – explosion proof vapourisers – H K L Gas Power Ltd
Alger Sanders – suppliers of diamond tip cutting tools – Trylon Ltd
Algon – Anglo Recycling Technology Ltd
Algram – prototype injection moulds, vacuum forming, injection moulding, assembly – Algram Groups
Ali – actuator range – Schneider Electric

Ali Studs – rugby and soccer boot studs – J V M Castings Ltd
Alice Collins – ladies knitwear and casualwear – Alice Collins
Alice Collins Junior – childrens casualwear – Alice Collins
Alice Soundtech – broadcast mixing consoles, broadcasting systems and equipment – Alice Soundtech plc
Aliflex – darts and shafts – Unicorn Products Ltd
Alimaster – aluminium modular shelving – Bedford Shelving Ltd
Alinabal – Mercury Bearings Ltd
Aliscaff Towers – Accesscaff International Ltd
Aliso – aluminium isopropoxide – Rhodia Ltd
Alistage – Accesscaff International Ltd
Alitec – darts and shafts – Unicorn Products Ltd
Alkaphot – water testing tablets – Palintest Ltd
Alkaprufe – plaster primer – Craig & Rose Ltd
Alkavis – water testing tablets – Palintest Ltd
Alki Furniture – The Winnen Furnishing Company
Alkin – high pressure compressors, parts and service – Airware International Ltd
Alko – Mowers – Loxston Garden Machinery
Alkon – processing chemicals for the rubber industry and industrial soaps – Stephenson Group Ltd
Alkorplan – fabricators of flexible water proof membranes, swimming pool, lake and resevoir liners – Aquaflex Ltd
Alkysil – gloss paint – Dacrylate Paints Ltd
All England Lawn Tennis Club – tennis club – The All England Lawn Tennis Club Championships Ltd
All Of Us – catalogues – Littlewoods Home Shopping Orders & Enquiries
All-One – plastic traps – Mcalpine & Company Ltd
***All Optik (Sweden)** – keystone and telebinocular – Warwick Evans Optical Co. Ltd
***All-Round Patent Band (Norway)** – banding for fixing pipes and cables – S A V UK Ltd
All Stars Darts – darts – Unicorn Products Ltd
Allan Dingle – heating engineers – Fleetwood Trawlers Supply Company
Allart – flush bolts – Frank Allart & Co. Ltd
allCLEAR the smarter flowcharter – Process mapping and analysis software – Proquis Ltd
AllClear© – glass and ceramics easy clean and protective coating – Lakes Bathrooms Ltd
Allcosil No 2 – silicone release agent - semi permanent – J Allcock & Sons Ltd
Alldrive Dumper – diesel dumper (4-wheel drive hydraulically controlled tip) – Thwaites Ltd
Allegheny Technologies Ltd – Allegheny Technologies Ltd (ATI)
Allen – keys and key sets – Danaher Tool Group
Allen – visual inspection equipment – Allen Vanguard Ltd
Allen – diesel engines – Rolls-Royce plc
Allen – Harrier Fluid Power Ltd
Allen Bradley – process equipment – Bearwood Engineering Supplies
Allen Davies – C P C Packaging
Allen-Vanguard – Allen Vanguard Ltd
Allen Ygnis Boilers – Twin Industries International Ltd
Allerban – Platt & Hill Ltd
Allermuir – Office Seating – Bucon Ltd
Allermuir Furniture – Capex Office Interiors
Allert (Germany) – hinge frame chains – Oetiker UK Ltd
Allerton – fabrications and overhead cranes – Allerton Steel Ltd
Allerton Mills Collection – bath sets – Melrose Textile Co. Ltd
Allett – horticultural machinery – Allett Mowers
Alleycat – welding generators – S I P Industrial Products Ltd
Allgaier – Incamesh Filtration Ltd
Allglas Ladders – Accesscaff International Ltd
Allgood – architectural ironmongery – Allgood
Alliance – Wealden Tyres Ltd
Alliance – Cyclops Electronics Ltd
ALLIANCE PLASTICS – Hydraulic & Offshore Supplies Ltd
Alliance Semi – M S C Gleichmann UK Ltd
Alliance Sterling – UK Office Direct
Allibin – Linpac Allibert Ltd
***Allied** – grabs – N R C Plant Ltd
***Allied Manufacturing Co (London) Ltd (Germany)** – Allied Manufacturing
Allied Pickfords – Pickfords Ltd
Allied Signal Automotive – turbo charger aftermarket,sales and marketing of turbo chargers – Honeywell
Allied Systems – Harrier Fluid Power Ltd
Allied Vision Technologies – Stemmer Imaging
Alligator – connector for subsea flowlines and risers – Oil States Industries UK Ltd
Alligator – saw grinding machinery for sawmills – Vollmer UK Ltd
Allinson – wholemeal flour – Allied Mills
Allis Chalmer – Team Overseas Ltd
ALLIS CHALMERS – Chaintec Ltd
Allis Chalmers – T V H UK Ltd
Allis Chambe – Harrier Fluid Power Ltd
Allis Mineral Systems – cone crusher – Metso Minerals UK Ltd
Allison – process and control engineers – Allison Engineering Ltd
Allison – Trowell Plant Sales Ltd
ALLISON HYDRAULICS – Hydraulic & Offshore Supplies Ltd
Allison Trans – Harrier Fluid Power Ltd
ALLMAN – Trafalgar Tools
Alloa Advertiser – newspaper – Dunfermline Press
Alloy 171 – Materion Brush Ltd
Alloy 174 – Materion Brush Ltd
Alloy 360 – Materion Brush Ltd
Alloy 60 – Materion Brush Ltd
Alloy 60, Alloy 171, Alloy 174, Toughmet, Moldmax, Protherm, Albemet, Alloy 360, Brush 60, Brush 390, Foramet, Moldmax, Toughmet. – Materion Brush Ltd
Alloy Tower Specials – Accesscaff International Ltd
Alloy Transport Bodies – alloy body panels and GRP bodies – Alloy Bodies Ltd
Alloymaster – Bandsaw – Dynashape Ltd
Allround – cricket and hockey balls – Kookaburra Reader Ltd
ALLS – Hydraulic & Offshore Supplies Ltd
ALLSHRED – Secure Shredding & Recycling – Allshred Ltd
***Allsopp Helikite Ltd** – Allsopp Helikites Ltd
Allspeeds – housemark – Allspeeds Ltd
Allstar Fuel Card – business fuel card – Arval UK Ltd
allthinshome.co.uk – Website – I P C Media Ltd
Alltmor – fishing tackle – Daiwa Sports Ltd
Allvac – Allegheny Technologies Ltd (ATI)
Ally – herbicide – Du Pont UK Ltd
Ally Deck – Accesscaff International Ltd
Allylift – Accesscaff International Ltd
Allytowers – Accesscaff International Ltd
Alma – Obart Pumps Ltd
***Almaco (U.S.A.)** – specialized agricultural equipment for plant breeding and research – Nickerson Bros Ltd
Almag Oil – lubricants – Chevron
Almatec – Air operated diagphram pumps – Axflow
Almatec - Wilden - Waukesha - Blackmer - Borger - Pulsafeeder - Mono - Zenith - ECO - Mouvex - Isochem - Coppus - AxFlow - Hermetic - Wernert - Bungartz - Burton Corblin - Tuthill - Lawrence - Slack & Parr - Carver - Eclipse - Apex – Axflow
Alodine – dairy chemicals – Delaval
Alouette – folding commode – Helping Hand Co.
Alpaca Select – Alpaca Select
Alpasonic SA (France) – ultrasonic cleaning systems – Haesler Machine Tools
Alpen – muesli – Weetabix Ltd
Alpha – 150-500g pp tubs and lids – R P C Containers Ltd
Alpha – fibre bonded carpet/tile – Warlord Contract Carpets Ltd
Alpha – partitioning systems – Service Partitions Ltd
Alpha – Cyclops Electronics Ltd
Alpha – disposable cutlery – Herald Plastics Ltd
Alpha – motor and motorcycle valves, valve guides and bearings – Alpha Bearings
Alpha – Compact kitchen – Anson Concise Ltd
Alpha – industrial gear oils available in a wide range of viscosity grades and a variety of additive packages – Castrol UK Ltd
***Alpha (United Kingdom)** – protective headwear – Helmet Integrated Systems Ltd
Alpha – domestic sinks – Carron Phoenix
Alpha – Expanded pupil stereo microscope – Vision Engineering Ltd
Alpha – Walter GB Ltd
Alpha – Hose and hydraulics – Holmes Hose Ltd
ALPHA – Grundfos Pumps Ltd
ALPHA+ – Grundfos Pumps Ltd
Alpha 2 – Walter GB Ltd
Alpha 20 – timber windows – Premdor Crosby Ltd
Alpha 200 – seating – Audience Systems Ltd
Alpha 22 – Walter GB Ltd
Alpha 4 – Walter GB Ltd
Alpha 4 Plus – Walter GB Ltd
Alpha 4 Plus Micro – Walter GB Ltd
Alpha 4 TFT 8XD – Walter GB Ltd
Alpha 44 – Walter GB Ltd
Alpha-80 – spirit based permanent marker – Industrial Services York Ltd
Alpha Bearings – motor cycle big end bearings – Alpha Bearings
Alpha CMMs – Status Metrology Solutions Ltd
Alpha Cord – fibre bonded carpet/tile – Warlord Contract Carpets Ltd
Alpha-File – document portfolios for schools – Corrugated Plastic Products Ltd
Alpha File, Cyclopak – Corrugated Plastic Products Ltd
Alpha HU-Al – laminated fabrics for thermal insulation – P D Interglas Technologies Ltd
Alpha Laval – European Technical Sales Ltd
Alpha Laval – spares & equipment – Bearwood Engineering Supplies
Alpha Maritex – coated & laminated materials for thermal insulation – P D Interglas Technologies Ltd
Alpha-Mix (United Kingdom) – hi shear & low shear liquid mixers for all industries – Farleygreene
Alpha Plus S – the ultimate electronic centre lathe – T S Harrison & Sons Ltd
Alpha Skimmer – recovery of oils and effluents in calm or sheltered waters – Megator Ltd
Alpha Supplies – industrial wipers & janitorial supplies – Bunzl Cleaning & Hygiene Supplies
Alpha Supplies – distributor of cleaning and hygiene supplies to the UK Away From Home (AFH) market – Bunzl Catering Supplies Ltd
Alpha T – Electronic touch screen lathe. – T S Harrison & Sons Ltd
Alpha Temp – building insulating & vapour barrier materials – P D Interglas Technologies Ltd
Alpha TFT 12XD – Walter GB Ltd
Alpha Therm Ltd – combustion boiler – Alpha Therm Ltd
Alpha U – Manual/Cnc lathe – T S Harrison & Sons Ltd
Alpha Weld – coated fabrics for welding trades – P D Interglas Technologies Ltd
ALPHA2 – Grundfos Pumps Ltd
Alphabet Blocks – signal conditioning instrumentation bulkhead mounting – Lee-Dickens Ltd
Alphabet Writing Desk – talking alphabet desk – Vtech Electronics UK plc
Alphacel – lenticular filter carriage – Flowtech Fluid Handling Ltd
Alphadew – moisture measuring instrument – M C M
AlphaDIN – signal conditioning instrumentation din rail mounting, mains powered – Lee-Dickens Ltd
Alphagage – A-scan thickness meter – Sonatest Ltd
Alphagrass – Synthetic Grass Carpet – Bishop Sports & Leisure Ltd
Alphajet – Walter GB Ltd
Alphalets – self adhesive sign making system – Polydiam Industries
Alphameric 100 – retail software solutions – Openbet Retail
Alphameric Broadcast Solutions – broadcast data networks, multimedia & satellite installation – Openbet Retail
Alphameric Red Onion – projectors, screens – Openbet Retail
Alphameric Solutions – custom made computer products - including keyboards and electronic point of sale – Openbet Retail
Alphameric Technologies – software and consultancy – Openbet Retail
Alphamin – hot melt adhesives – Darent Wax Co.
AlphaMINI – signal conditioning instrumentation din rail mounting, dc powered – Lee-Dickens Ltd
Alphamost – insecticide – Hockley International Ltd
Alphasol – disposable respirators – Alpha Solway Ltd
Alphasyn – industrial gear oils based on synthetic base oils for high performance operation – Castrol UK Ltd
Alphatrail (United Kingdom) – C M D Ltd
Alphi 11 – antifreeze – Fernox
Alphos – dairy chemicals – Delaval
Alpina – canister cleaners – Hoover Ltd
Alpine – Jet Mills – Hosokawa Micron Ltd
Alpine Collection – solid & engineered floors – Wood & Floors Com
***Alpine Westfalia (Germany/Austria)** – tunnelling equipment – Burlington Engineers Ltd
Alplas – range of shelf sales promotional material – Alplus
Alpoco – Aluminium Powder Co. Ltd
Alpro – aluminium and zinc sand/gravity die castings – Aluminium Products Ltd
Alpro – milk recording systems – Delaval
***Alps (Japan)** – meters – Servo & Electronic Sales Ltd
Alps Keiki – panel meters – Servo & Electronic Sales Ltd
ALR 40 – industrial sectional door – Hörmann (UK) Ltd
ALR Vitraplan – industrial sectional door – Hörmann (UK) Ltd
Alreflex 2L2 – thermal insulation membrane vapour barrier – Thermal Economics Ltd
Alrot – rot eradicationand damp proofing – Morris & Spottiswood Ltd
ALS 40 – industrial sectional door – Hörmann (UK) Ltd
Alsa – Harrier Fluid Power Ltd
Alsec – aluminium formwork systems – RMD Kwikform Limited
Alsford Timber – timber merchants – Alsford Timber Ltd
Alshor Plus – aluminium shoring systems – RMD Kwikform Limited
Alsident – Broen Valves Ltd
Alsop – Harrier Fluid Power Ltd
Alspa 8000 – Programmable Logic Controllers – Converteam UK Ltd
Alspa GD4000 – high performance AC drive – Converteam UK Ltd
Alspa MV1000 – variable speed drives – Converteam UK Ltd
Alspa MV3000 – variable speed drives – Converteam UK Ltd

Alspa MV500 – Variable Speed Drivers – Converteam UK Ltd

Alsthorn – Harrier Fluid Power Ltd

Alstom – equipmen/spares – Bearwood Engineering Supplies

Alstone – shower trays – Kohler Mira Ltd

Alta Brescia – Harrier Fluid Power Ltd

Altai – electrical components – Electrovision Group Ltd

Altaroute – variable message road signs – Altaroute Ltd

Altene – trichloroethylene – Atosina UK Ltd

Altera – Cyclops Electronics Ltd

Alterlux – lighting systems – Luxonic Lighting plc

Alterna – cross-head tap – Armitage Shanks Ltd

Altex – anti vibration gloves – Bennett Safetywear

Althea – Althea range from Heidrun Europlastic – Lunex Ltd

Althon – Althon Ltd

Altima Lighting – low voltage lighting systems – Altima Ltd

Altima, Orli, Geni – Altima Ltd

*Altinex (U.S.A.) – computer interfaces, cables & other computer peripherals – A V M Ltd

Altistart – soft starters – Schneider

Altivar – variable speed drive – Schneider

Altivar – Proplas International Ltd

Altivar ATV11 – Proplas International Ltd

Altivar ATV31 – Proplas International Ltd

Altivar ATV61 – Proplas International Ltd

Altivar ATV71 – Proplas International Ltd

Alto – lighting and electrical installation equipment – W F Electrical

Alto – Kranzle UK Ltd

Alto – Cleaning Equipment – Precious Washers Stafford Ltd

Alto – Trafalgar Tools

ALTO – industrial floor cleaning equipment – C S A Cleaning Equipment

Alto – industrial cleaning equipment – B & G Cleaning Systems Ltd

Alto – supply & service copiers, fax's etc – Alto Digital Networks Ltd

Alto – aluminium scaffold towers – Alto Tower Systems

Alto Mineral Oils – mineral oils with anti rust and antioxidant additives – Morris Lubricants

*Alto-Shaam – Equipline

Alto Towers – Accesscaff International Ltd

Alton – Ruxley Manor Garden Centre

Alton – cedar greenhouses – Compton Buildings

Alton – wooden greenhouses – Compton Buildings

Alton Greenhouses – cedar framed greenhouses – Compton Buildings

alton greenhouses robinsons greenhouses – Suppliers of renowned and long established brands such as Alton, Robinsons and Halls Greenhouses – Greenhouse Supply Ltd

Altora – polyester/cotton shoe upper material – J B Broadley

Altrans – acidic metal cleaner – Deb R & D Ltd

Altro – The Winnen Furnishing Company

Altro Flexiwall – acrylic wall & ceiling coating – Altro

*Altro Mipolam (Germany) – pvc flooring – Altro

*Altro Mondo Rubber (Italy) – rubber flooring – Altro

Altro Resin Systems – industrial resin flooring systems – Altro

Altro Resins – We install Altro Resin Systems – Nottingham Industrial Flooring Ltd

Altro safety flooring – slip resistant pvc flooring – Altro

Altro Whiterock cladding – pvc wall & ceiling cladding – Altro

Altrofix – flooring adhesive – Altro

Altrosmooth Concorde – smooth vinyl flooring – Altro

Altura Gloss & Satin – paper – Fenner Paper Co. Ltd

Altymid – high strength Polyimide parts – Greene Tweed & Co. Ltd

AluChef – premier & kitchen quality aluminium foil – Terinex Ltd

AluCurve – C P Cases Ltd

Aludip – hot-dipped aluminium-silicon alloy coated steel – Corus U K Ltd

*Alufix (Germany) – modular fixture system for metrology and aluminium clamping elements – Thame Engineering Co. Ltd

Alufluid – Fluid for aluminium – Tapmatic Engineers' Merchants

Aluglaze – powder crated aluminium panels – Panel Systems Ltd

Alulift – portable aluminium gantry crane – Metreel Ltd

Aluma – refractory cement – Vitcas Ltd

Alumaglass – special blasting media – Wheelabrator Group

Alumasc – guttering and piping – Ashworth

Alumaster – bandsaw – Dynashape Ltd

Alumatic – aluminium recessed access covers and frames – Norinco UK Ltd

Alumec 79 – tooling plate – Alcoa Europe Flat Rolled Products Ltd

Alumec 89 – tooling plate – Alcoa Europe Flat Rolled Products Ltd

Alumec 99 – tooling plate – Alcoa Europe Flat Rolled Products Ltd

Aluminique – aluminium conditioning system – Wrightbus Ltd

Aluminium Beams – Accesscaff International Ltd

aluminium curtain walling – showrooms, hospitals, shopfronts, aluminium windows. – North Aluminium

Aluminium Sulphate – for industrial use – Feralco UK Ltd

Aluminus – Forward Chemicals Ltd

Alumnasc Aluminium – guttering and rainwater pipes – Cembrit Ltd

Alumon D – zincate process – Cookson Electronics Ltd

Alumon EN – zincate process – Cookson Electronics Ltd

ALUP – compressors, parts and service – Airware International Ltd

Alup – Harrier Fluid Power Ltd

Alupro – Hofbauer (UK) Ltd

Alus Chalmers – transformers – Bearwood Engineering Supplies

Alusec – additives for high solids paints – Rhodia Ltd

Alushield – industrial gases – Boc Gases Ltd

Aluval – step ladders & combination ladder – Abru Ltd

AluWeld – C P Cases Ltd

Aluzink (Sweden) – aluzink coated steel sheet – S S A B Swedish Steel Ltd

Alvan Blanch – driers, agricultural industrial and waste materials, product handling equipment, feed milling and mixing machinery, food processing plant, specialist crop processing machinery – Alvan Blanch Development Co. Ltd

Alveolen – continuous cross-linked closed cell polyethylene foam – Sekisui Alveo Ag

Alveolit – continuous cross-linked closed cell polyethylene foam – Sekisui Alveo Ag

Alveolux – batch moulded cross-linked closed cell polyethylene foam – Sekisui Alveo Ag

Alvin – key clamps, animal drinking bowls & troughs – Fisher Alvin Ltd

Alwych – all weather covered flexible books – Reid Printers

AM Tech – Mobile Printers & Kiosk Printers – M-Tech Printers

Ama Drainer – K S B Ltd

Ama Porter – K S B Ltd

Ama Porter ICS – K S B Ltd

AMAACON – AMAACON CENTRE FOR LEARNING AND TRAINING – Amaacon Centre for Management & Marketing Education

Amacast – stainless steel shot – Ervin Amasteel Ltd

Amacast, Amasteel, Amacut, Excalibur, Amamix – Ervin Amasteel Ltd

AMACONEDU – AMAACON CENTRE FOR MANAGEMENT AND MARKETING EDUCATION – Amaacon Centre for Management & Marketing Education

Amada – Amada UK Ltd

Amada – Laser Trader Ltd

Amadausa – Harrier Fluid Power Ltd

Amajet – K S B Ltd

Amakasyn – AMK Drives & Controls Ltd

Amal – spares & equipment – Bearwood Engineering Supplies

Amal – pressure/vacuum valve – Safety Systems UK Ltd

Amalgamated – supply, installation & maintenance of fire detection and emergency lighting – Amalgamated Ltd

Amalgams – Roxspur Measurement & Control Ltd

Amamix – Mixture of steel, shot & grit to customer specification. – Ervin Amasteel Ltd

Amanda Hutson Ltd – Amanda Hutson Ltd

Amarex KRT – K S B Ltd

Amarex N – K S B Ltd

Amasteel – steel abrasives, shot and grit – Ervin Amasteel Ltd

Amaster – Kempston Controls Ltd

Amat – Office Seating – Bucon Ltd

Amateur Gardening – I P C Media Ltd

Amateur Photographer – I P C Media Ltd

Amazing Parties – Themed event providers – Amazing Parties Ltd

Amazon – ironers, folders, bagging machines – Armstrong Commercial Laundry Systems

Amazon 256 Cu – super duplex stainless steel – Columbia Metals Ltd

*Amazone – Ben Burgess Beeston

AMB 90 – polycrystalline CNB cutting tool inserts for the machining of hard ferrous materials – Diamond Detectors

Ambac – Harrier Fluid Power Ltd

*Ambach – Cooking ranges – Exclusive Ranges Ltd

Ambassador – UK Office Direct

Ambassador – roller blind & vertical blind fabrics – Faber Blinds UK Ltd

Ambassador – multi-purpose timber buildings – Browns of Wem Ltd

Ambassador – refrigerated supermarket display cases – Hussmann Refrigeration Ltd

Ambassador – locker – Link Lockers

Ambassador – postcards, diaries, greeting cards, notelets, caldendars and books – J Salmon Ltd

Ambassadors Bloomsbury – Ambassadors Bloomsbury Hotel

*Amber (Poland) – Arctic Paper UK Ltd

Amber 2000 – industrial protective footwear – Amber Safetywear Ltd

Amber Booth – vibration control products – Designed For Sound Ltd

Amber Vehicle Solutions Ltd – Simulation Solutions

Amber Waves – Interface Europe Ltd

Amberlyn – perfume speciality – Quest International UK Ltd

Amberol collection – street furniture – Amberol Ltd

Ambersil – Trafalgar Tools

Amberwood Publishing Ltd – healthcare publications, aromatherapy titles, books on herbs, vitamins and therapies – Amberwood Publishing Ltd

Ambesta Fuel Additives – special oils for running-in petrol and diesel engines – Morris Lubricants

Ambiance – vinyl flooring – Gerflor Ltd

Ambic – manufacturers and suppliers of quality dairy equipment – Ambic Equipment Ltd

Ambiente (Portugal) – cork floor tiles, acrylic sealed; designs and colours in cork – Siesta Cork Tile Co.

*Ambis – radio planar detectors – Lablogic Systems Ltd

Ambisan – speedy hard surface cleaner – Deb R & D Ltd

Ambler – S J Wharton Ltd

AMBORITE – polycrystalline CNB cutting tool inserts for the machining of hard ferrous materials – Diamond Detectors

AMBRAZITE – brazeable form of amborite for smaller tools and special applications – Diamond Detectors

Ambre – ladies and gents comfort casuals – UK Distributors Footwear Ltd

Ambrose Wilson – mail order catalogue – J D Williams Mail Order Group

*Ambrosio (Italy) – handlebars, stems and rims – Rsi

Ambus – Capex Office Interiors

AMC – Harrier Fluid Power Ltd

*Amco – Shelfspan Shelving Systems

AMCO VEBA – Hydraulic & Offshore Supplies Ltd

Amcor – R G K UK Ltd

Amcor – UK Office Direct

Amcor – commercial/domestic appliances – Amcor Ltd

AMCourierServices – Airfreight Carriers and ADR Specialists – AMCourierServices

AMD – Cyclops Electronics Ltd

Amdega – custom built western red cedar conservatories and garden buildings – Amdega Ltd

AMECaL – Gloss – Amecal

Amefa – cutlery – Amefa

AMEISE – Chaintec Ltd

Amenity Bark Mulch – mulch – Melcourt Industries

Ameprene – PureSil Technologies Ltd

Amergy – fuel additives – Ashland UK

America Oil – for oil based liquids – Merlett Plastics UK Ltd

American – tour operator – American Roundup

American Car Wash – car washing and valeting – American Carwash

*American Electrical (U.S.A.) – resistance soldering tools – Welwyn Tool Group Ltd

American Golf Discount Centre – golf retailers – American Golf

American Hoist – Team Overseas Ltd

American-Lincoln – Forresters Pressure Washer Services Ltd

American Parts – Harrier Fluid Power Ltd

*American Pro (U.S.A.) – Jack Sealey Ltd

American Range – Euro Catering Equipment

Americardan Universal Joints – G M B Associates

Ameridrives International – mechanical power transmission products – G M B Associates

Ameriflex – high performance couplings – G M B Associates

Ameriflex Couplings – G M B Associates

Amerigear – standard gear couplings – G M B Associates

Amerigear Couplings and Spindles – G M B Associates

AMEROID – Hydraulic & Offshore Supplies Ltd

Ameron – protective coating – Andrews Coatings Ltd

Amerscan – G E Healthcare

Amerscent – reodorants – Ashland UK

Amersep – flocculants – Ashland UK

Amersham – G E Healthcare

Amersham – Biochrom Ltd

Amersham & Flying A – G E Healthcare

Amersite – oxygen scavengers – Ashland UK

Amertec – G E Healthcare

Ames Precision Hardness Testers (Portable) – Electro Arc Co. Ltd

Amesil – PureSil Technologies Ltd

AMETEK – A global manufacturer of electronic instruments and electromechanical devices. – Lloyd Instruments Ltd

Ametek – Harrier Fluid Power Ltd

Ametek – Alpha Electronics Southern Ltd

Amethyst – luxury motor caravan – Auto Sleepers Ltd

Amey Vectra Ltd – engineering safety and management consultancy services – Vectra Group Ltd

Amguard – B P plc

AMI – Encoders UK

AMI – Shawcity Ltd

AMI-GFV – spares & equipment – Bearwood Engineering Supplies

Amica – leather goods – Modrec International Holdings Ltd

Amicus – Kratos Analytical Ltd

Amiflex – large bore hoses – Holmes Hose Ltd

AMIFLEX LARGE BORE HOSE ASSEMBLIES – Hydraulic & Offshore Supplies Ltd

Amine D – dehydroabietylamine – Hercules Holding Ii Ltd

Amine F,N and X – amine based corrosion inhibitors boiler treatment – Feedwater Ltd

Amine N & X – vapour phase corrosion inhibitor for condensate systems – Feedwater Ltd

Amipaque – G E Healthcare

Amitex – polyester filter fabric – Madison Filter

Amity – moulders & extruders of plastics – Warden Plastics Luton Ltd

AMK – European Technical Sales Ltd

Ammann – A T Wilde & Son Ltd

Ammeraal – process and conveyor belting – Ammeraal Beltech Ltd

Ammeraal Beltech – Conveyor belting – Sprint Engineering & Lubricant

Ammonium Nitrate – fuel oil explosives – E P C UK

Ammox – range of foam cleaners – Agma Ltd

Amopave – geotextile roads – Cordek Ltd

Amore – tufted carpet – Brockway Carpets Ltd

Amorini – current – Harlequin

Amot – spares & equipment – Bearwood Engineering Supplies

Amot – diesel engine safety controls and protection systems, pneumatic controls, electronic systems & instrument control panels – AMOT

*****Amoxinsol** – Pigs, chickens, Ducks and turkeys – Vetoquinol Ltd

*****AMP (U.S.A.)** – connectors – Amelec Ltd

AMP – connectors – Anglia

AMP – Tyco Electronics Ltd

AMP – Therma Group

AMP - Aspera - Bitzer - Bock - Bristol - Carrier - Chrysler - Copeland - Copelametic - Daikin - Danfoss - Dorin - Dunham Bush - Frigipol - Frascold - Frigidaire - Gelphametic - Grasso - Hall APV - Hitachi - Hubbard - Kobe - L'Unite Hermetique - Maneurop - McQuay - Mitsubishi - Prestcold - Refcomp - Sabroe - Tecumseh - Thermoking - Toshiba - Trane - York – Therma Group

AMP of Great Britain – registered trade name of company products – Tyco Electronics Ltd

Ampco – safety tools and copper based alloys – A M P C O Metal Ltd

Ampcoloy – high conductivity copper based alloys – A M P C O Metal Ltd

Ampcotrode – welding wires (MIG.TIG and coated elecrtrodes) – A M P C O Metal Ltd

Amperex – electronic tubes – Richardsons R F P D Ltd

*****Ampex (U.S.A.)** – magnetic tape equipment, for data storage – Ampex Great Britain Ltd

Amphenol – Selectronix Ltd

Amphenol – cable connectors and fibre optics – Amphenol Ltd

Amphenol – Contacts – Dax International Ltd

Amphenol – Connectors – Dax International Ltd

Amphenol – Cyclops Electronics Ltd

Amphenol - Bendix – Connectors – Dax International Ltd

Amphoclens – Forward Chemicals Ltd

Amphoram – amine derivative – Atosina UK Ltd

Ampire – M S C Gleichmann UK Ltd

Amplitaq – PCR product – Roche Diagnostics Ltd

Ampreg 20 – epoxy laminating system – Gurit UK Ltd

Ampreg 22 – epoxy laminating system – Gurit UK Ltd

Ampreg 26 – epoxy laminating system – Gurit UK Ltd

Ampreg Pregel – thixotropic resin additive – Gurit UK Ltd

Ampro – Lamphouse Ltd

Ampro – Hand Tools – Erro Tool Co. Ltd

Amprobe – Alpha Electronics Northern Ltd

Amprobe – Alpha Electronics Southern Ltd

AMRI BUTTERFLY VALVES (United Kingdom) – Ultravalve Ltd

Amstrad – consumer electronics – Amstrad Ltd

AMT – Review Display Systems Ltd

Amtec – threaded inserts for plastics – Bollhoss Fastenings Ltd

Amtech Solder Paste (U.S.A.) – Plimto Ltd

*****Amtex** – Amtex

Amtico – N W Flooring

*****Amtico** – Flooring – The Winnen Furnishing Company

Amtico Company – amtico luxury vinyl tiles – The Amtico Co. Ltd

Amtico Company Ltd – manufacture luxury vinyl floors – The Amtico Co. Ltd

Amtronic – K S B Ltd

Amtru – tools – Tatem Industrial Automation Ltd

AMX – control systems – Medbrook Services Ltd

Amylotex – starch ether – Hercules Holding Ii Ltd

ANACO – Hydraulic & Offshore Supplies Ltd

ANACO DISK SPRINGS – disk springs to DIN 2093, ball bearing disk springs – Spirol Industries Ltd

Anacomp – Formscan Limited

Anacon – thermal conductivity analyser – Systech Instruments Ltd

Anacure – industrial adhesive product range – Chemence Ltd

Anacure, Kwik-Fix, Verbatim, Mitre Mate, Anaseal. – Chemence Ltd

Anadurm – leather dyestuffs – Brenntag Colours Ltd

Anagas – electronic flue gas analyser – Colwick Instruments Ltd

Anaglypta – wall covering – Akzo Nobel Decorative Coatings Ltd

ANALITE – Turbidity probes – Halcyon Solutions

Analog Devices – Cyclops Electronics Ltd

Analyser – battery analyser – P A G Ltd

Anaseal – anaerobic sealants for gas main repair. – Chemence Ltd

Anatec-Pro – Emergi Lite Safety Systems Ltd

Ancamide – curing agents for epoxy resins – Air Products PLC

Ancamine – curing agents for epoxide resins – Air Products PLC

Ancarez – modifiers of epoxy resins – Air Products PLC

Anchor – needlecraft kits – Coats Ltd

Anchor – embroidery fabrics – Coats Ltd

Anchor – embroidery threads – Coats Ltd

Anchor pumps – Anchor Pumps Co. Ltd

Ancit – types of fuel – C P L Distribution

Ancol – dog collars, leads, comb and pet accessories – Ancol Pet Products Ltd

Ancor – wire and wire rope – Webster & Horsfall Ltd

AND LETHEM – Hydraulic & Offshore Supplies Ltd

Anda Crib – precast concrete crib retaining walls – P H I Group Ltd

Andantex – epicyclic gear units and differentials – Andantex Ltd

Andantex – European Technical Sales Ltd

Andean Wineries (Argentina) – Pol Roger Ltd

Anders Kern – Lamphouse Ltd

Anderson – cranes and stone cutting machines – Ladco

*****Anderson (Sweden)** – sanitary fittings in stainless steel, urinals, WCs, washing troughs, baths, mirrors, sluices and drinking fountains – G E C Anderson Ltd

Anderson – felt – Mells Roofing Ltd

Anderson Bradshaw & Co. – Anderson Bradshaw

Anderson Hearn Keene – direct marketing agency – Anderson Hearn Keene Ltd

ANDERSON HUGHES LTD – Hydraulic & Offshore Supplies Ltd

*****Anderson & Vreeland (U.S.A.)** – thermosetting matrix board – Plastotype

Andersons of Shetland – knitwear – Anderson & Co.

Anderton – Cirteq Ltd

Andor – Andor Technology Ltd

*****Andreas Zeller (Romania)** – violins, violas, cellos and double basses – Stentor Music Co. Ltd

ANDREW FRASER – Hydraulic & Offshore Supplies Ltd

Andrew Textiles – industrial synthetic felts – Andrew Webron Ltd

Andrews – Baxi Group

Andrex – UK Office Direct

Andria – eastern WC – Armitage Shanks Ltd

*****Andromat (Germany)** – manipulators – Pearson Panke Ltd

Anemosonic – ultrasonic anemometer – Airflow Developments Ltd

Anemosonic Humidivent Maxivent Miniloovent supervent – Airflow Developments Ltd

Angalok – fishing-angling-locking elbow joint – C B Frost & Co. Ltd

ANGAR – Hydraulic & Offshore Supplies Ltd

*****Angel (Korea, Republic of)** – school percussion instruments – John Hornby Skewes & Co. Ltd

Angel – Procter Machinery Guarding Ltd

Angel Hair – christmas decoration – Palmer Agencies Ltd

Angel Kids – babies, childrenswear and teenage fashions – Shenu Fashions

Angelery – hot water generators, heat exchangers – B S S Pipe Fitting Stockholders Head Office

*****Angelito** – ice cream – Kerry Foods Ltd

*****Anger (Austria)** – high speed cnc milling machines, high speed cnc machining centres – Citizen Machinery UK Ltd

Angle – urinal – Ideal Standard Ltd

Angle Ring – section bending enqineers – The Anglering Company

Anglepoise – lighting products – Anglepoise Ltd

Anglers Mail – I P C Media Ltd

Anglgear – power take off right angle drives – Varatio Holdings plc

Anglgear Industrial Bevel Units – gear boxes – Varatio Holdings plc

Anglia – metal stapling machine – Office Depot UK

Anglia Television – independent television contractor – Anglia Television Ltd

Anglicon – bioreactor control systems, temperature controllers, ph controllers, dissolved oxygen controllers, peristaltic pumps, heaters, thermocouples, RT probes, PH probes, dissolved oxygen probes – Brighton Systems Ltd

Angling Plus – magazine – Emap Ltd

Angling Times – magazine – Emap Ltd

Angling Times Yearbook – Emap Ltd

Anglo – Wigan Timber Ltd

Anglo American Eyewear – spectacle frames, cases, chains and sunglasses – Anglo American Optical

Anglo American Optical – spectacle frames, cases, chains and sunglasses – Anglo American Optical

Anglo-German Translation Services – German & English translation and interpreting service. – Anglo German Business & Finance Translation Services

*****Anglosew (Japan)** – industrial sewing machines and spare parts, cutting machinery, needles and attachments – Anglo American Sewing Machine

*****Anglospeed (Japan)** – industrial sewing machine clutch motors – Anglo American Sewing Machine

Angst+Pfister – European Technical Sales Ltd

Angus – stainless steel sink – Armitage Shanks Ltd

Angus – fire fighting equipment – Angus Fire

Angus – firefighting equipment – Bearwood Engineering Supplies

ANGUS HOSE – Hydraulic & Offshore Supplies Ltd

Angus Wellmaster – Water Rising Main – Mason Price Fluid Solutions Ltd

Anilam – HEIDENHAIN GB LTD

*****Animal Health** – Badcock & Evered

Animal Seats, Benches & Tables – hardwood animal shapes – S M P Playgrounds

Animalintex – veterinary poultice dressing – Robinson Healthcare Ltd

Animals and You – D C Thomson & Co. Ltd

Animo – Coffeetech

*****Animo** – Tudor Tea & Coffee

Ankor Corrosion Preventives – rust proofing treatment – Morris Lubricants

Ann Reeves – garments – Ann Reeves & Co. Ltd

Anna French – co-ordinated furnishing fabrics, wallpapers and lace – Anna French Ltd

Annabelle Classique – carpets - axminster – Brintons Carpets Ltd

Annefield Supplies (Gmc Corsehill Ltd) – Cleaning, Hygiene and Packaging Suppliers – Corsehill Packaging Ltd

Annefield Supplies (Gmc Corsehill Ltd) – Cleaning, Hygiene and Packaging Suppliers – G M C Corsehill

Annith – concrete roof tiles manufacturing machinery – Vortex Hydra UK Ltd

Announce Manager – telephone announcers – Storacall Engineering Ltd

Annubar – liquid level controllers – Emerson Process Management

Anobel – ammonium nitrate and fuel oil explosive – Orica UK Ltd

Anolite – anodising treatments – Metal Finishing Ltd

Anomark – anodising and printing – Alpha Anodising UK Ltd

Anopol – electropolishing processes & cleaning products for stainless steel – Anopol Ltd

Anopril – annonium nitrate – Orica UK Ltd

Anotec – metal finishing, anodising – Colour Anodising Ltd

Another Successful Transaction – Goldenberg Real Estate LLP

Anquamides – water based curing agents for epoxy resins – Air Products PLC

Anquamines – water-based curing agents for epoxy resins – Air Products PLC

Ansaldo – European Drives & Motor Repairs

*****Ansamac (Far East)** – answering machines – Geemarc Telecom S A

Ansamaster – small call sequences – Storacall Engineering Ltd

Anscombe & Ringland – estate agency services; management, rental, property and buildings; financial services, all letting of residential properties, property and buildings; insurance, mortgage and investment services – Chancellors

Ansley – connectors – Anglia

Anson – high pressure valves, swivel joints – Anson

Anson – business systems – Anson Systems Ltd

Anson Hoselifter – hose lifter – Anson

ANSON LTD – Hydraulic & Offshore Supplies Ltd

Anstone – reconstructed stone walling – Forticrete Ltd

Ansul – Kitchen fire suppression – Telegan Protection Ltd

Answer – enterprise resource planning solution for process industry – Kalamazoo - Reynolds Ltd

Antartex – sheepskin coats, leather products and knitwear – Antartex Village

Anteco – consumer products – Yule Catto & Co plc

Antel – protective coating – Andrews Coatings Ltd

Antelope (United Kingdom) – bandfacer on dust extraction unit – R J H Finishing Systems Ltd

Antelope – cafe chair – Race Furniture Ltd

Antennas – Micro-strip – Huber+Suhner (UK) Ltd

Antex – Pyrography tools – The Toolpost

Antex – soldering irons and accessories – Antex Electronics Ltd
Anther – perfume speciality – Quest International UK Ltd
***Anti con Finland (Finland)** – anti-condensation sarking membrane – Alumasc Exterior Building Products
Anti Glarecare – screen filters – Acco UK Ltd
Anti Kaspersky Personal Spam – Tekdata Distribution Ltd
Anti-Luce – truck side and tail board fasteners – Albert Jagger Ltd
Anti Ram Post – Aremco Products
Anti Spam – Tekdata Distribution Ltd
Anti Spam Filter – Tekdata Distribution Ltd
Anti Spam Services – Tekdata Distribution Ltd
Anti Spam Tool – Tekdata Distribution Ltd
Anti Spam Virus – Tekdata Distribution Ltd
Anti Virus and Firewall – Tekdata Distribution Ltd
Anti Virus Protection – Tekdata Distribution Ltd
Anticip – B P plc
Anticip-8 – B P plc
Antiference – TV and radio aerials and communication equipment – Antiference Ltd
Antifoam 86/013 – Basildon Chemical Co. Ltd / KCC
Antifoam 86/013 – Granada Cranes & Handling
Antifoam 96/071 – Granada Cranes & Handling
Antifoam 96/071 – Basildon Chemical Co. Ltd / KCC
Antifoam AP – Basildon Chemical Co. Ltd / KCC
Antifoam AP – Granada Cranes & Handling
Antifoam AR – Granada Cranes & Handling
Antifoam AR – Basildon Chemical Co. Ltd / KCC
Antifoam AR20 – Basildon Chemical Co. Ltd / KCC
Antifoam AR20 – Granada Cranes & Handling
Antifoam AR30 – Granada Cranes & Handling
Antifoam AR30 – Basildon Chemical Co. Ltd / KCC
Antifoam C100 – Basildon Chemical Co. Ltd / KCC
Antifoam C100 – Granada Cranes & Handling
Antifoam C100F – Granada Cranes & Handling
Antifoam C100F – Basildon Chemical Co. Ltd / KCC
Antifoam C100N – Basildon Chemical Co. Ltd / KCC
Antifoam C133 – Basildon Chemical Co. Ltd / KCC
Antifoam C133 – Granada Cranes & Handling
Antifoam E6 – Granada Cranes & Handling
Antifoam E6 – Basildon Chemical Co. Ltd / KCC
Antifoam ED5 – Basildon Chemical Co. Ltd / KCC
Antifoam ED5 – Granada Cranes & Handling
Antifoam FD – Granada Cranes & Handling
Antifoam FD – Basildon Chemical Co. Ltd / KCC
Antifoam FD20P – Basildon Chemical Co. Ltd / KCC
Antifoam FD20P – Granada Cranes & Handling
Antifoam FD30 – Granada Cranes & Handling
Antifoam FD30 – Basildon Chemical Co. Ltd / KCC
Antifoam FD50 – Basildon Chemical Co. Ltd / KCC
Antifoam FD50 – Granada Cranes & Handling
Antifoam FDP – Granada Cranes & Handling
Antifoam FDP – Basildon Chemical Co. Ltd / KCC
Antifoam FG10 – Basildon Chemical Co. Ltd / KCC
Antifoam FG10 – Granada Cranes & Handling
Antifoam FG50 – Granada Cranes & Handling
Antifoam FG50 – Basildon Chemical Co. Ltd / KCC
Antifoan C100N – Granada Cranes & Handling
Antique – luxury bathroom taps – Samuel Heath & Sons plc
Antique – ironwork – Kirkpatrick Ltd
antique furniture restoration, antique restoration, french polish, french polishers – We offer antique furniture restoration, french polish, wood restoration and painting decorating etc. – Colourfast Decorating - French Polish
Antique Pine Shelves – Plaut International
Antiquity – current – Harlequin
Antiquity Pewter – pewter ware – Goldsmiths Jewellers Ltd
Antiscale – beer scale preventative – Murphy & Son
Antisocial Stud – skateboard damage prevention product – Sportsmark Group Ltd
Antistat – Anti-static fabric – Carrington Career & Work Wear
Antivac – anti-syphon valves – Sheardown Engineering Ltd
Antivlam – fire retardant chipboard – Rex Bousfield Ltd
Antler – travel and leather goods – Antler Ltd
Antoinette – WC suite – Armitage Shanks Ltd
Anton Piller – UPS systems – Piller UK Ltd
***Antoni (China and Korea)** – violins and cellos – John Hornby Skewes & Co. Ltd
Antonio Carra – Harrier Fluid Power Ltd
Antron – nylon carpet fibre – Du Pont UK Ltd
Anutex – modelling wax – Kemdent
Anvil R – extreme sports safety gear – Ventura Corporation
Anville Inst – electronic temperature measurement – Anville Instruments
Anvol – fire resistant hydraulic oils – Castrol UK Ltd
Anwest Iwata – Aztech Components Ltd
Anya Larkin – Tektura plc
ANYCAST HIRE – SPECIALIST ANYCAST HIRE DIVISION – Surtees Southern Ltd
Anytec – Aluminium Boats – Wave Seven Marine Ltd
Aoki – Proplas International Ltd
AP Pumps – Alfa Laval Eastbourne Ltd
AP200 Series – UPS power supply – Emerson Network Power Ltd
AP400 Series – UPS power supply – Emerson Network Power Ltd
AP4300 Series – Emerson Network Power Ltd
Apac – associated packaging – Eurohill Traders Ltd
Apache – pipe clamps – Ellis Patents Ltd
Apaseal – tyre repair materials/ equipment – Apaseal Ltd
Apaseal – wheel balance weights – Apaseal Ltd
APD Pumps – AESpump
Apetito – Apetito Ltd
Apex – unique rubber compound food cutting boards – Partwell Cutting Technology Ltd
Apex – – Storage Direct
Apex – Apex Enterprises
APEX – inductive devices – Telcon Ltd
Apex – lighting products – Anglepoise Ltd
Apex Cranes – J Barnsley Cranes Ltd
Apex - Way's with Doorways – Apex Enterprises
Apexx – I M I Cornelius UK Ltd
APG – Aldridge Print Group
API 547 – Severe Duty Motor – Baldor UK
***API Delevan** – Wavelength Electronics Ltd
API Tenza – packing list envelopes book covering film labelling tape self adhesive labels, laminates – Tenza Technologies Ltd
Apico – motor cycle products – Apico International
APICOM – Dynamometers – Dynamometer Services Group Ltd
Apiezon (United Kingdom) – vacuum lubricants and sealants – M & I Materials Ltd
Apiezon – oils waxes and greases – AESpump
Apiezon – adhesives – Bearwood Engineering Supplies
Apiezon - Metrosil - Midel - Wolfmet – M & I Materials Ltd
APITECH – Hydraulic & Offshore Supplies Ltd
Aplha 3 – constant flow air sampling pump – Shawcity Ltd
Apogee – workflow software – Agfa Gevaert
Apolco Skates & Accessories – M V Sport & Leisure Ltd
Apollo – spares & equipment – Bearwood Engineering Supplies
Apollo – franchise window blinds – Luxaflex
***Apollo (Far East)** – casualwear – Remys Ltd
Apollo – Nortech Control Systems Ltd
Apollo – B D K Industrial Products Ltd
APOLLO – Hydraulic & Offshore Supplies Ltd
Apollo (United Kingdom) – sheeters – Atlas Converting
Apollo – intruder detectors – Chubb Electronic Security Ltd
Apollo – infrared detector – Guardall Ltd
***Apollo (U.S.A.)** – non-invasive blood pressure meter – Linton & Co Engineering Ltd
Apollo – Lamphouse Ltd
Apollo – HVLP turbine spraying systems – Bambi Air Compressors Ltd
Apollo – hospital furniture – Hoskins Medical Equipment Ltd
Apollo – architectural facing masonry – Lignacite Ltd
Apollo – solar cells – B P plc
Apollo R.T. – label print and apply system – Weyfringe Labelling Systems
Apollo Series 60 – conventional smoke and heat detectors – Apollo Fire Detectors Ltd
Apollo Sound – music – Apollo Sound
Apollo XP95 – I.S. (BASEEFA) approved analogue addressable – Apollo Fire Detectors Ltd
Apollo XP95 – analogue, addressable smoke and heat detectors – Apollo Fire Detectors Ltd
Apparelmaster – rental service for garments – Johnson Apparel Master Ltd
APPH – precision engineering, landing gear – B B A Aviation plc
Appla Macintosh – Core Tech sell, install, service and repair Appla computers and components. – Core Technical Solutions
***Applause (Korea, Republic of)** – roundback guitars – John Hornby Skewes & Co. Ltd
Appleby – luminaires and adaptable boxes – Electrium Sales Ltd
Appleyard Safety – UK's No1 Lockout Tagout Specialists – Appleyard Locksmith
Applied Clinical Trials – magazine – Advanstar Communications
Applied Enzyme Technology – protein stabilisation systems – University Of Leeds
Applied Holographics – Opsec Security Ltd
Applied Kilovolts – Applied Kilovolts
Applied Magnetic Systems – Magnetic conveyors, magnetic separators and aerosol palletising magnets. Electro permanent magnetic chucks. Pick and place magnets. Specially designed magnetic equipment guaranteed to perform to design specification. – Eclipse Magnetics Ltd
Applied Photophysics – scientific instruments – Applied Photophysics Ltd
Applikator – Kemet International Ltd
Applinal – perfume speciality – Quest International UK Ltd
Appryl – polypropylene (PP) – Atosina UK Ltd
Apra-norm – din panel instrument cases – Perancea Ltd
Apranorm – din panel instrument cases – Perancea Ltd
APT – electrical distribution – Electro Replacement Ltd
APTA – M S C Gleichmann UK Ltd
Aptcard – access control system – Apt Controls Ltd
Aptcard – barrier using card – A P T Controls Ltd
APTEC – manufacture and marketing of textiles and friction materials principally for industrial applications – Aptec Textiles Ltd
Apti – Lamphouse Ltd
Apticote – advanced plating and coating technology – Poeton Gloucester
Apticote, Nedox, Tufram – Poeton Gloucester
Aptkey – barrier using key – A P T Controls Ltd
APV – Petre Process Plant Ltd
AQ Seal – seal designs – Trelleborg Ceiling Solutions Ltd
***Aqata** – Cameo Bathrooms
Aqua – plastic bathroom accessories – Coram Showers Ltd
Aqua-Ban – water elimination tablets – G R Lane Health Products Ltd
Aqua Billboard – water based U.V. screen printing ink – Small Products
Aqua-Clear – water filter for particle, odour and taste removal – Aldous & Stamp Ltd
Aqua Cure – domestic & industrial water treatment equipment – Aqua Cure
Aqua-Dish – drainage covers – Technocover
Aqua-Drain – drainage covers – Technocover
Aqua Legion UK – Aqua Legion UK Ltd
Aqua Paste – aluminium paste for waterborne coatings – Silberline Ltd
Aqua-Safe – waterproof plug and socket – Elkay Electrical Manufacturing Co. Ltd
Aqua -Safe, Conclamp, Conta-Op, Ensto, HPM, Multiplug – Elkay Electrical Manufacturing Co. Ltd
Aqua-Slot – recessed drainage covers – Technocover
Aquabase – external water based decorative coating – Akzo Nobel Packaging Coatings Ltd
Aquabatten – sail batten – Bainbridge Aqua-Marine
AquaBeam – Divex
Aquabelt – gravity belt thickener – Ashbrook Simon Hartley Ltd
Aquabrand – water based floor coating systems – Tor Coatings Ltd
Aquabrome – pool chemicals and water treatment equipment. – Biolab UK Ltd
Aquabutt – plastic rainwater container with lid, tap and diverter – Richard Sankey & Son Ltd
Aquacal 2000 – pure water conductivity calibration system – L T H Electronics Ltd
AquaCEL – sodium carboxymethyl cellulose – Hercules Holding Ii Ltd
Aquachem – protective coating composition – Rotafix Ltd
Aquacoat SP – wood coating – Smith & Roger Ltd
Aquacolor QL – water based screen printing ink for paper and board – Fujifilm Sericol Ltd
Aquacube – a low inclusion pellet binder – Agil Chemicals Products
Aquaculture Equipment Ltd – Fisheries and fish farming equipment – Aquaculture Equipment Ltd
Aquadome – Speed Plastics Ltd
Aquadome; Solar Still; Medimask; Layflat; Supa Support – Speed Plastics Ltd
Aquadose – range of products designed to control mineral disorders in beef and dairy cattle by accurate dosing of the drinking water – Lambson Fine Chemicals Ltd
Aquafast – flange adaptors and couplings for PVC pipe connections – Viking Johnson
Aquafil – British Vita plc
Aquaflex – drinking water hose – Richards Hose Ltd
AquaFLO – polyanionic cellulose – Hercules Holding Ii Ltd
Aquaflow – modular adsorption systems for liquid – Jacobi Carbons
Aquafoil – clothing – Berghaus Ltd
Aquaforce – centrifugal pump – Aqualisa Products Ltd Head Office
Aquafresh – extractor fan – Aqualisa Products Ltd Head Office
Aquafun – outdoor toys – P M S International Group plc
Aquafusion – teacher training courses for exercise in water and related educational resources and equipment swimwear & pool equipment – Professional Fitness & Education
Aquagen – gas fired industrial water heaters – The Aerogen Co. Ltd
Aquagene – high performance hygiene coating system – Tor Coatings Ltd
Aquaglide – flume systems waterslides – Design & Display Structures Ltd
Aquaglide Interactive (United Kingdom) – interactive game system for above – Design & Display Structures Ltd
AquaGrip – flange adaptors for polyethylene pipe – Viking Johnson

Aquagrip – water based adhesive – Bostik Ltd
Aquaguard – B P plc
Aquajack (United Kingdom) – Hydraulically operated subsea bolt tensioner – Hydratight Morpeth
AquaJet – Mechline Developments Ltd
Aquajet – automatic topping up equipment – Chloride Motive Power C M P Batteries Ltd
Aquakeep – superabsorbant polymers – Atosina UK Ltd
Aquakinetic – water repellent fabric processing for marine, vehicle, hardward cover protection – J T Inglis & Sons Ltd
Aqualand – dry suits – Aqualand Ltd
Aqualife – anti graffiti system – Tor Coatings Ltd
Aqualight – shower light – Aqualisa Products Ltd Head Office
Aqualisa – Aqualisa Products Ltd Head Office
Aqualisa – Baxi Group
Aqualon – drinking fountain – Armitage Shanks Ltd
Aqualure – water based internal protective can coating – Akzo Nobel Packaging Coatings Ltd
Aqualux – shower enclosures and screens – Aqualux Products Holdings Ltd
Aquamac – weatherseal for timber window and doors – Schlegel UK
Aquaman – WRAS approved drinking water hose – Richards Hose Ltd
Aquamaster – anti spray vehicle mudflaps – Albert Jagger Ltd
Aquamaster – wetting agent – Scotts Co. Ltd
Aquamatic (U.S.A.) – ppo diaphragm valves – Everyvalve Ltd
Aquametro (Switzerland) – oil and heat meter – Bayham Ltd
Aquamixa – thermostatic shower/bath filler – Aqualisa Products Ltd Head Office
Aquanol – aerosol lubricant, electrical contact cleaner, rust inhibitor and water displacer – Keen World Marketing Ltd
Aquanox – a range of antioxidants for the stabilisation and protection of synthetic and natural water based polymers – Aquaspersions Ltd
Aquantraal 50% DPG – perfume speciality – Quest International UK Ltd
Aquanyl – nylacast 612 – Nylacast
Aquanyl Blue – heat stabilise grade cast nylon – Nylacast
Aquanyl Yellow – marine application grade cast nylon – Nylacast
AquaPAC – polyanionic cellulose – Hercules Holding Ii Ltd
Aquapac – waterproof casings – Aquapac International Ltd
Aquapac – packaged potable water treatment plant – Ovivo UK Ltd
Aquapak – 10-20 litre fold flat polethylene water carrier – Weltonhurst Ltd
Aquapak – pigmented water soluble dispersions – Tennants Inks & Coating Supplies Ltd
Aquapel – alkylketene dimer emulsions – Hercules Holding Ii Ltd
Aquaprint (United Kingdom) – design & type setting business – Sembcorp Bournemouth Water Ltd
AquaPro, – Autoamtic topping – Charger Bay Solutions
Aquapulse – underwater metal detector – Aquascan International Ltd
Aquapulse - underwater metal detector AX2000 - proton magnetometer – Aquascan International Ltd
Aquapure – Harrier Fluid Power Ltd
aquaquell – water filtration for commercial use – Brita Water Filter Systems Ltd
Aquaquest – water analysis spectrophotoniers – Cecil Instruments Ltd
Aquarec – Fistreem International Ltd
Aquarian – thermostatic shower valve – Aqualisa Products Ltd Head Office
Aquarius – low cost double beam spectrophotometers – Cecil Instruments Ltd
Aquarius – range of ten water filters and conditioners – Aldous & Stamp Ltd
Aquarius – water boiler – Marco Beverage Systems Ltd
Aquarius – Pledge Office Chairs Ltd
Aquarius Metals – Metalweb Ltd
Aquaroll – 29 or 40 litre polyethylene water carrier with rubber tyres and detatchable handle for caravanners and camping – F L Hitchman
Aquasan – laboratory water bath bacteriostat tablet – Guest Medical Ltd
AquaSave – wash water recycling system – Mecwash Systems Ltd
Aquasaver – spray mixing taps – Sheardown Engineering Ltd
Aquascutum – clothing and accessories for men and women – Aquascutum Pension Plan
Aquaseal – paramelt
Aquaseal – County Construction Chemicals Ltd
Aquaseat – shower seat – Aqualisa Products Ltd Head Office
Aquasil – chemical treatment for scale and corrosion control – Aldous & Stamp Ltd
Aquasil – aluminium paste for waterborne coatings – Silberline Ltd
Aquaskil – aquatic consultant – C J Skilton Aquarist
Aquasol – waterproof clothing – Alpha Solway Ltd
Aquasol – water based epoxy coating – Conren Ltd
Aquasol – salt for water softening purposes – British Salt Ltd
Aquasolv – Forward Chemicals Ltd
Aquasolv – aqueous metal cleaners – Mykal Industries Ltd
AquaSorb – activated carbons for water treatment. – Jacobi Carbons
***Aquasorb (France)** – water soluble polymers – Hercules Holding Ii Ltd
Aquaspeed Flute FZ – gloss finish water based ink for corrugated board – Fujifilm Sericol Ltd
Aquaspeed Ultra Display AS – water based UV screen printing ink for paper and board – Fujifilm Sericol Ltd
Aquastream – power shower system – Aqualisa Products Ltd Head Office
Aquastyle – electric shower system – Aqualisa Products Ltd Head Office
Aquastyle – bath sets – Melrose Textile Co. Ltd
Aquasystem – piping system, hot & cold heating – George Fischer Sales Ltd
Aquatack – paramelt
Aquatare (United Kingdom) – domestic plumbing & heating – Sembcorp Bournemouth Water Ltd
***Aquatet** – Pharmaq Ltd
Aquatex – lubricants – Chevron
Aquatique – victorian shower system – Aqualisa Products Ltd Head Office
Aquatread – water based floor coating systems – Tor Coatings Ltd
Aquatron – cabinet water stills – Bibby Scientific Ltd
Aquavalve 605 – thermostatic shower valve – Aqualisa Products Ltd Head Office
Aquavap – vapour-phase water based corrosion preventive (solvent free) for protection of internal parts, also testing of pumps, heat exchangers and pressure vessels etc – Vapor Tek Ltd
AquaVend Water Hoses – Mechline Developments Ltd
Aquavex – soft granule for waterborne inks & coatings – Silberline Ltd
Aquavex - Aqua Paste - Aquasil - EternaBrite - Sparkle Silver - Silvet - Silcroma - SilBerCotes – Silberline Ltd
Aquicide – industrial lubricants – B P plc
Aquigrind – industrial lubricants – B P plc
***Aquila (Denmark)** – high pressure washer – Tensid UK Ltd
Aquilon – nebuliser compressors for hospital & domestic use (mains only) – A F P Medical Ltd
Aqvavend – WRC approved drinking water hose – Copely Developments Ltd
AR 5000 – Househam Sprayers Ltd
AR1000 Rheometer – stress testing equipment – Ta Instruments
Aracon – metal clad aramid fibres – Du Pont UK Ltd
Araldite – adhesives – Bearwood Engineering Supplies
Araldite – Bostik Ltd
Aramid – ballistic protection, reinforcement fabrics – Fothergill Engineered Fabrics Ltd
Aran – yarn – Stylecraft
ARB – 4X4 Accessories – G K N Driveline Services Ltd
Arbardeck – Vastern Timber Co. Ltd
Arbeco – threading and knotting machines and paper converting equipment – A B Graphics International Ltd
Arbo – general – Adshead Ratcliffe & Co. Ltd
Arbo – County Construction Chemicals Ltd
Arbo U.B.C. – u.b.c bedding mastic – Adshead Ratcliffe & Co. Ltd
Arbocaulk – water based acrylic sealants – Adshead Ratcliffe & Co. Ltd
Arboflex – non setting glazing compound – Adshead Ratcliffe & Co. Ltd
Arbofoam – single pack polyurethane foam – Adshead Ratcliffe & Co. Ltd
Arbofoam R – single pack polyurethane foam – Adshead Ratcliffe & Co. Ltd
Arbokol – polysulphide rubber sealants – Adshead Ratcliffe & Co. Ltd
Arbolite – putty for wood and metal frames – Adshead Ratcliffe & Co. Ltd
Arbomast – gun grade sealing compounds – Adshead Ratcliffe & Co. Ltd
Arbomast – general purpose and butyl sealant – Adshead Ratcliffe & Co. Ltd
Arbomast – intumescent sealant – Adshead Ratcliffe & Co. Ltd
Arbomast BR – butyl sealant – Adshead Ratcliffe & Co. Ltd
Arbomast GP – gun grade sealing compounds – Adshead Ratcliffe & Co. Ltd
Arbomast Intumescent – intumescent sealant – Adshead Ratcliffe & Co. Ltd
Arbomeric – mspolymer sealants – Adshead Ratcliffe & Co. Ltd
Arbor – Maxa Technologies Ltd
Arbor Compost – soil conditioner – Melcourt Industries
Arbor-Slot – recessed tree grids – Technocover
Arboseal – pre-formed mastic strip – Adshead Ratcliffe & Co. Ltd
Arbosil – silicone sealant – Adshead Ratcliffe & Co. Ltd
Arbostrip – foam tapes – Adshead Ratcliffe & Co. Ltd
Arbothane – polyurethane sealants – Adshead Ratcliffe & Co. Ltd
Arburg – European Technical Sales Ltd
Arburg – Proplas International Ltd
Arburg – Harrier Fluid Power Ltd
Arcaboa – refrigeration – Interlevin Refrigeration Ltd
Arcade – bottom roller gear for glass shop fronts – P C Henderson Ltd
Arcadia – Printed fabrics – Zoffany
Arcadia Pantile – clay – Sandtoft Holdings Ltd
Arcadian – axminster saxony – Victoria Carpets Ltd
Arcasolve – Cleansorb Ltd
Arcasolve Orca – Cleansorb Ltd
Arcato – compressor lubricants for refrigerators – Morris Lubricants
ArcGen – Independent Welding Services Ltd
Arch – tar & bitumen boilers & sprayers – Thomas Coleman Engineering Ltd
Arch Master – preformed arch frame – Simpson Strong-Tie International Inc
archCAD+ – computer aided design software – Cadlogic Ltd
Archdale – Red House Industrial Services Ltd
Archer – tapping attachments, quick change drill chucks and ancillary tooling – Herbert Tooling Ltd
Archer – traffic monitoring systems – Golden River Traffic Ltd
Architect 2000 – computer aided design software – Cadlogic Ltd
Architection – vinyl flooring – Gerflor Ltd
Archive – current – Harlequin
Archive Box – storage box – Acco East Light Ltd
Archive Collection – handprinted wallpapers – Zoffany
Archive Folio – handprinted wallpapers – Zoffany
Archive Imaging – Genus Group
Archive Prints – printed fabric – Zoffany
Archo-Rigidon – corrosion resistant lining materials – Archco Rigidon Ltd
Archway Sheet Metal Works Ltd – Archway Sheet Metal Works Ltd
Arclex – glass bonded mica electrical engineering laminate – Tenmat Ltd
Arcol – polyol – I M C D UK Ltd
Arcolectric Switches PLC – E Preston Electrical Ltd
Arcoroc – Ascot Wholesale Ltd
Arcotronics – capacitors – Anglia
***Arctic (Sweden)** – woodfree coated paper and board – Arctic Paper UK Ltd
Arctic Spray – disposable aerosol pipe freezers – Arctic Products Ltd
Ardac – Money Controls Ltd
Arden – The Winnen Furnishing Company
Arden – N W Flooring
Arden – cycles – Professional Cycle Marketing
Arden Fleet Management – contract hire and leasing – Arden Garages Ltd
Arden Garage Finance – hire purchase finance for motor vehicles – Arden Garages Ltd
Arden Garages – Ford main dealer and self-drive hire – Arden Garages Ltd
Ardenbrite – decorative metallic paint systems – Tor Coatings Ltd
Ardex 25 – mortar admix – Ardex UK Ltd
Ardex aggregate – aggregate – Ardex UK Ltd
Ardex degreaser – degreaser – Ardex UK Ltd
Ardex Neoprene – primer – Ardex UK Ltd
Ardicol D20 – ready for use wall tile adhesive – Ardex UK Ltd
Ardion 100 – admixture to improve screeding, rendering and repair mortar s – Ardex UK Ltd
Ardion 101 – grout admix – Ardex UK Ltd
Ardion 51 – dispersion primer – Ardex UK Ltd
Ardion 82 – primer – Ardex UK Ltd
Ardion 90 – adhesive mortar admix – Ardex UK Ltd
Ardipox WS – epoxide tile adhesive and grout for walls and floors – Ardex UK Ltd
Ardit 300 – fast setting concrete resurfacer – Ardex UK Ltd
Ardit 55 – ultra rapid drying, self levelling sub-floor smoothing compound – Ardex UK Ltd
Ardit 880 – sub floor smoothing and levelling compound – Ardex UK Ltd
Ardit K15 – pumpable self levelling sub floor smoothing compound – Ardex UK Ltd
Ardit K15-B – pumpable smoothing compound base mix – Ardex UK Ltd
Ardit PK150 – pumpable protein free self-levelling sub-floor smoothing compound – Ardex UK Ltd
Ardit SD-T – rapid hardening and drying concrete topping – Ardex UK Ltd
Ardit SD-TB – pumpable sub-floor pre-levelling base mix – Ardex UK Ltd
Ardit Z8 – smoothing compound – Ardex UK Ltd
Arditex – latex based sub floor smoothing compound – Ardex UK Ltd
Arditex RS – latex-based sub-floor smoothing compound – Ardex UK Ltd

Ardu-Flex 5000 – flexible cement-based tile adhesive – Ardex UK Ltd
Ardu-Flex 6000 – rapid setting flexible cement-based tile adhesive – Ardex UK Ltd
Ardu-Flex FL – rapid setting flexible cement-based tile grout – Ardex UK Ltd
Ardu-Flex FS – flexible cement-based tile grout – Ardex UK Ltd
Arducem B2 – fast setting bonding cement – Ardex UK Ltd
Arducem EB2 – rapid setting cement for floor screens – Ardex UK Ltd
Ardurapid 35 – rapid hardening and drying cement for floor screeds – Ardex UK Ltd
Ardurapid 45 – rapid hardening and drying internal repair mortar – Ardex UK Ltd
Ardurit Am100 – rapid hardening one coat tiling render – Ardex UK Ltd
Ardurit C2 – cement-based tile grout for floor and walls – Ardex UK Ltd
Ardurit F4 – cement-based tile grout for walls – Ardex UK Ltd
Ardurit GK – rapid setting tile grout for walls and floors – Ardex UK Ltd
Ardurit S16 – rapid hardening setting and drying tile adhesive – Ardex UK Ltd
Ardurit S21 – rapid setting pourable floor tile bedding mortar – Ardex UK Ltd
Ardurit X7 – versatile tile adhesive for walls and floors – Ardex UK Ltd
ArduritS38 – rapid hardening flexible and pourable floor tile bedding mortar – Ardex UK Ltd
Area Data – consumer information reporting – C A C I
Arel – refractory materials – Robert Lickley Refractries Ltd
***Arelec (France)** – magnets – Magnet Applications Ltd
Arena – Display Wizard Ltd
Arena – Pledge Office Chairs Ltd
Arena Meeting Point – seating and meeting zone for public areas. Canopied semi-circular seats – S M P Playgrounds
Arena Sports System – ball games arena for football, basketball etc in outdoor public spaces, modular system – S M P Playgrounds
Ares Line – Office Seating – Bucon Ltd
***Arex** – Capital Refrigeration Services Ltd
***Arfe** – Burton Safes Ltd
Argent-Architects – Architects – Argent Architects
Argenta – silver furnishers – I M C
Argentina Autentica – Argentina bespoke travel specialists. Tailor-made holidays. – Argentina Autentica Ltd
ARGO – Hydraulic & Offshore Supplies Ltd
ARGO – Harrier Fluid Power Ltd
ARGO ECOTEC – Hydraulic & Offshore Supplies Ltd
ARGO FILTERS – Hydraulic & Offshore Supplies Ltd
Argon Sniffer – Pipestoppers
Argonaut – powder coating – Argonaut Powder Coating Ltd
Argonaut – silver plating process – P M D UK Ltd
Argonaut Armosystems – manufacturers related to the building industry – Argonaut Powder Coating Ltd
Argoneon Limited – Argoneon Ltd
Argoshield – industrial gases – Boc Gases Ltd
Argox – Label Printers & Barcode Scanners – M-Tech Printers
Argus – European Technical Sales Ltd
Argus – thermal imaging camera – E 2 V Technologies Ltd
***Argus (Germany)** – bar code verifier – Romaco Holdings UK Ltd
Argus 55 – motors for use in arduous enviroments. – Brook Crompton UK Ltd
Argweld – Pipestoppers
Argyll Deerstalker – Try & Lilly Ltd
ARI ARMATUREN COMPLETE RANGE INCLUDING 2 PORT, 3 PORT CONTROL VALVES (United Kingdom) – Ultravalve Ltd
Ariabel – cosmetic colourings – Sensient
Ariana – Roodsafe Ltd
Arianex – UK Office Direct
***Arianne (Portugal)** – canister cleaners – Hoover Ltd
Arianor – hair colourings – Sensient
Aric Wardbrooke – temperature contoller for transformers – Foundrometers Instrumentation Ltd
Aridian Waterless – urinal – Armitage Shanks Ltd
Ariel – quilts & pillows – Fogarty Filled Products Ltd
Ariens – Harrier Fluid Power Ltd
Aries – lubricants – Chevron
Aries – Pledge Office Chairs Ltd
Aries Design – contemporary fine art greeting cards – Great British Card Company plc
ARIES ENGINEERING CO. INC 'HYPERCYL' – Hydraulic & Offshore Supplies Ltd
Ariflex – showerhose – Merlett Plastics UK Ltd
ARIFLEX FLEXIBLE TUBES LTD – Hydraulic & Offshore Supplies Ltd
ARINC 404 – Dax International Ltd
ARINC 600 – Dax International Ltd
Aristarco – Traders Coffee Ltd
***Aristarco** – Euro Catering Equipment
Aristo – Applied Cutting Systems Ltd
Aristocat – brushes – Harris Cleaning Services
Aristomat – Applied Cutting Systems Ltd
Ariston – Stacatruc
Arizona – Windfall Brands Ltd
Arizona – rotary dryers – Abru Ltd
Arizona Superelastic – sludge and slurry hose – Merlett Plastics UK Ltd
Arjo – patient handling, bathing and disinfection equipment for use in hospitals, nursing homes and private homes – Arjo Med AB Ltd
Arjo Ambulift Power (United Kingdom) – battery powered patient handling system which lifts patients in and out of bath as well as assisting carers to transport and toilet them – Arjo Med AB Ltd
Arkady – extensive range of dough conditioners in 3 formats: liquid, paste & powder – C S M UK Ltd
Arlington Court – current – Harlequin
Arlon – high performance thermoplastic – Greene Tweed & Co. Ltd
ARLON ATLAS AUTOMATION – Hydraulic & Offshore Supplies Ltd
Arm – M S C Gleichmann UK Ltd
Arm Sangyo – Sebakmt UK Ltd
***Arma (France)** – metal faced bituminous based roofing sheets – Axter Ltd
Arma – Agricultural adjuvant – Interagro UK Ltd
Arma Ware – pottery – H G Stephenson Ltd
Armacoil – Trafalgar Tools
Armada – Belcom Cables Ltd
Armadillo – armoured security units and vaults – Extra Space Industries
Armadillo - armoured security units .Extra Cab - Jack Leg Cabin.Extra Mod - modular building systemTranspak - flat pak transportable system.Extraspan - industrial ware house building – Extra Space Industries
Armaflex – melamine edgebanding – Bauschlinnemann UK
Armaflex – insulation – Tool & Fastener Solutions Ltd
Armaform – plastic profiles extrusions – Bauschlinnemann UK
***Armag (Switzerland)** – profiling heads – Brunner Machine Tools Ltd
Armageddon – games, toys and playthings – Games Workshop Ltd
Armakleen – liquid cleaners – Brotherton Esseco Ltd
ARMANNI – Chaintec Ltd
***Armater (France)** – soil erosion geocell – A G A Group
Armatex – cut resistant clothing – Bennett Safetywear
Armatrim – laminated edgings, wrapping foils, surfacing materials – Bauschlinnemann UK
Armco – Berry Systems
Armet – armour steel welding electrode – Metrode Products Ltd
Armex – cleaning systems – Brotherton Esseco Ltd
Armex - cleaning systems Safegrip - runway de-icer – Brotherton Esseco Ltd
Armid – slip and/or anti blocking agents for polyolefins – Akzo Nobel Chemicals Holdings Ltd
Armillatox – agrochemical – Link-A-Bord Ltd
Armillatox - Link-a-bord – Link-A-Bord Ltd
Armitage Venesta – washroom systems – Armitage Shanks Ltd
Armor – Therma Transfer ribbons – Lancer Labels Ltd
Armor – UK Office Direct
Armor Forensics – Drug Test Kits – Crackdown Drug Testing
***Armorflex** – cable tied concrete block revetment system – A G A Group
***Armorloc** – hand placed interlocking concrete revetment block system – A G A Group
Armorvin – wire reinforced hose – Merlett Plastics UK Ltd
Armoslip – slip and/or anti blocking agents for polyolefins – Akzo Nobel Chemicals Holdings Ltd
Armostat – antistatic agent for polyolefins – Akzo Nobel Chemicals Holdings Ltd
Armour-Knit – cut-resistant clothing – Bennett Safetywear
Armourcote – metal finishing – Surface Technology plc
Armourcrete – British Vita plc
Armourface – gear pumps – Midland Pump Manufacturing Co. Ltd
Armourgard – Accesscaff International Ltd
Armourite – waterway equipment – Angus Fire
Armoursheet – load retention curtains – Lawrence David Ltd
Armowax – processing aid for filled polyolefins – Akzo Nobel Chemicals Holdings Ltd
Armox – range of armour steel plates – Swedish Steel
Armspan – G R P tank covers – Armfibre Ltd
Armstrong – S K Interiors Ltd
ARMSTRONG – Barber Pumps Ltd
Armstrong – Trafalgar Tools
Armstrong (United Kingdom) – ceilings – Scotwood Interiors Ltd
Armstrong – suspended ceiling – Service Partitions Ltd
Armstrong – The Winnen Furnishing Company
Armstrong – Red House Industrial Services Ltd
Armstrong Atlas – industrial fasteners – Caparo Atlas Fastenings Ltd
Armstrongs – The Winnen Furnishing Company
Army Navy – Harrier Fluid Power Ltd
Arne – BS4659 B01 general purpose oil hardening steel – Uddeholm Steel Stockholders
Arneson – propulsion system – M I T Ltd
Arno – Precision Tools
Arno – grooving tooling – Cromwell Group Holdings
***Arno** – carbide – Turner Tools Ltd
Arno Arnold – telescopic springs and concertina covers – M. Buttkereit Ltd
Arnold Barton – greetings cards – Hambledon Studios
Arnold Engineering Plastics – plastic fabrication and machining – Arnold Engineering Plastics Ltd
Arnolfini – contemporary arts centre – Arnolfini
Arnos – UK Office Direct
Aro – fluid handling pumps air operated – Air Power Centre Limited
ARO – European Technical Sales Ltd
Aro – Gustair Materials Handling Equipment Ltd
Aro Corporation – Gustair Materials Handling Equipment Ltd
Aro Hoists – Gustair Materials Handling Equipment Ltd
Aro Pneumatics – Gustair Materials Handling Equipment Ltd
Aro Pumps – Gustair Materials Handling Equipment Ltd
Aro Tools – Gustair Materials Handling Equipment Ltd
Aroma Guard – odour neutralisers – C P L Aromas Ltd
Aromagas – gases – Boc Gases Ltd
Aromat – relays, switches – Panasonic Electric Works
Aromat – Cyclops Electronics Ltd
Aromet – car/truck tyre repair patches, plugs & rubber moulding – Tech Europe
ARON – Hydraulic & Offshore Supplies Ltd
Aron – Hydraulic Component & Systems Ltd
ARON CETOP VALVES – Hydraulic & Offshore Supplies Ltd
Arosta – stainless steel welding electrodes – Lincoln Electric UK Ltd
Arpa – laminates – Rex Bousfield Ltd
Arpal – industrial and commercial cleaning chemicals – R P Adam Ltd
Arpax – anti carbonation masonry coating – Leighs Paints
Arqadia – mountboards and picture frame mouldings – Arqadia Ltd
Arrago – safety spectacle frames – Parmelee Ltd
Arrel Plastics – pvc products – Ariel Plastics Ltd
ARRI – Projects Department Ltd
Arriba! – uncoated paper & board – Howard Smith Paper Ltd
Arrid – anti-perspirant deodorant – Church & Dwight UK Ltd
***Arris** – Euro Catering Equipment
Arriva – safety spectacle frames – Parmelee Ltd
Arriva – public transport – Arriva North West
Arriva Cymru – buses – Arriva North West
ARRIVA Fox County – bus operators – Arriva Midlands North Ltd
Arriva The Shires – bus and coach service – Arriva The Shires & Essex Ltd
ARRM – automatic remote resistance sheath monitoring – Radio Detection
Arroboard – corrugator belts – P & S Textiles Ltd
Arrodrive – polyester conveyor belt – P & S Textiles Ltd
Arrol – medium duty D/T cover and frame – Norinco UK Ltd
Arrolink – polyester belting – P & S Textiles Ltd
Arromex – needle felt – P & S Textiles Ltd
Arropak – polyester packing flannel – P & S Textiles Ltd
Arroproof – polyester silicone coated – P & S Textiles Ltd
Arrow – step ladders – Abru Ltd
Arrow – Gem Tool Hire & Sales Ltd
Arrow – Sebakmt UK Ltd
Arrow – plastic push to lock fastener – Southco Manufacturing Ltd
Arrow – Quarter turn fasteners – Zygology Ltd
Arrow Imaging Limited – arrow imaging – Arrow Imaging Ltd
Arrow Staples – S J Wharton Ltd
Arroweb – polyester needle felt – P & S Textiles Ltd
Arrowsmith Marketing – marketing and eBusiness consultancy – Arrowsmith Marketing Ltd
Arrowtags – identification tag – Hellermann Tyton
Arrt International – Kumi Solutions Ltd
Art Americaine – paper – Paperun Group Of Companies
Art & Craft – monthly magazine – Scholastic School Book Fairs
Art Deco – door, window and electrical furniture – Frank Allart & Co. Ltd
Art of Silk, The – Tie Rack Ltd
Artcam – Delcam plc
Artcare – UK Office Direct
Arte – ladies clothing – Jon Adam
Artec – architectural flourescent systems – Selux UK Ltd
Artemis II – laboratory data handling system – Instem LSS
Artesyn – Cyclops Electronics Ltd
Artesyn – Power supplies & power conversion equipment – Emerson Network Power

Artex – D.I.Y. home improvement products – Artex Ltd
Artfoil – Kitfix Swallow Group Ltd
Artform – paint – Creative Art Products Ltd
Artform – washroom cubicle system – Premdor Crosby Ltd
Artform – gold electroform – Cookson Electronics Ltd
Artguard – art and graphic products – Mcivor Plastics Ltd
Arthur Webb Test Stands – test equipment – Hydrapower Dynamics Ltd
ARTI – Hydraulic & Offshore Supplies Ltd
ARTI INSTRUMENTS – Hydraulic & Offshore Supplies Ltd
***Artic** – Euro Catering Equipment
Artic Extreme – coated paper – Howard Smith Paper Ltd
Artic Matt – coated paper & board – Howard Smith Paper Ltd
Artic Silk – coated paper & board – Howard Smith Paper Ltd
Artic Volume – coated paper & board – Howard Smith Paper Ltd
Artifex (United Kingdom) – s.s metallic hose – Hydrasun Ltd
Artifex – speciality elastic bonded abrasives – Finishing Aids & Tools Ltd
Artificial Grass – Rose Hill Polymers Ltd
Artifort – Office Seating – Bucon Ltd
Artikula – lighting products – Anglepoise Ltd
Artile – ceramic glazed wall tiles decorated with digital images – Johnson Tiles Ltd
ARTIOS – CAD systems – Esko-Graphics
Artis – Ascot Wholesale Ltd
Artis – Worktops – Plasman Laminate Products Ltd
Artisan – potters wheel – Potclays Ltd
Artisan – tungsten carbide products – Artisan Sintered Products Ltd
ARTISON – Chaintec Ltd
Artlights – exhibition and gallery lighting, remote and automatic control – Selux UK Ltd
Artline – UK Office Direct
Artmill – Taegutec UK Ltd
Artoflex – synthetic rubber – Arto Chemicals Ltd
Artoleum Scala (Netherlands) – sheet linoleum – Forbo
Artonyl – nylon – Arto Chemicals Ltd
Artstart – chunky chalks – Creative Art Products Ltd
***Arturo Rossi (Spain)** – ladies shoes and boots – Cheshire Style Ltd
Artwood Collage – Kitfix Swallow Group Ltd
ArtWorks – graphics illustration program – Xara Ltd
Arty – stationery and childrens books – Holland Publishing Ltd
Arven – industrial chemicals – Arven Industrial Chemicals Ltd
Arvex – weavers of technical industrial fabrics – Arville Textiles
Arvis – plummer blocks and bearing housings – Criptic Arvis Ltd
AS-TEC – coating & lamination – William Clark & Sons Ltd
AS400 – Mid Blue International Ltd
AS5 – hardened & tempered boron steel – Wearparts UK Ltd
ASA – auto steering axle trailed sprayer – Cleanacres Machinery Ltd
Asahi – Mercury Bearings Ltd
ASB – Motor Technology Ltd
ASC Finance for Business – Aims Partnership plc
ASCA – Hydraulic & Offshore Supplies Ltd
ASCA JOUCOMATIC – Hydraulic & Offshore Supplies Ltd
Ascent – RMD Kwikform Limited
Aschenbrenner – European Technical Sales Ltd
***Aschrott'sche Gutsverwaltung (Germany)** – German wines – O W Loeb & Co. Ltd
Asco – B L Pneumatics Ltd
ASCO – Asco Numatics
ASCO – Hydraulic & Offshore Supplies Ltd
Asco Joucomatic – solenoid valves, pressure and temperature switches – Asco Numatics
Asco-Joucomatic – Gustair Materials Handling Equipment Ltd
ASCO NUMATIC – Asco Numatics
Asco Process – control valves – Asco Numatics
***Ascot (Taiwan)** – sports shoes – Ascot International Footwear Ltd
Ascot – bath – Ideal Standard Ltd
Ascot – decorators products – Stanley Decorating Products
ASD Norfolk Steel – steel stockholders – A S D
Asda – general stores – Asda Stores Ltd
Asda Brand – general products – Asda Stores Ltd
Asdon – office products, computer and business equipment suppliers – Asdon Group
ASEA – Chaintec Ltd
Asentra – B P plc
Aseptic Sweets – clean rooms – Medical Air Technology Ltd
AsepticSU – single use sterile bag assembly – Watson Marlow Pumps Ltd
ASF thomas – AESpump
Ashbourne Collection – bed linen – Pin Mill Textiles Ltd
Ashbrook – Ashbrook Simon Hartley Ltd
Ashbrook Simon-Hartley – registered Company No. 05259072 – Ashbrook Simon Hartley Ltd
Ashcroft – brand capacitors – M P E Ltd
Ashcroft – thermometers – Bearwood Engineering Supplies
Ashdene (Australia) – tablemats & coasters – Western House
Ashdown – wool blankets – John Horsfall & Sons Ltd
Ashfab – flashings & fabrications for the metal roofing & cladding industry – Ash & Lacy Building Systems Ltd
Ashfield – aluminium impact extrusions – Ashfield Extrusion Ltd
ASHFIELD SPRINGS LTD – Hydraulic & Offshore Supplies Ltd
Ashfix – fasteners and related accessories for the metal roofing & cladding industry – Ash & Lacy Building Systems Ltd
Ashford Adscene – newspaper title – Kent Regional News & Media
Ashford KM Extra – newspaper – Kent Messenger Group Ltd
Ashford Moulding – injection moulding – Plasticom Ltd
Ashgrid – support bar and spacer system for metal roofing & cladding new & refurbishment work – Ash & Lacy Building Systems Ltd
Ashi Japan – Harrier Fluid Power Ltd
Ashjack – flat to pitch roof conversion system – Ash & Lacy Building Systems Ltd
Ashley – wiring accessories – Hager Engineering Ltd
Ashley House – The Winnen Furnishing Company
Ashley Iles – Woodturning and woodworking tools – The Toolpost
Ashley Mill – cleaning cloths, impregnated cleaning cloths and artificial chamois – Lees Newsome Ltd
Ashmond – process control equipment and industrial engravers – Ashmond Electronics Ltd
Ashton – single skinned GRP up and over garage door – P C Henderson Ltd
Ashtons-of-Salford – Pressure and Vacuum Gauges – Valves Instruments Plus Ltd
***Ashursts** – A P B Trading Ltd
Ashzip - Ashtech - Ashfab - Ashflow - Ashgrid - Ashjack - Ashfix. – Ash & Lacy Building Systems Ltd
ASI – M S C Gleichmann UK Ltd
ASIZ – interface between sas software and cas idms – Business & Decision Ltd
Ask – Lamphouse Ltd
Askari (United Kingdom) – buzzers – Fulleon
ASLH – A S L
asm dimatec – sealant application – Bead Technologies Ltd
ASME – Funke
ASME U Stamp – Funke
ASP – Thomas Jacks Ltd
ASP – Bespoke solutions for all antivibration needs – Fibet Rubber Bonding UK Ltd
ASP 40 – industrial sectional door – Hörmann (UK) Ltd
ASP Powder Metallurgy High Speed Tool Steels – Taylor Special Steels Ltd
Aspec – anti static film cleaner – M C D Virtak Ltd
Aspect – M K Electric Ltd
Aspects – ceramic wall & floor tiles – Johnson Tiles Ltd
Aspen Adsim – software products for process engineering – Aspentech Ltd
Aspen Custom Modeler – software products for process engineering – Aspentech Ltd
Aspen Dynamics – software products for process engineering – Aspentech Ltd
Aspen Engineering Suite – software products for process engineering – Aspentech Ltd
Aspen Pinch – software products for process engineering – Aspentech Ltd
Aspen Plus – software products for process engineering – Aspentech Ltd
Aspen RT-Opt – software products for process optimization – Aspentech Ltd
Aspen Split – software products for process engineering – Aspentech Ltd
Aspen Watch – software products for process manufacturing operations – Aspentech Ltd
Aspen Zyqad – software products for process engineering – Aspentech Ltd
Aspera – Therma Group
Aspera – document management software – C H Jones Walsall Ltd
Aspivenin – Safety Assured Ltd
Asplit – chemical resistant coatings – Permatex Protective Coatings UK Ltd
Asquith – Red House Industrial Services Ltd
ASR 40 – industrial sectional door – Hörmann (UK) Ltd
***ASR Servotron** – European Drives & Motor Repairs
ASSA (Sweden) – cylinder, handles, hinges and high security cylinder locks – Assa Abloy Security Solutions
***ASSA Distinction (Portugal)** – door furniture – Assa Abloy Security Solutions
***ASSA Solid (Sweden)** – high security electric strikes, code locks and access control – Assa Abloy Security Solutions
Assab – laboratory furnishings – Morris & Spottiswood Ltd
Assassin – computer software – Associated Knowledge Systems Ltd
Assembly Hall – multi purpose assembly hall lighting – Designplan Lighting Ltd
Assessment Vunerability – Tekdata Distribution Ltd
Asset Collector – fixed asset tracking and recording system – Deaf Alerter plc
Assidoman Packaging UK Limited – corrugated containers – Smurfit Kappa Composites
Assimilate – Redsky It
Assistance International – recovery service – Fortis UK Ltd
Assmann – Desks – Bucon Ltd
Assured Transcription – Digital transcription, audio typing and word processing – Assured Transcription & Typing Services
***Astacon** – antistatic garment fabrics – Carrington Career & Work Wear
Astaroth Solutions – Astaroth Solutions
Astec – Power supplies & power conversion equipment – Emerson Network Power
Astec – Cyclops Electronics Ltd
Asterix – books – Hachette UK Ltd
Astley Court – Carpets-Axminster – Brintons Carpets Ltd
ASTON – Hydraulic & Offshore Supplies Ltd
Aston Martin DB7 – hand built, high performance motor cars – Aston Martin Works
Aston Martin V8 Coupe – hand built, high performance motor cars – Aston Martin Works
Aston Martin V8 Volante Car – hand built, high performance motor cars – Aston Martin Works
Aston Martin Vantage – hand built, high performance motor cars – Aston Martin Works
Astor – paramelt
Astore (Europe, Western) – pvc valves & fittings – Everyvalve Ltd
Astoria – Traders Coffee Ltd
Astoria – bathrooms – The Imperial Bathroom Company Ltd
Astra – polypropelene staple fibres – Drake Extrusion Ltd
Astra – presswork and sheetmetalwork, up to 500T presses, power systems - buss-bar systems, contract assembly - assembly and testing of mechanical and electrical, pneumatic products, toolmaking and machining – Astra Engineering Products Ltd
Astra – dual technology detector – Guardall Ltd
Astra – seat – Armitage Shanks Ltd
Astra-Star – polypropelene staple fibres – Drake Extrusion Ltd
Astra Veic Ind – Harrier Fluid Power Ltd
Astracast – Potter Cowan & Co Belfast Ltd
Astracast – Domestic kitchen sink workcentres – Astracast P.L.C.
Astrafoil – plastic sheeting – D E P
Astral – cast lever on pressed plate – Dortrend International Ltd
Astral (Europe, Western) – pvc valves & fittings – Everyvalve Ltd
Astral – finishes & waxes – F Ball & Co. Ltd
astral hygiene – Cleaning products – Astral Hygiene Ltd
Astralite – rooflights – Stoakes Systems Ltd
Astralux – fire retardant fabrics for use in window blinds – Dearnleys Ltd
Astralux Card – Coated Paper – Mcnaughton James Paper Group Ltd
Astralux Care – Mcnaughton James Paper Group Ltd
Astraroof – roof systems – Stoakes Systems Ltd
Astraseal – double glazing windows, doors, conservatories and glass sealed units – Graham Holmes Astraseal Ltd
Astrawall – curtain walling & structural glazing systems – Stoakes Systems Ltd
AstraZeneca – Astrazeneca
Astrea – educational violin string also for viola, cello and double bass – J P Guivier & Co. Ltd
Astric Dry-Bed – enuresis alarm – Astric Medical
Astro – sports and leisure footwear – D Jacobson & Sons Ltd
Astro – Machine Guard Solutions Ltd
ASTRO BATT (United Kingdom) – fire rated batt – Astroflame Fire Seals Ltd
ASTRO CF DRAINAGE SEAL (United Kingdom) – intumescent drainage seal – Astroflame Fire Seals Ltd
ASTRO CLAD (United Kingdom) – intumescent cladding – Astroflame Fire Seals Ltd
ASTRO COLLAR (United Kingdom) – intumescent pipe sleeve – Astroflame Fire Seals Ltd
ASTRO DL COVER (United Kingdom) – intumescent downlight cover – Astroflame Fire Seals Ltd
ASTRO DUCT WRAP (United Kingdom) – intumescent duct wrap – Astroflame Fire Seals Ltd
ASTRO EJ SEAL (United Kingdom) – intumescent expansion joint seal – Astroflame Fire Seals Ltd
Astro, Falcon, Planet, Bantam – T S Technology
ASTRO FINGERKEEPER COMMERCIAL (United Kingdom) – finger protection device – Astroflame Fire Seals Ltd
ASTRO FINGERKEEPER COMMERCIAL REARGUARD (United Kingdom) – finger protection device – Astroflame Fire Seals Ltd
ASTRO FINGERKEEPER INDUSTRIAL (United Kingdom) – finger protection device – Astroflame Fire Seals Ltd
ASTRO FM COMPOUND (United Kingdom) – fire rated cement/mortar – Astroflame Fire Seals Ltd

ASTRO FR ACOUSTIC FOAM (United Kingdom) – UK fire rated acoustic expanding foam – Astroflame Fire Seals Ltd
ASTRO FR EC FOAM (United Kingdom) – fire rated expanding foam – Astroflame Fire Seals Ltd
ASTRO GRILLE (United Kingdom) – intumescent air transfer grille – Astroflame Fire Seals Ltd
ASTRO LINER (United Kingdom) – intumescent letter box system – Astroflame Fire Seals Ltd
ASTRO LUMI CANOPY (United Kingdom) – fire rated luminaire canopy – Astroflame Fire Seals Ltd
ASTRO LUMI COVER (United Kingdom) – intumescent luminaire cover – Astroflame Fire Seals Ltd
ASTRO MASTIC (United Kingdom) – intumescent acoustic mastic – Astroflame Fire Seals Ltd
ASTRO PILLOW (United Kingdom) – intumescent fire pillow – Astroflame Fire Seals Ltd
ASTRO PROTECTA (United Kingdom) – intumescent hinge and lock protection – Astroflame Fire Seals Ltd
ASTRO PUTTY (United Kingdom) – intumescent putty – Astroflame Fire Seals Ltd
ASTRO SLEEVE (United Kingdom) – intumescent acoustic thermal pipe cover – Astroflame Fire Seals Ltd
ASTRO STRIP BS (United Kingdom) – intumescent door seals – Astroflame Fire Seals Ltd
ASTRO STRIP FO (United Kingdom) – intumescent fire only door seals – Astroflame Fire Seals Ltd
ASTRO STRIP FS (United Kingdom) – intumescent fire & smoke door seals – Astroflame Fire Seals Ltd
ASTRO STRIP SB (United Kingdom) – intumescent door seals – Astroflame Fire Seals Ltd
ASTRO STRIP TB (United Kingdom) – intumescent door seals – Astroflame Fire Seals Ltd
ASTRO TAPE (United Kingdom) – intumescent glazing tape – Astroflame Fire Seals Ltd
ASTRO THERMAL (United Kingdom) – intumescent pipe protection – Astroflame Fire Seals Ltd
ASTRO THERMAL FIRE PS (United Kingdom) – intumescent pipe protection – Astroflame Fire Seals Ltd
ASTRO U CHANNEL (United Kingdom) – intumescent glazing U channel – Astroflame Fire Seals Ltd
ASTRO WRAP (United Kingdom) – intumescent pipe wrap – Astroflame Fire Seals Ltd
Astrofade – National Door Co.
Astron – enamel topcoat – Du Pont UK Ltd
Astronaut Food – Edu-Sci Ltd
Astronaut Foods – Edu-Sci Ltd
Astronaut Ice Cream – Official Astronaut Ice Cream – Edu-Sci Ltd
Astrosyn – electrical rotating components & associated drives & controls – Astrosyn International Technolgy Ltd
***Asuka (Japan)** – lawnmowers spare parts – Danarm Machinery Ltd
Asulox – herbicide to control bracken – Bayer Crop Science
ASV (Europe, Western) – pvc/pp/pvdf valves – Everyvalve Ltd
ASYPOR – highly asymmetrical pore structured membrane filters – Parker Dominic Hunter Ltd
Asys – Biochrom Ltd
AT&T – Cyclops Electronics Ltd
AT150 – Thermo Electrical
AT188 – Thermo Electrical
AT257 – Thermo Electrical
AT557 – Thermo Electrical
AT757 – Thermo Electrical
Ata Abrasives – sander bands, flap wheels, abrasive belts, fan grinders and abrasive caps – A T A Grinding Processes Ltd
ATA Polifan – abrasive flap disc – A T A Grinding Processes Ltd
ATA Scrulok – abrasive quick change fibre discs – A T A Grinding Processes Ltd
Atabands – abrasive bands and holders – A T A Grinding Processes Ltd
Atabrite – polishing disc on quick change system and composite wheel for surface finishing – A T A Grinding Processes Ltd
Atabrushes – rotary wire brushes – A T A Grinding Processes Ltd
Ataburrs – tungsten carbide cutters – A T A Grinding Processes Ltd
Atac – gas separating equipment – Boc Gases Ltd
Atadisc – quick change abrasive surface conditioning and polishing discs – A T A Grinding Processes Ltd
Ataflex – polishing and grinding points – A T A Grinding Processes Ltd
Ataka – bath stain remover and kettle descaler – Laboratory Facilities Ltd
Atapoints – abrasive mounted, grinding points – A T A Grinding Processes Ltd
Atarolls – abrasive cartridge rolls – A T A Grinding Processes Ltd
Atastik – abrasive finishing discs – A T A Grinding Processes Ltd
Atcab Copco – A T Wilde & Son Ltd
Atchison Topeka – warehousing and distribution – Gullivers Sports Travel
Atco Admiral 16 Push – petrol rotary mowers – Bosch Lawn & Garden Ltd
Atco Admiral 16 S. – petrol rotary mowers – Bosch Lawn & Garden Ltd
Atco Admiral 16 S.E. – petrol rotary mowers – Bosch Lawn & Garden Ltd
Atco Balmoral 14 S. – petrol cylinder mower – Bosch Lawn & Garden Ltd
Atco Balmoral 14 S.E. – petrol cylinder mower – Bosch Lawn & Garden Ltd
Atco Balmoral 17 S. – petrol cylinder mower – Bosch Lawn & Garden Ltd
Atco Balmoral 17 S.E. – petrol cylinder mower – Bosch Lawn & Garden Ltd
Atco Balmoral 20 S. – petrol cylinder mower – Bosch Lawn & Garden Ltd
Atco Balmoral 20 S.E. – petrol cylinder mower – Bosch Lawn & Garden Ltd
Atco Club B.20 – petrol cylinder mower – Bosch Lawn & Garden Ltd
Atco Q.X. 10 x Blade Cylinder Cassette – 14in, 17in and 20in cassette – Bosch Lawn & Garden Ltd
Atco Q.X. 5 x blade Cylinder Cassette – 14in electric cassette – Bosch Lawn & Garden Ltd
Atco Q.X. 6 Blade Cylinder Cassette – 14in, 17in and 20in petrol cassette – Bosch Lawn & Garden Ltd
Atco Q.X. Lawn Scarifier Cassette – 14in, 17in and 20in Cassette – Bosch Lawn & Garden Ltd
***Atco Quiet Shredder 1600 (Germany)** – shredder – Bosch Lawn & Garden Ltd
***Atco Quiet Shredder 1800 (Germany)** – shredder – Bosch Lawn & Garden Ltd
***Atco Quiet Shredder 2000 (Germany)** – shredder – Bosch Lawn & Garden Ltd
Atco Royale B.20 E. – petrol cylinder mower – Bosch Lawn & Garden Ltd
Atco Royale B.24 E. – petrol cylinder mower – Bosch Lawn & Garden Ltd
Atco Royale B.24 R. V.C. – petrol cylinder mower – Bosch Lawn & Garden Ltd
Atco Royale B.30 F. – petrol cylinder mower – Bosch Lawn & Garden Ltd
Atco Viscount 19 S. – petrol rotary mowers – Bosch Lawn & Garden Ltd
Atco Viscount 19 S.E. – petrol rotary mowers – Bosch Lawn & Garden Ltd
Atco Windsor 12 S. – electric cylinder lawnmower – Bosch Lawn & Garden Ltd
Atco Windsor 14 S. – electric cylinder lawnmower – Bosch Lawn & Garden Ltd
ATCOMS – air traffic control operations management systems – Bytron
ATD – automated tool dispenser – Kardex Systems UK Ltd
Ateco Access – Access platform enabling work at height. – Ateco Ltd
Atela – B P plc
Ateso – Harrier Fluid Power Ltd
Athena (United Kingdom) – polyester cotton workwear fabric – Carrington Career & Work Wear
Athena LF – inset living flame gas fire – Robinson Willey
Athena RS – balanced flue gas fire – Robinson Willey
Athene – electron microscope grids – Agar Scientific
ATHEY – Harrier Fluid Power Ltd
Athlon – gymnasium lighting – Designplan Lighting Ltd
Athpol – all Athlone products – Athlone Extrusions (UK) Ltd
ATI-Europe Distribution – Allegheny Technologies Ltd (ATI)
ATI-Ladish – Allegheny Technologies Ltd (ATI)
ATI Tank Hire – A T I Tank Hire Ltd
ATIS – computer software for real time analysis phase eddy current inspection of non ferrous condenser/heat exchanger tubing. – Silverwing UK Ltd
Atkin – automated production equipment – Atkin Automation Ltd
Atkin, BHP – coil processing machines – Atkin Automation Ltd
***Atkinsons** – Tradelinens Ltd
Atkinsons All Silk – ties – Richard Atkinson
Atkinsons All Wool – ties – Richard Atkinson
Atkinsons Polyester – ties – Richard Atkinson
Atkinsons Royal Irish Poplin – ties – Richard Atkinson
Atlac – corrosion resistant resins – DSM UK Ltd
***Atlanta (Germany)** – standard driving elements for servo assisted systems, racks and pinions – Andantex Ltd
Atlanta – indoor multi storey car park luminaire – Holophane Europe Ltd
Atlanta – UK Office Direct
Atlantic – conveying systems – Atlantic Rubber Company Ltd
Atlantic – wire and wire rope – Webster & Horsfall Ltd
Atlantic Electric and Gas – electricity & gas supplier – Scottish & Southern Energy P.L.C.
Atlantis – archival supplies & artists materials – Atlantis European Ltd
Atlas – machine sewing threads – William Gee Ltd
Atlas – self propelled cropsprayers – Cleanacres Machinery Ltd
ATLAS – blind threaded inserts – Zygology Ltd
Atlas – automatic fire protection – Tyco Fire & Integrated Solutions
Atlas (United Kingdom) – slitter rewinders – Atlas Converting
Atlas – cable cleat – Ellis Patents Ltd
Atlas – tent pegs – The Hampton Works Ltd
Atlas – Harrier Fluid Power Ltd
Atlas (United Kingdom) – cotton rich workwear fabric – Carrington Career & Work Wear
ATLAS – acetabular cup – Surgicraft Ltd
Atlas – chromatography data systems – Thermo Fisher Scientific
ATLAS AUTOMATION – Hydraulic & Offshore Supplies Ltd
Atlas (Cable Cleat) Emperor (Cable Cleat) Elite (Cable Cleat) Vulcan (Cable Cleat) Vari-Cleat (Cable Cleat) Apache (Pipe Clamps) – Ellis Patents Ltd
Atlas Copco – QAS Generators – Power-Rite UK Ltd
Atlas Copco – construction and mining equipment and compressors – Service Engines Newcastle Ltd
ATLAS COPCO – Hydraulic & Offshore Supplies Ltd
***Atlas Copco (Germany)** – electric & cordless power tools – Harrow Tool Co. Ltd
Atlas Copco – Air Compressors Sales and Service – Atlas Copco Compressors Ltd
Atlas Copco – compressors, parts and service – Airware International Ltd
Atlas Copco – Sandhurst Plant Ltd
Atlas Copco – compressed air equipment – Scot J C B Ltd
Atlas Copco – compressors – Bearwood Engineering Supplies
Atlas Copco – Harrier Fluid Power Ltd
Atlas-Copco – Gustair Materials Handling Equipment Ltd
Atlas Copco – Midland Air Tools Ltd
Atlas Copco – Team Overseas Ltd
Atlas Copco Electric Tools – power tools for industry – Atlas Copco Tools Ltd
***Atlas Solar (Switzerland)** – manufacture solar equipment – Sundwel Solar Ltd
ATLET – Chaintec Ltd
Atlet – Stacatruc
Atlet – T V H UK Ltd
Atlet – Harrier Fluid Power Ltd
Atmel – Cyclops Electronics Ltd
Atmel – M S C Gleichmann UK Ltd
Atocan 16 – Thermo Electrical
Atocan 25 – Thermo Electrical
Atocan Advantage – Thermo Electrical
Atocan Advantage AP – Thermo Electrical
Atomod – atom parts – Spiring Enterprises Ltd
Atonal Heat Transfer Oils – refined mineral oils with heat resisting oxidation inhibitors – Morris Lubricants
Atorn – Premium Quality Brand of Engineering Consumables – Monks & Crane Industrial Group Ltd
ATOS – Hydraulic & Offshore Supplies Ltd
Atos – Harrier Fluid Power Ltd
Atotech – manufacturers of electroplating chemicals – Cannock Chemicals Ltd
Atox – biocide treatment – Aldous & Stamp Ltd
ATP tm – continous tracking technique – Millward Brown
ATP9 Traction Machine – fixed and variable height tables with a variety of accessories – Akron
Atplas – fibre glass reinforced plastic – Torgy Atlantic Engineering
Atracks – Mass Consultants Ltd
Atral, Daitem – Wireless intercom systems – Seamless Aluminium International Ltd
Atriavent – ventilation unit – Powermatic Ltd
Atriflo – kitchen taps – Avilion
Atriloy – metal alloy – Atritor Ltd
Atritor – drying & pulverising machine – Atritor Ltd
Atrixo – handcare products – Lil-lets UK Ltd
Attache – bright white laser/offset paper – Davies Harvey & Murrell
Attagel – thickener – Lawrence Industries Ltd
Attamat – polyester glass laminates – Attwater Group Ltd
Attamex – flexible composite insulations – Attwater Group Ltd
Attamica – micanite products – Attwater Group Ltd
Attane – Resinex UK Ltd
Attaply – flexible composite insulation – Attwater Group Ltd
Attapulgus – clays – Lawrence Industries Ltd
Attasurf – organic surfactant – Lawrence Industries Ltd
Attersall & Rothwell & Deva – Deva Tap Co
***ATV** – Reeth Garage Ltd
Atwood & Morrill – 3 way valves, check valves, wye globe valves, gate valves, atmospheric relief valve, spring relief valve, valve service – Weir Valves & Controls
AUBERT – non-contact optical metrology products of Switzerland – Mapra Technik Co.
AUBURN GEAR – Hydraulic & Offshore Supplies Ltd
Aubusson Prints – Printed fabrics – Zoffany
Aubusson Wallpaper – Wallcovering collection – Zoffany

Audi – L M C Hadrian Ltd

Audio Dopplex – traditional audio only obstetric pocket doppler – Huntleigh Healthcare

Audio Visual – hi-fi choice, home entertainment – Dennis Publishing

AudioFile – disk based editing system – A M S Neve Ltd

Audiotek – Accoustic consultants – Veale Associates Ltd

AudioWorks – audio editing software – Xara Ltd

Audit – ultrasonic thickness gauges – Baugh & Weedon Ltd

Audit – bespoke system for inventory control – R G I S Inventory Specialists

Auditmaster – call generator – Storacall Engineering Ltd

Auditor – portable collection device for data pak and compak – Barcrest Group

AUDUREAU – Chaintec Ltd

Augat – connectors – Anglia

Augat – Cyclops Electronics Ltd

Augener – Stainer & Bell Ltd

Auger Filler 4000 Series – powder filling machine – Riggs Autopack Ltd

Augusta – mens golf trousers & casual shirts – D Gurteen & Sons Ltd

*Augustine (U.S.A.) – guitar strings – John Hornby Skewes & Co. Ltd

Ault & Wiborg – vehicle refinishing paints systems – Permatex Protective Coatings UK Ltd

Aultograph – marking machines and stencils cutting machines – Pyramid Engineering & Manufacturing Co. Ltd

Aultra 2K – vehicle refinish paint – Spies Hecker UK

Aultratuff – commercial vehicle paint – Spies Hecker UK

Aurantion – perfume speciality – Quest International UK Ltd

Auratone – ceiling systems (suspended) – U S G UK Ltd

Aurobond – range of gold plating processes – Cookson Electronics Ltd

Aurocard – Graphic Board – Mcnaughton James Paper Group Ltd

Aurora – Rod Ends, Spherical Bearings – Rota Precision Ltd

Aurora – rucsac – Karrimor Ltd

Aurora – UK Office Direct

Aurora Coat – Sumitomo Electric Hardmetal Ltd

Aurora Conservatories – manufacture and design conservatories – Aurora Conservatories

Ausa – A T Wilde & Son Ltd

AUSA – Chaintec Ltd

Ausa – Border Industrial Services

AUSCO – Hydraulic & Offshore Supplies Ltd

Austen Brush Co – rubberised rotary wire brushes – Scaleaway Tools & Equipment Ltd

Austin – L M C Hadrian Ltd

Austin – vintage cars – British Motor Heritage Ltd

Austin Healey – vintage cars – British Motor Heritage Ltd

Austin Healey – Ashley Competition Exhausts Ltd

Austin Taylor – telecommunications equipment – Austin Taylor Communications

Austin Western – Harrier Fluid Power Ltd

Auto 3000 – auto parts shelving systems – S S I Schaefer Ltd

Auto-air – emergency breathing valve for divers – A P Valves

*Auto-Auger (U.S.A.) – mechanical post hole borer – Drivall Ltd

Auto Bar – pre-packed automotive parts – D L Products Ltd

Auto-Cup – vending in-cup drinks – Chequer Foods Ltd

Auto Imagination – Auto Imagination

Auto Leasing Europa – alliance of European vehicle leasing and management companies – Leaseplan UK Ltd

Auto Magic – B P plc

Auto-Sleeper – luxury motor caravans – Auto Sleepers Ltd

Auto-Sparks – harnesses, automotive wiring systems – Auto Sparks Ltd

Auto-Sprint – Emi-Mec Ltd

Auto-Trace – industrial trace heating systems – Tyco Electronics UK Ltd

Auto Trail – motor homes – Auto Trail V R Ltd

Auto Trust – breakdown warranties – Car Care Plan Ltd

Auto-Veri-Si – moisture measuring instrument – M C M

*Auto Well Safeway (Taiwan) – power vices – Abwood Machine Tools Ltd

Autobar – Autobar Group Ltd

Autobar, Pelican Rouge, King, Veriplast, Cafebar, Fibracan, Mono, James Aimar, Chequen Foods – Autobar Group Ltd

*Autobev – self-service water boiler – Marco Beverage Systems Ltd

Autoblok – European Technical Sales Ltd

Autoblok – S M W Autoblok

Autobomb – Fistreem International Ltd

Autobomb – calorimetry systems – Sanyo Gallenkamp plc

Autobox – short run corrugated box making machinery – Autobox Machinery Ltd

Autobrator – semi-automatic operator controlled, compressed air motivated and tube cleaning equipment – Airnesco Group Ltd

Autobronze – flux impregnated brazing rod – Weldability S I F

AutoClassic – Dometic UK Ltd

Autoclave (U.S.A.) – ultra high pressure tube, fittings and valves – Hydrasun Ltd

Autoclave, Firegard, I.V.G, Manuli, Offshore 850, Parker Hannifin, Seco, Snaptite, Synflex, Firemaster, Ponsloc. Action, Artifex, Bourdon Sedeme, Gates, ITR SPA, Jaymac, McDonald, Norgren, Oglaend, RSB, Polyflex, Titeflex, Tungum, Wade – Hydrasun Ltd

Autoclean – sample tube washer – Broker Ltd

Autoclenz – consumer products – Yule Catto & Co plc

Autoclimb – hydraulic self climbing formwork system – RMD Kwikform Limited

Autoclude – peristaltic pumps – Victor Marine

Autocone – stone crushers, pumps, crushers and vibrating screens, scalping screens and grizzly feeders – Terex

Autocraft Industries UK – automotive component – Autocraft Drivetrain Solutions Ltd

Autofast – envelopes – Eagle Envelopes Ltd

Autofeed – Hydrafeed Ltd

Autofil – automatic topping up equipment – Chloride Motive Power C M P Batteries Ltd

Autofilm – gravure resist films – Macdermid Autotype Ltd

Autofin (United Kingdom) – heavy duty automatic industrial grinding and polishing machines – R J H Finishing Systems Ltd

Autoflex – couplings – British Autogard Ltd

Autoflex – flexible crash doors, strip PVC curtains and rapid rise doors – Neway Doors Ltd

Autoflex IMD – hard coated films for IMD applications – Macdermid Autotype Ltd

Autoframe – sign material for aluminium posts – Bribex

Autofreway – horizontal pumps – Tuke & Bell Ltd

Autogard – torque limiters – British Autogard Ltd

Autogas – Calor Gas Ltd

Autogil – Hanbury Autogil

Autogil – Hanbury Autogil

Autoheat – greenhouse fan heater, parts and service – Findlay Irvine

Autokool – air conditioning service tools – R.J. Doran & Co. Ltd

Autoland – Autoland Ltd

Autolane – high speed pop up bollard for highways – Apt Controls Ltd

Autolec – electric steam boilers – Ormandy Rycroft

Autolift (United Kingdom) – mechanically operated bath lift for elderly and disabled persons – Arjo Med AB Ltd

Autoloader – automatic vehicle loading boom conveyor – Newland Engineering Co. Ltd

Autolock – shaft lock – Bruntons Propellers Ltd

Autologic – Vehicle diagnostics computer – Autologic Diagnostics

Autolok – car security device – Autolok Security

Autolok 2000 – steering wheel lock – Autolok Security

Autolok Driveshield – lockable, collapsible post – Autolok Security

Autolok Original – handbrake to gearstick lock – Autolok Security

Autolok protector – handbrake to gearstick lock – Autolok Security

Automa – small piece folders – Armstrong Commercial Laundry Systems

Automask – masking films for printing industry – Macdermid Autotype Ltd

Automate – mechanical indexing gearbox – Estuary Automation Ltd

Automate Major – mechanical indexing gearbox – Estuary Automation Ltd

Automate Super – mechanical indexing gearbox – Estuary Automation Ltd

Automatic I.D. News Europe – magazine – Advanstar Communications

Automatic Liquid Filling Systems – liquid filling machine – Riggs Autopack Ltd

Automatic Pick and Place Machines – flex4 – Elite Engineering Ltd

Automatic Rotary Filling Machine 3000 Series – rotary filling machine – Riggs Autopack Ltd

Automatic 'S' Mat – filter – Waterloo Air Products

Automation control manufrs – Crouzet Ltd

Automation Equipment – di-humidifiers – A B Precision Poole Ltd

Automation Technology – solutions for industry – Robert Bosch Ltd

Automax – stone crushers etc – Terex

Automech 3 – zone 1 and 2 diesel flameproofing – Pyroban

Automist – mist propagation for horticulture – Access Irrigation Ltd

Automite – pneumatic indexing gearbox – Estuary Automation Ltd

Automotive – aftermarket and service – Robert Bosch Ltd

Automotive Emission Control Carbons – Norit UK Ltd

Automotive Floor Systems – car carpets and heatshields – Rieter Automotive Great Britain Ltd

Automotor – materials handling systems – Fata Automation Ltd

*Autonics (Korea, Republic of) – controls – Tempatron Controls

Autopack – weighing and packing machines – Riggs Autopack Ltd

Autophoretic Paint Plant – A B T Products Ltd

*Autoplus (Italy) – mig welders – S I P Industrial Products Ltd

Autoprime – range of contractor pumps – S P P Pumps

Autoproducts – disposable services protection products – Autoproducts

Autoprop – propeller – Bruntons Propellers Ltd

Autopulit – bright polishing, brushing & graining machines for flat & shaped components. – Ellesco Ltd

Autosafe – car and truck mirrors and replacement glass kits – Thames Valley Pressings Ltd

Autosan – auto urinal/wc sanitizing system – Vectair Systems Ltd

AUTOSAN – H & H Commercial Truck Services Ltd

Autosand – stone crushers etc – Terex

Autoscan – Computerised used car valuation system – Kalamazoo - Reynolds Ltd

Autoscript – television prompting – Autoscript Ltd

AutoSeal – casting impregnation system – Mecwash Systems Ltd

AutoSec – high security revolving door – Gunnebo Entrance Control Ltd

Autoset – B P plc

Autoset (Production) (United Kingdom) – ball transfer units – Omnitrack Ltd

Autosheen – Forward Chemicals Ltd

Autosol – Cleaning and polishing products – Erro Tool Co. Ltd

Autosol – S J Wharton Ltd

AutoSpec (United Kingdom) – Sector mass spectrometer (GC-MS) – Waters

Autospin – Oil seals – Autospin (Oil Seals) Ltd

Autospot – spot welding guns – Sureweld UK Ltd

Autostack – flexible moving wall systems for dividing large areas – Union Industries

AUTOSTAR – Hydraulic & Offshore Supplies Ltd

Autostat – heat stabilized polyester – Macdermid Autotype Ltd

Autostat – analytical test for detecting auto antibodies in human – Hycor Biomedical Ltd

Autoswabbing – automatic lubrication of blank moulds on is machines – Graphoidal Developments

AutoTest - FastStart - Emergipack - TwinStart - Q Start - Smart Start - UniStart – Mackwell Electronics Ltd

Autotex – textured polyester – Macdermid Autotype Ltd

Autothane – microcellular polyurethane elastomer for impact, shock, vibration automotive – Dow Hyperlast

Autothane & Autothane Logo – British Vita plc

Autotint – aerosol paints and lacquers – Tetrosyl

Autotrack (Birmingham) (United Kingdom) – ball transfer units – Omnitrack Ltd

Autotrans – automatic work transporter unit – Guyson International Ltd

Autotutor – basic driver trainer – Simtech Simulation Techniques

Autovac – vacuum control unit – Heimbach UK

Autoval – principle automotive cleaning products – Quadralene Ltd

*Autoview 200 (Ireland) – keyboard video mouse PC Server switches – Techland Group Ltd

*Autoview Commander (U.S.A.) – keyboard video mouse multi PC-server switches – Techland Group Ltd

Autran – industrial lubricants – B P plc

Autronex – alloy acid gold electroplating processes – Cookson Electronics Ltd

Autumn Sun – bread mixes – E D M E Ltd

Auximax – servo-assisted pilot valves – Parker Hannifin Ltd

AV PNEUMATICS – Hydraulic & Offshore Supplies Ltd

Avac – Voice alarm system – C-Tec Security Ltd

Avada – B P plc

AVALCO – Hydraulic & Offshore Supplies Ltd

Avalon – Uncoated Paper – Mcnaughton James Paper Group Ltd

Avalon – comedy promotions – Avalon P R Ltd

Avalon and Lynwood – Avalon and Lynwood

Avalon Management Group Ltd – talent management – Avalon P R Ltd

Avalon Press & Publicity – publicity services – Avalon P R Ltd

Avalon Television Ltd – TV production – Avalon P R Ltd

Avalone M – perfume speciality – Quest International UK Ltd

Avancia – office furniture – Quantum Industries Ltd

Avant – digital film console – Red Lion 49 Ltd

Avante – shaft clamping elements – Cross & Morse

Avante – software system – Epicor Software UK Ltd

Avanti – Lusso Interiors

Avanti Eclipse – Lusso Interiors

Avanti Eclipse Plus – Lusso Interiors

Avanti Elite – Lusso Interiors

Avanti Fireshield – Lusso Interiors

Avanti Glass Doors – Lusso Interiors

Avanti Legno – Lusso Interiors

Avanti Matrix – Lusso Interiors

Avanti Solare – Lusso Interiors

Avanti Unity – Lusso Interiors

Avantra – imagesetters – Agfa Gevaert

Avaya – Telephone System – Alecto Solutions Ltd

Avaya – IP Office Business Communications, Installation, Support Services – CCV Telecom

AVAYA – Direct Voice & Data Ltd

Avaya Communications – Direct Voice & Data Ltd

Avaya Telephone Systems – Direct Voice & Data Ltd

Avbolt – a blind fastener with the strength of a bolt – Avdel UK Ltd

Avdel – blind rivet systems – Zygology Ltd

Avdel – Gustair Materials Handling Equipment Ltd

Avdel - Avdelok - Avex - Avibulb - Avinox - Avbolt - Avlug - Avmatic - Avseal - Briv - Bulbex - Chobert - Grovit - Hemlok - Hydra - Jo-Bolt - Jo-Lok - Maxlok - M B C - Monobolt - Stavex - Nutsert - Pip Pin - T-Lok - Rivscrew - TX2000 - Hexsert - Klamptite – Avdel UK Ltd

Avdel SR – sealed breakstem fastener – Avdel UK Ltd

Avdelok – high strength vibration resistant bolt type fastener – Avdel UK Ltd

Avdelok – structural rivet system – Zygology Ltd

Avec – hair cosmetics – Salon Services Hair & Beauty Supplies Ltd

AVELAIR – Hydraulic & Offshore Supplies Ltd

Aveling Bar – Harrier Fluid Power Ltd

Aveling Barford – Trowell Plant Sales Ltd

Avery – Anubis Label Technology Ltd

Avery – UK Office Direct

Avery Dennison – B D K Industrial Products Ltd

Avery Labels – Anubis Label Technology Ltd

Avex – blind rivets – Zygology Ltd

Avex – versatile multi-grip breakstem rivet – Avdel UK Ltd

Avey – D T L Broadcast Ltd

Aviator – optical frames and sunglasses – Hilton International Eye Wear Ltd

Avibulb – high strength blind breakstem fastener for thin sheet materials – Avdel UK Ltd

Avibulb – blind rivet for strong joints in thin materials – Zygology Ltd

Avica Products – rigid and flexible metallic ducting systems for aerospace – Meggitt Control Systems

AVIMID – polymide composite – Cytec Engineered Materials Ltd

Avinox – stainless steel versatile breakstem rivet – Avdel UK Ltd

Avinox – stainless steel blind rivets – Zygology Ltd

Avio – Lamphouse Ltd

Avision – Genus Group

Avitex – surface active agents/softeners/static control agents – Du Pont UK Ltd

Avitone – softener/dyeing assistants – Du Pont UK Ltd

AVL Zollner – Dynamometers – Dynamometer Services Group Ltd

Avlug – terminal posts – Zygology Ltd

Avlug – terminal posts – Avdel UK Ltd

Avmatic – automatic feed, breakstem fastener tool – Avdel UK Ltd

Avo – Alpha Electronics Northern Ltd

AVO – analogue and digital multimeters – Megger Ltd

Avo – Alpha Electronics Southern Ltd

Avoca – wart & verruca treatment – Bray Group Ltd

Avocet Hardware (Pacific Rim) – design, development and procurement of architectural ironmongery for use on doors and window and its sale and distribution – Avercet Hardware Ltd

Avometer - analogue digital multimeters Megger - electrical testing instruments, telecomms testing instruments Foster - high voltage and heavy current test equipment Ducter - low resistance ohmmeters Biddle - high voltage and cable fault location equipmen – Megger Ltd

Avon – non-con tap – Armitage Shanks Ltd

Avon – Wealden Tyres Ltd

Avon – medium duty rectangular side hinged grating and frame – Norinco UK Ltd

Avon – aero engines – Rolls-Royce plc

Avon Impact Management – Manufacturer of rubber extruded products including speed ramps, chocks... – Avon Impact Management

Avondale – Red House Industrial Services Ltd

Avonmeter – analogue digital multimeters – Megger Ltd

Avonride – axle and suspension systems for trailed vehicles – Knott-Avonride Ltd

Avoplaten – Crosland Laser Guarding Ltd

Avrolux – paper – Fenner Paper Co. Ltd

AVS Valves Ltd – distribution of valves – Bonomi UK Ltd

Avseal – plug for sealing redundant holes – Avdel UK Ltd

Avseal – sealing plug – Zygology Ltd

Avsert – stand-off pillar – Zygology Ltd

Avsert – versatile stand-off pillar – Avdel UK Ltd

Avtainer – low profile headed bolt for joining composite materials – Avdel UK Ltd

Avtainer – strong assembly of composite materials – Zygology Ltd

Avtronic – speed rivet system – Zygology Ltd

Avtronic – high speed fastener for joining edge and DIN connectors to printed circuit boards – Avdel UK Ltd

Avventura – incentive travel, conferences and corporate events – Avventura

AVX – Cyclops Electronics Ltd

Awac – Wholesale Welding Supplies Ltd

AWARD – projected display systems – Thales Training & Consultancy

Award Toolmakers – Wax injection tooling – Mckenna Group Ltd

AWEK – Linear & Radial Metal Trip Dogs, Rails & Drums – Francis and Francis Ltd

AWEK NORD – Trip Dogs, Rails & Drums – Francis and Francis Ltd

AWEK NORD – Francis and Francis Ltd

AWT Range Actuator – Electric multi-turn actuator – Rotork plc

*Awuko (Germany) – coated abrasive wide belts – Naylors Abrasives

AX05 boron nitride – Precision Ceramics

AX2000 – proton magnetometer – Aquascan International Ltd

Axa – European Technical Sales Ltd

Axair – Axair Fans UK Ltd

Axal – demountable ceiling tiles – Armstrong World Industries Ltd

Axcent 2 – low noise mixed-flow fans – Flakt Woods Ltd

Axcess – side opening tambour filing cabinets – Rackline Ltd

Axess – linking, stacking and multi-purpose chairs – Stage Systems Ltd

Axflow – metering and proportioning systems – Axflow

Axholme Herald, The – newspaper – Grimsby Telegraph

AXIAL PUMP SPA – Hydraulic & Offshore Supplies Ltd

Axico – variable pitch-in-motion fans – Flakt Woods Ltd

Axiflo 6000 (United Kingdom) – low nox burners – Hamworthy Combustion Engineering Ltd

Axijet – fans for tunnel ventillation – Flakt Woods Ltd

AXIM – Redsky lt

Axima – Kratos Analytical Ltd

*Aximaster (U.S.A.) – brushless digital servo and motion controller – European Drives & Motor Repairs

Axiom – digital production console – Red Lion 49 Ltd

Axiom – adjuvant oils – B P plc

Axiom – Thermo Electrical

Axiom-MT – digital multi - track consule – Red Lion 49 Ltd

Axiom SP&N – consumer unit – Schneider

Axis – Kratos Analytical Ltd

Axminster Power Tools – Woodturning accessories and chucks – The Toolpost

AXO Shredders Ltd – Manufacturers of mobile and stationary shredding machines for the confidential destruction, waste re – Axo Shredders Ltd

*Axona (Sweden) – glass sided pool provides ideal environment for treating patients who require hydrotherapy and rehabilitation – Arjo Med AB Ltd

*Axopatch (U.S.A.) – patch clamp amplifiers – Linton & Co Engineering Ltd

Axor – Motor Technology Ltd

Axseal – heavy duty truck and trailer seals – Pioneer Weston

*Axtep (France) – roof walkway system – Axter Ltd

Axus – axial fan – Nuaire Ltd

Aylesbury Float Valves – Keraflo Ltd

Aylesbury K type float valve – Keraflo Ltd

Aylesbury KAX float valve – Keraflo Ltd

Aylesbury KB float valve – Keraflo Ltd

Aylesbury KP float valve – Keraflo Ltd

Aylesbury Valves – Keraflo Ltd

Aynsley – fine bone china tableware and giftware – Aynsley China Ltd

Ayreid – precision hydraulic & mechanical work holding equipment – Acugrip Ltd

AyreidOmnigauge – Acugrip Ltd

Aysis Air – digital broadcast mixer – Red Lion 49 Ltd

Ayton Fabrication – pipe and steelwork fabrications – Pruce Newman Pipework Ltd

Ayton Fabrications – Pruce Newman Pipework Ltd

AZ – air operated high pressure pumps – Hydratron Ltd

Azarbre – perfume speciality – Quest International UK Ltd

Azatin – purified neem extract – Agrisense B C S Ltd

Azatin Align, Neemix – purified neem extract (azadirachtin) – Agrisense B C S Ltd

Azelis - Pioner Salt - Scansmoke - Sweetmaster – Broste Ltd

Aziz Sharpquips – Butchers Equipment – Aziz Sharpquips

Azizoff – premium and business gifts and product sourcing internationally – Azizoff Co.Ltd

Azlon – re-usable laboratory plastic ware – Bibby Scientific Ltd

Azo – European Technical Sales Ltd

Azobul – azodicarbonamide – Atosina UK Ltd

Azonine – direct dye stuffs – Town End Leeds plc

Aztec – A-Z of tamper evident closures on plastic pots – R P C Containers Ltd

Aztec – brake blocks for bicycles and cycle accessories – Madison

Aztec – electric – Trianco Heating Products Ltd

Aztec – vandal and weather resistant bulkhead lighting – Designplan Lighting Ltd

Aztec Range – metallic and lustre colours – Colourcraft C & A Ltd

Aztex – coagulated shoe upper material – J B Broadley

*Aztex – Duncan Stewart Textiles

Azur – two post electro-mechanical lifts for vehicles – Tecalemit Garage Equipment Co. Ltd

Azurtex – Madison Filter

B

B & A – Cordials – Flavour Master Ltd

B.A. – connectors, high voltage – F C Lane Electronics Ltd

B.A.3 – dining chair, with and without arms – Race Furniture Ltd

B.A.S. – banners aromatic solvent – Banner Chemicals Ltd

B.A.S.F. – nyloflex photopolymer printing plateu – Plastotype

B.A.T. Lantern Globes – glass bottles – Allied Glass Containers Ltd

B.B.B – pipes & lighters – Cadogan

B. (Ball) Blocks – ball-bearing v-blocks – Rubert & Co. Ltd

B Brand – Beeswift Ltd

B-Brand – safety equipment – Bearwood Engineering Supplies

B. Braun Medical – manufacturers and distributors of surgical and medical devices instruments and equipment – B Braun Medical Ltd

B.C.B. International – survival and military equipment, provisions and first aid equipment – B C B International Ltd

B.C. Barton – steel pressings & fabrication – B C Barton & Son Ltd

B C I – mechanically commutated DC motors – Ebm-Papst

B.C.I. – Chamber of Commerce – Birmingham Chambers Of Commerce & Industry

B.C.K. – granules for veterinary use – J M Loveridge

B & C VANE PUMPS – Hydraulic & Offshore Supplies Ltd

B & C vane pumps – J B J Techniques Ltd

B Click – First Aid – Beeswift Ltd

B-Click – safety boots – Bearwood Engineering Supplies

B Click Cut Resistant – Beeswift Ltd

B Click Fire Retardent – Beeswift Ltd

B Click Footwear – Beeswift Ltd

B Click Heavyweight – Beeswift Ltd

B Click Kutstop – Beeswift Ltd

B Click Once – Beeswift Ltd

B Click Traders – Beeswift Ltd

B Click Workwear – Beeswift Ltd

B.D. (Europe, Western) – pp hose fittings – Everyvalve Ltd

B.D.P. – multi profession design consultants – Building Design Partnership

B.D.T. – gold plating process – Cookson Electronics Ltd

B.D.W.D. – wire drawing dies, extruder dies, die repair machinery – British Diamond Wire Die Co. Ltd

B-Dri – safety clothing – Bearwood Engineering Supplies

B DRI Weatherproof – Beeswift Ltd

B&E Boilers – Twin Industries International Ltd

B.E.C. – sensors and electronic controls – Sigma Industries Ltd

B.E.M.A. – hydraulic systems – Bucher Hydraulics Ltd

B.E.M.A - Barmag Hydraulic - Beringer Hydraulic - Bucher Hidroirma - Bucher Hydraulik - HTF Frutigen AG – Bucher Hydraulics Ltd

B.F. 061 – heat resistant alloy-iron castings – Bradken UK Ltd

B.F. 1105 – low alloy steel castings – Bradken UK Ltd

B.F. 122 – high cr-iron wear resistant castings – Bradken UK Ltd

B.F. 123 – high cr-iron wear resistant castings – Bradken UK Ltd

B.F. 15/55 – heat-resisting alloy-iron castings – Bradken UK Ltd

B.F. 151 – high cr-iron wear resistant castings – Bradken UK Ltd

B.F. 152 – High cr-iron castings – Bradken UK Ltd

B.F. 153 – high cr-iron wear resistant castings – Bradken UK Ltd

B.F. 18/37 – heat-resisting alloy-iron castings – Bradken UK Ltd

B.F. 183 – high cr-iron wear resistant castings – Bradken UK Ltd

B.F. 200 – high cr-iron wear resistant castings – Bradken UK Ltd

B.F. 201 – heat resistant alloy-iron castings – Bradken UK Ltd

B.F. 202 – high cr-iron castings – Bradken UK Ltd

B.F. 203 – high cr-iron wear resistant castings – Bradken UK Ltd

B.F. 204 – high cr-iron wear resistant castings – Bradken UK Ltd
B.F. 2108 – low alloy steel castings – Bradken UK Ltd
B.F. 25/12 – heat-resisting alloy-iron castings – Bradken UK Ltd
B.F. 25/20 – heat-resisting alloy-iron castings – Bradken UK Ltd
B.F. 25/6 – heat resistant alloy-iron castings – Bradken UK Ltd
B.F. 253 – high cr-iron castings and wear resistent castings – Bradken UK Ltd
B.F. 254 – high cr-iron wear resistant castings – Bradken UK Ltd
B.F. 281 – heat-resisting alloy-iron castings – Bradken UK Ltd
B.F. 282 – heat-resisting alloy-iron castings – Bradken UK Ltd
B.F. 303 – high cr-iron wear resistant castings – Bradken UK Ltd
B.F. 423 – nickel-chromium-iron wear resistant castings – Bradken UK Ltd
B.F. 683 – nickel-chromium-iron resistant castings – Bradken UK Ltd
B.F.M. Motors – electric motors and fans – Beatson Fans & Motors Ltd
B.F.S. – brass fittings for the gas industry – Brass Fittings & Supplies Ltd
B Flex – Beeswift Ltd
B. Flute – corrugated cardboard – Calpack Ltd
B.G. Europa – Asphalt making machinery – B G Europa UK Ltd
B. & G. Lock – padlock – B & G Lock & Tool Company Ltd
B-Gas (United Kingdom) – refrigerants – Rabtherm International Ltd
B & H – range of decorative castings – Bruce & Hyslop Brucast Ltd
B.H. – leather seals and packings – Pioneer Weston
B.I.C.S. – bureau identity card service – Identilam plc
B.I.S. – high pressure fluid controls – B I S Valves Ltd
B.I.S. – spares & equipment – Bearwood Engineering Supplies
B.I.S. (Trent) – specialists in the manufacture of rosettes for all types of occasions – B I S Trent Rosettes
B.K. – rotary gear pumps – Albany Standard Pumps
B&K Precision (U.S.A.) – test & measuring instruments – Metrix Electronics
B. Label – castor oil – Bell Sons & Co. Ltd
B'Light – interior lighting – Crescent Lighting Ltd
B.-Line – plastic garden, houseware and childrens nursery products – T S R Plastics Ltd
B-Line – auto electrical company – Wood Auto Supplies Ltd
B.M.C. – vintage cars – British Motor Heritage Ltd
B.M.E. – industrial machine knives – Mastercut Cutting Systems Ltd
B.M.L Charisma – software – Electronic Data Processing plc
B.N.A. – caring concern home care and nursing services – B N A British Nursing Association
B.N.M. – fasteners manufacturers of precision machine parts – Bolt & Nut Manufacturing
B.N.R. – research and development – Nortel Networks UK Ltd
B O C – industrial gases, vacuum equipment, medical gases, medical equipment, fuel gases, welding equipment, storage and transportation services – Boc Gases Ltd
***B.O.C.M. Pauls** – Badcock & Evered
B O C Sureflow – industrial gases – Boc Gases Ltd
B P D Heating Controls – heating controls – B P Dempsey Ltd
B&Q – hand-power tools – B & Q Head Office Customer Service Line
B.R.H. – grain equipment – Blair Engineering
B.R.M. – primary lead and silver refiner secondary lead recycling – Britannia Refined Metals Ltd
***B.-ram** – radio hplc detectors – Lablogic Systems Ltd
B.S. 1452/1977 – grey iron grades 150, 180, 220, 260 and 300 for brake disc and drum castings – Precision Disc Castings Ltd
B.S.A. – bicycles – Raleigh UK Ltd
B.S.A. Pylarm – pellets – B S A Guns UK Ltd
B S A Tools – multi and single spindle automatic lathes – B S A Machine Tools
B.S. Executive Travel – travel company – B S Executive Travel Ltd
B.S.L. – bearing power transmission and allied products – Brammer Ltd
B.S.L B.S.B. – sheet metal pressings – Birmingham Specialities Ltd
B.S.S. Manor – copper tubes, fittings and plumbing products – B S S
B Safe – Beeswift Ltd
B Seen – Beeswift Ltd
B Sure – Beeswift Ltd
B-Sure – safety gloves – Bearwood Engineering Supplies
B & T – jig bushes/drill bushes, dowel pins, standard jig and fixture parts, shims, press tool parts, sealing plugs – Boneham & Turner Ltd
B.T. – T V H UK Ltd
B T X & NBTX/CTX (United Kingdom) – self-contained units for telephone exchanges – Eaton-Williams Group Ltd
***B.V.M. Brunner (Germany)** – packaging machinery – Advanced Dynamics Ltd
B.V.R.L.A. – initials of Association – British Vehicle Rental & Leasing Association
B & W – Proplas International Ltd
B & W – photographic creative filters – Johnsons Photopia Ltd
B.Y.D. – yarn dyers and sizers of cotton & cotton blends and man made fibres – Blackburn Yarn Dyers Ltd
B Y P Y – Hydraulic & Offshore Supplies Ltd
B Y P Y – hydraulics and transmission components – BYPY Hydraulics & Transmissions Ltd
B2B International (United Kingdom) – business to business market research specialist – B 2 B International Ltd
B2B International (United Kingdom) – Market Research, consultancy and training – B 2 B International Ltd
B60 – digital readout – Newall Measurement Systems Ltd
Ba components – Replacement made to measure kitchen and bedroom doors – Basically Doors
Ba.compressor – Bauer Group
BA, D2, LMA, LMF, LMG, LMH, LMHF, LMJ, LMV, SM, SMA, SMC. – F C Lane Electronics Ltd
Babcock B 380 Egglayer – Bird – Tom Barron Isa Ltd
Babe-eze – maternity back supports – Remploy Ltd
Babtie Group – technical and management consultants – Jacobs Engineering UK Ltd
Baby Bear Phone – Vtech Electronics UK plc
Baby Buck – clothing leather – Charles F Stead & Co. Ltd
Baby Driver – Vtech Electronics UK plc
Baby Sense – baby toiletries in unique finger grip bottles – F M C G Ltd
Baby Shapes 'N Things – Vtech Electronics UK plc
Baby Time 3 & 4 Ply – yarns – Stylecraft
Baby Time D.K. – yarns – Stylecraft
Baby Time DK Prints – yarn – Stylecraft
***Baby Vision (The Far East)** – toys – Tomy International
Baby wet ones – baby wipe tissues – Jeyes
Babybasics – children and baby wear – O S R International Ltd
Babydoll – childrens clothing – Gobina London Ltd
Babylon (United Kingdom) – fibre glass plant container – Christian Day Ltd
Babyrendel – baby changing tables – Vectair Systems Ltd
Babywise – all baby products – The Co Op
Bac-Det – bactericidal detergent for cleaning crockery, kitchen utensils and general surfaces – Evans Vanodine International plc
***Bacaware (United Kingdom)** – wireware & fireside equipment – Parasene
Bach – Kuwait Petroleum International Lubricants UK Ltd
***Bacharah Fyrite (U.S.A.)** – combustion testing equipment – Shawcity Ltd
Back DVD Up – Tekdata Distribution Ltd
Back Sounder – vehicle reversing alarms – O W L Electronics Ltd
Back Up – Tekdata Distribution Ltd
Backer – sheathed electric heating elements – Backer Electric Co. Ltd
Backup Data Data Storage – Tekdata Distribution Ltd
Backup Data Online Storage – Tekdata Distribution Ltd
Bacloc – stitch bonded crepe paper for secondary backing of tufted carpets – Scott & Fyfe Ltd
Bacsafe – password system – Vocalink Ltd
Bacstel – telecommunications link – Vocalink Ltd
BACT.A.CID – selective pig bactericide – Agil Chemicals Products
Bact-a-start – creep feed acidifier for piglets – Agil Chemicals Products
Bactericidal Hand Soap – blended natural soap, synthetic cleanser, moisturiser and bactericide – Premiere Products Ltd
Bactericidal Springclean – general purpose non-scratch hard surface cleaning detergent – Premiere Products Ltd
Bacteruritest – sterile paper strips for the quantitative estimation of bacteria present in urine – The Mast Group Ltd
Bactiram – bactericide – Atosina UK Ltd
Bactogel – germicidal floor jelly – Unico Ltd
Bactol – range of alkaline detergents – Agma Ltd
Bader – leisure wear – Rinku Group plc
Badge + (no words) – outer clothing, T-shirts and socks – St Andrews Link Trust
Badge + Words – stationery and printed matter; outer clothing, T-shirts and socks; wines, spirits and liqueurs and food – St Andrews Link Trust
Badgeworx (United Kingdom) – badge making kits – London Emblem Plc "All About Badges"
***Badott** – water – Danone Ltd
Badu – pumps – Speck Pumps UK Ltd
Baelz – pumps and lubrication equipment – Hartle I G E Ltd
Bafco – Harrier Fluid Power Ltd
BAFE – Fire Extinguisher Servicing and Maintenance registered – R B Health & Safety Solutions Ltd
***Bagda (United Kingdom)** – british advertising gifts distributors association – Galpeg Ltd
Bagged Aggregates – Brand & Rae
Bahco – Gem Tool Hire & Sales Ltd
Bahco – S J Wharton Ltd
Bahco – wrenches – Bearwood Engineering Supplies
Baigish – Thomas Jacks Ltd
Bailey – J & S Lewis Ltd
***Baileys** – Badcock & Evered
Bainbridge – sail cloth – Bainbridge Aqua-Marine
Bak-Fin – precision pressings, spring clips, wireforms, tension washers – Baker & Finnemore Ltd
BAKA – Chaintec Ltd
Bakasan – seat – Armitage Shanks Ltd
Bakaware – domestic and garden wire goods, fireguards, hearthside accessories and coal buckets/hods – A Mir & Co. Ltd
Bake-A-Matic – MacIntyre Chocolate Systems Ltd
Bake Master – bakery equipment – Acrivarn Ltd
Baker – Harrier Fluid Power Ltd
Baker Boy – Try & Lilly Ltd
Baker Browne – gloves – Chester Jefferies Ltd
Baker Horseshoes – horseshoe manufacturer – Vaughans Hope Works Ltd
Baker Horseshoes (horseshoe manufacturer) - Sterling farriers tools) - Alcosa (forges) - Brooks (anvils) - Vaughans (blacksmiths and foundry hand-tools). – Vaughans Hope Works Ltd
Baker Hughes Inteq – measurement while drilling, drilling fluid sand control – Baker Hughes
Baker Oil Tools – downhole permanent and retrievable completion systems for oil and gas wells – Baker Hughes
Bakers Oven – bread savouries & confectionery – Greggs plc
***Bakery Level 2** – Brooklands College
Bakewell – non-stick baking parchment – Terinex Ltd
***Balacron (Netherlands)** – book covering – B N International
Balancing Internet Load – Tekdata Distribution Ltd
Balco – jewellery equipment – A G Thomas Bradford Ltd
***Balcom (Germany)** – door entry and communications systems – A-Belco Ltd
***Baldor** – European Drives & Motor Repairs
Baldor – Proplas International Ltd
Baldor – Drives – Sprint Engineering & Lubricant
Baldor – Mercury Bearings Ltd
Baldor – ac & dc motors – Betech 100 P T Ltd
Baldor Motors – European Technical Sales Ltd
Baldwin – Harrier Fluid Power Ltd
BALDWIN DAVIS – Hydraulic & Offshore Supplies Ltd
Balemate – film wrapped bale handler – John C Collins
Bales – tour operators – Bales Worldwide Ltd
Balflo – A full range of pressure reducing valves with balanced inlet, for use on all types of medium, and duties available screwed or flanged to all recognised international standards in sizes 1/2" to 6" – Broady Flow Controller Ltd
Balguard – architectural metalwork – Balguard Engineering Ltd
BALKANCAR – Chaintec Ltd
Balkancar – Stacatruc
Ball Lock – Kennametal UK Ltd
Ball-Lok – ties – Band-It Co. Ltd
Ball Track – Kennametal UK Ltd
Ball Valve Sales – division of valvestock specialsing in the supply of ball valves – Valvestock
Ball Valves UK – maufacture gaskett valves pheonolic lominates & sheet jointing – Novus Sealing
Ballamore – office chairs – Top Office Equipment Ltd
Ballantyne – cashmere knitwear & clothing – Dawson International plc
Balloons – casual shoes – D Jacobson & Sons Ltd
Ballrace – G S F Promount
Balluff – Balluff Ltd
Balluff – Aztech Components Ltd
Balluff – European Technical Sales Ltd
BALLUFF – Hydraulic & Offshore Supplies Ltd
Balluft – Encoders UK
Bally – footwear, leather handbags and watches – Bally UK Sales Ltd
Bally Leather Jackets – hosiery and leather coats – Bally UK Sales Ltd
Balmix – trichloroethane – Atosina UK Ltd
Balmoral – merino wool blankets – John Horsfall & Sons Ltd
Balmoral – Hotel Complimentary Products
Balmoral Furniture – The Winnen Furnishing Company
Balon – Valves – Protective Supplies & Services Ltd
Balsham – steelwork and cladding for industrial and agricultural buildings – Balsham Buildings Ltd
BALSTON – Hydraulic & Offshore Supplies Ltd
Baltane – trichloroethane 111 – Atosina UK Ltd
Baltec Electro Press – electric presses – Baltec UK Ltd
Baltec FPS – aluminium extrusion – Baltec UK Ltd
Baltec Presses – pneumatic/manual/hydro presses – Baltec UK Ltd
Baltec Radial Riveting Machines – radial riveters – Baltec UK Ltd
Baltoro – clothing – Karrimor Ltd

Baltronic – lighting & lighting components – Coughtrie International Ltd

Balzers – general vacuum suppliers – AESpump

***Bamatec (Switzerland)** – wire machine – Embassy Machinery Ltd

Bambi – small, quiet and oil free air compressors – Bambi Air Compressors Ltd

BAMBI – Hydraulic & Offshore Supplies Ltd

Banbury – internal batch mixer – Farrel Ltd

Banbury Citizen – newspaper – Leamington Spa Courier

Banbury Guardian – newspaper – Leamington Spa Courier

Banca Woolwich – The Woolwich

Bancelamp – R Bance & Co. Ltd

***Band Clip (Worldwide)** – low pressure large hose fasteners – Oetiker UK Ltd

BAND-IT – Hydraulic & Offshore Supplies Ltd

Band-It – stainless steel clamping systems – Band-It Co. Ltd

Band-Seal – repair couplings – Naylor Drainage Ltd

Bandit – cable ties and markers – Wellhead Electrical Supplies

Bandit (United Kingdom) – fisnhing/regraining tool – Seco Engineering Co. Ltd

Bandmaster – horizontal bandsawing machines – Addison Saws Ltd

***Bandrift** – B A S F

Bang – magazine – Future Publishing Ltd

Bang-The-Door – pet baskets – Linden Textiles Ltd

Bangalol – perfume speciality – Quest International UK Ltd

***Banjo (U.S.A.)** – polypropylene ball valves and fitters – Dual Pumps Ltd

Banka – Agricultural adjuvant – Interagro UK Ltd

Banker – pens – Tallon International Ltd

Bankers' Almanac, The – international banking reference book – The Bankers' Almanac Reed Business Information

Bankers' Almanac World Ranking, The – top 3,000 international banks – The Bankers' Almanac Reed Business Information

Bankers' Almanc.com (BANKERSalmanac.com) – The most up to date source of Global banking information available on the internet – The Bankers' Almanac Reed Business Information

Banner – Harrier Fluid Power Ltd

Banner – schoolwear – Banner Ltd

Banner-Mag – Anchor Magnets Ltd

Banner Scafolding – contractors' plant hire & rental – Banner Plant Ltd

BANNER SERVICES – Hydraulic & Offshore Supplies Ltd

Bannons Ltd – Bannons

Banque Woolwich UK – The Woolwich

Banson Tool Hire – hire & sales of power tools, small plant and access equipment – Banson Tool Hire Ltd

Banswara – synthetic knitting and weaving yarn and fabrics – A P Y

Bantam – switchgear – Ellison Switchgear

Bantam Compack 2 – gas wallheater – Robinson Willey

Bantam Weight – textile piece goods – Reid & Taylor Ltd

Bantex – communications aerials – Renair Ltd

Bantex – UK Office Direct

BAOLI – Chaintec Ltd

bar – European Technical Sales Ltd

BAR – switches (rocker/push button) – Saia Burgess (Gateshead) Plc

Bar Harbour – half and long sleeve woven leisure shirts – Double Two Ltd

Barafoam – British Vita plc

Barb conelock – terminals plugs and sockets – Oxley Developments Company Ltd

Barbarian – rugby footballs – Gray Nicolls

Barbecue King – manufacturing catering equipment – B K I Europe Ltd

Barbican – carpets – Bond Worth

Barbican – textiles – Maurice Phillips

Barbican Lasermatt – coated paper – Howard Smith Paper Ltd

Barblues – spades, shovels and draining tools – Chieftain Forge

Barbour – M&ES Flexilope

Barbour – motor-cycling wear and waterproof clothing – J Barbour & Sons Ltd

Barbour ABI – Barbour - A B I

Barbour Thornproof – watertight fishing, shooting and motor cycle wear – J Barbour & Sons Ltd

Barcelona Chairs – The Winnen Furnishing Company

Barclays Vehicle Management Services – vehicle leasing and management for Barclays bank business customers – Leaseplan UK Ltd

BARCO – graphic design systems – Esko-Graphics

Barco – Lamphouse Ltd

Barco – Rotary Unions – Hamer Stevenson Ltd

Barcoat – paint isolator – U-Pol Ltd

Barcocim – (CIM) computer integrated management system for rubber and plasticss – B M S Vision Ltd

Barcode – barcoder – Avery Dennison

Barcode Systems – N S D International Ltd

Barcoder – barcoder – Avery Dennison

Barcooler – modular bar refrigeration units – I M C

Bard – urological catheters and collection systems; surgical urology product; cardiovascular and cardiopulmonary products – Bard Ltd

Barden – Mercury Bearings Ltd

Barden – super precision ball bearings – Barden Corporation (UK) Limited

Bardia – foley catheters – Bard Ltd

Bardyke – copper chemicals – Bardyke Chemicals Ltd

BAREISS – hardness testers of Germany – Mapra Technik Co.

Barern – cycle accessories – Witcomb Cycles

Barfield Travel and Tours – garden tours, patchwork & quilting – Agricultural Travel Bureau Ltd

Barflo – flo restriction value – Drainage Center Ltd

***Barford** – Dennis Barnfield Ltd

Barford – P J P Plant Hire

Barford – A T Wilde & Son Ltd

***Barframe** – bar building system – Servaclean Bar Systems Ltd

Barger Seals – European Technical Sales Ltd

Bari – steel bath – Ideal Standard Ltd

Barifine – minerals – Viaton Industries Ltd

Bariotrast – G E Healthcare

Bark Nuggets – mulch – Melcourt Industries

Barkeller – top loading can and bottle cooler – I M C

Barker Shoes – ladies and mens shoes – Barker Shoes

Barkers – POS Display Shop

Barko – Harrier Fluid Power Ltd

Barksdale – thermostats – Bearwood Engineering Supplies

Barley Hall – York Archaeological Trust For Excavation & Research Ltd

Barmac – Barmac-VSI crusher – Metso Minerals UK Ltd

Barmag Hydraulic – Bucher Hydraulics Ltd

***Barmobility** – Cantilever bar on wheels – Cantilever Bar Systems Ltd

Barnard – wholesale confectioners – E W Barnard Ltd

BARNES HYDRAULICS – Hydraulic & Offshore Supplies Ltd

Barnes & Woodhouse – ISPM 15 Timber, Wooden Crates & Packaging Specialists – Timber Packing Cases

Barnett – boxer shorts – Barnett The Factory

Barnsley Chronicle – The Barnsley Chronicle Ltd

Barnsley Chronicle Newspaper Group, The – The Barnsley Chronicle Ltd

Barnsley Independent – The Barnsley Chronicle Ltd

Barocel – vacuum gauges – B O C Edwards

Baromec – aneroid survey barometer – Meggitt Avionics

Baron – C E S Hire Ltd

***Baron Pen (Italy)** – a very successful retractable ballpen in attractive barrel colours – Hainenko Ltd

Baron Pils – lager – Temple Wines Ltd

Baron & Warren – patent and trade mark attorneys – Barron Warren & Redfern

Baroness – combining pea variety marketed – Limagrain UK Ltd

Baronet – Vi Spring Ltd

Baronet Supreme – Vi Spring Ltd

***Barr (U.S.A.)** – marine exhaust manifolds – Lancing Marine

Barraclough – soft drinks – Princes Soft Drinks

Barracuda – Display Wizard Ltd

Barracuda (Taiwan) – Bicycles – Moore Large & Co. Ltd

Barrie – fully-fashioned knitwear – Barrie Knitwear

Barrie – knitwear – Dawson International plc

Barrie Witcomb – lightweight framesets and cycles – Witcomb Cycles

Barrier Cream – wet or dry use cream – Evans Vanodine International plc

Barrier Rail – Berry Systems

Barrier Systems – Accesscaff International Ltd

Barrierflex – PVDC coated films – Printpack Enterprises Ltd T/A Printpack

Barrikade – machinable flame and heat resistant material – T W I

Barrow Bold Roman – clay – Sandtoft Holdings Ltd

Barrowmix – S J Wharton Ltd

Barry Controls – Specialty Fasteners & Components Ltd

Barry Controls – vibration, shock & noise control – Stop Choc Ltd

Barry Controls - Camloc - Hydraflow - Rosan - Pinet - Accuride, - Arvin - Lisi - Stop-choc - Spiralock - Tridair – Specialty Fasteners & Components Ltd

Barry M – cosmetics – Barry M Cosmetics

Barry Twomlow – darts – Unicorn Products Ltd

Barrycase – transit case shock protected – Stop Choc Ltd

Barryflex – anti-vibration mounting – Stop Choc Ltd

Barrymount – vibration, shock isolators – Stop Choc Ltd

Bartender – underbar units – I M C

Bartholomew – maps, atlases and other cartographic material – Harpercollins Publishers Ophelia House

Barton – UK Office Direct

Barton Conduit – Caparo Precision Tubes

Barton Willmore Partnership – architects and town planners & environment consultants – Barton Willmore LLP

Bartrak – adjustable pallet racking – Barton Storage Systems Ltd

Bartran – industrial lubricants – B P plc

Bartspan – heavy duty long span shelving – Barton Storage Systems Ltd

Barwick Group, The – Independent financial advisors – Merchant House Financial Services

Barwil – non-concussive self closing valves, sanitary fittings – Barber Wilson & Company Ltd

Barytes – minerals – Viaton Industries Ltd

BAS 2800+ – building management systems – Schneider Electric

BAse Design – ophthalmic tables – Base Design Ltd

Base Model Management – Fashion Show Production – Base Model

Base Modeler – sound system design – Bose Ltd

Base Models – Model hire – Base Model

Baseline – Bushboard Ltd

Baselite – base illumunated bollard – Haldo Developments Ltd

Baselock – roof glazing – Yule Catto & Co plc

Basex – tooling aids-index bases, trunnion units, bar drilling jigs, depth stop drill holders and toolmakers – C B Powell Ltd

***BASF** – Rutherfords

Basic Food Hygiene – Facilities Staff Training

Basildon Bond – UK Office Direct

Basildon Recorder – free weekly newspaper – Newsquest Essex Ltd

BaSiX – Mechline Developments Ltd

Basix – harnesses, belts and lanyards – Capital Safety Group Ltd

Baskerville – scientific research equipment, reaction vessels, high pressure apparatus, autoclaves and installations – Baskerville Reactors Autoclaves Ltd

Basket Platforms – Accesscaff International Ltd

***Basketshelf** – shelf for glass washer baskets – Servaclean Bar Systems Ltd

Basler – M&ES Flexilope

Basotect – Malamine foam – Custom Foams Ltd

Basotect - Malamine FoamNovada - Polyurethane foam – Custom Foams Ltd

Bassaire – clean rooms and laminar flow clean air equipment, micro-biological safety cabinets, validation and service. – Bassaire Ltd

Bassetts – Soft and chewy vitamins – Ernest Jackson & Co. Ltd

Bassetts soft & Chewey Vitamins – Ernest Jackson & Co. Ltd

Bastion – slimline vandal and weather resistant lighting – Designplan Lighting Ltd

Bat – metal straps, structural fixings, carpenters metal work and joist hangers – Expamet Building Products Ltd

BAT – tobacco (export) – British American Tobacco plc

***Batch Weighing** – weighing equipment – Procon Engineering Ltd

Batchfrac – software products for process engineer – Aspentech Ltd

Batchmatic – CNC lathes slide lathes – B S A Machine Tools

Batchpac – mixing plant – B G Europa UK Ltd

Batchplus – software products for batch process engineering – Aspentech Ltd

Bath Bubble – bath lift – R B F Healthcare

Bath Bubble - bath lift – R B F Healthcare

Bath Buddy – bath lift – R B F Healthcare

Bath Wizard – bath lift – R B F Healthcare

Bathard – gloves – Chester Jefferies Ltd

Bathmat (Portugal) – traditional cork bath mat – Siesta Cork Tile Co.

Bathstore.Com – bathroom equipment and furniture – Bathstore.com Ltd

Batley Valve – isolation butterfly valves, control butterfly valves – Weir Valves & Controls

Batson – B P plc

Battenfeld – Proplas International Ltd

Battenfield – Harrier Fluid Power Ltd

BATTIONI PAGANI – Chaintec Ltd

Battlemaniacs – games – Rare

Battleship – fibre bonded carpet – Heckmondwike FB

Battletoads – games – Rare

Baty – dial gauges, profile projectors and vision systems – Baty International

Baudouin – Harrier Fluid Power Ltd

Bauer – Southern Valve & Fitting Co. Ltd

Bauer – Submarine Manufacturing & Products Ltd

Bauer – electric motors – Bearwood Engineering Supplies

BAUER – Hydraulic & Offshore Supplies Ltd

Bauer – gearboxes – Potteries Power Transmission Ltd

***Bauer (Germany)** – horizontal bandsaws – Prosaw Ltd

BAUER COUPLINGS – Hydraulic & Offshore Supplies Ltd

Bauer GB – European Technical Sales Ltd

Bauer Gearboxes – Potteries Power Transmission Ltd

Bauer Kompressoren – Bauer Group

Baumann (Switzerland) – flexible shaft couplings – Lenze UK Ltd

BAUMANN – Chaintec Ltd

Baumann Side Loaders – Barloworld Handling C M S Lift Trucks Ltd

Baumer – Encoders UK

Baumer Electric (Switzerland) – proximity switches, encoders, photo electrics, ultrasonics, capacitives, my-com connectors, pressure and asi interface and fibre optics, laser sensors – Baumer Electric Ltd

Baumer Optronics (Germany) – vision systems – Baumer Electric Ltd

Baumgartner – European Technical Sales Ltd

Baumuller – European Drives & Motor Repairs

Bauromat – European Technical Sales Ltd

Bauser – Harrier Fluid Power Ltd

Bavaria Ladders – Accesscaff International Ltd

Bavaria Towers – Accesscaff International Ltd

Bavtrak – Digbits Ltd

Baxi – Baxi Group

Baxi boilers – energy efficient boilers – Elite Heating Ltd

*Baxter (Worldwide) – health products – Baxter Healthcare Ltd

Bay-bee – Eurocell Building Plastics Ltd

Bay Networks (U.S.A.) – Kingston Communications

Baya – Rutherfords

*Bayco (U.S.A.) – tanker fittings – Dixon Group Europe Ltd

Baydee – Tank contents gauge switch – Bayham Ltd

Baygal – polyol – I M C D UK Ltd

Baymak – Baxi Group

Baynell – bedding & mattresses – Baynell Ltd

Bayonet – tacks, nails and pins – Frank Shaw Bayonet Ltd

Bayrol – pool chemicals and water treatment equipment. – Biolab UK Ltd

Baysend – Remote reading tank contents gauge switch – Bayham Ltd

Baystack – enterprise LAN systems – Nortel Networks UK Ltd

BazaarBuilder.com – Sure Names Internet Solutions Ltd

BBA – sheep shear – Burgon & Ball Ltd

BBC – Arun Pumps Ltd

BBN – sheep shear – Burgon & Ball Ltd

BBQ – charcoal – Swift-Lite Charcoal

BC 2105 – Granada Cranes & Handling

BC 2105 – Basildon Chemical Co. Ltd / KCC

BC 2153 – Basildon Chemical Co. Ltd / KCC

BC 2153 – Granada Cranes & Handling

BC 2191 – Granada Cranes & Handling

BC 2191 – Basildon Chemical Co. Ltd / KCC

BC 2211 – Basildon Chemical Co. Ltd / KCC

BC 2211 – Granada Cranes & Handling

BC 2231 – Granada Cranes & Handling

BC 2231 – Basildon Chemical Co. Ltd / KCC

BC 2262 – Basildon Chemical Co. Ltd / KCC

BC 2262 – Granada Cranes & Handling

BC 2275 – Granada Cranes & Handling

BC 2275 – Basildon Chemical Co. Ltd / KCC

BC 2335 – Basildon Chemical Co. Ltd / KCC

BC 2335 – Granada Cranes & Handling

BC 2366 – Granada Cranes & Handling

BC 2366 – Basildon Chemical Co. Ltd / KCC

BC 2398 – Basildon Chemical Co. Ltd / KCC

BC 2398 – Granada Cranes & Handling

BC 2421 – Granada Cranes & Handling

BC 2421 – Basildon Chemical Co. Ltd / KCC

BC 2426 – Basildon Chemical Co. Ltd / KCC

BC 2426 – Granada Cranes & Handling

BC 2440 – Granada Cranes & Handling

BC 2440 – Basildon Chemical Co. Ltd / KCC

BC 30EPHV – Granada Cranes & Handling

BC 330/60 – Granada Cranes & Handling

BC 330/60 – Basildon Chemical Co. Ltd / KCC

BC 330EPHV – Basildon Chemical Co. Ltd / KCC

BC 330LV – Basildon Chemical Co. Ltd / KCC

BC 330LV – Granada Cranes & Handling

BC 338 – Granada Cranes & Handling

BC 338 – Basildon Chemical Co. Ltd / KCC

BC 361 – Basildon Chemical Co. Ltd / KCC

BC 361 – Granada Cranes & Handling

BC 380E – Granada Cranes & Handling

BC 380E – Basildon Chemical Co. Ltd / KCC

BC 380S – Basildon Chemical Co. Ltd / KCC

BC 380S – Granada Cranes & Handling

BC 403 – Granada Cranes & Handling

BC 403 – Basildon Chemical Co. Ltd / KCC

BC 404 – Basildon Chemical Co. Ltd / KCC

BC 404 – Granada Cranes & Handling

BC 83/132 – Granada Cranes & Handling

BC 83/132 – Basildon Chemical Co. Ltd / KCC

BC 85/76 – Basildon Chemical Co. Ltd / KCC

BC 85/76 – Granada Cranes & Handling

BC 88/161 – Granada Cranes & Handling

BC 88/161 – Basildon Chemical Co. Ltd / KCC

BC 89/175 – Basildon Chemical Co. Ltd / KCC

BC 89/175 – Granada Cranes & Handling

BC 90/080 – Granada Cranes & Handling

BC 90/080 – Basildon Chemical Co. Ltd / KCC

BC 91/023 – Basildon Chemical Co. Ltd / KCC

BC 91/023 – Granada Cranes & Handling

BC 93/018 – Granada Cranes & Handling

BC 93/018 – Basildon Chemical Co. Ltd / KCC

BC 96/004 – Basildon Chemical Co. Ltd / KCC

BC 96/004 – Granada Cranes & Handling

BC 96/042 – Granada Cranes & Handling

BC 96/042 – Basildon Chemical Co. Ltd / KCC

BC 96/061 – Basildon Chemical Co. Ltd / KCC

BC 96/061 – Granada Cranes & Handling

BC 98/073 – Granada Cranes & Handling

BC 98/073 – Basildon Chemical Co. Ltd / KCC

BC 99/012 – Basildon Chemical Co. Ltd / KCC

BC 99/012 – Granada Cranes & Handling

BC 99/099 – Granada Cranes & Handling

BC 99/099 – Basildon Chemical Co. Ltd / KCC

BC Components – Cyclops Electronics Ltd

BC Silicone Fluids – Basildon Chemical Co. Ltd / KCC

BC Silicone Fluids – Granada Cranes & Handling

BC Volatile Silicone 4 – Granada Cranes & Handling

BC Volatile Silicone 4 – Basildon Chemical Co. Ltd / KCC

BC Volatile Silicone 5 – Basildon Chemical Co. Ltd / KCC

BC Volatile Silicone 5 – Granada Cranes & Handling

BCE – ceramic capacitors – Anglia

BCH Ltd – food machinery – Coates Engineering International Ltd

BCMS – Buckhill Content Management System – Buckhill Ltd

BCT – Woodturners hollowing tools – The Toolpost

BCTC-CAMRASO – technical and advisory services for the carpet and cleaning and maintenance industries – B T T G Ltd

BD & CD – dehumidifiers for commercial & industrial applications – Ebac

BD Range – R M Sealers Ltd

BD SERIES – signal conditioning equipment din rail mounting. AC Powered – Lee-Dickens Ltd

BDO – darts promoters – British Darts Organisation Ltd

BDS – UK Office Direct

BEA Branches – name adopted by network of voluntary groups – Epilepsy Action

BEA filters – compressed air in line filtration – Airware International Ltd

Bea Filtri – Harrier Fluid Power Ltd

BEA Trading – Epilepsy Action

Beach Club – menswear – Saville Heaton Ltd

*Beach Management Systems (Denmark) – accretion of sandy beaches – A G A Group

Beacon – petite fleur carpets - axminster – Brintons Carpets Ltd

Beacon – waterproof and protective clothing – J Barbour & Sons Ltd

Beacon – services connected with monetary affairs class 36 – Beacon Private Trust

Beacon – remould truck tyres – Tyre Renewals Ltd

Beacons Leisure – outdoor and leisure division – Functional Foam Beacons Products Ltd

Beaded Gel – gel containing glycerine and polymer beads – Evans Vanodine International plc

Beakaprene – flameproof synthetic rubber coated fabric used to manufacture moulded bellows – Beakbane Ltd

Beakaprene - Plastichain - Centry Covers. – Beakbane Ltd

Beakbane – machine covers, connectors, joints and bellows, metal laser cutting/punching and fabrications – Beakbane Ltd

Beall – Buffing systems, Pen Wizard – The Toolpost

Bealon – N G K Berylco UK Ltd

BEAM – gas carburation equipment – H K L Gas Power Ltd

Beam-Rider™ – Extra Heavy Duty Cable/Hose Trolley System – Metreel Ltd

BeamClad Systems – floors, structural steelwork, doors, ceilings, pipes and ducts – Rockwool Rockpanel B V

BeamClamp – FastClamp

Beamer – radio and infra red control equipment – Cattron Theimeg UK Ltd

Beamish Black – ale & stouts – Scottish & Newcastle Pub Co.

Beamish Red – ale & stouts – Scottish & Newcastle Pub Co.

Beammaster – fire detector – Guardall Ltd

Beammaster – Bandsaw – Dynashape Ltd

Beamstroker – manual vertical honing machine – Equipment For You

Bean – drinking fountain valve – Sheardown Engineering Ltd

Beano – comic – D C Thomson & Co. Ltd

Beano Superstars – D C Thomson & Co. Ltd

Beanstalk – UK Office Direct

Beanstalk Marketing – B2B lead generation and market research telemarketing agency – Beanstalk Marketing Services

Bear (United Kingdom) – chisel, gouge and plane blade sharpener – R J H Finishing Systems Ltd

*Bear Family (Germany) – record company – Rollercoaster Records Ltd

Bear USA – gents winter clothes – FOCUS International Ltd

Bearcat – band saw blade teeth – L S Starrett Co. Ltd

Beardson – plumbers merchant, brass foundry specialist valves – Fraser & Ellis

*Beargrip (Czech Republic) – hex keys, riveters and driver bits – Castle Brook Tools Ltd

Bearing Oils – oil for use in bearing applications of steam equipment – Morris Lubricants

Bearwood – air conditioning – Bearwood Engineering Supplies

Beast 3860 – wood waste recycling – Spalding Pallets Ltd

*Beasy (United Kingdom) – analysis and simulation software products – C M Beasy Ltd

Beata – flash dryer and disintegrator – Atritor Ltd

Beatrix Potter – needlecraft – Coats Ltd

Beatrix Potter's Country World – Chorion plc

Beatsafe – slash - resistant police gloves – Bennett Safetywear

Beatson – glass bottles and jars – Beatson Clark Ltd

Beatson Fans and Motors – electric motors and allied equipjment, also including air-moving equipment – Beatson Fans & Motors Ltd

Beaufix – self adhesive nylon hook and loop fasteners – Sydney Beaumont Leeds Ltd

Beaufort – waterproof clothing – J Barbour & Sons Ltd

Beaufort – air-sea rescue equipment – Beaufort Air Sea Equipment Ltd

Beaufort – centrifugal fan – Halifax Fan Ltd

Beaumel – laminated plastics – Allied Manufacturing

Beauplas – rigid P.V.C. sheet white and clear – Sydney Beaumont Leeds Ltd

Beaustik – self cling window stick P.V.C. clear and colours – Sydney Beaumont Leeds Ltd

Beautabs – self adhesive foam pads – Sydney Beaumont Leeds Ltd

Beautape – gummed kraft sealing tape – Sydney Beaumont Leeds Ltd

Beautiful kitchens – I P C Media Ltd

Beautiful Landscapes Ltd – Gardening and Landscaping Services – Beautiful Landscapes Ltd

Beauty Without Cruelty – animal compassionate cosmetics and skincare – Vivalis Ltd

Beauvertate – perfume speciality – Quest International UK Ltd

Beaver – eyelets & rings, brass sail – Opas Southern Limited

Beaver – Submarine Manufacturing & Products Ltd

Beaver – hydraulic/pneumatic air operated pumps – Hydraulic Pneumatic Services

Beaver – hire and sale of scaffolding, building equipment, piling and non-mechanical plant and equipment including temporary security fencing – Beaver 84

Beaver Brand – domestic hardware and sail eyelets – H Hipkiss & Co. Ltd

Beaver Bureau – employment agency – Gullivers Sports Travel

Beaver Spaceliner – for litter collection or transporting equipment – Glasdon International Ltd

Beaverbrooks – jewellers – B J Ltd

Beaverclad – Beaver 84

Beavernet – Beaver 84

Bebco – Harrier Fluid Power Ltd

Beberod – hot melt lasting adhesive – Bostik Ltd

*Beche (Germany) – forging hammers and presses – Pearson Panke Ltd

Bechet Productique Cluses SA (France) – sliding head automatics and magazine barloaders – Haesler Machine Tools

*Beck (Germany) – reamers – Macinnes Tooling Ltd

Beck Greener – Beck Greener

BECK IPC Gmbh – Hydraulic & Offshore Supplies Ltd

Beck's – lager – Scottish & Newcastle Pub Co.

Beckarnley – Harrier Fluid Power Ltd

Becker – Harrier Fluid Power Ltd

Becker – dry carbon and other types of pump – AESpump

Becker Green Line - environmentally friendly coatings Beckqua - water based primers and finishes Beckrysol - high solids primers &and finishes – Becker Industrial Coatings Ltd

Beckett Expression – G F Smith

*Beckett Paper (U.S.A.) – high quality paper and board – G F Smith

Beckett Ridge – G F Smith

Beckqua – water based primers and finishes – Becker Industrial Coatings Ltd

Beckside Mills (United Kingdom) – Worsted Mens Suiting Fabric – John Foster Ltd

Beclawat – aluminium windows and door gear for rail and automotive vehicles – Percy Lane Products Ltd

*Beco (Germany) – filter sheets, filter cartridges – Fleximas Ltd

Becofil – non wettable fibre filters – Begg Cousland & Co. Ltd

Becoflex – rotating dust removal systems – Begg Cousland & Co. Ltd
Becoil – demisters – Begg Cousland & Co. Ltd
Becoknit – knitted wire products – Begg Cousland & Co. Ltd
Becone – coalescing unit – Begg Cousland & Co. Ltd
Becosolve – solvent recovery systems – Begg Cousland & Co. Ltd
Becosorb – gas absorption systems – Begg Cousland & Co. Ltd
Bed & Breakfast Insurance – specialist insurance – M M A Insurance plc
Bedale – waterproof jackets – J Barbour & Sons Ltd
Beddington – British Vita plc
Bedfords – dishwasher racks – Bedford Shelving Ltd
Bedloc – Fixfirm Ltd
Bedroom Classic – Ryalux Carpets Ltd
Bedroom Collection – Ryalux Carpets Ltd
Bedstead Mattress – Vi Spring Ltd
Bedstead Supreme Mattress – Vi Spring Ltd
Bee-bump – speed humps – Sportsmark Group Ltd
Bee Hive Bin – grit/salt bin – Sportsmark Group Ltd
Bee Secure – Bridgwater Electronics Ltd
Beech – Wood Burning Ovens – Exclusive Ranges Ltd
Beechfield Cap – baseball caps – Beechfield Brands Ltd
Beechwood – footwear – The Gammidge
Beechwood Appointments Register – recruitment service for all experienced engineers, scientists, technologists, sales, marketing and software-computing professionals – Beechwood Recruitment Ltd
Beechwood Recruitment – recruitment service for all experienced engineers, scientists, technologists, sales, marketing and software-computing professionals – Beechwood Recruitment Ltd
Beefeater – gin – Chivas Bros Holdings Ltd
Beefeater – fixing system – Allgood
Beehive (United Kingdom) – sugar confectionery – Bysel Ltd
Beel Boilers – Twin Industries International Ltd
Beemul – emulsion paint – Emusol Products Ltd
Beerline – valve and beerlines cleaner – Evans Vanodine International plc
Beesafe – safety wear – Bearwood Engineering Supplies
Beesure – safety gloves – Bearwood Engineering Supplies
Beeswift – safety boots – Bearwood Engineering Supplies
Beeswift – D S Safety
Beethoven – Kuwait Petroleum International Lubricants UK Ltd
Beetleback – metal finishing – Surface Technology plc
Begg of Ayr – scarves and stoles – Alex Begg & Co.
Beggars Banquet – record company – Beggars Group Ltd
***Bego (Germany)** – dental products – Metrodent Ltd
Begornia – sheep shear – Burgon & Ball Ltd
***Beha (Germany)** – test and measurement equipment – Electro Group Ltd
Behringer – Harrier Fluid Power Ltd
***Beier Variodrive** – variable speed drives – Centa Transmissions
***Beka (Germany)** – lubricating equipment – Lumatic Ga Ltd
Beka-max – L E K Sales
Bekaert – commercial and industrial wirework, plastic and nylon coatings – K Hartwall Ltd
BEKO – Hydraulic & Offshore Supplies Ltd
Beko – Fridge Freezer Direct Company Ltd
Beks – gents outfitters – Len Beck
Bekum – Proplas International Ltd
***Bel** – Michael Stevens & Partners Ltd
Bel Canto – loudspeaker – Lowther Loudspeaker Systems Ltd
Bel-Mix – continious mix plant machinery – B X Plant Ltd
Bel-Spray – bitumin & concrete cure machinery – B X Plant Ltd
Bel Valves – engineering components manufacturers for industry – British Engines Ltd
Belbro – sheet metalwork – Bell Bros Pudsey Ltd
Belden – Cyclops Electronics Ltd
Belden Communications – communication cables – B3 Cable Solutions
Beldon – Lusso Interiors
BELET – Chaintec Ltd
Belfast – fireclay sink – Armitage Shanks Ltd
Belfast Telegraph – newspaper publishers – Independent News & Media (NI) Ltd
Belfuse – Cyclops Electronics Ltd
Belgaarde – U C D Ltd
Belgravia – fan convectors – S & P Coil Products Ltd
***Belgravia International** – Hocaps Ltd
Belkin – UK Office Direct
Bell Autoparts – motor vehicle componants – M & F Components
Bell Equipment – Bell Equipment UK
Bell Travel – travel agents – Travelcare Uk Ltd
Bell Twist Woven Wilton – carpets - wilton – Brintons Carpets Ltd
Bell & Webster Concrete – precast concrete component – Bell & Webster Concrete Ltd
Bella – magazine – H Bauer Publishing
Bella by Ba – Replacement made to measure kitchen and bedroom doors – Basically Doors
***BELLALUX (France)** – photographic lamps – Osram Ltd
***BELLAPHOT (Germany)** – photographic lamps – Osram Ltd
BELLE – Hydraulic & Offshore Supplies Ltd
Belle – A T Wilde & Son Ltd
Belle Isle – fabric collection – Brian Yates
BELLE MAISONS – HOME DECOR , LIGHTING , FURNITURE MAINLY REPRO – Discount Leisure UK ltd
Bellier B Jacket – Birmingham Barbed Tape Ltd
Belling Lee – Cyclops Electronics Ltd
Bellinge Lee – Ets-Lindgren Ltd
Bellinge Lee - Rantec - Ray Proof - Emco - Holday - Euroshield - Lindgren - ETS – Ets-Lindgren Ltd
Bellingham and Stanley – Bellingham & Stanley Ltd
Bellis & Morcom – Red House Industrial Services Ltd
Bellofram – spares & equipment – Bearwood Engineering Supplies
BELLOFRAM – Hydraulic & Offshore Supplies Ltd
Bellows – PVC and neoprene – Plastic Mouldings Ltd
Bellows - Boots Electrical - Dust Covers - End Caps - Gaiters - Neoprene - P.V.C. - Shrouds. – Plastic Mouldings Ltd
BELLROPHON – ERP/MRP Software – Argonaut Systems Ltd
***Bells of Coldstream (Germany)** – Mercedes car dealership – Bell Truck Sales Ltd
Bellway – house builders – Bellway PLC
Belper Express – newspaper – Derby Telegraph Media Group
***Belt Weighing** – weighing equipment – Procon Engineering Ltd
Beltafine – sewage and industrial effluent screen – Higgins & Hewins Ltd
Beltit (United Kingdom) – belt grinder – Seco Engineering Co. Ltd
Beltlife – Forward Chemicals Ltd
Belts and Carrying Pouches – Michael Lupton Associates Ltd
Belvedere Electric – electric inset fire – Robinson Willey
Belvedere LF – inset living flame gas fire – Robinson Willey
Belvedere RS – inset balanced flue gas fire – Robinson Willey
Belzona – S J Wharton Ltd
Belzona – adhesives – Bearwood Engineering Supplies
***BemaTec (Germany/Switzerland)** – pulpers and refiners – Pulp & Paper Machinery Ltd
***Bematec (Switzerland)** – coating machines – S & P Spanarc Ltd
Bembo – typeface – Monotype Imaging Ltd
Bemco – electrical installation materials – Bemco Ltd
Bemis – toilet seats – Bemis Ltd
Ben – charity fund for motor industry – Ben - Motor & Allied Trades Benevolent Fund
Ben Alder – Scotch whisky blended – Gordon & Macphail
Benati – Harrier Fluid Power Ltd
Bench-Cut – compact cutting machine for plastic extrudate – Peter Gillard Company Ltd
Bench Hone – small manual horizontal honing machine for bench type applications – Equipment For You
Benchcote – Solmedia Laboratory Supplies
Benchmark – GRP bench seating – Sarena
Benchmarq – Cyclops Electronics Ltd
Benchrad – AEL Heating Solutions Ltd
Benchtidy – storage box – Radleys
Benco – Manipulators and engine stands – Brixworth Engineering
Bend-Eze – printed circuit aids – Welwyn Tool Group Ltd
Bendini – Harrier Fluid Power Ltd
Bendix – Harrier Fluid Power Ltd
Bendix – Cyclops Electronics Ltd
***Benecel (Belgium)** – methylcellulose and methylhydroxpropylcellulose – Hercules Holding li Ltd
***Benedikt & Jager (Austria)** – motor control gear – I M O Electronics Ltd
Beneflect – aluminised gloves – Bennett Safetywear
Benford – construction equipment – Service Engines Newcastle Ltd
Benford – dumpers, compaction rollers and concrete mixers – Terex UK Ltd
Benford – Custom Brakes & Hydraulics Ltd
Benford – P J P Plant Hire
BENFORD – Harrier Fluid Power Ltd
Benford – dumpers, rollers mixers & vibratory equipment – Scot J C B Ltd
Benford – A T Wilde & Son Ltd
Benford – Trowell Plant Sales Ltd
Benfra – Harrier Fluid Power Ltd
Benitex – Bennett Safetywear
Benito – Benito UK
Benjy – ladies fashions & gents – Fernan Trading Ltd
Benjywear – Fernan Trading Ltd
Benn's Media Directory – United Business Media Ltd
Benn's Mohair (United Kingdom) – Worsted Mens Suiting Fabric – John Foster Ltd
Bennett (United Kingdom) – spring grinding and spring coiling machines – Bennett Mahler
Bennett Controls – Froude Hofmann Ltd
Bennison – fabrics for interiors (curtains, blinds, walling and upholstery) – Bennison Fabrics
Bennite – limestone fillers – Ben Bennett JR Ltd
Bennite, Drill-carb – Ben Bennett JR Ltd
Benq – Lamphouse Ltd
Benrath – Cemb Hofmann UK Ltd
Benross – fancy goods importers – Benross Marketing Ltd
Benson – linear solenoids – H.E. & B.S. Benson Ltd
Benson – trowels – Benson Industries Ltd
Benson – Cabinet Heaters – L S Systems Ltd
Benson Exhausts – exhaust silencers – Benson Components Ltd
Benson Pleasurecraft – cruising holidays – Richardsons Stalham Ltd
Bentalls Express – fashions – The Bentall Centre
Bentalls Final Touches – fashions – The Bentall Centre
Bentalls Spectator – fashions – The Bentall Centre
Bentalls Trail Finder – fashions – The Bentall Centre
Bentley – optical frames and sunglasses – Hilton International Eye Wear Ltd
Bentley – Rhodes Bentley presses – Joseph Rhodes Ltd
Bentley-Nevada – probes – Bearwood Engineering Supplies
***Bentonil (France)** – bentonite – Sud-Chemie UK Ltd
Bentrade Ltd – trading company supporting the main charity – Ben - Motor & Allied Trades Benevolent Fund
Benum – Cogne UK Ltd
Benum Plus – Cogne UK Ltd
Benzini – boys and gents jeans and sweat shirts – A & J Menswear Retail Ltd
Benzler – Mercury Bearings Ltd
Benzyl Acetate – perfume speciality – Quest International UK Ltd
Benzyl Isoeugenol Forte – perfume speciality – Quest International UK Ltd
Benzyl Propionate – perfume speciality – Quest International UK Ltd
Benzyl Salicylate – perfme speciality – Quest International UK Ltd
***Bepco** – A P B Trading Ltd
Bepex – Dryers – Hosokawa Micron Ltd
Beral – brake linings and brake disc pads – Roadlink International Ltd
Beramic – beryllia technical ceramics – C B L Ceramics Ltd
BERARMA – Hydraulic & Offshore Supplies Ltd
BERARMA S R L – Hydraulic & Offshore Supplies Ltd
Berber Twist – tufted carpet – Brockway Carpets Ltd
Berco – World Leaders in Undercarriage – Midland Steel Traders Ltd
Berendsen Pumps – European Technical Sales Ltd
Berg (Germany) – grippers and die clamping tools – Ringspann UK Ltd
Berg Mixers – D D Hire
Berga – UK Office Direct
Bergen – recessed vandal and weather resistant lighting – Designplan Lighting Ltd
Bergen – cedarwood T+G panel garage door – P C Henderson Ltd
Bergen – gas engines – Rolls-Royce plc
Bergen – Rolls Royce
Bergen Chevron – cedarwood panel garage door – P C Henderson Ltd
Bergeon – tools and equipment – Time Products UK Ltd
Berger Tools – European Technical Sales Ltd
Bergquist – thermal interface materials – Anglia
Beringer Hydraulic – lift equipment, control valves – Bucher Hydraulics Ltd
Berkefeld – water treatment plant & systems – S P P Pumps
Berkeley – carpets – Bond Worth
Berkeley & Co. – Leonardt Ltd
Berkeley Variations – carpets – Bond Worth
Berkertex – bridal wear – Bridal Fashions Ltd
Berkshire Gravure – C P C Packaging
Bermaq – fabricating machines – Awltech Plastic Fabrication Sales Ltd
Bernard (France) – electric actuators – Zoedale plc
Bernard – engines – Brimotor Ltd
***Bernina (Germany)** – animal grooming tools – Diamond Edge Ltd
Bernstein (Germany) – ESD tools – Henri Picard & Frere
Bernstein switches – European Technical Sales Ltd
Berol – UK Office Direct
Berry Beam – Berry Systems
Berry Systems – safety barrier – Hill & Smith Ltd
Berthiez – high speed vertical turning and grinding machines – D S Technology UK Ltd
Berthoud – knapsack sprayers – Hypro Eu Ltd
Berto's – Contact grills – Nisbets plc
Bertos – Equipline
***Bertrand et Fils** – brandy (cognac) – O W Loeb & Co. Ltd
Beru – European Technical Sales Ltd

Berwick – stainless steel sink – Armitage Shanks Ltd

Berwin – tailored clothing – Berwin & Berwin Ltd

Berwyn – marine and agricultural products – Jepway Associates Ltd

Berwyn Engineering - Now owned by Jetway. – Jepway Associates Ltd

BERYLCO – beryllium/copper – N G K Berylco UK Ltd

BERYLCO 10 – N G K Berylco UK Ltd

BERYLCO 14 – N G K Berylco UK Ltd

BERYLCO 165 – N G K Berylco UK Ltd

BERYLCO 25 – N G K Berylco UK Ltd

*Beryvac (Germany) – beryllium-nickel spring alloy – Rolfe Industries

*Besam (Sweden) – automatic door systems – Besam Ltd

Besley & Copp – business forms and computer stationery printers – Besley & Copp Ltd

Bespoke Sliding Rooflights – Glazing Vision Ltd

Bespoke wheels Limited – Bespoke Wheels Ltd

*Bessey (Germany) – clamps for woodworking, steel fabrication and special purposes – L J Hydleman & Co. Ltd

Bessey – clamps – Arrow Supply Co. Ltd

BEST DYES – dyes – European O G D Ltd

Best Operations Practice – Bourton Group Ltd

Best Power (United Kingdom) – ups systems – Powersense Technology

Besta – liquid level switches – Able Instruments & Controls Ltd

Bestec – power supply – Stontronics Ltd

Bestem – tool & die steel – Somers Forge Ltd

*Bestmann Range (Germany) – coir erosion control products – A G A Group

Besto – bleach and pine disinfectant – Unico Ltd

Bestobell – liquid level controllers – Emerson Process Management

Bestobell – gate, globe, swing check, safety relief, ball, butterfly, bronze and stainless steel cryogenic valves – Flowgroup Ltd Bestobell Valves & Conflow

Bestobell Birflo – automatic constant flow control valves – Flowgroup Ltd Bestobell Valves & Conflow

Bestobell-Mowbrey – level switches – Bearwood Engineering Supplies

Bestobell Valves – cryogenic valves for industrial gas – Flowgroup Ltd Bestobell Valves & Conflow

Bestwelds – own brand mig, tig & plasma, torches, spares & consumables. – Weldspares Ltd

Beta – plumbers brass foundry – F W Hipkin Ltd

Beta – conventional eyepiece microscope – Vision Engineering Ltd

Beta-Probe – averaging pitot primary flow sensor – Tamo Ltd

Beta Skimmer – small clean-up operations where space is limited – Megator Ltd

Beta Tools – Trafalgar Tools

BetaBasic – high purity silica based columns with increased pH stability for HPLC and LC/MS – Thermo Fisher Scientific

BETABITE – Hydraulic & Offshore Supplies Ltd

Betabite – compression fittings and valves, non return and shut off – Betabite Hydraulics Ltd

Betabite – stainless steel and carbon steel high pressure couplings and valves – Betabite Hydraulics Ltd

Betabite Hydraulics – Trafalgar Tools

Betabric – Poundfield Products Ltd

Betabric Walling system – Poundfield Products Ltd

Betacom S.P. – electronic news gathering industrial format – Sony Head Office

Betacontrol – thickness measurement systems and density measuring equipment – Apropa Machinery Ltd

Betaflow – Harrier Fluid Power Ltd

BetaMax – highly retentive silica based columns for HPLC and LC/MS – Thermo Fisher Scientific

Betamesh – high performance filter mesh – G Bopp & Co. Ltd

Betapril – ammonium nitrate – Orica UK Ltd

Betasil – high purity, base deactivated silica columns – Thermo Fisher Scientific

Betathane – solid polyurethane products – Hallam Polymer Engineering Ltd

Betazyme – B-Glucanese – Murphy & Son

Beterprufe – rubber/bitumen liquid d.p.c. – Cavity Trays Ltd

Bethan – training and consultancy – University Of Leeds

Betico – service and parts for compressors for fairground rides – Airware International Ltd

Betoatlas – retaining wall – Grass Concrete Ltd

Betoconcept – retaining wall range – Grass Concrete Ltd

Betoflor – retaining wall – Grass Concrete Ltd

Betojard – noise barriers – Grass Concrete Ltd

Betonac – industrial flooring aggregate – Don Construction Products Ltd

Betonap – geotextiles – Grass Concrete Ltd

Betonol – protective coatings – Permatex Protective Coatings UK Ltd

Betotitan – retaining wall – Grass Concrete Ltd

Bettamix – plastic bottles – Bettix Ltd

Better Balance – Life & Work Coaching – Better Balance Coaching

Betterbox – datacommunications equipment – Betterbox Communications Ltd

Betterware – homeware and homecare products – Betterware Ltd

Bettinson Wheels – wheels – Terry Johnson Ltd

Bettis (United Kingdom) – valve actuators – Paladon Systems Ltd

Bettis – Orbinox UK Ltd

Betwixt – Marketing Company – Carnation Designs Ltd

Bevan Funnell – The Winnen Furnishing Company

Bevan Funnell Furniture – The Winnen Furnishing Company

Bevelled Lags – pipes, ducts and industrial noise control – Rockwool Rockpanel B V

Beveller (United Kingdom) – bevelling/chamfering – Seco Engineering Co. Ltd

Beverley – Beverley Environmental Ltd

Beverley – thermal oil heaters – Twin Industries International Ltd

Beverley Turbocoil – packaged thermal fluid heater – Beverley Environmental Ltd

Bevilacqua – bopp overwrapping film – A B L Perpack 1985 Ltd

Bevilacqua Lovetilene – p.e non fusion pallet covers – A B L Perpack 1985 Ltd

Bevpor – liquid stabilisation filter for beverage industry – Parker Dominic Hunter Ltd

Bevwhite – coffee whitener – A A K Bakery Services

Bewo – Peter Rushton Ltd

Bexley Borough Mercury – South London Press

Bexloy – automotive engineering resin – Du Pont UK Ltd

Beyeler – Bystronic UK Ltd

Beyschlag – Cyclops Electronics Ltd

Bezora – industrial lubricants – B P plc

*Bezzera – Maidaid Halcyon

BF Entron – resistance welding timers – Quality Manufacturing Services Ltd

BFF Nonwovens – nonwoven fabric – B F F Nonwovens

BFT – Eagle Automation Systems Ltd

BFT, – High End, Quality Automatic Gate Kits – C P A Ironworks

Bg Removals – Man and Van Nottingham Home and Office Removals company in Nottingham – Removals In Nottingham

BG710 – non contact measurement of moisture in biscuits – N D C Infra-Red Engineering Ltd

BGCMAP – LPR Corrosion Meter – Testconsult Ltd

BGMS – Buckhill Groupware and Mail Server – Buckhill Ltd

BGP – record label – Ace Records Ltd

Bhardwaj – offshore companies and marketing – Bhardwaj Insolvency Practitioners

BHC Aerovox – Cyclops Electronics Ltd

BHRA – technical information services in fluid and process engineering – B H R Group

Bi-Fi – internal radio aerial devices – B S H Industries Ltd

Bi-Fold Doors – Plaut International

Bi-Sonic – fans & blowers – G D Rectifiers Ltd

BI Technologies – Cyclops Electronics Ltd

Bianca – Turner Bianca

Bianca (United Kingdom) – unobtrusuve, aestically designed over head hoist available as either a room covering or single track system – Arjo Med AB Ltd

Bianchi – Aspen International Ltd

Bias Binding – W Attwood Ltd

Biasyde – bias binding – J B Broadley

Biax (Germany) – pneumatic tools, scrapers and flexible shaft machines – R J H Finishing Systems Ltd

Bibbigard – torque limiters, safety elements and backstops – Bibby Transmissions Ltd

Bibby – resilient and gear couplings – Bibby Transmissions Ltd

Bibby Distribution (United Kingdom) – distribution company – Bibby Lion Group

*Bibby Feeds – Curtis & Co Oundle Ltd

Bibbyflex – disc couplings – Bibby Transmissions Ltd

*Bic – Pens – Hospitality A V

BIC – UK Office Direct

BICAT – catalysts – I M C D UK Ltd

Biccotest – test equipment – Bearwood Engineering Supplies

Bicester Review – newspaper – Leamington Spa Courier

Bicester System – squash & racketball courts – Bicester Products Squash Court Manufacturers Ltd

Bicesterwall – squash court play wall systems – Bicester Products Squash Court Manufacturers Ltd

BICKERS – Hydraulic & Offshore Supplies Ltd

Bicobond 180 – polyester imide with thermosetting bond coat, biconesterproperties. bondable at 180 - 200 degrees c. replaces needfor varnishing/lacing & binding operations. spec IEC 317-N.NEMA MW 26C – Essex UK Ltd

Biconester – polyester - imide suitable for 180 degrees c class h spec.BS 6811part 3, 2 and IEC 317-8 – Essex UK Ltd

Biconester – polyester enamelled copper wire – Essex UK Ltd

Bicor – loudspeaker enclosure – Lowther Loudspeaker Systems Ltd

Bicosol – solderable enameled copper wire – Essex UK Ltd

Bicosol – quick soldering polyurethane base suitable for 130 degreesc classb. spec. BS 6811 part 3, 1 and IEC 317-4 – Essex UK Ltd

Bicotest – Alpha Electronics Southern Ltd

Bicotherm – high temperature dual coat enamelled copper wire – Essex UK Ltd

Bicotherm – modified polyester base with polyamide - imide top coats. suitable for 200 degrees c class 200. spec. no BS 6811 part 3,3. IEC 317-13. NEMA MW 1000 - 1973 section 35c and 36c – Essex UK Ltd

Bicycles – land rover – Pashley Cycles Ltd

Bicycles – traditional – Pashley Cycles Ltd

Bicycles – all purpose – Pashley Cycles Ltd

Biddle – Alpha Electronics Southern Ltd

Biddle – high voltage and cable fault location equipment – Megger Ltd

Biddy Pioneer – A P Valves

Bienfang – foamboard – Seal UK Ltd

Bifix – Seco Tools UK Ltd

Bifold – bifolding sliding door gear for wardrobes – P C Henderson Ltd

BIG A – Harrier Fluid Power Ltd

Big Beat – record label – Ace Records Ltd

Big Dipper – twin axle version of the Dipper for larger boats – Indespension Ltd

Big Head – USBL acoustic transceiver designed for deepwater applications and high vessel noise environments – Sonardyne International Ltd

Big John Drum – cardboard cylindrical container – Robinson Healthcare Ltd

Big Time Books – Peter Haddock Ltd

Big Tom – Windfall Brands Ltd

Big Value – Robinson Young Ltd

Big Weaves – fabric collection – Zoffany

Bighead – perforated metal fasteners with studs or nuts centrally located – Bighead Bonding Fasteners Ltd

Biglia – Machine Tool Supplies Ltd

Biglia – Whitehouse Machine Tools Ltd

BIGLIA – multiaxis CNC lathes – R K International Machine Tools Ltd

BigMouth – electronic speech safety, security and information systems – O W L Electronics Ltd

Bijou – cubicles for young children – Premdor Crosby Ltd

Bijou by Bianca – Turner Bianca

Bijou Chameleon – cubicles for changing areas – Premdor Crosby Ltd

*Bik Bouwprodkiten (Netherlands) – building products – Yule Catto & Co plc

BikeMinder – motor cycle alarms – O W L Electronics Ltd

Bilitene – PE/Card laminated pack – Index

BILL – Cralec Electrical Distributors Ltd

Billa – hosiery – M Comar & Sons Ltd

Billbo (Badge) – badges – Billbo UK Ltd

Billericay Recorder – free weekly newspaper – Newsquest Essex Ltd

*Billing (Denmark) – wooden boat kits – Amerang Group Ltd

Billows-Protocol – Billows Protocol Ltd

Bilopaque – G E Healthcare

BILSOM – Hydraulic & Offshore Supplies Ltd

Bima (Italy) – agricultural gear boxes – BYPY Hydraulics & Transmissions Ltd

Bimagrip – water-proof, anti-slip surface treatment product – R S Clare & Co. Ltd

Bimax – Bruderer UK Ltd

*Bimax (Switzerland) – automatic sawing machines – Brunner Machine Tools Ltd

BiMos – structurally intergrated bipolar/mosfet – Diodes Zetex Semiconductors Ltd

Binder – Mercury Bearings Ltd

Binder – Selectronix Ltd

Binder Magnets – European Technical Sales Ltd

Bindfast – plastic slide binding bars – Gilmex International Ltd

Bindi Cakes – Olympia Foods Ltd

*Binding Site (United Kingdom) – medical diagnostic products – The Binding Site Ltd

Binelace – Rotadex Systems Ltd

Bingovision – games-designs – Europrint Promotions Ltd

Binisil – silicone fluid masterbatches – Micropol Ltd

BinKeeper – litter bin fixing kit – Amberol Ltd

Binks Bullows – paint spraying equipment – Air Power Centre Limited

Binneys – engineers merchants – Binney & Son Ltd

Binnlock – wire fencing – Binns Fencing Ltd

Binns and Berry lathes – Phil Geesin Machinery Ltd

Binns and Berry trident lathes – Phil Geesin Machinery Ltd

Binwall – bin storage walls – Grass Concrete Ltd

Binzel – European Technical Sales Ltd

Binzel – Mig torches – Premier Welding Services Scotland Ltd

Binzel Torches & Spares – Wessex Welding & Industrial Supplies Ltd

BIO 2+ – microbiological safety cabinet – Envair Ltd

*Bio-Boost – Micron Bio-Systems

*Bio-Chlor – Micron Bio-Systems

Bio-Gard (United Kingdom) – range of bursting discs for hygienic/aseptic service – Elfab Ltd

Bio-Gard – Advanced Hygiene PVC Strip curtains with SteriTouch – Seymour Manufacturing International Smi Ltd

Bio-Guard (United Kingdom) – metal bursting disc for hygienic/aseptic fittings – Elfab Ltd

Bio-Kult – Probiotics International Ltd

Bio-Lapis – Probiotics International Ltd

*Bio-Mos – Alltech UK Ltd

Bio-Tel (United Kingdom) – burst-disc detector for hygienic/aseptic fittings – Elfab Ltd

BIO-X – high efficiency air sterilisation filters – Parker Dominic Hunter Ltd

BioBasic – silica based columns for Biomolecular separations – Thermo Fisher Scientific

Biocath – hydrogel encapsulated foley catheters – Bard Ltd

Biochiom – Biochrom Ltd

Biochrom 30 – pc controlled amino acid analyser – Biochrom Ltd

Biochrom 30 - PC controlled amino acid analyser, Genequant II - RNA & DNA calculator, GeneQuant pro - RNA & DNA calculator, Ultrospec 2100 pro - UV and visible, Novaspec III, Novaspec plus, visible spectrophotometer, Ultrospec 3100 pro - UV and visible spectrophotometer, Ultrospec 3300 pro - UV and VIS scanning narrow bandwidth spectrophotometer, Ultrospec 4300,5300,6300 pro - UV and VIS scanning narrow bandwidth spectrophotometer, Ultrospec 500 and 1100 pro - low cost UV and Visible Spectrophotometers - Libra S4, Libra S6, Libra S11, Libra S12, Libra S21, Libra S32, Libra S32PC, Libra S35 and Libra S35PCLightwave II, Biowave II, TOPAS Analyzer, WPA S800 and WPA S1200 – Biochrom Ltd

Bioclene – Forward Chemicals Ltd

Bioclinique (United Kingdom) – mnfrs & suppliers of beauty therapy & medical equipment – Bio Clinique

Biocode Sscuri Print – anti counterfeiting – C C L Labels Decorative Sleeves

Biodeck – trickling filter media – Munters Ltd

Biodyne – filter medium – Pall Europe Corporate Services

Bioflex (United Kingdom) – smoothbore flexible PTFE hose – Aflex Hose Ltd

*BioFlo (U.S.A.) – fermentation equipment – New Brunswick Scientific UK Ltd

Bioflon (United Kingdom) – smoothbore flexible PTFE hose. – Aflex Hose Ltd

Biogard – water based epoxy coating for hygienic areas – Leighs Paints

BioGuard – pool chemicals and water treatment equipment. – Biolab UK Ltd

Biolan – biocide – Blackburn Chemicals Ltd

Biological Crop Protection Ltd – Biological Controller – L S Systems Ltd

Biological Laundry Powder 100 – multi-purpose detergent powder – Premiere Products Ltd

*BIOLUX (Germany) – photographic lamps – Osram Ltd

*Biomass Grease Trap – Progressive Product Developments Ltd

Biomat – Althon Ltd

Biomat 2 – class II microbiological safety cabinet – Medical Air Technology Ltd

Biomatic – grease separators – F C Frost Ltd

Biomembrat – Wehrle Environmental

Biomet – additive for anti fouling paints – Atosina UK Ltd

Biometric Fingerprint Reader – Tekdata Distribution Ltd

Biometrics – Tekdata Distribution Ltd

Biometrics Fingerprint – Tekdata Distribution Ltd

Biometrics Hardware – Tekdata Distribution Ltd

Biometrics Identity Reader – Tekdata Distribution Ltd

Biometrics Precise – Tekdata Distribution Ltd

Biometrics Reader – Tekdata Distribution Ltd

Biometrics Reader UK – Tekdata Distribution Ltd

Biometrics Recognition – Tekdata Distribution Ltd

Biometrics Recognition Technology – Tekdata Distribution Ltd

Biometrics Security – Tekdata Distribution Ltd

Biometrics System – Tekdata Distribution Ltd

Biometrics UK – Tekdata Distribution Ltd

Biomulch – mulch – Melcourt Industries

Bionaire – UK Office Direct

*Bioplex Mineral Proteinates – Alltech UK Ltd

Bioprene – long life peristaltic tubing for the biotechnology and pharmaceutical industries – Watson Marlow Pumps Ltd

*Biopro – E D F Man

Biopty – automatic biopsy instument – Bard Ltd

Biopur – biological aerated flooded filter – Aker Kvaerner Engineering Services Ltd

Biorock – Non-Electric sewage treatment plant – Waste Tech Environmental Ltd

Bioscan – radio TLC detectors – Lablogic Systems Ltd

Biosperse – reodorants – Ashland UK

BIOSPOT (United Kingdom) – effervescent chlorine tablets for hospital and janitorial disinfection – Hydrachem Ltd

Biostat – package sewage treatment plant – Tuke & Bell Ltd

*Biosuper – Harbro Ltd

Biosystem – starch based biodegradable foam packaging – Caledonian Industries Ltd

Biotal – hydroxyapatite coatings for orthopaedic implants – Plasma Biotal Ltd

Biotec – package sewage treatment plant – Titan

Biotest – Air Sampling Equipment – Biotest UK Ltd

Biotop Colour (Austria) – vast range of coloured paper for copiers/lasers – Davies Harvey & Murrell

Bioventures – researching antenatal testing – University Of Leeds

BioWare – Environmentally Friendly Packaging – Huhtamaki UK Ltd

Bipra Limited – For All Your IT Needs! – Bipra Ltd

Birch – cleaners sink – Armitage Shanks Ltd

Bircher Reglomat – Safety edges, mats & relays. Sensing products for pedestrians & vhicles – Motion29 Ltd

Bird Balls – Euro Matic Ltd

Bird & Bird – corporate solicitors – Bird & Bird

Bird Chain – totally flexible, anti-perch birdwire system, for the protection of structures against roosting birds (pigeons and gulls) – Deben Group Industries Ltd

*Bird Precision (U.S.A.) – precision orifices – The West Group Ltd

Bird's – custard and dry mix deserts – Kraft Foods UK Ltd

Bird's Nest – Huck Nets UK Ltd

Bird Watching – magazine – Emap Ltd

Birkdale – washbasin and closet – Ideal Standard Ltd

Birketts – bread savouries & confectionery – Greggs plc

Birmingham Midshires First Response – banking and insurance and investment services – Birmingham Midshires Financial Services Ltd

Birmingham Midshires Mastercheque – banking, insurance and financial services – Birmingham Midshires Financial Services Ltd

Birmingham Safety Glass – glass – Auto Windscreens

Birns – Submarine Manufacturing & Products Ltd

Birthday Bed – Hoskins Medical Equipment Ltd

BIS – Business information service – Business Information Service

Bisandet – Forward Chemicals Ltd

BISAZZA – Leading glass mosaic brand – World's End Couriers Ltd

Bisca-Fuse (United Kingdom) – Anti static PTFE coated glass fabric – Biscor Ltd

Bisca-Pak (United Kingdom) – PTFE coated glass fabric – Biscor Ltd

Bisca-Sil (United Kingdom) – silicone coated glass fabrics – Biscor Ltd

Bisca-Stic (United Kingdom) – PTFE coated glass fabric tape – Biscor Ltd

Bisca-Tex (United Kingdom) – PTFE coated glass fabric – Biscor Ltd

Bisco cellular silicones – C B Frost & Co. Ltd

Bisco cellular silicones - BF 1000 HT800 – C B Frost & Co. Ltd

Bishop's Adamant – gauge glasses – J B Treasure & Co. Ltd

Bishopsgate – general insurance – Fortis UK Ltd

*Bishore (Germany) – paving supports – Alumasc Exterior Building Products

Bisiflex – magnetic materials in sheet and strip, all being flexible – Bisbell Magnetic Products Ltd

Bisigrip – magnetic knife racks – Bisbell Magnetic Products Ltd

Bisimag – magnetic blocks and discs – Bisbell Magnetic Products Ltd

Bisimag – rubber covered magnets – Bisbell Magnetic Products Ltd

Bisley – office equipment – F C Brown Steel Equipment Ltd

Bisley – Storage – Bucon Ltd

Bisley – UK Office Direct

Bisley – office furniture – E W Marshall Ltd

Bisley Office Equipment – office furniture – BBI Business Interiors Ltd

Bismuth metal and Chemicals – M C P Ltd

Bisoflex – B P plc

Bisoflex – chemicals (speciality plasticisers) – Cognis Performance Chemicals Ltd

Bisol – B P plc

Bisolube – B P plc

Bisolube – Cognis Performance Chemicals Ltd

Bisomer – chemicals (speciality monomers) – Cognis Performance Chemicals Ltd

Bisomer – B P plc

Bison (United Kingdom) – double-ended pedestal grinder – R J H Finishing Systems Ltd

Bison – remould truck tyres – Tyre Renewals Ltd

*Bistec (Hong Kong) – import and export calculator – Broughton & Co Bristol Ltd

Bistim – dual magnetic nerve stimulator module – Magstim Co. Ltd

Bitelli – Harrier Fluid Power Ltd

Bitex – reinforced leather gloves – Bennett Safetywear

Bitrex – bitter chemical – Macfarlan Smith Ltd

Bitstream – high quality fonts – Fontware Ltd

Bittner Collection – spectacle frames – Pennine Optical Group Ltd

Bituclean – Proteus Equipment Ltd

Bitucrete – instant road repair storage macadam – Colas Ltd

Bitukleen – Proteus Equipment Ltd

Bitukold – cold applied thixotropic bitumen emulsion for sealing vertical joints – Colas Ltd

Bitumac – polymer modified slurry surfacing – Colas Ltd

Bitumak – bitumen paints – Thomas Howse Ltd

Bitumen – emulsions – Tenants Bitumen

Bitumine – enamel paints – Witham Oil & Paint Lowestoft Ltd

Bituslip – Proteus Equipment Ltd

Bitutex FP – rapid setting hand applied slurry seal for footways, car parks and playgrounds – Colas Ltd

Bituthene – waterproof membranes – Grace Construction Ltd

Bituticton – heavy duty protective film – Cavity Trays Ltd

Bitzer – Therma Group

Biz Presentation – Presentation for business – Lightsource Event Technology Ltd

Bizarre – Magazine – John Brown Publishing

Bizcare Consult – Business Development Management Systems – Bizcare Ltd

Bizzarri – The Winnen Furnishing Company

BK – spinning aprons – Brooksbank Holdings

BKC – Stacatruc

Black – energy controls – Black Teknigas & Electro Controls Ltd

Black and Decker – power tools – Campbell Miller Tools Ltd

Black Basalt – giftware, jewellery and characterware – Wedgewood Travel Ltd

Black Book, The – wallpaper collection – Zoffany

Black Bush – whiskey – Old Bushmills Distillery Co. Ltd

Black Carbon – Corporate identity – Black Carbon Limited

Black Cat – fireworks – Black Cat Fireworks Ltd

Black Cherry Keyboard – Tekdata Distribution Ltd

BLACK & DECKER – Fieldway Supplies Ltd

Black & Decker – UK Office Direct

Black & Decker – Gem Tool Hire & Sales Ltd

Black & Decker – S J Wharton Ltd

Black & Decker – Red House Industrial Services Ltd

Black Diamond – dental products – Prima Dental Group Ltd

*Black Diamond – cheese slices – Kerry Foods Ltd

Black Diamond – processed cheese slices for fast food industry – Dairy Produce Packers Ltd

Black Diamond – panelling structures with lighting for exhibitions – Pinewood Associates

BLACK DIAMOND – Hydraulic & Offshore Supplies Ltd

Black Fibre – high quality black master batches for tape and fibre extrusion – Hubron Speciality Ltd

Black jack – flashing tape and bitumens – Everbuild Building Products Ltd

Black Knight 2 Gas – inset living flame gas fire – Robinson Willey

Black Knight Classic Collection – inset living flame gas fire – Robinson Willey

Black Knight Electric – electric inset fire – Robinson Willey

Black N'Red – UK Office Direct

Black Prince – boat holidays – Harlow Agricultural Merchants Ltd

Black Sheep – pure wool jerseys – Black Sheep Ltd

Black Silk – technical black plastic masterbatches for demanding applications – Hubron Speciality Ltd

Black Tek – polymer specific masterbatches for engineering thermoplastics – Hubron Speciality Ltd

*Blackalloy (U.S.A.) – toolbits and parting blades – Brunner Machine Tools Ltd

Blackalloy – Bruderer UK Ltd

Blackboard Plus – innovative blackboard – Barconwood Ltd

Blackedge – pencil – Cumberland Pencil Company

Blackfoot – action vehicles, remote, radio controlled and friction driven – P M S International Group plc

BLACKMER – pumps – H K L Gas Power Ltd

Blackmer – sliding vane positive displacement pumps – Axflow

Blackpool Pleasure Beach – amusement park and recreational facilities – Blackpool Pleasure Beach Ltd

Blackspur – DIY goods – Hamble Distribution Ltd

BLACKWATER HYDRAULICS – Hydraulic & Offshore Supplies Ltd

Bladerunner – indoor/outdoor spike/saktes/stud resistant flooring – Jaymart Roberts & Plastics Ltd

Blagden Chemicals – general chemicals – Blagden Specialty Chemicals Ltd

Blagdon Pumps – Air operated Double diaphragm – Fluid Pumps Ltd

Blaggy – cold roll formed steel metal sections – Blagg & Johnson Ltd

BLAGO – Hydraulic & Offshore Supplies Ltd

Blair – grain equipment – Blair Engineering

*Blak-ray (U.S.A.) – UV lamps - long wave – Ultra-Violet Products Ltd

Blake – sewage distributor – Tuke & Bell Ltd

Blakeborough Controls, Batley Valve, Hopkinsons, MAC Valves – Weir Valves & Controls

Blakeacre Bolt-Lok – fastening system – Blackacre Ltd

Blakeborough – globe/angle control valves, severe service control valves, choke valves, desuperheaters – Weir Valves & Controls

Blaken piling system – Hercules Holding Ii Ltd

Blakey – marble fireplaces – Colin Blakey's Fireplace Galleries Ltd

Blakey's Boot Protectors – heel plates, toe tips and 9 sizes of shoe protectors – Pennine Castings Ltd

Blakley – site electrics – Robert Craig & Sons Ltd

Blanca Press – Fast Systems Ltd

Blancapress – Fast Systems Ltd

Blanco Y Negro – record company – Rough Trade Management

Blanella – domestic heating and electrical appliances – Glen Electric Ltd

BLANKE ARMATUREN – Hydraulic & Offshore Supplies Ltd

*Blanose (France) – cellulose gum (sodium carboxymethylcellulose and CMC) – Hercules Holding Ii Ltd

Blast N'Vac (United Kingdom) – vacuum blast cleaning and recovery system ideal for the removal of toxic coatings – Jedtec Finishing Equipment

Blastaway (Switzerland) – Airless systems – Exitflex UK Ltd

Blastite – aluminium oxide – Washington Mills Electro Minerals Ltd

Blastmaster – abrasive blast cabinet – Wheelabrator Group

Blastrac – U S F Blastrac

Blaupunkt – in car communications – Robert Bosch Ltd

Blaw Knox – Harrier Fluid Power Ltd

Blaze – sailboat – Topper International

Blaze Design – Office Seating – Bucon Ltd

Blazemaster – firefighters' gloves – Bennett Safetywear

Blazemaster – cpvc – F L D Chemicals Ltd

Blazer – winter maintenance gritter – Whale Tankers Ltd

*Blazon (U.S.A.) – spray pattern indicator – Farmura Ltd

Bleach – strong – Evans Vanodine International plc

Blease – medical suction apparatus – Space Labs Healthcare

Blendworth Fabric – The Winnen Furnishing Company

Blenheim – 80% wool/ 20% nylon twist pile broadloom – Adam Carpets Ltd

Blenheim – Dixon Turner Wallcoverings Ltd

Blick – UK Office Direct

Blickle – Mercury Bearings Ltd

Blickle - Extrathane - Softhane - Besthane – Blickle Castors & Wheels Ltd

Blighline – refrigeration, catering concepts & checkouts – Blighline Ltd

Blind System Selection – The eclipse guide for windows blinds for architects and commercial specifiers – Eclipse Blind Systems

Bliss – woollen and worsted cloth – Fox Brothers & Company Ltd

Blitz – torque wrench – Hytorc Unex Ltd

Blitz Interative – interactive control systems for AV – Blitz Communications Ltd

Blitz Vision – audio visual presentation equipment – Blitz Communications Ltd

*Blizzard – Pentland Wholesale Ltd

BLM – B L M Group UK Ltd

BLM-Adige – Laser Trader Ltd

Bloc – street furniture – Townscape Products Ltd

Blocan – aluminium profile system, modular assembly system – Rose & Krieger

Block Detection Intrusion Ping – Tekdata Distribution Ltd

Block & Mesh – Accesscaff International Ltd

Block Paving – flagstone paving – Thakeham Tiles Ltd

Blocklift – gas spring - can be stopped at any position during operation – Camloc Motion Control Ltd

Blockware – open systems design methodology – New Information Paradigms Ltd

Blocnail Slimline Clasp – nail for lightweight building block – Glasgow Steel Nail Co. Ltd

Blodgett Convection – Middleby UK Ltd

Blodgett Conveyor – Middleby UK Ltd

Blogg – lifting bench – Blagg & Johnson Ltd

*Blom & Maters (Netherlands) – jar and bottle cleaning machines (air cleaning or rinsing) and bottle conveyor systems – A M J Maters Partnership Ltd

Blond Coat – Packaging Products Ltd

Blond Union – Packaging Products Ltd

Blood Bowl – games, playthings, miniatures and models – Games Workshop Ltd

Bloodhound Sensors – electronic nose sensors and instrumentations – University Of Leeds

Bloomsbury (United Kingdom) – traditional light switch – R Hamilton & Co. Ltd

Blount – Harrier Fluid Power Ltd

Blow Thru Sieve – Russell Finex Ltd

Blowdown Vessels – Abbott & Co Newark Ltd

Blowers (Roots) – G V E Ltd

Blown Loft Insulation – ceilings – Rockwool Rockpanel B V

BLP Components – Cyclops Electronics Ltd

BLT&C – Procurement and International Trade Training and Consultancy – BLT&C Ltd

Blu-Tack – re-usable adhesive – Bostik Ltd

Blue Anchor Line – forwarding & logistics – Kuehne & Nagel UK Ltd

Blue Arrow – employment agency – Blue Arrow Personnel Services Ltd

Blue Book, The – wallpaper collection – Zoffany

Blue Chip – vending ingredients and ambient food – Bunzl Vending Services Ltd

Blue Diamond – fast exit stalls – Delaval

Blue Dragon Dry Cleaners – dry cleaners launderers – Blue Dragon Dry Cleaners Ltd

Blue Dragon Hillingdon – Blue Dragon Dry Cleaners Ltd

Blue Eyetec – waterproof plaster (electronically detectable) – Robinson Healthcare Ltd

Blue Flame – firelighters – Tiger Tim Products Ltd

Blue Flash – masonry drill bits – Rawlplug Ltd

Blue Grass – perfumes – Elizabeth Arden

Blue Hawk – D.I.Y. home improvement products – Artex Ltd

Blue Line – screen chemicals – Macdermid Autotype Ltd

Blue Moon – childrens wear – David Charles Childrens Wear Ltd

Blue Moon – polypropylene baler twine – Steve Orr Ltd

Blue Pages – directory for British boat owners – Geraldine Flower Publications

Blue Ram Lavatory Cleaner – quick action lavatory cleanser – Premiere Products Ltd

Blue Ripple – stainless steel heat exhangers and swimming pool equipment – Jetform Services Ltd

Blue Roller – Textile sleeve for use in the aluminium extrusion industry – Marathon Belting Ltd

*Blue Royale – Anitox

*Blue Seal – Blue Seal Ltd

*Blue Seal – Crown Catering Equipment Ltd

Blue Seal – colouring and flavours – Cargill Flavor Systems UK Ltd

Blue Seal – step ladders & combination ladder – Abru Ltd

*Blue Seal – Capital Refrigeration Services Ltd

Blue Seal – Catercraft Catering Equipment

Blue Seal – Ascot Wholesale Ltd

Blue Star – hermetic condensing units by maneurop – Thermofrost Cryo plc

Blue Star Battery – lead acid battery distributors – Dynamic Battery Services Ltd

Blue Streak Europe – remanufacturers of electronic control units – Standard Motor Products Europe Ltd

Blue Streak II – cloth cutting machine – Eastman Staples Ltd

Blue Sulphur – Compsoft plc

Blue Tooth – Anritsu Ltd

Blue Triangle – brake equipment – Forster & Hales Ltd

Blue Wrapper – sash cord waxed – James Lever & Sons Ltd

Bluebird 'Pidion' – Maxa Technologies Ltd

Blueblur – childrens and baby wear – O S R International Ltd

Bluecrest – food service frozen – Youngs Seafood

Bluedeta – Trade name – Bluedelta

Blueparrot Media – Blueparrot Production & Events Ltd

Bluestripe – hacksaw blades (bi-metal high speed steel edge) – L S Starrett Co. Ltd

Bluetooth – UK Office Direct

Blum – European Technical Sales Ltd

Blusyl – neutral detergent – Evans Vanodine International plc

BM SERIES – signal conditioning equipment din rail mounting. DC Powered – Lee-Dickens Ltd

BMC – H & H Commercial Truck Services Ltd

BMD-GARANT – dust & fume extraction equipment – Dantherm Filtration Ltd

BMG Classics UK – produce, record, manufacture and distribute classical and non – Sony BMG Music Entertainment

BMM – Compact gas fired heaters – Barkair Ltd

BMW – Ashley Competition Exhausts Ltd

BMW – L M C Hadrian Ltd

BMW – Harrier Fluid Power Ltd

BNR – Blast and recovery systems – Jedtec Finishing Equipment

Bo Concept – The Winnen Furnishing Company

Boa – K S B Ltd

Boa (United Kingdom) – dust extraction – R J H Finishing Systems Ltd

Boardman – wholesalers of gloves – Boardman Bros Ltd

BoardMaster – universal diagnostic system – A B I Electronics Ltd

Boat Angler – magazine – Emap Ltd

Boat Level – Fieldway Supplies Ltd

Boatcoat – Tufcoat

Boax – K S B Ltd

Boax B – K S B Ltd

Bob Anderson – darts flights – Unicorn Products Ltd

Bob Martin – pet healthcare – Bob Martin UK Ltd

Bobbinet – woven tulle – Swisstulle UK Ltd

Bobcat – A T Wilde & Son Ltd

Bobcat – Border Industrial Services

BOBCAT – Chaintec Ltd

Bobcat – P J P Plant Hire

Bobcat – T V H UK Ltd

Bobolowski – European Technical Sales Ltd

BOC – industrial hoses – C C H Hose & Rubber

BOC Edwards High Vacuum – AESpump

BOC Gases – Wessex Welding & Industrial Supplies Ltd

Bock – Therma Group

Bock Workholding (U.S.A.) – Machine Vices – Roemheld UK Ltd

Bockingford – watercolour papers – Exaclair Ltd

BOCS – box office computer system – Seatem

Boden Timber Frame – prefabricated timber buildings – Boys & Boden Ltd

*Bodge The Badger (Far East) – functional outdoor gear for kids – Flitterman Investments Ltd

*Bodine (U.S.A.) – fractional geared motors – Micro Clutch Developments Ltd

Body Prints – ladies underwear – Westbridge International Group Ltd

Body Spray – classix bodyspray – L E C Liverpool Ltd

Bodybuilt – Sitsmart Ltd

Bodyguards – S J Wharton Ltd

*Bodymaster (France) – crash repair equipment – Bodyshop Solutions

Bodyshop Services – Akzo Nobel Coatings Ltd

Bodywise – cosmetics and perfumery - printed matter and clothing – Bodywise Ltd

Boelube – metal working lubricants – ATA Engineering Processes

Boen – N W Flooring

Boen Parkett – The Winnen Furnishing Company

Bofi – Equipline

Bofusion – Silhouette Beauty Equipment

Boge – Harrier Fluid Power Ltd

Boge – compressors, parts and service – Airware International Ltd

BOGE COMPRESSORS – Hydraulic & Offshore Supplies Ltd

Bogen Electronics – Selectronix Ltd

Bohl & Kirk – Harrier Fluid Power Ltd

Bohler Cutting Steel – knife making steels, also cutting and creasing rules – Partwell Cutting Technology Ltd

Bohler Dur – welding consumables – Bohler Welding Group Ltd

Bohler Fox – welding consumables – Bohler Welding Group Ltd

Bohler Ledurit – welding consumables – Bohler Welding Group Ltd

Bohler Steel – knife making steels, also cutting and creasing rules – Partwell Cutting Technology Ltd

Bohler Thyssen (Germany) – welding electrodes, wires & fluxes – John Davies 2001 Ltd

Bohrbuchsen (Switzerland) – Drill bushes – Berger Tools Ltd

Boilerclave – steam raising autoclave – L B B C Technologies

Boilertan – organic tannin - boiler treatment – Feedwater Ltd

Boilie Bayonet – fishing tackle class 28 – Drennan International Ltd

Bola (United Kingdom) – cricket ball delivery machine – Sportsmark Group Ltd

Bold Roll – concrete – Sandtoft Holdings Ltd

Bolehill Delph – sandstone – Realstone Ltd

Bolens – grass cutting machines and ancillary products – Claymore

BOLENZ & SCHAFFER – Hydraulic & Offshore Supplies Ltd

Bolero – kitchen furniture – Moores Furniture Group

Boley (Germany) – CNC lathes & turning centres – Citizen Machinery UK Ltd

Boliden Brass – Mckechnie Brass

*Bolivar (Cuba, Jamaica, Europe and Honduras) – cigars – Hunters & Frankau Ltd

Bolltex (Range) – indoor tennis surface – Verde Sports Cricket Ltd

Boltawall – vinyl wallcoverings – Tektura plc

Bolted Trusses – Roof trusses – R T E UK Ltd

BOLZONI – Chaintec Ltd

Bomac – heating elements for domestic and industrial applications – Bomac Electric Ltd

Bomag – P J P Plant Hire

Bomag – earthmoving equipment – Gunn J C B

Bomag – A T Wilde & Son Ltd

Bomag – Harrier Fluid Power Ltd

Bomag – Mawsley Machinery Ltd

Bombard – Plastic Bollard – Alto Bollards UK Ltd

Bombardier – Harrier Fluid Power Ltd

Bombardier – premium bitter ale – Wells & Young's Brewing Co.

Bombardier Transportation – Bombardier Transportation Rolling Stock UK Ltd

BombTec – Allen Vanguard Ltd

Bomford – Murley Agricultural Supplies Ltd

Bomford – Mike Garwood Ltd

Bomford – Joe Turner Equipment Ltd

Bon Appetit – disposable catering equipment – Plastico Ltd

Bon Vivant – savoury snack range – C S M UK Ltd

Bona Fide Technology – LCD displays – Anglia

Bonafil – artificial grass yarn – Bonar Yarns & Fabrics Ltd

Bonagrass – artificial grass yarn – Bonar Yarns & Fabrics Ltd

Bonagrass - Bonar Yarns – Bonar Yarns & Fabrics Ltd

Bonaire – baths – Jendico Ltd

Bonar Yarns – fibrillated polypropylene yarn for carpet industry – Bonar Yarns & Fabrics Ltd

Bonaslide – artificial grass yarn – Bonar Yarns & Fabrics Ltd

Bonasoft – artificial grass yarn – Bonar Yarns & Fabrics Ltd

Bonbiglioli – shearing and baling machinery – M M H Recycling Systems Ltd

Boncaster – insurance brokers – Equity Insurance

Bonda – expanding foam – Bondaglass Voss Ltd

Bonda Wood Fill – polyester wood fillers – Bondaglass Voss Ltd

Bondafiller – polyester filler – Bondaglass Voss Ltd

Bondaglass – glass fibre and resins – Bondaglass Voss Ltd

Bondax – carpet tiles – Bond Worth

Bondhus – S J Wharton Ltd

Bondina – NBC materials – Vilene Interlinings

*Bondioli and Pavesi (Italy) – agricultural PTO shafts and gearboxes – BYPY Hydraulics & Transmissions Ltd

Bondit – sealants – Arrow Supply Co. Ltd

Bondwave – nylon reinforced PVC sheetings – Flexible Reinforcements Ltd

Boneham Metal Products (BMP) (U.S.A.) – jig bushing/drill bushing, dowel pins, standard jig and fixture parts, shims, press tool parts, sealing plugs – Boneham & Turner Ltd

Bonfab – lace curtains & theatrical screens – Filigree Ltd

Bonfiglioli – Mercury Bearings Ltd

Bonfiglioli – power transmission products – Amir Power Transmission Ltd

Bonfiglioli Components – DC motors, AC motors and servo motors – Bonfiglioli UK Ltd

Bonfiglioli Gearboxes – gearboxes – Potteries Power Transmission Ltd

Bonfiglioli Riduttori – gear boxes and geared motors, variable speed drives – Bonfiglioli UK Ltd

BONFIGLIOLI TRASMITAL – Hydraulic & Offshore Supplies Ltd

Bongrape – premium low alcohol drinks – Bottle Green Drinks Co.

Bonhams – fine art autioneers – Bonhams Auctioneers

Bonito – 16 seater coaches – Optare Group Ltd

*Bonkote (Japan) – soldering/desoldering equipment – Electro Group Ltd

Bonnet – carrier for multipack of cartons for milk and juice – Nampak Carton

*Bonnet – heavy duty catering equipment – Asterix Catering Equipment Ltd

Bonnie – knitwear – Novinit Ltd

Bonocryl – water based coating – A G Stuart Holdings Ltd

Bonomi – Southern Valve & Fitting Co. Ltd

BONOMI – Hydraulic & Offshore Supplies Ltd

BONSER – Chaintec Ltd

Bonsoir – mens and ladies pyjamas, dressing gowns, nightshirts – Bonsoir Of London Ltd

Bontite – pallet stretch film – bpi.agri

Bonus – shower enclosures – Coram Showers Ltd

Bonus – Georgia Pacific GB Ltd

Bonus 180 – account – Furness Building Society

Bonusbond – vouchers – Grass Roots

Bonzer (United Kingdom) – caterers can openers, portioners and bar items, thermometers – Mitchell & Cooper Ltd

Boodles – jewellery – Boodles

Book2net – Genus Group

Boom Lifts – Accessscaff International Ltd

Boomslang – cranes – Panavision Grips Ltd

Boostamatic – pressure pumps – Stuart Turner Ltd

Boosted – boosted plumbing unit – Harton Services Ltd

Booster – agricultural wetting agent containing 100% polyalkylene oxide modified heptamethyl trisiloxane – Lambson Fine Chemicals Ltd

Booster Rad – supplement radiator – Kenlowe Accessories & Co. Ltd

Boostermat – K S B Ltd

Booth – post mix soft drink dispensers, carbonated vending modules and water chillers – Booth Dispensers

Booth Doors and Shutters – aircraft hangar doors and heavy industrial doors – Booth Industries

Booth Offshore Doors and Systems – fire and blast doors/wall systems – Booth Industries

Booth Repairs and Maintenance – door repair and maintenance service – Booth Industries

Booth Security – security doors – Booth Industries

Bootle Times – newspaper – Liverpool Daily Post & Echo

Boots Electrical – PVC and neoprene – Plastic Mouldings Ltd

Boplas – plastic components – Bolton Plastic Components Ltd

Boplicity – record label – Ace Records Ltd

BOPNav – remote BOP mounted acoustic transceiver – Sonardyne International Ltd

Bopp – wire cloth weavers and fabricators – G Bopp & Co. Ltd

Bopp & Reuther – Kee Valves

Bopp S D – screen printing mesh – G Bopp & Co. Ltd

Bopp SI – sieving/sizing mesh – G Bopp & Co. Ltd

Boracol B10RH – fungal growth steriliser and masonry biocide for dry rot – Channelwood Preservation Ltd

Boracol B20RH – wood preservative (high penetration inorganic boron) – Channelwood Preservation Ltd

Boracol B8.5RH – surface biocide (mould growth) and wood preservative – Channelwood Preservation Ltd

Boraxo – Gresolvent Ltd

Bordalok – needled bonded insulator – W E Rawson Ltd

Bordatex – bonded wadding – W E Rawson Ltd

Bordeaux Mixture – controls potato blight and other diseases – Vitax Ltd

Border – waterproof clothing – J Barbour & Sons Ltd

Borehole – centrifugal multistage shaft driven bowl pumps – Weir Group Senior Executives Pension Trust Ltd

BORELLI – Hydraulic & Offshore Supplies Ltd

Boremaster – Red House Industrial Services Ltd

Borg – Gate Locks – Steel Product Supplies

Borg Warner (Germany) – cage free wheels – Ringspann UK Ltd

Borg Warner – Team Overseas Ltd

Borger – rotary lobe positive displacement pumps – Axflow

Borghi – Dynamometers – Dynamometer Services Group Ltd

Boride – engineered abrasives - boride diemaker stones – Marcon Diamond Products Ltd

Boris Nets – trawl nets and fish farm cage nets – Boris Net Co. Ltd

Bormer – Twinmar Ltd

Borocilk – granular total herbiside – Bayer Crop Science

Boron Nitride – powder – Kennametal

Boron Rods – timber steriliser – Channelwood Preservation Ltd

*Borrebond – binding agent – Borregaard UK

*Borresperse (Norway) – lignosulphonates – Borregaard UK

Bosal – exhaust system – Bosal UK Ltd

Bosanova – Tekdata Distribution Ltd

Boscarol – Range of Emergency Products – Wel Medical Services

Bosch – power tools – Campbell Miller Tools Ltd

Bosch – power tools – Arrow Supply Co. Ltd

BOSCH – power tools – M B K Motor Rewinds Ltd

Bosch – Power Tools – Linacre Plant & Sales Ltd

Bosch – power tool – Robert Craig & Sons Ltd

Bosch – power tools – Brilec Power Tools Ltd

*Bosch (Germany) – electric & cordless power tools – Harrow Tool Co. Ltd

Bosch – Oxon Fastening Systems Ltd

*Bosch (Germany) – pneumatic control equipment – The West Group Ltd

BOSCH – European Drives & Motor Repairs

Bosch – Knighton Tool Supplies

Bosch – European Technical Sales Ltd

Bosch – SCARA Robots and Pallet Handling Systems. – S P Technology Ltd

BOSCH – Hydraulic & Offshore Supplies Ltd

Bosch – Pressure Design Hydraulics Ltd

Bosch – D D Hire

Bosch – UK Office Direct

Bosch – hydraulic equipment – Oddy Hydraulics Ltd

Bosch – Wessex Welding & Industrial Supplies Ltd

Bosch – Gustair Materials Handling Equipment Ltd

*Bosch (Germany) – Injection specialists – Watson Diesel Ltd

Bosch – S J Wharton Ltd

Bosch – Harrier Fluid Power Ltd

Bosch – Gem Tool Hire & Sales Ltd

Bosch – Encoders UK

Bosch – electrical equipment – Bearwood Engineering Supplies

*Bosch A.H.S. 3 (Switzerland) – hedgecutter, mains and cordless – Bosch Lawn & Garden Ltd

*Bosch A.H.S. 4 (Switzerland) – hedgecutter, mainsand cordless – Bosch Lawn & Garden Ltd

Bosch A.H.S. 40 - 24 (Switzerland) – hedgecutter – Bosch Lawn & Garden Ltd

Bosch A.H.S. 48 - 24 (Switzerland) – hedgecutter – Bosch Lawn & Garden Ltd

Bosch A.H.S. 55 - 24 – hedgecutter – Bosch Lawn & Garden Ltd

Bosch A.H.S. 60 - 24 (Switzerland) – hedgecutter – Bosch Lawn & Garden Ltd

Bosch A.H.S. 6000 Pro (Switzerland) – hedgecutter – Bosch Lawn & Garden Ltd

Bosch A.H.S. 7000 Pro (Switzerland) – hedgecutter – Bosch Lawn & Garden Ltd

Bosch A.K.E. 30 - 17 (Germany) – chain saw – Bosch Lawn & Garden Ltd

Bosch A.K.E. 35 - 17 (Germany) – chain saw – Bosch Lawn & Garden Ltd

Bosch A.K.E. 40 - 17 – chainsaw – Bosch Lawn & Garden Ltd

Bosch A.L.M. 28 – lawnmower – Bosch Lawn & Garden Ltd

Bosch A.L.M. 34 – lawnmower – Bosch Lawn & Garden Ltd

Bosch A.R.T. 23 – trimmer – Bosch Lawn & Garden Ltd

Bosch A.R.T. 25 – trimmer – Bosch Lawn & Garden Ltd

Bosch A.R.T. 30 – trimmer – Bosch Lawn & Garden Ltd

Bosch A.S.M. 32 – lawnmower – Bosch Lawn & Garden Ltd

Bosch A.X.T. 1600 (Germany) – shredder – Bosch Lawn & Garden Ltd

Bosch A.X.T. 1800 (Germany) – shredder – Bosch Lawn & Garden Ltd

*Bosch A.X.T. 2000 (Germany) – shredder – Bosch Lawn & Garden Ltd

Bosch Aquatak 100 (Italy) – pressure washer – Bosch Lawn & Garden Ltd

Bosch Aquatak 120i (Italy) – pressure washer – Bosch Lawn & Garden Ltd

Bosch Aquatak 1300 si (Italy) – pressure washer – Bosch Lawn & Garden Ltd

Bosch Aquatak 1500 si (Italy) – pressure washer – Bosch Lawn & Garden Ltd

Bosch Group – Trafalgar Tools

BOSCH POWER TOOLS – Fieldway Supplies Ltd

Bosch Power Tools – Drills, grinders, saws, sanders and a full range of rechargeable and cordless tools – R & M Electrical Group Ltd

BOSCH REXROTH – Hydraulic & Offshore Supplies Ltd

Bosch Rexroth – Southern Valve & Fitting Co. Ltd

Bosch-Rexroth Hydraulics – hydraulic parts – A C Hydraulics Ltd

Boscom – Tekdata Distribution Ltd

Boscotex – latex adhesive – Bostik Ltd

Bose – stereo speakers – Bose Ltd

Bose 802 – full range, portable PA speakers – Bose Ltd

Bose Lifestyle – hi-fi and home entertainment music systems – Bose Ltd

Bosello – Euroteck Systems UK Ltd

Boss – threading taps – Turner Tools Ltd

Boss – Stacatruc

Boss – T V H UK Ltd

BOSS – Business Operations System and Support – Bizcare Ltd

*Boss (U.S.A.) – industrial high pressure hose coupling for pneumatic and steam applications – Dixon Group Europe Ltd

Boss – Trafalgar Tools

BOSS – Chaintec Ltd

Boss – cycle – Falcon Cycles Ltd

Boss – pipe fittings, valves, gauges, jointing compounds and metallic cements – B S S Pipe Fitting Stockholders Head Office

Boss – sailboat – Topper International

Boss Design – Office Seating – Bucon Ltd

Boss-Flamco – pipe support systems – B S S Pipe Fitting Stockholders Head Office

Boss Green – jointing compounds – B S S Pipe Fitting Stockholders Head Office

Boss Lab – Broen Valves Ltd

Boss Minivent – automatic air vents – B S S Pipe Fitting Stockholders Head Office

Boss Towers – Accessscaff International Ltd

Boss Valves – F W Sibley Ltd

Bossblue – portable water pipe jointing compound – B S S Pipe Fitting Stockholders Head Office

Bossmatic – manually and power operated valves – B S S Pipe Fitting Stockholders Head Office

Bossmatic – control valves – Northvale Korting Ltd

*Bosspak (Australia) – tablet filling lines – Romaco Holdings UK Ltd

Bosswhite – jointing compounds and P.T.F.E. tape – B S S Pipe Fitting Stockholders Head Office

Bostik – Gem Tool Hire & Sales Ltd

Bostik – S J Wharton Ltd

Bostik – Austen Tapes Ltd

Bostik – B D K Industrial Products Ltd

Bostik – adhesives and sealants – Bostik Ltd

Bostik – UK Office Direct

Bostik – Bostik Ltd

Bostik – European Technical Sales Ltd

Bostik (UK) (United Kingdom) – adhesives – R D Taylor & Co. Ltd

Bostitch – Tri Pack Supplies Ltd

Bostitch – Gem Tool Hire & Sales Ltd

Boston – European Drives & Motor Repairs

BOSTON – Hydraulic & Offshore Supplies Ltd

Boston Gear – Motion Drives & Controls Ltd

Boston Gear – speed reducers, electric motors, bearings, gears & shaft accessories – G M B Associates

Boston Gear Motion Control Products – G M B Associates

Boston Gear - Watt Drive - Magpowr - Nexen Horton - Horton - Sitema - Coil Technology. – Motion Drives & Controls Ltd

Boston Matthews – extruders, dies, take-offs, auto saws, coilers, extrusion lines for pipes profiles and wire and cable insulation – Boston Munchy Ltd

*Boston Whaler (U.S.A.) – whaler boat – Dorset Lake Shipyard Ltd

Bostrand – mig wires – Murex Welding Products Ltd

Bosuns locker – ships chandler – Bosuns Locker

Boswell – root harvesters and feeders – Blair Engineering

Botek – Mollart Engineering

Botlin – fuse holders – Lawsons Fuses Ltd

Botra – bowls – Gunn & Moore

*Bottle Green Drinks – Mercia Fine Foods

Bottlegreen – premium adult drinks – Bottle Green Drinks Co.

Bouchard L'Escaut – U C D Ltd

Boughton – vehicle bodywork and cranes – Reynolds Boughton

Boughton Reynolds – waste handling and transportation equipment – Reynolds Boughton

Boulton – Incamesh Filtration Ltd

Bounce – hair preparations – Salon Services Hair & Beauty Supplies Ltd

Bounds Brand Scrumpy, – H Weston & Sons Ltd

*Bouquet Collection – Geerings Of Ashford Ltd

Bourdon – gauges – Bearwood Engineering Supplies

Bourdon Haenni – instrumentation – System Control Solutions Ltd

Bourdon Sedeme (France) – pressure gauges – Hydrasun Ltd

Bourgeonal – perfme speciality – Quest International UK Ltd

Bournemouth Daily Echo – daily newspaper – The Bournemouth Daily Echo

Bourns – Cyclops Electronics Ltd

Bourns – variable resistors inductors – Anglia

Bourns – multiuse - Prc resettable overcurrent protector – Hawco

Bowak – hygiene and disposable products – Bowak Ltd

Bowcourt – accountancy pads – Quicks Ltd

Bowdry – pitch dryer – Sportsmark Group Ltd

Bowens International – manufacturers of photographic flash lighting equipment – Bowens International Ltd

Bower – couplings & spares – Bearwood Engineering Supplies

Bower Roebuck and Co Ltd – woollen and worsted piece goods – Bower Roebuck & Co. Ltd

Bowex – couplings & spares – Bearwood Engineering Supplies

Bowex – Mercury Bearings Ltd

Bowker – W H Bowker Ltd

Bowley'S Of Bedford – Central Soucre Ltd

Bowleys – materials handling equipment – Central Soucre Ltd

Bowman – heat exchangers – Bearwood Engineering Supplies

Bowman – export stout – Wells & Young's Brewing Co.

Bowser Briggs – Harrier Fluid Power Ltd

BowTie – stainless steel tie for stabilising bowed walls and joists – Helifix Ltd

Boxall Industrial – design & manufacture industrial tank cleaning – Boxall Engineering Ltd

BoxBolt – FastClamp

*Boxer – Berthoud Sprayers

Boxer Boxer – boxer shorts – Barnett The Factory

Boxer Briefs – boxer shorts – Barnett The Factory

Boxford – Red House Industrial Services Ltd

Boxford – lathes,(standard and CNC) – Boxford Ltd

Boxford – drilling machines – Boxford Ltd

Boxford – milling machines (standard and CNC) – Boxford Ltd

Boxing News – magazine – Newsquest Group

Boxlight – Lamphouse Ltd

Boxmaker (United Kingdom) – Autobox Machinery Ltd

Boxpak – colour printers, cartons, paper baking cases, aluminium foilcontainers and foil blocking – Boxpak Ltd

Boy – Harrier Fluid Power Ltd

Boy – Proplas International Ltd

BP – B P plc

BP – Lubricants – Sprint Engineering & Lubricant

Bp – Hammond Lubricants & Chemicals Ltd

BP – range of steam boilers 2 Kw-30 Kw – Electrolux Laundry Systems

BP Amoco – B P plc

BP Carwash – B P plc

BP Domesticol – B P plc

BP Energy – B P plc

BP Express Shopping – B P plc

BP Gas – B P plc

BP Gas – S J Wharton Ltd

BP-in-Shield – B P plc

BP Lubricants – Race Industrial Products Ltd

BP Plus – B P plc

BP Response – B P plc

BP Shop – B P plc

BP Super – B P plc

BP Transform – B P plc

BPA – vacuum pumps – B P A UK Ltd

BPA International – The Winnen Furnishing Company

BPA - Vacuum Pumps. – B P A UK Ltd

BPCA – British pest control association – British Wood Preserving & Damp Proofing Association

*BPMA (United Kingdom) – british promotional merchanise assoc – Galpeg Ltd

BPR – Transcend Group Ltd

BPRV – BS&B Safety Systems (UK) Ltd

BPT – Door Entry System – Eagle Security Solutions Ltd

BPT – Eagle Automation Systems Ltd

BPW – trailer axle and suspension components – Roadlink International Ltd

BR – potting compound – Cytec Engineered Materials Ltd

Brabazon Art & Matt – paper – Fenner Paper Co. Ltd

Braby & Waller – solicitors – Irwin Mitchell Solicitors

Braces – belts, leather goods, bags etc – Heritage Belt Company

Brackett Green – spares & equipment – Bearwood Engineering Supplies

Brackla Engineering – darts, dart cabinets and accessories – Nodor International Ltd

Bracknell Standard – newspapers – Surrey & Berkshire Media Ltd

Bracol – thermal and acoustic insulation materials – Ainsworth Acoustics, Thermal & Building Insulation

Brad Harrison – Industrial automation waterproof connector systems – Motion29 Ltd

Bradbury – vehicle lifts – Spraybake Ltd

Bradbury – vehicle lifts – Bearwood Engineering Supplies

Bradco – sanitary washrooms – Franke Sissons Ltd

Braden – winches – Koppen & Lethem Ltd

Bradford – Hygienic couplings, fittings and valves – Dixon Group Europe Ltd

Bradford Traveller – buses – First Group plc

Bradlee Boilers – Twin Industries International Ltd

Bradley – CBM Logix

Bradley Hercules – airswept mill – Bradley Pulverizer Co.

Bradleys – traditional English furniture – J. S. Bradley Ltd

Bradrad – step drill for thin materials – G & J Hall Ltd

Bradtool – engineers' cutting tools – Bradford Tool Group

Bradwell Aggregates – sand and gravel – Bardon Concrete Ltd

Brady – shooting and fishing bags – E Jeffries & Sons Ltd

*Braemar (United Kingdom) – automotive upholstery leather – Bridge Of Weir Leather Co.

Braemar – WC & bidet – Armitage Shanks Ltd

Braemar – loop pile carpet tile – Warlord Contract Carpets Ltd

Braemar – yarns – Stylecraft

Braemar (Space Dyed Shades) – yarns – Stylecraft

Braham Millar – Niagara-Screen – Metso Minerals UK Ltd

*Brahma (Italy) – ignition transformers – Anglo Nordic Burner Products Ltd

Brahms – Kuwait Petroleum International Lubricants UK Ltd

Braime (United Kingdom) – elevator buckets and components – Braime Elevator Components Ltd

Brains Bitter – Bitter – S A Brain & Co. Ltd

Brains Dark – Bitter – S A Brain & Co. Ltd

Brains S.A. – Bitter – S A Brain & Co. Ltd

BrainStorm – software system – Independent Power Systems

Bramah – locks – Bramah Alarms

Brambly Hedge – Chorion plc

Bramet – self adhesive waterproof silicon carbide discs – Kemet International Ltd

Brand – Avalon and Lynwood

Brand Dynamics tm – brand equity evaluation – Millward Brown

Brand & Heinz – Haesler Machine Tools

BRAND HYDRAULICS – Hydraulic & Offshore Supplies Ltd

Brand X – paper – Fenner Paper Co. Ltd

Brandauer – Brandauer Precision Pressings

Brandenburg – Applied Kilovolts

Branding Consultants and Designers Worldwide – Landor Associates

Brandmoo – Baby & Infant Wear – BRANDMOO

Brandy Crag – natural slate – Burlington Slate Ltd

Brandy Crag Silver/Grey Slate – architectural slate – Burlington Slate Ltd

Brano – Antalis Mcnaughton

Branscombe – woven carpets in 100% pure new wool – Axminster Carpets Ltd

Brantham Engineering – electronic assembly – Brantham Engineering Ltd

Brantome – fabrics – Today Interiors Ltd

Brantwood – bed linen and towels – Pin Mill Textiles Ltd

Brass Inter-lock – hose connectors – Carl Kammerling International Ltd

Brasspol – chemical polish for brass – P M D UK Ltd

Brattvaag – Rolls Royce

Braudepumps – Chemical service pump – E Braude London Ltd

Brauer – toggle clamps and pneumatic clamping products – Brauer Ltd

BRAUER – Hydraulic & Offshore Supplies Ltd

Brauer – Trafalgar Tools

Brauer Air Movers/Air Amplifiers – Brauer Ltd

BRAUKMANN WATER PRODUCTS (United Kingdom) – Ultravalve Ltd

Braunston Marina – inland marina operators – Braunston Marina Ltd

Bravalar – Ackwa Ltd

Bray – electric heater – Chromalox UK Ltd

Bray Cattle Calendar – management system for farmers – Nicholas Bray & Son Ltd

Bray Electro Gate – electric gate acess system for electric fences – Nicholas Bray & Son Ltd

Bray H & L – care packs – Bray Group Ltd

Braylec – strip, ring, elements, cartridge heaters, and circulation heaters – Chromalox UK Ltd

BRAYSTOKE – Valeport Ltd

Brazcor – honeycomb with integral braze alloy – Neomet Ltd

Brazing – frame repairs – Witcomb Cycles

*Brazing (USA and Scandinavia) – anti corrosion products – B A C Corrosion Control Ltd

*Break-Line – Pentland Wholesale Ltd

Breakell Lifts – lifts – H Breakell Company Ltd

Breakir Centrifugal Disintegrator – crushing machine – John Leach Spares & Equipment

Breckmoor – woollen coates – Karpelle Ltd

Breco – European Technical Sales Ltd

Brecon – Prima Care

Brecon cubicle – Designed for children – Cubicle Centre

Brecon Water – Mercia Fine Foods

Bredel – high pressure hose pumps – Watson Marlow Pumps Ltd

Breeza – fans – The London Fan Co. Ltd

Breeza - industrial fans Breezax - impellers – The London Fan Co. Ltd

Breezax Impellers – fan blades – The London Fan Co. Ltd

Breeze – sailboat – Topper International

BREFCO – Barber Pumps Ltd

*Brema – Ice makers – Middleby UK Ltd

Bremag – rare earth magnets – Magnet Applications Ltd

Brembo – brake discs, calipers and pads – Roadlink International Ltd

Bremor SA (Switzerland) – sandblasting and deburring – Haesler Machine Tools

Brencliffe – consumer products – Yule Catto & Co plc

Brennenstuhl – Gem Tool Hire & Sales Ltd

Brentmere Leisure – static caravans – Omar Park Homes Ltd

Brentwood Gazette, The – newspaper – Essex Chronicle Media Group

Breox – chemicals, synthetic fluids, lubricants – Cognis Performance Chemicals Ltd

Breox – B P plc

Bret Technology GmbH – hydro/pneumatic cylinders-metal joining – Tox Pressotechnik

Bretford – UK Office Direct

Breton – Lead Precision Machine Tools Ltd

*Bretshaw (United Kingdom) – dust bins and buckets (galvanised and plastic) holloware – Parasene

Bretton – gas L.F.E. for class one or class two flues – Dunsley Heat Ltd

Bretton – bricks – Ibstock Brick Ltd

Bretton Red – Ibstock Brick Ltd

Breviglieri – J & S Lewis Ltd

*Breville (Hong Kong) – snack & sandwich toasters – Pulse Home Products Ltd

*Breville Pie Magic (Hong Kong) – pie maker – Pulse Home Products Ltd

*Breville Pizza Wizard (Hong Kong) – pizza maker – Pulse Home Products Ltd

Brevini – Brevini Power Transmissions

BREVINI – Hydraulic & Offshore Supplies Ltd

BREVINI FLUID POWER – Hydraulic & Offshore Supplies Ltd

BREVINI HYDRAULICS – Hydraulic & Offshore Supplies Ltd

Brevini Winches/PIV Drives – Brevini Power Transmissions

Brevis – Capex Office Interiors

Brewer Aerodyne – chimney cowl – Brewer Metalcraft Ltd

Brewer Chimney Capper – chimney covering for disused chimneys – Brewer Metalcraft Ltd

Brewer Ulitimate Flue Outlet (U.F.O.) – gas cowl – Brewer Metalcraft Ltd

Brewmaster – nylon beer tube – Valpar Industrial Ltd

Brian Mills – catalogues – Littlewoods Home Shopping Orders & Enquiries

Brian Yates Fabric – The Winnen Furnishing Company

Bricesco – kilns – Bricesco Ltd

Brickhouse – access covers and gratings – Ashworth

Brickhouse – security access covers – Steelway

Brickies Mate – workability aid for use in brick mortar – Building Chemical Research Ltd

Brickleen – Forward Chemicals Ltd

Brickman – briquetter – K K Balers Ltd

Brickseal – refractory cement – Darcy Products Ltd

Bridec – melamine boards – Bridec

Bridela (United Kingdom) – fire protective and insulation products – I C International
Bridge (United Kingdom) – carpet tiles – Checkmate Industries Ltd
Bridge Foundry – aluminium gravity die castings – Bridge Aluminium Ltd
Bridgemere Garden World – mixed retailer all form of leisure mainly gardening related – Bridgemere Nursery & Garden World
Bridgeport – Peter Rushton Ltd
Bridgestone – Wealden Tyres Ltd
Bridgestone/Firestone U.K. – car tyres, truck tyres, earthmover tyres, motor cycle tyres industrial tyres and agricultural tyres – Bridgestone UK Ltd
Bridlington Free Press – newspaper – Yorkshire Regional Newspapers Ltd
***Briel (Portugal)** – espresso coffee machines – Fairfax Coffee Ltd
Brietling – watches – Goldsmiths Jewellers Ltd
Brigadier – BS 6391 type 3 fire hose – Richards Hose Ltd
Brigadier – Steel Bollard – Alto Bollards UK Ltd
Briggs – safety boots – Arrow Supply Co. Ltd
Briggs & Strat – Harrier Fluid Power Ltd
Briggs & Stratton – A T Wilde & Son Ltd
Briggs & Sutton – Woodleigh Power Equipment Ltd
Bright Ideas – UK Office Direct
Bright Ideas – carpets – Interface Europe Ltd
Bright Wipe – multi purpose cloth – Ramon Hygiene Products
Brightflow – electronic peristaltic pump for dishwashers and laundries, water treatments and drain dosing – Brightwell Dispenser Ltd
BrighthandIT – Brighthand Web Design
Brighton – Try & Lilly Ltd
Brighton Marina – boat marina – Premier Marinas Brighton
Brightside – Brightside Print & Design
Brightspark – EDM cartridge filter – Microtech Filters Ltd
Brightstaltic – disposable peristaltic pump head – Brightwell Dispenser Ltd
Brightwater Grates – grates – Brightwater Engineering
Brightwater Product – sewage & water treatment – Brightwater Engineering
Brightwell – soap dispensers and paper dispensers – Brightwell Dispenser Ltd
***Brigon (Germany)** – combustion kits – Anglo Nordic Burner Products Ltd
Brijonate – isocyanates – I M C D UK Ltd
Brijonol – polyols – I M C D UK Ltd
BRILIANT POLISHES – BRILIANT METAL POLISHES – Briliant Polishes
Brilliant – paper – G F Smith
Brillite – fluorescent paint – Witham Oil & Paint Lowestoft Ltd
Brillo – UK Office Direct
Brimac – Adsorption media – Brimac Environmental Services Ltd
Brimar – cathode ray tubes and allied products – Brimar Ltd
Brimotor – generators, pumps and engines – Brimotor Ltd
Brindley – medium duty rectangular slide-out cover and frame – Norinco UK Ltd
Brink – best known for swan neck bars – Indespension Ltd
Brinkmann – European Technical Sales Ltd
Brinscan – fully automatic brinell hardness testing machine – Foundrax Engineering Products Limited
***Brio (France)** – decorative wood mouldings – Winther Browne & Company Ltd
Brisco Engineering – well-head and sub-sea control system – I C S Triplex
Briscol – bristle mixture – D S Commodities Ltd
Brise Soleil – D J B Projects
Brisol – Forward Chemicals Ltd
Bristol – fire protection clothing for professional volunteer fire fighters – Bristol Uniforms Ltd
Bristol – manufacture cars – Bristol Cars
Bristol – Therma Group
Bristol Chinese Pain relief acupuncture – acupuncture for back pain relief – Bristol Chinese Pain Relief Acupuncture
Bristol Maid – hospital equipment including trolleys, drug storage, cabinets, couches and nursing accessories – Bristol Maid Hospital Equipment
Bristol Street (Birmingham) – car dealers – Bristol Street Birmingham
Bristol Zak Back Pain Therapy – Back pain treatment – Bristol Chinese Pain Relief Acupuncture
Brit-Am – venture marketing – I A S Smarts Ltd
Brita – UK Office Direct
Brita Water Filter Systems Ltd – water filter systems and replacement cartridges all imported – Brita Water Filter Systems Ltd
Britaclean – water filtration for commercial use – Brita Water Filter Systems Ltd
Britaclean Extra – water filtration for commercial use – Brita Water Filter Systems Ltd
Britain Taco – micro embossed films for hygiene and disposable applications – Britton Taco Ltd
Britan – Red House Industrial Services Ltd
Britan – capstan lathes – Andrew Engineering Leigh Ltd
Britannia (United Kingdom) – corded brass track – Integra Products
Britannia Continental – holiday insurance – Civil Service Motoring Association
Britannia Jetspray – wheel and chassis washing plants - lorries, buses and cars – Smith Bros & Webb Ltd
Britannia product ltd – greeting cards and asssociated products – Hallmark Cards
Britannia Spray – brushless vehicle washer – Smith Bros & Webb Ltd
Britannia Streamline – vehicle washing plants - buses – Smith Bros & Webb Ltd
Britannia Strong – vehicle washing plants - lorries, buses and cars – Smith Bros & Webb Ltd
Britannia Supreme – vehicle washing plant - buses – Smith Bros & Webb Ltd
Britannia Train Wash – rail carraige & rolling stock washing plants – Smith Bros & Webb Ltd
Britannia Water Fittings – taps and mixers – Marflow Engineering Ltd
Britannic Travel – travel agency and business house – F C M Travel Solutions
Britannica CD – Encyclopaedia Britannica UK Ltd
Britannica Online – Encyclopaedia Britannica UK Ltd
BRITAX – Hydraulic & Offshore Supplies Ltd
Britax – child car seats, prams and pushchairs – Britax Excelsior Ltd
Britax Vega – lighting for car industry – Koito
Brite-Lite – reflective safety garments and accessories – Ronhill Sports
Britink – industrial inks, inkjet, bubble jet inks and associated marking devices – Roger Needham & Sons Ltd
British Berkefeld – domestic water filter – Fairey Industrial Ceramics
British Chemical Standard – certified reference materials, EURONORM certified reference materials – Bureau Of Analysed Samples Ltd
British Drawing – pencil – Cumberland Pencil Museum
British Eagle – cycle – Falcon Cycles Ltd
British Encoder Company – Encoders UK
British Filters – Harrier Fluid Power Ltd
British Filters – filter for beverage, process, industrial, aerospace and compression air – British Filters Ltd
British Gas Springs – Alrose Products British Gas Springs Ltd
British Gypsum – P F T Central
British Gypsum – S K Interiors Ltd
British Indicators – contact gauging – Baty International
British Library – vouchers – Bearwood Engineering Supplies
British livestock genetics – UK Sire Services Ltd
British Monomarks – fax broadcast service, post boxes and telephone answering services – British Monomarks
British Museum – publishing and retailing, tour operations, connections and press – British Museum Press Publications & Merchandise Ltd
British Museum The – Chorion plc
British Rema – crushing grinding & drying classifying plant – British Rema Manufacturing Co. Ltd
British Rema - crushing grinding, drying & classifying plant; Aerosplit - powder classifier; Rema - Rotary impact mill /classifier mill; Minisplit - powder classifier - lab size. – British Rema Manufacturing Co. Ltd
British School of Motoring, The – national driving tuition services – R A C
British Seals & Rubber Mouldings – gaskets, seals, washers and mouldings – British Gaskets Ltd
British Springs – Newburgh Engineering Co. Ltd
British Strongart – Coated Paper – Mcnaughton James Paper Group Ltd
British Telecom – Callsure Business Telephone & Fax Numbers
British Thornton – furniture for educations and libraries – British Thornton E S F Ltd
British Van Heusen – shirt brands – Morrison McConnell Ltd
British Vita & Group Symbol – British Vita plc
BritLock – reconstituted slates – Sandtoft Holdings Ltd
Britmac – cable management – Electrium Sales Ltd
Britomya – whiting fillers – Omya UK Ltd
Britool – automotive tools – Arrow Supply Co. Ltd
Britool – S J Wharton Ltd
Britool – Gem Tool Hire & Sales Ltd
Britseal – expanding sealant for sheet piles – Conren Ltd
BritSlate – reconstituted slates – Sandtoft Holdings Ltd
Britspace Modular – prefabricated buildings – Britspace Modular Buildings Ltd
Brittany Ferries – Brittany Ferries
Britvic – UK Office Direct
Briv – high speed, high clamp fastener for thin sheet metal – Avdel UK Ltd
Briv – speed rivet system – Zygology Ltd
Broadband Router – Tekdata Distribution Ltd
broadband services – Complete guide to mobile broadband, detailing the pros and cons of 3 G broadband. Broadband from mob – Accuracast Ltd
Broadbent Drives – industrial clutches – Wetherby Engineering Co. Ltd
Broadfield – acidulating unit – Bradley Pulverizer Co.
Broadheath – fruit pies, dairy cream, fruit fillings, steam puddings, – Elisabeth The Chef Ltd
Broadley J.B. – P.V.C. – J B Broadley
Broadrib – fibre bonded carpet – Heckmondwike FB
Broads Holidays – cruising holidays – Richardsons Stalham Ltd
Broadstone HE – Power flame cast iron sectional boilers – Hamworthy Heating Ltd
Broadstone House Ltd – processing garments – Broadstone Mill Shopping Outlet
Broadsword – Lusso Interiors
Broady Flow Control – Valves pressure reducing, pressure sustaining, relief and safety relief – Broady Flow Controller Ltd
Broag Remeha – boiler makers – Broag Ltd
Broaster – FFS Brands Ltd
Brobat – bleach – Jeyes
Broby – Kee Valves
Brocade Filigree Axminster – Victoria Carpets Ltd
Brocade Plain Wilton – Victoria Carpets Ltd
Brockway – The Winnen Furnishing Company
Brockway – conveyor roller manufacturers – Stourbridge Lion Ltd
Broco – Submarine Manufacturing & Products Ltd
Broderie III – fabrics wallpapers & borders – Today Interiors Ltd
Brodeur A Plus – Ketchum Pleon
Brodeur Worldwide – Ketchum Pleon
Brodifacoum – Sorex Ltd
Broens – manufacture lighting – Glamox Luxo Lighting Ltd
Brokk – Robotic Demolition – Elmcrest Diamond Drilling Ltd
Brolac – paint – Akzo Nobel Decorative Coatings Ltd
Bromgard – bromine based redox controlled inhibitor and biocide treatment for cooling towers – Feedwater Ltd
Bromgard – bromine based cooling water treatment system which gives redox control of inhibitors and biocide with only two liquids – Feedwater Ltd
Bromley – taps – Armitage Shanks Ltd
Brompton – ventilator – Space Labs Healthcare
Bronalin – linctus – Reckitt Benckiser plc
Bronnley – soaps & toiletries – H Bronnley & Co. Ltd
Bronte – The Winnen Furnishing Company
Bronte – insoles – A Algeo Ltd
Bronto Platforms – Accesscaff International Ltd
Brontoguard – heat resistant leather – Charles F Stead & Co. Ltd
Bronx Engineering – metalworking machinery – Bronx Engineering Ltd
Bronx England – Bronx Engineering Ltd
Brook – motor control gear – City Electrical Factors Ltd
Brook Crompton – Proplas International Ltd
Brook Crompton – electric motors in general and special purpose types including hazardous atmosphere up to 400KW – Brook Crompton UK Ltd
Brook Crompton – motors – Bearwood Engineering Supplies
Brook Hansen – motors gears transmissions – Invensys PLC
BROOK HYDRAULIC CUTTERS – Hydraulic & Offshore Supplies Ltd
Brook Roof Units – roof extract units – Systemair G M P H
***Brook Trout (U.S.A.)** – Intelligent fax PC boards – Techland Group Ltd
Brooke – ladies shoes for the more mature consumer – The Florida Group
Brooke – rotary gear pumps – Albany Pumps
Brooke Pumps – Albany Pumps
Brookes Forklift Service – fork lift truck rental – Gaylee Ltd
Brookfield – Fullbrook Systems Ltd
Brookite – kites – Brookite Ltd
Brooklands Brass Lighting – Light Fantastic
Brooks – anvils – Vaughans Hope Works Ltd
Brookside – metal ingots, copper based & copper sulphate – Brookside Metal Co. Ltd
Brooktree – Cyclops Electronics Ltd
Broom & Wade – Red House Industrial Services Ltd
Broomwade – Trowell Plant Sales Ltd
Broomwade – Harrier Fluid Power Ltd
Broomwade – compressors, parts and service – Airware International Ltd
Broomwade – air compressors – Motivair Compressors Ltd
Brophy, Thames Water and Metro Rod – ground maintenance & unblocking drains – Enterpride P.L.C.
Bros MFG – Harrier Fluid Power Ltd
Brother – Kone Cranes Machine Tool Services
Brother – typewriters, knitting machines, industrial sewing machines, colour copiers, facsimiles, printers and labelling machines – Brother International Europe Ltd
Brother – UK Office Direct

Brother – Brother inkjet cartridges, laser toners & printers – Inkxperts
Brother – M L P S
Brother – Whitehouse Machine Tools Ltd
Brother, HP, Lexmark, Samsung – inkjet cartridges / laser toner cartridges – inkstinx
Brother P-Touch Electronic labelling – laminated adhesive labels and stencil tapes – Universal Marking Systems Ltd
Brothers Pear Ciders – Windfall Brands Ltd
Brötje – Baxi Group
Broughton – Portable coolers – Beatson Fans & Motors Ltd
Broughton Crangrove – Wolseley UK
Broughton Moor – natural slate – Burlington Slate Ltd
Broughton Moor Green Slate – natural slate – Burlington Slate Ltd
Broughton Moor Slate – roofing and architectural slates – Burlington Slate Ltd
Brown Group – Trafalgar Tools
Brown Knight & Truscott – financial, colour & commercial printers – Brown Knight & Truscott Ltd
Brown Owl – Engineering – Delta Fluid Products Ltd
Brown Pestell – European Technical Sales Ltd
Brown Roof – Althon Ltd
Brown & Sharpe – Status Metrology Solutions Ltd
Brownall – Trafalgar Tools
Brownell – spares & equipment – Bearwood Engineering Supplies
Browning – chain & conveyor equipment – Bearwood Engineering Supplies
Brownridge Plastics – Cox Wokingham Plastics Ltd
Browns – bespoke steel buildings with clear spans upto 140 – Browns of Wem Ltd
Browns – clothes retailers – Browns S M S Ltd
Browns Buildings – industrial, agricultural and equestrian buildings – Browns of Wem Ltd
Brucast – range of decorative street furniture – Bruce & Hyslop Brucast Ltd
Bruce – mooring equipment manufacturers – Bruce Anchor Ltd
Bruce Oldfield – clothes designers – Bruce Oldfield Ltd
Brueninghaus – Harrier Fluid Power Ltd
BRUENINGHAUS – Hydraulic & Offshore Supplies Ltd
BRUFMA – trade association – British Rigid Urethane Foam Manufacturers Association Limited
Brugarolas – Lubricants – I K V Tribology Ltd
Brunel – weather and vandal resisting lighting – Designplan Lighting Ltd
Brunel – rigid litter bin free standing – Glasdon International Ltd
Brunel – heavy duty D/T non-rock cover and frame – Norinco UK Ltd
*Bruni Bear (Italy, Portugal & USA) – PVC tablecovers – Emko Consumer Products Ltd
*Bruni Bear (China) – cotton hand crochet tablecovers – Emko Consumer Products Ltd
BRUNILIFT – Chaintec Ltd
*Brunitec (Sweden) – local dust filters – Orthos Engineering Ltd
Brunmesh – welded & woven mesh – F H Brundle
*Brunner (Switzerland) – filament lamps – Baumer Electric Ltd
Brunnschweiler – batik textile piece goods – Cosmopolitan Textile Company Ltd
Brunperf – perforated metals – F H Brundle
Brunperf - Perforated metals. Brunmesh - Welded & woven mesh. – F H Brundle
Brunswick Tooling – engineers cutting tools – Brunswick Tooling Ltd
Brush – generators, controls, power management systems – Brush Electrical Machines Ltd
*Brush – European Drives & Motor Repairs
Brush 390 – Materion Brush Ltd
Brush 60 – Materion Brush Ltd
Brush N Dry – pvc backed olefin & polyprop scraper barriers mats – Jaymart Roberts & Plastics Ltd
*Brush N Wash (U.S.A.) – carpet cleaner – Hoover Ltd
Brush-Off – PVC backed coir entrance matting – Jaymart Roberts & Plastics Ltd
Brushed Plains – current – Harlequin
Brushmate – rear mounted sweeper – Danline International Ltd
Brusho – dyes and paints (educational), brusho lustre powders – Colourcraft C & A Ltd
Brushwood – woodstains and varnishes – Akzonobel
Brute – cloth cutting machine – Eastman Staples Ltd
Brutt Bars – County Construction Chemicals Ltd
Brutt Helical – structural repair system – Target Fastenings Ltd
Brutus – jewellery – W B Muddeman & Son Ltd
Bruynzeel Aqualine – Building Additions Ltd
*Bry-Kol (Spain and S. Korea) – commercial refrigeration and air conditioning equipment – Bry-Kol Developments Ltd
Bryans Aeroquipment – test and calibration equipment for aircraft instrument – Meggitt Avionics

Bryant – telescoper conveyor take up system – R A Rodriguez UK Ltd
Bryant – Red House Industrial Services Ltd
Brycham – synthetic chamois leathers – Lancashire Sock Manufacturing Co.
Bryden – riveting machines & tools – Roadlink International Ltd
BS & B – BS&B Safety Systems (UK) Ltd
BS EN3 – fire extinguishers – Adm Services UK Ltd
BSH Management – on site door fitters – Humphrey & Stretton plc
BSL – Proplas International Ltd
BSM C-Series – Servo Motor – Baldor UK
BSM N-Series – Servo Motor – Baldor UK
BSM R-Series – Servo Motor – Baldor UK
BSO – Hydraulic & Offshore Supplies Ltd
BSquare – Aspen International Ltd
BSS02A – borehole magnetic susceptibility system – Bartington Instruments Ltd
BT – Duplex Corporate Communications
BT – Chaintec Ltd
BT – UK Office Direct
BT Rolatruc – Stacatruc
BT's – pipette tips – Radleys
BTAL – Training Services and Room Hire – B T A L Incorporating Kadtal
BTC – tube bending machinery – Whitelegg Machines Ltd
BTech Inc (U.S.A.) – battery validation systems – I M H Technologies Ltd
BTP – magazine – Progressive Media Group
BTR – engineering products – Invensys PLC
BTTG – technical and advisory services for the textile and related industries – B T T G Ltd
Buamann – Harrier Fluid Power Ltd
Bubbleflex – air bubble cushioning packaging – Total Polyfilm
Bubbles – cycles – Professional Cycle Marketing
Bubenzer Bremsen (Germany) – industrial brakes and spreaders – Metool Products Ltd
Bucentaur Gallery – C C A Group Ltd
*Buchador (Germany) – saw sharpening machine – Brunner Machine Tools Ltd
Buchanan – terminal blocks – Anglia
BUCHER – Hydraulic & Offshore Supplies Ltd
Bucher – Harrier Fluid Power Ltd
Bucher Hidroirma – control valves & pumps – Bucher Hydraulics Ltd
BUCHER HYDRAULICS – Hydraulic & Offshore Supplies Ltd
Bucher Hydraulik – hydraulic systems & pumps – Bucher Hydraulics Ltd
BUCHI – Manufacturers of glass and glass lined steel equipment/glass & metal pressure reactors. – Ken Kimble Reactor Vessel Ltd
Buckenier – paint brushes – Whitaker & Sawyer Brushes Ltd
Buckhill DRPS – Buckhill Dynamic Resource Planning System – Buckhill Ltd
Buckingham – timber up and over garage door – P C Henderson Ltd
Buckingham – casement window internally beaded, shootbolt locking as standard – Coastal Aluminium
Buckingham Advertiser – newspaper – Leamington Spa Courier
Buckle My Shoe – childrens fashion shoes – R J Draper & Co. Ltd
Buckley Lamb – health care textiles – Buckley Lamb Ltd
Buckleys – spark testing equipment – Buckleys Uvral Ltd
Buckleys (UVRAL) Ltd – Buckleys Uvral Ltd
*Buckray (Netherlands) – bookcloth – Winter & Co UK Ltd
Bucks Advertiser – newspaper – Leamington Spa Courier
Bucks Herald – newspaper – Leamington Spa Courier
Bucyrys-Erie – Harrier Fluid Power Ltd
Budd – shirts – Budd Shirt Makers Ltd
*Buddy (Taiwan) – cycle accessories – Madison
Buddy – divers adjustable buoyancy jackets – A P Valves
Buddy Arctic – divers adjustable buoyancy jacket - for drysuited and wetsuited divers – A P Valves
Buddy Commando – divers adjustable buoyancy jacket - jacket style – A P Valves
Buddy Commando Profile – divers adjustable buoyancy jacket – A P Valves
Buddy Double Gold – divers adjustable buoyancy jacket - collar style – A P Valves
Buddy Explorer – Divers adjustable buoyancy jacket - for drysuit and wetsuited divers – A P Valves
Buddy Inspiration – Closed circuit rebreather – A P Valves
Buddy Pacific – divers adjustable buoyancy jacket - collar style – A P Valves
Buddy Sea King – divers adjustable buoyancy jacket - jacket style – A P Valves
Buddy Trident – A P Valves
Buddy Trimix – Divers adjustable buoyancy jacket - for drysuit and wetsuited divers – A P Valves
Budenberg – pressure gauges, thermometers, calibration and metrological calibration equipment – D H Budenburg

Budenberg – Direct Instrument Hire Ltd
Budenberg – spares & equipment – Bearwood Engineering Supplies
Budenberg - Desgranges et Huot – D H Budenburg
*Buderus (Germany) – heating equipment – Clyde Energy Solutions Ltd
Budget Tyres – Wealden Tyres Ltd
Budit – Melamine Polyphophates & Phosphate Esters – Mineral & Chemical Services Ltd
Buehler (Germany) – motors – Bancroft & Co.
*Buena Vista (U.S.A.) – videos and films – The Disney Store Ltd
*Buena Vista Home Entertainment (U.S.A.) – videos, dvd's, tapes etc – The Disney Store Ltd
*Buena Vista International (U.S.A.) – films – The Disney Store Ltd
Buendia Coffee – Aimia Foods
Buessing – Harrier Fluid Power Ltd
Buffalo – fencing gates of all types, plus timber garden buildings and garages intended for industrial or domestic use – Buffalo Timber Buildings
Buffalo – acoustic barriers for highways and railways – Buffalo Timber Buildings
Buffalo (United Kingdom) – double-ended pedestal polisher – R J H Finishing Systems Ltd
Buffel – pumps – Speck Pumps UK Ltd
Buffer Bead – fishing tackle class 28 – Drennan International Ltd
Buffer Vessels – Abbott & Co Newark Ltd
Buffer-Zone – aluminium entrance matting systems – Jaymart Roberts & Plastics Ltd
Buffodine – fish farming disinfectant – Evans Vanodine International plc
Buflex – flexible plastic hoses – Plastiflex UK Ltd
*Bug Fluid – Progressive Product Developments Ltd
Bug Jam – event – Santa Pod Raceway
*Bug Socks – Progressive Product Developments Ltd
Buggie – Manitou Site Lift Ltd
Buggiscopic – Manitou Site Lift Ltd
Buhl – European Technical Sales Ltd
Bühler – European Technical Sales Ltd
Buhler (Germany) – motors – Bancroft & Co.
Builder – software system – Attunity UK Ltd
Builder Center – Wolseley UK
Builders – ironmongery – Kirkpatrick Ltd
Buildex – I T W Constructions Productions
Bulb-Tite – Gesipa Blind Riveting Systems Ltd
Bulbex – blind breakstem fastener for soft materials – Avdel UK Ltd
Bulbex – special blind rivets – Zygology Ltd
Bulgin – connectors – Anglia
Bulgin – E Preston Electrical Ltd
Bulgin – Cyclops Electronics Ltd
Bulk Aluminium Sulphate – water filtration acid – Ferelco UK Ltd
Bulk Sulphuric Acid – industrial acid – Ferelco UK Ltd
Bulkigloss – paper – Paperun Group Of Companies
Bulkloader – telescopic boom conveyor for bulk materials – Newland Engineering Co. Ltd
Bull (United Kingdom) – twin motor pedestal polisher – R J H Finishing Systems Ltd
Bull – European Drives & Motor Repairs
Bull Cutter – Taegutec UK Ltd
Bull Motor – motors,generators – Bearwood Engineering Supplies
Bull Rubber – precision rubber mouldings – B G Technical Mouldings Ltd
Bull (Smithfield) – catering and butchers knives – Rotary Engineering UK Ltd
Bullard – Harrier Fluid Power Ltd
Bulldog – letter clips – Setten Ixl Ltd
Bulldog – Gem Tool Hire & Sales Ltd
Bulldog – Padlocks & Mortice Locks – T Morgan & Sons Ltd
Bulldog – games, sporting articles, outer clothing and footwear – Oxbridge
Bulldog – tent pegs and poles – The Hampton Works Ltd
Bulldog – powder paints – Thomas Howse Ltd
Bullet Proof Capsule – Birmingham Barbed Tape Ltd
*Bulletin Board (Netherlands) – noticeboard material – Forbo
Bullfighter – extra duty wide rib/fine rib hoof/skate/spike/dumbbell resistant rubber matting – Jaymart Roberts & Plastics Ltd
BULLFINCH – Hydraulic & Offshore Supplies Ltd
BULLI KAHL – Chaintec Ltd
Bullit – washing machines – Oliver Douglas Ltd
bullwings – website & logo name – Winged Bull Aviation Ltd
Bulroc – rock drilling equipment – Bulroc Ltd
*Bultmann (Germany) – tube draw benches – British & Continental Traders Ltd
Bumf-Lugger – suspension file carrier – Hamster Baskets
Bumotec – Rowan Precision Ltd
Bump Guard Products – Double Gee Hair Fashions Ltd
Bumpa Hoddi Boxa – Elevators – Mace Industries

Bumper Posts – Boston corner guards, The Protector, The Post Sleave – Boston Retail Products

Bumper Rails – Boston bumper series 1000, 1750, 2000, 3300, 6000, 8000 range – Boston Retail Products

Bumpers – casual shoes and shoes – D Jacobson & Sons Ltd

Bumperseal – rubber seal for bottom of rollershutter doors – Kleeneze Sealtech Ltd

Bunce – towed and tractor mounted sweepers, sweepers and snow ploughs – Bunce Ashbury Ltd

*Bunce Epoke (Denmark) – salt and sand spreaders and sweepers – Bunce Ashbury Ltd

Bunce Maxi – tractor mounted brush – Bunce Ashbury Ltd

Bundy – B L Pneumatics Ltd

Bungartz – special applications centrifugal pumps – Axflow

Bunker Lances – compressed air operated percussion lances for cleaning bunkers, silos, etc – Airnesco Group Ltd

Bunnie – hand and face driers – Wandsworth Group Ltd

Bunny bags – bin liners with handles – Cedo Ltd

Bunting – equipment for metal finishing industry – Bemco

Bunty – D C Thomson & Co. Ltd

Bunzl Disposables – Bunzl Catering Supplies Ltd

Bunzl Fine Paper – The Paper Company Ltd

Buoyant – upholstery furniture – Buoyant Upholstery Ltd

Buoylite L41 – emergency lifebuoy marker – Pains Wessex Ltd

Buoysmoke – marine lifebuoy marker – Pains Wessex Ltd

BUPA Cash Plan – cash plan provider – B U P A

Burberry – classic clothing and clothing accessories – Burberry Ltd

Burbury & Scott – Potter Cowan & Co Belfast Ltd

Burcas – engineers and tool specialists – Burcas Ltd

Burco – UK Office Direct

Burco – domestic heating and electrical appliances – Glen Electric Ltd

Burda World Wide Technologies – Global Parasols Ltd

BURGAFLEX – Hydraulic & Offshore Supplies Ltd

Burger King – fast food restaurants – Moto Hospitality Ltd

Burgess – air conditioning - service and commissioning – Burgess C R Commissioning Ltd

Burgess – hotel furniture - dining, banqueting and conference – Burgess Furniture Ltd

Burgess – Cyclops Electronics Ltd

Burgess – spares & equipment – Bearwood Engineering Supplies

BURGESS – switches/sensors – Saia Burgess (Gateshead) Plc

Burghley – waterproof clothing – J Barbour & Sons Ltd

Burgmann – spares & equipment – Bearwood Engineering Supplies

Burgmaster – Red House Industrial Services Ltd

Burgvogel – Continental Chef Supplies Ltd

Burkard – air sampling equipment and entomological equipment – Burkard Manufacturing Company Ltd

Burkert – Southern Valve & Fitting Co. Ltd

Burkert – easy fluid control systems – Burkert Controlmatics Ltd

Burkert – Trafalgar Tools

Burkert Fluid Control Systems – solenoid and process valves, fluid control sensors, transmitters and programmable controllers for the process industry – Burkert Controlmatics Ltd

BURKETT – Hydraulic & Offshore Supplies Ltd

Bürkle – European Technical Sales Ltd

Burleigh – earthenware, tableware, kitchenware and bathroom accessories – Burgess Dorling & Leigh Ltd

Burlen – general carburettors parts – Burlen Fuel Systems Ltd

Burlen – carburetters, fuel pumps and components – Burlen Fuel Systems Ltd

Burlington – shaving brushes – Progress Shaving Brush Vulfix Ltd

Burlington – natural slate – Burlington Slate Ltd

Burlington – catalogues – Littlewoods Home Shopping Orders & Enquiries

Burlington Slate – roofing and architectural slates – Burlington Slate Ltd

*Burlodge – Burlodge Ltd

Burmalex – The Winnen Furnishing Company

Burmatex 2200 Antistat – a low cost fibre bonded carpet – The Burmatex

Burmatex 4200 Sidewalk – a fibre bonded carpet with an extra fine rib – The Burmatex

Burmatex 4400 Broadway – a broad rib fibre bonded carpet – The Burmatex

Burmatex 5500 Luxury – a velour pile fibre bonded carpet – The Burmatex

Burmatex 7700 Grimebuster – fibre bonded dirt barrier in tile and sheet – The Burmatex

Burmatex Academy – fibre bonded carpet tile – The Burmatex

Burmatex Equity – cut pile carpet tile – The Burmatex

Burmatex Sport – fibre bonded carpet – The Burmatex

Burmatex Tivoli – a tufted carpet tile with a loop pile – The Burmatex

Burmatex Toreador – a loop pile patterned carpet tile – The Burmatex

Burmatex Tuff Plus – fibre bonded sheet carpet – The Burmatex

Burmatex Velour – a fibre bonded carpet tile in 18 colours – The Burmatex

Burnaid – cream – Reckitt Benckiser plc

Burnbright – solid fuels – Burnbright Fuels

Burnco – pattern & model shop supplies – John Burn & Co Birmingham Ltd

Burnco - John Burn & Co (B'ham) Ltd. – John Burn & Co Birmingham Ltd

Burnet (United Kingdom) – hair care accessories & headwear – Aburnet Ltd

Burnett – body support – R B F Healthcare

Burnett – panel products, timber and doors – N R Burnett Ltd

BURNETT & HILLMAN – Hydraulic & Offshore Supplies Ltd

Burnett & Hillman – Trafalgar Tools

Burnett Hillman – Southern Valve & Fitting Co. Ltd

Burnhamsigns – vitreous enamel signs – Stocksigns Ltd

Burns Country – travel rugs – Alex Begg & Co.

Buroflex – office furniture – Metalliform Holdings

Burrafirm – commercial vehicle fittings manufacturer, presswork, turning, assembly and injection mouldings – Burrafirm Ltd

Burraway – engineering tools – C L A Tools Ltd

Burroughes and Watts – manufacturers of cues – B & W Billiards Ltd

Burroughs and Watts – Burroughes & Watts

Burroughs & Watts – Burroughes & Watts

Burrqwik – engineering tools – C L A Tools Ltd

Burshaw – water boilers – Cona Ltd

Burshaw - Cona - Conamatic – Cona Ltd

Burson-Marsteller – public relations company – Burson Marsteller

Burst-Tel (United Kingdom) – burst-disc detector – Elfab Ltd

Burster (Germany) – electrical measuring instruments – The Seaward Group

Bursting Stone – natural slate – Burlington Slate Ltd

*Burton – Burton Safes Ltd

Burton Corblin – gas compressors – Axflow

Burton McCall – import and distribution of goods – Burton Mccall Ltd

Burton Wood Turnery – shive and spile manufacturers, wood turners and plastic injection moulders – W H Mason & Son Ltd

Burvill – wrought iron gates – Burvills

Bury Boot & Shoe – mail order catalogue – J D Williams Mail Order Group

Bury Times – publishers – Bury Times Ltd Classified Advertising

Bus UK – bus and coach services – East Yorkshire Motor Services Ltd

Busak Shamban – Mayday Seals & Bearings

BUSAK & SHAMBAN – Hydraulic & Offshore Supplies Ltd

*Busch (Germany and Switzerland) – vacuum pumps, pressure pumps, pumps – Busch UK Ltd

Busch – Harrier Fluid Power Ltd

Busch – general pumps/vacuum – AESpump

Buschjost – B L Pneumatics Ltd

BUSCHJOST – Hydraulic & Offshore Supplies Ltd

Buschjost – process valves – Norgren Ltd

Bush Nelson – commercial/industrial domestic fan heaters – B N Thermic

Bushboard – toilet cubicles – Bushboard Ltd

Bushmills – whiskey – Old Bushmills Distillery Co. Ltd

Bushmills Malt – whiskey – Old Bushmills Distillery Co. Ltd

*Busicom (Taiwan, Hong Kong, Malaysia and Japan) – import and export calculators and cash registers, manufacture POS and cash register systems – Broughton & Co Bristol Ltd

Busicom Cash Registers – Cash Register Services

Business Control Systems – software – Cincom Systems UK Ltd

Business Desk – software package – Paxton Computers Ltd

Business @ The Mitchell – part of The Mitchell Library – The Mitchell Library

Business West – G W E Business West

BusinessExpress – telecommunications systems and services – Nortel Networks UK Ltd

BUSPAD – Raised bus boarding platform – Rediweld Rubber & Plastics Ltd

Buss Kneader (Switzerland) – plastic compounding – Coperion Ltd

Bussmann – European Technical Sales Ltd

Bussmann – E Preston Electrical Ltd

Bussmann – fuses & fuse holders – Anglia

Bussmann – Cyclops Electronics Ltd

Buster – B L Pneumatics Ltd

Buster – traffic film removers – Agma Ltd

*Buta-Cup – U F A C UK Ltd

Butacite – polyvinyl butyral sheeting – Du Pont UK Ltd

Butaclor (France) – Polychloropreme rubber – Polimeri Europa Ltd

Butanox – methyethyl ketone peroxide – Akzo Nobel Chemicals Holdings Ltd

Butcher & Baker – Apetito Ltd

Butchers – dog food – Butchers Pet Care

*Butchers (U.S.A.) – chemicals & polishes – C S A Cleaning Equipment

Butchers Choice – small dog food – Butchers Pet Care

Bute Fabrics – dobby weave, contemporary upholstery fabrics for the furniture, office systems and interior furnishings market – Bute Fabrics

Butech – Butech – Haskel Europe Ltd

Butech – High pressure needle and ball valves – Hydratron Ltd

Butler Newall boring machines – Phil Geesin Machinery Ltd

Butlerib – trapezoidal roof and wall panel – Lindab Building Systems

Butterfield & Frazer (United Kingdom) – Worsted mens Suiting Fabric – John Foster Ltd

Butterfly valves – AESpump

*Butterick (U.S.A.) – paper patterns for dressmaking – Butterick Co. Ltd

*Butterick Greetings – greeting cards and social stationery – Butterick Co. Ltd

*Buttersoft (United Kingdom) – upholstery leather – Bridge Of Weir Leather Co.

Butterworths – manufacturing opticians – Butterworths Lenses

Buttle's – timber and builders merchants – Buttle plc

Buttress – professional management computer packages for architects, qualitysurveyors and consulting engineers – Definitive Computing Ltd

Butyl – W Mannering London Ltd

Butyl – rubber and plastic – Butyl Products Ltd

Buxton Insulation – import & processes of mica components, mica powder ceramic metal parts – Dean & Tranter

Buy Data Storage – Tekdata Distribution Ltd

Buy Floppy Disk Drive – Tekdata Distribution Ltd

Buzi – footwear – A P Y

Buzz – sailboat – Topper International

Buzzard – bale loader – Brown's Agricultural Machinery Company Ltd

BV Vestergaard – T V H UK Ltd

BV VESTERGAARD – Chaintec Ltd

BV Vestergaard – Stacatruc

BVC – blowers – Beatson Fans & Motors Ltd

BWC Textiles – filtration felt manufacturers – William Clark & Sons Ltd

BWH – Cases – Protechnic

BXL – bottles & closures – B P plc

By Design – ladies knitwear and leisure wear – By Design plc

Byco – food and pharmaceutical grades of hydrolysed gelatins – Croda Europe Ltd

Byepac – Grundfos Pumps Ltd

Byepac – Grundfos Pumps Ltd

Bygone Era – old style motor drivers clothing – Holden Vintage & Classic Ltd

Byron – flo-raters & distributors – Parker Hannifin UK plc

Byscoop – take-off probe for bypass loop sampling or analysis systems – Jiskoot Ltd

Bystronic – Bystronic UK Ltd

Bystronic – Laser Trader Ltd

Byte – sailboat – Topper International

Bytel – solid polyester for food handling – Fenner Drives Ltd

BZB Smoothies – Aimia Foods

C

C. – printing equipment – Cooper Printing Machinery Ltd

C-10 – Industrial Hydraulic Cylinders – Air Power & Hydraulics Ltd

C.4 Carbides – tungsten carbide gritted tools – C 4 Carbides Ltd

C.A.L. – printed circuit board assembly, product assembly, functional electronic testing and component procurement – Mode Lighting

C.A.S.E. – chemically assisted surface engineering – Metal Improvement Company LLC

C.A.S.E. – chemically assisted surface engineering – Metal Improvement Co.

C.A.S.E. – chemically assisted surface engineering – Metal Improvement Co.

C.A. Series – self priming pumps – Calpeda Ltd

C A T – cable avoiding tool – Radio Detection

C.A.T - Cable Avoiding Tool; RADIODETECTION - Buried Pipe and Cable Locators by Radiodetection; RD PRECISION LOCATORS - Locating Underground Services; RL 200 - High Voltage Cable Identifier; PHASOR - Phase and feeder identification instrument. Gatorcam - Inspection Calleras Duct & Pipe. – Radio Detection

C.A.W. – aluminium and PVCu windows, doors and conservatories – C A W Cornwall Ltd
C.A. Weidmuller – terminals etc – Weidmuller Ltd
C.B. – washers and bellville type – Industrial Trading Co. Ltd
C.B. Ferrari – CNC vertical machining centres – Halifax Numerical Controls Ltd
***C box (Germany)** – cassette and CD storage systems for automobiles – Fischer Fixings UK Ltd
C.C.C. Contacts (United Kingdom) – Ametek Prestolight
C C JENSEN – Hydraulic & Offshore Supplies Ltd
C-call – Waiting room call system – C-Tec Security Ltd
C. & D. – cricket helmets – Kookaburra Reader Ltd
C D A – synthetic diamond - carbide diamond abrasives – Diamond Detectors
C.D.L.C – telecommunications & telephonic equipment – Vodafone Retail Ltd
C.D. Series – air conditioners – Tev Ltd
***C & D Technologies (U.S.A.)** – lead acid batteries – Pulsar Developments Ltd
C-Ducer – accoustic transducer microphone – A M G Electronics
C.E.I.A. S.p.A – metal detectors - hand held and walk through – Pulsar Developments Ltd
***C.E.S. (Germany)** – architectural ironmongery – Groupco Ltd
C.E. Set – fan motors, fan blades and assemblies – Thermofrost Cryo plc
C.F.P. – communications protocol – Wordcraft International Ltd
C.F.W. – seals and moulded parts – Freudenberg Simrit LP
C-Flex Moulded Manifolds – PureSil Technologies Ltd
C-Flow – contained flow cabinet – Envair Ltd
C&G – Cheltenham & Gloucester plc
C & G Fast Foods – fast foods – Spud U Like
C-Gard – Impalloy
C-Guard – Impalloy
C.I. – overhead conveyors – Conveyors International (CI Logistics)
C.I. Corporate Insignia – Corporate Insignia Ltd
***C.I. Systems (Israel)** – infrared radiometers – Metax Ltd
C.I. Systems – manufacture software – C I Precision
C.K.D. CORPORATION – Hydraulic & Offshore Supplies Ltd
C & K Switches – Cyclops Electronics Ltd
C.L.S. – lightly perfumed hand soap – Evans Vanodine International plc
C/Line – shakers – New Brunswick Scientific UK Ltd
C.-Liner and C.-Board – marine and offshore – Rockwool Rockpanel B V
C-Lube – Forward Chemicals Ltd
C.M.C. – motion and process control systems for factory and machinery automation – European Drives & Motor Repairs
C.M.H.E.C. – carboxymethyl hydroxethyl cellulose – Hercules Holding Ii Ltd
C M L – 3 dimensional PVC presentation boxes, vacuum formed products and multi CD packaging – Vycon Products Ltd
C M S – specialist connectors and cabling systems – Betterbox Communications Ltd
C.M.S. 400 – wave soldering machine equipment – Blundell Production Equipment
C M S (Kent) – home market guaranteed used commercial vehicles & spare parts – C M S Kent Ltd
C.M.T.S. – cable modem terminal system – Nortel Networks UK Ltd
C-MAC – I Q D Frequency Products Ltd
C-MAC Frequency Products Ltd – I Q D Frequency Products Ltd
C-MAC Quartz Crystals – I Q D Frequency Products Ltd
C-Matic – Gustair Materials Handling Equipment Ltd
C.Matic – B L Pneumatics Ltd
C-MATIC – Hydraulic & Offshore Supplies Ltd
C-Max – contollers – Bearwood Engineering Supplies
C.O.H. Baines – suppliers of rubber extrusions to industrial sectors – C.O.H. Baines Ltd
***C.O.M.E.L (Italy)** – heated suction vacuum ironing tables and electric and steam boilers – Danor Engineering Ltd
C.P.A. – music P.A. loudspeakers – Tannoy Group Ltd
C.P.A 'combi' Gates – High End, Wrought iron and White Oak Gates – C P A Ironworks
C.P.C. – training courses for bus and lorry operators – Friendberry Ltd
C.P.L. Fragrances – fragrances – C P L Aromas Ltd
C P M – Designers & manufacturers of precision mould tools. – C P M Moulds Solutions Ltd
C-Panel – Hörmann (UK) Ltd
C Plus – Helman Workwear
C.Q.R. – bellboxes and cable for the security alarm industry – C Q R Ltd
C.R. – felt and asphalt roofing – Capital Roofing Co. Ltd
C. & R. – paints – Craig & Rose Ltd
C.R.A. – cloth spreading machine – Eastman Staples Ltd
C.R.A.C. – learning and development materials and programmes – Careers In Recruitment
C R C – C R Clarke & Co UK Ltd
C R Clarke – thermoforming and plastic fabrication equipment – C R Clarke & Co UK Ltd
C.R.D. – classical recording producers – C R D Records Ltd
C R M Marine Engines – marine engines – Watermota Ltd
C.R.P. 01 – Cogne UK Ltd
C-Reality – real time multi-standard film scanner including colour vector image processing – Cintel International Ltd
C.S.8 – dry foam carpet shampoo – Premiere Products Ltd
C S A – blasting equipment – C S A Cleaning Equipment
C S C – computer software house for construction industry – Computer Services Consultants UK Ltd
C S C CAD – computer aided drafting system – Computer Services Consultants UK Ltd
C S C Fasteel – steelwork analysis and design – Computer Services Consultants UK Ltd
C.S.L. Rheometer – versatile controlled stress rheometer for product development and R and D work – Ta Instruments
C S Products (Testing Equipment) – Meddings Machine Tools
C-Scan – buried pipeline insulation inspection – Ie-Ndt Manufacturer
C-Scope – metal detectors – C-Scope International Ltd
C-Scope – Alpha Electronics Northern Ltd
C-Scope – Alpha Electronics Southern Ltd
C-Sentry – Impalloy
C Series – digital readout – Newall Measurement Systems Ltd
C. Series – open impeller pumps and centrifugal pumps – Calpeda Ltd
C-Shield – impressed current cathodic protection systems for ship's hulls – Cathelco Ltd
C-Shrink (United Kingdom) – ctl c-shrink heatshrink cable joints & terminals – C T L Components plc
C-Solve – Non-Chlorinated Solvent – Unicorn Chemicals Ltd
***C.T.E. Chem-Tec (U.S.A.)** – flow monitors, flow meters and excess flow valves – Boiswood LLP
C.T.I Cryogenics – AESpump
C.T.L. Card Tech – computer software – Tsys
C.T.S. Corporation UK Ltd – press fit and surface mount backplanes, custom design or industry standard, electro-mechanical sub-assembly, resistor networks, automotive position sensors and frequency control devices – C T S Corporation
C.T.W. Cement – for mixed acids and alkalies, water wipeable – R I W Ltd
C.T.W. Screed – acid and corrosion resisting floor screed – R I W Ltd
C Teq – Helman Workwear
C-Through – videowall products – Electrosonic Ltd
C.V.A. – dieing presses – T M A Engineering Ltd
C.V.X. – access switch – Nortel Networks UK Ltd
***C. Von Schubert (Germany)** – German wines – O W Loeb & Co. Ltd
C.W. Fletcher – sheet metal work and engineering to aircraft and nuclear industries – C W Fletcher & Sons Ltd
C.X. & C.S. – mobile cold water power washing equipment – Rhinowash Ltd
C&Y INDUSTRIES – IDLER ROLLERS & DRUMS JOINT VENTURE – Q P I Ltd
***C-Y (R.O.C.) (China)** – battery holders – Servo & Electronic Sales Ltd
C11 – Relays – Dax International Ltd
C2C – water and wastewater operations and management services – C2C Services Ltd
C2K – electronic security seals – Unisto Ltd
C3DU – Cockpit Control and Display Unit – Specialist Electronics Services Ltd
C400 Series – electronic coin validators – Money Controls Ltd
C6 Extra – dairy chemicals – Delaval
CAB – M S C Gleichmann UK Ltd
Cab Co – casual menswear – Saville Heaton Ltd
Cab Glazing – glaze construction plant and machinery – Cab Glazing Services
Cabana – soft drinks dispense system – Nichols plc
Cabaret – snack tub with spoon in lid – R P C Containers Ltd
***Cabe** – Flail Mower – Active Grounds Maintenance Ltd
Cabelec – electrically conducting thermoplastic compounds – Cabot Plastics Ltd
Caber Decor – laminated and veneer boards – Norbord Europe Ltd
Caberboard – chipboard – Norbord
Caberfloor – chipboard flooring – Norbord
Caberwood – medium density fibreboard – Norbord
Cable Glands – cable glands to mod (n) spec, EMP glands general engineers, light engineers – Fairless Engineering
Cable Hive (United Kingdom) – Floor Gromett – C M D Ltd
Cable & Wireless – Callsure Business Telephone & Fax Numbers
Cableduct – cable trunking systems and cable tray – Cableduct Ltd
CableEase – information technology disaster recovery/temporary modular cabling system – Royce Communications Ltd
Cableeater – split harness wrap – Richco International Co. Ltd
Cableform Controls (United Kingdom) – controls for electric vehicles – Zodion Ltd
Cablegard – rust preventive grease for overhead electricity transmission conductors. – Vapor Tek Ltd
Cableman – Marking systems – Weidmuller Ltd
CableMate – Sebakmt UK Ltd
Cablemiser – system panel, supply & install – B B C Fire Protection Ltd
Cabra – bonded leather – Intercover (E Hampson) Ltd
Cabria – luxury washbasins, closet and bidet – Ideal Standard Ltd
Cacharel – spectacle frames – Pennine Optical Group Ltd
Cachebox – distribution server – Quantel Ltd
Cachet Cachet – chess sets – Traditional Games Co.
Cachet Furniture Direct – Anderson Bradshaw
CACI – database marketing software and bureau services – C A C I
Cacti – Anti scaling device – Hercules Security Fabrications Ltd
Cadbury – UK Office Direct
Caddetc – consultancy in CAD-Cam data exchange – University Of Leeds
***Caddie** – Caddie Products Ltd
***Caddie Valet** – Caddie Products Ltd
***Caddinox** – Caddie Products Ltd
Caddy – Trafalgar Tools
Cadence – cleaning agent for pressure and steam cleaners – Morris Lubricants
Cadet – portable diagnostic equipment – Crypton Ltd
Cadet – bath – Armitage Shanks Ltd
Cadet – desk with trueline parallel motion system – Blundell Harling Ltd
Cadfix – locates and fixes dirty geometry problems prior to exporting cleaned and healed geometry to acis and cad/cam/cae systems – Transcendata Europe Ltd
Cadis – magazines – Newhall Publications Ltd
Cadisac – economic replacement for traditional tea chest – Segezha Packaging
Cadnit – kettle fur collectors and scourers – La Cafetiere
Cadox – benzoyl peroxide slurry – Akzo Nobel Chemicals Holdings Ltd
Cadraw – software program for the construction industry – Arup
Cadre Quadra – ornate plaster ceiling tiles – U S G UK Ltd
CAESOR – Redsky It
Cafco 300 – fireproofing gypsum plaster – Promat UK Ltd
Cafe Direct – UK Office Direct
Cafe Hag – filter and instant coffee – Kraft Foods UK Ltd
***Cafe Maid** – coffee creamer – Pritchitts
Cafebar – Autobar Group Ltd
Caffini pumps – Anchor Pumps Co. Ltd
Caffyns Wessex – motor vehicles dealers – Caffyns plc
***Cafina (Switzerland)** – Coffee machines (Trade) – Melitta System Service
***Cafitesse** – Douwe Egberts UK
Cafm – computer aided facilities management – F M X Ltd
Cafsmaster Foam Systems – foam – Godiva Ltd
Cage – M S C Gleichmann UK Ltd
Cage & Aviary Birds – I P C Media Ltd
Cage Clamp – technology for gastight connections – WAGO Ltd
Caged Ball – T H K UK
CAICO (Columbus McKinnon) – Hawk Lifting
Cains – beer – Robert Cain Brewery
Cairngorm cubicles – Ultimate durability – Cubicle Centre
Cakes By Ann – Design and decoration of cakes for all occasions – Cakes By Ann
CAL – E Preston Electrical Ltd
Cal-Chip – Cyclops Electronics Ltd
Cal-m – organic mineral drink cal-made – G & G Food Supplies
Cal-Sol-Calcium – chloride solution for cheese – Chr. Hansen (UK) Ltd
Cal-Vac – rupture disc – Continental Disc UK Ltd
Calabrese Sink – a sink chopping board, rubbish chute & waste disposal - all in one – Cantilever Bar Systems Ltd
Calando Pine Disinfectant – powerful phosphate free disinfectant – Morris Lubricants
CalCheck – calibrator – Ion Science Ltd
Calcia – calcium and vitamin and iron supplement – Perrigo UK
Calciject – indicated in the treatment of hypocalcaemia – Norbrook Research
Calcium Aluminates Cements – cements – Kerneos Ltd
Calder – stainless steel washing trough – Armitage Shanks Ltd
Calder – turbines – Calder Ltd
Calder Line – buses – First Group plc
Calderdale – concrete – Sandtoft Holdings Ltd
caldi castle hire – bouncy castle hire – Caldi Castle Hire
Caldo – Trafalgar Tools
Caledonian – Caledonian Cables Ltd
Caledonian – roofing paint – Craig & Rose Ltd

*Caledonian (United Kingdom) – upholstery leather – Bridge Of Weir Leather Co.

*Caledonian Collection – Geerings Of Ashford Ltd

Calellafest – University sports tournament – Teamlink Sports Tours

Calfmate – calf feeding systems – John C Collins

Calfos – natural calcium phosphate – Croda Europe Ltd

Calibre – Rubber bands – Calibre Ltd

Calibre – Resinex UK Ltd

Calibris – rotary polishing brushes – Attenborough Dental Ltd

California Miss – footwear – Whyte & Son Nottingham Ltd

Caligen – British Vita plc

Caligraving – lithographers – Caligraving

Calinar – heatsinks – Anglia

Calisto – typeface – Monotype Imaging Ltd

Calivac & Sterigest – CSSD Traceability Systems – Amcor Flexibles

Call IP Over Voice – Tekdata Distribution Ltd

call navigator – Callsure Business Telephone & Fax Numbers

Call Pilot – unified messaging software – Nortel Networks UK Ltd

Callender-Hamilton – steel bridging – Painter Bros Ltd

Callenders – felt – Mells Roofing Ltd

Callisto (United Kingdom) – Scada – Remsdaq Ltd

Callisto – low voltage semi recessed architectural lighting – Designplan Lighting Ltd

Callsure – Callsure Business Telephone & Fax Numbers

Calm Down – Relieves stress, helps sleep, prevents travel sickness – Supplements For Pets Ltd

Calmark – Tekdata Distribution Ltd

Calmax – high toughness presswork tool steel – Uddeholm Steel Stockholders

Calmote – limestone powders – Omya UK Ltd

Calomax – Boilers – Calomax Ltd

Calor – aerosol propellants – Calor Gas Ltd

Calor – Gem Tool Hire & Sales Ltd

Calor Gas – butane gas – Calor Gas Ltd

Calor Natural Gas – Calor Gas Ltd

Calor Propane – propane gas – Calor Gas Ltd

Calor Refrigerants – Calor Gas Ltd

Calorettes – Prices Patent Candles Ltd

Calorex – heat pumps dehumidifiers & environment control – Certikin International Ltd

Caloxol – calcium oxide desiccants – Omya UK Ltd

Calpeda – Arun Pumps Ltd

Calpeda – pumps – Allpumps Ltd

Calrec Audio – professional broadcast sound equipment – Calrec Audio Ltd

CALTEC – hydrocarbon production boosting systems – B H R Group

Calvin Klein – Perscent

Calvinac – heat and catalyst cured synthetic resin coatings and linings – Lithgow Saekaphen Ltd

Calxite – building blocks – Thakeham Tiles Ltd

Calypso – Fistreem International Ltd

Calypso – Zeiss

Calypso – waterstill – Sanyo Gallenkamp plc

Calyxol – perfume speciality – Quest International UK Ltd

CALZONI – Hydraulic & Offshore Supplies Ltd

Calzoni – hydraulic motors – Parker Hannisin plc

CAM AUTOS – Hydraulic & Offshore Supplies Ltd

Cam Vac – Dust extractors – The Toolpost

Camargue – carpets – Bond Worth

Camargue – spring barley variety – Limagrain UK Ltd

Camargue – WC suite – Armitage Shanks Ltd

Camargue – boats – Sunseeker Poole Ltd

Camaster, Safeloc, Redspot, Safe Clip, Microswitch – Kempston Controls Ltd

Camatic – Camlock Systems Ltd

Camax – Alpha Electronics Southern Ltd

*Camber (U.S.A.) – cymbals – John Hornby Skewes & Co. Ltd

Camberley – 535mm double oven – Indesit Company UK Ltd

Cambi Lathes – Colchester Lathe Co. Ltd

Cambio – brokers and distributors of products in biotechnology – Cambio Ltd

Cambion – IC sockets, connectors, cage jacks, solder terminals, hardware, air coils, toroid and machine wound inductive products, coil forms, custom RF connectors. – Wearnes Cambion Ltd

Cambrain – interlocking slate – Monier Ltd

Cambrian – paving – Welsh Slates

Cambric – high quality fine linen paper – G F Smith

Cambridge – 600mm double oven – Indesit Company UK Ltd

Cambridge – UK Office Direct

Cambridge Connectors – manufacturer of electronic and electro-mechanical connectors and network products – Cambridge Electronic Industries Ltd

Cambridge Evening News – newspapers – Cambridge Newspapers Ltd

Cambridge Numerical Control – Cambridge Numerical Control

Cambridge Park – Tables – Bucon Ltd

Cambridge Solar – Cambridge Solar Ltd

Cambridge Weekly News – newspapers – Cambridge Newspapers Ltd

Camdata – computer equipment and industrial hardware – Camdata Ltd

Camdeboo – Freedown Food Co.

Came – Gate automation equipment – Essex Gate Systems

Came – Eagle Automation Systems Ltd

Camelot – axminster – Brintons Carpets Ltd

Cameo – electric instantaneous shower – Heatrae Sadia

Cameo – Genuine plaster decorative mouldings, ceiling centres and coving – Vencel Resil Ltd

Cameo – seat – Armitage Shanks Ltd

Cameo – saddlery, horse blankets, webbing and belts – Ollard Westcombe

Cameracolour – postcards, diaries, calendars and books – J Salmon Ltd

Cameras – Andor Technology Ltd

Cameron 2000 – maintenance of petrol pumps, and installation of pipe works – Cameron Forecourt Ltd

CamIR Range – CAMIR – Applied Scintillation Technologies

Camloc – Specialty Fasteners & Components Ltd

Camlock – tungsten carbide cutting tools – Hallamshire Hardmetal Products Ltd

Camlock – Hawk Lifting

Camlock – cutting tools – Hill Cliffe Garage

Camlock Couplings – Quick connect & disconnect couplings – Gall Thomson Environmental Ltd

Camouflage – dirt barrier carpet/tile – Warlord Contract Carpets Ltd

Camozzi – Mercury Bearings Ltd

Camozzi – Southern Valve & Fitting Co. Ltd

Camozzi – Aztech Components Ltd

CAMOZZI – Hydraulic & Offshore Supplies Ltd

Camozzi – Trafalgar Tools

CAMOZZI PNEUMATIC – Hydraulic & Offshore Supplies Ltd

Camozzi Pneumatics – comprehensive range of pneumatic components – Camozzi Pneumatics Ltd

Campbell – chains, ropes and accessories – Apex Tools

Camper & Nicholsons – yacht brokers and builders, charter brokers, yacht management, crew selection – Camper & Nicholsons Mayfair Ltd

Campini (Italy) – thermostats – A T C Semitec Ltd

Campus – Pledge Office Chairs Ltd

Camro – catering wireware – Cameron Robb Ltd

Camtainer – strong assembly of composite materials – Zygology Ltd

Camtek – Camtek Ltd

CAMWARE – manufacturing software – Yamazaki Machinery UK Ltd

Can flo – Harrier Fluid Power Ltd

Canacert – food colourings – Sensient

Canalis – busbar trunking – Schneider

Canalta – Jenex Ltd

Canary Wharf – property development – Canary Wharf Holdings Ltd

Canasta (United Kingdom) – carpet tiles – Checkmate Industries Ltd

Canberra – partitioning board – Eleco Timber Frame Ltd

CancerBoss – Custom Brakes & Hydraulics Ltd

Candid – mail order catalogue – J D Williams Mail Order Group

Candy Pile – redriven circular precast concrete pile – Balfour Beatty Living Places

Canesa – Heat shrinkable PVC tubing – Shrink Sleeve Ltd

Canford – broadcasting equipment – Canford Audio

CANGURU – Chaintec Ltd

Canister Pumps – multistage borehole pump (canned) – Weir Group Senior Executives Pension Trust Ltd

Cannon – computer printers – Micro Peripherals Ltd

Cannon – cabinets and enclosures for 19" 23": ETS I and other equipment and accessories, including fibre optic support products – Cannon Technologies Ltd

Cannon – beverage dispense equipment – I M I Cornelius UK Ltd

Cannon – Gem Tool Hire & Sales Ltd

Cannon Shelley – Shelley Thermoformers International Ltd

Cannon Silverplated Sports Cups – Cannon.Co.Uk

Canon – UK Office Direct

Canon (Japan) – micromotors DC – Trident Engineering Ltd

Canon – Lamphouse Ltd

Canon – Canon inkjet cartridges, laser toners, printers, cameras & photo paper – Inkxperts

Canon – Photocopier – Alecto Solutions Ltd

Canon Business Service – maintenance of canon small office products – Canon UK Ltd

Canon / Invu – I T @ Spectrum Ltd

Canon Photocopiers – Clarity Copiers

Canpa – boat hatches – Navimo UK Ltd

Cantalou – O P Chocolate Ltd

Cantaluppi (Italy) – production surface grinding machines – R K International Machine Tools Ltd

Cantata – software verification toolset for C C++ – I P L Information Processing Ltd

Cantata – kitchen furniture – Moores Furniture Group

Canterbury – tilt-n-turn window – Coastal Aluminium

Canterbury – automated food vender – Bunzl Vending Services Ltd

*Canterbury Foods – Tranfield Of Cumbria Ltd Vion Foods

Canterbury KM Extra – newspaper – Kent Messenger Group Ltd

Cantherm – thermal cutouts and miniature thermostats – Hawco

Canti-Clad – Rack supported roofs and canopies – Hi-Store

Canti Frame – a frames for cantilever racking – Hi-Store

Canti-Guide – heavy duty mobile cantilever/pidgeon hole racking – Hi-Store

Canti-lec – cable drum storage – Hi-Store

Canti-track – heavy duty racking and display – Hi-Store

Canti-Triever – storage racking – Rack International UK Ltd

Cantilever – taillifts – Joloda Hydraroll Ltd

Cantilever – stainless steel underbar – Cantilever Bar Systems Ltd

Cantilever Towers – Accesscaff International Ltd

Cantilevered Sliding Gate – heavy duty – Zeag UK Ltd

Cantilite – lightweight racking – Hi-Store

Cantilock – heavy duty canti-lever racking – Hi-Store

Cantoria – typeface – Monotype Imaging Ltd

CANUSA – Aztech Components Ltd

Cap Fruit – Fruit Puree – Classic Fine Foods Ltd

CAPA – polyols – I M C D UK Ltd

Capa – Harrier Fluid Power Ltd

Caparo Coldform – structural hollow sections – Caparo Tubes

Caparo Coldform - structural hollow sections – Caparo Tubes

Caparo Tubes (United Kingdom) – precision steel tube for furniture and automotive and general engineering purposes – Caparo Precision Tubes

Capco – repetition machining screws – C A P Group Of Companies

Cape Butts – shoe suede – Charles F Stead & Co. Ltd

Capella – diamond surface and semi recessed vandal resistant architectural lighting – Designplan Lighting Ltd

Capella Oil – lubricants – Chevron

Caperns – pet products – Bob Martin UK Ltd

Capex – vacuum pumps – Charles Austen Pumps Ltd

Capillex – photo stencil film – Macdermid Autotype Ltd

Capilure – insect attractants – International Pheromone Systems Ltd

Capita Education Services – educational management software, training, consultancy and support services, managed service – Capita Business Services Ltd

Capital Advertising – Global Radio

Capital Aluminium Extrusions Ltd / Capalex – Capalex

Capital Bonds – Capital World Travel

Capital Experiences – Capital World Travel

Capital Exposure Meters – Kauser International Trading Ltd

Capital Grade – roofing tiles and slates – Welsh Slates

Capital Incentives – Capital World Travel

Capital Radio London – Global Radio

Capital World Travel – Capital World Travel

Capitol – Harrier Fluid Power Ltd

Capitol – AESpump

Capitox – treatment of sewage – Ashbrook Simon Hartley Ltd

CAPLUGS – Caplugs Ltd

Capolago – steel bath – Ideal Standard Ltd

Capper P-C – thermoplastic pipework distribution – Glynwed Pipe Systems Ltd

Capps (China) – safety footwear – L H Safety Ltd

Cappuccino Cool – Dinkum Products Ltd

CAPRARI – J P Whitter Ltd

CapRescue – Capnograph – Wel Medical Services

Caprice – kitchen furniture – Moores Furniture Group

Capricorn – presensitised offset plates – Kodak Morley

Capricorn – digital console – A M S Neve Ltd

Caprin Tabs – enteric coated aspirin – Sinclair I S Pharma

Capris – ultra violet (UV) laser cable marking systems – Spectrum Technologies Ltd

Capsela Science Toys – introductory, starter, explorer, intermediate, advanced, expert and remote control – Vtech Electronics UK plc

Capstan Full Strength – plain cigarettes – Imperial Tobacco Group PLC

Capstan Ready Rubbed – pipe tobacco – Imperial Tobacco Group PLC

Captain – Stainless Steel Bollard – Alto Bollards UK Ltd

Captain Card – white tinted copier and desk top laser card – International Paper Equipment Finance LP

Captain Colours – tinted copier and desk top laser paper – International Paper Equipment Finance LP

Captain Tolley's Creeping Crack Cure – penetrating sealant – Captain Tolley Ltd

Captain White Copier – white copier and desk top laser paper – International Paper Equipment Finance LP

Capteur – City Technology Ltd

CAPTON – Proximity, Multi-Limit, Flow, Hot Material Detecting (Infrared), Machine Guard, Solenoid, Inter-Lock Safety Switches – Francis and Francis Ltd
Car Care Plan – breakdown warranties – Car Care Plan Ltd
Car-Plan – car care products – Tetrosyl
Caradale – clay bricks facing common and engineering – Caradel Brick Ltd
Caradon Plumbing Solutions – ideal boilers-domestic, industrial and commercial – Ideal Heating
Caradon Terrain – soil, drain, rainwater and waste systems – Ashworth
***Caran D'Ache (Switzerland)** – pens and artists materials – Jakar International Ltd
***Caran D'Ache** – lighters, pens and artists – Jakar International Ltd
Caranaudmetalbox – packaging – Crown Packaging
CarAseal – sealant – Carafax Ltd
Caravan – I P C Media Ltd
Caravan Brill – all American style bread & confectionery products – C S M UK Ltd
Carballoy – grey iron for general disc requirements – Precision Disc Castings Ltd
Carbide Wear Parts – Ceratizit UK Ltd
Carbofrax – high temperature refractories – Saint Gobain Industrial Ceramics Ltd
Carbon – reinforcement fabrics – Fothergill Engineered Fabrics Ltd
Carbon CMS – Online Content Management Software Package – 3E UK Ltd
Carbon CRM – Customer Relationship Management Software Package – 3E UK Ltd
Carbon Ecom – Online Electronic Commerce Software Package – 3E UK Ltd
Carbon Guerrilla – Carbon Management and Accounting – Carbon Guerrilla
Carbon Property – 3E UK Ltd
Carbon-X – vending machine conditioner filters – Flowtech Fluid Handling Ltd
Carbonex 250 – Forward Chemicals Ltd
Carbostore – liquid Co2 system – Cryoservice Ltd
Carbotec – activated charcoal impregnated reticulated foam and non-woven fibre wadding – Vitec
Carbowind – Electrical components for wind turbine maintenance – Electrical Carbon UK Ltd
***Carboxymethylcellulose (France)** – Hercules Holding Ii Ltd
Carbrax – Osborn Unipol Ltd
Card – computerised assended rating data – Chinal Management Services Ltd
Card & Party Store – greeting card and stationery wholesalers – Card & Party Store Ltd
Card Saver – The Woolwich
Cardforth – microprocessor development software – Computer Solutions Ltd
Cardinal – hearse – Coleman Milne Ltd
Cardinal – standard and bespoke timber and metal shopfittings and shopfitting contractors – Cardinal Shopfitting Ltd
Cardiotrol – instrument kits – Roche Diagnostics Ltd
***Cardlok (U.S.A.)** – PCB guides – Tekdata Distribution Ltd
Cardmaster – horizontal wheel card filing – Rotadex Systems Ltd
Cardoc – twines – Kent & Co Twines Ltd
Cardoc Three Fishes – Kent & Co Twines Ltd
Cardvendor – ticket vending machines – Coinage Limited
***Carel (Italy)** – thermostats etc – Starkstrom Ltd
Careline – linear actuators – Linak UK
Caremix – thermostatic mixing valves – Reliance Water Controls Ltd
CARER – Chaintec Ltd
Carescreen – Fixed standing screen – Contour Showers Ltd
Caress Royale – insert living flame effect fire – Indesit Company UK Ltd
Carex – liquid soap – P Z Cussons International Ltd
Carex – UK Office Direct
Carfax – case cards – Carfax Cards Ltd
***Cargo Auto Electrics (Denmark)** – Holger Christiansen UK Ltd
Caribbean – carpets – Interface Europe Ltd
Caribe – outdoor architectural post top luminaire – Holophane Europe Ltd
Caribe MarinExpress Lines Salaco Express Line – Ocean Express Ltd
Carina – vanity basin – Armitage Shanks Ltd
Caring UK – The Barnsley Chronicle Ltd
Carini Spa (Germany) – Centa Transmissions
Cariphalte Primer – primer for priming concrete surface prior to filling with Cariphalte JS or applying Colas Preformed – Colas Ltd
Carisma – domestic sinks – Carron Phoenix
Carl Schlenk – copper foils – Nemco Metals International Ltd
***Carl Wezel (Germany)** – precision rolling mills – British & Continental Traders Ltd
***Carl Zeiss (Germany)** – optical instruments – Carl Zeiss Ltd
Carlite Bonding Coat – undercoat for low suction – Bristish Gypsum
Carlite Browning – undercoat plaster, moderate suction – Bristish Gypsum
Carlite Finish – final coat for Carlite undercoats – Bristish Gypsum
Carlite Tough Coat – undercoat for high suction – Bristish Gypsum
Carlo Gavazzi (Denmark) – automation components and sensing products – Carlo Gavazzi UK Ltd
Carlo Gavazzi – Selectronix Ltd
Carlton – bicycles – Raleigh UK Ltd
Carlton – sewage distributor – Tuke & Bell Ltd
Carlton – standard ale blend – Charles H Julian Ltd
Carlyle Bus & Coach – bus & coach parts distribution – Carlyle Parts Ltd
Carlyle Bus Parks – division of Carlyle Bus & Coach – Carlyle Parts Ltd
Carlyle Export – division of Carlyle Bus & Coach – Carlyle Parts Ltd
Carlyle Service – divisions of Carlyle Bus & Coach – Carlyle Parts Ltd
Carmen – personal care equipment – Russell Hobbs Ltd
Carmene – textile processing aid – Benjamin R Vickers & Sons Ltd
Carminol – textile processing aid – Benjamin R Vickers & Sons Ltd
Carmo – high hardness, high toughness and presswork tool steel – Uddeholm Steel Stockholders
Carnation – corn caps and foot comforts – Cuxson Gerrard & Company Ltd
Carnation Professional Paddings – chiropody products – Cuxson Gerrard & Company Ltd
Carnhill Transformers – transformers and inductors – Carnhill Transformers Ltd
CARNICHROME – Lonza Biologics plc
CARNIPURE 50% IN WATER – Lonza Biologics plc
CARNIPURE ALC – Lonza Biologics plc
CARNIPURE CRYSTALLINE – Lonza Biologics plc
CARNIPURE MO CITRATE – Lonza Biologics plc
CARNIPURE TARTRATE – Lonza Biologics plc
Caro – square stud anti-slip rubber flooring – Jaymart Roberts & Plastics Ltd
Carolina – Graphic Board – Mcnaughton James Paper Group Ltd
Carousel – parallel synthesiser – Radleys
Carousel – washing machines – Oliver Douglas Ltd
Carousel – electric instantaneous shower – Heatrae Sadia
***Carpet Cleaning** – Nova Contract Cleaners
Carpet & Flooring Midlands – C F S Carpets
Carpet & Flooring South West – C F S Carpets
Carpet King – carpet cleaning liquids – Clantex Ltd
Carpet Loader – telescopic boom conveyor for carpet rolls – Newland Engineering Co. Ltd
Carpet Mousse – A Mousse for the spot removal of dirt and stains from carpets – Premiere Products Ltd
Carpmaels & Ransford – patent and trademark agents – Carpmaels & Ransford
Carquest – Harrier Fluid Power Ltd
CARREFFE – Chaintec Ltd
Carrelli – Sports Seats, Auto Carpet Sets & Mats – Cover-Zone
Carrera – spectacles, sunglasses and goggles – Safilo UK Ltd
Carrick – detonator for coal mines – Orica UK Ltd
Carrier – Therma Group
Carrier – air conditioning systems – Carrier Air Conditioning
***Carrier** – stubble cultivator – Vaderstad Ltd
Carrier – Apex Commercial Refrigeration & Aircon
Carrier – mobile air conditioners – Air & Water Centre
Carrier Kheops – contractors – Bearwood Engineering Supplies
Carrington – The British Millerain Company Ltd
Carringtons – Helman Workwear
Carrtech – finishing plant, ancilliaries, titanium jigs and fixings – Carrtech Engineering Products
CARSTOPPERS – Improving site safety to provide restriction in both car parks and commercial and industrial apps. – Rediweld Rubber & Plastics Ltd
Carter – Carter Controls UK Ltd
Carter-ADB – adiabatic coolers – Carter Thermal Industries Ltd
Carter-Doucet – automatic and continuous water filters – Carter Thermal Industries Ltd
Carter-Drycool – air blast coolers – Carter Thermal Industries Ltd
Carter-Midac – air pollution abatement – Carter Thermal Industries Ltd
Carter-Visco – water cooling tower (industrial) – Carter Thermal Industries Ltd
Carters – Richard Carter Ltd
Carters Pills – laxative – Church & Dwight UK Ltd
Cartier – watches and giftware – Goldsmiths Jewellers Ltd
Cartokote – paramelt
Carton Excel – Graphic Board – Mcnaughton James Paper Group Ltd
Carton Silkia – Graphic Board – Mcnaughton James Paper Group Ltd
***Carvela (Italy and UK)** – ladies and mens shoes and handbags – Kurt Geiger Ltd
Carver – Api 610 centrifugal pumps – Axflow
Carville – machining and fabrication of plastics – Carville Ltd
CASA DOLCE – Innovative Italian tile – World's End Couriers Ltd
Casablanca – current – Harlequin
Casabond – adhesion promoters – Thomas Swan & Co. Ltd
Casagrande – Harrier Fluid Power Ltd
Casaire – direct and indirect gas fired warm air space heating system for both industrial and commercial use – Constant Air Systems Ltd
***Casale (U.S.A.)** – marine vee-drives – Lancing Marine
Casali Electric Gates – Electric Gates – G8 Systems
***Casalinga** – Donatantonio
Casamance Fabric – The Winnen Furnishing Company
Casamid – non-reactive polyamides for inks and lacquers – Thomas Swan & Co. Ltd
Casamid – curing agents for epoxy powder coatings – Thomas Swan & Co. Ltd
Casamine – aminoethyl and hydroxyethyl alkyl imidazolines – Thomas Swan & Co. Ltd
***Casana (Switzerland)** – silent humidifiers – Air & Water Centre
Casappa – hydraulic – V H S Hydraulic Components Ltd
Casappa – Fairway Hydraulics Ltd
CASAPPA – Hydraulic & Offshore Supplies Ltd
Casappa – (hydraulic pumps & motors) – Harrier Fluid Power Ltd
***Casappa (Italy)** – hydraulic pumps and motors – BYPY Hydraulics & Transmissions Ltd
CASAPPA SPA – Hydraulic & Offshore Supplies Ltd
Casarez – bis-amine A and F epoxy resins and epoxy novolacs – Thomas Swan & Co. Ltd
Casastab – thickening agents for latex – Thomas Swan & Co. Ltd
Casathane – polyurethane prepolymers for castings and surface coatings – Thomas Swan & Co. Ltd
Cascade – high pressure washers – Delaval
Cascade – detergent – Delaval
Cascade – record label – Ace Records Ltd
Cascade – agricultural machinery – Horstine Farmery
Cascade System – Ellesco Ltd
Cascamite – powdered urea resin glues for boat building – Wessex Resins & Adhesives Ltd
Casco – dental materials – Plandent
Cascorez – PVA adhesives – Wessex Resins & Adhesives Ltd
Cascover – nylon sheathing for boats – Wessex Resins & Adhesives Ltd
Casdon – toy & nursery products – Caston PLC
Case – P J P Plant Hire
***Case** – Dennis Barnfield Ltd
Case – Harrier Fluid Power Ltd
Case Communications Ltd – Manufacturer, supplier of voice and data networking solutions by case communications in UK. – Case Communication
Case Poclain – Harrier Fluid Power Ltd
Case Sumitomo – C J Plant Ltd
CaseLite – Artillus Illuminating Solutions Ltd
Casella – Halcyon Solutions
***Casement (Belgium)** – cotton casement – Bryan & Clark Ltd
Cash – humane killer stunners – Accles & Shelvoke Ltd
Cash Electrical Stunner – Accles & Shelvoke Ltd
Cash Management Solutions – cash management safes – Air Tube Technologies Ltd
Cash Master – money counting machine – Cashmaster International
Cash-Rail – ticket rail for cash & carries – Alplus
Cash Registers Direct – Richard Smith Cash Registers
Cashbase – The Woolwich
Cashcade – games - designs – Europrint Promotions Ltd
Cashlines – games - designs – Europrint Promotions Ltd
Cashtronic – pneumatic tube conveyors – Air Tube Technologies Ltd
Casio – Lamphouse Ltd
***Casio** – Shelfguard Systems
Casio – UK Office Direct
***Casio** – Tayside Cash Registers
***Casio** – Cash & EPOS registers – I C R Touch LLP
Casio – M L P S
Casio Cash Registers – Cash Register Services
CASIUS – Calibration of attitute sensors in USBL systems – Sonardyne International Ltd
Casoron G4 – preemergent and total weedkiller – Vitax Ltd
Caspar – Global Parasols Ltd
Caspian – baths – Ideal Standard Ltd
Casque – computer access security systems – Distributed Management Systems Ltd
Cassandra – hot water bottles – Paul Murray plc

Cassettair – ceiling mounter heater – Biddle Air Systems Ltd
Cassini – IP65 ambient fitting – Concord Marlin Ltd
CAST COMPRESSION FITTINGS – Hydraulic & Offshore Supplies Ltd
Cast Refrax – abrasion resistant ceramic linings – Saint Gobain Industrial Ceramics Ltd
Cast Rooflight, The – Clement Windows Ltd
CAST-X – circulation heater – Watlow Ltd
Castaway – wine cooler – Scottish & Newcastle Pub Co.
Casteels – Wiper Equipment – Isla Components Ltd
Castel Mowers – Mike Garwood Ltd
Castelanotti – Olive Oil Spain – Classic Fine Foods Ltd
Castelanotti – Olive Oil – Classic Fine Foods Ltd
Castelco – Potentiometers and switches – Omeg Ltd
Castell – trapped key safety interlocking systems – Castell Safety International Ltd
Castell / Static Systems / Emerson – Safety lock-out systems / Nurse call equipment / Uninteruptible Power Supplies – Alfred J Hurst Ltd
Castella Panatella – british cigars – Imperial Tobacco Group PLC
Castelo – Cesol Tiles Ltd
Casting Wax – dental wax – Prima Dental Group Ltd
Castle – pension series – Standard Life plc
Castle – garment display units – Havelock Europa plc
Castle – continuous hinges and purpose made pressed hinges in all materials – Gold & Wassall Hinges Ltd
Castle – high speed steel drills, wood cutting bits, s.d.s masonry drills – Castle Brook Tools Ltd
Castle Group Ltd – manufacturers of precision sound level meters, dose meters, vibration meters and entertainment noise control meters, training, rental, and consultancy services – Castle Group Ltd
Castlebond – aggregate bonding resin – Hexham Sealants Ltd
Castlecoat – flexible epoxy coating – Hexham Sealants Ltd
Castlemead – 80% wool/ 20% nylon plain twist pile, 4 & 5m wide – Adam Carpets Ltd
Castleseal – porous surface sealer – Hexham Sealants Ltd
Castlestat – electric thermostats and switches, apparatus and instruments – Otter Controls Ltd
***Castoldi (Italy)** – jet unit – Lancing Marine
Castomer – urethane elastomers – Baxenden Chemicals Ltd
CASTROL – Hydraulic & Offshore Supplies Ltd
***Castrol** – machine cutting lubricants – Turner Tools Ltd
Castrol LMX – lithium complex grease with excellent load carrying characteristics and working temperature range – Castrol UK Ltd
Castrol Lubricants – Race Industrial Products Ltd
CASTROL TECHNOLOGY CENTRE – Hydraulic & Offshore Supplies Ltd
Casuma Pumps – high pressure water pumps – Alan Dale Pumps Ltd
Caswick – plastic encapsulated steps – Caswick Ltd
Cat – Avalon and Lynwood
Cat – Global Fasteners Ltd
Cat – C J Plant Ltd
CAT – Custom Brakes & Hydraulics Ltd
Cat & Genny – Alpha Electronics Southern Ltd
Cat Mate – pet accessories – Pet Mate Ltd
Cat Specialist – The Winnen Furnishing Company
Catalyst – Cyclops Electronics Ltd
Cataphoresis – Protective Finishing Group
Cataphos – white lining paint – Sportsmark Group Ltd
Catapult – catamaran – Topper International
Catarrh Eeze – herbal remedy for the relief of catarrh – Perrigo UK
Catch One – outerwear – Dineshco Textiles Ltd
Catchwell – Maxa Technologies Ltd
Category Lighting – C P D Distribution
***Catep (France)** – multi-speed and bevel gearboxes – Andantex Ltd
***Cater-Bake** – Cater Bake UK Ltd
Cater Care – cleaning material – Brakes
Caterbridge – Metalweb Ltd
Catercart – stainless steel catering trolleys – Craven & Co. Ltd
Caterclad – wall cladding – Interclad Ltd
Caterclean 50 – odourless bactericidal alkaline detergent degreaser for catering establishments – Premiere Products Ltd
Caterclean Spray – spray on wipe off odourless bactericidal alkaline degreaser for catering establishments – Premiere Products Ltd
CaterConneX – Mechline Developments Ltd
Caterers Linen Supply – Hire of linen and chefswear to caterers nationwide. – London Linen Supply Ltd
CaterGuard – Mechline Developments Ltd
Caterham – fireplaces – Caterham Fireplaces
Caterham 21 – two seater convertible sports car – Caterham Cars Ltd
Caterham 7 – two seater convertible sports car – Caterham Cars Ltd
Catering – charcoal – Swift-Lite Charcoal
Caterlux – Ascot Wholesale Ltd
Caterpi – A T Wilde & Son Ltd
Caterpillar – Harrier Fluid Power Ltd
Caterpillar – S J Wharton Ltd
Caterpillar – Melitzer Safety Equipment
Caterpillar – Custom Brakes & Hydraulics Ltd
Caterpillar – Central Plant Hire
CATERPILLAR – Hydraulic & Offshore Supplies Ltd
Caterpillar – T V H UK Ltd
Caterpillar – parts for caterpillar tractors – Husco International Ltd
Caterpillar – John Moore Tractor Parts Ltd
Caterpillar – Stacatruc
Caterpillar – Bison Plant Hire Ltd
CATERPILLAR – Chaintec Ltd
Caterpillar – Knighton Tool Supplies
Caterpillar – D S Safety
Caterpillar – earthmoving equipment, lift trucks, marine engines, generator sets, compaction, paving and agricultural equipment – Finning UK Ltd
Caterpiller – Team Overseas Ltd
Caterpiller – Marine & General Engineers Ltd
CaterTap – Mechline Developments Ltd
Caterware – black round bowls with clear lids – Pregis Rigid Packaging Ltd
Caterwrap – flexible packaging materials for food use and associated equipment – Wrap Film Systems Ltd
CaterZap – Mechline Developments Ltd
Catflax – Imp UK Ltd
Cathcart – Scottish knitwear – R A Young & Abercairn Of Scotland Ltd
Cathedral – insert living flame affect fire – Indesit Company UK Ltd
Cathedral Oak – kitchen furniture – Moores Furniture Group
Cathedral Shop, The, Canterbury – gifts – Canterbury Cathedral Shop
Cathelco – anti-fouling systems for the protection of ships pipework – Cathelco Ltd
Cathodeon – spectral light sources – Heraeus Noble Light Analytic Ltd
CATIC – C A T I C Trading Development UK Ltd
Catinair – cyclo filters – Dustraction Ltd
Cativa – B P plc
Caton – high voltage connectors and cable assemblies. – Glassman Europe Ltd
Catop – computer software – K B C Process Technology Ltd
Catron – hygiene and cleaning chemicals – Confederate Chemicals Ltd
Cats Eyes – Lightdome Road Products
Cats Eyes – night vision goggles – B A E Systems Ltd
Catseye – traffic markings etc – Reflecting Roadstuds Ltd
Cattell – special pressings for automotive industry – Jenks & Cattell Engineering Ltd
Cattle's – finance – Cattles Ltd
***Cattlemaster** – Armstrong & Holmes Ltd
Causeway – The Winnen Furnishing Company
Causeway – steel products – Causeway Steel Products Ltd
Cavalier – Steel Bollard – Alto Bollards UK Ltd
Cavalier – The Winnen Furnishing Company
Cavalier – darts and flights – Unicorn Products Ltd
Caveman – B P plc
Cavendish – insoles – A Algeo Ltd
Cavendish French Recollections – antique style costume jewellery – Cavendish French Ltd
Cavern City Tours – city tours (Beatles related) – Cavern City Tours Ltd
Cavern Club, The – night club, cavern pub, decoubertins sports bar and grill – Cavern City Tours Ltd
Caversham – single skinned GRP up and over garage door – P C Henderson Ltd
***Caves des Vinsde Sancerre (France)** – Loire wines – O W Loeb & Co. Ltd
CaveTab – colour coded filing systems – Civica UK Ltd
CAVGUARD – Suction Dampener/Cavitations Preventer – Pulsation Dampers At Pulseguard Ltd
Cavicloser – damp course and insulated closure for cavity walls – Cavity Trays Ltd
Cavilintel – lintel with security shutter – Cavity Trays Ltd
Caviroll – DPC in roll – Cavity Trays Ltd
Cavitray – preformed dampcourses etc – Cavity Trays Ltd
Cavity – cavity wall insulation in slab form – Rockwool Rockpanel B V
Cavivent – perr-joint cavity ventilator – Cavity Trays Ltd
Caviweep – perr-joint cavity weep – Cavity Trays Ltd
Caw – gaskets – Copper & Automotive Washer Co. Ltd
Cawflo – filters for automotive and motor cycle engines – Copper & Automotive Washer Co. Ltd
Cawfold – folded metal gaskets for sealing high pressure fluids and gases – Copper & Automotive Washer Co. Ltd
Cawo – Kenex Electro Medical Ltd
Caxton – O P Chocolate Ltd
Caxton – copier paper – W L Coller Ltd
Cazal – spectacle frames – Pennine Optical Group Ltd
Cazzaniga – Watts Industries UK Ltd
CBF – Hydraulic & Offshore Supplies Ltd
CBF Group – Advertising agency – C B F
CC – cutting formes – Crosland Cutters Ltd
CCD – Halcyon Solutions
CCS – Stemmer Imaging
CCS – Custom Control Sensors International
CCS1 – conservation glass – Rankins Glass Company Ltd
CD 220 – handfed optical mark reader – D R S Data Services Ltd
CD 400 – automatic optical mark reader – D R S Data Services Ltd
CD 800 Series – automatic optical mark reader – D R S Data Services Ltd
CD Changer Teac – Tekdata Distribution Ltd
CD Data Storage – Tekdata Distribution Ltd
CD Driver Rom Teac – Tekdata Distribution Ltd
CD210 – handfed optical mark reader – D R S Data Services Ltd
CD360 – automatic optical mark reader – D R S Data Services Ltd
CDC – Southern Valve & Fitting Co. Ltd
CDC 'C' – cytotoxic dispensing cabinet – Envair Ltd
CDL – Egg trays – Dispak Ltd
CE – sand blasting equipment – C S A Cleaning Equipment
CE – Stacatruc
Ce Gold – G E Healthcare
Ceag – miners lamps and industrial hazardous lighting – Ceag Ltd
Ceandess – metal presswork – Ceandess Wolverhampton Ltd
Ceasefire – flame retardent dispersions for various industries – Aquaspersions Ltd
***Ceax (Sweden)** – Ovako Ltd
Cebora – Independent Welding Services Ltd
Cecagel – silica gel – Atosina UK Ltd
Cecaperl – expanded perlite – Atosina UK Ltd
Cecaperl 40 – expanded perlite – Atosina UK Ltd
Cecarbon – activated carbon – Atosina UK Ltd
Cecasol – synthetic calcium silicate – Atosina UK Ltd
Ceccato – Harrier Fluid Power Ltd
Cecon (U.S.A.) – housing free wheels – Ringspann UK Ltd
Cedar – personal health scheme – Western Provident Association Ltd
Cedec – lime-free porous self binding footpath gravels – C E D Ltd
Cedenza (United Kingdom) – brass valance pole – Integra Products
***Cedit (Italy)** – ceramic floor & wall tiles – Bernard J Arnull & Co. Ltd
Ceejay – construction joint formers – Simpson Strong-Tie International Inc
Cefco – electrical product wholesalers; security and fire alarms; hazardous area electrical products – City Electrical Factors Ltd
Cegelec – Euroteck Systems UK Ltd
Cegelec – equipment spares – Bearwood Engineering Supplies
Cejn – Southern Valve & Fitting Co. Ltd
CeKa – cutlery – Carl Kammerling International Ltd
CeKa – tools – Carl Kammerling International Ltd
CEL – cable accessories, pcb hardware & solder – Anglia
Celandine – lumbo-sacral back supports – The Ashcroft Clinic
Celanese nylon 66 P.A. – Ticona UK Ltd
Celanex – thermoplastic polyester P.B.T. – Ticona UK Ltd
***Celatom (U.S.A.)** – filter powder – Fleximas Ltd
***Celavita** – Agrico UK Ltd
Celazole – Merseyside Metal Services
Celcoat – plasma flame and arc sprayed coatings – Celcoat Ltd
Celebration – metal specialist ceiling systems - bespoke systems – U S G UK Ltd
Celebrations Colours – paper – Fenner Paper Co. Ltd
***Celebrity (Korea, Republic of)** – roundback guitars – John Hornby Skewes & Co. Ltd
Celebrity Motion Furniture – The Winnen Furnishing Company
Celef – speakers – Celef Audio Ltd
Celerate – high solid resin paint driers – Rockwood Pigments
Celeste – roof windows – Ubbink UK Ltd
Celestia – metallic finish organic coated steel for cladding – Corus U K Ltd
Celflex – British Vita plc
Cellabrite – auxiliary finings – Murphy & Son
Cellarsafe – Combined sensor and control system for carbon dioxide and oxygen detection – Crowcon Detection Instrument Ltd
Cellartemp – packaged cellar cooling equipment – Thermofrost Cryo plc
Cellax – seat filler for footwear – Livingston & Doughty Ltd
Cellcore – Lemon Groundworks
Cellcore – ground floor slabs – Cordek Ltd
Cellex – mechanical heat tracing products – Thermon Electrical Heating Equipment

Cellflex – foam dielectric coax cable – R F S UK Ltd
Cellform – Permenent formwork with protection against gravel movement – Cordek Ltd
Cellhire – global mobile phone hire – Cellhire plc
Cellmill – fine grinding mechanical mill – Atritor Ltd
Cellnet – Mobile phones – Champ Telephones Ltd
Cello – bottom filler – Livingston & Doughty Ltd
Cellobond – phenolic resin – Momentive Specialty Chemicals UK Ltd
Cellolyn – resins – Hercules Holding Ii Ltd
Cellophane(tm) (United Kingdom) – a range of Cellulose films with unique attributes for packaging applications – Innovia Films Ltd
CelloTherm(tm) (United Kingdom) – Cellulose film that is microwaveable and ovenable – Innovia Films Ltd
Cellplus – antennas – Nortel Networks UK Ltd
Cellsafe – Solmedia Laboratory Supplies
Celltex – County Construction Chemicals Ltd
Cellular Phones – Champ Telephones Ltd
Cellux – self-adhesive packaging tapes – Scappa UK Ltd
CELLWATCH – battery monitoring – N D S L Ltd
***Cellwood Fractionators (Sweden)** – fibre recovery systems – Pulp & Paper Machinery Ltd
***Cellyte (Europe, The Far East and USA)** – sealed maintenance free deep cycle industrial batteries for standby (telecoms, ups) 10 year design life – S E C Industrial Battery Co. Ltd
Celmar – British Vita plc
Celotex – Ainsworth Acoustics, Thermal & Building Insulation
Celsio – Heat shrinking toolholders – Schunk Intec Ltd
Celstran – long strand fibre technology – Ticona UK Ltd
Celt – boots and slippers in sheepskin – Celtic Sheepskin Company Ltd
Celtic – batteries – Supac Ltd
Celtic – tiles – William Blyth Ltd
***Celtic Collection** – Geerings Of Ashford Ltd
Celulon – tough wear and cut resisting cellular ulons – Trelleborg Applied Technology
Celvin – British Vita plc
***Celwave RF (U.S.A.)** – antennas; mobile, base station, marine, portable: transmitter combiners, receiver multicouplers, dummy loads and circulators – Pulsar Developments Ltd
CEM – Bronkhorst UK Ltd
Cemairin 3 – air entraining admixture – Don Construction Products Ltd
CEMB – Cemb Hofmann UK Ltd
CEMB - Hofmann - Benrath – Cemb Hofmann UK Ltd
Cemcol – system of ground stabilisation – Cementation Skanska
Cemcore – continuous flight auger construction of grouted piles – Cementation Skanska
Cementone – Bostik Ltd
Cemfound – system of ground treatment using an enlarged base – Cementation Skanska
Cemloc – Device for accurate location of plunged columns – Cementation Skanska
Cemoi – O P Chocolate Ltd
Cemoil – oilwell cement – Cebo UK Ltd
Cemp – Mercury Bearings Ltd
***Cemp S.r.l. (Italy)** – flameproof electric motors – Micro Clutch Developments Ltd
Cempatch L.W. – lightweight cementitious repair mortar containing migrating corrosion inhibitor – Don Construction Products Ltd
Cempatch N – cementitious repair mortar – Don Construction Products Ltd
Cempatch Primer – primer for cementitious repairs – Don Construction Products Ltd
Cemset – computer program for pile behaviour – Cementation Skanska
Cemsolve – computer program for back analysis of test result – Cementation Skanska
CemTie – stainless steel tie for stabilising solid walls – Helifix Ltd
Cendris – computer services – T N T Document Services
Cengar – Gustair Materials Handling Equipment Ltd
Cengar (United Kingdom) – portable pneumatic saws – Cengar Ltd
Ceno – crankshaft balancing machine – Schenck Ltd
Cenpaq – automatic positive pressure self contained breathing apparatus – Scott International Ltd
Censtretch – rubber bands – Calibre Ltd
Centa Servogear – Centa Transmissions
Centaflex (Germany) – flexible shaft couplings – Centa Transmissions
Centaflex – Albert Jagger Ltd
Centafoam – foam centred display board – West Design Products Ltd
Centaline – self centering clutch release bearings – N S K Europe
Centalink (Germany) – flexible shafts and couplings – Centa Transmissions
Centaloc (Germany) – shaft and spline clamping devices – Centa Transmissions
Centamax (Germany) – flexible shaft couplings – Centa Transmissions
Centari – enamels – Du Pont UK Ltd
Centastart (Germany) – centrifugal clutches – Centa Transmissions
Centaur – commercial vehicle body parts and fittings – Albert Jagger Ltd
Centaur – low voltage group motor control centres – A T B Laurence Scott Ltd
Centaur – low voltage recessed architectural lighting – Designplan Lighting Ltd
Centaur – president cable management trunking, power post and pole system; PVC conduit, trunking and accessories – City Electrical Factors Ltd
Centaur 2 – benchtop centrifuge – Sanyo Gallenkamp plc
Centax (Germany) – flexible shaft couplings – Centa Transmissions
Centenary – appeal – Christie Hospital N H S Foundation Trust
Centennial (U.S.A.) – pc cards – Premier Engineering
Center line (U.S.A.) – Butterfly valve – Crane Process Flow Technology Ltd
Centerline – Crane Stockham Valve Ltd
Centillion – ATM switch – Nortel Networks UK Ltd
Centinel – stainless steel sanitary equipment – Franke Sissons Ltd
***Centon (Far East)** – cameras, camera lenses and camera accessories – Jessops plc
Centoplas – Albert Jagger Ltd
Central Fife Times – newspaper – Dunfermline Press
Central Semi – Cyclops Electronics Ltd
Central Spraysafe – Spraysafe Automatic Sprinklers
Central Steels – steel fabrication – Luton Steels Ltd
CentrAlert – Geoquip Ltd
Centrator – pipe alignment clamps – Centrator UK Ltd
Centrator – Weldlogic Europe Ltd
CENTRE FOR POWER TRANS & MOTION CONTROL – Hydraulic & Offshore Supplies Ltd
Centreclean – ring main power washing system – Rhinowash Ltd
Centreglow – Trafalgar Tools
Centreline – Coventry Toolholders Ltd
Centrelink – micro and mainframe link software – N C C Group
Centrepoint – static high pressure hot and cold water for single user operation – Rhinowash Ltd
Centresoft – computer games distributors – Centresoft Ltd
Centrestyle – The Barnsley Chronicle Ltd
***Centret (Netherlands)** – automatic blasting cabinet – C S A Cleaning Equipment
Centrex – feature card for the DMS – Nortel Networks UK Ltd
Centriboard – extruded plastic board – Centriforce Products Ltd
Centric Clutch – mechanical & pneumatic overload protection devices – G M B Associates
Centrifugal Transfer Pumps – G V E Ltd
Centrilux – artificial teeth – WHW Plastics Ltd
Centrimat – automatic pressure and water pressure sets – Calpeda Ltd
Centripal EU – centrifugal fans – Flakt Woods Ltd
Centriquip – registered Company No 05259072 – Ashbrook Simon Hartley Ltd
Centrisep – air cleaner – Pall Europe Corporate Services
Centritile – Centriforce Products Ltd
Centromat – pipe alignment clamps – B S A Tube Runner
Centron – Komet Ltd
Centronic – electronic and nuclear components and systems – Centronic Ltd
Centrurion Rugby Training Equipment – Sportsmark Group Ltd
***Centry Cover (U.S.A.)** – helically-wound tempered steel metal ribbon for protecting machinery shafts – Beakbane Ltd
Centura Pearl – decorative packaging – Slater Harrison & Co. Ltd
Centurian – blinds – V B S Centurion Blinds
Centurian – storage units for gas cylinders – Tri Metals Ltd
Centurion – industrial safety helmets, ear muffs and head and eye protection, cycle helmets – Centurion Safety Products Ltd
Centurion – pulp forming fabric – Heimbach UK
Centurion – Steel Bollard – Alto Bollards UK Ltd
Centurion DIY Conservatories – Centurion DIY Conservatories Llp
Centuro – litter bin free standing – Glasdon International Ltd
Century – security locks – Assaabloy Group
Century – mining lubricants – Fuchs Lubricants UK plc
Century – ferrous & non ferrous castings – Noirit Ltd Newman & Field Ltd
Centuryan Security – security guards – O C S Group Ltd
CEP Cumbria – plaster ceiling tiles – C E P Ceilings Ltd
CEP Echostop – plaster ceiling tile – C E P Ceilings Ltd
CEP Fastrack – system ceiling metal tiles – C E P Ceilings Ltd
CEP Heritage – high humidity calcium silicate ceiling tiles – C E P Ceilings Ltd
CEP Solitex 90RH – high humidity mineral fibre ceiling tiles – C E P Ceilings Ltd
CEP Solitude – mineral fibre grid panels – C E P Ceilings Ltd
CEP Solitude Cumulus – acoustic mineral fibre tiles – C E P Ceilings Ltd
CEP Solitude Nelson – acoustic mineral fibre tiles – C E P Ceilings Ltd
CEP Solitude Rilled – acoustic mineral fibre tiles – C E P Ceilings Ltd
CEP Tonico – acoustic mineral fibre tiles – C E P Ceilings Ltd
Cepac – Subsea Cylinders – Air Power & Hydraulics Ltd
CEPAC – tennis-multiuse sports coating – Emusol Products Ltd
Cepas (Democratic People's Republic of Korea) – Butterfly valve manufacture – Trimline Valves
Cepheus Oil – lubricants – Chevron
CEPO – cellulose powders – Omya UK Ltd
Cequra – external sounder – C Q R Ltd
Cerabar – overload resistant pressure transmitter – Endress Hauser Ltd
Cerafil – equipment for ceramics industry – Madison Filter
CERAM – consultancy, r & d and testing laboratory for materials and products – Ceramic Industry Certification Scheme Ltd
Ceramaguard – acoustic tiles – Armstrong World Industries Ltd
Ceramate – varistors – Anglia
Cerambeta – plumbers brass foundry – F W Hipkin Ltd
Ceramic – scale reducers – B W T Ltd
Ceramic Collection – The Amtico Co. Ltd
***Ceramic Foam Filters (U.S.A.)** – for cast shops and foundries – Porvair plc
***Ceramic Technologies (U.S.A.)** – razor blades – Engelmann & Buckham Ltd
Ceramide – skin range – Elizabeth Arden
Ceramique Internationale – ceramic tiles – Ceramique International Ltd
Ceramix – single lever mixer fittings - bathroom and kitchen – Ideal Standard Ltd
Ceramotherm – electric kilns – Ramsell Naber Ltd
Ceramox – ceramic capacitors – Oxley Developments Company Ltd
Ceramtex – ceramic effect colour masterbatch – Colloids Ltd
***Ceran (Germany)** – glass ceramic hobs – Schott UK Ltd
Ceratizit – Precision Tools
Cerawool – ceramic fibre products – Thermal Ceramics UK Ltd
Ceretec – G E Healthcare
Cerev (Portugal) – ceramic wall floor tiles – Pavigres UK Ltd
Cerezyme – enzymes – SCA Newtec
Cerifil – equipment for ceramics industry – Madison Filter
***Cerit (Brazil)** – synthetic and vegetable waxes – Industrial Waxes
Cerl – roller and cylinders – Cope Engineering Ltd
CERMAX – portable hygrometer – Michell Instruments Ltd
CERMET II – On-line hygrometer – Michell Instruments Ltd
Cerraro – Harrier Fluid Power Ltd
Certa (Switzerland) – automation systems – Rem Systems Ltd
Certificated 316 Welding – Fastec Engineering Ltd
Certificated Carbon Steel Welding – Fastec Engineering Ltd
Certificated Stainless Steel Welding – Fastec Engineering Ltd
Certikin – swimming pool equipment – Certikin International Ltd
Certipak – carrier for multi pots - desserts and yoghurts – Nampak Carton
***Certis Europe** – Horticultural pesticides – L S Systems Ltd
Certuss – steam generators – Certus UK Ltd
Certuss Generators – Twin Industries International Ltd
Cerunert – chemical resistant industrial vibration tiling system – J L Lord & Son Ltd
Cervolide – perfume speciality – Quest International UK Ltd
CES – Critical Environment Solutions Ltd
Cesab – Stacatruc
CESAB – Chaintec Ltd
***Cesar (France)** – carnival masks – Palmer Agencies Ltd
Cesclean – septic tank conditioner – Sorex Ltd
Cesco Magnetics – Magnetic separators, metal detectors – Bestpump
Cessna – Harrier Fluid Power Ltd
CESTILENE – Merseyside Metal Services
Cestra – surgical facemask – Robinson Healthcare Ltd
Cestretan – retan leather for hydraulic packings – Joseph Clayton & Sons Ltd
Cetecoil – H R S Heat Exchanges Ltd
Cetetherm – H R S Heat Exchanges Ltd
Cetincoat – abrasion resistant coating material for glass – Atosina UK Ltd

Cetriad – veterinary udder cream – J M Loveridge

Cetron – electronic tubes – Richardsons R F P D Ltd

Cetronic – European Technical Sales Ltd

Cetyl – floral disinfectant – Evans Vanodine International plc

CEWEL – Hydraulic & Offshore Supplies Ltd

Ceylamix – Seasoning Blends – Synergy Food Ingredients Ltd

CF – Hydraulic & Offshore Supplies Ltd

CFG – lockers – Link Lockers

CFIT – B L Pneumatics Ltd

CFP – LPCB approved 2-8 zone conventional fire panel – C-Tec Security Ltd

CFP Alarmsense – 2-8 zone two-wire fire panels – C-Tec Security Ltd

CFR ITALY – Hydraulic & Offshore Supplies Ltd

cg16 – AESpump

'CH' – hydraulic crawler cranes – R B Cranes Ltd

Chadpac – vapour phase inhibitors – Thompson & Capper Ltd

*Chadwick Ebert Hoeveler (Germany) – Chadwick International

*Chadwick Ledieu Oger (Paris and UK) – Chadwick International

*Chadwick South Africa Pty (South Africa) – Chadwick International

Chadwick Textiles – textile merchants – Chadtex Limited

Chafer 418 Spraypack – Self propelled agricultural crop sprayer – Chafer Machinery Ltd

Chafer 618 Spraypack – Self propelled agricultural crop sprayer – Chafer Machinery Ltd

Chafer Guardian – Trailed agricultural crop sprayer – Chafer Machinery Ltd

Chafer JCB demount Spraypack – Demountable agricultural crop sprayer – Chafer Machinery Ltd

Chafer Multidrive demonnt spraypack – Demountable agricultural crop sprayer – Chafer Machinery Ltd

Chafer Sentry – Trailed agricultural crop sprayer – Chafer Machinery Ltd

Chafer Unimog Spraypack – Demountable agricultural crop sprayer – Chafer Machinery Ltd

Chain & Post – Accesscaff International Ltd

Chainflex. – Igus (UK) Ltd

Chainflex Coupling – Renold Clutches & Couplings Ltd

Chair People, The – Wallis Office Furniture Ltd

Chaletpool – swimming pool enclosed in wooden building – Pinelog Ltd

Challenge – Challenge Power Transmission Ltd

Challenge – tacks, nails and pins – Frank Shaw Bayonet Ltd

Challenge – UK Office Direct

Challenge – industrial fastenings – Challenge Europe Ltd

Challenger – Stacatruc

Challenger – tennis trainer – Bishop Sports & Leisure Ltd

Challenger – goods trailer – Indespension Ltd

Challenger – agricultural machinery – Agco International Ltd

Challenger Art – Coated Paper – Mcnaughton James Paper Group Ltd

Challenger Feeds – BOCM Pauls Ltd

Challenger Offset – Uncoated Paper – Mcnaughton James Paper Group Ltd

Challenger Superbank – Uncoated Paper – Mcnaughton James Paper Group Ltd

Challenger Supertac – Self Adhesive – Mcnaughton James Paper Group Ltd

Challenger Tinted Offset – Uncoated Paper – Mcnaughton James Paper Group Ltd

Challenger Velvet – Coated Paper – Mcnaughton James Paper Group Ltd

Challenger White Postcard – Uncoated Paper – Mcnaughton James Paper Group Ltd

Challenger White Pulpboard – Uncoated Paper – Mcnaughton James Paper Group Ltd

Challow – agricultural buildings – Challow Products

Chalmit – industrial, zone 1/2 hazardous area and marine lighting fittings,submersible lighting – Chalmit Lighting

Chamber of Commerce (LCCI) – Lincolnshire Chamber Of Commerce & Industry

Chambo – babies, childrenswear and teenage fashions – Shenu Fashions

Chambrelan – G S F Promount

Chambrelan – European Technical Sales Ltd

Chamcoat – metallised films & laminates for adhesive coating – Chamberlain Plastics Ltd

Chamdrill – Iscar Tools

Chamette – expanded vinyl material in roll form – J B Broadley

Chamex – synthetic chamois leathers – Lancashire Sock Manufacturing Co.

Chamgroove – Iscar Tools

Chammill – Iscar Tools

Chamois (United Kingdom) – double ended bench, pedestal and dust extraction mounted polishers. – R J H Finishing Systems Ltd

Chamolux – textile material in roll form coated with plastics – J B Broadley

Chamotan – tanning oil for chamois leather – Seven Sea's Ltd

Champagne de Castelnau – Patriarche Wine Agencies

Champion – security rising arm barrier – Zeag UK Ltd

Champion – flour – Whitworth Holdings Ltd

Champion – Harrier Fluid Power Ltd

Champion Coaching – coaches – Sports Coach UK

Champion Hire (United Kingdom) – hire services – Champion Hire Ltd

Championship Manager – computer game – Square Enix Ltd

Champneys – health and fitness club – Champneys

Champneys Brussells – heath & fitness club – Champneys

Champneys Health Resort – health & fitness club – Champneys

Chancellors – estate agency services; management, rental, letting leasing of residential properties and buildings; financial services all relating to real estate, property and buildings; insurance and investment, appraisal, valuation and administration – Chancellors

Chancellors Associates – surveying, all relating to property – Chancellors

Chandler – Jenex Ltd

Chandos – record distributors and producers – Chandos Records

Channel Events – Demonstration and event teams – Channel Advantage Ltd

Channel Four – Channel Four Television Co. Ltd

Channel Four International – Channel Four Television Co. Ltd

Channel Games – Specialist field marketing team representing the games industry – Channel Advantage Ltd

Channel InStore – Tactical field marketing and merchandising team – Channel Advantage Ltd

Channel Knowledge – Data capture, collation, analysis and research – Channel Advantage Ltd

Channel Safety Systems – Fire alarm panels and detectors – R & M Electrical Group Ltd

Channel Specialists – Dedicated field marketing and merchandising teams – Channel Advantage Ltd

Channelwood Rechargeable System – patent insitu timber preservation process – Channelwood Preservation Ltd

Chantal – bed linen – Kipfold Ltd

Chantelle – tailor made caravan awning – Kingswood Canvas Ltd

Chantry Bollard – fully automatic hydraulic bollard – Apt Controls Ltd

Chap – construction, civil engineering contractors, building contractors, sand and gravel quarriers house builders, readymix mortar producers, utilities contractors – Chap Construction Aberdeen Ltd

Chapel Hill – Elgate Products Ltd

Chapman Envelopes – envelopes – Chapman Envelopes Ltd

Chappée – Baxi Group

CHAR-LYNN – Hydraulic & Offshore Supplies Ltd

Character – UK Office Direct

Charcuti – Leathams Ltd

Chargepac – coagulants – Ashland UK

CHARLATTE – Chaintec Ltd

Charles Austin – small diaphragm units – AESpump

Charles Blyth – suppliers to the upholstery and bedding trade of springs, wooden frames, upholstery materials and fabrics – Charles Blyth & Company Ltd

Charles Horrell – fashion footwear for men – Sanders & Sanders Ltd

*Charles Joguet (France) – Loire wines – O W Loeb & Co. Ltd

Charles Sheraton – CD/audio storage furniture – Frostholme Furniture Ltd

Charles Sowden (United Kingdom) – Worsted Mens Suiting Fabric – John Foster Ltd

Charles Walker – conveyor and transmission belting – Habasit Rossi Ltd

Charlie Miller – hairdressers – Charlie Miller Hairdressing

Charlotte – WC suite – Armitage Shanks Ltd

Charlotte Watson's Country Collection – Henry Watson Potteries Ltd

Charlynn – Harrier Fluid Power Ltd

Charmilles – Agie Charmilles Ltd

Charnley – artificial hip joint – Depuy International

Charnwood – handmade bricks, briquettes & special shapes – Charnwood Forest Brick Ltd

Charringtons – B P plc

Chartered Building Company Scheme – Chartered Institute of Building

Chartered Institute of Building, The – Chartered Institute of Building

Chartered Institute of Marketing (CIM) – professional body for marketing/sales training, education, information, consultancy and recruitment – Chartered Institute Of Marketing

Chartpak – drafting and design materials – Ashley Industrial Ltd

Chartwell – professional graph & survey pads, books & tachograph charts & accessories – Exaclair Ltd

Chartwell – UK Office Direct

Chase Blend 14 – seaweed animal food supplement – Chase Organics

Chase For Windows (United Kingdom) – environmental auditing software package – H A S T A M

Chasefeed – Taegutec UK Ltd

Chasemill – Taegutec UK Ltd

Chasemould – Taegutec UK Ltd

Chaseocto – Taegutec UK Ltd

Chaseside – Harrier Fluid Power Ltd

*Chasseur (France) – cast iron cookware – Dexam International

Chat – Chat It's Fate – I P C Media Ltd

Chat-Forum.com – Internet Chat Room Services – Ascii Software Ltd

Chat - It's Fate – I P C Media Ltd

Chat Passion – I P C Media Ltd

Chatanienrich – Lamphouse Ltd

Chateau – Turner Bianca

Chateau – kitchen furniture – Moores Furniture Group

Chateau Lamothe de Haux – wine – Rodney Densem Wines Ltd

Chateau Royale – axminster, with banded border – Victoria Carpets Ltd

CHATSWORTH – Wolds Engineering Services Ltd

Chatterfree – tungsten based alloys – Thermal Spray Material Services Ltd

Chatterfree - tungsten based alloys – Thermal Spray Material Services Ltd

Chaurin Arnoux – Alpha Electronics Southern Ltd

Chauvin Arnoux – Alpha Electronics Northern Ltd

Check-a-Note – forgery tester – Volumatic Ltd

Check Rite – Kee Valves

Checkbox – Calibration/Service Station monitor – Crowcon Detection Instrument Ltd

Checkloop NY (United Kingdom) – carpet tiles – Checkmate Industries Ltd

Checkmate – code reader – Crypton Ltd

Checkmate – A&S Lifting and Safety Ltd

Checkout – dart flights – Unicorn Products Ltd

Checkpoint – cheque writers, cheque signers, hologram holosealers, mailroom, forms handling and cheque handling equipment – Twofold Ltd

Checkpoint – Charlton Networks

Checkrib Plus (United Kingdom) – carpet tiles – Checkmate Industries Ltd

Checkrib Plus (United Kingdom) – broadloom – Checkmate Industries Ltd

Checkstar (United Kingdom) – carpet tiles – Checkmate Industries Ltd

Checkstat Cut (United Kingdom) – carpet tiles – Checkmate Industries Ltd

Checkstat Extra (United Kingdom) – carpet tiles – Checkmate Industries Ltd

Checkstat Two (United Kingdom) – carpet tiles – Checkmate Industries Ltd

Chedder Valley – Thatchers Cider Company Ltd

Cheek Colour Naturals – eye make-up – Elizabeth Arden

Cheetah (United Kingdom) – barrier systems – Motivation Traffic Control Ltd

Cheetah – Pressure washers – B & G Cleaning Systems Ltd

Cheetah – computer accessories – Electrovision Group Ltd

Cheetah – connector for oil well casing – Oil States Industries UK Ltd

Chef Set – aluminium & s/steel cookware – Catering Suppliers

Chefaire – combination ovens – Manitowoc Food Service UK

Chefs Brigade – Leathams Ltd

Cheiftan Towers – Accesscaff International Ltd

Chell – high vacuum gauges – AESpump

Chelmer Valve – electronic valves and semiconductor devices – C V C Chelmer Valve Co. Ltd

Chelmix Concrete – ready mixed concrete – Chelmix Concrete Ltd

Chelsea – building society – Chelsea Building Society

Chelsea – casement window, thermally broken, externally or internally beaded, choice of vent profile, choice of locking – Coastal Aluminium

Chelsea – Prices Patent Candles Ltd

Chelsea – colour filter – The Gemmological Association Of Great Britain

Chelsea Classics – wallpapers, fabrics, borders – Today Interiors Ltd

Chelsing – printed circuit boards assembly, product assembly functional electronic testing and component procurement – Mode Lighting

Cheltenham & Gloucester P.L.C. – Cheltenham & Gloucester plc

Chelton – aircraft antennas – Cobham Antenna Systems

Chelwood Brick – BS special shapes and bespoke shapes-Clay facing bricks-stock bricks – W H Collier Ltd

Chem-Gard – corrosion resistant horizontal centrifugal pump – Vanton Pumps Europe Ltd

Chem-Rez – industrial chemical – Ashland Specialties UK Ltd

Chemcast – precision cast special refractory shapes – D S F Refractories & Minerals Ltd

Chemclad – chemical resistant flooring – Addagrip Surface Treatments Ltd
Chemclad Mortar – industrial and chemical-resisting flooring and lining products – Addagrip Surface Treatments Ltd
Chemcoat 90 – Forward Chemicals Ltd
Chemcon – PTFE pipeline components – Production Techniques Ltd
Chemetator – scraped surface heat exchangers – Chemtech International Ltd
Chemexol – Forward Chemicals Ltd
Chemflo – PP & PVDF corrosion resistant pressure pipe systems – C P V Ltd
CHEMFLO – Flotronic Pumps Ltd
Chemical Industry Europe – United Business Media Ltd
Chemicarb – Activated Carbon Filter for the removal of toxic gases eg Arsine and Phosgene in the production of microchips and other electronic semiconductor devices – Emcel Filters Ltd
Chemicoil – fuel hose – Angus Fire
Chemisorb – carbon filter masks – E X X Projects
Chemisorb – carbon filter masks – Safelab Systems Ltd
Chemist & Druggist Directory – United Business Media Ltd
Chemmaster – chemical resitant clothing – Alpha Solway Ltd
Chemotronic – Fullbrook Systems Ltd
Chempac – chemical waste management service – Cleanaway Ltd
Chempac – carton filling machines for margarines and shortenings – Chemtech International Ltd
Chempac MK IV – brick wrapping machines for butter and margarines – Chemtech International Ltd
Chemplex – G K N Aerospace Transparancy Systems Ltd
Chemprint – single unique label printing system and material safety data sheets to comply with chemical legislation – Episys Group Ltd
Chemraz – perfluoroelastomer 'o' ring seal – Greene Tweed & Co. Ltd
Chemseal – Forward Chemicals Ltd
Chemset – thermosetting resin systems – R F Bright Enterprises Ltd
Chemsol – chemical resistant clothing – Alpha Solway Ltd
Chemsol Plus – chemical resitant clothing – Alpha Solway Ltd
Chemsolve – degreasing and cleaning solvents – C K Chemicals
Chemsure – PureSil Technologies Ltd
Chemtech – margarine processing systems, bone treatment plants, gelatine production plants, cocoa butter deodorisers – Chemtech International Ltd
Chemtube – hydraulically operated tubular diaphragm – Wallace & Tiernan Ltd
Chemvac – liquid ring vacuum pumps, centrifugal process pumps, gear pumps – Chemvac Pumps Ltd
Chemview – Safety Goggles – Scott International Ltd
Chenille Book – fabric collection – Zoffany
Chenille DK – Sirdar Spinning Ltd
Chep UK – pallet and container pool – Chep UK Ltd
Chequen Foods – Autobar Group Ltd
Cherco – agricultural and animal foodstuffs – Cherwell Valley Silos Ltd
Cherish – C C A Group Ltd
Cheriton (United Kingdom) – switches, sockets, dimmers, etc. – R Hamilton & Co. Ltd
Cherry Blossom – shoe polishes and waxes – Cherry Blossom Ltd
Cherry Blossom Original – shoe paste – Cherry Blossom Ltd
Cherry Bomb – performance exhaust silencer – Custom Chrome Ltd
Cherry Cherry Electrical Keyboard Mini ml4100 – Tekdata Distribution Ltd
Cherry Cherry Electrical Keyboard Mini ml4100 ps2 usb – Tekdata Distribution Ltd
Cherry Cherry Electrical Keyboard PC Standard – Tekdata Distribution Ltd
Cherry Keyboard UK – Tekdata Distribution Ltd
Cherry Semi – Cyclops Electronics Ltd
Cherry Switches – Foremost Electronics Ltd
Cherry Valley – duckling producers, chilled and frozed cooked foods and ready meals – Cherry Valley Farms Ltd
Cherub Baby 3 and 4 ply – yarns – Stylecraft
Cherub Baby D.K. – yarns – Stylecraft
Cherub Sparkle D.K. – yarns – Stylecraft
Cherwell – vanity basin – Armitage Shanks Ltd
Chess – complete office furniture range – Flexiform Business Furniture Ltd
Chester – bath – Ideal Standard Ltd
Chester Chronicle – weekly title – Flintshire Chronicle Newspapers
Chester Mail – free newspaper – Flintshire Chronicle Newspapers
Chesterfield Computer Repair Services – computer repairs and services maintenance sales in chesterfield – Chesterfield P C Support
Chesterfield Steel Services – fasteners industry – Stemcor Special Steels
Chestnut Products – Wood finishing products and adhesives – The Toolpost
Cheterfields Fine Foods – Childrens character baking kits gift sets – Kinnerton Confectionery Co. Ltd
***Chevalier (Taiwan)** – surface grinding and turret milling machines – C Dugard Ltd Machine Tools
Chevin – work and toolholdy equipment – Craftsman Tools Ltd
Cheviot – Try & Lilly Ltd
CHEVRON TEXACO TECHNOLOGY – Hydraulic & Offshore Supplies Ltd
Chewing Gum remover – freezes chewing gum to permit easy removal – Premiere Products Ltd
Chianti – ladies woven separates – Emreco International Ltd
Chiara – shower enclosure – Armitage Shanks Ltd
Chic – kitchens – Potter Cowan & Co Belfast Ltd
Chicago Miniature – Cyclops Electronics Ltd
Chicago Pneumatic, CP – Midland Air Tools Ltd
CHICAGO-RAWHIDE – Hydraulic & Offshore Supplies Ltd
Chicago Steel Tape CST – Sebakmt UK Ltd
Chichester – stainless steel tableware – Dexam International
Chichester – stainless steel trays and spiked carving dishes – Goodwood Metalcraft Ltd
***Chick n Ferno** – hot & spicy coated chicken – Moy Park Ltd
Chick n Teddies – Moy Park Ltd
CHICO – Hook and loop fastener. – Stretch Line UK Ltd
CHICO - Hook and loop fastener. – Stretch Line UK Ltd
Chief UK – Display Equipment – Carrier Refrigeration & Retail Systems Ltd
Chieftain – Emmerson Doors Ltd
Chieftain – spades and shovels – Chieftain Forge
Chieftain – planting tools and planting bags – Chieftain Forge
Chieftain Forestry – tool specialist – Chieftain Forge
Child Education – monthly magazine – Scholastic School Book Fairs
Child's Play – books, games and audio-visual materials – Childs Play International Ltd
Childcare Solutions – Accor Services
Childcare Vouchers – Accor Services
Childcraft – childrens paddling pools constructed from steel rigid frames, PVC flexible liners, wooden chalkboards and toy garages – Pot Black UK
Childrens hi-viz – Avalon and Lynwood
Childrens hi-viz vests/tabards – Avalon and Lynwood
Childrens high visibility – Avalon and Lynwood
Childrens high visibility vests/tabards – Avalon and Lynwood
Childwise – market research in conjunction with a panel of schools – Childwise
Chilkwell – sheepskin footwear – R J Draper & Co. Ltd
Chill n Win – cold revealing game cards – B & H Colour Change Ltd
Chillchecker – hand operated low temperature indicator – Thermographic Measurements Ltd
CHILTERN TOOLING – WEB SITE SALES chilterntooling.co.uk – SANO TOOLS
Chilton – Capex Office Interiors
Chimneyscaff – Accesscaff International Ltd
***Chinacite (China)** – anthracite – Rudrumholdings
Chinese Channel – Chinese television satellites – Chinese Channel
Chinet – Paper Packaging (Plates & Bowls) – Huhtamaki UK Ltd
Chinfong – presses – Worcester Presses
Chinook – centrifugal fan – Halifax Fan Ltd
Chint – E Preston Electrical Ltd
Chiorino PVC & PU – belting – Chiorino UK Ltd
Chipfast – chipboard/M.D.F. castor fixing – British Castors Ltd
Chipforth – microprocessor development software – Computer Solutions Ltd
Chipguard – Rotadex Systems Ltd
ChipMaster Compact – 40 channel digital IC tester (handheld) – A B I Electronics Ltd
ChipNet – smartcard operated cashless payment solution for point of sale vending, copying and network printing. – Emos-Infineer Ltd
Chipnet Quickstart – smartcard application – Emos-Infineer Ltd
Chippa – ship scaling equipment – Rotatools UK Ltd
Chippendale Electrical – Also Electrical Installations – Jack Electrical Ltd
Chipper – knife steel – Uddeholm Steel Stockholders
Chips & Tech – Cyclops Electronics Ltd
Chipsaway – Vehicle Bdy repairs – Chips Away International
Chiquitta – ladies footwear – Russell & Bromley Ltd
Chirofix – chiropody retention dressings – Cuxson Gerrard & Company Ltd
Chiroform Gel With Mineral Oil – advanced gel system fine relief of pressure and friction – Cuxson Gerrard & Company Ltd
Chiron – Birchfield Engineering Ltd
Chiropody Couches – Akron
Chiswick – record label – Ace Records Ltd
Chivalry – games, models, miniatures and war games – Games Workshop Ltd
Chloe – washbasin, closet, bidet and bath – Ideal Standard Ltd
***Chlorsol** – Pigs and chickens – Vetoquinol Ltd
Chobert – controlled expansion fastener for light weight fabrications – Avdel UK Ltd
Chobert – repetition riverting systems – Zygology Ltd
Choc-o-Nut – Stute Foods Ltd
Choc Roll Clamp – Tentec Ltd
Chockfast – epoxy resins – Hamworthy Waste Water plc
Choices – estate agents and lettings agents – Choice Properties
CHOISE – Integrated Software Solution for Retail and Wholesale – In-Tech Solutions UK Ltd
Choose-Hosting – Hosting Services for Personal and Business Websites – Choose-Hosting
Chopmaster – straw chopper – Brown's Agricultural Machinery Company Ltd
Chorus – accessories – Armitage Shanks Ltd
CHOTMERICS – Hydraulic & Offshore Supplies Ltd
Chris Craft – window blinds and furniture covers – Stevens Scotland Ltd
Christ – Freeze Dryers – Pauley Equipment Solutions
***Christen (Switzerland)** – drill grinding machines, cutter grinding machines and edge chamfering machines – Brunner Machine Tools Ltd
Christen – Bruderer UK Ltd
Christian Dior – spectacles and sunglasses – Safilo UK Ltd
Christie – business agents handling the sale, aquisition and valuation of businesses across the hotel, leisure, licensed, catering and retail sectors – Christie & Co. Ltd
Christie – Lamphouse Ltd
Christmas Gold – C C A Group Ltd
Christmas Greetings – C C A Group Ltd
***Christmas Presence (United Kingdom)** – christmas company – Universal Display Fittings
Chroma plus – polished chrome wiring accessories – M K Electric Ltd
Chromajet – electrochemical detector for HPLC – E D T Direct Ion Ltd
Chromalite – microbeads – Purolite International Ltd
Chromalox – strip, ring, cartridge and tubular heaters – Chromalox UK Ltd
***Chromatec** – Michael Stevens & Partners Ltd
***Chromato-vue (U.S.A.)** – UV viewing cabinets – Ultra-Violet Products Ltd
Chromazone – reversible colour changing ink – Thermographic Measurements Ltd
Chromet – chromium-molybdenum alloy steel welding electrodes – Metrode Products Ltd
Chromzirc 3 – copper chromium – Columbia Metals Ltd
Chromzirc 328 – copper chromium zirconium – Columbia Metals Ltd
Chronicle – software package that allows users to create and view timelines, using text, graphics, sound and digital video – Learning & Teaching Scotland
Chronicle ,The (Flintshire Editions) – weekly title – Flintshire Chronicle Newspapers
Chrysalid – building within a building – M S S Clean Technology
Chrysalis – music publishers – Chrysalis Entertainments Ltd
Chrysanthal – perfume speciality – Quest International UK Ltd
Chrysler – Therma Group
Chrysler – L M C Hadrian Ltd
***Chs Epoxy (Czech Republic)** – epoxy resins – J Allcock & Sons Ltd
Chubb – UK Office Direct
Chubb – Fieldway Supplies Ltd
Chubb – Secure Holidays
Chubb – locks – J L M Security
Chubb Atmosfire – high sensitivity smoke detection – Chubb Electronic Security Ltd
Chubb Controlmaster – fire control panel – Chubb Electronic Security Ltd
Chubb Vigil – intruder alarm system – Chubb Electronic Security Ltd
Chubb Windsor – intruder alarm system – Chubb Electronic Security Ltd
Chubb Zonemaster – fire control panel – Chubb Electronic Security Ltd
Chubbi-Stumps – hard to break crayons for infants – Creative Art Products Ltd
Chublets – crayons – Creative Art Products Ltd
Chuch – doctor blades – William Pinder & Sons Ltd
Chuck-Eez – S J Wharton Ltd
Chuckleprint – promotional clothes printer – Chuckleprint
Chudleys – dog food – Dodson & Horrell Country Store
Chumpit – waste pump – The Haigh Group Ltd
Chunki-Chalks – chunky chalks – Creative Art Products Ltd
Chunky – yarn – Stylecraft
Chunky Polo – shirt – Charterhouse Holdings plc
***Churchill** – Churchill China UK Ltd
Churchill – Red House Industrial Services Ltd

Churchill – quality brass carriage clocks and high class watches – L C Designs Ltd
*Churchill – Bob Crosby Agencies Ltd
Churchill – CNC lathes and gear hobbers – B S A Machine Tools
Churchill – UK Office Direct
*Churchill – tableware – Keemlaw Ltd
Churchill Denham lathes – Phil Geesin Machinery Ltd
Churchill lathes – Phil Geesin Machinery Ltd
Churchill Tooling – cut off blades and holders – J J Churchill Ltd
Churchtown – Churchtown Buildings Ltd
Churchtown Europa – Churchtown Buildings Ltd
*Chute (U.S.A.) – cutlery retrievers – Robot Coupe UK Ltd
CHV – direct fired gas fired unit heater – Nordair Niche
CHV – direct fired gas fired unit heater – Nordair Niche
Chy-max – vegetarian rennet – Chr. Hansen (UK) Ltd
*Ciak (Italy) – quality stickpen in attractive barrel colours – Hainenko Ltd
Ciat – HVAC Products – Barkair Ltd
CiBAS – Concentric Internal Bypas & Silencer – Citech Energy Recovery Systems UK Ltd
Cibie – car electrics – L A E Valeo Ltd
Cicely Mary Barker's As In Heaven – Chorion plc
Cico – cast in-situ refractory flue linings – Cico Chimney Linings Ltd
Cico chimney linings – Linings for chimneys – Cico Chimney Linings Ltd
Cico Flex – stainless steel flexible flue linings – Cico Chimney Linings Ltd
CICS – ceramic industry certification scheme – Ceramic Industry Certification Scheme Ltd
CIDS – compact integrated distribution switchroom – Schneider
CIEH – Rgistered Training Centre – R B Health & Safety Solutions Ltd
CIF – UK Office Direct
CIFA – Harrier Fluid Power Ltd
Cifer – computer terminals P.C.s and telex machines – Cifer Data Systems Ltd
Cig Arrete – Cigarette smoke Alarm – 03 Solutions Ltd
Cilbond – bonding agents for rubber or polyurethane to substrates, especially metal – Chemical Innovations Ltd
Cilcast – coldcuring polyurethane resin systems – Chemical Innovations Ltd
Cilcoat – in mould paint finishes – Chemical Innovations Ltd
Cilora – industrial lubricants – B P plc
Cilrelease – mould release agents – Chemical Innovations Ltd
Cim/21 – software products for process manufacturing operations – Aspentech Ltd
*Cimberio (Italy) – bronze gate valves & ball valves – S A V UK Ltd
Cimbria – grain handling equipment – Danagri - 3 S Ltd
Ciment Fondu Lafarge – cement – Kerneos Ltd
Cimjet – print and apply labelling systems – Markem-Imaje Ltd
*Cimm (Italy) – vessels – S A V UK Ltd
Cimtech – provides impartial information, advice, publications, consultancyand courses on all aspects of corporate information management – Cimtech
Cimtek – Harrier Fluid Power Ltd
Cinapse – high speed high density interconnections – Cinch Connectors Ltd
Cinbins – disposable burn bins – Labco
*Cinca (Portugal) – ceramic mosaic – A Elder Reed & Co. Ltd
*Cinca Nova Arquitectura (Portugal) – ceramic tiles – A Elder Reed & Co. Ltd
*Cincasolo (Portugal) – ceramic tiles – A Elder Reed & Co. Ltd
Cinch – Cyclops Electronics Ltd
Cinch – connectors & interconnect systems – Cinch Connectors Ltd
Cinch – Connectors – Dax International Ltd
Cinch – concentrated portion packed hard surface cleaner – Agma Ltd
Cinch Pattern 110 – subminiature multiple connectors – Cinch Connectors Ltd
Cincinnait – Red House Industrial Services Ltd
Cincinnati – Proplas International Ltd
Cincinnati – European Technical Sales Ltd
Cincinnati Mil – Harrier Fluid Power Ltd
Cincinnati Milacron – Proplas International Ltd
*Cincla (Italy) – weaving loom accessories – Pilkingtons Ltd
*Cincom (Japan) – Citizen cnc sliding head lathes – Citizen Machinery UK Ltd
Cincom Encompass – call centre solutions – Cincom Systems UK Ltd
*Cinders – Court Catering Equipment Ltd
Cintique – The Winnen Furnishing Company
Cintique Furniture – The Winnen Furnishing Company
CIOCCA – Hydraulic & Offshore Supplies Ltd
Ciocca Flanges – SAE pipe flanges – Stauff Anglia Ltd
Ciocco – hot chocolate machine – Marco Beverage Systems Ltd

Circaframe – particle filter any size, shape, resistance and efficiency to order – Emcel Filters Ltd
*Circle Seal (U.S.A.) – zero leakage valves and regulators – Tamo Ltd
Circo – slimline weather and vandal resistant bulkhead lighting – Designplan Lighting Ltd
Circo – circular surface and recessed vandal resistant architectural lighting – Designplan Lighting Ltd
*Circotherm (Germany) – ovens – B S H
Circron – technical synthetic tubular needlefelt fabrics – Andrew Webron Ltd
Circuit – managed laundry systems – J L A
Circuit Assembly – Selectronix Ltd
Circuit Brand – cored solder wire, solders and fluxes for the electronics industry – Plimto Ltd
Circular Polytanks – Kitemarked plastic cold water cisterns – Polytank Ltd
Circulux – commercial circular fluorescent lighting – Poselco Lighting Ltd
*Circutor (Spain) – electrical network, measurement and analysis energy management – Starkstrom Ltd
Cirgold 90 – alloy gold plating processes for P.C. – P M D UK Ltd
Cirgold 965 – immersion gold for surface mount in conjunction with procirc 964 – P M D UK Ltd
Cirkcaldy Herald – newspaper – Strachan & Livingston
Cirnedol – knitting machine needle oil – Benjamin R Vickers & Sons Ltd
Ciros ICP Systems – CCD Spectrometer – Spectro Analytical UK Ltd
Cirrus – Alpha Electronics Southern Ltd
Cirrus – Infrared flammable gas detector – Crowcon Detection Instrument Ltd
Cirrus – unit heater – S & P Coil Products Ltd
Cirrus GIIIx – Aerotech Engineering Ltd
Cirrus Logic – Cyclops Electronics Ltd
Cirscale – Record Electrical Associates
CIRTEQ UK – Hydraulic & Offshore Supplies Ltd
Cisaplast – Dual & triple glazed door systems – Showmaster Ltd
Cisco (U.S.A.) – Kingston Communications
Cisco Systems – Charlton Networks
Citadel – insulated fire safes – Kardex Systems UK Ltd
Citadel – S G System Products Ltd
Citadel – same day courier service, overnight express service, local, national and international deliveries and storage – City Sprint
Citadel – rule books, magazines, manuals, painting materials, miniatures and models for use with war games – Games Workshop Ltd
Citadel – cash protection systems – Spinnaker International
Citco – Cinetic Landis Ltd
CiTicel – City Technology Ltd
Citidel – stainless steel w/c – Franke Sissons Ltd
Citifone – telephone apparatus & instruments – Vodafone Retail Ltd
Citilites – ladies and childrens garments – Citilites Ltd
Citipak – roadside advertising package service mark – J C Decaux UK Ltd
CiTipel – City Technology Ltd
Citisoft – financial systems consultants – Citisoft
Citizen – Cyclops Electronics Ltd
Citizen – small graphic and video LCD modules, notebook floppy disk drives – Display Solutions Ltd
Citizen (Japan) – cnc sliding head lathes – Citizen Machinery UK Ltd
Citizen – UK Office Direct
Citizen – Rowan Precision Ltd
Citizen – Lamphouse Ltd
Citral Ex Litsea – perfume speciality – Quest International UK Ltd
Citrand – non-solvent beaded hand gel – Evans Vanodine International plc
Citrathal – perfume speciality – Quest International UK Ltd
Citrazine – worming tablets – J M Loveridge
Citreatt, Treattarome – R C Treatt & Co. Ltd
Citrix – gold reseller – Data Systems Computers Ltd
Citrix – Remote Communications Software – D P M Electronics Ltd
Citroen – L M C Hadrian Ltd
Citroen – Ashley Competition Exhausts Ltd
*Citron (Far East) – watch – J & K Henderson Enterprises Ltd
Citronellyl Nitrile – perfume speciality – Quest International UK Ltd
*Citrox P. – Agralan Ltd
City – remould truck tyres – Tyre Renewals Ltd
City – brass whistles – J Hudson & Co Whistles Ltd
City Bears – character merchandising license – Ulkutay & Co.
City Life – newspapers – Middleton Guardian
City Lights – European Lamp Group
City Master – industrial sweeping machine – Hako Machines Ltd

City Mini Golf – mini golf equipment – Bishop Sports & Leisure Ltd
City of London Courier Service – City Of London Courier Ltd
City Pumps – Italian domestic water pumps – Pedrollo Distribution
City Service – city service for garments – Johnson Apparel Master Ltd
City Style – Ryalux Carpets Ltd
Citybag – Instrument equipment computer tool – Hofbauer (UK) Ltd
*Citylights (Germany) – low voltage display lighting – Selux UK Ltd
CIVIC Chemi Hood – Filtering Device – Scott International Ltd
CJ Associates – CJ Associates Training
CJC – Hydraulic & Offshore Supplies Ltd
CJWT Solutions – Graphic Design & Printing – C J W T Solutions
CK Pump Station – K S B Ltd
CK Tools – hand tools – Carl Kammerling International Ltd
CKD – Southern Valve & Fitting Co. Ltd
*Claas (Germany) – combine harvesters, pick-up balers, forage harvesters, loaderwagons and mowers – Claas UK Ltd
Claas – Harrier Fluid Power Ltd
Cladding – thermoplastic extrusions – Russell Plastics
Cladding 280 – metal wall cladding system – Eleco Timber Frame Ltd
*Cladding Cleaning – Stayclean Contract Cleaning Services Ltd
Cladding Roll – prefabricated and moveable buildings and elements, external walls and pitched roofs – Rockwool Rockpanel B V
Cladrill – tool – C L A Tools Ltd
Cladshield – A Proctor Group Ltd
Claims Plus – vehicle maintenance – Arval UK Ltd
Claire dolls – P M S International Group plc
Clairefontaine – UK Office Direct
*Clairex – Wavelength Electronics Ltd
Clamcleat (United Kingdom) – rope cleats – Clamcleats Ltd
Clamflo – catalyst handling and maintenance shutdown – Dialog Technivac Ltd
Clamprite – Tests spindle drawbar pressure in less than one minute. – Tapmatic Engineers' Merchants
*Clampzyme – Forum Products Ltd
Clan – software packages – Schlumberger Oilfield UK plc
Clan – sports equipment, playground equipment – Clan Marketing Co.
Clan Douglas – high quality knitwear – Clan Douglas
Clanacric – tartan fabrics – J Bradbury & Co. Ltd
Clansman – Try & Lilly Ltd
Clarafile – suspended filing system – Office Depot UK
Clarcel – filter aid – Atosina UK Ltd
Clarcel – diatomaceous earth – Atosina UK Ltd
Clarcel Flo – perlite – Atosina UK Ltd
Clare – milling cutter, chucks, taps & drills and ancilliary equipment – Clare Fishers Ltd
Clare – lubricating oils & grease – R S Clare & Co. Ltd
Clare – slop hopper suite – Armitage Shanks Ltd
Clare – Alpha Electronics Southern Ltd
Clare Bechem – special lubricants for mining, automotive, cement and environmental uses – R S Clare & Co. Ltd
Clare Lube – industrial conventional oils & greases – R S Clare & Co. Ltd
Clare Tech – high performance and 'bespoke' lubricants – R S Clare & Co. Ltd
Clarehill – Rotational mouldings – Clarehill Plastics Ltd
Claremont & May Fragrance & Home – home fragrance products – Claremont & May
CLARIFIAR – Hydraulic & Offshore Supplies Ltd
Clarifire (United Kingdom) – voice alarm sounder – Fulleon
Clarion – typeface – Monotype Imaging Ltd
Clarion – mens footwear – UK Distributors Footwear Ltd
Clarion Print – recycled paper – Fenner Paper Co. Ltd
CLARIS – Hydraulic & Offshore Supplies Ltd
Claris – Pall Europe Corporate Services
Clariscan – G E Healthcare
CLARISEP – Hydraulic & Offshore Supplies Ltd
Clarital – chemical products for use in agriculture and horticulture – Fargro
Clariteyes – eye drops – M S D Animal Health
Clarity – Lamphouse Ltd
Clarity – rectangular flush meters with transparent front – Elektron Components Ltd
Clarity – reusable/unbreakable plastic glassware – Plastico Ltd
'Clarity cap' – audio grade capacitors – Industrial Capacitors Wrexham Ltd
Clarity Focus – rectangular flush meters with transparent front and bezel – Elektron Components Ltd
Clarityn Allergy – tablets – M S D Animal Health
Clarityn Allergy Syrup – M S D Animal Health
Clark – T V H UK Ltd
Clark – Stacatruc

CLARK – Chaintec Ltd
Clark – Harrier Fluid Power Ltd
Clark Michigan – Harrier Fluid Power Ltd
Clark's Chimney Cowls – stainless and mild steel cowls to overcome down draughts – Ascott Clark
Clarke – Red House Industrial Services Ltd
Clarke – spares & equipment – Bearwood Engineering Supplies
Clarke – Forresters Pressure Washer Services Ltd
Clarke – Custom Brakes & Hydraulics Ltd
CLARKE – Hydraulic & Offshore Supplies Ltd
Clarke – industrial cleaning equipment – B & G Cleaning Systems Ltd
***Clarke (U.S.A.)** – industrial floor cleaning equipment – C S A Cleaning Equipment
Clarke – permanent floor finish – Hire Technicians Group Ltd
Clarke Rendall – Reception Desks – Bucon Ltd
Clarke Transport – general haulage – Clarke Translift Ltd
Clarke (U.K) – moulded plugs – Cliff Electronic Components Ltd
Clarkson – Red House Industrial Services Ltd
Claro – subcontract precision machined parts and assemblies, conventional and CNC facilities – Claro Precision Engineering Ltd
Claro – Tekdata Distribution Ltd
CLARON – Hydraulic & Offshore Supplies Ltd
ClaronPolyseal – Mayday Seals & Bearings
Clarsol – bentonite – Atosina UK Ltd
Class – single lever fittings amd shower valves – Ideal Standard Ltd
CLASS 150-2500 FLOATING BALL VALVE USUALLY CLASS 150-600 1/2.-8. (United Kingdom) – Ultravalve Ltd
class conservatories – Builds domestic conservatories – Class Building Services
Classic – pumps – Wrightflow Technologies Ltd
Classic – Dometic UK Ltd
Classic – filing products range – Acco East Light Ltd
Classic – lighting equipment – Powerlite Lighting Solutions Ltd
Classic – british cigars – Imperial Tobacco Group PLC
Classic – motive power batteries & chargers – Chloride Motive Power C M P Batteries Ltd
Classic – Ascot Wholesale Ltd
Classic – sailboat – Topper International
Classic – cast aluminium handles – Paddock Fabrications Ltd
Classic – CCD imaging and spectroscopy cameras – Andor Technology Ltd
Classic – Vi Spring Ltd
Classic – compact suction sweepers – A B Schmidt UK Ltd
***Classic** – Crown Catering Equipment Ltd
CLASSIC – cat food – Butchers Pet Care
Classic – bathrooms – The Imperial Bathroom Company Ltd
Classic Badges – robust industrial wash heat seal badge – J & A International Ltd
Classic Boat – I P C Media Ltd
Classic Collection – rugs – Melrose Textile Co. Ltd
Classic Combination – mail order catalogue – J D Williams Mail Order Group
Classic Covers – fitted covers and curtains – Plumbs
***Classic Crystal** – Ecopure Waters
***Classic Crystal Ireland** – Ecopure Waters
Classic Crystal Scotland – Ecopure Waters
Classic FM – music magazine for classic FM radio – John Brown Publishing
Classic Imperial – vinyl flooring – Gerflor Ltd
Classic Ladders – Accesscaff International Ltd
Classic Laid – uncoated paper & board – Howard Smith Paper Ltd
Classic Reproductions (Indonesia) – furniture – Signal Business Systems Ltd
Classic Rib – uncoated paper & board – Howard Smith Paper Ltd
Classic Rock – magazine – Future Publishing Ltd
Classic Royale – Yara UK lt Ltd
Classic Superwove – uncoated paper & board – Howard Smith Paper Ltd
Classic Supreme – Vi Spring Ltd
Classic White – Snopake Ltd
Classic Wove – uncoated paper & board – Howard Smith Paper Ltd
Classica – sign blanks – Spandex plc
Classica – shower surround – Matki plc
Classique – ladies fashion shoes – D Jacobson & Sons Ltd
Classix – bodysprays and roll-on deodorant and anti-perspirant – L E C Liverpool Ltd
Classix (United Kingdom) – wireless alarm system – Bosch Security Systems
Classix Hairspray and Mousse – L E C Liverpool Ltd
Claud Butler – cycle – Falcon Cycles Ltd
Claude Lyons – Voltage and power control products – Claude Lyons Ltd
Claudgen (United Kingdom) – industrial and commercial heating appliances – Consort Equipment Products
Claudius Ash – dental product retail – Plandent
Claxton – V.S.R. and general vibraton test equipment, vibrating tables – Vibratory Stress Relieving Company
Clay Bulley – hand operated clay extrusion machines – Dragon Ceramex
Clayboard – Lemon Groundworks
Clayboard – void former to counter clay heave – Dufaylite Developments Ltd
Claymaster – Lemon Groundworks
Claymaster – foundations of buildings – Cordek Ltd
Claymore – calcium plumbate primer – Craig & Rose Ltd
Claymore – Uncoated Paper – Mcnaughton James Paper Group Ltd
CLAYMORE LUBRICANTS – Hydraulic & Offshore Supplies Ltd
Claymore Tools – Trafalgar Tools
Clayton (Belgium & USA) – steam generators and waste heat boilers – Clayton Thermal Products Ltd
Clayton Boilers – steam generators and waste heat boilers – Clayton Thermal Products Ltd
Clayton Dewandre – air brake components and systems – Wabco Automotive UK Ltd
Clayton Generators – Twin Industries International Ltd
Clayton Industries – steam generators and waste heat boilers – Clayton Thermal Products Ltd
***Clean Air Blanket (United Kingdom)** – brownfield site restoration – A G A Group
Clean-Flow – I A C Company Ltd
Clean Hands – pink heavy duty liquid hand cleaner – Evans Vanodine International plc
Clean Metals – Anti Friction Bushings – Sprint Engineering & Lubricant
Clean-Off – biocided contamination control mats – Jaymart Roberts & Plastics Ltd
Clean Room Installation Services – Installation of Partitions – Stodec Products Ltd
Clean rooms – Envair Ltd
Clean-Shield – clean room doors – Accent Hansen
Clean & Shine – floor maintainer for use with high speed machines – Evans Vanodine International plc
Clean-Zone – contamination control flooring material – Dycem Ltd
Cleanacres – advanced crop technology – Masstock Arable UK Ltd
Cleanapack – the cleanaway waste packaging compliance scheme – Cleanaway Ltd
Cleaners Sink – Ideal Standard Ltd
Cleanflo – enclosed belt conveyor – Geo Robson & Co Conveyors Ltd
Cleanflo – Class 100 Dryer Air Systems – Greenbank Technology Ltd
Cleanflow – clean air – Johnson & Starley Ltd
Cleanline – Broen Valves Ltd
***Cleanmaster (U.S.A.)** – hot water extraction carpet cleaning equipment and acoustic tile cleaning equipment – Host Von Schrader Ltd
Cleanroom – ceiling systems (suspended) – U S G UK Ltd
Cleansteam – electric clean steam boilers – Fulton Boiler Works Ltd
Cleantrack – overhead chain conveyor system for food processing – Stewart Gill Conveyors Ltd
Clear – window and glass cleaner c/w 2 hand spray – Evans Vanodine International plc
Clear Span – aluminium structures, rooflights, atria, swimming pool closures – Hartley Botanic Ltd
Clear-Spin – Seward Ltd
Clear-Tite – shrink barrier film and bags – Bemis Swansea
Clearbore – quick disconnect coupling – Cobham Mission Equipment Ltd
Clearcast (United Kingdom) – ctl clearcast resin cable joints – C T L Components plc
Clearclad – specialist electrophoretic coatings – L V H Coatings Ltd
Clearco – Refills – Isla Components Ltd
Clearcut – scissors – Office Depot UK
Clearedge – mineral based soluble cutting oils with or without EP additives – Castrol UK Ltd
Clearfire – smoke vent – McKenzie Martin Ltd
Cleargo – medium duty conveying and power transmission – Fenner Drives Ltd
Clearguard – Forward Chemicals Ltd
Clearlite – rooflight – McKenzie Martin Ltd
Clearlyte – range of electrophoretic lacquers – Cookson Electronics Ltd
Clearothene – materials and products in polythene – Clear View Ltd
ClearSec – full height stainless steel turnstile with polycarbonate rotor panels – Gunnebo Entrance Control Ltd
Clearspace – UK Office Direct
Clearspan – Peritys Greenhouses
Clearspring – natural vegetable based household products including liquid laundry detergent, washing up liquid, dishwasher liquid and rinse aid ecological biased – Faith Products Ltd
Clearstart – control gear – Schneider
Clearstor – adjustable office shelving – Link 51 Ltd
Cleartex – UK Office Direct
Cleartex Oil – lubricants – Chevron
Clearview – wiper range – Cosmic Automotives
Clearview Linbins – Storage Direct
Clearweld – system for laser welding plastics and fabrics – T W I
Cleaver Brooks Boilers – Twin Industries International Ltd
Cleenol – UK Office Direct
Cleenol – cleaning materials – Cleenol Group Ltd
Clemco – abrasive blast cleaning equipment – Hodge Clemco Ltd
Clemcote – airless paint spray units – Hodge Clemco Ltd
Clement Clarke – headsets – Hayward & Green Aviation Ltd
Clemvac – portable vacuum recovery system – Hodge Clemco Ltd
Clenaware – Catercraft Catering Equipment
Cleo – distributors of confectionery – Thornycroft Ltd
Cleopatra – countertop basin – Ideal Standard Ltd
Clevedon – fasteners – Clevedon Fasteners Ltd
Clever Cloggs – baby footwear – O S R International Ltd
Clever Kloggs – childrens shoes and sandals – UK Distributors Footwear Ltd
Clevis Ends – engineering components – Illston & Robson Ltd
Click – safety equipment – Bearwood Engineering Supplies
Click Footwear – Avalon and Lynwood
Click & Lock – gas spring - locks or stops in any position (button actuated) – Camloc Motion Control Ltd
Click Workwear – Safety Clothing – Parquip Of Somerset
***Clickflex (Germany)** – thermostatic bimetals – Rolfe Industries
ClickStorm – Search Engine Marketing – Adstorm
Clico – router cutters, straight and spiral flute in HSS and solide carbide, countersinks, woodworking cutting tools – Clico Sheffield Tooling Ltd
Clico – Central C N C Machinery Ltd
Clif Mock – Jenex Ltd
Cliff – plugs, sockets, connectors, knobs – Cliff Electronic Components Ltd
Cliff – sports accessories, golf bags, sportsballs – Jabez Cliff Company Ltd
Cliff-Barnsby – riding saddles, bridles and accessories – Jabez Cliff Company Ltd
Cliff Lanzarenco – darts – Unicorn Products Ltd
Clifford – car alarms – Quicksilver Automotive
Clifford Brothers – british made brass – Dortrend International Ltd
Clifford & Snell – alarm sounders, strobes, relays – Clifford & Snell
Clifton – planes, scrapers cap irons and spoke shaves – Clico Sheffield Tooling Ltd
Clifton (United Kingdom) – Temperature control laboratory equipment – Nickel Electro Ltd
Clifton Bollard – traditional style bollard maintenance free – Glasdon International Ltd
Clifton Enterprises – trade name – Vanasyl 2000
Climafan – fans for heat transfer oem applications – Flakt Woods Ltd
Climafan Aerofoil – metric axial flow fans – Flakt Woods Ltd
Climalight Towers – Accesscaff International Ltd
ClimAlloy Towers – Accesscaff International Ltd
Climatair – fan coil units – Waterloo Air Products
Climatic Test Chambers – climatic test rooms – Sanyo Gallenkamp plc
Climatronic – heating controllers – Schneider Electric
Climatronic Controllers – stand-alone controllers – Schneider Electric
CLIMAX – Hydraulic & Offshore Supplies Ltd
Climax – Stacatruc
***Clinac (U.S.A.)** – Radiotherapy linear accelerator – Varian Medical Systems UK Ltd
Clinaxys – clinical pathology data acquisition system – Clinical Systems Ltd
Clinch – a range of tube joints (welding not required) – Birmingham Stopper Ltd
Clinch Tube Joints – Birmingham Stopper Ltd
Cling Film – Cedo Ltd
Clingorap – PVC clingfilm – Terinex Ltd
Clingtex – lubricants – Chevron
Clini-Board – chart holder – Hampson Composites Ltd
Clinibin – storage bin – Adroit Modular Buildings plc
Cliniclean (United Kingdom) – Colour-coded disposable cleaning & wiping cloths – Wiper Supply Services Ltd
Clinicol – disposable hospital theatre equipment – P3 Medical Ltd
Clinicut – cryostat microtome – Bright Instrument Co. Ltd
Clinispin Horizon Centrifuges – Horizontal spin Centrifuges – Woodley Equipment Co. Ltd
Clinoblock – ceramic fibre furnace lining block – Dyson Thermal Technologies
Clinotherm – ceramic fibre furnace linings – Dyson Thermal Technologies
Clintex – textured coating – C J Enterprises

Clio – cosmetic bags and holdalls – Paul Murray plc
Clip – Portable and Modular Displays – Ace Exhibitions Displays & Installation
Clip – design and manufacture exhibition boards and stands – Clip Display
Clip Box – Clip Box range Heidrun Europlastic Products – Lunex Ltd
Clip-In – Petrel Ltd
Clip-In – labour saving electrical installation equipment – Petrel Ltd
Clipatrave – PVC door frames – Boomer Industries Ltd
Clipbox – true random access server – Quantel Ltd
Clipfiles – Snopake Ltd
Clipfit – fuse – Lawsons Fuses Ltd
Clipfix – Chorus Panel & Profiles
Clippa-Safe – child safety harnesses, babycarriers and webbing strap assemblies – Clippa Safe Ltd
Clippaplug – Electrocomponents plc
***Clippard (U.S.A.)** – miniature pneumatic equipment – The West Group Ltd
CLIPPARD – Hydraulic & Offshore Supplies Ltd
Clippard – B L Pneumatics Ltd
Clipper – A T Wilde & Son Ltd
Clipper – paint brushes – Whitaker & Sawyer Brushes Ltd
Clipper – General Fabrications Ltd
Clipper – stud welding equipment – Cutlass Fasteners Ltd
Clipper Series – Perancea Ltd
Clips – partitioning systems – Service Partitions Ltd
Clipwell Collection – spectacle frames – Pennine Optical Group Ltd
Clissold – textiles manufacturers – J H Clissold & Son Ltd
Clittall Composite – timber and aluminium composite windows – Crittall Windows Ltd
Cliveden – WC suite – Armitage Shanks Ltd
Clock Audio – professional microphones – Tukans Ltd
Clock Box II – complete plug-in time and temperature control pack – Sunvic Controls Ltd
Clone – relay adaptor – Ryder Towing Equipment
Clor-O-Cote – chlorinated rubber paint – Witham Oil & Paint Lowestoft Ltd
Clorius – meters and controls – Switch2 Energy Solutions
Closedtrack – overhead safety conveyor systems for industrial applications manufacturing, finishing and assembly operations – Stewart Gill Conveyors Ltd
Clothescare – clean and reproof gortex garments – S P H Europe plc
Cloud 7 – British Vita plc
Cloud 9 – British Vita plc
Cloud 9 – carpet underlays – Ball & Young Division Of Vitafoan Ltd
Clover – M S C Gleichmann UK Ltd
***Clover Sheep** – Harbro Ltd
Clovotox – selective herbicide with excellent turf safety; a single application controls clovers and many other broad-leaved weeds – Bayer Crop Science
Cloww Podium Platform – Accesscaff International Ltd
Club – unique database, word processing, and desktop publishing software package for IBM and compatible personal computers. – Bristol Office Machines
Club Casuals – menswear – Saville Heaton Ltd
Club Class – PVC binders – Phillips Plastics Ltd
Club Concrete (United Kingdom) – prefabricated bowling ditch channels – Sportsmark Group Ltd
Club GRC (United Kingdom) – prefabricated bowling ditch channels – Sportsmark Group Ltd
Club Green – indoor bowls carpets – Sportsmark Group Ltd
Club Special – darts – Unicorn Products Ltd
Club Strobeflower – entertainment stroboscope – Optikinetics Ltd
Clubdecor – web name – LUCID PRODUCTIONS
Clubman – luxury motor caravan – Auto Sleepers Ltd
Clubman – darts – Unicorn Products Ltd
Clubman – cameras, binoculars and lenses – Swains International plc
Clubman Accessories – photographic accessories – Swains International plc
ClubStile – half height stadia turnstyle – Gunnebo Entrance Control Ltd
Clugston – haulage, storage and distribution – Clugston Distribution Services Ltd
clunk click total backup solutions – online and onsite data backup, restore and storage – The Risc Group Ltd
Clustan – computer software, cluster analysis, statistics and marketing – Clustan Ltd
Clyde – sturtevant blowers – AESpump
Clyde – stainless steel plaster sink – Armitage Shanks Ltd
Clyde – soot blowers – Clyde Bergmann Ltd
Clyde Bergenmann – soot blowers – Clyde Bergmann Ltd
Clyde Combustions – heating equipment – Clyde Energy Solutions Ltd
Clyde Forest – soot blowers – Clyde Bergmann Ltd
Clyde Rail Spike – rail spikes for light gauge track – Glasgow Steel Nail Co. Ltd
Clydspin – lubricant – Clyde Bergmann Ltd
***Clynol (Germany and Holland)** – hair care products – Schwarzkopf Ltd
Clysar – polyolefin shrink film – Du Pont UK Ltd
CM Srl – RF Connectors – Select Cables Ltd
CM20 – Hydraulic & Offshore Supplies Ltd
CM710 – for the measurement of moisture in adverse industrial environments. eg. mining – N D C Infra-Red Engineering Ltd
CMA CGM – Worldwide Shipping Company – Macandrews & Co.
CMC – Motion and process control systems – European Drives & Motor Repairs
CME – large vertical m/cg cents – C Dugard Ltd Machine Tools
CMG – electric motors – Beatson Fans & Motors Ltd
CMG Electric Motors – electric motors – Potteries Power Transmission Ltd
CMI Healthcare Services – Service, Maintenance, Installation, Validation and distribution to Sterile Services Sector. – CMI Healthcare Services Ltd
CML – E Preston Electrical Ltd
CMO – Kee Valves
CMOS – Halcyon Solutions
CMS Vocational – training consultancy delivery – C M S Vocational Training Ltd
Cmt – diagnostic equipment trolley – Crypton Ltd
***CMZ (Spain)** – cnc turning centres – Citizen Machinery UK Ltd
CMZ – sheet metal & fabricating machinery – C M Z Machinery Ltd
CNC ROUTER – S R B Joinery Ltd
CNC Training – CNC programmer and setter training – Forelink Limited
Cnomo – B L Pneumatics Ltd
CNS Systems – Green Island (UK) Ltd
CO-PO – Harrier Fluid Power Ltd
Co seals – AESpump
Co-tron – coaxial connectors – Anglia
Coachkem – water soluble sachets for coach toilets – Elsan Ltd
Coachline – private hire and excursions – Stagecoach Ltd
Coachlinks – inter-urban coach services – Stagecoach Ltd
Coachwise – coaches – Sports Coach UK
Coalbrookdale GS1I – gas domestic heating appliance – AGA Rayburn
Coalbrookdale GS2i – gas domestic heating appliance – AGA Rayburn
Coalbrookdale GS3i – domestic heating appliance – AGA Rayburn
Coalbrookdale Little Wenlock – multi-fuel domestic heating and water heating appliance – AGA Rayburn
Coalbrookdale Much Wenlock – multi-fuel domestic heating and central heating appliance – AGA Rayburn
Coalbrookdale Rembrandt – solid fuel open fire – AGA Rayburn
Coalbrookdale Severn – multi-fuel domestic heating and central heating appliance – AGA Rayburn
Coalport – fine bone china giftware and figurines – Wedgewood Travel Ltd
Coastal – conservatories, victorian, edwardian, georgian, modern/contempary PVC-U/aluminium, windows casement, aluminium, PVC-U, windows ti lt-n-turn aluminium, PVC-U, windows vertical slide, PVC-U, doors hinged residential, PVC-U, aluminium and kitform – Coastal Aluminium
Coastal Conservatories – aluminium and PVC-U conservatories – Coastal Aluminium
Coastal doors and windows – aluminium hinged doors, sliding doors, windows and secondary glazing; PVC-u hinge doors and windows; double glazing sealed units – Coastal Aluminium
Coaster – the entry level easy launch trailer for smaller craft – Indespension Ltd
Coastguard – anti pollution device (propeller shaft) – Deep Sea Seals Ltd
Coastguard – inflatable booms – Oil Pollution Environmental Control Ltd
Coastline – secondary glazing – Coastal Aluminium
Coat-A-Sole – enamels, finishes & stains – F Ball & Co. Ltd
Coat Boost – Improve dull coats and maintain gloss – Supplements For Pets Ltd
Coatest – Elcometer Instruments Ltd
Coatex – polyurethane based associative thickeners – Omya UK Ltd
Coatosol – stone preservative – Craig & Rose Ltd
Coatostone – liquid stone – Craig & Rose Ltd
Coats – sewing threads and zips – William Gee Ltd
Coats – haberdashery – Coats Ltd
***Cob** – free range strains – P D Hook Hatcheries Ltd
Cobamat – antifatigue and non-slip safety matting – Coba Plastics Ltd
Cobar Wire, Fluxes & Solder Paste (Netherlands) – Plimto Ltd
Cobas – instruments – Roche Diagnostics Ltd
Cobble – carpet tufting machines – Cobble Blackburn Ltd
Cobex – Rigid PVC – Sallu Plastics
Cobra – powered helmet respirator – M S A Britain Ltd
Cobra – tactical gloves – Bennett Safetywear
Cobra – airport crash tenders – Carmichael Support Services
Cobra – stud welding equipment and fasteners – Cutlass Fasteners Ltd
Cobra – manilla files – Acco East Light Ltd
Cobra – Nd:YAG and Nd: Vanadate laser makers – Electrox
Cobra – pump – Torres Engineering & Pumps Ltd
Cobra – pipe bevelling machines – B S A Tube Runner
Cobra (United Kingdom) – dust extraction unit – R J H Finishing Systems Ltd
Cobra – flexible fibre glass rodding – T T UK Ltd
Cobra - E-Box - MaxBox - Maxbox Plus - Maxim - Raptor - Razor - Scorpion - Scorpion Rapide - Scriba. – Electrox
Cobra, Kirisun, Motorola – Walkie Talkie Radios – Amherst Walkie Talkie Radio Centre
Cobra Optics – Thomas Jacks Ltd
Cobra Seats – automotive seats & trim – Cobra Seats Ltd
Cobstel – cobalt-base alloy welding electrodes – Metrode Products Ltd
Cobuild – dictionaries/reference books – Harpercollins Publishers Ophelia House
Cochran Boilers – Twin Industries International Ltd
Cochrane – razor wire – Birmingham Barbed Tape Ltd
Cockett Bunker Market Report – bi weekley – Cockett Marine Oil Ltd
Cockett Bunker Price Index – daily index – Cockett Marine Oil Ltd
Cocksedge & Kither – gloves – Chester Jefferies Ltd
Coco Childrenswear – childrens fashion wear – Banner Ltd
Coda-Pin – Coda Systems Ltd
Code Red Distribution – labels and barcoding – Kelgray Products Ltd
Code Scape – cross pattern debugging software – Imagination Technology
Codeflat – PVC layflat pumping hose – Copely Developments Ltd
Codeflex – reinforced p.v.c. products – Copely Developments Ltd
Codemaster – tubing for identification purposes – Valpar Industrial Ltd
Codes – diagnostic equipment trolley – Crypton Ltd
Codex – electronic games, publications, rule books, magazines, books, games, models, miniatures and war games – Games Workshop Ltd
***Codicount (Switzerland)** – counting, storing & digital display modules – Oem - Automatic Ltd
***Codisplay (Switzerland)** – LED digital display modules – Oem - Automatic Ltd
Coelver (Switzerland) – microminiature coaxial electrical connectors – Lemo UK Ltd
Coffeaco – Combined Catering Services
Coffee Bay – Traders Coffee Ltd
***Coffilta Coffee** – Coffilta Coffee & Spring Water Services
COFMO – power presses – T M A Engineering Ltd
Cogenix – test equipment for rubber and plastics – Hartest Precision Instruments Ltd
Cogent – professional services – Nortel Networks UK Ltd
Cognitive TPG – Maxa Technologies Ltd
Cognito – mobile data communications solutions – Cognito Ltd
Cogsdill – engineering tools – C L A Tools Ltd
Cohen & Wilks International – ladies & mens fashions – Cohen & Wilks International Ltd
Cohfast – cohesive bandage – Robinson Healthcare Ltd
***Cohiba (Cuba, Jamaica, Europe and Honduras)** – cigars – Hunters & Frankau Ltd
COHLINE – Hydraulic & Offshore Supplies Ltd
Coil Technology – Motion Drives & Controls Ltd
Coilcraft – Cyclops Electronics Ltd
Coilthread – threaded wire insert – Advanex Europe
Coiltronics – Cyclops Electronics Ltd
Coiltronics – inductors & transformers – Anglia
Coin Controls – Money Controls Ltd
Coin Transfer – eurograded & office sales – Air Tube Technologies Ltd
Coinart – Pobjoy Mint Ltd
Cointaner – polythene bag for packaging coins – Britton Decoflex
Cokin – filters – Johnsons Photopia Ltd
***COL (Sweden)** – balancers – Atlas Copco Tools Ltd
COL.O.RING – Hydraulic & Offshore Supplies Ltd
Colab – photographic processors – One Vision Imaging
Colacryl – acrylic polymers – Lucite International Speciality Polymers & Resins Ltd
Colade Masterbatch – as Colade TPF but can be added to the bitument at the coating plant – Colas Ltd
Colade TPF – tar free bituminous binder for high performance defered set macadam production – Colas Ltd
Colaquex – high scrub emulsion paint – Emusol Products Ltd

Colas Blown Bitumen – 85/25 oxidised bitumen to BS3690 – Colas Ltd
Colas Filled Bitumen – filled bitumen grout for bedding reflective road studs, granite sets etc – Colas Ltd
Colbronze – high performance phosphor bronze – Columbia Metals Ltd
Colchester – Lathes & CNC turning machines – R K International Machine Tools Ltd
Colchester – touring caravans for the home and export market – Fleetwood Group Holdings Ltd
Colchester – Peter Rushton Ltd
Colchester – 600 Group plc
Colchester – Red House Industrial Services Ltd
Colchester lathes – Phil Geesin Machinery Ltd
Colchester Lathes – Colchester Lathe Co. Ltd
Colchester lathes spares – Phil Geesin Machinery Ltd
Colchester magnum lathes – Phil Geesin Machinery Ltd
Colchester mascot lathes – Phil Geesin Machinery Ltd
Colchester master lathes – Phil Geesin Machinery Ltd
Colchester mastiff lathes – Phil Geesin Machinery Ltd
Colchester Range – roof extract units – Flakt Woods Ltd
Colchester Student 1800 lathes – Phil Geesin Machinery Ltd
Colcryl/Colcolour – coloured surfacing for demarcation – Colas Ltd
***Cold Front (U.S.A.)** – heat barrier paste – Gray Campling Ltd
Cold Stop Curtains – Thermal curtains containing Tempro – Seymour Manufacturing International Smi Ltd
Coldbreak – cavity closure insulating D.P.C. – Thermal Economics Ltd
Coldflex – coldseal coated films – Printpack Enterprises Ltd T/A Printpack
Coldflow – drinks dispense equipment – I M I Cornelius UK Ltd
Coldpoint (United Kingdom) – for auto indexing, archive and retrieval of as400 spoolfiles – Pacific Solutions International Ltd
Coldstream – coolant – Comma Oil & Chemicals Ltd
Colduplex - CS – duplex stainless steel – Columbia Metals Ltd
Coldur-A – high silicon bronze – Columbia Metals Ltd
Cole Metal Products – manufacture of thermic lance and thermal lances – Cole Metal Products Ltd
Cole metal products - thermal lance manufrs – Cole Metal Products Ltd
Colebrook Bosson Saunders – Capex Office Interiors
Colefax & Fowler – interior design – Colefax & Fowler Ltd
Coleford – handmade bricks, paviors and briquettes – Coleford Brick & Tile
Coleman – M&ES Flexilope
Coleman's – spraying machines – Thomas Coleman Engineering Ltd
COLER SUPPLY – Component supply – Coler Supply Solutions
Coleraine – whiskey – Old Bushmills Distillery Co. Ltd
Coleraine – cheddar cheese & retail processed products – Dairy Produce Packers Ltd
Coles – Harrier Fluid Power Ltd
COLES – Chaintec Ltd
Coles Crane Parts – Anbar Trading Company
Colester – PVC beltings – Cozens & Cole Ltd
COLEX – Hydraulic & Offshore Supplies Ltd
COLEX INTERNATIONAL – Hydraulic & Offshore Supplies Ltd
COLEY – Hydraulic & Offshore Supplies Ltd
Colfit-DZR – dezincification-resistant brass – Columbia Metals Ltd
Colflex – water based laminating adhesives – Atosina UK Ltd
Colgrout – colloidal sand-cement grout – Keller Geo Technique
Colibri – mobile vehicle lifts – Universal Air Tool Company Ltd
Colilert – water testing reagents – Palintest Ltd
Colink – vee link belting – Cozens & Cole Ltd
Collafix – sew-in and fuisible interlinings for the shirtmaking and furnishing industry – Evans Textiles Sales Ltd
Collapad – undercollar materials – William Clark & Sons Ltd
Collapsible Gates – security gates – Bolton Gate Co. Ltd
Collator-Matic – collating machine – K A S Paper Systems Ltd
Collecta – stamp albums – Stanley Gibbons Ltd
College – sliding door gear and hardware for bottom roller folding partitions – P C Henderson Ltd
College Collection – spectacle frames – Pennine Optical Group Ltd
Collins – publishers of fiction and non-fiction books in various interest areas – Harpercollins Publishers Ophelia House
Collins – UK Office Direct
Collins and Hayes – washable loose cover range – Collins & Hayes Furniture
Collins and Hayes – modern upholstery – Collins & Hayes Furniture
Collins and Hayes – fixed cover and leather range – Collins & Hayes Furniture
Collins book bus – paperback children's books, fiction and non-fiction – Harpercollins Publishers Ophelia House
Collins Educational – fiction and non-fiction educational books – Harpercollins Publishers Ophelia House
Collins Trailers (Marston) – agricultural trailers – Marston Agricultural Services Ltd
Collins Walker Boilers – Twin Industries International Ltd
Collomix – Fullbrook Systems Ltd
Colman – grilles, diffusers & louvres – Eaton-Williams Group Ltd
Colmono – grouting machines – Keller Geo Technique
Colmonoy – hardfacing alloy (nickel base) – Wall Colmonoy Ltd
Colmonoy, Fusewelder, Nicrobraz, Nicrocoat, Nicrogap, Spraywelder, Stop-Off, Wallex – Wall Colmonoy Ltd
Colnago (Italy) – Frames – Pennine Cycles Whitaker & Mapplebeck Ltd
Cologne & Cotton – pure cotton bed linen and eau de cologne – Cologne & Cotton
Colonade – shower surrounds – Matki plc
Colop – supply mounts – Mark C Brown Ltd
Color-Brate – nozzle tips – Delavan Ltd
Color Plan – paper – G F Smith
Colorado – playground equipment – Russell Play Ltd
Colorama Collection – rugs – Melrose Textile Co. Ltd
Colorana – micronised red and black iron oxide pigments – Viaton Industries Ltd
Colorclear – low reflective glass – Rankins Glass Company Ltd
Colorcoat – pre-finished organic coated steel with liquid applied paint system for roofing and cladding applications – Corus U K Ltd
Colorcoat Connection – construction and design enquiry line – Corus U K Ltd
Colorcoat HPS200 – Chorus Panel & Profiles
Colorcopy (Austria) – high resolution paper for colour lazers – Davies Harvey & Murrell
Colorduct – coloured ductwork for exposed applications – Hotchkiss Air Supply
***Colorex A.S. (Switzerland)** – anti-static pressed vinyl tiles – Forbo
***Colorex E.L. (Switzerland)** – static conductive pressed vinyl tiles – Forbo
Colorfarm – Chorus Panel & Profiles
Colorit – Uncoated Paper – Mcnaughton James Paper Group Ltd
Colorjet CO – matt finish solvent ink for paper and board – Fujifilm Sericol Ltd
Colorline – wall lining glass – Rankins Glass Company Ltd
Colorlites – Registered Trade Mark – Colorlites Ltd
ColorMOS – unique colour imaging based on CMOS technology – S T Microelectronics
Colorplus Fluorescent CF – solvent fluorescent ink for paper and board – Fujifilm Sericol Ltd
Colorset – coloured papers – Fenner Paper Co. Ltd
***ColorSorb** – Jacobi Carbons
Colorstar CS – satin finish and solvent based ink for paper and board – Fujifilm Sericol Ltd
Colorstelve – pre-finished steel with liquid-applied paint system topped with polymer film laminate – Corus U K Ltd
Colotemp – Crayons changing colour with temperature – Thermographic Measurements Ltd
Colour Badging Systems – Corporate Insignia Ltd
Colour Creations – carpet tiles - axminster – Brintons Carpets Ltd
Colour Cut – material – Charterhouse Holdings plc
Colour Dimensions – decorative paint mixing systems – Akzonobel
Colour Express – full colour printers – Interprint Ltd
Colour Mastic – County Construction Chemicals Ltd
Colour Palette – decorative paint mixing systems – Akzonobel
***Colour Palette (U.S.A.)** – vinyl wallcoverings – Tektura plc
Colour Percha – colour coded gutta percha points – Prima Dental Group Ltd
Colour Points – colour coded paper points – Prima Dental Group Ltd
Colour Sealant – County Construction Chemicals Ltd
Colour Silicone – County Construction Chemicals Ltd
***Colour-Step (Sweden)** – slip resistant vinyl sheet – Forbo
Colour Studio – bed linen – Pin Mill Textiles Ltd
Colourdex – filing supplies – Kardex Systems UK Ltd
Coloured Mastic – County Construction Chemicals Ltd
Coloured Sealant – County Construction Chemicals Ltd
Coloured Silicone – County Construction Chemicals Ltd
Colourfreedom – cosmetics – Molton Brown Ltd
Colourful Novelty/Promotional Sponges – sponges to your own design – Recticel Corby
Colouring Club – childrens activity set – Tallon International Ltd
Colourmatch – floor, furniture and kitchen range – Everbuild Building Products Ltd
ColourMesh – Architectural wall covering – Marathon Belting Ltd
Colourmount – picture mount boards – Slater Harrison & Co. Ltd
Coloursafe – antislip coating – Sportsmark Group Ltd
Colphos 90 – free-machining phosphor bronze – Columbia Metals Ltd
Colplus – concrete plasticiser – Keller Geo Technique
Colron – wood dyes and furniture care products – Ronseal Ltd
Colsibro – high performance copper nickel silicon alloy – Columbia Metals Ltd
Colson – industrial and hospital castors – Colson Castors Ltd
Colspeed AB – free-machining aluminium bronze – Columbia Metals Ltd
***Colt Car Co (Japan)** – importers for Mitsubishi motors, cars, trucks, vans and parts – Colt Car Company Ltd
Coltide FP – hydrolysed protein – Croda Europe Ltd
Coltrisub – Submarine Manufacturing & Products Ltd
Columbia 310 – heat-resisting stainless steel – Columbia Metals Ltd
Columbus – energy efficient lighting products – Fern-Howard Ltd
***Columbus McKinnon (U.S.A.)** – electric chain hoists – Pfaff-Silberblau Ltd
Columbus McKinnon – R F Lifting & Access Ltd
Columbus McKinnon – Gustair Materials Handling Equipment Ltd
Columbus Minor – energy efficient lighting products – Fern-Howard Ltd
ColumnClad Systems – floors, structural steelwork, doors, ceilings, pipes and ducts – Rockwool Rockpanel B V
COM – carbon fiber material – Cytec Engineered Materials Ltd
COM 3 – A4 through the wall aluminium mailbox – Safety Letter Box Company Ltd
Com.Bine.Lace – Rotadex Systems Ltd
COM1 & SRX1 – A4 vertical aluminium mailboxes – Safety Letter Box Company Ltd
COM2 & SRX2 – A4 horizontal aluminium mail boxes – Safety Letter Box Company Ltd
Comag – magazine marketing & distribution – Comag
***Comar (Italy)** – capacitors – Cliff Electronic Components Ltd
Comar – optical components – Comar Instruments
Comark – electronic measurement instrumentation, accesories and services – Comark Ltd
Comark – Alpha Electronics Northern Ltd
Comark – Direct Instrument Hire Ltd
Comark – Alpha Electronics Southern Ltd
***Comasec (France)** – industrial safety handware – Marigold Industrial Ltd
Comasec Yate – rubber gloves – Marigold Industrial Ltd
Comato – Trepanning, grooving and parting-off systems. – Tapmatic Engineers' Merchants
COMATROL – Hydraulic & Offshore Supplies Ltd
COMATROL SRL – Hydraulic & Offshore Supplies Ltd
Comb Bind – comb binding machine – Securit World Ltd
Combat – warm air heaters – Robert Gordon Europe Ltd
Combat – food hygiene industry – Cleenol Group Ltd
Combat – Molyslip Atlantic Ltd
***Combi** – Armstrong & Holmes Ltd
Combi – synthetic wool combing apron – Brooksbank Holdings
Combi – water temperature controllers up to 95°C and oil to 150°C – Tricool Thermal
Combi-care Compact Scale Inhibitor – polyphosphate dosing unit – B W T Ltd
Combi Fab – fans – Dantherm Filtration Ltd
Combi-Flow – Bronkhorst UK Ltd
Combi-Flow Filters – Bronkhorst UK Ltd
Combi-Pak – large scale, reusable made to measure boxes. – D S Smith Correx
***Combibox** – electromagnetic clutch brake units – K E B UK Ltd
Combidrive – power transmission distribute equipment – Combidrive Ltd
***Combigear** – helical geared motors – K E B UK Ltd
***Combilok (Netherlands)** – vehicle restraint – Stertil UK Ltd
Combimeter – electromagnetic flow and energy meters – Switch2 Energy Solutions
Combination Ladders – Accesscaff International Ltd
Combined Smart Card Fingerprint Reader – Tekdata Distribution Ltd
Combined Trading Exports – fabric importers quality fabrics – Combined Trading Garments Ltd
Combinorm – electromagnetic clutch/brake – K E B UK Ltd
Combiperm – permanent magnet brake – K E B UK Ltd
Combirex CXA – profile cutting machine – Easab Cutting Systems
Combisafe – Accesscaff International Ltd
***Combistop** – spring-applied brakes – K E B UK Ltd
Combisystem – end suction centrifugal pumps – S P X Flow Technology
***Combitron** – power supply modules – K E B UK Ltd
***Combivert** – open loop and closed loop frequency inverters – K E B UK Ltd
Combivert - Open loop and closed loop frequency inverters. Combigear - Helical geared motors. Combistop - Spring applied brakes. Combinorm - Electromagnetic clutches and brakes. Combibox - electromagnetic clutch brake units. Combiperm -

permanent magnetic brakes. Combitron - Power supply modules. – K E B UK Ltd
Combizyme – multiple activity enzyme formulations – Biocatalysts Ltd
Combs – UK Office Direct
Comcall – mobile radio receiving & transmitting equipment – Vodafone Retail Ltd
Comcat – keyboard video mouse KVM switches – Techland Group Ltd
Comcen – computers and computer consumables (disks/toners/ink carts etc) – Comcen Computer Supplies Ltd
Comec (Italy) – Engine rebuilding machines – Fondera Ltd
COMEDIL – Tower Cranes – Skyline Tower Crane Services Ltd
Comef – compressors – Bearwood Engineering Supplies
Comeld – System for joining composites to metals – T W I
***Comelle** – ice cream & thick shake mixes – Pritchitts
***Comersa** – Nisbets plc
Comet – Euroteck Systems UK Ltd
***Comet (Taiwan)** – turret milling machines – Capital Equipment & Machinery Ltd
***Comet (Spain)** – high pressure pumps and agricultural – Dual Pumps Ltd
***Comet (Italy)** – shrink film – Engelmann & Buckham Ltd
Comet – diagnostic unit – Crypton Ltd
***Comet** – conveyor belt fasteners & machines – Mato Industries Ltd
Comet – labelling machine – Harland Machine Systems Ltd
Comet – decorators products – Stanley Decorating Products
Comet – apparatus for distributing sewage to filter beds – Ashbrook Simon Hartley Ltd
Comet Catering – catering equipment – Comet Catering Equipment Co. Ltd
Comev – CNC & conventional lathes – R K International Machine Tools Ltd
Comex – Submarine Manufacturing & Products Ltd
Comfi-sit Range – recliner chair with matching reclining settee, fixed chair and fixed settees – Sherborne Upholstery Ltd
Comfitts – comfort shoes – D B Shoes Ltd
Comfitts Nice "N' Easy – comfort shoes – D B Shoes Ltd
Comfitts Soft 'N' Easy – comfort shoes – D B Shoes Ltd
Comflex – flexible bellows, expansion joints & wraps – James Walker Townson Ltd
Comfort – Grundfos Pumps Ltd
Comfort – own brand for clothing, protective & safety – Weldspares Ltd
Comfort Front Entrance Door – Hörmann (UK) Ltd
Comfortable Options – bed linen – Ottoman Textiles Ltd
Comforts – hospital theatre footwear, foam slippers, bracelets and hospital drapes – P3 Medical Ltd
Comfortseal – aircraft seat cushions and backs – Recticel Corby
Comi Condor – centrifuges – A J G Waters Equipment Ltd
COMISA – World animal health industry organisation – National Office Of Animal Health Ltd
Comma Europa – 15W/50 multigrade oil – Comma Oil & Chemicals Ltd
Comma Premium – 2OW/50 multigrade oil – Comma Oil & Chemicals Ltd
Comma Super Coldmaster – antifreeze – Comma Oil & Chemicals Ltd
Comma Xstream – coolant – Comma Oil & Chemicals Ltd
COMMAND CONTROL CARTRIDGES – Hydraulic & Offshore Supplies Ltd
Command Gloss – Coated Paper – Mcnaughton James Paper Group Ltd
Command Matt – Coated Paper – Mcnaughton James Paper Group Ltd
Commander – stud welding equipment – Cutlass Fasteners Ltd
Commander – ac inverter – Control Techniques
Commander – Emmerson Doors Ltd
Commander Model – caravans – Carlight Caravans Ltd
Commander SE – Proplas International Ltd
***Commander UXP (U.S.A.)** – keyboard video mouse multi PC-sever switches – Techland Group Ltd
Commando – mens socks – H J Sock Group Ltd
Commando – Timber Bollard – Alto Bollards UK Ltd
Commando – BS 6391 type 2 fire hose – Richards Hose Ltd
Commando – industrial plugs and connectors – M K Electric Ltd
Commando Combi – industrial RCD sockets – M K Electric Ltd
Commandos – computer game – Square Enix Ltd
Commercial – Harrier Fluid Power Ltd
COMMERCIAL – Hydraulic & Offshore Supplies Ltd
Commercial Furniture Supplies (United Kingdom) – budget furniture – Severn Business Interiors Ltd
Comminutor – sewage disintegrators – Higgins & Hewins Ltd
commissioner – stacker cranes – T G W Ltd
Commodore – gas wallheater – Robinson Willey
Commodore – paint brushes – Whitaker & Sawyer Brushes Ltd
Commodore 2000 – Heavy duty catering equipment – Manitowoc Food Service UK
Common Sense – turnbutton fastener – Opas Southern Limited
commsandsound – pro audio & broadcast – Commsandsound.Com Ltd
Commslogic – IT and telecommunications consultancy – The Logic Group
Commtel – telephone accessories – Electrovision Group Ltd
Communication – range of RF based products – Air Tube Technologies Ltd
***Communications Specialities (U.S.A.)** – computer to video converters – A V M Ltd
Community Range (United Kingdom) – safe-free standing-grades o-v with L.P.C.B. & VdS certification – S M P Security Ltd
Community Re-Paint – paint re-use systems – Akzonobel
Community Telegraph – newspaper publishers – Independent News & Media (NI) Ltd
Como – Harrier Fluid Power Ltd
Como – precision injection mouldings – Component Moulders
Comoy – briar pipes – Cadogan
Compac – air cooled package chiller units – Tricool Thermal
Compac – Apex Computer Services Wales Ltd
Compac – close control air conditioning – Clivet UK
Compac Climafan – fans for heat transfer oem applications – Flakt Woods Ltd
CompacPRO – instrument case – Schroff UK Ltd
Compact (United Kingdom) – security lockcases – Assa Abloy Security Solutions
COMPACT – Hydraulic & Offshore Supplies Ltd
Compact – steam boilers – Hartley & Sugden
Compact – automotive recovery system – Eka Ltd
Compact – short hydraulic cylinders with integrated switching – Eland Engineering Company
Compact – stainless steel in-floor drainage channel – Webster-Wilkinson Ltd
Compact – folding shopblind – Deans Blinds & Awnings UK
Compact – sectional doors – B I S Door Systems Ltd
Compact – magnetic catches – Magnet Applications Ltd
Compact – pushbuttons and indicator units – Dewhurst plc
Compact – Alpha Electronics Southern Ltd
Compact 3in1 Sieve – Russell Finex Ltd
COMPACT-AIR (Italy) – Telecommunications air conditioning – Stulz UK Ltd Epsom
Compact Airlock Sieve – Russell Finex Ltd
Compact Airswept Sieve – Russell Finex Ltd
COMPACT CONTROLS – Hydraulic & Offshore Supplies Ltd
COMPACT CW (Germany) – Close Control Air Conditioning – Stulz UK Ltd Epsom
Compact Door – The new Folding door – Door Loading Services UK Ltd
COMPACT DX (Germany) – Close Control Air Conditioning – Stulz UK Ltd Epsom
Compact Gas – atmospheric gas boiler – Hartley & Sugden
Compact Hopper – coin payout mechanism – Money Controls Ltd
Compact NS – current limiting device – Schneider
Compact Sieve – Russell Finex Ltd
Compact Towers – Accesscaff International Ltd
***COMPACTA (Germany and Italy)** – lamps – Osram Ltd
Compacta – wedge belts – James Dawson & Son Ltd
Compactor – bale accumulator – Brown's Agricultural Machinery Company Ltd
Compactrol – valve – Delavan Ltd
Compacy – ladder stabilizing device for window cleaners – Ladderfix Ltd
Compaddress – software house – Buhrs UK Ltd
Compair – compressors, parts and service – Airware International Ltd
CompAir – Mawsley Machinery Ltd
Compair – Trowell Plant Sales Ltd
Compair air machines – Gustair Materials Handling Equipment Ltd
Compair Broomwade – Gustair Materials Handling Equipment Ltd
Compair Broomwade – compressors – Bearwood Engineering Supplies
Compair BroomWade – compressors – Air Power Centre Limited
Compair Hydrovane – compressors – Air Power Centre Limited
Compair Maxam – pneumatic control equipment – Air Power Centre Limited
Compair Maxam – spares & equipment – Bearwood Engineering Supplies
Compair Power Tools – automatic & hand tools, air/electric operated – Air Power Centre Limited
Compair Reavell – compressors – Air Power Centre Limited
Compair Reavell – compressors/spares – Bearwood Engineering Supplies
Compak – printout binders – London Letter File Company Ltd
Companies House – 750,000 business – Acxiom Ltd
Companion – wireless PBX – Nortel Networks UK Ltd
Company – magazine – National Magazine Company Ltd
Company on Net – brand protection online, internet verification, identity protection online – Connet UK Ltd.
Company Supercover – health insurance scheme for a group of 5 or more people – Western Provident Association Ltd
Compaq – Lamphouse Ltd
Compare – Gustair Materials Handling Equipment Ltd
Compare Holman – Harrier Fluid Power Ltd
COMPARE HYDROVANE – Hydraulic & Offshore Supplies Ltd
Compass – agricultural grass and clover mixtures – Limagrain UK Ltd
Compass – paints – Colour-Therm Ltd
Compasso – suspension trim for - grid – U S G UK Ltd
Compatt – computing and telemetering transponder underwater acoustic navigation and positioning transponder – Sonardyne International Ltd
Compaveyor – passenger conveyor – Schindler
Compel – end feed and solder ring fittings – Marflow Engineering Ltd
Compendium – woven fabrics – Zoffany
Competitor Ladders – Accesscaff International Ltd
Compex – envelope adhesive – Forbo Adhesives UK Ltd
Compic – computer photo identity card system – Identilam plc
Complete Guide Series – magazine – Future Publishing Ltd
Complete Office Interiors – total turn key operations ranging from: partitions, cellings, carpets, electrical, print and stationery – E W Marshall Ltd
Complete Tool Boxes – Accesscaff International Ltd
CompleteSource – Turnkey eAuction package – Sourcing Vantage Ltd
Compoflex – industrial hose & composite & rubber hose fittings – Amnitec Ltd
Compomac (Italy) – Cone clamping & torque limiters – Ringspann UK Ltd
Components in Electronics – magazine – Newsquest Group
Compress – pelleting machines – Andritz Seed & Bio Fuel Ltd
Compression – compression utility to save disc space – Xara Ltd
Compressor Products International – reciprocating compressor components manufacturer – Compressor Products International Ltd
Compressor Valve Engineering – compressor valves and components – Cook Compression Ltd
Comprite – computer software and machines – Thomas Wright-Thorite
Compsec – conference (annual) – Elsevier Publishers Ltd
Comptec – 19" equipment case – Schroff UK Ltd
Compton – Ruxley Manor Garden Centre
Compton – precast concrete garages, workshops and sheds – Compton Buildings
Compton – prefabricated garages/buildings – Compton Buildings
Compton Garages – sectional garages – Compton Buildings
Compucessory – UK Office Direct
COMPUMOTOR – Hydraulic & Offshore Supplies Ltd
Compupak IV – average weight control – Stevens Group Ltd
Compuprint – self adhesive computer labels on various materials – Sessions Of York
Computar – Stemmer Imaging
Computeach International (C.I.L.) – computer programming and systems training – Computeach International Ltd
Computer Arts – magazine – Future Publishing Ltd
Computer Arts Special – magazine – Future Publishing Ltd
Computer Data Storage – Tekdata Distribution Ltd
Computer Distributor – Tekdata Distribution Ltd
Computer Music – magazine – Future Publishing Ltd
Computertel – digital voice recording systems – Computertel Ltd
Computex – UK Office Direct
Computrac – moisture, hydrogen sulphide and mercury analysers – Able Instruments & Controls Ltd
Computronic Controls – manufacturers of industrial battery chargers -dc power supplies-dc standby systems – Computronic Controls Ltd
Comsecpack – communication equipment – Marlborough Communications Ltd
Comsol – computer software serivces – Computer Solutions Ltd
Comware – computer wiring accessories – Castle Dataware Ltd
Comyn Ching – panel heating and cooling – Comyn Ching
***Comyns (Malaysia)** – sterling silver – Royal Selangor Ltd
Con Amore – British Vita plc
Cona – coffee machine, rotary toaster, sandwich toaster, water boilers and jacketed urns – Cona Ltd
Conair – B L Pneumatics Ltd
Conair – Harrier Fluid Power Ltd
Conamatic – pour on coffee machines – Cona Ltd
CONAX TECHNOLOGIES (U.S.A.) – Techni Measure
Conbraco – back flow preventing – Northvale Korting Ltd
***CONCENTRA (France and Germany)** – lamps – Osram Ltd
Concentrate – Forward Chemicals Ltd

Concept – Gem Tool Hire & Sales Ltd

Concept – paper – Fenner Paper Co. Ltd

Concept 21/60 – Stainless steel rotary lobe pumps – Wrightflow Technologies Ltd

Concept 90 – aluminium sign systems – Universal Components

Concept Handwash – waterheater – Heatrae Sadia

Concept Laminates – Potter Cowan & Co Belfast Ltd

Concept Systems Design – silicon water/semi conductors – Concept Systems Design Ltd

Conceptor – research services – Research International Group Ltd

CONCERTINA – Injector for pressurised systems – Primalec

*Concerto (Sweden) – shower and procedure trolley allows patients to be cleansed and changed while laying in a supine position – Arjo Med AB Ltd

Concerto – kitchen furniture – Moores Furniture Group

Concise – business papers – Howard Smith Paper Ltd

Conclamp – cable entry and clamping device in one unit – Elkay Electrical Manufacturing Co. Ltd

Concoat – application engineers in chemical compounds, automatic dip and spray coating systems – Humiseal Europe Ltd

Concoat Auto-SIR – testing system – Humiseal Europe Ltd

Concor – honeycomb and plasterboard partitioning panel – Eleco Timber Frame Ltd

Concord – Terminals – Warwick Test Supplies

Concord – display lighting system – W F Electrical

Concord – UK Office Direct

Concorde Express – John Menzies plc

Concorde Matte Ivory – paper – Fenner Paper Co. Ltd

Concorde Pure Brilliance – paper – Fenner Paper Co. Ltd

Concorde Pure Silk – paper – Fenner Paper Co. Ltd

Concore – continuous flight auger construction of concrete piles – Cementation Skanska

Concourse Lantern – vandal and weather resistant area lighting – Designplan Lighting Ltd

Concrex – epoxy resin concrete floor repair compound – Watco UK Ltd

*Condensamax (Netherlands) – commercial condensing gas boiler – Stertil UK Ltd

Condensate Cleaners – limits environmental damage caused by poor condensation management – Condensate systems Ltd

Condense-A-Cure – condensation control, positive pressure ventilation unit – Channelwood Preservation Ltd

Conder – Wendage Pollution Control Ltd

Condor – rucsacs – Karrimor Ltd

Condor – Versalift Distributors UK Ltd

Condor – profile cutting machine – Easab Cutting Systems

Condor – envelopes – Eagle Envelopes Ltd

Condor – custom built and stock frames & cycles – Condor Cycles Ltd

Condor – diesel engines for military and marine applications – Perkins Engines Group Ltd

Condor – Harrier Fluid Power Ltd

Condor – Money Controls Ltd

CONDUMAX – hydrocarbon dew-point-analyser – Michell Instruments Ltd

Cone Blanchard – European Technical Sales Ltd

Cone Ranger – mobile cone crushing plant – Parker Plant Ltd

Conect – scheme offering students at FE colleges the flexibility of NEC courses – National Extension College

Conecut – taper drill for thin materials – G & J Hall Ltd

ConeLITE – motorway warning lamp – Doormen

CONEPT POWER – Hydraulic & Offshore Supplies Ltd

Conesep – condensate polishing system – Ovivo UK Ltd

Conex (Italy) – cone clamping elements – Ringspann UK Ltd

Conexant – Cyclops Electronics Ltd

Conexel – Terminals – Weidmuller Ltd

Conference Blue & Green – directory – United Business Media Ltd

Conference Manager – conference recording system – Storacall Engineering Ltd

Confetti – C C A Group Ltd

Confidex – guarentee for roofing and gladding products – Corus U K Ltd

Conflex – conduit screening suppression components and systems – Icore International

Confreight Group – sea freight consolidators – Vanguard Logistics Ltd

Confreight Group - Sea freight consolidators – Vanguard Logistics Ltd

Congrip – heavy duty epoxy resin antislip safety coating – Conren Ltd

CONGSBERG – CAM systems – Esko-Graphics

Conic-Flow – duct silencer – I A C Company Ltd

Conical Settlement – GRP upward flow settlement tank – Armfield Ltd

Coniston – shower tray – Armitage Shanks Ltd

Conlift – Grundfos Pumps Ltd

Conncert – automated fibre detection system – Prior Scientific Instruments Ltd

Connect – industrial head protection accessories – Centurion Safety Products Ltd

Connect-2 Technology – Connect 2 Technology Ltd

Connection – Office Seating – Bucon Ltd

Connection Seating – Capex Office Interiors

Connections – Interface Europe Ltd

Connections – connection design suite – Computer Services Consultants UK Ltd

Connectors – Stainless steel vee and band clamps – Teconnex Ltd

Connel of York – leather tool pouches, holsters and belts – Electro Group Ltd

Connell of York – leather tool pouches, holsters and belts – Electro Group Ltd

Connoisseur – fishing tackle – Daiwa Sports Ltd

Connor & Graham – bus and coach services – East Yorkshire Motor Services Ltd

Conpol 80 Polymer Additive – polymer additive for cementitious screeds – Conren Ltd

Conqueror – UK Office Direct

Conqueror – heavy duty rising arm barrier – Zeag UK Ltd

Conquest – Torches – K B Import & Export Ltd

Conquest Sheds – garden buildings and prefabricated garages & fencing – E L M Construction

Conren Joint Filler – rounded closed cell foam back-up rod for insertion into expansion joints – Conren Ltd

Conrico International Ltd – Land Rover Export Distributor – Conrico Service Centre

Conservation – uncoated paper & board – Howard Smith Paper Ltd

Consler – Harrier Fluid Power Ltd

Console – Livebookings Ltd

Consolodated Pneumatic Tools – Gustair Materials Handling Equipment Ltd

Consolidated Spinners & Manufacturers Ltd – yarn suppliers – Consolidated Spinners & Manufacturers Ltd

Consort – taps and mixers – Marflow Engineering Ltd

Consort – mole drainers & subsoilers – Brown's Agricultural Machinery Company Ltd

Consort (United Kingdom) – valance rail – Integra Products

Consort (United Kingdom) – domestic heating appliances – Consort Equipment Products

Consort – water temperature controllers up to 95 – Tricool Thermal

Consort – single skinned GRP up and over garage door – P C Henderson Ltd

Consort Complement – uncoated paper & board – Howard Smith Paper Ltd

Consort Royal Brilliance – coated paper and board – Howard Smith Paper Ltd

Consort Royal Satin – coated paper and board – Howard Smith Paper Ltd

Consort Royal Satin Tint – coated paper and board – Howard Smith Paper Ltd

Consort Royal Silk – coated paper and board – Howard Smith Paper Ltd

Consort Royal Silk Tint – coated paper and board – Howard Smith Paper Ltd

Constaflo – automatic constant flow valves – Flowgroup Ltd Bestobell Valves & Conflow

Constant Force (United Kingdom) – fall arrest post – Latchways plc

Construction Select – complete contractor – Allianz Insurance plc

Contact Bleach – concentrated viscous sodium hypochlorite solution – Premiere Products Ltd

Contact Gauge – Halcyon Solutions

Contact PKG – Chequer Foods Ltd

Contact Rivets – Samuel Taylor Ltd

Contactum – electrical accessories manufacturers – Contactum Ltd

Contec – Pulse Oximeters – Wel Medical Services

Contect Duck Oil – service spray – Deb R & D Ltd

Contemporary Furniture – The Winnen Furnishing Company

Contemporary Vinyls – vinyl wallcoverings – Today Interiors Ltd

Contempra – telephone sets – Nortel Networks UK Ltd

Contender Laser Offset – Uncoated Paper – Mcnaughton James Paper Group Ltd

Content Filtering Mail – Tekdata Distribution Ltd

ContentMaster – Content Management System Software for Internet/Intranet/Extranets/Websites – Web Labs Ltd

Contessa Natural Slate (Spain) – Cembrit Ltd

Conti – laminated and veneered boards – Norbord Europe Ltd

Conti Board – DIY board – Norbord

Conti Cotton Soft – patient cleansing wipes – Synergy Healthcare plc

Conti Moist – moist patient cleansing wipe – Synergy Healthcare plc

CONTI-TECH – Hydraulic & Offshore Supplies Ltd

Conti Washcloth – patient cleaning cloth – Synergy Healthcare plc

Conti Wipe – disposable medical wipes – Synergy Healthcare plc

Contiki – travel company – Contiki Travel UK Ltd

CONTINENTAL – Hydraulic & Offshore Supplies Ltd

Continental – Wealden Tyres Ltd

*Continental (France, Germany) – tyres – Continental Tyre Group Ltd

Continental – shower trays – Matki plc

Continental – tyres – National Tyre Service Ltd

Continental HY – Harrier Fluid Power Ltd

Continental Microwave – broadcast and television transmitting system – Vidlink International Ltd

Continental Modeller – worldwide magazine for model railway information – Peco Publications & Publicity Ltd

Continuline – acoustic louvre – I A C Company Ltd

Continuous Flight Auger Piles – Simplex Westpile Limited

Continuum – Bushboard Ltd

Contirun – foundry gateing system – Castings Technology International Ltd

Contisure – absorbent adult incontinent pads – Synergy Healthcare plc

ContiTech – air springs – Roadlink International Ltd

*Contitech (Germany, France) – rubber products – Continental Tyre Group Ltd

Contitech – European Technical Sales Ltd

Contivac – vacuum pumps – AESpump

Contivity – extranet switch – Nortel Networks UK Ltd

Contor 300/Contor 500 – Scott International Ltd

Contour – self contained breathing apparatus – Scott International Ltd

Contour – WC & washbasin – Armitage Shanks Ltd

Contour – emergency lighting range – Lab Craft Ltd

Contour 100 – Scott International Ltd

Contour 2000 – laterally operated fire shutter – Bolton Gate Co. Ltd

CONTOUR LINE CURVED ROOF CANOPIES – Living Space Ltd

Contra – Grundfos Pumps Ltd

Contract – Pledge Office Chairs Ltd

Contract (Portugal) – cork floor tiles - unsealed heavy density for contracts – Siesta Cork Tile Co.

Contract Flooring Suppliers – C F S Carpets

Contract Master – scrubber driers – Hako Machines Ltd

Contract Range, The – porcelain ceramic tiles – A Elder Reed & Co. Ltd

Contract Upholstery Tweeds – J Bradbury & Co. Ltd

Contractors Combined Insurance – turnover-related insurance for construction companies – M M A Insurance plc

Contractors Insurance Services – Genesis Risk Solutions Ltd

Contramate – Accesscaff International Ltd

Contraqua – Forward Chemicals Ltd

Contraves – European Drives & Motor Repairs

Contraves Drives – European Technical Sales Ltd

Contraves Motors – European Technical Sales Ltd

Contrec – spares & equipment – Bearwood Engineering Supplies

Contrepel – water repellent system – Contract Chemicals Ltd

*Contrinex (Switzerland) – sensors – Sensortek

Control – FM Radio Earmuff - Electronic Hearing Protection – Scott International Ltd

*Control Air (U.S.A.) – precision air regulators – The West Group Ltd

CONTROL DEVELOPMENTS – Hydraulic & Offshore Supplies Ltd

Control Knobs – Elektron Components Ltd

Control Master – temperature controller – Rayleigh Instruments Ltd

CONTROL TECHNIQUES – European Drives & Motor Repairs

Control Techniques – Proplas International Ltd

Control Technology Centre Ltd – Development of advanced process control systems tailored to clients control problems – University Of Manchester Incubator Company Ltd

Controlesta RCO – Controlesta is a modern building automation system which masters installations of all categories and – Elesta

Controlled Flame Boilers – Twin Industries International Ltd

Controller – peroxide stabilisers – Texchem

Controlobe – effective stitch lubricants – Contract Chemicals Ltd

Controlok – tape rules – L S Starrett Co. Ltd

Controlotron – non-contact flow meters – Able Instruments & Controls Ltd

Controls Center – Wolseley UK

Controvel – textile softening agents – Contract Chemicals Ltd

Controwet – non re wettable foaming agents – Contract Chemicals Ltd

Contura – adult disposable brief – Synergy Healthcare plc

*Conturan (Germany) – V.D.U. contrast enhancement filters – Schott UK Ltd

Conturbex – continuous screen/scroll centrifuge – Tema Machinery Ltd

Convac – toner vacumm cleaners – Longs Ltd

Convection – reflow machinery ovens – Elite Engineering Ltd

CONVENTRY CLIMAX – Chaintec Ltd

ConvertaBin – plastic compost making container with lid and optional ventilation – Richard Sankey & Son Ltd

CONVEYANCER – Chaintec Ltd

Conveyors International – overhead and garment handling conveyors – Conveyors International (CI Logistics)

Convocan – straight sided pot system - ice cream – Nampak Carton

Convosection – ceramic fibre lining system – Studweldpro UK Ltd

Convotherm – Axon Enterprises Ltd

*Convotherm – Convotherm Ltd

Convotherm – B B C S Ltd

Convowall – ceramic fibre lining system – Studweldpro UK Ltd

Conway – aircraft gas turbine engines – Rolls-Royce plc

Conway – Prima Care

Conway – Conway Trailer Division

Conway Cardinal – Conway Trailer Division

Conway Century – Conway Trailer Division

Conway Challenger – Conway Trailer Division

Conway Classic – Conway Trailer Division

Conway Conquest – Conway Trailer Division

Conway Countryman – Conway Trailer Division

Conway Cruiser – Conway Trailer Division

Conway Crusader – Conway Trailer Division

Conway Mirage – Conway Trailer Division

Conway Voyager – Conway Trailer Division

Conyl – textile coning oil – Benjamin R Vickers & Sons Ltd

Coo-Var – paints, primers & specialised coatings – Co-Var Ltd

Cooch – self propelled crane – Henry Cooch & Son Ltd

Cook – bale handling equipment including accumulators, grabs and handlers for conventional, round or large squares bales. Round bale unrollers available for tractor or forklift mounting capable of handling all sizes of round bale – David Ritchie Implements Ltd

Cook, Hammond & Kell – cartographers – Cook Hammond & Kell Ltd

Cook-Tite – heat treatable shrink films – Bemis Swansea

Cookson & Zinn – storage tanks and pressure vessels – Cookson & Zinn PTL Ltd

*Cooktek – M C S Technical Products Ltd

Cool-A-Zone – evaporative cooling units – Mellor Bromley

Cool case co uk ltd – jewelry cases – Pollards International

Cool Eyed Kids – spectacle frames – Pennine Optical Group Ltd

Cool Feet – cream, lotion, spray and gel for feet and legs – F M C G Ltd

Cool N Easy – portable air conditioning for the home – Ebac

Cool T – thermal wear – Sub Zero Technology Ltd

Cool-X – ice cold plaster – Robinson Healthcare Ltd

Cool Yule – C C A Group Ltd

Coolair – Osborn Unipol Ltd

Coolant Fed Rotating Toolholders – rotating metal toolholders – Hammond & Co. Ltd

Coolant Recycling Machines – industrial vacuum unit for cleaning, filtering and recycling contents of machine tool sumps – Freddy Products Ltd

Coolbor – oil fed twist drills – Metalbor Ltd

*Coolcat (United Kingdom) – racing & cruising catamaran – Cornish Crabbers LLP

*Coolcentre (Italy) – vending machines – Westomatic Vending Services Ltd

Coolcut – Forward Chemicals Ltd

Coolfit – pre-insulated pipework for refrigeration applications – George Fischer Sales Ltd

Coolflow – fan coil units – Biddle Air Systems Ltd

CoolFlow – Hydra Technologies ltd

Coolguard – corrosion protection and scale inhibitors for cooling systems – Feedwater Ltd

Coolicious Frozen Yoghurt – Coolicious Frozen Yogurt

Coolicious Frozen Yogurt – Coolicious Frozen Yogurt

Coolicious Fruit Smoothie – Coolicious Frozen Yogurt

Coolicious Iced Coffee – Coolicious Frozen Yogurt

Coolicious Shakes – Coolicious Frozen Yogurt

CoolLine – Cloakroom Solutions Ltd

Coolmation – industrial water chillers, cooling towers – Coolmation Ltd

Coolmax – performance fabrics – Du Pont UK Ltd

Coolplex – packaged cooling water dosing systems – Feedwater Ltd

Coolstar – cryogenic pump – Technical Vacuum Services Ltd

Coolstar OT – fast drying, satin finish screen printing ink for paper and board – Fujifilm Sericol Ltd

Coolsteel – Chorus Panel & Profiles

Coolstream – heavy duty fusing machinery – Reliant Machinery Ltd

Cooltex (United Kingdom) – high comfort fabric – Carrington Career & Work Wear

Cooper – pavement lights – H W Cooper

Cooper – power transmission products and split roller bearings – Cooper Roller Bearings Co. Ltd

Cooper Atkins – M C S Technical Products Ltd

Cooper Bussman – industrial & semi conductor fuses – G D Rectifiers Ltd

Cooper Man – printing equipment – Cooper Printing Machinery Ltd

Cooper & Turner – railway structural and general engineering fastenings – Anixter Ltd

Cooperheat (United Kingdom) – heat treatment equipment, furnaces and ovens, on site heat treatment services – Cooperheat UK Ltd

Coopers – spares & equipment – Bearwood Engineering Supplies

Coopers – Harrier Fluid Power Ltd

CooperTools – electronics equipment – Welwyn Tool Group Ltd

Coot – shirts – Polyfashions Ltd

Copa – sewage treatment – Copa Ltd

Copacabana – luxury bath – Ideal Standard Ltd

Copaclarifiers – polishing filter system – Copa Ltd

Copalmat – matt varnish – Akzo Nobel Packaging Coatings Ltd

Copar – Control Systems – C K Tech Serve Ltd

Copas – European Technical Sales Ltd

Copasacs – sewage filter system – Copa Ltd

Copaslip – Molyslip Atlantic Ltd

Copelametic – Therma Group

Copeland – Therma Group

Copeland – compressors – Bearwood Engineering Supplies

*Copeland (Germany & USA) – refrigeration and air conditioning compressors and condesing units – Emerson Climate Technologies Ltd

COPELEY – Hydraulic & Offshore Supplies Ltd

Copes & Timmings Pole – The Winnen Furnishing Company

Copimax – Office Products – Mcnaughton James Paper Group Ltd

*Copisil (Germany) – clays for carbonless copy paper – Sud-Chemie UK Ltd

Coplexel – reinforced p.v.c. patented hose products – Copely Developments Ltd

Copley Decor Mouldings – decorative architectural mouldings, rigid polyurethane cornices, dados, panel moulding, ceiling roses etc – Copley Decor Ltd

Copol – deodorising compound – C P L Aromas Ltd

*Copor (Italy) – air silencers – The West Group Ltd

Coppard – Coppard Plant Hire Ltd

Copper State Rubber – hose – Cebo UK Ltd

Coppercol – water testing tablets – Palintest Ltd

Coppernob – fashion ladies wear – Coppernob

Coppus – portable ventilators & air movers – Axflow

Coprel – fan motors and assemblies – Thermofrost Cryo plc

Copsil – Compensating mats for use in the press production of laminated board – Marathon Belting Ltd

Copy – media copying – D P T S Group Holdings Ltd

Copycad – Delcam plc

Copydex – S J Wharton Ltd

Copytec (Austria) – revolutionary triotech copier paper – Davies Harvey & Murrell

Cor-Ten A – high-strength low-alloy weldable structural steel – Corus U K Ltd

Cora Cutting Oils – Morris Lubricants

Coral – domestic sinks – Carron Phoenix

Coral brush Activ (United Kingdom) – entrance clean off zones – Checkmate Industries Ltd

Coral Brush Activ FR (United Kingdom) – entrance clean off zones – Checkmate Industries Ltd

Coral Classic (United Kingdom) – entrance clean off zones – Checkmate Industries Ltd

Coral Classic FR (United Kingdom) – entrance clean off zones – Checkmate Industries Ltd

Coral Duo (United Kingdom) – entrance clean off zones – Checkmate Industries Ltd

Coral Duo FR (United Kingdom) – entrance clean off zones – Checkmate Industries Ltd

Coral Luxe (United Kingdom) – entrance clean off zones – Checkmate Industries Ltd

Coral Luxe FR (United Kingdom) – entrance clean off zones – Checkmate Industries Ltd

Coralite – cathodic protection anodes – Cumberland Cathodic Protection

Corax – high tensile fence fittings – J B Corrie & Co. Ltd

Corbelform – A P T

Corbrite – organic pigments – European Colour plc

Corbusier – The Winnen Furnishing Company

Cordaflex (SMK) – tough rubber sheathbed reeling cable – Industrial Friction Materials Ltd

Cordaflex (SMK) - V – reinforced spreader reeling cable – Industrial Friction Materials Ltd

Cordent – dental instruments and accessories – Plandent

Cordex – round section driver belts – James Dawson & Son Ltd

Cordings of Piccadilly – Cordings Ltd

Cordon Vert – cookery school – Vegetarian Society UK Ltd

CORDS Duaflex – UK Precision Piston Ring Manufacturer – CORDS Duaflex Ltd

Cordtex – detonating cord – Orica UK Ltd

Cordura – nylon yarn – Du Pont UK Ltd

Core 2000 – highspeed event management network system – Amatek Precision Instruments UK Ltd

*Core-Cell Foam (Canada) – structural foam core – Gurit UK Ltd

Core, Central Reservation System – Softbrands

Core1 – Core 1

Corebond – polyester sealing fibres – Du Pont UK Ltd

CORELESS – Hydraulic & Offshore Supplies Ltd

Coresil – natural cork plates – Christie & Grey Ltd

Corex – cut and heat-resistant gloves – Bennett Safetywear

Corex – corner basin – Armitage Shanks Ltd

Corfast – organic pigments – European Colour plc

Corfiplaste (Portugal) – polypropylene ropes – Cotesi UK Ltd

*Corghi (Italy) – garage equipment – Apaseal Ltd

*Corghi – tyrefitting/ balancing – Apaseal Ltd

*Corgi – D P I Services

Cori-Flow – Bronkhorst UK Ltd

Corian – acrylic-based solid surface material – Du Pont UK Ltd

Coriflon (Portugal) – nylon ropes – Cotesi UK Ltd

Corinthian – laminated timber core flush doors – Mid-Ven Doors Ltd

Cork-A-Bond (Portugal) – adhesive – Siesta Cork Tile Co.

Cork Master (Portugal) – cork floor tiles, natural, all designs and colours; clear PVC surface for heavier areas – Siesta Cork Tile Co.

Corkboard (Portugal) – 3/8" thick dark cork wall tiles – Siesta Cork Tile Co.

CORKEN – pumps, compressors – H K L Gas Power Ltd

Corkscrew Co – the leaping frog – La Cafetiere

Corkscrew Co., The – bullpulls & legpulls – La Cafetiere

Corkwallpaper (Portugal) – Siesta Cork Tile Co.

Corlar – polyamide epoxy tank lining/enamels/primers – Du Pont UK Ltd

Corman – mens clothing – Cormans

Cormar – The Winnen Furnishing Company

CorMax – electrodeposition primers – Du Pont UK Ltd

Cormet – CR/MO alloy steel fluxed cored wires – Metrode Products Ltd

Corn Cob – abravies & carriers – Lawrence Industries Ltd

Corndell – pine domestic and contract furniture – Corndell Furniture Company Ltd

Cornelia James Neckwear (United Kingdom) – manufacturers of ties and scarves – Toye Kenning Spencer Stadden

Cornelius – drinks dispense equipment – I M I Cornelius UK Ltd

*Cornell Dubilier Electronics – Wavelength Electronics Ltd

Cornercare – manufacturers of plaster beads & expanded metal products – Protekor UK Ltd

Cornerfoot/Sidefoot (United Kingdom) – machine mounting pads – Farrat Isolevel

Cornerfoot/Sidefoot - Far-mat - HM Hamamat - Isolevel - Isomat - Isomount - Jackmount - Levalator - Squaregrip - Vidam - Wedgemount – Farrat Isolevel

Cornerstone – carpets - wilton – Brintons Carpets Ltd

Cornerstone – cable access solution – Nortel Networks UK Ltd

Cornerstone Spotlight – carpet - wilton – Brintons Carpets Ltd

Cornerstone Trading Partners Ltd t/a Cornerstone D – Make your presentations work as hard as you - we are presentations consultants. – Cornerstone Trading Partners Ltd

Cornette – exhaust ejectors – Exhaust Ejector Co. Ltd

Corney & Barrow Ltd – wine merchants – Corney & Barrow Ltd

Corniche – spring barley variety – Limagrain UK Ltd

Corniche – pump – Torres Engineering & Pumps Ltd

Corning – Precision Ceramics

Corning Gilbert – Wavelength Electronics Ltd

*Cornish Clam (United Kingdom) – cruisers – Cornish Crabbers LLP

*Cornish Coble (United Kingdom) – open day sales – Cornish Crabbers LLP

*Cornish Cormorant (United Kingdom) – open day sales – Cornish Crabbers LLP

*Cornish Crabber 17 (United Kingdom) – open day sales – Cornish Crabbers LLP

*Cornish Crabber 22 (United Kingdom) – cruisers – Cornish Crabbers LLP

*Cornish Crabber 24 (United Kingdom) – cruisers – Cornish Crabbers LLP

*Cornish Shrimper (United Kingdom) – open day sales – Cornish Crabbers LLP

Cornthian – Georgian styled metal up and over garage door – P C Henderson Ltd

Corofil – Flux cored wires – Murex Welding Products Ltd

Coroline – corrugated bitumen sheets – Ariel Plastics Ltd

Corolux – p.v.c. roof sheeting – Ariel Plastics Ltd

Corolux 2000 – high impact pvc roofing sheet – Ariel Plastics Ltd

Corona – sheep shear – Burgon & Ball Ltd

Coronation (United Kingdom) – corded brass track – Integra Products
Coronet – load indicating washers – Cooper & Turner
Coronet (United Kingdom) – bed canopy track – Integra Products
Coronet – steel lacing – Cozens & Cole Ltd
***Coronet** – 3663
Coronet – fasteners – Anixter Ltd
Coronet Paperbacks – books – Hachette UK Ltd
Corotherm – polycarbonate insulated roofing – Ariel Plastics Ltd
Corporal – Plastic Bollard – Alto Bollards UK Ltd
Corporate – Hainenko Ltd
Corporate 2000 – purpose-made steel windows and doors – Crittall Windows Ltd
Corporate Deopsit Account – Deposit account for businesses – West Bromwich Building Society
Corporate Lawclub – tailor-made protection and legal advice for employees, affinity groups and financial institutions – Allianz Legal Protection
Corporate W2O – steel windows and doors – Crittall Windows Ltd
Corracide – range of biocides – Roquette UK Ltd
Corrakote – coloured coatings for corrugating – Roquette UK Ltd
Corrax – stainless precipitation hardening steel – Uddeholm Steel Stockholders
Correlux P1 – Sebakmt UK Ltd
Correx – polypropylene protection sheet - windows floors - flame retardant LPS 1207 – Cordek Ltd
Correx – plastics corrugated extruded board, light hygienic containers and packaging solutions. – D S Smith Correx
Correx – Mar Deb
Correx – correction liquid and papers – Office Depot UK
Correx SM – high quality corrugated plastic for graphics and display markets – D S Smith Correx
Corriboard – twin-wall polypropylene re-cyclable board – Northern Ireland Plastics Ltd
Corrie – fencing – J B Corrie & Co. Ltd
Corrie Products – garden equipment – J B Corrie & Co. Ltd
Corriewise – fencing panels – J B Corrie & Co. Ltd
Corrigo – Seating – Bucon Ltd
Corrina – kitchenware – K B Import & Export Ltd
Corripol CR – solvent gloss ink for polythene signs – Fujifilm Sericol Ltd
Corroban – range of corrosion inhibitors for water systems – Feedwater Ltd
Corroflon (United Kingdom) – convoluted flexible PTFE hose – Aflex Hose Ltd
Corromide – cast nylon products and materials – I A C Plastics Ltd
Corromide - Cast nylon products and materials, Corroplas - Thermoplastic materials, Corrothene - UHMW polyethylene products and materials. – I A C Plastics Ltd
Corroplas – thermoplastic materials – I A C Plastics Ltd
Corrosperse – organic non-acid chemical cleaning agent – Feedwater Ltd
Corrothene – UHMW polyethylene products and materials – I A C Plastics Ltd
Corruchip – waste-based chip liner – Kappa Paper Recycling
Corruflute – waste-based fluting medium – Kappa Paper Recycling
Corrugasket – flange gasket – V I P-polymers
Corruliner – waste-based test liner 2 – Kappa Paper Recycling
Corsair – catering equipment – Corsair Engineering Ltd
Corstag – high tensile fence droppers – J B Corrie & Co. Ltd
CORTECO – Hydraulic & Offshore Supplies Ltd
Corteco – hub oil seal kits – Roadlink International Ltd
Cortone – organic pigments – European Colour plc
Cortx – British Vita plc
Corus – strip plates and structural steel sections – Corus
CORUS – Hydraulic & Offshore Supplies Ltd
Corus – Trafalgar Tools
Corvision – software system – Attunity UK Ltd
Corwrap – protected borosilicate glass process plant and pipeline – De Dietrich Process Systems Ltd
Corxley Script – UK Office Direct
Cory Freight – shipping and forwarding agents – Portman Travel Ltd
Cosalt Premier – life jackets – Cosalt Kenmore
Cosecure – mineral supplements for ruminant livestock – University Of Leeds
Cosimo – cards – The Medici Galleries
Cosmetal – Desks – Bucon Ltd
Cosmic – car security – Cosmic Automotives
Cosmic Software – microcontroller support – Anglia
***Cosmicar (Japan)** – Pentax UK Ltd
Cosmix – pharmaceutical and cosmetic machinery – T Giusti Ltd
Cosmo – Maingate Ltd
Cosmo Bingo & Social CLub – bingo & social club – Cosmo Bingo Club
Cosmopolitan – magazine – National Magazine Company Ltd
Cosmos & Orion – Glazing Vision Ltd
Cossack – men's grooming – Church & Dwight UK Ltd
Cost Reduction Associates – Cost reduction services for businesses of all sizes. – Lawson Consulting
***Costa Verde (Portugal)** – ladies sandals – Cheshire Style Ltd
Costain – oil gas and process – Costain Energy & Process
Costain Oil, Gas & Process Limited – process engineering contractors – Costain Energy & Process
Cosy-Carrier – baby carrier and rain cape – Clippa Safe Ltd
Cosy Tots – childrens slippers – D Jacobson & Sons Ltd
Cosybug – unvented package – Harton Services Ltd
Cosycoke and Sunbrite – industrial and domestic coke – Monckton Coke & Chemical Co.
Cosyfloor – R & D Marketings Ltd
Cosyskin – slippers – D Jacobson & Sons Ltd
Cotech – reinforcement material, multiaxial reinforcement materials for composites – Saint-Gobain Limited
Cotel – plastic mouldings – J G Coates Ltd
Coterie – dresses and suits – Frank Usher Group
Cotlene – synthetic replacement for cotton – Independent Twine Manufacturing Co. Ltd
Cotswold – window hardware (handles and hinges) – Cotswold Architectural Products
Cotswold – steel & aluminium windows – The Cotswold Casements
Cotswold Golf – golf shoes – Gardiner Bros & Co.
cotswold seeds ltd – Cotswold Seeds Ltd
***Cotswold Spring** – Cotswold Spring Water
Cotswold Woollen Weavers – weavers specialising in special commission and small scale development work – Cotswold Woollen Weavers
Cottage – WC Suite – Armitage Shanks Ltd
Cottage Craft – equestrian accessories – Matchmakers International Ltd
Cottam – horseshoes, tools and horseshoe nails – Arthur Cottam & Co.
Cottam & Preedy – C.P.90 - valves – Cottam & Preedy Ltd
COTTAM & PREEDY LTD – Hydraulic & Offshore Supplies Ltd
Cotton Look DK – yarn – Stylecraft
Cotton Lookalike Aran – yarns – Stylecraft
Cotton Lookalike DK – yarns – Stylecraft
Cottontails – cotton wool range – Robinson Healthcare Ltd
Coty – fragrance & toiletries – Coty UK Ltd
Coudoint – diodes – Bearwood Engineering Supplies
Cougar (United Kingdom) – pneumatic tensioned heavy duty backstand machine – R J H Finishing Systems Ltd
Coughtrie – lighting & lighting components – Coughtrie International Ltd
Council – sliding door gear and hardware for top-hung folding partitions – P C Henderson Ltd
Countdown (United Kingdom) – broadloom – Checkmate Industries Ltd
Countec – photometric test equipment – Sargrove Automation
Counterbact – Forward Chemicals Ltd
Counterchoice – household and haberdashery – Bray Group Ltd
Counterflow – high tech queue systems – Lonsto Insternational Ltd
Counterline – manufacturers of food servery equipment – Counterline
Counterplus – B P plc
Countourail – shower rails aluminium – Jendico Ltd
Country – decorative fire – Indesit Company UK Ltd
Country Cable – carpets – Cormar Carpets
Country Cooking – Turner Bianca
Country Flower – household textiles – Linden Textiles Ltd
Country Fresh – liquid air freshener – Premiere Products Ltd
Country Hamper – food hamper – Park Group plc
Country Homes & Interiors – I P C Media Ltd
Country Life – I P C Media Ltd
Country Living – magazine – National Magazine Company Ltd
Country Memories – Turner Bianca
Country Style 4 Ply – Sirdar Spinning Ltd
Country Style Aran – Sirdar Spinning Ltd
Country Style Double Knitting – Sirdar Spinning Ltd
Country Style Highlands & Islands – Sirdar Spinning Ltd
Country Walking – magazine – Emap Ltd
Country Wear – leisurewear – Countrywear Ltd
Countryman Power – G & M Power Plant Ltd
Countryside – touring caravans for the home and export market – Fleetwood Group Holdings Ltd
Countryside Range – outdoor furniture tables and seating – S M P Playgrounds
Countrywide Mobility – relocation and rental – H C R Ltd
County – counter – Link Hamson Ltd
County – classic looking garden tools – Spear & Jackson plc
County – car spares – Premier Supply Co.
County Concrete (United Kingdom) – prefabricated bowling ditch channels – Sportsmark Group Ltd
County Copier – business papers – Howard Smith Paper Ltd
County Dogs Feeds – Burnhill Services Ltd
County Game Feeds – Burnhill Services Ltd
County Grade – roofing tiles and slates – Welsh Slates
County GRC (United Kingdom) – prefabricated bowling ditch channels – Sportsmark Group Ltd
County Green (United Kingdom) – prefabricated bowling ditch channels – Sportsmark Group Ltd
County Horse Feeds – Burnhill Services Ltd
County II – category 2 low brightness louvre fitting – Designplan Lighting Ltd
County Orthopedic Footwear – orthopedic footwear – County Footware
County Pantile – clay – Sandtoft Holdings Ltd
Courage Best Bitter – ale & stouts – Scottish & Newcastle Pub Co.
Courier – telephones – Nortel Networks UK Ltd
Court Weaves – woven fabrics – Today Interiors Ltd
Courtenay – specialists in human resources search and selection – Courtenay Stewart Ltd
Courtiers Financial Services – wealth managment – Courtiers Investment Services Limited
***Cousino Macul (Chile)** – Pol Roger Ltd
***Couth (Spain)** – marking machines, presses etc, – Brandone Machine Tool Ltd
Cove – sandstone (red) – Realstone Ltd
Covemaster – Superior lightweight coving – Vencel Resil Ltd
Coventry – Harrier Fluid Power Ltd
Coventry Colletts – colletts and feeders for all machine tools – Herbert Tooling Ltd
Cover 2 Cover – childrens book club – Scholastic School Book Fairs
Cover Clear – book covering – Tenza Technologies Ltd
Cover Guard – Temporary Flame retardent protection syste, – Bainbridge Aqua-Marine
Cover-Structure – Lightweight roofing and clackling system – Cover Structure
Cover-Ups – disposable DIY coverall – Orvec International Ltd
cover-zone – Fully Tailored Car Covers – Cover-Zone
Coverclear – Wholesale Welding Supplies Ltd
Coverdale – management consultancy and training – The Coverdale Organisation Ltd
Coverflow – emulsion paint – T & R Williamson Ltd
Coverite – asphalt roofing contractors – Coverite Asphalters Ltd
Coversure Insurance Services – Insurance Broker – Coversure Insurance Services Ltd
Covrad Dravo – space heaters, process heaters NDS systems – Cov Rad Heat Transfer
Covrad Heat Transfer – commercial vehicle radiators and intercoolers power generation radiators, heat exchangers cooler groups – Cov Rad Heat Transfer
Cow Gum – rubber solution – Duco International Ltd
Cow Proofing – printers' blanket – Duco International Ltd
Cowen Flowline – Oil spill control equipment – Cowens Ltd
Cowenester – thermally bonded Polyester Wadding – Cowens Ltd
Cowie – PTFE laboratory products, temperature sensors and PTFE engineered products – Cowie Technology Group Ltd
Cowpuncher – humane slaughtering equipment – Accles & Shelvoke Ltd
Cox – County Construction Chemicals Ltd
Cox – heavy duty underwater bolt driver – Accles & Shelvoke Ltd
Cox – Cox Building Products Ltd
***Cox (U.S.A.)** – model aeroplanes – Amerang Group Ltd
Coxdome – roof lights – Yule Catto & Co plc
Coxdomes – Cox Building Products Ltd
Coxdomes – National Door Co.
COXREELS – Hydraulic & Offshore Supplies Ltd
Coxspan – Cox Building Products Ltd
Cozirc – paint drier – Rhodia Ltd
CP Clare – Cyclops Electronics Ltd
CP Range Actuator – Pneumatic linear or rotary quarter turn actuator – Rotork plc
CP Series II – plastics compounding machines – Farrel Ltd
CPA Electrical – Smith & Prince Ltd
CPC – Plenty Mirrlees Pumps
CPC – Hydraulic & Offshore Supplies Ltd
CPE – Hughes Pumps Ltd
CPK-N – K S B Ltd
CPL – the professional image providers – In Practice Systems Ltd
Cpmat – integrating cathodic protectioninto concrete stabilisationmattresses, cp mat leverages installation costs – Hockway
CPOAC – Hydraulic & Offshore Supplies Ltd
Cpoac – cylinders – Bearwood Engineering Supplies
CPP – Ovivo UK Ltd
CPPD – The CPPD suite of software products – Cobwebb Communications Ltd

CPTrak – storage and interactive reporting system for the analysis of time series data in the VAX and VMS environment – Business & Decision Ltd

CPV-Bulk – plastic tanks, bunds, fume scrubbers – C P V Ltd

CPV-df – PVDF pipes and fittings – C P V Ltd

CPV-Safeflo – Dual containment pipe systems – C P V Ltd

CPV-Zurn – laboratory and chemical waste above ground drainage systems, mechanical and electrofusion – C P V Ltd

CQR Security – Newburgh Engineering Co. Ltd

CR Seals – Mayday Seals & Bearings

cr2 – AESpump

CR3400 – in-mould epoxy gelcoat – Gurit UK Ltd

Cra-Cro International Personnel – a division of Stafforce Personnel Ltd, suppliers of temporary and permanent technical personnel to work overseas – Stafforce

Cra-Cro Personnel – a division of Stafforce Personnel Ltd, personnel consultants specialising in the supply of construction, engineering, industrial and trades – Stafforce

Crabtree – weaving machines and looms – Cobble Blackburn Ltd

Crabtree – industrial electrical wiring accessories, circuit breakers and control equipment – Electrium Sales Ltd

Crabtree Textile Machines – suppliers axminster & industrial loom suppliers. – Cobble Blackburn Ltd

Crack Bond TE – eopxy resin for crack injection – Helifix Ltd

Crackdown – Cocaine ID Swabs – Crackdown Drug Testing

Crackmeter – geotechnical instruments – Itm Soil Ltd

Crackwise – fatique design calculations – T W I

Cradle – computer aided systems and software engineering – Structured Software Systems Ltd 3sl

Cradle Clip – clip for cables – Hellermann Tyton

Cradley Boilers – Twin Industries International Ltd

Craft Collection – rugs – Melrose Textile Co. Ltd

Craft Cotton – yarns – Stylecraft

Craft Crank – heavily grogged clay body – Potclays Ltd

Crafticubes – tool holding equipment – Craftsman Tools Ltd

Craftitools – tool holding equipment – Craftsman Tools Ltd

Craftsman – mouthblown stemware and tumblers – Nazeing Glassworks Ltd

Craftsman Elite – tufted carpet – Brockway Carpets Ltd

Craftsman Twist – tufted carpet – Brockway Carpets Ltd

Craigavon – carpets – Ulster Carpet Mills Ltd

Craigmillar – cake mixes, fudges, icings, bakery fats & glazes – C S M UK Ltd

Crane – Ruxley Manor Garden Centre

CRANE – Hydraulic & Offshore Supplies Ltd

Crane – valves and pipe fitting – Crane Business Services & Utilities Ltd

***Crane** – Saffron – Trade Link London Ltd

CRANE – Cambridge Vending

Crane – Trafalgar Tools

Crane – Southern Valve & Fitting Co. Ltd

Crane – pumps – Allpumps Ltd

Crane-In-A-Box – kitform workstation crane system – Metreel Ltd

Crane Valves – engineers merchants – F W Sibley Ltd

Cranes Today – magazine – Progressive Media Group

Cranfield Precision – Cinetic Landis Ltd

Crastin – Resinex UK Ltd

Crater – lubricants – Chevron

Craven A – cigarettes – British American Tobacco plc

Craven Aluminium – aluminium shelving system – Craven & Co. Ltd

Craver – Harrier Fluid Power Ltd

Crawford Collets – 600 Group plc

Crawford Swift lathes – Phil Geesin Machinery Ltd

Crayola – coloured pencils – Binney & Smith Europe Ltd

Crayola Anti-Dust Chalks – white and coloured – Binney & Smith Europe Ltd

Crayola Creative Activity Products – creative products – Binney & Smith Europe Ltd

Crayola Fibre Pens – washable – Binney & Smith Europe Ltd

Crayola Poster Paints – washable paints – Binney & Smith Europe Ltd

Crayola Water Colour – paint sets - washable – Binney & Smith Europe Ltd

Crayola Wax Crayons – wax crayons – Binney & Smith Europe Ltd

Crazy String – carnival spray streamer – Palmer Agencies Ltd

CRC – Computer Room Consultants – Computer Room Consultants

Cre@te Online – magazine – Future Publishing Ltd

Creaseys – chartered accountants – Creaseys Chartered Accountants

Creatif – Creatif Leven Displays Ltd

Creation – vinyl flooring – Gerflor Ltd

Creative Colours – bed linen – Pin Mill Textiles Ltd

Creative FX – design - B C G Creative FX

Creda – Applied Energy Products Ltd

credhedz – Credhedz CREDIBILITY Cards. Brand. People. – Straight Talk In

Cree – WC – Armitage Shanks Ltd

***Crema** – Smiths Coffee Co. Ltd

Cremer Whiting – hand made bricks – W T Lamb Holdings Property Services

Cremer Whiting & Co. – hand made red facing bricks – Lambs Crener Whiting

Cremont (Italy) – arc, mig & tig welders – John Davies 2001 Ltd

Crenette – non woven scrims – Fothergill Crenette Ltd

Creoseal – Timber preservative – Creoseal Ltd

Crepetrol – creping aids for paper – Hercules Holding Ii Ltd

Crescent – five lever mortice deadlocks and sashlocks – Worrall Locks Ltd

Crescent – wrenches and multi function tools – Apex Tools

Crescent – lighting – Crescent Lighting Ltd

Crescent Bee – cooked meat presses – Selo UK Ltd

***Cresco (Germany)** – expanding waterstop – Max Frank Ltd

Cressanther – perfme speciality – Quest International UK Ltd

Crest – canned lager – Wells & Young's Brewing Co.

Crest Management System – management of settlement and custody in a Crest environment – D S T Global Solutions

Cresta – close control industrial water chillers – Coolmation Ltd

Cresta – cylinder oils – Castrol UK Ltd

Cresta – powered respirator – M S A Britain Ltd

Cresta Files – Rotadex Systems Ltd

Crestaflakes – flaked fats – A A K Bakery Services

Crestaflow – cryogenically powdered fats – A A K Bakery Services

Crestamix – emulsifier blends – A A K Bakery Services

Crestawhip – cake emulsifiers – A A K Bakery Services

Crestex – regimental and club, corporate ties – A R T GB Ltd

Crestomer – urethane acrylate resins – Scott Bader Co. Ltd

Crestron – control systems – Medbrook Services Ltd

Cretange – C E S Hire Ltd

Creteco – spacers and construction accessories – Max Frank Ltd

Crevette – Southend United Football Club Superstore

Crewe Chronicle – weekly title – Flintshire Chronicle Newspapers

Crewe Chronicle Sandbach Edition – weekly title – Flintshire Chronicle Newspapers

Crewe Mail – free newspaper – Flintshire Chronicle Newspapers

Crewfit – life jacket – Crewsaver Ltd

Cribmaster – professional tool crib automation – Kardex Systems UK Ltd

Cric and Croc – childrens clothing – Sarah Louise Ltd

Cricket – Turner Bianca

Crime Guard – Security Shutters – Shading Systems Ltd

Crimeshield – Keytrak Lock & Safe Company

Crimplene – mail order clothing – Chums Ltd

Crimploc – jump rings and fitting tools – Time Products UK Ltd

Criocabin (Italy) – refrigeration – Interlevin Refrigeration Ltd

Crios Bank – Servo Counters – Carrier Refrigeration & Retail Systems Ltd

Crisco – hair accessories – M Criscuolo & Co. Ltd

Crista – Hawksley & Sons Ltd

Cristel – computer furniture – Cristel Paint Finishers Ltd

Cristel Graphics – time management systems & time recorders – Cristel Paint Finishers Ltd

Cristel Paint Finishers – sheet metal work & powder coating – Cristel Paint Finishers Ltd

Criterion – Criterion Ices

Critical Incident Service – FOCUS Eap

Crittall – National Door Co.

CRL Control & Readout – temperatures and process instrumentation – Gefran UK

Croaker – Construction – Winget Ltd

Croboride – hard facing and metal facing – Croboride Engineering Ltd

Crockett & Jones – high quality footwear manufacturers – Crockett & Jones Ltd

***Croco (Far East)** – premium gifts suppliers and product sourcing – Croco Worldwide Ltd

Crocodile – wall connectors – Simpson Strong-Tie International Inc

Crodacid – fractionated fatty acids – Croda Chemicals Europe Ltd

Crodaclear – antifogging additives – Croda Chemicals Europe Ltd

Crodacoat – coating adhesives – Henkel Ltd

Crodafat – distilled fatty acids – Croda Chemicals Europe Ltd

Crodafix – emulsion adhesives – Henkel Ltd

Crodaglu – protein glues – Henkel Ltd

Crodagrip – pressure sensitive adhesives – Henkel Ltd

Crodalam – laminating adhesives – Henkel Ltd

Crodamelt – hot melt adhesives – Henkel Ltd

Crodamide – fatty acid amides – Croda Chemicals Europe Ltd

Crodamix – spray dried fats – A A K Bakery Services

Crodaseal – coldseal adhesives – Henkel Ltd

Crodastat – antistatic additives – Croda Chemicals Europe Ltd

Croderol – glycerine – Croda Chemicals Europe Ltd

Crodroit CS – chondroitin sulphate – Croda Europe Ltd

Croeckett Marine Oil Ltd – marine oil suppliers – Cockett Marine Oil Ltd

Croeso – Geerings Of Ashford Ltd

Croform – cobalt chromium alloy – Schottlander Dental Equipment Supplies

Croft – plummer blocks and bearing housings – Criptic Arvis Ltd

Croftair Clutches – Renold Clutches & Couplings Ltd

Crofton Engineering – structural steelwork and general fabrication, anti corrosion finishing (shot blast, hot metal spray and painting) fire drill training towers – Crofton Engineering Ltd

Crofts – Renold Clutches & Couplings Ltd

Crofts and Assinder – manufacturers & suppliers of handles, castors and furniture fittings in brass and mazak (zamak) diecastings, stainless steel and cast iron, and ceramic and glass knobs – Croft & Assinder Ltd

CROMA – CNC EPS hot wire cutting machines – Apropa Machinery Ltd

Croma Chain Saw Oils – cutter bar oils to meet all wood cutting requirements, mineral or vegetable based and biodegradable – Morris Lubricants

Cromalin – proofing film, toners and equipment – Du Pont UK Ltd

Cromaloy – electrical resistance wires and spiral elements – I M I Scott Ltd

Cromard – cylinder liners – Laystall Engineering Company Ltd

Cromarty – Try & Lilly Ltd

Cromax – general purpose leather gloves – Bennett Safetywear

Cromer Crab Co., The – seafood processors – Cromer Crab Company

Cromford – catering trolleys – Franke Sissons Ltd

Crompton Controls – control gear – Beatson Fans & Motors Ltd

Cromwell – protective headwear – Helmet Integrated Systems Ltd

Cromwells Madhouse – mens casual wear & jeans – Madhouse

Cromylite – range of chrome plating processes – Cookson Electronics Ltd

Cronapress – bell push continuous contact strip switch for use in security applications, public service vehicles, sheltered housing, machinery operations, police cell corridors, interview rooms, maintenance tunnels and security/affray systems – Cronapress Ltd

Cronar – polyester photographic film and base – Du Pont UK Ltd

Croner Reward – Croner Reward

***Cronifer (Germany)** – non-ferrous metals – Thyssenkrupp V D M UK Ltd

Cropelle – tube to tube D.I.P. process machines – Elite Engineering Ltd

Cropico – electrical measuring instruments – The Seaward Group

Cropico – Alpha Electronics Southern Ltd

Cropmatic – printed circuit board lead cutting machine – Blundell Production Equipment

Cropsafe – agro chemicals – Certis Europe

Cropsaver – range of trailers and mounted sprayers – Cleanacres Machinery Ltd

Croptex – agro chemicals – Certis Europe

***CropWalker** – Crop management system for farmers and agronomists – Muddy Boots Software Ltd

Crosby – Gustair Materials Handling Equipment Ltd

Crosby Group PLC – Hawk Lifting

Crosby Herald – newspaper – Liverpool Daily Post & Echo

Crosby Laughlin – valves – Bearwood Engineering Supplies

Crosland – Harrier Fluid Power Ltd

Crosland – Crosland Laser Guarding Ltd

CROSLAND FILTERS – Hydraulic & Offshore Supplies Ltd

Crosland Platen – handfed cutting and creasing machinery – Crosland Laser Guarding Ltd

Cross – Harrier Fluid Power Ltd

Cross – free wheel clutches – Cross & Morse

Cross – UK Office Direct

Cross and morse – transmission manufrs – T D Cross Ltd

***Cross Country (Far East)** – casualwear – Remys Ltd

CROSS HYDRAULICS – Hydraulic & Offshore Supplies Ltd

Cross & Morse – Transmission products – Sprint Engineering & Lubricant

Cross & Morse – Mercury Bearings Ltd

Cross Stitch Collection – magazine – Future Publishing Ltd

Cross Stitcher – magazine – Future Publishing Ltd

Cross-Ties – installation of remedial cavity wall ties – John R Crossland Construction Ltd

Crossbore (United Kingdom) – rebored sprockets and pulleys – Cross & Morse

Crossbow (United Kingdom) – demolition tools – Thomas Turton Ltd

Crossfire 480 – control of leatherjackets and frit fly in turf – Bayer Crop Science

Crossgard (Japan) – ball detent overload clutches – Cross & Morse

Crossgrip (United Kingdom) – roof walkways for maximum slip resistance and membrane protection – Plastic Extruders Ltd
Crossguard – Keytrak Lock & Safe Company
Crossley – diesel engines – Rolls-Royce plc
Crossley & Davis – management consultants and cerified accountants – Crossley & Davis
Crosslink – database service for polymer industries – Whitehall Recruitment Ltd
Crossorter – automated sorting conveyor systems – Van Der Lande Industries
Crosterene – stearic acid – Croda Chemicals Europe Ltd
CROUZET – Hydraulic & Offshore Supplies Ltd
Crouzet – switches, timers, counters, electric motors, pneumatic control, photo-electrics and inductive proximity switches, programmable controllers, solid state relays, control relays, limit switches, switches and sensors for aerospace – Crouzet Ltd
Crouzet – Proplas International Ltd
Crouzet – Trafalgar Tools
Crouzet – E Preston Electrical Ltd
Crouzet – Southern Valve & Fitting Co. Ltd
Crouzet – Gustair Materials Handling Equipment Ltd
Crouzet – contractors – Bearwood Engineering Supplies
***Crovac (Germany)** – malleable permanent magnet – Rolfe Industries
Crovisa – transformers – Bearwood Engineering Supplies
Crowborough Courier – newspaper – Kent Regional News & Media
Crowcon – Alpha Electronics Southern Ltd
Crowd Barriers – Accesscaff International Ltd
Crowd Control Barriers – barriers – Stage Systems Ltd
Crowguard – stain repellant – Crowson Fabrics Limited
Crowley – Genus Group
Crown – Derbyshire Building Society
Crown – glass mineral wool insulation – Knauf Insulation Ltd
Crown – Stacatruc
Crown – coinchanger – Coinage Limited
CROWN – Chaintec Ltd
Crown – Www.Safetysignsonline.Co.Uk
Crown – T V H UK Ltd
Crown – surface tables, precision inspection and metrology equipment, twoand three dimensional measuring and marking-out machines – Eley Metrology Ltd
Crown – Albany Pumps
Crown – bedroom and kitchen furniture – Allied Manufacturing
Crown 100 Roll – thermal and acoustic insulation – Knauf Insulation Ltd
Crown Class – airlines – Monarch Airlines
Crown Comfort – Quality slippers (all genders) – UK Distributors Footwear Ltd
Crown Cork and Seal Inc – Crown Packaging
Crown Dritherm – cavity wall insulation – Knauf Insulation Ltd
Crown Factoryclad – thermal and acoustic insulation for roofs and walls of profiled metal clad buildings – Knauf Insulation Ltd
Crown Factoryclad S.E. – thermal and acoustic insulation for roofs and walls of profiled metal clad buildings specifically for use in high humidity environments – Knauf Insulation Ltd
Crown Floor Slab – thermal and acoustic insulation for floors – Knauf Insulation Ltd
Crown Foiltherm – thermal insulation for pitched roof spaces and vertical studwork – Knauf Insulation Ltd
Crown Frametherm Batt – thermal and acoustic insulation and fire resistance for timber frame construction – Knauf Insulation Ltd
Crown Frametherm Roll U.F. – thermal insulation for fire resistance for timber frame construction – Knauf Insulation Ltd
Crown Frametherm Roll V.B. – thermal insulation and fire resistancefor timber frame construction – Knauf Insulation Ltd
Crown Lamella – thermal insulation for large diameter pipework and vessels – Knauf Insulation Ltd
Crown Memorials – monumental masonry – Crown Memorials Ltd
Crown Navy Board – thermal and acoustic insulation for applications in admiralty surface ships – Knauf Insulation Ltd
Crown Pipe Insulation – thermal and acoustic insulation for pipework – Knauf Insulation Ltd
Crown Polymer – render – P E Hines & Sons Ltd
Crown Rigid Duct Insulation – thermal and acoustic insulation for ducting – Knauf Insulation Ltd
***Crown & Rose (Malaysia)** – cast pewter – Royal Selangor Ltd
Crown Slabs – thermal and acoustic insulation – Knauf Insulation Ltd
Crown Sticky Wax – dental wax – Prima Dental Group Ltd
Crown Tools – Woodturning and woodworking tools – The Toolpost
Crown Trade – paint – Akzo Nobel Decorative Coatings Ltd
Crown Universal Ductwrap – thermal and acoustic insulation for ductwork – Knauf Insulation Ltd
Crown Velvet – Ryalux Carpets Ltd
Crown Wool – thermal acoustic insulation for general purpose use – Knauf Insulation Ltd
Crown Wool Combi-Roll – thermal and acoustic insulation for general purpose use – Knauf Insulation Ltd
Crowncast – foundry parting fluids – D A Stuart Ltd
Crowncote – rust preventatives – D A Stuart Ltd
Crowncut – neat cutting oils – D A Stuart Ltd
Crowndip – quenching oils – D A Stuart Ltd
Crowndraw – tube, bar and wire drawing oils – D A Stuart Ltd
Crownease – mould release oils – D A Stuart Ltd
Crownforge – hot metal forming lubricants – D A Stuart Ltd
Crownform – pressworking lubricants – D A Stuart Ltd
Crowngrease – greases – D A Stuart Ltd
Crownloc – Seco Tools UK Ltd
Crownlube – lubricating oils – D A Stuart Ltd
Crownpin – couplings – Renold Clutches & Couplings Ltd
Crownpin Coupling – Renold Clutches & Couplings Ltd
Crownpress – hydraulic oils – D A Stuart Ltd
Crownroll – rolling oils – D A Stuart Ltd
Crowther Marine – marine propellers and sterngear – J Crowther Royton Ltd
Croxley Script – Uncoated Paper – Mcnaughton James Paper Group Ltd
Croy – M L P S
Croydon Range – oak reproduction furniture – D F Webber & Harrison Ltd
Crrunch – mini wheat biscuits – Weetabix Ltd
CRT – continously regenrating tap – Eminox Ltd
Crucial (U.S.A.) – Memory Upgrades – Micron Europe Ltd
Crucible Technologies (United Kingdom) – telephone equipment for small businesses – Tele-Products Ltd
Cruise – computer software – K B C Process Technology Ltd
Cruise Control – childrens clothing – Gobina London Ltd
Cruiser – fishing tackle – Daiwa Sports Ltd
Crumcote – Rough coated plastic gloves – Bennett Safetywear
Crunchy Bran – bran – Weetabix Ltd
Crusade – The Paper Company Ltd
Crusader – fishing tackle – Daiwa Sports Ltd
Crusader – motor caravans – Leisuredrive Ltd
Crusader – radiator valves – Crane Business Services & Utilities Ltd
Crusader – polyethelene hand blast suction cabinet – Hodge Clemco Ltd
Crush-Ranger – mobile screening and crushing plant – Parker Plant Ltd
Crusilite – silicon carbide heating elements – Sandvik
Cruz – sailboat – Topper International
Crydom – Cyclops Electronics Ltd
Crydom International – E Preston Electrical Ltd
Cryo-M-Bed – fissue embedding compound – Bright Instrument Co. Ltd
Cryo Products – liquid nitrogen, s/steel storage vessels, repairs and servicing – Goodwood Metalcraft Ltd
Cryo sect – Seward Ltd
Cryobank – preservation system for long term storage of micro organisms at low temperature on glass beads – The Mast Group Ltd
Cryoclad – fire & insulation panels – Cryotherm Insulation Ltd
Cryogenic Deflashing Systems – Cryogenic deflash equipment for rubber and plastics industry – CDS UK
***Cryoperm (Germany)** – cryogenic magnetic shielding alloys – Rolfe Industries
Cryosafe – safety inspection scheme – Cryoservice Ltd
Cryosafe, Cryospec, Dial-a-flow, Fix-a-Flow, Ultracert - gas mixtures with UKAS certification – Cryoservice Ltd
Cryoshield – cryogenic refrigeration apparatus – Boc Gases Ltd
Cryosil – fire protection system-structured steel – Cryotherm Insulation Ltd
Cryospeed – industrial gases – Boc Gases Ltd
Cryospray – rapid freezing aerosol – Bright Instrument Co. Ltd
Cryostat – Solmedia Laboratory Supplies
Cryostop – fire penetration system – Cryotherm Insulation Ltd
Cryostop – Bishop Pipe Freezing Ltd
Cryovials – cryogenic vials – Radleys
Crypta – data – Unisto Ltd
Cryptocard – card operated access control system – Allgood
Cryptocode – push button access control system – Allgood
Crypton – automotive diagnostic equipment – Crypton Ltd
Crystal – X-ray films and accessories – Schottlander Dental Equipment Supplies
Crystal – fishing tackle – Drennan International Ltd
Crystal – plastic trachael tubes – Teleflex Medical
Crystal – quartz crystal – Pulsar Developments Ltd
Crystal – circulation powder and detergent sanitizer – Evans Vanodine International plc
Crystal – polish – Cleenol Group Ltd
Crystal Biodigester – 5year emptying interval, tertiary treatment. – Waste Tech Environmental Ltd
Crystal ECO – 5 year emptying interval – Waste Tech Environmental Ltd
Crystal Glassine – paper – H V Sier Ltd
Crystal Light/Heavy Liquid Paraffin – highly refined medicinal white oils – Morris Lubricants
Crystal Palace FC – football club – Crystal Palace FC
Crystal Semi – Cyclops Electronics Ltd
Crystalbrite – laundry systems – Cleenol Group Ltd
Crystaline – lighting equipment – Powerlite Lighting Solutions Ltd
Crystalite – 12v fluorescent lighting – Lab Craft Ltd
Crystalox – high temperature furnace systems for crystal growth – PV Crystalox Solar PLC
Crystaltile – suspension files – Acco UK Ltd
Crystaltype – nylon typewriter ribbon – Office Depot UK
Crystic – unsaturated polyester resins, strand related products and pigment pastes – Scott Bader Co. Ltd
Crystic Envirotec – low styrene content gelcoats and resins – Scott Bader Co. Ltd
Crystic Fireguard – intumescent fire retardant coating – Scott Bader Co. Ltd
Crystic Impreg – low pressure moulding compounds – Scott Bader Co. Ltd
Crystic Protec – mould coating – Scott Bader Co. Ltd
Crystic - unsaturated polyester resins, gelcoats and Strand related products Crystic Fireguard - intumescent fire retardant coating Crystic Impreg - low pressure sheet moulding compounds Crystic - pigment pastes Crestomer - urethane acrylate resins Crystic Envirotec - low styrene content resins and gelcoats. Polidene - vinylidene chloride copolymer emulsions Sobral - alkyds and epoxy esters Texicote - polyester powder coatings and PVA emulsions Texicryl - acrylic and styrene-acrylate emulsions (Texicryl is known in North America as Texigel) Texigel - water soluble polyacrylate thickeners Texipol - inverse emulsions – Scott Bader Co. Ltd
Cryston – high temperature refractories – Saint Gobain Industrial Ceramics Ltd
CS-SAFI – Cleansorb Ltd
CS2 Cure and Seal – single pack solvent based resin seal – Conren Ltd
CS24 – Forward Chemicals Ltd
CSA Ltd – wireless antennas – Jaybeam Ltd
CSM – Motor Technology Ltd
CSO Screening – combined sewer overflow – Copa Ltd
***CSR** – European Drives & Motor Repairs
CT – Proplas International Ltd
CT Marine – marine engine – Watermota Ltd
CTBF – charity – The Cinema & Television Benevolent Fund
CTC – ceramic capacitors – Anglia
CTC – Chaintec Ltd
CTC – Stacatruc
CTDI – imaging systems – Civica UK Ltd
CTI – AESpump
CTP-C.O.I.L. – low-vision aid magnifiers, plastic lenses, light guides, visors and telephone windows – Carclo Technical Plastics
CTS – Hydraulic & Offshore Supplies Ltd
***CTS (Motorola) (U.S.A.)** – piezo electric tweeter – Pulsar Developments Ltd
CTUK – Chaintec Ltd
CTX – Lamphouse Ltd
Cub (United Kingdom) – minor backstand idler – R J H Finishing Systems Ltd
CuB – chemical polish for copper and copper alloys – Lea Manufacturing Co.
***Cub Cadet (U.S.A.)** – garden tractors and rotary mowers – E P Barrus
Cube – Team Corporation UK Ltd
Cubeair (Denmark) – Safety blow gun – Berger Tools Ltd
Cubic-Casing – S R S Product plc
Cubic-Casing, Versirak - Sub-frame, Eurorack - Sub-frame - Netcase - Intermas – S R S Product plc
Cubit (United Kingdom) – steam generator – Eaton-Williams Group Ltd
Cubit – steam generator – Vapac Humidity Control Ltd
Cubitainer – polyethylene collapsible bottle – A Latter & Co. Ltd
Cuboid – CNC metalfolding machine – Joseph Rhodes Ltd
Cuccolini – Incamesh Filtration Ltd
cuddle factory – Best Years Ltd
Cuddledoon – wool blankets – John Horsfall & Sons Ltd
Cudos – diagnostic equipment – Crypton Ltd
CUE – Grundfos Pumps Ltd
Cue-Lure – insect attractants – International Pheromone Systems Ltd
***Cuisine Schmidt (France)** – kitchens – Potter Cowan & Co Belfast Ltd
CULLIGAN – Hydraulic & Offshore Supplies Ltd
Culm Valley – tinted papers – St Regis Paper Co. Ltd
Culmbrite – manilla – St Regis Paper Co. Ltd
***Culminal (Belgium)** – methylcellulose and hydroxypropylmethylcellulose and methylhydroxyethylcellulose – Hercules Holding Ii Ltd
Culmo – bright acid tin plating solutions – Schloetter Co. Ltd

Culpitt – food decorations – Culpitt Ltd

Cumberland – single skinned GRP up and over garage door – P C Henderson Ltd

Cumberland – cathodic protection systems – Cumberland Cathodic Protection

Cumberland Europe Ltd – plastic recycling machinery (grinders, pelletisers) – Cumberland Europe Ltd

Cumberland Premier – carpet – Cormar Carpets

Cumberland Twist – carpets – Cormar Carpets

Cumbria Limoscene – Limos in Cumbria – Cumbria Limoscene

Cumbrian Goat Experience – RARE BREED ANIMALS – Cumbrian Goat Experience

Cumin Nitrile – perfume speciality – Quest International UK Ltd

Cummins – Team Overseas Ltd

Cummins – Harrier Fluid Power Ltd

Cumulus – fibre bonded carpet – Heckmondwike FB

Cumulus – automatic weather station – Ele International

Cuno – Harrier Fluid Power Ltd

*Cuno Europe (France) – industrial filters – Flowtech Fluid Handling Ltd

*Cuno Filters (U.S.A.) – industrial filters – Flowtech Fluid Handling Ltd

Cup Carousel – heated cup carousel – Marco Beverage Systems Ltd

Cupanol – suspension – Reckitt Benckiser plc

Cuplok – Accesscaff International Ltd

Cupola – eliptical surface and semi recessed vandal resistant architectural lighting – Designplan Lighting Ltd

Cuponal – copper clad aluminium busbar – Hydro Static Extrusions Ltd

*Cuppone – Maidaid Halcyon

Cuprinol – woodcare products – Akzonobel

Cuprisil – oils – Bearwood Engineering Supplies

Cuprofen – tablets – Reckitt Benckiser plc

Cupromet – copper-base alloy welding electrodes – Metrode Products Ltd

Curastat – static eliminators – N V Tools Ltd

Cure C Cure – cycle patches for repairing tyres – Tech Europe

*Curioni Sun (Italy) – paper bag machinery – Engelmann & Buckham Ltd

*Curosurf (Switzerland) – babies respiratory aid – Merck Serono Ltd

Current Transformers – Telcon Ltd

Curricula – cosmetics and perfumery – Bodywise Ltd

Curry Sauce Co. – Olympia Foods Ltd

Currys – domestic appliances – Dixons Retail

Curso – low voltage semi recessed architectural lighting – Designplan Lighting Ltd

Curtain Styling – curtain making services – Thomas French Ltd

*Curti (Italy) – carton filling machines – Engelmann & Buckham Ltd

Curtiss Wright – high performance – Eaton Valve Products Limited

Curvatura – specialist ceiling systems - 3 dimensional – U S G UK Ltd

Curveline – Chorus Panel & Profiles

Curzate – fungicide – Du Pont UK Ltd

Curzon – Baxi Group

Cushion Adhesive Backing – flexo plate mounting material – Plastotype

Cushion Grip – denture fixture – M S D Animal Health

Cushionflex – goggles – Parmelee Ltd

Cushionfloor Classic – cushioned vinyl sheet – Forbo

Cushionfloor Deluxe – cushioned vinyl sheet – Forbo

Cushionfloor Elite – cushioned vinyl sheet – Forbo

Cushionfloor Super Glass – cushioned vinyl sheet – Forbo

Cushionfloor Super Luxury – cushioned vinyl sheet – Forbo

Cushionfloor Supreme – cushioned vinyl sheet – Forbo

Cushionfloor Ultima – cushioned vinyl sheet – Forbo

Cushman – Ransomes Jacobsen Ltd

Cushyfloat – anti-vibration mountings – Trelleborg Industrial A V S Ltd

Cushyfoot – anti-vibration mountings – Trelleborg Industrial A V S Ltd

Cushylevel – Trelleborg Industrial A V S Ltd

Cushymount – anti-vibration mountings – Trelleborg Industrial A V S Ltd

Cuski – Original and award winning Baby comforter – Totslots

Custodian – cash protection systems – Spinnaker International Ltd

CUSTOM – Hydraulic & Offshore Supplies Ltd

Custom 2000 – real time scheduling and control of vehicles for express collection and delivery – Lorien Resourcing Ltd

*Custom Accessories (USA and Asia) – car accessories – Custom Accessories Europe Ltd

Custom Filters – for equipment manufacturers – M P E Ltd

Custom Hose & Fittings – flexible hose and fittings, rubber, pvc, ptfe and stainless steel for hydraulic, automotive and industrial applications – Custom Hose & Fitting Ltd

*Custom Lift (Italy) – electro hydraulic scissor lift – Southworth Handling Ltd

Custom Print – Elite Papers Ltd

Custom Transformers – transformers – Custom Transformers Ltd

Custom Wrap – multi ply tissue cushioning – Jiffy Packaging Company Ltd

Customer Dynamics – management consultants – Marketing Dynamics Ltd

Customer Zone – Own labels – M A Rapport & Co. Ltd

CUT 8 – At home vehicle body repairs North East – CUT 8 Smart repairs

Cut-Grip – Iscar Tools

Cut Off Walls – to contain contaminated waste – Simplex Westpile Limited

Cutan Alcohol Gel – for rapid disinfection of skin – Deb R & D Ltd

Cutan Dispenser – sealed system soap dispenser for health care – Deb R & D Ltd

Cutan Multi Surface Wipes – moist wipes for damp dusting and general cleaning – Deb R & D Ltd

Cutan Soaps – high quality soaps for health care – Deb R & D Ltd

Cutback – bitumens – Tenants Bitumen

*Cuter (Italy) – machine vices – Abwood Machine Tools Ltd

Cutex – nail enamel – Coty UK Ltd

Cutipen – Mentholatum Co. Ltd

Cutler-Hammer – electrical equipment – Bearwood Engineering Supplies

Cutonic – agricultural chemicals – Lambson Fine Chemicals Ltd

Cutora – industrial lubricants – B P plc

*Cutting Mats and Knives (Taiwan) – Jakar International Ltd

Cutting Presses – new and secondhand cutting presses – Partwell Cutting Technology Ltd

*Cuvee St Martin – St Martin Vintners Ltd

CV IN-LINE FLEXIBLE COUPLINGS – Francis and Francis Ltd

CV3 – Switchbox – Cee Vee

CVA Range Actuator – Linear and quarter turn process control valve actuator – Rotork plc

CVR – manufacture lorry spares – Taylor Precision Plastics Ltd

CVS FERRARI – Chaintec Ltd

CVT – uhv supplies – AESpump

CWM-2000 – cold end coating system – Graphoidal Developments

Cwm Coke – types of foundry coke – C P L Distribution

Cwmni Twristiaeth Canolbarth Cymru – tourism company – Mid Wales Tourism

Cwt-y-Bugail – quarries – Welsh Slates

CX Call Point – Manual call point for fire alarm systems – Fulleon

CY – wear resisting white iron – Wearparts UK Ltd

Cyanolit – superglue (cynanoacrylate) – Euro Bond Adhesives Ltd

Cyanotec – Adhesives, cyanoacrylate, superglue – The Toolpost

CYBER GRINDING – test software for grinding processes – Walter Machines UK Ltd

Cyber machine monitor – manufacturing software – Yamazaki Machinery UK Ltd

Cyber Scheduler – manufacturing software – Yamazaki Machinery UK Ltd

Cyber tool management – manufacturing software – Yamazaki Machinery UK Ltd

CYBERAIR (Germany) – Close Control Air Conditioning – Stulz UK Ltd Epsom

CYBERCOOL (Germany) – Precision Chillers – Stulz UK Ltd Epsom

Cyberoptics – Stemmer Imaging

Cyberstar – Office Products – Mcnaughton James Paper Group Ltd

Cybex – video peripheral equipment – Betterbox Communications Ltd

Cycle Sport – I P C Media Ltd

Cycles Gladiator (California) – Patriarche Wine Agencies

Cycling Plus – magazine – Future Publishing Ltd

Cycling Weekly – I P C Media Ltd

Cyclists Touring Club – C T C National Cyclists Organisation

Cyclo (Germany) – speed reducers – Centa Transmissions Ltd

Cyclon – waterstill – Sanyo Gallenkamp plc

Cyclon – Fistreem International Ltd

Cyclone – concrete mixers – The Howard Group

Cyclone – cnc lathe – Denford Ltd

Cyclone – test chambers – Sharetree Ltd

Cyclone – Harrier Fluid Power Ltd

Cyclone – water based lubricant – Bodywise Ltd

Cyclone – fans – Systemair G M P H

Cyclonox – cyclohexanone peroxide – Akzo Nobel Chemicals Holdings Ltd

Cyclopak – intermediate bulk containers – Corrugated Plastic Products Ltd

Cyclopax – dust & fume extraction equipment – Dantherm Filtration Ltd

Cyclops – rucsacs – Berghaus Ltd

*Cyclotech (Sweden) – hydrocyclones – Pulp & Paper Machinery Ltd

Cyclus Copy – Recycled Paper – Mcnaughton James Paper Group Ltd

Cyclus Offset – Recycled Paper – Mcnaughton James Paper Group Ltd

Cyclus Print – Recycled Paper – Mcnaughton James Paper Group Ltd

Cycolac – Resinex UK Ltd

Cycoloy – Resinex UK Ltd

Cydopac – dust & fume extraction equipment – Dantherm Filtration Ltd

CYFORM – tooling prepreg – Cytec Engineered Materials Ltd

Cygnus Instruments Ltd – Euroteck Systems UK Ltd

CYL – Kee Valves

Cylindrical 26500 – Cinch Connectors Ltd

Cylindrical Air Intake – Cylindrical filter elements and purpose built cases for use on compressor, blower and engine air intakes for the removal of fine and course dust particles – Emcel Filters Ltd

Cymotion – Tekdata Distribution Ltd

Cynergy3 components – E Preston Electrical Ltd

*Cyngenta – Rutherfords

Cypherlock – standalone access control lock – Abloy UK

Cypress – Cyclops Electronics Ltd

Cyrel – photopolymer flexographic printing plates and equipment – Du Pont UK Ltd

Cystoleve – powder – Reckitt Benckiser plc

Cytoplan – food state vitamins and minerals dedicated to practitioners. – Natures Own Ltd

Cytox – cytotoxic protection packs – Synergy Healthcare plc

CZerbide (U.S.A.) – for mixture of SIC and Zr foundry moltern castings – Porvair plc

C³M (United Kingdom) – MOCVD TiN chamber – Aviza Technology UK Ltd

D

D. – (logo) smokers requisites, leather goods, mens clothing and jewelery – Alfred Dunhill Ltd

D.2. – connectors, stackable – F C Lane Electronics Ltd

D.A.S. – legal expenses insurance – D A S Legal Expenses Insurance Co. Ltd

D.A. Series – valves – David Auld Valves Ltd

*D'Aquisto (U.S.A.) – strings for musical instruments – John Hornby Skewes & Co. Ltd

D.B. – multi-purpose stacking linking chair – Race Furniture Ltd

D B C 50 – polycrystalline CBN cutting tool blanks for finished machining hard ferrous materials – Diamond Detectors

D.B.C. 80 – polycrystalline CRN cutting tool blanks for machining hard ferrous metals – Diamond Detectors

D.C.230EX – dust free diamond cutting system and angle grinder – Hilti GB Ltd

D.C. Connect – powerful software enabling tool which simplifier the integration of barcoded shopfloor data with any AS-400 system – Crown Computing Ltd

D.C.E. – Red House Industrial Services Ltd

D.C. Flex – a data collection engine designed to integrate a network of automated data acquisition devices into any host system – Crown Computing Ltd

D.C.M.1 – compact diamond drilling system to produce accurate holes – Hilti GB Ltd

D.C.M.1.5 – diamond core drilling system for fast, precise and clean drilling of installation through-holes in reinforced concrete – Hilti GB Ltd

D.C.M.2 – diamond core drilling equipment of modular design for through-holes and breaches in heavily reinforced concrete – Hilti GB Ltd

D.C.S – digital communication system – Samsung Telecom UK Ltd

D. Core – core spun thread – American & Efird GB Ltd

D.D. – computer systems, modules and related products – Double D Electronics Ltd

D.D.100 – hand held professional diamond coring system suitable for dry diamond coring into brickwork and masonry or wet diamond coring into reinforced concrete – Hilti GB Ltd

D.D.A. – telecom computer systems – Double D Electronics Ltd

D.D.H. – golf equipment – Dunlop Slazenger International Ltd

D.D.K. – connectors – Servo & Electronic Sales Ltd

*D D M Agriculture – Rural consultants, valuers & auctioneers – D D M Agriculture

D.D.S. – industrial computer systems – Double D Electronics Ltd

D-Drill – diamond drilling and sawing of concrete and ashfelt mini soil investigations – D Drill Master Drillers Ltd

D E B – S J Wharton Ltd

D.E.P.20 – heavy duty detergent powder, degreaser and decarboniser – Premiere Products Ltd

D.F.D. – rolling or sliding shutters and grilles, fire shutters, flexible crash doors and PVC strip curtains – Dudley Factory Doors Ltd
D.F.R. (United Kingdom) – low nox burners – Hamworthy Combustion Engineering Ltd
D.F.S. – micro electronic assembly equipment – G Bopp & Co. Ltd
D-Flex – Couplings – Baldor UK
D&G – Perscent
D.H. Dryfil – desiccant material – Parker Dominic Hunter Ltd
D.H. Puredri – compressed air dryer (sterile air) – Parker Dominic Hunter Ltd
D H River Conveyors – D H Industries Ltd
D.I.S.C. – door information sign combinations – Masson Seeley & Co. Ltd
D.-Line – Flowserve
D.M.C. – advanced process control – Aspentech Ltd
D.M.C. – embroidery, tapestry and crochet threads, cross stitch publications, needles and needlework collection – DMC Creative World
D.M.C. – parts for aeroplanes – Glenair UK
D.M.C. Plus – advanced process control – Aspentech Ltd
D&M MACHINERY LTD – D & M Machinery
D.M.S. – public digital multiplexed switch – Nortel Networks UK Ltd
D.M.S. Supernode – telecommunications switching equipment – Nortel Networks UK Ltd
D.P. Compak – data capture system for amusement arcades – Barcrest Group
D.P.N. – WAN switch – Nortel Networks UK Ltd
D.P.N.S.S. – network signalling systems – Nortel Networks UK Ltd
D.P.R. – mechanical handling – M C M Conveyor Systems
D.R. 20 – live storage shelving & racking – S S I Schaefer Ltd
D & R England (United Kingdom) – Worsted Mens Suiting Fabric – John Foster Ltd
D-Rainclean – Hoofmark UK Ltd
D-Raintank – Hoofmark UK Ltd
D.S. – office cleaning and hygiene service, janitorial supplies – L P M Cleaning
D.S. 1 – double sided presses – Joseph Rhodes Ltd
D.S. 2 – double sided presses – Joseph Rhodes Ltd
D.S.D. – Dead Sea discovery professional skincare – Finders International Ltd
D.S.F. – high alumina refractory bricks – D S F Refractories & Minerals Ltd
D.S.M. Engineering Plastics – nylatron and delrin etc – Righton Ltd
D.S.P. – dead sea professional products – Finders International Ltd
D-Tex – Anti theft alarm – Hot A V Ltd
D.V.S.T. – transmission systems – Dedicated Micros Ltd
D Visor – industrial deodorant – C P L Aromas Ltd
D.W.B. – dry water treatment – Murphy & Son
D.W.M. Copeland – refrigeration and air conditioning compressors and condensing units – Emerson Climate Technologies Ltd
D.X.3 – technical fish oil – Seven Sea's Ltd
D.X./S.L. – hob limiters – Sunvic Controls Ltd
D.Y.N – castings – D Y N Metal Ltd
D.Y.N. Gz 10 – castings – D Y N Metal Ltd
D.Y.N. Gz 14 – castings – D Y N Metal Ltd
D.Y.N. Rm – castings – D Y N Metal Ltd
D. Young – trade mark attorneys – D Young & Co.
D1236 – Telemetry outstation – Halcyon Solutions
D4 – Display Wizard Ltd
D400 – Display Wizard Ltd
D4140 – Telemetry outstation – Halcyon Solutions
D4150 – Telemetry outstation – Halcyon Solutions
D7000 – Telemetry outstation – Halcyon Solutions
D7140 – Telemetry outstation – Halcyon Solutions
D7150 – Telemetry outstation – Halcyon Solutions
Daas Organic Beer – Blond and Witte Belgian beer certified by the UK Soil Assoc – Daas Organic Beer
DAB – J P Whitter Ltd
DAB – Arun Pumps Ltd
Dab – Wyatt Bros Water Services Ltd
DABCO – catalysts – I M C D UK Ltd
Dac-Crete – floor paints – Dacrylate Paints Ltd
Dac-Pol 9 – urethane alkyd – Dacrylate Paints Ltd
Dac-Pol V.8 – polyurethane lacquer – Dacrylate Paints Ltd
Dac-Roc Smooth – masonry finish – Dacrylate Paints Ltd
Dac Varnish – clear varnishes – Dacrylate Paints Ltd
Dacafix – insulated cavity closer (PVC-U) for snapin window fixing – Quantum Profile Systems
Dacaform – insulated cavity closer (PVC-U) sub frames – Quantum Profile Systems
Dacaproof – insulated cavity closer – Quantum Profile Systems
Dacatie – insulated cavity closer damp proof window fixings – Quantum Profile Systems
Dachs – Baxi Group
Dacier – import & processes of mica components, mica powder ceramic metal parts – Dean & Tranter
Dacromet – highly protective zinc-based coating for steel components giving total coverage with no embrittlement – Wolverhampton Electro Plating Ltd
Dacromet – Protective Finishing Group
Dacron – polyester fibre – Du Pont UK Ltd
Dacsil – silicone enamel gloss – Dacrylate Paints Ltd
DAEDAL – Hydraulic & Offshore Supplies Ltd
Daewoo – Custom Brakes & Hydraulics Ltd
DAEWOO – Hydraulic & Offshore Supplies Ltd
Daewoo – C J Plant Ltd
Daewoo – Stacatruc
Daewoo – Machine Tool Supplies Ltd
Daewoo – L M C Hadrian Ltd
Daewoo – Sandhurst Plant Ltd
***Daewoo Marine Engines** – marine engines – Watermota Ltd
DAF – Bailey Morris Ltd
DAHL – Harrier Fluid Power Ltd
Dahle – UK Office Direct
***Daiei Manufacturing (Japan)** – chinese food manufacturing equipment – Selo UK Ltd
Daiglen of Scotland – kiltmakers – Daiglen
Daihatsu – L M C Hadrian Ltd
Daikin – Therma Group
Daikin – air conditioning – Bearwood Engineering Supplies
Daiko – Carbide disposable saw blades – Accurate Cutting Services Ltd
Daily Mail – newspapers – Associated Newspapers
Daines – C E S Hire Ltd
Dainichi – Birchfield Engineering Ltd
Dairy Industries International – magazine – Progressive Media Group
Dairy Seal – induction sealed cap for dairy industry – Bericap UK Ltd
Dairymaster – Harrier Fluid Power Ltd
Daisy D – Drainage bale handling tree plants machinery – Daisy D
Daiwa Specialist – fishing tackle – Daiwa Sports Ltd
Dal – light fittings – Designed Architectural Lighting Ltd
Dalau – PTFE rod tube film sheet components – Dalau Ltd
Dalcon PTFE – rod tube film sheet components – Dalau Ltd
Dale – Review Display Systems Ltd
Dale – plumbers and electricians-tinsmiths – R M Easdale
Dale – design and manufacture mining and tunnelling equipment, subcontract machining ISO 9001 accredited – Dale Mansfield Ltd
Dale – paints, wallpapers, decorators equipment & sundries – Robinson & Neal Ltd
Dale Brand – solders – R M Easdale
Dalen – Dalen Ltd
Dales – frozen seafoods – Dales Of Liverpool Ltd
Dales Decor Ceiling Roses – rigid polyurethane ceiling roses, dado, panel moulding – Copley Decor Ltd
Dalesman Aran – yarns – Stylecraft
Dalex – expanding wallet – Acco East Light Ltd
Dalex – drinks dispense equipment – I M I Cornelius UK Ltd
DALIAN – Chaintec Ltd
DALLAI – Hydraulic & Offshore Supplies Ltd
Dallas – 3 piece mixer taps – Ideal Standard Ltd
Dallas – Cyclops Electronics Ltd
Dallas Dream – bed linen and towels – Pin Mill Textiles Ltd
DALMAR – Hydraulic & Offshore Supplies Ltd
Dalmore Bluestone – polishing stones – Water Of Ayr
DALSA – Stemmer Imaging
Dalsouple – The Winnen Furnishing Company
Dalsuple – The Winnen Furnishing Company
***Dalter** – Parmesan cheese, whole, grated, catering – Baselica Ltd
Daltex – spun bonded non-woven polypropylene – Don & Low
Daltex Allershield – anti allergy bedding fabric – Don & Low
Daltex Cladshield – industrial roofing breather membrane – Don & Low
Daltex Covershield – protection fabrics for bedding – Don & Low
Daltex Frameshield – wall breather membrane – Don & Low
Daltex Gro-Shield – agricultural crop protection – Don & Low
Daltex Roofshield – specialist breathable under slate roofing membrane – Don & Low
Daltex Workshield – specialist fabrics for protective garments – Don & Low
***Dalva Ports** – The Vintners Selection Ltd
DAM (France) – Feluspar and Kastin – Hostombe Group Ltd
***Damart Thermolactyl (France)** – thermal underwear, clothes and household goods – Damart Thermal Wear Ltd
Damask Book – handprinted wallpapers collection – Zoffany
Damask Vol II – Wallcovering collection – Zoffany
DAMBACH – Chaintec Ltd
Damixa – Damixa Ltd
Dammit – leak & drain seating equipment – Darcy Products Ltd
Dampco – rising damp timber tretment and condensation control – Dampco UK Ltd
Dampcoat – Darcy Products Ltd
Dampers – provide a controlled arrest of a weight or lid across a variety of industrial applications – Camloc Motion Control Ltd
Dan – Hydraulic Power Units – Air Power & Hydraulics Ltd
Danaher Motion – Motor Technology Ltd
Danais – K S B Ltd
***Danarm (Japan)** – hedgetrimmers and brushcutters – Danarm Machinery Ltd
Dance Floor – portable dance floor-lite step and quickstep – Stage Systems Ltd
Danchem – chemical transfer hose – Dantec Ltd
Danchem - Danoil - Danflex – Dantec Ltd
Dando (United Kingdom) – top drive rotary hydraulic drilling rigs, cable percussion drilling rigs and all ancillary equipment – Dando Drilling International
Dandy – comic – D C Thomson & Co. Ltd
Dandy – Georgia Pacific GB Ltd
***Dandy Lift (Japan)** – pedestrian operated mobile scissor lift – Southworth Handling Ltd
Dane Board – sign blanks – Spandex plc
Danelectro (China) – electric guitars & FX pedals – John Hornby Skewes & Co. Ltd
Danesmoor – oil fired domestic boilers – Worcester Bosch Group Ltd
Danflex – flexible ducting hose – Dantec Ltd
Danflon – Dantec Ltd
Danfoss – electromagnetic vortex and coriolis flow meters – Able Instruments & Controls Ltd
Danfoss – Proplas International Ltd
Danfoss – hydraulic – V H S Hydraulic Components Ltd
DANFOSS – Hydraulic & Offshore Supplies Ltd
Danfoss – Harrier Fluid Power Ltd
Danfoss – Therma Group
Danfoss – electrical equipment – Bearwood Engineering Supplies
DANFOSS FLUID POWER – Hydraulic & Offshore Supplies Ltd
Danfoss Randall – central heating time controls and motorised valves – Danfoss Randall
DANFOSS SOCLA PRODUCTS (United Kingdom) – Ultravalve Ltd
Dangleflex Black – pendant suspension cable – Metreel Ltd
Dani – childrens clothing – Sarah Louise Ltd
Dania – seat – Armitage Shanks Ltd
Daniel – flowmeters & computers for gas & oil industry – Daniel Europe Ltd
***Daniel Koeman (India)** – Jeans – Prizeflex Ltd
Daniel Swarovski – objets d'art and fashion accessories – Swarovski UK Ltd
Danielson – advanced membrane and panel assemblies, electroluminescent lamps, touch screens – Danielson Ltd
Danks Boilers – Twin Industries International Ltd
***Danobat (Spain)** – bandsaws – Prosaw Ltd
Danobat – R K International Machine Tools Ltd
Danobat – Newall UK Ltd
Danoil – oil transfer hose – Dantec Ltd
***Danone Activ** – water – Danone Ltd
Danor – self contained electric and steam boilers and electric steam irons – Danor Engineering Ltd
DANTRUCK – Chaintec Ltd
Danubia – satin/polyester lining 60" – William Gee Ltd
Dapper – impulse heat sealers – Fischbein-Saxon
Dapta-gear – worm geared motors – Opperman Mastergear Ltd
Dar Lighting – Light Fantastic
Darco – activated carbon – Norit UK Ltd
Darda – Elmcrest Diamond Drilling Ltd
Dark Angels – electronic games, games, playthings, board games, minatures and models and fantany games – Games Workshop Ltd
Dark Future – playthings, board games, miniatures and models, war games and hobby games – Games Workshop Ltd
Dark Matter – Bespoke Carbon Fibre Products – Dark Matter Composites Ltd
Darlex – digital video recorder – Tecton Ltd
Darley – CNC press brakes and shears – Press & Shear Machinery Ltd
Darley Forms – business forms – Darley Ltd
Darley Labels – wet glue labels – Darley Ltd
Darley Leaflets – pharmaceutical and healthcare leaflets – Darley Ltd
Darnett – pressure testing – Bearwood Engineering Supplies
Darnot – cushion hose sheild – A Algeo Ltd
Darrowdale (United Kingdom) – Worsted Mens Suiting Fabric – John Foster Ltd
Dart – rucsacs – Berghaus Ltd
Dart – aero engines – Rolls-Royce plc
Dart – pump – Torres Engineering & Pumps Ltd
Dart 15 – catamarans – LaserPerformance
Dart 16 – catamarans – LaserPerformance
Dart 18 – catamarans – LaserPerformance

Dart Hawk – catamarans – LaserPerformance

Dartford and Swanley Informer Extra – newspaper – Kent Messenger Group Ltd

Dartmoor – woven carpets in 100% pure new wool pile – Axminster Carpets Ltd

Dartsak – wallet – Unicorn Products Ltd

Darvic – Rigid PVC – Sallu Plastics

Daryl – shower doors, enclosures, bath screens, all with safety glass (BS 6206) and shower trays bespoke design for made to measure units also available – Kohler Daryl Ltd

Dasco – industrial oils – D A Stuart Ltd

Dasco – shoe care products (shoe trees, shoe and boot stretchers, boot shapers, shoe horns, shoe laces, insoles, shoe cleaners, shoe polishes and aerosols – Dunkelman & Son Ltd

Dascolene – neat cutting oils – D A Stuart Ltd

Dascool – synthetic oils – D A Stuart Ltd

DASH – high throughput LC/MS columns – Thermo Fisher Scientific

Dashes – carpets – Interface Europe Ltd

Data Back Up – Tekdata Distribution Ltd

Data Care – cleaning preparations and equipment for electronic apparatus – Helix Trading Ltd

Data Carrier – Respiratory protection – Scott International Ltd

***Data Clear (U.S.A.)** – utp and stp cables – Huber+Suhner (UK) Ltd

Data Clip 2000 – multi clip for signs on datastrip for retail display – Alplus

Data Collector – data collection system – Deaf Alerter plc

Data Converters – Greenwich Instruments Limited

Data Device Portable Storage – Tekdata Distribution Ltd

Data Device Storage – Tekdata Distribution Ltd

Data Device Storage USB – Tekdata Distribution Ltd

Data Discman – portable CD electronic book player – Sony Head Office

Data DVD Storage – Tekdata Distribution Ltd

Data External Storage – Tekdata Distribution Ltd

Data Gage – gauging processors – Intra Ltd

Data Image – character and graphic LCD modules – Display Solutions Ltd

Data Logic – P C F Secure Document Systems Ltd

Data Logic – Photoelectric sensors – William Teknix

Data Mail – postal scale – Stevens Group Ltd

Data Matrix Systems (DMx) – 2D DMx marking and reading/verifying – Universal Marking Systems Ltd

Data Networking Division – specialist data network division – Newey & Eyre

Data Optical Storage – Tekdata Distribution Ltd

Data Pak – electronic data capture system (for amusement machines) – Barcrest Group

Data PC Storage – Tekdata Distribution Ltd

Data Product Storage – Tekdata Distribution Ltd

Data Raid Storage – Tekdata Distribution Ltd

Data Storage – Tekdata Distribution Ltd

Data Storage Solution – Tekdata Distribution Ltd

Data Storage Tape – Tekdata Distribution Ltd

Data Storage USB – Tekdata Distribution Ltd

Data Taker – Direct Instrument Hire Ltd

Data track – StrainSense Ltd

Databond – Emerson Network Power Ltd

Datac – industrial adhesives, hot melt adhesives, water based adhesives – H B Fuller

Datacard – ID Card Printer Manufacturer – Plastic ID

DataCard Ltd – plastic card personalisation systems – Data Card Ltd

Datacheck CBS 1 – Security Paper – Mcnaughton James Paper Group Ltd

Datacheck CBS 2 – Security Paper – Mcnaughton James Paper Group Ltd

Datacopy – UK Office Direct

Dataday – diaries, address, visitors, birthday and other social books and keepsake albums – Neale Dataday Ltd

Datafile – colour coded filing systems – Civica UK Ltd

Datafind – visible edge record card filing – Rotadex Systems Ltd

Dataflo – telecommunications cables and installation services – Nortel Networks UK Ltd

Dataflow – polling service – Arval UK Ltd

Dataglo – fluorescent marker for highlighting – Hainenko Ltd

DataGuard – Armoured BUS and Data cables – Belcom Cables Ltd

DataLife – CD-R – Verbatim Ltd

DataLifePlus – CD-R, CD-RW and DVD-Rs etc, Magnetic and optical storage media – Verbatim Ltd

Dataline – UK Office Direct

Datalogic – Barcode Readers and Mobile Computers – Barcodemania.Com

Datamax – Datamax labels, printers & ribbons – Lancer Labels Ltd

Datamax – Allcode UK Ltd

Datamonitor – international market analysis – Datamonitor plc

Datamoon – lighting effect – Premier Solutions Nottingham Ltd

DATAPAK (United Kingdom) – weld monitor - quality assurance – B F Entron Ltd

Datapron – B P plc

Dataputer – Statistical process control systems – Elcometer Instruments Ltd

***Datasouth (U.S.A.)** – serial impact dot matrix printers – Datatrade Ltd

DataStack – automated filing system – Kardex Systems UK Ltd

Datastat Plus – SPC Software – Elcometer Instruments Ltd

Datataker – Direct Instrument Hire Ltd

Datatech – pressure transduce – Bearwood Engineering Supplies

Datatemp – Radir Ltd

DataWorks – computer software and graphical database interface – Global Graphics Software Ltd

Datel – Cyclops Electronics Ltd

Datex – apparatus for simultaneous transmission of speech and data – Nortel Networks UK Ltd

Datona Rubbish Chutes – Accesscaff International Ltd

Datox – plastic file for storing computer printout – London Letter File Company Ltd

DATS For Windows – data acquisition analysis and display – Prosig Ltd

Datscan – G E Healthcare

Datsun – L M C Hadrian Ltd

DATSUN – Chaintec Ltd

Datsun – T V H UK Ltd

***Datum** – Procon Engineering Ltd

Datum – vaporiser – Space Labs Healthcare

Datum Ireland – Datum Monitoring Ireland

DatumPro – Datum Conversion Software – Geomatix Ltd

***DAU (Austria)** – heat sinks & heat pipes – Rolfe Industries

Dauntless – builders castings – Thomas Dudley Ltd

Dauphin – Office Seating – Bucon Ltd

DAV – Rolfe Industries

Davall Gears – Mercury Bearings Ltd

Davan – caravan retailers, awnings and accessories – Davan Caravans Ltd

Davan Caravans Limited – Davan Caravans Ltd

DAVENPORT – Polymer test instruments including melt flow indexers, melt viscometers, density columns, HDT/VICAT, falling dart impact testers etc – Lloyd Instruments Ltd

Davenport & Burgess – lock key manufacturer & distributor – Davenport Burgess

Davenport Packaging (United Kingdom) – manufacturers & main distributors of packaging – Davpack

Daventry Express – newspaper – Leamington Spa Courier

David Brown – Gears, motors – Bearwood Engineering Supplies

David Brown – Harrier Fluid Power Ltd

DAVID BROWN HYDRAULICS LTD – Hydraulic & Offshore Supplies Ltd

David Brown Radicon – gearboxes and geared motors – Disco Drive Kings Lynn Ltd

David Charles – childrens wear – David Charles Childrens Wear Ltd

David Harrison & Sons – electrical wholesalers – David Harrison & Sons Ltd

David Hunt Lighting – Light Fantastic

David Latimer – shirts – Rael Brook Group Ltd

David Morbey Timpani Sticks – professional timpani sticks – David Morbey Timpani & Percussion

David Nieper – lingerie – David Nieper

David Peterson – 8 day carriage clocks and quartz clocks – David Peterson Ltd

David S Smith – holding company – D S Smith Ukraine

Davidoff – filter cigarettes – Imperial Tobacco Group PLC

Davidoff Gold – filter cigarettes – Imperial Tobacco Group PLC

Davies – Harrier Fluid Power Ltd

Davigulli – high density polyethylene road gully BBA 91/66 – John Davidson Pipes Ltd

Davis – Lamphouse Ltd

Davis – Harrier Fluid Power Ltd

Davis and Hill – aluminium bronze, chrome copper, copper, manganese bronze, brass,gunmetal, phosper bronze, zinc and machining facilities – Davis & Hill

Davis and Oliver – silk ties – D P T Wear Ltd

Davis Derby – control and communication equipment – Davis Derby Ltd

Davison Highley – Office Seating – Bucon Ltd

Davment – rapid setting/hardening bedding mortars – Parex Ltd

Davol – suction, irrigation and wound drainage products; vascular access catheter and ports – Bard Ltd

Davpack (United Kingdom) – manufacturers & main distributors of packaging and printed packaging – Davpack

Davpack; Davenport Packaging. – Davpack

Davy – abseil fire escape – Lampitt Fire Escapes

Davy – Siemens plc

Davy McKee – spares – Bearwood Engineering Supplies

Dawbarn Evertaut – tarpaulins – Dawbarn & Sons Ltd

Dawes – cycles – Dawes

Dawson – special purpose conveyor belts – James Dawson & Son Ltd

***Dawson** – Court Catering Equipment Ltd

Dawson & Downie – Dawson Downie Lamont Ltd

Daxara – europe's largest selling camping and leisure trailers – Indespension Ltd

Day-Glo – papers and boards – Slater Harrison & Co. Ltd

***Day Labels** – Food Safety – Planglow Ltd

Day-Lite – Emergi Lite Safety Systems Ltd

DAYCO – Hydraulic & Offshore Supplies Ltd

Dayco – timing belt – C T P Wipac Ltd

Dayco – Belts – Sprint Engineering & Lubricant

Dayco – Mercury Bearings Ltd

Daymaster – barometer movements – Day Impex Ltd

Days Guides – books – Tudor Journals Ltd

Dayton – Harrier Fluid Power Ltd

Dazor – lamps and magnifiers – Time Products UK Ltd

DB Shoes – D B Shoes Ltd

DB™ – GGB UK

DBA – Money Controls Ltd

DBA 80 – polycrystalline CBN cutting tool blanks for machining hard ferrous metals – Diamond Detectors

DbArchive – Enterprise-wide Document Management Solution – Version One Ltd

DbAuthorise – Enterprise-wide Document Authorisation Module – Version One Ltd

DbCapture – Automated Invoice Capture Solution – Version One Ltd

DbChequePrint – Secure, efficient, cost-effective cheque printing solution – Version One Ltd

DbForm – Enterprise-wide Laserforms Solution – Version One Ltd

DBN 45 – polycrystalline CBN cutting tool blanks for machining hard ferrous metals – Diamond Detectors

DBox – Emulator adaption box – Hitex UK Ltd

Dc Brushless Motors – electronically commutated DC external and internal rotor motor – Ebm-Papst

DC230-S/EX – dust free diamond cutiing system and angle grinder – Hilti GB Ltd

DCB-GS Coupling – Renold Clutches & Couplings Ltd

DCC – direct cylinder conditioning – Garbuiodickinson

DCP – business papers – Howard Smith Paper Ltd

DCT – Selectronix Ltd

DD160-E – diamond core drilling system for fast, precise and clean drilling of installation through holes in re-inforced concrete. – Hilti GB Ltd

DD250-E – modular design diamond core drilling system for through holes and breaches into heavily reinforced concrete – Hilti GB Ltd

DD80-E – compact diamond drilling system to produce accurate holes – Hilti GB Ltd

DDS Collections – Business Debt Collections – D D S

DDS Fuels – UK Fuel Cards – D D S

DDS VAT – European VAT Recovery – D D S

De-Aerator – aerjec22 + aerjec 28 – Circulating Pumps Ltd

De-aerators – in line de-gassing – Netzsch Mastermix Ltd

De Beers – industrial diamonds – Diamond Detectors

***De Beleyr (Belgium)** – automatic & semi-atuomatic yarn conditioning machines – Robert S Maynard Ltd

***De Berkel** – Russums

De Berkel – Continental Chef Supplies Ltd

DE Cartes – computer software – Associated Knowledge Systems Ltd

De-Icer – Forward Chemicals Ltd

***De Jong Duke** – Coffeetech

De La Rue – A T M Parts

De Limon – grease blocks – Bearwood Engineering Supplies

De Longhi – R G K UK Ltd

De-Scale 10 – Forward Chemicals Ltd

De.Solv.It – solvent replacement – Mykal Industries Ltd

De-Sta-Co – European Technical Sales Ltd

De Ville – bed linen and towels – Pin Mill Textiles Ltd

De-walt – Fieldway Supplies Ltd

De Walt – Avalon and Lynwood

De Walt – power tools – Arrow Supply Co. Ltd

DE5000 – roller brake tester for heavy duty commercials – Tecalemit Garage Equipment Co. Ltd

DE7195 – roller brake tester for motorcycles – Tecalemit Garage Equipment Co. Ltd

DE7200 – roller brake tester for cars – Tecalemit Garage Equipment Co. Ltd

DE8232 – roller brake tester for light commercial vehicles – Tecalemit Garage Equipment Co. Ltd

DEA – Tesa Technology UK Ltd

***Deacondale (Worldwide)** – menswear – Newross Impex Ltd

Dead Sea Magik – Dead Sea skincare products – Finders International Ltd

Dead Sea Spa Magik – dead sea skincare and professional products – Finders International Ltd

Dealer Desk Towers – Accesscaff International Ltd

Dean – Dean Smith & Grace Lathes Ltd

Dean Smith and grace lathes – Phil Geesin Machinery Ltd

Dean Smith & Grace type 13, 1307, 1609, 1709, 2112, 25, 30 – Phil Geesin Machinery Ltd
Deanes – office furniture – Service Partitions Ltd
Deanlite – illuminated awning – Deans Blinds & Awnings UK
Deanston – electrics – Deanston Electrical Wholesalers Ltd
Dearman – pipe alognment clamps – Campbell Miller Tools Ltd
Death Trap Dungeon – computer game – Square Enix Ltd
Deathwing – games, playthings, miniatures and models for use in playing games – Games Workshop Ltd
Deb – Precision Tools
Deb 1000 – 1 litre cartridge dispensing system – Deb R & D Ltd
Deb 2000 – 2 litre cartridge dispensing system – Deb R & D Ltd
Deb Apple – apple lotion soap – Deb R & D Ltd
Deb Green – mild antibacterial soap – Deb R & D Ltd
Deb Lime – non solvent lime hand cleansing cream – Deb R & D Ltd
Deb Natural – powerful heavy duty hand cleanser for removing resins, paints, inks, bitumen, oil and grease – Deb R & D Ltd
Deb Peach – peach lotion soap – Deb R & D Ltd
Deb Printers Hand Wipes – hand cleaning wipes for the print industry – Deb R & D Ltd
Deb Protect – multi-purpose barrier cream – Deb R & D Ltd
Deb Pure – golden gel soap – Deb R & D Ltd
Deb Restore – reconditioning cream – Deb R & D Ltd
Debbonair Dynamics – High Risk Air Cushion for Wheelchairs – Dan Medica South Ltd
Debenhams – In Store Magazine – John Brown Publishing
Debra – ADME software – Lablogic Systems Ltd
Debretta – childrens fashion wear – Banner Ltd
Debtco – Arrears management software – Iris Group
Debtflow – solicitors – Brindley Twist Tafft & James LLP
DECA – Chaintec Ltd
Decade – load measuring and monitoring systems – Davis Decade Ltd
Decadex – seamless weather proofing membrane for walls and roofs – Sika Liquid Plastics
Decadry – pre printed designer paper – Pelltech Ltd
Decafil – filter aids – Ashland UK
Decalux – non-combustible decorative veneered panels – Panel Systems Ltd
Decanter – I P C Media Ltd
Decarock – natural stone chippings – Rowebb Ltd
Decayeux – DAD – D A D UK
***Dececco** – pasta-fine quality italian – Donatantonio
Deck Screed – offshore industry - floor screed to metal decks – R I W Ltd
***Deckdrain (United Kingdom)** – drainage geocomposite for below ground applications – A G A Group
***Deckel (Germany)** – CNC and conventional universal milling and boring machines – D M G UK Ltd
Deckel-Maho – CNC milling and boring machines, horizontal, vertical and universal machining centres – D M G UK Ltd
Deckshield – car park decking system – Flowcrete UK
DECLAR – thermoformable sheets – Cytec Engineered Materials Ltd
Deco – cable hose reeling drums and collector columns and slip rings – Metreel Ltd
Deco – Rowan Precision Ltd
Deco – Tornos Technologies UK Ltd
Deco - Tornos deco sliding head automatics. – Rowan Precision Ltd
Decobrik – lighting equipment – Powerlite Lighting Solutions Ltd
Decofloc – synthetic decorative flocks – John Peel & Son Ltd
Decograin – Hörmann (UK) Ltd
Decon – tunnelling equipment and associated equipment for the civil engineering industry: metal fabrication – Delta Civil Engineering Group Holdings Ltd
Deconite – form of plastic for furniture knobs – James Grove & Sons Properties Ltd
Deconyl – nylon plastic coating material – Plascoat
Decooflair – soft furnishings – Fulwith Textiles
Decopierre – Bespoke creative wall coating – Decopierre UK Ltd
Decora Collection – rugs – Melrose Textile Co. Ltd
Decora, Sunwood – Quality Blinds – Seaton Blinds
Decorail (United Kingdom) – plastic curtain track – Integra Products
Decoral – aluminium colouring processes – Lea Manufacturing Co.
Decorative Biomulch – mulch – Melcourt Industries
Decorative Finals – Marley Eternit Ltd
Decorative Truss – The Boston Beam – Boston Retail Products
Decorator 1st – decorator advisory services – Akzonobel
Decordrum – lighting equipment – Powerlite Lighting Solutions Ltd
Decorline – lighting equipment – Powerlite Lighting Solutions Ltd
Decorpole (United Kingdom) – wood curtain pole – Integra Products
Decorscreed – decorative pigmented aggregate expoxy floor screed – Conren Ltd
Decorseal – low gloss, clear and solvent based expoxy coating – Conren Ltd
Decorsquare – lighting equipment – Powerlite Lighting Solutions Ltd
Decoslim – lighting equipment – Powerlite Lighting Solutions Ltd
Decothane – seamless polyurethane waterproofing roof membrane – Sika Liquid Plastics
Decotherm A/S/E – roller shutters and grilles – Hörmann (UK) Ltd
Decotrim – lighting equipment – Powerlite Lighting Solutions Ltd
Decra-Led – self adhesive lead and ancillary products for converting glass into simulated stained glass – North Western Lead Company
Decramerse – immersion gold plating process for decorative coatings – P M D UK Ltd
Decrotex – powders for paint, plastics and artistic colours – Lanxess Ltd
Decsa – cooling towers – A J G Waters Equipment Ltd
Decyl Acetate Rectified – perfume speciality – Quest International UK Ltd
Dedsert – compression limiter – Tappex Thread Inserts Ltd
Dedust – re-cleanable panel filter – Waterloo Air Products
Dee – stainless steel slop hopper suite – Armitage Shanks Ltd
Dee Valley Water – water distribution – Dee Valley Water plc
Deed Mark – secure magnetic foil for paper – T S S I Sytems
Deep Clean Cleaning – We are the kitchen-cleaning specialists who offer a cost-effective professional deep cleaning servic – Deep Clean Cleaning Ltd
***Deep Cleaning** – Stayclean Contract Cleaning Services Ltd
Deep Fjord – frozen seafoods – Dales Of Liverpool Ltd
Deep Heat – Mentholatum Co. Ltd
Deep Kleen – odourless stripper and cleaner – Evans Vanodine International plc
Deep Relief – Mentholatum Co. Ltd
Deep Shaft – high intensity aerobic biological treatment process for BOD reductions of biodegradeable effluents – Aker Kvaerner Engineering Services Ltd
Deep Strip – metallised polish stripper – Evans Vanodine International plc
***Deepak Sareen Associates (U.S.A.)** – software distributors – Deepak Sareen Associates Ltd
Deepcoat – spray putty – U-Pol Ltd
Deer (United Kingdom) – bench and pedestal bandfacers – R J H Finishing Systems Ltd
Deerstalker – Try & Lilly Ltd
Deescan – dynamic weighing and measuring – Newland Engineering Co. Ltd
Defence Manufacturers Association – L M L Products Ltd
Defender – stainless steel friction hinges – Securistyle Ltd
Defender, The – double locking padlock – Henry Squire & Sons Ltd
Defendor – steel hinged fire and security doors – Kaba Door Systems
Defensor – Geoquip Ltd
Defesi – stabilised (degassed) ferrosilicon for use in the manufacture of welding electrodes – Hostombe Group Ltd
Defiance – contractors tools – Parker Merchanting Ltd
Defiance – contractors tools – Parker Merchanting Ltd
Defiance – contractors tools – Parker Merchanting Ltd
Defiance – contractors tools – Parker Merchanting Ltd
Defiance – contractors tools – Parker Merchanting Ltd
Defiance – Gem Tool Hire & Sales Ltd
Defiance – contractors tools – Parker Merchanting Ltd
Defiance – contractors tools – Parker Merchanting Ltd
Defiance – contractors tools – Parker Merchanting Ltd
Defiant, The – close shackle insurance rated padlock – Henry Squire & Sons Ltd
Defining Mascara – new formulae – Elizabeth Arden
Definition – paint brush, putty knife, chisel knife, shavehook, wallpaper seam roller, filling knife, stripping knife, brush comb, wallpaper stripper, paint roller – L G Harris & Co. Ltd
Definition Series – loudspeakers – Tannoy Group Ltd
Definitions – decorative paint mixing schemes – Akzonobel
Deflecto – UK Office Direct
Defontaine (France) – Hygienic valves manufacture – Trimline Valves
Deglas – extruded acrylic sheet – Stockline Plastics Ltd
Degraffit – Forward Chemicals Ltd
DEGUSSA LTD – Hydraulic & Offshore Supplies Ltd
Deha – Concrete lifing and fixings – Halfen Ltd
Dehn / Phoenix Contact / Salzer – Surge & Lightning protection / Innovation in connection technology / Rotary cam switches & isolators – Alfred J Hurst Ltd
Deightons – embroidery transfers – Coats Ltd
Deionised Water – high purity water – Morris Lubricants
Dejay Distribution – precision balls, solid carbide cutting tools, workholding equipment and machine tool accessories and rotor live centres, tools solid carbide. – Dejay Distribution Ltd
Dek – sports wear – UK Distributors Footwear Ltd
Dek Printing Machines – screen printers for use in surface mount electronics industry – Dek Printing Machines Ltd
***Dekocord (Belgium)** – exhibition cord carpet – Bryan & Clark Ltd
***Dekofelt (Germany)** – display felt – Bryan & Clark Ltd
Dekohm – applied to decade resistance boxes, inductance and capacitance – Cam Metric Holdings
***DEKOLUX (Germany)** – lamps – Osram Ltd
DekorLux – Minelco Ltd
***Dekosuede (Belgium)** – synthetic display suede – Bryan & Clark Ltd
Dela-Fit – nozzle fittings – Delavan Ltd
***Delabie** – Mechline Developments Ltd
***Delachaux (France)** – crane wheels and rails – British & Continental Traders Ltd
Delaval – Harrier Fluid Power Ltd
Delavan – eight & six roller pump – Delavan Ltd
Delcam – Central C N C Machinery Ltd
delcarmen , slate ni, aluminium and iron – roofing slate – J long & Son
Delco – Ecolab
Delco Remy – Team Overseas Ltd
Delcommerce (Contract Services) Ltd – Plant hire & services – Emcor UK plc
Delcrome – iron base hard facing alloys and cast components – Deloro Stellite Ltd
Delegate 628T – seating – Audience Systems Ltd
Delfin, Thuricide, Agree, Turex, CoStar, Teknar HP-D – bioinsecticides based on bacillus thuringiensis – Agrisense B C S Ltd
Delfloc – flocculant and retention aid – Hercules Holding Ii Ltd
Délifrance – Bakery – Delifrance UK Ltd
Déliquick – Frozen Bread – Delifrance UK Ltd
Delivery Bicycles and Tricycles – bicycles & tricycles – Pashley Cycles Ltd
Delkim – angling equipment – Delkim Ltd
Delkor – European Technical Sales Ltd
Dell – Lamphouse Ltd
Dell Computers – Status Metrology Solutions Ltd
Della Rovere Furniture – Capex Office Interiors
***Delmag (Germany)** – foundation equipment – Burlington Engineers Ltd
Delmex – hand care products – Apaseal Ltd
Delonghi – UK Office Direct
Delonghi – Gem Tool Hire & Sales Ltd
Deloro – nickel base hard facing alloys and cast components – Deloro Stellite Ltd
Deloro Stellite (United Kingdom) – Quay Surface Engineering Metalblast Ltd
Delphi – a human resource management solution addressing in a single database the functions required for payroll personnel and their associated disaplines – Midland HR
***Delphi (U.S.A.)** – Injection specialists – Watson Diesel Ltd
Delphic – filling material and artificial teeth – Schottlander Dental Equipment Supplies
Delphin Ware – wire ware – Wire & Plastic Products Ltd
***Delpiano (Italy)** – woollen and sem-worsted ring spinning frames – Robert S Maynard Ltd
Delrin – acetal resin – Du Pont UK Ltd
Delrin – W Mannering London Ltd
Delrin – Resinex UK Ltd
Delrin – Merseyside Metal Services
Delrin – Aaron Metal & Plastic Supplies Ltd
Delroyd Worm Gear – G M B Associates
Delsey – suitcases and travel goods – Pelham Leather Goods Ltd
Delta – sports garments and in particular football clothing – Star Sportswear Ltd
Delta – marking machines, stencil cutting machines and accessories – Pyramid Engineering & Manufacturing Co. Ltd
Delta – folding and fire folding shutters – Kaba Door Systems
Delta – Monier Ltd
Delta – footballs – Mitre Sports International Ltd
***Delta (Italy)** – oil pumps – Anglo Nordic Burner Products Ltd
Delta (Canada) – Pressure testers – Fondera Ltd
Delta – C M Machinery
***Delta (Japan)** – pipe cutting machines – B S A Tube Runner
Delta – watergel explosives – E P C UK
Delta – Lamphouse Ltd
Delta – paint brush, dusting brush, paperhanging brush, stripping knife, filling knife, putty knife, chisel knife, seam roller, shavehooks, scissors, paint roller, extension poles, wall brush – L G Harris & Co. Ltd
Delta 100 – ISO 100 film – Harman Technology Ltd
Delta 3200 – ISO 3200 speed film – Harman Technology Ltd
Delta 400 – ISO 400 speed film – Harman Technology Ltd
Delta 5 – condensation ovens – Humiseal Europe Ltd
Delta Activator – Multi-purpose liquid graffiti remover – Delta A G Ltd
***Delta Cafès** – Portugalia Wines UK

Delta Civil Engineering – underground civil engineering contractors directional drilling and builders – Delta Civil Engineering Group Holdings Ltd
Delta Controls – process control instrumentation – Delta Controls Ltd
Delta Cord – fibre bonded carpet/tile – Warlord Contract Carpets Ltd
Delta Dampacure – damp and timber treatment specialist – Delta Dampacure Fakenham Ltd
Delta Doc Johnson – marital aids – Scala Agenturen UK
Delta DP200 – Liquid chewing gum and glue remover – Delta A G Ltd
Delta Electrical Systems – electrical distribution switchboards – Eaton Electric Ltd
Delta F – oxygen analysers – Able Instruments & Controls Ltd
Delta Fasteners – honeycomb sandwich fasteners – J R Technology
DELTA FLUID PRODUCTS – Hydraulic & Offshore Supplies Ltd
Delta Graffi-gard – Water based sacrificial anti-graffiti coating – Delta A G Ltd
Delta Mag – Flowline Manufacturing Ltd
Delta Mag, Demi Mag, MiniSonic, DigiSonic P/E, Vortex PhD, Flo-Gage, Deltaflow, Multi-Mag, Hydro-Flow, V-Bar,Master Touch, Flo-System, Flo-Tote, Flo-Dar, Flo-Tracer, Flo-Mate, Ultraflux. – Flowline Manufacturing Ltd
Delta Microblitz – Biological stain and odour remover – Delta A G Ltd
Delta Plus – fibre bonded carpet/tile – Warlord Contract Carpets Ltd
DELTA POWER – Hydraulic & Offshore Supplies Ltd
Delta Rapid-strip – Heavy duty gel graffiti remover – Delta A G Ltd
Delta Seal – anti-corrosive finishes – Delta GB N Ltd
Delta series – Delta series of LCD monitor arms – Ergomounts Ltd
Delta-T Logger – data acquisition unit – Delta T Devices
Delta Tone – anti-corrosive finishes – Delta GB N Ltd
Deltabar – differential pressure transmitter – Endress Hauser Ltd
Deltabond – polymeric coated silica columns for HPLC – Thermo Fisher Scientific
Deltacoll – anti-corrosive finishes – Delta GB N Ltd
DELTADYNE – Hydraulic & Offshore Supplies Ltd
Deltadyne – pressure switches – Pall Europe Corporate Services
Deltaflex – electrical conduits – Icore International
Deltaflow – Flowline Manufacturing Ltd
Deltaloc – anti-corrosive finishes – Delta GB N Ltd
Deltaloc Nut – anti-corrosive finishes – Delta GB N Ltd
Deltalog – Pall Europe Corporate Services
DELTALOG – Hydraulic & Offshore Supplies Ltd
Deltamoist – moisture meter – James H Heal & Co. Ltd
Deltamost – insecticide – Hockley International Ltd
Deltapack – inks for corrugated cases – Hillbrook Printing Inks Ltd
Deltasack – low slip inks for paper sacks – Hillbrook Printing Inks Ltd
DELTASENSE – Hydraulic & Offshore Supplies Ltd
Deltasense – Pall Europe Corporate Services
Deltatone – Protective Finishing Group
Deltaweld – European Technical Sales Ltd
Deltech – Harrier Fluid Power Ltd
Deltight – weld nuts – B A S Components Ltd
Deltos – glass chalkboards – Charles Lightfoot Ltd
Deltrin AF – Merseyside Metal Services
Deltrol – Harrier Fluid Power Ltd
Deltrol – process control instrumentation – Delta Controls Ltd
DELTROL PRODUCTS – Hydraulic & Offshore Supplies Ltd
Deluxe – Harrier Fluid Power Ltd
Deluxe Chauffeurs of London – The Finest Chauffeur company in London – Deluxe Chauffeurs of London
Deluxe London – film processing laboratories London, Toronto and Hollywood – Deluxe London
DEMA – Redsky It
Demag (Germany) – Demag Cranes & Components Ltd
Demag – Proplas International Ltd
Demag – vibrating rollers – Metso Minerals UK Ltd
Demag – Harrier Fluid Power Ltd
Demag – spares – Bearwood Engineering Supplies
Demag Cranes – European Technical Sales Ltd
Demag Ergotech – injection moulding machines – Demag Hamilton Guarantee Ltd
Demand – insecticide – Sorex Ltd
DeMarcit – Safety Works & Solutions Ltd
Demco – hand grip – Plastic Mouldings Ltd
Demeon D – dimethy ether 99.9% – Akzo Nobel Chemicals Holdings Ltd
***Demeyere** – Pans – Continental Chef Supplies Ltd
Demi Mag – Flowline Manufacturing Ltd
Demi-Slot – architectural vandal and weather resistant lighting – Designplan Lighting Ltd
Deminos HR – HR Outsourcing – Deminos HR
Deminos HR – HR Outsourcing – Deminos
Deminpac – water demineralisation plant – Feedwater Ltd
Demise – residual insecticide – Sorex Ltd
demista – R & D Marketings Ltd
Demolition Insurance Services – Genesis Risk Solutions Ltd
Demon – financial modelling and reporting – Data Command Ltd
Demon for windows – financial modelling and reporting – Data Command Ltd
Demountable Partitiions Ltd (United Kingdom) – total office refurbishment – Demountable Partitions Ltd
Demtruk – collapsible transport trolley for heavy and sensitive machines/ equipment – Kentinental Engineering Ltd
Demux – seismic data demultiplexing – D P T S Group Holdings Ltd
Denamarin – Probiotics International Ltd
Denbeigh – books and ledgers (rigid covers) – Reid Printers
Denbigh – Red House Industrial Services Ltd
Denbigh – Prima Care
Denco – Harrier Fluid Power Ltd
Denco-Farval – grease blocks – Bearwood Engineering Supplies
***Dendritics (U.S.A.)** – portable carat balances – The Gemmological Association Of Great Britain
Denduct – clay conduits – Naylor Drainage Ltd
Dengie – horse feed – Dengie Crops Ltd
Denham lathes – Phil Geesin Machinery Ltd
Denholm – stainless steel basin – Armitage Shanks Ltd
Denholm Shipping Services – freight forwarders – Denholm Barwil
Denholme – dress velvet material, box and display velvets – Denholme Velvets Ltd
Denison – Pressure Design Hydraulics Ltd
Denison – Harrier Fluid Power Ltd
DENISON HYDRAULICS – Hydraulic & Offshore Supplies Ltd
Denison Hydraulics – hydraulic equipment, pumps, motors and valves – Parker Hannisin plc
Denison Mayes Group – manufacture service and calibration of materials testing, systems and software – Denison Mayes Group Ltd
Denko Platforms – Accesscaff International Ltd
Denline – plain end sleeve jointed half perforated pipes – Naylor Drainage Ltd
Denlok – clay jacking pipe system for trenchless sewer replacement – Naylor Drainage Ltd
Denman – haircare products including styling brushes, combs and hand held blow dryers – Denman International Ltd
Denmar – inflatable pipeline stoppers – Thomas Bugden & Co. Ltd
Dennis – motor mowers and rollers & turf maintenance equipment powered barrows – Howardson Ltd
Dennis Eagle – Harrier Fluid Power Ltd
Dennison – Solmedia Laboratory Supplies
Denny's – Avalon and Lynwood
Denny's aprons – Avalon and Lynwood
Denny's catering clothing – Avalon and Lynwood
Denny's chef jackets – Avalon and Lynwood
Denny's chefs clothing – Avalon and Lynwood
Denny's chefs whites – Avalon and Lynwood
Denny's scull caps – Avalon and Lynwood
***Denon (Japan)** – desoldering guns – Electro Group Ltd
Denplan – private dental health plan – Denplan Ltd
Denrod – clay access chamber for underground rodding – Naylor Drainage Ltd
Densal – for the densification of aluminium castings, by hot isostatic processing – Bodycote H I P Ltd
Dense Concrete – masonary, paint grade – Brand & Rae
Denseal – polyester joint vitrified clay pipes – Naylor Drainage Ltd
DENSION BERI – Hydraulic & Offshore Supplies Ltd
Densleeve – plain-end vitrified clay pipes with sleeve joints – Naylor Drainage Ltd
Denso Steelcoat System – anti-corrosion system – Winn & Coales Denso Ltd
Denso Tape – anti-corrosion tape – Winn & Coales Denso Ltd
Denso Therm – anti-corrosion tape – Winn & Coales Denso Ltd
Densoclad Tapes – cold applied anti-corrosion tapes – Winn & Coales Denso Ltd
Densofil – filling and packing for low temperature thermal insulation – Winn & Coales Denso Ltd
Densopol – anti-corrosion tapes – Winn & Coales Denso Ltd
Densyl – anti-corrosion tape, petrolatum based – Winn & Coales Denso Ltd
Dent – yarn break detection systems for the textile industry – Dent Instrumentation Ltd
Dent Instruments (U.S.A.) – energy loggers – I M H Technologies Ltd
Dentiplus – alcohol free mouthwashes, dental floss and fresh breath spray – F M C G Ltd
Dentogen – oil gel – Reckitt Benckiser plc
Denton – expanding wallet – Acco East Light Ltd
Denton Clark – Denton Clark Rentals
Dents – fashion gloves, non-slip palm, stretch nylon back driving gloves and shetland wool gloves – Dents
Denturax – brushes – Stoddard Manufacturing Co. Ltd
Denver – co-ordinated amenity lighting family – Holophane Europe Ltd
Denver Sala – Orion-Slurry pump – Metso Minerals UK Ltd
Deodamate – Forward Chemicals Ltd
Deodasan – Forward Chemicals Ltd
Deodis – Forward Chemicals Ltd
Deodorant Blocks – Forward Chemicals Ltd
DEOS – strater for lamps – Osram Ltd
Depa (Germany) – diaphragm pump – Crane Process Flow Technology Ltd
DEPA Pumps – Air operated diaphragm pumps – Bestpump
DEPA Pumps – Alfa Laval Eastbourne Ltd
Depeche – fashion boots and shoes – D Jacobson & Sons Ltd
Dependable – paper bags – Dempson Crooke Ltd
Dependable – pipe & cable clamps, springs & pressings – Dependable Springs & Pressings Ltd
Depocyte – Napp Pharmaceutical Group Ltd
Depol – multiple carbohydrase enzyme formulations – Biocatalysts Ltd
Depolox – oxidant residual and ph monitors – Wallace & Tiernan Ltd
Depotrol – chemical treatment of swimming pool water – Wallace & Tiernan Ltd
Deprag – pneumatic screwdrivers & hand tools – Baltec UK Ltd
Dept of Army – Harrier Fluid Power Ltd
Deptich – bed frames – Relyon Ltd
Deputy – programmable controllers – Nortel Networks UK Ltd
Depuy International – orthopaedic implant manufacturers – Depuy International
***Dequesa Natural (Spain)** – slates – Cembrit Ltd
***Derakane (Germany)** – glassflake lining systems – Lithgow Saekaphen Ltd
Deray – heat shrink tubing – D S G Canusa GmbH & Co.
***Derbigum (Belgium)** – high performance roofing – Alumasc Exterior Building Products
Derby – horse races derby – Epsom Downs Racecourse
Derby Evening Telegraph – newspaper – Derby Telegraph Media Group
Derby Express – newspaper – Derby Telegraph Media Group
Derby Panel Green – bone china tableware – The Royal Crown Derby Porcelain Company Ltd
Derby Top – textile piece goods – Reid & Taylor Ltd
Derbyshire (United Kingdom) – sugar confectionery – Bysel Ltd
Derbyshire Capital Reserve, The – Derbyshire Building Society
Derbyshire Deal Check, The – Derbyshire Building Society
Derbyshire Direct – Derbyshire Building Society
Derbyshire Harvester, The – Derbyshire Building Society
Derbyshire Life – Derbyshire Building Society
Derbyshire Manx Bond – Derbyshire Building Society
Derbyshire Memberloan, The – Derbyshire Building Society
Derbyshire Moneylink, The – Derbyshire Building Society
Derbyshire Mortgagecover – Derbyshire Building Society
Derbyshire Paymentscover, The – Derbyshire Building Society
Derbyshire, The – Derbyshire Building Society
Derbyshire Total Homecover, The – Derbyshire Building Society
Derbyshire Travelcover – Derbyshire Building Society
Derbystar – textile piece goods – Reid & Taylor Ltd
Derbysure – Derbyshire Building Society
Derek Roberts Antiques – antique clocks – Derek Roberts Antiques
Deritend Induction Services (United Kingdom) – engineering specialists in induction heating and melting – Deritend
***Derix (Germany)** – healds, drop wires and heald frames – Pilkingtons Ltd
Derkado – spring barley variety – Limagrain UK Ltd
Dermafusion – Silhouette Beauty Equipment
Dermagel – Forward Chemicals Ltd
Dermalift – Silhouette Beauty Equipment
Dermalogica – Skincare products researched and developed by the International Dermal Institute – Pure Beauty Online
Dermasol – hand soap – Agma Ltd
Dermatone – Silhouette Beauty Equipment
Dermine – biocidal hand soap – Agma Ltd
Dermo Vedic Products – Double Gee Hair Fashions Ltd
Dermol – alcohol based biocidal hand rinse – Agma Ltd
Dermos – anti-bacterial gloves – Bennett Safetywear
Dernier & Hamlyn – design, manufacture of contemporary and traditional customised lighting for the international project market - restoration and reputation of tradition luminaires – Dernier & Hamlyn Ltd
Derris Dust – insecticide – Vitax Ltd
Derwent – pencil – Cumberland Pencil Museum
Derwent – plaster sink – Armitage Shanks Ltd

Derwent – UK Office Direct

Des Case – Hygroscopic Breathers for Reservoirs and Gearboxes – J B J Techniques Ltd

Descalene – descalers for washing and dishwashing – Kilrock Products Ltd

Desch – Clutches and Power Transmission Equipment – J R Technical Services UK Ltd

Desch Plantpak – Pots & Trays – L S Systems Ltd

Desco – packaging machinery – Apropa Machinery Ltd

Desco – Submarine Manufacturing & Products Ltd

Design for Living – 3 piece suite – Forest Sofa

Design S – standard design passenger lifts – Schindler

Designer – swing door – Kawneer UK Ltd

Designer – amenity grass mixtures – Limagrain UK Ltd

Designer Collection – axminster velvet – Brintons Carpets Ltd

Designer Collection – bed linen – Pin Mill Textiles Ltd

Designer Tweed Chunky – yarns – Stylecraft

Designline – filing cabinets – Railex Filing Ltd

Designs J.C. – contracting – Carter Synergy

Desire – fashions – The Bentall Centre

Desize – enzyme desizing agents for removal of starch size – Brenntag Colours Ltd

Desk Files – portable desk files for cards – Rotadex Systems Ltd

Desklift – Linak UK

Deskline – linear actuators – Linak UK

Deskplus – UK Office Direct

Deskpower – Linak UK

Desktex – UK Office Direct

*Desktop (Netherlands) – desktop linoleum – Forbo

Desmodur – isocyanates – I M C D UK Ltd

Desmophen – polyol – I M C D UK Ltd

Desoprime – 2 pack high solids primers – PPG Aerospace

Desothane – 2 pack high solids polyurethane topcoat – PPG Aerospace

DeSoto – coatings for aerospace and defence – PPG Aerospace

DESOUTTER – Hydraulic & Offshore Supplies Ltd

Desoutter – Midland Air Tools Ltd

Desoutter – Gustair Materials Handling Equipment Ltd

DESTA – Chaintec Ltd

Desta – Stacatruc

Desta – T V H UK Ltd

Detect-A-Tag – metal detectable labels – Piroto Labelling Ltd

Detecta – B P plc

Detectamesh – detectable warning mesh – Boddingtons Ltd

Detectapen – BST Products

Detectatape – detectable warning tape – Boddingtons Ltd

Detectatape, Euromesh, Eurotape, Overlord, Sentree, Superstrong, Ultra-strong, Wavelay. – Boddingtons Ltd

Detection Intrusion Managed Service – Tekdata Distribution Ltd

Detection Intrusion Unit – Tekdata Distribution Ltd

Detective + – Transportable multi-gas monito – Crowcon Detection Instrument Ltd

DeTeWe Shipton – varied product range – Nine Shipton

Detex – Gamma ray irradiation indicators – Sessions Of York

Detizor – range of biocidal detergents – Agma Ltd

Detroit – ducting for fumes – Merlett Plastics UK Ltd

Detroit Diesel – Team Overseas Ltd

Detroit Diesel – Trowell Plant Sales Ltd

Dettox – UK Office Direct

Deutsch – Contacts – Dax International Ltd

Deutsch – Relays – Dax International Ltd

Deutsch – Connectors – Dax International Ltd

Deutsch – high and medium density push pull connectors; heavy duty connectors for earth moving vehicles, trucks and tractors; superscreen connecting devices; EMC connectors, fibre optic connectors, systems and components, hermetic connectors – Deutsch UK

Deutsch – Cyclops Electronics Ltd

Deutsche Asset Management – asset management – Deutscha Asset Management Ltd

DEUTSCHE STAR – Hydraulic & Offshore Supplies Ltd

Deutsche Techna – European Technical Sales Ltd

Deutz – Aktion Automotive Ltd

Deutz – engine spares – Service Engines Newcastle Ltd

Deutz – Team Overseas Ltd

Deutz – diesels & spares – Bearwood Engineering Supplies

Deutz – Harrier Fluid Power Ltd

DEUTZ DIESEL ENGINES – Hydraulic & Offshore Supplies Ltd

Deutz Fahr – J & S Lewis Ltd

*Deutz-Farr – George Colliar Ltd

Deva (United Kingdom) – screw conveyors – Astwell Augers Ltd

Deva – leather insoles – A Algeo Ltd

Deva – fashion boots – D Jacobson & Sons Ltd

Develop solutions for the automotive industry – Borgers Ltd

Developer (United Kingdom) – carpet tiles – Checkmate Industries Ltd

Development Securities – Development Securities Investments plc

Deveron – stainless steel urinal – Armitage Shanks Ltd

Device Only – scarves – Foster Enterprises

Devil Biss – Letchford Supplies Ltd

Devilbiss – Spray Guns and equipment. – Car Paint Warehouse Ltd

Devlieg – European Technical Sales Ltd

Devlieg – tooling products – Microbore Tooling Systems

Devlin Electronics – custom keyboards & electromechanical components – Devlin Electronics Ltd

Devol – engineering – Devol Engineering Ltd

Devon Contractors – building contractors and civil engineers – Devon Contractors Ltd

Devon Lady – timber frame prefabricated buildings – Allwood Buildings Ltd

Devonshire Axminster – Ryalux Carpets Ltd

Devonshire Twist – Ryalux Carpets Ltd

Devualt – Global Fasteners Ltd

Devweld – excellent impact strength adhesive – I T W Devcon

Dewalt – Oxon Fastening Systems Ltd

Dewalt – D D Hire

Dewalt – Knighton Tool Supplies

*Dewalt (United Kingdom) – electric & cordless power tools – Harrow Tool Co. Ltd

Dewalt – Gem Tool Hire & Sales Ltd

Dewalt – S J Wharton Ltd

Dewalt – Wessex Welding & Industrial Supplies Ltd

Dewdicator – moisture measuring instrument – M C M

Dewhirst – clothing manufacturers - men's suits and shirts, ladies trousers, skirts and blouses, and childrenswear – Dewhirst Group Ltd

Dewhirst Childrenswear – importers & traders in childrens clothing – Dewhirst Group Ltd

Dewhirst Ladieswear – importers & traders of ladieswear – Dewhirst Group Ltd

Dewhirst Menswear – Importers & traders of mensclothes – Dewhirst Group Ltd

DeWitt – Jenex Ltd

Dewluxe – moisture measuring instrument – M C M

DEWMET – cooled-mirror dew-point-hygrometer – Michell Instruments Ltd

Dewtex – non-woven industrial textiles – James Dewhurst Ltd

Dewulf – Full range of harvesting equipment for all root crops – Niagri Engineering Ltd

Dexine – rubber compound – Dexine Rubber Co. Ltd

Dexion – Warewashing & Refrigeration – Nisbets plc

Dexion (United Kingdom) – partitioning – Scotwood Interiors Ltd

Dexonite – reinforced ebonite – Dexine Rubber Co. Ltd

Dexoplas – plastics – Dexine Rubber Co. Ltd

Dextram – thin supported gloves in nitrile – Mapa Spontex

Dextramalt – stone ground malt flour – E D M E Ltd

Dextrol – paramelt

Dextrolin – paramelt

DF/IDF – direct fired gas fired unit heater – Nordair Niche

DF/IDF – direct fired gas fired unit heater – Nordair Niche

DFL – www.deepakafasteners.com – Deepak Fasteners

DG by Dancing Girl – Fashion Tights, Stockings, & Lifestyle Accessories, etc. – Pak Nylon Hosiery Co.

dh Electrolink – control system – D H Industries Ltd

DHOLLANDIA – Chaintec Ltd

Di-Cup – dicumyl peroxide – Hercules Holding Ii Ltd

Di-Log – Alpha Electronics Southern Ltd

Di-Vita – knitwear ensemble – Karpelle Ltd

Dia-Link – flexible diamond material – D K Holdings Ltd

Dia Malt – malt extracts – British Diamalt

*Diablo Chafing Fuel – Neville UK plc

*Diacel (Germany) – cellulose – Fleximas Ltd

Diacrome – chrome (hard) deposit – Firma Chrome Ltd

Diacryl – methacrylate monomers – Akzo Nobel Chemicals Holdings Ltd

Diacure – Akzo Nobel Packaging Coatings Ltd

Diaflex – Akzo Nobel Packaging Coatings Ltd

Diagen – laboratory testing equipment – Diagnostic Reagents Ltd

Diagnetics – Harrier Fluid Power Ltd

Diagraph – Manual Marking & Stencilling Products – Diagraph Products

Diagrit – electroplated diamond and C.B.N. tools – D K Holdings Ltd

DIAJET – direct injection abrasive jetting, powerful and precise abrasive waterjet cutting equipment – B H R Group

Dial-A-Flow – adjustable flow gas regulator – Cryoservice Ltd

Dial Accident Management – accident management and insurance services – Leaseplan UK Ltd

Dial Contracts – vehicle leasing – Leaseplan UK Ltd

Dial-Glass – special composition glasses – Plowden & Thompson Ltd

Dial House – general interest books, sporting titles – Ian Allan Publishing Ltd

Dial-Redrawn – redrawn capillaires and precision bores – Plowden & Thompson Ltd

Dialafile – multivendor communications package – Intech Ltd

*Dialatron (Far East) – telephones & cordless telephoning (applicable to continental Europe only) – Geemarc Telecom S A

Dialight – Cyclops Electronics Ltd

Dialog 300 – data logging support software – Ele International

Dialog 900 – data logging support software – Ele International

Dialog ADU – data logging support software – Ele International

Dialog EMS – data logging support software – Ele International

Dialux – Osborn Unipol Ltd

Diamant – glass shower enclosures – Novellini UK Ltd

Diamant Boart – concrete saws and diamond blades – Trenchex Garden Machinery

Diamard R – chlorinated rubber paint - floors – Emusol Products Ltd

Diamet HF5 – hard facing weld – Fospat Industrial Ltd

Diamex – malt extracts – British Diamalt

Diamic in a Diamond – carpenters' edge and tools high speed turning tools – Henry Taylor Tools Ltd

Diamond – fire doors – Drawn Metal Ltd

Diamond – Cooks Brushes

*Diamond (Japan) – portable cutters and straighteners – La Roche

Diamond – farrier tools – Apex Tools

Diamond – Antifriction Components Ltd

Diamond – bread improvers blends of enzymic active soya flour, fats and emulsifiers – C S M UK Ltd

Diamond – fibre bonded carpet – Heckmondwike FB

*Diamond (Japan) – rebar cutters – Welwyn Tool Group Ltd

Diamond – Engis UK Ltd

*Diamond (Italy) – fan assisted gas heater – Drugasar Service Ltd

Diamond – Ground Products – Weldlogic Europe Ltd

Diamond Art Series – Drugasar Service Ltd

Diamond Blades – A T Wilde & Son Ltd

Diamond Bonewrap – Grantham Manufacturing Ltd

Diamond Collection – spectacle frames – Pennine Optical Group Ltd

Diamond Cruisers – Richardsons Stalham Ltd

Diamond Edge – hairdressing scissors, razors, razor straps and dog grooming equipment – Diamond Edge Ltd

Diamond, excel, greenline, Norwich – Cooks Brushes

Diamond Facia Cladding (United Kingdom) – facia & soffit systems – Kedek Ltd

Diamond Glass – ionomer restorative material – Kemdent

Diamond Gripkraft – Grantham Manufacturing Ltd

Diamond Jaws – chuck jaws – Thame Engineering Co. Ltd

Diamond Joe – hand hammers – Visa Hand Tools Ltd

Diamond M.P.I. – Grantham Manufacturing Ltd

Diamond Polishing Compounds – diamond tool manufacturers – Abrasive Technology Ltd

Diamond Stylus – replacement styli, audio leads, cassettes, headphones, microphones, record and cassette accessories, video accessories, radios, calculators, personal HiFis and security products – The Diamond Stylus Company Ltd

*Diamond Super (Italy) – fan assisted forced flue gas heater – Drugasar Service Ltd

Diamond Super Style Series – Drugasar Service Ltd

Diamond Tester – The Gemmological Association Of Great Britain

Diamond Tools and Abrasive Solutions – Yokota UK

Diamond Twistwrap – Grantham Manufacturing Ltd

Diamondback – polyester/cotton processed fabric for animal cover use – J T Inglis & Sons Ltd

Diamondback (U.S.A.) – arch-breaking hoppers – Orthos Engineering Ltd

Diamondback – bicycles – Raleigh UK Ltd

DiamondBite – Chip-It

DiamondFaces – Eagleburgmann Industries UK Llp

DIAMONDSPIR – Hydraulic & Offshore Supplies Ltd

Diamondstar – paper – Paperun Group Of Companies

Diapaque – G E Healthcare

*Diaproof-K – Forum Products Ltd

DiaryCard – Cardinal Health U.K. 232 Ltd

Diastar – industrial diamonds – Star Industrial Tools Ltd

Diastat – medical diagnostic kits – Axis Shield Ltd

Diatest – measuring equipment – Verdict Gauge Ltd

DIATOOL – reamers – Drill Service Horley Ltd

Diatsol – industrial lubricants – B P plc

Dibo – hot cold water washers – Wilms Heating Equipment

Dibro – moulding & metalising – Dibro Ltd

Dicam – environmental control system for livestock production and crop storage indludes networked and modem linked remote building management and monitoring facilities – Farm Energy & Control Services Ltd

Dicera – paramelt

Dicercy White – Wine For Spice Ltd

DICHTOMATIK GMBH – Hydraulic & Offshore Supplies Ltd

DICKIES – Wolds Engineering Services Ltd

Dickies – Avalon and Lynwood

Dickies – Workwear Hi Visibility – A4 Apparel Ltd

Dickies – Workwear – Protective Supplies & Services Ltd

Dickies – industrial workwear, corporate clothing and footwear country clothing, safety wear – Dickies Workwear

Dickies 22 – Dickies Workwear

Dickies Portwest – Spyra Distribution

Dicopac – G E Healthcare

Dicotox Extra – selective herbicide which is specially suited to outfield turf giving economical control of at least 17 broad-leaved weeds – Bayer Crop Science

DIDCOT – Tipping bucket rain gauge – Halcyon Solutions

Didos – Retailers invoice matching solution – Iris Group

Die-Tough – low alloy steel die repair welding electrodes – Metrode Products Ltd

DieBold – A T M Parts

DIECI – Chaintec Ltd

Dieci Telehandlers – J E Buckle Engineers Ltd

Dielectric Analyser (D.E.A.) – heat analyser – Ta Instruments

Dieltest – range of oil test products – Baur Test Equipment Ltd

Dielube – B P plc

Diesel Direct – commerical diesel bunkering card – C H Jones Walsall Ltd

Dieslip – Molyslip Atlantic Ltd

DIESSE – Hydraulic & Offshore Supplies Ltd

Dievar – hot work die steel for diecasting, forging, extrusion – Uddeholm Steel Stockholders

Diexa – Harrier Fluid Power Ltd

Difenacoum – Sorex Ltd

Differential Scanning Calorimeter (D.S.C.) – Ta Instruments

Diffstak – integrated pumping system – B O C Edwards

diffstak – AESpump

*Digi (Japan) – digital scales – Marsden Weighing Machine Group

Digi Greeting Card – Digital Products - Indigo - Coated – Howard Smith Paper Ltd

DIGI PLAN – Hydraulic & Offshore Supplies Ltd

Digi-Speak – speak-out unit for the blind enabling them to use micrometers etc – Vaultland Engineering

Digicon – electronic control system – Rolls Royce Marine Electrical Systems Ltd

Digifill – G Webb Automation Ltd

Digiheat – L M K Thermosafe

Digimag – portable magnetic power packs – Baugh & Weedon Ltd

DigiMet (Germany) – digital measuring instruments – Preisser UK Ltd

DigiSonic P/E – Flowline Manufacturing Ltd

Digisound – Selectronix Ltd

Digitac – access control – Raytel Security Systems Ltd

Digital Camera Magazine – magazine – Future Publishing Ltd

Digital Dosing – Grundfos Pumps Ltd

Digital EI CID – test equipment for stator cores of generators and large motors – Adwel International Ltd

Digital Labels – N S D International Ltd

Digital Mail – Callsure Business Telephone & Fax Numbers

Digital Mercury (United Kingdom) – lighting control systems – R Hamilton & Co. Ltd

Digital Projection – Lamphouse Ltd

Digital Sprite – CCTV – Dedicated Micros Ltd

Digital Technology Intl – publishing software and electronic publishing for newspapers – Digital Technology International Ltd

Digital Zone Gloss – Digital Products - Toner Sheet Fed - Coated – Howard Smith Paper Ltd

Digital Zone Silk – Digital products - Toner Sheet Fed - Coated – Howard Smith Paper Ltd

Digitape – electronic tape rules – L S Starrett Co. Ltd

Digitrol – industrial electronic computer systems, design and engineering – Digitrol Ltd

Digitron – Alpha Electronics Southern Ltd

Dihart – Komet Ltd

Dihydroeugenol – perfume speciality – Quest International UK Ltd

Dihydrojasmone – perfume speciality – Quest International UK Ltd

Dihydromyrcenol – perfme speciality – Quest International UK Ltd

Dihydromyrcenol Acetate – perfume speciality – Quest International UK Ltd

Dijell – paramelt

Dik Guerts – gas wall heaters – Drugasar Service Ltd

DIL 402 C – Netzsch-Instruments

Dilatoflex – Interflex Hose & Bellows Ltd

DILATOFLEX – rubber bellows – Mercia Flexibles

Dilvac – vacuum flasks – Day Impex Ltd

Dimar – Manufacturer and supplier of anodised and powder coated extruded aluminium profiles – Dimar Ltd

Dimension – Briefcase Instrument Equipment Tool Computer Carrying cases – Hofbauer (UK) Ltd

Dimethicone 1000cs – Granada Cranes & Handling

Dimethicone 1000cs – Basildon Chemical Co. Ltd / KCC

Dimethicone 350cs – Basildon Chemical Co. Ltd / KCC

Dimethicone 350cs – Granada Cranes & Handling

Dimex – consumer products – Yule Catto & Co plc

Dimple Liner – ditchliners for bowling greens – Sportsmark Group Ltd

Dimple Marker – g m machine – Sportsmark Group Ltd

Dimplex – spares & equipment – Bearwood Engineering Supplies

Dimplex – domestic heating and electrical appliances – Glen Electric Ltd

Dimplex, – Glen Dimplex UK Ltd

Dimplex,Glen,Berry,Unidare,EWT,Electricaire – Glen Dimplex UK Ltd

DIN-A-MITE – power controllers – Watlow Ltd

Dina Relays – European Technical Sales Ltd

DINAMIC OIL – Hydraulic & Offshore Supplies Ltd

Dinex – Foodcare Systems Ltd

Dinn (United Kingdom) – ceilings – Scotwood Interiors Ltd

Dino Lift Platforms – Accesscaff International Ltd

Dino Platforms – Accesscaff International Ltd

DINOIL – Hydraulic & Offshore Supplies Ltd

DINOLIFT – Chaintec Ltd

Dinoram – diamines – Atosina UK Ltd

Dinoramac – diamine acetates – Atosina UK Ltd

Dinoramox – ethoxylated diamines – Atosina UK Ltd

*Dinse (Germany) – welding and cutting tools – Olympus Technologies Ltd

Diodes Inc. – Cyclops Electronics Ltd

Diodes Inc. – semiconductors – Anglia

Diodrast – G E Healthcare

Diolpate – British Vita plc

Dionic – brewing water treatment – Murphy & Son

Diorez – British Vita plc

Diotec – Cyclops Electronics Ltd

Diotec – M S C Gleichmann UK Ltd

DioxSorb – products for flue gas treatment – Jacobi Carbons

Dipal – dairy chemicals – Delaval

Diplomat – Thyssenkrupp Elevator UK Ltd

Diplomat – plastic cistern – Thomas Dudley Ltd

Diplomat – classic footwear for men – Sanders & Sanders Ltd

Diplomat – tilt and slide sunroof electric – Webasto Products UK Ltd

Diplomat Holidays – coach holidays – East Yorkshire Motor Services Ltd

Diplomat Tm Multistore – project management & database maintenance – D P T S Group Holdings Ltd

Diplomatic – Machine Tool Supplies Ltd

DIPMETER – For measuring water level – Halcyon Solutions

Dipper – traditional bunk boat trailer but with a triple-pivoted keel roller to help lauch and recovery – Indespension Ltd

Diprane – polyurethane casting and spray systems, polyester – Dow Hyperlast

Diprane – British Vita plc

Diptex – latex compound for dipped surgical goods etc – Vita Liquid Polymers

DIPTONE – Water level measurement – Halcyon Solutions

Diptronics – switches – Anglia

Dirasol – direct photostencil emulsions – Fujifilm Sericol Ltd

Direct Adhesive – hot melt and aqueous products – Direct Adhesives Ltd

Direct DNC – Seiki Systems Ltd

Direct Line – petrol pricing unit – Bribex

Direct Line Accident Management – Direct Line Insurance plc

Direct Line Financial Services – Direct Line Insurance plc

Direct Line Insurance – insurance – Direct Line Insurance plc

Direct Line ISA – Direct Line Insurance plc

Direct Line Life – Direct Line Insurance plc

Direct Line Mastercard – Direct Line Insurance plc

Direct Line Pensions – Direct Line Insurance plc

Direct Line Rescue – Direct Line Insurance plc

Direct Line Unit Trust – Direct Line Insurance plc

Direct Manufacturing Supply Co – craftsman brass giftware and brass table lamps and fireplace accessories – Direct Manufacturing Supply Co

Direct Packaging Solutions – Direct Packaging Solutions Ltd

Direct Reflecting – wide stereo image – Bose Ltd

Direct Salt – UK's leading salt distributor – INEOS Enterprises Ltd

Directional Data Systems Ltd – Directional Data Systems Ltd

Directions – The Woolwich

Director – rectangular flush meters in matt black – Elektron Components Ltd

Directors Bitter – ales & stout – Scottish & Newcastle Pub Co.

Directory To The Furniture & Furnishing Industry – United Business Media Ltd

Direx – aluminium sign systems – Universal Components

*Diro (Germany) – tube notching machines – Brandone Machine Tool Ltd

Dirt Driver – industrial cleaning equipment – B & G Cleaning Systems Ltd

Dirt-Fuse – Pall Europe Corporate Services

DIRT-FUSE – Hydraulic & Offshore Supplies Ltd

Disano – exterior, amenity and industrial lighting – City Electrical Factors Ltd

Disaster Response Network – Merryhill Envirotec Ltd

Disatac – electronic tachometers for ships – Dantec Dynamics Ltd UK

Disbocrete – concrete repair materials – Permarock Products Ltd

Disbon – range of protective and decorative coatings for concrete structures – Permarock Products Ltd

Disc – circular surface and semi recessed vandal resistant architectural lighting – Designplan Lighting Ltd

Discalloy – grey iron for high performance disc brakes – Precision Disc Castings Ltd

Discflex Coupling – Renold Clutches & Couplings Ltd

Discflo – disc pumps – P & M Pumps

Discman – portable CD player – Sony Head Office

Discmaster – multiple position dispenser for placement of antibiotic discs for susceptibility testing – The Mast Group Ltd

Discmaster – Saturn Spraying Systems Ltd

Discmatic – Saturn Spraying Systems Ltd

DISCO – mechanical variable speed drives – A T B Laurence Scott Ltd

Disco – mechanical variable speed drives – Disco Drive Kings Lynn Ltd

Discount – mortgage scheme – Market Harborough Building Society

*Discount Radio & Watch Co. Ltd (Hong Kong & Far East) – importers and wholesalers of watches, clock radios and radios – D R Warehouse Ltd

Discover – pregnency test – Church & Dwight UK Ltd

Discovery – Display Wizard Ltd

Discovery – Dead Sea vitamin and mineral supplements – Finders International Ltd

Discovery Foods – Olympia Foods Ltd

Discpac – The London Fancy Box Company Ltd

Discpan (United Kingdom) – circular access panels – Panelcraft Access Panels

Discreen (United Kingdom) – dynamic screen to solve modern screening problems in the waste water industry – Mono Pumps Ltd

Discretely Different – Registered design knickers for disabled ladies – Discretely Different

Disglaign – M S C Gleichmann UK Ltd

Dish Wash Extra – automatic cabinet machines in hard water areas which removes tannin – Evans Vanodine International plc

Dished ends – Abbott & Co Newark Ltd

Disk Drive External Floppy USB – Tekdata Distribution Ltd

Disk Drive Floppy USB – Tekdata Distribution Ltd

Disklabs, Disklabs Data Recovery, Disklabs Compute – Disklabs Ltd

DiskShred – On site Hard Drive Shredding service in UK & Ireland – Diskshred

Dismantling Joints – built in adjustability to flanged pipe systems – Viking Johnson

*Disney Holidays (U.S.A.) – holidays – The Disney Store Ltd

*Disney Land Paris (France) – theme park – The Disney Store Ltd

*Disoric (Germany) – sensors – Sensortek

Dispelair – Antifoam – Blackburn Chemicals Ltd

Dispensa – vending bottles – Chequer Foods Ltd

*Dispense-Rite – Range of cup, lid, straw & condiment dispensers – Taylor Foodservice Facilities

Dispensit – precision metering and dispense valves – Liquid Control Ltd

Dispenstech – time and pressure dispensing andpositive deplacement dispensing – Liquid Control Ltd

Dispercab – pigmented dispersion in various resin media – Tennants Inks & Coating Supplies Ltd

Dispercap – pigmented dispersion in various resin media – Tennants Inks & Coating Supplies Ltd

Dispercel – pigmented dispersion in various resin media – Tennants Inks & Coating Supplies Ltd

Disperchlor – pigmented dispersion in various resin media – Tennants Inks & Coating Supplies Ltd

Dispercryl – pigmented dispersion in various resin media – Tennants Inks & Coating Supplies Ltd

Disperkyd – pigmented dispersion in various resin media – Tennants Inks & Coating Supplies Ltd

Dispermat – Fullbrook Systems Ltd

Dispermid – pigemented dispersion in various resin media – Tennants Inks & Coating Supplies Ltd

Dispervyn – pigmented dispersion in various resin media – Tennants Inks & Coating Supplies Ltd

Dispette – disposable esr pipettes – Guest Medical Ltd

Display Outer – printed outer carton to hold individual cartons, bottles etc – Beamglow Ltd

Displays – Boston lighting merchandising displays, Boston: Rug, Tile, Door, Appliance displays – Boston Retail Products

Displays – Imex Print Services Ltd

Disposa – clinical waste control – Amcor Flexibles

Disposable Overalls – S J Wharton Ltd

Disposamatic – commercial foodwaste disposal units – The Haigh Group Ltd

Disposapad – Incontinence pad disposer – Franke Sissons Ltd

Dissolvine – chelating agent range – Akzo Nobel Chemicals Holdings Ltd

Dissolvo – Pipestoppers

Disston – Gem Tool Hire & Sales Ltd

Distec – vertical balancing machine – Schenck Ltd

Distinction Laid & Wove – Digital Products - Indigo - Uncoated – Howard Smith Paper Ltd

Distinctive Casuals – canvas casual shoes – Bacup Shoe Co. Ltd

Distinctive D – ties – D P T Wear Ltd

Distinctive Slippers – slippers – Bacup Shoe Co. Ltd

Disto – Fieldway Supplies Ltd

Distoleum – B P plc

Distop – computer software – K B C Process Technology Ltd

Distributor DVD – Tekdata Distribution Ltd

Distributors for: Tol-O-Matic Inc.,(USA); Hayes Brake LLC.,(USA); Zero-Max Inc.,(USA) – Robert Cupitt Ltd

Distrimex Pumps – centrifugal selfpriming water pumps – Alan Dale Pumps Ltd

Distrisorter – automated sorting conveyor systems – Van Der Lande Industries

Ditchwitch – Harrier Fluid Power Ltd

Ditech Range – Modular rack-based control system – Crowcon Detection Instrument Ltd

Ditel – London Electronics Ltd

Diva – ladies wear – Remys Ltd

Diva Eicon – Tekdata Distribution Ltd

Diva Eicon Technology – Tekdata Distribution Ltd

***Divanette (Netherlands)** – stacking and twin beds – Golden Plan Ltd

Divator MK11 – self contained under water breathing apparatus – Interspiro Ltd

Divator MKII – professional diving apparatus – Interspiro Ltd

DiveceL – City Technology Ltd

DiveDynamics – Divex

DIVER – Self contained water level data logger – Halcyon Solutions

Diverco – company brokers – Diverco Ltd

Divers – car accessories - ashtrays, clocks, compasses, jacks etc – Custom Accessories Europe Ltd

Diversey Lever – Proctor & Gamble – M & D Cleaning Supplies Ltd

Divex – under water engineering – Divex

Divice – clothing and headwear – St Andrews Link Trust

Divis – hydrated lime – Kilwaughter Chemical Co. Ltd

Dixell – electronic controls, monitoring systems and instruments, including thermometers, thermostats, humidity controls, defrost contols, pressure controls, pressure sensors, step controls, fan speed controls, probes – Thermofrost Cryo plc

Dixi – balers – K K Balers Ltd

Dixon – department store – J Dixon & Son Ltd

DIXON-ADFLOW – Hydraulic & Offshore Supplies Ltd

DIXON-ADFLOW COUPLINGS – Hydraulic & Offshore Supplies Ltd

Dixon Boss (U.S.A.) – Industrial high pressure hose couplings for pneumatic & steam applications – Dixon Group Europe Ltd

Dixons – domestic electronic products – Dixons Retail

Dixons On-line – internet store – Dixons Retail

Dizzolv – Forward Chemicals Ltd

Dizzolv Viscous – Forward Chemicals Ltd

DJ AZ – various cd albums for sale – D J Az Productions

Dk-Lok – Tube & Instrument thread fittings, valves. – Staffordshire Hydraulic Services Ltd

DLI – Hydraulic & Offshore Supplies Ltd

DLI – Mayday Seals & Bearings

dLine – ironmongery – Allgood

DLiner – waste-based test liner 3 – Kappa Paper Recycling

DM Series Sprag Clutch – Renold Clutches & Couplings Ltd

DMS – Dometic UK Ltd

DMS – standardised components for injection moulding tools – D M S-Diemould

DNH – Ex loudspeakers – Wellhead Electrical Supplies

DNP QUICK RELEASE COUPLINGS – Hydraulic & Offshore Supplies Ltd

DNV – Hydraulic & Offshore Supplies Ltd

Do-Grip – Iscar Tools

Do Stone – Granite Kitchen Worktop Specialists and all projects relating to Stone – Kitchen Worktops London

DoALL – Utility and automatic bandsaw machines – Accurate Cutting Services Ltd

DoALL – carbide and metal band saw blades – Accurate Cutting Services Ltd

DoAll - band saw blades & machines - Pedrazzoli - circular & bandsaws machines - Soitaab - Julia circular sawbaldes - Daiko disposable carbide sawbaldes – Accurate Cutting Services Ltd

***Dobel (Sweden)** – aluzink – S S A B Swedish Steel Ltd

Dobel 200 XT (United Kingdom) – Plastisol coated steel sheet-coil – S S A B Swedish Steel Ltd

Dobelshield – stucco embossed aluzink sheet for civil insulation cladding – S S A B Swedish Steel Ltd

Dobi – hydraulic and pneumatic seals – Polyurethane Progress Ltd

Dobi Cable Safe – Polyurethane Progress Ltd

Doble Dew – textiles – Maurice Phillips

DoBoy – R M Sealers Ltd

Docbox – Snopake Ltd

Docklands Light Railway – Light railway – Docklands Light Railway Ltd

Docmix – Broen Valves Ltd

Doctorcall – Doctorcall

Dod's – parliamentary reference book – Dod's Parliamentry Communications Ltd

Dodd's Group – 21st Century Logistics – Dodd's Group

DODGE – Wolds Engineering Services Ltd

Dodge – Bearings, Power Transmission Units – Sprint Engineering & Lubricant

Dodge – Mercury Bearings Ltd

Dodge – Harrier Fluid Power Ltd

Dodge – Baldor UK

Dodge Bearings – Race Industrial Products Ltd

Dodgebox – automated attendants – Storacall Engineering Ltd

***Dodson & Horrell** – Badcock & Evered

Dodson & Horrell Ltd – horse feed specialists – Dodson & Horrell Country Store

Doe – tennis courts and sports equipment – Doe Sport Ltd

Doeflex – British Vita plc

***Doepke (Germany)** – R.C.D.'s & M.C.B.'s – Doepke UK Ltd

Dog Bite – Slush Puppie Ltd

Dog Cages – vehicle dog cages – Hamster Baskets

Dog Magic – mechanical handling systems – Jervis B Webb Co. Ltd

Dog Mate – pet accessories – Pet Mate Ltd

Doga – torque reaction and measurement equipment – Baltec UK Ltd

Doherty Medical – medical & first aid furniture – Siddall & Hilton

Dolciano – steel bath – Ideal Standard Ltd

Dolling – Harrier Fluid Power Ltd

Dollinger – Harrier Fluid Power Ltd

Dolofil – dolomites – Omya UK Ltd

Dolphin – marine pumps – Hamworthy Waste Water plc

Dolphin – paint brushes – Whitaker & Sawyer Brushes Ltd

Dolphin Floating Strainers – land, sump, quarry drainage and pump protection – Megator Ltd

Dolplas – British Vita plc

Dom – door furniture – Allgood

Dom-Nemef-Corbin – patented cylinder systems – Ronis-Dom Ltd

Domae – consumer units – Schneider

Domain Guard – Mass Consultants Ltd

***Domaine Abel Garnier (France)** – Burgundy wines – O W Loeb & Co. Ltd

***Domaine Armand Rousseau (France)** – Burgundy wines – O W Loeb & Co. Ltd

Domaine Balland – wine – Rodney Densem Wines Ltd

Domaine Chatelus de la Roche – wine – Rodney Densem Wines Ltd

***Domaine de Courcel (France)** – Burgundy wines – O W Loeb & Co. Ltd

***Domaine de Montille (France)** – Burgundy wines – O W Loeb & Co. Ltd

***Domaine Dujac (France)** – Burgundy wines – O W Loeb & Co. Ltd

***Domaine Etienne Sauzet (France)** – Burgundy wines – O W Loeb & Co. Ltd

***Domaine Gagnard-Delagrange (France)** – Burgundy wines – O W Loeb & Co. Ltd

***Domaine Henri Gouges (France)** – Burgundy wines – O W Loeb & Co. Ltd

***Domaine Jean Pascal (France)** – Burgundy wines – O W Loeb & Co. Ltd

Domaine Juliette Avril – wine – Rodney Densem Wines Ltd

Domaine le Verger – wine – Rodney Densem Wines Ltd

Domaine les Chatelaines – wine – Rodney Densem Wines Ltd

Domaine Loberger – wine – Rodney Densem Wines Ltd

***Domaine Louis Michel (France)** – Chablis wines – O W Loeb & Co. Ltd

Domaine Masson Blondelet – wine – Rodney Densem Wines Ltd

Domaine Michel Mallard – wine – Rodney Densem Wines Ltd

***Domaine Michel Niellon (France)** – Burgundy wines – O W Loeb & Co. Ltd

Domaine Michel Servin – wine – Rodney Densem Wines Ltd

Domaine Prieure – wine – Rodney Densem Wines Ltd

***Domaine Ramonet (France)** – Burgundy wines – O W Loeb & Co. Ltd

***Domaine Saier (France)** – Burgundy wines – O W Loeb & Co. Ltd

***Domaine St. Pierre** – The Vintners Selection Ltd

Domange – Harrier Fluid Power Ltd

Dome – insulating bricks – D S F Refractories & Minerals Ltd

Domena – R G K UK Ltd

Domestic Circulators – compact/CP pumps – Circulating Pumps Ltd

Dometic InSight – Dometic UK Ltd

Domex 5 – low carbon bolster steel – Uddeholm Steel Stockholders

Domi – single lever or dual control mixers and twin flow fillers – Ideal Standard Ltd

Dominance – carpets – Penthouse Carpets Ltd

Dominator – CNC surface and creepfeed grinder – Jones & Shipman Grinding Ltd

Dominator – hose reels – Knowsley S K Ltd

***Dominici (Italy)** – ladies shoes – Ramostyle Ltd

Dominio – creative compositor for film – Quantel Ltd

Dominion – B P plc

Dominion – Harrier Fluid Power Ltd

Domino – jewellery castings – Weston Beamor Ltd

Domino – emergency lighting range – Lab Craft Ltd

Domino – rubber cistern – Thomas Dudley Ltd

DOMNICK HUNTER – Hydraulic & Offshore Supplies Ltd

Domnick Hunter – Trafalgar Tools

Domnick Hunter – Gustair Materials Handling Equipment Ltd

Domnick Hunter – Parker Dominic Hunter Ltd

***Don Ramos (Cuba, Jamaica, Europe and Honduras)** – cigars – Hunters & Frankau Ltd

Don Springs – springs & shapework – Don Springs Sheffield Ltd

Donald & Taylor – organic cotton wool – Synergy Healthcare plc

Donaldson – Harrier Fluid Power Ltd

DONALDSON FILTER COMPONENTS LTD/ULTRAFILTER – Hydraulic & Offshore Supplies Ltd

Donarbon – skip sales – Frimstone Ltd

Donati – Dale Lifting and Handling Equipment Specialists

Doncaster – field shelters – Browns of Wem Ltd

Doncasters Bramah – aircraft and aeroengineering fabrications in titanium and nickel alloys – Doncasters Structures Ltd

Doncasters Paralloy – centricast tubes and static fittings in specialist alloys – Doncasters Paralloy Ltd

DONGHUA – Chaintec Ltd

Donisthorpe – threads – William Gee Ltd

Donlite – building blocks – The Howard Group

Donn – S K Interiors Ltd

Donn – ceiling systems (suspended) – U S G UK Ltd

Donn DX Screw Fix – ceiling systems (suspended) – U S G UK Ltd

Donn Grid – suspension grid system – U S G UK Ltd

DONNOLDSON – Hydraulic & Offshore Supplies Ltd

Donny Mac – greetings cards – Hambledon Studios

Dontlock – safety device – L B B C Technologies

Dooby Duck – character – Roger Stevenson Ltd

Doodle Sticks – stencils – Helix Trading Ltd

Doodlebug – Ribbons, Buttons, Sequins – Art2Craft

Doon – stainless steel sink – Armitage Shanks Ltd

Door to Door Second Hand Clothes – Collecting door to door in West Midlands, East Yorkshire, North East England – College For International Cooperation & Development

Door to Door Second Hand Shoes – Collecting door to door in West Midlands, East Yorkshire, North East England – College For International Cooperation & Development

Doorfit – stockists and suppliers of architectural door fittings and garage doors, locksmiths and general builders, ironmongers – Doorfit Products Ltd

Doors & partition manufrs – Building Additions Ltd

Doortek – Enhanced security system – Pentagon Protection plc

Doosan – Birchfield Engineering Ltd

Doosan Daewoo – Mills C N C

Doosan,Merlo,Sanvik Rammer,Ausa – Plant and Construction Machinery sales and Service – Promac Solutions Ltd

Dopag – Aztech Components Ltd

Doppie – Direct on plastic printer with imaging electronics – Identilam plc

Dopplex Assist Range – Huntleigh Healthcare

Dopplex Printa – for use with Rd2, MD2 and FD2 – Huntleigh Healthcare

Dorchester – Atmospheric gas fired water heaters – Hamworthy Heating Ltd

Dorchester – limousine – Coleman Milne Ltd

Dorex – basin – Armitage Shanks Ltd

Dorgard – Safety Assured Ltd

***DORI (France)** – grass maintenance equipment and power barrows – Industrial Power Units Ltd

Dorian Soluble Oils – soluble oils synthetic and mineral based for metal cutting – Morris Lubricants

Doric – impression materials and modelling wax – Schottlander Dental Equipment Supplies

Dorin – semi-hermetic compressors and condensing units – Thermofrost Cryo plc

Dorin – Therma Group

Dorling Kindersley – children's and adults fiction and non-fiction - hardback and paperback – Penguin Books Ltd

Dorlux Beds – beds and mattresses – Dorlux Beds

Dorma – bed linen – Dawson Home Group Limited

Dorman – Trowell Plant Sales Ltd

Dorman Long Lintels – steel lintels – Wade Building Services Ltd

*Dormen Nuts – Mercia Fine Foods

Dormer – S J Wharton Ltd

Dormer – cutting tools – Bearwood Engineering Supplies

*Dormont – Mechline Developments Ltd

Dormy – UK Office Direct

Doro – UK Office Direct

Doro – lubricants – Chevron

Dörries – vertical turning machines, vertical machining centers – D S Technology UK Ltd

Dörries Scharmann – European Technical Sales Ltd

Dorsalure – insect attractants – International Pheromone Systems Ltd

Dorset – Try & Lilly Ltd

*Dorset Metal Spinning Services (United Kingdom) – sub-contract metal spinners – Dorset Metal Spinning Services

DORT – Depp oceanographic release transponder – Sonardyne International Ltd

Dorvic – shifting skates, ratchet jacks – Dorvic Engineering Ltd

Dosamatic – Mactenn Systems Ltd

Dosimag – electromagnetic flowmeter for high speed filling and batching – Endress Hauser Ltd

Dosmatic – Fertiliser Injectors – L S Systems Ltd

DOT – brand fasteners – Opas Southern Limited

Dot Markers (dot peen) – indent marking metals/plastics – Universal Marking Systems Ltd

Dots – carpets – Interface Europe Ltd

Double Delta – seal design – Trelleborg Ceiling Solutions Ltd

Double Disc Pumps – Alfa Laval Eastbourne Ltd

Double Duty (United Kingdom) – contract metal curtain track – Integra Products

Double Form – display and exhibition systems – RTD Systems Limited

Double Image Design Ltd – Complete Graphic Service – UK Safety Signs

Double Knitting 100g – Sirdar Spinning Ltd

Double Maxi – smoking kiln – Afos Ltd

Double Pantile – concrete – Sandtoft Holdings Ltd

Double R – foam core insulation boards – Celotex Ltd

Double R CW2000 – cavity wall insulation – Celotex Ltd

Double-R GA2000 – timber frame insulation and Pitched roof insulation – Celotex Ltd

Double Roman – concrete – Sandtoft Holdings Ltd

Double-safe – P D Interglas Technologies Ltd

Double Season – Yara UK It Ltd

Double Sharp – knives – Egginton Bros Ltd

Double Top – straight sliding door gear for wardrobe or cupboard doors – P C Henderson Ltd

Double Two – formal and evening shirts – Double Two Ltd

Double Two – shirts – The Wakefield Shirt Company Limited

Double Two – ladies – The Wakefield Shirt Company Limited

Double Two Collections – ladies blouses, dresses and soft suits – Double Two Ltd

Doublestore – rotating cabinets – Railex Filing Ltd

Douce-Hydro – spares – Bearwood Engineering Supplies

DOUGHBOY POOLS – SWIMMING POOLS – Discount Leisure UK ltd

Doughmaker – improvers – Allied Mills

Douglas – transformers and power supplies, DC and AC inverters, battery chargers and uninterruptable power supplies – Douglas Electronic Industries Ltd

Douglas Gill Ltd – lace manufacturers – Douglas Gill Ltd

Douglas Jackson Limited – Executive and Management Contact Centre, Call Centre and Customer Service recruitment consultancy – Douglas Jackson Ltd

Douglas-Kalmar – towbarless aircraft handling tractors – Douglas Equipment

Douglas-Kalmar - Douglas Tugmaster – Douglas Equipment

Douglas Tugmaster – towing tractors for the aircraft, airport, sea port, distribution & warehousing, industrial applications industries – Douglas Equipment

Doulton – domestic water filter – Fairey Industrial Ceramics

*Douwe Egberts – Aimia Foods

*Douwe Egberts – Douwe Egberts UK

Dove Tail – Monier Ltd

Dover Adscene – newspaper title – Kent Regional News & Media

Dover Express – newspaper title – Kent Regional News & Media

Doves Farm – Doves Farm Foods Ltd

Dow – County Construction Chemicals Ltd

Dow Corning – R W Greeff

Dow Corning – County Construction Chemicals Ltd

*Dow Corning (Belgium) – silicones and fluids – R D Taylor & Co. Ltd

Dow Corning – oils waxes and greases – AESpump

Dow Corning - sealants, Firestop - fire protection sealants, Painters Mate - decorators filler, Plumba - sealants, Trade Mate - sealants, QuickGrip - gap filling adhesive. – Dow Corning Ltd

Dow HDPE – Resinex UK Ltd

Dow LDPE – Resinex UK Ltd

DOWCLENE – Standard Industrial Systems Ltd

Dowlex – Resinex UK Ltd

DOWMAX – Hydraulic & Offshore Supplies Ltd

Down & Francis – structural, secondary fabricated steelwork – Down & Francis Industrial Products Ltd

Downel – fixed and variable angle SWASN plate hydraulic pumps and motors – Moog Aircraft Group

Downflow Containment Booths – dust booth – Extract Technology

Downland – pillows and duvets – Downland Bedding Co. Ltd

Downland – machinery and materials for glass fibre industry – K & C Mouldings England Ltd

Downland – concrete plain tile – Monier Ltd

Downlights – high efficiency and low glare down lighting – Selux UK Ltd

Downs Syndrome Screening Service – fetal testing service – University Of Leeds

Downtown – furnishing superstores – Oldrids Co. Ltd

Dowty – Hydraulic Component & Systems Ltd

DOWTY – Hydraulic & Offshore Supplies Ltd

*Dox (Germany) – brush polishers, spray dampers and reel handling equipment – Pulp & Paper Machinery Ltd

Dox Anode – inorganic zinc silicate primers – Leighs Paints

Doza – fishing tackle – Drennan International Ltd

DP10™ – GGB UK

DP11™ – GGB UK

DP31™ – GGB UK

DP4-B™ – GGB UK

DP4™ – GGB UK

DPC II – digital console – Digico UK Ltd

DPC Pumps – Alfa Laval Eastbourne Ltd

DPG – Capex Office Interiors

DProbe – Emulator – Hitex UK Ltd

DPU – industrial sectional door – Hörmann (UK) Ltd

DR BREIT – Hydraulic & Offshore Supplies Ltd

Dr. Daq – Pico Technology Ltd

Dr Marten – S J Wharton Ltd

Dr Martens – D S Safety

Dr Martins – Knighton Tool Supplies

Dr Martins – Global Fasteners Ltd

Dr Plumb – briar pipe – Cadogan

Dr Whites – sanitary protection – Lil-lets UK Ltd

Dr Whites Allnights – sanitary protection – Lil-lets UK Ltd

Dr Whites Contour – sanitary protection – Lil-lets UK Ltd

Dr Whites Maxi – sanitary protection – Lil-lets UK Ltd

Dr Whites Panty Pads – sanitary protection – Lil-lets UK Ltd

Dr Whites Secrets – sanitary protection – Lil-lets UK Ltd

DR128 – digital zone mixer – Allen & Heath Ltd

DR66 – digital zone mixer – Allen & Heath Ltd

Draefern – employment business contract labour – Right For Staff

Draeger – Brathalyzer Direct

Draftex – European Technical Sales Ltd

Drager – Brathalyzer Direct

Dragon – electric steam boilers – Fulton Boiler Works Ltd

Dragon – screens – Metso Minerals UK Ltd

Dragon – logo, fire and smoke seals and other fire protection products – Intumescent Seals

Dragon – firelighters – Tiger Tim Products Ltd

Dragonair HLO – industrial oil fired warm air heaters – Elan-Dragonair Ltd

Dragonair HNG – industrial gas fired warm air heaters – Elan-Dragonair Ltd

Dragoon – fibre bonded carpet – Heckmondwike FB

Dragoon – export ale – Wells & Young's Brewing Co.

Drain and Gas Bagstoppers – pipe stopper – Sarco Stopper Ltd

Drain-medic – Drain cleaning & Plumbing repairs – Drain-Medic plumbing

Drain Pan Pump – Condensate Removal Pump – E D C International Ltd

Drainage Center – Wolseley UK

Drainaway – Grundfos Pumps Ltd

Drainseal – Darcy Products Ltd

Drais (Germany) – milling – Orthos Engineering Ltd

Draka Cel Label (1) – British Vita plc

Draka Cel Label (2) – British Vita plc

Draka Cel Sterschuim – British Vita plc

Draka Polyaether & Logo – British Vita plc

Draka Welding Cables – European Technical Sales Ltd

Drakacel – British Vita plc

Drake International – human resources consultancy – Drake Medox Nursing

Drake & Scull Airport Services Ltd – Facilities management – Emcor UK plc

Drake & Scull Engineering – building services engineers – Emcor UK plc

Drake & Scull Engineering (north) Ltd – Building Services Engineers – Emcor UK plc

Drake & Scull International – building services engineers – Emcor UK plc

Drake & Scull Technical Services Ltd – facilities management – Emcor UK plc

Drakes – UK Office Direct

Drakes Pride – bowling green bowls, bowls bags and accessories – E A Clare & Son Ltd

Dralo – Huck Nets UK Ltd

Dranetz-BMI (U.S.A.) – power quality analysers – I M H Technologies Ltd

DRANETZ-BMI Power Quality Analysers, Electrotek - software, Satec - digital energy meters, Dent Instruments, energy loggers, BTech Inc Battery Validation Systems – I M H Technologies Ltd

Draper – Gem Tool Hire & Sales Ltd

*Draper (U.S.A.) – projection screens – A V M Ltd

Draper – hand tools – Arrow Supply Co. Ltd

Draper – Central C N C Machinery Ltd

DRAPER – Hydraulic & Offshore Supplies Ltd

Draper Glastonbury – sheepskin footwear, casual walking shoes and sandals – R J Draper & Co. Ltd

DRAPER TOOLS – Hydraulic & Offshore Supplies Ltd

Draper Tools – tool distributors – Draper Tools Ltd

Draper Tools – Trafalgar Tools

Draper Tools – Fieldway Supplies Ltd

Drawbars – range 3.STGTU 24T GTW – Abel Demountable Systems Ltd

Drawlock – gas pipe fittings from mains to meter – George Fischer Sales Ltd

Drawmer – professional audio equipment manufacturers – Drawmer Electronics Ltd

Drawmet – stainless steel clad aluminium profiles – Drawn Metal Ltd

Drawn Metal – stainless steel, bronze, brass and copper clad timber sections – Drawn Metal Ltd

Drawsol – drawing oils – D A Stuart Ltd

Drawspin – textile processing aid – Benjamin R Vickers & Sons Ltd

Drawstring Bags – bin liners with draw tape closures – Cedo Ltd

DRAX17 – video multiplexer for CCTV systems – Tecton Ltd

Dreadnought – high speed steel bars and forgings – Abbey Forged Products Ltd

Dreadnought – fibre bonded carpet – Heckmondwike FB

Dreadnought – plain clay roofing tiles – Hinton Perry Davenhill

Dream Lovers – bed linen – Kipfold Ltd

Dream Vision – Lamphouse Ltd

Dreamcast – video game consoles – Sega Europe Ltd

Dreamnight – spring interior and divan – Airsprung Furniture Group plc

Dreams 'N' Drapes – ready made curtains and bed linen – J Rosenthal & Son Ltd

Dreamscene – bed linen – Pin Mill Textiles Ltd

Dreh – Baxi Group

*Drei-s (Germany) – piercing punches and ejector pins – Welwyn Tool Group Ltd

Drenchwear – clothing – Drennan International Ltd

Drennan – fishing tackle class 28 – Drennan International Ltd

Dresinate – emulsifiers – Hercules Holding Ii Ltd

Dresinol – dispersions – Hercules Holding Ii Ltd

Dresser Clar – Harrier Fluid Power Ltd

*Dreumex (Netherlands) – hand cleaners - industrial – Cleenol Group Ltd

Drewclean – descalants – Ashland UK

Drewfloc – flocculants – Ashland UK

Drewgard – scale preventers – Ashland UK

Drewplus – anti-foaming agents – Ashland UK

Drewsperse – scale inhibitor – Ashland UK

Drexelbrook Engineering – RF admittance level systems – Able Instruments & Controls Ltd

Dri – Avalon and Lynwood

Dri – safety clothing – Bearwood Engineering Supplies

Dri-Foam – dry foam shampoo for rotary machines – Evans Vanodine International plc

DRI Pumps – Alfa Laval Eastbourne Ltd

Driffield Times – newspaper – Yorkshire Regional Newspapers Ltd

Drift Beta – drift reducing venturi – Hypro Eu Ltd

DriftBETA – drift reducing venturi nozzle – Hypro Eu Ltd

Drill-Carb – drilling mud – Ben Bennett JR Ltd

Drill Track – Horizontal boring tracking system – Radio Detection

Drimaster – anti-condensation unit – Nuaire Ltd

DrinkPac – instant drink capsule – Drinkmaster Ltd

Drivall – post and stake driver and hand tools – Drivall Ltd

***Drivall (New Zealand)** – electric fence systems – Drivall Ltd

Drivall – wire strainers – Drivall Ltd

Drive – current and voltage transducers – Northern Design Ltd

Drive-Ins – shoes – Newmans Footwear Ltd

Drive2arrive – 24 hour Light Haulage Services – Drive2arrive Light Haulage Services Ltd

Drivesert – fastenings – Tappex Thread Inserts Ltd

Drivesert - Flexiarm - Himould - Malesert - Multisert - Pushert - Foamsert - Microbarb - Sonicert - Suresert - Tappex - Trisert - Vandlgard - Trisert 3 - Dedsert – Tappex Thread Inserts Ltd

Driving force leisure – chemical seed and fertilizer (07071) 226622 – Pareto Golf Ltd

Drivloc – electronic DC injection braking system – R D M Industrial Services Ltd

Drizit – Cullen Metcalfe & Co. Ltd

Drizit – chemical, oil and maintenance absorbents – Darcy Products Ltd

Drizit - Serviron - Tracklube - Wetlube - Wirelube - Drainseal - Hydrotemp - Brickseal - Dammit – Darcy Products Ltd

DRM Pumps – Alfa Laval Eastbourne Ltd

Dromana Estate – House Of Townend

Dron Dickson Abacus – steel lighting columns, steel raising and lowering columns, shelters and covered walkways, steel fencing, illuminated and non-illuminated bollards, outdoor lighting design, street furniture, flood lights, luminears and amenity lighting – Abacus Lighting Ltd

Droop & Rein – portal machining centers, high speed machining centers – D S Technology UK Ltd

Drop Brim Panama – Try & Lilly Ltd

Drop Stop – Waiter's Friend Company Ltd

Drop Stop – Birchgrove Products

Drott – Harrier Fluid Power Ltd

***DRS Infoscan System (U.S.A.)** – complete desktop data capture solution (OHR,OCR,ICR) – D R S Data Services Ltd

Drube – Forward Chemicals Ltd

Druces & Attlee – solicitors – Druces LLP

Druces International – an alliance of independent European law firms offering business worldwide a one stop law shop doorway to Europe – Druces LLP

Druck – Halcyon Solutions

Druck – pressure measuring equipment – G E Sensing

Druck – Direct Instrument Hire Ltd

Drugalysers; Nicoscreen;Draeger alcohol tests – Drug and alcohol testing, training and consultancy services for occupational health services – Modern Health Systems

Drum – roll-your-own tobacco – Imperial Tobacco Group PLC

Drum Closures – Drum Closures Ltd

Drum Gold – roll-your-own tobacco – Imperial Tobacco Group PLC

Drum Major – tap – Worldwide Dispensers

Drum Tap – tap – Worldwide Dispensers

DrumKart – made from 100% polyethylene; the drum trolley is an ideal mobile dispensing unit and sump with a total capacity of 250 litres. – Jonesco (Preston) Ltd

Drummer Boy – hand sheep shears – Burgon & Ball Ltd

Drury – The Coffee Machine Company

DRX – fishing tackle – Drennan International Ltd

Dry-Cargo – Cullen Metcalfe & Co. Ltd

Dry-Cargo, Drizit, Hatch Tape. – Cullen Metcalfe & Co. Ltd

Dry Dek – floating stage (demountable) – Stage Systems Ltd

Dry Gloves – sailing, waterskiing and windsurfing gloves – Yachting Instruments Ltd

Dry Gummed – Mcnaughton James Paper Group Ltd

Dry Honer – fine abrasive blast mk – Wheelabrator Group

Dry Mitts – sailing, waterskiing and windsurfing mitts – Yachting Instruments Ltd

Dry Ram Cements – high temperature refractories – Saint Gobain Industrial Ceramics Ltd

Dry Tech – Monier Ltd

Drycol – leather dressing oil – Benjamin R Vickers & Sons Ltd

Dryerpac – dryer and dust collecting equipment – B G Europa UK Ltd

***Dryfat** – U F A C UK Ltd

DryFix – stainless steel remedial masonry connector – Helifix Ltd

Dryflex (U.S.A.) – teat sealant – Delaval

Drygen – G E Healthcare

Drylens – footwear – Russell & Bromley Ltd

Drylin – Igus (UK) Ltd

Drylok – glazing gasket system – Tremco Illbruck Ltd

Drylon – microcellular waterproof film with breathing properties, incorporating in glove linings – Michael Lupton Associates Ltd

Drysdale Heather Twist – Ryalux Carpets Ltd

Drysdale Twist – Ryalux Carpets Ltd

Drysocks – sailing, waterskiing and windsurfing socks – Yachting Instruments Ltd

Drystar – high vacuum pump – B O C Edwards

Drystar – vacuum pumps – Boc Gases Ltd

Drystick – screen printing adhesives – Fujifilm Sericol Ltd

Drytek – low melt films for encapsulation & lamination – D & K Europe Ltd

Drytek - Accufeed - Accumatic – D & K Europe Ltd

Drywite – peeled potato preservative – Drywite Ltd

DS Aircraft – machining centers – D S Technology UK Ltd

DS™ – GGB UK

DS2000 - ICCS Product – Integrated communications control system – Capita Secure Information Solutions

DS2000 - ICCS Product: Integrated communications control system. – Capita Secure Information Solutions

DSC – Wireless alarm system – Eagle Security Solutions Ltd

DSC 204 F1 Phoenix – Netzsch-Instruments

DSG lathes – Phil Geesin Machinery Ltd

DSi (United Kingdom) – Deep Si etching for MEMS & wafer level packaging – Aviza Technology UK Ltd

DSN – synathetic diamond - saw diamond abrasives – Diamond Detectors

DST – Driver Safety Training (Defensive, Off road, Desert Driving) – HR4 Ltd

DTAS – Yokota UK

DTS 2000 – pipeline communications and renewable power supplies – Eaton Aerospace Ltd

DTS LTD – Dispense Technology Services Ltd

DU – GGB UK

DU B – GGB UK

Du Pont – Letchford Supplies Ltd

Du Pont – Helman Workwear

du-Pre P.L.C. – supply, install and maintain telephone systems and networks – Du Pre plc

Dual Concentric – loudspeakers – Tannoy Group Ltd

Dual-Melt – medium frequency simultaneous power control units for induction furnaces – Inductotherm Europe Ltd

Dual Perfection – eye/brow shaper – Elizabeth Arden

Dual-Snap (U.S.A.) – pressure & temperature switches – Custom Control Sensors International

***Dual Stage Filtration Systems (U.S.A.)** – ceramic foam systems for cast shops and foundries – Porvair plc

Dual-Trak – medium frequency simultaneous power control units for induction furnaces – Inductotherm Europe Ltd

DualAir – heating and cooling unit – Robert Gordon Europe Ltd

Dualcase – aluminium sign systems – Universal Components

Dualcom – Christie Intruder Alarms Ltd

Dualcom Plus – Christie Intruder Alarms Ltd

Dualform – instant tooling concept – Joseph Rhodes Ltd

Dualine – Lubeline Lubricating Equipment

***Dualit** – Court Catering Equipment Ltd

Dualit – automatic commercial toasters – Dualit Ltd

Dualok – pulleys-drives – The Zerny Engineering Co. Ltd

Dualscan (United Kingdom) – flame viewing system – Hamworthy Combustion Engineering Ltd

Dualstat – immersion heater thermostat – Otter Controls Ltd

Dualstrip – intumescent smoke and fire strip – Dufaylite Developments Ltd

Dualway – Hughes Pumps Ltd

Duba – office furniture – Railex Filing Ltd

Dubilier – brand capacitors – M P E Ltd

DuBOIS – Dubois Ltd

DucaPlex – solid polythylene custom extruded sheet. – D S Smith Correx

***Ducarbo (Denmark)** – carbide tipped drills – Tekmat Ltd

Ducati – Harrier Fluid Power Ltd

Ducato – Printed fabrics – Zoffany

Duchess – washbasin and closet – Ideal Standard Ltd

Duchess – tufted velour – Victoria Carpets Ltd

Duchy Original – biscuit – Walkers Shortbread Ltd

Duck – UK Office Direct

Duckfoot – garden cultivator – Burgon & Ball Ltd

Duckhams – B P plc

Duckhams QTT – motor lubricants – B P plc

Ducktile Stourbridge Coldmills – cold rolled steel – Ductile Stourbridge Cold Mills Ltd

Duct QF – Dantherm Filtration Ltd

DUCTER – electrical measuring devices - low resistance ohmmeters – Megger Ltd

Ductgard – combined smoke and fire damper for air conditioning ductwork – Gilberts Blackpool Ltd

Ductile & Grey – Iron Pipework – Glenfield Valves Ltd

Ductmaster – axial fan – Nuaire Ltd

Ductmate – air ducting accessories – Ductmate (Europe) Ltd

Ductwrap and Ductslab – pipes, ducts, industrial noise control and original equipment – Rockwool Rockpanel B V

Dudley – cisterns – Thomas Dudley Ltd

Dudley – Secure Holidays

Duette – kitchen furniture – Moores Furniture Group

Duette – special effect paint rollers and paints – Akzonobel

Duetto – luxury motor caravan – Auto Sleepers Ltd

Dufaylite – honeycomb core – Dufaylite Developments Ltd

***Dufour (France)** – universal milling machines – Capital Equipment & Machinery Ltd

Dugard Eagle – CNC lathes – C Dugard Ltd Machine Tools

Dugard Eagle – V.M.C. – C Dugard Ltd Machine Tools

Dugdale – woollen and trimming merchants – Dugdale Bros & Co. Ltd

Dukane – Lamphouse Ltd

Duke Brand Herb Tea – laxative – Bell Sons & Co. Ltd

Dukes – sandstone – Realstone Ltd

Dulcotest – testing equipment – Bearwood Engineering Supplies

Dulevo – Harrier Fluid Power Ltd

Dulux – decorative paints – Akzonobel

Dulux – Www.Safetysignsonline.Co.Uk

Dulux Dog, The – decorative paints – Akzonobel

Dulwich design – leather jewel boxes – L C Designs Ltd

Duncan Baraclough (United Kingdom) – Worsted Mens Suiting Fabric – John Foster Ltd

Duncan street enterprises – logistics and rail terminal operations – Creative Logistics

Dundas Building Co. – Walker Timber Ltd

Dundee Courier – D C Thomson & Co. Ltd

Dunfermline Building Society – lending & investing – Dunfermline Building Society

Dunfermline Press & West of Fife Advertiser – newspaper – Dunfermline Press

Dung – European Technical Sales Ltd

Dungeonquest – games, models, miniatures and war games – Games Workshop Ltd

Dunham Bush – Therma Group

Dunhill – cigarettes – British American Tobacco plc

Dunhill (Longtail) – lighters, smokers requisites, toiletries, leather goods, watches and jewellery – Alfred Dunhill Ltd

Duni Banquet Line – most exclusive and heavy weight material – Duni Ltd

Dunilin – a unique material with a woven effect – Duni Ltd

Dunira Strategy – Tourism Consultants – Dunira Strategy Ltd

Dunisilk – a core product in a wide choice of sizes, colours and designs – Duni Ltd

Dunitex – a long life wipeable textile material – Duni Ltd

Dunkeld Atholl Brose – Scotch whisky liquer – Gordon & Macphail

Dunks – shoe care products – Dunkelman & Son Ltd

Dunlop – hose – Cebo UK Ltd

Dunlop – Wealden Tyres Ltd

Dunlop – golf equipment – Dunlop Slazenger International Ltd

Dunlop – guitar accessories and effects units – John Hornby Skewes & Co. Ltd

Dunlop – slippers, sandals & shoes – D Jacobson & Sons Ltd

Dunlop – spares & equipment – Bearwood Engineering Supplies

Dunlop Carry Bags – golf bags – Dunlop Slazenger International Ltd

Dunlop D D H 110 – golf balls – Dunlop Slazenger International Ltd

Dunlop D D H-O C G – club – Dunlop Slazenger International Ltd

Dunlop D D H Tour – Club – Dunlop Slazenger International Ltd

Dunlop Graphic Products – printers' blanket – Duco International Ltd

DUNLOP HIFLEX HYDRAULICS FITTINGS – Hydraulic & Offshore Supplies Ltd

DUNLOP HYDRAULIC HOSE – Hydraulic & Offshore Supplies Ltd

DUNLOP INDUSTRIAL HOSE – Hydraulic & Offshore Supplies Ltd

Dunlop Insertouch – Putter – Dunlop Slazenger International Ltd

Dunlop Stand Bag – golf bags – Dunlop Slazenger International Ltd

Dunlop Titanium – golf balls – Dunlop Slazenger International Ltd

Dunlop Tyres – Goodyear Dunlop UK Ltd

Dunlop Vision Putter – Putter – Dunlop Slazenger International Ltd

Dunlow – oil heaters – Ormandy Rycroft

Dunphy – oil and natural gas, LPG and waste and sludge gas burners and dual fuel burners, boiler control panels, gas boosters, fuel oil pumps, electronic fuel and air ratio controllers and data read-out – Dunphy Combustion Ltd

Dunsley – domestic central heating equipment – Dunsley Heat Ltd

Duo-Cam (United Kingdom) – sprag clutches – Cross & Morse

Duo-Chek – valves – Crane Process Flow Technology Ltd

Duo-Chek – Crane Stockham Valve Ltd

Duo-Chek/Flow Seal/Centerline/Noz-Chek – Crane Stockham Valve Ltd

***Duo-Fast (Worldwide)** – nailers, staplers, screwdrivers and collated fastenings – Duo-Fast

Duo-Firm – spring interior and divan – Airsprung Furniture Group plc

Duo heat – Glen Dimplex UK Ltd

Duo Plan – paper – G F Smith

Duodeck – timber boardings – R T E UK Ltd

Duodex – soft and hard laminated rubber lining – Dexine Rubber Co. Ltd

Duodisc – Exaclair Ltd
Duoduct – laboratory equipment – Leec Ltd
Duofast – I T W Constructions Productions
Duoflo – double chambered low vacuum dewatering unit – Heimbach UK
Duoflow – central heating control system with 3 port valve and wiring centre – Sunvic Controls Ltd
Duofold – performance clothing – Dawson International plc
Duoglide – two stage, split casing, centrifugal pumps for water supply and distribution and general pumping duties – Weir Group Senior Executives Pension Trust Ltd
Duojet – K S B Ltd
Duolaser – high white laser and copier paper – International Paper Equipment Finance LP
Duolastik – Trelleborg Industrial A V S Ltd
Duoloc – compression fitting (single ring - stainless steel) – Waverley Brownall Ltd
Duon – Komet Ltd
Duoplex – engines – Quality Monitoring Instruments Q M I
Duopress – Grundfos Pumps Ltd
DuoRock Roofing Boards – flat roofing boards – Rockwool Rockpanel B V
Duotex – double palm leather gloves – Bennett Safetywear
Duothane – multi component heat cure polyurethane resins – Chemical Innovations Ltd
Duovac 300 – dual vacuum milking system – Delaval
Dupar – lift products – Dewhurst plc
Dupical – perfume speciality – Quest International UK Ltd
Duplex – double spring unit – Airsprung Furniture Group plc
Duplex – modular building system – Portakabin Ltd
Duplex XC – premium quality engine oils – Morris Lubricants
Duplex-Z Blades – Morton Mixers & Blenders Ltd
Duplo – motor driven siren – Signals Ltd
***Duplo (Japan)** – graphic arts and office machinery – Duplo International Ltd
***DUPLO (Denmark)** – pre-school constructional toys – Lego UK Ltd
Duplo – sliding partitions – Becker Sliding Partitions Ltd
Duplo International Ltd – Head distribution company for Duplo products across EMEA region.
DUPLOMATIC SRL – Hydraulic & Offshore Supplies Ltd
Duplon – Komet Ltd
Duplus Domes Lightspan – roof lights – Duplus Architectural Systems Ltd
Dupont – Rutherfords
Dupont – performance chemical – G B R Technology Ltd
dupont – AESpump
Dupont Clysar – Packaging films – Wrapid Manufacturing Ltd
DupreVermiculite – Minelco Ltd
Dura – UK Office Direct
Dura fencing – Security – Darfen Durafencing Ltd
DURA INDUSTRIAL HOSE – Hydraulic & Offshore Supplies Ltd
Dura TEC – solid-state sealed peltier devices range from 28w to 70w heat pumping – Marlow Industries Europe
Durabla (U.S.A.) – axial guided check valve – Alexander Cardew Ltd
Durable – UK Office Direct
Durable – roofing & structural waterproofing – Durable Contracts Ltd
Durable Dot – press stud fastener – Opas Southern Limited
Duraboot (United Kingdom) – CV boot kit (stretchy) – Bailcast Ltd
Duracell – S J Wharton Ltd
Duracell – Gem Tool Hire & Sales Ltd
Duracell – batteries – John Hornby Skewes & Co. Ltd
Duracell – UK Office Direct
Duracell – Alkaline batteries – Halcyon Solutions
DURACELL – Groves Batteries
Duracet – disperse dyes – Town End Leeds plc
Duraclean – long lasting, durable coating for public access areas – Tor Coatings Ltd
Duraclean – hard surface cleaner – Unico Ltd
Duraclean Aseptic – hygiene coatings – Tor Coatings Ltd
Duracon – connectors, micro miniature and cable assemblies – Cinch Connectors Ltd
Duractive – reactive dyes – Town End Leeds plc
DURAD – Hydraulic & Offshore Supplies Ltd
Duradec – polyurethane shaped & contoured edgilgs – Havelock Europa plc
Duradec – textured wall finish – Duradec Wales Ltd
Duradon – 100% synthetic sailcloth – The British Millerain Company Ltd
Durafan – industrial plastic fan – APMG Ltd
Durafill – magnesium silicate paper filler – Akzo Nobel Chemicals Holdings Ltd
***Durafoam (Netherlands)** – wall covering – B N International
Durafoil – wear-resistant foil blade – Heimbach UK
***Durafort (Netherlands)** – wall covering – B N International
Durafrax – high temperature refractories – Saint Gobain Industrial Ceramics Ltd
Duraglas – reinformed thermoplastic substate – Bribex
DuraGrade – high wear resistant steel gauge blocks – Alan Browne Gauges Ltd
Duragrit – Abrasive burrs for wood carvers – The Toolpost
Duragun – air operated CV boot fitting tool – Bailcast Ltd
Durahide – binders polypropylene – Office Depot UK
Duralac – jointing compound – Llewellyn Ryland Ltd
Duralan – pre-metallised dyes – Town End Leeds plc
Duralast – filters/equipment – Bearwood Engineering Supplies
Duralife – polyester finish – Crittall Windows Ltd
Duralin – Publishing Paper – Mcnaughton James Paper Group Ltd
Duraline – spares & equipment – Bearwood Engineering Supplies
Duraline – fire hose – Angus Fire
Duraline – asbestos-free coreless induction melting furnace – Inductotherm Europe Ltd
Duraloft – British Vita plc
Duralon – plastic folders binders – Office Depot UK
Duralon – hair combs and sundry items – John Dobson Milnthorpe Ltd
Duralum – aluminium oxide – Washington Mills Electro Minerals Ltd
Duralum - Blastite - Silcaride - Dynamag - Duramul - Durazon. – Washington Mills Electro Minerals Ltd
Durameter – electric metering pump – Haskel Europe Ltd
Duramic – ceramic wear resistant dewatering elements – Heimbach UK
Duramine – acid dye stuffs – Town End Leeds plc
Duramould – British Vita plc
Duramould – polyurethane for mould making – Dow Hyperlast
Duramul – fused white mullite – Washington Mills Electro Minerals Ltd
***Duran (Germany)** – laboratory glassware, glass tubing and glass process plant and pipeline – Schott UK Ltd
Durantine – direct dye stuffs – Town End Leeds plc
Durap – British Vita plc
Durapac – co-polymer foam packaging – Foam Engineers Ltd
***Durapack (Germany)** – glass structured packing – Schott UK Ltd
Durapave – concrete block paving – Brooke Concrete Products Ltd
Durapel – leather dyes – Town End Leeds plc
Durapipe – thermoplastic pipe fittings & valve manufacturers – Glynwed Pipe Systems Ltd
Durapipe – Southern Valve & Fitting Co. Ltd
Durapipe – pipework systems – Davis Industrial Plastics Ltd
***Duraplac (Brazil)** – decorative hardboard – Price & Pierce Softwoods Ltd
Duraplas – Wholesale Welding Supplies Ltd
Duraplug – plug adaptors – M K Electric Ltd
Duraseal – sealing film – Radleys
Duraspring System – spring interior and divan – Airsprung Furniture Group plc
Durastrength – pvc impact modifier – Atosina UK Ltd
***Durasystems (U.S.A.)** – floor cleaning machines – C S A Cleaning Equipment
Duratax – John Hunt Bolton Ltd
Duratec – industrial sectional door – Hörmann (UK) Ltd
***Duratex (Brazil)** – standard hardboard – Price & Pierce Softwoods Ltd
***Duratherm (Germany)** – high temperature and corrosion resistant spring alloy – Rolfe Industries
Durazec – zinc-nickel alloy electro-coated steels with one micrometre of organic coating – Corus U K Ltd
Durazon – monoclinic zirconia – Washington Mills Electro Minerals Ltd
Durbal – European Technical Sales Ltd
Durbar – non-slip raised-pattern steel plates – Corus U K Ltd
Durehete – high strength bolting and stainless steel high temperature application – Corus Engineering Steels
Durelast – British Vita plc
Durelast – polyurethanes for table edging – Dow Hyperlast
Durham – paint driers – Rockwood Pigments
Durham – waterproof clothing – J Barbour & Sons Ltd
Durham CA – coatings additives – Rockwood Pigments
Durham-Duplex – industrial razor blades and machine knives – Durham Duplex
Durite – automotive electrical parts – Gordon Equipments Ltd
Durite Canterbury Spar – multi-coloured calcined flint – Brett Specialised Aggregates
Durive Instant-Lay Macadams – bagged macadams – Brett Specialised Aggregates
Durnburg – spares & equipment – Bearwood Engineering Supplies
Duro – paper for computer plotting/marking/pattern – Eastman Staples Ltd
Duro-Pallet – general industrial plastic pallet. – D S Smith Correx
Durocast – castable refractories – D S F Refractories & Minerals Ltd
Durogloss (United Kingdom) – Acrylic Capped ABS for Furniture Industry – Athlone Extrusions (UK) Ltd
Duropaque – screen printed self adhesive labels – Sessions Of York
Durosan – indoor (bathroom grade) acrylic capped ABS – Athlone Extrusions (UK) Ltd
Durosil – plastic mouldable refractory materials – D S F Refractories & Minerals Ltd
Durostone (Germany) – composite laminates – Roechling Engineering Plastics Ltd
Durosun – outdoor acrylic capped ABS – Athlone Extrusions (UK) Ltd
Dursley – luxury motor caravan – Auto Sleepers Ltd
***Durunyl (Netherlands)** – wall paper – B N International
Durus – gauge glasses – J B Treasure & Co. Ltd
Durwood – weaving loom shuttles – Pilkingtons Ltd
Duscovent – dust extraction and ventilation equipment – Duscovent Engineering Ltd
Dusfilt – shake cleaning collectors – Duscovent Engineering Ltd
Dusjet – reverse air collectors – Duscovent Engineering Ltd
Dusk – cream – Reckitt Benckiser plc
Dusk – special occasion and evening wear for younger set – Frank Usher Group
Dusmatic – dust control units – Duscovent Engineering Ltd
Duspray – wet collectors – Duscovent Engineering Ltd
Dust Covers – PVC and neoprene – Plastic Mouldings Ltd
Dusterloh – Slow Speed/High Torque Radial Piston Motors – J B J Techniques Ltd
Dusterloh – hydraulic motors – Parker Hannisin plc
DUSTERLOH Gmbh – Hydraulic & Offshore Supplies Ltd
Dustguard – heavy duty solvent based epoxy dustproofing sealer – Conren Ltd
Dustguard Antistat – heavy duty solvent based antistatic epoxy sealer – Conren Ltd
Dustmaster – refuse collectors – Tipmaster Ltd
Dustrap – particle filter for electronic and electrical enclosures – Emcel Filters Ltd
Dustrax – dust collectors – Dustraction Ltd
Dutch Light – Peritys Greenhouses
Dutral (Italy) – ethylene propylene rubber – Polimeri Europa Ltd
Dutton Forshaw – motor factor – Dutton Forshaw Ltd
Dutyman – hinged gate actuator – Frontier Pitts Ltd
Duxbak – waterproof maps – Harvey Map Services Ltd
DV/DH – direct fired gas fired unit heater – Nordair Niche
DV/DH – direct fired gas fired unit heater – Nordair Niche
DVD RW Teac – Tekdata Distribution Ltd
DVDiscpac – The London Fancy Box Company Ltd
DVE – power supply – Stontronics Ltd
DVON Audio – pro quality Hand held and Tie clip radio mics, Push to talk conference mics – Turnaround 360
DX – GGB UK
DX 10 with DuraStrong™ technology – GGB UK
DX-B™ – GGB UK
DX2000 – dairy chemicals – Delaval
Dyacid – equalising dyes for wool fibre – Brenntag Colours Ltd
Dyactive – reactive dyestuffs for cellulosic fibres – Brenntag Colours Ltd
Dyalan – premetallised dyes for wool, nylon and leather – Brenntag Colours Ltd
Dyckerhoff Black Label – oilwell cement – Cebo UK Ltd
Dyckoff Shackleton (United Kingdom) – Worsted Mens Suiting Fabric – John Foster Ltd
Dyclear/Hydroclear – reduction cleaning agents for polyester – Brenntag Colours Ltd
Dycon – valves – Dynamic Controls Ltd
Dyebrick – Color stain for Brick – Dyebrick
Dyescan – fluorescent tracer liquid used in peenscan process for coverage determination – Metal Improvement Co.
Dykor – Chemical resistant coatings – Whitford Ltd
Dylachem – textile auxiliary chemicals – S T R UK Ltd
Dylan – washable shrink-resistant wool – S T R UK Ltd
Dylan Works – programming language – Global Graphics Software Ltd
Dylev – levelling agents for acid dyestuffs applied to nylon fabric – Brenntag Colours Ltd
Dymax – pumps – Charles Austen Pumps Ltd
Dymel – aerosol propellant – Du Pont UK Ltd
Dymerex – dimerised rosin acid – Hercules Holding Ii Ltd
Dymet – manufacturera of tungsten carbide as sintered and finish ground wear parts & cutting tools to customer requirements – Dymet Alloys
Dymo – UK Office Direct
Dyna – slide up to date control boards – Signal Business Systems Ltd
Dyna-Fog – thermal fogging machine and machine for converting chemicals into mists, fogs and sprays – Fargro
Dyna Mobe – Office Seating – Bucon Ltd
Dynabraid – Sal Abrasives Technologies
Dynadrive – fuel efficient gearbox and final drive semi synthetic lubricant – Castrol UK Ltd
Dynafile – Gustair Materials Handling Equipment Ltd
***Dynafor (France)** – L.C.D. load indicators – Tractel UK Ltd
Dynagex – P5 permitted explosive – Orica UK Ltd

Dynahoe – Harrier Fluid Power Ltd

Dynalec – marine control system – Rolls Royce Marine Electrical Systems Ltd

Dynalight – R Bance & Co. Ltd

Dynallox – Dynamic Ceramic Ltd

Dynamag – mag oxide – Washington Mills Electro Minerals Ltd

Dynamax – SAE 10W/40 part synthetic fuel efficient heavy duty diesel engine oil – Castrol UK Ltd

Dynamic – Harrier Fluid Power Ltd

Dynamic Controls – valves and BVMI process engineering valves – Dynamic Controls Ltd

Dynamic Logic (ITT Flygt) – Halcyon Solutions

DYNAMIC VALVES - DYVAL SERVOS – Hydraulic & Offshore Supplies Ltd

Dynamics – Interface Europe Ltd

Dynamik – Gem Tool Hire & Sales Ltd

Dynamite – darts – Unicorn Products Ltd

Dynapac – A T Wilde & Son Ltd

Dynapac – Harrier Fluid Power Ltd

Dynapac – asphalt pavers, vibrating rollers and other light vibrating plant – Metso Minerals UK Ltd

Dynapar – Encoders UK

Dynasaw – band saw – Dynashape Ltd

Dynascope – Microscopes-projected image – Vision Engineering Ltd

Dynashape – all saw blades – Dynashape Ltd

Dynathane – microcellular polyurethane elastomer – Dow Hyperlast

Dynathane – British Vita plc

Dynatork – air motors – Huco Dynatork

Dynatron – ACVV regulated drive lift motor – Schindler

Dynaweld – electron beam welders – Cambridge Vacuum Engineering

Dyno Glazing – glaziers – The Zockoll Group Ltd

Dyno-Kil – pest prevention/ eradication – The Zockoll Group Ltd

Dyno-Kil – pest prevention – Dyno Rod Ltd

Dyno-Locks – lock-outs, lock changes, key cutting, safe opening and security installations – Dyno Rod Ltd

Dyno Locks – locksmiths – The Zockoll Group Ltd

Dyno Plumbing – plumbing service – The Zockoll Group Ltd

Dyno-Plumbing – all plumbing repairs and installations – Dyno Rod Ltd

Dyno-Rod – drain and pipework blockages, CCTV drain inspection surveys, drain repair and emergency services – Dyno Rod Ltd

Dyno-Rod – drain cleaning service – The Zockoll Group Ltd

Dyno Roofing – The Zockoll Group Ltd

Dyno-Roofing – all roof repairs and refurbishments – Dyno Rod Ltd

Dynobear – Kuwait Petroleum International Lubricants UK Ltd

Dynol – paramelt

Dyrect – direct dyestuffs for cellulosic fibres – Brenntag Colours Ltd

Dysoft – textile softener and lubricating agent – Brenntag Colours Ltd

Dyson – R G K UK Ltd

Dyson – UK Office Direct

Dysperse – dispersed dyestuffs for polyester, acetate & polyamide – Brenntag Colours Ltd

Dytek – fabric dyes, easifix dyes, printing systems – Colourcraft C & A Ltd

DYTRAN (U.S.A.) – Techni Measure

Dytran Instruments – scientific instruments – Sandhurst Instruments Ltd

Dywet – wetting agents for dyeing and preparation of textile fabrics – Brenntag Colours Ltd

Dzus – Quick access fasteners – Zygology Ltd

Dzus – quick release fasteners – Southco Manufacturing Ltd

Dzus Dart – quick release fasteners in plastic – Southco Manufacturing Ltd

E

E. – switchgear – Ellison Switchgear

e 3 Fibres – Phoenix Weighing Services Ltd

E A Combs – UK Office Direct

E A Matthews (United Kingdom) – Worsted Mens Suiting Fabric – John Foster Ltd

E.A.O. – equipment/spares – Bearwood Engineering Supplies

***E.A.O. (Switzerland)** – illuminated push button switches – E A O Ltd

E and G – electrical relays and switches – Polaron Cortina Ltd

E.B. 450/530 – scrubber driers – Hako Machines Ltd

E.B.A.C. – air conditioning for military and railway – Ebac

E.B.C. – brakes for motorcycles and cars – Freeman Automotive UK Ltd

E.B.P.G. 5000 – electron beam lithography system – Leica Microsystems

E.B.S. – Safety netting contractors – E B S Safety Netting

E.B.T. – incandescent lamps and multi chip leds – E A O Ltd

E B T Lamps & LED's – E Preston Electrical Ltd

E-Box – packaged laser marking systems – Electrox

E.C.G.D. – insurance – E C G D

E.C. Hopkins (United Kingdom) – flexible cables, flocking, sunroof cables and window-regulator cables – E C Hopkins Ltd

E.C.O. Paint – water based, air drying stoving paints – Thomas Howse Ltd

E.C.S. – on board cleaner – E C Smith & Sons Ltd

E-Carbon – Carbon brushes and graphite products for traction and industry – Electrical Carbon UK Ltd

E-Chains – Igus (UK) Ltd

E Christian & Company (Holdings) Limited – E C Group Ltd

E Christian & Company Limited – E C Group Ltd

E-Coat – East Midland Coatings Ltd

E.D.C. – traction motors - DC – A T B Laurence Scott Ltd

E.D.L. – industrial and commercial lighting fittings – E D L Lighting Ltd

E D P Merchant – software – Electronic Data Processing plc

E.D.S – Bailey Morris Ltd

***E&E Engineering (U.S.A.)** – automotive tooling equipment – The West Group Ltd

E.E.V. – valves electronic – E 2 V Technologies Ltd

E.F.O. – oil mist filtration unit – Plymovent Limited

E.F.S. – emergeny flotation systems for aircraft full design, development, manufacture and qualifications – G K N Aerospace Ltd

E.F.S.I.S – european food safety inspection service & food inspection services – Agriculture & Horticulture Development Board

E-Filtering Mail – Tekdata Distribution Ltd

E. Flute – corrugated cardboard – Calpack Ltd

***E G & G Controls** – European Drives & Motor Repairs

E.G.R. – exhaust gas recirculatory valves and systems – Interlube Systems Ltd

E.-Gel – floor gel – Evans Vanodine International plc

E.H. Smith – heavy building materials-manufacturers, stockists and – E H Smith

E.K. Williams – management consultancy – EK Williams Limited

E.L.E. – Ele International

E.L.M. – easy listening music – K R L

E.-Line – miniature TO-92 high temperature semiconductors – Diodes Zetex Semiconductors Ltd

E.-Line – epoxy resin – Flowserve

E.M.A.S. – publications – Bearwood Engineering Supplies

***E.M. and F.** – E M & F Group Ltd

E M B – natural diamond - engineered metal bond abrasives – Diamond Detectors

E M B S – natural diamond - engineered metal bond special abrasives – Diamond Detectors

E M C Advertising Gifts – E M C Advertising Gifts Ltd

E.M. Coatings – metal finishing, PTFE and dry film lubricants – E M Coating Services

E.M. Richford – rubber stamps, art stamps, pre-inkstamps and trodat selfinkers – E M Richford Ltd

E.M.S. – medical suppliers – EMS Physio Ltd

E-Max – bottled water cooler – Ebac

E-Mil – volumetric glassware – Bibby Scientific Ltd

E N M – numbering machines & daters – Acco UK Ltd

E.P.B. – Seco Tools UK Ltd

E P O S – electronic point of sale – XN Hotel Systems Ltd

E.P. Signature – Chorus Panel & Profiles

E.-Phos – thickened toilet cleaner, sanitiser and deodoriser – Evans Vanodine International plc

E.-Pine – general purpose q.a.c – Evans Vanodine International plc

E. Plan – modular retail display and shelving systems, dispensary shelving and storage range, counters and display cases and greeting card fittings – E Plan Solutions Ltd

E-Portfolio – NVQ evidence management – V3 Technologies

E.R.F. Ltd – commercial vehicles – E R F Ltd

E.R.F. Select – used trucks – E R F Ltd

***E & R Moffat** – Court Catering Equipment Ltd

E-Rack – C P Cases Ltd

E.S.A. – European Technical Sales Ltd

E.S.A. – educational and domestic furniture – Esa Mcintosh Ltd

e.s. active – engelbert strauss brand – Engelbert Strauss

e.s. image – engelbert strauss brand – Engelbert Strauss

e.s. motion – engelbert strauss brand – Engelbert Strauss

E S P – anatomical teaching models, skeletons, prepared microslides – Educational & Scientific Products Ltd

E.S.T.A. – digital audio systems – Electrosonic Ltd

E-SAFE – II hybrid power switch – Watlow Ltd

E Series – digital readout – Newall Measurement Systems Ltd

E. Series – 4-72 tonne oil mop skimmer systems – Oil Pollution Environmental Control Ltd

E-Signs – E-Signs Cheshire Ltd

E-Switch – Wavelength Electronics Ltd

E-T-A – circuit protection & control – E T A Circuit Breakers Ltd

E.T.A. – Energy Networks Association Ltd

E T A Circuit Protection & Control – E Preston Electrical Ltd

E.T.A. Electricity Training Association – Energy Networks Association Ltd

***E.T.G. (Switzerland)** – special steel – Ovako Ltd

E.T.P. (Sweden) – locking bushes – Lenze UK Ltd

E.T.U. – stainless steel gullies and channels – Wade International Ltd

E-Tag – electronic tagging – Oxley Developments Company Ltd

E-Vend UK – Vending Machines for Modern Lifestyles – E-Vend UK

***E. Walters (United Kingdom)** – Albion Ltd

E.X.4 – loudspeaker – Lowther Loudspeaker Systems Ltd

E.X.L. Shrink – shrink films – Sanders Polyfilms Ltd

E.X.L. Stretch – stretch films – Sanders Polyfilms Ltd

E.Y.M.S. – bus and coach services – East Yorkshire Motor Services Ltd

E.Y.M.S. Group – bus and coach services – East Yorkshire Motor Services Ltd

E.Z. – displacer and electronic liquid level transmitter – Magnetrol International UK Ltd

E-Z- Fit – Prestige Industrial Pipework Equipment

***E.Z. Form Cable Corp (U.S.A.)** – semi-rigid products – Huber+Suhner (UK) Ltd

E-Z-GO – Ransomes Jacobsen Ltd

E-Z Tec – metal detectors – Eriez Magnetics Europe Ltd

e1 – Tekdata Distribution Ltd

E1000 – Equipment For You

E2 – racking system – Cooper B Line Ltd

E2000 – single spindle C.N.C. controlled horizontal honing maching – Equipment For You

E2T – Impac Infrared Ltd

e3 Fibres – graded fibres with 3 way engineering (length, thickness & mix ratio) – Propex Concrete Systems Ltd

E3000 – single and twin spindle, C.N.C. controlled vertical honing machines – Equipment For You

E3500 – Equipment For You

eaga Insulation – the UKs leading installer of cavity wall and loft insulation – Carillion Plant Maintenance

Eagle – pump – Torres Engineering & Pumps Ltd

***Eagle (U.S.A.)** – containers for imflammable liquids – Safety Unlimited

Eagle – non-contact laser height and thickness gauging – Cortex Controllers Ltd

Eagle – industrial cleaning equipment – C S A Cleaning Equipment

Eagle – public address equipment, electrical accessories & cable – Electrovision Group Ltd

***Eagle (Indonesia)** – paper overlay plywood – Price & Pierce Softwoods Ltd

Eagle – bitter – Wells & Young's Brewing Co.

Eagle – Red House Industrial Services Ltd

Eagle – envelopes – Eagle Envelopes Ltd

Eagle – diesel engines vehicle and marine – Perkins Engines Group Ltd

Eagle 160 – Thermal Imaging – Scott International Ltd

***Eagle C H G (Malaysia)** – plywood – Price & Pierce Softwoods Ltd

Eagle O'Hawe Warrington – leather hides – Eagle Ottawa UK Ltd

eagle pack – pet food – Family Pet Services

Eagle Security – Intruder Alarm System – Eagle Security Solutions Ltd

Eagle Star Home Insurance – home insurance – Zurich Assurance

Eagle Star Motor Insurance – motor insurance – Zurich Assurance

Eagle Star Travel Insurance – travel insurance – Zurich Assurance

EagleBurgmann – Eagleburgmann Industries UK Llp

Eames Chairs – The Winnen Furnishing Company

***EAO Secme (France)** – tactile, pcb switches and keypads – E A O Ltd

***EAO Swisstac (Germany)** – illuminated push button switches – E A O Ltd

Earl – mattresses – Vi Spring Ltd

Earl Supreme – Vi Spring Ltd

Earlex – Gem Tool Hire & Sales Ltd

Early Bird – pregnancy testing kit – Kent Pharmaceuticals Ltd

Early Learning Centre – toy & game retailers – John Menzies plc

Earlybird – Procter Machinery Guarding Ltd

Earlydrive – driving tuition – MotorSport Vision

Earth Energy – geothermal heating and cooling systems for buildings – Geoscience Ltd

Earth tab Rivet – fast provision of earth terminals – Zygology Ltd

Earth Wear – leisure footwear – D Jacobson & Sons Ltd

***Earthway (U.S.A.)** – precision garden seeder – Danarm Machinery Ltd

Easat – antennas and sensor systems for communications and radar – Easat Antennas Ltd

Ease-E-Load – UK Office Direct

Ease-E-Load – trucks and trollies – Ease-E-Load Trolleys Ltd

Easergy – telecontrol interface – Schneider

Easi-Build Towers – Accesscaff International Ltd
Easi Fill – plasterboard jointing material – Bristish Gypsum
Easi-Glide – garage doors – Easifix
Easi-pave – traditional paths and driveways – Easifix
Easi Stitch – Kitfix Swallow Group Ltd
Easi-up-lifts – Accesscaff International Ltd
EasiClamp, Tap – fast, economical and permanent repair clamps for water mains pipe work – Viking Johnson
EasiCollar – repair system for socket and spigot joints – Viking Johnson
Easifile – files – Railex Filing Ltd
Easifill – G Webb Automation Ltd
Easifix – conservatory roofing systems, ready to fit upvc windows, doors and ancillary profiles – Easifix
Easifoam – latex foam compound for backing carpet etc – Vita Liquid Polymers
Easigo – industrial plugs and sockets to BS 196 – A-Belco Ltd
Easikleen – detergent powder – Evans Vanodine International plc
Easipark – pay on foot and pay from vehicle systems – Alfia Services Ltd
Easipeel – laminated sheet metal (in aluminium, steel, stainless steel and brass for the production of laminated metal components) – Ford Component Manufacturing Ltd
Easipool – portable above ground swimming pool, water store – Aquaflex Ltd
EasiRental – 98% Funding Acceptance – Max Web Solutions Ltd
EasiTee – universal tapping tees - 3" - 12" – Viking Johnson
East Fife Mail – newspaper – Strachan & Livingston
East Grinstead Courier – newspaper – Kent Regional News & Media
East Kent Mercury – newspaper – Kent Messenger Group Ltd
East Sussex Courier – newspaper – Kent Regional News & Media
East Yorkshire – bus and coach services – East Yorkshire Motor Services Ltd
East Yorkshire Buses – bus and coach services – East Yorkshire Motor Services Ltd
East Yorkshire Coaches – bus and coach services – East Yorkshire Motor Services Ltd
East Yorkshire Diplomat – coach services – East Yorkshire Motor Services Ltd
East Yorkshire Investments – investment – East Yorkshire Motor Services Ltd
East Yorkshire Motor Services – bus and coach services – East Yorkshire Motor Services Ltd
East Yorkshire Properties – property management – East Yorkshire Motor Services Ltd
East Yorkshire Railways – railway services – East Yorkshire Motor Services Ltd
East Yorkshire Tours – bus and coach services – East Yorkshire Motor Services Ltd
East Yorkshire Travel – bus and coach services – East Yorkshire Motor Services Ltd
***Eastbrook Farm Organic Meats** – Helen Browning's Totally organic – Eastbrook Farm Organic Meat Ltd
***Easterby Trailers** – Easterby Trailers Ltd
Eastern – Harrier Fluid Power Ltd
Eastern Carbide – tungsten carbide rod & strip – Hallamshire Hardmetal Products Ltd
Eastern Water Treatment – Eastern Water Treatment Ltd
***Eastern Wireless Telecommunications Inc** – Wavelength Electronics Ltd
Eastlight – UK Office Direct
Eastlight – lever arch files, box files, ring binders – Acco East Light Ltd
Eastman – cloth cutting machines, sewing machines, cloth spreading equipment and cad systems and software and computers – Eastman Staples Ltd
Easy – Jones & Shipman Grinding Ltd
Easy-Air – footpumps and nebulisers – Cameron Price Ltd
Easy Arches – preformed arch frames – Simpson Strong-Tie International Inc
Easy Breather – inhalant – Robinson Healthcare Ltd
Easy Breathers – inhalant tissues – Robinson Healthcare Ltd
EASY CABLE – Watlow Ltd
Easy-Cals (United Kingdom) – self-adhesive anodised aluminium foil labels – London Name Plate Manufacturing Co. Ltd
Easy Change – Coventry Toolholders Ltd
Easy Chute Rubbish Chutes – Accesscaff International Ltd
Easy Dot – adhesive dot for mounting posters – Alplus
Easy Eggs – egg products for catering – Framptons Ltd
Easy Fit Dome – High density polyethylene diffuser – Porvair plc
Easy Fit Dome – high density polyethylene diffuser – Porvair Sciences Ltd
Easy FM – community radio station used twice a year – Stroud College Of Further Education
Easy Label – label over printing system – Weyfringe Labelling Systems
Easy-Link – Rose & Krieger
Easy Move – computers and financial services – Birmingham Midshires Financial Services Ltd
Easy Net – magazine – Insitive Media
Easy Scale – stainless steel band – Band-It Co. Ltd
Easy Sign – self cling window lettering kits – Repro Arts Ltd
Easy-Slide – PE and PP bag/wallet with plastic slider – Index
Easy-Stik – adhesives for the consumer – Bostik Ltd
Easy Strip – strips polish with or without the use of a floor machine – Evans Vanodine International plc
Easyb's – leisure shoes – D B Shoes Ltd
Easybusiness (United Kingdom) – Kompass (UK)Ltd
Easycare Twist – Ryalux Carpets Ltd
EasyClean – paint brush, paint roller, roller sleeve cleaner – L G Harris & Co. Ltd
Easycom – Communications – Scott International Ltd
Easycomfort – bedlinen and pillows – Ottoman Textiles Ltd
Easycooler – bottled water coolers – Ebac
Easyguard – Safety Works & Solutions Ltd
Easyguard – Sponmech Safety Systems Ltd
Easymark – aerosol lining system – Sportsmark Group Ltd
EasyOrder (United Kingdom) – ECi Software Solutions Limited
Easyshine – dual purpose floor polish and cleaner – Evans Vanodine International plc
EasySnap – Unique Monodose Sachet Concept – PACK Innovation Ltd
Eaton – Trafalgar Tools
Eaton – E Preston Electrical Ltd
Eaton – Cyclops Electronics Ltd
Eaton – electrical equipment – Bearwood Engineering Supplies
Eaton – Harrier Fluid Power Ltd
EATON-AEROQUIP – Hydraulic & Offshore Supplies Ltd
EATON CORPORATION – Hydraulic & Offshore Supplies Ltd
Eaton/Cutler Hammer – Relays – Dax International Ltd
Eaton filtration – Anchor Pumps Co. Ltd
Eaton-Hydroline – hydraulic cylinders – A C Hydraulics Ltd
Eaton Walterschied – Southern Valve & Fitting Co. Ltd
Eaton-Williams Service (United Kingdom) – air conditioning service & maintenance – Eaton-Williams Group Ltd
Eau Fraiche – perfume – Elizabeth Arden
Eavy Metal – games, playthings, minatures and models – Games Workshop Ltd
Eazistrip – Lemon Groundworks
EBAC – commercial air conditioning – Ebac
EBAC 2000 Series – dehumidifiers for domestic applications – Ebac
EBARA – Hydraulic & Offshore Supplies Ltd
***EBARA** – Barber Pumps Ltd
Ebara – Arun Pumps Ltd
Ebara – Pumps – Wendage Pollution Control Ltd
Ebara – pumps – Allpumps Ltd
Ebara – vacuum pumps – AESpump
EBC , MINTEX, FIRSTLINE – CAR PARTS AND ACCESORIES WHOLESALE – AZCARPARTS UK
Ebel – watches – Goldsmiths Jewellers Ltd
***Eberhard (Germany)** – punches, ejector pins and drill bushes – Berger Tools Ltd
Eberle – spares & equipment – Bearwood Engineering Supplies
EBEST DYES – dyes – European O G D Ltd
Ebm – fan motors and assemblies – Thermofrost Cryo plc
Ebonol C – black on copper – Cookson Electronics Ltd
Ebonol S 34 – black on steel – Cookson Electronics Ltd
Ebonol Z80 – black on zinc plate – Cookson Electronics Ltd
***Ebony Collection** – Geerings Of Ashford Ltd
Ebor – concrete outdoor furniture, planters, litter bins, concrete fenciing, post and panel, pallisade, picket fencing – Ebor Concrete Ltd
Eborcraft – Desks – Bucon Ltd
Eborcraft – office furniture manufacturers – Eborcraft Ltd
EBT – Selectronix Ltd
EC – air handling unit – Flakt Woods Ltd
EC Group – E C Group Ltd
EC Logistics – E C Group Ltd
EC10 – Passive Hearing Protection – Scott International Ltd
EC12 – Passive Hearing Protection – Scott International Ltd
EC4 – Passive Hearing Protection – Scott International Ltd
EC8 – Passive Hearing Protection – Scott International Ltd
EC80 – phosphine monitor for fumigation – Bedfont Scientific Ltd
Ecco – Allied Meat Importers
Ecco 5000 (Belgium) – gas fired unit heaters – Reznor UK Ltd
Eccobond – adhesive – Resin Technical Systems
Ecepox – epoxidised soya bean oil – Atosina UK Ltd
Echelon – clothing lockers – Link Lockers
echo KLM – Wenaas Ltd
Echo Sounders – ships equipment – A B Precision Poole Ltd
Echomaster – sound absorbing masonry blocks – Tarmac Topblock Ltd
Echotel – ultrasonic level switch – Magnetrol International UK Ltd
ECIS – engineering careers information service – Science Engineering & Manufacturing Technologies
ECKERLE – Hydraulic & Offshore Supplies Ltd
***Eckold (Germany)** – sheet metal working machines – Eckold Ltd
Eclipse – hand refractometer – Bellingham & Stanley Ltd
Eclipse – Telephone management system – Data Track Technology plc
Eclipse – manual-cnc mills & lathes – Gate Machinery International Ltd
Eclipse – engineers tools – Arrow Supply Co. Ltd
***Eclipse** – hacksaw blades and frames – Spear & Jackson plc
Eclipse – building preservation equipment and garden sprayers – Eclipse Sprayers Ltd
Eclipse – engineers hand and cutting tools – Spear & Jackson plc
***Eclipse** – Shelfspan Shelving Systems
ECLIPSE – eRecords management – Stortext Ltd
Eclipse – Coatings reinforced with a blend of ceramic particles – Whitford Ltd
Eclipse – 180 ml-920 ml pp evoh bottles – R P C Containers Ltd
Eclipse – software packages – Schlumberger Oilfield UK plc
Eclipse – S J Wharton Ltd
Eclipse Magnetics – Permanent magnets in the following magnetic materials; cast alnico, ferrite rare earth, neodymium iron boron, complete range of magnetic equipment. Magnetic assemblies, magnetic sub assemblies. – Eclipse Magnetics Ltd
Eclipse - Spear & Jackson - Elliott Lucas - WHS - Tyzack - Spiralux - Neverbend - Heritage - Razorsharp – Spear & Jackson plc
Eclipse - Tracker – Data Track Technology plc
ECM – Kennametal Extrude Hone Ltd
***ECM** – Coffeetech
Eco – electronic controller – Vent Engineering
Eco – H T S Direct Ltd
ECO – external gear pumps – Axflow
Eco Compost – peat alternatives – Woodgrow Horticulture
Eco Fine Press GmbH – hydro/pneumatic cylinders – Tox Pressotechnik
Eco Promo2u – Promo2u Ltd
Eco Separator – Russell Finex Ltd
Eco Solutions – environment biotechnology – Symbio
ECO-Static Hot Pressure Cleaners – Pressure washers – B & G Cleaning Systems Ltd
Ecoair – Harrier Fluid Power Ltd
Ecoat – Protective Finishing Group
Ecobag – Injection moulded carrying cases – Hofbauer (UK) Ltd
***Ecobra (Germany)** – drawing instruments – Technical Sales Ltd
Ecocool – water soluble cutting fluids – Fuchs Lubricants UK plc
Ecocryl/Repolem – acrylic emulsions – Atosina UK Ltd
Ecocut – neat cutting fluids – Fuchs Lubricants UK plc
Ecocut Drill Turn – Ceratizit UK Ltd
Ecodrum – all fibre 100% recycled drum – Rexam Holding plc
***Ecofelt (United Kingdom)** – biodegradable revegetation mat – A G A Group
Ecofile – manilla – St Regis Paper Co. Ltd
Ecofile – The Woolwich
Ecoflex (GEA) – brazed plate heat exchangers (BHPE) by tau – Thermofrost Cryo plc
Ecoflex System – pre-insulated all plastic pipe – Durotan Ltd
Ecofloor – R & D Marketings Ltd
EcoFlow – modular adsorption for gas treatment – Jacobi Carbons
Ecofusion – glass coating system – Permastore Ltd
EcoJoist – Open web floor joist system – Gang-Nail
Ecojoist – Aspect Roofing
Ecojoist – Crendon Timber Engineering Ltd
Ecojoist – D W B Anglia Ltd
Ecojoist – Wrekin Frame & Truss
Ecojoist – Solent Roof Trusses Ltd
Ecojoist – Aber Roof Truss Ltd
Ecojoist – Arnold Laver Call Collect
Ecojoist – Roe Ltd
Ecojoist – Stevenson & Kelly Grampian
Ecojoist – Donaldson & Mcconnell Ltd
Ecojoist – Anglian Timber Ltd
Ecojoist – Normans
Ecolay – pe foam nxlpe flooring underlay – Functional Foam Beacons Products Ltd
Ecolec (United Kingdom) – class 11 heating apparatus; electric panel heaters; electric heating jackets; convection heaters; air conditioning apparatus; air cooling apparatus; all included in class 11 – Ecolec Ltd
ECOLIFT – Chaintec Ltd
Ecoline – Forward Chemicals Ltd
Ecom – Alpha Electronics Southern Ltd
Ecomat – R & D Marketings Ltd
***Ecomax (Germany)** – gas condensing boilers – Vaillant Ltd

Econ – Joe Turner Equipment Ltd

Econ – bookcases – E F G Matthews Office Furniture Ltd

Econ 40/75 – lightweight casement window – Kawneer UK Ltd

Econ 75 T.S. – top swing window – Kawneer UK Ltd

Econ Door – Kawneer UK Ltd

Econ-O-Matic – paint heater – Valco Cincinnati

*Econabator (U.S.A.) – catalytic incinerator for fumes – Higgins & Hewins Ltd

Econo-D – range of crimp-D connectors – Cinch Connectors Ltd

Econobord – food cutting boards – S J H Row & Son Ltd

Econocast – cast iron sectional boiler – Stertil UK Ltd

Econoclense – metal cleaners and picklers – P M D UK Ltd

Econofix – photographic chemicals – Jessops plc

*Econoflame (Netherlands) – commercial gas boiler – Stertil UK Ltd

Econoloc – gas spring - eliminates the need for separate safety rods in critical lift-assist applications – Camloc Motion Control Ltd

*Economatic (Germany) – dual fuel boiler – Stertil UK Ltd

Economix – wall mounted mixers – Sheardown Engineering Ltd

Economy – incubators – Sanyo Gallenkamp plc

Economy 7 – Energy Networks Association Ltd

Economy Cover – paper – H V Sier Ltd

Econoneb – nebuliser systems for the treatment of respiratory disorders – Clement Clarke International Ltd

Econopic – additive for mineral acid pickler – P M D UK Ltd

Econoplate – plate heat exchangers – Stertil UK Ltd

Econoprint – photographic chemicals – Jessops plc

*Econorad (Germany) – radiators – Stertil UK Ltd

Econostop – photographic chemicals – Jessops plc

Econotol – photographic chemicals – Jessops plc

*Econotwin (Germany) – commercial dual fuel boiler – Stertil UK Ltd

Econovate – dry acid pickling salts – P M D UK Ltd

Econowet – photographic chemicals – Jessops plc

Ecopet (United Kingdom) – recycled polyester strapping – Plastic Extruders Ltd

Ecophon – Ecophon Acoustic Ceiling and Panelling Products – ReSpace Acoustics Ltd

Ecophon – S K Interiors Ltd

Ecophon – acoustic tile – Acousticabs Industrial Noise Control Ltd

Ecopower – a range of control panels – V E S Ltd

*Ecorel (U.S.A.) – bookbinding materials – Winter & Co UK Ltd

Ecosack – Segezha Packaging

Ecosafe – Forward Chemicals Ltd

Ecoshaw – precision steel castings – Bonds Precision Casting Ltd

Ecoshaw - ceramic moulding process. – Bonds Precision Casting Ltd

EcoSorb – products for gas treatment – Jacobi Carbons

Ecostar – Hörmann (UK) Ltd

Ecostrip – depainting & degreasing system – N A Robson Ltd

Ecotechnics (Italy) – Aire conditioning units – Lumatic Ga Ltd

Ecotect – Forward Chemicals Ltd

EcoTerm – econet terminal software for unix – Cambridge Systems Design

Ecovent – V E S Ltd

Ecover – UK Office Direct

Ecowarm Cavity T & G – EPS partial fill cavity wall insulation – Springvale Insulation Ltd

Ecowarm Cavity Tag – EPS partial fill cavity wall insulation – Springvale E P S Ltd

Ecowarm Flat Roofs – EPS flat roof insulant – Springvale Insulation Ltd

Ecowarm Fulfil T & G – EPS full fill cavity wall insulation – Springvale Insulation Ltd

Ecowarm Fulfil Tag – EPS full fill cavity wall insulation – Springvale E P S Ltd

Ecowarm Warmboard – EPS general purpose insulant – Springvale E P S Ltd

Ecowarm Warmboard – EPS general purpose insulant – Springvale Insulation Ltd

Ecowarm Warmclad – EPS external wall insulant – Springvale Insulation Ltd

Ecowarm Warmclad – EPS external wall insulant – Springvale E P S Ltd

Ecowarm Warmfloor – EPS flooring insulation – Springvale E P S Ltd

Ecowarm Warmfloor – EPS floor insulation – Springvale Insulation Ltd

Ecowarm Warmlath – EPS board with batten recess for internal insulation – Springvale Insulation Ltd

Ecowarm Warmlath – EPS board with batten recess for internal insulation – Springvale E P S Ltd

Ecowarm Warmroof – EPS flat roof insulant – Springvale E P S Ltd

Ecowarm Warmsark – EPS sarking insulant for pitched roofs – Springvale E P S Ltd

Ecowarm Warmsark – EPS sarking insulant for pitched roofs – Springvale Insulation Ltd

Ecowarm Warmsqueez – EPS compressible between rafter insulant – Springvale Insulation Ltd

Ecowarm Warmsqueez – EPS compressible between rafter insulant – Springvale E P S Ltd

Ecozyme – Forward Chemicals Ltd

ECP – Canteen Furniture – Bucon Ltd

ECS – lighting controls – Camlar Ltd

Ectquote – Simbec Research Ltd

Ecudex – G E Healthcare

Ecuscan – G E Healthcare

EDA Radio Fire Alarm Systems – Leading Radio Fire Alarm Manufacturer – R V Fire Systems

*Edalco (Switzerland) – tapping attachments – Macinnes Tooling Ltd

Edalco SA (Switzerland) – "rotocoupe" chip breaking attachments for lathes – Haesler Machine Tools

Edalmatic – tapping attachments – Macinnes Tooling Ltd

Edaplan – levelling agents – Lawrence Industries Ltd

Edbro – Hydraulic Press – ECO Hydraulic Presses Ltd

Edbro hydraulic tipping systems – hydraulic tipping systems, telescopic and single stage, pump manufacture – Edbro plc

Edbro steel tipping bodies – steel tipping bodies - end, three-way and demountables – Edbro plc

Edding – UK Office Direct

Edding – pens, markers – Edding UK Ltd

Eddy – the home water cooler – Ebac

Eddystone – Perancea Ltd

Edeco Engineering – steam, control, sales and service – Edeco Petroleum Services Ltd

Edeco Power Systems – Diesel Engines transmissions and generators sales and service – Edeco Petroleum Services Ltd

Edeco Pressure Systems – wellhead, valve, actuator sales and refurbishment, pipeline repair composite reinforcement system – Edeco Petroleum Services Ltd

Eden – dense building block – Brand & Rae

*Eden Collection Organic Wines – Vinceremos Wines & Spirits Ltd

Eden Mirror – mirror manufrs – Gardner & Newton Ltd

Eden Rose Lifestyle – Eden Rose Lifestyle

Edenaire – customised air conditioning units – Eaton-Williams Group Ltd

Edenbridge Courier – newspaper – Kent Regional News & Media

Eder – Harrier Fluid Power Ltd

EDER – Hydraulic & Offshore Supplies Ltd

Edgcumbe – Alpha Electronics Southern Ltd

Edge – magazine – Future Publishing Ltd

Edge – M K Electric Ltd

Edge – industrial cleaning equipment – B & G Cleaning Systems Ltd

Edge - industrial cleaning equipment – B & G Cleaning Systems Ltd

EdgeCAM (United Kingdom) – CAM software for manufacturing – Pathtrace plc

Edgecub 100 – Pressure washers – B & G Cleaning Systems Ltd

Edgecub 90 – Pressure washers – B & G Cleaning Systems Ltd

Edgesweep Ride-On – Pressure washers – B & G Cleaning Systems Ltd

Edgesweep S Range – Pressure washers – B & G Cleaning Systems Ltd

Edgwick – Red House Industrial Services Ltd

EDI (Italy) – solenoid valves – Bosch Rexroth Ltd

EDI – Yokota UK

Edi – high voltage diodes – G D Rectifiers Ltd

EDI - Oil Sistem - Oil Control - OLEODINAMICA LC – Bosch Rexroth Ltd

EDI SYSTEM – Hydraulic & Offshore Supplies Ltd

Edicron – electronic valves and tubes, CRTs and components thereof, semiconductors and electronic components – Edicron Ltd

Edinburgh – sink – Armitage Shanks Ltd

Edison – heavy duty rectangular slide-out cover and frame – Norinco UK Ltd

Edistir – polystyreme – Polimeri Europa Ltd

Editbox – on-line non-linear editor – Quantel Ltd

Edlund – stainless steel can openers, can crushers, scales, knife sharpeners. – Metcalfe Catering Equipment Ltd

EDM – Consumables – Agie Charmilles Ltd

EDM Fluid – Race Industrial Products Ltd

Edmas – Harrier Fluid Power Ltd

Edme – malt products – E D M E Ltd

Edmolift – Edmolift UK Ltd

Edmund Bell – soft furnishings – Edmund Bell & Co. Ltd

Edmundson Electrical – electrical goods distributer – Edmundson Electrical Ltd

Edpac – multiple choice assessment package (computer software) - D R S Data Services Ltd

Educational and Scientific Products – anatomical teaching models, skeletons, prepared microslides – Educational & Scientific Products Ltd

Educational Wallcharts – Francis Chichester Ltd

Educraft – papers and boards – Slater Harrison & Co. Ltd

Eductoblast – portable closed circuit blast cleaning system – Hodge Clemco Ltd

Eductomatic – hand held closed circuit blast cleaning unit – Hodge Clemco Ltd

Edward Arnold – books – Hachette UK Ltd

Edward Pryor – stamping/marking – Bearwood Engineering Supplies

Edwardian – carpets - axminster – Brintons Carpets Ltd

Edwards – vacuum pumps and systems – Boc Gases Ltd

Edwards – vacuum equipment – Bearwood Engineering Supplies

Edwards – high vacuum pumps and plant – AESpump

Edwards High Vacuum – high vacuum pumps and plant – AESpump

Edwards high vacuum – Technical Vacuum Services Ltd

Edwards & Jones – Veolia Water Solutions & Technologies

Eeco – corner baths, caravan windows, shower trays and towing brackets – Exhaust Ejector Co. Ltd

Eel – scientific instruments – Diffusion Systems Ltd

Eesiban – stockinette bandage – Sallis Healthcare Ltd

Eesilas – anti-embolism hosiery – Sallis Healthcare Ltd

Eesilite – compression hosiery – Sallis Healthcare Ltd

Eesiness – two way stretch surgical hose – Sallis Healthcare Ltd

Eesinet – nylon net surgical hose – Sallis Healthcare Ltd

EEV (United Kingdom) – electronic industrial & transmitting tubes – Edicron Ltd

Eezifit – nozzle holders – Hypro Eu Ltd

Eezispray Valve – flow control – Hypro Eu Ltd

Eezitray – Wright Dental Group

Efast (Europe, Western) – pvc valves & fittings – Everyvalve Ltd

Effast – pipework systems – Davis Industrial Plastics Ltd

*Effbe (Germany) – rubber springs – Berger Tools Ltd

Effer – Harrier Fluid Power Ltd

Efina (Japan) – APS compacts – Pentax UK Ltd

Eflex – flexible couplings – Bibby Transmissions Ltd

EFP – Single zone conventional fire panel – C-Tec Security Ltd

EFS – electric flash steam boilers – Fulton Boiler Works Ltd

Ega-Kut – diestocks – Tom Carrington & Co. Ltd

Ega Mini – mini trunking – M K Electric Ltd

Egaclean (Switzerland) – alcohol solvent cleaning systems – Haesler Machine Tools

EGE – Powelectrics Ltd

*Egertec (United Kingdom) – straw archery targets and accessories – Quicks Archery

Eggbox Graphics – Eggbox Graphics

Egger Laminates (Austria) – laminable sheets – Egger UK Ltd

Egis – scooter controller – P G Drive Technology

*Egli (Switzerland) – butter processing equipment – Engelmann & Buckham Ltd

Eglo Lighting – Light Fantastic

Egoluce – Light Fantastic

*Egon Muller (Germany) – German wines – O W Loeb & Co. Ltd

Egrat – electronic video crosswire generator – Cortex Controllers Ltd

Egston – Relec Electronics Ltd

EGT – Sandhurst Plant Ltd

eh – series boosters – AESpump

EH10 – Passive Hearing Protection – Scott International Ltd

EH12 – Passive Hearing Protection – Scott International Ltd

EH4 – Passive Hearing Protection – Scott International Ltd

EH8 – Passive Hearing Protection – Scott International Ltd

EHF – General Vacuum Equipment Ltd

EHG SL10 – process controller and safety limit – Watlow Ltd

EHRCO – Hydraulic & Offshore Supplies Ltd

EI – electronic valves and semiconductors – Edicron Ltd

Eicon – Tekdata Distribution Ltd

Eicon Modem – Tekdata Distribution Ltd

Eiffel – medium duty rectangular slide-out cover and frame – Norinco UK Ltd

Eiger Deck – Accesscaff International Ltd

Eiger Towers – Accesscaff International Ltd

Eiki – Lamphouse Ltd

Eikon – Recyc/Disposable Single Gas Monitor – Crowcon Detection Instrument Ltd

Eimac (U.S.A.) – electronic industrial & transmitting tubes – Edicron Ltd

Einhell – Gem Tool Hire & Sales Ltd

Einhell – S J Wharton Ltd

Eins – Robot Gripper parts – Star Automation Uk Ltd

Eirich (Germany) – milling & mixing machinery – Orthos Engineering Ltd

Eisele – Motor Technology Ltd

Eisele – Gea Westfalia Seperator UK Ltd

Eisenhower – Dickies Workwear

Eitec – link apron covers and slideway wipers – M. Buttkereit Ltd

Eizo – Lamphouse Ltd

EJ – filter press – Veolia Water Solutions & Technologies

*Ejectadip (U.S.A.) – electronic components – Flair Electronics Ltd

Ekaland – rubber additive – Atosina UK Ltd

Ekalift – automotive recovery system – Eka Ltd

Ekamant – coated abrasives for wood working – Finishing Aids & Tools Ltd

Ekamant – Woodworking abrasives – The Toolpost

EKD – Hörmann (UK) Ltd

EKD GELENKROHR – M. Buttkereit Ltd

Ekins – The Woolwich

Ekins Homefile – The Woolwich

Ekins Professional – The Woolwich

Ekins Property Doctor – The Woolwich

Ekom-50 – 50mm thick aluminium partition system – Komfort Workspace plc

Ekornes – The Winnen Furnishing Company

EL CID – stator core condition testing – Adwel International Ltd

El-Flow Controllers – Bronkhorst UK Ltd

El-Flow Digital – Bronkhorst UK Ltd

El-Flow Meters – Bronkhorst UK Ltd

El-O-Matic – Frenstar

El-O-Matic – Orbinox UK Ltd

El-Press – Bronkhorst UK Ltd

El vac vacuum – AESpump

ELAFLEX – Flexible 'Spider' Shaft & Spacer Shaft Couplings – Francis and Francis Ltd

Elan – registered trade name – Elan Digital Systems Ltd

Elan – European Technical Sales Ltd

Elan – venetian blind system – Eclipse Blind Systems

Elan – wheel balancer for cars & commercials – Tecalemit Garage Equipment Co. Ltd

Elan-Dragonair – air heaters – Elan-Dragonair Ltd

Eland – hydraulic cylinders, actuators and systems, test rigs and simulators – Eland Engineering Company

Elanders Hindson Ltd – commercial printers – Elanders

Elasia – Harrier Fluid Power Ltd

Elastaseal – waterproofing systems for flat roofs – Tor Coatings Ltd

Elastimond – high voltage connectors – Wellhead Electrical Supplies

Elasto Valves – European Technical Sales Ltd

Elastomeric Joint Sealant – two component self smoothing polyurethane based joint sealant – Conren Ltd

Elastoplast – first aid dressing and airstrip first aid dressing – Lil-lets UK Ltd

Elation – felt mark paper – James Cropper plc

Elba – UK Office Direct

Elbaron – oil mist filters – M. Buttkereit Ltd

ELBE – Bailey Morris Ltd

Elco – Cyclops Electronics Ltd

Elco – washing soda crystals – East Lancs Chemical Co. Ltd

Elcock Power – tools – Elcock's Ltd

*Elcold (Denmark) – refrigeration – Interlevin Refrigeration Ltd

Elcometer – thickness gauge, worldwide for coating testing instruments and other instruments for quality control of surface coatings – Elcometer Instruments Ltd

Elcomponent – Alpha Electronics Southern Ltd

Elcon – Vertical Panel Saws – A L Dalton Ltd

Elcontrol – Elcontrol Ltd

Elda Scandinavian Recycling – tyre shredding and electronic recycling – M M H Recycling Systems Ltd

Eldar – games, toys, board games, miniatures and models for use in fantasy games – Games Workshop Ltd

Eldonian – stainless steel bits, spurs, stirrups and accessories – E Jeffries & Sons Ltd

Elec & Eltek – M S C Gleichmann UK Ltd

Elecolit – silver conductive adhesives and epoxy – Euro Bond Adhesives Ltd

Elecsols – Forward Chemicals Ltd

Elect 17 – Western Provident Association Ltd

Electem – tool & die steel – Somers Forge Ltd

Electol – anti-static solution for textile fibres – Benjamin R Vickers & Sons Ltd

Electrace – Cut length self limiting tape – Flexelec UK Ltd

Electrafil – Resinex UK Ltd

Electrak – cable management – Electrak Holdings Ltd

Electric Label – fashion clothing – P S Gill & Sons

Electricaire – Glen Dimplex UK Ltd

Electrical Enclosure Manufacturers – Tegrel Ltd

Electrical Equipment – magazine – Progressive Media Group

Electrical Testing and Inspection FWT Ltd – Electrical Testing and Inspection Provider – Electrical Testing & Inspection FWT Ltd

Electricar – battery electric road vehicles – Electricars Ltd

Electricar – heavy duty battery electric tow tractors and platform trucks – Electricars Ltd

Electricar – Stacatruc

Electricity Association – trade association – Energy Networks Association Ltd

Electricold – refrigeration – Electricold Refrigeration

Electrion – air cleaner – Trion The Division Of Ruskin Air Management Ltd

Electro – Gem Tool Hire & Sales Ltd

Electro Adaptor – Dax International Ltd

Electro Arc – Electro Arc Co. Ltd

Electro Cables Inc. – Belcom Cables Ltd

Electro Carbon – Morganite

Electro-Fence – a powerful intruder deterrent – Advanced Perimeter Systems Ltd

Electro Flow – spares & equipment – Bearwood Engineering Supplies

Electro Kabuki – special effect curtain operating system1 – Magnet Schultz Ltd

Electro-Mechano (U.S.A.) – drilling machines – Drill Service Horley Ltd

Electro-Medical Supplies (Greenham) Ltd – medical suppliers – EMS Physio Ltd

Electro Plasma – Review Display Systems Ltd

Electro-Wand (United Kingdom) – removal of weld discolouration – Seco Engineering Co. Ltd

Electrobolt – power bolt extension or retraction, robust construction and monitoring switches and wide operating voltage range – Castell Safety International Ltd

Electrocraft – European Drives & Motor Repairs

Electrode Dressers Inc – Yokota UK

*Electrodynamic Crystal – Wavelength Electronics Ltd

Electroflex – flexible diamond material – D K Holdings Ltd

Electrohome – Lamphouse Ltd

Electrol Roll – consumer database – Acxiom Ltd

Electrolene – Belcom Cables Ltd

Electrolevel (United Kingdom) – tilt transducer – Tilt Measurement Ltd

Electrolocation – Radio Detection

Electrolube – contact lubricants (elec), conformal coatings (PCB's), surface amount produce (PCB's), cleaning solvents service aids (freezer), oduction aids (photoresist) electro-conductive coatings, heat transfer pastes and epoxy & polyurethane resin systems – Electrolube

Electrolux – Clean Machine UK Ltd

*Electrolux Commercial Laundry Equipment – Brewer & Bunney

Electrolux Wascator – washing machines and hydro extractors – Electrolux Laundry Systems

Electromag – fine powder for use in ceramics – U C M Magnesia Ltd

Electromatic – sewage ejector – Tuke & Bell Ltd

*Electromatic (Denmark) – electronic components and data transmission equipment – Carlo Gavazzi UK Ltd

Electromotiv – Harrier Fluid Power Ltd

Electron – electronic water conditioning unit – B W T Ltd

Electronic equipment & instruments suppliers – Powertron Converters Ltd

Electronic Office – photocopies fax machines etc – lot PRC

Electronics – Progressive Media Group

Electronics Buyers Guide, The – electrical – United Business Media Ltd

Electropack – electric steam boilers – Fulton Boiler Works Ltd

ElectropaK – diesel generators – Perkins Engines Group Ltd

Electropatent Modular Power Tracking – Advanced Ergonomic Technologies Ltd

Electroplating Diamond Products – diamond tool manufacturers – Abrasive Technology Ltd

Electropower – gearboxes and geared motors – Disco Drive Kings Lynn Ltd

Electropower – standard gear-motor units – A T B Laurence Scott Ltd

Electrorava (Italy) – Dynamic balancing machines – Schmitt Europe Ltd

Electrotex Sales Co. – tv, videos, hi-fi accessories, sales & repair – Electrotex Sales Co.

Electrotorque – Norbar Torque Tools Ltd

ElectroVap – steam humidifiers – J S Humidifiers plc

Electrovision – audio amplification – Premier Solutions Nottingham Ltd

Electroway – back bar catering equipment – Manitowoc Food Service UK

Electrox – 600 Group plc

Electrum – entry level standard definition telecine including primary/secondary colour correction – Cintel International Ltd

Elegance – digitally printed wall & floor tiles – Johnson Tiles Ltd

Elegance – vinyl flooring – Gerflor Ltd

*Elegant (Philippines) – hardwood garden furniture – Gardencast

Elegant Homes – furniture – Elegant Homes Ltd

Elegant Touch – nail care products & false eyelashes – Original Addidtions

Eleganza – bath screens – Matki plc

Elektrabeckum – Oxon Fastening Systems Ltd

Elektro-Kohl – European Technical Sales Ltd

Elektron – telephone sets – Nortel Networks UK Ltd

Elektron – magnesium alloys – Magnesium Elektron

Elektron - MEL - Melmag - Zirmax - Melrasal – Magnesium Elektron

Elektrosafe – ceramic coated bearings for electrical insulation – N S K Europe

Elementory Watson – Global Graphics Software Ltd

Elementri – display systems for graphics & conferences – Clip Display

Elements – ceramic wall & floor tiles – Johnson Tiles Ltd

Elements – general health, mind body & spirit titles, lifestyle & special – Harpercollins Publishers Ophelia House

Elements – Tektura plc

Elements of Spice – Spices – Landauer Ltd

Elephant Planners (United Kingdom) – Year Planners – Libran Laminations Ltd

Elephante – design and manufacture of standard and purpose made industrial lifts and work platforms – Elephante Service & Maintenance Ltd

Elephantide – electrical insulating presspapers and pressboards – Weidmann Whiteley Ltd

Elesa – standard machine elements (plastic) – Elesa (UK) Ltd

Elesa-Clayton – Analogue/digital, mechanical/electronic indicators for positional setting of lead screws & shafts – Elesa (UK) Ltd

Elesa CLEAN – handles, lobed & knurled knobs for sanitary applications – Elesa (UK) Ltd

Elesa ESD – in special conductive techopolymer (ESD-C Electrostatic Discharge Conductive) – Elesa (UK) Ltd

Elesa SAN – with antimicrobial additives preventing the build up of microbes, bacteria, mildew & fungi – Elesa (UK) Ltd

Elesa Self Extinguish – meet the flame proof material requirements of UL-94 V0 – Elesa (UK) Ltd

Elesa SOFT – for a safer, more stable grip – Elesa (UK) Ltd

Elesta – European Technical Sales Ltd

*Elettrobar – Maidaid Halcyon

Elettrorava (Italy) – dynamic balancing machines – Schmitt Europe Ltd

Elettrotec – pressure switches, temperature switches, level switches – P V L Ltd

Elf – Online Lubricants

Elf – Lubricants – Sprint Engineering & Lubricant

Elfit – bright silver plating solutions – Schloetter Co. Ltd

*Elframo – Maidaid Halcyon

*Elftone – radios, tape recorders, clock radio, car radios – Omega Import Export Ltd

Elga – CNC hydraulic pressbrakes, CNC hydraulic shears – Press & Shear Machinery Ltd

Elga – Electrodes and wires – Premier Welding Services Scotland Ltd

Elga-Synchro – Press & Shear Machinery Ltd

Elgar – kitchen furniture – Moores Furniture Group

Elge – European Technical Sales Ltd

Elges – European Technical Sales Ltd

Elges – Mercury Bearings Ltd

Elgin – Harrier Fluid Power Ltd

Elgin Court – contemporary fine art greeting cards – Great British Card Company plc

Elia – Ascot Wholesale Ltd

Eligor (France) – die cast formula one trucks – Amerang Group Ltd

Elinca – antifouling device – Microtech Filters Ltd

Elintaal – perfume speciality – Quest International UK Ltd

Elintaal Forte – perfume speciality – Quest International UK Ltd

Elite – Vi Spring Ltd

Elite – breakdown warranties – Car Care Plan Ltd

Elite – medium sized fusing machinery – Reliant Machinery Ltd

Elite – beds – Elite Bedding Co. Ltd

Elite – Resinex UK Ltd

Elite – disposable cutlery – Plastico Ltd

Elite – filing product range – Acco East Light Ltd

Elite – panel cistern – Thomas Dudley Ltd

Elite – Flexible Edge Retention Profile – Pentagon Protection plc

Elite – Office Furniture – Bucon Ltd

ELITE – Chaintec Ltd

Elite – dealer management system (retail motor trade) – Kalamazoo - Reynolds Ltd

Elite – cable cleat – Ellis Patents Ltd

Elite Biscuits – U C D Ltd

Elite Energy – Elite Energy - The Specialist Energy Consultancy

Elite Energy – Elite Energy - The Specialist Energy Consultancy

Elite Portable Oxygen Systems (United Kingdom) – oxygen conserving device – Intermedical UK Ltd

Elite Video – Lamphouse Ltd

Elitebag Astro – Hofbauer (UK) Ltd

Elitebag Enduro – Hofbauer (UK) Ltd

Elitebag Pro – Hofbauer (UK) Ltd

EliteXecutive Travel – Airport, Ferry Port and Business Travel – EliteXecutive Travel

*Elith (France) – slates – Cembrit Ltd

*Elivero Porcelain – Porcelain, Glassware & Cutlery – La Porcellana Tableware International Ltd

Eliwell (Invensys) – electronic controls, monitoring systems and instruments including thermometers, thermostats, temperature alarms, humidity controls, defrost controls, pressure controls, pressure sensors, step controls, fan speed control data records, probes, transformers – Thermofrost Cryo plc

Elixair (UK) (United Kingdom) – PRC remover – R D Taylor & Co. Ltd

Elizabethan – Electrical – K B Import & Export Ltd

Eljon – organic pigments in dry form and as aqueous dispersions – European Colour plc

Elk (United Kingdom) – unmotorised bench bandfacer – R J H Finishing Systems Ltd

Elka – amenity dwarf perennial ryegrass – Limagrain UK Ltd

ELKA Rainwear – Waterproofs – L S Systems Ltd

Elkington – access covers & frames – GATIC

Elkington Coex – access covers & frames – GATIC

Elkington Cubic – access covers & frames – GATIC

Elkington-Gatic – access covers & frames – GATIC

Ellesco Diamond Paste – Ellesco Ltd

Ellesco Diamond Products – aqueous diamond lapping products – Ellesco Ltd

Ellesco Machines – Ellesco Ltd

Ellesmere – storage case – Acco East Light Ltd

Ellesmere – Prima Care

Ellesmere Port Pioneer – weekly title – Flintshire Chronicle Newspapers

Elliot – Red House Industrial Services Ltd

*Elliott (U.S.A.) – flexible drive shafts – Huco Dynatork

Elliott – contractors – Bearwood Engineering Supplies

Elliott Bear – Elgate Products Ltd

Elliott Lucas – pliers – Spear & Jackson plc

Ellis – production and sale of fancy woollen cloth – Joshua Ellis & Co.

Ellis – kitchen furniture – J T Ellis & Co. Ltd

Ellis Bridals – bridal dresses – Alandar Park

Ellis-Hotel Collection – hotel bedroom furniture – J T Ellis & Co. Ltd

Ellis-Scholar – school furniture – J T Ellis & Co. Ltd

Ellis-Solo Graduate – residential furniture – J T Ellis & Co. Ltd

Ellis-Vanity Flair – vanity units and bathroom furniture – J T Ellis & Co. Ltd

Ellison – circlips and retaining rings for automotive & industrial – Cirteq Ltd

Ellison – beds – Siddall & Hilton

Ellison – switchgear – Ellison Switchgear

Ellor – graphite spark erosion electrodes – Mersen UK

*Ellora – Saffron – Trade Link London Ltd

ELM – receiver – Armitage Shanks Ltd

Elma – watch cleaning machines – Time Products UK Ltd

Elmag – Apex Computer Services Wales Ltd

Elmatear Tautex – tear tester digital crimp tester – James H Heal & Co. Ltd

Elmelec – regn no 1-141-160 mica for foundries – Elmelin Ltd

Elmelin – regn no 1-141-161 elec insulation – Elmelin Ltd

Elmflex – regn no 1-154-045 flexible micanite – Elmelin Ltd

Elmo – Lamphouse Ltd

Elmtube – regn no 1-154-046 mica tubes – Elmelin Ltd

Elmwood – design consultants – Elmwood

Elobau – Relec Electronics Ltd

Elolegic – security lock systems – Kaba Ltd Head Office

Elora – S J Wharton Ltd

Elora Tools – Trafalgar Tools

*Elotest – Rohmann UK Ltd

*Elotip – Rohmann UK Ltd

Elox – Harrier Fluid Power Ltd

Elpec – metal bathroom accessories and metal giftware – Pascal & Co. Ltd

Elpower – lead acid batteries – Pulsar Developments Ltd

Elpress – crimp lugs and tools – Wellhead Electrical Supplies

ELPRO – Radio links – Halcyon Solutions

Elridge, Pope & Co. – managed, tenancy public houses – Marstons plc

ELRO (Germany) – pump – Crane Process Flow Technology Ltd

ELRO Pumps – Alfa Laval Eastbourne Ltd

Elsa – emergency life support apparatus – Scott International Ltd

Elsafe – Assa Abloy Hospitality Ltd

Elsan – portable toilets and sanitary chemicals – Elsan Ltd

ELSEC – metal detectors, magnetometers and UV monitors – Littlemore Scientific

*Elsner (U.S.A.) – roll wrapping equipment – Wrapid Manufacturing Ltd

Elson – Baxi Group

Elson – combination tanks, integrated plumbing units and mains pressure hotwater systems – Elsy & Gibbons

Elstar – refrigeration – Interlevin Refrigeration Ltd

Elstead Lighting – Light Fantastic

Elster Jeavons – OEM – Elster Kromschroder

Elsyl Range – Hotel Complimentary Products

Elta Fans – Northern Fan Supplies Ltd

Elterwater – natural slate – Burlington Slate Ltd

Elterwater Slate – roofing and architectural slates – Burlington Slate Ltd

*Eltex (United Kingdom) – greenhouse heaters and poultry equipment – Parasene

Eltex – Resinex UK Ltd

Eltra – Encoders UK

Eltron – thermal/thermal transfer printers – Datatrade Ltd

Eltron – Plastic ID card printers – Lancer Labels Ltd

Elu – Central C N C Machinery Ltd

*Elumatec (Germany) – machinery for aluminium and UPVC window and door fabrications – Elumatec UK Ltd

Elux – Lamphouse Ltd

Elvaloy – resin modifers – Du Pont UK Ltd

Elvamide – nylon multipolymer resin – Du Pont UK Ltd

Elvanol – polyvinyl alcohol resins – Du Pont UK Ltd

Elvax – vinyl resins – Du Pont UK Ltd

Elvax – EVA copolymers – Omya UK Ltd

ELVD – end of life vehicle directive - legislation – Protective Finishing Group

Elvetham Hall – conference centre – Elvetham Hotel Ltd

ELVO – Link Hamson Ltd

*Elvox (Italy) – video and audio door porters – Raytel Security Systems Ltd

Elwood Clamp (United Kingdom) – picture frame clamp – Lemsford Metal Products 1982 Ltd

ELWOOD CORPORATION – Hydraulic & Offshore Supplies Ltd

ELY ENERGY – waterbath vapourisers – H K L Gas Power Ltd

Ely Weekly News – newspapers – Cambridge Newspapers Ltd

Elysium – UK Office Direct

EM&S – Hydraulic & Offshore Supplies Ltd

EMA – punches – Pryor Marking Technology Ltd

email to fax – Callsure Business Telephone & Fax Numbers

EMB – Hydraulic & Offshore Supplies Ltd

Embassy Blue – filter cigarettes – Imperial Tobacco Group PLC

Embassy Filter – filter cigarettes – Imperial Tobacco Group PLC

Embassy Leisure Breaks – Jarvis Hotels Ltd

Embassy Number 1 – filter cigarettes – Imperial Tobacco Group PLC

Embedded Returning Wall – to provide vertical support to basements etc – Simplex Westpile Limited

Embee (France) – slate – Cembrit Ltd

Emblem – fishing tackle – Daiwa Sports Ltd

Embond – flooring adhesive – Tarkett Ltd

Embra – instruments – Canongate Technology Ltd

Embroidery Badges – Unique individually created embroidery badges – J & A International Ltd

Emcel – air filtration, purification and clean air equipment – Emcel Filters Ltd

Emcel-X Replacement Carbon Cells – emcels economy range of Activated Carbon Filter cells and panels to suit any existing filter installation – Emcel Filters Ltd

Emco – Ets-Lindgren Ltd

Emco Hobbymachines – lathes and mills for model engineering – Pro Machine Tools Ltd

EMCO-TEST – Hardness testers – Struers Ltd

Emco-Wheaton – fluid handling equipment, tank truck valves and fittings – Emco Wheaton

Emcoat – East Midland Coatings Ltd

Emcom Emcom Plus – software – East Midland Computers Ltd

Emcor – reinforcement fibre – Lawrence Industries Ltd

Emcron – custom built, absolute HEPA panel and radial filters – Emcel Filters Ltd

Emde GmnH (Germany) – industrial brakes – Centa Transmissions

Emdithene – polyurethane that offers a wider temperature range than standard polyurethane and improved moisture resistance – Robnor Resins Ltd

Emerald – chemicals – Kodak Morley

Emerald – portable filter unit – P M D UK Ltd

Emerald f&b – Softbrands

Emerald Golf – Softbrands

Emerald Spa – Softbrands

*Emerald Spoiler Soft Touch (Netherlands) – spoiler roof electric – Webasto Products UK Ltd

Emerlux – lighting & lighting components – Coughtrie International Ltd

Emerson – Asco Numatics

Emflex – unique flexible cleanable filter pads – Emcel Filters Ltd

Emflex – rubber flexible connectors – N Minikin & Sons Ltd

Emflon – filter medium – Pall Europe Corporate Services

Emgee – UK Office Direct

Emguard – earth continuity monitor – F D B Electrical Ltd

EMI-MEC – automatic lathes, CNC platen lathes and 2, 3 and 4axes CNC lathes and suppliers of vertical machining centres – Emi-Mec Ltd

Emiflex – Akzo Nobel Packaging Coatings Ltd

Eminox – stainless steel exhaust systems – Eminox Ltd

Emir – work benches, wood and plastic hand tools – Emmerich Berlon Ltd

Emissa (Switzerland) – multispindle drilling and tapping machines and heads – Haesler Machine Tools

Emistop – filter connectors – Selectronix Ltd

Emix – electromagnetically inducted, stirrer – Solois Thermal Ltd

EMM – electrochemical micro machining – Loadpoint Ltd

Emma – various electrical products – Inman & Co Electrical Ltd

Emmark – agricultural parts supply – Emmark UK Ltd

EMMEGAS – automotive LPG equipment – H K L Gas Power Ltd

EMMEGI – Hydraulic & Offshore Supplies Ltd

Emmegi – Air Blast, Water/Oil and Off-line Cooling Systems – J B J Techniques Ltd

Emmegi – non-ferrous circular sawing machines – Addison Saws Ltd

*Emmelle (Taiwan) – cycles – Moore Large & Co. Ltd

EMMERGI – Hydraulic & Offshore Supplies Ltd

Emmevi – tangential fan motors – Thermofrost Cryo plc

Emo – mainspring and waved washers – George Emmott Pawsons Ltd

EMP – M P E Ltd

EMP Intelligence Service – consultants in competitor intelligence – E M P Intelligence Service

Empera – polystyrene – B P plc

Emperor – cable cleat – Ellis Patents Ltd

Empetal – perfume speciality – Quest International UK Ltd

Emphasis – industrial felt tip markers – Roger Needham & Sons Ltd

Empire – ladders – J Gorstige Ltd

*Empire Bow (Worldwide) – mail order catalogue – Redcats UK

Empire Tooling – cut off blades and holders – J J Churchill Ltd

Employee Counselling – FOCUS Eap

Employee Management System – Topaz Computer Systems Ltd

Employees Assistance Programmes – FOCUS Eap

Emporio – casual wear – Raves Clothing Ltd

Emprep – non-silicated cleaner – Cookson Electronics Ltd

Empress – towel rail – Hampshire Electroplating Co. Ltd

Empress – bathroom accessories – Ideal Standard Ltd

Empteezy – waste handling equipment and drum storage equipment – Empteezy Ltd

EMR Company – Specialist in scrap metal – E M R Ltd

Emralon – East Midland Coatings Ltd

Emreco – ladies fashion separates – Emreco International Ltd

EMS – C P Cases Ltd

EMS – software package – Paxton Computers Ltd

Emsa – UK Office Direct

*Emsens (France) – kebab machines – Selo UK Ltd

Emslie Fallows – barrel burnishing and polishing equipment, media and compounds – Lea Manufacturing Co.

Emsworth Yacht Harbour – marina operators – Emsworth Yacht Harbour Ltd

EMT – Kone Cranes Machine Tool Services

EMT – Hydraulic Press – ECO Hydraulic Presses Ltd

EMTA – short form for engineering training authority – Science Engineering & Manufacturing Technologies

EMTA Awards Ltd – awarding body – Science Engineering & Manufacturing Technologies

Emuflo – vinyl floor convering systems – Emusol Products Ltd

Emuge – Precision Tools

Emulation Technology Inc – Jacarem Ltd

Emupad – underlay & shockpads for sports flooring – Emusol Products Ltd

Emupol – polyurethane sports flooring system – Emusol Products Ltd

Emuseal – floor sealants – Emusol Products Ltd

En Colline – wine – Rodney Densem Wines Ltd

EN397 – Head Protection – Scott International Ltd

EN795 – Rapid Rail GB Ltd

EN812 – Bump Cap or Safety baseball caps – Scott International Ltd

Ena Shaw – Ena Shaw Ltd

Enalon – plastic injection moulders – Enalon Ltd

Enamelcoat – high build solventless epoxy coating – Conren Ltd

Enamelling – chroming and all special finishes – Witcomb Cycles

*Enarco (Spain) – vibration equipment – La Roche

Enbond 808 – electro de-oxodising cleaner – Cookson Electronics Ltd

Enbond HD 162 – heavy duty soak cleaner – Cookson Electronics Ltd

Encad – Graphtec GB Ltd

Encase Ltd – corrugated fibreboard packaging – Encase Ltd
Encaustic – Cesol Tiles Ltd
Enclosures – electrical enclosures and junction boxes – Hawke International
Encoders – Encoders UK
Encopanel – heat conservation for steel mills – Encomech Engineering Developments Ltd
*****Encore (South Korea, Romania India, Taiwan and Slovenia)** – electric and acoustic guitars – John Hornby Skewes & Co. Ltd
Encore – range of recycled plastics – Luxus Ltd
Encore – steel circular saw blades – Dynashape Ltd
Encore (United Kingdom) – standing, raising and transferring hoist for the hospital environment – Arjo Med AB Ltd
Encore – K3 Business Technology Group plc
Encore – mechanical diaphragm metering pumps – Wallace & Tiernan Ltd
Encore – automation system – A M S Neve Ltd
Encore 434 – seating – Audience Systems Ltd
Encyclopaedia Britannica – Encyclopaedia Britannica UK Ltd
End Caps – PVC and neoprene – Plastic Mouldings Ltd
Endat – Encoders UK
Endat – HEIDENHAIN GB LTD
ENDECOTTS – Hydraulic & Offshore Supplies Ltd
Endomix – industrial gases – Boc Gases Ltd
*****Endon (Italy and Spain)** – domestic lighting – Endon Lighting Ltd
Endon Lighting – Light Fantastic
Endox 214 – de-rusting agent – Cookson Electronics Ltd
Endox L 76 – lacquer removal – Cookson Electronics Ltd
Endress & Hauser – European Technical Sales Ltd
Endura – industrial lubricant – B P plc
Endura Transfers – Long life commercially laundering work wear transfers – J & A International Ltd
Enduraflex – ducting – James Dawson & Son Ltd
Endurance – decorative paints – Akzonobel
Endurance Plate – silver plate wear – Goldsmiths Jewellers Ltd
Enduro – pre-fabricated timber fence panel system with steel posts, for industrial or domestic use – Buffalo Timber Buildings
ENDURO – high performance macro-synthetic fibres – Propex Concrete Systems Ltd
ENDURO – Phoenix Weighing Services Ltd
Ener – B P plc
ENER-G – Ener-G Combined Power
Enerbio – B P plc
Enercare – B P plc
Enercoat – B P plc
Enerflex – B P plc
Energas – industrial gas supply – Engineering & Welding Supplies Ltd
Energas – industrial gas filling distribution – Energas Ltd
Energaz – B P plc
Energear – B P plc
*****Energi Roof (Sweden)** – insulted aluminium roofing – Plannja Ltd
Energia – Electricity Utility – Viridian Group Ltd
Energilite – Emergi Lite Safety Systems Ltd
Energiser 4:19 – high quality, palm oil-based feed – Quality Liquid Feeds Ltd
Energol – B P plc
ENERGOS – Ener-G Combined Power
Energrease – B P plc
Energy – forage maize variety – Limagrain UK Ltd
Energy – Stream Measurement Ltd
Energy Chain – Igus (UK) Ltd
Energy Efficient – IsoCool Ltd
Energy-Lok – roof insulation – Celotex Ltd
ENERGY PROCESS – Hydraulic & Offshore Supplies Ltd
Energy Saving – IsoCool Ltd
EnergySaver Blown Cavity Wall Insulation – injected cavity wall insulation in loose form – Rockwool Rockpanel B V
*****Enerpac (U.S.A.)** – lifting equipment – Worlifts Ltd
Enerpac – hydraulic parts – A C Hydraulics Ltd
Enerpac – Enerpac UK
ENERPAC – Hydraulic & Offshore Supplies Ltd
Enerpac – Hydraulic Component & Systems Ltd
ENERPAC INDUSTRIAL TOOLS – Hydraulic & Offshore Supplies Ltd
ENERPAC PRODUCTION AUTOMATION – Hydraulic & Offshore Supplies Ltd
ENERPAC TORQUE WRENCHES – Hydraulic & Offshore Supplies Ltd
Enerpar – B P plc
Enerprint – B P plc
Enersyn – B P plc
Enertec – electronic equipment – Bearwood Engineering Supplies
Enerthene – B P plc
*****Enertrols (U.S.A.)** – shock absorbers – A C Hydraulics Ltd
Enfil – engineered fibre products – Thermal Ceramics UK Ltd
Engage – polyethylene elastomers – Omya UK Ltd

Engel – Proplas International Ltd
Engelhard – spares & equipment – Bearwood Engineering Supplies
Engelmotoren – European Technical Sales Ltd
Engelsberg – Kee Valves
Engine's Choice, The – B P plc
Engineering – special products – Ceratizit UK Ltd
Engis – Engis UK Ltd
Englemere Ltd – Chartered Institute of Building
English Abrasives – Sal Abrasives Technologies
English Lavender, The – lavender toiletry preparations (soap, talc, perfume etc) – Norfolk Lavender Trading Ltd
Enham Candles (United Kingdom) – candles – Enham Charity Shop
Enhance – modern high gloss super polish – Evans Vanodine International plc
Enhanced Memory – M S C Gleichmann UK Ltd
ENIDINE – Hydraulic & Offshore Supplies Ltd
Enigma Teeth – Schottlander Dental Equipment Supplies
Enlyte – electroless nickel – Cookson Electronics Ltd
ENM (United Kingdom) – counters and numbering machines – Zodion Ltd
Enodis – Catercraft Catering Equipment
Enots – tube fittings and tubing – Norgren Ltd
ENOTS – Hydraulic & Offshore Supplies Ltd
Enots – Southern Valve & Fitting Co. Ltd
Enots – B L Pneumatics Ltd
ENOTTS – Hydraulic & Offshore Supplies Ltd
Enpac – Safety Unlimited
Enplate – electroless plating solutions – Cookson Electronics Ltd
Enplate 432 – sensitisation of non-conducting surfaces – Cookson Electronics Ltd
Enplate 473 – conditioner for plastics – Cookson Electronics Ltd
Enplate 498 – neutralizer following 497 – Cookson Electronics Ltd
Enplate Accelerator 860 – post activator for plastics – Cookson Electronics Ltd
Enplate Act. 443 – activator for pc boards – Cookson Electronics Ltd
Enplate Activator 850 – activator for plastics – Cookson Electronics Ltd
Enplate AD 481 – etching of copper laminate – Cookson Electronics Ltd
Enplate AD 485 – etch for copper – Cookson Electronics Ltd
Enplate CU 406 – electroless copper for plastics & printed circuits – Cookson Electronics Ltd
Enplate CU 83 – high speed electroless copper – Cookson Electronics Ltd
Enplate Cu 872 – electroless copper for plastics – Cookson Electronics Ltd
Enplate Initiater 582 – activator for copper – Cookson Electronics Ltd
Enplate MB 435 – high peel strength black oxide – Cookson Electronics Ltd
Enplate MB 436 – black oxide for polymide and epoxy – Cookson Electronics Ltd
Enplate MB 6365 – high peel strength black oxide – Cookson Electronics Ltd
Enplate MLB 495 – polarize and swell – Cookson Electronics Ltd
Enplate MLB 497 – permanganate etch – Cookson Electronics Ltd
Enplate MLB 7268 – neutraliser/conditioner after 497 – Cookson Electronics Ltd
Enplate Neutraliser 835 – neutraliser for chromic acid – Cookson Electronics Ltd
Enplate NI 414 – electroless nickel for plastics – Cookson Electronics Ltd
Enplate NI 415 – electroless nickel – Cookson Electronics Ltd
Enplate NI 418 Special – bright stable electroless nickel – Cookson Electronics Ltd
Enplate NI 422 – electroless nickel high phosphorous – Cookson Electronics Ltd
Enplate NI 426 – electroless nickel for metals and plastics – Cookson Electronics Ltd
Enplate NI 429 – low phosphorus electroless nickel for pit free heavy deposit – Cookson Electronics Ltd
Enplate NI 434 – bright stable electroless nickel – Cookson Electronics Ltd
Enplate PC 451 – cleaner for printed circuits – Cookson Electronics Ltd
Enplate Pre Etch 3489 – solvent etch for plastics – Cookson Electronics Ltd
Enprep – immersion & electro cleaner – Cookson Electronics Ltd
Enprep – heavy duty electrolytic cleaner – Cookson Electronics Ltd
Enprep – satin etch – Cookson Electronics Ltd
Enpro – Harrier Fluid Power
Enreco – Head recovery and ventilation – Tev Ltd
ENROL – Electronic National Remote On-Line Learning – Its Training Services

ENSACO – Timcal Graphite & Carbon
Enshu – Warwick Machinery Ltd
Ensign – lighting equipment – Powerlite Lighting Solutions Ltd
Ensine Driven Pumps – Denton Pumps Ltd
*****Ensival-Moret** – centrifugal pumps – A J G Waters Equipment Ltd
Ensove Concrete Products – channel drainage high capacity – R Swain & Sons
*****Ensto (Finland)** – 3-5 way connectors – Elkay Electrical Manufacturing Co. Ltd
Enstrip 165S – strips nickel, tin, lead, zinc, cadmium – Cookson Electronics Ltd
Enstrip A – strips nickel, copper, zinc, cadmium, silver & tin – Cookson Electronics Ltd
Enstrip NP – strips nickel – Cookson Electronics Ltd
Enstrip S – as Enstrip A but needs cyanide addition – Cookson Electronics Ltd
Enstrip TL 107 – peroxide based tin lead stripper – Cookson Electronics Ltd
Enstrip TL 142 – peroxide based tin lead stripper – Cookson Electronics Ltd
Enstrip TL Conc – strips tin-lead – Cookson Electronics Ltd
Enstrips – metal strippers – Cookson Electronics Ltd
Entech – architectural products – Environmental Technology
Entek – anti-corrosion & drying aids – Cookson Electronics Ltd
Entek CU 56 – drying & protection aids for copper and alloys – Cookson Electronics Ltd
Entek NR 37 – rust preventative – Cookson Electronics Ltd
Entek NR 47 – rinsing aid for metal parts – Cookson Electronics Ltd
Entek RSO – soluble rust preventative oil – Cookson Electronics Ltd
Enterasys Networks – Charlton Networks
Enterprise – solid fuel heating equipment – Dunsley Heat Ltd
Enterprise – flexible benefits – Western Provident Association Ltd
Enterprise – ultra-high speed rotary system – Harland Machine Systems Ltd
ENTERTROLS – Hydraulic & Offshore Supplies Ltd
Enthobrite CAD 900 – cadmium deposit – Cookson Electronics Ltd
Enthobrite CLZ 938 – fully bright chloride zinc processes – Cookson Electronics Ltd
Enthone – Cookson Electronics Ltd
Enthox 8450 – irridescent passivate for chloride zinc deposits – Cookson Electronics Ltd
Enthox 986 – zinc passivation – Cookson Electronics Ltd
Enthox ZB 992 – black conversion coating for zinc – Cookson Electronics Ltd
Enthox ZB992 – black conversion coating for zinc – Cookson Electronics Ltd
Entivity VLC – Steeplechase Visual Logic Controller (VLC) is the fastest control software for manufacturing – Easymatics Ltd
Entonox – medical gases – Boc Gases Ltd
Entra-Lok – connector backshell locking device – Icore International
ENTRAN – StrainSense Ltd
Entrance Matting – Boston Links entrance matting – Boston Retail Products
Entrico – lighting & lighting components – Coughtrie International Ltd
Entrust – network security functions – Nortel Networks UK Ltd
Envetron – ancilliary printing equipment – N V Tools Ltd
Envioroclean – consumer products – Yule Catto & Co plc
Enviraclean – finishing systems – Hodge Clemco Ltd
Enviraclean - Clemco - Clemcote - Holloblast. – Hodge Clemco Ltd
Enviro-Tech – paper – Fenner Paper Co. Ltd
Enviro-weld – Assured Solutions Ltd
Enviro-X – hollow fibre membrane waste treatment unit – Kalsep UK
Envirocote Plus – paper products – Mcnaughton James Paper Group Ltd
Envirofast – fast acting roller doors – Envirohold Ltd
Enviroflex – valve stem sealing system – Flexitallic Ltd
Enviroflex – British Vita plc
Envirogard – dust and fume control hire – Envirogard Specialist Hires Ltd
Envirogard – water based high performance coatings – Leighs Paints
Envirogreen – special waste disposal – Envirogreen Special Waste Services Ltd
Envirolator – ceiling mounted power diffuser – Envirotec Ltd
Envirolats – environmentally friendly catalysts for alylation, alkmation, benzoylation, benzylation, esterifilation and oxidation realmond – Contract Chemicals Ltd
Envirolite – industrial stacking doors – Envirohold Ltd
Enviromat – heavy duty rubber industrial flooring – Linatex Ltd
Enviromat – Q Lawns In The Midlands
Enviromix 2000 (United Kingdom) – low nox burners – Hamworthy Combustion Engineering Ltd
Environmental Consultancy University of Sheffield – environment assessment, audit, planning, landscape design

and management, habitat assessment, ecological survey, pollution management and analysis, waste management and environmental engineering – E C U S

Environmental Street Furniture (ESF) – lighting, bollard & other highway items – Burden Ltd

Enviropak – Gas Fired Heating, Ventilation & Cooling Units – Reznor UK Ltd

Enviroplac Helps Save The Forests – wood plaques, trophies and silverware – Cannon.Co.Uk

Enviroplast – hygiene doors – Envirohold Ltd

Enviroquest – multi-purpose biodegradable sequestering agent – Contract Chemicals Ltd

Enviroscreen – overdoor warm air curtain – Envirotec Ltd

Enviroshield – transparent security shutter – Envirohold Ltd

Envirosol – Forward Chemicals Ltd

Envirostart – Proplas International Ltd

Envirovalve – Darcy Products Ltd

Envizion – pretreatment chemicals for printed circuits – Cookson Electronics Ltd

Envo-Flap – Anglo Adhesives & Services Ltd

Envo-Patch – Anglo Adhesives & Services Ltd

Envo-Seal – adhesives for envelope manufacture – Anglo Adhesives & Services Ltd

Envo-Seam – Anglo Adhesives & Services Ltd

Envo-Tack – Anglo Adhesives & Services Ltd

Envop – B P plc

Envoy – Communications – Scott International Ltd

Envoy – envelopes – Office Team

Envoy – teleprinters and packet switching equipment – Nortel Networks UK Ltd

Envoy – lockers, cubicles and bench seating – Link Lockers

Envron – B P plc

Envydro – Forward Chemicals Ltd

Enzieflex – paramelt

EO – Hydraulic & Offshore Supplies Ltd

EO2 – Hydraulic & Offshore Supplies Ltd

EP™ – GGB UK

EP12™ – GGB UK

EP202 – I T W Plexus

EP203 – C-Tec Security Ltd

EP205 – I T W Plexus

EP22™ – GGB UK

EP225 – I T W Plexus

EP250 – I T W Plexus

EP43™ – GGB UK

EP44™ – GGB UK

EP63™ – GGB UK

EP64™ – GGB UK

EP73™ – GGB UK

EP79™ – GGB UK

Epanoil – pharmaceutical fish gel – Seven Sea's Ltd

epc – Link Hamson Ltd

Epcos – Cyclops Electronics Ltd

EPCOS – passive components – Anglia

EPDM – W Mannering London Ltd

EPE – Hydraulic & Offshore Supplies Ltd

EPE – E P E UK Ltd

EPG – speed reducers and geared motors – A T B Laurence Scott Ltd

Epic – manufacture golf driving range equipment (01795) 427333 – Pareto Golf Ltd

Epic – games, playthings, miniatures and models all for use in playing games – Games Workshop Ltd

Epicon – enamels and lacquers – Craig & Rose Ltd

Epidek – epoxy deck coatings – Leighs Paints

Epidox – epoxy enamel paints – Witham Oil & Paint Lowestoft Ltd

Epidox 1 – epoxy enamel – Witham Oil & Paint Lowestoft Ltd

Epidox 2 – epoxy enamel – Witham Oil & Paint Lowestoft Ltd

Epidox Metacote – zinc rich primer – Witham Oil & Paint Lowestoft Ltd

Epigrip – epoxy high performance coatings for chemical resistance – Leighs Paints

Epimet – metallurgical mircroscope – Prior Scientific Instruments Ltd

Episcan – portable inspection microscope – Prior Scientific Instruments Ltd

Episode 4 – paper – Fenner Paper Co. Ltd

Epitag 2400 – heavy duty reel to reel label printers – Episys Group Ltd

Epitag Elite – label design and printing software – Episys Group Ltd

Epitag Elite Lite – low cost label design and printing software – Episys Group Ltd

Epitex – reinforced hide palm leather gloves – Bennett Safetywear

Epitome PMS – Softbrands

Epitome Res Portal – Softbrands

Epobond – high ductility pre-bonding zin plating – T W B Finishing Ltd

Epoc – plastic film capacitors – Anglia

Epocel – filter medium – Pall Europe Corporate Services

Epodils – diluants for epoxy resins – Air Products PLC

Epoil – oil additive – Hornett Bros & Co. Ltd

Epophen – epoxide resins for boatbuilding – Wessex Resins & Adhesives Ltd

Epos – Tekdata Distribution Ltd

Epos – supplier of EPOS tills and systems – Torex Retail Holdings Ltd

Epos Hardware – Tekdata Distribution Ltd

Eposeal – metal coating by electrophoresis included in class no.40 – T W B Finishing Ltd

Eposeal 300 – universal epoxy primer – Gurit UK Ltd

Epoxy Resin Flooring Systems – Addagrip Surface Treatments Ltd

Epoxytect – Forward Chemicals Ltd

EPP-MAGNUS – Hydraulic & Offshore Supplies Ltd

EPP Magnus – high pressure hydraulics – A C Hydraulics Ltd

*Eprinex – Merial Animal Health Ltd

EPS-Dricase – longterm storage and transport of high value equipment – E P S Logistics Technology Ltd

EPS-Driclad – flexible environmental protection system – E P S Logistics Technology Ltd

EPS-Dripak – reuseable, flexibly jointed, tough container – E P S Logistics Technology Ltd

Epsilon – paper – Fenner Paper Co. Ltd

Epsom – Try & Lilly Ltd

Epsom – steel bath – Ideal Standard Ltd

Epsom – UK Office Direct

Epsom Buses – local bus operation – Epsom Quality Line

Epsom Cash Registers – Cash Register Services

Epsom Coaches – coach hire – Epsom Quality Line

Epsom Holidays – tour operating – Epsom Quality Line

Epsom Salt – magnesium sulphate crystals and powder – Harris Hart & Co. Ltd

Epsom Salt Crystals – magnesium sulphate – Harris Hart & Co. Ltd

Epsom Travel – retail travel agency – Epsom Quality Line

Epson – Cyclops Electronics Ltd

Epson – Lamphouse Ltd

EPSON – Forever Scotland IT Consultancy

Epson – Epson inkjet cartridges & laser toners – Inkxperts

Epson – printer, scanner and electronic component supplier, video projector, consumables – Epson

EPU – sectional garage door – Hörmann (UK) Ltd

Equate – automatic call distribution system – Storacall Engineering Ltd

Equatherm – heating and cooling rolls – Cope Engineering Ltd

Equbond (United Kingdom) – items for equestrian trade – Vale Brothers

Equichip – equestrian surface – Melcourt Industries

Equichips – equestrian surface – Melcourt Industries

Equifall – equestrian surface – Melcourt Industries

Equifax (United Kingdom) – providers of information services to all industries. – Equifax plc

Equifax Cheque Solutions – providers of information services to all industries. – Equifax plc

Equifax HPI – providers of information services to all industries. – Equifax plc

Equifax Payment Services – providers of information services to all industries. – Equifax plc

Equifibre – equestrian surface – Melcourt Industries

EquiGran – granules for horse arenas – J Allcock & Sons Ltd

Equila – label design and printing software – Episys Group Ltd

Equilon – I.B.S. (irrable bowel syndrome) – Chefaro UK Ltd

Equimat – high tec box matting for horses – Davies & Company

*Equimax – Wormer paste, horses – Virbac Ltd

*Equinox (Far East) – watches – Zeon Chemicals Europe Ltd

Equinox – multi-platform data management system – Compsoft plc

Equinoxe – short-platform wheel-free scissor lift for vehicles – Tecalemit Garage Equipment Co. Ltd

Equip Trans – Betterbox Communications Ltd

Equipcare – repairs to all types of outdoor equipment, rucksacks, gaiters etc – S P H Europe plc

Equipment IP Over Voice – Tekdata Distribution Ltd

Equisand – equestrian surface – Melcourt Industries

EquiShred – shred for horse arenas – J Allcock & Sons Ltd

Equitree – riding boot tree – Dunkelman & Son Ltd

Equity – softleather ladies fashion and comfort footwear – Equity Shoes Ltd

Equiwrap – veterinary tissues, bandage, equiplast-adhesive bandage – Robinson Healthcare Ltd

*Eqvalan – Merial Animal Health Ltd

ERA – transformers – Stontronics Ltd

Eradicate – A deodorizer for eliminatig unpleasant odours in kitchens, toilets & washrooms – Hilti GB Ltd

Eraser – A cleaner and deodorizer for use in toilet and washroom areas – Hilti GB Ltd

Erasit – A low hazard graffitic remover – Premiere Products Ltd

Eratron – electronic valves and semiconductors – Edicron Ltd

*Erben J. Fischer (Germany) – German wines – O W Loeb & Co. Ltd

Ercol – furniture – Ercol Furniture Ltd

Erebus – Kuwait Petroleum International Lubricants UK Ltd

Erecta Switch – plastic level & flow switches – Tamo Ltd

Erem – cutters, pliers & tweezers – Welwyn Tool Group Ltd

Erem – cutter, pliers & tweezers – Apex Tools

ERG – M S C Gleichmann UK Ltd

Ergo – industrial safety harnesses – Spanset Ltd

ERGO / MEGA/COMPACT – Tool Presetting Equipment – Royal Tool Control Ltd

*ErgoPulse (Sweden) – impulse nutrunners – Atlas Copco Tools Ltd

Ergorex EXA – profile cutting machine – Easab Cutting Systems

ErgoScan – motorised microscope stage – Prior Scientific Instruments Ltd

Ergostyle – for aesthetic user-friendliness – Elesa (UK) Ltd

Eric the Penguin – Humorous Cards – Great British Card Company plc

Erico – Lower voltage components electrical panels – Wellhead Electrical Supplies

Ericom – Remote Communications Software – D P M Electronics Ltd

Ericsson – Cyclops Electronics Ltd

Eriez – magnetic separators (ferrous and non-ferrous); superconducting magnets – Eriez Magnetics Europe Ltd

*Eriks (Netherlands) – 'o' rings, seals, gaskets – E A P International Ltd

ERL – electrical distribution – Electro Replacement Ltd

Erma (United Kingdom) – hand and hydraulic crimping equipment – Sicame Electrical Developments Ltd

Ermaf – Hot Air Heaters – L S Systems Ltd

Ermatic – gas and airtight access covers – Norinco UK Ltd

Ernest Erbe – Trafalgar Tools

*Erosamat – soil erosion geomatting – A G A Group

Erowa (Switzerland) – EDM tooling systems – Rem Systems Ltd

Erro – Tool Stroage products – Erro Tool Co. Ltd

Errut – Belle Engineering Sheen Ltd

Ersta – coated abrasive products – Starcke Abrasives Ltd

ERTA-PC – Merseyside Metal Services

ERTACETAL – Merseyside Metal Services

ERTALON – Merseyside Metal Services

ERTALYTE – Merseyside Metal Services

Erwin Sick – European Technical Sales Ltd

ES – Ease Electrical Goods

ESA Encoders – European Technical Sales Ltd

Esab – Independent Welding Services Ltd

ESAB – welding manufrs & distbtrs – E S A B Group UK Ltd

Esab – S J Wharton Ltd

Esab Products – Wessex Welding & Industrial Supplies Ltd

Esbrid – ceramic reinforced polyamides – Asahi Thermofil UK Ltd

Escalator Safetystrip – escalator brushstrip deflector device – Kleeneze Sealtech Ltd

Escalator Shutters – rolling shutters non fire – Bolton Gate Co. Ltd

Escapism – Equipline

Escenti – tea tree products for body and hair, also a head lice repellent range – F M C G Ltd

*Eschenbach (Germany) – hotel porcelain – Bunzl Lockhart Catering Equipment

Esco – silicone rubber products – Bibby Scientific Ltd

Esco – vanity unit – Armitage Shanks Ltd

Esco – scouring pads – Murphy & Son

Esco – chemicals – Murphy & Son

ESCO – GET & Wear parts – Midland Steel Traders Ltd

Escol – vitreous enamel frits – Escol Products Ltd

Escor – constructional and other high grade wooden toys – Escor Toys Limited

Escort Elite – carpet cleaner – Clantex Ltd

Escort Mediclean – medical cleaning products – Clantex Ltd

Escort Pro System – carpet cleaning machine (industrial) – Clantex Ltd

ESD Floor Scruber Drier Range – Pressure washers – B & G Cleaning Systems Ltd

Esdash – polypropylene compounds – Asahi Thermofil UK Ltd

Esdash – Resinex UK Ltd

ESE Direct – E S E Direct

eserver – Mid Blue International Ltd

Esher News Series – Times Review Series Of Newspapers

ESI – sensors – Anglia

ESK – slop hopper – Armitage Shanks Ltd

Eskbank – textile piece goods – Reid & Taylor Ltd

eski – janitorial and personal protective equipment supplies – Parker Merchanting Ltd

eski – janitorial and personal protective equipment supplies – Parker Merchanting Ltd

eski – janitorial and personal protective equipment supplies – Parker Merchanting Ltd

eski – janitorial and personal protective equipment supplies – Parker Merchanting Ltd

eski – janitorial and personal protective equipment supplies – Parker Merchanting Ltd

Eski – Gem Tool Hire & Sales Ltd

eski – janitorial and personal protective equipment supplies – Parker Merchanting Ltd

Eski – janitorial and personal protective equipment supplies – Parker Merchanting Ltd

eski – janitorial and personal protective equipment supplies – Parker Merchanting Ltd

Eskimo – anti-freeze – Fuchs Lubricants UK plc

Eskimo Ice – Eskimo Ice

Eskimo Joe – Slush Puppie Ltd

Eslinx – audio visual control products – Electrosonic Ltd

Esmerk – business information services – Esmerk

Esop – revision hips – Surgicraft Ltd

ESP – Fife Tidland Ltd

ESP – Lightning protection – Halcyon Solutions

*ESPA – Barber Pumps Ltd

ESPA – Arun Pumps Ltd

Espa Pumps – Denton Pumps Ltd

Espace 628 – seating – Audience Systems Ltd

ESPEC – Unitemp Ltd

ESPEC Corp – Unitemp Ltd

Espero – sliding/folding partitions – Envirohold Ltd

Espha – lighting equipment – Powerlite Lighting Solutions Ltd

Espia – lighting equipment – Powerlite Lighting Solutions Ltd

Espio (Japan) – Compacts – Pentax UK Ltd

*Espresso Warehouse – Matthew Algie & Co. Ltd

Esprit – accounting & finance – Kalamazoo - Reynolds Ltd

Esprit IV – pump action auto airfreshener – Vectair Systems Ltd

Esquire – magazine – National Magazine Company Ltd

*Ess (Germany) – MIG and TIG welding equipment, plasma cutters – Olympus Technologies Ltd

Essar – woodfinishes – Smith & Roger Ltd

Essdee – British scraperboard – Oasis Art & Craft Products Ltd

Esse – Uncoated Paper – Mcnaughton James Paper Group Ltd

Esselte – UK Office Direct

Essemtec – Pick & Place – Turner Electronics

Essential – tools/adhesives/stationery – P M S International Group plc

Essential Auto Accessories – P M S International Group plc

*Essential Cuisine – Essential Cuisine Ltd

ESSENTIAL TRAINING SOLUTIONS – TRAINING CD ROMS – Emergency Planning Solutions

Essentials – I P C Media Ltd

Essentials – Tektura plc

Essento – UK Office Direct

Essepiu – Seating – Bucon Ltd

Essex – cardboard boxes – Connect Packaging

Essex – Red House Industrial Services Ltd

Essex – filing cabinets – Railex Filing Ltd

Essex Chronicle, The – newspaper – Essex Chronicle Media Group

Essex Upholstery – Euro Group UK

Esshete – high alloy steels for high temperature applications – Corus Engineering Steels

*Essno (Norway) – white Norwegian marble – Rowebb Ltd

Esso – lubricants – Bearwood Engineering Supplies

Esso – Hammond Lubricants & Chemicals Ltd

Esso – Lubricants – Sprint Engineering & Lubricant

Essonia – vending syrups – Chequer Foods Ltd

*Estarta (Spain) – centreless grinders – Takisawa UK Ltd

Estarta – Newall UK Ltd

Estasan – medium chain triglycerine oils – Croda International plc

Estate – wire fencing – Arce Lormittal

ESTEEM – Redsky It

Esteram – suppository base materials – Croda International plc

Esterpeel – printed and unprinted lidding films for fresh and frozen convenience foods – F F P Packaging Solutions Ltd

*Estima – Agrico UK Ltd

Estol – esters – Croda International plc

Estomid – nylon compounds – Asahi Thermofil UK Ltd

Estwing – Gem Tool Hire & Sales Ltd

Estyrene – styrenic compounds – Asahi Thermofil UK Ltd

ESWA – electric floor and ceiling designers, installers – Eswa Ltd

Etabloc – K S B Ltd

Etadry – moisture testing oven – James H Heal & Co. Ltd

Etaline – K S B Ltd

Etalon (Switzerland) – calipers, gauge blocks, co-ordinate measuring machines – Tesa Technology UK Ltd

Etalon – Status Metrology Solutions Ltd

Etanorm – K S B Ltd

Etatron – European Technical Sales Ltd

ETCi – Redsky It

ETE – sectional garage door – Hörmann (UK) Ltd

Etel – HEIDENHAIN GB LTD

Eternabrite – leafing paste pigment – Silberline Ltd

Eternit – Fieldway Supplies Ltd

Ethafoam – frost protection mats for concrete curing – Union Industries

Ethafoam – British Vita plc

Ethernet – Tennco Distribution Ltd

Ethical office recycling – Paperchasers Ltd

Ethomid – ethoxylated long chain aliphatic amide – Akzo Nobel Chemicals Holdings Ltd

Ethos – Dixon Turner Wallcoverings Ltd

Ethyl Safranate – perfume speciality – Quest International UK Ltd

*Ethylcellulose (U.S.A.) – Hercules Holding Ii Ltd

Ethysorb – impregnated alumina – Molecular Properties Ltd

Eti – Alpha Electronics Southern Ltd

ETI – Trafalgar Tools

ETI – electrical testing instruments for electricity transmission systems – Adwel International Ltd

ETNA Mundo – E T N A Assist UK

ETNA Vega – E T N A Assist UK

Etri – Cyclops Electronics Ltd

ETS – Ets-Lindgren Ltd

Ettore Cella – Pressure Switches – Coulton Instrumentation Ltd

EU – central air conditioning plant – Flakt Woods Ltd

Eu Vision – identity card system – T S S I Sytems

Eubama – Bruderer UK Ltd

*Eubama (Germany) – automatic transfer and indexing drum machines – Brunner Machine Tools Ltd

Euchner – Euchner UK Ltd

*Euchner (Germany) – sensors – Sensortek

Euchner – European Technical Sales Ltd

EUCHNER – Multi-Limit Switches – Francis and Francis Ltd

EUCHNER – Multi limit switches – Francis and Francis Ltd

Euchner – Encoders UK

Euchner Connectors – European Technical Sales Ltd

Euchner Electronic Handwheels – European Technical Sales Ltd

Euchner Enabling Switches – European Technical Sales Ltd

Euchner Joystick Switches – European Technical Sales Ltd

Euchner Limit Switch – European Technical Sales Ltd

Euchner Pendant Stations – European Technical Sales Ltd

Euchner Plunger Limit Switch – European Technical Sales Ltd

Euchner Position Switch – European Technical Sales Ltd

Euchner Safety Relay – European Technical Sales Ltd

Euchner Safety Switch – European Technical Sales Ltd

Eudec – fire retardant emulsion – Craig & Rose Ltd

Eudecryl – acrylic paint – Craig & Rose Ltd

Eugenol – perfume speciality – Quest International UK Ltd

Euler Hermes Collections UK Ltd – Euler Hermes

Euler Hermes Risk Services UK Ltd – Euler Hermes

Euler Hermes UK plc – Euler Hermes

Euraqua (UK) – water treatment equipment and components – Ferex Ltd

Eurastyle – quartz mantel and wall clocks – L C Designs Ltd

Eureka – Central vacuum – Strathvac

Euro C – gas fired unit heaters – Reznor UK Ltd

Euro Car Parks – car park management company – Euro Car Parks Ltd

EURO CHAIN – Iwis Drive Systems

Euro Grade – free standing safes offering up to £100,000 recommended overnight cash cover – Securikey Ltd

Euro-Grill – Equipline

EURO HI-TEMP – Hydraulic & Offshore Supplies Ltd

Euro-HYGIA – Grundfos Pumps Ltd

Euro-Lube – lubricant – Scientific Lubricants Ltd

Euro-Matic – floating plastic balls, for energy conservation, liquid loss, and odour control: gas scrubber tower packing ulitizing fluidizationtechnology: precision solid plastic balls: oil skimming booms – Euro Matic Ltd

*Euro-Matic (Denmark) – hollow plastic balls, floating cover for energy conservation and odour control, precision solid plastic balls valves-bearings etc, oil pollution control, oil absorbing booms and gas scrubbing media – Euro Matic Ltd

Euro-Merchandisers – Equipline

Euro Motors – fan motors and assemblies – Thermofrost Cryo plc

Euro-Ovens – Equipline

Euro-Plus – Euro Matic Ltd

Euro R.S.C.G. – direct marketing – Arnold K L P

Euro Seating UK – Euro Group UK

Euro T – gas fired unit heaters – Reznor UK Ltd

Euro Test Lane – computerised automatic brake, suspension & alignment testing – Tecalemit Garage Equipment Co. Ltd

Euro Towers – Accessscaff International Ltd

Euro X – gas fired unit heaters – Reznor UK Ltd

Eurobar – continental bar system – I M C

Eurobench – steel work benches & work stations – Q M P

Euroblend – food colourings – Sensient

Eurobond – Eurobond Laminates Ltd

*Eurobord (France) – recovery board – Alumasc Exterior Building Products

Eurobox – A4 domestic mailbox – Safety Letter Box Company Ltd

Eurobraze – specialist welding comsumables – Weldability S I F

Eurobulk – Coated Paper – Mcnaughton James Paper Group Ltd

Eurocall – radiopaging, radio facsimile apparatus & instruments – Vodafone Retail Ltd

Eurocare – one stop solution to the fashion industry – Incair Ltd

*Eurocastors (Germany) – wheels and castors – Eurocastors

*Eurocave – Wine storage systems – Around Wine

Eurocell – Eurocell Building Plastics Ltd

Eurocert – food colourings – Sensient

Eurocert Instant – food colourings – Sensient

Eurocham – synthetic chamois leathers – Lancashire Sock Manufacturing Co.

Eurocoaches – H & H Commercial Truck Services Ltd

Eurocoin – supplier of spare parts to leisure, casino and vending industry – Eurocoin Ltd

Eurocol – food colourings – Sensient

Eurocowl – Simplefit Ltd

Eurocraft – enclosures – Eurocraft Trustees Ltd

Eurocure – Akzo Nobel Packaging Coatings Ltd

Eurodekor (United Kingdom) – melamine faced chipboard – Egger UK Ltd

Eurodigit – digital equipment – Bearwood Engineering Supplies

Euroduct – PVC ducting – Davico Industrial Ltd

EuroFile – R W S Group plc

Eurofire – Emergi Lite Safety Systems Ltd

EUROFLARE – Hydraulic & Offshore Supplies Ltd

Euroflex – disc couplings – Bibby Transmissions Ltd

EuroFlex – Baldor UK

Eurofloor – prefinished, laminated, hardwood flooring – Atkinson & Kirby Ltd

*Euroflow (Sweden) – duct fan – Roof Units Ltd

EUROFLOW – Hydraulic & Offshore Supplies Ltd

Euroflow - duct fan - Eurofoil - plate and duct axial fan - Europak - roof extract unit - Europitch - adjustable pitch cased axial fan - Euroseries - plate and duct axial fan - Gemini - twin ventilation - Powerline - duct fan - Slimpack - duct fan - Viking - air handling units – Roof Units Ltd

*Eurofoil (Germany) – plate and duct axial fan – Roof Units Ltd

Eurofold – folding shutter and lift doors – Bolton Gate Co. Ltd

Eurogauge – manufacturers level control and instrumentation – Afriso Eurogauge Ltd

Euroglow – food colourings – Sensient

Eurogran – food colourings – Sensient

Eurohike – camping equipment and leisure wear – Blacks Leisure Group plc

Eurohm – fixed resistors – Anglia

Eurolake – food colourings – Sensient

EUROLIFT – Chaintec Ltd

Euroline – Autron Products Ltd

Eurolines – scheduled coach travel to over 450 destinations throughout Europe and Ireland – Eurolines UK Ltd

Eurologic – Eurocell Building Plastics Ltd

Eurologic ovolo – Eurocell Building Plastics Ltd

Eurolok – nylon cable ties – Davico Industrial Ltd

EUROLOK – Hydraulic & Offshore Supplies Ltd

Eurolon – nylon (polyamide) tubing – Copely Developments Ltd

Euromach – Harrier Fluid Power Ltd

Euromay (Italy) – electro magnetic flowmeters – Litre Meter Ltd

Euromedica – executive search in healthcare – Euromedica plc

Euromesh – barrier fencing mesh – Boddingtons Ltd

Euromet – surveyors tapes – Fisco Tools Ltd

Euromotori – explosion proof motors – Amir Power Transmission Ltd

Europ Hydro – Harrier Fluid Power Ltd

Europa – Alpha Electronics Southern Ltd

Europa – files, folders, spiral notebooks & cash books – Exaclair Ltd

Europa – wall mounted closet – Ideal Standard Ltd

EUROPA – CNC & conventional milling machines – R K International Machine Tools Ltd

Europa – venetian blind system – Eclipse Blind Systems

Europa – grinding machines - surface, cylindrical and centreless - milling machines – R K International Machine Tools Ltd

Europa – UK Office Direct

Europa Tile – clay – Sandtoft Holdings Ltd

Europack – electric steam boilers – Fulton Boiler Works Ltd

EuropacPRO – subrack – Schroff UK Ltd

Europage – radiopaging apparatus & instruments – Vodafone Retail Ltd

Europak – roof extract unit – Roof Units Ltd

Europanel – Eurobond Laminates Ltd

European Antenna – Cobham Antenna Systems, Microwave Antennas
European Boatbuilder – I P C Media Ltd
European Fuel Cell – Baxi Group
Europitch – adjustable pitch cased axial fan – Roof Units Ltd
Europoint – The Paper Company Ltd
EUROPOWER HYDRAULICS – Hydraulic & Offshore Supplies Ltd
Europreme N (Italy) – acrylomitrile butadiene rubber – Polimeri Europa Ltd
Europreme SOLT (U.S.A.) – styreme isopreme styreme rubber – Polimeri Europa Ltd
Europreme SOLT (Italy) – Styreme butadiene styreme rubber – Polimeri Europa Ltd
***Europrene CIS (Italy)** – polybutadine rubber – Polimeri Europa Ltd
Europrene Neocis (Italy) – high CIS polybutadine – Polimeri Europa Ltd
Europress – hydraulic presses – Mackey Bowley International Ltd
Europressmen – hydraulic presses – Mackey Bowley International Ltd
EUROPULSE – Hydraulic & Offshore Supplies Ltd
Europurge – purging agent – Euro Bond Adhesives Ltd
Eurorack – 19" cabinet – Schroff UK Ltd
Eurorack – S R S Product plc
***Euroroof AA Solar Coating** – solar reflective paint – Alumasc Exterior Building Products
***Euroroof Barrel Rooflights (Germany)** – continous barrel and triangular rooflighting – Alumasc Exterior Building Products
Euroroof Solar White – solar reflective emulsion paint – Alumasc Exterior Building Products
Eurosalad – range of salad containers – Pregis Rigid Packaging Ltd
***Euroseries (Germany)** – plate and duct axial fan – Roof Units Ltd
Eurosert – anchor nut – Zygology Ltd
Euroservo – Motor Technology Ltd
Euroshield – Ets-Lindgren Ltd
Euroshop – metal shopfitting fixtures – Havelock Europa plc
EUROSLEEVE – Hydraulic & Offshore Supplies Ltd
Euroslide – storage drawer cabinets – Q M P
Eurosol – food colourings – Sensient
***Eurosonic (Hong Kong)** – Electrical electronics telecommunication accessories – Europasonic UK Ltd
Eurospan (United Kingdom) – raw chipboard – Egger UK Ltd
Eurosprint – fast acting overhead stacking door – Envirohold Ltd
Eurostar – clocks and watches – L C Designs Ltd
Eurostar – range of domestic free standing and wall mounted oil fired boilers. – Trianco Heating Products Ltd
Eurostar W.M – domestic wall hung oil fired boiler (internal & external) – Trianco Heating Products Ltd
Eurosteam – steam boiler – Babcock Wanson UK Ltd
Eurostrand OSB (Germany) – orientated strand board – Egger UK Ltd
Eurostud System 30 – round stud rubber flooring – Jaymart Roberts & Plastics Ltd
Eurostyle – The Winnen Furnishing Company
Eurosuits – mens wear – Eurosuits Ltd
Euroswap – intermodal swap bodies – Abel Demountable Systems Ltd
Eurotainer – 20-25 litre Square Round high density polyethylene container – Weltonhurst Ltd
Eurotape – road barrier tape – Boddingtons Ltd
Eurotec – Melitzer Safety Equipment
Eurotek – Desks – Bucon Ltd
Eurotek Office – Capex Office Interiors
EUROTEL – Versalift Distributors UK Ltd
Eurotex – lubricants – Chevron
Eurotherm – temperature regulators – Bearwood Engineering Supplies
Eurotherm – Watts Industries UK Ltd
Eurotherm – Radir Ltd
Eurotherm – Motor Technology Ltd
Eurotherm 650 – Proplas International Ltd
Eurotherm Drives – Proplas International Ltd
Eurotherm Drives – Parker
***Eurotile (Finland)** – lightweight metal tilesheets – Alumasc Exterior Building Products
Eurotrak – track mounted primery jaw crushing plant – Terex
Eurotrucker – ratchet lashings – Spanset Ltd
Eurotype – type – Pryor Marking Technology Ltd
Eurovent – breather vent – Alumasc Exterior Building Products
Eurovit – food colourings – Sensient
EUROWASH – Hydraulic & Offshore Supplies Ltd
Euroweb – lashing systems – G T Factors Ltd
Euroweb - lashing systems – G T Factors Ltd
***Eutrac (Germany)** – 3 circuit and low voltage lighting track – Selux UK Ltd
EV – heat resisting steel – Wearparts UK Ltd
EVA – Naylor Specialists Plastics
Evabrite – post dip lacquer after plating – Cookson Electronics Ltd
Evac+Chair – evacuation chairs – Evac+Chair International Ltd
Evamix – prepackers of aggregates - evamix LTD – Evamix Aggregates
Evans – bespoke concrete products for the construction industry – Evans Concrete Products Ltd
Evans & Brown – Tektura plc
Evans Extraction Cleaner – carpet cleaner – Evans Vanodine International plc
Evans Spray Polish – aerosol with cfc free perfume – Evans Vanodine International plc
Evantech – tube bending machines, equipment and tooling – Silkmead Tubular Ltd
Evasperse – pigmented dispersion in various resin media – Tennants Inks & Coating Supplies Ltd
Evatane – ethylene vinyl acetate copolymers (EVA) – Atosina UK Ltd
Evazote – EVA copolymer foam – Zotefoams plc
Evazote – W Mannering London Ltd
Eve (Europe, Western) – Everyvalve Ltd
EvE - 85 Mfd Lines - Everyvalve Ltd – Everyvalve Ltd
Eve Barriers – safety barriers, mesh panel fencing – Eve Trakway Ltd
Eve Shieldtrack – temporary roadways, high security fencing, temporary bridges and pedestrian walkways – Eve Trakway Ltd
Eve Trakway – temporary roadways, high security fencing and temporary bridges and pedestrian walkways – Eve Trakway Ltd
Evening Echo – evening newspaper – Newsquest Essex Ltd
Evening Gazette – Gazette Media Company
Evening Herald – paid newspaper – Western Morning News Co. Ltd
Evening Post – newspapers – Surrey & Berkshire Media Ltd
Evening Post Group – newspapers – Nottingham Evening Post
Evening Standard – newspapers – Associated Newspapers
Evening Telegraph – D C Thomson & Co. Ltd
Evenmist – controlled spray for propagation – Evenproducts Ltd
Evenmore Opaque – Publishing Paper – Mcnaughton James Paper Group Ltd
Evenproducts – water storage tanks – Evenproducts Ltd
Evenshower – outdoor and glasshouse spraylines – Evenproducts Ltd
Evenstorm – sprinkler irrigation system – Evenproducts Ltd
Event – photographic mounts – Denis Wright Ltd
Event Based Automation – software feature (logic series) – A M S Neve Ltd
Event Series – Belcom Cables Ltd
Event Series – wedding albums – Denis Wright Ltd
Eventa (United Kingdom) – items for equestrian trade – Vale Brothers
Eventing – I P C Media Ltd
Eventrickle – low pressure drip irrigation – Evenproducts Ltd
Events – Corporate hospitality & themed events – Pinewood Associates
Eventscaff – Accesscaff International Ltd
EVER SLIK – Coating – E M Coating Services
Everbond – fusible interlinings – William Clark & Sons Ltd
Everbright Stainless – stainless steel fasteners – Everbright Stainless
Everbuild – sealants – Arrow Supply Co. Ltd
Everbuild – expanding foam, mitre fast adhesive. cleaners and lubricants, quck scrim tape, decorating fillers, all purpose wood adhesive, pva & sbr bonding agents, surface treatments, building chemicals, compounds and expoxies, tile adhesives – Everbuild Building Products Ltd
Everbuild – Gem Tool Hire & Sales Ltd
***Evercion (Taiwan)** – reactive dyestuffs for the textile industry – Magna Colours Ltd
Everdry – cavity trays – Timloc Building Products
Everest – gas cutting and welding equipment – J Weston & Partners Ltd
Everest – knitwear – Anderson & Co.
Everest – mobile fall arrest devices – Capital Safety Group Ltd
Everest – Lamphouse Ltd
***Everett Masson and Furby** – E M & F Group Ltd
Everflex – flexible wallcoating – Everlac GB Ltd
Everfresh – environmentally safe daily toilet cleaner with apple perfume – Evans Vanodine International plc
Evergreen – office supplies – Evergreen Office Supplies
Evergreen – office plants – Office Depot UK
Evergreen Laid & Wove – Uncoated Paper – Mcnaughton James Paper Group Ltd
Everink – pre-inked rubber stamps – Mark C Brown Ltd
Everising – horizontal bandsaw machines – Addison Saws Ltd
Everlasto – ropes, twines, cords – James Lever & Sons Ltd
Everlight – M S C Gleichmann UK Ltd
Everlight – Cyclops Electronics Ltd
Everline – line marking spray – Everbuild Building Products Ltd
Everlube – E M Coating Services
Everseal – water based polyurethane seals and coatings – Everlac GB Ltd
Eversheds – solicitors – Eversheds
Eversheds – solicitors – Eversheds
Eversheds – solicitors – Eversheds
Evertex – very long life textured wallcoating – Everlac GB Ltd
Everyman's Library – trade mark for books – Everymans Library Ltd
Everything A Pound – household, fancy and stationery goods – Pound World Ltd
Evferflex – professional sealants, just the job sealants, DIY sealants – Everbuild Building Products Ltd
Evian – UK Office Direct
Evo-Plas – adhesives for bonding of all plastics – Anglo Adhesives & Services Ltd
Evo-Stik – adhesives for general industry – Anglo Adhesives & Services Ltd
Evo-Stik – Bostik Ltd
Evo-Stik – S J Wharton Ltd
Evode – B D K Industrial Products Ltd
Evolis – vacuum circuit breaker – Schneider
Evolis – ID Card Printer Manufacturer – Plastic ID
Evollution – Display Wizard Ltd
Evolution – A P T
Evolution – All saw blades – Dynashape Ltd
Evolution – Solicitors software – Iris Group
Evolution – rubber flooring, flexible skirting – Gerflor Ltd
Evolution Glass Ltd – Glazing Contractors – Evolution Glass Ltd
Evolve – UK Office Direct
Evolve – Budget Desking Range – Flexiform Business Furniture Ltd
Evopower – Quality Power Equipment - Petrol Generators, Diesel Generators – Genpower Ltd
Evox Rifa – Cyclops Electronics Ltd
Evrite – UK Office Direct
Evro – applied to galvanometers (DC) – Cam Metric Holdings
Evroglas Steps – Accesscaff International Ltd
Evron – milling dye stuffs – Town End Leeds plc
***EW (United Kingdom)** – architects – Ellis Williams Architects Ltd
EW – Mass Consultants Ltd
***EWA (United Kingdom)** – architects – Ellis Williams Architects Ltd
Ewab – automated materials handling systems – E W A B Engineering Ltd
Ewart – conveying and rotary drive, chains and sprockets for all industries, including steel, combination and malleable chains – Ewart Chain Ltd
***Ewenz (Germany)** – bending and cutting machines – Welwyn Tool Group Ltd
EWOS – Mass Consultants Ltd
Ewos – Ewos Ltd
Ewplas – plastic chain and wheels for food and bottling industries, special plastic chains on request – Ewart Chain Ltd
EWT – Eastern Water Treatment Ltd
EWT – Glen Dimplex UK Ltd
Ex Connectors – electrical power and control cable connections – Hawke International
Ex-Flow – Bronkhorst UK Ltd
Exacompta – UK Office Direct
Exact – cultures for fermented milks manufacture – Chr. Hansen (UK) Ltd
EXACTSENSE™ – thermocouple – Watlow Ltd
Exalign – self aligning plain bearing units – Criptic Arvis Ltd
Exalign – premounted self aligning bearings – Mahle Engine Systems
EXAPORE ELEMENTS – Hydraulic & Offshore Supplies Ltd
***Exar (U.S.A.)** – high temperature wire – Huber+Suhner (UK) Ltd
Exar – Cyclops Electronics Ltd
Exar (USA) – high temp wire – Huber+Suhner (UK) Ltd
Exbond – computer readable database of over 10,000 euro and international bonds – Interactive Data
Excal – inverters – Beatson Fans & Motors Ltd
Excalabur – Lusso Interiors
Excalibur – granite sawing steel grit (special) – Ervin Amasteel Ltd
Excalibur – light control system – Guardall Ltd
Excalibur – high security window locking systems – Archibald Kenrick & Sons
Excalibur – screwbolts/manufacturers and distributors – Excalibur Screwbolts Ltd
Excalibur – arsenic analyser – P S Analytical Ltd
Excalibur – Coatings reinforced with stainless steel for use in industry and consumer markets – Whitford Ltd
Excel – Harrier Fluid Power Ltd
***Excel (France)** – bituminous based built up roof waterproofing membranes and acoustic systems – Axter Ltd

Excel – architectural draftproofing – Kleeneze Sealtech Ltd
EXCEL – Machine Tools – Excel Machine Tools Ltd
Excel – 36-48 seater bus – Optare Group Ltd
Excel – Cooks Brushes
Excel Cell – switches & mosfet relays – Anglia
Excelastic – flexible geomembrane lining – Geosynthetic Technology Ltd
***Excelda Ivory Board (Netherlands)** – paper – H V Sier Ltd
***Excelflex (France)** – single-ply roof water proofing membrane – Axter Ltd
Exceliner – flexible geomembrane lining – Geosynthetic Technology Ltd
Excellac – french polish – Smith & Roger Ltd
Excellence – Kent Frozen Foods Ltd
Excellose – french polish – Smith & Roger Ltd
Excelon – B L Pneumatics Ltd
Excelon – pneumatic filtering, regulating and lubricating apparatus – Norgren Ltd
EXCELON – Hydraulic & Offshore Supplies Ltd
***Excelsior (Europe and The Far East)** – sales of textile fabrics – Excelsior Textiles Ltd
Excelsior – shoes – Patrick Shoes Ltd
Excelsior Charcoal – charcoal – Swift-Lite Charcoal
Excelsior Coachways – private coach hire – Excelsior Tours Ltd
Excelsior Holidays - Bournemouth – continental and British coach package holidays – Excelsior Tours Ltd
Excelsiur – luxury motor caravan – Auto Sleepers Ltd
Excelta – paramelt
Excelthene – blended polymer medium density – Gelpack Excelsior Ltd
***Excelto (France)** – hubs and tandem hubs – Rsi
Excelvayor – accumulating roller conveyor systems – Exmac
Exceptional Lipsticks – new lipstick range – Elizabeth Arden
Excess 2000 – boats – Sunseeker Poole Ltd
Exchem Mining – strata control systems for mines & tunnels – 2 K Polymer Systems Ltd
Excluder – seal designs – Trelleborg Ceiling Solutions Ltd
Exclusive – artificial flowers, plants, haberdashery and Christmas decorations – Sehlbach & Whiting Ltd
***Exclusive Heritage Venues** – marketing of heritage properties for corporate entertaining – Consilium ltd
Exe – grinders – The Exe Engineering Company Limited
Executel – telephone equipment – Nortel Networks UK Ltd
Executive – mens socks – H J Hall
Executive – modular accommodation – Rollalong Ltd
***Executive (Worldwide)** – women's headties and textiles piece goods – Metro Textiles Ltd
Executive – mobile air cleaner – Trion The Division Of Ruskin Air Management Ltd
Executive – luxury motor caravan – Auto Sleepers Ltd
Executive Occasions – corporate hospitality – Kuoni Travel Ltd
Exel – Cyclops Electronics Ltd
Exel – shock tube detonator – Orica UK Ltd
exel vets – Chapelfield Veterinary Surgeons
Exelite – lightweight PVC face display board – Strata Panels UK
ExerTherm (United Kingdom) – non contact thermal monitoring of electrical switchgear – Q H I Group Ltd
Exetainer – evacuated and non evacuated blood collection vials – Labco
Exeter – woven carpets in 100% pure new wool pile – Axminster Carpets Ltd
Exicon (United Kingdom) – lateral power audio mosfets – Profusion plc
Exit R – all terrain boards and accessories – Ventura Corporation
EXITFLEX HOSE/FITTINGS – Hydraulic & Offshore Supplies Ltd
Exmet Brickwork Reinforcement – brick reinforcement – Expamet Building Products Ltd
Exmoor – woven carpets in 100% pure new wool pile – Axminster Carpets Ltd
Exodor – Forward Chemicals Ltd
Exor – lighting management and control systems – Ex Or Ltd
Exotics – salad dressings and dips – A A K Ltd
Expamet – metal beads, metal laths, arch formers, metpost, wall starters & steel lintels, joist hangers, straps & structural fixings movement ties – Expamet Building Products Ltd
Expamet – expanded metal mesh – Genwork Ltd
Expand – Display Wizard Ltd
Expanda – self expanding tube cleaning brushes and scrapers – Rotatools UK Ltd
Expander – Expanding bolts for any pivot problem – Midland Steel Traders Ltd
Expandia – electro plated reaming tool – Winterthur Technology UK Ltd
Expanding Barriers – Accesscaff International Ltd
Expandol – foam compound – Angus Fire
Expansion Vessels – Abbott & Co Newark Ltd
Expel C – chemical cleaner – Anglo Nordic Burner Products Ltd
Explosimeter – gas detector – M S A Britain Ltd
Expo-Telektron Safety Systems Ltd – industrial control systems and components for use in potentially explosive atmospheres – Expo Technologies Ltd
Expobrick – external wall insulation – Saint-Gobain Weber Ltd
Expofin – export service – G M A C
Expolath – external wall insulation – Saint-Gobain Weber Ltd
Expomesh – external wall insulation – Saint-Gobain Weber Ltd
Exponent – UK Office Direct
Export Sales Training Ltd – Chamber Of Commerce East Lancashire
ExpoTherm – external wall insulation – Saint-Gobain Weber Ltd
Expowest Displays – suppliers of portable display systems and accessories with a full graphics service – Exhibitions South West Ltd
Expowest Exhibitions – exhibition and event organisers, organisers of hotel, catering and hospitality exhibitions in the UK – Exhibitions South West Ltd
Express – supercritical fluid extraction and analysis service – University Of Leeds
Express – water heater – Heatrae Sadia
Express & Echo – newspaper – The Express & Echo
Express Moulds – plastic injection moulds and tooling, screen printing – Express Moulds Ltd
Express & Star – newspaper – Express & Star
Expression – software package that allows users to plan, organise, report and present information, aimed at the education market – Learning & Teaching Scotland
Expressway – switchgear – Ellison Switchgear
Exprexorter – automated sorting conveyor systems – Van Der Lande Industries
Exquisite – souvenirs and gifts – Watson Group Ltd
Exquisite Form (Philippines) – ladies underwear garments - brassieres, control briefs and all-in-ones – V F Intimates Ltd
Exshare – computer readable database of over 100,000 securities, available online – Interactive Data
Exstrong (Belgium) – bridge deck waterproofing – Alumasc Exterior Building Products
Extender Range – Electro optics – Applied Scintillation Technologies
Extendor – Keytrak Lock & Safe Company
Extensometers – geotechnical instruments – Itm Soil Ltd
Exterior Guard – textured wallcoating – Everlac GB Ltd
Extermisect – aircraft disinsecting spray – John Horsfall & Sons Ltd
External Building Services Ltd – E B S Safety Netting
External Floppy Disk Drive – Tekdata Distribution Ltd
Extir – expandable polystyreme – Polimeri Europa Ltd
EXTOL – budgetary control/commitment accounting package – Delta Computer Services
Extra – ladder stabilizer for walls – Ladderfix Ltd
Extra – sheet that replaces cartridges – Smurfit Kappa Townsend Hook
Extra Cab – jack leg cabin – Extra Space Industries
Extra Grass – Yara UK lt Ltd
Extra Mad – modular building system – Extra Space Industries
Extra Sensory Perception – fishing tackle – Drennan International Ltd
Extrac – exhaust gas waste heat recovery – Babcock Wanson UK Ltd
Extractor – mens clothing – Fashion Spinners
Extractor – storage racking – Rack International UK Ltd
Extractor Crane – combined fume extractor and tool suports system – Plymovent Limited
Extran – Yara UK lt Ltd
Extran PLan – Yara UK lt Ltd
Extraspace – Accesscaff International Ltd
Extraspan – industrial warehouse building – Extra Space Industries
Extratone – brown bread malt flour – E D M E Ltd
Extrem – clothing (waterproof) – Berghaus Ltd
eXtreme LOCKERS – Heavy Duty Weatherproof Lockers Ideal for Schools, Outdoor Use or extreme environments. – Action Storage Systems
eXtreme lockers, Action Storage Online – Action Storage Systems
Extremultus Miraclo – flat drive belts with leather or synthetic coatings used for power tranmission and box folding etc – Forbo Siegling
Extronics – M&ES Flexilope
Extru-Clean – purging compounds – Clariant UK Ltd
Extrude Honing – Kennametal Extrude Hone Ltd
Extrusions – Boston custom extrusions: Bumper, Ticket Strip, T moulds, edge trim – Boston Retail Products
Exxon – lubricants – Bearwood Engineering Supplies
Exypaque – G E Healthcare
Exytrast – G E Healthcare
EYE 2 EYE – optician's – Eye 2 Eye Gartshore Optical Centre
Eye for Marketing – Eye for Marketing
Eye Wash – eye wash fountain – Armitage Shanks Ltd
Eye Zone Fade Cream – reduces dary shadows under the eyes – Vivalis Ltd
Eyecare Vouchers – Accor Services
Eylure – nail care products & false eye lashes – Original Addidtions
***EZ-901E (U.S.A.)** – harmonic distortion analyser – Northern Design Ltd
Ez-Dock – Pontoons – Wave Seven Marine Ltd
Ez-form cable corp (USA) – semi-rigid products – Huber+Suhner (UK) Ltd
Ez-Hook – Test probes – Warwick Test Supplies
EZ-ZONE – integrated controllers – Watlow Ltd
Ezecal – F G H Controls Ltd
Ezeebox – Stackable packing case for fastank – Fast Engineering Ltd
Ezeewebsite.co.uk – Content Management System branch – Sidetrack Solutions
Ezeled – indicator lamps – Oxley Developments Company Ltd
Ezestrand – welding wire – Sureweld UK Ltd
Ezetrode – welding electrodes – Sureweld UK Ltd
Ezi-Lift – manhole cover lifters – Didsbury Engineering Ltd
EZO (Japan) – radial and axial ball bearings – S M B Bearings Ltd
EZstrip™ – Mono Pumps Ltd
***Ezt** – water boiler – Marco Beverage Systems Ltd
Ezykleen – ribbed indoor/outdoor vinyl matting – Jaymart Roberts & Plastics Ltd

F

F.A.M. 30 – iodophor disinfectant and detergent steriliser – Evans Vanodine International plc
F.B.M. – cistern type water heater – Heatrae Sadia
F.D.M.X. – digital multiplexers – Nortel Networks UK Ltd
F Darton & Co – Mercury barometers – Russell Scientific Instruments Ltd
F.F.E. – fire extinguishing systems-avation extinguishers – Fire Fighting Enterprises
F.F.F. – automotive hand tools – F F Franklin & Co. Ltd
F.G. Wilson – generators – Service Engines Newcastle Ltd
F H – multistage pumps – Weir Group Senior Executives Pension Trust Ltd
F.H. Jung – European Technical Sales Ltd
F.I.L. – Research Services – Facts International Ltd
F.I.P (Italy) – Mathew C Blythe & Son Ltd
F.I.R.A. International – furniture industry research association – Fira International
F.ILLI DIECI – Harrier Fluid Power Ltd
F.J.C. – flue jointing compound – Vitcas Ltd
F.K. Box – folding storage & transport container – S S I Schaefer Ltd
F.L.B. – facing bricks – Freshfield Lane Brickworks Ltd
***F. Leutert GmbH (Germany)** – engine indicators – Smail Engineers Glasgow Ltd
F.LLI TOGNELLA – Hydraulic & Offshore Supplies Ltd
F-Log (United Kingdom) – temperature monitoring system – Feedback Data Ltd
F M B – Star Micronics GB Ltd
***F.P. (Worldwide)** – agricultural spareparts – Gwaza Ltd
F.P. – flat pack preforming machines – Elite Engineering Ltd
F.P. (Italy) – bronze seawater pumps – Cleghorn Waring & Co Pumps Ltd
F P Mortgage No.1 – The Woolwich
F&S Electronik – M S C Gleichmann UK Ltd
F.S.L. – food safe lubricant – Action Can Ltd
F.S. Screed – rapid setting general purpose epoxy mortar and screed – Conren Ltd
F T – multistage pumps – Weir Group Senior Executives Pension Trust Ltd
F.T. Actuaries World Indices – Financial Times
F.T. Analysis Business Information – Financial Times
F.T. Annual Report Service – Financial Times
F.T. Cityline – Financial Times
F.T.L. – control systems – F T L Foundry Equipment Ltd
F.T. Profile Business Information – Financial Times
F. Werner – Red House Industrial Services Ltd
F.X. Surfacing – impact absorbing safer surfacing tiles of various depths and colours – S M P Playgrounds
F7000 – Pilot operated safety relief valves, ASME approved, both full bore design and API orifice designation. Sizes 1" x 2" to 12" x 16" – Broady Flow Controller Ltd
F8000 – Pilot operated safety relief valves, ASME approved, both full bore design and API orifice designation. Sizes 1" x 2" to 12" x 16" – Broady Flow Controller Ltd
FA Manager – computer game – Square Enix Ltd
Fab 1,2,3 – Designer Papers – Smurfit Kappa Townsend Hook
Fab-Mate – Accesscaff International Ltd
FABA – Chaintec Ltd
Fabaloy Fibre Glass Towers – Accesscaff International Ltd
Fabdec Ltd – stainless steel tanks – Fabdec Ltd
Faber – venetian blinds, vertical blinds and roller blinds – Guildford Shades
Faber 1800 Blackout Blind – blackout roller blind with FR fabric – Faber Blinds UK Ltd

Faber 2000 Blackout Blind – blackout roller blind with FR fabric – Faber Blinds UK Ltd
Faber Autostop – decelerating spring roller blind – Faber Blinds UK Ltd
Faber Cartell – art stationery & drawing instruments – West Design Products Ltd
Faber Charleston – venetian blind 50mm slat – Faber Blinds UK Ltd
Faber Escalade – vertical blind with sloping headrail, 89mm and 127mm louvres – Faber Blinds UK Ltd
Faber Gallery – venetian blind with printed slats, head and bottom rail, 25mm slat – Faber Blinds UK Ltd
Faber Illusion – venetian blind with 25mm, 35mm or 50mm perforated slat – Faber Blinds UK Ltd
Faber Maximatic – external venetian blind 65mm and 80mm slat – Faber Blinds UK Ltd
Faber Metalet 16/25/43/61 – internal venetian blinds 16mm, 25mm, 35mm and 50mm slat – Faber Blinds UK Ltd
Faber Metalet 61AV – internal dim-out venetian blind 50mm slat – Faber Blinds UK Ltd
Faber Metalet SV35 – internal rooflight venetian blind 35mm slat – Faber Blinds UK Ltd
Faber Metamatic – internal monocommand venetian blind 50mm slat – Faber Blinds UK Ltd
Faber Metamatic AV – internal monocommand dim-out venetian blind 50mm slat – Faber Blinds UK Ltd
Faber Midimatic – internal monocommand venetian blind 16mm, 25mm, 35mm and 50mm slat – Faber Blinds UK Ltd
Faber Minimatic – internal monocommand venetian blind 25mm slat – Faber Blinds UK Ltd
Faber Multistop – roller blind with friction stop control – Faber Blinds UK Ltd
Faber Nizza Awning – folding arm awning – Faber Blinds UK Ltd
Faber Rollotex – internal and external roller blind system with visually transparent FR sunscreening fabric – Faber Blinds UK Ltd
Faber Series One Blackout Blind – blackout roller blind with FR fabric – Faber Blinds UK Ltd
Faber Softline – venetian blind, 16mm, 25mm and 35mm slat – Faber Blinds UK Ltd
Faber Uprite – vertical blind with 50mm aluminium louvres – Faber Blinds UK Ltd
Faber Vertibay 40 – vertical blind with hinge corner joint for bay windows, 127mm louvres – Faber Blinds UK Ltd
Faber Vertical 30 – vertical blind, 63mm, 89mm and 127mm louvres – Faber Blinds UK Ltd
Faber Vertical 40 – vertical blind 89mm and 127mm louvres – Faber Blinds UK Ltd
Fabframe – Display shelving – Idea Showcases Ltd
Fabmax – semi-conductor manufacturing services – Boc Gases Ltd
Fabprene – British Vita plc
Fabric – perfumed viscous fabric conditioner – Evans Vanodine International plc
Fabric-Care – Fabric Care Dry Cleaners
Fabric Conditioner – liquid fabric conditioner – Premiere Products Ltd
Fabricast – non ferrous castings, machinists and pattern makers, coppersmiths, tube manipulators, manufacturers of heat exchangers and calorifiers, stockists of non-ferrous metals, stainless steels, plastics, valves and fittings – Fabricast Multi Metals Ltd
FabriClean - Pulse-Jet Fabric and Ceramic Filters - SmartPulse Controller - for optimisation of APC control – Lodge Cottrell Ltd
Fabriform – seat cushions process – Sears Manufacturing Company Europe Ltd
Fabrique – paper – Fenner Paper Co. Ltd
***Fabris Lane (Italy)** – hand made sunglasses – Fabris Lane Ltd
Fabritec – Desks and Storage – Bucon Ltd
Fabritex – industrial fabric gloves – Bennett Safetywear
Fabrizio – ladies fashions – Fabrizio Fashions Ltd
FabTrol – management information system for fabricators – Computer Services Consultants UK Ltd
Facc – Eagle Automation Systems Ltd
Facet – Harrier Fluid Power Ltd
***Faci (Italy)** – metallic stearates – Omya UK Ltd
Facom – hand tools – Arrow Supply Co. Ltd
Facom – S J Wharton Ltd
FACOM TOOLS – Wolds Engineering Services Ltd
***Facsys (U.S.A.)** – network fax server – Techland Group Ltd
Factair – air-line filtration units – Factair Ltd
Factor 4 – carpets – Interface Europe Ltd
***Factory Cleaning** – Stayclean Contract Cleaning Services Ltd
Factory Equipment – magazine – Progressive Media Group
Factory Monitoring & Control – a set of applications for time and attendance, activity management, access control and data collection. – Crown Computing Ltd
Factorylink – software for automation products – Schneider
Factotum – soldering machine – Time Products UK Ltd
Faculty – Hosokawa Micron Ltd
Fade-Out – treatment cream for unwanted brown marks on the skin – Vivalis Ltd
FAE – switches – C T P Wipac Ltd
Faema Bean to Cup Espresso Machines – M I K O Coffee Ltd
Faema Espresso Machines – M I K O Coffee Ltd
Fafnir – Mercury Bearings Ltd
FAG – Mercury Bearings Ltd
Fag – Team Overseas Ltd
Fag – Bearings – Sprint Engineering & Lubricant
FAG – Wolds Engineering Services Ltd
***Fage** – Cater Bake UK Ltd
Faggiolati – Italian submersible pumps – Pedrollo Distribution
Fagor – Cyclops Electronics Ltd
Fahr Butcher – Harrier Fluid Power Ltd
FAI – Harrier Fluid Power Ltd
Faience – (Architectural) - tiles and blocks – Shaws Of Darwen Ltd
Failsworth – hats – Failsworth Hats Ltd
Faint – knitwear – Vinola Knitwear
Fair Lady – hosiery – Swift J & R Ltd
Fair Trade Coffee – M I K O Coffee Ltd
Fair Trades Member – Somerglaze Windows Ltd
Fairbanks – childrens wear – David Charles Childrens Wear Ltd
Fairchild – Cyclops Electronics Ltd
Fairchild – p.c.b's – Bearwood Engineering Supplies
Fairchild – fasteners – Specialty Fasteners & Components Ltd
FAIRCHILD – Hydraulic & Offshore Supplies Ltd
Fairchild Semi – M S C Gleichmann UK Ltd
FAIREY ARLON – Hydraulic & Offshore Supplies Ltd
Fairey Arlon – Harrier Fluid Power Ltd
Fairey Arlon – switches – Bearwood Engineering Supplies
Fairline – luxury yachts – Fairline Boats Ltd
Fairline – taps – Armitage Shanks Ltd
Fairline Phantom – 38ft/42ft/43ft/46ft yachts – Fairline Boats Ltd
Fairline Squadron – 52ft/55ft/59ft/62ft/65ft – Fairline Boats Ltd
***Fairtex (Worldwide)** – imitation leather and textiles – Robert Werner Ltd
Fairtrade Organic Wines from Stellar Organics & La Riojana – Vinceremos Wines & Spirits Ltd
***Fairway** – Bri-Ton Fine Foods Ltd
Fairway – Capex Office Interiors
FAIRWAY SEALS – Hydraulic & Offshore Supplies Ltd
Fairy – UK Office Direct
Fairyworld – Chorion plc
Faith Footwear Ltd – ladies footwear – Faith Footwear Holdings Ltd
Faith In Nature – soaps and natural skin and hair care products using herbal extracts and essential oils, bath foams, guest sizes, contract manufrs – Faith Products Ltd
Faithfull – S J Wharton Ltd
Faithfull – Gem Tool Hire & Sales Ltd
Fakeham – Gem Tool Hire & Sales Ltd
Falcon – boots, shoes, slippers, leggings and gaiters – Twinmar Ltd
***Falcon** – Crown Catering Equipment Ltd
Falcon – envelopes – Eagle Envelopes Ltd
***Falcon** – prime cooking equipment – Keemlaw Ltd
Falcon – Nibbler – Biddle & Mumford Gears Ltd
Falcon – saddles – E Jeffries & Sons Ltd
Falcon – Axon Enterprises Ltd
Falcon – profile cutting machine – Easab Cutting Systems
Falcon – cycle – Falcon Cycles Ltd
***Falcon** – Oven ranges – Court Catering Equipment Ltd
Falcon Carbolic Soap – Kays Ramsbottom Ltd
Falcon Fire Ltd – Fire Protection – Falcon Fire Ltd
Falcon Sole Trader – Twinmar Ltd
Falconbridge – Nickel and copper products – Cannock Chemicals Ltd
Falconet – remotely piloted target aircraft – Eaton Aerospace Ltd
Falk – Couplings – Sprint Engineering & Lubricant
Falk – Harrier Fluid Power Ltd
Falkirk Council – signs – The Sign Factory
Fallguard – vertical fall arrest track system – Metreel Ltd
Fallguard – Safety Works & Solutions Ltd
Falling on Your Feet – videos educational – Utopia Records Ltd
Faltex – A M C Rollers Ltd
***Faltex (Switzerland)** – folding machines – Graphics Arts Equipment Ltd
Family Care – Steroplast Ltd
Family Continental Motoring – motoring and personal travel insurance – Europ Assistance Holdings Ltd
Family Continental Travel Assistance – personal and medical travel insurance – Europ Assistance Holdings Ltd
Family Lawclub – consumer personal injury dispute, employment disputes and a medical helpline – Allianz Legal Protection
Family Life Solutions – Accor Services
Famora – soap – John Gosnell Ltd
Famot – D M G UK Ltd
Fampla – Precision Tools
Fane – sluice sink – Armitage Shanks Ltd
Fanflex – anti-vibration mountings – Trelleborg Industrial A V S Ltd
Fanjet – fan assisted variable volume terminals for air conditioning systems – Gilberts Blackpool Ltd
Fanjet – nozzles – Delavan Ltd
Fanstat – thermostat for automotive industry – Otter Controls Ltd
***Fantasia (Taiwan)** – ceiling fans – Fantasia Distribution Ltd
Fantasia Ceiling Fans – Light Fantastic
Fantasie – bras, co-ordinating lingerie and bra-sized swimwear – Eveden Ltd
Fantasy – record label – Ace Records Ltd
Fantasy Island – family entertainment centre – Fantasy Island
***Fantasy Parchment (Netherlands)** – paper – H V Sier Ltd
Fantini Cosmi – Banico Ltd
Fantuzzi – Custom Brakes & Hydraulics Ltd
FANTUZZI – Chaintec Ltd
fantuzzi industrial equipment – sideloaders – F T M Materials Handling Ltd
Fanuc – European Technical Sales Ltd
***Fanuc** – European Drives & Motor Repairs
Fanuc – Encoders UK
Fanuc Boards – European Technical Sales Ltd
Fanuc Control PCBs – European Technical Sales Ltd
Fanuc Drive Cases – European Technical Sales Ltd
Fanuc Drives – European Technical Sales Ltd
Fanuc Encoders – European Technical Sales Ltd
Fanuc Fuses – European Technical Sales Ltd
Fanuc Input Units – European Technical Sales Ltd
Fanuc Linear Motors – European Technical Sales Ltd
Fanuc Machine Tool Controls – European Technical Sales Ltd
Fanuc Membranes – European Technical Sales Ltd
Fanuc Memory – European Technical Sales Ltd
Fanuc Monitors – European Technical Sales Ltd
Fanuc Motors – European Technical Sales Ltd
Fanuc Power Supply – European Technical Sales Ltd
Fanuc Servo Drives – European Technical Sales Ltd
Fanuc Servo Motors – European Technical Sales Ltd
Fanuc Spindle Motors – European Technical Sales Ltd
Fanuc Spindles – European Technical Sales Ltd
Fapsacks – paper sacks – Segezha Packaging
Faqtor – Lamphouse Ltd
Far East Travel Centre (F.E.T.C.) – travel agent and tour operator – Kuoni Travel Ltd
***Far-Manifolds/Maddalena (Italy)** – watermeters – S A V UK Ltd
Far-Mat (United Kingdom) – full area foundation vibration isolators – Farrat Isolevel
Far Ridge – Avalon and Lynwood
Faral – Zhender Group UK Ltd
Farameter – electricity and gas meters – Switch2 Energy Solutions
Faraoudja – Lamphouse Ltd
Farb – ladies' and children's overalls and dresses – Norland Burgess Ltd
Fare Catering – Principal Catering Consultants Ltd
Farecla – Letchford Supplies Ltd
Fargo – strong ale – Wells & Young's Brewing Co.
Farleygreene – Incamesh Filtration Ltd
***Farm Electric** – F E C Services Ltd
Farm Feed Blends – BOCM Pauls Ltd
Farm Fluid S – disinfectant – DuPont Animal Health Solutions
Farm Supplies (Dorking) Ltd – agricultural and horticultural goods retail and service – Farm Supplies Dorking Ltd
***Farmer Counts** – F C G Software Solutions Ltd
Farmers – polypropylene and baler twines, ropes, wrapping twines and big bale net wrap – Steve Orr Ltd
Farmgate – BOCM Pauls Ltd
Farmgran – soil conditioner – Farmura Ltd
Farmguard – sealant for concrete and masonary silage stores to prevent erosion of concrete and masonary – Spaldings Ltd
Farmhouse – Monier Ltd
***Farmhouse Biscuits** – Mercia Fine Foods
Farmura – liquid organic fertiliser – Farmura Ltd
Farnell – power supplies – Bearwood Engineering Supplies
Farnell – Proplas International Ltd
Farnham Castle International Briefing and Conference Centre – specialised intercultural skills training workshops, pre-departure and business briefings for every country and intensive tuition in any language. conference, meeting and training venue. – Farnham Castle Briefings Ltd
Farr – Harrier Fluid Power Ltd
FARRIS – S W Industrial Valves Services Ltd
Farymann – A T Wilde & Son Ltd
Fas – Southern Valve & Fitting Co. Ltd
Fascat – esterification catalysts – Atosina UK Ltd
Fascinating Finishes – paint effect – Kingstonian Paints Ltd

Fascol – polyester pigments – West & Senior Ltd

Fascol - polyester pigments, **Fastint** - mono pigment tinters, **Faspak, Corflow** - polyester flocoats, **Corgel** - isophthalic polyester gelcoats. – West & Senior Ltd

Fashion World – mail order catalogues – J D Williams Mail Order Group

fashy – hot water bottles – fashy UK Ltd

FASOP – Powelectrics Ltd

Faspak – packaging materials, corrugated boxes – Faspak Containers Ltd

Fasson – B D K Industrial Products Ltd

*Fast – Fast International Inc

Fast-Aid – wound dressings, adhesive plasters, heat pads – Robinson Healthcare Ltd

Fast Auto – A T E Technology Ltd

Fast Bid – A T E Technology Ltd

Fast-Binda – binding bars loading device – Gilmex International Ltd

Fast Chrome – after chrome dyes – Town End Leeds plc

Fast Clamp – Safety Works & Solutions Ltd

Fast Fit – patio door lock – Schlegel UK

Fast Foodfax – food and prime market intelligence – Cambridge Market Research Ltd

*Fast Fret (U.S.A.) – lubricant – John Hornby Skewes & Co. Ltd

Fast Lane Training – Accelerate Your Success – Fast Lane Training Ltd

Fast Paper – UK Office Direct

Fast Press – Fast Systems Ltd

Fast Thaw – radio frequency, defrosting machines for food industry – Petrie Technologies Ltd

Fast-Track – vinyl wallcoverings – Tektura plc

Fast trans – distribution transformer and package substations with fast delivery – Schneider

Fast Twist – spikes/cleats for golf shoes – Trisport Ltd

Fast Twist Systems – unique replaceable golf cleat fixing system – Trisport Ltd

Fastank – portable emergency storage container – Fast Engineering Ltd

Fastapine – pine sanitising gel – Deb R & D Ltd

Fastashelf – filing system – Railex Filing Ltd

Fastasleep – Fire proof & vandal proof bedding – Fast Engineering Ltd

Fastclamp – handrail fittings & tubes – Arrow Supply Co. Ltd

Fastec Engineering (United Kingdom) – precision engineers – Fastec Engineering Ltd

fastel – Emergency equipment – P4 Ltd

FASTENERS. – Arrow Supply Co. Ltd

FASTER – Hydraulic & Offshore Supplies Ltd

Fastgate – high speed bi-folding gate – Apt Controls Ltd

Fasti – standard & CNC folding machines – Press & Shear Machinery Ltd

*Fastimer – Fast International Inc

Fastintoman – Simbec Research Ltd

Fastlane – swimwear and beachwear – Westbridge International Group Ltd

Fastlay – Hoofmark UK Ltd

*FASTMIX – Dry flowable/powdered products – Nutrel Products Ltd

Fastmove – The Woolwich

*FASTPHITE – Phosphite based formulations – Nutrel Products Ltd

Fastpress – Fast Systems Ltd

Fastrak 5950 – steelwork design to BS5950 – Computer Services Consultants UK Ltd

Fastrak Multi Storey – multi storey building design – Computer Services Consultants UK Ltd

Fastrak Portal Frame – design/analysis multi span portal frames – Computer Services Consultants UK Ltd

Fastreact – Specialist planning and sourcing software – Fast React Systems Ltd

*Fastron – Fast International Inc

Fastscan – laser scanner for automatic on-line inspection – Sira Test & Certification Ltd

FastStrap – buckle - free tension curtain system – Lawrence David Ltd

Fatigue-Checker – rubber anti-fatigue standing mat system – Jaymart Roberts & Plastics Ltd

Faulhaber (Germany) – DC micromotors, gearheads,encoders,tachogenerators Importer – Electro Mechanical Systems (EMS) Ltd

Faun/Frisch – Harrier Fluid Power Ltd

Faversham News – newspaper – Kent Messenger Group Ltd

FAW – industrial folding door – Hörmann (UK) Ltd

Fawcett – Harrier Fluid Power Ltd

Fawcett Accumulator – Fawcett Christie Hydraulics Ltd

FAWCETT CHRISTIE – Hydraulic & Offshore Supplies Ltd

FAWCETT CHRISTIE HYDRAULICS – Hydraulic & Offshore Supplies Ltd

Fax Canning Oil – canning oil – Seven Sea's Ltd

fax to email – Callsure Business Telephone & Fax Numbers

FaxByNet – Fax software – Plain Sailing Communications Ltd

Faxfry – vegetable frying oil – Seven Sea's Ltd

Faxlead – computer software – Wordcraft International Ltd

FBN – Harrier Fluid Power Ltd

FBO – Harrier Fluid Power Ltd

FCH – Trafalgar Tools

FCI Framatone – Cyclops Electronics Ltd

fdb line – Benito UK

FE 227 – Fike Protection Systems Ltd

FE 25 – Fike Protection Systems Ltd

*FE Iron Foundry Filters (U.S.A.) – ceramic foam filters for cast shops and foundries – Porvair plc

Feather Finish – rapid drying smoothing and patching compound – Ardex UK Ltd

Featherpost – Tri Pack Supplies Ltd

Featherwing – plastic mudguards & spray suppression systems – Boydell & Jacks Ltd

FeB – chemical polish for ferrous based materials – Lea Manufacturing Co.

Feb MBT – County Construction Chemicals Ltd

Febo-flex – printers rollers for flexography – Bottcher UK Ltd

Febo-Grav – printers rollers for gravure – Bottcher UK Ltd

Febo-Lith – printers rollers for offset – Bottcher UK Ltd

Febo-Pren – hard polyurethane roller coverings for industrial use – Bottcher UK Ltd

Febo-Press – printers rollers for newspapers – Bottcher UK Ltd

Febo-Print – printers rollers for letterpress – Bottcher UK Ltd

*Fed Pizza Ovens – Nisbets plc

Fedaro – B P plc

Federal Bell – spare & equipment – Bearwood Engineering Supplies

Federal Mogul – Aerotech Engineering Ltd

FEDERAL MOGUL – Hydraulic & Offshore Supplies Ltd

FEDESA – European animal health industry federation – National Office Of Animal Health Ltd

Fedrex – X-ray equipment – Ie-Ndt Manufacturer

Feedback – trade publication – Food & Drink Federation

Feeder vision – P B S I Group Ltd

Feedex Nutrition – BOCM Pauls Ltd

FeedFloc – chemical effluent treatments for control of C.O.D. and suspended solids – Feedwater Ltd

Feedmaster – Hydrafeed Ltd

Feeds Marketing – BOCM Pauls Ltd

Feeler – Emi-Mec Ltd

Feet First – childrens footwear – Russell & Bromley Ltd

Feinmess (Germany) – In-Process Guaging – Schmitt Europe Ltd

Felcon Ltd – Felcon Ltd

Feldbinder GmbH (Germany) – tanker manufacturers – Feldbinder UK Ltd

Felisatti – Polishing Mop Electric, Grinders, Sanders – Car Paint Warehouse Ltd

Fellowes – UK Office Direct

Fells carpetss – Distributer of carpets – Roger Fell Ltd

Fellside Recordings – compact discs-folk/roots music – Fellside Recordings Ltd

Fellsongs – music publishing – Fellside Recordings Ltd

*Felss (Germany) – swage forming machines – Pearson Panke Ltd

Felthams – cotton bags – C P L Felthams

Felvinone – perfume speciality – Quest International UK Ltd

*Feme (Italy) – PCB relays – Carlo Gavazzi UK Ltd

Feminine Glow – cosmetics and perfumery – Bodywise Ltd

*Femo (Sweden) – illuminated magnifiers – Viking Optical Ltd

Fencecoat – wood preservative stain – Tor Coatings Ltd

FenceHire – Accesscaff International Ltd

Fenceman – electric fencing – Agrihealth

Fencing Direct – Accesscaff International Ltd

Fenda-Sox – covers for boat fenders – Nicholas Bray & Son Ltd

Fendolite M11 – fireproofing cementitious plaster – Promat UK Ltd

Fendress – turf top dressing for use on golf greens – Banks Amenity Products Ltd

Fendress Greentop – soilfree top dressing for use on golf greens – Banks Amenity Products Ltd

Fendt – tractors and farm machinery – Agco International Ltd

Fendt – Harrier Fluid Power Ltd

*Fendt – Agricultural Machinery – J J Farm Services Ltd

Fendt – Walling UK Ltd

Fenland – clean clothing for the food trades – Fenland Laundries Ltd

Fenn – office stationery and supplies, printing and vinyl graphics – J G Fenn Ltd

Fenn-O – typewriters, word processors, micro-computers – J G Fenn Ltd

Fenn-O-Furniture – office furnishings – J G Fenn Ltd

Fenn - Torin (U.S.A.) – spring coiling machinery – Bennett Mahler

FENNER – Hydraulic & Offshore Supplies Ltd

Fenner – European Technical Sales Ltd

Fenner – Mercury Bearings Ltd

Fenner Gearboxes – shaft mounted gearboxes – Potteries Power Transmission Ltd

Fensa Registered Company – Somerglaze Windows Ltd

Fensecure – Fenescure design, fabricate and install; Metal Security fencing, Amenity fencing, sports and playground fencing and multiball courts. Bowtop fencing, ballcourts, tubular fencing systems and gates, palisade Korapal security and gates. – Steelway

FENTEX – Hydraulic & Offshore Supplies Ltd

Fentex – Protim Solignum

Fentox – biocide treatment – Aldous & Stamp Ltd

*Fenwal (Worldwide) – health products – Baxter Healthcare Ltd

FENWICK – Chaintec Ltd

Fenwick – T V H UK Ltd

Fenwick – Harrier Fluid Power Ltd

Fepcare – service of central heating installations – F E P Heat Care Ltd

Fepheat – sale of central heating installations – F E P Heat Care Ltd

Fepstor – sale of central heating equipment – F E P Heat Care Ltd

FER HYDRAULICS – Hydraulic & Offshore Supplies Ltd

Ferex – low hydrogen electrodes – Murex Welding Products Ltd

Ferex – water softeners and filtration plant – Ferex Ltd

Fergatac – resin tackifier – Ferguson & Menzies Ltd

Ferguson – L M C Hadrian Ltd

Feripol – specialised ferric sulphate for potable water treatment – E A West

*Ferlea – Pira Ltd

Fermentose – brewing syrups – Tate & Lyle Public Ltd Company

*Fermod – Fermod Ltd

*Fermoflex – Fermod Ltd

*Fermos – Micron Bio-Systems

*Fermostock – Modular shelving – Fermod Ltd

Fern Plastics – precision injection mouldings in all thermoplastic materials – Fern Plastic Products Ltd

Fernbank – piece goods & articles – Fernbank Shed Company Ltd

Ferndale – wax country clothing – Blacks Leisure Group plc

Ferndale – Prima Care

Fernite – machine knives, shear blades, doctor blades – Fernite Of Sheffield Ltd

Fernox – water treatment chemicals – Fernox

Ferobestos – fibre reinforced engineering laminates – Tenmat Ltd

Ferochek – metal detector for detecting ferrous metals in foil packaging – Lock Inspection Systems Ltd

Ferodo – brake linings, clutch facings and fanbelts, disc brake pads, brake discs, brake fluid – Federal Mogul Friction Products

Ferodo – Custom Brakes & Hydraulics Ltd

Feroform – fibre reinforced engineering laminates – Tenmat Ltd

Feroglide – composite faced bearings – Tenmat Ltd

Feroxascan – G E Healthcare

Ferquatac – resins emulsions dispertions – Ferguson & Menzies Ltd

Ferraris – pocketpeak flow meters – Enspire Health

Ferraz – fuses – Bowers Ltd

Ferraz Shawmut – industrial & semi conductor fuses – G D Rectifiers Ltd

Ferret – automatic tube cleaning system compressed air operated – Airnesco Group Ltd

Ferret Platforms – Accesscaff International Ltd

Ferrett (United Kingdom) – trim tool grinder – R J H Finishing Systems Ltd

Ferri (Italy) – universal joints – Lenze UK Ltd

Ferri – Mercury Bearings Ltd

Ferribox – A low cost, made to measure, reusable, lightweight, high performance thermally insulating container for the distribution of temperature sensitive goods. – Excel Packaging & Insulation Company Ltd

Ferriplex – high ph stable chelated iron micronutrients for agriculture – Contract Chemicals Ltd

Ferriplus – high ph stable chelated iron micronutrients for agriculture – Contract Chemicals Ltd

*FERRIS (U.S.A.) – grass maintenance equipment – Industrial Power Units Ltd

Ferrite Inc – continuous industrial microwave systems for cooking and tempering – Selo UK Ltd

Ferro Alloys – all types of grades and sizes – West Brook Resources Ltd

Ferrochem – smoothing & deburring process for carbon steel – Anopol Ltd

Ferrofluid – Fluid for tapping steel, thread-rolling, broaching, boring, milling and turning. – Tapmatic Engineers' Merchants

Ferrolux – Sebakmt UK Ltd

Ferromatik Milacron – Proplas International Ltd

Ferromex – Omex Environmental Ltd

*Ferrosol (U.S.A.) – liquid iron – Farmura Ltd

FERROTRON – Merseyside Metal Services

Ferryline Cruisers – cruising holidays – Richardsons Stalham Ltd

Ferryman – open reversible liferaft – R F D Beaufort Ltd

Ferteco – Keith Mount Liming Ltd

Fertilizers Feed Fuel Minerals – Agricultural Central Trading

Ferumelt – paramelt

Festival – carpets – Interface Europe Ltd

*Festival (Netherlands) – make-up and aerosols for fun – Palmer Agencies Ltd

Festival – race meeting – The Steeplechase Co Cheltenham Ltd

Festival Satir – Coated Paper – Mcnaughton James Paper Group Ltd

Festival Superart – Coated Paper – Mcnaughton James Paper Group Ltd

Festo – Southern Valve & Fitting Co. Ltd

Festo – cylinders/valves – Bearwood Engineering Supplies

Festo – European Technical Sales Ltd

FESTO – Hydraulic & Offshore Supplies Ltd

Festo – Air Technics Ltd

Festo – Trafalgar Tools

Festo – pneumatics – A C Hydraulics Ltd

FESTO DIDACTC – Hydraulic & Offshore Supplies Ltd

Festo (Pneumatics) – control solutions – Air Power Centre Limited

Festool – power tools – Campbell Miller Tools Ltd

Fetal Dopplex 11 – advanced obstetric doppler – Huntleigh Healthcare

Feverscan – forehead thermometer – Robinson Healthcare Ltd

Fexmo – European Technical Sales Ltd

Fezer – Granada Material Handling Ltd

Ffestiniog – quarries – Welsh Slates

FFM non-drip/anti condensation coating – North West Sheeting Supplies

FG Workspace – Office Furniture – Bucon Ltd

FGA – rucsacs – Berghaus Ltd

FGH – company name – M Squared Instrumentation

FHG (United Kingdom) – holiday guide publishers – F H G Guides Ltd

FI – Roxspur Measurement & Control Ltd

Fi-Glass – glass fibre moulders & engineers – Fi Glass Developments Ltd

*Fiaam (Italy) – automotive filters – So-Gefi Filtration Ltd

Fiaam – Harrier Fluid Power Ltd

FIAC – Hydraulic & Offshore Supplies Ltd

Fiam – Gustair Materials Handling Equipment Ltd

Fiat – Ashley Competition Exhausts Ltd

FIAT – Chaintec Ltd

Fiat – L M C Hadrian Ltd

Fiat – Stacatruc

Fiat – C J Plant Ltd

Fiat Allis – Harrier Fluid Power Ltd

Fiat Allis – Team Overseas Ltd

FIAT-HITACHI – Hydraulic & Offshore Supplies Ltd

Fiat-Om – T V H UK Ltd

Fibar – glass fibre surveyors tape – Fisco Tools Ltd

Fibel – bushings & mountings – Fibet Rubber Bonding UK Ltd

Fiber-Tone – paper – Fenner Paper Co. Ltd

Fibercast – range of fine fibrillated micro-synthetic fibres – Propex Concrete Systems Ltd

Fibercast – Phoenix Weighing Services Ltd

Fibercill – medium density fibreboard windowboard – Fibercill

Fibermesh – Phoenix Weighing Services Ltd

Fibermesh – range of fibrillated and monofilament micro-synthetic fibres – Propex Concrete Systems Ltd

Fibershield – rolling fire curtain – Bolton Gate Co. Ltd

Fiberskirt – medium density fibreboard skirting – Fibercill

Fiberstran – garden furniture – Gardencast

Fibertherm – ceramic fibre high temperature insulation – W G Eaton Ltd

Fibertrave – medium density fibreboard architrave – Fibercill

Fibolite – ultra lightweight building block – Plasmor Ltd

Fibox – IP rated enclosures – Perancea Ltd

Fibox – Selectronix Ltd

Fibracan – Autobar Group Ltd

Fibral – glass fibre repair paste – U-Pol Ltd

Fibralene – spun polyester sewing thread – Amann Oxley Threads Ltd

Fibre-Data – fibre optic components – Opto Electronic Manufacturing Corporation Ltd

Fibre Fillings – manufacturers of polyester wadding – Fibre Fillings

Fibre-Locked – fabric filter media for dust and fume filtration – Andrew Webron Ltd

Fibre-Lyte – carbon fibre motorcycle accessories – Michael Brandon Ltd

Fibre Optic Modems – Greenwich Instruments Limited

Fibre-Plex – Probiotics International Ltd

Fibre-Tech – Fibre-Tech Industries LLP

Fibreblok – British Vita plc

Fibredec – high tensile strength surface and stress absorbing membrane ideal for cracked and crazed surfaces – Colas Ltd

*Fibreforce (U.S.A.) – manufacturers of fibre reinforced profiles – Exel Composites

Fibregrip – Specialist GRP rockbolts and soil nails – Minova Weldgrip Ltd

Fibrelite – glassfibre signs – Hi-Lite Signs Ltd

Fibrelite – fibreglass composite manufacturer of petrol station equipment – Fibrelite Composites Ltd

Fibrelite – external wall overcoating – Saint-Gobain Weber Ltd

Fibrelux – optical telecommunications connector kits – Nortel Networks UK Ltd

Fibrene – jointing paste – B & G Machining

Fibresand – reinforced sand surfac – Fibresand International Ltd

Fibreseal – GRP encapsulations – Hi-Lite Signs Ltd

Fibrespan – decking system for tanks, channels and baffles – Armfibre Ltd

Fibreturf – sports surfaces – Fibresand International Ltd

Fibro – European Technical Sales Ltd

*Fibro Sacco (Italy) – polypropylene, polyethylene extruded and woven bale sheeting and bags – Robert S Maynard Ltd

Fibrocom – Underwater communications cables – Cortland Fibron B X Ltd

Fibrodata – Cortland Fibron B X Ltd

Fibrodata – underwater data and instrumentation cables – Cortland Fibron B X Ltd

Fibroflex – underwater diving hoses – Cortland Fibron B X Ltd

Fibrohyd – Cortland Fibron B X Ltd

Fibrolife – Cortland Fibron B X Ltd

Fibroline – hoses for breathing and diving – Cortland Fibron B X Ltd

Fibromanta – European Technical Sales Ltd

Fibrophos – Keith Mount Liming Ltd

Fibropower – underwater power cables – Cortland Fibron B X Ltd

Fibroptic – Cortland Fibron B X Ltd

Fibrorov – Cortland Fibron B X Ltd

Fibrotex – fully automatic backwashable depth filter – Kalsep UK

Fibrotow – Cortland Fibron B X Ltd

Fibrovision – underwater television cables – Cortland Fibron B X Ltd

Fibroweld – Cortland Fibron B X Ltd

Fichefile – microfiche filing system – Railex Filing Ltd

Fichet – safes, fire safes, data safes, locks, security doors, vaults, vault doors, safety deposit boxes, fire doors and open banking equipment – Fbh-Fichet Ltd

FICS – manufacturing, distribution, financials and service system – Datapro Software Ltd

Fiddes – Vastern Timber Co. Ltd

Fiddes Payne – herbs and spices – Fiddes Payne

Fidelio – wallcoverings, borders and fabrics – Brian Yates

Fidelity – alloys and alginates – Schottlander Dental Equipment Supplies

Fidenter – textile piece goods – Reid & Taylor Ltd

Fidgit – fishing tackle – Drennan International Ltd

Fidus – quality control instruments – Cerulean

Fiebing – Abbey England Ltd

Field Classics – embroidered and printed leisurewear, sportswear & industrial clothing – Sutcliffe Farrar & Co. Ltd

Fieldbus ROUTE-MASTER – device connection and power supplies – Hawke International

FieldLink – BUS data communication cables – Belcom Cables Ltd

Fiesta – UK Office Direct

Fiesta – daylight fluorescent pigments – Swada London

Fiesta – darts and shafts – Unicorn Products Ltd

Fiesta – G F Smith

Fiesta Fibre Optic Panel – Manufactured and developed by litetec ltd, our fiesta fibre optic panels are an innovative product – Lite-Tec

Fife – Harrier Fluid Power Ltd

Fife Advertiser, The – newspaper – Strachan & Livingston

Fife Free Press – newspaper – Strachan & Livingston

Fife Herald – newspaper – Strachan & Livingston

Fife & Kinross Directory – yearly directory – Dunfermline Press

Fife & Kinross Extra – newspaper – Dunfermline Press

Fife Leader – newspaper – Strachan & Livingston

Fifelon – rubber coating – Fife Engineering Co. Ltd

Fifth Avenue – WC suite – Armitage Shanks Ltd

Fifth Avenue – fragrance – Elizabeth Arden

Fifty Plus – mail order catalogue – J D Williams Mail Order Group

*Figgio – Porcelain China Tableware – Continental Chef Supplies Ltd

Fike – Fike UK

Filamic – electrical and thermal insulation materials and products – Langtec Ltd

*Filarmonica (Spain) – haircutting scissors – Diamond Edge Ltd

File Back Up – Tekdata Distribution Ltd

File Holder – file holder – Acco East Light Ltd

*File Room (U.S.A.) – document imaging-management software – Techland Group Ltd

File Tracker – barcode file tracking – Civica UK Ltd

Fileguide – stationery manillas and pressboards – Weidmann Whiteley Ltd

FileMagic (U.S.A.) – as fortis but for application on lan only – Pacific Solutions International Ltd

Filetab – general applications software – N C C Group

Filetab – software for report generation – N C C Group

Filey & Humamby Mercury – newspaper – Yorkshire Regional Newspapers Ltd

Filigree – lace and net curtains, printed curtains – Filigree Ltd

Filigree Finesse – custom made sheer curtains including fire retardent – Filigree Ltd

Fill In Fun – magazine – H Bauer Publishing

Fillis – natural jute twine – Nutscene

Fillite – light weight filler – Trelleborg Offshore Ltd

Fillmaster – For mass ground fill, ie road embankment – Vencel Resil Ltd

Film Four Ltd – Channel Four Television Co. Ltd

Filmaster – combination boiler filling loop – Reliance Water Controls Ltd

Filmax – Harrier Fluid Power Ltd

Filmsec – Dry Film Lubricants – I K V Tribology Ltd

Filmtel – machine for changing tape to films – Moving Picture Co. Ltd

Filmwire – flexible printed circuits – Edo M B M Technology Ltd

Filofax – UK Office Direct

Filofax – organisers – Connect Two Promotions Ltd

Filofax – personal organisers – Filofax Stationary Suppliers

Filofax Time Management – time management systems – Filofax Stationary Suppliers

Filon – signmakers sheet – Righton Ltd

Filplastic – shelving and racking – Filplastic UK Ltd

Filpro – Harrier Fluid Power Ltd

Filseal – Pall Europe Corporate Services

FILSEAL – Hydraulic & Offshore Supplies Ltd

Filtalux – British Vita plc

Filter D – connectors, subminiature – Cinch Connectors Ltd

Filter Fog – electrostatic filters – Filtermist International Ltd

Filter Produ – Harrier Fluid Power Ltd

Filter Star (United Kingdom) – filterstar pressure guage – Star Instruments Ltd

Filterbed Distributors – Copa Ltd

Filterdyne – Harrier Fluid Power Ltd

Filtering Mail – Tekdata Distribution Ltd

Filterlite – Wholesale Welding Supplies Ltd

Filtermart – Harrier Fluid Power Ltd

Filtermist – dust filtration and air filtration – Filtermist International Ltd

FILTERPAC – combined high efficiency filter stages in a cabinet – Parker Dominic Hunter Ltd

Filterpak – filtration trollers – Fawcett Christie Hydraulics Ltd

Filterrite – Harrier Fluid Power Ltd

Filters – Harrier Fluid Power Ltd

Filters – A T Wilde & Son Ltd

Filtersoft – Harrier Fluid Power Ltd

FILTERTECHNIK – Hydraulic & Offshore Supplies Ltd

Filtertramp – tramp oil filter – Filtermist International Ltd

Filtex – dust filter units and extractors – Filtex Filters Ltd

Filto-Bench – work bench with integral extraction/filtration to remove dust and fumes – Horizon Mechanical Services International Ltd

Filtometers – filter pressure drop indicator – Airflow Measurements Ltd

Filtram – non-metallic materials for drainage in building and road-making – Terram Ltd

Filtrasol – window blinds – Luxaflex

Filtrasorb – granular activated carbon – Chemviron Carbon Ltd

Filtratio – Harrier Fluid Power Ltd

Filtration – Hydrotechnik UK Ltd

Filtre – Harrier Fluid Power Ltd

*Filtrec (Italy) – hydraulic filters – Harrier Fluid Power Ltd

FILTREC S R L – Hydraulic & Offshore Supplies Ltd

Filtrex – filter media – Heath Filtration Ltd

Filtrex – Harrier Fluid Power Ltd

Filtro – Small batch brewers – Marco Beverage Systems Ltd

Filtro Shuttle – Bulk coffee brewer – Marco Beverage Systems Ltd

Filtron – British Vita plc

Filtrona – quality control instruments – Cerulean

Filtrona – cigarette filters – Filtrona plc

Filtronic – British Vita plc

Filtronic AB (Sweden) – fume extraction equipment – Electro Group Ltd

Filu – Harrier Fluid Power Ltd

Fimet – Dental Chairs – North West Dental Equipment

Fina – Online Lubricants

Finaflex – modified binder – Total Bitumen

Finaids – grinding wheels vitrified-resinoid-discs, cutting wheels, points, flapdiscs, flapwheels spirobands and abrasive belts – Finishing Aids & Tools Ltd
Finalist Sportswear – Cofit T Shirts Deals
FinalTouch – germicidal wash room cleaner – Evans Vanodine International plc
Financial ACORN – C A C I
Financial Times Electronic Publishing – 24hr media monitoring – Interactive Data
Finaseal – modified slurry seal binder – Total Bitumen
Finasrain – brass faced watering can roses (plastic or rubber backs) – Eclipse Sprayers Ltd
Finasrain – spray roses – Haws Watering Cans
Finatex – road surfacing system – Total Bitumen
Fincantieri – Harrier Fluid Power Ltd
FINCLASS – Welding Wire and Electrodes – Finlex International Ltd
Fincline – shower trays – Matki plc
Finder – Cyclops Electronics Ltd
Finder Driver – attachement for cordless or power drills – Makita UK Ltd
Finder Relays – E Preston Electrical Ltd
Finders – Dead Sea products – Finders International Ltd
Fine Grind Colours – food colourings – Sensient
Fine Point Textured Velvet – carpets - wilton – Brintons Carpets Ltd
FINE TUBES LTD – Hydraulic & Offshore Supplies Ltd
Fine Upland Heathers – 80% wool/10% polyester/10% nylon twist or saxony pile 4 & 5m wide – Adam Carpets Ltd
Fine Velvet – Ryalux Carpets Ltd
Fine Worcester Twist – 80% wool/20% nylon 4 & 5m wide – Adam Carpets Ltd
Fineblade – paper – Smurfit Kappa Townsend Hook
Fineblade Satin Webb – Paper – Smurfit Kappa Townsend Hook
Fineblade Smooth – paper – Smurfit Kappa Townsend Hook
Finecast Aluminium Division – Aluminium castings – Mckenna Group Ltd
Finechip – paper – Smurfit Kappa Townsend Hook
Finefin – Osborn Unipol Ltd
Fineflute – paper – Smurfit Kappa Townsend Hook
Fineline – insulated glazed fire resistant doors, screens and atria – Fendor Ltd
Fineline – Fineline Environmental Ltd
Fineline – Fine Line
Fineline Asbestos Solutions – Asbestos Removal – Fine Line
Fineline Asbestos Solutions – Asbestos Removal – Fineline Environmental Ltd
Fineliner – paper – Smurfit Kappa Townsend Hook
Finers Stephen Innocent – solicitors – Finers Stephens Innocent LLP
Finesse – shower doors – Matki plc
Finetwist – Ryalux Carpets Ltd
Finex Separator – Russell Finex Ltd
Finger Phonics books 1-7 – childrens books for learning to read and write – Jolly Learning Ltd
Finger Protector – Safety Assured Ltd
Fingerprint Identification Reader – Tekdata Distribution Ltd
Fingerprint Reader – Tekdata Distribution Ltd
Fingerprint Reader Security System – Tekdata Distribution Ltd
Finglands Coachways – bus and coach services – East Yorkshire Motor Services Ltd
Finglands Travel Agency – travel agency – East Yorkshire Motor Services Ltd
Finings Adjunct – anxiliary finings – Murphy & Son
Finish – UK Office Direct
FINITE – Hydraulic & Offshore Supplies Ltd
Finlay BME – Sandvik
Finlay Foods – James A S Finlay Holdings Ltd
Finlay's – tea producers – James Finlay Limited
Finlays – James A S Finlay Holdings Ltd
Finlays – tobacconists and newsagents – Finlays Ltd
Finmere – Pledge Office Chairs Ltd
Finn – childrens shoes – D B Shoes Ltd
Finn Filter – Harrier Fluid Power Ltd
Finn-Power – CNC hole punching machines and FMS systems – Press & Shear Machinery Ltd
Finnpower – swaging machines – Hydrapower Dynamics Ltd
Finnsonic – industrial ultrasonic component cleaning equipment – Turbex Ltd
Finseal Pile – weather stripping for high performance aluminium windowsand doors – Schlegel UK
Finsys – financial planning system – Lorien Resourcing Ltd
Fintalc – talc – Omya UK Ltd
Fintec – quarrying machinery – Sandvik
Finweb – synthetic fibre wheels, discs, roll, sheets – Finishing Aids & Tools Ltd
***Fiocut (Germany)** – schott OPC ampoules – The Adelphi Group
Fioptic – detection for valves using fibre optics – Amri UK
Fiorivert ABQ7046 – speciality compound – Quest International UK Ltd
FIPIO – communications protocol – Schneider
***Fipro (Slovenia)** – non-combustible board – Rex Bousfield Ltd
Fira (Italy) – oil coolers – BYPY Hydraulics & Transmissions Ltd
Firaqua – water based paints – Firwood Paints Ltd
Fire Barrier – fireproofing system – Promat UK Ltd
Fire Barrier Systems – fire protection for use in ceilings and voids – Rockwool Rockpanel B V
Fire Barrier Transits – effective sealing for multiple cables – Hawke International
Fire Duct Systems – pipes, ducts and industrial noise control – Rockwool Rockpanel B V
Fire Protection – Hotchkiss Ltd
Fire Protection Services Ltd – Fire Protection Services Ltd
Fire Scribe – system panel, supply & install – B B C Fire Protection Ltd
Fire Security – automatic sprinkler systems – Fire Security Sprinkler Installations Ltd
Fire-Shield – fire doors – Accent Hansen
Fire Spray – Hotchkiss Ltd
Fire Tube – floors, structural steelwork, doors, ceilings, pipes and ducts – Rockwool Rockpanel B V
***Fireball (Italy)** – space heaters – S I P Industrial Products Ltd
FIREBAR – flat tubular heating elements – Watlow Ltd
Firebeam – obscuration smoke detector – U T C Fire & Security
FireBird – Gesipa Blind Riveting Systems Ltd
Firebird – Cabinets – Jo Bird & Co. Ltd
Firebird – profile cutting machine – Easab Cutting Systems
Firebird, Tough Store – Jo Bird & Co. Ltd
Fireblock – fire dampers for ductwork – Dufaylite Developments Ltd
Fireboard Systems – gypsum based building board with excellent fire resistant properties – Knauf Drywall
Firebrake – zinc borate flame retardant – Omya UK Ltd
Firebrand – rolling shutters and doors with up to 4 hour fire rating – Hart Door Systems
Firecall – monitoring of fire alarms & security alarms – A V R Group Ltd
FireCarb – Minelco Ltd
Firecharm LF – outset living flame gas fire – Robinson Willey
Firecharm RS – balanced flue gas fire – Robinson Willey
Firecheck – fire retardant membrane coating, asbestos encapsulant – Sika Liquid Plastics
Firecold – fireproof insulated panels – Stancold plc
Firecrest – Rotadex Systems Ltd
Firecrest Design – graphic & web designers – Interprint Ltd
Firecrest Photography – photographers – Interprint Ltd
Fired Refractory Shapes – Magna Industrials Ltd
FireFighter – Low Smoke Zero Halogen BUS data and control cables – Belcom Cables Ltd
Firefly – solid fuel heating equipment – Dunsley Heat Ltd
Firefly – Gesipa Blind Riveting Systems Ltd
Firefly – passive fire protection – T B A Textiles
***Firefly (Sweden)** – fire safety – Orthos Engineering Ltd
Firefly – Helman Workwear
Firefly – electronic controls for amusement and gaming machines – Heber Ltd
Firefly – throw out escape ladders – Lampitt Fire Escapes
FireFox – Gesipa Blind Riveting Systems Ltd
Firegard – fire damper for air conditioning system – Gilberts Blackpool Ltd
Firegem Visa 2 – radiant gas fire – Robinson Willey
Firegem Visa Deluxe Highline – radiant gas fire – Robinson Willey
Firegem Visa Highline – radiant gas fire – Robinson Willey
Firegem Visa Super Deluxe – radiant gas fire – Robinson Willey
Firegem Visa Super Deluxe Highline – radiant gas fire – Robinson Willey
Fireglow – fire lighter – Euroliters Ltd
Fireguard – boiler house and zonal gas control equipment – T C W Services Controls Ltd
Fireguard – Fireguard safety equipment co ltd
Fireguard Sack Holders – fire retardant sack holders for use in hospitals and in factories and offices – Wybone Ltd
Fireking – Secure Holidays
Firemac – smoke vent – McKenzie Martin Ltd
Firemaster – one hour fire door – Premdor Crosby Ltd
***Firemaster (Germany)** – B.O.P. control hoses – Hydrasun Ltd
Firemaster – Eurobond Laminates Ltd
Firemaster – fire protection products and systems – Thermal Ceramics UK Ltd
Firepak – pumps – Armstrong Holden Brooke Pullen Ltd
Firepan (United Kingdom) – fire rated access panels – Panelcraft Access Panels
Firepan Magna (United Kingdom) – double door fireproof access panels – Panelcraft Access Panels
Fireplan System – partitioning – Interior Property Solutions
Fireplank – upgrading ceilings for fire protection – Cryotherm Insulation Ltd
Fireray – smoke beam detectors – Fire Fighting Enterprises
FIREROD – cartridge heaters – Watlow Ltd
FIRESAFE – Dantec Ltd
Fireshield – half hour fire rated door – Premdor Crosby Ltd
Firesleeve – fire stop for plastic pipes – Dufaylite Developments Ltd
Firespec – fire retardant bonded board range – Rex Bousfield Ltd
Firespy – system panel, supply & install – B B C Fire Protection Ltd
Firestat – protex, cotton, antistatic, flame retardant – Carrington Career & Work Wear
Firestone – E.P.D.M. single ply roof membranes – Stephens Plastics Ltd
Firestone – Air Rides & Cylinders – Hi-Power Hydraulics
Firestone – Wealden Tyres Ltd
firestone epdm – rubber roofing – Retrofit Rubberroofing
Firestore – cylindrical water storage tanks – Franklin Hodge Industries Ltd
Firestream – controlled air incinerators – Incinco
***Fireswiss (Switzerland)** – fire resistant safety glass – C G I International Ltd
Firetainer – rectangular water storage tanks – Franklin Hodge Industries Ltd
Firetec – fire performance cables – A E I Cables
Firetec – Emergi Lite Safety Systems Ltd
Firetex – intumescent fire protection coatings for steelwork – Leighs Paints
Firetex – rolling steel fire shutters – Kaba Door Systems
Firetherm – County Construction Chemicals Ltd
Firetile – H & E Smith
Firetracer – multi point asperated high sensitivity smoke detector system – Icam Ltd
Firetwist Heather – Ryalux Carpets Ltd
FIREWALL – Dax International Ltd
Firewall Intrusion Detection – Tekdata Distribution Ltd
Firewatch – laboratory and kitchen gas isolating and testing system – T C W Services Controls Ltd
FireworkGuy – www.fireworkguy.co.uk – FireworkGuy.Co.Uk
Firglo – fast drying metal finish – Firwood Paints Ltd
Firlene – high flash, fast dyring paints – Firwood Paints Ltd
Firlex – decorative and maintenance paints – Firwood Paints Ltd
Firma-Loy – electro-less nickel – Firma Chrome Ltd
Firma-Pol – electropolishing of stainless steel – Firma Chrome Ltd
Firmagrip (United Kingdom) – Open grid drainage in roll format yet suitable for small wheeled traffic – Plastic Extruders Ltd
Firmashelf – modular shelving system – Craven & Co. Ltd
Firmatch – range of paints from a tinting system – Firwood Paints Ltd
Firmflex – drain rods and equipment – Wakefield Brush UK Ltd
Firmtwist Elite – tufted twist – Victoria Carpets Ltd
Firmwall – British Vita plc
Firpavar – chemical resisting paints – Firwood Paints Ltd
First 5 Towers – Accesscaff International Ltd
First Ascent – banking, insurance and investment services – Birmingham Midshires Financial Services Ltd
First Base Timber – Wolseley UK
First Beeline – bus company – First Bus
First Data Europe – F D R Ltd
First Financial Consultancy – management consultancy – The First Financial Consultancy Ltd
First Personnel – employment agency – First Personnel Group plc
First Point Assessment – oil and gas industry database of suppliers and contractors – First Point Assessment Ltd
First Quality – H Weston & Sons Ltd
First Quality Draught – H Weston & Sons Ltd
First Response – pregnency/ovulation tests – Church & Dwight UK Ltd
First Source – Euler Hermes
First Stop Safety – Tele-Products Ltd
Firstbase+ – baseball style bump & scrape head protection – Scott International Ltd
Firstlight – Light Fantastic
Firstplus Financial Group – The Woolwich
Firstplus Management Services – The Woolwich
Firstplus Services – The Woolwich
Firsyn – stoving industrial paints – Firwood Paints Ltd
Firth – stainless steel casting – Doncasters F B C Ltd
Firth – stainless steel washing trough – Armitage Shanks Ltd
Firth Rixon Rings – open die forgings – Firth Rixson Ltd
Firwood – miscellaneous range of industrial paints – Firwood Paints Ltd
***Fischer Fixings (Germany)** – fixing systems – Fischer Fixings UK Ltd
***Fischer Plug (Germany)** – nylon wallplug for woodscrews – Fischer Fixings UK Ltd

***Fischer System (Germany)** – hooks and brackets for complete garage and home storage systems – Fischer Fixings UK Ltd
***Fischerbolts (Germany)** – steel through bolts for concrete – Fischer Fixings UK Ltd
Fischerscope – coating thickness measuring instrument – Fischer Instrumentation GB Ltd
FISCO – Fieldway Supplies Ltd
Fisco – Fisco Tools Ltd
Fisco – Gem Tool Hire & Sales Ltd
Fish food manufrs – Ewos Ltd
Fish Mate – aquatic accessories – Pet Mate Ltd
Fisher – Gem Tool Hire & Sales Ltd
Fisher – valves & spares – Bearwood Engineering Supplies
Fisher – yachts – Northshore Yachts Ltd
Fisher Clark – UK Office Direct
Fisher Controls – Wilson UK Ltd
Fisher Plastics – precision trade injection moulders – Fisher
Fisher Price – toys – Mattel
Fisherbrand – AESpump
Fispa – Harrier Fluid Power Ltd
FISTREEM – Fistreem International Ltd
Fistreem – water purification – Sanyo Gallenkamp plc
Fistreem Multipure – Sanyo Gallenkamp plc
Fistreem Puri-Fi – Sanyo Gallenkamp plc
FIT – Hydraulic & Offshore Supplies Ltd
Fitness Pro-mat – aerobic mat – Functional Foam Beacons Products Ltd
Fitotron – plant growth chambers and rooms – Sanyo Gallenkamp plc
Fittapanel – lightweight panels for exhibitions, shopfitting and displays – Dufaylite Developments Ltd
Fitter & Poulton – electrical installation equipment – Petrel Ltd
Fitzpatrick – civil engineering and building contractors – Volkerhighways Ltd
Five Star – pencil – Cumberland Pencil Museum
Five Star – gelatine indirect photo stencil film – Macdermid Autotype Ltd
Fivex – protected protein – Rumenco Ltd
Fivilever – levelling feet – Fibet Rubber Bonding UK Ltd
Fivistop – anti-vibration products – Fibet Rubber Bonding UK Ltd
***Fix (Sweden)** – window espagnolettes and door bolts – Assa Abloy Security Solutions
Fix – used for relaxing all types of pastry – C S M UK Ltd
Fix-a-Flow – Fixed flow gas regulator. – Cryoservice Ltd
Fix Lock – fasteners and plastic buckles – I T W Nexus Europe
Fixatile – heat resistant adhesive – Vitcas Ltd
Fixecure – display card bagged product fixing system – CPC Packaging Ltd
Fixed Blade – louvres – H W Cooper
Fixed Rate – mortgage scheme – Market Harborough Building Society
Fixitol – dyestuff fixing agents to improve wet fastness of nylon and cotton fabrics – Brenntag Colours Ltd
Fixtured tools – Gustair Materials Handling Equipment Ltd
Fizz 'C' – effervescent vitamin c and mineral drink – G & G Food Supplies
FK – rod ends & spherical bearings – R A Rodriguez UK Ltd
FK 25 – Dantherm Filtration Ltd
FKSII (Germany) – sap r/3 interface – Feedback Data Ltd
Flackt – blowers & spares – Bearwood Engineering Supplies
Flag Brand – paint and wax polish – Flag Paints
Flags & Standards Ltd – bunting and raycot flags and standards – Flags & Standards Ltd
Flagship – holiday & travel insurance – M M A Insurance plc
***Flagship (Far East)** – binoculars – Jessops plc
Flair – darts, flights and shafts – Unicorn Products Ltd
Flair – luxury motor caravan – Auto Sleepers Ltd
Flair – Cloakroom Solutions Ltd
Flakt Woods – Northern Fan Supplies Ltd
Flamatrol – fireproof covering – G K N Aerospace Ltd
Flamcor – fire retardant decorative foil board – Rex Bousfield Ltd
Flame – magazines, books, manuals, rule books for playing games, stationery, artists materials for painting models, games and accessories, playthings, miniatures and models for use in fantasy games – Games Workshop Ltd
Flame-Fighter – fire hose – Angus Fire
Flame & Fume – flame and fume treatment of all fabrics and soft furnishings – House Of Flags
Flame Upholstery – The Winnen Furnishing Company
Flamefast – fire lighter – Euroliters Ltd
Flamefast – Vaughans Hope Works Ltd
Flamegard – flame retardant finished fabrics – Carrington Career & Work Wear
Flamenco – ballpoint pen ideal for advertising slogans – Hainenko Ltd
Flameshield (United Kingdom) – cotton satin flame retardant fabric – Carrington Career & Work Wear
Flamestat (United Kingdom) – flame retardant and anti static fabric – Carrington Career & Work Wear
Flametex – flame retardant treatment for felt pads – Airsprung Furniture Group plc
Flametex Fibre Pad – coir fibre insulating pad for sprung-interior – Airsprung Furniture Group plc
Flametuff – cotton/nylon flame retardant fabric – Carrington Career & Work Wear
Flamgard – B O B Stevenson Ltd
Flamgard Plus – Flammable gas detector with display – Crowcon Detection Instrument Ltd
Flaminaire – butane soldering torch – Time Products UK Ltd
Flamingo – paperback fiction and non-fiction books – Harpercollins Publishers Ophelia House
Flamrad – gas fired infra-red heaters and burners – Infraglo Sheffield Ltd
Flangeform – high strenghth captive fastener system – B A S Components Ltd
Flanges – pipe flanges of all types and materials – Flanges Ltd
Flapmaster – combination letterplatess – Paddock Fabrications Ltd
FlapStile – entrance gates – Gunnebo Entrance Control Ltd
Flare Free Device – fabrics – Heathcoat Fabrics Ltd
Flare Free & Head Dev – fabrics and clothing – Heathcoat Fabrics Ltd
Flare Seals (United Kingdom) – flare stack sealing device – Hamworthy Combustion Engineering Ltd
Flarescan (United Kingdom) – control system – Hamworthy Combustion Engineering Ltd
Flarestream (United Kingdom) – flare tip – Hamworthy Combustion Engineering Ltd
Flash (United Kingdom) – din rail and 72mm time switches – Sangamo Ltd
Flash – UK Office Direct
Flash – time clocks, defrost clocks, room thermostats – Thermofrost Cryo plc
Flash Connectors – Michael George Manufacturing Ltd
Flash Vessels – Abbott & Co Newark Ltd
Flash Welder – welding equipment – Bearwood Engineering Supplies
Flashband – Bostik Ltd
***Flashchanger (U.S.A.)** – combination flasher/lampchanger – A B Pharos Marine Ltd
Flashertape – self-adhesive flashing tape – Cavity Trays Ltd
Flashlight – brands sold under Turbosound name – Turbosound Ltd
Flashni (United Kingdom) – audio visual products – Fulleon
Flashpoint – sparking plugs and auto bulbs – Flashpoint England Ltd
Flashpoint – Bridgwater Electronics Ltd
Flashpoint Computer Parts – computers, hardware, software and other components – Flashpoint England Ltd
Flashpoint England – sparkplug & computer components – Flashpoint England Ltd
Flashpoint Infrared Testing – Emergi Lite Safety Systems Ltd
Flashpoint Security – City Of London Courier Ltd
Flashpoint UK & Europe – sparkplugs, computers and accessories – Flashpoint England Ltd
Flat-Flex – wire processing conveyor belting – Wire Belt Co. Ltd
Flat Jacks – hydraulic low-height load transfer jacks – Fagioli Ltd
Flat Jacks - Towerlift - Strand Jacks – Fagioli Ltd
Flat Pocket File – pocketed manilla file – Acco East Light Ltd
Flatau Dick – timber brokers – Flatau Dick UK Ltd
Flatau Dick & Co – brokers in wood & plywood – Flatau Dick UK Ltd
Flatau Dick Overseas – brokers in timber – Flatau Dick UK Ltd
Flatdeck 1 – baby piglet feed – A One Feed Supplements Ltd
Flatdeck 2 – baby piglet feed – A One Feed Supplements Ltd
Flatford – steel fabricators – Flatford
Flatlift – sub surface cultivators – Spaldings Ltd
Flatmaster – anti-condensation unit for flats – Nuaire Ltd
Flatwrap – barbed tape – Birmingham Barbed Tape Ltd
Flava Major – water filter – British Filters Ltd
***Flavorburst** – Taylor Scotland Ltd
Flavorpac – in-cup ingredients – Chequer Foods Ltd
Flawless Finish – pressed powder, loose powder and sponge-on cream make-up – Elizabeth Arden
Flawless Finish Mousse Make-Up – make-up – Elizabeth Arden
Flecked Stoneware – stoneware body with flechs & dapple markings – Potclays Ltd
Fleet – line marking machines and materials for sports grounds – Fleet Line Markers Ltd
Fleet Guard – Harrier Fluid Power Ltd
Fleet Lawclub – uninsured loss recovery motor contract and prosecution defence – Allianz Legal Protection
Fleet Track – vehicle tracking system – Golden River Traffic Ltd
Fleetarc – Supply the welding industry – Wilkinson Star
Fleetcard – business vehicle maintenance management card – Arval UK Ltd
Fleetfit – B L Pneumatics Ltd
Fleetfit – pipe fittings for vehicles – Norgren Ltd
FLEETFIT – Hydraulic & Offshore Supplies Ltd
Fleetguard – Team Overseas Ltd
Fleetmaster – lubricant – B P plc
Fleetnet – enhance group call service – Inmarsat Global Ltd
Fleetol – B P plc
Fleetweld – welding electrodes – Lincoln Electric UK Ltd
Fleetwood Blacksmith – wrought ironwork, trawl door – Fleetwood Trawlers Supply Company
Fleetwood Industrial Sack – fabric workers, tent awnings, coal sacks – Fleetwood Trawlers Supply Company
Fleetwood Port Services – stevedores – Fleetwood Trawlers Supply Company
Fleetwood Sheet Metal – sheet metal work – Fleetwood Trawlers Supply Company
Fleisch – pneumotachograph – Linton & Co Engineering Ltd
Flemimg Homes – individually designed timber frame homes, medical, commercial and recreational buildings – T Fleming Homes Ltd
Flemish Tile – clay – Sandtoft Holdings Ltd
Flenco – European Technical Sales Ltd
Flender – European Technical Sales Ltd
Flender – hydraulics/spares – Bearwood Engineering Supplies
Fletcher Smith – designers and suppliers of sugar factories and equipment (consultants for sugar industries) – Fives Fletcher Ltd
Fletcher Smith Ltd – consultants for sugar industries – Fives Fletcher Ltd
Fletol – lubricant – B P plc
Fleuroxene – Quest International UK Ltd
Fleury SA (Switzerland) – incline transfer machines annd unit heads & slides – Haesler Machine Tools
Flex-A-Seal – vapour saving seals – H M T Rubbaglas Ltd
Flex Beam Guard Rail – Berry Systems
FLEX-display – Display Wizard Ltd
Flex+Drive – Baldor UK
Flex-I-Liner – seal-less rotary plastic pump – Vanton Pumps Europe Ltd
Flex Max – maximum flexibility extraction arm with 5 angle joints – Plymovent Limited
Flex-Plate – spring loads pinion into mesh to eliminate backlash – Reliance Precision
FLEX-PVC – Naylor Specialists Plastics
Flex-Seal – couplings to joint pipes in low pressure sewarage and drainage systems – Flex Seal Couplings Ltd
Flex-Turn – 90° & 180° powered conveyers – Wire Belt Co. Ltd
Flex-Xel – needle punch bi-component felt – Imp UK Ltd
Flexa – flexible electrical conduit – M. Buttkereit Ltd
Flexair – air suspension units for trailers – Meritor HVS Ltd
Flexam – magnetic rubber – Magnet Applications Ltd
Flexane – liquid urethane for moulding and protective coatings – I T W Devcon
Flexaulic Ltd – hydraulic fittings hydraulic presses – A E L Flexaulic Ltd
Flexax – tolerance compensation fasteners – Bollhoss Fastenings Ltd
Flexbond – polyester wadding – W E Rawson Ltd
Flexcase – aluminium sign systems – Universal Components
Flexcell – expansion joint filler – Celotex Ltd
Flexcut – Wood carving tools – The Toolpost
Flexcut – material – Charterhouse Holdings plc
Flexdek – flexible rubber screen decks – Linatex Ltd
FlexDrive – Baldor UK
Flexel – radiant ceiling heating system and panels – Flexel International Ltd
Flexello – castors and wheels – Flexello Ltd
Flexello – Mercury Bearings Ltd
Flexello Polynyl – injection polyurethane nylon centre wheel – Flexello Ltd
Flexello Superthane – polyurethane elastomer tyred cast iron wheel – Flexello Ltd
FLEXEQUIP HYDRAULICS LTD – Hydraulic & Offshore Supplies Ltd
Flexetta – bias bindings – J B Broadley
Flexfelt – bonded felt – W E Rawson Ltd
Flexfit – spinal supports, heel cushions and waist supports – Remploy Ltd
Flexflyte (United Kingdom) – neoprene or silicone-coated glass-fibre fabric ducts with steel helix – Flexible Ducting Ltd
Flexflyte Super (United Kingdom) – axially and helically-reinforced tpe ducting with spring steel helix – Flexible Ducting Ltd
Flexi-Brush – reversible corrugated/pebbled vinyl matting – Jaymart Roberts & Plastics Ltd
Flexi-Dock – vehicle docking equipment – Envirohold Ltd
Flexi-Door – flexible crash door – Envirohold Ltd
Flexi G4, Flex, Euro – Narrow Aisle Ltd
Flexi-Hoops – embroidery hoops and frames – Coats Ltd

Flexi Label – label overprinting system – Weyfringe Labelling Systems

Flexi Mats – Flexi dot/coin/button.line/ridge/tred, sheet vinyl supplied in rolls with various surface patterns for most applications – Plastic Extruders Ltd

Flexi MDF – Flexible MDF – The Tambour Company Ltd

Flexi Ply – Flexible Plywood – The Tambour Company Ltd

Flexi-Post – Berry Systems

Flexi-Stretch – cohesive bandage – Robinson Healthcare Ltd

Flexi-Tile – pvc interlocking floor tiles – Quantum Profile Systems

Flexiarm – specialist installation machine for self-tapping inserts – Tappex Thread Inserts Ltd

Flexible Lacquers – paints – Colour-Therm Ltd

Flexible Mortgage – mortgage scheme – Market Harborough Building Society

Flexible, Semi-Rigid and Flexible Slabs – flexible light weight insulation slabs – Rockwool Rockpanel B V

Flexiburo – storage system – Flexiform Business Furniture Ltd

Flexicap – Syfer Technology Ltd

Flexicarb – flexible graphite – Flexitallic Ltd

Flexichuck – lathe chuck for thin walled components – Craftsman Tools Ltd

Flexicon – Aseptic filling systems – Watson Marlow Pumps Ltd

Flexicon – flexible conduits and connectors – Flexicon Ltd

Flexicon Europe – Flexicon Europe Ltd

Flexicover – flexible ceiling paints – Akzonobel

Flexicut – grinding wheels – ATI Garryson Limited

Flexideck – Safety Works & Solutions Ltd

Flexider – Harrier Fluid Power Ltd

Flexidisc – abrasive disc – ATI Garryson Limited

Flexidrip – landscape drip systems for hanging baskets & tubs – Access Irrigation Ltd

Flexiflair – wooden storage system – Flexiform Business Furniture Ltd

Flexiform – Storage – Bucon Ltd

Flexiform – systems office furniture – Flexiform Business Furniture Ltd

Flexiform – grommet strip – Hellermann Tyton

Flexiform – unique spring system – Dorlux Beds

Flexiframe – PVC door frames – Boomer Industries Ltd

Flexiglide – side-opening tambour storage systems – Flexiform Business Furniture Ltd

Flexigrid (United Kingdom) – 20mm high open grid rolls for extra heavy liquid spillage – Plastic Extruders Ltd

Flexiguard – an intruder detection system – Advanced Perimeter Systems Ltd

Flexijoint – flexible epoxy resin floor joint sealant for heavy duty traffic situations – Conren Ltd

Flexiline – preformed thermoplastic road marking – Sportsmark Group Ltd

Flexilink – budget office storage systems – Flexiform Business Furniture Ltd

Flexiloader – trade name for mobile-loader – Vanriet UK Ltd

FLEXILOPE – self seal polythene envelopes and packaging bags – M&ES Flexilope

*Flexim (Germany) – time of flight flowmeter – Tamo Ltd

Fleximas – Fleximas Ltd

Fleximetric – office storage and screens – Flexiform Business Furniture Ltd

Flexion – flexible doors – Envirohold Ltd

Flexipak – G E Healthcare

Flexipark – fully automatic car park system's – Zeag UK Ltd

Flexipatch – flexible circuit boards for jack fields – Mosses & Mitchell Ltd

Flexiperm – flexible permanent service – Whitehall Recruitment Ltd

Flexipol – Flexipol Packaging Ltd

FLEXIQUIP – Hydraulic & Offshore Supplies Ltd

Flexiring – tool holding equipment – Craftsman Tools Ltd

Flexirol – multidirectional sliding and folding door hardware system – P C Henderson Ltd

Flexiseal – waterproof membrane – R I W Ltd

Flexishaft – Mono Pumps Ltd

Flexishaft (United Kingdom) – connects the pump drive shaft to the orbiting rotor – Mono Pumps Ltd

Flexistor – modular storage systems – Flexiform Business Furniture Ltd

Flexistrong – Flexipol Packaging Ltd

FlexiStudy – scheme combining NEC open learning materials with tutorial support & facilities of the FE college – National Extension College

Flexitallic – spiral wound gaskets – Flexitallic Ltd

Flexite – non-asbestos, gasket filler material – Flexitallic Ltd

Flexitec – cellular polymer seals and gaskets with double sided adhesive tape – Vitec

Flexitex FE – plastisol textile ink for sports garments – Fujifilm Sericol Ltd

Flexiveyor – portable extendable gravity conveyor – Vanriet UK Ltd

*Flexilift (Germany) – low profile scissor lift – Southworth Handling Ltd

FlexLine – Antenna feeder coaxial cables – Belcom Cables Ltd

FlexLock – self-anchoring pipe couplings – Viking Johnson

Flexmaster – flexible beverage tubing – Valpar Industrial Ltd

Flexmaster – portable valve actuators/mechanical – Trelawny S P T Ltd

Flexmaster – Aeroquip Couplings – Hamer Stevenson Ltd

Flexmount – print stereo mounting tapes for the flexographic printing industry – Vitec

FLEXO – Pulsation Dampener – Pulsation Dampers At Pulseguard Ltd

Flexocare – UK Office Direct

Flexocel – flexible cold cure foam systems – Baxenden Chemicals Ltd

FLEXOCRAT – Liquid in bladder, high frequency, pressure response stabilizer – Pulsation Dampers At Pulseguard Ltd

Flexocrepe – cotton crepe bandage – Robinson Healthcare Ltd

Flexofil – bottom filler for footwear – Livingston & Doughty Ltd

Flexolite – timber windows – I D Products Ltd

Flexopads – adhesive pads – Robinson Healthcare Ltd

Flexoplast – elastic adhesive bandage – Robinson Healthcare Ltd

FLEXOR – Flange faced unit to ANSI B16.5 or metric PN/DN standards – Pulsation Dampers At Pulseguard Ltd

Flexor – magnetic rubber – Magnet Applications Ltd

FLEXORBER – PTFE Process System Damper/Protector – Pulsation Dampers At Pulseguard Ltd

*Flexoseal (U.S.A.) – adhesive application equipment for corrugated industry – Valco Cincinnati

*Flexotecnica (Italy) – flexographic printing presses – Engelmann & Buckham Ltd

FLEXOTEE – Pulsation damper with integral t-piece – Pulsation Dampers At Pulseguard Ltd

Flexotone – process flexographic printing – Printpack Enterprises Ltd T/A Printpack

Flexovit – abrasive discs & wheels – John Davies 2001 Ltd

Flexovoss – concrete moulding materials – Bondaglass Voss Ltd

Flexpanda – tube cleaning tools and brushes – Rotatools UK Ltd

Flexpro (TM) – serrated metal core – Flexitallic Ltd

Flexsol – liner manufacturing division – Ceva Container Logistics

Flextract (United Kingdom) – polyurethane and pvc ducting with spring steel helix – Flexible Ducting Ltd

Flextract - Superflextract - Flexflyte Super - Wyrem - Flexflyte - Kehroflex-S – Flexible Ducting Ltd

Flextuft – brushed nylon-on-rubber indoor/outdoor flooring/entrance matting – Jaymart Roberts & Plastics Ltd

Flexus – self adhering bandage – Robinson Healthcare Ltd

Flexwell – air dielectric coax cable – R F S UK Ltd

Flexy-Glass – disposable plastic glassware – Plastico Ltd

Flight – Capex Office Interiors

Flight Fabrications (United Kingdom) – screw conveyors – Astwell Augers Ltd

Flightcard – aviation payment services – B P plc

Flintag – crushed flint – Brett Specialised Aggregates

Flipflap – polyethylene hygiene door – Envirohold Ltd

Flipper – fishing tackle – Daiwa Sports Ltd

Flips for Windows – OMR forms design package (computer software) – D R S Data Services Ltd

FLIR – Insteng Process Automation Ltd

Flir – Thermal Imaging – Alpha Electronics Northern Ltd

FLIR Systems – manufacturer of Thermal Imaging Cameras – Flir Systems Ltd

Flir Systems – Express Instrument Hire Ltd

Flir (Thermal Imaging) – Fieldway Supplies Ltd

Flite – airline breathing apparatus, with rapid escape cylinder – Scott International Ltd

Flite Escape – airline/escape breathing apparatus – Scott International Ltd

Flitebag – Bespoke hand made transit cases – Hofbauer (UK) Ltd

Fliteline – flexible pressure hose – Icore International

Flitetop – Regina International Ltd

Flitetop - Matveyor - Ultop – Regina International Ltd

*Flitz (U.S.A.) – polish – John Hornby Skewes & Co. Ltd

Flixborough – bulk cargo handling services – Flixborough Wharf Ltd

Flli Dieci – Harrier Fluid Power Ltd

*Flo Control (Italy) – solenoid valves for gas or liquid brass or stainless body – Valeader Pneumatics Ltd

*Flo-Coupling (U.S.A.) – hose couplings in plastic – Dual Pumps Ltd

*Flo-Cut – sizer halver for potatoes – Flo Mech Ltd

Flo-Dar – Flowline Manufacturing Ltd

Flo-Filter – frying oil filtration system – Flo Mech Ltd

Flo-Gage – Flowline Manufacturing Ltd

Flo-Gro – liquid chemical fertiliser – Farmura Ltd

Flo-Grout – high strength grout – Don Construction Products Ltd

Flo-Grow – soil improver – Woodgrow Horticulture

Flo-Matic – Britax P S V Wypers Ltd

Flo-Pak – free flow polystyrene packaging material – F P International UK Ltd

Flo-System – Flowline Manufacturing Ltd

Flo-tech – Trafalgar Tools

*Flo-Therm – frying oil heater with pollution control – Flo Mech Ltd

Flo-Tote – Flowline Manufacturing Ltd

FLOATOLATOR – Hydraulic accumulator of capacities in excess of 5,000 litres – Pulsation Dampers At Pulseguard Ltd

Flobox – intermediate bulk containers – Flomotion Rental Ltd

Flochill – scraped surface heat exchanger – T Giusti Ltd

Flockage Litho – paper – Fenner Paper Co. Ltd

Flocon (Parker) – solenoid valves and pressure regulators, including suction regulators, discharge regulators, crankcase regulators, differential regulators, hot gas bypass regulators – Thermofrost Cryo plc

Flocrete – range of admixtures for concrete – Don Construction Products Ltd

Flofast – intermediate bulk containers – Flomotion Rental Ltd

Flofast 2 – intermediate bulk containers – Flomotion Rental Ltd

Flofold – intermediate bulk containers – Flomotion Rental Ltd

Floguard – double check valve – Reliance Water Controls Ltd

Flohr – European Technical Sales Ltd

*Flojet (U.S.A.) – diaphragm pumps – Dual Pumps Ltd

Flojet – pumps – ITT Industries Jabsco Pumps

Flojet - Jabsco - Rule - Danforth - Sudbury - Aquameter – ITT Industries Jabsco Pumps

Floline – hydraulic valves and components – The Vapormatic Co. Ltd

Flomark – ball paint markers – Walters & Walters Ltd

Flomat – sheet moulding compound – DSM UK Ltd

Flomat – Menzolit

Floodjet – nozzles – Delavan Ltd

Floodlight – brands sold under Turbosound name – Turbosound Ltd

Floor-cel, Floor-Cell, Floorcell – British Vita plc

Floor Talkers – Ritrama UK Ltd

Floor Talkers - Polytex - RI-Barrier - RI-Mark - RI-Triplex - RI-Cote - RI-Print - RI-Flex. – Ritrama UK Ltd

Floor Team – floor sanding machine and all accessories – Hire Technicians Group Ltd

Floor & Wall Cleaning Powder – mildly alkaline low foaming multi-purpose cleaner – Premiere Products Ltd

Floorbor Systems – floor and roof joist treatment preservation process – Channelwood Preservation Ltd

Floorcote – polyurethane finish – Spencer Coatings Ltd

Floorcote – rubberised floor paint – Co-Var Ltd

Floorcraft – design service – Tarkett Ltd

Floorfast – fixings for steel chequer plate flooring – Lindapter International

Flooring services – Vita Liquid Polymers

Flooritall – mezzanine floor – Space Way Self

Floorline (United Kingdom) – Single layer tubular construction roll format for light duty applications – Plastic Extruders Ltd

Floorline & Device – British Vita plc

Floormap – computerised MFL floorscanner for the detection, quantification and graphical reporting of underfloor corrosion in above ground storage tanks – Silverwing UK Ltd

Floorplate Non Metallic – non oxidizable synthetic trowelled-in cementitious surface – Conren Ltd

Floorplate S – non oxidizable metallic trowelled-in cementitious – Conren Ltd

Floortex – latex compound for latex cement flooring compositions – Vita Liquid Polymers

Floortex – UK Office Direct

Floozy – fishing tackle – Drennan International Ltd

Flopak – loose fill polystyrene – Ambassador Packaging Ltd

Flopax – intermediate bulk containers – Flomotion Rental Ltd

Floppy Disk Drive – Tekdata Distribution Ltd

Flor – carpets – Interface Europe Ltd

*Flora (Italy) – paper – Fenner Paper Co. Ltd

*Floradrain (Germany) – drainage layer – Alumasc Exterior Building Products

Florafree – anti bacterial soap – Deb R & D Ltd

Florafresh – fragrant disinfectant cleaner – Deb R & D Ltd

Floral Disinfectant – disinfectant based on biodegradable surfactants – Premiere Products Ltd

Florane – perfume speciality – Quest International UK Ltd

Floranyl AB 256 – speciality compound – Quest International UK Ltd

Florazol – spraying essence – Evans Vanodine International plc

Florette – carpets – Bond Worth

Florex – floor coatings systems – Tor Coatings Ltd

Flori-Stoon – 110 volt fluorescent lighting – Blakley Electrics Ltd

Florida – suction and discharge of foodstuffs and drinks – Merlett Plastics UK Ltd

*Floringo – Tradelinens Ltd

Floris – perfumery – J Floris Ltd

Florocyclene – perfume speciality – Quest International UK Ltd

Florosa (Q) – perfume speciality – Quest International UK Ltd

Florplast – polyester plasticiser/grinding aid – Kromachem Ltd

Florstab – anti skinning stabiliser for UV inks – Kromachem Ltd

Flos Lighting – The Winnen Furnishing Company

Flostax – intermediate bulk containers – Flomotion Rental Ltd

FloSystem – production optomisation software – Weatherford Edinburgh Petroleum Services Ltd

Flotanks – polypropylene and HDPE free standing tanks to DVS 2205 – Ian Flockton Developments Ltd

Flotbel – flotation aid – Ashland UK

*Flotect (U.S.A.) – Texcel Division

Flotrip – intermediate bulk containers – Flomotion Rental Ltd

Flotronic – air driven one nut double diaphragm pumps – Flotronic Pumps Ltd

Flourish – Vegetable Oil Spray – Velox Ltd

Flow Calculations – Bronkhorst UK Ltd

Flow Ezy – Uk agent hydraulic filters & accessories – Harrier Fluid Power Ltd

Flow-line – Harrier Fluid Power Ltd

Flow-Mon – flow indicators – Bearwood Engineering Supplies

Flow Science – flow consultancy and analysis – University Of Manchester Incubator Company Ltd

Flow Seal – Crane Stockham Valve Ltd

Floway – chemical waste underground drainage systems – C P V Ltd

Flowball – fine handwriting pen – Office Depot UK

Flowbits – Roxspur Measurement & Control Ltd

Flowbond Special – welding filler metal for high copper alloys – Columbia Metals Ltd

Flowcoat SF41 – water based, coloured epoxy sealer – Flowcrete UK

Flowcrete – We install Flowcrete Resin Systems – Nottingham Industrial Flooring Ltd

*Flowdata (Germany) – gear tube flow meter – Tamo Ltd

*Flowdrill (Netherlands) – flowdrilling equipment – Flowdrill UK Ltd

Flower Fairies – Chorion plc

Flowersharp – Air freshener – Statestrong Ltd

FLOWEZY – Hydraulic & Offshore Supplies Ltd

Flowfill and low-k Flowfill (United Kingdom) – gap-fill dielectric process, std and low-k oxide – Aviza Technology UK Ltd

Flowflex – type 'a' brass and DZR brass compression fittings – Flowflex Components Ltd

Flowguard – remote flow switches – Black Teknigas & Electro Controls Ltd

Flowmeca – ultra high purity gasket free fittings – Boiswood LLP

Flowmeters – Hydrotechnik UK Ltd

Flowmeters – Stream Measurement Ltd

Flowpac – intermittent compression system – Huntleigh Healthcare

Flowpac – water treatment – Barr Wray Ltd

Flowprime – solvent free, clear, low viscosity epoxy resin primer for cementitious substrates. – Flowcrete UK

Flowright – vibratory conveying systems – Wright Machinery Ltd

Flowrite – pipes & tubes – I P P Mardale

Flowseal – gear mechanisms – Bearwood Engineering Supplies

Flowseal (U.S.A.) – Butterfly valve – Crane Process Flow Technology Ltd

Flowseal WD – water based eopxy sealer – Flowcrete UK

Flowshield – epoxy resin self smoothing flooring system – Flowcrete UK

Flowstream – portable water flow meter – Ele International

Flowtec – B L Pneumatics Ltd

FLOWTECH – Hydraulic & Offshore Supplies Ltd

FLOWTECHNIK – Hydraulic & Offshore Supplies Ltd

FlowTek HDD (UK) Ltd – Horizontal Directional Drilling – Flowtek H D D Ltd

Flowtron Plus – intermittent compression system – Huntleigh Healthcare

Floyd – mechanical variable speed drive – Allspeeds Ltd

*Flubacher (Switzerland) – measuring eyeglasses – Vaultland Engineering

Flue & Chimney Systems – Prefabricated systems – Hamworthy Heating Ltd

FLUE FREE – chimney cleaning chemicals – Hydrachem Ltd

Fluical Calibrators – Bronkhorst UK Ltd

Fluid System Technologies (Scotland) Ltd – Swagelok Scotland is a trading name of Fluid System Technologies (Scotland) Ltd. – Swagelok Scotland

Fluidfill – vehicle fluid dosing machine – Schenck Ltd

Fluidiram – anti-caking agent for fertilisers – Atosina UK Ltd

Fluidpower – Harrier Fluid Power Ltd

Fluidrive – fluid couplings – Bearwood Engineering Supplies

Fluidtech – Harrier Fluid Power Ltd

Fluitek – Harrier Fluid Power Ltd

Fluitron – Harrier Fluid Power Ltd

Fluke – Alpha Electronics Southern Ltd

Fluke – Direct Instrument Hire Ltd

Fluke – multi meter test equipment – Longs Ltd

Fluke – European Technical Sales Ltd

Fluke – Radir Ltd

Fluke – Fieldway Supplies Ltd

Fluke – Alpha Electronics Northern Ltd

Fluke, Robin, AVO Megger, Chauvin Arnoux, Martindale, Kewtech, KewTechnik, Alphatek, ACT Meters, Seaward. – Sercal Electronics Ltd

Fluon (U.S.A.) – ptfe, ptfe compounds & lubricants, etfe, lm-etfe, pfa, ultra pure pfa & fluoroelastomer – AGC Chemicals Ltd

Fluophase – perfluorinated silica based columns offering unique selectivity for HPLC – Thermo Fisher Scientific

Fluor – Fluorinated Lubricants – I K V Tribology Ltd

*FLUORA (Germany) – lamps – Osram Ltd

Fluorat – PTFE labware – Portex Technologies Ltd

Fluoraz – elastomeric compound for extreme environments – Greene Tweed & Co. Ltd

Fluorel – Fluorel Ltd

Fluoromelt (U.S.A.) – melt processable compounds (fep, etfe, pfa, pvdf & ectfe based – AGC Chemicals Ltd

Fluoroseal – plastic container barrier treatment – Bettix Ltd

Fluorosint – Aaron Metal & Plastic Supplies Ltd

Fluorosint – Merseyside Metal Services

Flupac – filters/elements – Bearwood Engineering Supplies

FLUPAC – Hydraulic & Offshore Supplies Ltd

Flurene – PTFE coatings – E M Coating Services

Flurene - Perma-Slik - Microseal - Lube-Lok - Everlube – E M Coating Services

Flurex – tablets/capsules – Reckitt Benckiser plc

FLUROSINT – Merseyside Metal Services

Flush Clamp – complete connection system – Lindapter International

Flushgaze – Glazing Vision Ltd

Flushnut – perforated metal female fasteners & nuts centrally located – Bighead Bonding Fasteners Ltd

FLUTEC – Hydraulic & Offshore Supplies Ltd

Fluthane – O'Neill Medicalia Ltd

Fly & Wasp Killer – insecticide for all insect pests – Premiere Products Ltd

Flydor Products – insect and sunscreening products – Vincents Norwich Ltd

Flyers – AMG Forwarding Ltd

Flygt – Pumps – Wendage Pollution Control Ltd

Flygt – pumps & spares – Bearwood Engineering Supplies

Flygt Pumps – Denton Pumps Ltd

Flying Eye – traffic report aircraft – Global Radio

Flying Start – Yara UK It Ltd

FM – film adhesive – Cytec Engineered Materials Ltd

FMAudit (United Kingdom) – ECi Software Solutions Limited

FMC Lithium – F M C Chemicals Ltd

FMEA – Transcend Group Ltd

FMI – industrial folding door – Hörmann (UK) Ltd

FMK 25 – Dantherm Filtration Ltd

Foam Carpet Cleaner – instant foaming cleaner and spot and stain remover for fabrics – Premiere Products Ltd

Foamalux – Foam PVC Sheet – Brett Martin Ltd

Foamalux (United Kingdom) – PVC foam – Righton Ltd

Foamalux Ultra – Gloss Foam PVC Sheet – Brett Martin Ltd

Foamfree – Forward Chemicals Ltd

Foampac – British Vita plc

Foampak – British Vita plc

Foamsert – insert for structured foam plastics and wood – Tappex Thread Inserts Ltd

Focal Point Audio Visual – educational video cassettes – Focal Point Audio Visual Ltd

Focal Point Audio Visual Slide Sets – multimedia resources for education and training – Focal Point Audio Visual Ltd

Focus – FM Radio Earmuff - Electronic Hearing Protection – Scott International Ltd

Focus EAP Limited – FOCUS Eap

Focus Group – marketing consultants – Ipsos Mori

Fodder – fishing tackle – Drennan International Ltd

Fodel – thick film photoprintable compositions – Du Pont UK Ltd

Foden – Harrier Fluid Power Ltd

Fogarty – quilts & pillow – Fogarty Filled Products Ltd

Fogco – High pressure cooling and misting products – Arcadia Irrigation UK

Foladraft – drafting and diffusion film – Folex Ltd

Folajet – inkjet printing films – Folex Ltd

Folamask – cut and peel masking film – Folex Ltd

Folaproof – inkjet printing papers – Folex Ltd

Folarex – a range of print on drafting films – Folex Ltd

Fold Easy Towers – Accesscaff International Ltd

Foldex – disposable hand towels for surgical procedure packs – I P S Converters Ltd

Folding Box Board – Atlantis European Ltd

Folding Panama – Try & Lilly Ltd

Folex A.N. – anti-newton ring, anti static planning film – Folex Ltd

Folex Digiprint – film for printing on digital printers – Folex Ltd

Folex Digiprint – Digital Products - Xeikon - Specialities – Howard Smith Paper Ltd

Folex Fotojet – Folex Ltd

Folic Plus – folic acid supplement – Perrigo UK

Folkespeare – ties – Rael Brook Group Ltd

Folkestone Adscene – newspapers title – Kent Regional News & Media

Folkestone & Dover KM Extra – newspaper – Kent Messenger Group Ltd

Folkestone Herald – newspaper title – Kent Regional News & Media

Follen Dor – p.e clingfilm – A B L Perpack 1985 Ltd

Folliard – European Technical Sales Ltd

Folscaf Towers – Accesscaff International Ltd

Fomblin – oils waxes and greases – AESpump

Fomebond – primer for in-situ foaming – Forbo Adhesives UK Ltd

Fomex – sponge strip, plain and adhesive backed – C B Frost & Co. Ltd

Fontana – paperback fiction and non-fiction books – Harpercollins Publishers Ophelia House

Fontana – label – Mercury Records

Fontargen – welding consumables – Bohler Welding Group Ltd

Fontek – Letraset Ltd

Fontenay Prints – Printed fabrics – Zoffany

Fontenay Wallpaper – Wallcovering collection – Zoffany

Fontenay Weaves – woven fabrics – Zoffany

Fontijne – hydraulic laboratory table presses – Mackey Bowley International Ltd

*Fontinella – Ivory & Ledoux Ltd

Fontshop – fonts from linotype – Heidelberg Graphic Equipment Ltd

Fontware – custom font solutions – Fontware Ltd

Food & Freezer Bags – Cedo Ltd

Food Hygiene – Brooklands College

Food Processing Blades – The Jewel Blade Ltd

Foodline – on-line databases for the food industry – Leatherhead Food Research

FOODOLATOR – Pulsation damper with crevasse free polished parts to the drug standard – Pulsation Dampers At Pulseguard Ltd

Foodshield – Ironsides Lubricants Ltd

Footlight – typeface – Monotype Imaging Ltd

Footlites – Corporate occupational and non safety footwear – L H Safety Ltd

FootPrint – Floor graphic system – Macdermid Autotype Ltd

Footprint – Gem Tool Hire & Sales Ltd

Footprint – S J Wharton Ltd

Footprints – bra-sized swimwear – Eveden Ltd

Footsure Western – safety shoes and boots – Gardiner Bros & Co.

Forac – rotary valve actuators – Forac Ltd

Forafac – poly and per-fluorinated organic surfactants – Atosina UK Ltd

Forager – molasses based liquid – Rumenco Ltd

Foral – hydrogenated rosin – Hercules Holding Ii Ltd

Foral ester – hydrogenated rosin esters – Hercules Holding Ii Ltd

Forane – chlorinated fluorocarbons – Atosina UK Ltd

Foraperle – water and dirt repellants – Atosina UK Ltd

Forbo-Nairn – The Winnen Furnishing Company

Force – A bactericidal heavy duty cleaner for removing grease on heavily soiled floors and in the catering environment – Premiere Products Ltd

*Force – Berthoud Sprayers

Force 3 – harbour barge skimmer – Oil Pollution Environmental Control Ltd

Force 5 – harbour pollution control and general work boat – Oil Pollution Environmental Control Ltd

Force 7 – single ship at sea mop skimmer system – Oil Pollution Environmental Control Ltd

Force tm – sales modelling technique – Millward Brown

Forceflow 800 Series – fan convector heater – Biddle Air Systems Ltd

Forcepack (United Kingdom) – AC Linear Induction Motors – Force Engineering International Ltd

Forcote 95 – protective coating for the control of corrosion – Agma Ltd

*Ford – Kenneth Robson Equipment Ltd

Ford – motor company – Ford Motor Company Ltd

Ford – Ashley Competition Exhausts Ltd

Ford – Walling UK Ltd

Ford – L M C Hadrian Ltd

FORD – Bailey Morris Ltd

Ford – motor/tractor – Bearwood Engineering Supplies

Ford – cars and commercial vehicles – Invicta Paints
Ford Main Dealer – single franchise – Richardson Ford Ltd
Ford Maindealer – car and van dealer – Invicta Paints
ford tractors – T C Richards & Sons
Forda Cal – finely ground calcites – Minelco
Forda Dol – finely ground dolomite – Minelco
FordaCal – Minelco Ltd
FordaDol – Minelco Ltd
FordaGard – Minelco Ltd
FordaTal – Minelco Ltd
Fordham – Domestic kitchen sink workcentres – Astracast P.L.C.
Fords (United Kingdom) – Fords Packaging Systems Ltd
Fore – magazine – Emap Ltd
Foredil – Harrier Fluid Power Ltd
Foreign & Colonial – investment managers – F & C Asset Management
Forelink – CNC Training and applications – Forelink Limited
Forensic Marketing – Really Useful Research & Development
Forepaste – used for relaxing all types of pastry – C S M UK Ltd
Foresight – wetting agent – Farmura Ltd
Forest – Landscaping products – Garden Retreat Ltd
Forest Glades – 50% wool/50% polypropylene graphics 4m wide – Adam Carpets Ltd
FOREST HYDRAULICS – Hydraulic & Offshore Supplies Ltd
Forest Offset – woodfree printing papers, twin wire board – Davies Harvey & Murrell
Forestsaver – stationery products – The Green Consultancy
Forget Brimont – wine – Rodney Densem Wines Ltd
Forgeworld – paints, publications, books, magazines, rule books, games, models, miniatures and war games – Games Workshop Ltd
FORGINEX – STEEL FLOORING – Alvin Industrial Limited
Fork Truck Centre – new and used fork lift trucks – Fork Truck Centre Ltd
Form Talysurf – dimension, form and texture measuring instruments – Taylor Hobson Ltd
Form3Fast – lv switchboard service delivered in 4 weeks – Schneider
Formaclad – metallic building materials – A G B Steel Products Ltd
Formamet – Materion Brush Ltd
Formaspill – Solmedia Laboratory Supplies
Format – component preforming machines – Elite Engineering Ltd
Format – CNC surface and cylindrical grinders – Jones & Shipman Grinding Ltd
Format – architectural ironmongery – James Gibbons Format Ltd
Format FXO – Tekdata Distribution Ltd
Formation Superfine Offset – paper – Fenner Paper Co. Ltd
Formawall – Chorus Panel & Profiles
Formax (U.S.A.) – food form machines – Meatec
Formbore – boring tools for non-cylindrical shapes – Microbore Tooling Systems
Formby Times – newspaper – Liverpool Daily Post & Echo
Formcote – Forward Chemicals Ltd
*Formdrill (Belgium) – flowdrilling equipment – Robert Speck Ltd
Formelle – tube to tube D.I.P. process machines – Elite Engineering Ltd
Formette – component preforming machines – Elite Engineering Ltd
Formica – lifeseal products – W H Foster & Sons Ltd
Formica – Preston Plywood Supplies
Formica – laminate – Petal Postforming Ltd
Formica Aura – kitchen worktops – Bushboard Ltd
Formline (Germany) – MDF – Egger UK Ltd
Formline (Austria) – MDF – Egger UK Ltd
Formline Dekor (Austria) – melamine faced MDF – Egger UK Ltd
Formline Dekor (Germany) – melamine faced MDF – Egger UK Ltd
Formline DHF (Germany) – vapour permeable woodbased fibreboard – Egger UK Ltd
Formodac – B P plc
FormsMaster – Electronic Forms Software System for Internet/Intranet/Websites – Web Labs Ltd
Formula 1 – baked plate cleaner – Kodak Morley
Formulix – formula and equation editing software – Xara Ltd
Formvar – Essex UK Ltd
Formwork – Accesscaff International Ltd
Forrester Ketley – patent attorneys and trade mark attorneys – Forrester Ketley & Co.
Forsheda – seal – Trelleborg Forsheda Pipe Seals
FORSHEDA – Hydraulic & Offshore Supplies Ltd
Forster – Lusso Interiors
Forster & Hales – air pressure equipment – Forster & Hales Ltd
Forston 200+400 – packaged fan dilution units – Hamworthy Heating Ltd
Fort – Maingate Ltd

Fort – tent pegs – The Hampton Works Ltd
*Fort Bryan (U.S.A.) – guitar straps and accessories – John Hornby Skewes & Co. Ltd
Fort-E-Vite – health products – G R Lane Health Products Ltd
Fort potmover – Maingate Ltd
Fortaglas – glass fabrics – T B A Textiles
Fortamid – aramid textiles – T B A Textiles
Fortean Times – journal of strange phenomena – John Brown Publishing
Forth – heavy duty rectangular end hinged grating and frame – Norinco UK Ltd
Forth – stainless steel plaster sink – Armitage Shanks Ltd
Forth Bridge – paint and stainers and varnishes – Craig & Rose Ltd
Forth Promenade – heavy duty grating and frame for pedestrian areas – Norinco UK Ltd
Fortis (U.S.A.) – Microsoft NT/2000 based document management for scanning, storage and retrieval of hard copy or p.c. created documents, application on desktop, Intranet, Internet. – Pacific Solutions International Ltd
Fortis – Hydraulic expansion mandrels/arbors – Schunk Intec Ltd
Fortis ERM (U.S.A.) – electronic report management for Computer generated reports and documents – Pacific Solutions International Ltd
*Fortrac (Germany) – soil-reinforcing geogrid – A G A Group
Fortress – cash boxes – Helix Trading Ltd
Fortress – rising security screens – Air Tube Technologies Ltd
Fortress – pneumatic tube conveyors – Air Tube Technologies Ltd
Fortrex – toughened glass – N J Bradford Ltd
Fortron – polyphenylene sulphide – Ticona UK Ltd
Fortum – animal glue – Forbo Adhesives UK Ltd
Fortune Engineering (United Kingdom) – screw jacks, linear actuators, roller screws – Power Jacks Ltd
Forum – corridor, office and classroom lighting – Designplan Lighting Ltd
Forum – spring balanced drafting stand – Blundell Harling Ltd
Forward Flat File – manilla file – Acco East Light Ltd
Fosclor – disinfectants – Ashland UK
Foseco – chemicals – Foseco International Limited
Fosfol – foliar phosphate for agricultural crops – Landowner Liquid Fertilizers Ltd
Fosnova – display lighting – City Electrical Factors Ltd
Fosol – fish feeding oil – Seven Sea's Ltd
Fospat – hot melt adhesives and gun applicators – Fospat Industrial Ltd
Fospat – industrial markers – Fospat Industrial Ltd
Fospat – magnetic grip thermometers – Fospat Industrial Ltd
Fospro – dewatering fluid – Hellermann Tyton
Fosroc – Trac Structural Ltd
FOSSE LIQUITROL – Hydraulic & Offshore Supplies Ltd
*Foster – Capital Refrigeration Services Ltd
Foster – commercial refrigeration – Foster Refrigerator UK Ltd
*Foster – Coldrooms – Court Catering Equipment Ltd
Foster – high voltage and heavy current test equipment – Megger Ltd
Foster – Alpha Electronics Southern Ltd
Foster Ray – infra-red heaters for livestock – Diamond Edge Ltd
Foster Refrigerator – Apex Commercial Refrigeration & Aircon
Foster's Ice – lager – Scottish & Newcastle Pub Co.
Fosters – lager – Scottish & Newcastle Pub Co.
*Fosters – Crown Catering Equipment Ltd
*Fosters – refrigerator – Asterix Catering Equipment Ltd
Fotek – studio and school portraits – Fotek School Portraits
Founders & finishers – Sheardown Engineering Ltd
Foundrax – metal hardness testing machines and accessories – Foundrax Engineering Products Limited
Fount – religious books, fiction and non-fiction – Harpercollins Publishers Ophelia House
Four Four – motor car – Morgan Motor Co. Ltd
Four Seasons – retail caravans – Four Seasons France Ltd
Four Seasons – quilts – Trendsetter Home Furnishings Ltd
Four Seasons France – mobile home holidays in France – Four Seasons France Ltd
Fourth Estates – paperback fiction and non-fiction books – Harpercollins Publishers Ophelia House
Fourth Passenger Film – Film and Television production – Fourth Passenger Ltd
Fourth passenger Music video – Music Video production and marketing – Fourth Passenger Ltd
Fox – woollen and worsted piece goods-fine Merino wool qualities and puttees – Fox Brothers & Company Ltd
Fox Cab – taxi operator – Arriva Midlands North Ltd
Fox equip – Harrier Fluid Power Ltd
Foxbury – The Woolwich
Foxconn – Selectronix Ltd
Foxfield – fabric collection – Brian Yates
Foxguard – Bridgwater Electronics Ltd
Foxriver Paper – coloured papers and boards – G F Smith

foxstandpipes – standpipe & hose union tap enclosures – foxstandpipes
Foylite – lightweight class O face display board – Strata Panels UK
FP – Conventional fire panel – C-Tec Security Ltd
FP4 Plus – ISO 125 speed film – Harman Technology Ltd
FP70 – foam compound – Angus Fire
FPC – Harrier Fluid Power Ltd
FPS – glove boxes – A J G Waters Equipment Ltd
FPU – industrial folding door – Hörmann (UK) Ltd
FR Cros – Ammonium polyphosphates – Mineral & Chemical Services Ltd
FR Trans Transfers – Tough transfers for flame retardant work wear garments – J & A International Ltd
Fraba – European Technical Sales Ltd
Frac – circular surface and semi recessed vandal resistant architectural lighting – Designplan Lighting Ltd
Fraggiolati – Arun Pumps Ltd
Fram – automotive filters – So-Gefi Filtration Ltd
Fram – Harrier Fluid Power Ltd
Fram Europe – oil, air and fuel filters – So-Gefi Filtration Ltd
Frama – Westmore Business Systems Ltd
Frame Work – Emerson Network Power Ltd
*Framec (Italy) – refrigeration – Interlevin Refrigeration Ltd
Framed Polytanks – Unique design of plastic cold water cisternms – Polytank Ltd
*Frames (United Kingdom) – laundry stock control systems – Micross Electronics Ltd
Frameshield – A Proctor Group Ltd
Franberlube – Francis W Birkett & Sons Ltd
Franberlube – self lubricating bearings – Francis W Birkett & Sons Ltd
France – Y S E Ltd
Franchise Development – services to prospective franchisors/franchisees, international licensing producers of the franchise magazine, franchise international, the UK franchise directory, the Scottish franchise exhibition and the Irish franchise exhibition – Franchise Development Services Ltd
FRANCI – Mechanical Power Transmission Products – Francis and Francis Ltd
FRANCI MECHANICAL POWER TRANSMISSION PRODUCTS – Francis and Francis Ltd
Francis – searchlights and signalling lamps – John Lilley & Gillie Ltd
Francis Birkett – non ferrous founders, engineers and stockists – Francis W Birkett & Sons Ltd
Francis Chichester's Pocket Map & Guide of London – map & guide – Francis Chichester Ltd
Francis Frith Collection, The – historic photographs of Britian – Francis Frith Collection
Franciscan – tableware – Wedgewood Travel Ltd
Frank – spacer blocks – Max Frank Ltd
Frank – machines for cleaning by water pressure – Wilms Heating Equipment
Frank and Pignard – cetop 3, 5 and 8 hydraulic valves and controls – Koppen & Lethem Ltd
Frank Usher – special occsaion and evening wear – Frank Usher Group
*Franke (Switzerland) – UK sink range and taps – Franke UK Ltd
*Franke – Tudor Tea & Coffee
Franke – bearing assemblies; linear and rotary tables; precision CNC positioning systems – Schleifring Systems Ltd
*Franke Compact (Switzerland) – multi inset bowl sinks – Franke UK Ltd
Franke Divida – coloured synthetic sinks – Franke UK Ltd
Franke Fragranite – coloured synthetic sinks – Franke UK Ltd
Franke Fraquartz – coloured synthetic sinks – Franke UK Ltd
Franke Rotondo – round inset bowls – Franke UK Ltd
Franke Sorter – waste seperation systems – Franke UK Ltd
Franke Triflow – water purification systems – Franke UK Ltd
Franke Undermounted Bowls – stainless steel – Franke UK Ltd
Franke WSS – washroom & sanitary systems – Franke Sissons Ltd
Franki – construction of patented driven piles – Cementation Skanska
Franklin – tents, shelter systems, concealment systems and personal equipment – J & S Franklin Holdings & Management Services Ltd
Franklin – Harrier Fluid Power Ltd
Franklite Lighting – Light Fantastic
Frappiato – Douwe Egberts UK
*Frascold (Italy) – refrigeration compressors semi hermetic and screw compressors – H T G Trading Ltd
Frascold – Therma Group
*Fraser – Reeth Garage Ltd
Fraser Dolly – cranes – Panavision Grips Ltd
Fraser & Ellis – plumbers merchants – Fraser & Ellis
Fraud Scanner – counterfeit detection system – Poselco Lighting Ltd
Fravol – Edgebanders – A L Dalton Ltd

Fre-Flow – self priming pumps – S P X Flow Technology

Frederick Allen – jewellers ltd – Frederick Allen Ltd

Frederick Warne – children's books (including Beatrix Potter and flower fairies) – Penguin Books Ltd

FREE-AIR – full fresh air free-cooling – Stulz UK Ltd Epsom

Free Flow Trays – open freezing trays – Hamster Baskets

Free Form Fabrication – Cambridge Vacuum Engineering

Free Wall – Storage – Bucon Ltd

Freebird – catamaran – Northshore Yachts Ltd

Freecom.Net – Internet and e-commerce – Red Technology

Freed of London Ltd – ballet dancewear manufacturers – Freed Of London Ltd

Freedom – ceramic wall & floor tiles – Johnson Tiles Ltd

Freefix – polyester adhesive paste – DSM UK Ltd

FREEFLEX – heated tubing – Watlow Ltd

Freefoam – antifoam and defoamers, silicone or non silicone types – Brenntag Colours Ltd

Freeit – Forward Chemicals Ltd

Freelance (United Kingdom) – heat exchanger/tube cleaning system – Calder Ltd

***Freelin-Wade** – pneumatic tubing – The West Group Ltd

Freelink – range of dual and multiple phoneline simulators for demonstration and local connection – Good Thinking

Freelisp – reduced implementation, lispworks common lisp development environment – Global Graphics Software Ltd

Freeman Hardy Willis – fashion footwear – D Jacobson & Sons Ltd

Freemix – dough moulding compound – DSM UK Ltd

Freemix – Menzolit

Freespace – business music systems – Bose Ltd

***Freespirit (Taiwan)** – cycles – Moore Large & Co. Ltd

Freeway – reisdual, total herbicide – Bayer Crop Science

Freeway Offset – uncoated paper & board – Howard Smith Paper Ltd

***Freewheels (Germany)** – industrial freewheels – Stieber Clutch

FreighterBase – software package for freight fowarders – Integer Micro Systems Ltd

Frem – Capex Office Interiors

Frem – Storage – Bucon Ltd

French and Jupp – malt for the brewery industry – French & Jupps

French Connection Group Plc – clothing – French Connection Ltd

French Prints – Printed fabrics – Zoffany

French Wallpapers – Wallcovering collection – Zoffany

French Weaves – Woven fabrics – Zoffany

Freon – refrigerant – Du Pont UK Ltd

FRES – future rapid effects systems – Mass Consultants Ltd

Frescile – perfume speciality – Quest International UK Ltd

Fresco – wallcovering – Graham & Brown Ltd

***Fresco (France)** – fire retardant insulation boards – Alumasc Exterior Building Products

Fresco – carpets - axminster – Brintons Carpets Ltd

Frescol – textile lubricant – Benjamin R Vickers & Sons Ltd

Frescolene – textile lubricant – Benjamin R Vickers & Sons Ltd

Frescotex – textile processing aid – Benjamin R Vickers & Sons Ltd

Fresh – apple freshaire c/w 2 hand sprays – Evans Vanodine International plc

Fresh Pasta – Cibo Ristorante

Fresh Shakes – Dinkum Products Ltd

Fresh-ups – lemon fragranced fresh wipe – Robinson Healthcare Ltd

Freshair – air conditioning plant and ductwork – Senior Hargreaves Ltd

Freshaloo – 5% sulphamic acid descaler, disinfectant and deodorant – Premiere Products Ltd

Freshcup – Bulk coffee brewer – Marco Beverage Systems Ltd

Freshers – vending ingredients range – Nichols plc

***Freshers** – Aimia Foods

FreshMarx – labelling, date coding for the catering industry – Avery Dennison

Freshtex, Hycare, Tumblefresh, Big 100 – B F F Nonwovens

Freshtracks – skiing holidays, instruction and guiding – Ski Club Of Great Britain

***Fresia (Italy)** – snow blowers, PTO driven and self propelled – Bunce Ashbury Ltd

***Fresmak (Spain)** – arnold power vices – Abwood Machine Tools Ltd

***Frette** – Tradelinens Ltd

***Freuden berg (Germany)** – Flooring – Static Safe Ltd

Freudenberg – European Technical Sales Ltd

FREUDENBERG SIMRIT – Hydraulic & Offshore Supplies Ltd

Freway – vertical spindle sewage pump – Tuke & Bell Ltd

Frezza – Desks – Bucon Ltd

***Fri-Jado** – Equipline

Fric – circular surface and semi recessed vandal resistant architectural lighting – Designplan Lighting Ltd

Friction Glide – Graphoidal Developments

Frida – VLF test set 20kV – Baur Test Equipment Ltd

Fridays – sandwich fillings and ready meals – Fridays Ltd

***Friedrich Wilhelm Gymnasium (Germany)** – German wines – O W Loeb & Co. Ltd

Friendly Hotels – Choice Hotels International

Friendly Soap – Organic Soap; sls & paraben free – Friendly Soap

Friends of the Earth – environmental campaign organisation – Friends Of The Earth

Frigidaire – Therma Group

Frigipol – Therma Group

Frigomeccania – IsoCool Ltd

Frigorex (Greece) – refrigeration – Interlevin Refrigeration Ltd

***Frihopress** – Jarshire Ltd

Frilixa – refrigeration – Interlevin Refrigeration Ltd

Frimeda – concrete lifting systems – Halfen Ltd

Frimocar – Harrier Fluid Power Ltd

Frise – carpets – Interface Europe Ltd

Frisil – sillimanite – D S F Refractories & Minerals Ltd

fristaad – Wenaas Ltd

Fristads – workwear – Pioner Fristads

Frisylen Plastics – special plastics for cutting boards for industrial and food cutting industries – Partwell Cutting Technology Ltd

Fritz Hanson – Office Seating – Bucon Ltd

Frixipaque – G E Healthcare

Frodingham – flag processors – Civil and Marine Ltd

Froggo – novelty frog bin – Glasdon International Ltd

Frogspawn Thermal Insulation – Floating ball blanket – E Braude London Ltd

fromm family – pet food – Family Pet Services

Fronius – welding equipment – T P S Fronius

Fronius – Welding equipment – T P S Fronius Ltd

Fronius – welding equipment – T P S Fronius

Frontline – anaesthetic machinery – Space Labs Healthcare

Frontline Genius – anaesthetic machinery – Space Labs Healthcare

Frontline Plus – anaesthetic machine – Space Labs Healthcare

Frontrunner (United Kingdom) – entrance matting – Plastic Extruders Ltd

Frontrunner – Entrance flooring system, open grid heel proof entrance flooring system that scrapes, dries and cleans – Plastic Extruders Ltd

Frost Drainage Products – roof and floor drainage products – F C Frost Ltd

Frost Electroplating – specialist electroplaters in the finishes listed – Frost Electroplating Ltd

Frostar – glass frosters – I M C

Froude Consine – Dynamometers – Dynamometer Services Group Ltd

Froude Hofmann – dynamometers and test equipment for engine and vehicle testing in r&d and production – Froude Hofmann Ltd

Froy – bathroom sanitary ware – N Froy & Son

***Fruibel** – Unifine Food & Bake Ingredients

Fruiss Iced Tea Syrups – U C D Ltd

Fruit of the Loom – T-Shirts Sweatshirts Poloshirts Hooded Sweatshirts Clothing – A4 Apparel Ltd

Fruit of the Loom – First Impressions Europe Ltd

Fruit of the Loom – Avalon and Lynwood

Fruit of The Loom – T-shirts and sweat shirts (youth and adult sizes) – Fruit Of The Loom Ltd

Fruit Tree Grease – Vitax Ltd

Frumalo – malt loaf mixes – E D M E Ltd

FRUTIGEN A G – Hydraulic & Offshore Supplies Ltd

Fry's – Solder and flux products – Fernox

Frydenbo – Rolls Royce

***Frymaster** – Enodis Group

FS – full height mild steel turnstile with integral operator housing for stadia use – Gunnebo Entrance Control Ltd

FS80 – Forward Chemicals Ltd

FSB – ironmongery – Allgood

FSD UK – timber folding sliding doors – Folding Sliding Doors

FSM – monitering systems – Iicorr Ltd

FSM - monitering systems RCP - (Resistor controlled cathodic protection) SenCorr - Multipurpose probe system. – Iicorr Ltd

FSN – industrial folding door – Hörmann (UK) Ltd

FSV (Europe, Western) – ss & steel class valves – Everyvalve Ltd

FT800 – Glass Containment Film – Pentagon Protection plc

FTC UK Ltd – Trading – Ferroalloy Trading Company UK Limited

Fu Sheng – Therma Group

Fuchs – Harrier Fluid Power Ltd

Fuchs Lubricants – European Technical Sales Ltd

Fuel IT – retail petrol card – C H Jones Walsall Ltd

Fuel Tanks – pressed and welded assemblies – Warwick & Bailey Engineering

Fuelguard – automotive diesel anti-freeze – Dasic International Ltd

FuelMaster – B P plc

Fuels – Stream Measurement Ltd

Fuelsafe – vehicle fuel issues recording systems – Centaur Fuel Management

Fuelscope – integrated fuel management software – C H Jones Walsall Ltd

Fuelslip – Molyslip Atlantic Ltd

***Fuermatic** – Manual automatic sliding door gear – Fermod Ltd

Fugro Survey Ltd – offshore survey and positioning services (including ROV) – Fugro Survey

Fuho – Red House Industrial Services Ltd

***Fuhr (Germany)** – architectural ironmongery – Groupco Ltd

Fuji – spring separators – Baltec UK Ltd

Fuji – European Technical Sales Ltd

Fuji – European Drives & Motor Repairs

Fuji – tranisistors – Bowers Ltd

Fuji – x-ray equipment – Fidgeon Ltd

Fuji Electric – Pressure and temperature recorders and controllers – Coulton Instrumentation Ltd

Fujifilm – UK Office Direct

***Fujimi (Japan)** – plastic model kits – Amerang Group Ltd

Fujinon – Stemmer Imaging

Fujisoku (Japan) – pc cards & switches – Premier Engineering

Fujitsu – Cyclops Electronics Ltd

Fujitsu – Genus Group

Fujitsu – dry batteries – Kauser International Trading Ltd

Fujitsu – Lamphouse Ltd

Fujitsu – UK Office Direct

***Fujitsu** – Tayside Cash Registers

Fujitsu – Air conditioning – Fujitsu General UK Co. Ltd

Fujitsu Cash Registers – Cash Register Services

Fujitsu-Siemens – Lamphouse Ltd

Fujitsu Siemens – Quintech Computer Systems Ltd

Fulbourn Medical – manufacturers of surgeons control panels & installation of surgical lighting – G K Wood & Sons Ltd

Fulcrum – Capex Office Interiors

***Fulcrum** – E D F Man

Fulda Tyres – tyres – Fulda Tyres

***Fuldapark (Germany)** – grass substitute floorcoverings – Bryan & Clark Ltd

Fulleon (United Kingdom) – fire alarm and security bells – Fulleon

Fullers Earth – mineral filters – Lawrence Industries Ltd

Fullersite – slate powder – Welsh Slates

Fullstop – testing kit for oil industries – Klargester Environmental Ltd

Fully accredited with major manufacturers. – Kingston Communications

FULMEN - - Motive Power Batteries and Chargers. – Chloride Motive Power C M P Batteries Ltd

Fulton Boilers – Twin Industries International Ltd

Fumaplas – reinforced fumigation sheeting – Power Plastics

Fumex – fan motors for smoke extraction at high temperatures – Brook Crompton UK Ltd

Fumyl-o-Gas – methyl bromide – I M C D UK Ltd

Fun Sport – toys – Halsall Toys Europe Ltd

Fun Sport & People – ladies fashions – Fabrizio Fashions Ltd

Fun World – halloween products – Palmer Agencies Ltd

Functional Foam – packaging division – Functional Foam Beacons Products Ltd

Fungex – agro chemicals – Certis Europe

***Fungex** – Anitox

Fungicidal, AntiCondensation & Protective Paint Coatings – paint for protection against mould growth and condensation problems – Channelwood Preservation Ltd

***Funki (Denmark)** – range of livestock feeding systems – Master Farm Services GB Ltd

***Funki** – Milling & mixing equipment – B D C Systems

Funnybones – Olympia Foods Ltd

FUNNYMAN – jokes – Jarroy Importers Ltd

***Funxion (Denmark)** – door furniture – Assa Abloy Security Solutions

Furacin – acid and alkaline resisting cement – R I W Ltd

Furecol – sand binder system for the foundry industry – Ashland Specialties UK Ltd

Furfix – wall connectors extension profiles – Simpson Strong-Tie International Inc

Furlex – yacht reefing systems – Selden Mast Ltd

Furmanite – European Technical Sales Ltd

Furmanite – industrial leak sealing compounds, system and onsite services – Furmanite International Ltd

Furnace Instruments – Roxspur Measurement & Control Ltd

Furness Controls Ltd – Pressure-flow measurement instrumentation – Furness Controls Ltd

Furnicel – British Vita plc

Furnifix – onsite upholstery repair – Lyn Plan Upholstery Ltd

Furniture Select – complete fleet – Allianz Insurance plc

FURNO – Michael Lupton Associates Ltd

Furnsafe – flame retardant backcoating for upholstery – P W Greenhalgh & Co. Ltd

***Furon (U.S.A.)** – teflon pumps, valves, fittings and accessories – Boiswood LLP

FURSE – Halcyon Solutions

Furukawa – Harrier Fluid Power Ltd
Furukawa (Japan) – hydraulic breakers – Marubeni Komatsu Ltd
Fusewelder – hardsurfacing torch – Wall Colmonoy Ltd
Fusillier – Steel Bollard – Alto Bollards UK Ltd
Fusion – bulk storage systems for the liquid and dry products processing industries – Permastore Ltd
Fusion – terrazzo tiles – Quiligotti Terrazzo Ltd
Fusion – Melitzer Safety Equipment
Fusion Accounts – Fusion Accounts allows accountants to have real-time, easy to use, anytime, anywhere access. – Stiona Software Ltd
Fusion10 – Seating – Bucon Ltd
Fussells – rubber soles and heels for shoe repairing trade – Fussell's Rubber Co. Ltd
Futuba – Review Display Systems Ltd
Futura – glass fibre surveyors tape – Fisco Tools Ltd
Future – Sub contractors – AMG Forwarding Ltd
Future Glass – Desks – Bucon Ltd
Future Music – magazine – Future Publishing Ltd
FWAG Farming & Wildlife Advisory Group – is a registered charity, set up with the purpose of offering advice to farmers on how they can protect the wildlife habatats and species on the farm without the commercial business – Farming & Wildlife Advisory Group Ltd
FX-Airport Service Ltd – Taxi-MiniCab Service – F X Airport Services Ltd
FXO – Tekdata Distribution Ltd
FXO FXS – Tekdata Distribution Ltd
FXO FXS Interface – Tekdata Distribution Ltd
Fyffes – Traders in bananas – Fyffes Group Ltd
FYH – Mercury Bearings Ltd
Fylde Sails – boat covers and sails – Fleetwood Trawlers Supply Company
Fyne – construction tools & equipment – Terex UK Ltd
Fyrex – firefighting nozzles – Knowsley S K Ltd
Fyrol – phosphorous based flame retardants chloroalkyl phosphates, alkyl phosphonates – Akzo Nobel Chemicals Holdings Ltd
Fyrol – flame retardants – I M C D UK Ltd
Fyrolflex – oligomeric aryl diphosphates – Akzo Nobel Chemicals Holdings Ltd
Fyrquel – phosphate ester flame retardant – Akzo Nobel Chemicals Holdings Ltd

G

G 2000 – Plenty Mirrlees Pumps
G.A.A. – Kennametal UK Ltd
G.A.C. (U.S.A.) – electronic governing equipment – Industrial Power Units Ltd
G.A.F.S.A. – fertilizer – Soil Fertility Dunns Ltd
G.A. Pindar & Son Ltd – print and electronic media specialists – Pindar plc
G.B. – import and export of childrens clothing – Gobina London Ltd
G B – cycle handlebars and stems – Burgess Furniture Ltd
G.B.D. – briar pipe smokers accessories – Cadogan
G & B Fuels – fuel suppliers – GB Fuels Ltd
G-Ban – general consumer electronics colour TV, audio, video & satellite sales and servicing – John Banner
G-Bulb – Gesipa Blind Riveting Systems Ltd
G.C.10 – maintenance product for floors – Premiere Products Ltd
G.C.20 – maintenance product for floors – Premiere Products Ltd
G.C.-Ram – radio gas detectors – Lablogic Systems Ltd
G.C. Supplies – Stainless steel tube fittings – G C Supplies UK Ltd
G.D. – electronics – Smiths Detection
G.E.C. – piercing saws – Henri Picard & Frere
G.E.C. – relays – Bearwood Engineering Supplies
G.E.C.Elliott – pcb/switches – Bearwood Engineering Supplies
G.E.C. Industrial Controls – contractors/fuses – Bearwood Engineering Supplies
G E Fanuk – Halifax Numerical Controls Ltd
G.E.I. – sheet metal work and fabrications – G E I Electronic Industries Ltd
G.E.R. (Spain) – grinders surface and cylindrical and CNC – Capital Equipment & Machinery Ltd
G.E.T. – electrical equipment distribution – G E T
G.F. – pipe fittings in malleable iron and plastics, plastics valves, – George Fischer Sales Ltd
G & G – sole distributors of cal-m, sublingual nutrition, trufil capsules and protein plus (vegan) – G & G Food Supplies
G&G Vitamins. – The full range of vitamins, minerals, herbal and probiotic products - no additives of any kind. – G & G Food Supplements
G.H.L. 1 – The Woolwich
G.H.L. 2 – The Woolwich
G.H.L. Technology – The Woolwich
G.H. Zeal – pressure gauges, thermometers, flometers, hydrometers and clinical division – Zeal Clean Supplies Ltd
G.I.I. Giustimix – food processing machines – T Giusti Ltd
G.I.I. Intermix – pharmaceutical and cosmetic machinery – T Giusti Ltd
G.I. Presses – Rhodes - HME presses – Joseph Rhodes Ltd
G I Products – filing and office products – Gilmex International Ltd
G. & J. Greenall – G & J Greenall
G.K.N. – universal prop shafts – G K N Driveline Walsall
G.L.F. – charitable purposes trading company limited – Greater London Fund For Blind
G.M. – cricket – Gunn & Moore
g m machine – grass marking paint – Sportsmark Group Ltd
G&M Power - Countryman Power – G & M Power Plant Ltd
G&M Power Plant – G & M Power Plant Ltd
G M Profiles & Supplies – Steel stockholder – Gareth Pugh Steel Framed Buildings
G.M.S. – background music systems and public address equipment – G M S Music
G.M. Series – submersible pumps – Calpeda Ltd
G-Man – handsaws – Atkinson-Walker Saws Ltd
G-Motion (Germany) – geared motors – Lenze UK Ltd
G.P. – Grosvenor Pumps Ltd
G.P. – firebricks and firebacks – R E Knowles Ltd
G.P.50 – scientific instruments – Sandhurst Instruments Ltd
G.P.C. 8 – glutaraldehyde disinfectant – Evans Vanodine International plc
G P & J Baker Fabrics – The Winnen Furnishing Company
G.R.D. – software packages – Schlumberger Oilfield UK plc
G.R.P. – glass reinforced plastics – Northshore Composites Ltd
G.R.P. – open grid flooring & ladders – Moseley Rubber Company Pty Ltd
G.R.P. – clock towers, vents, access panels, housing, covers, hoppers, tanks, boxes, enclosures, kiosks, vehicle panels, mouldings, containers and construction. – Coe's Derby Ltd
G.R.P Steps & Ladders – Accesscaff International Ltd
G.S.L. – securit equipment distribution – Adi Gardiner Emea Ltd
G.S.R. Platforms – Accesscaff International Ltd
G.S. Robinson – sheet metalwork and fabrication – G S Robinson & Co. Ltd
G.S. Wheels – wheels – Terry Johnson Ltd
'G' SERIES (Netherlands) – gas wall heaters – Drugasar Service Ltd
G.T.B. Bandseal – rubber energised PFTE capseal – Greene Tweed & Co. Ltd
G.T. Foulis – specialist motoring and motor sport books – J Haynes Ltd
G.T.I. – interlocking floor tiles – Gerflor Ltd
G.T. Rings – high grade elastomer seal – Greene Tweed & Co. Ltd
G.T.S. Slipseal – rubber energised PFTE capseal – Greene Tweed & Co. Ltd
G.U.D. – Harrier Fluid Power Ltd
G.W. – magazines, books, manuals, rule books all relating to fantasy games – Games Workshop Ltd
G.W.F. (Switzerland) – gas and water meters – Switch2 Energy Solutions
G.W.S. Engineers – vacuum loading system for handling and conveying of waste material – G W S Engineers Ltd
G.Y.R.D. – switches – Polaron Cortina Ltd
G & Y SERVICES – STOCKTAKERS AND VALUERS – G & Y Services Stocktakers & Valuers
G103 – duplex steel castings – Gabriel & Co. Ltd
G39 – Safety Goggles – Scott International Ltd
G4 – 316 stainless steel castings – Gabriel & Co. Ltd
G4 – floor and damp sealer – Bondaglass Voss Ltd
G5 – gas sampler – Jiskoot Ltd
G64 – Capex Office Interiors
GA Town & Country – Your Move
Gabicci – classical menswear – gabicci
Gabriel Contractors – civil engineering contractors – Gabriel Contractors Ltd
GACO – Mayday Seals & Bearings
Gaco – Mercury Bearings Ltd
Gadgeter.com – gadgets and gizmos sold on the internet – Alternative Gifts
Gaebridge – Encoders UK
Gaebridge Encoders – Encoders UK
Gaelic – clay – Sandtoft Holdings Ltd
Gaffa Tape – a range of tapes for the leisure and entertainment industries – Advance Tapes Group Ltd
Gage Chek – HEIDENHAIN GB LTD
Gaggenau (Germany) – built in electrical kitchen appliances – Gaggenau UK Ltd
Gaines – marine stern gear propellers – Lancing Marine
Gainsborough – fabrics and furnishing fabrics – Gainsborough Silk Weaving Co. Ltd
Gainsborough – Dixon Turner Wallcoverings Ltd
Gainsborough – G F Smith
Gainsborough – Baxi Group
Gainsborough – mattresses and convertable bed settees – Gainsborough Ltd
Gainsborough Sofabeds – The Winnen Furnishing Company
Gaiters – PVC and neoprene – Plastic Mouldings Ltd
Gala Rope – synthetic and natural fibre ropes – Independent Twine Manufacturing Co. Ltd
Galactasol – guar products – Hercules Holding Ii Ltd
Galaxy – intruder alarms – ADT
Galaxy – vanity basin – Armitage Shanks Ltd
Galaxy – Aimia Foods
Galaxy (Portugal) – cork wall tiles in 4 coloured backgrounds – Siesta Cork Tile Co.
Galdabini – Tensile and Impact testing equipment – Struers Ltd
Galerie – Harman Technology Ltd
Galileo – vacuum pumps – AESpump
Galileo – ctp platesetters – Agfa Gevaert
Galiso (U.S.A.) – pressure test equipment – Bancroft & Co.
Gall Thomson Marine Breakaway Couplings – anti-pollution/safety marine breakaway couplings – Gall Thomson Environmental Ltd
Gall Thomson - Marine Breakaway Couplings, Camlock Couplings; Klaw Breakaway Couplings, Flip-flap Breakaway Couplings. – Gall Thomson Environmental Ltd
Gallenkamp – temperature control technology – Sanyo Gallenkamp plc
Gallenkamp – furnaces – Sanyo Gallenkamp plc
Gallenkamp Climatic Test Chambers – Sanyo Gallenkamp plc
Gallenkamp 'OMT' – microprocessor controlled ovens – Sanyo Gallenkamp plc
Gallenkamp Pharmaceutical Test Chambers – Sanyo Gallenkamp plc
Gallenkamp Plus – ovens and incubators – Sanyo Gallenkamp plc
Gallenkamp Prime – ovens – Sanyo Gallenkamp plc
Galleria – carpets - axminster – Brintons Carpets Ltd
Galleria – sign blanks – Spandex plc
Galleria 80/20 – Interface Europe Ltd
Galleria Antron – Interface Europe Ltd
Galletti (Italy) – air conditioning, fan coil units – Thermal Technology Sales Ltd
Galliard – Stainer & Bell Ltd
Galloway – Sco-Fro Group Ltd
Galt – audiovisual aids for education & training – James Galt & Co. Ltd
GALTECH – Hydraulic & Offshore Supplies Ltd
Galvalloy – hot-dip coated strip steel with eutectic alloy of 95% zinc, 5% aluminium, and other elements (substrate for colorcoat HPS200) – Corus U K Ltd
Galvanofix – plating outfits – Time Products UK Ltd
Galvatite – hot-dip zinc and iron-zinc alloy coated steel – Corus U K Ltd
Galvatite – mild flat steels – Corus
Galvosil – 1 and 2 pack inorganic zinc silicates – Hempel UK Ltd
Gamak Motors – AC motors – System Control Solutions Ltd
Gamasco – G M S Co.
Gamefair – waterproof jackets – J Barbour & Sons Ltd
Games 2 Play – board games – P M S International Group plc
Games Workshop – books, magazines, stationery, computer hardware, computer software, games, toys, board games, miniature and models for use in fantasy games – Games Workshop Ltd
Gamesfax – computer game organiser – Logax Ltd
Gamesman – Money Controls Ltd
Gamesmaster – magazine – Future Publishing Ltd
Gamet – precision taper roller bearings, precision angular contact ball bearings, ballscrew support bearings and cartridge units, precision roller assemblies and rotating centres – Gamet Bearings
Gamet Bearings – 600 Group plc
Gamgee Tissue – surgical dressings – Robinson Healthcare Ltd
Gamko – Apex Commercial Refrigeration & Aircon
Gamko – Fridge Freezer Direct Company Ltd
Gamma srl – crimping presses and mini applicators – Automated Cable Solutions Ltd
Gammons (U.S.A.) – taper reamers – Drill Service Horley Ltd
Gandlake Computer Services – computer software – Gandlake Computer Services Ltd
Gang Nail – ROOF TRUSS SYSYEMS – Gang-Nail
Gang-Nail Systems Limited – manufacturer of punched metal connector plates and specialist products for roof truss manufacture, pallet repair, crate and care construction and other applications. supplier of builders' products. Manufacturer of standard & bespoke mechanical machinery – Gang-Nail
Ganntri-Tilt – stillage for barrell handling and heavy plate fabricators – Geoffrey Maskell Engineering Ltd
Ganter – standard machine elements (metal) – Elesa (UK) Ltd
Ganter (Germany) – standard parts, handwheels and levers – Berger Tools Ltd
Gantres – Accesscaff International Ltd
Gantrex – rail fixings systems – Cranequip Ltd
Gantrex – motorised lifting equipment – Cranequip Ltd
Ganymed – prints – The Medici Galleries

Gap Group – plant hire – G A P Group Ltd

GAPI – Hydraulic & Offshore Supplies Ltd

GAR-FIL – GGB UK

GAR-FIL – GGB UK

GAR-MAX – GGB UK

Garage – specialising in volkswagon & audi cais – G & P Autocare

Garbeflex – pvc plasticiser – Atosina UK Ltd

Garcima Paella Pans – Paella Co. Ltd

Gard – a range of triboelectric dust monitors – Codel International Ltd

Gardamide – perfume speciality – Quest International UK Ltd

GardaPat 13 Digital – Digital Products - Toner Sheet Fed - Coated – Howard Smith Paper Ltd

Garden Bark – mulch and soil conditioner – Melcourt Industries

Garden City Coachworks – Body Shop – Spire Peugeot Ltd

Garden Gold – frozen vegetables – K H Taylor Ltd

Garden Rack – twine & accessory product merchandiser – Nutscene

Gardencast – cast aluminium garden furniture – Gardencast

Gardener Denv – Harrier Fluid Power Ltd

gardener denver – air compressors – Quinton Dental Air Services

Gardener Denver – air compressors-new compressors+ parts and service – Airware International Ltd

Gardens Illustrated – gardens magazine – John Brown Publishing

Gardiner of Selkirk – woollen weaving and knitting yarn – Gardiner Of Selkirk Ltd

Gardisette – Philip Cowan Interiors

Gardman – hanging baskets, moss poles, plastic and wire netting, plastic and multi mesh, bamboo, fencing, plant support, handy packs and furniture coverings – Gardman Ltd

Gardner – Cinetic Landis Ltd

Gardocyclene – perfume speciality – Quest International UK Ltd

Gardtec – Christie Intruder Alarms Ltd

Gardtex – chemical splash resistant finish – Heathcoat Fabrics Ltd

Gareth Pugh Steel Framed Buildings – Structural Steel Manufacturer – Gareth Pugh Steel Framed Buildings

Garfil – active carbon filter materials – Purification Products Ltd

Garg Wire – Gargsales (UK) Ltd

Garioni Boilers – Twin Industries International Ltd

Garland – ferrules and deep drawn pressings – Stroud Metal Co. Ltd

Garland – Axon Enterprises Ltd

Garland – touring caravans for the home and export market – Fleetwood Group Holdings Ltd

*****Garland** – Court Catering Equipment Ltd

Garlock – equipment/spares – Bearwood Engineering Supplies

Garoflam – range of fire retardant additives – Omya UK Ltd

Garolite – high activity magnesium oxide – Omya UK Ltd

Garr Tool – Precision Tools

Garran (United Kingdom) – Steel Lockers – Garran Lockers Ltd

Garret – Harrier Fluid Power Ltd

Garrison – manual barrier, manual roadcloser, wagon stopper – Frontier Pitts Ltd

Garryflex – abrasive blocks – ATI Garryson Limited

Garryson – carbide cutting tools and toggle clamps – ATI Garryson Limited

Garryson – carbide rotary tools and abrasive finishing products – ATI Garryson Limited

Garside – removal contractors – James Garside & Son Ltd

*****Garvens (Germany)** – dynamic check weighers – Romaco Holdings UK Ltd

GAS – Hydraulic & Offshore Supplies Ltd

Gas Arc Welding Equipment – Wessex Welding & Industrial Supplies Ltd

Gas-Check – gas leak detector – Ion Science Ltd

Gas Industry Directory – United Business Media Ltd

Gas industry manufrs – Brass Fittings & Supplies Ltd

Gas & Leachate Wells – system for releasing methane gas and contaminated water from refuse taps – Simplex Westpile Limited

Gas Safe – leak detection instruments – Anglo Nordic Burner Products Ltd

Gas Safety Workshop – Competency based practical training on compressed and cryogenic industrial gases, pressure systems, – Teksol Training & Technology Ltd

Gas Tec – F.I.D survey monitor – Crowcon Detection Instrument Ltd

Gascat – soldering iron – Antex Electronics Ltd

GasCheck R – refrigerant detector – Ion Science Ltd

GasCheck SF6 – SF6 detector – Ion Science Ltd

Gascut – soldering iron – Antex Electronics Ltd

Gaseeker – Purge/Leak monitor – Crowcon Detection Instrument Ltd

Gasflag – Single channel control unit – Crowcon Detection Instrument Ltd

Gasgard II – multigas portable monitor – M S A Britain Ltd

GASK-O-SEAL – Hydraulic & Offshore Supplies Ltd

Gaskell – The Winnen Furnishing Company

Gaskell & Chambers – I M I Cornelius UK Ltd

Gaslight – water taps – Rudge & Co UK

Gasman – Personal single gas monitor – Crowcon Detection Instrument Ltd

Gasmaster – One to one channel control system – Crowcon Detection Instrument Ltd

Gasmonitor Plus – 16 channel rack-based control system – Crowcon Detection Instrument Ltd

Gasoline – childrens clothing – Gobina London Ltd

gassense – gas specification calculator – Specialty Gases Ltd

Gast – smaller general engineering vacuum pumps – AESpump

Gast – Gustair Materials Handling Equipment Ltd

GAST – Hydraulic & Offshore Supplies Ltd

Gastracer – multi point multi component gas detector system – Icam Ltd

Gastrolyzer – hydrogen breath monitor for the diagnosis of gastrointestinal disorders – Bedfont Scientific Ltd

GastroTechniX – Mechline Developments Ltd

*****Gastrovac (Germany)** – vacuum packaging machinery – Multivac UK Ltd

Gatcombe – luxury motor caravan – Auto Sleepers Ltd

Gate Ayce – horizontal boring mills – Gate Machinery International Ltd

Gate Delta – vertical spindle grinding machines – Gate Machinery International Ltd

Gate Elliot – grinding and shaping machines – Gate Machinery International Ltd

Gate Giewont – milling machines – Gate Machinery International Ltd

GATE HYDRAULICS – Hydraulic & Offshore Supplies Ltd

Gate Milko – universal milling machines – Gate Machinery International Ltd

Gate Nodo – bench mounted centre lathes – Gate Machinery International Ltd

Gate Profitdrill – radial arm drilling machines – Gate Machinery International Ltd

Gate Profitmill – turret milling machines – Gate Machinery International Ltd

Gate Proth – surface grinding machines – Gate Machinery International Ltd

Gate Rigidturn – centre lathes – Gate Machinery International Ltd

Gate Sovereign – CNC milling machines – Gate Machinery International Ltd

Gate Stefor – surface grinding machines – Gate Machinery International Ltd

Gate Sturditurn – centre lathes – Gate Machinery International Ltd

Gate Unimill – vertical and horizontal milling machines – Gate Machinery International Ltd

Gate Urpe – slotting machines – Gate Machinery International Ltd

Gatedrives – industrial gate opener – Clarke Instruments Ltd

Gatehouse – waste management software – Isys Interactive Systems Ltd

Gatekeeper – parquet olefin-on-rubber indoor/outdoor barrier entrance mats – Jaymart Roberts & Plastics Ltd

Gatelocks – electric lock – Clarke Instruments Ltd

Gates (Belgium) – powerbraid slimline rotary hose & motion compensator hose – Hydrasun Ltd

Gates – Cambridgeshire Hydraulics Ltd

Gates – Mayday Seals & Bearings

Gates – Trafalgar Tools

GATES AUTOMOTIVE PRODUCTS – Hydraulic & Offshore Supplies Ltd

Gates Hose Fittings – Race Industrial Products Ltd

Gates Hydraulics – Race Industrial Products Ltd

Gateway – The Woolwich

Gateway – Lamphouse Ltd

Gatic 2000 – access covers & frames – GATIC

Gatic Hydralift – Hydraulically operated access covers & frames – GATIC

Gatic Slotdrain – Surface water drainage system – GATIC

Gatorcam – Inspection cameras duct & pipe – Radio Detection

Gaugetools – statistical analysis package for data gathered by on line or at line gauges – N D C Infra-Red Engineering Ltd

Gausstat – flexible and semi-rigid conductive foam and conductive foam packages – Vitec

GAV 8000 – Gesipa Blind Riveting Systems Ltd

Gavin Kenning Engineering – Market Stall manufacturer and supplier – Gavin Kenning Engineering

Gayc – refrigeration – Interlevin Refrigeration Ltd

Gaylets – pet products – Bob Martin UK Ltd

Gazelle – Try & Lilly Ltd

Gazelle – vertical blind system – Eclipse Blind Systems

GB Filtri – Harrier Fluid Power Ltd

*****GB Seeds** – Bodle Bros Ltd

GBC – UK Office Direct

GBM – Gesipa Blind Riveting Systems Ltd

GCGE Cylinders – high security cylinder designed to meet insurance industry guide lines – Kaba Ltd Head Office

GCT (United Kingdom) – Exact mass benchtop GC-MS – Waters

GDB – Furniture – Bucon Ltd

GDR/GDA – Nylon & Steel Sleeve Gear Couplings – Francis and Francis Ltd

GDV2 – distribution switchgear – Schneider

GE – Lamphouse Ltd

GE Druck – Direct Instrument Hire Ltd

GE Thermometrics – Nobel Electronics Ltd

Gear Pumps – G V E Ltd

Gearflex – gear couplings – Renold Clutches & Couplings Ltd

Gearflex DA Coupling – Renold Clutches & Couplings Ltd

Gearflex HDB Coupling – Renold Clutches & Couplings Ltd

Gearlube – Forward Chemicals Ltd

Gearmatic – hoists – Koppen & Lethem Ltd

Geartex – lubricants – Chevron

Geberit – HDPE pipes and fittings – Ashworth

Gebrol – fuel & lubricants – George Broughton & Co. Ltd

*****GEC** – European Drives & Motor Repairs

Gedore – hand tools – Arrow Supply Co. Ltd

*****Gedore (Germany)** – sockets, spanners, wrenches, pliers, screwdrivers, trolleys and benches – L J Hydleman & Co. Ltd

Gee Bee – soft drinks – Princes Soft Drinks

Gee-Jay – originals-schoolwear – Graham Winterbottom Ltd

*****Geemarc (Far East)** – cordless telephones – Geemarc Telecom S A

Geemarc Clear Sound – telephone & cordless telephone equipment – Geemarc Telecom S A

Geemarc Safety Line – telephone & cordless telephone equipment – Geemarc Telecom S A

Geepol – linings and accessories to the textile manufacturing trades and polyester/lining 60" – William Gee Ltd

Geesink Norba – refused waste collection equipment – Geesink Norba Ltd

Geha – Lamphouse Ltd

*****Gehl (U.S.A.)** – feeding equipment – Westmac Ltd

Gehl – Harrier Fluid Power Ltd

*****Geka (Germany)** – karasto horticultural fittings – Connectomatic

Geka – steel workers – R K International Machine Tools Ltd

*****Geku (Germany)** – formwork clamp system – Max Frank Ltd

Gel Hand Clean – premium grade gel hand clean – Premiere Products Ltd

Gel Kilrock – for descaling urinals, pools, machines, sanitary ware and baths – Kilrock Products Ltd

Gelamex – explosives – E P C UK

Gelbond – thixotropic contact adhesives – Forbo Adhesives UK Ltd

*****Gelec (Worldwide)** – electronic components – G English Electronics Ltd

Gelectrix – batteries using electro-active polymers – University Of Leeds

Geller – Oasis Systems

*****Geller** – Shelfguard Systems

Geller Cash Registers – Cash Register Services

Geller Cash Registers – New Horizon Systems Ltd

Geller CX-200 – New Horizon Systems Ltd

Geller ET-6800 – New Horizon Systems Ltd

Geller EX-300 – New Horizon Systems Ltd

Geller ML-780 – New Horizon Systems Ltd

Geller SX-580 – New Horizon Systems Ltd

Geller SX-680 – New Horizon Systems Ltd

Geller TS-600 – New Horizon Systems Ltd

Geller Vectron Pos Colour Touch – New Horizon Systems Ltd

Geller Vectron Pos Mini Colour – New Horizon Systems Ltd

Geller Vectron Pos Mobile – New Horizon Systems Ltd

Geller Vectron Pos Vario – New Horizon Systems Ltd

Gelphametic – Therma Group

Geltrack – waxed synthetic riding surface – Martin Collins Enterprises Ltd

Gem – aero engines – Rolls-Royce plc

GEM – Sal Abrasives Technologies

Gem – dictionaries and non-fiction reference books – Harpercollins Publishers Ophelia House

Gem – butterfly valves – Crane Business Services & Utilities Ltd

*****Gem** – Ice Cool Services Ltd

Gem – pump – Torres Engineering & Pumps Ltd

Gem Aquariums – aquariums – John Allan Aquariums Ltd

GEMELLI CHILDCARE VOUCHERS – Gemelli Childcare Vouchers Ltd

Gemi – hose clips – General Hoseclips Ltd

Gemini – seat – Armitage Shanks Ltd

Gemini – bulkhead lighting – Designplan Lighting Ltd

Gemini – twin ventilation – Roof Units Ltd

Gemini – full face mask respirator – Scott International Ltd

Gemini – offset plate conversion unit – Kodak Morley

Gemini – labelling system – Harland Machine Systems Ltd

Gemini – process filtration – British Filters Ltd

Gemini – Pledge Office Chairs Ltd

Gemini C2/S Montrose – Graphic Board – Mcnaughton James Paper Group Ltd

***Gemini Mannequins (United Kingdom)** – mannequin company – Universal Display Fittings

Gemline – lighter – Alfred Dunhill Ltd

Gemmological Text Books – gem text books – The Gemmological Association Of Great Britain

Gemo – magnetic catches – Magnet Applications Ltd

Gemstar – virus insecticide – Agrisense B C S Ltd

GEMU VALVES (United Kingdom) – Ultravalve Ltd

Gen 2000 – ultrasonic flaw detector – Baugh & Weedon Ltd

Genco Burners – packaged burners for the aggregate drying industry – Beverley Environmental Ltd

Gencor Beverley – incinerators, soil remediation and thermal fluid heating – Beverley Environmental Ltd

Genefoam – British Vita plc

Geneis – Dixon Turner Wallcoverings Ltd

Genelay – British Vita plc

Genequant II – RNA & DNA calculator – Biochrom Ltd

GeneQuant pro – RNA & DNA calculator – Biochrom Ltd

General (United Kingdom) – metallizing machinery – Atlas Converting

General Accident – land, new homes, residential lettings and connexions – Your Move

General Accident Property Services – Your Move

General Digital Corporation – touch screens – Bearwood Engineering Supplies

General Eastern – humidity instrumentation – Able Instruments & Controls Ltd

General Electric – European Drives & Motor Repairs

General Electric – brake coils – Bearwood Engineering Supplies

General Electric – Harrier Fluid Power Ltd

General Filter – spun copper driers – Thermofrost Cryo plc

General Finishes – Wood finishing products – The Toolpost

General Grant – jeans – Blacks Leisure Group plc

General Kinematics Ltd (United Kingdom) – vibratory process equipment for the foundry, re-cycling, chemical, mining, power generation and food processing industries – General Kinematics Ltd

***General Machinery Corp (U.S.A.)** – dicers, frozen block breakers, flakers, guillotines – Selo UK Ltd

General Packaging – Packaging – The General Packaging Company Ltd

General Purpose Undercoat – Spencer Coatings Ltd

General Vacuum – Harrier Fluid Power Ltd

Generation – flageolets – John Hornby Skewes & Co. Ltd

Generator set manufrs – Cummins Power Generation Ltd

Generator sets diesel-electric – Henry Cooch & Son Ltd

Generators – A T Wilde & Son Ltd

Genesis – cash protection systems – Spinnaker International Ltd

Genesis – Genesis V Systems Ltd

Genesis – Thermo Electrical

Genesis – DDC Controllers – Innotech Controls UK Ltd

GENESIS – Groves Batteries

Genesis – rivet placing tools – Zygology Ltd

Genesis bread – Manufacture bread – Mcerlains Bakery

Genestealer – games, toys, board games, miniatures and models for use in fantasy games – Games Workshop Ltd

Genesys – purified water generation plant – Puretech Process Systems Ltd

Genevac – pumps/centrifuges – AESpump

Genevac – laboratory vacuum pumps and evaporation systems – Genevac Ltd

Geni Downlight – Altima Ltd

Genicom – UK Office Direct

Genie – distribution switchgear – Schneider

Genie – Display Wizard Ltd

Genie – bathroom & toilet extract unit – Nuaire Ltd

Genie – R F Lifting & Access Ltd

GENIE – Chaintec Ltd

Genie – Dale Lifting and Handling Equipment Specialists

Genie – A leading manufacturer of Access Equipment – Caunton Access Ltd

Genie Lifts – Accesscaff International Ltd

Genie Platforms – Accesscaff International Ltd

Genius – Eagle Automation Systems Ltd

Genius – CNC control system – Gate Machinery International Ltd

Genius Electric Gates – Electric Gates – G8 Systems

GENKINGER – Chaintec Ltd

Genlab – Large range of standard and custom built industrial ovens and incubators. – Genlab Ltd

Genneg – Genus Group

Genny – signal transmitter – Radio Detection

Genorma – European Technical Sales Ltd

Genpol – general purpose lubricating oils – Benjamin R Vickers & Sons Ltd

GenSet – Independent Welding Services Ltd

Genstage – Accesscaff International Ltd

Gent – fire detection alarm and emergency lighting – Honeywell

Gentech (United Kingdom) – Manufacturer of sensors for liquid level, flow, proximity, motion and inertia and produce a range of reedswitches. With a specialist capability providing customise solutions to meet many applications, with ecad and prototype facilities. – Gentech International Ltd

Genu – pectin – C P Kelco Ltd

Genu Gum – locust bean (carob) gum (refined) – C P Kelco Ltd

Genu Pectin – pectin, high methoxyl and pectin, amidated – Hercules Holding Ii Ltd

Genuagar – agar – Hercules Holding Ii Ltd

Genugel – carrageenan and carrageenan blends for water-gel systems – Hercules Holding Ii Ltd

Genugel – carrageenan (for gelling applications) – C P Kelco Ltd

Genuine Haws – watering cans and spray roses – Haws Watering Cans

Genulacta – carrageenan (for dairy systems) – C P Kelco Ltd

Genulacta – carrageenan and carrageenan blends for dairy system – Hercules Holding Ii Ltd

Genus – Genus Group

Genus Eco-Matt – paper – Fenner Paper Co. Ltd

Genutine – carrageenan (gelatin alternative for food applications) – C P Kelco Ltd

Genuvisco – carrageenan (for thickening applications) – C P Kelco Ltd

Genuvisco – carrageenan for visosity applications – Hercules Holding Ii Ltd

Genware – Neville UK plc

Genweld – welding products – Wescol

Geo. Kingsbury Machine Tools Ltd – machine tools, asssembly machines and functional test equipment – George Kingsbury Ltd

Geobox – Linpac Allibert Ltd

Geocel – County Construction Chemicals Ltd

Geoflex – Sacrificial lining material – Tiflex Ltd

Geographics – UK Office Direct

***Geolon (Netherlands)** – woven geotextile range – A G A Group

GeoManager – Vehicle Tracking & Management – CAL-Logistics Ltd

GeoMEM Consultants (United Kingdom) – Scientific and technical software with emphasis on geological, geoenvironmental, geoscience, earth science, bioscience and mapping products. Technical software development and software training services. Established 1985. – Geomem Ltd

Geomevary – HSS circular saws – Dynashape Ltd

Geopuzzle – educational puzzles – V I P

Georg Jordan (Germany) – Mathew C Blythe & Son Ltd

George Cox – goodyear welted and cemented mens and youths footwear – Cox Geo J Ltd

***George Dennis (Czech Republic)** – effects pedals and amplifiers for musical instruments – John Hornby Skewes & Co. Ltd

George Dyke – press and drop forgings – George Dyke Ltd

George Fischer – pipework systems – Davis Industrial Plastics Ltd

George Fisher – Southern Valve & Fitting Co. Ltd

***George Muller Stiftung (Germany)** – German wines – O W Loeb & Co. Ltd

George Renault – Midland Air Tools Ltd

George Wilson Industries – gas meters – George Wilson Industries Ltd

George Wostenholm – knives – Egginton Bros Ltd

George Wright – components for orthoses – Gilbert & Mellish Ltd

Georges Renault – Gustair Materials Handling Equipment Ltd

Georgia – WC suite – Armitage Shanks Ltd

Georgian – luxury bathroom taps – Samuel Heath & Sons plc

GeoScience – geotechnical consultants – Geoscience Ltd

Geosoft – registered trade mark in UK – Graticule

Geothechnical Instruments – Halcyon Solutions

GeoTide – Tidal Analysis and Prediction Software – Geomatix Ltd

Gerb – European Technical Sales Ltd

***Geref (Switzerland)** – growth hormones – Merck Serono Ltd

Gerflor – The Winnen Furnishing Company

Gerhardt – Digestors, Distillation, Milling, Particle Sizing – Pauley Equipment Solutions

Gerken – Carbon brushes and related components for traction and industry – Electrical Carbon UK Ltd

Germain's – international seed pelleters – Germains Seed Technology

germazap – Air Steriliser - odour and germ control – 03 Solutions Ltd

***Gern Optik (Switzerland)** – keystone and telebinocular – Warwick Evans Optical Co. Ltd

Gerni – industrial cleaning equipment – B & G Cleaning Systems Ltd

Gerol – gear lubricating oils – Benjamin R Vickers & Sons Ltd

Gerrardhouse – herbal remedies & essential oils – Perrigo UK

GES – Hydraulic & Offshore Supplies Ltd

Gesipa – Gesipa Blind Riveting Systems Ltd

Gesipa – blind rivet systems – Zygology Ltd

Gesipa – Gustair Materials Handling Equipment Ltd

Gesipa – S J Wharton Ltd

GESPA – Portable Transfer Pumps for Dietel – Stephens Midlands Ltd

Gesswein – abrasive stones and mounted points – Kemet International Ltd

***Gestetner (EU & Japan)** – photocopiers and facsimiles – N R G Group Ltd

Gesto – Harrier Fluid Power Ltd

Get Yourself Connected – cables – John Hornby Skewes & Co. Ltd

Getaway Executive Travel – travel agent – Getaway Executive Travel Ltd

Getech – continental mapping and analysis services which involve the reprocessing of gravity and aeromagnetic data – University Of Leeds

GETi – Manufacture of Titanium wedding rings – Geti Ltd

***Gettys** – European Drives & Motor Repairs

Gettys Fanuc – European Drives & Motor Repairs

***Gettys Gould** – European Drives & Motor Repairs

GEWES – Bailey Morris Ltd

GF2K – innovative fashion briefcases, folios and travel bags – Modrec International Holdings Ltd

GGF – GALLOWAY GLASSFIBRE – Galloway Eggs Ltd

GGI – UK Office Direct

GH Range Actuator – Hydraulic scotch yoke actuator – Rotork plc

Ghidine Lighting – Light Fantastic

Ghost – fishing tackle class 28 – Drennan International Ltd

Ghurka – Steel Bollard – Alto Bollards UK Ltd

Giada – glass shower enclosures – Novellini UK Ltd

Gianni Ferrari – Professional Mowers – Loxston Garden Machinery

Gianni Vitorio – mens casualwear – Remys Ltd

Giant – extra thick felt tip marker – Office Depot UK

Giant Steps – carpets – Interface Europe Ltd

Giavelli – The Winnen Furnishing Company

Giazoid – G E Healthcare

Giclee – Imex Print Services Ltd

Gierre Life Limehaus Gibson – mens clothing – Cormans

Giesse Filtri – Harrier Fluid Power Ltd

***Gifu (Japan)** – decorative plywood panels and fire retardant decorative plywood panels – Plaut International

GIGANT – lamps – Osram Ltd

Gigawave – Vidlink International Ltd

***Gilbos (Belgium)** – medium and course count automatic and manual winding machines – Robert S Maynard Ltd

Gilchrist & Soames – toiletries and home fragrances – Gilchrist & Soames

Gildan – T-Shirts Sweatshirts Poloshirts Hooded Sweatshirts Clothing – A4 Apparel Ltd

Gildan – Avalon and Lynwood

***Gildemeister (Germany and Italy)** – CNC turning machines from 2 to 8 axis control – D M G UK Ltd

Gildemeister CNC lathes – Phil Geesin Machinery Ltd

Giletta – Harrier Fluid Power Ltd

Gilkes pumps – Anchor Pumps Co. Ltd

Gill Sans – typeface – Monotype Imaging Ltd

Gillardon – European Technical Sales Ltd

Gillhams Intellectual Property Lawyers – Qualified and Experienced Specialist Practitioners – Gillhams

Gillie – sestrel commercial compasses and nautical instruments – John Lilley & Gillie Ltd

Gills Cables – control cables for motor vehicles – Gills Cables Ltd

Gilmex – loose leaf mechanisms and systems – Gilmex International Ltd

Gilpa Pup – puppy food – Gilbertson & Page Ltd

Gimbal – gimbal joints for aircraft ducting – Senior Aerospace Bird Bellows

Gina – ladies shoes – Gina Shoes Ltd

Gino Ferrari – leathergoods - handbags, luggage and small leathergoods – Modrec International Holdings Ltd

Gino Polli – watches – Sherwood Agencies Ltd

Giovani Milan – Hotel Complimentary Products

Gipgloss – vehicle refinish paint – Spies Hecker UK

Gipsy – ladies hosiery – Textiliana Ltd

Giraffe – floodlighting units – Brimotor Ltd

***Giraffe Classic (South Africa)** – cranes – Panavision Grips Ltd

GIRAIR – Hydraulic & Offshore Supplies Ltd

Girair – Trafalgar Tools

Girard – Motor Technology Ltd

Girbil (United Kingdom) – irda interface – Greenwich Instruments Limited

Giroflex – office furniture – E W Marshall Ltd

Giroform – carbonless – Howard Smith Paper Ltd

Girvan – baby bath – Armitage Shanks Ltd

Gis – R F Lifting & Access Ltd

*Gis (Switzerland) – electric chain hoists, vacuum lifting equipment, Gis system - lightweight crane system – Pfaff-Silberblau Ltd

Gital – D M G UK Ltd

Gitram – valve service – Weir Valves & Controls

Giustimix – food processing machines – T Giusti Ltd

Giving at Christmas – C C A Group Ltd

Gizmo – Chip-It

GK – Frenstar

GKN – Bailey Morris Ltd

GKN Motorsport – Driveshafts & propshafts for racing & special vehicles – G K N Driveline Services Ltd

GKN Sinter Metals – GKN Sinter Metals Ltd

*GKS Perfekt (Germany) – toe jacks and trolleys for machinery movement – Southworth Handling Ltd

GL 2200 – live mixing consoles – Allen & Heath Ltd

GL 3300 – live mixing consoles – Allen & Heath Ltd

GL 4000 – live touring consoles – Allen & Heath Ltd

GL Designs Ltd – G L Designs Ltd

Glacetal – thrust washers and strip in acetal co-polymer for minimal lubrication – Mahle Engine Systems

GLACETAL KA – GGB UK

Glacia Granulite – salt for water softening purposes – British Salt Ltd

Glacia PDV – pure dried vacuum salt and granules for water softening purposes – British Salt Ltd

Glade – Capex Office Interiors

Gladiator – shirts – J M C Q Huston & Son

Gladiator Towers – Accesscaff International Ltd

*Glamos (Japan) – glazed ceramic mosaics – Udny Edgar & Co. Ltd

Glasdek – humidity control – Munters Ltd

Glasgow prestwick bond ltd – bond operations company – Glasgow Prestwick Airport Parking

GlasModul – Cloakroom Solutions Ltd

Glasroc Multiboard – glass reinforced gypsum boards – Bristish Gypsum

Glasroc S – frameless fire encasement system – Bristish Gypsum

Glass – ballistic protection, reinforcement fabrics – Fothergill Engineered Fabrics Ltd

Glass Bends – curved glass bends (annealed, laminated, toughened and double glazed) – Gardner & Newton Ltd

Glass Fibre – clock towers, vents, access panels, housing, covers, hoppers, tanks, boxes, enclosures, kiosks, vehicle panels, mouldings, containers and construction. – Coe's Derby Ltd

Glass Technology – Glass Renovation and Windscreen Repair Equipment – Windscreen Repair Service

Glass Wash – germicidal detergent for hand use – Evans Vanodine International plc

*Glasshelf – glass storage shelf with drip tray – Servaclean Bar Systems Ltd

Glassrack – Cloakroom Solutions Ltd

GlasStile – low to medium level flow controller – Gunnebo Entrance Control Ltd

Glassveyor – For the Glass and double glazing industry – Newland Engineering Co. Ltd

*Glastonbury Spring Water – Glastonbury Spring Water Co.

Glasurit – automotive refinish paints and associated products – B A S S Hydro Coatings Ltd

Glaze – dishwashing powder – Evans Vanodine International plc

Glazepta – British Vita plc

Glazpart – glazing accessories – Glazeparts UK Ltd

Glazpart over Glaz – vents – Glazeparts UK Ltd

Glazy – textile piece goods – Reid & Taylor Ltd

Gleam – Forward Chemicals Ltd

Gleason – European Technical Sales Ltd

Gleave – watches, clocks and materials – Gleave & Co.

Glen – domestic heating and electrical appliances – Glen Electric Ltd

Glen – Glen Dimplex UK Ltd

Glen Avon – malt Scotch whisky – Gordon & Macphail

Glen Calder – Scotch whisky blended – Gordon & Macphail

Glenair – parts for aeroplanes – Glenair UK

Glenair – Dax International Ltd

Glenair – Cyclops Electronics Ltd

Glenavy – carpets – Ulster Carpet Mills Ltd

Glenavy Donard – carpets – Ulster Carpet Mills Ltd

Glenavy Tara – carpets – Ulster Carpet Mills Ltd

Glenco – horticultural plastic growing units – Desch Plantpak Ltd

Glencoe – loop pile carpet tile – Warlord Contract Carpets Ltd

Glendale – flower design s/s table cutlery – Amefa

Glendun – carpets – Ulster Carpet Mills Ltd

*Glendyne Slate (Canada) – slate – Cembrit Ltd

Glenfield – wooden window and door frames – Benlowe Windows

Glenhusky – knitwear gents – Alice Collins

Glenmac – knitwear – Dawson International plc

Glenmoy figured – carpets – Ulster Carpet Mills Ltd

Glenmuir – sports knitwear – Glenmuir Ltd

Glenrothes Gazette – newspaper – Strachan & Livingston

Glenshane – carpets – Ulster Carpet Mills Ltd

Glensheske – carpets – Ulster Carpet Mills Ltd

GLENTHORPE – Hydraulic & Offshore Supplies Ltd

Glentone – carpets – Ulster Carpet Mills Ltd

Glentree Estates – estate agents – Glentree Estates

Glentronic – phase and frequency converters – A T B Laurence Scott Ltd

*Gleptosil – Alstoe Ltd

Glevum – edm machine – S E S Glos Ltd

Glidalong – Conway Trailer Division

Glidden – decorative paints – Akzonobel

Glide-Out – storage racking – Rack International UK Ltd

Glidebolt – nylon door bolts – Paddock Fabrications Ltd

Glidetrak – mobile storage and filing system – Rackline Ltd

Glidevale – ventilation and specialist building products – Building Product Design

Glimakra – Kee Valves

Glitterati – dress hire, sell evening wear, bride, bridesmaid and special occasion wear made to order and hire – Glitterati Dresswear Hire

Glo-Flame – gas D.F.E. open fire – Dunsley Heat Ltd

Glo-Leak (United Kingdom) – UV-fluorescent leak tracer fluids and dyes – Primalec

Glo-Leak – uv-fluorescent leak detection fluids – R.J. Doran & Co. Ltd

Glo-Marka – reflective and fluorescent shoulder belts, tabards and waistcoats, self adhesive dots and tapes – Glo-Marka

Glo-Tape – fluorescent hazard tape – I R S Ltd

Glo-Tex – heat-protective glove textile – T B A Textiles

Global – nylon castor – British Castors Ltd

Global – measurement machinery – Hexagon Metrology

*Global – Russums

*Global (USA and Scandinavia) – anti corrosion products – B A C Corrosion Control Ltd

Global – export of vehicle spare parts – Global Industries Ltd

Global CMMs – Status Metrology Solutions Ltd

Global Enviromental – solid (municipal) and liquid waste disposal – Kelda Group

Global Gourmet – spice blends – Fiddes Payne

Global Home Loans – The Woolwich

Global-Mix – software system – Format International Ltd

Global Towers – Accesscaff International Ltd

Global Yuasa Battery Co Ltd – battery manufacturer – Battery Distribution Group

Globalmaster Range – Accesscaff International Ltd

Globar – silicon carbide heating elements – Sandvik

GLOBE – Hydraulic & Offshore Supplies Ltd

Globe Frieght Ltd – freight – Pat Freight Ltd

Globe-King – VHF and SW amateur radio construction kits – John Banner

Globe Trotters (Italy) – safety footwear – L H Safety Ltd

GlobeStyle – record label – Ace Records Ltd

Glocote – fluorescent paint – Co-Var Ltd

Glopak – metallized floor seal – Agma Ltd

Glopol – germicidal cleaner/polish – Agma Ltd

Gloria & Pat – needlework publications – DMC Creative World

Gloriette – ladies hosiery – Textiliana Ltd

*Glorik – Euro Catering Equipment

Glory Glory Man United – magazine – Future Publishing Ltd

Gloss – Gloss – Amecal

Gloster – ductile iron heavy duty non-rock cover and frame – Norinco UK Ltd

Gloucester – timber up and over garage door – P C Henderson Ltd

Glover – marine lighting fittings and accessories – Stephen Glover & Co. Ltd

Glovia – enterprise resource planning (ERP) package – Northgate & Arinso

Glow-Worm Chatsworth And Dovedale – inset fire fronts & back boiler units – Heatcall Group Services

Glow-Worm Compleat – gas fire wall mounted system boiler range – Heatcall Group Services

Glow-Worm Energy Saver Combi – wall hung – Heatcall Group Services

Glow-Worm Energysaver – high energy wall mounted boiler – Heatcall Group Services

Glow-Worm Fuelsaver – economy plus gas fired wall mounted boiler – Heatcall Group Services

Glow-Worm Hideaway – gas fired floor mounted boiler – Heatcall Group Services

Glow-Worm Melody – Heatcall Group Services

Glow-Worm Miami – Heatcall Group Services

Glow-worm Micron – wall hung – Heatcall Group Services

Glow-Worm Opulence – gas fired back boiler – Heatcall Group Services

Glow-Worm Opus – gas fired back boiler – Heatcall Group Services

Glow-Worm Saxony – fire front & back boiler unit – Heatcall Group Services

Glow-Worm Swift Flow – gas fire wall mounted combination boiler – Heatcall Group Services

Glow Worm Ultimate – wall hung – Heatcall Group Services

Glowbug – pigment powders for paints – Glowbug Ltd

Glowman – aerosol all purpose cleaner polish – Keen World Marketing Ltd

Glowtex (United Kingdom) – high visibility fabric – Carrington Career & Work Wear

Glowworm boilers – energy efficient boilers – Elite Heating Ltd

GLpKa – instrument for pKa, logP, logD, solubility and dissolution measurement – Sirius Analytical Instruments

Glucolyte – powder – Reckitt Benckiser plc

Glucovis – Chesham Chemicals Ltd

Glue Dots (United Kingdom) – Austen Tapes Ltd

Gluelam – laminated beams – Kingston Craftsmen Timber Engineering Ltd

Glulam – timber beams – R T E UK Ltd

Glycair – Forward Chemicals Ltd

Glycool – Cooling Systems – I C S

Glyd Ring – seal designs – Trelleborg Ceiling Solutions Ltd

Glydring – seal designs – Trelleborg Ceiling Solutions Ltd

GLYDRING "T" – Hydraulic & Offshore Supplies Ltd

Glytex – lubricants – Chevron

GM – Harrier Fluid Power Ltd

GM set – 33kv switchgear – Schneider

GM6 – 33 kv indoor switchgear – Schneider

GMC – Harrier Fluid Power Ltd

Gmc – Alpha Electronics Southern Ltd

Gmeinder – final drive gear units for railways – M. Buttkereit Ltd

GN Netcom – Duplex Corporate Communications

GN Roof – Structural design and estimating software package – Gang-Nail

GN Truss – Structural design and estimating software package – Gang-Nail

Gnome – aero engines – Rolls-Royce plc

GNPD – global FMCG new product watch and procurement – Mintel Group Ltd

*Go (U.S.A.) – pressure regulator and valves, high purity pressure regulators – Boiswood LLP

Go Green – agricultural products – Amega Sciences plc

Go Power (U.S.A.) – dynamometers and controllers for engine test – Froude Hofmann Ltd

Go-Wipe – Georgia Pacific GB Ltd

*Goachers – P & D J Goacher

Goardian Led (United Kingdom) – A S D Lighting plc

GoBoPro – lighting effects projector – Optikinetics Ltd

GoBoShow – lighting effects projector – Optikinetics Ltd

Godiva – impression composition material – Kemdent

Godiva – fire pumps (portable, trailer, stationary, floating and vehicle mounted) compressed air foam systems – Godiva Ltd

Godstone – stock bricks, pavors and cutting service – W T Lamb Holdings Property Services

Godwin Crop Bag – gro-bag – E J Godwin Peat Industries Ltd

GOE – Guernsey Online Enterprise – GO Enterprise

Gogglebox – spectacle dispenser – Radleys

Gogglelox – glasses protection equipment – Plescon Security Products

Going Places – travel agents – Going Places

*Goiya Kgeisje (South Africa) – wine – Raisin Social

Gola – sports and leisure footwear – D Jacobson & Sons Ltd

Gold – textile piece goods – Reid & Taylor Ltd

Gold Block – pipe tobacco – Imperial Tobacco Group PLC

Gold Cash Registers – Cash Register Services

Gold Dot – immersion heater – Heatrae Sadia

Gold Flight – handsaws – Atkinson-Walker Saws Ltd

Gold Industry News – Emap Ltd

Gold Leaf Concept – make your own – Imperial Tobacco Group PLC

Gold Ring – general purpose solenoid valves – Parker Hannifin UK plc

Gold Roller – Textile sleeve for use in the aluminium extrusion industry – Marathon Belting Ltd

Gold Seal – flavourings and colourings – Cargill Flavor Systems UK Ltd

Gold Star – air rifle – B S A Guns UK Ltd

Gold Strand – agricultural baler twine – Independent Twine Manufacturing Co. Ltd

Gold wrap – agricultural netting for the big round bale – Independent Twine Manufacturing Co. Ltd

Gold X – Kuwait Petroleum International Lubricants UK Ltd

Goldammer – European Technical Sales Ltd

Goldbata – fish batter colouring – Drywite Ltd

Golden CeKa – hedge shears – Carl Kammerling International Ltd

Golden Days – merchandising agency – Chorion plc

Golden Fleece – buttons – Jason Buttons Ltd

Golden Glide (United Kingdom) – corded brass track – Integra Products

Golden Goal – games - designs – Europrint Promotions Ltd

Golden Match – darts – Unicorn Products Ltd

*Golden Tip Tea – Matthew Algie & Co. Ltd

Golden Unicorn – darts and flights – Unicorn Products Ltd

*Golden Vale – butter – Kerry Foods Ltd

Golden Velvet – Ryalux Carpets Ltd

Golden Virginia – roll-your-own tobacco – Imperial Tobacco Group PLC

GOLDENBLAST – Hydraulic & Offshore Supplies Ltd

Goldflam – Antimony Trioxide – Mineral & Chemical Services Ltd

Goldline – UK Office Direct

Goldline – graphic art pads, paper, paintbrushes, coloured paper & board & presentation cases – Exaclair Ltd

Goldline & Nera – egg layers – Johnstons Of Mountnorris

Goldone – PVC business books and organisers – Exaclair Ltd

Goldmaster – coated carbide – Ceratizit UK Ltd

Goldring – cartridges and hi-fi accessories – Goldring Products Ltd

Goldsmiths – jewellery, silverware, china, glass, watches and leather goods – Goldsmiths Jewellers Ltd

GoldSorb – precious metal recovery – Jacobi Carbons

Goldstrike – adhesion of subsequent gold plating – P M D UK Ltd

Golf Days – books – Tudor Journals Ltd

Golf Monthly – I P C Media Ltd

Golf Weekly – Emap Ltd

Golf World – Emap Ltd

Goliath – lifting equipment – Lifting Gear Products

Goliath – thread cutting – Bearwood Engineering Supplies

Goliath – portable lighting – Ses Sterling Ltd

Goliath – Goliath International Ltd

Goliath – boots and shoes – The Co Op

Goliath – threading specialists – Arrow Supply Co. Ltd

Golkem – speciality chemicals – Goldcrest Chemicals Ltd

Golmatic – Universal Milling machines including CNC vesions – Pro Machine Tools Ltd

Golpla – Hoofmark UK Ltd

Gomax – flexible hose and fittings by transfer oil – Thermofrost Cryo plc

Gomex - T.C.T. – saw blades & tooling – Gomex Tools Ltd

Gonker – Harrier Fluid Power Ltd

Good Honest Ales – beer – George Bateman & Son Ltd

Good Housekeeping – magazine – National Magazine Company Ltd

Good to Go Safety – Equipment inspection and tagging systems – Good to Go Safety Ltd

Good Woodworking – magazine – Future Publishing Ltd

GOOD YEAR – Hydraulic & Offshore Supplies Ltd

Goodfellow Cambridge – metals and materials for research and industry – Goodfellow Cambridge Ltd

Goodley Twist – carpets – Cormar Carpets

Goodridge – Hampshire Hose Services Ltd

GOODRIDGE – Hydraulic & Offshore Supplies Ltd

Goodridge – Trafalgar Tools

*Goodsmaster – 11ft 500kg-750kg and 1000kg-1500kg – Stannah Microlifts Ltd

Goodtoknow.co.uk – Website – I P C Media Ltd

Goodwin Barsby – Goliath-jaw crusher – Metso Minerals UK Ltd

Goodwin Barsby – Trowell Plant Sales Ltd

Goodwood – Try & Lilly Ltd

Goodyear – Trafalgar Tools

Goodyear – Wealden Tyres Ltd

Gopak – lightweight folding tables and contract furnishings – Gopak Ltd

Gopher – excavators – Neuson Ltd

Gordon – automotive electrical parts – Gordon Equipments Ltd

GORDON – Hydraulic & Offshore Supplies Ltd

Gordon Beningfield – Chorion plc

Gore – fabric – Lojigma International Ltd

Goretex – Fieldway Supplies Ltd

Gorilla – Glue – The Toolpost

Gorilla – Gem Tool Hire & Sales Ltd

Gossen – European Technical Sales Ltd

*Gotec (Germany) – knee and leg protective pads – Gotec Trading Ltd

Gotec – NDT products and apparatus, personal and general safety clothing, measuring, testing and inspection apparatus, instruments and welding spatter release spray, compressed air and gas leak detection spray – Gotec Trading Ltd

Gough – Incamesh Filtration Ltd

GOULDS – J P Whitter Ltd

Goulds – pumps – Robert Craig & Sons Ltd

GOULDS/LOWARA – Barber Pumps Ltd

Goulds Pumps – Goulds Pumps a Division of ITT Industries Ltd

Gourmet – mini kitchen – Anson Concise Ltd

Government Watchdog Service – customer watchdog customers in the Yorkshire water and york waterworks region – The Consumer Council For Water

Goxhill handmade clay plain tile – clay – Sandtoft Holdings Ltd

Goya – body sprays – Coty UK Ltd

*Goyen (Australia) – solenoid valves, diaphragm pulse valves, emission monitoring equipment for dust – Goyen Controls Co UK

Gozin – leather softener, mulling liquid – F Ball & Co. Ltd

GP Batteries – batteries – Anglia

GP Professionial – software for general practice – Seetec

GP Professionial - software for general practice – Seetec

GP Pumps – Alfa Laval Eastbourne Ltd

GP Range Actuator – Pneumatic scotch yoke actuator – Rotork plc

GPA. – Automation elements – William Teknix

GPS (United Kingdom) – PDA interface – Greenwich Instruments Limited

GPS Agencies – Ploymer pen blanks – The Toolpost

GPW Appointments – research – G P W Recruitment

GPW Construction – research – G P W Recruitment

GPW Research & Development – research – G P W Recruitment

GPW Secretarial – research – G P W Recruitment

GPW Trade – research – G P W Recruitment

GR – fan motors and assemblies – Thermofrost Cryo plc

GR1 – installation conference mixer – Allen & Heath Ltd

Grab-O-Matic – auto-mechanical drum handlers – St. Clare Engineering Ltd

Grabs Priestman – R B Cranes Ltd

Grace – Dean Smith & Grace Lathes Ltd

Grace – construction chemicals – Grace Construction Products Ltd

*Graco (U.S.A.) – paint spray equipment (airless HVLP) – Lion Industries UK Ltd

Graco – Trafalgar Tools

Grad – spray equipment – Graphoidal Developments

Grade Application Advisor – Kennametal UK Ltd

Graded Bark Flakes – mulch – Melcourt Industries

Gradex – B P plc

Gradmatic – spray equipment – Graphoidal Developments

Graduate – progressive lenses – Carlzeiss Vision

Gradwood – heating ventilation & air conditioning – Gradwood Ltd

*Graebener (Germany) – presses – Embassy Machinery Ltd

Graeme Lawton – picture frames – Denis Wright Ltd

Graffex – Forward Chemicals Ltd

Graffiti Remover – removes graffiti, aerosol spray and other difficult stains – Premiere Products Ltd

Graffsolve – Graffiti removal products – Solvent Solutions Ltd

Grafila – combining pea variety – Limagrain UK Ltd

*Grafit – crucibles for metal melting – Ramsell Naber Ltd

Grafix – stationery – R M S International Ltd

Grafo-therm – anti condensation products, factory applied or site applied onto steel/ aluminium roof sheeting – Grafo Products Ltd

Grafter – Dickies Workwear

Grafter – tools – Sherwood Agencies Ltd

Grafters – Melitzer Safety Equipment

Grafters – workwear – UK Distributors Footwear Ltd

Grafylon – copy transfer sheets and carbon papers – Office Depot UK

*Graham – refreigeration – Keemlaw Ltd

Graham Precision – liquid ring and other pumps – AESpump

Graham's – plumbing and heating – Jewson Ltd

Grahl – Sitsmart Ltd

Grainger – American Catalogue Products – Protective Supplies & Services Ltd

Grainliner – Curtainsider for grain transport – Boalloy Industries Ltd

Grainlock – cold abrasive cements – Lea Manufacturing Co.

*Gram – Court Catering Equipment Ltd

*Gram – Gram UK

Grammer – T E K Seating Ltd

Gramos – paint shop products – Orapi Ltd

Gramos – Car Body Consumables – Car Paint Warehouse Ltd

*Grampian (United Kingdom) – upholstery leather – Bridge Of Weir Leather Co.

Grampian cubicles – Wide design options – Cubicle Centre

*Grampian Minerals – Harbro Ltd

Granada (Portugal) – light/dark granules cork wall tiles – Siesta Cork Tile Co.

Granada Forecourts – diesel and petrol and shop – Moto Hospitality Ltd

Granada Lodge – budget accommodation – Moto Hospitality Ltd

Granada Shopping – retail shops – Moto Hospitality Ltd

Granada TV & Video – rental TV and video – Boxclever

*Granant – Granant Precast Concrete

Grandage – business name product designers – Grand Age Engineering Ltd

Grandee – paper – G F Smith

*Grandma Batty – Greencore Frozen Foods

Grandma Moses – Chorion plc

Grandmaster (United Kingdom) – broadloom – Checkmate Industries Ltd

Grandstand Seating – Accesscaff International Ltd

Grandsweep – park & road vacuum sweepers – Grand Age Engineering Ltd

Granduer Pure Silk Ivory – Digital Products - Indigo - Coated – Howard Smith Paper Ltd

Grane – through-hardening plastic mould steel – Uddeholm Steel Stockholders

Granfix – adhensives and building accessories – Granwood Flooring Ltd

Grange – fencing – Grange Fencing Ltd

*Grange Marketing – Grange Marketing

Grange Supafence – fencing – Grange Fencing Ltd

Granger's 1210 – colourless waterproofing solution for brickwork stonework concrete masonry and timber – Grangers International Ltd

Granger's Boot Deodorant – Anti-bacterial footwear deodorant – Grangers International Ltd

Granger's Boot 'N' Shoe Glue – Powerful adhesive designed to repair soles as well as holes and tears – Grangers International Ltd

Granger's Cemcol – chlorinated rubber paint for cement etc – Grangers International Ltd

Granger's Country Sports Range – Waterproofing and maintenance products designed for Country Sports clothing-footwear and accessories including equestrian accessories – Grangers International Ltd

Granger's Damp Sealer – sealer for rising damp in walls, seals floors and basement walls – Grangers International Ltd

Granger's Extreme Superpruf – Waterproofing spray for (breathable) clothing and paper – Grangers International Ltd

Granger's Fabsil – waterproofing and rotproofing treatment for canvas and nylon – Grangers International Ltd

Granger's Fabsil Gold – waterproofing high silicone product for clothing and rucksacks – Grangers International Ltd

Granger's G-Sport – waterproofing for leather, suede boots and shoes including breathable lined footwear – Grangers International Ltd

Granger's Gore-Tex Approved Range for Footwear – Footwear care range approved for use on Gore-Tex footwear – Grangers International Ltd

Granger's Mesowax – coloured and colourless waterproofer for porous and weathered canvas – Grangers International Ltd

Granger's Nubuck Conditioner – Water repellent and conditioning spray for nubuck-suede and oiled leather including footwear and breathable linings – Grangers International Ltd

Granger's Tent and Awning Cleaner – pure soap for tents and awnings – Grangers International Ltd

Granger's Wax – waterproofing for leather boots and shoes – Grangers International Ltd

Grangers Extreme Wash-in – waterproofing for natural and synthetic fabrics – Grangers International Ltd

Grangers Extreme Wash-In Cleaner – Pure soap cleaner for waterproof garments – Grangers International Ltd

*Granit (Germany) – sidecutters and pliers – Welwyn Tool Group Ltd

Granit - Leister - Drei-S - Welwyn Hot Knife - Simonds - H.K.Porter - Impacto - Cooper Tools - Zangl - Saltus - Owoco - Herbst - Ewenz - Strack - Diamond - Ripley - Kerry - Weller/Ungar. Sole agents for leading Continental, American and Japanese precisio – Welwyn Tool Group Ltd

Granite – domestic sink material – Carron Phoenix

Granite Collection – The Amtico Co. Ltd

Granite Setts – B.S435/1975 – Harris & Bailey Ltd

Granny-Ann – dairy replacement food – Potters

Granny's Original – vegetable derived pure natural soap flakes for the washing of wool and delicate items of clothing – F M C G Ltd

Gransprung – area elastic sports hall flooring – Granwood Flooring Ltd

GRANT – C A Grant Ltd

GRANT – C A Grant Ltd

Grant Barnett – umbrellas and sun umbrellas – Grant Barnett & Co. Ltd

Grant Lyon Eagre – international railway track manufacturers – Corus Cogier

Granton – cutlery of all kinds, giftware items and surgical and scientific knives – Granton Medical Ltd

*Granuldisk – Holmes Catering Equipment Ltd

Granwax – cleaners, polishes and maintenance products – Granwood Flooring Ltd

Granwax – Vastern Timber Co. Ltd

Granwood – composition block flooring, coved skirtings etc – Granwood Flooring Ltd

*Grapevine International (HK) Ltd – Grapevine International

*Grapevine International Ltd – Grapevine International

*Grapevine International Services Ltd – Grapevine International

GRAPHCAD – CAD/CAM Solutions for the upholstery, furniture, automotive, boat industries – Vetigraph CAD/CAM Ltd

graphElite – Artillus Illuminating Solutions Ltd

Graphiart Card – coated paper & board – Howard Smith Paper Ltd

Graphiart Duo – coated paper & board – Howard Smith Paper Ltd

Graphic Paintbox – creative system for print design – Quantel Ltd

Graphics Unlimited – large format digital printing – T P S Visual Communications Ltd

Graphilor – chemical carbons – Mersen UK

Graphtec Corporation – Graphtec GB Ltd

Grasam Samson Tools – engineering cutting tools and equipment – Grasam Samson Ltd

Graseby – electronics – Smiths Detection

Graseby Specac – scientific instrument accessories comprising 1.R accessories, optical components and testing instrumentation – Specac Ltd

Grass Roots – travel awards – Grass Roots

Grass Roots Travel Services – ABTA, IATA bonded travel agency – Grass Roots

Grassair – compressors, parts and service – Airware International Ltd

Grassblock – pre-cast paving – Grass Concrete Ltd

Grasscrete – reinforced grassed paving – Grass Concrete Ltd

Grasskerb – Plastic Kerb Edge Systems – Grass Concrete Ltd

Grasso – Therma Group

Grassroad – plastic grassed paving – Grass Concrete Ltd

Grassroof – Grass Concrete Ltd

Grate-Fast – fixings for open-grate flooring – Lindapter International

Grateful Dead – record label – Ace Records Ltd

Gratnell – storage frames, trolleys and plastic trays – Gratnells Ltd

Grattan – catologue – Grattan plc

Gratte Brothers (GB) – electrical contractors and engineers – Gratte Brothers Ltd

Grau – lamination – Rainer Schneider & Ayres

Grauff – upholstery and bedding machinery – Apropa Machinery Ltd

Gravesend KM Extra – newspaper – Kent Messenger Group Ltd

Gravesend Messenger – newspaper – Kent Messenger Group Ltd

Gravitex – anti stonechip coating – U-Pol Ltd

Gravity Internet – Gravity Internet Ltd

*****Gravograph (France)** – pantograph and computerised engraving machines and accessories – Gravograph Ltd

Gravure – printing – Printpack Enterprises Ltd T/A Printpack

*****Grayhill (U.S.A.)** – rotary, dual inline switches – E A O Ltd

Grayhill – Cyclops Electronics Ltd

grazeon – Northern Crop Driers Ltd

Graziano – D M G UK Ltd

Grd-03-12 – three axis fluxgate gradiometer – Bartington Instruments Ltd

Gre-Sol Jelly – Gresolvent Ltd

*****Grease Bugs** – Progressive Product Developments Ltd

Grease Guzzler – Wendage Pollution Control Ltd

GreasePaK – Mechline Developments Ltd

Great Eastern Ale – cask beer – Woodforde's Norfolk Ales

Great Oak Lifestyles – housewares – P M S International Group plc

Great Outdoors, The – magazine – Newsquest Group

Great White – powerful heavy duty hand cleanser for resins, paints, bitumen, inks – Deb R & D Ltd

Great Yarmouth Port Authority – port authority – Great Yarmouth Port Company Ltd

Greaves – Petre Process Plant Ltd

Greaves Portmadoc Slate – natural roofing & architectural slate – Greaves Welsh Slate Co. Ltd

Greblon – East Midland Coatings Ltd

Green Book – printed fabric and wallcoverings – Zoffany

Green Card, The – card holders – V I P

Green Cladding – cladding – D A Green & Sons Ltd

Green Door – Cold room insulated flip flap dors – Seymour Manufacturing International Smi Ltd

Green Line – coach service operations – First Bus

Green Pages – directory of agriculture for the UK – Geraldine Flower Publications

Green Roller – Textile sleeve for use in the aluminium extrusion industry – Marathon Belting Ltd

Green Roof – Althon Ltd

Green's – restaurant and oyster bar – Green's Restaurant

Green SRL – Seating – Bucon Ltd

Green Stripe – hacksaw blades (high speed steel flexible) – L S Starrett Co. Ltd

Green Structural – build structural steel framed buildings – D A Green & Sons Ltd

Green Sulphur – mildew control – Vitax Ltd

Green Team, The – live insects for the control of pests – Fargro

Green Up – liquid lawn feed – Vitax Ltd

Green Up Feed & Weed & Moss Killer – combined fertiliser, weedkiller and moss killer for lawns – Vitax Ltd

Green Up Weedfree – selective weed killer – Vitax Ltd

Greenacres – equestrian clothing – J Wood & Son Bilsdale Ploughs Ltd

Greenback – ledgers, handbound – Reid Printers

Greencat – range of emission control devices – Eminox Ltd

Greencoat Digital Gloss – Digital Products - Toner Sheet Fed - Coated – Howard Smith Paper Ltd

Greencoat Digital Velvet – Digital Products - Toner Sheet Fed - Coated – Howard Smith Paper Ltd

Greengages Limited – Caterers – Greengages Limited

Greenhill – consumer products – Yule Catto & Co plc

Greenhouse & garage manufrs – Compton Buildings

Greening Cable Support Systems – Cablofil

Greenjackets – roofing services – Greenjackets Roofing Services Ltd

Greenland Houchen – solicitors – G H P Solicitors Greenland Houchen Pomeroy

Greenleaves – recycled papers – Exaclair Ltd

Greenlign – plastic bearing housings – R A Rodriguez UK Ltd

Greenlign – stainless steel bearing inserts – R A Rodriguez UK Ltd

Greenline – moulded printed circuit edge connectors – Cinch Connectors Ltd

Greenline – Cooks Brushes

Greenmaster – fine turf solid and liquid fertiliser – Scotts Co. Ltd

Greenpar – coaxial connectors – Anglia

Greenshires – printers and publishers – Greenshires Group Ltd

Greenstar – Condensing Boiler – Worcester Bosch Group Ltd

Greenthane – power transmission belting – Polyurethane Products Ltd

GreenTwist – green jute garden twine – Nutscene

Greenvale – pea colouring – Drywite Ltd

Greenwich – Selectronix Ltd

Greenwich Borough Mercury – South London Press

Greenwich Instruments – non-volatile memory – Greenwich Instruments Limited

Greenwood Magnetics – Greenwood Magnetics Ltd

Greenwood pantile – clay – Sandtoft Holdings Ltd

Greenwoods – mens clothing – Greenwood Menswear

Greetin – bread release agent – A A K Bakery Services

Greeting Cards – Digital Products - Toner Sheet Fed - Coated – Howard Smith Paper Ltd

Greggs – bread savouries & confectionery – Greggs plc

Gregoire Besson – J E Buckle Engineers Ltd

Gregoire Besson – Ploughs/Discourdon – Paul Tuckwell Ltd

Gregomatic Cleaning Machines (Switzerland) – surface cleaning systems – Crofton House Associates

Grenadier – coat hooks – Allgood

Grenadier – Steel Bollard – Alto Bollards UK Ltd

Grenson – for men – Grenson Shoes Ltd

Grenson Feathermaster – for men – Grenson Shoes Ltd

Grenson Footmaster – for men – Grenson Shoes Ltd

Gresen – Harrier Fluid Power Ltd

GRESEN – Hydraulic & Offshore Supplies Ltd

Gresham – The Woolwich

Gresham Insurance – The Woolwich

Gresham Insurance Company – The Woolwich

Gresolvent Paste – Gresolvent Ltd

Grespania – ceramic wall and floor tiles – Northern Wall & Floor Ltd

Grespor (Portugal) – ceramic wall floor tiles – Pavigres UK Ltd

Gresso – Distributor of Induction,LED Lights – Gresso Ltd

GRESSWELL SAFETY VALVES (United Kingdom) – Ultravalve Ltd

Grey-Flex – hacksaw blades – L S Starrett Co. Ltd

Greyboards – uncoated paper & board – Howard Smith Paper Ltd

Greycar – Motoring clothing and accessories – Greycar Ltd

Greyfriars – Harrier Fluid Power Ltd

GreyHawk – greyscale digitiser – Xara Ltd

Grid – software packages – Schlumberger Oilfield UK plc

Grid-Line – Couplings – Baldor UK

Grid Liner – ditchliners for bowling greens – Sportsmark Group Ltd

Grid Plus – modular switching and control system – M K Electric Ltd

Gridlap – Morton Mixers & Blenders Ltd

Grieve – needles and knitting elements for use in industrial knitting machines – Mitchell Grieve

Griff – agricultural 8 chains – Griff Chains Ltd

Griffin – pump – Torres Engineering & Pumps Ltd

Griffin – screen mill – Bradley Pulverizer Co.

Griffiths Trailers – agricultural trailers – Marston Agricultural Services Ltd

Grifinguard – Keytrak Lock & Safe Company

Griflex – B L Pneumatics Ltd

Grigsby Barton – files/engravers – Bearwood Engineering Supplies

Grilamid (Switzerland) – nylon 12 and elastomers – E M S-Chemie UK Ltd

*****Grilamid (Switzerland)** – PA12 – E M S-Chemie UK Ltd

Grilamid TR (Switzerland) – transparent nylon – E M S-Chemie UK Ltd

Grilbond (Switzerland) – bonding agents – E M S-Chemie UK Ltd

Grilon (Switzerland) – nylon 6 and elastomers – E M S-Chemie UK Ltd

*****Grilon (Switzerland)** – PA6 & PA66 – E M S-Chemie UK Ltd

Grilon C (Switzerland) – copolyamides – E M S-Chemie UK Ltd

Grilon T (Switzerland) – nylon 66 – E M S-Chemie UK Ltd

Grilon TS – nylon 66/6 alloy – E M S-Chemie UK Ltd

*****Grilonit (Switzerland)** – epoxy resins – E M S-Chemie UK Ltd

Grilpet (Switzerland) – polyester – E M S-Chemie UK Ltd

Griltex (Switzerland) – hot melt adhesives – E M S-Chemie UK Ltd

Grime Grabber – aluminium and olefin entrance matting – Jaymart Roberts & Plastics Ltd

Grime Stopper – aluminium and polypropylene entrance matting – Jaymart Roberts & Plastics Ltd

Grimebuster – Pressure washers – B & G Cleaning Systems Ltd

Grimme – Ben Burgess Beeston

*****Grimme** – George Colliar Ltd

Grimme – J & S Lewis Ltd

Grimsby Evening Telegraph, The – newspaper – Grimsby Telegraph

Grimsby Target – newspaper – Grimsby Telegraph

Grind Fresh – range of grinding mils with high quality ingredients & spice blends – Fiddes Payne

Grindex – Arun Pumps Ltd

Grindingmaster – wide abrasive belt and brush finishing and deburring machines – Ellesco Ltd

Gringos – basics and western types – UK Distributors Footwear Ltd

Grinnell – sprinkler systems – Ansul Fabrication

Grip – bushes, drill jig – Talbot Tool Co. Ltd

Grip-A-Disc – Power sanding products – The Toolpost

Grip EV HD (United Kingdom) – entrance clean off zones – Checkmate Industries Ltd

Grip EV MD (United Kingdom) – entrance clean off zones – Checkmate Industries Ltd

Grip HD (United Kingdom) – entrance clean off zones – Checkmate Industries Ltd

Grip House – camera cranes – Panavision Grips Ltd

Grip-It-Hold – non-slip products – Dycem Ltd

Grip MD (United Kingdom) – entrance clean off zones – Checkmate Industries Ltd

Grip Tight – Bearings – Baldor UK

Gripcast – epoxy resin based seamless flooring screeds – J L Lord & Son Ltd

Gripchocks – rubber chocks – Rediweld Rubber & Plastics Ltd

Gripforce – BBA approved GRP rockbolts and soil nails – Minova Weldgrip Ltd

Gripmesh – fishing tackle class 28 – Drennan International Ltd

Grippa – secure cycle parking racks – Dixon Bate Ltd

Gripper – dart shafts and darts – Unicorn Products Ltd

Gripper – vehicle drinks holder – Custom Accessories Europe Ltd

Gripso – adhesives – F Ball & Co. Ltd

Gripsotex – adhesives – F Ball & Co. Ltd

Gripsotite – adhesives – F Ball & Co. Ltd

Gripstar – glazed ceramic tiles – A Elder Reed & Co. Ltd

Gripsure 8 Panel – rugby balls – Gray Nicolls

Gripsure-All Weather – netball – Gray Nicolls

*****Griptech (Germany)** – workholding products – Thame Engineering Co. Ltd

Griptester – skid resistance tester for roads, runways and helidecks – Findlay Irvine

Grisburger – Office Seating – Bucon Ltd

*****Grisol V** – Horses – Vetoquinol Ltd

Grit (Denmark) – industrial grinding and polishing machines – R J H Finishing Systems Ltd

*****Grivory (Switzerland)** – PA6I/6T – E M S-Chemie UK Ltd

Grivory GV (Switzerland) – polymers for metal replacement – E M S-Chemie UK Ltd

Grivory HT – polymers for high temperature applications – E M S-Chemie UK Ltd

Grizzly – garments – Charterhouse Holdings plc

Grizzly Activewear – garments – Charterhouse Holdings plc

Grizzly Golf Wear – garments – Charterhouse Holdings plc

Gro-Aid Products – Double Gee Hair Fashions Ltd

Gro-Cone – tree protection – Acorn Planting Products Ltd

Gro-Tank – hydroponic unit for growers and gardeners – Nutriculture

Gro-Well – horticultural product – Codnor Horticultural Ltd

Grobet – files/engravers – Bearwood Engineering Supplies

GroMaster – 50 watt pre-set thermostat propagator – Richard Sankey & Son Ltd

GROMELLE – Hydraulic & Offshore Supplies Ltd

Groovy Glitz – body and hair glitter – F M C G Ltd

Gropots – professional quality, matt black containers for outside growing – Richard Sankey & Son Ltd

Gros – installation mixed – Allen & Heath Ltd

Groshong – vascular access catheters – Bard Ltd

Grossmann Lighting – Light Fantastic

GroStart – unheated propagator with ventilated clear polystyrene top and watertight base – Richard Sankey & Son Ltd

Grosvenor – Metering Pumps – Robert Craig & Sons Ltd

Grosvenor – limousine – Coleman Milne Ltd

Grosvenor – shaving brushes – Progress Shaving Brush Vulfix Ltd

Grosvenor – install & manufr windows and conservatories – Grosvenor Windows Ltd

Grosvenor Gallery – art gallery – Grosvenor Gallery

Grosvenor Packaged Systems – complete custom designed and built chemical dosing systems – Grosvenor Pumps Ltd

Grosvenor plus – brass rope edge wiring accessories – M K Electric Ltd

Grosvenor Pumps – reciprocating positive displacement, diaphragm, fixed and variable pumps – Grosvenor Pumps Ltd

Groudform – Permanent formwork shuttering system – Cordek Ltd

Ground Work Equipment – Accesscaff International Ltd

Groundforce – trench shoring equipment – V P plc

Groundforce Horticultural Range – oils – Morris Lubricants

Groundform – Lemon Groundworks

Groundmate – ground protection mats – Centriforce Products Ltd

Groundsman Field Handbook – standard dimensions chart, wall chart – Sportsmark Group Ltd

Groundwork – environmental regeneration and awareness specialists – Groundwork UK

Group 4 Total Security – comprehensive security service – Group 4 Total Security Ltd

Group Five – shoes – Gardiner Bros & Co.

Group Schneider – Proplas International Ltd

Group Symbol – British Vita plc

Groutation – C E S Hire Ltd

GROVE – Chaintec Ltd

Grove – Team Overseas Ltd

Grove – Jones Cranes Parts

Grove Coles – Harrier Fluid Power Ltd

Grove - Jones - NCK – Jones Cranes Parts

Grovebury – Monier Ltd

***Grover (U.S.A.)** – guitar machine heads – John Hornby Skewes & Co. Ltd

Grovit – blind rivet for wood, plastic and other softer materials – Zygology Ltd

Grovit – for fastening wood, plastics, aluminium alloy – Avdel UK Ltd

***Grow Electric** – F E C Services Ltd

Growbark – soil conditioner – Melcourt Industries

Growing Companies – 80,000 companies – Acxiom Ltd

***Groz (Czech Republic)** – engineers small tools – Castle Brook Tools Ltd

***Groz-Beckert (Germany)** – needles for sewing and hosiery machines – Groz-Beckert UK

Grumac – re-tread equipment – Vacu Lug Traction Tyres Ltd

Grundair – portable air compresser – T T UK Ltd

Grundfos – Wyatt Bros Water Services Ltd

GRUNDFOS – J P Whitter Ltd

Grundfos – industrial, commercial and domestic pumps – Grundfos Pumps Ltd

Grundfos – Arun Pumps Ltd

Grundfos – Flow Mech Products Ltd

Grundfos Pumps – Pumps for Irrigation – L S Systems Ltd

Grundfos pumps – Anchor Pumps Co. Ltd

Grundoburst – hydraulic pipe bursting system – T T UK Ltd

Grundocrack – pipe cracking hammers – T T UK Ltd

Grundodrill – hydraulic dynamic impact combination steerable boring system – T T UK Ltd

Grundohit – steerable dry and wet combination boring system – T T UK Ltd

Grundomat – soil displacement hammers – T T UK Ltd

Grundopile – vertical piling hammers – T T UK Ltd

Grundopit – compact steerable boring system – T T UK Ltd

Grundoram – steel pipe ramming hammers – T T UK Ltd

Grundosleeve – PVC cable and pipe ducting – T T UK Ltd

Grundotug – conventional and cable pulling winches – T T UK Ltd

Grundotug – Phoenix Utility Services Ltd

Gryphon (United Kingdom) – double-ended bench, pedastal and dust extraction mounted grinders – R J H Finishing Systems Ltd

GS Industrie – European Technical Sales Ltd

GS3000 – studio recording mixed – Allen & Heath Ltd

GSF – G S F Promount

GSR – King Vehicle Engineering Ltd

GT-X (United Kingdom) – Software – Sword Ciboodle

***GTG (Sweden)** – grinders – Atlas Copco Tools Ltd

GTH Photography – Commercial Services including Advertising, PR, Architectural and Editorial – GTH Photography

GTX – timber soffit support beam – RMD Kwikform Limited

Guard-Dog – fluorescent bulkheads – Poselco Lighting Ltd

Guardex – pool chemicals and water treatment equipment – Biolab UK Ltd

Guardian – stainless steel sanitary equipment – Franke Sissons Ltd

***Guardian (Italy)** – bullet and impact resistant glass – C G I International Ltd

Guardian – staff safety systems, staff attack systems – Lismore Instruments Ltd

Guardian – Nederman Ltd

Guardian – Harrier Fluid Power Ltd

Guardian – range of automated robotic liquid handling systems – H T Z Ltd

Guardian 1 & 2 – Mail/Provisions box – Safety Letter Box Company Ltd

Guardian Barrier – light weight economic rising arm parking barrier – Apt Controls Ltd

Guardian, The – newspapers – Middleton Guardian

Guardian Weekly, The – newspapers – Middleton Guardian

GUARDINN – Hydraulic & Offshore Supplies Ltd

Guardmaster – Proplas International Ltd

***Guardscan (U.S.A.)** – manufacturer of industrial machine guarding systems – Tapeswitch Ltd

Guardsman – cash boxes – Helix Trading Ltd

Guardsman – door handles – Allgood

Guardwire – Geoquip Ltd

Gucci – optical frames and sunglasses – Hilton International Eye Wear Ltd

Guernsey Suite – aluminium garden furniture – Arrow Butler Castings

Guhring – Precision Tools

Guide to Good Living in London – map & guide – Francis Chichester Ltd

Guidograph (United Kingdom) – whitelining paint machine – Sportsmark Group Ltd

Guilbert – general office products – Office Depot UK

Guild Of Master Craftsmen, The – The Guild Of Mastercraftsmen G M C Publications Ltd

Guildhall – flat files, shelf filing wallets, stationery cabinets, upright pocket files, letter trays, pocket flat files, slipfiles, analysis books and pads, guide cards, dividers, accounting systems and business books – Exaclair Ltd

Guildhall – UK Office Direct

Guildhall Spiral Files – fitted files – Exaclair Ltd

Guilford Europe – high performance fabrics for a variety of automotive end uses – Guilford Europe Ltd

Guilford International – UK sales and marketing of US and UK production - knitted fabrics for apparel, domestic and industrial end uses – Guilford Europe Ltd

Guinness – guinness book of records publishers – Guinness World Records

Guiot – Harrier Fluid Power Ltd

Guitar & Bass – I P C Media Ltd

Guitar Techniques – magazine – Future Publishing Ltd

Guitarist – magazine – Future Publishing Ltd

GuJiBA – general consumer electronics sales and servicing, especially gloe-king vhf & sw amateur radio construction kits – John Banner

GUK – A M C Rollers Ltd

Gul – wetsuits and watersport accessories – Gul Watersports Ltd

Gul – watches – Gul Watersports Ltd

Gulf – Lubricants – Oiluk

Gulfgate – Harrier Fluid Power Ltd

Gullivers Sports Travel – tour operators – Gullivers Sports Travel

Gully Whale – gully emptying tanker – Whale Tankers Ltd

Gullywhale – standard specification gully emptier – Whale Tankers Ltd

Gun Drills – gun drills – Hammond & Co. Ltd

Gun Reamers – gun reamers – Hammond & Co. Ltd

Gunanail – multi-purpose building adhesive – Everbuild Building Products Ltd

Guncare – gun manufacturers – Holland & Holland Holdings Ltd

Gunn JCB – JCB and earthmoving equipment – Gunn J C B

Gunnebo – chains & lifting equipment – Gunnebo Industries Ltd

***Gunze (Japan)** – plastic kits and modelling paint – Amerang Group Ltd

Gurteen – clothing mens outwear – D Gurteen & Sons Ltd

Gusher – bilge pump – Munster Simms Engineering Ltd

Gusher – pump, valve and filters – Birmingham Pump Supplies

Gusmer – urethane spray equipment – Baxenden Chemicals Ltd

Gustafs – Halcyon Building Systems

***Gustafson (U.S.A.)** – sampling machinery – Orthos Engineering Ltd

Gustair – Gustair Materials Handling Equipment Ltd

***Gustav Emil Ern** – Chefs Knives – Gilberts Food Equipment Ltd

***Gustav Gessert (Germany)** – German wines – O W Loeb & Co. Ltd

Gutbrod – Harrier Fluid Power Ltd

Gutekunst – European Technical Sales Ltd

Guy-Raymond – tube and furniture fittings – Guy Raymond Engineering Company Ltd

GUYSON – Hydraulic & Offshore Supplies Ltd

Guyson – shot blast cabinets – R K International Machine Tools Ltd

GUYSON INTERNATIONAL – Hydraulic & Offshore Supplies Ltd

gv – dry pumps – AESpump

GWB – Bailey Morris Ltd

GWInstek – Test & Measurements Instruments – StanTronic Instruments

GX – Lubeline Lubricating Equipment

GXS2000 – rugby balls – Gray Nicolls

Gy-Roll – drilling heads – Gy-Roll Ltd

Gy-roll – Gustair Materials Handling Equipment Ltd

***Gym Sports (Far East)** – sports wear – Remys Ltd

Gymlene – polypropelene staple fibres – Drake Extrusion Ltd

Gymlene H T – high tenacity polypropylene or polyethelene fibres – Drake Extrusion Ltd

Gympro – fibre bonded carpet – Heckmondwike FB

Gyplyner – column and beam protection steel encasement systems – Bristish Gypsum

Gyplyner Ceiling – non-load bearing ceiling system – Bristish Gypsum

Gyplyner Walls – dry lining system for domestic use – Bristish Gypsum

Gyproc – tools, accessories and jointing products for plasterboard – Bristish Gypsum

Gyproc Baseboard – baseboard for plastering – Bristish Gypsum

Gyproc Core Board – board used in Gyproc shaftwall system – Bristish Gypsum

Gyproc Cornice Range – decorative mouldings – Bristish Gypsum

Gyproc Cove – coving – Bristish Gypsum

Gyproc Dri Wall Systems – plasterboard fixing systems – Bristish Gypsum

Gyproc Duoedge – edge profiled plasterboard – Bristish Gypsum

Gyproc Duplex Wallboard – reflective foil backed plasterboard – Bristish Gypsum

Gyproc Duraline – high impact resistant wallboard – Bristish Gypsum

Gyproc Easi-Fill – two-coat plasterboard jointing compound – Bristish Gypsum

Gyproc Fireline – fire resistant plasterboard – Bristish Gypsum

Gyproc Gypwall – internal partition system – Bristish Gypsum

Gyproc Joint Trims – UPVC alternative to jointing – Bristish Gypsum

Gyproc Jumbo Stud – separating walls – Bristish Gypsum

Gyproc Laminated – partition and wall lining system – Bristish Gypsum

Gyproc Lath – baseboard and plastering – Bristish Gypsum

Gyproc Lite-Mix Joint Cement – jointing material for plasterboard – Bristish Gypsum

Gyproc M/F Suspended Ceilings – jointless suspended ceiling – Bristish Gypsum

Gyproc Metal Stud Partition – non loadbearing fire resistant partition – Bristish Gypsum

Gyproc Moisture Resistant Fireline Board – moisture resistant, fire resistant, wallboard – Bristish Gypsum

Gyproc Paramount Dry Partition – pre-fabricated internal partition system – Bristish Gypsum

Gyproc Plank – gypsum plasterboard 19mm – Bristish Gypsum

Gyproc S I Floor System – insulating floor system – Bristish Gypsum

Gyproc Shaftwall System – fire resistant shaft enclosures – Bristish Gypsum

Gyproc Sheathing – Bristish Gypsum

Gyproc SoundBloc – sound resistant wallboard – Bristish Gypsum

Gyproc Thermal Board EHD – wallboard with a backing of extra high density expanded polystyrene – Bristish Gypsum

Gyproc Thermal Board LD – wallboard with backing of low density expanded polystyrene – Bristish Gypsum

Gyproc Thermal Board Plus – wallboard with backing of extruded polystyrene – Bristish Gypsum

Gyproc Thermal Board Super – wallboard with backing of phenolic foam board – Bristish Gypsum

Gyproc Triline – insulating plasterboard – Bristish Gypsum

Gyproc Wallboard – gypsum plasterboard – Bristish Gypsum

Gyptone – decorative sound performance plasterboard – Bristish Gypsum

Gyrane – perfume speciality – Quest International UK Ltd

Gyro Switches – Polaron Cortina Ltd

Gyrotest – gyratory compactor for asphalt – Ele International

Gyrowash – wash wheel – James H Heal & Co. Ltd

H

H 3530 – high speed door – Hörmann (UK) Ltd

H.4 – hot poured bitumen for painting joints – Colas Ltd

H. 77 – Harlow Printing Ltd

H.A. Birch (United Kingdom) – heating elements – Zodion Ltd

H.A.C. – pulleys – Cozens & Cole Ltd

H.B. Fuller Coatings Ltd – powder paints – Valspar Powder Coatings Ltd

H.B. Switchgear (United Kingdom) – Ametek Prestolight

H.C. Starck Ltd – molybdenum and tungsten components for semiconductors – H C Starck Ltd

H.D. – hydraulic cylinders – Eland Engineering Company

H.D.88 (Portugal) – acrylic sealed domestic or contract cork floor tiles – Siesta Cork Tile Co.

H.D.A. – white bread – E D M E Ltd

H. D. Howden Ltd – domestic and industrial immersion heaters, storage water heaters - domestic storage water heaters - industrial, electric heating elements, electric air heater batteries, electric boilers – Howden Electro Heating

H.D. Liquid – solvent wax polish – Premiere Products Ltd

H.D.P. 105 – blanket and roller wash – Dynamic Drawings Ltd

H.D.P. Swell – blanket repair – Dynamic Drawings Ltd

H.D.S. – high density stacking linking chair – Race Furniture Ltd

H.D.S. – standard hydraulic servo actuators – Eland Engineering Company

H.D.S. – hydraulic double sided presses – Joseph Rhodes Ltd

H-D-Sperse – pigment dispersions – Gemini Dispersions Ltd

H.D. Towers – Accesscaff International Ltd

H.E. – electricity – Scottish & Southern Energy plc

H.E.C.T. – hall effect current transformers – Telcon Ltd

H.E. Olby – builders merchants – H E Olby & Co. Ltd

H.E.S. – sales and service of hydraulic equipment – H E S Sales Ltd

H.F.C. – insurance services – H F C Bank

H.F.C. Bank – H F C Bank

H.F.D. – fire resisting duct products – Senior Hargreaves Ltd

H.G.A. – mechanical and electrical designs for building services – Halcrow Group Ltd

H G I – Castle Brook Tools Ltd

H&H – A M C Rollers Ltd

H.H.B. – professional audio and broadcast specialists – H H B Communications Ltd

*H.H. Eser (Germany) – German wines – O W Loeb & Co. Ltd

H.H.Hancocks Clasped Hand – tailors marking media and industrial markers – Rowland Sandwith Ltd

H.I. – Hellermann Tyton

H.I.E. – business support (grants, loans equity and training assistance) – Highlands & Islands Enterprise

H.J. Countryman – mens socks – H J Sock Group Ltd

H.J. Executive – mens socks – H J Sock Group Ltd

H.J. Immaculate – mens socks – H J Sock Group Ltd

H.J. Indestructible – mens socks – H J Sock Group Ltd

H.J. Rambler – mens socks – H J Sock Group Ltd

H.J. Softop – mens socks – H J Sock Group Ltd

H K Laser Marking Systems – H K Technologies Ltd

H K Laser Systems – marking machine – H K Technologies Ltd

*H.K. Porter (U.S.A.) – heavy duty cutting tools – Welwyn Tool Group Ltd

H.K. Porter – bolt cutters – Apex Tools

H K Porter – European Drives & Motor Repairs

H.K. Technologies – H K Technologies Ltd

H & L – mains filters – Anglia

H+L HYDRAULIC – Hydraulic & Offshore Supplies Ltd

H L Planar – StrainSense Ltd

H. & L. Russel – coathangers and kitchenware – H & L Russell

H.L.S. Higlow – photoluminous products – Hi-Lite Signs Ltd

H.M.C. – wheels and castors – Brauer Ltd

H.M.E. – Joseph Rhodes Ltd

H.M.E. – custom semiconductors, hybrid microcircuits and electronic systems connectors – Raytheon UK

H.M.G. – paint – H M G Paints Ltd

H M Hamamat (United Kingdom) – highload shock absorbing material – Farrat Isolevel

*H.M.I. (Germany) – lamps – Osram Ltd

H.M.L. – component machining – Sigma Industries Ltd

H.M.S. – high mast systems – Holophane Europe Ltd

H.M.T. Inc – tank maintenance and repair, fabrication engineering, floating roof seals and roof drain systems – H M T Rubbaglas Ltd

*H. Maihak A.G. (Germany) – bin level indicators – Smail Engineers Glasgow Ltd

H N C – Halifax Numerical Controls Ltd

H.O.S – Hydraulic & Offshore Supplies Ltd

H & P – Mamelok Holdings Ltd

H.P.-007 – cellulose – Hercules Holding Ii Ltd

H P C – Hydraulic & Offshore Supplies Ltd

H.P.G. (High Precision Ground) – tipped wide bandsaws – Ernest Bennett & Co Darlington Ltd

H.P.I. – gear pumps, motors and power packs – Koppen & Lethem Ltd

*H.P.M. (Australia) – weatherproof switches and lighting – Elkay Electrical Manufacturing Co. Ltd

H & R Johnson - Cristal - Campbell's - Minton Hollins - H & R Johnson International - Prismatics - Prismafit - Sensations - Freedom - Kerastar -Elements - Spirit - Aspects - Artile - Johnson Professional - Norcros Adhesives – Johnson Tiles Ltd

H. R. P. – wholesales refrigeration & air conditioning products – H R P Ltd

H R Smith – dischargers and antennas – Hayward & Green Aviation Ltd

H Range Actuator – Hydraulic linear or rotary quarter turn actuator – Rotork plc

H & S – aircraft engine overhaul – B B A Aviation plc

H.S.C. – high speed milling – Ceratizit UK Ltd

H.S.C. – multi-purpose cleaner – Evans Vanodine International plc

H.S. & H.X. – mobile hot water and steam power washing equipment – Rhinowash Ltd

H S I – Hospitality Search International Ltd

H.S.L.-B(-TZ) – automatic torque control version – Hilti GB Ltd

H.S.M. – tungsten carbide products – Marshalls Hard Metals

H.S. Pilot 2000 – auto pilot power boat – B & G Ltd

H.S.S. – distributer to building merchants – Henry Shaw & Sons Ltd

H.S.T. 46 – sailcloth – Heathcoat Fabrics Ltd

H.T. – hot tanks – Harton Services Ltd

H & T – H & T Bellas Ltd

H.T.B. – cricket and hockey balls – Kookaburra Reader Ltd

H.T. Bellas – timber and plywood importers, sawmillers and builders merchants – H & T Bellas Ltd

H T Collection – The Winnen Furnishing Company

H.T.F.H. – fluid mixers, canned glandless, magnetically-coupled and ceramic lined pumps – Hayward Tyler Fluid Handling

*H.T.I. (Germany) – lamps – Osram Ltd

H.T.I. – refrigeration/air-conditioning compressor spares – J & E Hall Ltd

H.T.P. – refrigeration/air-conditioning compressor spares – J & E Hall Ltd

H.T.V. – high temperatures and velocity space heating systems – Babcock Wanson UK Ltd

H.T.V. Group – I T V Wales plc

*H. Upmann (Cuba, Jamaica, Europe and Honduras) – cigars – Hunters & Frankau Ltd

H.V. – vertical oil mop skimmer – Oil Pollution Environmental Control Ltd

H. & V. and Process Pipe Sections – pipes, ducts, industrial noise control, marine and offshore – Rockwool Rockpanel B V

H.V.R. – resistors fixed high voltage, resistors fixed carbon non-inductive, resistors fixed ceramic – H V R International Ltd

H.W. 33 – hand wipes – Oil Pollution Environmental Control Ltd

H.W.A.T. – heating system for hot water service pipework – Tyco Electronics UK Ltd

H.W. Wallace – test equipment for rubber and plastics – Hartest Precision Instruments Ltd

H.Y.-C – plating lines with cantilever transporter – P M D UK Ltd

H.Y.-Trac – plating lines with twin-track transporters – P M D UK Ltd

H1100 Systems – hydrocarbon fire protection for steel pipes and vessels – Rockwool Rockpanel B V

H2Office or Floating Offices – An office built to fit into marina berths, lakes, rivers, that floats on the water – Waterspace Developments Limited

Ha - Vis – Harting Ltd

Ha - Vis RFID – Harting Ltd

Habasit – conveyor and transmission belting – Habasit Rossi Ltd

*Hach (U.S.A.) – water testing equipment – Camlab Ltd

HACH ULTRA ANALYTICS – Hydraulic & Offshore Supplies Ltd

*Hackman (Finland) – stainless steel cookware – Dexam International

Hadax – network switching systems – Betterbox Communications Ltd

Haddon-Tecstone – reconstructed ornamental and architectural stonework – Haddonstone Ltd

Haddonstone – reconstructed ornamental and acrhitectural stonework – Haddonstone Ltd

Haefely – transformers & spares – Bearwood Engineering Supplies

Haemasol – Solmedia Laboratory Supplies

*Hafsil (Norway) – atomised ferro silicone – Tennant Metallurgical Group Ltd

Hag Seating – Capex Office Interiors

*Hagemann (Germany) – packaging machinery – Advanced Dynamics Ltd

Hager – electrical distribution equipment & systems – Hager Engineering Ltd

Hagerty – jewellery care products – A G Thomas Bradford Ltd

Hagglunds – multi terrain vehicle – Traction Equipment Stafford Ltd

HAGGLUNDS-DENISION – Hydraulic & Offshore Supplies Ltd

Hagglunds-Denison – hydraulic equipment, pumps, motors and valves – Parker Hannisin plc

HAGGLUNDS DRIVES – Hydraulic & Offshore Supplies Ltd

Hago – UK Office Direct

Hahn Estates (California) – Patriarche Wine Agencies

Haier – UK Office Direct

Hailer Matt Extra – Mcnaughton James Paper Group Ltd

Hainbuch – Leader Chuck Systems Ltd

HAINZL – Hydraulic & Offshore Supplies Ltd

Hair – I P C Media Ltd

Hair Vadic Products – Double Gee Hair Fashions Ltd

Haith – food processing and agricultural machinery – Tickhill Engineering Co. Ltd

Haka-woks – Chinese cookers – Nisbets plc

Hakko – Touch Panel displays – Coulton Instrumentation Ltd

HAKO – Chaintec Ltd

Hako – Harrier Fluid Power Ltd

Hako-Flipper – manual sweeper – Hako Machines Ltd

Hako-Hamster 1050 – suction sweeper – Hako Machines Ltd

Hako Hamster 600/700 – suction sweeper – Hako Machines Ltd

Hako-Hamster 800 – suction sweeper – Hako Machines Ltd

Hako-Jonas 1100 – hydraulic suction sweeper – Hako Machines Ltd

Hako Jonas 1450 – hydraulic suction sweeper – Hako Machines Ltd

Hako-Jonas 1700 – high performance suction sweeper – Hako Machines Ltd

Hako-Jonas 950 – suction sweeper – Hako Machines Ltd

Hakomatic 100/130 – scrubber driers – Hako Machines Ltd

Hakomatic 1100B – scrubber-drier – Hako Machines Ltd

Hakomatic 1500B – scrubber-drier – Hako Machines Ltd

Hakomatic B900 – scrubber-drier – Hako Machines Ltd

*HaKRon (Germany) – powder iron composite cores & chokes – Rolfe Industries

HAL – Allen Vanguard Ltd

Hal – Video design suite – Quantel Ltd

Halamid – sodium chloro P toluene, sulphonamide – Akzo Nobel Chemicals Holdings Ltd

Halberg – process, clean, waste water pumps & sludge mixers – S P P Pumps

Halbro Sportswear – sports clothing – Halbro Sportswear Ltd

Halco – masons chisels with tungsten carbide tips – Marshalls Hard Metals Ltd

Halcyon – electronic repeater compass – B & G Ltd

Halcyon – science fiction models – Amerang Group Ltd

HALDEX AB – Hydraulic & Offshore Supplies Ltd

Haldex Barnes – Gear Pumps, Gear Motors, DC Mini Hydraulic Power Units, Gear Flow Dividers – J B J Techniques Ltd

HALDEX GMBH – Hydraulic & Offshore Supplies Ltd

HALDEX LTD – Hydraulic & Offshore Supplies Ltd

Haldolite – sign lights – Haldo Developments Ltd

Haldopillar – switchgear housing – Haldo Developments Ltd

Haldopost – enlarged basepost – Haldo Developments Ltd

Haldoset – offset bracketry – Haldo Developments Ltd

Hale Foam Systems – foam – Godiva Ltd

Halfen – concrete fixings and reinforcement – Halfen Ltd

Hall – HSS threading tools – G & J Hall Ltd

Hall APV – Therma Group

Hall Service – refrigeration service – J & E Hall Ltd

Hall Thermotank – marine systems-Marine refrigeration and air conditioning systems – J & E Hall Ltd

Hall Thermotank – refrigeration/air-conditioning compressor spares – J & E Hall Ltd

Halla – Harrier Fluid Power Ltd

HALLA – Chaintec Ltd

Hallden – shearing m/c's – Bearwood Engineering Supplies

Haller – Harrier Fluid Power Ltd

Hallfield – UK Office Direct

Hallite – reciprocating hydraulic seals and high performance polymeric components for engineering applications – Hallite Seals International Ltd

Hallite – Mayday Seals & Bearings

HALLITE SEALS INTERNATIONAL – Hydraulic & Offshore Supplies Ltd

Hallmarc – abrasives – Marcrist International Ltd

Hallmark – refrigeration/air-conditioning compressor spares – J & E Hall Ltd

Hallmark Cards UK – greeting cards – Hallmark Cards

Hallscrew – screw compressor for refrigeration – J & E Hall Ltd

Hallscrew – refrigeration/air-conditioning compressor spares – J & E Hall Ltd

Halltherm – refrigeration/air-conditioning compressors, remanufacturing – J & E Hall Ltd

Halltherm – spares and remanufactured compressors for refrigeration – J & E Hall Ltd

Halo – anti-theft mirrors and safety mirrors – Volumatic Ltd

Halo – slimline flexible bollard – Haldo Developments Ltd

Halo Plus – rechargeable halogen torch – Furneaux Riddall & Co. Ltd

Halo Plus 2-IS – intrinsically safe rechargeable halogen torch – Furneaux Riddall & Co. Ltd

*Haloflex (Germany) – flexible arm luminaire – E D L Lighting Ltd

HALOMET – lamps – Osram Ltd

Haloscale – Mechanical Respirometers – Enspire Health

*HALOSTAR (Germany) – energy saving low voltage T.H. lamps for display lighting – Osram Ltd

Halothane – O'Neill Medicalia Ltd

HALOTRONIC – lamps electronic ballast lamps – Osram Ltd

Halox – anticorrosive pigments and tannin stain inhibitors – Lawrence Industries Ltd

Haltron – electronic tubes – Richardsons R F P D Ltd

Halver Ltd – wheels & castors – Halver Ltd

Ham – chemical fertilisers & seed – Harlow Agricultural Merchants Ltd

Ham Baker Adams – Ham Baker Pipelines Ltd

Ham-let – Bristol Fluid System Technologies Ltd

HAM-LET – Hydraulic & Offshore Supplies Ltd

Ham-let – Southern Valve & Fitting Co. Ltd

HAM-LET ADVANCED CONTROL TECHNOLOGY – Hydraulic & Offshore Supplies Ltd

Ham-Let Hattersley – Trafalgar Tools

Hamada – printing machines – P P S Rotaprint Ltd

Hamamatsu – Euroteck Systems UK Ltd

*Hamba (Germany) – cup filling and sealing machines – Engelmann & Buckham Ltd

*Hambi (Germany) – mesh bending and cutting equipment – La Roche

Hamech – Stacatruc

Hamech – reach trucks, counter balance fork trucks and tow tractors – Crown Lift Trucks Ltd

Hameg – Fieldway Supplies Ltd

Hameg – Alpha Electronics Southern Ltd

Hamelin Stationery – children's colouring and activity – Hamelin Stationery Ltd

Hamelin Stationery – educational and commercial stationery – Hamelin Stationery Ltd

Hamil – wire and wire rope – Webster & Horsfall Ltd

Hamilton – brucshes, tools, rollers & decorating sundries – Hamilton Acorn Ltd

Hamilton Beach – Ascot Wholesale Ltd

Hamilton Beach – Kitchen, bar blenders & drinks mixers – Metcalfe Catering Equipment Ltd

Hamilton Litestat (United Kingdom) – switches, sockets, dimmers, etc – R Hamilton & Co. Ltd

Hamish Hamilton – adult fiction and non-fiction - hardback and paperback – Penguin Books Ltd

Hamlet Craft Tools – Woodturning and woodcarving tools – The Toolpost

Hamlin – reed switches, reed relays, proximity switches and shock sensors – Hamlin Electronics Europe Ltd

Hamlin – Cyclops Electronics Ltd

Hamlin - Reed switches, Reed relays, proximity switches, shock sensors – Hamlin Electronics Europe Ltd

Hamm – Harrier Fluid Power Ltd

Hammell – The Winnen Furnishing Company

Hammell Furniture – The Winnen Furnishing Company

Hammelmann – pumps – Calder Ltd

Hammercote – hammered enamel – Co-Var Ltd

Hammercote – hammer finish enamel – Spencer Coatings Ltd

Hammerite – metalcare products – Akzonobel

Hammerite Garage Door Enamel – garage door enamel – Hammerite Products Ltd

Hammerite Metal Finish – rust preventative paint – Hammerite Products Ltd

Hammerite Radiator Enamel – radiator enamel – Hammerite Products Ltd

Hammerite Underbody Seal – underseal – Hammerite Products Ltd

Hammerite Waxoyl – rustproofer – Hammerite Products Ltd

Hammersley – fine bone china tableware and giftware – Aynsley China Ltd

Hammond – Selectronix Ltd

Hammond – Perancea Ltd

Hammond – vacuum – AESpump

Hampshire – Review Display Systems Ltd

Hampshire Press – Design Print Copy Southampton – Hampshire Press

Hamptons – estate agents – Hamptons International

Hamra – clothing – Delaval

Hamster Baskets – freezer storage system – Hamster Baskets

HAMWORTHY – Hydraulic & Offshore Supplies Ltd

Hamworthy Belliss and Morcom – air and gas compressors – Gardner Denver Ltd

Han – Harting Ltd

Han – UK Office Direct

Han Axial Screw Module – Harting Ltd

Han DD – Harting Ltd

Han DD Module – Harting Ltd

Han E – Harting Ltd

Han - Eco – Harting Ltd

Han HC – Harting Ltd

Han - Modular – Harting Ltd

Han - Port – Harting Ltd

Han - Power – Harting Ltd

Han - Power S – Harting Ltd

Han - Power T – Harting Ltd

Han - Q – Harting Ltd

Han Q 4/2 – Harting Ltd

Han Q 5/0 – Harting Ltd

Han Q 7/0 – Harting Ltd

Han Q 8/0 – Harting Ltd

Han - Snap – Harting Ltd

Han - Yellock – Harting Ltd

*Han Young (Korea, Republic of) – controls – Tempatron Controls

Hancommander – profile cutting machine – Easab Cutting Systems

Hand Held Steam Gun – Pressure washers – B & G Cleaning Systems Ltd

*Hand in Glove (U.S.A.) – clean room vinyl gloves – Cravenmount Ltd

Hand Over Fist – Forward Chemicals Ltd

Hand Stamps – marks metals – Universal Marking Systems Ltd

Handell – Therma Group

Handguard (United Kingdom) – barrier cream – David Somerset Skincare

Handi Pumps – Alfa Laval Eastbourne Ltd

Handi-Spin – Seward Ltd

Handibags – polythene bags – Palco Industries Ltd

HandiBand – mini stainless steel repair clamps for all types of small bore pipes size 1/2" - 2" nominal bore – Viking Johnson

Handibit – the countersink with the handle – Q E P Ltd

Handiburr – reamers and chamferbits – G & J Hall Ltd

HandiClamp – stainless steel repair clamp – Viking Johnson

Handies – impregnated wipes – Branova Cleaning Services

Handiloo – self contained portable toilets – William G Search Ltd

Handipack – multi-purpose epoxy system – Gurit UK Ltd

Handipark – single bay parking bollard – Apt Controls Ltd

Handitrack (United Kingdom) – plastic curtain track (coil) – Integra Products

Handiwype – wiping product (paper) – Staples Disposables Ltd

Handle-Tie – polythene bags – Palco Industries Ltd

Handles – wood – Pilkingtons Ltd

Handoll – rotary gear pumps – Albany Pumps

Handrinse – basin – Armitage Shanks Ltd

Hands & Feet – coloured pumices – Vivalis Ltd

Hands of Wycombe – Boardroom Furniture – Bucon Ltd

Hands On – Forward Chemicals Ltd

Hands Soap Shop – Manufacture of soaps, body butters, creams, lotions, lip balms, bath products, and room scenters – Hands Industries Ltd

Handscan – miniature hand propelled MFL scanner for detection of underfloor corrosion in above ground storage tanks – Silverwing UK Ltd

Handsmoke – distress smoke signal – Pains Wessex Ltd

Handy – instantaneous handwash unit – Heatrae Sadia

Handy Dri – warm air hand drier – Heatrae Sadia

Handy Gas – S J Wharton Ltd

Handy Mains – inveter – Smet Ltd

handy rollers – Printmaker rollers – Hawthorn Printmaker Supplies

Handy Scan – EOBD scan tool – Crypton Ltd

HandyGuard – rubber gloves – Paul Murray plc

Handypack – flexible container for paint – Akzonobel

Handyshine – quick shoe polish – Cherry Blossom Ltd

Hanes – T-Shirts Sweatshirts Poloshirts Hooded Sweatshirts Clothing – A4 Apparel Ltd

Hang-Strip – Display strip for multiple packs, point of sale – Index

Hang up Bags – PP bag with adhesive hook pre applied – Index

Hang-Ups – Self adhesive die cut hooks – Index

HANGCHA – Chaintec Ltd

Hangglider Suspension File – Snopake Ltd

*Hangsterfer's (U.S.A.) – cutting oils – Macinnes Tooling Ltd

HANGZHOU – Chaintec Ltd

Hankinson – Harrier Fluid Power Ltd

HANKISON – Hydraulic & Offshore Supplies Ltd

Hankook – T W Ward CNC Machinery Ltd

Hann – Harrier Fluid Power Ltd

Hanna – winter barley variety – Limagrain UK Ltd

*Hannabach (Germany) – classic guitar strings – John Hornby Skewes & Co. Ltd

Hannay (U.S.A.) – hose and cable reels – Metool Products Ltd

HANNIFIN – Hydraulic & Offshore Supplies Ltd

Hannilase – vegetarian rennet – Chr. Hansen (UK) Ltd

Hannoart Gloss – Coated Paper – Mcnaughton James Paper Group Ltd

Hannoart Matt – Coated Paper – Mcnaughton James Paper Group Ltd

Hannoart Silk – Coated Paper – Mcnaughton James Paper Group Ltd

Hanomag – Harrier Fluid Power Ltd

Hanovia – manufacturer of ultra violet disinfection equipment – Hanovia Ltd

Hansen – quick release hose couplings – Guyson International Ltd

Hansen – Bristol Fluid System Technologies Ltd

HANSER HYDRAULIC – Hydraulic & Offshore Supplies Ltd

Hansil – County Construction Chemicals Ltd

Hanson – Gem Tool Hire & Sales Ltd

Hanson – international building materials company – Hanson Building Products

*Hanson Brass – Equipline

Hanson White – cards, gift wrap, ribbon, badges, bows and stationery related products – Gibson Hanson Graphics Ltd

Hanta – Harrier Fluid Power Ltd

*Hantarex (Italy) – video monitors, information display monitors, presentation monitors, video games monitors – Hantarex International Ltd

Hanwha (Korea, Republic of) – cnc swiss type turning centres – Citizen Machinery UK Ltd

*HAPA (Switzerland) – on-line printing systems – Romaco Holdings UK Ltd

Hapla – adhesive paddings for surgical and chiropadial use – Cuxson Gerrard & Company Ltd

Happy Hands – gloves – Peshawear UK Ltd

Har-bus – Harting Ltd

Har-bus HM – Harting Ltd

har-flex connectors – Harting Ltd

har-link – Harting Ltd

Har-mik – Harting Ltd

Harax – Harting Ltd

Harben – jetting equipment – Robert Craig & Sons Ltd

Harben & Neolith – high pressure water jetting equipment – Flowplant Group Ltd

Harben & Neolith - Aqua – high pressure water jetting equipment – Flowplant Group Ltd

Harbex – plumbing goods, sanitary ware and ironmongery – Harris & Bailey Ltd

Harbex-Ware – baths, plumbers' brassware and copper tubes – Harris & Bailey Ltd

Harbormaster – Sykes Marine Hydromaster Ltd

Harbourguard – solid buoyancy booms – Oil Pollution Environmental Control Ltd

Harbourite – Phoenix Weighing Services Ltd

Harbourite – fine fibrillated polypropylene fibres – Propex Concrete Systems Ltd

*Harbro Ruminant – Harbro Ltd

Harbuilt – Stacatruc

Harco (U.S.A.) – cathodic protection systems – Alexander Cardew Ltd

Harco Pack – plumbing unit – Harton Services Ltd

Harcon – refuse and clinical waste containers – Hardall International Ltd

Hardall – refuse chutes and linen chutes – Hardall International Ltd

Hardall Bergmann – refuse compactors – Hardall International Ltd

Hardall Gannet – refuse compactors – Hardall International Ltd

Hardall Ise – sink waste disposers and kitchen compactors – Hardall International Ltd

Hardall Trident – refuse compactors – Hardall International Ltd

Hardcore – processed natural drill diamond – Diamond Detectors

HARDENED & TEMPERED – HIGH TENSILE CARBON SPRING STEEL STRIP – Cold Rolled Strip Stock

Hardicoat – road surfacings – Miles Macadam Ltd

Hardicrete – road surfacings – Miles Macadam Ltd

Hardigg – C P Cases Ltd

Hardigrip – road surfacings – Miles Macadam Ltd

Hardinge Bridgeport – R K International Machine Tools Ltd

Hardipave – road surfacings – Miles Macadam Ltd

Hardman – S J Wharton Ltd

Hardox – abrasion resistant steel plate – Swedish Steel

Hardox - Weldox - Armox – Swedish Steel

Hardrive – pre-cast jointed pile – Simplex Westpile Limited

Hardrive Precast Piles – Simplex Westpile Limited

Hardrock Dual Density Range – flat roofs – Rockwool Rockpanel B V

hardware.com – Reseller of IT networking equipmentISO 9001:2000 accredited and BS7799 Part 1 and Part 2 compliant. – Hardware.com
HARDWEB BRIDGEWEB – machining centres – R K International Machine Tools Ltd
Hardwood Dimensions – laminated wood products, panels and machined products, hardwood dimension stock – Hardwood Dimensions Holdings Ltd
Hardy – cabin cruisers, fishing and work boats – Hardy Marine Ltd
Hardy Advanced Composites – bespoke composite tubing – Hardy & Greys Ltd
Hardy Amies – dress designers, sunglass designers, leather goods designers and general designers – Hardy Amies London Ltd
Hardy & Hanson (United Kingdom) – woollen and synthetic felt – Hardy & Hanson Ltd
Harefield – flexible rubber doors – B I S Door Systems Ltd
Harewood – bricks – Ibstock Brick Ltd
Harewood Burgundy Rustic – Ibstock Brick Ltd
Harewood Charcoal Grey – Ibstock Brick Ltd
Harewood Russet Buff – Ibstock Brick Ltd
Harewood Russet Cream – Ibstock Brick Ltd
Harewood Russet Orange – Ibstock Brick Ltd
Harewood Sunset Multi Red – Ibstock Brick Ltd
Harford Control – production of quality systems – Harford Control Ltd
Hargreaves – embroidery and screen printing of workwear/leisure clothing and promotional business gifts – Hargreaves Promotions
HARLAN – Chaintec Ltd
Harland Europa – High speed rotary labelling system – Harland Machine Systems Ltd
Harland Simon – electric drive and control equipment and computer systems UPS and battery support systems, process and machine automation – Harland Simon plc
Harlech – Prima Care
Harlequin – articles of clothing – Norland Burgess Ltd
Harlequin – Fuel storage products – Clarehill Plastics Ltd
Harlequin – bricks – Blockleys Brick Ltd
Harlequin – The Paper Company Ltd
Harlequin Chenille – Sirdar Spinning Ltd
Harlequin Fabrics – The Winnen Furnishing Company
Harlequin Intelligence – suite of products for investigation management and intelligence analysis – Global Graphics Software Ltd
Harlequin Screening Library – speciality halftone screening options for scriptworks – Global Graphics Software Ltd
Harlestone Wooden Gates – Dr A J Burch - Harlestone Road Surgery
Harley – Capex Office Interiors
***Harley (U.S.A.)** – cushion adhesive backing – Plastotype
Harlow Bros – poultry houses, ventilation fans and evaporative cooling systems – Harlow Brothers Ltd
Harman Motive – loudspeakers for the international automotive industry – Harman International
Harmer – roof outlets – Ashworth
Harmer AV Retro-gully – refurbishment roof outlet – Alumasc Exterior Building Products
Harmer Deck Uni-Ring – paving supports – Alumasc Exterior Building Products
***Harmer Insulated Outlets (Germany)** – roof outlets – Alumasc Exterior Building Products
Harmer Products – Cembrit Ltd
Harmonika in vinyl – sliding partitions – Becker Sliding Partitions Ltd
Harmonika in Wood – sliding partitions – Becker Sliding Partitions Ltd
Harmony – carpets – Penthouse Carpets Ltd
Harmony – glass and acrylic shower enclosures – Novellini UK Ltd
Harmony – shower curtains and panels – Jendico Ltd
Harmony – 600mm double oven – Indesit Company UK Ltd
Harmony – porcelain and fine china – Horwood Homeware Ltd
Harmony – luxury motor caravan – Auto Sleepers Ltd
Harmony – stationery manillas and pressboards – Weidmann Whiteley Ltd
Harmony – milking machine cluster/liners – Delaval
Harmony – pushbutton & control solution – Schneider
Harmony Extra – herbicide – Du Pont UK Ltd
Harmsco – Harrier Fluid Power Ltd
Harnessflex – conduit systems for vehicle industry – Harness Flex Ltd
Harnessflex – Adaptaflex Ltd
Haro (Taiwan) – Bicycles – Moore Large & Co. Ltd
Harpac – refuse compactors – Hardall International Ltd
Harpac Centaur – refuse compactors – Hardall International Ltd
Harpac Jenpak – refuse compactors – Hardall International Ltd
Harper Collins – publishers of fiction and non-fiction books in various interest areas – Harpercollins Publishers Ophelia House
Harper's & Queen – magazine – National Magazine Company Ltd
Harpon – supported latex gloves – Mapa Spontex
***Harpoon (United Kingdom)** – men's and ladies overall protective clothing and workwear, civic and super civic brands – Harveys Nursery
Harpoon – hardware screening accelerator – Global Graphics Software Ltd
Harrier – envelopes – Eagle Envelopes Ltd
Harrier – fishing tackle – Daiwa Sports Ltd
HARRIER – Hydraulic & Offshore Supplies Ltd
Harrier – cycle – Falcon Cycles Ltd
Harrier – top access lighting – Designplan Lighting Ltd
HARRIER FILTERS – Hydraulic & Offshore Supplies Ltd
Harries Board - Food preparation boardsHygienplas - Wall cladding – A B G Rubber & Plastics Ltd
HarriesBoard – A B G Rubber & Plastics Ltd
Harrington – S J Wharton Ltd
Harris – paint brushes, paint rollers, painters tools, shoe brushes & paint pads – L G Harris & Co. Ltd
Harris – gas welding equipment and accessories – Lincoln Electric UK Ltd
Harris – Trafalgar Tools
Harris County – Try & Lilly Ltd
Harris Looms – hand weaving equipment – Emmerich Berlon Ltd
Harris- paint brushes, paint rollers, paint pads, painters tools,decorative brushes and rollers, household & shoe brushes. – L G Harris & Co. Ltd
Harris-Walton Lifting Gear – lifting tackle – Harris Walton Lifting Gear Ltd
Harrison – metal turning lathes – T S Harrison & Sons Ltd
Harrison – 600 Group plc
Harrison – centre lathes, manual & CNC – R K International Machine Tools Ltd
Harrison – consulting geotechnical materials and environmental engineers – Harrison Group Enviromental Ltd
Harrison – Red House Industrial Services Ltd
Harrison m250 lathes – Phil Geesin Machinery Ltd
Harrison m300 lathes – Phil Geesin Machinery Ltd
Harrison m400 lathes – Phil Geesin Machinery Ltd
Harrison m500 lathes – Phil Geesin Machinery Ltd
Harrison - metal turning lathes, Alpha Plus S - the ultimate turning machine. – T S Harrison & Sons Ltd
Harrison V 350 lathes – Phil Geesin Machinery Ltd
Harrison V 390 lathes – Phil Geesin Machinery Ltd
Harrison V460 lathes – Phil Geesin Machinery Ltd
Harrison V550 lathes – Phil Geesin Machinery Ltd
Harrod Industrial – Harrod UK Ltd
Harrod Sport – Harrod UK Ltd
Harrow – bath – Ideal Standard Ltd
Harry Hall – equestrian clothing – Matchmakers International Ltd
Harry West – agricultural buildings, welding services – H West Prees Ltd
Harsh – hydraulic tipping gears/mechanical sheets/on board weighing – Harsh Ltd
Hart – Radir Ltd
Hart – graphites recarburisers, carbon charcoal and foundry products – David Hart Alcester Ltd
Hart Coating Technology – metals and chemicals for specialised technical areas of the coating industry – Hart Materials Ltd
Hart Scientific – Radir Ltd
Hartford – T W Ward CNC Machinery Ltd
Harting – connectors – Anglia
Harting – European Technical Sales Ltd
Harting – Cyclops Electronics Ltd
Harting – connectors – Bearwood Engineering Supplies
Harting Integrated Solutions (HIS) – Harting Ltd
Harting Push Pull LC Duplex, IP67 – Harting Ltd
Harting Push Pull RJ45, IP67 – Harting Ltd
Hartingdon House – mail order catalogue – J D Williams Mail Order Group
Hartland (United Kingdom) – switches, sockets, dimmers, etc. – R Hamilton & Co. Ltd
Hartley Botanic – aluminium structures, greenhouses – Hartley Botanic Ltd
Hartman – Relays – Dax International Ltd
Hartmann – Egg boxes – Dispak Ltd
Hartmann&Braun – European Technical Sales Ltd
HARTMANN & LAMMLE – Hydraulic & Offshore Supplies Ltd
***Hartner (Germany)** – drills – Macinnes Tooling Ltd
Harton Metro – unvented package – Harton Services Ltd
Hartonaut – boiler packaged unit – Harton Services Ltd
Hartonstore – combination tanks hot and cold – Harton Services Ltd
Hartshill – spinal fixation system – Surgicraft Ltd
Hartwell – vehicle conversion – Hartwell plc
Hartwell – Access fasteners – Zygology Ltd
Harvard – Harrier Fluid Power Ltd
Harvest – Portman Building Society
Harvest – carpets – Cormar Carpets
Harvest Aran – yarns – Stylecraft
Harvest Chunky – yarns – Stylecraft
Harvest DK – yarns – Stylecraft
Harvest Gold – Portman Building Society
Harvest Star – polypropylene baler twine – Steve Orr Ltd
Harvester – bread flour – Allied Mills
Harvey – office furniture – E W Marshall Ltd
Harvey Softeners – water softeners – Harvey Water Softeners Ltd
Harvey Wire – A Harvey & Co. Ltd
Harvie & Hudson – shirtmakers and tie specialists – Harvie & Hudson Ltd
Harwell – Rotadex Systems Ltd
Harwood Sandal Rustic – Ibstock Brick Ltd
Hasa (Export) – export used commercial vehicles & spare parts – C M S Kent Ltd
Hasbro – toys – Hasbro UK Ltd
Hasco – European Technical Sales Ltd
***Hasegawa (Japan)** – plastic model kits – Amerang Group Ltd
Hasflex – comprehensive range of flexible ducting – Hotchkiss Air Supply
Haskel – air driven pumps and boosters – Haskel Europe Ltd
Haskel – Pumps – Hi-Power Hydraulics
Haskins – souvenir and general giftware – Shaw Munster Ltd
Hasler – Helman Workwear
***Hassia (Germany)** – thermo forming, filling and sealing machines – Engelmann & Buckham Ltd
Hastelloy (U.S.A.) – high performance nickel base alloys for corrosive and high temperature service – Haynes International Ltd
Hastings – Harrier Fluid Power Ltd
Hatch – Aspen International Ltd
Hatch Tape – Cullen Metcalfe & Co. Ltd
Hatfield-Gasparinl – press brakes and guillotines – Hatfields Machine Tools Ltd
Hatfield Precision – press brake tooling – Hatfields Machine Tools Ltd
Hathaway – taps – Armitage Shanks Ltd
Hatt Kitchens – kitchen units – Pembar Ltd
HATTERSLEY – Hydraulic & Offshore Supplies Ltd
Hattersley - Macart – warping and weaving machines – Macart Textiles Machinery Ltd
Hattersley Valves – F W Sibley Ltd
Hatz – Aktion Automotive Ltd
Hatz – A T Wilde & Son Ltd
Haug – European Technical Sales Ltd
HAUHINCO – Hydraulic & Offshore Supplies Ltd
Haulmark – remould truck tyres – Tyre Renewals Ltd
Haulotte – Harrier Fluid Power Ltd
HAULOTTE – Chaintec Ltd
Hauloutte Platforms – Accesscaff International Ltd
Hava Shapiro – Process Equipment and Machinery – Hava Shapiro 1878 Ltd
Havana – sink – Armitage Shanks Ltd
Havelocktagou – modular partitioning system – Havelock Europa plc
Haven – Direct Instrument Hire Ltd
Haven – bathroom sets, shower curtains – Fogarty Filled Products Ltd
Haven Leisure – summer holidays and short breaks – Bourne Leisure
Haverhill – generators and welders – Robert Craig & Sons Ltd
Haverhill Weekly News – newspapers – Cambridge Newspapers Ltd
Havit – Port/Pipe Flanges for SAE 3000 & 6000 Series, Cetop, DIN, and ISO – J B J Techniques Ltd
HAVIT HYRAULIK – Hydraulic & Offshore Supplies Ltd
Havoline – Chevron
Havoline Motor Oil – lubricants – Chevron
HAWE – European Technical Sales Ltd
HAWE – Hydraulic & Offshore Supplies Ltd
Hawe – high pressure controls & hyd systems – Koppen & Lethem Ltd
Hawe – Aztech Components Ltd
HAWK – Data logger – Halcyon Solutions
Hawk – Jointing compound products for threaded joints – Fernox
Hawk – cycles – Professional Cycle Marketing
Hawk – carpets – Interface Europe Ltd
Hawk – non contact 3 axis measuring system – Vision Engineering Ltd
Hawk – envelopes – Eagle Envelopes Ltd
Hawk – Alpha Electronics Southern Ltd
Hawk I – programmable controller – AMOT
Hawke – cable glands, junction boxes, transit systems and connectors – Wellhead Electrical Supplies
Hawker – batteries – Invensys PLC
Hawkesworth Appliance Testing – PAT Testing Services / Portable Appliance Testing from Hawkesworth PAT Testing – Hawkesworth Appliance Testing
Hawkridge – solicitors – Hawkridge & Co.
Hawksley – medical equipment – Hawksley & Sons Ltd
Haworth – office furniture – BBI Business Interiors Ltd

Haworth - office furniture Senator International - office furniture Bisley Office Equipment - office furniture – BBI Business Interiors Ltd
Haws – watering cans, brass spray roses and planters – Eclipse Sprayers Ltd
Haws – watering cans and spray roses – Haws Watering Cans
Haws watering cans – watering cans, brass spray roses and planters – Eclipse Sprayers Ltd
Hay 2000 – preservative of hay – Agil Chemicals Products
Haydn – Kuwait Petroleum International Lubricants UK Ltd
Hayes Brake LLC (U.S.A.) – hydraulic & mechanical disc brakes – Robert Cupitt Ltd
Haynes (U.S.A.) – high performance nickel and cobalt base alloys for high temperature and corrosive service – Haynes International Ltd
Haynes & Cann – boots for military aircrews, fire crash crews and parachute jumping instructors, fabric flying helmets and corresponding ear capsules and rapid fastening devices for footwear – Haynes & Cann Ltd
Haynes Owners Workshop Manual – cars and motorcycle collection workshop diy manuals – J Haynes Ltd
Hayporter – Harrier Fluid Power Ltd
Hayruard – Harrier Fluid Power Ltd
Hayter – grass cutting equipment – Hayter Ltd
***Hayter** – Route V J Horticultural
Hayter Professional and Domestic Range – grass cutting equipment – Hayter Ltd
Hayward Tyler – boiler circulation pumps, submersible subsea pumps and electric motors, turbines and process pumps – Hayward Tyler Ltd
HAYWARD TYLER – J P Whitter Ltd
Haz-Mat Stak – storage racking – Rack International UK Ltd
Haz-Tab Granules – absorbent disinfectant granules – Guest Medical Ltd
Haz-Tabs – chlorine disinfectant tablets – Guest Medical Ltd
Hazardous Area Product Review – An industry publication reviewing products and services for the industry – 21st Century Energy Publications Ltd
Haze – UK Office Direct
HBE (Germany) – flexible shaft couplings – Centa Transmissions
HBE – Harrier Fluid Power Ltd
HBS – Hydraulic & Offshore Supplies Ltd
HC – Chaintec Ltd
HD – rising arm barriers – Apt Controls Ltd
HD Power – marine diesel engines – Perkins Engines Group Ltd
HD Security Barrier – heavy duty rising arm parking barrier – Apt Controls Ltd
HD Signal – standard hydraulic cylinders with integrated electrical switching to signal piston rod position, adjustable on extension and retraction – Eland Engineering Company
HDLT – A A T I Ltd
HDPE – Naylor Specialists Plastics
HDYRAULIC NORD – Hydraulic & Offshore Supplies Ltd
Head Funk – the funkiest hair styling range – F M C G Ltd
Head Girl – hair accessories – Paul Murray plc
Headcracker – cask beer – Woodforde's Norfolk Ales
Headliner – analysis books – Exaclair Ltd
Headlines – hair care products – P M S International Group plc
***Headway** – brand name – Headway Music Audio Ltd
Headway – books – Hachette UK Ltd
Heal's – home furnishings and furniture – Heal's
Heald – Red House Industrial Services Ltd
Heals Of Halifax – textile testing and quality control equipment – James H Heal & Co. Ltd
Health Boost – Health tonic – Supplements For Pets Ltd
Health & Homeopathy – magazine – British Homeopathic Association
Health & Hygiene – Facilities Staff Training
Health & Safety Product Review – An industry publication reviewing products and services for the industry. – 21st Century Energy Publications Ltd
Health & Sickness Cash Benefit Plan – Western Provident Association Ltd
Health & Spa – Hotel Complimentary Products
Healthcrafts – vitamin & mineral range – Perrigo UK
Healthwise – Western Provident Association Ltd
Healthy Eating – Facilities Staff Training
Heart – flavourings – Cargill Flavor Systems UK Ltd
Heart Brand – flavourings – Cargill Flavor Systems UK Ltd
Heartbeat – point of sale display hooks and fittings – Heartbeat Manufacturing Ltd
Hearts Cruisers – cruising holidays – Richardsons Stalham Ltd
Heat-Rad – gas fired, tubular and overhead radiant heaters – Horizon Mechanical Services International Ltd
Heat-Saver – warm air re-cycling units – Horizon Mechanical Services International Ltd
Heat Transfer Technology – Fabdec Ltd
Heat treatment – Oceaneering Asset Integrity
***Heat-Wave (Far East)** – leisureware – Remys Ltd
Heatcraft – evaporators – Bearwood Engineering Supplies
Heater/Mixers – bituminous compounds (LPG fired) white/yellow line materials – Thomas Coleman Engineering Ltd
Heatex – Manufacturer of electric process heating equipment and controls for safe and hazardous areas – EXHEAT Ltd
Heatguard – temperature control valve – Reliance Water Controls Ltd
Heath DK – yarn – Stylecraft
Heath Wines (Australia) – Patriarche Wine Agencies
Heathcoat 1808 with Portrait of J.H. – textiles – Heathcoat Fabrics Ltd
Heathcoat Fabrics – industrial fabrics and corporate workwear – Heathcoat Fabrics Ltd
Heather Berber – carpets - wilton – Brintons Carpets Ltd
Heather Cameron Foods – meringue manufacturer – Lees Of Scotland Ltd
Heather DK – yarn – Stylecraft
Heather Valley – mail order catalogue – J D Williams Mail Order Group
***Heathfield (Belgium)** – slate – Cembrit Ltd
Heathylee Guanaco – Heathylee House Farm
Heatkeeper Homes – Walker Timber Ltd
Heatomatic – fan assisted heater – Kenlowe Accessories & Co. Ltd
Heatovent – Glen Dimplex UK Ltd
***Heatpak (Netherlands)** – packaged boiler house – Stertil UK Ltd
Heatpipes – Thermacore Ltd
Heatrae – electric showers and water heaters – Heatrae Sadia
Heatrae Sadia – electric instantaneous water heaters and electric showers – Heatrae Sadia
Heatrae Sadia – electric water heaters and electric showers – Heatrae Sadia
Heatrae Sadia – Baxi Group
Heatrunner – UK Office Direct
Heatslave – oil combi – Worcester Bosch Group Ltd
Heatslave - Highflow – floor standing gas combination boilers – Worcester Bosch Group Ltd
Heatstore – space heating and electric showers – City Electrical Factors Ltd
Heavenly Delights – Kent Frozen Foods Ltd
Heavithane – solid tyred wheels – Brauer Ltd
Heavy Duty anchors – heavy duty sleeve anchors with automatic torque control. – Hilti GB Ltd
Heavy Duty Corolux – p.v.c. roof sheeting – Ariel Plastics Ltd
Heavy Duty Glide-Out – storage racking – Rack International UK Ltd
Heaxagon R Save & Prosper – Client investment administration – J P Morgan Ltd
Hebor – European Technical Sales Ltd
Hebridean – Try & Lilly Ltd
***Hechinger (Germany)** – quartz clock movements – A G Thomas Bradford Ltd
Hecnum – 55% Cu/45% Ni electric resistance alloy – Omega Resistance Wire Ltd
Hectavator – ridgid, hinged & trailed cultivators – Brown's Agricultural Machinery Company Ltd
Hedelios – multiaxis VMC – C Dugard Ltd Machine Tools
HEDEN-DANTRUCK – Chaintec Ltd
Hedgemaster – Econ Engineering Ltd
Hedges L260 – snuff – Imperial Tobacco Group PLC
Heenan – PWM AC inverters, eddy current drives and dynamometers – A T B Laurence Scott Ltd
Heenan – European Technical Sales Ltd
Hefty – range of polyethelane trays – Pregis Rigid Packaging Ltd
Heid – Red House Industrial Services Ltd
Heidelberg – A M C Rollers Ltd
Heidelberg – Merlin Precision Engineering Ltd
***Heidelberg (Germany)** – printing machines – Heidelberg Graphic Equipment Ltd
***Heidelberg Harris (France)** – web offset printing machines – Heidelberg Graphic Equipment Ltd
Heidenhain – C & H Precision Measuring Systems Ltd
Heidenhain – HEIDENHAIN GB LTD
Heidenhain – digital readout equipment – Halifax Numerical Controls Ltd
Heidenhain – Encoders UK
Heidra – 4" and 6" hydraulically driven dirty water submersible pumps – Godwin Pumps Ltd
Heidrun – Heidrun Europlastic Products – Lunex Ltd
Heil – Harrier Fluid Power Ltd
Heinemann – educational book publishers – Pearson Eduction Ltd
***Heinrich Wagner Sinto (Germany)** – mould making and casting lines – Pearson Panke Ltd
Heinz – UK Office Direct
Heinz 57 – food manufacturers – H J Heinz Co. Ltd
Heinz Mayer Clamps – European Technical Sales Ltd
Heinzmann – Heinzmann UK Ltd
Heiress – hair and body shampoo – Deb R & D Ltd
Heirloom – baby wool, knitting yarns, wholly or mainly of wool for making up into babies clothing – Norland Burgess Ltd
Heiss – European Technical Sales Ltd
Heito – Selectronix Ltd
Helafos – fibre optic joint enclosures – Hellermann Tyton
Helagaine – braided cable sleeving – Hellermann Tyton
Helagrip – (PVC and LFH) cable markers – Hellermann Tyton
Helashrink – heat shrink sleeving – Hellermann Tyton
Helatemp – (PTFE) and sleeving cable markers – Hellermann Tyton
Helawrap – cable protection and routing – Hellermann Tyton
Heldite – jointing compound for petrol, diesel, oil, hydraulic fluids, water, steam and gases – Heldite Ltd
***Helen Browning's Totally Organics** – Eastbrook Farm Organic Meat Ltd
Helen David English Eccentrics – Luxurious beaded silk, velvet devoke & cashmere evening, occasionwear and scarves for women – Helen David
Helene – 18/8 s/s table cutlery – Amefa
Helerman – Hellermann Tyton
HELI – Chaintec Ltd
Heli – Stacatruc
Heli-Ball – Iscar Tools
Heli-Face – Iscar Tools
Heli-Grip – Iscar Tools
Heli-Mill – Iscar Tools
Heli Octo – Iscar Tools
Heli Pile – underpinning system – Target Fastenings Ltd
Heli Quad – Iscar Tools
Heli-Tang – Iscar Tools
Heli-Turn – Iscar Tools
Helibeam System – stainless steel rods for crack stitching, lintel repairs, creating masonry beams and structural repairs and reinforcement – Helifix Ltd
HeliBond MMZ – cementitious, injectable grout – Helifix Ltd
Helical – Helical Technology
Helical – actuators, valve rotators & other engineering components – Helical Technology
HELICHECK – optoelectronic measuring machines – Walter Machines UK Ltd
Helicoil – Screws, thread insert systems (UK) – Emhart Teknologies
HELIDEBS CONTROL – Hydraulic & Offshore Supplies Ltd
Helifix – Trac Structural Ltd
Heligear – helical geared motors – Opperman Mastergear Ltd
Helilaps – expanding internal and external laps – Kemet International Ltd
Helios – grease blocks etc – Bearwood Engineering Supplies
Helios – switched power supplies – Nortel Networks UK Ltd
Heliox – Submarine Manufacturing & Products Ltd
Helipebs – hollow grinding media for fine cement – Helipebs Controls Ltd
Helipot – BI Technologies Ltd
Heliraft – raft for helicopters – R F D Beaufort Ltd
Heliraft XDS – jettisonable liferaft systems for helicopters – R F D Beaufort Ltd
Helita – J Lacey Steeplejack Contractors Ltd
HELITECH – Hydraulic & Offshore Supplies Ltd
Helitrim – BI Technologies Ltd
Helitronic - Helicheck - Helitronic Tool Studio - Cyber Grinding – Walter Machines UK Ltd
HELITRONIC TOOL STUDIO – software for tools – Walter Machines UK Ltd
Helitune – rotor tuner vibration analysis equipment for helicopters, fixed wing and industry – Ultra Electronics
Helix – stationery, drawing instruments, cash boxes etc – Helix Trading Ltd
Helix – UK Office Direct
Helix Crystal – drawing instruments – Helix Trading Ltd
Helix Images – writing instruments – Helix Trading Ltd
Helix Lock-Down – cash boxes – Helix Trading Ltd
Helix Tanks – Linpac Allibert Ltd
Helixchanger – Helical baffle design – Wellman Thermal Services Ltd
Helixorter – automated sorting conveyor systems – Van Der Lande Industries
Hell-Cat – lubricant and cycle computers – Rsi
Heller Machine Tools Ltd – machine tools – Heller Machine Tools
Hellerine – Sleeve fitting lubricant – Hellermann Tyton
Hellerman – Hellermann Tyton
Hellerman – cable ties and markers – Wellhead Electrical Supplies
Hellerman – draughting supplies and graphic equipment suppliers – Esmond Hellerman Ltd
Hellermann – Hellermann Tyton
Hellermann Tyton – European Technical Sales Ltd
Hellermark – stainless steel identification system – Hellermann Tyton
Helmsman – lockers, cubicles & changing room furniture – Helmsman
Helmsman – Storage – Bucon Ltd
Helmsman – mainframe workload scheduling software – Fox It Ltd

Heloderm – Dead Sea medicinal products – Finders International Ltd

Helofile – twinlock filing system – Office Team

Help The Aged – national charity number 272786 – Age UK

Help the Aged – help schemes for the elderly and supply minibuses – Age UK

Help the Aged Insurance Services – Insurance Services – Age UK

Helping Hand – reaching aid for the elderly and disabled – Helping Hand Co.

Helping Hands – Derbyshire Building Society

Helsyn – synthetic rubber sleeving – Hellermann Tyton

Helter Skelter DK – yarn – Stylecraft

Heltex – Helman Workwear

HELTRONIC – tool grinding machines – Walter Machines UK Ltd

Helvar – lighting controls – Camlar Ltd

Helvin – (PVC) cable markers – Hellermann Tyton

Hema – European Technical Sales Ltd

Hemcore – horse bedding – Harlow Agricultural Merchants Ltd

Heme – test equipment – Longs Ltd

Hemel Hempstead Gazette – newspaper – Leamington Spa Courier

Hemel Hempstead Herald Express – newspaper – Leamington Spa Courier

Hemelite – lightweight concrete blocks – Tarmac Topblock Ltd

Hemlok – special blind fasteners – Zygology Ltd

Hemlok – high performance blind bolt for thin gauge materials – Avdel UK Ltd

Hempadur – 2 pack epoxy coal tars, primers, high builds, M.I.O. and finishes – Hempel UK Ltd

Hempalin – alkyd and modified alkyd, primers, undercoats and emamels – Hempel UK Ltd

Hempanyl – 1 pack vinyl primers, high builds and enamels – Hempel UK Ltd

Hempatex – 1 pack chlorinated rubber, primers, high builds and finishes – Hempel UK Ltd

Hempathane – 2 pack polyurethane enamels – Hempel UK Ltd

Hempatone – emulsion paint – Hempel UK Ltd

Hempinol – high build bituminous coatings – Hempel UK Ltd

Hemsby Holiday Centre – Richardsons Stalham Ltd

Hemsec – insulated panel systems for use in controlled temperature applications – Hemsec Group

Hen doo printed t shirts – Avalon and Lynwood

Hen doo t shirts – Avalon and Lynwood

Hen night printed t shirts – Avalon and Lynwood

Hen night t shirts – Avalon and Lynwood

Henbury – First Impressions Europe Ltd

Henderson – sliding door gear – Till & Whitehead

Hendrickson – trailer axle and suspension components – Roadlink International Ltd

Hendy Body – repair of motor vehicles at bodyshops – Hendy Ford Southampton

Hendy Ford (United Kingdom) – distribution of ford motor cars – Hendy Ford Southampton

Hendy Hire (United Kingdom) – hire of cars and commercial vehicles – Hendy Ford Southampton

Hendy Lennox Honda – distribution of honda motor cars – Hendy Ford Southampton

Hendy Truck (United Kingdom) – distribution of ford and iveco ford commercial vehicles – Hendy Ford Southampton

Hengst – Harrier Fluid Power Ltd

Hengstler – Encoders UK

Hengstler – European Technical Sales Ltd

Henkovac – vacuum packaging for meats – The Scobie & Junor Group Ltd

HENLEY – Chaintec Ltd

Henley Centre – international consulting agency – The Futures Company

Henley Vinyls – vinyl wallcoverings – Today Interiors Ltd

Hennig – European Technical Sales Ltd

Henry – air conditioning and refrigeration components – Henry Technologies Ltd

Henry – commercial cleaning equipment – Numatic International

Henry – effects editor – Quantel Ltd

Henry Nuttall – Manitowoc Food Service UK

Henry's – electronic components – Henry's Electronics Ltd

Henry Taylor – Wood turning, wood carving and woodworking tools – The Toolpost

Henschel – Harrier Fluid Power Ltd

Hensley – GET & Wear parts – Midland Steel Traders Ltd

Hensoldt – European Technical Sales Ltd

Hep20 – Wavin UK

Hepa-Air-Deluxe – hepa air cleaner for the home – Ebac

Hepco – European Technical Sales Ltd

Hepco – engineering, manufacturing and distribution of linear motion products – Hepco Motion

Hepco – Mercury Bearings Ltd

Hepworth (United Kingdom) – underground cable jointing accessories and connectors – Sicame Electrical Developments Ltd

Heraeus – European Technical Sales Ltd

Herald – electronic alarms for liquid levels – Armstrong Holden Brooke Pullen Ltd

Herald – Vi Spring Ltd

Herald Supreme – mattresses – Vi Spring Ltd

Heraldry – manufacturers of quality wax and outdoor garments – Premier World Trading Ltd

Heras – Heras Ready Fence Service

Heras Fencing – Accesscaff International Ltd

Heras Readyfence – Heras Ready Fence Service

Herbert – Red House Industrial Services Ltd

Herbi – portable CDA herbicide applicator – Micron Sprayers Ltd

Herbie – casual wear – Raves Clothing Ltd

Herbline Ayurvedic Cosmetics – Ladies herbal beauty products – Think Mortgage Solutions

Herboxane – speciality compound – Quest International UK Ltd

Herbst – toggle clamps – Welwyn Tool Group Ltd

Herbulax – herbal laxative – Perrigo UK

Hercat – cationic rosin emulsion (paper size) – Hercules Holding Ii Ltd

Hercobond – CMC solution – Hercules Holding Ii Ltd

Hercofloc – flocculants – Hercules Holding Ii Ltd

Hercolyn – resins – Hercules Holding Ii Ltd

Hercosett – wool shrinkproofing agent – Hercules Holding Ii Ltd

Hercotac – modified hydrocarbon resins – Hercules Holding Ii Ltd

Hercules – marine data system – B & G Ltd

Hercules – industrial chemicals – Hercules Holding Ii Ltd

Hercules – Berry Systems

Hercules – bicycles – Raleigh UK Ltd

HERCULES HYDRAULICS – Hydraulic & Offshore Supplies Ltd

Hercules Piling – Balfour Beatty Living Places

Hercules Piling System – driven precast concrete pile – Balfour Beatty Living Places

*Herd Care – Cattle Information Services

Herfurth – high frequency, plastic welding equipment, radio frequency and ultrasonics – Xfurth Ltd

Herfurth Laser Technology – laser welding equipment – Xfurth Ltd

Herga – footswitches – Herga Electric

Hergair – remote control air switches – Herga Electric

Hergalite – intrinsic fibre optic sensors – Herga Electric

HERION – Hydraulic & Offshore Supplies Ltd

Herion – control valves – Norgren Ltd

Herion – European Technical Sales Ltd

Herion – Southern Valve & Fitting Co. Ltd

Herion – B L Pneumatics Ltd

Heritage – damask print wallpapers & borders – Today Interiors Ltd

Heritage – wooden window and door frames – Benlowe Windows

Heritage – bricks – Blockleys Brick Ltd

Heritage – paints of historic colours – Akzonobel

Heritage – Atlantis European Ltd

Heritage – carpet – Cormar Carpets

Heritage – soffits cladding – L B Plastics Ltd

Heritage – luxury touring caravans for the home & export markets – Fleetwood Group Holdings Ltd

Heritage fairway – Same as epic (01273) 220116 – Pareto Golf Ltd

Heritage Small Prints – wallpapers & borders – Today Interiors Ltd

*Herkules (Germany) – roll lathes and grinding machines – British & Continental Traders Ltd

Herman Miller – Capex Office Interiors

Herman Miller – Furniture – Bucon Ltd

Hermann Sewerin GmbH – Sewerin Ltd

*Hermes (Germany) – fibre discs – Indasa Abrasives UK Ltd

Hermetic – canned motor centrifugal pumps – Axflow

Hermetite – gasket compounds and sealants – Hammerite Products Ltd

Hermetite – adhesives – Bearwood Engineering Supplies

Hermicoat – Graphic Board – Mcnaughton James Paper Group Ltd

Hero – purification equipment – Ovivo UK Ltd

*Hero – Shelfguard Systems

Heron (United Kingdom) – PVC duckboard – Plastic Extruders Ltd

Heron International – property developers – Heron Cardiff Properties Ltd

Heronair – Open grid tubular construction rolls that offer an economical alternative – Plastic Extruders Ltd

Herongripa – 15mm high, wide spaced open grid rolls for food processing applications – Plastic Extruders Ltd

Heronrib – Multi directional drainage matting with Sanatized additives for 100% barefoot hygiene – Plastic Extruders Ltd

Herontile – Open grid hygienic EVA tiles with Sanitized additives – Plastic Extruders Ltd

Herontred – Vulcanised rubber tiles for sports & play flooring – Plastic Extruders Ltd

Herringbone – carpets – Cormar Carpets

Herritage cashmeer – Heritage Cashmere UK Ltd

Herrmidifer – humidification systems – Trion The Division Of Ruskin Air Management Ltd

Hertbert Equipment – spares for alfred herbert machines – Herbert Tooling Ltd

Herz – Rural Energy

HESSELMAN – Hydraulic & Offshore Supplies Ltd

Hesston – Harrier Fluid Power Ltd

Hetak – European Technical Sales Ltd

Heuft Basic – automatic on-line quality assurance system – Heuft Ltd

Heuft Spectrum – automatic on-line quality assurance system – Heuft Ltd

Heversham – fabric collection – Brian Yates

Hew Kabel – electric cables – Bearwood Engineering Supplies

Hewden – tool hire and tool sales – Hewden Hire Centres Ltd

*HEWI (Germany) – architectural ironmongery – Hewi UK Ltd

HEWI Nylon – door furniture balustrade, bathroom and cloakroom accessories – Hewi UK Ltd

Hewitt & May, Classic V1 – Hewitt & May (Shirtmakers) Ltd

Hewlett Packard – Lamphouse Ltd

Hewlett-Packard – Zones4U Ltd

Hewlett Packard – software/hardware – Bearwood Engineering Supplies

Hewlett-Packard – Cyclops Electronics Ltd

Hewlett Packard – Quintech Computer Systems Ltd

HEX-AIR – Elastomer Engineering Ltd

Hexacompact – Grundfos Pumps Ltd

HexaFlex (Germany) – flexible shaft couplings – Lenze UK Ltd

Hexaflex – elastomeric coatings and sealants – Hexham Sealants Ltd

Hexibit – power tool accessories – G & J Hall Ltd

Hexquisite – hexagonal range black base with clear lid – Pregis Rigid Packaging Ltd

Hexsert – one sided threaded fastener to provide high torque strength – Avdel UK Ltd

Hexsert – anchor nut – Zygology Ltd

Hexware – hinged hexagonal range black base clear top – Pregis Rigid Packaging Ltd

Hexyl Benzoate – perfume speciality – Quest International UK Ltd

Hexyl Crotonate – perfume speciality – Quest International UK Ltd

*Hey Pesto! – Tideford Organic Foods Ltd

Hey Presto – Compact Discs – K B Import & Export Ltd

Heypac – Hydraulic Component & Systems Ltd

HEYPAC – Hydraulic & Offshore Supplies Ltd

Heypac Pumps – hydraulic power units – A C Hydraulics Ltd

*Hezel (Germany) – wire cropping – Brandone Machine Tool Ltd

HFO – Bearings – Baldor UK

HG-1 – humidity calibrator – Michell Instruments Ltd

HG-A/-V/-S/-E/-L – roller shutters and grilles – Hörmann (UK) Ltd

HGPS – Head and gun positioning system – Sonardyne International Ltd

HGW – propeller shaft balancing machines – Schenck Ltd

Hi-access – patented compact junior saw – Q E P Ltd

Hi Black Trinitron – televisions – Sony Head Office

Hi-Brites – small coloured cords – Marlow Ropes Ltd

Hi-Build – extra high build textured wallcoating – Everlac GB Ltd

Hi-Combat – foam equipment – Angus Fire

Hi Connect – as-interface – Belden UK Ltd

Hi Cor – chrome plated bar – Chromebar

Hi-deck flooring – secondary flooring – Hi-Store

Hi-Den – alumina grinding media – P E Hines & Sons Ltd

Hi Device – sensor connectors & actuator connectors – Belden UK Ltd

HI-EX – GGB UK

Hi Fi Choice – magazine – Future Publishing Ltd

Hi-Fi News – I P C Media Ltd

HI-FORCE – Hydraulic & Offshore Supplies Ltd

Hi-Force – hydraulics – Smail Engineers Glasgow Ltd

Hi-Form – Business Forms – Mcnaughton James Paper Group Ltd

Hi-frame – Free standing A frames – Hi-Store

Hi-Gear – gears & spares – Bearwood Engineering Supplies

Hi-glo – fluorecent board and paper display material for retailers to write their prices on – Powell Marketing Ltd

Hi-Grade – protein concentrates for growing and finishing pigs – A One Feed Supplements Ltd

Hi-Heat – infra-red elements – Hassett Industries

Hi-Heat – withdrawble core element assemblies – Hassett Industries

Hi Lo – thermal wear – Sub Zero Technology Ltd

Hi-Lo – step dimming system – Luxonic Lighting plc

Hi-Mech CNC Mechanical Shears – CNC mechanical shear – Joseph Rhodes Ltd

Hi-Mod (United Kingdom) – quality rigging components – Petersen Stainless Rigging Ltd
Hi-Phase – cationic rosin emulsion - paper size – Hercules Holding Ii Ltd
Hi-Phorm – surface size - paper – Hercules Holding Ii Ltd
HI-Phos – bactericdal toilet cleaner – Evans Vanodine International plc
Hi-Ply – abrasive base paper and industrial papers – Weidmann Whiteley Ltd
Hi-Power – low vision aid magnifiers-microscopic and prismatic spectacles-industrial magnifiers-popular magnifiers-spectacle binoculars – Carlo Technical Plastics
Hi Power – passive active splitter boxes – Belden UK Ltd
Hi-Presflex – welded diaphragm metal bellows – Palatine Precision Ltd
Hi-Pro Range – high productivity floor maintenance machines – Truvox International Ltd
Hi-Procon – protein concentrate for growing and finishing pigs – A One Feed Supplements Ltd
Hi-Proof – damp proof course – Premier Coatings Ltd
Hi-Py – polyetheline tarpaulin – Pritchard Tyrite
Hi-Racker – Narrow Aisle Ltd
Hi Rel – Connectors – Dax International Ltd
Hi-Score – darts – Unicorn Products Ltd
Hi-Slim – lighting tubes – Oldham Lighting Projects Ltd
Hi Speed Gemini – offset plate conversion unit – Kodak Morley
Hi Sprint – oil containment systems – Vikoma International Ltd
Hi Stack – Insulation cages – Hi-Store
Hi Tec – water softener – B W T Ltd
Hi Tec Meter – water softener – B W T Ltd
***Hi-Tech (Democratic People's Republic of Korea)** – radio control equipment – Amerang Group Ltd
Hi Tech – Audio video tapes – K B Import & Export Ltd
Hi Tech – Snopake Ltd
Hi-Tech – cleaning apparatus and kits for electrical apparatus – Helix Trading Ltd
Hi-Temp – warning system – Kenlowe Accessories & Co. Ltd
Hi-Temp Pump – pump to specifically handle high temperature thermal fluids – Beverley Environmental Ltd
HI-Tempreze – Forward Chemicals Ltd
Hi-Ten Bond – universal base layer – Alumasc Exterior Building Products
Hi-Ten Elastomeric – pour and roll roofing – Alumasc Exterior Building Products
Hi Ten Taping Strip – 100mm joint tape – Alumasc Exterior Building Products
Hi-Throw PC 339 – acid copper for printed circuits – Cookson Electronics Ltd
Hi Tone – plate cleaner – Kodak Morley
Hi-Trolley – Heavy duty timber carriage – Hi-Store
Hi vis – Avalon and Lynwood
Hi-viz – Avalon and Lynwood
Hi-Way Towers – Accesscaff International Ltd
Hi=Fi – horse feed – Dengie Crops Ltd
HIAB – Hydraulic & Offshore Supplies Ltd
Hiab Foco – Harrier Fluid Power Ltd
Hiactive – detergent – Delaval
Hiatt – Aspen International Ltd
Hibass – Machine Guard Solutions Ltd
Hibass - Optoscan - Safety Scan - Astro – Machine Guard Solutions Ltd
Hibon – liquid ring pumps and pressure blowers – B O C Edwards
Hibuild 302 – epoxy surfacer and undercoat – Gurit UK Ltd
Hick Hargreaves – industrial pumps – AESpump
Hick Hargreaves – liquid ring pumps and boosters – B O C Edwards
Hickman – adult vascular access catheters – Bard Ltd
Hickstead Feeds – BOCM Pauls Ltd
HICOM – telephone systems – Integra I C T Ltd
HID – Access Control Manufacturer – Plastic ID
Hidden Valley – bean/pulse meals and rice/pasta dishes – Fiddes Payne
Hide-A-Way – promotional labels – C C L Labels Decorative Sleeves
Hide It Roller – Snopake Ltd
Hidentity Ltd – Hidentity Ltd
Hidro-Thermal – steam equipment – Bearwood Engineering Supplies
HIDROIRMA – Hydraulic & Offshore Supplies Ltd
***Hield (Europe)** – worsted suitings, furnishing fabric – Gamma Beta Holdings Ltd
Hifi – UK agent replacement filters – Harrier Fluid Power Ltd
Hiflo – G E Healthcare
Hiflo – Bostik Ltd
Higgns – drawing inks – West Design Products Ltd
High Class – neutral multi purpose cleaner - environmentally free – Evans Vanodine International plc
High Colour Control Cream – cream for helping to reduce redness on face and neck areas – Vivalis Ltd
High Containment Barrier Isolators – dust booth – Extract Technology
High Cool – Wolseley UK
High Impact Liner Board – high impact thermal insulation to concrete soffits/under-decks – Rockwool Rockpanel B V
***High Level Cleaning** – Nova Contract Cleaners
***High Level Cleaning** – Stayclean Contract Cleaning Services Ltd
High Performance Installation Filters – for shielded rooms, RFI, EMC, EMP – M P E Ltd
High Performance Partial Fill Cavity Slab – completely reliable and cost effective method of insulating new brick or masonry cavity walls whilst maintaining a minimum 25mm clear cavity – Rockwool Rockpanel B V
High Point Rendel – business, management and technology consultants – High-Point Rendel Ltd
High pressure air compressors – Bauer Group
High Pressure Coolant Pumps – coolant pumps (high pressure) – Hammond & Co. Ltd
High pressure optical cells – . – Hi-Pro Pressure Products Ltd
High Street – aluminium and olefin entrance matting – Jaymart Roberts & Plastics Ltd
High Strength Grout – high compressive strength grout – Conren Ltd
High Style Furnishings – curtain manufacturer – High Style Furnishings
High Table – food service management, staff restaurants, executive dining and beverage services, consultancy and design – Avenance
High Tech – Cloakroom Solutions Ltd
High Thrust – anti-vibration mounting – Trelleborg Industrial A V S Ltd
Higher & Higher – Accesscaff International Ltd
Highfield – gears & spares – Bearwood Engineering Supplies
Highflo – UPVC half round rainwater system (170mm) – Hunter Plastics
HIGHFLOW TETPOR – PTFE membrane filter cartridges – Parker Dominic Hunter Ltd
Highgard – a strong durable mudguard made from high density polyethylene – Jonesco (Preston) Ltd
Highgate – water taps – Rudge & Co UK
Highguard - High density plastic Sologuard - Mudguard incorporating anti spray – Jonesco (Preston) Ltd
Highland Antique Linen – Coated Paper – Mcnaughton James Paper Group Ltd
Highland Chromo – Coated Paper – Mcnaughton James Paper Group Ltd
Highland Fusilier – malt Scotch whisky – Gordon & Macphail
***Highland Game** – Harbro Ltd
Highland Laid – Uncoated Paper – Mcnaughton James Paper Group Ltd
Highland Piper – toiletries and cleaning materials – Superfine Manufacturing Ltd
Highland Sandgrain – Coated Paper – Mcnaughton James Paper Group Ltd
Highland Superwhite – Uncoated Paper – Mcnaughton James Paper Group Ltd
Highlande – polythene clad green houses – Clovis Lande Associates Ltd
Highlander – prepacked snacks and crisps (manufacturers) – Highlander Snacks Ltd
Highlander – BS 6391 type 2 fire hose – Richards Hose Ltd
Highlander Aran – Sirdar Spinning Ltd
Highlander Chunky – Sirdar Spinning Ltd
Highlead – Highlead Sewing Machines – Highlead Ltd
Highlighters – fluorescent highlighting markers/pens – Office Depot UK
Highline – insulated sectional garage door – P C Henderson Ltd
Highlite – rotary screen printing – C C L Labels Decorative Sleeves
Highlite Led (United Kingdom) – A S D Lighting plc
Highseal – cold applied fuel resistant dressing for bituminous/asphalt surfaces – Conren Ltd
Highseal F1 – elastomeric fuel resistant joint sealant – Conren Ltd
Highstreet Vouchers – vouchers – Park Group plc
Highway – windscreens and glass installers – Homeserve Emergency Services
Highway Led (United Kingdom) – A S D Lighting plc
Hihos – proprietary steel grade – Oil States Industries UK Ltd
Hijack – Cellar systems – Hijack Systems
Hikers – Footwear – Boot Tree
Hilco – arc welding electrodes – Weldability S I F
Hilco – Harrier Fluid Power Ltd
Hilco - Eurobraze - Sifbronze - Sifserrate - Sifredicote - SIFMIG - Super Silicon – Weldability S I F
Hilex – British Vita plc
Hilfex – Harrier Fluid Power Ltd
Hilflex – expandable braided sleeving – Hilltop Products
Hilger Crystals – Hilger Crystals Ltd
Hiline – pre-insulated pipe - district heating, chilled water – C P V Ltd
Hilite – disposable cutlery – Plastico Ltd
HiLites – dart flights – Unicorn Products Ltd
Hilka – Gem Tool Hire & Sales Ltd
Hill – oil drum pumps, lubrication equipment and hose clips – Ernest H Hill Ltd
Hill & Smith – safety barrier – Hill & Smith Ltd
Hillard – Harrier Fluid Power Ltd
Hillarys – blinds – Hillarys Blinds Northern Ltd
Hillflex S300 – silicone coated glass – Hilltop Products
Hilliard – Printed fabrics – Zoffany
Hilliard Wallpaper – Wallcovering collection – Zoffany
Hillman Newby – rotary seals – Aldona Seals
***Hillsider (China)** – Corston Sinclair Ltd
***Hilltop (U.S.A.)** – quarries – Welsh Slates
Hilly – sports and active wear clothing and accessories – Sweatshop
Hilma – hydraulic clamping – A C Hydraulics Ltd
***Hilma Romheld (Germany)** – machine vices and quick die changing equipment – Roemheld UK Ltd
Hilo Gas Equipment – Gas equipment – Premier Welding Services Scotland Ltd
Hiload – masonry joist manager – Simpson Strong-Tie International Inc
Hilson – trolleys and cloakroom equipment – Hilson Ltd
Hilson – filter bag cages and standard wirework – Hilson Ltd
Hilti – Hilti GB Ltd
Hilti – Gem Tool Hire & Sales Ltd
Hilti – anchor bolts – Traction Equipment Stafford Ltd
Hilti – drills & spares – Bearwood Engineering Supplies
Hilti Bolt – traditional high expansion anchor – Hilti GB Ltd
Hilti Ceiling hanger – simple fixing for suspended ceiling installation – Hilti GB Ltd
Hilti DBZ – metal tap in anchor for permanent light duty fixings – Hilti GB Ltd
Hilti DBZ-X – metal tap in anchor for permanent light duty fixings – Hilti GB Ltd
Hilti DD100 – hand held professional diamond coring system suitable for dry diamond coring into brickwork and masonry or wet diamond coring into reinforced concrete. – Hilti GB Ltd
Hilti DX A40/41 – semi-automatic cartridge operated fastening tools - universal, economical and safe – Hilti GB Ltd
Hilti DX A40-M/41-M – fully automatic cartridge operated fastening tools for repetitive fixings – Hilti GB Ltd
Hilti DX-E 37/72 – cartridge operated fastening tool – Hilti GB Ltd
Hilti DX351 – fully automatic cartridge operated fastening tools for repetitive drywall fixings – Hilti GB Ltd
Hilti DX36M – semi-automatic cartridge operated fastening tool, universal, economical and safe – Hilti GB Ltd
Hilti DX36MX – fully automatic cartridge operated fastening tool for repetitive fastenings – Hilti GB Ltd
Hilti DX450 – universal semi-automatic cartridge operated fastening tool – Hilti GB Ltd
Hilti DX600N – heavy duty single action cartridge operated fastening tool – Hilti GB Ltd
Hilti DX750 – semi-automatic cartridge operated tool for fastening profiled metal sheets, modified versions available for more specialised applications. – Hilti GB Ltd
Hilti DX750MX – fully automatic cartridge tool for fastening profiled metal sheets, modified versions available for more specialised applications – Hilti GB Ltd
Hilti Firestop Range – a range of graphite based product for passive fire protection of all industrial and commercial buildings – Hilti GB Ltd
Hilti HA8 – fixing with large eyelet for suspension work – Hilti GB Ltd
Hilti HDA – heavy duty undercut design anchor for maximised loads – Hilti GB Ltd
Hilti HEH – threaded anchor suitable for light duty applications – Hilti GB Ltd
Hilti HGN – nylon plug for use in low density lightweight block – Hilti GB Ltd
Hilti HGT – tap in fixing for plasterboard walls – Hilti GB Ltd
Hilti HHD – metal cavity fixing – Hilti GB Ltd
Hilti HHD-2 – pre-assembled metal cavity fixing – Hilti GB Ltd
Hilti Hit Resin Systems – medium and heavy duty self mixing resins for use with anchor rods or threaded sockets in all base materials – Hilti GB Ltd
Hilti HKD – medium duty internally threaded wedge anchor – Hilti GB Ltd
Hilti HKD-S – medium duty internally threaded wedge anchor – Hilti GB Ltd
Hilti HLD – nylon toggle fixing for plasterboard walls – Hilti GB Ltd
Hilti HMDS – medium duty sleeve expansion anchor – Hilti GB Ltd
Hilti HPF – nylon frame fixing with screw for uPVC window and door installation. – Hilti GB Ltd
hilti HPS Hammascrew – nylon plug and screw – Hilti GB Ltd
Hilti HRD – nylon frame fixing comprising of anchor body and suitable screw – Hilti GB Ltd
Hilti HSA – medium duty anchor range for through fastenings. – Hilti GB Ltd
Hilti HSC – medium duty undercut anchor – Hilti GB Ltd

Hilti HSL/HSL-TZ – heavy duty sleeve expansion anchor – Hilti GB Ltd

Hilti HST-R – stainless steel stud anchor – Hilti GB Ltd

Hilti HT – all metal frame fixing for window and door installation – Hilti GB Ltd

Hilti HUC-2 – heavy duty undercut anchor – Hilti GB Ltd

Hilti HUD – nylon plug for use with woodscrew – Hilti GB Ltd

Hilti HUS – for screw fastening straight into concrete without using an anchor – Hilti GB Ltd

Hilti HVA – heavy duty chemical anchor systems comprising of glass capsule and either anchor rod or threaded anchor socket – Hilti GB Ltd

Hilti HVB Shear Connectors – utilising Hilti's DX650 – Hilti GB Ltd

Hilti HVU – heavy duty chemical anchor system comprising of foil capsule and either anchor or threaded anchor socket – Hilti GB Ltd

Hilti IDMR – stainless steel insulation fastener – Hilti GB Ltd

Hilti IDP – propopylene insulation fastener – Hilti GB Ltd

Hilti IZ – positive expansion insulation fastener – Hilti GB Ltd

Hilti PD25 – laser measuring tool for measuring distances and calculating areas and volumes – Hilti GB Ltd

Hilti PHB – medium and light duty sleeve anchor – Hilti GB Ltd

Hilti PM10 – multi-directional laser tools for simultaneous plumb, level and square measurements – Hilti GB Ltd

Hilti PR20 – self levelling rotating laser – Hilti GB Ltd

Hilti PR60 – self levelling surveyors rotating laser – Hilti GB Ltd

Hilti SD45 – drywall screwdriver – Hilti GB Ltd

Hilti SF100 / 120-A – 9.6v and 12v cordless screwdrivers (respectively) – Hilti GB Ltd

Hilti ST18 – metal construction screwdriver – Hilti GB Ltd

Hilti SU 25 – universal screwdriver – Hilti GB Ltd

Hilti TE 1 – light duty rotary hammer drill for holes into concrete and masonry 4 - 18 diameter – Hilti GB Ltd

Hilti TE 104 – lightweight breaker and scaler – Hilti GB Ltd

Hilti TE 15C – rotary hammer drill for holes into concrete, masonry and stone 4 - 28mm. Also with light duty chiselling function. – Hilti GB Ltd

Hilti TE 25 – heavy duty hammer drill for 12 - 20mm holes into concrete, stone and masonry, can also drill steel up to 13mm – Hilti GB Ltd

Hilti TE 35 – universal lightweigh combi hammer – Hilti GB Ltd

Hilti TE 5 – medium duty rotary hammer drill for holes into concrete and masonry 4 - 20mm (also with dust extraction as extra) – Hilti GB Ltd

Hilti TE 505 – light to medium duty breaker for universal chiselling – Hilti GB Ltd

Hilti TE 55 – medium duty universal combi hammer – Hilti GB Ltd

Hilti TE 6A – battery rotary hammer drill for holes into concrete, masonry and stone 4 - 16mm – Hilti GB Ltd

Hilti TE 706 – powerful chiselling, ideal for building renovation work, repairs and plumbing installations – Hilti GB Ltd

Hilti TE 76-ATC – high performing combi hammer with additional built in operator protection in drilling mode – Hilti GB Ltd

Hilti TE 805 – removal and demolition work to concrete, masonry, stone and asphalt – Hilti GB Ltd

Hilti TE 905 – heavy duty demolition breaker for removal and demolition work to concrete, masonry, stone and asphalt – Hilti GB Ltd

Hilti TE15 – rotary hammer drill for holes into concrete, masonry and stone 4 - 28mm – Hilti GB Ltd

Hilti TKD3000 – universal rapid construction screwgun for dry wall applications – Hilti GB Ltd

Hilti TKD5000 – rapid construction screwgun for dry wall applications – Hilti GB Ltd

Hilti TKT2000 – screwgun for self drilling screws for universal applications – Hilti GB Ltd

Hilti Transformers – safety isolating for use with Hilti machines and other equipment – Hilti GB Ltd

Hilti WFE 150 – random orbital sander – Hilti GB Ltd

Hilti WSC 55 – 6" hand held circular saw – Hilti GB Ltd

Hilti WSC 85 – 8" hand held circular saw – Hilti GB Ltd

Hilti WSJ 110-ET – orbital action D handle jigsaw – Hilti GB Ltd

Hilti X-IE – DX36M cartridge operated tool – Hilti GB Ltd

Hilton – optical frames and sunglasses – Hilton International Eye Wear Ltd

Hilton Banks – UK Office Direct

Hilton's – DIY wholesalers and importers – Hilton Banks Ltd

*Hiltons (Italy) – decorative plaster coving, dust sheets – Hilton Banks Ltd

HIMA – Hima Sella Ltd

HIMA-SELLA – Hima Sella Ltd

Himalayan – Global Fasteners Ltd

Himaro – B P plc

Himod – high modulus thermoplastic compounds – Trelleborg Ceiling Solutions Ltd

Himould – high performance brass inserts for moulding in – Tappex Thread Inserts Ltd

Hindes – hollow ground blade – Burgon & Ball Ltd

*Hindusthan (Czech Republic) – engineers files and rasps – Castle Brook Tools Ltd

Hinomoto – Harrier Fluid Power Ltd

Hinton – Passive Monitoring Probe Product – Telesoft Technologies Ltd

HIP – High pressure valves, fittings, tubing & components – Staffordshire Hydraulic Services Ltd

HIPAK – corrugated box making machinery – Autobox Machinery Ltd

HIPATH – telephone system – Integra I C T Ltd

HIPIC – tweezers – Henri Picard & Frere

Hipic Pliers – pliers and cutters – Henri Picard & Frere

Hipkiss – hardware and eyelets – H Hipkiss & Co. Ltd

Hiplok – instantaneous coupling glass filled nylon one and quarter-2 inch – Industrial Hose & Pipe Fittings Ltd

HiPortfolio/2 – multi user pc/unix network investment management system – D S T Global Solutions

Hippo – mobile dust extraction unit with automatic cleaning – Horizon Mechanical Services International Ltd

Hippo – fibre bonded carpet – Heckmondwike FB

Hippo – paperback book publishing imprint – Scholastic School Book Fairs

HiPro – Dometic UK Ltd

HiPro Vision – Dometic UK Ltd

HiPromatic – Dometic UK Ltd

HIPS – Naylor Specialists Plastics

Hira – consumer electronics, radios, calculators, watches etc – The Hira Company Ltd

Hireburgess – function furniture hire – Burgess Furniture Ltd

HireCall – Allianz Insurance plc

Hirestar – carpet cleaner and carpet shampoo – Hire Technicians Group Ltd

Hiretech – floor sanding & edging machines 110 & 240 volt – Hire Technicians Group Ltd

Hiretech – steam wallpaper stripper electric 110 & 240 volt – Hire Technicians Group Ltd

Hirose – M S C Gleichmann UK Ltd

Hirose – Cyclops Electronics Ltd

Hiross – Parker Hannifin

Hiross Flexible Space Systems – Advanced Ergonomic Technologies Ltd

Hirschmann – rod ends & spherical bearings – Mantek Manufacturing Ltd

Hirschmann – Connectors – Warwick Test Supplies

Hirschmann - Bearings & Axial Shaft Seals. – Mantek Manufacturing Ltd

Hirsh – hand made 18 carat gold & platinum diamond & gem set fine jewellery – Hirsh Diamonds

Hit RE 500 – for professional fastening of reinforcing bars – Hilti GB Ltd

HITACHI – Hydraulic & Offshore Supplies Ltd

Hitachi – displays – M S C Gleichmann UK Ltd

Hitachi – Proplas International Ltd

*Hitachi (Japan) – electric & cordless power tools – Harrow Tool Co. Ltd

Hitachi – P J P Plant Hire

Hitachi – Videonations Ltd

Hitachi – Oxon Fastening Systems Ltd

Hitachi – TV – Sertronics Ltd

Hitachi – C J Plant Ltd

Hitachi – Lamphouse Ltd

*Hitachi – Kenneth Robson Equipment Ltd

Hitachi – Therma Group

Hitachi – Gem Tool Hire & Sales Ltd

HITACHI – Harrier Fluid Power Ltd

Hitachi – S J Wharton Ltd

Hitachi – frequency inverters, programmable logic controllers & servo systems – System Control Solutions Ltd

Hitachi – Cyclops Electronics Ltd

Hitachi Denshi – broadcasting and television equipment – Hitashi Kokusai

Hitachi Displays – LCD displays – Anglia

HiTec – high performance additives for lubricating oils and fuels – Afton Chemical

HiTec – Ethyl Product Range – Afton Chemical

Hitech – low voltage lighting – W F Electrical

Hitemp – minilock, clearbore and metaseal – Cobham Mission Equipment Ltd

Hiten – tensional steel strapping – Gordian Strapping Ltd

Hiti WFO 280 – orbital sander for a superior finish on all surfaces – Hilti GB Ltd

Hitide – B P plc

Hitli TKT 1300 – screwgun for thread forming screws - for profile sheet applications – Hilti GB Ltd

HiTOP – Operating Software – Hitex UK Ltd

hiTran (United Kingdom) – Heat exchanger tube insert (turbulator) – Cal Gavin Ltd

Hitzmann – Harrier Fluid Power Ltd

Hiway – four point lift flexible intermediate bulk container – Rexam Holding plc

Hiways by Episys – platform independent label printing – Episys Group Ltd

Hiyasun – deck chair canvas – Mitchell Interflex Ltd

Hizorb – disposable patient wipes – I P S Converters Ltd

*HK Audio (Germany) – pro audio equipment – John Hornby Skewes & Co. Ltd

*HKR (Germany) – powder iron composite cores & chokes – Rolfe Industries

HKS GMBH – Hydraulic & Offshore Supplies Ltd

HM – Peter Rushton Ltd

HMP – M S C Gleichmann UK Ltd

HMT – Hydraulic & Offshore Supplies Ltd

Hmv – sheet metal – R K International Machine Tools Ltd

*Hoaf (Netherlands) – infrared weed control systems – Industrial Power Units Ltd

Hobart – B B C S Ltd

Hobart – warewashing-cooking equipment, food preparation equipment – Hobart UK

*Hobart – Dishwashers & mixers – Court Catering Equipment Ltd

Hobart – Ascot Wholesale Ltd

Hobart Battery Chargers (U.S.A.) – Ametek Prestolight

Hobbs – ladies shoes and clothes – Hobbs Ltd

Hobbylite – European Lamp Group

Hobnail – fibre bonded carpet – Heckmondwike FB

Hobut – panel meters, current transformers, shunts, power transducers and protection relays – Howard Butler Ltd

*HOCAPS International – Hocaps Ltd

Hockley – chemical products for agriculture and veterinary use – Hockley International Ltd

Hockley - Mostyn - Permost - Alphamost - Deltamost – Hockley International Ltd

Hocus – simulation system with colour graphics – Lorien Resourcing Ltd

Hoddle – wheelbarrow tool rack – Hamster Baskets

Hodge Close – roofing & architectural slates – Burlington Slate Ltd

Hodgson – elec.measuring – Bearwood Engineering Supplies

Hoebeek – D G Heath Ltd

*Hoerauf (Germany) – erection and sealing of paper cups – Engelmann & Buckham Ltd

HOERBIGER – Hydraulic & Offshore Supplies Ltd

Hoerbiger – compressor valves, rings and packings, check valves, compressor regulation equipment. – Hoerbiger UK

HOERBIGER ORIGA – Hydraulic & Offshore Supplies Ltd

Hoerbiger Origa – Glamair Supplies Ltd

Hoerbiger Rings & Packings – sealing components for reciprocating compressors – Hoerbiger Rings & Packings Ltd

Hoes – Harrier Fluid Power Ltd

Hoesch Woodhead – coil springs – Thyssenkrupp Bilstein Woodhead

Hofbauer – C P Cases Ltd

Hofbauer – blow moulding – Hofbauer (UK) Ltd

Hoffer (U.S.A.) – turbine flow meters – Litre Meter Ltd

Hoffman – Harrier Fluid Power Ltd

Hofmann – Cemb Hofmann UK Ltd

*Hofmann Karl (Germany) – rive making machine – Brunner Machine Tools Ltd

Hoganasmobler – Sitsmart Ltd

Hogfors – Control valves – Cee Vee

Hoggs of Fife – footwear and country clothing. Protective clothing. – Hoggs of Fife Ltd

Hohner – Encoders UK

Hohner – incremental, absolute, linear and rotary encoders – Hohner Automation Ltd

Hohner – European Technical Sales Ltd

*Hokada (Romania) – guitar – Stentor Music Co. Ltd

Hoke – Southern Valve & Fitting Co. Ltd

HOKE – Hydraulic & Offshore Supplies Ltd

Hoke – Bristol Fluid System Technologies Ltd

Hokuetsu – Harrier Fluid Power Ltd

Holaday – Ets-Lindgren Ltd

Holborn Direct Mail – direct mail producer - full service offered from creation to posting – Holborn Direct Mail

HOLBURY – Hydraulic & Offshore Supplies Ltd

Hold-o-mat – Continental Chef Supplies Ltd

Holdax – pre-hardened bolster steel – Uddeholm Steel Stockholders

Holden Hydroman – advanced plastics – Polytec Holden Ltd

Holdfast – fixing technology – Rex Bousfield Ltd

*Holdridge (U.S.A.) – radius turning attachment – Drill Service Horley Ltd

Holdtite – Mercury Bearings Ltd

HOLDTITE INDUSTRIAL ADHESIVES – Hydraulic & Offshore Supplies Ltd

Holedall – Offshore and pressure hose fittings – Dixon Group Europe Ltd

Holemasters – diamond drilling – Holemasters Scotland

Holex Diabetic Chocolate – diabetic chocolate – A L Simpkin Co. Ltd

Holidaywise – The Woolwich

Holland and Barrett – health products – Holland & Barrett Ltd

Holland & Sherry – cloth merchants – Holland & Sherry

Holledge – instruments – Canongate Technology Ltd

Hollingsworth & Vose – filter speciality papers – Hollingsworth & Vose Co UK Ltd

Hollington – sandstone quarries and masonry works – J Oldham & Co. Ltd

Hollo-Bolt – steel cavity fixing – Lindapter International

Hollomate – Hollowing tool – The Toolpost

Holloplas – extruded plastic profiles – Centriforce Products Ltd

Hollywell – mining and industrial equipment, pressings – Holywell Engineering Ltd

Holman – Trowell Plant Sales Ltd

HOLMBURY – Hydraulic & Offshore Supplies Ltd

Holmbury – Holmbury Ltd

Holmes – blowers & spares – Bearwood Engineering Supplies

Holo-Krome – fasteners – Danaher Tool Group

Holofilm – transparent holograms – Opsec Security Ltd

Holoflex – holographic film – Opsec Security Ltd

Holofoil – holographic hot stamping foil – A P I Holographics Ltd

Holographic – film – Printpack Enterprises Ltd T/A Printpack

Holokrome – socket screws – Arrow Supply Co. Ltd

Holosec – General Vacuum Equipment Ltd

Holotrans – transparent holographic hot stamping foil – A P I Holographics Ltd

Holset – turbo chargers – Cummins Turbo Technologies Ltd

Holsten Pils – lager – Scottish & Newcastle Pub Co.

Holts – Gem Tool Hire & Sales Ltd

Holts – care products – Holt Lloyd International Ltd

Holts/Simoniz – car care products – Holt Lloyd International Ltd

*Holz Her (Germany) – pneumatic nailers, power tools, panel saws edge banders, and machining centres – Smeaton Hanscomb & Co. Ltd

Holzer – Diamond sharpening products – The Toolpost

Homag – European Technical Sales Ltd

Home Booster – Grundfos Pumps Ltd

Home Entertainment – magazine – Future Publishing Ltd

Home Gold – home insurance for proposers aged 50 & over – M M A Insurance plc

Home Loc – housing grade polymeric DPC – Timloc Building Products

Home 'N" Dry – whole crop additive – Dugdale Nutrition Ltd

Home of the Pudding Club – evening when customers can try puddings – Three Ways House Hotel

Home Seeker – newspaper – Western Morning News Co. Ltd

Home Show – the magazine – Newsquest Group

Home Smart – The Woolwich

HomeAid – DIY products – P M S International Group plc

HomeCover – Allianz Insurance plc

Homedry – dehumidifiers for domestic applications – Ebac

Homefile – The Woolwich

Homefire – types of fuel – C P L Distribution

Homefire Ovals – types of fuel – C P L Distribution

Homelight – standard steel windows and doors – Crittall Windows Ltd

Homeline – linear actuators – Linak UK

Homely Loop – carpets – Cormar Carpets

Homemaker – furnishing fabrics – Associated Home Fabrics Ltd

Homer-Pro – Diver navigation system – Sonardyne International Ltd

Homes & Gardens – I P C Media Ltd

Homestyle – carpets – Cormar Carpets

HOMESTYLE MULTI PURPOSE CANOPIES – Living Space Ltd

Hometrim – cellular building profiles – L B Plastics Ltd

homme rock – Men's Jewellery And Accessories – Tye Mann Limited

Honamat – CNC honing machines – Jones & Shipman Grinding Ltd

Honamould – abrasives for honing tools – Jones & Shipman Grinding Ltd

Honda – generators – Campbell Miller Tools Ltd

Honda – Ashley Competition Exhausts Ltd

*Honda – J Paterson & Sons

Honda – L M C Hadrian Ltd

Honda – lawnmowers – Small Engine Services Ltd

Honda – Obart Pumps Ltd

Honda – A T Wilde & Son Ltd

Honda Connectors – Selectronix Ltd

Honda Generators and Industrial Engines – D D Hire

Honer – pipe bevelling machine – B S A Tube Runner

Honermaster – fine abrasive blast cabinet – Wheelabrator Group

Honermatic – fine abrasive wheel m/c – Wheelabrator Group

Honeybells – ladies and gents fashion knitwear – B S Attwall & Co. Ltd

Honeycomb – planned maintenance system – Signal Business Systems Ltd

Honeywell – control equipment – Bearwood Engineering Supplies

Honeywell – Cyclops Electronics Ltd

Honeywell – Trafalgar Tools

Honeywell – E Preston Electrical Ltd

Honeywell – Proplas International Ltd

Honeywell – UK Office Direct

Honeywell – European Technical Sales Ltd

Honeywell – R G K UK Ltd

Honeywell Normalair-Garrett Ltd – control systems for the defence, aerospace, marine and high technology markets, environmental control, life support, hydraulic and weapon launch and guidance systems and equipment, investment castings. – Honeywell Aerospace

HONEYWELL PRODUCTS (United Kingdom) – Ultravalve Ltd

Honsberg – flow switches, flow meters – P V L Ltd

Hood – circular surface and semi recessed vandal resistant architectural lighting – Designplan Lighting Ltd

Hood One Design – dinghy sails – Hood Sailmakers

Hood Sailmakers Ltd – sail manufacturers – Hood Sailmakers

Hook & Loop – cable tie – Richco International Co. Ltd

Hookit – abrasive sheets – North British Tapes Ltd

Hoopro – Sheet metal work – Hooper Engineering Products Ltd

HOPA – suppliers of guest amenities, foodservice disposables and hygiene & cleaning products to the hotel and catering industries in the Netherlands and Belgium – Bunzl Catering Supplies Ltd

Hopflex (United Kingdom) – flexible cables, flocking, sunroof cables and window-regulator cables – E C Hopkins Ltd

Hopflex – E C Hopkins Ltd

Hopflex - Hopgen – E C Hopkins Ltd

Hopgen – E C Hopkins Ltd

Hopkins – catering and refrigeration equipment – Hopkins Catering Equipment Ltd

Hopkinsons – cutlery, special purpose knives, diving knives, hunting knives, ceremonial swords, machine knives – F E & J R Hopkinson Ltd

Hopkinsons – parallel slide gate valves, globe valves, check valves, isolation devices – Weir Valves & Controls

Hopper Window – ventilation unit – Powermatic Ltd

Horatio Myers & Co – manufacturers of beds and mattresses – Staples Uk Ltd

Horauf Pots – taper sided pots – Nampak Carton

Hörbiger-Origa – European Technical Sales Ltd

Horiuchi Cylinders – European Technical Sales Ltd

*Horizon (Japan) – collators, cutters, binders and folding machines – Graphics Arts Equipment Ltd

*Horizon, (Netherlands) – gas wall heaters – Drugasar Service Ltd

*Horizon (U.S.A.) – science fiction models – Amerang Group Ltd

Horizon (United Kingdom) – ECi Software Solutions Limited

Horizon – modular multi-activity fitness and activity centre – S M P Playgrounds

Horizon Craft – cruising holidays – Richardsons Stalham Ltd

Hörmann Dobo system – loading technology – Hörmann (UK) Ltd

Hormone Rooting Powder – Vitax Ltd

Horn – wire and wire rope – Webster & Horsfall Ltd

Hornby – model railways – Hornby Hobbies Ltd

Hornby Skewes – musical tutor books – John Hornby Skewes & Co. Ltd

Horne – thermostatic mixing valves – Horne Engineering Ltd

Horni Monkey – Schuh Ltd

Horning – pipe forming machines – Eckold Ltd

Horning Pleasurecraft – cruising holidays – Richardsons Stalham Ltd

Horse – I P C Media Ltd

Horse Brand – rotary cutters – A T A Grinding Processes Ltd

Horse Elastic – grinding discs, cutting discs, flap discs – A T A Grinding Processes Ltd

Horse & Hound – I P C Media Ltd

Horse's Head (United Kingdom) – scissors, knives and hand tools – Kutrite Of Sheffield Ltd

HorseHage – dustfree forage for horses – Horsehage Manufacturers Mark Westaway & Son

Horseley Bridge – GRP & Steel sectional water tanks and steel tanks – Horseley Bridge

*Horsleys (United Kingdom) – disposable textiles and airline supplies – Horsleys Ltd

Horstine Farmery – agricultural machinery and subcontract engineering – Horstine Farmery

Horstmann – central heating programmers, immersion heater controls and electricity metering equipment – Horstmann Group Ltd

Horstmann Timers & Controls – timeswitches etc – Horstmann Group Ltd

Horticultural Bark – Woodgrow Horticulture

Horticultural plastic products & plastic mouldings manufrs – Desch Plantpak Ltd

*Horton (U.S.A.) – air clutches and brakes – Micro Clutch Developments Ltd

Horton – Motion Drives & Controls Ltd

Horwood – cookware – Horwood Homeware Ltd

Hoseguard – hose union bib tap with double check valve – Reliance Water Controls Ltd

Hosemobile – 24 hour hosemobile workshops – Hydrapower Dynamics Ltd

Hoshazaki – Ascot Wholesale Ltd

Hosokawa – Hosokawa Micron Ltd

Hosokawa bepex – Hosokawa Micron Ltd

Hosokawa Rietz – Disintegrators – Hosokawa Micron Ltd

Hospital Development – magazine – Progressive Media Group

Hospital Equipment & Supplies – magazine – Progressive Media Group

*Hospitality Skills – Hospitality & Leisure Manpower

Hostaform – acetal copolymer – Ticona UK Ltd

Hostalen GUR – ultra high molecular weight high density polyethylene (UHMW HDPE) – Ticona UK Ltd

Hostess – heated food servers – Crosslee plc

Hot Air – inflight magazine – John Brown Publishing

Hot Asphalt – bodies – Econ Engineering Ltd

Hot Pot – soup kettle – Dualit Ltd

Hot Shots – childrens shoes – D Jacobson & Sons Ltd

Hot Water Static Pressure Cleaners – Pressure washers – B & G Cleaning Systems Ltd

HotAV – Hot A V Ltd

Hotbox – economy ovens – Sanyo Gallenkamp plc

Hotchkiss – heavy engineers – John D Hotchkiss Ltd

Hotchkiss Air Supply – Hotchkiss Ltd

Hotchkiss Ductwork – Hotchkiss Ltd

Hotel Inspector – Inspection on the Standards of Hotels Worldwide – Hotel Inspector

*Hotel - Minders – P C Paramedics

Hotelscene Conference Plus – Conferences, venues, and event management service – Hotelscene

Hotelscene Corporate Xtranet – Online hotel booking tool – Hotelscene

Hotfix – hot melt applicator – Power Adhesives Ltd

Hotline – diesel fuel filter heater kits – Exhaust Ejector Co. Ltd

Hotline – Magazine – John Brown Publishing

Hotlock Food Conveyors – heated food containers – Corsair Engineering Ltd

Hotmate – heat packs – Thermo Packs

Hotrace – self regulating domestic hot water temperature maintenance system – Flexelec UK Ltd

HOTSPOT – specialist stove and fireplace maintenance products – Hydrachem Ltd

HotSpotter – infra red hand held sensor – Product Innovation Ltd

Hotspur – Rotadex Systems Ltd

Hotspur Hussar (United Kingdom) – armoured vehicle – Penman Engineering Ltd

Hotstart – pre heater – Kenlowe Accessories & Co. Ltd

*Hotter Comfort Shoes (India and Thailand) – mens & ladies casual shoes – Beaconsfield Footwear Ltd

Hottinger – European Technical Sales Ltd

Hotwire – DSL access multiplexer – Nortel Networks UK Ltd

Hotwork – industrial burners, combustion & control systems, furnace modernisation – Hotwork Combustion Technology

Houlotte – R F Lifting & Access Ltd

Hoults – removal service – Hoults Group

Hounsfied H10ks (T) – materials testing machine – Tiniusolsen Ltd

Hounsfield 100R/S – extensometer – Tiniusolsen Ltd

Hounsfield 500L – laser extensometer – Tiniusolsen Ltd

Hounsfield H100kS (T) – materials testing machine – Tiniusolsen Ltd

Hounsfield H1KS (T) – materials testing machine – Tiniusolsen Ltd

Hounsfield H25kS (T) – materials testing machine – Tiniusolsen Ltd

Hounsfield H50KS (T) – materials testing machine – Tiniusolsen Ltd

Hounsfield H5KS T – materials testing machine – Tiniusolsen Ltd

House Beautiful – magazine – National Magazine Company Ltd

House Mouse – Chorion plc

House of Colour – image consultants – House Of Colour Ltd

House of Flags – Promotional items – House Of Flags Ltd

House of Flags – regional sales offices for company and national flag, flag poles and banners and associated items – House Of Flags

House of natural food Ltd – Production of organic & vegetarian food – Stanborough Press Ltd

House of Valentina, The – Elgate Products Ltd

House Plant – leaf shine & pest killer aerosols – Vitax Ltd

Housekeepers (United Kingdom) – range of gel air fresheners & carpet products. – A E Adams Ltd

Housesafe – underfloor safes – Securikey Ltd

housetohome.co.uk – Website – I P C Media Ltd

Hoval – pressure vessels, air receivers – Hoval Ltd

Hoval – industrial and commercial boilers, incinerators, industrial ventilators systems and heat recovery – Hoval Ltd

Hoval Boilers – Twin Industries International Ltd

Hovicon – Stainless Steel Sauce dispensers – Mitchell & Cooper Ltd

Hovis – bread and flour confectionery – Hovis

*****Howa (Japan)** – power operated lathe chucks – Thame Engineering Co. Ltd

Howard Bros – joinery – Howard Bros Joinery Ltd

*****Howard Miller** – M S S Watch Company

Howard Smith – tug operators - river Humber nd Medway areas – Svitzer Humber Ltd

Howden – Therma Group

Howden Electro Heating – Domestic and industrial immersion heaters, electric heating elements, electric air heater batteries, electric boilers, calorifiers and storage water heaters for industrial and commercial applications – Howden Electro Heating

Howdon (United Kingdom) – shearpin protection equipment – Howdon Power Transmission Ltd

Howe – Desks – Bucon Ltd

howecool – air conditioning – Howe Cool

Howmet – investment casting process, gas turbine components – Howmet Ltd

Howse's – paints, varnishes, powders – Thomas Howse Ltd

Howse's Rust Convertor – rust convertor – Thomas Howse Ltd

Howson – printing plates – Agfa Gevaert

Hoya Filters – Galvoptics Optical Goods

HOZELOCK – Hydraulic & Offshore Supplies Ltd

Hozelock – Trafalgar Tools

HP – Charlton Networks

HP – Supply HP Servers and Workstaions – UVFish Ltd

HP – UK Office Direct

HP – All HP servers, storage, software and desktop systems – Server Parts Ltd

HP – Apex Computer Services Wales Ltd

HP – Hewlett Packard inkjet cartridges, laser toners, printers – Inkxperts

HP boron nitride – Precision Ceramics

HP Hydrali – Harrier Fluid Power Ltd

*****HP Hydraulic (Italy)** – variable displacement hydraulic pumps and motors – BYPY Hydraulics & Transmissions Ltd

HP HYDRAULICS – Hydraulic & Offshore Supplies Ltd

HP Technik – Oil pumps – Anglo Nordic Burner Products Ltd

HP200 – organic coated steel for roof and wall cladding with leathergrain emboss – Corus U K Ltd

HP400/HP500 Series – relative humidity temperature probes – Lee-Dickens Ltd

HP5 Plus – ISO 400 speed film – Harman Technology Ltd

HPC – Harrier Fluid Power Ltd

HPC – compressors, parts and service – Airware International Ltd

HPC – compressor – Thorite

HPF™ – GGB UK

HPI – Hydraulic & Offshore Supplies Ltd

HPI – StrainSense Ltd

HPI – providers of information services to all industries. – Equifax plc

HPM – M P E Ltd

HPM™ – GGB UK

Hpnotiq – Windfall Brands Ltd

HPS200 – pre-finished organic coated steel for roof and wall cladding – Corus U K Ltd

HR 116 A/S – roller shutters and grilles – Hörmann (UK) Ltd

HR 120 A/S – roller shutters and grilles – Hörmann (UK) Ltd

HR 120 aero – roller shutters and grilles – Hörmann (UK) Ltd

HRODC Ltd – H R O D C

HRPC – Wolseley UK

HRS – M S C Gleichmann UK Ltd

HSE – HSE registered No 11/04 – R B Health & Safety Solutions Ltd

HSG™ – GGB UK

HSL-G-TZ – Hilti GB Ltd

HSL-TZ – Hilti GB Ltd

HSLB – Hilti GB Ltd

HSM – UK Office Direct

HSOP – computer consultants - hardware and software – H S O P Text Processing Services

HSP – Hydraulic & Offshore Supplies Ltd

HSP Gloss Board – Digital Products - Indigo - Coated – Howard Smith Paper Ltd

HSP Silk Board – Digital Products - Indigo - Coated – Howard Smith Paper Ltd

HSS 6530 – high speed door – Hörmann (UK) Ltd

*****HTBasic (U.S.A.)** – rocky mountain basic for PC – Lyons Instruments

HTEC – terminals and display systems for retail financial markets – Htec Ltd

HTF Frutigen AG – cartridge valves – Bucher Hydraulics Ltd

HTS – connectors – Anglia

HU seris – housed condensing units – Thermofrost Cryo plc

HUBA (Switzerland) – Techni Measure

Hubbard – Therma Group

Hubbard Commercial – commercial refrigeration systems multi compressor pack systems – H T G Trading Ltd

Hubbard Transport – transport refrigeration for medium low and multi-temperature vehicles – H T G Trading Ltd

Hubble Bubble – washing machines – Oliver Douglas Ltd

Huber – Ken Kimble Reactor Vessel Ltd

*****Huber & Suhner AG (Switzerland)** – R.F. and microwave products – Huber+Suhner (UK) Ltd

Huber-Warco – Harrier Fluid Power Ltd

Hübnel (Germany) – encoders, tachogenerators – Baumer Electric Ltd

Hubner – Encoders UK

Hübner Tachos – European Technical Sales Ltd

Hubron – Monopigments – Hubron Speciality Ltd

Hubron – black, white, colour master batches – Hubron Speciality Ltd

Hubtex – Stacatruc

Huck – fastening systems – Bearwood Engineering Supplies

Hucklecote – country clothing outwear – D Gurteen & Sons Ltd

Huco Dynatork – air motors – Huco Dynatork

Huco-Flex – miniature shaft misalignment couplers – Huco Dynatork

Huco - Huco-Flex - Huco-Pol - Uni-Lat - Vari-Tork - Oldham - Huco-Teleshaft - Poly-Flex - Placid Industries - Kerk - Inertia Dynamics - Hysteresis - Magnetic Technologies. – Huco Dynatork

Huco-Pol – zero backlash miniature universal joints – Huco Dynatork

Huco-Teleshaft – stock telescopic drive shaft assys – Huco Dynatork

Hudson – crystals & resonators – Anglia

Hudson Major – machines for drenching various fruit and vegetables prior to storage to prevent storage ailments and to prolong storage capabilities – John Wilson & Sons Industrial Engineer Blacksmith

Hudson Middleton – beakers and plaques - fine bone china – Hudson Of England Ltd

Huebsch – coin operated and on-premise washing machines and tumble dryers – Armstrong Commercial Laundry Systems

Huebsh – Clean Machine UK Ltd

*****Huedig (Germany)** – drainage and irrigation manufacturers – Connectomatic

Hufcor – sliding and folding acoustic partitions and operable walls – Kaba Door Systems

Hufcor – Style South

*****Hugel Et Fils** – Alsace wine – O W Loeb & Co. Ltd

Hughes – Cyclops Electronics Ltd

Hughes JVC – Lamphouse Ltd

Hughes Safety Showers – industrial safety shower and eyebath/facewash equipment – Hughes Safety Showers Ltd

Huhtamaki – Plastic & Paper Food Packaging (Food Service) – Huhtamaki UK Ltd

Hull and District Motor Services – bus and coach services – East Yorkshire Motor Services Ltd

Hull Daily Mail – newspaper – Mail News Media

Human Computer Interface – technical writing – Human Computer Interface Ltd

Human Factors – Bourton Group Ltd

Human Scale – Office Seating – Bucon Ltd

*****Humate (U.S.A.)** – humic acid products used in horticulture and agriculture for growth enhancement – Viresco UK Ltd

Humber – heavy duty non rock D/T grating and frame – Norinco UK Ltd

Humber – inflatable boats – Humber Fabrications Hull Ltd

Humber Fabrications – inflatable boats and fibreglass fabrications – Humber Fabrications Hull Ltd

Humber plain tile – clay – Sandtoft Holdings Ltd

Humbug – hum resector and passive isolator mainly for use on 50 and 75 impedance video systems – Tecton Ltd

HumEvap – evaporative humidifier – J S Humidifiers plc

Humidcoil – high humidity storage cooler – Thermal Engineering Systems Ltd

Humidicare – classic car storage system – E P S Logistics Technology Ltd

Humidivent – automatically ventilates when humidity is above set level – Airflow Developments Ltd

HumiPac – ceiling mounted humidifier – J S Humidifiers plc

*****Humiseal (U.S.A.)** – conformal coatings for pcbs – Humiseal Europe Ltd

Humour Factory – humorous cards – Great British Card Company plc

HUMPHREY – Hydraulic & Offshore Supplies Ltd

Hunger – cylinders/spares – Bearwood Engineering Supplies

Hunky-T – garments – Charterhouse Holdings plc

Hunt – plummer blocks and bearing housings – Criptic Arvis Ltd

Huntalloy – commercial bodies – Hunter Vehicles Ltd

Huntaplex – commercial bodies – Hunter Vehicles Ltd

Hunter – mobile crushing and screening outfit – Parker Plant Ltd

Hunter – Carbide tipped turning tools – The Toolpost

Hunter – above & below ground drainage systems (general entry) – Hunter Plastics

Hunter – web-offset press – L & M Ltd

Hunter Douglas – wholesale division, window blind components – Luxaflex

Hunter Fans – The Hunter Fan Company Ltd

Hunter Gears – gear cutters and machinists – Hunter Hields Gearcutting Ltd

Hunting – Hunting Plc

Huntingdon Weekly News – newspapers – Cambridge Newspapers Ltd

Hunton – flypress tooling and bolster outfits – Hartle I G E Ltd

Huntsman – tailors – H Huntsman & Sons Ltd

Hurco – edm machine – S E S Glos Ltd

Hurculace – shoe laces – Faire Bros & Co. Ltd

Huron Milling Machine – Phil Geesin Machinery Ltd

Huron Mu4 – Phil Geesin Machinery Ltd

Huron MU6 – Phil Geesin Machinery Ltd

Huron Nu4 – Phil Geesin Machinery Ltd

Hurricane – catamaran – White Formula Ltd

Hurricane – catamaran – Topper International

Hurricane – K-Tron Great Britain Ltd

Hurstridge – growing media – Sporting Surface Supplies Ltd

Hurth – European Technical Sales Ltd

Hurtz – printing frames – G Bopp & Co. Ltd

HUSCO INTERNATIONAL LTD – Hydraulic & Offshore Supplies Ltd

Hush Button – C-Tec Security Ltd

Hushair – Fill Stations – Scott International Ltd

Hushbox – acoustic cabinets – E F G Matthews Office Furniture Ltd

Hushvent – V E S Ltd

*****Husky** – Refrigeration – Export Ltd

Husky – Central vacuum – Strathvac

Husky Folding 25 and 40 – top hung gear for lightweight partitioning – P C Henderson Ltd

Husqvarna – D D Hire

Hustler – darts and flights – Unicorn Products Ltd

Husun – radio, marine VHF and UHF – Kelvin Hughes Ltd

Hutchins – Harrier Fluid Power Ltd

Huyck – roll coverings-paper technology – Invensys PLC

Huyundai – Stacatruc

*****HVB Burner Systems (U.S.A.)** – ceramic foam systems for cast shops and foundries – Porvair plc

HVD – Heron vinyl duckboard. Smooth top open grid matting for comfort & hygiene – Plastic Extruders Ltd

Hwacheon – Lead Precision Machine Tools Ltd

Hy-Bar – packaging Film – B P plc

Hy-Bond – tap washers – Slatebond Ltd

Hy-Dan – front mounted sweeper – Danline International Ltd

Hy-Fitt – Trafalgar Tools

Hy-lok – Twin Ferrule Instrument Fittings and Valves – Advanced Fluid Technologies Ltd

*****Hy Mac** – Kenneth Robson Equipment Ltd

HY-Rib Permanent Formwork – formwork – Expamet Building Products Ltd

Hya Solo – K S B Ltd

Hyamat – K S B Ltd

Hybild – B P plc

Hybright – optical brightening agents for various textile substraites – Brenntag Colours Ltd

Hybro Broilers – chicken – Johnstons Of Mountnorris

Hycadamp – metal-rubber-metal anti-vibration laminate – G K N Aerospace Ltd

Hycaflex – heavy duty neoprene-nylon fabric laminate for flexible containers, hovercraft skirts etc – G K N Aerospace Ltd

Hycalite – polyurethane/kevlar light weight flotation material – G K N Aerospace Ltd

Hycalite – polyurethane fueltank material – G K N Aerospace Ltd

Hycan – B P plc

HYcarb (U.S.A.) – for silicon carbide molten castings – Porvair plc

Hycatrol – nitrile and nitrile-P.V.C. based material for flexible fuel tanks – G K N Aerospace Ltd

Hycatrol HE-4 – rubber compound – G K N Aerospace Ltd

Hycatrol HG. 334 – modified nitrile rubber – G K N Aerospace Ltd

Hycatrol HP. 257 – nitrile rubber – G K N Aerospace Ltd

Hyclad – rubber-metal-rubber laminate for gaskets and seals – G K N Aerospace Ltd

Hyclad – manual plating lines – P M D UK Ltd

Hyclad – solid coating of flurocarbon on stainless steel sheet or coil – Corus U K Ltd

HYCO – Hydraulic & Offshore Supplies Ltd

Hycolin – Solmedia Laboratory Supplies

Hycon – Harrier Fluid Power Ltd

Hycon – Air Sampling Equipment – Biotest UK Ltd

HYCON – Hydraulic & Offshore Supplies Ltd

Hycontrol – valves, switches and ultrasonic level and flow instruments – Hycontrol Ltd

HYcor (U.S.A.) – for aluminium molten castings – Porvair plc

HyCore – Baldor UK

Hycover – distribution systems – Sewaco Ltd

Hydac – accumulators – Bearwood Engineering Supplies

Hydac – Harrier Fluid Power Ltd
Hydac – Trafalgar Tools
*Hydac (Germany) – hydraulic components – Hydac Technology Ltd
Hydac – hydraulic – V H S Hydraulic Components Ltd
HYDAC – Hydraulic & Offshore Supplies Ltd
Hydac – Pressure Design Hydraulics Ltd
HYDAC-FLUPAC – Hydraulic & Offshore Supplies Ltd
Hydac/Flupac – hydraulic parts – A C Hydraulics Ltd
Hydac International – Fairway Hydraulics Ltd
Hyde – Precision Components & Equipment Ltd
Hyde – building tools – Brian Hyde Ltd
Hyde Park – shaving brushes – Progress Shaving Brush Vulfix Ltd
Hyde Sails – manufacturing of sails and provider of laser cutting services – Hyde Sails Ltd
Hydema – Harrier Fluid Power Ltd
HYDERCO – Hydraulic & Offshore Supplies Ltd
Hydie – tool & die steel – Somers Forge Ltd
Hydis – M S C Gleichmann UK Ltd
*Hydome (France) – rooflights – Axter Ltd
Hydra – hydraulic portable valve actuator – Trelawny S P T Ltd
Hydra – instrument system - sail boats – B & G Ltd
Hydra – multi headed fastener placing system – Avdel UK Ltd
Hydra Towers – Accesscaff International Ltd
HYDRACLAMP – Hydraulic & Offshore Supplies Ltd
Hydraclaw – head or toe lift jack, 5 tonnes capacity – Tangye
Hydracushion – Fawcett Christie Hydraulics Ltd
HYDRADYNE – Hydraulic & Offshore Supplies Ltd
Hydrafeed – Hydrafeed Ltd
Hydraflex – ships hold cleaning gun – Trelawny S P T Ltd
Hydraflow – Specialty Fasteners & Components Ltd
HYDRAFORCE – Hydraulic & Offshore Supplies Ltd
*Hydragloss (U.S.A.) – high brightness clay for paper coating – Omya UK Ltd
HydraGRIP – application of plastics and non-slip coatings to grip or grab handles, lifting platforms, ramps for wheelchairs and aids for the disabled – Hydralon Coatings Ltd
Hydrainer – hydraulic submersible pumps – Hydrainer Pumps Ltd
Hydrakerb – small rising parking kerb – Apt Controls Ltd
Hydrakerb – rising kerbs – A P T Controls Ltd
Hydraline FX (United Kingdom) – smoothbore flexible PTFE hose – Aflex Hose Ltd
Hydralite – jacks, aluminium lightweight, from 20-130 tonnes – Tangye
Hydralogger – skidder loader – Malcolm W Shaw
Hydralok – connecting device for couplings to hoses, pipes and tubes, machines for applying connectors and/or couplings to hoses, pipes and to tubes – Endeavour International Ltd
Hydram – Allspeeds Ltd
Hydramac – Harrier Fluid Power Ltd
Hydramite – jacks, aluminium compact, for any position use, 6.5 tonnes – Tangye
Hydrangea Colourant – Vitax Ltd
Hydraotechni – Harrier Fluid Power Ltd
HYDRAOVANE – Hydraulic & Offshore Supplies Ltd
Hydrapak – manual high pressure pump for various fluids – Tangye
Hydrapilot – auto pilot sailboat – B & G Ltd
Hydrar – Newburgh Engineering Co. Ltd
HYDRASCAND – Hydraulic & Offshore Supplies Ltd
Hydraseal – British Vita plc
Hydraseal DPM – solvent and water free epoxy resin, liquid applied surface damp proof membrane – Flowcrete UK
Hydrasearch – Fluid conveying products for marine and aerospace industries – Dixon Group Europe Ltd
Hydrastart – fluid coupling – Renold Clutches & Couplings Ltd
Hydrastart Fluid Coupling – Renold Clutches & Couplings Ltd
HYDRASTORE – Hydraulic & Offshore Supplies Ltd
Hydrastumper – tree extractor – Malcolm W Shaw
Hydrasun – spares & equipment – Bearwood Engineering Supplies
Hydratex – British Vita plc
Hydratone – Dead Sea professional face and body products – Finders International Ltd
Hydratron – Air operated high pressure pumps – Hydratron Ltd
Hydratruck – tool and die handler – Stanley Handling Ltd
Hydraulic Drive – downhole pump – Weir Group Senior Executives Pension Trust Ltd
HYDRAULIC PROJECTS LTD – Hydraulic & Offshore Supplies Ltd
Hydraulic Tanks – pressed and welded assemblies – Warwick & Bailey Engineering
HYDRAULIK RING – Hydraulic & Offshore Supplies Ltd
Hydraulikring – European Technical Sales Ltd
Hydraumatec – Harrier Fluid Power Ltd
HYDRAUTO – Hydraulic & Offshore Supplies Ltd
Hydraversal Shears – hydraulic shear – Joseph Rhodes Ltd

Hydreco – Harrier Fluid Power Ltd
Hydrel – Holophane Europe Ltd
Hydro Aluminium – aluminium alloy extruded sections, bars, tubing, design assistance, drawing and profit typing also provide tubing, anodising, painting fabrication. – Hydro Aluminium Extrusion
Hydro Aluminium Extrusion – aluminium alloy extruded sections, bars and tubing, design assistance, drawing & prototyping also provided anodising, painting of fabrication. – Hydro Aluminium Extrusion
Hydro-Flow – Flowline Manufacturing Ltd
HYDRO-LINE – Hydraulic & Offshore Supplies Ltd
Hydro-Logic – Halcyon Solutions
Hydro-Mist Range – spray extraction carpet cleaning machines – Truvox International Ltd
Hydro Precise – Yara UK lt Ltd
Hydro-Thermal – steam equipment – Bearwood Engineering Supplies
HYDRO-VACUUM – LPG pumps – H K L Gas Power Ltd
Hydro-X – membrane for potable water treatment – Kalsep UK Ltd
Hydroban – bituminous roof waterproofing products – T R C Midlands Ltd
HYDROBELLO – Hydro pneumatic compresator for high and low temperature fluids – Pulsation Dampers At Pulseguard Ltd
Hydrocar – hydraulic – V H S Hydraulic Components Ltd
Hydrocarb – calcite filler – Omya UK Ltd
Hydrocare Fizzy – protein remover tablets for soft, hard, and gas permeable lenses – Allergan Ltd
Hydrocide SX – transparent solvent based aluminium stearate water repellent – Conren Ltd
Hydrocol – liquid colours – Lanxess Ltd
Hydrocompact – grease interceptor – Norinco UK Ltd
HYDROCONTROL – Hydraulic & Offshore Supplies Ltd
Hydrocraft – Harrier Fluid Power Ltd
Hydrodet – detergent-bottle wash. mach. & process plant – The Proton Group Ltd
*Hydrodrive (Italy) – marine hydraulic steering – Lancing Marine
Hydroferrox – liquid colours – Lanxess Ltd
Hydrofilt – Harrier Fluid Power Ltd
Hydrofilter – hydro carbon inteceptor – Norinco UK Ltd
*Hydrofit (Italy) – hose fittings – Hydrasun Ltd
Hydroflex – Harrier Fluid Power Ltd
HYDROFLEX – Accumulator with a one piece moulded bladder available from highly inert elastomerformulations – Pulsation Dampers At Pulseguard Ltd
Hydroflute – twin-wall polypropylene – Corrugated Plastic Products Ltd
Hydroform – ceiling panels – Celotex Ltd
Hydrogrip Machine Vices – Pharos Engineering Ltd
*Hydrohil (France) – air handling units – Thermal Technology Sales Ltd
Hydrokompenser – Schmitt Europe Ltd
HYDROKRAFT – Hydraulic & Offshore Supplies Ltd
Hydrol – hydraulic oils – Benjamin R Vickers & Sons Ltd
Hydroleca – expanded clay – Silvaperl
Hydrolite – flawless finish – Elizabeth Arden
Hydroluminium Extrusion – Hydro Aluminium Extrusion
HYDROLUX – Hydraulic & Offshore Supplies Ltd
Hydrolux – Sebakmt UK Ltd
Hydromac – Harrier Fluid Power Ltd
Hydromaster – Sykes Marine Hydromaster Ltd
Hydromatik – piston pumps – Bearwood Engineering Supplies
HYDROMATIK – Hydraulic & Offshore Supplies Ltd
Hydromet – propeller shaft material – Bruntons Propellers Ltd
HYDRONIT-EOS – Hydraulic & Offshore Supplies Ltd
Hydronox – antioxidant spray – Dynamic Drawings Ltd
Hydropac – power systems – B S P International Foundations Ltd
Hydropak – pumps – Armstrong Holden Brooke Pullen Ltd
Hydropile – piling systems – B S P International Foundations Ltd
Hydrosoft – water softening – INEOS Enterprises Ltd
Hydrospring – Stromag Ltd
Hydrostatically Pressed Crucible – Magna Industrials Ltd
Hydrosteel – Hydrogen inside steel detector – Ion Science Ltd
Hydrotech – wetsuits, drysuits and semi-dry suits, diving equipment and accessories – Stoney Cove Diver Training Centre Ltd
Hydrotech – automatic high pressure washing service – Hydrotech Systems Ltd
*Hydrotech Monolithic (Membrane 6125) (U.S.A.) – hot melt rubber modified bitumen waterproofing – Alumasc Exterior Building Products
HYDROTECHECNIK – Hydraulic & Offshore Supplies Ltd
Hydrotechnic – Trafalgar Tools
Hydrotechnik – Pressure Design Hydraulics Ltd
HYDROTECHNIK TEST EQUIPMENT – Hydraulic & Offshore Supplies Ltd
Hydrotemp – high temperature anti corrosive coating – Darcy Products Ltd

Hydrothane Screed – polyurethane screed with excellent chemical resistance – Conren Ltd
Hydrovane – air compressors – Motivair Compressors Ltd
Hydrovane – compressor – Thorite
HYDROVANE – Hydraulic & Offshore Supplies Ltd
Hydrovane – compressors, parts and service – Airware International Ltd
Hydrovane – compressors – Bearwood Engineering Supplies
Hydrovane – Red House Industrial Services Ltd
HYDROWA – Hydraulic & Offshore Supplies Ltd
Hydrowave 2000 – natural home perm – Vivalis Ltd
Hydrox – underwater protective lubricant – Benjamin R Vickers & Sons Ltd
*Hydroxyethylcellulose (Netherlands) – Hercules Holding Ii Ltd
*Hydroxypropylcellulose (U.S.A.) – Hercules Holding Ii Ltd
Hyfen – heavy duty conveying – Fenner Drives Ltd
Hyfex – Divex
Hyfin – Osborn Unipol Ltd
Hyflex (U.S.A.) – flexible shaft couplings – Centa Transmissions
Hyfoam – luxury foaming soap – Deb R & D Ltd
Hyfoam Antibac – antibacterial foaming soap – Deb R & D Ltd
Hyfoam Cartridge Dispensers – Deb R & D Ltd
Hyform – drilling chemicals – B P plc
Hyfrac – B P plc
Hygemics Cleaning Systems – Delaval
Hygenius Ultra – dairy chemicals – Delaval
Hygenus – hand sanitizing gel – Elsan Ltd
HygieNet (United Kingdom) – industrial head nets – Aburnet Ltd
Hygienics – anti-bacterial hand gel, requiring no water or towels in use – F M C G Ltd
Hygimat – antifatigue and non-slip safety matting for the food industry – Coba Plastics Ltd
Hygiplas – plastic storage and handling for food industry – Hygiplas Containers Ltd
Hykleen – B P plc
Hylamor – universal gasket and jointing compound – Hammerite Products Ltd
*Hyland (Worldwide) – health products – Baxter Healthcare Ltd
Hylo – budget equipment for plating – P M D UK Ltd
HYLOK – Hydraulic & Offshore Supplies Ltd
Hylomar – S J Wharton Ltd
Hylosan – B P plc
Hyma – foam production and conversion machinery – Hyma UK Ltd
Hymac – Harrier Fluid Power Ltd
Hymod – copper powder – Makin Metal Powders UK Ltd
Hynix – M S C Gleichmann UK Ltd
Hynix – Cyclops Electronics Ltd
Hyox – Divex
Hypablast – range of chemical dosing and washing equipment – Agma Ltd
Hypac – B P plc
Hypacage – collapsible cage pallets (wireformed) – Palletower GB Ltd
Hypaject – injection moulding machine – Magnum Venus Plastech Ltd
Hypal – pallets – British Polythene Industries plc
Hypalon – synthetic rubber – Du Pont UK Ltd
Hypalon – W Mannering London Ltd
Hypalon – elastomers from Du Pont – Omya UK Ltd
Hypam – developer – Harman Technology Ltd
Hypaque – G E Healthcare
Hyparflex – Metallic Hose – Dixon Group Europe Ltd
Hypec – Lightweight hydraulic jacks – Allspeeds Ltd
HyperBGA – http://www.endicottinterconnect.com/Products_hyperBGA.php – Endicott Interconnect UK Ltd
HyperCarb – Minelco Ltd
Hypercarb – porous graphitic carbon offering unique retention for H.P.L.C and LC/MS – Thermo Fisher Scientific
Hypercrete – British Vita plc
Hyperfil – pre-imp pregnated materials – Jones Stroud Insulations Ltd
Hyperform – heating and cooling rolls – Cope Engineering Ltd
HyperGEL – aqueous and organic polymeric columns for size exclusion cheomatography – Thermo Fisher Scientific
Hypergrade – B P plc
Hypergrade Plus – B P plc
Hyperion – B P plc
Hyperkote – polyurethane coatings – Dow Hyperlast
Hyperkote – British Vita plc
Hyperlam – glass fabric laminates – Jones Stroud Insulations Ltd
Hyperlast – polyether-based polyurethane spray and cast system – Dow Hyperlast
Hyperlast – British Vita plc
HyperLine – Road/Highway and Airport Runway Marking – Quality Marking Services Ltd

Hyperlyn – high performance octene based cast pallet wrap material (Stretch Film) – M J Maillis UK Ltd
Hyperm – gas permeable lenses – David Thomas Ltd
HyperREZ – polymeric columns for reversed phase, carbohydrate and ion exchange – Thermo Fisher Scientific
Hypersack – Segezha Packaging
Hyperseal – sealing and finishing tapes – Jones Stroud Insulations Ltd
HyperSEP – solid phase extraction columns – Thermo Fisher Scientific
Hypersil – spherical silica based columns for HPLC and LC/MS – Thermo Fisher Scientific
Hypersil B D S – base deactivated silica columns – Thermo Fisher Scientific
Hypersil Duet – mixed mode columns for the separation of ionic and hydrophobic analytes in one analysis – Thermo Fisher Scientific
Hypersil Green – HPLC columns for environmental analytes – Thermo Fisher Scientific
Hypersol Macronet – adsorbent resins – Purolite International Ltd
Hypertape – varnished fabrics – Jones Stroud Insulations Ltd
Hyperten – resin impregnated unidirectional banding tape – Jones Stroud Insulations Ltd
Hypertex – flexible polyester (non woven) paper-polyester film composites – Jones Stroud Insulations Ltd
Hypertherm – flexible nomex paper-polyester film and nomex paper-kapton film composites – Jones Stroud Insulations Ltd
Hyperthern – Independent Welding Services Ltd
Hyperware – Genus Group
Hyperx – Nortech Control Systems Ltd
Hyphos – dairy chemicals – Delaval
Hyplex – polypropylene strapping – Gordian Strapping Ltd
Hypneumat – European Technical Sales Ltd
Hypnos – domestic beds, divans & mattresses – Hypnos Ltd
Hypnos Contracts – hotel beds, divans & mattresses, sofa beds – Hypnos Ltd
Hypocell – water purification equipment for swimming pools – Hypocell Ltd
Hypochloros – detergent – Murphy & Son
Hypogear – B P plc
Hypor – cartridge soap dispenser system – Deb R & D Ltd
Hypor – dispenser – Appor Ltd
Hypot – cable testers – Bearwood Engineering Supplies
Hypotherm – Messer Cutting Systems
Hyprez – diamond products – Engis UK Ltd
Hyprint – B P plc
***Hypro (U.S.A.)** – pumps – Dual Pumps Ltd
Hypro – roller vane pumps & centrifugal pumps – Hypro Eu Ltd
Hypro – Harrier Fluid Power Ltd
HYPRO CORPORATION – Hydraulic & Offshore Supplies Ltd
Hyprosteps – Dale Lifting and Handling Equipment Specialists
Hyprosteps – Accesscaff International Ltd
Hypure – demineraliser systems – Kinetico UK Ltd
Hypuremate (United Kingdom) – Topside torque wrenches and bolt tensioners – Hydratight Morpeth
HyPURITY – high purity silica based columns with increased pH stability for HPLC AND lc/ms – Thermo Fisher Scientific
HYR-APP – Hydraulic & Offshore Supplies Ltd
HyRack – rackable high hygiene plastic pallet. – D S Smith Correx
***Hyranger (France)** – bituminous based built up roof waterproofing membranes – Axter Ltd
Hyrate Bio Filters – Sewaco Ltd
Hyreel – equipment for reel-to-reel plating – P M D UK Ltd
Hysa – B P plc
Hyseal – British Vita plc
Hysoft – range of softeners for finishing and printing of cellulosics and cellulosic blends – Brenntag Colours Ltd
Hysol – B P plc
Hysol – long life semi synthetic soluble cutting oils covering all applications – Castrol UK Ltd
Hyspin – hydraulic oils from ISO VG5 - ISO VG 150 offering both standard and high viscosity index, anti-wear and non anti-wear properties – Castrol UK Ltd
Hystacker – Stacatruc
Hystar HY – gloss finish ink for trichromatics on paper & board – Fujifilm Sericol Ltd
Hystep – hydraulic control valve – Rolls Royce Marine Electrical Systems Ltd
Hyster – Stacatruc
HYSTER – Chaintec Ltd
Hyster – T V H UK Ltd
Hyster – Team Overseas Ltd
Hyster – Harrier Fluid Power Ltd
Hyt – Radio Relay
HYT – Corby Radio Services Ltd
HYTAR – Hydraulic & Offshore Supplies Ltd
HYTEC – Hydraulic & Offshore Supplies Ltd
Hytecinformation Systems Ltd – Network project services provider – Hytec Information Security
Hytex – knitted cut resistant gloves – Bennett Safetywear
Hytex – lubricants – Chevron
HYTHANE – Hydraulic & Offshore Supplies Ltd
Hythane – high performance polyurethane compound used in hydraulic sealing applications – Hallite Seals International Ltd
Hythe Herald – newspaper title – Kent Regional News & Media
Hytherm – rigid foamed insulation boards – Axter Ltd
HYTHOS VALVES – Hydraulic & Offshore Supplies Ltd
HYTOS – Hydraulic & Offshore Supplies Ltd
Hytrac – overhead conveyors – M C M Conveyor Systems
Hytrel – polyester elastomers – Du Pont UK Ltd
Hytrel – Resinex UK Ltd
Hytrex – Harrier Fluid Power Ltd
Hytuf – hot work tool steel – Somers Forge Ltd
***Hyundai (Korea, Republic of)** – CNC lathes – C Dugard Ltd Machine Tools
***Hyundai (Korea, Republic of)** – cars – Hyundai Motor UK Ltd
HYUNDAI – Chaintec Ltd
Hyundai – L M C Hadrian Ltd
HYUNDAI – Welding Wire and Electrodes – Finlex International Ltd
Hyundai – Harrier Fluid Power Ltd
HYUPDONG – Hydraulic & Offshore Supplies Ltd
Hyvar – herbicide – Du Pont UK Ltd
Hyvis – polybutenes – B P plc
Hyviz – G K N Aerospace Transparancy Systems Ltd
HYZYME – drain and septic tank maintenance products – Hydrachem Ltd

I

I-125 Rapid Strund – G E Healthcare
I-125 Seeds – G E Healthcare
I.A.L. – marketing and management consultants in chemical, plastics and related industries – I A L Consultants
I.A.S. – advertising – I A S Smarts Ltd
I.A. Series Micronet – building management system – Schneider Electric
I.B.D.N. – integrated building distribution networks – Nortel Networks UK Ltd
I.B.S. – intelligent belt steering – Qualter Hall & Co. Ltd
I.B. System – drilling tools – Cromwell Group Holdings
I.C.N. Biomedicals – Icn Pharmaceuticals Ltd
I.C.S. – solutions builder accessories – Scientific Computers Ltd
I C S Robotics & Automation Ltd – I C S Robotics & Automation Ltd
I.C.S. Scotland – control and safety systems – I C S Triplex
***I.C.T.C. (France, Italy and Germany)** – inter-continental cookware and tableware – I C T C Ltd
I Cut My Way – pocket knives and trade knives – Egginton Bros Ltd
I.D.M. Electronics – precision slip ring assemblies, sliding contact devices, fibre optic rotary joints and rotary switches – Moog Components
I.D.T. – diamond tools and wheels – Indusmond Diamond Tools Ltd
I.E.C. Engineering – precision parts and mechanisms – I E C Engineering Ltd
I.E.E. – professional engineering society – Institution Of Engineering & Technology
***I.E.F. Werner (Germany)** – linear guideways and systems – R A Rodriguez UK Ltd
i-Frame – Goulds Pumps a Division of ITT Industries Ltd
I.G. – galvanised and stainless steel lintels – Ig Ltd
I.G. Cavity Trays – pre-creased cavity tray system for gable abutment and flat roof refurbishment applications – Ig Ltd
I.G.U.S. – middle of the road music – K R L
I Hate School – stationary sets for school – Padgett Bros A To Z Ltd
I.K.O. – bearings – Bearwood Engineering Supplies
I.L.C. – in-line centrifugal fans – Flakt Woods Ltd
I-Line – panelboard – Schneider
I.M.C. – waste compactors, silver burnishing machines, potato peelers, potato chippers, universal peelers, vegetable preparation machines, pot scrubbing machines, pre-rinse sprays, food waste disposers and systems and incontinence pad disposer – I M C
***I.M.E.A.S. (Italy)** – wide abrasive belt satin finishing machines – British & Continental Traders Ltd
I.M.I.Bailey Birkett – valves – Bearwood Engineering Supplies
I.M.O. – European Technical Sales Ltd
I.M.O. – housemark and meter and relay trade mark – I M O Electronics Ltd
I.M.S. – computers – S T Micro Electronics Ltd
I.M.S. – I M S International Marketing Services Ltd
I.M.S. Interanational Marketing Services – I M S International Marketing Services Ltd
i-Meta Manager – optimization Product – Information Strategies Key Intangible Value
I.N.A. – bearings – Bearwood Engineering Supplies
I.O.C.M. – G E Healthcare
I.O Shen Mastergrade Triplex Steel Knives – Knife Wizard
I.P.A. – computer software and systems solutions for newspaper publishers – I P A Systems Ltd
I.P. Connect – IP telephony solution – Nortel Networks UK Ltd
***I.P.S. Imperia (Italy)** – imperia pasta and noodle rollers – Fairfax Coffee Ltd
I.P.U. – air starting systems – Industrial Power Units Ltd
I PAK – inverter system – B F Entron Ltd
I.Q. Range – video overlay image quantifier and dimensioning gauging – Cortex Controllers Ltd
I Q Technologies – network accessories – Betterbox Communications Ltd
***I.Q. Video (Far East)** – video accessories – Jessops plc
I-R – Gustair Materials Handling Equipment Ltd
I-R Aro – Gustair Materials Handling Equipment Ltd
***I.R.C. (U.S.A.)** – resistors – T T Electronics Welwyn Components Ltd
I. & R. Standard – engineering components – Illston & Robson Ltd
I.S. 128/400 – tele communications systems – Nine Shipton
I.S.C.S. – structured cabling system – I T T Ltd
I.S.D.N – terminating units – Telspec plc
I.S.N.S. – structural networking system – I T T Ltd
I.S.R.I. – commercial vehicle seats – Isringhausen GB Ltd
I.S. Stocklines – promotional clothing, caps and bags – I S Enterprises International
I.S.T.D. – professional examination board – Imperial Society Of Teachers Of Dancing
I SAVE tax with the Woolwich – The Woolwich
I-SFT – M S C Gleichmann UK Ltd
I.T.C. – notch nuts and related lockwashers – Industrial Trading Co. Ltd
I.T.E. – fuses – Bearwood Engineering Supplies
I.T.L. – high and U.H.V. components, fabrications, chambers and vacuum engineering – MDC Vacuum Products Ltd
I.T.M.A. – Centre For Contemporary British History
I.T.N. – Independent Radio News Ltd
I.T.T. – elec.indic – Bearwood Engineering Supplies
***I.V.G. (Italy)** – industrial hose – Hydrasun Ltd
I.V.M. 1000 – tele communication systems – Nine Shipton
***I.V.O. (Germany)** – timers and counters (electronic) – I V O C M S
***I V V** – Decorative Hand-Made Glass – La Porcellana Tableware International Ltd
I.XL – pocket knives – Egginton Bros Ltd
i5 – Mid Blue International Ltd
i5os – Mid Blue International Ltd
iAccess – Our unique low maintenance access control system for apartment blocks – Timeit Software Distribution Ltd
IAD – Versalift Distributors UK Ltd
Ian Allan Publishing – transport and aviation books and magazines road rail aviation light transit – Ian Allan Publishing Ltd
Ian Leach Plumbing & Heating – Bathroom design and tiling, Central Heating and Boiler installation, Solar Panel Hot Water Systems – Ian Leach Plumbing & Heating
IARP (Italy) – refrigeration – Interlevin Refrigeration Ltd
Ibarmia – Lead Precision Machine Tools Ltd
IBC Mixers – Euromixers
Ibcol – disinfectant – Jeyes
Iberia Airlines – airline – Iberia Airlines
***Iberital** – Jaguar Epresso Systems
Ibex – brushes – Industrial Brushware Ltd
Ibex Pumps – Alfa Laval Eastbourne Ltd
Ibico – UK Office Direct
IBM – All IBM servers, storage, software and desktop systems – Server Parts Ltd
IBM – A T M Parts
IBM – Forever Scotland IT Consultancy
IBM – Apex Computer Services Wales Ltd
IBM – Lamphouse Ltd
IBM – Mid Blue International Ltd
IBM – IBM Servers and Storage – ibm247
IBM – Hardware – Moorgate Ltd
IBM Business Cards – business papers – Howard Smith Paper Ltd
IBM CD Case Labels – business papers – Howard Smith Paper Ltd
IBM CD/DVD Gloss Labels – business papers – Howard Smith Paper Ltd
IBM CD/DVD High Resolution Labels – business papers – Howard Smith Paper Ltd
IBM CD/DVD Labelling Kit – business papers – Howard Smith Paper Ltd
IBM Color Paper – business papers – Howard Smith Paper Ltd
IBM Color Pro – business papers – Howard Smith Paper Ltd
IBM computers – Mid Blue International Ltd
IBM Copy Pro – business papers – Howard Smith Paper Ltd
IBM Digital Photo Inkjet Paper – business papers – Howard Smith Paper Ltd
IBM Document Pro – business papers – Howard Smith Paper Ltd

IBM Gloss Coated Inkjet Paper – business paper – Howard Smith Paper Ltd

IBM Greeting Cards – business papers – Howard Smith Paper Ltd

IBM Inkjet Pro – business papers – Howard Smith Paper Ltd

IBM Inkjet Transparencies – business papers – Howard Smith Paper Ltd

IBM Laser Pro – business papers – Howard Smith Paper Ltd

IBM Matt Coated Inkjet Paper – business papers – Howard Smith Paper Ltd

IBM Multi-Functional Labels – business papers – Howard Smith Paper Ltd

IBM Office Pro – business papers – Howard Smith Paper Ltd

IBM Print Pro – business papers – Howard Smith Paper Ltd

IBM T-shirt Transfer Paper – business papers – Howard Smith Paper Ltd

Iboflor (United Kingdom) – carpet tiles – Checkmate Industries Ltd

ICAP 61 – Thermo Electrical

ICAP 61e – Thermo Electrical

Icarus S.N. (Belgium) – exotic alloy valves – Alexander Cardew Ltd

ICC – exhibition & conference centre – Nec Group

Ice Bank – ice building and storage systems – Thermal Engineering Systems Ltd

Ice Cream Tricycles – tricycles – Pashley Cycles Ltd

Ice'n'easy – Ice packs – Radleys

Ice Queen – paper – Paperun Group Of Companies

***Icechest** – ice/condiment storage – Servaclean Bar Systems Ltd

Icelander – thermal protective clothing for low temperature working environments – Vacuum Reflex

Icelert – road heating controller and road ice prediction systems – Findlay Irvine

Icem – T V H UK Ltd

ICEM – Chaintec Ltd

Icematic – refrigeration compressor lubricants for all models of compressor - mineral and synthetic based – Castrol UK Ltd

Iceni – bedroom furniture – Quantum Industries Ltd

iceni – company's registered trade mark – Iceni Productions Ltd

Iceni Cadet – bedroom furniture – Quantum Industries Ltd

Icerock Ductwork – rock mineral wool insulation for ductwork – Knauf Insulation Ltd

Icerock Rolls – thermal and acoustic insulation – Knauf Insulation Ltd

Icerock Slabs – thermal and acoustic insulation – Knauf Insulation Ltd

Icestop – heater for roof and gutter de-icing – Tyco Electronics UK Ltd

Icevent – remote cleaning of HVAC and kitchen extract ductwork affected by grease – System Hygienics Ltd

ICF – Office Furniture – Bucon Ltd

Icimar – Akzo Nobel Packaging Coatings Ltd

Icm – Euroteck Systems UK Ltd

ICMA – S M W Autoblok

Icom – Radio Relay

Icom – Servicom High Tech Ltd

ICOM – Corby Radio Services Ltd

Icon – digital live mixer – Allen & Heath Ltd

Icotek – cable gland systems – M. Buttkereit Ltd

ICP-MS Systems – Spectro Analytical UK Ltd

***ICR Touch** – I C R Touch LLP

ICR100 – fuel card reader – C H Jones Walsall Ltd

ICS – Image capture system – Vysionics

ICS Robotics & Automation – I C S Robotics & Automation Ltd

ICT – Cyclops Electronics Ltd

ICT (South Africa) – Morpho Cards UK Ltd

Icy – vodka – Charles H Julian Ltd

ID – UK Office Direct

ID/IDT Series – digital process indicators panel mounting – Lee-Dickens Ltd

ID-MARK – Imaging material – Dalesway Print Technology

ID Series – digital process indicators panel mounting – Lee-Dickens Ltd

***IDDF (U.S.A.)** – data base of pharmaceutical products – First Databank Europe Ltd

Idea Machine – Standard Industrial Systems Ltd

Ideagen Software Ltd – Software House – Ideagen Software Ltd

Ideal – welding machinery – Vollmer UK Ltd

Ideal – self dosing sewage distributor – Tuke & Bell Ltd

***Ideal (Italy)** – mig welders – S I P Industrial Products Ltd

Ideal Air Europe – portable heating systems, temporary heating, pest elimination – The Ideal Cleaning Company

Ideal Bean Bags – Ideal Bean Bags

Ideal Cleaning – commercial and domestic cleaning services – The Ideal Cleaning Company

Ideal Home – I P C Media Ltd

Ideal Industries – Alpha Electronics Southern Ltd

Ideal Lawn – brushes – Harris Cleaning Services

Ideal Manufacturing – chemicals for various industries, UK and overseas – Ideal Manufactures

Ideal Response – emergency rasponse for flood and fire damage, decontamination – The Ideal Cleaning Company

Ideal Standard – Baxi Group

Ideal-Standard – Ideal Standard Ltd

Ideal Studios – Web, Graphic design, photograhy and Marketing – Ideal Studios

ideal Studios Print – Ideal Studios

Ideal Studios Promotional Merchandise – Ideal Studios

Ideal-Tek – tweezers pliers – Time Products UK Ltd

Idealair – laboratory air conditioning equipment – James H Heal & Co. Ltd

Idealarc – arc welding transformers and rectifiers – Lincoln Electric UK Ltd

Ideas Furnace – Quality Website design and Development – Ideas Furnace Ltd

IDEASBYNET (United Kingdom) – the UK's one stop shop for promotional printed business gifts - free design, artwork & virtual samples – Ideasbynet Promotional Items

Idenden – Bostik Ltd

Identa Tape – Heat seal identification tape – J & A International Ltd

IDER – international disaster and emergency response – Andrich International Ltd

Idex – internally ducted exhaust – Solois Thermal Ltd

Idromat – flow and pressure pump controller – Calpeda Ltd

IDS – Stemmer Imaging

IDS – refrigerants, heat transfer fluids, oils, cleaning chemicals – Thermofrost Cryo plc

IDT – Cyclops Electronics Ltd

IDT (&ICS) – semiconductors – Anglia

IEF Werner – linear modules & controllers – R A Rodriguez UK Ltd

IEF Werner – custom built assembly & automation equipment – R A Rodriguez UK Ltd

IEF Werner – dosing & soldering systems – R A Rodriguez UK Ltd

IEF Werner – linear guideways, slides & systems – R A Rodriguez UK Ltd

IFM – Aztech Components Ltd

***Ifor Williams** – Reeth Garage Ltd

Ifor Williams – A T Wilde & Son Ltd

IFR Ltd – Manufacturer of test & measurement equipment – Aeroflex Ltd

***Igarashi (Japan)** – micromotors DC – Trident Engineering Ltd

Igel 38 – 38% filcon 1A hydrophilic contact lens material with and without UV inhibitor – Ultra Vision International Ltd

Igel 58 – 58% filcon 4A hydrophilic contact lens material with and without UV inhibitor – Ultra Vision International Ltd

Igel 67 – 67% filcon 4A hydrophilic contact lens material with and without UV inhibitor – Ultra Vision International Ltd

Igel 77 – 77% filcon 4A hydrophilic contact lens material with and without UV inhibitor – Ultra Vision International Ltd

Igel CD – 38% water contact lens, tinted or clear – Ultra Vision International Ltd

Igel Delta Toric – 54% water content, non-ionic, moulded soft toric contact lens for Astigmatism, with handling tint and UV inhibitor for monthly replacement – Ultra Vision International Ltd

Igel Hi-Tints – tinted soft contact lens – Ultra Vision International Ltd

Igel Kerasoft – 58% water content, non-ionic, lathed soft toric/spherical lens with UV Inhibitor for keratoconus cases – Ultra Vision International Ltd

Igel Omega - 38 – moulded soft contact lens, UV inhibitor, clear and handling tint – Ultra Vision International Ltd

Igel Omega 56 – 56% water content, non-ionic, moulded soft contact lens with handling tiny and UV inhibitor for monthly replacement – Ultra Vision International Ltd

Igel Presto – 58% water content soft contact lens, tinted or clear with UV inhibitor – Ultra Vision International Ltd

Igel Prima – 67% water content soft contact lens, tinted or clear with UV inhibitor – Ultra Vision International Ltd

Igel RX Sphere – 38%, 58%, 67% and 77% spherical lenses to own design, manufactured from Igel material – Ultra Vision International Ltd

Igel Rx Toric – 38%, 58% and 67% soft toric lens for astigmatism with UV inhibitor – Ultra Vision International Ltd

Igel SA Multifocal – 38% soft multifocal contact lens, spherical and toric for presbyopia – Ultra Vision International Ltd

Igel Stock Toric – 38% soft toric lens for astigmatism with UV inhibitor – Ultra Vision International Ltd

Igel Therapeutic – 77% soft contact lenses for prosthetic use – Ultra Vision International Ltd

Igel Therapeutic bandage – lenses manufactured from Igel 67 and 77 materials – Ultra Vision International Ltd

***IGF** – Cater Bake UK Ltd

Iglidur – Igus (UK) Ltd

Iglidur, Igubal, Drylin, Polysorb, Chainflex, E-Chains, Energy Chain, Readychain, Triflex – Igus (UK) Ltd

Igloo – B P plc

Igloo – sleeping bags – Comfy Quilts Ltd

Igloo RPO Ltd – Recruitment Management – Igloo RPO Ltd

Ignition – The Woolwich

Igranic – igranic motor control equipment – Igranic Control Systems Ltd

IGS – Softbrands

Igubal – Igus (UK) Ltd

Igus – Mercury Bearings Ltd

IHC – Harrier Fluid Power Ltd

IHC – intelligent home control solutions – Schneider

IHI – Harrier Fluid Power Ltd

***Iittala (Finland)** – glassware – Dexam International

Iiyama – Lamphouse Ltd

***Ikegami (Japan)** – broadcast and closed circuit television equipment – Ikegami Electronics

IKO – Antifriction Components Ltd

IKO – Mayday Seals & Bearings

IKO – Mercury Bearings Ltd

iKon – large area CCD camera – Andor Technology Ltd

Ikon – the writing edge – Hainenko Ltd

Ikon Office Solutions Plc – supply, install and service photocopiers – Ricoh UK Ltd

Ikon - The Writing Edge – Hainenko Ltd

Ikron – UK agent hydraulic filters & accessories – Harrier Fluid Power Ltd

Ikron (Italy) – hydraulic filters – BYPY Hydraulics & Transmissions Ltd

IKRON – Hydraulic & Offshore Supplies Ltd

Ikron – Fairway Hydraulics Ltd

Ikron – hydraulic – V H S Hydraulic Components Ltd

IKS – Antalis Mcnaughton

Ilfobrom – developer – Harman Technology Ltd

Ilfochrome – Harman Technology Ltd

Ilfoclean – Harman Technology Ltd

Ilfocolor – Harman Technology Ltd

Ilfofix – fixing agent – Harman Technology Ltd

Ilfoguard – mounting and laminating materials – Harman Technology Ltd

Ilfojet – inkjet media – Harman Technology Ltd

Ilfolab – Harman Technology Ltd

Ilford – photographic materials – Harman Technology Ltd

Ilford XP2 – C41 processed black & white film – Harman Technology Ltd

Ilfosol – Harman Technology Ltd

Ilfospeed – Harman Technology Ltd

Ilfostar – digital imaging equipment – Harman Technology Ltd

Ilfotec – Harman Technology Ltd

Ilfotol – Harman Technology Ltd

iLIght – lighting controls – Camlar Ltd

Ilkeston Express – newspaper – Derby Telegraph Media Group

Illig – plastics thermoforming machinery – Illig UK Ltd

Ilmor – racing engines – Mercedes A M G

Ilmvac – vacuum – AESpump

Ilobroach – neat broaching oils – Castrol UK Ltd

Ilocut – neat cutting oils with a wide range of viscosites and additive combinations – Castrol UK Ltd

Iloform – neat and soluble pressing and forming oils – Castrol UK Ltd

Ilogrind – neat grinding oils – Castrol UK Ltd

Ilumitex – dry spray multicolour wall coating – Pittaway Sempol Ltd

Ilumitextra – dry spray multicolour metallic wall coating – Pittaway Sempol Ltd

Image – shoes – D Jacobson & Sons Ltd

Image – G E Healthcare

Image – pop-up display system – Clip Display

IMAGE – computed generated imagery systems – Thales Training & Consultancy

Image – plastic jerrycan 1-5 ltrs – RPC Containers Ltd

Image 4 Colour copier – Office Paper – Mcnaughton James Paper Group Ltd

Image Automation – automatic inspection systems for quality control – Sira Test & Certification Ltd

Image Executive – Office Paper – Mcnaughton James Paper Group Ltd

Image Leader – Office Paper – Mcnaughton James Paper Group Ltd

Image Office – Office Paper – Mcnaughton James Paper Group Ltd

Image Premium – Office Paper – Mcnaughton James Paper Group Ltd

Image Star – videowall products – Electrosonic Ltd

Imagefarm – frozen and chilled food products – Imagefarm Ltd

Imagemag – videowall products – Electrosonic Ltd

Images – boating magazine – Sunseeker Poole Ltd

Imagination Access – Accesscaff International Ltd

Imagine – Display Wizard Ltd

Imago – building structure – M S S Clean Technology

Imagopaque – G E Healthcare

***Imai (Japan)** – plastic model kits – Amerang Group Ltd

Imak siccar – co logo-moto – Kirkpatrick Ltd

Imari – bone china tableware and giftware – The Royal Crown Derby Porcelain Company Ltd
Imastrip 122 – tin lead stripper – Cookson Electronics Ltd
Imastrip Conditioner 144 – copper conditioner following 122 – Cookson Electronics Ltd
Imastrip conditioner 147 – copper conditioner following 122 – Cookson Electronics Ltd
Imation – UK Office Direct
Imatronic – Global Laser Technology Solutions
***IMC** – Court Catering Equipment Ltd
Imco – thermoplastic and thermosetting trade mouldings for industry – Avalon Plastics Ltd
***Imco (U.S.A.)** – solid carbie cutting tools – Tekmat Ltd
IMEK Precision – Encoders UK
***Imet (Italy)** – sawing machines – Meddings Machine Tools
IMI – electrical resistance wires, spiral elements; thermocouple wires and cables – I M I Scott Ltd
IMI – air conditioners – Tev Ltd
IMI – pressure/vacuum valve – Safety Systems UK Ltd
IMI – hydraulic pneumatic and electric components – Norgren Ltd
IMI – pneumatic pressure regulators and electro-pneumatic interface equipment – I M I Watson Smith Ltd
IMI NORGREN – Hydraulic & Offshore Supplies Ltd
Immediacy – a leading UK Web Content Management System (WCMS) now owned by Alterian – Fusion Workshop
Immediacy – a leading UK Web Content Management System (WCMS) now owned by Alterian – Fusion Workshop
IMO – Hydraulic & Offshore Supplies Ltd
IMO – European Technical Sales Ltd
IMO – Proplas International Ltd
IMO – Cyclops Electronics Ltd
IMP – chimney cleaning chemicals – Hydrachem Ltd
Imp – portable flame cutting machine – Easab Cutting Systems
Impac – Impac Infrared Ltd
Impac, Mikron, Kleiber E2T, Quantum Technology – Impac Infrared Ltd
Impact – standard plastic container similar custom moulded bottle – RPC Containers Ltd
Impact Encore – K3 Business Technology Group plc
IMPACT JOINERS – JOINERY SERVICES – IMPACT JOINERS
Impacta – Impacta Ltd
Impacto – wire rope cutters – Welwyn Tool Group Ltd
Impactoflex – adhesives and sealants for use in industry – PPG Aerospace
Impacton – in line homgeniser – T Giusti Ltd
Impactor – Geoquip Ltd
Impactor – waste compactors – I M C
Impactor – masonry drill bits – Rawlplug Ltd
Impalloy – Impalloy
Impart/2 – PC-based investment management computer system – D S T Global Solutions
Impax – AISI P20 type pre-toughened plastic mould steel – Uddeholm Steel Stockholders
Impax Seals – mechanical seals – Pioneer Weston
Impbins.com – Own brand of products-waste bins-catering bins and grit salt bins – Imagenta Moulding plc
Impbond – PVA sealer/adhesive – Everlac GB Ltd
IMPCO – gas carburation equipment – H K L Gas Power Ltd
Impel – plumbing and heating fittings – Marflow Engineering Ltd
Impera – composite sanitary ware product – Franke Sissons Ltd
Imperial – B B C S Ltd
Imperial – punches & type – Pryor Marking Technology Ltd
***Imperial** – Imperial Catering Equipment Ltd
Imperial – Telescopic Bollard – Alto Bollards UK Ltd
Imperial Comfort – James Walker Textiles Ltd
Imperial Ladders – Accesscaff International Ltd
Imperial Leather – toiletries and soap – P Z Cussons International Ltd
Imperval – paint – Craig & Rose Ltd
Impet – thermoplastic polyester – Ticona UK Ltd
Imporient – UK Office Direct
Importech Ltd – King Builders
***Imposil** – Alstoe Ltd
Impregnawood – weaving loom shuttles – Pilkingtons Ltd
IMpress – Grundfos Pumps Ltd
Impress – Halcyon Solutions
Impression – 100mm thick system withe radiused profiles – Komfort Workspace plc
Impression Publiser – word processor/dtp software – Xara Ltd
Impression Style – word processor/dtp software – Xara Ltd
Improcel – general purpose impregnated filtration materials – Vitec
Improve Your Coarse Fishing – magazine – Emap Ltd
Improve Your Sea Angling – magazine – Emap Ltd
Improved True Dentalloy – dental products – Prima Dental Group Ltd
Imps – licquorice pellets – Ernest Jackson & Co. Ltd
Impsil – silicone based wall treatment – Everlac GB Ltd
Impulse – power nailers – I T W Constructions Productions
Impulse Cordless – brad, strip and coil nailers – I T W Constructions Productions
Imron – polyurethane enamel – Du Pont UK Ltd
In Attendance – 32 page, high quality magazine of the British Firefighter with national UK distribution – Gateacre Press Ltd
In Case Solutions, Custom ProductsAlulite, HiGloss ABS, Full Fight – In Case Solutions
In-Check – Peak Inspiratory Flow Meter for Measuring Pulmanory Function – Clement Clarke International Ltd
In Cup Vending Machines – Chequer Foods Ltd
In-Flow – Bronkhorst UK Ltd
In-Line Filters – Bronkhorst UK Ltd
In Shops – Ashtenne Ltd
In Style – I P C Media Ltd
IN4MA – Powelectrics Ltd
INA – Antifriction Components Ltd
INA – Mayday Seals & Bearings
INA – Mercury Bearings Ltd
Inalways – mains connectors – Anglia
***Inamet (Spain)** – heating replacement thermocouples – Anglo Nordic Burner Products Ltd
Inbis – robotics system builders and integrators advance manufacturing technology, aero-structures design, consultants, nuclear engineering and project management, C.A.D. & C.A.E. – Assystem UK Group
Inca Geometric – special purpose machines and tools – Inca Geometric Ltd
INCAB – Chaintec Ltd
Incamesh Filtration – Filtration equipment – Incamesh Filtration Ltd
Incentive Award Card – Capital World Travel
Inchbrook Printing Services Ltd – security bureau printing – Orchestra Wotton Group Ltd
Inchwrap – Dead Sea professional cellulite treatments – Finders International Ltd
Incinco – housemark and incinerators – Incinco
Inciner8 – incinerators – Inciner8 Ltd
Incinex – Gaseus effluent incineration – Babcock Wanson UK Ltd
Incite – G E Healthcare
Inclinometers – geotechnical instruments – Itm Soil Ltd
Inco – incontinence garments and pads – Robinson Healthcare Ltd
Inco Care – incontinence garments and pads – Robinson Healthcare Ltd
Inco Readiwipes – nonwoven textile for wiping – Robinson Healthcare Ltd
Incomaster – incontinence pad disposal unit – The Haigh Group Ltd
Incompak – provides electronic data capture facilities for video machines – Barcrest Group
Incon – Inspection Consultant Ltd
Incon – Incon (Inspection Consultants) Ltd
Incotes – International representatives – Incotes Ltd
Incremental – Encoders UK
INDACC – Hydraulic accumulator for use in hazard class vapor environments by mechanical valve actuation – Pulsation Dampers At Pulseguard Ltd
Indair – independant air suspension for trailers – Meritor HVS Ltd
***Indasa (Portugal)** – abrasives – Indasa Abrasives UK Ltd
Indentec – indentation hardness testing machines – Indentec Hardness Testing Machines Ltd
Independent Community Pharmacist – magazine – Newsquest Group
Independent Electrical Retailer – magazine – Newsquest Group
Indequip – Industrial Supplies – Parquip Of Somerset
INDEQUIP – Hydraulic & Offshore Supplies Ltd
Indespension – the trading names for all the trailers and related products plus the patented suspension units – Indespension Ltd
Indespension.com – the retail brand centred on the website – Indespension Ltd
Indestructable – UK Office Direct
***Index (U.S.A.)** – capsule fillers – Romaco Holdings UK Ltd
Index Extra – catalogues – Littlewoods Home Shopping Orders & Enquiries
Indexa – engineering specialist tooling – Cromwell Group Holdings
Indexia – stock market and options software specialists – Updata plc
Indi-cards – Digital Products - Indigo - Coated – Howard Smith Paper Ltd
India – Gem Tool Hire & Sales Ltd
India Tyres – Goodyear Dunlop UK Ltd
Indiana General – European Drives & Motor Repairs
Indic-8 – B P plc
Indicator – Stream Measurement Ltd
Indiclor – G E Healthcare
Indisplay – furniture hire – Indisplay Ltd
Inditherm – modular, re-usable, heated, lagging system – Inditherm
Indium – metal and compounds – M C P Ltd
Individual Crafts Range – Kitfix Swallow Group Ltd
Indomab – G E Healthcare
Indoor – cricket and hockey balls – Kookaburra Reader Ltd
INDOS – Chaintec Ltd
***Indra (Far East)** – breathable jackets – Flitterman Investments Ltd
Indramat – Encoders UK
***Indramat** – European Drives & Motor Repairs
INDRAMAT – Hydraulic & Offshore Supplies Ltd
Indramat Motors – European Technical Sales Ltd
Inductoheat Banyard – induction heaters – Inductotherm Heating & Welding Technologies Ltd
Indufil – Harrier Fluid Power Ltd
InduKey UK Ltd – Company Trading Name – Indukey UK Ltd
Indulge – bath soak in three superb fragrances – F M C G Ltd
InduMedical – IP65 Keyboard with impregnated Microban polyester frontsheet, suitable for medical industry – Indukey UK Ltd
InduProof – IP68 Keyboard for the Medical and other Industrial Applications – Indukey UK Ltd
InduSteel – Ruggedised vandal-proof Stainless Steel Keyboard – Indukey UK Ltd
Industria – road and amenity lanterns and road tunnel lighting systems – W R T L Exterior Lighting Ltd
Industrial – Pledge Office Chairs Ltd
Industrial Aluminium Towers – Accesscaff International Ltd
Industrial Automotive Lubricants – Race Industrial Products Ltd
Industrial C.C.T.V. Systems – high temperature viewing – Ist Ltd
Industrial Computers Ltd – Industrial-grade computers in a variety of form-factors and specifications, designed for reliability – Industrial Computers Ltd
Industrial Control Services – control and safety systems – I C S Triplex
Industrial Crank – heavily grogged clay body – Potclays Ltd
Industrial Encoders – Encoders UK
Industrial fabric producers – Industrial Textiles & Plastics Ltd
Industrial Filter – Harrier Fluid Power Ltd
Industrial Line – ethernet and fibre interfaces – Belden UK Ltd
Industrial P.U. Enamel – Spencer Coatings Ltd
Industrial power transmission distributors – Combidrive Ltd
Industrial Process – Stream Measurement Ltd
Industrial Pulpit Steps – Accesscaff International Ltd
Industrial refrigeration distributors – George Barkers
Industrialla spa – IsoCool Ltd
Industriever – automated vertical carousel – Kardex Systems UK Ltd
inea - Selecta PAM UTILITY: Opt-Emax - Tri-Glide - Guardsman - Warrior PAM TELECOM: SHD Briton -Opt-Emax - BT Precinct Cover PAM COMMERCAIL & INDUSTRIAL: Pametic - Bri-Pave - Broadstel - Bristeel ESTATE RANGE: Non-Rock Access Cover - Solid single Seal - Gully Grates PAM INTERNATIONAL: Inter-Ax - Watershed - Autolinea - Siltseal - Warrior SOIL & DRAIN ABOVE GROUND: Ensign - Timesaver - Roof Outlet BELOW GROUND: Ensign - Timesaver - Floor Drainage RAINWATER: Classical - Classical Plus - Classical Express – Saint Gobain P A M UK
***Ineco (Italy)** – gas appliance control systems – Anglo Nordic Burner Products Ltd
Inergen – gaseous extinguishing systems – ADT
Inergi – Beacon – Fulleon
***Inertia Dynamics** – electromegnetic brakes – Huco Dynatork
Infant Projects – bi-monthly magazine – Scholastic School Book Fairs
Infantryman – Steel Bollard – Alto Bollards UK Ltd
Infast – nuts, bolts and fasteners – Anixter Ltd
Infineer Chipcard Systems – vending 7500, point of sale 8500, copier control 6500, access control 1500 – Emos-Infineer Ltd
Infineon – Cyclops Electronics Ltd
INFINEUM PARATAC – Hydraulic & Offshore Supplies Ltd
INFINEUM SYNACTO – Hydraulic & Offshore Supplies Ltd
INFINEUM VISTONE – Hydraulic & Offshore Supplies Ltd
Infiniti – fashion shoes – D Jacobson & Sons Ltd
Infinity – fishing tackle – Daiwa Sports Ltd
Inflatable Collars for Rigid Hull Inflatable Boats – Henshaw Inflatables Ltd
Inflatek Valve – Mactenn Systems Ltd
Inflo Bulk Control – handling equipment – Bearwood Engineering Supplies
***Inflo Resometric** – belt weighing equipment – Procon Engineering Ltd
info carte – Oscar Press Ltd
Info Plus.21 – software for process operations – Aspentech Ltd
Infobook – executive information system – Data Command Ltd
Infocurve – modular sign systems – Signscape Systems Ltd

Infocus – Lamphouse Ltd

infoGenerics Ltd. – Software Development, Management and Marketing – Infogenerics Ltd

Infold – shower doors – Matki plc

Infopanel – aluminium sign systems – Spandex plc

Inform – clinical trials patient communication – Cohn & Wolfe Ltd

Informate (United Kingdom) – Software package for bolt load calculation – Hydratight Morpeth

Infosign – information board – Acco UK Ltd

Infotec – Copycare Office Equipment Ltd

Infotex – modular sign systems – Signscape Systems Ltd

Infraglo – gas fired infra-red heaters and burners – Infraglo Sheffield Ltd

Infralab – for the non contact multicomponent measurement of moisture, nicotine, sugars and temp in tobacco and moisture, and fat protein, oil in foods and bulk powders either in the lab or at line – N D C Infra-Red Engineering Ltd

Infranor – European Drives & Motor Repairs

*Infrico – Pentland Wholesale Ltd

Ingemat – European Technical Sales Ltd

Inger Rose – designer and manufacturer of top quality corporate clothing – Inger Rose

Ingersol-Dresser – pumps – Robert Craig & Sons Ltd

Ingersol Rand – Fisher Offshore

*Ingersoll (Far East) – watches – Zeon Chemicals Europe Ltd

Ingersoll – Harrier Fluid Power Ltd

Ingersoll – security products – Assaabloy Group

Ingersoll-Rand – Trafalgar Tools

Ingersoll Rand – compressors, parts and service – Airware International Ltd

INGERSOLL RAND – Hydraulic & Offshore Supplies Ltd

Ingersoll Rand – A T Wilde & Son Ltd

Ingersoll Rand – compressors & spares – Bearwood Engineering Supplies

Ingersoll Rand – Submarine Manufacturing & Products Ltd

Ingersoll-rand – Gustair Materials Handling Equipment Ltd

Ingersoll Rand – Team Overseas Ltd

Ingersoll-Rand – Southern Valve & Fitting Co. Ltd

Ingleby Trice Kennard – Ingleby Trice

Ingram Bros – bakery ingredients, suppliers to bakery & catering trades – Ingram Bros Ltd

Ingstrom Chute – fire escape chute system – Lampitt Fire Escapes

Inheritance – Turner Bianca

Inhibiter – soil conditioner – Farmura Ltd

Inipol – diamine salts – Atosina UK Ltd

Initial Washroom Management Service – air freshners, warm air dryers, paper disposable products, cabinet towels, sanitary towel dispenser and disposal soap dispensers – Rentokil Initial plc

Injectoid – injection and blow moulded plastics – Measom Freer Company

Inkmun – refill kit for bubble jet and ink jet printers – System Insight

INKOCROSS – Flexible Axially Loadable Shaft Couplings – Francis and Francis Ltd

Inkoff – Forward Chemicals Ltd

INKOFLEX – Flexible Disc Shaft Couplings – Francis and Francis Ltd

INKOMA – 'PK' Offset, 'LINEFLEX' In-line, 'INKOTURN' Encoder Shaft (SCHMIDT Alternatives), & Other Flexible CV Couplings – Francis and Francis Ltd

INKOMA 'ELAFLEX' – Flexible 'Spider' Shaft & Spacer Shaft Couplings – Francis and Francis Ltd

INKOMA 'INKOCROSS' – Flexible Axially Loadable Shaft Couplings – Francis and Francis Ltd

INKOMA 'INKOFLEX' – Flexible Disc Shaft Couplings – Francis and Francis Ltd

INKOMA 'INKOTURN' – Shaft Encoder High Speed Couplings – Francis and Francis Ltd

INKOMA 'Inkoturn' Encoder Couplings – (SCHMIDT Alternative) – Francis and Francis Ltd

INKOMA 'KSO' CRUCIFORM – CV Flexible Disc Element 'Oldham Design' Shaft Couplings – Francis and Francis Ltd

INKOMA 'LINEFLEX' – CV In-line Variable Offset Flexible Shaft Couplings – Francis and Francis Ltd

INKOMA 'Lineflex' Couplings – (SCHMIDT Alternative) – Francis and Francis Ltd

INKOMA 'PK' OFFSET – CV Large Variable Offset Flexible Shaft Couplings – Francis and Francis Ltd

INKOMA 'PK' Offset Couplings – (SCHMIDT Alternative) – Francis and Francis Ltd

INKOTURN – Shaft Encoder High Speed Couplings – Francis and Francis Ltd

Inkstinx – Compatible laser cartridges – inkstinx

*Inland – European Drives & Motor Repairs

Inlay Wax – dental wax – Prima Dental Group Ltd

Inline – sign blanks – Spandex plc

Inliners R – inline skates, safety gear and skating accessories – Ventura Corporation

Inmarset – Inmarsat Global Ltd

Innershield – self shielded flux cored wire – Lincoln Electric UK Ltd

Innesenti – cafe and leisure furniture – Metalliform Holdings

*Innocard (Malaya) – card access controls – Raytel Security Systems Ltd

Innotech – Control Range – Innotech Controls UK Ltd

Innotool – Vargus Tooling Ltd

Innotool – carbide – Turner Tools Ltd

*Innova (U.S.A.) – shakers – New Brunswick Scientific UK Ltd

Innovair – intelligent fan convector – Biddle Air Systems Ltd

innovations-tech – providing solutions for our customer needs – innovations-tech Ltd.

*Innovative displays – sign and design – Signconex Ltd

Innovene – B P plc

Innovex – B P plc

Inoac – air conditioning accessories, including trunking, brackets, hangers, security guards, saddles, mounting blocks – Thermofrost Cryo plc

*Inomak – Pentland Wholesale Ltd

Inonyl Acetate – perfume speciality – Quest International UK Ltd

Inonyl Formate Extra – perdume speciality – Quest International UK Ltd

InoTec – Genus Group

Inotec (Germany) – liquid mixers – Orthos Engineering Ltd

*Inotech – Rotisseries – Exclusive Ranges Ltd

inoventi – Artillus Illuminating Solutions Ltd

*Inox Pran (Italy) – stainless steel coffee makers – Fairfax Coffee Ltd

Inoxtrend – Euro Catering Equipment

Inoxyform – Catering Investments Ltd

Inpace – UK Office Direct

InPrint – Fife Tidland Ltd

Inrekor – Inrekor Ltd

insectazap – fly killers, fly screens etc – 03 Solutions Ltd

Insectocutor – R G K UK Ltd

Insett Air Freshner – insette air freshener – L E C Liverpool Ltd

Insette – hairdressing toiletry products - hairspray and mousse – L E C Liverpool Ltd

Insette Furniture Polish – L E C Liverpool Ltd

Insette Smells Nice Toilet Freshener – L E C Liverpool Ltd

Insette Spikey – spray gel and gel in tubs – L E C Liverpool Ltd

Inshore – Inshore Fisheries Ltd

INSIDEIR – Radir Ltd

Insight – electronic catalogue – Fisher Scientific UK Ltd

Insight 2000 – flow computer for blending and sampling – Jiskoot Ltd

Insight Controller – process controller for blending, additive injection and sampling applications – Jiskoot Ltd

Insiplas – repair of valuable ceilings – Cotswold Treatment P P Ltd

InSite – geographical information system – C A C I

InSite Europe – C A C I

InSite Fieldforce – territory planning and optimisation software – C A C I

Insitex – formliner system for textured concrete – Max Frank Ltd

Insitimb – repair of valuable timbers – Cotswold Treatment P P Ltd

InSkew – stainless steel structural batten fixing for fixing counterbattens through insulation in warm roof – Helifix Ltd

Insley – Harrier Fluid Power Ltd

Inspec – information services for the physics and engineering communities – Institution Of Engineering & Technology

Inspection Consultants – Incon (Inspection Consultants) Ltd

Inspection Consultants – Inspection Consultant Ltd

Inspection management – inspection services – Oceaneering Asset Integrity

InSpectra – Fife Tidland Ltd

InspeX Range – x-ray NDT – Applied Scintillation Technologies

Inspirations – decorative paints – Akzonobel

Inspire – components for wound dressings – Exopack Advanced Coatings Ltd

Instabill – multipe bill and credit slip payment document – The Computastat Group Ltd

Instabox – packaging materials, corrugated boxes – Faspak Containers Ltd

Instacem – concrete repair and special mortars etc – David Ball Group plc

Instacom – modular accommodation – Rollalong Ltd

Instaflex – PB water distribution piping system – George Fischer Sales Ltd

Instaflex - Signet - Primofit - GF - Coolfit. – George Fischer Sales Ltd

Instamac – permanent and instant pothole repair material – David Ball Group plc

Instant Nails – multi-use DIY adhesive – Everbuild Building Products Ltd

Instanta – B B C S Ltd

*Instanta – Court Catering Equipment Ltd

Instanta – Ackwa Ltd

Instapak – foam in place packaging – A Latter & Co. Ltd

Instapass – P C F Secure Document Systems Ltd

Instapruf – pre-mixed fully water repellant mortar – David Ball Group plc

Instarite Glue – glue tape applicator – Fuji Copian

Instarite II – correction applicator – Fuji Copian

Instarite S – correction applicator – Fuji Copian

Instaset – rapid hardening waterproof cement – David Ball Group plc

Instasupascreed – rapid curing and drying floor screed – David Ball Group plc

Institute of chartered accountants in England & Wales – Institute Of Chartered Accountants

Institute of Personnel and Development – Chartered Institute Of Personnel & Development

Institute of Practitioners – trade association – Institute Of Practitioners In Advertising Ltd

Instron – Materials testing systems – Instron

*Instructor System, The – Sound Dynamics Ltd

*Instrument Systems (Germany) – instruments for measurement of light – Metax Ltd

Insu-Loc – insulation retaining discs – Timloc Building Products

*Insudoor (Sweden) – insulated side folding doors – Stertil UK Ltd

Insugard – steel insulated rollling shutters – Kaba Door Systems

Insuglaze – resoplan insulated panels – Panel Systems Ltd

Insulated Composite Panels – North West Sheeting Supplies

Insulex – insulation – B S K Laminating Ltd

Insulflex – British Vita plc

Insuliner – curtainsider for chilled temperature controlled transport – Boalloy Industries Ltd

Insulite FR – Chorus Panel & Profiles

Insuloid – cable ties – Hellermann Tyton

Insulok – cable ties – Hellermann Tyton

Insulotube – electrical insulation tubes designed for protecting & repairing damaged wire insulation – Lamina Dielectrics Ltd

Insultite – heat shrink tubing – Hellermann Tyton

Insulux – British Vita plc

Insupak – roof insulation – Grace Construction Ltd

*Insuroll (Netherlands) – insulated roller shutter – Stertil UK Ltd

Intac – gas separating equipment – Boc Gases Ltd

Intacab – taxi operator and couriers – Intacab Ltd

Intalite – Light Fantastic

*Intec (Germany) – watertight sealing for concrete joints – Max Frank Ltd

Intech – software house – Intech Ltd

Intech – Agie Charmilles Ltd

Integi – Precision Tools

Integra – dustless powders – Lanxess Ltd

Integra – Amcor Flexibles

Integra – taps – Armitage Shanks Ltd

Integral – combined contractor & motor circuit breaker – Schneider

INTEGRAL – Hydraulic & Offshore Supplies Ltd

Integral Accumulator – accumlators – Freudenberg Simrit LP

Integral Flo-Tel (United Kingdom) – non-invasive ATEX approved burst-disc and panel detector – Elfab Ltd

Integrate360 – Online 360 Degree Feedback Survey Tool – Integrate HR Ltd

Integrated – valves & spares – Bearwood Engineering Supplies

Integrated Ducting Solutions (IDS) – Ducting for highways lighting etc. – Burden Ltd

INTEGRATED HYDRAULICS – Hydraulic & Offshore Supplies Ltd

Integrated Plumbing System – washroom system – Armitage Shanks Ltd

Integrated Systems Network (ISN) – building management system – Johnson Controls Ltd

IntegrateOS – Online Employee/Organisational Survey Tool – Integrate HR Ltd

IntegrateRecruit – Web Recruitment Tool – Integrate HR Ltd

Integrex Colourjet – IT solutions, electronic research & development – Integrex

Integrity – self-sealing penile sheath with applicator – Bard Ltd

Integro – litter bin with ash containers – Glasdon International Ltd

Intek 300 – industrial gas manifold 300 bar – Black Teknigas & Electro Controls Ltd

Intel – Desktop Computers – Savannah Estates Ltd

Intel – Cyclops Electronics Ltd

Intelect – Intergrated Electronics Ltd

Inteliheat – L M K Thermosafe

Intelligent Access – Access Control Software – I S Y S Ltd

Intelligent HR – Human Resources software – I S Y S Ltd

Intelligent Job Costing – Job Costing software – I S Y S Ltd

Intelligent Solutions – complete text production – Cincom Systems UK Ltd

Intelligent Time – Time and Attendance software – I S Y S Ltd

Intellinet – workflow software – Agfa Gevaert
Intellistream – Equipline
Intellitherm – Banico Ltd
Intene – polybutadiene rubber – Polimeri Europa Ltd
***Intensiv (Switzerland)** – dental diamonds – Metrodent Ltd
Inter-Active (1.A.) – waterproof clothing – Berghaus Ltd
Inter Clamp – Safety Works & Solutions Ltd
Inter-Loc – horizontal cavity tray system – Timloc Building Products
Inter Partner Assistance – provider of emergency medical, vehicle, legal and household assistance and services – Axa Assistance UK Ltd
Inter Stuhl – Office Seating – Bucon Ltd
Interactive Data – Interactive Data
Interactive Property Log Book – Property Log Book Company Ltd
Interagro – agriculture, adjuvants – Interagro UK Ltd
***Interal** – specialist aluminium diffusion coatings – Diffusion Alloys Ltd
Interapid (Switzerland) – gauges and micrometers – Tesa Technology UK Ltd
Interbond – specialised coatings – International Paint Ltd
Interbook – international bookbinding accessories – Gilmex International Ltd
Interbuild – exhibition organisers – Montgomery Exhibitions
Intercall – nurse call systems – Lismore Instruments Ltd
Intercar – private hire and couriers – Intacab Ltd
Intercepta – call sequencers – Storacall Engineering Ltd
Intercepta Range – call sequencers – Storacall Engineering Ltd
Interceptor – sports garments and in particular football clothing – Star Sportswear Ltd
Interchlor – chlorinated polymers – International Paint Ltd
***Interchrome** – specialist chromium diffusion coatings – Diffusion Alloys Ltd
Intercide – microbiocide – Akcros Chemicals Ltd
Interclad – supply internal hygienec wall and ceiling cladding – Interclad Ltd
Interclamp – Interclamp is a versatile range of malleable iron galvanised slip-on pipe / tube fittings. Typical c – Grainger Tubolt Ltd
Interconnect 200 – hybrid PABX – Samsung Telecom UK Ltd
Interconnect 3000 – open telephone system – Samsung Telecom UK Ltd
Intercrete – building blocks – Interfuse Ltd
***Intercure (Italy)** – curative for fluoroelastomers – J Allcock & Sons Ltd
Interdens – intumescent strip for doors – Dufaylite Developments Ltd
Intereurope – technical document service to the commerce and defence industry, creative graphics, technical translations – Intereurope Ltd
Intereurope Regulations – worldwide supply of motor manufacturing regulations to motor manufacturing industry – Intereurope Ltd
Interface – The Winnen Furnishing Company
Interface, Heuga, Firth, Bentley, Solenium, Intercell, Image, Renovisions. – Interface Europe Ltd
Interface Toolkit – software – Chaucer Group Ltd
Interfel SA Machines (Switzerland) – Haesler Machine Tools
Interfibre – cellulose fibres – Lawrence Industries Ltd
INTERFIRE (United Kingdom) – infrared interferometers – Precision Optical Engineering
Interflex – flexible crash doors, strip PVC curtains and rapid rise doors – Neway Doors Ltd
Interflex Hose & Bellows – Interflex Hose & Bellows Ltd
Interflon – P.T.F.E. stopcocks – Bibby Scientific Ltd
Interfoam – British Vita plc
Intergard – two component epoxies – International Paint Ltd
Intergrator – software package – N C C Group
Interiorcooler – interior fan – Kenlowe Accessories & Co. Ltd
Interiorheater – interior heater – Kenlowe Accessories & Co. Ltd
Interiors 1900 – Light Fantastic
Interkey – interchangeable stopcocks – Bibby Scientific Ltd
Interlac – oil modified undercoats and finishes – International Paint Ltd
Interland Newell and Sorrell – Corporate Design Company – Interbrand
Interline – fishing tackle – Daiwa Sports Ltd
Interlink Direct – The easiest way to ship a parcel online – Interlink Express Parcels Ltd
Interlite – solid mixed metal soap stabilisers – Akcros Chemicals Ltd
Interlock – Interface Europe Ltd
Interlock – flexible foam packaging corner block, converters of foam – Foam Engineers Ltd
Interlock – plastic binding bar for punched sheets – Gilmex International Ltd
Interlock – structural blind rivet – Zygology Ltd
Interlock Ceiling – hygienic ceiling system – Interclad Ltd
Interlocking 1 metre L-bloc – Poundfield Products Ltd
Interlocking 2 metre L-bloc – Poundfield Products Ltd
Interlocking L-bloc – Poundfield Products Ltd
Interlube – manual & automatic lubrication systems – Interlube Systems Ltd
Interlube – Trafalgar Tools
INTERLUBE – Hydraulic & Offshore Supplies Ltd
Interlube – Harrison Lubrication Engineering Ltd
Interlyte – building blocks – Interfuse Ltd
Intermas – S R S Product plc
Intermec – P C F Secure Document Systems Ltd
Intermec – Allcode UK Ltd
Intermec ck30 – Allcode UK Ltd
Intermec ck31 – Allcode UK Ltd
Intermec cn3 – Allcode UK Ltd
Intermec sf51 – Allcode UK Ltd
Intermes – Watts Industries UK Ltd
INTERMOT – Hydraulic & Offshore Supplies Ltd
Intermotor – original equipment and replacement parts for motor vehicles – Standard Motor Products Europe Ltd
International – decorative coatings – International Paint Ltd
International – snooker tables – Thurston
***International (United Kingdom)** – snooker tables – Thurston
International – air conditioning – Burgess C R Commissioning Ltd
International Boat Industry – I P C Media Ltd
International Damage Management – Merryhill Envirotec Ltd
International Environmental Technology – environmental tabloid – International Labmate Ltd
International Labmate – scientific publication (journal) – International Labmate Ltd
International Leather Guide – United Business Media Ltd
International Light Inc – radiometers and photometers – Able Instruments & Controls Ltd
International Power Presses – International Power Presses
International Rectifier – Cyclops Electronics Ltd
International Sport – public relations services, corporate hospitality and sports events – Read Management Services Ltd
Internet Advisor – magazine – Future Publishing Ltd
Internet Data Storage – Tekdata Distribution Ltd
Internet Works – magazine – Future Publishing Ltd
Internor/Sachn – Harrier Fluid Power Ltd
Internormen – Harrier Fluid Power Ltd
INTERNORMEN – Hydraulic & Offshore Supplies Ltd
Interpact – switch disconnector – Schneider
INTERPAK – manufacturer of presentation packaging – International Packaging Corporation
Interpark – Double Parking Systems
Interplan System – partitioning – Interior Property Solutions
Interplate – preconstruction primers – International Paint Ltd
Interpower – generator sets – Interpower International
Interprime – oil modified primers – International Paint Ltd
Interprint – full colour printers – Interprint Ltd
***Interpump Spa (Italy)** – piston pumps – Dual Pumps Ltd
Interset – high performance cavity fixing – Rawlplug Ltd
Intersil – Cyclops Electronics Ltd
Interslim – Silhouette Beauty Equipment
Interstab – mixed metal soap stabilisers – Akcros Chemicals Ltd
Interswage – hose – Cebo UK Ltd
Intertec Data Solutions T/a Prospect 360 – List Broker – Prospect 360
***Intertech (Germany)** – drawing instruments – Blundell Harling Ltd
Interthane – polyurethanes – International Paint Ltd
Intertuf – bituminous and hydrocarbon coatings – International Paint Ltd
Intertype – linecasting machines – L & M Ltd
Intervalve – Frenstar
Interventus – Occupational Psychologists – Interventus Business Psychologists
Intervinux – vinyl and vinyl acrylic coatings – International Paint Ltd
Interwax – lubricants for PVC – Akcros Chemicals Ltd
Interzinc – metallic zinc coatings – International Paint Ltd
Interzone – chevron ribbed polprop/aluminium entrance matting – Jaymart Roberts & Plastics Ltd
Intex – styrene butadiene rubber latex – Polimeri Europa Ltd
Intimus – UK Office Direct
Intimus – shredding machines – Martin Yale International Ltd
Intio – M S C Gleichmann UK Ltd
Intoco – engineering – Independent Tool Consultants Ltd
Intol – styrene butadiene rubber – Polimeri Europa Ltd
Intourist – travel to conferences, exhibitions and trade events in Russia and the C.I.S. – Intourist Ltd
Intourist Travel – tours to Russia, the former republics, Eastern Europe – Intourist Ltd
Intra – notch nuts & lock washers – Industrial Trading Co. Ltd
Intra-Automation – magnetic level gauges and pitot tube flow meters – Able Instruments & Controls Ltd
Intrabonded – diamond wheels – Indusmond Diamond Tools Ltd
Intracast – low cement castables – Calderys UK Ltd
Intrad – PVC handrails, wall protection, cladding – Intrad Ltd
Intrad Reflex – surface protection materials – Intrad Ltd
Intrad System 545 – aluminium handrails and balustrades – Intrad Ltd
Intrad TSM – stainless steel grab bars and shower seats for the disabled and elderly – Intrad Ltd
***INTRAFOL** – Stabilised liquid nitrogen formulations – Nutrel Products Ltd
Intralactam – rapid strip method for the detection of beta-lactamase producing bacteria – The Mast Group Ltd
Intravit 12 – maintenance of metabolic functions – Norbrook Research
Intrigue – Capex Office Interiors
Intrum Justitia Ltd – Stirling Park LLP
Intrusion Detection – Tekdata Distribution Ltd
Intrusion Detection Software Firewall – Tekdata Distribution Ltd
Intrusion Detection System – Tekdata Distribution Ltd
Intrusion Managed Prevention – Tekdata Distribution Ltd
Intrusion Prevention – Tekdata Distribution Ltd
Intufoam – expansion gap and joint sealer - fire resistant – Quelfire Ltd
Intuitive – London Electronics Ltd
Intumescent 2000 (United Kingdom) – wide range of passive fire protection products – Amberley Security
Inturbine – large rotor insertion turbine – Jiskoot Ltd
Invac – rectifier diodes & bridges – Anglia
Invacare – E P C
Invar – Maher Ltd
Invensys Sigma – building management system – Schneider Electric
Inversale – British Vita plc
Invertec – low voltage fluorescent light fittings and inverters – Invertec Ltd
Invertec – arc welding and rectifiers – Lincoln Electric UK Ltd
Investalist – Cheap property – Investalist Ltd
Investment Tooling International – injection moulding tools – Investment Tooling International Ltd
***Invicta (France)** – cast iron cookware – Dexam International
Invictalux (United Kingdom) – inspection and detection system – Primalec
Invisirung – vertical safe access ladder with foldaway rungs – Metreel Ltd
Ioma – uniforms and protective clothing – Ioma Clothing Co. Ltd
Iomega – UK Office Direct
ion gauges – AESpump
ION Information Technology – I.T, Software Solutions – Ion Information Technologies Ltd
Iona – records, tapes and compact discs – Lismor Recordings
Ionacure – electrically conductive adhesive, fixing and repair materials for the electronics industry – Chemence Ltd
Ionfab 300 Series – ion beam machines – Oxford Instruments
Ionfab 500 Series – ion beam machines – Oxford Instruments
Ionix – high performance wiring systems – Volex Group Ltd
Ionol – anti oxidant – F L D Chemicals Ltd
Ionone – perfume speciality – Quest International UK Ltd
Ionovax – film cleaner – M C D Virtak Ltd
Ionox – antioxidant – F L D Chemicals Ltd
IOSH – IOSH Working safely and managing safely – R B Health & Safety Solutions Ltd
Iowa Mold – Harrier Fluid Power Ltd
IP IP Over Telephony Voice – Tekdata Distribution Ltd
IP Over Phone Solution Voice – Tekdata Distribution Ltd
IP Over Solution Voice – Tekdata Distribution Ltd
IP Over System Voice – Tekdata Distribution Ltd
IP Over Telephony – Tekdata Distribution Ltd
IP Over UK Voice – Tekdata Distribution Ltd
IP Product Telephony – Tekdata Distribution Ltd
IP Specialist Telephony – Tekdata Distribution Ltd
IP Telephony – Tekdata Distribution Ltd
IP Telephony Solution – Tekdata Distribution Ltd
IP Telephony System – Tekdata Distribution Ltd
IP Telephony Voip – Tekdata Distribution Ltd
Ipacoll – waterbased adhesives – H B Fuller
IPAF Training – Accesscaff International Ltd
IPD – Stemmer Imaging
IPL – Hydraulic & Offshore Supplies Ltd
IPO – CNC lathes – Gate Machinery International Ltd
iProjects – project consultancy, project management – iPRT Group Ltd
IPSA – International Professional Security Association – Sonic Security Services Ltd
Ipso – Clean Machine UK Ltd
iPtest – electrical test equipment – Ip Test Ltd
IQ – building control systems – Trend Control Systems Ltd
IQ Allround – business papers – Howard Smith Paper Ltd
IQ Allround Triotec – business papers – Howard Smith Paper Ltd
IQ Economy – business papers – Howard Smith Paper Ltd
iq management systems – training and consultacncy – I Q Management Systems
IQ Premium – business papers – Howard Smith Paper Ltd

IQ Range Actuator – Electric multi-turn and quarter turn intelligent valve actuator – Rotork plc
IQ Selection – business papers – Howard Smith Paper Ltd
IQ750 – Eurocell Building Plastics Ltd
IQI – Lamphouse Ltd
IQT Range Actuator – Electric quarter turn, direct drive intelligent valve actuator – Rotork plc
Iram – Leader Chuck Systems Ltd
***Irazola (Spain)** – screwdrivers – Electro Group Ltd
IRCON – Insteng Process Automation Ltd
Ircon – Radir Ltd
***Irega (Spain)** – adjustable wrenches – Electro Group Ltd
iRegeneration – Regeneration, Land Development, Industrial, commercial, residential – iPRT Group Ltd
Ireland FX – Foreign Exchange Specialists. – Ireland FX
Irelands Saturday Night – newspaper publishers – Independent News & Media (NI) Ltd
Irena – ladies casualwear – Remys Ltd
Iridex – X-Ray and gamma ray crawlers – Ie-Ndt Manufacturer
IRidium – City Technology Ltd
***Irinox** – Capital Refrigeration Services Ltd
IRION – Chaintec Ltd
IRIS – Integrated Radio Information Systems – Scott International Ltd
Iris – flame monitoring system – J B Systems Ltd
Iris Stop – pipe sealing systems – A L H Systems Ltd
Irish ACORN – C A C I
Irish Cabin – household, fancy and kitchen linens, linen and cotton handkerchiefs – Mccaw Allan Ltd
Irish Road Motors – main Ford franchise – Lindsay Ford
Irisys – Alpha Electronics Southern Ltd
Irod – integrated pipE support system to eliminate crevice corrosion at pipe supports in all pipework situations – Hockway
Iron-Duke – hot dip galvanizing – W Corbett & Co Galvanizing Ltd
Iron Duke – fibre bonded carpet – Heckmondwike FB
IronGear Pickups – Guitar Pickups – Axetec Guitar Pickups & Parts
***Ironmaster (Italy)** – electric and steam irons – Danor Engineering Ltd
Ironmongery 2000 – comprehensive range of architectural ironmongery in all materials and suitable for all projects – Amberley Security
IronOr – Micaceous Iron Oxide – Mineral & Chemical Services Ltd
Ironsword – games – Rare
Irontite (U.S.A.) – Pressure testers & crack repair equipment – Fondera Ltd
Ironworkers – universal hydraulic – Kingsland Engineering Company Ltd
***Irox (Germany)** – reflective solar control glass – Schott UK Ltd
Irrigation Systems – design & supply of plants – Flowering Plants Ltd
***Irrimec** – Ben Burgess Beeston
Irritec (Italy) – pp fittings – Everyvalve Ltd
IRSbar – portable extendible road barriers – I R S Ltd
Irvine – slop hopper suite – Armitage Shanks Ltd
Irwin – Gem Tool Hire & Sales Ltd
Irwins – builders and specialist joinery – Irwins Ltd
Isabella – WC suite – Armitage Shanks Ltd
***Isap** – Regalzone LLP
ISAVE – The Woolwich
ISAVE tax – The Woolwich
Isawarren Brown Egglayer – Tom Barron Isa Ltd
ISC – Hydraulic & Offshore Supplies Ltd
Iscatex – modular sign systems – Signscape Systems Ltd
ISE – Waste disposals – Allied Manufacturing
Iseki – Ransomes Jacobsen Ltd
Iseki – Harrier Fluid Power Ltd
Isenr – Precision Tools
iSeries – Mid Blue International Ltd
Isinglass Finings – Murphy & Son
Isipaque – G E Healthcare
Isis – battens with acrylic prismatic controller – Designplan Lighting Ltd
Isis – garden pumps – Stuart Turner Ltd
Isis – Expanded pupil eyepiece accessory – Vision Engineering Ltd
Isis – countertop basin – Ideal Standard Ltd
ISIS – ink security imaging systems (for banknote) – Opsec Security Ltd
ISIS FLUID CONTROL – Hydraulic & Offshore Supplies Ltd
iSk-Portal – Internet portal – Information Strategies Key Intangible Value
iSkiv – Company acronys – Information Strategies Key Intangible Value
Iskra – starters, alternators, dc motors – Iskra UK Ltd
Iskra – electronic components – Iskra UK Ltd
Island Records – Universal Island Music Ltd
Islander – frozen seafoods – Dales Of Liverpool Ltd
Isle of Bute Candles – hand-made ornate candles – Orissor Trust Ltd
Isle of Bute Jewellery – costume jewellery – Orissor Trust Ltd
ISN – Bearings – Baldor UK
ISN Advantage – temperature control system – Johnson Controls Ltd
Iso – sailboat – Topper International
Iso – B L Pneumatics Ltd
ISO Couers – insulation jacket, tailor made for values, flanges, pipes etc – I S O Covers Ltd
Iso-Cure – sand binder system for the foundry industry – Ashland Specialties UK Ltd
ISO Design Venitian Blind – venitian blind for fitting to recess of tilt and turn windows – Eclipse Blind Systems
iso fittings – AESpump
Iso Fluthane – O'Neill Medicalia Ltd
Iso-Jasmone Pure – perfume speciality – Quest International UK Ltd
Isobar 4 SP&N – type a distribution board – Schneider
Isobar TP&N – type b distribution board – Schneider
Isobond – isophthalate bonded micapaper composites glass backed – Jones Stroud Insulations Ltd
Isobutavan – perfume speciality – Quest International UK Ltd
Isocab – Frimatec UK Ltd
Isochem – external gear pumps – Axflow
Isoclad – anti corrosive membrane coating – Sika Liquid Plastics
Isocom – Cyclops Electronics Ltd
Isocool – anti-freeze/coolant – B P plc
Isodam – non-latex dental dam – Four D Rubber Co. Ltd
Isodam – latex dental dam – Four D Rubber Co. Ltd
Isodaq – Halcyon Solutions
Isodesign Blind – The mono control venetian blind specially for glazed door and tilt n turn windows – Eclipse Blind Systems
Isoeugenol – perfume speciality – Quest International UK Ltd
Isoflex – liquid rubber waterproofer – Ronseal Ltd
Isoflexit – electrical conduits – Icore International
Isoflo – patented paper machine dewatering unit for quality improvements – Heimbach UK
Isoflux – European Drives & Motor Repairs
Isofoam – polyurethane foam system – Baxenden Chemicals Ltd
Isofon – B P plc
Isofusion – glass coated system – Permastore Ltd
Isoglide – single stage, end-suction, centrifugal pumps to ISO 2858 – Weir Group Senior Executives Pension Trust Ltd
Isojets – mould tools heat transfer – Thermacore Ltd
Isola – rubber bands – Isola Manufacturing Co Wythenshawe Ltd
Isola – marble and granite tiles – A Elder Reed & Co. Ltd
Isolast – perfluoroelastomer – Trelleborg Ceiling Solutions Ltd
ISOLAST – Hydraulic & Offshore Supplies Ltd
Isolemail (France) – heat cured synthetic resin lining – Lithgow Saekaphen Ltd
Isolevel (United Kingdom) – low frequency self-levelling air mounts – Farrat Isolevel
Isolok – security controlled padlock locking off systems – Castell Safety International Ltd
Isolok - Mistura – Castell Safety International Ltd
Isolongifolanone – perfume speciality – Quest International UK Ltd
Isomat – containment isolators – Medical Air Technology Ltd
Isomat (United Kingdom) – low frequency rubber anti-vibration material – Farrat Isolevel
Isomax – ISO pnuematic control valves – Parker Hannifin Ltd
Isomount (United Kingdom) – adjustable machine mounting – Farrat Isolevel
Isomune – instrument kits – Roche Diagnostics Ltd
Isopaque – G E Healthcare
ISOPIPES – mould tools heat transfer – Thermacore Ltd
Isoplas – crosslinkable polyethylene for extrusion and injection moulding – Micropol Ltd
Isoplast – Resinex UK Ltd
Isoplat – flame retardent braid for cable re-inforcement – Icore International
Isopon P38 – polyester filler paste – U-Pol Ltd
Isopon P40 – glass fibre repair paste – U-Pol Ltd
Isoria – K S B Ltd
Isostar – B L Pneumatics Ltd
Isosweet – high fructose glucose syrup – Tate & Lyle Public Ltd Company
Isothane - Agrispray - Foamshield - Technitherm - Duratherm - Bodymould - Ecofil - Reprocell - Armour-Flex - Armour -Lyte - Exoset - Pirthane - Themespray - Thermadek – Isothane Ltd
Isotherm – fan coils units – Biddle Air Systems Ltd
Isotta Franschini – Harrier Fluid Power Ltd
***Isovac (Germany)** – mineral insulated cables – Rolfe Industries
Isover – Ainsworth Acoustics, Thermal & Building Insulation
Isowool – mineral fibre insulation – Bristish Gypsum
ISP – all garden timber rproducts pallet makers – I P S Fencing
Isri (Isringhausen) – T E K Seating Ltd
ISS Ltd – International Scientific Supplies Ltd
ISSI – Cyclops Electronics Ltd
iStar – ICCD camera – Andor Technology Ltd
ISTAR – Mass Consultants Ltd
Isuzu – L M C Hadrian Ltd
Isuzu – Harrier Fluid Power Ltd
Isuzu – multi-purpose four wheel drive vehicles – Isuzu (UK) Ltd
It s done! Studio – It s done! Studio - is a creative web design company, providing professional website design services – It's Done
IT Bytes – electronic publishing, internet web-page design – B C G Creative FX
IT Jobs for Graduates – IT jobs for graduates from leading employers in The United Kingdom from the IT Jobs For Graduates. – It Job Board
IT Jobs in the Clty – Banking and finance IT jobs from leading employers in The United Kingdom from IT Jobs In The City. – It Job Board
It's Apple – Stute Foods Ltd
It Security – Tekdata Distribution Ltd
It Security Solution – Tekdata Distribution Ltd
IT Security Training – Tekdata Distribution Ltd
Itag – computerised cable identification system – Siegrist-Orel Ltd
***Italexpress (Italy)** – espresso coffee makers – Fairfax Coffee Ltd
Italia Range – Shower enclosures, doors & bath screens – Lakes Bathrooms Ltd
ITALMACHINE – Chaintec Ltd
Italpresse – hydraulic presses – Mackey Bowley International Ltd
Italvalvole – Zella Instrumentation & Control Ltd
Itap – Southern Valve & Fitting Co. Ltd
Itap – Trafalgar Tools
iteco – Link Hamson Ltd
Item (Germany) – aluminium machine construction system – Machine Building Systems Ltd
ITI – Information Technology Infrastructure Ltd
ITL – high vacuum components – AESpump
ITM – vacuum pumps – AESpump
ITM – inserters – Buhrs UK Ltd
ITM Dryers – dryers – Garbuiodickinson
Itochu – trading house – Itochu Europe plc
***Itoh (Japan)** – microprocessor guillotines – Graphics Arts Equipment Ltd
Itohnar – photo, video accessories – Kauser International Trading Ltd
ITR – Hydraulic & Offshore Supplies Ltd
ITR SPA (Italy) – air hose – Hydrasun Ltd
iTransport Group – Transport Planning, Transport Assessments, Travel Plans, Transport Consultant, Transport Consultancy – iPRT Group Ltd
iTransport Planning – Transport Planning, Transport Assessments, Travel Plans, Transport Consultant, Transport Consultancy – iPRT Group Ltd
ITS – International Training Service Ltd
ITT Cannon – Cyclops Electronics Ltd
ITT Cannon – Contacts – Dax International Ltd
ITT Cannon – Connectors – Dax International Ltd
ITT Cannon – electro-mechanical connectors and harnesses – I T T Ltd
ITT LOWARA – J P Whitter Ltd
ITW – Tri Pack Supplies Ltd
ITW – Cyclops Electronics Ltd
IV – Frenstar
IVC – Frenstar
Ivco Aifo – industrial engines – Iveco UK Ltd
Iveco – Harrier Fluid Power Ltd
IVECO – Bailey Morris Ltd
Iveco – Ford trucks – Invicta Paints
Iveco Ford – heavy truck specialist dealer – Invicta Paints
Iveco Ford Truck Ltd – truck manufacturers – Iveco UK Ltd
Ivepaque – G E Healthcare
IVEX – Frenstar
IVF – Frenstar
IVG – Hydraulic & Offshore Supplies Ltd
IVG – Hose – Holmes Hose Ltd
IVG – industrial hoses – C C H Hose & Rubber
***IVO (Germany)** – encoders, electronic tachometers & counters, operating time meters & electronic positioning devices – Baumer Electric Ltd
***Ivomec** – Merial Animal Health Ltd
Ivory Cats – Chorion plc
IVR – Frenstar
IVTFE – Frenstar
IVTL – Frenstar
Ivy – belting belts – J A Harrison & Co Manchester Ltd
Ivy – UK Office Direct
Iwaki Pumps – Denton Pumps Ltd

Iwanta – shoe mercery – A Algeo Ltd

IWIS – Chaintec Ltd

IWIS CHAIN – Wolds Engineering Services Ltd

IWM – milling cutters and hand tools for foam – Apropa Machinery Ltd

Iwox – oxidised waxes – Industrial Waxes

Ixef – Resinex UK Ltd

Ixenon – Lamphouse Ltd

IXL – UK Office Direct

IXL Premier Grip – UK Office Direct

iXon – CCD camera – Andor Technology Ltd

IXYS – Cyclops Electronics Ltd

Ixys – semiconductors – G D Rectifiers Ltd

Ixys – M S C Gleichmann UK Ltd

Izal – toilet paper and disinfectant – Jeyes

J

*J.A. Henckles (Germany) – cooks knives – Dexam International

*J. Aulanier (France) – Loire wines – O W Loeb & Co. Ltd

J B Furnace Engineering Ltd – J B Furnace Engineering Ltd

J B S-Systems GmbH – Star Micronics GB Ltd

J.C.B. – equipment/spares – Bearwood Engineering Supplies

J.C.B. – maintain and sell JCB machines – Scot J C B Ltd

J C B – Hydraulic & Offshore Supplies Ltd

J.C. Rennie & Co. Ltd – wool & yarn – Smiths Of Peter Head

J Connectors – multiple plugs & sockets – Cinch Connectors Ltd

J.D.2 – multi-purpose detergent powder – Premiere Products Ltd

J.D. Williams – mail order catalogue – J D Williams Mail Order Group

J E Hall – hermetic low noise units – Thermofrost Cryo plc

J & E Hall – refrigeration/air-conditioning compressor spares – J & E Hall Ltd

J.E.M. – smoke machines for the entertainment industry – Martin Manufacturing UK plc

J E Morgan – thermal wear – Dawson International plc

*J.F. (Denmark) – grassland machinery – Westmac Ltd

*J.G. Durand Cristal (France) – frosted cut contemporary crystal glassware – Western House

J.G. Speedfit – push in plumbing fittings – John Guest

*J & H Bunn Fertilisers – Bodle Bros Ltd

J H Richards – J H Richards & Co.

J.H.S. – amplifiers, PA systems and accessories, effects pedals and radio microphones, skin wrapped musical instrument accessories – John Hornby Skewes & Co. Ltd

J & H Wilson SP No 1 – snuff – Imperial Tobacco Group PLC

J & H Wilson Top Mill No 1 – snuff – Imperial Tobacco Group PLC

J & H Wilsons Medicated No 99 – snuff – Imperial Tobacco Group PLC

J.H. Witzel – Kee Valves

*J.J. Preum (Germany) – German wines – O W Loeb & Co. Ltd

J.J.S. – castings also spheroidal graphite – Joseph & Jesse Siddons Ltd

J.K. 700 – industrial Nd YAG laser systems – G S I Group Ltd

J.K. 700 Series – industrial Nd YAG laser systems – G S I Group Ltd

J.K.H. – drainage units – J K H Drainage Units Ltd

J.K. Lasers – industrial Nd YAG laser systems – G S I Group Ltd

J.K.O. – woodworking tooling – Smeaton Hanscomb & Co. Ltd

J.L.G. Accessmaster – aluminium personnel lifts – JLG Industries, Inc.

J.L.G. Boom Lifts – telescopic aerial work platforms self propelled – JLG Industries, Inc.

J.L.G. Scissor Lifts – self propelled scissor lifts – JLG Industries, Inc.

J.P.I. Tools – tools for D.I.Y. use – M & F Components

J.R.D. Mouldings (United Kingdom) – rubber mouldings – J R D Rubber Mouldings Ltd

J.R.D. Mouldings. and J.R.D. Pressings – J R D Rubber Mouldings Ltd

J.R.D. Pressings (United Kingdom) – metal pressings – J R D Rubber Mouldings Ltd

J.R. Industries Ltd – roller shutter door – J R Industries Ltd

J.R. Prepreg – preimpregnated resin prods & coated fabrics – J R Technology

J.R. Seal Strip – vacuum bag sealant – J R Technology

J.R. Vac Film – nylon vacuum bag film & elastomeric – J R Technology

*J. Reynaud (France) – Rhone wines – O W Loeb & Co. Ltd

J. & S. – machine tools and equipment – Jones & Shipman Grinding Ltd

J S BARNES – Hydraulic & Offshore Supplies Ltd

J.S. Clayton – first aid kits, surgical and adhesive dressings, first aid room equipment, stretchers, furniture and first aid training services – Clayton First Aid Ltd

J & S Davis – dental product wholesale – Plandent

J.S.R. Arable Farms – farming & contract farming – J S R Farming Group

J.S.R. Healthbred – advanced pig genetics, breeding pigs and semen – J S R Farming Group

J. & S. Small Tools – vices, centres, toolholders and production equipment – W D S

J. Suits – dust and acid resistant coveralls – Synergy Healthcare plc

J.T. – ceramic tile stockists – Just Tiles Ltd

J-Tech – Connectors – Dax International Ltd

*J.V.C. (Worldwide) – audio equipment, video equipment, digital video, colour televisions, audio and video blank tapes – J V C Forex UK Ltd

*J.W.L. (Denmark) – pneumatic (air) couplings and fittings, blow guns, cleaning guns,undersea guns, spiral recoil hoses – Stephens Midlands Ltd

J W & S – potato bag and box weigher – John White & Son Weighing Machines Ltd

J.W.T. – advertising and related services – J W T

J. Walter Thompson – advertising and related services – J W T

J Willi (Switzerland) – packaging machinery – Advanced Dynamics Ltd

J. Wood & Son – sale of agricultural and horticultural machinery parts and service – J Wood & Son Bilsdale Ploughs Ltd

J2 – M C R Systems Ltd

J2000 (Spain) – coin mechanisms – Jofemar UK

*Ja Ja – Ivory & Ledoux Ltd

Jab Fabrics – The Winnen Furnishing Company

Jabclad – external wall cladding – Vencel Resil Ltd

Jabcore – hardcore replacement material – Vencel Resil Ltd

Jabcork – Flat roof insulation panel – Vencel Resil Ltd

Jabdec – Flat roof insulation panel – Vencel Resil Ltd

Jablina – insulated panels – Vencel Resil Ltd

Jablite – insulation board – Vencel Resil Ltd

Jablite Cavity – Wall insulation – Vencel Resil Ltd

Jablite Flooring – floor insulation – Vencel Resil Ltd

Jablite Fulfil – Cavity wall insulation – Vencel Resil Ltd

Jablite Insulink – insulating eaves ventilator – Vencel Resil Ltd

Jablite Roof Element – Structural Insulated Roof Panel Element – Vencel Resil Ltd

Jablite Roof Panel – Warm pitched roof insulation – Vencel Resil Ltd

Jablite Thermacel – EPS loose fill beads for cavity insulation – Vencel Resil Ltd

Jablite WallLok – Cavity wall insulation – Vencel Resil Ltd

Jabperl – Flat roof insulation panel – Vencel Resil Ltd

Jabro – Seco Tools UK Ltd

Jabroll – Rollable roof insulation – Vencel Resil Ltd

Jabsco – marine pumps and associated products – Cleghorn Waring & Co Pumps Ltd

Jabsco – pumps – Robert Craig & Sons Ltd

Jabsco – barrel emptying pumps – Cleghorn Waring & Co Pumps Ltd

Jabsco – dc pumps for diesel fuel transfer – Cleghorn Waring & Co Pumps Ltd

Jabsco – marine water pumps – Lancing Marine

Jabsco – pumps – ITT Industries Jabsco Pumps

Jabsco – equipment & spares – Bearwood Engineering Supplies

Jabsqueeze – Pitch roof insulation – Vencel Resil Ltd

Jabsueeze – pitch roof insulation – Vencel Resil Ltd

Jabugo – Classic Fine Foods Ltd

JAC – Self-adhesive – Mcnaughton James Paper Group Ltd

Jack – Gem Tool Hire & Sales Ltd

Jack – S J Wharton Ltd

Jack-King – trolley jacks – Machine Mart

Jack Nut – Fixing for plastics – Torque Control Ltd

*Jack Nut (U.S.A.) – blind screw anchor – Emhart Teknologies

Jackaman, Smith & Mulley – solicitors – Jackaman's

Jackel – Tommee Tippee and Maws baby accessories – Jackel International Ltd

Jackel International – Tommee Tippee and Maws baby accessories – Jackel International Ltd

Jackes Evans (Parker) – solenoid valves, 3 way defrost valves – Thermofrost Cryo plc

Jackmount (United Kingdom) – anti-vibration machine mounting – Farrat Isolevel

Jackson – water boilers – Manitowoc Food Service UK

Jackson – S J Wharton Ltd

Jackson-Stops – chartered surveyors and estate agents – Jackson Stops & Staff

Jacksons Fencing – fencing and timber preservers – Jacksons Fine Fencing Ltd

Jacksons Fine Fencing – fencing and timber preservers – Jacksons Fine Fencing Ltd

Jacobs – chucks – Danaher Tool Group

Jacobsen – Harrier Fluid Power Ltd

Jacobson – taps – Sheardown Engineering Ltd

Jacoflute – corrugated cardboard – Calpack Ltd

*Jacques Depagneux (France) – Beaujolais wines – O W Loeb & Co. Ltd

Jade – soft toys – R M S International Ltd

Jade – production console – Digico UK Ltd

Jadever – Sole UK agent for Jadever scales – Midland Scales

JAE – connectors – Anglia

Jaeger Looms – European Technical Sales Ltd

Jag Hond Made In England – TCT saw blades – Ernest Bennett & Co Darlington Ltd

Jagalok – truck sideboard fastening system – Albert Jagger Ltd

Jagger – commercial vehicle body parts and fittings – Albert Jagger Ltd

Jaguar – IDC connector – Selectronix Ltd

Jaguar – pressure washers – B & G Cleaning Systems Ltd

Jaguar – rucsacs – Karrimor Ltd

Jaguar – speed converters – I M O Electronics Ltd

Jaguar – L M C Hadrian Ltd

Jaguar – print inspection systems – Tectonic International Ltd

Jahns – European Technical Sales Ltd

JAI – Stemmer Imaging

Jak-Bilt – cabins jack-legged – Boyton B R J System Buildings Ltd

*Jakar (Germany) – drawing instruments – Jakar International Ltd

*Jakar Erasersharp (Germany) – Jakar International Ltd

Jakarta – carpets – Interface Europe Ltd

Jakarta – vanity unit – Armitage Shanks Ltd

Jakemans Confectioners – G R Lane Health Products Ltd

*Jakes (Far East) – unisex jeans – Flitterman Investments Ltd

Jakob Boss – Turner Tools Ltd

Jalite – photoluminescent signs, tape, paints, waymarkers and fire fighting equipment identification symbols – Jalite plc

Jaltex – photoluminescent clothing material – Jalite plc

Jamaica – layflat delivery hose – Merlett Plastics UK Ltd

*Jamaican Best (Jamaica) – bottled sauces & canned foods – Dole Fresh UK Ltd

*Jamaican Pride (Jamaica) – bottled sauces & canned foods – Dole Fresh UK Ltd

Jamak – high strength mouldings and extrusions in silicone rubber – Jamak Fabrication Europe Ltd

Jambo Products – Double Gee Hair Fashions Ltd

James Aimar – Autobar Group Ltd

*James Aimer – Coffilta Coffee & Spring Water Services

James Aimer – teas, ground coffees – Chequer Foods Ltd

James Barry – jackets, suits and trousers – J B Armstrong & Co. Ltd

James Brindley Fabric – The Winnen Furnishing Company

James Durrans – foundry coating products – James Durrans & Sons Ltd

James Hare Silks – silk fabrics – James Hare Ltd

James Hare Silks – The Winnen Furnishing Company

James Herriot – needlecraft – Coats Ltd

James Neill – hand tools – Bearwood Engineering Supplies

James Tobias – Storage – Bucon Ltd

James White – Windfall Brands Ltd

James White Organic Joices – Windfall Brands Ltd

Jamette – woven industrial textiles – James Dewhurst Ltd

Jamicon – Cyclops Electronics Ltd

Jane Greenoff's Cross Stitch – magazine – Future Publishing Ltd

*Jane Shilton (China) – handbags – Shilton plc

Janet Frazer – catalogues – Littlewoods Home Shopping Orders & Enquiries

Jangy Engineering (U.S.A.) – magnetic based millers & milling cutters – John Davies 2001 Ltd

Janitol Original – degreasant detergent – Deb R & D Ltd

Janitol Plus – heavy duty degreaser – Deb R & D Ltd

Janitol Rapide – alkaline cleaner & degreaser – Deb R & D Ltd

Janitol Sanitiser – cleaning & sanitising detergent – Deb R & D Ltd

Janmak Ro-Ro – storage racking – Rack International UK Ltd

Janspeed – manifold systems and motor sport – Janspeed Technologies Ltd

Janus – domestic water heaters – Johnson & Starley Ltd

Janus (United Kingdom) – access control systems – Grosvenor Technology Ltd

*Japan Servo (Japan) – motors – Cliff Electronic Components Ltd

Japara – 100% cotton dyed, cupra and wax fabrics – The British Millerain Company Ltd

Japinda – GRP travel goods – Constellation Luggage Ltd

Japtic – 9 litre plastic syphon – Thomas Dudley Ltd

Jaques – rubber catheters and tubes – Teleflex Medical

Jaques Estier – ties – D P T Wear Ltd

Jar Opener – bottle & jar opener – Dycem Ltd

Jardin – WC suite – Armitage Shanks Ltd

Jardin – corrugated cases – Jardin Corrugated Cases Ltd

Jardine – cast aluminium metalwork, street furniture & lamp-posts(victorian design) – Gardencast

Jarlite Roof Element – structural insulated roof panel – Vencel Resil Ltd

Jarocol – temporary semi-permanent & permanent hair dye intermediates – Vivimed Labs Europe Ltd

***Jarshire** – Jarshire Ltd

Jarvis Breaks – Jarvis Hotels Ltd

Jarvis Group – Electronic information display systems manufactres – Techspan Systems Ltd

Jarvis Hotels – Jarvis Hotels Ltd

Jarylec – dielectric fluid – Atosina UK Ltd

Jarysol – thermal fluid – Atosina UK Ltd

Jarzon Plastics Ltd – Pentagon Plastics Ltd

Jasmacyclene – perfume speciality – Quest International UK Ltd

Jasmatone – perfume speciality – Quest International UK Ltd

Jasmopyrane – perfume speciality – Quest International UK Ltd

Jasmopyrane Forte – perfume speciality – Quest International UK Ltd

Jason – buttons – Jason Buttons Ltd

Jasons' Cradle – Man overboard recovery device – Jason's Cradle

Jaspa – wax polish stripper and cleaner – Evans Vanodine International plc

Jasper – jewellery, giftware and characterware – Wedgewood Travel Ltd

Jasper Conran – womens wear – Jasper Conran Ltd

Jassino – clothing – Fashion Spinners

Jastex – British Fabriks – J & S Taylor Ltd

Javac – vacuum – AESpump

JAVELIN – direct connection guard columns – Thermo Fisher Scientific

Jaxa – paints, lacquers, stains, powders – Fujichem Sonneborn Ltd

Jaxacel – cellulose finishes – Fujichem Sonneborn Ltd

Jaxacryl – stoving enamel and acrylic – Fujichem Sonneborn Ltd

Jaxafil – woodfillers – Fujichem Sonneborn Ltd

Jaxagard – strippable coating – Fujichem Sonneborn Ltd

Jaxakote – epoxy finishes – Fujichem Sonneborn Ltd

Jaxalac – polyurethane finishes – Fujichem Sonneborn Ltd

Jaxamel – melamine finishes – Fujichem Sonneborn Ltd

Jaxpal – palletised containers – A Latter & Co. Ltd

Jay-Be – folding beds, adjustable tables, tubular furniture, bunk and sofabeds, mattresses and cast iron bedsteads – Jay Be Ltd

Jay-Cincinatti – thermometers – Bearwood Engineering Supplies

Jay Dee – quick change tapping chucks – Herbert Tooling Ltd

Jay Electronque – Radio remote control systems – Motion29 Ltd

Jay Mac – Southern Valve & Fitting Co. Ltd

Jayblo – blowing agent – J Allcock & Sons Ltd

Jaycat – B P plc

Jaycee – hand operative paper guillotines – Mastercut Cutting Systems Ltd

Jayem – bicycle accessories – Adcal Labels Ltd

Jayex – electronic signs and programmable led electronic signs – Jayex Technology Ltd

Jaylon – janitorial maintenance products – Naylors Abrasives

JAYMAC – Hydraulic & Offshore Supplies Ltd

Jaymac (Germany) – industrial hose couplings – Hydrasun Ltd

Jaymart – The Winnen Furnishing Company

Jazz – UK Office Direct

Jazz Direct – Smooth Radio

Jazz Enterprises – Smooth Radio

Jazz FM 100.4 – Northwest jazz station – Smooth Radio

Jazz FM 102.2 – London's jazz station – Smooth Radio

JB Diego – Senova Ltd

JB Masters Ltd – sergical instrument manufts – J B Masters Ltd

JBH PROPERTY – J B H Property Consulting Ltd

JBJ – J B J Techniques Ltd

JBJ - Marzocchi - Mintor - Raja - Dentex - Spidex - Technodrive - Havit - SIEM - SMEI - Dusterloh - Haldex - Haldex Barnes - NewCool - Lovejoy - JoyTork - DesCase - Tranter - Emmegi - Swep - Scanwill - Emmegi – J B J Techniques Ltd

JBO – threaded gauges – Turner Tools Ltd

JC (Spain) – Ball valve manufacture – Trimline Valves

JCB – Central Plant Hire

JCB – Custom Brakes & Hydraulics Ltd

JCB – Coppard Plant Hire Ltd

JCB – P J P Plant Hire

JCB – Chaintec Ltd

JCB – parts for JCB vehicles – Husco International Ltd

JCB – Harrier Fluid Power Ltd

jComply – Policies and procedures management system – Tabaq Software Limited

JCS – Trafalgar Tools

JCS – Zero Clips Ltd

JDN – Gustair Materials Handling Equipment Ltd

***Jean-Jacques Vincent (France)** – Macon wines – O W Loeb & Co. Ltd

Jean Michel – feeders and folders – Armstrong Commercial Laundry Systems

***Jean Pierre (Switzerland)** – watch and clock importers – Topical Time Ltd

Jean Pierre – ladies and gents watches – A G Thomas Bradford Ltd

***Jeantil (France)** – feeding and bedding equipment – Westmac Ltd

Jecudex – G E Healthcare

Jeeves – dry cleaners – Jeeves Of Belgravia

Jeffries – saddlery – E Jeffries & Sons Ltd

***Jegs Electrical (Worldwide)** – Jegs Electrical Ltd

Jel – Komet Ltd

Jeld-Wen – doors, windows and staircases – Jeld Wen UK Ltd

Jeldis – Forward Chemicals Ltd

jeldwyn – Preston Plywood Supplies

Jellif Hydrau – Harrier Fluid Power Ltd

Jem – floodlighting – Brimotor Ltd

JENA – disposable products – Jena UK Ltd

Jena-Tec – Jena Rotary Technology Ltd

'Jenag' – automatic straining machine – D H Industries Ltd

Jendico – Jendico Ltd

Jendiwhirl – whirlpool systems for baths – Jendico Ltd

Jenilube – textile machine lubricant – Benjamin R Vickers & Sons Ltd

Jenoseel – D G Protective Coatings

Jensen – toolkits and tools – Longs Ltd

Jentech Computers Ltd – Shiloh Computers Ltd

Jentex Fuel Oils – fuels – Anthony Jenkins Fuel Oil Ltd

Jeol – electron microscopes and spectrometers – Jeol UK Ltd

Jepson – signs and number plates – Jepson & Co. Ltd

***Jerome Delahay** – The Vintners Selection Ltd

Jerribags – flexible 4 gal containers for fuels or water – G K N Aerospace Ltd

Jersetlite – thin supported glove in natural latex – Mapa Spontex

Jersette – supported natural latex gloves – Mapa Spontex

Jerzees – First Impressions Europe Ltd

Jesco – valves – Bearwood Engineering Supplies

Jespro – hydraulic engineering – Jespro 2000 Ltd

Jessate – perfume speciality – Quest International UK Ltd

Jessops – photo, video, digital and optical products – Jessops plc

Jesta – Ladies heavyweight cardigans knitwear – Novinit Ltd

Jesuscan – G E Healthcare

Jet – Central C N C Machinery Ltd

Jet – jeanswear – The Wakefield Shirt Company Limited

Jet Europe – Photopolymer printing plates – Plastotype

Jet-Flow – furnaces – Ajax Tocco International Ltd

***Jet Kunststofftechnik (Germany)** – building products – Yule Catto & Co plc

***Jet Line** – reverse jet dust filter – Delta Neu Ltd

Jet Line - reverse jet dust filter. – Delta Neu Ltd

Jet Melt – hot melt adhesive systems – North British Tapes Ltd

***Jet N Wash (Germany)** – multi function cleaner – Hoover Ltd

***Jet Nut (Ireland)** – Teenut – Jet Press Ltd

Jet Set – darts – Unicorn Products Ltd

Jet Stem – shafts – Unicorn Products Ltd

Jet-Vac – industrial air operated vacuum systems – K & A Furness Ltd

Jeta – sewage and industrial effluent grit separator – Higgins & Hewins Ltd

JeTan – dressing leather – Joseph Clayton & Sons Ltd

Jetcem – rapid setting cement – Vitcas Ltd

***Jetcleaner (Sweden)** – tool for cleaning bores of flexible hoses and rigid pipes – Applications Engineering Ltd

Jetfan – fan – Thermal Engineering Systems Ltd

Jetflo – Impingement or conveyorised dryer – Greenbank Technology Ltd

Jetfloor 300 – pre-cast concrete floors – Hanson Concrete Products plc

Jetfloor Plus – pre-cast concrete floors – Hanson Concrete Products plc

Jetfloor Slab – pre-cast concrete floors – Hanson Concrete Products plc

Jetfloor Standard – pre-cast concrete floors – Hanson Concrete Products plc

Jetfloor Super – pre-cast concrete floors – Hanson Concrete Products plc

Jethete – aircraft steel with high creep and rupture strength – Corus Engineering Steels

Jetin – Hughes Pumps Ltd

Jetin, Dualway, CPE. – Hughes Pumps Ltd

Jetline – bathroom mixers and taps – Ideal Standard Ltd

JetLite – shafts – Unicorn Products Ltd

Jetloc – bonding fasteners – Jet Press Ltd

Jetomat – automatic pressure sets – Calpeda Ltd

Jetpress – Jet Press Ltd

Jetrone – bituminous coating systems – Leighs Paints

Jetsetter – stationery – Davies Products Liverpool Ltd

Jetspray – I M I Cornelius UK Ltd

Jetspray AHU – atomising nozzle humidifier – J S Humidifiers plc

Jetspray Direct Air – atomising nozzle humidifier – J S Humidifiers plc

Jetstream – electrical laundry dosing systems – Christeyns UK Ltd

Jettsetter – jetsetter DTP software – Polydiam Industries

Jetvac – vacuum tanker with high pressure jetting – Whale Tankers Ltd

Jetvent – remote cleaning of HVAC ductwork affected by dust – System Hygienics Ltd

Jewel – razor blades, surgical blades, trimming knife blades and industrial blades – The Jewel Blade Ltd

***Jewellery World (Worldwide)** – jewellery, watches, hair accessories, hats and scarves, 9ct gold and sterling silver – Jewellery World Ltd

Jeyes – cleaning bleach – Jeyes

Jeyes Bloo – toilet block – Jeyes

***Jeyma (Spain)** – copy milling machines – Capital Equipment & Machinery Ltd

JFS – electric flash steam boilers – Fulton Boiler Works Ltd

Jidenco – powder coating machines – Robnor Resins Ltd

Jiffee Jet – mining equipment for cutting drums – Eskro Hydra Mining Divison

Jiffee Systems – mining equipment spares for cutting drums – Eskro Hydra Mining Divison

Jiffex Files – manilla files – Acco East Light Ltd

Jiffex Pocket File – pocketed manilla file – Acco East Light Ltd

Jiffy – Padded Bags – Jiffy Packaging Company Ltd

Jiffy – Tri Pack Supplies Ltd

Jiffy – Davpack

Jiffy – UK Office Direct

Jiffy – Mar Deb

Jiffy – dart sharpeners – Unicorn Products Ltd

Jiffy Bags – padded envelopes – Ambassador Packaging Ltd

Jiffy Bubble – polythene bubble cushioning – Ambassador Packaging Ltd

Jiffy Bubble – bubble wrapping and cushioning material sold in rolls and sheets – Jiffy Packaging Company Ltd

Jiffy Foam – lightweight polyethylene foam sold in rolls and sheets, interleaving and general wrapping and packaging applications – Jiffy Packaging Company Ltd

Jiffy Foam – expanded polyethylene foam – Ambassador Packaging Ltd

Jiffy Mounts – pre-curved brass backed rubber stereos – Plastotype

Jiffy Superlite – lightweight foam and paper laminate – Jiffy Packaging Company Ltd

Jiffy Utility Bags – tough lightweight postal bags – Jiffy Packaging Company Ltd

Jiffycel – L.D.P.E. foam plank – Jiffy Packaging Company Ltd

JiffyFoam – foam packaging material – A Latter & Co. Ltd

Jiffylite – lightweight bubble lined postal bag – Jiffy Packaging Company Ltd

Jiglets – childrens magnetic spelling jigsaw puzzles – Jolly Learning Ltd

Jigsaw Plus – Capex Office Interiors

Jigtool – vacuum pumps – AESpump

Jill Piers – Sanding systems – The Toolpost

Jimi-Heat – Flexelec UK Ltd

Jimmore – Precision Tools

JIMMY JOE – mens and boys wear – Magill Henshaw Ltd

Jinlogic – Sourcing Engineered Products and Components from China – Jinlogic Ltd

JIT – Transcend Group Ltd

Jizer – solvent degreaser – Deb R & D Ltd

Jizer Bio – non-solvent degreaser – Deb R & D Ltd

Jizon Marine – marine solvent degreaser – Deb R & D Ltd

JJ (Slovakia) – electronic valves, tubes and capacitators – Edicron Ltd

JK 700 Series – industrial Nd YAG laser systems – G S I Group Ltd

JK Lasers – industrial Nd YAG laser systems – G S I Group Ltd

***JKO Panelmaster (Austria)** – panel drilling sawing and edgeing machines, drilling and inserting machines, drilling, glueing – Smeaton Hanscomb & Co. Ltd

***JL Burgers** – Tranfield Of Cumbria Ltd Vion Foods

JLA – commercial laundry machine distributors – J L A

Jlfas – Harrier Fluid Power Ltd

JLG – Chaintec Ltd

JLG – R F Lifting & Access Ltd

Jlume – high brightness photoluminescent plastics – Jalite plc

JM Aerofoil – high efficiency axial flow fans for hvac applications – Flakt Woods Ltd

JM Aerofoil - Series 2100 - Aerofoil Climafan - Colchester Range - Axcent - Airpac - KB Series 28 - Compac Climafan - Varofoil. – Flakt Woods Ltd

JM Insulating Firebricks – high temperature insulation bricks – Thermal Ceramics UK Ltd

JME3D – Land & Engineering Surveyors – J M E Civils

JN1003 (Eurofighter/Typhoon) – Dax International Ltd

JNC – suppression capacitors – Anglia

Jo-Bolt – high strength blind bolt (aerospace industry) – Avdel UK Ltd

Jo-Lok – high strength blind bolt (aerospace industry) – Avdel UK Ltd

Joanna – typeface – Monotype Imaging Ltd

Job – cigarette papers – Imperial Tobacco Group PLC

Job Collector – work in progress tracking system – Deaf Alerter plc

Job Southeast – classified paper – Kent Messenger Group Ltd

Job Spot – employment agency – The G I Group

Joblite Roof Panel – warm pitched roof insulation – Vencel Resil Ltd

Jobworld – magazine – Insitive Media

Joca – manilla letter file – Civica UK Ltd

Jockey Mates – towbar ball hitch covers – Ascott Clark

JOD – fine beauty accessories – John O'Donnell Ltd

*Joda (Pakistan) – manicure instruments – John O'Donnell Ltd

*Jodine (China) – cosmetic purses and toilet holdalls – John O'Donnell Ltd

Jodozyme (U.S.A.) – pre milking disinfectant – Delaval

Joe Bloggs – up market casual wear – Juice Coperation Ltd

Joewell (Japan) – haircutting scissors – Diamond Edge Ltd

Jofra – Alpha Electronics Southern Ltd

Johanson – Cyclops Electronics Ltd

John Aird – net curtains – John Aird Holdings Ltd

John Ardern – Really Useful Research & Development

John Arderne – Really Useful Research & Development

*John Artis – Bob Crosby Agencies Ltd

John Banner – general consumer colour tv, audio, video & satellite sales & servicing – John Banner

John Bull – malt extracts – British Diamalt

John Charles – ladies evening wear – Alandar Park

John Clarke – pocket knives and sheath knives. – Egginton Bros Ltd

JOHN CRANE – Hydraulic & Offshore Supplies Ltd

John Deere – tractors, loaders, combines, balers, forage harvesters, mower conditioners and groundscare equipment – John Deere Ltd

*John Deere – Ben Burgess Beeston

John Deere – Garden Tractors – Loxston Garden Machinery

*John Deere – Route V J Horticultural

John Deere – Harrier Fluid Power Ltd

John Deere – Team Overseas Ltd

John Deere – A T Wilde & Son Ltd

John Deere Credit – financial service – John Deere Credit

John E Coyle – The Winnen Furnishing Company

John E Coyle Furniture – The Winnen Furnishing Company

John Foster (United Kingdom) – Worsted Mens Suiting Fabric – John Foster Ltd

John George – fastener distributors – John George & Sons Ltd

JOHN GUEST – Hydraulic & Offshore Supplies Ltd

John Guest – Gustair Materials Handling Equipment Ltd

John Guest – Southern Valve & Fitting Co. Ltd

John Guest – B L Pneumatics Ltd

John Halliday (United Kingdom) – Worsted Mens Suiting Fabric – John Foster Ltd

John Hanna Ltd – bleaching, dyeing and finishing textiles – John Hanna Ltd

John Lowe – darts and flights – Unicorn Products Ltd

John Menzies Wholesale – news,books & games retailers – John Menzies plc

John Moores – catalogues – Littlewoods Home Shopping Orders & Enquiries

*John O'Donnell (Korea, Republic of) – fine beauty accessories, cosmetic brushes – John O'Donnell Ltd

John Player Special King Size – filter cigarettes – Imperial Tobacco Group PLC

John Player Special White – filter cigarettes – Imperial Tobacco Group PLC

JOHN S BARNES – Hydraulic & Offshore Supplies Ltd

John Smedley – mens and ladies fine gauge knitwear using extra fine Merino wool and John Smedley's sea Island cotton, spinners of worsted yarns – John Smedley Ltd

John Smith's – ales & stouts – Scottish & Newcastle Pub Co.

John Tann Ltd – cash safes, fire safes, deposit lockers, strongroom doors, strongrooms and cash handling equipment – Gunnebo UK Ltd

John Walker – tuning forks of every description – Granton Medical Ltd

John Wigfull – industrial pipe work and LPG vessel maintenance – John Wigfull & Co. Ltd

John Wilson – engineering – John Wilson & Sons Industrial Engineer Blacksmith

Johnscliffe – ladies footwear – UK Distributors Footwear Ltd

Johnson Brothers – tableware – Wedgewood Travel Ltd

*Johnson Controls (U.S.A.) – lead acid batteries – Pulsar Developments Ltd

Johnson Elevanja – brakes and couplings, industrial and steelworks drum and disc brakes; sella, shaft and drum couplings – Johnson Elevanja Ltd

Johnson Gears – angular gear drive – S M I

Johnson-Matthey – platinum wire – Bearwood Engineering Supplies

Johnson & Phillips – capacitors – Eaton Electric Ltd

Johnson Professional – tile fixing systems – Johnson Tiles Ltd

Johnson Pump – Rotay Lobe pumps – Bestpump

Johnson's Coffee – Coffee – Stute Foods Ltd

Johnson Tiles – wall & floor tiles – Johnson Tiles Ltd

Johnson Wax – M & D Cleaning Supplies Ltd

Johnsons – UK Office Direct

Johnsons – dry cleaning service – Johnson Apparel Master Ltd

Johnsons Radio – VHF and SW amateur radio construction kits – John Banner

Johnsons Seeds – packeted seeds (for use by the hobby gardener) – Mr Fothergills Seeds Ltd

Johnstone/Manders – decorating centre (Kalon P.L.C.) – Johnstone's Paints Ltd

Johnstones Paints – decorating materials – Johnstone's Paints Ltd

JOINERY – S R B Joinery Ltd

JoinIT – on-line knowledge database on welding and joining – T W I

Joint Boost – Help with stiff joints and mobility – Supplements For Pets Ltd

Jointgrip 55 – anti-skid overbanding sealant – Colas Ltd

JOJO – Hydraulic & Offshore Supplies Ltd

Jolly – Novellini UK Ltd

Jolly Phonics Box – complete set of Jolly Phonics programme for children learning to read and wright – Jolly Learning Ltd

Jolly Phonics Videos 1 And 2 – childrens videos for learning to read and write – Jolly Learning Ltd

Jolly Phonics Wall Frieze – childrens frieze of letter sounds – Jolly Learning Ltd

Jolly Phonics Workbooks 1-7 – childrens workbooks for learning to read and write – Jolly Learning Ltd

Jolly Roger – agriculture produce – Fred Hartley Estates Ltd

Jolly's Drinks – soft drinks – Jolly's L W C

Joloda – trade name for all company products – Joloda Hydraroll Ltd

*Jomro (Germany) – hosiery machine accessories – Groz-Beckert UK

Jonathan James – shoe retailers – Jonathan James Ltd

Jonathan Wren – specialist recruitment consultants to the banking & financial services industry – Jonathan Wren & Co. Ltd

Jones and Shipman 1011 grinder – Phil Geesin Machinery Ltd

Jones and Shipman 1300 grinder – Phil Geesin Machinery Ltd

Jones and Shipman 1302 grinder – Phil Geesin Machinery Ltd

Jones and Shipman 1305 grinder – Phil Geesin Machinery Ltd

Jones and Shipman 1307 grinder – Phil Geesin Machinery Ltd

Jones and Shipman 1310 grinder – Phil Geesin Machinery Ltd

Jones and Shipman 1314 grinder – Phil Geesin Machinery Ltd

Jones and Shipman 1400 grinder – Phil Geesin Machinery Ltd

Jones and Shipman 1415 grinder – Phil Geesin Machinery Ltd

Jones and Shipman 310 tool and cutter – Phil Geesin Machinery Ltd

Jones and Shipman 540 grinder – Phil Geesin Machinery Ltd

Jones and Shipman rise & fall grinders – Phil Geesin Machinery Ltd

Jones & Attwood – machinery/spares – Bearwood Engineering Supplies

Jones Cranes – Jones Cranes Parts

Jones Electrical – Jones Steel Ltd

Jones Lang LaSalle – chartered surveyors – Jones Lang LaSalle

Jones Marine – Jones Steel Ltd

Jones Metals – Jones Steel Ltd

Jones & Palmer – printers of financial reports and colour brochures – Jones & Palmer Ltd

Jones & Shipman – machine tools and equipment – Jones & Shipman Grinding Ltd

Jones & Shipman – Peter Rushton Ltd

Jones & Shipman – Red House Industrial Services Ltd

Jones Steel – Jones Steel Ltd

Jonrad – general consumer electronics sales and servicing especially globe-king vhf & sw amateur radio construction kits – John Banner

Jorc – compressed air condensate management and drains – Airware International Ltd

Jord-Rotary Drum Filters – filters – Mahle Industrial Filteration UK Ltd

*Jordan Valve (U.S.A.) – pressure and temperature regulating and control valves – Tamo Ltd

Jordans – company registration, company administration and related software, conveyancing support and commercial and residential environmental reports, trade mark registration and name protection, co information, sealing devices & stamping for office use, engraved – Jordans Ltd

Jorvik Viking Centre – York Archaeological Trust For Excavation & Research Ltd

*Josef Schmitt (Germany) – German wines – O W Loeb & Co. Ltd

Joseph – retailer and designer ladies and mens fashion – Joseph & Co

Joseph Bramah – locks – Bramah Alarms

Joseph Kielberg – Tri Pack Supplies Ltd

Joseph Rodgers – pocket knives – Egginton Bros Ltd

Joseph Williams – Stainer & Bell Ltd

Josery – sportswear and leisure fabrics – Josery Textiles Ltd

Joshua Row – Bespoke Chipping Blocks – S J H Row & Son Ltd

*Josmeyer (Alsace) – Pol Roger Ltd

Jost – ball bearing turntables, fifth wheel couplings, trailer king pins, trailer landing gear, hubdometers – Jost Great Britain Ltd

Joucomatic – Southern Valve & Fitting Co. Ltd

Joucomatic – equipment & spares – Bearwood Engineering Supplies

Joucomatic – B L Pneumatics Ltd

JOUCOMATIC – Hydraulic & Offshore Supplies Ltd

Joucomatic – Aztech Components Ltd

Joucomatic - Air Automation - Trinorm - Circlair - Red Hat - Tripoint – Asco Numatics

Jouret – vanity unit – Armitage Shanks Ltd

Jowett & Sowry – stationery products – Jowett & Sowry Ltd

Jowitt Grinding Wheels – manufacturers of grinding wheels – George Jowitt & Sons Ltd

Joy – Harrier Fluid Power Ltd

Joy – plastic wood – Hammerite Products Ltd

Joy – Capex Office Interiors

Joy Mining Machinery – mining machinery – Joy Mining Machinery Ltd

Joyce Montague Contracts Ltd – Electrical Contractor and Energy Management – Electrical Testing & Inspection FWT Ltd

Joyners – timber joinery systems – Abru Ltd

Joysonic – housewares – Vitco Ltd

*JP (Costa Rica) – bananas – Dole Fresh UK Ltd

JPL Comms – Duplex Corporate Communications

JProbe – emulator – Hitex UK Ltd

JPS – JENNINGS PLANT HIRE – Jennings Building & Civil Engineering Ltd

JRK Imagingraphics – Genus Group

JS Air Curtains – air curtains – J S Humidifiers plc

JSB HESSELMAN – Hydraulic & Offshore Supplies Ltd

JSP – Powered respirators, PPE – The Toolpost

JSP Pollution Control – Fieldway Supplies Ltd

JSP Spillage Kits – Fieldway Supplies Ltd

JST – Cyclops Electronics Ltd

Jubilee – S J Wharton Ltd

Jubilee – Southern Valve & Fitting Co. Ltd

Jubilee – modular drainage system – Wade International Ltd

Jubilee – bandsaw machines – Addison Saws Ltd

Jubilee – snooker tables – Thurston

Jubilee – ditchliners for bowling greens – Sportsmark Group Ltd

Jubilee – W Mannering London Ltd

JUBILEE – Hydraulic & Offshore Supplies Ltd

Jubilee – Trafalgar Tools

Jubilee – luxury bathroom taps – Samuel Heath & Sons plc

Jubilee (United Kingdom) – brass curtain pole – Integra Products

Jubilee – worm drive hose clips – L Robinson Company Gillingham Ltd

Jubilee Bollard – classically styled architectural bollard – Glasdon International Ltd

Jubilee Clipdriver – hose clip tightening tool – L Robinson Company Gillingham Ltd

Jubilee Flexidriver – hose clip tightening tool – L Robinson Company Gillingham Ltd

Jubilee Wingspade – hose clip with spade – L Robinson Company Gillingham Ltd

Jucee – soft drinks – Princes Soft Drinks

*Jud (Liechtenstein) – felt and wire guides and tensioners – Pulp & Paper Machinery Ltd

Judge – cookware and knives – Horwood Homeware Ltd

Judo Valves – European Technical Sales Ltd

Judo Water Filters – self cleaning backflush water filters – Alan Dale Pumps Ltd

Jugstat – kettle and jug thermostat – Otter Controls Ltd

JuiCees – chewy sweet strip – A L Simpkin Co. Ltd

Juju – jelly shoes and wellingtons – Rushton Ablett Ltd

Julabo – Ken Kimble Reactor Vessel Ltd

Julia – Cloakroom Solutions Ltd

Julia – HSS and coated circular saw blades – Accurate Cutting Services Ltd

Julilee – Gustair Materials Handling Equipment Ltd

*Julius (Germany) – strip edge trimming machines – British & Continental Traders Ltd

JUMBO – Chaintec Ltd

Jumbo – pasture toppers – Brown's Agricultural Machinery Company Ltd

Jumbo – tap – Worldwide Dispensers

Jumbo – decorators products – Stanley Decorating Products

Jumbo – Linak UK

Jumbo Art and Velvet – paper – Fenner Paper Co. Ltd

Jumbo Home – Linak UK

Jumbo Markers – thick felt tip marker – Office Depot UK

Jumbo Weigher – digital crane/scales with extra large displays, capacities 2 tonnes to 20 tonnes – Straightpoint UK Ltd

JUMBOFLEX – Hydraulic accumulator for large diameter pipeline water hammer prevention of non-corrosive liquids – Pulsation Dampers At Pulseguard Ltd

Jumbox – Linpac Allibert Ltd

Jumburry – Try & Lilly Ltd

Jumo Instrument Co. – measurement & control instrumentation for temperature, pressure, humidity, conductivity and ph – Jumo Instrument Co. Ltd

Jumo Instruments – European Technical Sales Ltd

Jumo Poressure Gauges – European Technical Sales Ltd

Jumo Pressure Switches – European Technical Sales Ltd

Jumo Rod Thermostats – European Technical Sales Ltd

Jumop Level Probes – European Technical Sales Ltd

JUN-AIR – Hydraulic & Offshore Supplies Ltd

JUN-AIR – Gast Group Ltd

June Productions – music production company – June Productions Ltd

Jung Baufix – package drainage pump – Pump Technical Services

Jung Compli – package floor mounted, drainage & sewage system – Pump Technical Services

Jung Hebefix – under sink drainage system – Pump Technical Services

*Jung Pompen GmbH (Germany) – pumps – Pump Technical Services

Jung Pumps – Denton Pumps Ltd

Jungheinrich – T V H UK Ltd

JUNGHEINRICH – Chaintec Ltd

Jungheinrich – Stacatruc

Jungheinrich – Harrier Fluid Power Ltd

JUNGHEINRICH – Premier Lift Trucks Ltd

*Jungle Formula (Netherlands) – insect repellant – Chefaro UK Ltd

Jungle Pops – lollipops – A L Simpkin Co. Ltd

Junia – WC – Armitage Shanks Ltd

Junifil – dispenser – Appor Ltd

Junior – upright vacuum cleaner – Hoover Ltd

Junior – dog food – Gilbertson & Page Ltd

Junior – benchwork fume extractor – Plymovent Limited

Junior Bind – hotmelt binding machine – Securit World Ltd

Junior Bloggs – up market casual wear for children – Juice Coperation Ltd

Junior Canaries – junior membership – Norwich City Football Club

Junior Education – monthly magazine – Scholastic School Book Fairs

Junior Focus – monthly magazine – Scholastic School Book Fairs

Junior Hercules – screen mill – Bradley Pulverizer Co.

Junior Macare – baby products – Paul Murray plc

Junior Prolatch – Protex Fasteners Ltd

Junior SCP – steel hot water boiler – Hartley & Sugden

Junipor – dispenser – Appor Ltd

Juno – small bore pipe couplings 1/2" - 2" for steel and polythene pipe – Viking Johnson

Jupiter – fishing tackle – Daiwa Sports Ltd

Jupiter – labelling machine – Harland Machine Systems Ltd

Jupiter – Glazing Vision Ltd

Jupiter – combined PIR and microwave detector – Guardall Ltd

Jupiter – automatic processor for offset plates – Kodak Morley

Jupiter – planetary concrete pan mixers – The Howard Group

Jury – kitchenware – Thomas Plant Birmingham

*Just Bouillon (Germany) – stock cubes – Kallo Foods Ltd

Just Diaries – Trade Name – Just Diaries

Just Essential – toiletries using aromatherapy oils, 10ml aromatherapy oils – Faith Products Ltd

Just Fiber – dietry fibres – Lawrence Industries Ltd

Just for you – Hotel Complimentary Products

Just in time – Transcend Group Ltd

Just Jamie – ladies clothes – Just Jamie & the Paulrich Ltd

Just Shelving – UK Office Direct

Just -T – U C D Ltd

Just Tax – personal taxation service – Seymour Taylor

Just Wood – laser engraved quality wooden and acrylic giftware/promotional items – W H Mason & Son Ltd

JVC – Lamphouse Ltd

JW – Mayday Seals & Bearings

JWIS – Iwis Drive Systems

JWL – Trafalgar Tools

K

K.060 – Kennametal UK Ltd

K.090 – Kennametal UK Ltd

K.1 – Kennametal UK Ltd

K 10 – High Pressure Cylinders – Air Power & Hydraulics Ltd

K.15, 16, 60 Open Gear Oils – water resistant black residual lubricants – Morris Lubricants

K.2 EPGX Grease – specially developed bearing grease for operating at high temperatures – Morris Lubricants

K.25 – component preforming machines – Elite Engineering Ltd

K.313 – Kennametal UK Ltd

K.383 Anti Seize Compound – lead free anti seize compound – Morris Lubricants

K.4000,400,40,41,42,43, EP Grease – multi purpose lithium based greases – Morris Lubricants

K.420 – Kennametal UK Ltd

K.48 Grease – lithium soap, refined mineral oil and molybdenum disulphide based grease – Morris Lubricants

K.57 Grease – mineral oil, calcium hydroxy sterate thickened grease – Morris Lubricants

K.62 Grease – smooth grease thickened with organo modified bentone clay – Morris Lubricants

K.68 – Kennametal UK Ltd

K.84 Grease – synthetic semi fluid grease – Morris Lubricants

K. 968 White Grease – high quality food machine grease – Morris Lubricants

K.A. – church organ components – Kimber Allen UK Ltd

K.A.C. – break glass call points – Kac Alarm Co. Ltd

K.A. Seals – mechanical seals – Pioneer Weston

K'Archer – industrial cleaning equipment – B & G Cleaning Systems Ltd

K.B. Refrigeration – 24hr service of refrigeration and air conditioning; complete installation of coldroom's, fridges etc – K B Refrigeration Ltd

K Bar – R K Printcoat

K Bar - Meteringbar, Rotary Koater - Pilot Coating Machine. – R K Printcoat

K-basic – Topaz Computer Systems Ltd

K-Bins – small parts storage bins manufactured from corrugated fibre board and low cost quality die-cut boxes plain or printed made to your own requirements – K Bins Ltd

K-Box – custom plastic and metal enclosure systems – Danielson Ltd

K.C.250 – Kennametal UK Ltd

K.C.710 – Kennametal UK Ltd

K.C.720 – Kennametal UK Ltd

K.C.725M – Kennametal UK Ltd

K.C.730 – Kennametal UK Ltd

K.C.740 – Kennametal UK Ltd

K.C.792M – Kennametal UK Ltd

K.C.810 – Kennametal UK Ltd

K.C.850 – Kennametal UK Ltd

K.C.910 – Kennametal UK Ltd

K.C.935 – Kennametal UK Ltd

K.C.950 – Kennametal UK Ltd

K.C.990 – Kennametal UK Ltd

K.C.992M – Kennametal UK Ltd

K-Cab – Thermal Designs UK Ltd

K-Clad – Kestrel B C E Ltd

K.D.050 – Kennametal UK Ltd

K.D.100 – Kennametal UK Ltd

K.D.120 – Kennametal UK Ltd

K.D.200 – Kennametal UK Ltd

K.D.G. – pressure instrumentation – Emerson Process Management

K.D.G. Instruments – thermostats – Bearwood Engineering Supplies

K.E.G. Checkweighers – weighing system – Stevens Group Ltd

K-FIT – Hydraulic & Offshore Supplies Ltd

K-Forms – Flexible semantic knowledge capture at the point of its generation – Knowledge Now Limited

K.G. Smoke Dispersal – automatic opening ventilators – West Leigh Ltd

K-Guard – Thermal Designs UK Ltd

K & H Eppensterner – E P E UK Ltd

*K.H.K. (Japan) – stock and custom gears – R A Rodriguez UK Ltd

K-Integrate – Integrating Knowledge – Knowledge Now Limited

K.J. Extrusion Press – backward extrusion press – Joseph Rhodes Ltd

K.K. Balers – waste balers – K K Balers Ltd

K & L Ltd – Kennett & Lindsell Ltd

K.L.T. – windows and windscreens – Kellett Engineering Co. Ltd

K-Line (United Kingdom) – range of photographic sprays by S.W. Kenyon – S W Kenyon

K.M.3 – storage wall – Komfort Workspace plc

*K.M.P. Brand (Germany) – computer consumables,ribbons, inkjet, toners – K M P Crusader Manufacturing Co. Ltd

K.M.V. – Cogne UK Ltd

K N F – diaphragm pumps – AESpump

K-Now – Knowledge Now – Knowledge Now Limited

K-Rain – Irrigation products – Arcadia Irrigation UK

K.-Range – multistage barrel casing pumps – Weir Group Senior Executives Pension Trust Ltd

K-Rend – P F T Central

K-Rend – external coloured render and internal render – Kilwaughter Chemical Co. Ltd

K.S. 100e – texturised rucsac fabric – Karrimor Ltd

K.S.B. – valves – Bearwood Engineering Supplies

K.S. Containers – storage & distribution containers – S S I Schaefer Ltd

K-Search – Semantic hybrid Search tool to find your needed insight – Knowledge Now Limited

K-Store – Hybrid Knowledge store – Knowledge Now Limited

K.T.125 – Kennametal UK Ltd

K.T.175 – Kennametal UK Ltd

K.T.3 – kevlar rope – Marlow Ropes Ltd

K.W.M. – bushes and bushing tools – Time Products UK Ltd

K1 – print inspection systems – Tectonic International Ltd

K2R/Project T/Concept – contract kitchen furniture – Moores Furniture Group

K3000 – General Vacuum Equipment Ltd

K4 – lighting effects projector – Optikinetics Ltd

K40 Slideover – insulated sectional overhead doors – Kaba Door Systems

K4000 – General Vacuum Equipment Ltd

K5000 – General Vacuum Equipment Ltd

K501 – clear masonry waterproofing solution – Sika Liquid Plastics

K7 – 67mm thick screen system – Komfort Workspace plc

*Kaaz (Japan) – lawnmowers, brushcutters, hedgetrimmers and blowers – Danarm Machinery Ltd

KAB – T E K Seating Ltd

KAB – Sitsmart Ltd

Kab Office Chairs – Office Chairs – Stanwell Office Furniture

Kaba 20 – high security registered key locking system – Kaba Ltd Head Office

Kaba Delta – motorised strike – Kaba Ltd Head Office

Kaba EXOS8000 – server based proximity access control systems with windows control software – Kaba Ltd Head Office

Kaba Legic – proximity key/card access control system, programmeable – Kaba Ltd Head Office

Kaba Macs – stand alone proximity access control system – Kaba Ltd Head Office

Kaba Mini S – high security registered 19mm diameter system for utility cylinder locks – Kaba Ltd Head Office

Kaba Quattro S – high security euro profile cylinder systems - key registration – Kaba Ltd Head Office

Kabelschlepp (Germany) – plastic and steel cable carriers – Metool Products Ltd

Kabelschlepp – European Technical Sales Ltd

Kabex – cable printer – Ses Sterling Ltd

Kaby Engineers – machined components, fabrications and tooling, multi-spindle to CNC capacity – Kaby Engineers Ltd

Kace – automatic spray & dip coating systems – Humiseal Europe Ltd

Kaercher – Harrier Fluid Power Ltd

Kaesar – compressors, parts and service – Airware International Ltd

Kaeser – Harrier Fluid Power Ltd

Kaessbohrer – Harrier Fluid Power Ltd

KAFER – dial gauges and dial indicators of Germany – Mapra Technik Co.

Kafon – conduit screening suppression components and systems – Icore International

*Kahla – Neville UK plc

Kahlig (Germany) – DC Motors, gearheads – Electro Mechanical Systems (EMS) Ltd

*Kahr (U.S.A.) – aerospace journal, spherical and rod-end bearings – R A Rodriguez UK Ltd

Kaiser-Kamo – Harrier Fluid Power Ltd

KAIZAN – Transcend Group Ltd

KAIZEN – Transcend Group Ltd

KALE MAKINA LTD – Pinstructure Ltd

Kaleidoscope – bright shades – St Regis Paper Co. Ltd

Kaleidoscope – electronic commerce messaging system – Multicom Products Ltd

Kalic – high reactivity milk of lime – Tarmac

*Kallo (Belgium) – rice cakes and rice cereals – Kallo Foods Ltd

Kallodoc – acrylic toothpowder – Metrodent Ltd

Kalmar – Harrier Fluid Power Ltd

KALMAR – Chaintec Ltd

Kalmar – Stacatruc

Kalmar – Custom Brakes & Hydraulics Ltd

KALMAR-CLIMAX – Chaintec Ltd
Kalmar-Climax – T V H UK Ltd
Kalmar-Irion – T V H UK Ltd
KALMAR-IRION – Chaintec Ltd
Kalmar-LMV – T V H UK Ltd
Kalmem LF – Low Fouling Hollow fibre membrane for water treatment – Kalsep UK
Kalms – Natural Remedy for Relief of Stress – G R Lane Health Products Ltd
Kaloric – Kaloric Heater Co. Ltd
Kalrez – perfluoroelastomer parts – Du Pont UK Ltd
Kalsafe – Roodsafe Ltd
Kam Conveyor Cleaners – powered brush chain, chevron and flat conveyor cleaners – Kleeneze Sealtech Ltd
Kamag – Harrier Fluid Power Ltd
Kamara – Drugasar Service Ltd
Kamara power flu – fan assisted forced flu gas heater – Drugasar Service Ltd
Kamasa – S J Wharton Ltd
Kamdeals – The Winnen Furnishing Company
Kameo – Lusso Interiors
Kameo 50 – 50mm thick stud partitioning system – Komfort Workspace plc
Kameo 75 – 75mm thick system with rounded corners – Komfort Workspace plc
Kamewa – Aquamaster – Rolls Royce
Kamokasier – Harrier Fluid Power Ltd
Kand-Air – air duster equipment – Arctic Products Ltd
Kandola Silks – The Winnen Furnishing Company
Kane May – Alpha Electronics Southern Ltd
Kane-May – electronic instrumentation accessories and services – Comark Ltd
Kango – power tools – Brilec Power Tools Ltd
Kansas – Wenaas Ltd
Kansas – workwear – Pioner Fristads
Kanthal Hot Rod – silicon carbide heating elements – Sandvik
KANTSEAL – Hydraulic & Offshore Supplies Ltd
Kao-C – suspension – Reckitt Benckiser plc
Kaowool – ceramic fibre products – Thermal Ceramics UK Ltd
KAPPA – robust, high sensitivity capillary columns – Thermo Fisher Scientific
Kapron – Thermal Reflections Ltd
Kaptech – flexible hoses – Guyson International Ltd
Kapton – polyimide film – Du Pont UK Ltd
Karatclad – gold electroplating processes – Cookson Electronics Ltd
Karate – darts and dart shafts – Unicorn Products Ltd
KARBERG & HENNEMANN – Hydraulic & Offshore Supplies Ltd
Karbon – friction precursors – Cytec Engineered Materials Ltd
Karcher – R G K UK Ltd
Karcher – Kranzle UK Ltd
Karcher – Trafalgar Tools
Karcher – Gem Tool Hire & Sales Ltd
Kardex – visible records systems – Kardex Systems UK Ltd
Kardex, Linvar, Linpic and Megamat Vertical carous – Secondhand and Re-furbished Vertical Storage carousels and Vertical Shuttle units. – Abbeydale Storage
Karir – clothing manufacturer – S Karir & Sons Ltd
***Karl Roll (Germany)** – ultrasonic cleaning plant – Embassy Machinery Ltd
Karnabax – food grade wax for coating confectionery mixing vessels – British Wax Refining Co.
Karndean – N W Flooring
Karndean – The Winnen Furnishing Company
Karnival – bright manilla range – Acco East Light Ltd
Karpelle – coats, jackets, dresses, trousers and skirts – Karpelle Ltd
Karramandi – Natural Soap and Skin Care – Karramandi
Karrimat – sleeping mats – Karrimor Ltd
Karrimix – readymix concrete – Bardon Concrete Ltd
Karrimor – rucsacs and cycle luggage – Karrimor Ltd
Karrson from Norway – Norwegian sweaters – R A Young & Abercairn Of Scotland Ltd
Kartofix – paramelt
Kaschke – inductive components – Anglia
Kasco – M Suleman & Co.
Kasfold – booklet maker – K A S Paper Systems Ltd
***Kason Contract Furniture** – Kestrel Design
Kaspersky anti virus – Tekdata Distribution Ltd
Kastl – European Technical Sales Ltd
KATAS – Hydraulic & Offshore Supplies Ltd
Katercarb – An Activated Carbon Filter Unit for the enhanced removal of food odours including catering, hotel and food processing areas – Emcel Filters Ltd
***Katerglass** – Disposable tumblers – Dispo International
Katkin – door furniture – Allgood
Kato – Harrier Fluid Power Ltd
Kato Entex – pressed metal parts – Advanex Europe Ltd
Katopark – Double Parking Systems
Kauser – cleaning cloths – Kauser International Trading Ltd
KAVAC – Hydraulic & Offshore Supplies Ltd
KAVAIR – Hydraulic & Offshore Supplies Ltd
KAWASAKI – Hydraulic & Offshore Supplies Ltd
Kawasaki – C J Plant Ltd
***Kawasaki** – J Paterson & Sons
Kawasaki – Mike Garwood Ltd
Kawasaki – A T Wilde & Son Ltd
Kawatatec – Kone Cranes Machine Tool Services
Kay-Cel – expanded polystyrene for packaging, insulation and building applications – Kay-Metzeler Ltd
Kay-Metzeler – polyurethane foam – Vita Group
Kay Optical Servicing – optical and ophthalmic instrument repairs (also binoculars, microscrope repairs etc), binocular and telescope sales – Kay Optical Servicing
Kayaba – C J Plant Ltd
Kayden – Mercury Bearings Ltd
Kaydon – Harrier Fluid Power Ltd
Kaydon – thin section tapered roller bearings – R A Rodriguez UK Ltd
Kaydon – thin section "reali-slim" ball bearings – R A Rodriguez UK Ltd
Kaydon – slewing rings & custom made bearings – R A Rodriguez UK Ltd
Kaydon, Spirolox, IEF Werner, KHK, Bryant, Schatz, A.R.B., FK, Greenlign, Kahr, MRC, RBC, Unitec, Valve Research, Zetassi. – R A Rodriguez UK Ltd
Kaylan – polyurethane – Kay Dee Engineering Plastics Ltd
Kaylee Transfers – self adhesive emblems, vehicle livery and transfers – Kaylee Transfers Ltd
Kaystol – scourable textile lubricants – Millers Oils Ltd
Kaytime – Clocks – K B Import & Export Ltd
KBK – Metal Bellows, Spider & Safety Overload Clutch-Couplings – Francis and Francis Ltd
KBK KB – Metal bellows couplings – Francis and Francis Ltd
KBK KBE – Flexible spider couplings – Francis and Francis Ltd
KBK KBK – Safety overload clutch couplings – Francis and Francis Ltd
kbos2 – KBOS2
KDMS – dealer management system – Kalamazoo - Reynolds Ltd
KE – Kentinental Engineering Ltd
KE-Burgmann – Eagleburgmann Industries UK Llp
Kearney & Treker – Red House Industrial Services Ltd
Kearns Richard boring machines – Phil Geesin Machinery Ltd
KEB – Mercury Bearings Ltd
Kebab T Disc Skimmer – industrial skimmers for oil recovery – Vikoma International Ltd
Keco – industrial castors and wheels – Keystone Castor Co.
Keco – industrial castors and wheels – Keystone Castor Co.
Keco - range of castors and wheels.Flexello - range of castors and wheels.Keystone - stockists and distributors of castors and wheels.Revvo - range of castors and wheels.Shepherd castors - range of castors.G-Dok Footmaster range - multifunctional castors. – Keystone Castor Co.
Kee access – FastClamp
Kee anchor – FastClamp
Kee dome – FastClamp
Kee guard – FastClamp
Kee Klamp – Safety Works & Solutions Ltd
Kee klamp – FastClamp
Kee Klamp – Accesscaff International Ltd
Kee Klamps – tube fittings – Kee Systems Ltd
Kee lite – FastClamp
Kee mark – FastClamp
Kee nect – FastClamp
Kee stainless – FastClamp
KEELARING – Hydraulic & Offshore Supplies Ltd
KEELAVITE – Hydraulic & Offshore Supplies Ltd
Keeler – opthalmic, optometric and general medical equipment and sub-miniature halogen bulbs – Keeler Ltd
Keeler Loupes – magnifiers for surgical and dental applications – Keeler Ltd
Keen – aerosols, insect killer, air fresheners, spray starch, window cleaner, wax furniture polish, oven cleaner and carpet cleaner – Keen World Marketing Ltd
Keen Superkill – ant and roach exterminator – Keen World Marketing Ltd
Keenan Klassik Bale Handler – mixer wagon – Richard Keenan UK Ltd
Keenan Refurb – wagons & boxes, mixer feeds, feeders, pret – Richard Keenan UK Ltd
Keene – Harrier Fluid Power Ltd
Keep-It – Keep-it Security Products
Keep It (United Kingdom) – Security products – George Dyke Ltd
Keepheat – hermatically sealed insulating glass units – A C Yule & Son Ltd
Keey Clothing – Inline London
KEF – loud speaker – K E F
KEF Uni-Q Technology – loud speaker – K E F
Kegscan – barcoding system – Deaf Alerter plc
Kehroflex-S (United Kingdom) – robust, heavy duty, black polyurethane ducting, hydrolysis and microbe resistant – Flexible Ducting Ltd
Keil – mortice chains – Leitz Tooling UK Ltd
KeilKraft – model aircraft kits – Amerang Group Ltd
***Keithley (U.S.A.)** – instruments test & measurement – Keithley Instruments Ltd
***Keithley (U.S.A.)** – data acquisition – Keithley Instruments Ltd
Kelco-Crete – welan gum (construction grade) – C P Kelco Ltd
Kelcogel – gellan gum – C P Kelco Ltd
Keldax – resins – Du Pont UK Ltd
Keldent – xanthan gum (toothpaste grade) – C P Kelco Ltd
Kelgray Products – labels and barcoding – Kelgray Products Ltd
Kelgum – specialty blends based on xanthan gum – C P Kelco Ltd
Keller – pressure transmitters – Tamo Ltd
Keller – equipment & spares – Bearwood Engineering Supplies
Kellog – Harrier Fluid Power Ltd
Kellysearch.co.uk – industrial search engine for industry, listing details of over 1million companies worldwide – The Bankers' Almanac Reed Business Information
***Kelpak (South Africa)** – liquid seaweed – Farmura Ltd
***Kelplant (South Africa)** – soil conditioner – Farmura Ltd
Kelsey Rose – bridal dresses – Alandar Park
Keltek – contract electronics manufacturers – Plexus Corp UK Ltd
Kelton – Woodturning tools – The Toolpost
Keltrol – xanthan gum, (food and personal care grade) – C P Kelco Ltd
Kelvin – Stacatruc
***Kelvin (Italy)** – Refrigeration unit – Total Process Cooling Ltd
Kelvin Top Set – safety observation and incident prevention programme system – Kelvin Top-Set Ltd
Kelvin Valley Properties – Brand – Kelvin Valley Properties
Kelzan – xanthan gum, (industrial grade) – C P Kelco Ltd
Kemco – impression composition material – Kemdent
Kemcut – industrial lubricant – B P plc
Kemdent – Kemdent
Kemesonic – Kemet International Ltd
KEMET – capacitors – Anglia
Kemet – Cyclops Electronics Ltd
Kemet 300 – metallurgical, geological and universal polishing machines – Kemet International Ltd
Kemfast 2 – chemical anchor – Rawlplug Ltd
Kemfix – chemical anchor – Rawlplug Ltd
***Kemira Fertilisers** – Bodle Bros Ltd
Kemmel – dog food – Gilbertson & Page Ltd
Kemnay – red oxide primer – Spencer Coatings Ltd
Kemp Engineering – Kemp Engineering & Surveying Ltd
Kempe's Engineers Year-Book – United Business Media Ltd
***Kemper** – Anker Machinery Company Ltd
KEMPF – Bailey Morris Ltd
Kemppi – Wessex Welding & Industrial Supplies Ltd
Kemps – publishers of business to business directories – Kemps Publishing Ltd
Kemps Film Television and Commercial Production Services Handbook – used by Production companies, it is the most comprehensive guide to the film, television and production services in the UK and world wide. www.kftv.com – The Bankers' Almanac Reed Business Information
Kempsafe – marine galley, heating and laundry equipment – Kempsafe Ltd
Kempton – pony boxes – Browns of Wem Ltd
Kempton – ticket boards – St Regis Paper Co. Ltd
Kemwall – cosmetic filling machine – Kemwall Engineering Co.
Kemwell – heat treatment equipment, metal heat treatment on site and in-house, design, supply and installation of surface heating products – Kemwell Thermal Ltd
Kenalev – dyestuff levelling for wool, cotton etc – Brenntag Colours Ltd
Kenamide – selected dyes for polyamide – Brenntag Colours Ltd
Kenanthrol – acid milling dyestuffs – Brenntag Colours Ltd
Kenbraid – carrier ropes and paper machine threading – William Kenyon & Sons Ropes & Narrow Fabrics Ltd
Kenco – roast, ground and instant coffee – Kraft Foods UK Ltd
Kenco – Alba Beverage Co. Ltd
Kenco – UK Office Direct
Kendal Cover – cover paper – James Cropper plc
Kendal Manilla – manilla board – James Cropper plc
Kendal Pressboard – coverboard – James Cropper plc
Kendall & Gernt – Red House Industrial Services Ltd
Kendex – tungsten carbide indexable inserts – Kennametal UK Ltd
Kendia – diamond grinding wheels – D K Holdings Ltd
Kendon Automotive – Test and Service Equipment – Oakmain Ltd

*Kendu Milling Cutters (Spain) – Macinnes Tooling Ltd

Kenex – Kenex Electro Medical Ltd

Kenfil – inclined separation screens – Pulp & Paper Machinery Ltd

Kengrip – Kennametal UK Ltd

Kenilworth Weekly News – Leamington Spa Courier

Kenloc – positive lock tungsten carbide tooling – Kennametal UK Ltd

Kenlofan – fans – Kenlowe Accessories & Co. Ltd

Kenlowemotor – motors D.C. – Kenlowe Accessories & Co. Ltd

Kennedy – valves – Bearwood Engineering Supplies

KennedyOH – Occupational health services – Kennedy Occupational Health

Kennedys – publishers of trade magazines and books – Kennedy's Publications Ltd

Kenneform – Kennett & Lindsell Ltd

Kenner – toys – Hasbro UK Ltd

Kennylbond – spindle tapes – William Kenyon & Sons Ropes & Narrow Fabrics Ltd

Kenrick – pastic injection moulding – Archibald Kenrick & Sons

Kenrick – builders hardware – Archibald Kenrick & Sons

Kensington – UK Office Direct

Kensington – fresh brew tea and coffee machine – Bunzl Vending Services Ltd

Kensington – residential door – Coastal Aluminium

Kenstack – roof vent – McKenzie Martin Ltd

Kent – record label – Ace Records Ltd

Kent – hairbrushes, bodybrushes, combs and shaving brushes, specialists in natural wool and bristle for retail and trade – GB Kent & Sons plc

Kent Business – monthly paper – Kent Messenger Group Ltd

Kent GB – wood profiling and shaping – GB Kent & Sons plc

Kent Messenger – newspaper – Kent Messenger Group Ltd

Kent Today – newspaper – Kent Messenger Group Ltd

Kentel – Business Telephone – Cost-A-Call Ltd

Kentinental – Kentinental Engineering Ltd

Kentish Express – newspaper – Kent Messenger Group Ltd

Kentish Gazette – newspaper – Kent Messenger Group Ltd

Kentmere – photographic paper and cardboard packaging – Kentmere Ltd

KENTRUCK – Chaintec Ltd

Kenwood – Tecstar Electronics Ltd

Kenwood – oscioscopes – Longs Ltd

Kenwood – Alpha Electronics Southern Ltd

Kenwood - Tecstar - Prism – Tecstar Electronics Ltd

Kenworth – Team Overseas Ltd

Kepac – panelling for exhibitions – Pinewood Associates

Keps – permanent insulating formwork, energy efficient building system – Springvale Insulation Ltd

Keraflow – Keraflo Ltd

Keraflow Ball Valves – Keraflo Ltd

Keral – traditional castables – Calderys UK Ltd

Keralox – ramming mixes – Calderys UK Ltd

Keram – ramming mixes – Calderys UK Ltd

Kerastar – ceramic, porcelain floor and cladding tiles – Johnson Tiles Ltd

Kerbfast – road kerb for traffic islands – Worms Eye Site Investigation Ltd

Kerbmaster – remould truck tyres – Tyre Renewals Ltd

Kerbsider – captive curtain sider bodywork – Lawrence David Ltd

Kercast – ultra low cement castables – Calderys UK Ltd

Kerex – ramming mixes – Calderys UK Ltd

Kergun – gunning mixes – Calderys UK Ltd

*Kerk – leadscrews – Huco Dynatork

Kerlite – insulating castables – Calderys UK Ltd

Kermag – gunning mixes – Calderys UK Ltd

Kermix – ramming mixes – Calderys UK Ltd

Kern Liebers – knitting machine elements – Groz-Beckert UK

Kerplast – plastics – Calderys UK Ltd

Kerr Bi-Lingual – language recruitment – Kerr Multilingual

Kerr Recruitment – administrative staff recruitment and temporary staff – Kerr Multilingual

Kerridge – Macclesfield Stone Quarries Ltd

Kerry – ultrasonic staking tool – Welwyn Tool Group Ltd

*Kerzolin – Flickers Ltd

Kessler – Custom Brakes & Hydraulics Ltd

Kessler – European Drives & Motor Repairs

Kesslers International – designers of point of sale display units – Kesslers International Ltd

Kestrel – commercial gas heater – Vulcana Gas Appliances Ltd

Kestrel – Gem Tool Hire & Sales Ltd

Kestrel – non contact measuring system – Vision Engineering Ltd

Keter – plastic garden furniture and plastic household/DIY goods/bathroom & storage – Keter UK Ltd

Ketjenblack EC – electrically conductive carbon black – Akzo Nobel Chemicals Holdings Ltd

Ketjenflex 8 – speciality suphonamides – Akzo Nobel Chemicals Holdings Ltd

Ketjenflex 9S – orthopara toluene sulfonamide – Akzo Nobel Chemicals Holdings Ltd

Ketjenflex MH – speciality sulphonamides – Akzo Nobel Chemicals Holdings Ltd

Ketjenflex MS80 – speciality sulphonamides – Akzo Nobel Chemicals Holdings Ltd

Ketjenlube – lube oil additives – Akzo Nobel Chemicals Holdings Ltd

Ketlene – descalers – Ashland UK

Ketonex – B P plc

Ketosaid – aids in the treatment of acetonaemia & ketosis in cattle & sheep – Norbrook Research

Ketovite – multi vitamin – Astellas Pharma Ltd

Ketron Peek – Merseyside Metal Services

Kett's Rebellion – cask beer – Woodforde's Norfolk Ales

Kettle Klear – kettle descaler – Thompson & Capper Ltd

*Kettler (Germany) – Fitness equipment, garden & home office furniture, toys and bicycles. – Kettler GB Ltd

Keuper Red – red firing clay body – Potclays Ltd

Kevlar – aramid fibre – Du Pont UK Ltd

*Kew – J Paterson & Sons

Kew – industrial cleaning equipment – B & G Cleaning Systems Ltd

*KEW (Denmark) – pressure washers/steam cleaners – C S A Cleaning Equipment

Kew – Kranzle UK Ltd

Kewanee Boilers – Twin Industries International Ltd

Kewtechnik – Alpha Electronics Southern Ltd

Kex – jeans and leisurewear – Regatta Ltd

KEY CLAMP – METAL BRACKETS – Alvin Industrial Limited

key edge – locksmiths – Invictus Locks & Security

Key Kap – protective device for keyboards – Box Factory Ltd

Key Stage – modular platform (demountable) – Stage Systems Ltd

Keybak – self retracting key reels – Securikey Ltd

Keyboard – air conditioning controls – Schneider Electric

Keyboard – DIY panels melamine faced-edged – Kronoplus Ltd

Keyboard Cavalcade – monthly newspaper by subscription only 16.00 per year – Sceptre Promotions Ltd

Keyboard Slidaway – slides under your PC when not in use – Acco UK Ltd

Keybold Vacuum – AESpump

Keycall – telephonic & radio paging apparatus & instruments incorporating keys – Vodafone Retail Ltd

Keyence – Aztech Components Ltd

Keyfuels – commercial diesel bunkering card – C H Jones Walsall Ltd

Keygrout – high strength polyester grout – Don Construction Products Ltd

Keylite – keyboard switches – N S F Controls Ltd

KeyMed – medical endoscopy and associated equipment – Keymed Ltd

Keymer – terracotta finiales, hand made clay roofing tiles and fittings, roof ventilation products – Keymer Tiles Ltd

Keyosk – Camlock Systems Ltd

Keyseater – keyseating machine – Lunn Engineering Co. Ltd

Keyston and Keyfix – chemical fixings – Don Construction Products Ltd

*Keystone (U.S.A.) – vision screener – Warwick Evans Optical Co. Ltd

Keystone – valves – Valve Spares Ltd

Keystone – battery holders & connectors – Anglia

Keystone – stockist and distributors of industrial castors and wheels – Keystone Castor Co.

Keystone – stockist and distributors of industrial castors and wheels – Keystone Castor Co.

Keystone – spherical silica based columns for HPLC and LC/MS – Thermo Fisher Scientific

Keyswitch – relays-cradle, custom built and miniature types, timers and solenoids – Clifford & Snell

*Keyview II (U.S.A.) – remote KVM switch network controller – Techland Group Ltd

*Keyvox-Benelux (Netherlands) – keystone and telebinocular – Warwick Evans Optical Co. Ltd

kf fittings – AESpump

KF200 – square cut folder – Acco East Light Ltd

KGE – grouting equipment – Keller Geo Technique

KHD – Harrier Fluid Power Ltd

KI – Storage – Bucon Ltd

Kia – L M C Hadrian Ltd

Kia-ora – fruit pastilles – Ernest Jackson & Co. Ltd

kic – Link Hamson Ltd

Kickers – Sports & leisure clothing – Pentland Group plc

Kidde – fire safety products – Hammerite Products Ltd

Kiddee Palm – Manchester Hosiery A Division Of Aikon Europe Group Ltd

Kiddicare – safety catches – Crittall Windows Ltd

Kiddie Kabin – playground equipment – Russell Play Ltd

Kiddie's Gro Aid Products – Double Gee Hair Fashions Ltd

*Kiddies Way – Hancocks Cash & Carry Ltd

Kidrel – bookbinding material – Intercover (E Hampson) Ltd

Kidrex – leather cloth – Intercover (E Hampson) Ltd

Kids hi-viz – Avalon and Lynwood

Kids hi-viz vests/tabards – Avalon and Lynwood

Kids high visibility – Avalon and Lynwood

Kids high visibility vests/tabards – Avalon and Lynwood

Kids of Wilmslow – private workplace nurseries and training providers – Kids Unlimited

Kidspeak tm – childrens market research – Millward Brown

KidZone – decorative paints – Akzonobel

Kieggen – static compaction – Geesink Norba Ltd

Kielder – shower tray – Armitage Shanks Ltd

Kikkers – UK Office Direct

Kilamic – steriliser – Murphy & Son

Kilbrock – drain cleaner – Kilrock Products Ltd

Kilburn & Strode – patent attorneys and trade mark agents – Kilburn & Strode

Kilkof – traditional cough remedy – Bell Sons & Co. Ltd

Killan Craft – import ceramics and terracotta – Elegant Homes Ltd

Killgerm – pest control products – Killgerm Group Ltd

Killgerm – pesticides – Conquer Pest Control Ltd

*Killy Sport – active outdoor clothing – Nevica Ltd

*Killy Technical Equipment (Far East) – ski wear – Nevica Ltd

*Kiln Furniture (U.S.A.) – ceramic foam filters and system for cast shops and foundries – Porvair plc

Kilner Vacuumation – vacuum lifting equipment – Kilner Vacuumation Co. Ltd

Kiloheat – centrifugal and axial flow fans – Nicotra-Gebhardt Ltd

Kilowhale – Vacuum tanker - high pressure – Whale Tankers Ltd

Kilowhale – vacuum tanker - high performance – Whale Tankers Ltd

Kilrock – multi purpose descaler for most water heating appliances and calorifiers – Kilrock Products Ltd

Kilrock CHC – central heating cleaner – Kilrock Products Ltd

Kilrock CHP – central heating protector – Kilrock Products Ltd

Kilrock Moisture Traps – removes moisture from atmosphere - chemical de-humidifiers – Kilrock Products Ltd

Kimberlely-Clark – UK Office Direct

Kimberley Clark – Nationwide – M & D Cleaning Supplies Ltd

Kimberly-Clarke – S J Wharton Ltd

*Kimmenade (Netherlands) – building products – Yule Catto & Co plc

Kind – cosmetics and perfumery – Bodywise Ltd

Kindercryl – orthodontic acrylic – Metrodent Ltd

Kinderman – Lamphouse Ltd

Kinergetics – Divex

Kinergetics - Ultrathermics - Stealth,Bauer Compressors, Aqua Beam, Hyox – Divex

Kinetico – non electric water softeners (industrial, domestic and commercial) automatic filters, reverse osmosis systems and deionisers – Kinetico UK Ltd

Kinetico – water softeners (domestic) – Harvey Water Softeners Ltd

KINETROL – Hydraulic & Offshore Supplies Ltd

Kinetrol – pneumatic equipment – Kinetrol Ltd

Kinetrol Actuators – Aztech Components Ltd

King – trailers and public utilities – King Trailers Ltd

King – Trafalgar Tools

King – Autobar Group Ltd

King – glass shower enclosure and bathroom accessories – Novellini UK Ltd

King – King Vehicle Engineering Ltd

KING & CO – Hydraulic & Offshore Supplies Ltd

King Dick – spanners – King Dick Tools

King Dick Tools – Trafalgar Tools

King Edward Coronets – british cigar – Imperial Tobacco Group PLC

King Edwards Crowns – british cigars – Imperial Tobacco Group PLC

King Highway Products – King Vehicle Engineering Ltd

King - King Trailers - Skyking - Traiload - Swingthru - Wumag - GSR - Zwiehoff - Lolode – King Trailers Ltd

*King Koil Beds – Tradelinens Ltd

King Long – H & H Commercial Truck Services Ltd

King Rail – road/rail vehicles – King Trailers Ltd

King Trailers – King Trailers Ltd

Kingbright – Selectronix Ltd

Kingbright – Cyclops Electronics Ltd

Kingdom Blinds – Suppliers and Installers of Window Blinds For Home or Office. – Kingdom Blinds

Kingfisher – architectural louvres and solar shading – Building Product Design

Kingfisher – grease fittings (grease nipples) – Kingfisher Lubrication

Kingfisher – hardened steel & stainless steel grease fittings – Kingfisher Lubrication

Kingfisher – toilet sponges – Recticel Corby

Kingfisher – fishmeal analogue for non-ruminants – A One Feed Supplements Ltd

Kingfisher - hardened steel & stainless steel grease fittings Kinglok - angle grease fittings – Kingfisher Lubrication
Kingfisher Huddersfield – buses – First Group plc
Kingfisher Stone – ornamental stone – Redwood Stone
Kingflo-Tanks – reinforced plastic free standing cylindrical vertical and horizontal tanks to BS 4994 – Ian Flockton Developments Ltd
Kingfrost – food service frozen – Youngs Seafood
Kingley – type 'b' fittings in DZR brass – Flowflex Components Ltd
KINGLIFTER – Chaintec Ltd
Kinglok – angle grease fittings – Kingfisher Lubrication
Kingmax Taiwan (Taiwan) – pc cards – Premier Engineering
Kings – Seeds – E W King & Co. Ltd
Kings – Connectors – Dax International Ltd
Kings and Queen Velvet – Ryalux Carpets Ltd
Kingsdown – exporter of agricultural & automotive spare parts. – Kingsdown
Kingsland – metal working machines, sheet metal working machines – Kingsland Engineering Company Ltd
Kingsland – steel workers – R K International Machine Tools Ltd
Kingsland iron workers – Phil Geesin Machinery Ltd
Kingsland machines – Phil Geesin Machinery Ltd
Kingsley – horizontal sliding window – Kawneer UK Ltd
Kingsman – Plastic Bollard – Alto Bollards UK Ltd
Kingsmead Publications – christmas card publishers – Kingsmead
Kingsmill Sugar – sugar paper – St Regis Paper Co. Ltd
KINGSPAN – ROOFING AND CLADDING – E S K Industrial Roofing Ltd
Kingspan – insulated roof and wall panels, cladding and roof lights – Kingspan Ltd
Kingspan – Ainsworth Acoustics, Thermal & Building Insulation
Kingspan Envirodek – Kingspan Ltd
Kingspan Lo-Pitch – Kingspan Ltd
Kingspan Longspan – Kingspan Ltd
Kingspan Optimo – Kingspan Ltd
Kingspan Purlcrete Chevron – Kingspan Insulation Ltd
Kingspan Purlcrete Promenade – Kingspan Insulation Ltd
Kingspan Rooftile – Kingspan Ltd
Kingspan Styrodur 3035 C.S. – Kingspan Insulation Ltd
Kingspan Styrodur 3035 N – Kingspan Insulation Ltd
Kingspan Styrodur 3500 L – Kingspan Insulation Ltd
Kingspan Styrodur 4000 S – Kingspan Insulation Ltd
Kingspan Styrodur 5000 S – Kingspan Insulation Ltd
Kingspan Tapercork – Kingspan Insulation Ltd
Kingspan Thermabrick – Kingspan Ltd
Kingspan Thermafloor T.F.70 – Kingspan Insulation Ltd
Kingspan Thermafloor T.F.72* – Kingspan Insulation Ltd
Kingspan Thermafloor T.F.73 – Kingspan Insulation Ltd
Kingspan Thermaliner T.L.63 – Kingspan Insulation Ltd
Kingspan ThermalinervT.L.60 – Kingspan Insulation Ltd
Kingspan Thermapitch T.P.10 – Kingspan Insulation Ltd
Kingspan Thermaroof T.R.20 – Kingspan Insulation Ltd
Kingspan Thermaroof T.R.21 – Kingspan Insulation Ltd
Kingspan Thermaroof T.R.22 – Kingspan Insulation Ltd
Kingspan Thermaroof T.R.23 – Kingspan Insulation Ltd
Kingspan Thermaroof T.R.24 – Kingspan Insulation Ltd
Kingspan Thermaroof T.R.25 – Kingspan Insulation Ltd
Kingspan Thermaroof T.R.26 – Kingspan Insulation Ltd
Kingspan Thermaroof T.R.26 F.M. – Kingspan Insulation Ltd
Kingspan Thermaroof T.R.27 – Kingspan Insulation Ltd
Kingspan Thermaroof TR27FM – Kingspan Insulation Ltd
Kingspan Thermaroof TR31 – Kingspan Insulation Ltd
Kingspan Thermastone – Kingspan Ltd
Kingspan Thermataper T.T.40 – Kingspan Insulation Ltd
Kingspan Thermataper T.T.42 – Kingspan Insulation Ltd
Kingspan Thermataper T.T.46 – Kingspan Insulation Ltd
Kingspan Thermataper TT47 – Kingspan Insulation Ltd
Kingspan Thermatile – Kingspan Ltd
Kingspan Thermawall T.W.50 – Kingspan Insulation Ltd
Kingspan Thermawall T.W.51 – Kingspan Insulation Ltd
Kingspan Thermawall T.W.52 – Kingspan Insulation Ltd
Kingspan Thermawall T.W.53 – Kingspan Insulation Ltd
Kingspan Thermawall TW55 – Kingspan Insulation Ltd
Kingspan Tile Support – Kingspan Ltd
Kingspan WoodTherm – Kingspan Ltd
Kingston – Best Wholesale Prices – Secure Telecom UK Ltd
Kingston – taps and mixers – Ideal Standard Ltd
Kingston Eclipse – network management system, open news – Kingston Communications
Kingston Messenger – voice processing system – Kingston Communications
***Kingstone (Hungary)** – tyres – Kings Road Tyres & Repairs Ltd
***Kingsway** – Hancocks Cash & Carry Ltd
Kingsway – footwear – The Gammidge
Kinky pin – compliant pc pins – Oxley Developments Company Ltd
Kinloch – stainless steel urinal – Armitage Shanks Ltd
Kinlock Waterless – stainless steel urinal – Armitage Shanks Ltd
Kinnerton – Novelty and character confectionery – Kinnerton Confectionery Co. Ltd
Kinney – industrial pumps – AESpump
Kinney (United Kingdom) – industrial vacuum pumps and systems – Girovac Ltd
Kinross – loop pile carpet tile – Warlord Contract Carpets Ltd
Kinsman (China) – instrument hardshell cases – John Hornby Skewes & Co. Ltd
Kintrella – soft expanded polyurethane coated fabric – J B Broadley
KIP – Hydraulic & Offshore Supplies Ltd
KIP – solenoid valves – Norgren Ltd
KIP (P & Zonen) – Alpha Electronics Southern Ltd
***Kir Opas (Norway)** – keystone and telebinocular – Warwick Evans Optical Co. Ltd
Kira – Warwick Machinery Ltd
Kirby Morgan – Submarine Manufacturing & Products Ltd
Kirin – premium bottled lager – Wells & Young's Brewing Co.
Kirk Rudy – inserters and feeders – Buhrs UK Ltd
Kirkby – roofing and architectural slates – Burlington Slate Ltd
Kirn – shower valve – Armitage Shanks Ltd
Kirsten – soldering machines and crimping machines – Turner Electronics
Kirton – kayaks – Kirton Kayaks Ltd
KIS – kardex imaging system – Kardex Systems UK Ltd
Kis Cosmetics – Double Gee Hair Fashions Ltd
Kisag (Switzerland) – Caterers preparation machinery Importer – Mitchell & Cooper Ltd
Kisag – Cream Whippers – Gilberts Food Equipment Ltd
Kismet – Topaz Computer Systems Ltd
Kissling – European Technical Sales Ltd
Kistler – supply transducers for measuring force acceleration and pressure – Kistler Instruments Ltd
Kitagawa – European Technical Sales Ltd
Kitchen and Walker – radial drills – R K International Machine Tools Ltd
***Kitchen Cleaning** – Nova Contract Cleaners
Kitchen Devils – housewares, knives etc – Fiskars Brands UK Ltd
***Kitchen Filtertrap** – Progressive Product Developments Ltd
Kitchen & Wade Radial arm Drills – Phil Geesin Machinery Ltd
Kitchen & Walker Pillar Drills – Phil Geesin Machinery Ltd
Kitchen & Walker radial arm drills – Phil Geesin Machinery Ltd
Kitchencraft – housewares – Thomas Plant Birmingham
Kitchenmate – chopping boards – Amefa
Kitfix – traditional games – Kitfix Swallow Group Ltd
Kittytracker – Alpha R F Ltd
Kitz – Kitz - ISO – Kitz Corporation
Kitz – European Technical Sales Ltd
Kiva – variable speed drives – Allspeeds Ltd
Kjellberg – Messer Cutting Systems
Kjeltabs – laboratory reagents in tablet form – Thompson & Capper Ltd
Klambush – bush clamp for domestic appliances – Hellermann Tyton
Klamklip – cable clip – Hellermann Tyton
Klampress – belt filter press – Ashbrook Simon Hartley Ltd
Klaschka – European Technical Sales Ltd
Klassic – modular timber partition system – Komfort Workspace plc
Klaus Parking System – Double Parking Systems
Klaxet – Moflash Signalling Ltd
Klaxet – motor driven hooter – Signals Ltd
Klaxon – audible signals and beacons – Signals Ltd
Klaxon – marine equipment & spares – Bearwood Engineering Supplies
Klaxon K Bell – bells – Signals Ltd
Klean Cut – corrugated packaging – D S Smith Packaging Ltd
KLEDIL – rubber bellows – Mercia Flexibles
Kleen (Denmark) – economy range of brushware – Vikan UK Ltd
KLEEN-CHANGE – Hydraulic & Offshore Supplies Ltd
Kleen-Line – B & W Mechanical Handling
Kleen-Screen – Forward Chemicals Ltd
Kleencoat – brushes – Harris Cleaning Services
Kleenex – UK Office Direct
Kleenfuel AS – fuel oil treatment – Dasic International Ltd
Kleengel – germicidal floor jelly – Unico Ltd
Kleenglass – machine glass wash – Unico Ltd
Kleenwash – clothes line – James Lever & Sons Ltd
Kleiber – Impac Infrared Ltd
***Kleim & Ungerer (Germany)** – single spindle automatic – Brunner Machine Tools Ltd
KLEIN GELENKWELLEN – Bailey Morris Ltd
Kleinknecht – European Technical Sales Ltd
***Klensorb (Europe)** – absorbent granules – B & D Clays & Chemicals Ltd
Klepper – kayaks – Kirton Kayaks Ltd
Klerat – rodenticide – Sorex Ltd
Klik – secure connection systems – Hager Engineering Ltd
Klik Fold Towers – Accesscaff International Ltd
Klik Lighting – Lighting Distribution System – R & M Electrical Group Ltd
Klik Microfold Tower – Accesscaff International Ltd
Klik Mini Fold Towers – Accesscaff International Ltd
Klik Stairwell Towers – Accesscaff International Ltd
Klik Towers – Accesscaff International Ltd
Kliklok – end and top load containing systems – Nampak Carton
Klilstak Unit – Accesscaff International Ltd
Klime-Ezee Steps – Accesscaff International Ltd
Kling-on Blue – Forum Products Ltd
Klingelhofer – circlips – Bearwood Engineering Supplies
Klingersil – gasket materials – Klinger Ltd
Klingspor – S J Wharton Ltd
Klippon – terminals and enclosures – Weidmuller Ltd
Klippon – European Technical Sales Ltd
Klober – Office Furniture – Bucon Ltd
Klockner Moeller – Proplas International Ltd
Kluber – Greases and Lubricants – Sprint Engineering & Lubricant
Kluber – Mercury Bearings Ltd
***Klucel (U.S.A.)** – hydroxypropylcellulose – Hercules Holding li Ltd
KM – Educational Furniture – Bucon Ltd
Km – disposable cutlery – Herald Plastics Ltd
KMA-Process – Glenvale Packaging
KMP Brand – K M Products Europe Ltd
KMT – High pressure and ball valves – Hydratron Ltd
Knaack – site security – Traction Equipment Stafford Ltd
Knapp – Universal Woodworking machines – Pro Machine Tools Ltd
Knapp – pipeline pigging equipment – Alexander Cardew Ltd
KNAUF – P F T Central
Knecht – Harrier Fluid Power Ltd
Knecht – oil, fuel, cabin and air dryer cartridges – Roadlink International Ltd
KNF Neuberger – diaphragm pumps – AESpump
Kniel – European Technical Sales Ltd
Knife Wizard – Knife Wizard
Knight – registered class 6 metals – Knight Strip Metals Ltd
Knight – Mike Garwood Ltd
Knight Imaging – Southern Scientific
Knight Kit – Midland Systems Ltd
Knight Paperbacks – books – Hachette UK Ltd
Knight X-Ray – Southern Scientific
Knightrum – soda blasters – Branova Cleaning Services
Knightsbridge – contract, hotel, leisure and office seating – Knightsbridge Ltd
Knippex – S J Wharton Ltd
Knitol – textile lubricant – Benjamin R Vickers & Sons Ltd
Knitter – Cyclops Electronics Ltd
Knitter-Switch – switches – Anglia
Knitters and Sewers World – wholesalers of wool and haberdashery Knitting yarns and tapestries. – Knit and Sew
Knoll – Lamphouse Ltd
Knoll Chip Reducers – European Technical Sales Ltd
Knoll Filters – European Technical Sales Ltd
Knoll Pumps – European Technical Sales Ltd
Knoll Pumps & Conveyors – European Technical Sales Ltd
Knoll Separators – European Technical Sales Ltd
Knollands Septic Tanks & Drainage – Septic Tanks and Drainage Products – Knollands
KnollExtraction Stations – European Technical Sales Ltd
Knorr Bremser – cylinders/spares – Bearwood Engineering Supplies
Knowledge, The – United Business Media Ltd
Knowledge Works – expert system toolkit – Global Graphics Software Ltd
Knowsley – firefighting systems – Knowsley S K Ltd
Knu Foil – tool steel heat treatment foil – Knight Strip Metals Ltd
Knufoil – tool steel heat treatment foil – Knight Strip Metals Ltd
Knurlcut – Precision Tools
KOA – Cyclops Electronics Ltd
KOA – passive components – Anglia
Kobblecork (Portugal) – 3/8" thick natural cork wall tiles – Siesta Cork Tile Co.
Kobe – Therma Group
Kobelco – Harrier Fluid Power Ltd
***Kobelco (Japan)** – quarry crushers – Marubeni Komatsu Ltd
Kobelco – P J P Plant Hire
Kobelco – Bison Plant Hire Ltd
Kobelco – C J Plant Ltd
***Kobird (Japan)** – encrusting machines, bakery equipment, extrusion and cutting systems – Selo UK Ltd
Koblend – Sol T – Polimeri Europa Ltd
Kobo – Kobo UK Ltd
Kobo – Mercury Bearings Ltd

Kobold – equipment & spares – Bearwood Engineering Supplies
Kobold Flow Meters – European Technical Sales Ltd
Kocour – Laboratory testing equipment – Cannock Chemicals Ltd
***KOCSIS (U.S.A.)** – hydraulic starting equipment – Industrial Power Units Ltd
Kodak – UK Office Direct
***Kodak** – Photo – Hospitality A V
Kodak Filters – Galvoptics Optical Goods
Kodax – Lamphouse Ltd
Koden – air conditioning and heating ventilation – Honeywell Control Systems Ltd
Kodiak – Dickies Workwear
Koehring – Harrier Fluid Power Ltd
Kohler – Harrier Fluid Power Ltd
Kohler – A T Wilde & Son Ltd
Kohler (U.S.A.) – petrol engines – E P Barrus
KOHLSWA ESSEM AB – Hydraulic & Offshore Supplies Ltd
Kokuyo – Office Seating – Bucon Ltd
Kolate – aluminium organics for grease manufacture – Rhodia Ltd
Kolbenseeger – European Technical Sales Ltd
koldblue – Abbey England Ltd
***Kolher (Germany)** – tube notching machines – Brandone Machine Tool Ltd
Köllmann – European Technical Sales Ltd
Kollmorgen – European Drives & Motor Repairs
Kollmorgen – European Technical Sales Ltd
Kollmorgen – Motor Technology Ltd
***Koloman Handler (Austria)** – loose leaf mechanisms – Gilmex International Ltd
Kolorcourt – waterbased acrylic sports surface paint – Emusol Products Ltd
Kolourcourt Porous Acrylic – tennis-multiuse sports coating – Emusol Products Ltd
Komac – Office Seating – Bucon Ltd
Komara – skimmers for oil pollution – Vikoma International Ltd
Komatsu – A T Wilde & Son Ltd
***Komatsu (Japan)** – construction machinery – Marubeni Komatsu Ltd
Komatsu – industrial forklifts – G Reekie Group Ltd
***Komatsu** – Kenneth Robson Equipment Ltd
Komatsu – Stacatruc
Komatsu – C J Plant Ltd
KOMATSU – Chaintec Ltd
Komatsu – Custom Brakes & Hydraulics Ltd
Komatsu – P J P Plant Hire
KOMATSU – Hydraulic & Offshore Supplies Ltd
Komatsu – John Moore Tractor Parts Ltd
Komatsu – T V H UK Ltd
Kombiflex – British Vita plc
Kombimatec – machinery for aluminium and UPVC profiles – Kombimatec Machines Ltd
Komet – Komet Ltd
Kometa – ambient 600 x 600 fitting – Concord Marlin Ltd
Komfie – Lusso Interiors
Komfire 100 – 100mm thick system with 1 hour fire protection – Komfort Workspace plc
Komfire-75 – 75mm thick stud partitioning system – Komfort Workspace plc
Komfort – Lusso Interiors
Komfort – S K Interiors Ltd
Komfort (United Kingdom) – partitioning – Scotwood Interiors Ltd
Komfort – partitioning systems – Service Partitions Ltd
Komori Oil – Harrier Fluid Power Ltd
Kompact – Kratos Analytical Ltd
Kompass Direct – individually tailored labels, listings or floppy disks from Reed Business Information databases. – The Bankers' Almanac Reed Business Information
Kompass Industrial Trade Names – 61,000 trade names and 20,000 lapsed trade names. – The Bankers' Almanac Reed Business Information
Kompass International Editions – in-depth data from around the world – The Bankers' Almanac Reed Business Information
Kompass Register CD – detailed information on 83,000 companies – The Bankers' Almanac Reed Business Information
Kompress – electrical accessories – Kompress Holdings Ltd
Komtronic – Komet Ltd
Koncert – hinge – Securistyle Ltd
Koncetta – Cloakroom Solutions Ltd
***Kondia Powermill (Spain)** – milling machines turret type – Capital Equipment & Machinery Ltd
Konditorei – ground coffee – Bunzl Vending Services Ltd
Konduct – temperature transfer cement – J L Lord & Son Ltd
Konfigure – office desking and seating systems – Komfort Workspace plc
Koni – shock absorbers for trucks, trailers and buses – Roadlink International Ltd
***Koni (Netherlands)** – shock absorber – J W E Banks Ltd
Konika – UK Office Direct
KONTAK – Hydraulic & Offshore Supplies Ltd
Kontec – Stationary Clamping Systems – Schunk Intec Ltd
Kontimag – continuous mineral cables production – Wrexham Mineral Cables Ltd
Kontrakt – office furniture – Pedley Furniture International Ltd
Kontron – M S C Gleichmann UK Ltd
Kooi – Harrier Fluid Power Ltd
KOOI AAP – Chaintec Ltd
Kook Kup – U C D Ltd
Kool N Krazy Gang – on knitwear (2-9yrs) and footwear – O S R International Ltd
Koolcolt – UK Solar Ltd
Koolman – temperature controlled trailer – Lynton Trailers UK Ltd
Koolmax – straight cutting oils & lubricants – Metal Working Lubricants Ltd
Koolmax N.F. (United Kingdom) – Metal finishing lubricants – Metal Working Lubricants Ltd
Kooltech – refrigeration and air conditioning – Kooltech Ltd
Kooltherm – timber frame board – Kingspan Insulation Ltd
Kooltherm K1 – roofboard – Kingspan Insulation Ltd
Kooltherm K10 – soffit board – Kingspan Insulation Ltd
Kooltherm K2 – roofboard – Kingspan Insulation Ltd
Kooltherm K3 – floorboard – Kingspan Insulation Ltd
Kooltherm K5 – roofboard – Kingspan Insulation Ltd
Kooltherm K5 E.W.B. – external wallboard – Kingspan Insulation Ltd
Kooltherm K7 – sarking board – Kingspan Insulation Ltd
Kooltherm K8 – cavity board – Kingspan Insulation Ltd
***Kop-Flex Inc (U.S.A.)** – gear couplings – Micro Clutch Developments Ltd
***Kopal (France)** – counter sinks & clamps – Hill Cliffe Garage
Kopp – variable speed drives – Allspeeds Ltd
Kopp – Mercury Bearings Ltd
Kopp Filters – Galvoptics Optical Goods
Kopp Variator – variable speed drives – Allspeeds Ltd
Koppen and Lethem – analogue, proportional valves and electric controls and filtration systems – Koppen & Lethem Ltd
Koppens (Netherlands) – food form machines – Meatec
***Kora Packmat (Germany)** – packaging machinery – Advanced Dynamics Ltd
Kores – UK Office Direct
Korex – aramid paper honeycomb core – Du Pont UK Ltd
***Korg UK (Japan)** – musical instruments – Korg UK Ltd
Korifit – white PVC pliable conduit system – Adaptaflex Ltd
***Korint (Italy)** – clip action ballpen with jumbo refill in atrractive barrel colours – Hainenko Ltd
***Korklite (Portugal)** – cork insulation – Alumasc Exterior Building Products
Korklite Gutter – removes ponding from box gutters – Alumasc Exterior Building Products
Korklite Plus – composite cork/polyurethane insulation – Alumasc Exterior Building Products
***Korklite Taper (Portugal)** – tapered cork insulation system – Alumasc Exterior Building Products
Korkpak – protection board – Grace Construction Ltd
KORLOY – Cutwel Ltd
Koroseal – Tektura plc
***Korrugal (Sweden)** – aluminium building sheet – Plannja Ltd
Kort Engineering – marine engineering – Kort Propulsion Co. Ltd
Kort Engineering - Marine engineering, Kort Propulsion - Marine engineering, Kort Nozzle - Marine engineering, – Kort Propulsion Co. Ltd
Kort Propulsion – marine engineering – Kort Propulsion Co. Ltd
Körting – European Technical Sales Ltd
Korting – fluid jet equipment – Northvale Korting Ltd
***Koruma (Germany)** – complete creme lines – Romaco Holdings UK Ltd
Kos – fire cement – Vitcas Ltd
Kostil – SAN – Polimeri Europa Ltd
***Kostyrka (Germany)** – hydraulic clamping sleeves and equipment – Roemheld UK Ltd
KOTHEA – Passionate About Fabrics – KOTHEA
Kotklite Drain – Localised ponding eliminator – Alumasc Exterior Building Products
Kotron – capacitance level transmitter – Magnetrol International UK Ltd
***Kottaus & Busch (Germany)** – tube expanders, tube expansion equipment – Brandone Machine Tool Ltd
KOve Pac – distributor of food packaging, disposable and hygiene supplies to caterers, hotels, restaurant, theme parks and high street bakeries and butchers in Germany – Bunzl Catering Supplies Ltd
Kowo – X-Ray accessories – Ie-Ndt Manufacturer
Kowolux – X-Ray film viewers – Ie-Ndt Manufacturer
Kowomat – gamma radiography isotope containers – Ie-Ndt Manufacturer
Koyo – Mercury Bearings Ltd
Koyo (UK) – ball and roller bearings – Koyo UK Ltd
***Kozako (Canada)** – range of Actuators – Electric Actuator Co. Ltd
KPM – Southern Valve & Fitting Co. Ltd
KR – Hydraulic & Offshore Supplies Ltd
KR FITTINGS – Hydraulic & Offshore Supplies Ltd
Kraft (Europe, Western) – al valves – Everyvalve Ltd
Kraft – cheeses – Kraft Foods UK Ltd
Kraft Manilla & Cover – Atlantis European Ltd
Kraftex – building, concreting and thermal insulation papers – Packaging Products Ltd
Krafty – UK Office Direct
Kral (Austria) – positive displacement meters – Litre Meter Ltd
Kral – triple screw pumps for lubricated liquids up to 100 bar – Selwood Pump Company Ltd
Kralinator – Harrier Fluid Power Ltd
Kramer – Harrier Fluid Power Ltd
Kramer – electro mag.brake – Bearwood Engineering Supplies
Kramer Allrad – Compact Loaders – Parkway Plant Sales Ltd
Kramplex – video multicamera recorder – Tecton Ltd
***Krantz (Germany)** – diffusers – Designed For Sound Ltd
***Krantz (Germany)** – exhaust air incineration – Engelmann & Buckham Ltd
Kranzle – industrial cleaning equipment – B & G Cleaning Systems Ltd
Kranzle – Kranzle UK Ltd
Kraus & Naimer – E Preston Electrical Ltd
Krauss Maffei – Proplas International Ltd
KRAUT KRAMER – Xstrahl Ltd
Krautkrämer – European Technical Sales Ltd
Kreg – Pocket hole jointing systems – The Toolpost
Kreis Dissolver – Fullbrook Systems Ltd
Kremlin – Aztech Components Ltd
Kremtect – Forward Chemicals Ltd
***Kreta (Italy)** – clip action ballpen in attractive barrel colours – Hainenko Ltd
***Kretzer (Germany)** – hairdressing and industrial scissors – Triumph Needle Co. Ltd
Krimpit – cable accessories – Davico Industrial Ltd
Kriscat – B P plc
***Kristal** – Regalzone LLP
Kristal – UK Office Direct
Kristalex – pure monomer hydrocarbon resin – Hercules Holding Ii Ltd
Kristalon – Yara UK It Ltd
***Krogab** – Krogab
***Krogab 100% Coffee** – Krogab
***Krogab Bag In Box Juice System** – Krogab
***Krogab Classic Pure Orange Juice** – Krogab
Krogab Toscane Coffee System – Krogab
Krom-Schroder – switches – Bearwood Engineering Supplies
Kromacryl – dispersed pigments in aqueous acrylic resin – Kromachem Ltd
Kromogel – Wright Dental Group
Kromschröder – European Technical Sales Ltd
Kronenbourg 1664 – lager – Scottish & Newcastle Pub Co.
***Kronenflex (Germany)** – grinding discs and cutting of wheels – Klingspor Abrasives Ltd
Kronofloor – moisture resistant and particleboard flooring tongued, grooved and square-edged – Kronoplus Ltd
Kronos 1001 – titanium dioxide – Kronos Ltd
Kronos 1014 – titanium dioxide – Kronos Ltd
Kronos 1071 – titanium dioxide – Kronos Ltd
Kronos 1074 – titanium dioxide – Kronos Ltd
Kronos 1075 – titanium dioxide – Kronos Ltd
Kronos 1077 – titanium dioxide – Kronos Ltd
Kronos 1080 – titanium dioxide – Kronos Ltd
Kronos 1171 – titanium dioxide – Kronos Ltd
Kronos 2044 – titanium dioxide – Kronos Ltd
Kronos 2047 – titanium dioxide – Kronos Ltd
Kronos 2056 – titanium dioxide – Kronos Ltd
Kronos 2059 – titanium dioxide – Kronos Ltd
Kronos 2063 – titanium dioxide – Kronos Ltd
Kronos 20635 – titanium dioxide – Kronos Ltd
Kronos 2073 – titanium dioxide – Kronos Ltd
Kronos 2081 – titanium dioxide – Kronos Ltd
Kronos 2160 – titanium dioxide – Kronos Ltd
Kronos 2190 – titanium dioxide – Kronos Ltd
Kronos 2220 – titanium dioxide – Kronos Ltd
Kronos 2222 – titanium dioxide – Kronos Ltd
Kronos 2225 – titanium dioxide – Kronos Ltd
Kronos 2230 – titanium dioxide – Kronos Ltd
Kronos 2257 – titanium dioxide – Kronos Ltd
Kronos 2300 – titanium dioxide – Kronos Ltd
Kronos 2310 – titanium dioxide – Kronos Ltd
Kronos 2330 – titanium dioxide – Kronos Ltd
Kronos 2400 – titanium dioxide – Kronos Ltd
Kronos 3000 – titanium dioxide – Kronos Ltd
Kronos 3025 – titanium dioxide – Kronos Ltd

Kronospan – medium density fireboard, melamine faced medium density fibreboard and melamine faced particleboard – Kronoplus Ltd
Kronospan – Wigan Timber Ltd
Kronospan – M D M Timber Ltd
Kroy – electronic labelling systems – Ashley Industrial Ltd
KRP – Hydraulic & Offshore Supplies Ltd
*Krunchy Fried Chicken – Pendle Frozen Foods Ltd
Krupp Kautex – Proplas International Ltd
KRV 2000 Turret Mills – Phil Geesin Machinery Ltd
KRV 3000 Turret Mills – Phil Geesin Machinery Ltd
KRV 4000 bed Mills – Phil Geesin Machinery Ltd
KRV Turret Mills – Phil Geesin Machinery Ltd
Krystal – bulked polyester thread – American & Efird GB Ltd
Krystal Plate – well format plates, with opaque walls and optically clear bases – Porvair plc
Krystal Plate- Micromass - Porvent - Spinmaster - Multi-Pore Ceramic Filters - Selee Foam Filters - Sinterflo - Super Dome - Vyon - Easy Fit Dome - Kiln Furniture - HVB Burner Systems - Dual Stage Filtration Systems - Ceramic Foam Filters - FE Iron Foundry Filters - Microlute - Porvair Fuel Cell Technologies - Mictofiltrex - Megga Gaz - Ultravap - Talvic - Hycor - Hycarb - CZerbide - Metpore - Metflome. – Porvair plc
Krytox – fluorinated oils & greases – Du Pont UK Ltd
Krytox – highly fluoronated oil – G B R Technology Ltd
krytox – AESpump
Krytox – Fluorinated Lubricants – I K V Tribology Ltd
KS1000 Kingzip – Kingspan Ltd
KSB – Pumps – Wendage Pollution Control Ltd
KSB Pumps – Denton Pumps Ltd
KSB VALVES (United Kingdom) – Ultravalve Ltd
'KSO' CRUCIFORM – CV Flexible Disc Element 'Oldham Design' Shaft Couplings – Francis and Francis Ltd
KTR – European Technical Sales Ltd
KTR – high strength aluminium fastener with large blind side bearing area – Avdel UK Ltd
Kub – Komet Ltd
Kuba (GEA) – evaporators (coolers), condensors and heat exchangers – Thermofrost Cryo plc
Kubic – flexible foam packaging – Foam Engineers Ltd
Kubitizer – impact breaker – Parker Plant Ltd
Kubitranger – mobile impact breaker – Parker Plant Ltd
Kübler – European Technical Sales Ltd
Kubota – Central Plant Hire
Kubota – Dennis Barnfield Ltd
Kubota – Woodleigh Power Equipment Ltd
Kubota – mini excavators – Service Engines Newcastle Ltd
Kubota – Harrier Fluid Power Ltd
Kubota – A T Wilde & Son Ltd
Kubota Submerged Membranes – membrane process for biological treatment of waste water, giving high purity treated effluent – Aker Kvaerner Engineering Services Ltd
*Kuchenprofi (Germany) – kitchenware – Dexam International
Kufner – last chance filters – G Bopp & Co. Ltd
Kuha – Mike Garwood Ltd
Kuhlmeyer – semi and automatic weld preparation and dressing machines and specialised wood finishing machines – Ellesco Ltd
*Kuhn – Reeth Garage Ltd
Kuhnke – Trafalgar Tools
KUHNKE – Hydraulic & Offshore Supplies Ltd
Kuhnke – Southern Valve & Fitting Co. Ltd
Kuhrt Leach LLP – Kuhrt Leach LLP
Kuka Robotics – Robots – Machines Automation Robotic Systems Ltd
Kuka Welding Equipment – European Technical Sales Ltd
Kullasigns – general commercial signs – Legend Signs Ltd
Kulorub – for finishing heels, edges & waists – F Ball & Co. Ltd
Küma – European Technical Sales Ltd
*Kumera (Finland) – geared motors, worm and helical gearboxes – Pulp & Paper Machinery Ltd
Kumfies – sitmats – Functional Foam Beacons Products Ltd
Kumzof – solvent for stripping cemented soles & heel covers – F Ball & Co. Ltd
Kuoni Schools – student travel – Kuoni Travel Ltd
Kuoni (Trade Fairs) – tour operator – Kuoni Travel Ltd
Kuoni Travel – tour operator – Kuoni Travel Ltd
Kuppersbusch – Cateringequipment – KFS Service Ltd
Kuraki CNC – boring machines – Mills C N C
Kuroma – pressure smoking kettle and pressure fryers – Pandet Ltd
*Kurt Geiger (Italy and UK) – ladies and mens shoes and handbags – Kurt Geiger Ltd
Kurt J Lesker – general vacuum supplies – AESpump
Kurt Salmon Associates – global management consultancy for retail and consumer product industries – Kurt Salmon
Kurust – rust converter – Hammerite Products Ltd
Kuschall – E P C
KUSEL – Bailey Morris Ltd

Kushion Kraft – multi ply paper cushioning – Jiffy Packaging Company Ltd
Kushion Kraft – embossed paper – Ambassador Packaging Ltd
Kushyfall – lias playground surface – Melcourt Industries
*Kustom (USA and China) – amplifiers, pa equipment for music instrument use – John Hornby Skewes & Co. Ltd
Kustom Kit – First Impressions Europe Ltd
Kustom kit – Clothing & Sports wear – Connect Two Promotions Ltd
Kutherm – electrical resistance wires and spiral elements – I M I Scott Ltd
Kutrite (United Kingdom) – scissors, knives and hand tools – Kutrite Of Sheffield Ltd
Kuwait Fuelcare (East) – fuels – Kuwait Petroleum GB Ltd
Kuwait Fuelcare (Edenbridge) – fuels – Kuwait Petroleum GB Ltd
Kuwait Fuelcare (Midlands) – fuels – Kuwait Petroleum GB Ltd
Kuwait Fuelcare (North & Scotland) – fuels – Kuwait Petroleum GB Ltd
Kuwait Fuelcare (South) – fuels – Kuwait Petroleum GB Ltd
KV – Hydraulic & Offshore Supplies Ltd
KV – Aztech Components Ltd
KV – Southern Valve & Fitting Co. Ltd
KV AUTOMATION – Hydraulic & Offshore Supplies Ltd
Kvaener Engineering & Construction – general & precision engineering & construction work – Aker Subsea Ltd
Kvaener Pulp & Paper – manufacturers & recyclers of paper – Aker Subsea Ltd
Kvaener Shipbuilding – manufacturers of ships & boats – Aker Subsea Ltd
Kvaerner – specialist piling and ground engineering contractors – Cementation Skanska
*Kverneland – Evergreen Tractors Ltd
Kverneland – Ploughs/Drills/Spreaders – Paul Tuckwell Ltd
Kwik-Case – audio and visual security cases – Plescon Security Products
Kwik Fit – tyres and exhausts – Kwik-Fit GB Ltd
Kwik Fix – hardware – Profast Ni Ltd
Kwik-Issue – library self-issue system – Plescon Security Products
Kwik-Way – grinding machines – Bearwood Engineering Supplies
Kwik-Way (U.S.A.) – Engine rebuilding & brake reconditioning machines – Fondera Ltd
Kwikastrip – reinforcement continuity system – Halfen Ltd
Kwikcova – sheeting system for open-topped bulk containers and lorry bodies – Reynolds Boughton
KwikFix – consumer adhesive range of mainly blister carded products, including super glue, clear glue and glue sticks. – Chemence Ltd
KwikForm Towers – Accesscaff International Ltd
Kwikprint – Hot foil printing equipment – Dalesway Print Technology
Kwikroll – rapid action fabric doors – Kaba Door Systems
Kwikstage – steel access/propping/decking/shoring systems – RMD Kwikform Limited
Kwiktip – retractable ballpen – Hainenko Ltd
Kwikvent – Britax P S V Wypers Ltd
Kwoffit – home-made beer ingredients – Potters
Kymene – neutral curing wet-strength resin – Hercules Holding Ii Ltd
Kynar – pvdf powders and granules – Atosina UK Ltd
Kyocera – Copiertec Ltd
Kyocera – UK Office Direct
Kyocera Fineceramics – Vargus Tooling Ltd
Kyomi – washbasins, closets, bidets, baths – Ideal Standard Ltd
Kyon – Kennametal UK Ltd
Kyosha Industries – Portable Printers – M-Tech Printers
Kyoto – Batteries, Brake Pads, Bearings,Tyres, – Wemoto Ltd World's End Motorcycles Ltd
Kyros – fodder beet variety – Limagrain UK Ltd
*Kyser (U.S.A.) – guitar accessories – John Hornby Skewes & Co. Ltd

L

L.A.C. – waterproof membrane – R I W Ltd
L-bloc – Poundfield Products Ltd
L.C. Automation – technical distributors – L.C. Automation Ltd
L.C.F. Bishop – Manitowoc Food Service UK
L.C. (LANcity) – cable access solutions – Nortel Networks UK Ltd
L.C. OLEODINAMICA – Hydraulic & Offshore Supplies Ltd
L-Carvone – perfume speciality – Quest International UK Ltd
L-CUP – Hydraulic & Offshore Supplies Ltd
L.D.O. Geodraft – drafting film, double or single matt, anti-static, plain or green tint – Service Point UK Ltd
L.D.O. Geofilm – clear and anti-static diazo film with ink receptive surface – Service Point UK Ltd
L.D.O. Geomatt – polyester diazo film, with drafting surface and effective UV light screen – Service Point UK Ltd

L.D.S. – vibration test equipment – L D S Test & Measurment Ltd
L.E.D. Technology – back lights special L.E.D.'s – Opto Electronic Manufacturing Corporation Ltd
*L.E.P. (United Kingdom) – vehicle lighting equipment ie. reflectors etc – Perei Group Ltd
L'Esprit Et Le Vin – Birchgrove Products
L.F.I. (United Kingdom) – wooden and alloy ladders, steps, stagings and trestles – Ladder & Fencing Industries Newent Ltd
L&G – M S C Gleichmann UK Ltd
L.G.V. – training courses for drivers – Friendberry Ltd
*L J Star (U.S.A.) – sight flow indicators – Visilume Ltd
L.M. – metal & chemical traders – London Metals Ltd
L.M.A. – accessories – F C Lane Electronics Ltd
L.M.F. – connectors, circular screw thread – F C Lane Electronics Ltd
L.M.G. – connectors, circular screw thread – F C Lane Electronics Ltd
L.M.H. – connectors, circular bayonet – F C Lane Electronics Ltd
L.M.H.F. – connectors-circular bayonet filtered – F C Lane Electronics Ltd
L.M.J. – connectors, circular screw thread – F C Lane Electronics Ltd
L.M.V. – connectors, mains voltage – F C Lane Electronics Ltd
L.N. E-Consulting Ltd – Web Agency, Search Engine Optimization,Web Marketing, Web Services & Consultancy – L.N. E-Consulting Ltd
L&N Furnace Equipment – J B Furnace Engineering Ltd
L.P. (Import Export) Supplies – plumbing and heating merchants – L P Import Export Supplies Ltd
L. & R. – cleaning fluids and machines – Time Products UK Ltd
*L.R. Baggs (U.S.A.) – pick-ups for musical instruments – John Hornby Skewes & Co. Ltd
L R spare Parts – Panaf & Company
L.R.T. Lothian Airlink – buses to airport – Lothian Buses plc
L.R.T. Lothian Talisman – coach holidays – Lothian Buses plc
L Ring Drum – 210li tight head – Fibrestar Drums Ltd
L Ronning (Sweden) – pressure test equipment – Bancroft & Co.
L.S.L. – suppliers of laboratory products – Laboratory Sales UK Ltd
L.S. Opticians Record System – carded record system for opticians – Holborn Direct Mail
*L.S.V (Sweden) – grinders – Atlas Copco Tools Ltd
*L. Schuler (Germany) – presses – Embassy Machinery Ltd
L-Strip – steel lintel – Naylor Drainage Ltd
L.T.S. – architectural lighting – Selux UK Ltd
*L.T.V (Sweden) – nut runners – Atlas Copco Tools Ltd
L U L – Specified suppliers – A A T I Ltd
*L'Unite Hermetique (France) – heremetic compressors and condensing units – H T G Trading Ltd
L'Unite Hermetique – Therma Group
La Brasserie – wine – Rodney Densem Wines Ltd
La Cafetiere – adjustable measures – La Cafetiere
La Cafetiere – plunger coffee maker – La Cafetiere
La Cafetiere Di Moda – unbreakable cafetieres – La Cafetiere
La Furnitura, Ltd. – Furniture For Life – La Furnitura, Ltd.
*La Maison des Sorbets – La Maison des Sorbets Foods Ltd
*La Man – compressed air filter dryers – Airware International Ltd
La Manda, Nuevo Extremo – wine – Rodney Densem Wines Ltd
*La Nature Organic Wines – Vinceremos Wines & Spirits Ltd
*La Pavoni (Italy) – cappuccino machines – Fairfax Coffee Ltd
La Pizza Co. – Olympia Foods Ltd
La Premiere Enhanced Graphic Tufted – Victoria Carpets Ltd
*La-Reine (Far East) – ladieswear – Remys Ltd
La Roche – reinforcement bar bending and cutting machinery – La Roche
*La Scala – ice cream – Kerry Foods Ltd
La Spaziate Espresso Machines – Espresso Machines – Cavendish Tea Coffee Ltd
La Toque Blanche – premium chefs' hats & headgear – Pal International Ltd
*La Tour Polignac – Ivory & Ledoux Ltd
*Lab (South America) – scientific publication for south and central America – International Labmate Ltd
Lab Africa – scientific publication for africa – International Labmate Ltd
Lab Asia – scientific publication for Asia – International Labmate Ltd
Lab-Craft – fluorescent lighting – Lab Craft Ltd
Label Applicators – Avery Dennison
Label Designer – software for printing labels from Apple MacIntosh on sheets via a postscript laser printer – Computalabel International Ltd
*Label Logic – Software – Planglow Ltd
Label Master – label overprinting system – Weyfringe Labelling Systems

Label printer – label printer – Avery Dennison
Label Printing – label software, thermal printers and foils – Universal Marking Systems Ltd
Labelfix – labelling adhesives – H B Fuller
Labello – lipcare – Lil-lets UK Ltd
Labelprinter – instant label maker – Office Depot UK
Labelsco – self adhesive labels and narrow web printers – Labelsco
Labguard – anti-microbial handsoap – Day Impex Ltd
Labino Lamps – European Technical Sales Ltd
Labmaster – calibration equipment – Intra Ltd
Labmite – high pressure gas regulator – Black Teknigas & Electro Controls Ltd
***Labmote (UK and Ireland)** – scientific publication for United Kingdom and Ireland – International Labmate Ltd
Labomix – laboratory development machines – T Giusti Ltd
Labotherm – laboratory furnaces – Ramsell Naber Ltd
LaBour – chemical & process pumps for specialised & hazardous materials – S P P Pumps
Labstar – high pressure gas regulator – Black Teknigas & Electro Controls Ltd
Labtech – UK Office Direct
Labtek – laboratory gas manifold – Black Teknigas & Electro Controls Ltd
LabVIEW – software product – National Instrument UK Corp Ltd
LabWindows/CVI – software product – National Instrument UK Corp Ltd
Lacey Hulbert – large piston units – AESpump
Laclube – textile processing aid – Benjamin R Vickers & Sons Ltd
Lacovyl – pvc suspension polymers – Atosina UK Ltd
Lacqrene – polystyrene (crystal and hips) – Atosina UK Ltd
Lacqtene – low density polyethylene (LDPE) – Atosina UK Ltd
Lacqtene HD – high density polyethylene ((hdpe) – Atosina UK Ltd
Lacsol – solvent-borne cleaner for removing contaminants, which inhibit adhesion, from rubber surfaces – SATRA Technology Centre
Lactabs – milk sample preserving tablets – Thompson & Capper Ltd
Lactec – calf milk replacer – A One Feed Supplements Ltd
Lacto-Calamine – sun and skin care products – M S D Animal Health
Lacto Calamine Lotion – M S D Animal Health
Lactomix – molasses based liquid – Rumenco Ltd
Lactosym – animal prophylactic – Multigerm Ltd
Lad Micrometer – calibration equipment – Intra Ltd
Lada – L M C Hadrian Ltd
Ladco Advanced Engineering – Sub contract engineering services. – Ladco
Ladder-Flex – conveyor chain – Wire Belt Co. Ltd
Ladder Frame Towers – Accesscaff International Ltd
Ladder Safety Devices – Accesscaff International Ltd
Ladder Stops – County Construction Chemicals Ltd
Ladder-X-it – folding fire escape ladder – Lampitt Fire Escapes
Ladderfix – ladder stabilizing devices (various) – Ladderfix Ltd
LadderLatch (United Kingdom) – mobile anchorage device (vertical systems) – Latchways plc
Ladders-Direct – Accesscaff International Ltd
Ladderscaff – ladder scaffold system with swing up handrail – Ladderfix Ltd
Ladderspan Towers – Accesscaff International Ltd
Ladsaf – cable based ladder safety systems – Capital Safety Group Ltd
Lady Clare Ltd – table mats, trays, waste paper tubs and pictures etc – Lady Clare Ltd
Lady Fayre (United Kingdom) – hair nets hairdressing – Aburnet Ltd
Ladybird – children's fiction and non-fiction - hardback and paperback – Penguin Books Ltd
Ladybird – childrens books and audio cassette packs – Ladybird Books Ltd
Ladymax – sportswear country knights country wear – Max Power Sports Co.
***Lafert (Italy)** – A.C. electric motors – Motovario Ltd
***Lafert S.r.l. (Italy)** – electric motors – Micro Clutch Developments Ltd
Lafis – T V H UK Ltd
LAFIS – Chaintec Ltd
LAG – Mercury Bearings Ltd
Lagan Finance – Bannons
Laguiole – Birchgrove Products
***Laier (Germany)** – vibration equipment – La Roche
Lainacomb – textile fibre processing aid – Benjamin R Vickers & Sons Ltd
Lainasil – yarn strengthening agent – Benjamin R Vickers & Sons Ltd
Lainaspin – wool processing aid – Benjamin R Vickers & Sons Ltd
Lainatwist – textile processing aid – Benjamin R Vickers & Sons Ltd
Lainchbury – grain handling equipment – Blair Engineering
Laird of Kilkelly, The – waxed clothing & non waxed clothing – P S Gill & Sons
Laird Technologies – thermal interface materials – Anglia
Lake Records – compact discs - jazz – Fellside Recordings Ltd
Lakeland – pencil – Cumberland Pencil Museum
Lakeland Limited – creative kitchenware & household goods – Lakeland
Lakes Collections – Coated shower enclosures, doors & bath screens. – Lakes Bathrooms Ltd
Laltesi – Harrier Fluid Power Ltd
Laman – compressed air in line filters and dryers – Airware International Ltd
Lamatherm – insulation – Siderise Insulation Ltd
Lamb Air Mover – ventilation equipment – M S A Britain Ltd
Lamb Mackintosh – Capex Office Interiors
Lambar – laminated busbar trunking – Ellison Switchgear
Lambert & Butler Gold – filter cigarettes – Imperial Tobacco Group PLC
Lambert & Butler King Size – filter cigarettes – Imperial Tobacco Group PLC
Lambert & Butler Menthol – filter cigarettes – Imperial Tobacco Group PLC
Lambert & Butler White – filter cigarettes – Imperial Tobacco Group PLC
LAMBORGHINI – Hydraulic & Offshore Supplies Ltd
Lamborghini – J & S Lewis Ltd
Lamborghini Pumps – European Technical Sales Ltd
Lambs Bricks & Arches – restoration specialist & genetal brick merchants including soft reds – W T Lamb Holdings Property Services
Lamella Mat – pipes, ducts and industrial plant – Rockwool Rockpanel B V
***Lamello (Switzerland)** – jointing systems – Smeaton Hanscomb & Co. Ltd
***Lamina Filtertraps** – Progressive Product Developments Ltd
Laminated Shim Material – 0.05mm or 0.075mm laminations, peeled off as required – Industrial Trading Co. Ltd
Laminex – leather laminate membrane – J B Broadley
Lamit – laminating machines for foam etc. – Apropa Machinery Ltd
Lamontite – type 'a' brass and DZR brass compression fittings – Flowflex Components Ltd
Lamp – financial and management control systems – Bensasson & Chalmers Ltd
Lampconserver – doubles lamp life – Multiload Technology
Lampmaster – modular, selv compatible dimming system for all dimmable lighting loads – Multiload Technology
Lampways – European Lamp Group
Lampways Lamp Shop – European Lamp Group
LAN Components – networking components – I T T Ltd
Lan Rover Shiva – Tekdata Distribution Ltd
Lanalux – finish for wool tops – S T R UK Ltd
Lanaquarelle – watercolour papers – Exaclair Ltd
Lanarkshire Welding – steelbridge fabricators, steelwork fabricators and electric welders – Lanarkshire Welding Co. Ltd
Lancashire Glass – replacement PVC doors, windows, conservatories and roofline – Lancashire Glass & Solar Ltd
lancashire school of welding – welding courses – lancashire school of welding
Lancaster & Winter – steel stockholders – Lancaster & Winter Ltd
Lance Spray-Hood Accessory – Pressure washers – B & G Cleaning Systems Ltd
Lancer – Timber Bollard – Alto Bollards UK Ltd
Lancer Boss – T V H UK Ltd
LANCER BOSS – Chaintec Ltd
Lancer Boss – Stacatruc
Lancers – trousers – J B Armstrong & Co. Ltd
Lancet, The – medical journal – The Lancet
Lanchor – surface dressing binder – Total Bitumen
Lancia – L M C Hadrian Ltd
Land Cruiser – Churchtown Buildings Ltd
Land & Marine Products Ltd – Maon overboard recovery device – Jason's Cradle
Land Rover World – I P C Media Ltd
Land that Job – ecourse – In the Hot Seat
***Landers (Germany)** – grabs – N R C Plant Ltd
Landis – Cinetic Landis Ltd
Landis Cincinnati – Cinetic Landis Ltd
Landis Gardner – Cinetic Landis Ltd
Landis Grinding Systems – Cinetic Landis Ltd
Landis Lund – Cinetic Landis Ltd
Landlife – wildlife registered charity – Landlife Ltd
Landlink – property developers – Landlink Ltd
Landloo – single flush self contained toilet – Landsmans Ltd
Landlords Insurance – specialist insurance – M M A Insurance plc
LANDMARKA – Low power radio telemetry system – E2I Ltd
Landmec – Land Machinery Ltd
Landrover – Team Overseas Ltd
Landscape – embossed door – Premdor Crosby Ltd
Landscape – Interface Europe Ltd
Landscape Bark – soil improver – Melcourt Industries
Landtrekka – daypacks and camping accessories – Regatta Ltd
Lanes – Health Products – G R Lane Health Products Ltd
Laney Heatstock – guitar amplifiers and speakers – Headstock Distribution
Lanfranchi – Bottle Unscramblers – Lanfranchi Uk
Lang – pneumatic equipment – Bearwood Engineering Supplies
Lang-Laru – European Technical Sales Ltd
Lang Spannwerkzeuge – European Technical Sales Ltd
Langdale - Duralon Solace - Shoe laces – John Dobson Milnthorpe Ltd
Langen – packaging machinery – Molins plc
Langstane Press – office and computer supplies, furniture and print – Langstane Press Ltd
Langtry – luxury bathroom taps – Samuel Heath & Sons plc
Language of Colour – collection of colours for decorative paints – Akzonobel
Lanier – photo copiers and facsimile machines – Unigraph UK Ltd
Lanimol – waterless hand cleanser – Deb R & D Ltd
Lankroflex – epoxy plasticisers – Akcros Chemicals Ltd
Lankromark – Akcros Chemicals Ltd
Lankroplast – rheozogy modifiers – Akcros Chemicals Ltd
Lankrostat – antistatic agents – Akcros Chemicals Ltd
Lanmix – delayed set binder – Total Bitumen
Lano – The Winnen Furnishing Company
Lansdowne – liquid soap – Elsan Ltd
Lansing – T V H UK Ltd
Lansing – Stacatruc
Lansing – Harrier Fluid Power Ltd
LANSING BAGNALL – Chaintec Ltd
Lansing/Linde – material handling equipment – Lancing Linde Creighton Ltd
Lansing Linde – electric powered reach trucks, floor trucks, tow tractors, turret trucks, order pickers, engined counter balance trucks, container handlers and side loaders – Lansing Linde Ltd
Lansing Linde (Blackwood) Ltd – fork lift trucks – Linde Heavy Truck Division
Lansky – Sharpening systems – The Toolpost
LanSolve Racking – Warwick Fraser & Co. Ltd
Lantana – tufted carpet – Brockway Carpets Ltd
LANTEC INDUSTRIES – Hydraulic & Offshore Supplies Ltd
***Lantech (U.S.A.)** – stretchwrapping machinery – Ambassador Packaging Ltd
Lantex – tubes and bobbins for textile and mechanical industries – Langtec Ltd
Lantex – modified surface dressing binder – Total Bitumen
Lantor – Anglo Recycling Technology Ltd
Lantor – nonwoven fabrics for military and industrial protective clothing, medical wound dressings, orthopaedic products and industrial areas such as filtration, clothing interlinings, bagstock, shoe felts, wipes and bleeder felt for composite moulding – Lantor UK
Lantor C-Knit – fabric for military protective clothing – Lantor UK
Lantor Cube – steriliser test cube for testing the effectiveness of steam sterilisers – Lantor UK
Lantor Equaliser – nonwoven breather felt for composite moulding – Lantor UK
Lantor Formflex – polyester orthopaedic undercast padding – Lantor UK
Lantor Formflex Duo – viscose/polyester orthopaedic undercast padding – Lantor UK
Lantor Formflex Natural – viscose orthopaedic undercast padding – Lantor UK
Lantor Synthetic – polyester orthopedic under cast padding – Lantor UK
Lanvin – spectacle frames – Pennine Optical Group Ltd
Lanway – pulverisers, hammermills and crushers – Lanway Ltd
Lapads – acoustic processing system – B A E Systems Ltd
Lapauw – washer extractors – Armstrong Commercial Laundry Systems
Lapidolith – flurosilicate liquid chemical case hardener and dustproofer – Conren Ltd
Lapmaster – range of lapping and polishing machines – Lapmaster International Ltd
Lapmaster - lapping and polishing machines. – Lapmaster International Ltd
LAPP – Mathew C Blythe & Son Ltd
Lapp Cables – European Technical Sales Ltd
Laptair Interlinings – interlinings – Mitchell Interflex Ltd
Laptop Screen Online – Offers replacement laptop screens for branded laptops including Dell, Acer, Tosh – Laptop Screen Online
Larch-Lap – feather edge panel fencing – Forest Garden plc
Larch/London – sink/sink – Armitage Shanks Ltd
LARGA – Hydraulic & Offshore Supplies Ltd

Large Character Inkjet Marking – metals / plastics /pckging / concrete / wood / fibreboard – Universal Marking Systems Ltd

Large Flange Nutsert – one sided fastener threaded with high load bearing feature – Avdel UK Ltd

Largo – Pledge Office Chairs Ltd

***Lark (China)** – violins, cornets, trumpets, clarinets, flutes and ukuleles – John Hornby Skewes & Co. Ltd

Larrykins – sueded lambskin gloves and mittens – Nursey Of Bungay

***Larsson (Sweden)** – pliers and cutters for electronics – Electro Group Ltd

Laryngographs – speech analysis systems and speech pattern audiometers – Laryngograph Ltd

LARZEP – Hydraulic & Offshore Supplies Ltd

Larzep – J V Hydraulics Ltd

Las Mobili – Desks – Bucon Ltd

Las Olas (Argentina) – Patriarche Wine Agencies

Laser – lighting equipment – Powerlite Lighting Solutions Ltd

Laser – Laser Transport International Ltd

Laser – desking systems – Flexiform Business Furniture Ltd

Laser – plastic container alternative to Jerry can – RPC Containers Ltd

Laser – dinghies – LaserPerformance

Laser 1000 – label overprinting system – Weyfringe Labelling Systems

Laser 16 – dinghies – LaserPerformance

Laser 2000 – dinghies – LaserPerformance

Laser 3000 – dinghies – LaserPerformance

Laser 4000 – dinghies – LaserPerformance

Laser 5000 – dinghies – LaserPerformance

Laser Eps – dinghies – LaserPerformance

LASER FIX – Hydraulic & Offshore Supplies Ltd

Laser Folio – personalised direct mail package in personalised folder – Lettershop Group

Laser II Regatta – dinghies – LaserPerformance

Laser marking – YAG and CO2 for metals/plastics – Universal Marking Systems Ltd

Laser Methane – Methane Detection Gun – Crowcon Detection Instrument Ltd

Laser Pico – dinghies – LaserPerformance

Laser Printers – Formscan Limited

Laser Radial – dinghies – LaserPerformance

Laser Royal – personalised 8 page direct mail brochure – Lettershop Group

Laser Tools – S J Wharton Ltd

Laserfab – Subcontract CNC Sheetmetal work. – Guttridge Ltd

Laserfax – computer software for PC fax – Wordcraft International Ltd

Lasergraphics – Lamphouse Ltd

LaserLab – Laser Trader Ltd

Laserline – Bridgwater Electronics Ltd

Laserlope – personalised direct mail package laser addressed envelope – Lettershop Group

Laserlyte – Global Laser Technology Solutions

Lasermark – Sebakmt UK Ltd

LaserMark – CO2 laser marker – G S I Group Ltd

Laserprint Premium – paper – Fenner Paper Co. Ltd

Lasersure – strip steels with stay-flat properties – Corus U K Ltd

Lasertech – paper – Fenner Paper Co. Ltd

Lasox – laser welding apparatus – Boc Gases Ltd

Lastu – knitted clothing – Norland Burgess Ltd

Latcocel – polythene film – A Latter & Co. Ltd

Lateral 80 – lateral file – Acco East Light Ltd

Lateral Model T – lateral file – Acco East Light Ltd

Lateralfile Storage – Capex Office Interiors

Latex-ite – acrylic sports surface system – Emusol Products Ltd

Lathamclad – wallcladding – James Latham plc

Latour (France) – wire toube and strip bending machines – Bennett Mahler

LATreat – ALWC anticorrision – B A C Corrosion Control Ltd

Latstock – full range of homebrew equipment – Bray Group Ltd

Lattam – limpet magnets – Magnet Applications Ltd

Lattenax – waterproof building membranes, foil – A Latter & Co. Ltd

Lattice – M S C Gleichmann UK Ltd

Lattice – Cyclops Electronics Ltd

Lattice Semiconductor – programmable logic – Anglia

Latty – gland packings, mechanical seals, jointing & gaskets, live loading systems – Latty International Ltd

Laudus – B P plc

Lauffer – UK Office Direct

Launa – windows – Launa Windows

***Laundrosil (Germany)** – laundry bentmites – Sud-Chemie UK Ltd

Laundry F.M. – commercial laundry facilities management – J L A

Laundry Fresh – biological liquid laundry detergent – Premiere Products Ltd

Laura – radio HPLC software – Lablogic Systems Ltd

Laura Ashley – ladies garments and accessories, soft furnishing etc, home furnishings and childrens garmen – Laura Ashley Ltd

Laureate – London Electronics Ltd

Laurel – UK Office Direct

Laurydol – lauroyl peroxide – Akzo Nobel Chemicals Holdings Ltd

Lauzon – prefinished, solid, hardwood flooring – Atkinson & Kirby Ltd

Lavella – domestic sinks – Carron Phoenix

Lavender Boxes – corrugated cartons – Boxes & Packaging Ltd

Laverda – Mike Garwood Ltd

Laverl – trailer hardware – Boyriven

Laverock – textile piece goods – Reid & Taylor Ltd

Lavette – Forward Chemicals Ltd

Law-Direct – Mills & Reeve LLP

Lawclub – Allianz Insurance plc

LawNet – federation of independent law firms – Lawnet

LawNet Quality in Law – law services – Lawnet

***Lawnflite (U.S.A.)** – garden tractors – E P Barrus

***Lawnflite (U.S.A.)** – rotary mowers & brushcutters – E P Barrus

Lawphone – Allianz Insurance plc

Lawrence – centrifugal pumps – Axflow

Lawson – fuse links – Lawsons Fuses Ltd

Lawson Consulting – Consulting proposition for change, project and programme management. – Lawson Consulting

Lawson Mardon Star – aluminium foil – Novelis Foil & Technical Products

Lawtel – legal information services – Yougovcentaur

Laybond – N W Flooring

Laycarb – silicon carbide impregnation – Laystall Engineering Company Ltd

Layflat – Speed Plastics Ltd

Layher Scaffolding – Accesscaff International Ltd

Layrub – flexible couplings and shafts – Twiflex Ltd

Lazer System – radio alarm (wire free) external detection system – Lazer Systems

Lazer Way – laser guided AGV systems – Exmac

LazerSharp – papers and films for photocopiers, laser printers and DTP – West Design Products Ltd

Lazonby – sandstone (red) – Realstone Ltd

LB Filters – Harrier Fluid Power Ltd

***LBB (Sweden)** – drills – Atlas Copco Tools Ltd

LBS Autodoor Systems – automatic entrance door systems – L B S Group

LBS Dagendor – security open grilles – L B S Group

LBS Diamondguard – sliding lattice gates – L B S Group

LBS Doorguard SD & FD – doorguard reinforced door – L B S Group

LBS Fastguard – high-speed rolling doors – L B S Group

LBS Fenceguard – L B S Group

LBS Fire Curtain – L B S Group

LBS Fireguard – L B S Group

LBS Heatguard – industrial door – L B S Group

LBS Homeguard 150 – domestic reinforced shutters – L B S Group

LBS Homeguard 38 – domestic reinforced shutters – L B S Group

LBS Induguard 75 – industrial shutters – L B S Group

LBS Insuguard 100 – insulated shutters – L B S Group

LBS Insuguard F100 – fire resistant shutters – L B S Group

LBS Permaguard – permanent security products – L B S Group

LBS Polyguard 90 – L B S Group

LBS Secureguard 150 – security sliding doors – L B S Group

LBS Secureguard 229 – security sliding doors – L B S Group

LBS Secureguard F150 – fire-rated security sliding doors – L B S Group

LBS Secureguard F229 – L B S Group

LBS Shopguard 178 – L B S Group

LBS Shopguard 230 – L B S Group

LBS Shopguard 75 – L B S Group

LBS Specialized Door Services – L B S Group

LBS Viewguard 75 – L B S Group

LBW Machines – Portable Line Boring and Welding Machines – LBW Machines

LBX – Frenstar

LC-65 – preservative free daily contact lense cleaner – Allergan Ltd

LC Oleddinamica – valves & diverters – Harrier Fluid Power Ltd

LC-Oledoinamica – Fairway Hydraulics Ltd

***LC Oleodinamica (Italy)** – cetop hydraulic valves – BYPY Hydraulics & Transmissions Ltd

LC Security Barrier – light duty high specification rising arm barrier – Apt Controls Ltd

LC35 – rising arm barriers – Apt Controls Ltd

LCGC International – magazine – Advanstar Communications

LCH - London Clearing House, The – financials and commodities futures and options clearing house – L C H Clearnet Group Ltd

LCH RepoClear – clearing house for interbank trades in European government repos – L C H Clearnet Group Ltd

LCH SwapClear – clearing house for interbank interest rate swaps – L C H Clearnet Group Ltd

LCSA – gas fired unit heaters – Reznor UK Ltd

LCT (United Kingdom) – Exact mass benchtop LC-MS – Waters

LCU – Lightweight command unit – Sonardyne International Ltd

LDPE – Naylor Specialists Plastics

Le Buffet – catering utensils – Samuel Groves

***Le Chef** – Russums

Le Club – optical frames & sunglasses – Hilton International Eye Wear Ltd

Le Coq Sportif – sports clothes – FOCUS International Ltd

Le Son By Maxim – audio products – Sherwood Agencies Ltd

Le winters – Bar & bistro – Strangfor Arms Hotel

Lea Compound – greaseless bar compounds for satin finishing – Lea Manufacturing Co.

Leach Lewis Plant Ltd – construction plant distribution and plant and engine spare part supply. – Leach Lewis Ltd

Leach/LRE – Relays – Dax International Ltd

Lead-T-Pren – gutter expansion joint – British Lead

Leader – newspaper – The Express & Echo

Leadership Development Ltd – training provider specialising in sales, customer service and management training – Leadership Development Ltd

Leadwell – Lead Precision Machine Tools Ltd

Leaflex – cotton reinforced grinding wheels – Lea Manufacturing Co.

League 6 Panel – rugby – Gray Nicolls

Leak Alert – cost effective gas leak detector – Scott International Ltd

Lealde – Newall UK Ltd

Leamington Spa Courier – Leamington Spa Courier

Leamington Spa Review – Leamington Spa Courier

Lean manufacturing – Transcend Group Ltd

Leap – B P plc

Leaptronix – Logic Analysers and power supplies – StanTronic Instruments

Lear – vehicle seats and seat mechanisms – Lear Corporation UK Ltd

***Learning Network** – Hospitality & Leisure Manpower

Learning Pad – electronic sketch pad/keyboard, connects to tv – Vtech Electronics UK plc

Learok Britelea – calcined alumina grease bars – Lea Manufacturing Co.

Learok Classic – general purpose grease bars – Lea Manufacturing Co.

Learok Ferrobrite – fused alumina grease bars – Lea Manufacturing Co.

Learok Tripolea – tripoli grease bars – Lea Manufacturing Co.

Leathawash – glove shampoo – A Algeo Ltd

Leather Food Cream – leather cleaner and conditioner, suitable for leather and furniture upholstery – Oakland Financial Advisors

Leather Groom – leather cleaner and conditioner – Oakland Financial Advisors

Leathercraft – UK Office Direct

Leatherette Paper – E Becker Ltd

Leathersmith – diaries, social books and leathergoods bound in leather and other high quality materials – Neale Dataday Ltd

LeaWeb – non-woven abrasives products – Lea Manufacturing Co.

Leay – aluminium windows, curtain walling, doors and shopfronts – Leay Ltd

***LEBA (Portugal)** – leather bags and accessories – Alami International Ltd

Lebtourneau – Harrier Fluid Power Ltd

Lechler – spray nozzles, valves, headers control systems and associated products for liquid spraying equipment – Lechler Ltd

Lecroy – Alpha Electronics Northern Ltd

Lectraglas – a range of epoxy glass tubing – Custom Composites Ltd

Lectraglas, Unilam – Custom Composites Ltd

Lectralevel – floatless liquid level control – Black Teknigas & Electro Controls Ltd

Lectrapearl – specialist electrophoretic coatings – L V H Coatings Ltd

Lectraseal – specialist electrophoretic coatings – L V H Coatings Ltd

Lectrobase – specialist electrophoretic coatings – L V H Coatings Ltd

Lectrobond – specialist electrophoretic coatings – L V H Coatings Ltd

Lectros – damp proofing material – Lectros International Ltd

Lectrotect – Forward Chemicals Ltd

LED 100 – downlighters – Concord Marlin Ltd

LED 150 – downlighters – Concord Marlin Ltd

LED Series – led marker lights – Holophane Europe Ltd
Led Trak – trevira underlay for metal sheet – British Lead
Leda – gang mowers, hydraulic and trailed – Lloyds & Co Letchworth Ltd
Ledasoft – soft lenses – David Thomas Ltd
Ledco – Gem Tool Hire & Sales Ltd
Ledex & Dormeyer – solenoids – Saia Burgess (Gateshead) Plc
Ledray – photoswitch – Black Teknigas & Electro Controls Ltd
Ledtech Europe – commodity light emitting diodes – Opto Electronic Manufacturing Corporation Ltd
Lee Lighting – hire of television, theatre and commercial lighting equipment – Panalux Ltd
Lee & Plumpton – Desks – Bucon Ltd
Lee Spring – high quality compression extension and torsion springs – Lee Spring Ltd
Leec – medical, laboratory and mortuary equipment – Leec Ltd
Leeds City Link – buses – First Group plc
Leeds & Northrup – controllers – Bearwood Engineering Supplies
Leeds & Northrup – J B Furnace Engineering Ltd
Leek United Building Society – financial services – Leek United Building Society
Lees' – confectionery & bakery product manufacturer – Lees Of Scotland Ltd
***Leeson (U.S.A.)** – D.C. electric motors – Motovario Ltd
Leeswood – zinc ingots – R M Easdale
Leeway – cereal seeds – Henry Bell & Co Grantham Ltd
Leezone – food trades deodourant – Drywite Ltd
Leg-O-Mat – looselay interlocking rubber flooring tiles – Jaymart Roberts & Plastics Ltd
Legacy Liberator – software – Transoft Ltd
Legacy Recycled Art & Matt – paper – Fenner Paper Co. Ltd
Legal Advice Call – Allianz Insurance plc
Legal-Direct – Mills & Reeve LLP
Legal & General – Legal & General Group P.L.C.
Legal & General Assurance Society Ltd (United Kingdom) – Legal & General Group P.L.C.
Legamaster – UK Office Direct
Legamaster – planning boards & visual presentation – Edding UK Ltd
Legend – dental products – Prima Dental Group Ltd
Legend – luxury motor caravan – Auto Sleepers Ltd
Legend Restorative – glass ionomer filling material – Prima Dental Group Ltd
Legend Silver – reinforced glass inomer material for posterior use & core build up – Prima Dental Group Ltd
LEGIRS – Hydraulic & Offshore Supplies Ltd
***LEGO (Denmark)** – building toys – Lego UK Ltd
Lego Mindstorms – Robotic Construction – Lego UK Ltd
***Lego Technic (Denmark)** – constructional toys – Lego UK Ltd
Legrand – Proplas International Ltd
Legrand – European Technical Sales Ltd
Legrand ATX/EEXE/EEXD – hazardous area control systems – J B Systems Ltd
Legris – Southern Valve & Fitting Co. Ltd
Legris – Gustair Materials Handling Equipment Ltd
Legris – Trafalgar Tools
LEGRIS CONNECTIC – Hydraulic & Offshore Supplies Ltd
LEIBHERR – Hydraulic & Offshore Supplies Ltd
Leica – photographic equipment – R G Lewis Ltd
Leica – Fieldway Supplies Ltd
***Leica (Germany)** – cameras, lenses, projectors, binoculars and enlargers – Leica Camera Ltd
Leica Microsystems Imaging Solutions – image analysers & processing systems – Leica Microsystems Cambridge Ltd
Leicester Mercury Group Ltd – news paper publishers – Leicester Mail Ltd
Leicester Square – carpets - axminster – Brintons Carpets Ltd
Leigh – Dovetail and tenon jigs – The Toolpost
Leigh – insurance company – Houlder Group
Leigh House – Leigh House Serviced Offices, Leeds – Leigh House Facilities Management Ltd
Leigh's – alkyd based coating systems – Leighs Paints
Leigh Spinners – carpet and needlepunch floorcovering & carpet tiles – Leigh Spinners Ltd
Leighs Roadline – road marking paint – Leighs Paints
Leighton Buzzard Citizen – newspaper – Milton Keynes Citizen
Leighton Buzzard Observer – newspaper – Leighton Buzzard Observer & Citizen
Leine & Linde – Encoders UK
***Leister (Switzerland)** – hot air tools and blowers – Welwyn Tool Group Ltd
Leisure Business – a free monthly full colour newspaper for leisure proffesionals – The Barnsley Chronicle Ltd
Leiten Berger – thermometers – E V O Instrumentation Ltd
Leitenberger – thermometers – E V O Instrumentation Ltd
***Leitner (Germany)** – Modular Exhibition SAystems – Duo GB Ltd
Leitz – UK Office Direct
Leitz – tungsten-tipped circular saws, window tooling sets, drills, router bits, thin planing knives and profile cutters – Leitz Tooling UK Ltd
Lektriever – automated filing system – Kardex Systems UK Ltd
Leltex – industrial safety wear – Longworth Ltd
Lem – Alpha Electronics Northern Ltd
Lem – Alpha Electronics Southern Ltd
LEM – Direct Instrument Hire Ltd
Lem Heme – Direct Instrument Hire Ltd
Lemag (Germany) – peak pressure indicators – Star Instruments Ltd
Lemark – universal replacement for motor vehicles – Standard Motor Products Europe Ltd
Lemco – stand off barrel insulators – Broanmain
Lemken – J & S Lewis Ltd
Lemo – European Technical Sales Ltd
***Lemo (Switzerland)** – connectors – Lemo UK Ltd
Lemo – Cyclops Electronics Ltd
Lemon Cream Cleanser – mildly abrasive general cleaner – Premiere Products Ltd
Lemon Disinfectant – cationic disinfectant – Premiere Products Ltd
Lemon Gel – lemon floor and wall gel – Evans Vanodine International plc
LEMP – M P E Ltd
Lemsford Cases (United Kingdom) – Lemsford Metal Products 1982 Ltd
Lennox – air-conditioning, heating and ventilation equipment – Lennox Industries
Lenon – optical frames and sunglasses – Hilton International Eye Wear Ltd
Lenor – UK Office Direct
Lenord + Bauer – Motor Technology Ltd
Lenord + Bauer - Ormec - Eurotherm - Seidel - Kollmorgen - R + W - Eisele - Girard - Euroservo - Zebotronics - Papst - CSM - ASB - Acroloop - Axor - Danaher Motion – Motor Technology Ltd
Lenz – Harrier Fluid Power Ltd
Lenze – equipment & spares – Bearwood Engineering Supplies
Lenze – Mercury Bearings Ltd
Lenze – European Technical Sales Ltd
Lenze (Germany) – AC and DC motor speed control, worm gear and helical worm gear boxes, electric geared motors, shaft mounted geared motors, helical gearboxes, servo & inverter variable speed drives – Lenze UK Ltd
***Lenze** – European Drives & Motor Repairs
Lenze Controls – European Technical Sales Ltd
Lenze Drive PLCs – European Technical Sales Ltd
Lenze Gearboxes – European Technical Sales Ltd
Lenze Geared Motors – European Technical Sales Ltd
Lenze Industrial PCs – European Technical Sales Ltd
Lenze LCU Motor Starters – European Technical Sales Ltd
Lenze Motors – European Technical Sales Ltd
Lenze Servos – European Technical Sales Ltd
LEO ELECTRIC – Hydraulic & Offshore Supplies Ltd
Leocatic Mix – bitument emulsion for manufacturing depot stock macadams – Colas Ltd
Leocatic Spray – cold applied bitumen cationic emulsion, ideal for surface dressing footways – Colas Ltd
Leochip VLS – thixoptropic heavy duty bitumen surfacing binder – Colas Ltd
Leoclean – cleans tools and equipment of most uncured epoxy products – Colas Ltd
Leonardt & Co – precision pressings for writing instruments, stationery products,leather goods and the electronics industry – Leonardt Ltd
Leoni – cable – Leoni-Temco Ltd
Leoni – Belcom Cables Ltd
Leopard – Pressure washers – B & G Cleaning Systems Ltd
Leopard (United Kingdom) – 2 hp single ended backstand machine – R J H Finishing Systems Ltd
Leopard – connector for oil-well conductor pipe – Oil States Industries UK Ltd
Leopard (auto start & stop) – Pressure washers – B & G Cleaning Systems Ltd
Leopave – hand applied ready to use slurry seal for sealing footpaths open textured patches or footpaths – Colas Ltd
Leoseal – bitumen emulsion with rubber latex used as a waterproof membrane – Colas Ltd
Leotak – rapid breaking cationic tack coating emulsion which has excellent adhesion in damp conditions – Colas Ltd
***Lerloy (U.S.A.)** – tweezers soldering aids – Henri Picard & Frere
Leroi – Harrier Fluid Power Ltd
Leromur – retaining wall – Grass Concrete Ltd
Leroy Somer – Proplas International Ltd
***Leroy Somer** – European Drives & Motor Repairs
Leroy Somer Electric Motors – electric motors – Potteries Power Transmission Ltd
Leroy Somer Gearboxes – gearboxes – Potteries Power Transmission Ltd
***Les Glaciers** – La Maison des Sorbets Foods Ltd
Les Lunettes Essilor – spectacle frames – Pennine Optical Group Ltd
***Les Pâtissiers** – La Maison des Sorbets Foods Ltd
Lesker – general vacuum supplies – AESpump
Lesney – die castings and plastic mouldings – Lesney Industries Ltd
Lesonal – Akzo Nobel Coatings Ltd
Lesu (France) – ladieswear – Prizeflex Ltd
Let Lok – twin ferrule compression fittings and valves – Betabite Hydraulics Ltd
Let's Cast – Kitfix Swallow Group Ltd
Let's Go With Katy – CD-ROM series for children aged 5-14 teaching orientation and bearings – Learning & Teaching Scotland
Letchworth – swim-pool cleaning brush kit – Stoddard Manufacturing Co. Ltd
Lethobarb – for veterinary euthanasia – J M Loveridge
Letraline – graphic arts supplies – Letraset Ltd
Letraset – graphics arts supplies – Letraset Ltd
Letraset – UK Office Direct
Letratone – graphic arts supplies – Letraset Ltd
Lettasafe – post boxes – Burvills
Letter Sounds Games – childrens books and games for reading and writing practice – Jolly Learning Ltd
Letts – diaries calendars – Charles Letts Group Ltd
Letts – UK Office Direct
Letts of London – diaries calendars and stationery – Charles Letts Group Ltd
Letts Year Plan – wall chart planner – Charles Letts Group Ltd
Leuze-Mayser – European Technical Sales Ltd
***Leuzer (Germany)** – sensors – Sensortek
***LEV Mini-stacker (France)** – adjustable width stacker – Southworth Handling Ltd
Levacide – broad spectrum anthelmintic – Norbrook Research
Levafas – broad spectrum anthelmintic – Norbrook Research
Levalator (United Kingdom) – machine levelling units – Farrat Isolevel
Levante – Thermal Reflections Ltd
Level 2 Food Safety – Facilities Staff Training
Level Control – K S B Ltd
Level-Line – level crossing panel marking tape – Sportsmark Group Ltd
Levelay – self smoothing jointless 2 component epoxy flooring – Conren Ltd
Levelay Antistat – antistatic self smoothing jointless 2 component epoxy flooring composition – Conren Ltd
Levelay H.D.T. – seamless flow applied epoxy flooring – Conren Ltd
Leveliser – ladder levelling device – Ladderfix Ltd
Levelling Switches – Polaron Cortina Ltd
Levelox Smoke Curtains – automatic smoke containment curtain – Levolux A T Ltd
Levelride – automatic rideheight reset – Meritor HVS Ltd
Leven – stainless steel slop hopper – Armitage Shanks Ltd
Leverpak – fibre drum with lever container – Rexam Holding plc
Leviathan – heavy duty commercial vehicle lifts – Tecalemit Garage Equipment Co. Ltd
Levin – refrigeration – Interlevin Refrigeration Ltd
Levington TPMC – Fertiliser for landscaping – Scotts Co. Ltd
Levolux – external sunbreaker fin systems – Levolux A T Ltd
Levolux – tension blind system-internal/external fabric blind – Levolux A T Ltd
Levolux – sheer blind and venetian blind – Levolux A T Ltd
Levolux – external fabric roller system – Levolux A T Ltd
Levolux – vertical blind – Levolux A T Ltd
Levolux Easi Hook – fabric curtains – Levolux A T Ltd
Levolux Easi Roller – roller blind – Levolux A T Ltd
Levolux External Sunbreaker Fin System – Levolux A T Ltd
Levolux Fascade – external blind – Levolux A T Ltd
Levolux Markisolette – fabric external blind – Levolux A T Ltd
Levolux Matrix – aluminium fixed louvre screens – Levolux A T Ltd
Levolux Rollscreen – external roller blind – Levolux A T Ltd
Levolux Skyvane – skylight venetian – Levolux A T Ltd
Levolux Slimgroove – blackout blinds – Levolux A T Ltd
Levolux Solashade – external louvred blinds – Levolux A T Ltd
Levolux Ventilation Louvre – ventilation louvre – Levolux A T Ltd
Levolux Walk-On Brise Soleil – Levolux A T Ltd
Levolux Window Curtains – fabrics – Levolux A T Ltd
***Levoni** – italian treats – Donatantonio
Levy Gems – gemstone dealers and diamond merchants – Levy Gems Ltd
Levy Hill MKVI – Radiometer – Applied Scintillation Technologies
Levy Hill MKVQ - Visualize Range - CamIR Range - SecureX Range - MedeX Range - InspeX Range - Extender Range - Scintillize Range – Applied Scintillation Technologies

Lewis Anglo – latches and hinges, harrows and iron forging – Samuel Lewis Ltd
***Lewis-Grip (United Kingdom)** – tubular support bandage – Lewis's Medical Supplies
Lewis&Hill – Furniture manufacturers and designers – Lewis & Hill
***Lewis-Plast (United Kingdom)** – first aid products – Lewis's Medical Supplies
***Lewis-Sauz (United Kingdom)** – tubular finger bandage – Lewis's Medical Supplies
Lewis & Taylor – patent and trade mark agents – Mark's & Clerk LLP
Lewis & Wood – The Winnen Furnishing Company
Lewisham Borough Mercury – South London Press
Lewisol – resins – Hercules Holding Ii Ltd
Lewmar Marine – marine equipment - winches, blocks, hatches, portlights, shackles and hydraulic equipment – Lewmar Ltd
Lex Browser – First Databank Europe Ltd
Lex Transfleet – Truck & van contract hire, fleet management, truck & van rental, vehicle management, fleet services, fuel card, mobile – Fraikin Ltd
Lexan – Resinex UK Ltd
Lexan – Sunlight Plastics Ltd
Lexcast – acrylic sheets – Lexcast Ltd
Lexmark – colour inkjet printers – Johnsons Photopia Ltd
Lexmark – Printers – Moorgate Ltd
Lexmark – laser printers – Datatrade Ltd
Lexmark – Lexmark inkjet cartridges, laser toners & printers – Inkxperts
Lexmark – UK Office Direct
***Lexsuco LP4 & LP6 (Canada)** – expansion joint – Alumasc Exterior Building Products
Lexy Collection – knitwear, t-shirts, sweatshirts and jogging suits – Paramount Knitwear Leicester Ltd
Leybold – Harrier Fluid Power Ltd
Leyburn – fabric collection – Brian Yates
Leyburn Blend – Ibstock Brick Ltd
LEYLAND – Bailey Morris Ltd
Leyland – Harrier Fluid Power Ltd
LFA 427 – Netzsch-Instruments
LG – Lamphouse Ltd
LG – LCD Televsions – Electrotec International Ltd
LG – Telephone System – Alecto Solutions Ltd
LG Electronics – air conditioners (split systems, cassettes, high walls, convertibles, window, rootop packages), hermetic compressors – Thermofrost Cryo plc
Lg Semicon – Cyclops Electronics Ltd
***LGB (Sweden)** – tappers – Atlas Copco Tools Ltd
LGC Executive Search – Senior Mgt and Board recruiters – L G C Executive Search
LGM – Chaintec Ltd
LGSAmarine (United Kingdom) – international marine & cargo surveyors engineers & consultants – L G S A Marine
LHA – Hydraulic & Offshore Supplies Ltd
LHA – Harrier Fluid Power Ltd
LI-COR (U.S.A.) – Glen Spectra Ltd
Libbey – Ascot Wholesale Ltd
Libby (USA) – Bar style drinkwater – Western House
Liberator – Derbyshire Building Society
Liberator – emergency escape window stay – Frank Allart & Co. Ltd
Liberator (United Kingdom) – broadloom – Checkmate Industries Ltd
Liberator – Large AC Motors – Baldor UK
Liberon – Wood finishes and restoration products – The Toolpost
Liberon – Vastern Timber Co. Ltd
***Libfer** – B A S F
Libra – range of spectrophotometers – Biochrom Ltd
Libra – digital console – A M S Neve Ltd
Libra – push-button water boiler – Marco Beverage Systems Ltd
Libra – Pledge Office Chairs Ltd
Libra Live – digital console – A M S Neve Ltd
Libran Laminators (United Kingdom) – Trade Encapsulators – Libran Laminations Ltd
***Librel** – B A S F
Librex – library and display equipment – Librex Ltd
***Libspray** – B A S F
Libvent – Britax P S V Wypers Ltd
Lichfield – WC suite – Armitage Shanks Ltd
Licon – switches – I T W Switches & Switch Panel Ltd
lidget garages, lidget concrete – concrete buildings workshops and store buildings from Britain s favourite range of concrete garages – The Garden Buildings Centre
Lidl – Supply Chain Solution Ltd
Lido – corner bath – Ideal Standard Ltd
Liebherr – Harrier Fluid Power Ltd
***Liebherr-Great Britain (Germany)** – construction machines – Liebherr-Great Britain Ltd
Liebig – anchor bolts – Arrow Supply Co. Ltd
Liesegang – Lamphouse Ltd
Lieutentant – Plastic Bollard – Alto Bollards UK Ltd
***Lievers (Netherlands)** – vibration equipment – La Roche
Life-Aid – reverses the process of dehydration – Norbrook Research
Life-size – Video conferencing equipment – Medbrook Services Ltd
Lifeline – emergency call unit – Tunstall Healthcare UK Ltd
Lifeline Fire Systems – vehicle fire protection – Lifeline Fire & Safety Systems Ltd
Lifemaster – life jackets – Vacuum Reflex
Lifeplan – nutritional supplements – Lifeplan Products Ltd
Lifeskills Smart Spender – CD-ROM about spending wisely for SEN and primary age group – Learning & Teaching Scotland
Lifeskills Time and Money – CD-ROM teaching telling the time and handling money for SEN and primary age group – Learning & Teaching Scotland
Lifesmoke – distress smoke signal – Pains Wessex Ltd
Lifestyles U.K. – lifestyle database – C A C I
Lift – heavy duty cleaner and degreaser – Evans Vanodine International plc
Lift – refillable trigger sprays – Cleenol Group Ltd
Lift And Force – sewage ejector – Tuke & Bell Ltd
Lift Guard – brushstrip safety sealing for elevators & lifts – Kleeneze Sealtech Ltd
Lift-Off – dart flights – Unicorn Products Ltd
Lift the Dot – canopy & awning fastener – Opas Southern Limited
Liftaway – Grundfos Pumps Ltd
Liftcon – Forward Chemicals Ltd
LIFTER – Chaintec Ltd
Lifting equipment manufrs – Saxon Lifts Ltd
Lifting Gear Hire – Accesscaff International Ltd
Liftkar – powered stair climber – Stanley Handling Ltd
Liftmaster – Easygates Ltd
Liftmate – powered access equipment – Terex UK Ltd
Lifton Dumpers – Parkway Plant Sales Ltd
LIFTRITE – Chaintec Ltd
Lig-Free – Conservation Resources UK Ltd
Ligantraal – perfume speciality – Quest International UK Ltd
Light Commercial Pumps – SE pumps – Circulating Pumps Ltd
Light Haulage Contractors – Landsmans Ltd
Light Show – carpets – Interface Europe Ltd
Light Source Digital Video – video production – Lightsource Event Technology Ltd
Light-Store – for lamps, tubes and bulbs, low energy saving lamps – MPW Group
Light Systems – Boston Powertrack – Boston Retail Products
Lightbox – W & Co Design Solutions Ltd
Lightboxes – W & Co Design Solutions Ltd
Lighthouse – Gem Tool Hire & Sales Ltd
Lighthouse SPC – Status Metrology Solutions Ltd
Lighting (United Kingdom) – photo electric street lighting controls, low voltage lights for caravans and commercial vehicles – Zodion Ltd
Lighting and floodlighting for motorways – Henry Cooch & Son Ltd
Lighting emergency, illuminated self powered – Henry Cooch & Son Ltd
Lighting equipment portable – Henry Cooch & Son Ltd
Lightnin – Petre Process Plant Ltd
Lightning – adjuvent oils – B P plc
Lightning Art & Silk – paper – Fenner Paper Co. Ltd
Lightning Ivory Board – board – Fenner Paper Co. Ltd
Lightning Stranglehold – steel banding and fixing systems – Seac Ltd
Lightrak – lighting control and power distribution – Electrak Holdings Ltd
Lightspan – wide area glazing – Duplus Architectural Systems Ltd
Lightware – Lamphouse Ltd
Lignacite – fine textured lightweight load bearing concrete building blocks – Lignacite Ltd
Lignacite – medium density building blocks – Lignacite Ltd
Lignacite – fair face blocks – Tarmac Topblock Ltd
Lignacrete – fine textured dense load bearing high strength concrete building blocks – Lignacite Ltd
***Ligne Rose** – Roset UK Ltd
Lignostone (Germany) – densified wood – Roechling Engineering Plastics Ltd
Ligntinh Crushers – Hunwick Engineering Ltd
Ligustral – perfume speciality – Quest International UK Ltd
Lil-lets – miniature tampons – Lil-lets UK Ltd
***Lillico Attlee** – Bodle Bros Ltd
Lilliput – nursery buildings – Portakabin Ltd
Lilliput – Atlantis European Ltd
Lilliput HE – Power flame cast iron sectional boilers – Hamworthy Heating Ltd
Lilliput Lane – needlecraft – Coats Ltd
Lillywhites – sports retailers – Lillywhites
Lily of the Valley – fragrant gifts and toiletries – Norfolk Lavender Trading Ltd
Lim, Paul – darts and flights – Unicorn Products Ltd
LIMAB – Limab UK
Limara – bodyspray – Lil-lets UK Ltd
Limarosta – stainless steel welding electrodes – Lincoln Electric UK Ltd
Limbar – disabled persons handles and rails – Allgood
Limbase – lime/cement products for soil stabilisation – Tarmac
Limbux – hydrated lime to BS890 – Tarmac
Lime – Technical Recruitment – Lime Technical Recruitment
Lime – lime perfume based on q.a.c. – Evans Vanodine International plc
Lime Scale Preventer – protection of hot water systems against limescale to be hung in water – Fernox
Limebond – cement for building mortars – Tarmac
Limelite – limescale remover – P Z Cussons International Ltd
Limex70 – Keith Mount Liming Ltd
***LIMINESTRA (Germany)** – lamps – Osram Ltd
Limo Darkglass – car window darkening process – Quicksilver Automotive
Limontamoquette – patterned vinyl sheet flooring – Jaymart Roberts & Plastics Ltd
Limpet – treatment process – Osborn Unipol Ltd
Limpet Pump – Condensate Removal Pump – E D C International Ltd
Limpetite – brushable & sprayable rubber coating – Bristol Metal Spraying & Protective Coatings Ltd
Limslip – B P plc
Lina Chirino – Ladies designer knitwear – Novinit Ltd
Linaclad – screen panels – Linatex Ltd
Linacut – cut end slurry hose – Linatex Ltd
Linadek – polyurethane screen panels – Linatex Ltd
Linaflex – abrasion resistant rubber hose – Linatex Ltd
Linaflow – air operated sleeve valve – Linatex Ltd
LINAK – Linak UK
Linak Power – Linak UK
Linapump – rubber lined slurry pump – Linatex Ltd
***Linard (Malaysia)** – abrasion resistant rubber – Linatex Ltd
***Linatex (Malaysia)** – abrasion resistant rubber – Linatex Ltd
***Linbide (New Zealand)** – sealants – Indasa Abrasives UK Ltd
Linbin Cabinets – Storage Direct
Linbins – Storage Direct
***Lincat** – Crown Catering Equipment Ltd
***Lincat** – Court Catering Equipment Ltd
***Lincat** – catering equipment – Asterix Catering Equipment Ltd
Lincat – Ascot Wholesale Ltd
Linco Beer – shampoo/conditioner – Church & Dwight UK Ltd
Lincoln – shower tray – Armitage Shanks Ltd
Lincoln – Harrison Lubrication Engineering Ltd
Lincoln – 500mm single oven – Indesit Company UK Ltd
Lincoln – pantiles – William Blyth Ltd
Lincoln – Ovens – Hugall Services Ltd
Lincoln – timber up and over garage door – P C Henderson Ltd
***Lincoln** – Viscount Catering Ltd
Lincoln – grease blocks – Bearwood Engineering Supplies
Lincoln Cleaning Machines – industrial floor cleaning machinery – Lincoln Cleaning Technology
Lincoln-Helios – grease blocks – Bearwood Engineering Supplies
Lincolnweld – sub arc flux and wires – Lincoln Electric UK Ltd
Linda – baths – Ideal Standard Ltd
Lindale – fabric collection – Brian Yates
Lindapter – structural steelwork fixing – Lindapter International
Lindapter – S J Wharton Ltd
Lindapter – steel connectors – Arrow Supply Co. Ltd
LINDE – Hydraulic & Offshore Supplies Ltd
Linde – C J Plant Ltd
Linde – pumps & motors – Linde Hydraulics Ltd
Linde – T V H UK Ltd
Linde – Stacatruc
LINDE – Chaintec Ltd
Linde – Harrier Fluid Power Ltd
Linde Heavy Truck Division Ltd – Linde Heavy Truck Division
LINDE HYDRAULICS – Hydraulic & Offshore Supplies Ltd
Lindemann – refuse shredders, Zerdirator-scrap metal shredders – Metso Minerals UK Ltd
Linden – lager – Temple Wines Ltd
Lindgren – Ets-Lindgren Ltd
Lindhaus Hepa Range – twin motored upright vacuum – Truvox International Ltd
Lindhaus Vacuum cleaners – Pressure washers – B & G Cleaning Systems Ltd
Lindibolt – self heading bolt suitable for cavity steel structures – Lindapter International
Lindiclip – beam clamp for services support – Lindapter International
Lindisfarne – mead, fruit wines, preserves, relishes, confectionery and biscuits – Lindisfarne Hotel
Lindor (Netherlands) – mixing machinery – Orthos Engineering Ltd

Lindos – spare parts – Linde Hydraulics Ltd
LINDOS – Hydraulic & Offshore Supplies Ltd
Lindstrom – cutters & pliers – Welwyn Tool Group Ltd
Lindum – concrete – Sandtoft Holdings Ltd
Lindy Electronics – computer accessories – Lindy Electronics Ltd
Line Drivers – Greenwich Instruments Limited
Line Lazer (U.S.A.) – whitelining paint machine – Sportsmark Group Ltd
Line-Lok – guy runner – Clamcleats Ltd
Line Paint – solvent based epoxy line paint – Conren Ltd
Linea (United Kingdom) – switches, sockets, dimmers, etc – R Hamilton & Co. Ltd
*Linea Arte – E T N A Assist UK
Linea Gastro – E T N A Assist UK
*Linea Piccola – E T N A Assist UK
LineaMatic – Hörmann (UK) Ltd
Linear – linear flourescent lighting – Selux UK Ltd
Linear – Linear Tools Ltd
Linear – Display Wizard Ltd
Linear and Trapezodal Firestop Systems – fire stopping at wall and ceiling junctions – Rockwool Rockpanel B V
Linear Planrad – AEL Heating Solutions Ltd
*Linear Pro (Germany) – P.A. systems – John Hornby Skewes & Co. Ltd
Linear Technology – Cyclops Electronics Ltd
Linear Weighing 3000 Series – fully automatic microelectronic controlled systems – Riggs Autopack Ltd
Linearform Thermoformers – high speed inline for refrigerator inner body liner manufacture – Shelley Thermoformers International Ltd
LinearMaster Compact – handheld analogue ic tester – A B I Electronics Ltd
Lineartechnik – European Technical Sales Ltd
Linebacker – self-adhesive – Howard Smith Paper Ltd
Linebloc – filter – Schurter Ltd
Linecall 2000 – nursecall system – Eclipse Nursecall Systems Ltd
Linecall 3000 – nursecall system – Eclipse Nursecall Systems Ltd
LINEFLEX – CV In-line Variable Offset Flexible Shaft Couplings – Francis and Francis Ltd
*Lineman (U.S.A.) – line test set – Lyons Instruments
Linemaster – digital drives controllers – Ultra Electronics Ltd
Linemelt – mains frequency holding and melting equipment – Inductotherm Europe Ltd
Linen Formula 1 – Try & Lilly Ltd
Linen Mesh Trilby – Try & Lilly Ltd
Liner Major – concrete mixer – Multi Marque Production Engineering Ltd
Liner Mini Handler – 4 wheel drive telescopic handler – Multi Marque Production Engineering Ltd
Liner Rolpaint – mortar mixers – Multi Marque Production Engineering Ltd
Liner Rough Rider – 2 and 4 wheel drive dumpers – Multi Marque Production Engineering Ltd
Linescan (EG & G) – security, x-ray inspection systems – L-3 Communications Security & Detection Systems
Linesman – skipless safety helmet – M S A Britain Ltd
LINESTRA – lamps – Osram Ltd
Linex – technical drawing instruments – Pelltech Ltd
Linex – UK Office Direct
Linfinity – Cyclops Electronics Ltd
Ling Design – greetings cards, social stationary, giftwrap, napkins – Ling Design Ltd
Ling Dynamic – vibration test equipment – L D S Test & Measurment Ltd
Ling Dynamic Systems – vibration test equipment – L D S Test & Measurment Ltd
Link – Vidlink International Ltd
Link – communications-mobile phases, faxes and organisers – Dixons Retail
Link 2 – fibre optic industrial systems communications – Parker
Link-a-bord – plastic modular system for composit bins, planters, window boxes, raised beds – Link-A-Bord Ltd
LINK-BELT – Chaintec Ltd
Link-bilt – volumetric relocatable buildings – Boyton B R J System Buildings Ltd
Link tm – pre-testing research technique – Millward Brown
Link Units – Accesscaff International Ltd
link2home – prior web site – neighbo
Linkflex – flexible couplings – S S White Technologies UK Ltd
Linkline – flexible conveyor system – Expert Tooling & Automation
Linkliner – sliding door van body – Boalloy Industries Ltd
LinkLite – MaxMax Ltd
Links 99 – computer game – Square Enix Ltd
Links and Badge – computer games – St Andrews Link Trust
Linnex – Mailing films – Sanders Polyfilms Ltd
Linney – headwear (or hats and caps) – Try & Lilly Ltd
Linonews – web-offset press – L & M Ltd
Linotype – typesetting machines – L & M Ltd

Linscan – Radir Ltd
Linshelf – Storage Direct
Linspace – Storage Direct
Linton – woollen cloth – Linton Tweeds Ltd
Linton – metal litter bins – Linton Metalware
LINTRA – Hydraulic & Offshore Supplies Ltd
Lintra – rodless pneumatic cylinders – Norgren Ltd
Lintra – B L Pneumatics Ltd
Lintronic – electronics – Linde Hydraulics Ltd
LINTRONIC – Hydraulic & Offshore Supplies Ltd
*Lintvalve – leak detection equipment – Procon Engineering Ltd
Linux Format – magazine – Future Publishing Ltd
Linvar – Storage Direct
Linvar – induction regulators and electromagnetic apparatus – Muirhead Aerospace
Linvic – carbon, alloy and stainless steel pipes, flanges and fittings – Linvic Engineering Ltd
Linx – continuous ink jet printers and ancillary equipment – Linx Printing Technologies plc
Lion – Pressure washers – B & G Cleaning Systems Ltd
Lion – herbs, spices and sauces – A A K Ltd
Lion (United Kingdom) – major backstand idler – R J H Finishing Systems Ltd
Lion – electron beam lithography system – Leica Microsystems
Lion 40% – 40% anionic bitumen emulsion – Colas Ltd
Lion 55% – sub-base sealant against loss of moisture and fines and for formation sealing to maintain optimal moisture and strength – Colas Ltd
Lion (auto start & stop) – Pressure washers – B & G Cleaning Systems Ltd
Liondoor – crash proof and resistant hi speed factory doors – Union Industries
LionHeart – oat bran bread mix – G R Wright & Sons Ltd
Liozan – activated hydrazine hydrate – Atosina UK Ltd
Lip Definer – lip pencil – Elizabeth Arden
Lip Gloss – gloss lipstick – Elizabeth Arden
Lipomod – lipolytic enzymes – Biocatalysts Ltd
Lipprite – Osborn Unipol Ltd
Lipprox – Osborn Unipol Ltd
Lippryll – Osborn Unipol Ltd
*Liptons – Hygiene Warehouse
LiqTec – Grundfos Pumps Ltd
Liquabrade Ferrospray – fused alumina liquid compounds – Lea Manufacturing Co.
Liquabrade Spraybrite – calcined alumina liquid compounds – Lea Manufacturing Co.
Liquabrade Tripospray – tripoli liquid compounds – Lea Manufacturing Co.
Liqualine – B P plc
Liqualube – bobbing greases – Lea Manufacturing Co.
Liqui-Flow – Bronkhorst UK Ltd
LIQUIBELLO – Hydro pneumatic compensator for high and low temperature fluids with stainless and other corrosion resistant metals – Pulsation Dampers At Pulseguard Ltd
Liquid Commom Lisp – independently supported common Lisp software programming environment – Global Graphics Software Ltd
Liquid Crystal Devices – colour changing products – B & H Colour Change Ltd
Liquid High Gloss – Spencer Coatings Ltd
Liquid Silk – water based lubricant – Bodywise Ltd
liquid Solid Separator – Russell Finex Ltd
Liquid Solutions – industrial filtration and separation equipment – Total Filtration Ltd
Liquid Spray Polish – non-aerosol furniture spray polish – Premiere Products Ltd
Liquidpure – water drum filter – Norit UK Ltd
Liquifil – liquid filtration material – Purification Products Ltd
LIQUIFLEX – Pulsation damper used for volumetric flow smoothing from stock in 316 stainless steel wetted metal parts – Pulsation Dampers At Pulseguard Ltd
Liquimatic 1-8 – quality zinc free hydraulic oils – Morris Lubricants
Liquimatic 17 37A & 47A – specially formulated multigrade hydraulic oils – Morris Lubricants
Liquimatic 33G – automotive transmission fluid – Morris Lubricants
Liquimatic BVG – biodegradable hydraulic oil – Morris Lubricants
Liquimatic C3 – high quality transmission and hydraulic oil – Morris Lubricants
Liquimatic DII – automatic transmission fluid – Morris Lubricants
Liquimatic E85 – transmission fluid to leyland spec E85 – Morris Lubricants
Liquimatic HY – transmission oil to case MS1207 specification – Morris Lubricants
Liquimatic JDF – transmission and hydraulic oil to john deere jd20c, Ford M2C-134D – Morris Lubricants
Liquimetrics – automatic metal pouring equipment – Inductotherm Europe Ltd
Liquipak – liquid carrying fibredrum – Rexam Holding plc

Liquiphant – vibrating level limit switch – Endress Hauser Ltd
Liquisafe 46 – fire resistant hydraulic fluid – Morris Lubricants
Liquistore – drinking water storage tanks – Franklin Hodge Industries Ltd
Liquisweet – water sweetner for pigs – A One Feed Supplements Ltd
Liquitherm – electric melting and holding furnaces – Ramsell Naber Ltd
Lirax – Linear Systems – Schunk Intec Ltd
Liros – Fullbrook Systems Ltd
Lismor – records tapes and compact discs etc – Lismor Recordings
Lispworks – computer software and programming language and programming environment – Global Graphics Software Ltd
Lisson – plastic sheets – H W Cooper
LISTA – storage solutions – R K International Machine Tools Ltd
Lister – locomotive spares – Alan Keef Ltd
Lister – A T Wilde & Son Ltd
Lister and Petter – diesel engines – Service Engines Newcastle Ltd
Lister Diesel Gensets – diesel driven generating sets – Lister Petter Ltd
Lister Marine Diesels – marine diesel engines – Lister Petter Ltd
Lister Petter – air and water cooled diesel engines – Lister Petter Ltd
Lister Petter – diesels & spares – Bearwood Engineering Supplies
Lister Petter – Trowell Plant Sales Ltd
Lister Petter – Harrier Fluid Power Ltd
Lister Petter Diesels – air and water cooled diesel engines – Lister Petter Ltd
Litao – printing on pvc and plastics product names – Reid Printers
Lite-Dialco – l.e.d./diodes – Bearwood Engineering Supplies
Lite-on – Cyclops Electronics Ltd
Liteglaze – clear acrylic sheet – Ariel Plastics Ltd
Litepile – Beaver 84
*Litepipe (U.S.A.) – 3 extended lightsource for aids to navigation application – A B Pharos Marine Ltd
Literacy for Life – Series of literacy books for Primary pupils – Egon Publishers Ltd
Litestat – R Hamilton & Co. Ltd
LiteTracker – personal visual flashing indicator – Wolf Safety Lamp Company Ltd
LiteTracker – bottom supported cantilevered gate – Frontier Pitts Ltd
Lithene – liquid polybutadienes – Frutarom UK Ltd
LITHOPURE – Hydraulic & Offshore Supplies Ltd
Lithoshield – Ironsides Lubricants Ltd
Lithotronic – Fullbrook Systems Ltd
Litoceramika – Cesol Tiles Ltd
Litre Meter (United Kingdom) – pelton wheel turbine flowmeters – Litre Meter Ltd
Litta Pikka – litter collection tool – Glasdon International Ltd
Littac – insecticide for litter beetle control – Sorex Ltd
Littelfuse – E Preston Electrical Ltd
Littelite – pilot lights – Bearwood Engineering Supplies
Litterbug – sweepers – Denis Rawlins Ltd
Litterpicker – reacher for street cleaning – Helping Hand Co.
*Little Aristocrat (Portugal and The Far East) – baby wear, childrens wear and baby shoes – O S R International Ltd
Little Book – wallpaper – Zoffany
Little Brown – The Little Brown Book Group
Little Bus – bus services – East Yorkshire Motor Services Ltd
Little Champion – John Hunt Bolton Ltd
Little Chef – waitress service restaurant – Moto Hospitality Ltd
Little Giant Stepladder – Accesscaff International Ltd
Little Giants – childrens wear – Little Giants Ltd
Little Glass House – Emerson Network Power Ltd
Little Grey Rabbit – Chorion plc
Little Leader – childrens wear – Little Giants Ltd
Little Logger – garden saw – Atkinson-Walker Saws Ltd
Little Nipper – Procter Machinery Guarding Ltd
Little Renown – babies, childrenswear and teenage fashions – Shenu Fashions
Little Smart Smarty Junior – Vtech Electronics UK plc
Littlefuse – Cyclops Electronics Ltd
Littlewoods – catalogues – Littlewoods Home Shopping Orders & Enquiries
Littlewoods Personal Finance – The Woolwich
Litton – mechanical, electrical, ventilation services, building contractor, ductwork manufacturer – Litton Group Ltd
Litton – Encoders UK
Live Lecture – Web based live lectures – V3 Technologies
Live Leeches – bio chemical and leech hyaluronidase – Biopharm Leeches
Live Load – Tentec Ltd
LiveGear – Vidlink International Ltd
Liverpool Football Club – merchandise – Liverpool Football Club Ticket Bookings

Liverpool Victoria Friendly Society – financial services – Liverpool Victoria
Liveryman – horse clippers & groomers – Agrihealth
LIVING SPACE GLAZING BARS – Living Space Ltd
Livingetc – I P C Media Ltd
Livingston – test equipment management solutions and computer products – Livingston UK
Liwell – flip flow screening machine – Tema Machinery Ltd
Lixetone – perfume speciality – Quest International UK Ltd
Lixetone Coeur – perfume speciality – Quest International UK Ltd
LJM – European Technical Sales Ltd
LJU Light Barriers – European Technical Sales Ltd
***Lladro (Spain)** – porcelain figurines – Dexam International
Llanrad – automotive and commercial radiator distributors and number plate component distributors – Llanrad Distribution plc
Llechwedd Slate Caverns – tourist attraction – Quarry Tours Ltd
LLOYD INSTRUMENTS – Materials testing equipment and polymer testing instruments – Lloyd Instruments Ltd
Lloyd Lawn & Leisure – gardening equipment – Lloyd Ltd
Lloyd Loom – furniture – Lloyd Loom Ltd
Lloyd Loom – The Winnen Furnishing Company
LLOYDS – Hydraulic & Offshore Supplies Ltd
Lloytron – consumer electronic, small electrical appliances, haircare products, security products, lighting and rechargeable batteries – Laltex & Co. Ltd
LM Guide – T H K UK
LMCF – Linear Motor – Baldor UK
LMDS – Linear Motor – Baldor UK
LMIC – Linear Motor – Baldor UK
***LMP (Sweden)** – nutrunners – Atlas Copco Tools Ltd
***LMS (Sweden)** – impact wrenches – Atlas Copco Tools Ltd
LMS – line management systems – Radio Detection
LMSS – Linear Motor – Baldor UK
Lo-Drift – drift reducing spray nozzles – Hypro Eu Ltd
Load Balancing – Tekdata Distribution Ltd
Load Cells – geotechnical instruments – Itm Soil Ltd
Load Link – digital tensile load indicators, 1 tonne to 500 tonnes – Straightpoint UK Ltd
Load Lugger – box trailers – Lynton Trailers UK Ltd
Loadascreen – mobile conveying and screening plant – Parker Plant Ltd
LoadCentre KQ2 – distribution board – Schneider
Loaded – I P C Media Ltd
Loadguard – safe load indicator – Thermo Scientific
Loadlink – T S M Ltd
Loadmaker – commercial vehicle bulkheads – J R Industries Ltd
Loadmaster – general purpose trailers – Lynton Trailers UK Ltd
Loadmaster – In motion weighing and volume measuring – Newland Engineering Co. Ltd
Loadmaster – hinges – Cooke Brothers Ltd
Loadrunner – box trailers – Lynton Trailers UK Ltd
Loadspeeder – hydraulic demount equipment – Abel Demountable Systems Ltd
Loadstar – tumble dryers – Armstrong Commercial Laundry Systems
Loadstar – Clean Machine UK Ltd
LoadSure – Pump tubing element – Watson Marlow Pumps Ltd
Loafer – fishing tackle – Drennan International Ltd
Loake Bros Shoemakers – footwear – Loake Shoemakers
Loans Direct – The Woolwich
Lobkowicz – czech premium lager – Temple Wines Ltd
Lobro – Driveshafts & CV Products – G K N Driveline Services Ltd
Lobster – Gustair Materials Handling Equipment Ltd
Lobster – tennis ball machine – Sportsmark Group Ltd
LOC – Chaintec Ltd
Loc-Line – coolant hose – Filtermist International Ltd
***Loc Strip (Australia)** – movement control joint brass and neoprene – MFS Stone Surfaces Ltd
Localiner – curtain and door combination vehicle bodywork – Boalloy Industries Ltd
Locate – aluminium sign systems – Universal Components
Locator – marketing services – Research International Group Ltd
Locator B – labelling machine – Harland Machine Systems Ltd
***Lochinvar (Netherlands)** – water heaters – William May Ltd
Lochrin – fencing – William Bain Fencing Ltd
Lochrin Classic Rivetless – William Bain Fencing Ltd
Lochrin Palisading – steel fencing – William Bain Fencing Ltd
Lochshore – Scottish music – K R L
Locinox – Locks and Access Protection – Steel Product Supplies
LOCITE – Hydraulic & Offshore Supplies Ltd
LOCITITE – Hydraulic & Offshore Supplies Ltd
Lock & Leave – Lookers plc
Lock On Plus – Gates Hydraulics Ltd
Locker Air Maze – breathers – Bearwood Engineering Supplies
Lockhart – hotel and restaurant catering equipment – Bunzl Lockhart Catering Equipment
LOCKINEX – METAL BRACKETS – Alvin Industrial Limited
Lockinlyne – folding table system – Morgan Contract Furniture Ltd
Lockmaster – 24hr mobile security (locksmiths, safe openings safes & grilles) – Lockmasters Mobile Safes & Locks
Lockmaster – multi point locks – Paddock Fabrications Ltd
Locksafe – cash boxes – Helix Trading Ltd
Lockseam – stainless steel systems, doors, entrances and shopfronts – Stewart Fraser Ltd
Lockstone – dry build block walling with natural stone look – P H I Group Ltd
Locktile – Evertile Ltd
Lockwell – Quick release pins – Zygology Ltd
Locopulsor – railway wagon shunting machines – E G Steele & Co. Ltd
Loctite – adhesives – Arrow Supply Co. Ltd
Loctite – adhesives & compounds – Anglia
Loctite – Trafalgar Tools
Loctite – UK Office Direct
Loctite – Gem Tool Hire & Sales Ltd
Loctite – S J Wharton Ltd
Loctite (UK) – adhesives – R D Taylor & Co. Ltd
Lodding – paper machine doctors and doctor blades steam foils for moisture addition and curl control – Kadant UK Ltd
Loddon – internal partitions, hinged and sliding doors to form loose boxes; external stables, external doors for blockwork, portable horse pens, horse stocks and equestrian accessories, cattle handling and feeding equipment – Loddon Engineering Ltd
LODEMATIC – Hydraulic & Offshore Supplies Ltd
Lodexol – industrial gear oils – Morris Lubricants
Lodexol SS43 – semi synthetic gear oil – Morris Lubricants
Lodexol W – fully synthetic gear oil – Morris Lubricants
Lodge Cottrell – environmental engineering – Lodge Cottrell Ltd
Lodge (Furniture) Limited – Furniture & Furnishings for Landlords & Property Investors – Lodge Furniture Ltd
Lodge Tyre Co – tyres – Lodge Tyre
Loersch – slide mounting systems and accessories – Johnsons Photopia Ltd
Loewe – pipes – Cadogan
Loewy Robertson – spares – Bearwood Engineering Supplies
Lofco – mine car controller – Qualter Hall & Co. Ltd
Loft Ladders – Accesscaff International Ltd
Loftpan (United Kingdom) – access to loft space, loft hatch – Panelcraft Access Panels
Log Chop – wood guillotine – Brown's Agricultural Machinery Company Ltd
Logan Fenamec (UK) – materials handling equipment (conveyor systems) – Logan Teleflex UK Ltd
Loganair – airline transport company – Loganair Ltd
Logax – personal organisers, diaries, planners and promotional stationery items – Logax Ltd
Logic – lighting control – Premier Solutions Nottingham Ltd
Logic – digital console – A M S Neve Ltd
***Logic** – J Paterson & Sons
Logic 1 – digital console – A M S Neve Ltd
Logic 2 – digital console – A M S Neve Ltd
Logic 3 – digital console – A M S Neve Ltd
Logic Plus – plug sockets – M K Electric Ltd
Logica – indirect method of printing via silicone pad known as pad printers or tampographic printers – Tampographic Ltd
Logicator – rotary control logic series – A M S Neve Ltd
Logicolor – Astell Scientific Holdings Ltd
Logitech – UK Office Direct
LOGITRANS – Chaintec Ltd
Logo Bugs – Logo Bugs Plus Ltd
Logobears – soft toys (promotional) – Billbo UK Ltd
LogoBugs – Logo Bugs Plus Ltd
Lohal – electrical conduit – Icore International
Loheat – coldstore floor and door heating equip, control panels and pressure relief valves, dairy water heaters and hygiene equip and pressurised water systems and parlour wash down systems – Loheat
Lohmann – Gawler Tapes & Plastics Ltd
***Lohmann (Germany)** – repulpable splicing tape – Stokvis Tapes UK Ltd
Lohmann – B D K Industrial Products Ltd
Lohmann GB Limited – Lohmann GB Ltd
LOHMANN ISTOLTERFOKT – Hydraulic & Offshore Supplies Ltd
Lojiclean – glass lens and clean room wipe – Lojigma International Ltd
Lok-bilt – sectional prefabricated buildings – Boyton B R J System Buildings Ltd
LOK-FIT – Keyless Pulley Mounting Conical Rings – Francis and Francis Ltd
LOKOMEC – Hydraulic & Offshore Supplies Ltd
Lola Cars – racing cars – Lola Cars Ltd
LOLER – Stacatruc
Lollipop – phase seperator – Radleys
Lollipop Safety Stick – childrens safety lollipop stick – Papersticks Ltd
Lolode – King Vehicle Engineering Ltd
Lombardini – Harrier Fluid Power Ltd
Lombardini – A T Wilde & Son Ltd
LOMBARDINI – Hydraulic & Offshore Supplies Ltd
***Lombardini (Italy)** – marine diesel engines – Lancing Marine
LOMBARDINI ENGINES – Hydraulic & Offshore Supplies Ltd
Lomer – hiking and treking boots and shoes – UK Distributors Footwear Ltd
***Londina** – Donatantonio
London Badge & Button Co. (United Kingdom) – manufacturers of badges, buttons & cufflinks – Toye Kenning Spencer Stadden
London Cargo Centre – John Menzies plc
London City Airport – London City Airport Ltd
London Clock Co. – quartz mantel and wall clocks – L C Designs Ltd
London Electricity (LE) – suppliers of electricity – E D F Energy
London Fan Company – fans & impellers – Beatson Fans & Motors Ltd
London Jazz – Smooth Radio
London Linen Supply – Linen hire/launder for restaurants – London Linen Supply Ltd
London Man – map & guide – Francis Chichester Ltd
London Market Information Link – London Stock Exchange plc
London Wall – Lusso Interiors
London Woman – map & guide – Francis Chichester Ltd
London Workwear Rental – Supply and launder of chefswear to restaurants, leisure sector, qsr and casual dining sector. – London Linen Supply Ltd
Londonlink – coach service operations – First Bus
Lone Wolf B2B Telemarketing – B2B Telemarketing service – Lonewolf B2b Tele Marketing
LONERTIA – Spigot & Socket Flexible Couplings – Francis and Francis Ltd
Long – Harrier Fluid Power Ltd
Long Handled Sponges – Helping Hand Co.
Long Life – G.R.P. cold water storage tanks – Nicholson Plastics Ltd
Long Life Copy Safe – Atlantis European Ltd
Long-roger Giraffe – cranes – Panavision Grips Ltd
Longcliffe – lime & limestone products – Longcliffe Quarries Ltd
Longcote – liquid applied coatings – Chase Protective Coatings Ltd
***Longflame (Columbia)** – anthracite – Rudrumholdings
Longlast – clothes line – James Lever & Sons Ltd
Longley Systems – pre-stressed concrete – The Howard Group
Longlife – catering cookware – Samuel Groves
Longlife – Ascot Wholesale Ltd
Longlife – wear resistant coater blades – Uddeholm Steel Stockholders
Longlife – brushware – Harris Cleaning Services
Longlife 2505 – disinfectant – DuPont Animal Health Solutions
Longs – precision rubber rollers and tool kits – Longs Ltd
Longseal – range of waterproof membranes – Chase Protective Coatings Ltd
Longshoreman – waterproof clothing – J Barbour & Sons Ltd
***Longshot (United Kingdom)** – archery accessories, targets, bows, arrows, bags, quivers, bowstringers etc – Quicks Archery
Longspan – Shelving – Stormor Systems Ltd
***Longview (U.S.A.)** – keyboard video mouse PC server switches – Techland Group Ltd
Longwrap – petrolatum tapes and mastics – Chase Protective Coatings Ltd
Lonsdale – carpet – Cormar Carpets
Lonsto – security retail equipment – Lonsto Insternational Ltd
Lonsto Security – anti-theft shop security – Lonsto Insternational Ltd
Lonsto Systems – ticket queue management systems – Lonsto Insternational Ltd
Look – design spectacle frames – Look Designs Ltd
Look – roasting film and bags – Terinex Ltd
Look – I P C Media Ltd
Lookout – software product – National Instrument UK Corp Ltd
Loop-a-Line – Sebakmt UK Ltd
Loopies (United Kingdom) – play equipment/toys – Mike Ayres Design Ltd
Loos Boilers – Twin Industries International Ltd
Loot – publishers of free-ads paper – Loot Ltd
Loovent – toilet extractor units – Airflow Developments Ltd
Loquid Spray Polish – non-aerosol furniture spray polish – Premiere Products Ltd
Loramatic – vertical flaskless moulding machines – Ramsell Naber Ltd

Lorch – feather and fibre filling machines – Apropa Machinery Ltd
Lorenzo – cover paper – James Cropper plc
Lorenzo – cards – The Medici Galleries
Loretto – bottom roller gear for sliding cupboard doors – P C Henderson Ltd
***Lorlin Electronics (United Kingdom)** – switch & connector and power supply manufacturers – Lorlin Electronics Ltd
Loro & Parisini – crushing & screening plant – Metso Minerals UK Ltd
Loroch – machinery for grinding saws – Vollmer UK Ltd
LoSalt – Klinge Chemicals Ltd
***Loss of Weight** – weighing equipment – Procon Engineering Ltd
Lotader – ethylene acrylic ester and maleic anhydride terpolymers – Atosina UK Ltd
Lothian Buses – public transport – Lothian Buses plc
Lotracker – bottom supported cantilevered gate – Frontier Pitts Ltd
Lotryl – ethylene-acrylic ester copolymers – Atosina UK Ltd
Lotto – football kit – FOCUS International Ltd
Lotus – UK Office Direct
Lotus Pond Filters – Denton Pumps Ltd
Lotus Pond Pumps – Denton Pumps Ltd
Lotus Professional – janitorial and hygeine products – Ambassador Packaging Ltd
Lotuslyke – drinking fountain (N.B. valve and ware) – Sheardown Engineering Ltd
Louis Santini – Watches – K B Import & Export Ltd
Louvamatic – automatic opener for greenhouse louvre windows – Eden Halls Greenhouses Ltd
Louvolite – components and fabrics for window blinds – Louver-Lite
Louvrelite – vertical drapes – Guildford Shades
Lovato – control solutions for industry – Lovato UK Ltd
Lovatt & Rickett – manufrs & wholesalers of saddles to retailers – L & R Saddles Ltd
Lovejoy (U.S.A.) – flexible couplings – Lenze UK Ltd
Lovell – Workwear, woodturners smocks and joiners aprons – The Toolpost
Loveson – shoes and boots – Thomas H Loveday
Low-ap-Flow – Bronkhorst UK Ltd
Low Cost – mortgage scheme – Market Harborough Building Society
Low DP Flow – Bronkhorst UK Ltd
Low Foam – combined bactericidal neutral low foaming detergent – Premiere Products Ltd
Low Foam Cleaner – cleaner for use with scrubber and dryer combination machines – Evans Vanodine International plc
Low Maintenance PB4 – building system – Rollalong Ltd
Low Profile – ladies fashion – Low Profile
Low Salt – Klinge Chemicals Ltd
Lowara – Arun Pumps Ltd
Lowara – Pumps – Wendage Pollution Control Ltd
Lowara – Flow Mech Products Ltd
Lowara – Wyatt Bros Water Services Ltd
Lowara pumps – Anchor Pumps Co. Ltd
Lowes Financial Management Limited – financial advisors – Lowes Financial Management Ltd
Lowzone – wheelchair cushion – Helping Hand Co.
Loxford – radiological dose assessment film holders (dosemeters),wine and beer testers – Loxford Equipment Co. Ltd
Loxton Lighting – Light Fantastic
Loxtons Cuisine Sous-Vide – Loxton Foods
***Loxtons Heat and Serve** – Loxton Foods
Loxtons Ready-t-cook – Loxton Foods
Lozaron – a unique material compounded by schlegel for weatherseals and glazing gaskets – Schlegel UK
LPA 386 Prolog for DOS – AI programming language for DOS – Logic Programming Associates Ltd
LPA DataMite – data mining toolkit – Logic Programming Associates Ltd
LPA Flex – expert system development toolkit – Logic Programming Associates Ltd
LPA FLINT – fuzzy logic development toolkit – Logic Programming Associates Ltd
LPA Intelligence Server – prolog interface to other windows applications – Logic Programming Associates Ltd
LPA MacProlog – AI programming language for macintosh – Logic Programming Associates Ltd
LPA Prolog++ – object-orientated development toolkit – Logic Programming Associates Ltd
LPA Prolog for Windows – AI programming language for windows 3.1, windows 95 & windows NT – Logic Programming Associates Ltd
LPA ProWeb Server – for developing Web based server applications – Logic Programming Associates Ltd
LPU – sectional garage door – Hörmann (UK) Ltd
LSD – direct fired gas fired unit heater – Nordair Niche
LSD – direct fired gas fired unit heater – Nordair Niche
***LSF (Sweden)** – grinders – Atlas Copco Tools Ltd
Lsi Logic – Cyclops Electronics Ltd
***LSR (Sweden)** – grinders – Atlas Copco Tools Ltd
LT Architect – computer aided design software – Cadlogic Ltd
Lt Engineer – computer aided design software – Cadlogic Ltd
LT Structural – computer aided design software – Cadlogic Ltd
LTH – sectional garage door – Hörmann (UK) Ltd
LTM (United Kingdom) – low temperature curing epoxy resin material systems – Umeco
LTR – Hydraulic & Offshore Supplies Ltd
***LTS (Sweden)** – impact wrenches – Atlas Copco Tools Ltd
LTW – Selectronix Ltd
LTW - Honda Connectors - Methode - Stratos Lightwave - Foxconn - DCT - Woodhead - RJ-Lnxx - Circuit Assembly - SAIA Bugess - Switchcraft - Rectron - ACPA - Greenwich - Heito - Widmaier - Bogen Electronics - Hammond - Fibox - Phoenix Contact - Binder - Omron - Carlo Gavazzi - Otto MEC - Digisound - Kingbright - EBT - Tyco - Weiland - Amphenol - Madison - EMISTOP. – Selectronix Ltd
***Lu-Ve Contardo (Italy)** – coolers, evaporaters and condensers – H T G Trading Ltd
Lubar – bobbing greases – Lea Manufacturing Co.
Lube-Lok – E M Coating Services
Lubemaster – vehicle mounted lubrication service unit – Tecalemit Garage Equipment Co. Ltd
Lubeplus – Lubeline Lubricating Equipment
Luberfiner – Harrier Fluid Power Ltd
Lubesaf – Forward Chemicals Ltd
Lublue – UK Office Direct
LubriCurve (United Kingdom) – rail lubricators and lubricants – Q H I Group Ltd
Lubrilox – bulk polyester – Amann Oxley Threads Ltd
LUBRIZOL INTERNATIONAL LABORATORIES – Hydraulic & Offshore Supplies Ltd
Lubysil – metal cutting fluid – John Clayden & Partners Lubysil Ltd
Lucalor – chlorinated pvc – Atosina UK Ltd
Lucas – components for aircraft – Goodrich Control Systems
Lucas – automotive components – T R W Ltd
Lucas Bryce – fuel injection equipment for diesel engines – Woodward Diesel Systems
Lucent – Cyclops Electronics Ltd
Lucid – company trade name – LUCID PRODUCTIONS
Lucidol – benzoyl peroxide compositions – Akzo Nobel Chemicals Holdings Ltd
Lucifer – general purpose & refrigeration valves – Parker Hannifin UK plc
LUCIFER – Hydraulic & Offshore Supplies Ltd
Lucipal – benzoyl peroxide compositions – Akzo Nobel Chemicals Holdings Ltd
Luckins – electric & machenical manuals – Luckins
Lucky Shirt – games-designs – Europrint Promotions Ltd
Lucoi – electronic control software – Goodrich Control Systems
Lucy Cousins - Maisy – Chorion plc
Lucy Lighting – Low Voltage cutouts, isolator units, fuse units, sheet steel and cast iron pillars and associated equipment. – Lucy Switchgear
Lucy Oxford – electrical switchgear for utilities, contractors and industrial use – Lucy Switchgear
Lucy Switchgear – MV ground and pole mounted switchgear and automation soultions for utilities, contractors and industrial use. – Lucy Switchgear
LUDECKE – Hydraulic & Offshore Supplies Ltd
Ludlow – linecasting machines – L & M Ltd
Ludo – playground equipment – Russell Play Ltd
Ludox – colloidial silica – Du Pont UK Ltd
LUEN – Hydraulic & Offshore Supplies Ltd
***LUF (Sweden)** – screwdrivers – Atlas Copco Tools Ltd
Lufkin – measuring tapes and spirit levels – Apex Tools
Lugall – portable winch hoist – Metreel Ltd
LUGLI – Chaintec Ltd
Lugli – T V H UK Ltd
***Luigi Bormioli (Italy)** – Italian crystal glassware – Western House
Luisiana – delivery hose liquids and foodstuffs – Merlett Plastics UK Ltd
Lullaby – toddlers shoes – D Jacobson & Sons Ltd
Lulworth – high efficiency steel boilers – Hamworthy Heating Ltd
***LUM (Sweden)** – screwdrivers – Atlas Copco Tools Ltd
Lumaro – B P plc
***Lumat (Germany)** – label presence scanning system – Romaco Holdings UK Ltd
Lumatic – lubricating equipment, grease guns, grease nipples, pumps for oil and gear pumps – Lumatic Ga Ltd
Lumatic – grease guns, pumps for oil and grease – Stephens Midlands Ltd
Lumax – bulbs for specialised needs and car accessories – Ceag Ltd
Lumberg – connectors – Anglia
Lumberg – European Technical Sales Ltd
Lumberjack – polyurethane wood adhesives, wood repair products, wood protection products – Everbuild Building Products Ltd
Lumenition – ignition leads, ignition systems and fuel systems, rev limiters – Autocar Electrical Equipment Company Ltd
Lumenox – translucent plastic printed symbols or words for use on instrument panels – John Mcgavigan Ltd
Lumens – Lamphouse Ltd
Lumeter – Trafalgar Tools
Lumex – Cyclops Electronics Ltd
***Lumiglas (Germany)** – process lighting & sight windows – Visilume Ltd
***LUMILUX (Germany)** – triphospher flourescent tubes – Osram Ltd
Lumina – Money Controls Ltd
Lumineri – Lumineri
Lumineux – for lamps, tubes and bulbs, low energy saving lamps – MPW Group
Luminex – metallic coated cloth for ironing board covers – Lancashire Sock Manufacturing Co.
Luminos – Kurt J Lesker Company Ltd
Luminous Wall – high temperate gas-fired combustion system – Maywick Ltd
Lumisty – Architectural Window Films
Lumitex, Inc. – Review Display Systems Ltd
Lumitron – lighting – Lumitron Lighting Services Ltd
LUMIWALL – Artillus Illuminating Solutions Ltd
Lumo (United Kingdom) – low voltage lighting (interior vehicle) – Zodion Ltd
Lumopaque – G E Healthcare
Lumsden – spares & service for surface grinding machines – Lumsden Grinders Ltd
Lumsden – Red House Industrial Services Ltd
Luna – laboratory air conditioning – Luwa UK Ltd
Lunatack – hot melt adhesives – H B Fuller
Luncase – instrument cases – Lunds
Luncheon Vouchers – Accor Services
Lundesk – desk for electronics – Lunds
***Lune** – Bob Crosby Agencies Ltd
Lunex – Plastic and other household products – Lunex Ltd
Lunn Davis – keyseating machines – Lunn Engineering Co. Ltd
Lunrac – instrument racks and cubicles – Lunds
***Lupa** – Donatantonio
Luranyl – Resinex UK Ltd
Lureflash – fly dressing and fishing equipment – Lureflash International
Lustrana – leather – Andrew Muirhead & Son Ltd
Lustre – Osborn Unipol Ltd
Lustrol – leather – Andrew Muirhead & Son Ltd
Lutz – stone fixings and support – Halfen Ltd
Lutz – European Technical Sales Ltd
Luwa – air conditioning equipment – Luwa UK Ltd
Luxaflex – window blinds – Luxaflex
Luxalay – British Vita plc
Luxalon – ceilings, cladding and sun louvres etc – Luxaflex
Luxan – British Vita plc
Luxara – natural gums, stabilisers and gelling agents for food production – Arthur Branwell & Co. Ltd
Luxbond – British Vita plc
Luxbond Fibreblok – British Vita plc
Luxeon – Lamphouse Ltd
Luxia/NCE – catering equipment, glasswashers, dishwashers and icemakers cooking ranges – Luxia Catering Equipment
Luxico – lighting & lighting components – Coughtrie International Ltd
Luxigrips – cushion heelgrips – A Algeo Ltd
Luxina – the wholesale lamp co ltd – International Lamps & Components
Luxina - The Wholesale Lamp Co Ltd – International Lamps & Components
Luxine – scumble stain – Craig & Rose Ltd
Luxonic – lighting systems – Luxonic Lighting plc
LuxStar – precision laser welder – G S I Group Ltd
Luxury Mohair – yarns – Stylecraft
Luxus – Luxus Loft Conversions
Luxwol – British Vita plc
Luytex – fibre/polyester resin engineered compounds – Trelleborg Ceiling Solutions Ltd
LVD – Laser Trader Ltd
LVD – L V D UK Ltd
LVG Voucher Handling – Accor Services
Lycidas – tufted carpet – Brockway Carpets Ltd
Lycra – lightweight tights and shorts – Ronhill Sports
Lycra – spandex – Du Pont UK Ltd
Lydian – water emulsifiable solvent degreaser – Morris Lubricants
Lyftman – Tawi UK
Lynavane – single stage vertical in-line pumps – Weir Group Senior Executives Pension Trust Ltd
Lyndella – ladies dresses, separates & evening wear – Norman Linton Ltd

Lyndon – taps & dies – Tom Carrington & Co. Ltd
Lyndon – S J Wharton Ltd
Lynester – display systems – Signscape Systems Ltd
Lynn Wood Designs – domestic upholstered furniture – Lyn Plan Upholstery Ltd
Lynplan – taylored zip-on covers and re-upholstery – Lyn Plan Upholstery Ltd
Lynton Exhibition/Demonstration Trailers – exhibition/demonstration trailers – Lynton Trailers UK Ltd
Lynton Hydraulic Tipping Trailers – hydraulic tipping trailers – Lynton Trailers UK Ltd
Lynton Mobile Works Units – mobile works units, messrooms, offices, specials – Lynton Trailers UK Ltd
Lynton Vending Trailers – vending trailers, standard & custom built – Lynton Trailers UK Ltd
Lynwood – DIY and decorating products – Lynwood Products Ltd
Lynx – print inspection systems – Tectonic International Ltd
Lynx – Pressure washers – B & G Cleaning Systems Ltd
Lynx – connector for oil-well conductor pipe – Oil States Industries UK Ltd
Lynx – fast food equipment – Lincat Ltd
Lynx – Eyepieceless stereo viewer – Vision Engineering Ltd
Lyomaster – freeze dryers – Boc Gases Ltd
Lyons – UK Office Direct
Lyrantion 50% DPG – perfume speciality – Quest International UK Ltd
Lyrex – adjuvent oils – B P plc
Lyro – B P plc
Lyrol – B P plc
Lysander – tufted carpet – Brockway Carpets Ltd
Lyta – plasterers' hawk – Benson Industries Ltd
Lytag – building blocks – Interfuse Ltd
Lytatype – Kenex Electro Medical Ltd
Lytatype, Kenex, Cawo, Rothband, Wardray Premise, PREMAC – Kenex Electro Medical Ltd
Lyte – aluminium and glass fibre ladders and steps, light trade tower and roof ladder, industrial rope and push-up ladders – Lyte Industries Wales Ltd
Lyte Ladders – Accesscaff International Ltd
Lyte Towers – Accesscaff International Ltd
LYTEFLEX – Hydraulic & Offshore Supplies Ltd
Lytespan – electrical lighting track – W F Electrical
Lytespan 1,2,3 – track – Concord Marlin Ltd
Lytespan LP – track – Concord Marlin Ltd
Lytetube 75, 90 – linear systems – Concord Marlin Ltd
Lyteze – heat cutting and sealing appliances – Lyteze Products Ltd

M

M.50 – mortise deadlock – Assaabloy Group
M.52 – mortise sashlock – Assaabloy Group
M/A Com – Cyclops Electronics Ltd
M.A. Garton-Smith Exclusive Commissions – pen & ink pastel, oil, engraving, water colours andframing and period moulds, live event artist-known locally for capturing the atmosphere of an event in waterwear and unusual pastel technique – Rake 'N' Lift & Co - Nottingham Rakes UK Rakes Specialists
M-A-M – Traditional Italian Ovens – Target Catering Equipment
M.A.R.C. – Manufacturing and Retail Corporation - Global Procurement Specialists – M A R C Co GB Ltd
*M.A.S. (Czech Republic) – automatic lathes – Citizen Machinery UK Ltd
*M.A.S. (Switzerland) – microprocessor applications systems – European Drives & Motor Repairs
M and D Drainage – M & D Drainage Ltd
M. and M. – flannelette sheets – Pin Mill Textiles Ltd
*M and M Installations – Satellite Television Contractors
M.B. – games and puzzles – Hasbro UK Ltd
M B C – high performance locked stem blind rivet (aerospace industry) – Avdel UK Ltd
M.C. Transport Ltd – ABEKO (UK) Ltd
M.D. – knitwear – Marshall Deacon Knitwear Ltd
M D A – synthetic diamond - metalbond diamond abrasives – Diamond Detectors
M.D.B. – modular self cleaning fume and dust filtration unit – Plymovent Limited
M.D.E. – diving equipment – Midland Diving Equipment Ltd
M.D.S. – container lift legs – Joloda Hydraroll Ltd
M.D. Towers – Accesscaff International Ltd
M Dickerson – sand & gravel – Frimstone Ltd
M.E.L. – chemicals – M E L Chemicals
M.E.S. – marine evacuation systems – R F D Beaufort Ltd
M.F. – plastic packaging – Measom Freer Company
M F Promotions (United Kingdom) – I M S International Marketing Services Ltd
M. Filter – Harrier Fluid Power Ltd
M & G – M & G Group plc
M.G.C. Lamps – lamps – M G C Lamps

M.G. Duff – design and supply of cathodic protection – M G Duff International Ltd
M.G.G. Lamps – micro lamps – Partex Marking Systems UK Ltd
M & G Life – M & G Group plc
M.G.M. Assurance – life pensions and unit trusts – M G M Advantage
M.H.A. – low speed, high torque hydraulic motors (radial piston HYD motors) – P S S
M.I.D.8 Mastring – Mastring used for identification of anaerobic bacteria – The Mast Group Ltd
M.I.E. Power Generators – diesel generators – Turner E P S Ltd
M.I.H. – oil preheaters and immersion heaters – EXHEAT Ltd
*M.I. Joint (Australia) – mechanical movement joint (major joint) – MFS Stone Surfaces Ltd
M.I.L.S. – modular interlink system – Bribex
M. & J. – waste reducers – M M H Recycling Systems Ltd
*M. J. & A. Owen – Animalscan Ltd
M.K. – figure ice skates – John Wilson Skates and MK Blades
M.K.11 Rising Arm Barrier – Zeag UK Ltd
*M.L. Gatewood (U.S.A.) – needle jet nozzles – Pulp & Paper Machinery Ltd
M.L.R. 2 – fully synthetic racing oils – Morris Lubricants
M.L.R. 2 Stroke Engine Oils – racing developed engine oils – Morris Lubricants
M.L.R. 30. 40 & 50 – castor oil based engine oils – Morris Lubricants
M.L.R. 4 Stroke Engine Oil – fully synthetic multigrade motor oil developed from motor cycle racing technology – Morris Lubricants
M.L.R. Chain Lube – aerosol packed lubricant for motor cycle chains – Morris Lubricants
M.L.R. Light/Medium Gear Oil – fully synthetic gear oil – Morris Lubricants
M.L.R. Motor Cycle Products – gear oils, racing grease and brake fluid for motor cycles – Morris Lubricants
M.L.R. Premium 4 – synthetic fortified mineral engine oil – Morris Lubricants
M.L.R. Racing Brake Fluid – high boiling brake fluid – Morris Lubricants
M.L.R. Racing Grease – greases for severe driving conditions – Morris Lubricants
M@LDI HT (United Kingdom) – Benchtop MALDI-TOF-MS – Waters
M. les Mutuelles du Mans – assurances – M M A Insurance plc
M. Lodge & Son – import textiles – M Lodge & Son
M & M – Stacatruc
*M. & M. (Switzerland) – spinning machines – Embassy Machinery Ltd
M&M – Southern Valve & Fitting Co. Ltd
M.M.900 – data logging equipment – Ele International
M.M.950 – data logging equipment – Ele International
M.M.D. – mineral sizing and crushing machines – M M D Mining Machinery Developments
M. & M. Redhead – forwarding agents – Redhead Freight Ltd
M/ntrx – Continental Disc UK Ltd
M.P.10 – less concentrated multi-purpose cleaner – Premiere Products Ltd
M.P.9 – concentrated multi-purpose cleaner – Premiere Products Ltd
M.P.C. Series – plastic pool pumps – Calpeda Ltd
M.P.M.S. – maintenance management software – Microsystems Technology
M.P.S.I. – computer software and information services – M P S I Systems Ltd
M.P.W. – mains adaptors, power supplies and transformers – MPW Group
M-Power – Measurement products, rules, squares – The Toolpost
M-Pro – terminals – Anglia
M.Q. Lubricant – cavity lining products – Prima Dental Group Ltd
M.R. – paints, sundries, and wallcoverings – Dulux Ltd
M.R.E. 557 – conveyor belt fasteners and machines – Mato Industries Ltd
M.R.P. – trucks, trolleys, trailers and mobile safety steps – M R P Trucks & Trolleys
M.R.T.T. – aerial towed target systems – Eaton Aerospace Ltd
M.S. – automatic voltage stabilisers – Claude Lyons Ltd
M.S.E. – modular supply equipment – Nuaire Ltd
M.S.E. Mistral Centrifuges – micro-bench-top general purpose refrigerated and floor standing refrigerated – Sanyo Gallenkamp plc
M.SP Ltd – Agricultural merchants – Mccreath Simpson & Prentice Ltd
M.S.S. – grooving systems, turning and threading – Ceratizit UK Ltd
M S T – Matsuura Machinery Ltd
M Series Balancer – Gustair Materials Handling Equipment Ltd
M.T.E. – commercial vehicle body builders – Massey Truck Engineering Ltd

M.T.S. 1000 – single phase meter tester – Northern Design Ltd
M.T.S. 3000 – 3 phase meter tester – Northern Design Ltd
M-Tec – P F T Central
M-Tec – C E S Hire Ltd
M@trix/Matrix – Suite of management programs – Gang-Nail
M-Type – fixed output, high flow pump – Grosvenor Pumps Ltd
M.U. Universal – master batch – Ampacet UK
M.V.C. – automatic voltage stabilisers – Claude Lyons Ltd
M.V.I. – mercury vapour indicator – Shawcity Ltd
M.V.X. – continuous compounding of rubber preblends – Farrel Ltd
*M. Von Othegraven (Germany) – German wines – O W Loeb & Co. Ltd
M.W. – chain mortice gear – M W Equipment
M W P – MWP Advanced Manufacturing
M Wolf (Germany) – high output horizontal and vertical transfer machines – Haesler Machine Tools
M.X.H. – horizontal multi-stage stainless steel pumps – Calpeda Ltd
M.X.S. – submersible multi-stage stainless steel pumps – Calpeda Ltd
M.X.V. – vertical multi-stage stainless steel pumps – Calpeda Ltd
M1 (United Kingdom) – ECi Software Solutions Limited
M20 – Telemetry outstation sewage pumping stations – Halcyon Solutions
M26 boron nitride – Precision Ceramics
M40 – Telemetry outstation sewage pumping stations – Halcyon Solutions
M5 – Thermo Electrical
M6 – Thermo Electrical
M98 – Full Face Respirators – Scott International Ltd
MA1020 – I T W Plexus
MA1021 – I T W Plexus
MA1023 – I T W Plexus
MA1025 – I T W Plexus
MA300 – I T W Plexus
MA310 – I T W Plexus
MA320 – I T W Plexus
MA3940 – I T W Plexus
MA3940LH – I T W Plexus
MA403 – I T W Plexus
MA420 – I T W Plexus
MA422 – I T W Plexus
MA425 – I T W Plexus
MA550 – I T W Plexus
MA556 – I T W Plexus
MA557 – I T W Plexus
MA615 – Mobile Applications Ltd
MA820 – I T W Plexus
MA821 – I T W Plexus
MA822 – I T W Plexus
MA922 – I T W Plexus
MA925 – I T W Plexus
MAAC (U.S.A.) – metal amino acid chelate – Thomson & Joseph Ltd
MAAC, Metalosate Foliar. – Thomson & Joseph Ltd
Maban – scottish knitwear – R A Young & Abercairn Of Scotland Ltd
Mabel Lucy Atwell – Chorion plc
Mabey – bridging – Mabey Holdings Ltd
Mablex – Resinex UK Ltd
Mac – throat lozenges – Ernest Jackson & Co. Ltd
MAC – Hydraulic & Offshore Supplies Ltd
Mac-Electrodes – welding electrodes – M W A International Ltd
mac tac avery – signmaking vinyl – The Vinyl Corporation
Mac-Trode – welding electrodes – M W A International Ltd
MAC Valves – ball valves – Weir Valves & Controls
Macadamat – macadam and polyethylene mesh for erosion control – Colas Ltd
MacBarcoda – software for originating bar codes as EPS files on Apple MacIntosh – Computalabel International Ltd
Macbro Services – electrical maintenance – Mcdonald Brown & Facilities Ltd
Macco – Coffeetech
Maccstone – Macclesfield Stone Quarries Ltd
Maccurat – B P plc
MacDonald – Trafalgar Tools
MACDONALD COUPLINGS – Hydraulic & Offshore Supplies Ltd
MacDonald Lindsay Pindar – print and electronic media specialists – Pindar plc
MacDoor – sectional doors – B I S Door Systems Ltd
Maceal – perfume speciality – Quest International UK Ltd
Macer 8 – standardised carbohydrate enzymes for natural product extraction – Biocatalysts Ltd
Macfarlanes – solicitors – Macfarlanes
MacFormat – magazine – Future Publishing Ltd
MacFS – reads & writes mac discs and acorn risc computers – Xara Ltd
Macgas – B P plc

MacGregor Global Services – Hydraulic and pipework services – Cargotec UK Ltd

*Machery-Nagel (Germany) – chromatography equipment – Camlab Ltd

Machin – aluminium conservatories and canopies – Amdega Ltd

Machinagraph – engraving, etching, screen printing and anodising – Machinagraph Ltd

Machine Dishwashing Liquid – liquid dishwashing detergent – Premiere Products Ltd

Machine Dishwashing Powder – dishwashing detergent with high alkalinity – Premiere Products Ltd

Machine Mart – retail outlet of powered equipment – Machine Mart

Machinery manufrs – K-Tron Great Britain Ltd

machines4sale.co.uk – web site name – Machines4sale

Machsize – Nairda Ltd

MacIntyre – chocolate refinery – Ladco

MacIntyre Chocolate Systems – Used since 1832 – MacIntyre Chocolate Systems Ltd

Macipump – centrifugal sewage pumps – The Haigh Group Ltd

*Mack – Berthoud Sprayers

Mack – Harrier Fluid Power Ltd

Mack – Team Overseas Ltd

Mackay's of St Andrews – golf themed food gift range – Mackays Ltd

Mackridge – roof vent – McKenzie Martin Ltd

Mackwell – emergency lighting modules, inverters, batteries and electronic products – Mackwell Electronics Ltd

Maclean Lighting – lighting fixtures and fittings – Maclean Electrical

Macnaught – Hydrotechnik UK Ltd

MACNAUGHT – Hydraulic & Offshore Supplies Ltd

Maco – automatic bandsaw – Prosaw Ltd

*Macofar (Italy) – powder filling systems; sterile lines – Romaco Holdings UK Ltd

Macomeudon – Harrier Fluid Power Ltd

Macor – Precision Ceramics

Macpactor – steel landfill compactor wheels – Bernard Mccartney Ltd

MacPhails – malt Scotch whisky – Gordon & Macphail

MacRoberts – solicitors – Macroberts LLP

Macroclean – cleaning pads – Denis Rawlins Ltd

Macron – 45 Kg industrial dryer – Electrolux Laundry Systems

Macronix – Cyclops Electronics Ltd

Macronix – M S C Gleichmann UK Ltd

Macsoft – wire tube strip bending machines – Bennett Mahler

Macstream – roof extract unit – McKenzie Martin Ltd

Mactac Imagin – Digital Products - Toner Sheet Fed - Self Adhesive – Howard Smith Paper Ltd

MacThermal – software for printing labels on reels via thermal printers from Apple MacIntosh – Computalabel International Ltd

Macwax – British Vita plc

*Madal (Spain) – Manufacture & distribute of air defusion – Tek Ltd

Madam's Choice – knitwear – Novinit Ltd

MADAN – Hydraulic & Offshore Supplies Ltd

Madan Pumps – hydraulic/pneumatic madan air operated pumps – Hydraulic Pneumatic Services

*Mademer (Brazil) – solid pine doors – Price & Pierce Softwoods Ltd

Madgecourt – curtain tapes, dress and upholstery trimmings – Madgecourt Curtains

Madico – Architectural Window Films

Madico - Opalux - V-Kool - Lumisty – Architectural Window Films

*Madison (Far East) – cycle accessories – Madison

*Madison – Selectronix Ltd

Madrigal – Turner Bianca

Maedler – European Technical Sales Ltd

Maelor – medical regulators and flowmeters – Wescol

Maersk – shipping – The Maersk Company UK Ltd

Maersk Line – shipping – The Maersk Company UK Ltd

Maestro – desktop telephones – Nortel Networks UK Ltd

Maestro – darts – Unicorn Products Ltd

Maestro Pallet – Linpac Allibert Ltd

Maestrowave – Ascot Wholesale Ltd

Mafco – motor spares and accessories – M & F Components

Mafill – Resinex UK Ltd

Maflex – Resinex UK Ltd

Maflowline – corrosion control wrapping tape – Chase Protective Coatings Ltd

Maflowrap – corrosion control wrapping tape – Chase Protective Coatings Ltd

*Mag-Edge – flexible self-adhesive magnetic tape – Anchor Magnets Ltd

Mag-Lite – UK Office Direct

*MAG.NET – Hocaps Ltd

MAG - TECH LIMITED – Fire alarms – Mag-Tech

Mag Vac – Anchor Magnets Ltd

MAG01/MAG01H – fluxgate magnetometers – Bartington Instruments Ltd

MAG01H – fluxgate declinometer/inclinometer – Bartington Instruments Ltd

MAG03MC/MAG03MS – three axis magnetic field sensors – Bartington Instruments Ltd

MAG03MSS – submersible three axis magnetic field sensor – Bartington Instruments Ltd

MAG03RC – three axis range magnetometer – Bartington Instruments Ltd

MAGANESE – Hydraulic & Offshore Supplies Ltd

Magazon – magnetic particle inspection benches and systems – Baugh & Weedon Ltd

MAGDACC – Hydraulic accumulator for compact remote telemetry stored volume indication and control – Pulsation Dampers At Pulseguard Ltd

Magelis – human machine interface equipment – Schneider

Magellan – organic synthesiser for new drug discovery – H T Z Ltd

Magellan – packet switches and network access products – Nortel Networks UK Ltd

Maggi – Central C N C Machinery Ltd

*Magiboards (United Kingdom) – white writing boards, flip charts, hanging rail systems, copy boards, pinboards, sign and display, planning systems, pens and accessories – Magiboards Ltd

Magic – UK Office Direct

Magic – Proplas International Ltd

Magic – files, tools, steels – Hill Cliffe Garage

Magic Box – sprayer computer – Cleanacres Machinery Ltd

Magic Letters – Vtech Electronics UK plc

Magic Platforms – Accesscaff International Ltd

Magic Power Technology Ltd – Standard and custom low voltage power supply solutions from Taiwan – Photon Power Technology Ltd

Magicard – ID Card Printer Manufacturer – Plastic ID

Magicfit – hosiery – Gregory Pollard Ltd

*Magikitch'n – Chargrills – Middleby UK Ltd

Maginin – Lamphouse Ltd

*Magis – Pira Ltd

Maglease – fire release – Clarke Instruments Ltd

Magline – Flowserve

MAGLINER – Chaintec Ltd

Maglite – high activity magnesium oxides – Omya UK Ltd

Maglite – Gem Tool Hire & Sales Ltd

Maglock – switches – Bearwood Engineering Supplies

Magmex – Omex Environmental Ltd

Magmo – Plenty Mirrlees Pumps

MAGMO – Plenty Mirrlees Pumps

MAGNA – Grundfos Pumps Ltd

Magna – general lubrication and special purpose grades – Castrol UK Ltd

Magna – radio frequency drying and heating equipment – Strayfield Ltd

Magna Interior Systems – PU trim components – Magna Exteriors & Interiors Ltd

Magna-Sight – magnifiers – Time Products UK Ltd

Magnabond – water based chemical binder – Magna Industrials Ltd

Magnacote – refractory cements – Magna Industrials Ltd

Magnacryl – pigmented acrylic resin universal tinters – Tennants Inks & Coating Supplies Ltd

Magnacut – disposable knive system – Bright Instrument Co. Ltd

Magnafleet SHPD – super high performance diesel oil – Millers Oils Ltd

Magnaflow – felt tip marker – Office Depot UK

Magnaflux – magnetic crack detection – Magnaflux

MagnaGear XTR – Gears – Baldor UK

Magnaglo – fluorescent magnetic inks – Magnaflux

Magnakyd – pigmented long oil decorative alykd preparations – Tennants Inks & Coating Supplies Ltd

Magnaloy – Couplings – Sprint Engineering & Lubricant

Magnamal – monolithic linings – Magna Industrials Ltd

Magnapaque – G E Healthcare

Magnaprint – chemical for the textile printing industry – Magna Colours Ltd

Magnarange – radio frequency drying and heating equipment – Strayfield Ltd

Magnaset – pigmented high colour concentrates – Tennants Inks & Coating Supplies Ltd

Magnastart – slipring motor starter – Adwel International Ltd

Magnasyn Tape – magnetic tape – Newall Measurement Systems Ltd

Magnatrol (U.S.A.) – heavy duty solenoid valves – Zoedale plc

Magnatube – radio frequency drying and heating equipment – Strayfield Ltd

Magnecol – water testing tablets – Palintest Ltd

Magnesium Sulphate Crystals – Harris Hart & Co. Ltd

Magnesium Sulphate Dryed Powder – Harris Hart & Co. Ltd

Magnesium Sulphate Exsiccated Powder – Harris Hart & Co. Ltd

*Magnesol – Filter aid – Fast International Inc

Magnet – brand glass paper – Naylors Abrasives

Magnet – jointing – J A Harrison & Co Manchester Ltd

Magnetek – European Drives & Motor Repairs

Magnetic AutoControl (Germany) – Traffic and pedestrian control barriers Importer – Electro Mechanical Systems (EMS) Ltd

Magnetic Paper – Abel Magnets Ltd

*Magnetic Technologies – permanent magnet brakes – Huco Dynatork

Magnetix – DC/DC convertors & inductors – Anglia

*Magnetoflex (Germany) – malleable permanent magnet – Rolfe Industries

Magnetone – sounders – Anglia

Magnia – WC – Armitage Shanks Ltd

*Magnier – Rotary screen cleaners – B D C Systems

MagniF – Minelco Ltd

*Magnifer (Germany) – non-ferrous metals – Thyssenkrupp V D M UK Ltd

Magnifin – flame retardant magnesium hydroxide fillers – Omya UK Ltd

Magnifol – foliar fertilizer for agricultural crops – Landowner Liquid Fertilizers Ltd

MagnifyB – Online Marketing and Website Management – Magnify B

Magnochem – K S B Ltd

Magnol – motor/tractor oils – Morris Lubricants

Magnum – Resinex UK Ltd

Magnum (United Kingdom) – tension control disc brake – Twiflex Ltd

Magnum – protective and safety wear – Lincoln Electric UK Ltd

Magnum – large stainless steel catering sinks – Franke Sissons Ltd

Magnum – high levelling, fast bright nickel process – Cookson Electronics Ltd

Magnum (U.S.A.) – shock absorbers for industrial use – Ace Controls International

Magnum – humane slaughtering equipment – Accles & Shelvoke Ltd

Magnum - tension control disc brake. Mistral - tension control disc brake. Wichita - disc brakes. Metana - hydraulic caliper brake. Modevo - tension control disc brake. – Twiflex Ltd

magnus – stacker cranes – T G W Ltd

MAGNUS – Hydraulic & Offshore Supplies Ltd

MAGNUS Imprints – personalised Christmas cards – Rupert Magnus Trading Co. Ltd

Magnus Power – Manufacturer of Power supplies and frequency converters – Magnus Power

Magpie – waste glass disposal – Amcor Flexibles

Magplastic – Proplas International Ltd

Magpowr – Motion Drives & Controls Ltd

Magsi – type – Pryor Marking Technology Ltd

Magstim 200 – magnetic nerve stimulator – Magstim Co. Ltd

Magstim 220 – magnetic nerve stimulators – Magstim Co. Ltd

Magstim 250 – magnetic nerve stimulators – Magstim Co. Ltd

Magstim Rapid – magnetic nerve stimulators – Magstim Co. Ltd

Magtrak – respiratory flow sensor and monitor – Enspire Health

MAHLE – Hydraulic & Offshore Supplies Ltd

Mahle – European Technical Sales Ltd

Mahle Purolator – Harrier Fluid Power Ltd

*Maho (Germany) – CNC milling and drilling machines, horizontal, vertical and universal machining centres – D M G UK Ltd

*Maidaid Halcyon – Brewer & Bunney

*Maidaid-Halcyon – Maidaid Halcyon

Maidenese – artificial silk fabrics and garments – John Maden & Sons Ltd

Maidline – cruising holidays – Richardsons Stalham Ltd

Maidstone KM Extra – newspaper – Kent Messenger Group Ltd

*Maier-Unitas (Germany) – knife grinding machine sewing parts – Triumph Needle Co. Ltd

Mail Miser – bubble lined postal bags – Jiffy Packaging Company Ltd

Mail on Sunday, The – newspapers – Associated Newspapers

*Mail Room (U.S.A.) – document imaging-management software – Techland Group Ltd

Mailer Matt Extra – Coated Paper – Mcnaughton James Paper Group Ltd

Mailforce 1 – Telescopic sloping through the wall mailbox – Safety Letter Box Company Ltd

Mailforce 2 – Telescopic through the wall mailbox – Safety Letter Box Company Ltd

Mailforce 3 – Lateral through the wall mailbox – Safety Letter Box Company Ltd

Mailite – postal bags – A Latter & Co. Ltd

Mailmaster – inserting machine – K A S Paper Systems Ltd

Main Agents for John Deere – Tractors/Combines – Paul Tuckwell Ltd

Main Ring – horse feed – Rumenco Ltd
Main Road (Sheet Metal) Ltd – sheet metalwork and fabrications – Main Road Sheet Metal Ltd
Maine – Storage – Bucon Ltd
Mainetti (UK) Ltd – garment hangers & accessories – Mainetti UK Ltd
Mainline – mains frequency melting equipment – Inductotherm Europe Ltd
Mainman – B P plc
Mainmast Books – international maritime booksellers – Focal Point Audio Visual Ltd
Mainmet – domestic heat meter systems – Switch2 Energy Solutions
Mainspray – internal pipe sealing systems – A L H Systems Ltd
Mainstay – Emmerson Doors Ltd
Mainstay – electrical switchboard safety matting – Jaymart Roberts & Plastics Ltd
Mainstay – cod liver oil – Seven Sea's Ltd
Maintenance Cleaner – general maintenance and spray cleaning – Evans Vanodine International plc
***Maison Champy (Burgundy)** – Pol Roger Ltd
Maisonneuve – furnishing fabrics – Maisonneuve & Co.
Majestic – O P Chocolate Ltd
Majestic – shower doors, enclosures, specials, bath screens and steam enclosures – Majestic Shower Co
Majestic – bottom roller gear for patio, showroom and interior doors – P C Henderson Ltd
Majestic Wilton Velvet – carpets - wilton – Brintons Carpets Ltd
***Major** – Berthoud Sprayers
Major Demi-Glace – Major International Ltd
Major Mari-Base – Major International Ltd
Major Stock Base – Major International Ltd
Majorca – footwear – Whyte & Son Nottingham Ltd
Makaton – language programmes for children & Adults with communication difficulties – The Makaton Charity
Makaurite – masonry paints – T & R Williamson Ltd
Make to Order Manufacture – Topaz Computer Systems Ltd
Makfil system srl – cable cut and stripping and crimping machines – Automated Cable Solutions Ltd
Making Computers Easy I.T - Visulizing – Computer Repair Teaching you how to use computers and programs Help recover files 24hrs Repair – Making Computers Easy I.T - Visulizing
Making Contact – printed publications – Nortel Networks UK Ltd
Making the link – Making the Link
Makino – European Technical Sales Ltd
Makino – Red House Industrial Services Ltd
Makino – Harrier Fluid Power Ltd
Makita – Gem Tool Hire & Sales Ltd
Makita – S J Wharton Ltd
Makita – Dickies Workwear
Makita – Wessex Welding & Industrial Supplies Ltd
Makita – power tools – Campbell Miller Tools Ltd
Makita – power tools – Brilec Power Tools Ltd
Makita – Knighton Tool Supplies
Makita – Global Fasteners Ltd
Makita – industrial power tools – Makita UK Ltd
Makita – power tools – Arrow Supply Co. Ltd
Makita – D D Hire
Makita – Oxon Fastening Systems Ltd
Makita – Fieldway Supplies Ltd
Makita – Power Tools – Linacre Plant & Sales Ltd
***Makita (Japan)** – electric & cordless power tools – Harrow Tool Co. Ltd
Makro – Supply Chain Solution Ltd
Makrolon – Sunlight Plastics Ltd
Makroswing – transparent, rigid traffic doors – Envirohold Ltd
Malabar – The Winnen Furnishing Company
Maldive – radiators – Novellini UK Ltd
Malem Alarm – enuresis (bedwetting) alarm, cures bedwetting) – Malem Medical
Malesert – self-tapping male threaded inserts for plastic – Tappex Thread Inserts Ltd
Malham – bricks – Ibstock Brick Ltd
Malham Blend – Ibstock Brick Ltd
Malkyl – Forward Chemicals Ltd
***Mall Herlan (Germany)** – collapsible tube machinery – Pearson Panke Ltd
***Mallein (France)** – textile beams and cloth rolls – Pilkingtons Ltd
Mallmaster – supermarket trolley castors – Flexello Ltd
Malloy – Cogne UK Ltd
Malmo – Vanity unit – Armitage Shanks Ltd
Maloney (U.S.A.) – pipeline equipment – Alexander Cardew Ltd
Maloto Property Consultants Ltd – Chartered Surveyors – Maloto Property Consultants Ltd
Maloya – tyre and rubber products – Vredestein UK Ltd
Malroy – ironing tables, shopping trolleys, kitchen stools, step stools, shelf brackets, folding tables, breakfast bar stools and radiator shelves – Malroy Products Dudley Ltd
Malt Cob – malted brown bread concentrate – E D M E Ltd
***Malteser (Germany)** – manicure implements – John O'Donnell Ltd
Maltflaven – essence for vinegar alternative – Drywite Ltd
Malton & Pickering Mercury – newspaper – Yorkshire Regional Newspapers Ltd
Maltone – dark fine malt flour – E D M E Ltd
Maltron – ergonomic computer keyboards – P C D Maltron Ltd
Malvern – testing equipment – Bearwood Engineering Supplies
Malvern – Ruxley Manor Garden Centre
Malvern cubicles – Fast-track – Cubicle Centre
Malvern Instruments – Malvern Instruments Ltd
***Mamas & Papas (Italy)** – distribution of nursery goods and toys – Mamas & Papas (Stores) Ltd
Mamiya – medium format cameras and accessories – Johnsons Photopia Ltd
Mamut – Business Software Solution – Synergiq
Man to Man – cosmetics and perfumery – Bodywise Ltd
MAN TRUCKS – Bailey Morris Ltd
Management Consultants to Industry – Bourton Group Ltd
Management Forum (United Kingdom) – conference, seminars, event managemnt and e-learning – Management Forum
Management of Change – Bourton Group Ltd
Manalox – aluminium organics for printing inks and water repellents – Rhodia Ltd
Manchester Conference Centre (United Kingdom) – city centre conference venue – The Manchester Conference Centre
Manchester Evening News – newspapers – Middleton Guardian
Manchester Informatics Ltd – IT consultancy and support services to the industrial community – University Of Manchester Incubator Company Ltd
Manchester Innovation – technology for licence – University Of Manchester Incubator Company Ltd
Manchester Morning Metro – newspapers – Middleton Guardian
Manchester United – magazine – Future Publishing Ltd
Mancini – The Winnen Furnishing Company
MANCON – fully automatic stretch wrapping machines – M J Maillis UK Ltd
Mandalay – roll-form round stud rubber flooring – Jaymart Roberts & Plastics Ltd
Mandarin – design and commercial photography – Mandarin Creative Solutions Ltd
Mandolite 550 – fireproofing cementitious plaster (offshore work) – Promat UK Ltd
Mandolite CP2 – fireproofing cementitious plaster – Promat UK Ltd
Mandricote – paper – Fenner Paper Co. Ltd
Manebar – propeller shaft seal – Deep Sea Seals Ltd
Manebrace – propeller shaft seal – Deep Sea Seals Ltd
Manecraft – propeller shaft seal – Deep Sea Seals Ltd
Maneguide – rudder stock seal – Deep Sea Seals Ltd
Manesafe – bulkhead seal – Deep Sea Seals Ltd
Maneseal – propeller shaft seal, stern shaft, line shaft and thrust bearings – Deep Sea Seals Ltd
Manesty – pharmaceutical, tablet presses and coaters and tablet tooling, fluid bed equipment – Manesty
Maneurop – Therma Group
Maneurop – hermetic compressors and condensing units (blue star) – Thermofrost Cryo plc
Manex – exhaust clips – Norma UK Ltd
Manfield – shoes, sandals & boots – D Jacobson & Sons Ltd
Mangar Air Flow Compressor – power source – Mangar International Ltd
Mangar Bathlift – powered elevating bathing seat – Mangar International Ltd
Mangar Booster – multi-purpose lifter with powered elevating seat – Mangar International Ltd
Mangar ELK – lightweight portable powered emergency floor lift – Mangar International Ltd
Mangar Freestyle and Freestyle Junior – powered elevating wheelchair – Mangar International Ltd
Mangar Handy Pillow Lift – pneumatic powered lift – Mangar International Ltd
Mangar Leg Lifter/Cotside – powered pneumatic lifts legs into bed & doubles as a cot – Mangar International Ltd
Mangar Leg Support – powered pneumatic elevating fits any chair or wheelchair – Mangar International Ltd
Mangar Lifting Cushion – pneumatic powered aid to enable standing up – Mangar International Ltd
Mangar Porter – attendant operated mobile chair with different seating backrests – Mangar International Ltd
Mangar School Porter – mobile chair with powered elevating seat for the less mobile – Mangar International Ltd
Mangar Situp – people lift & turning – Mangar International Ltd
Mangar Surf Bather – prevents moving & handling risks – Mangar International Ltd
Mangar Therapy Wedge – moving handling & transfer of children at floor level for treatment & floor exercises – Mangar International Ltd
Mangaroo – portable battery powerpack – Mangar International Ltd
Manhattan – boats – Sunseeker Poole Ltd
Manhattan – web tracking product – Technical Direct Ltd
Manhattan II – software (property management) – Raindrop Information Systems Ltd
Manhattan Series 5 Bathrooms – Manhattan Furniture
Manhattan Series 7 Kitchens – 60 door styles ranging from simple square edged melamine to top of the range solid wood and handpainted finishes – Manhattan Furniture
Manhole Buddy – Magnetic Manhole Cover Lifter – PWM Distribution
Mani-Flow – Bronkhorst UK Ltd
Maniaccess – Manitou Site Lift Ltd
Manilec – Manitou Site Lift Ltd
***Maniloader (France)** – fork lift trucks – Manitou Site Lift Ltd
***Maniscopic (France)** – fork lift trucks – Manitou Site Lift Ltd
Manista – hand cleanser – Comma Oil & Chemicals Ltd
Manita – textile articles – Dryer & Hoffman Ltd
Manitou – A T Wilde & Son Ltd
***Manitou (France)** – fork lift trucks – Manitou Site Lift Ltd
Manitou – Mawsley Machinery Ltd
Manitou – Harrier Fluid Power Ltd
Manitou – Stacatruc
Manitou – T V H UK Ltd
Manitou – fork lift trucks – Service Engines Newcastle Ltd
manitou industrial handling equipment – telescopic forklifts – F T M Materials Handling Ltd
Manitou Platforms – Accesscaff International Ltd
***Manitou Telescopic Handlers** – Murley Agricultural Supplies Ltd
Manitransit – Manitou Site Lift Ltd
MANITU – Chaintec Ltd
Mankind – cosmetics and perfumery – Bodywise Ltd
Manley – medical ventilator – Space Labs Healthcare
Mann & Hummel – Harrier Fluid Power Ltd
Manna – textile articles excluding tablecloths – Dryer & Hoffman Ltd
Manner (Finland) – quality castors – Effortec Ltd
Mannesmann Demag – European Drives & Motor Repairs
MANNESMANN REXROTH – Hydraulic & Offshore Supplies Ltd
Manomet – metal organic compounds – Rhodia Ltd
Manor – living flame effect fire – Indesit Company UK Ltd
Manor – paints – Manor Coating Systems
Manor – filter plate press – Ashbrook Simon Hartley Ltd
Manor B.F. – living flame effect fire – Indesit Company UK Ltd
Manor E.F. – living flame effect fire – Indesit Company UK Ltd
Manor P.F. – living flame effect fire – Indesit Company UK Ltd
Manosec – driers for paints and inks – Rhodia Ltd
Manosperse – predispersed sulphur for rubber – Rhodia Ltd
Manoverboard – marine lifebuoy marker – Pains Wessex Ltd
ManPharm – Development of pharmaceutical and healthcare technologies – University Of Manchester Incubator Company Ltd
Manpower – Oceaneering Asset Integrity
Manro – chemicals – Stepan UK Ltd
***Manrose (Spain)** – domestic ventilation fans and equipment – Manrose Manufacturing Ltd
Mansafe (United Kingdom) – fall arrest system – Latchways plc
Mansafe – Safety Works & Solutions Ltd
Mansell – building contractors – Mansell Construction Services Ltd
Manser (Switzerland) – CNC slotting machines – Haesler Machine Tools
Mansion – bottom roller gear for sliding windows and interior doors – P C Henderson Ltd
Manta – electronic security seals (rfid) – Unisto Ltd
Manta - C2K – Unisto Ltd
Mantair – below ground packaged sewage treatment plants – Mantair
Mantis – application development software – Cincom Systems UK Ltd
Mantis – First Impressions Europe Ltd
Mantis – Team Corporation UK Ltd
Mantis – Optical viewers – Vision Engineering Ltd
Mantra – plant management software – B M S Technology Ltd
***Manuel Rodriguez (Spain)** – guitars – John Hornby Skewes & Co. Ltd
Manufacture hydraulic bolt tensioning equipment – Tentec Ltd
***Manuli (Italy)** – hydraulic hose and fittings – Hydrasun Ltd
MANULI – Hydraulic & Offshore Supplies Ltd
Manuli – Tri Pack Supplies Ltd
MANULI HAYDRAULICS – Hydraulic & Offshore Supplies Ltd
MANULI HOSE & FITTINGS – Hydraulic & Offshore Supplies Ltd

Manuli Hydraulics – Trafalgar Tools
MANULI POWERTEAM – Hydraulic & Offshore Supplies Ltd
Manumix – manual shower mixer – Sheardown Engineering Ltd
Manumold – Red House Industrial Services Ltd
Manurhin – Red House Industrial Services Ltd
Manurhin – Whitehouse Machine Tools Ltd
Manx Independent Carriers – Isle of Mans Premier Transport Operator – Manx Independent Carriers
Manzanate – perfume speciality – Quest International UK Ltd
*Map (Worldwide) – import and export, specialize in basmatic rice, lentils and spices – Map Trading Ltd
Map & Guide to European Cities – map & guide – Francis Chichester Ltd
Map Marketing – UK Office Direct
Map Server 4 – development tools in microsoft windows – Graticule
Mapa – protective gloves – Mapa Spontex
*Maped (France) – drawing instruments and rules – West Design Products Ltd
Mapei – County Construction Chemicals Ltd
Mapinfo – software & digital data for improved business – Pitney Bowes Software Ltd
*Maplelite Pumice (Greece and Italy) – pumice for the construction industry – Maple Aggregates UK Ltd
Maps Sales – ordnance survey, road, public information and reference maps – Cook Hammond & Kell Ltd
Maptools – development tools for mapping in mircosoft windows – Graticule
Marabu – Tampographic Ltd
Maranitz – Lamphouse Ltd
Maranyl – nylon 6/6 resin – Du Pont UK Ltd
Marathon – Cloakroom Solutions Ltd
Marathon – heavy duty visual and acoustic barrier system and gates with steelposts and anti-vandal features intended for industrial use – Buffalo Timber Buildings
Marathon – Radir Ltd
Marathon – top hung ball race system for sliding doors – P C Henderson Ltd
Marathon Fire Door – top hung system for 1/2 hour fire doors – P C Henderson Ltd
*Marathon Hi-vent (Canada) – high level vent – Alumasc Exterior Building Products
Marathon MM – Radir Ltd
Marathon Seals – PTFE lip seals – Pioneer Weston
Marathron Pumps – AESpump
Marauder – games, playthings, miniatures and models for use in fantasy games – Games Workshop Ltd
Marban – specialist spray coating – L V H Coatings Ltd
*Marble Chippings (Greece and Italy) – chippings for the decorative industry – Maple Aggregates UK Ltd
Marble Collection – The Amtico Co. Ltd
Marbo – electrical wiring accessories – Electrium Sales Ltd
*Marcaddy (Germany) – cable reeling systems – W F Electrical
MARCEL AUBERT – non-contact optical metrology products of Switzerland – Mapra Technik Co.
Marcfi – Catersales Ltd
Marchioness – pillows & duvets – Downland Bedding Co. Ltd
Marcia Cutting Oils – Morris Lubricants
Marclean – anti-graffiti remover – Dacrylate Paints Ltd
Marco (United Kingdom) – professional range of bingo m/c's with plug-in slace displays (electronic) – Park Lane News Ltd
Marco Leer – leather restoration – Lyn Plan Upholstery Ltd
Marco Polo – frames and sunglasses – Hilton International Eye Wear Ltd
Marcon – diamond abrasive products – Marcon Diamond Products Ltd
Marcrist – surface preparation – Marcrist International Ltd
Marcrist – wire brushes – Marcrist International Ltd
Marcrist – diamonds – Marcrist International Ltd
Marcryl – Extruded Acrylic Sheet & Extruded – Brett Martin Ltd
Marden Edwards (United Kingdom) – Designers, manufacturers and suppliers of packaging machinery and product handling systems – Marden Edwards Ltd
Mardi Gras – Georgia Pacific GB Ltd
Mardlers Mild – cask beer – Woodforde's Norfolk Ales
Marelli Electric Motors – electric motors – Potteries Power Transmission Ltd
Marfak – lubricants – Chevron
Marflex MB – precast chimney block system – P D Edenhall
Marflex ML – precast multifuel flue liners – P D Edenhall
Marflex QL – high performance pumice flue liner – P D Edenhall
Marflex Typex HP – gas flue block system – P D Edenhall
*Marfona – Agrico UK Ltd
Margard – anti-graffiti remover and coatings – Dacrylate Paints Ltd
Margard W.B. – water based anti-graffiti remover and coatings – Dacrylate Paints Ltd
*Marghestone (Italy) – assimilated granite tiles and slabs – MFS Stone Surfaces Ltd

Marglass – glass scrim – A Latter & Co. Ltd
Margot De Paris – tapestries and embroideries – DMC Creative World
Marie – radio isotope stock control – Lablogic Systems Ltd
Marie Claire – I P C Media Ltd
Marin Ark – marine evacuation systems – R F D Beaufort Ltd
Marina – yacht marina – Gosport Marina
Marine – BS 6391 type 1 fire hose – Richards Hose Ltd
Marine H.D. Enamel – Spencer Coatings Ltd
Marine Hydrocarbon Firewall Slab – marine and offshore – Rockwool Rockpanel B V
Marine & Industrial Heat – industrial heating and control equipment – EXHEAT Ltd
Marine Underlays – flame retardant underlays; sound insulation underlays – Ball & Young Division Of Vitafoan Ltd
Marinecall – telephone services – Weather Call
Marineline – Alrose Products British Gas Springs Ltd
*Mariner (U.S.A.) – outboard motors – E P Barrus
Mariner – WC – Armitage Shanks Ltd
Marinol – biodegradable marine degreaser – Deb R & D Ltd
Mario Pinto – S M W Autoblok
Marion – Harrier Fluid Power Ltd
Mariotti – Stacatruc
Mark – Harrier Fluid Power Ltd
Mark 1 Pool Lift (United Kingdom) – transfers disabled swimmers into and out of water – Arjo Med AB Ltd
Mark-It – UK Office Direct
Mark Paterson & Associates – literacy agents – The Marsh Agency Ltd
Mark5 – Cox Building Products Ltd
Markal – paint/crayons – Bearwood Engineering Supplies
MarketForce – sales and marketing software system – Onyx Software
Marketpoint – database marketing – Marketpoint Europe Ltd
Markforce – trade mark agent – Markforce
Markies – Agrico UK Ltd
Markilux – awnings – Deans Blinds & Awnings UK
Markitwise – Tyden Brooks
Marklab – laboratory fittings – Armitage Shanks Ltd
Markloc – fail safe heavy duty locking bolt – Qualter Hall & Co. Ltd
Marks – equjpment & spares – Bearwood Engineering Supplies
Marksman – traffic monitoring systems – Golden River Traffic Ltd
Marktronic – dot marking machines – Pryor Marking Technology Ltd
Markus – cold-store, hygiene and sound-proof doors – Envirohold Ltd
Markwik – hospital fittings – Armitage Shanks Ltd
Marl – opto electronics – Marl International Ltd
Marl Creative Arc – architect, retail and commerical lighting specilist – Marl International Ltd
Marl International Limited – opto electronics design & manufacture – Marl International Ltd
Marl Optosource – distribution of high quality led's products – Marl International Ltd
Marland (U.S.A.) – freewheels – Ringspann UK Ltd
Marland – UK Office Direct
Marlborough – internal panel door – Premdor Crosby Ltd
Marlborough Studio Collection – 80% wool/20% nylon – Adam Carpets Ltd
Marlborough Tiles – ceramic tiles wall & floor glazed terracotta masolica handpainting – Marlborough Tiles
Marler Haley – Portable and Modular Displays – Ace Exhibitions Displays & Installation
Marlex G.F. – twin wall metal gas flue system – P D Edenhall
Marley Bold Roll – roof tiles – Marley Eternit Ltd
Marley Cloak Verge System – for mendip and bold roll and double roman tiles – Marley Eternit Ltd
Marley Conductive – static conductive vinyl flooring system – Tarkett Ltd
Marley Dry Ridge and Dry Mono Ridge System – ridge system – Marley Eternit Ltd
Marley Eaves Ventilation System – ventilation system – Marley Eternit Ltd
Marley Eclipse PUR – non-directional heavy duty vinyl flooring – Tarkett Ltd
Marley Eclipse SD – static dissipative vinyl flooring – Tarkett Ltd
Marley Elite PUR – non-directional heavy duty vinyl flooring – Tarkett Ltd
Marley Esteem – domestic prestige flooring – Tarkett Ltd
Marley Europa – semi-flexible floor tiles – Tarkett Ltd
Marley Gas Vent Ridge Tiles – ridge tiles – Marley Eternit Ltd
Marley HD Synergy PU – heavy duty vinyl flooring – Tarkett Ltd
Marley Interlocking Dry Verge System – dry verge system – Marley Eternit Ltd
Marley Ludlow Major – roof tiles – Marley Eternit Ltd
Marley Marlden – rooftiles – Marley Eternit Ltd
Marley Marquess – roof tiles – Marley Eternit Ltd

Marley Marvent Roof Ventilating Tiles – ventilating tiles – Marley Eternit Ltd
Marley Matrix – high performance decorative vinyl flooring – Tarkett Ltd
Marley Matrix Naturals – heavy duty natural effect flooring – Tarkett Ltd
Marley Mendip – roof tiles – Marley Eternit Ltd
Marley Modern – roof tiles – Marley Eternit Ltd
Marley Plain – roof tiles – Marley Eternit Ltd
Marley Plain Tile Cloak Verge – Marley Eternit Ltd
Marley Plain Tile Dry Ridge System – tile – Marley Eternit Ltd
Marley Reflections – natural effect vinyl flooring – Tarkett Ltd
Marley Ridge Vent Terminal – vent terminal – Marley Eternit Ltd
Marley Ventilated Dry Ridge System – dry ridge system – Marley Eternit Ltd
Marley Ventilating Ridge Tiles – vent ridge terminal roof tiles – Marley Eternit Ltd
Marley Vylon Plus – flexible floor tiles – Tarkett Ltd
Marley Wessex – roof tiles – Marley Eternit Ltd
Marleyflex – semi-flexible floor tiles – Tarkett Ltd
Marleyflor Plus PU – flexible vinyl flooring – Tarkett Ltd
Marleyfold – Building Additions Ltd
marleyrail polyrail mipolam rehau – plastic handrails – W Brighton Handrails
Marleytred – acoustic underlay – Tarkett Ltd
Marlin Leek – webbing, slings and lifting equipment – Marling Leek Ltd
Marlmarque – marble type paper and board – G F Smith
Marlon – Sunlight Plastics Ltd
Marlon (United Kingdom) – polycarbonate – Righton Ltd
Marlon CS Longlife – Profiled Polycarbonite Sheet – Brett Martin Ltd
Marlon FSX Longlife – Solid Plycarbonate Sheet – Brett Martin Ltd
Marlon ST Longlife – Profiled PVC Sheet & Profiled – Brett Martin Ltd
Marlon - Trilite – Brett Martin Ltd
Marlone – gents, ladies and childrens' fine footwear – UK Distributors Footwear Ltd
Marlow – Harrier Fluid Power Ltd
Marlow – vanity basin – Armitage Shanks Ltd
Marlow Ropes – yachting, industrial ropes climbing ropes – Marlow Ropes Ltd
Marlow Ropes – shipping, towing and oilfield ropes – Marlow Ropes Ltd
Marlowbraid – yacht rope – Marlow Ropes Ltd
Marltone – marble two toned paper – G F Smith
Marlux – Akzo Nobel Packaging Coatings Ltd
Marmara – corner bath – Ideal Standard Ltd
Marmarino – Type of Decorative Plaster – Armourcoat Ltd
*Marmofloor (Netherlands) – marbled lindem banded to melt planks – Forbo
Marmoleum – The Winnen Furnishing Company
Marmoleum Dual – marbled sheet and tile linoleum – Forbo
*Marmoleum Fresco – sheet linoleum – Forbo
*Marmoleum Real (Netherlands) – sheet linoleum – Forbo
Marmox – Thermal Reflections Ltd
Marplan – marketing services – Research International Group Ltd
Marples – Gem Tool Hire & Sales Ltd
Marplug – operation at low working pressures (typically 2bar) hence safer than other pigging systems – Martec Of Whitwell Ltd
Marprene – long life peristaltic pump tubing – Watson Marlow Pumps Ltd
Marquee World – Accesscaff International Ltd
Marquees – (patent) continental awnings – Guildford Shades
Marquis – carpets - axminster – Brintons Carpets Ltd
*Marquis d'Angerville (France) – Burgundy wines – O W Loeb & Co. Ltd
Marrakesh – carpets - axminster – Brintons Carpets Ltd
Marrill – machine tool – Marrill Engineering Co Ltd
Mars – planetary concrete pan mixers – The Howard Group
*Mars (Germany) – animal grooming tools – Diamond Edge Ltd
Marsden Feeds – BOCM Pauls Ltd
Marseline – gaskets and seals – Scandura
MARSH – Hydraulic & Offshore Supplies Ltd
MARSH BELLOFRAM – Hydraulic & Offshore Supplies Ltd
MARSH BELLOFRAM EUROPE – Hydraulic & Offshore Supplies Ltd
MARSH PRESSURE GAUGES – Hydraulic & Offshore Supplies Ltd
Marshall – modular boiler sequence controllers – Hamworthy Heating Ltd
Marshall – amplification equipment – Marshall Amplifications plc
Marshall Arts – Marshall Arts
Marshall Cavendish Books – Marshall Cavendish Ltd
Marshall Cavendish Multimedia – Marshall Cavendish Ltd

Marshall Pickering – bibles and other religious books, fiction and non-fiction – Harpercollins Publishers Ophelia House

Marshall Town – Fieldway Supplies Ltd

Marshall Tufflex – Eurocell Building Plastics Ltd

Marshalls – Pasta – Pasta Foods Ltd

Marshalls – Thornbury Surfacing Chippenham Ltd

Marshaltown – Gem Tool Hire & Sales Ltd

Marstair – cellar cooling, close control air conditioning – Thermofrost Cryo plc

Marstair – Air conditioning equipment – Banfield Refrigeration Supplies Ltd

Marstair – air conditioners – Tev Ltd

Marston – automotive heat exchangers and radiators – Denso Marston Ltd

Martec – retail consultants – Martec International Ltd

Martech – market research – Metra Martech Ltd

Martech Publications – specialist guides and directories on technical subjects – Metra Martech Ltd

Martech Software – business information systems – Metra Martech Ltd

Martello – door interlock with 2 pole switch – Castell Safety International Ltd

Martin – brass furniture fittings – Martin Co. Ltd

Martin – smoke machines, audio visual equipment – Martin Manufacturing UK plc

martin – Link Hamson Ltd

Martin – saws – Bearwood Engineering Supplies

Martin Electric – resistance welding products/consumables – Obara UK

Martin Luck Group – Martin Luck Group - Office Supplies and Stationery, Office Interiors and Print Management – Martin Luck Group Ltd

*Martin & Lunel (France) – plugs and sockets – W F Electrical

Martin Sprocket & Gear – Couplings, Pulleys, Taper Bushes, Screw Conveyors – Sprint Engineering & Lubricant

Martin Wells (U.S.A.) – Valve seat inserts – Fondera Ltd

Martin Yale – UK Office Direct

Martin Yale – folding machines – Martin Yale International Ltd

Martinal – alumina trihydrate flame retardants – Omya UK Ltd

Martindale – respiratory protection equipment – Centurion Safety Products Ltd

Martindale – safety equipment – Bearwood Engineering Supplies

Martindale – Alpha Electronics Southern Ltd

Martinique – baths – Jendico Ltd

Marton Forge (United Kingdom) – furniture (metal) – Febland Group Ltd

Marton Weaver – wicker furniture – Febland Group Ltd

MARTONAIR – Hydraulic & Offshore Supplies Ltd

Martonair – hydraulic pneumatic and electric components – Norgren Ltd

Martonair – Aztech Components Ltd

Martonair – pneumatic equipment – Bearwood Engineering Supplies

Martonair – B L Pneumatics Ltd

Martor – European Technical Sales Ltd

Martred – fibre bonded carpet/tile – Warlord Contract Carpets Ltd

*Marui (Japan) – plastic model kits – Amerang Group Ltd

Marvec – Profiled PVC Sheet & Profiled – Brett Martin Ltd

Marvel – Harrier Fluid Power Ltd

Marvel – shaving brushes – Progress Shaving Brush Vulfix Ltd

Marvel Comics – spectacle frames – Pennine Optical Group Ltd

Marving – Exhaust Systems – Wemoto Ltd World's End Motorcycles Ltd

MARWEL – Conveyors – Marwel Conveyors

Marwel - conveyors – Marwel Conveyors

Marwin – Red House Industrial Services Ltd

Marwood – non mechanical plant hire and sales – Marwood Group Ltd

Marxo – machinery – Marcrist International Ltd

Marzak – Harrier Fluid Power Ltd

Marzocchi – Hydraulic Component & Systems Ltd

Marzocchi – High Pressure Gear Pumps, Gear Motors – J B J Techniques Ltd

MARZOCCHI – Hydraulic & Offshore Supplies Ltd

Mascani – Senova Ltd

Mascoprint – Masco Print Developments Ltd

*Mascot (Norway) – chargers/psu/inverters – Pulsar Developments Ltd

Masey Ferguson – Harrier Fluid Power Ltd

Maskador – pharadichlorobenzene – Chance & Hunt Ltd

Masocare – iodophor teat dip – Evans Vanodine International plc

Masodine – iodophor teat dip – Evans Vanodine International plc

Masodip – chlorhexidine teat dip – Evans Vanodine International plc

Mason Coatings – Akzo Nobel Coatings Ltd

Mason Graphics – Akzo Nobel Coatings Ltd

Mason Master – drill bits and hand tools – Rawlplug Ltd

Mason's Ironstone – earthenware, tableware and giftware – Wedgewood Travel Ltd

Mason Safeflex – Interflex Hose & Bellows Ltd

Mason Superflex – Interflex Hose & Bellows Ltd

*Mason Switch (U.S.A.) – switch's – Amelec Ltd

Masoshistigs – plastic educational toys – Willis Toys Ltd

MasoSine – sinusoidal pumps – Watson Marlow Pumps Ltd

Masport – domestic grass cutting machines – Claymore

Mass Fax – bulk fax transmissions – Breeze Ltd

Mass-Sieve – vibrating screen – Parker Plant Ltd

Masseeley – group trade name – Masson Seeley & Co. Ltd

*Massen (Switzerland) – vision systems – Baumer Electric Ltd

Massey – Walling UK Ltd

Massey Ferguson – Ross Farm Machinery Ltd

Massey-Ferguson – compact tractors – G Reekie Group Ltd

Massey Ferguson – agricultural machinery – Agco International Ltd

*Massey Ferguson – Agricultural machinery – J J Farm Services Ltd

Massey Ferguson - Fendt - Challenger – Agco International Ltd

Massflo Feeders – screw conveyors and elevators – Ajax Equipment Ltd

MassLynx 4.0 (United Kingdom) – Global Mass-Informatics Platform – Waters

MassPREP Station (United Kingdom) – Protein Digestion Robot – Waters

Mast – management and skills training, personnel development and consultancy – M A S T International Group Ltd

Mast Assure – a range of antisera – The Mast Group Ltd

Mast ID – dehydrated biochemical agar media for bacterial identification – The Mast Group Ltd

Mast Redipac – dehydrated culture media in preweighed amounts in foil sachets – The Mast Group Ltd

Mast Rediprep – sterile blood culture, egg media and urine screening plates – The Mast Group Ltd

Mast Towers – Accesscaff International Ltd

Masta – equestrian clothing – Matchmakers International Ltd

*Mastabar – conveyor care equipment – Mato Industries Ltd

Mastabar 'C' Type – conveyor belt fastener and rotary cam lacing machine – Mato Industries Ltd

Mastafil – dispenser – Appor Ltd

Mastafluor – immunofluorescence test – The Mast Group Ltd

Mastascan – automated zone reader – The Mast Group Ltd

Mastascanelite – computerised plate reading-reporting system for microbiology – The Mast Group Ltd

Mastascrape – conveyor belt cleaning devices – Mato Industries Ltd

Mastazyme – enzyme immunoassay test kits for infectious diseases and other clinical conditions – The Mast Group Ltd

Mastenbroek – Mastenbroek Ltd

Master – mobile grain driers – Master Farm Services GB Ltd

Master – security padlocks and chains – Securikey Ltd

Master Build Insurance – insurance for builders – M M A Insurance plc

Master Casters – pressure diecastings – J V M Castings Ltd

Master Class – cookware, knives – Thomas Plant Birmingham

Master Curl Products – Double Gee Hair Fashions Ltd

Master Grid – magnetic planning boards – Acco UK Ltd

Master Grip – kitchen gadgets – Thomas Plant Birmingham

Master Lock – UK Office Direct

Master Magnets – magnetic separation equipment – Master Magnets Ltd

Master Palette – decorative paint mixing systems – Akzonobel

*Master Plastics – Regalzone LLP

Master Shear – garden shear – Burgon & Ball Ltd

Master-Style – luxury bathroom taps – Samuel Heath & Sons plc

Master Suites (United Kingdom) – master keyed cylinders, in all major cylinder types – Amberley Security

Master Touch – Flowline Manufacturing Ltd

Master Vac – vacuum cleaners (net pick up and spray extraction) – Denis Rawlins Ltd

Master Video Painter – electronic sketch pad, connects to tv – Vtech Electronics UK plc

Masterbloc – modular switchboard – Schneider

Masterblok – wood substitute for pattern making – J R Technology

Masterchef – catering equipment – Manitowoc Food Service UK

Masterclass Series – magazine – Future Publishing Ltd

Mastercote – food colour dispersion – Sensient

Mastercraft – period bathroom water fittings – Barber Wilson & Company Ltd

Mastercraft – full gloss and lustre enamels – T & R Williamson Ltd

MasterCraftsman – tufted carpet – Brockway Carpets Ltd

Mastercube – a low inclusion pellet binder – Agil Chemicals Products

Mastercut – Industrial machine knives – Mastercut Cutting Systems Ltd

Masterdor – doors of wood fitted into PVC or metal frames – Manse Masterdor Ltd

Masterfile – stationery – William Pollard & Company Ltd

Masterflex – Southern Valve & Fitting Co. Ltd

Masterflex – flexible drives and couplings – S S White Technologies UK Ltd

Masterflex – Trafalgar Tools

Masterflor+ (United Kingdom) – carpet tiles – Checkmate Industries Ltd

Masterflor + (United Kingdom) – broadloom – Checkmate Industries Ltd

Mastergear – valve actuators – Opperman Mastergear Ltd

Mastergreen Indoor – permanent indoor bowling green surface – Verde Sports Cricket Ltd

Mastergreen Outdoor – permanent outdoor bowling green surface – Verde Sports Cricket Ltd

Masterline – pre-terminated fibre optic systems – Huber+Suhner (UK) Ltd

Masterlock – padlocks – Acco UK Ltd

MasterMark – ram harness & crayows, animal markers, sheep halters and cattle shackles – Rowland Sandwith Ltd

Mastermask – kraft masking paper – Staples Disposables Ltd

Mastermeasure – Glenvale Packaging

Masterpact – circuit breaker – Schneider

*Masterpiece – Tudor Tea & Coffee

Masterpiece – acrylic and oil painting kit, colour shading, bonny beads, silk painting, artwood collage, 3D sequin art – Kitfix Swallow Group Ltd

Masterpiece XL (United Kingdom) – carpet tiles – Checkmate Industries Ltd

Masterpiece XL (United Kingdom) – broadloom – Checkmate Industries Ltd

Masterplug – Gem Tool Hire & Sales Ltd

Masterpoint – remote data capture system – Barcrest Group

MasterPump – Condensate Removal Pump – E D C International Ltd

Masters – UK Office Direct

Masterscan – ultrasonic flaw detectors – Sonatest Ltd

Masterseal – weatherproofed 1856 rated wiring accessories – M K Electric Ltd

MasterSharp – modular home sharpening system – Plasplugs

Mastershield – Mar Deb

MasterSizer – particle sizer – Malvern Instruments Ltd

Mastertex – textured coating – C J Enterprises

Masterwash – Manitowoc Food Service UK

Masterwash – Manitowoc Foodservice UK Limited

Mastiff Hands Free – total hands-free access control system – Mastiff Electronic Systems Ltd

Mastiff Network – integrated access control and monitoring network and database – Mastiff Electronic Systems Ltd

Mastiff Viewcard – optically coded card, tag and contactless access control and I.D. systems – Mastiff Electronic Systems Ltd

Mastral – general purpose grease bars – Lea Manufacturing Co.

Mastring – multiple ring device – The Mast Group Ltd

Mastring S – multiple antibiotic susceptibility testing device – The Mast Group Ltd

Mat-A-Chek – to assess quality of iron – Baugh & Weedon Ltd

Matabi – Gem Tool Hire & Sales Ltd

Matadoor – crash proof and resistant hi speed factory doors – Union Industries

Matador – coated abrasive products – Starcke Abrasives Ltd

*Matamic (Japan) – unglazed ceramic mosaics – Udny Edgar & Co. Ltd

MATARA – Hydraulic & Offshore Supplies Ltd

MATBRO – Chaintec Ltd

Matbro – Harrier Fluid Power Ltd

Match – rugby, soccer, netball and basketball balls – Gray Nicolls

Match Bigshots – Emap Ltd

Match Weekly – magazine – Emap Ltd

Match Yearbook – Emap Ltd

*Matchbox (U.S.A.) – aerial matching instrument – Lyons Instruments

Matchmaker – decorative paint mixing systems – Akzonobel

Matchmaker – bonding porcelain – Schottlander Dental Equipment Supplies

Matchmaster – Kitfix Swallow Group Ltd

Matchmate – alloys – Schottlander Dental Equipment Supplies

Matchpoint – Office Paper – Mcnaughton James Paper Group Ltd

Matcon – Matcon discharger valves, for discharging powder and granular materials from silos or hoppers; Matcon intermediate bulk container system, for storage and transportation of powders and discharge to process of powders – Matcon Ltd

Matech – European Technical Sales Ltd

Mateline – automatic pie and tart machines, pastie and sausage roll machines and all ancillary equipment – Mateline Engineering Ltd

Matfer-Bourgeat (France) – utensils, cooking and pastry – Mitchell & Cooper Ltd

Mather & Platt – Harrier Fluid Power Ltd
Maths Cubes – cubes – Abceta Playthings Ltd
Maths Made Easy – Series of maths books for Primary pupils – Egon Publishers Ltd
Mathys – Off The Wall Graffiti Solutions
Matic – Obart Pumps Ltd
Matkandu – broad rib anti-slip rubber flooring – Jaymart Roberts & Plastics Ltd
Matki – shower surround – Matki plc
Matlocker – looselay interlocking rubber flooring tiles – Jaymart Roberts & Plastics Ltd
Matlows (United Kingdom) – manufacturer of sugar confectionery – Swizzels Matlow Ltd
MATRAL – Chaintec Ltd
Matral – T V H UK Ltd
Matrex – Terrapin Ltd
Matrisse – paper and board – Fenner Paper Co. Ltd
***Matrix (Germany)** – paver – Farmura Ltd
Matrix – Red House Industrial Services Ltd
Matrix – face shield – Parmelee Ltd
Matrix – industrial power transmissions – Matrix International Ltd
Matrix – Dixon Turner Wallcoverings Ltd
Matrix – clutches & brakes, mechanical, electromagnetic, hydraulic, pneum atic, face tooth couplings – Matrix International Ltd
***Matrix (Italy)** – high speed solenoid valves – The West Group Ltd
MATRIX – Hydraulic & Offshore Supplies Ltd
Matryx (U.S.A.) – pneumatic vane type actuators – Induchem
Matsui – T.V. videos and hi-fi – Dixons Retail
Matsuo (Japan) – thermostats – A T C Semitec Ltd
Matsuo – Cyclops Electronics Ltd
Matsushita – Cyclops Electronics Ltd
Matsushita – relays, switches, programmable logic controllers, vision recognition systems, sensing and detection components, fans, solenoids, encoders – Panasonic Electric Works
Matsuura – Matsuura Machinery Ltd
Mattei – compressors, parts and service – Airware International Ltd
Mattei – Rotary Vane Compressors – Mattei Compressors Ltd
Mattel – toys – Mattel
***Matthew Algie** – Matthew Algie & Co. Ltd
Matthew Norman – clocks – M A Rapport & Co. Ltd
Matthews – posture chairs – E F G Matthews Office Furniture Ltd
Mattke – European Technical Sales Ltd
Mattplat MG – matt solvent ink for plastics – Fujifilm Sericol Ltd
Matveyor – Regina International Ltd
Maul – UK Office Direct
Maurice Phillips – textiles – Maurice Phillips
Mauser (Switzerland) – measuring instruments – Tesa Technology UK Ltd
Mavilor – European Drives & Motor Repairs
Mavitta – engineering support services – Mavitta Division Morson Projects
***Mawbeef** – Tranfield Of Cumbria Ltd Vion Foods
Mawdsley – European Drives & Motor Repairs
Mawson Triton Mouldings – compression plastic mouldings – M T M Ltd
Max – Tri Pack Supplies Ltd
Max – V E S Ltd
Max Appliances – waste disposals manufrs – Max Appliances Ltd
Max-E Boost – Grundfos Pumps Ltd
Max-Econ – range of radiant heating automatic controls – Horizon Mechanical Services International Ltd
MAX In-Line – robotic selective coater – Humiseal Europe Ltd
***Max Mueller (Germany)** – CNC turning machines from 2 to 8 axis control – D M G UK Ltd
Max - Playstation 2 Gaming – magazine – Future Publishing Ltd
Max Power – unisex clothing – Max Power Sports Co.
Max Power Sports – unisex sports clothing – Max Power Sports Co.
Max-Rapide – V E S Ltd
Max St – sanitary towel disposal unit – Max Appliances Ltd
Maxam – building maintenance products, property protection products and window films – Maxam
Maxam – pneumatic equipment – Bearwood Engineering Supplies
Maxam – fluid power equipment – Parker Hannifin Ltd
MAXAM – Hydraulic & Offshore Supplies Ltd
MaxBox – packaged laser marking systems – Electrox
MaxBox plus – laser marking workstations – Electrox
Maxcess – maximum access bodywork – Lawrence David Ltd
Maxell – UK Office Direct
Maxfit – safety eye shield – Parmelee Ltd
Maxfli – golf equipment – Dunlop Slazenger International Ltd
Maxfli Australian Blade – golf clubs – Dunlop Slazenger International Ltd

Maxfli Briefcase – Accessory – Dunlop Slazenger International Ltd
Maxfli Carryall – Bag – Dunlop Slazenger International Ltd
Maxfli Deluxe Carry Bag – golf bags – Dunlop Slazenger International Ltd
Maxfli Deluxe Stand 1 – golf bags – Dunlop Slazenger International Ltd
Maxfli Dual Purpose – golf bags – Dunlop Slazenger International Ltd
Maxfli Executive Umbrella – golfing umbrella – Dunlop Slazenger International Ltd
Maxfli Head Covers – golf club covers – Dunlop Slazenger International Ltd
Maxfli HT – golf balls – Dunlop Slazenger International Ltd
Maxfli JT Glove – golf club – Dunlop Slazenger International Ltd
Maxfli Junior Staff – club set – Dunlop Slazenger International Ltd
Maxfli Practise Ball Bag – accessories golf bag – Dunlop Slazenger International Ltd
Maxfli Pro Umbrella – golfing umbrella – Dunlop Slazenger International Ltd
Maxfli Revolution – baseball caps, golf balls and golf clubs – Dunlop Slazenger International Ltd
Maxfli Staff Bag – 9 1/2inch and 11 inch golf bags – Dunlop Slazenger International Ltd
Maxfli Stand Bag – golf bags – Dunlop Slazenger International Ltd
Maxfli Tour Textured – baseball caps – Dunlop Slazenger International Ltd
Maxfli Tour Twill Caps – baseball caps – Dunlop Slazenger International Ltd
Maxfli Travel Cover – cover for golf clubs – Dunlop Slazenger International Ltd
Maxfli Vision – golfing viser – Dunlop Slazenger International Ltd
Maxfli XD All Weather – golf club – Dunlop Slazenger International Ltd
Maxfli XF Maxflex – golf glove – Dunlop Slazenger International Ltd
Maxfli XS Distance – golf balls – Dunlop Slazenger International Ltd
Maxfli XS Tour – golf balls – Dunlop Slazenger International Ltd
Maxfli XS Tour Ltd – golf glove – Dunlop Slazenger International Ltd
Maxfli XS Towel – towel – Dunlop Slazenger International Ltd
Maxfli XT All Cabretta – golf glove – Dunlop Slazenger International Ltd
Maxflo – Mactenn Systems Ltd
Maxflo - MaxSandflo - MultiAshflo - Inflatek Valve - SuperMaxflo - Dosamatic – Mactenn Systems Ltd
Maxi – smoking kiln – Afos Ltd
Maxi 6 – tumble dryer – Hoover Ltd
Maxibag – Injection moulded carrying cases – Hofbauer (UK) Ltd
Maxiboot (United Kingdom) – CV boot kit (large joints 90mm+) – Bailcast Ltd
***Maxibrew** – bulk coffee brewer – Marco Beverage Systems Ltd
Maxicarb – Activated Carbon Filter for high efficiency filtration and heavy duty performance – Emcel Filters Ltd
Maxicon – angle bead – Expamet Building Products Ltd
Maxidrill Short Hole Drills – Ceratizit UK Ltd
MaxiFit – universal couplings, stepped couplings, flange adaptors and special fittings, size range 40mm (1 1/2") to 600mm (24") – Viking Johnson
Maxifleet MP – multi-use diesel/petrol oil – Millers Oils Ltd
Maxiflex – wire rope and fittings – Tractel UK Ltd
Maxiflex Universal Tooling System – Ceratizit UK Ltd
Maxiflo – dispenser – Appor Ltd
Maxiflow – Harrier Fluid Power Ltd
Maxilock – toolholders – Ceratizit UK Ltd
Maxilock F.X. Parting Tools – Ceratizit UK Ltd
Maxim – laser marking workstations – Electrox
Maxim – magazine publishing systems – 5 Fifteen Ltd
Maxim – DDC Controllers – Innotech Controls UK Ltd
Maxim – audio, video, clocks and household – Sherwood Agencies Ltd
Maxim – Cyclops Electronics Ltd
Maxim Lamps – Electric lamps & electrical accessories – J F Poynter Ltd
Maxima – UK Office Direct
Maxima – large formwork panel system – RMD Kwikform Limited
Maximag – high permeability low carbon refines iron – West Brook Resources Ltd
Maximair – extruded louvre – McKenzie Martin Ltd
Maximal – contacts for the security alarm industry – C Q R Ltd
Maximill – range of milling cutters – Ceratizit UK Ltd
Maximill – spindle nose cutters – Ceratizit UK Ltd
Maximus – water based lubricant – Bodywise Ltd
Maxipor – dispenser – Appor Ltd
Maxipor – cartridge soap dispenser system – Deb R & D Ltd

Maxithen – A wide range of colour and additive masterbatches supplied for use in polyolefins and styrenic polymers together with polymer specific masterbatches, particularly suitable for use in the engineering polymers. – Gabriel Chemie UK Ltd
Maxivent – kitchen extraction fans – Airflow Developments Ltd
Maxlok – versatile high strength, vibration resistant, bolt type fastener – Avdel UK Ltd
Maxlok – structural rivet system – Zygology Ltd
Maxmatic – domestic waste disposal units – Max Appliances Ltd
Maxon – Radio transmitters, receivers and transceivers – Maxon C I C Europe Ltd
MaxSandflo – Mactenn Systems Ltd
Maxseal – hydraulic actuators – Truflo Gas Turbines Ltd
Maxum – Concentric speed reducer – Baldor UK
Maxwell House – UK Office Direct
Maxwell House – instant coffee – Kraft Foods UK Ltd
Maxwell House – Alba Beverage Co. Ltd
***Maxxor** – Berthoud Sprayers
May Fair – bed linen/towels – Kipfold Ltd
May Field – lager – Batleys Cash & Carry
May Gibbs – Chorion plc
Maybrey – aluminium alloy castings – Maybrey Reliance
Mayfair – electric heaters – Kaloric Heater Co. Ltd
Mayfair – accessories – Armitage Shanks Ltd
Mayfair – shaving brushes – Progress Shaving Brush Vulfix Ltd
Mayfair Match – optical frames and sunglasses – Hilton International Eye Wear Ltd
Mayflex – cables – Mayflex UK Ltd
Mayflower – QD enamels, hammer finishes, epoxy enamels, industrial primers, chlorinated rubber finishes and pre-catalysed lacquers – Kingstonian Paints Ltd
Maynard – textile machinery and accessories; consultants to the textile industry – Robert S Maynard Ltd
Maypole – trailer parts – Maypole Ltd
Mayr – European Technical Sales Ltd
Maytag – Clean Machine UK Ltd
Maywood – Double Parking Systems
Mazak – Harrier Fluid Power Ltd
Mazak – Laser Trader Ltd
Mazak – machine tools – Yamazaki Machinery UK Ltd
Mazak – Rowan Precision Ltd
Mazak, Mazatrol, CAMWARE, Cyber Tool Management, Cyber Machine Monitor – Yamazaki Machinery UK Ltd
Mazatrol – CNC systems – Yamazaki Machinery UK Ltd
Mazda – L M C Hadrian Ltd
Mazda – Ashley Competition Exhausts Ltd
Mazda – cars – M C L Group Ltd
Mazzle – map jigsaw puzzle – Harvey Map Services Ltd
MB-1 – Central Heating Protection – Fernox
MB Dynamics – Manufacturer of Vibration Test & Calibration and Modal Excitation Systems – Calibration Dynamics
MBB – Chaintec Ltd
MBO – A M C Rollers Ltd
MBUK – magazine – Future Publishing Ltd
MC Security Barrier – rising arm parking barrier – Apt Controls Ltd
MC set – indorr withdrawable mv switchgear – Schneider
McAlpine – traps – Mcalpine & Company Ltd
McArthurs – safety workwear and janitorial products – Mcarthur Group Ltd
McBean's – orchids – Mcbean's Orchids
McCann Erickson – advertising agents with specialists in advertising, design, sales promotion & direct marketing – Mccann Erickson Ltd
McCarthy & Stone – Mccarthy & Stone Ltd
***McConnel** – Hedge/grasscutting – Paul Tuckwell Ltd
McConnell – Joe Turner Equipment Ltd
McCormick – Mike Garwood Ltd
McDonagh Furniture – The Winnen Furnishing Company
McDonald Couplings (United Kingdom) – air hose couplings – Hydrasun Ltd
McEwan's Export – ales & stouts – Scottish & Newcastle Pub Co.
McEwans Larger – lager – Scottish & Newcastle Pub Co.
McEwens of Perth – clothing – Mcewens Of Perth
McGeoch – electronic equipment – Mcgeoch Technology Ltd
McGill Heating & Plumbing – heating & plumbing – Mcgill Security
McGill Security – security – Mcgill Security
McGregor-Rutland – high quality polythene film and printed polythene bags – Skymark Packaging Solutions Ltd
MCIB – compressed air refrigerant dryers – Airware International Ltd
McLaren – cardboard and packaging – Mclaren Packaging Ltd
McLaren – formula 1 racing team – Mclaren Racing
McLean Lighting – lighting fixtures and fittings – Maclean Electricals
MCM – European Technical Sales Ltd
McMaster – fastenings – Bearwood Engineering Supplies

McMaster Carr – American Catalogue Products – Protective Supplies & Services Ltd

Mcmastercar – Harrier Fluid Power Ltd

Mcminn – gardening and houseware product – Mcminn Hardware Wholesalers

McNaughton – Centre saver system for woodturners – The Toolpost

MCP – low melting point fusible alloys, metals and alloys – M C P Ltd

MCP Metal – metal spray equipment – MCP Group

McQuay – refrigeration/air-conditioning compressor spares – J & E Hall Ltd

McQuay – Therma Group

McQuay Service – air conditioning service – J & E Hall Ltd

MCR – Maxa Technologies Ltd

MCR – rising arm farriers – Apt Controls Ltd

MCS – rising arm barriers – Apt Controls Ltd

MCT – test equipment for medium sized motor stators and rotor bars – Adwel International Ltd

McVan Instruments Pty Ltd – Halcyon Solutions

McVitie's – UK Office Direct

MD Asia – business strategies for China & Asia – Concept Systems Design Ltd

MDA Scientific – low level toxic gas monitoring – Honeywell Analytics Ltd

MDF-Bonder – two part adhesive for mdf or similar materials – C G P Chemicals Ltd

MDPE – Naylor Specialists Plastics

MDS – metalclad distribution substation – Schneider

me* – Mobile Expertise Ltd

Mead – Aztech Components Ltd

Mead – Southern Valve & Fitting Co. Ltd

Meadow – washbasin, closet and bidet – Ideal Standard Ltd

*Meadow Cottage – farmhouse ice cream – Blackburne & Haynes

*Meadow Cottage Untreated – Channel Island milk – Blackburne & Haynes

Meadowbank Associates – recruitment consultants – Meadowbank Associates Ltd

Meadows Bridal Shoes Ltd – bridal shoe manufrs – Meadows Bridal Shoes Ltd

Mealmaster – a range of hmr containers with fog gard – Pregis Rigid Packaging Ltd

Meanwell – power supply – Stontronics Ltd

Measom Freer – plastic bottles and caps – Measom Freer Company

Measure-Mark – steel tape rules – Fisco Tools Ltd

Measurement Studio – software product – National Instrument UK Corp Ltd

Measuremeter – distance measuring wheel – Trumeter Co Ltd

Mebasol – eurogreen system – Farmura Ltd

MECA INOX VALVES (United Kingdom) – Ultravalve Ltd

*Mecagrav (France) – marking mechanisms – Brandone Machine Tool Ltd

Mecal – non-ferrous saw & cnc machining centres – Addison Saws Ltd

Mecalac – Harrier Fluid Power Ltd

Mecanocaucho – European Technical Sales Ltd

MECG – MECG Ltd

Mechadyne – automotive research and development – Mechadyne International Ltd

Mechanical Seals – John Crane UK Ltd

Mechanical Testing – Oceaneering Asset Integrity

Mechanofusion – Hosokawa Micron Ltd

*Mechatronic (Germany and USA) – fans and motors – Ebm-Papst

Mechelle – spectrograph – Andor Technology Ltd

*Mechline – Mechline Developments Ltd

MechoShade – internal roller sunscreening system with visually transparent FR fabric – Faber Blinds UK Ltd

Mecloran – trichlorethane 1,1,1 – Atosina UK Ltd

MECMAN – Hydraulic & Offshore Supplies Ltd

Mecman – Bosch Rexroth Ltd

Mecman – equipment/spares – Bearwood Engineering Supplies

*Mecmar – Mecmar Driers 2000 Ltd

Mectron – Harrier Fluid Power Ltd

MecWash – cleaning and degreasing systems for metal parts – Mecwash Systems Ltd

MED E – Solmedia Laboratory Supplies

Med Info Sys – pharmaceutical system mehodology – New Information Paradigms Ltd

Medal Duck – Popular, Reliable and Value for money – Chi Yip Group Ltd

Medallion – luxury motor caravan – Auto Sleepers Ltd

Medallion PMS – Softbrands

Medallion Twist – carpets – Penthouse Carpets Ltd

Medallion, Web Booking Engine – Softbrands

Meddings – drilling machines – Meddings Machine Tools

Meddings – Red House Industrial Services Ltd

Meddings – Peter Rushton Ltd

Meddings – drilling machines – R K International Machine Tools Ltd

Meddings Flott – Meddings Machine Tools

Meddings-Ibarmia (Spain) – drilling machines – Meddings Machine Tools

Meddings Machine Tools – Meddings Machine Tools

Meddings Thermalec – Meddings Machine Tools

Medel Nebulisers (Italy) – nebulisers for medical use – Intermedical UK Ltd

MedeX Range – x-ray medical – Applied Scintillation Technologies

Medi-Bed – horse feed – Dengie Crops Ltd

Medi+Physics – G E Healthcare

Media & Marketing Services – Media & Marketing Services

Media Print (Sweden) – woodfree coated papers & boards – Davies Harvey & Murrell

Media Screen – Display Wizard Ltd

Mediacraft – commissioning and returns systems – Buhrs UK Ltd

MediaStar – solution for networked video conferencing – Cabletime Ltd

Mediation & Conciliation – FOCUS Eap

Mediavision – Lamphouse Ltd

Medicaid – insurance policy – P S H A

Medical Device Technology – magazine – Advanstar Communications

Medical Laboratory World – magazine – Progressive Media Group

Medicar – medical transportation service – Great Western Ambulance Sevice N H S Trust

Medicarb – joint resurfacing device – Surgicraft Ltd

Medicare – insurance policy – P S H A

Medicare – medical storage systems – Craven & Co. Ltd

Medicel – City Technology Ltd

Medici – prints, greetings cards, postcards, stationery, books and calendars – The Medici Galleries

Mediclad – sall system for pharmaceutical and medical industry – Interclad Ltd

Mediclad H D – pressed PVC sheet – Interclad Ltd

Mediclinics – R G K UK Ltd

Medico – pipes – Cadogan

Medicom – medical publishing – Medicom UK Ltd

Medicover – insurance policy – P S H A

Mediguard – nursing and patient gowns – Synergy Healthcare plc

Medimask – Speed Plastics Ltd

Medina – shoes, boots and handbags – Courtesy Shoes Ltd

Medion – Lamphouse Ltd

Mediplus – Mediplus Ltd

Medisafe – Medisafe UK Ltd

Medisure – healthcare benefits – Simply Health

Medite MDF – M D M Timber Ltd

Meditek – medical gas manifold – Black Teknigas & Electro Controls Ltd

Meditelle – Meditelle Medical Equipment (sub-division of Beautelle Equipment Ltd) – Meditelle

Meditherm – heat packs – Thermo Packs

Medium – Lamphouse Ltd

Medium Champion – John Hunt Bolton Ltd

Mediwaste – medical waste management software – Isys Interactive Systems Ltd

Medley – telecommunciation switching equipment and software – Nortel Networks Ltd Ltd

Medline – linear actuators – Linak UK

Medmaw – Meadows & Passmore Ltd

MEDO – linear shuttle & diaphragm air and vacuum pumps – Nitto Kohki Europe Co. Ltd

Medo – canker cure – Vitax Ltd

Medsonic HS – hospital instrument cleaning system – Guyson International Ltd

Medusa – generators – S I P Industrial Products Ltd

Medway KM Extra – newspaper – Kent Messenger Group Ltd

MEECH – Hydraulic & Offshore Supplies Ltd

Meech Air Technology – air technology product – Meech Static Eliminators Ltd

Meech S C T – web cleaning product – Meech Static Eliminators Ltd

Meech Static Eliminators – static – Meech Static Eliminators Ltd

Mefranal – perfume speciality – Quest International UK Ltd

MEGA – B L Pneumatics Ltd

*Mega (Taiwan) – horizontal bandsaws – Prosaw Ltd

Mega – thread rolling machine – R K International Machine Tools Ltd

Mega – fourth generation language – Blanewood Andrews Computing plc

Mega choc – O P Chocolate Ltd

Mega-Grip – Gesipa Blind Riveting Systems Ltd

Mega Line – industrial shock absorber, high-energy – Weforma Daempfungstechnik GmbH

Megabag – Instrument equipment tool carrying cases – Hofbauer (UK) Ltd

Megadyne – Mercury Bearings Ltd

Megafan (Germany) – new generation fans – Ebm-Papst

Megafil – dispenser – Appor Ltd

Megafilm – floor protection film product – British Polythene Industries plc

Megafit – universal couplings, stepped couplings and flange adaptors, size range 50 mm (2") to 300mm (12") – Viking Johnson

Megaflex – Gates Hydraulics Ltd

Megaflo – unvented hot water storage cylinder – Heatrae Sadia

Megahorn – cycle safety device – Product Innovation Ltd

Megaject – injection moulding machine – Magnum Venus Plastech Ltd

Megajet – Walter GB Ltd

Megajet Hochleistungbohrer – Walter GB Ltd

Megalife – hot water storage cylinder – Heatrae Sadia

MEGALIFE XT – GGB UK

Megalite – hangar doors – Envirohold Ltd

Megallium – cobalt chromium alloy – Attenborough Dental Ltd

*Megaperm (Germany) – nickel iron soft magnetic alloys – Rolfe Industries

Megapower – Lamphouse Ltd

Megarad – Resinex UK Ltd

Megas II Monitor – sound reinforcement console – Digico UK Ltd

Megas II Stage – sound reinforcement console – Digico UK Ltd

Megascrape – Slurry scraper – Brown's Agricultural Machinery Company Ltd

Megashor – heavy duty shoring system – RMD Kwikform Limited

Megasl – disposable respirators – Alpha Solway Ltd

Megasol – zenon arc light fastness tester – James H Heal & Co. Ltd

Megaspiral Hose – Gates Hydraulics Ltd

MEGAsys – a computer based security management system – Advanced Perimeter Systems Ltd

Megatherm – thermal storage boiler – Ormandy Rycroft

Megator Sliding – shoe pumps and packaged sets – Megator Ltd

Megatron – European Technical Sales Ltd

Megatuff – Gates Hydraulics Ltd

Megavac – Gates Hydraulics Ltd

megazorb – Northern Crop Driers Ltd

Megga Gaz – gas filters and elements – Porvair plc

Megger – Direct Instrument Hire Ltd

Megger – Alpha Electronics Southern Ltd

MEGGER – electrical measuring devices - insulation/continuity – Megger Ltd

Megger – Range of electrical / electronic test instruments – Pennine Instrument Services Ltd

Megger – Alpha Electronics Northern Ltd

Meggezones – throat pastells – M S D Animal Health

Meggitt – Cyclops Electronics Ltd

Meggitt Marsh Guardian Systems – security alarms – Chris Lewis

Megnam – heating elements – L P C Elements Ltd

Meighs – aluminium bronze castings – Langley Alloys Ltd

*Meiko – Meiko UK Ltd

*Meiko – dishwashers – Asterix Catering Equipment Ltd

Meiko – B B C S Ltd

Meiller – Harrier Fluid Power Ltd

Meillor – gaskets and washers – Freudenberg Simrit LP

MEILLOR – Hydraulic & Offshore Supplies Ltd

MEKANO – REMTV AGENCY LTd

MEL – European Technical Sales Ltd

MEL – magnesium alloys – Magnesium Elektron

Mel Gibsons Braveheart – computer game – Square Enix Ltd

*Melafac – fire retardant melamine faced chipboard – Rex Bousfield Ltd

*Melafac Flame (Belgium) – fire retardant melamine faced chipboard – Rex Bousfield Ltd

Melamaster – high quality melamine giftware & catering products – Coleshill Plastics Ltd

MELAMASTER - High quality melamine giftware and tableware – Coleshill Plastics Ltd

MelCat – Zirconium chemicals for catalysis – M E L Chemicals

MELCHIORRE – fine grinding & super finishing solutions – R K International Machine Tools Ltd

Melco – tools (hand tools and garage equipment) – Thomas Meldrum Ltd

Melcourt – Melcourt Industries

Meleco – melamine foam sponge pad – Branova Cleaning Services

*Melegari (Italy) – carbonated drinks filling equipment – Engelmann & Buckham Ltd

Meleto – solid grade laminate cubicles – Panel Systems Ltd

Melfab – non-clothing textile materials – Terram Ltd

Mellobase – Helman Workwear

Melloguard – Helman Workwear

Melmag – magnesium alloys – Magnesium Elektron

Melnotte & Fils – champagne – O W Loeb & Co. Ltd

Melody – kitchen furniture – Moores Furniture Group

Melody – Pledge Office Chairs Ltd

Melova – cotton lace babywear – Smith & Archibald Ltd

Melox – zirconium oxides – M E L Chemicals
Meloxide – zirconium chemicals – M E L Chemicals
Melram – metal matrix composite – Magnesium Elektron
Melrasal – fluxes – Magnesium Elektron
Melrose – WC & bidet – Armitage Shanks Ltd
Melting Point – apparatus – Sanyo Gallenkamp plc
Melton – bricks – Ibstock Brick Ltd
Melton Antique Blend – Ibstock Brick Ltd
Melton Blend – Ibstock Brick Ltd
Meltus – linctus – Reckitt Benckiser plc
MEM – Cralec Electrical Distributors Ltd
MEM – Proplas International Ltd
Membrel – Triogen Ltd
***Memco (U.S.A.)** – brass fittings – The West Group Ltd
Memolub – self lubricating bearing – Square Two Lubrication Ltd
Memoquartz – multi countdown digital chronographs, multi alarm digital chronographs – Yachting Instruments Ltd
***Memorase (U.S.A.)** – eprom erasors – Ultra-Violet Products Ltd
Memorilok – access control systems – Abloy UK
Memory – photographic films, frames and albums, single use – Swains International plc
MEMS Power Generation – Generator Hire and Rental – Mems Power Generation
Men of England – mens toiletries – Norfolk Lavender Trading Ltd
Men's Magazine – maxim, stuff – Dennis Publishing
Mengle – Harrier Fluid Power Ltd
***Menlo (U.S.A.)** – solid carbide cutting tools – Tekmat Ltd
Mensa – testing of IQ – British Mensa Ltd
Mensor Corporation – Manufacturer of Pressure Test, Measurement & Calibration Instruments – Calibration Dynamics
Menthodex – cough syrups, lozenges and chest rubs – Bell Sons & Co. Ltd
Mentholatum – Mentholatum Co. Ltd
Mentor – Tyco
Mentor – dc variable speed convertor – Control Techniques
MENTOR Enterprise – Redsky It
Menzerna – special purpose polishing waxes and barrelling pastes – Lea Manufacturing Co.
Menzies Transport Services – John Menzies plc
Menzimuck – Harrier Fluid Power Ltd
Merano – glazed ceramic tiles – A Elder Reed & Co. Ltd
Mercatus – refrigeration – Interlevin Refrigeration Ltd
Mercedes – ambulance spares – Bearwood Engineering Supplies
Mercedes – L M C Hadrian Ltd
Mercedes Benz – medallion luxury motorcaravan – Auto Sleepers Ltd
***Mercedes-Benz (Germany)** – passenger cars and commercial vehicles – Mercedes Benz UK Ltd
Mercedes Benz – car showroom, service and parts – Western Automobile Co.
MERCEDES BENZ – Bailey Morris Ltd
Mercedes Benz – Harrier Fluid Power Ltd
Mercedez Benz – montana luxury motorcaravan – Auto Sleepers Ltd
Mercer (Switzerland) – quality dial and lever gauges – Tesa Technology UK Ltd
Mercer Rubber Bellows – Interflex Hose & Bellows Ltd
Merchandome – National Door Co.
Merchants Gourment Chef's – Leathams Ltd
Mercian Masterplan – hire and sale of portable buildings – Mercian Masterplan Ltd
Merculume – recessed commercial HID. luminaire – Holophane Europe Ltd
Mercuri Urval – management consultants – Mercuri Urval ltd
***Mercury (Far East)** – Sports Footwear – G H Warner Footwear plc
Mercury – label – Mercury Records
Mercury (United Kingdom) – UV lamp – Primalec
Mercury – flowhead, manometer, spirometer, audiometer, rhinomanometer and acoustic rhinometer – G M Instruments Ltd
Mercury – planetary concrete pan mixers – The Howard Group
Mercury Distribution – Leicester Mail Ltd
Mercury Litestat – R Hamilton & Co. Ltd
Mercury Mark 5 – automatic processor for offset plates – Kodak Morley
Mercury Series – loudspeakers – Tannoy Group Ltd
Mericbrand – rubber product branding – Polymeric Labels Ltd
Meridian – business telecommunications equipment – Nortel Networks UK Ltd
Meridian – energy efficient lighting products – Fern-Howard Ltd
Meridian – propeller design – Stone Marine Propulsion Ltd
Meridian 1 – digital PBX equipment – Nortel Networks UK Ltd
Meridiana – bathroom accessories – Paul Murray plc
***Meristem** – Agrico UK Ltd
Merit – a range of budget priced trailers for small boats – Indespension Ltd
Merit – UK Office Direct
***Meritena 100 (Netherlands)** – maize starch – Tate & Lyle Public Ltd Company
Meritena 200 – wheat starch – Tate & Lyle Public Ltd Company
Meritor – brake components – Roadlink International Ltd
Meritose – dextrose – Tate & Lyle Public Ltd Company
Merkel – Mayday Seals & Bearings
Merkel – fluid seals, hydraulic and pneumatic – Freudenberg Simrit LP
MERKEL – Hydraulic & Offshore Supplies Ltd
Merlett – Hampshire Hose Services Ltd
MERLETT – Hydraulic & Offshore Supplies Ltd
Merlett – Pvc hose and Ducting – Parquip Of Somerset
Merlett – Southern Valve & Fitting Co. Ltd
MERLETT PLASTICS – Hydraulic & Offshore Supplies Ltd
Merlin – metal up and over garage door – P C Henderson Ltd
Merlin – super silent generators – Harrington Generators International Ltd
Merlin – connector for oil-well conductor pipe – Oil States Industries UK Ltd
Merlin – Mono Pumps Ltd
Merlin – lighting control – Premier Solutions Nottingham Ltd
Merlin – polythene carrier bag with drawstrap handle – Britton Decoflex
Merlin – mercury analyser – P S Analytical Ltd
Merlin – envelopes – Eagle Envelopes Ltd
Merlin Gerin – process equipment – Bearwood Engineering Supplies
Merlin Gerin – Schneider Electric Ltd
Merlin Gerin – brand name for electrical distribution products – Schneider
Merlo – J & S Lewis Ltd
***Merlo** – Dennis Barnfield Ltd
Merlo – G T Lifting Solutions Ltd
MERLO – Chaintec Ltd
Merlo – Harrier Fluid Power Ltd
Merlo Telescopic – G T Lifting Solutions Ltd
Mermaid – Ascot Wholesale Ltd
Mermaid – catering bakeware – Samuel Groves
***Merobel (France)** – magnetic particle clutches – Andantex Ltd
Meropa – lubricants – Chevron
Merpol – surface active agent – Du Pont UK Ltd
Merrill – lifting clamps – Apex Tools
Merrychef – B B C S Ltd
***Merrychef** – Court Catering Equipment Ltd
Mersea – powered input units – Flakt Woods Ltd
Mersey – heavy duty rectangular end hinged grating and frame – Norinco UK Ltd
Mersey Ferris – passenger transport – Merseytravel
Merseylink – passenger transport – Merseytravel
Merseytravel – passenger transport – Merseytravel
Mervene – epoxy and acrylic two pack paints – Firwood Paints Ltd
Mesa – UK Office Direct
Mesh & Pin Fencing – Accesscaff International Ltd
Mesh Tracks – Hoofmark UK Ltd
Message – paper – Fenner Paper Co. Ltd
Message makers – flourscent shapes for writing messages on – Powell Marketing Ltd
Messageware - X400 – a range of mission-critical electronic messaging and directory software solutions for high assurance applications – Nexor Ltd
Messdoch – thermostats – Bearwood Engineering Supplies
Messenger – Vodafone Retail Ltd
Messer – Harrier Fluid Power Ltd
Messer – Messer Cutting Systems
Messer Greishiem – Messer Cutting Systems
Messersi Tracked Carriers – Parkway Plant Sales Ltd
Messier-Dowty – complete landing gear systems for military and commercial aircraft – Messier Dowty Ltd
Messr Greisham – Laser Trader Ltd
Met-Boom™ – Outreach Boom Systems – Metreel Ltd
Met-Hard – hardfacing welding electrodes – Metrode Products Ltd
Met-Jet – high velocity HVOF system – Metallisation Ltd
Met-Max – High recovery stainless steel electrodes – Metrode Products Ltd
***Met-Pump (U.S.A.)** – Magneco Metrel UK Ltd
Met-Track – enclosed track systems – Metreel Ltd
Met-Trak™ – steel drag chain system – Metreel Ltd
Metabin – S J Wharton Ltd
Metablen – polystyrene additives – Atosina UK Ltd
Metabo – Oxon Fastening Systems Ltd
Metabo – S J Wharton Ltd
Metabs – preservative – Murphy & Son
Metacone – anti-vibration mountings – Trelleborg Industrial A V S Ltd
Metadure – machinery enamel – Craig & Rose Ltd
Metadyne – anechoic rooms – I A C Company Ltd
Metaflex – spiral wound gaskets – James Walker Moorflex Ltd
Metaflood – lighting equipment – Powerlite Lighting Solutions Ltd
Metafour – computer s/w environment, networks and workstations – Metafour UK Ltd
Metagard – prefabrication primers for steel – Leighs Paints
***Metaglas (Germany)** – glass fused to metal sight glass – Visilume Ltd
Metagrip – anti corosive alkyd primers – Leighs Paints
Metair – air conditioning, heating and ventilating – Metair Mechanical Services
Metal Barriers – Accesscaff International Ltd
Metal Bells – interlink chain mail – Screen Systems Wire Workers Ltd
Metal Belts – wire conveyor belts – Screen Systems Wire Workers Ltd
Metal-Cut – cutting machine for metal reinforced profiles – Peter Gillard Company Ltd
Metal Drum – Metal Drum
Metal Hammer – magazine – Future Publishing Ltd
Metal Work – Southern Valve & Fitting Co. Ltd
METAL WORK – Hydraulic & Offshore Supplies Ltd
Metalarm – metal detectors and separators – Eriez Magnetics Europe Ltd
Metalastik – anti-vibration mountings, flexible couplings, flexible bearings and rubber suspension – Trelleborg Industrial A V S Ltd
Metalchek – metal detector for detecting/rejecting ferrous/non-ferrous metals – Lock Inspection Systems Ltd
Metalchek, Ferochek & Needlechek manufrs – Lock Inspection Systems Ltd
Metalclad Plus – industrial surface mount metal plate, wiring accessories – M K Electric Ltd
Metaletch – universal marking systems – Universal Marking Systems Ltd
***Metallack (Sweden)** – aluminium pigmented paint – Plannja Ltd
Metallic Collection – The Amtico Co. Ltd
Metallica – lever arch & ring binders – Acco East Light Ltd
Metalliform – tubular furniture, stadium and arena seating – Metalliform Holdings
METALLOGEN – lamps – Osram Ltd
Metalon – PVC/polyester metallised film – Chamberlain Plastics Ltd
Metalosate Foliar (U.S.A.) – crop micro-nutrient sprays – Thomson & Joseph Ltd
Metaltech Electrochemical – oxide and etch marking metals – Universal Marking Systems Ltd
Metaltex – plastic and metal kitchen tools – Metaltex UK Ltd
Metalube – lubricants for fibre processing – Brenntag Colours Ltd
Metalweb – Metalweb Ltd
Metalweb Shapes – Metalweb Ltd
Metalwork – air filter, regulators and lubricators – Stephens Midlands Ltd
Metalwork Pneumatic – Hampshire Hose Services Ltd
Metamax – meta-kaolin – Lawrence Industries Ltd
Metana (United Kingdom) – spring applied/hydraulic release caliper brake – Twiflex Ltd
Metapas – range of zinc passivates – Schloetter Co. Ltd
Metapex – detergents, various, anonic and non anonic blends – Brenntag Colours Ltd
Metaplex – slow release biocide – Witton Chemical Co. Ltd
Metapor (Switzerland) – microporous aluminium – Aegis Advanced Materials Ltd
Metapraxis Business Control Cycle – consultancy methodology and business management service – Metapraxis Ltd
Metapraxis EKS (Enterprise Knowledge Server) – software products – Metapraxis Ltd
Metapraxis Empower – software product – Metapraxis Ltd
METARIS HYDRAULICS – Hydraulic & Offshore Supplies Ltd
Metaseal – metallic sealing ring – Cobham Mission Equipment Ltd
Metaseal – apparatus for distributing sewage to filter beds – Ashbrook Simon Hartley Ltd
Metastron – G E Healthcare
Metatec & Metaflux – corrosion protection, lubrication, chemical cleaning, adhesives, sealants, welding consumables and accessories – Metatec Metaflux Ltd
Metavent – slate roof ventilation – Cembrit Ltd
Metavision – Lamphouse Ltd
Metcalfe – Catering Equipment - food slicing, potato chipping, potato peeling, vegetable preparing and dicing, food mixing machines and waste disposal units – Metcalfe Catering Equipment Ltd
***Metco (U.S.A.)** – sintered metal components – Aegis Advanced Materials Ltd
Metco (United Kingdom) – Quay Surface Engineering Metalblast Ltd
Metdeck – metal decking products – Expamet Building Products Ltd
Meteor – high capsulation system – D & K Europe Ltd
Meteor – nylon transmission belts – Chiorino UK Ltd

Meteor – air rifle – B S A Guns UK Ltd
Meteor – scissors – Acme United Europe
Meteor – steel surveyors tape – Fisco Tools Ltd
Meteor – colour pigments (high temperature) – Lawrence Industries Ltd
Meteor Carbine – air rifle – B S A Guns UK Ltd
Meterate – glass flowmeters – G P E Scientific Ltd
Meterbox Systems – boundary boxes – Sewaco Ltd
Meterflow – flowmeters – Emerson Process Management
Meteringbar – R K Printcoat
Meterman – Warwick Test Supplies
Meters – Stream Measurement Ltd
meters uk HCM4 TOMi & MAXi Water Meters – Product brands – Meters UK Ltd
Metfix – Alderdale Fixing Systems
Metflame (U.S.A.) – burner plates – Porvair plc
Metflex – reinforced synthetic rubber diaphragms for gas meters and a rangeof compression mouldings for gas, hi-fi, automobile and – Metflex Precision Moulding Ltd
***Metglas (U.S.A.)** – nickel-base brazing foil – Neomet Ltd
Methode – Cyclops Electronics Ltd
Methode – Selectronix Ltd
Methodist – transact property, liability, personal accident, consequential loss insurance – Methodist Insurance plc
Methyl Ionone – perfume speciality – Quest International UK Ltd
Methyl Ionone Alpha ISO – perfume speciality – Quest International UK Ltd
Methyl Myrisate – perfume speciality – Quest International UK Ltd
Metiflash – zinc alloy strip in 10m coils for flashings, weatherings etc – Metra Non Ferrous Metals
Metizinc – zinc-titanium alloy in sheets, strips or coils for roofing, flashings and all weatherings – Metra Non Ferrous Metals
Metlex – bathroom accesories – Triton Showers
Meto-Fer – Automation elements, sensors – William Teknix
Metoid – bonding system for diamond and C.B.N. wheels – D K Holdings Ltd
Metolat – wetting & dispersing agents – Lawrence Industries Ltd
Metool – motorised and spring operated cable and hose reels and collector columns – Metool Products Ltd
Metpore EFCS – Diesel Exhaust filtration and catalyst support – Porvair plc
Metpost – metal fence spikes – Expamet Building Products Ltd
Metra – consultancy – Metra Martech Ltd
Metra Martech – marketing consultancy – Metra Martech Ltd
Metrawatt – Alpha Electronics Southern Ltd
Metric-E – Baldor UK
Metrix – Alpha Electronics Southern Ltd
Metrix – C E S Hire Ltd
Metro – dental laboratory equipment – Metrodent Ltd
Metro – train – Nexus
Metro Active – playground equipment – Russell Play Ltd
Metro Era – radiator valves – Midland Brass Fittings Ltd
Metro Movie Centre Ltd – cinema & amusement centre – Cosmo Bingo Club
Metro Play – playground equipment – Russell Play Ltd
Metro Rooflights – National Door Co.
Metro Sport – playground equipment – Russell Play Ltd
Metrocall – Vodafone Retail Ltd
Metrocryl – denture base – Metrodent Ltd
Metrode – arc welding electrodes – Metrode Products Ltd
Metrode Welding Consumables – Wessex Welding & Industrial Supplies Ltd
Metrodent – teeth – Metrodent Ltd
***Metrodin High Purity (Switzerland)** – infertility drug – Merck Serono Ltd
Metrofil – dispenser – Appor Ltd
Metrohm – electrical test equipment – Spirent plc
Metrohm – Alpha Electronics Southern Ltd
Metrolux – teeth – Metrodent Ltd
Metrolux – dicast luminiare with borascilicate glass for tunnel lighting – Holophane Europe Ltd
Metromec – Wenzel UK Ltd
Metromold – Injection moulding – Metromold Ltd
Metron – circulation powder and detergent steriliser – Evans Vanodine International plc
Metronic – pneumatic tube conveyors for hospitals/commerce/industry – Air Tube Technologies Ltd
Metronics – HEIDENHAIN GB LTD
Metropolis – Turner Bianca
Metropolitan – brass whistles – J Hudson & Co Whistles Ltd
Metropolitan – plunger coffee maker – La Cafetiere
Metrose – cast iron boilers – Hartley & Sugden
Metrosil (United Kingdom) – non-linear resistors and varistors – M & I Materials Ltd
Metrotech Corporation – Sebakmt UK Ltd
Metrotest – electrical testing instruments – City Electrical Factors Ltd
Metrotherm – unvented/boiler systems – Harton Services Ltd
Metrotone – teeth – Metrodent Ltd
Metrotrak – track mounted primary jaw crushing plant – Terex
METRULOK – Hydraulic & Offshore Supplies Ltd
Metsec – Halcyon Building Systems
Metsol – Forward Chemicals Ltd
Metspeed – concrete producing machines – The Howard Group
Mettler Toledo – pH, conductivity, DO meters – Pauley Equipment Solutions
Metu System – duct support and jointing systems – Hotchkiss Air Supply
Metway – jug kettle – Metway Electrical Industries Ltd
***Metway (Malaysia)** – traditional Kettle – Metway Electrical Industries Ltd
Metway – terminal block connectors – Metway Electrical Industries Ltd
Metway – mini jug kettle – Metway Electrical Industries Ltd
Mevantraal – perfume compound – Quest International UK Ltd
MEWP – Versalift Distributors UK Ltd
Mexapol – metallised polish high solids – Evans Vanodine International plc
Mexica – branded carpets,underlays etc – Flooring Trade Supplies
***Meyer (Germany)** – specialist industrial lighting – Gray Campling Ltd
Meyer – Bruderer UK Ltd
Meynell – showers – Kohler Mira Ltd
Mez+za+nine – Mezzanine floors – Llonsson Ltd
Mezzanine – Hi-Store
Mezzdek – Preston Plywood Supplies
Mezzdek p5 – Preston Plywood Supplies
Mezzdek p6 – Preston Plywood Supplies
Mezzstore – mezzanine floors, platforms and components – European Mezzanine Systems Ltd
MF 2200 Series – tractor – Agco International Ltd
MF 3200 Series – tractor – Agco International Ltd
MF-4000 – Hydraulic & Offshore Supplies Ltd
MF 4200 Series – tractor – Agco International Ltd
MF 6200 Series – tractor – Agco International Ltd
MF 8200 Series – tractor – Agco International Ltd
MF Cerea – combine harvester – Agco International Ltd
MF2000 – Hydraulic & Offshore Supplies Ltd
MF3000 – Hydraulic & Offshore Supplies Ltd
MFP – Conventional fire panel – C-Tec Security Ltd
MG – vintage cars – British Motor Heritage Ltd
MG – L M C Hadrian Ltd
MG – Ashley Competition Exhausts Ltd
MG Process Valves – tank outlet valves – A J G Waters Equipment Ltd
MGM – brake motors – Amir Power Transmission Ltd
MGM – pump – Allpumps Ltd
MGN – A M C Rollers Ltd
MHA – Southern Valve & Fitting Co. Ltd
MHA – Hydraulic & Offshore Supplies Ltd
MHG – linear encoder – Newall Measurement Systems Ltd
MHS – Hydraulic Component & Systems Ltd
Mi-Va – workshop circular & bandsaw – Addison Saws Ltd
Mia Romanoff – Tektura plc
MIAG – Chaintec Ltd
Miatex – heat resisting leather – Bennett Safetywear
MIC – T V H UK Ltd
MIC – Chaintec Ltd
MICa – software systems, education business systems – Fretwell-Downing Hospitality Ltd
Mica – mineral filler – Lawrence Industries Ltd
Mica Supplys – import & processes of mica components, mica powder ceramics metal parts – Dean & Tranter
Micaclad – coloured pigments for plastic – Lawrence Industries Ltd
Micafil – Minelco Ltd
Michael Joseph – adult fiction and non-fiction - hardback and paperback – Penguin Books Ltd
Michael Leather Clothing – leather clothing – Michael Clothing Co
Michael Owens World League Soccer – computer game – Square Enix Ltd
Michelin – Michelin Tyre plc
Michelin – Wealden Tyres Ltd
Michigan – Harrier Fluid Power Ltd
***Mico (United Kingdom)** – panic hardware – Assa Abloy Security Solutions
MicoNav – precision underwater acoustic measuring instrument – Sonardyne International Ltd
Miconic – 16 bit microprocessor lift control system – Schindler
Micracall – Vodafone Retail Ltd
Micrel – Cyclops Electronics Ltd
Micro – water softener – B W T Ltd
Micro – small programmable logic controller – Schneider
Micro – custom carpet tiles – Brintons Carpets Ltd
Micro-Beam – flexible coupling – Huco Dynatork
Micro Crusher – Digbits Ltd
Micro Dicing Systems – dicing machine – Loadpoint Ltd
Micro Diet – diet food – Uni Vite Healthcare
Micro-Em – small portable filter pump – P M D UK Ltd
MICRO-FAG – Hydraulic & Offshore Supplies Ltd
Micro-Felt – fabric filter media for high filtration efficiency – Andrew Webron Ltd
Micro Focus Cobol (United Kingdom) – Application analysis – Micro Focus Ltd
Micro-Loft – polyester performance insulations – Du Pont UK Ltd
Micro-Lub – PTFE and hard chrome deposit – Firma Chrome Ltd
MICRO-REGCAROUSELS – SCREEN PRINTING MACHINES – Micro-Reg Carousels
Micro Sandwich – corrugated cardboard – Calpack Ltd
Micro Sandwich Display – corrugated cardboard – Calpack Ltd
Micro Scalextric – pre-school motor racing – Hornby Hobbies Ltd
***Micro Spire** – Wavelength Electronics Ltd
Micro-Thermal Analyser (M.T.A.) – heat testing equipment – Ta Instruments
Micro-Ulva – portable CDA insecticide and fungicide applicator – Micron Sprayers Ltd
Micro X – 2 phase only signal controller – Pike Signals Ltd
Micro x – rupture disc – Continental Disc UK Ltd
MicroAce – dicing machine – Loadpoint Ltd
Microair – aerial atomisers – Micron Sprayers Ltd
Microband – agricultural machinery – Horstine Farmery
MicroBar – Minelco Ltd
Microbarb – press fit brass insert for thin section plastics – Tappex Thread Inserts Ltd
Microblock – Solmedia Laboratory Supplies
***MICROBOOSTERS** – Crop specific mixers – Nutrel Products Ltd
Microbore – fine boring tools and spindle tooling – Microbore Tooling Systems
MICROBORE – Hydraulic & Offshore Supplies Ltd
Microbuild – super strength admixtures – Everbuild Building Products Ltd
Microcall – Vodafone Retail Ltd
Microcans – non-refillable cylinders – Specialty Gases Ltd
MicroCarb – Minelco Ltd
MICROcel – City Technology Ltd
Microcene – Polyethylene (Metallocene) powders for rotational mouldings. – Micropol Ltd
Microcentric – Leader Chuck Systems Ltd
MicroChamber – Conservation Resources UK Ltd
Microchip – Cyclops Electronics Ltd
Microchip – semiconductors – Anglia
Microclean – ultrasonic aqueous and semi-aqueous cleaning systems – Guyson International Ltd
Microclene – Ambient air filtration units – The Toolpost
Microcoat – LD and HD PE powders for fluidised bed-coating – Micropol Ltd
Microcoat – Polyethylene and nylon powders for dipcoating – Micropol Ltd
Microcreation – high volume reference text data base publishers – Page Bros Norwich Ltd
Microcut – Lead Precision Machine Tools Ltd
MicroDin – programmable signal conditioner-din rail mounting – Lee-Dickens Ltd
Microdol – dolomite – Omya UK Ltd
Microdot – connectors – Anglia
Microdot – precision dispenser – Humiseal Europe Ltd
Microdress – grinding wheel thinning attachment – P G T Ceewrite Ltd
Microdynamics – ignition systems and turbo products, rev limiters performance meter – Autocar Electrical Equipment Company Ltd
Microelectrica Scientifica (Italy) – Mathew C Blythe & Son Ltd
Microface – computer aided test systems, automation systems and robotics – Microface Ltd
Microfast – organic pigments – Kromachem Ltd
Microfeeder – high accuracy and low rate volumetric feeder – Gericke Ltd
Microfile – personal organisers – Filofax Stationary Suppliers
Microfilm Shop, The – microfilm supplies and equipment – Microfilm Shop
Microfilter – Harrier Fluid Power Ltd
Microfiltrex – design and manufacture specialist microfiltration and separation products for the aerospace and defence nuclear, polymer, pharmaceutical and industrial markets. – Porvair plc
Microfine 2 – L N S Turbo UK Ltd
Microfit – modular portable CDA sprayer for herbicide applications – Micron Sprayers Ltd
MicroFlex – Baldor UK
Microflex – wood treatment – Spencer Coatings Ltd
Microflex – servo drive couplings – British Autogard Ltd
MicroFlex e100 – Servo Drive – Baldor UK
Microflow – beer dispense equipment – Microflow Europe T/A Total Celler Systems
Microflow – Bronkhorst UK Ltd

Microfoam Cavity – partial fill cavity wall insulation – Springvale Insulation Ltd

Microfoam EPS – partial fill and flooring insulation – Springvale E P S Ltd

Microfoam Flooring – floor insulation – Springvale Insulation Ltd

Microfog – pneumatic equipment – Norgren Ltd

MicroGage – precision thickness meter – Sonatest Ltd

Microgard – hazard protection workwear – Orvec International Ltd

MicroGas – Cardinal Health U.K. 232 Ltd

MicroGel – Minelco Ltd

Microguard – access control system to protect personnel from dangerous machinery or other hazards – Castell Safety International Ltd

Microlase – diode laser – Keeler Ltd

MicroLazer – printer – Texas Instruments Ltd

*Microlift – service lift 50kg-100kg – Stannah Microlifts Ltd

Microlin – Linear polyethylenes for rotational mouldings – Micropol Ltd

Microlink – Crosslinkable polyethylenes for rotational moulding – Micropol Ltd

Microlite – powdered ion-exchange resins – Purolite International Ltd

Microlite – ladder stabilizer for walls or roof access – Ladderfix Ltd

Microload – weighing system – Thermo Scientific

Microloc – workholding system – A C Hydraulics Ltd

*MicroLoc – Micron Workholding Ltd

Micrologic – control unit – Schneider

Microlook – acoustic ceiling tiles – Armstrong World Industries Ltd

MicroLoop – Cardinal Health U.K. 232 Ltd

MicroLoop - DiaryCard - MicroGas - PulseTrace - SmokeCheck - PrinterNOX - Spida - MicroRint - MicroPeak - SpiroUSB. – Cardinal Health U.K. 232 Ltd

Microlute – 96 well solid phase extraction system – Porvair plc

Microlux – lighting equipment – Powerlite Lighting Solutions Ltd

*Microlyte (The Far East) – sealed maintainace free deep cycle industrial batteries for standby (telecoms, ups) 5 year design life – S E C Industrial Battery Co. Ltd

Micromag – Trafalgar Tools

Micromark – UK Office Direct

*Micromass (U.S.A.) – ceramic foam filters and systems for cast shops and foundries – Porvair plc

Micromax – CDA atomiser for agrochemical application from vehicles – Micron Sprayers Ltd

Micromax – Microcellular rail pad – Tiflex Ltd

Micromax – energy efficient lighting products – Fern-Howard Ltd

Micromax – miniature pneumatic cylinders – Parker Hannifin Ltd

Micromax – oval microwave containers with fog gard – Pregis Rigid Packaging Ltd

MicroMed – drop & volumetric infusion controller – Malem Medical

Micromill – cnc milling machine – Denford Ltd

MICROMIST – Fike Protection Systems Ltd

Micromist – nebulisers & nebuliser compressors – A F P Medical Ltd

*Micron (Italy) – anodyzed aluminium straight edges, tee squares and set squares – Technical Sales Ltd

Micron – excavators – Neuson Ltd

Micron – the professional Office Pen – Hainenko Ltd

Micron – M S C Gleichmann UK Ltd

Micron – Hosokawa Micron Ltd

Micron/X1 – CDA atomiser for use on aircraft or ground air-assisted sprayers – Micron Sprayers Ltd

Micron/X15 – CDA atomiser for use on helicopters – Micron Sprayers Ltd

Micronair – aerial atomisers – Micron Sprayers Ltd

Micronas – Cyclops Electronics Ltd

Micronclean – supply and cleaning of cleanroom garments – Micronclean Laundry

Micronet – building management system – Schneider Electric

MicroNex – Minelco Ltd

Micronex – CDA attachment for knapsack mistblowers – Micron Sprayers Ltd

Microniser – fluid energy mill – Atritor Ltd

Micronizer – infra red heat processing systems for cocoa, cereals, pulses, beans and oilseeds for consumer products, animal feed and pet food – Micronizing UK Ltd

Micropac – hydraulic pump – Sarum Hydraulics Ltd

MICROPAC PUMPS – Hydraulic & Offshore Supplies Ltd

Micropak – backpack liquid container for use with CDA sprayers – Micron Sprayers Ltd

Micropak – Sevcon Ltd

MICROPAK 16 (United Kingdom) – weld timer – B F Entron Ltd

MICROPAK 8 (United Kingdom) – weld timer – B F Entron Ltd

MicroPeak – Cardinal Health U.K. 232 Ltd

MICROpel – City Technology Ltd

Microphen – Harman Technology Ltd

Micropilot – non-contact radar level measurement – Endress Hauser Ltd

Micropol – Low density polyethylene, polypropylene and nylon for rotational moulding – Micropol Ltd

Micropore – Harrier Fluid Power Ltd

Microporous PTFE Products – Portex Technologies Ltd

Microprofile – BLD trimetal tapes – Samuel Taylor Ltd

MicroRint – Cardinal Health U.K. 232 Ltd

Microsales – electrical components – Akhter Computers Ltd

Microsave – extra low voltage control system – Nuaire Ltd

Microscaff – Accesscaff International Ltd

Microscan – ultrasonic flaw detector – Sonatest Ltd

Microscraper 500 – L N S Turbo UK Ltd

*Microseal (U.S.A.) – adhesive application control – Valco Cincinnati

Microseal – E M Coating Services

Microsemi – Cyclops Electronics Ltd

Microset – tool presetting machines – Microbore Tooling Systems

Microset – D M G UK Ltd

Microshift – bridge controls for engine speed and gearbox clutches – Radamec Control Systems Ltd

Microsil – single in-line reed relays – Pickering Electronics Ltd

Microslim – emi suppression filter – Oxley Developments Company Ltd

Microsoft – Quintech Computer Systems Ltd

Microsoft – Microsoft – First Stop Computer Group Ltd

Microsoft – UK Office Direct

Microsoft – Supply & Support Microsoft Software and Solutions – UVFish Ltd

Microsoft – Charlton Networks

Microsoft – Forever Scotland IT Consultancy

Microsoft – Apex Computer Services Wales Ltd

Microsoft – Akita Systems Ltd

Microsoft – Microsoft Small Business Specialist – D P M Electronics Ltd

Microsoft Windows XP – magazine – Future Publishing Ltd

Microsolve – cleaning systems for use with organic solvents – Guyson International Ltd

MicroSpar – Minelco Ltd

Microsplit – British Rema Process Equipment Ltd

Microsplit – powder classifier – British Rema Manufacturing Co. Ltd

Microsplit – air separators – British Rema Manufacturing Co. Ltd

Microsprint – Emi-Mec Ltd

MICROSTAR (United Kingdom) – weld timer – B F Entron Ltd

Microstat – semi-conductive PE powders – Micropol Ltd

Microstat – agricultural machinery – Horstine Farmery

MICROSTRAIN (U.S.A.) – Techni Measure

Microswitch – Kempston Controls Ltd

MICROSYN – linear encoder – Newall Measurement Systems Ltd

*Microtap (Germany) – bench top tapping machines-microprocessor control – Robert Speck Ltd

Microtech – Engis UK Ltd

Microtech – software development – Microsystems Technology

Microtech – filter element cartridges – Microtech Filters Ltd

Microtech (Invensys) – chiller controls – Thermofrost Cryo plc

Microtech Software – procurement management software – Microsystems Technology

Microtek – flatbed and film scanners – Johnsons Photopia Ltd

Microtel – traffic data telemetry systems – Golden River Traffic Ltd

Microtest – marketing services – Research International Group Ltd

Microtherm – pasteurisers – Delaval

*Microtherm (Germany) – thermal cutouts and miniature thermostats – Hawco

Microtint – dispersed pigments for emulsions – Kromachem Ltd

Microtouch – M S C Gleichmann UK Ltd

Microtrak (United Kingdom) – access control – Feedback Data Ltd

Microtrend – B P plc

Microtrol – pneumatic equipment – Norgren Ltd

Microturn – cnc lathe – Denford Ltd

Microview – M C M

Microviper – video microscope compact – Allen Vanguard Ltd

Microway – parts for aeroplanes – Glenair UK

Microweb – membrane coated filter fabrics – Andrew Webron Ltd

Mid Bar Collapsible Gates – Bolton Gate Co. Ltd

Mid Devon Gazette – newspapers – North Devon Journal

Mid Sussex Citizen – newspapers – Mid Sussex Times & Citizen

Mid Sussex Times – newspaper – Mid Sussex Times & Citizen

Mid-Ven – veneered panels and doors – Mid-Ven Doors Ltd

Mid Wales Tourism – tourism company – Mid Wales Tourism

Midaco – Kone Cranes Machine Tool Services

MIDAS – Valeport Ltd

Midbras – brass valves etc – Midland Brass Fittings Ltd

*MidcomInc – Wavelength Electronics Ltd

Middleby Marshall – Ovens – Hugall Services Ltd

Middlesbrough Football & Athletic Co. (1986) Ltd – Middlesborough Football Club

Middlesex County Cricket Club – Middlesex County Cricket Club

Middleton – engineers and tools supplies – A J Middleton & Co. Ltd

Middlewich Chronicle – weekly title – Flintshire Chronicle Newspapers

Midel (United Kingdom) – low flammability, environmentally friendly transformer fluid – M & I Materials Ltd

Midgi-Toilet – one seat flush toilet – Landsmans Ltd

Midi (United Kingdom) – alu foil slitters & separators – Atlas Converting

Midi – medium sized stainless steel catering sinks – Franke Sissons Ltd

Midi Star – glandless solenoid valves – Norgren Ltd

Midi Star – B L Pneumatics Ltd

Midicraft – Polytronics Design Ltd

MidiMax – midi card for acorn risc computers – Xara Ltd

MIDISTAR – Hydraulic & Offshore Supplies Ltd

Midland Automation – supply monitoring relays – Midland Automation Ltd

Midland Industrial Glass Ltd – glass components for industry – Midland Industrial Glass

Midland Pneumatic – equipment/spares – Bearwood Engineering Supplies

MIDLAND PNEUMATIC – Hydraulic & Offshore Supplies Ltd

Midland Publishing – aviation publishing – Ian Allan Publishing Ltd

Midland Red – local bus and coach services in Warwickshire, Oxfordshire and surrounding areas – Stagecoach Ltd

Midlands – East Midlands – AMG Forwarding Ltd

Midlands Electricity – supply and distribution of electricity – R W E Npower

Midlock – filing cabinet – Railex Filing Ltd

Midnight Deluxe – insert living flame effect fire – Indesit Company UK Ltd

Midshires – banking, insurance and investment services – Birmingham Midshires Financial Services Ltd

Midweek Visiter – newspaper – Liverpool Daily Post & Echo

Midwife – relay adaptor – Ryder Towing Equipment

Miele – fitted kitchens and built in appliances, domestic and commercial laundry appliances, vacuum cleaners and domestic and commercial dishwashing appliances – Miele

Miele – Clean Machine UK Ltd

*Miele (Germany) – laboratory and hospital washing machines – Scientific Instrument Centre Ltd

*Miele Laundry and Dishwasher – Brewer & Bunney

*Miester (Germany) – flow switches & indicators – Tamo Ltd

Miflex – heating elements – L P C Elements Ltd

Mig Pak – industrial MIG equipment – Murex Welding Products Ltd

Migatronic – Independent Welding Services Ltd

MIGL – consulting engineers – Manderstam International Group Ltd

*Migmate (Italy) – portable mig welders – S I P Industrial Products Ltd

Mijno – Aztech Components Ltd

Mikalor – Trafalgar Tools

MIKALOR – Pinstructure Ltd

Mike Henson Presentations Ltd – multi-A.V. – Mike Henson Presentations Ltd

Mike Whitley – Mike Whitley Leather Goods

Miko Coffee – M I K O Coffee Ltd

Mikram – heating elements – L P C Elements Ltd

Mikro – Air Classifier Mills – Hosokawa Micron Ltd

Mikron – Impac Infrared Ltd

Mikron – gear hobbers – Turner Electronics

Mikron – precision moulded gears and technical components – Forteq UK Ltd

MIKROSPIN – Hydraulic & Offshore Supplies Ltd

MIL-C-24308 – Dax International Ltd

MIL-C-26482 (Series 1, Crimp) – Dax International Ltd

MIL-C-26482 (Series 1, Solder) – Dax International Ltd

MIL-C-26482 (Series 2) – Dax International Ltd

MIL-C-26500 – Dax International Ltd

MIL-C-38999 (Series 1) – Dax International Ltd

MIL-C-38999 (Series 2) – Dax International Ltd

MIL-C-38999 (Series 3) – Dax International Ltd

MIL-C-38999 (Series 4) – Dax International Ltd

MIL-C-39012 – Dax International Ltd

MIL-C-39029 – Dax International Ltd

MIL-C-5015 – Dax International Ltd

MIL-C-81511 (Series 1,2,3 & 4) – Dax International Ltd

MIL-C-83723 (Series 3) – Dax International Ltd

MIL-C-83733 – Dax International Ltd

MIL-C-85049 – Dax International Ltd

MIL'S (France) – medium vacuum pumps & systems – Girovac Ltd

***Mila (United Kingdom)** – hardware for double glazed windows and doors – Mila Hardware

Milair – waterproof and breathable pu coated fabrics – The British Millerain Company Ltd

Milano – carpet – Cormar Carpets

Milano – boots – D Jacobson & Sons Ltd

Milaproof – synthetic waterproof, FR and UV finish. – The British Millerain Company Ltd

Milborne – SMS, USSD Messaging Gateway Product – Telesoft Technologies Ltd

***Milco** – Brewer & Bunney

MILD STEEL STRIP – LOW CARBON MILD STEEL STRIP – Cold Rolled Strip Stock

***Mildly Mad Pub Company** – York Brewery Co. Ltd

Mildothane Turf Liquid – systemic fungicide – Bayer Crop Science

Mildsteel – tubulars and fittings to BS1387 and BS1740 – C M T Tube Fittings Ltd

Milecoat – road surfacings – Miles Macadam Ltd

Mileflex – road surfacings – Miles Macadam Ltd

Milegrip – road surfacings – Miles Macadam Ltd

Mileguard – road surfacings – Miles Macadam Ltd

Milepave – road surfacings – Miles Macadam Ltd

Miles Royston – Dax International Ltd

Miles Roystone – parts for aeroplanes – Glenair UK

Mileseal – road surfacings – Miles Macadam Ltd

Milestone – antiques, porcelain, books – Goss & Crested China Ltd

Milestone – record label – Ace Records Ltd

Milestone – Brand – Bluedelta

Mileta – waterproof golf clothing & sportsbags – Mileta Ltd

Miletac – road surfacings – Miles Macadam Ltd

Miletex – road surfacings – Miles Macadam Ltd

Milford – Red House Industrial Services Ltd

Milford – uplighter – Designplan Lighting Ltd

***Milfresh** – Aimia Foods

Milgear EP – gear oils – Millers Oils Ltd

***Militta (Germany)** – Coffee machines (Trade) – Melitta System Service

Milk Tippler – bird-safe milk carrier for doorstep – Hamster Baskets

***Millac** – milk powder – Pritchitts

***Millac Gold** – cream alternatives – Pritchitts

Millac Maid – one cup portion whiteners – Pritchitts

Millair – compressor oils – Millers Oils Ltd

Millar – Merlin Precision Engineering Ltd

***Millathane 300 (U.S.A.)** – synthetic rubber – Notedome Ltd

***Millathane E-34 (U.S.A.)** – synthetic rubber – Notedome Ltd

Millenia – taps – Armitage Shanks Ltd

Millenicut – files – Bearwood Engineering Supplies

Millenium – skin care – Elizabeth Arden

Millenium press metal – press work,metal forming – Midland Power Press Services Ltd

Millenium Text & Cover – paper – Fenner Paper Co. Ltd

Millennium – vinyl flooring sheet – Gerflor Ltd

Millennium – casualwear – Remys Ltd

Millennium – fishing tackle class 28 – Drennan International Ltd

Millennium – pallet wrap equipment for every industry – M J Maillis UK Ltd

Millennium – range of air-operated grease & oil pumps – Tecalemit Garage Equipment Co. Ltd

***Millennium (U.S.A.)** – Pine oil – Ferguson & Menzies Ltd

***Millennium (U.S.A.)** – solvents and cleaners – Ferguson & Menzies Ltd

Millennium Laser – paper – Fenner Paper Co. Ltd

Millennium Real Art – paper – Fenner Paper Co. Ltd

Millennium Real Silk – paper – Fenner Paper Co. Ltd

Miller – Gem Tool Hire & Sales Ltd

Miller – Welding transformers and rectifiers – Premier Welding Services Scotland Ltd

Miller – Independent Welding Services Ltd

Miller Genuine Draft – lager – Scottish & Newcastle Pub Co.

Miller Pattison – cavity wall insulation, fire barriers and loft insulation, draught proofing, wall ties – Miller Pattison Ltd

Miller Pilsner – lager – Scottish & Newcastle Pub Co.

Millerain – textile finishes for industrial fabrics – The British Millerain Company Ltd

MILLERS – Hydraulic & Offshore Supplies Ltd

Millers – musical instruments, pianos electric and traditionaland sheet music – Millers Music Centre Ltd

Millers Black Moly – dry film lubricants – Millers Oils Ltd

Millers Classic 20W-50 – for classic cars – Millers Oils Ltd

Millers Classic Mini – for mini engines and gear boxes – Millers Oils Ltd

Millers Classic Mini Sport – mini competition cars – Millers Oils Ltd

Millers Classic Sport – for classic competition cars – Millers Oils Ltd

Millers Dieselclean Plus – diesel fuel treatment – Millers Oils Ltd

Millers Hi-Wax – car shampoo – Millers Oils Ltd

Millers Injectoclean – petrol fuel treatment – Millers Oils Ltd

Millers Panolin – environmentally friendly – Millers Oils Ltd

Millers TRX – semi-synthetic transmission oil – Millers Oils Ltd

Millers XFE – diesel exclusive engine oil – Millers Oils Ltd

Millers XFS – full synthetic petrol engine oil – Millers Oils Ltd

Millers XSS – semi-synthetic petrol engine oil – Millers Oils Ltd

Milletts – leisure wear, camping equipment, mens and boys clothing, footwear, industrial clothing and sportswear – Blacks Leisure Group plc

Millicarb – micronized crystalline calcite – Omya UK Ltd

Milliken Carpet – contract carpet tiles – Milliken Industrials Ltd

Milliken Carpet - contract carpet tiles. – Milliken Industrials Ltd

Millimat – Eswa Ltd

Millinemum – Potter Cowan & Co Belfast Ltd

Millingford – Allspeeds Ltd

Millipak – Sevcon Ltd

Millipore – Harrier Fluid Power Ltd

Millipore (UK) – filtration and water purification – Millipore UK Ltd

Milliput – cold setting epoxy putty – The Milliput Co.

Millitex – scourable textile oils – Millers Oils Ltd

Millmax AW – hydraulic oils – Millers Oils Ltd

***Mills & Co (Textiles) (India and The Far East)** – indicator, bookcloth, label and filter cloths – Evans Textiles Sales Ltd

MillTech – double chain and flight conveyor – Andritz Seed & Bio Fuel Ltd

Milltest – pipe stoppers and pressure testing large diameter pipeline device – Henshaw Inflatables Ltd

Millube – gear purpose oils – Millers Oils Ltd

Millward Brown – market research – Millward Brown

Millway – slideway oils – Millers Oils Ltd

Mils – vacuum pumps – AESpump

Milton – precast concrete mainly for drainage – Milton Pipes Ltd

Milwalkee – Oxon Fastening Systems Ltd

Milward – knitting accessories – Coats Ltd

Milwaukee – Gem Tool Hire & Sales Ltd

Milwaukee – S J Wharton Ltd

Milwaukee – Knighton Tool Supplies

Mimiplex – video multiplexer for CCTV systems – Tecton Ltd

Mimram – 8 and 11 pin plug in housings – Perancea Ltd

Min-Stretch Thin – wire conveyor belts – George Lane & Sons Ltd

Minac – air cooled package chiller units – Tricool Thermal

Mindray – Ultrasound scanners – Caiyside Imaging Ltd

Mindray – Patient Monitors – Wel Medical Services

***Mineralight (U.S.A.)** – short wave ultra violet lamps – Ultra-Violet Products Ltd

***Minerprint (Italy)** – chemical for the textile printing industry – Magna Colours Ltd

Minerva – software for dealing rooms – Collaborative Solutions Ltd

***Minerva (France)** – stencils – Jakar International Ltd

Minerva – fire alarm – ADT

Minerva Football Co Ltd – association footballs, rugby balls and other sports equipment – Minerva Football Company Ltd

Minewatch – remote control and monitoring systems for mines – Davis Derby Ltd

Minfil – carboniferous limestone – Omya UK Ltd

***Mingardi (Italy)** – electric linear actuator – Electro Mechanical Systems (EMS) Ltd

Mini – small stainless steel catering sinks – Franke Sissons Ltd

Mini – Ashley Competition Exhausts Ltd

Mini – smoking kiln – Afos Ltd

Mini – L M C Hadrian Ltd

MINI – Valeport Ltd

MINI-AIR (Italy) – telecommunication air conditioning – Stulz UK Ltd Epsom

Mini Arch – lever arch with slim spine – Acco East Light Ltd

Mini-Bar – vending machine – Drinkmaster Ltd

Mini-Bar – machine tool-special purpose – Grampian Motors

Mini Biomulch – mulch – Melcourt Industries

Mini Booms – designed for concentrating oils and effluents – Megator Ltd

Mini Bus 160 – 160 amp tap of bus-bar system – Astra Engineering Products Ltd

Mini Card – Rotadex Systems Ltd

Mini-circuits – Cyclops Electronics Ltd

Mini Coker – stoker – James Proctor Ltd

Mini Compack – electric steam boilers – Fulton Boiler Works Ltd

Mini Dopplex – low cost pocket doppler – Huntleigh Healthcare

Mini Haz-Tabs – baby feeding bottle sterilization tablets – Guest Medical Ltd

***Mini Logger (U.S.A.)** – human ambulatory monitor – Linton & Co Engineering Ltd

Mini Loovent – small toilet extractor unit – Airflow Developments Ltd

Mini New Line – shopfitting – RTD Systems Limited

Mini-Plas – plastic injection moulders, mould makers – Miniplas Ltd

Mini Plaza – compact litter bin free standing – Glasdon International Ltd

Mini Quad – energy saving bulk head lighting – Designplan Lighting Ltd

Mini ROVNav – compact remote LBL acoustic transceiver – Sonardyne International Ltd

Mini SA – flexible portable single gas monitor – Scott International Ltd

Mini Seal – non-concussive taps – Sheardown Engineering Ltd

Mini Sifter – Russell Finex Ltd

***Mini-Stacker (Sweden)** – portable electric lifter – Southworth Handling Ltd

Mini Star – glandless solenoid valves – Norgren Ltd

MINI STAR – Hydraulic & Offshore Supplies Ltd

Mini Vac – beach cleaning systems – Vikoma International Ltd

Mini Weigher – lightweight digital crane scales with capacities 500kg to 10 tonnes – Straightpoint UK Ltd

Mini Wheel – conveyor wheel system – Atlantic Rubber Company Ltd

Mini-Wright – peak flow meter for measuring pulmonary function – Clement Clarke International Ltd

Mini-Wright AFS – peak flow meter for measuring pulmonary funtion – Clement Clarke International Ltd

Mini-Xtra – radiator valves – Midland Brass Fittings Ltd

Miniature – soldering iron – Antex Electronics Ltd

Miniature Corolux – lightweight p.v.c. sheets – Ariel Plastics Ltd

Minibag – Injection moulded carrying cases – Hofbauer (UK) Ltd

Minibel – sound-dampened tct circular sawblades – Gomex Tools Ltd

Minibix with banana – whole wheat flakes in biscuit form with banana – Weetabix Ltd

Minibix with chocolate – whole wheat flakes in biscuit form with chocolate – Weetabix Ltd

Minibix with fruit – whole wheat flakes in biscuit form with fruit & nuts – Weetabix Ltd

Minibloc – mains outlet – Schurter Ltd

Minibooster (Denmark) – hydraulic intensifiers – A C Hydraulics Ltd

MINIBOOSTER – Hydraulic & Offshore Supplies Ltd

Minical Mk III – MV/MA calibrator – Haven Automation Ltd

Minicall – MV/MA Calibrator – Haven Automation Ltd

Minicastor – castors – Archibald Kenrick & Sons

Minicentral – air conditioning units – Eaton-Williams Group Ltd

***Minichamps (Germany)** – diecast model cars – Amerang Group Ltd

Minicheck – Hydrotechnik UK Ltd

MINICHEF – temperature controllers – Watlow Ltd

MINICUB (United Kingdom) – mini portable incubator – Cherwell Laboratories Ltd

Minidee – Tank contents gauge switch – Bayham Ltd

Minifill – G Webb Automation Ltd

Miniflare – distress signal kit – Pains Wessex Ltd

Miniframe – aluminium sign systems – Spandex plc

Minigraph – profile cutting machine – Easab Cutting Systems

Minilift – hoists, (safety man-riding and goods lifting), hoists for aircraft ground support, weapon loading, forklift and jib trucks and handling systems – Didsbury Engineering Ltd

Minilock – quick disconnect coupling, self sealing – Cobham Mission Equipment Ltd

Minilux – lightmeters – Airflow Measurements Ltd

MINIMA – light formwork panel system – RMD Kwikform Limited

Minimaster – Seco Tools UK Ltd

Minimat – automatic pressure and water pressure sets – Calpeda Ltd

Minimatic – control valves – Northvale Korting Ltd

MiniMax – Rubber tracks and undercarriage for Mini Excavators – Midland Steel Traders Ltd

Minimax – energy efficient lighting products – Fern-Howard Ltd

Minimax Folding Tower – Accesscaff International Ltd

MiniMaxflo – Mactenn Systems Ltd

Minimeasuremaxx – distance measuring wheel – Trumeter Co Ltd

Minimess – Hydrotechnik UK Ltd

Minimess - Minicheck Schroeder, Filtration, Macnaught, Flowmeters PC 9000 – Hydrotechnik UK Ltd

Minimotor (Switzerland) – Ironless rotor DC motors and gearheads Importer – Electro Mechanical Systems (EMS) Ltd

MiniMoves – Removals and Storage – Minimoves

***Minipa (Hong Kong)** – meters – Servo & Electronic Sales Ltd

Minipact – circuit breaker – Schneider

Minipol – British Vita plc

Miniscrub – Pressure washers – B & G Cleaning Systems Ltd

Minisend – Remote reading tank contents gauge – Bayham Ltd

Minisender – dense phase pneumatic conveying system – Gericke Ltd

Minisil – single in-line reed relays – Pickering Electronics Ltd

MiniSIV – Normesh Ltd

MiniSonic – Flowline Manufacturing Ltd

MINISPACE (Germany) – close control air conditioning – Stulz UK Ltd Epsom

Minisplit – powder classifier (lab size) – British Rema Manufacturing Co. Ltd

Minisplit – British Rema Process Equipment Ltd

Minit Work Platform – Accesscaff International Ltd

MiniTemp – Radir Ltd

Minitemp – temperature controls – Rayleigh Instruments Ltd

Minitran – lightweight semitrailers – Lynton Trailers UK Ltd

MINITROL – An instrument transient peak pressure isolator – Pulsation Dampers At Pulseguard Ltd

Minival – 2 port motor open and close valve – Sunvic Controls Ltd

MINIWATT – lamps – Osram Ltd

MiniWorld – I P C Media Ltd

Minlon – Resinex UK Ltd

Minlon – engineering thermoplastic resins – Du Pont UK Ltd

Minni-Die – press brake punching equipment – Minni-Die Ltd

Minni-Die – Minni-Die Range of Press Tooling – MINNI-DIE LIMITED

Minnimatic – pumps – Walter Hill Plant Ltd

Minnkota Electric Outboards – outboard motors – Navimo UK Ltd

Minolta – UK Office Direct

Minox – Incamesh Filtration Ltd

*Minox (Germany) – cameras and binoculars – Leica Camera Ltd

Minpack – Tri Pack Supplies Ltd

Minpack, Signode, Tesa, 3M, Jiffy, ITW, Featherpost, Bostitch, Max, Joseph Kielberg, Manuli, Vibac. – Tri Pack Supplies Ltd

Minster – Victorian panelled metal up and over garage door – P C Henderson Ltd

Minster – limousine – Coleman Milne Ltd

Minster Balustrading – reconstructed natural stone balustrading – Minsterstone Ltd

Minster Fireplaces – reconstructed natural stone fireplace – Minsterstone Ltd

Minster Garden Ornaments – reconstituted limestone, seats, vases, urns and water features – Minsterstone Ltd

Minster Link – bus and coach services – East Yorkshire Motor Services Ltd

Minster Paving – reconstructed natural stone smooth, riven, country house, mosaic – Minsterstone Ltd

MINSUP – Hydraulic & Offshore Supplies Ltd

Mint – Baldor UK

Mint – Pobjoy Mint Ltd

Mint - MintDrive - FlexDrive - Flex+Drive - MicroFlex - EuroFlex - NextMove PCI - NextMove ESB - NextMove ES - NextMove ST - NextMove BX - NextMove PC - SmartMove - Super-E - Metric-E - VersaFlex - SmartMotor - HyCore – Baldor UK

Mintaurus – Harrier Fluid Power Ltd

Mintax – cameras – P M S International Group plc

MintDrive – Baldor UK

Mintech – M S C Gleichmann UK Ltd

Mintel International – market research analysts – Mintel Group Ltd

Mintex – Custom Brakes & Hydraulics Ltd

Minton Hollins – ceramic wall tiles and period designs – Johnson Tiles Ltd

MINTOR – Hydraulic & Offshore Supplies Ltd

Mintor – Reservoir and Gearbox Accessories – J B J Techniques Ltd

Mintrx – rupture disc – Continental Disc UK Ltd

Minuet – kitchen furniture – Moores Furniture Group

Minuteman Press – Minuteman Press Ltd

Minwa – battery charger – Stontronics Ltd

Miodox – micaceous oxide paints – Witham Oil & Paint Lowestoft Ltd

Miofol Roofshield 125 – tile underlay, vapour barrier and breather membrane – Thermal Economics Ltd

Mipex – crucible ramming media – Magna Industrials Ltd

MIRA – motor research – Mira Ltd

Mira – showers – Kohler Mira Ltd

Mira Showers, whirlpool baths, Triton Mixer Shower – Get bathrooms, taps, showers, accessories, sanitaryware and radiators online from purebathrooms.net. – Pure Bathrooms

Mirac – cnc bench lathe – Denford Ltd

Miracle – hammer mills, disintegrator – Miracle Mills Ltd

Miracle Tape – invisible adhesive tape – Office Depot UK

Miracoil – chrome nylon transmission belts – Chiorino UK Ltd

Miracoil Rino – synthetic drive belts, carrier belts & tapes – Chiorino UK Ltd

Miracon – sectional conveyor systems, conveyors and elevators for all industries – Miracon Conveyors Ltd

Mirada – safety spectacle frames – Parmelee Ltd

Mirage – Lusso Interiors

Mirage – roller blind system – Eclipse Blind Systems

Mirage – 75mm thick hung panel partitioning system – Komfort Workspace plc

Mirage – plastic concealed cistern – Thomas Dudley Ltd

Mirage – cover paper – James Cropper plc

Mirage – sports and leisure footwear – D Jacobson & Sons Ltd

Mirage – shower surround – Matki plc

Mirage – hardware/software realtime Cd emulation and development tool – Imagination Technology

Miranda – cameras and photographic equipment – Dixons Retail

*Miranti (Sweden) – mobile bathing stretcher – Arjo Med AB Ltd

MIRD-G – P B S I Group Ltd

MIRD-T – P B S I Group Ltd

MIRI-E – P B S I Group Ltd

MIRI-ES – P B S I Group Ltd

MIRI-I – P B S I Group Ltd

MIRI-IE – P B S I Group Ltd

*Mirogard (Germany) – non reflecting glass – Schott UK Ltd

MIRP-1 – P B S I Group Ltd

Mirrlees – Plenty Mirrlees Pumps

Mirrolene – materials and products in clear polypropylene film – Clear View Ltd

Mirropack – materials and products in transparent film – Clear View Ltd

Mirrophane – materials and products in cellulose transparent film – Clear View Ltd

Mirror Trim – Designs In Aluminium

Mirrospot – ultra sonic metal to glass bonding system – Havelock Europa plc

Mirrothene – materials and products in polythene – Clear View Ltd

MIRV-0 – P B S I Group Ltd

MIRV-NVD – P B S I Group Ltd

MIRV-U – P B S I Group Ltd

MIRV-U0 – P B S I Group Ltd

Miscol – oil additive – Hornett Bros & Co. Ltd

*Miscross Laundry Systems (United Kingdom) – control systems (laundry) – Micross Electronics Ltd

Miss Navita – cardigans/fashion wear – Kentex Jeans & Casuals

Miss Sparks – knitwear – Vinola Knitwear

Mission – books – Childs Play International Ltd

Mission T.R.W. – valves – Bearwood Engineering Supplies

Mist-X – exhaust silencer mist eliminator – Parker Dominic Hunter Ltd

Mistaire – nozzles – Delavan Ltd

Mister Pig – pig cooling systems – Access Irrigation Ltd

Mistral – Hoisery – Swift J & R Ltd

Mistral – partitioning systems – Service Partitions Ltd

*Mistral (Taiwan) – woodwind instruments – Stentor Music Co. Ltd

Mistral – Lusso Interiors

Mistral – directional roadside signage – Bribex

Mistral – centrifugal fan – Halifax Fan Ltd

Mistral – single and double door bottle coolers – I M C

Mistral (United Kingdom) – tension control disc brake – Twiflex Ltd

Mistral By Metway – electric kettle – Metway Electrical Industries Ltd

Mistrale – special grades of ferric sulphate for sewage treatment – E A West

*Misura (Italy) – systems furniture – Ergonom Ltd

Misys – software and hardware for insurance companies – Open G I

MIT – marine industrial transmissions – M I T Ltd

MIT (Multiple Insert Tooling) – process – Magnum Venus Plastech Ltd

Mita – UK Office Direct

Mitac Consultancy & Training – R L Polk UK Ltd

Mitchell and Cooper – Ascot Wholesale Ltd

Mitchell Cotts Transmissions – automotive drive-line assemblies – M C T Reman Ltd

Mitchinol – manufacturers of resins – Tennants Inks & Coating Supplies Ltd

Mitco – canvas and plastic goods – Andrew Mitchell & Co. Ltd

MITECON – Progressive Technical Development – Mitecon Ltd

MiTek – builders products, connector plates and designers – Mitek

Mitel – Cyclops Electronics Ltd

Mitotoyo – measuring equipment – Verdict Gauge Ltd

*Mitralux International (Switzerland) – hand lamps and searchlights – Pulsar Developments Ltd

Mitre – sweets – Barnetts Confectioners Ltd

*Mitre (Worldwide) – brand name sporting goods – Mitre Sports International Ltd

Mitre – countertop basin – Ideal Standard Ltd

Mitre Mate – 2-part instant adhesive system for bonding mdf and wood mitres – Chemence Ltd

Mitsubishi – Premier Lift Trucks Ltd

Mitsubishi – Cyclops Electronics Ltd

Mitsubishi – equipment & spares – Bearwood Engineering Supplies

Mitsubishi – a/c drives – Betech 100 P T Ltd

Mitsubishi – Harrier Fluid Power Ltd

Mitsubishi – Therma Group

Mitsubishi – L M C Hadrian Ltd

Mitsubishi – semiconductors, intelligent power modules – Bowers Ltd

Mitsubishi – TV. video, audio, security products, business software, industrial sewing machines, circuit protection devices, motor control gear system control equipment, robots, automotive equipmentuctors – Mitsubishi Electric Europe BV Power Systems Group

Mitsubishi – T V H UK Ltd

Mitsubishi – CBM Logix

Mitsubishi – European Drives & Motor Repairs

Mitsubishi – Stacatruc

Mitsubishi – C balance fork trucks I.C. engined and electric warehousing – Crown Lift Trucks Ltd

MITSUBISHI – Chaintec Ltd

Mitsubishi – Catercraft Catering Equipment

Mitsubishi – Merlin Precision Engineering Ltd

Mitsubishi – Ashley Competition Exhausts Ltd

Mitsubishi – Proplas International Ltd

Mitsubishi – Lamphouse Ltd

Mitsubishi Carbide – cutting tools – Mitsubishi Carbide

Mitsubishi Carbide – Precision Tools

Mitsubishi F500 – Proplas International Ltd

Mitsubishi S500 – Proplas International Ltd

Mitsubishi S500 FR-F700 – Proplas International Ltd

Mitsubishi Video Paper – video paper – Chartrite Ltd

Mitsy – ladies fashion – K & A Fashions

Mitutoyo – Precision Tools

Mitutoyo – measuring equipment – Bearwood Engineering Supplies

Mitutoyo – Emics Calibration Services

Mityvac – obstetric products – Surgicraft Ltd

Mix – Lamphouse Ltd

Mix 'N' Bake – premixes – Allied Mills

Mixaco (Germany) – mixing of solids – Coperion Ltd

Mixmeter – the smallest in-line multiphase meter in the world – Jiskoot Ltd

MixTender – U C D Ltd

Miyano – Birchfield Engineering Ltd

Miyano Machinery Inc (Japan) – cnc barworking lathes turning centres & drilling/tap centres – Citizen Machinery UK Ltd

Mizar Gloss Digital – Digital Products - Xeikon - Coated – Howard Smith Paper Ltd

Mizar Matt Digital – Digital Products - Xeikon - Coated – Howard Smith Paper Ltd

MK – ice skates – H D Sports Ltd

MK10B – 2/3/4 multi phase signal controller – Pike Signals Ltd

MKS – vacuum capacitance manometers – AESpump

*MKS (U.S.A.) – nutcracker - porting unix to windows tool – Scientific Computers Ltd

ML. Works – programming Language/environment – Global Graphics Software Ltd

ML1/K1 – C-Tec Security Ltd

MLG – GGB UK

MLG™ – GGB UK

MLine – Catering Equipment – Manitowoc Food Service UK Ltd

MLK hoist – Gustair Materials Handling Equipment Ltd

MM2000 – T M Electronics Ltd

MM710 – for the non contact on line measurement of moisture, fat, oil and protein in foods and bulk materials – N D C Infra-Red Engineering Ltd

MML McGeoch Marine – Fire doors , accommodation units for offshore – MML Ltd

MMT000 – T M Electronics Ltd

Mo-El – Mechline Developments Ltd

Mobex – mobile lincompex equipment – Nortel Networks UK Ltd

Mobi – UK Office Direct

Mobi-Deque Discotheques – Arranging Discotheques for almost 40 years – First Light London

Mobil – Hammond Lubricants & Chemicals Ltd

Mobile Exhibition Units – Landsmans Ltd

Mobile laser tag arena – Inflatable laser tag hire – Xtreme Vortex

Mobile Mains Toilets – Landsmans Ltd

Mobile Mess Rooms – Landsmans Ltd

Mobile rock climbing wall – Mobile rock climbing wall hire - portable trailer – Xtreme Vortex

Mobile Security Barrier – Birmingham Barbed Tape Ltd

mobiles – S.C.L Mobile Communications

Mobilfile – storage system – Railex Filing Ltd

Mobili Office – Office Furniture – Bucon Ltd

Mobius – mobile and portable two way radio – Motorola Ltd

Mobrey – liquid level switches – Emerson Process Management

Mod-bilt – sectional timber hutting – Boyton B R J System Buildings Ltd

Mod Comfys – ladies comfort sandals – UK Distributors Footwear Ltd

Modairflow – comfort control for air systems – Johnson & Starley Ltd

Modbore – Kennametal UK Ltd

Modbus – communications protocol – Schneider

Modbus Plus – communications protocol – Schneider

Mode – mens fashion jackets & trousers – D Gurteen & Sons Ltd

Mode Lighting – environmental lighting controller and electronic transformers for low voltage lighting – Mode Lighting UK Ltd

Model 3000 – in situ gas analyser – Codel International Ltd

Model Collector – I P C Media Ltd

Model Makers lathe – Phil Geesin Machinery Ltd

Modelling Wax – dental wax – Prima Dental Group Ltd

Modelmark – steel stamps – Pryor Marking Technology Ltd

Modelmark – punches & type – Pryor Marking Technology Ltd

Models 1 – model agency – Models One Ltd

Models Direct – modelling agency – Models Direct-National Model Register Men/Women Children Centre

***Modentic** – Yateson Stainless

Modeq – modular PC-based education system for use in teaching of power electronics or engineering – Haven Automation Ltd

Modern Art Society – prints – The Medici Galleries

Modern Classics – The Winnen Furnishing Company

Modern Furniture – The Winnen Furnishing Company

Modern Industrie SA (France) – auto parts handling, drilling and turning machines – Haesler Machine Tools

Modern Power Systems – magazine – Progressive Media Group

Modern Screws – nut, bolt and industrial fasteners – Modern Screws Ltd

Modern Skin Care – skin care range – Elizabeth Arden

Moderncross – golf buggy hire and sale – William G Search Ltd

Modernfold – folding and flat wall partitions – Guildford Shades

Modernfold 800 – vinyl concertina range – Brockhouse Modernfold Ltd

Modevo (United Kingdom) – tension control disc brake – Twiflex Ltd

Modicon – range name of automation components – Schneider

Modicon – Schneider Electric Ltd

Modicon TSX – automation PLC product – Schneider

Modified Silane – County Construction Chemicals Ltd

Moditorque (Germany) – spring applied brakes – Lenze UK Ltd

Modligiani – Digital Products - Indigo - Uncoated – Howard Smith Paper Ltd

Modo Pre-print – Business Forms – Mcnaughton James Paper Group Ltd

Modric – door furniture – Allgood

Moducel FLEXaire – AHU's & roof-top package airconditioners, fan coil units – Eaton-Williams Group Ltd

Modugrid – Modular mezzanine floors – Llonsson Ltd

MODUL AIR – Hydraulic & Offshore Supplies Ltd

Modula – shower tray – Armitage Shanks Ltd

Modulair – Modular fan coil unit – Biddle Air Systems Ltd

Modulair – airline trolley and supply system – Scott International Ltd

Modulair – Applied Energy Products Ltd

Modular – glazed ceramic tiles – A Elder Reed & Co. Ltd

Modular 2000 – multi-link glazing panels – Alumasc Exterior Building Products

MODULAR CONTROLS – Hydraulic & Offshore Supplies Ltd

Modular Fixturing – customised gauging at low cost – Intra Ltd

Modular Rooflights – daylighting systems – Alumasc Exterior Building Products

Modular Wiring – Boston security arms for retail racking displays – Boston Retail Products

Module 2000 – interchangeable sign system – Masson Seeley & Co. Ltd

Module 60 – interchangeable sign system – Masson Seeley & Co. Ltd

Module 600 – wall or pole mounted luminaire – Holophane Europe Ltd

MODULE-MOUNT – ceramic fiber furnace system – Watlow Ltd

ModuleDryer – non contact turning and drying of coated webs – Spooner Industries Ltd

Modulevel – displacer operated liquid level controller – Magnetrol International UK Ltd

Moduline – acoustic panelling – I A C Company Ltd

Modulink – conveyor modules and elements – Interroll Ltd

Modulink – manufacturers of educational and office furniture – Educational & Municipal Equipment Scotland Ltd

***Modulock (Germany)** – modular tooling system for machining centres – Macinnes Tooling Ltd

***Moduloval (France)** – elliptical concrete drainage pipes – Stanton Bonna Concrete Ltd

Modulus – carpet tile and broadloom carpeting – Bonar Floors Ltd

modulyo – freeze dryers – AESpump

Modupack – onshore accommodation – Ferguson Group Ltd

Modus – flushing valve – Armitage Shanks Ltd

***Moebius & Rupert (Germany)** – pencil sharpeners – Jakar International Ltd

Moeller – E Preston Electrical Ltd

Moeller – Proplas International Ltd

MOFFET MOUNTY – Hydraulic & Offshore Supplies Ltd

MOFFETT-KOOI – Chaintec Ltd

Mohawk – Red House Industrial Services Ltd

Mohel Nice – electric motors – Bearwood Engineering Supplies

Moistrex MX8000 – for the easy and rapid moisture analysis of paper and board samples either at line or in the lab – N D C Infra-Red Engineering Ltd

Moists – toilet tissues – Jeyes

Mojo – paper – Fenner Paper Co. Ltd

Moklansa – European Technical Sales Ltd

Mokro – high cr-iron wear resistant castings – Bradken UK Ltd

Mokveld – high pressure engineered valves – S P P Pumps

***Molasses** – E D F Man

Moldanized Shapes – heat shrink mouldings – Hellermann Tyton

Moldmax – Materion Brush Ltd

Moldmax – high conductivity alloy – Uddeholm Steel Stockholders

Mole Post – Aremco Products

Moleculite – transition metal oxidation catalyst – Molecular Properties Ltd

Molex – Cyclops Electronics Ltd

Molex – pump – Whale Tankers Ltd

Molfit – wheels equipment – Terry Johnson Ltd

***Moli International** – Range of insulated drop-in ice bins and bar sinks – Taylor Foodservice Facilities

Molins – tobacco machinery – Molins plc

Mollart – Mollart Engineering

Mollasine – mollased meal – Rumenco Ltd

Mollichaff – dust free chaff for horses – Horsehage Manufacturers Mark Westaway & Son

Molton Brown – cosmetics – Molton Brown Ltd

Moly Slip – Molyslip Atlantic Ltd

MOLYCOTE – Wolds Engineering Services Ltd

Molydome – atom parts – Spiring Enterprises Ltd

Molykote – greases – Bearwood Engineering Supplies

***Molykote (Germany)** – speciality lubricants – R D Taylor & Co. Ltd

Molykote – R W Greeff

Molykote – East Midland Coatings Ltd

Molymod – molecular model parts and system – Spiring Enterprises Ltd

Molyneux – rail fixings – Cranequip Ltd

Molyslip – Molyslip Atlantic Ltd

Molytex – lubricants – Chevron

***Moment (Sweden)** – wallcovering – Tektura plc

Momentim Packaging (United Kingdom) – Foilco Ltd

Moments – pillows & bathroom sets – Fogarty Filled Products Ltd

Momentum – control products, i/o modules – Schneider

Monaco – scissors and knives – Acme United Europe

Monarch – airlines – Monarch Airlines

Monarch – marking systems – Avery Dennison

Monarch – piping music – K R L

Monarch – agricultural grass and clover mixtures – Limagrain UK Ltd

***Monarch (U.S.A.)** – oil burner nozzles – Anglo Nordic Burner Products Ltd

Monarch – offset blankets – Kodak Morley

Monarch – extension ladders – J Gorstige Ltd

Monarch Ladders – Accesscaff International Ltd

Monarflex – Fieldway Supplies Ltd

Monax – borosilicate glass/flat gauge glass – Monax Glass Ltd

Monckton Sunbrite – industrial and domestic coke – Monckton Coke & Chemical Co.

Mondas – business process software & consultancy – Corero Systems Ltd

Mondéco – seamless terrazzo flooring – Flowcrete UK

Mondeo – European Technical Sales Ltd

Mondi Packaging – corrugated cartons – Boxes & Packaging Ltd

Mondial Assistance – 24 hour recovery service, help line – Mondial Assistance Ltd

***Mondial Elite** – Pentland Wholesale Ltd

***Mondo (Italy)** – sunglasses – Fabris Lane Ltd

Mondolux – lighting equipment – Powerlite Lighting Solutions Ltd

Moneyfacts – provider of financial information – Moneyfacts Group plc

Moneywise – The Woolwich

Monica – age classification – C A C I

Monicon – equipment & spares – Bearwood Engineering Supplies

MONITOR – Valeport Ltd

Monitor – rectangular flush meters in matt black – Elektron Components Ltd

Monitor – vandal resistant lighting – Designplan Lighting Ltd

Monitor – various high technology ceramic coatings – Monitor Coatings Ltd

Monitor Audio – loudspeakers – Monitor Audio Ltd

Monitor III – prison cell lighting – Designplan Lighting Ltd

Monitorq – torque monitoring systems – British Autogard Ltd

Monkey – land clearing winch – Trewhella Brothers Ltd

Monkey Borer – hand operated post hole borer – Trewhella Brothers Ltd

Monkey Jack – hand operated jack – Trewhella Brothers Ltd

Monkey - Monkey Borer - Monkey Jack - Monkey Winch - Monkey Strainer - Wallaby Winch - Trulift – Trewhella Brothers Ltd

Monkey Strainer – wire strainer for fencing – Trewhella Brothers Ltd

Monkey Winch – land clearing winch – Trewhella Brothers Ltd

Monkwell – expanding file – Acco East Light Ltd

Monnier & Zahner AG – Haesler Machine Tools

Monninghoff (Germany) – tooth clutches – Lenze UK Ltd

Mono – motor driven siren – Signals Ltd

Mono – progressing cavity pumps – Mono Pumps Ltd

Mono – Arun Pumps Ltd

Mono – Autobar Group Ltd

Mono – hinge – Medway Galvanising & Powder Coating Ltd

Mono – progressing cavity rotary displacement pumps – Axflow

Mono – subsoiler – Simba International Ltd

Mono-Link – firing module for power controllers – United Automation Ltd

Mono-Muncher – equipment/spares – Bearwood Engineering Supplies

Mono-Pump – pumps/spares – Bearwood Engineering Supplies

Mono pumps – Anchor Pumps Co. Ltd

Mono Pumps – Denton Pumps Ltd

Mono pumps – Progressing cavity – Fluid Pumps Ltd

Monobloc – folding arm awnings – Guildford Shades

Monobolt – structural breakstem fastener with multi-grip capability – Avdel UK Ltd

Monobolt – blind bolt system – Zygology Ltd

***Monoceram (Italy)** – ceramic tiles – A Elder Reed & Co. Ltd

Monocompact – Grundfos Pumps Ltd

***Monocoque Trailers** – Easterby Trailers Ltd

Monocouche – P F T Central

MONODIE – synthetic monocrystalline diamond wire-drawing die blanks – Diamond Detectors

MONODITE – synthetic monodite crystalline diamond tool blanks – Diamond Detectors

MONODRESS – synthetic monodite crystalline diamond dressers – Diamond Detectors

Monoflex – forming fabric – Heimbach UK

Monoframe – aluminium sign systems – Spandex plc

Monogram – cutlery – Amefa

Monogrid – wire conveyor belts – George Lane & Sons Ltd

Monolastex Smooth – high performance decorative masonry finish – Sika Liquid Plastics

Monolyn – high performance blown pallet wrap material (Stretch Film) – M J Maillis UK Ltd

Monomig – single phase M.I.G. machines – Sureweld UK Ltd

MONOPAK (United Kingdom) – weld timer – B F Entron Ltd

Monoplan – moveable wall system – Becker Sliding Partitions Ltd

Monopoly Two (United Kingdom) – broadloom – Checkmate Industries Ltd

***Monoprene** – Anitox

Monopress – Grundfos Pumps Ltd

Monopty – disposal biopsy instrument – Bard Ltd

Monorail (United Kingdom) – plastic curtain track – Integra Products

Monoskin – high tech sports and outdoor socks – Sweatshop

Monostrut Rail – Berry Systems

Monotex ML – water based textile ink – Fujifilm Sericol Ltd

Monothane (United Kingdom) – single component polyurethane elastomers for rollers, seals and gaskets – Dow Hyperlast

Monothane – single component heat cure polyurethane resins – Chemical Innovations Ltd

Monotrak – mobile shelving systems – Rackline Ltd

Monotype C.D. 6.0. – typeface resource – Monotype Imaging Ltd

Monovec – schilling rudder – Hamworthy Waste Water plc

MonoWhale – one man operated gully emptier – Whale Tankers Ltd

Monrox – self flow castables – Calderys UK Ltd

***Monsanto** – Rutherfords

Monsieur – optical frames and sunglasses – Hilton International Eye Wear Ltd
Monsoon – motors for use in tropical conditions – Brook Crompton UK Ltd
Monsoon – fragrance & toiletries – Coty UK Ltd
Monsoon – shower pumps – Stuart Turner Ltd
Montage – energy monitoring & targeting – Schneider Electric
Montana – WC suite – Armitage Shanks Ltd
Montana Syrups – U C D Ltd
Montanal (Germany) – sodium/potassium chloride – Hostombe Group Ltd
Montecatini – shoes – Patrick Shoes Ltd
***Montecristo (Cuba, Jamaica, Europe and Honduras)** – cigars – Hunters & Frankau Ltd
Montevideo – sheep shear – Burgon & Ball Ltd
MONTINI – Chaintec Ltd
***Montmere (Worldwide)** – importers and exporters of textile goods – Simportex Ltd
Montrose – loop pile carpet tile – Warlord Contract Carpets Ltd
Montrose – Try & Lilly Ltd
Monument – Gem Tool Hire & Sales Ltd
Monument – plumbers tools – Monument Tools Ltd
***Mood (Italy)** – executive furniture – Ergonom Ltd
Moody Sigma Yachts – Princess Yachts International plc
Moog – Harrier Fluid Power Ltd
Moog – equipment/spares – Bearwood Engineering Supplies
MOOG – Pressure Design Hydraulics Ltd
MOOG – Hydraulic & Offshore Supplies Ltd
MOOG ATCHLEY – Hydraulic & Offshore Supplies Ltd
MOOG PEGASUS – Hydraulic & Offshore Supplies Ltd
MOOG WHITTON – Hydraulic & Offshore Supplies Ltd
Mookow – Baby & Infant Wear – BRANDMOO
Moonbag – sleeping bag – Comfy Quilts Ltd
Moonlight – energy efficient lighting products – Fern-Howard Ltd
Moonraker – fishing tackle – Daiwa Sports Ltd
Moonstone – wallcovering – Graham & Brown Ltd
Moorcroft – hand made ornamental pottery giftware and table lamps – W Moorcroft Ltd
Moore & Wright – measuring equipment – Bearwood Engineering Supplies
Moorepay – payroll processing services – Moorepay Ltd
Moorish – Cesol Tiles Ltd
Moorland – waterproof clothing – J Barbour & Sons Ltd
Moorside – ring joint gaskets & specialist metal machining – James Walker Moorflex Ltd
***Moorwood Vulcan** – medium & heavy duty catering equipment – Moorwood Vulcan
Moorwood Vulcan – combination ovens, catering equipment and water boilers – Manitowoc Food Service UK
Moorwood Vulcan – B B C S Ltd
Moose (United Kingdom) – pedestal bandfacer – R J H Finishing Systems Ltd
Mopar – Harrier Fluid Power Ltd
MOPLANT – thorn guard and nail guard anti puncture tyre liners – Moplant
MOPS – the national newspapers' mail order protection scheme – National Newspaper Safe Home Ordering Protection Scheme
MORA – Chaintec Ltd
Moraine – Interface Europe Ltd
Morane – portable I.D. systems, security lamintor machines and materials – Payne Security Ltd
MORAVIA – Hydraulic & Offshore Supplies Ltd
Moravia – Trafalgar Tools
Morbank – volumetric glassware – Bibby Scientific Ltd
More O'Ferrall – outdoor advertising hoardings – Clear Channel International Ltd
Moreophos – granulated fertilizer – Soil Fertility Dunns Ltd
Moreplene – types of rope – Cotesi UK Ltd
Moreplon – types of rope – Cotesi UK Ltd
Moreprop – types of ropes – Cotesi UK Ltd
Moresecure – slotted angle – Moresecure Ltd
Moresecure British Standard – bolt together medium duty shelving system – Moresecure Ltd
Moresecure Clearstor 2 – clip together standard duty shelving system – Moresecure Ltd
Moresecure Clip-on Longspan – clip-together heavy duty longspan shelving system – Moresecure Ltd
Moresecure Containers – plastic small-parts storage system – Moresecure Ltd
Moresecure Euro Shelving – clip-together medium duty shelving system – Moresecure Ltd
Moresecure Palletstor – heavy duty pallet racking system – Moresecure Ltd
Moresecure Rolled Edge – bolt together standard duty shelving system – Moresecure Ltd
Moresecure Square Tube – knock together square tube construction system – Moresecure Ltd
***Moretti Forni** – Pizza equipment – Middleby UK Ltd
Morey Boogie – body boards – Gul Watersports Ltd
Morflex (U.S.A.) – couplings – Cross & Morse
Morflex – Mercury Bearings Ltd
Morgan – R K International Machine Tools Ltd
Morgan – lift out crucible furnace type L.O. – Molten Metal Products Ltd
Morgan Central – axis tilting furnace – Molten Metal Products Ltd
Morgan Dual Energy Bale Out Furnace – MKIV – Molten Metal Products Ltd
Morgan Electric – resistance bale out furnace – Molten Metal Products Ltd
Morgan Electric – resistance basin tilting furnace MKIV – Molten Metal Products Ltd
Morgan Electric Resistance Bale Out Furnace – MKIV – Molten Metal Products Ltd
Morgan Gas Fired Bale Out Furnace – MKIX – Molten Metal Products Ltd
Morgan HE – electric ladle – Molten Metal Products Ltd
Morgan High Efficiency – bale out furnace – Molten Metal Products Ltd
Morgan Miniature – crucible furnace – Molten Metal Products Ltd
Morgan Rekofa – European Technical Sales Ltd
Morgan's – screen printing services, contract manufacturers and contract fillers – Morgans Pomade Company Ltd
Morgan's Dark Secret – darkens grey hair; formulated for women – Morgans Pomade Company Ltd
Morgan's Hair Darkening Cream – darkens grey hair – Morgans Pomade Company Ltd
Morgan's Perfumed Pomade – darkens grey hair – Morgans Pomade Company Ltd
Morgan's Pomade – darkens grey hair – Morgans Pomade Company Ltd
Morgan's Revitalising Shampoo – shampoo which helps to revitalise dry hair – Morgans Pomade Company Ltd
Morganite – carbon brushes and current collectors – Morganite
Morgardshammar – equipment/spares – Bearwood Engineering Supplies
MORI (United Kingdom) – high density etch source for polysilicon & dielectrics – Aviza Technology UK Ltd
Mori Seiki – Machine Tool Supplies Ltd
Morlands – sheepskin and sheepskin coats, jackets, boots and slippers, lambswool car rugs – Morlands Glastonbury
Morning Fresh – dishwasher products and washing-up liquid – P Z Cussons International Ltd
Moro – gully emptier – A B Schmidt UK Ltd
***Moroccan Wines From Celliers Meknes** – Vinceremos Wines & Spirits Ltd
Morooka – Harrier Fluid Power Ltd
Moros – shearing and baling machinery – M M H Recycling Systems Ltd
Morphy Richards – electrical appliances – Morphy Richards Ltd
Morphy Richards – domestic heating and electrical appliances – Glen Electric Ltd
Morplan – Morplan
***Morray (Japan)** – robot palletizing systems – W J Morray Engineering Ltd
Morray – bagging and weighing equipment, sack sealing and handling systems – W J Morray Engineering Ltd
Morris – Gustair Materials Handling Equipment Ltd
Morris – vintage cars – British Motor Heritage Ltd
Morris – S J Wharton Ltd
Morris – adhesives, lubricants/ steam engine oils – Arrow Supply Co. Ltd
Morris – L M C Hadrian Ltd
MORRIS – Hydraulic & Offshore Supplies Ltd
Morris Brake Fluid – high molecular weight polyalkylene glycol ether and ether borates fluid – Morris Lubricants
MORRIS LUBRICANTS – Wolds Engineering Services Ltd
Morris Lubricants – oils, lubricants and coolants for all compressors – Airware International Ltd
***Morris Lubricants** – machine cutting lubricants – Turner Tools Ltd
Morris Material Handling – Dale Lifting and Handling Equipment Specialists
Morris Minor – vintage cars – British Motor Heritage Ltd
Morris Office Furniture – Capex Office Interiors
Morris Tooling – CNC and automotive shank tool holder – Bilz Tool
Morris Universal Antifreeze – engine frost protection to -34 degress C – Morris Lubricants
Morrisflex (United Kingdom) – tungsten carbide and high speed steel burrs, contact wheels and mounted points – R J H Finishing Systems Ltd
Morrison – equipment & spares – Bearwood Engineering Supplies
MORRISON-ITI – Hydraulic & Offshore Supplies Ltd
Morrison Sale Purchase – Cory Logistics Ltd
Morrison Shipping – Cory Logistics Ltd
Morrison Tours – Cory Logistics Ltd
Morrisons – Supply Chain Solution Ltd
Morse (United Kingdom) – roller chain & torque limiters – Cross & Morse
Morse – S J Wharton Ltd
Morse – equipment/spares – Bearwood Engineering Supplies
Morso – Baxi Group
Morspot – painting and decorating contractors – Morris & Spottiswood Ltd
Mortadd – Forward Chemicals Ltd
MorTie – stainless steel masonry wall tie (new build) – Helifix Ltd
Morton Ploughshares – Morton Mixers & Blenders Ltd
Morton Youngs Borland Ltd – window furnishings – Morton Young & Borland Ltd
Mortons – herbal remedies – Lifeplan Products Ltd
Mosa – equipment & spares – Bearwood Engineering Supplies
Mosa – Independent Welding Services Ltd
Mosa – welding & electric generatores – John Davies 2001 Ltd
Mosail – video multiplayer – Tecton Ltd
Moser-Glaser (Switzerland) – Mathew C Blythe & Son Ltd
Mosfet – surface mount electronic devices – Diodes Zetex Semiconductors Ltd
Moss – Red House Industrial Services Ltd
Moss – Abbey England Ltd
Mosses & Mitchell – audio and video jackfields, jacks and accessories for studio and broadcast applications – Mosses & Mitchell Ltd
MOSTANA – B S A Machine Tools
Mostana 165 lathes – Phil Geesin Machinery Ltd
Mostana 1m63 centre lathes – Phil Geesin Machinery Ltd
Mostana heavy duty lathes – Phil Geesin Machinery Ltd
Mostyn – chemical products for agriculture and public health – Hockley International Ltd
Motak – lubricants – Chevron
Motex – lubricants – Chevron
Mothercare – retail stores & merchandise for the family – Mothercare plc
Mothers Pride – bread and flour confectionery – Hovis
Motherwell Control Systems – equipment/spares – Bearwood Engineering Supplies
Motic – Motic Microscopes & Motic Digital Camera Kits – G D C Microscopes
Moticam – Digital Camera Kits – G D C Microscopes
Motiflex – Baldor UK
MotiFlex e100 – Servo Drive – Baldor UK
Moto Lita – steering wheels – Moto-Lita Ltd
MOTOFLOW – Hydraulic & Offshore Supplies Ltd
***Motoman (AB) (Sweden)** – robot welding and turn key suppliers – Motoman Robotics UK Ltd
Motor Boat & Yachting – I P C Media Ltd
Motor Boats Monthly – I P C Media Ltd
Motor Caravan – I P C Media Ltd
Motor Cycle City – retail motor cycles, clothing parts and accessories and servicing – Infinity Motorcycles Ltd
Motor Lawclub – motor uninsured loss recovery – Allianz Legal Protection
Motor Lawclub "Elite" – uninsured loss recovery, recovery of the insured vehicle anywhere in europe following an inmobilising accident. – Allianz Legal Protection
Motor Sport – magazine – Haymarket Media Group
Motor Trade Select – complete office – Allianz Insurance plc
Motorbase – The Woolwich
***Motorbooks Int (U.S.A.)** – car, motoring and aviation books – J Haynes Ltd
MotorCall – Allianz Insurance plc
MotorCover – Allianz Insurance plc
Motorcraft – Harrier Fluid Power Ltd
Motorcycle Lawclub – uninsured loss recovery, recovery of the insured mmotorcyle anywhere in europe following an immobilising accident discount on datatag – Allianz Legal Protection
Motorfax – motoring organisers – Logax Ltd
Motorguard – Harrier Fluid Power Ltd
Motoring News – magazine – Haymarket Media Group
Motorola – Cyclops Electronics Ltd
Motorola – Servicom High Tech Ltd
Motorola – Radio Relay
Motorola – UK Office Direct
Motorolla – Harrier Fluid Power Ltd
Motorplan – software computer systems – R L Polk UK Ltd
Motorvision – P B S I Group Ltd
Motovario – Mercury Bearings Ltd
***Motovario (Italy)** – gear units and geared motor units – Motovario Ltd
Motovario – gearboxes – Betech 100 P T Ltd
Motovario Gearboxes – gearboxes – Potteries Power Transmission Ltd
Mouette – folding mobile commode – Helping Hand Co.
Mould-Dry – injection moulding systems – Munters Ltd
Mouldable – firebrick – Vitcas Ltd
Mouldex – S J Wharton Ltd
Mouldings – Plaut International
Mouldmaster – footballs, netballs, rugby balls and basketballs – Mitre Sports International Ltd
Mouldspeed – Cox Wokingham Plastics Ltd

*Moulin – Ivory & Ledoux Ltd

Moulton – bicycles – The Moulton Bicycle Co. Ltd

Mount Riley (New Zealand) – Patriarche Wine Agencies

Mount Royal – pocket & pendant watches – Topical Time Ltd

Mountain Bike Rider – I P C Media Ltd

Mountain House – Freeze Dried Meals – European Freeze Dry

Mountfort – superior saddlery – E Jeffries & Sons Ltd

Mourn Range – Candle – Northern Candles

Mouse – three wheeled road vehicle with petrol and diesel engine – Combidrive Ltd

Mouse Training – IT Training for Business – Mouse Training

Mousebreaker.com – I P C Media Ltd

Mouthcare – periodontal product distribution – Plandent

Mouvex – oscillating disc pumps – Axflow

MoveAway – security products – O W L Electronics Ltd

Movicol – isosmotic laxative – Norgine International Ltd

Movidrive – Drive Invertors – S E W Eurodrive Ltd

Movidyn – Servo Controller – S E W Eurodrive Ltd

Movimot – For geared motor with integrated frequency inverter – S E W Eurodrive Ltd

Moving Floor – automatic truck loading system – Joloda Hydraroll Ltd

Moving Picture Co. – facility house – Moving Picture Co. Ltd

Movinord Partitioning – Advanced Ergonomic Technologies Ltd

*Moviret (Germany) – DC thyristor control – S E W Eurodrive Ltd

Movistrob – stroboscopes – James H Heal & Co. Ltd

Movitec – K S B Ltd

Movitrac – inverter – S E W Eurodrive Ltd

Movitron – S E W Eurodrive Ltd

Movline (Portugal) – composite fibre ropes – Cotesi UK Ltd

Movlon (Portugal) – polypropylene ropes – Cotesi UK Ltd

Movsplit (Portugal) – beaded ropes – Cotesi UK Ltd

Movspun (Portugal) – polypropylene staple – Cotesi UK Ltd

Movstar (Portugal) – yacht ropes – Cotesi UK Ltd

*Moxie (Canada) – thermistors and thermal switches – Hawco

*Moxy (Norway) – dump trucks – Marubeni Komatsu Ltd

MP 75 – P F T Central

MP Filtri – Harrier Fluid Power Ltd

MPAC – Telephony Boards (CTI) – Telesoft Technologies Ltd

MPACS – intergrated into cloted loops – Intra Ltd

MPL – Mamelok Holdings Ltd

mPm – Solenoid valve and pressure transducer connector – Motion29 Ltd

Mpoptions – G E Healthcare

MPR10 – P B S I Group Ltd

MPR20 – P B S I Group Ltd

MPR2000 And MPC2000D – P B S I Group Ltd

MPR3E5 – P B S I Group Ltd

MPS (Switzerland) – Precision miniature bearings and ballscrews – Electro Mechanical Systems (EMS) Ltd

MPSI – mineral grinding equipment – Metso Minerals UK Ltd

MQZ – Thermo Electrical

MR-24 – standing seam roof cladding – Lindab Building Systems

Mr Fothergill's Seeds – packeted seeds (for use by the hobby gardener) – Mr Fothergills Seeds Ltd

Mr Fothergills – packeted seeds (for use by the hobby gardener) – Mr Fothergills Seeds Ltd

MR-Memex – system for managing mixed distributed data resources using data compression and parellel processing principles to provide realtime data management and full content search access – Memex Technology Ltd

Mr. Muscle – UK Office Direct

Mr. Sheen – UK Office Direct

Mr Superspray Lube – aerosol lubricant for cycle, car and home – Superspray Lube

MRAMS – marine riser angle monitoring system – Sonardyne International Ltd

MRAR – P B S I Group Ltd

MRAU – P B S I Group Ltd

MRAW – P B S I Group Ltd

MRC – full range of mectric & inch ball bearings – R A Rodriguez UK Ltd

MRC – Vidlink International Ltd

MRCS – P B S I Group Ltd

MRD Magnets – manufacturer of Magnetic Products – Magnetic Rubber Direct Ltd

MRDG – P B S I Group Ltd

MRDT-T2/T3 – P B S I Group Ltd

MREF-1/3 – P B S I Group Ltd

MRFF – P B S I Group Ltd

MRI-E – P B S I Group Ltd

MRI-ED – P B S I Group Ltd

MRI-EX – P B S I Group Ltd

MRI-I – P B S I Group Ltd

MRI-ID – P B S I Group Ltd

MRI-IDS – P B S I Group Ltd

MRI-IE – P B S I Group Ltd

MRI-IED – P B S I Group Ltd

MRI-V – P B S I Group Ltd

MRMF – P B S I Group Ltd

MRNS – P B S I Group Ltd

MROS – P B S I Group Ltd

MRP Trucks & Trolleys – M R P Trucks & Trolleys

MRRP-1/3 – P B S I Group Ltd

MRS – C H L Equipment Ltd

Mrs Beeton – Chorion plc

Mrs Dales Garden – frozen vegetables and fruit – Dales Of Liverpool Ltd

Mrs Ultra Skates – M V Sport & Leisure Ltd

MRTR – P B S I Group Ltd

MRTS – P B S I Group Ltd

MRVT – P B S I Group Ltd

MS2 – magnetic susceptibility equipment – Bartington Instruments Ltd

MSC Coupling – Renold Clutches & Couplings Ltd

MSC Vertriebs GmbH, Gleichmann Electronics – M S C Gleichmann UK Ltd

MSE – metal spring energised seal – Greene Tweed & Co. Ltd

MSE – European Technical Sales Ltd

MSE Harrier – benchlop centrifuge – Sanyo Gallenkamp plc

MSP – motor systems protection – F D B Electrical Ltd

MSP – Fife Tidland Ltd

MSP Planet – Arun Pumps Ltd

MSS SP 44 – Hydraulic & Offshore Supplies Ltd

MST Continus – analgesic – Napp Pharmaceutical Group Ltd

MT 30 – marine engine, industrial gas turbine – Rolls-Royce plc

MTA (Switzerland) – pick and place components – Machine Building Systems Ltd

MTC – Harrier Fluid Power Ltd

MTC – Multi telescopic vehicle loading conveyor – Newland Engineering Co. Ltd

MTD (U.S.A.) – garden tractors & rotary mowers – E P Barrus

MTE – Hydraulic & Offshore Supplies Ltd

MTE – Proplas International Ltd

MTG – multi test gravelometer chip resistance tester. – Q-Lab Corporation

MTL100 Series – Shunt-diode safety barriers – Measurement Technology Ltd

MTL2000 Series – Isolating IS interface units – Measurement Technology Ltd

MTL3000 Series – Isolating IS interface units – Measurement Technology Ltd

MTL400 Series – Isolating IS interface units – Measurement Technology Ltd

MTL4700 Series – Shunt diode safety barriers – Measurement Technology Ltd

MTL4840 Series – Hart Maintenance system – Measurement Technology Ltd

MTL5000 Series – Isolating IS interface units – Measurement Technology Ltd

MTL611B – IS Pocket data terminal and accessories – Measurement Technology Ltd

MTL630 Series – 3 and 4 digit IS Indicators – Measurement Technology Ltd

MTL643 – IS Text Display – Measurement Technology Ltd

MTL644 – IS Text Display – Measurement Technology Ltd

MTL645 – Interactive Terminal – Measurement Technology Ltd

MTL650 Series – Interactive operator terminals – Measurement Technology Ltd

MTL670 Series – Process PCs – Measurement Technology Ltd

MTL680 Series – 3 and 4 digit loop-powered indicators – Measurement Technology Ltd

MTL700 Series – Shunt diode safety barriers – Measurement Technology Ltd

MTL7000 Series – Shunt diode safety barriers – Measurement Technology Ltd

MTL800 Series – IS Multiplexer systems – Measurement Technology Ltd

MTL8000 Series – Modular I/O – Measurement Technology Ltd

MTL8800L Series – Block I/O – Measurement Technology Ltd

MTL901 System – Ship to shore ESD Link – Measurement Technology Ltd

MTL920 Series – Hazardous area power supplies – Measurement Technology Ltd

MTM – Roxspur Measurement & Control Ltd

MTM (United Kingdom) – medium temperature curing epoxy resin material systems – Umeco

MTM (Made To Measure) – multi-storage systems – Railex Filing Ltd

Mu-Meter – runway friction measuring equipment – Douglas Equipment

MUA – direct fired gas fired unit heater – Nordair Niche

MUA – direct fired gas fired unit heater – Nordair Niche

Muck Boot – The Welly Shop Ltd

Mudie – fashion shirt, knitwear, trousers, – Double Two Ltd

Mudie – casualwear – The Wakefield Shirt Company Limited

*Muehlhauser (Germany) – tunnelling equipment – Burlington Engineers Ltd

Mueller – line components, stop valves, check valves, relief valves, fusible plugs, copper fittings and flare fittings – Thermofrost Cryo Ltd

*Mufax (Japan) – Office machines – Uniter Group Ltd

Muilty Link Cubes – cubes – Abceta Playthings Ltd

Mujur – indonesian plywood – Plaut International

Mulcare – industrial hygiene products – Mullett & Company UK Ltd

Mulcare & Multex – disposable industrial paper products – Mullett & Company UK Ltd

Mulchip – mulch – Melcourt Industries

*Muleskinner (U.S.A.) – epoxy encapsulated wire wheel – Gray Campling Ltd

muli – satellite vehicles – T G W Ltd

Muller – leak proof oilers – Longs Ltd

*Muller (Germany) – forms guillotines – Buhrs UK Ltd

Müller Co-Ax – European Technical Sales Ltd

Muller & Pesant – spares – Bearwood Engineering Supplies

Muller & Weigert (Germany) – panel meters & accessories – Metrix Electronics

Muller Weingarten – forging equipment – Pearson Panke Ltd

Mullfrax – high temperature refractories – Saint Gobain Industrial Ceramics Ltd

Mulsine – textile processing aid – Benjamin R Vickers & Sons Ltd

Mult Five Way Ladders – Accesscaff International Ltd

Multex – leather palm-cotton backed gloves – Bennett Safetywear

Multi-Amp – high current and protective relay test equipment – Megger Ltd

Multi-Amp – Alpha Electronics Southern Ltd

Multi-Axis Filament Winding Machinery – Pultrex Ltd

Multi-Beam – flexible coupling – Huco Dynatork

*Multi Caddie – Caddie Products Ltd

Multi-Dek – modular stage and tiering (demountable) – Stage Systems Ltd

Multi Digital Gloss – Digital products - Indigo - Coated – Howard Smith Paper Ltd

Multi Digital Silk – Digital Products - Indigo -Coated – Howard Smith Paper Ltd

Multi Dopplex 11 – bi-directional, vascular and obstetric, pocket doppler – Huntleigh Healthcare

Multi-Fit – fan motors – Thermofrost Cryo plc

Multi-Form – lv switchboard – Schneider

Multi-Guard (United Kingdom) – cross-scored reverse-acting metal bursting disc – Elfab Ltd

Multi Installations Ltd – Supplier and Installer of SBD PAS 23/24 FD30 Flat Entrance, Communal Entrance, High Security Doors – Multi Installations

Multi-level – floor drains and gullies – Wade International Ltd

Multi-Mag – Flowline Manufacturing Ltd

Multi Mark Heat Seal Machine – Hand operated heat seal machine 6 x 4 platen and also available as 10 x 10 platen – J & A International Ltd

Multi-Mill – grinder – Andritz Seed & Bio Fuel Ltd

Multi-Mix – software system – Format International Ltd

Multi-Peel – labels – Field Box More Labels

*Multi-pore Ceramic Filters (U.S.A.) – for cast shops and foundries – Porvair plc

Multi-Pouch – sterilisation reel made up of pouches – Amcor Flexibles

Multi-Purpose Ladders – Accesscaff International Ltd

MULTI-SAS (United Kingdom) – air monitoring system – Cherwell Laboratories Ltd

Multi-Seat Swing – swing with two or more seats – S M P Playgrounds

Multi-Shear – garden shear – Burgon & Ball Ltd

Multi-Shield – general purpose – Accent Hansen

Multi-Stor – storage cupboards – Acco UK Ltd

Multi-trip Insurance – annual travel insurance – M M A Insurance plc

Multi-wing – fan impellers – Beatson Fans & Motors Ltd

MultiAshflo – Mactenn Systems Ltd

Multibag – Instrument equipment tool carrying cases – Hofbauer (UK) Ltd

Multibase – mineral filled polyolefin masterbatches – Omya UK Ltd

Multiblend – bulk blasting system – E P C UK

Multichuck and Multivice Leader Gamet – Leader Chuck Systems Ltd

Multiclene 100 – Forward Chemicals Ltd

Multiclene 200 – Forward Chemicals Ltd

Multicom – pc communications software – Multicom Products Ltd

Multicore – soldering products – Anglia

Multicrom – paint – Creative Art Products Ltd

Multicut – step drills for thin materials – G & J Hall Ltd

Multicut Universal – soluble cutting fluid – Millers Oils Ltd

*Multicyl (Canada) – air hydraulic power units – Berger Tools Ltd

Multideck – Metal Deck Ltd

Multideco – Tornos Technologies UK Ltd

Multidrill – Sumitomo Electric Hardmetal Ltd

Multifak – lubricants – Chevron
Multifan (Germany) – DC equipment fans – Ebm-Papst
Multifeed – Hydrafeed Ltd
MULTIFIL™ – GGB UK
Multifire – smoke vent – McKenzie Martin Ltd
Multifit – plastic traps and fittings – Mcalpine & Company Ltd
Multifix – motors and accessories – Time Products UK Ltd
Multiflex – flexible crash doors, strip PVC curtains and rapid rise doors – Neway Doors Ltd
Multiflux mixer – high speed batch mixer – Gericke Ltd
Multiform – UK Office Direct
Multiform Technologies – Halcyon Solutions
Multigauge 3000 – Underwater Multiple Echo Ultrasonic Thickness Gauge – Tritex NDT Ltd
Multigauge 5500 – Hands Free Multiple Echo Ultrasonic Thickness Gauge – Tritex NDT Ltd
Multigauge 5600 – General Purpose Multiple Echo Ultrasonic Thickness Gauge – Tritex NDT Ltd
Multigerm – animal feed – Multigerm Ltd
Multigrade IV – variable graded paper with various backings & coatings – Harman Technology Ltd
Multigram – multi-image holograms – Opsec Security Ltd
Multiguard – flame retardant, antistatic, chemical splash and high visibility – Carrington Career & Work Wear
Multigully – multidirectional roof outlet – Alumasc Exterior Building Products
MultiJet (United Kingdom) – high pressure pump units – Calder Ltd
Multilase – diode laser – Keeler Ltd
Multilex Drug Data Files – data base of pharmaceutical products – First Databank Europe Ltd
Multilife – fully synthetic multigrade motor oil – Morris Lubricants
Multiline – Flowserve
Multiload – lighting control technology – Multiload Technology
MULTILUBE – GGB UK
Multimat – camping mat – Functional Foam Beacons Products Ltd
Multimatic – Standard Industrial Systems Ltd
Multimould – footballs, netballs, rugby balls and basketballs – Mitre Sports International Ltd
MultipacPRO – chassis – Schroff UK Ltd
Multipet – B P plc
MultiPharma – Glenvale Packaging
Multiplait – nylon tree surgery, towing and mooring rope – Marlow Ropes Ltd
Multiplan System – partitioning – Interior Property Solutions
Multiplex – micro processor control and data acquisition system – U T C Fire & Security
Multiplex – footballs & rugby balls – Mitre Sports International Ltd
*Multiplier Industries (U.S.A.) – nickei cadmium rechargeable batteries – Pulsar Developments Ltd
Multipoint (United Kingdom) – it provides selectable multi-mode detection to suit the environment in which it is installed and includes a built-in isolator and optional sounder – Fike Safety Technology Ltd
Multipoint – PCB assembly machines – Elite Engineering Ltd
Multipoint Connections – Videoconferencing Management Services – Direct Visual Ltd
Multipointelite – automated multipoint inoculator – The Mast Group Ltd
Multiprofile – A P T
Multiquip – Harrier Fluid Power Ltd
MultiSEP – 96-Well plate solid phase extraction system – Thermo Fisher Scientific
Multisert – proven performer in thermoplastics, headed & unheaded in two lengths, press-in, ultrasonic insert – Tappex Thread Inserts Ltd
Multisperse – range of rubber chemical dispersions – Omya UK Ltd
Multisprint CNC – Emi-Mec Ltd
Multistar – Devaco International Ltd
*MultiStep (Sweden) – heavy duty vinyl sheet – Forbo
Multistrike – Pipestoppers
*Multiswitch (Switzerland) – thumb wheel operated switches – Oem - Automatic Ltd
Multiswitch – European Technical Sales Ltd
Multiswitch – Balluff Ltd
MultiSync – monitors – Nec Europe Ltd
Multitec – K S B Ltd
*Multitherm – electric furnaces for heat treatment – Ramsell Naber Ltd
Multitrak – mobile shelving system – Rackline Ltd
*Multivac (Germany) – vacuum packing machinery – Multivac UK Ltd
Multiview – surveillance and cable TV transmission systems – Nortel Networks UK Ltd
Multivis – motor oils – Morris Lubricants
Multivitamin Injection – prevention & treatment of vitamin deficiencies in animals – Norbrook Research
Multiwash – scrubber dryer – Truvox International Ltd
MultiWave – industrial Nd YAG laser system – G S I Group Ltd

Multix – wiper-slot circular sawblades for multiple ripping – Gomex Tools Ltd
Multuvision – Lamphouse Ltd
Muncher (United Kingdom) – range of twin shaft, slow speed, high torque grinders for the waste water industry – Mono Pumps Ltd
Munck – equipment/spares – Bearwood Engineering Supplies
Mundesley Holiday Centre – over 50's holidays – Richardsons Stalham Ltd
*Munkebo Beholder-Fabrik Trading A/S (Denmark) – vacuum recovery systems – Hodge Clemco Ltd
*Munken (Sweden) – uncoated book and graphical papers – Arctic Paper UK Ltd
Munken Lynx – uncoated paper & board – Howard Smith Paper Ltd
Munken Print – uncoated paper & board – Howard Smith Paper Ltd
Munken Print Extra Vol 15 – uncoated paper & board – Howard Smith Paper Ltd
Munken Print Extra Vol 18 – uncoated paper & board – Howard Smith Paper Ltd
Munken Print Extra Vol 20 – uncoated paper & board – Howard Smith Paper Ltd
Munken Pure – uncoated paper & board – Howard Smith Paper Ltd
Munro – Halcyon Solutions
Munro Corbett Chart – wallchart showing Scottish mountains – Harvey Map Services Ltd
Munro & Miller Fittings – welding fittings and expansion joints – Munro & Miller Fittings Ltd
Mupem SA (Spain) – CNC turret lathes, cam autos, multispindles, magazine bar loaders – Haesler Machine Tools
Mupor – engineered products – Portex Technologies Ltd
Mupor Plus – surface treatment service – Portex Technologies Ltd
Mupor tm – PTFE microporous membrane – Portex Technologies Ltd
Murata – Cyclops Electronics Ltd
Murata – ceramic capacitors, inductors & sounders – Anglia
Muratec – UK Office Direct
Muratec Murata – Matsuura Machinery Ltd
Muratec Wiedemann (Japan) – CNC turret punch presses & laser combination machines – Tower Machine Tools Ltd
Murco – petroleum products – Murco Petroleum Ltd
Murco Shopstop – service station convenience store – Murco Petroleum Ltd
Murder One – book shop – Murder One
Murex – industrial hoses – C C H Hose & Rubber
Murex – Independent Welding Services Ltd
*Muro (France and The Far East) – binding and laminating equipment – Murodigital
Murphy Broth – Harrier Fluid Power Ltd
Murphy Yeast Aid – Murphy & Son
Murr – European Technical Sales Ltd
Murrayfield – rugby footballs – Gray Nicolls
Murrays Manicure – manicure products – Paul Murray plc
Muscovite Mica – Minelco Ltd
Museum Board – Atlantis European Ltd
Music Limited – Chrysalis Entertainments Ltd
Music Magazine – metal hammer – Dennis Publishing
Music Minus One – classical backing tape – Forsyth Bros Ltd
Music Process Engravers & Printers – music and reel label printers – Caligraving
Musicon Range – music on hold machines – Storacall Engineering Ltd
Musk R-1 – perfume speciality – Quest International UK Ltd
Musks – sausages – Musks Ltd
Musonic – audio products – Musonic UK Ltd
*Musso (Italy) – sorbet and ice cream machines – Robot Coupe UK Ltd
Mustang – Harrier Fluid Power Ltd
mustang – stacker cranes – T G W Ltd
Mustang – pump – Torres Engineering & Pumps Ltd
Mustang – radiator valves – Midland Brass Fittings Ltd
Mustang Communications – sound systems – Mustang Communications Ltd
Mustang Tools – clay pipe cutters, building profiles, roof tile croppers, floor tile cutters, lifting tools, mortar rakes, slaters tools, tackers kits, bricklayers tools, brick and sack barrows and platform tru cks – Mustang Tools Ltd
Mustek – Lamphouse Ltd
Mustlock – safety devices – L B B C Technologies
Musto Yachting – sailing, leisure and country wear – Musto Ltd
MUT – Banico Ltd
Mute Records – record company – Mute A & R
Muti-Master – Iscar Tools
*Muva (Germany) – sewing machine needles – Triumph Needle Co Ltd
MV Digistart – Medium Voltage Motor Starter – Soft Start UK
mwponline.com – MWP Advanced Manufacturing
MXIC – M S C Gleichmann UK Ltd

*MXR (U.S.A.) – effects pedals – John Hornby Skewes & Co. Ltd
My Cinema – Euro Group UK
My Fair Lady – soap talc – P Z Cussons International Ltd
My First Words – Vtech Electronics UK plc
My Toy – toys – Halsall Toys Europe Ltd
My Weekly – D C Thomson & Co. Ltd
My Weekly Puzzeltime – D C Thomson & Co. Ltd
Myatts – Criterion Ices
Mycom – generation of analytical instruments – Endress Hauser Ltd
Mycom – Therma Group
Mycostat – an in-feed mould inhibitor – Agil Chemicals Products
Mycroply – paramelt
Myflo – V E S Ltd
Myford – Red House Industrial Services Ltd
Myford – European Technical Sales Ltd
Myford – metal turning lathes, vertical milling machines, woodturning lathes and cylindrical grinding machines and CNC cylindrical grinding machines – Myford Ltd
myholidayideas.co.uk – Website – I P C Media Ltd
Mykal – R W Greeff
Mylar – polyester film – Du Pont UK Ltd
*Mylbond (Belgium) – modified starch – Tate & Lyle Public Ltd Company
Mylox Technologies – Panel Mounted & Portable Printers – M-Tech Printers
*Myobock (Germany) – electronically controlled upper limbs – Otto Bock Healthcare plc
Myotex – environmental control window blind fabric – Eclipse Blind Systems
Myoview – G E Healthcare
Myriad IV – downlighters – Concord Marlin Ltd
Myron – orthopaedic footwear – Remploy Ltd
Mysolv – workshop degreasers – Mykal Industries Ltd
Mystrol – liquid maintenance cleaner – Evans Vanodine International plc
Mytec (Germany) – hydraulic workholding chucks & mandrels – Ringspann UK Ltd
Mytec - RCS - Borg Warner - Compomac - Conex - Tollok - Sikumat - Rimostat - Cecon - Marland – Ringspann UK Ltd
MZ (Japan) – SLRS – Pentax UK Ltd
MZR (United Kingdom) – lighting management system – Sangamo Ltd

N

N.A.C.C. – promotion of research into treatment and causes of inflamatory bowel desease – Crohn's & Colitis UK
N.A.G. – numerical, statistical & visualisation software – N A G Ltd
N.A.I.S. – relays, switches, programmable logic controllers, vision recognition systems, sensing and detection components – Panasonic Electric Works
N.A.T.S. – national air traffic services – Civil Aviation Authority
N.B. Mouldings – injection moulders (Trade) – Osprey Ltd
N.B.S. – Nottingham Building Society
*N.B.T. (U.S.A.) – furriers sewing thread – William Gee Ltd
N.C.A. Series – liquid ring pumps – Calpeda Ltd
N.C.C. – IT consultancy, open systems and training – N C C Group
N.C. Conveyor – transfer belt conveyor – Parker Plant Ltd
N.C.H.A. – national care homes association – National Care Association
N.C.P. – car parks – National Car Parks Ltd
N.C.T. Leather – wet blue hides – N C T Leather Ltd
N.D.B.1. – copper finings – Murphy & Son
N.D.B.3. – enzymic chillproofer – Murphy & Son
N.D.T. – certification and training – Oceaneering Asset Integrity
N.E. – refined iron ingots – Metabrasive Ltd
N.E.C. – relays – I M O Electronics Ltd
N.E.C. – car telephones, printers, monitors and PC's – Nec Europe Ltd
N.E.C. phones – mobile and car telephones – Nec Europe Ltd
N.E.R.C. – to promote and support basic strategic and applied research – Natural Environment Research Council
N.E.T.C. – design and development of motor vehicles – Nissan Technical Centre Europe Ltd
N.G.C. Series – compact jet pumps – Calpeda Ltd
N.G.D., N.R.D., N.F.D. – Kennametal UK Ltd
N.G.K. – spark plugs and accessories – N G K Spark Plugs UK Ltd
N.G. Series – jet pumps – Calpeda Ltd
N.J.D. – electronic equipment – Premier Solutions Nottingham Ltd
N.L. – shirtmakers, hosiery and shoemakers – New & Lingwood Ltd
N.L. Accelerators – cobalt and amine curing agents for UP resins – Akzo Nobel Chemicals Holdings Ltd
N.M. Series – centrifugal pumps – Calpeda Ltd

N.O.A.H. – National Office of Animal Health - representing animal medicine industry in UK – National Office Of Animal Health Ltd

*N.O.K. (Japan, Singapore and USA) – seals and moulded parts – Freudenberg Simrit LP

N.P.C. – cutex nail polish remover – Coty UK Ltd

N.P.L. – Norton Plastics

N.P. Series – pool pumps – Calpeda Ltd

N. Peal & Co. – knitted outerwear, cashmere and lambswools fully fashioned knitwear – N Peal

n-power – R W E Npower

N.R.C. – crawler cranes, grabs, trench sheets and strutts, skips, crane spares, crane testing and test weights hire, mobile access platform hire, specialist steelwork design, fabrication and erection – N R C Plant Ltd

N.R.S. – measures the readership of newspapers & magazines – National Readership Surveys

N.R. Series – in-line pumps – Calpeda Ltd

N.S.F.-Cutler-Hammer – switches – N S F Controls Ltd

N.S.F.-Rotary wafer – switches – N S F Controls Ltd

N. Series – bare-shaft centrifugal pumps – Calpeda Ltd

N. Series – numotor piston actuator – Severn Glocon Ltd

N.T. – all products and services – Nortel Networks UK Ltd

N.T.G. – precision gears – Northern Tool & Gear Co. Ltd

N.T.K. – technical ceramics – N G K Spark Plugs UK Ltd

N.T.N. – bearing sales & distribution – N T N Bearings UK Ltd

N.T. Series – turbine pumps – Calpeda Ltd

N U M – Halifax Numerical Controls Ltd

N.V. Tools – N V Tools Ltd

N.W. – development agency – North West Development Agency

N800 – Hörmann (UK) Ltd

NA Range Actuator – Electric actuator for use in Nuclear environments – Rotork plc

*Nabertherm – electric furnaces for metal melting and heat treatment – Ramsell Naber Ltd

NABIC – Hydraulic & Offshore Supplies Ltd

Nabic – Engineering – Delta Fluid Products Ltd

Nabic – Trafalgar Tools

Nacco – Stacatruc

Nachi – Mercury Bearings Ltd

Naegelen valves (Germany) – fully teflon lined ball valves and accessories – Induchem

Naf – Kee Valves

Naf-Check – non return valves – Northvale Korting Ltd

Nafion – perfluorinated membranes – Du Pont UK Ltd

Nagel – Permat Machines Ltd

Naim – hi-fi & audio components – Naim Audio Ltd

Nair – depilatories – Church & Dwight UK Ltd

Nairn – urinal – Armitage Shanks Ltd

Nairn 1600 – cushioned vinyl sheet – Forbo

Nairn 1800 – cushioned vinyl sheet – Forbo

Nairn 2000 – cushioned vinyl sheet – Forbo

Nairn 2500 – cushioned vinyl sheet – Forbo

Nairn Classic 1400 – cushioned vinyl sheet – Forbo

Nairn Cushionfloor – cushioned vinyl sheet – Forbo

*NAIS (Japan) – sensors – Sensortek

Naish Felt – compressed wool felt – Naish Felts Ltd

Naish Felts – compressed wool felt and needlefelt technical textiles – Naish Felts Ltd

NAITeC – UK network of I.T. training centres – Itec North East Ltd

*Najet (U.S.A.) – micro drilling machines – Drill Service Horley Ltd

NAK – Hydraulic & Offshore Supplies Ltd

Nakamura – Machine Tool Supplies Ltd

Nakan – pvc rigid and flexible compounds – Atosina UK Ltd

Nakan S – pvc engineering alloys – Atosina UK Ltd

Nalg – Harrier Fluid Power Ltd

*Namaqua (South Africa) – wine – Raisin Social

Namco – European Technical Sales Ltd

Namelet – patient identity band – Robinson Healthcare Ltd

*Namjai – Montien Spice Co. Ltd

NAMUR – B L Pneumatics Ltd

*Nann (Germany) – pneumatically operated clamping and indexing devices – Brunner Machine Tools Ltd

Nano – small programmable logic controllers – Schneider

NanoAce – dicing machines – Loadpoint Ltd

Nanocular – Hosokawa Micron Ltd

Nanostep – nanometric surface measuring instruments – Taylor Hobson Ltd

Nantwich Chronicle – weekly title – Flintshire Chronicle Newspapers

*Nao (Spain) – porcelain figurines – Dexam International

Napa – Harrier Fluid Power Ltd

Napelec – B P plc

NAPEX – Resin Bonded Surfacing

Napgel – B P plc

Nappigon – disposable nappy disposer – Franke Sissons Ltd

Nappigon – disposable nappy disposer – I M C

Nappy sacks – Cedo Ltd

Naptel – B P plc

Napvis – polybutanes – B P plc

*Narex (Czech Republic) – machine tool equipment – Castle Brook Tools Ltd

Narite 300 – extra-hard high strength aluminium bronze – Columbia Metals Ltd

Narite 400 – extra-hard high strength aluminium bronze – Columbia Metals Ltd

Narrow Platforms – Accesscaff International Ltd

Nash – vacuum – AESpump

Nash Hytor (U.S.A.) – steam ejector systems – Gardner Denver Nash UK

Nash Kinema – steam ejector systems – Gardner Denver Nash UK

Nashuatec – Copyrite Ltd

*Nashuatec (EU & Japan) – photocopiers and facsimiles – N R G Group Ltd

nash_elmo (Germany) – liquid ring vacuum pumps and compressors – Gardner Denver Nash UK

Nasserheider – Glenvale Packaging

National – B P plc

National – relays, switches, programmable logic controllers, vision recognition systems, sensing and detection components, fans, solenoids, encoders – Panasonic Electric Works

National – Morganite

National Autoparts – clutch components, brake discs and brake drums – National Auto Parts

National Cert. for personal License Holders – Brooklands College

National Clamps – wheelclamps – National Clamps

National Counties – financial services – National Counties Building Society

National Electronics – electronic tubes – Richardsons R F P D Ltd

National Gallery London, The – The National Gallery

National Machinery – European Technical Sales Ltd

National Monitoring – intruder alarm & plant monitoring – A V R Group Ltd

National Nuclear Corporation (United Kingdom) – Multi-disciplined engineering, project management, safety and technical consultancy company. – Amec Ltd

National Semiconductor – Cyclops Electronics Ltd

National Telebank – pay as you view TV and video rental – Boxclever

National Warranty Bond – warranties – Car Care Plan Ltd

National Windscreens – automotive glass replacement service - nationwide – National Windscreens Ltd

Nationwide Access Platforms – Accesscaff International Ltd

Natmar – marking machines and identification tape – Armstrong Commercial Laundry Systems

Natracalm – herbal tranquilliser – Perrigo UK

Natrasleep – herbal remedy used to encourage natural sleep – Perrigo UK

Natratex – Thornbury Surfacing Chippenham Ltd

natrix – high capacity sorting systems – T G W Ltd

*Natrosol (Netherlands) – hydroxyethylcellulose – Hercules Holding Ii Ltd

*Natrosol Plus (Netherlands) – modified hydroxyethylcellulose – Hercules Holding Ii Ltd

Natty – babies, childrenswear and teenage fashions – Shenu Fashions

Natura Teeth – Schottlander Dental Equipment Supplies

Natural Dimensions – decorative paint mixing systems – Akzonobel

Natural Flair – machine made in 100% wool – Brintons Carpets Ltd

Natural Harvest – Ryalux Carpets Ltd

Natural Hints – decorative paints – Akzonobel

*Natural Loofah – in a variety of sizes – Recticel Corby

*Natural Palette (Switzerland) – vinyl wallcoverings – Tektura plc

Natural Pine Shelves – Plaut International

NaturaLight Systems – National Door Co.

Nature's Own – suppliers of food state vitamin and mineral supplements. – Natures Own Ltd

Nature's Own – suppliers of food state vitamin and mineral supplements – Natures Own Ltd

Nature's Way – multi-purpose cleaner – Premiere Products Ltd

Nature SKO – Footwear – Boot Tree

NatureFlex(tm) (United Kingdom) – certified biodegradable and compostable films manufactured from sustainable/renewable resources – Innovia Films Ltd

Natureform – Bacup Shoe Co. Ltd

Naturelle Pure Wool DK – yarn – Stylecraft

Naturelli – Manufacturers and Distributors of Natural Stone Products – Naturelli Stone

NATURELOOK WOVEN FLOORING – FLOORING FOR SWIMMING POOL SURROUNDS , BOATS ETC – Discount Leisure UK ltd

Naue Fasertechnik – Hoofmark UK Ltd

Nautica – routers – Nortel Networks UK Ltd

Nauticalia – maritime gifts, artefacts & brassware & mail order – Nauticalia Ltd

Nautilus – business papers – Howard Smith Paper Ltd

Nautilus – LIMS – Thermo Fisher Scientific

Nautilus Beta – industrial water softeners – Aldous & Stamp Ltd

Naval – Kee Valves

Navico – marine electronics equipment – Navico UK

Navigator – UK Office Direct

Navigator – toys – Halsall Toys Europe Ltd

Navitar – Lamphouse Ltd

Naxos – European Technical Sales Ltd

Naylobon – resin bonded coated abrasives – Naylors Abrasives

Nayloflex – cutting and grinding discs – Naylors Abrasives

Naylon – non woven abrasives – Naylors Abrasives

Naylor – S J Wharton Ltd

Naylors – abrasives – Naylors Abrasives

Naylorsafe – safety products – Naylors Abrasives

Nayprint – printed products – Nayler Group Ltd

NBK – counterflow cooler – Andritz Seed & Bio Fuel Ltd

NC Program Manager – Seiki Systems Ltd

NC951 – Disabled persons toilet alarms – C-Tec Security Ltd

NCC Escrow International – software source code protection service – N C C Group

NCK – Trowell Plant Sales Ltd

NCK – Jones Cranes Parts

NCR – A T M Parts

NCR 5070 – A T M Parts

NCR 5084 – A T M Parts

NCR 5085 – A T M Parts

NCR 5088 – A T M Parts

NCR 5670 – A T M Parts

NCR 5674 – A T M Parts

NCR 5675 – A T M Parts

NCR 5685 – A T M Parts

NCR 5688 – A T M Parts

NCR 5870 – A T M Parts

NCR 5874 – A T M Parts

NCR 5875 – A T M Parts

NCR 5879 – A T M Parts

NCR 5884 – A T M Parts

NCR 5885 – A T M Parts

NCR 5886 – A T M Parts

NCR 5888 – A T M Parts

NCR Cash Registers – Cash Register Services

NDD Pulomary Function Systems (United Kingdom) – spirometers and hospital equipment – Intermedical UK Ltd

NDK – Cyclops Electronics Ltd

NDK Europe – crystals, oscillators & SAW devices – Anglia

NDT Radiography – x-rays on casting for aircraft – James Fisher Inspection & Measurement Services Ltd

Neal Pestforce – environmental services – Neal Pestforce Ltd

Neale Atkinson – A well renowned and respected commercial photographic expert. – PR Photographer London

Near Nett Shape – Cambridge Vacuum Engineering

Neata Lever – non-concussive taps – Sheardown Engineering Ltd

Neata Seal – non concussive taps – Sheardown Engineering Ltd

Neata Spray – spray taps – Sheardown Engineering Ltd

Neata Tap – taps – Sheardown Engineering Ltd

Neata Toggle – non-concussive taps – Sheardown Engineering Ltd

Neata Turn – non-concussive taps – Sheardown Engineering Ltd

Neataturn – non-concussive taps – Sheardown Engineering Ltd

*Neatform (United Kingdom) – curved mdf – Neat Concepts Ltd

Neatmatch – Neat Concepts Ltd

*Neatmould (United Kingdom) – decorated mdf – Neat Concepts Ltd

Neatrout – Neat Concepts Ltd

*Neatrust (United Kingdom) – perforated mdf – Neat Concepts Ltd

Neatslot – Neat Concepts Ltd

Neatstain – rapid haematology and gram stain – Guest Medical Ltd

Neban – grade 20/20, 1mm to 25mm cork – Charles Cantrill Ltd

NEBAR – Cork Elastomer Jointing – Tiflex Ltd

Nebraska Boilers – Twin Industries International Ltd

NEBS Management – national examining board for supervision and management – City & Guilds Of London Institute

Nebular – architectural bulkhead, weather and vandal resisting lighting – Designplan Lighting Ltd

*NEC – Hospitality A V

NEC – UK Office Direct

NEC – Lamphouse Ltd

NEC – Videonations Ltd

NEC – M S C Gleichmann UK Ltd

NEC – Review Display Systems Ltd

Nec – Cyclops Electronics Ltd

NEC – telephone equipment – Cobus Communications

NEC Arena – exhibition & conference centre – Nec Group
NEC Ltd – exhibition centre – Nec Group
NEC Schott (Japan) – thermal fuses – A T C Semitec Ltd
Necchi (ERC) – hermetic compressors – Thermofrost Cryo plc
Neckline – carrier for multi bottle packs – Nampak Carton
NECO – customised/special AC & DC motors, geared motors and controllers – A T B Laurence Scott Ltd
Necrons – electronic games, publications, rule books, magazines, books, games, models, miniatures and war games – Games Workshop Ltd
***Nectar (Netherlands)** – worldwide mobile bagging commodities – Nectar Group Ltd
Nederman – Southern Valve & Fitting Co. Ltd
Nederman – fluid/air hose reels – Air Power Centre Limited
Nedox – Poeton Gloucester
Needlechek – detects ferrous metals in clothing that incorporates non-ferrous zips or trimmings – Lock Inspection Systems Ltd
Needlecraft – magazine – Future Publishing Ltd
Needlestop – needle-resistant gloves – Bennett Safetywear
Neenah Environment – writing, text and cover – Howard Smith Paper Ltd
Neeter Drive (United Kingdom) – bevel gearboxes – Power Jacks Ltd
Nefax – facsimile machines – Nec Europe Ltd
***Neff (Germany)** – built-in kitchen appliances – B S H
Neff Lineartechnik – European Technical Sales Ltd
***Negahban Gas Co. (Iran)** – gas valves – Anglo Nordic Burner Products Ltd
Negator – chemical enzymes to simulate stone washing effect on denim – Brenntag Colours Ltd
Neggretti – Roxspur Measurement & Control Ltd
Negretti Aviation – aircraft and engine instruments, controls, transducers and recorders, precision aneroid barometers, aircrew oxygen and NBC protection systems and ground support equipment – Meggitt Avionics
Negri Bossi – Proplas International Ltd
NEI – mineral grinding equipment – Metso Minerals UK Ltd
Neil Robertson Stretcher (United Kingdom) – rescue stretcher & use in marine & offshore situations – B C I Stretchers Ltd
Neill – Gem Tool Hire & Sales Ltd
Nelco – special purpose electric motors, moulded commutators, power and control electronics – Cooper Controls Ltd
Nellie – brewery filtration – British Filters Ltd
Nelson – three strand polypropylene rope – Marlow Ropes Ltd
Nelson Burgess – silencing and filtration systems – Burgess Architectural Products Ltd
Nelson Hurst – insurance brokers – Alexander Forbes Risk Services Ltd
Nelson Winslow – Harrier Fluid Power Ltd
Nelsons Revenge – cask beer – Woodforde's Norfolk Ales
Nemco – Food Preparation Equipment – Gilberts Food Equipment Ltd
***Nemetnejad (Far East)** – oriental carpets – I Nemetnejad Ltd
Nemo Q – queue control systems – Lonsto Insternational Ltd
NEMP – M P E Ltd
Nendle – noise and vibration control equipment – Nendle Acoustics Ltd
Nenplas – plastic extrusions, handles, carpet savas and glides – Homelux Nenplas
Nenplas - Amerock (die cast handles and knobs) – Homelux Nenplas
NEO Trims – knitted flat bed trims, cuffs, collars and welts and woven ribbons, mirror and sequins items – The Neoknitting & Trim Ltd
Neobergomate Forte – perfume speciality – Quest International UK Ltd
Neocare – piglet energiser – SCA Newtec
Neoflex – rigid and flexible exhaust clamps – Neophix Engineering Co. Ltd
Neogene – specialised industrial paints, stoving enamels, lacquers and paints for plastics – Neogene LLP
Neokil – rodenticide – Sorex Ltd
Neolith – jetting equipment and chemicals – Robert Craig & Sons Ltd
Neolyn – resins – Hercules Holding Ii Ltd
Neopolitan Bollard – maintenance free bollard – Glasdon International Ltd
Neopolitan Plaza – litter bin free standing – Glasdon International Ltd
Neoprene – elastomers from Du Pont – Omya UK Ltd
Neoprene – W Mannering London Ltd
Neoprene – flex mouldings – Plastic Mouldings Ltd
Neoscan – G E Healthcare
Neosorexa – rat packs – Sorex Ltd
Neotex – nylon filter fabric – Madison Filter
Neotex – supported neoprene or gloves – Mapa Spontex
Neotex – high performance fire retardent vertical blind fabric – Eclipse Blind Systems
Neotronics – portable gas detection – Honeywell Analytics Ltd
Neowave – Telephone based intercoms BT or Mobile phone – Seamless Aluminium International Ltd
Neox – protective sterntube oil – Benjamin R Vickers & Sons Ltd
Nephroflow – G E Healthcare
Neptronic – resistive and gas humidifiers – J S Humidifiers plc
Neptune – multiway bayonet connectors – I T T Ltd
Neptune – microprocessor generator control – Guyson International Ltd
Neptune – paint brushes – Whitaker & Sawyer Brushes Ltd
Neptune – IP65 rated labelling machine – Harland Machine Systems Ltd
Neptune DK – yarn – Stylecraft
Neptune Unique – paper – Fenner Paper Co. Ltd
NER – Stemmer Imaging
Nera – dry blend vinyl flooring – Gerflor Ltd
Nera Telecommunications – satellite communications service – N S S L Ltd
Nero Stop – vinyl duckboard matting for wet areas – Jaymart Roberts & Plastics Ltd
Nervanaid – sequestering agents and micronutrients and agriculture – Contract Chemicals Ltd
***Nervar (France)** – chainsets, rings and bottom brackets – Rsi
Nerve Bone Liniment – liniment – Bell Sons & Co. Ltd
Nescafe – UK Office Direct
Nescot College – North East Surrey College Of Technology
Nesite Raised Access Flooring – Advanced Ergonomic Technologies Ltd
Ness Furniture – contract furniture office chairs, desking/storage, reception/waiting, dining/bistro, hospital furniture, airport seating – Ness Furniture Ltd
Nessco – Nessco Group Ltd
Nessie – water hydraulics – Danfoss Ltd
Nessie – Harrier Fluid Power Ltd
NESSIE WATER HYDRAULICS – Hydraulic & Offshore Supplies Ltd
Nester – automatic nesting software for fabric, foam and wood industries – Apropa Machinery Ltd
Nestle – UK Office Direct
Nestledown – mattress, divan and bunk beds and latex foam mattresses – Nestledown Beds
.net – magazine – Future Publishing Ltd
Neta Bar – plastic cover to prongs for binding – Gilmex International Ltd
Netcargo International – Logistics Provider – Netcargo International UK Ltd
Netcase – S R S Product plc
Netfoam – polyethylene foam net – A Latter & Co. Ltd
Netgear – small/home office LAN's – Nortel Networks UK Ltd
Netline – Linak UK
Netstal – Harrier Fluid Power Ltd
Netstal – Proplas International Ltd
Netto – Supply Chain Solution Ltd
Netvue – Netvue
Network – instrumentation and auto pilot systems – B & G Ltd
Network Intrusion Detection – Tekdata Distribution Ltd
Network Intrusion Detection System – Tekdata Distribution Ltd
Network Load Balancing – Tekdata Distribution Ltd
Network Vehicles – network of franchises providing financing and management for vehicle fleets – Leaseplan UK Ltd
NETWORK VEKA AND FENSA – M P N Upvc Windowsdoors & Conservatories
Networked DNC – Seiki Systems Ltd
Netzsch Mastermix (United Kingdom) – horizontal continuous wet grinding mills, dispersers, dissolvers and large batch mixers, agitated holding tanks, filling machines, modules, turn key projects – Netzsch Mastermix Ltd
***Neuenkamp (Germany)** – British & Continental Traders Ltd
Neuling Translations – German & English translation and interpreting service. – Anglo German Business & Finance Translation Services
Neuma-Torq – cutting machine for plastic extrudate – Peter Gillard Company Ltd
Neurology Products – selection of wide "bobath" plinths and tilt tables – Akron
Neurosign 100 – intraoperative nerve monitor – Magstim Co. Ltd
Neurosign 800 – intra operative nerve monitor – Magstim Co. Ltd
***Neurostim (Germany)** – regional anaesthesia stimulator – Linton & Co Engineering Ltd
Neusiedler – UK Office Direct
Neuson – C J Plant Ltd
Neuson – Harrier Fluid Power Ltd
Neutralac – lime for effluent treatment – Lhoist UK
Neutralle – UK Office Direct
Neutrasol – Forward Chemicals Ltd
Neutrogena – UK Office Direct
Neutronex – pure gold process – Cookson Electronics Ltd
NEVA – Cambridge Vending
Nevada (Portugal) – light granules cork wall tiles – Siesta Cork Tile Co.
Nevada – suction and discharge of foodstuffs, wine and beer – Merlett Plastics UK Ltd
Nevada – rotary dryers – Abru Ltd
Neve – professional audio equipment – A M S Neve Ltd
Neverbend – carbon steel, and stainless steel garden tools – Spear & Jackson plc
***Nevica (Far East)** – ski-wear – Nevica Ltd
New Century – software system – Format International Ltd
New Decade – carpet accessories and underlays – Salesmark Ltd
New England – envelopes – G F Smith
New England – carpets – Interface Europe Ltd
New English Library – books – Hachette UK Ltd
New Era – wooden window and door frames – Benlowe Windows
New Guard – protective coatings – Andrews Coatings Ltd
New Guardian – UK Office Direct
New Haden Pumps – pumps & pumping solutions – New Haden Pumps Ltd
new holland – Turney Group
New Holland – Harrier Fluid Power Ltd
New Holland Kobelco – P J P Plant Hire
***New-Holland Tractors** – Murley Agricultural Supplies Ltd
New Image – greetings cards – Hambledon Studios
New Image – fashion footwear – D Jacobson & Sons Ltd
New Life – fertilizer – Soil Fertility Dunns Ltd
New Life 2 – fertilizer – Soil Fertility Dunns Ltd
New Life 3 – fertilizer – Soil Fertility Dunns Ltd
New Life 4 – fertilizer – Soil Fertility Dunns Ltd
New Life 5 – fertilizer – Soil Fertility Dunns Ltd
New Life 6 – fertilizer – Soil Fertility Dunns Ltd
New Pentwist – carpets – Penthouse Carpets Ltd
New Pro Foundries – non-ferrous sand castings – New Pro Foundries Ltd
New Ryalux – Ryalux Carpets Ltd
New Studio – carpets – Penthouse Carpets Ltd
New Technology Snacks – snack pellets for snack manufacture – Pasta Foods Ltd
New World – modular multi-activity play system for young children – S M P Playgrounds
Newage Stamford – Trowell Plant Sales Ltd
Newall – Red House Industrial Services Ltd
Newall – Encoders UK
Newall – Newall UK Ltd
Newall – digital readout – R K International Machine Tools Ltd
Newaplas – melamine faced chipboard – F W Mason & Sons Midland Ltd
Neway – flexible crash doors, strip PVC curtains and rapid rise doors – Neway Doors Ltd
Neway – flexible rubber doors – B I S Door Systems Ltd
Newbridge (U.S.A.) – Kingston Communications
Newburgh – precision engineers, fabricators, iron founders and design engineers – Newburgh Engineering Co. Ltd
Newbury – Try & Lilly Ltd
Newcastle Brown Ale – ale – Scottish & Newcastle Pub Co.
Newcomen Society, The – The Newcomen Society
NewCool – Water/Oil Coolers, Air/Oil Coolers – J B J Techniques Ltd
Newdome – flat top burglar resistant rooflights, glass barrel lights, lantern lights, one piece glass domes, hinged ventilated rooflights and segmented (spherical) domelights – Gardner & Newton Ltd
Newland – specialist belt conveyors – Newland Engineering Co. Ltd
Newland – Try & Lilly Ltd
Newlec – lighting, wiring accessories, fixings and fastenings and commerical electrical equipment – Newey & Eyre
***Newlong (Japan)** – portable and fixed head stitchers – W J Morray Engineering Ltd
Newman – labelling and capping machines – Newman Labelling Systems Ltd
Newman & Field – ship chandlery – Noirit Ltd Newman & Field Ltd
Newman's – shoes – Newmans Footwear Ltd
Newman's Bambinos – shoes – Newmans Footwear Ltd
Newman's Corkers – shoes – Newmans Footwear Ltd
Newman's Mama Mia – shoes – Newmans Footwear Ltd
***Newmar (U.S.A.)** – electrical equipment (marine) – Aquapac International Ltd
Newmarket Weekly News – newspapers – Cambridge Newspapers Ltd
***Newpack (Italy)** – form-fill-seal packaging machines – Chemtech International Ltd
Newpark – Automated Car Park Systems – Newpark Security Ltd
Newport – butane gas lighter refills, pipecleaners, petrol lighter fluid, universal flints and wicks – Keen World Marketing Ltd
Newport Mini-Filters – cigarette filters – Keen World Marketing Ltd
News in Focus – newspaper – Kent Regional News & Media
Newsmith – industrial washing machines and handling equipment, detergents and servicing – Newsmith Stainless Ltd
Newspoint – public relations consultants – Sales Point

Newstreet – automatic plate production system – Kodak Morley
NewTeam – showers and shower accessories – Damixa Ltd
Newton Derby – alternators and frequency converters, permanent magnet generators, exciters and motors – Newton Derby Ltd
Nexan – Cobus Communications
Nexans – Eswa Ltd
Nexans Cable (France) – industrial cables – Metool Products Ltd
Nexen Horton – Motion Drives & Controls Ltd
Nexis – Pall Europe Corporate Services
NEXIS – Hydraulic & Offshore Supplies Ltd
Nexon – Cables – Dax International Ltd
NEXOR – software – Nexor Ltd
Next – Next plc
***Next Day Fans (United Kingdom)** – fan manufrs – Westmid Fans
Next Directory – Next plc
Next Retail – Next plc
NextMove BX – Baldor UK
NextMove ES – Baldor UK
NextMove ESB – Baldor UK
NextMove PC – Baldor UK
NextMove PCI – Baldor UK
NextMove ST – Baldor UK
***Nexton (Netherlands)** – Hercules Holding Ii Ltd
Nextwaveit – RideThe Wave – Nextwave It Ltd
Nexun – Stacatruc
Nexus – fasteners and plastic buckles – I T W Nexus Europe
Nexus – Wessex Welding & Industrial Supplies Ltd
***Nexygen** – Lloyd instruments advanced machine control and data analysis software package for materials testing – Lloyd Instruments Ltd
NF 2000 – Dantherm Filtration Ltd
NFK 2000 – modulised wood filler – Dantherm Filtration Ltd
NFREN – M S C Gleichmann UK Ltd
NGC Magazine – magazine – Future Publishing Ltd
NGK – spark plugs – N G K Spark Plugs UK Ltd
NGN – vacuum – AESpump
NGV (United Kingdom) – ECi Software Solutions Limited
Ni-Trax – mens safety shoes and boots – Bunzl S W S
NIA – exhibition & conference centre – Nec Group
Niagara – files, tools, steels – Hill Cliffe Garage
Nibbler – size reduction equipment – Gericke Ltd
Nibron Special – extra high strength nickel bronze – Columbia Metals Ltd
Nic – Cyclops Electronics Ltd
Nica – pharmaceutical mixer/extruder/spheronizer system – Aeromatic Fielder Ltd
Nicerol – foam compound – Angus Fire
Nichicon – Cyclops Electronics Ltd
NICHIYU-NYK – Chaintec Ltd
Nicholas Associates – construction personnel consultants. A division of nicholas associates limited – Stafforce
Nicholson – files, rasps, hacksaw blades and frames – Apex Tools
Nick Munro – Continental Chef Supplies Ltd
Nicklon – Pobjoy Mint Ltd
Niclene – Forward Chemicals Ltd
Niclube – Forward Chemicals Ltd
Nico – butt hinges, cabinet hinges, window friction hinges, cabinet stays, castors and espagnolette bolts – Nico Manufacturing Co. Ltd
Nicodome – netting clad enclosures – Clovis Lande Associates Ltd
***Nicofence (Netherlands)** – woven netting fabrics – Clovis Lande Associates Ltd
Niconico – ladies leisurewear – Banner Ltd
***Nicorros (Germany)** – non-ferrous metals – Thyssenkrupp V D M UK Ltd
***Nicotarp (Netherlands)** – geomembrane for pond and lake lining – A G A Group
Nicrex – stainless steel electrodes – Murex Welding Products Ltd
Nicrobraz – brazing alloy, high temperature – Wall Colmonoy Ltd
Nicrocoat – high temp oxidation resistance coatings – Wall Colmonoy Ltd
***Nicrofer (Germany)** – non-ferrous metals – Thyssenkrupp V D M UK Ltd
Nicrogap – aids for brazing wide gap joints – Wall Colmonoy Ltd
Nidec (Germany) – Electro Mechanical Systems (EMS) Ltd
Nidec Servo (Japan) – Electro Mechanical Systems (EMS) Ltd
***Nieco** – Equipline
Nifco – Nifco UK Ltd
Niftilds – Solmedia Laboratory Supplies
Niftylift – hydraulic access platforms – Niftylift Ltd
NIFTYLIFT – Chaintec Ltd
NiftyLift – R F Lifting & Access Ltd
Niftylift – UK based manufacturer of Access Platforms – Caunton Access Ltd
Niftylift Platforms – Accesscaff International Ltd
Nigel Mansell – racing school, four wheel drive karting, rally school and supercar experience – MotorSport Vision
Night Scented Jasmine – jasmine fragrance toiletries – Norfolk Lavender Trading Ltd
Nightstar – darts – Unicorn Products Ltd
Niika – Quality core gripping and transmission components – Machineco Ltd
Nikalium – alloy metals – Stone Marine Propulsion Ltd
Nikken – Precision Tools
Nikko – Harrier Fluid Power Ltd
Nilbite – anti-nailbiting liquid – Laboratory Facilities Ltd
Nilco – vacuum cleaner/polisher/scrubbers – Denis Rawlins Ltd
Nilfisk – industrial cleaning equipment – B & G Cleaning Systems Ltd
Nilfisk – Trafalgar Tools
NILFISK – vacuum cleaners – M B K Motor Rewinds Ltd
Nilflan – technology process – Kingspan Insulation Ltd
Nilos – European Technical Sales Ltd
Nilperm – vapour barrier – Alumasc Exterior Building Products
Niltox – breathing air purifier – Willpower Breathing Air Ltd
Niluent – breath membrane – Kingspan Insulation Ltd
Nim Winches – oceanographic and umbilical winches and material handling systems – Rotrex Winches
Nimar – 18% Ni maraging steel – Corus Engineering Steels
Nimax – high efficiency nickel base alloy welding electrodes – Metrode Products Ltd
Nimbus – taps – Armitage Shanks Ltd
Nimbus – Infrared flammable gas detector – Crowcon Detection Instrument Ltd
Nimbus – pumps and compressors – Rolls-Royce plc
Nimbus G11 – Aerotech Engineering Ltd
Nimbus Lite – Aerotech Engineering Ltd
Nimbus Records – compact discs and record label in own right – Wyastone Estate Ltd
Nimline – diesel dumper (2 wheel drive) – Thwaites Ltd
Nimlok – Display Wizard Ltd
Nimlok – modular display system and exhibition stands – Nimlok Ltd
Nimplant – nitrogen ion implantation – Tecvac Ltd
Nimrod – nickel base alloy welding electrodes – Metrode Products Ltd
Nimrod – typeface – Monotype Imaging Ltd
Nimrod Plus Gloss Paper and Board – woodfree blade coated paper – Premier Paper Group Ltd
Nimrod Plus Matt Paper – woodfree blade coated paper – Premier Paper Group Ltd
Nimrod Plus Silk Paper and Board – woodfree blade coated paper – Premier Paper Group Ltd
Ninja Corporation, The – childrens leisure products – Finecard International Ltd
Nippon – starter and alternators injection – Nippon Distribution
Nippon – ant, fly and wasp killer sprays and ant powder – Vitax Ltd
Nippon – Harrier Fluid Power Ltd
Nippon – Stacatruc
***Nippon (Japan)** – liquid level switches & floats – Applications Engineering Ltd
Nippon Chemi-con – Cyclops Electronics Ltd
Nippondenso – Harrier Fluid Power Ltd
***Niro (Switzerland)** – unglazed ceramic tiles – A Elder Reed & Co. Ltd
Niron – nickel iron alloy plating solution – Cookson Electronics Ltd
Nisa – steel bath – Armitage Shanks Ltd
Nisa – food buying consortium – Nisa
Nisermatic Deluxe – fires – Indesit Company UK Ltd
NISSAN – Chaintec Ltd
Nissan – Ashley Competition Exhausts Ltd
Nissan – Stacatruc
Nissan – T V H UK Ltd
Nissan – L M C Hadrian Ltd
Nissan – Custom Brakes & Hydraulics Ltd
Nissan – Harrier Fluid Power Ltd
Nissan – Premier Lift Trucks Ltd
Nissan – Apollo Plant Holdings Ltd
Nissei – Proplas International Ltd
Nistac – home office desks – Kettler GB Ltd
Nistan – tin nickel plating process – P M D UK Ltd
Nistar – bright nickel plating process – P M D UK Ltd
Nistelle – nickel base hard facing alloys and cast components – Deloro Stellite Ltd
Nitex – industrial gloves, nitrile synthetic rubber with cotton liner – Specialised Latex Services Ltd
Nitra-Clear – water filter for nitrate removal, drinking water – Aldous & Stamp Ltd
Nitrasil – silicon nitride engineering ceramics – Tenmat Ltd
Nitrazone – industrial gases – Boc Gases Ltd
Nitricol – water testing tablets – Palintest Ltd
Nitrile – W Mannering London Ltd
***Nitro (Far East)** – unisex jeans – Flitterman Investments Ltd
***Nitrocellulose (U.S.A.)** – Hercules Holding Ii Ltd
Nitron – patented process involving strengthening and hardening of titanium and stainless steel substrates followed by titanium nitride coating – Tecvac Ltd
Nitrotop – Yara UK It Ltd
NITROX – nitrogen gas generators – Parker Dominic Hunter Ltd
***Nitto (Japan)** – tools – Indasa Abrasives UK Ltd
Nitto – B D K Industrial Products Ltd
Nitto – Gawler Tapes & Plastics Ltd
NITTO – Hydraulic & Offshore Supplies Ltd
Nitto – General Fabrications Ltd
Nitto Kohki Europe – quick release coupling, air compressor-oil free, vacum pump-oil free, pneumatic hand tool, portable hydraulic punching machine and portable magnetic cutting unit – Nitto Kohki Europe Co. Ltd
Nituff – hard anodised film impregnated with P.T.F.E. – Aluminium Surface Engineering Ltd
Nivea – skincare, bath, hair and sun products – Lil-lets UK Ltd
Nivea Facials – skin lotion – Lil-lets UK Ltd
NIVEC (Italy) – portable nebuliser – M G Electric
***NK Networks Coaxial & TV Camera Cables (TRIAX) (Germany)** – Radiall Ltd
NL Special Treatments – bodycare toiletries – Norfolk Lavender Trading Ltd
NMAE – emulation and testing software for a TMN manager – N C C Group
NMB – StrainSense Ltd
NMCE – emulation and testing software for an agent device – N C C Group
NME – I P C Media Ltd
Nnonskin Linseed inks – vegetablebased inks for printmakers – Hawthorn Printmaker Supplies
No-climb – smoke & heat detector testers – No Climb Products Ltd
No Logo! – jackets and jeans – Kentex Jeans & Casuals
No Loss – household and outdoor brooms, protective gloves, clothing and masks, protective glasses – L G Harris & Co. Ltd
NO SKIVE – Hydraulic & Offshore Supplies Ltd
No-Tarn – tarnish inhibitor for silver and gold plated parts – P M D UK Ltd
No1 Rustbeater – metal primer – Hammerite Products Ltd
***Noack (Germany)** – blister packaging machines – Romaco Holdings UK Ltd
Nobex – Gem Tool Hire & Sales Ltd
Nobilta – Hosokawa Micron Ltd
Nobo – Lamphouse Ltd
***Nobo** – Hospitality A V
Nobo – UK Office Direct
Nocchi Pumps – Denton Pumps Ltd
Noctula – B P plc
Noddy – spectacle frames – Pennine Optical Group Ltd
Nodor – dart boards – Nodor International Ltd
Noflote – conductivity level probe/controller – Lee-Dickens Ltd
Noirit – yacht & boat chandlery – Noirit Ltd Newman & Field Ltd
Noise-Foil – sound absorption panel – I A C Company Ltd
Noise-Lock Panel – acoustic panel – I A C Company Ltd
Noishield Louvre – weather louvre – I A C Company Ltd
Noishield Panel – acoustic panel – I A C Company Ltd
Noja Power – Mathew C Blythe & Son Ltd
Nokia – UK Office Direct
Nolten – automotive battery testers – Gordon Equipments Ltd
***Noltina** – crucibles for metal melting – Ramsell Naber Ltd
***Noltina-Stabil** – crucibles for melting metal – Ramsell Naber Ltd
***Noma (China)** – decorative electric lights and christmas tree lights - indoor and outdoor – Noma Lites
***Noma Moonrays (Canada)** – low voltage garden lighting – Noma Lites
Nomad – infra red heater – Robinson Willey
Nomad – matting systems for dirt control – North British Tapes Ltd
Nomapack – Davpack
***Nomar (France)** – french oven to tableware – Bunzl Lockhart Catering Equipment
Nomex – aramid fibre/paper presboard – Du Pont UK Ltd
Non destructive testing – Oceaneering Asset Integrity
Non-Oxide – ceramic materials – Kennametal
Non Stop – fashion – Novinit Ltd
None Destructive Test Equipment – test piece simulation – J R Technology
Nonskin Ettching Inks – Etchink inks for printmakers – Hawthorn Printmaker Supplies
NOP Research Group – market research – N O P Research Group Ltd
***Nor Reg norway (Norway)** – wraparound packaging machinery – Waller Eurosel
NORAC – induction motors for industrial and marine applications – A T B Laurence Scott Ltd
Noram – amines – Atosina UK Ltd

Noram – industrial and karting clutches – Wetherby Engineering Co. Ltd

Noramac – amine acetates – Atosina UK Ltd

Noramium – quaternary ammonium compounds – Atosina UK Ltd

Noramox – ethoxylated primary amines – Atosina UK Ltd

Norba – Harrier Fluid Power Ltd

Norbar – Gem Tool Hire & Sales Ltd

Norbar – Gustair Materials Handling Equipment Ltd

Norbar – torque equipment – Bearwood Engineering Supplies

Norbar – torque equipment – Norbar Torque Tools Ltd

Norclad – roofing and cladding material – Firth Steels Ltd

Norco – Harrier Fluid Power Ltd

*Norcool (Norway) – refrigeration – Interlevin Refrigeration Ltd

Norcor – corrugated board – Smurfit Kappa Sheetfeeding

Norcros Adhesives – tile fixing systems – Johnson Tiles Ltd

NORD – Hydraulic & Offshore Supplies Ltd

Nord – Mercury Bearings Ltd

Nord Gears – European Technical Sales Ltd

Nordac – microporous wood stains and varnishes – Dacrylate Paints Ltd

*Nordale – Greencore Frozen Foods

Nordberg – crushing and screening – Metso Minerals UK Ltd

Nordel IP – metallocene EPDM – Omya UK Ltd

Nordfab – dust and fume extraction equipment – Dantherm Filtration Ltd

Nordic – 12v fluorescent lighting – Lab Craft Ltd

Nordic Green Plus – rolled copper for building work – Luvata Sales Oy (UK)

Nordic Style – Scandinavian furniture – Nordic Style Ltd

Nordiko Coaters – AESpump

*Nordisk (Denmark) – column boards & training room systems – A V M Ltd

Nordson – Adhesive Application Systems – Nordson UK Ltd

*Nordson (Reg) (U.S.A.) – hot-melt adhesive applicators – Nordson UK Ltd

Nordstar – prefinished, crosslaminated, hardwood flooring – Atkinson & Kirby Ltd

*Norelem (France) – tooling parts – A C Hydraulics Ltd

NORELEM – Hydraulic & Offshore Supplies Ltd

Noremat – Tractor mounted reacharm mowers & hedge trimmers – Bunce Ashbury Ltd

Norfine – aquarium nets, aviary nets, pond nets and koi nets – Norfine Nets

Norfloat – buoys, fenders and navigation aids – Norfloat International Ltd

Norfolk – in line patio door – Coastal Aluminium

Norfolk – portable stand, roads and warning signs etc – I R S Ltd

Norfolk Brushes – Brushes – Harris Cleaning Services

Norfolk Greenhouses – greenhouses and sheds – Norfolk Greenhouses Ltd

Norfolk Lavender – lavender toiletry preparations (soap, talc, perfume etc) – Norfolk Lavender Trading Ltd

Norfolk Nog – cask beer – Woodforde's Norfolk Ales

Norfran – Norfran Ltd

Norgren – pneumatic controls – Thorite

NORGREN – Hydraulic & Offshore Supplies Ltd

Norgren – Aztech Components Ltd

Norgren (United Kingdom) – pneumatic equipment – Hydrasun Ltd

Norgren – Hydraulic Component & Systems Ltd

Norgren – Trafalgar Tools

Norgren – B L Pneumatics Ltd

Norgren – Southern Valve & Fitting Co. Ltd

Norgren - Asco - Joucomatic - Clippard - Griflex, Enots, Martonair - Excelon - Adams Lubtech - Herion - Lintra - Iso - Vdma - Cnomo - Excel - Isostar - Pneufit - C.Matic - Piezotronic - Sentronic - Airmover - Olympian - FFLuft.Fast. – B L Pneumatics Ltd

Norgren Martonair – pneumatic equipment – Bearwood Engineering Supplies

Norgren Martonair – hydraulic pneumatic and electric components – Norgren Ltd

Norit – activated carbon – Norit UK Ltd

Norithene – carbon filters – Norit UK Ltd

Norkie – cask beer – Woodforde's Norfolk Ales

Norland – heating ventilation & air conditioning maintenance – Norland Managed Services Ltd

Norlin – linseed variety – Limagrain UK Ltd

Norlyn Shopfittings – shelving, garment rails, fashion systems for clothing and footwear, basket units for shops, stores, warehouses etc – F & G Smart Shopfittings Ltd

Norma – Southern Valve & Fitting Co. Ltd

NORMA – Hydraulic & Offshore Supplies Ltd

Norma – Trafalgar Tools

Norma – Hampshire Hose Services Ltd

NORMA – Wide band power analysers – The Seaward Group

Normacol – bulk laxative – Norgine International Ltd

Normalair-Garrett – Honeywell Aerospace

Norman – Harrier Fluid Power Ltd

Norman Filters – UK agent hydraulic filters & accessories – Harrier Fluid Power Ltd

Norman Linton – ladies dresses, two pieces & separates – Norman Linton Ltd

Norman Linton Petite – ladies clothing – Norman Linton Ltd

NORMAND - – AC & DC motors, geared motors and controllers – A T B Laurence Scott Ltd

Normesh – Normesh Ltd

*Normet (Finland) – tunnelling equipment – Burlington Engineers Ltd

Norris Brothers – property management – Norris Brothers Ltd

Norriseal – Teamco International Ltd

NORSEMAN – Hydraulic & Offshore Supplies Ltd

Norsocryl – speciality acrylate – Atosina UK Ltd

Norsorex – oil absorbant – Atosina UK Ltd

Norstar – key telephone equipment and software – Nortel Networks UK Ltd

Nortech (Italy) – refrigeration – Interlevin Refrigeration Ltd

Nortel – all products and services – Nortel Networks UK Ltd

Nortel A World of Networks – all products and services – Nortel Networks UK Ltd

North Devon Journal – newspapers – North Devon Journal

North Exposure – Interface Europe Ltd

*North Pacific (U.S.A.) – flying toys and gliders – Amerang Group Ltd

North Star – air handling unit – Waterloo Air Products

North West Telegraph – newspaper publishers – Independent News & Media (NI) Ltd

Northcot Bricks Ltd – bricks, handmade & wirecut – Northcot Brick

Northern Design – Alpha Electronics Southern Ltd

*Northern Feather – Tradelinens Ltd

Northern Hotel & Restaurant – The Barnsley Chronicle Ltd

Northern jackson equipment – hydraulic repairs – Scope Engineers Ltd

Northern Joinery – staircases – Northern Joinery

Northern Marine – ship managers and marine services – Northern Marine Management Ltd

Northern Telecom – all products and services – Nortel Networks UK Ltd

Northey – compressors – Bearwood Engineering Supplies

Northshore – GRP laminates – Northshore Composites Ltd

Northumbria – waterproof clothing – J Barbour & Sons Ltd

Northwich Chronicle – weekly title – Flintshire Chronicle Newspapers

Northwich Herald & Post – free newspaper – Flintshire Chronicle Newspapers

Norton – Red House Industrial Services Ltd

Norton – Saint-Gobain Abrasives Ltd

Norton – plastic injection moulding – Norton Plastics

Norton Flypresses – fly and arbor presses – T Norton Ltd

Norust – corrosion inhibitor – Atosina UK Ltd

Norval – non return valves – Northvale Korting Ltd

Norwe – transformer bobbins – Rainer Schneider & Ayres

*norwesco – Norwesco Coffee

Norwest Holst – specialist construction and civil engineering products and services – Vinci plc

Norwich – Cooks Brushes

Noryl – Aaron Metal & Plastic Supplies Ltd

Noryl – Resinex UK Ltd

Notary – papers – Office Team

Notcutts – nurseries garden centre – Notcutts Ltd

Notestix – repositionable adhesive notes – Paragon Group UK Ltd

Notifier Fire Alarm Equipment – Leading Fire Alarm System Manufacturer – R V Fire Systems

Nottingham Property Services – estate agency – Nottingham Building Society

Notts Sport – synthetic surfaces and systems for sports and play – Notts Sport Ltd

Nourycryl – methacrylate monomers – Akzo Nobel Chemicals Holdings Ltd

Nourymix – additive concentrates for plastics – Akzo Nobel Chemicals Holdings Ltd

Nouryset – allyl based monomers – Akzo Nobel Chemicals Holdings Ltd

Nouveau – fires – Indesit Company UK Ltd

Nouvelle – UK Office Direct

Nouvelle – Georgia Pacific GB Ltd

Nova – small sized fusing machinery – Reliant Machinery Ltd

Nova – industrial cleaning equipment – B & G Cleaning Systems Ltd

Nova Challenger – windows – Nova Group Ltd

Nova-Glo – fluorescent pigments – Dane Colour UK

Nova-Mag – Anchor Magnets Ltd

Nova Star – carpet – Cormar Carpets

Novacap Inc – Cyclops Electronics Ltd

Novada – polyurethane foam – Custom Foams Ltd

Novaflex – silicone bonded flexible micapaper composite – Jones Stroud Insulations Ltd

Novakey – key telephone equipment – Nortel Networks UK Ltd

Novalastic – modified surface dressing binder – Total Bitumen

*Novamet (U.S.A.) – metallic particulate products – Hart Materials Ltd

Novamill – cnc bench milling machine – Denford Ltd

Novaset – sand binder system for the foundry industry – Ashland Specialties UK Ltd

Novasil – antacid – Reckitt Benckiser plc

Novaspec II – low cost visible spectrophotometer – Biochrom Ltd

Novaspec Plus – Biochrom Ltd

Novastar – 19" cabinet for office – Schroff UK Ltd

Novatex (United Kingdom) – Non - woven cleaning & wiping cloths – Wiper Supply Services Ltd

Novatex Grease – lubricants – Chevron

Novatip – pen – Office Depot UK

Novatone – ceiling tiles – U S G UK Ltd

Novaturn – cnc bench lathe – Denford Ltd

Novax – Solid oak furniture ash furniture pine furniture distribution – Nova Comex Ltd

Novel Industrie SA (France) – parts baskets and trolleys – Haesler Machine Tools

Nover – electrolytic capacitors – Anglia

Novex – B P plc

Novibra – anti-vibration mountings – Trelleborg Industrial A V S Ltd

Novo – litter bin with fire safety feature – Glasdon International Ltd

Novobond – epoxy bonded resin rich glass backed mica composite – Jones Stroud Insulations Ltd

Novocon – range of steel fibre reinforcement – Propex Concrete Systems Ltd

Novocon – Phoenix Weighing Services Ltd

Novojet – gas fired unit heaters – Reznor UK Ltd

*Novolam Securite (France) – fire retardant melamine faced chipboard – Rex Bousfield Ltd

Novomesh – Phoenix Weighing Services Ltd

Novomesh – combined system of steel & polypropylene fibres – Propex Concrete Systems Ltd

Novor 950 – crosslinking agent for high temperature cure of rubbers – Rubber Consultants

Novoston – alloy metals – Stone Marine Propulsion Ltd

Novotex – high performance steel fibres – Propex Concrete Systems Ltd

Novotex – Phoenix Weighing Services Ltd

Novox – gas separation apparatus – Boc Gases Ltd

Novus – UK Office Direct

Now – I P C Media Ltd

"Now" – kitchens & bedrooms – Potter Cowan & Co Belfast Ltd

Nowax – paramelt

Nowills – cutlery, special purpose knives, diving knives, hunting knives, ceremonial swords, machine knives – F E & J R Hopkinson Ltd

Noxamine – amine oxide – Atosina UK Ltd

Noxamium – ethoxylated quaternary ammonium chlorides – Atosina UK Ltd

NOxBox+ – inhaled nitric oxide therapy monitor – Bedfont Scientific Ltd

Noxol – textile processing aid – Benjamin R Vickers & Sons Ltd

Noyna – protective clothing – Noyna School Aprons

Noyna Safety – high visibility and reflective clothing and reflective material for vehicles – Noyna School Aprons

Noz-Chek – Crane Stockham Valve Ltd

Noz-Chek – valves – Crane Process Flow Technology Ltd

NP Aerospace Defence & Composite Products – ballistic products – N P Aerospace Ltd

NP2000 – Cost effective auto-pay solution – Newpark Security Ltd

NP3000 – Cashier based parking system – Newpark Security Ltd

NP3000 – Our most advanced Pay on Foot System – Newpark Security Ltd

NPK – Yokota UK

NPK – Gustair Materials Handling Equipment Ltd

NRG – Proplas International Ltd

*NRG flow – Wholebake Ltd

NRS – reads number plates for traffic applications – Vysionics

NRSA Training – C & G Services Ltd

NRSWA – C & G Services Ltd

NS Feeder pillar – low voltage distribution feeder pillars – Schneider

NSF- Slimline - Keylight Keyboard Switches – N S F Controls Ltd

NSI NACOSS Gold – National Security Inspectorate - National Approval Council for Security Systems – Sonic Security Services Ltd

NSK – ball and roller bearings, ball screws and linear positioning – N S K Europe

NSK – Mercury Bearings Ltd

NSK Nakanishi – T S Technology

NSK-RHP – Antifriction Components Ltd

NSS – Screws – Non Standard Socket Screws Ltd

NTK – oil seals – Action Seals Ltd

NTK – ceramic products, sensors – N G K Spark Plugs UK Ltd
NTMAIL – Gordano Ltd
NTN – Mercury Bearings Ltd
Nu-Lec – pole mounted switchgear – Schneider
Nu-Lip Rings – quad. section type rings – Pioneer Weston
Nu-Martindale – abrasion and pilling tester – James H Heal & Co. Ltd
Nu-Swift – fire fighting equipment – Nu Swift International Ltd
Nu-Swift ABC Multy-Purpose – dry powder extinguishers – Nu Swift International Ltd
Nu-T-Link – transmission belting (V-link) – Fenner Drives Ltd
NU TOOL – Hydraulic & Offshore Supplies Ltd
Nu-Type – metal type products for office machinery and marking equipment – Nu-Type Ltd
Nu-Way – oil, gas & dual fuel burner equipment – Nu Way
Nuage – dermatologically tested skincare products plus shaving oil for men – F M C G Ltd
NuAire – ventilation equipment – Nuaire Ltd
Nuance – bathroom & bedroom worktops – Bushboard Ltd
Nuastyle – taps – Armitage Shanks Ltd
*NuBuck (United Kingdom) – upholstery leather – Bridge Of Weir Leather Co.
Nucana – drain rods – Wardsflex Ltd
NUCAP EUROPE – Mapra Technik Co.
*Nuclear (Germany) – isotope containers – Ie-Ndt Manufacturer
Nuclepore – Harrier Fluid Power Ltd
Nucleus – marine radar navigator – Kelvin Hughes Ltd
Nucleus - Huson – Kelvin Hughes Ltd
NuDelta – The Woolwich
NuDelta Company – The Woolwich
Nufinf – Manufacture & sales – Universal Sealents UK Ltd
Nuflex – polypropylene drain rods – Wardsflex Ltd
NuFrame – PVC lattice panels – L B Plastics Ltd
Nugent – Harrier Fluid Power Ltd
Nugget – B L Pneumatics Ltd
Nugget – pneumatic equipment – Norgren Ltd
NUGGET – Hydraulic & Offshore Supplies Ltd
Nuggets – dog biscuits – Gilbertson & Page Ltd
Nulectrohms – Roxspur Measurement & Control Ltd
Nulene – piping cord – L B Plastics Ltd
Nullifire – County Construction Chemicals Ltd
Nulon – emulsion paints – Leighs Paints
Num – CNC, TELENUMERICS, SERVOMAC – N U M UK Ltd
Numatic – industrial cleaning equipment – B & G Cleaning Systems Ltd
Numatic – commercial and industrial cleaning machines – Numatic International
Numatic – industrial cleaning equipment – C S A Cleaning Equipment
Numatic – UK Office Direct
Numatic – R G K UK Ltd
NUMATICS – Hydraulic & Offshore Supplies Ltd
Numatics – B L Pneumatics Ltd
Numatics – Southern Valve & Fitting Co. Ltd
Numerik Jena – HEIDENHAIN GB LTD
Numorex NXA – profile cutting machine – Easab Cutting Systems
NUN-CNC TELENUMERICS SERVOMAC – N U M UK Ltd
NuNale Cream – Nail care cream for split and flaking nails – Laboratory Facilities Ltd
NuNale Sapphire Nail File – Used for shaping nails, especially useful to the elderly – Laboratory Facilities Ltd
NUOVA DETAS – Chaintec Ltd
Nuova FIMA – pressure gauges & process thermometers – E V O Instrumentation Ltd
Nuova Simonelli – espresso machines – Coffeetech
Nuovo Pignone – Harrier Fluid Power Ltd
Nupro – Harrier Fluid Power Ltd
Nupro – Southern Valve & Fitting Co. Ltd
Nursery Projects – magazine – Scholastic School Book Fairs
Nursery Window, The – nursery fabrics and wallpapers – Nursery Window Ltd
Nursey's – leather and sheepskin clothing – Nursey Of Bungay
Nursey's Lamb & Sheepskin Products – shearling coats, hats, gloves, mitts and slippers – Nursey Of Bungay
Nustrip 93 – nickel stripper – P M D UK Ltd
*Nutracell – Micron Bio-Systems
*Nutrak (Taiwan) – cycle inner tubes – Madison
Nutran – Yara UK It Ltd
*Nutri Logic – Software Nutrition – Planglow Ltd
*NUTRICHEL – Complexed formulation – Nutrel Products Ltd
Nutriculture – nutrients for growing plants in water – Nutriculture
Nutrish – probiotic cultures for fermented milks – Chr. Hansen (UK) Ltd
Nutrition Training – Facilities Staff Training
Nutromex – Omex Environmental Ltd
Nutromex, Ferromex, Magmex – Omex Environmental Ltd
Nuts – I P C Media Ltd
Nutsert – rivet nut – Zygology Ltd

Nutsert (Standard) – one sided threaded fastener for thicker materials – Avdel UK Ltd
Nuttall – shelving – Alan Nuttall Ltd
Nuttall Gear – G M B Associates
Nuttall Gear Corporation – Reducers, gearmotors, speed reducers – G M B Associates
Nuttall Gear Motors and Drives – G M B Associates
Nuval – neutral detergents – Quadralene Ltd
Nuvelle – 27 seat upwards coaches – Optare Group Ltd
Nuway – combustion controls and burners – O E M Group Ltd
NVG Friendly – night vision lighting product – Oxley Developments Company Ltd
NView – Lamphouse Ltd
Nvmatics – Glamair Supplies Ltd
*NVQ Catering & Hospitality – Brooklands College
nw – fittings – AESpump
Ny-Bias – bias bindings – J B Broadley
Nya Nordiska – The Winnen Furnishing Company
Nycoil – Southern Valve & Fitting Co. Ltd
NYCOIL – Hydraulic & Offshore Supplies Ltd
Nyfast – Nylon fasteners – Nylon Fasteners Ltd
NYK-Nichiyu – T V H UK Ltd
Nyl-Cut – material – Charterhouse Holdings plc
Nylacast – polymerised cast nylons – Nylacast
Nylacast Bigfoot – outrigger support pads – Nylacast
Nylacast H.S. Blue – Nylacast
Nylacast Moly – mos2 filled grade – Nylacast
Nylacast Nylube – compound lubricated high pressure grade cast nylon – Nylacast
Nylacast Nylube – 0.08 coefficient of friction – Nylacast
Nylacast Oilon – the original oil lubricant (premier grade) cast nylon – Nylacast
Nylatch – Panel fasteners – Zygology Ltd
Nylatron – modified nylons – Davis Industrial Plastics Ltd
Nylatron – Resinex UK Ltd
Nylatron MC901 – Merseyside Metal Services
Nylfloor – carpets – Interface Europe Ltd
Nylind PA6, PA66 (Ind. Quality) – Resinex UK Ltd
*Nyliners (Holland and Germany) – nylon bearings – Kellett Engineering Co. Ltd
Nylobag NB – solvent based opaque ink for nylon – Fujifilm Sericol Ltd
Nylon – East Midland Coatings Ltd
Nylon-D – nylon coating powder for application by fluidised bed – Nylon Colours Ltd
Nylon-R – nylon coating powder for application by electrostatic spray – Nylon Colours Ltd
Nylon-RNylon-D – Nylon Colours Ltd
Nylon R-Ag+ – Omnikote Ltd
Nylon R-AG – Omnikote Ltd
Nylon R-AM – Nylon Colours Ltd
Nylotex NX – solvent based ink for many proofed synthetic fabrics – Fujifilm Sericol Ltd
Nylotron – Merseyside Metal Services
NYPOR – high performance nylon membrane cartridge filters – Parker Dominic Hunter Ltd
Nyrex – UK Office Direct
Nytarp – PVC materials – Andrew Mitchell & Co. Ltd
*Nz – cultivator – Vaderstad Ltd

O

O.B. – automated sound control systems – Out Board
O.B.C. – record label – Ace Records Ltd
O'Brien Corporation – pre-insulated tubing bundles – Boiswood LLP
O.C.C.A.M. – computers – S T Micro Electronics Ltd
*O-Clip (Worldwide) – hose clips – Oetiker UK Ltd
O.D. Wheels – ladder wheels with automatic anti-roll facility – Ladderfix Ltd
O'Donnell – Sharpening systems for woodturners – The Toolpost
O.E.B. – auto electrical company – Wood Auto Supplies Ltd
O.H. Evans – furnishings for furnishing industry, blackout curtain lining – Evans Textiles Sales Ltd
O'Hagan's Sausage – Freedown Food Co.
O.J.C – record label – Ace Records Ltd
O.J's – Quality experienced service – Range Choice
O&K – Chaintec Ltd
O.K. – jazz – K R L
O&K – Harrier Fluid Power Ltd
O.Kay – handling solutions for waste recycling – O Kay Engineering Services Ltd
O-LOK – Hydraulic & Offshore Supplies Ltd
O.M.C. – LCD's and accessories – Opto Electronic Manufacturing Corporation Ltd
O.M.C.- Fibredata – Opto Electronic Manufacturing Corporation Ltd
*O.M.G. (Italy) – cast aluminium kitchen gadgets and coffee makers – Fairfax Coffee Ltd
*O.M.P. (Italy) – coldsaws – Prosaw Ltd
*O.M.S.O. (Italy) – silk screen and offset printing of bottles and containers – Engelmann & Buckham Ltd

*O.M.V. (Italy) – Thermoforming machinery and sheet extrusion machinery – Engelmann & Buckham Ltd
O.P.C. – specialist railway publishers – J Haynes Ltd
O.P.Q. – occupational personality questionaire – S H L Group Ltd
*O. Quitmann (Czech Rep, Slovak Rep and Malaysia) – kitchen, dining and occasional furniture importers – Quitmann Furniture
O.R.B. – combining pea variety – Limagrain UK Ltd
O.S.C.O.L. – laundry division products – Christeyns UK Ltd
O.S.C.R.E.T.E. – concrete division products – Christeyns UK Ltd
O.S.E.C. – on-site electrolytic chlorination – Wallace & Tiernan Ltd
O2 – Premier Mobiles
Oak – personal health scheme – Western Provident Association Ltd
Oak Furniture – The Winnen Furnishing Company
Oak Glade – Globally recognized major brand - a fantastic free service for our clients to add extra value – M A R C Co GB Ltd
Oakes Bros Ltd – agricultural and horticultural machinery – Oakes Bros Ltd
Oakland – passenger lifts passenger goods and sercuce lifts maintenance repair and modernisation – Oakland Excelsior
Oakman Menswear – trousers casual – Saville Heaton Ltd
Oaks Lighting – Light Fantastic
Oaks, The – horse races – Epsom Downs Racecourse
Oasis – ladies fashions – Oasis Fashions Limited
Oasis – can puncher – Henry Squire & Sons Ltd
OASIS (United Kingdom) – effervescent chlorine tablets for emergency water purification and sterilisation of baby bottles and feeding equipment – Hydrachem Ltd
Oasis SAF – Technical Absorbents
Oasters – eggs and egg products – Fridays Ltd
OASYS – purified water generation plant – Puretech Process Systems Ltd
Oban – Try & Lilly Ltd
Obara – European Technical Sales Ltd
Obara Europe – resistance welding products/consumables – Obara UK
Obara Europe - Martin Electric – Obara UK
Obelisk Music – music publishing – Obelisk Music
*Oberburg (Switzerland) – bottle cap making machinery, trimming, thread rolling and beading machines – Pearson Panke Ltd
Oberdorfer (U.S.A.) – bronze centrifugal and gear pumps – Cleghorn Waring & Co Pumps Ltd
Oberg – files – Bearwood Engineering Supplies
Oblique – Capex Office Interiors
Observer – network management monitoring software – N C C Group
Observer, The – newspapers – Middleton Guardian
Occasion – motor caravans – Leisuredrive Ltd
OCCO – Hydraulic & Offshore Supplies Ltd
OCCO COOLERS – Hydraulic & Offshore Supplies Ltd
Occutest – test for detection of occult blood in faeces – The Mast Group Ltd
Ocean – Watts Industries UK Ltd
Ocean – Cloakroom Solutions Ltd
Ocean – wire and wire rope – Webster & Horsfall Ltd
Ocean Magic – surfboards – Ocean Magic Surf Boards
Ocean Treasure – Popular, Reliable and Value for money – Chi Yip Group Ltd
OCEE Design – Office Seating – Bucon Ltd
OCS Support Services – office,window & building cleaning – O C S Group Ltd
Octabin – Quadwall Ltd
Octabin – Mar Deb
Octacut – diamond forming tools – Star Industrial Tools Ltd
*Octagon – incubators – Brinsea Products Ltd
Octagon – Camlock Systems Ltd
Octane – paper – Fenner Paper Co. Ltd
Octanorm – display and exhibition systems – RTD Systems Limited
Octanorm – Display Wizard Ltd
Octanorm – Aluminium Exhibition Materials – Ace Exhibitions Displays & Installation
Octanorm-Newline – display and exhibition systems – RTD Systems Limited
OCTAPENT – Rain gauge – Halcyon Solutions
Octavie – paper – Fenner Paper Co. Ltd
Octo 250 Towers – Accesscaff International Ltd
Octobin – Quadwall Ltd
Octomill – Seco Tools UK Ltd
Octopus – connector for subsea flowlines and risers and TLE applications – Oil States Industries UK Ltd
octopus pressure washer – beach cleaning system – Vikoma International Ltd
Octopus Toilet Arms – toilet arms – Helping Hand Co.
Octoral – Water Car Paint - Basecoat, Solvent Polyester Basecoat, Two Pack Lacquers, Hardener, Primers, Etch – Car Paint Warehouse Ltd

Octos – Kurt J Lesker Company Ltd

Octyl Acetate – perfume speciality – Quest International UK Ltd

Odasorb – odour absorbing material – Purification Products Ltd

ODE – Hydraulic & Offshore Supplies Ltd

ODE SOLENOID VALVES (United Kingdom) – Ultravalve Ltd

Odell – gas and charcoal barbecues – Crosslee plc

Odeon – fashion footwear – D Jacobson & Sons Ltd

ODESSE – Hydraulic & Offshore Supplies Ltd

Odin – broaching machines – Odin

Odlo – Provides temperature regulation without compression, a leading base layer manufacturer. – Baselayer Ltd

Odo-Vent – odour elimination filter – Waterloo Air Products

Odorgard – chemical wet scrubber for odour control – Higgins & Hewins Ltd

Odoron – odourless disinfectant – Evans Vanodine International plc

Odyssey – kitchen worktops – Bushboard Ltd

ODYSSEY – Groves Batteries

Odyssey Superfine – paper – Fenner Paper Co. Ltd

Oelikon – Red House Industrial Services Ltd

OEM Design – magazine – Progressive Media Group

OEMER – European Drives & Motor Repairs

OEO (Open Electronic Office) – software exchange – Transoft Ltd

Oerlikon – S J Wharton Ltd

Oerlikon Leybold – high vacuum pumps & plant – AESpump

Oetiker – B L Pneumatics Ltd

Oetiker – S J Wharton Ltd

Oetiker – Southern Valve & Fitting Co. Ltd

OETIKER – Hydraulic & Offshore Supplies Ltd

*Oetiker (Worldwide) – hose clips, self-sealing quick release couplings and pincers – Oetiker UK Ltd

OFCOM – Mass Consultants Ltd

Offenbach Bible – paper – Fenner Paper Co. Ltd

Office Chairs Direct – suppliers of office chairs – Brent Cross Office Furniture

Office Electrics – Capex Office Interiors

Office Equipment News – magazine – Progressive Media Group

Office Furniture Distributors Ltd – office furniture distribs – Woodstock Leabank Ltd

Office Match Ball – irish football assoc (football) – Gray Nicolls

Office Options Interiors – interior fit-out division, UK – Office Options

Office Speciality – Storage – Bucon Ltd

Officemake – Churchtown Buildings Ltd

Offices & Surgeries Insurance – specialist insurance – M M A Insurance plc

officetalk – SharePoint Specialists – Business Resources Development Ltd

Official Match Ball – league of Wales (football) – Gray Nicolls

Official Playstation 2 Special Edition – magazine – Future Publishing Ltd

Official Playstation 2 Tips – magazine – Future Publishing Ltd

Official UK Playstation 2 Magazine – magazine – Future Publishing Ltd

Official UK Playstation Magazine – magazine – Future Publishing Ltd

Official World Championship Netball – Gray Nicolls

Official World Cup – rugby – Gray Nicolls

Officine Rami – Night blinds – Showmaster Ltd

Offshore 850 – layflat supply hoses – Hydrasun Ltd

Offshore Oil & Gas Directory – United Business Media Ltd

Ofrahide – 2 and 4 ring binders – Office Depot UK

Ofrex – general office products – Office Depot UK

Ofrex Slim – pen – Office Depot UK

Ogden (Transteel) Ltd – steel stockholders and merchants – Ogden Transteel Ltd

OGEE – PVCU rainwater system – Hunter Plastics

Ogihara – automotive, press tools, assembly lines, sub-assemblies – Stadco Telford

Oglaend Systems (Norway) – cable tray & clamping systems – Hydrasun Ltd

Ogle Design – industrial design consultants and model makers, rapid prototyping and low volume prototypes – Ogle Models & Prototypes Ltd

Ogniebene – linear acctuaters – Amir Power Transmission Ltd

Ohaus – Weighing Equipment – Pauley Equipment Solutions

Ohmart – density, weight, moisture, level and thickness meters for – Able Instruments & Controls Ltd

Ohmega – applied to decade resistance boxes, inductance and capacitance – Cam Metric Holdings

Ohmite – Cyclops Electronics Ltd

OHP – Lamphouse Ltd

OIL CONTROL – Hydraulic & Offshore Supplies Ltd

Oil Control (Italy) – pressure, flow and motion control valves – Bosch Rexroth Ltd

Oil De Naturelle Products – Double Gee Hair Fashions Ltd

Oil & Gas Product Reveiw – An industry publication reviewing products and services for the industry – 21st Century Energy Publications Ltd

OIL GEAR – Hydraulic & Offshore Supplies Ltd

OIL GEAR TOWLER – Hydraulic & Offshore Supplies Ltd

OIL SISTEM – Hydraulic & Offshore Supplies Ltd

Oil Sistem (Italy) – power packs – Bosch Rexroth Ltd

OIL SISTEM SRL – Hydraulic & Offshore Supplies Ltd

OIL-X – high efficiency compressed air filters – Parker Dominic Hunter Ltd

Oilcooler – transmission oil cooling – Kenlowe Accessories & Co. Ltd

Oilfield Equipment – Schoeller Bleckmann & Darron

Oilheater – heater – Kenlowe Accessories & Co. Ltd

Oilite – sintered bearings – Bowman International Ltd

Oilsorb-Ultra – oil absorbent material for cleaning up oil spills – Cowens Ltd

OILTECH – Hydraulic & Offshore Supplies Ltd

Oily Water Seperator – the removal of hydrocarbons and settable solids from water – Megator Ltd

Oiseaux de Paradis – Woven fabrics – Zoffany

Okartek (Finland) – plastic conveyor rollers – Effortec Ltd

Okeford – Media Platform, IVR, Media Server, MRF, IMS Product – Telesoft Technologies Ltd

Okerin – paramelt

Oki – UK Office Direct

OKI – Cyclops Electronics Ltd

Okk – Whitehouse Machine Tools Ltd

OKO Relays – relays – Anglia

Okuma – Machine Tool Supplies Ltd

OKW Enclosures – O K W Enclosures Ltd

Olab (Italy) – solenoid valves – Zoedale plc

OLAB – Hydraulic & Offshore Supplies Ltd

OLAER – Hydraulic & Offshore Supplies Ltd

Olbas Oil – Decongestant – G R Lane Health Products Ltd

Old Charm – furniture – Wood Bros Furniture Ltd

Old Course St Andrews – computer games – St Andrews Link Trust

Old English – Prices Patent Candles Ltd

Old English Pantile – clay – Sandtoft Holdings Ltd

Old Father Time – clocks – Goldsmiths Jewellers Ltd

Old Miners Lozenges – medicated lozenges – A L Simpkin Co. Ltd

Old Park – Old Park Engineering Services

Old Rosie – H Weston & Sons Ltd

Old Town Canoe – canoe – Navimo UK Ltd

Oldbury Chain Grate – stoker – James Proctor Ltd

Oldham – miniature shaft misalignment couplers – Huco Dynatork

Oldham X-Y – servo shaft misalignment couplers – Huco Dynatork

OLEDINAMICA – Hydraulic & Offshore Supplies Ltd

Oleo – industrial energy absorbing equipment – Oleo International Ltd

OLEO DINAMICA L.C. – Hydraulic & Offshore Supplies Ltd

Oleo Resinous Seal – 48% solids and highly slip resistant penetrating seal – Premiere Products Ltd

Oleo Tecno – Orbital Hydraulic Motors – J B J Techniques Ltd

OLEODINAMICA (Italy) – cetop valves – Bosch Rexroth Ltd

OLEODINAMICA REGGIANA – Hydraulic & Offshore Supplies Ltd

Oleostar – Fairway Hydraulics Ltd

OLEOSTAR – Hydraulic & Offshore Supplies Ltd

Oleostar – hydraulic – V H S Hydraulic Components Ltd

*Oleostar (Italy) – hydraulic circuit valves – BYPY Hydraulics & Transmissions Ltd

Oleostar – hyrdraulic circuit valves – Harrier Fluid Power Ltd

OLEOTECHNICA – Hydraulic & Offshore Supplies Ltd

Olexobit – B P plc

Olga – British Vita plc

Olga Device – British Vita plc

Olga Eurocel – British Vita plc

Olga Sanocel – British Vita plc

Olimpic – European Technical Sales Ltd

*Olis – Euro Catering Equipment

Olive – hair accessories – Bray Group Ltd

Oliver James – special occasion and evening wear in larger sizes – Frank Usher Group

Olivers – bread savouries & confectionery – Greggs plc

Olivetti – Photocopier – Alecto Solutions Ltd

Olivetti – UK Office Direct

Olivetti Cash Registers – Cash Register Services

OLLI – cat food – Butchers Pet Care

Olma Leduc – European Technical Sales Ltd

Olsen Shutters – manufacturers of rolling shutters – Russell Shutters Ltd

Olten – European Technical Sales Ltd

Olympi Castor – castors – Archibald Kenrick & Sons

Olympia – UK Office Direct

Olympia II – ceiling tiles – U S G UK Ltd

Olympian – Commercial refrigeration manufacturers – Carter Retail Equipment

Olympian – hydraulic pneumatic and electric components – Norgren Ltd

Olympian – solid chipboard core – Mid-Ven Doors Ltd

Olympian – B L Pneumatics Ltd

Olympic – Pobjoy Mint Ltd

Olympic – Gem Tool Hire & Sales Ltd

Olympic 580 – carpets – Interface Europe Ltd

Olympic Blinds Ltd – venetian, roller, vertical and wood venetian blinds and exterior canopies – Olympic Blinds Ltd

Olympus – aero engines – Rolls-Royce plc

Olympus – MIG welding and plasma cutting equipment – Olympus Technologies Ltd

Olympus – UK Office Direct

Olympus – carpets – Bond Worth

Olympus – Lamphouse Ltd

Olympus – pump – Torres Engineering & Pumps Ltd

Olympus Distribution – fasteners for industry – Olympus Distribution Ltd

Olympus Industrial – industrial endoscopy and related equipment for remote usual inspection – Keymed Ltd

Olympus-KeyMed – medical endoscopy and associated equipment – Keymed Ltd

Olys – Twinmar Ltd

OM – Chaintec Ltd

OM CNC – vertical turning machines – Mills C N C

*Omaka Springs (New Zealand) – Pol Roger Ltd

Omal (Italy) – pneumatic actuators – Zoedale plc

Omal – cash counting equipment – Volumatic Ltd

Omal – Southern Valve & Fitting Co. Ltd

Omar – park homes – Omar Park Homes Ltd

Omar Leisure – holiday homes – Omar Park Homes Ltd

Omar UPVC – windows – Omar Park Homes Ltd

OMAX – Water jet profile cutting machines – Sciss Ltd

OMC – Harrier Fluid Power Ltd

OMdeSIGN London Partnership – Omdesign London Ltd

Omeg – potentiometers and switches – Omeg Ltd

Omega – range of laboratory furniture – APMG Ltd

Omega – K S B Ltd

*Omega (China) – hydraulic lifting equipment – S I P Industrial Products Ltd

Omega – kitchen worktops – Bushboard Ltd

*Omega – radios, tape recorders, car stereos, speakers, headphones, telephones and torches – Omega Import Export Ltd

Omega – four loop flexible intermediate bulk container – Rexam Holding plc

Omega – Valspar Powder Coatings Ltd

Omega – Polyester litho plater. – Macdermid Autotype Ltd

Omega 201 and fxP (United Kingdom) – single chamber and cluster plasma etch tools – Aviza Technology UK Ltd

Omega Complete – kitchen worktops – Bushboard Ltd

Omega Optical – Glen Spectra Ltd

Omega Systems – slitter inspection rewinders – A B Graphics International Ltd

Omegadeck Tower – Accesscaff International Ltd

Ometron – instruments for analysing stress and vibration – Sira Test & Certification Ltd

OMG – Chaintec Ltd

OMG – Stacatruc

OML – S M W Autoblok

Omme PLatforms – Accesscaff International Ltd

Ommemog Platforms – Accesscaff International Ltd

OMNI+ – speciality interface – P G Drive Technology

OMNI-BALL – Omnitrack Ltd

OMNI-FLOAT – Omnitrack Ltd

OMNI-GLIDE – Omnitrack Ltd

Omni-Guard (United Kingdom) – peripherally-scored reverse-acting metal bursting disc – Elfab Ltd

OMNI-SLIDE – Omnitrack Ltd

OMNI-SWEEP – Omnitrack Ltd

Omnia – paper – Fenner Paper Co. Ltd

Omniball (United Kingdom) – ball transfer units – Omnitrack Ltd

Omnidirectional (United Kingdom) – ball transfer units – Omnitrack Ltd

OMNIDOX – e records management – Stortext Ltd

Omniflex – equipment for boats – R W O Marine Equipment Ltd

Omnigauge – linear slide gauges for O/D, I/D width & centre distance measurement, dial or digital readout. – Acugrip Ltd

Omnigraf – G E Healthcare

*Omniledger (U.S.A.) – computer systems – Omniledger Ltd

Omnilux – lighting equipment – Powerlite Lighting Solutions Ltd

Omnimat (United Kingdom) – ball transfer units – Omnitrack Ltd

Omnimax – directional caravan aerial – Maxview Ltd

OmniMix – digital sound and picture mixing console/editor – Red Lion 49 Ltd

Omnipaque – G E Healthcare

Omnipro – Harman Technology Ltd

Omnis – lubricants – Chevron

Omniscan – G E Healthcare

Omnithane – high strength polyurethane formulation – Pipeline Engineering & Supply Company Ltd
Omnitone – G E Healthcare
Omnitrack Ltd (United Kingdom) – ball transfer units – Omnitrack Ltd
Omnitrast – G E Healthcare
Omniwheel (United Kingdom) – ball transfer units – Omnitrack Ltd
***Omori Machinery (Japan)** – tray stretch wrapping, shrink wrappers, horizontal form fill and seal, controlled atmosphere sealing systems, cartoners – Selo UK Ltd
Omron – Cyclops Electronics Ltd
Omron – Encoders UK
Omron – Computer hardware – Torex Retail Holdings Ltd
Omron – CBM Logix
Omron – Selectronix Ltd
Omron – Proplas International Ltd
Omron – M S C Gleichmann UK Ltd
Omron – European Technical Sales Ltd
Omron – relays, switches, sensors & connectors – Anglia
Omron Counters – European Technical Sales Ltd
Omron Digital Panel Indicators – European Technical Sales Ltd
Omron Electromechanical Relays – European Technical Sales Ltd
Omron Fibre Optic Sensor – European Technical Sales Ltd
Omron Frequency Converrters – European Technical Sales Ltd
Omron Inductive Sensors – European Technical Sales Ltd
Omron Limit Switches – European Technical Sales Ltd
Omron Low Voltage Switch Gear – European Technical Sales Ltd
Omron Machine Interfaces – European Technical Sales Ltd
Omron Measurement Sensor – European Technical Sales Ltd
Omron Monitoring Products – European Technical Sales Ltd
Omron Motion Controllers – European Technical Sales Ltd
Omron Photo Electric Sensors – European Technical Sales Ltd
Omron PLCs – European Technical Sales Ltd
Omron Power Supplies – European Technical Sales Ltd
Omron Programmable Logic Controllers – European Technical Sales Ltd
Omron Pushbutton Switches – European Technical Sales Ltd
Omron Relays – European Technical Sales Ltd
Omron Rotary Encoder – European Technical Sales Ltd
Omron Sensors – European Technical Sales Ltd
Omron Servo Systems – European Technical Sales Ltd
Omron Solenoids – European Technical Sales Ltd
Omron Solid State Relay – European Technical Sales Ltd
Omron Temperature Controller – European Technical Sales Ltd
Omron Timers – European Technical Sales Ltd
Omron Vision Sensor – European Technical Sales Ltd
OMT – Harrier Fluid Power Ltd
Omya – extenders and fillers – Omya UK Ltd
On Business – business papers – Howard Smith Paper Ltd
On-Call Receptionist – Vodafone Retail Ltd
On Demand Technology – On Demand Technology
On Line – pumps – Wrightflow Technologies Ltd
On Offset – uncoated paper & board – Howard Smith Paper Ltd
On-Site Access – Accesscaff International Ltd
On the Bell – magazine for emergency services with national UK distribution – Gateacre Press Ltd
On Top – leisure headwear – P M S International Group plc
Onan – compressors – Bearwood Engineering Supplies
Onan – Harrier Fluid Power Ltd
ONCA – S M W Autoblok
Once – decorative paints – Akzonobel
oncology – Napp Pharmaceutical Group Ltd
Oncopro – G E Healthcare
Oncoseed – G E Healthcare
One 2 One – mobile communications – T-Mobile UK
One 2 One Mobile Phones – Champ Telephones Ltd
One 7 Liner – 17 tonne curtainsider bodywork – Boalloy Industries Ltd
One Five One – Cogne UK Ltd
One For Me (United Kingdom) – hair nets hairdressing – Aburnet Ltd
One In Seven – magazine – Rnid
One Nut – Flotronic Pumps Ltd
One Step – childrens shoes – D Jacobson & Sons Ltd
Onecup – range of foam cups and lids – Pregis Rigid Packaging Ltd
Oneflow – electronic peak flow meters – Enspire Health
Oneway – Woodturning tools, lathes, chucks – The Toolpost
Oniachlor – trichloroisocyanuric acid – Atosina UK Ltd
Onsrud Cutters – CNC router cutters – ATA Engineering Processes
OnTrack – Vascular Access kits for Hemodialysis – Scottish Health Innovations
Onx Range – cements for high temperature applications – David Ball Group plc
Onyx – high temperature tank-mounting filter unit – P M D UK Ltd
***Onyx Spoiler (Netherlands)** – spoiler roof manual or electric – Webasto Products UK Ltd
Oocide – disinfectant – DuPont Animal Health Solutions
Opal – dishwasher powder – East Lancs Chemical Co. Ltd
Opal computors – it specialists – Owen & Palmer Ltd
OPALINA – lamps – Osram Ltd
Opalux – Architectural Window Films
Opec - Oil Pollution Environmental Control – Oil Pollution Environmental Control Ltd
Opedic – hospital theatre footwear, foam slippers, bracelets and hospital drapes – P3 Medical Ltd
Opel – L M C Hadrian Ltd
Opel – Ashley Competition Exhausts Ltd
Open Box Beam – Berry Systems
Open Business School – Open University Worldwide
Open Date – hot foil and thermal printing equipment – Open Date Equipment Ltd
Open Front Office – strategic application for fund managers worldwide – D S T Global Solutions
Open Messenger – solution for automatic trade confirmation, settlement and reconciliation – D S T Global Solutions
Open Options – real-time application with attendance clockings and work-booking data applied immediately to the system database, enabling users to get up-to-the-minute information on the status of employees and work tasks. – Crown Computing Ltd
Open Plan Borrowing – The Woolwich
Open Plan Mortgage – The Woolwich
Open Plan Private Bank – The Woolwich
Open Plan Protecting – The Woolwich
Open Plan Saving – The Woolwich
Open Plan Services – The Woolwich
Open Plan Shop – The Woolwich
Open Planners – UK Office Direct
Open Process – enterprise scheduling and control software – Fox It Ltd
Open Sky – ventilation unit – Powermatic Ltd
Open The Box – games – S E Jones & Son
Open Top Wallets – manilla wallet – Acco East Light Ltd
Open University Press, The – Open University Worldwide
Open Unversity, The – Open University Worldwide
Openair by Proudhart – waxed clothing – P S Gill & Sons
OpenBase – software – Prismtech Ltd
Opendoor – human resource/payroll software – Northgate H R Ltd
Openlaw – Oxford Law & Computing Ltd
OPENRAM – Hydraulic & Offshore Supplies Ltd
Opera/Tempo (United Kingdom) – powered sling lifter with unique tilting spreader bar lifts from the floor if required and from high beds – Arjo Med AB Ltd
Opico – agricultural machinery distributors – Opico Ltd
Opium DK – Sirdar Spinning Ltd
Opmaster – Operating Theatre Trolley & Table – Swift Medical Trolleys Ltd
Opsigal – Counting System – C K Tech Serve Ltd
Optare – buses – Optare Group Ltd
Optare Coach Sales – coaches – Optare Group Ltd
Optek – Cyclops Electronics Ltd
Optel – Open University Worldwide
OPTera – DWDM systems – Nortel Networks UK Ltd
***Opti (Worldwide)** – spectacle frames – Optiquality Holdings Ltd
Opti-Gard (United Kingdom) – high specification reverse-acting metal bursting disc range – Elfab Ltd
***Optia (Germany)** – slide storage cabinets – A V M Ltd
Optibelt – Mercury Bearings Ltd
Optibelt – V-pulleys for taper bushes, V-belts, timing pulleys, sprockets – Optibelt UK Ltd
OPTIBELT – Wolds Engineering Services Ltd
Optibelt – belting – Arntz Belting Co. Ltd
Optibelt D.K. – double V-belts – Optibelt UK Ltd
Optibelt DK – double V-belts – Optibelt UK Ltd
Optibelt K.B. – kraftbands – Optibelt UK Ltd
Optibelt KB – Kraftbands – Optibelt UK Ltd
Optibelt KR – V-belts with patterned top surfaces – Optibelt UK Ltd
Optibelt P.K. – V-belts with patterned top surfaces – Optibelt UK Ltd
Optibelt R.B. – ribbed belts – Optibelt UK Ltd
Optibelt RB – ribbed belts – Optibelt UK Ltd
Optibelt S.K. – wedge belts to BS 3790 – Optibelt UK Ltd
Optibelt SK – wedge belts to BS 3790 – Optibelt UK Ltd
Optibelt SVX – variable speed belts – Optibelt UK Ltd
Optibelt V.B. – V belts – Optibelt UK Ltd
Optibelt V.X. – variable speed belts – Optibelt UK Ltd
Optibelt VB – V belts – Optibelt UK Ltd
Optibelt Z.R. – timing belts – Optibelt UK Ltd
Optibelt Z.R.M. – timing belts metric – Optibelt UK Ltd
Optibelt ZR – timing belts – Optibelt UK Ltd
Optiblet ZRM – timing belts metric – Optibelt UK Ltd
Optica – lighting & lighting components – Coughtrie International Ltd
Optichain – chain – Optibelt UK Ltd
Opticoat – General Vacuum Equipment Ltd
Optidress – grinding wheel dressing attachment – P G T Ceewrite Ltd
OPTIFLAME – Glen Dimplex UK Ltd
Optiflex – V-belts poly 60 – Optibelt UK Ltd
Optiflex – Illumiated Magnifier – Anglepoise Ltd
***Optiflo (Germany)** – rheological additive – Sud-Chemie UK Ltd
***Optigel (Germany)** – rheological additives – Sud-Chemie UK Ltd
Optigland – bulkhead penetrator – Icore International
Optik 1 – infra red heater – Robinson Willey
Optik 2 – infra red heater – Robinson Willey
Optilab – General Vacuum Equipment Ltd
Optima (United Kingdom) – integrated rollstock – Escada Systems Ltd
Optima – dry air in-line control valves – Parker Hannifin Ltd
OPTIMA – Groves Batteries
Optima – Lusso Interiors
Optima – earth fault protection equipment – F D B Electrical Ltd
Optima – Facade Rainscreen Cladding Solutions – Sotech Ltd
Optima 117 – single glazed partition system – Optima Ltd
Optima 217 – double glazed partition system – Optima Ltd
Optima 97 – advanced drywall partition system – Optima Ltd
Optima Badges – high definition screen printed heat seal badge – J & A International Ltd
Optima Bi-Panel – steel relocatable office partitioning – Optima Ltd
Optima Elements – composite partition system – Optima Ltd
Optima Spacewall – acoustically sound and flexible working partition – Optima Ltd
Optimale – recycled paper – Fenner Paper Co. Ltd
Optimat – open end V-belting (with connectors) – Optibelt UK Ltd
Optimax – belts – Optibelt UK Ltd
Optimo – arch well cladding – Kingspan Ltd
Optimol – Greases and Lubricants – Sprint Engineering & Lubricant
Optimum – conduit end termination for cable – Icore International
Optimum 50 Towers – Accesscaff International Ltd
Options – kitchen worktops – Bushboard Ltd
Options – decorative paints – Akzonobel
Options – Georgia Pacific GB Ltd
Options Complete – kitchen worktops – Bushboard Ltd
Optipaque – G E Healthcare
Optipark – automatic number plate recognition system – Alfia Services Ltd
Optipath – C G Tech Ltd
Optipot – horticultural plastic growing units – Desch Plantpak Ltd
Optirail – high visibility predestrian guardrial – Alpharail Ltd
OptiScan – motorised microscope stage – Prior Scientific Instruments Ltd
Optivity – data network management – Nortel Networks UK Ltd
Opto – shop fitting equipment – Opto International Ltd
Optoflex – rubber sheathbed flexible fibre-optic cable – Industrial Friction Materials Ltd
Optolite – contrast enhancement and EMI shielded filter windows for electronic displays – Instrument Plastics Ltd
Optoma – Lamphouse Ltd
Optomer – high purity monomers for optical & medical use – Vickers Laboratories Ltd
Optoscan – Machine Guard Solutions Ltd
Optosign – production of colour changing led illuminated panels & signs – Marl International Ltd
Optrex – Review Display Systems Ltd
Optronic Laboratories (U.S.A.) – Glen Spectra Ltd
Opus – lubricants and hydrocarbon waxes – Ferguson & Menzies Ltd
Opus – low voltage fuseway – Schneider
Opus – bathroom & toilet extract unit – Nuaire Ltd
Opus – kitchen furniture – Moores Furniture Group
Opus – Pledge Office Chairs Ltd
Opus – UPVC windows, doors and conservatories, aluminium windows and doors – Opus Windows
Opus – piano – Forsyth Bros Ltd
Opus 700 – medium/heavy duty catering equipment – Lincat Ltd
Opus Business Customers – - provide SME businesses with cheap electricity – Opus Energy Ltd
Opus Combis – combi steamer ovens – Lincat Ltd
Opus Consultancy Services – Opus Consultancy Service
Opus Corporate Solutions – - develop flexible and tailored electricity products – Opus Energy Ltd
Opus Education & Research – Opus Consultancy Service

Opus P.C.F. – polycarbonate cement – Schottlander Dental Equipment Supplies

Opus-Silver – reinforce glass ionomer core build up material – Schottlander Dental Equipment Supplies

Opus Software Limited – Halcyon Solutions

Opus Weaves – woven fabrics – Today Interiors Ltd

Opuscem – glass ionomer fixing cement – Schottlander Dental Equipment Supplies

Opusfil – glass ionomer restorative – Schottlander Dental Equipment Supplies

OR-X (Israel) – test & measuring instruments – Metrix Electronics

*Oralla (Spain) – Stainless bar mills – Amodil Supplies

*Oramec – Merial Animal Health Ltd

Oranfresh – Traders Coffee Ltd

Orange – Premier Mobiles

Orange – Mobile phones – Champ Telephones Ltd

Orange Box – Seating – Bucon Ltd

Orangebox – Capex Office Interiors

Orapol – prophylaxis pastes – Prima Dental Group Ltd

Oraproph – prophylaxis pastes – Prima Dental Group Ltd

Orascan – G E Healthcare

Orbinox (Spain) – Knife gate valves manufacture – Trimline Valves

Orbis – UK Office Direct

Orbis – security screens & alarm systems – Sitexorbis plc

Orbis Range – rotary polisher/scrubber – Truvox International Ltd

Orbit – vanity basin – Armitage Shanks Ltd

Orbit – The Little Brown Book Group

Orbit Developments – property developers – Orbit Developments

Orbit Distribution – Orbit Distribution Ltd

Orbit GmbH – European Technical Sales Ltd

Orbit Irrigation – Irrigation products – Arcadia Irrigation UK

Orby – livestock feeders and feeding systems – Orby Engineering Ltd

Orby Ezi-Fit – manger systems for herringbone milking parlours – Orby Engineering Ltd

Orbyveyor – helical flight (auger) conveyor systems – Orby Engineering Ltd

Orchard – Orchard Drawing Boards

Orchard Farm – own brand food products – Brakes

Orchard Laid and Wove – paper – Fenner Paper Co. Ltd

Orchard Superfine – paper – Fenner Paper Co. Ltd

Orderman – M C R Systems Ltd

Oregon – bath – Armitage Shanks Ltd

Oregon – flexible ducting hose – Merlett Plastics UK Ltd

Orelf – mineral flotation agent – Atosina UK Ltd

Orevac – modified eva and grafted polyolefines – Atosina UK Ltd

Orgal – acrylic resins – Lawrence Industries Ltd

Orgalloy – Resinex UK Ltd

Orgalloy – polymide 6/6 polypropylene – Atosina UK Ltd

Organic Cider – H Weston & Sons Ltd

Organic Vintage – H Weston & Sons Ltd

Organisational Modelling International – architectural design and space projects – Chadwick International

*Orgapack (Switzerland) – strapping tools, spares, seals and repairs – SATCO Tapes

Orgasol – pa 6 - 12 fine powder – Atosina UK Ltd

Orglas – hygenic wall lining – R I W Ltd

Oria Airspring Bellows – Interflex Hose & Bellows Ltd

ORIEN CARDS – Customised Print Jobs of High Quality at Lower Costs with prompt delivery – Orien Cards LLP

Orient – Display Wizard Ltd

Orient – clothes line – James Lever & Sons Ltd

ORIGA – Hydraulic & Offshore Supplies Ltd

Origa – Southern Valve & Fitting Co. Ltd

ORIGA SYSTEM PLUS – Hydraulic & Offshore Supplies Ltd

Origina Watermarked – paper – Fenner Paper Co. Ltd

Original – water taps – Rudge & Co UK

Original Cordings, The – traditional country clothing – Cordings Ltd

Original Suffolk Collection, The – Henry Watson Potteries Ltd

Origins – ceramic glazed wall tiles – Johnson Tiles Ltd

Orima – acid gold plating process – Cookson Electronics Ltd

Orima – steel bath – Armitage Shanks Ltd

Orinal Art – The Winnen Furnishing Company

Orion – automatic test equipment – B A E Systems Ltd

Orion – roof windows – Ubbink UK Ltd

ORION (United Kingdom) – SiCOH damascene dielectric process with k<2.5 – Aviza Technology UK Ltd

Orion – flexible tube labelling machine – Harland Machine Systems Ltd

Orion – seat – Armitage Shanks Ltd

Orion – videos and televisions – Orion Electric UK Co. Ltd

Orion - Comet - Gemini - Neptune - Proteus - Saturn - Sirius - Jupiter - Pulsar - Titan - Enterprise - Harland Europa – Harland Machine Systems Ltd

Orissor – printed publications and books related to matters of mind, body and the environment – Orissor Trust Ltd

Orissor Productions – printed and recorded music, particulary musicals – Orissor Trust Ltd

ORKOT – Hydraulic & Offshore Supplies Ltd

Orkot – reinforced plastics etc – Trelleborg Ceiling Solutions Ltd

*Orlando (Portugal) – ladies shoes – Cheshire Style Ltd

Orlando Rui – ladies shoes – Cheshire Style Ltd

Orlando the Marmalade Cat – Chorion plc

Orli Downlight – Altima Ltd

Orlik – briar pipes – Cadogan

Orline – diesel dumper (2 wheel drive) – Thwaites Ltd

Orman Risk Analysts – Orman Risk Analysts

Ormec – Motor Technology Ltd

Ormerod – Red House Industrial Services Ltd

Ormon – European Technical Sales Ltd

Oroglas – Resinex UK Ltd

Orsi – Joe Turner Equipment Ltd

Orsogril – grating system – Alpharail Ltd

ORT – Oceanographic release transponder – Sonardyne International Ltd

Ortak – jeweller – Ortak Jewellery Ltd

Orthoban – wadding & padded bandage for use under plaster – Cowens Ltd

Orthoban - Orthopaedic Bandage, Oilsorb-Ultra - Oil Absorbents, Wetsorb - high capacity water soaking media. – Cowens Ltd

*Orthocryl (Germany) – clear lacquer – Otto Bock Healthcare plc

Orthoflo – low vacuum dewatering unit – Heimbach UK

Ortholate – perfume speciality – Quest International UK Ltd

*Orthologic (U.S.A.) – orthodontic appliances – Plandent

Orthomat – carpets – Interface Europe Ltd

Orthopaedic solutions – CE marked products – Mckenna Group Ltd

Orthos – mechanical handling and process engineers to the foundry industry – Orthos Projects Ltd

Orthosport – semi-orthopaedic footwear – Gilbert & Mellish Ltd

Orthotrek – Modular Footwear – Gilbert & Mellish Ltd

Orthowrap – Textile Orthoses – Gilbert & Mellish Ltd

Orthtek – ThermoplasticComposit – Greene Tweed & Co. Ltd

Ortlinghaus – brakes, clutches – Ortlinghaus UK Ltd

Ortlinghaus – European Technical Sales Ltd

Ortlinghaus - brakes, clutches – Ortlinghaus UK Ltd

Orvar Supreme – BS4659 BH13 hot work die steel – Uddeholm Steel Stockholders

Orvec – passenger care products – Orvec International Ltd

Orwak – European Technical Sales Ltd

OS400 – Mid Blue International Ltd

Osborne – commercial refrigerators, beer and wine coolers – Osborne Refrigerators Ltd

OSG – Precision Tools

Osiris – sensors – Schneider

OSL Seals and Numatics – Newburgh Engineering Co. Ltd

OSL Stock Holders – Newburgh Engineering Co. Ltd

Oslo Lift and Slide – Park Farm Design

Osma – rainwater – Wavin UK

Osmocote – controlled release fertilizer – Scotts Co. Ltd

Osmonics – Harrier Fluid Power Ltd

Osmose Celbrite – Protim Solignum

Osmose Lifewood – copper chrome based wood preservative system (pretreat) – Protim Solignum

Osmose Naturewood – copper based wood preservative system (pretreat) – Protim Solignum

Ospbar 4c – distribution board – Schneider

Osprey – gas-atomised metal powders including M.I.M powders and spray deposited shapes and coatings – Sandvick Osprey Ltd

Osprey – fishing tackle – Daiwa Sports Ltd

Osprey – envelopes and paper – Eagle Envelopes Ltd

Osram – Cyclops Electronics Ltd

Osram – car electrics – L A E Valeo Ltd

*OSRAM DULUX (Germany) – compact fluorescent,energy-efficient lamps for long service life – Osram Ltd

*OSRAM GMBH (Germany) – lamps and lighting products – Osram Ltd

Ostopore – stoma care range – Teleflex Medical

OTC – Hydraulic & Offshore Supplies Ltd

Otehall – E Preston Electrical Ltd

Otehall – Microswitches – Saia Burgess (Gateshead) Plc

OTI – Optical test equipment – Optical Tools For Industry Ltd

Otis – lifts and escalators – Otis Ltd

OTT Hydrometry – Halcyon Solutions

Ott-Jakob – European Technical Sales Ltd

Otter (United Kingdom) – pool chair hoist – Arjo Med AB Ltd

Otter Controls Ltd – Thermostates & safety cut outs – Otter Controls Ltd

Otter Manilla – manilla – St Regis Paper Co. Ltd

Otter Pumps – Denton Pumps Ltd

Otterbrite – manilla – St Regis Paper Co. Ltd

Otterburn – baby rugs, tweeds etc and textiles – Otterburn Mills Ltd

Otterguard – safety cut-out device for kettles – Otter Controls Ltd

Otterstat – thermostat – Otter Controls Ltd

*Otto Bock (Germany) – artificial limbs – Otto Bock Healthcare plc

Otto Holland GmbH – European Technical Sales Ltd

Otto MEC – Selectronix Ltd

Ouchless – plasters – Robinson Healthcare Ltd

OULTON – switched reluctance/brushless DC drives – A T B Laurence Scott Ltd

Out and About – artificial grass matting – Bruce Starke & Co. Ltd

*Outdoor Scene (Far East) – technical outdoor clothing – Flitterman Investments Ltd

OutdoorExteriot – simes – Concord Marlin Ltd

Outershield – gas shielded flux cored wire – Lincoln Electric UK Ltd

Outlaw – shoes – D Jacobson & Sons Ltd

Outlaw – boats – Sunseeker Poole Ltd

Outrage – boots – D Jacobson & Sons Ltd

Outsource Ireland – Outsource Ireland Ltd

Ova-Easy – Brinsea Products Ltd

Ovablend – egg based food ingredients – Framptons Ltd

Ovacryl – buffable acrylic polish – Evans Vanodine International plc

Oval – under countertop basin – Ideal Standard Ltd

Ovalgrip – (PVC) and LFH) cable markers – Hellermann Tyton

*Ovation (U.S.A.) – roundback guitars – John Hornby Skewes & Co. Ltd

Oven Cleaner – cold oven cleaner spray – Premiere Products Ltd

Oven Cleaner – thickened cleaner to emulsify baked on grease – Evans Vanodine International plc

Ovenable Board – microwave dishes – Rexam Holding plc

Ovenclean – concentrated odourless caustic based cold oven cleaner – Premiere Products Ltd

Ovencut – Forward Chemicals Ltd

Overbeck – Newall UK Ltd

Overland kincardine – carvan retail – Overland Leisure & Caravans

Overlord – early warning alarm system – Boddingtons Ltd

Overlord – suspension files – Acco East Light Ltd

Overton – aluminium windows and door gear rail and automatic vehicles – Percy Lane Products Ltd

Owatonna – Harrier Fluid Power Ltd

*Owlet Apple Juice – Owl House Fruit Farm

Owoko – electronic assembly tools – Welwyn Tool Group Ltd

Owon – Handheld Oscilloscopes – StanTronic Instruments

OWON – handheld and Portable Digital color LCD display Oscilloscope – Owon Technology Ltd

Oxascan – G E Healthcare

Oxbridge – tea, confectionery, biscuits, preserved fruits, meat products, and pickles – Oxbridge

Oxbridge Cricket – Tiflex Ltd

Oxelene – cotton and polyester corespun – Amann Oxley Threads Ltd

Oxelene DP – polyester and polyester corespun – Amann Oxley Threads Ltd

Oxella – glace cotton polyester corespun – Amann Oxley Threads Ltd

Oxendales – mail order catalogue – J D Williams Mail Order Group

Oxford – bathrooms – The Imperial Bathroom Company Ltd

Oxford – portable chemical toilet – Elsan Ltd

Oxford – 500mm single oven – Indesit Company UK Ltd

Oxford – UK Office Direct

Oxford – maths sets – Helix Trading Ltd

Oxford Chemicals – speciality and aroma chemicals – Frutarom UK Ltd

Oxford Illustrated Press – outdoor activities – J Haynes Ltd

Oxford Innovation – technical, economic and management consultants, specialists in technology assessment and audits, innovation and technology transfer, manager of several innovation centres premises for new technology based firms – Oxford Innovation Ltd

oxford neckties – quality silk neckties – Oxford Neckties

Oxford Welders – Welding plant & electric arc – Pickhill Engineers Ltd

OxiMag – Minelco Ltd

Oxistat – a blended anti-oxidant – Agil Chemicals Products

oxizone – Air Steriliser - odour and germ control – 03 Solutions Ltd

Oxoid – culture media powder – Oxoid Holdings Ltd

Oxone – monopersulfate compound – Du Pont UK Ltd

Oxycontin – analgesic – Napp Pharmaceutical Group Ltd

Oxycontin - analgesic, Transtec - analgesic, Adizem XL - hypertension and angina, Zanidip - hypertension, MST Continus - analgesic, Depocyte - oncology – Napp Pharmaceutical Group Ltd

Oxygen Sniffer – Pipestoppers

Oxypic – leak sealer industrial and domestic boilers – Dunsley Heat Ltd

Oxysept 1 – disinfecting solution for soft contact lenses – Allergan Ltd
Oxysept 1 Step – disinfecting, neutralizing system for soft contact lenses – Allergan Ltd
Oxysept 2 – rinsing, neutralizing and storage solution for soft contact lenses – Allergan Ltd
Oxysept Saline – preservative free, sterile, buffered, aerosol saline – Allergan Ltd
Oxysolve – oxygenated solvents – B P plc
Oyez – stationery – Office Team
Oyez Copier – plain paper copier paper – Office Team
Oyez Legal Support Systems – computer softwear – Office Team
Oyez Multicopier Laser Plus – multi purpose paper – Office Team
Oyez Stronghold – files – Office Team
Oyez Strongmail – envelopes – Office Team
Oyez Supertype – typewriter ribbons – Office Team
Oyez Trifilm – carbons – Office Team
Oyez Wills – wills software package – Office Team
Oysterette – baths – Jendico Ltd
Ozaphan – Genus Group
***Ozark (S.Korea and Japan)** – banjos and mandolins – Stentor Music Co. Ltd
Ozat – Triogen Ltd
Ozocap – bag filter – Waterloo Air Products
Ozoflo – bag filter – Waterloo Air Products
Ozokleen – bag filter – Waterloo Air Products
***Ozone** – Smiths Coffee Co. Ltd
Ozopleat – disposable panel filter – Waterloo Air Products
Ozotex – disposable panel filter – Waterloo Air Products
Ozzie – Oswald Bailey Group

P

P 2000 – Plenty Mirrlees Pumps
P.43 – desludging submerged rotary jet mixer – Veolia
P.A.C.E. – cooker hoods/electrical fittings – Potter Cowan & Co Belfast Ltd
P.A. Finlay & Co. – building contractors – Pa Finlay & Company Ltd
P.A.L. (Taiwan) – plastic bagmaking machinery – Kween B Ltd
P.A.N. 7 – castings – D Y N Metal Ltd
P.A.N. Al 7 – castings – D Y N Metal Ltd
P.A.N. Al10 – castings – D Y N Metal Ltd
P.A.N. B – castings – D Y N Metal Ltd
P.A.N. Soms – castings – D Y N Metal Ltd
P.A.S.S. – poly-aluminium silicate sulphate coagulant for water treatment – Feralco UK Ltd
P A Testing – PAT Testing Specialists – P A Testing Ltd
P & B – instruments and transducers – P B S I Group Ltd
P & B Engineering – motor protection relays – P B S I Group Ltd
P & B Power Engineering – general protection relays – P B S I Group Ltd
P.B.T.I. – toner and ink jet cartridges – P B T International
P & B Technical Services – manufacture control panels – P B S I Group Ltd
P & B Weir Electrical – soft start for motors – P B S I Group Ltd
P & C – motor vehicle spares – Panaf & Company
P.C.A. – cavity lining products – Prima Dental Group Ltd
P.C.D. Tooling – diamond tool – Leitz Tooling UK Ltd
***P.C. Glassblocks (U.S.A.)** – Pittsburgh Corning UK Ltd
P.C.L. – couplings & hose – Air Power Centre Limited
P.C.M.S. – personal computer - production monitoring system (SFDC) for plastics, packaging, pharmaceutical and pressings etc – B M S Vision Ltd
P.C.P. – conversion kits for gaming and AWP machines (worldwide) – P C P Micro Products Ltd
P.C. Pro – Dennis Publishing
P.C. Publishing – publishers – Jones & Palmer Ltd
P.C.S./P.A.S. – fire alarm control systems – U T C Fire & Security
P.C.S. Superbox – Storage City Ltd
P C T – Gustair Materials Handling Equipment Ltd
P.C.V. – training courses for drivers – Friendberry Ltd
P C World – PCs and software – Dixons Retail
P.D. – pumps – Wrightflow Technologies Ltd
P.D.M.X. – digital multiplexers – Nortel Networks UK Ltd
P.E.S. (United Kingdom) – mechanical/constriction products and services – P E S UK Ltd
P F E – P C F Secure Document Systems Ltd
P F P E – G B R Technology Ltd
P.F.S. – pressure zinc die castings – Archibald Kenrick & Sons
P.G. Series – silver soldered fittings – Tungum Ltd
P.G. SERIES – Hydraulic & Offshore Supplies Ltd
P & H – violin bows – Stentor Music Co. Ltd
P.H.C. – tungsten carbide products – Triten International Ltd
P.H.C. Building Supplies – Travis Perkins plc
***P.H. Gerbaud** – The Vintners Selection Ltd
P.H.L.S. – test specimens – Health Protection Agency
P.H.S. - Material Handling Systems – conveyors, magazines and measuring systems for steel and heavy duty applications – Prosaw Ltd
P.I.C – instant foaming non abrasive general cleaner – Premiere Products Ltd
P.I.V. – positive infinitely variable speed gears – Bibby Transmissions Ltd
P K – Power Access Systems Ltd
P & M – drying machinery for chemicals, foods and textile machinery – Petrie Technologies Ltd
P.M.301 – panel mounted kwh/VAL/VArh/MD meter – Northern Design Ltd
P.M. 303 – low cost miniature electricity meter – Northern Design Ltd
P.M.305 – panel mounted multi-function electricity meter – Northern Design Ltd
P.M.390 – panel mounted multi-function electricity meters – Northern Design Ltd
P.M.4 – loudspeaker – Lowther Loudspeaker Systems Ltd
P.M.6 – loudspeaker – Lowther Loudspeaker Systems Ltd
P.M.A. Group – automotive radiators and vehicle registration plates – P M A Group
***P.M.C. (U.S.A.)** – can fillers, food formers – Selo UK Ltd
P.M.D. 505 – non-etch cleaner for aluminium and non-ferrous metals – P M D UK Ltd
P.M.D. 606 – heavy duty, long life cleaner for brass and steel – P M D UK Ltd
P.M.D.C. – ca-idms performance management package – Business & Decision Ltd
P M Oils – Process oils – Nynas UK Ab
P.O.D.S. – Hydraulic & Offshore Supplies Ltd
P.P.G. – gear units, mill gears, cylindrical grinding mills, kilns and dryers – Power Plant Gears
P.P.G. – producers of glass fibre reinforcement & yarn – P P G Industries UK Ltd
P.P.I – Power Products International Ltd
P.P M A Show – trade association for UK and overseas, manufacturers of process and packaging machines; publishers, exhibition and conference orgaisers and machinery consultants. – P P M A Ltd
P.P.P. – water-hammer arrestors – Wade International Ltd
P.R. 600 – pallet racking – S S I Schaefer Ltd
P.R.C. – protected rack channel – Reliance Precision
P.R.M. – marine gear boxes – Lancing Marine
P. Rayner – transmission engineers geared motor units – Pumps & Gear Boxes Ltd
P.S.5 – 15% solids and acrylic based plastic emulsion floor seal – Premiere Products Ltd
P.S.C. – contrast enhancement filters – Optical Filters
P.S.F. – extremely gentle dense phase conveyor – Gericke Ltd
***P.S.I (Germany)** – prasent service institut – Galpeg Ltd
P.S.S. – stainless steel medium – Pall Europe Corporate Services
P.S. Vibro Screen – vibratory screens – Filter Screen Supply Ltd
P Series – double acting, spring failsafe, actuator – Severn Glocon Ltd
P.T.E. – plastic components, wearstrips, change parts – Sigma Industries Ltd
P.T.I. – Precision Technology International – Precision Technologies International Ltd
P.T.S. Foulmaster – package foul & surface drainage – Pump Technical Services
P.T.S. Sumo – heavy duty floor drainer – Pump Technical Services
P.T.S. Trashmaster – industrial & commercial drainage – Pump Technical Services
***P. Tirfor (France)** – lifting equipment – Worlifts Ltd
P.U.L.S.I. – analytical instruments – Kittiwake Procal Ltd
P.U. Poles – lighting poles for various applications – Painter Bros Ltd
P&V (United Kingdom) – rock drilling bits, extension rods and ancillary equipment, contractors tools and demolition tools. – Padley & Venables Ltd
P.V.C. – casting and welding – Plastic Mouldings Ltd
P.V.C. Strip Curtains – Bolton Gate Co. Ltd
P.V.C. Vendo – service mark – Vendo plc
P.V.T. – software packages – Schlumberger Oilfield UK plc
P.W. Merkle – leather-rubber, plastics machinery – P W Merkle Ltd
P.W.S. Distributors Ltd – distributors of furniture components – P W S Distributors
P2000 Pyramid – Glazing Vision Ltd
P3 – Molecular Control Systems Ltd
P5 – Molecular Control Systems Ltd
P5125 – Bostik Ltd
P5600 – 8 channel mobile data acquisition system – Prosig Ltd
P7 – Molecular Control Systems Ltd
PAC – sodium carbonate hydrated lime – Ferelco UK Ltd
Pace – folding openers – Caldwell Hardware Ltd
Pacemaker – uncoated paper & board – Howard Smith Paper Ltd
Pacemaker – instant accommodation units – Portakabin Ltd
Pacemaker Laid – uncoated paper & board – Howard Smith Paper Ltd
Pacer – open frame steel surveyors tape – Fisco Tools Ltd
Pacer – convertor – Ajax Tocco International Ltd
Pacer – electronic pulsation system – Delaval
***Pacer (U.S.A.)** – centrifugal pumps – Dual Pumps Ltd
Pacer Components – specialist distributor for opto-electronic components – Pacer Components plc
Pacesetter – postoperative knee braces – Remploy Ltd
Pacesetter Ivory Board – uncoated paper & board – Howard Smith Paper Ltd
Pacestter Pulp Board – uncoated paper & board – Howard Smith Paper Ltd
Pacet – roof & vent fans – Pacet Manufacturing Ltd
Pacific – Display Wizard Ltd
Pacific Corp (Taiwan) – card cameras – Premier Engineering
Pacific Jeans – jeans wear – Gobina London Ltd
Pacific Pump – Condensate Removal Pump – E D C International Ltd
***Pacific Scientific** – European Drives & Motor Repairs
Packaged Air Blast – dry air water coolers – Thermal Engineering Systems Ltd
Packaged Water Chillers – water induction generator coolers – Thermal Engineering Systems Ltd
Packaging Directory – industrial and commercial specialist packaging – Davpack
Packaging distributors – Antalis Mcnaughton
Packaging Industry Directory – United Business Media Ltd
PackagingTeam – Software Application packaging and setup authoring – Packaging Team Ltd
Packer – machines and equipment used for packaging and wrapping – Lea Valley Packaging Ltd
Packfab – Harrier Fluid Power Ltd
Packless – fibre-free silencer – I A C Company Ltd
***Packmat (Germany)** – packaging machinery – Advanced Dynamics Ltd
Packpoint – packaging machines and materials – Lea Valley Packaging Ltd
Paco Marcos (Spain) – designer shoes ladies – Cheshire Style Ltd
***Paco Molina (Portugal)** – ladies shoes – Cheshire Style Ltd
Pacrim Audio – German designed Line array active flying PA system – Turnaround 360
Pacton – Sallu Plastics
Pacwright – vertical form fill and seal machinery – Wright Machinery Ltd
Padana – Airedale Environmental Services Ltd
Padawax – shoe wax in a sponge – Cherry Blossom Ltd
Padblocks – printed memo block – Irvin Brothers Ltd
Paddington Bear – Chorion plc
Paddington Bear – neadlecraft – Coats Ltd
Paddock – DIY hardware – Paddock Fabrications Ltd
Paddock Royale – Yara UK lt Ltd
Paddock Wood Courier – newpaper – Kent Regional News & Media
Paddy Hopkirk – car accessories – Mont Blanc Industry UK Ltd
Padmex – Resinex UK Ltd
Pag ACS – fast chargers – P A G Ltd
Pag AR Series – auto-ranging fast chargers – P A G Ltd
Pag Belt – rechargeable battery products – P A G Ltd
Pag Light – battery lighting – P A G Ltd
Pag LOK – battery connector – P A G Ltd
Pag Pac – rechargeable battery products – P A G Ltd
Pag RTI – battery run time information – P A G Ltd
Page – paint boxes – Oasis Art & Craft Products Ltd
Pageant Range – 6 single axle clubman touring caravans – Bailey Of Bristol
Pageantry II – fabrics, wallpapers & borders – Today Interiors Ltd
Paine Manwaring – general heating and plumbing installation and service engineers – Paineman Waring
Paines – malt extracts – British Diamalt
Pains-Wessex – marine distress signals – Pains Wessex Ltd
Paint By Numbers – art products – Oasis Art & Craft Products Ltd
Paint Shop – UK Office Direct
Paint Star – Hydravalve Ltd
paintbox – complete graphics system – Quantel Ltd
Paintjet Systems – single dot paint marking – Universal Marking Systems Ltd
Pair Gain Equipment – digital carrier systems – Telspec plc
Pak-bilt – "knock-down" overseas units – Boyton B R J System Buildings Ltd
Pakord – rayon cord strapping – Gordian Strapping Ltd
Pakprint – printed self-adhesive tapes – SATCO Tapes
Pakscan – 2 wire microprocessor based actuator control system – Rotork plc
Paksol – Grip Seal Resealable Zip Lock Bags – Grays Packaging Ltd
Pal – hygiene and barrier protection products for food, industrial and healthcare markets – Pal International Ltd

Pal – CNC machine tool retrofit and rebuild – Pennine Automation Spares Ltd
Pal Bond – Palram Europe Ltd
Pal Clear – Palram Europe Ltd
***Pal Disc (Australia)** – low profile turntable – Southworth Handling Ltd
Pal Door – Palram Europe Ltd
Pal Gard – Palram Europe Ltd
Pal Glas – Palram Europe Ltd
Pal Grass – artificial display grass – Support In Sport Ltd
Pal-Lift Stacker (Italy) – pedestrian powered stacker for pallets and cages – Southworth Handling Ltd
Pal Opaque – Palram Europe Ltd
Pal Rapper – Semi automatic stretch wrapping machines – M J Maillis UK Ltd
Pal Ruf – Palram Europe Ltd
Pal Shield – Palram Europe Ltd
Pal Sun – Palram Europe Ltd
Palace – building material chemicals – Palace Chemicals Ltd
Palace Belvedere – carpets - axminster – Brintons Carpets Ltd
Palace Cinema (Stalybridge) Ltd – cinema – Cosmo Bingo Club
Palace Design – carpets - axminster – Brintons Carpets Ltd
Palace Series 2 – electrical switches and accessories – Wandsworth Group Ltd
Palace Series 3 – electrical switches and accessories – Wandsworth Group Ltd
Palace Velvet Wilton – carpets - axminster – Brintons Carpets Ltd
Paladign – AS/400 investment management computer system – D S T Global Solutions
Paladin – fine turf and bowling green motor mower – Lloyds & Co Letchworth Ltd
Paladin – pelleting machines – Andritz Seed & Bio Fuel Ltd
Paladio – ctp platesetters – Agfa Gevaert
Palair – Gustair Materials Handling Equipment Ltd
Palantype – computer aided transcription systems – Possum
Palastrong – extruded polythene film, bags & sacks – Palagan Ltd
Palatine – plate – H G Stephenson Ltd
Palazzo – kitchen furniture – Moores Furniture Group
Palazzo – cover paper – James Cropper plc
PalestrinA – tufted carpet – Brockway Carpets Ltd
Palette 2000 – carpets – Interface Europe Ltd
Palette 3000 – carpets – Interface Europe Ltd
Palette 4000 Flecks – carpets – Interface Europe Ltd
Palette 4000 Tweeds – carpets – Interface Europe Ltd
Palfinger – Harrier Fluid Power Ltd
Palight – Palram Europe Ltd
Palintest – water testing and environmental testing equipment – Palintest Ltd
Pall – Harrier Fluid Power Ltd
Pall – filters & spares – Bearwood Engineering Supplies
PALL – Hydraulic & Offshore Supplies Ltd
Pall – filters – Pall Europe Corporate Services
Pall Mall – household textiles – Linden Textiles Ltd
Pall Trinity – Harrier Fluid Power Ltd
Palladex – palladium plating process – Cookson Electronics Ltd
Palladian – taps and mixers – Ideal Standard Ltd
Palladium Chunky – yarn – Stylecraft
Pallas – prints – The Medici Galleries
Pallecon – returnable containers – Ceva Container Logistics
Pallet Pal – manual palletiser and de palletiser – Southworth Handling Ltd
Palletower – converter frames for stacking pallets – Palletower GB Ltd
Palletruck – hydraulic hand pallet trucks – Palletower GB Ltd
Palletsupremo – Bandsaw – Dynashape Ltd
PALLSORB – Hydraulic & Offshore Supplies Ltd
Palm – Review Display Systems Ltd
Palm – UK Office Direct
Palm – men's ladies' and children's knitted underwear – Manchester Hosiery A Division Of Aikon Europe Group Ltd
Palm Beach – spectacle frames – Pennine Optical Group Ltd
Palma (China) – classical guitars – John Hornby Skewes & Co. Ltd
PALMER CHENARD – Hydraulic & Offshore Supplies Ltd
Palmers – supply and erection, hire and sale of scaffolding and access equipment – Palmer & Harvey Ltd
Palmers Industrial Services – multidisciplines maintenance & construction services incorporating access, industrial coatings, insulation, passive fire protection and industrial cleaning – Palmer & Harvey Ltd
Palmit – hygiene product – B P plc
Palms Tropical Oasis, The – miniature zoo – Stapeley Water Gardens Ltd
Palmyco – sandfilled synthetic sports grass – Support In Sport Ltd
***Palnut (U.S.A.)** – locknut – Jet Press Ltd
***Palsys (Netherlands)** – palletisers for cardboard boxes, bags and trays – A M J Maters Partnership Ltd
Palvini – jeans and trousers – Kentex Jeans & Casuals
Pama – Windfall Brands Ltd
PAMA, COBRA, KRUSELL, BLUETOOTH, PLUG N GO – MOBILE PHONE ACCESSORIES BLUETOOTH PRODUCTS MULTI-MEDIA PRODUCTS – Pama & Co. Ltd
Pamak – tall oil fatty acids – Hercules Holding Ii Ltd
PAMARGAN – Hydraulic & Offshore Supplies Ltd
Pamargan Products – bonded seals – Pamargan Products Ltd
Pamela Mann – ladies hosiery – Nylon Hosiery
Pamma Rugs – Top brand designer modern and ethnic traditional rugs – Pamma Rugs
***PAMOdrive** – electronically commutated DC external rotor motor – Ebm-Papst
***PAMOdyn** – electronically commutated DC servo motor – Ebm-Papst
Pamolyn – fatty acids – Hercules Holding Ii Ltd
***PAMOtronics** – modular motor drive and control systems – Ebm-Papst
Pamper – underwater hull cleaning machine – U M C International
Pamphlox – cardboard boxes – J T Sawyer & Co. Ltd
PAN – programmable acoustic navigator-acoustic transceiver dedicated to the transmission and decoding of subsea acoustic signals – Sonardyne International Ltd
Pan Hire – trailer hire – Panema Trailer Engineering Ltd
PAN6432 (602 Series) – Dax International Ltd
PAN6433 – Dax International Ltd
Panacase – aluminium sign systems – Universal Components
***Panache (Spain)** – ladies shoes – Cheshire Style Ltd
Panache – A range of coordinated lingerie – Panache Lingerie
Panache Atlantis – Liquid Filled Bra – Panache Lingerie
Panache Interiors – Commercial and Residential interior design service – panache interiors
Panache Special Occasions – Bridal Lingerie – Panache Lingerie
Panache Sport – high impact sports bra – Panache Lingerie
Panache Superbra – For the larger cup sizes (DD to G) – Panache Lingerie
Panache Swimwear – Cup sized swimwear – Panache Lingerie
Panalarm – annunciator and sequential event recorder – Amatek Precision Instruments UK Ltd
Panalpina – freight forwarders – Panalpina World Transport Ltd
Panama – PVC coated blind, awning and canopy fabrics – Somic Textiles
Panama – british cigars – Imperial Tobacco Group PLC
Panamatic – washing machines – Oliver Douglas Ltd
Panamech – flexible coupling – Huco Dynatork
Panaseal – full facemask respirator – Scott International Ltd
Panasolve – solvent – Euro Bond Adhesives Ltd
Panasonic – computer printers – Micro Peripherals Ltd
Panasonic – LCD and Plasma Televisions – Electrotec International Ltd
Panasonic – geared motors, servo motors – Lenze UK Ltd
***Panasonic** – Court Catering Equipment Ltd
Panasonic – Review Display Systems Ltd
Panasonic – Programmable controllers, sensors, vision systems. – William Teknix
Panasonic – Tekdata Distribution Ltd
Panasonic – Oxon Fastening Systems Ltd
Panasonic – capacitors, inductors, fans & transducers – Anglia
Panasonic – Lamphouse Ltd
Panasonic – UK Office Direct
Panasonic – Cyclops Electronics Ltd
Panasonic – Cobus Communications
Panasonic – welding equipment – Olympus Technologies Ltd
Panasonic Photocopiers – Clarity Copiers
Panasonic, Samsung – Installation, Support Services – CCV Telecom
Panasonic Telephone Systems – Direct Voice & Data Ltd
Panatrim – aluminium sign systems – Universal Components
Panavise – vices – Longs Ltd
Panaz – Philip Cowan Interiors
Panaz – furnishing and upholstery fabrics – Panaz Ltd
Pancrex – pancreatin enzyme – Astellas Pharma Ltd
Panda – optical frames and sunglasses – Hilton International Eye Wear Ltd
Panda – mobile dust extraction unit – Horizon Mechanical Services International Ltd
Pandect Instrument Laboratories – repair and recertification of aircraft instruments – Pandect Instrument Laboratories Ltd
Pandora – B P plc
Pandora – cards – The Medici Galleries
Pandrol – Tunnel Steels
Panduit – Cyclops Electronics Ltd
Panel-Vue – wide angle floodlight luminaire – Holophane Europe Ltd
Panelflex – panelling for exhibitions – Pinewood Associates
Panelmate – graphic workstation – Schneider
Panelmix – panel mounted mixing valve – Sheardown Engineering Ltd
Paneltex – modular sign systems – Signscape Systems Ltd
Panema – service, general repair, re-furbishments – Panema Trailer Engineering Ltd
Panex – quarter turn fasteners quick release – Southco Manufacturing Ltd
Panex – Quarter turn fasteners – Zygology Ltd
Pangea Iron Oxides – Pangea Ltd
Panisco Pack Bux – corrugated fibreboard containers & sheet, specialist supplier to the trade – Mondi Packaging Limited
Panko – breadcrumbs – Griffith Laboratories Ltd
Panoflam – fire retardant chipboard – Rex Bousfield Ltd
Panoflex – flat rubber sheathbed festoon cable – Industrial Friction Materials Ltd
Panoptica – film and video post production software – Global Graphics Software Ltd
Panorama – Interface Europe Ltd
Panorama – finger collar system – Bribex
***Panorama D.T.V.** – Michael Stevens & Partners Ltd
Panoramic – glazed sectional overhead doors – Kaba Door Systems
Panorex – radio opaque marking tape – Prima Dental Group Ltd
Panotex – inherently flame resistant textiles – Universal Carbon Fibres Ltd
PanSystem – well test analysis software – Weatherford Edinburgh Petroleum Services Ltd
Pant Pumps – footwear – Russell & Bromley Ltd
PANTAK – Xstrahl Ltd
***Pantec (Italy)** – test and measuring instruments – Carlo Gavazzi UK Ltd
Panter Platforms – Accesscaff International Ltd
Pantex – garment presses – Armstrong Commercial Laundry Systems
Pantheon – floodlighting – Designplan Lighting Ltd
Panther – vertical blind system – Eclipse Blind Systems
Panther – Pressure washers – B & G Cleaning Systems Ltd
Panther – generators – T P S Fronius
Panther – Campbell International
Panther – Generators – T P S Fronius Ltd
Panther – mobile and static hot cupboards – Lincat Ltd
Panther – generators – T P S Fronius
Panther – Harrier Fluid Power Ltd
Panther – channels & ties – Simpson Strong-Tie International Inc
Panther (United Kingdom) – barrier systems – Motivation Traffic Control Ltd
Panther Int' – Belle Engineering Sheen Ltd
Pantone – Letraset Ltd
Pantone – UK Office Direct
Pantone Books (U.S.A.) – graphic art supplies – Letraset Ltd
Pantrac – Pantograph carbons and carbon brushes for traction and industry – Electrical Carbon UK Ltd
Pantrak – curtain sided body – Panema Trailer Engineering Ltd
Papadopoulous – U C D Ltd
Paper House – humorous greeting cards – Great British Card Company plc
Paper-Masters – Mamelok Holdings Ltd
Paper Mate – UK Office Direct
Paper Sculture – Kitfix Swallow Group Ltd
Paperblanks – quality bound hand stitched books – Birmingham Business Supplies Ltd
Paperchase – high quality stationery and greeting cards retailer – Paperchase
Paperflow – paper and stationery – Paper Flow Ltd
Papermaster – conditioner – Greenbank Technology Ltd
Papersafe – files – Office Depot UK
Papersafe Neon Notes – fluorescent sticky notes – Office Depot UK
Papersafe Removeable Notes – yellow sticky notes – Office Depot UK
Papersticks – cotton buds pharmaceutical and confectionery sticks – Papersticks Ltd
***Papillon (Italy)** – domino masks – Palmer Agencies Ltd
Papoose – child carrier – Karrimor Ltd
PAPR - Proflow SC – Powered Air Purifying Respirations – Scott International Ltd
PAPR-Tornado – Powered Air Purifying Respirations – Scott International Ltd
Papst – Motor Technology Ltd
***Papst (Germany)** – fans and motors – Ebm-Papst
Papst – Cyclops Electronics Ltd
Papst (Ebm) – fan motors (axial) – Thermofrost Cryo plc
PAPVR – natural paper – Winter & Co UK Ltd
Papyex – expanded graphite paper – Mersen UK
Papyrobord – drawing board covering – Pelltech Ltd
Papyrus – modular sign systems – Signscape Systems Ltd
Paqualab – water testing laboratory – Ele International
***Par Aide (Canada)** – Golf course accessories (Canadian) (01424) 819008 – Pareto Golf Ltd

PARA-FLEX – Couplings – Baldor UK

Para Red – distress rocket – Pains Wessex Ltd

ParaCAD+ – computer aided design software – Cadlogic Ltd

Paracera – paramelt

Paracoat – paramelt

Paracol – wax emulsions – Hercules Holding Ii Ltd

Paradigm – M S C Gleichmann UK Ltd

Paradip – paramelt

Paradox – games and puzzles – Pentangle Puzzles & Games

*Paradur (Germany) – taps – Macinnes Tooling Ltd

Parafil – plastic extrusions – Linear Composites

*Paraflam (Austria) – fire resistant safety glass – C G I International Ltd

Paraflex – paramelt

Paraglas – cast acrylic sheeting – Stockline Plastics Ltd

Paragon Products, Paragon Hygiene Specialists – Paragon Products UK Ltd

Paragrid – geogrid for soil reinforcement – Terram Ltd

Paraid – stretchers and rescue medical equipment – Evac+Chair International Ltd

Paraline – Bushboard Ltd

Paraline – revetment and winch rope – Marlow Ropes Ltd

Paraline – ceiling systems (suspended) – U S G UK Ltd

Paraline – linear metal ceiling systems – U S G UK Ltd

Paralink – plastic extrusions – Linear Composites

Paralink – geogrid for soil reinforcement – Terram Ltd

Parallax – software systems and financial accounting software – Sherwood Systems Ltd

Paraloop – plastic extrusions – Linear Composites

Paramelt – paramelt

Paramo Clay – tools – F W Sibley Ltd

Paramount – carpet – Cormar Carpets

Paramount – cycle and motorcycle locks – Henry Squire & Sons Ltd

Paramount – oil measures, funnels and safety cans – Hartle I G E Ltd

Paramount – cattle yards – Browns of Wem Ltd

Paramour – knitwear, t-shirts, sweatshirts, jogging suits and underwear – Paramount Knitwear Leicester Ltd

Parapet – circular surface vandal resistant architectural lighting – Designplan Lighting Ltd

Paraplast – Solmedia Laboratory Supplies

Paraplex – polymeric plasticiser – Omya UK Ltd

Parasol – water taps – Rudge & Co UK

Paraweb – plastic extrusions – Linear Composites

Parazone – UK Office Direct

Parcels to Ireland – Delivery to Ireland from England – Parcels To Ireland

Parch Marque – paper and card – G F Smith

Parchment Book – wallpaper collection – Zoffany

*Pardini – Neville UK plc

*Parentini (Italy) – cycle clothing – Rsi

Pareto (United Kingdom) – ball dispensors, washers, pickers & golf course accessories – Pareto Golf Ltd

Parexel MMS – medical communications – Parexel M M S Europe Ltd

PARFLEX – Hydraulic & Offshore Supplies Ltd

Parflu – chimneys (metal) – William May Ltd

Paris – Fole Gras – Classic Fine Foods Ltd

Park Hampers – food hamper – Park Group plc

Park Home & Holiday Caravan – I P C Media Ltd

Park Pack – rigged ceiling or wall mounted outdoor luminaire – Holophane Europe Ltd

Parkeblock – hardwood block flooring – Atkinson & Kirby Ltd

Parker – UK Office Direct

Parker – Mayday Seals & Bearings

PARKER – Hydraulic & Offshore Supplies Ltd

Parker – Hydraulic Component & Systems Ltd

Parker – Aztech Components Ltd

Parker – toys – Hasbro UK Ltd

Parker – Southern Valve & Fitting Co. Ltd

Parker – control valves and line components, including driers, cores, sightglasses, moisture indicators, suction accumulators, expansion valves, constant pressure valves, solenoid valves, stop valves, check valves, automotive products and flexible hose – Thermofrost Cryo plc

Parker – Harrier Fluid Power Ltd

PARKER ARLON – Hydraulic & Offshore Supplies Ltd

PARKER CAD – Hydraulic & Offshore Supplies Ltd

PARKER CYLINDERS – Hydraulic & Offshore Supplies Ltd

PARKER DAYCO – Hydraulic & Offshore Supplies Ltd

Parker & Farr – upholstery and occasional pieces for contract and domestic use – Parker & Farr Furniture Ltd

PARKER FILTRATION – Hydraulic & Offshore Supplies Ltd

Parker Filtration – Trafalgar Tools

PARKER FLUID CONNECTORS – Hydraulic & Offshore Supplies Ltd

Parker (Hannifin) – Bristol Fluid System Technologies Ltd

PARKER HANNIFIN – Hydraulic & Offshore Supplies Ltd

*Parker Hannifin (U.S.A.) – tube fittings and adapters – Hydrasun Ltd

Parker Hannifin – European Technical Sales Ltd

Parker Hannifin – equipment/spares – Bearwood Engineering Supplies

PARKER HANNIFIN FLUID CONNECTORS – Hydraulic & Offshore Supplies Ltd

PARKER HANNIFIN INDUSTRIAL – Hydraulic & Offshore Supplies Ltd

PARKER ILUCIFER – Hydraulic & Offshore Supplies Ltd

PARKER MAXAM – Hydraulic & Offshore Supplies Ltd

Parker Maxam – pneumatic parts – A C Hydraulics Ltd

PARKER MOBILE – Hydraulic & Offshore Supplies Ltd

Parker Packaging – heavy duty cartons and packaging materials – Parker International Ltd

PARKER PNEUMATIC – Hydraulic & Offshore Supplies Ltd

PARKER PNEUMATIC CONNECTORS – Hydraulic & Offshore Supplies Ltd

PARKER PNEUMATIV FILTRATION DIVISION – Hydraulic & Offshore Supplies Ltd

PARKER PUMP & VALVE DIVISION – Hydraulic & Offshore Supplies Ltd

parker seeds – Adams & Howling Ltd

Parker Store (Redding) – hydraulic hose distributors – M F Hydraulics Ltd

PARKER UCC – Hydraulic & Offshore Supplies Ltd

PARKERTRONIC – Hydraulic & Offshore Supplies Ltd

Parkestrip – hardwood strip flooring – Atkinson & Kirby Ltd

Parkheath Estates – estate agents – Parkheath

Parkline – steel, timber and concrete prefabricated buildings – Parklines Buildings Ltd

PARKRIMP – Hydraulic & Offshore Supplies Ltd

Parkway – marine, boats & small craft – Parkway Marine

PARL – Hydraulic & Offshore Supplies Ltd

Parlok – tamper proof plastic closure – Bericap UK Ltd

Parmask – dust mask – Parmelee Ltd

Parmeko – transformers – Parmeko plc

Parmet – air heaters – William May Ltd

Parmigiani – hydraulic presses – Mackey Bowley International Ltd

Parnassus Gallery – traditional fine art greeting cards – Great British Card Company plc

Paroc Pipe Insulation – rock mineral wool insulation for pipework – Knauf Insulation Ltd

Parozone – bleach/bleach block – Jeyes

Parque – reprographics – Service Point UK Ltd

Parquet – flooring – Pilkingtons Ltd

Parquet Collection – The Amtico Co. Ltd

Parr – buffer for DNA polymerisation – Cambio Ltd

Parrot – hands free telephone kits – Fast Fit Nationwide Ltd

Parry – Ascot Wholesale Ltd

Parry – Crown Catering Equipment Ltd

Parsec – linear surface and semi recessed vandal resistant architectural lighting – Designplan Lighting Ltd

Parsell – punching products – Minni-Die Ltd

Parspout – pourer for tins and drums – Bericap UK Ltd

*Partagas (Cuba, Jamaica, Europe and Honduras) – cigars – Hunters & Frankau Ltd

Partech Electronics – water quality instrumentation – Partech Electronics Ltd

Partex – cable markers – Partex Marking Systems UK Ltd

Partial Fill Cavity Slabs – external walls – Rockwool Rockpanel B V

Partmaker – Star Micronics GB Ltd

Partner – A T Wilde & Son Ltd

Partner – Power Cutters – Robert Craig & Sons Ltd

Partner Tech – Partner Tech UK Corp Ltd

Partslift – Forklift Division – Sparex International Ltd

Party Ice – ice cube packs – Packaged Ice Co. Ltd

Party Time – Robinson Young Ltd

Partygear – party novelty itemes – Palmer Agencies Ltd

Parvalux – fractional H.P. electric motors and geared units – Parvalux Electric Motors Ltd

Parvalux – motors – Beatson Fans & Motors Ltd

Parvex – European Drives & Motor Repairs

Parvula – B P plc

Parweld – welding torch and consumable manufacturers – Parweld Ltd

PAS – UK Office Direct

*PAS (Netherlands) – filing system – Gilmex International Ltd

Pasio – horizontal balancing machine – Schenck Ltd

Pasio – Schenck Ltd

Paslode – D D Hire

Paslode – Gem Tool Hire & Sales Ltd

Paslode – I T W Constructions Productions

Pasma Training – Accesscaff International Ltd

Pasquali – Harrier Fluid Power Ltd

Pass – protection & authentication security system – Opsec Security Ltd

Passenger Lifts – lifts for mini and midi buses and ambulances – Ratcliff Palfinger

Passenger Step Lifts – passenger lifts for buses, coaches and libraries – Ratcliff Palfinger

Passion Knitwear – knitted garments – Passion Knitwear Ltd

Passivent – natural ventilatioin systems – Building Product Design

Passport – multi service WAN switch – Nortel Networks UK Ltd

Password ABCD – accountancy books – B P P Professional Education

Pasta Foods – dried pasta products – Pasta Foods Ltd

Pasta Fresca – Cibo Ristorante

Pastelle – G F Smith

Pastiche Art – Kitfix Swallow Group Ltd

Pastimes Crafts Range – Kitfix Swallow Group Ltd

Pat Says Now – Swiss novelty computer mouse company – Sleepy Weasel Ltd

PAT Testing – portable appliance testing – Essex Pat Testing

PataMates – budget soft toys – P M S International Group plc

Patay – a range of hand pumps – Pump International Ltd

PatBase – online patent database – R W S Group plc

Patch N Match – Heat seal fabric repair systems – J & A International Ltd

Patchfast – fast setting ready to use epoxy concrete repair kit – Conren Ltd

Patchmac – Aggregate Industries Ltd

Patchouli Oil Acid Washed – perfume speciality – Quest International UK Ltd

Pathfinder Ultra - the world's first data collector/ scanner / printer, Platform label design software, and the new 9800 series of tabletop bar code printers, Monarch - Marking Systems.Easy Loader - Hand held labelling systemsFreshMarx - labelling, date coding for the catering industry – Avery Dennison

Pathlite – path lights – Haldo Developments Ltd

Pathtrace (United Kingdom) – software house for engineering – Pathtrace plc

Pathway – The Woolwich

Patience (United Kingdom) – carpet tiles – Checkmate Industries Ltd

Patina / Lutron / Emergi-Lite – Energy efficient lighting / Dimming control systems / Emergency lighting – Alfred J Hurst Ltd

Patio Door Rollers – multifit or tandem – Schlegel UK

Patlite – LED signal light towers and beacons – Motion29 Ltd

Patlite (Japan) – signal towers & beacons – Lenze UK Ltd

Patons – hand knitting yarns – Coats Ltd

PATRIA – Chaintec Ltd

Patriarche (France) – Patriarche Wine Agencies

Patricia Roberts – yarns, pattern books and ready to wear sweaters (hand knitted) – Patricia Roberts Knitting Ltd

Patrick Eggle Guitars – guitars – Patrick Eggle

Patrick Stephens – aviation, motor sport, maritime and military – J Haynes Ltd

Patrizio – shoes – Patrick Shoes Ltd

Pattern 3 – fibre drum with slip on lid – Rexam Holding plc

Pattisson – Golf course accessories (01342) 301849 – Pareto Golf Ltd

Patton Electronics – line drivers – Betterbox Communications Ltd

*Paul Jaboulet Aine – Rhone wine – O W Loeb & Co. Ltd

Paul Smith – retailer, designer and wholesaler of mens, womens and childrens wear – Paul Smith Ltd

Paul Smith – Perscent

Paula Designs – ladies fashion – Paula Designs Ltd

Paula Rosa – kitchen furniture and bathroom furniture – Paula Rosa Kitchens

Paulrich – ladies clothes – Just Jamie & the Paulrich Ltd

Pauraqua – drinking fountain – Rudge & Co UK

Paus – Harrier Fluid Power Ltd

Pavigres (Portugal) – ceramic wall floor tiles – Pavigres UK Ltd

Pavilion – bed canopy systems – Pavilion Textiles Ltd

Pavilion – cards – The Medici Galleries

Pavior – recessed covers for block infill – Norinco UK Ltd

Pavisolo (Portugal) – ceramic wall floor tiles – Pavigres UK Ltd

Paxorter – automated sorting conveyor systems – Van Der Lande Industries

Paxton – medium duty circular cover and frame – Norinco UK Ltd

Pay as you go Projectors – Hot A V Ltd

Pay-Off-Pak – fibre drum for wire – Rexam Holding plc

Paycare – cash benefit health insurance schemes used throughout the United Kingdom by all industries – Paybare

Payemaster – system for payroll records – Acco UK Ltd

Paylor Controls – electronic component distribution – Paylor Controls Ltd

Paytrack – Money Controls Ltd

PBN – pyrolytic boron nitride components and crucibles – Kennametal

PBR – Harrier Fluid Power Ltd

PC 9000 – Hydrotechnik UK Ltd

PC Answers – magazine – Future Publishing Ltd

PC Dmis – measurement software – Hexagon Metrology

PC-DMIS – Status Metrology Solutions Ltd

*PC Extender Plus (U.S.A.) – keyboard video mouse multi PC-sever switches – Techland Group Ltd

PC Format – magazine – Future Publishing Ltd

PC Gamer – magazine – Future Publishing Ltd
PC Gamer Presents – magazine – Future Publishing Ltd
PC Plus – magazine – Future Publishing Ltd
PC Power Pad – Vtech Electronics UK plc
PC Software – magazine – Future Publishing Ltd
PC9000 – Hydraulic & Offshore Supplies Ltd
PCF – counterflow cooler – Andritz Seed & Bio Fuel Ltd
PCI Membranes – PCI Membranes
PCL – B L Pneumatics Ltd
PCL – Glamair Supplies Ltd
PCL – Gustair Materials Handling Equipment Ltd
PCL – Southern Valve & Fitting Co. Ltd
PCL – Hydraulic & Offshore Supplies Ltd
PCL – Trafalgar Tools
PCL AIR TECHNOLOGY – Hydraulic & Offshore Supplies Ltd
PCL Machinery – P C L Machinery
PClab – automated chemical reactor – Spectrum Computer Supplies Ltd
PCM – Hydraulic & Offshore Supplies Ltd
PCM – pipeline current mapper – Radio Detection
PCPump – Automated fluid handling system – Spectrum Computer Supplies Ltd
PDA – premadia diamond abrasives – Diamond Detectors
PDA – Range of induction loop amplifiers – C-Tec Security Ltd
PDA – on-line partial discharge test equipment for HV electrical machines – Adwel International Ltd
PDA Range – C-Tec Security Ltd
PDA102 – C-Tec Security Ltd
PDA2000 – photo metric dispersion analyser – Rank Brothers Ltd
PDA200E – C-Tec Security Ltd
PDFlex – flexible dry chrome hydraulic leather – Joseph Clayton & Sons Ltd
PDG Helicopters – Aircharter-helicopters – P D G Helicopters
PDMS – plant design management system – Aveva Solutions Ltd
PDP – Gem Tool Hire & Sales Ltd
Peabody – equipment/spares – Bearwood Engineering Supplies
Peabody Holmes – blowers/spares – Bearwood Engineering Supplies
Peacock Garden – 80% wool/20% nylon graphics – Adam Carpets Ltd
Peak – light trailer undergear equipment – Peak Trailers Ltd
Peak – Derbyshire Building Society
Peak Moor – sandstone – Realstone Ltd
Pearl – Pearl Assurance public limited company – Pearl Assurance plc
Pearl – 12V fluorescent lighting – Lab Craft Ltd
Pearl – fat concentrates containing bread improvers – C S M UK Ltd
Pearl – soap and toiletries – P Z Cussons International Ltd
Pearl Drops – tooth polish – Church & Dwight UK Ltd
Pearl Duo – 600mm double oven – Indesit Company UK Ltd
Pearlex – pearlised ironing board fabrics – Lancashire Sock Manufacturing Co.
Pearlised Liquid Hand Soap – blend of synthetic cleansers and moisturisers – Premiere Products Ltd
Pearpoint – CCTV drain inspection equipment – Robert Craig & Sons Ltd
Pearson Challenger – one row harvester – Richard Pearson Ltd
Pearson Enterprise Plus 2000 – potato, vegetable and root crop harvesters 2 row – Richard Pearson Ltd
Pearson Jumbo – bedformer – Richard Pearson Ltd
Pearson machines – Phil Geesin Machinery Ltd
Pearson Maverick – 2 row potato and vegetable harvesters – Richard Pearson Ltd
Pearson Megastar – soil separation and stone clod separators – Richard Pearson Ltd
Pearson Mini Jumbo – bedformer – Richard Pearson Ltd
Pearson Quality Master – two row harvester – Richard Pearson Ltd
Pearson Rapier – haulm topper – Richard Pearson Ltd
Pearson Rotaforma – rotary cultivation 1.8m – Richard Pearson Ltd
Pebax – polyether and polyamide block copolymers – Atosina UK Ltd
Pebax – Resinex UK Ltd
PECAS – intergrated management information systems for printers and packaging organisations – Radius Solutions Ltd
Peco – model railway specialities in all gauges – Pritchard Patent Product Co. Ltd
Peco – Harrier Fluid Power Ltd
Peco Big Bore & Sport – high performance silencer ranges stainless steel – A & I (Peco) Acoustics Ltd
Peco HDR – heavy duty rally and competion big bore manifolds and skidded exhaust systems – A & I (Peco) Acoustics Ltd
PECVD – General Vacuum Equipment Ltd
PED – Funke
Pedestal – theatre seating – Race Furniture Ltd

*Pedilan (Germany) – expanded polyurethane foam – Otto Bock Healthcare plc
*Pedilen (Germany) – liquid component to produce rigid foam – Otto Bock Healthcare plc
*Pedilin (Germany) – expanded polyethylene thermoplastic foam sheet – Otto Bock Healthcare plc
*Pedilon (Germany) – thermoplastic rigid sheet – Otto Bock Healthcare plc
PEDRAZZOLI – Band and circular sawing machines – Accurate Cutting Services Ltd
Pedrette Engineering Ltd – Target Catering Equipment
PEDRO – Hydraulic & Offshore Supplies Ltd
Pedro Gold – meat and cereal dog food – Pedro Pet Foods Ltd
Pedro Original – meat and cereal dog food – Pedro Pet Foods Ltd
*PEDROLLO – Barber Pumps Ltd
Pedrollo – Italian water pumps – Pedrollo Distribution
Pedrollo Pumps – Denton Pumps Ltd
Pedrotti (Italy) – Demountable bushes, pressfit pillars & bushes – Berger Tools Ltd
Pee-Pod – remote control camera heads – A & C Ltd
Pee Wee – European Technical Sales Ltd
Peebles – Try & Lilly Ltd
Peeco (U.S.A.) – flow switches – Alexander Cardew Ltd
Peek – high performance material – Davis Industrial Plastics Ltd
PEEK – Merseyside Metal Services
Peek (U.S.A.) – metal polish – Mitchell & Cooper Ltd
Peek Elite (United Kingdom) – LED and tungsten halogen traffic signal head – Peek Traffic Ltd
Peek Elive – Peek Traffic Ltd
Peek Elive – Peek Traffic Ltd
Peek Guardian – Peek Traffic Ltd
Peek Guardian – Peek Traffic Ltd
Peek Guardian (United Kingdom) – red light, speed and bus lane enforcement systems – Peek Traffic Ltd
Peek Traffic – Peek Traffic Ltd
Peek Traffic – Peek Traffic Ltd
Peek Traffic – Peek Traffic Ltd
Peel Jones – tuyere and copper plates for blast furnaces – Peel Jones Copper Products Ltd
Peelseal – laminate with peelable seal – Printpack Enterprises Ltd T/A Printpack
Peenflex – flexible urathene mouldings – Metal Improvement Company LLC
Peenflex – flexible urathene mouldings – Metal Improvement Co.
Peenflex – flexible urathene mouldings – Metal Improvement Co.
PEENSCAN – fluorescent tracer liquid used in peening process for coverage determination – Metal Improvement Co.
PEENSCAN – fluorescent tracer liquid used in shot peening process for coverage determination – Metal Improvement Co.
PEENSCAN – fluorescent tracer liquid used in shot peening process for coverage determination – Metal Improvement Company LLC
Peentex – textured architectural finishes – Metal Improvement Company LLC
Peentex – textured architectural finishes – Metal Improvement Co.
Peentex – textured architectural finishes – Metal Improvement Co.
Peerafilter – contrast enhancement filter – Peerless Plastics & Coatings
Peeraguard – UV abrasion resistant hard coating – Peerless Plastics & Coatings
Peeraguard Exterior – UV abrasion resistant hand coating for outdoor USG – Peerless Plastics & Coatings
Peeramist – Semi-Hard anti-mist coating – Peerless Plastics & Coatings
Peerashield – RFI shielded optical filters – Peerless Plastics & Coatings
Peerless – Harrier Fluid Power Ltd
Peerless – clean & waste water & fire protection pumps & packages – S P P Pumps
Peerless Pump – equipment/spares – Bearwood Engineering Supplies
*Peerless/Winsmith – European Drives & Motor Repairs
Peerless Winsmith – European Technical Sales Ltd
Peg – T V H UK Ltd
Peg (Italy) – Valve seat grinders – Fondera Ltd
PEG-FENWICK – Chaintec Ltd
Pegasus – tufted carpet – Brockway Carpets Ltd
Pegasus – UK Office Direct
Pegasus – mens leisure wear and swimmear – Banner Ltd
Pegasus – pump – Torres Engineering & Pumps Ltd
Pegasus – rubber belting – Chiorino UK Ltd
Pegasus – denture base and repair marterials – Schottlander Dental Equipment Supplies
Pegasus – aero engines – Rolls-Royce plc
Pegasus Partitioning – C P D Distribution

Pegg Whiteley - Macart – dyeing & finishing spares – Macart Textiles Machinery Ltd
Pegler – Mechline Developments Ltd
PEGS – project engineering system – Aveva Solutions Ltd
*PEI (France) – plastic forming presses – Pearson Panke Ltd
PEI – Merseyside Metal Services
*Peiniger (Germany) – industrial scissors – Aegis Advanced Materials Ltd
Peko – laundry equipment – G & E Automatic Equipment Ltd
Pekos (Spain) – Ball valve manufacture – Trimline Valves
Pektron – electronics – Pektron
Pelargene – perfume speciality – Quest International UK Ltd
Pelaspan – expanded polystyrene loose-fill – A Latter & Co. Ltd
Peli – C P Cases Ltd
Peli – Cases – Protechnic
Pelican – disposable medical products – Pelican Healthcare Ltd
*Pelican (U.S.A.) – rigid water tight cases & torches – Aquapac International Ltd
Pelican – automatic grease removal system – Tuke & Bell Ltd
Pelican Rouge – Autobar Group Ltd
Peljob – Harrier Fluid Power Ltd
Pellafino – polyurethane coated fabric – J B Broadley
Pellethane – Resinex UK Ltd
Pelloby – cranes and hoists – Pelloby Engineering Ltd
Pelltech – UK Office Direct
PEM – self clinching nuts, studs, standoffs, panel fasteners – Zygology Ltd
Pembroke – drinks dispenser – Bunzl Vending Services Ltd
PEMSERTER – Installation equipment for PEM fasteners – Zygology Ltd
*Pen-ray (U.S.A.) (U.S.A.) – UV sources – Ultra-Violet Products Ltd
Penang (United Kingdom) – fibre glass plant container – Christian Day Ltd
Pencon – power cord assemblies – Volex Group Ltd
Pencyl – Stainless Steel Cylinders – Air Power & Hydraulics Ltd
Pendaflex – UK Office Direct
Pendata – printout binders – London Letter File Company Ltd
Pendle Cold Store – Pendle Frozen Foods Ltd
Pendock Profiles – Fieldway Supplies Ltd
Pendragon Contracts – contract hire and vehicle leasing – Pendragon Contracts Ltd
Pendred – moisture maintenance systems – Norman Pendred & Co. Ltd
Penecert – penetrant certification testing chemical – Magnaflux
Penetration – bitumens – Tenants Bitumen
Penfold – manufacturer of gold corporate gift packs, golf clubs & golf accessories (01342) 324404 – Pareto Golf Ltd
Penguin – adult fiction and non-fiction - paperback – Penguin Books Ltd
Penguin – swimming pools – Penguin Swimming Pools Ltd
Penhard – chrome carbide deposited wear resisitant steel plates – Triten International Ltd
Penistone – carpets – Penthouse Carpets Ltd
Penlite – miniature pen sized pocket torch – Wolf Safety Lamp Company Ltd
Penloc – acrylic – Euro Bond Adhesives Ltd
Penlon – anaesthetic machines, ventilators, vaporizers and laryngoscopes, gas pipeline systems – Penlon Ltd
Penn Athletic – tennis fashion clothing for gents – FOCUS International Ltd
Pennine – spectacle frames – Pennine Optical Group Ltd
Pennine – transformers, sheet metal work and electronics, computer business systems – Pennine Radio Ltd
Pennine Castings – general castings in black heart malleable and grey iron – Pennine Castings Ltd
Pennine cubicles – Practical & Economical – Cubicle Centre
Pennine Cycles – racing cycles and frames – Pennine Cycles Whitaker & Mapplebeck Ltd
Pennine Industries Ltd – pet & garden products – Pennine Products
Pennine Slate – concrete – Sandtoft Holdings Ltd
penning – gauges – AESpump
Penning gauges – Technical Vacuum Services Ltd
Pennodorant – gas odourant – Atosina UK Ltd
Penny & Giles – Halcyon Solutions
Penny & Giles – measuring equipment – Bearwood Engineering Supplies
Penobel – P4/5 coal mining explosive – Orica UK Ltd
Penrhyn – quarries – Welsh Slates
Pensense – pens and diaries – Tallon International Ltd
Penta – Orbinox UK Ltd
Penta-Cut – Iscar Tools
Pentaclear – UPVC for the box industry – Klockner Pentaplast Ltd
Pentacompact – Grundfos Pumps Ltd
Pentacut – Camtek Ltd
Pentad Titan – hydraulic gang mower – Lloyds & Co Letchworth Ltd

Pentaflex – blendex series of explosives – E P C UK

Pentafood – UPVC and PVC.PE for the food industry – Klockner Pentaplast Ltd

Pentag – oilwell pumping units – Pentag Gears & Oil Field Equipment Ltd

Pentag – gearing – Pentag Gears & Oil Field Equipment Ltd

Pentag Gearbelt – tooth belt drive – Pentag Gears & Oil Field Equipment Ltd

Pentag Hubdriva – speed reducer – Pentag Gears & Oil Field Equipment Ltd

Pentag Milldriva – heavy duty gear couplings – Pentag Gears & Oil Field Equipment Ltd

Pentag Mitredriva – angle gear units – Pentag Gears & Oil Field Equipment Ltd

Pentag Universal – taper bushes – Pentag Gears & Oil Field Equipment Ltd

Pentagon Ltd – car dealers, parts & accessories – Reeve (Derby) Ltd

Pentagram Design Ltd – Pentagram Design

Pentalyn – resins – Hercules Holding Ii Ltd

Pentapharm – UPVC for the pharmaceutical industry – Klockner Pentaplast Ltd

Pentaprint – UPVC for the screen and litho print industry – Klockner Pentaplast Ltd

Pentaprop – polypropylene in sheet and reel form – Klockner Pentaplast Ltd

Pentax – Stemmer Imaging

Pentel – UK Office Direct

pentic – humidifications systems – Norman Pendred & Co. Ltd

Pentos – office furniture – E W Marshall Ltd

People U.K. – individual level geo-lifestyle segmentation system – C A C I

Peoples Friend – D C Thomson & Co. Ltd

Pep N Spice – dip spice blends - just add yoghurt – Fiddes Payne

Pep-Set – sand binder system for the foundry industry – Ashland Specialties UK Ltd

Pepe – jeans and fashion casualwear including shirts, pants, knitwear, jackets, T-shirts, sweatshirts, shoes and belts – Pepe Jeans London

Pepe Penalver – fabrics – Brian Yates

Pepi (U.S.A.) – thermostats – A T C Semitec Ltd

PEPLYN – all polypropylene filter cartridges – Parker Dominic Hunter Ltd

Pepper Lee (United Kingdom) – Worsted Mens Suiting Fabric – John Foster Ltd

Pepperl and Fuchs – Proplas International Ltd

Pepperl+Fuchs – E Preston Electrical Ltd

Pepperl & Fuchs – switches – Bearwood Engineering Supplies

Peps – Camtek Ltd

Pepton – peptisers for rubber and polymer applications – Thomas Swan & Co. Ltd

PER Design – PER Design is a multi-award winning product design group based in the UK and China. We provide a one – P E R Design UK Ltd

Peradon – snooker and pool cue manufacturers and accessories – E A Clare & Son Ltd

Perama – marine diesel engines – Perkins Engines Group Ltd

Perancea – custom & standard enclosures – Perancea Ltd

Perceptol – developer – Harman Technology Ltd

Percol – Aimia Foods

Percol – UK Office Direct

Percom – polyprosylone compounds – Perrite

Percy Lane – aluminium windows and doors for automotive, rail, bus, coach and prefabricated building industries; security assault doors for bus and coaches; security screens for windows and doors in vehicle and buses – Percy Lane Products Ltd

Percy Lane Products – aluminium windows and doors for automotive, rail, bus, coach and prefabricated building industries; security assault doors for bus and coaches; security screens for windows and doors in vehicles – Percy Lane Products Ltd

Peregrine – envelopes – Eagle Envelopes Ltd

Peregrine – diesel fuel heaters – Preheat Engineering Ltd

Peregrine – sump heaters for engines – Preheat Engineering Ltd

Peregrine – engine heaters – Preheat Engineering Ltd

Peregrine – coolant heaters for engines – Preheat Engineering Ltd

Peregrine – battery chargers on board – Preheat Engineering Ltd

Perennis – marketing consultants – Perennis Ltd

Perfect – leather watch straps – Perfect Leather Sales Ltd

PERFECT – surface grinding machines – R K International Machine Tools Ltd

Perfect Covering Concealer – everyday blemishes – Elizabeth Arden

Perfect Partners – fabrics, bedding and wall paper – Ena Shaw Ltd

Perfectaset – durable finish for wool textile piece goods – W T Johnson & Sons Huddersfield Ltd

Perfecting (U.S.A.) – Quick disconnect, self sealing and dry break couplings. – Dixon Group Europe Ltd

Perfection – painters cutlery, paint rollers, and paint brushes – Hamilton Acorn Ltd

Perfecto HT – heat transfer oils – Castrol UK Ltd

Perfecto T – turbine oils – Castrol UK Ltd

Perfectum – textile piece goods – Reid & Taylor Ltd

Perflex – tpr – Perrite

Perflex – shrink barrier film and bags – Bemis Swansea

Perfolatex – British Vita plc

Perforelm – perforated mica – Elmelin Ltd

Perform Europe – tour operator – Kuoni Travel Ltd

Performa – automatic washing machine – Hoover Ltd

Performa Eco – automatic washing machine – Hoover Ltd

Performance Pensions – personal pensions products – Clerical Medical Investment Group Ltd

Performance Percussion – percussion instruments – John Hornby Skewes & Co. Ltd

Performance Semi – Cyclops Electronics Ltd

Performax – Seco Tools UK Ltd

Performex – corrosion inhibitors – Ashland UK

Perfume – ladies casualwear – Remys Ltd

Perfuscan – G E Healthcare

pergo – N W Flooring

*Pergonal (Switzerland) – infertility drugs – Merck Serono Ltd

Pericom Semiconductor – Cyclops Electronics Ltd

Periflex – expandable braided sleevings – Relats UK Ltd

Periflex – flexible couplings – Stromag Ltd

Periflex (Spain) – expandable sleeving – Croylek Ltd

Period Embossed Tiles – H & E Smith

Perisil – silicone rubber coated, glass braided sleeving – Relats UK Ltd

Perkadox – organic peroxides solid – Akzo Nobel Chemicals Holdings Ltd

Perkins – Team Overseas Ltd

Perkins – engines & spares – Bearwood Engineering Supplies

Perkins – Trowell Plant Sales Ltd

Perkins – diesel engines – Perkins Engines Group Ltd

Perkins – Harrier Fluid Power Ltd

Perkut – rodenticide – Sorex Ltd

Perlac – range of abs compounds – Perrite

Perlene – polyemylene – Perrite

Perlex – polycarbonates – Perrite

Perlosol – emulsifiers and detergent for bleaching – S T R UK Ltd

Perloy – pc abs blends – Perrite

Perm-a-fix – stainless steel stick-on corner guards – Webster-Wilkinson Ltd

Perm Kare Products – Double Gee Hair Fashions Ltd

Perma – Harrison Lubrication Engineering Ltd

Perma – European Technical Sales Ltd

Perma Core – American & Efird GB Ltd

Perma-Slik – E M Coating Services

Perma Spun – spun polyester thread – American & Efird GB Ltd

Permabond – adhesives – Arrow Supply Co. Ltd

Permabond – range of adhesives – Zygology Ltd

PERMABOND ENGINEERING ADHESIVES – Hydraulic & Offshore Supplies Ltd

*Permacel (U.S.A.) – speciality self adhesive tape – Stokvis Tapes UK Ltd

Permaclips – terne coated fixing clips – British Lead

Permacor – protective coatings – Permatex Protective Coatings UK Ltd

Permacrib – B.B.A. approved timber crib walling – P H I Group Ltd

Permadeck – anti skid flooring – Permadeck Systems Ltd

Permadrip – landscape trickle irrigation – Access Irrigation Ltd

Permadryve – powder couplings – Bibby Transmissions Ltd

Permadure – water paint – Craig & Rose Ltd

Permafilter – Althon Ltd

Permafix – Wall-mounted small tools/parts storage – Adfield Harvey Ltd

Permafresh – finishing resin for cottons and viscose – Contract Chemicals Ltd

Permagard – Anti-bacteria fabric – Carrington Career & Work Wear

Permaglass – glass reinforced laminates & mouldings – Permali Gloucester Ltd

Permaglass-X – high strength glass fibre reinforced laminate – Permali Gloucester Ltd

Permagrip – anti skid flooring – Permadeck Systems Ltd

Permaguard Conductive Coatings – primary element of a cathodic protection system for combatting corrosion within reinforced concrete structures – Permarock Products Ltd

Permalux – flame retardant gloss – Craig & Rose Ltd

Permalyn – pale ester resin – Hercules Holding Ii Ltd

Permanoid – PVC electric wires, cables and insulating sleevings, armoured cables, data and instrumentation cables – Permanoid Ltd

Permapass – zinc post treatment after plating – Cookson Electronics Ltd

Permaply – technical laminates – Weidmann Whiteley Ltd

Permapol – polymer system combining advantages of urethane and polysulphide polymers for sealant applications – PPG Aerospace

Permaprint – overprint receptive nameplates for computer imprinting – Sessions Of York

Permaquip – Harsco Rail Ltd

PermaRend – render-only external rendering and maintenance system – Permarock Products Ltd

PermaRock – external wall insulation systems – Permarock Products Ltd

Permascreed – proprietary cement based screeding system – D P C Screeding Ltd

Permasep – reverse osmosis for water desalination – Du Pont UK Ltd

Permastamp – pre-inked rubber stamps – Mark C Brown Ltd

Permastic – bituminous composition – Craig & Rose Ltd

Permastore – glass coated steel tanks and silos – Permastore Ltd

Permat – honing, polishing and specialised machines – Permat Machines Ltd

*Permate (Canada) – non-bituminous vapour barrier – Alumasc Exterior Building Products

Permatex – waterproof membrane – J B Broadley

Permavel – permanent cotton softener – S T R UK Ltd

Permavoid – Althon Ltd

PERMCO – Hydraulic & Offshore Supplies Ltd

*Permenorm (Germany) – nickel iron soft magnetic alloys – Rolfe Industries

Permknap – blue flints for exposed aggregate concrete – C E D Ltd

Permost – insecticides – Hockley International Ltd

Permox – permeation analyser for film and moulded packaging materials – Systech Instruments Ltd

*Permwhite Calcined Flint (France) – white calcined flint – Brett Specialised Aggregates

*Pernifer (Germany) – non-ferrous metals – Thyssenkrupp V D M UK Ltd

Pernix – chromate processes, solder brighteners – Cookson Electronics Ltd

Perrin & Rowe – bathroom taps and showers – Avilion

Perriprene – British Vita plc

*Perrot (Germany) – sprinklers – Connectomatic

Perrot – brake components – Roadlink International Ltd

Perry – Harrier Fluid Power Ltd

Perry Lane Products – aluminium windows and doors for automotive, rail, bus, coach and prefabricated building industries; security assault doors for bus and coaches; security screens for windows and doors in vehicles and buildings – Percy Lane Products Ltd

Perryform – aluminium windows & doors for prefabricated modular buildings – Percy Lane Products Ltd

Perrys – Alfa Romeo, Fiat, Hyundai & Seat main dealer car sales, vehicle repairs, servicing body repairs and part sales – Perrys

Pers-pex – Plastic for display boards – H L N Supplies

*Persada (Indonesia) – solid timber doors – Price & Pierce Softwoods Ltd

Persil – UK Office Direct

Perske Motors – European Technical Sales Ltd

Personafile – personnel records – Anson Systems Ltd

Personal Travel Insurance – medical and personal insurance – Europ Assistance Holdings Ltd

Personnel Lifts – Accesscaff International Ltd

Personnel Relations – management training via e-Learning – The P R Organisation

Perspex – Sunlight Plastics Ltd

Perstorp Axiom – laminates and boards – Potter Cowan & Co Belfast Ltd

Pertal – acetals – Perrite

Pertemps – employment agency – Jobs@Pertemps

Pertene – perchloroethylene – Atosina UK Ltd

Pertex Windsuits – specially designed windproof garments for running, biking and hiking – Ronhill Sports

Perth – stainless steel WC – Armitage Shanks Ltd

PES – Merseyside Metal Services

Pesca – curtainsider and trailer hardware – Boyriven

Pesco – knitwear – Gloverall PLC T/A Peter Scotts

Pest Control – Contract – Pest Help Ltd

pest west fly killers – B P C Anglia Ltd

Pestcatcher – Pestcatcher

Pestroy – pet products – Bob Martin UK Ltd

Pet Mate – pet accessories – Pet Mate Ltd

Pet-Pick – Injection moulded carry handle for bottles – Index

PETA – Personal electronic torque analyser – Torque Leader

Peta Easi-Grip – self opening scissors and hand tools – Peta UK Ltd

Peta Fist-Grip – garden hand tools – Peta UK Ltd

Peta Wide-Grip – scissors – Peta UK Ltd

Petbow Cogeneration – Ener-G Combined Power

Petch Elliot – voltage transformer test sets – Airflow Measurements Ltd

Peter Craig – catalogues – Littlewoods Home Shopping Orders & Enquiries

Peter England – shirt brands – Morrison McConnell Ltd

Peter Hall – building trade – Fleetwood Trawlers Supply Company

Peter Hoar – special laminating and cutting machines for PE and other foams – Apropa Machinery Ltd

Peter Pan – Chorion plc

Peter Paul (U.S.A.) – stainless steel solenoid valves – Zoedale plc

Peter Rayner – gears – Bearwood Engineering Supplies

***Peter Reed** – Tradelinens Ltd

Peter Scott – knitwear – Gloverall PLC T/A Peter Scotts

Peter Storm – waterproof and breathable jackets – Blacks Leisure Group plc

Peter Stuyvesant – cigarettes – British American Tobacco plc

Peterkin – dolls, power force – Peterkin UK Ltd

Peters – bus and coach doors – Spraybake Ltd

Petersgate – paper – W L Coller Ltd

Peterson Spring – springs, pressworks, wire shapes, multi-slide parts and sub assemblies – Peterson Spring Europe Ltd

Petguard – The Woolwich

Petheleyne – radon/mathane barrier material – Cavity Trays Ltd

Petiole – perfume speciality – Quest International UK Ltd

***Petit-Jean SA (France)** – swarf processing equipment – Haesler Machine Tools

Petitjean Swarf Processing Plant (France) – Haesler Machine Tools

Petra (United Kingdom) – fibre glass plant container – Christian Day Ltd

Petrel – explosion protected electrical equipment – Petrel Ltd

Petrel – explosion protected electrical lighting and control gear – Petrel Ltd

Petrie & McNaught – food machinery – Petrie Technologies Ltd

Petrocel – open cell foam - anti explosion medium – Foam Engineers Ltd

Petrochem Aluzink (United Kingdom) – ribbed aluzink sheet for petrochem ical market – S S A B Swedish Steel Ltd

PETROCHEMICAL – Hydraulic & Offshore Supplies Ltd

Petrofine – computer software – K B C Process Technology Ltd

Petrolier – supported nitrile gloves – Mapa Spontex

***Petromatic (U.S.A.)** – Automatc Greease feeder – Adfield Harvey Ltd

Petroplan – Petroplan

Petroplast – industrial chemicals – Petroplastics & Chemicals Ltd

Petroseal – foam compound – Angus Fire

Petxina – architectural amenity luminare – Holophane Europe Ltd

Petzetakis – Plastic hoses – Holmes Hose Ltd

Petzl – D D Hire

Peugeot – pollensa luxury motorcaravan – Auto Sleepers Ltd

Peugeot – L M C Hadrian Ltd

Peugeot – ravenna luxury motorcaravan – Auto Sleepers Ltd

Peugeot – pescara luxury motorcaravan – Auto Sleepers Ltd

Peugeot – Ashley Competition Exhausts Ltd

***Peugeot (France)** – cycles – Pennine Cycles Whitaker & Mapplebeck Ltd

Pevac – anti-terrorist vehicle access control – Apt Controls Ltd

Pevicon – pyroelectric vidicon TV camera tube – E 2 V Technologies Ltd

Pewag – Dale Lifting and Handling Equipment Specialists

Pex – zips – Zipex UK Ltd

Pexalyn – modified hydrocarbon resins – Hercules Holding Ii Ltd

***Pexapipe (Germany)** – advanced heating and plumbing products – I P P E C Systems Ltd

***Pexatherm (Germany)** – advanced heating and plumbing products – I P P E C Systems Ltd

PF400 – power ventilator – Ebac

PFAFF – Dale Lifting and Handling Equipment Specialists

Pfaff – R F Lifting & Access Ltd

***Pfaff Silberblau (Germany)** – lifting and handling equipment and worm gear screw jacks – Pfaff-Silberblau Ltd

***Pfankuch (Germany)** – stationery wrapping machinery – Wrapid Manufacturing Ltd

Pfauter – Red House Industrial Services Ltd

Pfauter – European Technical Sales Ltd

Pfeiffer – general vacuum suppliers – AESpump

Pferd Brand – cut off and grinding discs – A T A Grinding Processes Ltd

pfpe – fluids – AESpump

PFT – C E S Hire Ltd

PFT – P F T Central

PG – Aimia Foods

PG 38 & PG 45 – patent glazing – Kawneer UK Ltd

PG Lighting – vehicle crash test lighting – Power Gems Ltd

PG Mix – Yara UK It Ltd

PG Tips – UK Office Direct

PG Tips – Alba Beverage Co. Ltd

PGS Production Services – Petrofac

PGS Production Services. – Petrofac

PGT – Programmable generic transponder – Sonardyne International Ltd

PH-CLEANTEC – universal hot cleaners for machines and parts cleaning – M. Buttkereit Ltd

***Ph Foreau (France)** – Loire wines – O W Loeb & Co. Ltd

Ph Horn Ph – Precision Tools

Phaidon – books on the arts – Phaidon Press Ltd

Phalcon – high technology racon – A B Pharos Marine Ltd

Phantom – pump – Torres Engineering & Pumps Ltd

Phantom – power assisted respirator – Scott International Ltd

Phantom – Asbestos Removal – Scott International Ltd

Phantom – top hung silent system for sliding doors – P C Henderson Ltd

Phantom Glossart & Satin – paper – Fenner Paper Co. Ltd

Phantom PVR – Brand – Bluedelta

Pharm-assist – flexible film isolator with zoned laminar flow – Envair Ltd

Pharma Filters – dust booth – Extract Technology

Pharma Matrix – pharmaceutical mixing machine – Aeromatic Fielder Ltd

Pharmaceutical Executive – magazine – Advanstar Communications

Pharmaceutical Technology Europe – magazine – Advanstar Communications

PHARMADRUM – Processing containers for a GMP environment – Drum Systems Ltd

Pharmaquipe – Contract manufacturer of nutraceutical products, vitamins and supplements. – Pharmarquip

Pharmix – pharmaceutical and cosmetic machinery – T Giusti Ltd

Pharoah – asset and facilities management system – Datapro Software Ltd

Phase 2 – G F Smith

Phasitron – power factor correction equipment – Sargrove Automation

Phelps Dodge – antennas – Pulsar Developments Ltd

Phenix – cameras – Kauser International Trading Ltd

Phenogel – veterinary tablets - phenyl butazone – J M Loveridge

Phenoxyethyl Isobutyrate Beta – perfume speciality – Quest International UK Ltd

Phenyl Ehtyl Formate – perfume speciality – Quest International UK Ltd

Phenyl Ethyl Acetate – perfume speciality – Quest International UK Ltd

Phetch – Forward Chemicals Ltd

Philadelphia – soft cheeses – Kraft Foods UK Ltd

***Philadelphia (Italy)** – polishing compound – British & Continental Traders Ltd

Philip – optical frames and sunglasses – Hilton International Eye Wear Ltd

Philip Cornes & Co Ltd – T W Metals Ltd

Philips – label – Mercury Records

Philips – Cyclops Electronics Ltd

Philips – LCD Televisions – Electrotec International Ltd

Philips – lighting controls – Camlar Ltd

Philips – Lamphouse Ltd

Phillip Dunbaven Acoustics – Accoustic Consultants – P D A Ltd

Phillips – bicycles – Raleigh UK Ltd

Phillips – UK Office Direct

Phillips Foils – hot press marking foils – Phillips Foils Ltd

Phillips International Paper Directory – United Business Media Ltd

Phlocast – rodding castables – Calderys UK Ltd

Phlogopite Mica – Minelco Ltd

Phlox – low cement castables – Calderys UK Ltd

PhoCheck – VOC detector – Ion Science Ltd

Phoenix – UK Office Direct

Phoenix – foundry coating products – James Durrans & Sons Ltd

Phoenix – safety spectacle frames – Parmelee Ltd

Phoenix – carpets – Interface Europe Ltd

PHOENIX – Phoenix Air Cargo

Phoenix – European Technical Sales Ltd

Phoenix – hinges – Cooke Brothers Ltd

Phoenix – concrete presses and take off machines – Morris Bros Ltd

Phoenix – sounders, strobes and buzzers for the security alarm industry – C Q R Ltd

Phoenix – grinding wheels – Phoenix Abrasive Wheel Co. Ltd

Phoenix contact – Cyclops Electronics Ltd

Phoenix Contact – Selectronix Ltd

PHOENIX HYDRAULIC – Hydraulic & Offshore Supplies Ltd

Phone Data – interactive voice recognition – F B H Associates Ltd

Phonemaster – small telephone answering equipment – Storacall Engineering Ltd

Phonics Handbook, The – teachers resource book for teaching reading and writing – Jolly Learning Ltd

Phoschromate – conversion coating for aluminium – P M D UK Ltd

Phosflex – phosphate based flame retardant plasticisers, triaryl, trialkyl, & trialkyl eryl phosphates – Akzo Nobel Chemicals Holdings Ltd

Phosmin – slow release phosphate fertilizers – Soil Fertility Dunns Ltd

Phosphate Range – phosphate based fertilizers – Soil Fertility Dunns Ltd

Phostex – lubricants – Chevron

Photec – used under licence from Hitachi Chemical Co. Japan – Cookson Electronics Ltd

Photec – tracer gas leak detector – Ion Science Ltd

Photina – typeface – Monotype Imaging Ltd

Photo Album Company – UK Office Direct

Photo-Me International Plc – photo-booths, childrens rides, leisure equipment, printing machines – Photo Me (International) plc

Photo Research (U.S.A.) – Glen Spectra Ltd

Photo Resists – specialist electrophoretic coatings – L V H Coatings Ltd

Photogen – nitrogen generators – Cryoservice Ltd

Photogold ecommerce solutions – web design , ecommerce solutions – Photogold Web Design

Photolabs – exhibition display & digital imaging – Warrens Display Ltd

Photon – solid state TV camera – E 2 V Technologies Ltd

Photon Beard – Projects Department Ltd

Photonfocus – Stemmer Imaging

Photonic – LED & Fibre Optic Light Sources For Microscope Illumination – G D C Microscopes

Phototone – Letraset Ltd

PHoxAir – personal phosphine monitor for fumigation – Bedfont Scientific Ltd

Phurnacite – types of fuel – C P L Distribution

Phycomp – Cyclops Electronics Ltd

Physical Properties – Bronkhorst UK Ltd

Physiopaque – G E Healthcare

Physiotherapy Packages – electro-therapy, intermittent compression and exercise equipment – Akron

Pi Tape – diameter measuring tape - high accuracy to 0.01 mm or 0.001" resolution – P I Tape Ltd

Piab – Southern Valve & Fitting Co. Ltd

Piab – European Technical Sales Ltd

PIAB – Hydraulic & Offshore Supplies Ltd

***Piazo Technology Ink** – Wavelength Electronics Ltd

***Piazza D'Oro** – Douwe Egberts UK

Pic Arc Welders – welding plant and electric arc – Pickhill Engineers Ltd

PICADOR PULLEYS – A ,Z, B SECTION PRESSURE AND DIE CAST PULLEYS – A B C Polishing & Engineering Supplies

Picard – tweezers, membrane boxes, optical aids – Henri Picard & Frere

Picardy – hand tools, builders and household ironmongery – D F Wishart Holdings Ltd

Picast – process for manufacture of investment castings – P I Castings Ltd

Picastings – precision investment castings – P I Castings Ltd

Picbloc – videowall products – Electrosonic Ltd

Piccadilly – shaving brushes – Progress Shaving Brush Vulfix Ltd

Picco – Iscar Tools

Picco – hydrocarbon resins – Hercules Holding Ii Ltd

Piccolastic – styrene resin elastomers – Hercules Holding Ii Ltd

Piccolo – taps – Armitage Shanks Ltd

Piccolyte – terpene resins – Hercules Holding Ii Ltd

Piccopale – hydrocarbon resins – Hercules Holding Ii Ltd

Piccotac – hydrocarbon resins – Hercules Holding Ii Ltd

Piccotex – vinyltoluene copolymer resins – Hercules Holding Ii Ltd

Piccovar – alkyl-aromatic resins – Hercules Holding Ii Ltd

Pick Me Up – I P C Media Ltd

Pickfords – Pickfords Ltd

Pickfords Records Management – Pickfords Ltd

Pickfords Vanguard – Pickfords Ltd

Pickwick – Uncoated Paper – Mcnaughton James Paper Group Ltd

***Pickwick** – Douwe Egberts UK

Pickxi – pick counter – James H Heal & Co. Ltd

Pico Technology – Pico Technology Ltd

PicoAce – grinding machine – Loadpoint Ltd

Picorex PXC – profile cutting machine – Easab Cutting Systems

Picosil – single in-line reed relays – Pickering Electronics Ltd

Picturebox – still store system – Quantel Ltd

Picturecolour – line or process printed self adhesive labels in up to eight colours – Sessions Of York

Pictureframe – modular graphics system – Quantel Ltd

Piedro – semi-orthopaedic footwear – Gilbert & Mellish Ltd

***Pieper (Germany)** – cutting dies – Engelmann & Buckham Ltd

Pierre Cardin – neck ties – Woodstock Neckwear Ltd

Pierre Cardin – uk licensee for leather goods & luggage – Modrec International Holdings Ltd

Piezometers – geotechnical instruments – Itm Soil Ltd

Piezomotor (Sweden) – Piezo electric motor (linear & rotary) – Electro Mechanical Systems (EMS) Ltd

Piezotronic – B L Pneumatics Ltd

Pifco – battery powered electrical equipment, torches, lighting, car accessories, fans, air treatment and travel products – Russell Hobbs Ltd

Pigeon Brand – wood boring tools – J E Morrison & Sons Ltd

Piggyback – forklift trucks – Joloda Hydraroll Ltd

Piglet Primer – peat piglet food – A One Feed Supplements Ltd

Piher – Cyclops Electronics Ltd

Piher – variable resistors – Anglia

Pikes – portable traffic signals – Pike Signals Ltd

Pilgrim – port – George Bateman & Son Ltd

Piling – Equipment – Piling Equipment Ltd

Piling hammers – air and hydraulic – B S P International Foundations Ltd

Pilkington – edge tech – Holdens Supaseal Ltd

Pilkington – safety glass – Pilkington Group Ltd

Pilkington Automotive – automotive safety glass – Pilkington Automotives

Pillar Mate – Frame for building brick pillars – Allum Fabrications

Piller – UPS Systems – Piller UK Ltd

Pillo-Sol – greenhouse insulation – A Latter & Co. Ltd

Pillomat (United Kingdom) – component protection matting – Plastic Extruders Ltd

Pillow Perfect – pillow raiser – R B F Healthcare

Pilot – T E K Seating Ltd

Pilot+ – wheelchair controller – P G Drive Technology

Pilot – Quarter turn fasteners – Zygology Ltd

Pilot – Hydraulic Press – ECO Hydraulic Presses Ltd

Pilot – push to lock fastener – Southco Manufacturing Ltd

Pilot – UK Office Direct

Pilot Coating Machine – R K Printcoat

*Pilot Cutter 30 (United Kingdom) – cruisers – Cornish Crabbers LLP

Pilz – Proplas International Ltd

Pilz – European Technical Sales Ltd

Pilz Control Relays – European Technical Sales Ltd

Pilz Monitoring Relays – European Technical Sales Ltd

Pilz Operator Display – European Technical Sales Ltd

Pilz Safety Relays – European Technical Sales Ltd

Pilz Sensors – European Technical Sales Ltd

Pilz Switches – European Technical Sales Ltd

PIMESPO – Chaintec Ltd

Pimespo – T V H UK Ltd

*Pin (USA and Scandinavia) – anti corrosion products – B A C Corrosion Control Ltd

Pin-Hi – soft drink range – Nichols plc

Pin-Up – home perms – Vivalis Ltd

Pin Yarn – Kitfix Swallow Group Ltd

Pinball Wizard – universal coupling – Dixon Bate Ltd

Pinboard (Portugal) – 1/4" thick light and dark cork wall tiles – Siesta Cork Tile Co.

Pinbrazing – B A C Corrosion Control Ltd

Pindar P.L.C. – print and electronic media specialists – Pindar plc

Pindar-Routel Ltd – print and electronic media specialists – Pindar plc

Pindar Systems Inc – print and electronic media specialists – Pindar plc

Pinder Set – print and electronic media specialists – Pindar plc

Pinders – business appraisors providing detailed repairs and valuations on all types of leisure, healthcare and retail businesses – Christie & Co. Ltd

Pine Disinfectant – chlorinated phenol disinfectant – Premiere Products Ltd

Pine Doors – Plaut International

Pine Gel – pine floor and wall gel – Evans Vanodine International plc

Pinefresh – Forward Chemicals Ltd

Pinelodge – pre-fabricated pine accommodation lodges – Pinelog Ltd

Pinelog – leisure buildings – Pinelog Ltd

Pinewood – flame retardant furnishing fabrics – Pinewood Drapilux UK Ltd

Pinewood – Philip Cowan Interiors

Pinflex – Renold Clutches & Couplings Ltd

Pinflex Coupling – Renold Clutches & Couplings Ltd

Pingon – Harrier Fluid Power Ltd

Pink – B P plc

Pink Pearl – pink perfumed liquid hand and body soap – Evans Vanodine International plc

Pinks Syrups – Pure and natural fruit syrups – Pinks Syrups

*Pinkus Muller Organic German Beers – Vinceremos Wines & Spirits Ltd

PINNACLE – Machine Tools – Excel Machine Tools Ltd

Pinnacle – bench trunking – M K Electric Ltd

Pinpanel (Portugal) – 1/4" thick, self-adhesive cork wall tiles – Siesta Cork Tile Co.

Pinpoint – distress handflare – Pains Wessex Ltd

PinPoint – Snopake Ltd

Pinpoint – medical record tracking software – Civica UK Ltd

Pinson – Padlocks (Specialised) – Securefast PLC

Pioneer – Lamphouse Ltd

Pioneer – dental lathe and general brushes – E. Berry & Sons

PIONEER – Hydraulic & Offshore Supplies Ltd

PIONEER – direct connection columns for LC/MS – Thermo Fisher Scientific

Pioneer – Harrier Fluid Power Ltd

Pioneer – insoles – A Algeo Ltd

Pioneer Marquees – Marquee hiring – Pioneer Marquees

Pioneer Oil Seals – rotary shaft seals in various rubber compounds – Pioneer Weston

Pioneer Pump – self priming pumps – P & M Pumps

PIONEER WESTON – Hydraulic & Offshore Supplies Ltd

Pioneer Weston Oil Seals – rotary shaft seals in various rubber compounds and leather – Pioneer Weston

Pionér – protective clothing – Pioner Fristads

Pioner Salt – Broste Ltd

Piovan Star – Injection Moulding machine robots – Star Automation Uk Ltd

Pip – swimwear – Pipminster Ltd

Pip Pin – quick release fastener – Avdel UK Ltd

Pipac – computer program for simulating pulsations inside pipe networks – Spectrum Acoustic Consultants Ltd

Pipe and Tube Group – pipe and tubing – Benteler Distribution Ltd

Pipe Section Mat – pipes, ducts, industrial noise control and industrial plant – Rockwool Rockpanel B V

Pipe Sections – pipe insulation – Rockwool Rockpanel B V

Pipe Testing Equipment - Sarco Inspectra – pipe lear testing – Sarco Stopper Ltd

Pipe Wizards – Prestige Industrial Pipework Equipment

Pipecheck – pipe contents discriminator (between water and gas) – Baugh & Weedon Ltd

PIPEGUARD – Membrane design slim, cost effective, accumulator for use in marine saline and other corrosive application – Pulsation Dampers At Pulseguard Ltd

PIPEHUGGER – Pulsation damper with large range of chemical compatibilities yet only using a low cost carbon steel vessel – Pulsation Dampers At Pulseguard Ltd

Pipeline Center – Wolseley UK

Pipemaster – plumbing tool – Antex Electronics Ltd

*Pipeprop (Canada) – pipe supports – Alumasc Exterior Building Products

*Piper (United Kingdom) – day races – Cornish Crabbers LLP

Pipescan – magnetic flux leakage adjustable scanner for detection of random I.D. corrosion pits in carbon steel piping. – Silverwing UK Ltd

*Pipeseal (U.S.A.) – pipe flashings – Alumasc Exterior Building Products

Pipestoppers – Pipestoppers

Pipework Kits – Purewell & Wessex 100m series – Hamworthy Heating Ltd

Pippin Products – fun learning kits basic literacy & numeracy for all ages – Pippin Products

*Piquant – Piquant Ltd

Pique (United Kingdom) – polyester cotton image wear fabric – Carrington Career & Work Wear

Piramid Valley Computers – installation of computers – Pyramid Valley Computers

*Piranha (U.S.A.) – hydraulic universal steelworker – Prosaw Ltd

Piranha (United Kingdom) – UV lamp – Primalec

Pirani – gauges – AESpump

Pirani gauges – Technical Vacuum Services Ltd

Pirelli – Wealden Tyres Ltd

Pirelli – tyres – National Tyre Service Ltd

Pirobloc – thermal oil heaters – Twin Industries International Ltd

Piroto – labels or tags on rolls, sheets and fan folds – Piroto Labelling Ltd

Pirouette – rotary storage and filing system – Rackline Ltd

Pisani – tools, machinery and accessories for stone processing; wholesalers of marble, granite and stone architectural hard landscaping products – Pisani plc

PISCO – Hydraulic & Offshore Supplies Ltd

Pista – sewage and industrial effluent grease separator – Higgins & Hewins Ltd

PISTER KUGLEHAEHNE – Hydraulic & Offshore Supplies Ltd

PISTOFLEX – Piston accumulator with ultra responsive frequency capability – Pulsation Dampers At Pulseguard Ltd

PISTOFRAM – Combination diafram and piston with no detectable break out stiction – Pulsation Dampers At Pulseguard Ltd

PISTOLITE – Hydraulic volume storage with long LD ratio and a wobble free, guided, piston – Pulsation Dampers At Pulseguard Ltd

*Pitco Frialator – Fryers – Middleby UK Ltd

Pitkin Unichrome Ltd – guide book publishers – Pitkin

Pitsham – hand made bricks, pavors and fireplaces – W T Lamb Holdings Property Services

Pittler – Red House Industrial Services Ltd

Pittler – European Technical Sales Ltd

Piusi – fluid handling equipment – Centre Tank Services

Piusi – Obart Pumps Ltd

PIV Drives – Brevini Power Transmissions

Pivacyclene – perfume speciality – Quest International UK Ltd

Pivarose – perfume speciality – Quest International UK Ltd

Pivatic – punching, folding & shearing machines from coil – Press & Shear Machinery Ltd

Pivi – spring steel fasteners – Springfast Ltd

*Pivot Master (U.S.A.) – roof drain systems – H M T Rubbaglas Ltd

Pixel Power – equipment for broadcast television – Pixel Power Ltd

'PK' OFFSET – CV Large Variable Offset Flexible Shaft Couplings – Francis and Francis Ltd

Pkus – Lamphouse Ltd

PL1/K1 – C-Tec Security Ltd

Plaaya – promotional clothing, printers and embroiderers – Lea Ray Retail Ltd

Placam – metal backed magnetic rubber – Magnet Applications Ltd

Place UK – soft fruit growers, processors, bean sprout growers & processors, contract freezers, importers & exporters of frozen fruit – Place UK Ltd

Placesetter – range of foam display packs and lids – Pregis Rigid Packaging Ltd

*Placid Industries – brakes – Huco Dynatork

Placor – metal backed magnetic rubber – Magnet Applications Ltd

Plaidcrete – cement colourings – Rowebb Ltd

Plain Tile – concrete – Sandtoft Holdings Ltd

Plains Collection – woven fabrics – Zoffany

Plalite – fire fighting equipment and precision engineers – Plalite Ltd

Plamar – HS and NS spirally-wound electrical insulation tubes manufactured from polyester film – Lamina Dielectrics Ltd

Plamar - Plamaron - Plamec - Plamide - Plamon - InsulOtube. – Lamina Dielectrics Ltd

Plamaron – HS and NS electrical insulation tubes manufactured from a combination of polyester film and Du Pont Nomex aramid paper – Lamina Dielectrics Ltd

Plamec – HS electrical insulation tubes manufactured from polyester film – Lamina Dielectrics Ltd

Plamide – Spirally wound electrical insulation tubes manufactured from Du Pont Kapton polyimide film – Lamina Dielectrics Ltd

Plamon – electrical insulation tubes manufactured from Du Pont Nomex – Lamina Dielectrics Ltd

"Plan D" – sinks – Potter Cowan & Co Belfast Ltd

Planar – Review Display Systems Ltd

Planar – Lamphouse Ltd

Planar fxP and 300 (United Kingdom) – dielectric CVD cluster tools up to 300mm – Aviza Technology UK Ltd

*Planatol (Germany) – adhesives bookbinding – Gilmex International Ltd

Pland – Domestic kitchen sink workcentres for the contract market. – Astracast P.L.C.

Plane Handling – air freight forwarders – Dnata

Planet – Lusso Interiors

Planet – locomotive spares – Alan Keef Ltd

Planet – vanity basin – Armitage Shanks Ltd

Planet – planetary concrete pan mixers – The Howard Group

Planet – aluminium windows & doors for prefabricated modular buildings – Percy Lane Products Ltd

Planet – recycled scissors and knives – Acme United Europe

Planet Nod – Duvets/Pillows – Iggesund Paperboard Ltd

Planet Plus – Woodturning accessories – The Toolpost

Planhorse – New Zealand Plan storage systems – Orchard Drawing Boards

*Planmeca (Finland) – dental equipment – Plandent

Plannette – fans for electronic cooling – AMETEK Airscrew Limited

Plannja – steel building sheet – Plannja Ltd

Plano – Gem Tool Hire & Sales Ltd

Plant & Build – Accesscaff International Ltd

Plant components – G R P weirs launders & scum barriers – Armfibre Ltd

Plant Lifedge – knives – Acme United Europe

Plant & Process Safety – Newson Gale Ltd

Plantation – sheen finish tubs, troughs, planters, saucers and windowsill and drip trays – Richard Sankey & Son Ltd

Plantation Direct – Coffee – Plantation Coffee Ltd

Plantfinder Platforms – Accesscaff International Ltd

Plantin – typeface – Monotype Imaging Ltd

PlantMaster 90 – electrically heated 50 watt propagator with variable thermostaticcontrol – Richard Sankey & Son Ltd

Planto – environmentally friendly fluids – Fuchs Lubricants UK plc

Plantpak – horticultural plastic growing units – Desch Plantpak Ltd

Plantronics – UK Office Direct

Plantronics – Duplex Corporate Communications
Plants of Distinction – seedsmen horticultural – Plants Of Distinction
Plasblak – carbon black thermoplastic masterbatches – Cabot Plastics Ltd
Plascoat – Thermoplastic coating powders – Plascoat
Plascon – building blocks – Plasmor Ltd
PLASFIT – Hydraulic & Offshore Supplies Ltd
Plasfit – pipe fittings – Norgren Ltd
Plasgard – liquid applied coatings – Chase Protective Coatings Ltd
Plaslite – lightweight building blocks – Plasmor Ltd
Plaslube – Resinex UK Ltd
Plasma 54 – Thermo Electrical
Plasma Technology – process equipment for semiconductor industry – Oxford Instruments
Plasmalab – flexible, compact and modular plasma processing equipment – Oxford Instruments
Plasmanite – decorative laminate and bonded wall boards – Plasman Laminate Products Ltd
PlasmaQuad 1 (PQ1) – Thermo Electrical
PlasmaQuad 2 (PQ2) – Thermo Electrical
PlasmaQuad 3 (PQ3) – Thermo Electrical
Plasmatrace 1 – Thermo Electrical
Plasmatrace 2 – Thermo Electrical
Plasmor Architectural Masonry – coloured fair faced units – Plasmor Ltd
Plaspal – plastic pallets – Rea Plasrack Ltd
Plaspave – concrete block pavers – Plasmor Ltd
Plasplugs – DIY tools and fixings – Plasplugs
Plasser – Harrier Fluid Power Ltd
Plastaline – extruded non refelctive thermoplastic road marking material – R S Clare & Co. Ltd
Plastalux Reflective – extruded reflective thermoplastic road marking material – R S Clare & Co. Ltd
Plastapan (United Kingdom) – access doors with plasterboard finish – Panelcraft Access Panels
Plastarib – raised rib thermoplastic road marking material – R S Clare & Co. Ltd
Plastaspray – spray reflective and nin reflective thermoplastic road marking material – R S Clare & Co. Ltd
Plastathix – extruded thermoplastic marking material – R S Clare & Co. Ltd
Plastazote – crosslinked polyethylene foam in LOPE/HOPE – Zotefoams plc
Plastazote – W Mannering London Ltd
Plastazote « - Evazote « - Supazote « - Propozote«. – Zotefoams plc
Plastestik – adhesive – Plastestrip Profiles Ltd
Plastestrip (Profiles) – PVC extrusions – Plastestrip Profiles Ltd
Plastex (United Kingdom) – Safety Matting – Plastic Extruders Ltd
Plastex – kayaks – Kirton Kayaks Ltd
Plastex Grid – Open grid and closed surface heavy duty tiles – Plastic Extruders Ltd
Plastexa – plastic-coated jointless bias binding – J B Broadley
Plasthall – polymeric plasticiser – Omya UK Ltd
Plasti-Cals (United Kingdom) – self-adhesive plastic labels – London Name Plate Manufacturing Co. Ltd
Plastibrade – flexible liquid satin finishing compound – Lea Manufacturing Co.
Plastic Cleaner – cleaning powder, stain remover and brightener – Premiere Products Ltd
Plastic moulding manufrs – Dubois Ltd
Plastic Steel – metal filled repair epoxy – I T W Devcon
Plasticell – unicellular pvc foam – Permali Gloucester Ltd
***Plastichain (France)** – cable carriers (drag chain) systems used to protect powerlines in motion – Beakbane Ltd
Plasticlad – cladding accessories – Plastestrip Profiles Ltd
Plastico – Ascot Wholesale Ltd
Plasticote – paramelt
Plasticpan (United Kingdom) – pop out plumbing access cover – Panelcraft Access Panels
Plasticsticks – cotton buds pharmaceutical and confectionery sticks – Papersticks Ltd
Plasticuet – moulders & extruders of plastics – Warden Plastics Luton Ltd
Plastiflor – round stud or leathergrain vinyl tiles – Jaymart Roberts & Plastics Ltd
Plastigauge (United Kingdom) – plastic precision clearance gauges for measurement of clearance in plain bearings, mould tools, shaft end floats, turbine tips and gland clearance – Plastigauge
Plastiglue – flexible liquid satin finishing compound – Lea Manufacturing Co.
Plastijet XG – gloss solvent ink for plastics – Fujifilm Sericol Ltd
***Plastimec (Italy)** – plastic yarn carriers, cones and tubes – Robert S Maynard Ltd
Plastipure Fluorescent FP – solvent fluorescent ink for plastics – Fujifilm Sericol Ltd
Plastisol – Chorus Panel & Profiles
Plastix – crayon – Creative Art Products Ltd
Plasto – embossing dies – Plastotype
Plastoflex – paramelt
Plastomelt – paramelt
Plastoshim – curved brass sleeves with tension bands – Plastotype
Plaswite – titanium dioxide thermoplastic masterbatches – Cabot Plastics Ltd
Platanex – platinum plating process – Cookson Electronics Ltd
Plate Heat Exchanger – H R S Heat Exchanges Ltd
***Plate-Mate** – Shelfspan Shelving Systems
Platemaster – axial fan – Nuaire Ltd
Platestreet – automatic plate production system – Kodak Morley
Platilon – hot melt adhesives – Atosina UK Ltd
Platinic – stainless steel finish – Allgood
Platinite – platinised titanium anodes – Cumberland Cathodic Protection
Platinum – fat concentrates containing bread improvers – C S M UK Ltd
Platinum 18 – emulsion floor polish – Premiere Products Ltd
Platinum 25 – emulsion floor polish – Premiere Products Ltd
Platipus – earth anchoring systems & solutions for civil engineering (tunnel linings, sheet pile retention, pipeline buoyancy, slope stabilisation, retaining walls, erosion control, scaffolding, temporary buildings, guyed structures) the landscaping industry – Platipus Anchors Ltd
Platon – hot melt adhesive – Atosina UK Ltd
Platon – Roxspur Measurement & Control Ltd
Platon Air Gap Technology – damp proofing membrane – Triton Chemical Manufacturing Co. Ltd
Platt UK Ltd - Macart – full range of platt spares – Macart Textiles Machinery Ltd
Plaut International – international agents for timber & other wood based industries – Plaut International
Play Chips – playground surface – Melcourt Industries
Play School – toys – Hasbro UK Ltd
Playa – corner bath – Ideal Standard Ltd
Playbark – lias playground surface – Melcourt Industries
Playchip – lias playground surface – Melcourt Industries
Playdale – playground equipment – Playdale Playgrounds Ltd
Players Navy Cut – plain cigarettes – Imperial Tobacco Group PLC
Players Navy Cut Flake – pipe tobacco – Imperial Tobacco Group PLC
Playgrounds – playground equipment – Playdale Playgrounds Ltd
Playing Mantis – licenced modelkits and die cast – Amerang Group Ltd
Playnes – tennis ball melton – Milliken Woollen Speciality Products
Playon – impact absorbing rubber wet pour play surfacing – Conren Ltd
Playsafe – thermometers for babycare – B & H Colour Change Ltd
Playtex – ladies underwear – Playtex Ltd
Plaza – rubber flooring – Gerflor Ltd
Plaza – washbasin, closet, bidet, bath, taps and mixers – Ideal Standard Ltd
PLC's – CBM Logix
Pledge – UK Office Direct
Pledge – Office Seating – Bucon Ltd
Pledge – chairs – Service Partitions Ltd
Pledge Seating – Capex Office Interiors
Pleiger – European Technical Sales Ltd
Plenty – Plenty Mirrlees Pumps
Plenty – mixers/spares – Bearwood Engineering Supplies
Plessey – Cyclops Electronics Ltd
Plex – portable display systems – P E P Ltd
Plex Display – Display Wizard Ltd
Plex Displays – Imex Print Services Ltd
Plex, portable display systems - Ultima, portable display systems – P E P Ltd
Plexiglam – Sunlight Plastics Ltd
Plexus – I T W Plexus
Pliaxseal Valves (U.S.A.) – butterfly valves – Induchem
Plinths & Couches – variable height models with a variety of accessories – Akron
Pliobord – grommet strip – Ses Sterling Ltd
Pliosil – expanded braiding – Ses Sterling Ltd
Pliospire – cable binding – Ses Sterling Ltd
Plipad – graduated demembraned polyurethane foam washable filter mats – Emcel Filters Ltd
PLM – Harrier Fluid Power Ltd
***Plover** – Scott & Newman Ltd
plug and grow – grow light – Online Electrical Wholesalers
Plugloc – Pigging safety system for compliance with ippc & pressure equipment directive – Martec Of Whitwell Ltd
Plugstat – electrical apparatus and instruments, switches and circuit breakers – Otter Controls Ltd
Plugway – plug-in power distribution bus-bar system – Astra Engineering Products Ltd
Plugway Minor – single phase plug in power supply system – Astra Engineering Products Ltd
Plumb – hammers – Apex Tools
Plumb Center – Wolseley UK
Plumb Centres – Plumbing and Heating – Builder Center Ltd
Plumbers Bits – traps & wc connectors & accessories (soil & waste systems) – Hunter Plastics
Plumbs – fitted covers and curtains – Plumbs
Plumbs Mail Order – stretch covers and curtains – Plumbs
***Plumtree Farm Foods** – Tranfield Of Cumbria Ltd Vion Foods
Plus – Lamphouse Ltd
Plus 4 – motor car – Morgan Motor Co. Ltd
Plus 8 – motor car – Morgan Motor Co. Ltd
Plus Direct Emulsions – Screen printing emulsions. – Macdermid Autotype Ltd
Plus Fabric – UK Office Direct
Plusaqua – water thinnable resins for electro deposition – Omya UK Ltd
Plustron – Lighting & calculators – K B Import & Export Ltd
Plustronic – servo electric gripping systems – Schunk Intec Ltd
Pluto – electronic controls for amusement and gaming machines – Heber Ltd
Plymouth Extra – newspaper – Western Morning News Co. Ltd
Plynyl Flooring – The Winnen Furnishing Company
PMI – Harrier Fluid Power Ltd
PMI – European Drives & Motor Repairs
PMR – Vidlink International Ltd
PNEUDRI – adsorption principle compressed air dryer – Parker Dominic Hunter Ltd
Pneufit – B L Pneumatics Ltd
PNEUFIT – Hydraulic & Offshore Supplies Ltd
Pneufit C – pipe fittings – Norgren Ltd
Pneuko – pneumatic seal – Freudenberg Simrit LP
Pneumablo – air conditioning equipment – Luwa UK Ltd
PNEUMADYNE – Hydraulic & Offshore Supplies Ltd
***Pneumadyne (U.S.A.)** – miniature pneumatic valves & fittings – The West Group Ltd
Pneumaid – high pressure logic elements – Parker Hannifin Ltd
Pneumasort – A C Automation
Pneumaster – air operated drum pump – Filtermist International Ltd
Pneumatech – Harrier Fluid Power Ltd
Pneumatic – hand tools – Elite Engineering Ltd
Pneumatic Control Equipment – associated panels – Asco Numatics
Pneumax – Gustair Materials Handling Equipment Ltd
Pneumax – Southern Valve & Fitting Co. Ltd
Pneumax – equipment & spares – Bearwood Engineering Supplies
PNEUMAX – Hydraulic & Offshore Supplies Ltd
Pneumax – J V Hydraulics Ltd
Pneumax Valves – Trafalgar Tools
Pneumo – Cogne UK Ltd
PNEUMOTUBE – Hydraulic & Offshore Supplies Ltd
Pneupac – ventilators – Smiths Medical International Ltd
Pneuride Airspring Bellows – Interflex Hose & Bellows Ltd
Pneutorque – Norbar Torque Tools Ltd
PNMsoft – Business Process Management – PNMsoft
PNUE-LOK – Hydraulic & Offshore Supplies Ltd
Pobjoy Crownfolio – Pobjoy Mint Ltd
Pobjoy mint – Pobjoy Mint Ltd
Pobjoy Mint Crownmedal – Pobjoy Mint Ltd
Pobjoy Mint Jewellery – Pobjoy Mint Ltd
Pobjoy silverclad – Pobjoy Mint Ltd
***Pocket Songs (U.S.A.)** – sing along tapes – Forsyth Bros Ltd
Pocketpeak – peak flow meters – Enspire Health
Pocklington Post – newspaper – Yorkshire Regional Newspapers Ltd
Poclain – Team Overseas Ltd
Poclain – Harrier Fluid Power Ltd
POCLAIN – Hydraulic & Offshore Supplies Ltd
***Poclain** – Kenneth Robson Equipment Ltd
Poclain Case – construction equipment, case poclain – Service Engines Newcastle Ltd
Pod Space Limited – Manufacturer of Eco Friendly, contemporary prefabricated buildings. – Pod Space Ltd.
Podium Deck – Althon Ltd
Podium Platforms – Accesscaff International Ltd
Podmores Engineers – bowl feeders, linear feeders, elevators, conveyors, robot feeding, and factory automation systems – Podmores Engineers Ltd
Podotech – shoe insole – A Algeo Ltd
Podotech – insole system for chyrodyes – A Algeo Ltd
Podowegde – insoles and orthopaedic devices – A Algeo Ltd
Poeppelmann – European Technical Sales Ltd
POGGI – 'Gleason' Spiral Bevel Gearboxes, Gear Couplings, 'System-P' Pulleys & Bushes & Other PT products – Francis and Francis Ltd
POGGI A2000 – Spiral Bevel Gearboxes – Francis and Francis Ltd

POGGI GDR/GDA – Nylon & Steel Sleeve Gear Couplings – Francis and Francis Ltd

POGGI LOK-FIT – Keyless Pulley Mounting Conical Rings – Francis and Francis Ltd

POGGI 'System-P' – Taper-locking Pulley Bushes – Francis and Francis Ltd

POGGI 'System-P' – Taper-locking Bush Pulleys – Francis and Francis Ltd

Point – paperback book publishing imprint – Scholastic School Book Fairs

Point Master – A P T

Pointmaster – Mortar Finishing Tool – PWM Distribution

Pokolm – die milling systems – Ceratizit UK Ltd

Polamco – Dax International Ltd

*Polar (Germany) – guillotines – Heidelberg Graphic Equipment Ltd

Polar – Lusso Interiors

Polar – glazed system with minimal frame work – Komfort Workspace plc

Polar – paper – Paperun Group Of Companies

Polar – new and used cars – Polar Ford York

Polar Bear – frozen seafoods – Dales Of Liverpool Ltd

Polar Bear – marine diesel engines and spares – Kelvin Diesels British Polar Engines Ltd

Polar Process – Pump feeder, ultrasonic cutters and extruders – Bestpump

POLAR SEALS – Hydraulic & Offshore Supplies Ltd

Polar System – pipe freezing equipment – Arctic Products Ltd

PolarBar – Assa Abloy Hospitality Ltd

Polarflow – I M I Cornelius UK Ltd

Polaris – fire safes – Warwick Fraser & Co. Ltd

*Polaris (U.S.A.) – petrol & diesel all terrain vehicles & water craft – E P Barrus

Polaris – tyre changer for cars & commercials – Tecalemit Garage Equipment Co. Ltd

Polaris Popular – Immersion heater for corrosive solutions – E Braude London Ltd

*Polaroid (U.S.A.) – polarising filters – Instrument Plastics Ltd

Polaroid – Lamphouse Ltd

Polaroid – UK Office Direct

Polaron – lighting controls – Camlar Ltd

Polaron – uhv supplies – AESpump

Polatrak (U.S.A.) – cathodic protection monitoring solutions for all applications – Hockway

Polatrak - Retropod - Cpmat - Irod. – Hockway

*Poldi (Czech Republic) – twist drills and tool sets – Castle Brook Tools Ltd

Polemaster – fishing tackle – Drennan International Ltd

Poli Film Adhesive Products – self-adhesive protective film – Poli Film UK Ltd

Police, Fire and Ambulance – gloves – Michael Lupton Associates Ltd

Policeman – quality control device for induction heat sealing – Bericap UK Ltd

Polidene – vinylidene chloride copolymer emulsions – Scott Bader Co. Ltd

Polido – compressed air – Merlett Plastics UK Ltd

Poliflex – polishing points – A T A Grinding Processes Ltd

Polisoft – Wiper Supply Services Ltd

Pollard – Red House Industrial Services Ltd

Pollux – Cloakroom Solutions Ltd

Polly Pig – foam pipeline pigs – Alexander Cardew Ltd

Polmark – information service/database system – Ecorys UK

Polo Diesel – diesel fuel injection pump parts – Dieselprods Ltd

Poltpro – Harrier Fluid Power Ltd

Polutef-PTFE – ptfe coated glass fabrics/sewing threads – Polux Ltd

"Polux" – dyed glass yarns – Polux Ltd

"Polux" – thermocouple cables/high temp cables – Polux Ltd

Poly BD – hydroxyl terminated polybutadiene – Atosina UK Ltd

Poly-Disc – Couplings – Baldor UK

Poly-Fine XLD – Pall Europe Corporate Services

Poly-pale – polymerised rosin acid – Hercules Holding Ii Ltd

Poly-Select Logo – British Vita plc

Poly-Tip – machine tool wheel dressing accessory – P G T Ceewrite Ltd

Poly-Toggle – hollow wall fixing – Rawlplug Ltd

Poly-Vu – safety security mirrors – Mirror Technology Ltd

Polyart – synthetic paper – B P plc

Polybags – polythene bags – Polybags Ltd

Polybox – Bespoke hand made polypropylene boxes – Hofbauer (UK) Ltd

Polycase – Snopake Ltd

Polycat – catalysts – I M C D UK Ltd

Polycell – pre-decorative products – Akzonobel

Polycham – synthetic chamois leathers – Lancashire Sock Manufacturing Co.

Polychannel – surface water drainage – Ashworth

*Polycling (U.S.A.) – PE clingfilm – Terinex Ltd

Polycold – AESpump

Polycolour Plastics – dispersed colour and additive master batches and compounds – Ampacet UK

Polycom – Videonations Ltd

Polycom – Ferguson Polycom Ltd

Polycom – Video conferencing equipment – Medbrook Services Ltd

Polycom – Polycom video and audio conferencing – Tukans Ltd

Polycore – liquid polymer controlled release formulation containing pheromones – Agrisense B C S Ltd

Polycryl – acrylic coated braided polyester sleeving – Relats UK Ltd

Polydekk – polycarbonate roofing and cladding system – Rockwell Sheet Sales Ltd

Polydiam – CNC engraving systems, embossing counterforce platemaking systems, design software, etching systems – Polydiam Industries

Polydiam – rubber stamp making systems & supplies – Polydiam Industries

Polydiam – photopolymer systems & resin – Polydiam Industries

Polydol – British Vita plc

Polydyne YD – multipurpose ink for papers, plastics etc – Fujifilm Sericol Ltd

Polyfast – Resinex UK Ltd

Polyfile – Snopake Ltd

Polyfile – UK Office Direct

Polyfile ID – Snopake Ltd

Polyfilla – fillers – Akzonobel

Polyflex – copolymer extruded weatherseals for timber and metal windows and doors – Schlegel UK

Polyflex – stretchfilm - hand and machine use – Total Polyfilm

Polyflex (Germany) – high pressure thermoplastic hose – Hydrasun Ltd

POLYFLEX – Hydraulic & Offshore Supplies Ltd

Polyflite – dart flights – Unicorn Products Ltd

Polyfoam Plus Agriboard 220 – thermal insulation for agricultural buildings – Knauf Insulation Ltd

Polyfoam Plus Cavity Closer – thermal insulation for use between inner and outer leafs of a masonry cavity wall at openings – Knauf Insulation Ltd

Polyfoam Plus Cavityboard – cavity wall insulation – Knauf Insulation Ltd

Polyfoam Plus Floorboard – thermal insulation for floors – Knauf Insulation Ltd

Polyfoam Plus I.D.P. System – insulation and DPC for thermal bridging problems – Knauf Insulation Ltd

Polyfoam Plus Laminating Board – insulation suitable for laminating to a range of facing materials – Knauf Insulation Ltd

Polyfoam Plus Liner Board – thermal insulation for walls by dry lining – Knauf Insulation Ltd

Polyfoam Plus Pitched Roofboard – thermal insulation for pitched roofs – Knauf Insulation Ltd

Polyfoam Plus R.V.B. – insulation suitable for laminating to a range of facing materials – Knauf Insulation Ltd

Polyfoam Plus Roofboard – thermal insulation of flat roofs – Knauf Insulation Ltd

Polyfoam Plus Sarking Board – thermal insulation of pitched roofs – Knauf Insulation Ltd

Polyfoam Raft-R-Vent – to maintain eaves ventilation airspace – Knauf Insulation Ltd

Polyfree – solvent free polyurethane – Forbo Adhesives UK Ltd

Polyfree – polyurethane adhesive – Forbo Adhesives UK Ltd

Polygold – polymers and flocculating agents – Goldcrest Chemicals Ltd

PolyGrip – Gesipa Blind Riveting Systems Ltd

Polyken (U.S.A.) – pipe wrapping tapes – Alexander Cardew Ltd

Polykraft – polythene-kraft papers – A Latter & Co. Ltd

Polylog – integrated pneumatic logic system – Parker Hannifin Ltd

Polylope – UK Office Direct

Polymat 'Hi-Flow' – A mechanically stitch bonded reinforcement consisting of a deformable ENGINEERED thermoplastic core sandwiched between two layers of chopped stand glass fibre. Designed for use in RTM, RTM light, VARTM and Vacuum Infusion – Scott & Fyfe Ltd

Polymatic – fusion tools for jointing thermoplastic pipes and fittings – C P V Ltd

Polymers Plus – software products for polymer process engineering – Aspentech Ltd

Polymex – colour-coded plastic shims – P S G Group Ltd

Polymica – flexible film covered integrated mica composite – Jones Stroud Insulations Ltd

Polymirror – virtually unbreakable safety mirrors – Volumatic Ltd

Polymit – economy covers and tarpaulins – Andrew Mitchell & Co. Ltd

Polynellie – beer stabiliser – British Filters Ltd

POLYPAC – Hydraulic & Offshore Supplies Ltd

Polypack – Polystyrene packaging – Polypack Packaging Supplies

Polypak – 10-30 litre blow moulded polyethylene circular drum – Weltonhurst Ltd

Polypenco – engineering plastics – Barkston Plastics Engineering Ltd

*Polyphem (Germany) – blister packaging fill control – Romaco Holdings UK Ltd

*Polyphem III (Germany) – print character verification system – Romaco Holdings UK Ltd

Polypin – 17 and 34 pint composite beer pack – Weltonhurst Ltd

Polyplast PY – gloss finish, solvent ink for plastics – Fujifilm Sericol Ltd

Polyplay – Playground Surfacing – Polytech International

PolyPlus – polyester resin system – Helifix Ltd

Polyprep – for preparing polyelectrolyte solution – Wallace & Tiernan Ltd

Polypress – British Vita plc

Polypropylene – Naylor Specialists Plastics

Polypropylene – Resinex UK Ltd

Polyprotec – plastic welding – Inform Plastics Ltd

Polyrad – detergents inhibitors – Hercules Holding Ii Ltd

Polyrad – cross linked polyethelene – Brand Rex Ltd

Polyram – polyamines – Atosina UK Ltd

*Polyrey (Germany) – work top and laminate – Allied Manufacturing

Polyrib – corrugated polypropylene sheet – Mcivor Plastics Ltd

Polyrod – pultruded sections – Jones Stroud Insulations Ltd

Polysafe – knitted heat and cut resistant gloves – Bennett Safetywear

Polyscreen PS – 2 pack ink for metals and industrial plastics – Fujifilm Sericol Ltd

Polyseal – hydraulic pressure seals – Claron Hydraulic Seals Ltd

Polyshield – sludge and metal ion conditioners for boiler/cooling systems – Feedwater Ltd

Polysorb – Igus (UK) Ltd

Polystone (Germany) – thermoplastic – Roechling Engineering Plastics Ltd

Polyswitch – circuit protection components – Tyco Electronics UK Ltd

Polytan – tannin based boiler treatment – Feedwater Ltd

Polytank Combination Tanks – Cold water storage cisterns and primary expansion cisterns – Polytank Ltd

Polytank Lofttanks – plastic cold water tanks – Polytank Ltd

Polytank Poly A30 – Hygenic Type A air gap – Polytank Ltd

Polytank Slimtanks – Unique design of coldwater cisterns – Polytank Ltd

Polytex – Ritrama UK Ltd

Polytop – polymer headed fasteners – Seac Ltd

Polytrak – waxed synthetic riding surface – Martin Collins Enterprises Ltd

Polytrak – Running Track systems – Polytech International

Polytwist – polypropylene garden twine – Nutscene

Polyu' – polycarbonate roofing and glazing systems – Rockwell Sheet Sales Ltd

PolyWally – Snopake Ltd

Polyweld – Conservation Resources UK Ltd

Polywrap – polyester and polyester thread – American & Efird GB Ltd

Pom Pom – grease guns – Lumatic Ga Ltd

Pom Pom Braids – Double Gee Hair Fashions Ltd

Pomegreat – Windfall Brands Ltd

Pomoma – Test accessories – Warwick Test Supplies

Pomosin – pectin, low methoxyl and pectin high methoxyl – Hercules Holding Ii Ltd

Pompadour – hair dressing and beauty suppliers – Pompadour Laboratories Ltd

Pomtava – Aztech Components Ltd

PONAR WADOWICE – Hydraulic & Offshore Supplies Ltd

Ponchotech (United Kingdom) – protective garment – Showers & Eyebaths Services Ltd

*Ponsloc (France) – CAM action couplings – Hydrasun Ltd

Pontoon (United Kingdom) – broadloom – Checkmate Industries Ltd

Pooch Pets – pet products – P M S International Group plc

Pool-Dry – swimming pool dehumidification – Munters Ltd

Pool Installers – Pool Installers

Pool-Vac – swimming pools and chemical servicing – Pool Vac Ltd

Poole lighting – lighting – Poole Lighting Ltd

PoolWise – pool chemicals and water treatment equipment. – Biolab UK Ltd

POP – rivets and riveting systems – Emhart Teknologies

Popinjay – UK Office Direct

Poplar – personal health scheme – Western Provident Association Ltd

Popsy – tops – Kentex Jeans & Casuals

Poptyser – software – Knowledge Software Ltd

Popular – interior paint grade flush door – Premdor Crosby Ltd

Popular – metal stapler (50/60) – Office Depot UK

Popular – refrigerated back bar bottle cabinets – Autonumis

Popular Range – linear fluorescent systems – Thorn Lighting Ltd
Por-A-Mold – mould making material – Chemical Innovations Ltd
Porcel – British Vita plc
***Porcupine** – mortarless concrete block retaining wall system – A G A Group
Porelon – pre-inked rubber stamps – Mark C Brown Ltd
Poremet/Absolta – sintered wire cloth – G Bopp & Co. Ltd
Porocel – activated aluminium – Lawrence Industries Ltd
Porofib – mouldabel felts and fully-cured for automobile industry, also felts for the bedding industry including flex-xel bi-component – Imp UK Ltd
Poroflex – Imp UK Ltd
Poroil – felt for soaking up oil spills – Imp UK Ltd
Poron (U.S.A.) – cellular urethane foams solutions for gasketing, sealing and energy absorption – Caledonian Industries Ltd
Poroprint – electronic measuring equipment – Fischer Instrumentation GB Ltd
POROUS PAVING – Resin Bonded Surfacing
Porpoise – on-line & laboratory rheometers/viscometers – Molecular Control Systems Ltd
Porsche – Ashley Competition Exhausts Ltd
Porsche – L M C Hadrian Ltd
Porspen – polyester sheeting – P & S Textiles Ltd
Port-A-Cart – cleaners janitorial trolly – Spraychem Ltd
Port of Workington – deep water port between Mersey and Clyde – Port Of Workington
Porta – module based building systems and services – Portakabin Ltd
Porta-Hire – network of Portakabin hire centres – Portakabin Ltd
Porta Ramp – vehicle speed restriction (speed bump) – Moseley Rubber Company Pty Ltd
Porta-Xtra – accessories for module based buildings – Portakabin Ltd
***Portabar** – Portable bar in a box – Cantilever Bar Systems Ltd
Portable Calibrator – Bronkhorst UK Ltd
Portacell – Relocatable Cell Site – Portastor Ltd
Portaclave – laboratory equipment – Astell Scientific Holdings Ltd
Portadisc – Saturn Spraying Systems Ltd
Portafix – Portable small tools/parts storage – Adfield Harvey Ltd
***Portaflash (Far East)** – photographic studio flash – Jessops plc
Portaflex – lightweight decontamination shower – Hughes Safety Showers Ltd
Portagauge – Portable Pre-Programmed Ultrasonic Thickness Gauge – Coltraco Ltd
Portakabin – Construction Industry Accountancy Ltd
Portakabin – instant building solutions – Portakabin Ltd
Portalevel – Coltraco Ltd
Portamarine – Coltraco Ltd
Portamatic – pressure testing – Walter Hill Plant Ltd
Portapath – Roland Plastics Ltd
Portapath - Technotile – Roland Plastics Ltd
Portascanner – Coltraco Ltd
Portasign – portable tubular tripod – Kingtools
Portastor Communications – Network Infrastructure Solutions Providers – Portastor Ltd
Portescap (Switzerland) – dc gearsheads – Trident Engineering Ltd
Portex – British Vita plc
Portex Vilum – British Vita plc
Portflo – catalyst handling and maintenance shutdown – Dialog Technivac Ltd
Portfolio – wallpapers – Today Interiors Ltd
PORTfolio PMS – Softbrands
PORTfolio, Web Booking Engine – Softbrands
Portia – essential healthcare products – Bray Group Ltd
Portia – dispenser – Appor Ltd
Portico – carpets - axminster – Brintons Carpets Ltd
Portico – insert living flame effect fire – Indesit Company UK Ltd
***Portion-aire (U.S.A.)** – small shot single component dispensers – R F Bright Enterprises Ltd
***Portionator (U.S.A.)** – two-component meter and mix dispensers – R F Bright Enterprises Ltd
Portionpak – single portion sachets – Chequer Foods Ltd
Portland – navigational aids – Blundell Harling Ltd
Portland – sealed system pressurisation sets – Hamworthy Heating Ltd
Portman – basin – Armitage Shanks Ltd
Portman – Portman Building Society
Portman Travel – business conference incentive and travel services – Portman Travel Ltd
Portman Travel – business travel agents – Portman Travel Ltd
Portobello – pressure vessels and heat exchangers – Portabello Fabrications
PortPhoenix – PU foam buoyancy pinch boom – Cowens Ltd
Portways – British Vita plc
Portwell – industrial and 19" rack chassis systems with power supplies. – Display Solutions Ltd
Portwest – workwear – Howsafe Ltd
Portwest – Workwear – Linacre Plant & Sales Ltd
Porvent – battery vent membranes – Porvair Sciences Ltd
Porvent – battery vent membranes – Porvair plc
Porweb – polyester needle felt – P & S Textiles Ltd
POS+ – monitor on-pack promotions – Mintel Group Ltd
Pos-A-Set – rupture disc – Continental Disc UK Ltd
Posalfilin – plantile warts treatment – Norgine International Ltd
Poseidon 2000 – deluge-proof cable glands – C M P UK Ltd
Poselco – fluorescent lighting fittings (luminaires) – Poselco Lighting Ltd
Posi-Guard (United Kingdom) – bursting disc for ultra-low pressure service – Elfab Ltd
Posi2orter – automated sorting conveyor systems – Van Der Lande Industries
Posidyne – filter medium – Pall Europe Corporate Services
Posie – bone china tableware and giftware – The Royal Crown Derby Porcelain Company Ltd
Posieden – Submarine Manufacturing & Products Ltd
Posifill – filling machines (liguid) – Liquid Control Ltd
Posiflow – continuous output pumps – Liquid Control Ltd
Posiload – positive displacement pump – Liquid Control Ltd
Posimixer – static mixers – Liquid Control Ltd
Posishot – micro-shot volumetric metering – Liquid Control Ltd
Positronic Industries – Jacarem Ltd
Posiva – Mercury Bearings Ltd
Posivalve – volumetric metering devices – Liquid Control Ltd
Possum – home automation systems for disabled and elderly people – Possum
Post Excel – Westmore Business Systems Ltd
Post-It – UK Office Direct
Postair – UK Office Direct
Postal Initiative – postal skills – Design Initiative Ltd
Poster Clamp – Imex Print Services Ltd
Poster Snap – Imex Print Services Ltd
Postillion – point of sale software – Carval Computing Ltd
Postlip Papers – filter media manufactured from cellulose, glass microfibres and synthetic non-woven and melt blown materials – Hollingsworth & Vose Co UK Ltd
Postman Pat – Chorion plc
Postmaster – letter boxes – Paddock Fabrications Ltd
Postmaster – UK Office Direct
Postmaster – Acco UK Ltd
Postsafe – UK Office Direct
Posturite – adjustable magnetic sloping writing board to ease neck and back pain associated with writing and reading – Posturite Ltd
Pot Black (UK) Ltd – snooker and pool tables, cues and accessories – Pot Black UK
Pot Boy – potwash system – I M C
Pot Noodle – UK Office Direct
Pot Pouree – pot water – Haws Watering Cans
Potter & Bromfield – relays – Bearwood Engineering Supplies
Potter & Brumfield – Cyclops Electronics Ltd
Potter & Moore – toiletries and home fragrances – Gilchrist & Soames
Potter's – catarrh pasilles – Ernest Jackson & Co. Ltd
Potterton – Baxi Group
Potterton boilers – energy efficient boilers – Elite Heating Ltd
Pottikem – fluids and sachets for chemical toilets – Elsan Ltd
Potts – earth moving equipment, buckets, blades, grabs, grapples and attachments – Potts Buckets & Attatchments Ltd
Potts Buckets – earth moving equipment, buckets, blades, grabs, grapples and attachments – Potts Buckets & Attatchments Ltd
Poulty First – suppliers of D.O. poultry and layers – Poultry First Ltd
Poundstretcher – retailers – Poundstretcher Ltd
Powaclene – Forward Chemicals Ltd
Powaclene Plus – Forward Chemicals Ltd
Powaclene T.F.R. – Forward Chemicals Ltd
Powafoam – Forward Chemicals Ltd
PowaKaddy (United Kingdom) – electrically powered golf trolleys, pull trolleys, and ancilliaryequipment – Powakaddy International Ltd
Powasol 10 – Forward Chemicals Ltd
Powasol 20 – Forward Chemicals Ltd
Powasteam 200 – Forward Chemicals Ltd
Powder Antifoam 2527 – Granada Cranes & Handling
Powder Antifoam 2527 – Basildon Chemical Co. Ltd / KCC
Powder Prime – water based primer for powder coatings – Thomas Howse Ltd
PowderVision – for the measurement of materials in enclosed ducting – N D C Infra-Red Engineering Ltd
PowderVision - for the measurement of materials in enclosed ductingInfralab - for the non contact multicomponent measurement of moisture, nicotine, sugars and temp in tobacco and moisture, and fat protein, oil in foods and bulk powders either in the lab or at lineTM710 - for the non contact on line measurement if nicotine, sugars, temperature and moisture in tobaccoMM710 - for the non contact on line measurement of moisture, fat, oil and protein in foods and bulk materials Gaugetools - statistical analysis package for data gathered by on line or at line gaugesMoistrex MX8000 - for the easy and rapid moisture analysis of paper and board samples either at line or in the lab. – N D C Infra-Red Engineering Ltd
Powel – roof tile machines – Powel Automation Ltd
Power – B P plc
Power 2 rack – power distribution unit – Schneider
Power-Belt – horizontal & incline belt conveyors – Vanriet UK Ltd
Power Commander – Moore Speed Racing Ltd
Power Cool – industrial water chillers – Coolmation Ltd
Power Dome – pneumatic equipment – Bearwood Engineering Supplies
Power Flood – lighting equipment – Powerlite Lighting Solutions Ltd
Power Gem – solar simulation/artificial daylight – Power Gems Ltd
Power Grip – worm drive hose clips – Norma UK Ltd
Power-Gro – liquid nutrient formulation for growing plants in water – Nutriculture
Power House Generators – standby generators – Scorpion Power Systems
Power Innovations – Cyclops Electronics Ltd
Power Integrations – power conversion ICs – Anglia
POWER JACK – Hydraulic & Offshore Supplies Ltd
Power Jacks (United Kingdom) – bevel gearboxes – Power Jacks Ltd
Power Jacks (United Kingdom) – screw jacks, linear actuators, bevel gearboxes & roller screws – Power Jacks Ltd
Power Jacks (United Kingdom) – linear actuators – Power Jacks Ltd
Power Jacks (United Kingdom) – roller screws – Power Jacks Ltd
Power Jacks - Screw Jacks, Linear Actuators & Gearboxes, Precision Actuation Systems, Neeter Drive Bevel Gearboxes, Spiracon Roller Screws, Rolaram Linear Actuators, Youngs Lifting, Duff-Norton Actuators , Duff-Norton Rotary Unions. – Power Jacks Ltd
Power Jammer – high load holding equipment – Spinlock Ltd
Power-Line by Reed – uk reo uk ltd – Reco-Prop UK Ltd
Power Makes Sense – electrical and audio accessories – P M S International Group plc
Power Master – Gem Tool Hire & Sales Ltd
***POWER-MEC** – Midland Power Machinery Distributors
Power Pact 4 – panel board – Schneider
Power Painting – paint application techniques – Lion Industries UK Ltd
Power Pod – remote control camera heads – A & C Ltd
Power Project – teamplan project management software – Asta Development plc
Power Quality – Radir Ltd
Power Rail 323 – din rail kw demanol & kwh meter – Northern Design Ltd
***Power Rangers (Far East)** – figures & accessories – Bandai UK Ltd
Power Rider – powered wheelchair – Remploy Ltd
Power Roller – powered roller conveyors – Vanriet UK Ltd
Power Sonic – lead acid batteries – Pulsar Developments Ltd
Power-Sonic – sealed lead acid batteries (rechargeable), nickel cadmium cells and batteries (rechargeable) – Power Sonic Europe
Power Strainer – paint strainer – Lion Industries UK Ltd
Power-Style 3 – form 3 lv switchboards – Schneider
Power-Style 4 – form 4 lv switchboards – Schneider
POWER TEAM – Hydraulic & Offshore Supplies Ltd
Power Tools – professional & DIY – Robert Bosch Ltd
Power Tower – high performance tape backup system – Cristie Software
Power Wall – protective coating – Powerwall Space Frame Systems Ltd
Powerail Vahle – electrification equipment – Powerail Ltd
Powerbase – geotextiles – Industrial Textiles & Plastics Ltd
PowerBird – Gesipa Blind Riveting Systems Ltd
PowerBird-Solar – Gesipa Blind Riveting Systems Ltd
Powerblast – pressure blast machines and accessories, self contained and portable blast rooms with automatic and semi automatic abrasive recovery – Power Blast International
Powerbond – heavy duty textile and composites laminating machinery – Reliant Machinery Ltd
Powerboss – Proplas International Ltd
Powerbox – Powerbox Group Ltd
Powercard – electrical power supplies – Nortel Networks UK Ltd

Powercase – Global Graphics Software Ltd
Powerchanger – tape backup auto changer – Cristie Software
Powerclad – reinforced scaffold sheeting – Industrial Textiles & Plastics Ltd
Powerclad DN – scaffold debris netting – Industrial Textiles & Plastics Ltd
Powerclad FR – flame retardant scaffold sheeting – Industrial Textiles & Plastics Ltd
Powerclean – reinforced coated films and tape fabrics – Industrial Textiles & Plastics Ltd
Powercleat – lower load holding equipment – Spinlock Ltd
Powerclene – reinforced coated films and tape fabrics – Industrial Textiles & Plastics Ltd
Powerclutch – rope holding equipment – Spinlock Ltd
Powercommand – control system – Cummins Power Generation Ltd
Powercut – B P plc
Powerdeck – Mezzanie Floors – Stormor Systems Ltd
Powerdis – Forward Chemicals Ltd
Powerdol – electrical power supplies – Nortel Networks UK Ltd
Powerdoor Electric Gates – Electric Gates – G8 Systems
Powerex – transistors – Bowers Ltd
Powerfect – electrical mains quality measuring equipment for voltage, current or power – Energy I C T
Powerfil – power cable filler yarns – Independent Twine Manufacturing Co. Ltd
Powerfin (United Kingdom) – heavy duty manual industrial grinding and polishing machines – R J H Finishing Systems Ltd
Powerfirm – combined heating power product (CHB) – Scorpion Power Systems
Powerflash – photographic studio equipment – Jessops plc
Powerflex – flexible crash doors, strip PVC curtains and rapid rise doors – Neway Doors Ltd
Powerflex – stretchfilm machine use 300% + stretch – Total Polyfilm
Powerflex 40 – Proplas International Ltd
Powerflex 70 – Proplas International Ltd
Powerflex 700 – Proplas International Ltd
Powerflex Expansion Joints – Interflex Hose & Bellows Ltd
Powerflexi – powered portable extendable conveyor – Vanriet UK Ltd
Powerfoil – vapour barriers and control layers – Industrial Textiles & Plastics Ltd
Powerform – thermoformers (general purpose) – Shelley Thermoformers International Ltd
Powerfresh – Forward Chemicals Ltd
Powerfusion – polyethylene pipeline welding – Harrington Generators International Ltd
Powergauge – Sevcon Ltd
Powergel – emulsion explosives – Orica UK Ltd
Powergem – lighting equipment – Powerlite Lighting Solutions Ltd
Powerglide – snooker/billiards/pool – Gunn & Moore
Powergrab – A P T
Powergrip – European Technical Sales Ltd
Powerhone – versatile vertical honing machine – Equipment For You
Powerinspect – Delcam plc
Powerkube – horizontal balers – Pakawaste
Powerkube Plus – horizontal balers – Pakawaste
Powerkube XL – horizontal balers – Pakawaste
Powerlab 8 – school science laboratory – S & B UK Ltd
Powerlift – fishing tackle – Daiwa Sports Ltd
Powerline – replacement parts for tractors and engines – The Vapormatic Co. Ltd
Powerline – sale of electricity – R W E Npower
Powerline – duct fan – Roof Units Ltd
Powerlink – busbar trunking – M K Electric Ltd
Powerlite – reinforced polyethylene tarpaulin material – Power Plastics
POWERLOCK – Hydraulic & Offshore Supplies Ltd
PowerLogic – electrical network monitoring & control – Schneider
Powerlon – reinforced roofing materials – Industrial Textiles & Plastics Ltd
Powerlon BM – breather membrane – Industrial Textiles & Plastics Ltd
Powerlon HP – reinforced roofing tiles – Industrial Textiles & Plastics Ltd
Powerlon SP – high permeable roofing membrane – Industrial Textiles & Plastics Ltd
Powerlon VCL – vapour barriers and control layers – Industrial Textiles & Plastics Ltd
Powermarc – abrasives – Marcrist International Ltd
***Powermaster Plus** – Sound Dynamics Ltd
PowerMate – powered stair climber – Stanley Handling Ltd
Powermax – Baxi Group
Powermax – golf equipment – Dunlop Slazenger International Ltd
Powermesh – fishing tackle – Daiwa Sports Ltd
Powermesh – open weave meshes – Industrial Textiles & Plastics Ltd
Powermex – open weave meshes – Industrial Textiles & Plastics Ltd
Powermill – Delcam plc
Powerminder – panel mounted power multimeter – Northern Design Ltd
Powermod – electrical power supplies – Nortel Networks UK Ltd
Powernet – scaffold debris netting – Industrial Textiles & Plastics Ltd
Powernet – B P plc
Powerpac – Sevcon Ltd
Powerpak – Sevcon Ltd
Powerpak – Asbestos Removal – Scott International Ltd
Powerpin – flexible couplings – Bibby Transmissions Ltd
Powerplas – reinforced PVC sheeting – Power Plastics
Powerplas – reinforced PVC tarpaulin material – Power Plastics
PowerPro (United Kingdom) – Our brand of diesel generators from 4-2000kva – Powersource Projects Ltd
Powerpull – bar puller – Thame Engineering Co. Ltd
Powersaver (United Kingdom) – Electric heating and hot water controller – Sangamo Ltd
Powersaver – talking motor cycle alarms – O W L Electronics Ltd
Powerscan – ultrasonic flaw detector – Sonatest Ltd
Powerseat – electro/hydraulic gas valves – Black Teknigas & Electro Controls Ltd
Powersense (United Kingdom) – mains disturbance monitors – Powersense Technology
Powershade – automatic and remote control vertical blinds – Eclipse Blind Systems
Powershape – Delcam plc
Powershare – power unit – Ajax Tocco International Ltd
Powershield – design, supply and installation of steel doors for fire, security, personnel blast, clean room applications and cell security products for prison authorities – Powershield Doors Ltd
Powershuttle – 4 wheel drive diesel dumper with torque converter transmissions – Thwaites Ltd
***PowerSoak** – S R L Countertech Ltd
Powerson – lighting equipment – Powerlite Lighting Solutions Ltd
Powersprays – C E S Hire Ltd
***POWERSTAR (Germany)** – metal halide lamps – Osram Ltd
Powerstay – voltage stabilisers – Claude Lyons Ltd
Powerstock – rapid recovery modular calorifiers – Hamworthy Heating Ltd
Powerstream – lighting equipment – Powerlite Lighting Solutions Ltd
Powersuite – Alpha Electronics Southern Ltd
Powersure – Emerson Network Power Ltd
Powerswivel – rotating skip - 4 wheel drive dumper – Thwaites Ltd
Powertarp – reinforced tarpaulins – Industrial Textiles & Plastics Ltd
POWERTEC – European Drives & Motor Repairs
Powerton HP – reinforced roofing materials – Industrial Textiles & Plastics Ltd
Powertrak – electronic mobile shelving systems – Rackline Ltd
Powertrak – power control units for induction furnaces – Inductotherm Europe Ltd
Powertron – switchmode power supplies and DC to DC converters – Powertron Converters Ltd
Powertronics – European Technical Sales Ltd
Powervac – beach cleaning systems – Vikoma International Ltd
***Powerware (U.S.A.)** – uninterruptable power systems – Eaton Electric Sales Ltd
Powerware (United Kingdom) – ups systems – Powersense Technology
Powerware Systems – Eaton Electric Sales Ltd
Powerwash – Gates Hydraulics Ltd
Powerwash T.F.R.'s – vehicle cleaners – Deb R & D Ltd
PowerWeb (U.S.A.) – web browser and search engine for nt based document management – Pacific Solutions International Ltd
Powlift – manufacture and design materials handling equipment – Powlift Handling Systems Ltd
Powmet – press ready bronze premix – Makin Metal Powders UK Ltd
Powrlock – tooling parts – A C Hydraulics Ltd
POWRLOCK – Hydraulic & Offshore Supplies Ltd
Pozi-Combi – bandsaw – Dynashape Ltd
Pozi-Pitch – bandsaw – Dynashape Ltd
Pozi-Rake – bandsaw – Dynashape Ltd
Pozi-Tooth – bandsaw – Dynashape Ltd
Pozi-Vari – bandsaw – Dynashape Ltd
Ppe – Avalon and Lynwood
PPS Plant Performance Services – Goulds Pumps a Division of ITT Industries Ltd
PPU – emulsion sprayer – Thomas Coleman Engineering Ltd
PQ – polycarbonate, acrylic and P.V.C. sheet – Righton Ltd
PQ Eclipse – Thermo Electrical
PQ Excell – Thermo Electrical
PQM – Power Quality Management products – Claude Lyons Ltd
PR2001 – range of garment presses – Electrolux Laundry Systems
Pr53, 23 & 103 – liquid sample receivers – Jiskoot Ltd
Practical – car and van rental – Practical Car & Van Rental
Practical Boat Owner – I P C Media Ltd
Practical Parenting – I P C Media Ltd
PracticeProfit – Profit enhancement services for professional practices. – Lawson Consulting
Practicon – electronic equipment for weighing, process controls and data logging; suppliers of process control and computer systems – Practicon Ltd
Practiplast – B P plc
PRADIFA – Hydraulic & Offshore Supplies Ltd
Pradifa – Mayday Seals & Bearings
***Praga (India)** – surface grinders – Capital Equipment & Machinery Ltd
Pramac – Stacatruc
PRAMAC – Chaintec Ltd
PRAT – Chaintec Ltd
Prat – T V H UK Ltd
Prater Roofing – Prater Ltd
***Pratissoli (Italy)** – pumps – Dual Pumps Ltd
Pratissoli Pumps – high pressure water pumps – Alan Dale Pumps Ltd
PRATT – Hydraulic & Offshore Supplies Ltd
Pratt Burnerd America – D M G UK Ltd
Praxair Metallisation (United Kingdom) – Quay Surface Engineering Metalblast Ltd
PRC – sealants for use in aerospace and insulated glass – PPG Aerospace
Pre Computer Graduate – Vtech Electronics UK plc
Pre Computer Notebook II – Vtech Electronics UK plc
Pre Computer Prestige – Vtech Electronics UK plc
Pre-fect – gut conditioner for swine and poultry – Agil Chemicals Products
***Pre-School (The Far East)** – toys – Tomy International
Precast – terrazzo units – Quiligotti Terrazzo Ltd
Precept Deluxe – insert living flame effect fire – Indesit Company UK Ltd
Preci-Dip – Cyclops Electronics Ltd
Precidor Bore Finishing Systems – European market – Permat Machines Ltd
Precious Gems – carpets – Bond Worth
Precis Marketing – Marketing Agency – Adstorm
Precisa (Germany) – colour print and side film and colour paper – Agfa Gevaert
Precise – alginate impression compounds – Prima Dental Group Ltd
precise pro audio hire – audio hire and sales – Precise Pro Audio Hire
Precision Actuation Systems (PAS) (United Kingdom) – roller screws – Power Jacks Ltd
Precision Actuation Systems (PAS) (United Kingdom) – screw jacks, linear actuators, roller screws – Power Jacks Ltd
Precision Actuation Systems (PAS) (United Kingdom) – linear actuators – Power Jacks Ltd
Precision Chains England – conveyor chains and wheels – Precision Chains Ltd
***Precision Dynamics (U.S.A.)** – solenoid valves – Tamo Ltd
Precision England – steel conveyor roller chains – Precision Chains Ltd
***Precision Fitting (U.S.A.)** – nylon fittingss – Dual Pumps Ltd
Precision Plan – Yara UK It Ltd
Precision Plus – AESpump
Precision Polymer Engineering – 'o' rings and technical mouldings in a full range of materials – Precision Polymer Engineering Ltd
Precision Series – loudspeakers – Tannoy Group Ltd
PRECISION STEP SYSTEMS - – electro-pneumatic clutch brakes – A T B Laurence Scott Ltd
Precision Technologies International – Precision Technologies International Ltd
Precision tools suppliers – Tesa Technology UK Ltd
Precista – hand tools – Time Products UK Ltd
Precistep (Switzerland) – Minature stepper motors – Electro Mechanical Systems (EMS) Ltd
Precitec – Laser Trader Ltd
Preco – broadcast audio products – Preco Ltd
Precolor – Precolor Sales Ltd
Preconceive – Folic Acid – G R Lane Health Products Ltd
Preconomy Ltd – injection and transfer moulds for plastics and high pressure diecasting dies – Preconomy
Predator – area floodlight luminaire – Holophane Europe Ltd
Predator – boats – Sunseeker Poole Ltd
Predator – lighting effect – Premier Solutions Nottingham Ltd
Predict – B P plc
Prediction – I P C Media Ltd

***Predictor (Netherlands)** – pregancy diagnosis – Chefaro UK Ltd
Prefect – Agil Chemicals Products
Preference – Georgia Pacific GB Ltd
Preform – plumbing unit – Harton Services Ltd
Preformed S.A.M. – preformed stress absorbing membrane which inhibits onset of reflective cracking – Colas Ltd
Preformed Surface Dressing – flexible preformed surface dressing, in rolls, with high PSV chippings. – Colas Ltd
Prekev – G M S Co.
Prelude – Interface Europe Ltd
***Prelude (Sweden)** – shower cabinet available with or without WC function – Arjo Med AB Ltd
Prelude – kitchen furniture – Moores Furniture Group
Prelude – textiles – Restmor Ltd
Prelude – fashion footwear – D Jacobson & Sons Ltd
Prelude Plus – kitchen furniture – Moores Furniture Group
Premac – clear radiation shielding acrylic – Wardray Premise Ltd
PREMAC – Kenex Electro Medical Ltd
Premac Super – emulsion floor polish – Premiere Products Ltd
Premadex – neutron absorbent material – Wardray Premise Ltd
Premadia – range of synthetic and natural diamond abrasives – Diamond Detectors
Prembond – liquid corrosion protection systems – Premier Coatings Ltd
Premcote – pipeline anti-corrosion tapes – Premier Coatings Ltd
Premcote Mould Dress – mould dressing – Huttenes-Albertus UK Ltd
Premdor – Preston Plywood Supplies
Premflex – band saw – Dynashape Ltd
PREMIAIR – Hydraulic & Offshore Supplies Ltd
Premier – refrigerated back bar bottle cabinets – Autonumis
Premier – Lamphouse Ltd
Premier – dental lathe and general brushes – E. Berry & Sons
Premier – UK Office Direct
Premier – shower enclosures – Coram Showers Ltd
Premier – mobile rock crushers – Terex
Premier – brake pads, shoes and clutches – Premier Braking Ltd
Premier – ultra marine and manganese violet pigments for plastics – Holliday Pigments Ltd
Premier – double glazing – Premier M & D Windows
Premier – free standing safes – Securikey Ltd
Premier – guillotines & timmers – Martin Yale International Ltd
Premier – linens - bed linens – Pin Mill Textiles Ltd
***Premier Choice** – Premierchoice Ltd
Premier Collection – prestige vinyl tile and planks – Tarkett Ltd
Premier Court – cushioned tennis court carpet system – Emusol Products Ltd
Premier-Grip – office sundries – Setten Ixl Ltd
Premier-Hangfile – suspension filing systems – Setten Ixl Ltd
Premier - HangfileBulldogPremier - Grip – Setten Ixl Ltd
Premier House – Choice Hotels International
Premier Housewares – kitchenware and housewares – Premier Housewares LLP
Premier Marina Brighton – boat marina – Premier Marinas Brighton
Premier Mix – animal feed – Burnhill Services Ltd
Premier Range – thickness meter – Fidgeon Ltd
Premier Storage and Office Solutions Ltd – Pallet Racking, Shelving, Mezzanine Floors, Office Partitioning / Furniture – Premier Storage & Office Solutions Ltd
Premier Vinyl Matt – Spencer Coatings Ltd
Premier Vinyl Silk – Spencer Coatings Ltd
Premiercard – B P plc
***Premiere** – Agrico UK Ltd
Premiere Antistatic – perfumed liquid antistatic – Premiere Products Ltd
Premiere Automatic – low foaming automatic detergent powder – Premiere Products Ltd
Premiere Bio Automatic – low foaming biological automatic detergent powder – Premiere Products Ltd
Premiere Clean & Buff – maintenance product for floors – Premiere Products Ltd
Premiere Cream Cleanser – mildly abrasive general cleaner – Premiere Products Ltd
Premiere Foam Cleanser – scouring powder containing bleach and abrasive – Premiere Products Ltd
Premiere Safestrip – a low hazard stripper for removing seals from wood, stone and metal – Premiere Products Ltd
Premiere Stone Vitrifier – cleaning treatment and rejuvenation of stone floors – Premiere Products Ltd
Premiertrak – track mounted primary jaw crushing plant – Terex
Premierzone – Vodafone Retail Ltd
Premisan – a cleaner disinfectant for destroying micro-organisms in washroom areas – Premiere Products Ltd
Premium – darts shafts – Unicorn Products Ltd
Premium – medium programmable logic controllers – Schneider
Premium 80 – high performance high solid content binder for stress sites – Colas Ltd
***Premium Halal Burgers** – Fakir Halal Doners
Premium MX – dart shafts – Unicorn Products Ltd
Prempol X – bactericidal neutral detergent – Premiere Products Ltd
Premseal – waterproof membrane – Premier Coatings Ltd
Premshield – flashing tape – Premier Coatings Ltd
Premstrip 90 – floor stripper – Premiere Products Ltd
Premtape – pipeline anti-corrosion tapes – Premier Coatings Ltd
Premturps – turpentine – Premiere Products Ltd
Preplan – instant accommodation – Rollalong Ltd
Prepufe – pre-applied waterproof member – Grace Construction Ltd
Presco – metal pressing & scaffold components – Presco Components
Presentation – white copier paper – International Paper Equipment Finance LP
Presentation Skills Workshop – Skills Workshop Ltd
Presentor – rectangular flush meters with interchangeable fronts and bezels – Elektron Components Ltd
Preside – network management software – Nortel Networks UK Ltd
President – office furniture – E W Marshall Ltd
***President (Germany)** – awning – Deans Blinds & Awnings UK
President – hinges for commercial aluminium systems – Securistyle Ltd
President – single skinned GRP up and over garage door – P C Henderson Ltd
***President Screens** – President Blinds Ltd
PresorVac (TM) – Waiter's Friend Company Ltd
Press N' Play Ball – Vtech Electronics UK plc
Press N' Play Block – Vtech Electronics UK plc
Press Tap – tap – Worldwide Dispensers
***Press:Air:Trol (U.S.A.)** – air sensors & switches – The West Group Ltd
Pressavon – press working of small components – Pressavon Ltd
Pressclene – Forward Chemicals Ltd
Pressflow – gantry robots – Expert Tooling & Automation
Pressfold – light gauge metal fabricators, specializing in stainless steel, aluminium and precision folding of sheet metal – Powershield Doors Ltd
Presslock – quick disconnect coupling, self-sealing – Cobham Mission Equipment Ltd
***PressMAir (Italy)** – stainless steel pneumatic equipment – The West Group Ltd
Pressmatic – laboratory liquid dispensers – Bibby Scientific Ltd
PressOn – adaptor – Hitex UK Ltd
Pressure Devices Inc. PDI (U.S.A.) – pressure & vacuum switches – Applications Engineering Ltd
Pressure Seal – one piece mailing – Paragon Group UK Ltd
Pressure Vessels – air receivers and expansion vessels – Abbott & Co Newark Ltd
Pressware – Dual ovenable packaging – Pregis Rigid Packaging Ltd
Prestbury – hospital furniture – Hoskins Medical Equipment Ltd
Prestcold – refrigeration compressors and condensing units – Emerson Climate Technologies Ltd
Prestcold – Therma Group
Prestex – Madison Filter
Prestige – record label – Ace Records Ltd
Prestige – glass shower enclosures – Novellini UK Ltd
Prestige – breakdown warranties – Car Care Plan Ltd
Prestige – ultra marine pigments for plastics – Holliday Pigments Ltd
Prestige – Copper Tiles – Matthew Hebden
Prestige 2com – surface trunking for data – M K Electric Ltd
Prestige Industrial – industrial baking pans – F B S Prestige
Prestige Plus – skirting and dado trunking – M K Electric Ltd
Prestige Power Poles and Posts – poles and posts – M K Electric Ltd
Prestige series – loudspeakers – Tannoy Group Ltd
Prestigious Textiles – The Winnen Furnishing Company
Prestik – preformed sealing strip – Bostik Ltd
Presto – cutting tools – Arrow Supply Co. Ltd
Presto Print – Press To Print
Prestolite – car electrics – L A E Valeo Ltd
Prestolite Contactors (United Kingdom) – Ametek Prestolight
PRESTOLOK – Hydraulic & Offshore Supplies Ltd
Preston Mills (United Kingdom) – Worsted Mens Suiting Fabric – John Foster Ltd
Preston Plywood – Preston Plywood Supplies
PrestoPac – corrugated packaging – D S Smith Packaging Ltd
Prestoplan – timber frame construction – Prestoplan Ltd
Pretty Polly, Aristoc, Elbeo, Golden Lady, Cindy – Tights & Stockings – Pak Nylon Hosiery Co.
Prevail – Resinex UK Ltd
Previews – paint selection software – Akzonobel
Prevul – prevulcanised latex – Vita Liquid Polymers
PRH – process refractometer – Bellingham & Stanley Ltd
Priadit – antistatic agents – Croda International plc
Priamus – Kuwait Petroleum International Lubricants UK Ltd
Pricerine – glycerines – Croda International plc
Prices – candles – Prices Patent Candles Ltd
Pricewaters Coopers – chartered accountants – Pricewaterhousecoopers LLP
Pricing Guns – Avery Dennison
Pride Of Strathspey – malt Scotch whisky – Gordon & Macphail
Pride of U.S.A. Products – Double Gee Hair Fashions Ltd
Priesser – verniers and micrometers – Verdict Gauge Ltd
Priestleys (United Kingdom) – Worsted Mens Suiting Fabric – John Foster Ltd
Priestman – Harrier Fluid Power Ltd
Priestman Grabs – R B Cranes Ltd
Prifac – fatty acids – Croda International plc
Prifat – industrial triglycerides – Croda International plc
PRIFORM – toughened resin infusion materials system – Cytec Engineered Materials Ltd
Prifrac – frationated fatty acids – Croda International plc
Prilect – domestic heating and electrical appliances – Glen Electric Ltd
Prima – urinal – Ideal Standard Ltd
Prima – European Technical Sales Ltd
Prima – Laser Trader Ltd
Prima Plus Tape – Garment identification labels – J & A International Ltd
Prima Tape – Garment identification labels – J & A International Ltd
Primabrand – rubber product branding – Polymeric Labels Ltd
Primacor – Resinex UK Ltd
Primalec – ultra-violet hand lamps – R.J. Doran & Co. Ltd
Primalec (United Kingdom) – ultra violet lamps for fluorescent exposure, leak detection and curing – Primalec
Primapor – Madison Filter
PRIMARY FLUID POWER – Hydraulic & Offshore Supplies Ltd
Primavera by Bianca – Turner Bianca
***Prime 100** – motor insurance – M M A Insurance plc
Prime 20 – epoxy infusion system – Gurit UK Ltd
Prime-Aid – first aid dressings – Campbell Medical Supplies
Prime Time – monthly 50+ paper – The Bournemouth Daily Echo
Primeaid – adhesive dressings, bandages, first aid kits and eye wash equipment – Campbell Medical Supplies
Primef – Resinex UK Ltd
Primeguard – protective overalls – Synergy Healthcare plc
Primeline – Office Chairs – Stanwell Office Furniture
Primelite – outdoor advertising agents – Primesight London Ltd
Primetex – disposable wipes and cloths – Synergy Healthcare plc
Primfil – core and pastes – Huttenes-Albertus UK Ltd
Primofit – malleable iron compression fittings – George Fischer Sales Ltd
Primox – waste treatment plant – Boc Gases Ltd
Primox – industrial gases – Boc Gases Ltd
Primrose Valley Coaches – bus and coach services – East Yorkshire Motor Services Ltd
Primweld – adheshives – Huttenes-Albertus UK Ltd
Prince – Harrier Fluid Power Ltd
Princes Soft Drinks – soft drinks – Princes Soft Drinks
Princess – combining pea variety – Limagrain UK Ltd
Princess – hospital ward beds – Hoskins Medical Equipment Ltd
Princess – optical frames and sunglasses – Hilton International Eye Wear Ltd
Princess – washbasin and closet – Ideal Standard Ltd
Princess Greenhouses – aluminium hobby greenhouse – Eden Halls Greenhouses Ltd
Princess International – motor yachts – Princess International Sales & Service Ltd
Princess Motor Cruisers – Princess Yachts International plc
Princestone – sand & gravel sales in Norfolk – Frimstone Ltd
Principality Building Society – Principality Building Society
Pringle – leisurewear – Dawson International plc
Pringles – UK Office Direct
Printa – Screen and pad printing equipment – Dalesway Print Technology
Printapot – cylindrical plastic container – Robinson Healthcare Ltd
Printasia – digital imaging products – Harman Technology Ltd
Printed Carton – glued, printed folded carton – Beamglow Ltd
Printel – aqueous dispersions of organic pigments for textile applications – European Colour plc
Printell – print management function to automatically generate the quantity of label types when triggered via operator, data

polling or automatic launch from another package – Episys Group Ltd
Printer & Pressman – natural citrus cleaners – Vindotco UK Ltd
Printerbox – Home Office, Small Office website – Glen Office Supplies Ltd
PrinterNOX – Cardinal Health U.K. 232 Ltd
Printers Choice – paper – Paperun Group Of Companies
Printex – Forward Chemicals Ltd
Printgard – spray – Lyson Ltd
Printing Trades Directory – United Business Media Ltd
Printmet – sheet metal manufacturers and engineers – Printmet Ltd
Printronix – Printer – Moorgate Ltd
Printscan – computer software – Wordcraft International Ltd
Priolene – oleines – Croda International plc
Priolube – lubricant base fluids – Croda International plc
Prior Diesel – Prior Diesel Ltd
Priorlab – laboratory microscope – Prior Scientific Instruments Ltd
PriorLux – laboratory microscope – Prior Scientific Instruments Ltd
PriorSpec – fibre optic inspection microscope – Prior Scientific Instruments Ltd
Priory – hand tools – Smith Francis Tools Ltd
Priory Castor – castors – The Priory Castor & Engineering Co. Ltd
Priplast – plasticisers – Croda International plc
Pripol – polymerised fatty acids – Croda International plc
Prisavon – soap base – Croda International plc
PRISECTER – sampling equipment, automatic – Eriez Magnetics Europe Ltd
***Prisinter (France)** – interlocked switch sockets – W F Electrical
PRISM – polar embedded spherical silica columns for HPLC – Thermo Fisher Scientific
Prism – Tecstar Electronics Ltd
Prism Glasses – Portable mirror therapy device for stroke and phantom limb pain rehabilitation – Scottish Health Innovations
Prism Projects – graphic designers specialising in signs, printing marketing – Rake 'N' Lift & Co - Nottingham Rakes UK Rakes Specialists
Prisma Evolution – indoor switchboard – Schneider
Prisma G – wall mounted functional system – Schneider
Prisma GK – wall mounted functional system – Schneider
Prisma GX – wall mounted functional system – Schneider
Prisma P – floor standing functional system – Schneider
Prisma PH – floor standing functional system – Schneider
Prismafit – ceramic fittings & coves – Johnson Tiles Ltd
Prismalume – enhanced industrial lighting luminaire – Holophane Europe Ltd
Prismasphere – outdoor prismatic post top luminaire – Holophane Europe Ltd
Prismatics – glazed wall tiles - plain colours – Johnson Tiles Ltd
Prismatron – energy saving – Holophane Europe Ltd
Prismertec – water softener – B W T Ltd
Prismo – Zeiss
Prismpack – industrial high bay luminaire – Holophane Europe Ltd
Prismpackette – low mount, industrial luminaire – Holophane Europe Ltd
Prisorine – isostearic acids – Croda International plc
Pristerene – stearines – Croda International plc
Pritex – polyurethane foam converters for industrial co's only – Pritex
Pritt – UK Office Direct
Private – Steel Bollard – Alto Bollards UK Ltd
Private label – O P Chocolate Ltd
Privilege Insurance – Direct Line Insurance plc
Prize Aran with Wool – Sirdar Spinning Ltd
Prize Baby DK – Sirdar Spinning Ltd
Prize Chunky – Sirdar Spinning Ltd
Prize DK – Sirdar Spinning Ltd
Pro 2000 – Scott International Ltd
Pro-Activ – Pledge Office Chairs Ltd
Pro-Active – dog food – Gilbertson & Page Ltd
Pro-Balance – Probiotics International Ltd
Pro-Bloc – seating fireblocking fabrics – T B A Textiles
Pro-Boot – Bunzl S W S
Pro-Carp – fishing tackle – Daiwa Sports Ltd
Pro-Co – photographic processing equipment – M C D Virtak Ltd
Pro-Dophilus – milk-free acidophilus powder – G & G Food Supplies
Pro Engineer – Linmech Technical Solutions Ltd
Pro Equine – Abbey England Ltd
Pro-Fibre – Probiotics International Ltd
***Pro-Form (U.S.A.)** – vacuum forming materials – Metrodent Ltd
Pro-Kolin – Probiotics International Ltd
Pro-Man – Value for money safety footwear range – Rock Fall UK Ltd
Pro-Mem – syringe filters – Radleys
Pro Pen (France) – Technifor
Pro Pike – fishing tackle – Daiwa Sports Ltd
***Pro-Quartz (Japan)** – Pentax UK Ltd
Pro-Railing – stainless steel hand railing system – F H Brundle
Pro-Set – epoxy laminating system – Wessex Resins & Adhesives Ltd
Pro-Sked – software for oil refinery operations – Aspentech Ltd
Pro Specialist – fishing tackle – Daiwa Sports Ltd
Pro Star – sports garments and in particular football clothing – Star Sportswear Ltd
Pro-Stik – DIY adhesives and sealants – Bostik Ltd
Pro-Tex – cut resistant gloves – Bennett Safetywear
Pro-Wynd – filter cartridges – M C D Virtak Ltd
Proactive Hire – Equipment Hire and Leasing – Proactive Test Solutions Ltd
Proactive Test – Test Consultancy – Proactive Test Solutions Ltd
ProBag – C P Cases Ltd
Proban – Helman Workwear
Proban (United Kingdom) – cotton flame retardant fabric – Carrington Career & Work Wear
Probase 3 Cream – M S D Animal Health
Probase 3 Lotion – M S D Animal Health
Probe – Devaco International Ltd
Probuild – A Proctor Group Ltd
Procare – barrier handcream – Day Impex Ltd
ProCase – C P Cases Ltd
ProCast – Goulds Pumps a Division of ITT Industries Ltd
***Procede COR (France)** – biofixations - EC.EFB grade 1 micro organisms fixed to a mineral support – Symbio
Proceine – disinfectant – Agma Ltd
Procelinc – A Proctor Group Ltd
***Proceq (Germany)** – company name – Abbey Spares & Supplies
PROCESS – Hydraulic & Offshore Supplies Ltd
Process Containment Systems – dust booth – Extract Technology
Process Control – magazine – Progressive Media Group
Process I/O – Modular and Block I/O – Measurement Technology Ltd
Processing Plant – hot bonding controllers and heater mats composited grp repair equipment – J R Technology
Procheck – A Proctor Group Ltd
***ProCheck** – An interactive decision support system for pesticide use – Muddy Boots Software Ltd
Prochem – industrial cleaning equipment – B & G Cleaning Systems Ltd
Prochem – industrial cleaning chemicals – C S A Cleaning Equipment
Prochem and ESP – advanced environmental simulation software – Aker Kvaerner Engineering Services Ltd
Prochinor – armines – Atosina UK Ltd
Prochinor – demulsifying agent – Atosina UK Ltd
Prociene 100JL – solid biocide – Agma Ltd
Procirc – printed circuit chemicals – P M D UK Ltd
Procirc 900 – chemical polish – P M D UK Ltd
Procirc 9001 – alkali cleaner – P M D UK Ltd
Procirc 9002 – alkali cleaner – P M D UK Ltd
Procirc 9003 – alkali cleaner – P M D UK Ltd
Procirc 901 – cleaner conditioner – P M D UK Ltd
Procirc 9010 – cleaner conditioner – P M D UK Ltd
Procirc 9020 – acid cleaner – P M D UK Ltd
Procirc 9021 – acid cleaner – P M D UK Ltd
Procirc 9022 – acid cleaner – P M D UK Ltd
Procirc 903 – printed circuit board cleaner – P M D UK Ltd
Procirc 905 – acid cleaner – P M D UK Ltd
Procirc 909 – flux residue remover – P M D UK Ltd
Procirc 911 – microetch cleaner – P M D UK Ltd
Procirc 9110 – microetch cleaner – P M D UK Ltd
Procirc 9121 – microetch cleaner – P M D UK Ltd
Procirc 9122 – microetch cleaner – P M D UK Ltd
Procirc 9130 – microetch cleaner – P M D UK Ltd
Procirc 9132 – microetch cleaner – P M D UK Ltd
Procirc 921 – microetch – P M D UK Ltd
Procirc 9342 – tin lead stripper – P M D UK Ltd
Procirc 9361 – tin lead stripper – P M D UK Ltd
Procirc 9362 – tin lead stripper – P M D UK Ltd
Procirc 9390 – high capacity jig stripper for copper – P M D UK Ltd
Procirc 9401 – aqueous developer – P M D UK Ltd
Procirc 9421 – resist stripper – P M D UK Ltd
Procirc 9422 – resist stripper – P M D UK Ltd
Procirc 945 – resist stripper – P M D UK Ltd
Procirc 952(80) – post treatment – P M D UK Ltd
Procirc 961 – anti tarnish – P M D UK Ltd
Procirc 963 – activator – P M D UK Ltd
Procirc 964 – electroless nickel – P M D UK Ltd
Procirc 965 – pure gold immersion plating process – P M D UK Ltd
Procirc 9691 – antifoam – P M D UK Ltd
Procirc 971M – acid copper – P M D UK Ltd
Procirc 980 – immersion tin – P M D UK Ltd
Procirc 981TK – tin lead – P M D UK Ltd
Procirc 985 – solder conditioner – P M D UK Ltd
Procirc 986 – solder conditioner – P M D UK Ltd
Procirc 987 – solder conditioner – P M D UK Ltd
Procirc 9870 – solder conditioner – P M D UK Ltd
Procirc 9902 – I R Flux – P M D UK Ltd
Procirc 9945 – H.A.L. flux – P M D UK Ltd
Procirc 9990 – hot oil – P M D UK Ltd
Procirc 9991 – hot oil flux – P M D UK Ltd
Procirc SP230 – black oxide – P M D UK Ltd
Procirc SP236 – resist stripper – P M D UK Ltd
Procirc SP237 – resist stripper – P M D UK Ltd
Procirc SP239 – resist stripper – P M D UK Ltd
Procirc SP240 – resist stripper – P M D UK Ltd
Procirc SP263 – microetch – P M D UK Ltd
Procirc SP264 – acid cleaner – P M D UK Ltd
PROCITY – Artillus Illuminating Solutions Ltd
Proclad – protective weld surfacing system – F T V Proclad International Ltd
Proclean – cleansing fluid – M C D Virtak Ltd
Procol – Ball valves – Cee Vee
Procor – liquid waterproofing – Grace Construction Ltd
Procostat – liquid anti static film cleaner – M C D Virtak Ltd
Procter – machinery guards and security fencing, gates and ornamental railings – Procter Fencing
Proctor Ash Crusher – ash handling – James Proctor Ltd
Proctor Masts – dinghy, dayboat and one design spars – Selden Mast Ltd
Proctor Screw Elevator – materials handling – James Proctor Ltd
Proctors Pinelyptus – pastilles – Ernest Jackson & Co. Ltd
***Procyon (U.S.A.)** – parallel arm tapping machines – Meddings Machine Tools
Prodeck – A Proctor Group Ltd
Prodifa – R G K UK Ltd
prodir – quality pens – Connect Two Promotions Ltd
Prodor bond '50' – latex cement admixture – R I W Ltd
Prodorbond – hardwearing, jointless and resilient floor finish – R I W Ltd
Prodorcrete G.T. – high performance PU floor screeds – R I W Ltd
Prodorfilm Easy Clean – wall coating – R I W Ltd
Prodorflor – corrosion resisting jointless flooring – R I W Ltd
Prodorglaze – textured wall finish – R I W Ltd
Prodorguard – floor coating – R I W Ltd
Prodorite – R I W Ltd
Prodorshield – self levelling floor finish - coloured – R I W Ltd
***Proface (Switzerland)** – touch panel operator terminals – Oem - Automatic Ltd
***Profasi (Switzerland)** – infertility drugs – Merck Serono Ltd
Professional – decorative paints – Akzonobel
Professional – citrus based hand cleaners, (degreaser, adhesive remover) – Vindotco UK Ltd
Professional – kitchenette – Anson Concise Ltd
Professional Fee Protection – insurance companies & individuals against being investigated by customs & excise, the inland revenue, DSS etc & if they abide by the terms & conditions of the policy we pay their accountancy fees – Professional Fee Protection Ltd
Professionaltouch – Hair sprays & mousse – Statestrong Ltd
Profi – Antalis Mcnaughton
PROFI*ICE – ice makers – Electro Refrigeration
Profibus – communications protocol – Schneider
PROFILE – Hydraulic & Offshore Supplies Ltd
Profile (United Kingdom) – closed loop process control – Escada Systems Ltd
Profile – insulated sectional garage doors – P C Henderson Ltd
Profile – WC & basin – Armitage Shanks Ltd
Profile – ceiling mounted air cleaner – Trion The Division Of Ruskin Air Management Ltd
Profile – filter medium – Pall Europe Corporate Services
Profile – dental products – Prima Dental Group Ltd
Profile – Silhouette Beauty Equipment
Profile – bedroom based home insurance – M M A Insurance plc
Profile – steel shelving system – Rackline Ltd
***Profile (Japan)** – Pentax UK Ltd
Profile 2 – Half mask-respiratory protector – Scott International Ltd
Profile 2tm – Half mask-respiratory protector – Scott International Ltd
Profile Gold – bedroom based home insured for proposers aged 50 & over – M M A Insurance plc
Profile Partitions – Trac Office Contracts
Profile Series – loudspeakers – Tannoy Group Ltd
Profile Style – ring bingers, lever arch files & box files, laminated – Acco East Light Ltd

Profile TLC – light cured composits – Prima Dental Group Ltd

Profile Universal – compsites – Prima Dental Group Ltd

Profiles – The Winnen Furnishing Company

Profiles – changing and toilet cubicles – Bushboard Ltd

Profiline – Quality range of protective carrying cases – Hofbauer (UK) Ltd

ProFin – polishing compounds, buffs and equipment for industrial and hobbyist applications – Lea Manufacturing Co.

Profit Controller – weighing control systems – Stevens Group Ltd

Profit Haven – retail canopies & buildings – Clovis Lande Associates Ltd

Profit Improvement Program – engineering service – K B C Process Technology Ltd

Profitlich – Harrier Fluid Power Ltd

Profix – sell fixings and fasteners – Eurofix Ltd

ProFLASH – high intensity rechargeable emergency lamp – Doormen

Profloor Dynamic – A Proctor Group Ltd

Proflow 2/Actoflow – Scott International Ltd

Proflow SC – Asbestos Removal – Scott International Ltd

Proflow SC – modular powered or airline respiratory system – Scott International Ltd

Proflow SC Asbestos – modular powered or airline respiratory system – Scott International Ltd

Profoil – A Proctor Group Ltd

Profoil – Custom made pre-grooved foil faced thermal insulation boards creating a radiant surface suitable for use with all hot water underfloor heating systems. – Excel Packaging & Insulation Company Ltd

Proforce – Professional PPE covering Head, Hearing, Eye & Face, Respiratory and Hand protection and Workwear. – Process & Plant Equipment Ltd

Proform – Redsky It

Proform – steel shelving system – Rackline Ltd

Progluer – Autobox Machinery Ltd

Prognox – G E Healthcare

Programma – Alpha Electronics Southern Ltd

*Programme 3 (Italy) – storage wall – Ergonom Ltd

Programs – shop lights and down lighting – Luxonic Lighting plc

Progreen – Progreen Weed Control Solutions Ltd

Progress – drilling machines – Gate Machinery International Ltd

Progress (United Kingdom) – ECi Software Solutions Limited

Progress – Red House Industrial Services Ltd

Progress – clock keys and parts – Henri Picard & Frere

Progress Accountancy – Robert Half Ltd

Progression AEC – Redsky It

Progressive – Lubeline Lubricating Equipment

Progrind – Jones & Shipman Grinding Ltd

Prohood – Capture hood air measuring instrument – Airflow Developments Ltd

proifinox – Electro Refrigeration

PROINERT – Fike Protection Systems Ltd

Proiv – rapid application development (RAD) tool – Northgate & Arinso

*Projecem (France) – render – P E Hines & Sons Ltd

Projectiondesign – Lamphouse Ltd

Projectioneurope – Lamphouse Ltd

Projector – Display Device – Touch A V Ltd

Projectordress – grinding wheel forming attachment – P G T Ceewrite Ltd

Projectorscope – optical measuring instrument for precision machining – P G T Ceewrite Ltd

Prokia – Lamphouse Ltd

Proklens – automatic printing press parts washing machine and solvent recovery unit – Cope Engineering Ltd

Prolink – plastic modular belting – Forbo Siegling

ProLITE – hand torch – Doormen

Prolite – carbon fibre rolls – Cope Engineering Ltd

Prolou Ltd – Beauty Products – Prolou Ltd

Promag – electromagnetic flowmeter – Endress Hauser Ltd

Promaize – molasses based liquid – Rumenco Ltd

Proman – project monitoring & contract tour selection – Bensasson & Chalmers Ltd

Promask – full face mask respirators positive or negative pressure – Scott International Ltd

Promass – coriolis mass flowmeter – Endress Hauser Ltd

Promat – CNC production cylindrical grinders – Jones & Shipman Grinding Ltd

Promatec SA (France) – oil filtration systems – Haesler Machine Tools

Promatic – oil emulsion seperation filters – Turbex Ltd

*Promatic (Italy) – cartoning and case packing machines – Romaco Holdings UK Ltd

ProMatic – Hörmann (UK) Ltd

ProMatic Akku – Hörmann (UK) Ltd

ProMatic P – Hörmann (UK) Ltd

Promel – explosion suppressant for in tank fitment – G K N Aerospace Ltd

PROMET – process moisture analysers – Michell Instruments Ltd

Prometec – European Technical Sales Ltd

Promethean Activboard – Interactive board – Touch A V Ltd

Promindsa – natural red iron oxides – Omya UK Ltd

Prominent – European Technical Sales Ltd

Promisan – A cleaner disinfectant for destroying micro-organisms in washroom areas – Premiere Products Ltd

Promix – thermostatic mixing valves – Reliance Water Controls Ltd

Promo2u – Promo2u Ltd

Promod – standardised proteolytic enzymes – Biocatalysts Ltd

Promol – protein concentrates – Rumenco Ltd

Promoline – Quality range of injection moulded carrying cases – Hofbauer (UK) Ltd

Promot – European Technical Sales Ltd

Promot-A-Pack – promotional labels – C C L Labels Decorative Sleeves

Promotional Bugs – Logo Bugs Plus Ltd

Promotional t shirts – Avalon and Lynwood

Promotivation – travel company – B S Executive Travel Ltd

Promtek – microprocessor weighing systems – Promtek Ltd

Proops – Accounts model supply company – Linic Products Ltd

Propack PVC (LMF) – shrink pvc/shrink polyolefin – A B L Perpack 1985 Ltd

PropacPRO – instrument case – Schroff UK Ltd

Propafilm(tm) (United Kingdom) – a range of high performance BOPP films for packaging applications – Innovia Films Ltd

PropaFresh(tm) (United Kingdom) – a range of BOPP films for fresh produce applications – Innovia Films Ltd

ProPak – self contained breathing apparatus – Scott International Ltd

Propaque – paste opaque – Schottlander Dental Equipment Supplies

Propaream(tm) (United Kingdom) – thick BOPP films for cut paper – Innovia Films Ltd

Propellers Sterngear & Associated Marine Hardwear – Teignbridge Propellers International

Properseal – paramelt

Property – newspapers – Surrey & Berkshire Media Ltd

Property Advertiser – free weekly newspaper – The Bournemouth Daily Echo

Property Log Book – Property Log Book Company Ltd

'Property Matters' – Property – Jonathan Berney

Property Owners Insurance – specialist insurance – M M A Insurance plc

Property Standard – newspapers – Surrey & Berkshire Media Ltd

Propex – polypropylene filter fabric – Madison Filter

Propex – geotextile – Cordek Ltd

Proplene – PP pipes and fittings – C P V Ltd

Propozote – 100% polypropylene foam – Zotefoams plc

Propyform – British Vita plc

Propylat – Borgers Ltd

Propylex – British Vita plc

PROQUIS – Business/Quality Management Software – Proquis Ltd

ProRack – C P Cases Ltd

ProSafe – Dometic UK Ltd

Prosaw – coldsaws, bandsaws, hacksaws, friction saws and saw blade sharpeners – Prosaw Ltd

Prosaw – horizontal and vertical band saws – R K International Machine Tools Ltd

ProScan – motorised microscope stage – Prior Scientific Instruments Ltd

Proscco – stone cleaning chemicals & paintstrippers – Tensid UK Ltd

ProSeal – sealants for use in aerospace – PPG Aerospace

PROSEP – Hydraulic & Offshore Supplies Ltd

PROSEP (R) – prosep affinity chromatography products for the purification of proteins – Merc Millipore

ProServe – cd-rom with smart designer, product locator and smart marking – WAGO Ltd

Proshield – Helman Workwear

Proshifter – active ACL brace – Remploy Ltd

Prosoc – prosthetic sock – Remploy Ltd

Prosol – polishing compound removers – Lea Manufacturing Co.

Prosonic – non-contact ultrasonic level and flow measurement – Endress Hauser Ltd

Prospector – open frame steel surveyors tape – Fisco Tools Ltd

Prospex – Terrapin Ltd

Prostar OS – satin finish ink for trichromatics on paper and board – Fujifilm Sericol Ltd

Prosteam – software – K B C Process Technology Ltd

Proswim – swimming pool chemicals – S I S Chemicals Ltd

Protag – retail security products – Protag Retail Security

Protal – liquid coatings – Winn & Coales Denso Ltd

Protec – fire detection systems, emergency lighting and security systems – Protec Fire Detection

Protec – A Proctor Group Ltd

Protec Fibre Glass Towers – Accesscaff International Ltd

Protect – heavy duty floor and wall coatings – J L Lord & Son Ltd

Protect – hard surface cleaner and powerful disinfectant deodoriser – Evans Vanodine International plc

Protect – protection system against over voltage damage – WAGO Ltd

Protect-a-Pad – fire protection welding pads – Fireprotect Chester Ltd

Protect-a-Shield – light weight, high temperature insulation – Fireprotect Chester Ltd

Protect-a-Tape – fire protection window tape – Fireprotect Chester Ltd

Protect-a-Wrap – high temperature exhaust wrap – Fireprotect Chester Ltd

Protecta – Roodsafe Ltd

Protecta – solvent-free epoxy coating system – Gurit UK Ltd

Protectamat – contamination control mats – Dycem Ltd

Protective clothing distributors – Mapa Spontex

Protective & site equipment manufrs – Parker Merchanting Ltd

Protectomuffs – padded transit covers – Andrew Mitchell & Co. Ltd

Protector – cycle and motorcycle locks – Henry Squire & Sons Ltd

Protector – range of head, hearing, eye, face & respirator protection products – Scott International Ltd

Protector – underfloor safes – Securikey Ltd

Protector AFU 300 – Compressed airline filtration units – Scott International Ltd

Protector AFU 600 – Compressed airline filtration units – Scott International Ltd

Protector Safety – safety equipment – Bearwood Engineering Supplies

Protector Torweld – Respiratory Protection – Scott International Ltd

Protector Vision 2 – Full Face Respirator – Scott International Ltd

*Protectoseal (U.S.A.) – containers for inflammable liquids – Safety Unlimited

Protein Plus – milk-free protein dring (vegan) – G & G Food Supplies

ProteinLynx GS 2.0 (United Kingdom) – Global Protein-Informatics Platform – Waters

Protema – Tawi UK

Proten Drills – drills – Hammond & Co. Ltd

ProteomeWorks System (United Kingdom) – H.T. Proteomics Discovery System – Waters

Proteous – aero engines – Rolls-Royce plc

Protest – computer language – Nortel Networks UK Ltd

Proteus – labelling machine – Harland Machine Systems Ltd

Proteus – tools – Tatem Industrial Automation Ltd

Proteus – modular consumer units, B-type boards and circuit protection accessories; industrial switchgear and distribution boards – City Electrical Factors Ltd

Proteus – single loop controller – F G H Controls Ltd

Protex – fasteners latches handles – Protex Fasteners Ltd

Protex – respirators – Cuxson Gerrard & Company Ltd

Protex – flameproof cable glands – C M P UK Ltd

Protex BANDCLAMP (TM) – quick action band clamp down to 25mm diameter and capable of pressures up to 6.5 bar (100 p.s.i.) – Protex Fasteners Ltd

Protex CatchBolt – Protex Fasteners Ltd

Protex CATCHBOLT (R) – unique fastener design ensures all round rigidity and alignment – Protex Fasteners Ltd

Protex ProLatch – Protex Fasteners Ltd

Protex ProLatch (TM) The – fastener forces a door or panel to close against a seal and holds firmly in place – Protex Fasteners Ltd

Protexin – probiotics for animals & humans, natural beneficial feed supplements – Probiotics International Ltd

Protherm – high conductivity alloy – Uddeholm Steel Stockholders

Protherm – Materion Brush Ltd

Protim Clearchoice – above ground optimised wood preservative system (pretreat) – Protim Solignum

Protim Prevac System – treatment plant for the double vacuum impregnation of timber with protim wood preservative – Protim Solignum

Protim Solignum Architectural – Protim Solignum

Protim Solignum Timbertone – Protim Solignum

Protim Wood Preservatives – Protim Solignum

Protistor – Fuses – Bowers Ltd

Protistor – fuses – Mersen UK

Protocol – Office Seating – Bucon Ltd

Protofish – fish based protein – Rumenco Ltd

Protoktor – Protekor UK Ltd

Protolon (FL) – flat H.V. reeling cable 3-30 kV – Industrial Friction Materials Ltd

Protolon (FL) LWL – flat H.V. reeling cables 3-30 kV with integrated fibre optics – Industrial Friction Materials Ltd

Protolon (SMK) – H.V. reeling cable 3-30 kV – Industrial Friction Materials Ltd

Protolon (SMK) LWL – H.V. reeling cables 3-30 kV with integrated fibre optics – Industrial Friction Materials Ltd

Proton – Gas Detection – Scott International Ltd

Proton – software – Clinical Computing

Proton – adjustable door hinges – Paddock Fabrications Ltd

Protoplex – keg washing & CIP cleaning – The Proton Group Ltd

Protor – turbine monitoring system – Prosig Ltd

***Protostar (Germany)** – milling cutter – Macinnes Tooling Ltd

***Prototex (Germany)** – taps – Macinnes Tooling Ltd

***Prototyp (Germany)** – taps for cutting internal threads – Robert Speck Ltd

Protrak – waxed synthetic riding surface – Martin Collins Enterprises Ltd

Provac – sinks – M C D Virtak Ltd

Provatech (Switzerland) – food form machines – Meatec

Provectron – Britannia Lightning Prevectron Ltd

***Provencette** – Grill – Delifrance UK Ltd

Provengas – automatic gas proving – Black Teknigas & Electro Controls Ltd

Provex Range – Health & Safety bathroom accessories – Lakes Bathrooms Ltd

Proviacal – lime for civil engineering – Lhoist UK

Provident – provision of credit – Provident Financial

Provident Financial – provision of credit – Provident Financial

Provident Financial – home collected credit – Greenwood Personal Credit

Providental Personal Dental Plan – Western Provident Association Ltd

***Provideo** – Michael Stevens & Partners Ltd

Provincial pantile – clay – Sandtoft Holdings Ltd

Provision – software systems – Fretwell-Downing Hospitality Ltd

Provoice – alarm systems, announcement systems and communication systems, voice-activated alarm, announcement and communication systems which emit a voice message – Protec Fire Detection

ProVQ Limited – Provq Ltd

Prowall – A Proctor Group Ltd

Prowirl – vortex flowmeter – Endress Hauser Ltd

PROXAL – Hydraulic & Offshore Supplies Ltd

Proxima – Lamphouse Ltd

Proximity – fixed wireless access – Nortel Networks UK Ltd

Proxistor – Aztech Components Ltd

Proxistor – sensors – Sensortek

PROXISTOR – Powelectrics Ltd

PROXITRON – Proximity & Electronic Flow Switches – Francis and Francis Ltd

Proxxon – Minature power tools – The Toolpost

Prozone – B P plc

Prudhomme – European Technical Sales Ltd

Pryor – punches, type, engraved dies & machinery – Pryor Marking Technology Ltd

Pryor – stamping/marking – Bearwood Engineering Supplies

Pryormark – marking machinery – Pryor Marking Technology Ltd

PS Assessa – plld tax software – Northgate H R Ltd

PS enterprise – human resource management & payroll software for client server architecture – Northgate H R Ltd

PS Financials – f. accounting software – Northgate H R Ltd

pSeries – Mid Blue International Ltd

PSF Terrain – Melitzer Safety Equipment

PSI – Hydraulic & Offshore Supplies Ltd

PSI – ultra-high efficiency filters and air/om separators compressed air and vacuum industries together with housings and silencers – P S I Global Ltd

PSI GLOBAL LTD – Hydraulic & Offshore Supplies Ltd

Psicon – Geoquip Ltd

Psion – Allcode UK Ltd

Psion (teklogik) – Allcode UK Ltd

PSM Antistick Graphite – tanged laminated graphite – Klinger Ltd

PSM2 – magazine – Future Publishing Ltd

PT 5 – range of industrial ironing units – Electrolux Laundry Systems

PT 6 – range of industrial ironing units – Electrolux Laundry Systems

PT 7 – range of industrial ironing units – Electrolux Laundry Systems

PT 9 – range of industrial ironing units – Electrolux Laundry Systems

PT4 4 – range of industrial ironing units – Electrolux Laundry Systems

PTBCHA – perfume speciality – Quest International UK Ltd

PTBCHA High-Cis – perfume speciality – Quest International UK Ltd

PTC's – for motor – Rainer Schneider & Ayres

PTFE – Merseyside Metal Services

PTFE – all types of trade names for paint product – Protective Finishing Group

PTFE HOSE – Hydraulic & Offshore Supplies Ltd

PTG 600 – mechanical steel tubing – Benteler Distribution Ltd

PTG 700 – high tensile cold finished seamless tubes – Benteler Distribution Ltd

PTI TECHNOLOGIES – Hydraulic & Offshore Supplies Ltd

PTI Technology – Harrier Fluid Power Ltd

PTI WATER FILTERS – Hydraulic & Offshore Supplies Ltd

PTO Line – drive shafts and components – The Vapormatic Co. Ltd

PU & Nylon Tube – Gustair Materials Handling Equipment Ltd

PU7000 – Thermo Electrical

PU701 – Thermo Electrical

PU9000 – Thermo Electrical

PU9200 – Thermo Electrical

Publi Test – marketing services – Research International Group Ltd

Publicis (France) – advertising agency – Publicis Chemistry

Publisher Plus – dtp software – Xara Ltd

Puckator – Duftöle – Puckator Ltd

Puddle Chucker – fishing tackle – Drennan International Ltd

Puddlemop – small clean-up operations in shallow puddles, drains and culverts etc – Megator Ltd

PUDF – Merseyside Metal Services

Pudlo – building admixtures (waterproofers) plasticisers – David Ball Group plc

Puffin – children's fiction and non-fiction - paperback – Penguin Books Ltd

Pujol – Mercury Bearings Ltd

Pukka Pads – UK Office Direct

Pulimat – Harrier Fluid Power Ltd

Pullcap – cartridge fuse assemblies – A-Belco Ltd

Pullcap – modular fuse holders – Lawsons Fuses Ltd

Pullen – pumps, parts and fittings – Armstrong Holden Brooke Pullen Ltd

Pullen – kessel drainage technology (partnership) – Armstrong Holden Brooke Pullen Ltd

Pullen – homa submersible pump (partnership) – Armstrong Holden Brooke Pullen Ltd

Pullen Boosterpak – pumps, parts and fittings – Armstrong Holden Brooke Pullen Ltd

Pullman – self-contained buildings – Portakabin Ltd

***Pullman (Far East and Europe)** – mens, ladies and childrens shoes – G H Warner Footwear plc

Pulltap – Birchgrove Products

Pulltex – Wine accessories – Mitchell & Cooper Ltd

Pullway – telephone accessories – Commtel

Pullwinding Machines – Pultrex Ltd

Pulpit Steps – Accesscaff International Ltd

Pulpress – pumps – Armstrong Holden Brooke Pullen Ltd

Puls-O-Rev – pulse transmitters for use with any type of flow meter or counter – Jiskoot Ltd

PULS-TAKT – pulse phase pneumatic conveyor – Gericke Ltd

PULSAFE – Hydraulic & Offshore Supplies Ltd

Pulsafeeder – diaphragm metering pumps – Axflow

Pulsair – tonometer – Keeler Ltd

PULSAR – Ultrasonic level measurements – Halcyon Solutions

Pulsar – theatre and disco lighting and controls and effects – Pulsar Light Of Cambridge Ltd

Pulsar – embossing coder – Fischbein-Saxon

Pulsar – J Lacey Steeplejack Contractors Ltd

Pulsar – Alpha Electronics Southern Ltd

Pulsar Instruments – Sound level meters, dosimetry equipment, real time analyzers – Dakat Ltd

Pulsatron – ultrasonic plastic assembly systems – Guyson International Ltd

Pulse – wire managed desking – Senator International Ltd

Pulse – Resinex UK Ltd

Pulse – Cyclops Electronics Ltd

Pulse-flow – pulse phase pneumatic conveying system – Gericke Ltd

Pulse II – aerosol dispenser – Vectair Systems Ltd

Pulse Plus – hot water boilers – Fulton Boiler Works Ltd

Pulse Tools – Gustair Materials Handling Equipment Ltd

PULSEGUARD – Pulsation Accumulator – Pulsation Dampers At Pulseguard Ltd

Pulseguard – Jenex Ltd

PulseTrace – Cardinal Health U.K. 232 Ltd

PULSETWIN – Twin ported in and out separated, flow through path interception damper – Pulsation Dampers At Pulseguard Ltd

Pulstrak – pulse transmitters for use with any type of flowmeter – Jiskoot Ltd

Pultrex – fibre reinforced plastics machinery for the composites industry – Pultrex Ltd

Pultrusion Machines – Pultrex Ltd

Pulverbond – Coat Dust Substitutes – James Durrans & Sons Ltd

Pulverite – ground coal dust – James Durrans & Sons Ltd

Puma – Callsure Business Telephone & Fax Numbers

Puma – work shoes – Engelbert Strauss

***Puma (Taiwan)** – forklifts trucks – G H L Liftrucks Ltd

Puma (United Kingdom) – barrier systems – Motivation Traffic Control Ltd

Puma Stationary – Prressure washers – B & G Cleaning Systems Ltd

***Puma UK (United Kingdom)** – sports & goods distributors – Puma UK Trustees Ltd

Pump Control – K S B Ltd

Pump Drive – K S B Ltd

Pump Expert – K S B Ltd

Pump Plan – Grundfos Pumps Ltd

PUMPGUARD – Flow through flex tube damper for viscosities through 1 million cP and heavy particulate slurries – Pulsation Dampers At Pulseguard Ltd

Pumping Sets – for industrial applications – Thermal Engineering Systems Ltd

Pumpsil – Platinum-cured silicone tubing with laser ethced traceability. – Watson Marlow Pumps Ltd

PumpSmart – Goulds Pumps a Division of ITT Industries Ltd

Pumptronics – electronic garage commercial fuel pump manufacturers – Pumptronics Europe Ltd

***Punch (Cuba, Jamaica, Europe and Honduras)** – cigars – Hunters & Frankau Ltd

***Punch** – Anitox

Punch Wizard – automatic punch – Acco UK Ltd

Punjana – tea distributors, importers, blenders and packers – Punjana Ltd

Pur-a-Gold – acid gold electroplating processes – Cookson Electronics Ltd

Pura – solid vegatable oil-vegatable lard – A D M Pura Foods Ltd

Pura Foods – liquid cooking oils for the retail and foodservice trades standard extended and long life frying oils for the foodservice market – A D M Pura Foods Ltd

Pura Foods Products – baking and catering fats and oils cake and pastry margarine shortenings bread fats and emulsions confectionery fats solid frying fats – A D M Pura Foods Ltd

Pura Frymax – solid vegatable frying fat – A D M Pura Foods Ltd

Pura Gold Cup – range of margarines and speards – A D M Pura Foods Ltd

Pura Light Touch – liquid low cholesterol alternative to butter – A D M Pura Foods Ltd

***Purafil (U.S.A.)** – odour and corrosive gas treatment – Higgins & Hewins Ltd

PURAIR – Range of 'stand alone' Anaesthetic Gas Scavenging Systems – MEC Medical Ltd

Purasorb – sorbent resins – Purolite International Ltd

Purchasing Management Services – purchasing, stock control and stores training courses – P M S York Ltd

Purcon – recruitment, training and consultancy services in the field of purchasing and supply chain management – Purcon Consultants Ltd

Pure Air (United Kingdom) – air purification & filtration and odour control. – Consort Equipment Products

Pure & Clear Collection – shampoo and conditioner – Alberto-Culver Co. (UK) Ltd

Pure Cotton Crepe DK – Sirdar Spinning Ltd

Pure Malt – malt extracts – Pure Malt Products Ltd

Pure Metals – West Brook Resources Ltd

Pure Power – uninterruptible power supplies – Claude Lyons Ltd

Pure Roast – malt extracts – Pure Malt Products Ltd

Pure Water Cooling – stainless steel low conductivity water cooling system – Thermal Engineering Systems Ltd

Purecoat – high quality arc spray coating – Metallisation Ltd

PureFlo – water treatment – J S Humidifiers plc

Pureflo – respiratory protection – Helmet Integrated Systems Ltd

Purelite Airshield – respiratory protection – Helmet Integrated Systems Ltd

PurePower – upright vacuum cleaners – Hoover Ltd

Pureprene – PureSil Technologies Ltd

Puresil – PureSil Technologies Ltd

Puretrans – PureSil Technologies Ltd

PureWeld XL – high quality weldable TPE tubing peristaltic pumps – Watson Marlow Pumps Ltd

Purewell – Atmospheric gas fired modular boilers – Hamworthy Heating Ltd

Purflux – Harrier Fluid Power Ltd

***Purgard (Germany)** – transparent MDI container – The Adelphi Group

Purge Dams – Pipestoppers

Purgex 2000 – purging compounds – Clariant UK Ltd

Purilan – skylights – Ubbink UK Ltd

Purimachos – refractory cements – Vitcas Ltd

Puripore – reticulated polyether and polyester polyurethanes – Vitec

Purisoure – nutrients for effluent treatment – Chance & Hunt Ltd

Purita – drinking fountain – Armitage Shanks Ltd

Puritabs – M S D Animal Health

Puritabs Maxi – water purification tablets – M S D Animal Health

Purity Plus – medicated lotions and skin cleansers – F M C G Ltd

Purlees – Window stickers – Purlfrost Ltd
Purlfrost – window film – Purlfrost Ltd
Puro – drinking fountain – Armitage Shanks Ltd
Purofine – narrow bead size range ion exchange resins – Purolite International Ltd
Purolator – filters – C T P Wipac Ltd
Purolite – synthetic ion-exchange resins – Purolite International Ltd
Puropack – packed bed systems – Purolite International Ltd
Purosep – powdered non exchange resins, analytical use – Purolite International Ltd
Purple Pineapple – Kent Frozen Foods Ltd
Push Flash – concealed flush tank actuator – Sheardown Engineering Ltd
PUSH-LOK – Hydraulic & Offshore Supplies Ltd
Push Purge – patented feature of moisture measuring equipment – M C M
Pushcorp – tools – Tatem Industrial Automation Ltd
Pushflush – concealed flush tank actuator – Sheardown Engineering Ltd
PushLock (United Kingdom) – safety eyebolt – Latchways plc
Pusila – B P plc
Putzmeister – C E S Hire Ltd
Putzmeister – Harrier Fluid Power Ltd
Puzzle Collection – magazine – H Bauer Publishing
PVC Profiles – Boomer Industries Ltd
PVDF – Merseyside Metal Services
PVR – rotant pumps – AESpump
PX – disinfectants – Killgerm Group Ltd
PX Filtration – Harrier Fluid Power Ltd
Py – powder, spray and aerosol containing natural pyrethrum – Vitax Ltd
Pygme – positive displacement fixed and variable output pump – Grosvenor Pumps Ltd
Pyle National – Connectors – Dax International Ltd
Pyle National – Dax International Ltd
Pynol – strong pine disinfectant – Evans Vanodine International plc
Pynolic – pine disinfectant – Evans Vanodine International plc
Pyraclean – lighting diffusers – Lamplighter Plastic Mouldings Ltd
Pyrakill – Forward Chemicals Ltd
Pyralin – polyimide coatings – Du Pont UK Ltd
Pyralux – flexible composites – Du Pont UK Ltd
Pyralvex – mouth ulcers treatment – Norgine International Ltd
Pyramark – consumables for marking and stencil cutting machines – Pyramid Engineering & Manufacturing Co. Ltd
Pyramat – pyramid vinyl safety matting – Jaymart Roberts & Plastics Ltd
Pyramid – vacuum ovens, welders and glove box systems – Pyramid Engineering Services Co. Ltd
Pyramid – investment account – Leek United Building Society
Pyramids – mosquito nets – Swisstulle UK Ltd
***Pyran S (Germany)** – fire resisting glass – Schott UK Ltd
Pyratak – fire resistant and anti bandit – Rankins Glass Company Ltd
Pyratox – chemical treatment for closed circuit heating and chilled water system – Aldous & Stamp Ltd
Pyrenees – shoes – Patrick Shoes Ltd
Pyrex – laboratory glassware – Bibby Scientific Ltd
Pyrex – flat head resistant glass – J B Treasure & Co. Ltd
Pyristor – laminating cement systems – Bowers Ltd
Pyro-Bloc – fibre modules – Thermal Ceramics UK Ltd
Pyro-lam – insulated fire resistant glass – Fendor Ltd
Pyro-lithic – integrity fire resistant glass – Fendor Ltd
Pyro-rest – fire engineered glass restraint, suspension and expansion system (patent pending) – Fendor Ltd
Pyroballistic – fire resistant and bullet resistant – Rankins Glass Company Ltd
Pyroban – permanent F.R. for curtain linings – P W Greenhalgh & Co. Ltd
Pyrobel – fire resistant glass – Rankins Glass Company Ltd
Pyrobelite – fire resistant glass – Rankins Glass Company Ltd
Pyroclear – fire resistant & low reflective glass – Rankins Glass Company Ltd
Pyrodry – non-permanent F.R. for curtain linings – P W Greenhalgh & Co. Ltd
Pyrofine – flame retardants for paper and cotton – Atosina UK Ltd
Pyroflex – fire retardant foam for contract furnishings – Vitec
Pyroforane 1211 – bromochlorodifluoromethane – Atosina UK Ltd
Pyroforane 1301 – bromotrifluoromethane – Atosina UK Ltd
Pyroguard Clear – fire resisting safety glass – C G I International Ltd
Pyroguard Wired – fire resisting safety glass – C G I International Ltd
Pyrolith – porous ceramic medias – Fairey Industrial Ceramics
Pyrometer – Radir Ltd
Pyronyl – nylon flame retardants – Perrite
Pyropress – pressure, temperature, flow level and speed sensing devices, valves and control panels and systems – Pyropress Engineering Co. Ltd
Pyrosilo – storage racking – Rack International UK Ltd
Pyrosorb – British Vita plc
Pyrosorb – fire resistant acoustic foam and composites to class 0 British Building Regulations – Vitec
Pyrosten – fire resistant glass – C G I International Ltd
Pyrotek Engineering – engineers materials for the aluminium industry – Pyrotek Engineering Materials Ltd
Pyrovent – smoke ventilation – Yule Catto & Co plc
Pyruma – fire cement – Vitcas Ltd
Python (United Kingdom) – water repellent outdoor fabric – Carrington Career & Work Wear
Python – cranes – Panavision Grips Ltd
Pyxel – variable output leak free diaphragm pump – Grosvenor Pumps Ltd

Q

Q – motor oil – B P plc
Q. – darts flights – Unicorn Products Ltd
Q.4 – quad video display system – Tecton Ltd
Q.8 – Kuwait Petroleum International Lubricants UK Ltd
Q-Build – modular stage and tiering (demountable) – Stage Systems Ltd
Q.C. Series – signal conditioning instrumentation 19" rack mounting – Lee-Dickens Ltd
Q.E.1 & Q.E.2 – electronic programmers – Grasslin UK Ltd
Q.E.D. – audio products – Armour Home Electronics
Q.E.D. Quorn Engine Developments – parts for the Lotus Ford twin cam, Vauxhall 16 valve 2 litre and Rover K Series engines, together with machining, building and testing services – Q E D
Q. Flights – Unicorn Products Ltd
Q Flow (United Kingdom) – a lotus notes bases document flow product – Pacific Solutions International Ltd
Q-Fog – cyclic corrosion testers – Q-Lab Corporation
Q.L. Conveyor – mobile or transportable belt conveyor – Parker Plant Ltd
Q-Lab – natural outdoor test facility in Florida and Arizona – Q-Lab Corporation
Q-Lon – seal for PVC-U windows and doors – Schlegel UK
Q M I Atmospheric Detector – for all machine rooms with fuel, lubricating or hydraulic oil lines; purifier rooms, bow thrusters, and steering gear. – Quality Monitoring Instruments Q M I
Q M I Engine Detector – for crankcases gear and chain cases, pumps, compressors, gear boxes, and thrust bearings. – Quality Monitoring Instruments Q M I
Q M I Multiplex – oil mist detection systems – Quality Monitoring Instruments Q M I
Q Mark – security thread – T S S I Sytems
Q.P. The Quotepanel – insurance brokers – Bromwich Insurance Brokers
Q-Panel – steel and aluminium substrates for testing applied coatings. – Q-Lab Corporation
Q-Phos – phosphate/phosphated pre-treated steel test panels. – Q-Lab Corporation
Q Plant & Haulage – plant & haulage – Notts Contractors Ltd
Q-Plus – modular tiering (demountable) – Stage Systems Ltd
Q'Preme – ladies' and children's underwear and slumberwear – Headen & Quarmby Ltd
Q.R. – compost activator – Chase Organics
Q.R.O. 90 Supreme – hot work die steel for forging and aluminium extrusion – Uddeholm Steel Stockholders
Q Range Actuator – Single-phase quarter-turn direct drive electric actuator – Rotork plc
Q.S. – B P plc
Q.S. – clothing – Store 21
Q'Sol – neutral detergent – Evans Vanodine International plc
Q-Sun – xenon based light fastness tester. – Q-Lab Corporation
Q.T.C. – quick tool change – Joseph Rhodes Ltd
***Q-Tech** – Wavelength Electronics Ltd
Q-Tof micro (United Kingdom) – Benchtop 'Q-TOF' LC-MS-MS – Waters
Q-Tof Ultima (United Kingdom) – High performance 'Q-TOF' MALDI/API – Waters
Q-Track – natural sunlight concentrator. – Q-Lab Corporation
Q.V.F. – borosilicate glass process plant and pipeline – De Dietrich Process Systems Ltd
Q.X.R. – premium motor oil – B P plc
Q8 – Hammond Lubricants & Chemicals Ltd
QAS Systems Ltd, The – QuickAddress range of addresss management software works interactivily finding an address from a postcode or finding a postcode from a partial addresss. All databased on the Royal Mail's Postcode Address File (PAF) – Experian Q A S
Qasar – range of automated blood grouping systems – H T Z Ltd
QD – nurse call systems – Wandsworth Group Ltd
QE XXX – structural reinforcement – Gurit UK Ltd
QHP – Hydraulic & Offshore Supplies Ltd
Qiang jang – vacuum pumps – AESpump
QM1 & QM2 – electro mechanical programmers – Grasslin UK Ltd
QPA – microwave components – Q-Par Angus Ltd
qsb – valves – AESpump
QTC – Cyclops Electronics Ltd
Quad – amplifiers, loud speakers, radio tuner units and compact disc players – Quad Electroacoustics Ltd
Quadbloc – 4-way mains outlet – Schurter Ltd
Quadbreak – fusegear – Schneider
Quadcare – hand washing preparations – Quadralene Ltd
***Quadco (U.S.A.)** – control levers – Ringspann UK Ltd
Quadcompact – Grundfos Pumps Ltd
Quadnet – 4-loop networkable (up to 250 panels) for large buildings eg. airports. – Fike Safety Technology Ltd
Quadoptic – vehicle head lamps – C T P Wipac Ltd
Quadpanel – quarter turn latch – Zygology Ltd
Quadra – four post electro-hydraulic platform lifts for vehicles – Tecalemit Garage Equipment Co. Ltd
Quadra Chek – HEIDENHAIN GB LTD
Quadraflex – triple layer forming fabric with flat strand – Heimbach UK
Quadralene – principle cleaning and hygiene products general trade – Quadralene Ltd
Quadraloc – synchronous digital drive locking system – Parker
Quadran – custom weave – Gurit UK Ltd
Quadrangle – circular recessed architectural lighting – Designplan Lighting Ltd
Quadrant – 2D bulkhead lighting – Designplan Lighting Ltd
Quadrant – plastic engineering materials – Davis Industrial Plastics Ltd
Quadrant – shower enclosures and trays – Ideal Standard Ltd
Quadrant Gas – natural gas – Shell Gas Direct
Quadrant Visual Solutions – audio visual hire & presentation sales & service – Quadrant Security Group Ltd
Quadratainer – square plastic containers – Greif UK Ltd
Quadring – energy saving bulk head lighting – Designplan Lighting Ltd
QUADRING – Hydraulic & Offshore Supplies Ltd
Quadro – Kranzle UK Ltd
Quadro – Cloakroom Solutions Ltd
QuadroPulse – highpower quadruple magnetic stimulator – Magstim Co. Ltd
Quadscan – Fixed System Gas Detection Range – Scott International Ltd
Quadvent – Britax P S V Wypers Ltd
Quadwall – intermediate bulk containers (ibc) – Quadwall Ltd
Quaestor – legal accounting time recording system – Professional Technology UK Ltd
Quaife – precision engineers – R T Quaife Engineering Ltd
QUAKER CHEMICAL LTD – Hydraulic & Offshore Supplies Ltd
qualatis – Quality and consultacncy – I Q Management Systems
Qualcast Classic Electric 30 – cylinder lawnmower – Bosch Lawn & Garden Ltd
Qualcast Classic Petrol 35 S – cylinder lawnmower – Bosch Lawn & Garden Ltd
Qualcast Classic Petrol 43 S – cylinder lawnmower – Bosch Lawn & Garden Ltd
Qualcast Cobra 32 – rotary lawnmower – Bosch Lawn & Garden Ltd
Qualcast Concorde 32 – cylinder lawnmower – Bosch Lawn & Garden Ltd
Qualcast Easi-Lite 28 – hover mower – Bosch Lawn & Garden Ltd
Qualcast Easi-Lite 34 – hover mower – Bosch Lawn & Garden Ltd
Qualcast Easi-trak 32 – rotary lawnmower – Bosch Lawn & Garden Ltd
Qualcast Elan 32 – cylinder lawnmower – Bosch Lawn & Garden Ltd
Qualcast Hedge Master 370 – garden care – Bosch Lawn & Garden Ltd
Qualcast Hedge Master 420 – garden care – Bosch Lawn & Garden Ltd
Qualcast Hedge Master 480 – garden care – Bosch Lawn & Garden Ltd
Qualcast Lawn Raker 32 – garden care – Bosch Lawn & Garden Ltd
Qualcast Panther 30 – cylinder lawnmower – Bosch Lawn & Garden Ltd
Qualcast Power-Line – extension cable – Bosch Lawn & Garden Ltd
Qualcast Powertrak 34 – rotary lawnmower – Bosch Lawn & Garden Ltd
QUALCAST POWERTRAK 400 – rotary lawnmower – Bosch Lawn & Garden Ltd
Qualcast Q.X. Lawn Scarifer Cassette – 12in, 14in and 17in cassettes – Bosch Lawn & Garden Ltd
Qualdis – Forward Chemicals Ltd
Qualicol – shirt & garment interlinings – P W Greenhalgh & Co. Ltd

Qualiprobe – ion-selective electrode – E D T Direct Ion Ltd

Qualitair – standard air conditioning units – Eaton-Williams Group Ltd

Qualitas – domestic suites – Armitage Shanks Ltd

Quality Catorpack – Robinson Young Ltd

Quality Equipment – agricultural engineers – G E Baker UK Ltd

QUALITY HYDRAULIC POWER LTD – Hydraulic & Offshore Supplies Ltd

Quality Irrigation – supply of automatic commercial and private landscape irrigation systems to include design, installation and supervisory package – Quality Irrigation Ltd

***Quality Lifts (Spain)** – passenger & goods lifts – Quality Lift Products Ltd

Quality Lighting Design – Light Fantastic

Quality Management Systems – weighing systems – Stevens Group Ltd

Quality & Quality 6556 – Popular, Reliable and Value for money – Chi Yip Group Ltd

Quality Semiconductor – Cyclops Electronics Ltd

Quality Tech – Cyclops Electronics Ltd

Quallafil – Extralife – Platt & Hill Ltd

Quallofil – Supreme – Platt & Hill Ltd

Quallofil – polyester performance insulation – Du Pont UK Ltd

Qualserv – methodology for measuring and assessing customers' perception of service quality – C I Research

Qualtec – UK Office Direct

Qualter & Smith Drilling machines – Phil Geesin Machinery Ltd

Qualtermatic – automatic bottom dump skip – Qualter Hall & Co. Ltd

Quantacure – photoiniators and co initiators – Pentagon Fine Chemicals Ltd

Quantaflex – electroluminescent illumination system – Danielson Ltd

QuanTanium – Coatings reinforced with titanium – Whitford Ltd

Quantase – medical diagnostic kits – Axis Shield Ltd

Quantec – Addressable call system – C-Tec Security Ltd

Quantec Surveyor – C-Tec Security Ltd

Quantic – ultrasonic flaw detector – Baugh & Weedon Ltd

QUANTIS – Gears – Baldor UK

QuantMuster – Monier Ltd

Quantum – cast aluminium lever furniture – Paddock Fabrications Ltd

Quantum – clock – E A Combs Ltd

Quantum – large programmable logic controllers – Schneider

Quantum 1 – circular surface and semi recessed vandal resistant architectural lighting – Designplan Lighting Ltd

Quantum 2 – circular surface and semi recessed vandal resistant architectural lighting – Designplan Lighting Ltd

Quantum 530 – carpets – Interface Europe Ltd

Quantum System – artificial limb – Ortho Europe Ltd

Quantum Technology – Impac Infrared Ltd

Quantum/V.S. – software – Electronic Data Processing plc

Quantum2 – Coatings reinforced with ceramic particles – Whitford Ltd

Quarry Products Association – quarry products association is the trade association for the aggregates, asphalt, surfacing, ready-mixed concrete, lime, silica sand, slag recycled aggregates and mortar industries – Mineral Products Association

Quarry Tours – Tourist attraction – Quarry Tours Ltd

Quartermaster – modular shelving – Bedford Shelving Ltd

Quartermate – pre milking teat dip spray – Delaval

Quartet – UK Office Direct

Quartet – fabrics – Today Interiors Ltd

Quartsan – composite material – Franke Sissons Ltd

Quartz – Roof Units Ltd

Quartz – turret punch presses – Joseph Rhodes Ltd

Quartz Auto – gas wallheater – Robinson Willey

Quartz Manual – gas wallheater – Robinson Willey

***Quartzo 88 (Italy)** – silicas quartz aggregate – MFS Stone Surfaces Ltd

Quasar – Quasar range Heidrun Europlastic Products – Lunex Ltd

Quash – sanitiser that removes grease & lipstick from drinking glasses – The Proton Group Ltd

Quasilan – adhesive – Baxenden Chemicals Ltd

Quatro brush – Claens channels in sewage treatment works – Quatroserve Ltd

Quatro clean – Portable washdown trailer – Quatroserve Ltd

Quatro lift – Lifting gear – Quatroserve Ltd

Quatro Maxi screen – Flitration material, sewage – Quatroserve Ltd

Quatron – Komet Ltd

Quatroscreen – Filtration material, sewage – Quatroserve Ltd

Quattrix – cut off blades and holders (parting off) – J J Churchill Ltd

Quattro – automatic washing machine/dishwasher – Hoover Ltd

Quattro Compact – label overprinting system – Weyfringe Labelling Systems

Quattro Easy Logic – automatic washing machine – Hoover Ltd

Quattro micro (United Kingdom) – Compact 'triple' quadrupole – Waters

Quattro Plus – label overprinting system – Weyfringe Labelling Systems

Quattro Ulitima (United Kingdom) – Very high performance 'triple' quadrupole – Waters

Quattromill – Seco Tools UK Ltd

Quaver – door handles – Allgood

Quay – circular surface and recessed vandal resistant architectural lighting – Designplan Lighting Ltd

Qube – modular airline equipment – Parker Hannifin Ltd

Qubic Fonts – typeface software – Monotype Imaging Ltd

QUD – Harrier Fluid Power Ltd

Queen Anne – silver plated tableware – Queen Anne Tableware Ltd

Queen's Ware – fine earthenware tableware and giftware – Wedgewood Travel Ltd

Queensbury Fabrics (United Kingdom) – Worsted Mens Suiting Fabric – John Foster Ltd

Queensbury Textiloes (United Kingdom) – Worsted Mens Suiting Fabric – John Foster Ltd

Quelfire – PVC pipe fire stop seal, fire stop expansion joint system, air transfer grilles, intufoam, QF1, QF4, steelcote intumescent coating for steel, intumescent varnish for timber, fire retardant emulsion SS system and mastic – Quelfire Ltd

Quell – Sound masking systems – Apple Dynamics Ltd

Quenchtex – lubricants – Chevron

Quendila – B P plc

Quendrila – industrial oil – B P plc

Quentin Books – book publisher and dealer in secondhand and antiquarian books – The Marsh Agency Ltd

Quenvhas – Business systems – RFDS Consultants

***Querciabella (Tuscany)** – Pol Roger Ltd

Querella – Softex-Permatex clothing fabrics – J B Broadley

Quest for Quality – quality improvement programme designed by carers for the healthcare industry – Christie & Co. Ltd

Quest-i – Intangible analysis suite – Information Strategies Key Intangible Value

Quester – management consultants – Quester Assessment Systems Ltd

Question Mark – computer software – Question Mark Computing Ltd

Questra – Resinex UK Ltd

Queue Management Systems – queue control – Lonsto International Ltd

Quevebuster – Queueing Systems – O W L Electronics Ltd

Quicher – screw sorters – Baltec UK Ltd

Quick-Change – moulds – Thermacore Ltd

Quick & Easy Cross Stitch – magazine – Future Publishing Ltd

Quick Fit – traffic management sign frame – Nationwide Signs Ltd

QUICK-FIT – Hydraulic & Offshore Supplies Ltd

Quick Fix – Display Wizard Ltd

Quick Serve – tap – Worldwide Dispensers

Quick-Strip – special bag used for removing asbestos – Quick-Strip Ltd

***Quick-Wedge (U.S.A.)** – screw-holding screwdrivers – Longs Ltd

***Quickfit** – inspectors test kit – Vernon Morris Utility Solutions Ltd

Quickfit – interchangeable jointed glassware – Bibby Scientific Ltd

QuickFit – couplings, flange adaptors and stepped couplings – Viking Johnson

Quickfix 2 – washroom cubicle system – Premdor Crosby Ltd

Quickie – E P C

Quickie – J & S Lewis Ltd

***QuickLink** – Mechline Developments Ltd

Quickloc – quick release fasteners – Bollhoss Fastenings Ltd

Quicklock – patent doors – L B B C Technologies

Quickmast – epoxy and polyester resins – Don Construction Products Ltd

***Quickmill (Canada)** – gantry milling machines – Meddings Machine Tools

***Quicks (United Kingdom)** – bowstrings, finger guards, archery clothing, target faces, and other accessories – Quicks Archery

Quicksafe.co.uk – Retail Websites Limited

Quickset – calibrated torque screwdrivers – Torque Leader

Quickshelf – bolt free heavy duty shelving – Barton Storage Systems Ltd

***Quicksilver (U.S.A.)** – inflatable ribs & dinghys – E P Barrus

Quicksilver – cellular telephone and car audio accessories – Quicksilver Automotive

Quicksilver and Alchemy – hot air levelling equipment for printed circuit board industry hot air levelling equipment – Circuit Engineering Marketing Company Ltd

Quickstep – N W Flooring

QuickStep – D G Heath Ltd

Quickstep Travel – buses – First Group plc

Quicktest – cliff connectors – Cliff Electronic Components Ltd

Quickwork – Red House Industrial Services Ltd

Quiet – pneumatic components – Bosch Rexroth Ltd

QUIET – Hydraulic & Offshore Supplies Ltd

Quiet-Duct – duct silencer – I A C Company Ltd

Quiet Life – Natural Remedy for Relief of Stress – G R Lane Health Products Ltd

Quiet-Vent – ventilating silencer – I A C Company Ltd

Quietaire – pneumatic silencers – Norgren Ltd

QUIETAIRE – Hydraulic & Offshore Supplies Ltd

Quietis – hermetic low noise condensing units and packs – Thermofrost Cryo plc

Quietwin – in line twin fan – Nuaire Ltd

Quietzone Acoustic Absorbers – sound absorption and control of reverberant noises – Knauf Insulation Ltd

Quietzone Acoustic Blanket – to improve the acoustic performance of timber stud walls and partitions – Knauf Insulation Ltd

Quietzone Acoustic Floor Slab – acoustic insulation of floors – Knauf Insulation Ltd

Quietzone Acoustic Sealant – improves sound performance of partitions – Knauf Insulation Ltd

Quietzone Acoustic Shield – acoustic insulation for roofs and walls – Knauf Insulation Ltd

Quietzone Floor Foam – to improve impact sound resistance of floors – Knauf Insulation Ltd

Quietzone Floorlam – acoustic insulation for floors – Knauf Insulation Ltd

Quietzone Liner Board – acoustic insulation for walls and ceilings – Knauf Insulation Ltd

Quietzone Mufti-Lag – acoustic sheet for lagging pipes and ducts – Knauf Insulation Ltd

Quietzone Partition Batt – acoustic insulation for general purpose use – Knauf Insulation Ltd

Quietzone Partition Roll – acoustic insulation for partitions – Knauf Insulation Ltd

Quietzone Resilient Channel – galvanised steel channel to improve the sound insulation of partitions – Knauf Insulation Ltd

Quietzone Sonic Liner – provides acoustic attenuation for air-conditioning ductwork and air handling units – Knauf Insulation Ltd

Quietzone Sound Deadening Quilt – to improve sound impact resistance of floors – Knauf Insulation Ltd

Quietzone Studio Mattress – sound absorption for studios and auditoria – Knauf Insulation Ltd

Quikaboard – Q K Honeycomb Products Ltd

Quikapanels – Q K Honeycomb Products Ltd

Quikfreeze – Bishop Pipe Freezing Ltd

Quikgo – hollow tube – Fenner Drives Ltd

Quikpoint – Mortar Repointing Gun – PWM Distribution

Quikref – yearly calendar – Charles Letts Group Ltd

Quiksteel – darts and shafts – Unicorn Products Ltd

Quillon – germicidal detergent – Evans Vanodine International plc

Quincy – Harrier Fluid Power Ltd

Quincy – air compressors – M I T Ltd

Quintas & Quintas – Offspring International

***Quintero (Cuba, Jamaica, Europe and Honduras)** – cigars – Hunters & Frankau Ltd

Quintessa Art Collection – prints – The Quintessa Art Collection

Quintesse – shower surround – Matki plc

Quintozene Wettable Powder – contact fungicide – Bayer Crop Science

Quitetite – valves – David Auld Valves Ltd

Quiz – female fashion – Tarak Manufacturing Co. Ltd

Qunicy – Submarine Manufacturing & Products Ltd

Quo Vadis – UK Office Direct

Quorna – narrow fabrics – M Wright & Sons Ltd

QUV – fluorescent UV accelerated weathering testers – Q-Lab Corporation

Qwicket – mororised pedestrian gate – Frontier Pitts Ltd

***Qwik Time (China)** – metronomes – John Hornby Skewes & Co. Ltd

***Qwik Tune (China)** – guitar tuners – John Hornby Skewes & Co. Ltd

***Qwikbrew** – bulk coffee brewer – Marco Beverage Systems Ltd

Qwikline II – consumer unit – Schneider

R

R.12 Epoxy Jointing Cement – jointing cement – J L Lord & Son Ltd

R & A – The Royal & Ancient Golf Club Of St Andrews

R.A.-Discharger – rotary arm bin discharger – Gericke Ltd

R.A.M. – plastic modular belts and slat top conveyor chains – Sigma Industries Ltd

R and A – The Royal & Ancient Golf Club Of St Andrews

R'ANGLE – strong right angle attachment in thin materials – Zygology Ltd

R.B. – civil engineers – Roger Bullivant Ltd

R.B.2 Airsporter – air rifle – B S A Guns UK Ltd

R.B.2 Airsporter - SS Carbine – air rifle – B S A Guns UK Ltd

R.B.2 Stutzen – air rifle – B S A Guns UK Ltd

R.B.211 – aero engines – Rolls-Royce plc

R.B. Booms – river booms – Oil Pollution Environmental Control Ltd

R-B International – cranes and excavators – R B Cranes Ltd

R. Bickley – pest control service – R Bickley & Co.

R.C. Brady – leather bookmarks, key fobs and a wide range of souvenirs and gifts – R C Brady & Co.

R.C.C. Business Mortgages – access to committed lines of finance for business purchase or refinance – Christie & Co. Ltd

R.C.C. Insurance Brokers – arranged bespoke business insurance including life assurance – Christie & Co. Ltd

R.C.C. Retaining Walls – retaining wall units, bulk storage units & universal temp & perm barriers – Tarmac Precast Concrete Ltd

R.C. Treatt – manufacture materials for aromatic fragrances – R C Treatt & Co. Ltd

R-Can Environmental – The manufacturer of the largest number of 'domestic' and 'smaller Industrial' UV units in the world. – U V O 3 Ltd

R.D. – precision locators – Radio Detection

R & D Laboratories – Parent Company – R & D Laboratories Ltd

R.D. Precision Locators – locating underground services – Radio Detection

R E Brown underwriting ltd – Markel UK Ltd

R.E. Forsters – upholsterers, furniture and cabinet makers – R E Forster Ltd

R.E.V. Gomm – badges & souvenir giftware – Shaw Munster Ltd

R.F. Gain – RF transistors – Richardsons R F P D Ltd

R.F. & R.M. Open Presses – open fronted presses – Joseph Rhodes Ltd

R.F.U. England – rugby – Rugby Football Union

***R.-Flex (Germany)** – flexible abrasives – Klingspor Abrasives Ltd

R.&G. – gauge-switches and instruments for indication and control of liquid levels and flows – Bayham Ltd

R.G. Engineering – injection moulders – R G Engineering

R.G.T. – reliance geared transducer – Reliance Precision

R.H.D.S. Double Sided Press – double sided presses – Joseph Rhodes Ltd

R H Form – Sitsmart Ltd

R.H.L. (United Kingdom) – hydraulic piston motors and pumps – Rotary Power Ltd

R.H. Open Front Presses – open fronted presses – Joseph Rhodes Ltd

R.I.T.B. – Stacatruc

R.I. VALVES – Hydraulic & Offshore Supplies Ltd

R. & J.M. Place – soft fruit growers, processors, bean sprout growers & processors, contract freezers, importers & exporters of frozen fruit – Place UK Ltd

R. & J. Partington – furnishing fabrics, cambrics sheetings, linings, satins and flame proof barrier fabrics – R & J Partington

R.M.303 – din rail low cost electricity meter – Northern Design Ltd

R.M.F. – micro filtration – Koppen & Lethem Ltd

R.M.J.M. – design consultants – R M J M Ltd

R & M Metal Finishing – R & M Metal Finishing Ltd

R.M.S.2000 – radiomicrophone systems – Audio Ltd

R.M.S. 2020 – radiomicrophone systems – Audio Ltd

R M Sealers – R M Sealers Ltd

R.M.T. – rail, maritime and transport workers trade union – National Union Of Rail Maritime & Transport Worker

R.M.X. 16 – digital reverberation effects unit – A M S Neve Ltd

R. Mould – custom brokers – R L M International Ltd

R.N. Metal Marker – Markers for metal – Roger Needham & Sons Ltd

R.N.S. – London Stock Exchange plc

R.O – Ovivo UK Ltd

R.o.S.P.A. – Royal Society For The Prevention Of Accidents Ltd

R.P. 18 – oil/chemical absorbent – Oil Pollution Environmental Control Ltd

R.P.A.S. – clinical trial random patient generator and label printing software – Episys Group Ltd

R.P.F. – Kennametal UK Ltd

R.P.P. – power, voice and data writing accessories – City Electrical Factors Ltd

R.P. Towing – towing equipment suppliers, trailer hire & manufacture – R P Towing

R.R.F.C. – football club – Raith Rovers Football Club

R. Range – plastic salad boxes – R P C Containers Ltd

R.S.A. – prioprietary urethane polymers – Greene Tweed & Co. Ltd

R.S.C. – learned and professional society of chemistry – Royal Society Of Chemistry

R & S Collectables – Trading name – lauctionshop Ltd

R.S.E. – reliance servo epicyclic – Reliance Precision

R.S.G. – reliance servo gearbox – Reliance Precision

***R.S.L. (China)** – nylon shuttlecocks and practice shuttlecocks – Reinforced Shuttlecocks Ltd

***R.S.L. Ace (China)** – nylon shuttlecock – Reinforced Shuttlecocks Ltd

***R.S.L. Official (China)** – feather shuttlecock – Reinforced Shuttlecocks Ltd

***R.S.L. Silver Feather (China)** – feather shuttlecock – Reinforced Shuttlecocks Ltd

***R.S.L. Tourney (China)** – feather shuttlecock – Reinforced Shuttlecocks Ltd

R.S.S. – Active Security Group Ltd

R Series – AC induction motors - medium range – A T B Laurence Scott Ltd

R + W – Motor Technology Ltd

R + W Antriebselemente GmbH (United Kingdom) – Tandler Precision Ltd

R.W.O. – sail boat fittings, in stainless steel and plastic – R W O Marine Equipment Ltd

R.X. Super Plus – SAE 15W/40 API CH-4/CG-4/SG specification mixed fleet high performance engine oil – Castrol UK Ltd

R40 – half face mask respirator negative pressure – Scott International Ltd

R60 – half face mask respirator negative pressure – Scott International Ltd

R700/H33 – heavy duty girder systems – RMD Kwikform Limited

RA XXX – structural reinforcement – Gurit UK Ltd

Raaco – UK Office Direct

Raak – architectural lighting – Electrak Holdings Ltd

Rabbitstat – selective rabbit bactericide – Agil Chemicals Products

Rabe (Germany) – tillage equipment – Westmac Ltd

***Rabi** – George Colliar Ltd

Rabit – injection moulding machines – MCP Group

Rabourdin Industrie (France) – Standard parts for mould tools, precision mould sets. Shoulder bolts, guide pillars & bushes, cartridge heaters – Berger Tools Ltd

***Rabourdin Picardie (France)** – Standard parts for press tools precision die sets, pillars, bushes, ball cages & wear plates – Berger Tools Ltd

Rabtherm (United Kingdom) – refrigeration test equipment – Rabtherm International Ltd

RAC Cable Gland – With unique multi-armour clamping system – Hawke International

RAC Trackstar – GPS stolen vehicle tracker – Fast Fit Nationwide Ltd

Racecall – telephone services – Weather Call

Racecar Engineering – I P C Media Ltd

***Racer** – Berthoud Sprayers

Racer – optical frames and sunglasses – Hilton International Eye Wear Ltd

Racetech – equipment and parts for racing cars – Raceparts

RaceTech – provision of technical service to race courses – Racetech

Racfil – Harrier Fluid Power Ltd

RACINE – Hydraulic & Offshore Supplies Ltd

Racinedana – Harrier Fluid Power Ltd

Rack – Desks – Bucon Ltd

Rack and Panel – Dax International Ltd

Rack and Shelf Labels – Warehouse Labels – Rack & Shelf Labels

RACOR – Hydraulic & Offshore Supplies Ltd

RAD – AEL Heating Solutions Ltd

RAD – radiopharmaceutical safety cabinet – Envair Ltd

Rad-Active – UV surface coating additives – Kromachem Ltd

Rad-Color – UV compatible pigment dispersions – Kromachem Ltd

Rad/Comm Systems Corp – radiation detection systems – M M H Recycling Systems Ltd

Rad-Flow – UV flow improvers for radiation curing systems – Kromachem Ltd

Rad-Line – radiant heating system – B S S Pipe Fitting Stockholders Head Office

Rad-Matt – UV matting compound – Kromachem Ltd

Rad-Start – photo initiators – Kromachem Ltd

Rad-Wax – wax dispersions in UV compatible media – Kromachem Ltd

Rada – thermostatic mixing valves, manual and electronic timed flow controls for showering and washing – Kohler Mira Ltd

Radar – ceiling tiles (suspended) – U S G UK Ltd

Radar – childrens clothing – Gobina London Ltd

Radar – signs – Radar Signs

Radcrete – polymer modified concretes – Radflex Contract Services Ltd

Radegast – Temple Wines Ltd

Räder Vogel – European Technical Sales Ltd

Radflex – expansion jointing systems – Radflex Contract Services Ltd

Radford – fashion jewellery – Radford Supplies Ltd

Radford Ezy Stumps – spring back cricket stumps – Sportsmark Group Ltd

Radford Retail Systems – Shop fitting & checkouts – Carrier Refrigeration & Retail Systems Ltd

Radi-Heat – highly efficient bumer systems for fish & chips frying ranges – Preston & Thomas Ltd

Radia – Medical examination lamp – Anglepoise Ltd

Radia El – Medical examination lamp – Anglepoise Ltd

Radiaflex – radiating cable – R F S UK Ltd

Radiall – Cyclops Electronics Ltd

Radiall – Connectors – Dax International Ltd

***Radiall (France)** – coaxial and multipin connectors – Radiall Ltd

Radiance – shower surrounds – Matki plc

Radiation Tolerant TV System – closed circuit TV system for nuclear and hazardous areas – Ist Ltd

Radicon – Mercury Bearings Ltd

***Radio coverage (Switzerland)** – cell enhancement products – Huber+Suhner (UK) Ltd

Radiodetection – buried pipe and cable locaters by radiodetection – Radio Detection

Radiodetection – Buried pipe & cable locators by radiodetection – Radio Detection

Radiodetection – Alpha Electronics Southern Ltd

Radiometrie – manufacturers of – Thermo Radiometrie Ltd

Radium – British Vita plc

Radius – radio communications equipment – Motorola Ltd

Radius Professional Office – Accounts Production, Practice Management, Payroll, FDS Taxpoint SA, Other Office Applications – Practice Net Ltd

Radix – Teamco International Ltd

Radjoint – epoxy sealant – Radflex Contract Services Ltd

Radlab – laboratory plastics – Radleys

Radmat – waterproofing and protective coating – Radflex Contract Services Ltd

Radol (United Kingdom) – low nox burners – Hamworthy Combustion Engineering Ltd

Radonbar – radon barriers – Cavity Trays Ltd

***Radox (Switzerland)** – high temperature resistant wire – Huber+Suhner (UK) Ltd

Radprofile – Radan

Radpunch – Radan

Rads – AEL Heating Solutions Ltd

Radsil – Molyslip Atlantic Ltd

Rael Brook – shirts – Rael Brook Group Ltd

Raffletech (United Kingdom) – range of raffle machines with tote/score & quiz timer functions (electronic) – Park Lane News Ltd

Rafid – Geoquip Ltd

Raflatac – self adhesive label stock – Raflatac Ltd

Raflex – sealing rim – Cobham Mission Equipment Ltd

Raftor – A liquid laundry destainer – Premiere Products Ltd

Raga Rose – Wine For Spice Ltd

Ragg – tuning forks of every description – Granton Medical Ltd

Raghi – Gem Tool Hire & Sales Ltd

Ragno – small bore hoses – Merlett Plastics UK Ltd

Rahnqvist UK – sell specialised stationery to education and commerce – Rahmqvist UK Ltd

RAID – MJM Data Recovery Ltd

Rail – tail lamp – Doormen

Rail – possession limit board – Doormen

Rail – marker board – Doormen

Rail – gate arm lamps – Doormen

Rail Air – coach service operations – First Bus

Railcar Loader – multi section belt conveyor for loading rail cars – Newland Engineering Co. Ltd

Railok – vertical rail safety systems – Capital Safety Group Ltd

Railscan – ultrasonic flaw detector – Sonatest Ltd

Railway Modeller – Great Britains model railway magazine – Peco Publications & Publicity Ltd

Raimondi-Tower Cranes – Skyline Tower Crane Services Ltd

Rain Forest – carpets – Interface Europe Ltd

Rainbow – dart flights – Unicorn Products Ltd

Rainbow Recruitment – employment agency and business – Rainbow Recruitment UK Ltd

rainbow woodchips, natures colourful compainion – Rainbow Woodchips

Raincheater – bicycle brake block – Fibrax Ltd

Raincoat – waterproofing coatings for flat and pitched roofs – Tor Coatings Ltd

Raindrop – nozzles – Delavan Ltd

Rainproof Heater – infra red heater – Robinson Willey

Rainscreen Duo-Slab – effective thermal insulation for rainscreen and overcladding applications – Rockwool Rockpanel B V

***Raja** – Raja Frozen Foods Ltd

RaJa – European Technical Sales Ltd

RAJA-Lovejoy – Spidex Couplings, Dentex Couplings, Bellhousings, Bellhousing Cooler, Noise Absorbtion Flanges, Aluminium Reservoir Accessories, Access Covers, Torsional Couplings, Torque Limiting Couplings – J B J Techniques Ltd

RAJA-LOVEJOY – Hydraulic & Offshore Supplies Ltd

RAK – Porcelain China Tableware – Continental Chef Supplies Ltd

Rake 'N' Lift, The Nottingham Rakes – ideal for golf club, private and landscape gardeners or contractors estates and local authorities, wildlife parks, equine market stables, use as a shovel or rake-dual purpose, hard wearing, also moss rakes, dog scoops and powerful hand tools – Rake 'N' Lift & Co - Nottingham Rakes UK Rakes Specialists

Rakguard – Berry Systems

Rako – Portable ventilators – Beatson Fans & Motors Ltd

Rakoll – woodworking adhesives – H B Fuller

Rakusen's – kosher food – Rakusens Ltd

Raleigh – bicycles and components – Raleigh UK Ltd

Ralspeed – Proplas International Ltd

Ralumac – polymer modified and cold applied micro asphalt road surface treatment – Colas Ltd

Raly – magnetic catches – Magnet Applications Ltd

Ralyester – L.V. switchgear – A-Belco Ltd

*Ram – Equipline

Ram – low cement castables – Calderys UK Ltd

Ram Power – hydraulic cylinders – A C Hydraulics Ltd

RAM POWER – Hydraulic & Offshore Supplies Ltd

RAM REMAN LTD – Hydraulic & Offshore Supplies Ltd

Ramax S – pre-hardened stainless bolster steel – Uddeholm Steel Stockholders

Rambaudi – Red House Industrial Services Ltd

Rambler – luxury motor caravan – Auto Sleepers Ltd

Ramco – corrosion control – Ramco Tubular Services Ltd

Ramco CNC Ltd – CNC Sub Contract Machining – Richard Alan Engineering Company Ltd

Ramdoor – crash proof & resistant hi speed factory doors – Union Industries

Ramesys CONSTRUCT – Redsky It

Ramesys SUMMIT – Redsky It

Rammax – A T Wilde & Son Ltd

Rammax – Harrier Fluid Power Ltd

Rammer – hydraulic hammers and cutter crushers – Metso Minerals UK Ltd

Ramon – quickwipe dishcloths etc – Ramon Hygiene Products

*Ramon Allones (Cuba, Jamaica, Europe and Honduras) – cigars – Hunters & Frankau Ltd

Ramoneur – cleaning services – Maclellan International Ltd

Rampart – vandal resistant lighting – Designplan Lighting Ltd

RAMPARTS – Hydraulic & Offshore Supplies Ltd

Rampmaster - hot/cold temperature forcing block - SlimLine – Sharetree Ltd

Rampower – Hydraulic Component & Systems Ltd

Ramset – I T W Constructions Productions

Ramsey – switches – Bearwood Engineering Supplies

Ramtron – M S C Gleichmann UK Ltd

Ranch Rider – Farm Tours

Rancilio – The Coffee Machine Company

Rand – compressors & spares – Bearwood Engineering Supplies

Rando Oil – lubricants – Chevron

Ranford Doors – manufacturer of doors – Russell Shutters Ltd

Range of Oak Conditioned Ciders – H Weston & Sons Ltd

Ranger – glass fibre surveyors tape – Fisco Tools Ltd

RANGER – Chaintec Ltd

Ranger – Pressure washers – B & G Cleaning Systems Ltd

Ranger – 7 touring caravans, (1 * twin axle, 6 * single axle) – Bailey Of Bristol

Rani Collection, The – Ladies Fashions – Variety Silk House Ltd

Rani Gold – Wine For Spice Ltd

Rank Taylor Hobson – sensors – Bearwood Engineering Supplies

Rankin McGregor Ltd – Cyberlux

Rankins – glass – Rankins Glass Company Ltd

*Rannock Smokery – Rannoch Smokery

Ransomes – Ransomes Jacobsen Ltd

Ransomes – potato and root crop diggers – Blair Engineering

Ransomes – Harrier Fluid Power Ltd

Rantec – Ets-Lindgren Ltd

Rapan – Mud, Blue Clay, Yellow Clay, Bath Salt - for masks, body wraps, baths, compresses, etc. – Medicina (UK) Ltd

*Rapco (U.S.A.) – cables – John Hornby Skewes & Co. Ltd

Rapesco – Gem Tool Hire & Sales Ltd

Rapesco – Gustair Materials Handling Equipment Ltd

Rapesco – UK Office Direct

RAPESCO – Hydraulic & Offshore Supplies Ltd

Rapid – UK Office Direct

*Rapid – drills – Vaderstad Ltd

Rapid – printer driver designed for flexibility - allows uses to choose between printing – Episys Group Ltd

Rapid – concrete pan mixers – Rapid International Ltd

Rapid Bar Tie 15/20mm – formwork tie systems – RMD Kwikform Limited

Rapid Hire Centres – tool and plant hire – Rapid Hire Centres Ltd

Rapid Metadure – machinery enamel – Craig & Rose Ltd

Rapid Reel – The Paper Company Ltd

*Rapid Roll (Sweden) – high speed roller doors – Stertil UK Ltd

Rapid Seal – fast drying non-flammable 34% solids water based seal with added urethane – Premiere Products Ltd

Rapid Shell Dry – Process Technology Europe Ltd

Rapid Strand – G E Healthcare

Rapidat – G E Healthcare

Rapidclimb – Climbing Formwork Systems. – RMD Kwikform Limited

Rapide – V E S Ltd

*Rapide (Sweden) – metal roof tile – Plannja Ltd

Rapide – inclined vibrating screen – Parker Plant Ltd

Rapidoc – hard copy documents – I H S Global

Rapidpurge – Resinex UK Ltd

Rapidroom – steel manufactured office units – Adroit Modular Buildings plc

Rapidshor – steel shoring system – RMD Kwikform Limited

Rapidus – marketing database software – Acxiom Ltd

Rapier – quarter turn fasteners quick release – Southco Manufacturing Ltd

Rapier – high security window locking systems – Archibald Kenrick & Sons

Rapier Tapes – weaving – Pilkingtons Ltd

RAPISARDA HOSE AND FITTINGS – Hydraulic & Offshore Supplies Ltd

*Rapitech (Sweden) – high speed sectional door – Stertil UK Ltd

Rapleys – Commercial property and planning consultants – Rapleys LLP

Rapport – clocks – M A Rapport & Co. Ltd

Raptor – EF technology laser makers – Electrox

Raptor – a liquid laundry destainer – Premiere Products Ltd

Raptor – fishing tackle – Drennan International Ltd

RAR – overhead tubular radiant heaters – Reznor UK Ltd

RAS Asbestos – Asbestos Removal – Scott International Ltd

Ras/Ras astestic – Scott International Ltd

Rascal – high and standard definition telecine for converting film to video – Cintel International Ltd

Rascals – promotional bugs (novelties) – Billbo UK Ltd

Rascals – Turner Bianca

Rassapron – non-selective weed killers – B P plc

Ratak – rodenticide – Sorex Ltd

Ratcliff Cantilever Lifts – cantilever style tail lifts 500kg-3000kg – Ratcliff Palfinger

Ratcliff Column Lifts – column style tail lifts 500kg-2000kg – Ratcliff Palfinger

Ratcliff Light Van Lifts – 300kg-500kg for mini vans – Ratcliff Palfinger

Ratcliff Tail lifts – tail lifts – Ratcliff Palfinger

Ratfischatlas – Harrier Fluid Power Ltd

*Rational – Combi ovens – Court Catering Equipment Ltd

Rational – B B C S Ltd

Rational – Ascot Wholesale Ltd

RatiopacPRO – subrack – Schroff UK Ltd

Ratiotronic TM – electronic air/gas ratio controller – Dunphy Combustion Ltd

Rauma – Rolls Royce

*Rautenstrauch (Germany) – German wines – O W Loeb & Co. Ltd

Ravago Off Grades – Resinex UK Ltd

Ravago Recycled Material – Resinex UK Ltd

Ravamid – Resinex UK Ltd

Ravatal – Resinex UK Ltd

RAVE – Risk and Value Engineering (R.A.V.E) is an in house software application developed by Ingen Ideas – Ingen Ideas Ltd

Ravendo – Maingate Ltd

Ravenna – washbasins, closets and bidets – Ideal Standard Ltd

Ravensburger Ltd – childrens jig saw puzzles and games – Ravensburger Ltd

Raves – fashion wear – Raves Clothing Ltd

Ravitex – tip dressers – Quality Manufacturing Services Ltd

Ravitex/Sinterleghe – European Technical Sales Ltd

Rawie GmbH and Co. KG (Germany) – friction buffers – H.J. Skelton & Co. Ltd

Rawlbloc – lightweight block fixing – Rawlplug Ltd

Rawlbolt – masonry anchor – Rawlplug Ltd

Rawlbolt – anchor bolts – Arrow Supply Co. Ltd

Rawldrill – manual drill – Rawlplug Ltd

Rawlnut – multi-purpose fixing – Rawlplug Ltd

Rawlok – sleeve anchor – Rawlplug Ltd

Rawlplug – registered company name – Rawlplug Ltd

Rawlplug – Gem Tool Hire & Sales Ltd

Rawlplug Fibre Plugs – wallplugs – Rawlplug Ltd

Rawlplug Plastic Plugs – wallplugs – Rawlplug Ltd

Rawlplug Plastic Wood – wood filler – Rawlplug Ltd

Rawlplug Rapid – staple guns and staples – Rawlplug Ltd

Rawlplug Self Drill Plasterboard Fixing – plasterboard fixing – Rawlplug Ltd

Rawlplug Spring Toggles – cavity fixings – Rawlplug Ltd

Rawlplug Throughbolt – masonry anchor – Rawlplug Ltd

Rawlplug Wedge Anchors – masonry anchors – Rawlplug Ltd

Rawltool – manual drill – Rawlplug Ltd

Ray Gold (Asia) – lighting range – Febland Group Ltd

Ray Proof – Ets-Lindgren Ltd

Raybloc (United Kingdom) – double slot shim for use on the most common types of bearing or plummer blocks housings – Rayhome Ltd

Rayburn 200G – gas-fired domestic cooking appliance – AGA Rayburn

Rayburn 200L – gas-fired domestic cooking appliance – AGA Rayburn

Rayburn 208G – gas-fired domestic cooking and hot water appliance – AGA Rayburn

Rayburn 208KN – oil-fired domestic cooking appliance – AGA Rayburn

Rayburn 208KV – oil-fired domestic cooking and hot water appliance – AGA Rayburn

Rayburn 208L – gas-fired domestic cooking and hot water appliance – AGA Rayburn

Rayburn 212SN – solid fuel domestic cooking appliance – AGA Rayburn

Rayburn 212SV – solid fuel domestic cooking and hot water appliance – AGA Rayburn

Rayburn 216M – multi-fuel domestic cooking, hot water and central heating appliance – AGA Rayburn

Rayburn 355S – solid fuel domestic cooking, hot water and central heating appliance – AGA Rayburn

Rayburn 360D – diesel domestic cooking, hot water and central heating appliance – AGA Rayburn

Rayburn 360K – oil-fired domestic cooking, hot water and central heating appliance – AGA Rayburn

Rayburn 368K – oil-fired domestic cooking, hot water and central heating appliance – AGA Rayburn

Rayburn 380G – gas-fired domestic cooking, hot water and central heating appliance – AGA Rayburn

Rayburn 380L – gas-fired domestic cooking, hot water and central heating appliance – AGA Rayburn

Rayburn 400G – gas-fired domestic cooking appliance – AGA Rayburn

Rayburn 400K – oil-fired domestic cooking appliance – AGA Rayburn

Rayburn 460K – oil-fired domestic cooking, hot water and central heating appliance – AGA Rayburn

Rayburn 460KB – oil-fired domestic cooking, hot water and central heating appliance – AGA Rayburn

Rayburn 480AG – gas-fired domestic cooking, hot water and central heating appliance – AGA Rayburn

Rayburn 480K – oil-fired domestic cooking, hot water and central heating appliance – AGA Rayburn

Rayburn 480KB – oil-fired domestic cooking, hot water and central heating appliance – AGA Rayburn

Rayburn 499K – oil-fired domestic cooking, hot water and central heating appliance – AGA Rayburn

Rayburn 499KB – oil-fired domestic cooking, hot water and central heating appliance – AGA Rayburn

Raychem – Cyclops Electronics Ltd

Raychem – resettable fuses, cables & accessories – Anglia

Raychem – Stabilag E S H Ltd

Rayco – Wylie Systems

Raydyot – car accessories – Truck-Lite Co. Ltd

Rayette – gas-fired radiant ovens fixedwall conveyorised – Maywick Ltd

Raylite Turbo Start – battery Manufr – Battery Distribution Group

Raymaster – gas fired radiant ovens (fully adjustable) - conveyorised – Maywick Ltd

RAYMAX – radiant heaters – Watlow Ltd

Raymond – Stacatruc

Rayner – opticians – Rayner Opticians

Raynger – Radir Ltd

Rayoface(tm) (United Kingdom) – high performance BOPP label substrates for pressure sensitive applications – Innovia Films Ltd

Rayofoil(tm) (United Kingdom) – metallised BOPP label substrates for the pressure sensitive label market – Innovia Films Ltd

Rayoform (tm) (United Kingdom) – clear & white BOPP film for in mould label application – Innovia Films Ltd

Rayovac – watch and clock cells – A G Thomas Bradford Ltd

Rayoweb(tm) (United Kingdom) – clear, BOPP film for release liner applications – Innovia Films Ltd

Rayshim (United Kingdom) – pre-cut precision shims – Rayhome Ltd

Raystoc (United Kingdom) – pre-packed shim steel stock in both metric and imperial sizes. – Rayhome Ltd

Raytek – Radir Ltd

Raytek – Insteng Process Automation Ltd

Raytek – Alpha Electronics Southern Ltd

Raytek – company name – M Squared Instrumentation

Raytek Corp – Radir Ltd

Raytek GmbH – Radir Ltd

Raytek Inc – Radir Ltd

Raytel – process control equipment and instrumentation – Rayleigh Instruments Ltd

Raytel - Generic – trade mark covering all goods – Raytel Security Systems Ltd

Raytheon – Cyclops Electronics Ltd
Razor – carbon dioxide laser makers – Electrox
Razor Mesh – barbed tape – Birmingham Barbed Tape Ltd
Razor Spike – Keytrak Lock & Safe Company
Razorsharp – cutting tools-secateurs, shears, loppers – Spear & Jackson plc
***Razzle** – Taylor Scotland Ltd
Ra'alloy ramps – Aluminium ramps – Ra'Alloy Ramps Ltd
RB – steam boilers – Fulton Boiler Works Ltd
RB – Trowell Plant Sales Ltd
RBC – heavy duty needle roller bearings – R A Rodriguez UK Ltd
RBC – cam followers – R A Rodriguez UK Ltd
RBC – heavy duty rod-ends and bushings – R A Rodriguez UK Ltd
RBF Healthcare – manufacturing services for healthcare industry – R B F Healthcare
RC XXX – structural reinforcement – Gurit UK Ltd
RCA – Lamphouse Ltd
RCC – Alpha Electronics Southern Ltd
RCD – Rugged Computing Device – Specialist Electronics Services Ltd
RCI – air flow meters – P V L Ltd
RCP – Resistor controlled cathodic protection – Iicorr Ltd
RCS – Ringspann UK Ltd
RCS Controls (Germany) – cables & control systems – Ringspann UK Ltd
RD4000 – buried pipe anc cable locators by radiodetection – Radio Detection
RDS 1600 – radar display systems – Eaton Aerospace Ltd
Re-Flex – reforming, pliable bodyshell for bollards – Haldo Developments Ltd
Re-Nu – kitchens – Re-Nu Kitchens Ltd
RE PAK ELEMENTS – Hydraulic & Offshore Supplies Ltd
RE XXX – structural reinforcement – Gurit UK Ltd
REA – plastic shelving – Rea Plasrack Ltd
Rea Fireact – fire proof doors and windows – R E A Metal Windows Ltd
Rea Firebreak – fire proof doors and windows – R E A Metal Windows Ltd
Rea Frame – metal windows and door – R E A Metal Windows Ltd
Rea Steel – W20 and W40 windows – R E A Metal Windows Ltd
Rea Therm – fire proof doors and windows – R E A Metal Windows Ltd
Reach-A-Height Ladders – Accesscaff International Ltd
ReactiVar – harmonic filtering system – Schneider
Reacto – Mcnaughton James Paper Group Ltd
Reader – C E S Hire Ltd
Reader – Optical character recognition – Vysionics
Reader's Digest Association Ltd – apparatus for reproducing sound from disc and tape – Vivat Direct Limited
Readers Digest – publishers – Vivat Direct Limited
Readi-Bake – sweet treats including cookies (M&Ms, Smarties, Simpsons), doughnuts, cakes & muffins – C S M UK Ltd
Readi Bed Pads/Seat Pads – reusable incontinence pads – Robinson Healthcare Ltd
Readibibs – reusable clothing protectors – Robinson Healthcare Ltd
Readibriefs – reusable incontinence briefs – Robinson Healthcare Ltd
Reading Standard – newspapers – Surrey & Berkshire Media Ltd
Readistretch – incontinence briefs – Robinson Healthcare Ltd
Readiwash – foam spray – Robinson Healthcare Ltd
Readiwipes – wipes – Robinson Healthcare Ltd
Ready Brek – hot oat cereal – Weetabix Ltd
Ready-Cals (United Kingdom) – self adhesive anodised aluminium foil labels in strips – London Name Plate Manufacturing Co. Ltd
Ready To Use TFR – multi-purpose traffic film remover – Deb R & D Ltd
Readybolt – threaded rod – Archibald Kenrick & Sons
Readychain – Igus (UK) Ltd
Readymade – Vaughans Hope Works Ltd
Readymade Companies – Shelf companies – Readymade Companies Worldwide.com
***Readyspex (Far East)** – readymade reading glasses – Readyspex Ltd
Readywax – liquid wax shoe polish – Cherry Blossom Ltd
Real – Genus Group
Real – microfilm silver and diazo duplicators – Microfilm Shop
Real, JRK Imagingraphics, Archive Imaging, Genneg, OIT, Genus. – Genus Group
Real Organic – Organic sauces, luxury conserves, chutneys, specialist foods – Real Organic Foods
Real Pop Up Company – Ninja Corporation Ltd
***Reali - Slim (U.S.A.)** – thin-section bearings – R A Rodriguez UK Ltd
Reality – operating systems and relational database – Northgate & Arinso
Reality Series M6000 – computer margins from 2 devices to 850 – Northgate & Arinso
Really Works – non-hazardous cleaning products – Vindotco UK Ltd
Realm – Vi Spring Ltd
Realm – stainless steel hygienic valves, valve systems and pipeline components – Inoxpa Ltd
Realm Monarch Valves – double and single sealing hygienic mixproof – Inoxpa Ltd
Realm RPRII Hygienic Pressure Relief Valves – manual and automatic spring override – Inoxpa Ltd
Realm Supreme – Vi Spring Ltd
Realslate – Cornish rustic and silver slate – Realstone Ltd
Realstone – six English sandstone quarries – Realstone Ltd
Rearguard – trailer lamps monitor – Ryder Towing Equipment
RebusHRonline – Human resource and payroll solution – Northgate H R Ltd
RECA – fixings & power tools to the building industry – Anchorfast Ltd
Recall – document management (archiving) – Kalamazoo - Reynolds Ltd
Recaro – T E K Seating Ltd
Recipe Formulation – weighing system – Stevens Group Ltd
Recirculating Toilets – Landsmans Ltd
Recital Corporation – web application, development & relational database software – Recital Corporation Ltd
Recliner Chairs – The Winnen Furnishing Company
Reco – agricultural machinery – Ruston's Engineering Co. Ltd
***Reco Complete Range** – Murley Agricultural Supplies Ltd
Recognition Express – personalised name badges, signs, corporate jewellery, plaques and recognition awards – Recognition Express
Recoil – S J Wharton Ltd
Record – S J Wharton Ltd
Record – Alpha Electronics Southern Ltd
Record – Central C N C Machinery Ltd
Record – Record Electrical Associates
Record – Chaintec Ltd
Record Pasta – dried pasta products – Pasta Foods Ltd
Record Power – Lathes, chucks, bandsaws – The Toolpost
Recording Technologies – exhibition – Association Of Professional Recording Services Ltd
Recordon – textile piece goods – Reid & Taylor Ltd
Recovery Text and Cover – paper – Fenner Paper Co. Ltd
Recruitment agency – S Com Group Ltd
Recruitment Consultants – for secretarial and financial recruitment – Meadowbank Associates Ltd
Recruitment Matters – magazine – Insitive Media
Rectangular Polytanks – Kitemarked plastic cold water cistens – Polytank Ltd
Rectella – soft furnishings and upholstery fabrics – Rectella
Rectiphase – power quality – Schneider
Rectivar – variable speed drive – Schneider
Rectory – insert living flame effect fire – Indesit Company UK Ltd
Rectory – interior period door – Premdor Crosby Ltd
Rectron – Cyclops Electronics Ltd
Rectron – Selectronix Ltd
Rectus – Trafalgar Tools
RECTUS – Hydraulic & Offshore Supplies Ltd
Rectus – Southern Valve & Fitting Co. Ltd
Recyclex – B P plc
Recycling – method of re-using ashphalt for paving – Colas Ltd
Recyclomat – asphalt recycling concept – B G Europa UK Ltd
***Recyconomic (Germany)** – coated recycled – John Heyer Paper Ltd
Red Alert – red mini trunking – M K Electric Ltd
Red Box Change Management – Software for implementing change processes – Fox It Ltd
Red Box Configuration Management – Software for cataloguing and controlling an organisation's infrastructure – Fox It Ltd
Red Box Help Desk & Problem Management – Software for logging, tracking and managing incidents and problems – Fox It Ltd
Red Care – signalling – Chubb Electronic Security Ltd
Red Door – perfumes – Elizabeth Arden
Red Flash – batteries, portable power packs – D M S Technologies Ltd
Red Fox – austenitic steels for furnace equipment – Corus Engineering Steels
Red Funnel – ferry and hi-speed service between Southampton, Cowes and the Isle of Wight – Red Funnel Ferries Ltd
Red Funnel Towage – towage services in port of Southampton – Red Funnel Ferries Ltd
Red Hat – solenoid valves – Asco Numatics
RED HAT – Hydraulic & Offshore Supplies Ltd
Red Kooga – ginseng supplement – Perrigo UK
Red Mosquito – Company Brand Name – Red Mosquito Ltd
Red Multi – Ibstock Brick Ltd
Red or Dead – fashions and design – Pentland Ltd
Red Point – photoelectric handheld tachometer – Foundrometers Instrumentation Ltd
Red Rad, Big Rad, Master Heater, Easiheat – Infrared space heaters – Infrared Heater UK
Red Ram – Premium protective clothing – Weldspares Ltd
Red Rock – clothing and footwear – D Jacobson & Sons Ltd
Red Roller – Textile sleeve for use in the aluminium extrusion industry – Marathon Belting Ltd
Red Rooster – Yokota UK
Red Rooster – Red Rooster Industrial UK Ltd
Red Rooster – Gustair Materials Handling Equipment Ltd
red ruby – Devon Cattle Breeders Society
Red Stripe – hacksaw blades (high speed steel NL hard) – L S Starrett Co. Ltd
Red Stripe – premium lager – Wells & Young's Brewing Co.
Red Tails – fishing tackle class 28 – Drennan International Ltd
Red Top – racing battery – D M S Technologies Ltd
Red Z – Energy Drink – Stute Foods Ltd
RedAnt Software – Production Control Software – Stone Technology Limited
Redashe – Trafalgar Tools
REDASHE – Hydraulic & Offshore Supplies Ltd
Redashe – Southern Valve & Fitting Co. Ltd
RedCare – Christie Intruder Alarms Ltd
Redcare – Eagle Security Solutions Ltd
Redcare GSM – Eagle Security Solutions Ltd
Redcare GSM – Christie Intruder Alarms Ltd
Redco – broaching tools – Pharos Engineering Ltd
Redco Hydrogip Machine Vices – Pharos Engineering Ltd
Redco Broaches – Pharos Engineering Ltd
***Redco LSP (U.S.A.)** – airless lubrications systems – Pharos Engineering Ltd
Redcrest – inflatable boats – Avon Inflatables Ltd
Reddihinge – window friction stays – Reddiplex Ltd
Reddilock – glazing wedges – Reddiplex Ltd
Reddipile – weather stripping – Reddiplex Ltd
Reddiprene – window gaskets – Reddiplex Ltd
Reddisealant – silicone sealants – Reddiplex Ltd
Reddish Joinery – UPVC and hardwood double glazing, conservatories and joinery – Reddish Joinery Ltd
Redditape – security glazing tape – Reddiplex Ltd
Reddiwire – Webster & Horsfall Ltd
Reddy – bus and coach services – East Yorkshire Motor Services Ltd
Redeem 100% Recycled – paper – Fenner Paper Co. Ltd
Redel (Switzerland) – plastic self-hatching electrical connectors – Lemo UK Ltd
***Redex (France)** – epicyclic gear units and steel processing machines – Andantex Ltd
Redford – Try & Lilly Ltd
Redgo – medium duty conveying – Fenner Drives Ltd
Redhawk – Dickies Workwear
Rediboard – circuit board – L P A Channel Electric
Rediform – stock non-computer forms and carbon rolls – Paragon Group UK Ltd
Redipave – Pedestrian Refuge Island – Rediweld Rubber & Plastics Ltd
REDIPOR (United Kingdom) – prepared culture media – Cherwell Laboratories Ltd
Redirack – pallet racking – Redirack Ltd
Redland – Monier Ltd
Redland 49 – Monier Ltd
Redline – Broen Valves Ltd
Redline – magazine – Future Publishing Ltd
Redline (Portugal) – compact netting – Cotesi UK Ltd
Redline – AEL Heating Solutions Ltd
Redlock – door lock – Allgood
Redpoint – Cyclops Electronics Ltd
Redrib – metal lathing – Expamet Building Products Ltd
Redring – Trafalgar Tools
Redring – Applied Energy Products Ltd
***Redskins (France)** – garments – Ramostyle Ltd
Redspot – Kempston Controls Ltd
Redstart – inflatable boats – Avon Inflatables Ltd
redstone – Callsure Business Telephone & Fax Numbers
Redthane – conveyor belting – Polyurethane Products Ltd
Reduced Pressure Electron Beam Welding – Cambridge Vacuum Engineering
Redvent – Monier Ltd
Redways – pipe lining materials – Project Building Company Ltd
Redwood (China) – safety footwear – L H Safety Ltd
Redwood – Safety footwear – L H Safety Ltd
Redwood (Portugal) – safety footwear – L H Safety Ltd
Redwood (Vietnam) – safety footwear – L H Safety Ltd
Redwood Stone – ornamental stone – Redwood Stone
Reed Educational & Professional Publishers – Pearson Eduction Ltd
REEDEX – Hydraulic & Offshore Supplies Ltd
Reekie – Reekie portable and transportable metal cutting machine tools, in situ and subcontract machining – Reekie Machining Ltd

REELFAST – surface mount nuts, standoffs and panel fasteners – Zygology Ltd

Reelstick – label printers – Euro Label Printers

Reena – childrens clothing and specialising school wear – M Comar & Sons Ltd

Ref-Sked – a scheduling tool for petroleum refineries – Aspentech Ltd

Refcomp – Therma Group

Refel – silicon carbide engineering ceramics – Tenmat Ltd

Refilco – Harrier Fluid Power Ltd

***Refit (Switzerland)** – multiple sclorosis – Merck Serono Ltd

Reflection – An ecologically friendly emulsion polish – Premiere Products Ltd

Reflections – traditional washbasin, closet and bidet – Ideal Standard Ltd

Reflections – greetings cards – Hambledon Studios

Reflections DK – yarn – Stylecraft

Reflectoware – sanitary ware – Shaws Of Darwen Ltd

Reflectra – Lamphouse Ltd

Reflex – mobile & fixed rail mounted headlamp beam testers – Tecalemit Garage Equipment Co. Ltd

Reflex – Lamphouse Ltd

Reflex – carpets – Interface Europe Ltd

Reflex – door furniture – Allgood

Reflex – British Vita plc

Reflex – flexible plastic hose – Plastiflex UK Ltd

Reflex – membrane touch switch-graphic overlay – Exopack Advanced Coatings Ltd

Reflex Flexitile – interlocking floor systems – Quantum Profile Systems

Reflex (Highviz) – irrigation hose – Richards Hose Ltd

Reflex R – high specification conference tabling and courtroom furniture, flexible in arrangement and demountable for storage – Fray Design Ltd

Reflex Trainer – rugby – Gray Nicolls

Reflex With Accents – carpets – Interface Europe Ltd

Reflexite – Helman Workwear

***Reform (Germany)** – CNC gear and spline grinding machines/CNC surface grinding machines – Takisawa UK Ltd

Reform – machinery for grinding knives – Vollmer UK Ltd

Reform Ladders – Accesscaff International Ltd

Reformat – seismic data reformatting – D P T S Group Holdings Ltd

Refrabloc – traditional castables – Calderys UK Ltd

Refraciment – motars and coatings – Calderys UK Ltd

Refractometer Fluid 1.79 – gem testing fluid – The Gemmological Association Of Great Britain

Refractory Glaze Wash – Vitcas Ltd

Refrax – high temperature refractories – Saint Gobain Industrial Ceramics Ltd

Refresh – opthalmic solution for tired, irritated and sore eyes – Allergan Ltd

Refrex – Yorkshire Refractory Products Ltd

Refrigerating Specialities (Parker) – Industrial solenoid valves and pressure regulators, including suction regulating discharge regulators, crankcase regulators, differential regulators, hot gas bypass regulators, gas powered valves, strainers. – Thermofrost Cryo plc

Refrigerating Specialties – industrial refrigeration control valves – Parker Hannifin UK plc

Refurbplus – tank refurbishment service – Franklin Hodge Industries Ltd

Regal – Vi Spring Ltd

Regal – fishing tackle – Daiwa Sports Ltd

Regal – offset blankets – Kodak Morley

Regal – masonry paint – Craig & Rose Ltd

Regal 3000 System – shelving system – S S I Schaefer Ltd

Regal 4000 System – shelving system – S S I Schaefer Ltd

Regal 7000 – shelving system – S S I Schaefer Ltd

Regal Filter – filter cigarettes – Imperial Tobacco Group PLC

Regal King Size – filter cigarettes – Imperial Tobacco Group PLC

Regal Oil – lubricants – Chevron

Regal Supreme – Vi Spring Ltd

Regal Tinted Ivory – U-Coated Paper – Mcnaughton James Paper Group Ltd

***Regal Tip (U.S.A.)** – drumsticks and malletts – John Hornby Skewes & Co. Ltd

Regal Ultrawhite – Uncoated Paper – Mcnaughton James Paper Group Ltd

RegaLead – window decoration products – Regalead Ltd

Regalian – property developers – Davstone Holdings Ltd

Regalite – hydrogenated resin – Hercules Holding Ii Ltd

Regalrez – hydrogenated resin – Hercules Holding Ii Ltd

RegaPaK – corrugated packaging – D S Smith Packaging Ltd

Regatta – outdoor clothing: anoraks, parkas, waterproofs, trousers, casual wear, socks, hats and gloves – Regatta Ltd

Regatta – cold & wet weather clothing – Howsafe Ltd

Regeltechnik – Harrier Fluid Power Ltd

Regenacell – Replacement Carbon Filter cells and panels of any size to suit any existing filter installation. – Emcel Filters Ltd

Regency – touring caravan – Bailey Of Bristol

Regency – lighting equipment – Powerlite Lighting Solutions Ltd

Regency – Portman Building Society

Regency – woven collection – Intercover (E Hampson) Ltd

Regency – concrete paving – Thakeham Tiles Ltd

Regency Collection – Hotel Complimentary Products

Regency Gloss – coated paper & board – Howard Smith Paper Ltd

Regency Satin – coated paper & board – Howard Smith Paper Ltd

Regency Superflo – high capacity rainwater system – Hunter Plastics

Regency & West of England – Portman Building Society

Regenerative – furnace – Molten Metal Products Ltd

Regent – period bathroom water fittings – Barber Wilson & Company Ltd

Regent – metal up and over garage door – P C Henderson Ltd

Regent – mole drainers & subsoilers – Brown's Agricultural Machinery Company Ltd

Regent – pressings and welded assemblies – Regent Engineering Company

Regent – 80% Cu/20% Ni electric resistance alloy – Omega Resistance Wire Ltd

Regent – Try & Lilly Ltd

Regent – equestrian footwear – Sanders & Sanders Ltd

Regent – Monier Ltd

Regent Chevron – metal up and over garage door – P C Henderson Ltd

Regent, Monarque, Emperor – Indespension Ltd

Regentex – polyestere/cotton processed fabric – J T Inglis & Sons Ltd

REGF Trapped Roller Freewheel – Renold Clutches & Couplings Ltd

***Reghin (Romania)** – cellos and double basses – John Hornby Skewes & Co. Ltd

Regimental Gloss – high gloss shoe polish – Cherry Blossom Ltd

Regina – Mercury Bearings Ltd

Regina – glass and plastics – Regina Industries Ltd

Regina – Transmission Chain – Sprint Engineering & Lubricant

REGINA – Chaintec Ltd

Regina International – carpets - axminster – Brintons Carpets Ltd

***Regine (Switzerland)** – tweezers – Electro Group Ltd

Regis Ovens (United Kingdom) – baked potato ovens-gas – Kedek Ltd

Registrac – photo electric control equipment – Sargrove Automation

Regloplas – temperature controllers – Motan Ltd

REGLP Trapped Roller Freewheel – Renold Clutches & Couplings Ltd

REGO – regulators & valves – H K L Gas Power Ltd

***Rego-Fix (Switzerland)** – collet chucks and collets – Brunner Machine Tools Ltd

Regubinder – spine binding machinery – Gilmex International Ltd

Regulator Cut (United Kingdom) – carpet tiles – Checkmate Industries Ltd

Regulator Loop (United Kingdom) – carpet tiles – Checkmate Industries Ltd

Regulator Pattern (United Kingdom) – carpet tiles – Checkmate Industries Ltd

Regulett – tablets – Reckitt Benckiser plc

Regulox K – grass growth regulator – Bayer Crop Science

***Regumaize** – E D F Man

Regus Office – furnished and serviced offices in business centres – Regus Management Ltd

Regutapes – spine binding tapes – Gilmex International Ltd

REGV Trapped Roller Freewheel – Renold Clutches & Couplings Ltd

Rehau – Gem Tool Hire & Sales Ltd

***Rehau (Germany)** – PVC handrails – Architectural Plastics Ltd

Reich – Couplings – Ringflex Drive Systems Ltd

Reich Couplings – Ringflex Drive Systems Ltd

Reichert-Jung – measuring equipment – Bearwood Engineering Supplies

Reihansl – European Technical Sales Ltd

Reiku – heat protection materials – Partex Marking Systems UK Ltd

***Reimu (Italy)** – friction bandsaws – Prosaw Ltd

Reiner – UK Office Direct

Reinforced Plastics – plant 2 consumables and vacuum systems – J R Technology

***Reinforced Turf (United Kingdom)** – pre-grown turf for erosion protection – A G A Group

Reinvent Your Career – Published by Hodder Mobius in 2005 – In the Hot Seat

***Reis (Germany)** – robots for welding, mechanical handling and plastics moulding – Olympus Technologies Ltd

Reiss Retail – fashion retailers menswear & ladies fashions – Reiss Retail Ltd

Rekofa – European Technical Sales Ltd

Rekord – Stacatruc

Rekord – agriculture machinery, parts, accessories and sundries related to agriculture, storage and crop drying – Rekord Sales

RELATED FLUID POWER – Hydraulic & Offshore Supplies Ltd

Relax – Pledge Office Chairs Ltd

Relaxair, Relax Air – British Vita plc

Relaxator – relaxing chair – Patterson Products Ltd

Release – combined water softener, low foam surface agent, deodorant and brightener – Premiere Products Ltd

Releaseflex – siliconised films – A C P Ltd

***Reli A Flex (U.S.A.)** – Flexible coupling – Reliance Precision

Reliability – chemicals – Bristol-Myers Squibb

Reliable Brand – handkerchiefs, antimacassars, embroidery, bindings, braids, dusters, curtains, galloons, tape trimmings, laces (boot and corset), bedspreads, quilts, blants, sheets, pillow cases, table cloths towels etc – Norland Burgess Ltd

Reliable Spring Manufactures – Spring & Wire Shapes – Frederick Spring Co.

Reliacath – nelaton catheters for intermittent self-catheterisation – Bard Ltd

RELIALINE – Watlow Ltd

Reliance – Drives – Sprint Engineering & Lubricant

Reliance – water controls – Reliance Water Controls Ltd

Reliance – Baldor UK

Reliance Worldwide – control valves – Reliance Water Controls Ltd

***Relief-Xtra (Japan)** – magnetic dot plaster – Robinson Healthcare Ltd

Relionmac – writing pads and note books – Mccormick John & Co. Ltd

Relisys – Lamphouse Ltd

Relyon – beds, sofabeds & bedframes – Relyon Ltd

Rema – British Rema Process Equipment Ltd

Rema – impact grinder and classifier mill – British Rema Manufacturing Co. Ltd

Rema Tip Top UK – industrial rubber linings, vulcanised products, tyre repair materials and tyre shop equipment – Rema Tip Top UK Ltd

Rembelt – range of back supports – Remploy Ltd

***Rembrandt (Netherlands)** – case erectors and loaders – A M J Maters Partnership Ltd

Remco Motors – European Technical Sales Ltd

Remcor – I M I Cornelius UK Ltd

Remedial Wall Ties – system for remedy of corroded cavity wall ties – Hilti GB Ltd

Remko – soft magnetic iron – Uddeholm Steel Stockholders

Remote Annex – terminal server – Nortel Networks UK Ltd

Remote Control – equipment & spares – Bearwood Engineering Supplies

Remote Control – for windows – H W Cooper

Remote Controls – for industrial and domestic – Zap Controls Ltd

Remote Estimating Ltd – Electrical Estimating Support – Remote Estimating Ltd

Removable Data Storage – Tekdata Distribution Ltd

RemovAll – Eco-friendly paint strippers for industry, aviation, marine, DIY etc – Cirrus Systems Ltd

REMTV – REMTV AGENCY LTd

Renaissance – ceramic tiles – Craven Dunnill & Co. Ltd

Renata – coin cells & holders – Anglia

Renate Bucone – lingerie – Scala Agenturen UK

***Renaud-Bossuat (France)** – Loire wines – O W Loeb & Co. Ltd

Renault – cars – Renault UK Ltd

RENAULT – Bailey Morris Ltd

Renault – Harrier Fluid Power Ltd

Renault – Ashley Competition Exhausts Ltd

Renault – L M C Hadrian Ltd

***Rench-Rapid (Germany)** – absorbent for oil and chemical spillages – Gotec Trading Ltd

Renco – HEIDENHAIN GB LTD

Renco – Encoders UK

Rencol – plastic handwheels, handles, knobs, levelling feet & toggle clamps – Rencol Components Ltd

Rendacrete – repair mortars – Rotafix Ltd

Rendit – repair of brickwork & masonry – Rendit Ltd

Renegade – cattle fly control – Sorex Ltd

***Reneka** – Tudor Tea & Coffee

Renelite – elastomeric weather proofing finish – Tremco Illbruck Ltd

Renesas – Cyclops Electronics Ltd

Renesas – M S C Gleichmann UK Ltd

Renfor – chemical-resisting lining – Addagrip Surface Treatments Ltd

Renfor Cement – chemical and wear resisting lining and repair products – Addagrip Surface Treatments Ltd

Renishaw – Status Metrology Solutions Ltd

Renishaw – measuring equipment – Renishaw plc

Renlok – square nylon insert lock nut – Cooper & Turner

Renlok – self locking nut – Cooper & Turner

Reno – Pressure Washers – W Bateman & Co.
Renoclean – cleaning products – Fuchs Lubricants UK plc
Renoir – motor caravans – Leisuredrive Ltd
Renold – Mercury Bearings Ltd
RENOLD – Wolds Engineering Services Ltd
RENOLD – Chaintec Ltd
Renold Chains – chain – Potteries Power Transmission Ltd
Renold Conveyor Chains – conveyor chain – Potteries Power Transmission Ltd
Renold Gearboxes – gearboxes – Potteries Power Transmission Ltd
Renoldflex – Torsionally rigid steel coupling (TRC) – Renold Clutches & Couplings Ltd
Renolin – machine lubricants – Fuchs Lubricants UK plc
Renolit – greases – Fuchs Lubricants UK plc
Renovate – detergent & sanitiser-to refurbish drinking glasses and clean glass wash machines – The Proton Group Ltd
Renovex – B P plc
Renown – water taps – Rudge & Co UK
Renown – soccer, netball, basketball balls – Gray Nicolls
Renown – Monier Ltd
***Renson (France)** – centrifugal pumps – Dual Pumps Ltd
Renson UK Ltd – aluminium louvre panels and ventilators – Renson Fabrications Ltd
Rentaweigh – weighing machines – Kinnersley Engineering Ltd
Renz – Desks – Bucon Ltd
REOLUBE – Hydraulic & Offshore Supplies Ltd
ReoVib – Reo UK Ltd
ReoVib - Vareotron - Reotron – Reo UK Ltd
Repave – carriageway regeneration to 30mm – Colas Ltd
Repco - Macart – self twist spinning machines – Macart Textiles Machinery Ltd
Repcoat – protective, decorative anti-carbonation coating – Don Construction Products Ltd
Repeat Laser – Office Paper – Mcnaughton James Paper Group Ltd
Repelicone – water repellent – Don Construction Products Ltd
Repertoire – woven fabrics – Today Interiors Ltd
Replay Matt – paper – Fenner Paper Co. Ltd
Replica – Digital Products - Toner Sheet Fed - Uncoated – Howard Smith Paper Ltd
Replica – teeth – Metrodent Ltd
Replica Digital Reels – Digital Products - Xeikon - Uncoated – Howard Smith Paper Ltd
Replicar – insurance – Car Care Plan Ltd
Replicast – moulding system polyester – Castings Technology International Ltd
Replin Fabrics – woven transport fabric manufacturers and contract furnishing fabric manufacturers – Replin Fabrics
Repropoint – reprographic services and design office supplies – Repropoint Ltd
Repsol – suplher products – Omya UK Ltd
Res-Q-Man – accessed rescue systems – Capital Safety Group Ltd
Resbuild (United Kingdom) – Resin Building Products Ltd
Rescueline – helpline – First Assist Group Ltd
Rescumatic – emergency escape devices – Capital Safety Group Ltd
Resdev – We install Resdev Resin Systems – Nottingham Industrial Flooring Ltd
Research in Focus – market research management and interpretation – Ipsos Mori
Research International – marketing services – Research International Group Ltd
Resi Wood – timber engineering resins – Rotafix Ltd
Resimetal – Engineering repair coatings for industrial equipment and components in agressive environments – Resimac Ltd
Resin – light rail embedment material, telecommunication jointing and sealing compounds and electrical potting compound and resin – A L H Systems Ltd
Resin Bond Diamond Products – diamond tool manufacturers – Abrasive Technology Ltd
Resin Size 249 – potassium soap – Hercules Holding Ii Ltd
Resinex – Resinex UK Ltd
***Resistamyl (Netherlands)** – modified starch – Tate & Lyle Public Ltd Company
Resistex – Leighs Paints
Resistol – dye resist agents for wool and nylon blends – Brenntag Colours Ltd
ResiTie – stainless steel resin-resin remedial wall tie system – Helifix Ltd
Resolver – Encoders UK
ResourceMaster – Booking system for Internet – Web Labs Ltd
Respect – casual wear – Raves Clothing Ltd
Respond – computer software for unified PC messaging fax email print – Wordcraft International Ltd
Response – instantaneous hot water units – Armstrong Holden Brooke Pullen Ltd
Resqhook – safety knives – Egginton Bros Ltd
Resque (United Kingdom) – Emergency Services – Remsdaq Ltd

Resta – Pledge Office Chairs Ltd
Restart – disaster response network – Merryhill Envirotec Ltd
Result – First Impressions Europe Ltd
Result – promotional clothing – I S Enterprises International
Retailbase – Retailers head office solution – Iris Group
Retailkey – Iris Group
Retell – UK Office Direct
Reten – flocculant and retention aid – Hercules Holding Ii Ltd
Retention Units – retaining frames for pallets – Palletower GB Ltd
Retread – revitalisation and shaping of existing macadam roads and footpaths – Colas Ltd
Retriever 55 – dog waste bin – Glasdon International Ltd
RetroBouy – an impressed current system to provide cost effective protection for larger structures – Hockway
Retrocat – servicing maintenance and cathodic protection of mains, pipes and conduits – Severn Trent Water
Retropaque – G E Healthcare
Retropod – rov installable life extension solution for insitu cathodic protection installations – Hockway
Retroseal – seal for existing timber windows and doors – Schlegel UK
RetroTie – stainless steel remedial wall tie system – Helifix Ltd
Retrowall – Preston Plywood Supplies
REUF Trapped Roller Freewheel – Renold Clutches & Couplings Ltd
REUK – Renold Clutches & Couplings Ltd
REUKC – Renold Clutches & Couplings Ltd
REUKCC – Renold Clutches & Couplings Ltd
Reunion – broadband wireless access solution – Nortel Networks UK Ltd
REUS Trapped Roller Freewheel – Renold Clutches & Couplings Ltd
REUSNU Trapped Roller Freewheel – Renold Clutches & Couplings Ltd
Revelation – travel goods – Antler Ltd
Revell Model Kits – Binney & Smith Europe Ltd
Reversacol – photochromic dyes – Vivimed Labs Europe Ltd
Reversacol - Jarocol – Vivimed Labs Europe Ltd
Reverso – flags, canvas covers and marine safety equipment – Speedings Ltd
Revertex – rubber latices – Yule Catto & Co plc
Revesorb – flame retardant Polyurethane foam and composites for acoustic absorption and insulation – Vitec
REVIEW – full colour design review – Aveva Solutions Ltd
***Revitex (Spain)** – insulating sleeving – Croylek Ltd
Revitex – insulating sleevings – Relats UK Ltd
Revmaster – variable speed drives – Opperman Mastergear Ltd
Revo (Germany) – actuator – Crane Process Flow Technology Ltd
Revol – belt treatments, high temperature graphite and molybdenum lubricants – Revol Ltd
Revolair – Compressors – Scott International Ltd
Revolution 500 – A heavy duty liquid laundry detergent – Premiere Products Ltd
Revolver – 2 sided rotating displays – T P S Visual Communications Ltd
Revometer (United Kingdom) – mechanical tachometer – Foundrometers Instrumentation Ltd
RevoSec – full height rotary security door – Gunnebo Entrance Control Ltd
Revue – traditional style washbasins, closet, and bidet – Ideal Standard Ltd
Revvo – Mercury Bearings Ltd
Reward – catering & commercial trolleys – Reward Manufacturing Co. Ltd
Rewarding Dogs – Dog Behaviour Modification System – Rewarding Dogs
Rewinders – C M Machinery
***Rewpovent (United Kingdom)** – ventilation/heat recovery units – Thermal Technology Sales Ltd
Rex – V E S Ltd
REX – Italian porcelain floor tile – World's End Couriers Ltd
***Rex (Germany)** – digital and analogue time switches – Starkstrom Ltd
Rex Rotary – Copiertec Ltd
***Rex Rotary (EU & Japan)** – photocopiers and facsimiles – N R G Group Ltd
Rex Rotary – copy duplicator – Unigraph UK Ltd
Rexaloy – laboratory metalware – R & L Enterprises Ltd
Rexam – print and packaging – Rexam Holding plc
Rexam – Amcor Flexibles
Rexam Cad – paper – Arjo Wiggins Chartham Ltd
Rexam - Inspire - StratFX – Exopack Advanced Coatings Ltd
Rexel – UK Office Direct
***Rexius** – Vaderstad Ltd
***Rexius Twin** – Vaderstad Ltd
Rexneed – metal disc couplings – Lenze UK Ltd
Rexnord – engineering products – Invensys PLC
REXNORD – Chaintec Ltd
Rexnord – transmission chain, conveyor chain – Rexnord NV UK

Rexnord – Mercury Bearings Ltd
Rexon – Peter Rushton Ltd
Rexroth – Trafalgar Tools
Rexroth – Pressure Design Hydraulics Ltd
Rexroth – hydraulic – V H S Hydraulic Components Ltd
REXROTH – Hydraulic & Offshore Supplies Ltd
Rexroth – Hydraulic Component & Systems Ltd
Rexroth – equipment/spares – Bearwood Engineering Supplies
Rexroth – Harrier Fluid Power Ltd
***Reynolds (U.S.A.)** – aluminium coloured foil sheets – Terinex Ltd
REYROLLE – Hydraulic & Offshore Supplies Ltd
Reznor – commercial air heaters – Johnson & Starley Ltd
Reznor. – Reznor UK Ltd
RF6 Cable Duty – heavy duty – Cablofil
RF7 Cable Tray – medium duty – Cablofil
RFM – digital refractometer – Bellingham & Stanley Ltd
RFM (United Kingdom) – workwear and coveralls – Corston Sinclair Ltd
RFM - digital refracometer.Eclipse - hand refractometerPRH - process refractometerADP - polarimeterAG - calibration materials – Bellingham & Stanley Ltd
RFT (Germany) – electronic valves and tubes, CRTs and semiconductors – Edicron Ltd
RG100 – traffic light – Dok Tek Systems Ltd
RGIS – retail & grocery inventory specialists – R G I S Inventory Specialists
RGK – E P C
RGR Fabricating – filtration & strainer manufacturers & designers, & plate work & piping – R G R Fabrications & Welding Services Ltd
Rhapsody – kitchen furniture – Moores Furniture Group
Rhapsody – key telephone system – Samsung Telecom UK Ltd
***Rhapsody (Sweden)** – bath with revolutionary shaped tub with automatic filling to a pre-set level at a pre-set temperature and features an equipment cleaning system – Arjo Med AB Ltd
RHC – gas fired unit heaters – Reznor UK Ltd
Rheinstahl – Harrier Fluid Power Ltd
Rheogel – paramelt
Rheopaque – G E Healthcare
Rheumasol – herbal remedy for the relief of rheumatic ache and pain – Perrigo UK
Rhino – security steel lockers for clothes and valuables – Link Lockers
Rhino – mine car controller – Qualter Hall & Co. Ltd
Rhino – GB Beverages
Rhino Doors – Chorus Panel & Profiles
Rhino Tough Glass – fibre Composite - has a very high impact strength, vandal resistance is corrosion proof and has complete rigidity – Wybone Ltd
Rhinoceros – hinges – London Pressed Hinge Co. Ltd
Rhinofloor – The Winnen Furnishing Company
Rhinohide – protective body armour for clothing – Foam Engineers Ltd
RHL – Hydraulic & Offshore Supplies Ltd
Rhobot – rhodes interpress transfer systems – Joseph Rhodes Ltd
Rhoburn – flammability tester – James H Heal & Co. Ltd
Rhodes – sheet metal working machinery, presses and shears – Joseph Rhodes Ltd
Rhodes – Engineering – Delta Fluid Products Ltd
RHODES – Trafalgar Tools
Rhodex – rhodium plating process – Cookson Electronics Ltd
Rhodius (Germany) – cutting and grinding disk – Brian Hyde Ltd
Rhofeed – rhodes roll feed – Joseph Rhodes Ltd
RHOMBOS TECHNOLOGIES – Specialist data storage system – Kenure Developments Ltd
Rhombus – Mercury Bearings Ltd
Rhomint – rhodes coining press – Joseph Rhodes Ltd
Rhos Dopplex – combined doppler and PPG system – Huntleigh Healthcare
Rhosort – rhodes coin sotring machine – Joseph Rhodes Ltd
RHP – Mercury Bearings Ltd
RHP – bearings – N S K Europe
Rhubafuran – perfume speciality – Quest International UK Ltd
Rhythm – paper – Fenner Paper Co. Ltd
Rhythm – magazine – Future Publishing Ltd
Rhythm – quartz mantel and wall clocks – L C Designs Ltd
***Rhythm-Tech (U.S.A.)** – tambourines and percussion products – John Hornby Skewes & Co. Ltd
RI-Barrier – Ritrama UK Ltd
RI-Cote – Ritrama UK Ltd
RI-Flex – Ritrama UK Ltd
Ri-Jac – automatic hose nozzle – W A Cooke & Sons
RI-Mark – Ritrama UK Ltd
RI-Print – Ritrama UK Ltd
RI-Triplex – Ritrama UK Ltd
RIA (Europe, Western) – hdpe valves – Everyvalve Ltd

Rialta – plunger coffee maker – La Cafetiere

Rialto – shower screen – Ideal Standard Ltd

Rialto – internet rating and billing – A T & T

Rib-Tone – board – Fenner Paper Co. Ltd

RIBA – A A T I Ltd

RIBBLE VALLEY HOG ROAST – HOG ROAST AND MACHINES – Ribble Valley Homes Ltd

Ribblelite – (plain lightweight and supercoated) general purpose fire hose – Richards Hose Ltd

Ribbon Blenders – Morton Mixers & Blenders Ltd

Ribline – material for road marking – Line Markings Ltd

Ric – ground compactors – B S P International Foundations Ltd

Rice Hydro – Hydrostatic Test Pumps – Hydratron Ltd

Richard Barrie – furnishing fabrics – Ena Shaw Ltd

Richard Burbidge Architectural Mouldings – skirtings, dado and cornices – Richard Burbidge Ltd

Richard Burbridge – D G Heath Ltd

Richard Grant – car accessories – Richard Grant Mouldings Ltd

Richard Hayward – sailcloth – Heathcoat Fabrics Ltd

Richard Newnham Project Management Services – Richard Newnham Project Management Services – Richard Newnham Project Management Services

Richard R Leader – Leader Chuck Systems Ltd

Richard Western Trailers – agricultural trailers, manure spreaders, silage feeders, slurry equipment and bowsers – Richard Western Ltd

Richards – J H Richards & Co.

Richardsons Stalham – cruising holidays – Richardsons Stalham Ltd

Richardwood – babywear, childrens wear, accessories and bedding – Richard Wood Babywear

Richmond – shirts and pyjamas – J M C Q Huston & Son

Richmond – Monier Ltd

Richmond – patio door, solid or thermally broken – Coastal Aluminium

Richmond – accessories – Armitage Shanks Ltd

Richmond Envoy drilling machines – Phil Geesin Machinery Ltd

Richmond House by Bianca – Turner Bianca

Richmond King Size – filter cigarettes – Imperial Tobacco Group PLC

Richmond King Size Menthol – filter cigarettes – Imperial Tobacco Group PLC

Richmond Smooth King Size – filter cigarettes – Imperial Tobacco Group PLC

Richmond Superkings – filter cigarettes – Imperial Tobacco Group PLC

Richmond Superkings Menthol – filter cigarettes – Imperial Tobacco Group PLC

Richmond Superkings Smooth – filter cigarettes – Imperial Tobacco Group PLC

RICHYPUCCI – The Prestige Pet Wear Company – Richypucci Ltd

Rickmeier – European Technical Sales Ltd

*Rico (U.S.A.) – clarinet and saxophone reeds – John Hornby Skewes & Co. Ltd

Ricoh – 35mm camerasand digital cameras – Johnsons Photopia Ltd

Ricoh – photo copiers – Unigraph UK Ltd

Ricoh – Copiertec Ltd

Ricoh – UK Office Direct

Ricoh Photocopiers – Clarity Copiers

Ricom – Copycare Office Equipment Ltd

Ride On – breakdown warranties – Car Care Plan Ltd

Rider – optical frames and sunglasses – Hilton International Eye Wear Ltd

Rider York – buses – First Group plc

Ridgeway – Portman Building Society

*Ridgid (U.S.A.) – pipe threading equipment – Harrow Tool Co. Ltd

Ridgid – pipe and bolt threading machines – Ridge Tool UK - Division Of Emerson

Ridgid Kollmann – pipe and drain cleaning machines – Ridge Tool UK - Division Of Emerson

Riduttori – Brevini Power Transmissions

Riedel – transformers – Amir Power Transmission Ltd

Riedel – European Technical Sales Ltd

RIETSCHLE – Hydraulic & Offshore Supplies Ltd

Rietschle – Harrier Fluid Power Ltd

Rietschle – general pumps/vacuum – AESpump

Rifle – Henry Shaw & Sons Ltd

Rifleman – Timber Bollard – Alto Bollards UK Ltd

Rigblast – multi discipline to oil, gas industries – R B G

Rigby & Peller – bras, co-ordinating lingerie – Eveden Ltd

Rigging – Accesscaff International Ltd

Righton – non ferrous metals and industrial plastics – Righton Ltd

Righton Fasteners – Fastener Management and Supply – Righton Fasteners Ltd

Rigi-Hooks – Injection moulded hooks, self adhesive – Index

Rigibore – boring tools and equipment – Rigibore Ltd

Rigid Coupling – Renold Clutches & Couplings Ltd

RIGIDAL – profiled aluminium building sheet – Rigidal Systems Ltd

Rigidal corogrid – bar and backet roof spacer system – Rigidal Systems Ltd

Rigidal Deadpan – rain drumming reduction system – Rigidal Systems Ltd

RIGIDAL LOKROLL – standing seam concealed fix sheeting – Rigidal Systems Ltd

Rigidal MicroMatt – pre-weathered finish to aluminium – Rigidal Systems Ltd

Rigidal - Rigidal Thermowall - Rigidal Ziplok - Rigidal Lokroll - Rigidal Deadpan - Rigidal Thermohalter - Rigidal Corogrid. – Rigidal Systems Ltd

Rigidal Safewire – fall restraint system – Rigidal Systems Ltd

Rigidal Themohalter – thermally efficient roof spacer system – Rigidal Systems Ltd

RIGIDAL THERMOWALL – architectural wall panel system – Rigidal Systems Ltd

Rigidal ZIPLOK – standing seam system – Rigidal Systems Ltd

Rigidamp – vibration damped structures – Stop Choc Ltd

Rigidax – Rigidax Tooling Compound – International Waxes

Rigideck – high density 38 mm sheet surfaces – Hi-Store

Rigidex – B P plc

Rigidgrid – Unbraced mezzanine floors – Llonsson Ltd

Rigidpak – 23-33 litre blow moulded polythene containers – Weltonhurst Ltd

Rigiflex – modular boring system – Rigibore Ltd

Rigigrip – milling cutter – Clare Fishers Ltd

Rigilene – B P plc

Rigilon – hard photopolymer for moulding – Plastotype

Rigilor – high modulus carbon fibre – Mersen UK

Rigimesh – steel filter medium – Pall Europe Corporate Services

RIGIMESH – Hydraulic & Offshore Supplies Ltd

Rigipore – B P plc

Rigor – BS4659 BA2 air and vacuum hardening general purpose steel – Uddeholm Steel Stockholders

Rigspray – external coating for corrosion protection of offshore structures – Archco Rigidon Ltd

RIKO – liquid level switches & floats – P V L Ltd

*Riko (Japan) – liquid level switches and floats – Applications Engineering Ltd

Riley – vintage cars – British Motor Heritage Ltd

Rilsan – Nylon colours distributor of the Rilsan range of products manufactured by ARKEMA – Nylon Colours Ltd

Rilsan A – nylon 12 granules (pa12) – Atosina UK Ltd

Rilsan B – nylon 11 granules, fine powders, monofilaments and copolymers (pa11) – Atosina UK Ltd

Rilsan B PA11 – Resinex UK Ltd

RIMCO – Tipping bucket rain gauges – Halcyon Solutions

Rimmel – cosmetics – Coty UK Ltd

Rimmel Silks – cosmetics – Coty UK Ltd

Rimostat – Ringspann UK Ltd

RIMSEAL – Hydraulic & Offshore Supplies Ltd

Rimso-50 – dinethyl sulphoxide – Britannia Health Products Ltd

Rin Tin Tin – ladies footwear – Faith Footwear Holdings Ltd

RING – Hydraulic & Offshore Supplies Ltd

Ring-Free – diesel engine oil – Morris Lubricants

Ring Free XHD – FE fuel efficient shpd oil – Morris Lubricants

Ring Free XHD Plus – oil for turbo charged diesel engines for long drain periods – Morris Lubricants

Ringcraft – rings – Goldsmiths Jewellers Ltd

Ringfeder – Ringflex Drive Systems Ltd

Ringflex – European Technical Sales Ltd

RINGLER – suction systems for the metal industry – M. Buttkereit Ltd

Ringlok – compression fitting (twin ring - stainless steel and other alloys) – Waverley Brownall Ltd

Ringmaster – fungicide – Bayer Crop Science

Ringmaster C – medium voltage switchgear – Schneider

Ringmaster compact – medium voltage switchgear – Schneider

Ringspann – star discs shaft clamping elements – Ringspann UK Ltd

*Ringspann (Germany) – workholding and power transmission products – Ringspann UK Ltd

Ringway signs Ltd – permanent & temporary traffic signs, flexible road signs, street furniture, associated fittings & veichle libery – Ringway Specialist Services Ltd

Rinktex – ice rink carpet – Verde Sports Cricket Ltd

Rinku – fashions – Rinku Group plc

Rinse Aid – liquid rinse additive – Premiere Products Ltd

Rinse-Clene – dairy chemicals – Delaval

Rinstead Adult Gel – mouth ulcer products – M S D Animal Health

Rinstead Contact Pastilles – mouth ulcer products – M S D Animal Health

Rinstead Sugar Free Pastilles – mouth ulcer products – M S D Animal Health

Rinstead Teething Gel – M S D Animal Health

Rio – K S B Ltd

Rio – hybrid PABX – Samsung Telecom UK Ltd

Riotec – K S B Ltd

Riotherm – K S B Ltd

RIP – interment package (burials/cemeteries) – Delta Computer Services

Riplex – plastic surgical catheter tubes and tubing – Teleflex Medical

Ripley – Harrier Fluid Power Ltd

*Ripley (U.S.A.) – cable preparation tools – Welwyn Tool Group Ltd

Ripp 'n' Flow – Flexipol Packaging Ltd

Rippatape – pressure-sensitive, self-adhesive tear tape used to open corrugated and folding cartons – Payne

Ripple Retail Concepts – retail display cabinets – Lynton Trailers UK Ltd

Risbridger – aircraft ground servicing equipment and garage forecourt equipment – Risbridger Ltd

Rise Hire Platforms – Accesscaff International Ltd

Riserbond – TDR equipment – Radio Detection

Rising Kerb – road blocker – Zeag UK Ltd

*Rising Paper (U.S.A.) – high quality paper and board – G F Smith

Riskwise – service and software for risk based inspection of process plant – T W I

Rislan A PA12 – Resinex UK Ltd

Riston – photopolymer film – Du Pont UK Ltd

Ritchie – yellow jacket – AESpump

Ritchie Agricultural – manufacturers of livestock feeding, handling and weighing equipment for cattle, sheep, pigs and deer. Bale handling, feeding and grassland management equipment. Seedbed consolidation equipment – David Ritchie Implements Ltd

Ritchie Industrial – design, manufacture and supply fabrications and mechanical equipment for the gas, materials handling (pallets, crates etc) offshore and aquaculture industries – David Ritchie Implements Ltd

Ritchie Water, Ritchie Industrial, Ritchie Agricultural, Cook. – David Ritchie Implements Ltd

Ritchlight Hartington Conway – National Door Co.

Rite Lok – Components Direct

Rittal – Proplas International Ltd

Rittal – Switch gear and close control cooling – Barkair Ltd

Rittal Coolers – European Technical Sales Ltd

Rittal Enclosures – European Technical Sales Ltd

Rittmeyer – wire stripping machines – Automated Cable Solutions Ltd

Ritz – centrifugal pumps – New Haden Pumps Ltd

Ritz – hotel – The Ritz Hotel

Ritz Atro – archimedean screw pumps – New Haden Pumps Ltd

RIV – robotic inspection vehicle to rotor-in-place generator testing – Adwel International Ltd

Riva – computer systems for retail, cash & carry and Hewlet-Packard – Torex Retail Holdings Ltd

RIVA CALZONI – Hydraulic & Offshore Supplies Ltd

Rivclinch – sheet metal clinching – Bollhoss Fastenings Ltd

River – record label – B G S Productions Ltd

River Accessories – accessories for bathrooms – Bathstore.com Ltd

River Mill Flags – flags, flag poles and advertising banners – House Of Flags

River Phoenix – PVC foam buoyancy fence boom – Cowens Ltd

Riveria RS – inset balanced flue gas fire – Robinson Willey

Riverside – record label – Ace Records Ltd

Rivertrace – equipment & spares – Bearwood Engineering Supplies

Rivetting Machines – radial – Turner Machine Tools

Riviera – fruit crush compounds – Cargill Flavor Systems UK Ltd

Riviera – vending machines – Westomatic Vending Services Ltd

Riviera Electric – electric inset fire – Robinson Willey

Riviera LF – inset living flame gas fire – Robinson Willey

Riviera Plus – vending machines – Westomatic Vending Services Ltd

Rivitex – riveted gloves and mitts – Bennett Safetywear

Rivkle (Rivnut) – blind rivet nuts and studs – Bollhoss Fastenings Ltd

Rivmatic – continuous feed high speed repetition rivet installation machine – Avdel UK Ltd

Rivo – machinery for grinding saws – Vollmer UK Ltd

Rivscrew – removable and reusable fastener for assembly of electronic components – Avdel UK Ltd

Rivscrew – screw and rivet fastener systems – Zygology Ltd

Rivset – blind rivets and self-piercing rivets – Bollhoss Fastenings Ltd

Rizistal – acid and alkali resisting cements – J L Lord & Son Ltd

Rizistalcrete polymer screed – J L Lord & Son Ltd

Rizla – roll-your-own papers and accessories – Imperial Tobacco Group PLC

Rizla King Size – cigarette papers – Imperial Tobacco Group PLC
Rizla Regular – cigarette papers – Imperial Tobacco Group PLC
RJ-Lynxx – Selectronix Ltd
RJE – Trowell Plant Sales Ltd
Rjh tool and equipment – grinding machines – R K International Machine Tools Ltd
RM 25 X Cable Tray – medium duty return flange – Cablofil
RM 50 X Cable Tray – heavy duty return flange – Cablofil
RM Automotive – Letchford Supplies Ltd
RM Power Trunking – single & multi compartment – Cablofil
RM6 – 24v indoor ring main unit – Schneider
RMB 30 Basket Tray – heavy duty – Cablofil
RMF – Hydraulic & Offshore Supplies Ltd
RML 100 Cable Ladder – medium duty – Cablofil
RML 125 Cable Ladder – heavy duty – Cablofil
RML 150 Cable Ladder – extra heavy duty – Cablofil
RML 60 Cable Ladder – light duty – Cablofil
RMS – Connectors – Dax International Ltd
Ro-Mil – power supply unit – Roband Electronics plc
Road – roadside space – J C Decaux UK Ltd
Road Runner Dispatch – same day couriers – Covelward Ltd
Roadall – concrete breaker – Drivall Ltd
Roadblocker – vehicle blocking device and hydraulic rising bollards – Frontier Pitts Ltd
Roadlink – brake shoes and rivets, disc brake calipers and steering and suspension components – Roadlink International Ltd
Roadway – Accesscaff International Ltd
Roalt – brown bread malt flour – E D M E Ltd
Rob Roy – Trowell Plant Sales Ltd
Robac – rubber accelerators – Robinson Brothers Ltd
Robant – rubber rolls for printing & textile industry – Robant Services Ltd
***Robax (Germany)** – heat resistant glass ceramic – Schott UK Ltd
Robay – air compressors – Rodwell H T B Ltd
Robbi (Italy) – cylindrical grinders – R K International Machine Tools Ltd
Robbi (Italy) – Engine rebuilding machines – Fondera Ltd
ROBBOLITE – Hydraulic & Offshore Supplies Ltd
***Robby** – Osprey Deep Clean Ltd
Robec – rotating biological contactor – Tuke & Bell Ltd
Roberson – artists materials – C Roberson & Co. Ltd
ROBERT BOSCH – Hydraulic & Offshore Supplies Ltd
Robert Burling – roofing supplies – Roberts & Burling Roofing Supplies Ltd
Robert Gord – Harrier Fluid Power Ltd
Robert Lloyd – The Winnen Furnishing Company
Robert Noble – textile piece goods of high quality wool and cashmere – Robert Noble
Robert Noble – woven apparel fabric manufacturers – Replin Fabrics
Robert Prettie – plumbing, heating & mechanical services – Mighty
Robert Sorby – woodturning tools and accessories, chisels and miscellaneous woodworking tools – Robert Sorby
Robert Sorby – Woodturning tools, chucks, sharpening products – The Toolpost
***Roberto Rossini (Worldwide)** – spectacle frames – Optiquality Holdings Ltd
***Roberts** – Greencore Frozen Foods
Roberts of Churchgate – jewellers and engravers – Roberts Of Churchgate
Roberts Radio – radio receivers – Roberts Radio Ltd
Robertshaw – fire fighting equipment – Bearwood Engineering Supplies
Robertson – marine electronics equipment – Navico UK
Robette – mini range of RBCS – Tuke & Bell Ltd
Robey Boilers – Twin Industries International Ltd
Robin – A T Wilde & Son Ltd
Robin – Direct Instrument Hire Ltd
Robin – Alpha Electronics Southern Ltd
Robin – strimmers & hedge trimmers cultuvators – Small Engine Services Ltd
Robin – Alpha Electronics Northern Ltd
Robinson – commercial and railway vehicle shutters – J R Industries Ltd
Robinson Activate – carbon dressing – Robinson Healthcare Ltd
Robinson Iron Work – steel fabricators – Robinson Engineering Ltd
Robinson Nugent – Cyclops Electronics Ltd
Robinson Pumps – Denton Pumps Ltd
Robinson Superflex – veterinary cohesive bandage – Robinson Healthcare Ltd
Robinson Young – UK Office Direct
Robinsons – UK Office Direct
Robinsons – Ruxley Manor Garden Centre
Robinsons – metal greenhouses – Compton Buildings
Robinsons – drinks and squashes – Robinsons Soft Drinks Ltd
Robinsons Greenhouses – aluminium greenhouses – Compton Buildings
Robocoope – Ackwa Ltd
robojet – high pressure water jetters – Robojet Ltd
***Robond (U.S.A.)** – adhesive application equipment for the printing industry – Valco Cincinnati
Robot Accessories – tools – Tatem Industrial Automation Ltd
Robot Coupe – Ascot Wholesale Ltd
Robot Coupe – B B C S Ltd
***Robot Coupe (France)** – food processors, vertical cutter mixers, high speed sieves and vegetable preparation machines – Robot Coupe UK Ltd
***Robots** – Pira Ltd
Robur – pallet trucks and stackers – Stanley Handling Ltd
Robust – stapling machines – Office Depot UK
Robust EL7 – antistatic vinyl flooring – Gerflor Ltd
Rocado – UK Office Direct
***Rocar (United Kingdom)** – buckets – Parasene
Rocbinda – Thornbury Surfacing Chippenham Ltd
Roch – Tesa Technology UK Ltd
Rochester – Alpha Electronics Southern Ltd
Rock Air – Midland Air Tools Ltd
Rock Deformation Research – analysis of rock faults from oil and gas reservoirs – University Of Leeds
Rock Fall – High quality safety footwear and safety clothing – Rock Fall UK Ltd
Rock-It Cargo – air and sea freighting for bands and groups – Rock-It Cargo Ltd
Rock-Ranger – mobile crushing plant – Parker Plant Ltd
Rock-Sledger – jaw crusher – Parker Plant Ltd
Rockclose – cavity closer, thermal and acoustic – Rockwool Rockpanel B V
Rockeater – hydraulic breaker steels (points and chisels for hydraulic hammers) – Caldervale Forge Co. Ltd
Rocket – label – Mercury Records
***Rocket** – batteries – Michael Brandon Ltd
Rocket – footwear – Whyte & Son Nottingham Ltd
***Rocket Burner** – high efficiency oil burner for central heating – Lion Industries UK Ltd
Rocket Fuel – UK Office Direct
Rockfloor – interlocking insulation board for floors of all types – Rockwool Rockpanel B V
Rockfon – S K Interiors Ltd
Rockie – shirts – Blacks Leisure Group plc
Rocklap – process pipe sections – Rockwool Rockpanel B V
Rockliner – external and internal walls – Rockwool Rockpanel B V
Rockliner – fire idea metal casings and panelling systems – Cryotherm Insulation Ltd
Rockliniser (U.S.A.) – hard face deposition equipment – Aegis Advanced Materials Ltd
ROCKMASTER – Hydraulic & Offshore Supplies Ltd
RockShield – external walls insulation – Rockwool Rockpanel B V
Rocksil – rock mineral wool insulation – Knauf Insulation Ltd
Rocksil Fire Protection Slabs – fire protection – Knauf Insulation Ltd
Rocksil Firetech 160 – fire protection – Knauf Insulation Ltd
Rocksil Firetech Ductslab – fire protection – Knauf Insulation Ltd
Rocksil Floor Slab – thermal and acoustic insulation for floors – Knauf Insulation Ltd
Rocksil Insulation Mat – thermal and acoustic insulation for general purpose use – Knauf Insulation Ltd
Rocksil Lamella – insulation for large diameter pipework and vessels – Knauf Insulation Ltd
Rocksil Pipe Insulation – thermal insulation for pipework – Knauf Insulation Ltd
Rocksil Roofmax – thermal insulation of "warm deck" flat roofs – Knauf Insulation Ltd
Rocksil Slabs – thermal and acoustic insulation for general purpose use – Knauf Insulation Ltd
Rocksil Smoke and Fire Barrier – fire protection – Knauf Insulation Ltd
Rocksizer – rock crushers – Parker Plant Ltd
Rockspan – Eurobond Laminates Ltd
***Rocktek (China)** – guitar effects pedals – John Hornby Skewes & Co. Ltd
Rockwell – upvc roofing and cladding sheets, twin and triplewall polycarbonate sheets – Rockwell Sheet Sales Ltd
Rockwell – typeface – Monotype Imaging Ltd
Rockwell – Cyclops Electronics Ltd
Rockwell – Proplas International Ltd
Rockwell – vertical machining centres – Takisawa UK Ltd
Rockwell Automation – Proplas International Ltd
Rockwell Twin-Pro – twinwall polypropylene sheet – Rockwell Sheet Sales Ltd
Rocla – Harrier Fluid Power Ltd
ROCLA – Chaintec Ltd
Rococo – sportswear – Rococo Style Ltd
Rococo – cobble setts – Plasmor Ltd
Rocol – S J Wharton Ltd
Rocon Foam Products Ltd – foam products – Rocon Foam Products Ltd
Rodatherm – fuel oil treatment – Rodol Ltd
Rodaviss – glass joint – Radleys
Rodex – clothing and accessories for men and women – Aquascutum Pension Plan
***Roditor (Italy)** – polishing mops – British & Continental Traders Ltd
Rodobal – Rod Ends, Spherical Bearings – Rota Precision Ltd
Rodobal, rodoflex, Rodogrip, Aurora. – Rota Precision Ltd
Rodoflex – Flexible Couplings – Rota Precision Ltd
Rodogrip – Precision Locking Nuts – Rota Precision Ltd
Rodol – water treatment – Rodol Ltd
Rodpak – chemical dosers – Rodol Ltd
Roederstein Capacitors – Vishay Ltd
Roemheld (Germany) – hydraulic clamping equipment – Roemheld UK Ltd
Roemheld – workholding systems – J V Hydraulics Ltd
Rofatop (Germany) – breather membrane – Cembrit Ltd
Rogers Chapman – chartered surveyors – Rogers Chapman plc
Rohan Design – adventure travel clothing – Rohan Designs Ltd
Röhm – Rohm Great Britain Ltd
Rohm – Cyclops Electronics Ltd
Rohm – resistors, semiconductors & optoelectronics – Anglia
Röhm – European Technical Sales Ltd
Röhm Adaptor Plates – European Technical Sales Ltd
Röhm Compact Vices – European Technical Sales Ltd
Röhm Drill Chucks – European Technical Sales Ltd
Röhm Driven Tools – European Technical Sales Ltd
Röhm Lathe Chucks – European Technical Sales Ltd
Röhm Machine Vices – European Technical Sales Ltd
Röhm Mandrels – European Technical Sales Ltd
Röhm Power Chucks – European Technical Sales Ltd
Röhm Tailstocks – European Technical Sales Ltd
ROK-IT Gauges – gauges – Hammond & Co. Ltd
Rokide – high temperature refractories – Saint Gobain Industrial Ceramics Ltd
Rol-Kleen – rolling oils – D A Stuart Ltd
Rol-Trac – industrial and security automatic door systems for sliding, fold ing and swing doors – Rol Trac Automatic Doors Ltd
Rola – locks – Bramah Alarms
Roladoor – roller doors – Stertil UK Ltd
Roland – Merlin Precision Engineering Ltd
***Roland (Italy)** – sheet thickness measuring equipment – Pearson Panke Ltd
Rolashield – Ironsides Lubricants Ltd
Rolawn – turf growers – Rolawn Ltd
Rolba – Harrier Fluid Power Ltd
Rolcork (Portugal) – cork in rolls, sheets – Siesta Cork Tile Co.
ROLEC Enclosures – O K W Enclosures Ltd
***Rolex (Belgium)** – catering trays – Bunzl Lockhart Catering Equipment
Rolex – watches – Goldsmiths Jewellers Ltd
Roline – distribute computers – Rotronic Distribution Services
***Roll (Germany)** – cleaning degreasing plants – Embassy Machinery Ltd
Roll-a-Ring – large steel rings for machinery and construction – J M R Section Benders Ltd
Roll Fed – labels – Printpack Enterprises Ltd T/A Printpack
Roll-Flex (Finland) – multi-directional rollers – Effortec Ltd
Roll-on Balls – Euro Matic Ltd
Rollagas – lighter – Alfred Dunhill Ltd
Rollajack – instant accommodation – Rollalong Ltd
Rollamat – Thermal Reflections Ltd
Rollaround Roadway – Accesscaff International Ltd
Rollaseal – clip on brushstrip sealing for side guid channels of rollershutter doors – Kleeneze Sealtech Ltd
Rollaskid – instant accommodation – Rollalong Ltd
Rollaway – inflatable boats – Avon Inflatables Ltd
Rollawheel – instant accommodation – Rollalong Ltd
Rollbatts – prefabricated, moveable buildings, elements, internal walls, floors, flat roofs, pitched roofs, ceilings and original equipment – Rockwool Rockpanel B V
Rollcovering – press rolls – Moseley Rubber Company Pty Ltd
Rolldamp – fountain solution – Kodak Morley
Rollei – Lamphouse Ltd
Rollem – perforating, slitting, cutting and numbering machines – Rollem Ltd
Roller, Access, Stowaway – manual wheelchairs – Remploy Ltd
Roller Coaster – the original easy launch trailer with patented rollers and swinging beam – Indespension Ltd
Roller Sider – vertical lift curtain sided bodywork – Lawrence David Ltd
***Rollerack** – Sound Dynamics Ltd
Rollerbarker – price tickets – Norman Pendred & Co. Ltd
Rollercoaster – record company – Rollercoaster Records Ltd
Rollerprice – price tickets – Norman Pendred & Co. Ltd

Rollers – rubber coated – James Dawson & Son Ltd
***Rolleston Vale Still and Australian** – St Martin Vintners Ltd
***Rollex** – rollers – Vaderstad Ltd
Rolling Center – Component Systems for Sliding Gates, Sliding and Folding Industrial Doors, and Cantilever Gates – Steel Product Supplies
Rollins – UK Office Direct
ROLLIT – Timcal Graphite & Carbon
RollMatic – roller garage door – Hörmann (UK) Ltd
Rolloff – cake release agent – A A K Bakery Services
Rollor – reusable plastic glassware – Plastico Ltd
Rolls – curtain rails and poles – Hallis Hudson Group Ltd
Rolls Emporium – fashion curtain poles – Hallis Hudson Group Ltd
Rolls Majorglide – heavy channel curtain rail – Hallis Hudson Group Ltd
Rolls Miniglide – small channel curtain rail – Hallis Hudson Group Ltd
Rolls-Nylastic – reinforced plastic curtain rail – Hallis Hudson Group Ltd
Rolls Retrospectives – MTM curtain poles – Hallis Hudson Group Ltd
Rolls-Rotary – sewage pump – Tuke & Bell Ltd
Rolls Statements – decorative accessories – Hallis Hudson Group Ltd
Rolls Staywite – aluminium curtain track – Hallis Hudson Group Ltd
Rolls Superglide – decorative curtain rail – Hallis Hudson Group Ltd
Rollscan – Surface and subsurface roll inspection equipment – Sarclad Ltd
ROLLSTAR AG – Hydraulic & Offshore Supplies Ltd
Rolltex – Electro discharge texturing equipment – Sarclad Ltd
Rollway – Mercury Bearings Ltd
Rolstak – commercial sliding doors or curtain bodies – Hunter Vehicles Ltd
Rolux – handheld stroboscope – Foundrometers Instrumentation Ltd
Roly-Poly – puzzles – Pentangle Puzzles & Games
Roma Medical Aids Ltd (United Kingdom) – manufacture of rehabilitation equipment for the elderly & disabled also tubular fabrications etc – Roma Medical Aids Ltd
Romag – magnetic conveyors – Geo Robson & Co Conveyors Ltd
Romag - magnetic conveyors; Cleanflo - enclosed belt conveyor, Airglide - enclosed, air supported belt conveyor. – Geo Robson & Co Conveyors Ltd
***Romano** – Agrico UK Ltd
Romax – Energy efficient lighting products – Fern-Howard Ltd
RomaxDesigner – knowledge-based computer program for modelling and design analysis of transmission systems and rotating equipment – Romax Technology Ltd
Rombouts – roast and ground coffee – Premier
Romco – bakery machines and equipment – Romco Equipment Ltd
***Romeo & Juliet (Cuba, Jamaica, Europe and Honduras)** – cigars – Hunters & Frankau Ltd
***Romheld (Germany)** – hydraulic tooling parts – A C Hydraulics Ltd
Römheld – European Technical Sales Ltd
Romheld - Hydraulic work holding equipmentF.T.W. - Rotary indexing tablesStark - Zero point mounting systems – Roemheld UK Ltd
Romi – Matsuura Machinery Ltd
Romino – Cloakroom Solutions Ltd
Romney Marsh Herald – newspaper title – Kent Regional News & Media
Romo Fabrics – The Winnen Furnishing Company
Rompa – terry napkins – Pin Mill Textiles Ltd
Rompa – products for people with learning disabilties – Robinson Healthcare Ltd
***Ron-Vik (U.S.A.)** – line strainers in plastic – Dual Pumps Ltd
Rondal – Cloakroom Solutions Ltd
Rondelux – compact fluorescent luminaires – Poselco Lighting Ltd
Rondis – disproportionated rosin esters – Akzo Nobel Chemicals Holdings Ltd
Rondoflex – round rubber sheathbed festoon cable – Industrial Friction Materials Ltd
Rondoflex (C) - FC – Sheilded EMC power cables – Industrial Friction Materials Ltd
Rondoflex (Chain) – rubber sheathbed chain cable – Industrial Friction Materials Ltd
Ronhill – Ronhill Sports
Roniair – vacuum pumps – AESpump
Ronseal – varnishes, wood stains and wood fillers – Ronseal Ltd
Ronson – lighters, watches, pen sets – Ronson Incorporated Ltd
Roof Units – industrial fans – Beatson Fans & Motors Ltd
***Roof Units Ltd (United Kingdom)** – fan manufrs – Westmid Fans
Roofab Scrim – synthetic fine mesh woven polyester fabric – Conren Ltd
Roofline – Kestrel B C E Ltd
Roofpave – glass reinforced concrete promenade tiles – Alumasc Exterior Building Products
Roofscape – Monier Ltd
Roofshield – A Proctor Group Ltd
Roofstat – non-metallic roofing materials – Terram Ltd
Rooftex – one component 'liquid rubber' tar – Conren Ltd
Rooftex GP Primer – general purpose one component solvent based special polyurethane primer – Conren Ltd
Rooftex Granules – fine graded flat granules – Conren Ltd
Rooftex Silver Coating – one component aluminium based reflective overcoating treatment – Conren Ltd
Rooftex Urethane Primer – one component solvent based polyurethane primer – Conren Ltd
Rooftile Clansman – Marley Eternit Ltd
Rooftile Heritage – Marley Eternit Ltd
Rooftile Mock Bond Modern – Marley Eternit Ltd
Rooftile Thaxden – Marley Eternit Ltd
Rooftrak 10 – anti-slip flat roof walkways – Alumasc Exterior Building Products
Rooksmere Recording Studios – Recording Studio – Rooksmere Studios
Room Scaffolds – Accesscaff International Ltd
Room Scents – gel air fresheners – F M C G Ltd
Rootfast – anti vandal, minimal maintenance park and street furniture with earth anchorage or concrete mounting fixings – Earth Anchors Ltd
Roots and Shoots – garden products – P M S International Group plc
Röperwerk – European Technical Sales Ltd
Ropeshield – Ironsides Lubricants Ltd
Ropetwist – washbasin, closet, bidet and bath – Ideal Standard Ltd
Roquet – Hydraulics – Hi-Power Hydraulics
Roquet – J V Hydraulics Ltd
***Rorgue** – Cooking ranges – Exclusive Ranges Ltd
Roro – Stacatruc
Rosaflex – footwear – Whyte & Son Nottingham Ltd
Rosalac – flame retardant wood finishes, polyurethane gloss – Craig & Rose Ltd
Rosan – Specialty Fasteners & Components Ltd
Rose – Mercury Bearings Ltd
Rose – bearings – Nmb-Minebea UK Ltd
Rose Eexe – terminal boxes – J B Systems Ltd
Rose Shoes – footwear – Whyte & Son Nottingham Ltd
Rose with English Lavender – fragrant gifts and toiletries – Norfolk Lavender Trading Ltd
Roseberry – interior feature door – Premdor Crosby Ltd
Rosejoint – bearings for racing cars – Nmb-Minebea UK Ltd
***Roselle Supreme** – cream alternatives – Pritchitts
Rosemary – clay plain tiles and fittings – Monier Ltd
Rosengrens – fire safes – Warwick Fraser & Co. Ltd
Rosengrens – Secure Holidays
Rosengrens Tann Ltd – cash safes, fire safes, deposit lockers, strongroom doors, strongrooms and cash handling equipment – Gunnebo UK Ltd
Rosenthal (J. Rosenthal & Son Ltd) – textile piece goods – J Rosenthal & Son Ltd
Rosetto – industrial hogring & stapling manufacturers – J & H Rosenheim & Co. Ltd
Roshni (United Kingdom) – sounders – Fulleon
Rosina – shower enclosure – Armitage Shanks Ltd
Rosinco – UK Office Direct
Roskel Contracts Ltd – suspended ceiling contractors – Roskel Contracts Ltd
ROSPA – Stacatruc
***Ross** – Organic strains – P D Hook Hatcheries Ltd
Ross – retail frozen fish – Youngs Seafood
Ross – valves – Bearwood Engineering Supplies
Ross – Gustair Materials Handling Equipment Ltd
Ross Care Centres – rehabiliation equipment supply, service and repair – Ross Care Cummunity Equipment Centre
Ross Engineering – high voltage relays and dividers. – Glassman Europe Ltd
***Ross Tools (Hong Kong and Taiwan)** – handtools and equipment – Benross Marketing Ltd
Ross Valves – European Technical Sales Ltd
Rossapol – detergent – Unico Ltd
Rossi – Mercury Bearings Ltd
Rossi – branded sportswear – Rossi Clothing
Rossi Cogeme – Harrier Fluid Power Ltd
Rossi Gearboxes – gearboxes – Potteries Power Transmission Ltd
Rosslite – customized expanded polystyrene – S C A Packaging
Rosta – Kobo UK Ltd
ROTA – Lathe chucks – Schunk Intec Ltd
Rota-Broach – magnetic drilling machines – Arrow Supply Co. Ltd
Rota Broach – Newburgh Engineering Co. Ltd
Rota Trim – rotary action cutters for boards, card, paper and film up to – Rotatrim
Rota Trim - rotary action cutters for boards, card, paper and film up to 20mm thickness. – Rotatrim
RotaBolt – tension control threaded fasteners – James Walker Rotabolt Ltd
Rotabroach – magnetic drilling machines – Campbell Miller Tools Ltd
Rotadex – UK Office Direct
Rotadex – rotary card index – Rotadex Systems Ltd
Rotadisc – lateral and vertical suspended filing – Rotadex Systems Ltd
Rotadisk – equipment/spares – Bearwood Engineering Supplies
Rotafine – rotating drum screen for sewage and industrial effluent – Higgins & Hewins Ltd
Rotafix – Trac Structural Ltd
Rotafix – Rotafix Ltd
Rotaflo – rotary valve stopcocks – Bibby Scientific Ltd
Rotaflow – flow signalling devices used in conjunction with volumeter – Nicotra-Gebhardt Ltd
ROTAFLOW (United Kingdom) – swivel joint – Rotaflow F V Ltd
Rotajet – darts, shafts and flights – Unicorn Products Ltd
Rotakit – brushes – Stoddard Manufacturing Co. Ltd
Rotaklenz – aspirator & spittoon sterilant & cleansing agent – Prima Dental Group Ltd
Rotakote – British Vita plc
Rotakote – rotational cast polyurethane – Dow Hyperlast
Rotalip – high speed rotary lip seal – Greene Tweed & Co. Ltd
RotaMatic – Hörmann (UK) Ltd
Rotameter – variable area flowmeter – Emerson Process Management
Rotanote – rotary card filing system – Rotadex Systems Ltd
Rotapol – rotary polishing brushes and mops – Stoddard Manufacturing Co. Ltd
Rotaprint – printing machines and consumables – P P S Rotaprint Ltd
Rotareach, Flexi, Easipick, Hi-Racker, Dambach, lexi GAS, Flexi AC, Flexi G3 – Narrow Aisle Ltd
Rotaro – combined contact and photoelectric handheld tachometer – Foundrometers Instrumentation Ltd
Rotary – filing systems – Railex Filing Ltd
Rotary Bored Piles – Simplex Westpile Limited
***Rotary Cultivator** – Grimme UK Ltd
Rotary Impact Mill – classifier mill – British Rema Manufacturing Co. Ltd
Rotary Jet – washing machines – Oliver Douglas Ltd
Rotary Koater – R K Printcoat
Rotas – programmable speed relay – Foundrometers Instrumentation Ltd
Rotascan – circular filing systems – Railex Filing Ltd
RotaSec – full height stainless steel turnstile with stainless rotor or mild steel with paint finish – Gunnebo Entrance Control Ltd
Rotashutter – blinds and shutters – Rotalac Plastics Ltd
Rotasift – sieve shaker – Ele International
Rotastep – clutch brake, electro - pneumatic – A T B Laurence Scott Ltd
Rotating Biological Contractors (RBC) – Copa Ltd
Rotatool – tube cleaning machines and tools, and flexible drives – Rotatools UK Ltd
Rotatrim – self sharpening rotary action cutters for card, paper boards and film up to 20mm thickness – Rotatrim
Rotavolt – continuously variable auto transformer – Watford Control Instruments Ltd
Rotavolt - variable transformers. – Watford Control Instruments Ltd
Rotawash Floor Cleaner – Pressure washers – B & G Cleaning Systems Ltd
Rotech – European Technical Sales Ltd
Rotecno – medical fabric (sole agent for Swiss item) and medical textile garments – Lojigma International Ltd
Rotex – Incamesh Filtration Ltd
***Rotex (Belgium)** – label makers and embossing tapes – Ashley Industrial Ltd
Rothenberger – Gem Tool Hire & Sales Ltd
Rothenberger – pipework tools – Arrow Supply Co. Ltd
Rothermix – shower valves – A & J Gummers Ltd
Rothmans – cigarettes – British American Tobacco plc
Roto – pumps – Allpumps Ltd
Roto-Processor – rotor coating – Aeromatic Fielder Ltd
Rotobac – general heavy duty disinfectant – D A W Enterprises Ltd
Rotocare – poultry house disinfectant – D A W Enterprises Ltd
Rotoclene – powerful liquid surface cleaner – D A W Enterprises Ltd
Rotocut – PCB lead cutting machines – Turner Electronics
Rotoflash – warning beacons – Moflash Signalling Ltd
Rotoflex – flexible couplings – Trelleborg Industrial A V S Ltd
Rotofloat – Trelleborg Industrial A V S Ltd
Rotogard – prevents re-contamination of eggs after washing and sanitizing – D A W Enterprises Ltd
Rotogrip (Germany) – automatic snow chain – Rud Chains Ltd

RotoLatch (United Kingdom) – temporary fall arrest system – Latchways plc
Rotolin – linear-rotary bearings doctor blade bearings – Brauer Ltd
Rotolok – Pall Europe Corporate Services
Rotomaid – egg washing and sanitizing machines for the poultry industry – D A W Enterprises Ltd
Rotomec (Italy) – gravure printing presses coating & laminating lines – Atlas Converting
Rotondo – vending machines – Drinkmaster Ltd
Rotoplant – G Webb Automation Ltd
Rotor Clip – industrial circlips – Rotor Clip Ltd
Rotorainer – irrigation machine – Briggs Irrigation
Rotorpostor – 3 sided rotating displays – T P S Visual Communications Ltd
Rotosan – egg washing and sanitizing powder & liquids – D A W Enterprises Ltd
Rotosoap – liquid soap with active bactericide & built-in skin care – D A W Enterprises Ltd
Rotostay – headsail reefing systems for sailing yachts – Rotomarine Boat Equipment
***Rototest** – Rohmann UK Ltd
Rototherm – equipment & spares – Bearwood Engineering Supplies
Rotovac – vacuum tanker with positive displacement pump – Whale Tankers Ltd
Rotoworm – drain rod rotating machine – Wardsflex Ltd
Rotox – rotating indicators – Oxley Developments Company Ltd
Rotring – UK Office Direct
Rougeite – multicoloured calcined flint for pebbledash and decorative uses – C E D Ltd
Rough Guides – travel, music and other reference guides – Rough Guides
Rough Guides – travel guides – Penguin Books Ltd
Rough Terrain Platforms – Accesscaff International Ltd
Rough Trade – record company – Rough Trade Management
Roulunds – Mercury Bearings Ltd
Roulunds – Belts – Sprint Engineering & Lubricant
Roundel – kitchens and bedrooms – Roundel Manufacturing Ltd
Roundhead – Steel Bollard – Alto Bollards UK Ltd
***Roundup** – Equipline
Roundup – desk tidy – Helix Trading Ltd
Roust-A-Bout – Accesscaff International Ltd
Route 21 – all gender fashion – UK Distributors Footwear Ltd
Routeco – Proplas International Ltd
Routemaster – D T L Broadcast Ltd
Router Cutters – cutters for the woodworking trade – Trend Machinery & Cutting Tools Ltd
Routin 1883 Syrups – U C D Ltd
ROV-Homer – ROV navigation system – Sonardyne International Ltd
ROV-TRAK – ROV navigation system – Sonardyne International Ltd
Rover – L M C Hadrian Ltd
Rover – Ashley Competition Exhausts Ltd
***Rover (Italy)** – marble tiles – A Elder Reed & Co. Ltd
Rover – inflatable boats – Avon Inflatables Ltd
***Rover Conglomerated (Italy)** – marble and granite – Bernard J Arnull & Co. Ltd
Rover Ribs – rigid inflatable boats – Avon Inflatables Ltd
ROVNav – remote long baseling (LBL) acoustic transceiver – Sonardyne International Ltd
Rovprobe – underwater flooded member detector – Baugh & Weedon Ltd
Rovral Green – contact fungicide for turf diseases – Bayer Crop Science
Row Fabrications – food preparation tables – S J H Row & Son Ltd
Rowblock – butchers chopping blocks – S J H Row & Son Ltd
Rowcrop – narrow tractor wheels for cropspraying – Standen Engineering Ltd
Rowlett – Ascot Wholesale Ltd
Rowplas – food cutting boards – S J H Row & Son Ltd
Roxascan – G E Healthcare
Roxio – UK Office Direct
Roxon – Gem Tool Hire & Sales Ltd
Roxsure – insurance products – J C Roxburgh & Co. Ltd
Royal – Harrier Fluid Power Ltd
Royal – Tool Presetting Equipment – Royal Tool Control Ltd
Royal – Secure Holidays
Royal – gun manufacturers – Holland & Holland Holdings Ltd
Royal Aeronautical Society – multi-disciplinary professional institution dedicated to the global aerospace community – Royal Aeronautical Society
Royal & Ancient – The Royal & Ancient Golf Club Of St Andrews
Royal and Ancient – The Royal & Ancient Golf Club Of St Andrews
Royal Antoinette – bone china tableware and giftware – The Royal Crown Derby Porcelain Company Ltd
Royal Ascot – carpets - axminster – Brintons Carpets Ltd
Royal Award – blended whisky – Charles H Julian Ltd
Royal Axminster – woven carpets in 100% pure new wool – Axminster Carpets Ltd
Royal Birkdale – golf club – Royal Birkdale Golf Club
Royal Brierley – glass crystal – Royal Brierley Crystal Ltd
Royal Clovelly – woven carpets in 100% pure new wool pile – Axminster Carpets Ltd
Royal Club – blended whisky – Charles H Julian Ltd
Royal Collection – spectacle frames – Pennine Optical Group Ltd
Royal Cozyfires – flame effect gas & electric fires – Crosslee plc
Royal Crest – Turner Bianca
Royal Dartmouth – woven carpets in 100% pure new wool pile – Axminster Carpets Ltd
Royal Deluxe – guns – Holland & Holland Holdings Ltd
Royal Double Rifle – guns – Holland & Holland Holdings Ltd
***Royal Doulton** – Bob Crosby Agencies Ltd
Royal Forest of Dean Blue – Forest Of Dean Stone Firms Ltd
Royal Forest of Dean Grey Sandstone – Forest Of Dean Stone Firms Ltd
Royal Garden – handcrafted iron garden furniture – Kettler GB Ltd
***Royal Genware** – Neville UK plc
Royal Incorporation of Architects in Scotland, The – association for architects – Royal Incorporation Of Architects In Scotland
Royal Liver Assurance – life assurance, endowment and pensions – Royal Liver Assurance
Royal Over and Under – guns – Holland & Holland Holdings Ltd
Royal Prestige Gloss – coated paper & board – Howard Smith Paper Ltd
Royal Prestige Matt – coated paper & board – Howard Smith Paper Ltd
Royal Prestige Print 500 – coated paper & board – Howard Smith Paper Ltd
Royal Seaton – woven carpets in 100% pure new wool pile – Axminster Carpets Ltd
***Royal Selangor (Malaysia)** – cast pewter – Royal Selangor Ltd
Royal Sovereign – UK Office Direct
Royal Standard – parafin – B P plc
Royal Worcester – domestic porcelain, fine bone china, ornamental and giftware – Portmeirion Group Ltd
Royald Herald & Shield Device – shoes – Newmans Footwear Ltd
Royale – toughened glass – Rankins Glass Company Ltd
***Royale (Sweden)** – metal roof tile – Plannja Ltd
Royale – quilts – Trendsetter Home Furnishings Ltd
Royalex – basin – Armitage Shanks Ltd
Royalite – British Vita plc
Royalle – distributors of confectionery – Thornycroft Ltd
Royce – rouges – Lea Manufacturing Co.
Royle Publications – greetings cards general – Great British Card Company plc
Royston – bricks – Ibstock Brick Ltd
Royston Brown – Ibstock Brick Ltd
Royston Golden Buff – Ibstock Brick Ltd
Royston Red – Ibstock Brick Ltd
Royston Weekly News – newspapers – Cambridge Newspapers Ltd
Roystons – patent and trade mark agents – Marks & Clerk LLP
RPC – Proplas International Ltd
RPM – AC HIgh Speed Motors – Baldor UK
RPS Group Plc – Environmental Consultancy – R P S Planning & Development Ltd
RPVE – gas fired unit heaters – Reznor UK Ltd
RQ Motor Range – Zella Instrumentation & Control Ltd
***RRC (Sweden)** – chipping hammers – Atlas Copco Tools Ltd
***RRD (Sweden)** – chipping hammers – Atlas Copco Tools Ltd
***RRF (Sweden)** – chipping hammers – Atlas Copco Tools Ltd
RS – equipment & spares – Bearwood Engineering Supplies
RS-100 – rainscreen system – Kawneer UK Ltd
RS Components – Proplas International Ltd
RSB (Germany) – tube clamps – Hydrasun Ltd
RSF – HEIDENHAIN GB LTD
RSF Encoders – European Technical Sales Ltd
RTD – temperature monitors – F D B Electrical Ltd
RTI APPLICATION DRYER – Hydraulic & Offshore Supplies Ltd
RTP – Rotary stainless steel tanker pumps – Wrightflow Technologies Ltd
RTP Company – Engineering Plastics & Speciality Plastic Compounds – P D L Solutions Europe Ltd
RTS Systems – adhesive encapsulants – Resin Technical Systems
RTY – First Impressions Europe Ltd
RUALTEC – Hydraulic & Offshore Supplies Ltd
RuB – Southern Valve & Fitting Co. Ltd
Rubber – stereo compounds – Plastotype
Rubber Bellows – Interflex Hose & Bellows Ltd
Rubber Design – anti-vibration mounts – M I T Ltd
Rubber Tracks – A T Wilde & Son Ltd
Rubberline – well-bottom cistern – Thomas Dudley Ltd
Rubbermaid – UK Office Direct
Rubbertrack – silica sand high grade soft rubber – Martin Collins Enterprises Ltd
Rubberwell – well-bottom cistern – Thomas Dudley Ltd
Ruberg (Germany) – grain cleaning and handling equipment, aspirators from 40-300 TPH, mixers, dust filters, silos – Nickerson Bros Ltd
Ruberoid – felt – Mells Roofing Ltd
Rubicon – multi-purpose cleaner – Evans Vanodine International plc
Rubino – glass shower enclosures and bath screens – Novellini UK Ltd
Rubout – rubber and latex deodorant – C P L Aromas Ltd
***Ruby** – Tea, saffron, poppodoms – Trade Link London Ltd
Ruby – fuel less confidential paper destroyer – J G Shelton & Co. Ltd
Rubycon – Cyclops Electronics Ltd
Ruckle – Rotary Indexing Tables – Roemheld UK Ltd
Rud Chains – Gustair Materials Handling Equipment Ltd
Rud Matic Disc (Germany) – Rud Chains Ltd
Ruda – holiday park – Ruda Holiday Park Ltd
***Rudd (U.S.A.)** – forestry marking paint – Chieftain Forge
Rudford Property Management – industrial property management company – Rudford Property Management
Rudge – bicycles – Raleigh UK Ltd
Rudge Whitworth – bicycles – Raleigh UK Ltd
RUELCO PRODUCTS – Hydraulic & Offshore Supplies Ltd
Ruez – European Technical Sales Ltd
Ruf 'N' Tumble – Ashtenne Ltd
Rugbeian – rugby footballs – Gray Nicolls
Rugby – oilwell cement – Cebo UK Ltd
Rugby Advertiser – newspaper – Leamington Spa Courier
Rugby Review – newspaper – Leamington Spa Courier
Rugby World – I P C Media Ltd
Rugeley Newsletter – Staffordshire Newspapers Ltd
Rugged Systems – Rugged Computer Supplier – Steatite Batteries
Ruggerini – Harrier Fluid Power Ltd
Ruggerini – A T Wilde & Son Ltd
Ruhle Inductosyn – European Technical Sales Ltd
***Ruko (Denmark)** – security cylinders – Assa Abloy Security Solutions
Ruland (U.S.A.) – flexible shaft couplings – Lenze UK Ltd
Rule – submersible pump – Cleghorn Waring & Co Pumps Ltd
Rule – pumps – ITT Industries Jabsco Pumps
Rumag – magnesium liquid – Rumenco Ltd
Rumevite – feed blocks – Rumenco Ltd
Ruminlix – mineral buckets – Rumenco Ltd
Rumins – minerals – Rumenco Ltd
Rumours – air fresheners – P Z Cussons International Ltd
Run-Around Coils – for heat recovery – S & P Coil Products Ltd
Runco – Lamphouse Ltd
Runcorn and Widnes Herald and Post – free newspaper – Flintshire Chronicle Newspapers
Runcorn Weekly News – weekly title – Flintshire Chronicle Newspapers
Runnymede Dispersions – Dispersions for plastic and rubber industries – Tennants Inks & Coating Supplies Ltd
Ruption – protective padding and BMX bicyles – Ruption Bikes
Ruralclad – organic coated steels for cladding low-humidity farm buildings – Corus U K Ltd
***Rusch (Italy)** – horizontal bandsaws – Prosaw Ltd
Rushtik Chequers – boadweave deluxe quality seagrass floorcovering – Jaymart Roberts & Plastics Ltd
Rushton – international and industrial sewing machine dealers (mainly second hand) – Wimbledon Sewing Machine Co. Ltd
Ruskin Air Management – Ruskin Air Management Ltd
Ruskins – Www.Safetysignsonline.Co.Uk
Russell – concrete roof tiles manufacturing machinery – Vortex Hydra UK Ltd
Russell Baldwin & Bright – estate agents – Chancellors
Russell Black – central heating systems – Russell Black Ltd
Russell Castings – BS5750 and ISO9002 - producers of grey and ductile castings and machined components – Russell Ductile Castings Ltd
Russell Eco Filter – Russell Finex Ltd
Russell Finex – Russell Finex Ltd
Russell Hobbs – kettles, toasters, coffee makers, irons, sandwich toasters, can openers and hot trays – Russell Hobbs Ltd
Russell Morehouse – compressed air refrigerant dryers – Airware International Ltd
Russell Rinex – Incamesh Filtration Ltd
Russell Shutters – rolling shutter manufrs – Russell Shutters Ltd
Russia Heavy lathes – Phil Geesin Machinery Ltd
***Russums** – Russums
Rust-Busters – anti corrosion products – F L D Chemicals Ltd

*Rust-Oleum (Netherlands) – anti-corrosive and specialised coatings – Andrews Coatings Ltd

Rustic Biomulch – mulch – Melcourt Industries

Rustilo – corrosion preventives – Castrol UK Ltd

Rustins – Gem Tool Hire & Sales Ltd

Rustkote – rust conversion paint – Thomas Howse Ltd

Rustoff – rust & scale remover – Deb R & D Ltd

Rustoleum – Off The Wall Graffiti Solutions

Rustoleum – Www.Safetysignsonline.Co.Uk

Rustoleum – Trafalgar Tools

RUSTON – Hydraulic & Offshore Supplies Ltd

Ruston – Trowell Plant Sales Ltd

Ruston Hornsby – locomotive spares – Alan Keef Ltd

Rustop – VCi papers – B S K Laminating Ltd

Rutax Pumps – Denton Pumps Ltd

Ruthenex – ruthenium plating process – Cookson Electronics Ltd

Rutherford (United Kingdom) – grain handling & cleaning – Astwell Augers Ltd

ruvac – pumps – AESpump

rv – pumps – AESpump

RV Live Steam – live steam humidifiers – J S Humidifiers plc

RX – Harrier Fluid Power Ltd

RX 2000 – dairy chemicals – Delaval

RX 400D2 – driving lamp – C T P Wipac Ltd

Ryadream – Ryalux Carpets Ltd

Ryasax – Ryalux Carpets Ltd

Ryasilk – Ryalux Carpets Ltd

Ryatwist Colour Collection – Ryalux Carpets Ltd

Ryatwist Royale – Ryalux Carpets Ltd

Ryatwist Tweed – Ryalux Carpets Ltd

Ryavelvet Royale – Ryalux Carpets Ltd

Ryaweave Natural Collection – Ryalux Carpets Ltd

Ryax – process pump – Sterling Fluid Systems UK Ltd

Ryblock – close coupled pump – Sterling Fluid Systems UK Ltd

Rycent – multi stage pump – Sterling Fluid Systems UK Ltd

*Rychiger (Switzerland) – ready meal filling equipment – Engelmann & Buckham Ltd

Ryco – Harrier Fluid Power Ltd

Rycom – combination pump – Sterling Fluid Systems UK Ltd

Rycroft – Baxi Group

Ryda – Agricultural adjuvant – Interagro UK Ltd

Rydal Engineering – punches and dies for turret machines – Rydal Precision Tool Ltd

Ryder – towbar electrical system – Ryder Towing Equipment

Rye-Pac Packaging Supplies – Wholesale Packaging Supplier – Ryepac Packaging

Ryecrete – seamless resin floor system – Ryebrook Resins Ltd

Ryend – long coupled DIN 24255 pump – Sterling Fluid Systems UK Ltd

Ryetone – rye malt flour – E D M E Ltd

Ryflex – belt driven pump – Sterling Fluid Systems UK Ltd

*Rygo (United Kingdom) – hydraulic control valves – The West Group Ltd

Ryheat – high temperature pump – Sterling Fluid Systems UK Ltd

Rykneld Metals – non ferrous scrap metal merchants – Rykneld Metals Ltd

Rykneld Tean – woven webbings, tapes and ribbons from natural and synthetic fibres(6-100mm) also braid and cords from 1-10mm – Rykneld Tean Ltd

Ryland – polyester gelcoats – Llewellyn Ryland Ltd

Rylands – polyester colour pastes – Llewellyn Ryland Ltd

Rymill Coonawarra (South Australia) – Pol Roger Ltd

Rynite – Resinex UK Ltd

Rynite – thermoplastic polyester resin – Du Pont UK Ltd

Ryobi – S J Wharton Ltd

Ryobi – Gem Tool Hire & Sales Ltd

*Ryobi (Japan) – electric & cordless power tools – Harrow Tool Co. Ltd

Ryobi – D D Hire

Ryobi – Oxon Fastening Systems Ltd

Ryomatic – booster set – Sterling Fluid Systems UK Ltd

Rypos – positive displacement pump – Sterling Fluid Systems UK Ltd

Rypulp – non clogging pump – Sterling Fluid Systems UK Ltd

Ryseal – pressurisation sets – Sterling Fluid Systems UK Ltd

Ryside – side channel pump – Sterling Fluid Systems UK Ltd

Rytherm – condensate sets – Sterling Fluid Systems UK Ltd

Rytor – canned motor and magnetic drive pumps – Sterling Fluid Systems UK Ltd

Ryvac – liquid ring vacuum pump – Sterling Fluid Systems UK Ltd

Ryval Roll Seal Control Valves – boiler bypass control/check valves – Sterling Fluid Systems UK Ltd

Ryvert – vertical pump and sludge mixers – Sterling Fluid Systems UK Ltd

Ryvin – vertical in line pump – Sterling Fluid Systems UK Ltd

S

S.A.21 – Rotadex Systems Ltd

S.A.E. J490 – engineering components – Illston & Robson Ltd

S.A.F.I. – safety spectacle frames – Parmelee Ltd

S.A. Florenza (France) – Haesler Machine Tools

S.A.M. – surgical suction equipment – M G Electric

*S.A.M. (Switzerland) – packaging machinery – Advanced Dynamics Ltd

S.A.P.A. – aluminium extrusions – Sapa Profiles Ltd

S.A.R. – search and rescue raft – R F D Beaufort Ltd

S.A.T. Sea-Air Transport – Cromac Smith Ltd

S & B – Highwood Engineering Ltd

S.B.1 – emulsion floor polish – Premiere Products Ltd

S.B.K. – brushwood killer – Vitax Ltd

S.B.S. – sound insulating raised floor system – Thermal Economics Ltd

S.B.S. – batteries & accumulators – Enersys Ltd

S.C.500 – beam mounted seating – Race Furniture Ltd

S.C.A. – sewage conditioner – E A West

S.C.P. – steel hot water boiler – Hartley & Sugden

S.D. 3 – dyneema core yacht racing rope – Marlow Ropes Ltd

S.D.A. – multi-axis DC transistor servo drive – European Drives & Motor Repairs

S D A Plus – synthetic diamond - saw diamond abrasives – Diamond Detectors

S.D.B. – single-axis DC transistor servo drive – European Drives & Motor Repairs

S/D.M.S. Accessnode – fibre optic and radio transmission equipment – Nortel Networks UK Ltd

S/D.M.S. Transportnode – digital telephone switching and transmission equipment – Nortel Networks UK Ltd

S.D.M.X. – digital multiplexers – Nortel Networks UK Ltd

S.D.M.X. – digital delay unit – A M S Neve Ltd

S.D.S. – finance – Colt Car Company Ltd

S.D.S. – stainless steel sanitaryware, catering and shower equipment – Stainless Design Services Ltd

S.D.-S.D.S. Series – bore-hole pumps – Calpeda Ltd

S.D.S-Relais – relays, fans and switches – Panasonic Electric Works

S.D.X. Index – tele-communication systems – Nine Shipton

S E A L – estate agents – Citywide Estate Agents

S.E.A.Q. International – London Stock Exchange plc

S.E.M. – controlled motor technology – Sem Ltd

S E P – service and support – Schneider Electric

S.E.S. – installation & commissioning of air conditioning – Shepherd Engineering Services Ltd

*S.E.W. (Germany) – electric motors – Power Plant & Drives

S.E.W. – speed drive, motor controlled – S E W Eurodrive Ltd

*S.F.C. Southern Fried Chicken – S F C Wholesale

S'Fill 400 – lightweight epoxy filler – Gurit UK Ltd

S-G-B Towers – Accesscaff International Ltd

S.G.M. – separation units – Cranequip Ltd

S.G.M. – lifting magnets – Cranequip Ltd

S.G.M. – permanent magnets, particularly sintered, alnico and bonded magnets – S G Magnets Ltd

S.H.I. Cashmere – designer Cashmere collection – Shi Cashmere

S.I.A. – abrasives – Arrow Supply Co. Ltd

S.I.F. Silver Solder – oxy-acetylene brazing rods – Weldability S I F

S.I.G.T.A. – professional training establishments – Sigta Ltd

S.I.M.A. – ceramic wall and floor tile cutting, mitring machines – Northern Wall & Floor Ltd

S.I.P. – industrial products – Arrow Supply Co. Ltd

*S.I.P. (Italy) – portable electric arc welders – S I P Industrial Products Ltd

S.J. – roofing contractors – S & J Roofing Ltd

S.J. Clarke – contract curtain makers to hotels etc – High Style Furnishings

S.L.4000 G + Master Studio System – sound mixing consoles – Red Lion 49 Ltd

S.L.9000 J – ultimate analogue mixing consoles – Red Lion 49 Ltd

S+L+H – Harrier Fluid Power Ltd

S.L.S. – syringes, bending springs, test plugs, brass ended poly cleaning rods & pressings – Skeldings Ltd

S.-Line – horizontal split case pumps – Flowserve

S.M. – connectors, plastic sub miniature – F C Lane Electronics Ltd

S.M.80 – sintered high speed steel – Ceratizit UK Ltd

S.M.A. – plastic subminiature connectors – F C Lane Electronics Ltd

S.M.A. – styrene-maleic anhydrid copolymers – Atosina UK Ltd

S.M.A.R.T. – customer satisfaction – Research International Group Ltd

S.M.B. (China) – radial and axial ball bearings – S M B Bearings Ltd

S M C – Alpha Electronics Southern Ltd

S.M.C. – plastic subminiature connectors – F C Lane Electronics Ltd

S M C – Hydraulic & Offshore Supplies Ltd

S.M.E. – precision pick-up arms and turntables, contract precision engineering and electroplating – S M E Ltd

*S.M.G. (Germany) – presses – Embassy Machinery Ltd

S.M.S. – fire detection, alarm and emergency lighting – Honeywell

S.O.R. – S O R Europe Ltd

S.O.S. Medecins – Doctorcall

S.P.3 – blanket and roller wash – Dynamic Drawings Ltd

S.P.66 – maintenance product for floors – Premiere Products Ltd

S.P.A. Series – spa pumps – Calpeda Ltd

S.P.A.T.A. – swimming pool and allied trades association – The Swimming Pool & Allied Trades Association Ltd

S.P CONSTRUCTION – IN CARPENTRY & JOINERY – S P Carpentry & Joinery

S.P. Glass Bubbles – filler – Gurit UK Ltd

S.P. Micro Balloons – filler – Gurit UK Ltd

S.P. Microfibres – filler – Gurit UK Ltd

S.P.S. Tech – fasteners aerospace and automotive – S P S Technologies Ltd

S P Snuff – snuff nasal – Wilson Company Sharrow Ltd

S.R.L. – acoustic consultancy and testing – S R L Technical Services Ltd

S.R.T.E. – demountable side loader – Eka Ltd

S Range Actuator – Hydraulic quarter turn & linear sub-sea actuator – Rotork plc

*S. & S. (Italy) – worsted suiting and jacketing – Schofield & Smith Huddersfield Ltd

S.S.80 – solvent based viscous product for stripping seal and paint – Premiere Products Ltd

*S.S.A.B. Dobel (Sweden) – aluzink (coated steel stockholders) – S S A B Swedish Steel Ltd

S.S.S. – saw sharpening service – Super Sharp Saw Service

S.S.S. – petroleum outlets – Shaws Petroleum Ltd

S.S.W. Automotive – manufacture dryers – S S White Technologies UK Ltd

S.S.W. Black Diamonds – diamond burs – Prima Dental Group Ltd

S.S.W. Diamonds – grey diamond burs – Prima Dental Group Ltd

S.S.W. Impression Paste – zinc oxide & eugenol impression material – Prima Dental Group Ltd

S.S.W. Impression Tray Adhesive – tray adhesive – Prima Dental Group Ltd

S.S.W. Instruments – hand instruments – Prima Dental Group Ltd

S.S.W. New True Dentalloy N T D A – dental alloy – Prima Dental Group Ltd

S.S.W. Steel Burs – steel burs – Prima Dental Group Ltd

S.S.W. TC Burs – tungsten carbide burs – Prima Dental Group Ltd

S.S.W. Tray Adhesive Solvent – adhesive solvent – Prima Dental Group Ltd

S.S. White – dental products – Prima Dental Group Ltd

S.S. White Industrial – flexible drives – S S White Technologies UK Ltd

S.T. – Severn Trent Water

S T G – specialist transport group – S T G Ltd

*S.T.M. (Italy) – geared motors – Micro Clutch Developments Ltd

S.T.S – Specialist Tube Supplies Ltd

S.T.-Size – hydrogenated rosin emulsion paper size – Hercules Holding Ii Ltd

S-Type – fixed & variflow positive displacement pump – Grosvenor Pumps Ltd

*S.V.M. (Switzerland) – electronic energy meters – Switch2 Energy Solutions

S W A L E C – electricity & gas supplier – Scottish & Southern Energy P.L.C.

S.W.C.S. – horological tools – Time Products UK Ltd

S0L0 – zero halogen low smoke cable glands, cleats and accessories – C M P UK Ltd

S2000 – Money Controls Ltd

S3DR – Solid State Data Recorder – Specialist Electronics Services Ltd

S3DR - Solid State Data Recorder; C3DU - Cockpit Control and Display Unit; RCD - Rugged Computing Device. – Specialist Electronics Services Ltd

S4000 – Reference standard cooled mirror dew-point-hygrometer – Michell Instruments Ltd

SA – cylinder & pipe thermostats – Sunvic Controls Ltd

SA 80 – adhesive film – Gurit UK Ltd

*Sa Ronix (U.S.A.) – crystal oscillators and quartz crystals – Pulsar Developments Ltd

SA Series Sprag Clutch – Renold Clutches & Couplings Ltd

SA100 Linear & Rotary – digital readout – Newall Measurement Systems Ltd

Saab – L M C Hadrian Ltd

Saacke – rotary cup pressure jet and steam atomising burners – Saacke Combustion Services Ltd

*Saacke (Germany) – NCI automatic and manual cutter grinding machines – Brunner Machine Tools Ltd

*Saarberg – Saarlander UK Ltd

*Saarlander – Saarlander UK Ltd

Sabertube – glass reinforced plastic tubing – St Bernard Composites Ltd

Sabex – PBX equipment – Nortel Networks UK Ltd

Sabo – domestic grass cutting machines – Claymore

Sabre – range of emergency breathing apparatus & medical products. – Scott International Ltd

Sabre (United Kingdom) – perimeter detection – Remsdaq Ltd

Sabre – Lusso Interiors

Sabre Arc – plasma cutting equipment – Murex Welding Products Ltd

Sabre Elsa – Emergency Life Support Apparatus – Scott International Ltd

SABRE EUROPA JAINNHER – centreless grinders – R K International Machine Tools Ltd

Sabrecom – Radio Communications Interface – Scott International Ltd

Sabreglaze – double glazed windows, doors and conservatories – Sabreglaze Window Repairs

Sabrex – computer blast simulation – Orica UK Ltd

Sabritec – Connectors – Dax International Ltd

Sabroe – Therma Group

Saburr – Rotary burrs for wood carving – The Toolpost

*Saccardo Arturo (Italy) – vacuum packaging systems, shrink tanks – Selo UK Ltd

Sacco – B P plc

Sachman – Lead Precision Machine Tools Ltd

Saco – D M G UK Ltd

Saddlecraft – clothes – Westgate Group Ltd

Saddlery World – equestrian accessories – E Jeffries & Sons Ltd

Sadia Refrigeration – upright service cabinets and chefs counters – Manitowoc Food Service UK

Sadia Senator – upright refrigerated service stainless steel cabinets – Manitowoc Food Service UK

Sadia Sovereign – upright refrigerated service cabinet stove enamel – Manitowoc Food Service UK

Sadia Sterling – upright refrigerated service cabinets in aluminium and stainless steel – Manitowoc Food Service UK

Sadler Range – Dortrend International Ltd

Sadolin Classic – a low to medium build exterior woodstain providing protection to timber substrates such as cladding, fascias, fencing etc. – Akzo Nobel Woodcare Ltd

Sadolin Extra – a medium to high build exterior woodstain for providing protection to timber substrates including all exterior softwood and hardwood joinery. For optimum protection on new wood use as a finish to Sadolin Classic. – Akzo Nobel Woodcare Ltd

Sadolin Fencing Woodstain – water-borne, high performance timber protection, formulated to provide a long lasting water-repellent stain for use on planed and rough sawn garden timbers. – Akzo Nobel Woodcare Ltd

Sadolin Floor Colours – an interior water-borne woodstain for decoration of interior timber floors. Requires finishing with Sadolin Hard Wearing Floor Varnish. – Akzo Nobel Woodcare Ltd

Sadolin Hard Wearing floor Varnish – a clear protective interior varnish for use on timber floors. Incorporates a one-component water-borne sealer to reduce darkening of the timber and grain raising. – Akzo Nobel Woodcare Ltd

Sadolin High Performance Varnish – a protective interior varnish for use on window frames, handrails, skirtings, wood panelling, doors, furniture etc. available in colours and colourless. – Akzo Nobel Woodcare Ltd

Sadolin PV67 Heavy Duty Varnich – a clear protective interior varnish for use on timber floors, bar tops and other timbers where a very hard wearing finish is required. – Akzo Nobel Woodcare Ltd

Sadolin Quick Drying Floor Varnish – a clear protective interior varnish for use on timber floors and other timbers where a quick drying and hard wearing finish is required. – Akzo Nobel Woodcare Ltd

Sadolin Quick Drying Varnish – a water-borne, interior protective varnish available in clear or coloured finishes. – Akzo Nobel Woodcare Ltd

Sadolin Quick Drying Wood Preserver – a water-borne timber preservative – Akzo Nobel Woodcare Ltd

Sadolin Shed and Fence Preserver – an organic solvent-borne decorative timber preservative formulated to provide long lasting protection on sheds, fences and other exterior garden timbers. (HSE No. 6821) – Akzo Nobel Woodcare Ltd

Sadolin Shed and Fence Protection – a low build woodstain providing economic timber protection for rough sawn timbers. – Akzo Nobel Woodcare Ltd

Sadolin Stainable Woodfiller – a two-part wood filler for timber in exterior and interior environments, formulated to accept most conventional woodstains and dyes. – Akzo Nobel Woodcare Ltd

Sadolin Supercoat – a medium to high build exterior woodstain offering superior absorption and greater durability benefits, resulting in reduced costs. – Akzo Nobel Woodcare Ltd

Sadolin Superdec – a medium to high build water-based opaque timber coating. – Akzo Nobel Woodcare Ltd

Sadolin Wood Effects – a water-borne woodstain for decoration of interior timbers. – Akzo Nobel Woodcare Ltd

Sadolin Wood Preserver – a colourless, organic, solvent-borne timber preservative. (HSE No. 5649) – Akzo Nobel Woodcare Ltd

Sadolin Woodfiller – a one-pack wood filler for small repairs such as nail holes and minor surface defects, to timber in exterior and interior environments. Available in 6 wood tones. – Akzo Nobel Woodcare Ltd

Sadtem (France) – Mathew C Blythe & Son Ltd

SAE – Hydraulic & Offshore Supplies Ltd

SAE FLANGES – Hydraulic & Offshore Supplies Ltd

SAF – aerated filter – Copa Ltd

Saf – Independent Welding Services Ltd

Saf – trailer axle and suspension components – Roadlink International Ltd

SAF 2507 – Sandvik Bioline

SAF 2507 – super duplex stainless steel – Columbia Metals Ltd

SAF/Apollo – steam air finisher/multiconditioners – Electrolux Laundry Systems

Saf-Twist – respirator – Parmelee Ltd

Safariland – Aspen International Ltd

Safe Access Solutions – Accesscaff International Ltd

Safe-Air – mobile breathing air units respiratory equipment – Factair Ltd

Safe-Air Tester – air quality tester – Factair Ltd

Safe Clip – Kempston Controls Ltd

Safe Flex – hacksaws – L S Starrett Co. Ltd

Safe-Guard (United Kingdom) – cross-scored forward-acting metal bursting disc – Elfab Ltd

Safe Return – Rescue Equipment – Task Masters UK Ltd

Safe & Sound – medical sundries (plasters etc) – Paul Murray plc

Safe-T-Guard – heavy duty rubber ring mat – Jaymart Roberts & Plastics Ltd

Safe-t-store – storage buildings – Adroit Modular Buildings plc

Safe-T-Zone – interlocking grease resistant rubber ring link flooring/matting – Jaymart Roberts & Plastics Ltd

SafeAir Tester – air quality tester to BS 4275 – Factair Ltd

Safebloc – mains connector – Schurter Ltd

Safebond – flooring adhesive – Tarkett Ltd

Safeco – service for compressors on fairground rides – Airware International Ltd

Safecontractor Approved – Safecontractor

Safecrest – British Vita plc

*Safed – electric furnaces – Ramsell Naber Ltd

Safedeko/Chip – round studded and smooth textured extra slip resistant vinyl safety floorings – Jaymart Roberts & Plastics Ltd

Safedeko/Diamond – extra heavy duty 3mm(1mm wear surface) diamond deckplate vinyl safety flooring – Jaymart Roberts & Plastics Ltd

Safedeko/Metal – embossed round stud/geometric chequeplate standard chequered metallic design vinyl safety floorings – Jaymart Roberts & Plastics Ltd

Safeflex – rulers – Helix Trading Ltd

Safeframe – Display Security – Destec Systems Ltd

Safegard – overload clutches – Cross & Morse

Safegas – leak detection fluid – Anglo Nordic Burner Products Ltd

Safegrip – hip protector – Robinson Healthcare Ltd

Safegrip – runway de-icer – Brotherton Esseco Ltd

Safeguard – underfloor safes – Securikey Ltd

Safeguard – County Construction Chemicals Ltd

Safeguard – anti pollution device (propeller shaft) – Deep Sea Seals Ltd

Safeguard – Accesscaff International Ltd

Safeguard – wandering alarm systems – Wandsworth Group Ltd

Safeguard Garages – battery garages – Compton Buildings

Safeguard Systems Europe – paperwork solutions for increased efficiency – S G World Ltd

Safehip – hip protector – Robinson Healthcare Ltd

Safelab – laboratory furniture – Safelab Systems Ltd

Safelab – laboratory furniture – E X X Projects

Safelift – hydraulic hoists – Rossendale Group Of Lifting Gear Co. Ltd

Safelite – 600mm signface bollard – Haldo Developments Ltd

Safeloc – Kempston Controls Ltd

*Safematic (Finland) – lubrication systems and mechanical seals – Pulp & Paper Machinery Ltd

Safepact 2 – switch disconnector – Schneider

Safepak Device – G E Healthcare

Safer Glaze – fire resistant glazing beads – C G I International Ltd

SaFeS-VII – unix and mini computer manufacturing control system – Safe Computing Ltd

Safes XI – windows bared manufactory systems – Safe Computing Ltd

Safeseat – toilet seat sanitizing system – Vectair Systems Ltd

*SafeStep (Sweden) – slip resistant vinyl sheet – Forbo

Safestore – storage buildings – Adroit Modular Buildings plc

Safestore – hazardous substance cabinets – Barton Storage Systems Ltd

Safestrip – p.v.c. insulation & door strip – Copely Developments Ltd

Safetrack – horizontal fall arrest track system – Metreel Ltd

Safetred Aqua – slip resistant vinyl flooring – Tarkett Ltd

Safetred Dimension – slip resistant vinyl flooring – Tarkett Ltd

Safetred Universal – slip resistant vinyl flooring – Tarkett Ltd

Safety Base – Ladder Levelling Device – Ladderfix Ltd

Safety Couplings – Oetiker UK Ltd

Safety Harnesses – Accesscaff International Ltd

Safety Kleen – supplies parts washers & offers a collection service of automotive and industrial waste streams – Safety Kleen UK Ltd

Safety Pipe – secondary containment pipe for fluids and gases – Durotan Ltd

Safety Scan – Machine Guard Solutions Ltd

Safety Services – gas detectors, tripods, hoists and breathing apparatus – V P plc

Safety Signs & Notices – Safety Signs & Notices

Safety Soft – skin degerming mousse – Day Impex Ltd

Safety walk Products – Tape – Austen Tapes Ltd

Safetynet – enhance group call service via - inmarset – Inmarsat Global Ltd

Safetyplus – high performance masonry anchor – Rawlplug Ltd

Safetyswitch – IP54/56 switch disconnectors – M K Electric Ltd

Safetywear – protective clothing and products – Premier World Trading Ltd

Safewire – flexible horizontal fall arrest – Metreel Ltd

Safewrap – kitchen disposables – Marchant Manufacturing Co. Ltd

Safewrap - Caterpack - Marchant - Big Value – Marchant Manufacturing Co. Ltd

Safex – load restraint systems – Andrew Mitchell & Co. Ltd

Saffire – gas welding equipment – Murex Welding Products Ltd

Saffron Walden Weekly News – newspapers – Cambridge Newspapers Ltd

Safi (Europe, Western) – pp valves – Everyvalve Ltd

Safilo – optical frames and sunglasses – Hilton International Eye Wear Ltd

Safire – sealed lead acid batteries – Anglia

Saflok – connecting hooks – Capital Safety Group Ltd

Saft (Sweden) – industrial nickel cadmium batteries – Alcad

Saft – industrial nickel cadmium batteries – Alcad

*Saft (France) – industrial nickel cadmium batteries – Alcad

Saftronic – soft starters – Thermofrost Cryo plc

Saga – acoustic foambacked looselay vinyl tiles – Gerflor Ltd

SAGE – Quintech Computer Systems Ltd

Sage – Logma Systems Design Ltd

SAGE – I T Works

Sage – UK Office Direct

SAGE CRM – I T Works

SAGE FORECASTING – I T Works

SAGE INSTANT ACCOUNTS – I T Works

SAGE INSTANT PAYROLL – I T Works

SAGE LINE 50 – I T Works

SAGE PAYROLL – I T Works

SAGE PERSONEL – I T Works

SAGE PIID – I T Works

Sagem – Lamphouse Ltd

Sagem – UK Office Direct

Saginomiya – electronic, electro-mechanical and mechanical controls and instruments, including thermostats, pressure control, oil pressure controls defrost control humidity controls, pressure transducers, step controls, fan speed controls, pressure controls – Thermofrost Cryo plc

Sahara – washable incontinent bed and chair pads – Synergy Healthcare plc

Sahara – rotary dryers – Abru Ltd

Sahara – Lamphouse Ltd

Sahara – electric dryers for animals – Diamond Edge Ltd

Sahara Deluxe – radiant gas fire – Robinson Willey

Sahara LF – outset living flame gas fire – Robinson Willey

Sahara Presentation Systems – manufacturers and distributors of presentation and training equipment – Sahara Presentation Systems plc

Sahara RS – balanced flue gas fire – Robinson Willey

Sahara Safeguard – radiant gas fire – Robinson Willey

SAHOS – machining centres – R K International Machine Tools Ltd

SAI – Hydraulic & Offshore Supplies Ltd

SAIA – motors – Saia Burgess (Gateshead) Plc

SAIA Bugess – Selectronix Ltd

Saia-Burgess – E Preston Electrical Ltd

SAIA - motors BURGESS - switches – Saia Burgess (Gateshead) Plc

SAIF feeder pillars – switched & insulated fusegear – Schneider

Sailman – Full batten systems – Bainbridge Aqua-Marine

Sainsburys – Supply Chain Solution Ltd

Saint Gobain – Stokvis Tapes UK Ltd
SAINT GOBAIN – World's End Couriers Ltd
SAINT GOBAIN PPL – Hydraulic & Offshore Supplies Ltd
Saisho – T.V. video and hi-fi – Dixons Retail
*Saizen (Switzerland) – growth hormones – Merck Serono Ltd
SAJ – Dynamometers – Dynamometer Services Group Ltd
Sakae (Japan) – Techni Measure
Sakai – Harrier Fluid Power Ltd
*Sakaphen (Germany) – heat and catalyst cured synthetic resin coatings and Linings – Lithgow Saekaphen Ltd
SAL – Sal Abrasives Technologies
SALA – B L M Group UK Ltd
Sala – retractable life line lock – Capital Safety Group Ltd
Sala Group – company logo – Capital Safety Group Ltd
Salaco Express Line – Ocean Express Ltd
Salamander Copperstar – High performance crucibles – Molten Metal Products Ltd
Salamander Excel – high performance crucibles – Molten Metal Products Ltd
Salamander Excel E – high performance crucibles – Molten Metal Products Ltd
Salamander Iso-Suprex – high performance crucibles – Molten Metal Products Ltd
Salamander Plumbago – graphitic refractories – Molten Metal Products Ltd
Salamander S.R. – high performance crucibles – Molten Metal Products Ltd
Salamander Super – high performance crucibles – Molten Metal Products Ltd
SALAMI – Hydraulic & Offshore Supplies Ltd
Salbak – Sallu Plastics
Salbex – Sallu Plastics
*Salco (Hong Kong) – toys and fancy goods – Salco Group plc
Salcombe – woven carpets in 100% pure wool pile – Axminster Carpets Ltd
Sale Systems – sale poster and ticket designs – Repro Arts Ltd
Sales Performance – sales training for the IT industry – Selling Sciences
Salespoint – telephone marketing and database analysis systems – Sales Point
SalesTalk – talking sales promotional aids – O W L Electronics Ltd
Salestrend – UK Office Direct
SALEV – Chaintec Ltd
Salev – T V H UK Ltd
Salicon – preservative – Murphy & Son
Salinas – vinyl wallcoverings and fabrics – Tektura plc
Salisbury – 535mm single oven – Indesit Company UK Ltd
Salisbury 2 LF – outset living flame gas fire – Robinson Willey
Salisbury 2 RS – balanced flue gas fire – Robinson Willey
Salisbury Turbo – power flue gas fire – Robinson Willey
Salkil – broad spectrum poultry bactericide – Agil Chemicals Products
Salmon – brushes – The Hill Brush Company Ltd
Salon Chic – hair straightening range – F M C G Ltd
Salonex – hairdressers basin – Armitage Shanks Ltd
Salop Trailers – agricultural trailers – Marston Agricultural Services Ltd
*Salopian Gold – Scott & Newman Ltd
Salt Abrasives – Wessex Welding & Industrial Supplies Ltd
Salter – UK Office Direct
Salto – Electronic Door Access – Style Tech
Salton – coffee machines, toasters, yogurt makers and bag sealers – Russell Hobbs Ltd
Salts Healthcare – mnfctr, dstrbr of ostomy and waindcare devices, dispensing appliance contractor, breast care – Salts Healthcare
Saltus – torque wrenches – Welwyn Tool Group Ltd
Salty Dog Crisps – Mercia Fine Foods
Salvador – Automaic Crosscuting – A L Dalton Ltd
Salvagnini – Laser Trader Ltd
SALVATORI – Italian natural stone – World's End Couriers Ltd
Salvis – Cooking Ranges – Exclusive Ranges Ltd
Sam – V E S Ltd
SAM DICK – explosion proof vapourisers – H K L Gas Power Ltd
SAM HYDRAULIK – Hydraulic & Offshore Supplies Ltd
Sam Sainz – mens casuals – Novinit Ltd
Sam Weller & Son – decatising or blowing wrappers together with jute and polypropylene with jute and polypropylene bags for presspacking and packaging for the textile trade and continuous belting/fabrics, industrial cotton manufacturers – Sam Weller Holdings Ltd
SAMAG – Chaintec Ltd
*Sambonet – 18/10 Stainless Steel Cutlery & Holloware – La Porcellana Tableware International Ltd
Sambron – rough terrain fork lifts – G Reekie Group Ltd
SAMBRON – Chaintec Ltd
Samco – glass test tubes surgical instruments – S Murray & Co. Ltd
Same – Harrier Fluid Power Ltd

Same – tractor spares – Bearwood Engineering Supplies
Same Tractors – Pigney H Son Agricultural Engineers
Samelco Web Technology – Samelco Automation Systems Ltd
Samiflex – flexible shaft couplings – British Autogard Ltd
Sammic – Ackwa Ltd
Samoa – lubrication equipment – Samoa Ltd
SampleManager – LIMS – Thermo Fisher Scientific
Sampletuft – tufting machine – Thom Engineering Ltd
Samrex Textiles – curtains – Samrex Textiles
Samson – metal reclamation machinery – Grasam Samson Ltd
Samson – metal repair system (rotten structural columns) in sectional timber buildings – Channelwood Preservation Ltd
Samson – safety footwear – M K Associates
Samson – vacuum pumps – AESpump
Samson – B & W Mechanical Handling
Samson – stubble turnip variety – Limagrain UK Ltd
Samson – tent pegs – The Hampton Works Ltd
Samson Column Repair Kit – mechanical jacking device for decaying structural timber columns in timber frame buildings – Channelwood Preservation Ltd
Samson, Stormajor, Shiploader, Kleen-Line, Sterling. – B & W Mechanical Handling
SAMSUNG – Hydraulic & Offshore Supplies Ltd
SAMSUNG – Chaintec Ltd
Samsung – LCD and Plasma Televisions – Electrotec International Ltd
Samsung – UK Office Direct
Samsung – Copiertec Ltd
Samsung – Ascot Wholesale Ltd
Samsung – Lamphouse Ltd
Samsung – Stacatruc
Samsung – Oasis Systems
*Samsung – Tayside Cash Registers
*Samsung – C J Plant Ltd
*Samsung – Shelfguard Systems
Samsung – M S C Gleichmann UK Ltd
SAMSUNG – Harrier Fluid Power Ltd
Samsung – Cobus Communications
Samsung – Cyclops Electronics Ltd
Samsung Cash Registers – Cash Register Services
samtec – Cyclops Electronics Ltd
Samuk – Stacatruc
SAMUK – Chaintec Ltd
Samurai – fishing tackle – Daiwa Sports Ltd
Samwha – Cyclops Electronics Ltd
Sanbrew – Hygienic hose – Dixon Group Europe Ltd
Sanburst – infra red heater – Robinson Willey
Sancell – bubble wrap – Sansetsu UK Ltd
Sanchez Romero Carvajal – Spanish cured ham – Classic Fine Foods Ltd
Sander and Kay – mail order catalogue – J D Williams Mail Order Group
Sanders – classic footwear for men – Sanders & Sanders Ltd
Sanders Pepper Smith RIBA Chartered Practice – Architects – Sanders Pepper Smith Ltd
SANDERSON – Hydraulic & Offshore Supplies Ltd
Sanderson – Custom Brakes & Hydraulics Ltd
SANDERSON – Chaintec Ltd
Sanderuft – wallcoverings – Arthur Sanderson Ltd
Sanderson – Harrier Fluid Power Ltd
Sanderson Fabrics – furnishing fabrics and made-up products – Arthur Sanderson Ltd
Sanderson Options – wallcoverings and fabrics – Arthur Sanderson Ltd
Sanderson Spectrum – paint – Arthur Sanderson Ltd
Sanderson Townend & Gilbert – chartered surveyors – Sanderson Weatherall Chartered Surveyors
Sandfield – Sandfield Engineering Co. Ltd
Sandfield Engineering – Sandfield Engineering Co. Ltd
Sandfield - Sandfield Engineering – Sandfield Engineering Co. Ltd
*Sandflex (Germany) – flexible abrasives – Klingspor Abrasives Ltd
Sandiacre – packaging machinery – Molins plc
Sandingmaster – T M Machinery Sales Ltd
Sandisk – M S C Gleichmann UK Ltd
Sandmaster – abrasive products – Sandmaster Ltd
Sandor – sand dewaterer – Parker Plant Ltd
Sandowheel – sand dewaterer – Parker Plant Ltd
*Sandoz (Switzerland) – precision carbide drills and tools – Brunner Machine Tools Ltd
Sandpiper pumps – Air operated Double diaphragm – Fluid Pumps Ltd
Sandretto – Proplas International Ltd
Sandringham – WC suite – Armitage Shanks Ltd
Sandringham – merino wool blankets – John Horsfall & Sons Ltd
Sandvik – tools/equipment – Bearwood Engineering Supplies
Sandvik – Precision Tools
Sandvik – S J Wharton Ltd
Sandvik Bioline Sanmac – Sandvik Bioline

SANDVIK MATERIALS TECHNOLOGY – Hydraulic & Offshore Supplies Ltd
Sandy Stone – Macclesfield Stone Quarries Ltd
Sanflex – Hygenic hose – Dixon Group Europe Ltd
Sanfood – Hygienic hose – Dixon Group Europe Ltd
Sanford – UK Office Direct
Sangamo (United Kingdom) – time switches – Sangamo Ltd
Sangamo – timers – Bearwood Engineering Supplies
SANGAMO - SUNTRACKER - MZR – Sangamo Ltd
Sangenic International – Nappy Disposal System – Jackel International Ltd
Sani-Fem – sanitary and washroom products – Unicorn Hygienics
Sani Safe – Elsan Ltd
Saniblanc D – Disinfectants – Lhoist UK
Sanico Building Services – Building Refurbishment London Company – Sanico Building Services Ltd
SaniFloor – Mechline Developments Ltd
Sanilav – toilet bowl cleanser – Jeyes
Sanimatic – disposal units – The Haigh Group Ltd
Sanistrel – sanitary towel disposer – I M C
Sanistrel – sanitary towel disposer – Franke Sissons Ltd
Sanitize – detergent sanitizing powder with chlorine – Evans Vanodine International plc
*Sanitized – bacteriostatic and fungistatic chemicals for the hygienic protection of textiles, plastics, rubber products, footwear etc against bacteria, associated odour formation, fungi and moulds – British Sanitized Ltd
Sanitrx – rupture disc – Continental Disc UK Ltd
Sanken – Cyclops Electronics Ltd
Sankyo – European Technical Sales Ltd
SANO TOOLS – MILLING TOOLS – SANO TOOLS
*Sanovo (Denmark) – egg breaking machinery – Lactosan UK Ltd
Santa Pod – raceway – Santa Pod Raceway
*Santarini – dried pasta products – Pasta Foods Ltd
*Sante – Agrico UK Ltd
Santon – Baxi Group
Santoprene – PureSil Technologies Ltd
Santoquin – antioxidant – F L D Chemicals Ltd
Santos – Blenders – Metcalfe Catering Equipment Ltd
Santos Martinez (Romania) – classical guitars – John Hornby Skewes & Co. Ltd
Sanura – urinal – Armitage Shanks Ltd
*Sanwa (Japan) – testing instruments – Servo & Electronic Sales Ltd
Sanyo – UK Office Direct
Sanyo – M S C Gleichmann UK Ltd
Sanyo – Videonations Ltd
*Sanyo (Japan) – television, microwaves etc – Sanyo Sales & Marketing Europe GmbH
Sanyo – TV – Sertronics Ltd
Sanyo – Lamphouse Ltd
Sanyo – PLR thermal cyclers – Sanyo Gallenkamp plc
Sanyo – refrigerators and freezers – Sanyo Gallenkamp plc
Sanyo – Cyclops Electronics Ltd
*Sanyo Denki (Japan) – fans and stepper motors – E A O Ltd
SAP Motor Factors – SAP Motor Factors
SAPA Profiles (United Kingdom) – Aluminium extrusion manufacturers and component supplier – Sapa Profiles UK Ltd
Sapelem – B L Pneumatics Ltd
Saphire, Ruby and Emerald (The Gem Collection) – investment funds for use with Clerical Medical's investment products – Clerical Medical Investment Group Ltd
SaPHuR – payroll and human resources management system – Safe Computing Ltd
Saphur Tempest – pay and till system for agencies offering temporay contract staff – Safe Computing Ltd
Sapona – datacare cleaning equipment – Helix Trading Ltd
Sapona – cleaning preparations and equipment – Helix Trading Ltd
Sapovis – liquid soap – Elsan Ltd
Sappar – pile rig positioning system – Balfour Beatty Living Places
Sapphire – 1-3ltr catering jars pp evoh – R P C Containers Ltd
Sapphire – commercial shutters and grilles – Kaba Door Systems
*Sapphire (Netherlands) – electric folding fabric sunroof – Webasto Products UK Ltd
Sapphire – water heater – Heatrae Sadia
Sapphire – hospital and industrial incinerator – J G Shelton & Co. Ltd
Sapphire – electronic tachometers – Sapphire Research & Electronics Ltd
Sapphire – blue teat dip – Evans Vanodine International plc
Sapphire – bread improvers - blends of enzyme active soya flour, fats and emulsifiers – C S M UK Ltd
Sapphire – lubrication equipment – Centre Tank Services
Sara – soil studies using radio tracer software – Lablogic Systems Ltd
Sarah Louise – childrens clothing – Sarah Louise Ltd
Sarapron – non-selective weed killers – B P plc

Saras Process – selective portable electroplating equipment sales and service work – Saras Process Ltd
Sarasin RSBD – ASME section VIII pilot operated safety valves, ASME section VIII spring loaded safety valves, ASME Section I safety valves – Weir Valves & Controls
Sarasota – Peek Traffic Ltd
Sarasota – Peek Traffic Ltd
Sarasota – Peek Traffic Ltd
Sarbe – search & rescue beacons – Clifford & Snell
Sarco Resistra Gas Bags – pipe stoppers – Sarco Stopper Ltd
Sarco Supra Gas Stoppers – Sarco Stopper Ltd
Sarco Ultra Twin Bags – twin bags for single entry into pipeline – Sarco Stopper Ltd
Sarel – brand name for enclosure range – Schneider
Sarel – Proplas International Ltd
Sarel / Canalis – Enclosure systems / Power & LIghting busbar trunking – Alfred J Hurst Ltd
Sarena – GRP cold water storage tanks and lids – Sarena
Sarenarap – wraparound insulation – Sarena
Sarginsons Precision Components – Sarginsons Industries
Sarginsons Precision Components - Advance Tooling. – Sarginsons Industries
Sari – full face mask respirators positive or negative pressure – Scott International Ltd
Sarina – round stud anti-slip rubber flooring and stair treads – Jaymart Roberts & Plastics Ltd
Sarita (United Kingdom) – compact standing, raising and transferring hoist for use in nursing and residential homes – Arjo Med AB Ltd
***SARP** – Midland Power Machinery Distributors
SARUM HYDRAULICS – Hydraulic & Offshore Supplies Ltd
Sasco – UK Office Direct
***Sasco Real Mayonnaise** – Sasco Sauces Ltd
Sasha Dolls – dolls – Abceta Playthings Ltd
Saskia – high vacuum – AESpump
Sassi – electrical equipment for hairdressing salons – Salon Services Hair & Beauty Supplies Ltd
Sata – Letchford Supplies Ltd
Satair – Test Rigs – Hi-Power Hydraulics
Satblast (United Kingdom) – variable pressure, fully saturdated wet blast cleaning system – Jedtec Finishing Equipment
Satco – cotton tying tapes & polypropylene ribbons – SATCO Tapes
Satcoprint Labels – SATCO Tapes
Satec (Israel) – digital energy meters – I M H Technologies Ltd
Satellite – steel surveyors tape – Fisco Tools Ltd
***Satelliti (Italy)** – computer tables – Ergonom Ltd
Satfone – airborne satellite telecommunications equipment for executive and commercial aircraft – Thales Avionics Ltd
Satin – paste concentrate – C S M UK Ltd
Satin Slims – darts – Unicorn Products Ltd
Satinex – greaseless bar compounds for satin finishing – Lea Manufacturing Co.
Satinlux – darts – Unicorn Products Ltd
Satintone – clay – Lawrence Industries Ltd
Satinwood – decorative paints – Akzonobel
Satis Coaters – AESpump
Satra Footwear Technology Centre – SATRA Technology Centre
Satreat – solution for priming, halogenating rubber surfaces to improve the adhesion thereto, or for rendering the surfaces smooth and tack free – SATRA Technology Centre
Satronic – equipment/spares – Bearwood Engineering Supplies
Saturn – labelling machine – Harland Machine Systems Ltd
Saturn – seat – Armitage Shanks Ltd
Saturn 95 – prestel terminal emulator for windows – Red Sky I T Ltd
Saturn Web – internet and intranet services, email, domain names, bureau services turnkey systems and bespoke programming – Red Sky I T Ltd
Saturno Steam Vapour Systems (Italy) – mobile steam generators – Crofton House Associates
Satylite – satin nickel plating solutions – Cookson Electronics Ltd
Saudi National Pump – pump – S M I
Sauer – hydraulic – V H S Hydraulic Components Ltd
Sauer – D M G UK Ltd
Sauer – Harrier Fluid Power Ltd
Sauer Sundstrand – gear pumps and piston pumps – Sauer-Danfoss Ltd
Sauerwein – Lamphouse Ltd
Sauflon Pharmaceuticals Ltd – full range of contact lenses & contact lens solutions. contract manufacture of pharmaceuticals – Sauflon Pharmaceuticals Ltd
Saunders – valves/spares – Bearwood Engineering Supplies
Saunders HC4 (United Kingdom) – diaphragm valves – Crane Process Flow Technology Ltd
SAUNDERS IDV – diaphragm Valves – Crane Process Flow Technology Ltd
Saunderson House – financial advisors – Saunderson House
Sauter & Barruffalid Turrets – Machine Tool Supplies Ltd
Sauvage – knitted dacron vascular grafts – Bard Ltd
Sav-Wire – true two wire fire alarm system – Protector Alarms UK Ltd
Savair – European Technical Sales Ltd
Savant – I.T. consultancy, education and bespoke software – Savant Ltd
Savant – vacuum – AESpump
Savara – Harrier Fluid Power Ltd
Save & Invest – financial advisors – Save & Invest Financial Planning
Saville AV – Lamphouse Ltd
Saville Heaton – menswear – Saville Heaton Ltd
Savo – Sitsmart Ltd
***Savoir Bed Company** – Tradelinens Ltd
Savona – washing up liquid – Premiere Products Ltd
Savose – cushion heel grip – A Algeo Ltd
Savox – dedicated communications interface – Interspiro Ltd
Savoy – brass plain edge wiring accessories – M K Electric Ltd
Savoy – bias bindings, trouser waistband and corded piping – W Attwood Ltd
Savoy - Bias Binding. – W Attwood Ltd
Sawtec – cutting components for brushcutters – Emak UK Ltd
Sawton – premier plus unvented hot water storage – Heatrae Sadia
Saxby – T V H UK Ltd
SAXBY – Chaintec Ltd
Saxon – hot air continuous heat sealers – Fischbein-Saxon
Saxon – Saxon Lifts Ltd
Saxon – Monier Ltd
Saxon Velours – fibre bonded carpet/tile – Warlord Contract Carpets Ltd
Sayfglida – horizontal lifelines – Capital Safety Group Ltd
Sayfguard – roofedge protection – Capital Safety Group Ltd
SB Booms – oil absorbent booms – Oil Pollution Environmental Control Ltd
SB Series Sprag Clutch – Renold Clutches & Couplings Ltd
SBB – European Technical Sales Ltd
SBC – EDDY Current Variators and servo drives – Amir Power Transmission Ltd
SBC™ – GGB UK
SBES LifeSaver – Man down alarm system for Aircraft refueling Vehicles – S B E S Ltd
SBQ Flexible – polypropline sack distributors – Smith Bros Quinton Ltd
SBS (U.S.A.) – Dynamic grinding wheel balancing – Schmitt Europe Ltd
SBS, SMS, Acuity Research. – Schmitt Europe Ltd
SBS Videos – transport, aviation & military videos – Ian Allan Publishing Ltd
SC – air operated high pressure pumps – Staffordshire Hydraulic Services Ltd
SCA – S M W Autoblok
SCA Tuscarora – moulders of expanded polystyrene, polypropylene, polyethylene and all known copolymers. – Sca Foam Products
Scaffbrite – Forward Chemicals Ltd
Scaffeze – Forward Chemicals Ltd
Scaffeze Plus – Forward Chemicals Ltd
Scaffold Boards – Accesscaff International Ltd
Scaffold Tower Hire – Accesscaff International Ltd
Scaffold Tower Sales – Accesscaff International Ltd
Scaffolding & Roofing Insurance Services – Genesis Risk Solutions Ltd
Scafpad – scaffolding steel & rubber base plates for upright scaffolding tube. – Polymer Products UK Ltd
Scafpad - scaffolding steel & rubber base plates for upright scaffolding tube. – Polymer Products UK Ltd
Scala – Scala Agenturen UK
Scala – black and white slide film – Agfa Gevaert
Scalamp – applied to galvanometers, fluxmeters, electrostatic voltmeters, microammeters and moving coil voltmeters – Cam Metric Holdings
Scaleaway Tools & Equipment Ltd – tube cleaning/polishing equipment – Scaleaway Tools & Equipment Ltd
Scalemaster – hardwater scale inhibiting units, electrolytic, magnetic electronic scale control central heating chemicals central heating corrosion master – D A W Enterprises Ltd
Scalextric – model racing car system – Hornby Hobbies Ltd
Scalink – connectors – Spiring Enterprises Ltd
Scalinks – scale system of molecular model – Spiring Enterprises Ltd
Scalomatic – coarse abrasive wheel m/c – Wheelabrator Group
Scama – message text ammunciators – Amatek Precision Instruments UK Ltd
Scan-Care – Barcode Scanner Repair and Maintenance contracts – Crosscheck Systems Ltd
***Scan Coin (Sweden)** – cash handling equipment – Scan Coin
Scanabowl – outdoor bowling surface – Verde Sports Cricket Ltd
Scanagrene – permanent (indoor) bowling green surface – Verde Sports Cricket Ltd
Scanagrene/Verde Mat/Verde '95 – roll-up bowling mats – Verde Sports Cricket Ltd
Scandura Seals – Newburgh Engineering Co. Ltd
ScanFlex (Denmark) – door furniture – Assa Abloy Security Solutions
Scania – Harrier Fluid Power Ltd
SCANIA – Bailey Morris Ltd
Scanivalve Corporation – Manufacturer of Intelligent Measurement Systems for Wind Tunnel & Turbine Apps. – Calibration Dynamics
***Scanlift (Denmark)** – mechanical and fork lift truck services – Scanlift Ltd
Scanlift Platforms – Accesscaff International Ltd
Scanlight – scanner software and hardware package – Xara Ltd
Scanmail – Screening and detection equipment – Scanna MSC
Scanmaster – web inspection – Vysionics
Scanmax – Screening and detection equipment – Scanna MSC
Scanna – Screening and detection equipment – Scanna MSC
Scanner Cadet, The – radio instrument systems – John Hornby Skewes & Co. Ltd
***Scanroof (Sweden)** – metal roof tile – Plannja Ltd
SCANSENSE – ScanSense
Scansmoke – Broste Ltd
Scantrak – Screening and detection equipment – Scanna MSC
ScanVision – CT scanning capability on the ximatron – Varian Medical Systems UK Ltd
SCANWILL – Hydraulic & Offshore Supplies Ltd
Scanwill – Hydraulic Pressure Intensifiers – J B J Techniques Ltd
SCAPA (United Kingdom) – speciality self adhesive tape – Stokvis Tapes UK Ltd
Scapa – Trafalgar Tools
Scapa (United Kingdom) – Tapes scapa tapes – R D Taylor & Co. Ltd
Scapa – Gawler Tapes & Plastics Ltd
Scapa – B D K Industrial Products Ltd
Scapa – Scappa UK Ltd
SCAPA GROUP – Hydraulic & Offshore Supplies Ltd
Scapa Tapes – Shand Higson & Co. Ltd
Scarab – electrical power supplies – Nortel Networks UK Ltd
Scarab – Harrier Fluid Power Ltd
Scaraweb – bird repellent – Chase Organics
Scarborough and District – bus and coach services – East Yorkshire Motor Services Ltd
Scarborough Evening News – newspaper – Yorkshire Regional Newspapers Ltd
Scarborough Mercury Series – newspaper – Yorkshire Regional Newspapers Ltd
Scarborough Skippers – bus services – East Yorkshire Motor Services Ltd
Scarem – Bird Scaring Device – CLT Innovations Ltd
Scarves Travel Rugs – J Bradbury & Co. Ltd
Scavenger – towed sweeper, collector – Danline International Ltd
SCEM (Parker) – solenoid valves – Thermofrost Cryo plc
Scenaria – digital sound mixing consoles/editors – Red Lion 49 Ltd
Scent-Off – training aids for cats and dogs – Vitax Ltd
Sceptre – Unoix and mainframe performance monitoring and reporting software – Fox It Ltd
Sceptre – hand and body lotion soap – Deb R & D Ltd
Sceptre – books – Hachette UK Ltd
Sceptre Promotions – keyboard cavalcade monthly newspapers, promoters of festivals and exhibitions, electronic organs – Sceptre Promotions Ltd
Sceptre Publishers – books on keyboard tuition – Sceptre Promotions Ltd
SCETNet – subject-specific CD-ROM series for teachers and students aged 16+, based on web resources – Learning & Teaching Scotland
SCETPioneer – secure online learning environment – Learning & Teaching Scotland
SCETWorks – administration package for schools and colleges – Learning & Teaching Scotland
Schabaver – slurry pump – Sterling Fluid Systems UK Ltd
Schaefer – Harrier Fluid Power Ltd
***Schaefer & Flottmann (Germany)** – downstream butter packaging, case erecting equipment – Engelmann & Buckham Ltd
Schaefer Technologies Inc. – Glenvale Packaging
Schaevitz – StrainSense Ltd
Schaffner – E Preston Electrical Ltd
Schaffner – European Technical Sales Ltd
Schaffner – Nemp filters, RFI and EMI filters and chokes, interference simulation test equipment, ATE for testing power supplies – Schaffner Ltd
Schaffner – suppression products – Anglia
Schaffner – Cyclops Electronics Ltd

Scharmann – Machining centers boring mills – D S Technology UK Ltd
Schat-Harding – equipment & spares – Bearwood Engineering Supplies
***Schatz (U.S.A.)** – aircraft control bearings – R A Rodriguez UK Ltd
Schaudt Mikrosa – European Technical Sales Ltd
Scheer (Germany) – pelletisers – Coperion Ltd
Schell – European Technical Sales Ltd
Schenck – Dynamometers – Dynamometer Services Group Ltd
Schenker Air Cargo – freight – Schenkers Ltd
Schenker Exhibitions – exhibition work – Schenkers Ltd
Schenker International – freight – Schenkers Ltd
Schenker Logistics – freight – Schenkers Ltd
Schenker Seacargo – freight – Schenkers Ltd
Schermuly – marine distress signals – Pains Wessex Ltd
Schiavi (Italy) – flexo printing presses coating & laminating lines – Atlas Converting
Schimmel – piano & forsyth music publications-sheet music warren & phillips-sheet music – Forsyth Bros Ltd
Schindler – lifts, escalators and passenger conveyors – Schindler
Schindler 100 – passenger lift – Schindler
Schindler 300 (Switzerland) – pre-engineered passenger lifts offering over 1200 variations – Schindler
***Schleicher (Germany)** – coilfeeders and profiling – Embassy Machinery Ltd
Schleicher Relays – European Technical Sales Ltd
Schleifring – European Technical Sales Ltd
Schlesurger – Cee Vee
Schleuniger – Used cutting,stripping and crimping machines – Automated Cable Solutions Ltd
Schleuniger – cutting leads and cable processing – Turner Electronics
Schloemann Siemag – equipment/spares – Bearwood Engineering Supplies
Schlumberger – electricity meters – Actaris Development UK Ltd
Schlumberger Neptune – Stream Measurement Ltd
Schmalenberger – European Technical Sales Ltd
Schmalz – European Technical Sales Ltd
Schmersal – European Technical Sales Ltd
Schmersal Interlock Switches – European Technical Sales Ltd
Schmersal Limit Switches – European Technical Sales Ltd
Schmersal Safety Controllers – European Technical Sales Ltd
Schmersal Safety Interlocks – European Technical Sales Ltd
Schmersal Safety Relays – European Technical Sales Ltd
***Schmetz (Germany)** – needles for sewing and hosiery machines – Groz-Beckert UK
SCHMIDT CONTROL-FLEX – Shaft Encoder Couplings – Francis and Francis Ltd
SCHMIDT IZ – Constant Velocity Universal Joints – Francis and Francis Ltd
SCHMIDT LOEWE – CV Axial push pull/Rotary couplings – Francis and Francis Ltd
SCHMIDT OFF-SET – CV Large Variable Offset Couplings – Francis and Francis Ltd
SCHMIDT OMNI-FLEX – Composite Lamina Flexible Couplings – Francis and Francis Ltd
SCHMIDT SEMI-FLEX – CV In-Line Flexible Couplings – Francis and Francis Ltd
SchmidtCare – contract maintenance – A B Schmidt UK Ltd
Schmitt – Schmitt Europe Ltd
Schmitz – trailers – Schmitz Cargobull UK Ltd
Schnapp Batteries – battery manufacturer – Battery Distribution Group
Schneeberger – Antifriction Components Ltd
Schneider – taking and enlarging lenses – Johnsons Photopia Ltd
Schneider – Schneider Electric Ltd
Schneider AG – Lamphouse Ltd
Schneider Inverters – inverters – Potteries Power Transmission Ltd
Schneider-Kreuznach – Stemmer Imaging
Schnell – Automated machines – La Roche
Schnyder – Hobs – Turner Electronics
Schoeller-Bleckmann – Schoeller Bleckmann & Darron
Schoeller-Bleckmann – stainless tubes, pipes and hollow bars, duplex/super duplex – Schoeller-Bleckmann UK
Scholastic – childrens books – Scholastic School Book Fairs
Scholatic Press – childrens books – Scholastic School Book Fairs
***Schonwald** – Hotel Porcelain & Glass – La Porcellana Tableware International Ltd
School Talk – Vtech Electronics UK plc
Schoolbuses – bus & coach service – Stagecoach Ltd
Schott Filters – Galvoptics Optical Goods
Schott Filters - Kopp Filters - Kodak Filters - Wratten Filters - Hoya Filters. – Galvoptics Optical Goods
***Schott Zwiesel (Germany)** – crystal stemware – Schott UK Ltd
Schrack – European Technical Sales Ltd
SCHRADER – Hydraulic & Offshore Supplies Ltd
SCHRADER BELLOWS – Hydraulic & Offshore Supplies Ltd
Schrader Bellows – equipment/spares – Bearwood Engineering Supplies
Schroder – Kee Valves
Schroder – edible fats processing plants – Engelmann & Buckham Ltd
SCHROEDER – Hydraulic & Offshore Supplies Ltd
Schroeder – Harrier Fluid Power Ltd
Schroeder – Hydrotechnik UK Ltd
SCHROEDER FILTRATION – Hydraulic & Offshore Supplies Ltd
Schubert – Kuwait Petroleum International Lubricants UK Ltd
Schugi – Agglomeration – Hosokawa Micron Ltd
Schuh Clothing for Feet – Schuh Ltd
Schultz – European Technical Sales Ltd
Schumacher Filter – European Technical Sales Ltd
Schumi – hair and beauty products – Schumi Hairdressers
SCHUNK – Hydraulic & Offshore Supplies Ltd
Schunk – European Technical Sales Ltd
Schunk – chucks, grippers, tool holders – A C Hydraulics Ltd
Schunk – tools – Tatem Industrial Automation Ltd
Schunk – Gripping systems – Schunk Intec Ltd
Schurter – E Preston Electrical Ltd
Schurter – fuses, fuseholders & connectors – Anglia
Schurter – Cyclops Electronics Ltd
SCHWA – alien defence products and alien head logo – John Brown Publishing
***Schwartz (Worldwide)** – spices – Mccormick Europe Ltd
***Schwarzkopf (Germany and Holland)** – hair products – Schwarzkopf Ltd
Schwarzpunkt – transformer bobbins (phenolic) – Rainer Schneider & Ayres
SCHWER – Hydraulic & Offshore Supplies Ltd
***Schwing (Germany)** – concrete pumps – Burlington Engineers Ltd
Schwing – Harrier Fluid Power Ltd
Sci-Q – peristaltic pumps for science, complete range from research pilot and proceeds – Watson Marlow Pumps Ltd
Sciaky electric Welding Machines – supplier of welding equipment for automotive, aerospace and body in white industries, standard resistance welding and automated machines and robotic systems. Spot seam and projection welders – Sciaky Electric Welding Machines Ltd
Scientific Data Management – magazine – Advanstar Communications
Scientific Optics Ltd – optical components, sub assemblies and instruments – Scientific Optical Ltd
Scigen – chemical product company – Scipac Ltd
Sciglass – laboratory and industrial glassware – Scientific Glass Blowing Co. Ltd
Scimitar – Lusso Interiors
Scimitar – mens basics - non leather soles – UK Distributors Footwear Ltd
Scimitar Motor Services PLC – www.scimitarmotorservices.co.uk – Barnet Service & Tuning Centre
Scintadren – G E Healthcare
Scintilla – micro-textured surface finish on colorcoat HPS200 material – Corus U K Ltd
Scintillize Range – settled screens – Applied Scintillation Technologies
Scintimab – G E Healthcare
Scissor Lifts – Accesscaff International Ltd
Scitec – G.703/G.704 converters – Betterbox Communications Ltd
SCM – stray current mapper – Radio Detection
***Sco-fro** – Sco-Fro Group Ltd
Scofa – soda bread flour – G R Wright & Sons Ltd
Scolaquip – stationery and educational sundries – Creative Art Products Ltd
Scolart – educational art materials – Creative Art Products Ltd
Scolefin – Resinex UK Ltd
Sconablend – Resinex UK Ltd
Scopemeter – Alpha Electronics Southern Ltd
Scopple – electronic test probe – Nortel Networks UK Ltd
***Scorbot (Israel)** – educational and industrial robots, cim systems & vision systems – Brandone Machine Tool Ltd
Scoremaster – darts – Unicorn Products Ltd
Scorpio – presensitised offset plate – Kodak Morley
Scorpion – diamond floor grinding system for marble and stone floors – D K Holdings Ltd
Scorpion – Yb:Fibre laser makers – Electrox
Scorpion – a remote operated ultrasonic crawler designed to allow thickness measurement on carbon steel above ground storage tanks, spheres, risers, rigs, steel work and ships without the need for costly scaffolding or rope access services. – Silverwing UK Ltd
Scorpion Model SS 360 – a remote operated ultrasonic crawler designed to allow thickness measurement on carbon steel above ground storage tanks, spheres, risers, rigs, steel work and ships without the need for costly scaffolding or rope access services – Silverwing UK Ltd
Scorpion Rapide – Yb:Fibre lasermakers – Electrox
Scotburster – hydraulic breaker steels (points and chisels for hydraulic hammers) – Caldervale Forge Co. Ltd
Scotbyte – furniture for computer systems – Specialist Computer Centres Ltd
Scotbyte supplies – furniture for computer systems – S C C
Scotch – UK Office Direct
Scotch – Austen Tapes Ltd
Scotch – adhesive tapes – North British Tapes Ltd
Scotch-Brite – surface cleaning and conditioning products – North British Tapes Ltd
Scotch-Brite – UK Office Direct
Scotch House *The – wool and cashmere knitwear and home textiles – Burberry Ltd
Scotchbrite – scouring pads – Murphy & Son
Scotchcast – electrical resins – Resin Technical Systems
Scotchcast – cable jointing, terminating, coding and taping systems – North British Tapes Ltd
Scotchlite – reflective materials – North British Tapes Ltd
Scotchlite – Helman Workwear
Scotchlite – reflective street nameplates and road signs – I R S Ltd
Scotcrest Uk Ltd – commission embroiderers – Scotcrest
Scotcut – cutting wheels – Build Centre
Scotdisc – record and video producers – B G S Productions Ltd
Scotia – Scotia Instrumentation Ltd
Scotknit – Single needle bed knitted fabric – Scott & Fyfe Ltd
Scotknit 3D – Double needle bed knitted fabric – Scott & Fyfe Ltd
Scotloop – Stitch bonded loop fabric for hoop engagement – Scott & Fyfe Ltd
***Scotman** – icemakers – Tillwise Cash Registers
Scotnet – netting for meats – The Scobie & Junor Group Ltd
Scots Magazine – D C Thomson & Co. Ltd
Scotsman – textile piece goods – Reid & Taylor Ltd
Scotsman – Try & Lilly Ltd
Scott – UK Office Direct
Scott – electrical resistance wires and spiral elements – I M I Scott Ltd
Scott – range of respiratory protection equipment powered & negative pressure – Scott International Ltd
Scott – M S C Gleichmann UK Ltd
Scott – Lamphouse Ltd
Scott M'95 NBC Respirator – Scott International Ltd
Scottish ACORN – C A C I
Scottish Curler – periodical – Dunfermline Press
Scottish Farmer, The – magazine – Newsquest Group
Scottish Hydro Electric – electricity & gas distributor and supplier – Scottish & Southern Energy P.L.C.
Scottish Print Employers Federation – association for printing companies – Scottish Daily Newspaper Society
Scottish Sweater Store – knitwear – Charles N Whillans Partnership
Scottish Youth Hostels Assoc – 80 youth hostels throughout Scotland – Scottish Youth Hostel
Scottlay – geotextile – Cordek Ltd
Scotts Feeds – animal feed – Fane Valley Feeds Ltd
Scotube – circular woven polypropylene FIBC fabrics – Scott & Fyfe Ltd
Scotweave – flat woven polypropylene FIBC fabrics – Scott & Fyfe Ltd
Scourmaster – textile washing machine – Philip Lodge Ltd
Scourmatic – textile washing machine – Philip Lodge Ltd
Scourtex – scouring, washing and wetting chemicals – Texchem
Scout – portable personal multigas monitor – Scott International Ltd
Scout Winter Wheat – Senova Ltd
Scouts – electronic remote monitoring and control equipment – W R T L I-Tunnel
Scovax – Osborn Unipol Ltd
SCPE – steel hot water boiler – Hartley & Sugden
Scramble Nets – Marine evacuation device – Jason's Cradle
Scraped Surface – H R S Heat Exchanges Ltd
Scraperfoil – art products – Oasis Art & Craft Products Ltd
Screen – a quarternary disinfectant with combined virucidal, bacterial and fungicidal properties – Premiere Products Ltd
***Screen (Japan)** – printing machinery – Dainippon Screen UK Ltd
Screen People, The – Wallis Office Furniture Ltd
Screen Stars – T-shirts, sweat shirts and other promotional clothing for the imprint market – Fruit Of The Loom Ltd
Screen Stars – First Impressions Europe Ltd
Screenbase – Lusso Interiors
Screenbase – building products – Yule Catto & Co plc
Screenranger – screening plant – Parker Plant Ltd
ScreenSound – digital audio recorder/editor – Red Lion 49 Ltd
Screentex – water sieve products – Screen Systems Wire Workers Ltd

***Screetons Agriculture** – Rural consultants, valuers & auctioneers – D D M Agriculture
ScrewFast Foundations Ltd (United Kingdom) – Designers and suppliers of screw (helical) piles and grillages for buildings adn tall structures Telecoms, Road and Rail – Screwfast Foundations Ltd
Screwlock – screwed QD coupling, self-sealing – Cobham Mission Equipment Ltd
Scriba – Nd:YAG laser makers – Electrox
Scriptworks – computer software and postscript language compatible RIP – Global Graphics Software Ltd
ScriptWorks MicroRip – postscript language compatable RIP for fast growing low resolution digital colour and large format printing markets – Global Graphics Software Ltd
***Scroll** – range of show cases and poster frames – Signconex Ltd
Scrounger – tramp oil skimmer – Master Chemical Europe Ltd
Scuba – leisure management system including Memberships and Access Control – Delta Computer Services
Scuba – Bauer Group
Sculptura – aluminium sign systems – Spandex plc
Sculpture Grain – natural timber beams and complimentary wood products – Sculpture Grain Ltd
Scunthorpe Evening Telegraph, The – newspaper – Grimsby Telegraph
Scunthorpe Target, The – newspaper – Grimsby Telegraph
Scuranate – isocyanates – I M C D UK Ltd
Scutches – Fieldway Supplies Ltd
Scyllan Diesel Fuel Additive – gas oil and derv additive which prevents cold filter plugging in cold conditions – Morris Lubricants
SC² Heavy Weight (U.S.A.) – shock absorbers for industrial use – Ace Controls International
sd plastering – plastering/building – S D Plastering
SDB – synthetic diamond - saw diamond abrasives – Diamond Detectors
SDC – Colour fastness testing products – James H Heal & Co. Ltd
SDMO – Generator Associates Ltd
SDSS – S D System Solutions Ltd
SE 130 – epoxy prepreg – Gurit UK Ltd
SE 135 – epoxy prepreg – Gurit UK Ltd
SE 84 – epoxy prepreg – Gurit UK Ltd
SE 85 – epoxy prepreg – Gurit UK Ltd
SE 90 – epoxy prepreg – Gurit UK Ltd
SE Labs – Calibration Laboratory – Scientific Electro Systems Ltd
Se'lux – exterior and interior lighting – Selux UK Ltd
SEA – Automatic gates and traffic barriers – Seamless Aluminium International Ltd
SEA – Eagle Automation Systems Ltd
Sea Angler – magazine – Emap Ltd
Sea-Col 760 – super duplex stainless steel – Columbia Metals Ltd
Sea Cove – frozen seafoods – Dales Of Liverpool Ltd
Sea Devil – beach cleaning systems – Vikoma International Ltd
Sea Gems – jewellery and pens – Seagems Ltd
Sea Harris – Sea Harris
Sea King – marine diesel engines – Perkins Engines Group Ltd
Sea Phoenix – PU air buoyancy curtain boom – Cowens Ltd
Sea Searcher & Retreaver – recovery magnets – Nauticalia Ltd
Seabourne Express Courier – international couriers – Seabourne Forwarding Group
SeaChange – Ener-G Combined Power
Seacon – equipment & spares – Bearwood Engineering Supplies
Seafarer – safety equipment – Beaufort Air Sea Equipment Ltd
Seafield – storage and distribution – Seafield Logistics Ltd
Seaflex (Portugal) – mooring ropes – Cotesi UK Ltd
Seaglow – frozen sea foods – Dales Of Liverpool Ltd
Seaguard – container (TEU) repaiar tapes – Chase Protective Coatings Ltd
Seaguard – marine hatch tape – Chase Protective Coatings Ltd
Seagull – ultra marine blue violet and pink pigments – Holliday Pigments Ltd
Seagull – cameras and accessories – Kauser International Trading Ltd
Seahorse – natural stone ceramic tiles and swimming pools – Seahorse Pools Ltd
Seaking Podmore – brokers in wood & plywood – Flatau Dick UK Ltd
Seal – mounting and laminating equipment and materials – Seal UK Ltd
SEAL – image finishing – Seal UK Ltd
Seal – merchandisers & display – Lincat Ltd
Seal Brand – woven elastic brand – H Seal & Co. Ltd
Seal-IT – Apex Commercial Refrigeration & Aircon
Seal-It – laminating systems – Securit World Ltd
Seal Jet – Mayday Seals & Bearings
Seal-Lock – sealing nuts – Bollhoss Fastenings Ltd
Seal Master – equipment & spares – Bearwood Engineering Supplies
Seal Trak – data download – Unisto Ltd
Sealant B – acrylic emulsion floor seal – Evans Vanodine International plc
***Sealed (Italy)** – partitioning – Ergonom Ltd
Sealex – expanded ptfe jointing – Klinger Ltd
Sealex – container sealing compounds – Vita Liquid Polymers
Sealey – Letchford Supplies Ltd
SEALEY – Wolds Engineering Services Ltd
Sealey – S J Wharton Ltd
Sealflex 2 – microwave cable assemblies – I T T Ltd
Sealgrip – PIB Seal Amalgamating Tape – Trafford Rubber Products
Sealine – fishing tackle – Daiwa Sports Ltd
SEALING PARTS – Hydraulic & Offshore Supplies Ltd
Sealkleen – filter assembly – Pall Europe Corporate Services
Sealmaster (U.S.A.) – bearings – Cross & Morse
Sealmaster – Mercury Bearings Ltd
Sealskin – shower curtains (textile and PVC) – Coram Showers Ltd
SEALTITE – Hydraulic & Offshore Supplies Ltd
Sealtron – Connectors – Dax International Ltd
***Sealtron (U.S.A.)** – connectors – Amelec Ltd
Seamaker – wave systems – Barr Wray Ltd
SeaMark Systems – offshore products and services – Foundocean Ltd
***Seamaster (Japan)** – compasses – Yachting Instruments Ltd
Seamount – vibration isolating mountings for marine engines – Stop Choc Ltd
***Seapak** – U F A C UK Ltd
Seaprobe – underwater ultrasonic thickness gauge – Baugh & Weedon Ltd
Seaq – London Stock Exchange plc
Search – liquid clothes wash – Evans Vanodine International plc
Search – contractors plant hire and sale, portable accomadation hire and sale, toilets and golf buggy hire and sale – William G Search Ltd
Search Engine Optimization – Creative Web Mall UK is one of the leading company in providing affordable services. – Creative Web Mall UK
Search Me – magazine – H Bauer Publishing
Searchlight Electric – Light Fantastic
SearchMaster – Advanced Search Engine for Categorisation on Internet – Web Labs Ltd
Seargent Welch – AESpump
Searider – rigid inflatable boats – Avon Inflatables Ltd
Searle – industrial and commercial refrigeration equipment – Searle Manufacturing
Sears – T E K Seating Ltd
SEAS Limited – Summer Schools, Group Placement, Seminars and Marketing for Schools – Shilcock Education Advisory Service Ltd
Seasava Plus – leisure life raft – R F D Beaufort Ltd
Seasons – carpets – Cormar Carpets
Seaspeed – sailcloth – Heathcoat Fabrics Ltd
Seasport De Luxe – rigid inflatable boats – Avon Inflatables Ltd
Seasport Jet – rigid inflatable boats – Avon Inflatables Ltd
***Seaspray** – Sco-Fro Group Ltd
Seat – L M C Hadrian Ltd
Seaward – Alpha Electronics Southern Ltd
Seawings – cabin cruisers and sports boats – Hardy Marine Ltd
Seawork – Fillets – Seawork UK Ltd
SebaKMT – Sebakmt UK Ltd
Sebalog – Sebakmt UK Ltd
Sebastian Coe Health Clubs – Jarvis Hotels Ltd
SEBIA – electrophrosesis – Analytical Technologies Ltd
SEBIM – nuclear pilot operated safety valves – Weir Valves & Controls
Sebo – upright carpet vacuums – Sebo UK Ltd
Secar Cements – cements – Kerneos Ltd
Seceuroglide Excel – Insulated roller garage door with Secured by Design licence and Police Preferred Specification – vertex barrier systems uk Ltd
Seceuroguard – Keytrak Lock & Safe Company
Seceuromesh – Perforated security screen with Secured by Design licence and Police Preferred Specification – vertex barrier systems uk Ltd
Seceuroshield 3801 – Continental roller shutter with Secured by Design licence and Police Preferred Specification – vertex barrier systems uk Ltd
Seceuroshield 7501 – Commercial roller shutter with Secured by Design licence and Police Preferred Specification – vertex barrier systems uk Ltd
Seceurovision 7501 – Vision roller shutter with Secured by Design licence and Police Preferred Specification – vertex barrier systems uk Ltd
Seckford Wine Agency – Seckford Wines
***Seco (U.S.A.)** – copper seals for flared fittings – Hydrasun Ltd
***Seco** – carbide – Turner Tools Ltd
Seco – Seco Tools UK Ltd
Seco – personal safety equipment and safety harnesses – Stenhouse Equipment Safety Co. Ltd
Seco – Precision Tools
***Seco-Flex (Sweden)** – machining centre tooling – Seco Tools UK Ltd
Secochem – K S B Ltd
***Secodex (Sweden)** – indexable insert toolholders – Seco Tools UK Ltd
***Secolor (Sweden)** – cutting tool inserts – Seco Tools UK Ltd
Secomax – Seco Tools UK Ltd
Second Nature – greetings card – Second Nature Ltd
Secondary Flight Display System – standby flight system that senses and displays altitude, attitude and airspeed – Meggitt Avionics
Secondary Navigation Display System – standby navigation display, interferes with ADF, VOR and DME radios together with the magnetic fluse gate, to provide a complete back up navigation display – Meggitt Avionics
***Seconomy (Sweden)** – computer data-cutting tools – Seco Tools UK Ltd
Secosim – European Technical Sales Ltd
Secure – heelgrips – A Algeo Ltd
Secure A Site – Brand Name – Secure A Site UK Ltd
Secure Mix – pressure balancing shower systems – F C Frost Ltd
Secure-Shield – security doors – Accent Hansen
Secure Touch – autoclave control system – Astell Scientific Holdings Ltd
Secure Transfer Systems – cash management, storage, movement, transfer – Air Tube Technologies Ltd
Securelock – security goods including locks and padlocks – P M S International Group plc
Secureseal – random number mechanical security seal – O E M Group Ltd
Securex – type 'b' fittings in DZR brass – Flowflex Components Ltd
SecureX Range – x-ray security – Applied Scintillation Technologies
Securfold – Emmerson Doors Ltd
Securi-Key Petromatic – fuel monitoring systems – Kelgray Products Ltd
Securicor – G 4 S Cash Solutions
Securifast – Mortice Locks – Securefast PLC
Securifire – incinerators for the destruction of security waste – Incinco
Securigrille – scissor folding security grilles – Hart Door Systems
Securikey – UK Office Direct
Securikey – key filing, storage cabinets, key security systems, wall underfloor safes self-retracting keyreels, cash boxes, fire resistant boxes, security and safety mirrors, domestic security hardware – Securikey Ltd
Securiseal – polythene bag with self-sealing adhesive strip – Britton Decoflex
Securishred – off site security shredding and waste paper recycling – P H S Datashred Ltd
Securistile – pitts external turnstile – Frontier Pitts Ltd
Securit – ID card system & visitor registration systems – Securit World Ltd
SECURITAS – Mobile Services – Securitas Mobile
Securitas Guarding Services – manpower security services, specialist services, security training, consulting and investigations, systems integration (inc - CCTV, access control) – Securitas Security Services
Securiticket – stationery – William Pollard & Company Ltd
Security – Boston security arms for retail racking displays – Boston Retail Products
Security Screen – rising security screens – Air Tube Technologies Ltd
Securoglide – Synektics Ltd
Sedgwick – Abbey England Ltd
Sedgwick – Central C N C Machinery Ltd
Sedgwick Independent Financial Consultants – The Woolwich
Sedis – Mercury Bearings Ltd
SEDIS – Chaintec Ltd
Sedis – European Technical Sales Ltd
***See & Sew (U.S.A.)** – paper patterns for dressmaking – Butterick Co. Ltd
SeeABILITY – residential, rehabilitation and day services for adults with a visual impairment and other disabilities – Seeability
Seeboard – regional electricity company – Edf Energy
Seebreez – vision systems – Baty International
***Seedburo (U.S.A.)** – testing and handling equipment for the grain, seed and feed industries – Nickerson Bros Ltd
***Seeka (Japan)** – sensors – Sensortek
Seeka Utility Surveying – Kemp Engineering & Surveying Ltd
Seekure – industrial wrapping/heavy duty – B S K Laminating Ltd

Seekure – polyethylene protection roll - flame retardant LPS 1207 – Cordek Ltd
Seen – Avalon and Lynwood
Seepex – equipment & spares – Bearwood Engineering Supplies
Seephose – glasshouse trickle irrigation – Access Irrigation Ltd
Seetru – Trafalgar Tools
Sefa – G E Healthcare
Sefar – sythetic woven products – G Bopp & Co. Ltd
Sefelec (France) – electrical safety testing instruments – The Seaward Group
Sefelec - Norma - Burster – The Seaward Group
Sefram (France) – instruments & recorders – Metrix Electronics
Sega Fredo Coffee – Ackwa Ltd
***Sega Lock-On (China)** – quazer style shooting game – Bandai UK Ltd
***Segno Lighting** – Pira Ltd
Segs – shoe protectors – Pennine Castings Ltd
Sehcat – G E Healthcare
Seidel – Motor Technology Ltd
SEIFERT – Xstrahl Ltd
SEIKETSU – Transcend Group Ltd
Seiko – Cyclops Electronics Ltd
***Seiko (Japan)** – electronic quartz metronomes and musical tuners – John Hornby Skewes & Co. Ltd
SEIL – Scotland Electronics
SEIL – Scotland Electronics
SEIRI – Transcend Group Ltd
Seismic – Bauer Group
SEISO – Transcend Group Ltd
Seistream – towed seismic array – Nortel Networks UK Ltd
SEITON – Transcend Group Ltd
Sekisui – Shand Higson & Co. Ltd
Seko Bono-Exacta – metering pumps,dosing pumps & systems – A J G Waters Equipment Ltd
Sekonic – light meters – Johnsons Photopia Ltd
Sekure Controls – Display Security – Destec Systems Ltd
Sel Biomat – Althon Ltd
Sel Permafilter – Althon Ltd
Sel Permavoid – Althon Ltd
***Sel-Plex** – Alltech UK Ltd
Seladin – Vertical suspended sump pumps – Selwood Pump Company Ltd
Selar – barrier resins – Du Pont UK Ltd
Selbourne – taps – Armitage Shanks Ltd
Selby (United Kingdom) – sugar confectionery – Bysel Ltd
Selby Pop (United Kingdom) – sugar confectionery – Bysel Ltd
Selclen Super – hard surface cleaner – Selden Research Ltd
Selco – builders merchants – Selco Builders Warehouse
Selco – M&ES Flexilope
Selden Mass – dinghy yacht spars – Selden Mast Ltd
Seleco – Lamphouse Ltd
Select – motor breakdown and assistance insurance – Europ Assistance Holdings Ltd
Select – Metal Edge Retention Profile – Pentagon Protection plc
Select – Emerson Network Power Ltd
Select – digital panel meter – Elektron Components Ltd
Select – domestic sinks – Carron Phoenix
Select – luxury furniture polish – Selden Research Ltd
Select – hotel bedroom furniture – Pedley Furniture International Ltd
Select Gauges – carbide slip gauges – Tesa Technology UK Ltd
***Select Golf** – Prime Appointments Ltd
Selecta-Speed – multi speed gearbox – Varatio Holdings plc
Selectatab – culture media supplements in convenient tablet form – The Mast Group Ltd
Selectavial – lyophilised culture media supplements in vials – The Mast Group Ltd
Selections – mail order catalogue – J D Williams Mail Order Group
selections – Selections Mail Order Ltd
Selective Travel Group – Selective Asia
Selecto Flash – plastic ventilators and other container parts – Selecto Part UK Ltd
Selector Europe (United Kingdom) – trading name for Spencer Stuart's selection services in UK – Spencer Stuart & Associates Ltd
Selectric – domestic circulator pump – Grundfos Pumps Ltd
Selectronic – bread, bun and sandwich toasters – Dualit Ltd
Selectronic – electronic remote control systems – Nortel Networks UK Ltd
Selects – electronic programmers – Sunvic Controls Ltd
Selectzone – Vodafone Retail Ltd
***Selee Foam Filters (U.S.A.)** – for cast shops and foundries – Porvair plc
Self Adhesive Labels – N S D International Ltd
Self Adhesive Sheets – Digital Products - Indigo - Self Adhesive – Howard Smith Paper Ltd
Self feed drill – Gustair Materials Handling Equipment Ltd
Self-Grip – Iscar Tools
Self-Lube – housed bearings – N S K Europe
Self-Shine – Forward Chemicals Ltd
Selfix 10 – DIY aerial – Maxview Ltd
Selfkep – Regalzone LLP
Selfseal (United Kingdom) – selfseal test plugs – Test Plugs Ltd
Selgiene – bactericidal cleaner concentrate – Selden Research Ltd
Selibate – solid polymer controlled release formulation containing pheromones – Agrisense B C S Ltd
Selite - Seladin - Selpack – Selwood Pump Company Ltd
Selkan – glandless circulating pumps – Armstrong Controls Ltd
Sell's Products & Services Directory – United Business Media Ltd
Sellarc – Pressure Washers and Compressors – W Bateman & Co.
Sellite – sellite block company – The Howard Group
Sellotape (United Kingdom) – tapes scapa tapes – R D Taylor & Co. Ltd
Sellotape – B D K Industrial Products Ltd
Sellotape – UK Office Direct
Sellotape – self-adhesive tapes, foam sealants and bonding materials and butyl sealants – Scappa UK Ltd
***Selmark (Malaysia)** – spun pewter – Royal Selangor Ltd
Selmat – filter foams for air and dust, water filtration and cosmetic applications (fire and non-fire retardent) – Recticel Corby
Selmex – water based concrete sealer – Selden Research Ltd
SELO – schnitzel presses, steam cooking tunnels – Selo UK Ltd
Selosol – detergent degreaser – Selden Research Ltd
Selpack Pumps – Packaged pumping stations – Selwood Pump Company Ltd
Seltek – electrical and electronic testing and measuring apparatus and instruments and electrical energy metering – Energy I C T
***Selter (Spain)** – magnetic chucks – Capital Equipment & Machinery Ltd
Seltex – lubricants – Chevron
Seltorque – Trowell Plant Sales Ltd
Selva – clock construction kits and accessories – Time Products UK Ltd
Selwood – A T Wilde & Son Ltd
SELWOOD "C" RANGE – chopper pump – Selwood Ltd
SELWOOD "D" RANGE – high flow general purpose self priming centrifugal pump – Selwood Ltd
SELWOOD "H" RANGE – high head and dewatering pumps – Selwood Ltd
SELWOOD "HS" RANGE – hydraulic submersible pump – Selwood Ltd
SELWOOD "PD" RANGE – automatic self priming positive displacement pump – Selwood Ltd
SELWOOD "S" RANGE – self priming solids handling pump – Selwood Ltd
SELWOOD SELPRIME – unique original selwood self priming system – Selwood Ltd
SELWOOD SELTORQUE – self priming vortex flow pump – Selwood Ltd
SELWOOD SIMPLITE – single diaphragm pump – Selwood Ltd
SELWOOD SPATE – automatic self priming pump – Selwood Ltd
Selwyn Thermography – raised letter heading dye stamping – DocuPrint Ltd
***SEM** – European Drives & Motor Repairs
Semco – Peter Rushton Ltd
Semco – packaging and application systems for multi-component sealants and adhesives – PPG Aerospace
Semens Transformers – European Technical Sales Ltd
Semfreeze – reactive or curable chemical materials for use in industry – PPG Aerospace
Semfreeze – service comprising the mixing, freezing and/or delivery (still frozen), of multi-component reactive chemicals to industrial users – PPG Aerospace
SEMI SRL – Hydraulic & Offshore Supplies Ltd
Semicell – Semikron UK Ltd
Semier – Harrier Fluid Power Ltd
Semikron – Cyclops Electronics Ltd
Semikron – electronic equipment – Bearwood Engineering Supplies
***Semikron (Germany)** – silicon rectifier products – Semikron UK Ltd
Semikron – semiconductors – G D Rectifiers Ltd
Semikron – European Technical Sales Ltd
Semin – B P plc
Seminar Authoring Tool – computer and web based training authoring system – Information Transfer LLP
Seminar Learning System – online learning management system – Information Transfer LLP
Semipack – Semikron UK Ltd
Semipont – Semikron UK Ltd
Semistack – Semikron UK Ltd
Semitec (Japan) – ntc Thermistors – A T C Semitec Ltd
Semitrans – Semikron UK Ltd
Semitron – Merseyside Metal Services
Semkit – storage and mixing device for 2 component sealants and adhesives – PPG Aerospace
SEMPAS – Hydraulic & Offshore Supplies Ltd
Sempen – storage and mixing device for 2 component coatings – PPG Aerospace
SEMPERIT – Hydraulic & Offshore Supplies Ltd
***Semperit (Austria & Eire)** – tyres – Continental Tyre Group Ltd
Sempra – tyres – National Tyre Service Ltd
SEMPRESS – Hydraulic & Offshore Supplies Ltd
Senarcom – strain viewer – Sharples Stress Engineers Ltd
Senator – interior sliding door gear and hardware – P C Henderson Ltd
Senator – commercial friction hinges – Securistyle Ltd
Senator – Capex Office Interiors
Senator – Furniture – Bucon Ltd
Senator – Portman Building Society
Senator – optical frames and sunglasses – Hilton International Eye Wear Ltd
Senator – office furniture – E W Marshall Ltd
Senator International – office furniture – BBI Business Interiors Ltd
Senator pens – Bic Pens – Co-Optimize Marketing Ltd
Senator Range – 4 twin axle endurance touring caravans – Bailey Of Bristol
SenCorr – Multipurpose probe system. – Iicorr Ltd
Sendas del Rey – wine – Rodney Densem Wines Ltd
Seneca Skates & Accessories – M V Sport & Leisure Ltd
Senertec – Baxi Group
Senflux – non-return valve – Armstrong Controls Ltd
Senia – WC – Armitage Shanks Ltd
***Senior Bind (U.S.A.)** – hotmelt binding machine – Securit World Ltd
Senior Line – free phone advice line – Age UK
Senior Options – Western Provident Association Ltd
Seniorlink – alarm service – Age UK
Senju – Solder paste – Link Hamson Ltd
Senlac – cast reconstructed stone and concrete mouldings, copings, balustrading etc – Senlac Stone Ltd
Sennebogen – Harrier Fluid Power Ltd
Sennheiser – headsets – Hayward & Green Aviation Ltd
Sennheiser – Duplex Corporate Communications
Senotherm – East Midland Coatings Ltd
Sensa – energy saving fluorescent fittings – Thorn Lighting Ltd
Sensaflush – automatic urinal control – Vectair Systems Ltd
Sensatap – automatic tap system – Vectair Systems Ltd
Sensation – darts – Unicorn Products Ltd
Senseal – annular pressure sensors – Texcel Division
Sensearound (United Kingdom) – sensory vehicle – Mike Ayres Design Ltd
Sensemaster – sensing devices and allied products – Sensemaster Ltd
Sensiq – cosmetics – Coty UK Ltd
Sensiq Skin Care – skin care – Coty UK Ltd
Sensistor – Sebakmt UK Ltd
SENSITUBE – Hydraulic & Offshore Supplies Ltd
SENSOCONTROL – Hydraulic & Offshore Supplies Ltd
***Sensopart (Germany)** – sensors – Sensortek
Sensor – marketing services – Research International Group Ltd
Sensor – fishing tackle – Daiwa Sports Ltd
Sensoreflow – electronic control – Armitage Shanks Ltd
Sensorflow Solo – electronic control – Armitage Shanks Ltd
Sensorium – Multi vendor system integration supervisor – Advanced Desktop Systems Ltd
Sensorium iBMS – Advanced Desktop Systems Ltd
SensorLine – surface velocity sensor for paper – Dantec Dynamics Ltd UK
Sensorlink – T S M Ltd
Sensory Studio (United Kingdom) – multi sensory equipment – Mike Ayres Design Ltd
SENSY – StrainSense Ltd
Sentinel – computer boiler house management – Saacke Combustion Services Ltd
Sentinel – type 2 covered fire hose – Richards Hose Ltd
Sentinel – two post electro-hydraulic lifts for vehicles – Tecalemit Garage Equipment Co. Ltd
Sentinel – low voltage circuit breakers – Ellison Switchgear
Sentinel – Prices Patent Candles Ltd
Sentinel – uninterruptable power supply – Key Source Ltd
Sentinel – oil containment systems – Vikoma International Ltd
Sentinel – cash protection systems – Spinnaker International Ltd
Sentinel 16 – Fixed System Gas Detection Range – Scott International Ltd
Sentinel Card Services – insurers of credit cards – Credit Card Sentinel UK Ltd
Sentinel Crankcase Oil – oil solely for use in the sumps of sentinel steam engines – Morris Lubricants

Sentinel II – Fixed System Gas Detection Range – Scott International Ltd
Sentinel Major – cardboard container for talc – Robinson Healthcare Ltd
Sentinel Minor – cardboard container for talc – Robinson Healthcare Ltd
Sentinel Sound Floor – impact sound absorbing 5mm thick polyethylene foam – Thermal Economics Ltd
Sentinel VI 6 – Fixed System Gas Detection Range – Scott International Ltd
Sentor – Wright Dental Group
Sentree – tree guard – Boddingtons Ltd
Sentri Site Boxes – Accesscaff International Ltd
Sentriboxes – A T Wilde & Son Ltd
Sentrico – lighting & lighting components – Coughtrie International Ltd
Sentrie – walk through metal detectors – L-3 Communications Security & Detection Systems
Sentrilock – high security window locking systems – Archibald Kenrick & Sons
Sentrix – wire managed desking – Senator International Ltd
SENTROL 1000 – supervisory and display systems – Silvertech Safety Consultancy Ltd
SENTROL 2000 – scada systems – Silvertech Safety Consultancy Ltd
SENTROL 3000 – industrial control systems – Silvertech Safety Consultancy Ltd
SENTROL 4000 – DCS systems – Silvertech Safety Consultancy Ltd
SENTROL 5000 – emergency shutdown systems – Silvertech Safety Consultancy Ltd
SENTROL 6000 – fire and gas systems – Silvertech Safety Consultancy Ltd
Sentronic – B L Pneumatics Ltd
Sentronic – Gustair Materials Handling Equipment Ltd
Sentry – uninterruptable power supply – Key Source Ltd
Sentry – circuit protection – M K Electric Ltd
Sentry – waxed threads with needles – F Ball & Co. Ltd
Sentry – UK Office Direct
***Sep (Italy)** – two wheeled tractor units and attachments – Bunce Ashbury Ltd
SEP – support & energy partnership – Schneider Electric
Sepam – protection, control & monitoring unit – Schneider
Separation Technology – Harrier Fluid Power Ltd
SEPTRA – Hydraulic & Offshore Supplies Ltd
Sepura – Condensate Cleaners – Condensate systems Ltd
Sequel II – sound re-inforcement console – Digico UK Ltd
Sequin Art – Kitfix Swallow Group Ltd
Sequin Stone Ltd T/A Contraband – gifts and interior accessories – Contraband
Sequoia Series M9000 – computer margins from 2 devices to 850 – Northgate & Arinso
SERA – Hydraulic & Offshore Supplies Ltd
Seraclone – Blood Grouping – Biotest UK Ltd
Serator – saw steel – Uddeholm Steel Stockholders
Serck – heat exchangers – Bearwood Engineering Supplies
Sereclone – Blood Grouping – Biotest UK Ltd
Serenade – kitchen furniture – Moores Furniture Group
Serenella – soft vinyl coated fabric – J B Broadley
Sergent – Plastic Bollard – Alto Bollards UK Ltd
Seri-Touch – Autron Products Ltd
Seriatim – masterclass case management & workflow system – Professional Technology UK Ltd
Seriatim – legal management and accounting time recording system – Professional Technology UK Ltd
Sericard CD – solvent laminating ink for credit cards – Fujifilm Sericol Ltd
Series 10 – 10 watt teaching microprocessors – Gillett & Sibert Ltd
Series 1000 – UV-Visible spectrophotometers – Cecil Instruments Ltd
Series 110 – mechanical indexing gearbox – Estuary Automation Ltd
Series 1100 – HPLC systems – Cecil Instruments Ltd
Series 19 – computers margins from 2 devices to 850 – Northgate & Arinso
Series 20 – 20 watt research microprocessors – Gillett & Sibert Ltd
Series 200 – vending machine – Drinkmaster Ltd
Series 2000 – split body valves – Severn Glocon Ltd
Series 2000 – UV-Visible spectrophotometers – Cecil Instruments Ltd
Series 2000 – solenoid valves gas – Black Teknigas & Electro Controls Ltd
Series 2000 – sectional garage doors – Hörmann (UK) Ltd
Series 2000 – up-over garage doors – Hörmann (UK) Ltd
Series 2000 and Series 3000 – refrigerated display cabinets and equipment – George Barkers
Series 3000 – UV-Visible spectrophotometers – Cecil Instruments Ltd
Series 3000/4000 – cryogenic valves – Severn Glocon Ltd
Series 3500/2600 – Total lift full nozzle safety relief valves to API specifications in sizes 1/2" x 1" through to 8" x 10" 'T' orifice. The 3500 series now carries the ASME 'UV' and 'NB' code approval stamps. – Broady Flow Controller Ltd
Series 400 – vending machine – Drinkmaster Ltd
Series 500 – Vending machine – Drinkmaster Ltd
Series 5000 – label applicator – Weyfringe Labelling Systems
Series 5000 – top entry valves – Severn Glocon Ltd
Series 5000 – fatigue rated hydraulic servo actuators, complete with co-axially mounted electrical feedback suitable for up to 345 Bar (5000 PSI) working pressure – Eland Engineering Company
Series 55 – mechanical indexing gearbox – Estuary Automation Ltd
Series 6 – pipe sealing systems – A L H Systems Ltd
Series 6000 – PTFE lined, bellows sealed globe valve – Severn Glocon Ltd
Series 70 – alarm annunciator – Amatek Precision Instruments UK Ltd
Series 7000 – Ultra high purity globe valve – Severn Glocon Ltd
Series 80 – mechanical indexing gearbox – Estuary Automation Ltd
Series 8000 – butterfly valves – Severn Glocon Ltd
Series 90 – alarm ammunciators – Amatek Precision Instruments UK Ltd
Series 9000 – control ball valves – Severn Glocon Ltd
Series 9000 – UV-Visible spectrophotometers – Cecil Instruments Ltd
Series E – steam boilers – Fulton Boiler Works Ltd
Series E 440LDC – steam boilers – Fulton Boiler Works Ltd
Series E-5700 – Bronkhorst UK Ltd
Series E-7000 – Bronkhorst UK Ltd
SERIES FOUR – Telemetry outstation sewage pumping stations – Halcyon Solutions
Series J – steam boilers – Fulton Boiler Works Ltd
Serifix – screen mesh adhesive – Fujifilm Sericol Ltd
Seringone 50% Benzyl Acetate – perfume speciality – Quest International UK Ltd
Serious PR – Public Relations Consultants – Serious P R
Serious Stuff Clothing – boys wear – Banner Ltd
Seripol SO – gloss solvent ink for pre-treated polythene bottles – Fujifilm Sericol Ltd
Seriprep – screen preparation chemicals – Fujifilm Sericol Ltd
Seristar SX – gloss solvent ink for paper and board – Fujifilm Sericol Ltd
Seritec TH – solvent ink for membrane switch printing – Fujifilm Sericol Ltd
Serjeants – chartered patent agents and trade mark attorneys – Serjeants
SermAlcote coating – Manufacture and apply SermAlcote Coating – Praxair
SermaLoy coating series – Manufacture and apply SermaLoy Coating range – Praxair
SermeTel coating series – Manufacture and apply SermeTel Coating range – Praxair
***Serono GPM (Spain)** – medium – Merck Serono Ltd
***Serophene (Switzerland)** – infertility drugs – Merck Serono Ltd
SERPAC Enclosures – O K W Enclosures Ltd
Sertis – B P plc
***Serv-o-Dex (Germany)** – automatic indexing tables – Meddings Machine Tools
SERV-RITE – thermocouple wire and cable – Watlow Ltd
***ServaClean** – stainless steel bar fitments – Servaclean Bar Systems Ltd
Server Load Balancing – Tekdata Distribution Ltd
***Serveview Plc (U.S.A.)** – keyboard video mouse multi PC-sever switches – Techland Group Ltd
Service – provision of spares, pump, valve repair & field maintenance services – S P P Pumps
Service Aid – aerosols & associated products for the service engineer – C G P Chemicals Ltd
Service & Systems Solutions – computers – Northgate Managed Services Ltd
Servicebag – Top opening tool case – Hofbauer (UK) Ltd
ServiceBuilder – intelligent networks – Nortel Networks UK Ltd
Serviced apartments – Serviced apartments in Milton Keynes and Northampton – Cotels Management Ltd
Serviceline – Quality range of tool cases – Hofbauer (UK) Ltd
Servidek – bridge waterproofing – Grace Construction Ltd
Servipak – protection board – Grace Construction Ltd
Serviron – Darcy Products Ltd
Servirufe – roof waterproofing – Grace Construction Ltd
Serviseal – external waterstops – Grace Construction Ltd
SERVITIR – FUEL CARDS, VAT RECOVERY, TOLL CARDS, CMR PADS – Servitir
Servitite – internal waterstops – Grace Construction Ltd
Serviwrap – pipe protection membranes – Grace Construction Ltd
ServIdent – cable marker service for heatshrink and PVC – Hellermann Tyton
***Servo (U.S.A.)** – micro drilling machines – Capital Equipment & Machinery Ltd
Servo-Torq – cutting machine for plastic and rubber extrusion – Peter Gillard Company Ltd
Servo (USA) – electronic feed units for turret mills – Capital Equipment & Machinery Ltd
Servofill – G Webb Automation Ltd
Servol – multigrade motor oils – Morris Lubricants
Servol EP Gear Oil – paraffinic mineral oil based gear oil – Morris Lubricants
SERVOMAC – European Drives & Motor Repairs
Servomax – equipment & spares – Bearwood Engineering Supplies
Servomech (Italy) – linear actuators and screwjacks – Lenze UK Ltd
***Servopress (Germany)** – automatic indexing tables – Meddings Machine Tools
Servostep – electronic bridge controls – Radamec Control Systems Ltd
***Sesam (Germany)** – electric strikes – Raytel Security Systems Ltd
Sesame – B P plc
SESINO – Hydraulic & Offshore Supplies Ltd
Sesquel – connectors – Servo & Electronic Sales Ltd
Sestrel – compasses and nautical instruments – John Lilley & Gillie Ltd
Set-Matic – collating machine – K A S Paper Systems Ltd
Seta – quality control instruments for petroleum and other industries – Stanhope Seta Ltd
Seta-Hot – electric heater – Stanhope Seta Ltd
Setaclean – total sediment tester – Stanhope Seta Ltd
Setaflash – flash point tester – Stanhope Seta Ltd
Setafoam 150 – foaming characteristic bath – Stanhope Seta Ltd
Setamatic – penetrometer – Stanhope Seta Ltd
Setapoint – filter flow of aviation fuels at low temperature – Stanhope Seta Ltd
Setasill – distillation apparatus – Stanhope Seta Ltd
SetaTime – electronic timer – Stanhope Seta Ltd
Setavap – vapour pressure tester – Stanhope Seta Ltd
Setavis – kinematic viscometer – Stanhope Seta Ltd
Setcim – software for process operations – Aspentech Ltd
Setcrete – surface treatments and waterproofers – Don Construction Products Ltd
SETEM (France) – Braime Elevator Components Ltd
Setex – Zella Instrumentation & Control Ltd
***Setra (U.S.A.)** – pressure transducers, accelerometers – Boiswood LLP
Setseal – cementitious waterproofing products – Don Construction Products Ltd
Settlement Gauges – geotechnical instruments – Itm Soil Ltd
Seuffer – Foremost Electronics Ltd
Sevcon – controls for electric vehicles – Sevcon Ltd
Seven 5 liner – 7.5 tonne curtainsider bodywork – Boalloy Industries Ltd
Seven Birmingham – Media & print manufactturer – Schawk
Seven Interactive – Media & print manufacturer – Schawk
Seven London – Media & print manufacturer – Schawk
Seven Manchester – Media & print manufacturer – Schawk
Seven Seas – cod liver oil – Seven Sea's Ltd
Seven Solutions – Media & print manufacturer – Schawk
Sevenfold & Ninefold Files – compartmented files – Acco East Light Ltd
Sevenoaks Chronicle – newspaper – Kent Regional News & Media
Severin Quick-Table – Global Parasols Ltd
Severn – heavy duty rectangular side hinged grating and frame – Norinco UK Ltd
Severn Trent Water – water and sewerage services – Severn Trent Water
Severn Trent Water ST – Severn Trent Water
Seville – WC suite – Armitage Shanks Ltd
Sevora – industrial lubricants – B P plc
SEW – Mercury Bearings Ltd
Sew Personal – Sew Personal Ltd
SEW - Varimot - Varibloc - Varidisc - Movitrac - Movidrive - Movimot - Movidyn Sales and Service Organisations throughout the world. – S E W Eurodrive Ltd
Seward – Alpha Electronics Northern Ltd
Sewatec – K S B Ltd
Sewoo – Maxa Technologies Ltd
***Sextons (Worldwide)** – in car audio systems – Sextons
SFC Express – FFS Brands Ltd
SFM Technology Ltd – engineering – S F M
SFR – Watts Industries UK Ltd
Sfu – Gustair Materials Handling Equipment Ltd
SFX – magazine – Future Publishing Ltd
SH1000 – Thermo Electrical
SH4000 – Thermo Electrical
(Shackleton System Drives) SSD – previous name for Eurotherm Drives – Parker
Shackman – ID card systems, ID cameras, instant print cameras, government registration products, general procurement – Chiltern I T Parts
Shadeacrete – cement colours – Lanxess Ltd

Shademakers – Global Parasols Ltd

Shades – screenprinters and mirror manufacturers – Shades Graphics Ltd

Shades of Light Roller Blind Fabrics Collection – An exclusive range of roller blinds and prints some with matching fabric for soft furnishings – Eclipse Blind Systems

Shades of Light Venetian Blind Collection – A range of venetian blinds in 4 vane widths for domestic and contract use – Eclipse Blind Systems

Shades of Light Vertical Blind Collection – An extensive range of vertical blinds for domestic and contract applications – Eclipse Blind Systems

Shades of Light Wooden Venetian Blind Collection – A collection of bass wood venetian blinds for domestic and contract applications – Eclipse Blind Systems

Shadomaster – profile projectors – Baty International

Shadowrib – trapezoidal wall panel – Lindab Building Systems

Shaftesbury H.E. – Power flame cast iron sectional boilers – Hamworthy Heating Ltd

*Shajah – Raja Frozen Foods Ltd

Shakespeare Monofilament – thermo plastic monofilament – Shakespeare Monofilament UK Ltd

Shaldon – woven carpets in 100% pure new wool pile – Axminster Carpets Ltd

*Shalovent (United Kingdom) – low height ventilation/heat recovery units – Thermal Technology Sales Ltd

SHAMBAN – Hydraulic & Offshore Supplies Ltd

Shamrock – spectrograph – Andor Technology Ltd

Shandals – Alan James Raddon

*Shanklin (U.S.A.) – shrink packaging machinery – Wrapid Manufacturing Ltd

Shanks – waste disposal by high temperature incineration waste management services and recovery/recycling of solvents – Shanks Group plc

*Shanks (Italy) – garden tractors and sweepers – E P Barrus

Shannon – fabricating machines – Awltech Plastic Fabrication Sales Ltd

Shapal – Precision Ceramics

Shapal – Precision Ceramics

Shape – cheese spreads, yoghurts – Uniq plc

Sharepoint – Core Technology Systems UK Ltd

Shark Hose – fish transport – Merlett Plastics UK Ltd

Shark They Bite – screws for wood – Fastbolt Distributors UK Ltd

*Sharkfin (Sweden) – plectra – John Hornby Skewes & Co. Ltd

Sharon Sloane – leather clothes – Scala Agenturen UK

Sharp – Cyclops Electronics Ltd

Sharp – Lamphouse Ltd

Sharp – Ascot Wholesale Ltd

Sharp – TV – Sertronics Ltd

Sharp – UK Office Direct

Sharp – Westmore Business Systems Ltd

*Sharp – Tayside Cash Registers

*Sharp – Cash register systems – I C R Touch LLP

*Sharp – Shelfguard Systems

Sharp Cash Registers – Cash Register Services

Sharp & Nickless – brandysnaps and brandsnap baskets – Sharp & Nickless Ltd

Sharp Photocopier – Westmore Business Systems Ltd

Sharp Photocopiers – Clarity Copiers

Sharpak – sharps disposal containers – Amcor Flexibles

Sharpie – UK Office Direct

Sharples – photoelastic stress analysis equipment and services – Sharples Stress Engineers Ltd

Sharples – Polariscopes – Sharples Stress Engineers Ltd

Sharples – strain viewers and training – Sharples Stress Engineers Ltd

Sharps Bin – Solmedia Laboratory Supplies

Sharpstuff – Sharpstuff Event & Business Development

Sharrow Bay – fabric collection – Brian Yates

Sharwood – Indian, Oriental and Chinese food – Centura Foods Ltd

Shatterproof – unbreakable plastic glassware – Plastico Ltd

Shaver 579 Brown Egglayer – Tom Barron Isa Ltd

Shaving Foam – classix shaving foam – L E C Liverpool Ltd

Shaw – precision steel castings – Bonds Precision Casting Ltd

Shaws – terracotta, faience and glazed bricks – Shaws Of Darwen Ltd

Shaws Twintiles – extruded vitrified frostprool tiles for walls – Shaws Of Darwen Ltd

She – magazine – National Magazine Company Ltd

Shear Connector System – equipment and fasteners to fix composite decks – Hilti GB Ltd

Shear N Spice – spice blends and candy sugar – Fiddes Payne

Sheargard (United Kingdom) – overload clutches – Cross & Morse

Shearguard – water and heat resistant leather – Charles F Stead & Co. Ltd

Shearline – CNC milling and turning, sheet metal, welding, vacuum bronzing and electro mechanical assembly – Shearline Precision Engineering Ltd

Shearsert – threaded fastener for low strength alloys – Tappex Thread Inserts Ltd

Shearstone – reconstructed stone walling – Forticrete Ltd

Shearwater – Akzo Nobel Packaging Coatings Ltd

Sheen Equipment – flame guns and cable laying equipment – Sheen Equipment

Sheer (United Kingdom) – switches, sockets, dimmers, etc. – R Hamilton & Co. Ltd

Sheer Luxury – net curtaining – Tyrone Textiles Ltd

Sheer Silk – toiletries – The Co Op

Sheerblend – high impact modified external grade PVC – L B Plastics Ltd

Sheercell – building products – L B Plastics Ltd

Sheerclad – external cladding – L B Plastics Ltd

Sheeredge – lipping – L B Plastics Ltd

Sheerframe – window and door system – L B Plastics Ltd

Sheerframe Curtain Walling System – L B Plastics Ltd

Sheerframe Louvre System – L B Plastics Ltd

Sheerframe System 5000 – window and door system – L B Plastics Ltd

Sheerframe System 6000 – newbuild window & door system – L B Plastics Ltd

Sheerglide – drawer system – L B Plastics Ltd

Sheerline – decking & fencing – L B Plastics Ltd

Sheerness Times Guardian – newspaper – Kent Messenger Group Ltd

Sheervent – ventilation system – L B Plastics Ltd

Sheerwater leisure – seed and chemical fetilzer (01403) 700073 – Pareto Golf Ltd

Sheetmaster – Storage racking – Rack International UK Ltd

Shefcut – engineering tools – C L A Tools Ltd

Sheffield United – professional football club – Sheffield United Football Club Ticket Office

Sheila Coombes – new botanicals fabric wallcovering – Brian Yates

Sheila Coombes 111 – wallpaper and borders – Brian Yates

Sheila Coombes Abbey Garden – fabric collection – Brian Yates

Sheila Coombes I – fabric wallpapers and borders – Brian Yates

Sheila Coombes II – fabric and wallpaper – Brian Yates

Sheila Coombes Tara – fabric collection – Brian Yates

SHEILDMASTER – Hydraulic & Offshore Supplies Ltd

Shelbourne Reynolds – farm machinery – Shelbourne Reynolds Engineering Ltd

Shelbourne Reynolds Hectolitre Measure – cereal hectolitre measure – Shelbourne Reynolds Engineering Ltd

Shelbourne Reynolds Rape Swather – oil seed rape cutter – Shelbourne Reynolds Engineering Ltd

Shelectric Ltd – Industrial Control Systems – Shelectric Control Panel Mnfrs

Shell – Hammond Lubricants & Chemicals Ltd

Shell Aviation Products (United Kingdom) – lubricants – R D Taylor & Co. Ltd

SHELL GLOBAL SOLUTIONS LTD – Hydraulic & Offshore Supplies Ltd

SHELL OILS AND LUBRICANTS – Hydraulic & Offshore Supplies Ltd

SHELL UK OIL PRODUCTS LTD – Hydraulic & Offshore Supplies Ltd

Shellawax – Woodfinishing products – The Toolpost

Shelley – Shelley Thermoformers International Ltd

Shelley – Female body spray – Statestrong Ltd

Shelley F.S.C.S. – kiln lining system – P E Hines & Sons Ltd

Shellwin Plc – property builders – Wessex & Co.

Shelterguard – tree protection – Acorn Planting Products Ltd

Shelters r us – Shelters 'R' Us - We are a Smoking shelter and cigarette bin manufacturer, supplying a large range – Shelters R Us

Shenstone – bricks – Ibstock Building Products Ltd

Shepard's Stain – kit for demonstration of HB-F in red cells – Clin-Tech Ltd

Shepherd – castors – Archibald Kenrick & Sons

Shepherd – casting machines – Bearwood Engineering Supplies

Shepherd Neame – brewers – Shepherd Neame Ltd

Shepherdette – castors – Archibald Kenrick & Sons

Shepherds – Yara UK It Ltd

Shepherds International – Furnishings – Pullingers Furnishers Ltd

Shepley – carpets – Penthouse Carpets Ltd

Sheppy – PVA adhesives, hot and cold dextrine and organic adhesives – Sheppy Ltd

Sheraplex – duplex coating – Bodycote Metallurgical Coatings Ltd

Sherardizing – zinc rustproofing process – Bodycote Metallurgical Coatings Ltd

Sherborne Occasional Range – upholstered occasional furniture – Sherborne Upholstery Ltd

Sherbourne – tilt-n-slide patio door – Coastal Aluminium

Sherbourne Upholstery – The Winnen Furnishing Company

Sheriden – Axminster carpet – Ulster Carpet Mills Ltd

Shering – road and rail weighbridges, platforms, scales and instrumentation – Shering Weighing Ltd

Sherlock – Try & Lilly Ltd

Sherpa Steps – Accesscaff International Ltd

Sherwood – Prices Patent Candles Ltd

Sherwood Interiors – suspended ceilings and interiors – Sherwood Interiors Ltd

Shetland – knitwear manufacture and wholesalers, also retail and outlets for all three brands – Anderson & Co.

Shetland Seafish – Shetland Seafish Ltd

Shetland Warehouse – knitwear – Anderson & Co.

Shev 30 – heat recovery ventilation – Dunsley Heat Ltd

SHG – linear encoder – Newall Measurement Systems Ltd

Shibaura – C J Plant Ltd

Shibaura – Harrier Fluid Power Ltd

Shield – Superior lubricating greases – Ironsides Lubricants Ltd

Shielded feeder pillars – shielded patern fusegear – Schneider

Shielded Liners – milking machine liner – Delaval

SHIELDFAST – screening & term cable braids – Resintech Ltd

Shift – power wash liquid – Evans Vanodine International plc

Shifter – materials handler – Neuson Ltd

Shilcock Education Advisory Service Limited – General Education Advice – Shilcock Education Advisory Service Ltd

*Shilton (China) – luggage – Shilton plc

Shin Nippon Koki – Matsuura Machinery Ltd

Shindengen – M S C Gleichmann UK Ltd

Shindengen – electronic components and semi-conductors – Shindengen

Shindengen – rectifier diodes – Anglia

Shindengen – Cyclops Electronics Ltd

Shine – paper – Fenner Paper Co. Ltd

*Shinko (Japan) – electronic temperature controllers – Testemp Ltd

Shinnihon Yuken – Harrier Fluid Power Ltd

*Shinohara (Japan) – offset presses – Graphics Arts Equipment Ltd

Shiploader – B & W Mechanical Handling

Shipmate – marine electronics equipment – Navico UK

Ships Monthly – I P C Media Ltd

Shiraz – ladies woven – Emreco International Ltd

Shire (United Kingdom) – diesel canal boat engines – E P Barrus

Shire Contract Furniture (United Kingdom) – systems furniture – Severn Business Interiors Ltd

Shire Design Consultants (United Kingdom) – Interior Design – Severn Business Interiors Ltd

Shire Pantile – concrete – Sandtoft Holdings Ltd

Shire Range – GRP doorway canopies – Torclad Ltd

Shirla – cable sheath testing system – Baur Test Equipment Ltd

Shirley – textile instruments and machinery – S D L Atlas

Shirley Technologies – textile, scientific and testing services – B T T G Ltd

Shirtmaster – mens casual shirts – Banner Ltd

Shirts – jerwyn street type quality shirts/mail order – Barnett The Factory

SHITSUKE – Transcend Group Ltd

Shiva – Tekdata Distribution Ltd

Shiva Lanrover – Tekdata Distribution Ltd

Shiva Site – Tekdata Distribution Ltd

Shivaru – dresses – Kentex Jeans & Casuals

Shockbox – membrane box – Henri Picard & Frere

SHOCKGUARD – Composite PTFE diaphragm damper with elastomeric resilient backing and encapsulated anti extrusion stiffener.pulsation dampener – Pulsation Dampers At Pulseguard Ltd

Shockguard – Jenex Ltd

Shockguard – protective corners – A Latter & Co. Ltd

Shocksafe – Insulated tools for civil engineering – Richard Carter Ltd

Shoe Findings – Livingston & Doughty Ltd

Shoeboxorter – automated sorting conveyor systems – Van Der Lande Industries

Shoecare – repairs to all types of outdoor footwear – S P H Europe plc

Shoflo – Stream Measurement Ltd

Shoon – footwear and clothing distributors – Shoon Trading Ltd

Shoot – I P C Media Ltd

Shooting Times & Country Magazine – I P C Media Ltd

*Shoplights (Germany) – retail display lighting – Selux UK Ltd

Shops, Restaurants & Public Houses Insurance – specialist insurance – M M A Insurance plc

Shore Guardian – oil containment systems – Vikoma International Ltd

Shorguard – Accesscaff International Ltd

Short-Offset 3D – high resolution seismic processing – Fugro Seismic Imaging Ltd

Short Stories – Short Stories of London Ltd

Shortlands – project accounting and financials software – Datapro Software Ltd
Shott Zwiesel – Ascot Wholesale Ltd
Shout – D C Thomson & Co. Ltd
Show Wall – panel for display purposes – Acco UK Ltd
Showa – S J Wharton Ltd
Showa Strain Gauges – Graphtec GB Ltd
Showbis – theatre booking ticketing – Delta Computer Services
Showboard – panel for display purposes – Acco UK Ltd
Showboard Foldaways – portable panel for display purposes – Acco UK Ltd
Showcase – clear bakery packaging – Pregis Rigid Packaging Ltd
Shower Pumps – aquaboost – Circulating Pumps Ltd
Showercare – Shower enclosures – Contour Showers Ltd
Showerclene – Forward Chemicals Ltd
Showerlux – shower enclosures, overbath screens, baths, whirlpools and spas, cabinets, mirrors & mirror cabinets – Showerlux UK Ltd
Showermate – shower equipment and systems – Stuart Turner Ltd
Showertub – bath – Armitage Shanks Ltd
Showman – software analysis package (traffic) – Golden River Traffic Ltd
Showmaster – display trailer – Lynton Trailers UK Ltd
Showpoint – exhibition and hospitality trailer rental – Lynton Trailers UK Ltd
Showscaff – Accesscaff International Ltd
Shrinktek – heat shrinkable sleeving – Shrinktek Polymers International Ltd
Shrouds – PVC and neoprene – Plastic Mouldings Ltd
SHS – Schmitt Europe Ltd
Shu Works – industrial protective footwear – Amber Safetywear Ltd
***Shubb (U.S.A.)** – capodastra for stringed musical instruments – John Hornby Skewes & Co. Ltd
Shur-Flo – draught inducer – Anglo Nordic Burner Products Ltd
Shuttle – cutters – Turner Tools Ltd
Shuttle – industrial storage system – Kardex Systems UK Ltd
Shuttles – weaving – Pilkingtons Ltd
Shuvholer – post hole digging tool – Drivall Ltd
SI – Alpha Electronics Southern Ltd
Si-AL-O-N – International Syalons Newcastle Ltd
Si-Gro Scan – moisture measuring instrument – M C M
Si-Grometer – collective name for all the instruments – M C M
SI INSERTS – inserts specifically for use in plastics – Zygology Ltd
sia – Kingdom Security Ltd
Siam (France) – freewheels – Ringspann UK Ltd
SIAT – Semi automatic stretch wrapping machines; case sealers, case errectors. – M J Maillis UK Ltd
SIBRE (Germany) – industrial brakes – Centa Transmissions
Sicame (France) – overhead line accessories – Sicame Electrical Developments Ltd
SICCATHERM – lamps – Osram Ltd
SICHELSMIDT – Chaintec Ltd
SICIS – Glass mosaic – World's End Couriers Ltd
Sick Colour Sensors – European Technical Sales Ltd
Sick Encoders – European Technical Sales Ltd
Sick Industrial Sensor – European Technical Sales Ltd
Sick Motors – European Technical Sales Ltd
Sick Positioning Drives – European Technical Sales Ltd
Sick Proximity Sensors – European Technical Sales Ltd
Sickens – Www.Safetysignsonline.Co.Uk
Sickle-Test – kit for demonstration of HB-S – Clin-Tech Ltd
***Siclean** – method for the successful cleaning of turbine hot section components during refurbishment and recoating – Diffusion Alloys Ltd
Sicma – Baxi Group
***Sicmo-Bendix (Monaco)** – mist free paint spray equipment – Gray Campling Ltd
Sico – equipment for use in multi-purpose areas in educational establishments, leisure facilities and hotels-portable dance floors, room service equipment, in-wall and rollaway beds, mobile, folding tables and stages. – Sico-Europe Ltd
Sicoflex – Resinex UK Ltd
Sicoklar – Resinex UK Ltd
Sicoma OMG – manufactuer of concrete mixers – Sicoma OMG
Sicomin (France) – Epoxy resin systems – Matrix Composite Materials Company Ltd
Sicoran – Resinex UK Ltd
Sicostirolo – Resinex UK Ltd
Sicotal – Resinex UK Ltd
Sicoter – Resinex UK Ltd
Sicurgas – Banico Ltd
Sideliner – striping tape range – Cosmic Automotives
Sidetrack Hosting – The Hosting / Server Management arm of Sidetrack Solutions – Sidetrack Solutions
Sidetrack Webdesign – The Website Design branch of Sidetrack Solutions – Sidetrack Solutions
Sidetracker – sideloader and multi direction fork lift trucks – Sidetracker Engineering Ltd
Sidetrak – mobile storage and filing system – Rackline Ltd
Sidewinder – escalator and contour horizontal fire shutters – Kaba Door Systems
Sidewinder – Display Wizard Ltd
Sidlock – Camlock Systems Ltd
Sidlock - Keyosk – Camlock Systems Ltd
***Siebe (U.S.A.)** – pneumatic heating equipment – O E M Group Ltd
SIEBE – Hydraulic & Offshore Supplies Ltd
SIEBE AUTOMOTIVE – Hydraulic & Offshore Supplies Ltd
Siebe Gorman – Submarine Manufacturing & Products Ltd
Siebe Pneumatics – pneumatic control products – Air Power Centre Limited
Siebert Head – package design specialists – Siebert Head Ltd
Siegar – fixed point and infrared gas detection & fire detection – Honeywell Analytics Ltd
Siegling (Germany) – transmission and conveyor belts – Forbo Siegling
Sielemann – European Technical Sales Ltd
Siemans – Proplas International Ltd
Siemens – European Drives & Motor Repairs
Siemens – telephone systems – Integra I C T Ltd
***Siemens (Germany)** – electric motors – Power Plant & Drives
Siemens – CBM Logix
Siemens – European Technical Sales Ltd
Siemens – Electric motors – Beatson Fans & Motors Ltd
Siemens – Halifax Numerical Controls Ltd
SIEMENS – Hydraulic & Offshore Supplies Ltd
Siemens – Encoders UK
Siemens – vacuum pumps – AESpump
Siemens – Cyclops Electronics Ltd
Siemens – equipment/spares – Bearwood Engineering Supplies
Siemens AC Converters – European Technical Sales Ltd
Siemens AC Drives – European Technical Sales Ltd
Siemens AC Motors – European Technical Sales Ltd
Siemens Acoustic Sensors – European Technical Sales Ltd
Siemens DC Drives – European Technical Sales Ltd
Siemens DC Motors – European Technical Sales Ltd
Siemens Dives – European Technical Sales Ltd
Siemens Drive Systems – European Technical Sales Ltd
Siemens Drives – European Technical Sales Ltd
Siemens Electric Actuators – European Technical Sales Ltd
Siemens Fans – European Technical Sales Ltd
Siemens Filters – European Technical Sales Ltd
Siemens Flamproof Motors – European Technical Sales Ltd
Siemens Flow Indicators – European Technical Sales Ltd
Siemens Flow Sensors – European Technical Sales Ltd
Siemens Flow Switches – European Technical Sales Ltd
Siemens Flow Transducers – European Technical Sales Ltd
Siemens Flowmeters – European Technical Sales Ltd
Siemens Frequency Inverter – European Technical Sales Ltd
Siemens Gear Controller – European Technical Sales Ltd
Siemens Geared Motor – European Technical Sales Ltd
Siemens Generators – European Technical Sales Ltd
Siemens High Efficiency Motors – European Technical Sales Ltd
Siemens High Voltage AC Motors – European Technical Sales Ltd
Siemens High Voltage Drives – European Technical Sales Ltd
Siemens High Voltage Motors – European Technical Sales Ltd
Siemens HV Drives – European Technical Sales Ltd
Siemens HV Motors – European Technical Sales Ltd
Siemens Induction Motors – European Technical Sales Ltd
Siemens Industrial PCs – European Technical Sales Ltd
Siemens Inverter Drives – European Technical Sales Ltd
Siemens Inverters – European Technical Sales Ltd
Siemens Isolation Transformers – European Technical Sales Ltd
Siemens Isolators – European Technical Sales Ltd
Siemens Laser Sensors – European Technical Sales Ltd
Siemens LCD Monitors – European Technical Sales Ltd
Siemens Low Voltage Motors – European Technical Sales Ltd
Siemens LV Motors – European Technical Sales Ltd
Siemens Machine Tool Controls – European Technical Sales Ltd
Siemens Machine Tools – European Technical Sales Ltd
Siemens Master Drives – European Technical Sales Ltd
Siemens Motion Sensors – European Technical Sales Ltd
Siemens Motor Spindle – European Technical Sales Ltd
Siemens Motor Starter – European Technical Sales Ltd
Siemens Motors – European Technical Sales Ltd
Siemens Network Systems – Kingston Communications
Siemens Operator Interface – European Technical Sales Ltd
Siemens Panel Boards – European Technical Sales Ltd
Siemens PLC Boards – European Technical Sales Ltd
Siemens Position Switch – European Technical Sales Ltd
Siemens Power Supplies – European Technical Sales Ltd
Siemens Pressure Gauges – European Technical Sales Ltd
Siemens Proximity Switches – European Technical Sales Ltd
Siena – cover paper – James Cropper plc
Sierra (U.S.A.) – thermal mass gas flowmeters – Litre Meter Ltd
Sierra Instruments – Litre Meter Ltd
Sierra Nevada – cycles – Universal Cycles
Sierrablen – fine turf slow release fertilisers – Scotts Co. Ltd
Sierrablen – outfield turf controlled release fertilizers – Scotts Co. Ltd
Siesta – furniture, upholstery, bedding, carpets and all floor coverings – N H Chapman & Co. Ltd
Siesta (Portugal) – hard wax finish domestic density cork floor tiles – Siesta Cork Tile Co.
Sievmaster – sieving machines for powder, liquids etc for food, pharmaceutical and chemcial industries vibratory, rotary, vacuum & linear models – Farleygreene
Sievmaster, Alpha-Mix – Farleygreene
Sifalumin – aluminium welding rods – Weldability S I F
Sifam – electrical measuring instruments – Elektron Components Ltd
Sifbronze – special brazing alloys – Weldability S I F
Sifcupron – copper/phosphorous brazing alloy – Weldability S I F
Sifflux – brazing flux powder – Weldability S I F
Sifmig – aluminium mig filler wire – Weldability S I F
Sifredicote – bronze brazing rods with full fluxcoating – Weldability S I F
Sifserrate – bronze brazing rod flux impregnated – Weldability S I F
Sifsteel – oxy-acetylene welding rods – Weldability S I F
Sifter – size separation equipment – Gericke Ltd
SIG – Proplas International Ltd
Sightline – A A T I Ltd
Sightline3 – A A T I Ltd
Sigloch&Schrieder – European Technical Sales Ltd
***Sigma** – European Drives & Motor Repairs
Sigma – protective coating – Andrews Coatings Ltd
Sigma – UK Office Direct
Sigma – Centrifuges – Pauley Equipment Solutions
Sigma – bridge type machining centres – C Dugard Ltd Machine Tools
SIGMA – Hydraulic & Offshore Supplies Ltd
SIGMA – PTPE based sealing material – Flexitallic Ltd
Sigma – Mercury Bearings Ltd
Sigma – Ex magnetic switches – Wellhead Electrical Supplies
Sigma 2 – automatic positive pressure self contained breathing apparatus – Scott International Ltd
Sigma fxP (United Kingdom) – magnetron sputtering cluster tool – Aviza Technology UK Ltd
Sigma Lutin – Arun Pumps Ltd
Sigma Skimmer – recovery of oils and effluents in calm or sheltered waters – Megator Ltd
Sigmadeck Tower – Accesscaff International Ltd
SIGMAGraF – Graphic displays films – Macdermid Autotype Ltd
Sigmascope – thread pitch measuring device – James H Heal & Co. Ltd
Sigmund Freud Copyrights – literary estate of Sigmund Freud – The Marsh Agency Ltd
Sign*A*Rama – Sign Franchise – Sign A Rama
Sign Design – sign making – A & E Plastic Fabrications Ltd
Sign Solutions Software – point of sale, shelf-edge labelling and in-store POS production system – Episys Group Ltd
Sign Systems Centre – aluminium frames flat signs – J & A Kay Ltd
***Signa Set Plus (Germany)** – part recycled – John Heyer Paper Ltd
Signal – knitwear – Passion Knitwear Ltd
Signal – blood culture system – Oxoid Holdings Ltd
Signatime – Signatime
Signatory – Vi Spring Ltd
Signatrol – Insteng Process Automation Ltd
Signature – UK Office Direct
Signature – C C A Group Ltd
Signature – telephone sets – Nortel Networks UK Ltd
Signature Technology – distributors – Davis Decade Ltd
Signatures – decorative paints and applicators – Akzonobel
Signax – sign products – Legend Signs Ltd
Signbiters – clip for shelf advertising – Alplus
Signcast – modular sign systems – Signscape Systems Ltd
***Signco** – sign manufrs – Signconex Ltd
Signet – flow monitoring equipment – George Fischer Sales Ltd
SigNext – Electronic products – Weidmuller Ltd
Signfix – stainless steel and aluminium sign fixings – Signscape Systems Ltd
Signlite – low profile, edge lit display unit – Spandex plc
Signode – Tri Pack Supplies Ltd

Signpost – guide to premier hotels in Great Britain & Ireland – Priory Publications Ltd
Signum Sign Studio – Signum Sign Studio
Sigtel – Fire telephone system – C-Tec Security Ltd
Sihi – process pumps & vacuum technology – S P P Pumps
Sihi – vacuum pumps – AESpump
Sihi – European Technical Sales Ltd
Sihl Digital Reels – Digital Products - Xeikon - Specialities – Howard Smith Paper Ltd
Sika – thermometers – Bearwood Engineering Supplies
Sika (Germany) – thermometers – Star Instruments Ltd
Sika – County Construction Chemicals Ltd
Sikabond – Vastern Timber Co. Ltd
Sikkens – Akzo Nobel Coatings Ltd
Sikkens AC Multiprimer – acrylic resin based primer with good adhesion properties to suitably prepared non-ferrous metal substrates. – Akzo Nobel Woodcare Ltd
Sikkens AK Primer – alkyd based rust inhibiting primer for use on suitably prepared ferrous metals in exterior and interior applications. – Akzo Nobel Woodcare Ltd
Sikkens BL Dêcor – an interior woodstain formulated to protect and aesthetically enhance interior hardwoods and softwoods. Ideal for use on areas not subject to abrasion. – Akzo Nobel Woodcare Ltd
Sikkens BL Primer – a water-borne acrylic primer, formulated to minimise extractive discoloration by hardwoods of opaque finishes, such as Sikkens Cetol BL Opaque. – Akzo Nobel Woodcare Ltd
Sikkens BL Unitop – a colourless protective interior varnish for use over Sikkens Cetol BL Decor. – Akzo Nobel Woodcare Ltd
Sikkens Cetol BL21 Plus (Europe) – an alkyd/acrylic water-based coating for providing protection to timber substrates such as cladding, fascias, soffits, fencing and garden timbers, or as a base stain prior to the application of Sikkens BL31 on joinery. – Akzo Nobel Woodcare Ltd
***Sikkens Cetol BL31** – a medium build, water borne woodstain for use with Cetol BL21 plus as a finish to new timbers or as a maintenance coat for existing decoration to door and window joinery. – Akzo Nobel Woodcare Ltd
***Sikkens Cetol Filter 7 (Europe)** – a solvent-based, semi-gloss finishing coat for window and door joinery. Contains ultraviolet light absorbers providing superior protection from the harmful effects of sunlight. – Akzo Nobel Woodcare Ltd
Sikkens Cetol HLS (Europe) – a low to medium build exterior woodstain. this product absorbs into the timber surface offering flexibility in areas of high timber movement. – Akzo Nobel Woodcare Ltd
Sikkens Cetol Novatech (Europe) – a high solids exterior woodstain for use as one-coat base stain to Sikkens Cetol Novatop, or as a two-coat system for large timber areas. – Akzo Nobel Woodcare Ltd
Sikkens Cetol Novatop – a one-coat finish over Sikkens Cetol Novatech. provides a level of durability normally associated with traditional three coat systems. – Akzo Nobel Woodcare Ltd
Sikkens Cetol Opaque – a water-borne, moisture vapour permeable, opaque timber coating to protect and decorate timber substrates. Available in a wide range of colours. – Akzo Nobel Woodcare Ltd
***Sikkens Cetol THB (Europe)** – a medium build durable woodstain – Akzo Nobel Woodcare Ltd
***Sikkens Cetol TS Interior (Europe)** – a medium build solvent-borne interior varnish to protect and aesthetically enhance interior hardwoods and softwoods. – Akzo Nobel Woodcare Ltd
Sikkens Componex WR – a timber repair system, consisting of an adhesion promoting two-pack primer and a two-pack filler, for refabricating damaged or decayed timber substrates. – Akzo Nobel Woodcare Ltd
Sikkens Kodrin Spachtel – a surface filler for open grained timbers, prior to overcoating with opaque finishes – Akzo Nobel Woodcare Ltd
Sikkens - Lesonal - Bodyshop Services - Mason Coatings - Mason Graphics – Akzo Nobel Coatings Ltd
Sikkens Onol Express – a medium-build, solvent-borne primer/undercoat for use on timber and suitably prepared and primed metal substrates. Fast drying. – Akzo Nobel Woodcare Ltd
***Sikkens Onol Primer/Undercoat (Europe)** – primer/undercoat, for use on timber in exterior and interior locations. Also as an undercoat on suitably primed metal and hard plastics. – Akzo Nobel Woodcare Ltd
Sikkens Redox AK Primer – a rust inhibiting primer for prepared ferrous metal substrates – Akzo Nobel Woodcare Ltd
***Sikkens Rubbol AZ (Europe)** – a premium quality high gloss finish for use on timbers in exterior and interior locations. – Akzo Nobel Woodcare Ltd
Sikkens Rubbol BL gloss/stain – a vapour permeable satin/gloss finish for use on timber in exterior or interior locations. – Akzo Nobel Woodcare Ltd
***Sikkens Rubbol Satura (Europe)** – a satin opaque finish for use on timber in exterior or interior locations. – Akzo Nobel Woodcare Ltd
Sikkufit – rotary and hydraulic seals – Freudenberg Simrit LP
Sikumat – Ringspann UK Ltd
***Sil-All** – Alltech UK Ltd
Silaflex – big bale wrapping film - silage – Total Polyfilm
Silage 2000 – silage additive – Agil Chemicals Products
Silbak – Wiper Blades – Isla Components Ltd
SilberCotes – coated metallic pigments for coatings, powder coatings – Silberline Ltd
***Silbury Boxed Fats** – Silbury Marketing Ltd
Silcabond – silicate masonry coating – Sika Liquid Plastics
Silcaride – silicon carbide – Washington Mills Electro Minerals Ltd
SILCOFAB – Hydraulic & Offshore Supplies Ltd
Silcoms – engineering, toolmaker, chain manufacturer – Silcoms
Silcroma – coloured metallic pigments for plastics – Silberline Ltd
Silectrom System – inverters – Bonfiglioli UK Ltd
Silent 700 – portable memory terminal – Texas Instruments Ltd
Silent Gliss – Philip Cowan Interiors
Silent Gliss – The Winnen Furnishing Company
Silent Gliss – curtain track systems, poles, roller blinde, stage and electric tracks, vertical blinds, hospital cubicle systems, austrian, roman, festoon and reefed blinds, venetian, dim-out and pleated blinds, wintergarden systems – Silent Gliss Ltd
Silent Knight – super silent generators – Harrington Generators International Ltd
Silentrap – plastic anti-syphon trap – Mcalpine & Company Ltd
Silesia – Camberley Catering Equipment
Silesia Velox – High Speed Grills – Velox Ltd
Silex – Camberley Catering Equipment
SILFAB – Jamak Fabrication Europe Ltd
Silfos – solder/equipment – Bearwood Engineering Supplies
Silhouette – household textiles – Linden Textiles Ltd
***Silhouette (Austria)** – spectacle frames – Silhouette UK Ltd
Silhouette – Silhouette Beauty Equipment
Silhouette – architectural fluorescents – Selux UK Ltd
Silhouette – bed linen – Thomas Frederick & Co. Ltd
Silicate Enriched – render – P E Hines & Sons Ltd
silicon oils – AESpump
Silicone – W Mannering London Ltd
Silicone – rubber products – James Dawson & Son Ltd
Silicone Hose – heat resistant hose – James Dawson & Son Ltd
Siliconix – Cyclops Electronics Ltd
Siliporite – molecular sieves – Atosina UK Ltd
Silit – high temperature refractories – Saint Gobain Industrial Ceramics Ltd
Silit ED – silicon carbide heating elements – Sandvik
Silitect – Forward Chemicals Ltd
Silk – portable machine tools – Furmanite International Ltd
***Silk FCO (Germany)** – coated recycled – John Heyer Paper Ltd
Silkair – lubricants for pneumatics – Fuchs Lubricants UK plc
Silkanray – stockings and socks – Norland Burgess Ltd
Silkgrain – Hörmann (UK) Ltd
Silkmead Tubular – tubular products and components – Silkmead Tubular Ltd
Silkolene – specialist motorcycle lubricants – Fuchs Lubricants UK plc
Silkskin – fishing tackle – Drennan International Ltd
Silkstart – electronic softstart clutch control module – Clark Electric Clutch & Controls Ltd
Silkstone & Millenium Acrylic – worktop – Potter Cowan & Co Belfast Ltd
Silky Look DK – Sirdar Spinning Ltd
SILL – high quality lighting – Sill Lighting UK Ltd
Sill Optics – Stemmer Imaging
***Sillem (Italy)** – polishing machinery – British & Continental Traders Ltd
***Silmax** – milling cutters – Turner Tools Ltd
Silner – half face mask respirator negative pressure – Scott International Ltd
Silner 12, Silner RG, Silner R40/R60 – Scott International Ltd
Silomate – dry silo mortar – Tarmac Quarry Products Ltd
Silotite – agricultural stretch film – bpi.agri
SilQdec – solid state radiation detectors – Q-Par Angus Ltd
Silquartz – domestic sink materials – Carron Phoenix
Silsilcopper – oxy-acetylene welding rods – Weldability S I F
Siltexol – Forward Chemicals Ltd
Siltye – packaging twine – Independent Twine Manufacturing Co. Ltd
Siluma – Vitcas Ltd
Silvalite – expander perlite – Silvaperl
Silvalite - expander perliteVermalite - exfoliated vermiculiteHydroleca - expanded claySilverslag - slag coagulare – Silvaperl
Silvapron – crop protection products – B P plc
SILVENT – Hydraulic & Offshore Supplies Ltd
Silvent – compressed air nozzles and silencers – Designed For Sound Ltd
Silver Bird – eucalyptus oil – Bell Sons & Co. Ltd
Silver Comet – darts – Unicorn Products Ltd
Silver Contacts – Samuel Taylor Ltd
Silver Fox – stainless steels with high resistance to corrosion – Corus Engineering Steels
Silver Link – Derbyshire Building Society
Silver Link – fast food equipment – Lincat Ltd
Silver-Lube – corrosion resistant housed bearings – N S K Europe
Silver Rinse – rinsing product removing all traces of tarnish and brightening silver – Premiere Products Ltd
***Silver Shield (United Kingdom)** – non-stick cookware – Pendeford Metal Spinnings Ltd
Silver Star – bailer twine – Marlow Ropes Ltd
Silverite – aluminium paint – Craig & Rose Ltd
SILVERLINE – Hydraulic & Offshore Supplies Ltd
Silverline – Storage – Bucon Ltd
Silverline – Clamps – The Toolpost
Silverline – Wessex Welding & Industrial Supplies Ltd
Silverline – Gem Tool Hire & Sales Ltd
Silverline Storage – Capex Office Interiors
Silverline Tools – Trafalgar Tools
Silverplatter – electronic publishing CD-Rom – Wolters Kluwer Health
Silversafe – Conservation Resources UK Ltd
Silversafe – Atlantis European Ltd
Silverslag – slag coagulare – Silvaperl
Silverson – Petre Process Plant Ltd
Silverson – high shear rotor stator mixers – Silverson Machines Ltd
Silverstone – pallet shuttle system - cnc machines – Robert Speck Ltd
Silverstone – Stacatruc
Silverstone – fluoropolymer coatings – Du Pont UK Ltd
Silverteam – Proplas International Ltd
Silvertronic – Alpha Electronics Southern Ltd
Silverwood Ladders – Accesscaff International Ltd
Silvet – polymer carried granules form for plastics, inks, coatings & powder coatings – Silberline Ltd
Silvine – note books, exercise books & writing pads – William Sinclair & Sons Stationers Ltd
Silvrex – silverplating process – Cookson Electronics Ltd
Sim-L-Bus – vehicle driver trainer – Simtech Simulation Techniques
Sim-L-Car – car driver trainer – Simtech Simulation Techniques
Sim Travelair (Italy) – portable oxygen concentrator – Intermedical UK Ltd
SIM2 – Lamphouse Ltd
Simalto Plus – research technique – Research For Today Ltd
Simas Filters – Harrier Fluid Power Ltd
***Simba** – Ben Burgess Beeston
SIMBAT – Dynamic Testing System – Testconsult Ltd
Simca – L M C Hadrian Ltd
Simcar – aeration – Ashbrook Simon Hartley Ltd
***Simco (Netherlands)** – static elimination equipment – Advanced Dynamics Ltd
SIME – Stromag Ltd
Sime Industrie – brakes/couplings – Bearwood Engineering Supplies
***Simel (Italy)** – burner motors – Anglo Nordic Burner Products Ltd
SIMEON – LED & Halogen Theatre Lighting – Swift Medical Trolleys Ltd
Simer – automatic metal sawing machnes – Addison Saws Ltd
Simethcone Antifoam C100EP – Granada Cranes & Handling
Simethicone – Granada Cranes & Handling
Simethicone Antifoam C100EP – Basildon Chemical Co. Ltd / KCC
Simethicone Antifoam C100F – Basildon Chemical Co. Ltd / KCC
Simethicone Antifoam C100F – Granada Cranes & Handling
Simethicone Antifoam PD30 – Basildon Chemical Co. Ltd / KCC
Simko – hydraulic piston seal – Freudenberg Simrit LP
Simkral – ABS polymers – Polimeri Europa Ltd
Simlex Chalmit – Ex Fluorescent lighting – Wellhead Electrical Supplies
Simmerring – radial shaft seals – Freudenberg Simrit LP
Simmerring – rotary shaft seal – Freudenberg Simrit LP
SIMMERRING – Hydraulic & Offshore Supplies Ltd
Simmm – pressure washers – Denis Rawlins Ltd
Simmonds Hobson – builders and developers – House Of Flags
Simon-Hartley – Ashbrook Simon Hartley Ltd
Simon Platforms – Accesscaff International Ltd
***Simonds (U.S.A.)** – electronic production tools – Welwyn Tool Group Ltd
Simone – ceramic tiles – Ceramic Tile Distributors Ltd

*Simonet (Switzerland) – centre lathes, capstan lathes and plug board capstans – Brunner Machine Tools Ltd

Simota – Reusable Air Filters – Wemoto Ltd World's End Motorcycles Ltd

Simpack – compactor – Skip Units Ltd

Simpack – waste compactors – Randalls Fabrications Ltd

Simpack - Waste Compactors – Randalls Fabrications Ltd

Simplabelt (Germany) – variable speed drives – Lenze UK Ltd

Simplabloc (Germany) – clutch brakes – Lenze UK Ltd

Simplafill – automatic sack filling & weighing equipment – A T Sack Fillers

Simplaflex (Switzerland) – flexible couplings – Lenze UK Ltd

Simplastic – PVC catheters – Teleflex Medical

Simplatroll (Germany) – electro-magnetic clutches and brakes – Lenze UK Ltd

Simplavolt – power units – Lenze UK Ltd

Simple – skincare, bath, hair and sun products – Lil-lets UK Ltd

Simple Signman – signs – 4site Implementation Ltd

Simplesse – microparticulated whey protein concentrate – C P Kelco Ltd

Simplex – new locomotives and spares – Alan Keef Ltd

*Simplex – universal milling & cutting tool – Brandone Machine Tool Ltd

Simplex – account, VAT record, wages and teachers record books – George Vyner Ltd

Simplex - Planet. – Alan Keef Ltd

Simplex Rapid (Italy) – spring coiling machines – Bennett Mahler

Simplicity – garden and lawn tractors – Claymore

Simplicity – Harrier Fluid Power Ltd

Simply Bio – laundry detergent for autodose application – The Proton Group Ltd

*Simply Chefs – Hocaps Ltd

Simply Cubicles – Mark Simpkin Ltd (Simply Group)

Simply Herbs – Registered trademark – Simply Herbs

Simply Hibi – Windfall Brands Ltd

Simply Lockers – Mark Simpkin Ltd (Simply Group)

*Simply Sauces – Piquant Ltd

Simply Seating – Mark Simpkin Ltd (Simply Group)

Simply Shelters – Mark Simpkin Ltd (Simply Group)

Simply Tables and Chairs – Mark Simpkin Ltd (Simply Group)

Simpson – Moore Speed Racing Ltd

Simpson – G F Smith

*Simpson Paper (U.S.A.) – high quality paper and board – G F Smith

Simpson's-in-the-Strand – restaurant – Simpsons In The Strand

Simrad – marine electronics equipment – Navico UK

Simrax – mechanical face seal – Freudenberg Simrit LP

Simrit – seals and precision mouldings – Freudenberg Simrit LP

Simrit – Mayday Seals & Bearings

Simritan – special polyurethane for hydraulic applications – Freudenberg Simrit LP

SIMRIZ – Hydraulic & Offshore Supplies Ltd

Sims Portex – plastic products for medical and surgical use – Smiths Medical

Simulator – Arjo Wiggins Chartham Ltd

Simunye – Allied Meat Importers

*Sinadder (U.S.A.) – FM test set – Lyons Instruments

Sinbar – herbicide – Du Pont UK Ltd

Sincerely Yours – stationery – Robinson Young Ltd

Sinclair Classical Rainwater – gutter pipes & fittings – Ashworth

Sinclair Collins – equipment spares – Bearwood Engineering Supplies

Sinclair Collins – diaphragm operated steam & process control valves – Parker Hannifin UK plc

Sinclair Ensign – soil, drain and waste systems – Ashworth

Sinclair Horticulture – Composts – L S Systems Ltd

*Sinclair McGill – Bodle Bros Ltd

Sinclair Timesaver – soil and drain systems – Ashworth

*Sincron (Spain) – geared motors and helical reduction gear boxes – Andantex Ltd

Sindanyo – reinforced cement for electrical and thermal insulation – Tenmat Ltd

Sindy – Hasbro UK Ltd

Sinewave – active harmonic filtering system – Schneider

Single Disc Pumps – Alfa Laval Eastbourne Ltd

Single-Mix – software system – Format International Ltd

Single Pak – in line centrifugal cabinet single fan – Nuaire Ltd

Single Top – straight sliding door gear for wardrobe or cupboard doors – P C Henderson Ltd

Singlestat – immersion heater thermostat – Otter Controls Ltd

Sinico (United Kingdom) – Accurate Cutting Services Ltd

Sink Box – Perancea Ltd

SINO-T – Expansion toolholders – Schunk Intec Ltd

Sinodor – perfume speciality – Quest International UK Ltd

Sinora – plywood – Plaut International

Sinpro – power supply – Stontronics Ltd

Sintec – intermetallic resistance heated evaporator sources for use with metallising equipment – Kennametal

Sintec Bearings – long life precision bearings – Ebm-Papst

Sinterflo – sintered porous stainless steel – Porvair Sciences Ltd

Sinterflo – sintered porous stainless steel – Porvair plc

Sioux Tools – Gustair Materials Handling Equipment Ltd

SIP – Gem Tool Hire & Sales Ltd

SIP – Hydraulic & Offshore Supplies Ltd

*Sipa (Italy) – stretch blowmoulding machines – Engelmann & Buckham Ltd

*Sipcut (Italy) – abrasives – S I P Industrial Products Ltd

Sipernat – precipitated silica – Lawrence Industries Ltd

Sipex – Cyclops Electronics Ltd

SIPLA – Grundfos Pumps Ltd

SIPS – Seismic integrated positioning system – Sonardyne International Ltd

SIPS 2 – Seismic integrated positioning system – Sonardyne International Ltd

SIPS Plus – Seismic integrated positioning system – Sonardyne International Ltd

Sipurtec – siliconised foam shoe and car care products – Vitec

Sir Galahad – mercury and gas analyser – P S Analytical Ltd

Sira Electro-Optics Limited – contract research and development – Sira Test & Certification Ltd

SIRA Smart Optics – advanced optical systems – Sira Test & Certification Ltd

Sira Technology Centre – collaborative multi-client research and postgraduate research programmes – Sira Test & Certification Ltd

Sira Test & Certification Ltd – test, calibration and quality assurance services – Sira Test & Certification Ltd

Sirai (Italy) – solenoid valves, brass, plastic, pinch – Zoedale plc

Sirai – Trafalgar Tools

Sirai Coils – European Technical Sales Ltd

Sirai Micro Solenoid Valves – European Technical Sales Ltd

Sirai Pressure Switches – European Technical Sales Ltd

Sirai Solenoid Valves – European Technical Sales Ltd

Sirai Valves – European Technical Sales Ltd

SIRAL – Hydraulic & Offshore Supplies Ltd

Sirco-Pressure Switches – Sirco Controls Ltd

Sirio – transformers/wound components – G D Rectifiers Ltd

Siris – pile rig instrumentation system – Balfour Beatty Living Places

Sirius – technical white oils – Fuchs Lubricants UK plc

Sirius – labelling machine – Harland Machine Systems Ltd

Sirius – vanity basin – Armitage Shanks Ltd

SiriusT3 – instrument for pKa, logP, logD, and solubility measurement – Sirius Analytical Instruments

Sirocco – Meiko UK Ltd

Siroflex – County Construction Chemicals Ltd

Sirofloc – process for enhanced removal of a significant number of legislatively important contaminants from water, wastewater and sewage – Aker Kvaerner Engineering Services Ltd

Sirovelle – textile softeners – S T R UK Ltd

Sirrus – shower valves – A & J Gummers Ltd

Sirtan – wax polish – Evans Vanodine International plc

SIS – UK Office Direct

Sistan – soil sterilant – Universal Crop Protection Ltd

SISU – Woodleigh Power Equipment Ltd

SISU – Chaintec Ltd

SIT (Italy) – flexible shaft couplings – Lenze UK Ltd

Sita 200 Plus (United Kingdom) – the sita 200 plus is an intelligent addressable system that allows up to 200 detectors and sounders on one loop – currently unmatched in the market place – Fike Safety Technology Ltd

Site Hoarding – Accesscaff International Ltd

Site Offices – mobile and jackleg – Landsmans Ltd

Site Safe – Accesscaff International Ltd

Siteblazer – Maingate Ltd

Sitecop – sleeping policeman/speed ramp – Rediweld Rubber & Plastics Ltd

Siteguard – security systems – ADT

Sitekem – site toilets and water soluble sachets for mobile site toilets – Elsan Ltd

Sitema – Motion Drives & Controls Ltd

Sitenet Software – Emerson Network Power Ltd

Siteplot – ultasonic plotting system – Sonatest Ltd

Sitescan – ultrasonic flaw detector – Sonatest Ltd

Sitewatch – telemetry and scada equipment – Lee-Dickens Ltd

Siti – Mercury Bearings Ltd

*Sitma (Italy) – overwrap, shrink wrapping and bindery equipment – Engelmann & Buckham Ltd

Sitoni – value for money, traditional pasta – Pasta Foods Ltd

Sitting Pretty – haemorrhoid wipe – Robinson Healthcare Ltd

Sittingbourne KM Extra – newspaper – Kent Messenger Group Ltd

Sittingbourne Print – commercial printers, photocopy bureau, rubber stamps and stationery – Stat Shop

Six Sigma – Claudius Consulting

Six Sigma – Transcend Group Ltd

Sjöberg – Benches for woodworking – The Toolpost

SK Pumps – Alfa Laval Eastbourne Ltd

*Skandia – Elevating and conveying equipment – B D C Systems

*Skanwood (Scandinavia) – wooden kitchen utensils – Dexam International

Skate & Track – manual truck loading system – Joloda Hydraroll Ltd

SKC Gleittechnik – anti-friction material and structural joint filler – M. Buttkereit Ltd

SKEGA – Hydraulic & Offshore Supplies Ltd

Skega – wear rubber products – Metso Minerals UK Ltd

Skeletorso – anatomical models for demonstration – Educational & Scientific Products Ltd

Skelton design – specialist design services for cellar systems – Hijack Systems

Sketchley – workwear rental & washroom services – Johnson Services Group

Skeye – Maxa Technologies Ltd

SKF – Mercury Bearings Ltd

SKF – Antifriction Components Ltd

SKF (Switzerland) – AC and DC linear actuators and columns – Electro Mechanical Systems (EMS) Ltd

SKF – Mayday Seals & Bearings

SKF (UK) LTD – Hydraulic & Offshore Supplies Ltd

Ski – Y S E Ltd

Ski – ski slope underlay – Verde Sports Cricket Ltd

Ski Web – ski & pole carrier – PSI Ltd (Skiweb UK)

Skibhoull – knitwear – Anderson & Co.

Skid-bilt – cabins-skidded – Boyton B R J System Buildings Ltd

Skidata – revenue generating access control vehicle – Apt Controls Ltd

Skidder – tricycles – Padgett Bros A To Z Ltd

Skiip – semikron intelligent integrated power – Semikron UK Ltd

Skilmatic Range Actuator – Electro-hydraulic actuators for quarter turn or linear applications – Rotork plc

Skimma – plastering trowel – Benson Industries Ltd

Skin Illuminating Complex – healthy glowing skin – Elizabeth Arden

Skinicles – treatment for brown pigmentation marks on the skin – Vivalis Ltd

Skinner – general purpose solenoid valves – Parker Hannifin UK plc

Skinner – Pipe Clamps – Protective Supplies & Services Ltd

*Skintact (Japan) – low adherent dressing – Robinson Healthcare Ltd

Skipper – bus services – East Yorkshire Motor Services Ltd

Skipper – washing machines – Oliver Douglas Ltd

Skipstar – 4 wheel drive dumper – Thwaites Ltd

Skipton – building society – Skipton Building Society plc

*Skira (Far East) – clothing manufacturer – S Karir & Sons Ltd

*Skittles (Italy) – ladies sandal – Cheshire Style Ltd

*Skivertex (U.S.A.) – bookbinding materials – Winter & Co UK Ltd

*Skoda (Czech Republic) – machine tool equipment – Castle Brook Tools Ltd

Skoda – L M C Hadrian Ltd

Skoda – Ashley Competition Exhausts Ltd

*Skopes (Worldwide) – tailored menswear – Newross Impex Ltd

Skopos Fabrics – The Winnen Furnishing Company

Sky Airports Direct – B Sky Cars

Sky Divers – waterproof and non waxed clothing – P S Gill & Sons

Sky Radio Cars – B Sky Cars

Sky Technologies Innerware Solution – Connects SAP to mobile devices – iQlink Ltd

Sky travel – travel agents – Glasgow Prestwick Airport Parking

Skycryl – paints, coatings and enamels, all in the nature of paints, varnishes (other than insulating varnish) and colouring matters (not for laundry or toilet use) – PPG Aerospace

Skydome – National Door Co.

Skye PXM Xantia – Mcnaughton James Paper Group Ltd

Skye PXM Xantur – Mcnaughton James Paper Group Ltd

Skye PXM Xenon – Mcnaughton James Paper Group Ltd

Skye Satin – Coated Paper – Mcnaughton James Paper Group Ltd

Skye Silk Natural White – Coated Paper – Mcnaughton James Paper Group Ltd

Skyegloss Ivory – Coated Paper – Mcnaughton James Paper Group Ltd

Skyelux 2000 – Coated Paper – Mcnaughton James Paper Group Ltd

Skyesilk – Coated Paper – Mcnaughton James Paper Group Ltd

Skyesilk Ivory – Coated Paper – Mcnaughton James Paper Group Ltd

Skyewhite Superior – Uncoated Paper – Mcnaughton James Paper Group Ltd
Skyflex – paints, coatings and enamels, all in the nature of paints and varnishes (other than insulating varnish) – PPG Aerospace
Skyfold – Style South
Skyglide – Glazing Vision Ltd
Skygloss – Coated Paper – Mcnaughton James Paper Group Ltd
Skyhigh – Versalift Distributors UK Ltd
SKYJACK – Chaintec Ltd
Skyjack – R F Lifting & Access Ltd
Skyjack Platforms – Accesscaff International Ltd
Skyjet High Performance Tank Pump – Condensate Removal Pump – E D C International Ltd
Skykem – water soluble sachets for aircraft toilets – Elsan Ltd
SkyKing – King Vehicle Engineering Ltd
SkyKing Equipment – aerial acccess platforms – King Trailers Ltd
Skylab – Alpha Electronics Southern Ltd
***Skylark (China)** – violins – John Hornby Skewes & Co. Ltd
Skylight – architectural aesthetic lighting – Selux UK Ltd
Skyline – V E S Ltd
Skyline – roof glazing – Yule Catto & Co plc
Skylite – mobile floodlighting towers – Henry Cooch & Son Ltd
Skyparks – Double Parking Systems
skype – Callsure Business Telephone & Fax Numbers
Skyport Handling – John Menzies plc
Skyscan (United Kingdom) – balloon aerial photography, aerial infa-red surveys & photo library – Skyscan Aerial Photography
Skyshield – paints, coatings and enamels, all in the nature of paints and varnishes (other than insulating varnish) – PPG Aerospace
Skythane – paints, coatings and enamels, all in the nature of paints and varnishes (other than insulating varnish) – PPG Aerospace
***Skytop 200 (Italy)** – glass hatch sunroof – Webasto Products UK Ltd
Skytronic – audio, video, disco, vehicle computer & communication products – Skytronic Ltd
***Skyview (Netherlands)** – Small HatchLatch handle – Webasto Products UK Ltd
Slack & Parr – External gear pumps – Axflow
Slade Packaging – C P C Packaging
Slate-Mate – plastic grip for holding roof tiles together – Maxview Ltd
Slater Menswear – menswear retailers – Slaters
Slaters – garage and services – Slaters Of Abergele Ltd
Slatesoil – soil pipe terminal – Ubbink UK Ltd
Slatevent – roof void ventilation – Ubbink UK Ltd
Slatevent II – slate roof ventilation – Cembrit Ltd
Slatwall – Preston Plywood Supplies
Slatz – aluminium sign systems – Spandex plc
Slave-Dor – garage door and gate controls – Apt Controls Ltd
Slave-Dor – car park doors – A P T Controls Ltd
Slazenger – golf equipment – Dunlop Slazenger International Ltd
Slazenger – Aimia Foods
Sledger-Kubit – limestone breaking plant – Parker Plant Ltd
Sleekline – telephone sets – Nortel Networks UK Ltd
Sleepmaster – British Vita plc
Sleeprite – beds – Elite Bedding Co. Ltd
Sleepsafe – quilts and pillows – Comfy Quilts Ltd
Sleepscene – bedlinen – Kipfold Ltd
Sleeve-Pak – reusable container system. – D S Smith Correx
Slendaur – vacuum contactor starters – A T B Laurence Scott Ltd
Slenderline – Autron Products Ltd
Slendid – specialty pectins (used as fat replacers) – C P Kelco Ltd
Slendid – fat replacer – Hercules Holding Ii Ltd
Slick Willies – rollerblades, skateboards and snowboards clothing – Slick Willies Ltd
Slickgone – oil dispersants – Dasic International Ltd
Slidax – sliding door bodywork – Lawrence David Ltd
Slide-A-Sign – changeable menu display system – Barconwood Ltd
Slide-up Planning – production scheduling, signal furniture and planning systems – Signal Business Systems Ltd
Slidesafe – Safety Assured Ltd
Slidewinder – fishing tackle – Daiwa Sports Ltd
Slik – silicone bakery paper and release paper – A C P Ltd
Slik 7 – jeans, trousers, jackets and outer wear – Kentex Jeans & Casuals
Slik Cinderella – Schuh Ltd
Slikstik – shafts – Unicorn Products Ltd
Slikstik MX – dart shafts – Unicorn Products Ltd
Slim – diary – Charles Letts Group Ltd
Slim Line – stainless butt hinges – Cooke Brothers Ltd
Slim Slatz – aluminium sign systems – Spandex plc
Slimaster – slimline combination letterplates – Paddock Fabrications Ltd
Slimglide (United Kingdom) – aluminium curtain track – Integra Products
Slimline – front tip, hi tip, power swivel, 2 wheel drive dumper – Thwaites Ltd
Slimline – drawer system – L B Plastics Ltd
Slimline – A general commercial grade Activated Carbon Filter system incorporated within a narrow depth – Emcel Filters Ltd
Slimline – Flotronic Pumps Ltd
Slimline – multi-purpose cistern – Thomas Dudley Ltd
SlimLine – environmental text chambers – Sharetree Ltd
Slimline – aluminium sign systems – Universal Components
Slimline – index mechanism – N S F Controls Ltd
Slimlock – lever arch file – Office Depot UK
Slimpack – duct fan – Roof Units Ltd
Slimpan (United Kingdom) – space critical access panels – Panelcraft Access Panels
Slimpick Long Flap – full flap document wallet – Acco East Light Ltd
Slimpick & Twinpick Wallets – manilla document wallets – Acco East Light Ltd
Slims – darts – Unicorn Products Ltd
Slimstile Range – stainless steel tripod turnstile – Gunnebo Entrance Control Ltd
Slindicator – metal bolts for doors – Allgood
Slingits – polythene bags – Palco Industries Ltd
Slip Radsil – Molyslip Atlantic Ltd
Slip Tuneslip – Molyslip Atlantic Ltd
SLIPFREE – universal connections for use in HPLC and LC/MS systems – Thermo Fisher Scientific
Slippa – Agricultural adjuvant – Interagro UK Ltd
Slipper – slide system for cupboard doors – P C Henderson Ltd
Slippy Bottom – marine anti foil paint – H M G Paints Ltd
Slipstrip – PFTE bearing material – Greene Tweed & Co. Ltd
Slitmaster – aerated for pasture land – Brown's Agricultural Machinery Company Ltd
Slitter – C M Machinery
SLO FLO – Waiter's Friend Company Ltd
Sloan & Davidson – cast iron rainwater and soil goods – J & J W Longbottom
Slogan – G E Healthcare
Sloppy Slipper – Bacup Shoe Co. Ltd
Slosyn – European Drives & Motor Repairs
Slot – architectural vandal and weather resistant lighting – Designplan Lighting Ltd
Slotanit – ductile bright acid zinc plating solutions – Schloetter Co. Ltd
Slotocoup – bright acid copper plating solutions – Schloetter Co. Ltd
Slotolet – M.S.A. based tin and tin lead plating solutions – Schloetter Co. Ltd
Slotoloy – Range of zinc alloy plating solutions – Schloetter Co. Ltd
Slotonik – bright nickel plating solutions – Schloetter Co. Ltd
Slotosit – pcb manufacturing process – Schloetter Co. Ltd
Slotworld Ltd – amusement centres – Cosmo Bingo Club
slube – puzzle – Toyk Design
Sludgebuster – Veolia
Sluicemaster – bedpan disposal unit – The Haigh Group Ltd
***Sluis (Netherlands)** – roasting, puffing and drying plant – Engelmann & Buckham Ltd
Slush Puppie – Slush Puppie Ltd
Slydlok – fuse holders – Lawsons Fuses Ltd
Slydring – bearing designs – Trelleborg Ceiling Solutions Ltd
SLYDRING – Hydraulic & Offshore Supplies Ltd
SLYDWAY – Hydraulic & Offshore Supplies Ltd
Slydway – linear bearing system – Trelleborg Ceiling Solutions Ltd
SM-3 – liquid seaweed plant nutrient SM3 and SM6 – Chase Organics
SM Range (NO3) – sliding partitions – Becker Sliding Partitions Ltd
SM6 – 24 or 36kv indoor switchgear – Schneider
SMA – Genus Group
Small Batch Plastics – Pentagon Plastics Ltd
Small Classic – british cigars – Imperial Tobacco Group PLC
Small Classic Filter – british cigars – Imperial Tobacco Group PLC
Small Weaves – fabric collection – Zoffany
Small Weaves II – fabric collection – Zoffany
Smallbone – kitchen, bedroom, bathroom and office furniture – Canburg
***Smaragd (Sweden)** – high performance vinyl sheet – Forbo
***Smart (U.S.A.)** – check valves – The West Group Ltd
Smart Card – Tekdata Distribution Ltd
Smart Card Application – Tekdata Distribution Ltd
Smart Card Reader – Tekdata Distribution Ltd
Smart Card Reader Writer – Tekdata Distribution Ltd
Smart Card Security – Tekdata Distribution Ltd
Smart Card Solution – Tekdata Distribution Ltd
Smart Card Technology – Tekdata Distribution Ltd
***Smart Choice** – 3663
Smart Fume Cupboard – fume cupboard – S & B UK Ltd
Smart-Hone – automatic horizontal honing machine with electronic management – Equipment For You
Smart Junior – de-soldering machine – Vysionics
Smart Keys – keyboard connecting to pc – Vtech Electronics UK plc
Smart Reflow – ICS surface mount bga rework machine – Vysionics
Smart scart – Brand – Bluedelta
Smart solutions – Central vacuum – Strathvac
Smart Start – ac softstart – Control Techniques
Smart Start Basic Plus – Vtech Electronics UK plc
Smart Start Elite – Vtech Electronics UK plc
Smart Start Premier – Vtech Electronics UK plc
Smart Track – cost recovery and expense management solutions for office equipment. – Emos-Infineer Ltd
Smart Truline – solder paste application and alignment – Vysionics
Smart View – Radir Ltd
Smartbalancer 3 – portable/field balancing machine – Schenck Ltd
Smartbalancer 3 – Schenck Ltd
Smartboard – Interactive Board – Touch A V Ltd
Smartboard – Lamphouse Ltd
Smartcell – Fast-track Cell Site – Portastor Ltd
Smartcom – controller – Reznor UK Ltd
SmartDate – thermal transfer coders – Markem-Imaje Ltd
SmartElec – controller – Airbloc
Smartkontrols – Ener-G Combined Power
Smartlock – foam hinge pack locking system – Pregis Rigid Packaging Ltd
SmartMotor – Baldor UK
SmartMove – Baldor UK
Smartply – Wigan Timber Ltd
Smartply OSB – M D M Timber Ltd
SmartPrint Central – network printer control – Emos-Infineer Ltd
Smartsign – temperature sensitive sign – Stocksigns Ltd
***Smash (Portugal)** – baby clothes – Alami International Ltd
SMC – Sandhurst Plant Ltd
SMC – Aztech Components Ltd
SMC – Air Technics Ltd
SMC – Hydraulic Component & Systems Ltd
SMC – Southern Valve & Fitting Co. Ltd
SMC – Gustair Materials Handling Equipment Ltd
SMC – Harrier Fluid Power Ltd
SMC Electronics – Cyclops Electronics Ltd
SMC PNEUMATICS – Hydraulic & Offshore Supplies Ltd
Smead – UK Office Direct
Smeaton – medium duty circular cover and frame – Norinco UK Ltd
Smei – Planetary Gearboxes – J B J Techniques Ltd
SMEL S.R.L. – Hydraulic & Offshore Supplies Ltd
Smiffys – Smiffy's
Smiffys, Smiffys USA – Smiffy's
Smiffys USA – Smiffy's
Smith – Jones Cranes Parts
Smith – G F Smith
Smith – Dean Smith & Grace Lathes Ltd
Smith Corona – UK Office Direct
Smith Gamblin Haworth – Development consultancy architectural technologies – Stripe Consulting Ltd
Smith & Johnson – stainless steel vee clamps – Teconnex Ltd
Smithbrook Lighting – Light Fantastic
Smiths Gore – farm management – Smiths Gore
SMITHS INDUSTRIES – Hydraulic & Offshore Supplies Ltd
SMJ – Gem Tool Hire & Sales Ltd
Smog-Eater – electrostatic precipitators for air cleansing – Horizon Mechanical Services International Ltd
Smog-Mobile – mobile fume extraction unit – Horizon Mechanical Services International Ltd
Smog-Rambler – self-supporting, flexible and fume extractor arms – Horizon Mechanical Services International Ltd
Smoke Clearer – ultra high temperature smoke extract fan – Nuaire Ltd
SmokeCheck – Cardinal Health U.K. 232 Ltd
Smokegard – combined smoke and fire damper for air conditioning systems – Gilberts Blackpool Ltd
Smokerlyzer – carbon monoxide monitor for smoking cessation – Bedfont Scientific Ltd
Smokey Eyes – eye pencil – Elizabeth Arden
Smometa – smoke alarm and indicator – U T C Fire & Security
Smooth Flow – tap – Worldwide Dispensers
Smooth Lining Eye Pencil – eye pencil – Elizabeth Arden
Smoothcat – catalyst handling and maintenance shutdown – Dialog Technivac Ltd
Smoothline – disposal container – Skip Units Ltd
Smoothline – floor mopping system – Spraychem Ltd
Smox – test points – Oxley Developments Company Ltd
SMP – Secure Holidays

SMS (U.S.A.) – Laser based measurements & alignment systems – Schmitt Europe Ltd
Smudge – T-shirt printers – Smudge Ink
Smurfit Print UK – promotional print and packaging – Dobson & Crowther
SMV-KONECRANES – Chaintec Ltd
SMW – Harrier Fluid Power Ltd
SMW – S M W Autoblok
SMW-Autoblok – S M W Autoblok
Snack manufrs – O P Chocolate Ltd
***Snackmart (U.S.A.)** – vending machines – Westomatic Vending Services Ltd
Snail – hand tools – Smith Francis Tools Ltd
Snakeboard – M V Sport & Leisure Ltd
Snale – PC pins – Oxley Developments Company Ltd
Snap Brim Panama – Try & Lilly Ltd
SNAP-FIT – Hydraulic & Offshore Supplies Ltd
Snap-Lay – Sub Sea 7 Ltd
Snap-On – hand tools – Bearwood Engineering Supplies
Snap-Pipe – Sub Sea 7 Ltd
Snap Rivet – plastic fastening rivot – Alplus
***Snap-Tap (Sweden)** – indexable insert threading tools – Seco Tools UK Ltd
SNAP TITE – Hydraulic & Offshore Supplies Ltd
Snap-Tite – Trafalgar Tools
Snap-tite – Southern Valve & Fitting Co. Ltd
SNAP-TITE EUROPE B.V. – Hydraulic & Offshore Supplies Ltd
Snaplock – push-on, pull-off reusable fastener – Bollhoss Fastenings Ltd
Snaplox – test points – Oxley Developments Company Ltd
Snappa Clips – Snopake Ltd
***Snapper** – Route V J Horticultural
Snapper – hose clip – Hellermann Tyton
Snappy Snaps – photo processing – Snappy Snaps Franchises Ltd
Snapron – filter sleeve fitting assembly – Andrew Webron Ltd
Snapshot – image capture/ID software – Delta Computer Services
Snaptite (U.S.A.) – quick release couplings – Hydrasun Ltd
Snaptte – Harrier Fluid Power Ltd
SNFA – Mercury Bearings Ltd
Snickers – Melitzer Safety Equipment
Snickers – Workwear Corporatewear – A4 Apparel Ltd
Sno-Lock – Hose and couplings for snow making equipment. – Dixon Group Europe Ltd
Sno Smoothie – Slush Puppie Ltd
Snoezelen – special care products – Robinson Healthcare Ltd
Snopake – Snopake Ltd
Snopake – UK Office Direct
Snow – ploughs – Econ Engineering Ltd
Snow Danobat Grinder – Phil Geesin Machinery Ltd
Snow Drift – handkerchief – Spence Bryson Ltd
Snow OS horizontal Grinders – Phil Geesin Machinery Ltd
Snow ring Grinders – Phil Geesin Machinery Ltd
Snow RT Ring grinder – Phil Geesin Machinery Ltd
Snow vertical spindle grinders – Phil Geesin Machinery Ltd
Snowcal – whiting fillers – Omya UK Ltd
Snowcard – insurance services - mountain sports and activity travel – Snowcard Insurance Services Ltd
Snowdon – Halcyon Solutions
Snowflake – christmas products including decorations, artificial trees, ornaments figurines and tableaux – P M S International Group plc
Snowflake Ivory BD's – paper – H V Sier Ltd
Snowfort – coated wollastonite fillers – Omya UK Ltd
***Snowhite (France)** – ultra white printing paper – Davies Harvey & Murrell
Snowqueen – ready made curtains – Kipfold Ltd
Snug – Mentholatum Co. Ltd
Snuggle-Dry by Bianca – Turner Bianca
Snuggly 2 ply – Sirdar Spinning Ltd
Snuggly 3 ply 100g – Sirdar Spinning Ltd
Snuggly 3 ply 50g – Sirdar Spinning Ltd
Snuggly Aran – Sirdar Spinning Ltd
Snuggly Double Knitting 50g – Sirdar Spinning Ltd
Snuggly Lustre 4 ply – Sirdar Spinning Ltd
Snuggly Lustre DK – Sirdar Spinning Ltd
Snuggly QK – Sirdar Spinning Ltd
SNUGS – sheepskin baby booties – Starchild Shoes
SO/SX Series Sprag Clutch – Renold Clutches & Couplings Ltd
Soak Up – Forward Chemicals Ltd
Soap Shop – soap packet vendor – Coinage Limited
Soaplife – I P C Media Ltd
Soaps, Perfumery & Cosmetics – magazine – Progressive Media Group
Sobral – alkyds and epoxy esters – Scott Bader Co. Ltd
Sobrom – methyl bromide – I M C D UK Ltd
Sobstad – sailmakers – Elvstrom Sails Ltd
Society Logo – banking, insurance & financial services – Birmingham Midshires Financial Services Ltd
Society Logo (Man & Woman) – banking, insurance and financial services – Birmingham Midshires Financial Services Ltd
Society of Motor Manufacturers & Traders – trade association – S M M T Ltd
Socks by Swift – mens socks – J Alex Swift Ltd
Socomef – Oil pot burners – Anglo Nordic Burner Products Ltd
***Socorex (Switzerland)** – liquid handling equipment – Camlab Ltd
Socumfi – shoes, sandals – D Jacobson & Sons Ltd
Soder-Wick – de soldering device – Time Products UK Ltd
Sodium Heptonate – sodium glucoheptonate – Croda Europe Ltd
Sofadi – display and exhibition systems – RTD Systems Limited
Sofame (France) – work benches and seating – Effortec Ltd
Soffit Lining Solutions – soffits, underpasses – Rockwool Rockpanel B V
Sofflo – catalyst handling and maintenance shutdown – Dialog Technivac Ltd
Sofima – Harrier Fluid Power Ltd
SOFIMA – Hydraulic & Offshore Supplies Ltd
SOFIMA FILTERS – Hydraulic & Offshore Supplies Ltd
Sofnocarb – activated carbon – Molecular Properties Ltd
Sofnocat – precious metal catalyst – Molecular Properties Ltd
Sofnofil – odour adsorbent – Molecular Properties Ltd
Sofnolime – granular carbon dioxide absorbent – Molecular Properties Ltd
Sofra – Harrier Fluid Power Ltd
Sofralub – Harrier Fluid Power Ltd
Sofrance – Harrier Fluid Power Ltd
Soft Cotton – yarns – Stylecraft
***Soft-Eft** – Commidea Ltd
Soft-Foot – vinyl foam anti-fatigue standing matting – Jaymart Roberts & Plastics Ltd
Soft Line – shoe lining materials – J B Broadley
Soft & Pure – cotton wool range – Robinson Healthcare Ltd
Softapads – drum head pads – John Hornby Skewes & Co. Ltd
Softbag – Bespoke hand made bags – Hofbauer (UK) Ltd
Softdock – pontoon fendering – Nicholas Bray & Son Ltd
Softec Microsystems – microcontroller support – Anglia
SOFTECS – Washtec UK Ltd
Softek Structural Office Suite – windows based 2D/3D analysis & design of steel and concrete – Computer Services Consultants UK Ltd
Softfall – lias playground surface – Melcourt Industries
Softfoam Surfboards – Movevirgo Ltd
Softfoam Surfboards- Swell – Movevirgo Ltd
Softinger – European Technical Sales Ltd
Softline Showers – D A W Enterprises Ltd
Softone – Georgia Pacific GB Ltd
Softop – mens socks – H J Hall
Softop Comfort Cover – soft, hygienic toilet seat cover – Helping Hand Co.
Softpatch – communications systems - parts and intercom systems – Speakerbus
Softsheen – decorative paints – Akzonobel
Softstart UK – Motor Soft Starters – Soft Start UK
Software Professionals – It recruitment agency, specialising in the supply of trainees – Computeach International Ltd
Softwash – Washtec UK Ltd
Softwash - SOFTECS – Washtec UK Ltd
Soho – small offices & home offices 200,000+ – Acxiom Ltd
Soil Panal – british designed green faced reinforced slope systems – P H I Group Ltd
***Soir De Paris (France)** – perfume – Bourjois Ltd
SOITAAB – Bandsaw, laser, plasma and waterjet cutting machines – Accurate Cutting Services Ltd
Sokleen – bleach – Unico Ltd
Sola – hard resin lenses – Carlzeiss Vision
SOLAAR – Thermo Electrical
Solace – Shoe laces – John Dobson Milnthorpe Ltd
Soladex – solvent based anti corrosive weatherproof membrane based on Dupont Hypalon – Sika Liquid Plastics
Solaglas Laminated – laminted & security glass – Solaglas Ltd
Solair G.R.P. – architectural products, garage doors, cottage and door canopies – Solair Group Architectural Products
Solair GRP Dormer Windows – Solair Group Architectural Products
Solar – Lusso Interiors
Solar – security film – H W Cooper
Solar 100C – lighting effects projector – Optikinetics Ltd
Solar 250 – lighting effects projector – Optikinetics Ltd
Solar Dome – polythene clad enclosures (500 ft plus) – Clovis Lande Associates Ltd
Solar Essence – The UK market leaders in solar thermal technologies that fully integrate with your central heating s – Solar Essence
Solar Sill – Speed Plastics Ltd
Solar System – programmable projector attachment – Optikinetics Ltd
SolaRay – solar powered active infrared wire free detection – Lazer Systems
Solarbo (Ecuador) – balsa wood – Amerang Group Ltd
Solarcaine – sun and skin care cream lotion and gel – M S D Animal Health
Solarcaine Spay – M S D Animal Health
Solare – Lusso Interiors
Solarfilm – plastic film covering for model aircraft – Solarfilm Sales Ltd
Solargard – UK Solar Ltd
SolarGrip – Gesipa Blind Riveting Systems Ltd
Solaris – mechanical coated heatset web offset magazine paper (M.F.C.) – Stora Enso UK Ltd
Solaro – fabric – M Howgate Ltd
Solartex – fabric covering for model aircraft – Solarfilm Sales Ltd
SOLAS – Fibre-Tech Industries LLP
Solberg – Harrier Fluid Power Ltd
Solcon 137 – degreaser with quick break properties – Agma Ltd
Solcon 80R – solvent based degreaser – Agma Ltd
Solder Resist – flux & cleaning media – Humiseal Europe Ltd
Sole Sister – Twinmar Ltd
Soled Out – Twinmar Ltd
Solenoid Valves – manufacturers of valves – Bifold Group
Solera – 27 seat upwards coaches – Optare Group Ltd
Solfuel – Tradebe Solvent Recycling Ltd
Solicut – Chef Knives – Gilberts Food Equipment Ltd
Solid Applied Technologies – Ultrasonic Level detection – Coulton Instrumentation Ltd
Solid Auto (UK) Ltd – import motor vehicle components – Solid Auto UK Ltd
Solid Contracts Ltd – SolidWorks, Pro-Engineer, Inventor, SolidEdge CAD Recruitment Consultancy – Solid Contracts Ltd
Solid Edge – Linmech Technical Solutions Ltd
Solid Fuel Association – promotes solid fuel for domestic heating and provides advisory services on all aspects of solid fuel heating – Solid Fuel Association
Solid Streak – marker – Office Depot UK
Solid Surfaces – corian, surell, avonite, antium – W H Foster & Sons Ltd
Solid Timber Doors – Plaut International
Solidair – British Vita plc
Solidcut – Camtek Ltd
Solignum – canned product range – Protim Solignum
Soliphant – level limit switch (bulk materials) – Endress Hauser Ltd
***Solis** – Coffeetech
Solitaire – production console – Digico UK Ltd
Solitaire – emergency lighting range – Lab Craft Ltd
Solmec – Sandhurst Plant Ltd
Solo – 32-36 seat bus – Optare Group Ltd
Solo – dental disposable (inc needles) – Plandent
Solo – scooter controller – P G Drive Technology
Solo – horticultual, agricultual and industrial spraying machines – Solo Sprayers Ltd
Solo – professional detector maintenance equipment – No Climb Products Ltd
Solo – vending machines – Westomatic Vending Services Ltd
Solo – T M Electronics Ltd
Solo 8 Live – sound reinforcement console – Digico UK Ltd
Solo and Duo – kitchen furniture – Moores Furniture Group
Solo Live – sound reinforcement console – Digico UK Ltd
Solo Logic – production console – Digico UK Ltd
Solo Monitor – sound reinforcement console – Digico UK Ltd
Solo Percussion Mallets – drumsticks and mallets – David Morbey Timpani & Percussion
Sologard – medium density plasic mudguards with integrated spray suppression – Jonesco (Preston) Ltd
Sololink – linkable suspension files – Acco East Light Ltd
Solomon Systech – display ICs – Anglia
Solotab – suspension files – Acco East Light Ltd
Solotab Colour Range – coloured suspension files – Acco East Light Ltd
Solovair – air-cushion soled footwear – N P S Shoes Ltd
Solray – panel heating and cooling – Comyn Ching
Solstice – single skinned GRP up and over garage door – P C Henderson Ltd
Solstis – paper – Fenner Paper Co. Ltd
Solstrip – Forward Chemicals Ltd
Solstuds – upholstery nails – Frank Shaw Bayonet Ltd
Solswiv – rigging and lifting tackle – Solid Stampings Ltd
Soltrend – B P plc
Solucote – polyurethane resins – Lawrence Industries Ltd
Solutions Direct – safes, electronic article surveillance systems, fog bandit, bespoke communication systems/helpfinder/stafffinder – Air Tube Technologies Ltd
Solutions Four – Solutions Four is a UK web design company based in London UK, providing branded web design – Solutions Four

Solvenol – terpene hydrocarbons – Hercules Holding Ii Ltd

Solvent Cleaner – cleaner for cleaning of uncured products – Conren Ltd

Solvex – chemical cleaning products covering applications from vehicle washes to machine tool system cleaners – Castrol UK Ltd

Solving – Solving Ltd

Solvit – paint stripper – Smith & Roger Ltd

Solvitax – cod liver oil (veterinary usage) – Seven Sea's Ltd

Solvitec – liquid vitamins – SCA Newtec

Solvol – soluble oils – D A Stuart Ltd

Solvol – various products – Hammerite Products Ltd

Solway Zipper – waterproof clothing – J Barbour & Sons Ltd

Somacel – wool blankets – John Horsfall & Sons Ltd

Somas – Orbinox UK Ltd

Somax – shirts, pyjamas, nightshirts, shorts and dressing gowns – J M C Q Huston & Son

Somband – kraft change over tape for paper mills – Somic Textiles

Somcord – kraft paper cords for tying and piping – Somic Textiles

Somdie – tool & die steel – Somers Forge Ltd

***Somdrain** – drainage geocomposite – Geosynthetic Technology Ltd

Somers Engineering – Somers Totalkare Ltd

Somers Supamold – plastic mould steel – Somers Forge Ltd

Somers Vehicle Lifts – mobile vehicle lifts for truck and PSV sectors – Somers Totalkare Ltd

Somerset – pole or wall mounted outdoor area luminaire – Holophane Europe Ltd

Somersets E-Z Shave (United Kingdom) – shaving preparation – David Somerset Skincare

Somersets Shaving Oil (United Kingdom) – shaving preparation – David Somerset Skincare

Somerton – office chairs – Top Office Equipment Ltd

Somet – Harrier Fluid Power Ltd

Something New – C C A Group Ltd

Something Special – embroidery kits – DMC Creative World

Somflex – Extruded plastic piping – Somic Textiles

Somfy – Synektics Ltd

Somnite – hypnotic suspension – Norgine International Ltd

Somos – Harrier Fluid Power Ltd

Somplas – Extruded PVC piping – Somic Textiles

Somplas 30 – tool & die steel – Somers Forge Ltd

Somtack – extruded PVC piping and edge trim for upholstery furniture – Somic Textiles

***Somtube** – drainage geocomposite – Geosynthetic Technology Ltd

Somweave – woven paper fabric for furniture, bags, lampshades and wallcoverings – Somic Textiles

Somyarn – paper yarn – Somic Textiles

Sonacoat – coating thickness gage – Sonatest Ltd

Sonagage – ultrasonic thickness Meter – Sonatest Ltd

Sonata – special effect coatings – Akzonobel

Sonata – vending machines – Westomatic Vending Services Ltd

Sonata – kitchen furniture – Moores Furniture Group

Sonata – Pledge Office Chairs Ltd

Sonatest – laboratory equipment – Bearwood Engineering Supplies

Sonatone – Ceiling tiles (acoustical) – U S G UK Ltd

Sonazoid – G E Healthcare

Songmaker Studios – 20 studios nationwide, providing customers with a unique experience,a perfect gift for young and old – Songmaker Ltd

Sonic – Mass Consultants Ltd

Sonic – speak-through security communication screens – Sonic Windows Ltd

Sonic – telecommunications equipment – Sonic Communications International Ltd

Sonic (United Kingdom) – Bicycles – Moore Large & Co. Ltd

Sonic Clearvox Windows – incorporate integral open duplex interiorly and induction loop to provide assistance for the hard of hearing – Sonic Windows Ltd

Sonic Drilling – Sonic – Sonic Drilling Supplies Ltd

Sonicleaners – Apollo

Sonicleaners, Sonifiers, and Totalsonic. – Apollo

Sonicsert – threaded inserts for ultrasonic insertion – Tappex Thread Inserts Ltd

Sonicwall – Charlton Networks

SonicWall (U.S.A.) – internet firewall – Tekdata Distribution Ltd

Sonifiers – Apollo

Soniprep – ultrasonic disintegrator – Sanyo Gallenkamp plc

Sonique – Sonique Ltd

Sonix – UK Office Direct

Sonix 2000 – nebuliser systems for the treatment of respiratory disorders – Clement Clarke International Ltd

Sonomatic – Langford Electronics UK Ltd

Sonoston – alloy metals – Stone Marine Propulsion Ltd

Sonoxcarb – high efficiency activated carbon air filter for removal of atmospheric pollutant gases – Emcel Filters Ltd

Sontara – spun-lace fabric – Du Pont UK Ltd

Sontay – Alpha Electronics Southern Ltd

Sony – Encoders UK

Sony (Japan) – cameras – Premier Engineering

Sony – Cyclops Electronics Ltd

Sony – electronic digital readout and precision measuring equipment for machine tools and machine applications – Stanmatic Precision UK Ltd T/A Axis Group

SONY – Stemmer Imaging

Sony – UK Office Direct

Sony – Videonations Ltd

Sony – Lamphouse Ltd

***Sony** – TV/Video Data Projectors – Hospitality A V

Sony – LCD Televisions – Electrotec International Ltd

***Sony Corporation (Japan)** – radio and TV – Sony Head Office

Sony Paper – video paper – Chartrite Ltd

Soot Master – vacuum cleaner – Anglo Nordic Burner Products Ltd

Sooth-Tan – lotion – Reckitt Benckiser plc

Sopap – European Technical Sales Ltd

Soparis – Harrier Fluid Power Ltd

Sophie – washbasin, closet, bidet and bath – Ideal Standard Ltd

Soraluce – T W Ward CNC Machinery Ltd

Sorbacal – lime for gas treatment – Lhoist UK

Sorbatox – mycotoxin absorber – Agil Chemicals Products

Sorbonorit – activated carbon – Norit UK Ltd

***Sorema (Italy)** – plastics washing and re-cycling – Engelmann & Buckham Ltd

Sorex Super Fly Spray – insecticide aerosol – Sorex Ltd

Sorex Wasp Nest Destroyer – insecticide – Sorex Ltd

Sorexa – rodenticide – Sorex Ltd

Sorexa CD – mouse killer – Sorex Ltd

Sorgene 5 – disinfectants – Sorex Ltd

Sorocco – 16 seater coaches – Optare Group Ltd

Sortex – electronic sorting machines, colour sorting machines, visionsystems, mechanical sorting machines and separators (colour) – Buhler Sortex Ltd

Sorting Code Numbers Electronic – provides sorting code numbers electronically. – The Bankers' Almanac Reed Business Information

SOSS – hinges, concealed – N V Tools Ltd

Sotfet – surface mount MOSFET – Diodes Zetex Semiconductors Ltd

Sotheby's – auctioneers – Sothebys

Sottini – Ideal Standard Ltd

Soudokay – welding consumables – Bohler Welding Group Ltd

Soudometal – welding consumables – Bohler Welding Group Ltd

Soulard – Foie Gras – Classic Fine Foods Ltd

Sound Activities – Series of books to support reading and spelling – Egon Publishers Ltd

Sound Alert – development of directional sirens and alarms – University Of Leeds

Sound Beam Trolley (United Kingdom) – mobile sound beam system – Mike Ayres Design Ltd

Sound-Check – acoustic wallcovering systems – Bridgeplex Ltd

Sound Control – hearing protection – M S A Britain Ltd

Sound Security ITD – Security Services – Sound Security Ltd

Sound-Shield – sound proof doors, fire shield, fire doors – Accent Hansen

Sound Support – induction loop amplifiers & systems – Sound Support

Sound Transfer – digital editing, remastering and location recording – Fellside Recordings Ltd

Sound Travels – coach services – East Yorkshire Motor Services Ltd

SoundBloc – higher performance sound reducing plasterboard – Bristish Gypsum

Soundlab – music and disco equipment – Electrovision Group Ltd

Soundpac – acoustic duct inserts and attenuators – Hotchkiss Air Supply

Soundranger – warning systems – Lowther Loudspeaker Systems Ltd

Souriau – Connectors – Dax International Ltd

Souriau – Contacts – Dax International Ltd

South Durham Herald & Post – Gazette Media Company

South Lincs Cladding – cladding – South Lincs Construction Ltd

South London Press Friday – South London Press

South London Press Tuesday – South London Press

South Seas – Ryalux Carpets Ltd

South Staffordshire Newsletter – Staffordshire Newspapers Ltd

South West Office Supplies – Discount Supplies of Everything Office – South West Office Supplies

South West One – public relations – South West One Ltd

South Wirral News – free newspaper – Flintshire Chronicle Newspapers

Southbend – Ranges – Middleby UK Ltd

Southbound – record label – Ace Records Ltd

Southco – latches and access hardware – Zygology Ltd

Southco – latches and access hardware – Southco Manufacturing Co.

Southend Standard – free weekly newspaper – Newsquest Essex Ltd

Southerly – yachts – Northshore Yachts Ltd

Southern Comfort – shirts – Rael Brook Group Ltd

Southern Electric – electricity & gas distributor and supplier – Scottish & Southern Energy P.L.C.

Southern Fried Chicken – FFS Brands Ltd

Southern Game Meat – Freedown Food Co.

Southern Spring Technologies – design spring technologies – Southern Springs & Pressings Ltd

Southport Visiter – newspaper – Liverpool Daily Post & Echo

Southworth – cotton fibre paper – Pelltech Ltd

SOV – unfired thermal fluid heated steaming calorfier – Babcock Wanson UK Ltd

Sovella – Human-Centred design, modular furniture (Finland) – Scandinavian Storage Group

Soveregin Silk Ivory – coated paper & board – Howard Smith Paper Ltd

Sovereign – yachts – Northshore Yachts Ltd

Sovereign – Autron Products Ltd

Sovereign – bread flour – Allied Mills

Sovereign – cricket bats – Kookaburra Reader Ltd

Sovereign – note & coin changer – Coinage Limited

Sovereign – County Construction Chemicals Ltd

Sovereign – double skinned GRP up and over garage door – P C Henderson Ltd

Sovereign Chemical Industries – damp-proofing, timber treatment and building products – Bostik Sovereign Chemicals

Sovereign Gloss – coated paper & board – Howard Smith Paper Ltd

Sovereign Silk – coated paper & board – Howard Smith Paper Ltd

Soveriegn Labels – self adhesives – Howard Smith Paper Ltd

Sovex Series 200 – lightweight monorail – M C M Conveyor Systems

Sovis Saint-Gobain – Toughened curved display glass – Showmaster Ltd

Sovtek (Russian Federation) – electronic valves & tubes – Edicron Ltd

Sow HiFertility – protein concentrate for sows – A One Feed Supplements Ltd

Soxon – sock and stocking aid – Helping Hand Co.

Soy-Grade – soya balancer for growing and finishing pigs – A One Feed Supplements Ltd

SP 106 – multi-purpose epoxy systems – Gurit UK Ltd

SP 115 – clear laminating systems – Gurit UK Ltd

SP 127 – epoxy gelcoat system – Gurit UK Ltd

SP 320 – clear epoxy coating system – Gurit UK Ltd

SP 531 – 100 degrees c epoxy gelcoat system – Gurit UK Ltd

SP 631 – 100 degrees c epoxy laminating system – Gurit UK Ltd

SP Firestop Systems – external walls, junctions with floor slabs, voids – Rockwool Rockpanel B V

SP Technology – S P Technology Ltd

SP™ – GGB UK

SP190 – Thermo Electrical

SP2900 – Thermo Electrical

SP9 – Thermo Electrical

SP91 – Thermo Electrical

Spa 2000 – adjustable posture support chair – R B F Healthcare

Spa Gelatin – edible and pharmaceutical gelatins – Croda Europe Ltd

Spa-Tan – waterproof chrome sole leather – Joseph Clayton & Sons Ltd

Spabond 120 – epoxy adhesive system – Gurit UK Ltd

Spabond 125 – epoxy adhesive system – Gurit UK Ltd

Spabond 130 – epoxy adhesive system – Gurit UK Ltd

Spabond 330 – epoxy adhesive system – Gurit UK Ltd

Spabond 335 – epoxy adhesive system – Gurit UK Ltd

Spabond 340 – epoxy adhesive system – Gurit UK Ltd

Spabond 345 – epoxy adhesive system – Gurit UK Ltd

Spabond 720 – rapid cure epoxy adhesive – Gurit UK Ltd

Spabond 735 – epoxy adhesive system – Gurit UK Ltd

Spabond 740 – corebond epoxy adhesive – Gurit UK Ltd

Spabond 765 – fire retardant epoxy adhesive – Gurit UK Ltd

Space – washbasins, closets, baths, shower screens, enclosure and trays – Ideal Standard Ltd

Space Hulk – electronic games, publications, rule books, magazines, books, games, models, miniatures and war games – Games Workshop Ltd

Space Marine – games, playthings, miniatures and models, all for use in fantasy games – Games Workshop Ltd

Space Oasis – Screens – Bucon Ltd

Space Ray – radiant heaters – Space-Ray UK

Space Saver – recessed ceiling air cleaner – Trion The Division Of Ruskin Air Management Ltd

Space Station – storage space facilities – Space Station Self Storage

Spacefleet – games, playthings, miniatures and models for use in fantasy games – Games Workshop Ltd

Spaceguard – five lever security, deadlocks, sashlocks and padlocks – Worrall Locks Ltd

Spacemaker – Double Parking Systems

Spacemasters – Boremasters

Spacesaver – collator – K A S Paper Systems Ltd

Spacetec – spacer fabrics – Heathcoat Fabrics Ltd

Spaceworx – UK Office Direct

Spafax – vehicle mirrors – Spafax International Ltd

Spaggiari (Italy) – ac & dc geared motors – Lenze UK Ltd

*Spaggiari (Italy) – geared motors – Micro Clutch Developments Ltd

*Spaggiari Transmission (Italy) – Micro Clutch Developments Ltd

SpaGuard – pool chemicals and water treatment equipment – Biolab UK Ltd

Spairo Shaft – pneumatically expanding mandrels – S & P Spanarc Ltd

Span – magazine – London City Mission

Spancan – mixtures of gases for use in calibration of safety and tox gas analysers and chromatographs – Spantech Products Ltd

Spandeck – Accesscaff International Ltd

Spanfloor – floating floor sound insulation system – Thermal Economics Ltd

Spanish Property – Your Key to Spain offers the very best advice on Spanish Property – Your Key To Spain

Spanset – webbing, cargo slings and lashings – Spanset Ltd

Spanset – load restraint system – Traction Equipment Stafford Ltd

Spantech – apparatus for analysing oxygen and flue gas, filters for scientific purposes and fuel efficiency monitoring apparatus – Spantech Products Ltd

Spar – grocers – Henderson Group Ltd

Sparcatron – electrical discharge machines – S E S Glos Ltd

Spare Moments – Kitfix Swallow Group Ltd

Sparex – Agricultural spare parts and accessories – Sparex International Ltd

*Sparex – A P B Trading Ltd

Spark – dry cell batteries and light bulbs – A P Y

Sparkal – copper and silver tungsten – Mersen UK

Sparkle – solder – Link Hamson Ltd

Sparkle Silver – aluminium paste pigment – Silberline Ltd

Sparkle Silver Premier – Silberline Ltd

Sparksafe – Heat & spark resstant rolls or modules with bonded rubber top to a rubber foam base – Plastic Extruders Ltd

Sparling – flowmeters – Emerson Process Management

Sparta – car-park lighting – Designplan Lighting Ltd

Spartherm – fan assisted gas heater – Drugasar Service Ltd

Spartox – weather and vandal resistant lighting – Designplan Lighting Ltd

Spasmonal – anti-spasmodic – Norgine International Ltd

Spasor – foliar applied translocated herbicide – Bayer Crop Science

Spasor Biactive – foliar applied translocated herbicide – Bayer Crop Science

Spata – soft drinks – Princes Soft Drinks

Spazone – designed system for commercial spa & hydro therapy pool water treatment – Triogen Ltd

Spear & Jackson – Gem Tool Hire & Sales Ltd

Spear & Jackson – builders tools, saws, D.I.Y hand tools – Spear & Jackson plc

Spear & Jackson – Fieldway Supplies Ltd

Spearhead – Joe Turner Equipment Ltd

Spearhead – control of broad-leaved weeds in turf – Bayer Crop Science

Spec-Cal – process calibrator – Haven Automation Ltd

Special 07/Zista 07 (Germany) – welded precision steel tubing – Benteler Distribution Ltd

Special Blends – Mykal Industries Ltd

Special Collections – mail order catalogue – J D Williams Mail Order Group

Special Day – C C A Group Ltd

Special K – Cogne UK Ltd

Special Recipe – diabetic chocolate and sugar free pastilles – Ernest Jackson & Co. Ltd

*Special Springs (Italy) – die springs of chrome vanadium spring steel, specific sprays – Berger Tools Ltd

Specialist Cables Division – cable distribution centre – Newey & Eyre

Specialist Lamps & Lighting Division – specialist lamps, lighting control gear and fuses – Newey & Eyre

Specialist screen printers – industrial and promotional graphics – Butchers Printed Products Ltd

Specialist Welded Products – . – S W P Welded Products Ltd

Specials – special machines – Varatio Holdings plc

Specibord – steel insulated panels – Laminated Supplies Ltd

Specimen Bark – soil conditioner – Melcourt Industries

Specitest – specimen collector – Armitage Shanks Ltd

Speck – triplex pumps – Speck Pumps UK Ltd

Speckletone – U-Coated Paper – Mcnaughton James Paper Group Ltd

SpecMaster – Monier Ltd

Specshield – industrial gases – Boc Gases Ltd

Spectra – audiofile feature - colour display – A M S Neve Ltd

Spectra – industrial gases, gas generators – Boc Gases Ltd

Spectra – colour coated architectural ironmonger – Allgood

Spectra – double deck bus – Optare Group Ltd

Spectra Seal – industrial gases – Boc Gases Ltd

Spectra VU – Safety Goggles – Scott International Ltd

Spectralite – lenses – Carlzeiss Vision

Spectralite – polyester pigment pastes – DSM UK Ltd

Spectralux 2000 – fibre optic projector – FOCUS International

Spectralux 3000 – fibre optic projector (conservation) – FOCUS International

Spectralux 3000M – fibre optic projector (conservation) – FOCUS International

Spectralux 6000 – fibre optic projector (high intensity) – FOCUS International

Spectralux 6000 IP65 – fibre optic projector (exterior rated) – FOCUS International

Spectralux 6000 IP68 – fibre optic projector (submersible). – FOCUS International

Spectro Foil – gift wrapping – Frith Flexible Packaging Ltd

Spectro Xepos – XRF spectrometer with extended polarization optical system – Spectro Analytical UK Ltd

Spectro Xlab 2000 – XRF spectrometer with polarised radiation – Spectro Analytical UK Ltd

SPECTROCAST – compact emission spectrometer – Spectro Analytical UK Ltd

Spectrocem – Gas Control Equipment for corrosive and toxic gases – Spectron Gas Control Systems Ltd

Spectrocom – Industrial Gas Control Equipment – Spectron Gas Control Systems Ltd

SPECTROFLAME – I.C.P. optical emission spectrometer – Spectro Analytical UK Ltd

SPECTROLAB – laboratory optical emission spectrometer – Spectro Analytical UK Ltd

Spectrolab – Laboratory Gas Control Equipment – Spectron Gas Control Systems Ltd

SPECTROLUX – automated cabin laboratory – Spectro Analytical UK Ltd

spectron – AESpump

Spectron – leakdetector service/repair – Technical Vacuum Services Ltd

Spectron – Gas Control Equipment – Spectron Gas Control Systems Ltd

Spectron – leak detectors – B O C Edwards

SPECTROPORT – portable optical emission spectrometer – Spectro Analytical UK Ltd

Spectros – Kurt J Lesker Company Ltd

Spectrosort – Portable Ark/Spark spectrometer – Spectro Analytical UK Ltd

Spectrotec – Industrial Gas Control Equipment – Spectron Gas Control Systems Ltd

SPECTROTEST – mobile optical emission spectrometer – Spectro Analytical UK Ltd

Spectrum – spectrum acoustic consultants – Spectrum Acoustic Consultants Ltd

Spectrum – 3/4 row sugar beet harvester – Standen Engineering Ltd

Spectrum – glazed ceramic tiles – A Elder Reed & Co. Ltd

Spectrum – European Technical Sales Ltd

Spectrum – microwave drying machine – Aeromatic Fielder Ltd

Spectrum Wheels – Metal Spinners Group Ltd

Spectrum600 – Moflash Signalling Ltd

Spectus Systems – PVC-U systems window and door – Spectus Windows Systems

Speed Genie – Bridgwater Electronics Ltd

Speed Glass Welding Products – Wessex Welding & Industrial Supplies Ltd

Speed Queen – laundry washers and dryers – Armstrong Commercial Laundry Systems

Speed Riveting – fast cartridge riveting system – Zygology Ltd

Speedal – non-ferrous metals and engineering plastics – Righton Ltd

Speedcure – photoinitiators and activators – Lambson Fine Chemicals Ltd

SpeedDeck – profiled metal cladding system for roofs and external walls – Eleco Timber Frame Ltd

Speedfeed – Hammond & Co. Ltd

SPEEDFIT – Hydraulic & Offshore Supplies Ltd

Speedfold – automatic horizontally folding doors – Envirohold Ltd

Speedform – high speed inline thermoformers for reel fed thin sheet products – Shelley Thermoformers International Ltd

Speedgard – aluminium insulated rolling shutters – Kaba Door Systems

Speedglass – Welding helmets – Premier Welding Services Scotland Ltd

Speedhone – Equipment For You

Speedhone Ea – semi automatic horizontal honing machine – Equipment For You

Speedhone Em – small manual horizontal honing machine – Equipment For You

Speedi-bilt – steel folding portal-framed buildings – Boyton B R J System Buildings Ltd

Speedi-Copies – A4 standard 2 and 3 part unit carbon sets – Paragon Group UK Ltd

Speedi-Memos – 3 part carbon interleaved sets – Paragon Group UK Ltd

SPEEDI-SLEEVES – Hydraulic & Offshore Supplies Ltd

Speedibook – unit sets in book form used in a PVC binder – Paragon Group UK Ltd

SpeediForm – sprocket holed continous forms for high speed printers – Paragon Group UK Ltd

Speedilabel – stock or spacually printer continuous labels – Paragon Group UK Ltd

Speedimailer – self contained mailing document system – Paragon Group UK Ltd

Speediseal – continuous sprocket-holed, and cut sheet, heat and pressure seal forms for mailing applications – Paragon Group UK Ltd

Speediset – carbon interleaved and carbon less unit sets – Paragon Group UK Ltd

Speedivac – vacuum pumps – Boc Gases Ltd

SpeediValves – vacuum isolation-valves – B O C Edwards

Speediweb – sprocket holed continous forms for computer terminals and small business machines – Paragon Group UK Ltd

Speedline – marine linethrower – Pains Wessex Ltd

Speedliner – Chip-It

*Speedmax (Germany) – drill and end mills – Macinnes Tooling Ltd

Speedo – swimwear – Speedo International Ltd

Speedograph Richfield – automotive equipment – Speedograph Richfield Ltd

Speedona – v-belts – James Dawson & Son Ltd

Speedor – high speed automatic energy saving door – Hart Door Systems

*Speedqueen – Brewer & Bunney

Speedqueen – Clean Machine UK Ltd

Speedspray Q.D. Enamel – Spencer Coatings Ltd

SpeedStile – entrance gates – Gunnebo Entrance Control Ltd

Speedtrap – speed switch operating from magnetic perception head – AMOT

Speedturn – CNC multi slide lathe – B S A Machine Tools

Speedway – rigid light duty gravity track – Vanriet UK Ltd

Speedway – office scissors – Acme United Europe

Speedy 80 Towers – Accesscaff International Ltd

Speedy-Diff – kit for rapid staining of blood films for differential counts – Clin-Tech Ltd

Speedy Hire – Accesscaff International Ltd

Speedy V (Switzerland) – Airless systems – Exitflex UK Ltd

*Speeflo (U.S.A.) – pneumatic airless paint spray equipment – Gray Campling Ltd

Spekabox – electronic intercom systems and modems – Speakerbus

SPENCER FRANKLIN – Hydraulic & Offshore Supplies Ltd

Spencer & Holstead – Red House Industrial Services Ltd

Spencer Liquid High Gloss – gloss paint – Spencer Coatings Ltd

Spencer Marine gloss – gloss paint – Spencer Coatings Ltd

Spencers Industrial PU enamel – enamel paint – Spencer Coatings Ltd

Spenco – Agricultural spare parts – Sparex International Ltd

Spendor – monitor loudspeakers – Spendor Audio Systems Ltd

SPENKLIN – Hydraulic & Offshore Supplies Ltd

Sperloplast – plastic pirns – Pilkingtons Ltd

Sperlowood – laminated picking sticks – Pilkingtons Ltd

Speroni – Obart Pumps Ltd

Sperrin Metal Products – steel storage equipment, shelving, pallet racking and lockers, office cupboards and mezzanine flooring – Sperrin Metal Products Ltd

Sperry Vickers – equipment/spares – Bearwood Engineering Supplies

Spey – waterproof clothing – J Barbour & Sons Ltd

Spey – aero engines – Rolls-Royce plc

Spey – sluice suite – Armitage Shanks Ltd

Spheerol – greases covering a wide range of applications with variety thickening soaps, additive packages and mineral or synthetic base oils – Castrol UK Ltd

Spheric-Trafalgar Ltd – High precision – Spheric Trafalgar Ltd

Spheriflex – Trelleborg Industrial A V S Ltd

Spherilastik – resilient bearings – Trelleborg Industrial A V S Ltd

SPHEROSYN – linear encoder – Newall Measurement Systems Ltd

Spice – sailboat – Topper International

Spice – Spice Girls Mag – John Brown Publishing

Spice is Nice – James A S Finlay Holdings Ltd

Spice Trader – herbs and spices – Fiddes Payne

SPICER – Bailey Morris Ltd

Spicer Hallfield – UK Office Direct

Spida – Cardinal Health U.K. 232 Ltd

Spidan – Aftermarket CV Products. Our range covers 40,000 vehicle applications – G K N Driveline Services Ltd

Spider Coupling – Renold Clutches & Couplings Ltd

Spider Platforms – Accesscaff International Ltd

*Spiderfix (Spain) – capped and uncapped push on fastener – Jet Press Ltd

Spiderflex – spider couplings – Renold Clutches & Couplings Ltd

Spiderflex Coupling – Renold Clutches & Couplings Ltd

*Spies Hecker (Germany) – vehicle refinish paint – Spies Hecker UK

Spies Hecker – vehicle refinishing paint systems – Permatex Protective Coatings UK Ltd

Spieth – European Technical Sales Ltd

*Spike 2000 (U.S.A.) – polycabonate bird deterrent system for protection of structures against roosting birds – Deben Group Industries Ltd

Spikey – hairdressing toiletry products - hairspray and mousse – L E C Liverpool Ltd

*Spildri (Europe) – absorbent granules – B & D Clays & Chemicals Ltd

Spill Pod – Spill Kit – Fentex Ltd

Spillaway – Forward Chemicals Ltd

*Spilsorb (Europe) – absorbent granules – B & D Clays & Chemicals Ltd

SPIN (United Kingdom) – SPIN Selling Skills – Huthwaite International

Spinblast and Holloblast – pipe internal cleaning tools – Hodge Clemco Ltd

Spinclean – self-cleaning disc filter – Premier Filtration

Spinflex – fishing tackle – Drennan International Ltd

Spink & Son – Dealers and numismatic auctioneers – Spink & Son Ltd

Spinlock – marine deck fittings – Spinlock Ltd

Spinmaster – A sintered filtration device for use in polymer production – Porvair plc

Spinmaster – a sintered filtration device for use in polymer productions – Porvair Sciences Ltd

Spinvol – textile processing aid – Benjamin R Vickers & Sons Ltd

Spir-o-lizer – downhole oilfield casing centralizer and torque reduction tool – Downhole Products plc

Spir Star – Ultra high pressure hose assemblies – Staffordshire Hydraulic Services Ltd

*Spirac (Sweden) – shaftless conveyors, de-watering and thickening equipment, classifier and compactor – Pulp & Paper Machinery Ltd

Spiral Guard – protective hose wrap – Moss Express

Spiralectric – flexible plastic hose with inbuilt electrical conductor – Plastiflex UK Ltd

Spiralift – spring balances – Caldwell Hardware Ltd

Spiralina – cable protector – Merlett Plastics UK Ltd

Spiralite – fire protection system-structured steel – Cryotherm Insulation Ltd

Spiralock – plastic flexible hoses – Plastiflex UK Ltd

Spiralock – Specialty Fasteners & Components Ltd

Spiralon – steel drum – Greif UK Ltd

Spirapool – plastic swimming pool vacuum hose – Plastiflex UK Ltd

Spiratube – shell and tube heat exchanger – H R S Heat Exchanges Ltd

Spiratube - Unicus - Cetecoil - Spiravap – H R S Heat Exchanges Ltd

Spirax Sarco – air regulators – Bearwood Engineering Supplies

Spires – relational database management suppliers – Bensasson & Chalmers Ltd

Spirette – Prices Patent Candles Ltd

Spirex – spring balances – Caldwell Hardware Ltd

Spirex – tubes for electrical and thermal applications – Langtec Ltd

Spirit – ceramic glazed wall tiles – Johnson Tiles Ltd

Spirits of Salt – cleaner for brickwork, concrete and metal – Kilrock Products Ltd

Spiro Bearings – Crawford Precision Engineering Ltd

Spirofil – weigh and fillers for FIBCs (1 tonne bags) – Spiroflow Ltd

Spiroflow – flexible screw conveyors (dry solids) – Spiroflow Ltd

Spirogal System – pre-insulated steel and copper pipe – Durotan Ltd

Spiroglide – multi stage ring suction pumps – Weir Group Senior Executives Pension Trust Ltd

Spiroglide – multi-stage centrifugal pumps for high pressure water duties – Weir Group Senior Executives Pension Trust Ltd

SPIROL INSERTS – inserts for plastics – Spirol Industries Ltd

SPIROL PINS – coiled spring pins, slotted spring pins, solid pins – Spirol Industries Ltd

Spirol Spacers – spacers, tubular products, rivets – Spirol Industries Ltd

SPIROL TUBULAR PRODUCTS – spacers, compression limiters, special bushings, alignment dowels – Spirol Industries Ltd

Spiroline – modular airline systems – Interspiro Ltd

*Spirolox (U.S.A.) – spiral wound retaining rings – R A Rodriguez UK Ltd

Spiromatic – high performance breathing apparatus – Interspiro Ltd

Spiromatic 90 – high performance breathing apparatus – Interspiro Ltd

Spiromatic Escape – short duration escape apparatus with full facemask – Interspiro Ltd

Spiroscape – short duration hooded escape apparatus – Interspiro Ltd

Spirotred – spiral staircase – Pedley Furniture International Ltd

Spirotroniq – computerised self test breathing apparatus – Interspiro Ltd

SpiroUSB – Cardinal Health U.K. 232 Ltd

Spiroweigh – ingredients weighing systems – Spiroflow Ltd

Spit – I T W Constructions Productions

Spitfire – vintage cars – British Motor Heritage Ltd

Spitfire – welder – Harrington Generators International Ltd

Spitznagel – European Technical Sales Ltd

Splash – umbrella – Sherwood Agencies Ltd

Splashinator – water guns and pistols – P M S International Group plc

Splashless – non splash machine lubricant – Benjamin R Vickers & Sons Ltd

SPLAYED BASE – Rain gauge – Halcyon Solutions

*Splendour Snacks – Splendour Snacks

Splice – system tables – E F G Matthews Office Furniture Ltd

Spline Masters – Precision Technologies International Ltd

Splintex – toughened glass components – Midland Industrial Glass

SPLIT-AIR (Italy) – telecommunications air conditioning – Stulz UK Ltd Epsom

Split Level – games-designs – Europrint Promotions Ltd

Split Mate – wire type plug gauge sets – Yorkshire Precision Gauges Ltd

Splitstone – split walling – Thakeham Tiles Ltd

*Splitz (Portugal) – ladies shoes – Cheshire Style Ltd

Spod-X – virus insecticide – Agrisense B C S Ltd

*SpohrGmbh (Germany) – water level recorders and dip meters – Smail Engineers Glasgow Ltd

Spoke – circular surface and semi recessed vandal resistant architectural lighting – Designplan Lighting Ltd

Sponge Blasting – Dust Free Abrasive Cleaning – Concrete Renovations

Spooner – tunnel dryers for paper, pulp, printing, textile, film, metal strip and foil production and converting industries including air flotation dryer systems, associated oxidiser and pollution control equipment – Spooner Industries Ltd

Spork – disposable cutlery – Plastico Ltd

Sport 14 – sailboat – Topper International

Sport 16 – sailboat – Topper International

Sport Abroad – tour operator – Kuoni Travel Ltd

Sport Engineering – fitness equipment & spares – Bearwood Engineering Supplies

Sport For All – Sport England Funding Page

Sport of Kings – sportswear – Charles N Whillans Partnership

Sportac – sporting gloves – Chester Jefferies Ltd

Sporting Gun – I P C Media Ltd

Sporting-Links – golf, bicycle and equestrian products – Martin Andrew Kearney

Sporting Model Over and Under – guns – Holland & Holland Holdings Ltd

Sporting Post – D C Thomson & Co. Ltd

Sportique – GRP inboard and outbourd tournament ski boats – Sportique Ski Boats

Sportiseat – seat stick (shooting stick) and folding walking sticks – Stroud Metal Co. Ltd

Sports Coating – coatings for tarmac, rubber and concrete tennis surfaces, coatings for netball, hockey, multi sport surfaces, full acrylic and polyurethane coatings – Everlac GB Ltd

Sports Mail – newspaper – Mail News Media

Sports Seat – benches – Audience Systems Ltd

Sportsman – footwear – Whyte & Son Nottingham Ltd

Sportsmaster – outfield turf fertilisers – Scotts Co. Ltd

Sportstar – Male body spray – Statestrong Ltd

Sportswell – garments for sport – Josery Textiles Ltd

Sportswise – sporting research consultancy – Childwise

Spot – Chorion plc

Spot-Mix – asphalt plant – Parker Plant Ltd

Spotcheck – red dye penetrant – Magnaflux

SPOTFAST – Flush rivet – Zygology Ltd

Spotkleen – spot removing cloth – House Of Dorchester

Spotless – scourable machine lubricants – Benjamin R Vickers & Sons Ltd

Spotlight CD – CD rom British actors and actresses database – Spotlight Casting Directories & Contacts

Spotlight Express – carpet tiles - wilton – Brintons Carpets Ltd

Spotlight, The – casting directories (film, TV and theatre) – Spotlight Casting Directories & Contacts

*Spotmatic (Italy) – spot welding guns – S I P Industrial Products Ltd

SPP – clean & waste water, fire protection & contractor pumps & packages – S P P Pumps

SPP Projects – major water project construction management services – S P P Pumps

Sprague – Cyclops Electronics Ltd

Sprague Capacitors – Vishay Ltd

Spray Grip – polyurethane, hand applied, anti-skid surfacing – Colas Ltd

Spray Inject – damp proofing pump – Midland Pump Manufacturing Co. Ltd

Spray 'N' Save Aerosol – for helping tp prevent christmas tree needle drop – Vitax Ltd

Spray Polish Cleaner – economy spray polish – Premiere Products Ltd

Spraybake – spraybooths and ovens for industrial and automotive applications – Spraybake Ltd

Spraycot – cotton processing aid – Benjamin R Vickers & Sons Ltd

Spraydet – powder detergent sanitiser for cleaning/de-scaling – The Proton Group Ltd

Spraygrip – premium anti-skid surface treatment for potential danger spots – Colas Ltd

Spraymaker – gas charged disposable spray gun – Trelleborg Applied Technology

Spraymar – paint and line marking machine – Patterson Products Ltd

Spraymar (United Kingdom) – whitelining paint machine – Sportsmark Group Ltd

Spraymist Pumps – fine spray pumps – Hammond & Co. Ltd

Spraymixa – spray tap – Armitage Shanks Ltd

Spraysafe – campaign to reduce use of residual herbicides – Severn Trent Water

Spraysheen – Forward Chemicals Ltd

Spraytec – cleaning products – Cleenol Group Ltd

Spraywash – Forward Chemicals Ltd

Spraywelder – spray welding pistol – Wall Colmonoy Ltd

Spreadbury Travel – retail travel agencies – Bath Travel

Spreaderflex – Cables for gravity-fed collector basket operation – Industrial Friction Materials Ltd

Spred – decorative paints – Akzonobel

Spred-Sert – expanding thread inserts for plastics – Bollhoss Fastenings Ltd

*Sprimag (Germany) – industrial spraying equipment – Pearson Panke Ltd

*Spring (Switzerland) – hotel and restaurant equipment – Bunzl Lockhart Catering Equipment

*Spring (Switzerland) – fondue equipment – Dexam International

*Spring Cleaning – Nova Contract Cleaners

Spring Master – spring interior and divan – Airsprung Furniture Group plc

Spring Oilseed Rape – Senova Ltd

Spring Steel – Berry Systems

SPRING STEEL STRIP – HIGH CARBON SPRING STEEL STRIP USED TO PRODUCE SPRINGS – Cold Rolled Strip Stock

Springbak – spring mounted bollard – Haldo Developments Ltd

*Springbank (United Kingdom) – scotch malt whisky – J & A Mitchell Co. Ltd

*Springbourne – 3663

Springco – springs, wireshapes and pressings in all materials – Springco N I Ltd

Springfix – European Technical Sales Ltd

Springflex – bonded felt pad – W E Rawson Ltd

Springham – laboratory stopcocks – Bibby Scientific Ltd

Springlok – needled insulator padding – W E Rawson Ltd

Springride Spring Bellows – Interflex Hose & Bellows Ltd

Springs Sterling – flat springs, coil springs and pressings – Sterling Springs Ltd

Springstop. Springs custom made to individual specification. – Springstop (UK) Ltd

Springvale Cavity Tag – EPS partial fill cavity wall insulant – Springvale E P S Ltd

Sprint – Walter GB Ltd

Sprint – manilla – James Cropper plc

Sprint – Multi-function Flue Gas Analyser – Crowcon Detection Instrument Ltd

Sprint – DC controllers – Beatson Fans & Motors Ltd

Sprint – dc drives – Betech 100 P T Ltd

Sprint – structural moulding material – Gurit UK Ltd

Sprint – sprung lever furniture – Paddock Fabrications Ltd

Sprint Gewindebohrer – Walter GB Ltd

Sprinty – range of self inking stock message rubber stamps – Mark C Brown Ltd

Sprite – CCTV – Dedicated Micros Ltd

Sprite – injection moulding machines – MCP Group

Sprite Lite – CCTV – Dedicated Micros Ltd

Sproscan – G E Healthcare
Sprush – suede and sheepskin and multi purpose brush – Oakland Financial Advisors
SPTMAN – SPT Hammer Energy Analyser – Testconsult Ltd
SPU 40 – industrial sectional door – Hörmann (UK) Ltd
Spudulike – filled jacket potatoes – Spud U Like
Spur – pump – Torres Engineering & Pumps Ltd
Spurlac – laquer UF – T & R Williamson Ltd
Spurseel – varnishes and floor paints – T & R Williamson Ltd
Sputagest – lyophilised additive for digestion of sputum specimens – The Mast Group Ltd
SPX – Hydraulic & Offshore Supplies Ltd
Spyda workstations – flexible and versatile as Reflex for all office areas – Fray Design Ltd
Spyder Engineering – chassis manufacturing and engineering – Spyder Cars Ltd
Spygas – CO/Freon/Natural Gas Leak Seeker – Crowcon Detection Instrument Ltd
Spysure – Keylogger Software with Powerful PC Monitoring – Spysure
SQ – Ultra hygenic rotary lobe pumps – Wrightflow Technologies Ltd
SQFlex – Grundfos Pumps Ltd
Squad – cleaner polish – Selden Research Ltd
Squadron Self Adhesive – paper – Fenner Paper Co. Ltd
Square Cut Folders – manilla folder – Acco East Light Ltd
Square D – European Technical Sales Ltd
Square D – brand name for electrical distribution products – Schneider
Square D – Schneider Electric Ltd
Square D AC Contactors – European Technical Sales Ltd
Square D Circuit Breakers – European Technical Sales Ltd
Square D Coils – European Technical Sales Ltd
Square D Heater Units – European Technical Sales Ltd
Square D Magnetic Starters – European Technical Sales Ltd
Square D Moulded Case Circuit Breakers – European Technical Sales Ltd
Square D Safety Switches – European Technical Sales Ltd
Square D Starters – European Technical Sales Ltd
Square D Transfer Switches – European Technical Sales Ltd
***Square Tap (U.S.A.)** – parallel arm tapping machines – Meddings Machine Tools
Squaregrip (United Kingdom) – anti-vibration pads – Farrat Isolevel
Squaremaster – axial fan – Nuaire Ltd
Squaresert – Zygology Ltd
Squaresert – one sided threaded fastener to provide additional high torque strength – Avdel UK Ltd
Squashni (United Kingdom) – platform sounders – Fulleon
Squawk – fishing tackle – Drennan International Ltd
***Squeeze Eze (U.S.A.)** – printed circuit aids – Welwyn Tool Group Ltd
Squeezer – bale transporter – Brown's Agricultural Machinery Company Ltd
Squelch – polyacrylamide crystals used in horticulture for water holding – Viresco UK Ltd
Squibb – chemicals – Bristol-Myers Squibb
Squiggle – circular surface and semi recessed vandal resistant architectural lighting – Designplan Lighting Ltd
Squire – padlocks, locks and vegetable peelers – Henry Squire & Sons Ltd
Squire – S J Wharton Ltd
Squire – Try & Lilly Ltd
Squire Blue Blade – can openers – Henry Squire & Sons Ltd
Squire Cablelocks – high security and standard cablelocks – Henry Squire & Sons Ltd
Squire Clam – hasps and staples – Henry Squire & Sons Ltd
Squire Cycle Shacks Locks UBX – cycle shackle locks – Henry Squire & Sons Ltd
Squire Hi-Security Lock-Sets – high security plastic covered cables with padlock (cable not incorporated within padlock body) – Henry Squire & Sons Ltd
Squire High Security XL70 – padlock – Henry Squire & Sons Ltd
Squire Lock-Set – heavy duty chain and lock – Henry Squire & Sons Ltd
Squire Miniciam – hasps and staples – Henry Squire & Sons Ltd
Squire Motorbike Shackle Locks UBXM – motorbike shackle locks – Henry Squire & Sons Ltd
Squire Mystic – combination padlocks – Henry Squire & Sons Ltd
Squire Old English – padlocks – Henry Squire & Sons Ltd
Squire Stonghold - HS4 – high security padlock – Henry Squire & Sons Ltd
Squire Stronglock – padlocks – Henry Squire & Sons Ltd
Squire Vulcan – high security hasp and staple – Henry Squire & Sons Ltd
Squirrel (United Kingdom) – band strapping machine – R J H Finishing Systems Ltd
Squrbo – inline fan – Nuaire Ltd
Sqware – UK Office Direct
SR Pumps – Alfa Laval Eastbourne Ltd
SR Rivet – Zygology Ltd
SR Series – electronic coin validators – Money Controls Ltd
SR3 – Money Controls Ltd
SR5 – Money Controls Ltd
SRA – clutch brake, electro - pneumatic – A T B Laurence Scott Ltd
SRCS Creative – A small marketing company offering practical marketing support services to SME – SRCS Creative
SRL – S R L Countertech Ltd
ssaib – Tops Security Solutions
SSAIB – Security Systems & Alarms Inspection Board – Sonic Security Services Ltd
SSD – Proplas International Ltd
SSE – Silkscreen Europe Ltd
SSF Design – S S F Design
SSP – Stacatruc
SSP Pumps – Alfa Laval Eastbourne Ltd
ST – range of spotting tables – Electrolux Laundry Systems
ST – M S C Gleichmann UK Ltd
St. Andrews Citizen – newspaper – Strachan & Livingston
St. Bruno Flake – pipe tobacco – Imperial Tobacco Group PLC
St. Bruno Ready Rubbed – pipe tobacco – Imperial Tobacco Group PLC
St. George – shoe laces, trimmings, straps elastic woven and braided, treasury tags tags (metal-plastic), bag handles, window blind components – Faire Bros & Co. Ltd
St. Ivel Gold – low fat spread – Uniq plc
St. Ives Weekly News – newspapers – Cambridge Newspapers Ltd
St James Blade – Coated Paper – Mcnaughton James Paper Group Ltd
St. James Collection – tap, mixers and accessories for the bathroom – Marflow Engineering Ltd
St. Mark's – clothing manufacturer – S Karir & Sons Ltd
ST Microelectronics – Cyclops Electronics Ltd
St. Neots Weekly News – newspapers – Cambridge Newspapers Ltd
St. Pauls Mix – one of a range of heritage grouts and mortars for historic building renovation – C M S Pozament
ST System – cutting tools & holders – J J Churchill Ltd
St Tanks – separator tanks – Oil Pollution Environmental Control Ltd
St Thomas – clay bodies for oxidation or reduction – Potclays Ltd
STA 449 C Jupiter – Netzsch-Instruments
Sta-Lock – padlock – B & G Lock & Tool Company Ltd
STA-SAF – BS&B Safety Systems (UK) Ltd
Sta-Secure – padlock – B & G Lock & Tool Company Ltd
***Staatliche Weinbaudomaene (Germany)** – German wines – O W Loeb & Co. Ltd
Stabiflex – cable conduits – Hennig UK Ltd
Stabila – spirit levels – Brian Hyde Ltd
Stabila – Fieldway Supplies Ltd
Stabila – Gem Tool Hire & Sales Ltd
***Stabilenka (Netherlands)** – soil-reinforcing woven geotextile – A G A Group
Stabilizer – stabilizing agent for hydrogen peroxide bleaching – Brenntag Colours Ltd
Stabilo – Fieldway Supplies Ltd
Stabilo – UK Office Direct
Stabiram – emulsifier – Atosina UK Ltd
Stabl-Levl-Air – air mount for vibration isolation – Stop Choc Ltd
Stablization Plants – stabalised road base materials – B G Europa UK Ltd
Stabor – composite ceramics – Kennametal
***Stabylia (U.S.A.)** – oil hole drilling equipment – Weatherford UK
Stacatruc – Stacatruc
Stackatruck – Stacatruc
Stackitall – cantilever racking – Space Way Self
Stadia – multi purpose and sports hall lighting – Designplan Lighting Ltd
Stadium – chalks and crayons – Stadium Crayons Ltd
Staedtler – UK Office Direct
Staeng – Backshell adaptors – Staeng Ltd
STAFFA – Hydraulic & Offshore Supplies Ltd
Staffa – hydraulic motors and high torque low speed hydraulic motors – Kawasaki Precision Machinery UK Ltd
Stafforce Recruitment – a division of Stafforce Personnel Ltd, suppliers of commercial, industrial, medical and catering personnel – Stafforce
***Stafford Leathergoods (China)** – purses, notecases,handbags, wallets, executive and pilot cases, conference folders, nylon backpacks, hard and soft luggage, belts & umbrella – G H Stafford & Son Ltd
Stafford Newsletter – Staffordshire Newspapers Ltd
Staffordshire – bricks – Ibstock Building Products Ltd
Staffordshire Life Magazine – Staffordshire Newspapers Ltd
Staffware – workflow automation tool designed to automate departmental and enterprise-wide business processes, intergrating with databases andother software products – Tibco Software Ltd
Stag – vintage cars – British Motor Heritage Ltd
Stag – Trafalgar Tools
Stag (United Kingdom) – motorised bench bandfacer – R J H Finishing Systems Ltd
Stag – jointing paste – Smail Engineers Glasgow Ltd
Stag doo printed t shirts – Avalon and Lynwood
Stag doo t shirts – Avalon and Lynwood
Stag night printed t shirts – Avalon and Lynwood
Stag night t shirts – Avalon and Lynwood
Stagecoach Busways – Stagecoach Ltd
Stagecoach Red & white – bus services – Stagecoach In South Wales
Stagecoach United Counties – bus and coach operator – Stagecoach Ltd
Stagger Feed Press – auto feed press – Joseph Rhodes Ltd
Stags – estate agents and auctioneers – Stags
Stahl – A M C Rollers Ltd
***Stahl (Germany)** – folders – Heidelberg Graphic Equipment Ltd
Stahl Hoist – Gustair Materials Handling Equipment Ltd
Stahlschluessel – steel standards comparisions book & cd-rom – Mito Construction & Engineering Ltd
Stainless Steel Cleaner – cleaner and polish for steel, chrome and other metal surfaces – Premiere Products Ltd
***Stainless Steel Heat Exchangers (France)** – heat exchangers for deionised water – Thermal Engineering Systems Ltd
Stainless Steel Mesh – Devaco International Ltd
Stainless Steel Twin Track – Stewart Gill Conveyors Ltd
Stainless Tube & Needle Co. – hypodermic needles and stainless tube stockists and manipulators – Stainless Tube & Needle Co. Ltd
Stainmaster – residential carpeting – Du Pont UK Ltd
Stainshield – industrial gases – Boc Gases Ltd
Stair-Deck – Accesscaff International Ltd
Stairbar – non-contact web stabiliser system – Spooner Industries Ltd
Stairmate – Accesscaff International Ltd
Stairmate (United Kingdom) – stairclimber appliance – Enable Access
Stairspan Towers – Accesscaff International Ltd
Stairway Towers – Accesscaff International Ltd
Stak A.S.R. – storage racking – Rack International UK Ltd
Stakapal – storage equipment – Stakapal Ltd
Stakker – office chairs – Top Office Equipment Ltd
Stal – Therma Group
Stalham Pleasure Craft – cruising holidays – Richardsons Stalham Ltd
STALIF – interbody fusion device – Surgicraft Ltd
***Stam (Italy)** – coil cut up and forming lines – Pearson Panke Ltd
Stama – Matsuura Machinery Ltd
Stamina – Agricultural adjuvant – Interagro UK Ltd
***Stamp (Europe and Asia)** – clothing – Dalco International Ltd
Stamp-Ever (R) – hand stamps - customised – Mark C Brown Ltd
Stamp Magazine – I P C Media Ltd
Stamylan P – Resinex UK Ltd
***Stanadyne (U.S.A.)** – Injection specialists – Watson Diesel Ltd
Stanair – industrial doors – Stanair Industrial Door Services Ltd
Stancold – insulated panels and door – Stancold plc
***Stand By (India & Pakistan)** – unisex clothing – Fashion Spinners
Standafile – Rotadex Systems Ltd
Standall Tools – paving breaker steels, hydraulic breaker steels rotary and percussive drill rods, electric tools – Standall Tools Ltd
Standard – Tesa Technology UK Ltd
Standard – washbasins, closets, steel bath – Ideal Standard Ltd
Standard Golf U K – golf course equipment – Envirogreen Special Waste Services Ltd
Standard Horizon – Radio Relay
Standard Life – Standard Life plc
Standard Life Bank – Standard Life plc
Standard Life Investments – Standard Life plc
Standard Lockers – locker – Link Lockers
Standard Pattern – concrete – Sandtoft Holdings Ltd
Standard Plus – ready assembled & custom built distribution, panel & switchboard service – Schneider
STANDARD POWER – Hydraulic & Offshore Supplies Ltd
Standard System – pre-insulated steel and copper pipe – Durotan Ltd
Standard T-link – transmission belting – Fenner Drives Ltd
Standard X Cable Tray – single flange – Cablofil
***Standardgraph (Germany)** – stencils – Blundell Harling Ltd
Standel Dawman – low load flexi wheels, electric motor driven gear boxes, worm reduction boxes, variable speed

controllers, complete drive modules, illuminated outdoor plastic decorations and plastic rotational moulding – Standel Dawman Ltd
Standen Clodmaster – destoner and declodder – Standen Engineering Ltd
Standen FM Flail Topper – potato topper – Standen Engineering Ltd
Standen Planter – 2 and 3 row potato planters – Standen Engineering Ltd
Standen Spectra – destoner and declodder – Standen Engineering Ltd
Standeven (United Kingdom) – Worsted Mens Suiting Fabric – John Foster Ltd
***Standfast (United Kingdom)** – snooker tables – Thurston
Standfast – snooker tables – Thurston
Standfast – valves – David Auld Valves Ltd
Standing Semam Roofing (UK) – Plannja Ltd
Standox – vehicle refinishing paint – Permatex Protective Coatings UK Ltd
Standox – Letchford Supplies Ltd
Stanhope – gear pumps – Albany Pumps
Stanhope – gear pumps – Albany Standard Pumps
Stanhope Barclay Kellett – rotary gear pumps – Albany Pumps
Stanko lathes – Phil Geesin Machinery Ltd
Stanler – European Technical Sales Ltd
Stanley – Wenaas Ltd
Stanley – hydraulic breakers – Service Engines Newcastle Ltd
Stanley – UK Office Direct
Stanley – Fieldway Supplies Ltd
Stanley – Cyclops Electronics Ltd
Stanley – hand tools – Bearwood Engineering Supplies
Stanley – Gem Tool Hire & Sales Ltd
Stanley – Submarine Manufacturing & Products Ltd
Stanley – S J Wharton Ltd
Stanley Gibbons – stamp albums, dealing & auctions – Stanley Gibbons Ltd
Stanley Hand Tools – D D Hire
Stanley Tools – surveyors equipment – Technical Sales Ltd
Stanomatic – greaseworker – Stanhope Seta Ltd
Stanostat – conductive powders – Keeling & Walker Ltd
Stanplan – Standard Life plc
Stanwell Office Furniture – Trading name – Stanwell Office Furniture
Stanwin – pumps – Albany Standard Pumps
Staple Wizard – automatic stapler – Acco UK Ltd
Stapleframe – PVC door frames – Boomer Industries Ltd
Staples – mattresses, bedsteads and divans – Staples Uk Ltd
Stapol – Osborn Unipol Ltd
Stapure – PureSil Technologies Ltd
Star – diamond tools – Star Industrial Tools Ltd
Star – UK Office Direct
STAR – Hydraulic & Offshore Supplies Ltd
STAR (Spain) – cigarett vending machines – Jofemar UK
Star – Antifriction Components Ltd
Star – profile cutting machine – Easab Cutting Systems
Star – glass shower enclosures – Novellini UK Ltd
Star – rucsacs – Berghaus Ltd
Star – Mercury Bearings Ltd
Star – Star Micronics GB Ltd
Star Attraction – yarn – Stylecraft
Star & Cross – pocket knives – Egginton Bros Ltd
Star-Light – cable TV products – Nortel Networks UK Ltd
Star Link Chains – jewellery – Cookson Precious Metals Ltd
Star Micronics (Japan) – L N S Turbo UK Ltd
Star Refrigeration – industrial refrigeration contractors for cold storage, food processing, petrochemical, ice plants, ice rinks, water chilling, export - design, installation and maintenance – Star Refrigeration Ltd
Star Seiki – Japanese Injection Moulding machine robots – Star Automation Uk Ltd
Star x – rupture disc – Continental Disc UK Ltd
***Starbide (U.S.A.)** – air grinders – Drill Service Horley Ltd
Starbird Satellite Services – satellite communications company – A P T N
Starbloc – process pumps – Armstrong Controls Ltd
Starburst – non gamma II alloys and capsules – Schottlander Dental Equipment Supplies
Starchem – Car Body Consumables – Car Paint Warehouse Ltd
STARCHILD – manufacturer and distributer of soft leather baby shoes – Starchild Shoes
Starconl – Tecstar Electronics Ltd
Starcut – neat cutting oils – Midland Oil Refinery Ltd
Stardome – National Door Co.
Stardrive – motor speed drives – Ultra Electronics Ltd
Stardust – pillows & duvets – Downland Bedding Co. Ltd
Starfish – Cambio Ltd
Starflex – belt driven pumps – Armstrong Controls Ltd
STARFLOW – Flow logger – Halcyon Solutions
Starfrost Helix – site built spirral freezing or chilling system – Starfrost UK Ltd
Starfrost Turbo – site built IQF in-line freezing or chilling system – Starfrost UK Ltd
Stargard – S G System Products Ltd
Stargard - Stronghold - Strading - Citadel - AL50 – S G System Products Ltd
Stargear – gear oils – Midland Oil Refinery Ltd
STARK – Hydraulic & Offshore Supplies Ltd
Stark – zero point mounting systems – Roemheld UK Ltd
Starlight – light cured composites direct delivery – Schottlander Dental Equipment Supplies
Starline – Southern Valve & Fitting Co. Ltd
Starline (Italy) – Ball valve manufacture – Trimline Valves
Starline – in line pumps – Armstrong Controls Ltd
Starline (Sales Ideas) – advertising calendars, diaries, pens, business gifts, motor trade items and promotional clothing. – Starline
Starlink – audiofile networking – A M S Neve Ltd
Starlite (U.S.A.) – cutting tools, grinders – Drill Service Horley Ltd
Starlite – taps – Armitage Shanks Ltd
Starlite – disposable cutlery – Plastico Ltd
Starlite Helix – factory pre-assembled spiral freezing or chilling system – Starfrost UK Ltd
Starlite Turbo – factory pre-assembled IQF in-line freezing or chilling system – Starfrost UK Ltd
Starlock – push-on fasteners – Baker & Finnemore Ltd
STARLOG – Flow logger software – Halcyon Solutions
Starlube – lubricating oils – Midland Oil Refinery Ltd
Starlux – lighting equipment – Powerlite Lighting Solutions Ltd
Starmaster – lighting equipment – Powerlite Lighting Solutions Ltd
Starmaster – coated carbide – Ceratizit UK Ltd
Starmaster – extension ladders – Abru Ltd
Starmax – sports garments & in particular football clothing – Star Sportswear Ltd
Starna – ultra violet and infra red lamps – Starna Industries Ltd
Starnorm – process pumps – Armstrong Controls Ltd
Starol – stage, television, film and disco lighting control equipment – Stage Control Ltd
Starpak – package booster sets – Armstrong Controls Ltd
Starpipe – pre-insulated steel and copper pipe – Durotan Ltd
Starpoint (Germany) – side loading swivel eyebolt – Rud Chains Ltd
Starpoint – component manufacturers for leisure and vending – Starpoint Electrics Ltd
Starpoint – fishing tackle – Drennan International Ltd
***Starpower (U.S.A.)** – marine diesel engines – Lancing Marine
Starpress – hydraulic oils – Midland Oil Refinery Ltd
Starpress - Starlube - Starquench - Starsol – Midland Oil Refinery Ltd
Starquench – quench oils – Midland Oil Refinery Ltd
Starrett – S J Wharton Ltd
Starrett – precision tools, gauges and saws – L S Starrett Co. Ltd
Starrett – precision products – Arrow Supply Co. Ltd
Starsoft – sports garments & in particular football clothing etc. – Star Sportswear Ltd
Starspray – bread release agent – A A K Bakery Services
Start – UK Office Direct
Startalk – key telephone system with voice messaging facility – Nortel Networks UK Ltd
Starteam – ERF all makers – E R F Ltd
Starter Motors – A T Wilde & Son Ltd
***Startmaster (Italy)** – battery booster and charger starters – S I P Industrial Products Ltd
Startpact – starters & control equipment – Schneider
***Startrek (Far East)** – figures & accessories – Bandai UK Ltd
Startrite – Red House Industrial Services Ltd
Startrite – Peter Rushton Ltd
Startrite – R K International Machine Tools Ltd
StartSource – Entry level eAuction package – Sourcing Vantage Ltd
StarTwist(tm) (United Kingdom) – clear and metallised cellulose films with ultra high performance twist retention – Innovia Films Ltd
Starwatch (United Kingdom) – integrated access control system – Remsdaq Ltd
Starweld – merchanised pta systems – Deloro Stellite Ltd
Statbrush – conductive anti static brushes – M C D Virtak Ltd
***State of the Art** – Wavelength Electronics Ltd
Statease – static dissipative products for the electronics industry – Vitec
Stately-Albion Ltd – residential park homes – Stately Albion Ltd
Statesman – 2 row potato harvesters - 1500 – Standen Engineering Ltd
Static L.S.K. – access/speleo rope – Marlow Ropes Ltd
Static Systems – equipment & spares – Bearwood Engineering Supplies
Statimeter – load cells and pressure gauges – A E L Flexaulic Ltd
Statstrip – antistatic brush strip – Kleeneze Sealtech Ltd
Status – darts and flights – Unicorn Products Ltd
Status – meths reduceable hydro carbon free inks for polythene – Hillbrook Printing Inks Ltd
Status Incentive Travel Programmes – M C I
Status Instruments – Status Instruments Ltd
Status Meetings – M C I
Status Seating – Capex Office Interiors
Status Seating – Office Seating – Bucon Ltd
Status - Smart Writers – Hainenko Ltd
Status Study Missions – M C I
Staubil – 6 Axis Robots – S P Technology Ltd
***Staubli (France)** – industrial robots/quick release couplings – Staubli UK Ltd
Stäubli – European Technical Sales Ltd
STAUBLI UNIMATION – Hydraulic & Offshore Supplies Ltd
Stauff – European Technical Sales Ltd
STAUFF – Hydraulic & Offshore Supplies Ltd
Stauff – hydraulic accessories – J V Hydraulics Ltd
Stauff – Southern Valve & Fitting Co. Ltd
stauff – Harrier Fluid Power Ltd
STAUFF CONNECT – Hydraulic & Offshore Supplies Ltd
STAUFF FILTRATION – Hydraulic & Offshore Supplies Ltd
STAUFF FLEX – Hydraulic & Offshore Supplies Ltd
STAUFF FORM – Hydraulic & Offshore Supplies Ltd
STAUFF LOGISTICS – Hydraulic & Offshore Supplies Ltd
Stauff Pipe Clamps – Tube/Cable clamps available im mild or stainless steel – Stauff Anglia Ltd
STAUFF PRESSURE TEST SYSTEMS – Hydraulic & Offshore Supplies Ltd
STAUFF TYPE – Hydraulic & Offshore Supplies Ltd
STAUFF TYPE CLAMPS – Hydraulic & Offshore Supplies Ltd
Stavax ESR – AISI 420 heat treatable stainless plastic mould steel – Uddeholm Steel Stockholders
Staveley Fine Worsteds (United Kingdom) – Worsted Mens Suiting Fabric – John Foster Ltd
Stavex – Zygology Ltd
Stavex – breakstem fastener with exceptional multi-grip capability – Avdel UK Ltd
Stavinor – pvc additives – Atosina UK Ltd
Stawell – water boilers – Cona Ltd
***Stax** – modular sign systems – Signconex Ltd
Stax – record label – Ace Records Ltd
Stay Dry – minerals – Rumenco Ltd
Stay Off – animal deterrent – Vitax Ltd
Stay open – non skin printmaker inks – Hawthorn Printmaker Supplies
Staybelite – partially hydrogenated rosin acid – Hercules Holding Ii Ltd
Staybelite Ester – partially hydrogenated rosin ester – Hercules Holding Ii Ltd
***Staycold (South Africa)** – refrigeration – Interlevin Refrigeration Ltd
Stayflex – pliable conduit – Adaptaflex Ltd
Stayform – bandages – Robinson Healthcare Ltd
STB Detector – Money laundering detection – Lombard Risk
STB GlobalView – Management reporting – Lombard Risk
STB Reporter – Financial reporting – Lombard Risk
STB Super Consolidator – Data consolidation & management – Lombard Risk
STB TaxMan – Inland revenue reporting – Lombard Risk
STD Boss Lab – Broen Valves Ltd
Steadfast – Emmerson Doors Ltd
Steadytec – Tennco Distribution Ltd
Stealaway – knitwear label – Passion Knitwear Ltd
Stealth – Divex
Stealth – Phoenix Weighing Services Ltd
Stealth – fine multi-filament polypropylene fibres – Propex Concrete Systems Ltd
Stealth Hopper – coin payout mechanism – Money Controls Ltd
Steam Cylinder Oils – single stage locomotive and stationary engine oil – Morris Lubricants
Steam Team – wallcovering removal system – Hire Technicians Group Ltd
Steambloc – steam boiler - Fire-Tube – Babcock Wanson UK Ltd
Steamstat – kettle thermostat – Otter Controls Ltd
Stearn – UK Office Direct
Stearns – electromagnetic clutches, brakes and disc brakes – Bibby Transmissions Ltd
Steatite Batteries – Industrial Battery Manufacturer – Steatite Batteries
Steatite Embedded – Embedded Systems and Mini-ITX – Steatite Batteries
Steb – silver-copper bimetal – Samuel Taylor Ltd
Stebmetal – silver and copper bimetal – Samuel Taylor Ltd
Stebweld – seam welded contact materials – Samuel Taylor Ltd
STECKO – Hydraulic & Offshore Supplies Ltd
***Stedy (Sweden)** – compact standing & transfer aid for nursing home and homecare use – Arjo Med AB Ltd

Steed Upholstery – upholstery manufrs – F & M Steed Upholstery Ltd
Steel 6/metal profile to match Big 6 – North West Sheeting Supplies
Steel Building Systems – cold rolled metal profiles for external and internal load bearing partition and floor elements – Knauf Drywall
Steel-in-Steel – pre-insulated pipe for high temperatures buried (400c max) – Durotan Ltd
Steel Security Containers – Landsmans Ltd
Steel World – steel fabrication – Luton Steels Ltd
Steelbrite – Osborn Unipol Ltd
Steelcase – Office Seating – Bucon Ltd
Steelclad – self-contained steel buildings – Adroit Modular Buildings plc
Steelgard – solvent deposited thin film rust preventives – Vapor Tek Ltd
Steelguard – temporary hording – Beaver 84
Steelite – Ascot Wholesale Ltd
***Steelite** – tableware – Keemlaw Ltd
***Steelite** – Bob Crosby Agencies Ltd
Steelite – the strongest name in tableware – Steelite International plc
Steelkane – steel drain rods – Wardsflex Ltd
Steelway (United Kingdom) – Light structural steel workers and specialised standard of walkways, open type flooring, handrails, balustrades, fire escapes – Steelway
Steelway - Fensecure – Steelway
Steelweld – Red House Industrial Services Ltd
Steely Products – Richardson & Co. Ltd
Steeplechase VLC – Steeplechase Visual Logic Controller (VLC) is the fastest control software for manufacturing – Easymatics Ltd
Steerflex – Trelleborg Industrial A V S Ltd
STEERFORTH – Hydraulic & Offshore Supplies Ltd
Steerman Load Moving Systems – Dale Lifting and Handling Equipment Specialists
STEFA – Hydraulic & Offshore Supplies Ltd
Stefani – European Technical Sales Ltd
Steff – Central C N C Machinery Ltd
Stegmann Encoders – European Technical Sales Ltd
Steiger – Harrier Fluid Power Ltd
STEINBOCK – Chaintec Ltd
Steinbock – T V H UK Ltd
Steinecker – European Technical Sales Ltd
Steinel – Alpha Electronics Southern Ltd
***Steinweg (Germany)** – company name – Abbey Spares & Supplies
Stellar – Commercial refrigeration – Carter Retail Equipment Ltd
Stellar – stainless steel cookware, teaware and knives – Horwood Homeware Ltd
Stellex – Stainless steel catering equipment – West Scomac Catering Equipment Ltd
Stellite – cobalt base wear resistant alloys – Deloro Stellite Ltd
Stellram – Precision Tools
Stellundum – tungsten carbide materials – Deloro Stellite Ltd
Stelrad Elite – steel panel/convector radiator – Stelrad Group Ltd
Stelrad LST – low surface temperature radiator – Stelrad Group Ltd
Stelrad Planar – steel panel/convector, flat fronted radiator – Stelrad Group Ltd
Stelrad Therma – tubular towel rail – Stelrad Group Ltd
Stelrad Towel Rail – steel panel/convector radiator with integral towel rail – Stelrad Group Ltd
Steltube – UK Office Direct
Stelvertite – laminate coating for steel – Color Steels Ltd
Stelvetite – pre-finished organic coated steel with polymer film laminate – Corus U K Ltd
***Stelvio (Italy)** – stems – Rsi
Stelzer – Gea Westfalia Seperator UK Ltd
Stemco – hub oil seals, hub caps & hubodometers – Roadlink International Ltd
Stemkor – industrial lubricants – B P plc
STEMMER IMAGING – Stemmer Imaging
StemTech Twim Ram ECM (United Kingdom) – ECM machine – Winbro Group Technologies
Stencilets – childrens stencils for writing and drawing – Jolly Learning Ltd
Stenhoj – hydraulic presses – Mackey Bowley International Ltd
Stenhouse – fire suit, air breathing apparatus and smoke mask – Stenhouse Equipment Safety Co. Ltd
Stenner – Band Resaws – A L Dalton Ltd
Stentor – strings – Stentor Music Co. Ltd
Stentor – electronic speech security systems – O W L Electronics Ltd
***Stentor Student (China)** – violins, violas and cellos – Stentor Music Co. Ltd
Stents – impression material – Schottlander Dental Equipment Supplies
Stentwall – interlocking piled wall – Balfour Beatty Living Places
Step-a-loft – loft access door – Timloc Building Products
Step Beam – flexible coupling – Huco Dynatork
Step In – shoes – D Jacobson & Sons Ltd
Stepanpol – polyols – I M C D UK Ltd
Stephens – grease guns, nipples, pumps for oil and grease, hose reels, coolant pumps and adjustable hoses, pneumatic equipment; air couplingsand fittings and blow guns – Stephens Midlands Ltd
Stephens – gaskets, washers, shims, jigs, fixtures, press tools and special purpose machines – Stephens Gaskets Ltd
Stephens – UK Office Direct
Stephens Pre-Cut Alignment Shims – in laminates, stainless steel, plastic, brass, aluminium – Stephens Gaskets Ltd
Stephens Shim Stock – standard size of close tolerance thickness shim in plastic, brass, stainless steel, steel – Stephens Gaskets Ltd
Stephenson – heavy duty rectangular slide-out cover and frame – Norinco UK Ltd
Stephilco – trim jet nozzles – S & P Spanarc Ltd
Stepper Motor Drivers – Greenwich Instruments Limited
Steppy – UK Office Direct
Steps – aluminium, bronze, pvcu and pvc stairnosings – Quantum Profile Systems
Stepseal – seal design – Trelleborg Ceiling Solutions Ltd
STEPSEAL – Hydraulic & Offshore Supplies Ltd
Stepsure (United Kingdom) – electric caravan step – Bailcast Ltd
Stera (United Kingdom) – Austen Tapes Ltd
Stera-Tape – Gawler Tapes & Plastics Ltd
Stera Tape – double sided tapes – North British Tapes Ltd
Steratape – B D K Industrial Products Ltd
Sterco Fabrics – shirtings corset & sail cloths – Fernbank Shed Company Ltd
Stereo Everywhere – stereo image width – Bose Ltd
***Stereoprint (Switzerland)** – thermosetting matrix board – Plastotype
Steribag – sterilisation bag – Amcor Flexibles
Steridex – water-based hygienic wall coating for breweries, food factories and hospitals – Sika Liquid Plastics
Sterilac – sterilising varnish – Akzo Nobel Packaging Coatings Ltd
Sterilight – Quality UV units from R-Can – U V O 3 Ltd
Sterilin – disposable laboratory plastic ware – Bibby Scientific Ltd
Sterilobe – stainless steel rotary lobe pumps – Wrightflow Technologies Ltd
Sterimate – laboratory equipment – Astell Scientific Holdings Ltd
Sterisept – water based polyurethane-based wall coating for hygiene sensitive areas – Sika Liquid Plastics
Sterisheen – water-based, hygienic wall coating with semi-gloss finish for hygiene sensitive areas – Sika Liquid Plastics
Sterithane – hygiene coating system – Tor Coatings Ltd
Sterling – ISO pump – Sterling Fluid Systems UK Ltd
Sterling – farriers tools – Vaughans Hope Works Ltd
Sterling – handle – Securistyle Ltd
STERLING – Hydraulic & Offshore Supplies Ltd
Sterling – Pressure Design Hydraulics Ltd
Sterling – bottom roller gear for timber or metal doors – P C Henderson Ltd
Sterling – castings – Doncasters Sterling Ltd
Sterling – Autron Products Ltd
Sterling – B & W Mechanical Handling
Sterling – European Technical Sales Ltd
Sterling – Bridgwater Electronics Ltd
Sterling Board – oriented strand board – Norbord
Sterling Farm – suppliers of livestock equipment – Poultry First Ltd
STERLING HYDRAULICS – Hydraulic & Offshore Supplies Ltd
Sterne – refrigeration/air-conditioning compressor spares – J & E Hall Ltd
Sternerblomqui – Harrier Fluid Power Ltd
Sternette – refrigeration/air-conditioning compressor spares – J & E Hall Ltd
***Sternpower (U.S.A.)** – sterndrive – Lancing Marine
Steroban – Steroplast Ltd
Sterochef – Steroplast Ltd
Sterocrepe – Steroplast Ltd
Steropad – Steroplast Ltd
Steroplast – plasters and strappings – Steroplast Ltd
Steroply – Steroplast Ltd
Sterowipe – Steroplast Ltd
Sterox – domestic water chlorination kit – Fernox
***Stetter (Germany)** – concrete mixing plants – Burlington Engineers Ltd
Stevedore – self loading trailer – Eka Ltd
Stevens & Williams – Royal Brierley Crystal Ltd
Stewart Buchanan Gauges – pressure and temperature gauges and needle valves – Stewart-Buchanan Gauges Ltd
Stewart Superior – UK Office Direct
Steyr – Harrier Fluid Power Ltd
Sthil – Mawsley Machinery Ltd
Stic Havroy – European Technical Sales Ltd
Stich – sportswear, outerwear & leisurewear – Max Power Sports Co.
Stick 2 – contact adhesives and superglue – Everbuild Building Products Ltd
Stick 'n' Hang – hanging fixing for signs – Alplus
Stickimalt – malt loaf mixes – E D M E Ltd
Stickyboot (United Kingdom) – CV boot kit (split) – Bailcast Ltd
Stiebel of Nottingham – knitted polyester, especially jacquard, curtain net – Filigree Ltd
Stieber – Mercury Bearings Ltd
Stieber – industrial freewheels – Stieber Clutch
Stiefel Laboratories (UK) Ltd – research in dermatology – Stiefel Laboratories (UK) Ltd
Stien – Peter Rushton Ltd
Stierli – hydraulic horizontal bending machines – Press & Shear Machinery Ltd
Stiga – Mowers – Loxston Garden Machinery
Stihl – D D Hire
Stihl – A T Wilde & Son Ltd
Stihl – Mike Garwood Ltd
STiK – paper – Fenner Paper Co. Ltd
Stikit – self-adhesive abrasive sheets and discs – North British Tapes Ltd
Stilcons – Poundfield Products Ltd
STILL – Chaintec Ltd
Still – T V H UK Ltd
Still – Harrier Fluid Power Ltd
Stillmuchtooffer – Professional development for mature people – Stillmuchtooffer Ltd
Sting – darts, flights and shafts – Unicorn Products Ltd
Stinger – vehicle arresting device – Spanset Ltd
Stirling – stainless steel slop hopper suite – Armitage Shanks Ltd
Stirling – hot and cold carbonated automatic drinks machine – Bunzl Vending Services Ltd
Stirling News – newspaper – Dunfermline Press
Stitched Edge – Flanged paper edge roll for upholstery – Somic Textiles
STIX (United Kingdom) – text & measuring instruments – Metrix Electronics
STM – Mercury Bearings Ltd
STM – Cyclops Electronics Ltd
STMicroelectronics – semiconductors – Anglia
Stoaway – UK Office Direct
Stobart Davies – Books – The Toolpost
Stock – Vargus Tooling Ltd
***Stockburger (Germany)** – clocks, barometers, hygometers, thermometers and anometers – Yachting Instruments Ltd
StockerYale – Stemmer Imaging
STOCKLIN – Chaintec Ltd
Stockline (Italy) – geared motors – Lenze UK Ltd
Stockmaster (Australia) – mobile platform ladders – Effortec Ltd
Stockmaster – modular shelving – Bedford Shelving Ltd
Stockshop – Animal husbandry products – Sparex International Ltd
Stocksigns – signs (safety and general) – Stocksigns Ltd
Stockvis – Double Parking Systems
Stoddard – brushes – Stoddard Manufacturing Co. Ltd
Stokbord – extruded plastic board – Centriforce Products Ltd
Stokes – Harrier Fluid Power Ltd
Stokes – industrial pumps – AESpump
Stokes – piston pumps – B O C Edwards
Stokes Interiors – tiles and interiors – R J Stokes Company Ltd
Stokesley Town Crier – Gazette Media Company
Stokke – Sitsmart Ltd
Stoklift – lift tables – Stertil UK Ltd
***Stoll (Germany)** – hay equipment – Westmac Ltd
Stomacher – Seward Ltd
Stomacher - Clear-Spin - Handi-Spin - Cryo sect – Seward Ltd
Stompers – insoles and orthopeadic devices – A Algeo Ltd
Stone – fasteners and foundries – Stone Foundries Ltd
STONE – Hydraulic & Offshore Supplies Ltd
Stone Boilers – Twin Industries International Ltd
Stone Collection – The Amtico Co. Ltd
Stone Fasteners – solid rivets and nails – Stone Fasteners Ltd
Stone Fasteners – ferrous and non ferrous nails and rivets – Stone Foundries Ltd
Stone Foundries – aluminium, magnesium and copper based castings, MOD approved BS5750 ISO 9002 – Stone Foundries Ltd
Stone Newsletter – Staffordshire Newspapers Ltd
Stone Platt – Variable Speed PIV Gear Box – Kearsley Precision Engineering
Stone Wallwork – Variable Speed PIV Gear Box and Chains – Kearsley Precision Engineering

Stoneage – ageing compound for Haddonstone – Haddonstone Ltd
Stonehose – compressed air hose – Merlett Plastics UK Ltd
Stonehouse Paper & Bag Mills Ltd – plain or printed bags pockets for photographic, nuclear industry & presentation. long end bags for canning industry. paper bands for bank stationery, film fronted bags for presentation & photographic prints, paper layflat tubing for protection. – Stonehouse Paper & Bag Mills Ltd
Stonesizer – granulator – Parker Plant Ltd
StoneTec Plus – Cloakroom Solutions Ltd
Stonewold – Monier Ltd
Stop – electric fencers – Delaval
Stop-choc – Specialty Fasteners & Components Ltd
Stop-N-Flow – mechanical handling systems – Jervis B Webb Co. Ltd
Stop'n Grow – Mentholatum Co. Ltd
Stop-Off – stopping off compounds – Wall Colmonoy Ltd
Stop Quick – brake cleaner – Deb R & D Ltd
Stop & Stay – gas spring - multi-position holding of a counter balanced weight over the entire stroke of the gas spring – Camloc Motion Control Ltd
Stopgap – floor preparation materials – F Ball & Co. Ltd
Stopslip Aggregate – anti-slip additives – Conren Ltd
Storafile – archive box – Office Depot UK
Storage Box – storage box – Acco East Light Ltd
Storall – records & storage systems – Acco East Light Ltd
Storall – UK Office Direct
Storall Quickfold – range of archival storage boxes – Acco East Light Ltd
Store a call voice systems Ltd – Telecommunications – Storacall Engineering Ltd
Store Pack – retail packaging & shop equipment, catering and food packaging – Davpack
Storeshield – distribution services – Boc Gases Ltd
Storflam – J Storey & Co. Ltd
Stork – upholstered office chairs – Race Furniture Ltd
Storlina – humidity controlled lining system for buildings – E P S Logistics Technology Ltd
Storm – sash cords – Ibex Marina Ropes
Storm – marine cordage – Ibex Marina Ropes
Storm – fashion watches – Sun 99 Ltd
Storm – model management agency – Storm
Stormajor – B & W Mechanical Handling
Stormcote – masonry paint – Spencer Coatings Ltd
Stormer – TN traffic generation and performance analysis software – N C C Group
Stormfleece – Bill Beaumont Textiles Ltd
Stormguard – clear wall seal – Everlac GB Ltd
Stormor – Shelving & Racking – Stormor Systems Ltd
Stormor Euroshelving – ajustable industrial shelving – Link 51 Ltd
Stormor Longspan – heavy duty adjustable shelving – Link 51 Ltd
Stormsafe – door mats – Bruce Starke & Co. Ltd
Stormscreen – Mono Pumps Ltd
Stormtex – Bill Beaumont Textiles Ltd
Storpick Steps – Accesscaff International Ltd
Stortrack – horizontal storage and retrieval carousel systems – Stewart Gill Conveyors Ltd
Storybook CD-ROM – software resource for young children based on stories by Scottish authors – Learning & Teaching Scotland
Stott – weighing – Hosokawa Micron Ltd
Stour – slop hopper suite – Armitage Shanks Ltd
Stoves – fan assisted gas heater – Drugasar Service Ltd
Stowaway – British Vita plc
Stowe Woodward – roll coverings-paper technology – Invensys PLC
Stowford Export – H Weston & Sons Ltd
Stowford Press – H Weston & Sons Ltd
Stowford Press, Stowford Export, Scrumpy Supreme, Old Rosie, Herefordshire Country Perry, Bounds Brand Scrumpy, First Quality, Traditional Scrumpy. Range of Oak Conditioned Ciders, Organic Cider, Vintage Cider, Organic Vintage Cider. 1880 Cider. – H Weston & Sons Ltd
stp – pumps – AESpump
STP – Harrier Fluid Power Ltd
STP – car care products – Clorox Car Care Ltd
STR Design & Print – S T R Designers & Lithographic Printers
Strachan – West of England billiards cloth – Milliken Woollen Speciality Products
Strachan - west of England billiards cloth; Playnes - tennis ball melton. – Milliken Woollen Speciality Products
***Strack (Germany)** – injection moulding plates & accessories – Welwyn Tool Group Ltd
Strack Normteilwerk (Germany) – Die sets, standard parts for press tools – Berger Tools Ltd
Strading – S G System Products Ltd
Stradis – total strategic distribution planning – Lorien Resourcing Ltd
***Strahman** – sampling tank drain & tank outlet valves, steam/water mixers & washdown equipment – A J G Waters Equipment Ltd
Strahman MG Valves – A J G Waters Equipment Ltd
Straight Sliding 280-307 Top Hung – door gear for domestic, commercial, industrial or argricultural applications – P C Henderson Ltd
Strain Gauging – load monitoring & measuring – Strainstall
Stramclad – profiled metal cladding for roofs and external walls – Eleco Timber Frame Ltd
Stramit – partitioning and roofing and cladding systems – Eleco Timber Frame Ltd
Stramliner – profiled metal roof liner panel – Eleco Timber Frame Ltd
StramTile – metal simulated tile roofing sheet – Eleco Timber Frame Ltd
Stranco – swimming pool chemical control – Wallace & Tiernan Ltd
Strand – Projects Department Ltd
Strand – shaving brushes – Progress Shaving Brush Vulfix Ltd
Strand Condition Monitor – Measurement equipment for continous casting machines – Sarclad Ltd
Strand Jacks – heavy lift jacking system – Fagioli Ltd
Strandek – glass fibre – Salty Yacht Productions Ltd
Stranlite – lightweight building blocks – Plasmor Ltd
Stranlite Thermalbond Blocks – high insulation building blocks – Plasmor Ltd
Strapack – strapping machines – Gordian Strapping Ltd
StrapTrap – Haberdashery garment trimming bra strap holder Strapatrap – Strap Trap
Strata – metal personnel door – Stertil UK Ltd
Strata – UK Office Direct
Strata – fires – Indesit Company UK Ltd
Strata-Color – profiled steel cladding and roofing for agricultural buildings – Strata Color (Coated Steels) Ltd
Stratabord – Chorus Panel & Profiles
Stratafil – quilts – Trendsetter Home Furnishings Ltd
Stratech Scientific – Distributor of specialist life science research tools. – Stratech Scientific Ltd.
Strategy – flipchart marker – Hainenko Ltd
Strategy Development – Bourton Group Ltd
Strategy in Focus – strategic marketing consultants – Ipsos Mori
Strateline – turning stand winch units and conveyor winch units – Varatio Holdings plc
Strateline – speed reducers – Varatio Holdings plc
StratFX – Exopack Advanced Coatings Ltd
Strathmore – americana high quality paper and board – G F Smith
Strathmore Element – G F Smith
Strathmore Papers – coloured textural papers and boards – G F Smith
Strathmore Renewal – G F Smith
Strathmore Writing – paper – G F Smith
STRATICA – flooring – The Amtico Co. Ltd
***Stratoflex (U.S.A.)** – rubber hydraulic hose – Hydrasun Ltd
Stratos – Sanitary accessories – Franke Sissons Ltd
Stratos Lightwave – Selectronix Ltd
Stratton – tubular drafting stand – Blundell Harling Ltd
stratus – stacker cranes – T G W Ltd
Stratus – IP Network Service – Direct Visual Ltd
STRAUB – Hydraulic & Offshore Supplies Ltd
Stream Measurement – Stream Measurement Ltd
Streamflo – flowmeters – Nixon Flowmeters Ltd
Streamline – shower tray – Armitage Shanks Ltd
Streamline – point of use water heater – Heatrae Sadia
Streamline – stainless steel grating – Wade International Ltd
Streamline Surgical – Specialist Obesity Surgery – Streamline Surgical LLP
Streatham, Clapham Mercury – South London Press
Strebord – heavy duty wood particle board – Falcon Panel Products Ltd
Street – overhead cranes, goliath cranes, electric wire rope hoists, electric chain hoists, jib cranes and vacuum lifting equipment – Street Crane Ltd
Street Case Notice Boards – Notice Board Company
Street Fighter – aluminium entrance matting – Jaymart Roberts & Plastics Ltd
Street King – aluminium and polypropylene entrance matting – Jaymart Roberts & Plastics Ltd
Street Shuttle – fast about town shuttle bus services – Stagecoach Ltd
Street Talkers – menu display characters – Barconwood Ltd
Stress Master – thermal stress screen – Sharetree Ltd
Stressless – The Winnen Furnishing Company
STRETCH-TO-LENGTH – gas line heater system – Watlow Ltd
STRICKSCREW – screws on a re-loadable cartridge – Zygology Ltd
***Stridhs (Sweden)** – beef, sheep and pig casing cleaning machinery – Selo UK Ltd
Striebig – T M Machinery Sales Ltd
***Striffler (Germany)** – routing equipment for UPVC and wood, window and door fabrications – Elumatec UK Ltd
Strika – sports and sking goods – M & T Crossley Tordoff
Strike – High Performance emulsion polish stripper – Premiere Products Ltd
Strikeforce – fishing tackle – Daiwa Sports Ltd
Striker – darts – Unicorn Products Ltd
Striker – firefighting nozzles – Knowsley S K Ltd
***String Swing (U.S.A.)** – hangers for musical instruments – John Hornby Skewes & Co. Ltd
Strip-Blade – special holder for rotogravure and flexographic printing presses – Uddeholm Steel Stockholders
Stripbloc – mains outlet – Schurter Ltd
Stripflex – flexible crash doors, strip PVC curtains and rapid rise doors – Neway Doors Ltd
Stripjet – nozzle – Delavan Ltd
Stripkwik – paint remover – Spencer Coatings Ltd
Strix – thermostatic controls – Strix UK Ltd
***Stromag** – European Drives & Motor Repairs
Stromberg – fuses – Bearwood Engineering Supplies
Stromberger – European Technical Sales Ltd
Strong Recycling Baler – W250 Cardboard Baler Equipment - For Cardboard, Plastic & Paper – Strong Recycling Balers Ltd
Strong Recycling Baler – W500 Cardboard Baler Equipment - For Cardboard, Plastic & Paper – Strong Recycling Balers Ltd
Strong Recycling Baler – W50 Cardboard Baler Equipment - For Cardboard, Plastic & Paper – Strong Recycling Balers Ltd
Strong Recycling Baler – W70 Cardboard Baler Equipment - For Cardboard, Plastic & Paper – Strong Recycling Balers Ltd
Strong Recycling Baler – W40 Cardboard Baler Equipment - For Cardboard, Plastic & Paper – Strong Recycling Balers Ltd
Strong-TIE – connectors for timber and masonry construction – Simpson Strong-Tie International Inc
Strongbank – Accesscaff International Ltd
Strongbox – DIY floorboard safes – Securikey Ltd
Strongboys – Accesscaff International Ltd
Stronghold – filing cases, safes and cash boxes – Helix Trading Ltd
Stronghold – extra heavy duty studded rubber safety flooring/mats – Jaymart Roberts & Plastics Ltd
Stronghold – overalls – J M C Q Huston & Son
Stronghold – plastic welding – Stronghold International Ltd
Stronghold – S G System Products Ltd
Stronglock – padlocks – Henry Squire & Sons Ltd
Struckmeier – European Technical Sales Ltd
Structural Detailing and drafting services – 3d modelling to the highest standards – Approved Fabricators
Structure – carpets – Interface Europe Ltd
Structure-Flex – fabricators in reinforced flexible plastic materials – Structure Flex
Structured Training – management & sales training & consultancy solutions – Structured Training Ltd
Struers – Metallographic preparation equipment and consumables – Struers Ltd
Struktur – display and exhibition systems – RTD Systems Limited
Struthers – relays – Bearwood Engineering Supplies
***STS (Germany)** – special transformers & chokes – Rolfe Industries
STS – stems expansion – Garbuiodickinson
Stuart – scientific equipment – Bibby Scientific Ltd
Stuart – pumps – Stuart Turner Ltd
Stuart Jones Headboards – The Winnen Furnishing Company
Stuart Peters – knitwear – Stuart Peters Ltd
Stuart Reducing Valve – shower valves – A & J Gummers Ltd
Stuart Turner – Arun Pumps Ltd
Stuart Turner Pond Pumps – Denton Pumps Ltd
Stuart Turner Pumps – Denton Pumps Ltd
Stuart Turner Shower Pumps – Denton Pumps Ltd
Stuarts Micrometer Blue – high spot bearing marker – B & G Machining
Stubbs – Abbey England Ltd
***Stüber (Germany)** – single and multi-end stop motion switches – Robert S Maynard Ltd
Stubs – silver steel & gauge plate – Arrow Supply Co. Ltd
STUCCHI – Hydraulic & Offshore Supplies Ltd
Stucco – Type of decorative plaster – Armourcoat Ltd
Stuckham (United Kingdom) – Duo-check valve manufacture – Trimline Valves
Student Stone Specimens – The Gemmological Association Of Great Britain
Studer – European Technical Sales Ltd
Studio – washbasins, bidets, closets, baths and accessories – Ideal Standard Ltd
Studio 2 – seating – Audience Systems Ltd
Studio Experience – Lamphouse Ltd
Studio Monitors – loudspeakers – Tannoy Group Ltd

Studio William – Cutlery – Continental Chef Supplies Ltd

Studiomate – connectors – Anglia

Stuewe – European Technical Sales Ltd

Stuma Plastics – Newburgh Engineering Co. Ltd

Sturaco – lubricants – D A Stuart Ltd

Sturdee – three strand polypropylene rope – Marlow Ropes Ltd

Sturge – Metool Products Ltd

*Sturtz (Germany) – joint welding and cleaning machinery for UPVC window and door fabrications – Elumatec UK Ltd

Stycast – electrical encapsulants – Resin Technical Systems

Styccobond – adhesive for decorative flooring materials – F Ball & Co. Ltd

Styccoclean – floor cleaner – F Ball & Co. Ltd

Styccoscreed – floor preparation materials – F Ball & Co. Ltd

Styccoseal – silicone sealant – F Ball & Co. Ltd

*Style (Netherlands) – CNC co-ordinate tables – Meddings Machine Tools

Style 300 – safety helmet – Scott International Ltd

Style 600 – safety helmet – Scott International Ltd

Stylemaster – headlight protectors and sun roof deflectors – Exhaust Ejector Co. Ltd

Stylemaster Cut (United Kingdom) – broadloom – Checkmate Industries Ltd

Stylemaster Loop (United Kingdom) – broadloom – Checkmate Industries Ltd

Styletech – Ironmongery of Distinction – Style Tech

STYLGRAPH – Design solutions for the fashion, upholstery, furniture industries – Vetigraph CAD/CAM Ltd

Stylite Cavity Wall – S P I Ltd

Stylite Cavity Wall Stylite Flooring – S P I Ltd

Stylite Flooring – S P I Ltd

Stylo – golf clothing & shoes – Matchmakers International Ltd

Stylo Matchmakers – golf clothing & shoes – Matchmakers International Ltd

Stylsafe – safety spectacle frames – Parmelee Ltd

Styroclad – masterclad and styrofoam insulated soffitt and ceiling system – Panel Systems Ltd

Styrofloor – chipboard and styrofoam insulated flooring system – Panel Systems Ltd

Styroglaze – insulated steel panel – Panel Systems Ltd

Styroliner – plasterboard and styrofoam insulated dry lining system – Panel Systems Ltd

Styron – Resinex UK Ltd

Styron A-Tech – Resinex UK Ltd

Styx 99 – Aircraft toilet deodorant – Agma Ltd

SU Fuel Systems – carburetters, fuel pumps and components – Burlen Fuel Systems Ltd

SU Fuel Systems – car and fuel injection components – Burlen Fuel Systems Ltd

SU-Zenith – carburetters, fuel pumps and components – Burlen Fuel Systems Ltd

Su/Zenith – fuel systems/fuel injection – Burlen Fuel Systems Ltd

Suave – Decorative soft-touch and silk-touch coatings – Whitford Ltd

Sub-frame – S R S Product plc

Sub-Mini – Sub miniature transponder-responder – Sonardyne International Ltd

Sub Surface – site investigation and specialist geotechnical and environmental consultants – Sub Surface Ltd

Sub Zero – thermal wear – Sub Zero Technology Ltd

Sub Zero Technology – thermal wear – Sub Zero Technology Ltd

*Subair (U.S.A.) – sportsturf/golfgreen aeration system – Industrial Power Units Ltd

Subaru – Ashley Competition Exhausts Ltd

Subaru – L M C Hadrian Ltd

Subaru UK – two and four wheel drive saloon cars and estates – Subaru (UK) Ltd

Sublift – Semi-Submersible Boat Lift – Wave Seven Marine Ltd

Sublime – Vi Spring Ltd

Subliscreen Aqua HQ – water based subliming transfer ink – Fujifilm Sericol Ltd

Submerged Ash Conveyor – ash handling – James Proctor Ltd

Submitomo – Harrier Fluid Power Ltd

Succession – packet switched network solution – Nortel Networks UK Ltd

Suchard – chocolate drink – Kraft Foods UK Ltd

Suchard – UK Office Direct

Suchard – Alba Beverage Co. Ltd

*Sucofit (Switzerland) – heat shrinkable products – Huber+Suhner (UK) Ltd

*Sucoflex (Switzerland) – microwave cable assembly – Huber+Suhner (UK) Ltd

*Sucoform (Switzerland) – microwave formable cable – Huber+Suhner (UK) Ltd

Sucoplate – connector plating, bright, non-tarnish finish – Huber+Suhner (UK) Ltd

*Sucoplate (Switzerland) – special R.F. connector plating – Huber+Suhner (UK) Ltd

*Sucorad (Switzerland) – radiating cables for tunnel communications – Huber+Suhner (UK) Ltd

*Sucrea – Unifine Food & Bake Ingredients

Sudpack UK Ltd – vacuum pouch manufacturers and supppliers of thermoforming film – Sudpack UK Ltd

*Suedel Luxe (France) – display and decorative covermaterials – Winter & Co UK Ltd

Suface Clean Radiators – Autron Products Ltd

Suffolk Herbs – seeds – E W King & Co. Ltd

Suffolk Tableware – Henry Watson Potteries Ltd

Suga Switches – European Technical Sales Ltd

*Sugarcraft Diploma – Brooklands College

Sugg Lighting – contemporary and traditional gas, electric and lighting equipment – Sugg Lighting Ltd

Sugino – high pressure waterjet deburring for machined components – Ellesco Ltd

Suhner – multi purpose flexible shaft machines and accessories, portable electric-pneumatic tools – Finishing Aids & Tools Ltd

Suhner Fiberoptic – fibre optic components & systems – Huber+Suhner (UK) Ltd

Suire – J J Westaby & Partners

Suisoplus – pliers and screwdrivers – Carl Kammerling International Ltd

Suitcon – QD plastic suit coupling, self-sealing – Cobham Mission Equipment Ltd

Sulfatine – food can lacquer – Akzo Nobel Packaging Coatings Ltd

Sullair – Harrier Fluid Power Ltd

Sulphurcut – Yara UK It Ltd

Sultex Oil – lubricants – Chevron

Sulto Oils – cutting oils – Morris Lubricants

Sumer SA (France) – Centa Transmissions

Sumiboron – Sumitomo Electric Hardmetal Ltd

Sumidia – Sumitomo Electric Hardmetal Ltd

Sumitomo – Precision Tools

Summer Lifts – Accesscaff International Ltd

Summit – domestic sinks – Carron Phoenix

Summit – UK Office Direct

Summit – Office Seating – Bucon Ltd

Summit – co-ordinate measuring machines (CMM) – Eastman Staples Ltd

Summit – UK conferences by Jarvis – Jarvis Hotels Ltd

Summit – Derbyshire Building Society

*Sumner (U.S.A.) – pipe fit-up tools – B S A Tube Runner

Sumo – Fluorescent light tube disposal – B K Safety

Sumo IT – Heavyweight IT Support – Sumo IT

Sump-Gard – suspended type sump pump in PP, PVDF and CPVC – Vanton Pumps Europe Ltd

Sump Pumps – G V E Ltd

Sumpclean – Darcy Products Ltd

Sumtak – Encoders UK

Sun – hydraulic cartridge valves – Anubis Label Technology Ltd

SUN CARTRIDGE VALVES – Hydraulic & Offshore Supplies Ltd

SUN HYDRAULICS LTD – Hydraulic & Offshore Supplies Ltd

Sun Lite – Palram Europe Ltd

Sun Microsystems – All Sun servers, storage, software and desktop systems – Server Parts Ltd

Sun Opak – Palram Europe Ltd

Sun Ripe – orange juice, apple juice and still lemonade and fresh fruit products – Daniels Group

Sun Top – Palram Europe Ltd

Sun Tuf – Palram Europe Ltd

Sun Vista – window blinds and furniture covers – Stevens Scotland Ltd

Sunbank – Dax International Ltd

Sunbeam – L M C Hadrian Ltd

Sunbeam – Harrier Fluid Power Ltd

SunBlush – Leathams Ltd

Sunburst – carpets – Cormar Carpets

Sunbury (United Kingdom) – sealed lead acid battery chargers – Sicame Electrical Developments Ltd

Suncell – solar panels and controls for swimming pool heating – C P V Ltd

Suncorite – East Midland Coatings Ltd

Sundance – tufted carpet – Brockway Carpets Ltd

Sunday Life – newspaper publishers – Independent News & Media (NI) Ltd

Sunday Post – D C Thomson & Co. Ltd

Sundeala – pinboard & notice boards – Celotex Ltd

Sundown – curtain lining finish – P W Greenhalgh & Co. Ltd

Sundown – dishcloth – Ramon Hygiene Products

Sundown - curtain lining, Furnsafe - F.R. back coating upholstery, Pyroban - permanent F.R. for curtain linings, Pyrodry - non-permanent F.R. for curtain linings. – P W Greenhalgh & Co. Ltd

Sundridge – Water proof clothing – Sundridge Holdings

Sundwel – solar collectors and ancillary equipment – Sundwel Solar Ltd

Sunfilm – anti-glare and non-reflective sunscreening film – Faber Blinds UK Ltd

SunFLASH – high intensity hazard lamp – Doormen

Sunflex – Park Farm Design

Sunflex – flexible plastic swimming pool hoses – Plastiflex UK Ltd

Sunflex – packaged goods, window finishing products – Luxaflex

Sunflex Folding Sliding Doors – Park Farm Design

Sunflex Sliding Door – Park Farm Design

Sunflower – dried apple mix, lemon pie fillings – James A S Finlay Holdings Ltd

Sunflowers – fragrance – Elizabeth Arden

Sunfold – glazed folding walls internal & external – Becker Sliding Partitions Ltd

Sunjet – spectacles and sunglasses – Safilo UK Ltd

Sunkist – Fruit Juices & Fruit Sectionisers – Metcalfe Catering Equipment Ltd

Sunlustre – full fat soya bean meal – A One Feed Supplements Ltd

*Sunmate (Netherlands) – small and medium-glass hatch – Webasto Products UK Ltd

Sunnen Products – Harrier Fluid Power Ltd

*Sunnex Products (Hong Kong) – stainless steel holloware – Zodiac Stainless Products Co. Ltd

Sunon – fan motors (axial square frame) – Thermofrost Cryo plc

Sunpack (Norway) – Manufacture polystyrene packaging – Sungerlitt Ltd

Sunprene – high molecular weight flexible pvc – Atosina UK Ltd

Sunseeker – Blinds – Guildford Shades

Sunset – bed linen – Thomas Frederick & Co. Ltd

Sunset – household textiles – Linden Textiles Ltd

Sunset Self Tanning Cream – sun cream – Bell Sons & Co. Ltd

Sunsetters – sunglasses – Paul Murray plc

Sunspel Boxer – men's boxer undershorts, pyjamas and dressing gowns – Sunspel Menswear Ltd

Sunspot – pool chemicals and water treatment equipment. – Biolab UK Ltd

Sunstoppers – sunglasses – P M S International Group plc

Sunstrand – Harrier Fluid Power Ltd

Sunstrand – piece goods, yarns, threads, fabrics and handkerchiefs made of artificial silk or in which artificial silk predominates – Norland Burgess Ltd

Sunstrand Hose – stockings and socks – Norland Burgess Ltd

Suntime – roller, venetian, vertical, pleated blinds and fabrics – Faber Blinds UK Ltd

Suntona – UVA goggles and lotions/gels – Bray Group Ltd

Suntoni – knitwear – Vinola Knitwear

Suntracker (United Kingdom) – din profile, electronic astronomical time clock/time switch – Sangamo Ltd

Sunwall – screen walling – Thakeham Tiles Ltd

Sunway – window blinds – Luxaflex

*Sunx (Japan) – sensors – Sensortek

Supa Support – Speed Plastics Ltd

Supac – batteries – Supac Ltd

Supacat – sand binder system for the foundry industry – Ashland Specialties UK Ltd

Supacat – multi terrain vehicle – Traction Equipment Stafford Ltd

Supacat – high mobility vehicles, glider launching winches and pallet trailers – Supacat

Supacord – fibre bonded carpet – Heckmondwike FB

Supadance International – luxury dance shoes – Supadance Ltd

Supafil – cavity wall insulation – Knauf Insulation Ltd

Supaflex – variable speed pulley drives – Disco Drive Kings Lynn Ltd

Supaflex – belt variable speed drives – A T B Laurence Scott Ltd

Supaflo – super plasticiser – Don Construction Products Ltd

Supajet – electric dryers for animals – Diamond Edge Ltd

Supalick – molassed mineral buckets – Rumenco Ltd

Supalux – Fieldway Supplies Ltd

Supamix – shower valve – Armitage Shanks Ltd

Suparflex – Metallic Hose – Dixon Group Europe Ltd

Supasafe – tube cleaning machines – Rotatools UK Ltd

Supaset – sand binder system for the foundry industry – Ashland Specialties UK Ltd

Supashoppa – Ashtenne Ltd

Supasol – Forward Chemicals Ltd

Supasol Hydro – Forward Chemicals Ltd

Supastor – storage box – Acco East Light Ltd

Supastor 24 – 24" storage box – Acco East Light Ltd

Supastrip – pressure sensitive, self-adhesive tear tape used to open flexible packaging – Payne

Supastrut – flexible framing system for construction – Anixter Ltd

supaTag – Solmedia Laboratory Supplies

Supatex – sheeting for latex fashionwear – Four D Rubber Co. Ltd

Supatex – natural latex rubber sheeting in various thickness and colours – Four D Rubber Co. Ltd
Supatex – sheeting for latex fashionwear – Four D Rubber Co. Ltd
Supathaw – Forward Chemicals Ltd
Supavits – nutritional supplements – G & G Food Supplies
Supaweb – technical synthetic filter fabrics – Andrew Webron Ltd
Supawrap Pinkplus – thermal insulation for pitched roofs at ceiling level – Knauf Insulation Ltd
Supazote – ethylene copolymer – Zotefoams plc
Supelec – luminaires & adaptable boxes – Electrium Sales Ltd
Super 40 – high protein feed for dairy cows – Quality Liquid Feeds Ltd
Super-Ajax – P1 coal mining explosive – Orica UK Ltd
Super Aquaduct – potable water hose – Angus Fire
Super Aquarius – high performance double beam spectrophotometers – Cecil Instruments Ltd
Super Batch Manager – point of print handling programme to enable multiple designs to be printed out in variable volumes at different locations – Episys Group Ltd
Super Blackmobile – mobile asphalt and tarmacadam plant – Parker Plant Ltd
Super Blades – wiper blade – C T P Wipac Ltd
Super Buzzard – big bale loader – Brown's Agricultural Machinery Company Ltd
Super C's – wholesalers of bedding, household linen, clothing, household fancy electrical goods – S Collins & Company Ltd
Super Colifax – solid fuel boiler – Hartley & Sugden
Super Compact – system for catering and food processing plants – Webster-Wilkinson Ltd
Super D – discrete wire IDC – Cinch Connectors Ltd
Super Dartmoor – woven carpets in 100% pure new wool pile – Axminster Carpets Ltd
Super Dome – high density polyethylene diffuser – Porvair Sciences Ltd
Super Dome – high density polyethylene diffuser – Porvair plc
Super Dopplex 11 – advanced bi-directional pocket doppler – Huntleigh Healthcare
SUPER DUPLEX – Hydraulic & Offshore Supplies Ltd
Super Duplex – High Tech Fabrications Ltd
Super Duplex (Uns32750) – S & N Stainless Pipeline Products Ltd
Super Duplex (Uns32760) – S & N Stainless Pipeline Products Ltd
Super-E – Baldor UK
Super Folders – plastic, open two sides and folders – Office Depot UK
Super Humus – soil conditioner – Melcourt Industries
Super Jersette – supported natural latex gloves – Mapa Spontex
Super-Light – Anchor Magnets Ltd
Super Lincoln Twist – tufted carpet – Brockway Carpets Ltd
Super Mirage – furniture spray polish – Premiere Products Ltd
Super Mosstox – mosskiller which is ideal for use both on fine turf and hard surfaces – Bayer Crop Science
Super N T Meteor – high speed encapsulation system – D & K Europe Ltd
Super NuNale Lotion – Nail care lothion for split and flaking nails – Laboratory Facilities Ltd
SUPER P – Timcal Graphite & Carbon
Super Penistone – carpets – Penthouse Carpets Ltd
Super Pentwist – carpets – Penthouse Carpets Ltd
Super Photon – solid state TV camera – E 2 V Technologies Ltd
Super Plus – Kuwait Petroleum International Lubricants UK Ltd
Super Point – Kennametal UK Ltd
Super Pro – sports garments and in particular football clothing – Star Sportswear Ltd
Super Roller Coaster – twin axle roller trailer for larger craft – Indespension Ltd
Super Seal – access covers – Wade International Ltd
Super Selectric – Grundfos Pumps Ltd
Super Shinobi – fishing tackle – Daiwa Sports Ltd
Super Silicon – cast iron gas welding rods – Weldability S I F
Super Slim Soldier/Slimshor – multi purpose steel beam system and accessories – RMD Kwikform Limited
Super Speed Fit – Gustair Materials Handling Equipment Ltd
Super Speedfit Centre – push in plumbing fittings – John Guest
Super Sport – air rifle – B S A Guns UK Ltd
Super Sport Custom – air rifle – B S A Guns UK Ltd
Super Star – air rifle – B S A Guns UK Ltd
Super Star – polypropylene baler twine – Steve Orr Ltd
Super Sub-Mini – Super sub miniature transponder/responder – Sonardyne International Ltd
Super Sward – Yara UK lt Ltd
Super Target – software – K B C Process Technology Ltd
Super-Tensile – flat belting – James Dawson & Son Ltd
Super Tracker – BMX cycles – Universal Cycles
***Super-Trapp (U.S.A.)** – marine intake and exhaust silencers – Lancing Marine
Super Trident – marine sewage treatment plant – Hamworthy Waste Water plc
Super Trix – lager – Temple Wines Ltd
Super Twosome (United Kingdom) – steel track & valance curtain track – Integra Products
Super V – B P plc
Super-V-Gard – safety helmet – M S A Britain Ltd
Super Verde Wilton Cricket Grass – artificial cricket wicket surface – Verde Sports Cricket Ltd
Super Versitrac – universal tractor oil – Morris Lubricants
Super VR – information kiosks – Cashmaster International
Super Woodlands – carpets – Penthouse Carpets Ltd
Super Wyndham – plain wilton – Victoria Carpets Ltd
Superac – Coventry Toolholders Ltd
Superails – clip on towel rails – Midland Brass Fittings Ltd
Superbarb – barbed tape – Birmingham Barbed Tape Ltd
SuperBike – Magazine – I P C Media Ltd
Superblend – washing up liquid – Jeyes
Superbraid – sash cord – James Lever & Sons Ltd
Supercash – humane slaughtering equipment – Accles & Shelvoke Ltd
Supercast – fishing tackle – Daiwa Sports Ltd
Supercharge – protected protein – Rumenco Ltd
Supercharge – B P plc
Supercoil – rolling smoke curtain – Bolton Gate Co. Ltd
Supercol – Manilla Board – Mcnaughton James Paper Group Ltd
Superconcentrate – Protector, restorer, silencer and leak-sealer for dosing via radiator vents – Fernox
Supercook – baking decorations – Dr Oetker
Supercore – stainless steel flux cored wires – Metrode Products Ltd
Supercut – Bowl turning tool – The Toolpost
Superdeck Platforms – Accesscaff International Ltd
Superdeluxe – veneered and fully finished door – Premdor Crosby Ltd
SuperDreadnought – fibre bonded carpet – Heckmondwike FB
Superdrug – toiletries, pharmaceutical & cleaning products – Superdrug Stores plc
Superdual P.A. – loudspeakers – Tannoy Group Ltd
Superedge – soluble cutting fluids – Castrol UK Ltd
Superfil – soft toy filling – W E Rawson Ltd
Superfine Velvet – Ryalux Carpets Ltd
Superfleet – vehicle refinishing paint – Permatex Protective Coatings UK Ltd
Superflex – flexible crash doors, strip PVC curtains and rapid rise doors – Neway Doors Ltd
Superflex – a range of polyurethane ductkings – Merlett Plastics UK Ltd
Superflex – high strength detonating cord – Orica UK Ltd
Superflexit – conduit screening suppression components and systems – Icore International
Superflexo – flexographic printing on polyethylene and polypropylene films – Amcor Flexibles UK Ltd
Superflextract (United Kingdom) – axially and helically-reinforced pvc ducting with spring steel helix – Flexible Ducting Ltd
Superflor – carpets – Interface Europe Ltd
Superfold – accoustic folding door – Bolton Gate Co. Ltd
Superform – preformer – Link Hamson Ltd
Superfresco – wallcovering – Graham & Brown Ltd
Superglide – storage racking – Rack International UK Ltd
Supergreen – B P plc
Supergrip – curing hot melt – Bostik Ltd
Supergrit – Ervin Amasteel Ltd
Superguard A.L. – aluminium/polyamide brush pile barrier carpeting/entrance matting – Jaymart Roberts & Plastics Ltd
Superhawk – boats – Sunseeker Poole Ltd
Superide – rubber coated textiles – Ferguson Polycom Ltd
***Superion (U.S.A.)** – solid carbide cutting tools – Tekmat Ltd
Superior – folding shutter and folding lift doors – Bolton Gate Co. Ltd
Superior Boilers – Twin Industries International Ltd
Superior Ribbons – range of decorative ribbons – Stribbons Ltd
Superior Ribbons - range of decorative ribbons. – Stribbons Ltd
Superjet – disposable cutlery – Plastico Ltd
Superjet – Jetchem Systems Ltd
Superkings – filter cigarettes – Imperial Tobacco Group PLC
Superkings Blue – filter cigarettes – Imperial Tobacco Group PLC
Superkings Menthol – filter cigarettes – Imperial Tobacco Group PLC
Superkings White – filter cigarettes – Imperial Tobacco Group PLC
Superkub – Tangye
Superlifts-Genie – Accesscaff International Ltd
Superlite – tin oxide – Keeling & Walker Ltd
Superloadascreen – mobile screening and conveying plant – Parker Plant Ltd
Superloc – compression fitting (single ring - carbon steel) – Waverley Brownall Ltd
Superloo – portable toilet – Adroit Modular Buildings plc
SUPERLUX – lamps – Osram Ltd
Supermat – R G K UK Ltd
SuperMaxflo – Mactenn Systems Ltd
Supermet – stainless steel welding electrodes – Metrode Products Ltd
Supermet – super alloy-nickel or cobalt based – Firth Rixson Metals Ltd
***Supermet (Worldwide)** – women's headties and textile piece goods – Metro Textiles Ltd
Supermicrometer – calibration equipment – Intra Ltd
Supermig – stainless steel MIG wires – Metrode Products Ltd
***Supermig (Italy)** – Jack Sealey Ltd
Supermin – pressure switches – Black Teknigas & Electro Controls Ltd
Supernode – telecommunications switching equipment – Nortel Networks UK Ltd
Supernova – Alpha Electronics Southern Ltd
Superose – paint – Craig & Rose Ltd
Superpar – lift pumps for diesel engines – Dieselprods Ltd
Superquiet – generating sets hire – Abird Ltd
Superquiet – extremely quiet AC and DC equipment fans – Ebm-Papst
SuperRide – axles with independent suspension units offering a softer, smoother ride – Indespension Ltd
Supersave – modular cold rooms – Hemsec Group
Supersave – insulted doors – Hemsec Group
Superscript – printers – Nec Europe Ltd
Superseal – solenoid valves – Black Teknigas & Electro Controls Ltd
Superseal – alkyd resin seal – Evans Vanodine International plc
Superseal – pu low Density Water Seal – Recticel Corby
SuperSeal – SuperSeal Tyre Sealants – Superseal Anglia Ltd
Superseal – draught proofing seals, sealants, PVC curtains, compression seals, fire and smoke seals – Kleeneze Sealtech Ltd
Supersensor – fishing tackle – Daiwa Sports Ltd
Supersert – anchor nut – Zygology Ltd
Supersert – one sided threaded fastener for thicker materials with locking facility – Avdel UK Ltd
***Supersnap (Taiwan)** – Jack Sealey Ltd
Supersoft – upholstery piping cord – Somic Textiles
Supersoft Logo – British Vita plc
Supersonic – quick release fasteners – Southco Manufacturing Ltd
Supersot – surface mount high dissipation semiconductors – Diodes Zetex Semiconductors Ltd
Superspa – taps – Armitage Shanks Ltd
Superspan – banded v and wedge belts – James Dawson & Son Ltd
Supersport – inflatable boats – Avon Inflatables Ltd
Supersport – rugby jerseys and leisure wear – Supersport Leisure Shirts Ltd
Supersport SS Carbine – air rifle – B S A Guns UK Ltd
Supersprint – Emi-Mec Ltd
Supersteam Vur – unfired thermal fluid heated steaming calorfier – Babcock Wanson UK Ltd
Superston – alloy metals – Stone Marine Propulsion Ltd
Superstore – large steel store – Adroit Modular Buildings plc
Superstrong – road barrier tape – Boddingtons Ltd
SuperTarget – pinch technology software – K B C Process Technology Ltd
Superteat – teat dip – Delaval
***Supertechno (Germany)** – cranes – Panavision Grips Ltd
SuperTEN – air rifle – B S A Guns UK Ltd
Supertex – Cyclops Electronics Ltd
Supertex – bakery hydrates – A A K Bakery Services
Supertherm – shower valve – Armitage Shanks Ltd
Supertouraine & Touraine – Wrightrain Environmental Ltd
Supertox 30 – broad spectrum selective herbicide for turf – Bayer Crop Science
Supertrol – Box Section (Internal) Rust Preventive – Action Can Ltd
Supervelour – shoe suede – Charles F Stead & Co. Ltd
Supervent – kitchen extraction fans – Airflow Developments Ltd
Supervisco Static – B P plc
SuperVision – Fife Tidland Ltd
Supervite – pet foods – Henry Bell & Co Grantham Ltd
Superwalker – waterproof map for walkers – Harvey Map Services Ltd
Superwheel – conveyor skate wheels – Atlantic Rubber Company Ltd
Superwhite – business papers & uncoated paper & baord – Howard Smith Paper Ltd
Superwood – weaving loom shuttles – Pilkingtons Ltd
Superwool 607 – high temperature insulation products – Thermal Ceramics UK Ltd
Superwool 607 Max – high temperature insulation products – Thermal Ceramics UK Ltd

Superwool 612 – high temperature insulation products – Thermal Ceramics UK Ltd
Superyacht business – I P C Media Ltd
SuperYacht World – I P C Media Ltd
Supol – materials - silicon, nylon, polyethylene, hypalon, EPDM, neoprene & nitrite – Hallam Polymer Engineering Ltd
Supoweis – suppository base materials – Croda International plc
Supplex – textile nylon/performance fabric – Du Pont UK Ltd
supplied systems – Oxford Software
Supplier Teac UK – Tekdata Distribution Ltd
Supply Chain Management – Bourton Group Ltd
Supra – advanced relational database management system – Cincom Systems UK Ltd
Supra – roundslings – Spanset Ltd
Suprabloc – recessed access covers – Technocover
Supraduct – dust covers – Technocover
Supragrid – gratings – Technocover
Supral – superplastic aluminium alloys – Superform UK
SupraMatic – Hörmann (UK) Ltd
SupraMatic E – Hörmann (UK) Ltd
SupraMatic H – Hörmann (UK) Ltd
SupraMatic P – Hörmann (UK) Ltd
Supramesh – filter medium – Pall Europe Corporate Services
Supramig – Welding wire – Lincoln Electric UK Ltd
Suprarex SXE-P – profile cutting machine – Easab Cutting Systems
Suprasteel – manhole covers and concrete filled access covers – Technocover
Suprega Plus – solvent free hand cleanser – Deb R & D Ltd
Suprema – CNC high speed CBN cylindrical grinders – Jones & Shipman Grinding Ltd
Supremacy – Display Wizard Ltd
Supreme – water boiler - instant hot water for beverages – Heatrae Sadia
Supreme – Wealden Tyres Ltd
Supreme – pig units – Browns of Wem Ltd
Supreme – Emmerson Doors Ltd
Supreme – ceiling mounted air cleaner – Trion The Division Of Ruskin Air Management Ltd
Supreme – carpets – Penthouse Carpets Ltd
Supreme Deluxe – carpets – Penthouse Carpets Ltd
Supreme Mohair – luxury yarn – Sirdar Spinning Ltd
Suprex – diesel engine oil – Millers Oils Ltd
Supromat – CNC production cylindrical grinders – Jones & Shipman Grinding Ltd
Suprox – reinforced leather gauntlet gloves – Bennett Safetywear
Surchlor – swimming pool chemical – Atosina UK Ltd
Sure – extension ladders – J Gorstige Ltd
Sure – equipment & spares – Bearwood Engineering Supplies
Sure Air Tools – Sureweld UK Ltd
Sure-Kut – manufacture scissors – Acme United Europe
***Sure Pos 500** – IBM Touch sales – I C R Touch LLP
Sure Strip – non-ammoniated polish stripper – Evans Vanodine International plc
Sure-Stroke – golf balls and golf equipment – Clan Marketing Co.
Surebuild – lightweight framing system in galvanised steel – Corus U K Ltd
Surefill – closed transfer system – Horstine Farmery
Surefire – closure plate tape for gas fire closure plates – Advance Tapes Group Ltd
Surefit – harnesses with elasticated panels – Capital Safety Group Ltd
Surefit – half round rainwater system (112mm) – Hunter Plastics
Surefit – plastic waste system – Mcalpine & Company Ltd
Surefit Squareflo – rectangular rainwater systems – Hunter Plastics
Surefit Stormflo – 200mm rainwater system (commercial/agricultural) – Hunter Plastics
Sureflow – gases and gas mixtures – Boc Gases Ltd
Sureflow – pumped instantaneous electric shower – Heatrae Sadia
Suregrip – anti-slip coating – Co-Var Ltd
Suregrip – anti-slip deck paint – Teal & Mackrill Ltd
Surelan – Belcom Cables Ltd
Surelift – single-point-lift flexible intermediate bulk container – Rexam Holding plc
Surelight – Belcom Cables Ltd
Surelock – door safety devices – L B B C Technologies
Surelux – lighting systems – Luxonic Lighting plc
Suremark – markers/crayons – Bearwood Engineering Supplies
Suremark – brand name of I.S. products – Industrial Services York Ltd
Suremark Drywype – for writing on dry wipe boards – Industrial Services York Ltd
Suremark Magnum – spirit based marking pens, large capacity for industrial use – Industrial Services York Ltd
Suremark Metal Marker – ball valve marking pen for marking all types of metal – Industrial Services York Ltd
Suremig – three phase M.I.G. machines – Sureweld UK Ltd
Sureseal – total systems for induction sealing closures to container necks, metal and plastic – Bericap UK Ltd
Suresert – press-fit threaded insert for plastics – Tappex Thread Inserts Ltd
Sureskills Ltd – Sureskills
***SureStep (Sweden)** – slip resistant vinyl sheet – Forbo
Suretest – high performance aerosol smoke detector tester – No Climb Products Ltd
Sureweb – polyester webbing lifting slings & lifting gear – Medway Sling Company
Surex 002 Oxysure – Surex International Ltd
Surex Voxsan – Surex International Ltd
SURFACE KERBING – lightweight surface mounted kerbing products – Rediweld Rubber & Plastics Ltd
SURFACE MASTER – next generation surface film – Cytec Engineered Materials Ltd
Surface-Walk – anti-slip surfacings – North British Tapes Ltd
Surfcast – fishing tackle – Daiwa Sports Ltd
SurfControl E-Mail filter – controls what e-mail content you recieve – Surfcontrol plc
SurfControl Web Filter – controls what web page content you recieve – Surfcontrol plc
Surfi-Sculpt – Cambridge Vacuum Engineering
Surfi Sculpt – fine surface treatment – T W I
Surfix – hot cationic bitumen emulsion for surface dressing – Colas Ltd
Surfix 80 – polymer reinforced high solids content bitumen emulsion for use on high speed roads – Colas Ltd
Surftech – solvent resistant, conductive bonded coating technology – Fibrestar Drums Ltd
Surge Vessels – Abbott & Co Newark Ltd
SURGEGUARD – Surge alleviator and shock attenuator for piping up to 600 millimeter diameter and six kilometer lengths – Pulsation Dampers At Pulseguard Ltd
Surgery Original Footwear Co. – Schuh Ltd
Surgicraft-Copeland – fetal scalp electrodes – Surgicraft Ltd
surin – beer and curry sauce – Surin Restaurant
Surlyn – ionomer resin – Du Pont UK Ltd
Surphalt – road surfacing systems – Total Bitumen
Surrey Advertiser – Times Review Series Of Newspapers
Surrey and Hants Courier Series – Times Review Series Of Newspapers
Surrey & Hants Star – Times Review Series Of Newspapers
Surtech – import machinery – Surface Technology Products Ltd
Surtronic – equipment/spares – Bearwood Engineering Supplies
Surtronic – portable surface roughness measuring instrument – Taylor Hobson Ltd
***Surveyor (USA and Scandinavia)** – anti corrosion products – B A C Corrosion Control Ltd
Surviva – liferaft (commercial) – R F D Beaufort Ltd
Survival – safety whistles – J Hudson & Co Whistles Ltd
Survivolite – emergency lighting – Oxley Developments Company Ltd
Survivor – rucksacks – Regatta Ltd
Survivor – UK Office Direct
Suspended Ceilings – M G H Interiors
***Sussex Classic** – Fish frying range – Sussex Catering Equipment Services Ltd
Sussex Innovation Centre – University Of Sussex Intellectual Property Ltd
SussexIP – University Of Sussex Intellectual Property Ltd
Sustain – metallised polish – Evans Vanodine International plc
Sustainable Drainage – Althon Ltd
Sutcliffe Furniture – dining room furniture and three piece suites, occasional furniture – Frostholme Furniture Ltd
***Sutus Far East (Hong Kong)** – watches – Rita Fancy Goods Ltd
***Suunto (Finland)** – compasses, surveying instruments & wristop computers – Viking Optical Ltd
Suva – refrigerant – Du Pont UK Ltd
Suxes – garments – Sherwood Agencies Ltd
Suzuki – L M C Hadrian Ltd
Suzuki ATV – Pigney H Son Agricultural Engineers
Svanehoj – deepwell cargo pumps – Hamworthy Waste Water plc
SVE Truck – T V H UK Ltd
***Svegma** – Continous mixed flow grain driers – B D C Systems
Sven – UK Office Direct
Sven – Capex Office Interiors
Sverker 3 & 21 – high carbon and high chromium tool steel – Uddeholm Steel Stockholders
Svetlana (Russian Federation) – electronic valves & tubes – Edicron Ltd
SVETRUCK – Chaintec Ltd
SVL – Bibby Scientific Ltd
Swade Aid – suede and sheepskin cleaner – Oakland Financial Advisors
Swade Groom – suede and sheepskin cleaner – Oakland Financial Advisors
Swade Guard – water repellent – Oakland Financial Advisors
Swagelock – Southern Valve & Fitting Co. Ltd
SWAGELOK / PARKER EQUIVALENT – Hydraulic & Offshore Supplies Ltd
Swagelok Tube Fittings – Twin ferrule tube fittings 316 Stainless steel – Stauff Anglia Ltd
Swallowglide – single stage end suction pumps – Weir Group Senior Executives Pension Trust Ltd
Swan – diesel generators – Swan Generators Ltd
Swan – range of trailers and mounted machines – Cleanacres Machinery Ltd
Swan – record company – Rollercoaster Records Ltd
Swanage & Wareham Advertiser – weekly free newspapers – The Bournemouth Daily Echo
Swanglide (United Kingdom) – steel curtain track – Integra Products
Swanlac – bleached shellacs – A F Suter Ltd
Swanlac - Bleached dewaxed shellac & waxy bleached shellac. – A F Suter Ltd
Swansea Industrial Components Ltd – electrical wiring harness manufacturers subcontracters – Swansea Industrial Components Ltd
Swansilk – Poly-coated tissue products – Swan Mill Paper Co. Ltd
Swansoft – air laid material – Swan Mill Paper Co. Ltd
Swantex – disposable tableware – Swan Mill Paper Co. Ltd
Swarfega – rapid hand cleanser – Deb R & D Ltd
Swarfega Orange – solvent free heavy duty hand cleansing cream – Deb R & D Ltd
Swarfega Power – powerful multi-purpose hand cleansing cream – Deb R & D Ltd
Swarfega Red Box – hand cleaning wipes – Deb R & D Ltd
Swarovski Crystal Components – transfers trimmings beads buttons – Swarovski UK Ltd
Swarovski Crystal Memories – miniature collectables – Swarovski UK Ltd
Swarovski Jewelers Collection – fashion jewellery – Swarovski UK Ltd
Swarovski Selection – crystal objets d'art – Swarovski UK Ltd
Swarovski Silver Crystal – giftware and collectables – Swarovski UK Ltd
SWC – Harrier Fluid Power Ltd
Sweco – Incamesh Filtration Ltd
Swedex – Central C N C Machinery Ltd
***Swedhouse (Sweden)** – swedish instant windows & doors – Inwido UK Ltd
Sweeney & Blocksidge – Highwood Engineering Ltd
Sweet 'N Dry – sileage additive – Dugdale Nutrition Ltd
***Sweet n Low** – Dietary Food Ltd
Sweetella – chemicals – Bristol-Myers Squibb
Sweetmaster – Broste Ltd
Sweetmore Engineering Holdings Ltd – Brass & Non-Ferrous Founders – J T Price & Co.
Swell – surf products – Movevirgo Ltd
***Swema (Sweden)** – temperature measuring instruments – S & P Spanarc Ltd
SWEP – Hydraulic & Offshore Supplies Ltd
Swep – Brazed Plate Oil Coolers, and Gasketed – J B J Techniques Ltd
SWF – Granada Material Handling Ltd
Swift – connector for oil well casing – Oil States Industries UK Ltd
Swift – 24 hour paint colour matching – Thomas Howse Ltd
Swift – multiaxis microstepping intelligent stepper motor controller – Cortex Controllers Ltd
Swift – office furniture, stationery and machines – Swift Business Solutions Ltd
Swift-Fix – Status Metrology Solutions Ltd
Swift Lift – potato, vegetable, grain and industrial elevators and conveyors – Terry Johnson Ltd
Swift Lite – charcoal – Swift-Lite Charcoal
Swift Maid – childrens tights – J Alex Swift Ltd
Swift & Sure – gas spring - self-contained solution for supporting, counterbalancing, tensioning and damping – Camloc Motion Control Ltd
Swiftak – bottle labelling adhesives aqueous – Forbo Adhesives UK Ltd
Swiftbond – solvent based adhesive – Forbo Adhesives UK Ltd
SwiftContext – Web based applications – Swift Computing
Swiftcut – textile accessories – W B Swift Ltd
Swiftic – Slitting Saws – www.tap-die.com
Swiftic – hacksaw blades and tool bits – Metalbor Ltd
Swiftlift – crane – Tipmaster Ltd
Swiftlock – laboratory equipment – Astell Scientific Holdings Ltd
Swindens – revolving head vices – Swindens Patents Ltd
Swindens Revolving Head Vices – revolving head vices – Swindens Patents Ltd
Swing – Harrier Fluid Power Ltd
Swing Amajet – K S B Ltd
Swing-Boom – adjustable horizontal dust and fume extraction boom – Horizon Mechanical Services International Ltd
Swing Couplings – Oetiker UK Ltd

Swinglift cranes – cranes – Penny Hydraulics Ltd

Swingline – integrity glazed fire resistant doors, screens and atria – Fendor Ltd

Swingo – compact suction sweepers – A B Schmidt UK Ltd

Swingthru' International – King Trailers Ltd

Swire Oilfield Services – offshore containers, tanks, chemical storage and helifuel services – Swire Oilfield Services

Swirl – WC toilet blue blocks and 2 in 1 liquid rim fresheners – F M C G Ltd

Swish – Concord Building Plasitcs – Oldham Trade Plastics

Swiss Diamond – Cookware – Gilberts Food Equipment Ltd

Swiss Net – netting – Swisstulle UK Ltd

Swisscam – Star Micronics GB Ltd

Swisscut – Iscar Tools

*Swisstool AG (Switzerland) – CNC slotting machines and CNC rotary tables – Haesler Machine Tools

Swissturn – Iscar Tools

Switch4 (United Kingdom) – Ipad sensory room control – Mike Ayres Design Ltd

Switchcraft – Selectronix Ltd

Switchcraft Inc – Cyclops Electronics Ltd

Switching Systems – Telspec plc

Switchpanels – membrane switchpanels – I T W Switches & Switch Panel Ltd

Switchtrack System – manual garment handling system for clothing and textile industry – Dearnleys Ltd

*Switchview (U.S.A.) – keyboard video mouse multi PC-sever switches – Techland Group Ltd

Swivelstat – equipment for boats – R W O Marine Equipment Ltd

Swizzels (United Kingdom) – manufacturer of sugar confectionery – Swizzels Matlow Ltd

Swizzels Matlow (United Kingdom) – manufacturer of sugar confectionery – Swizzels Matlow Ltd

Swops – liquid waste management software – Isys Interactive Systems Ltd

Swordfish – UK Office Direct

Swordfish – patented process giving variety of toeshapes – Cox Geo J Ltd

SY™ – GGB UK

Sybase – management consultancy – Sybase UK Ltd

Sycotex – (CIM) computer integrated management system for textiles – B M S Vision Ltd

Sydewynder – snakeboards, helmets, cones and rider protection – P M S International Group plc

Sydney Packett and Sons – insurance brokers, underwriters – Sydney Packett & Sons Ltd

Sydney Packett (Life & Pensions) – independent financial advisers – Sydney Packett & Sons Ltd

Syfer – multi-layer ceramic capacitors – Syfer Technology Ltd

Syfer Technology – ceramic capacitors – Anglia

Syfer Technology – Cyclops Electronics Ltd

Sykes – information support services – Sykes Global Service

Sykes-Pickavant – S J Wharton Ltd

Sykes-Pikavant – Gem Tool Hire & Sales Ltd

Sylbert – handcrafted skeleton clocks – Kemmel Ltd

Sylglas – weatherproofing products – Winn & Coales Denso Ltd

Syloguard – concrete protection products – Milbury Systems Ltd

Syloseal – polyurethane, acrylic, bituminous and cementitious joint sealants – Milbury Systems Ltd

Sylvan Shadows – 80% wool/20% polyproylene graphics – Adam Carpets Ltd

Sylvefibre – growing media additive – Melcourt Industries

Symalit – fluoroplastics – Davis Industrial Plastics Ltd

Symantec – UK Office Direct

Symat – Fife Tidland Ltd

Symat - InPrint - MSP - ESP. – Fife Tidland Ltd

Symbio – biotechnical cleaning solutions to replace, bleach acids, alkalies and solvents – Symbio

Symbio – Office Paper – Mcnaughton James Paper Group Ltd

Symbio Biofilter – biological filtration incorporating biofixtation for waste water and industrial effluent – Symbio

Symbio BLT – biological removal of black layer on sports pitches – Symbio

Symbio Drainclean – biological drain and sewer maintenance – Symbio

Symbio Green Circle – biological maintenance of fine and sports turf to replace chemical fertilisers and fungicides – Symbio

Symbio Living Water – bioremdiation service for polluted lakes, ponds and rivers – Symbio

Symbois Logic – Cyclops Electronics Ltd

Symbol – luxury motor caravan – Auto Sleepers Ltd

Symbol – Allcode UK Ltd

Symbol – Barcode Readers and Mobile Computers – Barcodemania.Com

Symbol Mc1000 – Allcode UK Ltd

Symbol Mc3000 – Allcode UK Ltd

Symbol Mc35 – Allcode UK Ltd

Symbol Mc50 – Allcode UK Ltd

Symbol Mc70 – Allcode UK Ltd

Symbol Mc9090 – Allcode UK Ltd

Symco Linings – Samuel Simpson & Co. Ltd

Symingtons – Dandelion Coffee – G R Lane Health Products Ltd

Symphoni (United Kingdom) – high effeciency sounders – Fulleon

Symphony – M C R Systems Ltd

Symphony – luxury motor caravan – Auto Sleepers Ltd

Symphony Hall – exhibition & conference centre – Nec Group

Symposium – call center solutions – Nortel Networks UK Ltd

Synarol – B P plc

Synbiotic DC – Probiotics International Ltd

*Syncarb-F – crucibles for metal melting – Ramsell Naber Ltd

Syncera – paramelt

Synchrochop – Rotating field synchronises current regulation – Phytron UK Ltd

*Synchrolub (France) – spray and oil mist systems – Lumatic Ga Ltd

Synchrome – vinyl gloves – Bennett Safetywear

SYNCHRON – Hydraulic & Offshore Supplies Ltd

Synchron – valve technology – Linde Hydraulics Ltd

Syncol – tissue and converting adhesive – Forbo Adhesives UK Ltd

Syncon – nylon pac and pace – Perrite

Syncro7 (United Kingdom) – supervisory corrigator control – Escada Systems Ltd

Syncroflex – pvc plasticisers – Croda Chemicals Europe Ltd

Syncrolift – ship lift systems – Rolls-Royce plc

Syncrolube – PVC lubricants – Croda Chemicals Europe Ltd

Syncurat – B P plc

Syncut – industrial lubricant – B P plc

SYNDAX – thermally stable polycrystalline diamond for rock drilling – Diamond Detectors

SYNDAX 3 – thermally stable polycrystalline diamond for rock drilling – Diamond Detectors

SYNDIE – polycrystalline diamond wire drawing die blanks – Diamond Detectors

SYNDITE – polycrystalline diamond blanks for cutting tools and wear resistant parts – Diamond Detectors

SYNDRILL – polycrystalline diamond for rock drilling – Diamond Detectors

Synelec – Lamphouse Ltd

Synergen 501 – protective coating for the control of corrosion – Agma Ltd

Synergen 718 – protective coating for the control of corrosion – Agma Ltd

Synergie – range of compatable solder pastes, wire – Humiseal Europe Ltd

Synergiq – Integrated Business Solutions – Synergiq

Synergy – less able bath – Armitage Shanks Ltd

Synflex – thermoplastic hose and fittings – Hydrapower Dynamics Ltd

Synflex – Hampshire Hose Services Ltd

SYNFLEX – Hydraulic & Offshore Supplies Ltd

*Synflex (U.S.A.) – thermoplastic hydraulic hose – Hydrasun Ltd

Syngene – gel electrophoresis systems – Synoptics Ltd

Synlube 90 – lubricants – Chevron

Synolite – unsaturated polyester resins – DSM UK Ltd

Synoptics – image processing and image analysis systems – Synoptics Ltd

Syntha Pulvin – polyester powder coating for aluminium and hot dip galvanised steel components – Birmingham Powder Coatings

Synthascreed – synthetic anhydrite screeding system – D P C Screeding Ltd

Synthastone – shower trays – Matki plc

Synthatec – Architectural Powder Coatings – Valspar Powder Coatings Ltd

SYNTHESIS – wall cladding – The Amtico Co. Ltd

Synthomer – rubber latices – Yule Catto & Co plc

Syntilo – soluble and synthetic cutting oils covering wide variety of application – Castrol UK Ltd

Syntran II – fuel efficient transmission oil – Millers Oils Ltd

Syntrend – B P plc

Synzintex – mild flat steels – Corus

Syphon – tap – Worldwide Dispensers

Syphons – u and ring syphons – C M T Tube Fittings Ltd

Syr – pressure reducing valves – Reliance Water Controls Ltd

Syrex – electronic sounders – Signals Ltd

Syrex – shrieker fire sounder – Signals Ltd

Syrex – mikro fire sounder – Signals Ltd

Sys2000 – food waste pulper system – I M C

Syscompact – cable fault locators – Baur Test Equipment Ltd

Syspro – K3 Business Technology Group plc

System 10 – pvc-u window and door systems – W H S Halo

System 2000 – Gabriel & Co. Ltd

System 290 – weighing systems – Stevens Group Ltd

System 3000 – computerized building energy management system – Inenco Ltd

System 32 10 – high speed lamination system – D & K Europe Ltd

System 3R – Agie Charmilles Ltd

System 4000 – zone 2 gas protection system – Pyroban

System 5000 – backbone inter WAN systems – Nortel Networks UK Ltd

System 6000 – high quality polymeric DPC – Timloc Building Products

SYSTEM 8 – low cost PCB functional test system – A B I Electronics Ltd

System 88 – pressure boosters for pressurisation of cold water and fire services – Megator Ltd

System 9000 – high quality polymeric DPC – Timloc Building Products

System B – fire barriers and penetration seals – Nullifire Ltd

System E – Nairda Ltd

System Fifty – conduit screening suppression components and systems – Icore International

System Hygienics – Hotchkiss Ltd

System J – intumescent seal for fire protection across joints and seals – Nullifire Ltd

System-Loc (United Kingdom) – disc holder orientation device – Elfab Ltd

System "M" – fire resistant mastic for fire protection gaps – Nullifire Ltd

System One – Bushboard Ltd

System-P – Taper-locking Bush Pulleys – Francis and Francis Ltd

System-P – Taper-locking Pulley Bushes – Francis and Francis Ltd

System "S" – intumescent coating for steel protection in internal and external and hydrocarbon environments – Nullifire Ltd

System Scaffolding – Accesscaff International Ltd

System Sixty – conduit screenind suppression components & systems – Icore International

System Sprite – CCTV – Dedicated Micros Ltd

System W – Intumescent coating for flame resistance to wood – Nullifire Ltd

System Zero – tamper proof screw driving system – B A S Components Ltd

System2000 (Sweden) – bath incorporating thermostatically controlled shower and a choice of manual or thermostatically control bath filling system – Arjo Med AB Ltd

Systeme – a pro-vitamin hair care and styling range for all hair types – F M C G Ltd

Systemfile Storage – Capex Office Interiors

Systemline – audio products – Armour Home Electronics

Systems Inc – M S C Gleichmann UK Ltd

Systems Technology Consultants – consultancy services in network design and audit, open communications/legal services including litigation support/computer strategy/security systems and disaster recovery – Systems Technology Consultants Ltd

Systemtray – UK Office Direct

T

T.90 – darts – Unicorn Products Ltd

T.95 – darts – Unicorn Products Ltd

T.A.B.-link – link transmission belting without studs – Fenner Drives Ltd

T-A-Line – Scott International Ltd

T.C. – building society – Tipton & Coseley Building Society

T.C.B. Cavity Barrier – barrier for timber frame dwellings to provide a fire stop in the cavity – Rockwool Rockpanel B V

T.C.I. Thyssen Control Integral – Thyssenkrupp Elevator UK Ltd

T.C.M. – T V H UK Ltd

T / C / X series – Kiosk Terminals – KT Technology

T-Cap – Taegutec UK Ltd

T-Cast – Taegutec UK Ltd

T-Clamp – Taegutec UK Ltd

T-Class – trade class product range – L G Harris & Co. Ltd

T.D.10 – acid descaler, disinfectant and deodorant – Premiere Products Ltd

T.D.30 – 18% orthophosphoric acid descaler, descaler and deodorant – Premiere Products Ltd

T.D.A.-VC30/60 – industrial vacuum cleaners for use with Hilti rotary hammers, cutting equipment and diamond drilling systems – Hilti GB Ltd

T.D. Board – fireproofing board – Promat UK Ltd

T&D HQS – Taps, Dies, Dienuts – www.tap-die.com

T&D, HQS, ZN, Trubor, Swiftic – Taps Dies Dienuts Drills Reamers Milling Cutters Toolbits – Tapdie

T D Industrial Covers – tools – Tatem Industrial Automation Ltd

T.D.M.X. – digital multiplexers – Nortel Networks UK Ltd

*T. de G. (Spain) – manual lathe chucks – Thame Engineering Co. Ltd

T-Drill – Taegutec UK Ltd

T.E.15 – electro-pneumatic hammer drilling machine – Hilti GB Ltd

T.E.18-M – universal rotary hammer drilling machine – Hilti GB Ltd

T.E.24 – powerful rotary hammer drilling machine – Hilti GB Ltd

T.E.5 – lightweight rotary hammer drilling machine – Hilti GB Ltd
T.E.504 – electro-pneumatic chiselling machine – Hilti GB Ltd
T.E.54 – electro-pneumatic combi-hammer for powerful drilling and chiselling performance – Hilti GB Ltd
T.E.74 – electro-pneumatic combi-hammer – Hilti GB Ltd
T.E. 804 – medium duty breaker – Hilti GB Ltd
T E C – P C F Secure Document Systems Ltd
T.E.C. – power transformers – Claude Lyons Ltd
T E L – transformer manufacturers & winders – Transformer Equipment Ltd
T.E.S. Jetfans – portable ventilation for agriculture, horticulture and industry – Thermal Engineering Systems Ltd
***T.G.I. (U.S.A.)** – threading systems – Marshalls Hard Metals Ltd
T.-Gage – ultrasonic thickness meter – Sonatest Ltd
T.H. Brown Distribution – general transport – T H Brown Employment Services Ltd
T.H.E. – John Menzies plc
T.H.E. Games – distributors of nintendo products – John Menzies plc
***T H R** – Total Herd Recording – Cattle Information Services
T.I.P.S. – heatshrink printing system for standard and LFH heatshrink and labels – Hellermann Tyton
T. & J. – reamers – Taylor & Jones Ltd
T.J. Filters – filtration equipment, automated oil, air and fuel filters – British Filters Ltd
T. J.'S – in house delicatessen – Avenance
T J Skelton – medal badge & sports trophy manufres – W H Darby Ltd
T.K. Chillers – scientific water coolers – Thermal Engineering Systems Ltd
T.K./R./D. – boiler thermostats – Sunvic Controls Ltd
T.L.M. – Kennametal UK Ltd
T.L.X./M. – room thermostats for all applications including digital – Sunvic Controls Ltd
T-lok – Zygology Ltd
T-Lok – fastener with high pull-out leads used to attach components to soft materials – Avdel UK Ltd
***T.M.C.I. Padovan (Italy)** – filters – Chemtech International Ltd
T.M.P.S. – services of registered trade mark agents – Trade Mark Protection Society
T.M.P Worldwide – recruitment advertising – T M P Worldwide Ltd
t-mass – thermal mass flowmeter – Endress Hauser Ltd
T.Mobile – Premier Mobiles
T Mobile – Callsure Business Telephone & Fax Numbers
T. Morley & Co – plate bending & fabrication services – The Anglering Company
T.N.-X. – SDH multiplexers – Nortel Networks UK Ltd
T.P.400 – lightweigh breaker – Hilti GB Ltd
T-Power – Scott International Ltd
T-Pren – Gutter Expansion Joint – Matthew Hebden
T.Q. – short for traditional quality - own brand products – Owlett Jaton
T.Q. Anker-u-fix – universal wallplugs – Owlett Jaton
T.Q. Ankercoach – coach screws, washers and wallplugs – Owlett Jaton
T.Q. Ankerdriva-screw – universal plasterboard fixing – Owlett Jaton
T.Q. Ankerframe – frame fixing – Owlett Jaton
T.Q. Ankerhammer – hammer fixing – Owlett Jaton
T.Q. Ankerit – anchor and cavity fixings – Owlett Jaton
T.Q. Ankermasonry-nail – masonry nails – Owlett Jaton
T.Q. Ankerplasta-Screw – nylon cavity wall fixings – Owlett Jaton
T.Q. Ankerplug – nylon wallplugs – Owlett Jaton
T.Q. Ankerset – hollow wall anchors – Owlett Jaton
T.Q. Ankershield – metal shield anchors – Owlett Jaton
T.Q. Ankersleeve – metal sleeve bolts – Owlett Jaton
T.Q. Ankertog – spring toggles for cavity walls – Owlett Jaton
T.Q. Ankerwindow – UPVC window frame fixings – Owlett Jaton
T.Q. Euroscrew – single threaded wood and chipboard screw – Owlett Jaton
T.Q. Fastascrew – slotted hardened, twinthreaded wood and chipboard screws – Owlett Jaton
T.Q. Keypsafe – locks and security fixings – Owlett Jaton
T.Q. Plusdriv – plusdriv recessed, hardened, twinthreaded wood and chipboard screws – Owlett Jaton
T.Q. Polypak – household fixtures and fittings sealed in polythene bags – Owlett Jaton
T.Q. TwinQwik – recessed twin threaded wood and chipboard screws – Owlett Jaton
T & R – Alpha Electronics Southern Ltd
T.R. 2000 – facing machines – B S A Tube Runner
T.R.G. Range – domestic anthracite free standing boiler – Trianco Heating Products Ltd
T.R.H.1800 – universal 2 speed cam-action drilling machine – Hilti GB Ltd
T.R.H. Range – domestic solid fuel roomheater – Trianco Heating Products Ltd
T.R.I. Hospitality Consulting – experts in hotels, tourism and leisure – Tri Hospitality Consulting Ltd
T.R.L. Technology – satellite communications equipment, mobile satcom terminal test equipment and radio receivers and systems – L-3 T R L Technology
T.R.X. – isolation transformers – Claude Lyons Ltd
T-RIM – E-glass warp knitted reinforcement fabric – Scott & Fyfe Ltd
T.-S. – drawing equipment – Technical Sales Ltd
T S M – promotion agency & relationship & trade marketing & advertising – Data Know How
T.S.S.D.P.S.C. Isolator Range – double pole isolater units, lockable – W R T L I-Tunnel
T. Series – peripheral impeller pumps – Calpeda Ltd
T-Shield – emi/rfi shielded windows – Optical Filters
T-Size 22 – fortified rosin emulsion paper size – Hercules Holding Ii Ltd
T.T.C. – blue-heavy duty bactericidal toilet cleaner and scale remover for porcelain – Evans Vanodine International plc
T.T.F. – in frame ventilator – R W Simon Ltd
T-Tech – threading tools – T-Tech Tooling Ltd
T.U.F. – mens safety boots and shoes – Bunzl S W S
T.U.S – sheep shear – Burgon & Ball Ltd
T.V.C.L. – lift control system – Liftstore Ltd
T.V. Guide Aylesbury – newspaper – Leamington Spa Courier
T.V. Guide (Hemel) – newspaper – Leamington Spa Courier
T.V.L. – European Technical Sales Ltd
T.V. Times – I P C Media Ltd
T.W. Franks – machines for cleaning by water pressure – Wilms Heating Equipment
T.X. Split Seals – rotary shaft split seals – Pioneer Weston
T.Y.J. – energy regulators – Sunvic Controls Ltd
T11 (Spain) – coin mechanisms – Jofemar UK
T2000 – Transparent Paper – Mcnaughton James Paper Group Ltd
T3 – magazine – Future Publishing Ltd
T303 – Bostik Ltd
TA – Lamphouse Ltd
Tab-seal – overseals for drum closures – Greif UK Ltd
Table Mats & Coasters – The Coaster Company
Tabo – Cremators – Facultatieve Technologies Ltd
Tabquick – file label system – Civica UK Ltd
Tabula – computer filing systems – Railex Filing Ltd
TAC – air treatmment, air conduction, cleaning, waste handling – Luwa UK Ltd
Tacho – Encoders UK
Tachograph – charts and accessories – Exaclair Ltd
Taco – fabrics – Brian Yates
Tacolin – micro embossed films for hygiene and disposable applications – Britton Taco Ltd
Tacolyn – resins dispersions – Hercules Holding Ii Ltd
Tactel – nylon textile fibre – Du Pont UK Ltd
Tactile Murals (United Kingdom) – bespoke interactive murals – Mike Ayres Design Ltd
Tactsense – tactile labels – C C L Labels Decorative Sleeves
Tadano – Harrier Fluid Power Ltd
TADOR – telephone based door entry system – Dorcom Ltd
Tafa Arc Spray – metal spray equipment – MCP Group
Tafelstern – Porcelain / bone china – W M F UK Ltd
Tafigel – polyrurethane thickeners – Lawrence Industries Ltd
Taftex – quiltweave bedspreads – Gailarde Ltd
Tag Semi – Cyclops Electronics Ltd
Tagax – electro-magnetic security tagging system for protecting goods against theft – Payne
Tagfresh – Harvey Waddington
Tagging – systems and tags – Air Tube Technologies Ltd
Tagytt-90 – G E Healthcare
Tahiti – WC suite – Armitage Shanks Ltd
Taicom – connectors – Anglia
TAILIFT – Chaintec Ltd
Tailormade – bespoke paper making service – Howard Smith Paper Ltd
Tairyfil – Carbon Fibre Yarn – Sage Zander Ltd
Taisei Kogyo – Harrier Fluid Power Ltd
Tait – Servicom High Tech Ltd
TAIT – Corby Radio Services Ltd
Taiwan Takaswai – T W Ward CNC Machinery Ltd
Tak Products – ancillary materials – Thomas Howse Ltd
Takahashi – Whitehouse Machine Tools Ltd
Takamaz – Warwick Machinery Ltd
Takamisawa – Cyclops Electronics Ltd
Take A Break – magazine – H Bauer Publishing
Take A Crossword – magazine – H Bauer Publishing
Take A Look – magazine – H Bauer Publishing
Take A Puzzle – magazine – H Bauer Publishing
Take-Off – promotional labels – C C L Labels Decorative Sleeves
Take-Out – promotional labels – C C L Labels Decorative Sleeves
TAKEUCHI – Hydraulic & Offshore Supplies Ltd
Takeuchi – P J P Plant Hire
Takeuchi – Harrier Fluid Power Ltd
Takeuchi – A T Wilde & Son Ltd
Takeuchi Mini Excavators – Parkway Plant Sales Ltd
***Takisawa (Japan)** – CNC lathes and machining centres – Takisawa UK Ltd
Takisawa – Birchfield Engineering Ltd
Takoma – record label – Ace Records Ltd
Takpave – tactile surface for visually impaired – Rediweld Rubber & Plastics Ltd
TAKrag – sticky impregnated cloth – Orapi Ltd
Takumi – large vertical m/cg cents – C Dugard Ltd Machine Tools
TAL – executive search & selection – Tal Talent
TAL Assessment – occupational psychology – Tal Talent
Talbot – Ashley Competition Exhausts Ltd
Talbot – L M C Hadrian Ltd
Talbot Blue – engineers layout fluid – Talbot Tool Co. Ltd
Talbot White – engineers layout fluid – Talbot Tool Co. Ltd
Talene – distilled oleines – Benjamin R Vickers & Sons Ltd
TalentBank – recruitment – Talentmark Ltd
Talentmark – pharmaceutical and health care recruitment consultants – Talentmark Ltd
TalentSearch – recruitment – Talentmark Ltd
Talisman – white and tinted offset and tinted boards – International Paper Equipment Finance LP
Talisman – games, miniatures and models for use in playing games, – Games Workshop Ltd
Talisman – corporate wear – Bunzl S W S
Talk 'N Smile Farm – Vtech Electronics UK plc
Talk 'N Tell Phone – Vtech Electronics UK plc
Talk 'N Type – Vtech Electronics UK plc
TalkDac (United Kingdom) – audio confirmation system – Bosch Security Systems
Talkin' Loud – club label – Mercury Records
Talking Alphabet Desk – Vtech Electronics UK plc
Talking Alphabet Picture Desk – Vtech Electronics UK plc
Talking Battleship Command – Vtech Electronics UK plc
Talking Driving School – Vtech Electronics UK plc
Talking Einstein – Vtech Electronics UK plc
Talking First Steps Baby Walker – Vtech Electronics UK plc
Talking Number Desk – Vtech Electronics UK plc
Talking Phone Pals – Vtech Electronics UK plc
Talking Smart Start Scholar – Vtech Electronics UK plc
Talking Whiz Kid Animated – Vtech Electronics UK plc
Talking Whiz Kid Mouse Pro – Vtech Electronics UK plc
Talking Whiz Kid Power Mouse – Vtech Electronics UK plc
TalkSheet CRM – Complete suite of software applications for customer relationship management – Knowledgewire Systems
Tallescope – Accesscaff International Ltd
Tallistag – paper – Fenner Paper Co. Ltd
Tallon – carpets – Penthouse Carpets Ltd
Tallon – christmas decorations, cards and sundries – Tallon International Ltd
Tally – UK Office Direct
Tally – computer printers – Tallygenicom
Talograft – bone graft substitute material containing hydroxyapatite – Plasma Biotal Ltd
Talon – rodenticide – Sorex Ltd
Talon – pipe clips, pipe cover and insulation spacers for 15mm, 22mm and 28mm pipe fixing plugs and compression olives/rings, firesleeves and wraps – Talon
Talon – connector for oil well conductor pipe – Oil States Industries UK Ltd
TALS – Torque activated loggin systems – Torque Leader
Talvic (U.S.A.) – inoculants ceramic foam filter for foundries – Porvair plc
Talyrond – roundness and cylindricity measuring instruments – Taylor Hobson Ltd
Talyrond - Talysurf - Nanostep - Surtronic - Talyscan - Form Talysurf - Talyvel – Taylor Hobson Ltd
Talyscan – 3D surface analysis system - non-contact – Taylor Hobson Ltd
Talystep – step height measuring system – Taylor Hobson Ltd
Talysurf – surface measuring instruments – Taylor Hobson Ltd
Talytrac – radius and form measuring system – Taylor Hobson Ltd
Talyvel – high precision electronic leveling instruments – Taylor Hobson Ltd
Tam O'Shanter – hone stones – Water Of Ayr
Tamar – heavy duty non rock D/T grating and frame – Norinco UK Ltd
Tamar – woven carpets in 100% pure new wool pile – Axminster Carpets Ltd
Tamara – silver & gold jewellery – W B Muddeman & Son Ltd
Tamashi – cameras, lighting – Sherwood Agencies Ltd
Tambour – Roller shutters, wooden – The Tambour Company Ltd
Tame – self lock cable ties – Perancea Ltd
***Tamfelt (Finland)** – filter fabrics, filter bags, deckers – Pulp & Paper Machinery Ltd

Tamlex – metal cable, screed and void trunking, cable tray, ladder and support systems and metal boxes – City Electrical Factors Ltd

Tamlite – luminaires for most industrial, commercial, amenity and display installations – City Electrical Factors Ltd

Tamp-A-Seal – tamper evident labels – C C L Labels Decorative Sleeves

Tamrock – air compressors, parts and service – Airware International Ltd

Tamrock – Harrier Fluid Power Ltd

Tamron – Stemmer Imaging

Tamrotor – air compressors, parts and service – Airware International Ltd

Tamsil – silicas – Lawrence Industries Ltd

Tamtec – emergency and security lighting; fire panels, alarms and detectors – City Electrical Factors Ltd

Tamura – thermal fuses – Anglia

Tamura – countertop basin – Ideal Standard Ltd

Tamura Europe – power supplies, telecom tx's power units, ac adaptors, battery chargers, thermal printheads piczo invertors, anorphas tx's – Tamura Europe Ltd

Tamura Hinchley – electrical transformers, power units, adaptors, battery chargers, thermal printheads, thermal printers – Tamura Europe Ltd

Tanaka – Gem Tool Hire & Sales Ltd

Tanda – stainless steel trays, hooks, shackles and balustrading – Tanda Engineering

Tandberg – Videonations Ltd

Tandee – Tooling equipment – Tooling & Equipment Engineers Ltd

Tandler – Mercury Bearings Ltd

Tandler Zahnrad Und Getriebefabrik Gmbh – Tandler Precision Ltd

Tanflex – waterproof and flexible vegetable sole leather – Joseph Clayton & Sons Ltd

Tangent – sliding door gear for folding or 'round-the-corner' doors – P C Henderson Ltd

Tangent – shower enclosures and trays – Ideal Standard Ltd

Tangent Furniture – Capex Office Interiors

Tangi-Flow – cutting tools, broaching heads, roller boxes – Tangi-Flow Products Limited

*Tanglewood (Korea, Republic of) – guitars and amplifiers – European Music Co. Ltd

Tangmill – Iscar Tools

Tango – helical worm geared motors – Opperman Mastergear Ltd

Tango (Finland) – castors with high performance plastic construction – Effortec Ltd

Tangye – hydraulic jacks, cylinders & pumps – Allspeeds Ltd

TANGYE – lightweight hydraulic jacks – Worlifts Ltd

Tangye – jacks – Bearwood Engineering Supplies

Tanita – electronic digital scales – Marsden Weighing Machine Group

Tank Breather – For the control of a wide variety of chemical vapour, gas and odorous discharges from liquid storage, processing tanks and vent lines/stack pipes – Emcel Filters Ltd

Tank Scrapers – Copa Ltd

Tanker – bulk powder – Feldbinder UK Ltd

Tankerbase – software package for fuel, oil, lubricants, gas and solid fuel distributors – Integer Micro Systems Ltd

Tankerling – for protection of tanker internals – Archco Rigidon Ltd

Tanklenz – dairy chemicals – Delaval

Tankmaster – sight gauges – Atkinson Equipment

Tannoy – all products – Tannoy Group Ltd

Tannoy – professional loudspeakers – Tukans Ltd

Tannoy Audix – communications, public address/voice alarm systems, amplifiers, loudspeakers – Audix Systems Ltd

Tansley Teak – Tansley Teak

Tansorite – door, drawer & window fittings (metal) – Allgood

Tantara (United Kingdom) – printed or plain blouse fabric – Carrington Career & Work Wear

Tantofex – taps and mixers for bathroom and kitchen – Ideal Standard Ltd

TAP 40 – industrial sectional door – Hörmann (UK) Ltd

Tapcut – Forward Chemicals Ltd

Tapley – electronic and mechanical brake meters and runaway friction testers – Tapley Instrumentation

Tapmate – Damixa Ltd

Tappex – specialist fastening systems – Tappex Thread Inserts Ltd

TAR 40 – industrial sectional door – Hörmann (UK) Ltd

Tara – polyethelene and polystyrene machines – Apropa Machinery Ltd

Tarabrook – ridgid box manufacturing – Benson Box Ltd

Taraflex Sport – sports flooring – Gerflor Ltd

Taralay Confort – acoustic vinyl flooring – Gerflor Ltd

Tarasafe – extra duty hi-vinyl antislip flooring – Gerflor Ltd

Tardex – non durable flame retardents – Contract Chemicals Ltd

Tardis Winter Oat – Senova Ltd

Targa – 30ft/34ft/37ft/43ft/48ft sport cruisers – Fairline Boats Ltd

*Target (U.S.A.) – mixer desks – John Hornby Skewes & Co. Ltd

Target – concrete saws and diamond blades – Trenchex Garden Machinery

Target – search and selection service – Whitehall Recruitment Ltd

Target – spray fluxer for soldering machines – Blundell Production Equipment

Target – traffic data analysis software – Golden River Traffic Ltd

Target Counters – Target Catering Equipment

Target Fixings – County Construction Chemicals Ltd

Target Kitchen Ventilation – Target Catering Equipment

Target Safety – Melitzer Safety Equipment

Target Stainless Fabrications – Target Catering Equipment

Targus – UK Office Direct

Tarifold – UK Office Direct

Tarkett – N W Flooring

Tarn-Pure – T P Technology plc

Taro – lubricants – Chevron

TARP – Hydraulic & Offshore Supplies Ltd

Tarpee – reinforced polythene tarpaulins – Power Plastics

Tarpen – hedge cutters and generators – Brimotor Ltd

Tarpey-Harris – toolmaking and machining specialists – Tarpey-Harris Ltd

Tarrant – cold water supply booster pump sets – Hamworthy Heating Ltd

Tartwist – tarred jute garden twine – Nutscene

TAS – wide angle traffic surveillance – Vysionics

TAS Schafer – Ringflex Drive Systems Ltd

TASC – eddy current drives and brakes – A T B Laurence Scott Ltd

Task – industrial workplace luminaires – E D L Lighting Ltd

Taskmaster – manufacturers of steel doors and glazed entrance systems – Doors & Hardware Ltd

Tastee Foods – Ethnic snack foods – Landauer Ltd

*Tasti-Grans – U F A C UK Ltd

Tatami – carpets – Interface Europe Ltd

Taurex – Gesipa Blind Riveting Systems Ltd

Taurus – Gesipa Blind Riveting Systems Ltd

Taurus – Pledge Office Chairs Ltd

Tautliner – loadbearing curtainsider bodywork – Boalloy Industries Ltd

Tavak – heat sealing machines, packaging, bags and carrier bags – Tavak Ltd

Tavern – darts – Unicorn Products Ltd

TAWI – Tawi UK

Tawlite – stainless steel holloware for caterers and hospitals – Goodwood Metalcraft Ltd

Tax-Direct – Mills & Reeve LLP

Taxan – Lamphouse Ltd

TaxiPay, MobilePOS, SmartPay, TonePay – Electronic Payment Solutions – Adelante Software Ltd

Tay – pump – Torres Engineering & Pumps Ltd

Tay – stainless steel urinal – Armitage Shanks Ltd

Tay – aero engines – Rolls-Royce plc

Taybrite – types of fuel – C P L Distribution

Taylor & Challen – power presses – T M A Engineering Ltd

*Taylor Freezer – Taylor Scotland Ltd

Taylor-Hobson – metrology equipment – Taylor Hobson Ltd

Taylor Hobson – equipment/spares – Bearwood Engineering Supplies

Taylor & Lodge – fine worsted suiting and jacketing cloths for gentlemen and ladies also clothes with cashmere, silk and summer kid mohair – Taylor & Lodge

Taylor Made Compounds – Resinex UK Ltd

Taylor of London – traditional English toiletries, and room sprays – Vivalis Ltd

Taylor of London - Natural Range – Hotel Complimentary Products

Taylor of London - Platinum Range – Hotel Complimentary Products

Taylor Valves Ltd – assortment of industrial valves to class 1500, all main alloys – Invictas Group

Taylors NewsForce – retail newsagents – R Taylor & Sons Ltd

TB SONIO – turbocharger core balancing machine – Schenck Ltd

TC 3 – dispersant spray system – Vikoma International Ltd

TCgard – Thermal conductivity sensor for % volume gas measurement – Crowcon Detection Instrument Ltd

TCH – Hydraulic & Offshore Supplies Ltd

TCM – Stacatruc

TCM – Chaintec Ltd

TCM – Premier Lift Trucks Ltd

TCM – Harrier Fluid Power Ltd

TD – tube developments – Tube Development

TDAPI – Protocol Stack Software – Telesoft Technologies Ltd

TDB – high performance pressed access doors – Hotchkiss Air Supply

TDK – UK Office Direct

TDK – recording media – John Hornby Skewes & Co. Ltd

TDK – Cyclops Electronics Ltd

TDR – Drill Grinders – Boremasters

TDR2 – Pile Integrity Tester – Testconsult Ltd

Teac – Tekdata Distribution Ltd

Teac CD Rom Drive – Tekdata Distribution Ltd

Teac CD RW – Tekdata Distribution Ltd

Teac DVD – Tekdata Distribution Ltd

Teac UK – Tekdata Distribution Ltd

Teach Yourself – books – Hachette UK Ltd

Teachers Book Club (Red House) – Scholastic School Book Fairs

Team Daiwa – fishing tackle – Daiwa Sports Ltd

TEAM SIMOCO – Corby Radio Services Ltd

*Team Sprayers – Team Sprayers Ltd

Teamac – marine and industrial coatings – Co-Var Ltd

Teamac – marine and industrial coatings – Teal & Mackrill Ltd

Teamalak – varnishes – Teal & Mackrill Ltd

Teamleader – management systems desking – E F G Matthews Office Furniture Ltd

Teamspirit – systems desking – E F G Matthews Office Furniture Ltd

Teamtalk – system desking – E F G Matthews Office Furniture Ltd

Teamwork – posture chairs & system desking – E F G Matthews Office Furniture Ltd

Teapigs – Teapigs

Tears of Scotland Liquer – Charles H Julian Ltd

Tec – hot melt applicators (hand held) – Power Adhesives Ltd

Tec – transformers – The Transformer & Electrical Co. (Engineering) Ltd

TEC – lathe chuck jaws – Thame Engineering Co. Ltd

TEC – TEC labels, printers & ribbons – Lancer Labels Ltd

Tec – air cooled package weather proof chillers – Tricool Thermal

Tec – Allcode UK Ltd

*Tec – Shelfguard Systems

Tec Cash Registers – Cash Register Services

Tec Cote – advanced epoxy & polymer based materials – Parex Ltd

Tec Roc Eprorange – mortars and waterproofing products – Parex Ltd

Tecalemit – breathers – Bearwood Engineering Supplies

Tecalemit – grease guns – Stephens Midlands Ltd

TECALEMIT – Hydraulic & Offshore Supplies Ltd

Tecaro AG (Switzerland) – Haesler Machine Tools

Tecbond – hot melt adhesive (shaped) – Power Adhesives Ltd

Teccor – Cyclops Electronics Ltd

TecEtch – acid etch material – Parex Ltd

TecFast – rapid setting cementitious mortars – Parex Ltd

TecFix – adhesives for civil engineering and construction – Parex Ltd

TecFlor – range of floor dressings – Parex Ltd

TecFlow – admixtures for various applications – Parex Ltd

Tecfrigo (Italy) – refrigeration – Interlevin Refrigeration Ltd

TecGrip – resin anchors for structural purposes – Parex Ltd

TecGrout – cement, epoxy and polyester based products – Parex Ltd

Tech Brush – specially designed industrial brushes – Kleeneze Sealtech Ltd

Tech-Style – drafting machines – Technical Sales Ltd

*Techcon (U.S.A.) – micro air dispense equipment – Liquid Control Ltd

Techdata – Tekdata Distribution Ltd

Techdec – fusion and laminate to GRP backing – Sarena

Techline – linear actuators – Linak UK

Techmaster – Jones & Shipman Grinding Ltd

Techmat – CNC creep feed grinders – Jones & Shipman Grinding Ltd

Technacell – lead acid batteries – Pulsar Developments Ltd

Techne – Alpha Electronics Southern Ltd

Technemab – G E Healthcare

Techner Vantrunk – ladder and channel cable support systems – Wellhead Electrical Supplies

Technibond – double sided bonding tapes – Technibond Ltd

Technic – unsupported neoprene gloves – Mapa Spontex

Technic ELS – static conductive vinyl tiles – Gerflor Ltd

Technical Ceramics – machining facility – Kennametal

Technifil – high technology fillers – Tetrosyl

Techniflam – fire retardent fabric system – Eclipse Blind Systems

Techniflex – solid & foamed acrylic tapes – Technibond Ltd

Technifor (France) – Technifor

Technigram – B P plc

Technik – UK Office Direct

Technik Art – commercial art pads and rolls – Exaclair Ltd

Techniprene – PureSil Technologies Ltd

Techniseal – self-adhesive foam sealants – Technibond Ltd

Technivac – catalyst handling and maintenance shutdown – Dialog Technivac Ltd

techno print – Link Hamson Ltd

Technobag – Injection moulded carrying cases – Hofbauer (UK) Ltd

Technobi – Hepco Motion

Technodrive – Splitter Gearboxes, Engine/Pump Adaptors, Overcentre Clutches, Speed Increasing/Reducing Gearboxes – J B J Techniques Ltd

TECHNODRIVE TWIN DISC – Hydraulic & Offshore Supplies Ltd

Technodrives (Netherlands) – DC electric motors – Transdrive Engineering Ltd

Technolaque – insulation materials and laminates – Attwater Group Ltd

Technolog – Halcyon Solutions

*Technomax – Burton Safes Ltd

Technomax – cylinders – Parker Hannifin Ltd

Technor – level guage back lighting and flashing beacons – Wellhead Electrical Supplies

Technostat – static dissipative laminates – Attwater Group Ltd

Technotile – Roland Plastics Ltd

Technotrend – security equipment – Power Stax plc

Technox – Dynamic Ceramic Ltd

*Techpap (France) – formation and other on-line sensors – Pulp & Paper Machinery Ltd

Techseal – Protective Finishing Group

Techsil. – Techsil Ltd

Techtron – Cleaning Chemicals – Precious Washers Stafford Ltd

Techviz – Technical & commercial illustration – Techviz

Techwax – Techsil Ltd

Techweld – Pipestoppers

Teckdata – Tekdata Distribution Ltd

*Teckpik (U.S.A.) – guitar plectra – John Hornby Skewes & Co. Ltd

Tecnocar – Harrier Fluid Power Ltd

TECNOCAR – Chaintec Ltd

*Tecnogres (Italy) – refined porcelain stoneware floor tiles – Bernard J Arnull & Co. Ltd

Tecnostyl – UK Office Direct

Tecnostyl – Italian-visual display – Orchard Drawing Boards

TECO – Pile Integrity Tester – Testconsult Ltd

*Teco (Netherlands) – tube expanders – B S A Tube Runner

Teco – timber connectors and joist hangers – Teco Ltd

Teco – equipment & spares – Bearwood Engineering Supplies

TecPatch – concrete and masonary repair products – Parex Ltd

Tecpro – professional intercom and communications systems – Canford Audio

Tecquipment – engineering lab equipment for educational purposes – T Q Education & Training Ltd

Tecreel (United Kingdom) – hydraulic hose reels – Interlube Systems Ltd

TecRoc – range of specialist products – Parex Ltd

TecRoc Appleby – advanced concrete repair product range – Parex Ltd

Tecstar – Tecstar Electronics Ltd

Tecstone – reconstructed ornamental and architectural stonework – Haddonstone Ltd

Tectonic – paper – Fenner Paper Co. Ltd

Tector – Resinex UK Ltd

Tectrite – phase failure relays, timers and thermistor control units – Midland Automation Ltd

Tectyl – rust preventives – Valvoline Oil Co.

Tectyl Valvoline – oils and wax protectives – Thomas Howse Ltd

Tecumsch – Therma Group

Tecumseh – Harrier Fluid Power Ltd

Tecvac – high vacuum coating process and equipment – Tecvac Ltd

Ted – mens shirts – Ted Baker Ltd

Ted – shirts – Ted Baker plc

Teddington Controls Limited – engine protection equipment and control and surveillance systems – Teddington Appliance Controls Ltd

TEDDS – the calculation pad for the professional engineer – Computer Services Consultants UK Ltd

Teddy Club – character merchandising license – Ulkutay & Co.

Tedeco – UK Office Direct

Tedimom – MDI and TDI – Polimeri Europa Ltd

Tedlar – polyvinyl fluoride film – Du Pont UK Ltd

Tee-Nuts – internally threaded wood fixing system – Jet Press Ltd

Teeda Hair Straightener – hair staightener – M S D Animal Health

Teedy – plastic fabricators – Talbot Designs Ltd

Teepol – detergents – Cleenol Group Ltd

Teepol ,Teepol HB7,Teepol Multipurpose,Teepol Gold,Teepol 30%,Teepol GD51,Teepol GD53,Teepol 310,Teepol L – Harvey Waddington

Tees – medium duty rectangular end hinged grating and frame – Norinco UK Ltd

Teesside Herald & Post – Gazette Media Company

Teesside Industrial Controls – transformer manufactures – Carroll & Meynell Transformers Ltd

Teesside Precision Engineering – Precision Engineering of small and medium components – Teesside Precision Engineering Ltd

Tefal (UK) – small electrical appliances – Group Seb Ltd

Tefcold – refrigeration – Interlevin Refrigeration Ltd

TEFEN – Hydraulic & Offshore Supplies Ltd

Tefen (Israel) – pneumatic fittings – Everyvalve Ltd

Teflon – East Midland Coatings Ltd

Teflon – fluoropolymer coatings – Du Pont UK Ltd

Teflon – W J P Engineering Plastics Ltd

Teflon – Resinex UK Ltd

Teflon PFA – Heating Cable – Cross Electrical Nottingham Ltd

Tefzel – Resinex UK Ltd

Tefzel – tetrafluoroethylene film – Du Pont UK Ltd

Tego dial – hmi construction solution – Schneider

Tego Power – motor starter construction solution – Schneider

Tegola – Versatile Tile – Matthew Hebden

Tegula – paving blocks – Tobermore Concrete Products Ltd

Tehalit – cable trunking – Ses Sterling Ltd

Tehalit – cable management systems – Hager Engineering Ltd

Teigler – European Technical Sales Ltd

Tek Data – Tekdata Distribution Ltd

Tekdata – computer products – Tekdata Distribution Ltd

Tekdata Defender – Tekdata Distribution Ltd

Tekfix – wallcovering adhesive – Tektura plc

Tekhaus – building system – Kingspan Insulation Ltd

Tekhniseal Ltd (United Kingdom) – mechanical seals & associated products – Tekhniseal Ltd

Tekmatic – Air Technics Ltd

Tekni – solenoid valves – Black Teknigas & Electro Controls Ltd

Tekni Kleen Computer Services – professional on site cleaning of all computer equipment – Tekni Kleen Computer Services Ltd

Teknilite – Yorkshire Refractory Products Ltd

Teknion – Office Seating, Desks – Bucon Ltd

Tektor – specialist electrophoretic coatings – L V H Coatings Ltd

Tektor – capacitance level probe/controller – Lee-Dickens Ltd

Tektronix – UK Office Direct

Tektronix – Fieldway Supplies Ltd

Tektronix – oscilloscopes – Longs Ltd

Tektronix – Alpha Electronics Southern Ltd

Tektura – wallcovering – Tektura plc

Tektura-Online – Tektura plc

*Teku – Pots & Trays – L S Systems Ltd

TEL-AIR (Italy) – telecommunications air conditioning – Stulz UK Ltd Epsom

Teladapt – plugs and jacks for telephone equipment – Nortel Networks UK Ltd

*Telco (Denmark) – sensors – Sensortek

Telcom Semi – Cyclops Electronics Ltd

Telcon – wound components – G D Rectifiers Ltd

Tele-call – t.v. bedside system – Wandsworth Group Ltd

TELE MECANIQUE – Hydraulic & Offshore Supplies Ltd

Tele-Products Limited (United Kingdom) – manufacturer of telephone test equipment – Tele-Products Ltd

Teleacoustics – telephone hoods, cabinets and kiosks – Storacall Engineering Ltd

*Telebinocular (U.S.A.) – vision screener – Warwick Evans Optical Co. Ltd

Telecommunications – public networks private networks, private networks mobile telephones – Robert Bosch Ltd

Telecomvision – surveillance and video equipment – Nortel Networks UK Ltd

Teleconcept – telephone products – Rocom

Telecrimp – cable jointing machine and equipment – Kembrey Wiring Systems Ltd

TELEDYNE – Hydraulic & Offshore Supplies Ltd

Teledyne – Relays – Dax International Ltd

*Teledyne (U.S.A.) – air-powered hydraulic pumps – The West Group Ltd

Teledyne – Cyclops Electronics Ltd

Teledyne Sprague – pumps – Allpumps Ltd

Telefunken – Cyclops Electronics Ltd

Telegen Generators – generators for Telecoms – Scorpion Power Systems

Telehouse – computer and telecommunications, housing, management and disaster recovery services – Telehouse International

Telelogic UK – computer software consultancy – I B M UK Ltd

Telemecanique – Schneider Electric Ltd

Telemecanique – Proplas International Ltd

Telemecanique – brand name for automation and control components – Schneider

Telemecanique – European Technical Sales Ltd

Telemecanique Inverters – inverters – Potteries Power Transmission Ltd

Telemecanique / Merlin Gerin – Industrial Control & Automation / High, Medium & Low voltage distribution systems – Alfred J Hurst Ltd

Telemechanique – equipment/spares – Bearwood Engineering Supplies

Teleologic – computer software development – Teleologic Ltd

Telepaque – G E Healthcare

Telepen – bar code system – S B Electronic Systems Ltd

telephone – Callsure Business Telephone & Fax Numbers

Telephone Answering Machine – Vtech Electronics UK plc

telephone numbers – Callsure Business Telephone & Fax Numbers

Telephone Sanitiser – telephone cleaner and disinfectant – Premiere Products Ltd

Telephone Short Stories of London – Short Stories of London Ltd

Teleplus – teleconverters – Johnsons Photopia Ltd

TELEPNEUMATIC – Hydraulic & Offshore Supplies Ltd

TelePorter – telephone based door entry system – Dorcom Ltd

Telerace – G S F Promount

Telerex TXB – profile cutting machine – Easab Cutting Systems

*Telescoper (U.S.A.) – conveyor take-up unit – R A Rodriguez UK Ltd

Telescopic Posts – Aremco Products

Teleseal – Mccomb Developments

Teleserv – bridge remote control system for small ships – Radamec Control Systems Ltd

Teleshare – telephone services – Weather Call

Telesteps – Accesscaff International Ltd

Teletech – Sebakmt UK Ltd

teletest 32 – emulator – Hitex UK Ltd

Televis – monitoring and control systems by eliwell – Thermofrost Cryo plc

Telex – Lamphouse Ltd

Telford – medium duty rectangular slide-out cover and frame – Norinco UK Ltd

Telios – canister cleaner – Hoover Ltd

TELL TALE – Hydraulic & Offshore Supplies Ltd

Tellabs – Telecommunications – Tellabs

TELLAFEDA – Pinstructure Ltd

Tellarini – Arun Pumps Ltd

Tellarinni – Obart Pumps Ltd

Tellenco – roller box tool 0.6 and 12.0 diameter – Portland Engineering Co. Ltd

Teller Inks & Coatings – pigment manufacturers – Tennants Inks & Coating Supplies Ltd

*Tellier (France) – canopeners, chipping machines and triturators (sieves) – Robot Coupe UK Ltd

Tellure Rota – Mercury Bearings Ltd

Telsan – PVC gloves – Mapa Spontex

Telstor – capacitance level probe/controller – Lee-Dickens Ltd

*Telsyn – Fire blankets – Telegan Protection Ltd

Telxon – mobile computing wireless lans – Symbol Technologies Ltd

TEM – Kennametal Extrude Hone Ltd

TEMA – Hydraulic & Offshore Supplies Ltd

Tema – Trafalgar Tools

TEMA – Funke

TEMA-UK – Hydraulic & Offshore Supplies Ltd

*Temafa (Germany) – fibre opening, cleaning and blending equipment – Robert S Maynard Ltd

Temcana – commercial gas heater – Vulcana Gas Appliances Ltd

Temet 25 – material for propeller shafts – Teignbridge Propellers International

Temp-Rite – melting indicators 'crayons' used mainly for the welding industry. – Thermographic Measurements Ltd

Tempa Glass – toughened glass – A C Yule & Son Ltd

Tempaflam – fire retardant glass – A C Yule & Son Ltd

Tempatrol – electronic water heaters – M C D Virtak Ltd

Tempatron – timers and controllers – Tempatron Controls

Tempcal – temperature dry-block calibrators – Haven Automation Ltd

Tempchek – floor & roof insulation – Celotex Ltd

Tempchek Deck – roof deck – Celotex Ltd

Tempest – emergency lighting range – Lab Craft Ltd

Temple Newsam – handprinted wallpaper collection – Zoffany

Tempo – countertop basin – Ideal Standard Ltd

Tempo – kitchen furniture – Moores Furniture Group

Tempo – running vests and shorts – Ronhill Sports

Tempo – helical geared motors – Opperman Mastergear Ltd

Temporary Fencing – Beaver 84

Tempory Fencing – Accesscaff International Ltd

Tempostatic – oil-heat exchanger (oil cooler) – Kenlowe Accessories & Co. Ltd

Temprano – vending machines – Westomatic Vending Services Ltd

Temprite – oil separators – Thermofrost Cryo plc

TempRite – cpvc – F L D Chemicals Ltd

Tempro – Helman Workwear

Tempro – Unique thermal insulation – Seymour Manufacturing International Smi Ltd

Tempus – modular connector system – I T T Ltd

Tempwall – Designs In Aluminium

Ten Form – mild flat steels – Corus

Tenacetin – modelling wax – Kemdent

Tenastic – printout binders – London Letter File Company Ltd

Tenasyle – modelling wax – Kemdent

Tenatex – modelling wax – Kemdent

Tenax – tool steel bars and forgings – Abbey Forged Products Ltd

Tenax – grafting wax – Vitax Ltd

Tenax – car hood & awning fastener – Opas Southern Limited

Tenax Wax – dental waxes – Prima Dental Group Ltd

Tenaz Rapitest – gardening & D.I.Y – Tenax UK Ltd

Tenbloc – in mold inoculants for foundries – Tennant Metallurgical Group Ltd

Tenby – wiring accessories – Legrand

Tencoat – bituminous paint – Tenants Bitumen

Tender Moments – mid-range soft toys – P M S International Group plc

Tender Touch – cotton wool – Lil-lets UK Ltd

Tendo – Hydraulic expansion tool holders – Schunk Intec Ltd

Tenet – filing and loose leaf binder systems – London Letter File Company Ltd

Tenet - Tenastic - Compak - Datox - Pendata. – London Letter File Company Ltd

Tenfjord – Rolls Royce

Tenform – micro-alloyed high-strength formable steels – Corus U K Ltd

Teng – S J Wharton Ltd

Teng – hand tools – Arrow Supply Co. Ltd

*Tenmag (Norway) – foundry treatment alloys – Tennant Metallurgical Group Ltd

Tennaglo – gas fire radiants – Thermal Ceramics UK Ltd

TENNANT – Chaintec Ltd

Tennant – Harrier Fluid Power Ltd

Tenniturf – artificial grass for sport – Anglian & Midland Sports Surfaces

Tenon – Lusso Interiors

Tenon – S K Interiors Ltd

Tenon (United Kingdom) – partitioning – Scotwood Interiors Ltd

Tenset – defer set binder – Tenants Bitumen

Tenside Electrical Ltd – Company name – Thameside Electrical Ltd

Tensil – foundry inoculants – Tennant Metallurgical Group Ltd

Tensil Seal – flow wrapping films – Sanders Polyfilms Ltd

Tension – Cloakroom Solutions Ltd

Tensolyn – high performance cast pallet wrap material (Stretch Film) – M J Maillis UK Ltd

Tensor – Team Corporation UK Ltd

*Tensor (Sweden) – nutrunners – Atlas Copco Tools Ltd

Tenspray – polymer modified binder – Tenants Bitumen

TENTE – Wolds Engineering Services Ltd

Tentec – Tentec Ltd

Tenthset – Kennametal UK Ltd

Tentwist – carpets – Cormar Carpets

Tenza – UK Office Direct

Tenza – packing list envelopes book covering film labelling tape self adhesive labels – Tenza Technologies Ltd

Tenzalopes – packing list envelope – Tenza Technologies Ltd

Tepco UK – Tepco Engineering International

Tepex – thermoplastic engineered preforms – Du Pont UK Ltd

*Teplast (Germany) – magnetic plugs, oil gauges – Meddings Machine Tools

*Tepro (Germany) – oil windows gauges – Meddings Machine Tools

TeQ Collection – spot and linear track lighting – Concord Marlin Ltd

*TER (Italy) – electrical control equipment – Metreel Ltd

Ter-Mate – electrical terminal blocks – Termate

Ter-Mate Master Frame – busbar support frames – Termate

Terathane – polyether glycols – Du Pont UK Ltd

Terathane – PTMEG polyols – I M C D UK Ltd

Tercarol – polyols – Polimeri Europa Ltd

Tercel – British Vita plc

Teredo (United Kingdom) – polyester cotton workwear fabric – Carrington Career & Work Wear

Terex – Trowell Plant Sales Ltd

Terex – Harrier Fluid Power Ltd

Terex – Custom Brakes & Hydraulics Ltd

TEREX – Chaintec Ltd

Terex – P J P Plant Hire

Terinda – polyester textile fibre – Du Pont UK Ltd

Termacon – Methode Connector – Selectronix Ltd

Termilock – circular connector bacushell – Icore International

*Termin-8 – Anitox

Terminal - Scanners – Avery Dennison

Terminator – roof extract fan – Nuaire Ltd

Terminator – Top specification Safety eyewear – Infield Safety UK Ltd

Termiscan – electrical testing apparatus – Nortel Networks UK Ltd

Termodeck – air conditioning system – Termodeck

Teroman – B P plc

Terra – textured anti-slip rubber floor tiles – Jaymart Roberts & Plastics Ltd

Terra Firma – trekking and climbing socks – Star Sportswear Ltd

Terra-Perma – plastic pots, chimney pots, troughs and bird baths – Richard Sankey & Son Ltd

Terrac – lubricant – B P plc

Terracotta – Shaws Of Darwen Ltd

Terrain – leisure footwear – D Jacobson & Sons Ltd

Terrain Blocker – all purpose anti ram blocker – Apt Controls Ltd

Terralin – Solmedia Laboratory Supplies

Terralux – lighting bollard – Holophane Europe Ltd

Terram – industrial and agricultural non-wovens and geotextiles – B B A Aviation plc

*Terram (United Kingdom) – non-metallic geotextile in roll form for use in drainage and roadmaking – Terram Ltd

Terraneo Intercoms – Intercoms – G8 Systems

Terrapin – leather and travel goods – H Gostelow Terapin Sales

Terrastrobe – entertainment stroboscope – Optikinetics Ltd

Terre Bormane – Olive Oil from Italy – Classic Fine Foods Ltd

Terreus – Uncoated Paper – Mcnaughton James Paper Group Ltd

Terri Brogan – spectacles and sunglasses – Safilo UK Ltd

Terry – S J Wharton Ltd

Terry – Trafalgar Tools

Terry – Norma UK Ltd

Terry Group Ltd – lifts for disabled and industry – Terry Lifts Ltd

Terry Stock Springs – Euro Stock Springs Ltd

Terylon – copying film – Office Depot UK

Tesa – flexo plate mounting – Plastotype

*Tesa (Switzerland) – measuring equipment – Vaultland Engineering

Tesa – General Fabrications Ltd

Tesa – Gawler Tapes & Plastics Ltd

tesa – Shand Higson & Co. Ltd

*Tesa – adhesive tapes – Tri Pack Supplies Ltd

*Tesa (Switzerland) – gauge blocks, calipers and micrometers – Tesa Technology UK Ltd

Tesa – B D K Industrial Products Ltd

Tesa (Switzerland) – precision measuring tools – Tesa Technology UK Ltd

Tesa – Anchor Magnets Ltd

Tesa – Austen Tapes Ltd

Tesch – European Technical Sales Ltd

Tesco – Supply Chain Solution Ltd

Tesl – CNC machine Centre – Gate Machinery International Ltd

Tesla (Czech Republic) – electronic valves and tubes, CRTs, semiconductors and electronic components – Edicron Ltd

Tesla Engineering Ltd – electro magnets & super conducting magnets – Tesla Engineering Ltd

Teslapaque – G E Healthcare

Teslascan – G E Healthcare

Teslatec – antistatic rubber bench and floor mats – Vitec

Tespa – stainless steel banding products – Signscape Systems Ltd

Tessa – account – Furness Building Society

Tessa – Status Metrology Solutions Ltd

Test Plugs (United Kingdom) – Test Plugs Ltd

Test-um – Test equipment – Select Cables Ltd

Test Weld – Pipestoppers

Testbourne – Scientific product for industry & research – Testbourne

Testing Times – magazine covering software verification – I P L Information Processing Ltd

Testo – Alpha Electronics Southern Ltd

Testrade – non destructive testing – Testrade Ltd

TestStand – software – National Instrument UK Corp Ltd

Testweld – Huntingdon Fusion Techniques

Tesys – motor starting system – Schneider

Tetcol – retort and contact thermometers, mercury switches – Russell Scientific Instruments Ltd

*Tethys (Italy) – a superb quality retractable pen with barrel action mechanism, gold and silver fittings – Hainenko Ltd

Teton – G F Smith

Tetra – Financial, distribution & manufacturing package – Kalamazoo - Reynolds Ltd

Tetra – brick and stone adhesives and polystyrene adhesives – Tetrosyl

Tetra – homecar products – Tetrosyl

Tetra – Portable Multi Gas Monitor – Crowcon Detection Instrument Ltd

Tetra 3 – Personal multi-gas monitor – Crowcon Detection Instrument Ltd

Tetra Brik – flat-top, rectangular paper and plastic laminate liquid food pack – Tetra Pak Ltd

Tetra Classic – tetrahedron paper and plastic laminate liquid food pack – Tetra Pak Ltd

Tetra Prisma – flat-top rectangular paper plastic laminate liquid food pack with fluted edges – Tetra Pak Ltd

Tetra Rex – gable and flat top paper plastic laminate liquid food pack – Tetra Pak Ltd

Tetra Top – paper and plastic laminate liquid food pack – Tetra Pak Ltd

Tetra Wedge – wedge shaped paper/plastic laminated liquid food pack – Tetra Pak Ltd

Tetrabond – wallpaper and wallcovering adhesives – Tetrosyl

Tetrabond – P.V.A. adhesives – Tetrosyl

Tetrad Plc – leather and fabric furniture – Tetrad plc

Tetrafix – tiling adhesive – Tetrosyl

Tetraform – Grinding Machine – Loadpoint Ltd

Tetragrout – tiling grout – Tetrosyl

Tetratainer – roll container – Tetra Pak Ltd

Tetratex – textured and exterior wall paints – Tetrosyl

Tetrion – fillers, adhesives and decorators sundries – Tetrosyl

TETROSYL – Hydraulic & Offshore Supplies Ltd

Teversham Motors – Teversham Motors

Tex – V E S Ltd

Tex – sealants – Indasa Abrasives UK Ltd

Tex – masking tape – Indasa Abrasives UK Ltd

Texaco – Harrier Fluid Power Ltd

Texaco – Hammond Lubricants & Chemicals Ltd

Texaco 4 Star – petrol – Chevron

Texaco Low Temp – lubricants – Chevron

Texaform – lubricants – Chevron

Texamatic Fluid – lubricants – Chevron

Texando – lubricants – Chevron

*Texas (U.S.A.) – i.cs – Amelec Ltd

Texas Instruments – UK Office Direct

Texas Instruments – Cyclops Electronics Ltd

*Texas Spectrum Electronics – Wavelength Electronics Ltd

Texassist – bleaching and dyeing auxilaries – Texchem

Texatherm – lubricants – Chevron

Texax Filtra – Harrier Fluid Power Ltd

Texbac – Underlay fabrics. – J & D Wilkie Ltd

Texcel – process controls – Texcel Division

Texcel (United Kingdom) – dynamometers and engine control systems – Froude Hofmann Ltd

Texcharge TC – water based screen printing ink for textile printing – Fujifilm Sericol Ltd

Texclad – lubricants – Chevron

Texdye – dyeing auxilaries – Texchem

Texecom – Registered Texacom Installers – Page Systems

Texet – calculators and office equipment and electronic data banks – The Hira Company Ltd

Texfin – finishing chemicals – Texchem

Texicote – polyester powder coatings and PVA emulsions – Scott Bader Co. Ltd

Texicryl – acrylic and styrene-acrylate emulsions (texicryl is known in North America as texigel) – Scott Bader Co. Ltd

Texiflock – Flock numbers, letters, logo's & badges – Imagine Transfers

Texifused – fusible interlinings for the shirt, blouse and garment making industries – Evans Textiles Sales Ltd

Texigel – water soluble polyacrylate thickeners – Scott Bader Co. Ltd

Texipol – inverse emulsions – Scott Bader Co. Ltd

Texipress Impressions – Heat Press – Imagine Transfers

Texkimp – unwinding and tensioning creels for all yarns, fibrs, cords and tapes, monofilaments and multifilament tows – Texkimp Ltd

Texnap – lubricants – Chevron

Texoil – suction and discharge of oil based liquids – Merlett Plastics UK Ltd

Texopaque OP – opaque platisol textile printing ink – Fujifilm Sericol Ltd

Texpar – lubricants – Chevron

Texplay – special macadam sports surface – Anglian & Midland Sports Surfaces

Texplus – pvc & polyester – Pritchard Tyrite

Texsoft – softeners for textile use – Texchem

Texsol – lubricants – Chevron

Texson – fans and calculators – Omega Import Export Ltd

Texspan – load restraint equipment – Pritchard Tyrite

Texton – cavity lining products – Prima Dental Group Ltd

Textra – textile converters – Textra

Textron – stitch bonded crepe paper underlay substrates – Scott & Fyfe Ltd

Textron – Harrier Fluid Power Ltd

Textron – Zygology Ltd

Textron - Scotweave - Scotube - Polymat - Polymat - "Hi-Flow" - Scotloop - Scotknit - Scotknit 3D - T-TRIM - Bacloc – Scott & Fyfe Ltd

Textures – Woven fabrics – Zoffany

Texturol – textile processing aid – Benjamin R Vickers & Sons Ltd

TF Groundworks – All Types of ground work – TF Groundworks

TFC Cable Assemblies Ltd – TFC have over 30 years experience supplying custom electrical & electronics sub assemblies to some of the worlds leading OEM's and CEM's – T F C Cable Assemblies Ltd

TG 209 F1 Iris – Netzsch-Instruments

TGM-Tower Cranes – Skyline Tower Crane Services Ltd

th Contact – push buttons – Saia Burgess (Gateshead) Plc

Thales – Euroteck Systems UK Ltd

Thales Acoustics – headsets – Hayward & Green Aviation Ltd

Thalheim (Germany) – encoders, tachogenerators – Baumer Electric Ltd
Thalheim (Germany) – tachogenerators – Lenze UK Ltd
Thame – lathe chuck jaws – Thame Engineering Co. Ltd
Thame Gazette – newspaper – Leamington Spa Courier
Thames Lubricants – lubricating oils, greases, transport, industrial and agricultural lubricants and ancilliary cleaning products,oil spill absorbant products – Thames Lubricants Ltd
Thanet KM Extra – newspaper – Kent Messenger Group Ltd
Thatchers Coxs – Thatchers Cider Company Ltd
Thatchers Gold – Thatchers Cider Company Ltd
Thatchers Heritage – Thatchers Cider Company Ltd
Thatchers Katy – Thatchers Cider Company Ltd
Thawalert – machine operated low temperature indicator – Thermographic Measurements Ltd
Thaxton (U.S.A.) – high pressure pipe stoppers – Alexander Cardew Ltd
The Acorn Account – childrens savings accounts – West Bromwich Building Society
*The Blues (Korea) – harmonies – John Hornby Skewes & Co. Ltd
The Bristol Kitchen Company – Bespoke furniture Makers – The Bristol Kitchen Company
The Canser Research Campaign – charity – Cancer Research Ventures Ltd
The Co-operative Bank P.L.C. – Co-Operative Banking Group
The Coffee Machine Company London – The Coffee Machine Company
The Coram Family – children's charity – Coram Family
The Country Diary of an Edwardian Lady – Chorion plc
The Electric Company – Electric Co.
The Engineering Industry Buyers Guide – United Business Media Ltd
The Field – I P C Media Ltd
The Floorline Collection (Austria) – laminate flooring for domestic & commercial applications – Egger UK Ltd
The Floorline Collection (Germany) – laminate flooring for domestic & commercial applications – Egger UK Ltd
The Folio Society – mail order club book – The Folio Society
The Fragrent Gardener – bodycare and toiletries – Norfolk Lavender Trading Ltd
The Granite Collection – Carved Granite Ornaments – Redwood Stone
The Herbert Group – weighing scales, wrapping & labelling systems – Herbert Retail Ltd
The Hire Network – Accesscaff International Ltd
The Hireman – Accesscaff International Ltd
The Incentive Works – The Incentive Works Ltd
The Independent Traveller – Farm Tours
The Institute of Chartered Accountants in England & Wales – Institute Of Chartered Accountants
The IT Job Board – IT jobs from leading employers in The United Kingdom from The IT Job Board. – It Job Board
The 'Jak' – A P T
The Little Nipper – Procter Machinery Guarding Ltd
The M.A.D. Virtual Assistant – Virtual marketing, admin and daily help – The M A D Virtual Assistant
The Machining Centre Ltd – precision engineering service – Machining Centre Ltd
The Mailing Business – T M B International Ltd
The Merchants Group – telephone management consultants – Merchants Ltd
The Mirror – Mirrorpix
The National Ladder Co – Accesscaff International Ltd
The Natural Look – tufted heather velour – Victoria Carpets Ltd
The Natural Rug Store – Sells high quality custom made natural rugs. – Style International Ltd
The News – Web rolling product. – Wordcraft International Ltd
The Nipper – Procter Machinery Guarding Ltd
The Oxford Duplication Centre – The Oxford Duplication Centre – The Oxford Duplication Centre
The Pay People – The Pay People www.thepaypeople.com – Thomas Elliot Associates
The People – Mirrorpix
The Quest Profiler – Personality Questionnaire – Eras Ltd
The Railway Magazine – I P C Media Ltd
The Red House – school book club – Scholastic School Book Fairs
The Retail Doctor – The Retail Doctor
The SAP Job Board – SAP jobs from leading employers in The United Kingdom. – It Job Board
The Saw Centre Ltd – saw – Saw Centre Ltd
*The Scanner (Taiwan) – radio microphones – John Hornby Skewes & Co. Ltd
The Secure-store – Letchworth self storage limited
The Secure-store – The Secure-Store
The Sentry – Procter Machinery Guarding Ltd
The Shooting Gazette – I P C Media Ltd
The Snowman – Chorion plc
The Sunday Mirror – Mirrorpix

The Tasting Game – Waiter's Friend Company Ltd
The Trader – newspaper – Yorkshire Regional Newspapers Ltd
The Translation People – Translation Services – The Translation People Limited
The Travel Collection – direct sell travel – Kuoni Travel Ltd
The Trevross Hotel – The hotel name – Trevross Hotel
The ultimate stainless steel cleaner – Cleans and polishes in one application – Stainless steel cleaner ltd
The Village Collectables – decorative ceramic teapots – Western House
The Waiters Friend – Waiter's Friend Company Ltd
*The White Light Room – Zoki UK Ltd
The Wind in the Willows – Chorion plc
The Windsor Bed Co – The Winnen Furnishing Company
The Wombles – Chorion plc
The Woolwich – The Woolwich
The World of Beatrix Potter – Chorion plc
The World of Lewis Carroll – Chorion plc
Theakston Best Bitter – ale & stouts – Scottish & Newcastle Pub Co.
Theakston Old Peculier – ale & stouts – Scottish & Newcastle Pub Co.
Theba – B P plc
*Themac (U.S.A.) – tool post grinders – Aegis Advanced Materials Ltd
Theo Fennell – jewellery – Theo Fennell plc
Theobald – sewing and knitting machines – Theobald Sewing Machines Ltd
Theracap – G E Healthcare
THERAPAX – Xstrahl Ltd
Therapod – Capex Office Interiors
THERATHERM – lamps – Osram Ltd
Therm – Kranzle UK Ltd
Therma-Stak – heat recovery equipment – Package Boiler Services Ltd
ThermaBlock – thermal guard aramids – Du Pont UK Ltd
Thermac – insulated louvre – McKenzie Martin Ltd
Thermacam – Express Instrument Hire Ltd
thermaCAM – Flir Systems Ltd
Thermacel – floating insulation material for swimming pools – Power Plastics
Thermadoor – insulated overhead doors – Stertil UK Ltd
Thermaglass – toughened glass for the domestic appliance industry – Solaglas Ltd
Thermaglaze – toughened glass for the architectural industry – Solaglas Ltd
Thermal – vacuum pumps – AESpump
Thermal Dynamics – Independent Welding Services Ltd
thermal Dynamis S – Wessex Welding & Industrial Supplies Ltd
Thermal Oxidiser – Gaseous effluent incineration – Babcock Wanson UK Ltd
Thermal Shield – 260C high temperature electrical connectors – D42 Thermal Ltd
*Thermalast (Germany) – constant modulus alloys – Rolfe Industries
Thermalert – Radir Ltd
Thermaline – gas/oil control panel – Harton Services Ltd
Thermalite – toughened glass for the automotive industry – Solaglas Ltd
Thermalite Coursing Bricks – meet building regulations by coursing in, closing the cavity and protecting against cold bridges – Marley Eternit Ltd
Thermalite Floorblock – insulating aircrete block to meet building regulations – Marley Eternit Ltd
Thermalite Hi-Strength 10 – compressive strength of 10N/mm2 – Marley Eternit Ltd
Thermalite Hi-Strength 7 – compressive strength of 7N/mm2 – Marley Eternit Ltd
Thermalite Hi-Strength Smooth Face – paint grade aircrete block for commercial and domestic projects with a compressive strength of 7N/mm2 – Marley Eternit Ltd
Thermalite Hi-Strength Trenchblock – lightweight foundation block with a compressive strength of 10N/mm2 – Marley Eternit Ltd
Thermalite Large Format Blocks – two and a half times the size of normal blocks but lightweight & compliant with CDM regulations – Marley Eternit Ltd
Thermalite Party Wall – excellent sound reduction properties – Marley Eternit Ltd
Thermalite Shield 2000 – moisture resistant aircrete block – Marley Eternit Ltd
Thermalite Smooth Face – paint grade aircrete block for commercial and domestic projects – Marley Eternit Ltd
Thermalite Thin Joint Mortar – benefit from faster build speed, increased productivity, improved thermal performance and airtightness, reduced site wastage – Marley Eternit Ltd
Thermalite Trenchblock – lightweight foundation block cuts construction time in half – Marley Eternit Ltd
Thermalite Turbo – high insulation aircrete block – Marley Eternit Ltd
Thermalloy – Cyclops Electronics Ltd

Thermally Insulated Bi-Folding Door – Bolton Gate Co. Ltd
Thermalux – Emmerson Doors Ltd
Thermapad – G M S Co.
Thermapad - Gamasco - Prekev – G M S Co.
Thermaquilt – floating insulation swimming pool covers – Power Plastics
Thermaresistant – air conditioning and fumes ducting – Merlett Plastics UK Ltd
Thermaroll – Emmerson Doors Ltd
Thermaroll – insulated roller doors – Stertil UK Ltd
THERMASLEEVE – nozzle heater – Watlow Ltd
Thermatek – Safeguard Electronic Systems Ltd
Thermatek, Thermatrad, Thermamod, Thermafoil, Thermaphase. – Safeguard Electronic Systems Ltd
Thermatop – toughened glass hob tops for the domestic and commercial use – Solaglas Ltd
Thermax – thermal indicating labels and paints and tlc thermochromic liquid chystal indicators – Thermographic Measurements Ltd
Thermet – high temperature austenitic electrodes – Metrode Products Ltd
Thermex – forging lubricants – D A Stuart Ltd
Thermic Ultra – co-extruded catering jar – R P C Containers Ltd
Thermic Welding – Rapid Rail GB Ltd
Thermiculite – high temperature non-asbestos sealing material – Flexitallic Ltd
Thermik Thermal Cutouts – cutouts – Rainer Schneider & Ayres
Thermimax – Industrial gas burner systems – Lanemark International Ltd
Thermit Welding – Rapid Rail GB Ltd
Thermo – manufacture heat exchangers – Sterling Thermal Technology Ltd
Thermo bar scan – T M Electronics Ltd
Thermo Jarrel Ash – Thermo Electrical
Thermo-Mechanical Analyser (T.M.A.) – heat testing equipment – Ta Instruments
Thermoalloy – Cyclops Electronics Ltd
Thermobloc – industrial warm air heaters/cabinet heaters – Babcock Wanson UK Ltd
Thermocast – heating/cooling structual system – Tarmac Precast Concrete Ltd
Thermochromic – paints – Colour-Therm Ltd
Thermochromic Photochromic – printing inks – Colour-Therm Ltd
Thermoclave – Dry Atmosphere Autoclave System – L B B C Technologies
*ThermoCompact (Germany) – gas boiler – Vaillant Ltd
Thermocool (Belgium) – gas fired unit heaters – Reznor UK Ltd
Thermodek – insulating roof-board, cut-to-falls – Vencel Resil Ltd
Thermodie – tool & die steel – Somers Forge Ltd
Thermodiffusion – industrial and commercial heating and ventilation engineers – Thermodiffusion Ltd
Thermodisc – Foremost Electronics Ltd
Thermodrum – drum mix asphalt plant – B G Europa UK Ltd
Thermodyne – Transit cases in HPDE – Hofbauer (UK) Ltd
Thermofit – heat-shrinkable tubing and moulded parts – Tyco Electronics UK Ltd
*Thermoflux (Germany) – nickel iron soft magnetic alloys – Rolfe Industries
Thermofoil – protective wear – Angus Fire
Thermoforce – tangential fan heaters for the heating of agricultural & horticultural premises – Thermoforce Ltd
Thermogel – heat packs – Thermo Packs
Thermogravimetric Analyser (T.G.A.) – heat test equipment – Ta Instruments
Thermogrip – extruded rod form hot melt adhesives – Bostik Ltd
Thermoguard – high temperature protective glass sleeving – Jones Stroud Insulations Ltd
Thermoject – hot runner systems (plastics) – D Y N Metal Ltd
Thermojet – adhesive application equipment – Valco Cincinnati
Thermoking – Harrier Fluid Power Ltd
Thermoking – Therma Group
Thermolite – Platt & Hill Ltd
Thermolite – polyester performance insulation – Du Pont UK Ltd
ThermoLoc – insulated cavity closer – Timloc Building Products
Thermoloft – polyester performance insulation – Du Pont UK Ltd
Thermomatic – electric radiator fan – Kenlowe Accessories & Co. Ltd
Thermomatic H.D. – electric radiator fan – Kenlowe Accessories & Co. Ltd
Thermomax – solar collectors – Thermomax Ltd
THERMOMISER/WTM – destratification fans – Babcock Wanson UK Ltd
Thermon – electrical heat tracing products – Thermon Electrical Heating Equipment

Thermopac – thermal fluid heaters – Babcock Wanson UK Ltd
Thermopol – hoses for trucks and automobiles – Thermopol Ltd
THERMOPOLYMER – polymer heating device or technology – Watlow Ltd
ThermoPro – Hörmann (UK) Ltd
Thermosafe (United Kingdom) – drum & process induction heater – L M K Thermosafe
Thermoscan – thermochromic liquid crystal thermometers – B & H Colour Change Ltd
Thermoscreens – warm ambient & cold store air curtains – Thermoscreens Ltd
Thermoseal – round section high temperature glass seals – Jones Stroud Insulations Ltd
Thermount – printed wiring board reinforcement – Du Pont UK Ltd
ThermoView – Radir Ltd
Thermox – oxygen analysers – Amatek Precision Instruments UK Ltd
Thermox – tin oxide – Keeling & Walker Ltd
TheSonicNet – Company Name – TheSonicNet
Thesscote – flux coated brazing rod – Thessco Ltd
Thesscote - brazing rods – Thessco Ltd
Theta-Probe – soil moisture sensor – Delta T Devices
Thicko – Slush Puppie Ltd
Thiel – Red House Industrial Services Ltd
Thielmann – European Technical Sales Ltd
***Thiessen (Germany)** – fat cubers – Selo UK Ltd
Thin Sheet Nutsert – one sided threaded fastener for thinner materials – Avdel UK Ltd
THINBAND – band heaters – Watlow Ltd
Think & Do – PC-based control and human machine interface (HMI) development software – Easymatics Ltd
Think & Do Live – PC-based control and human machine interface (HMI) development software – Easymatics Ltd
Think & Do Studio – PC-based control and human machine interface (HMI) development software – Easymatics Ltd
Thirst Aid – Waiter's Friend Company Ltd
This Is Motor – newspaper – Mail News Media
This Is Property – newspaper – Mail News Media
Thistle – Halcyon Solutions
Thistle Board Finish – final coat plaster – Bristish Gypsum
Thistle Dri-Coat – cement based renovating plaster – Bristish Gypsum
Thistle Hardwall – undercoat plaster with higher impact resistance – Bristish Gypsum
Thistle Multi Finish – multi purpose finishing plaster – Bristish Gypsum
Thistle Projection – one coat machine applied plaster – Bristish Gypsum
Thistle Renovating – undercoat plaster for re-plastering – Bristish Gypsum
Thistle Universal One Coat – one coat plaster – Bristish Gypsum
Thistle X-Ray Plaster – pre-mixed barium gypsum plaster for x-ray protection – Bristish Gypsum
Thom Lamont – Dawson Downie Lamont Ltd
***Thomas (Italy)** – coldsaws and bandsaws – Prosaw Ltd
Thomas – Harrier Fluid Power Ltd
Thomas & Betts – Cyclops Electronics Ltd
Thomas Burberry – clothing and accessories – Burberry Ltd
Thomas Cook Holidays – tour operator – Thomas Cook Ltd
Thomas Coulter Building Services – electrical and plumbing services – Morris & Spottiswood Ltd
Thomas Flinn – Saws and cabinet scrapers – The Toolpost
Thomas Frederick – bed linen – Thomas Frederick & Co. Ltd
Thomas Frederick – household textiles – Linden Textiles Ltd
Thomas Goode – Cavers Wall China Ltd
Thomas Hosking & Sons – coach building and hydraulics – Thomas Hosking Ltd
Thomas Regout – G S F Promount
Thomas Ross – fine art publishers of engravings and etchings – Thomas Ross Ltd
Thomas Sanderson – blinds – Thomas Sanderson Ltd
Thomas Turton (United Kingdom) – contractors and industrial tools – Thomas Turton Ltd
Thome – European Technical Sales Ltd
***Thommen (Switzerland)** – thread rolling machines – Brunner Machine Tools Ltd
Thompson – welding machines – Bearwood Engineering Supplies
Thompson Damp Seal – stain blocking damp seal to mark mask water staining – Ronseal Ltd
Thompsons Drive Seal – water based decorative waterproofer for tarmac and concrete drives – Ronseal Ltd
Thompsons Patio Seal – water based waterprofer for use on patios and block paving – Ronseal Ltd
Thompsons Roof Seal – water based roof seal for flat or felt roofs – Ronseal Ltd
Thompsons Water Seal – solvent based waterproofer – Ronseal Ltd
Thomsen – C E S Hire Ltd
Thomson – Antifriction Components Ltd
Thomson – Lamphouse Ltd
Thomson – Danaher Motion UK Company
Thomson Directories Database – 1.8 million businesses – Acxiom Ltd
***Thomson Industries Inc (U.S.A.)** – nylon bearings – Kellett Engineering Co. Ltd
Thomson-Thorn Missile Electronics – defence electronic missiles – Thales Missile Electronics
Thor – rawhide and copper hammers and mallets – Thor Hammer Company Ltd
Thorace – dead-blow nylon hammers – Thor Hammer Company Ltd
Thorex – plastic and nylon hammers – Thor Hammer Company Ltd
Thorite – compressed air specialists – Thomas Wright-Thorite
Thorite Diamond – Range of compressors – Thorite
Thorlite – soft-faced hammers – Thor Hammer Company Ltd
Thorn Lighting – Team Overseas Ltd
Thorn Security – equipment & spares – Bearwood Engineering Supplies
Thoroughbred – Vaughans Hope Works Ltd
Thorp Modelmakers – model making, architectural, engineer and prototype models, computer visualisation/walk throughs – Thorp Modelmakers Ltd
Thorpe Park – family leisure Park – Thorpe Park Ski Shop
***Thorpe Trees** – Thorpe Trees
Thorsons – general health, mind, body and spirit titles, lifestyle and special – Harpercollins Publishers Ophelia House
Thorub – rubber-faced hammers and mallets – Thor Hammer Company Ltd
Thought Train – creative thinking program system – Kelvin Top-Set Ltd
Thovex – ointment – Delaval
Threadneedle – corporate wear – The Wakefield Shirt Company Limited
Thredol – sewing thread lubricants – Benjamin R Vickers & Sons Ltd
Three 5 liner – 3.5 tonne bodywork – Boalloy Industries Ltd
Three-five systems – Cyclops Electronics Ltd
Three Hands – disinfectant – Jeyes
Three Nuns – pipe tobacco – Imperial Tobacco Group PLC
Three's Company – ladies fashion – Justina Of London Ltd
Threesome (United Kingdom) – corded track and valance and dress curtain rail – Integra Products
Threshold T32 (United Kingdom) – entrance clean off zones – Checkmate Industries Ltd
+ **Threshold T32/Marine (United Kingdom)** – entrance clean off zones – Checkmate Industries Ltd
Threshold T80/20 (United Kingdom) – carpet tiles – Checkmate Industries Ltd
Threshold T80/20 (United Kingdom) – entrance clean off zones – Checkmate Industries Ltd
Thrige-Titan – European Drives & Motor Repairs
Thripstick – controls thrip as part of an intergrated pest management system in glasshouses – Aquaspersions Ltd
Thrislington – toilet cubicles – Thrislington Cubicles Ltd
***Thrive (Japan)** – electric clippers – Diamond Edge Ltd
Throaties – throat pastilles – Ernest Jackson & Co. Ltd
Throwol – soaking oil for silk – Benjamin R Vickers & Sons Ltd
Thrust Petroleum – petroleum – Bayford & Co. Ltd
***Thunder Tiger (Taiwan)** – model aeroplane engines – Amerang Group Ltd
Thurbon – Mass Consultants Ltd
Thurlby Thandar – Alpha Electronics Southern Ltd
Thurrock Gazette – free weekly newpaper – Newsquest Essex Ltd
Thurston – snooker and pool table makers and accessories – E A Clare & Son Ltd
Thwaites – Trowell Plant Sales Ltd
Thwaites – Mawsley Machinery Ltd
Thwaites – Harrier Fluid Power Ltd
Thwaites – earthmoving equipment – Gunn J C B
Thwaites – Custom Brakes & Hydraulics Ltd
Thwiates – A T Wilde & Son Ltd
Thyodene – indicator for iodine and iodometry – Sherman Chemicals Ltd
Thyssen – welding consumables – Bohler Welding Group Ltd
Thyssen Escalators – Thyssenkrupp Elevator UK Ltd
***Thyssen Henschel (Germany)** – andromat manipulators – Pearson Panke Ltd
Thyssen Krupp – Sandhurst Plant Ltd
Thyssen Modernization – Thyssenkrupp Elevator UK Ltd
Ti-Pure – titanium dioxide rutile – Du Pont UK Ltd
Tiara – Vi Spring Ltd
Tiara Supreme – Vi Spring Ltd
Tibbo Technology – serial device servers – Anglia
Tibs – Bob Martin UK Ltd
tic – controllers – AESpump
Tic Tac – circular surface and recessed vandal resistant architectural lighting – Designplan Lighting Ltd
Tickhill – agricultural, food processing and bulk handling equipment – Tickhill Engineering Co. Ltd
TICO – clip strip, machinery mounting products, off-shore pipe support products, resilient seatings and structural bearings – Tiflex Ltd
Tico Pad – W Mannering London Ltd
TICS – Tics International Ltd
Tidco – Barmac-VSI crusher – Metso Minerals UK Ltd
Tide Tables – Tide Tables for the UK – Douglas Press
Tidemaster – clocks, watches and tidal computers – Yachting Instruments Ltd
Tidenet – plastic protection netting extruded and knitted; geotextiles, spunbond fabrics for agriculture and horticulture, construction amennity and leisure and fish farming applications – Tildenet Ltd
Tidibin – storage bin – Adroit Modular Buildings plc
Tie-Dex – stainless steel tie – Band-It Co. Ltd
Tie-Lok – stainless steel tie – Band-It Co. Ltd
Tie Rack – silk ties, scarves and accessories – Tie Rack Ltd
Tiede – Euroteck Systems UK Ltd
Tien Ying – Wahoo Enterprises Limited
Tiffany – tiffany – Armitage Shanks Ltd
Tiffany – casual shoes – D Jacobson & Sons Ltd
Tiflex Performance Polymer Components – Tiflex Ltd
TIGEAR – Gears – Baldor UK
Tiger (United Kingdom) – barrier systems – Motivation Traffic Control Ltd
Tiger (United Kingdom) – backstand double ended grinder – R J H Finishing Systems Ltd
Tiger – hydraulic presses – Mackey Bowley International Ltd
Tiger – Pressure washers – B & G Cleaning Systems Ltd
Tiger Gloves – S J Wharton Ltd
Tiger Super – Pressure washers – B & G Cleaning Systems Ltd
Tiger T. – artificial grass golf mats – Exclusive Leisure Ltd
Tigi Wear – fashion – Rinku Group plc
Tik Tok – terry napkins – Pin Mill Textiles Ltd
Tilda – rice – Tilda Ltd
TILE – trends in leisure and entertainment – Andrich International Ltd
Tilepan (United Kingdom) – access panel that can be tiled – Panelcraft Access Panels
Tilesafe – tile bonding system – Premier Coatings Ltd
Tileshack – ceramic tile retailer – Craven Dunnill & Co. Ltd
Till Rolls – New Horizon Systems Ltd
Tillsafe – range of secure accessories – Air Tube Technologies Ltd
Tillwite – appears on architectural ironmongery, engineer and building products – Till & Whitehead
Tilt Sensors – geotechnical instruments – Itm Soil Ltd
Tiluma – heat resistant adhesive – Vitcas Ltd
Tim Skilton – Abrasive finishing systems – The Toolpost
Timb-a-tilt – timber tiltback vertical sliding systems – Caldwell Hardware Ltd
Timber Masterclass – modular timber building – Adroit Modular Buildings plc
Timber Trades Address Book – United Business Media Ltd
Timbercolour – wood-stains and varnish for wood – Akzonobel
Timberex – wood finishing product – Watco UK Ltd
Timberflex – undercarriage systems for use with Parkestrip strip flooring – Atkinson & Kirby Ltd
Timberjack – Harrier Fluid Power Ltd
Timberland – S J Wharton Ltd
Timberland – D S Safety
Timberland – Knighton Tool Supplies
Timberland – Global Fasteners Ltd
Timberlast Frames – new window joinery/window frames incorporating the Timberlast preservative system frames guaranteed for life – Channelwood Preservation Ltd
Timberlast System – wood preservative system for the pre-treatment of manufactured joinery extends the life of treated timber indefinitely – Channelwood Preservation Ltd
Timberset – adhesives – Rotafix Ltd
Timbertex – modular sign systems – Signscape Systems Ltd
Timberworld – retailers of timber and building supplies – Wenban Smith Ltd
Time – The Little Brown Book Group
Time Chain – fashion watches – Sun 99 Ltd
Time Collector – time and attendance system – Deaf Alerter plc
Time-Compression – magazine for rapid products – Rapid Newscommunications Group
Time Export – Versalift Distributors UK Ltd
Time Lamp – neons – Anglia
Time Manager – time recording and management system – Bensasson & Chalmers Ltd
Time Manufacturing – Versalift Distributors UK Ltd
Time Out – magazine – Time Out Group
TimeFlex – digital delay unit – A M S Neve Ltd
Timeform Racing Publications – racing publications – Portway Press Ltd

TimeIT – our brand of leading time and attendance entry level software – Timeit Software Distribution Ltd

TimeIT Ultra – Our comprehensive integrated T&A, Access control and HR software – Timeit Software Distribution Ltd

TimeLox (Sweden) – digital locking – Assa Abloy Security Solutions

Timelox – Assa Abloy Hospitality Ltd

Timemaster – quartz mantel and wall clocks – L C Designs Ltd

Timemaster – Derbyshire Building Society

Timeplan – fuel monitoring equipment – Timeplan Ltd

Timeplan – desk diary – Charles Letts Group Ltd

*Timeplex (U.S.A.) – computer networking – K Com

Times 2 – speedfiles – Kardex Systems UK Ltd

Times Books – atlases and special interest reference books – Harpercollins Publishers Ophelia House

Times Microwave – E M J Management Ltd

Times Microwave – RF cable & connectors – Select Cables Ltd

Times New Roman – typeface – Monotype Imaging Ltd

Times Review Series – Times Review Series Of Newspapers

Times, The – newspaper publisher – The Times Newspaper Classified

Timesaver – Ellesco Ltd

Timesaver – drawer system – L B Plastics Ltd

Timescape – coach tour operators – Island Getaways

Timeset – computer program for pile settlement prediction – Cementation Skanska

Timet UK Ltd – titanium manufacturers – Timet UK Ltd

Timex – watches – UK Time Ltd

Timken – bearings etc – Bearwood Engineering Supplies

Timken – truck, trailer & PCV wheel bearings – Roadlink International Ltd

Timloc – building products – Timloc Building Products

Timonta – Relec Electronics Ltd

Timonta, Egston, Varitronix, Elobau, Electrodynamics. – Relec Electronics Ltd

TIMREX – Timcal Graphite & Carbon

TIMROC – Timcal Graphite & Carbon

Timson – printing machinery – Timsons Ltd

TimTie – stainless steel timber frame wall tie (new build) – Helifix Ltd

Tinaderm Cream – M S D Animal Health

Tinaderm Plus Powder Aerosol – M S D Animal Health

Tinderm Plus Powder – M S D Animal Health

Tinite – toughened version of titanium nitride coating – Tecvac Ltd

Tinite, Nitron, Nimplant – Tecvac Ltd

Tinker – range of inflatable sailing dinghies – Henshaw Inflatables Ltd

Tinstab – tin stabilisers – Akcros Chemicals Ltd

Tiny Touch Camera – Vtech Electronics UK plc

Tiny Touch Phone – Vtech Electronics UK plc

TINYLOG – Data logger – Halcyon Solutions

Tiocco – Harrier Fluid Power Ltd

Tip Top – knitwear steaming tables – Electrolux Laundry Systems

*Tipco Inc (Canada) – standard punches and dies to catalogue and/or drawings in metric and imperial – Berger Tools Ltd

Tipform – shuttering system for landfill sites – Cordek Ltd

Tipmaster – tipping trucks – Tipmaster Ltd

Tipnology – tipping equipment – Tipmaster Ltd

Tipp-ex – UK Office Direct

Tipper – bale accumulator – Brown's Agricultural Machinery Company Ltd

Tippkemper - Matrix – Incotech Ltd

Tiptoe – galley and caravan pump – Munster Simms Engineering Ltd

Tiptone – B P plc

Tiptone Alba – B P plc

Tiptonic – B P plc

*Tirak (Germany) – lifting and pulling machines, suspended cradle and platform machines – Tractel UK Ltd

*Tirfor (France) – pulling, lifting and handling equipment – Tractel UK Ltd

Tirion – seat stick & umbrella – Noirit Ltd Newman & Field Ltd

Tiris – identification system – Texas Instruments Ltd

Tiro-Clas (France) – production workstations for industry – Electro Group Ltd

Tirrobond – newspaper print blanket – P & S Textiles Ltd

Tirropeen – printers blanket – P & S Textiles Ltd

TIRSAN – Bailey Morris Ltd

*Tirtiaux (Belgium) – fractionation of vegtable fats – Engelmann & Buckham Ltd

Tisserand – aromatherapy products – Tisserand Aromatherapy

Tital – titanium alloy – Hytorc Unex Ltd

Titan – garden stores – Tri Metals Ltd

Titan – press and assembly – Berck Ltd

Titan – universal strength tester – James H Heal & Co. Ltd

*Titan (U.S.A.) – spray equipment – Gray Campling Ltd

Titan – bilge pump – Munster Simms Engineering Ltd

*Titan (U.S.A.) – airless tips – Gray Campling Ltd

Titan – supported nitrile gloves – Mapa Spontex

Titan – heavy duty gear for sliding gates – P C Henderson Ltd

Titan (United Kingdom) – slitter rewinders – Atlas Converting

Titan – PTFE micro titer plates – Radleys

Titan – high speed linear labelling system – Harland Machine Systems Ltd

Titan – Gem Tool Hire & Sales Ltd

*Titan (U.S.A.) – paint spray equipment (airless) HVLP – Lion Industries UK Ltd

Titan – aluminium and timber access equipment, ladders, steps, trestle stagings and accessories – Titan Ladders Ltd

Titan – automotive lubricants – Fuchs Lubricants UK plc

Titan Distribution UK Ltd – Titan Distribution Ukltd

Titan Gate Barriers – Accesscaff International Ltd

Titan Hydraulic Wrenches – Torque Solutions Ltd

Titan opto – LED and LED displays – Anglia

Titan Raodblocker – anti ram impact tested road blocker – Apt Controls Ltd

Titan Tanks – Storage tanks for fuel – L S Systems Ltd

Titan Towers – Accesscaff International Ltd

Titanium Diboride – powders – Kennametal

Titanlite – thin supported gloves in nitrile – Mapa Spontex

Titebond – Adhesives for wood – The Toolpost

Titeflex (U.S.A.) – PTFE lined flexible hoses – Hydrasun Ltd

Titertek – produce biologicals – Icn Pharmaceuticals Ltd

Titex Plus – Walter GB Ltd

Titex Plus – precision cutting tools – Precision Tools

Titley & Marr – The Winnen Furnishing Company

Titman – Central C N C Machinery Ltd

Tiwst – Display Wizard Ltd

*Tixogel (Germany) – organoclay gellants – Sud-Chemie UK Ltd

*Tixoton (Germany) – bentonites – Sud-Chemie UK Ltd

Tizit – hardmetal products – Ceratizit UK Ltd

TK Steel – Melitzer Safety Equipment

TLC – thermochromic liquid crystals – Thermographic Measurements Ltd

*TLC-4 Brooder – brooder – Brinsea Products Ltd

TLR – Zygology Ltd

TM – Harrier Fluid Power Ltd

TM3 – methyl bromide and sulphuryl fluoride (Vikane) monitor for fumigation – Bedfont Scientific Ltd

TM710 – for the non contact on line measurement if nicotine, sugars, temperature and moisture in tobacco – N D C Infra-Red Engineering Ltd

TMB International – T M B International Ltd

Tmoa – trade mark agents – Hallmark Ip Ltd

TMS – tunnel management systems - computer controlled management systems – Delta Civil Engineering Group Holdings Ltd

TMT – linear motion products – R A Rodriguez UK Ltd

TNC – HEIDENHAIN GB LTD

TNM – multiples sealed and screwed connectors – I T T Ltd

TNT Network Logistics – Ceva Network Logistics Ltd

TNT Newsfast – Ceva Network Logistics Ltd

*Toastmaster – Toasters & food holding equipment – Middleby UK Ltd

Toastywarm – Churchtown Buildings Ltd

Tobacconists – sundries – Wilson Company Sharrow Ltd

Tobbletag – The Bottle Bag – Tobbletag Ltd

Toby – footwear – Russell & Bromley Ltd

Today's Golfer – magazine – Emap Ltd

Today's Runner – magazine – Emap Ltd

Todd – sugar beet cleaner loaders – Terry Johnson Ltd

Todo – couplings – Cebo UK Ltd

Toe Foot Cleaner – Helping Hand Co.

Toesavers – Global Fasteners Ltd

Toflife T.P. – anti graffiti system – Tor Coatings Ltd

Toftejorg – tank and vessel cleaning unit – Pulp & Paper Machinery Ltd

Tog 24 – waterproof hiking clothing & thermal wear – Mileta Ltd

Tog-L-Loc – metal joining system – B T M UK Automation Products

Together – mail order fashion design – Together Ltd

Toil – Agricultural adjuvant – Interagro UK Ltd

TOK Switches – E Preston Electrical Ltd

Tokin – M S C Gleichmann UK Ltd

Toko – coils & filters – B E C Distribution Ltd

Toko – B E C Distribution Ltd

Toko – Cyclops Electronics Ltd

Tokstrip – waterproof sealing strip for pre-cast concrete units – Winn & Coales Denso Ltd

Toku – Red Rooster Industrial UK Ltd

Toku – Yokota UK

Tol-O-Matic (U.S.A.) – all power transmission products – Robert Cupitt Ltd

Tolite – blocks concrete – Tobermore Concrete Products Ltd

Tollok (Italy) – Cone clamping – Ringspann UK Ltd

Tollok (Italy) – locking brushes – Lenze UK Ltd

Tolni – thermometers, hygrometers and barometers – Russell Scientific Instruments Ltd

Tolomatic – Mercury Bearings Ltd

Tom Tom – Radio Relay

Tomahawk – masonry connectors – Simpson Strong-Tie International Inc

Tombow – UK Office Direct

Tomboy (United Kingdom) – polyester cotton workwear fabric – Carrington Career & Work Wear

Tomburn – Powder coating services – Birmingham Powder Coatings

Tomcat – High quality safety footwear range – Rock Fall UK Ltd

Tomco – Quick Connect Couplings – Advanced Fluid Technologies Ltd

Tomco – Trafalgar Tools

Tomco – Southern Valve & Fitting Co. Ltd

*Tomica World (The Far East) – toys – Tomy International

Tommylift – hydraulic taillifts – Tipmaster Ltd

Tomorrows World Travel – travel agents – Midlands Co Op Food

Tompion – 9ct gold, silver and fashion jewellery – A G Thomas Bradford Ltd

Tomtech – control equipment for horticulture – Tomtech UK Ltd

Tomy – toys – Tomy International

*Tomy Games (The Far East) – toys – Tomy International

Tonbridge Courier – newspaper – Kent Regional News & Media

Tonecall – Vodafone Retail Ltd

Tonks Book Case Strip – adjustable bookcase strip, used for shopfitting, units and library systems – J Crowther Royton Ltd

Tönshoff – European Technical Sales Ltd

*Tonsil (Germany) – bleaching earths – Sud-Chemie UK Ltd

Too Can – anti graffiti – T & R Williamson Ltd

Tool Box Direct – Accesscaff International Ltd

Tool boy – Tool Assembly / dismantling handling equipment – Royal Tool Control Ltd

Tool Connection – S J Wharton Ltd

Tool-King – hand tools – Machine Mart

Tool Location Management – Kennametal UK Ltd

Tool Store – silhouette tool board overlay system – Repro Arts Ltd

Toolbank – multi-purpose metal hand power tools – Curtis Holt Southampton Ltd

Toolbin – storage bin for tools – Adroit Modular Buildings plc

ToolBox – Accesscaff International Ltd

Tooldyne – machine tool balancing machine – Schenck Ltd

Toolfast – hand tools – Anixter Ltd

Toolite – power tools, hand tools – Toolite Co.

Toolmaster – Tool Preseeting Equiment and accesories – Royal Tool Control Ltd

Toolpro – Kennametal UK Ltd

Tools & Dies – Manufacture tools – West Midlands Foundry Co. Ltd

Toolsafe – safety equipment brand name – Kingtools

Toolstream – Measurement and workholding products – The Toolpost

Toom Raider – laracroft computer game – Square Enix Ltd

Tootella (United Kingdom) – shirting/blouse fabric – Carrington Career & Work Wear

Top Comfort Entrance Door – Hörmann (UK) Ltd

Top-Deck – Accesscaff International Ltd

Top Executive – office chairs – Top Office Equipment Ltd

Top Gear – internal gear pumps – S P X Flow Technology

Top Gourmet – Pepper & Salt Mills – Gilberts Food Equipment Ltd

Top Gourmet – Cutting Boards – Gilberts Food Equipment Ltd

Top-Grip – Iscar Tools

Top News – retail newsagents – R Taylor & Sons Ltd

Top Notch – toolholder system – Kennametal UK Ltd

Top Office – office equipment – Top Office Equipment Ltd

Top Plan – office furniture – Top Office Equipment Ltd

Top Prestige Entrance Door – Hörmann (UK) Ltd

Top Prestige Plus Entrance Door – Hörmann (UK) Ltd

Top Safe – safety observation and incident prevention programme – Kelvin Top-Set Ltd

Top Secret – stationery storage holders and book ends – Helix Trading Ltd

Top Set – incident investigation programme – Kelvin Top-Set Ltd

Top-Spot – sign frame system – Alplus

Top Table – kitchen textiles – Linden Textiles Ltd

Top Tec – Physical computer security, TV consoles/stands – Dalen Ltd

Top Tech – office furniture – Top Office Equipment Ltd

Top Tier – sugercraft training for the bakery and catering profession both for the UK and overseas market – Top Tier Sugarcraft

Top Tilth – seeded cultivator – Simba International Ltd

Top Tower – Accesscaff International Ltd

Topanol – anti oxidant – F L D Chemicals Ltd

Topanol – antioxidants – Chance & Hunt Ltd

Topas – cycloolefin copolymers – Ticona UK Ltd

TOPAS Analyzer – Biochrom Ltd

Topaz – range of mixing consoles – Digico UK Ltd

Topaz – luxury motor caravan – Auto Sleepers Ltd

Topaz – software – Topaz Computer Systems Ltd

Topaz – sailboat – Topper International

Topaz Insight – Topaz Computer Systems Ltd

*Topcon (Japan) – opto-electronic instruments – Metax Ltd

Topcover – trade emulsions – Everlac GB Ltd

Topcrete – dense aggregate concrete blocks – Tarmac Topblock Ltd

Topdeck – rubber ring anti-fatigue safety mats – Jaymart Roberts & Plastics Ltd

TopDeck – Temporary Car Park – TopDeck Parking

Topdown – Vaderstad Ltd

Topflight – workwear – The Wakefield Shirt Company Limited

Topfoam – inverted roof insulation – Alumasc Exterior Building Products

Topgro – Yara UK It Ltd

Topgrow – tree and shrub planting mix – Melcourt Industries

Tophoven – Global Parasols Ltd

Topjob S – terminal blocks, up to 30% smaller – WAGO Ltd

Toplite – aircrete building blocks – Tarmac Topblock Ltd

Toplite – hand held portable searchlight for hazardous areas – Wolf Safety Lamp Company Ltd

Toplobe – pumps – S P X Flow Technology

Toplon – building services fieldbus system – WAGO Ltd

Topmatic – Polypropylene Top Slide Zip Pouches – Grays Packaging Ltd

Topmesh – mesh security systems – Barton Storage Systems Ltd

Topmesh – sintered wire mesh – G Bopp & Co. Ltd

Toppa – carrier for multipacks of plastic bottles for milk or juice – Nampak Carton

Topper – sailboat – Topper International

Topper – business and industrial cases – Topper Cases Ltd

Topper Ovens (United Kingdom) – baked potato ovens-electric – Kedek Ltd

Toprax – bolt free shelving – Barton Storage Systems Ltd

Tops 8D – Transcend Group Ltd

tops8d – Transcend Group Ltd

*Topslider Spoiler (Italy) – spoiler roof manual or electric – Webasto Products UK Ltd

Topsoft – finish for wool tops – S T R UK Ltd

Topstar – UK Office Direct

Topstore – small parts storage – Barton Storage Systems Ltd

Topsy – Glasdon International Ltd

Topsy 2000 – Glasdon International Ltd

Topsy Jubilee – victoriana style litter container free standing – Glasdon International Ltd

Toptech – Toptech Europe Ltd

Toptower – scaffold towers, trestles, portable floodlights and fume extractors – Top Tower Ltd

*Toptrim (Belgium) – GRP roof edge trim – Alumasc Exterior Building Products

Topwing – pumps – S P X Flow Technology

Tor Anti Climb Paint – stops climbing by vandals and intruders – Tor Coatings Ltd

Tor Anti Graffiti Systems – high performance and decorative coating systems which provide surfaces enabling efficient and long term graffiti removal – Tor Coatings Ltd

Tor Specialist Floor Coating Systems – coatings which provide long term maintenance free flooring applications – Tor Coatings Ltd

Tor Specialist Hygiene Systems – high performance and tile-like coating systems providing long term hygienic joint-free surfaces – Tor Coatings Ltd

Tor Specialist Masonry Systems – masonry systems which provide long term maintenace free protection – Tor Coatings Ltd

Tor Wood Preservative Stains – stains to suit all applications – Tor Coatings Ltd

Torapron – non-selective weed killers – B P plc

Torassen Reactive – Capex Office Interiors

Torbay – woven carpets in 100% pure new wool pile – Axminster Carpets Ltd

Torch – PC-compatible commercial, industrial and educational computer systems and computer parts – Torch Computers Ltd

*Torchtite (Belgium) – torch applied roofing system – Alumasc Exterior Building Products

Torclad – fibreglass mouldings, fibreglass doors, and GRP doorway canopies – Torclad Ltd

Torclad – waterproofing coatings for roofs – Tor Coatings Ltd

Torclean – range of graffiti removal systems – Tor Coatings Ltd

Torcote – masonry coating system – Tor Coatings Ltd

Torcrete – masonry system – Tor Coatings Ltd

Torcure – floor coating systems – Tor Coatings Ltd

Tordeck – balcony refurbishment coatings – Tor Coatings Ltd

Torfirth – holding company – East Yorkshire Motor Services Ltd

Torgem – room heater – Arleigh International Ltd

Torglow – room heater – Arleigh International Ltd

Torguard – anti graffiti system – Tor Coatings Ltd

Torit Donald – Harrier Fluid Power Ltd

Torite – Harrier Fluid Power Ltd

*Tork Classic – S C A Hygiene Products UK Ltd

Tork Comfort – S C A Hygiene Products UK Ltd

*Tork Cuisine – S C A Hygiene Products UK Ltd

*Tork Exclusiv Softline – S C A Hygiene Products UK Ltd

*Tork Matic – S C A Hygiene Products UK Ltd

Torkam – Pan and Tilt Actuator System – Air Power & Hydraulics Ltd

Torko – Rotary Actuators – Air Power & Hydraulics Ltd

Torlife WB – high performance anti graffiti system – Tor Coatings Ltd

TORLON – Merseyside Metal Services

Torlon – high performance material – Davis Industrial Plastics Ltd

Tormek – Sharpening systems – The Toolpost

Tormo – precision turned parts, industrial jewels and fine springs and pressings – Tormo Ltd

Tornado – fishing tackle – Daiwa Sports Ltd

Tornado – cartridge hammers and concrete anchors – Tornado Construction Products

Tornado – diamond floor grinding system for marble and stone floors – D K Holdings Ltd

Tornado – modular powered or airling respiratory system – Scott International Ltd

Tornado – plastic whistles – J Hudson & Co Whistles Ltd

Tornado Bedpan Washers (Sweden) – thermal disinfection bedpan washers – Arjo Med AB Ltd

Tornado CNC Lathes – Colchester Lathe Co. Ltd

Tornos Deco – sliding head automatics – Rowan Precision Ltd

Toro – Harrier Fluid Power Ltd

Torpress Airspring Bellows – Interflex Hose & Bellows Ltd

Torprufe C.M.F. – high performance masonry coatings – Tor Coatings Ltd

Torprufe C.R.C. – waterproofing coatings for pitched roofs – Tor Coatings Ltd

Torprufe EMF – high performance masonry coatings – Tor Coatings Ltd

Torq-Master – soft starter – Ralspeed Ltd

Torqair – self locking nuts – B A S Components Ltd

Torqlok – self locking nuts – B A S Components Ltd

TORQUE-ARM II – Gears – Baldor UK

Torque Safe – production torque wrenches – Torque Leader

Torquebreaker – miniature torque handles – Torque Leader

Torqueleader – torque control equipment – Torque Leader

Torquemaster – production torque screwdrivers – Torque Leader

Torquemeter – dial indicating torque wrenches – Torque Leader

Torqueslipper – production torque wrenches – Torque Leader

Torquetronic – torque meters – Torquemeters

Torres – pumps – Allpumps Ltd

Torrex – fire upgrading coatings – Tor Coatings Ltd

Torrington – Mayday Seals & Bearings

Torry – mechanical smoking kiln – Afos Ltd

Torsan A Enamel – chlorinated rubber paint – Tor Coatings Ltd

Torsan P Gloss Finish – mould, damp and fungi resistant gloss – Tor Coatings Ltd

Torshield – anti-carbonation masonry coatings – Tor Coatings Ltd

Torso – spring balances – Caldwell Hardware Ltd

Torstone – masonry system – Tor Coatings Ltd

Torstrip – chemical stripping systems – Tor Coatings Ltd

Tortread – long life floor paint, non slip safety floor paint – Tor Coatings Ltd

Torus – Kurt J Lesker Company Ltd

Torusmill – Fullbrook Systems Ltd

Torvac – electron beam/furnaces – Cambridge Vacuum Engineering

Torvac Furnaces – vacuum furnaces – Cambridge Vacuum Engineering

Torvale Fisher – overhead conveyors – M C M Conveyor Systems

*Tos (Czech Republic) – lathe chucks – Castle Brook Tools Ltd

TOS – European Technical Sales Ltd

*Tos Varnsdorf (Czech Republic) – Horizontal Borders – C Dugard Ltd Machine Tools

*Tos Varnsdrof (Czech Republic) – horizontal borers – C Dugard Ltd Machine Tools

Toshiba – Lamphouse Ltd

Toshiba – transistors – Bowers Ltd

Toshiba – C J Plant Ltd

Toshiba – semiconductors & optoelectronics – Anglia

Toshiba – TV – Sertronics Ltd

Toshiba – UK Office Direct

Toshiba – CBM Logix

Toshiba – Cyclops Electronics Ltd

Toshiba – hardware/software – Bearwood Engineering Supplies

Toshiba – Therma Group

Toshiba Air Conditioning – Apex Commercial Refrigeration & Aircon

Toshiba Machine – T M Robotics (Europe) Ltd

Toshiba Strata DK Range – tele-communication systems – Nine Shipton

Toshiba tec – Allcode UK Ltd

Toshulin – T W Ward CNC Machinery Ltd

Tot – washing-up liquid – Deb R & D Ltd

Total Access – Accesscaff International Ltd

Total Dynamic Automation – software feature (logic series) – A M S Neve Ltd

Total Film – magazine – Future Publishing Ltd

Total Framework – business solution software – Cincom Systems UK Ltd

Total Guitar – magazine – Future Publishing Ltd

Total Recall – computer system – Red Lion 49 Ltd

Total Recruitment Solutions – S Com Group Ltd

Total Refrigeration – commercial refrigeration contractors – Total Refrigeration Ltd

Total Solutions Total Eclipse – The eclipse solutions based approach to window shading problems – Eclipse Blind Systems

Totalkare Prolift – mobile vehicle lifts for truck, rail & PSV sectors – Somers Totalkare Ltd

TOTALLIFTER – Chaintec Ltd

TotalSealCare – Eagleburgmann Industries UK Llp

TotalStone – Not all walls are made of stone – Total wall

TotalWall – Not all walls are made of stone – Total wall

Totavit – capsules – Reckitt Benckiser plc

Tote Heater – L M K Thermosafe

Totem – Taps, Dies, Dienuts – www.tap-die.com

Totem Glue Stick – Hainenko Ltd

Totem Towers – Accesscaff International Ltd

Totnoll Promotions – promotional merchandise – Sonata Ltd

Totton Pumps – totton magnetically coupled, plastic and centrifugal pumps – Xylem

Toucan Platforms – Accesscaff International Ltd

Touch and Reveal – thermochromic ink products – B & H Colour Change Ltd

Touch Dry – hot melt ink coders – Markem-Imaje Ltd

Touch 'N Turn Book – Vtech Electronics UK plc

Touchbase – The Woolwich

*Touchstone Movies (U.S.A.) – films – The Disney Store Ltd

Tough Store – Cabinets – Jo Bird & Co. Ltd

Tough Tags – labels – Radleys

Toughmet – Materion Brush Ltd

Toughseal – waterproof membrane – R I W Ltd

Tourer Lite – nebuliser compressors for domestic use (portable for 12V & mains) – A F P Medical Ltd

Tournament – fishing tackle – Daiwa Sports Ltd

Tow A Van – box trailer – Indespension Ltd

Tow-a-Van – a range of van/box trailers from 2.8 to 6.6m3 capacity – Indespension Ltd

Tow-bilt – wheeled towable offices and toilets – Boyton B R J System Buildings Ltd

Tow-it – trailer hire company operating through all Indespension stores – Indespension Ltd

*Towe Lamps – Flickers Ltd

Tower – Grasslin UK Ltd

Tower – pans and pressure cookers – Russell Hobbs Ltd

Tower Domestic – domestic heating controls – T F C Group

Tower Flue – terminal guards – T F C Group

Tower Lift – heavy lift temporary support system – Fagioli Ltd

Tower Motorised – valves – T F C Group

Tower Repairs & Spares – Accesscaff International Ltd

Tower Water – water treatment products – T F C Group

Toweracks – tubular post pallets for racking pallets – Palletower GB Ltd

Towerchron – time switches and programmers – T F C Group

Towerstat – Grasslin UK Ltd

Towmotor – Harrier Fluid Power Ltd

Town & Country Homebuilders – The Woolwich

Town & Country Property Services (East Anglia) – The Woolwich

Town & County – The Woolwich

Town & County Homecare – The Woolwich

Townscape – street furniture and paving – Townscape Products Ltd

Townsend – cycle – Falcon Cycles Ltd

Townson & Mercer – Record Electrical Associates

Towsweep – towed sweeper – Danline International Ltd

Towveyer – mechanical handling systems – Jervis B Webb Co. Ltd

Tox – aerosol insect killer – Keen World Marketing Ltd

Tox-Pressotechnik – European Technical Sales Ltd

toxCO+ – carbon monoxide breath monitor for diagnosis of carbon monoxide poisoning – Bedfont Scientific Ltd

Toyburn – toy flammability tester – James H Heal & Co. Ltd

Toye Kenning & Spencer (United Kingdom) – manufacturers of badges, medals, civic & society regalia, enamel giftware, trophies & long service awards. – Toye Kenning Spencer Stadden

*Toyo Jidoki (Japan) – stand up retortable pouch packaging machinery – Selo UK Ltd

*Toyo Machine Manufacturing Co (Japan) – sachet & stick packaging machinery – Selo UK Ltd

Toyota – Premier Lift Trucks Ltd

Toyota – Harrier Fluid Power Ltd

TOYOTA – Chaintec Ltd

Toyota – Stacatruc

Toyota – L M C Hadrian Ltd

Toyota – T V H UK Ltd

Toyota – Ashley Competition Exhausts Ltd

toyota industrial equipment, – forklifts and other material handling – F T M Materials Handling Ltd

Toys 2 Play – pocket money toys – P M S International Group plc

*Tozer Seeds – Vegetable seeds for professional growers – Tozer Seeds Ltd

TP POWER SERVICES – T P Power Services Ltd

TP Sound Services – prof conference & theatre sound systems – Blitz Communications Ltd

TPC – thermal fluid heaters – Babcock Wanson UK Ltd

TPC Pneumatics – Southern Valve & Fitting Co. Ltd

Traccess – curtain sider bodywork – Lawrence David Ltd

Traceable calibration services – Stream Measurement Ltd

Tracescan – Thermo Electrical

Tracetek – leak detecting and locating systems – Tyco Electronics UK Ltd

TraceTek – Stabilag E S H Ltd

Track-Marshall – tractors – T M S Gainsborough Ltd

Trackalign – portable wheel alignment gauge – Tecalemit Garage Equipment Co. Ltd

Trackelast – Resilient Track Support materials – Tiflex Ltd

Tracker – name and address data enhancement software – Acxiom Ltd

Tracker – open frame steel surveyors tape – Fisco Tools Ltd

Tracker – mens and boys clothing – Blacks Leisure Group plc

Tracker – Data Track Technology plc

Tracker 2 – high speed pattern recognition – Vysionics

Tracker UK – vehicle tracking devices – Fast Fit Nationwide Ltd

Tracker Vehicle Recovery Systems – Parkway Plant Sales Ltd

Tracklube – anti corrosive and lubrication for railway ancillary equipment – Darcy Products Ltd

*Tracknet 2000 (United Kingdom) – laundry conveyor control system – Micross Electronics Ltd

*Tracknet Pro (United Kingdom) – laundry production manament systems – Micross Electronics Ltd

Trackranger – tracked primary crushing plant – Parker Plant Ltd

Trackster – lightweight training trouser for running, biking and hiking – Ronhill Sports

Tracktex – indoor athletics track surface – Verde Sports Cricket Ltd

Trackwall – acoustic room divider – I A C Company Ltd

Tracoinsa – European Technical Sales Ltd

Tract Seating – Capex Office Interiors

Tractel – Hawk Lifting

Tractel – Dale Lifting and Handling Equipment Specialists

Tractive Power – Push or pull loads from a few kg to 50,000kg – Tractive Power Ltd

*Tractor Panels – A P B Trading Ltd

Tractran – lubricant – B P plc

TRADA – research consultancy and testing for timber and construction industries – Trada Technology

Trade 1st – 1st Choice for Professionals – Trade 1st Ltd

Trade Kitchen Appliances – Trade division supplying builders, construction companies and independent joiners – Contract Kitchens Ltd

Trade Mark Consultants – Trade Mark Attorneys – Trademark Consultants

Trade Mark Intelligence – Trade Mark searching and watching service – Trademark Consultants

Trade Plate Holder – number plates – Bisbell Magnetic Products Ltd

Trade Pulpit Steps – Accesscaff International Ltd

Trade Towers – Accesscaff International Ltd

Trademarc – abrasives – Marcrist International Ltd

Trademark Transfers – Transfers for ownership marking and simple corporate imaging – J & A International Ltd

Trademaster Towers – Accesscaff International Ltd

Trader (United Kingdom) – manual handling equipment – Effortec Ltd

Trader – sack trucks and trolleys – Redhill Manufacturing

Tradesman Steps & Ladders – Accesscaff International Ltd

Tradesmig – light duty MIG welding equipment – Murex Welding Products Ltd

Tradesource – printers of direct mail stationery – Mail Solutions Ltd

Tradestig – light duty TIG equipment – Murex Welding Products Ltd

Tradewinds Parasol – Global Parasols Ltd

Tradewise – market research within industry – Childwise

Tradex Instruments – gears, splines, serrations, C.N.C., C.A.M. auto, repetition turning, and cylindrical grinding – Tradex Instruments Ltd

Tradical – lime for building – Lhoist UK

Trading Place – Ashtenne Ltd

Traditional – taps and mixers and V.C. accesories – Ideal Standard Ltd

Traditional Scaffolding – Accesscaff International Ltd

Traditional Scrumpy – H Weston & Sons Ltd

Tradlym – lime putty, mortars, renders, washes and pigments and hydraulic lime (France) – Chelmix Concrete Ltd

Tradpan (United Kingdom) – access panels – Panelcraft Access Panels

Trafag – European Technical Sales Ltd

Trafag Pressure Switches – European Technical Sales Ltd

Trafag Pressure Transmitters – European Technical Sales Ltd

Trafag Temperature Transmitter – European Technical Sales Ltd

Trafag Thermostats – European Technical Sales Ltd

Trafalgar Bearing Co. – Spheric Trafalgar Ltd

Traffaid – clay conditioner – Borregaard UK

Traffic Flow Plate – one way vehicle control – Frontier Pitts Ltd

Traffic Management – Accesscaff International Ltd

Traffic Range – combined scrubber/dryers (mains and battery type) – Truvox International Ltd

Traffic Soil Remover – vehicle soil remover – Evans Vanodine International plc

Traffic Stopper – Aremco Products

Traffic Zone – loop pile carpet – Warlord Contract Carpets Ltd

Traffideck – British Vita plc

Traffideck – polyurethane systems for waterproofing and anti-skid surfacing – Dow Hyperlast

Traffigrip – British Vita plc

Traffolyte – Able Engraving & Design

TrafiBEACON – emergency beacon for use on vehicle – Doormen

Traficop – traffic calming products – Rediweld Rubber & Plastics Ltd

TrafiLAMP E – hazard warning road lamp – Doormen

TrafiLITE – warning road lamp – Doormen

Trail – cable management software – I T T Ltd

Trail – magazine – Emap Ltd

Trailer Barrow – versatile load movers and wheelbarrows – Elsan Ltd

Trailer-Mount Lifts – Accesscaff International Ltd

Traiload – traffic managment solutions – King Trailers Ltd

Traiload – King Vehicle Engineering Ltd

*Traiteur – Wilson Sloane Street Ltd

Trak Crusher – Digbits Ltd

Trak Wheel – wheels for conveyor curves – Atlantic Rubber Company Ltd

Trakatak – cycles – Professional Cycle Marketing

Trallnor – Maingate Ltd

*Tram (U.S.A.) – microphone – Audio Ltd

Tramivex – British Vita plc

*Tramontina (Brazil) – kitchen knives – Zodiac Stainless Products Co. Ltd

Tramspread – range of slurry handling equipment – Master Farm Services GB Ltd

Trandos – vehicle scheduling and routing system – Lorien Resourcing Ltd

Trane – Therma Group

*Trangia (Sweden) – cooking stoves – Karrimor Ltd

Tranicase – aluminium sign supplies – Universal Components

Tranilamp – E Preston Electrical Ltd

Tranquilitie – James Walker Textiles Ltd

Trans-Marque – translucent paper – G F Smith

TRANS TECHNOLOGY (GB) LTD – Hydraulic & Offshore Supplies Ltd

Transarc – industrial mma equipment – Murex Welding Products Ltd

Transax – providers of information services to all industries. – Equifax plc

Transbus PT – B P plc

Transcable – cable test vans – Baur Test Equipment Ltd

Transcal – industrial oils – B P plc

Transcend – Largest Transcend Flash Distributor in UK – Secure Telecom UK Ltd

Transclean – B P plc

Transclear – G F Smith

Transcoat – micro porous wood stain – Tor Coatings Ltd

Transcote – P.U. coach finish – Spencer Coatings Ltd

Transcut – industrial lubricants – B P plc

TRANSDEV – Wolds Engineering Services Ltd

Transducer – Encoders UK

*Transducer Systems – Procon Engineering Ltd

*Transducers Data Sense – weighing equipment – Procon Engineering Ltd

*Transducers Data Weigh – weighing equipment – Procon Engineering Ltd

*Transducers (UK) – Procon Engineering Ltd

Transend – Tank contents gauge switch – Bayham Ltd

*TransEra HT Basic (U.S.A.) – computer software chip – Lyons Instruments

Transfastener (United Kingdom) – mobile anchorage device (horizontal systems) – Latchways plc

Transfeed – rubber faced feed belts – Chiorino UK Ltd

Transfeed – stretchless conveyor belts – Chiorino UK Ltd

Transfer Oil – gomax flexible hose, fittings and vibration eliminators – Thermofrost Cryo plc

Transfluid – all transmission systems – M I T Ltd

Transfluid - all transmission systemsTwin disc - transmission systemArneson - propulsion systemMIT - Marine Industrial Transmissions Quincy - Air Compressors – M I T Ltd

Transformation – ladies clothing and lingerie – Transformation

Transformers – safety isolating for use with all Hilti machines and other equipment – Hilti GB Ltd

Transheat – continuous furnaces for the electronics industry – B T U Europe Ltd

Transhield – distribution services – Boc Gases Ltd

Transilon – light to medium duty conveyor belting – Forbo Siegling

Transit Specialist Dealer – Invicta Paints

Transit Wrap – protective cover for machines while in transit – C P L Felthams

*Transition Cow – E D F Man

Translations – Translation into and from any language of the world. – Global Translators UK Ltd

Translet – colostomy bags – Teleflex Medical

Translift – Stacatruc

Translink – aluminium silicates – Lawrence Industries Ltd

Transloc – gazetteer for determining grid references from addresses – Lorien Resourcing Ltd

Transmation – portable pressure calibration – Able Instruments & Controls Ltd

TRANSMET – dew-point transmitter – Michell Instruments Ltd

Transmig – industrial mig equipment – Murex Welding Products Ltd

Transmix – asphalt plant – Parker Plant Ltd

*Transnorm System (Germany) – TS1500 belt curve conveyor (patented) and all conveyor modules for unit handling – Smart Stabilizer Systems

*Transonic (U.S.A.) – transit time flowmeters – Linton & Co Engineering Ltd

Transpak (Austria) – flat pack buildings – Extra Space Industries

Transpalite – acrylic products – Stanley Plastics Ltd

Transparent building – web enabled technology in plc control – Schneider

Transparent factory – web enabled technology in plc control – Schneider

Transparent infrastructure – web enabled technology in plc control – Schneider

Transparent Ready – web enabled technology across all automation product platforms & industries – Schneider

Transpath – computerised road network of Great Britain – Lorien Resourcing Ltd

Transpeed – one pack PU transport finish, primer & undercoats – T & R Williamson Ltd

Transpeed – two pack acrylic – T & R Williamson Ltd

Transpillars – Insulated stand off pillars – Schurter Ltd

Transplan – depot location package – Lorien Resourcing Ltd

Transplastix – roof glazing – Yule Catto & Co plc

Transputer – computers – S T Micro Electronics Ltd

Transradio – coaxial cable RF and fibre optics connectors and devices – Radiall Ltd

Transtec – analgesic – Napp Pharmaceutical Group Ltd

Transtech Sys Inc – Non Nuclear Density Meters – J R Technical Services UK Ltd

Transthane – conveyor belting – Polyurethane Products Ltd

Transtig – industrial tig equipment – Murex Welding Products Ltd

Transtrip – routing software – Lorien Resourcing Ltd

Transuit – safety equipment – Beaufort Air Sea Equipment Ltd

Transultex – lubricants – Chevron

Transwheel – multi-directional wheels – Atlantic Rubber Company Ltd

Transym OCR (TOCR) – ocr software – Transym Computer Services Limited

Tranter – Gasketed Plate Heat Exchangers – J B J Techniques Ltd

Trap – Mass Consultants Ltd

Trappit – insect pest traps and house plant cart products – Agrisense B C S Ltd

Traratchet – heavy duty ratchet spanners – F & R Belbin Ltd

Traseolide – perfume speciality – Quest International UK Ltd

Trasmital Bonfiglioli – planetary gear boxes and hydraulic motors – Bonfiglioli UK Ltd

Traspark – Double Parking Systems

Tratto – single lever mixer taps – Ideal Standard Ltd

Trav-O-Lator – moving cover escalator – Otis Ltd

Travel Bug – luggage and accessories – P M S International Group plc

Travel Note – notebook computer – Texas Instruments Ltd
Travel Rugs – J Bradbury & Co. Ltd
Travel Well Range – personnel water purifiers – Pre Mac International Ltd
Travelcaps – herbal product to relieve the symptoms of travel sickness – Perrigo UK
Traveller Products – for luggage – K B Import & Export Ltd
Travelmate – notebook computer – Texas Instruments Ltd
Travers Smith Braithwaite – solicitors – Travers Smith Ltd
Travis perkins – builders mechants – Keyline Builders Merchants
Travol – ring traveller lubricant – Benjamin R Vickers & Sons Ltd
Travolene – ring traveller lubricant – Benjamin R Vickers & Sons Ltd
TRAX – Trax
Trax Active – sports and leisurewear – Rococo Style Ltd
Tray-Pak – reusable tray container system. – D S Smith Correx
Tray Shifters – seed tray carriers – Hamster Baskets
Treadlock – interlock rubber ring anti-fatigue/anti-slip matting – Jaymart Roberts & Plastics Ltd
Treadmaster – Twinmar Ltd
Treadmaster – specialised halogen free safety flooring for transport industry and public buildings – Tiflex Ltd
Treadmaster Marine – anti-slip yacht decking – Tiflex Ltd
TREADSAFE (United Kingdom) – abrasive-coated, stainless-steel, anti-slip treads, nosings, decking, cleats and ladder-rung covers designed to withstand high volume pedestrian traffic and extremes of temperature – Porcher Abrasive Coatings Ltd
Treasure Chest – storage boxes – Helix Trading Ltd
Treblegem – outerwear – Dineshco Textiles Ltd
Tree Logo – Portman Building Society
Tree Pit – Althon Ltd
Tree Tops – Christmas lights – K B Import & Export Ltd
Treesaver – envelopes – Eagle Envelopes Ltd
Treespat – weed prevention matting – Acorn Planting Products Ltd
Treetop – disinfectant – Deb R & D Ltd
Treker – fork lift trucks – Sidetracker Engineering Ltd
Trekker – monobloc and compact batteries – Chloride Motive Power C M P Batteries Ltd
Trelawny Surface Preparation Technology – needle scalers, long reach scalers, scaling hammers, long reach scabblers, large area de-scalers and concrete scabblers, vibration reduced compactors – Trelawny S P T Ltd
Trelleborg – Hose – Holmes Hose Ltd
Trelleborg Teguflex – Interflex Hose & Bellows Ltd
Trellex – wear resistant rubber products, dust protection systems, conveyor belting & accessories – Metso Minerals UK Ltd
TrellExtreme – anti-vibration mountings for off highway – Trelleborg Industrial A V S Ltd
Trellidor – Keytrak Lock & Safe Company
Tremain Textiles – textiles – Maurice Phillips
Tremco 440 Tape – glazing tape for timber windows & doors – Tremco Illbruck Ltd
Tremco 900 – tape sealant system for sloped glazing – Tremco Illbruck Ltd
Tremco Aluminiser – roof coating reflective – Tremco Illbruck Ltd
Tremco Burmastic – cold applied roof felt adhesive – Tremco Illbruck Ltd
Tremco Dymeric – building sealant – Tremco Illbruck Ltd
Tremco Fibremat – roof repair – Tremco Illbruck Ltd
Tremco Mono – building sealant – Tremco Illbruck Ltd
Tremco Penefelt – roof revitaling compound – Tremco Illbruck Ltd
Tremco Proglaze – silicone building sealant – Tremco Illbruck Ltd
Tremco Proshim – pre-shimmed glazing tape – Tremco Illbruck Ltd
Tremco Small Joint Sealant – building sealant for narrow joints – Tremco Illbruck Ltd
Tremco SST 800 – high performance glazing tape – Tremco Illbruck Ltd
Tremco Swiggle Strip – insulating glass sealant system – Tremco Illbruck Ltd
Tremco Tremcoveral – roof repair – Tremco Illbruck Ltd
Tremco Tremfil – building sealant – Tremco Illbruck Ltd
Tremco Tremflex – polyurethane sealant – Tremco Illbruck Ltd
Tremco Tremlok – tape security glazing – Tremco Illbruck Ltd
Tremco Weathermat – roof coating – Tremco Illbruck Ltd
Tremfoam – expanding polyurethane foam – Tremco Illbruck Ltd
Tremgrip – multi-purpose building adhesive – Tremco Illbruck Ltd
Tremroof 118 – asbestos cement roof treatment – Tremco Illbruck Ltd
Tremsil – silicone glazing sealant – Tremco Illbruck Ltd
Trench (Austria) – Mathew C Blythe & Son Ltd
Trench Plate – Fieldway Supplies Ltd
Trenchex – trenching machines – Trenchex Garden Machinery
Trend – access control systems – Trend Control Systems Ltd
Trend – cutting tools – Trend Machinery & Cutting Tools Ltd
Trend – Gem Tool Hire & Sales Ltd
Trend – S J Wharton Ltd
Trend – Personal respirators, router cutters – The Toolpost
Trend – cutters – Campbell Miller Tools Ltd
Trend – Central C N C Machinery Ltd
Trend Router Cutters – D D Hire
Trend to Beauty – Fernan Trading Ltd
Trendline – UK Office Direct
Trendsetter – quilts – Trendsetter Home Furnishings Ltd
Trenomat – big shed doors – Envirohold Ltd
Trent – precast concrete engineering products – Trent Concrete Ltd
Trent – aero engines – Rolls-Royce plc
Trent Cladding – architectural cladding – Trent Concrete Ltd
Trent-Midland Software Enterprise – Wide HR management solution which combines ease of use with high level functionality – Midland HR
Trent T6 – multi storey framed buildings – Trent Concrete Ltd
Trentino Systems – Printer Interfaces and Controllers – M-Tech Printers
Trenton Box Co. – printed cardboard cartons – Trenton Box Co. Ltd
Trentside Recycling Ltd – cardboard and paper – D S Smith Recycling PLC
Trespa – Fieldway Supplies Ltd
***Trespa (Netherlands)** – acid resistant solid laminate – Rex Bousfield Ltd
Trespass – skiwear and sportswear – Jacobs & Turner Ltd
Trestles – Accesscaff International Ltd
Treston – Desks – Bucon Ltd
Tretocrete – latex based additive for cementitious mixes – Tremco Illbruck Ltd
Tretodek – flexible car deck waterproofing – Tremco Illbruck Ltd
Tretoflex – flexible waterproofing – Tremco Illbruck Ltd
Tretolastex – bitumen/rubber solution – Tremco Illbruck Ltd
Tretoplast – clean zone coating sterile areas – Tremco Illbruck Ltd
Tretoshield – concrete repair system protection – Tremco Illbruck Ltd
Trevi Showers – Ideal Standard Ltd
Trevitest – system for testing safety and relief valves on-line and off-line – Furmanite International Ltd
Trexus – UK Office Direct
Tri A – Airless air assist systems – Exitflex UK Ltd
Tri-Fold – Gesipa Blind Riveting Systems Ltd
Tri Force – fishing tackle – Daiwa Sports Ltd
Tri-Guard – corner protectors - polycarbonate – Tektura plc
Tri-Lite – 12v fluorescent lighting – Lab Craft Ltd
Tri-Lok – steel tape rules – Fisco Tools Ltd
Tri-Lok – metal joining system – B T M UK Automation Products
Tri-matic – steel tape rules – Fisco Tools Ltd
Tri-Point – darts and shafts – Unicorn Products Ltd
Tri-Shell – sandwich foam cistern – Thomas Dudley Ltd
Tri-Star – Contacts – Dax International Ltd
Tri-Star – Connectors – Dax International Ltd
Tri-Sure – drum closures – Greif UK Ltd
Tri-Tech – liquid filling machines – Riggs Autopack Ltd
Tri-Zone – spring unit with 12>1/2 gauge springs across centre section to provide extra support – Airsprung Furniture Group plc
TRIA – Letraset Ltd
Tria Marker – graphic arts supplies – Letraset Ltd
Triac – cnc bench milling machine – Denford Ltd
Triac-fanuc – cnc milling machine – Denford Ltd
TRIAD – connectors – Anglia
Triad Group plc – data base management – Triad Group plc
Triad Hydraulic Oils – Morris Lubricants
Triag (Switzerland) – workholding systems – Rem Systems Ltd
Triangle – equipment & spares – Bearwood Engineering Supplies
Triangle Sports – scarves – Foster Enterprises
Triangles – Portman Building Society
Tribaloy – intermetallic materials – Deloro Stellite Ltd
TribeACE – dust monitoring equipment – Pcme
Triboguard – Harrier Fluid Power Ltd
Tribolite (United Kingdom) – ignition system – Hamworthy Combustion Engineering Ltd
Tribore – boring tools – Microbore Tooling Systems
Tribos – Power shrinking tool holders – Schunk Intec Ltd
Tribune – shower enclosure – Armitage Shanks Ltd
Tricast – cast resin transformer range – Schneider
Tricentric – isolation butterfly valves – Weir Valves & Controls
Tricho Tech – drug analysis/hair analysis – Tricho-Tech
Triclean – multi purpose floor maintainer – Unico Ltd
Tricompact – Grundfos Pumps Ltd
Tricool – process cooling equipment including air and water cooled chillers, cooling towers and temperature controllers – Tricool Thermal
Tricycles – special needs – Pashley Cycles Ltd
Tricycles – folding – Pashley Cycles Ltd
Tricycles – electrically assisted – Pashley Cycles Ltd
Tricycles – childrens – Pashley Cycles Ltd
Tridair – Specialty Fasteners & Components Ltd
Tridecene-2-Nitrile – perfume speciality – Quest International UK Ltd
Tridek – Harrier Fluid Power Ltd
Trident – dart holders – Unicorn Products Ltd
Trident (United Kingdom) – polyester cotton workwear fabric – Carrington Career & Work Wear
Trident – Solmedia Laboratory Supplies
Trident – luxury motor caravan – Auto Sleepers Ltd
Trident – micromotors-geasheads-controllers-encoders – Trident Engineering Ltd
Trident – multipin connector system – I T T Ltd
Trident – steel strip – J B & S Lees
Trident Blinds – energy saver blinds and awnings, specialising in energy saver conservatory blinds – Trident Blinds Ltd
Trident Broadcord – fibre bonded carpet/tile – Warlord Contract Carpets Ltd
***Trident Feeds** – Curtis & Co Oundle Ltd
Trident-Neptune – marine de-scaling equipment – Trelawny S P T Ltd
Tridentum,Dolomiten,Itaglia,Salvador,Mondini,Victo – The Knife Sharpening Company
Tridex – 3 ply sandwich rubber lining – Dexine Rubber Co. Ltd
Tridex – resistive exercise band and Digiband exercise bands – Four D Rubber Co. Ltd
Tridon – Zero Clips Ltd
TRIDON – Pinstructure Ltd
Triefus – diamond blades – Robert Craig & Sons Ltd
Trifast P.L.C. – holding company – Trifast
Trifid – B P plc
Trifid – Alpha Electronics Southern Ltd
***Triflex (Germany)** – Borgers Ltd
Triflex – Igus (UK) Ltd
Triflo – dispenser – Appor Ltd
Triflow – domestic water filter systems – Avilion
Trifusion – glass coating system – Permastore Ltd
TRIGGERFISH – mens and womens indoor loungewear shoes – Starchild Shoes
Trigon – white perrlised visous germicidal hand soap – Evans Vanodine International plc
Trigon – Komet Ltd
Trigonal – UV catalyst for polyester resins – Akzo Nobel Chemicals Holdings Ltd
Trigonfm – catering – Castle View International Holdings Limited
Trigonox – liquid organic peroxides – Akzo Nobel Chemicals Holdings Ltd
Trihal – cast resin transformer range – Schneider
Triklamp – bush clamp – Hellermann Tyton
Trikon (United Kingdom) – Aviza Technology UK Ltd
Trilite – aluminium structural system – Optikinetics Ltd
Trilite, truss, opti, trussing – The Trilite Zone
Trim – UK Office Direct
Trim – air cooled package chiller units – Tricool Thermal
Trim – cutting fluids & coolants – Master Chemical Europe Ltd
Trim Boost – Weight management – Supplements For Pets Ltd
Trimapanel – Chorus Panel & Profiles
Trimat – brake linings for industry – Trimat Ltd
Trimawall – Chorus Panel & Profiles
Trimax – reciprocating pumps – Armstrong Controls Ltd
Trimaz Transfers – Transfers for leisure wear and waterproof garments – J & A International Ltd
***Trimediazine** – Horses – Vetoquinol Ltd
***Trimediazine B.M.P.** – Pigs, chickens and turkeys – Vetoquinol Ltd
Trimesh – space frame system – Clip Display
Trimite (Scotland) – paints – Trimite Scotland Ltd
***Trimmaster (U.S.A.)** – trim tabs and hatch lifters – Lancing Marine
Trimod Besta – liquid level switches – Able Instruments & Controls Ltd
Trimseal – upvc and plastic building profile stockist – Trimseal Ltd
Trimvent – slot & glaze ventilators for timber, UPVC & aluminium windows and doors – Titon Hardware Ltd
Trinadol – knitting machine oil – Benjamin R Vickers & Sons Ltd
Trinitron – TV – Sony Head Office
Trinity – aircraft control systems – B B A Aviation plc
Trinivol – scourable machine lubricant – Benjamin R Vickers & Sons Ltd
Trinkets – dog food – Gilbertson & Page Ltd
Trinoram – triamines – Atosina UK Ltd
Trio – ride on golf buggy – Patterson Products Ltd

Trio – industrial controller (Floorcare) – P G Drive Technology

Trio – fishing tackle – Daiwa Sports Ltd

Trio – kitchen furniture – Moores Furniture Group

Triogen (United Kingdom) – ultra violet systems and ozone generators for water purification – Triogen Ltd

Triohmic – electrically conductive rubber bench and floor mats – Vitec

Trion – electrostatic air cleaners – Thermofrost Cryo plc

Trionic – Solmedia Laboratory Supplies

Trionic – protective glove for clean rooms – Mapa Spontex

TRIP DOGS & RAILS – Francis and Francis Ltd

Trip-L-Grip – timber connectors – Teco Ltd

Trip-Trap – Procter Machinery Guarding Ltd

Tripak – refuse compactors – Hardall International Ltd

Triple A – anodised aluminium alloy clothes lockers and changing and toilet cubicles – Link Lockers

Triple A International – interim management – Triple A International

Triple A Plus – Rope and sling protection sleeve – Marathon Belting Ltd

Triple Crown – rugby footballs – Gray Nicolls

*Triple Crown (Spain) – triple coated silk papers and boards (also gloss & ivory) – Davies Harvey & Murrell

Triple Gold – Derbyshire Building Society

Triple King – point of sale equipment – Thomas Hopkinson & Son Ltd

Triple Life – long life wire fencing – Arce Lormittal

Triple Plus + – Full Function/Purge handheld multi monitor – Crowcon Detection Instrument Ltd

Triple-Plus – European Lamp Group

TripleLock – security coupling heads 'you can't forget to triplelock it' – Indespension Ltd

Triplex – laminated vehicle glass – Pilkington Agr UK Ltd

Tripod Bored Piles – Simplex Westpile Limited

Tripoint – pressure and temperature switches – Asco Numatics

TRIRO – Plenty Mirrlees Pumps

Triseal – Pharmaceutical plate seoler – Porvair plc

Trisert – self tapping high performance insert for engineering plastic (brass) – Tappex Thread Inserts Ltd

Trisert-3 – self-tapping high performance insert for metal alloys & composites (steel, 303 & 316 stainless steel) – Tappex Thread Inserts Ltd

Triskell – roofing contractors – Chemplas Ltd

Trisomet – Chorus Panel & Profiles

Trisport – plastic golf cleat fixing systems – Trisport Ltd

Tristar – anti-vandal taps and mixer showers – Ideal Standard Ltd

Tristar GT – matt trichromatic ink for paper and board – Fujifilm Sericol Ltd

Tristile – tripod turnstile – Gunnebo Entrance Control Ltd

Tritainer – small capacity tanks – Franklin Hodge Industries Ltd

Tritap – trilobular screws – Fastbolt Distributors UK Ltd

Tritech – computer software – Tritech Computer Services Ltd

TriTech (U.S.A.) – dual technology detector – Bosch Security Systems

Triticale – Senova Ltd

Triton – screwdrivers – Carl Kammerling International Ltd

*Triton – Ice Cool Services Ltd

Triton (Italy) – British & Continental Traders Ltd

Triton – pumps – Albany Standard Pumps

Triton – electric, mixer and power showers – Triton Showers

Triton – cable gland – C M P UK Ltd

Triton – Gem Tool Hire & Sales Ltd

Triumph – vintage cars – British Motor Heritage Ltd

Triumph – L M C Hadrian Ltd

Triumph – wall mounted and ceiling mobile air cleaner – Trion The Division Of Ruskin Air Management Ltd

Triumph – Storage – Bucon Ltd

Triumph – bicycles – Raleigh UK Ltd

Triumph Business systems – Metal filing Cabinets – Triumph Furniture

Triventek – Hotchkiss Ltd

Trix – clothing for the young at heart – Fashion Spinners

Trixene – polyurethane pre polymers – Baxenden Chemicals Ltd

Trixie Lift (United Kingdom) – powered general purpose hoist ideal for nursing homes and domestic use – Arjo Med AB Ltd

Trixol – loom oil – Benjamin R Vickers & Sons Ltd

Trizyme – composite mash enzyme – Murphy & Son

Troax – S K Interiors Ltd

*Troax UK (Sweden) – industrial wall mesh – Troax UK Ltd

Trockenperlen – absorbents for gas drying – Lawrence Industries Ltd

Trodat – UK Office Direct

Troikal – B P plc

Troikene – B P plc

Trojan – Batteries – Charger Bay Solutions

Trojan – wheel-free jacking beams/pit jacks – Tecalemit Garage Equipment Co. Ltd

Trojan – H P P UK Ltd

Trojan – underground hydraulic gate actuator – Frontier Pitts Ltd

Trojan Ladders – Accesscaff International Ltd

Trojan XIV – beryllium-free high strength copper alloy – Columbia Metals Ltd

Trokene – B P plc

Trokyd – B P plc

Trokyl – B P plc

Trolex – sensors for pressure-flow, gas level temperature and vibration and control systems – Trolex Ltd

Trolley (United Kingdom) – mobile sensory resource – Mike Ayres Design Ltd

Trolley Duct – mobile power distribution system – Astra Engineering Products Ltd

Trolley Guidance Rails – The Boston Boss, The Barricade, UBS Rail – Boston Retail Products

*Trolley Lift – goods lift 250kg-300kg – Stannah Microlifts Ltd

Trolleymaster – guarded mobile power collector track – Astra Engineering Products Ltd

Trollop – fishing tackle – Drennan International Ltd

Tron – precision engineers – Tron

Troon – stainless steel countertop basin – Armitage Shanks Ltd

Trooper – luxury motor caravan – Auto Sleepers Ltd

Trophies for Tities – Trophies – Goodwill Trophy Company Ltd

Trophy – luxury motor caravan – Auto Sleepers Ltd

Trophy Range – floor polishers and scrubbing machines – Truvox International Ltd

Tropical medicine microscope – specially developed overseas microscope – Gillett & Sibert Ltd

Tropicoir – wall to wall matting – Bruce Starke & Co. Ltd

Trout Fisherman – magazine – Emap Ltd

Trout & Salmon – magazine – Emap Ltd

Trowel – machine sewing threads – William Gee Ltd

Trowel Trades – builders and plasterers – Morris & Spottiswood Ltd

Trowelette – machine sewing threads – William Gee Ltd

Trowelite – mortar plasticiser – Don Construction Products Ltd

Troy (United Kingdom) – cotton rich workwear fabric – Carrington Career & Work Wear

Troy – P C F Secure Document Systems Ltd

Troyke – Kone Cranes Machine Tool Services

TRP Perar – ball valves – Eaton Valve Products Limited

Tru-Lift – core self climbing formwork system – RMD Kwikform Limited

Tru-Lok – tape rules – L S Starrett Co. Ltd

*Tru-Test (New Zealand) – electronic livestock weighers – Drivall Ltd

Trubeam – decorative timber beams – Winther Browne & Company Ltd

Trubor – Drills Reamers Cutters – www.tap-die.com

Trubor – twist drills, reamers and milling cutters – Metalbor Ltd

Trucard – coated paper & board – Howard Smith Paper Ltd

Trucast – precision investment castings – Trucast Ltd

Trucker – Melitzer Safety Equipment

Truckline – Brittany Ferries

Trucklog – data loggers for electric trucks – Davis Derby Ltd

Truckmaster – diesel engine oil – Millers Oils Ltd

Truckmaster – commercial vehicle weathershields – Exhaust Ejector Co. Ltd

Truckmaster XHFE – fuel efficient high performance diesel engine oil – Millers Oils Ltd

Truckmaster XHPD – extra high performance diesal engine oil – Millers Oils Ltd

Truckstops – B P plc

True – paper – Fenner Paper Co. Ltd

True-Angle – adjustable set square – Blundell Harling Ltd

True-Cut – Jenex Ltd

True Knit – hobby graph papers – Exaclair Ltd

True Refrigeration – Apex Commercial Refrigeration & Aircon

True Type – fonts – Fontware Ltd

True2Life – software services / Interactive media – True2Life Ltd

Trueborer – jaw boring fixture – Thame Engineering Co. Ltd

*Truecraft (Far East) – agricultural workshop tools including air tools, electric saws, socket and spanner sets, also fasteners packs including nuts, bolts, washers, clips, pins etc – Spaldings Ltd

Trueform – shoes & sandals – D Jacobson & Sons Ltd

Truegrip BT – BBA/HAPAS approved high friction anti-skid for roads – Conren Ltd

Truegrip TCD – expoxy anti-skid coloured finish for external application – Conren Ltd

Trueline – parallel motion system A3/A2 and A1 – Blundell Harling Ltd

Truetreads – tyres – Lodge Tyre

Truflo – automatic switches to guard against excessive or inadequate flow – Flowgroup Ltd Bestobell Valves & Conflow

Truflo – Casing Dryer – Greenbank Technology Ltd

Truflo – Air suspension/Air flotation systems – Greenbank Technology Ltd

Truflo – non ferrous ball, check and plug valves – Truflo Gas Turbines Ltd

Truflote – floating reamer holder – F & R Belbin Ltd

Trufold – flat work folding machines – Armstrong Commercial Laundry Systems

Trulift – lifting jacks – Trewhella Brothers Ltd

Truly – M S C Gleichmann UK Ltd

Trumans Business Consulting – Business and Management Consultancy – Trumans Business Consulting

Trumatic – industrial machinery – Trumpf Ltd

Trumatic - CNC punches and profiling machines – Trumpf Ltd

Trumech – close tolerance cold finished steel tube – Benteler Distribution Ltd

Trumeter – counting timing and measuring machines – Trumeter Co Ltd

Trumf – fishing tackle – Daiwa Sports Ltd

Trumpf™ – Laser Trader Ltd

Truninger – internal gear pumps – Bucher Hydraulics Ltd

TRUNNION MOUNTED 1/2.-36. CLASS 150-2500 (United Kingdom) – Ultravalve Ltd

*Trupart (Worldwide) – spare parts for automobiles – Truepart Ltd

Trusstray – Chorus Panel & Profiles

Trusswall – structural curtainwall – Kawneer UK Ltd

Trusteam – Conservation Resources UK Ltd

TrustedReviews.com – Website – I P C Media Ltd

TRUSTMARK – Resin Bonded Surfacing

Trutest – smoke detector tester – No Climb Products Ltd

Trutex – suppliers of boys and girls schoolwear leisurewear and sportswear – Trutex plc

Truvox – industrial cleaning equipment – B & G Cleaning Systems Ltd

Truxorter – automated sorting conveyor systems – Van Der Lande Industries

TRV400 – thermostatic radiator valve – Sunvic Controls Ltd

TRW – Cyclops Electronics Ltd

Try and Hire – recruitment – Grafton Recuitment

Trysin – specified virus-free trypsin – Biocatalysts Ltd

TS – automatic voltage stabilisers – Claude Lyons Ltd

TS 5000 – DAT drive that uses the parallel printer port – Cristie Software

TSC – Maxa Technologies Ltd

Tschan – European Technical Sales Ltd

Tsingtao – Windfall Brands Ltd

Tsubaki – Antifriction Components Ltd

Tsubaki – Mercury Bearings Ltd

Tsubakimoto Chains – chain – Potteries Power Transmission Ltd

*Tsukasa (Japan) – DC motors – Cliff Electronic Components Ltd

TSURUMI – Arun Pumps Ltd

Tsurumi – Obart Pumps Ltd

TT (Europe, Western) – steel class valves – Everyvalve Ltd

TT – Pumps – Wendage Pollution Control Ltd

*TT PUMPS – Barber Pumps Ltd

TT Pumps – Denton Pumps Ltd

TT33 – Portable temporary cold room – Seymour Manufacturing International Smi Ltd

TTarr – roofing contractors – Morris & Spottiswood Ltd

TTG Directory – United Business Media Ltd

TTO – oil seals – Action Seals Ltd

TTURA (United Kingdom) – Resin Building Products Ltd

TTW – direct fired gas fired unit heater – Nordair Niche

TTW – direct fired gas fired unit heater – Nordair Niche

Tub-Box – column formers – Max Frank Ltd

Tubalox – heating elements – Chromalox UK Ltd

Tubarad – AEL Heating Solutions Ltd

Tube Aid – vaginal examination and delivery simulator – Educational & Scientific Products Ltd

Tube Developments – suppliers and exporters of all types of tube and tube fittings – Tube Development

Tubecut – Camtek Ltd

TUBEGUARD – Two stage, pipggy back mounted, high pressure liquid chromatography (hplc)food and drug science flow control – Pulsation Dampers At Pulseguard Ltd

Tubes – computer software – Chris Naylor Research Ltd

TubeSec – full height two door booth suitable for high security applications – Gunnebo Entrance Control Ltd

Tubetest – effluent testing reagents – Palintest Ltd

Tubex – manufacturers of tree shelters and vine shelters – Tubex Ltd

Tubocadet – profile cutting machine – Easab Cutting Systems

Tubus (Germany) – emergency elastomer buffer – Ace Controls International

*Tudor – Tudor Tea & Coffee

Tudor Labels – reel fed self address labels and promotion labelling products – Field Box More Labels

Tuf – Melitzer Safety Equipment

Tuf-Met – high strength low alloy electrodes – Metrode Products Ltd

Tufanega – heavy duty hand cleanser – Deb R & D Ltd
Tufchrome – high re-iron wear resistant castings – Bradken UK Ltd
Tufcoat – Tufcoat
Tufcon 80 Screed – polymer modified cementitious screed – Conren Ltd
Tufcote – enamels – Du Pont UK Ltd
Tuff Nette – expanding wallet – Acco East Light Ltd
Tuff Spun – Economical ribbed vinyl foam in rolls or modules for general purpose use – Plastic Extruders Ltd
Tuff Spun Wear – Vinyl foam in rolls or modules with dual density for improved wear layer – Plastic Extruders Ltd
Tuff Stuff – Bushboard Ltd
Tuffa – 100% polyurethane floor seal – Evans Vanodine International plc
Tuffa Bobbin – plastics injection mouldings – Barr Mason Ltd
Tuffbank – Accesscaff International Ltd
Tuffcoat – Gates Hydraulics Ltd
Tuffjack – book jacket – Premier Paper Group
Tuffking – Melitzer Safety Equipment
Tuffking – safety footwear – M K Associates
Tuffmaster – safety helmets – Scott International Ltd
Tuffmaster/Style 600/style 300/First Base – Scott International Ltd
Tuffnells – express parcel delivery – Tuffnelln Parcels Express
tuffply – plastic plywood alternative – Adapt Formwork Ltd
Tuffy – float operated level switch – Magnetrol International UK Ltd
Tufkut – manufacture scissors – Acme United Europe
Tuflex – flexible plastic hoses with inbuilt services – Plastiflex UK Ltd
Tuflex – v-belts – The Zerny Engineering Co. Ltd
Tuflin Valves (United Kingdom) – PTFE sleeved plug valves and teflon lined plug valves – Induchem
Tuflok – removable and reusable two piece plastic rivet – Jet Press Ltd
Tufram – Poeton Gloucester
Tuftex – natural and synthetic latex compounds for backing tufted and woven carpets – Vita Liquid Polymers
Tuftex – sporting goods – Phillips Tuftex Ltd
Tuftop – Glass cutting boards – Tuftop
Tuftrax – mens safety footwear – Bunzl S W S
Tufty – Royal Society For The Prevention Of Accidents Ltd
Tugboat – record company – Rough Trade Management
Tugite – hockey balls – Kookaburra Reader Ltd
***Tugmaster** – Douglas Equipment
Tula – Desks – Bucon Ltd
Tulip – washbasins, bidets, closets and baths – Ideal Standard Ltd
Tully Perimeter Security – security and car park traffic control barriers and gates, motorised electro-mechanical actuators and turnstiles – Zeag UK Ltd
Tumi – Latin American craft centres – Tumi
Tunbo – toolbits and cutters – P G T Ceewrite Ltd
Tunbridge Wells Courier – newspaper – Kent Regional News & Media
Tunbridge Wells & Tonbridge KM Extra – newspaper – Kent Messenger Group Ltd
Tuneslip – Molyslip Atlantic Ltd
Tungsten Intert Gas (TIG) – Pipestoppers
Tungstone – glazed ceramic tiles – A Elder Reed & Co. Ltd
Tungum – high pressure tubes for clean systems, corrosion resistant and thermal fatigue resistant castings – Tungum Ltd
Tungum (United Kingdom) – alloy tubing – Hydrasun Ltd
Tungum Alloy – complex alpha brass alloy – Tungum Ltd
Tünkers – European Technical Sales Ltd
Turbair – portable, air assisted, CDA applicators for pest control, poultry vaccination etc – Micron Sprayers Ltd
Turbex – industrial spray washing machines for component cleaning – Turbex Ltd
Turbex – foam generator – Angus Fire
Turbi-Tech – self cleaning sensor suitable for measurement of suspended solids turbidity – Partech Electronics Ltd
Turbinol – B P plc
Turbiscan – Fullbrook Systems Ltd
Turbo – two part easy maintenance syphons – Thomas Dudley Ltd
***Turbo (Switzerland)** – coolant oil centrifugal clarifiers – Brunner Machine Tools Ltd
Turbo-Flo – air assisted breathing apparatus – M S A Britain Ltd
Turbo-Jet – L N S Turbo UK Ltd
Turbo Rapid – plastics mixing machine – Aeromatic Fielder Ltd
TurboDriver – a range of fast printer drivers – Xara Ltd
***Turbofan** – Blue Seal Ltd
TurboFast – stainless steel fixings for securing timber to low density blocks – Helifix Ltd
Turboflex – disc couplings and composite fibre shafts – Bibby Transmissions Ltd
Turboflex – couplings – Bearwood Engineering Supplies
Turbolite – compressed air operated flood/bay lights – Wolf Safety Lamp Company Ltd
Turbolite – diamonds – Marcrist International Ltd
Turbomat – automatic pressure sets – Calpeda Ltd
Turbomax – SAE 15W/40 - SHPD engine oil has D. Benz 228.3 and CCMC D5 approvals – Castrol UK Ltd
***TurboMax (Germany)** – gas combination boiler – Vaillant Ltd
Turboneb – nebuliser systems for the treatment of respiratory disorders – Clement Clarke International Ltd
Turbopower – upright vacuum cleaners – Hoover Ltd
TURBOSEP – fermentation offgas filtration system – Parker Dominic Hunter Ltd
Turbosol – C E S Hire Ltd
Turbosound – manufacturers of professional audio equipment – Turbosound Ltd
Turbostream – thermostatic power shower – Aqualisa Products Ltd Head Office
TurboTie – stainless steel brick-aircrete wall tie (new build) – Helifix Ltd
***Turboweld (Italy)** – fan-cooled wheel mounted welder – S I P Industrial Products Ltd
Turcite – engineered thermoplastic compounds – Trelleborg Ceiling Solutions Ltd
Turck – European Technical Sales Ltd
Turck – switches – Bearwood Engineering Supplies
Turcon – engineered thermoplastic compound – Trelleborg Ceiling Solutions Ltd
Turcon - Turcite - Zurcon – Trelleborg Ceiling Solutions Ltd
Turf chemicals – wide range of fungicide and herbicide products – Scotts Co. Ltd
***Turf Iron (Australia)** – fine turf rollers – Farmura Ltd
Turf Royale – Yara UK lt Ltd
Turfandstuff.com – Turf N Stuff Ltd
Turfex – agricultural products – Amega Sciences plc
Turlon – Merseyside Metal Services
***Turmix (Switzerland)** – silent humidifiers – Air & Water Centre
***Turn-Act (U.S.A.)** – rotary actuators – The West Group Ltd
Turnbull & Asser – shirts – Turnbull & Asser Ltd
Turner chilled Rose – Newburgh Engineering Co. Ltd
Turngrove – B O B Stevenson Ltd
Turning Point – Streamlined Propeller Repairs
Turnings – wood – Pilkingtons Ltd
Turton (United Kingdom) – tools – Thomas Turton Ltd
Tuscan – vandal resistant and hoseproof lighting – Designplan Lighting Ltd
Tuscan – European Drives & Motor Repairs
Tushingham – windsurfing sails and accessories – Tushingham Sails Ltd
Tusker – safety footware – Howsafe Ltd
Tuskers – Footwear – Linacre Plant & Sales Ltd
Tuthill – blowers – Axflow
Tuthill Energy Systems – steam turbines – Axflow
Tuuci – Global Parasols Ltd
Tuxco – Harrier Fluid Power Ltd
Tuxford & Tebbutt – stilton cheese – Tuxford & Tebbutt
Tuxton – Foodcare Systems Ltd
TV easy – I P C Media Ltd
TV One – Video and audio distribution and switching – Tukans Ltd
TV Quick – television guide – H Bauer Publishing
TV & Satellite week – I P C Media Ltd
TV50 – Dust Extractor – PWM Distribution
TVA Corona Probe – probe used for off-line location of PD discharges in HV machine windings – Adwel International Ltd
TVS – knee brace – St. Clare Engineering Ltd
***TVS Glass (Netherlands)** – inbuilt sunroof – Webasto Products UK Ltd
TVX Hoists – Street Crane Ltd
TW Metals – pipe tube fittings & flanges, stainless steel aluminium & special alloys – T W Metals Ltd
Twang.net Ltd – IT – Timico Ltd
Tweed – stainless steel WC – Armitage Shanks Ltd
Tweedie Evans Consulting – Contaminated Land, ground engineering and construction phase monitoring – Tweedie Evans Consulting
Tweeny – domestic kitchen foodwaste disposer – Tweeny Ltd
Tweeny – waste disposers – Potter Cowan & Co Belfast Ltd
Twido – high functionality, compact plc – Schneider
Twiflex – Custom Brakes & Hydraulics Ltd
Twiflex – disc brakes, clutch couplings and air-start clutches – Twiflex Ltd
Twiflex – brakes – Bearwood Engineering Supplies
Twilight D.K. – yarns – Stylecraft
Twin Cap – twin nozzle holder – Hypro Eu Ltd
***Twin Combi (Sweden)** – cylinder locks – Assa Abloy Security Solutions
Twin Disc – equipment & spares – Bearwood Engineering Supplies
Twin disc – transmission system – M I T Ltd
Twin Frame – True Carbon Zero building method – Solo Timber Frame Ltd
Twin Set – electronic instrument cases – Lunds
Twin-Skin – anti blister double socks for sport and outdoor – Sweatshop
***Twin-Tec (U.S.A.)** – pneumatic connectors – The West Group Ltd
Twin Tip Tooling – cut off blades and holders – J J Churchill Ltd
Twin Track – freeline and power free overhead conveyor systems for loads upto 750kgs – Stewart Gill Conveyors Ltd
Twin Unival – central heating control system with 2 x 2 port valves including digital – Sunvic Controls Ltd
Twin Wheel – castors – Archibald Kenrick & Sons
Twinbloc – mains outlet – Schurter Ltd
Twinbore – boring tools – Microbore Tooling Systems
Twinbreak – fusegear – Schneider
Twindrive – Linak UK
Twineline/Lexium – motion control solutions - integrated and stand alone – Schneider
Twinfile – rotating filing cabinets – Civica UK Ltd
TwinFLASH – school crossing beacon – Doormen
Twinflex (United Kingdom) – the revolutionary 2 wire conventional fire detection system that saves upto 40% on installation costs – Fike Safety Technology Ltd
Twinflex – brakes – Bearwood Engineering Supplies
Twinflex Plus (United Kingdom) – incorporating "checkpoint" technology which filters nuisance alarms on a conventional system. Meets BS 5839 and EN54 standards – Fike Safety Technology Ltd
Twinflow – metering, mixing and dispensing equipment – Liquid Control Ltd
TWINFO – two materials on same backing liner – T P L Labels Ltd
Twinimum – compact twin fan units for ventilation extract from toilet areas – V E S Ltd
***Twinings** – Mercia Fine Foods
Twinings Classic – tea – R. Twining & Co. Ltd
Twinings Earl Grey Tea – Alba Beverage Co. Ltd
TwinLITE – warehouse traffic light – Doormen
Twinlock – UK Office Direct
Twinloop (United Kingdom) – broadloom – Checkmate Industries Ltd
TWINRO – Plenty Mirrlees Pumps
Twinskin – anti blister double socks for sport and outdoor – Sweatshop
Twinspot – emergency lighting – Lab Craft Ltd
Twintex – cable markers – Hellermann Tyton
Twintop – manilla wallet – Acco East Light Ltd
Twinwall – cladding – L B Plastics Ltd
Twisco – Manitou Site Lift Ltd
***Twist (Sweden)** – screwdrivers – Atlas Copco Tools Ltd
Twister – Burroughes & Watts
TWK Transducers – European Technical Sales Ltd
Two Ticks – toys and fancy goods – M Gordon & Sons
Twose – Joe Turner Equipment Ltd
Twose – agricultural machinery-hedgecutters-flail mowers-yard scrapers, cultivators – Twose of Tiverton Ltd
***Twose** – Reeth Garage Ltd
Twosome (United Kingdom) – corded track and valance – Integra Products
Twyman – Joe Turner Equipment Ltd
TX – Chillton Agricultural Equipment Ltd
TX – telescopic platforms – Audience Systems Ltd
TX2000 – battery powered tool for breakstem fasteners – Avdel UK Ltd
TXgard-IS+ – Toxic and oxygen gas detector with display – Crowcon Detection Instrument Ltd
TXgard Plus – Toxic and oxygen gas detector with display – Crowcon Detection Instrument Ltd
TY-D – cable tie mount hardware – Zygology Ltd
Tychem – Helman Workwear
Tyco – Connectors – Dax International Ltd
Tyco – Selectronix Ltd
Tyco – Relays – Dax International Ltd
Tyco (U.S.A.) – process valves – Orthos Engineering Ltd
Tyco – Cyclops Electronics Ltd
Tyco Electronics – connectors, switches & fibre optic products – Anglia
Tyco Electronics UK Ltd – registered trade name of company products – Tyco Electronics Ltd
Tycoons – mens basics - leather soles – UK Distributors Footwear Ltd
Tycord – synthetic tying twine – Gordian Strapping Ltd
Tydisan – pet products – Bob Martin UK Ltd
Tyeband – rayon strapping and tapes – SATCO Tapes
Tygashield – welding and fire blankets – Fothergill Engineered Fabrics Ltd
Tygasil – thermal insulation, welding and fire blankets – Fothergill Engineered Fabrics Ltd
Tyglas – thermal insulation, welding and fire blankets – Fothergill Engineered Fabrics Ltd
Tyglas 1000 C – welding and fire blankets – Fothergill Engineered Fabrics Ltd

Tylex – modified polyurethane coating for interior walls – Tremco Illbruck Ltd
Tylor – positive displacement – Emerson Process Management
Tylors – poitive displacement rotary piton flowmeters – Emerson Process Management
Tylose – HEC thickeners – Omya UK Ltd
Tyne – aero engines – Rolls-Royce plc
Tynes – Stacatruc
Tyneside – glass toughened, laminated, glass polycarbonate – Tyneside Safety Glass
Tyneside Printers – print on metal for can manufacture – Crown Speciality Packaging
Tyneside-System MSR – glass bullet resistant – Tyneside Safety Glass
Tynex – nylon filaments – Du Pont UK Ltd
Typar – polypropylene non-woven – Du Pont UK Ltd
***Type I Plus (Germany)** – silica coated vials – The Adelphi Group
Type L – cold emulsion sprayer – Thomas Coleman Engineering Ltd
Typhoon – positive pressure ventilation fans – Godiva Ltd
Typhoon – B L Pneumatics Ltd
Typhoon International – wetsuits, drysuits, life jackets, diving equipment, thermal footwear, immersion suits, military crysuits and helicopter and passenger suits – Typhoon International Ltd
Tyranid – electronic games, computer software, computer apparatus, cassettes, compact discs, video cassettes, films, magnetic data carriers, recording discs and cartoons, games, playthings, miniatures and models – Games Workshop Ltd
Tyreflex – tyre couplings – Renold Clutches & Couplings Ltd
Tyreflex Coupling – Renold Clutches & Couplings Ltd
Tyrfil – polymer filling system for puncture proof tyres – Chemical Innovations Ltd
Tyril – Resinex UK Ltd
Tyrin – chlorinated polyethylene – Omya UK Ltd
***Tyro (France)** – plate saws, abrasive cut-off machines, friction saws – Prosaw Ltd
Tyrocane – lozenges – Reckitt Benckiser plc
Tyrolit – S J Wharton Ltd
Tyrone – net curtaining – Tyrone Textiles Ltd
Tyropaque – G E Healthcare
Tytape – rayon cord tying tape – Gordian Strapping Ltd
TYVEK – Fieldway Supplies Ltd
Tyvek – UK Office Direct
Tyvek – overalls – Bearwood Engineering Supplies
Tyvek – S J Wharton Ltd
Tyvek – spun-bonded olefin – Du Pont UK Ltd
Tyvek Protech – Helman Workwear
Tyzack – plastering trowels – Spear & Jackson plc
Tyzack Turner – scythe blades, grass hooks, silage and hay knives – Burgon & Ball Ltd
Tyzor – organic titanate – Du Pont UK Ltd

U

U 2000 – Plenty Mirrlees Pumps
U'Beaut – Wood finishes – The Toolpost
U/BL – software – Transoft Ltd
U-Bond – Bonded watchhouse keepers suite – Iris Group
U-Flow – Bronkhorst UK Ltd
U/Gi – software – Transoft Ltd
U.H.B. – the prefix for certain uddeholm tool and strip grades of steel – Uddeholm Steel Stockholders
U.H.B. 11 – medium carbon bolster steel – Uddeholm Steel Stockholders
U.H.L. – hydraulic equipment – Universal Hydraulics Ltd
U.K. Kompass Register – in-depth industrial and commercial information reference book – The Bankers' Almanac Reed Business Information
U.K. Platforms – Accesscaff International Ltd
U.K. Sierra – gas overhead radiant heater – Drugasar Service Ltd
U.K. Towers – Accesscaff International Ltd
U.K. Waste – recycling, collection and disposal waste – Biffa Waste Services Ltd
U.L.I.S. – developing and marketing company of Leeds University's innovation and provisions of technology service, to industry (consultancy, testing, product and process development research) and expert witness sourcing – University Of Leeds
U.N.I. – conveyor chains and accessories – Sigma Industries Ltd
U.N.O. Drafting Templates – lettering guides and allied supplies – West Design Products Ltd
U.P.M. Kymmene – paper – U P M Kymmene Ltd
U.S. Army Tank – Harrier Fluid Power Ltd
U/SQL Client Server – software – Transoft Ltd
U.T. – pneumatic tools – Universal Air Tool Company Ltd
U.T.C. – under sink electric water heaters – Heatrae Sadia
U.T.M.C. – hard and anti reflection lens coating – Carlzeiss Vision
U.V.G. – vehicle spares – Bearwood Engineering Supplies
U.V.R.A.L. – pinhole detectors, DC and AC, high and low voltage – Buckleys Uvral Ltd
UAXXX – structural reinforcement – Gurit UK Ltd
Ubbink – Ubbink UK Ltd
Ubbink – National Door Co.
Ubiflo – Ubbink UK Ltd
Ubifresh – Ubbink UK Ltd
Ubigas – Ubbink UK Ltd
Ubisoil – soil pipe terminal – Ubbink UK Ltd
Ubivent – roof void vent – Ubbink UK Ltd
ubm – Unified Bandwidth Management - The catchworrd for our unified communications solution - Xrio Ltd
UBMi – UBM with integrated ADSL Modems – Xrio Ltd
UCA (Belgium) – gas fired unit heaters – Reznor UK Ltd
UCC – Harrier Fluid Power Ltd
UCD – Harrier Fluid Power Ltd
Uchida Rexroth – C J Plant Ltd
***Uchida Yoko (Japan)** – duplicating machines – Unigraph UK Ltd
UCI – freight forwarders – U T I Worldwide UK Ltd
Uckfield Courier – newspaper – Kent Regional News & Media
UCMS – Managed services for IT departments – Fox It Ltd
UCXXX – structural reinforcement – Gurit UK Ltd
UDAL – manufacture & install machine guards – Jones & Wilson Ltd
Udylite – electroplating processes – Cookson Electronics Ltd
UESA – Condensing Gas Fired Unit Heaters – Reznor UK Ltd
UEXXX – structural reinforcement – Gurit UK Ltd
UFCXXX – structural reinforcement – Gurit UK Ltd
UFEXXX – structural reinforcement – Gurit UK Ltd
Uffix – Desks – Bucon Ltd
UFI – Harrier Fluid Power Ltd
UFL – Walter GB Ltd
UFO – Sumitomo Electric Hardmetal Ltd
***Ufoxane (Norway)** – lignosulphonate – Borregaard UK
***Ugarola (Spain)** – auto rod straightening and cutting machines – La Roche
Ugly Bug – childrens plaster – Robinson Healthcare Ltd
UHU – UK Office Direct
UK Clearings Directory – (formerly known as Sorting Code Numbers) Lists over 14,500 sorting code numbers for UK bank branches and 8,300 CHAPS Euro BICS allocated to UK financial institutions. – The Bankers' Almanac Reed Business Information
UK Connection – student travel – Kuoni Travel Ltd
UK Distributor – Tekdata Distribution Ltd
UK Licensee for Camel Travel Bags & Luggage – Modrec International Holdings Ltd
Ukalene – methylene chloride (for aerosols) – Atosina UK Ltd
UKAS – united kingdom accreditation service – UK Accreditation Service
***Ukidan (Switzerland)** – thrombolytic – Merck Serono Ltd
Ulcaid – gel/lozenges – Reckitt Benckiser plc
Ulectriglide – centrifugal multistage submersible pumps – Weir Group Senior Executives Pension Trust Ltd
***Ulma (Spain)** – food packaging machinery – Wrapid Manufacturing Ltd
Ulon – highest quality polyurethane elastomers – Trelleborg Applied Technology
Ulster Classic Wilton – plain velvet Wilton – Ulster Carpet Mills Ltd
Ulster Velvet – woven Wilton – Ulster Carpet Mills Ltd
Ulster Weavers – tea towels, PVC aprons and bags, kitchen co-ordinates, giftware and fine linens – Ulster Weavers Home Fashions
Ultem – Resinex UK Ltd
Ultim8 – metal tube and component connector range primarily 25mm box section tube, connectors re-configurable to enable multi-angled constructions – B C G Creative FX
Ultima – portable display systems – P E P Ltd
Ultima – 19" racking system – Cooper B Line Ltd
Ultima – paint brush, dusting brush, paperhanging brush, stripping knife, filling knife, putty knife, chisel knife, seam roller, shavehooks, scissors, paint roller, extension poles – L G Harris & Co. Ltd
Ultima Display – Display Wizard Ltd
Ultima heat seal machine – Air operated heat seal machine – J & A International Ltd
Ultima Lite – nebuliser compressors for domestic use (portable for 12v & mains)and battery – A F P Medical Ltd
Ultimate – Georgia Pacific GB Ltd
Ultimation – console automation/moving fader package – Red Lion 49 Ltd
Ultimix – pharmaceutical and cosmetic machinery – T Giusti Ltd
Ultimo – mens contemporary clothing - suits & jackets – D Gurteen & Sons Ltd
Ultimum 584 – carpets – Interface Europe Ltd
Ultipleat – Pall Europe Corporate Services
Ultipor – filter medium – Pall Europe Corporate Services
Ultop – Regina International Ltd
Ultra – up and over door gear for timber doors – P C Henderson Ltd
Ultra (United Kingdom) – polyester cotton hospital fabric – Carrington Career & Work Wear
Ultra – polythene bags – Palco Industries Ltd
Ultra Board – Lightweight Honeycomb Board – Dufaylite Developments Ltd
Ultra-boom – oil absorbent boom – Cowens Ltd
Ultra Brilliant – dairy chemicals – Delaval
Ultra-Coating – radial spray coating – Aeromatic Fielder Ltd
Ultra Four – four layer bandage for leg – Robinson Healthcare Ltd
Ultra-Lok – clamp, stainless steel clamping system – Band-It Co. Ltd
***Ultra Matrix (U.S.A.)** – keyboard video mouse multi PC-sever switches – Techland Group Ltd
Ultra-Slim – ultra thin section bearings – R A Rodriguez UK Ltd
Ultra-strong – detectable warning tape – Boddingtons Ltd
Ultra Tape – adhesive tape – Bruce Douglas Marketing Ltd
ULTRA-VITALUX – lamps – Osram Ltd
Ultrabag – Instrument equipment tool carrying cases – Hofbauer (UK) Ltd
UltraCarb – Minelco Ltd
Ultracare – A commercial framework for fulfilling resource requirements within IT – Fox It Ltd
Ultracast – ultra low cement castables – Calderys UK Ltd
Ultraclean Systems, X-treme Blue, X70 – Blue Rubber Cleaning Rollers, Adhesive Rolls, Wipes, Cleanroom Supplies – Ultraclean Systems UK Ltd
***Ultrafilter (Germany)** – filters/compressed air dryers – Donaldson Filteration GB Ltd
Ultrafilter – air, condensate treatment products – Air Power Centre Limited
Ultraflex – adhesive coated tapes and metal plastic film laminates – G T S Flexible Materials Ltd
Ultraflow – theatre ultra clean air enclosures – Medical Air Technology Ltd
Ultraframe Works – A framework for integrating point products for cohesive systems management – Fox It Ltd
Ultraglide (United Kingdom) – corded metal track – Integra Products
ultragrade oil – AESpump
Ultragrain – polished stainless steel sheet – Righton Ltd
Ultrahide – decorative paints – Akzonobel
Ultraire – hydraulic pneumatic and electric components – Norgren Ltd
Ultrakan – straight sided pot system – Nampak Carton
Ultralastik – Trelleborg Industrial A V S Ltd
Ultralift – Eclipse Magnetics Ltd
Ultralift – spring balances – Caldwell Hardware Ltd
Ultralift Plus – Eclipse Magnetics Ltd
Ultralite – nickel plating processes – Cookson Electronics Ltd
Ultralux – lighting & lighting components – Coughtrie International Ltd
Ultramat – CNC and microprocessor grinders – Jones & Shipman Grinding Ltd
***Ultramax** – boiler optimisation software – Procon Engineering Ltd
ULTRAMED – lamps – Osram Ltd
Ultramet – positional stainless steel welding electrodes – Metrode Products Ltd
Ultramet B – stainless steel pipe welding electrodes – Metrode Products Ltd
ULTRAMIC – 600 advanced ceramic heaters – Watlow Ltd
Ultranitril – unsupported nitrile gloves – Mapa Spontex
***Ultraperm (Germany)** – nickel iron soft magnetic alloys – Rolfe Industries
Ultrarex – profile cutting machine – Easab Cutting Systems
ULTRASCAN – compressed air leak detector – E2l Ltd
Ultrasil – high performance siliconised release paper – A C P Ltd
Ultrasizer – particle sizing at high concentrations – Malvern Instruments Ltd
Ultrason – Resinex UK Ltd
Ultrasound & Gynaecology – specialist couches for coposcopy, ultrasound scanning and TV treatment – Akron
Ultratec – Inspection Consultant Ltd
Ultratec – Incon (Inspection Consultants) Ltd
Ultrathane Plus – products made from polyurethane elastomers – Watts Urethane Products Ltd
Ultrathemics – Divex
ULTRAtherm – baking solution – Kodak Morley
ULTRAthin – finishing solution – Kodak Morley
Ultratone TN – solvent trichromatic ink for paper and board – Fujifilm Sericol Ltd
ULTRAVALVE CAST STEEL TRUNNION BALL VALVE (United Kingdom) – Ultravalve Ltd
Ultravalve Check Valve (United Kingdom) – Ultravalve Ltd
Ultravalve complete range of fire protection products :- UL/FM fire protection valves (United Kingdom) – Ultravalve Ltd
Ultravalve Fireriser Butterfly Valve (United Kingdom) – Ultravalve Ltd

Ultravalve Fireriser gate valves (United Kingdom) – Ultravalve Ltd

ULTRAVALVE FLOATING BALL VALVE/TRUNNION IN CAST STEEL (United Kingdom) – Ultravalve Ltd

ULTRAVALVE FORGED STEEL TRUNNION BALL VALVE (United Kingdom) – Ultravalve Ltd

ULTRAVALVE SPECIAL ALLOY VALVES (United Kingdom) – Ultravalve Ltd

Ultravalve Y Strainer (United Kingdom) – Ultravalve Ltd

Ultravanil ABQ7012 – speciality compound – Quest International UK Ltd

Ultravap – solvent removal from microplates – Porvair plc

Ultravar 2000 – polyurethane varnish – Gurit UK Ltd

*Ultraview (U.S.A.) – keyboard video mouse multi PC-sever switches – Techland Group Ltd

Ultravis – polybutenes – B P plc

Ultravolt – power line conditioners – Douglas Electronic Industries Ltd

*Ultrazine (Norway) – lignosulphonate – Borregaard UK

Ultrazyme – protein remover tablets for soft contact lenses – Allergan Ltd

Ultril – supported nitrile gloves – Mapa Spontex

Ultrospec 1100 pro – UV and visible low cost spectrophotometer – Biochrom Ltd

Ultrospec 2100 pro – UV and visible spectophotometer – Biochrom Ltd

Ultrospec 3000 pro – UV & visible spectrophotometer – Biochrom Ltd

Ultrospec 3100 pro – UV and visible spectrophotometer – Biochrom Ltd

Ultrospec 3300 pro – UV and visible spectrophotometer – Biochrom Ltd

Ultrospec 4300 pro – UV and visible spectrophotometer – Biochrom Ltd

Ultrospec 500 pro – UV and visible spectrophotometer – Biochrom Ltd

Ultrospec 5300 pro – UV and VIS scanning narrow bandwidth – Biochrom Ltd

Ultrospec 6300 pro – UV and VIS scanning narrow bandwidth spectrophotometer – Biochrom Ltd

ULTRWEAR – Merseyside Metal Services

Ultrx – rupture disc – Continental Disc UK Ltd

Ulva – portable CDA insecticide and fungicide applicator – Micron Sprayers Ltd

Ulvac – vacuum pumps – AESpump

Ulvafan – portable, air assisted, CDA applicator for indoor pest control – Micron Sprayers Ltd

Ulvamast – vehicle-mounted CDA insecticide and fungicide applicator – Micron Sprayers Ltd

Ulvapron – B P plc

Um-Matic – B P plc

Umami – cat food – Gilbertson & Page Ltd

Umax – Lamphouse Ltd

Umbra – Obart Pumps Ltd

Umbro – active sports and leisure clothing – Umbro International Ltd

Umc – Cyclops Electronics Ltd

Unbar – seasoning blends – Unbar Rothon Ltd

Unbar – seasoning blends – World Of Spice Ltd

UNBRAKO – It has name in fasteners industry worlwide. for more info. log on to www.unbrako.in – Deepak Fasteners

Unbrako – fastners – S P S Technologies Ltd

Unbrako – S J Wharton Ltd

Uncle Bobtail – chalks and crayons, modelling clay and face paints – Stadium Crayons Ltd

Uncle Lukes – cough sweets – Barnetts Confectioners Ltd

Uncle Mick – babies, childrenswear and teenage fashions – Shenu Fashions

Uncut – I P C Media Ltd

Undelac – paint – Craig & Rose Ltd

Under Armour Allseason Gear – Regulates core body temperature in changing environmental conditions, providing maximum comfort. – Baselayer Ltd

Under Armour Cold Gear – High performance clothing for cold and winter weather conditions, ideal for skiing and snowboarding – Baselayer Ltd

Under Armour Heat Gear – Draws moisture away fropm the skin, keeping you cool and comfortable in hot conditions – Baselayer Ltd

Underbridge Platforms – Accesscaff International Ltd

Undercover – Umbrellas – K B Import & Export Ltd

Understanding Industry – courses in schools and colleges for 16-19 year olds about the importance of industry and commerce – Enterprise Education Trust

Uneek – First Impressions Europe Ltd

Ungar – soldering equipment – Apex Tools

Ungerer – European Technical Sales Ltd

Uni-Belt – belt conveyors – Conveyor Units Ltd

Uni-Cage – hydraulic cages for unit tool punching – Minni-Die Ltd

Uni-Cardan Service – Repair and manufacture of propshafts for the automotive & industrial sector – G K N Driveline Services Ltd

UNI CHAINS – Wolds Engineering Services Ltd

Uni-Dry – Monier Ltd

Uni-Form – precision bore tubing – G P E Scientific Ltd

Uni-Guard (United Kingdom) – scored reverse-acting metal bursting disc – Elfab Ltd

Uni-hinge Packs – range of universal foam containers – Pregis Rigid Packaging Ltd

Uni-Lat – miniature shaft misalignment couplers – Huco Dynatork

Uni-Mix – software system – Format International Ltd

Uni-Pak – reusable pallet container system. – D S Smith Correx

Uni-Ram – hydraulic punching cylinders – Minni-Die Ltd

Uni-Shel – portable shelters – Andrew Mitchell & Co. Ltd

Uni-Sport – folding cycles – Universal Cycles

Uni-Trex – Terrapin Ltd

Uni-Trex, Prospex, Matrex – Terrapin Ltd

Uni-Xu 1000 – pallet singulation powered roller conveyor – Conveyor Units Ltd

UNI-XU Series – powered roller accumulation conveyor – Conveyor Units Ltd

Unibacs – computer software systems – Carval Computing Ltd

Unibag – Injection moulded carrying cases – Hofbauer (UK) Ltd

Unibar Cutting Machines – Wessex Welding & Industrial Supplies Ltd

Unibilt – mechanical handling systems – Jervis B Webb Co. Ltd

Unibind – document bindings – Unibind Systems Ltd

Unibloc – unified gas valve – Dunphy Combustion Ltd

Uniblue – paper wiping product – Staples Disposables Ltd

Unibond – Gem Tool Hire & Sales Ltd

UNIBOOT – CV boot kit (universal) – Bailcast Ltd

Unibrain – Stemmer Imaging

Unibrand – rubber product branding – Polymeric Labels Ltd

Unicam AA – Thermo Electrical

Unicap – pipe fittings for gas and waterboard – Atlantic Plastics

Unicase – aluminium sign systems – Universal Components

Unicell – chemical blowing agents – Omya UK Ltd

Unichain – Mercury Bearings Ltd

Unichema – fatty acids, esters, oleine, stearine, amides and nickel catalyst – Croda International plc

Unico – wholesale quality furniture fittings – Unico Components Ltd

Unicol – audio visual stands, trolleys and brackets – Unicol Engineering

Unicol – pipe fittings for gas and waterboard – Atlantic Plastics

Unicon – universal conveyor control system for mines – Davis Derby Ltd

Unicon Connectors – oil pollution control equipment – Vikoma International Ltd

Unicone – flexible joints – C M T Tube Fittings Ltd

Unicorn – universal masterbatched ex stock – Begg & Co Thermoplastics Ltd

Unicorn (United Kingdom) – band grinder and polisher – R J H Finishing Systems Ltd

Unicorn – Trafalgar Tools

Unicorn – darts – Unicorn Products Ltd

Unicorn Products – refuse sack holders, fire retardant bins trolleys and cabinets – Unicorn Hygienics

UNICORNM CHEMICALS SPECIALIST SOLUTIONS – Hydraulic & Offshore Supplies Ltd

Unicost – contract cost ledger – Blanewood Andrews Computing plc

Unicover – banking insurance and investment services – Birmingham Midshires Financial Services Ltd

Unicrane – Red House Industrial Services Ltd

Unicrop – crop protection – Universal Crop Protection Ltd

Unicryl – water based coatings – Witham Oil & Paint Lowestoft Ltd

Unicube – asbestos nuclear and chemical personnel decontamination and controlled access systems – Union Industries

Unicup – pipe fittings for gas and waterboard – Atlantic Plastics

Unicup – aluminium foil cup – Rexam Holding plc

Unicus – H R S Heat Exchanges Ltd

Unicut – semi-severed cable identification system – Hellermann Tyton

Unicycles – unicycles – Pashley Cycles Ltd

Unidap – pipe fittings for gas and waterboard – Atlantic Plastics

Unidare – Glen Dimplex UK Ltd

Unidox – primer – Witham Oil & Paint Lowestoft Ltd

Unidox – metal primers, non-oxidising paint – Witham Oil & Paint Lowestoft Ltd

Unidrain – pipe connector – Naylor Drainage Ltd

Unidrive – Proplas International Ltd

Unifact – room controllers – Schneider Electric

Unifact PRO – Schneider Electric

Unifan – electric fan – Kenlowe Accessories & Co. Ltd

Unifan O/E – electric fan – Kenlowe Accessories & Co. Ltd

Unifarm Fertilizer – Carrs Billington Agriculture Sales Ltd

Unifelt – fibre felt – Thermal Ceramics UK Ltd

Unifibre Reinforcement – unidirectional fabric – Gurit UK Ltd

Unified Bandwidth Management – The catchworrd for our unified communications solution – Xrio Ltd

Uniflex – Trelleborg Industrial A V S Ltd

Uniflex – Broen Valves Ltd

Uniflex – aluminium sign systems – Universal Components

Uniflo – air handling units – Uniflo Systems Ltd

Uniflow – unit heater – Biddle Air Systems Ltd

Unifoil – aluminium foil container – Rexam Holding plc

Uniform – caps – Try & Lilly Ltd

Uniform – precision bore glass tubing – G P E Scientific Ltd

Uniform Express – stock service same day dispatch – Uniform Express Ltd

Uniformity – desks – E F G Matthews Office Furniture Ltd

Uniformity Steel – housemark – Cogne UK Ltd

Unigas – oil, gas and dual fuel burners – G P Burners C I B Ltd

Unigas - gas and oil burner. – G P Burners C I B Ltd

Unigel – P3 coal mining explosive – Orica UK Ltd

Uniglaze – eggshell lustre – Witham Oil & Paint Lowestoft Ltd

Uniglide – single stage, split casing, centrifugal pumps for water supply – Weir Group Senior Executives Pension Trust Ltd

Uniglow – photoluminescent paint – Witham Oil & Paint Lowestoft Ltd

Unigrab – silage forks – Brown's Agricultural Machinery Company Ltd

Unigraph – reprographic products – Unigraph UK Ltd

Unigraphics – Linmech Technical Solutions Ltd

Unigrip – blind rivets for building and panel work – Anixter Ltd

Uniguard – emulsion polish – Unico Ltd

UNIGUARD – guard cartridge holder – Thermo Fisher Scientific

Unikool – multi-product cooler – Andritz Seed & Bio Fuel Ltd

Unilam – a range of carbon epoxy & glass epoxy sheet & plate – Custom Composites Ltd

Unileaf – thin ulon sheetings – Trelleborg Applied Technology

UniLED – LED lighting – PLM Illumination Ltd

Uniledg – financial ledgers – Blanewood Andrews Computing plc

Unilight – aluminium sign systems – Universal Components

Uniline – road marking paint – Witham Oil & Paint Lowestoft Ltd

Uniline – accessories for the agricultural retailer – The Vapormatic Co. Ltd

Uniline – Safety Works & Solutions Ltd

UNILITE – Fieldway Supplies Ltd

Unilite – photoluminescent signs – Allgood

Uniload – weighing system for fork trucks – Thermo Scientific

Unilock – Zero Point Clamping System – Schunk Intec Ltd

Unilock – access control – Blanewood Andrews Computing plc

Unilock – building products – Yule Catto & Co plc

Unilok – adhesives and bonding agents – Trelleborg Applied Technology

Uniluwa – air conditioning equipment – Luwa UK Ltd

Unimac – Clean Machine UK Ltd

Unimac – washer extractors – Armstrong Commercial Laundry Systems

Uniman – MRP 2 based manufacturing computer system – Blanewood Andrews Computing plc

Unimat – clean air equipment for hospital laboratories – Medical Air Technology Ltd

Unimatic – steel tape rules – Fisco Tools Ltd

Unimatic – European Technical Sales Ltd

Unimatt – flat oil paint – Witham Oil & Paint Lowestoft Ltd

Unimax (United Kingdom) – natural draft and low nox burners – Hamworthy Combustion Engineering Ltd

Unimax – bases on a universal carrier system, the Universal range of colour masterbatches is compatible with most thermoplastic polymers. – Gabriel Chemie UK Ltd

*Unimec (Italy) – screwjack and gear units – Motovario Ltd

Unimesh – safety protection debris netting – Union Industries

Unimesh – liner system for bearings – Nmb-Minebea UK Ltd

Unimess – reed switch operated float switches, magnetic level gauges and pitot tube flow meters – Able Instruments & Controls Ltd

Unimessage Pro – computer software for unified PC messaging fax email print copy scan and internet fax. – Wordcraft International Ltd

Unimix – coolant proportioner – Master Chemical Europe Ltd

*Unimog (Germany) – all purpose tractor – Mercedes Benz UK Ltd

Union – security products – Assaabloy Group

Union Briketts – types of fuel – C P L Distribution

Union Hardwear – industrial workwear – Regatta Ltd

Union Logo – British Vita plc

Union Special – Sewing Machines – Union Special (UK) Limited

Unior – S J Wharton Ltd

***Unipac (Italy)** – tube fillers – Romaco Holdings UK Ltd
***Unipac (Denmark)** – diy, home improvement products, pet care products – D-Pac Ltd
Unipage – radio pagers – Intercity Telecom Ltd
Unipak – fibre drum for platen discharge – Rexam Holding plc
Unipak – polyurethane wood lacquer – Craig & Rose Ltd
UNIPAK – weld timer and control system – B F Entron Ltd
UNIPHASE – universal packing media for use in guard cartridges – Thermo Fisher Scientific
Uniplas – steel tape rules – Fisco Tools Ltd
Unipleat – uniform pleat retention system for pleated blinds – Eclipse Blind Systems
Uniplex – CCTV equipment – Dedicated Micros Ltd
Uniplex – engines – Quality Monitoring Instruments Q M I
Uniplus – free flow nylon wheel chain – Conveyor Units Ltd
UNIPOD – welfare unit – McNealy Brown Ltd
Unipol UF – catalysed solvent ink for pretreated polythene containers – Fujifilm Sericol Ltd
Uniport – Uniport Business Systems Ltd
Unipre – multi component casting/hot spraying machines – R F Bright Enterprises Ltd
Unipulse flowmeter – Stream Measurement Ltd
Unique – writing boards and display boards, information boards, planner boards, notice boards, roller boards, whiteboards, flipcharts and projection screens. Audio and visual systems, projectors, multi media packages. Touch control panels – Spaceright Europe Ltd
Unique – lighters – Alfred Dunhill Ltd
Unique – Chamber Of Commerce East Lancashire
Unique Languages – Language Training Agency – Unique Languages
Uniregal – WC – Armitage Shanks Ltd
***Uniroyal (UK, France, Germany, Belgium)** – tyres – Continental Tyre Group Ltd
Uniroyal – M S C Gleichmann UK Ltd
Uniroyal – Wealden Tyres Ltd
Uniscol – pipe fittings for gas and waterboard – Atlantic Plastics
Uniseal – slip resistant floor seal – Unico Ltd
Uniseis – seismic data processing system – Fugro Seismic Imaging Ltd
Unishare – central heating control system with 3 port valve – Sunvic Controls Ltd
Unishop – shop floor data collection – Blanewood Andrews Computing plc
Unisil – silicone waterproof solution – Witham Oil & Paint Lowestoft Ltd
Unislate – universal lead slate – British Lead
Unislip/Uniwax – fatty acid amides – Croda International plc
Unisok – pipe fittings for gas and waterboard – Atlantic Plastics
Unison Soluble Oils – soluble cutting oils – Morris Lubricants
Unisop – sales order processing – Blanewood Andrews Computing plc
Unispare – domestic electric appliance spares, manufacturer of vacuum cleaner paper bags – Unispare Domestic Appliances
Unistaff – personnel system – Blanewood Andrews Computing plc
Unistaff – computer software systems – Carval Computing Ltd
Unistar – housewares – Vitco Ltd
Unisteel – stainless steel urinal – Armitage Shanks Ltd
Unistor – assymetric electrical resistors – Nortel Networks UK Ltd
Unistrut – Veronalder Ltd
Unistrut Cable Management – Cable support systems for the world's Oil, Gas and Petrochemical industries – R & M Electrical Group Ltd
Unistrut Channel – Metal Framing System – R & M Electrical Group Ltd
Unistuc – masonry finish – Witham Oil & Paint Lowestoft Ltd
Uniswop – pnuematic demount equipment – Abel Demountable Systems Ltd
Unisys – computer hardware and software consultants and systems integrators, network equipment suppliers and implementors – Unisys Ltd
Unit Manager – sealed unit order processing invoicing software – Clear Thinking Software Ltd
Unit Pallets – timber pallets pallet repairs timber recycling & Heat Treatment for export services – Unit Pallets Ltd
Unit Two Systems – plumbing and heating contractors – Unit Two Systems
Unitair – Unit Products Ltd
Unitas – super gloss paints – Witham Oil & Paint Lowestoft Ltd
Unitec – Harrier Fluid Power Ltd
Unitec – fine powder for use in ceramics – U C M Magnesia Ltd
Unitec – high precision machine tool bearings – R A Rodriguez UK Ltd
Unitec – spares for buses and coaches – Optare Group Ltd
Unitec Rotherham – Bus and coach repair facilities – Optare Group Ltd
United Automation – electronic equipment – Bearwood Engineering Supplies
United Chemi-con – Cyclops Electronics Ltd
United Distillers – export administration – The Diageo
United Electric Controls – pressure and temperature switches and controls – Able Instruments & Controls Ltd
United Engines – Harrier Fluid Power Ltd
United Flexible – vibration eliminators – Thermofrost Cryo plc
United Flexible – corrugated & stripweld metallic hose and assemblies – Amnitec Ltd
United Paper – graphic and paper suppliers to the printing trade, industry and education – United Paper Merchants Ltd
United Skates R – skateboards, all terrain skateboards, longboards and accessories – Ventura Corporation
United Utilities P.L.C – electricity and water suppliers – United Utilities Water plc
Unitend – computer software systems – Carval Computing Ltd
Unitend – time and attendance system – Blanewood Andrews Computing plc
Unitest – Alpha Electronics Southern Ltd
Unitex Reinforcement – unidirectional fabric – Gurit UK Ltd
Unitherm – conditioning equipment – Andritz Seed & Bio Fuel Ltd
Unitherm – thermal insulation products – Maineport Ltd
Unitherm – fire protection coatings – Permatex Protective Coatings UK Ltd
Unitor – marine refrigeration spares, chemicals and refrigeration services and spares, welding consoles, fire and safety products and services. – Wilhelmsen Ship Service
Unitrac – gravity roller conveyor – Conveyor Units Ltd
UNITRAC – Chaintec Ltd
Unitrim – aluminium sign systems – Universal Components
Unitrode – Cyclops Electronics Ltd
Unitronix – production control systems – Andritz Seed & Bio Fuel Ltd
Unitrunk – trunking – Uni Trunk Ltd
Unitrust – security protection services – Unitrust Protection Services Ltd
Unity II – telecommunications instruments – Nortel Networks UK Ltd
Univ – power supply – Stontronics Ltd
Unival – 2 port spring return valve – Sunvic Controls Ltd
Univap – coolers (evaporators) – Thermofrost Cryo plc
Univar – pressure switches – Black Teknigas & Electro Controls Ltd
Univer – hydraulic cylinders – A C Hydraulics Ltd
Univer – Pneumatic cylinders and valves – William Teknix
Univer – Southern Valve & Fitting Co. Ltd
Univerbar – Catersales Ltd
Universal – incinerators – Facultatieve Technologies Ltd
Universal – WC – Armitage Shanks Ltd
Universal – Popular, Reliable and Value for money – Chi Yip Group Ltd
***Universal (Germany)** – dog brushes – Diamond Edge Ltd
Universal – Batteries – Charger Bay Solutions
Universal – quick release fasteners – Southco Manufacturing Ltd
Universal – air tools – Arrow Supply Co. Ltd
Universal – pharmaceutical and cosmetic machinery – T Giusti Ltd
Universal – shower trays – Matki plc
***Universal** – Armstrong & Holmes Ltd
Universal – Sal Abrasives Technologies
Universal Air Tools – Universal Air Tool Company Ltd
Universal Boltforgers – bolts – Universal Boltforgers Ltd
Universal Cable Gland – the cable gland for the offshore industry – Hawke International
Universal Display (United Kingdom) – company – Universal Display Fittings
Universal - Dowson & Mason - Evans Universal - Tabo Inex - Evans Tabo Universal - Fours Delot International – Facultatieve Technologies Ltd
Universal Drum – 30li, 60li, 120li, 150li, 220li open top – Fibrestar Drums Ltd
Universal Edge – high speed copper access platform – Nortel Networks UK Ltd
Universal Glazing – aluminium windows, roof lights, curtain walling, barrell glazing and patent glazing – Universal Glazing Ltd
Universal Hopper – coin payout mechanism – Money Controls Ltd
Universal Hydr – Harrier Fluid Power Ltd
Universal Impex – confirming and trading house – Universal Impex Ltd
Universal Locks – locksmiths supply and installation of security systems including grilles, alarms and access control nationwide – Universal Locks Ltd T/A Universal Security Group
Universal Milling – electrical and contract work – Andritz Seed & Bio Fuel Ltd
Universal - R – dixell service replacement electronic controller – Thermofrost Cryo plc
Universal Towel – continuous cabinet roller towels-wash room products (janitorial) – Universal Towel Company Ltd
Universe – carpets – Interface Europe Ltd
University of London – University Of London
University of Sussex – University Of Sussex Intellectual Property Ltd
Univision D B M S – software – Electronic Data Processing plc
Uniwage – payroll – Blanewood Andrews Computing plc
Uniwage – computer software systems – Carval Computing Ltd
***Uniwell** – Shelfguard Systems
Uniwell – Cube Epos Ltd
Uniwell – M C R Systems Ltd
Uniwell Cash Registers – Cash Register Services
Unix Reinforcement – unidirectional fabric – Gurit UK Ltd
Unizone – component burn-in – Sharetree Ltd
Uno – sliding partitions – Becker Sliding Partitions Ltd
Uno Systems – Vortex Hydra UK Ltd
UNOFRAM – Small one piece membrane dampening accumulators – Pulsation Dampers At Pulseguard Ltd
Unomat – Direct Instrument Hire Ltd
UNS – fishing tackle – Drennan International Ltd
***Unsink (United Kingdom)** – offshore buoyancy system for displacement yachts & power boats – Adec Marine Ltd
Up and Under – electric floor and ceiling heating – Eswa Ltd
Up-n-Away – Forward Chemicals Ltd
UP Station GX – Emerson Network Power Ltd
UPA (Belgium) – gas fired unit heaters – Reznor UK Ltd
Uplec Industries – telecommunications, test and transmission equipment – Uplec Industries Ltd
UPOL – Letchford Supplies Ltd
Upol A – polyester filler pastes – U-Pol Ltd
Upol B – glass fibre repair paste – U-Pol Ltd
Upol C – polyester filler pastes – U-Pol Ltd
Upol D – polyester filler pastes – U-Pol Ltd
Upol E – polyester filler pastes – U-Pol Ltd
Upol Top-Stop – body filler – U-Pol Ltd
UPRIGHT – Chaintec Ltd
Uptix – unix-based investment management computer system – D S T Global Solutions
Urad – coating additives – DSM UK Ltd
Uradil – water thinnable & water dispersed alkyds & polymers – DSM UK Ltd
Uradur 2P – blocked NCO resins – DSM UK Ltd
Uraflex – polyurtehanes; 2 pack & elastomers – DSM UK Ltd
Uragard – urethane resin based heavy duty flooring screeds – J L Lord & Son Ltd
Uragum – resin maleic & resin esterified phenolics – DSM UK Ltd
Uralac – polyester/alkyds, straight & modified – DSM UK Ltd
Uramex – melamine/benzoguanamine/urea curing agents – DSM UK Ltd
Uramol – polymer dispersions – DSM UK Ltd
Uranox – aliphatic oxirane/epoxy esters & epoxy ester emulsions – DSM UK Ltd
Urathix – thixotropic alkyds – DSM UK Ltd
Uravar – phenolic resins & precondensates – DSM UK Ltd
Urbis – lighting and public furniture – Urbis Lighting Ltd
Urch Harris – stamp mail order – Stanley Gibbons Ltd
Urimeter – urine drainage meters – Bard Ltd
Uriplan – incontinence products - foley catheters, leg bags, overnight drainage bags, urinals, penile sheaths and accessories – Bard Ltd
Uristat – medical diagnostic kits – Axis Shield Ltd
Urko – Gem Tool Hire & Sales Ltd
Urospec – specialised surgical urology products – Bard Ltd
Urquhart – gas and oil burners, incinerators and fired heaters – Sterling Thermal Technology Ltd
Urquhart-Dykes & Lord – patents and trade mark agents – Urquhart Dykes & Lord
URS – Sears Manufacturing Company Europe Ltd
Ursa Oils – lubricants – Chevron
Ursa Super L.A. – lubricants – Chevron
Ursa Super T.D. – lubricants – Chevron
URT – LCD displays – Anglia
Usacert – food colourings – Sensient
Usagran – food colourings – Sensient
Usalake – food colourings – Sensient
Usborne – childrens books – Usborne Publishing
Uscan – pipe & cable location equipment – C-Scope International Ltd
Used Direct – Lookers plc
Used Systems Exchange – second hand business telephones – Cost-A-Call Ltd
Used Towers – Accesscaff International Ltd
Useful Labels – stock range of plain white self-adhesive labels for laser and computer printers – Sessions Of York
USF – Eurometals UK Ltd
Using Jolly Phonics – teachers video for teaching reading and writing – Jolly Learning Ltd
Usit – bonded seal – Freudenberg Simrit LP
Uster – yarn cutters and clamps – Dent Instrumentation Ltd
USX – ultrasonic detection devices – Primalec
UT (China) – 1-18th scale die castcars – Amerang Group Ltd

Utax – Copiertec Ltd
Utax – Lamphouse Ltd
UTCXXX – structural reinforcement – Gurit UK Ltd
Utex – Euroteck Systems UK Ltd
UTI – international freight fowarders – U T I Worldwide Ltd
Utile – compressors-air and gas (rotary), vacuum pumps (rotary) – Utile Engineering Co. Ltd
Utility – media remastering project QC toolkit – D P T S Group Holdings Ltd
Utility Sink – Ideal Standard Ltd
Utilux – Utilux UK Ltd
Utopia – computer software – K B C Process Technology Ltd
Utopia – record company – Utopia Records Ltd
UTP – welding consumable – Bohler Welding Group Ltd
Uttoxeter Newsletter – Staffordshire Newspapers Ltd
UV – Ovivo UK Ltd
UV Techniek – U V O 3 Ltd
Uvacure – ultra violet light curing adhesives and fixing range – Chemence Ltd
UVAZONE – Triogen Ltd
Uvex – non chemical water management system – System Uvex Ltd
Uvibond UV – curing varnishes – Fujifilm Sericol Ltd
Uviclad – specialist electrophoretic coatings – L V H Coatings Ltd
Uvipak NG – UV curing ink for polythene bottles – Fujifilm Sericol Ltd
Uviplast UP2000 – UV ink for plastic signs – Fujifilm Sericol Ltd
Uvispeed Gloss UX – UV curing ink for paper and plastics – Fujifilm Sericol Ltd
***Uviterno (Switzerland)** – ultra violet curing – Engelmann & Buckham Ltd
UVivid CN – flatbed screen - narrow web ink – Fujifilm Sericol Ltd
UVivid Flexo FL – narrow web label printing ink – Fujifilm Sericol Ltd
Uvivid RN – rotary screen - narrow web ink – Fujifilm Sericol Ltd
Uzin – N W Flooring

V

V. – endorsement for vegetarian products – Vegetarian Society UK Ltd
V 10008 – high speed door – Hörmann (UK) Ltd
V 1401 Atex – high speed door – Hörmann (UK) Ltd
V. 18 – iodophor disinfectant – Evans Vanodine International plc
V 2515 Food L – high speed door – Hörmann (UK) Ltd
V 2715 SE R – high speed door – Hörmann (UK) Ltd
V 3009 Conveyor – high speed door – Hörmann (UK) Ltd
V 3015 Clean – high speed clean – Hörmann (UK) Ltd
V 3015 RW – high speed door – Hörmann (UK) Ltd
V 3515 Iso – high speed door – Hörmann (UK) Ltd
V 5015 SE – high speed door – Hörmann (UK) Ltd
V. & A. – museum trading company – V & A Enterprises Ltd
V.A.L.-S.C. Series – vertical shaft pumps – Calpeda Ltd
V.A.M.P. – In Practice Systems Ltd
V.A.M.P. Data – In Practice Systems Ltd
V.A.M.P. Links – In Practice Systems Ltd
V & A Twist – Ryalux Carpets Ltd
V-Bar – Flowline Manufacturing Ltd
V C Long Reach Excavators – R B Cranes Ltd
V.C.M. 80 – vibratory non thermal stress reduction equipement - portable and metal stabilisation – Vibratory Stress Relieving Company
V.C.M. 90 – vibratory non thermal stress reduction equipment - portable and metal stabilisation – Vibratory Stress Relieving Company
V.C.M. 905 – vibratory non thermal stress reduction equipment - portable and metal stabilisation – Vibratory Stress Relieving Company
V-Coil – S J Wharton Ltd
V.F. – fuses and plugtaps – Dencon Accessories Ltd
V.-Flange – Kennametal UK Ltd
V.G. – grocers – Henderson Group Ltd
V & G Anchorage – cage type anchorage for metal parapet posts – Varley & Gulliver Ltd
V.I.A. Contract Hire – commercial contract hire – Petit Forestier
V.I.A. Countryside – commercial vehicle rental – Petit Forestier
V.I.L. – paint and ink media – V I L Resins Ltd
V.I.P. – medium frequency melting equipment – Inductotherm Europe Ltd
V.K./L. – immersion thermostats – Sunvic Controls Ltd
V-Koo – Architectural Window Films
V.L.I./V.C.I. – single stage and vertical in-line pumps for general water and oil pumping duties – Weir Group Senior Executives Pension Trust Ltd
V-Line – marine starting air compressor – Hamworthy Waste Water plc
V.M. – hydrant flow gauges, quickfit inspectors kits, mains static pressure testing kit and flow and pressure test kit and monitor – Vernon Morris Utility Solutions Ltd
V.M.A.C.S. – Vodafone Retail Ltd
V.M.C. – tool & die steel – Somers Forge Ltd
V-Notch – chlorine or sulphur dioxide dosing unit – Wallace & Tiernan Ltd
V.-Notch – Kennametal UK Ltd
V.P.I. – vibration pattern imaging – Sira Test & Certification Ltd
V Rack – analogue effects rack – A M S Neve Ltd
V.S. Bevel Units – 90 degree drives – Varatio Holdings plc
V*S Drives – Baldor UK
V.S.I. Vacational Studies (International) Ltd – residential English language courses – Vacational Studies
V.S.M. – abrasives – Arrow Supply Co. Ltd
V Series – analogue console – A M S Neve Ltd
V-Smart – Capex Office Interiors
***V.T. (U.S.A.)** – microphone – Audio Ltd
V-Thane – polyurethane products – Hallam Polymer Engineering Ltd
v-trans – vinyl designs – Imagine Transfers
V.V.V.F. -ISOSTOP 60M – Thyssenkrupp Elevator UK Ltd
V.W.M.C. – tool & die steel – Somers Forge Ltd
V200MD – Pressure washers – B & G Cleaning Systems Ltd
V3 (Belgium) – gas fired unit heaters – Reznor UK Ltd
VAC – acrylic coated glass braided sleaving – Relats UK Ltd
***VAC (Germany)** – alloys; parts and components with special magnetic, electrical & physical properties – Rolfe Industries
Vac-Guard (United Kingdom) – bursting disc for ultra-low pressure service – Elfab Ltd
Vac-Mat – vacuum workholding system – Thame Engineering Co. Ltd
Vac-U-Torq – cutting machine for plastic extrudate – Peter Gillard Company Ltd
VAC - Vacuumschmelze - Vacomax - Vacodym - Vitrovac - Ultraperm - Vitroperm - DAU - HKR - Hakron-STS – Rolfe Industries
Vacation Travel Centre – travel company – B S Executive Travel Ltd
Vacational Studies – residential English language courses – Vacational Studies
Vacflo – Suction or through drying (conveyorised) – Greenbank Technology Ltd
Vacflo, The – industrial dryer – Greenbank Technology Ltd
Vacherin Limited – Vacherin Ltd
Vacman Specialist Cleaning – Vacman Specialist Cleaning
Vacmaster – air operated vacuum gun – Filtermist International Ltd
Vacmaster – suction loading equipment – Tipmaster Ltd
Vacmetal – engineering solutions – S M S Mevac UK Ltd
***Vacodil (Germany)** – nickel iron glass to metal sealing alloys – Rolfe Industries
***Vacodur (Germany)** – cobalt-iron alloy for high speed machines – Rolfe Industries
***Vacodym (Germany)** – neodymium-boron-iron magnets – Rolfe Industries
***Vacoflex (Germany)** – thermostatic bimetals – Rolfe Industries
***Vacoflux (Germany)** – cobalt iron soft magnetic alloys – Rolfe Industries
VACOHUB (Germany) – vacuum lifting beams and stackers – British & Continental Traders Ltd
***Vacomax (Germany)** – rare earth-cobalt magnets – Rolfe Industries
***Vacon** – nickel iron cobalt glass to metal sealing alloys – Rolfe Industries
Vacon – Proplas International Ltd
Vacon 10 – Proplas International Ltd
Vacon Drives – Potteries Power Transmission Ltd
Vacon Inverters – inverters – Potteries Power Transmission Ltd
Vacon NXL – Proplas International Ltd
Vacon NXS – Proplas International Ltd
***Vacoperm (Germany)** – nickel iron soft magnetic alloys – Rolfe Industries
Vacrel – photopolymer film solder mask – Du Pont UK Ltd
Vacrol – textile processing aid – Benjamin R Vickers & Sons Ltd
Vacspin – spinning lubricant – Benjamin R Vickers & Sons Ltd
Vactech – Techsil Ltd
Vacu-Beads – glass beads – Wheelabrator Group
Vacu-Blast – blast equipment – Wheelabrator Group
Vacu-Blaster – closed circuit blast m/c – Wheelabrator Group
Vacu-Brasive – blast abrasive – Wheelabrator Group
Vacu-Dapt – specialist blast machine adaption service – Wheelabrator Group
Vacu-Grit – angular blast abrasive – Wheelabrator Group
Vacu-Honer – ultra fine abrasive blast m/c – Wheelabrator Group
Vacu-Lox – aluminium oxide abrasive – Wheelabrator Group
Vacu-Lug Traction Tyres Ltd – Vacu Lug Traction Tyres Ltd
Vacu-Peener – shot peening m/c – Wheelabrator Group
Vacu-Rack – vacuum cleaner tool rack – Hamster Baskets
Vacu-Shot – peening quality steel shot – Wheelabrator Group
***VACU-Systems (Germany)** – vacuum clamping systems – Thame Engineering Co. Ltd
Vacu-Teach – controls and special software for blasting and peening machines – Wheelabrator Group
Vacu-Trol – controls and special software for blasting and peening machines – Wheelabrator Group
Vacu-Veyor – abrasive recovery system – Wheelabrator Group
Vacueasy – Tawi UK
Vacuhoist – Harrier Fluid Power Ltd
Vacupress (Food Quality) – suction & discharge for foodstuffs – Merlett Plastics UK Ltd
Vacupress Oil – for oil based products – Merlett Plastics UK Ltd
vacustat – AESpump
Vacuubrand – diaphragm pumps – AESpump
Vacuum Fittings – G V E Ltd
Vacuum Gauges – G V E Ltd
Vacuum Generators – uhv supplies – AESpump
Vacuum Pumps – G V E Ltd
***Vacuumschmelze (Germany)** – alloys; parts and composites with special magnetic, electrical & physical properties – Rolfe Industries
Vacuvin – Birchgrove Products
Vadarex – heat rub – Bell Sons & Co. Ltd
Vaddio – PTZ cameras and control/tracking systems – Tukans Ltd
***Vaderstad** – Drills/cultivators – Paul Tuckwell Ltd
***Vaderstad Drills** – Murley Agricultural Supplies Ltd
Vag – Harrier Fluid Power Ltd
Vahle – European Technical Sales Ltd
***Vaihinger (Germany)** – liquid level indicators – Visilume Ltd
Vaillant – Split system air conditioning – Banfield Refrigeration Supplies Ltd
Vairox – waste water effluent treatment plant – Boc Gases Ltd
Vakstat – M C D Virtak Ltd
VakTape – tear tape used to open hermetically - sealed packaging – Payne
Val d'Isère – Y S E Ltd
val fabrications – M G Trevett Ltd
Valachrome – illuminated signs – Colyer London
VALAIR DATA – mobile air sterilisation filter integrity tester – Parker Dominic Hunter Ltd
Valbruna – stainless steel, nickel alloy and titanium long products – Valbruna UK Ltd
Valencia – basin – Armitage Shanks Ltd
***Valentine** – Court Catering Equipment Ltd
Valeo – car electrics – L A E Valeo Ltd
Valeport – Halcyon Solutions
Valerex – plastic drums – Greif UK Ltd
Valerie Vole – printed matter and toys for water safety campaign – Severn Trent Water
***Valet Aqua Range** – wet pick-up floor drying machines – Truvox International Ltd
Valet Range – dry pick-up vacuum cleaners (canister and back pack types) – Truvox International Ltd
Valethene – plastic drums – Greif UK Ltd
Valiant Satin – paper – Fenner Paper Co. Ltd
Validyne – scientific instruments – Sandhurst Instruments Ltd
Valla Cranes U.K. – sells & services Valla cranes – Peter Hird & Sons Ltd
Vallectric Ltd – electric, mechanical and plumbing installation contractors and tele communications contractors – Vallectric Ltd
Valleda – UK Office Direct
Valley Spring – compression springs, extension springs, disc springs, die springs, wave spring washers, torsion springs and all spring components – Valley Spring Co. Ltd
Vallon – Euroteck Systems UK Ltd
Vallorbe – files – Bearwood Engineering Supplies
***Vallorbe Usines (Switzerland)** – files – Electro Group Ltd
Valmet – Harrier Fluid Power Ltd
***Valmet (Finland)** – stock preparation equipment, pulpers, pressure screens – Pulp & Paper Machinery Ltd
VALMET – Chaintec Ltd
Valmicro (Brazil) – Ball valve manufacture – Trimline Valves
Valor – Baxi Group
Valox – Resinex UK Ltd
VALPAR T.C.S. – liquid temperature control system – Valpar Industrial Ltd
Valpes (France) – electric actuators – Zoedale plc
VALPRES, VALBIA RANGE OF PNEUMATIC ELECTRIC, MANUAL OPERATED VALVES (United Kingdom) – Ultravalve Ltd
Valradio – inverters – Valradio Electronic Ltd
Valrhona – Pastry – Classic Fine Foods Ltd
Valu Mix – dog food – Gilbertson & Page Ltd
Value 100 – low cost motor insurance – M M A Insurance plc
Value Guard – insurance – Car Care Plan Ltd
Value Home – low cost home insurance – M M A Insurance plc
Value Management – S Com Group Ltd

Value Rite – Tools – K B Import & Export Ltd
VALUE RIVET NUT – Range of rivet nuts for all applications – Zygology Ltd
Valufare – vending ingredient and plastic cups – Bunzl Vending Services Ltd
Valupax – Robinson Young Ltd
***Valvan Baling Systems (Belgium)** – automatic baling machines – Robert S Maynard Ltd
VALVE – Blackhall Engineering Ltd
Valve Art (China) – Electronic valves & tubes – Edicron Ltd
Valve Guide Reamers – reamers – Hammond & Co. Ltd
Valve Healthcare Services – Edeco Petroleum Services Ltd
Valve Research – aircraft quality hydraulic valves – R A Rodriguez UK Ltd
Valve Testing Centre – independent certification and accreditation service for the gas, oil and petrochemical industries Worldwide – University Of Leeds
Valveoil – hydraulic directional control valves – Harrier Fluid Power Ltd
Valvestock – industrial valves distributor with specialised actuation division – Valvestock
Valvoline – lubricating oils – Valvoline Oil Co.
Valvoline – oils and wax protectives – Thomas Howse Ltd
Vam Soli – Inks – Plastotype
Vamac – ethylene/acrylic elastomers – Du Pont UK Ltd
Vamac – ethylene acrylic elastomers – Omya UK Ltd
Van-Dal – ladies footwear for all ocassions – The Florida Group
Van Delft – ceramic wall, floor, fireplace tiles, refractory firebricks, special shapes fireclay, victorian reproduction and restoration tiles – H & E Smith
Van Dijck – typeface – Monotype Imaging Ltd
***Van Dommele (Belgium)** – flax and hemp processing machinery, dust extraction systems – Robert S Maynard Ltd
Van Houten – U C D Ltd
Van Leeuwen – tubular steel products – Van Leeuwen Wheeler Ltd
Van Nelle – Douwe Egberts UK
***Van Pamel (Belgium)** – R.B.G. systems, video web viewing systems – Engelmann & Buckham Ltd
Van Remmen UV Techniek – high specification UV units for all commercial and industrial applications. Available with a wide range of features and add-ons to suit every application. high quality and still very competitive. – U V O 3 Ltd
Van Vaults – Fieldway Supplies Ltd
Vanadis 10 – powder metallurgical high performance tool steel – Uddeholm Steel Stockholders
Vanadis 23, 30 & 60 – powder metallurgical high performance high speed steel – Uddeholm Steel Stockholders
Vanadis 4 – powder metallurgical high performance tool steel – Uddeholm Steel Stockholders
Vanair – Harrier Fluid Power Ltd
Vanard – vanadium treated micro alloyed steels – Corus Engineering Steels
Vanco – Hydrafeed Ltd
Vancouver – yachts – Northshore Yachts Ltd
Vandaele – PTO & engine driven woodchippers – Bunce Ashbury Ltd
Vandalene – anti climb paint – Co-Var Ltd
Vandalite – Security & Anti-Vandal Glazing – Architectual Fibre Glass Mouldings Ltd
Vandar – thermoplastic alloys – Ticona UK Ltd
Vanderlande Industries – materials handling systems – Van Der Lande Industries
Vanderlande Industries - materials handling systems – Van Der Lande Industries
Vandervelde – import & proccesses of mica components, mica powder ceramic metal parts – Dean & Tranter
Vandex – County Construction Chemicals Ltd
Vandlgard – tamper proof fastener – Tappex Thread Inserts Ltd
Vanellus – lubricants – B P plc
Vangroenweghe – narrow belt machines for metal & woodworking – Ellesco Ltd
Vanguard – removal packaging materials – Jiffy Packaging Company Ltd
Vanguard – UK Office Direct
Vanguard – record label – Ace Records Ltd
Vanguard Carpets – C F S Carpets
Vanguard Products – furniture packing products – Ambassador Packaging Ltd
***Vanisperse (Norway)** – oxylignin – Borregaard UK
Vanloader – small vehicle loading conveyor/unloading conveyor – Newland Engineering Co. Ltd
Vanodox – peracetic acid based disinfectant – Evans Vanodine International plc
Vanorinse – pipeline cleaner and sterilant for dairies – Evans Vanodine International plc
Vanosan – dx tank sanitizer – Evans Vanodine International plc
Vanquish – glyphosote biactive based total CDA herbicide – Bayer Crop Science
Vanroyce – caravans – Auto Trail V R Ltd
Vanson – battery charger – Stontronics Ltd
***Vantage (Germany)** – unvented hot water cylinder – Vaillant Ltd
Vantage – office chairs – Top Office Equipment Ltd
Vantage – IP65 food factory – Holophane Europe Ltd
Vantico (United Kingdom) – Epoxies – R D Taylor & Co. Ltd
Vantis – Cyclops Electronics Ltd
Vapac – humidifiers – Vapac Humidity Control Ltd
Vapac – humidifiers – Eaton-Williams Group Ltd
VapaNet – microprocessor controlled steam humidifier. – Eaton-Williams Group Ltd
Vaporax – steam boilers – Babcock Wanson UK Ltd
Vapormat – Vapormatt Ltd
Vapormatic – replacement parts for agricultural and industrial tractors, hydraulic components, PTO parts and accessories – The Vapormatic Co. Ltd
Vapormatic – Harrier Fluid Power Ltd
Vapormatt – Vapormatt Ltd
Vaporol – vapour-phase corrosion preventive oils for the protection of internal parts, such as engines, gearboxes, fuel tanks etc – Vapor Tek Ltd
Vapour boosters – Technical Vacuum Services Ltd
vapour boosters – AESpump
***Vapourmatic** – A P B Trading Ltd
Vapourstat – kettle thermostat – Otter Controls Ltd
Vapro-Tek – vapour phase inhibitor paper (VCI paper) – Vapor Tek Ltd
Varcap – PFC equipment – S D C Industries Ltd
Varcon – heat-cleaned glass braid impregnated with silicone varnish – Relats UK Ltd
Vardex – Vargus Tooling Ltd
Varedplan – museum showcases – A Edmonds & Co. Ltd
Vargull – parapet railings in steel and aluminium – Varley & Gulliver Ltd
Vari-Cleat – cable cleat – Ellis Patents Ltd
Vari-flow – the ultimate overhead handling system for the sewing industry. – Richardson & Co. Ltd
Vari-level – floor drains and gullies – Wade International Ltd
Vari-Lift – gas spring - adjustable force gas spring (fitted with a valve) – Camloc Motion Control Ltd
***Vari-Phi (France)** – belt type speed variators – Andantex Ltd
Vari-Purpose – modular corridor building services system – F C Frost Ltd
VARI RAIL – STELL HANDRAILING – Alvin Industrial Limited
Vari-Tite Clip – multi-purpose aluminium clip for retail display – Alplus
Vari-Tork – miniature friction slip clutches – Huco Dynatork
Vari-Warm – British Vita plc
Varian – uhv and turbo pumps – AESpump
Varian – Red House Industrial Services Ltd
***Varibloc (Germany)** – mechanical variable speed drives – S E W Eurodrive Ltd
***Varidisc (Germany)** – mechanical variable speed drives – S E W Eurodrive Ltd
Variflo – dispenser – Appor Ltd
Varilip – seal design – Trelleborg Ceiling Solutions Ltd
***Varimot (Germany)** – mechanical variable speed drives – S E W Eurodrive Ltd
Vario – Display Wizard Ltd
Vario Stage – stage products – Audience Systems Ltd
Variocut – chlorine free neat oils for flute and form grinding – Castrol UK Ltd
Variodrive – electronically commutated DC external rotor motors – Ebm-Papst
Variofan – variable speed fans-high performance – Ebm-Papst
Variohm Transducers – European Technical Sales Ltd
Varioplanter – modular timber planter system – Russell Play Ltd
Variopro – programmable cooling fans – Ebm-Papst
Variostore – mini load systems – Van Der Lande Industries
Various Alloys – grey iron fpr higher tensile requirements and increased crack resistance – Precision Disc Castings Ltd
***Various Trade Names (Taiwan)** – Motor cycles batteries – Staniforth Motor Cycles Wholesale Ltd
Variprop – propeller – Bruntons Propellers Ltd
Variseal – seal designs – Trelleborg Ceiling Solutions Ltd
Variset – Tool Presetting Equipment & Toolmanagement software – Royal Tool Control Ltd
Variset – cloakroom equipment – A.J. Binns Ltd
VariSource – high dose rate after loader – Varian Medical Systems UK Ltd
Varispray – variable spray pattern shower head – Aqualisa Products Ltd Head Office
Varistar – 19" cabinet for industrial applications – Schroff UK Ltd
VarisVision – image management system completing the vision environment – Varian Medical Systems UK Ltd
***Varitex** – signmakers – Signconex Ltd
Varitone – sound absorption panel – I A C Company Ltd
Varitroix – Relec Electronics Ltd
Varitronix – Cyclops Electronics Ltd
Varivap – variable output steam humidifier – Eaton-Williams Group Ltd
Varley – alarm sounder – Clifford & Snell
Varley – pumps – Varley Pumps Ltd
Varley – gear pumps – Hayward Tyler Ltd
Varley - pumps. – Varley Pumps Ltd
Varlogic – power factor correction and harmonic filtering – Schneider
Varmatic Lightmaster – Energy Efficiency Lighting Controller – S D C Industries Ltd
Varmatic Senator – power factor correction equipment – S D C Industries Ltd
Varpac – power factor correction equipment – S D C Industries Ltd
Varplus – capacitors – Schneider
Varscan – seismic data vectorising – D P T S Group Holdings Ltd
VARTA – Groves Batteries
***Varta** – automotive batteries – Varta Automotive Batteries Ltd
VARTA – Batteries – Halcyon Solutions
VASCAT – European Drives & Motor Repairs
Vasco – British Vita plc
Vascutherm – electrical heated gloves and socks for medical applications – Vacuum Reflex
Vast – Zeiss
VAT – vacuum valves – AESpump
Vaughan – chopper pumps – P & M Pumps
Vaughans – blacksmiths tools – Vaughans Hope Works Ltd
Vauxhall – L M C Hadrian Ltd
Vauxhall – Ashley Competition Exhausts Ltd
Vauxhall/Opel parts – H & M Automotive UK Ltd
Vax Cleaning Solutions and Dust Bags – Vax Ltd
Vax Luna 1300 – multi purpose cleaner – Vax Ltd
Vax Luna 1400 – multi purpose cleaner – Vax Ltd
Vax Sahara – hard floor cleaner – Vax Ltd
Vazo – free radcial sources/chemical additive – Du Pont UK Ltd
VB241 – Sallu Plastics
VBond – Virtualization based ADSL bonding solution – Xrio Ltd
VC & Group Symbol – British Vita plc
VCH – Cyclops Electronics Ltd
***VDB (France)** – microphone carbon fibre boom poles – Audio Ltd
VDMA – B L Pneumatics Ltd
Veba – ladies fashions – High Society
Vecs – public address close circuit tv intercom & professional sound – Toa Corperation UK Ltd
Vecta – pumps and equipment for dairy farming, water treatment equipment – Loheat
***Vectis 500** – Touch screens – I C R Touch LLP
Vector – videowall products – Electrosonic Ltd
Vector – Global Laser Technology Solutions
Vector – ac flux reactor – Control Techniques
Vector – automatic blasting equipment – Wheelabrator Group
Vector – hinge – Securistyle Ltd
Vector – packet switches and network access products – Nortel Networks UK Ltd
Vectorbeam – electron beam lithography system – Leica Microsystems
Vectra – wholly aromatic polyester; liquid crystal polymer – Ticona UK Ltd
Vectron – Oasis Systems
Vectwin – Hamworthy Waste Water plc
VEE BEE – filters, strainers and separators – Vee Bee Filtration UK Ltd
***Vee-ray** – Blue Seal Ltd
***Veenstra (Netherlands)** – tube and wire bending machines – Brandone Machine Tool Ltd
***Veetee Brand** – Veetee Rice Ltd
Veevers Carter – flowers – Veevers Carter Flowers Ltd
***Vega (Italy)** – hydraulic cylinders – A C Hydraulics Ltd
Vehicle – awnings – Deans Blinds & Awnings UK
Vehicle Control – A range of vehicle control products – Gunnebo Entrance Control Ltd
Velbex – Sallu Plastics
Velcon – Harrier Fluid Power Ltd
VELCRO – hook and loop fastening – Opas Southern Limited
Velcro – touch and close – William Gee Ltd
Velcro – Gawler Tapes & Plastics Ltd
Vellotape – Campbell International
Vellotape, Panther – Campbell International
***Velma** – Cater Bake UK Ltd
Velo Sport – clothing, cycles and frames – Witcomb Cycles
Velometers – swinging vane anemometer – Airflow Measurements Ltd
Velopost – folding and inserting machine – K A S Paper Systems Ltd
Velotak – envelope adhesive – Forbo Adhesives UK Ltd
Velox – Camberley Catering Equipment
Velox – High Speed Grills – Velox Ltd
Veltex – chamois leather – Hutchings & Harding Ltd
Velux – Wigan Timber Ltd
Velux – Velux recognised installer: we only use Velux windows not cheaper alternatives – G&M Loft Conversions

Velvawax – extra smooth wax crayons – Creative Art Products Ltd
Velvet Book II – fabric – Zoffany
Velvets – woven fabrics – Zoffany
VEM – Mercury Bearings Ltd
VendaGuard – vending machine alarms – O W L Electronics Ltd
Vender – Harrier Fluid Power Ltd
Vending Tricycles – tricycles – Pashley Cycles Ltd
Vendor – Kingston Communications
Vendor Inspection – Oceaneering Asset Integrity
Venetian – Prices Patent Candles Ltd
Venicelux Digital – Digital Products - Toner Sheet Fed - Coated – Howard Smith Paper Ltd
Venieri – Harrier Fluid Power Ltd
Venners – licensed stock audit and inventory and retail – Christie & Co. Ltd
Venners Computer Systems – provision of stock control & EPOS software for organisations managing food and beverage operations worldwide – Christie & Co. Ltd
Venom – car alarms – Quicksilver Automotive
Vent Air – UK Office Direct
***Vent-Axia** – Industrial Fans – Beatson Fans & Motors Ltd
Vent Axia – Northern Fan Supplies Ltd
***Vent Axia Ltd (United Kingdom)** – fan manufrs – Westmid Fans
Vent King – Combined Catering Services
Ventair – Chorus Panel & Profiles
Ventamatic – passive controllable and static window ventilators – R W Simon Ltd
Ventapipe – air admittance valve – Mcalpine & Company Ltd
Ventatank – Atkinson Equipment
Ventcroft – security products – Ventcroft Ltd
Ventec – range of electrion controllers. – Vent Engineering
Ventec – deep hole drill – Hammond & Co. Ltd
Ventec Drills – deep hole drills – Hammond & Co. Ltd
Ventex – grease filter – Waterloo Air Products
Ventform – ground floor slabs where methane gas is a problem – Cordek Ltd
Ventilex (Netherlands) – fluid bed dryers – Orthos Engineering Ltd
Ventmist – nebulisers & nebuliser compressors – A F P Medical Ltd
Ventomatic – automatic opener for greenhouse roof vents – Eden Halls Greenhouses Ltd
Ventrolla – Ventrolla Ltd
Ventsafe – dust and fume (non-hazardous) – Envirogard Specialist Hires Ltd
Ventura – rooflight – McKenzie Martin Ltd
Ventura – National Door Co.
Ventura – Safety Goggles – Scott International Ltd
Ventura – WC – Armitage Shanks Ltd
Venture – vision systems – Baty International
Venture Brand – butcher catering and trade knives – Herbert M Slater Ltd
Venture Tapes – B D K Industrial Products Ltd
Venturi 5000 (United Kingdom) – low nox burners – Hamworthy Combustion Engineering Ltd
Ventus – abrasive blast cabinet – Wheelabrator Group
Venue – Pledge Office Chairs Ltd
Venus – bonded nylon – Amann Oxley Threads Ltd
***Venus** – Tea, saffron, poppodoms, spices – Trade Link London Ltd
Venus – flexible packaging films, polyethylene, polypropylene and E.V.A. – Amcor Flexibles UK Ltd
Verbatim – photopolymer resins and systems for flexographic plate manufacture – Chemence Ltd
Verco – office furniture – E W Marshall Ltd
Verco – office furniture – Verco Office Furniture Ltd
Verco – Office Seating – Bucon Ltd
Verco – Sitsmart Ltd
Verco – Capex Office Interiors
Verdalia A – perfume speciality – Quest International UK Ltd
Verde Artificial Grass – Verde Sports Cricket Ltd
Verde Golf Driving Mat – mats and inserts for golf ranges – Verde Sports Cricket Ltd
Verde Tee Frame – portable all-weather golf tee – Verde Sports Cricket Ltd
Verde Weave – woven permanent indoor bowling green surface – Verde Sports Cricket Ltd
Verde WinterTee – all-weather tee surfaces – Verde Sports Cricket Ltd
Verdemat – indoot bowls carpets – Sportsmark Group Ltd
Verdepitch – outdoor cricket wicket and indoor roll-up wicket – Verde Sports Cricket Ltd
***Verdestan** – Evergreen Tractors Ltd
Verdeturf – sand-filled artificial grass – Verde Sports Cricket Ltd
Verdi – kitchen furniture – Moores Furniture Group
Verdi Collection – Geerings Of Ashford Ltd
Verdict – precision measuring equipment – Verdict Gauge Ltd
Verdict Gauge Ltd – Verdict Gauge Ltd
Verdigreen – Melcourt Industries
Verdilyn – perfume speciality – Quest International UK Ltd
Verdinal – perfume speciality – Quest International UK Ltd
Verdoracine – perfume speciality – Quest International UK Ltd
Verglo – conduit fittings and wiring accessories, and cable management products – Stephen Glover & Co. Ltd
VeriBox – Barcode Validation System – Crosscheck Systems Ltd
Verid – fingerprint verification – T S S I Sytems
Veridia – precision bore glass tubing – Chance Glass Ltd
Veriplast – Autobar Group Ltd
Veritas – Planes, measuring tools, calipers – The Toolpost
Verivide – Colour Assessment cabinets – James H Heal & Co. Ltd
VeriVide – cabinets for the visual assessment of colour – Verivide Ltd
Vermalite – exfoliated vermiculite – Silvaperl
Vermeer – Harrier Fluid Power Ltd
Vermeer – trenchers, trench compactors, impact moles, guided boring equipment, tree spades, stump cutters and brushwood chippers – Vermeer UK
Vermeer – Yacht Cranes – Wave Seven Marine Ltd
Vermiculite – sprayed coatings – Promat UK Ltd
Vermor – pressure recorders – Vernon Morris Utility Solutions Ltd
Verone – impression materials – Schottlander Dental Equipment Supplies
Versa – a range of wheelchair access vehicles – Windes Car Centre
Versa Frame – frame pack for farm and industrial straight sliding doors – P C Henderson Ltd
Versa Lifting – King Lifting Ltd
Versaduct – sheet metal fabricating, CNC plasma cutting and dust extraction – Versaduct Sheet Metal Ltd
VersaFlex – Baldor UK
Versaflex – flexible tubing – Bolton Plastic Components Ltd
Versailles – WC suite – Armitage Shanks Ltd
Versalar – routers – Nortel Networks UK Ltd
Versalift – Versalift Distributors UK Ltd
Versalite – Harrier Fluid Power Ltd
Versamatic pumps – Air operated Double diaphragm – Fluid Pumps Ltd
Versanut – anchor nut – Zygology Ltd
Versapak – UK Office Direct
Versapak – re-usable mailing pouches, mail sacks, consumable paper envelopes, mail room furniture, security products and security systems for doping control – Versapak International
Versarray – semiconductor integrated circuits – Nortel Networks UK Ltd
Versatemp – applied and packaged energy reclaim heat pump air conditioning – Clivet UK
Versatile – tile cutter – Q E P Ltd
Versatile – multi purpose cleaner with lemon odour – Evans Vanodine International plc
Versatool – Hollowing tool – The Toolpost
Versi-Dredge – Self Propelled Dredger – Wave Seven Marine Ltd
Version 7.50 – spring design software – Institute Of Spring Technology
version 8 – spring design software – Institute Of Spring Technology
Version A.I. – welding equipment – Bearwood Engineering Supplies
Versiplan – sliding partitions – Becker Sliding Partitions Ltd
Versirak – S R S Product plc
Versitile Construction – purchasing storage and racking systems – Atol Racking & Building Ltd
Vertamet – Stainless steel electrodes for vertical down welding – Metrode Products Ltd
Vertelon – perfume speciality – Quest International UK Ltd
Vertex Standard – Radio Relay
Vertical Drop Rolling Shutters – Bolton Gate Co. Ltd
Vertical Mixers – Morton Mixers & Blenders Ltd
Vertical Strong Box – storage case – Acco East Light Ltd
Vertiforce – fibre system designed for wall applications – Propex Concrete Systems Ltd
Vertiforce – Phoenix Weighing Services Ltd
Vertigo – label – Mercury Records
Vertiseal – polysulphide sealant – Grace Construction Ltd
Vertisorter – automated sorting conveyor systems – Van Der Lande Industries
Verto – tiling trims and accessories – Verto Ltd
Verto Data – Single point of contact for all the UK Insternet Service Providers – Verto Data
Vertrel – R W Greeff
Verulam – 300mm/150mm prof. scale rules – Blundell Harling Ltd
Vervis – B P plc
Vescor – Harrier Fluid Power Ltd
Vesipaque – G E Healthcare
Vespel – Aaron Metal & Plastic Supplies Ltd
Vespel – parts & shapes – Du Pont UK Ltd
Vessel – Harrier Fluid Power Ltd
***Vesta (Italy)** – pneumatic control equipment – The West Group Ltd
Vestale – washing station – Armitage Shanks Ltd
Vesteel – vitreous enamelling quality steel strip – Corus U K Ltd
Vestfrost – Fridge Freezer Direct Company Ltd
Vestr – Cambridgeshire Hydraulics Ltd
Vestry – UK Office Direct
VETIGRAPH – CAD/CAM for the fashion and apparel industries – Vetigraph CAD/CAM Ltd
Vetiveryl Acetate Subst. ABX7062 – speciality compound – Quest International UK Ltd
***Vetremox** – Pharmaq Ltd
Vexve – Kee Valves
VF Coupling – Renold Clutches & Couplings Ltd
VF1 – Data logger – Halcyon Solutions
VG – Ellesco Ltd
VG – uhv supplies – AESpump
VG 9000 – GD-MS – Thermo Electrical
VG Elemental – Thermo Electrical
VG9000 – Thermo Electrical
Vi-King – concrete drainage pipes and manholes – Stanton Bonna Concrete Ltd
Via-Sit – Office Seating – Bucon Ltd
Via Technologies – Cyclops Electronics Ltd
Viacem – pigment – Viaton Industries Ltd
Viaduct – software – Electronic Data Processing plc
Vials – Solmedia Laboratory Supplies
***VIALUX (Germany and UK)** – high pressure sodium discharge lamps – Osram Ltd
Viasat – scandinavian satellite television company – Viasat Broadcasting Group Ltd
Viaseed – G E Healthcare
***VIB (Germany)** – spraydampers, steam and condensate systems – Pulp & Paper Machinery Ltd
Vibac – Tri Pack Supplies Ltd
Vibac – General Fabrications Ltd
Vibia Lighting – Light Fantastic
Vibixa – breakfast cereal – Weetabix Ltd
Vibraclamp – tube clamping systems, wall brackets, anti-vibration mounts – Thermofrost Cryo plc
Vibradex – anti vibration matting – Dexine Rubber Co. Ltd
***Vibram (Italy)** – moulded rubber soles (vibram s.p.a. milan) – Davies & Company
Vibrasonics – Russell Finex Ltd
Vibratom – vibrating ball mills – Tema Machinery Ltd
Vibreaker – aircraft ducting joints – Senior Aerospace Bird Bellows
***Vibrex (U.S.A.)** – Environmental Equipments Ltd
Vibro Pile – piling systems – B S P International Foundations Ltd
Vibrodynamics – separation equipment – S W G Process Engineering Ltd
Vibrolators – B L Pneumatics Ltd
Vibromax – Harrier Fluid Power Ltd
Vibroplant – dumpers, mixers, rollers, compressors, tractors, generators, lighting equipment, rough terrain forklifts and mini excavators – V P plc
Vibroplant - Compressed Air – compressors and ancillary equipment; large compressors for offshore equipment – V P plc
Vibroplant P.L.C. – V P plc
Vibroplant - Power Generation – super silenced generator – V P plc
Vibroplant - Powered Access – power aerial access equipment – V P plc
Vibroplant-Recycling Division – Screens and crushers – V P plc
Vibroplant- Welding Division – welding equipment – V P plc
VIC Tavlic – Pipework – Tunnel Steels
Vican – internal gear pumps for use on oils, solvents, paints and resins – Selwood Pump Company Ltd
Vice Roy – solid fuel control pannel – Harton Services Ltd
Vicel – British Vita plc
Vicentini (Italy) – clay making equipment – Orthos Engineering Ltd
Viceroy – molt drainers & subsoilers – Brown's Agricultural Machinery Company Ltd
Vickerlube – scourable machine lubricants – Benjamin R Vickers & Sons Ltd
Vickers – Red House Industrial Services Ltd
Vickers – equipment/spares – Bearwood Engineering Supplies
Vickers – Harrier Fluid Power Ltd
Vickers – Hydraulic Component & Systems Ltd
Vickers – Pressure Design Hydraulics Ltd
Vickers On-Line – precision solutions for automatic analysers – Vickers Laboratories Ltd
Vickery – paper machine doctors and doctor blades – Kadant UK Ltd
Vickery – sheetmetal working equipment and machinery – Hartle I G E Ltd
Vicon – J & S Lewis Ltd

Vicon – 3 dimensional movement analysis system – Vicon Motion Systems Ltd

Vicon – reconnaisance & CMPS systems – Thales Optronics Ltd

Vicrin (Portugal) – polypropylene multifilament – Cotesi UK Ltd

Vicrtex – luxury vinyl wallcoverings – Tektura plc

Victa – cricket and hockey balls – Kookaburra Reader Ltd

Victa (Australia) – domestic & professional rotary mowers – E P Barrus

Victa – lawnmowers – Small Engine Services Ltd

Victan – dry chrome leather – Joseph Clayton & Sons Ltd

Victaulic – pipe joints and fittings – Midland Tube & Fabrications

Victaulic – mechanical pipe jointing systems – Glynwed Pipe Systems Ltd

Victor – hazardous area lighting, mine lighting, connectors and couplers – Victor Products Ltd

Victor – equipment & spares – Bearwood Engineering Supplies

Victor – Central C N C Machinery Ltd

Victor – Ascot Wholesale Ltd

Victor – Axon Enterprises Ltd

Victor Hugo, Steven Daniels, and Ruffino – quality giftware – P M S International Group plc

Victor Manufacturing Ltd – commercial catering equipment – Victor Manufacturing Ltd

Victor Pyrate – tank washing machines and gas-freeing fans (portable) – Victor Marine

Victor Vodac Device – Vodafone Retail Ltd

Victoria-Milford Grinders – double ended grinding machines – Gate Machinery International Ltd

Victoria-Velox Hacksaw – hacksawing machines – Gate Machinery International Ltd

*Victorian (United Kingdom) – snooker tables – Thurston

Victorian – snooker tables – Thurston

Victorinox – Russums

Victory – shower trays – Novellini UK Ltd

Victory – brushes – Harris Cleaning Services

"Victory Flush Valves" – naval brass flushing valves – Victory Valve Sales Ltd

Victory V – throat lozenges – Ernest Jackson & Co. Ltd

Vidacord – impregnated & unimpregnated braided and twisted cords – Jones Stroud Insulations Ltd

Vidaflex XGR – expandable glass braid sleeving – Jones Stroud Insulations Ltd

Vidaflex XGS – expandable glass braid silicone elastomer coated sleeving – Jones Stroud Insulations Ltd

Vidaflex XNF – braided sleeving from Nomex yarn – Jones Stroud Insulations Ltd

Vidam (United Kingdom) – rubber cork anti-vibration material – Farrat Isolevel

Vidaseal – oven door seals – Jones Stroud Insulations Ltd

Vidatape – woven glass polyester and nomex tapes – Jones Stroud Insulations Ltd

Videcom – hardware design and production, software design and development – Videcom International Ltd

Video 7 – Lamphouse Ltd

Video Arts Interactive Learning – producers and distributors of interactive training programmes on CD-I and CD-ROM – Video Arts Group Ltd

Video Vortex – videos – Scala Agenturen UK

Videofax – TV and video organiser – Logax Ltd

Videoflex – steel tape rules – Fisco Tools Ltd

Videogauge – modular machine vision system – Vysionics

Videoguard – closed circuit television equipment – Volumatic Ltd

Videoscope – inspection/alignment systems – Loadpoint Ltd

Videx – High End, Intercomms, Videocomms Etc – C P A Ironworks

Videx – Wired audio and video intercom – Seamless Aluminium International Ltd

Vidikron – Lamphouse Ltd

*Vidmar (Switzerland) – tool cabinets storage systems – Brunner Machine Tools Ltd

Vieler – Aluminium extrusions & display case hardware – Showmaster Ltd

Viennaline – spectacles and sunglasses – Safilo UK Ltd

Viessmann Boilers – Twin Industries International Ltd

View From – sportswear apparel – Nova International

Viewbase Link – financial and communication control of public house estates – F B H Associates Ltd

Viewbox – light boxes for graphics, printing, photography, signs and medical – D W Group Ltd

Viewcomp – digital VMS user control system – Savant Ltd

Viewpack – photographic storage systems, photography – D W Group Ltd

Viewpack – sterilisation pouches – Amcor Flexibles

Viewpoint (United Kingdom) – AS 400 based system to enable scanning, storage and retrieval of hard copy documents – Pacific Solutions International Ltd

Viewsonic – Lamphouse Ltd

Vifil – British Vita plc

*Vifrifrigo (Italy) – marine refrigeration – Aquapac International Ltd

Vigen Ltd – pc networks & solutions – Viglen Technology Ltd

Vigilant – valves – David Auld Valves Ltd

Vignal – car electrics – L A E Valeo Ltd

Vigor – tools and equipment – Time Products UK Ltd

Vigortronix – name – Vigortronix Ltd

Vijeo Look – entry level SCADA software – Schneider

*Vikan Hygiene System (Denmark) – cleaning and hygiene equipment – Vikan UK Ltd

Vikan Transport System (Denmark) – commercial vehicle cleaning equipment – Vikan UK Ltd

Vikan UK (Denmark) – chemical cleaning products etc – Vikan UK Ltd

Viking – binoculars, telescopes, magnifiers and low vision aids – Viking Optical Ltd

Viking – paint brushes – Whitaker & Sawyer Brushes Ltd

Viking – adult fiction and non-fiction - hardback and paperback – Penguin Books Ltd

Viking – exhibition portable stand – RTD Systems Limited

*Viking (Denmark) – Jack Sealey Ltd

Viking – air handling units – Roof Units Ltd

Viking – steel bath – Armitage Shanks Ltd

Viking – Weights and weighing equipment – Barr & Grosvenor Ltd

Viking – wall plugs – Bostik Ltd

Viking 360 – continuous feed breakstem riveting system suitable for robotic adaption – Avdel UK Ltd

Viking-Johnson – pipe couplings and adaptors; new unused and secondhand steeltubes, welding fittings and fabrications – Midland Tube & Fabrications

Viking Johnson – metal pipe jointing systems – Glynwed Pipe Systems Ltd

Viking Johnson – pipe couplings, flange adaptors and pipe repair clamps – Viking Johnson

Viking Mowers – D D Hire

Viking pumps – Anchor Pumps Co. Ltd

Vikotank – oil storage tank – Vikoma International Ltd

Vikotanks – oil containment systems – Vikoma International Ltd

Vikro Steel – Doncasters F B C Ltd

Vilamin – amino resins – V I L Resins Ltd

Vilaqua – water thinnable resins – V I L Resins Ltd

Vileda – Freudenberg Household Products

Viledon – gas liquid filtration materials and other non woven material – Vilene Interlinings

Vilene – interlinings (non woven) – Vilene Interlinings

ViLITE – high indensity warning road lamp – Doormen

Vilkyd – alkyd resins – V I L Resins Ltd

Villa Owners Club – property managers – H P B Management Ltd

Villiers – engines & pumps spare parts – Power Assemblies Ltd

*Villiger (Cuba, Jamaica, Europe and Honduras) – cigars – Hunters & Frankau Ltd

Vilmed – non woven medical materials – Vilene Interlinings

Vilosyn – maleic and phenolic resins – V I L Resins Ltd

Vilton Cars – Car Sales – Spire Peugeot Ltd

*Vimto – Aimia Foods

Vimto – soft drink range – Nichols plc

Vina Bondad – wine – Rodney Densem Wines Ltd

Vina Cantaluna (Chile) – Patriarche Wine Agencies

Vinachem – Micro-repellent – Rotafix Ltd

Vinadac – high build maintenance coatings – Dacrylate Paints Ltd

Vincents – shopfitters – Vincents Norwich Ltd

Vincit – range of protective coatings and rust converters – Agma Ltd

Viners – cutlery and cookware – Oneida International Ltd

Vingcard – Assa Abloy Hospitality Ltd

Vinilflex – flexible conduit – Merlett Plastics UK Ltd

Vinoseal – clamp flange for sealing vinyl and other sheet floorings around manholes, gullies and channels – Webster-Wilkinson Ltd

Vinsol – resin – Hercules Holding Ii Ltd

Vintage (India) – electric & acoustic guitars – John Hornby Skewes & Co. Ltd

Vintage Cider – H Weston & Sons Ltd

Vinyl Book I – wallcovering collection – Zoffany

Vinyl Book II – wallcovering collection – Zoffany

Vinyl Book III – wallcovering collection – Zoffany

Vinyl Book IV – wallcovering collection – Zoffany

Vinyl Fencing – Vinyl Fencing Ltd

Vinyl v – Wallcovering collection – Zoffany

Vinyl VI – Wallcovering collection – Zoffany

Vinylac – plastic protection materials – Harrison Thompson & Co. Ltd

Viola – VLF test set 40kV – Baur Test Equipment Ltd

Viomedex – enteral feeding products and surgical skin markers – Viomedex Ltd

Viotril ABQ5770 – speciality compound – Quest International UK Ltd

VIP 300 – overcurrent & earth fault protection devices – Schneider

Viper – pump – Torres Engineering & Pumps Ltd

Viper – fire fighting vehicle – Carmichael Support Services

Viper – automated sorting conveyor systems – Van Der Lande Industries

Viper (United Kingdom) – cotton nylon high abrasion fabric – Carrington Career & Work Wear

Viper – aero engines – Rolls-Royce plc

Virage – handle – Securistyle Ltd

Virago – The Little Brown Book Group

Virbamec – Endectocide injection for cattle, pigs and sheep – Virbac Ltd

Virbamec Pour-On – Endectocide for cattle – Virbac Ltd

Virbamec Super – Endectocide and flukicide injection for cattle – Virbac Ltd

Virenium – Pobjoy Mint Ltd

Viresco – micro-organism product which suppresses disease and banishes certain leaf pests – Viresco UK Ltd

Virex – mucus extractor – Surgicraft Ltd

Virio – vertical balancing machine – Schenck Ltd

Virisite Wills Diamond – diamond tool manufacturers – Abrasive Technology Ltd

Virkon – virulidal disinfectant – Day Impex Ltd

Virkon – disinfectant – DuPont Animal Health Solutions

Virkon – Solmedia Laboratory Supplies

Virtua – digital console – Digico UK Ltd

Virtual Bench – software product – National Instrument UK Corp Ltd

Virtual Showroom – new & used car locator (internet) – Kalamazoo - Reynolds Ltd

Visa – twin tank portable toilets – Elsan Ltd

Visa – vacuum in-situ application for applying cladding – U M C International

VISA ENERGY ELECTRICITY GENERATORS – VISA NERGY ELECTRICITY GENERATORS – Visa Energy GB Ltd

Visclair Tabs – mucolytic – Sinclair I S Pharma

Visco – B P plc

Visco 2000 – lubricants – B P plc

Visco 5000 – B P plc

Visco 7000 – B P plc

Visco-Led – red lead paint – Witham Oil & Paint Lowestoft Ltd

Visco Nova – lubricants – B P plc

Viscoatex – acrylic based thickeners – Omya UK Ltd

Viscoform – casting patterns – Attenborough Dental Ltd

Viscol – lubricating oils and petroleum products – Rock Chemicals Ltd

Visconol – textile processing aid – Benjamin R Vickers & Sons Ltd

Viscount – Axon Enterprises Ltd

Viscount – drainers – Brown's Agricultural Machinery Company Ltd

Viscount – handle – Securistyle Ltd

Vise Grip – S J Wharton Ltd

Visegrip – Gem Tool Hire & Sales Ltd

Vishay – Cyclops Electronics Ltd

Vishay – European Technical Sales Ltd

Vishay Sfernice – Nobel Electronics Ltd

Vishay Spectrol – Nobel Electronics Ltd

Visible Difference – cosmetics – Elizabeth Arden

Visicard – Rotadex Systems Ltd

Visimask – medical personnel protection – Synergy Healthcare plc

Vision (United Kingdom) – ECi Software Solutions Limited

Vision – battery and mains operated pay and display machines – Alfia Services Ltd

Vision – handling system control software – Van Der Lande Industries

Vision – 2 row potato harvesters - 1750 – Standen Engineering Ltd

Vision – Lamphouse Ltd

Vision (United Kingdom) – post corrigator logistics – Escada Systems Ltd

Vision – overhead tubular radiant heaters – Reznor UK Ltd

Vision – full face mask respirators positive or negative pressure – Scott International Ltd

Vision – architectural bollards – Designplan Lighting Ltd

VISION 93 – plug in refrigerated display cabinets – Hussmann Refrigeration Ltd

Vision Engineering Ltd – microscopes – Vision Engineering Ltd

Vision Express (UK) Ltd – optical lense retail stores – Vision Express UK

Vision now – Contact lenses – Peekay National Eyecare Group Ltd

Vision Strip – complete composite glazing strip – Tremco Illbruck Ltd

Vision-wall – acoustic window system – I A C Company Ltd

Vision Work Surface – Potter Cowan & Co Belfast Ltd

Vision ZPS – warehouse picking control software – Van Der Lande Industries

Visiongard – perforated steel rolling shutters – Kaba Door Systems

Visionhire – rental and retails TV and video – Boxclever

VisionPro – VisionPro series of LCD monitor arms – Ergomounts Ltd

Visions – quilts and bedding – Comfy Quilts Ltd

VisionTrack – digital video recorder – Red Lion 49 Ltd

Visionvent – Glazing Vision Ltd

Visipanel – Rotadex Systems Ltd

Visipaque – G E Healthcare

Visipaye – magazine machine for payroll – Anson Systems Ltd

Visiplant – G E Healthcare

Visipoint – edge and body punched cards – Anson Systems Ltd

Visipost – vertical visible systems – Anson Systems Ltd

Visisizer – spray sizing systems – Oxford Lasers Ltd

Visit – multimedia products – Nortel Networks UK Ltd

Visitape – cellotape – Office Team

Visitor Days – books – Tudor Journals Ltd

Viskproof – aluminium roll-on pilfer proof caps – Viscose Closures Ltd

Viskring – self shrink cellulose rings and tubing – Viscose Closures Ltd

*Visloux (Germany) – sensors – Sensortek

Visopaque – G E Healthcare

Visqueen (United Kingdom) – polythene film, sacks & bags – British Polythene Industries plc

Visqueen – damp proof membrane - polyethylene – Visqueen Building Products South Wales Ltd

*Vista (U.S.A.) – keyboard video mouse multi PC-sever switches – Techland Group Ltd

Vista – window blind components – Luxaflex

Vista – Eurocell Building Plastics Ltd

Vista (U.S.A.) – aluminium plant container – Christian Day Ltd

Vista (Germany) – colour print and slide film and colour paper – Agfa Gevaert

Vista – exterior amenity luminaire – Holophane Europe Ltd

*Vista Alegre (Portugal) – ceramic tableware – Dexam International

Vistafile – filing systems – Anson Systems Ltd

Vistalux – pvc roof sheeting – Ariel Plastics Ltd

Vistar – Noel Village Steel Founder Ltd

Vistop – computer software – K B C Process Technology Ltd

Vistra – B P plc

Vistrain – interactive video training and applications – N C C Group

Visual Automation – develop image analysis, process control, security and visual recognition systems – University Of Manchester Incubator Company Ltd

Visualize Range – visualize – Applied Scintillation Technologies

Visurgis Optibelt – Transmission Belts – Sprint Engineering & Lubricant

Vita – British Vita plc

Vita-Bark – soil improver – Woodgrow Horticulture

Vita Flex – Anchor Magnets Ltd

VITA & Group Symbol – British Vita plc

Vita-Lenton – British Vita plc

Vita-one – British Vita plc

Vitableach – wood bleach – Smith & Roger Ltd

Vitabond – British Vita plc

Vitacal – British Vita plc

Vitacare – British Vita plc

Vitachem – British Vita plc

Vitachem – latex technology – Vita Liquid Polymers

Vitafeeds – soluble feeds – Vitax Ltd

Vitafibre – British Vita plc

Vitafil – British Vita plc

Vitaflight – British Vita plc

Vitafoam – British Vita plc

Vitafresh – antimicrobial food quality conveyor belting – Ammeraal Beltech Ltd

Vitaglo – safety coatings – Leighs Paints

Vitalac – external decorative coating – Akzo Nobel Packaging Coatings Ltd

Vitalair – Containment systems – Hosokawa Micron Ltd

Vitalam – British Vita plc

Vitalay – British Vita plc

Vitalegs – skin care – Chefaro UK Ltd

Vitaline – British Vita plc

Vitality – British Vita plc

Vitalograph – medical instrumentation, respiratory measurement – Vitalograph UK Ltd

Vitalon – nylon belting and rubber-nylon beltings – Ammeraal Beltech Ltd

Vitalure – protective internal can coating – Akzo Nobel Packaging Coatings Ltd

Vitaluxan – British Vita plc

Vitaluxe – British Vita plc

Vitamat – British Vita plc

*Vitamax – Pharmaq Ltd

Vitamol – British Vita plc

Vitamousse – British Vita plc

Vitapad – British Vita plc

Vitapedic – British Vita plc

Vitapet – cod liver oil pet food suppliment – Seven Sea's Ltd

Vitaphram – British Vita plc

Vitaplas – PVC plastisols – Vita Liquid Polymers

Vitaply – polyurethene and PVC conveyor beltings – Ammeraal Beltech Ltd

Vitapol – British Vita plc

Vitapol – french polish – Smith & Roger Ltd

Vitaprene – British Vita plc

Vitapruf – British Vita plc

Vitaquilt – British Vita plc

*Vitari (Italy) – straightening and cutting to lengths, barbed wire machines, chain forming and welding machines and chainlink fence machines – Embassy Machinery Ltd

Vitaseal – British Vita plc

Vitaseal – impregnated foam slow recovery sealants for automotive and building applications – Vitec

Vitasoft – British Vita plc

Vitasol – British Vita plc

Vitasorb – British Vita plc

Vitastic – chrome-nylon beltings – Ammeraal Beltech Ltd

Vitastretch – British Vita plc

Vitatex – British Vita plc

Vitathane – British Vita plc

Vitatherm – British Vita plc

Vitathone – cream – Reckitt Benckiser plc

Vitatread – British Vita plc

Vitaweb – British Vita plc

Vitawrap – British Vita plc

Vitax – compost maker – Vitax Ltd

Vitax Blood, Fish and Bone – Vitax Ltd

Vitax Bonemeal – Vitax Ltd

Vitax Claybreaker – Vitax Ltd

Vitax Conifer & Shrub – Vitax Ltd

Vitax Garden Lime – Vitax Ltd

Vitax Growmore – Vitax Ltd

Vitax Irish Moss Peat – Vitax Ltd

Vitax Q4 – fertiliser – Vitax Ltd

Vitax Q4 Multipurpose Compost – Vitax Ltd

Vitax Q4 Rose Food – Vitax Ltd

*Vitco (Far East) – housewares – Vitco Ltd

Vitec – British Vita plc

Vitech (United Kingdom) – coated keular and carbon fibre fabrics for clothing – Carr Reinforcements

Vitelec – Cyclops Electronics Ltd

Viternus – metal protective paints – Crosbie Casco Coating

Vitesse – contact & systemic fungisde for turf – Bayer Crop Science

Vitesta – British Vita plc

Vitex (Germany) – quality coated abrasives – V S M Abrasives Ltd

*Vitmos (Italy) – vitreous glass mosaics – Udny Edgar & Co. Ltd

Vitolane – sol-gel scratch resistant coating – T W I

Vitomag – mobile magnetic power packs – Baugh & Weedon Ltd

Viton – vehicle refinishing paints – Permatex Protective Coatings UK Ltd

Viton – fluoroelastomer – Du Pont UK Ltd

Viton – W Mannering London Ltd

Vitox – water/effluent, treatment plant – Boc Gases Ltd

Vitra – Desks – Bucon Ltd

Vitraglaze – vitreous enamel steel bonded to insulate – Panel Systems Ltd

Vitralit – U.V. curable – Euro Bond Adhesives Ltd

Vitramon – capacitors – Vishay Ltd

Vitratex – modular sign systems – Signscape Systems Ltd

Vitrex – tile and glass cutter – Q E P Ltd

Vitrex – Gem Tool Hire & Sales Ltd

Vitrex – S J Wharton Ltd

Vitrocoat – material for renovating sanitary ware – Renubath Services Ltd

Vitropac – Rolfe Industries

*Vitroperm (Germany) – nano crystalline alloy – Rolfe Industries

*Vits (Germany) – driers, incinerators, coating and impregnating lines, sheeters – Engelmann & Buckham Ltd

Vitsmart – Windfall Brands Ltd

VIVA – Decorative Italian tile supplier – World's End Couriers Ltd

Vivak – Sunlight Plastics Ltd

Vivante – motor caravans – Leisuredrive Ltd

Vivid – security,x-ray inspection systems – L-3 Communications Security & Detection Systems

Vivid (EG & G) – security, x-ray inspection systems – L-3 Communications Security & Detection Systems

Vivitar – Lamphouse Ltd

Vivo – grocers – Henderson Group Ltd

Vivoseed – G E Healthcare

Viz – comic – John Brown Publishing

Viz-a-Viz – fashion – Rinku Group plc

Vizlite – Helman Workwear

VIZU – FFS Brands Ltd

Vlsi – Cyclops Electronics Ltd

VLT – frequency converters (electronic) – Danfoss Ltd

VM1 Ventilometer – hand held spirometer for measuring pulmonary function – Clement Clarke International Ltd

VME – Harrier Fluid Power Ltd

VMS – voluntary milking systems – Delaval

VNU Net – magazine – Insitive Media

VO5 – shampoo and conditioner, hot oil range, styling range, colour range – Alberto-Culver Co. (UK) Ltd

Voda – telecommunications equipment – Vodafone Retail Ltd

Vodabase – Vodafone Retail Ltd

Vodabit – Vodafone Retail Ltd

Vodabreak – Vodafone Retail Ltd

Vodac GSM – Vodafone Retail Ltd

Vodac PCN – Vodafone Retail Ltd

Vodacall – Vodafone Retail Ltd

Vodacard – Vodafone Retail Ltd

Vodacare – Vodafone Retail Ltd

Vodacarte – Vodafone Retail Ltd

Vodacom – data communication services – Vodafone Retail Ltd

Vodaconnect – Vodafone Retail Ltd

Vodafax – data communication, telephone and facsimile services – Vodafone Retail Ltd

Vodafone – telecommunications & telephonic apparatus and instruments – Vodafone Retail Ltd

vodafone – Callsure Business Telephone & Fax Numbers

Vodafone – Premier Mobiles

Vodafone – Mobile phones – Champ Telephones Ltd

Vodafone Call Manager – Vodafone Retail Ltd

Vodafone Creditcall – telephone apparatus & instruments adapted for use on credit – Vodafone Retail Ltd

Vodafone Creditfone – Vodafone Retail Ltd

Vodafone Euro Digital – mobile phone – Vodafone Retail Ltd

Vodafone GSM – radiopaging, message sending, receiving and forwarding services – Vodafone Retail Ltd

Vodafone Metro Digital – mobile phone – Vodafone Retail Ltd

Vodafone PCN – telecommunications equipment – Vodafone Retail Ltd

Vodafone Recall – Vodafone Retail Ltd

Vodahire – hiring and rental of data communications & telecommunications equipment – Vodafone Retail Ltd

Vodalert – message sending, receiving & forwarding services – Vodafone Retail Ltd

Vodaline – Vodafone Retail Ltd

Vodalink – data communication services – Vodafone Retail Ltd

Vodalux – Vodafone Retail Ltd

Vodamap – Vodafone Retail Ltd

Vodanational – Vodafone Retail Ltd

Vodanet – Vodafone Retail Ltd

Vodapage – telephone, radio telephone, radio facsimile & radio communication services – Vodafone Retail Ltd

Vodapage Codecall – Vodafone Retail Ltd

Vodapoint – mobile telephones, radiopaging apparatus & instruments – Vodafone Retail Ltd

Vodarent – Vodafone Retail Ltd

Vodaservice – telecommunication equipment maintenance services – Vodafone Retail Ltd

Vodashop – Vodafone Retail Ltd

Vodassure – insurance services relating to telecommunications equipment – Vodafone Retail Ltd

Vodastream – Vodafone Retail Ltd

Vodastream Fax – Vodafone Retail Ltd

Vodata – Vodafone Retail Ltd

Vodatel – Vodafone Retail Ltd

Vodatelcom – Vodafone Retail Ltd

Vodawatch – Vodafone Retail Ltd

Vodex – rutile industry standard grade 3 MMA electrode – Murex Welding Products Ltd

Voe – aluminium work boats – Malakoff Ltd

Voegele – Harrier Fluid Power Ltd

Voest Alpine (Austria) – Bushes, brass with graphite inserts – Berger Tools Ltd

Vogel – Harrison Lubrication Engineering Ltd

Vogel (Germany) – bevel gearboxes – Lenze UK Ltd

Vogel – L E K Sales

Vogel Gearboxes – European Technical Sales Ltd

Vogue – soft drinks – Princes Soft Drinks

*Vogue Patterns (U.S.A.) – paper patterns for dressmaking – Butterick Co. Ltd

Vogue - radiator valves kwik pack prepacked plumbing products – Primaflow Ltd

Vohran – shower hose – Merlett Plastics UK Ltd

Voice + – magazine – Advanstar Communications

Voice-on-Hold – electronic speech promotional replacement for telephone music on hold – O W L Electronics Ltd

Voice Over IP – Tekdata Distribution Ltd

Voice Over IP Company – Tekdata Distribution Ltd

Voice Over IP Gateway – Tekdata Distribution Ltd
Voice Over IP Phone – Tekdata Distribution Ltd
Voice Over IP Phone System – Tekdata Distribution Ltd
Voice Over IP Provider – Tekdata Distribution Ltd
Voice Over IP Software – Tekdata Distribution Ltd
Voice Over IP Technology – Tekdata Distribution Ltd
Voice Over IP Telephony – Tekdata Distribution Ltd
Voice Over IP Voip – Tekdata Distribution Ltd
Voiplex – VoIP telephone systems – Voiplex
VOITH – Bailey Morris Ltd
Voith – couplings/spares – Bearwood Engineering Supplies
Voith – Harrier Fluid Power Ltd
VOITH ENGINEERING – Hydraulic & Offshore Supplies Ltd
Vokes – Harrier Fluid Power Ltd
Volac – laboratory glassware – Poulten & Graf Ltd
Voler – lubricant – Revol Ltd
Volex – electrical and electronic interconnect products and systems – Volex Group Ltd
Volex – electrical wiring accessories – Electrium Sales Ltd
Volex Group – electrical and electronic interconnect products and systems – Volex Group Ltd
Volex Powercords – powercords and connectors for electrical products – Volex Group Ltd
Volex Wiring Systems – wiring systems for specialist automotive and agricultural and commercial vehicles – Volex Group Ltd
Volkmann – Vacuum conveying equipment – Volkmann UK Ltd
Volkswagen – L M C Hadrian Ltd
Volkswagen – Ashley Competition Exhausts Ltd
VolksWorld – I P C Media Ltd
***Vollmer (Germany)** – strip gauging systems – British & Continental Traders Ltd
Vollmer – machinery for grinding saws – Vollmer UK Ltd
Vollmer Kegel-Sport – bowling alleys – Vollmer UK Ltd
Volpi – Stemmer Imaging
***Volstro (U.S.A.)** – milling machine attachments – Capital Equipment & Machinery Ltd
Voltelef – polychlorotrifluoroethylene (pctfe) granules and powders – Atosina UK Ltd
Voltmaster – self regulating 'intelligent transformer' for low voltage lighting systems – Multiload Technology
Volumatic – counter cache-cash security system – Volumatic Ltd
Volumeter – fan flow measuring device – Nicotra-Gebhardt Ltd
***Volvic Touch of Fruit** – water – Danone Ltd
Volvo – L M C Hadrian Ltd
Volvo – Central Plant Hire
Volvo – P J P Plant Hire
Volvo – marine engines and parts – Robert Craig & Sons Ltd
Volvo – Custom Brakes & Hydraulics Ltd
Volvo – C J Plant Ltd
Volvo – Harrier Fluid Power Ltd
***Volvo (Switzerland)** – watches – Gus Jones
Volvo – Mawsley Machinery Ltd
VOLVO – Bailey Morris Ltd
Volvo Penta – Trowell Plant Sales Ltd
Volvo Penta – Marine & General Engineers Ltd
Volvo Penta – marine & industrial engines – Volvo Penta UK
Volvo Penta & Caterpiller – Marine & General Engineers Ltd
***Von Hoevel (Germany)** – German wines – O W Loeb & Co. Ltd
***Von Kesselstatt (Germany)** – German wines – O W Loeb & Co. Ltd
Von Roll – Kee Valves
VON RUDEN – Hydraulic & Offshore Supplies Ltd
Vonax – Osborn Unipol Ltd
***Vortec (U.S.A.)** – compressed air operated products – Advanced Dynamics Ltd
Vortex – Twelve channel control system – Crowcon Detection Instrument Ltd
Vortex – bagless upright vacuum cleaner – Hoover Ltd
Vortex – lighting effect – Premier Solutions Nottingham Ltd
Vortex Hydra – concrete roof tiles manufacturing machinery – Vortex Hydra UK Ltd
Vortex PhD – Flowline Manufacturing Ltd
Vortice – Northern Fan Supplies Ltd
Vortok – The design and manufacture of maintenance products for timber railway sleepers and railway related products – Vortok International
Vortox – Harrier Fluid Power Ltd
Voss – Trafalgar Tools
VOSS – Hydraulic & Offshore Supplies Ltd
Voss – Fairway Hydraulics Ltd
Votex – agricultural machinery manufacturers & precision engineers – Votex Hereford Ltd
Voxmail – voice mail – Storacall Engineering Ltd
Voyager – playground equipment – Russell Play Ltd
Voyager – science-fiction and fantasy books – Harpercollins Publishers Ophelia House
Voyager – long term travel insurance (up to 18 months) – Europ Assistance Holdings Ltd
VPS BREVINI – Hydraulic & Offshore Supplies Ltd
VPX – steam generators – Babcock Wanson UK Ltd
VR Claymaster – Compressible fill (to accommodate clay heave) – Vencel Resil Ltd
VR Floatmaster – Pontoons & boons – Vencel Resil Ltd
VR Interiors – Decorative ceiling, ceiling centres, coving and wall veneer – Vencel Resil Ltd
VR Legend – analogue console – A M S Neve Ltd
VR Voidmaster – Insulating in-fill panel for concrete beam floors & void forming for internal & external shuttering – Vencel Resil Ltd
VR Warmaline – Wall and ceiling veneer – Vencel Resil Ltd
Vracron – acrylic copolymers – DSM UK Ltd
Vredestein – tyre and rubber products – Vredestein UK Ltd
***Vredo** – Anker Machinery Company Ltd
Vrieco-Nauta – Mixers & dryers – Hosokawa Micron Ltd
VRS – mobile shelving system – S S I Schaefer Ltd
VS1 GV – AC Vector Drive – Baldor UK
VS1 MX – AC IP66 Drive – Baldor UK
VS1 PF – AC Pump & Fan Drive – Baldor UK
VS1 PM – AC Permanent Magnet Motor Drive – Baldor UK
VS1 ST – AC Micro Drive – Baldor UK
VSI – wheelchair controller – P G Drive Technology
VSM (Germany) – quality coated abrasives – V S M Abrasives Ltd
VT – Techsil Ltd
VTM – fixed resistors – Anglia
VTM (United Kingdom) – intermediate service temperature vacuum processable systems – Umeco
Vuba-Coat – Best Selling Epoxy Floor Paint – Vuba Industrial Supplies
Vuba-Patch Repair – Best Selling Concrete Repair Mortar – Vuba Industrial Supplies
Vul-Cup – organic peroxides – Hercules Holding Ii Ltd
Vulcabond – bonding agent – Akcros Chemicals Ltd
Vulcan – cable cleat – Ellis Patents Ltd
***Vulcan** – Fellows
Vulcan – aluminized protective clothing for high temperatures – W G Eaton Ltd
Vulcan – fishing tackle – Daiwa Sports Ltd
Vulcan – sewage distributor paddle type – Tuke & Bell Ltd
Vulcan – impervious loop pile carpet – Warlord Contract Carpets Ltd
Vulcasil – silcon carbide high alumina and zircon refractories – Vulcan Refractories Ltd
Vulcatherm – ceramic and quartz infra-red emitters – Vulcan Refractories Ltd
Vulco Spring – Vulco Spring & Presswork Co. Ltd
Vulfix – shaving brushes – Progress Shaving Brush Vulfix Ltd
Vulfix Service – shaving brushes – Progress Shaving Brush Vulfix Ltd
Vulfix Travel – shaving brushes – Progress Shaving Brush Vulfix Ltd
Vulkollan – polyurethane elastomers – Trelleborg Applied Technology
VV – permanent merchant finish for worsted piece goods of superior quality – W T Johnson & Sons Huddersfield Ltd
VW – Bailey Morris Ltd
VW Golf+ – I P C Media Ltd
Vybak – Flexible PVC – Sallu Plastics
VYC (Spain) – Relief/control/check valves manufacture – Trimline Valves
Vycon – DIY swimming pool – Certikin International Ltd
Vydate – insecticide – Du Pont UK Ltd
Vydex – pvc coated steel posts – Signscape Systems Ltd
Vyella Rocola – shirt brand – Morrison McConnell Ltd
Vyklene – scouring aids – Benjamin R Vickers & Sons Ltd
Vymol – machine lubricant – Benjamin R Vickers & Sons Ltd
Vymox – machine lubricant – Benjamin R Vickers & Sons Ltd
Vynagrip (United Kingdom) – Open grid welded construction rolls with very high slip resistance – Plastic Extruders Ltd
Vynalast – Sallu Plastics
Vynastat – ESD, open grid electro static dissipative (ESD) matting - IEC1340-4-1 – Plastic Extruders Ltd
Vyon – sintered porous HDPE and PP plastic material – Porvair plc
Vyon – sintered porous HDPE and PP plastic material – Porvair Sciences Ltd
Vystat. P – processing aid for polypropylene – Benjamin R Vickers & Sons Ltd

W

W.A.C. – poly aluminium chloride – Atosina UK Ltd
W.B. – unvented cylinder – Worcester Bosch Group Ltd
W.B.S. Acrylic Sealer – building products – Addagrip Surface Treatments Ltd
W.C.F. – food, distributors and fuel stations and mail order catalogues – W C F Ltd
W.D.E. 436 pigmented – coloured top coats – Addagrip Surface Treatments Ltd
W.D.E. 436 Primer – cold applied epoxy compounds – Addagrip Surface Treatments Ltd
W.D. Membrane and Bonder – high strength epoxy resin adhesive for concrete – Conren Ltd
W.D. Patching Kits – epoxy resin patching material – Conren Ltd
W.D.S. Production Equipment – vices, centres, toolholders and production equipment – W D S
W.D.V. – Graphtec GB Ltd
W & Design – products – Watlow Ltd
W.E. – Alpha Electronics Southern Ltd
W.E.C.S Tools – Precision engineers – W E C S Precision Ltd
W.H. Collier – handmade bricks & briquettes – W H Collier Ltd
W.H.S. – brick and hand trowels – Spear & Jackson plc
W.H. Smith – retailers – WH Smith Retail Ltd
W.H.T. – drop forgings up to 50kgs – W H Tildesley Ltd
W.ISA – The Woolwich
W.J.S. – hall marked jewellery and findings – W J Sutton Ltd
W J White – Desks – Bucon Ltd
W. Logan – European Technical Sales Ltd
W.M. – provider of decision support information to pension funds and fund managers – The World Markets Company Public Limited Company
W.M.302 – kwh meter wall mounted – Northern Design Ltd
W.M.305 – wall mounted multi-function electricity meter – Northern Design Ltd
***W.P.R. (Germany)** – lateral location studs – Roemheld UK Ltd
W.P. Thompson – patent agents – W P Thompson & Co
W.R. 325 – domestic water heater – Worcester Bosch Group Ltd
W.S. 230 – angle grinder – Hilti GB Ltd
W.S.70 – solvent type stripper containing active emulsifier and detergent – Premiere Products Ltd
W.S.K. Machines – knife making machines and accessories – Partwell Cutting Technology Ltd
W.S.P. – rubber plastic and silicone surgical products – Teleflex Medical
W.S. & W.S.K. – tool drawer cabinets – S S I Schaefer Ltd
W. Sahlberg – European Technical Sales Ltd
W. Series – spring opposed diaphragm actuator – Severn Glocon Ltd
W.T.S. – The Woolwich
W. Wereldhave – property management & developers – Wereldhave Property Management
W100 – special metal finishes – Watson & Lewis Ltd
W200 – special metal finishes – Watson & Lewis Ltd
W500 – special metal finishes – Watson & Lewis Ltd
Wabco – Harrier Fluid Power Ltd
Wabco – pneumatics – Bosch Rexroth Ltd
WABCO – air brake components and systems – Wabco Automotive UK Ltd
Wabco UK – braking systems – Wabco Automotive UK Ltd
Wabeco – Professional Mills and lathes including CNC versions – Pro Machine Tools Ltd
Wachs – pipe bevelling machines – Campbell Miller Tools Ltd
Wacker – Harrier Fluid Power Ltd
Waddington – leather motorcycle gloves and gauntlets – Michael Lupton Associates Ltd
Waddingtons – games & puzzles – Hasbro UK Ltd
Wade – Southern Valve & Fitting Co. Ltd
Wade – roof outlets – Wade International Ltd
Wade – Trafalgar Tools
Wade – Engineering – Delta Fluid Products Ltd
Wade – Aztech Components Ltd
Wade (United Kingdom) – compression couplings – Hydrasun Ltd
Wade Upholstery – The Winnen Furnishing Company
Wadec – textured wall finish – Duradec Wales Ltd
Wadkin – Red House Industrial Services Ltd
Wadkin – Classical Woodworking Machinery – A L Dalton Ltd
Waeschle (Germany) – bulk plastics handling – Coperion Ltd
Waferscale – Cyclops Electronics Ltd
Waffle Floor – pneumatic recovery blast room – Wheelabrator Group
Wagner – T V H UK Ltd
WAGNER – Chaintec Ltd
Wagner – line tap valves – Thermofrost Cryo plc
Wagner – pumps – Allpumps Ltd
Wago – Proplas International Ltd
Wago Connectors – European Technical Sales Ltd
Wahoo – Wahoo Enterprises Limited
***Waiko (Germany)** – office furniture – Trademark Interiors Ltd
Waircom – Banico Ltd
Waitrosse Food Illustrated – Food Magazine – John Brown Publishing
***Waka (Japan)** – connectors – Cliff Electronic Components Ltd
Wakefield – chimney sweep equipment brushes – Wakefield Brush UK Ltd
Wako – Harrier Fluid Power Ltd
Walbrad – Heritage Cashmere UK Ltd
Walcon Marine – floating pontoons – Walcon Marine Ltd
Waldens – Dale Lifting and Handling Equipment Specialists
Waldens Wiltshire Foods – Apetito Ltd

Waldes Truarc – fasteners – Bearwood Engineering Supplies
Waldron – industrial power transmissions – Matrix International Ltd
Waldron – gear couplings – Matrix International Ltd
***Walk & Surf (Italy)** – sailing shoes – Yachting Instruments Ltd
Walkchips – walk surface – Melcourt Industries
Walker – equipment & spares – Bearwood Engineering Supplies
Walker and Hall – cutlery and silvergoods – Goldsmiths Jewellers Ltd
Walker Magnetic – Rotobux Magnetic Boring Machines – Robert Craig & Sons Ltd
Walker Timber Frame – Walker Timber Ltd
Walker Windows – canopy, pivot, dual turn and slide side windows – Walker Timber Ltd
Walker Woodstock – Walker Timber Ltd
Walkers – Walkers Shortbread Ltd
Walkman – personal stereo – Sony Head Office
Walksafe – Safety Works & Solutions Ltd
Walkwell Flooring Supplies – C F S Carpets
WALL-AIR (Italy) – telecommunications air conditioning – Stulz UK Ltd Epsom
Wall Mount Brunel – vandal and weather resistant wall mounting perimeter lighting – Designplan Lighting Ltd
Wall Spike – wall spikes – Birmingham Barbed Tape Ltd
Wallaby Creek – wine – Rodney Densem Wines Ltd
Wallaby Ridge – wine – Rodney Densem Wines Ltd
Wallaby Winch – hand operated winch – Trewhella Brothers Ltd
Wallace (United Kingdom) – Worsted Mens Suiting Fabric – John Foster Ltd
Wallace Cameron – UK Office Direct
Wallace Instruments – test equipment for rubber and plastics – Hartest Precision Instruments Ltd
***Wallbolts (Germany)** – expansion anchors for masonry – Fischer Fixings UK Ltd
Wallcord – fibre bonded wallcovering – Heckmondwike FB
***Walldrive (Taiwan)** – Jack Sealey Ltd
Wallex – hardfacing alloy (cobalt base) – Wall Colmonoy Ltd
Wallgate – combined handwashing and drying systems consisting of instantaneous water heating, electronic soap, dispensing and high power hot air drying or paper towels and urinal flush controllers and sterilising waste traps and hand driers-sensor operated taps – Wallgate
Wallis Seating – Capex Office Interiors
Wallpackette – wall mounted luminaire – Holophane Europe Ltd
Wallpackette III – architectural wall mounted luminaire – Holophane Europe Ltd
Wallpaper – I P C Media Ltd
Walltalkers – project-on and write-on/wipe off wallcovering – Tektura plc
Wallways – Accesscaff International Ltd
Walmey – bricks – Ibstock Building Products Ltd
Walnut Flake – pipe tobacco – Imperial Tobacco Group PLC
Walpres – sheet metal pressing and welded assemblies – Walsall Pressings Co. Ltd
WALPRO – Hydraulic & Offshore Supplies Ltd
Walrad (United Kingdom) – low nox burners – Hamworthy Combustion Engineering Ltd
Walrus – tamper-evident polythene envelope with self-sealing adhesive strip – Britton Decoflex
Walsall – lever mortice locks and padlocks – Walsall Locks Ltd
***Walt Disney Consumer Products (U.S.A.)** – consumer products – The Disney Store Ltd
***Walt Disney Parks & Resorts (U.S.A.)** – theme parks & resorts – The Disney Store Ltd
Walter – Precision Tools
Walters – industrial marking paints, industrial crayons, industrial chalks and engineers French chalk talc sticks – Walters & Walters Ltd
Walters – woven silk fabrics – Stephen Walters & Sons Ltd
WALTERSCHEID – Hydraulic & Offshore Supplies Ltd
Walton – temperature control systems and optical projectors – Walton Engineering Co. Ltd
***Walton (Netherlands)** – sheet linoleum – Forbo
Waltons – R K International Machine Tools Ltd
WALVOIL – Hydraulic & Offshore Supplies Ltd
Walvoil – hydraulic – V H S Hydraulic Components Ltd
Walvoil – Fairway Hydraulics Ltd
***Walvoil (Italy)** – hydraulic valves – BYPY Hydraulics & Transmissions Ltd
WAM – Wam Engineering
Wandsworth – electrical switches and sockets, medical exam lamps and patient to nurse call systems – Wandsworth Group Ltd
***Wanit (Germany)** – slates – Cembrit Ltd
***Wanit Repro (Germany)** – slates – Cembrit Ltd
Wanner – greape group – Stephens Midlands Ltd
***Wanner (Switzerland)** – grease guns – Lumatic Ga Ltd
***Wanner (U.S.A.)** – high pressure diaphragm pumps – Cleghorn Waring & Co Pumps Ltd
Wansbeck – sink – Armitage Shanks Ltd
Wanson Generators – Twin Industries International Ltd
Wanson Thermal Oil Heaters – Twin Industries International Ltd
Wap – industrial cleaning equipment – B & G Cleaning Systems Ltd
Wapora – special machines for foam – Apropa Machinery Ltd
Ward – Red House Industrial Services Ltd
Ward CNC Retrofit – T W Ward CNC Machinery Ltd
Wardpower (United Kingdom) – diesel driven generating sets 1-3000 KVA – Sheafpower Ltd
Wardray – radiation shielding products – Wardray Premise Ltd
Wardray Premise – Kenex Electro Medical Ltd
Wardwinch – sewer winching system – Wardsflex Ltd
Warehouse Rail – Berry Systems
Warehousing Storage – industrial storage – Parker International Ltd
Warfarin – rodenticide – Sorex Ltd
Warhammer – magazines, books, manuals, rule books for playing games, miniatures and models for use in fantasy games, video and computer games, computer software, toys and games – Games Workshop Ltd
***Waring (U.S.A.)** – bar and kitchen blenders, drink mixers and juice extractors – Robot Coupe UK Ltd
Warlord Carpet – Advanced Ergonomic Technologies Ltd
***Warmacite (South Africa)** – anthracite – Rudrumholdings
Warmaster – games, plaything, minatures, models – Games Workshop Ltd
WarmMelt – packaging adhesive – H B Fuller
Warmplan XX Auto – gas wallheater – Robinson Willey
Warmplan XX Manual – gas wallheater – Robinson Willey
Warmwell H.E. – Atmospheric Gas Fired modular & condensing boiler – Hamworthy Heating Ltd
Warne – surgical products and devices – Teleflex Medical
Warner – The Little Brown Book Group
Warner – clutches & brakes – Betech 100 P T Ltd
Warnitol – machine lubricant – Benjamin R Vickers & Sons Ltd
Warren-Morrison – valves & spares – Bearwood Engineering Supplies
Warren-Morrison (United Kingdom) – Pinch Valves manufacture – Trimline Valves
Warrior Trucks – Dale Lifting and Handling Equipment Specialists
Warth – thermal interface materials – Anglia
Warwick – industrial cleaning equipment – B & G Cleaning Systems Ltd
Warwick – carpet – Cormar Carpets
Warwick – timber up and over garage door – P C Henderson Ltd
Warwick – rotary gear pumps – Albany Pumps
Warwick – 500mm single oven – Indesit Company UK Ltd
Warwick – casement window internally or externally beaded, shootbolt locking as standard – Coastal Aluminium
Warwick Fabric – The Winnen Furnishing Company
Warwick Pumps – Albany Pumps
Wascator – Programmable automatic washing machine – James H Heal & Co. Ltd
***Wasco (U.S.A.)** – miniture pressure switches – Tamo Ltd
Wash Angel – retail store laundry concept – J L A
Wash Vac – Wolseley UK
Wash & Wax – car shampoo with special wax – Deb R & D Ltd
Wash 'n' Wear 4 Ply – Sirdar Spinning Ltd
Wash 'n' Wear Aran Crepe – Sirdar Spinning Ltd
Wash 'n' Wear Double Crepe DK – Sirdar Spinning Ltd
Washford – manilla paper for envelopes – St Regis Paper Co. Ltd
***Washguard (U.S.A.)** – motors for hostile applications – Motovario Ltd
Washpactor – sewage screenings processor – Higgins & Hewins Ltd
Washpoint – Cleaning Machine – Loadpoint Ltd
Washpoint – static high pressure hot and cold water washing unit for single or multi user operation – Rhinowash Ltd
Wask-RMF – gas transition fittings – Glynwed Pipe Systems Ltd
Wasp – low current and membrane switches rotary solenoids BS900 approval – W A S P Ltd
Wasp – M L P S
Wasteflow – plastic fitting for bath and cistern overflow – Mcalpine & Company Ltd
Wastemaster, The – 38 litre dual purpose polyethylene waste carrier for caravanners – F L Hitchman
WasteMate – Grundfos Pumps Ltd
WasteMate Plus – Grundfos Pumps Ltd
Wastematic – commercial waste disposal units – Max Appliances Ltd
Watasava – spray mixing taps – Sheardown Engineering Ltd
Watchdog – vehicle fuel issues recording systems – Centaur Fuel Management
Watchguard – cctv & alarms – RhinoCo Technology
Watco – treatments for the coating and renovation of concrete – Watco UK Ltd
Water Bird – parascending parachutes – Waterbird Parakites
Water Bunnie – macerators – Wandsworth Group Ltd
Water Champ (U.S.A.) – high performance mixer – Wallace & Tiernan Ltd
Water Fun – toys – Halsall Toys Europe Ltd
Water in fuel detection capsules – Water in fuel detection capsules – A Searle & Co. Ltd
Water Nymph – pumps – Stuart Turner Ltd
Water of Ayr – polishing stones – Water Of Ayr
Water Pinch – software – K B C Process Technology Ltd
Water point – Hot water dispenser – Drinkmaster Ltd
Water Soluble Dam, Dissolvo – Pipestoppers
Water Storage & Engineering – supply and installation of liner for water, chemical and effluent; water service includes design and engineering; earth moving, pumping, electric, fabrication and construction design & construction – Miles Waterscapes Ltd
Water systems manufrs – T P Technology plc
Water Tracker – software – K B C Process Technology Ltd
Water Wizard – Surex International Ltd
Waterbook, The – waterproof notebooks – V I P
Waterfall – carpet manuf – Phoenox Textiles Ltd
Waterfield – decorative & hygienic wall cladding – Interclad Ltd
Waterfords – Glass ware – Connect Two Promotions Ltd
Waterguard – corrosion inhibitor for potable water systems – Feedwater Ltd
Waterguard – Harrier Fluid Power Ltd
Waterhog – mats – Denis Rawlins Ltd
Waterhog – High performance mats and matting. – Mats4U
Waterjet – Precision Waterjet Ltd
Waterkey – prepayment meters and usage recording system – Severn Trent Water
Waterline Envirotech – Halcyon Solutions
Waterloo – Air movement equipment – Barkair Ltd
Waterloo – Tool Storage products – Erro Tool Co. Ltd
Waterloo – G S F Promount
Waterman – Harrier Fluid Power Ltd
Waterman – UK Office Direct
Watermark – secure magnetic stripe for plastic cards – T S S I Sytems
WaterMate – Grundfos Pumps Ltd
Watermota – engines & accessories – Watermota Ltd
Watersaver – spray mixing taps – Sheardown Engineering Ltd
Waterscreen – vibrating screens – Parker Plant Ltd
Watershield – Hampshire Hose Services Ltd
Watershield – hydraulic fittings – J V Hydraulics Ltd
Waterstones – booksellers – H M V & Waterstones
Waterstop – waterproofing spray – Cherry Blossom Ltd
WaterStore – plastic rainwater container with lid and tap – Richard Sankey & Son Ltd
Watertimer – slow closing spray taps – Sheardown Engineering Ltd
Waterways – taps and mixers (twin flow or mono flow) – Ideal Standard Ltd
Wathen Gardiner – country clothing – C & D King Ltd
Watkins Boilers – packaged and mobile boilers large industrial boilers for liquid storage – Watkins Hire
Watkins Hire Ltd – Mobile Boiler Plantrooms – Watkins Hire Ltd
WATLOW – design services – Watlow Ltd
WATLOW – temperature sensors, thermocouples, etc for controlling temperature, pressure, humidity and other conditions – Watlow Ltd
WATLOW.COM – Internet web site address – Watlow Ltd
Watrous – stainless steel washroom equipment – F C Frost Ltd
Watson – Global Graphics Software Ltd
Watson – intestinal biopsy capsule – Enspire Health
Watson Mapping – Global Graphics Software Ltd
Watson Pro – Global Graphics Software Ltd
Watson Smith – I/P converters – Coulton Instrumentation Ltd
Watson Smith – electro-pneumatic interface equipment and pneumatic pressure regulators – I M I Watson Smith Ltd
Watson Smith – proportional control valves – Norgren Ltd
Watt – heavy duty non rock D/T cover and frame – Norinco UK Ltd
Watt Drive – Motion Drives & Controls Ltd
Wattflow – Watts Industries UK Ltd
Wattisfield Ware – pottery – Henry Watson Potteries Ltd
Watts – Watts Industries UK Ltd
Watts – Harrier Fluid Power Ltd
Watts and Partner Management – Watts Group plc
Watts and Partners – Watts Group plc
Watts Cliff – sandstone (lilac) – Realstone Ltd
Watts Valves – Flow Mech Products Ltd
wau boosters – AESpump
Waukensha – Harrier Fluid Power Ltd
Waukesha – circumferential piston and centrifugal pumps – Axflow

WAVEGUARD – Bladderless no moving parts dampner for hertz (Hz) in excess of 200 – Pulsation Dampers At Pulseguard Ltd
Wavelay – detectable warning tape – Boddingtons Ltd
Wavelene – nylon reinforced polythene laminate – Flexible Reinforcements Ltd
Wavelock – nylon reinforced PVC laminate – Flexible Reinforcements Ltd
Wavemill – Sumitomo Electric Hardmetal Ltd
Waveney Mills Semolina – durum semolina millers – Pasta Foods Ltd
Wavespan – PVC strip curtain system (industrial & cold store) – Flexible Reinforcements Ltd
Wavetek – Alpha Electronics Southern Ltd
Wavetek Meterman – Alpha Electronics Southern Ltd
Wavin Apollo - Bi-axial PVC-U – water systems – Wavin Ltd
Wavin Ducting - Polyethylene and PVC – ducting systems – Wavin Ltd
Wavin SupaGas - Polyethylene (P.E.100) – gas pipe system – Wavin Ltd
Wavin SupaSure - Polyethylene (P.E.100) – potable water systems – Wavin Ltd
WavinCoil - PVC – land drainage systems – Wavin Ltd
Wavindrain – underground drainage pipes and fittings – Wavin UK
WavinGas - Polyethylene (P.E.80) – gas pipe system – Wavin Ltd
WavinSafe - PVC-U – pressure pipe systems – Wavin Ltd
Wavinsewer – sewer pipes and fittings – Wavin UK
WavinSure - Polyethylene (P.E.80) – potable water systems – Wavin Ltd
Wax County – Try & Lilly Ltd
Waxaid – drops – Reckitt Benckiser plc
Waxemul – textile wax emulsion – Benjamin R Vickers & Sons Ltd
Waxpersion – wax dispersions in solvents – Kromachem Ltd
Waxsol – ear wax dissolvant – Norgine International Ltd
Waxtrack – waxed synthetic riding surface – Martin Collins Enterprises Ltd
Way – Arun Pumps Ltd
Way Lubricant – lubricants – Chevron
Wayne – Harrier Fluid Power Ltd
WD-40 – Gem Tool Hire & Sales Ltd
WD-40 – S J Wharton Ltd
WDT – crimping tools/machines – Welwyn Tool Group Ltd
Weald Courier – newspaper – Kent Regional News & Media
Wearhard – hardened & tempered boron steel – Wearparts UK Ltd
Wearparts – earthmoving and quarry wear resisting parts – Wearparts UK Ltd
***Weatherbeater Doors (Canada & USA)** – high performance residential entrance doors – Ig Ltd
***Weatherbeater Garage Doors (U.S.A.)** – steel sectional garage doors in raised panel and horizontal ribbed styles – Ig Ltd
Weathercall – telephone services – Weather Call
Weathered Masonry – shotblasted block – Tarmac Topblock Ltd
***Weatherford (U.S.A.)** – oil hole drilling equipment – Weatherford UK
Weatherguard – smooth wallcoating – Everlac GB Ltd
WEATHERGUARD CANTILEVER CANOPIES – Living Space Ltd
Weathermarque – processed white fabric for marques/tentage – J T Inglis & Sons Ltd
Weathermaster – V E S Ltd
Weathershield – decorative paints – Akzonobel
Weatherstrip – insertion tool for automotive window frames – Pressavon Ltd
Weathertop – single point lift flexible intermediate container – Rexam Holding plc
Weatherwriter – weatherproof clipboards – V I P
Weaves Vol II – jacquard & dobby weaves – Today Interiors Ltd
Weavetop – polyester reinforced PVC for blinds & awnings – Flexible Reinforcements Ltd
Weavexx – roll coverings-paper technology – Invensys PLC
Web conferencing – Web based videoconferencing – V3 Technologies
Web-labs – Supplier of Internet or Intranet or Extranet Systems to the Public Sector – Web Labs Ltd
Webb Ivory – greeting cards and gifts – The Webb Group
Webber – solenoid valves – Norgren Ltd
Webcon – carburettor and engine management components for motor vehicles – Standard Motor Products Europe Ltd
Webpoint (United Kingdom) – web browser for the retrieval and viewing of documents via internet of intranet – Pacific Solutions International Ltd
Webron – technical synthetic needlefelt fabrics – Andrew Webron Ltd
website design website development website hosting – website design website development website hosting website seo domain name registration – LatestSol Website Design & Development
Webster and Bennett DH type vertical boring machines – Phil Geesin Machinery Ltd
Webster and Bennett elevating rail vertical boring machines – Phil Geesin Machinery Ltd
Webster and Bennett EV vertical boring machines – Phil Geesin Machinery Ltd
Webster and Bennett M type vertical boring machines – Phil Geesin Machinery Ltd
Webster and Bennett V type vertical boring machines – Phil Geesin Machinery Ltd
Webster and Bennett vertical lathes – Phil Geesin Machinery Ltd
Webster & Bennet – Red House Industrial Services Ltd
Webster Drives – ancillary transmissions for commercial vehicles – Webster Drives (A Gardner Denver Product)
Webster Instruments – instruments for the measurement of flow, pressure and temperature – Webtec Products
Webster Instruments - instruments for the measurement of flow pressure & temperature. – Webtec Products
Webtec – Harrier Fluid Power Ltd
Webtec Hydraulics – hydraulic valves and pumps – Webtec Products
WEBTECH – Hydraulic & Offshore Supplies Ltd
Webtex – polyester/cotton waterproof fabric – The British Millerain Company Ltd
Webtool – lightweight hydraulic jacks – Allspeeds Ltd
Webuser – I P C Media Ltd
Weda – submersible pump – Metso Minerals UK Ltd
Weda – Atlas Copco Compressors Ltd
Wedding – I P C Media Ltd
Wedding Bells – C C A Group Ltd
Wedding Flowers – I P C Media Ltd
Wedding Ring Company – manufacture jewellery – Brown & Newirth Ltd
Wedge – Cloakroom Solutions Ltd
Wedge Group Galvanizing – a complete and comprehensive hot dip galvanizing service – Acrow Galvanising Ltd
Wedge Group Galvanizing – a complete and comprehensive hot dip galvanizing service – Wedge Galvanizing Group Ltd
Wedge Group Galvanizing – a complete and comprehensive hot dip galvanizing service – Edward Howell Galvanizers Ltd
Wedge Group Galvanizing – a complete and comprehensive hot dip galvanizing service – Worksop Galvanising Ltd
Wedge Group Galvanizing – a complete and comprehensive hot dip galvanizing service – Merseyside Galvanising Ltd
Wedge Group Galvanizing – a complete and comprehensive hot dip galvanizing service – Pillar Wedge Ltd
Wedge Group Galvanizing – a complete and comprehensive hot dip galvanizing service – Wessex Galvanisers Ltd
Wedge Group Galvanizing – a complete and comprehensive hot dip galvanizing service – South East Galvanizers Ltd
Wedge Group Galvanizing – a complete and comprehensive hot dip galvanizing service – Humber Galvanising Ltd
Wedge Group Galvanizing – a complete and comprehensive hot dip galvanizing service – Metaltreat Ltd
Wedgeform Scaffolding – Accesscaff International Ltd
Wedgegard (United Kingdom) – protection device – Howdon Power Transmission Ltd
Wedgelock – Kennametal UK Ltd
Wedgemount (United Kingdom) – anti-vibration mounts for machinery – Farrat Isolevel
Wedgewire – looped and welded types – Screen Systems Wire Workers Ltd
Wedgwood – fine bone china, ovenware tableware and giftware – Wedgewood Travel Ltd
***Wedgwood** – Bob Crosby Agencies Ltd
Wedo – UK Office Direct
Weedwiper – applicator – Certis Europe
Weekes – Stainer & Bell Ltd
Weekly News – D C Thomson & Co. Ltd
Weeks Trailers – agricultural and local authority tipping trailers – Richard Western Ltd
***Weeren (Germany)** – facing & centering machine – Robert Speck Ltd
Weetabix – whole wheat flakes in biscuit form – Weetabix Ltd
Weetabix - Vibixa - Alpen - Crunchy Bran - Weetos - Ready Brek - Advantage - Minibix - Crrrunch. – Weetabix Ltd
Weetos – chocolate flavoured wheat hoops – Weetabix Ltd
Weforma – industrial shock absorber – Weforma Daempfungstechnik GmbH
WEG (Brazil) – electric motors – Weg Electric Motors UK Ltd
WEG – Proplas International Ltd
WEG Motors – European Technical Sales Ltd
Weholite – structured walk HDPE drainage pipes to 2.2m diameter – Asset International Ltd
Weidermann – Harrier Fluid Power Ltd
Weighcare – medical scales – Marsden Weighing Machine Group
Weighload – Wylie Systems
Weighload Systems Ltd – rated capacity indicator manufacturer – Midland Safe Load Indicators
Weighman – traffic monitoring systems – Golden River Traffic Ltd
Weighmaster – G Webb Automation Ltd
Weighmaster - Easifill - Minifill - Servofill - Digifill - Rotoplant – G Webb Automation Ltd
Weiland – Selectronix Ltd
Weimar – Harrier Fluid Power Ltd
Weir Electrical Instrument – electrical instrumentation (analogue and digital) for industrial and educational establishments of all types; buchholz relays for protection of mineral filled power transformers and earthing equipment – P & B Weir Electrical
Weir Pacific – weir ball valve spares – Valve Spares Ltd
Weirboom – oil containment systems – Vikoma International Ltd
Weitronic – M S C Gleichmann UK Ltd
***Weitzer (Austria)** – parquet flooring – Pilkingtons Ltd
Weko – European Technical Sales Ltd
WEL – Own Brand – Wel Medical Services
Welbeck – school sportswear and sweatshirts – Josery Textiles Ltd
Welchs – sugar confectionary – House Of York
Weld Grip – prefabricated steel – B R C Southampton
Weld Purge – Pipestoppers
Weld Purging Dams – Pipestoppers
Weldability – Welding Consumables – Steel Product Supplies
Weldability – Gem Tool Hire & Sales Ltd
Weldcraft – Tig torches – Premier Welding Services Scotland Ltd
Welderqual – software for storing welder qualifications – T W I
Weldex – welders gauntlets – Bennett Safetywear
Weldex – heat resistant leather gauntlet gloves – Bennett Safetywear
Weldfit – pipe and tube fittings – Norgren Ltd
Weldgrip – Company name – Minova Weldgrip Ltd
Welding Bags – purge welding bag (inert gas) – Sarco Stopper Ltd
Weldlogic – Weldlogic Europe Ltd
WELDMATIC (United Kingdom) – adaptive control timer – B F Entron Ltd
Weldmesh – wire mesh distributors. – Genwork Ltd
WeldOffice – comprehensive range of software for welded fabrication – T W I
Weldox – extra high strength steel plate – Swedish Steel
Weldshield – flame retardant fabric for welding – Carrington Career & Work Wear
Weldshield – P D Interglas Technologies Ltd
Weldspec – storage of welding procedures – T W I
Weldspeed – Weldspeed Ltd
WELDSTAR (United Kingdom) – weld timer and control system – B F Entron Ltd
Weldstop – thermal protection fabric – T B A Textiles
Weldtite – cycle maintenance products – Weldtite Products Ltd
Weleda – natural medicines and toiletries – Weleda UK Ltd
Welfold – folding insulated overhead door – Senior Hargreaves Ltd
Welift – lifting insulated overhead door – Senior Hargreaves Ltd
Welin – Camlock Couplings – Gall Thomson Environmental Ltd
Welin Davits – marine life saving equipment (boat launches) – Welin Lambie
Welka – Gate Locks – Steel Product Supplies
***Well Nut (U.S.A.)** – blind screw anchor – Emhart Teknologies
Well Pumps – Denton Pumps Ltd
Welland – generating sets – Welland Engineering Ltd
Welland – sluice suite – Armitage Shanks Ltd
Weller – soldering equipment – Longs Ltd
Weller – soldering equipment – Apex Tools
Weller-Ungar – soldering tools/machines – Welwyn Tool Group Ltd
Wellin – Turnell & Odell Ltd
Wellington – cordage – Kent & Co Twines Ltd
Wellington – fibre bonded carpet – Heckmondwike FB
Wellman – well log data vectorising – D P T S Group Holdings Ltd
Wellman Bibby – Variable Speed PIV Gear Box – Kearsley Precision Engineering
Wellman Booth – high integrity and severe process and industrial type cranes – Wellman Booth
WELLMASTER – Hydraulic & Offshore Supplies Ltd
Wellmaster – flexible rising main – Angus Fire
***Wells** – Equipline
Wells & Edwards – Stacatruc
Wells Valves – High pressure valves – Endeavour International Ltd
Welltest – software packages – Schlumberger Oilfield UK plc
Welmade – domestic water storage units – Q M P
Welmegox – resistors – T T Electronics Welwyn Components Ltd
Welmex – Wholesale Welding Supplies Ltd
Welpower – inverters & uninterruptable power supply – Valradio Electronic Ltd
***Weltex (Sweden)** – fluting aid – Borregaard UK
Welwyn – Cyclops Electronics Ltd

Welwyn – general trade name – T T Electronics Welwyn Components Ltd

Wembley – saddlery – E Jeffries & Sons Ltd

Wembley Laminations (United Kingdom) – Trade Encapsulators – Libran Laminations Ltd

WEMOTO – Motorcycle Parts and Accessories – Wemoto Ltd World's End Motorcycles Ltd

Wemyss Fabrics – fabrics (furnishing) – Wemyss Weavecraft Ltd

Wenaas – Wenaas Ltd

Wenban-Smith Joinery – joinery – Wenban Smith Ltd

Wendt – Winterthur Technology UK Ltd

Wenglor – European Technical Sales Ltd

*Wenglor (Germany) – sensors – Sensortek

*Wenking (Germany) – potentiostats – Linton & Co Engineering Ltd

Wensleydale – carpets – Bond Worth

Wensleydale Longwool Sheepshop – commission manufacturers of Wensleydale wool products, hand knitting yarns, hand and machine knitted garments, exclusive worsted fabric hand knitting patterns – Wensleydale Longwool Sheep Shop

*Wentelbed (Netherlands) – vertical and horizontal wall folding beds – Golden Plan Ltd

Wentgate – electron beam/furnaces – Cambridge Vacuum Engineering

Wentgate Dynaweld – Electron beam machines – Cambridge Vacuum Engineering

Wentworth – WC – Armitage Shanks Ltd

Wentworth – Gas LFE for class one or class two flues – Dunsley Heat Ltd

Wentworth – golf and country club – Wentworth Club Ltd

Wenzel – Wenzel UK Ltd

Wenzel – European Technical Sales Ltd

Wenzel Geartec – Wenzel UK Ltd

Wepuko Hydraulic Pumps – high pressure water pumps and compressors – Alan Dale Pumps Ltd

Werie – Harrier Fluid Power Ltd

*Werie – vacuum pumps, compressors and blowers – Gardner Denver Ltd

Werma – Signal Towers – Saia Burgess (Gateshead) Plc

Werma – E Preston Electrical Ltd

Werner & Pfleiderer (Germany) – compounding plastics chemical and food – Coperion Ltd

Wernert – plastic lined centrifugal pumps – Axflow

Wescol – welding products – Wescol

Wesley Group – Pressure Washers – Precious Washers Stafford Ltd

Wesper – refrigeration/air conditioning compressor spares – J & E Hall Ltd

Wessex – plastic stapler – Office Depot UK

Wessex 100m – High efficiency pre-mix gas fired modular boilers – Hamworthy Heating Ltd

Wessex HE – high efficiency pre-mix gas fired modular boilers – Hamworthy Heating Ltd

West – J & S Lewis Ltd

*West (Switzerland) – Conductive boxes – Static Safe Ltd

West – agricultural machinery – H West Prees Ltd

West Hyde – Perancea Ltd

West Meters – thermometers, hygrometers, soil meters and associated products – Outside In Designs UK Ltd

West System – epoxy resin system – Wessex Resins & Adhesives Ltd

Westad – Kee Valves

Westaim – speciality nickel powders – Neomet Ltd

Westat – standby battery charger – P E Systems Ltd

Westbere Spar – grey calcined flint – Brett Specialised Aggregates

Westbound – record label – Ace Records Ltd

Westcode – semiconductors – G D Rectifiers Ltd

Westcode, Hind, International Rectifier, IXYS – Harmsworth Townley & Co. Ltd

Westdale – vanity unit – Armitage Shanks Ltd

Westech – suspended ceiling cleaning and coating – Crofton House Associates

Westerbeke – marine engines – Watermota Ltd

Westermo (Elpro) – Halcyon Solutions

Western – Harrier Fluid Power Ltd

Western Buses – bus and coach service – Stagecoach Ltd

Western Digital – Cyclops Electronics Ltd

Western Electric (U.S.A.) – electronic valves & tubes – Edicron Ltd

Western Morning News – paid newspaper – Western Morning News Co. Ltd

Western Telematics – Betterbox Communications Ltd

Western Welding – tanks/pressure vessals/general engineering – Western Welding & Engineering Co. Ltd

Westex – Westley Plastics Ltd

Westex Carpets – The Winnen Furnishing Company

Westfalia – Gea Westfalia Seperator UK Ltd

Westfalia – Double Parking Systems

Westinghouse – Harrier Fluid Power Ltd

Westinghouse – equipment/spares – Bearwood Engineering Supplies

Westland Casting – non-ferrous founders – Westland Casting Co. Ltd

Westlon – Westley Plastics Ltd

Westminster – residential door – Coastal Aluminium

Westminster – bathrooms – The Imperial Bathroom Company Ltd

Westminster Chemicals – anodising furniture – Redditch Anodising

Westminster Range – fireside chair, high seat chair and matching settee – Sherborne Upholstery Ltd

Westmorland – waterproof clothing – J Barbour & Sons Ltd

Weston Oil Seals – rotary shaft seals in rubber and leather – Pioneer Weston

Westpoint – combs – Paul Murray plc

Westra – Rotadex Systems Ltd

Westward – Services, refrigeration – Carrier Refrigeration & Retail Systems Ltd

*Westward Ho (Portugal) – handkerchiefs, socks and linen – Alami International Ltd

Westwood – automatic recessing heads – Cogsdill Nuneaton Ltd

wet n view – specialist ink – B & H Colour Change Ltd

Wet ones – refreshing tissue wipes – Jeyes

WET Sensor – pore water conductivity sensor – Delta T Devices

Wexas – travel club – Wexas Travel

*Wexiodisk – Holmes Catering Equipment Ltd

Weycon – weigh conveyors – Garbuiodickinson

*Weydown – Jersey cream (untreated) – Blackburne & Haynes

Weyers – precision gearboxes and instruments – Weyers Bros Ltd

Weymouth – parallel motion system – Blundell Harling Ltd

Weyroc HDX (United Kingdom) – heavy duty chipboard for use in mezzanine industrial flooring applications – Egger UK Ltd

Weyroc PCX (United Kingdom) – flooring grade chipboard with removable polythene film laminated to top surface – Egger UK Ltd

Weyroc PFB (United Kingdom) – phenolic faced flooring grade chipboard – Egger UK Ltd

Weyroc U313 (United Kingdom) – flooring grade chipboard with enhanced moisture resistance – Egger UK Ltd

WGB – Harrier Fluid Power Ltd

WH – iron & steel metal merchants – Walter Heselwood Ltd

Whale – pumps – Munster Simms Engineering Ltd

Whale Flipper – galley and caravan pump – Munster Simms Engineering Ltd

Whale Henderson – Munster Simms Engineering Ltd

Whale Tankers – Whale Tankers Ltd

Whaler – knitwear – Stevenage Knitting Co. Ltd

Whalevac – range of vacuum tankers – Whale Tankers Ltd

Wharfedale – loudspeakers – Wharfedale International Ltd

Wharncliffe Publishing – The Barnsley Chronicle Ltd

What Digital Camera – I P C Media Ltd

What guitar? – magazine – Future Publishing Ltd

What Mountain Bike? – magazine – Future Publishing Ltd

What's On – leisure and entertainment guide (weekly) – Kent Messenger Group Ltd

Whats on T.V. – I P C Media Ltd

WHC 20 – hand crimper – Wrexham Mineral Cables Ltd

Wheatley (U.S.A.) – swing check valve – Alexander Cardew Ltd

Wheatone – wheat malt flour – E D M E Ltd

Wheatsheaf – Jewellers Ring Sizing Tools – Wheatsheaf Jewellers Tools

Wheel Barrows – Fieldway Supplies Ltd

Wheel driven & portable shot blasting equipment suppliers for floor surfaces – Wheelabrator Allevard

Wheelabrator – abrasive cleaning equipment and air pollution control – Wheelabrator Allevard

Wheelmeal – mobile stacking baskets – Craven & Co. Ltd

Wheelchair Lifts – lifts used on road vehicles – Ratcliff Palfinger

Wheelie Bins – Fieldway Supplies Ltd

Wheelsets UK – Noel Village Steel Founder Ltd

Wheelsets UK - Vistar – Noel Village Steel Founder Ltd

Wheelwash – Wheel Wash Ltd

Wherry Best Bitter – cask beer – Woodforde's Norfolk Ales

Whessoe – engineers to energy industries – Whessoe Oil & Gas Ltd

Whifords – mail order catalogue – J D Williams Mail Order Group

*Whipper – Taylor Scotland Ltd

WHIPTRUCK – Chaintec Ltd

Whirline – rotary clothes line – F W Hipkin Ltd

*Whirlpool – Pentland Wholesale Ltd

*Whirlpool – icemakers – Tillwise Cash Registers

Whirlpool – appliances – Allied Manufacturing

Whirlpool – Novellini UK Ltd

*Whirlpool "BauKnecht" Ignis (Germany & Italy) – built-in and free standing appliances – Potter Cowan & Co Belfast Ltd

Whirlpool Professional – Equipline

Whirlwind – fast acting traffic doors – Envirohold Ltd

Whirpool – Ideal Standard Ltd

Whiskey Ready Rubbed – pipe tobacco – Imperial Tobacco Group PLC

*Whispers (World Wide) – household textiles – Linens Direct

Whispex – Forward Chemicals Ltd

Whistles – ladies clothes – Whistles Ltd

Whitby Gazette – newspaper – Yorkshire Regional Newspapers Ltd

Whitchurch Herald – weekly title – Flintshire Chronicle Newspapers

Whitcomp (U.S.A.) – ptfe compounds – AGC Chemicals Ltd

Whitcon (U.S.A.) – ptfe lubricants – AGC Chemicals Ltd

*White and Newton Furniture – White & Newton Furniture Ltd

White Cross Systems – development, manufr and supply of database servers – Kognitio Ltd

White Disinfectant – powerful disinfectant particularly suitable for outdoor use – Premiere Products Ltd

White Dwarf – magazines, books, manuals, rule books for playing games – Games Workshop Ltd

White & Gold Collection – Hotel Complimentary Products

White Knight – gas and charcoal barbecues – Crosslee plc

White Knight – tumble dryers – Crosslee plc

White knight – washing machine, freezer and fan gas and electric cookers – Crosslee plc

White Knight – rechargeable handlamp for emergency services use – Furneaux Riddall & Co. Ltd

White & Newton Furniture – dining room furniture, upholstery and occasional furniture – Frostholme Furniture Ltd

*White Rhino (Netherlands) – high grade ivory board – Davies Harvey & Murrell

White Rose Environmental – medical/clinical waste collection and disposal – Kelda Group

White Spot, The – pipes – Alfred Dunhill Ltd

White-Westinghouse – appliances – Allied Manufacturing

Whiteboard Plus – innovative whiteboard – Barconwood Ltd

Whiteflex – electrical dryers – S S White Technologies UK Ltd

Whitehill – Central C N C Machinery Ltd

Whitehill – cutter heads – Whitehill Spindle Tools Ltd

Whitehot Creative – Company name and logo – Whitehot Creative

Whitelegg – wire machinery – Whitelegg Machines Ltd

Whitemetal – J H Richards & Co.

Whiterox – INEOS Enterprises Ltd

Whitesales – National Door Co.

Whiting – commercial and railway vehicle shutters – J R Industries Ltd

Whitmore's Lubricants – Square Two Lubrication Ltd

Whitsed – potato, vegetable, grain and industrial elevators and conveyors – Terry Johnson Ltd

Whittaker Xyplex (U.S.A.) – Kingston Communications

Whittingdales Solicitors – Whittingdales Solicitors

Whittle – light duty recessed rectangular cover and frame – Norinco UK Ltd

Whitworth Bros – flour millers – Whitworth Holdings Ltd

Who Cares – charitable organisation – The Who Cares Trust

Wholesale – blinds – Hillarys Blinds Northern Ltd

Wholesale Select – complete retailer – Allianz Insurance plc

WHS – domestic central heating equipment – Worcester Bosch Group Ltd

Wibalin – bookbinding materials – Winter & Co UK Ltd

Wichita – equipment/spares – Bearwood Engineering Supplies

Wichita – clutches & brakes – Betech 100 P T Ltd

Wichita (United Kingdom) – pneumatic clutches and brakes – Twiflex Ltd

Wichita – European Technical Sales Ltd

Wick Machinery – Glenvale Packaging

Wicke – Mercury Bearings Ltd

Wickford Recorder – free weekly newspaper – Newsquest Essex Ltd

Wickhams – fishing tackle – Lureflash International

Wickman – fuses – Bearwood Engineering Supplies

Wickman – machine tool spares – P B K Micron Ltd

Wicksteed – playground equipment – Wicksteed Leisure Ltd

*Wicotex (Netherlands) – bookbinding materials – Winter & Co UK Ltd

Wide Ram – stoker – James Proctor Ltd

Widerlite – prismatic bulkhead luminaire – Holophane Europe Ltd

Widia Magnetic Materials – magnets – Rainer Schneider & Ayres

Widma – machinery for grinding saws – Vollmer UK Ltd

Widmaier – Selectronix Ltd

Widnes Weekly News – weekly title – Flintshire Chronicle Newspapers

Widney – windows, roller blinds and telescopic slides – Widney Manufacturing Ltd

Wieland – bronze components – J Roberts Ltd
Wieland Electrical Connections – E Preston Electrical Ltd
Wieland Werke – non-ferrous semi products – Nemco Metals International Ltd
Wieser – punches and design tools – Partwell Cutting Technology Ltd
Wiesner Hager – Furniture – Bucon Ltd
***Wiess (Germany)** – indicating pressure switches – Tamo Ltd
WIG 20 – insulated gland – Wrexham Mineral Cables Ltd
Wika – measuring equipment – Bearwood Engineering Supplies
WIka Calibration Line – Manufacturer of Pressure & Temperature Measurement & Calibration Instruments – Calibration Dynamics
***Wika Instruments (Germany)** – pressure & vacuum gauges – B K W Instruments Ltd
Wikai – Southern Valve & Fitting Co. Ltd
Wike Mills (United Kingdom) – Worsted Mens Suiting Fabric – John Foster Ltd
Wilcanders – The Winnen Furnishing Company
Wilcolite – aluminium tipper bodies – Wilcox Commercial Vehicles Ltd
Wilcox – commercial vehicle bodies – Wilcox Commercial Vehicles Ltd
Wilcox – Status Metrology Solutions Ltd
Wild – forged and rolled rings – Thomas C Wild
Wild Rose – hand made spun lead crystal tableware – Nazeing Glassworks Ltd
Wild Trax – sports and leisurewear – Rococo Style Ltd
Wildcat – bulked polyester thread – American & Efird GB Ltd
Wildcat – Pressure washers – B & G Cleaning Systems Ltd
Wilden – architectural door fittings, aluminium-stainless steel and brass fittings – Dortrend International Ltd
Wilden – air operated double diaphragm pumps – Axflow
Wilden pumps – Air operated Double diaphragm – Fluid Pumps Ltd
Wiles Group Ltd – stationery and graphic supply – Wiles Group
***Wilevco (U.S.A.)** – batter mixing and control machinery – Selo UK Ltd
Wilfred Scruton – agricultural engineers and farm machinery distributors – Wilfred Scruton Ltd
Wilj – medical diagnostic equipment – Integrated Technologies Ltd
WILKA – Hydraulic & Offshore Supplies Ltd
Wilkenson – Harrier Fluid Power Ltd
Wilkinson Furniture – The Winnen Furnishing Company
Wilkinson Hardware – homes and gardens stones – Wilkinson Hardware Stores Ltd
Wilkinson Sword – garden tools – Fiskars Brands UK Ltd
Wilkinsons – shears & scissors – William Gee Ltd
Wilko – products for home and garden – Wilkinson Hardware Stores Ltd
Will&Hahnenstein – European Technical Sales Ltd
***Will & Hahnestein (Germany)** – drum heating cabinets – British & Continental Traders Ltd
Willan Building Services – ventilation – Willan
Willbrandt Expansion Joints – Interflex Hose & Bellows Ltd
Willcox Hose – industrial hose and composite and rubber hose fittings – Amnitec Ltd
Willemin-Macodel SA – Haesler Machine Tools
Willetts – equipment & spares – Bearwood Engineering Supplies
***Willi Haag (Germany)** – German wines – O W Loeb & Co. Ltd
Willi Vogel AG – European Technical Sales Ltd
***Willi Wader (Germany)** – blast furnace tapping equipment and tooling – British & Continental Traders Ltd
William Brown – high quality wool, wool and silk and wool linen piece goods – Robert Noble
William Hall & Co. – fancy yarn suppliers – William Hall & Company
William Hill Organization – turf accountant – William Hill
William Jones Packaging – printing paper & polythene carrier bags – William Jones Packaging
William Laycock (United Kingdom) – Worsted Mens Suiting Fabric – John Foster Ltd
William Lockie of Hawick – knitwear – William Lockie & Co. Ltd
William M. Mercer – human resource and employee benefit consultancy – Mercer
Williams – grand prix engineering – Williams F1
***Williams** – Capital Refrigeration Services Ltd
Williams – Catercraft Catering Equipment
***Williams** – Refrigeration – Court Catering Equipment Ltd
Williams Brothers of Sheffield – stockholders of nuts and bolts and all other fasteners – Williams Fasteners
Williams Superslim – hand tools – Smith Francis Tools Ltd
Willow – sports and leisure references books, fiction and non-fiction – Harpercollins Publishers Ophelia House
Willpower – manufacturer of breathing air purifiers – Willpower Breathing Air Ltd
Wills Rings – seal design – Trelleborg Ceiling Solutions Ltd
Wilmat – fork lift trucks, electric vehicles and mechanical handling equipment – Wilmat Ltd
Wilmot Dickson – Construction – E Turner & Sons
Wilms – industrial heating – Wilms Heating Equipment
WILMS – Hydraulic & Offshore Supplies Ltd
WILO Pumps – Flow Mech Products Ltd
Wilro ASSY – Diffused Light – Global Doors Ltd
Wilro BZS – Light – Global Doors Ltd
Wilshire – I M I Cornelius UK Ltd
***Wilshire** – Ice Cool Services Ltd
Wilson Blades – ice skates – H D Sports Ltd
Wiltex – Coated Fabrics – J & D Wilkie Ltd
Wilton 125 – transfer case – Acco East Light Ltd
Wilton 2000 – carpets – Ulster Carpet Mills Ltd
Wilton Royal – The Winnen Furnishing Company
Wiltshire Farm Foods – Apetito Ltd
Wim Hemmink – cocktail and evening wear, suits, day dresses – Wim Hemmink
Wima – Cyclops Electronics Ltd
Wimborne H.E. – Power flame cast iron sectional boilers – Hamworthy Heating Ltd
Wimpey Homes – house builders – Taylor Wimpey UK Ltd
Wimpy – restaurants – Wimpy Restaurants Group Ltd
Wimstrip – weigh-in motion sensors – Golden River Traffic Ltd
Winbond – Cyclops Electronics Ltd
Winbuild – Redsky It
Winchester – CNC multi slide lathes – B S A Machine Tools
Winchester – 535mm single oven – Indesit Company UK Ltd
Wincor – A T M Parts
Wincro – stainless steel building components – Wincro Metal Industries Ltd
Wincro Brickwork Support Systems – Wincro Metal Industries Ltd
Wincro Clip – nylon clip for retaining cavity wall insulation – Wincro Metal Industries Ltd
Wincro Safe Tie – Wincro Metal Industries Ltd
Wincro Stainless Steel Reinforcing Bar – Wincro Metal Industries Ltd
Wincro-Suregrip – stainless steel flooring systems – Wincro Metal Industries Ltd
WIND-AIR (Italy) – telecommunications air conditioning – Stulz UK Ltd Epsom
Windfarer – truck streamlining kits, truck air deflectors – Aerodyne Equipment
Windian – play balls – Kookaburra Reader Ltd
Windles – watch clock oils – Henri Picard & Frere
Windmaster – compasses and anometers – Yachting Instruments Ltd
Windmaster – car weathershields – Exhaust Ejector Co. Ltd
Window Book – printed fabrics – Zoffany
Window Cleaners Ladders – Accesscaff International Ltd
***Window Cleaning** – Nova Contract Cleaners
***Window Cleaning** – Stayclean Contract Cleaning Services Ltd
Window Spirit – non abrasive cleaner to produce smear-free shine – Premiere Products Ltd
Window Spray – foam cleaner for windows and mirrors – Premiere Products Ltd
windowborn horsebox company – M G Trevett Ltd
Windowgard – steel and aluminium security shutters – Kaba Door Systems
Windows XP Answers – magazine – Future Publishing Ltd
Windposts – G A Fixings Ltd
Windsor – limousine – Coleman Milne Ltd
Windsor – security control panel – Guardall Ltd
Windsor – taps, showers and accessories – Deva Tap Co
Windsor – residential door, solid or thermally broken – Coastal Aluminium
Windsor – bathrooms – The Imperial Bathroom Company Ltd
Windsor Castle (United Kingdom) – Mitre Linen
Windsor Life – life assurance – Windsor Life Assurance
Winflex – drive couplings – British Autogard Ltd
***Winflo Brand** – Giro Food Ltd
Winget – Construction – Winget Ltd
Winget – Harrier Fluid Power Ltd
Winget – A T Wilde & Son Ltd
Winget – Trowell Plant Sales Ltd
Wingo – games - designs – Europrint Promotions Ltd
***Wings (India)** – guitar bags – John Hornby Skewes & Co. Ltd
Wings Furniture – Capex Office Interiors
WingStile – glass entrance gate – Gunnebo Entrance Control Ltd
Winguard – The Woolwich
Winguard Insurance – The Woolwich
Winguard Insurance Company – The Woolwich
Winkel – European Technical Sales Ltd
Winklepress – filter presses – Ashbrook Simon Hartley Ltd
Winkworth – mixing and blending machines – Winkworth Machinery Ltd
Winopaque – G E Healthcare
Winpac – G E Healthcare
Winsford Chronicle – weekly title – Flintshire Chronicle Newspapers
Winslow – Harrier Fluid Power Ltd
Winslow – Adaptors – Warwick Test Supplies
Winsta – the new customer connector system for building installion – WAGO Ltd
Winsta, Toplon, Protect. – WAGO Ltd
Wintec – Harrier Fluid Power Ltd
Winter – Saint-Gobain Abrasives Ltd
***Winterbotham Darby & Co. (Worldwide)** – delicatessen products, confectionery, patisserie, biscuits, organic products and snacks – Winterbotham Darby & Co. Ltd
Wintercure – rapid curing epxoy coatings – International Paint Ltd
***Winterhalter** – warewashing – Keemlaw Ltd
***Winterhalter** – Court Catering Equipment Ltd
Winther Browne & Co Ltd – period moulding, architectural moulding, fire surrounds and radiator cabinets, screening panels, furniture legs, room divders and staircasing – Winther Browne & Company Ltd
Winton Environmental Management Ltd – environmental services – Bureau Veritas
Wipedown – surface cleaning wipe – Robinson Healthcare Ltd
Wipedowns – surface cleaning wipe – Robinson Healthcare Ltd
Wiperstat – automotive safety cut-out device – Otter Controls Ltd
Wippermann – European Technical Sales Ltd
Wiratec – textile testing services – B T T G Ltd
Wire Bind – wire comb binding machine – Securit World Ltd
Wire-wrap – tools – Welwyn Tool Group Ltd
Wire Wrap – tools – Apex Tools
Wired Mat – insulation mat faced with wire mesh – Rockwool Rockpanel B V
Wireless Broadband Router Distributor – Tekdata Distribution Ltd
***Wirelok (New Zealand)** – fence line connectors – Drivall Ltd
***Wirtgen (Germany)** – road milling machines – Colas Ltd
Wirtgen – Harrier Fluid Power Ltd
***Wirth & Gruffat (France)** – rotary transfer machines & CNC turning Centre – Haesler Machine Tools
Wisconsin – engines – Trenchex Garden Machinery
Wisden – Cricket Mag – John Brown Publishing
Wisewear – clothing – C & D King Ltd
Wispay for Windows TM – the definitive payroll system for PCs – Wisbech Payroll Services
Wiss – Gem Tool Hire & Sales Ltd
Wiss – scissors & snips – Apex Tools
Witamwas – European Technical Sales Ltd
Witch – pipe hangers - supports – Carpenter & Paterson Ltd
WITCH – soot and smoke abater – Hydrachem Ltd
Witcomb – lightweight cycles and framesets, junior cycles, trikes, BMX tandems and ATB mountain bikes – Witcomb Cycles
Witcomb Cycles – renovations of all types of cycles and antiques restored as new, wheelchair repairs and new wheelchairs – Witcomb Cycles
Witech (Switzerland) – CNC high speed sliding head automatic – Haesler Machine Tools
With – The Woolwich
Withers & Rogers – patent and trade mark attorneys – Withers & Rogers LLP
Without – The Woolwich
Witness – R G K UK Ltd
***Wittenborg Easy Vend (U.S.A.)** – refrigerated food merchandiser – N & W Global Vending Ltd
Wittenborg FB50 – semi-automatic coffee dispensing machine – N & W Global Vending Ltd
Wittenborg FB55 – Semi-automatic coffee dispensing machine – N & W Global Vending Ltd
Wittenborg FM4000 – refrigerated food merchandiser – N & W Global Vending Ltd
***Wittenborg Instant 5100 (U.S.A.)** – instant drinks merchandiser – N & W Global Vending Ltd
Wittenborg Snack – drilled glass fronted snack merchandiser – N & W Global Vending Ltd
Witter – britain's best selling towbar sold at all Indespension stores – Indespension Ltd
Witter Towbars – car and light commercial towbars – C P Witter Ltd
***Wittner (Germany)** – violin, viola and cello accessories; metronomes – John Hornby Skewes & Co. Ltd
Wix – Harrier Fluid Power Ltd
Wizard & Mini Wizard – Vtech Electronics UK plc
Wizard System – auto urinal and WC dosing system – Vectair Systems Ltd
WiZZBiKE.com – Bicycle Retailer and Service Provider – Evans Cycles Ltd
WIZZOO Limited – Wizzoo
Wm Clowes – printers, book binders and diary publishers, digital print, pre-press rfacilities, software applications and CD preperation – C P I William Clowes Ltd
WM Web Design – Your Local Web Design & SEO Service - Solihull, Birmingham and Coventry – W M Web Design
WMD – Motorcycle Parts Distribution – Wemoto Ltd World's End Motorcycles Ltd

*WMF – Coffee machines/tableware – W M F UK Ltd

WMG – plastic bearings – Bowman International Ltd

WMI-6 – ball bearings – Bowman International Ltd

WMP – industrial warm air heaters/cabinet heaters – Babcock Wanson UK Ltd

WMU – dry PTFE lined wrapped bearings – Bowman International Ltd

WMX – wrapped bearings - acetal lined – Bowman International Ltd

WNS – Rollforming Machinery – W Neal Services

Woburn – casement window internally beaded, shootbolt locking as standard – Coastal Aluminium

*Wohler – Michael Stevens & Partners Ltd

Wohlhaupter – Precision Tools

Woking Funeral Service – funeral directors, memorials and pre-needed funerals arranged – Woking Funeral Service

Woking News & Mail Series – Times Review Series Of Newspapers

Wokingham Times Series – newspapers – Surrey & Berkshire Media Ltd

Wolf – safety equipment – Bearwood Engineering Supplies

Wolf – Red House Industrial Services Ltd

Wolf – radiator valves – Marflow Engineering Ltd

Wolf – intrinsically safe torches – Wolf Safety Lamp Company Ltd

Wolfcraft – Gem Tool Hire & Sales Ltd

Wolflite – safety handlamp, rechargeable battery powered – Wolf Safety Lamp Company Ltd

Wolfmet (United Kingdom) – tungsten-based components – M & I Materials Ltd

Wolseley – vintage cars – British Motor Heritage Ltd

Wolseley Centres – Complete building trade merchants – Builder Center Ltd

Wolstenholme Machine Knives Ltd – machine knives – Wolstenholme Machine Knifes Ltd

Wolverhampton Handling – conveyor roller – Wolverhampton Handling Ltd

Woman – I P C Media Ltd

Woman & Home – I P C Media Ltd

Womans Own – I P C Media Ltd

Womans Weekly – I P C Media Ltd

Women & Golf – I P C Media Ltd

Wonderfire – Baxi Group

Wondersoft Baby D.K. – yarns – Stylecraft

Wonderwall Water Features – Stainless steel water features for architects and designers – Mena Engineering UK Ltd

Wonsover – parting fluid for foundry use – Ernest B Westman Ltd

Wontlock – safety device – L B B C Technologies

Wood Collection – The Amtico Co. Ltd

Woodauto – auto electrical company – Wood Auto Supplies Ltd

Woodbine – plain cigarettes – Imperial Tobacco Group PLC

Woodbury Leisure – wooden lodge carvans – Omar Park Homes Ltd

Woodchuck – wooden puzzles and playthings – Pentangle Puzzles & Games

Woodcoat – wood preservative stain – Tor Coatings Ltd

Woodcote – wood stain – Witham Oil & Paint Lowestoft Ltd

Woodfibre – walk surface – Melcourt Industries

Woodfield Systems – loading arms, swivel units, truck and rail car loading systems – Woodfield Systems Ltd

Woodgate – Harrier Fluid Power Ltd

Woodgrip – school craft benches – Pedley Furniture International Ltd

Woodhead – Selectronix Ltd

*Woodland (Far East) – casualwear – Remys Ltd

Woodlands – carpets – Penthouse Carpets Ltd

Woodman Twist – tufted carpet – Brockway Carpets Ltd

Woods (United Kingdom) – switches, sockets, dimmers, etc – R Hamilton & Co. Ltd

*Woods Air Movement Ltd (United Kingdom) – fan manufrs – Westmid Fans

Woodsheen – wood-stains and varnish for wood – Akzonobel

Woodstock – neck ties – Woodstock Neckwear Ltd

Woodstock – cut pile carpet – Warlord Contract Carpets Ltd

Woodstock Classic – 100% zeftron contract broadloom & tiles – Adam Carpets Ltd

Woodstock Leabank – Woodstock Leabank Ltd

Woodweld – repair and filler compound for new and weathered timber – Channelwood Preservation Ltd

Woodwelder – radio frequency generator for rapid glue curing – Gibbs Sandtech Ltd

Woodworker – saw bench – Brown's Agricultural Machinery Company Ltd

Woof Wear – equestrian protection and accessories – Gul Watersports Ltd

Woollen Blankets – J Bradbury & Co. Ltd

Woolmoss – pure wool hanging basket liner – Vitax Ltd

Woolspring – Anglo Recycling Technology Ltd

Woolwich – The Woolwich

Woolwich Agency Services – The Woolwich

Woolwich Asset Management – The Woolwich

Woolwich Assured Homes – The Woolwich

Woolwich Broking Services – The Woolwich

Woolwich Card Save – The Woolwich

Woolwich Card Services – The Woolwich

Woolwich Consumer Finance – The Woolwich

Woolwich Contracts – The Woolwich

Woolwich Conveyancing Services – The Woolwich

Woolwich Credit Services – The Woolwich

Woolwich Developments – The Woolwich

Woolwich Direct – The Woolwich

Woolwich Easy Step – The Woolwich

Woolwich Electronic Shopping – The Woolwich

Woolwich Enterprises – The Woolwich

Woolwich Estate Agency Services – The Woolwich

Woolwich Executors – The Woolwich

Woolwich Finance – The Woolwich

Woolwich Financial Advisory Services – The Woolwich

Woolwich Financial Brokers – The Woolwich

Woolwich Financial Services – The Woolwich

Woolwich Fund Managers – The Woolwich

Woolwich Group – The Woolwich

Woolwich Group Funding – The Woolwich

Woolwich Guernsey – The Woolwich

Woolwich Holdings – The Woolwich

Woolwich Home Services – The Woolwich

Woolwich Home Shopping – The Woolwich

Woolwich Homes – The Woolwich

Woolwich Housing – The Woolwich

Woolwich Housing Management – The Woolwich

Woolwich Ignition – The Woolwich

Woolwich Independent Financial Advisory Services – The Woolwich

Woolwich Individual Savings Account Managers – The Woolwich

Woolwich Insurance Services – The Woolwich

Woolwich International Trustees – The Woolwich

Woolwich Internet Bank – The Woolwich

Woolwich Internet Services – The Woolwich

Woolwich Investment Services – The Woolwich

Woolwich (Isle of Man) – The Woolwich

Woolwich Life – The Woolwich

Woolwich Life Assurance – The Woolwich

Woolwich Lifestyle – The Woolwich

Woolwich Loan Services – The Woolwich

Woolwich Monitor – The Woolwich

Woolwich Mortgage Services – The Woolwich

Woolwich Motorbase – The Woolwich

Woolwich Nominees – The Woolwich

Woolwich Open Plan – The Woolwich

Woolwich Open Plan Borrowing – The Woolwich

Woolwich Open Plan Private Bank – The Woolwich

Woolwich Open Plan Protecting – The Woolwich

Woolwich Open Plan Saving – The Woolwich

Woolwich Open Plan Services – The Woolwich

Woolwich Open Plan Shop – The Woolwich

Woolwich Pension Fund Trust – The Woolwich

Woolwich Pension Services – The Woolwich

Woolwich Personal Equity Plan Managers – The Woolwich

Woolwich Personal Finance – The Woolwich

Woolwich Plan Managers – The Woolwich

Woolwich Plan Nominees – The Woolwich

Woolwich Property Services – The Woolwich

Woolwich Property Shop – The Woolwich

Woolwich Sharestore – The Woolwich

Woolwich Shop – The Woolwich

Woolwich Spa – The Woolwich

Woolwich Surveying Services – The Woolwich

Woolwich Surveying Services Property Management – The Woolwich

Woolwich Switch and Save – The Woolwich

Woolwich Unit Trust Managers – The Woolwich

Wooster – crystallographic instruments – Crystal Structures Ltd

Woosung – vacuum – AESpump

Wooton – Trailers – Paul Tuckwell Ltd

Worcester – power presses – Higgins & Hewins Ltd

Worcester boilers – energy efficient boilers. - Elite Heating Ltd

WordFile – R W S Group plc

Wordgrove – UK Office Direct

Wordsworth – Industrial Computer Manufacturer and System Integrator – Steatite Batteries

Wordsworth – moulded and embossed door – Premdor Crosby Ltd

WordWorks – thesaurus and dictionary software – Xara Ltd

Work-Hard – work hardening hardfacing welding electrodes – Metrode Products Ltd

Work Out – The Barnsley Chronicle Ltd

Work Platforms – Accesscaff International Ltd

*Work Zone (U.S.A.) – Heavy duty contamination control/industrial flooring – Dycem Ltd

Worka-B – Print estimating, costing, MIS computer software – Honeycomb Computer Technology

Workbikes – industrial cycles and tricycles – Pashley Cycles Ltd

Workflow Analyser – Core Technology Systems UK Ltd

Workforce – Melitzer Safety Equipment

Workhorse Communications – public relations – Workhorse Communications

Working from Home Insurance – specialist insurance – M M A Insurance plc

Worklink – people management system – Kalamazoo - Reynolds Ltd

Workmate 95 – prestel terminal emulator for Window 95/NT – Red Sky I T Ltd

Workmate Executive – prestel terminal emulator for MS Dos – Red Sky I T Ltd

Workmats PVS – private viewdate system for prestel and interactive teletext – Red Sky I T Ltd

Workshop – air compressors – S I P Industrial Products Ltd

World – hand dryers (warm air) – W F Electrical

World – range of molasses-based feeds for all classes of livestock – Quality Liquid Feeds Ltd

World Acceptor – Money Controls Ltd

World Alpha – carpets – Interface Europe Ltd

World Beta – carpets – Interface Europe Ltd

World Delta – Interface Europe Ltd

World Epsilon – Interface Europe Ltd

World Footwear – international magazine covering all aspects of footwear – World Trade Publishing Ltd

World Gamma – carpets – Interface Europe Ltd

World Is Your Oyster, The – recruitment agency – Park Street People Ltd

World Lambda – Interface Europe Ltd

World Leather – international magazine covering all aspects of leather, leather making and leather products – World Trade Publishing Ltd

World Omega – carpets – Interface Europe Ltd

World Sigma – Interface Europe Ltd

World Soccer – I P C Media Ltd

World Sports Activewear – international magazine covering all aspects of technology and news for sports and leisure wear – World Trade Publishing Ltd

World Squash – European Squash Federation

World Traveller – nebuliser systems for the treatment of respiratory disorders – Clement Clarke International Ltd

World-valve – Kee Valves

World Wizard Traveller – Vtech Electronics UK plc

*Worldteam (Far East) – leisurewear – Remys Ltd

Worldwide – wallcovering – Tektura plc

Worldwide Support Services – Softbrands

Worms Eye – sevice trade name - ground investigation services – Worms Eye Site Investigation Ltd

Worson – die cushion equipment – Worson Die Cushions Ltd

Worswick – equipment/spares – Bearwood Engineering Supplies

Worthington – Harrier Fluid Power Ltd

WORTHINGTON – Hydraulic & Offshore Supplies Ltd

Worwick – equipment/spares – Bearwood Engineering Supplies

Woven Wire – woven wire mesh – Screen Systems Wire Workers Ltd

Wovina – woven labels, name tapes, embroidery – Wovina Woven Labels

WP – premium efficiency, electric motor – Brook Crompton UK Ltd

WPA Biowave – Biochrom Ltd

WPA Lightwave – Biochrom Ltd

WPA S800/S1200 – Biochrom Ltd

WPA Spectroware – Biochrom Ltd

WR-21 – marine engine – Rolls-Royce plc

WR525 – carbon fibre reinforced Polyetheretherketone – Greene Tweed & Co. Ltd

Wrangler – jeans lee-jeans luggage – V F Northern Europe Ltd

Wrap a tag – golf security tag – Air Tube Technologies Ltd

Wrap-it-Ties – cable ties – Richco International Co. Ltd

Wraps UK (United Kingdom) – Shrinkwrap machinery – Marden Edwards Ltd

Wratten Filters – Galvoptics Optical Goods

Wrekin – briar bricks – Blockleys Brick Ltd

Wren – light duty rectangular cover and frame – Norinco UK Ltd

Wren – infra-red heaters for livestock – Diamond Edge Ltd

Wright – Mechanical Respirometers – Enspire Health

Wright – peak flow meters – Enspire Health

Wright Pump – Positive displacement circumferential piston pumps – Bestpump

*Wright Rain (Italy) – irrigation equipment for agricultural applications, field scale horticulture and industrial dust suppression – Wrightrain Environmental Ltd

Write First Time – word-based manual writing system – Information Transfer LLP

Write-in-Light – illuminated display systems – Barconwood Ltd

Write'n'Light – Barconwood Ltd
Writer's Toolkit – software package that helps users structure their imaginative, functional & personal writing – Learning & Teaching Scotland
Writing 90 G.S.N. – G F Smith
Writing Text Cover – G F Smith
WRT-100 – winding resistance test set for transmission transformers – Adwel International Ltd
WT/WTR/WTN/WTO – industrial themostats/programmable & R.F. controlled – Sunvic Controls Ltd
WTD 501 – wedge tightness detector for large motors and generators – Adwel International Ltd
WUH – unit heaters – Babcock Wanson UK Ltd
Wulftec – Stretch wrapping machines – M J Maillis UK Ltd
Wumag – aerial platforms from 30m up to 85m – King Trailers Ltd
Wumag – King Vehicle Engineering Ltd
Wumag Platforms – Accesscaff International Ltd
Wundrol – bread divider oil – A A K Bakery Services
WV (Europe, Western) – ci butterfly valves – Everyvalve Ltd
WVM – 4 hole automotive tanks – H K L Gas Power Ltd
WWMPS – wetwell mounted pump station – Kalsep UK
www.chem-distribution.com – Online web sales of chemicals – Lindchem Ltd
www.newcastle-pat-testing.co.uk – Portable Appliance Testing, PAT tests in newcastle – North East Observation Ltd
www.sleepersdirect.co.uk – Railway Sleepers – Rustic Touch Ltd
Wybone – litter bins, grit and salt bins, fire retardant sack holders and planters – Wybone Ltd
Wychwood – cut pile carpet – Warlord Contract Carpets Ltd
Wydos – drawing office equipment and supplies including C.A.D. systems – West Yorkshire Drawing Office Services Ltd
Wyercentor – clothes line – James Lever & Sons Ltd
Wyercentor - Clothes Line, Superbraid - Sash Cord, Orient - Clothes line, Longlast - Clothes Line, Everlasto - Ropes, twines, cord, Blue Wrapper - Sash Cord Waxed – James Lever & Sons Ltd
***Wyko** – Unifine Food & Bake Ingredients
Wyko – Proplas International Ltd
Wyle X – circuit protection – Electrium Sales Ltd
***Wylie** – crane safty equipment manufrs – Wylie Systems
Wylie – safeload indicators – N R C Plant Ltd
Wyman-Gordon – manifolds, sphere tees, special fabrications, fittings and flanges – Wyman Gordon
Wyndol – textile processing aid – Benjamin R Vickers & Sons Ltd
WYNITE – heat resisting white iron – Wearparts UK Ltd
Wynsors World of Shoes – shoes boots and handbags – Courtesy Shoes Ltd
Wyptex Plus – speciality wipers – C G P Chemicals Ltd
Wyrem (United Kingdom) – robust ducting made from 2-ply rubber-coated fabric – Flexible Ducting Ltd
Wyseplant – general plant hire including electrical and mechanical plant, scaffolding, temporary fencing, accommodation units, passengers and goods construction hoists, powered access equipment – WyseGroup Ltd
Wysepower – provision of temporary electrical installations – WyseGroup Ltd
Wyvern – scaffolding erectors – Wyvern Scaffolding
Wyvern Cargo – general haulage, freight forwarding and storage – Wyvern Cargo Distribution Ltd
WZ12 2DX – compact live mixing console – Allen & Heath Ltd
WZ14 4 2+ – live mixing console – Allen & Heath Ltd
WZ16 2DX – compact live mixing console – Allen & Heath Ltd

X

X. – picture hooks, pins and wire – Frank Shaw Bayonet Ltd
X.C.16 – Cogne UK Ltd
X-CELL (United Kingdom) – portable lighting products – Nitech Ltd
X-Com – plugs and terminal blocks – WAGO Ltd
X.D.10/19 – current transducers – Northern Design Ltd
X.D. 80 Degreaser – highly efficient detergent cleaner – Conren Ltd
X.F.P. – Formscan Limited
X.H.P.D. Engine Oil – engine oil – Millers Oils Ltd
X.L. – fire cement – Vitcas Ltd
X.L. – progressive lenses – Carlzeiss Vision
X.L. Shafts – dart shafts and darts – Unicorn Products Ltd
X-LINE (Italy) – telecommunications heat exchangers – Stulz UK Ltd Epsom
***X.P. 4000 (U.S.A.)** – keyboard video mouse PC server switches – Techland Group Ltd
X-Pol – Forward Chemicals Ltd
X.R. – cylinders, rams and pumps from 4.5-900 tonnes – Tangye
X-Ray and Isotope – non contact thickness gauges and profile gauges – Thermo Radiometrie Ltd
X. Signs Express – franchised sign making business – Signs Express Ltd
X Stamper – UK Office Direct
X-Stat – static elimination equipment – M C D Virtak Ltd
X.T.K.T. 2000 Single Speed Screwgun – driving self-tapping and self-drilling construction screws – Hilti GB Ltd
X Test – Precious metal analysers – Spectro Analytical UK Ltd
X-TRACOAT – Hydraulic & Offshore Supplies Ltd
X-Tract – Hydrafeed Ltd
X.V. Mirror Ring – mastring for identification of haemophilus – The Mast Group Ltd
X10 – Capex Office Interiors
X9 – Digital Products - Toner Sheet Fed - Coated – Howard Smith Paper Ltd
X9 Digital Reels – Digital Products - Xeikon - Coated – Howard Smith Paper Ltd
XACTEMP – hand-held temperature probes – Watlow Ltd
XACTPAK – mineral insulated, metal-sheathed cable – Watlow Ltd
Xanadu – dircon/glyphosote based total CDA herbicide – Bayer Crop Science
Xanto – steel bath – Ideal Standard Ltd
Xantrex – Alpha Electronics Southern Ltd
Xantural – xanthan gum (pharmaceutical grade) – C P Kelco Ltd
Xbox Gamer – magazine, published by FXM International – Future Publishing Ltd
Xbox UK – official magazine, published by FXM International – Future Publishing Ltd
Xcelite – cutters & pliers – Welwyn Tool Group Ltd
Xcelite – tools – Apex Tools
XCXXX – structural reinforcement – Gurit UK Ltd
xds – pumps – AESpump
Xenacryl – acrylic resin – Baxenden Chemicals Ltd
Xenalak – acrylic resin – Baxenden Chemicals Ltd
Xennal – write disinfectant – Bell Sons & Co. Ltd
Xennol – antiseptic disinfectant – Bell Sons & Co. Ltd
***XENOPHOT (Germany)** – lamps – Osram Ltd
Xenoy – Resinex UK Ltd
Xerox – Lamphouse Ltd
Xerox – UK Office Direct
Xerox Business – Mcnaughton James Paper Group Ltd
Xerox, Epson, Canon, Kyocera – Multifunction printers and supplies – inkstinx
Xerxes – Ladies Fashions – Variety Silk House Ltd
XEXXX – structural reinforcement – Gurit UK Ltd
XFM – Global Radio
XFP – Networkable analogue addressable fire panel – C-Tec Security Ltd
Xgard – Detectors for oxygen, toxic and flammable gases – Crowcon Detection Instrument Ltd
XGard – a durable mudguard range which offers technical and optical improvements to meet the high quality demanded by modern vehicle builders and customers – Jonesco (Preston) Ltd
Xi series – Allcode UK Ltd
Xicor – Cyclops Electronics Ltd
Xidex – Formscan Limited
Xilinx – Cyclops Electronics Ltd
Ximatron – radiotherapy simulator and treatment planning unit – Varian Medical Systems UK Ltd
XimaVision – digital imaging system with image manipulation capability – Varian Medical Systems UK Ltd
Xinox – Sanitary accessories – Franke Sissons Ltd
Xinruilian (Japan) – dc/ac axial fans – Trident Engineering Ltd
Xinrvilian (Japan) – dc/ac axial fans – Trident Engineering Ltd
xited uk ltd – tops – West Village Ltd
Xixin – cabinets for housing computer and electronic equipment – Xixin Ltd
XL Drum – 120li, 210li, 220li tight head – Fibrestar Drums Ltd
XL Pallet Racking – adjustable racking system – Link 51 Ltd
XlCut – low carbon resulphurised free cutting steels – Corus Engineering Steels
XLerator – Hand Dryer – 03 Solutions Ltd
XM – Compterised Control Systems – AMET (Europe) Ltd
Xmaster – computer software – Chris Naylor Research Ltd
Xodus Group, oil and gas, consultants, subsea, dri – Xodus Group - Oil and Gas consultants; subsea & process engineering – Xodus Group Ltd
XONDO – turbocharger compressor wheel/turbine wheel/shaft assembly balancing machine – Schenck Ltd
Xpelair – Trafalgar Tools
Xpelair – Applied Energy Products Ltd
Xpertrule – system development tool with a formalised knowledge engineering methodology and utlilising rule induction-xpertrule miner, advanced data minings technologies – Expert Rule Software Ltd
Xplore – Maxa Technologies Ltd
Xporta – worldwide accommodation service – Portakabin Ltd
Xpose – Pledge Office Chairs Ltd
Xpres – trading name – Charterhouse Holdings plc
Xpress – Display Wizard Ltd
Xpressions – Display Wizard Ltd
Xpressions Card & Gift Co – Gibson Hanson Graphics Ltd
***XR2 & XR5 (U.S.A.)** – geomembrane for waste pits and water courses – A G A Group
xSeries – Mid Blue International Ltd
XSRS – Cross streamer ranging system – Sonardyne International Ltd
XTD-4 – stereo microscope – Gillett & Sibert Ltd
XTL-1 – zoom stereo microscope – Gillett & Sibert Ltd
Xtra Flex – highly flexible PVC conduit – Adaptaflex Ltd
Xtra Protection – sublingual vitamin and mineral powder – G & G Food Supplies
Xtrabag – Injection moulded carrying case – Hofbauer (UK) Ltd
***Xtraflex** – polyester cotton mechanical stretch fabric – Carrington Career & Work Wear
Xtralite – National Door Co.
Xtratherm XTCW – polyisocyanurate cavity wall board – Xtratherm
Xtratherm XTPR – poyisocyanurate pitched roof board – Xtratherm
Xtratherm XTSP – poyisocyanurate flat roof board – Xtratherm
Xtratherm XTUF – poyisocyanurate under floor board – Xtratherm
Xtratuff – Gates Hydraulics Ltd
Xtreme – SCSI Cables Assemblies – Selectronix Ltd
Xtreme Vortex – Mobile events and activity hire – Xtreme Vortex
Xuron – microshears – Welwyn Tool Group Ltd
Xybex – coolant recycling system – Master Chemical Europe Ltd
XYit – Map Digitizing Software – Geomatix Ltd
Xylac – Decorative coatings – Whitford Ltd
Xylan – One - two - and three coat fluoropolymer coatings – Whitford Ltd
Xylan – organic coating which gives good corrosive resistance, containin g PTFE and polymer binder, providing high adhesion to substrate – Wolverhampton Electro Plating Ltd
Xylan – Protective Finishing Group
Xylan – East Midland Coatings Ltd
Xylan - Teflon - Molykote - Suncorite - Greblon - Senotherm - Emralon - Nylon - E-Coat - Emcoat – East Midland Coatings Ltd
Xylan - Xylar - Xylac - Quantum2 - QuanTanium - Eclipse - Excalibur - Dykor - Suave (fluoropolymer coatings) – Whitford Ltd
Xylar – High temperature inorganic coatings – Whitford Ltd
Xymark – laser coders – Linx Printing Technologies plc
Xyron – UK Office Direct
XYShield – conductive/non conductive gasketing – Shielding Solutions Ltd
XYZ lathes – Phil Geesin Machinery Ltd
Xzit GB – Darcy Products Ltd

Y

Y.A.K. – canoe equipment – Crewsaver Ltd
Y-Tack – textile warp treatments – S T R UK Ltd
Yachting Monthly – I P C Media Ltd
Yachting World – I P C Media Ltd
Yageo – Cyclops Electronics Ltd
Yakari (Italy) – Bicycles – Moore Large & Co. Ltd
***Yakpak (Taiwan)** – Cycle luggage – Madison
Yale – Premier Lift Trucks Ltd
Yale – Harrier Fluid Power Ltd
Yale – Stacatruc
Yale – security products – Assaabloy Group
Yale – A&S Lifting and Safety Ltd
Yale – locks – J L M Security
YALE – Chaintec Ltd
Yale – T V H UK Ltd
Yale Fork Lift Trucks – fork lift counterbalanced, pallet and trucks – Yale
Yale Industrial Products – Dale Lifting and Handling Equipment Specialists
Yale Industrial products – Hawk Lifting
Yale Industrial Trucks – fork lift truck – Yale
Yale lift trucks – counterbalanced fork lift trucks – Yale
Yamaha – Lamphouse Ltd
Yamaha – golf cars – G Reekie Group Ltd
Yamaha – Cyclops Electronics Ltd
Yamaichi – Cyclops Electronics Ltd
Yamashin – Harrier Fluid Power Ltd
***Yamauchi (Japan)** – spinning aprons, cots – Brooksbank Holdings
Yang-Yam – T V H UK Ltd
YANG-YAM-PUMA – Chaintec Ltd
Yanmar – P J P Plant Hire
Yanmar (Japan) – diesel tractors & engines – E P Barrus
Yanmar – Harrier Fluid Power Ltd
Yanmar – A T Wilde & Son Ltd
Yanmar Excavators – A T Wilde & Son Ltd
Yard-Man – garden tractors and rotary mowers – E P Barrus

Yard-O-Led – writing instruments – Filofax Stationary Suppliers

Yardmaster – muck scraper – Brown's Agricultural Machinery Company Ltd

Yarmo – industrial overalls and cotton leisure wear – Yarmouth Stores Ltd

Yarmor – pine oils – Hercules Holding Ii Ltd

Yarnemul – textile processing aid – Benjamin R Vickers & Sons Ltd

Yarnol – textile processing aid – Benjamin R Vickers & Sons Ltd

Yasda – Whitehouse Machine Tools Ltd

Yashkawa – Proplas International Ltd

YBW.com – I P C Media Ltd

***Yea-Sacc** – Alltech UK Ltd

Yeast Aid – yeast food – Murphy & Son

Yellow Marketing Information – consultancy – Geoplan Spatial Intelligence Ltd

Yellow Sulphur – mildew control – Vitax Ltd

Yener – Glenvale Packaging

Yeoman – Steel Bollard – Alto Bollards UK Ltd

Yeoman Rainguard – guttering – Harrison Thompson & Co. Ltd

Yeoman Shield – plastic protection material – Harrison Thompson & Co. Ltd

Yeomanshield - Rainguard - Anticlimb - Custom Mouldings - Formula One - Colourcap – Harrison Thompson & Co. Ltd

Yeti – gaiters – Berghaus Ltd

Yew Tree Fabric, A – worsted piece goods, fancy and plain fabrics for mens and ladies in all wool, polyester and wool, silk and wool, tartans/corporate wear cloths – Butterworth & Roberts Ltd

YF – Alpha Electronics Southern Ltd

Yippy Yippy Yum Yum – Popular, Reliable and Value for money – Chi Yip Group Ltd

YKK – zips – William Gee Ltd

Yodac – alarm sounders – Clifford & Snell

Yodalarm – alarm sounders – Clifford & Snell

Yodalarm - Yodalex - Yodac - Yodalight - Clifford & Snell - Keyswitch - Sarbe – Clifford & Snell

Yodalex – alarm sounders – Clifford & Snell

Yodalight – alarm sounders/strobes – Clifford & Snell

Yodel – Criterion Ices

Yoga – Pre and post surgical garments/ compression garments and post natal girdles – Yoga Model London Limited

Yokogawa – Lamphouse Ltd

Yokota – Red Rooster Industrial UK Ltd

Yokota – Yokota UK

Yokota – Gustair Materials Handling Equipment Ltd

Yokota Airtools – Yokota UK

Yokudo – microswitches – Anglia

Yoo J – vertical boring/turning cents – C Dugard Ltd Machine Tools

York – Split system air conditioning – Banfield Refrigeration Supplies Ltd

York – Therma Group

York – residential door – Coastal Aluminium

***York House The Taste Of Excellence** – York House Meat Products Ltd

York Shipley Boilers – Twin Industries International Ltd

Yorkleen – Central C N C Machinery Ltd

Yorkon – single source building service and steel framed building system – Yorkon Ltd

Yorkshire Building Society – Yorkshire Building Society

Yorkshire by Post – Yorkshire Building Society

Yorkshire Evening Post, The – newspapers – Yorkshire Post

Yorkshire Guernsey – Yorkshire Building Society

Yorkshire Post, The – newspapers – Yorkshire Post

Yorkshire Rider – buses – First Group plc

Yorkshire Water Projects – joint venture and other business developments in home and overseas markets – Kelda Group

Yorkshire Water Services – yorkshire's major utility supplier of drinking water and waste disposal to 4.5 million residents and 160,000 business users – Kelda Group

Yorkshire Web Offset – The Barnsley Chronicle Ltd

Yorkshire Windows – manufacture & install windows – Yorkshire Window Co. Ltd

Yorkway – pharmaceutical and cosmetic machinery – T Giusti Ltd

You – magazine – Associated Newspapers

Youle – non ferrous casting, street furniture and nameplates – J Youle & Co. Ltd

Young – glass shower enclosures – Novellini UK Ltd

Young Headway – books – Hachette UK Ltd

Young Lions – paperback childrens books, fiction and non-fiction – Harpercollins Publishers Ophelia House

Young savers – account – Furness Building Society

Youngmans – Accesscaff International Ltd

Youngs – retail frozen fish – Youngs Seafood

Youngs Lifting (United Kingdom) – mechanical jacks – Power Jacks Ltd

***Youngs Talbot** – General Catering Supplies Ltd

Your Horse – magazine – Emap Ltd

Your Local Property Shop – Brand – Kelvin Valley Properties

Your Stationary – UK Office Direct

YPG – precision gauges – Yorkshire Precision Gauges Ltd

YRL 105 (United Kingdom) – abrasion resistantsoft natural rubber with good resistance to abrasive slurries - 45 shore 'A' – Yorkshire Rubber Linings Ltd

YRL 106 (United Kingdom) – abrasion resistant soft natural rubber - 60 shore 'A' – Yorkshire Rubber Linings Ltd

YRL 110 (United Kingdom) – high quality nitrile rubber - 57 shore 'A' – Yorkshire Rubber Linings Ltd

YRL 120 (United Kingdom) – high quality bromobutyl rubber resists hot acids and chemicals - 55 shore 'A' – Yorkshire Rubber Linings Ltd

YRL 138 (United Kingdom) – premium grade non-black, non-conductive, flexible ebonite suitable for acids and chemicals – Yorkshire Rubber Linings Ltd

YRL 146 (United Kingdom) – premium grade neoprene rubber resists hot acids and chemicals, oils and greases and seawater – Yorkshire Rubber Linings Ltd

YRL 178 (United Kingdom) – white food quality natural rubber FDA and BGA approved - 50 shore 'A' – Yorkshire Rubber Linings Ltd

YRL 200 (United Kingdom) – WRC approved EPDM rubber suitable for potable water 60 shore 'A' – Yorkshire Rubber Linings Ltd

YRL121 (United Kingdom) – premium grade drab hypalon for use with sodium hypochlorite – Yorkshire Rubber Linings Ltd

YRL136 (United Kingdom) – premium grade ebonite rubber sheet – Yorkshire Rubber Linings Ltd

YRL137 (United Kingdom) – premium grade ebonite rubber sheet silica free high temp grade – Yorkshire Rubber Linings Ltd

YSF6 – withdrawable indoor switchgear – Schneider

YUASA – Batteries – Halcyon Solutions

YUASA – Groves Batteries

Yuasa – sealed lead acid battery – Anglia

Yuasa – Yuasa Batteries – The Battery Shop UK LTD

Yuasa – Cyclops Electronics Ltd

YUATANAI – Hydraulic & Offshore Supplies Ltd

Yuill Homes – private house building developers and building contractors – Cecil M Yuill Ltd

YUKEN – Hydraulic & Offshore Supplies Ltd

Yuken – J V Hydraulics Ltd

Yukon – instrument connection software – Thermo Fisher Scientific

Yukon – Thomas Jacks Ltd

Yuleplus – lowe glass – A C Yule & Son Ltd

Yuzuzest ABJ 7091 – speciality compound – Quest International UK Ltd

Yves Saint Laurent – lighters & pens – Ronson Incorporated Ltd

Z

***Z.A.B. (Netherlands)** – sliding tables – Brandone Machine Tool Ltd

Z Bloc – fibre modules – Thermal Ceramics UK Ltd

Z.C.I. – cavity lining products – Prima Dental Group Ltd

Z F Industrial Drives – hysteresis - clutches and brakes – Clark Electric Clutch & Controls Ltd

Z-Laser Optoelektronik GmbH – Headquarters – Z-Laser Uk Sales Office

Z-Mill – Taegutec UK Ltd

Z'Nap – Building Toys – Lego UK Ltd

Z.O.E. – zin oxide & eugenol BP – Prima Dental Group Ltd

Z.S. – multi-purpose stacking linking chair – Race Furniture Ltd

Zaandam – plastic and paper mail wrapping – Buhrs UK Ltd

ZAK system – roller shutters and grilles – Hörmann (UK) Ltd

Zal – disinfectant – Jeyes

Zal Bath Cleaner – cream bath cleaner – Jeyes

Zalutite – mild flat steels – Corus

***Zambello (Italy)** – helical and gear and worm gearboxes – Andantex Ltd

Zamo – disinfectant, bleach, washing up liquid, top-up de-ionised water – Zamo Household Products Ltd

***Zanchetta (Italy)** – powder handling systems – Romaco Holdings UK Ltd

Zander – Parker Hannifin

Zanderlon – Water Soluble Yarn – Sage Zander Ltd

Zanidip – hypertension – Napp Pharmaceutical Group Ltd

***Zanolli** – Cater Bake UK Ltd

Zante – Pledge Office Chairs Ltd

Zanzibar – vinyl wallcoverings and fabrics – Tektura plc

Zap Controls – electronic design developments – Zap Controls Ltd

Zarges Ladders – Accesscaff International Ltd

Zarox – Fluorinated Lubricants – I K V Tribology Ltd

Zasche – European Technical Sales Ltd

Zassenhaus – Pepper & Salt Mills – Gilberts Food Equipment Ltd

ZAVOLI Antom – automotive LPG injection kits – H K L Gas Power Ltd

ZBA Services – electron beam lithography system – Leica Microsystems

Zebex – Maxa Technologies Ltd

Zebotronics – Motor Technology Ltd

Zebra – M L P S

Zebra – P C F Secure Document Systems Ltd

Zebra – ID Card Printer Manufacturer – Plastic ID

Zebra – Zebra labels & printers & ribbons – Lancer Labels Ltd

Zebra – Printers – Moorgate Ltd

Zebra 105sl – Allcode UK Ltd

Zebra 2844 – Allcode UK Ltd

Zebra ql220 – Allcode UK Ltd

Zebra ql320 – Allcode UK Ltd

Zebra ql420 – Allcode UK Ltd

Zebra rw220 – Allcode UK Ltd

Zebra rw420 – Allcode UK Ltd

Zebra s4m – Allcode UK Ltd

Zebra z4m – Allcode UK Ltd

Zebra zm400 – Allcode UK Ltd

Zecom – photocopyable waterproof paper – V I P

Zed Chex – Checker plate vinyl top fused to patented foam base in rolls or modules – Plastic Extruders Ltd

Zed Land – Patented foam construction in rolls or modules with anti-fatigue properties – Plastic Extruders Ltd

Zed Tred – Hardwearing vinyl ribbed top fused to patented foam base in rolls or modules – Plastic Extruders Ltd

Zedex – High performance DPC – Visqueen Building Products South Wales Ltd

Zedflo – burners for glass forehearths – Dyson Thermal Technologies

Zedmark – precision cast refractories – Dyson Thermal Technologies

Zedstrip – steel lintels – Naylor Drainage Ltd

Zedtec – glass conditioning requirements – Dyson Thermal Technologies

Zedwedge – V-belts – The Zerny Engineering Co. Ltd

Zeeospheres – spherical ceramic extenders – Lawrence Industries Ltd

Zeiss – Zeiss

ZEITLAUF antriebstechnik – Zeitlauf

Zelec – antistatic agents/chemical additive – Du Pont UK Ltd

Zelig Platforms – Accesscaff International Ltd

Zelio – electronic timers & control relays – Schneider

Zemdrain – thermally bonded 100% polypropylene – Du Pont UK Ltd

***Zemdrain (Luxembourg)** – controlled permeability formliner – Max Frank Ltd

Zen – brake drums, disc, hubs and flywheels – Roadlink International Ltd

Zeni – cylinder brass padlock range – Walsall Locks Ltd

Zenite – Resinex UK Ltd

Zenith – seating – Audience Systems Ltd

Zenith – carburetters and components – Burlen Fuel Systems Ltd

Zenith – fuel systems car components – Burlen Fuel Systems Ltd

Zenith – Lamphouse Ltd

Zenith – Aztech Components Ltd

Zenith – external gear pumps – Axflow

Zenith – general purpose grease bar and liquid compounds – Lea Manufacturing Co.

Zenith cases – exterior notice boards and display cases – Pinpoint Presentation

Zenith Club Class – carpets - axminster – Brintons Carpets Ltd

Zentech/Xtech/Midirobo Tech/Duotech/Maxirobo Tech (United Kingdom) – EDM machines – Winbro Group Technologies

***Zentrofix (Switzerland)** – centre locators – Vaultland Engineering

***Zeon Chich (Far East)** – watches – Zeon Chemicals Europe Ltd

Zephlex – plastic flexible vacuum hose – Plastiflex UK Ltd

Zephron – technical synthetic needlefelt filter fabrics – Andrew Webron Ltd

Zephur/Alpha/Zeta/Delta/Theta (United Kingdom) – laser machines – Winbro Group Technologies

Zephyr Rib – fibre bonded carpet – Heckmondwike FB

Zepkyr/Hypha/Zeta/Delta/Theta (United Kingdom) – lasermachines – Winbro Group Technologies

Zeraloy – stainless steel alloy – Weir Materials & Foundries

Zermatt – kitchen vapour proof lighting – Designplan Lighting Ltd

Zero – circular recessed architectural lighting – Designplan Lighting Ltd

Zero 88 – lighting control equipment – Cooper Controls Ltd

Zero-Max (U.S.A.) – all power transmission products – Robert Cupitt Ltd

ZeroC – gritters – Econ Engineering Ltd

Zeroclad – cladding system to support purpose-made panels in any plane – Gillespie UK Ltd

Zeroclips – Zero Clips Ltd

Zeroclips - JCS - Tridon. – Zero Clips Ltd

Zerodec – element made in glass reinforced gypsum – Gillespie UK Ltd

Zerohal – halogen-free cable jacket material – Tyco Electronics UK Ltd

*Zeroll (U.S.A.) – caterers ice cream scoops – Mitchell & Cooper Ltd

Zeron – stainless steel alloys – Weir Materials & Foundries

Zeron 100 – super duplex stainless steel – Weir Materials & Foundries

Zeron 25 – stainless steel alloy – Weir Materials & Foundries

*Zeroset-Servo (France) – gearboxes – Andantex Ltd

Zerospan – ceiling tiles made in grg, size 600x600 mm – Gillespie UK Ltd

Zest – magazine – National Magazine Company Ltd

Zest – desks – E F G Matthews Office Furniture Ltd

Zeste – aerosol body deodorant, room freshener – Keen World Marketing Ltd

Zetaclad – specialist electrophoretic coatings – L V H Coatings Ltd

Zetanite – mens safety boots and shoes (with non-metallic toe caps) – Bunzl S W S

Zetasassi – belt and chain tensioners, overload clutches – R A Rodriguez UK Ltd

Zetascan – yarn examining machine – James H Heal & Co. Ltd

Zetasizer – zeta potential measurement – Malvern Instruments Ltd

Zetatron – electronic water conditioner for scale control in hard water – Aldous & Stamp Ltd

Zetex – semiconductors – Anglia

Zetex – Cyclops Electronics Ltd

Zettelmeyer – Harrier Fluid Power Ltd

Zettler – Cyclops Electronics Ltd

Zeus – trouser finisher – Electrolux Laundry Systems

ZF – Harrier Fluid Power Ltd

ZF – European Technical Sales Ltd

Zheng Mao – Offspring International

Ziehl Abeg – European Technical Sales Ltd

Ziehl Abegg – fan motors and assemblies – Thermofrost Cryo plc

Ziehl-ABM – European Technical Sales Ltd

Zig Zag – toddlers shoes, sports and leisure footwear – D Jacobson & Sons Ltd

Zig-Zag Towers – Accesscaff International Ltd

Zigazaga 2000 – chevron ribbed polypropylene foyer/entrance matting – Jaymart Roberts & Plastics Ltd

Ziggurat – commercial and decorative energy saving luminaires – Poselco Lighting Ltd

Ziggy – diamond surface vandal resistant architectural lighting – Designplan Lighting Ltd

Zika – swimwear – Rococo Style Ltd

Zilmet Vessels – Flow Mech Products Ltd

Zilog – Cyclops Electronics Ltd

Zin – bushes for sheet metal jigs – Talbot Tool Co. Ltd

Zincaslot – cyanide free alkaline zinc plating solutions – Schloetter Co. Ltd

Zincrolyte – zinc alloy plating process – Cookson Electronics Ltd

Zinga – Harrier Fluid Power Ltd

Zingalv – Forward Chemicals Ltd

Zinloy – zinc nickel alloy plating – Cookson Electronics Ltd

Zinnatine – food can lacquer – Akzo Nobel Packaging Coatings Ltd

Zintec – electrolytic zinc coated steel – Corus U K Ltd

Zintek – Protective Finishing Group

Zip Clip – metal fastening mechanism – Office Depot UK

Zip Grip – B P plc

Zip-Patch – quick cure and adhesive impregnated repair kit – I T W Devcon

Zip-Up Towers – Accesscaff International Ltd

*Zippo (U.S.A.) – cigarette lighters, rules, keyholders, knives, greenskeepers and writing instruments – Zippo UK Ltd

Ziptubes – slotted tubs – Rollform Sections Ltd

Zircomplex – thixutrope for latex paints – Rhodia Ltd

Zircon – Zirconium Silicates – Mineral & Chemical Services Ltd

Zircon – industrial lubricant – B P plc

Zircon – Kramp UK Ltd

Zircosol – chemicals for paper – M E L Chemicals

Zircozon – zirconium silicate – P E Hines & Sons Ltd

Zirgel – thixatropic agents – M E L Chemicals

Zirmax – zirconium hardener – Magnesium Elektron

Zirmel – chemicals for paper – M E L Chemicals

ZMD – Cyclops Electronics Ltd

Zodiac – screw gauge – Zodiac Screw Gauge Ltd

Zodiac – cutlery and holloware – Zodiac Stainless Products Co. Ltd

Zodion (United Kingdom) – street lighting controls – Zodion Ltd

Zofanny Paints – paints – Zoffany

Zoffany – Philip Cowan Interiors

Zoffany Trimmings – Trimmings – Zoffany

Zoketts – construction toys – Broanmain

Zollern – European Technical Sales Ltd

Zon – Seating – Bucon Ltd

Zone 1 Towers – Accesscaff International Ltd

Zonemaster – air conditioning controls – Schneider Electric

Zonoson – G E Healthcare

Zonyl – micropowders/fluoroadditives – Du Pont UK Ltd

Zoom-Whip – fishing tackle – Daiwa Sports Ltd

ZOOMATIC – Hydraulic & Offshore Supplies Ltd

Zopla – adhesive paddings for surgical and chiropodial use – Cuxson Gerrard & Company Ltd

Zorzettig – wine – Rodney Densem Wines Ltd

Zotefoams – W Mannering London Ltd

ZPREG (United Kingdom) – striped impregnation, variable temperature curing epoxy resin material systems – Umeco

Zschimmer & Schwarz (France) – Chemical Additives – Hostombe Group Ltd

Ztec – LXI Oscilloscopes – StanTronic Instruments

ZTV Electronics – Cameras – Halcyon Solutions

Zubes – throat lozenges – Ernest Jackson & Co. Ltd

Zurcon – engineered thermoplastic compound – Trelleborg Ceiling Solutions Ltd

Zurn – Harrier Fluid Power Ltd

*Zuzazz (Germany) – record company – Rollercoaster Records Ltd

Zweifel – Leader Chuck Systems Ltd

Zweigart – needlework fabrics and canvas – DMC Creative World

Zwiehoff-Zagro – King Trailers Ltd

ZX Coat – Sumitomo Electric Hardmetal Ltd

ZX Hoists – Street Crane Ltd

ZX - range of overhead cranes, ZX Hoists, TX Hoists, CX Chain Hoists. – Street Crane Ltd

Zybax – microbiological cleaning solutions – Branova Cleaning Services

Zycomm – supply and service 2-way radio equipment – Zycomm Electronics Ltd

Zyglo – fluorescent penetrant materials – Magnaflux

Zygo – safety footwear – Amber Safetywear Ltd

Zygology – Zygology Ltd

*Zykon (Germany) – stress free, undercut anchors for concrete – Fischer Fixings UK Ltd

*Zyliss (Switzerland) – gadgets – Dexam International

Zymax – diastatic malt flour – E D M E Ltd

Zymax – Lightning protectors – Halcyon Solutions

Zymaxx – chemical & creep resistant parts – Du Pont UK Ltd

Zymolene – solvent scours – Brenntag Colours Ltd

Zytel – nylon resins – Du Pont UK Ltd

Zytel – Resinex UK Ltd

COMPANY INFORMATION

This section shows the addresses and telephone communication details for entries listed in the trade name section. A summary of trade names in use is given for each company.

2

2 K Polymer Systems Ltd Venture Crescent Nixs Hill Indl-Est, Alfreton DE55 7RA Tel. *01773 540440* Fax. *01773 607638* E-mail. *info@2kps.net* Web. *www.2kps.net Exchem Mining*

3

3663 Buckingham Court Kingsmead Business Park, London Road, High Wycombe HP11 1JU Tel. *0370 3663251* E-mail. *advice_centre@3663.co.uk* Web. *www.3663.co.uk* *Coronet – *Smart Choice – *Springbourne*

3D Sports (a division of Kookaburra Reader Ltd) 3 Brakey Road Weldon North Industrial Estate, Corby, Northampton NN17 5LU Tel. *0845 6760099* Fax. *01536 209211* E-mail. *info@3dsports.co.uk* Web. *www.3dsports.co.uk 3D Sports Ltd (India)*

3E UK Ltd 14 Free Trade House Lowther Road, Queensbury, Stanmore HA7 1EP Tel. *0844 8849739* E-mail. *solutions_3e@hotmail.com* Web. *www.3esolutions.net 3E – Carbon CMS – Carbon CRM – Carbon Ecom – Carbon Property*

3g Foodservice Ltd 30 West Dock Street, Hull HU3 4HL Tel. *01482 593700* Fax. *01482 324550* E-mail. *info@3gfoodservice.co.uk* Web. *www.3gfoodservice.co.uk 3G Breaded Scampi – 3G Desserts – 3G Food Service – 3G Individual Entrees – 3G Prawns – 3G Ready Meals – 3G Sausages – 3G Seafood Solutions – 3G Select – 3G Select Premium Desserts*

3 M Healthcare Ltd 3 M House 1 Morley Street, Loughborough LE11 1EP Tel. *01509 611611* Fax. *01509 613253* E-mail. *jsmith123@mmm.com* Web. *www.3m.com 3M Health Care*

4

4mation Educational Software Ltd PO Box 282, Barnstaple EX31 1HG Tel. *01271 325353* Fax. *01271 322974* E-mail. *rob@4mation.co.uk* Web. *www.4mation.co.uk 4 Mation – 4 Mation Educational Resources*

4site Implementation Ltd 22 Hemmells, Basildon SS15 6ED Tel. *01268 540081* Fax. *01268 541624* E-mail. *sales@4site-implementation.com* Web. *www.4site-implementation.com Simple Signman*

5

5 Fifteen Ltd 180 Bedford Avenue, Slough SL1 4RA Tel. *01753 440515* Fax. *01753 440550* E-mail. *info@5fifteen.com* Web. *www.5fifteen.com Maxim*

6

600 Group plc PO Box 20, Heckmondwike WF16 0HN Tel. *01924 415000* Fax. *01924 415015* E-mail. *mail@600group.com* Web. *www.600group.com Colchester – Crawford Collets – Electrox – Gamet Bearings – Harrison*

A

A4 Apparel Ltd Unit 1 Velator, Braunton EX33 2DX Tel. *01271 816158* Fax. *01905 755885* E-mail. *info@a4apparel.co.uk* Web. *www.a4apparel.co.uk Dickies – Fruit of the Loom – Gildan – Hanes – Snickers*

A A H Pharmaceuticals Sapphire Court Paradise Way, Coventry Walsgrave Triangle, Coventry CV2 2TX Tel. *024 76432000* Fax. *024 76432001* E-mail. *it@aah.co.uk* Web. *www.aah.co.uk A.A.H. Pharmaceuticals*

A A K Ltd Davy Road Astmoor Industrial Estate, Runcorn WA7 1PZ Tel. *01928 565221* Fax. *01928 561172* E-mail. *jon.devine@aak.com* Web. *www.aak.com Exotics – Lion*

A A K Bakery Services Falcon Street, Oldham OL8 1JU Tel. *0161 6526311* Fax. *0161 6272346*

E-mail. *steve.hamilton@aak.com* Web. *www.aak.com Bevwhite – Crestaflakes – Crestaflow – Crestamix – Crestawhip – Crodamix – Greetin – Rolloff – Starspray – Supertex – Wundrol*

A Algeo Ltd Unit 14 Sheridan House Speke Hall Road, Liverpool L24 9HB Tel. *0151 4481228* Fax. *0151 4481008* E-mail. *sales@algeos.com* Web. *www.algeos.com Bronte – Cavendish – Darnot – Deva – Iwanta – Leathawash – Luxigrips – Pioneer – Podotech – Podotech – Podowegde – Savose – Secure – Stompers*

A&A Lifting and Safety Ltd 28 Churchward Drive Stretton, Burton on Trent DE13 0AU Tel. *01785 318239* E-mail. *sales@aslifting.co.uk* Web. *www.aalifting.co.uk A&A Lifting and Safety*

A&S Lifting and Safety Ltd 28 Churchward Drive Stretton, Burton On Trent DE13 0AU Tel. *07530 040476* E-mail. *sales@aslifting.co.uk* Web. *www.aslifting.co.uk Yale – Checkmate*

Aardvark Clear Mine Ltd Shevock Estate, Insch AB52 6XQ Tel. *01464 820122* Fax. *01464 820985* E-mail. *office@aardvarkclearmine.com* Web. *www.aardvarkclearmine.com Aardvark*

Aarhuskarlshamn Hull Ltd Aarhus Karlshamn King George Dock, Hull HU9 5PX Tel. *01482 701271* Fax. *01482 709447* E-mail. *john.hart@aak.com* Web. *www.aak.com AKO*

Aaron Metal & Plastic Supplies Ltd Unit 7-8 Barnack Trading Centre Novers Hill, Bedminster, Bristol BS3 5QE Tel. *0117 9231988* Fax. *0117 9231469* E-mail. *info@aaronmetals.co.uk Delrin – Fluorosint – Noryl – Vespel*

A A T I Ltd 11 Swinbourne Drive Springwood Industrial Estate, Braintree CM7 2YP Tel. *01376 346278* Fax. *01376 348480* E-mail. *info@aati.co.uk* Web. *www.aati.co.uk HDLT – L U L – RIBA – Sightline – Sightline3*

A & A Wines Ltd 13 Manfield Park, Cranleigh GU6 8PT Tel. *01483 274666* Fax. *01483 268460* E-mail. *info@aawines.co.uk* Web. *www.aawines.co.uk A & A Foods Ltd – A & A Wines Ltd*

Abacus Lighting Ltd Oddicroft Lane, Sutton In Ashfield NG17 5FT Tel. *01623 511111* Fax. *01623 552133* E-mail. *sales@abacuslighting.com* Web. *www.abacuslighting.com Abacus – Dron Dickson Abacus*

Abal Engineering UK Unit 6 Parkway 4 Trading Estate, Trafford Park, Manchester M17 1SW Tel. *0161 8743100* Fax. *0161 8743101* E-mail. *sales@abal.co.uk* Web. *www.abal.co.uk Abal*

Abbey Board Cromwell House Altendiez Way, Burton Latimer, Kettering NN15 5YZ Tel. *01536 420055* Fax. *01536 421726* E-mail. *julie.coles@abbey.dssp.com* Web. *www.abbeycorrugated.co.uk AbbeyFlex – AbbeyLite – AbbeyScreen*

Abbeydale Storage 51 Springfield Road, Sheffield S7 2GE Tel. *0114 2819299* Fax. *0114 2819399* E-mail. *sales@abbeydalestorage.co.uk* Web. *www.abbeydalestorage.co.uk Kardex, Linvar, Linpic and Megamat Vertical carous*

Abbey England Ltd Haig Road Parkgate Industrial Estate, Knutsford WA16 8DX Tel. *01565 650343* Fax. *01565 633825* E-mail. *gb@abbeysaddlery.co.uk* Web. *www.abbeysaddlery.co.uk Abbey Bits – Fiebing – koldblue – Moss – Pro Equine – Sedgwick – Stubbs*

Abbey Forged Products Ltd Beeley Wood Works Beeley Wood Lane, Sheffield S6 1ND Tel. *0114 2312271* Fax. *0114 2324980* E-mail. *lee.thomas@abbeyfp.co.uk* Web. *www.abbeyforgedproducts.co.uk Admiral – Dreadnought – Tenax*

Abbey Current Accounts (Head Office) 2-3 Triton Square, London NW1 3AN Tel. *0800 5875045* Fax. *020 76124010* Web. *www.abbey.com Abbey National*

Abbey Pynford plc Second Floor Hille House 132 St Albans Road, Watford WD24 4AQ Tel. *01923 211160*

Fax. *01923 234434* E-mail. *vicki.highcock@abbeypynford.co.uk* Web. *www.abbeypynford.co.uk Abbey Pynford*

Abbey Spares & Supplies Unit 17 Top Barn Business Centre Worcester Road, Holt Heath, Worcester WR6 6NH Tel. *01905 621666* Fax. *01905 621866* E-mail. *sales@abbeyspares.co.uk* Web. *www.abbeyspares.co.uk *Proceq (Germany) – *Steinweg (Germany)*

Abbey Masterbatch Ltd Whitelands Mill Whitelands Road, Ashton Under Lyne OL6 6UG Tel. *0161 3082550* Fax. *0161 3442345* E-mail. *office@abbeymb.com* Web. *www.abbeymasterbatch.com Abbey Thermosets*

Abbicoil Springs 21 Carn Road Portadown, Craigavon BT63 5WG Tel. *028 38333245* Fax. *028 38335997* E-mail. *sales@abbicoil.co.uk* Web. *www.abbicoil.co.uk Abbicoil*

Abbott & Co Newark Ltd Newark Boiler Works Northern Road, Newark NG24 2EJ Tel. *01636 704208* Fax. *01636 705742* E-mail. *henryp@air-receivers.co.uk* Web. *www.air-receivers.co.uk Pressure Vessels – Air Receivers – Expansion Vessels – Buffer Vessels – Flash Vessels – Surge Vessels – Blowdown Vessels – Dished ends*

A B C Catering & Party Equipment Hire Ltd 2 Wealdstone Road Kimpton Indus Park, Sutton SM3 9QN Tel. *020 86416700* Fax. *020 86419300* E-mail. *hire@abchire.co.uk* Web. *www.abchire.co.uk ABC Glass Box*

Abceta Playthings Ltd (Denton Agencies-Sven Carlson Ltd) 19 Torkington Road Hazel Grove, Stockport SK7 4RG Tel. *0161 4834500* Fax. *0161 4566896* E-mail. *sir.terry.john.denton@dicksystem.com* Web. *www.dicksystem.com Maths Cubes – Muilty Link Cubes – Sasha Dolls*

A B C Polishing & Engineering Supplies Picador Engineering 103 Louth Road Holton-Le-Clay, Grimsby DN36 5AD Tel. *01472 824520* Fax. *01472 824520* E-mail. *sales@abcpolishing.co.uk* Web. *www.abcpolishing.co.uk PICADOR PULLEYS*

A B C Selfstore Unit 3 Wandsworth Trading Estate 118-120 Garratt Lane, London SW18 4DJ Tel. *0800 0150787* E-mail. *wandsworth@abcselfstore.co.uk* Web. *www.abcselfstore.co.uk ABC Selfstore*

ABEKO (UK) Ltd Viking Haven Inghams Road, Tetney, Grimsby DN36 5LW Tel. *01472 210054* Fax. *01472 210484* E-mail. *enquiries@abeko.uk.com* Web. *www.abeko.uk.com M.C. Transport Ltd*

A-Belco Ltd The A-Belco Group Factory No1 Jubilee Industrial Estate Jubilee Industrial Estate, Ashington NE63 8UG Tel. *01670 813275* Fax. *01670 851141* E-mail. *sales@cortem.co.uk* Web. *www.a-belco.co.uk *Balcom (Germany) – Easigo – Pullcap – Ralyester*

Abel Demountable Systems Ltd Station Road Old Tupton, Chesterfield S42 6DA Tel. *01246 851175* Fax. *01246 855506* E-mail. *sales@abelsystems.co.uk* Web. *www.abelsystems.co.uk 737 – Abel bodies – Abelmatic – Airlite – Drawbars – Euroswap – Loadspeeder – Uniswop*

Abel Magnets Ltd Balaclava Road, Sheffield S6 3BG Tel. *0114 2495949* Fax. *0114 2495950* E-mail. *info@magnetic-paper.com* Web. *www.magnetic-paper.com Magnetic Paper*

R G Abercrombie Caledonian Road, Alloa FK10 1NB Tel. *01259 222500* Fax. *01259 222528* E-mail. *info@diageo.com Abercrombie*

Aber Roof Truss Ltd (Gang-Nail Systems Ltd) Off Babbage Road Engineer Park, Sandycroft, Deeside CH5 2QD Tel. *01244 539165* Fax. *01244 539166* E-mail. *sales@aberrooftruss.co.uk* Web. *www.aberrooftruss.co.uk Ecojoist*

A B Graphics International Ltd Carnaby Industrial Estate Lancaster Road, Carnaby, Bridlington YO15 3QY
Tel. *01262 671138* Fax. *01262 606359*
E-mail. *info@abgint.com* Web. *www.abgint.com* Arbeco – Omega Systems

A B G Rubber & Plastics Ltd 10 Sketty Close Brackmills Industrial Estate, Northampton NN4 7PL Tel. *01604 700880*
Fax. *01604 766113* E-mail. *sales@abgrp.co.uk*
Web. *www.abgrp.co.uk* Harries Board - Food preparation boardsHygienplas - Wall cladding – HarriesBoard

A B I Electronics Ltd Unit 2 Dodworth Business Park, Dodworth, Barnsley S75 3SP Tel. *01226 207420*
Fax. *01226 207620* E-mail. *sales@abielectronics.co.uk*
Web. *www.abielectronics.co.uk* BoardMaster – ChipMaster Compact – LinearMaster Compact – SYSTEM 8

Abird Ltd Ramsgate Road, Sandwich CT13 9ND
Tel. *01304 613221* Fax. *01304 614833*
E-mail. *info@abird.co.uk* Web. *www.abird.co.uk* Superquiet

A B L Aluminium Components Ltd Premier House Garretts Green Trading Estate Valepits Road, Birmingham B33 0TD
Tel. *0121 7898686* Fax. *0121 7898778*
E-mail. *stephen.richardson@ablcomponents.co.uk*
Web. *www.ablcomponents.co.uk* ABL Heatsinks

Able Direct Centre Ltd 5 Mallard Close Earls Barton, Northampton NN6 0LS Tel. *01604 810781*
Fax. *08704 442766* E-mail. *sales@able-labels.co.uk*
Web. *www.able-labels.co.uk* Able

Able Engraving & Design Unit D1-D2 Haysbridge Business Centre Brickhouse Lane, South Godstone, Godstone RH9 8JW Tel. *01342 843211* Fax. *01342 844209*
E-mail. *a.douglas@able-engraving.co.uk*
Web. *www.able-engraving.co.uk* Traffolyte

Able Instruments & Controls Ltd (Level Division) Danehill Lower Earley, Reading RG6 4UT Tel. *0118 9311188*
Fax. *0118 9312161* E-mail. *analytical@able.co.uk*
Web. *www.able.co.uk* Besta – Computrac – Controlotron – Danfoss – Delta F – Drexelbrook Engineering – General Eastern – International Light Inc – Intra-Automation – Ohmart – Transmation – Trimod Besta – Unimess – United Electric Controls

Able Internet Payroll Ltd Unit 101, China House 395 Edgware Road, London NW2 6LN Tel. *020 84389791*
Fax. *0871 9896099*
E-mail. *sally.wells@ableinternetpayroll.com*
Web. *www.ableinternetpayroll.com* Able Internet Payroll Ltd

Abloy UK Abloy House Hatters Lane, Watford WD18 8QY
Tel. *01923 255066* Fax. *01923 230281*
E-mail. *rrice@abloysecurity.co.uk* Web. *www.abloy.co.uk*
*ABLOY (Finland) – ABLOY Disklock Pro – ABLOY Exec – ABMAGS – Cypherlock – Memorilok

A B L Perpack 1985 Ltd 7 Baron Avenue Telford Way Industrial Estate, Kettering NN16 8UW Tel. *01536 412744*
Fax. *01536 412752* E-mail. *christine@ablperpack.co.uk*
Web. *www.ablperpack.co.uk* Ajover (Darnelwrap) – Bevilacqua – Bevilacqua Lovetilene – Follen Dor – Propack PVC (LMF)

A B Pharos Marine Ltd Steyning Way, Hounslow TW4 6DL
Tel. *020 85381100* Fax. *020 85774170*
E-mail. *sales@pharosmarine.com*
Web. *www.pharosmarine.com* *Flashchanger (U.S.A.) – *Litepipe (U.S.A.) – Phalcon

A B Precision Poole Ltd 1 Fleets Lane, Poole BH15 3BZ
Tel. *01202 665000* Fax. *01202 675965*
E-mail. *enquiries@abprecision.co.uk*
Web. *www.abprecision.co.uk* Aemoti Operated Vehicles – Automation Equipment – Echo Sounders

Abrasive Technology Ltd Roxby Place Fulham, London SW6 1RT Tel. *020 74710200* Fax. *020 74710202*
E-mail. *customerservices@abrasive-tech.com*
Web. *www.abrasive-tech.com* Diamond Polishing Compounds – Electroplating Diamond Products – Resin Bond Diamond Products – Virisite Wills Diamond

Abril Industrial Waxes Ltd Sturmi Way Village Farm Industrial Estate, Pyle, Bridgend CF33 6BZ Tel. *01656 744896*
Fax. *01656 744887* E-mail. *info@abrilindustrialwaxes.co.uk*
Web. *www.abril.co.uk* Abrilflo – Abrilube – Abriwax

Abru Ltd Derwentside Industrial Park Derby Road, Belper DE56 1WE Tel. *01773 525730* Fax. *01773 828059*
E-mail. *sales@abru.co.uk* Web. *www.abruladders.co.uk*
Aluval – Arizona – Arrow – Blue Seal – Joyners – Nevada – Sahara – Starmaster

Absolute Search Ltd Hamilton House 39 Hookstone Road, Harrogate HG2 8BT Tel. *01423 544785*
E-mail. *info@absolutesearch.co.uk*
Web. *www.absolutesearch.co.uk* Absolute Search

A B T Products Ltd Ashburton Industrial Estate, Ross On Wye HR9 7BW Tel. *01989 563656* Fax. *01989 566824*
E-mail. *nigel.mummery@abtproducts.com*
Web. *www.abtproducts.com* ABT Products Ltd – Autophoretic Paint Plant

Aburnet Ltd Walter Street Draycott, Derby DE72 3NU
Tel. *01332 874797* Fax. *01332 875284*
E-mail. *info@aburnet.co.uk* Web. *www.aburnet.co.uk* Abur (United Kingdom) – Burnet (United Kingdom) – HygieNet (United Kingdom) – Lady Fayre (United Kingdom) – One For Me (United Kingdom)

ABUS Crane Systems Ltd Unit 1 1 Business Village, Yateley GU46 6GA Tel. *01252 749000* Fax. *01252 749001*

E-mail. *info@abuscranes.co.uk* Web. *www.abuscranes.co.uk*
ABUS

Abwood Machine Tools Ltd (Division of Atlanta Trust Ltd) 615 Princes Road, Dartford DA2 6DY Tel. *01322 225271*
Fax. *01322 291862* E-mail. *sales@abwoodcnc.co.uk*
Web. *www.abwoodcnc.co.uk* Abwood – *Auto Well Safeway (Taiwan) – *Cuter (Italy) – *Fresmak (Spain)

A & C Ltd 83 Headstone Road, Harrow HA1 1PQ
Tel. *020 84275168* Fax. *020 88612469*
E-mail. *info@powerpod.co.uk* Web. *www.powerpod.co.uk*
Pee-Pod – Power Pod

Academy Class Ltd 99 Waterloo Road, London SE1 8UL
Tel. *0800 0438889* Fax. *0870 3305722*
E-mail. *info@academyclass.com*
Web. *www.academyclass.com* Academy Class

A C Automation (Agents For Koberlein Gmbh) Hartland Avenue Tattenhoe, Milton Keynes MK4 3DN
Tel. *01908 501796* Fax. *01908 501796*
E-mail. *a.child@ac-automation.co.uk*
Web. *www.ac-automation.co.uk* Pneumasort

A C Bedrooms Carders Corner White Horse Business Park, Trowbridge BA14 7DT Tel. *01225 340388*
E-mail. *acbedrooms@yahoo.co.uk*
Web. *www.acbedrooms.co.uk* AC bedrooms

Accelerated Learning Systems Ltd 50 Aylesbury Road Aston Clinton, Aylesbury HP22 5AH Tel. *01296 631177*
Fax. *01296 631074* E-mail. *info@acceleratedlearning.com*
Web. *www.acceleratedlearning.com* Accelerated Learning Systems

Accent Hansen (Sales Office) Unit 2 Chadderton Industrial Estate Greenside Way, Middleton, Manchester M24 1SW
Tel. *0161 2844100* Fax. *0161 6553119*
E-mail. *sales@accenthansen.com*
Web. *www.hansengroup.biz* Clean-Shield – Fire-Shield – Multi-Shield – Secure-Shield – Sound-Shield

Accesscaff International Ltd 37 Croydon Road, Beckenham BR3 4AB Tel. *08448 487784* Fax. *0844 8487785*
E-mail. *mraccess@mraccessuk.com*
Web. *www.accesscaffinternational.com* Access All Areas – Access Brands Towers – Access Direct – Access Mate Towers – Access Platforms – Access Pod Towers – Access Rental Platforms – Access Systems – Acrow Props – Aerial Platforms – Aichi Platforms – Aliscaff Towers – Alistage – Allglas Ladders – Alloy Tower Specials – Ally Deck – Allylift – Allytowers – Alto Towers – Aluminium Beams – Armourgard – Barrier Systems – Basket Platforms – Bavaria Ladders – Bavaria Towers – Block & Mesh – Boom Lifts – Boss Towers – Bronto Platforms – Cantilever Towers – Chain & Post – Cheiftan Towers – Chimneyscaff – Classic Ladders – Climalight Towers – ClimAlloy Towers – Cloww Podium Platform – Combination Ladders – Combisafe – Compact Towers – Competitor Ladders – Complete Tool Boxes – Contramate – Crowd Barriers – Cuplok – Datona Rubbish Chutes – Dealer Desk Towers – Denko Platforms – Dino Lift Platforms – Dino Platforms – Easi-Build Towers – Easi-up-lifts – Easy Chute Rubbish Chutes – Eiger Deck – Eiger Towers – Euro Towers – Eventscaff – Evroglas Steps – Expanding Barriers – Extraspace – Fab-Mate – Fabaloy Fibre Glass Towers – FenceHire – Fencing Direct – Ferret Platforms – First 5 Towers – Fold Easy Towers – Folscaf Towers – Formwork – G.R.P Steps & Ladders – G.S.R. Platforms – Gantres – Genie Lifts – Genie Platforms – Genstage – Gladiator Towers – Global Towers – Globalmaster Range – Grandstand Seating – Ground Work Equipment – H.D. Towers – Hauloutte Platforms – Heras Fencing – Hi-Way Towers – Higher & Higher – Hydra Towers – Hyprosteps – Imagination Access – Imperial Ladders – Industrial Aluminium Towers – Industrial Pulpit Steps – IPAF Training – Kee Klamp – Klik Fold Towers – Klik Microfold Tower – Klik Mini Fold Towers – Klik Stairwell Towers – Klik Towers – Klilstak Unit – Klime-Ezee Steps – KwikForm Towers – Ladder Frame Towers – Ladder Safety Devices – Ladders-Direct – Ladderspan Towers – Layher Scaffolding – Lifting Gear Hire – Link Units – Little Giant Stepladder – Loft Ladders – Lyte Ladders – Lyte Towers – M.D. Towers – Magic Platforms – Manitou Platforms – Marquee World – Mast Towers – Mesh & Pin Fencing – Metal Barriers – Microscaff – Minimax Folding Tower – Minit Work Platform – Monarch Ladders – Mult Five Way Ladders – Multi-Purpose Ladders – Narrow Platforms – Nationwide Access Platforms – Niftylift Platforms – Octo 250 Towers – Omegadeck Tower – Omme PLatforms – Ommemog Platforms – On-Site Access – Optimum 50 Towers – Panter Platforms – Pasma Training – Personnel Lifts – Plant & Build – Plantfinder Platforms – Podium Platforms – Protec Fibre Glass Towers – Pulpit Steps – Reach-A-Height Ladders – Reform Ladders – Rigging – Rise Hire Platforms – Roadway – Rollaround Roadway – Room Scaffolds – Rough Terrain Platforms – Roust-A-Bout – S-G-B Towers – Safe Access Solutions – Safeguard – Safety Harnesses – Scaffold Boards – Scaffold Tower Hire – Scaffold Tower Sales – Scanlift Platforms – Scissor Lifts – Sentri Site Boxes – Sherpa Steps – Shorguard – Showscaff – Sigmadeck Tower – Silverwood Ladders – Simon Platforms – Site Hoarding – Site Safe – Skyjack Platforms – Spandeck – Speedy 80 Towers – Speedy Hire – Spider Platforms – Stair-Deck – Stairmate – Stairspan Towers – Stairway Towers – Storpick Steps – Strongbank – Strongboys –

Summer Lifts – Superdeck Platforms – Superlifts-Genie – System Scaffolding – Tallescope – Telesteps – Tempory Fencing – The Hire Network – The Hireman – The National Ladder Co – Titan Gate Barriers – Titan Towers – Tool Box Direct – ToolBox – Top Tower – Top-Deck – Total Access – Totem Towers – Toucan Platforms – Tower Repairs & Spares – Trade Pulpit Steps – Trade Towers – Trademaster Towers – Tradesman Steps & Ladders – Traditional Scaffolding – Traffic Management – Trailer-Mount Lifts – Trestles – Trojan Ladders – Tuffbank – U.K. Platforms – U.K. Towers – Underbridge Platforms – Used Towers – Wallways – Wedgeform Scaffolding – Window Cleaners Ladders – Work Platforms – Wumag Platforms – Youngmans – Zarges Ladders – Zelig Platforms – Zig-Zag Towers – Zip-Up Towers – Zone 1 Towers

Access Controlled Solutions Ltd Pine Drive Lower Wokingham Road, Crowthorne RG45 6BX
Tel. *01344 771569* E-mail. *sales@acsltd.eu*
Web. *www.acsltd.eu* ACT

Access Garage Doors Ltd Genesis House Priestley Way, Crawley RH10 9PR Tel. *01293 652472* Fax. *01293 843417*
E-mail. *sales@accessgaragedoors.com*
Web. *www.accessgaragedoors.com* A Access garage doors – A Access Garage Doors & Gates Ltd

Access Irrigation Ltd 17 Yelvertoft Road Crick, Northampton NN6 7XS Tel. *01788 823811* Fax. *01788 824256*
E-mail. *sales@access-irrigation.co.uk*
Web. *www.access-irrigation.co.uk* Access Garden Products – Access Irrigation – Advantage – Automist – Flexidrip – Mister Pig – Permadrip – Seephose

Accles & Shelvoke Ltd Selco Way Off First Avenue Minworth Industrial Estate, Minworth, Sutton Coldfield B76 1BA
Tel. *0121 3134567* Fax. *0121 3134569*
E-mail. *stewartmorris@eley.co.uk*
Web. *www.acclesandshelvoke.co.uk* Acvoke – Cash – Cash Electrical Stunner – Cowpuncher – Cox – Magnum – Supercash

Acco East Light Ltd Ashton Road Denton, Manchester M34 3LR Tel. *0161 3369431* Fax. *0161 3208012*
E-mail. *mark.winstanley@acco-eastlight.co.uk*
Web. *www.accoeastlight.com* Archive Box – Classic – Cobra – Dalex – Denton – Eastlight – Elite – Ellesmere – File Holder – Flat Pocket File – Forward Flat File – Jiffex Files – Jiffex Pocket File – Karnival – KF200 – Lateral 80 – Lateral Model T – Metallica – Mini Arch – Monkwell – Open Top Wallets – Overlord – Profile Style – Sevenfold & Ninefold Files – Slimpick & Twinpick Wallets – Slimpick Long Flap – Sololink – Solotab – Solotab Colour Range – Square Cut Folders – Storage Box – Storall – Storall Quickfold – Supastor – Supastor 24 – Tuff Nette – Twintop – Vertical Strong Box – Wilton 125

Accor Services 50 Vauxhall Bridge Road, London SW1V 2RS
Tel. *020 78346666* Fax. *020 79310700*
E-mail. *webmaster@accor-services.com*
Web. *www.accor-services.com* Childcare Solutions – Childcare Vouchers – Eyecare Vouchers – Family Life Solutions – Luncheon Vouchers – LVG Voucher Handling

Acco UK Ltd Oxford House Oxford Road, Aylesbury HP21 8SZ Tel. *01296 397444* Fax. *01296 392303*
E-mail. *peter.munk@acco.com* Web. *www.acco.co.uk* Anti Glarecare – Crystaltile – E N M – Infosign – Keyboard Slidaway – Master Grid – Masterlock – Multi-Stor – Payemaster – Postmaster – Punch Wizard – Show Wall – Showboard – Showboard Foldaways – Staple Wizard

Accuracast Ltd 64 Elmshurst Crescent, London N2 0LP
Tel. *0800 0196813* E-mail. *b.simon@accuracast.com*
Web. *www.accuracast.com* broadband services

Accuramatic Laboratory Equipment 42 Windsor Road, Kings Lynn PE30 5PL Tel. *01553 777253* Fax. *01553 777253*
E-mail. *info@accuramatic.co.uk*
Web. *www.accuramatic.co.uk* Accuramatic

Accurate Cutting Services Ltd Units 44-45 Crossgate Rd, Park Farm Industrial Estate, Redditch B98 7SN
Tel. *01527 527058* Fax. *01527 527541*
E-mail. *sales@accurate-cutting.co.uk*
Web. *www.accurate-cutting.co.uk* Daiko – DoALL – DoALL – DoAll - band saw blades & machines - Pedrazzoli - circular & bandsaws machines - Soitaab - Julia circular sawbaldes - Daiko disposable carbide sawblades – Julia – PEDRAZZOLI – SOITAAB – Sinico (United Kingdom)

Accurist Watches Asher House Blackburn Road, London NW6 1AW Tel. *020 74473900* Fax. *020 74473946*
E-mail. *sales@accurist.co.uk* Web. *www.accurist.co.uk*
Accurist

A C D C Led Ltd Innovation Works Gisburn Road, Barrowford, Nelson BB9 8NB Tel. *08458 626400* Fax. *01282 608401*
E-mail. *sales@acdclighting.co.uk*
Web. *www.acdclighting.co.uk* AC/DC Lighting Systems

ACDOCO Ltd Mallison Street, Bolton BL1 8PP
Tel. *01204 600500* Fax. *01204 600501*
E-mail. *specialist@acdo.co.uk* Web. *www.acdo.co.uk*
ACDOCO

Ace Controls International 404 Haydock Lane Haydock, St Helens WA11 9TH Tel. *01942 727440* Fax. *01942 717273*
E-mail. *info@ace-controls.co.uk*
Web. *www.acecontrols.co.uk* Magnum (U.S.A.) – SC² Heavy Weight (U.S.A.) – Tubus (Germany)

Ace Exhibitions Displays & Installation Church House Wrexham Road, Bulkeley, Malpas SY14 8BW Tel. *07767 258958* E-mail. *aceexhibit@aol.com* Web. *www.britishamericandisplays.com Abex – Ace – Clip – Marler Haley – Octanorm*
Ace Records Ltd 42-50 Steele Road, London NW10 7AS Tel. *020 84531311* Fax. *020 89618725* E-mail. *sales@acerecords.co.uk* Web. *www.acerecords.co.uk Ace – BGP – Big Beat – Boplicity – Cascade – Chiswick – Fantasy – GlobeStyle – Grateful Dead – Kent – Milestone – O.B.C. – O.J.C – Prestige – Riverside – Southbound – Stax – Takoma – Vanguard – Westbound*
Acer UK Ltd Acer House Poyle Road, Colnbrook, Slough SL3 0QX Tel. *020 82833000* Fax. *01753 699201* E-mail. *sales@acer-euro.com* Web. *www.acer.co.uk *Acer (Germany and Holland) – Acer Acros – *Acer Altos (U.S.A.)*
Ace Signs Group 1 Bentalls, Basildon SS14 3BS Tel. *01268 706800* Fax. *01702 294325* E-mail. *enquiries@asg.co.uk* Web. *www.acesigns.co.uk Ace Signs Group Ltd*
A C Hydraulics Ltd 12 Mandervell Road Oadby, Leicester LE2 5LQ Tel. *0116 2710561* Fax. *0116 2720561* E-mail. *sales@achydraulics.co.uk* Web. *www.achydraulics.co.uk A.C.H. – Bosch-Rexroth Hydraulics – Eaton-Hydroline – Enerpac – *Enertrols (U.S.A.) – EPP Magnus – Festo – Heypac Pumps – Hilma – Hydac/Flupac – Microloc – Minibooster (Denmark) – *Norelem (France) – Parker Maxam – Powrlock – Ram Power – *Romheld (Germany) – Schunk – Univer – *Vega (Italy)*
Acketts Group Ltd Molyneux Court 4 Radford Way, Billericay CM12 0BT Tel. *01277 655178* Fax. *01277 632121* E-mail. *info@ackettsgl.co.uk* Web. *www.ackettsgl.co.uk A T D*
Ackwa Ltd Unit 2a Trevanth Road, Leicester LE4 9LS Tel. *0116 2460880* Fax. *0800 6348121* E-mail. *jackie@ackwa.co.uk* Web. *www.ackwa.co.uk Bravalar – Instanta – Robocoope – Sammic – Sega Fredo Coffee*
Acme United Europe Estate Office Thorncliffe Park Estate Newton Chambers Road, Chapeltown, Sheffield S35 2PH Tel. *0114 2203709* Fax. *0114 2203706* E-mail. *sales@acmeunited.co.uk* Web. *www.acmeunitedeurope.co.uk Meteor – Monaco – Planet – Plant Lifedge – Speedway – Sure-Kut – Tufkut*
Acorn Marketing Ltd 105 London Road River, Dover CT16 3AA Tel. *01304 827330* Fax. *01304 827080* E-mail. *sales@acorn.uk.net* Web. *www.acorn.uk.net Action Transfers*
Acorn Planting Products Ltd Little Money Road Loddon, Norwich NR14 6JD Tel. *01621 874200* Fax. *01508 528775* E-mail. *sales@acorn-p-p.co.uk* Web. *www.acorn-p-p.co.uk Gro-Cone – Shelterguard – Treespat*
Acousticabs Industrial Noise Control Ltd Unit 52 Pocklington Industrial Estate Pocklington, York YO42 1NR Tel. *01759 305266* Fax. *01759 305268* E-mail. *info@acousticabs.com* Web. *www.acousticabs.com Acousticurtain – Acoustifoam – Acoustilouvre – Acoustislab – Ecophon*
A C P Ltd The Vineyards Gloucester Road, Cheltenham GL51 8NH Tel. *01242 512345* Fax. *01242 576633* E-mail. *enquiries@adcoat.co.uk* Web. *www.api-cop.com Releaseflex – Slik – Ultrasil*
Acquisitions Victorian Edwardian Fireplaces 24-26 Holmes Road, London NW5 3AB Tel. *020 74822949* Fax. *020 72674361* E-mail. *sales@acquisitions.co.uk* Web. *www.acquisitions.co.uk Acquisitions*
Acrivarn Ltd South Park Mills Hare Lane, Pudsey LS28 8DR Tel. *0113 2578875* Fax. *0113 2577564* E-mail. *sales@acrivarn.co.uk* Web. *www.acrivarn.co.uk Bake Master*
Acrokool Ltd 1 Veerman Park Thaxted Road, Saffron Walden CB10 2UP Tel. *01799 513631* Fax. *01799 513635* E-mail. *roger.moore@acrokool.com* Web. *www.acrokool.com Acrokool*
Acrow Galvanising Ltd (Wedge Group Galvanizing) Unit 4 Commercial Centre Ashdon Road, Saffron Walden CB10 2NH Tel. *01799 522219* Fax. *01799 522447* E-mail. *nick.hasler@wedge-galv.co.uk* Web. *www.wedge-galv.co.uk Wedge Group Galvanizing*
Actaris Development UK Ltd Langer Road, Felixstowe IP11 2ER Tel. *01394 694000* Fax. *01394 276030* E-mail. *csaunders@actaris.co.uk* Web. *www.felixstowe.actaris.com Schlumberger*
Action Can Ltd (Formerly Plow Products Ltd) Dixon Close Old Boston Trading Estate, Haydock, St Helens WA11 9SF Tel. *01942 713667* Fax. *01942 716235* E-mail. *sales@actioncan.com* Web. *www.actioncan.com Action Can – Action Can AC-90 – Action Can Amaze – Action Can AS-90 – Action Can CT-90 – F.S.L. – Supertrol*
Action Handling Equipment Ltd Maltings Industrial Estate Station Road, Sawbridgeworth CM21 9JY Tel. *01279 724989* Fax. *01279 600224* E-mail. *sales@actionhandling.co.uk* Web. *www.actionhandling.co.uk Action Handling Equipment*
Action Medical Research 31 North Parade, Horsham RH12 2DP Tel. *01403 210406* Fax. *01403 210541* E-mail. *info@action.org.uk* Web. *www.action.org.uk Action Research*
Action Seals Ltd Westfield Road, Wallasey CH44 7JA Tel. *0151 6526661* Fax. *0151 6534994* E-mail. *steve.quail@actionseals.co.uk* Web. *www.actionseals.com NTK – TTO*
Action Storage Systems 6 Fitzhamon Court Wolverton Mill, Milton Keynes MK12 6LB Tel. *01908 525700* Fax. *01908 321650* E-mail. *sales@action-storage.co.uk* Web. *www.action-storage.co.uk eXtreme LOCKERS – eXtreme lockers, Action Storage Online*
Active Grounds Maintenance Ltd Pollingfold Works Rudgwick, Horsham RH12 3AS Tel. *01403 823344* Fax. *01403 822458* E-mail. *active@grasstex-active.com* Web. *www.activegm.co.uk *Active – *Cabe*
Active Security Group Ltd 5-7 Horsecroft Place, Harlow CM19 5BT Tel. *01279 420016* Fax. *01279 444491* E-mail. *administration@activesecuritygroup.co.uk* Web. *www.activesecuritygroup.com R.S.S.*
Activ Web Design 8 Mayden House, Long Bennington Business Park Main Road, Long Bennington, Newark NG23 5DJ Tel. *0845 0940497* Fax. *0870 7515574* E-mail. *info@activwebdesign.com* Web. *www.activwebdesign.com/hu17/ Activ Web Design*
Acugrip Ltd Unit 7 Executive Park Hatfield Road, St Albans AL1 4TA Tel. *01727 845225* Fax. *01727 845345* E-mail. *mail@acugrip.co.uk* Web. *www.acugrip.co.uk Acugrip – AyreidOmnigauge – Ayreid – Omnigauge*
Acumedic Centre Ltd 101-105 Camden High Street, London NW1 7JN Tel. *020 73885783* Fax. *020 73875766* E-mail. *courses@acumedic.com* Web. *www.acumedic.com Acumedic Centre*
A C W A Services Ltd Acwa House Acorn Business Park Keighley Road, Skipton BD23 2UE Tel. *01756 794794* Fax. *01756 790898* E-mail. *pripley@acwa.co.uk* Web. *www.acwa.co.uk ACWa*
Acxiom Ltd Dominican Court 17 Hatfields, London SE1 8DJ Tel. *020 75265100* Fax. *020 82135588* Web. *www.acxiom.com Acxiom Directors At Home Database – Acxiom Directors At Home Database – Companies House – Electrol Roll – Growing Companies – Rapidus – Soho – Thomson Directories Database – Tracker*
Adam Carpets Ltd Birmingham Road, Kidderminster DY10 2SH Tel. *01562 822247* Fax. *01562 751471* E-mail. *info@adamcarpets.com* Web. *www.adamcarpets.com Blenheim – Castlemead – Fine Upland Heathers – Fine Worcester Twist – Forest Glades – Marlborough Studio Collection – Peacock Garden – Sylvan Shadows – Woodstock Classic*
Jon Adam Second Floor 184-192 Drummond Street, London NW1 3HP Tel. *020 73875384* Fax. *020 73834065* E-mail. *reception@jonadam.co.uk* Web. *www.jonadam.co.uk Arte*
R P Adam Ltd Arpal Works Riverside Road, Selkirk TD7 5DU Tel. *01750 21586* Fax. *01750 21506* E-mail. *salesinfo@rpadam.co.uk* Web. *www.rpadam.co.uk Arpal*
Adamsez NI Ltd 766 Upper Newtownards Road Dundonald, Belfast BT16 1TQ Tel. *028 90480465* Fax. *028 90480485* E-mail. *info@adamsez.com* Web. *www.adamsez.com Adamsez*
Adams & Howling Ltd Granary Offices Manor Farm The Green, Little Plumstead, Norwich NR13 5EL Tel. *01603 722372* Fax. *01603 722472* E-mail. *enquiries@adamsandhowling.co.uk* Web. *www.adamsandhowling.co.uk parker seeds*
Adams Lubetech Ltd Unit 6 Binns Close, Coventry CV4 9TB Tel. *024 76467941* Fax. *024 76694002* E-mail. *info@adamslube.com* Web. *www.adamslube.com Adams*
Adaptaflex Ltd C M G House Station Road Industrial Estate Station Road, Coleshill, Birmingham B46 1HT Tel. *01675 468222* Fax. *01675 462090* E-mail. *duncan.mckinlay@adaptaflex.co.uk* Web. *www.adaptaflex.co.uk Adaptalok – Adaptaring – Adaptaseal – Adaptasteel – Harnessflex – Korifit – Stayflex – Xtra Flex*
Adaptainer Ltd Long Meadow Flaunden Lane, Bovingdon, Hemel Hempstead HP3 0PA Tel. *01442 834566* Fax. *01442 834335* E-mail. *office@adaptainer.co.uk* Web. *www.adaptainer.co.uk Adaptainer*
Adapt Formwork Ltd Forward Works Bridge Lane, Woolston, Warrington WA1 4BA Tel. *0151 3450297* E-mail. *info@adaptformwork.com* Web. *www.adaptformwork.com tuffply*
Adcal Labels Ltd Jayem Works Gomm Road, High Wycombe HP13 7DJ Tel. *01494 530761* Fax. *01494 461651* E-mail. *sales@adcal-labels.co.uk* Web. *www.adcal-labels.co.uk Jayem*
Adcutech Ltd P A C M House Blackworth Estate, Highworth, Swindon SN6 7NA Tel. *01793 765405* Fax. *01793 766060* E-mail. *sales@adcutech.co.uk* Web. *www.adcutech.com Alcomax*
Addagrip Surface Treatments Ltd Bell Lane Bellbrook Industrial Estate, Uckfield TN22 1QL Tel. *01825 761333* Fax. *01825 768566* E-mail. *sales@addagrip.co.uk* Web. *www.addagrip.co.uk 1000 System Resin – Addaclenz Floor Cleaner – Addacrete – Addaflex – Addaflor – Addagrip Heavy Duty Mortar – Addalevel – Addamortar – Addamortar Colour Pack – Addapatch – Addaprime – Addaseal 20 (clear) – Addaseal 50 (clear) – Addaseal Colour Pack – Addasol Primer – Addasol Top Coat – Addastone Adhesive – Addastone Primer – Addastone Sealer – Addawall (Wall Coating) – Chemclad – Chemclad Mortar – Epoxy Resin Flooring Systems – Renfor – Renfor Cement – W.B.S. Acrylic Sealer – W.D.E. 436 pigmented – W.D.E. 436 Primer*
Addison Saws Ltd Attwood Street, Stourbridge DY9 8RU Tel. *01384 264950* Fax. *01384 456331* E-mail. *sales@addisonsaws.co.uk* Web. *www.addisonsaws.co.uk Bandmaster – Emmegi – Everising – Jubilee – Mecal – Mi-Va – Simer*
Addstone Cast Stone Addstone Way Off Anchor Road, Stoke On Trent ST3 5BL Tel. *01785 878402* Fax. *01785 819958* E-mail. *admin1@addstone.co.uk* Web. *www.addstone.co.uk Addstone*
Adecco UK Ltd 44 Shenley Road, Borehamwood WD6 1DR Tel. *020 89536700* Fax. *020 82074686* E-mail. *1493.borehamwood@adecco.co.uk* Web. *www.adecco.co.uk Addeco Alfred Marks*
Adec Marine Ltd 4 Masons Avenue, Croydon CR0 9XS Tel. *020 86869717* Fax. *020 86809912* E-mail. *sales@adecmarine.co.uk* Web. *www.adecmarine.co.uk *Unsink (United Kingdom)*
Adelante Software Ltd Unit 22 Grove Park Industrial Estate Waltham Road, White Waltham, Maidenhead SL6 3LW Tel. *01628 820500* Fax. *01628 820509* E-mail. *darrellb@adelante.co.uk* Web. *www.adelante.co.uk TaxiPay, MobilePOS, SmartPay, TonePay*
The Adelphi Group Adelphi Group of Companies Olympus House Mill Green Road, Haywards Heath RH16 1XQ Tel. *01444 472300* Fax. *01444 472329* E-mail. *sales@adelphi.uk.com* Web. *www.adelphi.uk.com *Fiocut (Germany) – *Purgard (Germany) – *Type I Plus (Germany)*
Adel Rootstein 9 Beaumont Avenue, London W14 9LP Tel. *020 73811447* Fax. *020 73813263* E-mail. *sales@adelrootstein.co.uk* Web. *www.rootstein.com Adel Rootstein*
adeptdoors Ltd 24-25 Squires Gate Industrial Estate Squires Gate Lane, Blackpool FY4 3RN Tel. *01253 403328* Fax. *01253 403329* E-mail. *enquiries@adeptdoors.co.uk* Web. *www.adeptdoors.co.uk Adept Doors Ltd*
Adfield Harvey Ltd The Granary Beckbury, Shifnal TF11 9DG Tel. *01952 752500* Fax. *01952 752510* E-mail. *info@adfield.co.uk* Web. *www.adfield.co.uk Permafix – *Petromatic (U.S.A.) – Portafix*
Adglow Ltd Ledbury House Alexandra Way, Ashchurch, Tewkesbury GL20 8NB Tel. *01684 272900* Fax. *01684 850729* E-mail. *dainge@adinstall.co.uk* Web. *www.adglow.co.uk Adglow*
Adi Gardiner Emea Ltd Transpennine Trading Estate, Rochdale OL11 2PX Tel. *01706 343343* Fax. *01706 646600* E-mail. *ehorton@gardinersecurity.co.uk* Web. *www.gardinersecurity.co.uk G.S.L.*
Adline Personalised Products Sterling House 20 Renfield Street, Glasgow G2 5AP Tel. *0141 2211491* Fax. *0141 2484411* E-mail. *sales@adlinepersonalised.com* Web. *www.adlinepersonalised.com Adline*
A D M Computing Chaucer Road, Canterbury CT1 1HH Tel. *01227 473530* Fax. *01227 473509* E-mail. *adrian@adm-computing.co.uk* Web. *www.admcomputing.co.uk ADM Computing*
Admiral 39 Chesterfield Road, Dronfield S18 2XG Tel. *01246 411764* Fax. *01246 290294* E-mail. *admin@admiralconstruction.co.uk* Web. *www.admiralconstruction.co.uk Admiral*
A D M Pura Foods Ltd Erith Oil Works Church Manorway, Erith DA8 1DL Tel. *01322 443000* Fax. *01322 443027* Web. *www.adm.com Pura – Pura Foods – Pura Foods Products – Pura Frymax – Pura Gold Cup – Pura Light Touch*
Adm Services UK Ltd Unit 422 Clifford House 7-9 Clifford Street, York YO1 9RA Tel. *01904 349400* Fax. *01904 337770* E-mail. *info@admfire.co.uk* Web. *www.admfire.co.uk BS EN3*
A D P Ltd 40-48 Pyrcroft Road, Chertsey KT16 9JT Tel. *08452 300237* Fax. *08452 302371* E-mail. *sales@adp-es.co.uk* Web. *www.uk.adp.com ADP (U.S.A.)*
Adroit Modular Buildings plc Trow Way, Worcester WR5 3BX Tel. *01905 356018* Fax. *01905 351868* E-mail. *mail@adroitgroup.co.uk* Web. *www.adroitmodular.com Rapidroom*
Adroit Modular Buildings plc Delta Way, Cannock WS11 0BE Tel. *01543 404040* Fax. *01543 404114* E-mail. *sales@elliott-algeco.com* Web. *adroitmodular.com Clinibin – Safe-t-store – Safestore – Steelclad – Superloo – Superstore – Tidibin – Timber Masterclass – Toolbin*
Adshead Ratcliffe & Co. Ltd Derby Road, Belper DE56 1WJ Tel. *01773 826661* Fax. *01773 821215* E-mail. *julian.miller@arbo.co.uk* Web. *www.arbo.co.uk Arbo – Arbo U.B.C. – Arbocaulk – Arboflex – Arbofoam – Arbofoam R – Arbokol – Arbolite – Arbomast – Arbomast – Arbomast – Arbomast BR – Arbomast GP – Arbomast Intumescent – Arbomeric – Arboseal – Arbosil – Arbostrip – Arbothane*

Adstorm Charter House Sandford Street, Lichfield WS13 6QA Tel. *08456 444567* E-mail. *enquiries@adstorm.co.uk* Web. *www.adstorm.co.uk AdStorm – Precis Marketing – ClickStorm*

Adsum Auxilium Limited Bouncers Bank Half Moon Lane, Tudeley, Tonbridge TN11 0PR Tel. *01892 836969* Fax. *01892 836969* E-mail. *info@adsumaux.co.uk* Web. *www.adsumaux.co.uk Adsum Life & Career Coaching*

ADT Security House Summit Business Park Hanworth Road, Sunbury On Thames TW16 5DB Tel. *01932 743456* Fax. *01932 743222* E-mail. *anton.alphonsus@adt.co.uk* Web. *www.adt.co.uk A.D.T. Fire and Security – Galaxy – Inergen – Minerva – Siteguard*

Advanced Desktop Systems Ltd 13 Ledgers Meadow Cuckfield, Haywards Heath RH17 5EW Tel. *01444 454487* Fax. *01444 448159* E-mail. *tony.elphick@advanceddesktop.com* Web. *www.advanceddesktop.com Sensorium – Sensorium iBMS*

Advanced Dynamics Ltd 250 Thornton Road, Bradford BD1 2LB Tel. *01274 220300* Fax. *01274 308953* E-mail. *malcolm@advanceddynamics.co.uk* Web. *www.advanceddynamics.co.uk *B.V.M. Brunner (Germany) – *Hagemann (Germany) – J Willi (Switzerland) – *Kora Packmat (Germany) – *Packmat (Germany) – *S.A.M. (Switzerland) – *Simco (Netherlands) – *Vortec (U.S.A.)*

Advanced Ergonomic Technologies Ltd 201-203 London Road, East Grinstead RH19 1HA Tel. *01342 310400* Fax. *01342 310401* E-mail. *gbt@flexiblespace.com* Web. *www.flexiblespace.com Electropatent Modular Power Tracking – Hiross Flexible Space Systems – Movinord Partitioning – Nesite Raised Access Flooring – Warlord Carpet*

Advanced Fluid Technologies Ltd 35 Finchwell Road, Sheffield S13 9AS Tel. *0114 2448560* Fax. *0114 2486997* E-mail. *info@advancedfluid.co.uk* Web. *www.advancedfluid.co.uk Hy-lok – Tomco*

Advanced Perimeter Systems Ltd 16 Cunningham Road, Stirling FK7 7TP Tel. *01786 479862* Fax. *01786 470331* E-mail. *admin@apsltd.net* Web. *www.apsltd.net Electro-Fence – Flexiguard – MEGAsys*

Advanced Polymers Ltd (t/a Adpol) Unit 20 Ham Bridge Trading Estate Willowbrook Road, Worthing BN14 8NA Tel. *01903 820475* Fax. *01903 820969* E-mail. *sales@adpol.co.uk* Web. *www.adpol.co.uk Adpol*

Advanced Technology Machines Ltd 4 Molly Millars Bridge, Wokingham RG41 2WY Tel. *0118 9770099* Fax. *0118 9892288* E-mail. *sales@atmmt.com* Web. *www.atmmt.com Advanced Technology Machines Ltd*

Advance Tapes Group Ltd PO Box 122, Leicester LE4 5RA Tel. *0116 2510191* Fax. *0116 2653070* E-mail. *info@advancetapes.com* Web. *www.advancetapes.com Advance – Agritape – Gaffa Tape – Surefire*

Advanex Europe Ltd Mill Park Industrial Estate Station Road, Southwell NG25 0ET Tel. *01636 815555* Fax. *01636 817725* E-mail. *sales@advanexeurope.co.uk* Web. *www.advanexeurope.co.uk Kato Entex*

Advanex Europe Glaisdale Drive East, Nottingham NG8 4JY Tel. *0115 9293931* Fax. *0115 9295773* E-mail. *enquiries@advanexeurope.co.uk* Web. *www.advanexeurope.co.uk Coilthread*

Advanstar Communications Poplar House Park West Sealand Road, Chester CH1 4RN Tel. *01244 378888* Fax. *01244 370011* E-mail. *mroberts@advanstar.com* Web. *www.advanstar.com Applied Clinical Trials – Automatic I.D. News Europe – LCGC International – Medical Device Technology – Pharmaceutical Executive – Pharmaceutical Technology Europe – Scientific Data Management – Voice +*

Adverc B M Ltd 245 Trysull Road, Wolverhampton WV3 7LG Tel. *01902 380494* Fax. *01902 380435* E-mail. *techsales@adverc.co.uk* Web. *www.adverc.co.uk Adverc (United Kingdom)*

Adwel International Ltd Park House, Greenhill CrescentWatford Business Park, Watford WD18 8PH Tel. *01923 254433* Fax. *01923 218278* E-mail. *info@adwel.co.uk* Web. *www.irispower.com Digital El CID – EL CID – ETI – Magnastart – MCT – PDA – RIV – TVA Corona Probe – WRT-100 – WTD 501*

A E Adams Ltd 4 Mackley Industrial Estate Henfield Road, Small Dole, Henfield BN5 9XR Tel. *01273 493936* Fax. *01273 494769* E-mail. *sales@aeadams.co.uk* Web. *www.aeadams.co.uk Housekeepers (United Kingdom)*

A Edmonds & Co. Ltd (Head Office) 89 Constitution Hill, Birmingham B19 3JY Tel. *0121 2368351* Fax. *0121 2364793* E-mail. *info@edmonds.uk.com* Web. *www.edmonds.uk.com Varedplan*

Aegis Advanced Materials Ltd Crundalls Farmhouse Crundalls Lane, Bewdley DY12 1NB Tel. *01299 404153* Fax. *01299 401468* E-mail. *jk@aegis-ceramics.co.uk* Web. *www.aegis-ceramics.co.uk Metapor (Switzerland) – *Metco (U.S.A.) – *Peiniger (Germany) – Rockliniser (U.S.A.) – *Themac (U.S.A.)*

A E I Cables Durham Road Birtley, Chester le Street DH3 2RA Tel. *0191 4103111* Fax. *0191 4108312* E-mail. *info@aeicables.co.uk* Web. *www.aeicables.co.uk Firetec*

A Elder Reed & Co. Ltd (t/a Reed Harris) Riverside House Unit 5 Carnwath Road Industrial Estate 27 Carnwath Road, London SW6 3HR Tel. *020 77367511* Fax. *020 77362988* E-mail. *martyn@reed-harris.co.uk* Web. *www.reedharris.co.uk Agglio – *Cinca (Portugal) – *Cinca Nova Arquitectura (Portugal) – *Cincasolo (Portugal) – Contract Range, The – Gripstar – Isola – Merano – Modular – *Monoceram (Italy) – *Niro (Switzerland) – *Rover (Italy) – Spectrum – Tungstone*

A E L Flexaulic Ltd Llay Hall Industrial Estate Mold Road, Cefn-Y-Bedd, Wrexham LL12 9YG Tel. *01978 761848* Fax. *01978 762340* E-mail. *flexaulic@btconnect.com* Web. *www.flexaulic.com Flexaulic Ltd – Statimeter*

AEL Heating Solutions Ltd 4 Berkely Court Manor Park, Runcorn WA7 1TQ Tel. *01928 579068* Fax. *01928 579523* E-mail. *healey@aelheating.com* Web. *www.aelheating.com AEL – AEL Heating Solutions – AELtherm – Benchrad – Linear Planrad – RAD – Rads – Redline – Tubarad*

A & E Plastic Fabrications Ltd 40 St. Peters Street Radford, Nottingham NG7 3FF Tel. *0115 9780048* Fax. *0115 9791351* E-mail. *info@aaep.co.uk* Web. *www.aeplastics.co.uk Sign Design*

Aerco Ltd Unit 16-17 Lawson Hunt Industrial Park, Broadbridge Heath, Horsham RH12 3JR Tel. *01403 260206* Fax. *01403 259760* E-mail. *rlaughton@aerco.co.uk* Web. *www.aerco.co.uk Aerco Ltd*

Aerodyne Equipment 67 Bideford Avenue Perivale, Greenford UB6 7PX Tel. *020 89985042* Fax. *020 89914321* E-mail. *sales@aerodyneuk.com* Web. *www.aerodyneuk.com Aeroboost – AerOver – Windfarer*

Aeroflex Ltd Six Hills Way, Stevenage SG1 2AN Tel. *01438 742200* Fax. *01438 727601* E-mail. *derek.smith@aeroflex.com* Web. *www.aeroflex.com IFR Ltd*

The Aerogen Co. Ltd Unit 3 Alton Business Centre, Alton GU34 2YU Tel. *01420 83744* Fax. *01420 80032* E-mail. *info@aerogen.co.uk* Web. *www.aerogen.co.uk Aerocin – Aerogen – Aquagen*

Aeromatic Fielder Ltd 15 Chandlers Ford Chandler's Ford, Eastleigh SO53 4ZD Tel. *023 80267131* Fax. *023 80253381* E-mail. *sales-uk@aeromatic-fielder.com* Web. *www.gea-ps.com Aerocoater – Nica – Pharma Matrix – Roto-Processor – Spectrum – Turbo Rapid – Ultra-Coating*

Aerotech Engineering Ltd Unit 40 Louis Pearlman Centre Goulton Street, Hull HU3 4DL Tel. *01482 586300* Fax. *01482 586303* E-mail. *john@aerotecheng.com* Web. *www.aerotecheng.com Cirrus GIIIx – Federal Mogul – Nimbus G11 – Nimbus Lite*

A E Southgate Ltd Station Road Coleshill, Birmingham B46 1HT Tel. *01675 463096* Fax. *01675 467455* E-mail. *rita@brushexpert.com* Web. *www.brushexpert.com A.E.S.*

AESpump Unit 30 Midsussex Business Park Folders LaneEast Ditchling Common, Hassocks BN6 8SE Tel. *01273 891450* Fax. *01273 891451* E-mail. *sales@absolutevacuum.co.uk* Web. *www.absolute-vacuum.com 306 coater – Adixen – Alcatel – Apiezon – ASF thomas – Balzers – Becker – BOC Edwards High Vacuum – Busch – Butterfly valves – Capitol – cg16 – Charles Austin – Chell – Clyde – Co seals – Contivac – cr2 – CVT – diffstak – Dow Corning – dupont – Ebara – Edwards – Edwards High Vacuum – eh – El vac vacuum – Fisherbrand – Fomblin – Galileo – Gast – Genevac – Graham Precision – gv – Hammond – Hick Hargreaves – Ilmvac – ion gauges – iso fittings – ITL – ITM – Javac – Jigtool – K N F – kf fittings – Kinney – KNF Neuberger – krytox – Kurt J Lesker – Lacey Hulbert – Lesker – Mils – MKS – modulyo – Nash – NGN – nw – Oerlikon Leybold – penning – Pfeiffer – pfpe – Pirani – Polaron – Precision Plus – PVR – Qiang jang – qsb – Rietschle – Ritchie – Roniair – ruvac – rv – Samson – Saskia – Savant – Seargent Welch – Siemens – Sihi – silicon oils – spectron – Stokes – stp – Thermal – tic – ultragrade oil – Ulvac – vacustat – Vacuubrand – Vacuum Generators – vapour boosters – Varian – VAT – VG – wau boosters – Woosung – xds – Keybold Vacuum – Satis Coaters – Nordiko Coaters – APD Pumps – Marathron Pumps – 40-30 Cryogenic Cryogenics – C.T.I Cryogenics – CTI – Polycold*

AETC Ltd Victoria Avenue Yeadon, Leeds LS19 7AW Tel. *0113 2505151* Fax. *0113 2386006* Web. *www.aetc.co.uk AETC*

Aflex Hose Ltd Spring Bank Industrial Estate Watson Mill Lane, Sowerby Bridge HX6 3BW Tel. *01422 317200* Fax. *01422 836000* E-mail. *rod.anderson@aflex-hose.co.uk* Web. *www.aflex-hose.co.uk Bioflex (United Kingdom) – Bioflon (United Kingdom) – Corroflon (United Kingdom) – Hydraline FX (United Kingdom)*

Afos Ltd Kingston House Saxon Way Priory Park, Hessle HU13 9PB Tel. *01482 372100* Fax. *01482 372150* E-mail. *peter.martin@afosgroup.com* Web. *www.afosgroup.com Afos – Double Maxi – Maxi – Mini – Torry*

A F P Medical Ltd 15 Arches Business Centre Mill Road, Rugby CV21 1QW Tel. *01788 579408* Fax. *01788 540199* E-mail. *info@afpmedical.com* Web. *www.afpmedical.com Aquilon – Micromist – Tourer Lite – Ultima Lite – Ventmist*

Afriso Eurogauge Ltd Unit 4 Satellite Business Village, Crawley RH10 9NE Tel. *01293 658360* Fax. *01293 528270* E-mail. *sales@eurogauge.co.uk* Web. *www.eurogauge.co.uk Eurogauge*

A F Suter Ltd 1 Beckingham Business Park Beckingham Street, Tolleshunt Major, Maldon CM9 8LZ Tel. *01621 869600* Fax. *08707 773959* E-mail. *afsuter@afsuter.com* Web. *www.afsuter.com Swanlac – Swanlac - Bleached dewaxed shellac & waxy bleached shellac.*

Afton Chemical London Road, Bracknell RG12 2UW Tel. *01344 304141* Fax. *01344 420666* E-mail. *barrie.horsted@aftonchemical.com* Web. *www.aftonchemical.com HiTec – HiTec*

A G A Group Merton Hall Ponds Merton, Thetford IP25 6QH Tel. *01953 886824* Fax. *01953 889644* E-mail. *ash@agagroup.org.uk* Web. *www.agagroup.co.uk *Armater (France) – *Armorflex – *Armorloc – *Beach Management Systems (Denmark) – *Bestmann Range (Germany) – *Clean Air Blanket (United Kingdom) – *Deckdrain (United Kingdom) – *Ecofelt (United Kingdom) – *Erosamat – *Fortrac (Germany) – *Geolon (Netherlands) – *Nicotarp (Netherlands) – *Porcupine – *Reinforced Turf (United Kingdom) – *Stabilenka (Netherlands) – *XR2 & XR5 (U.S.A.)*

AGA Rayburn PO Box 30, Telford TF8 7DX Tel. *01952 642000* Fax. *01952 243138* E-mail. *info@aga-web.co.uk* Web. *www.aga-rayburn.co.uk Aga C – Aga CB – Aga E – Aga EC – Aga ECM – Aga EE – Aga GC – Aga GCB – Aga GCBM – Aga GCM – Aga GE – Aga GEB – Aga GEBM – Aga GEM – Aga OC – Aga OCB 135 – Aga OCB 90 – Aga OCBM 135 – Aga OCBM 90 – Aga OCM – Aga OE – Aga OEB – Aga OEBM – Aga OEM – Coalbrookdale GS1I – Coalbrookdale GS2i – Coalbrookdale GS3i – Coalbrookdale Little Wenlock – Coalbrookdale Much Wenlock – Coalbrookdale Rembrandt – Coalbrookdale Severn – Rayburn 200G – Rayburn 200L – Rayburn 208G – Rayburn 208KN – Rayburn 208KV – Rayburn 208L – Rayburn 212SN – Rayburn 212SV – Rayburn 216M – Rayburn 355S – Rayburn 360D – Rayburn 360K – Rayburn 368K – Rayburn 380G – Rayburn 380L – Rayburn 400G – Rayburn 400K – Rayburn 460K – Rayburn 460KB – Rayburn 480AG – Rayburn 480K – Rayburn 480KB – Rayburn 499K – Rayburn 499KB*

Agar Scientific Unit 7 M11 Business Link Parsonage Lane, Stansted CM24 8GF Tel. *01279 813519* Fax. *01279 815106* E-mail. *sales@elektron-technology.com* Web. *www.elektronplc.com Agar Scientific – Athene*

A G B Steel Products Ltd 146 Crownpoint Road, Glasgow G40 2AE Tel. *0141 5567551* Fax. *0141 5561516* E-mail. *info@agbsteelproducts.co.uk* Web. *www.agbsteelproducts.co.uk Formaclad*

AGC Chemicals Ltd Hill House International, Thornton Cleveleys FY5 4QD Tel. *01253 861800* Fax. *01253 861950* E-mail. *susie.claridge@fluon.co.uk* Web. *www.fluon.co.uk Aflas (Japan) – Aflon (Japan) – AG Fluoropolymers (U.S.A.) – Fluon (U.S.A.) – Fluoromelt (U.S.A.) – Whitcomp (U.S.A.) – Whitcon (U.S.A.)*

Agco International Ltd Abbey Park Stareton, Kenilworth CV8 2TQ Tel. *024 76694400* Fax. *024 76852495* E-mail. *info@masseyferguson.com* Web. *www.masseyferguson.com Challenger – Fendt – Massey Ferguson – Massey Ferguson - Fendt - Challenger – MF 2200 Series – MF 3200 Series – MF 4200 Series – MF 6200 Series – MF 8200 Series – MF Cerea*

Age UK York House 207-221 Pentonville Road, London N1 9UZ Tel. *020 87657200* Fax. *020 72781116* E-mail. *info@acent.co.uk* Web. *www.efa.org.uk Help the Aged – Help The Aged – Help the Aged Insurance Services – Senior Line – Seniorlink*

Agfa Gevaert Eleventh Floor Vantage West Great West Road, Brentford TW8 9AX Tel. *020 82314983* Fax. *020 82314951* E-mail. *laurence.roberts@agfa.com* Web. *www.agfa.com *AGFA. (Belgium) – *Agfacolor (Germany) – Apogee – Avantra – Galileo – Howson – Intellinet – Paladio – Precisa (Germany) – Scala – Vista (Germany)*

Aggregate Industries Ltd Smithhall Lane Hulland Ward, Ashbourne DE6 3ET Tel. *01335 372222* Fax. *01909 568780* E-mail. *alan.smith@aggregate.com* Web. *www.brookeconcrete.co.uk Patchmac*

Agie Charmilles Ltd North View Coventry Walsgrave Triangle, Coventry CV2 2SJ Tel. *024 76538666* Fax. *024 76530023* E-mail. *info@uk.gfac.com* Web. *www.gfac.com Agie – Charmilles – EDM – Intech – System 3R*

Agil Chemicals Products Hercules 2 Calleva Park, Aldermaston, Reading RG7 8DN Tel. *0118 9813333* Fax. *0118 9810909* E-mail. *david@kiotechagil.com* Web. *www.kiotechagil.com Aquacube – Bact-a-start – BACT.A.CID – Hay 2000 – Mastercube – Mycostat – Oxistat – Pre-fect – Prefect – Rabbitstat – Salkil – Silage 2000 – Sorbatox*

Agma Ltd Gemini Works Haltwhistle Industrial Estate, Haltwhistle NE49 9HA Tel. *01434 320598* Fax. *01434 321650* E-mail. *mfranklin@agma.co.uk* Web. *www.agma.co.uk 0 S D 569 – Agmacote – Agmapak – Agmasol – Ammox – Bactol – Buster – Cinch – Dermasol – Dermine – Dermol – Detizor – Forcote 95 – Glopak – Glopol – Hypablast – Proceine – Prociene 100JL – Solcon 137 –*

Solcon 80R – Styx 99 – Synergen 501 – Synergen 718 – Vincit
Agralan Ltd The Old Brickyard Ashton Keynes, Swindon SN6 6QR Tel. *01285 860015* Fax. *01285 860056* E-mail. *sales@agralan.co.uk* Web. *www.agralan.co.uk* **Agralan Envirofleece – *Agralan Enviromesh – *Agralan Revive – *Citrox P.*
Agrico UK Ltd Castleton of Eassie Eassie, Forfar DD8 1SJ Tel. *01307 840551* Fax. *01307 840245* E-mail. *archiegibson@agrico.co.uk* Web. *www.agrico.co.uk* **Celavita – *Estima – *Marfona – Markies – *Meristem – *Premiere – *Romano – *Sante*
Agricultural Central Trading 90 The Broadway, Chesham HP5 1EG Tel. *01494 784931* Fax. *01494 791553* E-mail. *sales@actionfarm.co.uk* Web. *www.actionfarm.co.uk* *Fertilizers Feed Fuel Minerals*
Agricultural Travel Bureau Ltd 14 Chain Lane, Newark NG24 1AU Tel. *01636 705612* Fax. *0870 4423291* E-mail. *info@agritravel.co.uk* Web. *www.agritravel.co.uk* *Barfield Travel and Tours*
Agriculture & Horticulture Development Board Board National Agricultural Centre, Stoneleigh Park, Kenilworth CV8 2TL Tel. *024 76692051* Fax. *01908 609221* E-mail. *info@ahdb.org.uk* Web. *www.ahdb.org.uk E.F.S.I.S*
Agrihealth 9 Silverwood Industrial Area Silverwood Road, Lurgan, Craigavon BT66 6LN Tel. *028 38314570* Fax. *01630 658280* E-mail. *info@agrihealth.co.uk* Web. *www.agrihealth.co.uk Fenceman – Liveryman*
Agripa Solutions 43 Colquhoun Avenue Hillington Park, Glasgow G52 4BN Tel. *0141 8108780* Fax. *08700 859001* E-mail. *info@agripa.com* Web. *www.agripa.com Agripa – Agripa Fleet Media – Agripa Holdings*
Agrisense B C S Ltd Unit 1 3 Taffs Mead Road, Treforest Industrial Estate, Pontypridd CF37 5SU Tel. *01443 841155* Fax. *01443 841152* E-mail. *sales@agrisense.co.uk* Web. *www.agrisense.co.uk Azatin – Azatin Align, Neemix – Delfin, Thuricide, Agree, Turex, CoStar, Teknar HP-D – Gemstar – Polycore – Selibate – Spod-X – Trappit*
A Harvey & Co. Ltd 2 Stockton End Sunderland Road, Sandy SG19 1SB Tel. *01767 684666* Fax. *01767 683111* E-mail. *sales@harveywire.co.uk* Web. *www.harveywire.co.uk Harvey Wire*
Aimer Products Ltd Unit 6 Plaza Business Centre, Enfield EN3 7PH Tel. *020 88048282* Fax. *020 88048821* E-mail. *sales@aimer.co.uk* Web. *www.aimer.co.uk Aimer*
Aimia Foods Penny Lane Haydock, St Helens WA11 0QZ Tel. *01942 272900* Fax. *01942 272831* E-mail. *customer.services@aimiafoods.com* Web. *www.aimiafoods.com Buendia Coffee – BZB Smoothies – *Douwe Egberts – *Freshers – *Galaxy – *Milfresh – Percol – PG – Slazenger – *Vimto*
Aims Partnership plc 3 Park Road, London NW1 6AS Tel. *020 76166629* Fax. *020 76166634* E-mail. *lara.frankel@asc.co.uk* Web. *www.aims.co.uk ASC Finance for Business*
Ainsworth Acoustics, Thermal & Building Insulation Old Grange Farm Bursledon, Southampton SO31 8GD Tel. *01489 885565* Fax. *01489 885258* E-mail. *enquiries@ainsworth-insulation.co.uk* Web. *www.ainsworth-insulation.co.uk Bracol – Kingspan – Celotex – Isover*
A & I (Peco) Acoustics Ltd 100 Sandford Street, Birkenhead CH41 1AZ Tel. *0151 6479015* Fax. *0151 6661805* E-mail. *sales@peco.co.uk* Web. *www.peco.co.uk A. & I. – Peco Big Bore & Sport – Peco HDR*
Airbloc AmbiRad Ltd (Airbloc Division) Fens Pool Avenue, Brierley Hill DY5 1QA Tel. *01384 489700* Fax. *01384 489707* E-mail. *marketing@airbloc.co.uk* Web. *www.airbloc.co.uk AB – AC – ACR – ACT – SmartElec*
Airclaims Group Ltd 2nd Floor Building 947 Cardinal Point Heathrow Airport, Hounslow TW6N 6EL Tel. *020 88971066* Fax. *020 88596294* E-mail. *info@airclaims.com* Web. *www.airclaims.com Airclaims*
John Aird Holdings Ltd Greenbank Mills East Main Street, Darvel KA17 0JB Tel. *01560 323600* Fax. *01560 323601* E-mail. *johnaird@compuserve.com* Web. *www.johnaird.co.uk John Aird*
Airdri Ltd Technology House Oakfield Industrial Estate Eynsham, Witney OX29 4AQ Tel. *01865 882330* Fax. *01865 881647* E-mail. *sales@airdri.com* Web. *www.airdri.com Airdri*
Airedale Environmental Services Ltd The Old Bank 7-9 Harrogate Road Rawdon, Leeds LS19 6HW Tel. *0113 2502459* Fax. *0113 2501858* E-mail. *jenny.markham@airedale-es.co.uk* Web. *www.airedale-cleanrooms.co.uk Airdale Cleanroom – Airedale Clean Room – Padana*
Airedale Springs The Spring Works Bridgehouse Lane, Haworth, Keighley BD22 8PA Tel. *01535 643456* Fax. *01535 645392* E-mail. *sales@airedalesprings.co.uk* Web. *www.airedalesprings.co.uk Airedale*
Airflow Developments Ltd Aidelle House Lancaster Road Cressex Business Park, High Wycombe HP12 3QP Tel. *01494 525252* Fax. *01494 461073* E-mail. *jkelly@airflow.co.uk* Web. *www.airflow.com Airflow – Anemosonic – Anemosonic Humidivent Maxivent Miniloovent supervent – Humidivent – Loovent – Maxivent – Mini Loovent – Prohood – Supervent*
Airflow Measurements Ltd 72 Manchester Road Kearsley, Bolton BL4 8NZ Tel. *01204 571499* Fax. *01204 571734* E-mail. *tony@airflowmeasurements.com* Web. *www.airflowmeasurements.com Filtometers – Minilux – Petch Elliot – Velometers*
Airgonomics Ltd Unit 17 Queensway Link Industrial Estate Stafford Park, Telford TF3 3DN Tel. *01952 299920* Fax. *01952 290063* E-mail. *sales@airgonomics.co.uk* Web. *www.airgonomics.co.uk Airgonomics – Airgonomics - Airfilm equipment M7ES07*
Airguard Filters Ltd Unit 9 Gill & Russell Business Park Pleck Road, Walsall WS2 9ES Tel. *01922 628782* Fax. *01922 645441* E-mail. *m.garrigan@airguard.co.uk* Web. *www.airguardfilters.co.uk Airguard*
Airmat Machinery Ltd 43 Bridgeman Terrace, Wigan WN1 1TT Tel. *01942 493563* Fax. *01942 496276* E-mail. *info@airmat-machinery.co.uk* Web. *www.airmat-machinery.co.uk Airmat*
Airnesco Group Ltd Unit 2 Bredgar Road Industrial Estate Bredgar Road, Gillingham ME8 6PL Tel. *01634 267070* Fax. *01634 267079* E-mail. *lorraine@airnesco.com* Web. *www.airnesco.com Airnesco – Autobrator – Bunker Lances – Ferret*
Airport Bearing Co. Ltd Unit 4d Blenheim Park Road, Nottingham NG6 8YP Tel. *0115 9757571* Fax. *0115 9273778* E-mail. *sales@abco.co.uk* Web. *www.abco.co.uk Abco*
Air Power Centre Limited Unit B4 Anchorage Business Park Chain Caul Way, Ashton-on-Ribble, Preston PR2 2YL Tel. *01772 728513* Fax. *01772 736506* E-mail. *apcpreston@airpowercentre.com* Web. *www.airpowercentre.com Aro – Binks Bullows – Compair BroomWade – Compair Hydrovane – Compair Maxam – Compair Power Tools – Compair Reavell – Festo (Pneumatics) – Nederman – P.C.L. – Siebe Pneumatics – Ultrafilter*
Air Power & Hydraulics Ltd 13-15 Watt Road, Glasgow G52 4PQ Tel. *0141 8104511* Fax. *0141 8833825* E-mail. *hydraulics@aph.co.uk* Web. *www.aph.co.uk C-10 – Cepac – Dan – K 10 – Pencyl – Torkam – Torko*
Air Products PLC (Head Office) 2 Millennium Gate Westmere Drive, Crewe CW1 6AP Tel. *0800 3890202* Fax. *0161 2234753* E-mail. *kuhnm@airproducts.com* Web. *www.airproducts.com Ancamide – Ancamine – Ancarez – Anquamides – Anquamines – Epodils*
Air Sea Containers 318 New Chester Road, Birkenhead CH42 1LE Tel. *0151 6450636* Fax. *0151 6449268* E-mail. *kstaniford@air-sea.co.uk* Web. *www.air-sea.co.uk Air Sea*
Airsprung Furniture Group plc Canal Road Industrial Estate Canal Road, Trowbridge BA14 8RQ Tel. *01225 754411* Fax. *01225 763256* E-mail. *info@airsprung-group.co.uk* Web. *www.airsprungbeds.co.uk Airsprung – Airsprung Beds and Airsprung & Reclining Figure Device – Airsprung Beds Relax Logo – Airsprung Super Coil – Dreamnight – Duo-Firm – Duplex – Duraspring System – Flametex – Flametex Fibre Pad – Spring Master – Tri-Zone*
Air Studios Lyndhurst Hall Lyndhurst Hall Lyndhurst Road, London NW3 5NG Tel. *020 77940660* Fax. *020 77948518* E-mail. *info@airstudios.com* Web. *www.airstudios.com Air Studios*
Air Technics Ltd Unit D3 Chaucer Business Park Watery Lane, Kemsing, Sevenoaks TN15 6YU Tel. *01732 760660* Fax. *01732 760661* E-mail. *sales@airtechnics.co.uk* Web. *www.airtechnics.co.uk Festo – SMC – Tekmatic*
Air Tube Technologies Ltd 5 Hartlebury Trading Estate Hartlebury, Kidderminster DY10 4JB Tel. *01299 254254* Fax. *01299 254299* E-mail. *sales@airtubegroup.co.uk* Web. *www.airtubegroup.co.uk Cash Management Solutions – Cashtronic – Coin Transfer – Communication – Fortress – Fortress – Metronic – Secure Transfer Systems – Security Screen – Solutions Direct – Tagging – Tillsafe – Wrap a tag*
Airvert Ghyll Road Industrial Estate Ghyll Road, Heathfield TN21 8AW Tel. *01323 444002* Fax. *01435 864838* E-mail. *sales@airvert.co.uk* Web. *www.airvert.co.uk Airvert*
Airware International Ltd Smithsway Saxon Business Park Stoke Prior, Bromsgrove B60 4AD Tel. *01527 870110* Fax. *01527 872388* E-mail. *andrew@awi.co.uk* Web. *www.awi.co.uk Alkin – ALUP – Atlas Copco – BEA filters – Betico – Boge – Broomwade – Compair – Gardener Denver – Grassair – HPC – Hydrovane – Ingersoll Rand – Jorc – Kaesar – *La Man – Laman – Mattei – MCIB – Morris Lubricants – Russell Morehouse – Safeco – Tamrock – Tamrotor*
Air & Water Centre Artex Avenue Rustington, Littlehampton BN16 3LN Tel. *01903 858657* Fax. *01903 850345* E-mail. *sales@airandwatercentre.com* Web. *www.airandwatercentre.com Carrier – *Casana (Switzerland) – *Turmix (Switzerland)*
Aish Electro-Mechanical Services Unit 2b 8 Cowley Road, Nuffield Industrial Estate, Poole BH17 0UJ Tel. *01202 677100* Fax. *01202 677233* E-mail. *service@aishpumps.co.uk* Web. *www.aishpumps.co.uk Aish*
Ajax Equipment Ltd Milton Works Mule Street, Bolton BL2 2AR Tel. *01204 386723* Fax. *01204 363706* E-mail. *sales@ajax.co.uk* Web. *www.ajax.co.uk Ajax – Massflo Feeders*
Ajax Tocco International Ltd (a division of AjaxTOCCO Magnethermic Corporation) 2 Dorset Road Saltley Business Park, Saltley, Birmingham B8 1BG Tel. *0121 3228000* Fax. *0121 3228080* E-mail. *phyland@ajaxtocco.com* Web. *www.ajaxtocco.co.uk Jet-Flow – Pacer – Powershare*
A J G Waters Equipment Ltd PO Box 1853, Croydon CR9 7AW Tel. *020 86899994* Fax. *020 86891715* E-mail. *sales@watersequip.co.uk* Web. *www.watersequip.co.uk 3V Cogeim – 3V Mabo – *Airflex – Comi Condor – Decsa – *Ensival-Moret – FPS – MG Process Valves – Seko Bono-Exacta – *Strahman – Strahman MG Valves*
A & J Menswear Retail Ltd Marathon House Olympic Business Park Drybridge Road, Dundonald, Kilmarnock KA2 9AE Tel. *01563 852200* Fax. *01563 851127* Web. *www.d2jeans.com Benzini*
Akcros Chemicals Ltd Lankro Way Eccles, Manchester M30 0LX Tel. *0161 7851111* Fax. *0161 7887886* E-mail. *webadmin@akcros.com* Web. *www.akcros.com Akcrostab – Intercide – Interlite – Interstab – Interwax – Lankroflex – Lankromark – Lankroplast – Lankrostat – Tinstab – Vulcabond*
A K D Engineering Ltd Horn Hill, Lowestoft NR33 0PX Tel. *01502 527800* Fax. *01502 527848* E-mail. *sales@akd-engineering.co.uk* Web. *www.akd-engineering.co.uk A K D*
Aker Kvaerner Engineering Services Ltd Phoenix House 3 Surtees Way, Surtees Business Park, Stockton On Tees TS18 3HR Tel. *01642 334000* Fax. *01642 334001* E-mail. *bus.dev@akersolutions.com* Web. *www.akersolutions.com Biopur – Deep Shaft – Kubota Submerged Membranes – Prochem and ESP – Sirofloc*
Aker Subsea Ltd Unit 12 Clivemont Road, Cordwallis Industrial Estate, Maidenhead SL6 7BZ Tel. *01628 506560* Fax. *01628 506501* E-mail. *info@kvaerner.com* Web. *www.akerkvaerner.com Kvaener Engineering & Construction – Kvaener Pulp & Paper – Kvaener Shipbuilding*
Akhter Computers Ltd Akhter House Perry Road, Harlow CM18 7PN Tel. *01279 821200* Fax. *01279 821300* E-mail. *sales@akhter.co.uk* Web. *www.akhter.co.uk Akhter – Microsales*
A K Industries Ltd Unit 1-2 Foxwood Court, Rotherwas Industrial Estate, Hereford HR2 6JQ Tel. *01432 375100* Fax. *01432 263532* E-mail. *sales@aki.co.uk* Web. *www.aki.co.uk A.K. Industries*
Akita Systems Ltd Unit 5 Chaucer Business Park Watery Lane Kemsing, Sevenoaks TN15 6PL Tel. *01732 762675* Fax. *01732 761741* E-mail. *info@akitasystems.com* Web. *www.AkitaSystems.com Microsoft*
Akron Unit 1 Penny Corner, Ipswich IP1 5AP Tel. *01473 461042* Fax. *01473 462924* E-mail. *cterry@akronproducts.co.uk* Web. *www.akronproducts.co.uk ATP9 Traction Machine – Chiropody Couches – Neurology Products – Physiotherapy Packages – Plinths & Couches – Ultrasound & Gynaecology*
Aktion Automotive Ltd Unit 18 Garonor Way Royal Portbury Dock, Portbury, Bristol BS20 7XE Tel. *029 20464668* Fax. *029 20464669* E-mail. *parts@rollopowersolutions.co.uk* Web. *www.rollouk.com Deutz – Hatz*
Akzonobel Wexham Road, Slough SL2 5DS Tel. *01753 550000* Fax. *01753 578218* E-mail. *richard.stuckes@akzonobel.com* Web. *www.dulux.com Brushwood – Colour Dimensions – Colour Palette – Community Re-Paint – Cuprinol – Decorator 1st – Definitions – Duette – Dulux – Dulux Dog, The – Endurance – Flexicover – Glidden – Hammerite – Handypack – Heritage – Inspirations – KidZone – Language of Colour – Master Palette – Matchmaker – Natural Dimensions – Natural Hints – Once – Options – Polycell – Polyfilla – Previews – Professional – Satinwood – Signatures – Softsheen – Sonata – Spred – Timbercolour – Ultrahide – Weathershield – Woodsheen*
Akzo Nobel Chemicals Holdings Ltd (Sales Office) 1-5 Queens Road Hersham, Walton On Thames KT12 5LT Tel. *01932 247891* Fax. *01932 231204* Web. *www.akzonobel.com Armid – Armoslip – Armostat – Armowax – Butanox – Cadox – Cyclonox – Demeon D – Diacryl – Dissolvine – Durafill – Ethomid – Fyrol – Fyrolflex – Fyrquel – Halamid – Ketjenblack EC – Ketjenflex 8 – Ketjenflex 9S – Ketjenflex MH – Ketjenflex MS80 – Ketjenlube – Laurydol – Lucidol – Lucipal – N.L. Accelerators – Nourycryl – Nourymix – Nouryset – Perkadox – Phosflex – Rondis – Trigonal – Trigonox*
Akzo Nobel Coatings Ltd 136 Milton Park Milton, Abingdon OX14 4SB Tel. *01235 862226* Fax. *01235 862236* E-mail. *cr@akzonobel.com* Web. *www.sikkenscr.co.uk Bodyshop Services – Lesonal – Mason Coatings – Mason Graphics – Sikkens – Sikkens - Lesonal - Bodyshop Services - Mason Coatings - Mason Graphics*
Akzo Nobel Decorative Coatings Ltd Hollins Road, Blackburn BB1 0BG Tel. *01254 704951* Fax. *01254 774414* Web. *www.akzonobel.com Anaglypta – Brolac – Crown Trade*
Akzo Nobel Packaging Coatings Ltd Bordesley Green Road Bordesley Green, Birmingham B9 4TQ Tel. *0121 7666600* Fax. *0121 7666601* E-mail. *enquiries@ici.com*

Web. *www.akzonobel.com/packaging Aquabase – Aqualure – Copalmat – Sterilac – Sulfatine – Vitalac – Vitalure – Zinnatine*

Akzo Nobel Packaging Coatings Ltd Rotterdam Road, Hull HU7 0XX Tel. *01482 825101* Fax. *01482 838231* E-mail. *alvin.wilson@akzonobel.com* Web. *www.akzonobel.com Diacure – Diaflex – Emiflex – Eurocure – Icimar – Marlux – Shearwater*

Akzo Nobel Woodcare Ltd Meadow Lane, St Ives PE27 4UY Tel. *01480 496868* Fax. *01480 496801* E-mail. *woodcare@sis.akzonobel.com* Web. *www.akzonobel.co.uk Sadolin Classic – Sadolin Extra – Sadolin Fencing Woodstain – Sadolin Floor Colours – Sadolin Hard Wearing floor Varnish – Sadolin High Performance Varnish – Sadolin PV67 Heavy Duty Varnich – Sadolin Quick Drying Floor Varnish – Sadolin Quick Drying Varnish – Sadolin Quick Drying Wood Preserver – Sadolin Shed and Fence Preserver – Sadolin Shed and Fence Protection – Sadolin Stainable Woodfiller – Sadolin Supercoat – Sadolin Superdec – Sadolin Wood Effects – Sadolin Wood Preserver – Sadolin Woodfiller – Sikkens AC Multiprimer – Sikkens AK Primer – Sikkens BL Dêcor – Sikkens BL Primer – Sikkens BL Unitop – Sikkens Cetol BL21 Plus (Europe) – *Sikkens Cetol BL31 – *Sikkens Cetol Filter 7 (Europe) – Sikkens Cetol HLS (Europe) – Sikkens Cetol Novatech (Europe) – Sikkens Cetol Novatop – Sikkens Cetol Opaque – *Sikkens Cetol THB (Europe) – *Sikkens Cetol TS Interior (Europe) – Sikkens Componex WR – Sikkens Kodrin Spachtel – Sikkens Onol Express – *Sikkens Onol Primer/Undercoat (Europe) – Sikkens Redox AK Primer – *Sikkens Rubbol AZ (Europe) – Sikkens Rubbol BL gloss/stain – *Sikkens Rubbol Satura (Europe)*

Alabaster & Wilson Ltd 9-11 Legge Lane, Birmingham B1 3LD Tel. *0121 2362356* Fax. *0121 2330774* E-mail. *info@alabasterandwilson.com* Web. *www.alabasterandwilson.com A. & W.*

Alami International Ltd 7 Dace Road, London E3 2NG Tel. *020 85337800* Fax. *020 85330026* E-mail. *sales@alami.co.uk* Web. *www.alami.co.uk *LEBA (Portugal) – *Smash (Portugal) – *Westward Ho (Portugal)*

Alanco Alamatic Ltd Wilton Street Denton, Manchester M34 3WH Tel. *0161 3364702* Fax. *0161 3350100* E-mail. *info@alanco-alamatic.com* Web. *www.alanco-alamatic.com Alamatic – Alanco*

Alandar Park 1 Guillemot Place Clarendon Road, London N22 6XG Tel. *020 88888833* Fax. *020 88884942* E-mail. *barry@ellisbridals.co.uk* Web. *www.ellisbridals.co.uk Ellis Bridals – John Charles – Kelsey Rose*

A Latter & Co. Ltd River Wharf Mulberry Way, Belvedere DA17 6AR Tel. *020 83100123* Fax. *020 83100868* E-mail. *admin@alatter.co.uk* Web. *www.alatter.co.uk Aircap – Cubitainer – Instapak – Jaxpal – JiffyFoam – Latcocel – Lattenax – Mailite – Marglass – Netfoam – Pelaspan – Pillo-Sol – Polykraft – Shockguard*

Alba Beverage Co. Ltd 4 Sauchiebank, Edinburgh EH11 2NN Tel. *0131 5392755* Fax. *0131 3468008* E-mail. *info@albabeverage.co.uk* Web. *www.albabeverage.co.uk Kenco – Maxwell House – PG Tips – Suchard – Twinings Earl Grey Tea*

Albacom George Buckman Drive Camperdown Industrial Estate, Dundee DD2 3SP Tel. *01382 889311* Fax. *01382 810171* E-mail. *sales@albacom.co.uk* Web. *www.albacom.co.uk Albacom*

Albany Pumps Church Road, Lydney GL15 5EQ Tel. *01594 842275* Fax. *01594 842574* E-mail. *sales@albany-pumps.co.uk* Web. *www.albany-pumps.co.uk Albany – Brooke – Brooke Pumps – Crown – Handoll – Stanhope – Stanhope Barclay Kellett – Warwick – Warwick Pumps*

Albany Standard Pumps (a division of Albany Engineering Co. Ltd) Richter Works Garnett Street, Bradford BD3 9HB Tel. *01274 725351* Fax. *01274 742467* E-mail. *john.bramley@albany-pumps.co.uk* Web. *www.albany-pumps.co.uk B.K. – Stanhope – Stanwin – Triton*

Albe England Ltd Newton Works 51 Bideford Avenue Perivale, Greenford UB6 7PR Tel. *020 89977282* Fax. *020 89982932* E-mail. *terry.roff@albe.com* Web. *www.albe.com ALBE*

Alberto-Culver Co. (UK) Ltd Lime Tree Way Hampshire International Business Park, Chineham, Basingstoke RG24 8ER Tel. *01256 705000* Fax. *01256 705001* Web. *www.alberto.co.uk Alberto Balsam – Pure & Clear Collection – VO5*

Albion Ltd Suite 12 Malvern Gate, Bromwich Road, Worcester WR2 4BN Tel. *01905 427555* Fax. *0845 2801716* E-mail. *info@albionltd.co.uk* Web. *www.albionltd.co.uk *E. Walters (United Kingdom)*

Albis UK Ltd 2-3 Montgomery Close Parkgate Industrial Estate, Knutsford WA16 8XW Tel. *01565 755777* Fax. *01565 755196* E-mail. *ian.mills@albis.com* Web. *www.albis.com Albis*

Albright International Ltd 125 Red Lion Road, Surbiton KT6 7QS Tel. *020 83905357* Fax. *020 83901927* E-mail. *nigeledwardlawrence@albright.co.uk* Web. *www.albright.co.uk Albright*

Albrissi Interiors 1 Sloane Square, London SW1W 8EE Tel. *020 77306119* Fax. *020 72599113* E-mail. *albrissiuk@aol.com* Web. *www.albrissi.net Aldrissi*

Alcad 5 Astra Centre Edinburgh Way, Harlow CM20 2BN Tel. *01279 772555* Fax. *01279 420696* E-mail. *carter.sarah@alcad.com* Web. *www.alcad.com *Alcad (Sweden and France) – Saft – *Saft (France) – Saft (Sweden)*

Alchemie Ltd Warwick Road Kineton, Warwick CV35 0HU Tel. *01926 641600* Fax. *01926 641698* E-mail. *sales@alchemie.com* Web. *www.alchemie.com Alchemie – Alchemix*

Alcoa Europe Flat Rolled Products Ltd PO Box 383, Birmingham B33 9QR Tel. *0121 2528000* Fax. *0121 2528001* E-mail. *info@alcoa.com* Web. *www.alcoa.com Alumec 79 – Alumec 89 – Alumec 99*

Alcohols Ltd Charringtons House The Causeway, Bishops Stortford CM23 2ER Tel. *01279 658464* Fax. *01279 757613* E-mail. *info@alcohols.co.uk* Web. *www.alcohols.co.uk Alcohols – Alcosol*

Alco Valves Mission Works Birds Royd Lane, Brighouse HD6 1LQ Tel. *01484 710511* Fax. *01484 713009* E-mail. *uk@alco-valves.com* Web. *www.alco-valves.com Alco*

A L Dalton Ltd Crossgate Drive Queens Drive Indl-Est, Nottingham NG2 1LW Tel. *0115 9865201* Fax. *0115 9862820* E-mail. *sales@daltonsmachines.com* Web. *www.daltonsmachines.com Elcon – Fravol – Salvador – Stenner – Wadkin*

Alderdale Fixing Systems New John Street, Halesowen B62 8HT Tel. *0121 5615500* Fax. *0121 5613535* E-mail. *sales@alderdale.com* Web. *www.alderdale.com Metfix*

Aldona Seals 1 Brindley Road South West Industrial Estate, Peterlee SR8 2LT Tel. *0191 5181555* Fax. *0191 5180555* E-mail. *gtsm@gtgroup.co.uk* Web. *www.gtsm.co.uk Aldona Seals Ltd – Hillman Newby*

Aldous & Stamp Ltd 90 Avenue Road, Beckenham BR3 4SA Tel. *020 86591833* Fax. *020 86769676* E-mail. *sales@aldous-stamp.co.uk* Web. *www.aldous-stamp.co.uk Aqua-Clear – Aquarius – Aquasil – Atox – Fentox – Nautilus Beta – Nitra-Clear – Pyratox – Zetatron*

Aldridge Print Group Unit 9 Mitcham Industrial Estate Streatham Road, Mitcham CR4 2AP Tel. *020 82394100* Fax. *020 82394120* E-mail. *aldridges@apgprint.com* Web. *www.apgprint.com Aldridge Print Group – Aldridge Print Group - APG. – APG*

Alecto Solutions Ltd 1 Ilex Close, Yateley GU46 6JP Tel. *0845 0261493* Fax. *0845 0261494* E-mail. *enquiries@alectosolutions.co.uk* Web. *www.alectosolutions.co.uk Canon – Olivetti – LG – Avaya*

Alembic Foods Ltd River Lane Saltney, Chester CH4 8RQ Tel. *01244 680147* Fax. *01244 680155* E-mail. *sales@alembicproducts.co.uk* Web. *www.alembicproducts.co.uk Alembicol D*

Aleph Europe Ltd 1 Newton Close Park Farm Industrial Estate, Wellingborough NN8 6UW Tel. *01933 679600* Fax. *01933 401165* E-mail. *info@alepheurope.com* Web. *www.alepheurope.com Aleph*

Alexander Forbes Risk Services Ltd Lockton House 6 Bevis Marks, London EC3A 7AF Tel. *020 79330000* Fax. *020 79330915* Web. *www.aforbes.co.uk Nelson Hurst*

Alexander Ramage Associates LLP Griffin House West Street, Woking GU21 6BS Tel. *01483 750701* Fax. *01483 740560* E-mail. *sandie@ramage.co.uk* Web. *www.ramage.co.uk Alexander Ramage Associates*

Alex Begg & Co. 17 Viewfield Road, Ayr KA8 8HJ Tel. *01292 267615* Fax. *01292 269510* E-mail. *enquiries@beggscotland.com* Web. *www.beggscotland.com Begg of Ayr – Burns Country*

Alexika Ltd Communication House 93 Main Street, Addingham, Ilkley LS29 0PD Tel. *01943 839227* Fax. *01943 830279* E-mail. *mail@alexika.com* Web. *www.alexika.com Alexika (United Kingdom)*

Alfa Laval Eastbourne Ltd Birch Road, Eastbourne BN23 6PQ Tel. *01323 412555* Fax. *01323 414515* E-mail. *barry.godfrey@alfalaval.com* Web. *www.alfalaval.com Alfa Laval – AP Pumps – DEPA Pumps – Double Disc Pumps – DPC Pumps – DRI Pumps – DRM Pumps – ELRO Pumps – GP Pumps – Handi Pumps – Ibex Pumps – Single Disc Pumps – SK Pumps – SR Pumps – SSP Pumps*

Alfia Services Ltd Unit 4 Fiston Centre, Kingswood, Bristol BS15 4GQ Tel. *0117 9181000* Fax. *0117 9475533* E-mail. *sales@alfia.co.uk* Web. *www.alfia.co.uk Easipark – Optipark – Vision*

Alfred Dunhill Ltd 5-7 Mandeville Place, London W1U 3AY Tel. *08454 580779* Fax. *020 78388333* E-mail. *customer.services@dunhill.com* Web. *www.dunhill.com D. – Dunhill (Longtail) – Gemline – Rollagas – Unique – White Spot, The*

Alfred J Hurst Ltd Unit 10 Graham Industrial Park Dargan Crescent, Belfast BT3 9LP Tel. *028 90770037* Fax. *028 90779749* E-mail. *admin@ajhurst.com* Web. *www.ajhurst.com Castell / Static Systems / Emerson – Dehn / Phoenix Contact / Salzer – Patina / Lutron / Emergi-Lite – Sarel / Canalis – Telemecanique / Merlin Gerin*

Matthew Algie & Co. Ltd 16 Lawmoor Road, Glasgow G5 0UL Tel. *0141 4292817* Fax. *0141 4293389* E-mail. *garynicol@matthewalgie.com* Web. *www.matthewalgie.com *Espresso Warehouse – *Golden Tip Tea – *Matthew Algie*

Algram Groups Eastern Wood Road Langage Business Park, Plympton, Plymouth PL7 5ET Tel. *01752 342388* Fax. *01752 342482* E-mail. *stephen.brown@algram.com* Web. *www.algram.com Algram*

A L H Systems Ltd 1 Kingdom Avenue Northacre Industrial Park, Westbury BA13 4WE Tel. *01373 858234* Fax. *01373 858235* E-mail. *sales@alh-systems.co.uk* Web. *www.alh-systems.co.uk Iris Stop – Mainspray – Resin – Series 6*

Alice Collins Middleton Business Park Cartwright Street, Cleckheaton BD19 5LY Tel. *01274 870600* Fax. *01274 870222* E-mail. *info@alicecollins.com* Web. *www.alicecollins.com Alice Collins – Alice Collins Junior – Glenhusky*

Alice Soundtech plc Unit 34d Hobbs Indl-Est Newchapel, Lingfield RH7 6HN Tel. *01342 833500* Fax. *01342 833350* E-mail. *sales@alice.co.uk* Web. *www.alice.co.uk Alice Soundtech*

AL-KO Kober Ltd South Warwickshire Business Park Kineton Rd, Southam CV47 0AL Tel. *01926 818500* Fax. *01926 818562* E-mail. *marketing@al-ko.co.uk* Web. *www.al-ko.co.uk AL-KO – AL-KO Kober*

Ian Allan Publishing Ltd Riverdene Business Park Molesey Road Persham, Walton On Thames KT12 4RG Tel. *01932 266600* E-mail. *sales@ianallanpub.co.uk* Web. *www.ianallanpub.co.uk Dial House – Ian Allan Publishing – Midland Publishing – SBS Videos*

John Allan Aquariums Ltd Eastern Way, Bury St Edmunds IP32 7AB Tel. *01284 755051* Fax. *01284 750960* E-mail. *tradeenquiries@johnallanaquariums.com* Web. *www.johnallanaquariums.com Gem Aquariums*

Frank Allart & Co. Ltd 15-35 Great Tindal Street, Birmingham B16 8DR Tel. *0121 4106000* Fax. *0121 4562234* E-mail. *sales@allart.co.uk* Web. *www.allart.co.uk Allart – Art Deco – Liberator*

J Allcock & Sons Ltd Oak Chemical Works Textile Street, Manchester M12 5DL Tel. *0161 2237181* Fax. *0161 2230173* E-mail. *ja@allcocks.co.uk* Web. *www.allcocks.co.uk Allcosil No 2 – *Chs Epoxy (Czech Republic) – EquiGran – EquiShred – *Intercure (Italy) – Jayblo*

Allcode UK Ltd Kamino House Stuart Road, Broadheath, Altrincham WA14 5GJ Tel. *0161 9298158* Fax. *0161 9294539* E-mail. *info@allcode.co.uk* Web. *www.allcode.co.uk Datamax – Intermec – Intermec ck30 – Intermec ck31 – Intermec cn3 – Intermec sf51 – Psion – Psion (teklogik) – Symbol – Symbol Mc1000 – Symbol Mc3000 – Symbol Mc35 – Symbol Mc50 – Symbol Mc70 – Symbol Mc9090 – Tec – Toshiba tec – Xi series – Zebra – Zebra 105sl – Zebra 2844 – Zebra ql220 – Zebra ql320 – Zebra ql420 – Zebra rw220 – Zebra rw420 – Zebra s4m – Zebra z4m – Zebra zm400*

Allegheny Technologies Ltd (ATI) Granby Avenue, Birmingham B33 0SP Tel. *0121 7898030* Fax. *0121 7898027* E-mail. *graeme.parkinson@atimetals.com* Web. *www.atimetals.com Allegheny Technologies Ltd – ATI-Europe Distribution – Allvac – ATI-Ladish*

Frederick Allen Ltd 24 Winchcombe Street, Cheltenham GL52 2LX Tel. *01242 514869* Fax. *01242 514869* E-mail. *enniskillen@allanarc.com* Web. *www.allanarc.com Frederick Allen*

The All England Lawn Tennis Club Championships Ltd Church Road, London SW19 5AE Tel. *020 89462244* Fax. *020 89478752* E-mail. *christine.tostevin@aeltc.com* Web. *www.wimbledon.org All England Lawn Tennis Club*

Allen & Heath Ltd Kernick Industrial Estate, Penryn TR10 9LU Tel. *01326 372070* Fax. *01326 377097* E-mail. *glenn.rogers@dmh-global.com* Web. *www.allen-heath.com DR128 – DR66 – GL 2200 – GL 3300 – GL 4000 – GR1 – Gros – GS3000 – Icon – WZ12 2DX – WZ14 4 2+ – WZ16 2DX*

Allen Vanguard Ltd (formerly P.W. Allen) Unit 700 Allen House Ashchurch Business Centre Alexandra Way, Ashchurch, Tewkesbury GL20 8TD Tel. *01684 851100* Fax. *01684 851101* E-mail. *tom.maher@allenvanguard.com* Web. *www.allenvanguard.com Allen – Allen-Vanguard – BombTec – HAL – Microviper*

Allergan Ltd 1st Floor Marlow International The Parkway, Marlow SL7 1YL Tel. *01628 494444* Fax. *01494 473593* Web. *www.allergan.com Hydrocare Fizzy – LC-65 – Oxysept 1 – Oxysept 1 Step – Oxysept 2 – Oxysept Saline – Refresh – Ultrazyme*

Allerton Steel Ltd Allerton House Thurston Road, Northallerton DL6 2NA Tel. *01609 774471* Fax. *01609 780364* E-mail. *reception@allertonsteel.co.uk* Web. *www.allertonsteel.co.uk Allerton*

Allett Mowers Baden-Powell Road Kirkton Industrial Estate, Arbroath DD11 3LS Tel. *01241 437740* Fax. *01241 431715* E-mail. *sales@allett.co.uk* Web. *www.allett.co.uk Allett*

Allgood 297 Euston Road, London NW1 3AQ Tel. *020 73879951* Fax. *020 73837950* E-mail. *info@allgood.co.uk* Web. *www.allgood.co.uk Allgood – Beefeater – Cryptocard – Cryptocode – dLine – Dom – FSB – Grenadier – Guardsman – Katkin – Limbar – Modric – Platinic – Quaver – Redlock – Reflex – Slindicator – Spectra – Tansorite – Unilite*

Allianz Insurance plc 57 Ladymead, Guildford GU1 1DB Tel. *01483 568161* Fax. *01483 300952* E-mail. *a.torrance@cornhill.co.uk* Web. *www.allianz.co.uk Construction Select – Furniture Select – HireCall – HomeCover – Lawclub – Lawphone – Legal Advice Call – Motor Trade Select – MotorCall – MotorCover – Wholesale Select*

Allianz Legal Protection Redwood House Brotherswood Court Great Park Road, Bradley Stoke, Bristol BS32 4QW Tel. *08702 434340* Fax. *01454 455601* E-mail. *phil.ruse@allianz.co.uk* Web. *www.allianz-ni.co.uk Corporate Lawclub – Family Lawclub – Fleet Lawclub – Motor Lawclub – Motor Lawclub "Elite" – Motorcycle Lawclub*

Allied Glass Containers Ltd 69 South Accommodation Road, Leeds LS10 1NQ Tel. *0113 2451568* Fax. *0113 2449349* E-mail. *admin@allied-glass.com* Web. *www.allied-glass.com B.A.T. Lantern Globes*

Allied Manufacturing Sarena House Grove Park Industrial Estate Grove Park, London NW9 0EB Tel. *020 89048844* Fax. *020 82009510* E-mail. *stephen.joseph@kingswood-allied.co.uk* Web. *www.kingswood-allied.co.uk *Allied Manufacturing Co (London) Ltd (Germany) – Beaumel – Crown – ISE – *Polyrey (Germany) – Whirlpool – White-Westinghouse*

Allied Meat Importers Windsor House Britannia Road, Waltham Cross EN8 7NX Tel. *01992 807950* Fax. *01992 807951* E-mail. *amiuk@alliedmeats.com* Web. *www.alliedmeats.com Ecco – Simunye*

Allied Mills Sunblest Flour Mill Tilbury Docks, Tilbury RM18 7JR Tel. *01375 363100* Fax. *01375 850706* E-mail. *customer.services@allied-mills.co.uk* Web. *www.allied-mills.co.uk Allinson – Doughmaker – Harvester – Mix 'N' Bake – Sovereign*

Allison Engineering Ltd 2 Capricorn Centre Cranes Farm Road, Basildon SS14 3JA Tel. *01268 526161* Fax. *01268 533144* E-mail. *sharwood@allison.co.uk* Web. *www.allison.co.uk Allison*

Alloy Bodies Ltd Jubilee Works Clifton Street, Miles Platting, Manchester M40 8HN Tel. *0161 2057612* Fax. *0161 2021917* E-mail. *accounts@alloybodies.co.uk* Web. *www.alloybodies.co.uk Alloy Transport Bodies*

Allpumps Ltd 448 Brightside Lane, Sheffield S9 2SP Tel. *0114 2442203* Fax. *0114 2425885* E-mail. *sales@torrespumps.co.uk* Web. *www.allpumps.co.uk Calpeda – Crane – Ebara – MGM – Roto – Teledyne Sprague – Torres – Wagner*

Allshred Ltd PO Box 240, Chipping Norton OX7 9BA Tel. *0800 3895155* E-mail. *admin@allshred.co.uk* Web. *www.allshred.co.uk ALLSHRED*

Allsopp Helikites Ltd South End Damerham, Fordingbridge SP6 3HW Tel. *01725 518750* Fax. *01725 518786* E-mail. *allsopp@helikites.com* Web. *www.allsopphelikites.com *Allsopp Helikite Ltd*

Allspeeds Ltd Royal Works Atlas Street Clayton Le Moors, Accrington BB5 5LW Tel. *01254 615100* Fax. *01254 615199* E-mail. *info@allspeeds.co.uk* Web. *www.allspeeds.co.uk Allspeeds – Floyd – Hydram – Hypec – Kiva – Kopp – Kopp Variator – Millingford – Tangye – Webtool*

Alltech UK Ltd Ryhall Road, Stamford PE9 1TZ Tel. *01780 764512* Fax. *01780 764506* Web. *www.alltech.com *Bio-Mos – *Bioplex Mineral Proteinates – *Sel-Plex – *Sil-All – *Yea-Sacc*

Allum Fabrications Wilden Industrial Estate, Stourport On Severn DY13 9JY Tel. *01299 821388* Fax. *01299 821389* E-mail. *sales@dallumfabrications.co.uk* Web. *www.dallumfabrications.co.uk Pillar Mate*

Allwood Buildings Ltd Talewater Works Talaton, Exeter EX5 2RT Tel. *01404 850977* Fax. *01404 850946* E-mail. *terry@allwoodtimber.co.uk* Web. *www.allwoodtimber.co.uk Devon Lady*

Alpaca Select 82 Frobisher Road, Coventry CV3 6NA Tel. *024 76411776* Fax. *024 76411776* E-mail. *sales@alpaca-select.co.uk* Web. *www.alpaca-select.co.uk Alpaca Select*

Alpha Anodising UK Ltd 54 Marlow Bottom, Marlow SL7 3ND Tel. *01494 535504* Fax. *01628 475949* E-mail. *sales@alphaanodising.demon.co.uk* Web. *www.alphaanodising.demon.co.uk Anomark*

Alpha Bearings Kingsley Street, Dudley DY2 0PZ Tel. *01384 255151* Fax. *01384 457509* E-mail. *info@alpha-bearings.com* Web. *www.alpha-bearings.com Alpha – Alpha Bearings*

Alpha Electronics Northern Ltd 35 Gibfield Park Avenue Atherton, Manchester M46 0SY Tel. *01942 886993* Fax. *01942 886450* E-mail. *north@alpha-electronics.com* Web. *www.alpha-electronics.com Amprobe – Avo – C-Scope – Chauvin Arnoux – Comark – Flir – Fluke – Lecroy – Lem – Megger – Robin – Seward*

Alpha Electronics Southern Ltd Unit 16 Wren Industrial Estate Coldred Road, Maidstone ME15 9YT Tel. *01622 690187* Fax. *01622 678827* E-mail. *sales@alpha-electronics.com* Web. *www.alpha-electronics.com Air Flow – Ametek – Amprobe – Avo – Bicotest – Biddle – C-Scope – Camax – Cat & Genny – Chaurin Arnoux – Cirrus – Clare – Comark – Compact – Cropico – Crowcon – Di-Log – Digitron – Ecom – Edgcumbe – Elcomponent – Eti – Europa – Fluke – Foster – Gmc – Hameg – Hawk – Ideal Industries – Irisys – Jofra – Kane May – Kenwood – Kewtechnik – KIP (P & Zonen) – Lem – Martindale – Megger – Metrawatt – Metrix – Metrohm – Multi-Amp – Northern Design – Powersuite – Programma – Pulsar – Radiodetection – Raytek – RCC – Record – Robin – Rochester – S M C – Scopemeter – Seaward – SI – Silvertronic – Skylab – Sontay – Steinel – Supernova – T & R – Techne – Tektronix – Testo – Thurlby Thandar – Trifid – Unitest – W.E. – Wavetek – Wavetek Meterman – Xantrex – YF*

Alpharail Ltd Urban Road Kirkby-in-Ashfield, Nottingham NG17 8AP Tel. *01623 750214* Fax. *01623 756596* E-mail. *mark.sipson@alpharail.co.uk* Web. *www.alpharail.co.uk Optirail – Orsogril*

Alpha R F Ltd 29 New Road Hextable, Swanley BR8 7LS Tel. *01322 666661* Fax. *01322 665828* E-mail. *info@alpharf.co.uk* Web. *www.alpharf.co.uk Kittytracker*

Alpha Solway Ltd Factory 1 Queensberry Street, Annan DG12 5BL Tel. *01461 202452* Fax. *01461 202452* E-mail. *sales@alphasolway.com* Web. *www.alphasolway.com Alphasol – Aquasol – Chemmaster – Chemsol – Chemsol Plus – Megasl*

Alpha Therm Ltd Nepicar House London Road, Wrotham Heath, Sevenoaks TN15 7RS Tel. *01732 783000* Fax. *01732 783080* E-mail. *info@alphatherm.co.uk* Web. *www.alpha-innovation.co.uk Alpha Therm Ltd*

Alplus Unit 1 Lancaster Business Park Aviation Way, Southend Airport, Southend On Sea SS2 6UN Tel. *01702 541000* Fax. *01702 541100* E-mail. *bhood@alplus.com* Web. *www.alplus.com Adgrips – Alplas – Cash-Rail – Data Clip 2000 – Easy Dot – Signbiters – Snap Rivet – Stick 'n' Hang – Top-Spot – Vari-Tite Clip*

Alrose Products British Gas Springs Ltd (British Gas Springs) 4 King St Industrial Estate Langtoft, Peterborough PE6 9NF Tel. *01778 561422* Fax. *01778 560400* E-mail. *sales@gas-springs.com* Web. *www.gas-springs.com British Gas Springs – Marineline*

Alsford Timber Ltd 63-69 Heath Road, Twickenham TW1 4AT Tel. *020 88922868* Fax. *020 88925474* E-mail. *r.paget@alsfordtimber.com* Web. *www.alsfordtimber.com Alsford Timber*

Alstoe Ltd 16-20 Dale Road Sheriff Hutton, York YO60 6RZ Tel. *01347 878606* Fax. *01347 878333* E-mail. *info@alstoe.co.uk* Web. *www.alstoe.co.uk *Gleptosil – *Imposil*

Altaroute Ltd 10 North Road Yate, Bristol BS37 7PA Tel. *01454 311475* Fax. *01454 273065* E-mail. *info@altaroute.com* Web. *www.altaroute.com Altaroute*

Alternative Gifts The Innovation Centre Mewburn Road, Banbury OX16 9PA Tel. *0870 2006272* Fax. *0870 2006282* E-mail. *info@alt-gifts.com* Web. *www.alt-gifts.com Gadgeter.com*

Althon Ltd Vulcan Road South, Norwich NR6 6AF Tel. *01603 488700* Fax. *01603 488598* E-mail. *sales@althon.co.uk* Web. *www.althon.co.uk Althon – Biomat – Brown Roof – Green Roof – Permafilter – Permavoid – Podium Deck – Sel Biomat – Sel Permafilter – Sel Permavoid – Sustainable Drainage – Tree Pit*

Altima Ltd 4 Chase Road, London NW10 6HZ Tel. *020 84538740* Fax. *020 89658010* E-mail. *sales@altima.co.uk* Web. *www.altima.co.uk Altima Lighting – Altima, Orli, Geni – Geni Downlight – Orli Downlight*

Alto Bollards UK Ltd Unit 1b Tudhoe Industrial Estate, Spennymoor DL16 6TL Tel. *01388 810782* Fax. *0800 4715242* E-mail. *paul@altobollards.com* Web. *www.altobollards.com Admiral – Bombadier – Brigadier – Captain – Cavalier – Centurion – Commando – Corporal – Fusillier – Ghurka – Grenadier – Imperial – Infantryman – Kingsman – Lancer – Lieutentant – Private – Rifleman – Roundhead – Sergent – Yeoman*

Alto Digital Networks Ltd 294-304 St James's Road, London SE1 5JX Tel. *020 77400700* Fax. *01268 561018* E-mail. *info@altodigital.com* Web. *www.altodigital.com Alto*

Alto Tower Systems 24 Walkers Road North Moons, Moons Moat North Industrial Estate, Redditch B98 9HE Tel. *01527 62946* Fax. *01527 597444* E-mail. *sales@alto-towers.co.uk* Web. *www.alto-group.co.uk Alto*

Altro Works Road, Letchworth Garden City SG6 1NW Tel. *01462 480480* Fax. *01462 707504* E-mail. *enquiries@altro.co.uk* Web. *www.altro.com Altro Flexiwall – *Altro Mipolam (Germany) – *Altro Mondo Rubber (Italy) – Altro Resin Systems – Altro safety flooring – Altro Whiterock cladding – Altrofix – Altrosmooth Concorde*

Alumasc Exterior Building Products White House Works Bold Road, St Helens WA9 4JG Tel. *01744 648400* Fax. *01744 648401* E-mail. *littlewoodr@alumasc-exteriors.co.uk* Web. *www.alumasc-exteriors.co.uk *Anti con Finland (Finland) – *Bishore (Germany) – *Derbigum (Belgium) – *Eurobord (France) – *Euroroof AA Solar Coating – *Euroroof Barrel Rooflights (Germany) – Euroroof Solar White – *Eurotile (Finland) – Eurovent – Exstrong (Belgium) – *Floradrain (Germany) – *Fresco (France) – Harmer AV Retro-gully – Harmer Deck Uni-Ring – *Harmer Insulated Outlets (Germany) – Hi Ten Taping Strip – Hi-Ten Bond – Hi-Ten Elastomeric – *Hydrotech Monolithic (Membrane 6125) (U.S.A.) – *Korklite (Portugal) – Korklite Gutter – Korklite Plus – *Korklite Taper (Portugal) – Kotklite Drain – *Lexsuco LP4 & LP6 (Canada) – *Marathon Hi-vent (Canada) – Modular 2000 – Modular Rooflights – Multigully – Nilperm – *Permate (Canada) – *Pipeprop (Canada) – *Pipeseal (U.S.A.) – Roofpave – Rooftrak 10 – Topfoam – *Toptrim (Belgium) – *Torchtite (Belgium)*

Aluminium Powder Co. Ltd Forge Lane Minworth Industrial Park, Minworth, Sutton Coldfield B76 1AH Tel. *0121 3516119* Fax. *0121 3517604* E-mail. *sales@alpoco.co.uk* Web. *www.alpoco.co.uk Alpoco*

Aluminium Products Ltd Alpro Foundry Haines Street, West Bromwich B70 7DA Tel. *0121 5531911* Fax. *0121 5005796* E-mail. *mike@alpro.co.uk* Web. *www.aluminiumproductsltd.co.uk Alpro*

Aluminium Surface Engineering Ltd Bodmin Road, Coventry CV2 5DX Tel. *024 76611921* Fax. *024 76602196* E-mail. *admin@ase4anodising.co.uk* Web. *www.ase4anodising.co.uk Nituff*

Alvan Blanch Development Co. Ltd Chelworth Manor Crudwell, Malmesbury SN16 9SG Tel. *01666 577333* Fax. *01666 577339* E-mail. *info@alvanblanch.co.uk* Web. *www.alvanblanch.co.uk Alvan Blanch*

Alvin Industrial Limited PO BOX 140, Bexhill On Sea TN39 3WG Tel. *01424 846962* Fax. *01424 848973* E-mail. *info@alvinindustrial.eu* Web. *www.alvin.net FORGINEX – KEY CLAMP – LOCKINEX – VARI RAIL*

Amaacon Centre for Management & Marketing Education Victory House 400 Pavilion Drive, Northampton Business Park, Northampton NN4 7PA Tel. *0844 8007307* Fax. *01604 410838* E-mail. *enquiries@amaaconedu.com* Web. *www.managementandmarketingcollege.com AMACONEDU – AMAACON*

Amada UK Ltd Spennells Valley Road, Kidderminster DY10 1XS Tel. *01562 749500* Fax. *01562 749510* E-mail. *info@amada.co.uk* Web. *www.amada.co.uk Amada*

Amalgamated Ltd Systems House Dawson Street Swinton, Manchester M27 4FJ Tel. *0161 7282228* Fax. *0161 7945102* Web. *www.amalgamatedltd.co.uk Amalgamated*

Amanda Hutson Ltd Studio 27 Townmead Business Centre, London SW6 2SZ Tel. *020 73719865* E-mail. *design@hutsonbespoke.com* Web. *www.amandahutson.com Amanda Hutson Ltd*

Amann Oxley Threads Ltd Guide Mills South Street, Ashton Under Lyne OL7 0PJ Tel. *0161 3396400* Fax. *0161 3431705* E-mail. *graham.hall@oxley-threads.com* Web. *www.oxley-threads.com Fibralene – Lubrilox – Oxelene – Oxelene DP – Oxella – Venus*

Amazing Parties Ltd 277 London Road, Burgess Hill RH15 9QU Tel. *01342 712233* Fax. *01444 240101* E-mail. *steve@amazingpartythemes.com* Web. *www.amazingpartythemes.com Amazing Parties*

Ambassador Packaging Ltd Road One Winsford Industrial Estate, Winsford CW7 3QB Tel. *01606 567000* Fax. *01606 567001* E-mail. *ambassador@ambassador-antalis.co.uk* Web. *www.ambassador-antalis.co.uk Flopak – Jiffy Bags – Jiffy Bubble – Jiffy Foam – Kushion Kraft – *Lantech (U.S.A.) – Lotus Professional – Vanguard Products*

Ambassadors Bloomsbury Hotel 12 Upper Woburn Place, London WC1H 0HX Tel. *020 76935400* Fax. *020 73889930* E-mail. *reservations@ambassadors.co.uk* Web. *www.ambassadors.co.uk Ambassadors Bloomsbury*

Amberley Security 185-187 Copnor Road, Portsmouth PO3 5BT Tel. *023 92660730* Fax. *023 92650349* E-mail. *info@amberley-security.co.uk* Web. *www.amberley-security.co.uk Intumescent 2000 (United Kingdom) – Ironmongery 2000 – Master Suites (United Kingdom)*

Amberol Ltd The Plantation King Street, Alfreton DE55 7TT Tel. *01773 830930* Fax. *01773 834191* E-mail. *sales@amberol.co.uk* Web. *www.selfwateringplanters.co.uk Amberol collection – BinKeeper*

Amber Safetywear Ltd 18 Howberry Close, Edgware HA8 6TA Tel. *020 89515868* E-mail. *amber@btconnect.com* Web. *www.ambersafetywear.co.uk Amber 2000 – Shu Works – Zygo*

Amberwood Publishing Ltd Unit 4 Stirling House, Sunderland Quay Culpeper Close, Medway City Estate, Rochester ME2 4HN Tel. *01634 290115* Fax. *01634 290761* E-mail. *info@amberwoodpublishing.com* Web. *www.amberwoodpublishing.com Amberwood Publishing Ltd*

Ambic Equipment Ltd Unit 1 Parkside Avenue Two, Witney OX28 4YF Tel. *01993 776555* Fax. *01993 779039* E-mail. *enquiries@ambic.co.uk* Web. *www.ambic.co.uk Ambic*

Amcor Ltd 9 Ryan Drive, Brentford TW8 9ER Tel. *020 85604141* Fax. *020 82328814* E-mail. *amcor@compuserve.com* Web. *www.amcorgroup.com Air Treatment Products – Amcor*

Amcor Flexibles Winterbourne Road Bradley Stoke, Bristol BS34 8PT Tel. *0117 9872000* Fax. *0117 9872002* E-mail. *keith.owen@amcor.com* Web. *www.amcor.com Calivac & Sterigest – Disposa – Integra – Magpie – Multi-Pouch – Rexam – Sharpak – Steribag – Viewpack*

Amcor Flexibles UK Ltd Digby Street, Ilkeston DE7 5TS Tel. *0115 9324391* Fax. *0115 9327506* E-mail. *paul.rodger@amcor.com* Web. *www.amcor.com Superflexo – Venus*

AMCourierServices 26 Easington Ave Hartford Green, Cramlington NE23 3HR Tel. *01670 735667* Fax. *01670 735667* E-mail. *andrew@amcourierservices.co.uk* Web. *www.amcourierservices.co.uk AMCourierServices*

A M C Rollers Ltd Unit 2 Polo Grounds, New Inn, Pontypool NP4 0TW Tel. *01495 769100* Fax. *01495 760111* E-mail. *tonysmith@amcomponents.co.uk* Web. *www.amcomponents.co.uk Faltex – GUK – H&H – Heidelberg – MBO – MGN – Stahl*

Amdega Ltd Faverdale Industrial Estate, Darlington DL3 0PW Tel. *01325 468522* Fax. *01325 489209* E-mail. *info@amdega.co.uk* Web. *www.amdega.co.uk Amdega – Machin*

Amec Ltd Amec Building 02 Booths Park, Knutsford WA16 8QZ Tel. *01565 652100* Fax. *01565 683200* E-mail. *marketing@nnc.co.uk* Web. *www.amec.co.uk National Nuclear Corporation (United Kingdom)*

Amecal Met-Cal House Fisher Street, Newcastle upon Tyne NE6 4LT Tel. *0191 2622266* Fax. *0191 2626622* E-mail. *sales@amecal.com* Web. *www.amecal.com aerospace metrology & electromechanical calibratio – AMECaL – Gloss*

Amefa 15 Orgreave Drive, Sheffield S13 9NR Tel. *0114 2542530* Fax. *0844 5553435* E-mail. *sales@amefa.co.uk* Web. *www.amefa.co.uk 1700 Series – 1800 Helpmates – 2370 Titan – Amefa – Glendale – Helene – Kitchenmate – Monogram*

Amega Sciences plc 17 Lanchester Way Royal Oak Industrial Estate, Daventry NN11 8PH Tel. *01327 704444* Fax. *01327 871154* E-mail. *admin@amega-sciences.com* Web. *www.amega-sciences.com Go Green – Turfex*

Amelec Ltd 101 Moreton Street, Cannock WS11 5HN Tel. *01543 466191* Fax. *01543 467339* E-mail. *info@amelec.co.uk* Web. *www.amelec.co.uk *AMP (U.S.A.) – *Mason Switch (U.S.A.) – *Sealtron (U.S.A.) – *Texas (U.S.A.)*

Amerang Group Ltd Commerce Way, Lancing BN15 8TA Tel. *01903 765496* Fax. *01903 765178* E-mail. *sales@amerang-group.com* Web. *www.amerang-group.com *Billing (Denmark) – *Cox (U.S.A.) – Eligor (France) – *Fujimi (Japan) – *Gunze (Japan) – Halcyon – *Hasegawa (Japan) – *Hi-Tech (Democratic People's Republic of Korea) – *Horizon (U.S.A.) – *Imai (Japan) – KeilKraft – *Marui (Japan) – *Minichamps (Germany) – *North Pacific (U.S.A.) – Playing Mantis – Solarbo (Ecuador) – *Thunder Tiger (Taiwan) – UT (China)*

American Carwash 68 York Way, London N1 9AG Tel. *020 72780600* Fax. *020 72788942* E-mail. *admin@americancarwash.co.uk* Web. *www.americancarwash.co.uk American Car Wash*

American & Efird GB Ltd Chapelfield Radcliffe, Manchester M26 1JF Tel. *0161 7661544* Fax. *0161 7669965* E-mail. *paul.dhenin@amefird.co.uk* Web. *www.amefird.co.uk D. Core – Krystal – Perma Core – Perma Spun – Polywrap – Wildcat*

American Golf 1030 Europa Boulevard Westbrook, Warrington WA5 7YW Tel. *01925 488400* Fax. *01925 488411* E-mail. *ged.gould@americangolf.co.uk* Web. *www.americangolf.co.uk American Golf Discount Centre*

American Roundup P O Box 2008, Pulborough RH20 1WA Tel. *01798 865946* Fax. *01798 865961* E-mail. *sales@americanroundup.com* Web. *www.americanroundup.com American*

AMETEK Airscrew Limited 111 Windmill Road, Sunbury On Thames TW16 7EF Tel. *01932 765822* Fax. *01932 761098* E-mail. *mail.airscrew@ametek.co.uk* Web. *www.airscrew.co.uk AC & DC Motors – Airscrew – Airscrew 1000 – Airscrew 2000 – Airscrew 3000 – Airscrew 4000 – Plannette*

Amatek Precision Instruments UK Ltd (AMETEK Precision Instruments (UK) Ltd) 21 Ridge Way Hillend, Dunfermline KY11 9JN Tel. *01383 825630* Fax. *01383 825715* E-mail. *steve.faulis@amatek.com* Web. *www.amatekpower.com Core 2000 – Panalarm – Scama – Series 70 – Series 90 – Thermox*

Ametek Prestolight Regal Works Ipswich Road, Cardiff CF23 9XP Tel. *029 20496763* Fax. *029 20462337* E-mail. *chris.jenkins@ametek.co.uk* Web. *www.ametek.co.uk C.C.C. Contacts (United Kingdom) – H.B. Switchgear (United Kingdom) – Hobart Battery Chargers (U.S.A.) – Prestolite Contactors (United Kingdom)*

AMET (Europe) Ltd 5 Cambridge Westpoint Stirling Way, Papworth Everard, Cambridge CB23 3GY Tel. *01480 831222* Fax. *08708 362118* E-mail. *info@ameteurope.co.uk* Web. *www.ameteurope.com Advent – XM*

A M F Polymers Ltd Avondale Way Avondale Industrial Estate, Pontrhydyrun, Cwmbran NP44 1TS Tel. *01633 873229* Fax. *01633 866600 A.M.F. Alloys – A.M.F. Polymers*

A M G Electronics Scotlands Midhurst Road, Haslemere GU27 2PT Tel. *01428 658775* Fax. *01428 658438* E-mail. *sales@c-ducer.com* Web. *www.c-ducer.com C-Ducer*

AMG Forwarding Ltd Unit S25 Hastingwood Industrial Park Wood Lane, Erdington, Birmingham B24 9QR Tel. *0121 3866780* Fax. *0121 3866785* E-mail. *andrew@amglogistics.co.uk* Web. *www.amglogistics.co.uk Air Freight – Flyers – Future – Midlands*

Amherst Walkie Talkie Radio Centre 70 Kingsgate Road, London NW6 4TE Tel. *020 73289792* Fax. *020 72092704* E-mail. *enquiries@walkie-talkie-radio.co.uk* Web. *www.walkie-talkie-radio.co.uk Cobra, Kirisun, Motorola*

A Mir & Co. Ltd Taylors Lane, Oldbury B69 2BN Tel. *0121 5441999* Fax. *0121 5444951* E-mail. *office@a-mir.co.uk* Web. *www.a-mir.co.uk Bakaware*

Amir Power Transmission Ltd Amir House Maxted Road, Hemel Hempstead Industrial Estate, Hemel Hempstead HP2 7DX Tel. *01442 212671* Fax. *01442 246640* E-mail. *saeed.khodadoost@amirpower.co.uk* Web. *www.amirpower.co.uk Bonfiglioli – Euromotori – MGM – Ogniebene – Riedel – SBC*

A M J Maters Partnership Ltd 12 Barley Road Great Chishill, Royston SG8 8SA Tel. *01763 838164* Fax. *01763 838871* E-mail. *sales@maters.co.uk* Web. *www.maters.co.uk *Blom & Maters (Netherlands) – *Palsys (Netherlands) – *Rembrandt (Netherlands)*

AMK Drives & Controls Ltd Moulton Park Business Centre Redhouse Road, Moulton Park Industrial Estate, Northampton NN3 6AQ Tel. *01604 497806* Fax. *01604 497809* E-mail. *patrick.amk@talk21.com* Web. *www.talk21.com Amakasyn*

Ammeraal Beltech Ltd John Tate Road Foxholes Business Park, Hertford SG13 7QE Tel. *01992 500550* Fax. *01992 553010* E-mail. *south@ammeraalbeltech.co.uk* Web. *www.ammeraalbeltech.com Ammeraal*

Ammeraal Beltech Ltd Parkwood Street, Keighley BD21 4PL Tel. *01535 667015* Fax. *01535 610250* E-mail. *keighley@ammeraalbeltech.co.uk* Web. *www.ammeraalbeltech.com Vitafresh – Vitalon – Vitaply – Vitastic*

Amnitec Ltd Abercanaid, Merthyr Tydfil CF48 1UX Tel. *01685 385641* Fax. *01685 389683* E-mail. *sales@amnitec.co.uk* Web. *www.amnitec.co.uk Compoflex – United Flexible – Willcox Hose*

Amodil Supplies Forest Park Cleobury Mortimer, Kidderminster DY14 9BD Tel. *01299 270771* Fax. *01299 270080* E-mail. *sales@amodil.co.uk* Web. *www.amodil.co.uk *Oralla (Spain)*

AMOT (Roper Industries Ltd) Western Way, Bury St Edmunds IP33 3SZ Tel. *01284 762222* Fax. *01284 760256* E-mail. *info@amot.com* Web. *www.amot.com Amot – Hawk I – Speedtrap*

Ampacet UK Unit F1 21 Halesfield Industrial Estate, Telford TF7 4NX Tel. *01952 581814* Fax. *01952 581815* Web. *www.ampacet.com M.U. Universal – Polycolour Plastics*

A M P C O Metal Ltd 17 Binns Close, Coventry CV4 9TB Tel. *024 76467011* Fax. *024 76461455* E-mail. *info@ampcometal.com* Web. *www.ampcometal.com Ampco – Ampcoloy – Ampcotrode*

Ampex Great Britain Ltd 5 Elmwood Chineham Business Park, Basingstoke RG24 8WG Tel. *01256 814410* Fax. *01256 814474* E-mail. *sales@ampexgb.co.uk* Web. *www.ampexdata.com *Ampex (U.S.A.)*

Amphenol Ltd Thanet Way, Whitstable CT5 3JF Tel. *01227 773200* Fax. *01227 276571* E-mail. *info@amphenol.com* Web. *www.amphenol.co.uk Amphenol*

Amri UK Mostyn Road, Holywell CH8 9DN Tel. *01352 717100* Fax. *01352 717171* Web. *www.amriglobal.com Fioptic*

A M S Neve Ltd Billington Road, Burnley BB11 5UB Tel. *01282 457011* Fax. *01282 417282* E-mail. *info@ams-neve.com* Web. *www.ams-neve.com 55 Series – A/V Sync – AudioFile – Capricorn – Encore – Event Based Automation – Libra – Libra Live – Logic – Logic 1 – Logic 2 – Logic 3 – Logicator – Neve – R.M.X. 16 – S.D.M.X. – Spectra – Starlink – TimeFlex – Total Dynamic Automation – V Rack – V Series – VR Legend*

Amstrad Ltd 130 Kings Road, Brentwood CM14 4EQ Tel. *01277 228888* Fax. *01277 211350* E-mail. *info@amstrad.com* Web. *www.amstrad.com Amstrad*

A M System UK Ltd 8 Watling Drive, Hinckley LE10 3EY Tel. *01455 250550* Fax. *01455 250072* E-mail. *sales@amsystem.co.uk* Web. *www.amsystem.co.uk A.M. System (UK)*

Amtex Kingsland, Leominster HR6 9QT Tel. *01568 720302* E-mail. *info@amtexltd.co.uk* Web. *www.amtexltd.co.uk *Amtex*

The Amtico Co. Ltd Kingfield Road, Coventry CV6 5AA Tel. *024 76861400* Fax. *024 76861552* E-mail. *info@amtico.com* Web. *www.amtico.co.uk Amtico Company – Amtico Company Ltd – Ceramic Collection – Granite Collection – Marble Collection – Metallic Collection – Parquet Collection – Stone Collection – STRATICA – SYNTHESIS – Wood Collection*

Analytical Technologies Ltd Lynchford House Lynchford Lane, Farnborough GU14 6JB Tel. *01252 514711* Fax. *01252 511855* E-mail. *analyticaltechnologies@aol.com SEBIA*

Anbar Trading Company 44 Belton Lane Great Gonerby, Grantham NG31 8NA Tel. *01476 571966* Fax. *01476 592093* E-mail. *anbar@globalnet.co.uk Coles Crane Parts*

Bruce Anchor Ltd Royston Road Deans Industrial Estate, Deans, Livingston EH54 8AH Tel. *01506 415454* Fax. *01506 461202* E-mail. *info@bruceanchor.myzen.co.uk* Web. *www.lineone.net Bruce*

Anchorfast Ltd Doranda Way, West Bromwich B71 4LU Tel. *0121 5250525* Fax. *0121 5803555* E-mail. *d.dobson@reca-uk.com* Web. *www.reca-uk.com RECA*

Anchor Magnets Ltd Bankside Works Darnall Road, Sheffield S9 5AH Tel. *0114 2441171* Fax. *0114 2426612* E-mail. *sales@anchormagnets.com* Web. *www.anchormagnets.co.uk Banner-Mag – Mag Vac – *Mag-Edge – Nova-Mag – Super-Light – Tesa – Vita Flex*

Anchor Pumps Co. Ltd Unit C2 Taylor Business Park Risley, Warrington WA3 6BL Tel. *01925 761120* Fax. *08707 779845* E-mail. *sales@anchorpumps.com* Web. *www.anchorpumps.com Anchor pumps – Caffini pumps – Eaton filtration – Gilkes pumps – Grundfos pumps – Lowara pumps – Mono pumps – Viking pumps*

Ancol Pet Products Ltd Ancol House 113 Leamore Lane, Walsall WS2 7DA Tel. *01922 402428* Fax. *01922 404983* E-mail. *sales@ancol.co.uk* Web. *www.ancol.co.uk Ancol*

Andantex Ltd Rowley Drive Baginton, Coventry CV3 4LS Tel. *0161 3305331* Fax. *0161 3440210* E-mail. *sales@andantex.co.uk* Web. *www.andantex-kinematic.com Andantex – *Atlanta (Germany) – *Catep (France) – *Merobel (France) – *Redex (France) – *Sincron (Spain) – *Vari-Phi (France) – *Zambello (Italy) – *Zeroset-Servo (France)*

Anderson & Co. The Shetland Warehouse Commercial Street, Lerwick, Shetland ZE1 0BD Tel. *01595 693714* Fax. *01595 694811* E-mail. *info@shetlandknitwear.com* Web. *www.shetlandknitwear.com Andersons of Shetland – Everest – Shetland – Shetland Warehouse – Skibhoull*

Anderson Bradshaw Unit 2-3 Woodlea Park Station Approach, Four Marks, Alton GU34 5AZ Tel. *01420 562645* Fax. *01420 561696* E-mail. *sales@andersonbradshaw.co.uk* Web. *www.andersonbradshaw.co.uk Anderson Bradshaw & Co. – Cachet Furniture Direct*

G E C Anderson Ltd Oakengrove Shire Lane, Hastoe, Tring HP23 6LY Tel. *01442 826999* Fax. *01442 825999* E-mail. *info@gecanderson.co.uk* Web. *www.gecanderson.co.uk *Anderson (Sweden)*

Anderson Greenwood Instrumentation (a division of Tyco Engineered Products (UK) Ltd) Sharp Street Worsley, Manchester M28 3NA Tel. *0161 7907741* Fax. *0161 7031859* E-mail. *info@stafetysytemsuk.com* Web. *www.andersongreenwood.com AGCO – AGCO - Anderson Greenwood*

Anderson Hearn Keene Ltd 5 Bridle Close, Kingston Upon Thames KT1 2JW Tel. *020 85414222* Fax. *020 85414518* E-mail. *david.hearn@andersonhearnkeene.co.uk* Web. *www.andersonhearnkeene.co.uk Anderson Hearn Keene*

Andor Technology Ltd 9 Millennium Way, Belfast BT12 7AL Tel. *028 90237126* Fax. *028 90310792* E-mail. *sales@andor-tech.com* Web. *www.andor-tech.com Andor – Cameras – Classic – iKon – iStar – iXon – Mechelle – Shamrock*

Andrew Engineering Leigh Ltd 14 Lodge Road Atherton, Manchester M46 9BL Tel. *01942 888848* Fax. *01942 888878* E-mail. *enquiries@andrew-engineering.co.uk* Web. *www.andrew-engineering.co.uk Britan*

Andrews Coatings Ltd Carver Building Littles Lane, Wolverhampton WV1 1JY Tel. *01902 429190* Fax. *01902 426574* E-mail. *info@andrewscoatings.co.uk* Web. *www.rustoleumaerosols.co.uk Ameron – Antel – New Guard – *Rust-Oleum (Netherlands) – Sigma*

Andrew Webron Ltd Walshaw Road, Bury BL8 1NG Tel. *0161 7611411* Fax. *0161 7631156* E-mail. *info@andrewwebron.com* Web. *www.andrewwebronltd.com Andrew Textiles – Fibre-Locked – Micro-Felt*

Andrew Webron Ltd Hareholme Mill Bacup Road Rawtenstall, Rossendale BB4 7JL Tel. *01706 214001* Fax. *01706 830003* E-mail. *sales@andrewwebron.com* Web. *www.andrewwebron.com Circron – Microweb – Snapron – Supaweb – Webron – Zephron*

Andrich International Ltd 10 Sambourne Road, Warminster BA12 8LJ Tel. *01985 846181* Fax. *01985 846163*

E-mail. *info@andrich.com* Web. *www.andrich.com IDER – TILE*
Andritz Seed & Bio Fuel Ltd Stockholm Road, Hull HU7 0XL Tel. *01482 825119* Fax. *01482 839806* Web. *www.andritz.com Compress – MillTech – Multi-Mill – NBK – Paladin – PCF – Unikool – Unitherm – Unitronix – Universal Milling*
Anglepoise Ltd A10 Railway Triangle Walton Road, Portsmouth PO6 1TN Tel. *023 92224450* Fax. *023 92385445* E-mail. *info@anglepoise.co.uk* Web. *www.anglepoise.com Anglepoise – Apex – Artikula – Optiflex – Radia – Radia El*
Anglia Sandall Road, Wisbech PE13 2PS Tel. *01945 474747* Fax. *01945 474849* E-mail. *info@anglia.com* Web. *www.anglia.com Aavid Thermalloy – Alcoswitch – AMP – Ansley – Arcotronics – Augat – BCE – Bergquist – Bona Fide Technology – Bourns – Buchanan – Bulgin – Bussmann – Calinar – CEL – Ceramate – Co-tron – Coiltronics – Cosmic Software – CTC – Diodes Inc. – Diptronics – EPCOS – Epoc – ESI – Eurohm – Excel Cell – GP Batteries – Greenpar – H & L – Harting – Hitachi Displays – HTS – Hudson – IDT (&ICS) – Inalways – Invac – JAE – JNC – Kaschke – KEMET – Keystone – Knitter-Switch – KOA – Laird Technologies – Lattice Semiconductor – Loctite – Lumberg – M-Pro – Magnetix – Magnetone – Microchip – Microdot – Multicore – Murata – NDK Europe – Nover – OKO Relays – Omron – Panasonic – Piher – Power Integrations – Raychem – Renata – Rohm – Safire – Schaffner – Schurter – Shindengen – Softec Microsystems – Solomon Systech – STMicroelectronics – Studiomate – Syfer Technology – Taicom – Tamura – Tibbo Technology – Time Lamp – Titan opto – Toshiba – TRIAD – Tyco Electronics – URT – VTM – Warth – Yokudo – Yuasa – Zetex*
Anglia Television Ltd Anglia House Agricultural Hall Plain, Norwich NR1 3JG Tel. *08448 816920* Fax. *01603 631032* E-mail. *neil.thompson@itv.com* Web. *www.itv.com Anglia Television*
Anglian Developments Ltd The Granary School Road, Neatishead, Norwich NR12 8BU Tel. *01692 630808* Fax. *01692 631591* E-mail. *angdev@btconnect.com* Web. *www.angdev A.D.*
Anglian & Midland Sports Surfaces Nene Valley Business Park Oundle, Peterborough PE8 4HN Tel. *01832 272449* Fax. *01832 272993* E-mail. *info@amss.co.uk* Web. *www.amss.co.uk Tenniturf – Texplay*
Anglian Timber Ltd The Sawmill Colchester Road, Wix, Manningtree CO11 2RS Tel. *01255 870881* Fax. *01255 870480* E-mail. *sales@angliantimber.co.uk* Web. *www.angliantimber.co.uk Ecojoist*
Anglo Adhesives & Services Ltd Anglo House Dalby Road, Melton Mowbray LE13 0BL Tel. *01664 480866* Fax. *0116 4480963* E-mail. *sales@anglo-adhesives.co.uk* Web. *www.anglo-adhesives.co.uk Envo-Flap – Envo-Patch – Envo-Seal – Envo-Seam – Envo-Tack – Evo-Plas – Evo-Stik*
Anglo American Optical 210 Archway Road, London N6 5AX Tel. *020 83400888* Fax. *020 83401888* E-mail. *mrt.aaoco@btconnect.com* Web. *www.aaoco.com Anglo American Eyewear – Anglo American Optical*
Anglo American Sewing Machine Unit 3 14a Burwell Road, London E10 7QG Tel. *020 85392220* Fax. *020 85392215* E-mail. *anglosewing@aol.com* Web. *www.anglosewing.co.uk *Anglosew (Japan) – *Anglospeed (Japan)*
Anglo Recycling Technology Ltd Bridge End Mills Tong Lane, Whitworth, Rochdale OL12 8BG Tel. *01706 853513* Fax. *01706 853625* E-mail. *simon.macaulay@anglofelt.com* Web. *www.anglorecycling.com Algon – Lantor – Woolspring*
Anglo German Business & Finance Translation Services 25 Grand Avenue, London N10 3BD Tel. *020 83653778* Fax. *020 83653778* E-mail. *sheelagh.neuling@btconnect.com* Web. *www.neulingtranslations.co.uk Anglo-German Translation Services – Neuling Translations*
Anglo Nordic Burner Products Ltd Units 12-14 Island Farm Avenue, West Molesey KT8 2UZ Tel. *020 89790988* Fax. *020 89796961* E-mail. *sales@anglonordic.co.uk* Web. *www.anglonordic.co.uk *Brahma (Italy) – *Brigon (Germany) – *Delta (Italy) – Expel C – Gas Safe – HP Technik – *Inamet (Spain) – *Ineco (Italy) – *Monarch (U.S.A.) – *Negahban Gas Co. (Iran) – Safegas – Shur-Flo – *Simel (Italy) – Socomef – Soot Master*
Angus Fire Thame Park Road, Thame OX9 3RT Tel. *01844 265000* Fax. *01844 265156* E-mail. *general.enquiries@kiddeuk.co.uk* Web. *www.angusfire.co.uk Alcoseal – Angus – Armourite – Chemicoil – Duraline – Expandol – Flame-Fighter – FP70 – Hi-Combat – Nicerol – Petroseal – Super Aquaduct – Thermofoil – Turbex – Wellmaster*
Animalscan Ltd 21 Hockers Lane Detling, Maidstone ME14 3JL Tel. *01622 737408* Fax. *01622 737408* E-mail. *m.jowen@onetel.net *M. J. & A. Owen*
Anitox Anitox House 80 Main Road, Earls Barton, Northampton NN6 0HJ Tel. *01604 811228* Fax. *01604 811013* E-mail. *james.burk@anitox.co.uk* Web. *www.anitox.com *Blue Royale – *Fungex – *Monoprene – *Punch – *Termin-8*
Anixter Ltd Brimington Road North, Chesterfield S41 9BE Tel. *01246 459300* Fax. *01246 455778* E-mail. *chris.tyrrell@anixter.com* Web. *www.anixter.com Adesco – Cooper & Turner – Coronet – Infast – Supastrut – Toolfast – Unigrip*
Anixter Industrial Ltd Fastener House 3 Edmund Road, Sheffield S2 4EB Tel. *0114 2738961* Fax. *0114 2697171* Web. *www.anixterindustrial.com Adesco*
Anker Machinery Company Ltd Church Walk House Farley Lane, Braishfield, Romsey SO51 0QL Tel. *01794 367722* Fax. *01794 369119* E-mail. *info@ankermachinery.co.uk *Kemper – *Vredo*
Anopol Ltd 70 Bordesley Street, Birmingham B5 5QA Tel. *0121 6326888* Fax. *0121 6312274* E-mail. *info@anopol.co.uk* Web. *www.anopol.co.uk Anopol – Ferrochem*
Anritsu Ltd 200 Capability Green, Luton LU1 3LU Tel. *01582 433200* Fax. *01438 740202* E-mail. *sales@anritsu.co.uk* Web. *www.anritsu.com 3G – 3G, Blue Tooth. – Blue Tooth*
Anson Seventh Avenue Team Valley Trading Estate, Gateshead NE11 0JW Tel. *0191 48200220* Fax. *0191 4878835* E-mail. *anson-gateshead@anson.co.uk* Web. *www.anson.co.uk Anson – Anson Hoselifter*
Anson Concise Ltd 1 Eagle Close Arnold, Nottingham NG5 7FJ Tel. *0115 9260911* Fax. *0115 9673398* E-mail. *info@ansonconcise.co.uk* Web. *www.ansonconcise.co.uk Access – Alpha – Gourmet – Professional*
Anson Systems Ltd (a division of G M Business Print & Systems Ltd) Unit 11 Glacier Buildings Harrington Road, Brunswick Business Park, Liverpool L3 4BH Tel. *0151 7090676* Fax. *0151 7090678* E-mail. *sales@gmbusinessprint.co.uk* Web. *www.gmbusinessprint.co.uk Anson – Personafile – Visipaye – Visipoint – Visipost – Vistafile*
Ansul Fabrication Downing Street, Smethwick B66 2JL Tel. *0121 5653108* Fax. *0121 5581339* E-mail. *ansulfabricationsuk@tyco-valves.com* Web. *www.tyco-bspd.com Grinnell*
Antalis Mcnaughton Gateway House Interlink Way West Bardon Hill, Coalville LE67 1LE Tel. *01530 505150* Fax. *08706 073160* E-mail. *contact@antalis-mcnaughton.co.uk* Web. *www.antalis-mcnaughton.co.uk Brano – IKS – Packaging distributors – Profi*
Antartex Village Lomond Industrial Estate, Alexandria G83 0TP Tel. *01389 754263* Fax. *01389 750656* E-mail. *enquiries@pondenhome.co.uk* Web. *www.ewm.co.uk Antartex*
Antex Electronics Ltd 2 Westbridge Industrial Estate, Tavistock PL19 8DE Tel. *01822 613565* Fax. *01822 617598* E-mail. *sales@antex.co.uk* Web. *www.antex.co.uk Antex – Gascat – Gascut – Miniature – Pipemaster*
Antiference Ltd Fradley Distribution Park Wood End Lane, Fradley, Lichfield WS13 8NE Tel. *01675 465487* Fax. *01675 463478* E-mail. *trevor.paintain@antiference.co.uk* Web. *www.antiference.co.uk Antiference*
Antifriction Components Ltd Unit 8-9 The Commercial Centre Days Road, St Philips, Bristol BS2 0QS Tel. *0117 9556678* Fax. *0117 9551287* E-mail. *sales@afc-uk.com* Web. *www.afc-uk.com Diamond – IKO – INA – NSK-RHP – Schneeberger – SKF – Star – Thomson – Tsubaki*
Antler Ltd Pilot Works Alfred Street, Bury BL9 9EF Tel. *0161 7640721* Fax. *0161 7640723* E-mail. *custserv@antler.co.uk* Web. *www.antler.co.uk Antler – Revelation*
Anubis Label Technology Ltd The Sanderson Centre Lees Lane, Gosport PO12 3UL Tel. *023 92511234* Fax. *023 92513322* E-mail. *sales@anubislabels.com* Web. *www.anubislabels.com Avery – Avery Labels – Sun*
Anville Instruments Bramble Orchard Folly Lane North, Farnham GU9 0HX Tel. *01252 351030* Fax. *01252 323492* E-mail. *sales@anvilleinstruments.com* Web. *www.anvilleinstruments.com Anville Inst*
A One Feed Supplements Ltd North Hill Dishforth Airfield, Thirsk YO7 3DH Tel. *01423 322706* Fax. *01423 323260* E-mail. *norman.gordon@a-one.co.uk* Web. *www.a-one.co.uk Flatdeck 1 – Flatdeck 2 – Hi-Grade – Hi-Procon – Kingfisher – Lactec – Liquisweet – Piglet Primer – Sow HiFertility – Soy-Grade – Sunlustre*
Apaseal Ltd Bowes House 25 Battle Road, Hailsham BN27 1DX Tel. *01323 842066* Fax. *01323 440450* E-mail. *sales@apaseal.co.uk* Web. *www.apaseal.co.uk Apaseal – Apaseal – *Corghi (Italy) – *Corghi – Delmex*
A P B Trading Ltd Unit 38 Hartlebury Trading Estate Hartlebury, Kidderminster DY10 4JB Tel. *01299 250174* Fax. *01299 251752* E-mail. *enquiries@apbtrading.co.uk* Web. *www.apbtrading.co.uk *Ashursts – *Bepco – *Sparex – *Tractor Panels – *Vapourmatic*
Apetito Ltd Canal Road, Trowbridge BA14 8RJ Tel. *01225 753636* Fax. *01225 777084* E-mail. *info@apetito.co.uk* Web. *www.apetito.co.uk Apetito – Butcher & Baker – Waldens Wiltshire Foods – Wiltshire Farm Foods*
Apex Commercial Refrigeration & Aircon Eton House 4 Waterside Drive, Langley, Slough SL3 6EZ Tel. *01689 892510* Fax. *0870 9985000* E-mail. *apexrefrigeration@apexonline.co.uk* Web. *www.carrieraircon.co.uk Carrier – Foster Refrigerator – Gamko – Seal-IT – Toshiba Air Conditioning – True Refrigeration*
Apex Computer Services Wales Ltd Unit 2 St Michaels Court Church Street, Newport NP20 2BY Tel. *01633 215123* Fax. *01633 215124* E-mail. *support@apexcs.co.uk* Web. *www.apexcs.co.uk Acer – Compac – Elmag – HP – IBM – Microsoft*
Apex Enterprises Kern House Corporation Road, Birkenhead CH41 1HB Tel. *0151 6479323* Fax. *0151 6050655* E-mail. *j.t.kern@btinternet.com* Web. *www.o2.co.uk Apex – Apex - Way's with Doorways*
Apex Tools (a division of Cooper Great Britain Ltd) Pennine House, Washington NE37 1LY Tel. *0191 4197700* Fax. *0191 4179421* E-mail. *michael.shaw@apextoolgroup.com* Web. *www.apextoolgroup.com Campbell – Crescent – Diamond – Erem – H.K. Porter – Lufkin – Merrill – Nicholson – Plumb – Ungar – Weller – Wire Wrap – Wiss – Xcelite*
Apico International Unit 2 Bridgewater Close Network 65 Business Park, Hapton, Burnley BB11 5TE Tel. *01282 473190* Fax. *08707 779202* E-mail. *sales@apico.co.uk* Web. *www.apico.co.uk Apico*
A P I Holographics Ltd Astor Road, Salford M50 1BB Tel. *0161 7898131* Fax. *0161 7075315* E-mail. *enquiries@apigroup.com* Web. *www.apigroup.com Holofoil – Holotrans*
APMG Ltd Mount Skip Lane Little Hulton, Manchester M38 9AL Tel. *0161 7992200* Fax. *0161 7992220* E-mail. *enquiries@apmg.co.uk* Web. *www.apmg.co.uk A.P. – Airform – Durafan – Omega*
Apollo Pond House Bulmer Lane, Holme-on-Spalding-Moor, York YO43 4HE Tel. *01430 860049* Fax. *01430 861550* E-mail. *sales@apolloultrasonics.co.uk* Web. *www.apolloultrasonics.co.uk Sonicleaners – Sonicleaners, Sonifiers, and Totalsonic. – Sonifiers*
Apollo Fire Detectors Ltd (A Halma Group Company) 36 Brookside Road, Havant PO9 1JR Tel. *023 92492412* Fax. *023 92492754* E-mail. *marketing@apollo-fire.co.uk* Web. *www.apollo-fire.co.uk Apollo Series 60 – Apollo XP95 – Apollo XP95*
Apollo Plant Holdings Ltd Redstone Industrial Estate, Boston PE21 8AL Tel. *01205 351722* Fax. *01205 360432* E-mail. *enquiries@apollo-plant.co.uk* Web. *www.impact-handling.com Nissan*
Apollo Sound 32 Ellerdale Road, London NW3 6BB Tel. *020 74355255* Fax. *020 74310621* Web. *www.apollosound.co.uk Apollo Sound*
Apple Dynamics Ltd 6 Well House Barns Chester Road, Bretton, Chester CH4 0DH Tel. *08707 415347* Fax. *01352 751565* E-mail. *info@applesound.com* Web. *www.appledynamics.com Quell*
Appleyard Locksmith 24 Norton Road, Stockton On Tees TS18 2BS Tel. *01642 880777* Fax. *01642 670298* E-mail. *info@lockout-tagout.co.uk* Web. *www.lockout-tagout.co.uk Appleyard Safety*
Applications Engineering Ltd 5 Horsted Square Bellbrook Industrial Estate, Uckfield TN22 1QG Tel. *01825 764737* Fax. *01825 768330* E-mail. *info@appeng.co.uk* Web. *www.appeng.co.uk *Jetcleaner (Sweden) – *Nippon (Japan) – Pressure Devices Inc. PDI (U.S.A.) – *Riko (Japan)*
Applied Cutting Systems Ltd Unit 4a Pickhill Business Centre Smallhythe Road, Tenterden TN30 7LZ Tel. *01580 761500* Fax. *01580 761700* E-mail. *sales@appliedcutsys.com* Web. *www.appliedcutsys.com Aristo – Aristomat*
Applied Energy Products Ltd Morley Way, Peterborough PE2 9JJ Tel. *01733 456789* Fax. *01733 310606* E-mail. *john.lee@applied-energy.com* Web. *www.applied-energy.com Creda – Modulair – Redring – Xpelair*
Applied Kilovolts Woods Way Goring-by-Sea, Worthing BN12 4QY Tel. *01903 502744* Fax. *01903 708851* E-mail. *sales@appliedkilovolts.com* Web. *www.appliedkilovolts.com Applied Kilovolts – Brandenburg*
Applied Photophysics Ltd Unit 21 Leatherhead Trade Park Station Road, Leatherhead KT22 7AG Tel. *01372 386537* Fax. *01372 386477* E-mail. *sales@photophysics.com* Web. *www.photophysics.com Applied Photophysics*
Applied Scintillation Technologies Unit 7-8 Roydenbury Industrial Estate Horsecroft Road, Harlow CM19 5BZ Tel. *01279 641234* Fax. *01279 413679* E-mail. *rhawkins@appscintech.com* Web. *www.appscintech.com CamIR Range – Extender Range – InspeX Range – Levy Hill MKVI – Levy Hill MKVQ - Visualize Range - CamIR Range - SecureX Range - MedeX Range - InspeX Range - Extender Range - Scintillize Range – MedeX Range – Scintillize Range – SecureX Range – Visualize Range*
Appor Ltd Duffield Road Industrial Estate Little Eaton, Derby DE21 5EG Tel. *01332 832455* Fax. *01332 834427* E-mail. *info@appor.com* Web. *www.appor.com Hypor – Junifil – Junipor – Mastafil – Maxiflo – Maxipor – Megafil – Metrofil – Portia – Triflo – Variflo*
Approved Fabricators 16 Debdale Lane Astley, Tyldesley, Manchester M29 7FL Tel. *08448 845213* E-mail. *info@approvedfabricators.co.uk*

Web. *www.approvedfabricators.co.uk Structural Detailing and drafting services*

Apropa Machinery Ltd Coburg House 5 Gloucester Road, Teddington TW11 0NS Tel. *020 89021114* Fax. *020 89021115* E-mail. *sales@apropa.co.uk* Web. *www.apropa.co.uk Albrecht Baumer – Betacontrol – CROMA – Desco – Grauff – IWM – Lamit – Lorch – Nester – Peter Hoar – Tara – Wapora*

A P T (Advanced Pro Tools Ltd) 27 Pant-Y-Fid Road Aberbargoed, Bargoed CF81 9DT Tel. *01443 835086* Fax. *01443 835086* E-mail. *sales@handtools.org.uk* Web. *www.handtools.org.uk Corbelform – Evolution – Multiprofile – Point Master – Powergrab – The 'Jak'*

Apt Controls Ltd The Power House Chantry Place, Harrow HA3 6NY Tel. *020 84212411* Fax. *020 84213951* E-mail. *sales@aptcontrols.co.uk* Web. *www.aptcontrols-group.co.uk Aptcard – Autolane – Chantry Bollard – Fastgate – Guardian Barrier – Handipark – HD – HD Security Barrier – Hydrakerb – LC Security Barrier – LC35 – MC Security Barrier – MCR – MCS – Pevac – Skidata – Slave-Dor – Terrain Blocker – Titan Raodblocker*

A P T Controls Ltd Unit 1 Bow Enterprise Park, London E3 3QY Tel. *020 75381871* Fax. *020 75382693* E-mail. *dholden@westminster.gov.uk* Web. *www.aptcontrols.co.uk Aptcard – Aptkey – Hydrakerb – Slave-Dor*

Aptec Textiles Ltd Darlington Road West Auckland, Bishop Auckland DL14 9PD Tel. *01388 832321* Fax. *01388 832200* E-mail. *enquiries@aptecproducts.co.uk* Web. *www.aptecproducts.co.uk APTEC*

A P T N The Interchange Oval Road, London NW1 7DZ Tel. *020 74827400* Fax. *020 74138302* E-mail. *ncampbell@ap.org* Web. *www.ap.org Starbird Satellite Services*

A P Valves (t/a A P Valves) Water-Ma-Trout, Helston TR13 0LW Tel. *01326 561040* Fax. *01326 573605* E-mail. *sales@apvalves.com* Web. *www.apvalvesdirect.com A.P. Valve – Airmaster – Airmaster 500 – Auto-air – Biddy Pioneer – Buddy – Buddy Arctic – Buddy Commando – Buddy Commando Profile – Buddy Double Gold – Buddy Explorer – Buddy Inspiration – Buddy Pacific – Buddy Sea King – Buddy Trident – Buddy Trimix*

A P Y 104 Uppingham Road, Leicester LE5 0QF Tel. *0116 2769200* Fax. *0116 2769200* E-mail. *office@apy2000.com* Web. *www.apy2000.co.uk Banswara – Buzi – Spark*

Aquaculture Equipment Ltd 36 Foxdenton Lane Middleton, Manchester M24 1QG Tel. *0161 6835869* Fax. *0161 6835869* E-mail. *sales@aquacultureequipment.co.uk* Web. *www.aquacultureequipment.co.uk Aquaculture Equipment Ltd*

Aqua Cure Aqua Cure House Hall Street, Southport PR9 0SE Tel. *01704 501616* Fax. *01704 544916* E-mail. *sales@aquacure.co.uk* Web. *www.aquacure.co.uk Aqua Cure*

Aquaflex Ltd 1 Edison Road Churchfields, Salisbury SP2 7NU Tel. *01722 328873* Fax. *01722 413068* E-mail. *info@aquaflex.co.uk* Web. *www.aquaflex.co.uk Alkorplan – Easipool*

Aqualand Ltd Stonebridge Mills Stonebridge Lane, Leeds LS12 4QL Tel. *0113 2631451* Fax. *0113 2792472* E-mail. *charlotte.hurdman@aqualandlimited.com* Web. *www.aqualandlimited.com Aqualand*

Aqua Legion UK Ltd Suite 335 Kemp House 152-160 City Road London EC1V 2NX, London EC1V 2NX Tel. *020 85553797* Fax. *020 85553797* E-mail. *enquiries@aqualegion.com* Web. *www.aqualegion.com Aqua Legion UK*

Aqualisa Products Ltd Head Office Westerham Trade Centre The Flyers Way, Westerham TN16 1DE Tel. *01959 560000* Fax. *01959 560030* E-mail. *enquiries@aqualisa.co.uk* Web. *www.aqualisa.co.uk Aquaforce – Aquafresh – Aqualight – Aqualisa – Aquamixa – Aquarian – Aquaseat – Aquastream – Aquastyle – Aquatique – Aquavalve 605 – Turbostream – Varispray*

Aqualux Products Holdings Ltd Universal Point Steelmans Road, Wednesbury WS10 9UZ Tel. *0121 5267600* Fax. *0121 5267601* E-mail. *enquiries@aqualux.co.uk* Web. *www.aqualux.co.uk Aqualux*

Aquapac International Ltd Unit 7 Bessemer Park 250 Milkwood Road, London SE24 0HG Tel. *020 77384466* Fax. *020 77386801* E-mail. *info@aquapac.net* Web. *www.aquapac.net Aquapac – *Newmar (U.S.A.) – *Pelican (U.S.A.) – *Vifrifrigo (Italy)*

Aquascan International Ltd Aquascan House Hill Street, Newport NP20 1LZ Tel. *01633 841117* Fax. *01633 254829* E-mail. *info@aquascan.co.uk* Web. *www.aquascan.co.uk Aquapulse – Aquapulse - underwater metal detector AX2000 - proton magnetometer – AX2000*

Aquascutum Pension Plan Ibex House 42 Minories, London EC3N 1DY Tel. *020 72651553* Fax. *020 76759099* E-mail. *customer.services@aquascutum.co.uk* Web. *www.aquascutum.co.uk Aquascutum – Rodex*

Aquaspersions Ltd Beacon Hill Road, Halifax HX3 6AQ Tel. *01422 386200* Fax. *01422 386239* E-mail. *info@aquaspersions.co.uk* Web. *www.aquaspersions.co.uk Aquanox – Ceasefire – Thripstick*

Arcadia Irrigation UK Kennel Cottage Hawthorn Lane, Rowledge, Farnham GU10 4DJ Tel. *01252 714986* Fax. *01252 821563* E-mail. *sales@arcadiairrigation.co.uk* Web. *www.arcadiairrigation.co.uk Fogco – K-Rain – Orbit Irrigation*

Arce Lormittal Birley Vale Close, Sheffield S12 2DB Tel. *0114 2392601* Fax. *0114 2642514* E-mail. *fencingsales@arcelormittal.com* Web. *www.arcelormittal.com Estate – Triple Life*

Archco Rigidon Ltd Denso House 33-35 Chapel Road, London SE27 0TR Tel. *020 86707511* Fax. *020 87612456* E-mail. *johnburtonb@benso.net* Web. *www.denso.net Archo-Rigidon – Rigspray – Tankerling*

Architectual Fibre Glass Mouldings Ltd Globe Works Richmond Street, Accrington BB5 0RH Tel. *01254 357000* Fax. *01254 357011* E-mail. *info@fibreglassmouldings.co.uk* Web. *www.fibreglassmouldings.co.uk Vandalite*

Architectural Plastics Ltd 1 St Roberts Mews, Harrogate HG1 1HR Tel. *01423 561852* Fax. *01423 520728* E-mail. *architecturalplastics@hotmail.co.uk* Web. *www.architecturalplastics.co.uk *Rehau (Germany)*

Architectural Window Films 45-47 Lancaster Road, Barnet EN4 8AR Tel. *08450 261125* Fax. *08450 261126* E-mail. *solutions@architecturalwindowfilms.com Lumisty – Madico – Madico - Opalux - V-Kool - Lumisty – Opalux – V-Koo*

Archway Sheet Metal Works Ltd 1-3 Paxton Road, London N17 0BP Tel. *020 83650760* Fax. *020 83659670* E-mail. *info@archwaysm.com* Web. *www.archwaysm.com Archway Sheet Metal Works Ltd*

Arctic Paper UK Ltd Quadrant House 47 Croydon Road, Caterham CR3 6PB Tel. *01883 331800* Fax. *01883 330560* E-mail. *info@arcticpaper.com* Web. *www.arcticpaper.com *Amber (Poland) – *Arctic (Sweden) – *Munken (Sweden)*

Arctic Products Ltd Nina Works Gelderd Road, Leeds LS12 6NA Tel. *08448 718461* Fax. *01536 264900* E-mail. *sales@arctic-products.co.uk* Web. *www.arctic-products.co.uk Arctic Spray – Kand-Air – Polar System*

Arden Garages Ltd Masons Road, Stratford Upon Avon CV37 9NF Tel. *01789 267446* Fax. *01789 414446* E-mail. *dt@ardengarages.com* Web. *www.ardengarages.co.uk Arden Fleet Management – Arden Garage Finance – Arden Garages*

Ardex UK Ltd Homefield Road, Haverhill CB9 8QP Tel. *01440 714939* Fax. *01440 716660* E-mail. *info@ardex.co.uk* Web. *www.ardex.co.uk Ardex 25 – Ardex aggregate – Ardex degreaser – Ardex Neoprene – Ardicol D20 – Ardion 100 – Ardion 101 – Ardion 51 – Ardion 82 – Ardion 90 – Ardipox WS – Ardit 300 – Ardit 55 – Ardit 880 – Ardit K15 – Ardit K15-B – Ardit PK150 – Ardit SD-T – Ardit SD-TB – Ardit Z8 – Arditex – Arditex RS – Ardu-Flex 5000 – Ardu-Flex 6000 – Ardu-Flex FL – Ardu-Flex FS – Arducem B2 – Arducem EB2 – Arduraplid 35 – Arduraplid 45 – Ardurit Am100 – Ardurit C2 – Ardurit F4 – Ardurit GK – Ardurit S16 – Ardurit S21 – Ardurit X7 – ArduritS38 – Feather Finish*

Aremco Products Foxoak Street, Cradley Heath B64 5DQ Tel. *01384 568566* Fax. *01384 634601* E-mail. *sales@aremco-products.co.uk* Web. *www.aremco-products.co.uk Telescopic Posts – Mole Post – Anti Ram Post – Traffic Stopper*

Argent Architects 1 Montrose Penally, Tenby SA70 7PU Tel. *01834 845440* Fax. *01834 845440* E-mail. *info@argent-architects.co.uk* Web. *www.argent-architects.co.uk Argent-Architects*

Argentina Autentica Ltd 68 Ennerdale Road, Richmond TW9 2DL Tel. *020 71936886* E-mail. *info@argentinaautentica.com* Web. *www.argentinaautentica.com Argentina Autentica*

Argonaut Powder Coating Ltd 13 Nutwood Way Totton, Southampton SO40 3SZ Tel. *023 80873455* Fax. *023 80872255* E-mail. *info@argonaut-uk.com* Web. *www.argonaut-uk.com Argonaut – Argonaut Armosystems*

Argonaut Systems Ltd Guildford House 3-4 Guildford Crescent, Cardiff CF10 2HJ Tel. *0845 6431881* E-mail. *mail@argonautsystems.com* Web. *www.argonautsystems.com BELLROPHON*

Argoneon Ltd Unit A6 Continental Approach Westwood Industrial Estate, Margate CT9 4JG Tel. *01843 226420* Fax. *01843 226420* E-mail. *michael@argoneon.co.uk* Web. *argoneon.co.uk Argoneon Limited*

Ariel Plastics Ltd Speedwell Industrial Estate Staveley, Chesterfield S43 3JP Tel. *01246 281111* Fax. *01246 561115* E-mail. *pat.williams@brettmartin.com* Web. *www.arielplastics.com Arrel Plastics – Coroline – Corolux – Corolux 2000 – Corotherm – Heavy Duty Corolux – Liteglaze – Miniature Corolux – Vistalux*

Arjo Med AB Ltd St. Catherine Street, Gloucester GL1 2SL Tel. *01452 428200* Fax. *01452 428344* E-mail. *uksales@arjo.co.uk* Web. *www.arjo.com *Alenti (Sweden) – Arjo – Arjo Ambulift Power (United Kingdom) – Autolift (United Kingdom) – *Axona (Sweden) – Bianca (United Kingdom) – *Concerto (Sweden) – Encore (United Kingdom) – Mark 1 Pool Lift (United Kingdom) – *Miranti (Sweden) – Opera/Tempo (United Kingdom) – Otter (United Kingdom) – *Prelude (Sweden) – *Rhapsody (Sweden) – Sarita (United Kingdom) – *Stedy (Sweden) – System2000 (Sweden) – Tornado Bedpan Washers (Sweden) – Trixie Lift (United Kingdom)*

Arjo Wiggins Chartham Ltd The Mill Station Road, Chartham, Canterbury CT4 7JA Tel. *01227 813500* Fax. *01227 738883* E-mail. *mark.hobday@arjowiggins.com* Web. *www.arjowiggins-tracingpapers.com Rexam Cad – Simulator*

Arleigh International Ltd Unit 1-5 Century Park Ballin Road, Nuneaton CV10 9GA Tel. *024 76390100* Fax. *024 76390810* E-mail. *info@arleigh.co.uk* Web. *www.arleigh.co.uk Torgem – Torglow*

Armfibre Ltd Unit 7 Wilstead Industrial Park, Kenneth Way, Wilstead, Bedford MK45 3PD Tel. *01234 741444* Fax. *01234 742095* Web. *www.productionglassfibre.co.uk Armspan – Conical Settlement – Fibrespan – Plant components*

Armitage Shanks Ltd (Ideal Standard) Old Road Armitage, Rugeley WS15 4KK Tel. *01543 490253* Fax. *01543 491677* E-mail. *merrickj1@aseur.com* Web. *www.armitageshanks.co.uk Admiral – Alder – Alterna – Andria – Angus – Antoinette – Aqualon – Aridian Waterless – Armitage Venesta – Astra – Avon – Bakasan – Belfast – Berwick – Birch – Braemar – Bromley – Cadet – Calder – Camargue – Cameo – Carina – Charlotte – Cherwell – Chiara – Chorus – Clare – Cliveden – Clyde – Coniston – Contour – Corex – Cottage – Cree – Dania – Dee – Denholm – Derwent – Deveron – Doon – Dorex – Edinburgh – ELM – Esco – ESK – Eye Wash – Fairline – Fane – Fifth Avenue – Firth – Forth – Galaxy – Gemini – Georgia – Girvan – Handrinse – Hathaway – Havana – Integra – Integrated Plumbing System – Irvine – Isabella – Jakarta – Jardin – Jouret – Junia – Kielder – Kinloch – Kinlock Waterless – Kirn – Larch/London – Leven – Lichfield – Lincoln – Magnia – Malmo – Mariner – Marklab – Markwik – Marlow – Mayfair – Melrose – Millenia – Modula – Modus – Montana – Nairn – Nimbus – Nisa – Nuastyle – Orbit – Oregon – Orima – Orion – Perth – Piccolo – Planet – Portman – Profile – Purita – Puro – Qualitas – Richmond – Rosina – Royalex – Salonex – Sandringham – Sanura – Saturn – Selbourne – Senia – Sensoreflow – Sensorflow Solo – Seville – Showertub – Sirius – Specitest – Spey – Spraymixa – Starlite – Stirling – Stour – Streamline – Supamix – Superspa – Supertherm – Synergy – Tahiti – Tay – Tiffany – Tribune – Troon – Tweed – Uniregal – Unisteel – Universal – Valencia – Ventura – Versailles – Vestale – Viking – Wansbeck – Welland – Wentworth – Westdale*

Armourcoat Ltd Morewood Close, Sevenoaks TN13 2HU Tel. *01732 460668* Fax. *01732 450930* E-mail. *sales@armourcoat.co.uk* Web. *www.armourcoat.co.uk Marmarino – Stucco*

Armour Home Electronics Unit B3 Kingswey Business Park Forsyth Road, Woking GU21 5SA Tel. *01483 747474* Fax. *01483 545600* E-mail. *bill.stanley@armourhome.co.uk* Web. *www.armourhome.co.uk Q.E.D. – Systemline*

Armstrong Commercial Laundry Systems Ampere Road, Newbury RG14 2AE Tel. *01635 33881* Fax. *01635 32434* E-mail. *enquiries@armstrong-laundry.co.uk* Web. *www.armstrong-laundry.co.uk Amazon – Automa – Huebsch – Jean Michel – Lapauw – Loadstar – Natmar – Pantex – Speed Queen – Trufold – Unimac*

Armstrong Controls Ltd Wenlock Way, Manchester M12 5JL Tel. *08444 145145* Fax. *0121 5501679* E-mail. *marketing@holdenbrooke.com* Web. *www.armstrongcontrols.co.uk Selkan – Senflux – Starbloc – Starflex – Starline – Starnorm – Starpak – Trimax*

Armstrong Holden Brooke Pullen Ltd Ormside House 21 Ormside Way, Redhill RH1 2BA Tel. *01737 378100* Fax. *01737 378140* E-mail. *salesuk@armlink.com* Web. *www.holdenbrookepullen.com Firepak – Herald – Hydropak – Pullen – Pullen – Pullen – Pullen Boosterpak – Pulpress – Response*

Armstrong & Holmes Ltd South Heath Lane Fulbeck, Grantham NG32 3HX Tel. *01400 261061* Fax. *01400 262289* E-mail. *sales@farmtrailers.co.uk* Web. *www.farmtrailers.co.uk *Cattlemaster – *Combi – *Universal*

J B Armstrong & Co. Ltd Middleton Street, Ilkeston DE7 5TT Tel. *0115 9324913* Fax. *0115 9300083* E-mail. *jacqueline@armstrongsmill.co.uk James Barry – Lancers*

Armstrong World Industries Ltd Armstrong House 38 Market Square, Uxbridge UB8 1NG Tel. *01895 251122* Fax. *01895 274284* Web. *www.gema-ceilings.com Axal – Ceramaguard – Microlook*

Arnold Engineering Plastics Ltd 2 Regal Close Kings Park Road, Moulton Park Industrial Estate, Northampton NN3 6LL Tel. *01604 499651* Fax. *01604 790057* E-mail. *info@arnold-aep.co.uk* Web. *www.arnoldplastics.com Arnold Engineering Plastics*

Arnold K L P 109 Wardour Street, London W1F 0UN Tel. *020 74783478* Fax. *020 74783578* Web. *www.arnoldklp.com Euro R.S.C.G.*

Arnolfini 16 Narrow Quay, Bristol BS1 4QA Tel. *0117 9172300* Fax. *0117 9172303* E-mail. *boxoffice@arnolfini.org.uk* Web. *www.arnolfini.org.uk Arnolfini*

Arntz Belting Co. Ltd Pennyburn Passage, Londonderry BT48 0AE Tel. *028 71261221* Fax. *028 71263386* E-mail. *abc@optibelt.com* Web. *www.optibelt.com Optibelt*

Bernard J Arnull & Co. Ltd 17-21 Sunbeam Road, London NW10 6JP Tel. *020 89656094* Fax. *020 89611585* E-mail. *bernard.arnull@easynet.co.uk* Web. *www.bernardarnull.co.uk *Cedit (Italy) – *Rover Conglomerated (Italy) – *Tecnogres (Italy)*

Around Wine 57 Chiltern Street, London W1U 6ND Tel. *020 79354679* Fax. *020 79350479* E-mail. *info@aroundwine.co.uk* Web. *www.aroundwine.co.uk *Eurocave*

Arqadia Ltd 2 Wolseley Road Wolburn Road Industrial Estate, Kempston, Bedford MK42 7AD Tel. *01234 857488* Fax. *01234 840190* E-mail. *michael.brown@arqadia.co.uk* Web. *www.arqadia.co.uk Arqadia*

Arriva Midlands North Ltd 852 Melton Road Thurmaston, Leicester LE4 8BT Tel. *01543 466123* Fax. *0116 2605605* Web. *www.arrivabus.co.uk ARRIVA Fox County – Fox Cab*

Arriva North West 6 St Andrews Square, Manchester M1 2NS Tel. *0161 2726565* Fax. *0161 2727333* Web. *www.arriva.co.uk Arriva*

Arriva North West 73 Ormskirk Road, Liverpool L9 5AE Tel. *0151 5222800* Fax. *0151 5222811* E-mail. *stonep@arrivanw.co.uk* Web. *www.arrivabus.co.uk Arriva Cymru*

Arriva The Shires & Essex Ltd 487 Dunstable Road, Luton LU4 8DS Tel. *01582 587000* Fax. *01582 587000* E-mail. *heathwilliams@arriva-shires.com* Web. *www.arriva.co.uk Arriva The Shires*

Arrow Butler Castings Station Road Whittington Moor, Chesterfield S41 9ES Tel. *01246 450027* Fax. *01246 261913* E-mail. *sales@arrowbutlercastings.co.uk* Web. *www.arrowbutlercastings.co.uk Guernsey Suite*

Arrow Imaging Ltd Unit 34 Pebble Close, Tamworth B77 4RD Tel. *01827 310350* Fax. *01827 313880* E-mail. *nick.hawkes@arrow-imaging.co.uk* Web. *www.arrow-imaging.co.uk Arrow Imaging Limited*

Arrowsmith Marketing Ltd Sunningdale Wollaston Road, Stourbridge DY7 6RX Tel. *01384 376299* E-mail. *info@arrowsmithmarketing.co.uk* Web. *www.arrowsmithmarketing.co.uk Arrowsmith Marketing*

Arrow Supply Co. Ltd Fastener House 7- 9 Sunbeam Rd, Kempston, Bedford MK42 7BZ Tel. *01234 840404* Fax. *01234 840374* E-mail. *information@arrow-supply.co.uk* Web. *www.arrow-supply.co.uk Bessey – Bondit – Bosch – Briggs – Britool – De Walt – Draper – Eclipse – Everbuild – Facom – Fastclamp – FASTENERS. – Gedore – Goliath – Holokrome – Liebig – Lindapter – Loctite – Makita – Morris – Permabond – Presto – Rawlbolt – Rota-Broach – Rothenberger – S.I.A. – S.I.P. – Starrett – Stubs – Teng – Universal – V.S.M.*

Artex Ltd Pasture Lane Ruddington, Nottingham NG11 6AE Tel. *0115 9405066* Fax. *0115 9405240* E-mail. *nathan.cole@bpb.com* Web. *www.artex-rawlplug.co.uk Artex – Blue Hawk*

A R T GB Ltd 231 Eldon Street Ashton-On-Ribble, Preston PR2 2BB Tel. *01772 204504* Fax. *01772 202283* E-mail. *sales@alisterreidties.com* Web. *www.alisterreidties.com Crestex*

Arthur Branwell & Co. Ltd 58-62 High Street, Epping CM16 4AE Tel. *01992 577333* Fax. *01992 561138* E-mail. *colincooper@branwell.com* Web. *www.branwell.com Luxara*

Arthur Cottam & Co. Carrwood Road, Chesterfield S41 9QB Tel. *01246 453672* Fax. *01246 260274* E-mail. *info@cottamhorseshoes.com* Web. *www.cottamhorseshoes.com Cottam*

Arthur Sanderson Ltd Chalfont House Oxford Road, Denham, Uxbridge UB9 4DX Tel. *08445 439500* Fax. *01895 830055* E-mail. *enquiries@a-sanderson.co.uk* Web. *www.sanderson-uk.com Sanderson – Sanderson Fabrics – Sanderson Options – Sanderson Spectrum*

Artillus Illuminating Solutions Ltd Unit 5 Bellman Gate Holcot Lane, Sywell, Northampton NN6 0BL Tel. *01604 678410* Fax. *01604 671335* E-mail. *j.elliott@artillus.com* Web. *www.artillus.com CaseLite – graphElite – inoventi – LUMIWALL – PROCITY*

Artisan Sintered Products Ltd Unit 15 Shepley Industrial Estate South Audenshaw, Manchester M34 5DW Tel. *0161 3365911* Fax. *0161 3350280* E-mail. *sales@artisnacarbide.co.uk* Web. *www.artisancarbide.co.uk A.S.P. – Artisan*

Arto Chemicals Ltd Arto House London Road, Binfield, Bracknell RG42 4BU Tel. *01344 860737* Fax. *01344 860820* E-mail. *sales@artochemicals.com* Web. *www.artochemicals.com Artoflex – Artonyl*

Art2Craft Studio 7 Britannia Centre Waterworks Road, Hastings TN34 1RT Tel. *01424 715701* E-mail. *sales@art2craft.co.uk* Web. *www.art2craft.co.uk Doodlebug*

Arun Pumps Ltd Unit D7 Dominion Way, Rustington Trading Estate, Rustington, Littlehampton BN16 3HQ Tel. *01903 776447* Fax. *01903 850709* E-mail. *arun.pumps@btconnect.com* Web. *www.arunpumps.com Alcon – BBC – DAB – Calpeda – Ebara – ESPA – Fraggiolati – Grindex – Grundfos – Lowara – Mono – MSP Planet – Sigma Lutin – Stuart Turner – Tellarini – TSURUMI – Way*

Arup (Head Office) 13 Fitzroy Steet, London W1T 4BQ Tel. *020 77553279* Fax. *020 77553716* E-mail. *london@arup.com* Web. *www.arup.com Cadraw*

Arval UK Ltd Arval Centre Windmill Hill Business Park Whitehill Way, Swindon SN5 6PE Tel. *01793 887000* Fax. *0870 4196688* Web. *www.arval.co.uk Allstar Fuel Card – Claims Plus – Dataflow – Fleetcard*

Arven Industrial Chemicals Ltd 12 Goddard Road Astmoor Industrial Estate, Runcorn WA7 1QF Tel. *01928 576262* Fax. *01928 575383* E-mail. *info@arven.co.uk* Web. *www.arven.co.uk Arven*

Arville Textiles Sandbeck Lane, Wetherby LS22 7DQ Tel. *01937 582735* Fax. *01937 580196* E-mail. *graham.ford@arville.com* Web. *www.arville.com Arvex*

Asahi Thermofil UK Ltd 28 New Lane, Havant PO9 2NQ Tel. *023 92486350* Fax. *023 92472388* Web. *www.thermofil.co.uk Esbrid – Esdash – Estomid – Estyrene*

Ascii Software Ltd PO BOX 4174,, Poole BH15 4PF Tel. *01202 258041* Fax. *023 92200833* E-mail. *sales@asciisoftware.com* Web. *www.asciisoftware.com Chat-Forum.com*

Asco Numatics 2 Pit Hey Place, Skelmersdale WN8 9PG Tel. *01695 713600* Fax. *01695 729477* E-mail. *steve.meadows@emerson.com* Web. *www.asconumatics.co.uk ASCO – Asco Joucomatic – ASCO NUMATIC – Asco Process – Emerson – Joucomatic - Air Automation - Trinorm - Circlair - Red Hat - Tripoint – Pneumatic Control Equipment – Red Hat – Tripoint*

Ascot International Footwear Ltd Kingfisher House Restmor Way, Wallington SM6 7AH Tel. *020 87737800* Fax. *020 87737815* E-mail. *sales@ascot-int.net* Web. *www.ascot-int.net *Ascot (Taiwan)*

Ascott Clark 42 Western Lane Buxworth, High Peak SK23 7NS Tel. *01663 734221* Fax. *01663 734318* E-mail. *c.clark@ascottclark.com* Web. *www.ascottclark.com Clark's Chimney Cowls – Jockey Mates*

Ascot Wholesale Ltd 5 Leafy Oak Farm Cobbetts Lane, Blackwater, Camberley GU17 9LW Tel. *01252 875555* Fax. *01252 876666* E-mail. *mike@ascotwholesale.co.uk* Web. *www.ascotwholesale.co.uk Arcoroc – Artis – Blue Seal – Caterlux – Classic – Elia – Hamilton Beach – Hobart – Hoshazaki – Libbey – Lincat – Longlife – Maestrowave – Mermaid – Mitchell and Cooper – Parry – Plastico – Rational – Robot Coupe – Rowlett – Samsung – Sharp – Shott Zwiesel – Steelite – Victor*

A S D Hamlin Way, Kings Lynn PE30 4LQ Tel. *01553 761431* Fax. *01553 692394* E-mail. *enquiries@asdmetalservices.co.uk* Web. *www.asdplc.co.uk ASD Norfolk Steel*

Asda Stores Ltd Asda House Southbank Great Wilson Street, Leeds LS11 5AD Tel. *0113 2435435* Fax. *0113 2418666* Web. *www.asda.com Asda – Asda Brand*

A S D Lighting plc Mangham Road Greasbrough, Rotherham S61 4RJ Tel. *01709 374898* Fax. *01709 830533* E-mail. *sales@asdlighting.com* Web. *www.asdlighting.com Highlite Led (United Kingdom) – Highway Led (United Kingdom) – Goardian Led (United Kingdom)*

Asdon Group Systems House Enterprise Crescent, Lisburn BT28 2BH Tel. *028 92675114* Fax. *028 92660256* E-mail. *sales@asdongroup.com* Web. *www.asdongroup.com Asdon*

A Shade Above Unit 5 Wellington House Camden Street, Portslade, Brighton BN41 1DU Tel. *01273 881130* Fax. *01273 880600* E-mail. *design@ashadeabove.co.uk* Web. *www.ashadeabove.co.uk A Shade Above (United Kingdom)*

Ashbrook Simon Hartley Ltd 10-11 Brindley Court Dalewood Road, Lymedale Business Park, Newcastle ST5 9QH Tel. *01782 578650* Fax. *01782 260534* E-mail. *enquiries@as-h.com* Web. *www.as-h.com Aquabelt – Ashbrook – Ashbrook Simon-Hartley – Capitox – Centriquip – Comet – Klampress – Manor – Metaseal – Simcar – Simon-Hartley – Winklepress*

Ashfield Extrusion Ltd B Field Industrial Estate Clover Street, Kirkby-In-Ashfield, Nottingham NG17 7LH Tel. *01623 757333* Fax. *01623 751771* E-mail. *ashfield.sales@btconnect.com* Web. *www.ashfield-extrusion.co.uk Ashfield*

Ash & Lacy Building Systems Ltd Bromford Lane, West Bromwich B70 7JJ Tel. *0121 5251444* Fax. *0121 5253444* E-mail. *sales@ashandlacy.com* Web. *www.ashandlacy.co.uk Ashfab – Ashfix – Ashgrid – Ashjack – Ashzip - Ashtech - Ashfab - Ashflow - Ashgrid - Ashjack - Ashfix.*

Ashland Specialties UK Ltd Vale Industrial Estate, Kidderminster DY11 7QU Tel. *01562 821300* Fax. *01562 740785* E-mail. *jgadd@ashland.com* Web. *www.ashland.com Chem-Rez – Furecol – Iso-Cure – Novaset – Pep-Set – Supacat – Supaset*

Ashland UK Wimsey Way Somercotes, Alfreton DE55 4LR Tel. *01773 604321* Fax. *01773 606901* Web. *www.ashland.com Advantage – Amergy – Amerscent – Amersep – Amersite – Biosperse – Chargepac – Decafil – Drewclean – Drewfloc – Drewgard – Drewplus – Drewsperse – Flotbel – Fosclor – Ketlene – Performex*

Ashley Competition Exhausts Ltd 1 New Street, Walsall WS1 3DF Tel. *01922 720767* Fax. *01922 721354* E-mail. *brian@ashleycompetitionexhausts.com* Web. *www.ashleycompetitionexhausts.com Austin Healey – BMW – Citroen – Fiat – Ford – Honda – Mazda – MG – Mini – Mitsubishi – Nissan – Opel – Peugeot – Porsche – Renault – Rover – Skoda – Subaru – Talbot – Toyota – Vauxhall – Volkswagen*

Ashley Industrial Ltd South Wraxall, Bradford On Avon BA15 2RL Tel. *01225 868083* Fax. *01225 868089* E-mail. *japapps@aol.com* Web. *www.ashley-group.co.uk Chartpak – Kroy – *Rotex (Belgium)*

Laura Ashley Ltd Design Centre 27 Bagleys Lane, London SW6 2QA Tel. *020 78805100* Fax. *020 78805200* E-mail. *sean.anglim@lauraashley.com* Web. *www.lauraashley.com Laura Ashley*

Ashmond Electronics Ltd 8 Gadwey House Leigh Street, High Wycombe HP11 2QU Tel. *01494 440925* Fax. *01494 446795* Web. *www.ashmond.demon.co.uk Ashmond*

Ashtenne Ltd 35 Spring Road Tyseley, Birmingham B11 3EA Tel. *0121 7782233* Fax. *0121 7021760* E-mail. *mcloughlin.c@ashtenne.co.uk* Web. *www.ashtenne-online.co.uk In Shops – Ruf 'N' Tumble – Supashoppa – Trading Place*

Ashworth Neachells Lane, Wolverhampton WV11 3QF Tel. *01902 867400* Fax. *01902 867499* E-mail. *carl.green@ashworth.eu.com* Web. *www.ashworth.eu.com Alumasc – Brickhouse – Caradon Terrain – Geberit – Harmer – Polychannel – Sinclair Classical Rainwater – Sinclair Ensign – Sinclair Timesaver*

A S K Group 2 Northgate Avenue, Bury St Edmunds IP32 6BB Tel. *01284 777900* Fax. *01284 764025* E-mail. *reception@translate.co.uk* Web. *www.askgroup.co.uk AGET Language Services*

A S L Spring Hill Farm Harborough Road, Pitsford, Northampton NN6 9AA Tel. *01604 883300* Fax. *01604 883881* E-mail. *sales@aslholdings.co.uk* Web. *www.aslh.co.uk ASLH*

Aspect Roofing Gang-Nail Systems Ltd The Old Mill Harling Road, Norwich NR16 2QW Tel. *01953 717777* Fax. *01953 717164* E-mail. *enquiries@aspectroofing.co.uk* Web. *www.aspectroofing.co.uk Ecojoist*

Aspen International Ltd 11 Apple Industrial Estate Whittle Avenue, Fareham PO15 5SX Tel. *01489 573888* Fax. *01489 584485* E-mail. *sales@aspen-international.com* Web. *www.aspen-international.com Safariland – Hatch – Hiatt – Bianchi – BSquare*

Aspentech Ltd C1 Reading International Business Park Basingstoke Road, Reading RG2 6DT Tel. *0118 9226400* Fax. *0118 9226401* E-mail. *info@aspentech.com* Web. *www.aspentech.com Adsim – Aspen Adsim – Aspen Custom Modeler – Aspen Dynamics – Aspen Engineering Suite – Aspen Pinch – Aspen Plus – Aspen RT-Opt – Aspen Split – Aspen Watch – Aspen Zyqad – Batchfrac – Batchplus – Cim/21 – D.M.C. – D.M.C. Plus – Info Plus.21 – Polymers Plus – Pro-Sked – Ref-Sked – Setcim*

Assaabloy Group Portebello Works School Street, Willenhall WV13 3PW Tel. *01902 366911* Fax. *01902 368535* E-mail. *john.middleton@assaabloyuk.com* Web. *www.assaabloyuk.com Century – Ingersoll – M.50 – M.52 – Union – Yale*

Assa Abloy Hospitality Ltd Unit 21 Stadium Way Tilehurst, Reading RG30 6BX Tel. *0118 9452200* Fax. *0118 9451375* E-mail. *uk@vcegroup.com* Web. *www.vingcardelsafe.com Elsafe – PolarBar – Timelox – Vingcard*

Assa Abloy Security Solutions Unit 3-4 Z K Park 23 Commerce Way, Croydon CR0 4ZS Tel. *020 86885191* Fax. *020 86880285* E-mail. *sales@assaabloy.co.uk* Web. *www.assa.co.uk *A/S Ruko (Denmark) – ASSA (Sweden) – *ASSA Distinction (Portugal) – *ASSA Solid (Sweden) – Compact (United Kingdom) – *Fix (Sweden) – *Funxion (Denmark) – *Mico (United Kingdom) – *Ruko (Denmark) – ScanFlex (Denmark) – TimeLox (Sweden) – *Twin Combi (Sweden)*

Asset International Ltd Stephenson Street, Newport NP19 4XH Tel. *01633 273081* Fax. *01633 290519* E-mail. *sales@assetint.co.uk* Web. *www.assetint.co.uk Weholite*

Associated Home Fabrics Ltd Hyline House Tilson Road, Roundthorn Industrial Estate, Manchester M23 9JD Tel. *0161 9981526* Fax. *0161 9460407* E-mail. *sales@a-h-f.co.uk* Web. *www.a-h-f.co.uk Homemaker*

Associated Knowledge Systems Ltd The Old Smithy Heaton House, Boroughbridge, York YO51 9HE Tel. *01423 321450* Fax. *01423 321451* E-mail. *roy.slater@aksbedale.co.uk* Web. *www.aksbedale.co.uk Assassin – DE Cartes*

Associated Newspapers Northcliffe House 2 Derry Street, London W8 5TT Tel. *020 79386000* Fax. *020 79373214* E-mail. *manchester@dailymail.co.uk* Web. *www.associatednewspapers.co.uk Daily Mail – Evening Standard – Mail on Sunday, The – You*

M K Associates 38 Chigwell Lane, Loughton IG10 3NY Tel. *020 85084001* Fax. *01494 775090* E-mail. *enquiries@mkcarlton.com* Web. *www.giffardnewton.com Samson – Tuffking*

Association Of Professional Recording Services Ltd PO Box 22, Totnes TQ9 7YZ Tel. *01803 868600* Fax. *01803 868444* E-mail. *sales@atrs.co.uk* Web. *www.atrs.co.uk Recording Technologies*

Assured Solutions Ltd Unit H Westminster Industrial Estate Measham, Swadlincote DE12 7DS Tel. *01530 272922* Fax. *01530 272921* E-mail. *sales@assuredsolutionsltd.co.uk* Web. *www.chemicalsuppliers.uk.com Enviro-weld*

Assured Transcription & Typing Services Teffont Long Mill Lane, Plaxtol, Sevenoaks TN15 0QR Tel. *01732 810502* E-mail. *mae@assuredtranscription.co.uk* Web. *www.assuredtranscription.co.uk Assured Transcription*

Assystem UK Group Club Street Bamber Bridge, Preston PR5 6FN Tel. *01772 645000* Fax. *01772 645001* E-mail. *lstewart@assystemuk.com* Web. *www.assystem.com Inbis*

Asta Development plc 10 Pearson Road Central Park, Telford TF2 9TX Tel. *01952 293491* Fax. *01952 293494* E-mail. *sales@astadev.com* Web. *www.astadev.com Power Project*

Astaroth Solutions Exchange Apartments Sparkes Close, Bromley BR2 9EX Tel. *08458 686914* E-mail. *sales@astarothsolutions.com* Web. *www.astarothsolutions.com Astaroth Solutions*

Astellas Pharma Ltd (Associated Co. Yamanouchi) Lovett House Causeway Corporate Centre Lovett Road, Staines TW18 3AZ Tel. *01784 419615* Fax. *01784 419401* Web. *www.astellas-europe.co.uk Ketovite – Pancrex*

Astell Scientific Holdings Ltd 19 - 21 Powerscroft Road, Sidcup DA14 5DT Tel. *020 83004311* Fax. *020 83002247* E-mail. *sales@astell.com* Web. *www.astell.com Logicolor – Portaclave – Secure Touch – Sterimate – Swiftlock*

Asterix Catering Equipment Ltd Unit 2 Brookdale Court, Chapeltown, Sheffield S35 2PT Tel. *0114 2329922* Fax. *0114 2403605* E-mail. *andrea@asterixcatering.co.uk* Web. *www.asterixuk.co.uk *Bonnet – *Fosters – *Lincat – *Meiko*

Aston Martin Works Tickford Street, Newport Pagnell MK16 9AN Tel. *01908 619264* Fax. *01908 216439* E-mail. *ubez@astonmartin.com* Web. *www.astonmartin.com Aston Martin DB7 – Aston Martin V8 Coupe – Aston Martin V8 Volante Car – Aston Martin Vantage*

Astracast P.L.C. Woodlands Roydsdale Way, Euroway Trading Estate, Bradford BD4 6SE Tel. *01274 475179* Fax. *01274 654176* E-mail. *sales@astracast.co.uk* Web. *www.astracast.co.uk Astracast – Fordham – Pland*

Astra Engineering Products Ltd Queens Road Aston, Birmingham B6 7NH Tel. *0121 3273571* Fax. *0121 3276381* E-mail. *hallj@astrapressings.co.uk* Web. *www.astrapressings.co.uk Astra – Mini Bus 160 – Plugway – Plugway Minor – Trolley Duct – Trolleymaster*

Astral Hygiene Ltd Charlesfield Industrial Estate St Boswells, Melrose TD6 0HH Tel. *01835 824342* Fax. *01835 824343* E-mail. *sales@astralhygiene.co.uk* Web. *www.astralhygiene.co.uk astral hygiene*

Astrazeneca Alderley Park, Macclesfield SK10 4TF Tel. *01625 582828* Fax. *01625 585022* E-mail. *david.brennan@astrazeneca.co.uk* Web. *www.astrazeneca.co.uk AstraZeneca*

Astric Medical 36 Blatchington Road, Hove BN3 3YN Tel. *01273 716516* Fax. *01273 716516* E-mail. *info@astric-medical.co.uk* Web. *www.astric-medical.co.uk Astric Dry-Bed*

Astroflame Fire Seals Ltd Unit 8 The I O Centre Stephenson Road, Fareham PO15 5RU Tel. *01329 844500* Fax. *01329 844600* E-mail. *sales@astroflame.com* Web. *www.astroflame.com ASTRO BATT (United Kingdom) – ASTRO CF DRAINAGE SEAL (United Kingdom) – ASTRO CLAD (United Kingdom) – ASTRO COLLAR (United Kingdom) – ASTRO DL COVER (United Kingdom) – ASTRO DUCT WRAP (United Kingdom) – ASTRO EJ SEAL (United Kingdom) – ASTRO FINGERKEEPER COMMERCIAL (United Kingdom) – ASTRO FINGERKEEPER COMMERCIAL REARGUARD (United Kingdom) – ASTRO FINGERKEEPER INDUSTRIAL (United Kingdom) – ASTRO FM COMPOUND (United Kingdom) – ASTRO FR ACOUSTIC FOAM (United Kingdom) – ASTRO FR EC FOAM (United Kingdom) – ASTRO GRILLE (United Kingdom) – ASTRO LINER (United Kingdom) – ASTRO LUMI CANOPY (United Kingdom) – ASTRO LUMI COVER (United Kingdom) – ASTRO MASTIC (United Kingdom) – ASTRO PILLOW (United Kingdom) – ASTRO PROTECTA (United Kingdom) – ASTRO PUTTY (United Kingdom) – ASTRO SLEEVE (United Kingdom) – ASTRO STRIP BS (United Kingdom) – ASTRO STRIP FO (United Kingdom) – ASTRO STRIP FS (United Kingdom) – ASTRO STRIP SB (United Kingdom) – ASTRO STRIP TB (United Kingdom) – ASTRO TAPE (United Kingdom) – ASTRO THERMAL (United Kingdom) – ASTRO THERMAL FIRE PS (United Kingdom) – ASTRO U CHANNEL (United Kingdom) – ASTRO WRAP (United Kingdom)*

Astrosyn International Technolgy Ltd The Old Courthouse New Road Avenue, Chatham ME4 6BE Tel. *01634 815175* Fax. *01634 826552* E-mail. *astrosyn@btinternet.com* Web. *www.astrosyn.com Astrosyn*

Astwell Augers Ltd A14 Huntingdon Road Thrapston, Kettering NN14 4PT Tel. *01832 735300* Fax. *01832 735533* E-mail. *sales@astwell.co.uk* Web. *www.astwell.co.uk Deva (United Kingdom) – Flight Fabrications (United Kingdom) – Rutherford (United Kingdom)*

ATA Engineering Processes 88 House Unit B Boundary Way, Hemel Hempstead Industrial Estate, Hemel Hempstead HP2 7SS Tel. *01442 264411* Fax. *01442 231383* E-mail. *sales@ataeng.com* Web. *www.ataeng.com Boelube – Onsrud Cutters*

A T A Grinding Processes Ltd 37 Dalsetter Avenue Drumchapel, Glasgow G15 8TE Tel. *0141 9404720* Fax. *0141 9404721* E-mail. *ata@atagrinding.co.uk* Web. *www.atagrinding.co.uk A.T.A. – Ata Abrasives – ATA Polifan – ATA Scrulok – Atabands – Atabrite – Atabrushes – Ataburrs – Atadisc – Ataflex – Atapoints – Atarolls – Atastik – Horse Brand – Horse Elastic – Pferd Brand – Poliflex*

A T B Laurence Scott Ltd PO Box 25, Norwich NR1 1JD Tel. *01603 628333* Fax. *01603 610604* E-mail. *admin@laurence-scott.com* Web. *www.laurence-scott.com Centaur – DISCO – E.D.C. – Electropower – EPG – Glentronic – Heenan – NECO – NORAC – NORMAND - – OULTON – PRECISION STEP SYSTEMS - – R Series – Rotastep – Slendaur – SRA – Supaflex – TASC*

A T C Semitec Ltd Unit 14 Cosgrove Business Park Daisy Bank Lane, Anderton, Northwich CW9 6FY Tel. *01606 871680* Fax. *08709 010888* E-mail. *sales@atcsemitec.co.uk* Web. *www.atcsemitec.co.uk Campini (Italy) – Matsuo (Japan) – NEC Schott (Japan) – Pepi (U.S.A.) – Semitec (Japan)*

Ateco Ltd Bulldozer House New Road, Sheerness ME12 1AU Tel. *01795 660666* Fax. *01795 661559* E-mail. *info@atecoaccess.com* Web. *www.atecoaccess.com Ateco Access*

A T E Technology Ltd 48 Green Meadows Westhoughton, Bolton BL5 2BN Tel. *01942 815603* Fax. *01942 815321 Fast Auto – Fast Bid*

Athlone Extrusions (UK) Ltd Equipoint Coventry Road, Birmingham B25 8AD Tel. *0121 7644848* Fax. *0121 7644443* E-mail. *sales@athloneuk.com* Web. *www.athloneextrusions.ie Athpol – Durosan – Durosun – Durogloss (United Kingdom)*

ATI Garryson Limited Spring Road, Ibstock LE67 6LR Tel. *01530 261145* Fax. *01530 262801* E-mail. *sales@garryson.co.uk* Web. *www.atigarryson.co.uk Flexicut – Flexidisc – Garryflex – Garryson – Garryson*

A T I Tank Hire Ltd Thamesfield Way Off Pasteur Road, Great Yarmouth NR31 0DW Tel. *01493 441747* Fax. *01493 442717* E-mail. *info@atitanks.co.uk* Web. *www.atitanks.co.uk ATI Tank Hire*

Atkin Automation Ltd 11 Howlett Way, Thetford IP24 1HZ Tel. *01842 753521* Fax. *01842 763614* E-mail. *sales@atkinautomation.com* Web. *www.atkinautomation.com Atkin – Atkin, BHP*

Atkinson Equipment Moat Road West Wilts Trading Estate West Wilts Trading Estate, Westbury BA13 4JF Tel. *01373 822220* Fax. *01373 826996* E-mail. *sales@atkinsonequipment.com* Web. *www.atkinsonequipment.com Tankmaster – Ventatank*

Atkinson & Kirby Ltd Unit 1 Atkinson Road, Ormskirk L39 2AJ Tel. *01695 573234* Fax. *01695 573859* E-mail. *sales@akirby.co.uk* Web. *www.akirby.co.uk Eurofloor – Lauzon – Nordstar – Parkeblock – Parkestrip – Timberflex*

Atkinson-Walker Saws Ltd 1 Cotton Mill Row, Sheffield S3 8RU Tel. *0114 2752121* Fax. *0114 2725065* E-mail. *sales@atkinson-walker-saws.co.uk* Web. *www.atkinson-walker-saws.co.uk G-Man – Gold Flight – Little Logger*

Atlantic Plastics Eddison Road Hams Hall Distribution Park Coleshill, Birmingham B46 1AB Tel. *01675 437900* Fax. *01675 437909* E-mail. *sdrain@tyco-valves.com* Web. *www.tmproducts.com Unicap – Unicol – Unicup – Unidap – Uniscol – Unisok*

Atlantic Rubber Company Ltd Castleton Works Atlantic Street, Broadheath, Altrincham WA14 5BX Tel. *0161 9283727* Fax. *0161 9269755* E-mail. *info@atlanticgb.co.uk* Web. *www.atlanticrubber.co.uk Atlantic – Mini Wheel – Superwheel – Trak Wheel – Transwheel*

Atlantis European Ltd 1st Floor Brittania House 68-80 Hanbury Street, London E1 5JL Tel. *020 73778855* Fax. *020 73778850* E-mail. *mail@atlantisart.co.uk* Web. *www.atlantisart.co.uk Atlantis – Folding Box Board – Heritage – Kraft Manilla & Cover – Lilliput – Long Life Copy Safe – Museum Board – Silversafe*

Atlas Converting Wolseley Road Kempston, Bedford MK42 7XT Tel. *01234 852553* Fax. *01234 851151* E-mail. *alan.johnson@bobstgroup.com* Web. *www.atlasconverting.com Apollo (United Kingdom) – Atlas (United Kingdom) – General (United Kingdom) – Midi (United Kingdom) – Rotomec (Italy) – Schiavi (Italy) – Titan (United Kingdom)*

Atlas Copco Compressors Ltd Swallowdale Lane Hemel Hempstead Indl-Est, Hemel Hempstead HP2 7EA Tel. *01442 261201* Fax. *01543 676501* E-mail. *kevin.prince@uk.atlascopco.com* Web. *www.atlascopco.co.uk Atlas Copco – Weda*

Atlas Copco Tools Ltd Swallowdale Lane Hemel Hempstead Industrial Estate, Hemel Hempstead HP2 7EA Tel. *01442 261202* Fax. *01442 240596* E-mail. *toolsuk._info@atlascopco.com* Web. *www.atlascopco.com AEG Electric Tools – Atlas Copco Electric Tools – *COL (Sweden) – *ErgoPulse (Sweden) – *GTG (Sweden) – *L.S.V (Sweden) – *L.T.V (Sweden) – *LBB (Sweden) – *LGB (Sweden) – *LMP (Sweden) – *LMS (Sweden) – *LSF (Sweden) – *LSR (Sweden) – *LTS (Sweden) – *LUF (Sweden) – *LUM (Sweden) – *RRC (Sweden) – *RRD (Sweden) – *RRF (Sweden) – *Tensor (Sweden) – *Twist (Sweden)*

A T M Parts 11-12 Admiralty Way, Camberley GU15 3DT Tel. *01276 607200* Fax. *01276 609040* E-mail. *info@atm-parts.com* Web. *www.atm-parts.com De La Rue – DieBold – IBM – NCR – NCR 5070 – NCR 5084 – NCR 5085 – NCR 5088 – NCR 5670 – NCR 5674 – NCR 5675 – NCR 5685 – NCR 5688 – NCR 5870 – NCR 5874 – NCR 5875 – NCR 5879 – NCR 5884 – NCR 5885 – NCR 5886 – NCR 5888 – Wincor*

Atol Racking & Building Ltd Unit A3 Wymeswold Industrial Park Wymeswold Road, Burton-on-the-wolds, Loughborough LE12 5TY Tel. *01509 881345* Fax. *01509 881064* E-mail. *keith.walker@atol.co.uk* Web. *www.atol.co.uk Versitile Construction*

Atosina UK Ltd Globe House Bayley Street, Stalybridge SK15 1PY Tel. *0161 3384411* Fax. *0161 3031908* Web. *www.petrochemicals.atofina.com Acticarbone – Adine – Alerton – Altene – Amphoram – Appryl – Aquakeep – Azobul – Bactiram – Balmix – Baltane – Biomet – Cecagel – Cecaperl – Cecaperl 40 – Cecarbon – Cecasol – Cetincoat – Clarcel – Clarcel – Clarcel Flo – Clarsol – Colflex – Dinoram – Dinoramac – Dinoramox – Durastrength – Ecepox – Ecocryl/Repolem – Ekaland – Evatane – Fascat – Fluidiram – Forafac – Forane – Foraperle – Garbeflex – Inipol – Jarylec – Jarysol – Kynar – Lacovyl – Lacqrene – Lacqtene – Lacqtene HD – Liozan – Lotader – Lotryl – Lucalor – Mecloran – Metablen – Nakan – Nakan S – Noram – Noramac – Noramium – Noramox – Norsocryl – Norsorex – Norust – Noxamine – Noxamium – Oniachlor – Orelf – Orevac – Orgalloy – Orgasol – Pebax – Pennodorant – Pertene – Platilon – Platon – Poly BD – Polyram – Prochinor – Prochinor – Pyrofine – Pyroforane 1211 – Pyroforane 1301 – Rilsan A – Rilsan B – S.M.A. – Siliporite – Stabiram – Stavinor – Sunprene – Surchlor – Trinoram – Ukalene – Voltelef – W.A.C.*

A T P Automatic Transmission Parts UK Ltd Victoria Street Hednesford, Cannock WS12 1BU Tel. *01543 870330* Fax. *01543 426581* E-mail. *alanrichards@atp-group.com* Web. *www.atp-group.com A.T.P.*

Atritor Ltd PO Box 101, Coventry CV6 5RE Tel. *024 76662266* Fax. *024 76665751* E-mail. *sales@atritor.com* Web. *www.atritor.com Atriloy – Atritor – Beata – Cellmill – Microniser*

A T Sack Fillers PO Box 434, Huntingdon PE26 2RB Tel. *01487 814002* Fax. *01487 814002* E-mail. *sales@simplafillsystems.co.uk* Web. *www.simplafillsystems.co.uk Accrafill – Simplafill*

A T & T Highfield House Headless Cross Drive, Redditch B97 5EQ Tel. *01527 518181* Fax. *01527 402408* E-mail. *paul.brazier@att.com* Web. *www.att.com Rialto*

Attenborough Dental Ltd Viscosa House George Street, Nottingham NG1 3BN Tel. *0115 9473562* Fax. *0115 9509086* E-mail. *info@attenborough.com* Web. *www.attenborough.com Calibris – Megallium – Viscoform*

Attunity UK Ltd Venture House 2 Arlington Square Downshire Way, Bracknell RG12 1WA Tel. *01344 742805* Fax. *0118 9753005* Web. *www.attunity.co.uk Builder – Corvision*

B S Attwall & Co. Ltd 14-20 Cannock Street, Leicester LE4 9HR Tel. *0116 2763800* Fax. *0116 2460139* E-mail. *noni@bsattwall.com* Web. *www.bsattwall.com Honeybells*

Attwater Group Ltd Hopwood Street, Preston PR1 1UN Tel. *01772 258245* Fax. *01772 203361* E-mail. *info@attwater.com* Web. *www.attwater.com Attamat – Attamex – Attamica – Attaply – Technolaque – Technostat*

A T Wilde & Son Ltd Station Yard Station Road, Dorrington, Shrewsbury SY5 7LH Tel. *01743 718777* Fax. *01694 723945* E-mail. *enquiries@atwildeplantparts.co.uk* Web. *www.atwildeplantparts.co.uk Ammann – Atcab Copco – Ausa – Barford – Belle – Benford – Bobcat – Bomag – Briggs & Stratton – Caterpi – Clipper – Diamond Blades – Dynapac – Farymann – Filters – Generators – Hatz – Honda – Ifor Williams – Ingersoll Rand – John Deere – Kawasaki – Kohler – Komatsu – Kubota – Lister – Lombardini – Manitou – Partner – Rammax – Robin – Rubber Tracks – Ruggerini – Selwood – Sentriboxes – Starter Motors – Stihl – Takeuchi – Thwiates – Winget – Yanmar – Yanmar Excavators*

Audience Systems Ltd 19b Washington Road West Wilts Trading Estate, Westbury BA13 4JP Tel. *01373 865050* Fax. *01373 827545* E-mail. *sales@audiencesystems.com* Web. *www.audiencesystems.com Accolade – Alpha 200 – Delegate 628T – Encore 434 – Espace 628 – Sports Seat – Studio 2 – TX – Vario Stage – Zenith*

Audio Ltd Audio House Progress Road, Sands Industrial Estate, High Wycombe HP12 4JD Tel. *01494 511711* Fax. *01494 539600* E-mail. *info@audioltd.com*

Web. www.audioltd.com R.M.S. 2020 – R.M.S.2000 – *Tram (U.S.A.) – *V.T. (U.S.A.) – *VDB (France)

Audix Systems Ltd Station Road Wendens Ambo, Saffron Walden CB11 4LG Tel. 01799 540888 Fax. 01799 541618 E-mail. sales@tepg.com Web. www.tepg.com Tannoy Audix

Aurora Conservatories The Old Station Naburn, York YO19 4RW Tel. 01904 653380 Fax. 01904 610318 E-mail. info@btconnect.com Aurora Conservatories

Charles Austen Pumps Ltd Royston Road Byfleet, West Byfleet KT14 7NY Tel. 01932 355277 Fax. 01932 351285 E-mail. info@charlesausten.com Web. www.charlesausten.com Capex – Dymax

Austen Tapes Ltd Ivy Arch Road, Worthing BN14 8BX Tel. 01892 832141 Fax. 01903 205515 E-mail. sarah.gamble@austen-tapes.co.uk Web. www.austen-tapes.co.uk 3M – 3M, Stera-tape, Lohman, Advance, Tesa, Rotunda, Evode, Jiffy, Velcro, Mima films.. – Advance (United Kingdom) – Bostik – Glue Dots (United Kingdom) – Safety walk Products – Scotch – Stera (United Kingdom) – Tesa

Autobar Group Ltd East Wing 14th Floor, 389 Chiswick High Road, London W4 4AJ Tel. 020 89876500 Fax. 020 89876501 E-mail. sales@autobar.com Web. www.autobar.com Autobar – Autobar, Pelican Rouge, King, Veriplast, Cafebar, Fibracan, Mono, James Aimar, Chequen Foods – Cafebar – Chequen Foods – Fibracan – James Aimar – King – Mono – Pelican Rouge – Veriplast

Autobox Machinery Ltd Unit 15 Youngs Industrial Estate Stanbridge Road, Leighton Buzzard LU7 4QB Tel. 01525 379359 Fax. 01525 382353 E-mail. b.tabor@autobox.co.uk Web. www.autobox.co.uk Autobox – Boxmaker (United Kingdom) – HIPAK – Progluer

Autocar Electrical Equipment Company Ltd 49-51 Tiverton Street, London SE1 6NZ Tel. 020 74034334 Fax. 020 73781270 E-mail. sales@autocar-electrical.com Web. www.autocar-electrical.com Lumenition – Microdynamics

Autocraft Drivetrain Solutions Ltd (t/a Autocraft Industries UK) Syston Lane Belton, Grantham NG32 2LY Tel. 01476 581300 Fax. 01476 70589 E-mail. sharris@autocraftds.com Web. www.autocraftds.co.uk Autocraft Industries UK

Auto Imagination The Courtyard Ranmore Manor Crocknorth Road, Dorking RH5 6SX Tel. 01483 284114 Web. www.autoimagination.com Auto Imagination

Autoland Ltd Prigee House 175 Bilton Road, Perivale, Greenford UB6 7BD Tel. 020 89988866 Fax. 020 89988869 E-mail. autoland@prigee.com Web. www.prigee.com Autoland

Autologic Diagnostics Autologic House London Road, Wheatley, Oxford OX33 1JH Tel. 01865 870050 Fax. 01865 870051 E-mail. info@autologic.com Web. www.autologic-diagnostics.com Autologic

Autolok Security 52 Park Lane Royton, Oldham OL2 6PU Tel. 0161 6248171 Fax. 0161 6273742 E-mail. david.brearley@autolok.co.uk Web. www.autolock.co.uk Autolok – Autolok 2000 – Autolok Driveshield – Autolok Original – Autolok protector

Automated Cable Solutions Ltd 44 A Tylers Green Road, Swanley BR8 8LG Tel. 0845 4288919 Fax. 01322 665718 E-mail. sales@automatedcablesolutions.co.uk Web. www.automatedcablesolutions.co.uk Gamma srl – Makfil system srl – Rittmeyer – Schleuniger

Autonumis Cirencester Road, Tetbury GL8 8SA Tel. 01666 502641 Fax. 01666 504397 E-mail. info@autonumis.co.uk Web. www.autonumis.co.uk Popular – Premier

Autoproducts Lon Parcwr Industrial Estate, Ruthin LL15 1NJ Tel. 01824 707555 Fax. 01824 707560 E-mail. autoproducts@office-mail.co.uk Web. www.autoproducts.co.uk Autoproducts

Autoscript Ltd Unit 2 Heathlands Close, Twickenham TW1 4BP Tel. 020 88918900 Fax. 020 75159529 E-mail. hire@autoscript.tv Web. www.autoscript.tv Autoscript

Auto Sleepers Ltd Orchard Works Industrial Estate Willersey, Broadway WR12 7QF Tel. 01386 853338 Fax. 01386 858343 E-mail. info@auto-sleepers.co.uk Web. www.auto-sleepers.co.uk Amethyst – Auto-Sleeper – Clubman – Duetto – Dursley – Excelsiur – Executive – Flair – Gatcombe – Harmony – Legend – Medallion – Mercedes Benz – Mercedez Benz – Peugeot – Peugeot – Peugeot – Rambler – Symbol – Symphony – Topaz – Trident – Trooper – Trophy

Auto Sparks Ltd 80-88 Derby Road Sandiacre, Nottingham NG10 5HU Tel. 0115 9497211 Fax. 0115 9491955 E-mail. sales@autosparks.co.uk Web. www.autosparks.co.uk Auto-Sparks

Autospin (Oil Seals) Ltd Birkdale Avenue Selly Oak, Birmingham B29 6UB Tel. 0121 4721243 Fax. 0121 4713348 E-mail. sales@autospin.co.uk Web. www.autospin.co.uk Autospin

Auto Trail V R Ltd Trigano House Genesis Way, Grimsby DN37 9TU Tel. 01472 571000 Fax. 01472 571001 E-mail. sales@auto-trail.co.uk Web. www.auto-trail.co.uk Auto Trail – Vanroyce

Auto Windscreens 112-116 Electric Avenue, Birmingham B6 7EB Tel. 0121 3222455 Fax. 0121 3222108 Web. www.racautowindscreens.co.uk Birmingham Safety Glass

Autron Products Ltd 17 Second Avenue, Halstead CO9 2SU Tel. 01787 473964 Fax. 01787 474061 E-mail. sales@autron.co.uk Web. www.autron.co.uk Euroline – Seri-Touch – Slenderline – Sovereign – Sterling – Suface Clean Radiators

A V A Ltd Unit 1 Monkton Park, Farnham GU9 9PA Tel. 01252 733040 Fax. 01252 722958 E-mail. srpentony@avamountings.co.uk Web. www.ava-antivibrationmountings.co.uk A.V.A.

Avalon and Lynwood P.O. Box 608, Altrincham WA15 7ZP Tel. 0161 9048642 E-mail. sales@avalonandlynwood.com Web. www.avalonandlynwood.com Avalon and Lynwood – Brand – Cat – Childrens hi-viz – Childrens hi-viz vests/tabards – Childrens high visibility – Childrens high visibility vests/tabards – Click Footwear – De Walt – Denny's – Denny's aprons – Denny's catering clothing – Denny's chef jackets – Denny's chefs clothing – Denny's chefs whites – Denny's scull caps – Dickies – Dri – Far Ridge – Fruit of the Loom – Gildan – Hen doo printed t shirts – Hen doo t shirts – Hen night printed t shirts – Hen night t shirts – Hi vis – Hi-viz – Kids hi-viz – Kids hi-viz vests/tabards – Kids high visibility – Kids high visibility vests/tabards – Ppe – Promotional t shirts – Seen – Stag doo printed t shirts – Stag doo t shirts – Stag night printed t shirts – Stag night t shirts

Avalon Plastics Ltd Morland Road Morlands Enterprise Park, Glastonbury BA6 9FZ Tel. 08703 891998 Fax. 01458 834384 E-mail. enquiries@avalonplastics.co.uk Web. www.avalonplastics.co.uk Imco

Avalon P R Ltd 4a Exmoor Street, London W10 6BD Tel. 020 75987222 Fax. 020 75987223 E-mail. enquiries@avalonuk.com Web. www.avalonuk.com Avalon – Avalon Management Group Ltd – Avalon Press & Publicity – Avalon Television Ltd

Avdel UK Ltd 2 Swiftfields Watchmead Industrial Estate, Welwyn Garden City AL7 1LY Tel. 01707 292000 Fax. 01707 292199 E-mail. salesavdel@acument.com Web. www.avdel-global.com Avbolt – Avdel - Avdelok - Avex - Avibulb - Avinox - Avbolt - Avlug - Avmatic - Avseal - Briv - Bulbex - Chobert - Grovit - Hemlok - Hydra - Jo-Bolt - Jo-Lok - Maxlok - M B C - Monobolt - Stavex - Nutsert - Pip Pin - T-Lok - Rivscrew - TX2000 - Hexsert - Klamptite – Avdel SR – Avdelok – Avex – Avibulb – Avinox – Avlug – Avmatic – Avseal – Avsert – Avtainer – Avtronic – Briv – Bulbex – Chobert – Grovit – Hemlok – Hexsert – Hydra – Jo-Bolt – Jo-Lok – KTR – Large Flange Nutsert – M B C – Maxlok – Monobolt – Nutsert (Standard) – Pip Pin – Rivmatic – Rivscrew – Squaresert – Stavex – Supersert – T-Lok – Thin Sheet Nutsert – TX2000 – Viking 360

Avenance Central House Balfour Road, Hounslow TW3 1HY Tel. 08450 300100 Fax. 020 85694069 E-mail. info@elior.co.uk Web. www.avenance.co.uk High Table – T. J.'S

Avercet Hardware Ltd Brookfoot Mills Elland Road, Brookfoot, Brighouse HD6 2RW Tel. 01484 711700 Fax. 01484 720124 E-mail. post@avocet-hardware.co.uk Web. www.avercet-hardware.co.uk Avocet Hardware (Pacific Rim)

Avery Dennison 7 Astra Centre Edinburgh Way, Harlow CM20 2BN Tel. 01279 786000 Fax. 01279 786100 E-mail. declan.quinn@eu.avery.dennison.com Web. www.monarch.averydennison.com Barcode – Barcoder – FreshMarx – Label Applicators – Label printer – Monarch – Pathfinder Ultra - the world's first data collector/ scanner / printer, Platform label design software, and the new 9800 series of tabletop bar code printers, Monarch - Marking Systems.Easy Loader - Hand held labelling systemsFreshMarx - labelling, date coding for the catering industry – Pricing Guns – Terminal - Scanners

Aveva Solutions Ltd High Cross Madingley Road, Cambridge CB3 0HB Tel. 01223 556655 Fax. 01223 556666 E-mail. info@aveva.com Web. www.aveva.com PDMS – PEGS – REVIEW

Avilion Unit 1 Gateway Xiii Industrial Estate Ferry Lane, Rainham RM13 9JY Tel. 01708 526361 Fax. 01708 550220 E-mail. steve.cole@avilion.co.uk Web. www.perrinandrowe.com Atriflo – Perrin & Rowe – Triflow

Aviza Technology UK Ltd Ringland Way, Newport NP18 2TA Tel. 01633 414000 Fax. 01633 414141 E-mail. sales@trikon.com Web. www.avizatechnology.com Advanced Hi-Fill (United Kingdom) – C^3M (United Kingdom) – DSi (United Kingdom) – Flowfill and low-k Flowfill (United Kingdom) – MORI (United Kingdom) – Omega 201 and fxP (United Kingdom) – ORION (United Kingdom) – Planar fxP and 300 (United Kingdom) – Sigma fxP (United Kingdom) – Trikon (United Kingdom)

A V M Ltd 6 Hawley Lane Industrial Estate Hawley Lane, Farnborough GU14 8EH Tel. 01252 510363 Fax. 01252 519874 E-mail. sales@avmltd.co.uk Web. www.avmltd.co.uk *Altinex (U.S.A.) – *Communications Specialities (U.S.A.) – *Draper (U.S.A.) – *Nordisk (Denmark) – *Optia (Germany)

Avon Impact Management Hampton Park West Semington Rd, Melksham SN12 6NB Tel. 01225 896421 Fax. 01225 896301 E-mail. sales@avon-impact.com Web. www.avon-impact.com Avon Impact Management

Avon Inflatables Ltd Dafen, Llanelli SA14 8NA Tel. 01554 882000 Fax. 01554 882039 E-mail. alan.morgan@zmp-zodiac.com Web. www.avoninflatables.co.uk Adventure – Redcrest – Redstart – Rollaway – Rover – Rover Ribs – Searider – Seasport De Luxe – Seasport Jet – Supersport

A V R Group Ltd (t/a National Monitoring) 16-24 Attenburys Park Estate Attenburys Lane, Timperley, Altrincham WA14 5QE Tel. 0161 9059998 Fax. 0161 9059988 E-mail. info@sonicalarm.com Web. www.sonicalarm.com Firecall – National Monitoring

Avventura 18 Lindfield Road, London W5 1QR Tel. 020 88108020 Fax. 020 89975353 E-mail. avventura@btconnect.com Web. www.avventura.co.uk Avventura

Awg plc Anglian House Ambury Road, Huntingdon PE29 3NZ Tel. 01480 323000 Fax. 01480 323115 Web. www.anglianwater.co.uk A.W.G

AWI Ltd AWI Ltd Cothey Way, Ryde PO33 1QT Tel. 01983 817220 Fax. 01983 616295 E-mail. paulw@awilmicrowaves.com Web. www.awilmicrowaves.com A.W.I.

Awltech Plastic Fabrication Sales Ltd 4 The Omni Business Centre Omega Park, Alton GU34 2QD Tel. 01420 525222 Fax. 01420 525226 E-mail. info@awltech.co.uk Web. www.awltech.co.uk Bermaq – Shannon

Axa Assistance UK Ltd 106-118 Station Road, Redhill RH1 1PR Tel. 08706 090023 Fax. 0870 6090024 E-mail. bob.ewers@axa-assistance.co.uk Web. www.axa-assistance.co.uk Inter Partner Assistance

Axair Fans UK Ltd Lowfield Drive Centre 500, Wolstanton, Newcastle ST5 0UU Tel. 01782 349430 Fax. 01782 349439 E-mail. grant.edwards@axair-fans.co.uk Web. www.axair-fans.co.uk Axair

Axetec Guitar Pickups & Parts Heath Close, Kendal LA9 5BW Tel. 01539 755015 E-mail. info@axetec.co.uk Web. www.axetec.co.uk IronGear Pickups

Axflow Orion Park Northfield Avenue, London W13 9SJ Tel. 020 85792111 Fax. 020 85797326 E-mail. info@axflow.co.uk Web. www.axflow.co.uk Almatec – Almatec - Wilden - Waukesha - Blackmer - Borger - Pulsafeeder - Mono - Zenith - ECO - Mouvex - Isochem - Coppus - AxFlow - Hermetic - Wernert - Bungartz - Burton Corblin - Tuthill - Lawrence - Slack & Parr - Carver - Eclipse - Apex – Axflow – Blackmer – Borger – Bungartz – Burton Corblin – Carver – Coppus – ECO – Hermetic – Isochem – Lawrence – Mono – Mouvex – Pulsafeeder – Slack & Parr – Tuthill – Tuthill Energy Systems – Waukesha – Wernert – Wilden – Zenith

Axis Shield Ltd Luna Place Dundee Technology Park, Dundee DD2 1XA Tel. 01382 422000 Fax. 01382 422088 E-mail. paul.henrickson@axis-shielduk.com Web. www.axis-shielduk.com Diastat – Quantase – Uristat

Axminster Carpets Ltd Woodmead Road, Axminster EX13 5PQ Tel. 01297 32244 Fax. 01297 35241 E-mail. sales@axminster-carpets.co.uk Web. www.axminster-carpets.co.uk Branscombe – Dartmoor – Exeter – Exmoor – Royal Axminster – Royal Clovelly – Royal Dartmouth – Royal Seaton – Salcombe – Shaldon – Super Dartmoor – Tamar – Torbay

Axon Enterprises Ltd 8a St Martins Street, Hereford HR2 7RE Tel. 01432 359906 Fax. 01432 352436 E-mail. sales@axon-enterprises.co.uk Web. www.axon-enterprises.co.uk Convotherm – Falcon – Garland – Victor – Viscount

Axo Shredders Ltd Unit 11 Kenneth Way Wilstead, Bedford MK45 3PD Tel. 01234 742400 Fax. 01234 742401 E-mail. uk@axo.cc Web. www.axo.cc AXO Shredders Ltd

Axter Ltd Unit 3 West Road Ransomes Europark, Ipswich IP3 9SX Tel. 01473 724056 Fax. 01473 232118 E-mail. info@axterltd.co.uk Web. www.axter.co.uk *Arma (France) – *Axtep (France) – *Excel (France) – *Excelflex (France) – *Hydome (France) – *Hyranger (France) – Hytherm

Aynsley China Ltd Sutherland Road, Stoke On Trent ST3 1HZ Tel. 01782 339400 Fax. 01782 339401 E-mail. admin@aynsley.co.uk Web. www.aynsley.co.uk Aynsley – Hammersley

Mike Ayres Design Ltd Unit 8 Shepherds Grove, Stanton, Bury St Edmunds IP31 2AR Tel. 01359 251551 Fax. 01359 251707 E-mail. enquiries@mikeayresdesign.co.uk Web. www.mikeayresdesign.co.uk Loopies (United Kingdom) – Sensearound (United Kingdom) – Sensory Studio (United Kingdom) – Sound Beam Trolley (United Kingdom) – Trolley (United Kingdom) – Tactile Murals (United Kingdom) – Switch4 (United Kingdom)

AZCARPARTS UK 2A DEWSBURY ROAD WESTGATE WAKEFIELD WF2 9BS 2A DEWSBURY ROAD, WESTGATE, Wakefield WF2 9BS Tel. 01924 369000 Fax. 01924 298625 E-mail. azar@azcarparts.vo.uk Web. WWW.AZCARPARTS.CO.UK EBC , MINTEX, FIRSTLINE

Azizoff Co. Ltd 2 Beechfield Road, London N4 1PE Tel. 020 88096902 Fax. 020 88005795 E-mail. azizoffco@tiscali.net Azizoff

Aziz Sharpquips 139 St Edmunds Road, London N9 7PS Tel. *020 82112400* Fax. *020 83283507* E-mail. *ashikaziz@hotmail.co.uk* Web. *www.sharpquips.co.uk Aziz Sharpquips*

Aztech Components Ltd 78 Atcham Close Winyates East, Redditch B98 0NZ Tel. *01527 500151* Fax. *01527 500151* E-mail. *sales@aztech.uk.net* Web. *www.aztech.uk.net Anwest Iwata – Balluff – Camozzi – CANUSA – Dopag – Hawe – IFM – Joucomatic – Keyence – Kinetrol Actuators – Kremlin – KV – Martonair – Mead – Mijno – Norgren – Parker – Pomtava – Proxistor – SMC – Wade – Zenith*

B

B 2 B International Ltd 14 Ack Lane East Bramhall, Stockport SK7 2BY Tel. *0161 4406000* Fax. *0161 4406006* E-mail. *info@b2binternational.com* Web. *www.b2binternational.com B2B International (United Kingdom) – B2B International (United Kingdom)*

B3 Cable Solutions Delaunays Road, Manchester M9 8FP Tel. *0161 7409151* Fax. *0161 7958393* E-mail. *info@b3cables.com* Web. *www.b3cables.com Belden Communications*

Babcock Wanson UK Ltd 7 Elstree Way, Borehamwood WD6 1SA Tel. *020 89537111* Fax. *020 82075177* E-mail. *info@babcock-wanson.co.uk* Web. *www.babcock-wanson.co.uk Eurosteam – Extrac – H.T.V. – Incinex – SOV – Steambloc – Supersteam Vur – Thermal Oxidiser – Thermobloc – THERMOMISER/WTM – Thermopac – TPC – Vaporax – VPX – WMP – WUH*

B A C Corrosion Control Ltd Unit C10-C11 Stafford Park 11, Telford TF3 3AY Tel. *01952 208500* Fax. *01952 290325* E-mail. *sales@bacgroup.com* Web. *www.bacgroup.com *Brazing (USA and Scandinavia) – *Global (USA and Scandinavia) – LATreat – *Pin (USA and Scandinavia) – Pinbrazing – *Surveyor (USA and Scandinavia)*

Backer Electric Co. Ltd Fitzwilliam Road Eastwood Trading Estate, Rotherham S65 1TE Tel. *01709 828292* Fax. *01709 828388* E-mail. *finance@backer.co.uk* Web. *www.backerelectric.com Backer*

Bacup Shoe Co. Ltd Atherton Holme Mill Railway Street, Bacup OL13 0UF Tel. *01706 873304* Fax. *01706 873216* E-mail. *stevensmith@bacupshoe.co.uk* Web. *www.bacupshoe.co.uk Distinctive Casuals – Distinctive Slippers – Natureform – Sloppy Slipper*

Badcock & Evered Washford Mill Washford, Watchet TA23 0JY Tel. *01984 640412* Fax. *01984 640160* E-mail. *enquiries@badcockevered.co.uk *Animal Health – *B.O.C.M. Pauls – *Baileys – *Dodson & Horrell*

Scott Bader Co. Ltd Wollaston Hall Wollaston, Wellingborough NN29 7RL Tel. *01933 663100* Fax. *01933 663028* E-mail. *info@scottbader.com* Web. *www.scottbader.com Crestomer – Crystic – Crystic - unsaturated polyester resins, gelcoats and Strand related products Crystic Fireguard - intumescent fire retardant coating Crystic Impreg - low pressure sheet moulding compounds Crystic - pigment pastes Crestomer - urethane acrylate resins Crystic Envirotec - low styrene content resins and gelcoats. Polidene - vinylidene chloride copolymer emulsions Sobral - alkyds and epoxy esters Texicote - polyester powder coatings and PVA emulsions Texicryl - acrylic and styrene-acrylate emulsions (Texicryl is known in North America as Texigel) Texigel - water soluble polyacrylate thickeners Texipol - inverse emulsions – Crystic Envirotec – Crystic Fireguard – Crystic Impreg – Crystic Protec – Polidene – Sobral – Texicote – Texicryl – Texigel – Texipol*

B A E Systems Ltd (Environmental & E M C Test Centre) Airport Works, Rochester ME1 2XX Tel. *01634 844400* Fax. *01634 203647* E-mail. *frank.ewen@baesystems.com* Web. *www.baesystems.com Cats Eyes – Lapads – Orion*

Bailcast Ltd Unit 8 Chorley North Industrial Pk, Chorley PR6 7BX Tel. *01257 266060* Fax. *01257 261034* E-mail. *enquiry@bailcast.com* Web. *www.bailcast.com Duraboot (United Kingdom) – Duragun – Maxiboot (United Kingdom) – Stickyboot (United Kingdom) – UNIBOOT – Stepsure (United Kingdom)*

Bailey Of Bristol South Liberty Lane, Bristol BS3 2SS Tel. *0117 9665967* Fax. *0117 9636554* E-mail. *sales@bailey-caravans.co.uk* Web. *www.bailey-caravans.co.uk Pageant Range – Ranger – Regency – Senator Range*

Bailey Morris Ltd Little End Road Eaton Socon, St Neots PE19 8GE Tel. *01480 216250* Fax. *01480 403045* E-mail. *sales@baileymorris.co.uk* Web. *www.baileymorris.co.uk A.K. Kardan – DAF – E.D.S – ELBE – FORD – GEWES – GKN – GWB – IVECO – KEMPF – KLEIN GELENKWELLEN – KUSEL – LEYLAND – MAN TRUCKS – MERCEDES BENZ – RENAULT – SCANIA – SPICER – TIRSAN – VOITH – VOLVO – VW*

Bainbridge Aqua-Marine Unit 8 Flanders Industrial Park Flanders Road Hedge End, Southampton SO30 2FZ Tel. *01489 776000* Fax. *01489 776005* E-mail. *info@bainbridgeint.co.uk* Web. *www.bainbridgemarine.co.uk Aquabatten – Bainbridge – Cover Guard – Sailman*

C.O.H. Baines Ltd Rubber Extrusions Unit 3 Buckingham House Longfield Road, Tunbridge Wells TN2 3EY Tel. *01892 543311* Fax. *01892 530682* E-mail. *sales@coh-baines.co.uk* Web. *www.coh-baines.co.uk C.O.H. Baines*

Baker & Finnemore Ltd 199 Newhall Street, Birmingham B3 1SN Tel. *0121 2362347* Fax. *0121 2367224* E-mail. *sales@bakfin.com* Web. *www.bakfin.com Bak-Fin – Starlock*

Baker Hughes Barclayhill Place Portlethen, Aberdeen AB12 4PF Tel. *01224 408000* Fax. *01224 408001* E-mail. *ian.gellie@bakerhughes.com* Web. *www.bakerhughes.com Baker Hughes Inteq*

Baker Hughes Woodside Road Bridge Of Don Industrial Estate, Aberdeen AB23 8BW Tel. *01224 223000* Fax. *01224 824015* E-mail. *info@bakerhughes.com* Web. *www.bakerhughes.com Baker Oil Tools*

Ted Baker plc The Glasshouse Princes Square 48 Buchanan Street, Glasgow G1 3JN Tel. *0141 2219664* Fax. *0141 2213544* Web. *www.tedbaker.com Ted*

Baldor UK Mint Motion Centre Unit 6 Bristol Distribution Park Hawkley Drive, Bradley Stoke, Bristol BS32 0BF Tel. *01454 850000* Fax. *01454 859002* E-mail. *sales.uk@baldor.com* Web. *www.baldor.com API 547 – BSM C-Series – BSM N-Series – BSM R-Series – D-Flex – Dodge – EuroFlex – Flex+Drive – FlexDrive – Grid-Line – Grip Tight – HFO – HyCore – ISN – Liberator – LMCF – LMDS – LMIC – LMSS – MagnaGear XTR – Maxum – Metric-E – MicroFlex – MicroFlex e100 – Mint – Mint - MintDrive - FlexDrive - Flex+Drive - MicroFlex - EuroFlex - NextMove PCI - NextMove ESB - NextMove ES - NextMove ST - NextMove BX - NextMove PC - SmartMove - Super-E - Metric-E - VersaFlex - SmartMotor - HyCore – MintDrive – Motiflex – MotiFlex e100 – NextMove BX – NextMove ES – NextMove ESB – NextMove PC – NextMove PCI – NextMove ST – PARA-FLEX – Poly-Disc – QUANTIS – Reliance – RPM – SmartMotor – SmartMove – Super-E – TIGEAR – TORQUE-ARM II – V*S Drives – VersaFlex – VS1 GV – VS1 MX – VS1 PF – VS1 PM – VS1 ST*

Bales Worldwide Ltd Bales House Junction Road, Dorking RH4 3HL Tel. *01306 732732* Fax. *01306 740048* E-mail. *enquiries@balesworldwide.com* Web. *www.balesworldwide.com Bales*

Balfour Beatty Living Places Balfour Beatty Group Pavilion B Ashwood Park Ashwood Way, Basingstoke RG23 8BG Tel. *01256 400400* Fax. *01256 400401* E-mail. *foundations@stent.co.uk* Web. *www.bblivingplaces.com Candy Pile – Hercules Piling – Hercules Piling System – Sappar – Siris – Stentwall*

Balguard Engineering Ltd Unit 8 Cherrycourt Way, Leighton Buzzard LU7 4UH Tel. *01525 373673* Fax. *01525 850287* E-mail. *steve.l@balguard.co.uk* Web. *www.balguard.co.uk Balguard*

David Ball Group plc Huntingdon Road Bar Hill, Cambridge CB23 8HN Tel. *01954 780687* Fax. *01954 782912* E-mail. *sales@pudlo.com* Web. *www.pudlo.com Instacem – Instamac – Instapruf – Instaset – Instasupascreed – Onx Range – Pudlo*

F Ball & Co. Ltd Churnetside Business Park Station Road, Cheddleton, Leek ST13 7RS Tel. *01538 361633* Fax. *01538 361622* E-mail. *mail@f-ball.co.uk* Web. *www.f-ball.co.uk Astral – Coat-A-Sole – Gozin – Gripso – Gripsotex – Gripsotite – Kulorub – Kumzof – Sentry – Stopgap – Styccobond – Styccoclean – Styccoscreed – Styccoseal*

Balluff Ltd 4 Oakwater Avenue Cheadle Royal Business Park, Cheadle SK8 3SR Tel. *0161 2824740* Fax. *0161 4365951* E-mail. *sales@balluff.co.uk* Web. *www.balluff.co.uk Balluff – Multiswitch*

Ball & Young Division Of Vitafoan Ltd (a division of Vitafoam Ltd) 53 Causeway Road Earlstrees Industrial Estate, Corby NN17 4DU Tel. *01536 200502* Fax. *01536 269554* E-mail. *sales@underlay.com* Web. *www.underlay.com Cloud 9 – Marine Underlays*

Bally UK Sales Ltd 116 New Bond Street, London W1S 1EN Tel. *020 74917062* Fax. *020 74089888* E-mail. *lhills@bally.ch* Web. *www.bally.com Bally – Bally Leather Jackets*

Balsham Buildings Ltd 7 High Street Balsham, Cambridge CB21 4DJ Tel. *01223 894404* Fax. *01223 892818* Web. *www.balsham.uk.com Balsham*

Baltec UK Ltd Danehill Lower Earley, Reading RG6 4UT Tel. *0118 9311191* Fax. *0118 9311103* E-mail. *design@baltecuk.com* Web. *www.baltecuk.com Baltec Electro Press – Baltec FPS – Baltec Presses – Baltec Radial Riveting Machines – Deprag – Doga – Fuji – Quicher*

Bambi Air Compressors Ltd 152 Thimble Mill Lane, Birmingham B7 5HT Tel. *0121 3222299* Fax. *0121 3222297* E-mail. *sales@bambi-air.co.uk* Web. *www.bambi-air.co.uk Apollo – Bambi*

Bancroft & Co. Unit 5 Bolney Grange Industrial Park Bolney, Haywards Heath RH17 5PB Tel. *01444 248884* Fax. *01444 242767* E-mail. *sales@bancroft.co.uk* Web. *www.bancroft.co.uk Buehler (Germany) – Buhler (Germany) – Galiso (U.S.A.) – L Ronning (Sweden)*

Bandai UK Ltd Jellicoe House Grange Drive, Hedge End, Southampton SO30 2AF Tel. *01489 790944* Fax. *01489 790643* E-mail. *info@bandai.co.uk* Web. *www.bandai.co.uk *Power Rangers (Far East) – *Sega Lock-On (China) – *Startrek (Far East)*

Band-It Co. Ltd Telford Crescent Speedwell Industrial Estate, Staveley, Chesterfield S43 3PF Tel. *01246 477333* Fax. *01246 476324* E-mail. *jbowmer@idexcorp.com* Web. *www.band-it-idex.eu Ball-Lok – Band-It – Easy Scale – Tie-Dex – Tie-Lok – Ultra-Lok*

Banfield Refrigeration Supplies Ltd 6 Wycombe Industrial Mall West End Street, High Wycombe HP11 2QY Tel. *01494 473330* Fax. *01494 473057* E-mail. *sales@banfield-refrigeration.com* Web. *www.banfield-refrigeration.com York – Vaillant – Marstair*

Banico Ltd Tilson Road Roundthorn Industrial Estate, Manchester M23 9GF Tel. *08451 700740* Fax. *0845 1700750* E-mail. *info@banico.co.uk* Web. *www.banico.co.uk Fantini Cosmi – Intellitherm – MUT – Sicurgas – Waircom*

The Bankers' Almanac Reed Business Information Windsor Court East Grinstead House, East Grinstead RH19 1XA Tel. *01342 326972* Fax. *01342 335612* E-mail. *information@reedinfo.co.uk* Web. *www.bankersalmanac.com Bankers' Almanac World Ranking, The – Bankers' Almanac, The – Bankers' Almanc.com (BANKERSalmanac.com) – Kellysearch.co.uk – Kemps Film Television and Commercial Production Services Handbook – Kompass Direct – Kompass Industrial Trade Names – Kompass International Editions – Kompass Register CD – Sorting Code Numbers Electronic – U.K. Kompass Register – UK Clearings Directory*

Banks Amenity Products Ltd 4 The Point, Market Harborough LE16 7QU Tel. *01858 464346* Fax. *01858 434734* E-mail. *sales@banksamenity.co.uk* Web. *www.banksamenity.co.uk Fendress – Fendress Greentop*

J W E Banks Ltd St Guthlacs Lodge Crowland, Peterborough PE6 0JP Tel. *01733 210123* Fax. *01733 210920 *Koni (Netherlands)*

Banner Ltd Banner House Greg Street, Stockport SK5 7BT Tel. *0161 4748000* Fax. *0161 4747655* E-mail. *nigel.plenderleith@bannergroup.co.uk* Web. *www.bannergroup.co.uk Banner – Coco Childrenswear – Debretta – Niconico – Pegasus – Serious Stuff Clothing – Shirtmaster*

Banner Chemicals Ltd Hampton Court Manor Park, Runcorn WA7 1TU Tel. *01928 597000* Fax. *01928 597001* E-mail. *reception@bannerchemicals.com* Web. *www.bannerchemicals.com B.A.S.*

John Banner Lydes Road, Malvern WR14 2BY Tel. *01684 569285* Fax. *01684 568946* E-mail. *jbworcs@hotmail.com G-Ban – Globe-King – GuJiBA – John Banner – Johnsons Radio – Jonrad*

Banner Plant Ltd Callywhite Lane, Dronfield S18 2XS Tel. *01246 299400* Fax. *01246 290253* E-mail. *dronfield@bannerplant.co.uk* Web. *www.bannerplant.co.uk Banner Scafolding*

Bannons 71 North Street, Belfast BT1 1NB Tel. *028 90329335* Fax. *028 90235152* E-mail. *tony.bannons@ukgateway.net* Web. *www.bannons.com Bannons Ltd – Lagan Finance*

Banson Tool Hire Ltd East Mount 125 Pellon Lane, Halifax HX1 5QN Tel. *01422 254999* Fax. *01422 254778* E-mail. *sales@banson.uk.com* Web. *www.banson.uk.com Banson Tool Hire*

Barber Pumps Ltd Jacksons Yard Douglas Road North, Fulwood, Preston PR2 3QH Tel. *01772 715502* Fax. *01772 712716* E-mail. *s.barber@barberpumps.co.uk* Web. *www.barberpumps.co.uk ARMSTRONG – BREFCO – *EBARA – *ESPA – GOULDS/LOWARA – *PEDROLLO – *TT PUMPS*

Barber Wilson & Company Ltd Crawley Road, London N22 6AH Tel. *020 88883461* Fax. *020 88882041* E-mail. *sales@barwil.co.uk* Web. *www.barwil.co.uk 1890's – Barwil – Mastercraft – Regent*

Barbour - A B I Hinderson Point, Ellesmere Port CH65 9HQ Tel. *0151 3533500* Fax. *0151 3533637* E-mail. *info@barbour-abi.com* Web. *www.barbour-abi.com Barbour ABI*

J Barbour & Sons Ltd Simonside, South Shields NE34 9PD Tel. *0191 4554444* Fax. *0191 4542944* E-mail. *info@barbour.com* Web. *www.barbour.com Barbour – Barbour Thornproof – Beacon – Beaufort – Bedale – Border – Burghley – Durham – Gamefair – Longshoreman – Moorland – Northumbria – Solway Zipper – Spey – Westmorland*

Barcodemania.Com Ver House London Road, Markyate, St Albans AL3 8JP Tel. *08455 085608* Fax. *0845 3370260* E-mail. *sales@barcodemania.com* Web. *www.barcodemania.com Datalogic – Symbol*

Barconwood Ltd Unit 2a Woolpit Business Park Windmill Avenue, Woolpit, Bury St Edmunds IP30 9UP Tel. *01359 242490* Fax. *01359 242468* E-mail. *sales@barconwood.co.uk* Web. *www.barconwood.co.uk Blackboard Plus – Slide-A-Sign – Street Talkers – Whiteboard Plus – Write'n'Light – Write-in-Light*

Barcrest Group Margaret Street, Ashton Under Lyne OL7 0QQ Tel. *0161 3441000* Fax. *0161 3082580* E-mail. *info@barcrestgroup.com* Web. *www.barcrestgroup.com Auditor – D.P. Compak – Data Pak – Incompak – Masterpoint*

Bard Ltd Forest House Brighton Road, Crawley RH11 9BP Tel. *01293 527888* Fax. *01293 552428* E-mail. *customer.services@crbard.com* Web. *www.crbard.com Bard – Bardia – Biocath – Biopty – Davol – Groshong – Hickman – Integrity – Monopty – Reliacath – Sauvage – Urimeter – Uriplan – Urospec*

Barden Corporation (UK) Limited Plymbridge Rd Estover, Plymouth PL6 7LH Tel. *01752 735555* Fax. *01752 733481* E-mail. *bardenbearings@schaeffler.com* Web. *www.bardenbearings.co.uk Barden*

Bardon Concrete Ltd Unit 7 Robert Way, Wickford SS11 8DD Tel. *01268 769696* Fax. *01268 769097* Web. *www.bardonconcrete.co.uk Bradwell Aggregates – Karrimix*

Bardyke Chemicals Ltd Hamilton Road Cambuslang, Glasgow G72 7XL Tel. *01698 823361* Fax. *01698 820535* E-mail. *sales@bardyke.com* Web. *www.bardyke.com Bardyke*

Barkair Ltd Auckland House 66 Kingsway, Bishop Auckland DL14 7JF Tel. *01388 607874* Fax. *01388 603050* E-mail. *paulbarker@barkair.co.uk* Web. *www.barkair.co.uk Ciat – BMM – Rittal – Waterloo*

Barker Shoes Station Road Earls Barton, Northampton NN6 0NT Tel. *01604 810387* Fax. *01604 812350* E-mail. *akalsi@btinternet.com* Web. *www.barker-shoes.co.uk Barker Shoes*

Barkston Plastics Engineering Ltd 221 Pontefract Lane, Leeds LS9 0DX Tel. *0113 2492200* Fax. *01942 842844* E-mail. *jenny.duxbury@barkstonltd.co.uk* Web. *www.barkstonltd.co.uk Polypenco*

Barloworld Handling C M S Lift Trucks Ltd 9 Michelin Road, Newtownabbey BT36 4PT Tel. *028 90842537* Fax. *028 90842947* E-mail. *info@handling.barloworld.co.uk* Web. *www.barloworld.co.uk Baumann Side Loaders*

E W Barnard Ltd 14 Alfreton Road, Sutton In Ashfield NG17 1FW Tel. *01623 555527* Fax. *01623 443781* E-mail. *r.barnard@btconnect.com* Web. *www.barnard-confectionery.co.uk Barnard*

Barnet Service & Tuning Centre 1 Motorway Margaret Road, Barnet EN4 8DW Tel. *020 84416667* Fax. *020 84417516* E-mail. *bstc@scimitarmotorservices.co.uk* Web. *www.scimitarmotorservices.co.uk Scimitar Motor Services PLC*

Barnett The Factory 61 Haliburton Road, Twickenham TW1 1PD Tel. *020 88910067* Fax. *020 88910067* E-mail. *peter_barnett@hotmail.com* Web. *www.barnettmanufacturing.co.uk Barnett – Boxer Boxer – Boxer Briefs – Shirts*

Grant Barnett & Co. Ltd Waterfront House 55 South Street, Bishops Stortford CM23 3AL Tel. *01279 758075* Fax. *01279 758095* E-mail. *enquiries@grantbarnett.com* Web. *www.grantbarnett.com Grant Barnett*

Barnetts Confectioners Ltd Stansfield Street, Nottingham NG7 2AE Tel. *0115 9784642* Fax. *0115 9449236* E-mail. *sales@barnettconfectioners.co.uk* Web. *www.barnettconfectioners.co.uk Mitre – Uncle Lukes*

Dennis Barnfield Ltd Lodge Quarry, Carnforth LA5 9DW Tel. *01524 733422* Fax. *01524 736450* E-mail. *info@dennisbarnfield.co.uk* Web. *www.dennisbarnfield.co.uk *Barford – *Case – Kubota – *Merlo*

J Barnsley Cranes Ltd Unit 1 The Wallows Indl-Est Wallows Road, Brierley Hill DY5 1QB Tel. *01384 484811* Fax. *01384 484333* E-mail. *sales@jbarnsleycranes.com* Web. *www.jbarnsleycranes.com Apex Cranes*

Barron Warren & Redfern 19 South End, London W8 5BU Tel. *020 79370294* Fax. *020 79374786* E-mail. *patags@baron-warren.co.uk* Web. *www.bwr-ip.co.uk Baron & Warren*

Barr & Grosvenor Ltd Jenner Street, Wolverhampton WV2 2AE Tel. *01902 352390* Fax. *01902 871342* E-mail. *sales@bargrosvenorwannado.co.uk* Web. *www.barrandgrosvenor.wanadoo.co.uk Viking*

Barrie Knitwear Burnfoot Industrial Estate, Hawick TD9 8RJ Tel. *01450 365500* Fax. *01450 365501* E-mail. *enquiries@barrie.co.uk* Web. *www.barrie.co.uk Barrie*

Barr Mason Ltd 10 Greycaine Road, Watford WD24 7GG Tel. *01923 212400* Fax. *01923 817024* E-mail. *sales@barrmason.co.uk* Web. *www.barr-mason.co.uk Tuffa Bobbin*

Barr Wray Ltd 324 Drumoyne Road, Glasgow G51 4DY Tel. *0141 8825757* Fax. *0141 8823690* E-mail. *sales@barrandwray.com* Web. *www.barrandwray.com Flowpac – Seamaker*

Barry M Cosmetics Unit 1 Bittacy Business Centre Bittacy Hill, London NW7 1BA Tel. *020 83492992* Fax. *020 83467773* E-mail. *info@barrym.co.uk* Web. *www.barrym.com Barry M*

Bartington Instruments Ltd 5 Thorney Leys Business Park, Witney OX28 4GE Tel. *01993 706565* Fax. *01993 774813* E-mail. *tessa.evans@bartington.com* Web. *www.bartington.com BSS02A – Grd-03-12 – MAG01/MAG01H – MAG01H – MAG03MC/MAG03MS – MAG03MSS – MAG03RC – MS2*

B C Barton & Son Ltd 1 Hainge Road Tividale, Oldbury B69 2NR Tel. *0121 5572272* Fax. *0121 5572276* E-mail. *website@bcbarton.co.uk* Web. *www.bcbarton.co.uk B.C. Barton*

Barton Storage Systems Ltd Mount Pleasant, Bilston WV14 7NG Tel. *01902 499500* Fax. *01902 353098* E-mail. *enquiries@bartonstorage.com* Web. *www.barton-storage-systems.co.uk Bartrak – Bartspan – Quickshelf – Safestore – Topmesh – Toprax – Topstore*

Barton Willmore LLP Beansheaf Farm House Bourne Close, Calcot, Reading RG31 7BW Tel. *0118 9430000* Fax. *0118 9430001* E-mail. *duncan.west@bartonwillmore.co.uk* Web. *www.bartonwillmore.co.uk Barton Willmore Partnership*

B A S Components Ltd Unit 9 Sevenoaks Business Centre Cramptons Road, Sevenoaks TN14 5DQ Tel. *01732 775820* Fax. *01732 775821* E-mail. *lroberts@bas-components.co.uk* Web. *www.bas-components.co.uk *A.V.K. Industrial Products (U.S.A.) – Deltight – Flangeform – System Zero – Torqair – Torqlok*

Base Design Ltd Bigods Hall Bigods Lane, Dunmow CM6 3BE Tel. *01371 876479* E-mail. *mark@base-design.co.uk* Web. *base-design.co.uk BAse Design*

Baselayer Ltd 11 Derry Downs, Orpington BR5 4DT Tel. *01689 603675* E-mail. *baselayer@newerainternet.com* Web. *www.baselayer.co.uk Under Armour Cold Gear – Under Armour Heat Gear – Under Armour Allseason Gear – Odlo*

Baselica Ltd (t/a Fine Italian Foods) 3 Somers Place, London SW2 2AL Tel. *020 86716622* Fax. *020 86786151* E-mail. *enquiries@fineitalianfoods.co.uk* Web. *www.fineitalianfoods.co.uk *Dalter*

Base Model PO Box 6709, Bournemouth BH11 0BW Tel. *08452 255015* Fax. *01202 301156* E-mail. *info@basemodels.co.uk* Web. *www.basemodels.co.uk Base Model Management – Base Models*

B A S F Cleckheaton Road Low Moor, Bradford BD12 0JZ Tel. *01274 417000* Fax. *01274 606499* E-mail. *info@cibasc.com* Web. *www.basf.com *Alcosorb – *Bandrift – *Libfer – *Librel – *Libspray*

Basically Doors Unit 1 Rookery Road, Barnoldswick BB18 6YH Tel. *01282 816434* Fax. *01200 445576* E-mail. *sales@basicallydoors.co.uk* Web. *www.basicallydoors.co.uk Ba components – Bella by Ba*

Basildon Chemical Co. Ltd / KCC Kimber Road, Abingdon OX14 1RZ Tel. *01235 526677* Fax. *01235 524334* E-mail. *sales@baschem.co.uk* Web. *www.baschem.co.uk Antifoam 86/013 – Antifoam 96/071 – Antifoam AP – Antifoam AR – Antifoam AR20 – Antifoam AR30 – Antifoam C100 – Antifoam C100F – Antifoam C100N – Antifoam C133 – Antifoam E6 – Antifoam ED5 – Antifoam FD – Antifoam FD20P – Antifoam FD30 – Antifoam FD50 – Antifoam FDP – Antifoam FG10 – Antifoam FG50 – BC 2105 – BC 2153 – BC 2191 – BC 2211 – BC 2231 – BC 2262 – BC 2275 – BC 2335 – BC 2366 – BC 2398 – BC 2421 – BC 2426 – BC 2440 – BC 330/60 – BC 330EPHV – BC 330LV – BC 338 – BC 361 – BC 380E – BC 380S – BC 403 – BC 404 – BC 83/132 – BC 85/76 – BC 88/161 – BC 89/175 – BC 90/080 – BC 91/023 – BC 93/018 – BC 96/004 – BC 96/042 – BC 96/061 – BC 98/073 – BC 99/012 – BC 99/099 – BC Silicone Fluids – BC Volatile Silicone 4 – BC Volatile Silicone 5 – Dimethicone 1000cs – Dimethicone 350cs – Powder Antifoam 2527 – Simethicone Antifoam C100EP – Simethicone Antifoam C100F – Simethicone Antifoam PD30*

Baskerville Reactors Autoclaves Ltd Unit 30 Long Wood Road, Trafford Park, Manchester M17 1PZ Tel. *0161 8485960* Fax. *0161 8882345* E-mail. *admin@baskervilleautoclaves.co.uk* Web. *www.baskervilleautoclaves.co.uk Baskerville*

Bassaire Ltd Duncan Road Park Gate, Southampton SO31 1ZS Tel. *01489 885111* Fax. *01489 885211* E-mail. *neil.thomas@bassaire.co.uk* Web. *www.bassaire.co.uk Bassaire*

B A S S Hydro Coatings Ltd Unit 101 Tenth Avenue Deeside Industrial Park, Deeside CH5 2UA Tel. *01244 281315* Fax. *01244 281316* Web. *www.bass.co.uk Glasurit*

Batchglow Ltd Units 3-4 Bookers Way Dinnington, Sheffield S25 3SH Tel. *01909 550966* Fax. *01909 550955* E-mail. *info@batchglow.co.uk* Web. *www.batchglow.co.uk Acclaim Powder Coaters*

George Bateman & Son Ltd Salem Bridge Brewery Mill Lane, Wainfleet, Skegness PE24 4JE Tel. *01754 880317* Fax. *01754 880939* E-mail. *info@bateman.co.uk* Web. *www.bateman.co.uk Good Honest Ales – Pilgrim*

Bathstore.com Ltd Unit 2a Felnex Trading Estate, Wallington SM6 7EL Tel. *01923 694740* Fax. *020 87735004* E-mail. *enquiries@bathstore.com* Web. *www.bathstore.com Bathstore.Com – River Accessories*

Bath Travel 4 High Street, Christchurch BH23 1AY Tel. *01202 484247* Fax. *01202 487144* Web. *www.bathtravel.com Spreadbury Travel*

Batleys Cash & Carry Skelton Grange Road, Leeds LS10 1RZ Tel. *0113 2771313* Fax. *0113 2720495* Web. *www.batleys.co.uk May Field*

Battery Distribution Group Unit 2 Fellows Court Lockside Anchor Brook Industrial Park, Aldridge, Walsall WS9 8BZ Tel. *01922 741710* Fax. *01922 741719* E-mail. *sales@batterydistribution.com* Web. *www.batterydistribution.com Global Yuasa Battery Co Ltd – Raylite Turbo Start – Schnapp Batteries*

The Battery Shop UK LTD Unit 20 Orbit Centre Ashworth Road, Bridgemead, Swindon SN5 7YG Tel. *01793 421509* Fax. *01793 432010* E-mail. *info@thebatteryshop.co.uk* Web. *www.thebatteryshop.co.uk Yuasa*

Baty International Victoria Road, Burgess Hill RH15 9LR Tel. *01444 235621* Fax. *01444 246985* E-mail. *sales@baty.co.uk* Web. *www.baty.co.uk Baty – British Indicators – Seebreez – Shadomaster – Venture*

Bauer Group (Bauer Compressors) Haydock Industrial Estate North Florida Road Haydock, St Helens WA11 9TN Tel. *01942 724248* Fax. *01942 270771* E-mail. *general@bauer.uk.com* Web. *www.bauergroup.co.uk Ba.compressor – High pressure air compressors – Bauer Kompressoren – Seismic – Scuba*

H Bauer Publishing Academic House 24-28 Oval Road, London NW1 7DT Tel. *020 72418000* Fax. *020 72418056* Web. *www.bauer.co.uk Bella – Fill In Fun – Puzzle Collection – Search Me – Take A Break – Take A Crossword – Take A Look – Take A Puzzle – TV Quick*

Baugh & Weedon Ltd Beech Business Park Tillington Road, Hereford HR4 9QJ Tel. *01432 267671* Fax. *01432 359017* E-mail. *sales@bandwndt.co.uk* Web. *www.bandwndt.co.uk Audit – Digimag – Gen 2000 – Magazon – Mat-A-Chek – Pipecheck – Quantic – Rovprobe – Seaprobe – Vitomag*

Baumer Electric Ltd 33-36 Majors Road Watchfield, Swindon SN6 8TZ Tel. *01793 783839* Fax. *01793 783814* E-mail. *sales.uk@baumer.com* Web. *www.baumer.com Baumer Electric (Switzerland) – Baumer Optronics (Germany) – *Brunner (Switzerland) – Hübnel (Germany) – *IVO (Germany) – *Massen (Switzerland) – Thalheim (Germany)*

Baur Test Equipment Ltd Unit C1 Connaught Business Centre Imperial Way, Croydon CR0 4RR Tel. *020 86610957* Fax. *020 86424801* E-mail. *sales@baurtest.com* Web. *www.baurtest.com Dieltest – Frida – Shirla – Syscompact – Transcable – Viola*

Bauschlinnemann UK Widow Hill Road Heasandford Industrial Estate, Burnley BB10 2TB Tel. *01282 686850* Fax. *01282 412361* E-mail. *info@uk.bauschlinnemann.com* Web. *www.uk.bauschlinnemann.com Armaflex – Armaform – Armatrim*

Baxenden Chemicals Ltd Paragon Works Rising Bridge, Accrington BB5 2SL Tel. *01254 872278* Fax. *01254 871247* E-mail. *mail@baxchem.co.uk* Web. *www.baxenden.co.uk Castomer – Flexocel – Gusmer – Isofoam – Quasilan – Trixene – Xenacryl – Xenalak*

Baxi Group 16 Stanier Way Wyvern Business Park, Chaddesden, Derby DE21 6BF Tel. *01332 545400* Fax. *01332 545410* E-mail. *info@baxipotterton.co.uk* Web. *www.baxigroup.com Alfer – Andrews – Aqualisa – Baxi – Baymak – Brötje – Chappée – Curzon – Dachs – Dreh – Elson – European Fuel Cell – Gainsborough – Heatrae Sadia – Ideal Standard – Morso – Potterton – Powermax – Rycroft – Santon – Senertec – Sicma – Valor – Wonderfire*

Baxter Healthcare Ltd Wallingford Road Compton, Newbury RG20 7QW Tel. *01635 206000* Fax. *01635 206115* E-mail. *enquiries@baxter.com* Web. *www.baxter.com *Baxter (Worldwide) – *Fenwal (Worldwide) – *Hyland (Worldwide)*

Bayer Crop Science 230 Camebridge Science Park Milton Road, Cambridge CB4 0WB Tel. *01223 226500* Fax. *01223 426240* E-mail. *w.welter@bayercropscience.com* Web. *www.bayercropscience.co.uk Actrilawn 10 – Asulox – Borocilk – Clovotox – Crossfire 480 – Dicotox Extra – Freeway – Mildothane Turf Liquid – Quintozene Wettable Powder – Regulox K – Ringmaster – Rovral Green – Spasor – Spasor Biactive – Spearhead – Super Mosstox – Supertox 30 – Vanquish – Vitesse – Xanadu*

Bayford & Co. Ltd Bowcliffe Hall Bramham, Wetherby LS23 6LP Tel. *01937 541111* Fax. *01937 841465* E-mail. *sales@bayford.co.uk* Web. *www.bayford.co.uk Thrust Petroleum*

Bayham Ltd Rutherford Road, Basingstoke RG24 8PG Tel. *01256 464911* Fax. *01256 464366* E-mail. *chris@bayham.demon.co.uk* Web. *www.tankgauges.co.uk Aquametro (Switzerland) – Baydee – Baysend – Minidee – Minisend – R.&.G. – Transend*

Baynell Ltd 85-86 Darlington Street, Wolverhampton WV1 4EX Tel. *01902 425616* Fax. *01902 311242 Baynell*

B B A Aviation plc 105 Wigmore Street, London W1U 1QY Tel. *020 75143999* Fax. *020 74082318* E-mail. *info@bbaaviation.com* Web. *www.bbaaviation.com APPH – H & S – Terram – Trinity*

B B C Fire Protection Ltd St Florian House Ayton Road, Wymondham NR18 0QH Tel. *01953 857700* Fax. *01953 857750* E-mail. *sales@bbcfire.co.uk* Web. *www.bbcfire.co.uk Cablemiser – Fire Scribe – Firespy*

B B C S Ltd Unit 9 Riverside Court Westminster Industrial Estate, Measham, Swadlincote DE12 7DS Tel. *01530 274933* Fax. *01530 515292* E-mail. *john.blount@bbcs-ltd.com* Web. *www.bbcs-ltd.com Convotherm – Hobart – Imperial – Instanta – Meiko – Merrychef – Moorwood Vulcan – Rational – Robot Coupe*

BBI Business Interiors Ltd Unit A Quinn Close, Coventry CV3 4LH Tel. *024 76303000* Fax. *024 76303099* E-mail. *david@bbiltd.co.uk* Web. *www.bbi.uk.com Bisley Office Equipment – Haworth – Haworth - office furniture Senator International - office furniture Bisley Office Equipment - office furniture – Senator International*

B Braun Medical Ltd Unit 8 Brookdale Road Thorncliffe Park Estate, Chapeltown, Sheffield S35 2PY Tel. *0114 2259000* Fax. *0114 2259111* E-mail. *deborah.darling@bbraun.com* Web. *www.bbraun.com B. Braun Medical*

B C B International Ltd Units 7-8 Clydesmuir Road Industrial Estate, Cardiff CF24 2QS Tel. *029 20433700* Fax. *029 20433701* E-mail. *info@bcbin.com* Web. *www.bcbin.com B.C.B. International*

B C G Creative FX 10 Bocking End, Braintree CM7 9AA Tel. *01376 323461* E-mail. *creativefx@virgin.net Aceframe – Creative FX – IT Bytes – Ultim8*

B C I Stretchers Ltd 386-388 South Eldon Street, South Shields NE33 5SY Tel. *0191 4553984* Fax. *0191 4569653* E-mail. *info@bci-stretchers.co.uk* Web. *www.bci-stretchers.co.uk Neil Robertson Stretcher (United Kingdom)*

B & D Clays & Chemicals Ltd 10 Wandle Way, Mitcham CR4 4NB Tel. *020 86409221* Fax. *020 86485033* E-mail. *sales@bdclays.co.uk* Web. *www.catlitters.co.uk *Klensorb (Europe) – *Spildri (Europe) – *Spilsorb (Europe)*

B D C Systems Prospect Farm Monxton, Andover SP11 7DA Tel. *01264 710900* Fax. *01264 710987* E-mail. *info@bdcsystems.com* Web. *www.bdcsystems.com *Akron – *Funki – *Magnier – *Skandia – *Svegma*

B D K Industrial Products Ltd (Adhesive Technology Specialists) Levington Park Bridge Road, Levington, Ipswich IP10 0JE Tel. *01473 659059* Fax. *01473 659104* E-mail. *sales@bdk.uk.com* Web. *www.bdk.uk.com 3M – Advance Tapes – Apollo – Avery Dennison – Bostik – Evode – Fasson – Lohmann – Nitto – Scapa – Sellotape – Steratape – Tesa – Venture Tapes*

Beacon Private Trust Ellerd House Amenbury Lane, Harpenden AL5 2EJ Tel. *01582 761125* Fax. *01582 761126* E-mail. *beacon@beacon-ifa.co.uk* Web. *www.beacon-ifa.com Beacon*

Beaconsfield Footwear Ltd 2 Peel Road, Skelmersdale WN8 9PT Tel. *01695 712720* Fax. *01695 712715* E-mail. *admin@hotter.co.uk* Web. *www.hottershoes.com *Hotter Comfort Shoes (India and Thailand)*

Bead Technologies Ltd 2 Union House Union Drive, Sutton Coldfield B73 5TN Tel. *0121 3543854* Fax. *0845 0176269* E-mail. *admin@beadtech.co.uk* Web. *www.beadtech.co.uk asm dimatec*

Beakbane Ltd Stourport Road, Kidderminster DY11 7QT Tel. *01562 820561* Fax. *01562 820560* E-mail. *info@beakbane.co.uk* Web. *www.beakbane.co.uk Beakaprene – Beakaprene - Plastichain - Centry Covers. – Beakbane – *Centry Cover (U.S.A.) – *Plastichain (France)*

Beamglow Ltd Somersham Road, St Ives PE27 3LP Tel. *01480 465012* Fax. *01480 494826* E-mail. *moirag@beamglow.co.uk* Web. *www.beamglow.co.uk Display Outer – Printed Carton*

Beanstalk Marketing Services Moulsham Mill Parkway, Chelmsford CM2 7PX Tel. *0845 4742047* E-mail. *info@beanstalkmarketing.co.uk* Web. *www.beanstalkmarketing.co.uk Beanstalk Marketing*

Bearwood Engineering Supplies (Inc. Bearwood Intl Ltd) 11 Vernon Road, Birmingham B16 9SQ Tel. *0121 4547227* Fax. *0121 4545991* E-mail. *jon.laxton@btconnect.com* Web. *www.bearwoodinternational.co.uk A.E.G. – A.I. Welders – A.V.O. – Acme – Aerovox – Air-Maze – Alfa Laval Saunders – Allen Bradley – Alpha Laval – Alstom – Alus Chalmers – Amal – AMI-GFV – Amot – Angus – Apiezon – Apollo – Araldite – Ashcroft – Atlas Copco – B-Brand – B-Click – B-Dri – B-Sure – B.I.S. – Bahco – Barksdale – Bauer – Bearwood – Beesafe – Beesure – Beeswift – Bellofram – Belzona – Bentley-Nevada – Bestobell-Mowbrey – Biccotest – Bosch – Bourdon – Bower – Bowex – Bowman – Brackett Green – Bradbury – British Library – Brook Crompton – Brownell – Browning – Budenberg – Bull Motor – Burgess – Burgmann – C-Max – Carrier Kheops – Cegelec – Clarke – Click – Comef – Compair Broomwade – Compair Maxam – Compair Reavell – Contrec – Coopers – Copeland – Coudoint – Cpoac – Crosby Laughlin – Crouzet – Crovisa – Cuprisil – Cutler-Hammer – Daikin – Danfoss – Darnett – Datatech – David Brown – Davy McKee – De Limon – Demag – Denco-Farval – Deutz – Dimplex – Dormer – Douce-Hydro – Dri – Dulcotest – Dunlop – Duralast – Duraline – Durnburg – E.A.O. – E.M.A.S. – Eaton – Eberle – Edward Pryor – Edwards – Electro Flow – Elliott – Enertec – Engelhard – Esso – Eurodigit – Eurotherm – Exxon – Fairchild – Fairey Arlon – Farnell – Federal Bell – Festo – Fisher – Flackt – Flash Welder – Flender – Flow-Mon – Flowseal – Fluidrive – Flupac – Flygt – Ford – G.E.C. – G.E.C. Industrial Controls – G.E.C.Elliott – Garlock – General Digital Corporation – General Electric – Goliath – Grigsby Barton – Grobet – Haefely – Hallden – Harting – Heatcraft – Helios – Hermetite – Hew Kabel – Hewlett Packard – Hi-Gear – Hidro-Thermal – Highfield – Hilti – Hodgson – Holmes – Honeywell – Huck – Hunger – Hydac – Hydrasun – Hydro-Thermal – Hydromatik – Hydrovane – Hypot – I.K.O. – I.M.I.Bailey Birkett – I.N.A. – I.T.E. – I.T.T. – Inflo Bulk Control – Ingersoll Rand – Integrated – J.C.B. – Jabsco – James Neill – Jay-Cincinatti – Jesco – Johnson-Matthey – Jones & Attwood – Joucomatic – K.D.G. Instruments – K.S.B. – Keller – Kennedy – Klaxon – Klingelhofer – Knorr Bremser – Kobold – Kramer – Krom-Schroder – Kwik-Way – Lang – Leeds & Northrup – Lenze – Lincoln – Lincoln-Helios – Lister Petter – Lite-Dialco – Littelite – Locker Air Maze – Loewy Robertson – Maglock – Malvern – Markal – Marks – Martin – Martindale – Martonair – Maxam – McMaster – Mecman – Mercedes – Merlin Gerin – Messdoch – Midland Pneumatic – Millenicut – Mission T.R.W. – Mitsubishi – Mitutoyo – Mohel Nice – Molykote – Monicon – Mono-Muncher – Mono-Pump – Moog – Moore & Wright – Morgardshammar – Morrison – Morse – Mosa – Motherwell Control Systems – Muller & Pesant – Munck – Norbar – Norgren Martonair – Northey – Oberg – Onan – Pall – Parker Hannifin – Peabody – Peabody Holmes – Peerless Pump – Penny & Giles – Pepperl & Fuchs – Perkins – Peter Rayner – Plenty – Pneumax – Potter & Bromfield – Power Dome – Protector Safety – Pryor – Ramsey – Rand – Rank Taylor Hobson – Reichert-Jung – Remote Control – Rexroth – Rivertrace – Robertshaw – Ross – Rotadisk – Rototherm – RS – Same – Sandvik – Sangamo – Satronic – Saunders – Schat-Harding – Schloemann Siemag – Schrader Bellows – Seacon – Seal Master – Seepex – Semikron – Serck – Servomax – Shepherd – Siemens – Sika – Silfos – Sime Industrie – Sinclair Collins – Snap-On – Sonatest – Sperry Vickers – Spirax Sarco – Sport Engineering – Stanley – Static Systems – Stromberg – Struthers – Sure – Suremark – Surtronic – Tangye – Taylor Hobson – Tecalemit – Teco – Telemechanique – Thompson – Thorn Security – Timken – Toshiba – Triangle – Turboflex – Turck – Twiflex – Twin Disc – Twinflex – Tyvek – U.V.G. – United Automation – Vallorbe – Version A.I. – Vickers – Victor – Voith – Waldes Truarc – Walker – Warren-Morrison – Westinghouse – Wichita – Wickman – Wika – Willetts – Wolf – Worswick – Worwick*

Beatson Clark Ltd The Glass Works Greasbrough Road, Rotherham S60 1TZ Tel. *01709 828141* Fax. *01709 835388* E-mail. *sales@beatsonclark.co.uk* Web. *www.beatsonclark.co.uk Beatson*

Beatson Fans & Motors Ltd 16 Newhall Road, Sheffield S9 2QL Tel. *0114 2449955* Fax. *0114 2449956* E-mail. *enquiries@beatson.co.uk* Web. *www.beatson.co.uk Airflow – B.F.M. Motors – Beatson Fans and Motors – Broughton – BVC – CMG – Crompton Controls – Excal – London Fan Company – Multi-wing – Parvalux – Rako – Roof Units – Siemens – Sprint – *Vent-Axia*

Beaufort Air Sea Equipment Ltd Beaufort Road, Birkenhead CH41 1HQ Tel. *0151 6529151* Fax. *0151 6536639* E-mail. *cgreen@rfdbeaufort.com* Web. *www.rfdbeaufort.com Beaufort – Seafarer – Transuit*

Bill Beaumont Textiles Ltd Unit 4 Chorley North Business Park Drumhead Road, Chorley PR6 7BX Tel. *01257 263065* Fax. *01257 241348* E-mail. *sales@billbeaumont.co.uk* Web. *www.billbeaumont.co.uk Stormfleece – Stormtex*

Beautiful Landscapes Ltd 55 Crondall court Pitfield streeet, Islington, London N1 6JH Tel. *07964 305410* E-mail. *info@beautifullansdapes.co.uk* Web. *www.beautifullandscapes.co.uk Beautiful Landscapes Ltd*

Beaver 84 Ellencroft House Harvey Road, Basildon SS13 1EP Tel. *08704 238584* Fax. *01268 727184* E-mail. *sales@beaver84.co.uk* Web. *www.beaver84.co.uk Beaver – Beaverclad – Beavernet – Litepile – Steelguard – Temporary Fencing*

B E C Distribution Ltd 20 Park Street, Princes Risborough HP27 9AH Tel. *08454 900405* Fax. *0845 4900406* E-mail. *sales@bec.co.uk* Web. *www.bec.co.uk Toko – Toko*

E Becker Ltd 2 Hazlemere View Hazlemere, High Wycombe HP15 7BY Tel. *01494 713777* Fax. *01494 713888* E-mail. *brian.white@onmedica.com Leatherette Paper*

Becker Industrial Coatings Ltd Goodlass Road, Liverpool L24 9HJ Tel. *0151 4481010* Fax. *0151 4482589* E-mail. *reception@beckers-bic.com* Web. *www.beckers-bic.com Becker Green Line - environmentally friendly coatings Beckqua - water based primers and finishes Beckrysol - high solids primers &and finishes – Beckqua*

Becker Sliding Partitions Ltd Wemco House 477 Whippendell Road, Watford WD18 7QY Tel. *01923 236906* Fax. *01923 236906* E-mail. *g-browne@becker.uk.com* Web. *www.becker.uk.com Duplo – Harmonika in vinyl – Harmonika in Wood – Monoplan – SM Range (NO3) – Sunfold – Uno – Versiplan*

Beck Greener Fulwood House 12 Fulwood Place, London WC1V 6HR Tel. *020 72422535* Fax. *020 74058113* E-mail. *sales@beckgreener.com* Web. *www.beckgreener.com Beck Greener*

Bedfont Scientific Ltd Station Yard Station Road, Harrietsham, Maidstone ME17 1JA Tel. *01622 851122* Fax. *01634 673721* E-mail. *ask@bedfont.com* Web. *www.bedfont.com EC80 – Gastrolyzer – NOxBox+ – PHoxAir – Smokerlyzer – TM3 – toxCO+*

Bedford Shelving Ltd 8 Greaves Way Industrial Estate Stanbridge Road, Leighton Buzzard LU7 4UB Tel. *01525 852121* Fax. *01525 851666* E-mail. *sales@bedfordshelf.com* Web. *www.bedfordshelf.co.uk Alimaster – Bedfords – Quartermaster – Stockmaster*

Beechfield Brands Ltd Unit 3 Warth Park Radcliffe Road, Bury BL9 9NB Tel. *0161 7629444* Fax. *0161 7629555* E-mail. *sales@beechfield.com* Web. *www.beechfield.com Beechfield Cap*

Beechwood Recruitment Ltd 221 High Street, London W3 9BY Tel. *020 89928647* Fax. *020 89925658* E-mail. *mail@beechwoodrecruit.com* Web. *www.beechwoodrecruit.com Beechwood Appointments Register – Beechwood Recruitment*

Beeswift Ltd West Wing Delta House Delta Point Greets Green Road, West Bromwich B70 9PL Tel. *0121 5242323* Fax. *0121 5242325* E-mail. *sales@beeswift.com* Web. *www.beeswift.com B Brand – B Click – B Click Cut Resistant – B Click Fire Retardent – B Click Footwear – B Click Heavyweight – B Click Kutstop – B Click Once – B Click Traders – B Click Workwear – B DRI Weatherproof – B Flex – B Safe – B Seen – B Sure*

Beggars Group Ltd 17 Alma Road, London SW18 1AA Tel. *020 88709912* Fax. *020 88711766* E-mail. *postmaster@beggars.com* Web. *www.beggars.com Beggars Banquet*

Begg Cousland & Co. Ltd Building 5 Studio 3 Templeton Business Centre 62 Templeton Street, Glasgow G40 1DA Tel. *0141 5565288* Fax. *0141 5547447* E-mail. *sales@beggcousland.com* Web. *www.beggcousland.com Becofil – Becoflex – Becoil – Beconit – Becone – Becosolve – Becosorb*

Begg & Co Thermoplastics Ltd 71 Hailey Road, Erith DA18 4AW Tel. *020 83101236* Fax. *020 83104371* E-mail. *info@beggandco.co.uk* Web. *www.beggandco.co.uk Unicorn*

F & R Belbin Ltd Back of 165-169 Whitley Road, Whitley Bay NE26 2DN Tel. *0191 2522875* Fax. *0191 2970812* E-mail. *sales@frbelbin.co.uk* Web. *www.frbelbin.co.uk Traratchet – Truflote*

Belcom Cables Ltd Warish Hall Takeley, Bishops Stortford CM22 6NZ Tel. *01279 871150* Fax. *01279 871129* E-mail. *sales@belcom.co.uk* Web. *www.belcom.co.uk DataGuard – FieldLink – FireFighter – FlexLine – Surelan – Event Series – Armada – Surelight – Leoni – Electro Cables Inc. – Electrolene*

Belden UK Ltd Manchester International Office Centre Styal Road, Manchester M22 5WB Tel. *0161 4983754* Fax. *0121 3295001* Web. *www.hirschmann.co.uk Hi Connect – Hi Device – Hi Power – Industrial Line*

H & T Bellas Ltd 12-14 Mountsandel Road, Coleraine BT52 1JD Tel. *028 70342205* Fax. *028 70352413* E-mail. *info@bellas.co.uk* Web. *www.bellas.co.uk H & T – H.T. Bellas*

Bell Bros Pudsey Ltd Green Lane, Pudsey LS28 8JN Tel. *0113 2565715* Fax. *0113 2569255* E-mail. *info@bellbros.com* Web. *www.bellbros.com Belbro*

Edmund Bell & Co. Ltd Euroway Industrial Estate, Bradford BD4 6SU Tel. *01274 680000* Fax. *01274 680699* E-mail. *sales@edmundbell.co.uk* Web. *www.edmundbell.co.uk Edmund Bell*

Belle Engineering Sheen Ltd Sheen, Buxton SK17 0EU Tel. *01298 84606* Fax. *01298 84722* E-mail. *sales@belle-group.co.uk* Web. *www.belle-group.co.uk Errut – Panther Int'*

Bell Equipment UK Unit 6c Graycar Business Park Barton Turns Barton Under, Barton Under Needwood, Burton On Trent DE13 8EN Tel. *01283 712862* Fax. *01283 712687* E-mail. *general@uk.bellequipment.com* Web. *www.bellequipment.co.uk Bell Equipment*

Bellingham & Stanley Ltd Longfield Road, Tunbridge Wells TN2 3EY Tel. *01892 500400* Fax. *01892 543115* E-mail. *sales@bellinghamandstanley.co.uk* Web. *www.bellinghamandstanley.com ADP – AG – Bellingham and Stanley – Eclipse – PRH – RFM – RFM - digital refracometer.Eclipse - hand refractometerPRH - process refractometerADP - polarimeterAG - calibration materials*

Bell Sons & Co. Ltd Cheshire House Gorsey Lane, Widnes WA8 0RP Tel. *0151 4221200* Fax. *0151 4221211* E-mail. *sales@bells-healthcare.com* Web. *www.bells-healthcare.com B. Label – Duke Brand Herb Tea – Kilkof – Menthodex – Nerve Bone Liniment – Silver Bird – Sunset Self Tanning Cream – Vadarex – Xennal – Xennol*

Bell Truck Sales Ltd Bellway Industrial Estate Whitley Road, Longbenton, Newcastle Upon Tyne NE12 9SW Tel. *0191 2700787* Fax. *0191 2664780* E-mail. *info@belltruckandvan.co.uk* Web. *www.belltruckandvan.co.uk *Bells of Coldstream (Germany)*

Bellway PLC Seaton Burn House Dudley Lane, Seaton Burn, Newcastle upon Tyne NE13 6BE Tel. *0191 2170717* Fax. *0191 2366230* E-mail. *peter.johnson@bellway.co.uk* Web. *www.bellway.co.uk Bellway*

Bell & Webster Concrete Ltd Alma Park Road, Grantham NG31 9SE Tel. *01476 562277* Fax. *01476 562944* E-mail. *shaun.brown@eleco.com* Web. *www.bellandwebster.co.uk Bell & Webster Concrete*

Bemco (t/a Bemco) 11-12 Carver Street, Birmingham B1 3AS Tel. *0121 2365868* Fax. *0121 2368211* E-mail. *info@bemco.com* Web. *www.bemco.uk.com Bunting*

Bemco Ltd Bridgend Road, London SW18 1TN Tel. *020 88740404* Fax. *020 88770153* E-mail. *bryan.barkes@bemco.co.uk* Web. *www.bemco.co.uk Bemco*

Bemis Ltd Farrington Road, Burnley BB11 5SW Tel. *01282 438717* Fax. *01282 412717* E-mail. *uksales@bemiseurope.com* Web. *www.bemiseurope.com Bemis*

Bemis Swansea Siemens Way Swansea Enterprise Park, Swansea SA7 9BB Tel. *01792 784700* Fax. *01792 784784* E-mail. *info@bemis.com* Web. *www.bemis.com Clear-Tite – Cook-Tite – Perflex*

Ben Bennett JR Ltd Lisle Road, Rotherham S60 2RL Tel. *01709 382251* Fax. *01709 369206* E-mail. *pudell@benbennettjr.co.uk* Web. *www.benbennettjr.co.uk Bennite – Bennite, Drill-carb – Drill-Carb*

Benito UK Unit 9 Bridge Mills Rochdale Road, Ramsbottom, Bury BL0 0RE Tel. *01706 821010* Fax. *01706 826324* E-mail. *bschofield@benitouk.com* Web. *www.benitouk.com Benito – fdb line*

Benlowe Windows Park Road Ratby, Leicester LE6 0JL Tel. *0116 2395353* Fax. *0116 2387295* E-mail. *sales@benlowe.co.uk* Web. *www.benlowe.co.uk Glenfield – Heritage – New Era*

Ben - Motor & Allied Trades Benevolent Fund Lynwood Rise Road, Ascot SL5 0AJ Tel. *01344 620191* Fax. *01344 622042* E-mail. *david.main@ben.org.uk* Web. *www.ben.org.uk Ben – Bentrade Ltd*

Bennett Mahler 2 Merse Road Moons Moat North Industrial Estate, Redditch B98 9HL Tel. *01527 64444* Fax. *01527 591668* E-mail. *bennettmahler@msn.com* Web. *www.bennettmahler.com Bennett (United Kingdom) – Fenn - Torin (U.S.A.) – Latour (France) – Macsoft – Simplex Rapid (Italy)*

Bennett Safetywear 11 Mersey Road Crosby, Liverpool L23 3AF Tel. *0151 9243996* Fax. *0151 9246548* E-mail. *sales@bennettsafetywear.co.uk* Web. *www.bennettsafetywear.co.uk Aintex – Ajax – Alco – Altex – Armatex – Armour-Knit – Beatsafe – Beneflect – Benitex – Bitex – Blazemaster – Cobra – Corex – Cromax – Crumcote – Dermos – Duotex – Epitex – Fabritex – Hytex – Miatex – Multex – Needlestop – Polysafe – Pro-Tex – Rivitex – Suprox – Synchrome – Weldex – Weldex*

Bennison Fabrics 16 Holbein Place, London SW1W 8NL Tel. *020 77308076* Fax. *020 78234997* E-mail. *sales@bennisonfabrics.com* Web. *www.bennisonfabrics.com Bennison*

Benross Marketing Ltd Benross House Speke Hall Road, Liverpool L24 9WD Tel. *0151 4481200* Fax. *0151 4481221* E-mail. *anil@benross.com* Web. *www.benross.com Benross – *Ross Tools (Hong Kong and Taiwan)*

Bensasson & Chalmers Ltd St Johns Innovation Centre Cowley Road, Cambridge CB4 0WS Tel. *01223 420048* Fax. *01223 420418* E-mail. *sales@benc.co.uk* Web. *www.benc.co.uk Lamp – Proman – Spires – Time Manager*

Benson Box Ltd Interlink Park Bardon Hill, Coalville LE67 1PE Tel. *01530 518200* Fax. *01530 518222* E-mail. *n.benson@bensonbox.co.uk* Web. *www.bensonbox.co.uk Tarabrook*

Benson Components Ltd Saxon Works South Street, Openshaw, Manchester M11 2FY Tel. *0161 9528888* Fax. *0161 2316866* E-mail. *sales@bensonexhausts.com* Web. *www.bensonexhausts.com Benson Exhausts*

H.E. & B.S. Benson Ltd 1 Laureate Industrial Estate School Road, Exning Road, Newmarket CB8 0AR Tel. *01638 663535* Fax. *01638 667434* E-mail. *sales@hebsbenson.co.uk* Web. *www.hebsbenson.co.uk Benson*

Benson Industries Ltd Valley Mills Valley Road, Bradford BD1 4RU Tel. *01274 722204* Fax. *01274 306319 Benson – Lyta – Skimma*

Benteler Distribution Ltd New Progress Works Crompton Way, Bolton BL1 8TY Tel. *01204 301611* Fax. *01204 593074* E-mail. *sales@benteler-distribution.co.uk* Web. *www.benteler-distribution.co.uk Pipe and Tube Group – PTG 600 – PTG 700 – Special 07/Zista 07 (Germany) – Trumech*

Berck Ltd Titan Works Pleasant Street, Lyng Industrial Estate, West Bromwich B70 7DP Tel. *0121 5532726* Fax. *0121 5531087* E-mail. *sales@bercklimited.co.uk* Web. *www.bercklimited.co.uk Titan*

Berger Tools Ltd Units B1 B2 Chaucer Business Park Watery Lane, Kemsing, Sevenoaks TN15 6QY Tel. *01732 763377* Fax. *01732 763335* E-mail. *sales@berger-tools.co.uk* Web. *www.berger-tools.co.uk Bohrbuchsen (Switzerland) – Cubeair (Denmark) – *Eberhard (Germany) – *Effbe (Germany) – *Ganter (Germany) – *Multicyl (Canada) – Pedrotti (Italy) – Rabourdin Industrie (France) – *Rabourdin Picardie (France) – *Special Springs (Italy) – Strack Normteilwerk (Germany) – *Tipco Inc (Canada) – Voest Alpine (Austria)*

Berghaus Ltd 12 Colima Avenue Sunderland Enterprise Park, Sunderland SR5 3XB Tel. *0191 5165600* Fax. *0191 5165601* E-mail. *reception@berghaus.com* Web. *www.berghaus.com Airfoil – Aquafoil – Cyclops – Dart – Extrem – FGA – Inter-Active (1.A.) – Star – Yeti*

Bericap UK Ltd Sutton Fields Industrial Estate Oslo Road, Hull HU7 0YN Tel. *01482 826666* Fax. *01482 832839* E-mail. *info@bericap.com* Web. *www.bericap.com Dairy Seal – Parlok – Parspout – Policeman – Sureseal*

E. Berry & Sons Unit 19 308A Melton Road, Leicester LE4 7SL Tel. *0845 1306862* Fax. *0845 3892144* E-mail. *info@premierpioneer.co.uk* Web. *www.premierpioneer.co.uk Pioneer – Premier*

Berry Systems Springvale Industrial Park, Bilston WV14 0QL Tel. *01902 491100* Fax. *01902 494080* E-mail. *sales@berrysystems.co.uk* Web. *www.optimumbarriers.co.uk A Rail – Armco – Barrier Rail – Berry Beam – Flex Beam Guard Rail – Flexi-Post – Hercules – Monostrut Rail – Open Box Beam – Rakguard – Spring Steel – Warehouse Rail*

Berthoud Sprayers Waterford Industrial Estate Mill Lane, Great Massingham, Kings Lynn PE32 2HT Tel. *01485 520626* E-mail. *sales@berthoud.co.uk* Web. *www.berthoud.co.uk *Boxer – *Force – *Mack – *Major – *Maxxor – *Racer*

Berwin & Berwin Ltd Roseville Road, Leeds LS8 5EE Tel. *0113 2442244* Fax. *0113 2424398* E-mail. *sales@berwinberwin.co.uk* Web. *www.berwinberwin.co.uk Berwin*

Besam Ltd Assa Abloy Group Washington House Brooklands Close, Sunbury On Thames TW16 7EQ Tel. *01932 765888* Fax. *01932 765864* E-mail. *info@besam.co.uk* Web. *www.besam.co.uk *Besam (Sweden)*

Besley & Copp Ltd Unit 7 Orchard Court Heron Road, Sowton Industrial Estate, Exeter EX2 7LL Tel. *01392 477137* Fax. *01392 432046* E-mail. *sales@besleyandcopp.co.uk* Web. *www.besleyandcopp.co.uk Besley & Copp*

Bespoke Wheels Ltd Unit 2 Block B Harriott Drive, Heathcote Industrial Estate, Warwick CV34 6TJ Tel. *01926 887722* E-mail. *sales@bespokewheels.co.uk* Web. *www.bespoketyres.co.uk Bespoke wheels Limited*

Bestpump 34 Commonhead Street, Airdrie ML6 6NS Tel. *08454 672378* Fax. *01236 728900* E-mail. *john@bestpump.co.uk* Web. *www.bestpump.co.uk Cesco Magnetics – DEPA Pumps – Johnson Pump – Polar Process – Wright Pump*

Best Years Ltd PO Box 6898, Daventry NN11 3WG Tel. *01327 262189* Fax. *01327 262189* E-mail. *sales@bestyears.co.uk* Web. *www.bestyears.co.uk cuddle factory*

Betabite Hydraulics Ltd Stuart Road Manor Park, Runcorn WA7 1TS Tel. *01928 594500* Fax. *01928 579818* E-mail. *sales@betabite.co.uk* Web. *www.betabite.co.uk Betabite – Betabite – Let Lok*

Betech 100 P T Ltd Four Square Building Thomas Street, Heckmondwike WF16 0LS Tel. *08707 573344* Fax. *08707 573388* E-mail. *sales@betech.co.uk* Web. *www.betech.co.uk Baldor – Mitsubishi – Motovario – Sprint – Warner – Wichita*

Better Balance Coaching Orchard Cottages Flushing, Falmouth TR11 5TR Tel. *01326 374114* E-mail. *info@betterbalance.co.uk* Web. *www.betterbalance.co.uk Better Balance*

Betterbox Communications Ltd 43 Burners Lane South Kiln Farm, Milton Keynes MK11 3HA Tel. *01908 560200* Fax. *01908 565533* E-mail. *info@betterbox.co.uk* Web. *www.betterbox.co.uk Betterbox – C M S – Cybex – Equip Trans – Hadax – I Q Technologies – Patton Electronics – Scitec – Western Telematics*

Betterware Ltd Stanley House Park Lane Castle Vale, Birmingham B35 6LJ Tel. *08451 294500* Fax. *08451 294654* E-mail. *r.way@betterware.co.uk* Web. *www.betterware.co.uk Betterware*

Bettix Ltd Lever Street, Bolton BL3 6NZ Tel. *01204 526241* Fax. *01204 521958* E-mail. *sales@bettix.co.uk* Web. *www.bettix.co.uk Bettamix – Fluoroseal*

Beverley Environmental Ltd (Head Office) Unit 2 Eagle Estate Brookers Road, Billingshurst RH14 9RZ Tel. *01403 782091* Fax. *01403 782087* E-mail. *info@beverley-environmental.co.uk* Web. *www.beverley-environmental.co.uk Beverley – Beverley Turbocoil – Genco Burners – Gencor Beverley – Hi-Temp Pump*

B F Entron Ltd Castle Mill Works Birmingham New Road, Dudley DY1 4DA Tel. *01384 455401* Fax. *01384 455551* E-mail. *sales@bfentron.co.uk* Web. *www.bfentron.co.uk DATAPAK (United Kingdom) – I PAK – MICROPAK 16 (United Kingdom) – MICROPAK 8 (United Kingdom) – MICROSTAR (United Kingdom) – MONOPAK (United Kingdom) – UNIPAK – WELDMATIC (United Kingdom) – WELDSTAR (United Kingdom)*

B F F Nonwovens Bath Road, Bridgwater TA6 4NZ Tel. *01278 428500* Fax. *01278 429499* E-mail. *enquiries@bff-technicalfabrics.co.uk* Web. *www.bff-technicalfabrics.co.uk BFF Nonwovens – Freshtex, Hycare, Tumblefresh, Big 100*

B & G Ltd 2 Premier Way, Romsey SO51 9DH Tel. *01794 518448* Fax. *01794 518077* E-mail. *info@navico.com* Web. *www.navico.com H.S. Pilot 2000 – Halcyon – Hercules – Hydra – Hydrapilot – Network*

B & G Cleaning Systems Ltd Abeles Way Holly Lane Industrial Estate, Atherstone CV9 2QZ Tel. *01827 717028* Fax. *01827 714041* E-mail. *martin@bgclean.co.uk* Web. *www.bgclean.co.uk Alto – Cheetah – Clarke – Dirt Driver – ECO-Static Hot Pressure Cleaners – Edge – Edge - industrial cleaning equipment – Edgecub 100 – Edgecub 90 – Edgesweep Ride-On – Edgesweep S Range – ESD Floor Scruber Drier Range – Gerni – Grimebuster – Hand Held Steam Gun – Hot Water Static Pressure Cleaners – Jaguar – K'Archer – Kew – Kranzle – Lance Spray-Hood Accessory – Leopard – Leopard (auto start & stop) – Lindhaus Vacuum cleaners – Lion – Lion (auto start & stop) – Lynx – Miniscrub – Nilfisk – Nova – Numatic – Panther – Prochem – Puma Stationary – Ranger – Rotawash Floor Cleaner – Tiger – Tiger Super – Truvox – V200MD – Wap – Warwick – Wildcat*

B G Europa UK Ltd Giffords Road Clopton, Wickhambrook, Newmarket CB8 8PQ Tel. *01440 821155* Fax. *01440 821156* E-mail. *parts@bgeuropa.co.uk* Web. *www.bgeuropa.co.uk B.G. Europa – Batchpac – Dryerpac – Recyclomat – Stablization Plants – Thermodrum*

B & G Lock & Tool Company Ltd Chapel Green, Willenhall WV13 1RD Tel. *01902 605946* Fax. *01902 633794* E-mail. *sales@bgpadlocks.co.uk* Web. *www.bgpadlocks.co.uk B. & G. Lock – Sta-Lock – Sta-Secure*

B & G Machining The Blacksmiths Shop Worthing Road, West Grinstead, Horsham RH13 8LW Tel. *01403 864471* Fax. *01403 865365* E-mail. *tony@bgmachining.co.uk* Web. *www.bgmachining.co.uk Fibrene – Stuarts Micrometer Blue*

B G S Productions Ltd Newtown Street Kilsyth, Glasgow G65 0LY Tel. *01236 821081* Fax. *01236 826900* E-mail. *info@scotdisc.co.uk* Web. *www.scotdisc.co.uk River – Scotdisc*

B G Technical Mouldings Ltd Fiddington, Tewkesbury GL20 7BJ Tel. *01684 299290* Fax. *01684 850198* E-mail. *sales@bgtechnical.co.uk* Web. *www.british-gaskets.co.uk Bull Rubber*

Bhardwaj Insolvency Practitioners 47-49 Green Lane, Northwood HA6 3AE Tel. *01923 820966* Fax. *01923 835311* E-mail. *info@bhardwaj.co.uk* Web. *www.bhardwaj.co.uk Bhardwaj*

B & H Colour Change Ltd 212 St Anns Hill, London SW18 2RU Tel. *08454 584121* Fax. *0845 4584131* E-mail. *gilly@colourchange.com* Web. *www.colourchange.com Chill n Win – Liquid Crystal Devices – Playsafe – Thermoscan – Touch and Reveal – wet n view*

B H R Group The Fluid Engineering Centre Wharley End, Cranfield, Bedford MK43 0AJ Tel. *01234 750422* Fax. *01234 750074* E-mail. *contactus@bhrgroup.co.uk* Web. *www.bhrgroup.com BHRA – CALTEC – DIAJET*

Bibby Lion Group 105 Duke Street, Liverpool L1 5JQ Tel. *0151 7088000* Fax. *0151 7941001* E-mail. *iain.speak@bibbydist.co.uk* Web. *www.bibbydist.co.uk Bibby Distribution (United Kingdom)*

Bibby Scientific Ltd Beacon Road, Stone ST15 0SA Tel. *01785 812121* Fax. *01785 813748* E-mail. *info@bibby-scientific.com* Web. *www.bibby-scientific.com Aquatron – Azlon – E-Mil – Esco – Interflon – Interkey – Morbank – Pressmatic – Pyrex – Quickfit – Rotaflo – Springham – Sterilin – Stuart – SVL*

Bibby Transmissions Ltd Cannon Way, Dewsbury WF13 1EH Tel. *01924 460801* Fax. *01924 457668* E-mail. *sales@bibbytransmissions.co.uk* Web. *www.bibbytransmissions.co.uk Bibbigard – Bibby – Bibbyflex – Eflex – Euroflex – P.I.V. – Permadryve – Powerpin – Stearns – Turboflex*

Bicester Products Squash Court Manufacturers Ltd 55 West End, Witney OX28 1NJ Tel. *01993 774426* Fax. *01993 779569* E-mail. *sales@squashcourts.co.uk* Web. *www.squashcourts.co.uk Bicester System – Bicesterwall*

Biddle Air Systems Ltd St Marys Road, Nuneaton CV11 5AU Tel. *024 76384233* Fax. *024 76373621* E-mail. *sales@biddle-air.co.uk* Web. *www.biddle-air.co.uk Cassettair – Coolflow – Forceflow 800 Series – Innovair – Isotherm – Modulair – Uniflow*

Biddle & Mumford Gears Ltd 8-18 Kings Place, Buckhurst Hill IG9 5EA Tel. *020 85054615* Fax. *020 85053718* E-mail. *mahendra@biddleandmumford.co.uk* Web. *www.biddleandmumford.co.uk Falcon*

Biffa Waste Services Ltd Rixton Old Hall Manchester Road, Rixton, Warrington WA3 6EW Tel. *0161 7751011* Fax. *0161 7757291* Web. *www.biffa.co.uk U.K. Waste*

Bifold Group Greengate Industrial Estate Middleton, Manchester M24 1SW Tel. *0161 3454777* Fax. *0161 3454780* E-mail. *gjacobson@bifold.co.uk* Web. *www.bifold.co.uk Solenoid Valves*

Bighead Bonding Fasteners Ltd Units 15-16 Elliott Road, Bournemouth BH11 8LZ Tel. *01202 574601* Fax. *01202 578300* E-mail. *info@bighead.co.uk* Web. *www.bighead.co.uk Bighead – Flushnut*

Billbo UK Ltd Saville Street, Macclesfield SK11 7LQ Tel. *01625 427010* Fax. *01625 511481* E-mail. *sales@billbo.co.uk* Web. *www.billbo.co.uk Billbo (Badge) – Logobears – Rascals*

Billows Protocol Ltd 11 Bridgeturn Avenue Old Wolverton, Milton Keynes MK12 5QL Tel. *01908 315539* Fax. *01908 311795* E-mail. *colin@billowsprotocol.com* Web. *www.billowsprotocol.com Billows-Protocol*

Bilz Tool 304 Bedworth Road, Coventry CV6 6LA Tel. *024 76369700* Fax. *024 76369701* E-mail. *dennis.butler@morristooling.com* Web. *www.morristooling.com Morris Tooling*

The Binding Site Ltd PO Box 11712, Birmingham B14 4ST Tel. *0121 4361000* Fax. *0121 4307061* E-mail. *info@bindingsite.co.uk* Web. *www.bindingsite.co.uk *Binding Site (United Kingdom)*

Binney & Smith Europe Ltd Bedford Heights Brickhill Drive, Bedford MK41 7PH Tel. *01234 266702* Fax. *01234 342110* E-mail. *vyoung@binneysmith.com* Web. *www.crayola.com Crayola – Crayola Anti-Dust Chalks – Crayola Creative Activity Products – Crayola Fibre Pens – Crayola Poster Paints – Crayola Water Colour – Crayola Wax Crayons – Revell Model Kits*

Binney & Son Ltd Unit H Spring Hill Industrial Park Steward Street, Birmingham B18 7AF Tel. *0121 4544545* Fax. *0121 4541145* E-mail. *binney.eng@btconnect.com Binneys*

A.J. Binns Ltd Harvest House Cranbourne Road, Potters Bar EN6 3JF Tel. *01707 855555* Fax. *01707 857565* E-mail. *enq@ajbinns.com* Web. *www.ajbinns.com Variset*

Binns Fencing Ltd Harvest House 2 Cranborne Industrial Estate Cranborne Road, Potters Bar EN6 3JF Tel. *01707 855555* Fax. *01707 857565* E-mail. *contracts@binns-fencing.com* Web. *www.binns-fencing.com Binnlock*

K Bins Ltd Westfield Mills Kirk Lane, Yeadon, Leeds LS19 7LX Tel. *0113 2509777* Fax. *0113 2506700* E-mail. *sales@kbins.com* Web. *www.kbins.com K-Bins*

Biocatalysts Ltd Unit 1 Cefn Coed Nantgarw, Cardiff CF15 7QQ Tel. *01443 843712* Fax. *01443 846500* E-mail. *sales@biocats.com* Web. *www.biocatalysts.com Combizyme – Depol – Lipomod – Macer 8 – Promod – Trysin*

Biochrom Ltd 22 Science Park Milton Road, Cambridge CB4 0FJ Tel. *01223 423723* Fax. *01223 420164* E-mail. *sales@biochrom.co.uk* Web. *www.biochrom.co.uk Amersham – Asys – Biochiom – Biochrom 30 – Biochrom 30 - PC controlled amino acid analyser, Genequant II - RNA & DNA calculator, GeneQuant pro - RNA & DNA calculator, Ultrospec 2100 pro - UV and visible, Novaspec III, Novaspec plus, visible spectrophotometer, Ultrospec 3100 pro - UV and visible spectrophotometer, Ultrospec 3300 pro - UV and VIS scanning narrow bandwidth spectrophotometer, Ultrospec 4300,5300,6300 pro - UV and VIS scanning narrow bandwidth spectrophotometer, Ultrospec 500 and 1100 pro - low cost UV and Visible Spectrophotometers - Libra S4, Libra S6, Libra S11, Libra S12, Libra S21, Libra S32, Libra S32PC, Libra S35 and Libra S35PCLightwave II, Biowave II, TOPAS Analyzer, WPA S800 and WPA S1200 – Genequant II – GeneQuant pro – Libra – Novaspec II – Novaspec Plus – TOPAS Analyzer – Ultrospec 1100 pro – Ultrospec 2100 pro – Ultrospec 3000 pro – Ultrospec 3100 pro – Ultrospec 3300 pro – Ultrospec 4300 pro – Ultrospec 500 pro – Ultrospec 5300 pro – Ultrospec 6300 pro – WPA Biowave – WPA Lightwave – WPA S800/S1200 – WPA Spectroware*

Bio Clinique The Exchange Mill Lane, Newbold on Stour, Stratford Upon Avon CV37 8DR Tel. *01789 450304* Fax. *01789 450892* Web. *www.bioclinique.co.uk Bioclinique (United Kingdom)*

Biolab UK Ltd Unit 4 Andoversford Industrial Estate Andoversford, Cheltenham GL54 4LB Tel. *01242 820969* Fax. *01242 820180* E-mail. *sales@biolabuk.com* Web. *www.biolabuk.com Aquabrome – Bayrol – BioGuard – Guardex – PoolWise – SpaGuard – Sunspot*

Biopharm Leeches 2 Bryngwili Road Pontarddulais, Swansea SA4 0XT Tel. *01792 885595* Fax. *01792 882440* E-mail. *sales@biopharm-leeches.com* Web. *www.biopharm-leeches.com Live Leeches*

Biotest UK Ltd Unit 28 Monkspath Business Park Highlands Road, Shirley, Solihull B90 4NZ Tel. *0121 7333393* Fax. *0121 7333066* E-mail. *chris_hyde@biotestuk.com* Web. *www.biotestuk.com Biotest – Hycon – Seraclone – Sereclone*

Bipra Ltd Northway House 1379 High Road, London N20 9LP Tel. *020 84453288* E-mail. *info@bipra.com* Web. *www.bipra.com Bipra Limited*

Birchfield Engineering Ltd Northfield Road Netherton, Dudley DY2 9JQ Tel. *01384 237171* Fax. *01384 237273* E-mail. *peter@birchfieldengineering.co.uk* Web. *www.birchfieldengineering.co.uk Chiron – Dainichi – Doosan – Takisawa – Miyano*

Birchgrove Products Unit 3c Merrow Business Park Merrow Lane, Guildford GU4 7WA Tel. *01483 533400* Fax. *01483 533700* E-mail. *sales@birchgrove.co.uk* Web. *www.birchgrove.co.uk Drop Stop – L'Esprit et Le Vin – Laguiole – Pulltap – Vacuvin*

Bird & Bird 15 Fetter Lane, London EC4A 1JP Tel. *020 74156000* Fax. *020 74156111* E-mail. *info@twobirds.com* Web. *www.twobirds.com Bird & Bird*

Jo Bird & Co. Ltd Factory Lane Bason Bridge, Highbridge TA9 4RN Tel. *01278 785546* Fax. *01278 780541* E-mail. *jobird@btinternet.com* Web. *www.jobird.co.uk Firebird – Firebird, Tough Store – Tough Store*

Francis W Birkett & Sons Ltd PO Box 16, Cleckheaton BD19 5JT Tel. *01274 873366* Fax. *01274 851615* E-mail. *info@fwbirkett.com* Web. *www.fwbirkett.com Franberlube – Franberlube – Francis Birkett*

Birmingham Barbed Tape Ltd Unit 11 Hartlebury Trading Estate Hartlebury, Kidderminster DY10 4JB Tel. *01299 251770* Fax. *01299 251776* E-mail. *rsmith@bbtltd.com* Web. *www.birminghambarbedtape.co.uk Bellier B Jacket – Bullet Proof Capsule – Cochrane – Flatwrap – Mobile Security Barrier – Razor Mesh – Superbarb – Wall Spike*

Birmingham Business Supplies Ltd 25 Adams Street, Birmingham B7 4LT Tel. *0121 3547881* Fax. *0121 3557288 Paperblanks*

Birmingham Chambers Of Commerce & Industry 75 Harborne Road, Birmingham B15 3DH Tel. *0121 4546171* Fax. *0121 4558670* E-mail. *enquiries@birminghamchamber.org.uk* Web. *www.birmingham-chamber.com B.C.I.*

Birmingham Midshires Financial Services Ltd PO Box 81, Wolverhampton WV9 5HZ Tel. *08456 022828* Fax. *01902 302811* E-mail. *info@birminghammidshires.co.uk* Web. *www.bmsavings.co.uk Birmingham Midshires First Response – Birmingham Midshires Mastercheque – Easy Move – First Ascent – Midshires – Society Logo – Society Logo (Man & Woman) – Unicover*

Birmingham Powder Coatings (a division of Tomburn Ltd) Clonmel Road Stirchley, Birmingham B30 2BU Tel. *0121 4594341* Fax. *0121 4511735* E-mail. *sales@tomburn.co.uk* Web. *www.tomburn.co.uk Syntha Pulvin – Tomburn*

Birmingham Pump Supplies 7 Network Park Industrial Estate Duddeston Mill Road, Saltley, Birmingham B8 1AU Tel. *0121 5033000* Fax. *0121 5033002* E-mail. *sales@birminghampumps.co.uk* Web. *www.birminghampumps.co.uk Gusher*

Birmingham Specialities Ltd Moor Lane, Birmingham B6 7HE Tel. *0121 3565026* Fax. *0121 3569198* E-mail. *sales@bhamspec.co.uk* Web. *www.bhamspec.co.uk B.S.L B.S.B.*

Birmingham Stopper Ltd Incorporating Hickton Pressings Ltd 235 Icknield Street Hockley, Birmingham B18 6QU Tel. *0121 5517781* Fax. *0121 5544567* E-mail. *info@birminghamstopper.co.uk* Web. *www.birminghamstopper.co.uk Clinch – Clinch Tube Joints*

Bisbell Magnetic Products Ltd Hillfield Lane Stretton, Burton On Trent DE13 0BN Tel. *01283 531000* Fax. *01283 534000* E-mail. *sales@bisbellmagnets.com* Web. *www.bisbellmagnets.com Bisiflex – Bisigrip – Bisimag – Bisimag – Trade Plate Holder*

Biscor Ltd Kingsmark Freeway Oakenshaw, Bradford BD12 7HW Tel. *01274 694684* Fax. *01274 694685* E-mail. *info@biscor.com* Web. *www.biscor.com Bisca-Fuse (United Kingdom) – Bisca-Pak (United Kingdom) – Bisca-Sil (United Kingdom) – Bisca-Stic (United Kingdom) – Bisca-Tex (United Kingdom)*

B I S Door Systems Ltd Unit 13-14 Hodgson Court Hodgson Way, Wickford SS11 8XR Tel. *01268 767566* Fax. *01268 560284* E-mail. *sales@bis-doors.co.uk* Web. *www.bis-doors.co.uk Compact – Harefield – MacDoor – Neway*

Bishop Pipe Freezing Ltd Pipefreezing & Hot Tapping 58a Shirley Road, Croydon CR0 7EP Tel. *0800 132750* Fax. *020 86545459* E-mail. *bishop@pipefreezingsales.com* Web. *www.pipefreezingsales.com Cryostop – Quikfreeze*

Bishop Sports & Leisure Ltd Bishops House Crown Lane, Farnham Royal, Slough SL2 3SF Tel. *01753 648666* Fax. *01753 648989* E-mail. *sales@bishopsport.co.uk* Web. *www.bishopsport.co.uk Alphagrass – Challenger – City Mini Golf*

Bison Plant Hire Ltd Unit 12 Broadway Trading Estate, South Cerney, Cirencester GL7 5UH Tel. *01285 862222* Web. *www.bisonplanthire.com Caterpillar – Kobelco*

B I S Trent Rosettes Unit 2 Railway Enterprise Centre Shelton New Road, Stoke On Trent ST4 7SH Tel. *01782 279797* Fax. *01782 279797* E-mail. *bistrent@gmail.com B.I.S. (Trent)*

B I S Valves Ltd Unit 17-23 Kingfisher Park Collingwood Road, West Moors, Wimborne BH21 6US Tel. *01202 896322* Fax. *01202 896718* E-mail. *salesadmin@bisvalves.co.uk* Web. *www.bisvalves.co.uk B.I.S.*

BI Technologies Ltd Telford Road Eastfield Industrial Park, Glenrothes KY7 4NX Tel. *01592 662200* Fax. *01592 662299* E-mail. *sales@bitechnologies.co.uk* Web. *www.bitechnologies.com Helipot – Helitrim*

Bizcare Ltd 19 St Vincent Court, Gateshead NE8 3DZ Tel. *0191 4209838* Fax. *08712 181954* E-mail. *enquiries@bizcare.co.uk* Web. *www.bizcare.co.uk Bizcare Consult – BOSS*

B J Ltd Adele House 32-34 Park Road, Lytham St Annes FY8 1RE Tel. *01253 721262* Fax. *01253 711765* E-mail. *david.corlton@beaverbrooks.co.uk* Web. *www.beaverbrooks.co.uk Beaverbrooks*

B K I Europe Ltd Theale Technology Centre Station Road Theale, Reading RG7 4AA Tel. *08709 904242* Fax. *0870 9904243* E-mail. *peterst@bkideas.co.uk* Web. *www.bkideas.co.uk Barbecue King*

B K Safety 20 Pembroke Rise, Doncaster DN5 8PP Tel. *01302 785063* Fax. *01302 785063* E-mail. *kevin-irwin@bksafety.co.uk* Web. *www.bksafety.co.uk Sumo*

B K W Instruments Ltd Weymouth Road Eccles, Manchester M30 8SH Tel. *0161 7074838* Fax. *0161 7877580* E-mail. *sales@bkwinstruments.co.uk* Web. *www.bkwinstruments.co.uk *Wika Instruments (Germany)*

Blackacre Ltd Austin Way Hampstead Industrial Estate, Birmingham B42 1DU Tel. *0121 3585066* Fax. *0121 3581721* E-mail. *sales@blackacre.co.uk* Web. *www.blackacre.co.uk Blakeacre Bolt-Lok*

Blackburn Chemicals Ltd Cunliffe Road Whitebirk Industrial Estate, Blackburn BB1 5SX Tel. *01254 52222* Fax. *01254 664224* E-mail. *sales@bbchem.co.uk* Web. *www.bbchem.co.uk Biolan – Dispelair*

Blackburne & Haynes Meadow Cottage Churt Road, Headley, Bordon GU35 8SS Tel. *01428 712155* Fax. *01428 714001 *Meadow Cottage – *Meadow Cottage Untreated – *Weydown*

Blackburn Yarn Dyers Ltd Blackburn Yarn Dyers Haslingden Road, Blackburn BB2 3HN Tel. *01254 53051* Fax. *01254 672233* E-mail. *info@bydltd.co.uk* Web. *www.bydltd.co.uk B.Y.D.*

Black Carbon Limited Rectory Barn Huntingdon Road, Wyton, Huntingdon PE28 2AD Tel. *01480 464914* E-mail. *nic@blackcarbon.co.uk* Web. *www.blackcarbon.co.uk Black Carbon*

Black Cat Fireworks Ltd Crosland Hill, Huddersfield HD4 7AD Tel. *01484 640640* Fax. *01484 658039* E-mail. *sales@blackcatfireworks.co.uk* Web. *www.blackcatfireworks.co.uk Black Cat*

Blackhall Engineering Ltd Cedar House 362 Bradford Road, Brighouse HD6 4DJ Tel. *01484 407080* Fax. *01484 400155* E-mail. *sales@blackhall.co.uk* Web. *www.blackhall.co.uk VALVE*

Blackpool Pleasure Beach Ltd Ocean Boulevard, Blackpool FY4 1EZ Tel. *08712 221234* Fax. *01253 401098* E-mail. *info@bpbltd.com* Web. *www.blackpoolpleasurebeach.com Blackpool Pleasure Beach*

Russell Black Ltd 399a Kenton Lane, Harrow HA3 8RZ Tel. *020 89077757* Fax. *020 89091055* E-mail. *sales@russellblack.co.uk* Web. *www.russellblack.co.uk Russell Black*

Black Sheep Ltd 9 Penfold Street Aylsham, Norwich NR11 6ET Tel. *01263 733142* Fax. *01263 735074* E-mail. *email@blacksheep.ltd.uk* Web. *www.blacksheep.ltd.uk Black Sheep*

Blacks Leisure Group plc Mansard Close Westgate Industrial Estate, Northampton NN5 5DL Tel. *01604 441111* Fax. *01604 441164* E-mail. *enquiries@blacks.co.uk* Web. *www.blacks.co.uk Eurohike – Ferndale – General Grant – Milletts – Peter Storm – Rockie – Tracker*

Black Teknigas & Electro Controls Ltd Orion Court Ambuscado Road Eaton Socon, St Neots PE19 8YX Tel. *01480 407074* Fax. *01480 407076* E-mail. *sales@blackteknigas.co.uk* Web. *www.blackteknigas.com ACTU – Black – Flowguard – Intek 300 – Labmite – Labstar – Labtek – Lectralevel – Ledray – Meditek – Powerseat – Provengas – Series 2000 – Supermin – Superseal – Tekni – Univar*

Blagden Specialty Chemicals Ltd Osprey House Black Eagle Square, Westerham TN16 1PA Tel. *01959 562000* Fax. *01959 565111* E-mail. *sales@blagden.co.uk* Web. *www.blagden.co.uk Blagden Chemicals*

Blagg & Johnson Ltd Newark Business Park Brunel Drive, Newark NG24 2EG Tel. *01636 703137* Fax. *01636 701914* E-mail. *info@blaggs.co.uk* Web. *www.blaggs.co.uk Blaggy – Blogg*

Blair Engineering Balmoral Road Rattray, Blairgowrie PH10 7AH Tel. *01250 872244* Fax. *01250 872098* E-mail. *sales@blairengineering.co.uk* Web. *www.blairengineering.co.uk B.R.H. – Blair – Boswell – Lainchbury – Ransomes*

Blakley Electrics Ltd 1 Thomas Road Crayford, Dartford DA1 4GA Tel. *08450 740084* Fax. *01920 464682* E-mail. *sales@blakley.co.uk* Web. *www.blakley.co.uk Flori-Stoon*

Blanewood Andrews Computing plc 5 Grove Ash Dawson Road, Bletchley, Milton Keynes MK1 1XL Tel. *01908 368001* Fax. *01908 641034* E-mail. *enquiries@blue-alligator.co.uk* Web. *www.bacuk.com Mega – Unicost – Uniledg – Unilock – Uniman – Unishop – Unisop – Unistaff – Unitend – Uniwage*

Blickle Castors & Wheels Ltd 30 Vincent Avenue Crownhill, Milton Keynes MK8 0AB Tel. *01908 560904* Fax. *01908 260510* E-mail. *sales@blickle.co.uk*

Web. *www.blickle.co.uk Blickle - Extrathane - Softhane - Besthane*

Blighline Ltd Unit 5-10 Sparrow Way Lakesview International Business Park, Hersden, Canterbury CT3 4JQ Tel. *01227 712000* Fax. *01227 719000* E-mail. *roy.corker@blighline.co.uk* Web. *www.blighline.co.uk Blighline*

Blitz Communications Ltd 100 Centennial Avenue Centennial Park, Elstree, Borehamwood WD6 3SA Tel. *020 83271000* Fax. *0870 1621111* E-mail. *enquiries@blitzcommunications.co.uk* Web. *www.blitzcommunications.co.uk Blitz Interative – Blitz Vision – TP Sound Services*

B L M Group UK Ltd Unit 4 Ampthill Business Park, Ampthill, Bedford MK45 2QW Tel. *01525 402555* Fax. *01525 402312* E-mail. *sales@blmgroup.uk.com* Web. *www.blmgroup.uk.com ADIGE – BLM – SALA*

Blockleys Brick Ltd Sommerfeld Road Trench Lock, Telford TF1 5RY Tel. *01952 251933* Fax. *01952 265377* E-mail. *sales@blockleys.com* Web. *www.blockleys.com Harlequin – Heritage – Wrekin*

B L Pneumatics Ltd Norris Way, Rushden NN10 6BP Tel. *01933 358822* Fax. *01933 410451* E-mail. *sales@blpneumatics.co.uk* Web. *www.blpneumatics.co.uk Adams Lubtech – Airmover – Asco – Bundy – Buschjost – Buster – C.Matic – CFIT – Clippard – Cnomo – Conair – Enots – Excelon – Fleetfit – Flowtec – Griflex – Herion – Iso – Isostar – John Guest – Joucomatic – Lintra – Martonair – MEGA – Midi Star – NAMUR – Norgren – Norgren - Asco - Joucomatic - Clippard - Griflex, Enots, Martonair - Excelon - Adams Lubtech - Herion - Lintra - Iso - Vdma - Cnomo - Excel - Isostar - Pneufit - C.Matic - Piezotronic - Sentronic - Airmover - Olympian - FFLuft.Fast. – Nugget – Numatics – Oetiker – Olympian – PCL – Piezotronic – Pneufit – Sapelem – Sentronic – Typhoon – VDMA – Vibrolators*

BLT&C Ltd 604 Southleigh Road, Emsworth PO10 7TA Tel. *07753 662602* E-mail. *keith.sparrow@bltandc.co.uk* Web. *bltandc.co.uk BLT&C*

Blue Arrow Personnel Services Ltd 154 Hatfield Road, St Albans AL1 4JA Tel. *01727 841433* Fax. *01727 844241* E-mail. *info@bluearrow.co.uk* Web. *www.bluearrow.co.uk Blue Arrow*

Bluedelta Unit 2 Saxon Way Melbourn, Royston SG8 6DN Tel. *01763 263120* Fax. *01763 261958* E-mail. *info@bluedelta.co.uk* Web. *www.bluedelta.co.uk Bluedeta – Milestone – Phantom PVR – Smart scart*

Blue Dragon Dry Cleaners Ltd Whiteleys Parade Uxbridge Road, Uxbridge UB10 0NZ Tel. *01895 236571* Fax. *01895 812950* Web. *www.bluedragon.uk.com Blue Dragon Dry Cleaners – Blue Dragon Hillingdon*

Blueparrot Production & Events Ltd Unit 5 Forth Industrial Centre, Sealcarr Street, Edinburgh EH5 1RF Tel. *0131 5103333* Fax. *0131 5103334* E-mail. *info@blueparrotevents.com* Web. *www.blueparrotproduction.com Blueparrot Media*

Blue Seal Ltd Unit 67 Gravelly Industrial Park, Birmingham B24 8TQ Tel. *0121 3275575* Fax. *0121 3279711* E-mail. *goconnell@blue-seal.co.uk* Web. *www.blue-seal.co.uk *Blue Seal – *Turbofan – *Vee-ray*

Blundell Harling Ltd (Incorporating Magpie Furniture) Granby Industrial Estate Albany Road, Weymouth DT4 9TH Tel. *01305 206000* Fax. *01305 760598* E-mail. *sales@blundellharling.co.uk* Web. *www.blundellharling.co.uk Academy – Cadet – Forum – *Intertech (Germany) – Portland – *Standardgraph (Germany) – Stratton – True-Angle – Trueline – Verulam – Weymouth*

Blundell Production Equipment Unit C-D Seven Stars Industrial Estate Quinn Close, Coventry CV3 4LH Tel. *024 76210270* Fax. *024 76694155* E-mail. *sales@blundell.co.uk* Web. *www.blundell.co.uk C.M.S. 400 – Cropmatic – Target*

Mathew C Blythe & Son Ltd The Green Tredington, Shipston On Stour CV36 4NJ Tel. *01608 662295* Fax. *01608 662006* E-mail. *sales@matthewcblythe.co.uk* Web. *www.mcblythe.co.uk F.I.P (Italy) – Georg Jordan (Germany) – LAPP – Microelectrica Scientifica (Italy) – Moser-Glaser (Switzerland) – Noja Power – Sadtem (France) – Trench (Austria)*

B M S Technology Ltd 10 Sandringham Close, Bournemouth BH9 3QP Tel. *0701 0700020* Fax. *0701 0700021* E-mail. *info@bmstech.com* Web. *www.bmstech.com Mantra*

B M S Vision Ltd Capricorn Park Blakewater Road, Blackburn BB1 5QR Tel. *01254 662244* Fax. *01254 267100* E-mail. *sales@barco.com* Web. *www.visionbms.com Barcocim – P.C.M.S. – Sycotex*

B N A British Nursing Association Tor Lodge 15 Park Hill Road, Torquay TQ1 2AL Tel. *08718 733324* Fax. *01803 299161* E-mail. *info@bna.co.uk* Web. *www.bna.co.uk B.N.A.*

B N International Metro Centre Dwight Road, Watford WD18 9YD Tel. *01923 219132* Fax. *01923 219134* Web. *www.bnint.nl *Balacron (Netherlands) – *Durafoam (Netherlands) – *Durafort (Netherlands) – *Durunyl (Netherlands)*

B N Thermic 34 Stephenson Way, Crawley RH10 1TN Tel. *01293 547361* Fax. *01293 531432* E-mail. *sales@bnthermic.co.uk* Web. *www.bnthermic.co.uk Bush Nelson*

Boalloy Industries Ltd Radnor Park Trading Estate West Heath, Radnor Park Industrial Estate, Congleton CW12 4QA Tel. *01260 275151* Fax. *01260 279696* E-mail. *sales@boalloyindustries.co.uk* Web. *www.boalloyindustries.co.uk Grainliner – Insuliner – Linkliner – Localiner – One 7 Liner – Seven 5 liner – Tautliner – Three 5 liner*

Boardman Bros Ltd 50 Red Bank, Manchester M4 4HF Tel. *0161 8322381* Fax. *0161 8332456* E-mail. *phil@boardmanbros.co.uk* Web. *www.boardmanbros.co.uk Boardman*

Bob Crosby Agencies Ltd Crosby House Field Close, Shieldfield, Newcastle Upon Tyne NE2 1AE Tel. *0191 2098000* Fax. *0191 2098001* E-mail. *roger@crosbys.co.uk* Web. *www.crosbys.co.uk *Churchill – *John Artis – *Lune – *Royal Doulton – *Steelite – *Wedgwood*

Bob Martin UK Ltd Wemberham Lane Yatton, Bristol BS49 4BS Tel. *01934 831000* Fax. *01934 831050* E-mail. *sales@bobmartin.co.uk* Web. *www.bobmartin.co.uk Bob Martin – Caperns – Gaylets – Pestroy – Tibs – Tydisan*

B O B Stevenson Ltd 5 Coleman Street, Derby DE24 8NL Tel. *01332 574112* Fax. *01332 757286* E-mail. *l.perrott@bobstevenson.co.uk* Web. *www.bobstevenson.co.uk Alcosa – Flamgard – Turngrove*

B O C Edwards (Head Office) Crawley Business Quarter Manor Royal, Crawley RH10 9LW Tel. *01293 528844* Fax. *01293 533453* E-mail. *carol.hunt@edwards.boc.com* Web. *www.edwardsvaccum.com Barocel – Diffstak – Drystar – Hibon – Hick Hargreaves – Spectron – SpeediValves – Stokes*

Boc Gases Ltd The Priestley Centre 10 Priestley Road, Surrey Research Park, Guildford GU2 7XY Tel. *01483 579857* Fax. *0800 136601* E-mail. *specialproducts@uk.gases.boc.com* Web. *www.boc.com Alushield – Argoshield – Aromagas – Atac – B O C – B O C Sureflow – Cryoshield – Cryospeed – Drystar – Edwards – Endomix – Entonox – Fabmax – Intac – Lasox – Lyomaster – Nitrazone – Novox – Primox – Primox – Specshield – Spectra – Spectra Seal – Speedivac – Stainshield – Storeshield – Sureflow – Transhield – Vairox – Vitox*

BOCM Pauls Ltd Mill Road, Radstock BA3 5TT Tel. *01761 438055* Fax. *01275 373828* E-mail. *info@bocmpauls.co.uk* Web. *www.bocmpauls.co.uk Challenger Feeds – Farm Feed Blends – Farmgate – Feedex Nutrition – Feeds Marketing – Hickstead Feeds – Marsden Feeds*

Boddingtons Ltd Blackwater Trading Estate The Causeway, Maldon CM9 4GG Tel. *01621 874200* Fax. *01621 874299* E-mail. *john@boddingtons-ltd.com* Web. *www.boddingtons-ltd.com Detectamesh – Detectatape – Detectatape, Euromesh, Eurotape, Overlord, Sentree, Superstrong, Ultra-strong, Wavelay. – Euromesh – Eurotape – Overlord – Sentree – Superstrong – Ultra-strong – Wavelay*

Bodle Bros Ltd Southdown Store Cuckfield Road, Burgess Hill RH15 8RE Tel. *01444 247757* Fax. *01444 870953* E-mail. *shop@bodlebros.co.uk* Web. *www.bodlebros.co.uk *GB Seeds – *J & H Bunn Fertilisers – *Kemira Fertilisers – *Lillico Attlee – *Sinclair McGill*

Bodycote H I P Ltd Carlisle Close Sheffield Road, Chesterfield S41 9ED Tel. *01246 260888* Fax. *01246 260889* E-mail. *lance.tidbury@bodycote.com* Web. *www.bodycote.com Densal*

Bodycote Metallurgical Coatings Ltd Shakespeare Street, Wolverhampton WV1 3LR Tel. *01902 452915* Fax. *01902 352917* E-mail. *sales.bmc@bodycote.co.uk* Web. *www.bodycote.co.uk Sheraplex – Sherardizing*

Bodyshop Solutions (t/a Celette) Stephenson Close Drayton Fields Industrial Estate, Daventry NN11 8RF Tel. *01327 300700* Fax. *01327 300586* E-mail. *enquiries@celetteuk.com* Web. *www.celetteuk.com *Bodymaster (France)*

Bodywise Ltd Unit 8 Enterprise Way, Cowes PO31 8AP Tel. *01983 248888* Fax. *01983 248899* E-mail. *sales@bodywise.biz* Web. *www.bodywise.biz 121 – 6 S – Aeolus – Bodywise – Curricula – Cyclone – Feminine Glow – Kind – Liquid Silk – Man to Man – Mankind – Maximus*

Bohler Welding Group Ltd European Business Park Taylors Lane, Oldbury B69 2BN Tel. *0121 5697700* Fax. *0121 5442876* E-mail. *sales@bwguk.co.uk* Web. *www.bwguk.co.uk Bohler Dur – Bohler Fox – Bohler Ledurit – Fontargen – Soudokay – Soudometal – Thyssen – UTP*

Boiswood LLP Unit A1 Spinnaker House Spinnaker Road, Hempsted, Gloucester GL2 5FD Tel. *01452 330011* Fax. *01452 330088* E-mail. *info@boiswood.co.uk* Web. *www.boiswood.co.uk *C.T.E. Chem-Tec (U.S.A.) – Flowmeca – *Furon (U.S.A.) – *Go (U.S.A.) – O'Brien Corporation – *Setra (U.S.A.)*

Bollhoss Fastenings Ltd Midacre Willenhall Trading Estate Midacre, Willenhall WV13 2JW Tel. *01902 637161* Fax. *01902 609495* E-mail. *enquiries@bollhoff.co.uk* Web. *www.bollhoss.com Amtec – Flexax – Quickloc – Rivclinch – Rivkle (Rivnut) – Rivset – Seal-Lock – Snaplock – Spred-Sert*

Bolt & Nut Manufacturing White Lee Road Swinton, Mexborough S64 8BH Tel. *01709 570212* Fax. *01709 584125* E-mail. *sales@tachart.com* Web. *www.tachart.com B.N.M.*

Bolton Gate Co. Ltd Waterloo Street, Bolton BL1 2SP Tel. *01204 871000* Fax. *01204 871049* E-mail. *general@boltongate.co.uk* Web. *www.boltongate.co.uk 1/2 Hour Fire Resisting Roller Shutter – Collapsible Gates – Contour 2000 – Escalator Shutters – Eurofold – Fibershield – Mid Bar Collapsible Gates – P.V.C. Strip Curtains – Supercoil – Superfold – Superior – Thermally Insulated Bi-Folding Door – Vertical Drop Rolling Shutters*

Bolton Plastic Components Ltd Lever Street, Bolton BL3 6NZ Tel. *01204 526241* Fax. *01204 521958* E-mail. *dbutler@boltonplastics.co.uk* Web. *www.boplas.co.uk Boplas – Versaflex*

Bomac Electric Ltd 13a & 13b Randles Road Knowsley Business Park, Prescot L34 9HX Tel. *0151 5464401* Fax. *0151 5491661* E-mail. *peter.bowen@bomac-elec.co.uk* Web. *www.bomac-elec.co.uk Bomac*

Bombardier Transportation Rolling Stock UK Ltd Derby Carriage Works Litchurch Lane, Derby DE24 8AD Tel. *01332 257500* Fax. *01332 266271* E-mail. *heidi.lee@uk.transport.bombardier.com* Web. *www.bombardier.com Bombardier Transportation*

Bonar Floors Ltd Unit 92 Seedlee Road Walton Summit Centre, Bamber Bridge, Preston PR5 8AE Tel. *020 70330335* Fax. *0870 8550535* Web. *www.bonarfloors.co.uk Modulus*

Bonar Yarns & Fabrics Ltd St Salvador Street, Dundee DD3 7EU Tel. *01382 227346* Fax. *01382 202378* E-mail. *info@bonaryarns.com* Web. *www.bonaryarns.com Bonafil – Bonagrass – Bonagrass - Bonar Yarns – Bonar Yarns – Bonaslide – Bonasoft*

Bondaglass Voss Ltd 158 Ravenscroft Road, Beckenham BR3 4TW Tel. *020 87780071* Fax. *020 86595297* E-mail. *bondaglass@btconnect.com Bonda – Bonda Wood Fill – Bondafiller – Bondaglass – Flexovoss – G4*

Bonds Precision Casting Ltd Clitheroe Works Potters Loaning, Alston CA9 3TP Tel. *01434 381228* Fax. *01434 381038* E-mail. *andrew.dodd@bondsprecisioncastings.com* Web. *www.bondsprecisioncastings.com Ecoshaw – Ecoshaw - ceramic moulding process. – Shaw*

Bond Worth Townshend Works Puxton Lane, Kidderminster DY11 5DF Tel. *01562 745000* Fax. *01562 732827* E-mail. *enquiries@bondworth.co.uk* Web. *www.bondworth.co.uk Afghan – Barbican – Berkeley – Berkeley Variations – Bondax – Camargue – Florette – Olympus – Precious Gems – Wensleydale*

Boneham & Turner Ltd Oddicroft Lane, Sutton In Ashfield NG17 5FS Tel. *01623 445450* Fax. *01623 621645* E-mail. *sales@boneham.co.uk* Web. *www.boneham.co.uk B & T – Boneham Metal Products (BMP) (U.S.A.)*

Bonfiglioli UK Ltd 3-7 Grosvenor Grange Woolston, Warrington WA1 4SF Tel. *01925 852667* Fax. *01925 852668* E-mail. *sales@bonfiglioli.com* Web. *www.bonfiglioli.com Bonfiglioli Components – Bonfiglioli Riduttori – Silectrom System – Trasmital Bonfiglioli*

Bonhams Auctioneers Montpelier Street, London SW7 1HH Tel. *020 73933900* Fax. *020 73933905* E-mail. *chris.watson@bonhams.com* Web. *www.bonhams.com Bonhams*

Bonomi UK Ltd Thomas Industrial Park, Nuneaton CV11 6BQ Tel. *024 76320768* Fax. *024 76354143* E-mail. *sales@bonomi.co.uk* Web. *www.bonomi.co.uk AVS Valves Ltd*

Bonsoir Of London Ltd 45 Broadwick Street, London W1F 9QW Tel. *020 74392050* Fax. *020 74392215* E-mail. *sophie@bonsoir-showroom.com* Web. *www.bonsoirdirect.com Bonsoir*

Boodles Boodles House 35 Lord Street, Liverpool L2 9SQ Tel. *0151 2272525* Fax. *0151 2551070* E-mail. *nicholaswainwright@boodles.com* Web. *www.boodles.com Boodles*

Boomer Industries Ltd Knockmore Hill Industrial Estate 6 Ferguson Road, Lisburn BT28 2FW Tel. *028 92662881* Fax. *028 92661119* E-mail. *orders@boomer.co.uk* Web. *www.boomer.co.uk Clipatrave – Flexiframe – PVC Profiles – Stapleframe*

Booth Dispencers Moor Park Avenue, Blackpool FY2 0LZ Tel. *01253 501800* Fax. *01253 501804* E-mail. *sales@booth-dispensers.co.uk* Web. *www.booth-dispensers.co.uk Booth*

Booth Industries PO Box 50, Bolton BL3 2RW Tel. *01204 366333* Fax. *01204 380888* E-mail. *marketing@booth-industries.co.uk* Web. *www.booth-industries.co.uk Booth Doors and Shutters – Booth Offshore Doors and Systems – Booth Repairs and Maintenance – Booth Security*

Boot Tree 1 Addison Bridge Place, London W14 8XP Tel. *020 76022866* Fax. *020 76022085* E-mail. *robertlusk@boottree.co.uk* Web. *www.birkinstock.co.uk Hikers – Nature SKO*

G Bopp & Co. Ltd (Registered Office) Grange Close Clover Nook Industrial Park, Somercotes, Alfreton DE55 4QT Tel. *01773 521266* Fax. *01773 521163* E-mail. *info@gbopp.com* Web. *www.boppmesh.co.uk Absolta – Betamesh – Bopp – Bopp S D – Bopp SI – D.F.S. – Hurtz – Kufner – Poremet/Absolta – Sefar – Topmesh*

Border Industrial Services (T/A Border Industrial Services Ltd) Unit 1 Darren Buildings Prince of Wales Industrial, Abercarn, Newport NP11 5AR Tel. *01495 237888* Fax. *01495 237900* E-mail. *sales@borderbobcat.com* Web. *www.borderbobcat.com Ausa – Bobcat*

Boremasters High Street Cleobury Mortimer, Kidderminster DY14 8DS Tel. *01299 270942* Fax. *01299 270212* E-mail. *alanrobins@boremasters.co.uk* Web. *www.boremasters.co.uk Spacemasters – TDR*

Borgers Ltd Hortonwood 30, Telford TF1 7LJ Tel. *01952 670345* Fax. *01952 670123* E-mail. *info@borgers-group.com* Web. *www.borgers-group.com Develop solutions for the automotive industry – Propylat – *Triflex (Germany)*

Boris Net Co. Ltd Copse Road, Fleetwood FY7 6RP Tel. *01253 779291* Fax. *01253 778203* E-mail. *john@borisnet.co.uk* Web. *www.borisnet.co.uk Boris Nets*

Borregaard UK Clayton Road Birchwood, Warrington WA3 6QQ Tel. *01925 285400* Fax. *01925 285434* E-mail. *marketing_europe@borregaard.com* Web. *www.borregaard.com Additive A – Additive A/Traffaid – *Borrebond – *Borresperse (Norway) – Traffaid – *Ufoxane (Norway) – *Ultrazine (Norway) – *Vanisperse (Norway) – *Weltex (Sweden)*

Bosal UK Ltd Unit 330 Four Oaks Road, Bamber Bridge, Preston PR5 8AP Tel. *01772 771000* Fax. *01772 312750* E-mail. *buk.marketing@eur.bosal.com* Web. *www.bosal.com Bosal*

Bosch Lawn & Garden Ltd Suffolk Works, Stowmarket IP14 1EY Tel. *01449 742000* Fax. *01449 742008* Web. *www.bosch.co.uk Atco Admiral 16 Push – Atco Admiral 16 S. – Atco Admiral 16 S.E. – Atco Balmoral 14 S. – Atco Balmoral 14 S.E. – Atco Balmoral 17 S. – Atco Balmoral 17 S.E. – Atco Balmoral 20 S. – Atco Balmoral 20 S.E. – Atco Club B.20 – Atco Q.X. 10 x Blade Cylinder Cassette – Atco Q.X. 5 x blade Cylinder Cassette – Atco Q.X. 6 Blade Cylinder Cassette – Atco Q.X. Lawn Scarifier Cassette – *Atco Quiet Shredder 1600 (Germany) – *Atco Quiet Shredder 1800 (Germany) – *Atco Quiet Shredder 2000 (Germany) – Atco Royale B.20 E. – Atco Royale B.24 E. – Atco Royale B.24 R. V.C. – Atco Royale B.30 F. – Atco Viscount 19 S. – Atco Viscount 19 S.E. – Atco Windsor 12 S. – Atco Windsor 14 S. – *Bosch A.H.S. 3 (Switzerland) – *Bosch A.H.S. 4 (Switzerland) – Bosch A.H.S. 40 - 24 (Switzerland) – Bosch A.H.S. 48 - 24 (Switzerland) – Bosch A.H.S. 55 - 24 – Bosch A.H.S. 60 - 24 (Switzerland) – Bosch A.H.S. 6000 Pro (Switzerland) – Bosch A.H.S. 7000 Pro (Switzerland) – Bosch A.K.E. 30 - 17 (Germany) – Bosch A.K.E. 35 - 17 (Germany) – Bosch A.K.E. 40 - 17 – Bosch A.L.M. 28 – Bosch A.L.M. 34 – Bosch A.R.T. 23 – Bosch A.R.T. 25 – Bosch A.R.T. 30 – Bosch A.S.M. 32 – Bosch A.X.T. 1600 (Germany) – Bosch A.X.T. 1800 (Germany) – *Bosch A.X.T. 2000 (Germany) – Bosch Aquatak 100 (Italy) – Bosch Aquatak 120i (Italy) – Bosch Aquatak 1300 si (Italy) – Bosch Aquatak 1500 si (Italy) – Qualcast Classic Electric 30 – Qualcast Classic Petrol 35 S – Qualcast Classic Petrol 43 S – Qualcast Cobra 32 – Qualcast Concorde 32 – Qualcast Easi-Lite 28 – Qualcast Easi-Lite 34 – Qualcast Easi-trak 32 – Qualcast Elan 32 – Qualcast Hedge Master 370 – Qualcast Hedge Master 420 – Qualcast Hedge Master 480 – Qualcast Lawn Raker 32 – Qualcast Panther 30 – Qualcast Power-Line – Qualcast Powertrak 34 – QUALCAST POWERTRAK 400 – Qualcast Q.X. Lawn Scarifer Cassette*

Bosch Rexroth Ltd 38 Herald Way Binley Industrial Estate, Coventry CV3 2RQ Tel. *024 76635711* Fax. *024 76635041* E-mail. *sales@boschrexroth.co.uk* Web. *www.boschrexroth.co.uk EDI (Italy) – EDI - Oil Sistem - Oil Control - OLEODINAMICA LC – Oil Control (Italy) – Oil Sistem (Italy) – OLEODINAMICA (Italy)*

Bosch Rexroth Ltd Broadway Lane South Cerney, Cirencester GL7 5UH Tel. *01285 863000* Fax. *01285 863003* E-mail. *info@boschrexroth.co.uk* Web. *www.boschrexroth.co.uk Mecman – Quiet – Wabco*

Robert Bosch Ltd PO Box 93, Uxbridge UB9 5HJ Tel. *01895 834466* Fax. *01895 838388* E-mail. *hermann.kaess@uk.bosch.com* Web. *www.bosch.co.uk Automation Technology – Automotive – Blaupunkt – Power Tools – Telecommunications*

Bosch Security Systems PO Box 750, Uxbridge UB9 5ZJ Tel. *01895 878088* Fax. *01895 878089* E-mail. *paul.wong@uk.bosch.com* Web. *www.boschsecurity.co.uk Abacus (United Kingdom) – Classix (United Kingdom) – TalkDac (United Kingdom) – TriTech (U.S.A.)*

Bose Ltd Unit 1 Ambley Green Gillingham Business Park, Gillingham ME8 0NJ Tel. *08707 414500* Fax. *08707 414545* E-mail. *philip_carpenter@bose.com* Web. *www.bose.com Acoustimass – Base Modeler – Bose – Bose 802 – Bose Lifestyle – Direct Reflecting – Freespace – Stereo Everywhere*

Bostik Ltd Ulverscroft Road, Leicester LE4 6BW Tel. *01785 272727* Fax. *0116 2689299* E-mail. *sales@bostik.co.uk* Web. *www.bostik.co.uk Aquagrip – Beberod – Blu-Tack – Boscotex – Bostik – Easy-Stik – Prestik – Pro-Stik – Supergrip – Thermogrip – Viking*

Bostik Ltd Common Road, Stafford ST16 3EH Tel. *01785 272727* Fax. *01785 257236* Web. *www.bostik.com Araldite – Bostik – Cementone – Evo-Stik – Flashband – Hiflo – Idenden – P5125 – T303*

Bostik Sovereign Chemicals Park Road Industrial Estate Park Road, Barrow In Furness LA14 4EQ Tel. *01229 870800* Fax. *01229 870500* E-mail. *henry@sovchem.co.uk* Web. *www.sovchem.co.uk Sovereign Chemical Industries*

Boston Munchy Ltd Navigation Road, Worcester WR5 3DE Tel. *01905 763100* Fax. *01905 763101* E-mail. *sales@bostonmatthews.co.uk* Web. *www.bostonmatthews.co.uk Boston Matthews*

Boston Retail Products PO Box 3564, Faringdon SN7 9AR Tel. *08707 706680* Fax. *08707 706681* E-mail. *sales@bostonretail.com* Web. *www.bostonretail.com Bumper Posts – Bumper Rails – Decorative Truss – Displays – Entrance Matting – Extrusions – Light Systems – Modular Wiring – Security – Trolley Guidance Rails*

Bosuns Locker 10 Military Road The Royal Harbour, Ramsgate CT11 9LG Tel. *01843 597158* Fax. *01843 597158* E-mail. *accounts@whitstablemarine.co.uk* Web. *www.whitstablemarine.co.uk Bosuns locker*

Bottcher UK Ltd Cwmdraw Industrial Estate Newtown, Ebbw Vale NP23 5AE Tel. *01495 350300* Fax. *01495 350064* E-mail. *stephen.hannon@bottcher-systems.com* Web. *www.boettcher.de Febo-flex – Febo-Grav – Febo-Lith – Febo-Pren – Febo-Press – Febo-Print*

Bottle Green Drinks Co. Frogmarsh Mill South Woodchester, Stroud GL5 5ET Tel. *01453 872882* Fax. *01453 872188* E-mail. *simonspeers@bottlegreen.co.uk* Web. *www.bottlegreen.co.uk Bongrape – Bottlegreen*

Bourjois Ltd Princess House 50-60 Eastcastle Street, London W1W 8EA Tel. *020 74366110* Fax. *020 74365490* E-mail. *claire.laurin@chanel.co.uk* Web. *www.boujois.co.uk *Soir De Paris (France)*

Bourne Leisure 1 Park Lane, Hemel Hempstead HP2 4YL Tel. *01442 230300* Fax. *01442 230368* E-mail. *jane.bentall@bourneleisuregroup.co.uk* Web. *www.haven.com Haven Leisure*

Bourton Group Ltd (Head Office) Bourton Hall Bourton, Rugby CV23 9SD Tel. *01926 633333* Fax. *01926 633450* E-mail. *info@bourton.co.uk* Web. *www.bourton.co.uk Best Operations Practice – Human Factors – Management Consultants to Industry – Management of Change – Strategy Development – Supply Chain Management*

Bowak Ltd Unit 5 Sterling Way, Reading RG30 6HW Tel. *0118 9415511* Fax. *0118 9451961* E-mail. *info@bowak.co.uk* Web. *www.bowak.co.uk Bowak*

Bowens International Ltd 355 Old Road, Clacton On Sea CO15 3RH Tel. *01255 422807* Fax. *01255 475503* E-mail. *info@bowens.co.uk* Web. *www.bowensinternational.co.uk Bowens International*

Bower Roebuck & Co. Ltd Glendale Mills New Mill, Holmfirth HD9 7EN Tel. *01484 682181* Fax. *01484 683469* E-mail. *info@bowerroebuck.com* Web. *www.bowerroebuck.co.uk A Laverton – Bower Roebuck and Co Ltd*

Bowers Ltd Unit 5 Longley Lane Sharston Industrial Area, Manchester M22 4WT Tel. *0161 9453126* Fax. *0161 9460384* E-mail. *mark@bowerssemiconductors.com* Web. *www.bowerssemiconductors.com Ferraz – Fuji – Mitsubishi – Powerex – Protistor – Pyristor – Toshiba*

W H Bowker Ltd Holme Road Bamber Bridge, Preston PR5 6BP Tel. *01772 628800* Fax. *01772 628801* E-mail. *enquiries@bowkergroup.co.uk* Web. *www.bowkertransport.co.uk Bowker*

Bowman International Ltd Unit 10 Isis Court Wyndyke Furlong, Abingdon OX14 1DZ Tel. *01235 462500* Fax. *01235 811234* E-mail. *enquiries@bowman.co.uk* Web. *www.bowman.co.uk Oilite – WMU – WMX – WMG – WMI-6*

Boxall Engineering Ltd Unit 50 Grace Business Centre 23 Willow Lane, Mitcham CR4 4TU Tel. *020 86488468* Fax. *020 86484162* E-mail. *info@boxall-industrial.co.uk* Web. *www.boxall-industrial.co.uk Boxall Industrial*

Boxclever Technology House 239 Ampthill Road, Bedford MK42 9QQ Tel. *01234 355233* Fax. *01234 226090* E-mail. *enquiries@boxclever.co.uk* Web. *www.boxclever.co.uk Granada TV & Video – National Telebank – Visionhire*

Boxes & Packaging Ltd 11 Uxbridge Road, Leicester LE4 7ST Tel. *0116 2662666* Fax. *0116 2662555* E-mail. *sales@boxesandpackaging.co.uk* Web. *www.boxesandpackaging.co.uk Lavender Boxes – Mondi Packaging*

Box Factory Ltd 2 Caswell Road, Leamington Spa CV31 1QD Tel. *01926 430510* Fax. *01926 430505* E-mail. *sales@boxfactory.co.uk* Web. *www.boxfactory.co.uk Key Kap*

Boxford Ltd Wheatley, Halifax HX3 5AF Tel. *01422 358311* Fax. *01422 355924* E-mail. *sales@boxford.co.uk* Web. *www.boxford.co.uk Boxford – Boxford – Boxford*

Boxpak Ltd 65 Church Road, Newtownabbey BT36 7LR Tel. *028 90365421* Fax. *028 90866731* E-mail. *mmaitland@boxpak.co.uk* Web. *www.boxpak.co.uk Boxpak*

Boydell & Jacks Ltd Marlborough Street, Burnley BB11 2HW Tel. *01282 456411* Fax. *01282 437496* E-mail. *sales@featherwing.com* Web. *www.featherwing.com Featherwing*

Boyriven 23 Wainman Road, Peterborough PE2 7BU Tel. *01733 361377* Fax. *01733 361334* E-mail. *sales@boyriven-uk.com* Web. *www.boyriven.com Laverl – Pesca*

Boys & Boden Ltd Mill Lane, Welshpool SY21 7BL Tel. *01938 556677* Fax. *01938 555773* E-mail. *dean@boysandboden.co.uk* Web. *www.pearstairs.co.uk Boden Timber Frame*

Boyton B R J System Buildings Ltd 1 Tyne Road, Sandy SG19 1SA Tel. *01767 692572* Fax. *01767 691268* E-mail. *paul@boyton-brj.co.uk* Web. *www.boyton-brg.co.uk Jak-Bilt – Link-bilt – Lok-bilt – Mod-bilt – Pak-bilt – Skid-bilt – Speedi-bilt – Tow-bilt*

B P plc 1 St James's Square, London SW1Y 4PD Tel. *020 74964000* Fax. *020 74964630* Web. *www.bp.com Actipron – Adco – Adcut – Adform – Adformal – Adformax – Adkemet – Adkriss – Admax – Aerowrap – Air BP – Amguard – Anticip – Anticip-8 – Apollo – Aquaguard – Aquicide – Aquigrind – Asentra – Atela – Auto Magic – Autoset – Autran – Avada – Axiom – Bartran – Batson – Bezora – Bisoflex – Bisol – Bisolube – Bisomer – BP – BP Amoco – BP Carwash – BP Domesticol – BP Energy – BP Express Shopping – BP Gas – BP Plus – BP Response – BP Shop – BP Super – BP Transform – BP-in-Shield – Breox – BXL – Cativa – Caveman – Charringtons – Cilora – Counterplus – Cutora – Datapron – Detecta – Diatsol – Dielube – Distoleum – Dominion – Duckhams – Duckhams QTT – Empera – Endura – Ener – Enerbio – Enercare – Enercoat – Enerflex – Energaz – Energear – Energol – Energrease – Enerpar – Enerprint – Enersyn – Enerthene – Engine's Choice, The – Envop – Envron – Fedaro – Fleetmaster – Fleetol – Fletol – Flightcard – Formodac – FuelMaster – Gradex – Himaro – Hitide – Hy-Bar – Hybild – Hycan – Hyform – Hyfrac – Hykleen – Hylosan – Hypac – Hypergrade – Hypergrade Plus – Hyperion – Hypogear – Hyprint – Hysa – Hysol – Hyvis – Igloo – Indic-8 – Innovene – Innovex – Isocool – Isofon – Jaycat – Kemcut – Ketonex – Kriscat – Laudus – Leap – Lightning – Limslip – Liqualine – Lumaro – Lyrex – Lyro – Lyrol – Maccurat – Macgas – Mainman – Microtrend – Multipet – Napelec – Napgel – Naptel – Napvis – National – Noctula – Novex – Olexobit – Oxysolve – Palmit – Pandora – Parvula – Pink – Polyart – Power – Powercut – Powernet – Practiplast – Predict – Premiercard – Prozone – Pusila – Q – Q.S. – Q.X.R. – Quendila – Quendrila – Rassapron – Recyclex – Renovex – Rigidex – Rigilene – Rigipore – Royal Standard – Sacco – Sarapron – Semin – Sertis – Sesame – Sevora – Silvapron – Soltrend – Stemkor – Super V – Supercharge – Supergreen – Supervisco Static – Synarol – Syncurat – Syncut – Syntrend – Technigram – Teroman – Terrac – Theba – Tiptone – Tiptone Alba – Tiptonic – Torapron – Tractran – Transbus PT – Transcal – Transclean – Transcut – Trifid – Troikal – Troikene – Trokene – Trokyd – Trokyl – Truckstops – Turbinol – Ultravis – Ulvapron – Um-Matic – Vanellus – Vervis – Visco – Visco 2000 – Visco 5000 – Visco 7000 – Visco Nova – Vistra – Zip Grip – Zircon*

B P A UK Ltd (Vacuum Pumps & Blowers) Unit A6 Astra Park Parkside Lane, Leeds LS11 5SZ Tel. *0113 2765000* Fax. *0113 2715880* E-mail. *sales@bpauk.com* Web. *www.bpauk.com BPA – BPA - Vacuum Pumps.*

B P C Anglia Ltd Unit 1 Brunel Business Court Brunel Way, Thetford IP24 1HP Tel. *01842 762670* Fax. *01842 762633* E-mail. *mail@bpc-anglia.co.uk* Web. *www.bpc-anglia.co.uk pest west fly killers*

bpi.agri Worcester Road, Leominster HR6 0QA Tel. *01568 617220* Fax. *01568 611435* E-mail. *sales@bpiagri.com* Web. *www.bpiagri.com Bontite – Silotite*

B P I Films Ltd Moor Road, Sevenoaks TN14 5EQ Tel. *01732 450001* Fax. *01732 740043* E-mail. *admin@bpipoly.com* Web. *www.bpifilms.com Advanced Films*

B P P Professional Education B P P House Aldine Place, London W12 8AA Tel. *020 87402222* Fax. *020 87402239* E-mail. *carl@bpp.com* Web. *www.bpp.com Password ABCD*

B & Q Head Office Customer Service Line Head Office 1 Hampshire Corporate Park Templars Way, Chandler's Ford, Eastleigh SO53 3YX Tel. *08456 096688* Fax. *023 80257480* E-mail. *customerservicedepartment@b-and-q.co.uk* Web. *www.diy.com B&Q*

J Bradbury & Co. Ltd Britannia Mills Stoney Battery, Huddersfield HD1 4TW Tel. *01484 648182* Fax. *01484 648669* E-mail. *sales@bradburyfabrics.com*

Web. *www.bradburyfabrics.com Aid Blankets – Clanacric – Contract Upholstery Tweeds – Scarves Travel Rugs – Travel Rugs – Woollen Blankets*

Bradford Tool Group Beta Works 1 Tong Street, Bradford BD4 9PW Tel. *01274 683902* Fax. *01274 651168* Web. *www.bradtool.co.uk Bradtool*

Bradken UK Ltd Box 4 Heath Road, Wednesbury WS10 8LZ Tel. *0121 5264111* Fax. *0121 5264174 B.F. 061 – B.F. 1105 – B.F. 122 – B.F. 123 – B.F. 15/55 – B.F. 151 – B.F. 152 – B.F. 153 – B.F. 18/37 – B.F. 183 – B.F. 200 – B.F. 201 – B.F. 202 – B.F. 203 – B.F. 204 – B.F. 2108 – B.F. 25/12 – B.F. 25/20 – B.F. 25/6 – B.F. 253 – B.F. 254 – B.F. 281 – B.F. 282 – B.F. 303 – B.F. 423 – B.F. 683 – Mokro – Tufchrome*

Bradley Pulverizer Co. 15 Kennet Road, Dartford DA1 4QN Tel. *01322 559106* Fax. *01322 528690* E-mail. *sales@bradleypulv.com* Web. *www.bradleypulverizer.co.uk Bradley Hercules – Broadfield – Griffin – Junior Hercules*

Braime Elevator Components Ltd Hunslet Road, Leeds LS10 1JZ Tel. *0113 2461800* Fax. *0113 2435021* E-mail. *4b-uk@go4b.com* Web. *www.go4b.com 4B (U.S.A.) – Braime (United Kingdom) – SETEM (France)*

Brakes Alpha Way Thorpe Industrial Park, Thorpe, Egham TW20 8RT Tel. *01784 485050* Fax. *01784 485040* Web. *www.brake.co.uk Cater Care – Orchard Farm*

Bramah Alarms 31 Oldbury Place, London W1U 5PT Tel. *020 79357147* Fax. *020 79352779* E-mail. *lock.sales@bramah.co.uk* Web. *www.bramah.co.uk Bramah – Joseph Bramah – Rola*

Brammer Ltd Unit 26 Westbrook Road Trafford Park, Manchester M17 1AY Tel. *0161 8488484* Fax. *0161 8728718* E-mail. *cm@brammer.plc.uk* Web. *www.brammer.co.uk/ B.S.L.*

Brandauer Precision Pressings 235 Bridge Street West, Birmingham B19 2YU Tel. *0121 3592822* Fax. *0121 3592836* E-mail. *aedwards@brandauer.co.uk* Web. *www.brandauer.co.uk Brandauer*

BRANDMOO (LONDON) 4 Cuthill Brae Willow Wood Park, West Calder EH55 8QE Tel. *01501 762082* E-mail. *molly@brandmoo.com* Web. *www.brandmoo.com Brandmoo – Mookow*

Brandone Machine Tool Ltd 48 Station Road, Harrow HA1 2SQ Tel. *020 88637141* Fax. *020 88613658* E-mail. *brandone@btconnect.com* Web. *www.brandonemarking.co.uk *Albert Otto (Germany) – *Couth (Spain) – *Diro (Germany) – *Hezel (Germany) – *Kolher (Germany) – *Kottaus & Busch (Germany) – *Mecagrav (France) – *Scorbot (Israel) – *Simplex – *Veenstra (Netherlands) – *Z.A.B. (Netherlands)*

Michael Brandon Ltd 15-17 Oliver Cresent, Hawick TD9 9BJ Tel. *01450 373333* Fax. *01450 375252* E-mail. *sales@brandonltd.co.uk* Web. *www.brandonltd.co.uk Fibre-Lyte – *Rocket*

Brand & Rae Russell Mills Springfield, Cupar KY15 5QX Tel. *01334 652828* Fax. *01334 655967* Web. *www.brandandrae.co.uk Albacrete – Albalite – Albatherm – Bagged Aggregates – Dense Concrete – Eden*

Brand Rex Ltd Viewfield Industrial Estate, Glenrothes KY6 2RS Tel. *01592 772124* Fax. *01592 775314* E-mail. *loswald@brand-rex.com* Web. *www.brand-rex.co.uk Polyrad*

Branova Cleaning Services Meadow Mills Carlton Road, Dewsbury WF13 2BA Tel. *01924 486000* Fax. *01924 486010* E-mail. *sales@branova.com* Web. *www.branova.com Handies – Knightrum – Meleco – Zybax*

Brantham Engineering Ltd 3l Moss Road, Witham CM8 3UQ Tel. *01376 518384* Fax. *01376 518900* E-mail. *mail@brantham.com* Web. *www.brantham.com Brantham Engineering*

Brass Fittings & Supplies Ltd Hawkshead Hope Street, Glossop SK13 7SS Tel. *01457 854415* Fax. *01457 855403* E-mail. *philbfs@btinternet.com B.F.S. – Gas industry manufrs*

Brathalyzer Direct The Old Farmhouse Kingham Road, Churchill, Chipping Norton OX7 6NE Tel. *01608 658935* Fax. *01608 658935* E-mail. *contactus@breathalyserdirect.co.uk* Web. *www.breathalyserdirect.co.uk AL6000 – AL7000 – Alcohawk – Draeger – Drager*

E Braude London Ltd (Head Office) Liberta House 17 Scotland Hill, Sandhurst GU47 8JR Tel. *01252 876123* Fax. *01252 875281* E-mail. *admin@braude.co.uk* Web. *www.braude.co.uk Braudepumps – Frogspawn Thermal Insulation – Polaris Popular*

Brauer Ltd Mount Farm Dawson Road, Bletchley, Milton Keynes MK1 1JP Tel. *01908 374022* Fax. *01908 641628* E-mail. *sales@brauer.co.uk* Web. *www.brauer.co.uk Brauer – Brauer Air Movers/Air Amplifiers – H.M.C. – Heavithane – Rotolin*

Braunston Marina Ltd The Wharf Braunston, Daventry NN11 7JH Tel. *01788 891373* Fax. *01788 891436* E-mail. *info@braunstonmarina.co.uk* Web. *www.braunstonmarina.co.uk Braunston Marina*

Bray Group Ltd Olive House 1 Regal Way, Faringdon SN7 7BX Tel. *01367 240736* Fax. *01367 242625* E-mail. *info@bray-healthcare.com* Web. *www.bray.co.uk Avoca – Bray H & L – Counterchoice – Latstock – Olive – Portia – Suntona*

Nicholas Bray & Son Ltd PO Box 4279, Wincanton BA9 0AB Tel. *01963 364240* Fax. *01963 364240* E-mail. *sales@nicholasbray.co.uk* Web. *www.nicholasbray.com Bray Cattle Calendar – Bray Electro Gate – Fenda-Sox – Softdock*

B R C Southampton 2 Belbins Business Park Cupernham Lane, Romsey SO51 7JF Tel. *01794 521158* Fax. *01794 521154* E-mail. *sales@brc.ltd.uk* Web. *www.selsa.com Weld Grip*

Breeze Ltd Breeze House Albert Close Trading Estate, Whitefield, Manchester M45 8EH Tel. *0161 7963600* Fax. *0161 7963700* E-mail. *info@breez.co.uk* Web. *www.breeze.co.uk Mass Fax*

Brenntag Colours Ltd High Level Way, Halifax HX1 4PN Tel. *01422 358431* Fax. *01422 330867* E-mail. *colours.sales@albionchemicals.co.uk* Web. *www.brenntag-colours.com Anadurm – Desize – Dyacid – Dyactive – Dyalan – Dyclear/Hydroclear – Dylev – Dyrect – Dysoft – Dysperse – Dywet – Fixitol – Freefoam – Hybright – Hysoft – Kenalev – Kenamide – Kenanthrol – Metalube – Metapex – Negator – Resistol – Stabilizer – Zymolene*

Brent Cross Office Furniture Sayer House Oxgate Lane, London NW2 7JN Tel. *020 82082626* Fax. *020 82082012* E-mail. *sales@brentxofficefurniture.co.uk* Web. *www.brentxofficefurniture.co.uk Office Chairs Direct*

Brett Specialised Aggregates Sturry Quarry Fordwich Road, Sturry, Canterbury CT2 0BW Tel. *08456 080572* Fax. *08456 080573* E-mail. *sales@brett-specialised-aggregates.co.uk* Web. *www.brett.co.uk Durite Canterbury Spar – Durive Instant-Lay Macadams – Flintag – *Permwhite Calcined Flint (France) – Westbere Spar*

Brevini Power Transmissions Planet House Centre Park, Warrington WA1 1QX Tel. *01925 636682* Fax. *01925 636682* E-mail. *sales@brevini.co.uk* Web. *www.brevini.co.uk Brevini – Brevini Winches/PIV Drives – PIV Drives – Riduttori*

Brewer & Bunney Unit 9 Barncoose Industrial Estate, Redruth TR15 3XX Tel. *01752 266444* Fax. *01209 313057* E-mail. *enquiries@brewerandbunney.co.uk* Web. *www.brewerandbunney.co.uk *Electrolux Commercial Laundry Equipment – *Maidaid Halcyon – *Miele Laundry and Dishwasher – *Milco – *Speedqueen*

Brewer Metalcraft Ltd Thicket Lane Halnaker, Chichester PO18 0QS Tel. *01243 539639* Fax. *01243 533184* E-mail. *sales@brewer-cowl.com* Web. *www.brewercowls.co.uk Brewer Aerodyne – Brewer Chimney Capper – Brewer Ulitimate Flue Outlet (U.F.O.)*

Bribex 10 North Road Yate, Bristol BS37 7PA Tel. *01454 310150* Fax. *01454 310191* E-mail. *info@bribex.com* Web. *www.bribex.com Autoframe – Direct Line – Duraglas – M.I.L.S. – Mistral – Panorama*

Bricesco Ltd (British Ceramic Service Co. Ltd) Lymedale Business Centre Hooters Hall Road, Lymedale Business Park, Newcastle ST5 9QF Tel. *01782 567300* Fax. *01782 344601* E-mail. *richard.bridgewater@bricesco.co.uk* Web. *www.bricesco.co.uk Bricesco*

Bridal Fashions Ltd Springfield Business Park Springfield Road, Grantham NG31 7BG Tel. *01476 593311* Fax. *01476 574396* Web. *www.berketexbride.com Berkertex*

Bridec West Bay Road, Bridport DT6 4EH Tel. *01308 456684* Fax. *01308 424255* E-mail. *general@bridec.co.uk* Web. *www.bridec.co.uk Bridec*

Bridge Aluminium Ltd 84 Bridge Street, Wednesbury WS10 0AN Tel. *0121 5560995* Fax. *0121 5569971* E-mail. *info@bridgealuminium.com* Web. *www.bridgealuminium.com Bridge Foundry*

Bridgemere Nursery & Garden World Bridgemere, Nantwich CW5 7QB Tel. *01270 521100* Fax. *01270 520215* E-mail. *info@bridgemere.co.uk* Web. *www.bridgemere.co.uk Bridgemere Garden World*

Bridge Of Weir Leather Co. Baltic Works Kilbarchan Road, Bridge Of Weir PA11 3RH Tel. *01505 612132* Fax. *01505 614964* E-mail. *iain.mcfadyen@bowleather.co.uk* Web. *www.bowleather.co.uk *Braemar (United Kingdom) – *Buttersoft (United Kingdom) – *Caledonian (United Kingdom) – *Grampian (United Kingdom) – *NuBuck (United Kingdom)*

Bridgeplex Ltd 1a Merivale Road, London SW15 2NW Tel. *020 87894063* Fax. *020 87854191* E-mail. *soundcheck@btinternet.com* Web. *www.fabritrak.co.uk Sound-Check*

Bridgestone UK Ltd Athena Drive Tachbrook Park, Warwick CV34 6UX Tel. *01926 488500* Fax. *01926 488600* E-mail. *john.mcnaught@bridgestone-eu.com* Web. *www.bridgestone.eu Bridgestone/Firestone U.K.*

Bridgwater Electronics Ltd Unit 9 Westmans Trading Estate Love Lane, Burnham On Sea TA8 1EY Tel. *01278 789552* Fax. *01278 789782* E-mail. *sales@bridgwater-electronics.co.uk* Web. *www.bridgwater-electronics.co.uk Bee Secure – Flashpoint – Foxguard – Laserline – Speed Genie – Sterling*

Briggs Irrigation Boyle Road Willowbrook East Industrial Estate, Corby NN17 5XU Tel. *01536 260338* Fax. *01536 263972* E-mail. *warrenbriggs@briggsirrigation.co.uk* Web. *www.briggsirrigation.co.uk Rotorainer*

Brighthand Web Design 7 Thorndown Lane, Windlesham GU20 6DD Tel. *01276 489004* E-mail. *info@brighthand.co.uk* Web. *www.brighthand.co.uk BrighthandIT*

Bright Instrument Co. Ltd St Margarets Way Stukeley Meadows Industrial Estate, Huntingdon PE29 6EU Tel. *01480 451980* Fax. *01480 456031* E-mail. *sales@brightinstruments.com* Web. *www.brightinstruments.com Clinicut – Cryo-M-Bed – Cryospray – Magnacut*

Brighton Systems Ltd Unit K Quarry Road, Newhaven BN9 9DG Tel. *01273 515563* Fax. *01273 611533* E-mail. *sales@brightonsystems.co.uk* Web. *www.brightonsystems.co.uk Anglicon*

W Brighton Handrails (Handrails) 55 Quarry Hill Wilnecote, Tamworth B77 5BW Tel. *01827 284488* Fax. *01827 250907* E-mail. *wbrightonhandrails@ntlworld.com* Web. *www.marleyrail.com marleyrail polyrail mipolam rehau*

Brightside Print & Design 112 Union Street, London SE1 0LH Tel. *020 79605111* E-mail. *mail@brightsideonline.com* Web. *www.brightsideonline.com Brightside*

Brightwater Engineering Unit 2 The Business Centre Avenue One, Letchworth Garden City SG6 2HB Tel. *01462 485005* Fax. *01462 485003* E-mail. *peter.gaynor@brightwater.uk.com* Web. *www.brightwater.co.uk Brightwater Grates – Brightwater Product*

Brightwell Dispenser Ltd Euro Business Park New Road, Newhaven BN9 0DQ Tel. *01273 513566* Fax. *01273 516134* E-mail. *sales@brightwell.co.uk* Web. *www.brightwell.co.uk Brightflow – Brightstaltic – Brightwell*

Brilec Power Tools Ltd 109 Grove Lane Handsworth, Birmingham B21 9HF Tel. *0121 5544989* Fax. *0121 5545488* E-mail. *brilecsales@btconnect.com A.E.G. – Bosch – Kango – Makita*

Briliant Polishes 2-4b Arrow Court Industrial Estate Hergest, Kington HR5 3ER Tel. *07789 286821* E-mail. *sales@briliant.biz* Web. *www.briliant.biz BRILIANT POLISHES*

Brimac Environmental Services Ltd 21 Dellingburn Street, Greenock PA15 4TP Tel. *01475 720273* Fax. *01475 720016* E-mail. *info@brimacservices.com* Web. *www.brimacservices.com Brimac*

Brimar Ltd Chadderton Industrial Estate Greenside Way, Middleton, Manchester M24 1SN Tel. *0161 6817072* Fax. *0161 6823818* E-mail. *gary.payne@brimar.ltd.uk* Web. *www.brimar-ltd.com Brimar*

Brimotor Ltd 10-12 Culverden Down, Tunbridge Wells TN4 9SA Tel. *01892 537588* Fax. *01892 527724* E-mail. *info@brimotor.co.uk* Web. *www.brimotor.co.uk Bernard – Brimotor – Giraffe – Jem – Tarpen*

Brindley Twist Tafft & James LLP Lowick Gate Siskin Drive, Middlemarch Business Park, Coventry CV3 4FJ Tel. *024 76531532* Fax. *024 76301300* E-mail. *enquiries@bttj.com* Web. *www.bttj.com Debtflow*

Brinsea Products Ltd Station Road Sandford, Winscombe BS25 5RA Tel. *01934 823039* Fax. *01934 820250* E-mail. *info@brinsea.co.uk* Web. *www.brinsea.co.uk *Octagon – Ova-Easy – *TLC-4 Brooder*

Brintons Carpets Ltd PO Box 16, Kidderminster DY10 1AG Tel. *01562 820000* Fax. *01562 634737* E-mail. *pjohansen@brintons.co.uk* Web. *www.brintons.co.uk Abbotsford Collection – Annabelle Classique – Astley Court – Beacon – Bell Twist Woven Wilton – Camelot – Colour Creations – Cornerstone – Cornerstone Spotlight – Designer Collection – Edwardian – Fine Point Textured Velvet – Fresco – Galleria – Heather Berber – Leicester Square – Majestic Wilton Velvet – Marquis – Marrakesh – Micro – Natural Flair – Palace Belvedere – Palace Design – Palace Velvet Wilton – Portico – Regina International – Royal Ascot – Spotlight Express – Zenith Club Class*

Bristish Gypsum Gypsum Head Office East Leake, Loughborough LE12 6HX Tel. *0115 9451000* Fax. *0115 9451901* E-mail. *bgtechnical.enquiries@bpb.com* Web. *www.british-gypsum.com Carlite Bonding Coat – Carlite Browning – Carlite Finish – Carlite Tough Coat – Easi Fill – Glasroc Multiboard – Glasroc S – Gyplyner – Gyplyner Ceiling – Gyplyner Walls – Gyproc – Gyproc Baseboard – Gyproc Core Board – Gyproc Cornice Range – Gyproc Cove – Gyproc Dri Wall Systems – Gyproc Duoedge – Gyproc Duplex Wallboard – Gyproc Duraline – Gyproc Easi-Fill – Gyproc Fireline – Gyproc Gypwall – Gyproc Joint Trims – Gyproc Jumbo Stud – Gyproc Laminated – Gyproc Lath – Gyproc Lite-Mix Joint Cement – Gyproc M/F Suspended Ceilings – Gyproc Metal Stud Partition – Gyproc Moisture Resistant Fireline Board – Gyproc Paramount Dry Partition – Gyproc Plank – Gyproc S I Floor System – Gyproc Shaftwall System – Gyproc Sheathing – Gyproc SoundBloc – Gyproc Thermal Board EHD – Gyproc Thermal Board LD – Gyproc Thermal Board Plus – Gyproc Thermal Board Super – Gyproc Triline – Gyproc Wallboard – Gyptone – Isowool – SoundBloc – Thistle Board Finish – Thistle Dri-Coat – Thistle Hardwall – Thistle Multi Finish – Thistle Projection – Thistle Renovating – Thistle Universal One Coat – Thistle X-Ray Plaster*

Bristol Cars Concorde Road Patchway, Bristol BS34 5TB Tel. *0117 9799444* Fax. *0117 9236356* E-mail. *sales@bristolcars.co.uk* Web. *www.bristolcars.co.uk Bristol*

Bristol Chinese Pain Relief Acupuncture 39 Cotham Hill, Bristol BS6 6JY Tel. *0117 9741199* Fax. *0117 9237266* E-mail. *hanzhentong@hotmail.com* Web. *www.backachetherapy.co.uk Bristol Chinese Pain relief acupuncture – Bristol Zak Back Pain Therapy*

Bristol Fluid System Technologies Ltd Fourth Way Avonmouth Way Avonmouth, Bristol BS11 8DL Tel. *0117 9821107* Fax. *0117 9826436* E-mail. *info@bristol.swagelok.com* Web. *www.swagelok.com/bristol Ham-let – Hansen – Hoke – Parker (Hannifin)*

The Bristol Kitchen Company 14 Redcross Street St Judes, Bristol BS2 0BA Tel. *0117 9140340* E-mail. *info@thebristolkitchencompany.co.uk* Web. *www.thebristolkitchencompany.co.uk The Bristol Kitchen Company*

Bristol Maid Hospital Equipment (t/a Bristol Maid) Blandford Heights, Blandford Forum DT11 7TG Tel. *01258 451338* Fax. *01258 455056* E-mail. *sales@bristolmaid.com* Web. *www.bristolmaid.com Bristol Maid*

Bristol Metal Spraying & Protective Coatings Ltd Payne's Shipyard Coronation Road, Bristol BS3 1RP Tel. *0117 9662206* Fax. *0117 9661158* E-mail. *sales@bmspc.co.uk* Web. *www.bmspc.co.uk Limpetite*

Bristol-Myers Squibb Unit 2 Uxbridge Business Park Sanderson Road, Uxbridge UB8 1DH Tel. *01895 523000* Fax. *01895 523010* Web. *www.bms.com Reliability – Squibb – Sweetella*

Bristol Office Machines Petherton Road, Bristol BS14 9BZ Tel. *01275 890140* Fax. *01275 890111* E-mail. *info@bom.co.uk* Web. *www.bom.co.uk Club*

Bristol Street Birmingham 156-182 Bristol Street, Birmingham B5 7AZ Tel. *0121 6666000* Fax. *0121 6666340* E-mail. *martin.leach@bristolstreet.co.uk* Web. *www.bristolstreetmotors.co.uk Bristol Street (Birmingham)*

Bristol Uniforms Ltd Wathen Street Staple Hill, Bristol BS16 5LL Tel. *0117 9563101* Fax. *0117 9565927* E-mail. *enquiries@bristoluniforms.com* Web. *www.bristol.uniforms.com Bristol*

Britannia Health Products Ltd Forum House 41-51 Brighton Road, Redhill RH1 6YS Tel. *01737 773741* Fax. *01737 762672* E-mail. *admin@britannia-pharm.co.uk* Web. *www.britannia-pharm.co.uk Rimso-50*

Britannia Lightning Prevectron Ltd 12 Longue Drive Calverton, Nottingham NG14 6QF Tel. *0115 8477113* Fax. *0115 8475185* E-mail. *mike@prevectron.co.uk* Web. *www.lightningconsultants.co.uk Provectron*

Britannia Refined Metals Ltd Britannia Works Botany Road, Northfleet, Gravesend DA11 9BG Tel. *01474 538200* Fax. *01474 538203* Web. *www.brm.co.uk B.R.M.*

Brita Water Filter Systems Ltd Brita House Granville Way, Bicester OX26 4JT Tel. *01932 770599* Fax. *0870 4870999* E-mail. *professional@brita.co.uk* Web. *www.brita.co.uk aquaquell – Brita Water Filter Systems Ltd – Britaclean – Britaclean Extra*

Britax Excelsior Ltd 1 Churchill Way West, Andover SP10 3UW Tel. *01264 333343* Fax. *01264 334146* E-mail. *sales_marketing_email@britax.com* Web. *www.britax.co.uk Britax*

Britax P S V Wypers Ltd Navigation Road, Worcester WR5 3DE Tel. *01905 350500* Fax. *01905 763928* E-mail. *paul.curry@psvwypers.com* Web. *www.psvwypers.com Flo-Matic – Kwikvent – Libvent – Quadvent*

British American Tobacco plc Globe House 4 Temple Place, London WC2R 2PG Tel. *020 78451000* Fax. *020 72400555* Web. *www.bat.com BAT*

British American Tobacco plc Oxford Road, Aylesbury HP21 8SZ Tel. *01296 335000* Fax. *01296 335999* E-mail. *info@aylesford-newsprint.co.uk* Web. *www.bat.com Craven A – Dunhill – Peter Stuyvesant – Rothmans*

British Autogard Ltd 2 Wilkinson Road Love Lane Industrial Estate, Cirencester GL7 1YT Tel. *01285 640333* Fax. *01285 659476* E-mail. *sales@autogard.co.uk* Web. *www.autogard.co.uk Airjustor – Autoflex – Autogard – Microflex – Monitorq – Samiflex – Winflex*

British Castors Ltd Golds Green Works Bagnall Street Hill Top West Bromwich, West Bromwich B70 0TZ Tel. *0121 5567221* Fax. *0121 5022658* E-mail. *info@colson-castors.co.uk* Web. *www.colson-castors.co.uk Chipfast – Global*

British & Continental Traders Ltd Oxford House North Bridge Road, Berkhamsted HP4 1EH Tel. *01442 877415* Fax. *01442 872782* E-mail. *sales@b-ct.co.uk* Web. *www.b-ct.co.uk *Bultmann (Germany) – *Carl Wezel (Germany) – *Delachaux (France) – *Herkules (Germany) – *I.M.E.A.S. (Italy) – *Julius (Germany) – *Neuenkamp (Germany) – *Philadelphia (Italy) – *Roditor (Italy) – *Sillem (Italy) – Triton (Italy) – VACOHUB (Germany) – *Vollmer (Germany) – *Will & Hahnestein (Germany) – *Willi Wader (Germany)*

British Darts Organisation Ltd 2 Pages Lane, London N10 1PS Tel. *020 88835544* Fax. *020 88830109* Web. *www.bdodarts.com BDO*

British Diamalt Maltkiln Lane, Newark NG24 1HN Tel. *01753 614730* Fax. *01753 614740* E-mail. *sales@diamalt.co.uk* Web. *www.diamalt.co.uk Dia Malt – Diamex – John Bull – Paines*

British Diamond Wire Die Co. Ltd 66 Old Wareham Road, Poole BH12 4QS Tel. *01202 745104* Fax. *01202 746125* E-mail. *sales@bdwd.freeserve.co.uk* Web. *www.balloffetdie.com B.D.W.D.*

British Engines Ltd St Peters, Newcastle Upon Tyne NE6 1BS Tel. *0191 2659091* Fax. *0191 2763244* E-mail. *info@bel.co.uk* Web. *www.bel.co.uk Bel Valves*

British Filters Ltd 11-12 Porsham Close Roborough, Plymouth PL6 7DB Tel. *01752 703900* Fax. *01752 703901* E-mail. *sales@britishfilters.co.uk* Web. *www.britishfilters.co.uk British Filters – Flava Major – Gemini – Nellie – Polynellie – T.J. Filters*

British Gaskets Ltd Unit 7 Childerditch Industrial Estate Childerditch Hall Drive, Little Warley, Brentwood CM13 3HD Tel. *01277 815300* Fax. *01277 815350* E-mail. *sales@british-gaskets.co.uk* Web. *www.british-gaskets.co.uk British Seals & Rubber Mouldings*

British Homeopathic Association 29 Park Street West, Luton LU1 3BE Tel. *01582 408675* Fax. *01582 723032* E-mail. *info@britishhomeopathic.org* Web. *www.britishhomeopathic.org Health & Homeopathy*

British Lead Peartree Lane, Welwyn Garden City AL7 3UB Tel. *01707 324595* Fax. *01707 328941* E-mail. *sales@britishlead.co.uk* Web. *www.britishlead.co.uk Lead-T-Pren – Led Trak – Permaclips – Unislate*

British Mensa Ltd St Johns House St Johns Square, Wolverhampton WV2 4AH Tel. *01902 772771* Fax. *01902 392500* E-mail. *enquiries@mensa.org.uk* Web. *www.mensa.org.uk Mensa*

The British Millerain Company Ltd Broad Shaw Farm Broad Shaw Lane, Milnrow, Rochdale OL16 4NR Tel. *01706 649242* Fax. *01706 527611* E-mail. *sales@britishmillerain.com* Web. *www.britishmillerain.com Carrington – Duradon – Japara – Milair – Milaproof – Millerain – Webtex*

British Monomarks Monomark House 27 Old Gloucester Street, London WC1N 3AX Tel. *020 74195000* Fax. *020 78319489* E-mail. *mail@monomark.co.uk* Web. *www.britishmonomarks.co.uk British Monomarks*

British Motor Heritage Ltd Cotswold Business Park Range Road, Witney OX29 0YB Tel. *01993 707200* Fax. *01993 707222* E-mail. *info@bmh-ltd.com* Web. *www.bmh-ltd.com Austin – Austin Healey – B.M.C. – MG – Morris – Morris Minor – Riley – Spitfire – Stag – Triumph – Wolseley*

British Museum Press Publications & Merchandise Ltd 38 Russell Square, London WC1B 3QQ Tel. *020 73231234* Fax. *020 73238616* E-mail. *reception@britishmuseum.co.uk* Web. *www.britishmuseum.org British Museum*

British Polythene Industries plc 96 Port Glasgow Road, Greenock PA15 2UL Tel. *01475 501100* Fax. *01475 743143* E-mail. *carolanderson@bpipoly.com* Web. *www.bpipoly.co.uk Hypal – Megafilm – Visqueen (United Kingdom)*

British Rema Manufacturing Co. Ltd The Image Works Foxwood Industrial Park, Chesterfield S41 9RN Tel. *01246 269955* Fax. *01246 269944* E-mail. *sales@britishrema.co.uk* Web. *www.britishrema.com Aerosplit – British Rema – British Rema - crushing grinding, drying & classifying plant; Aerosplit - powder classifier; Rema - Rotary impact mill /classifier mill; Minisplit - powder classifier - lab size. – Microsplit – Microsplit – Minisplit – Rema – Rotary Impact Mill*

British Rema Process Equipment Ltd Unit 4, Traso Business Park Cally Lane, Dronfield S18 2XR Tel. *01246 269955* Fax. *01246 269944* E-mail. *sales@britishrema.com* Web. *www.britishrema.co.uk Aerosplit – Microsplit – Minisplit – Rema*

British Rigid Urethane Foam Manufacturers Association Limited 12a High Street East, Glossop SK13 8DA Tel. *01457 855884* Fax. *0161 2369292* E-mail. *brufma@brufma.co.uk* Web. *www.brufma.co.uk BRUFMA*

British Salt Ltd Cledford Lane, Middlewich CW10 0JP Tel. *01606 832881* Fax. *01606 835999* E-mail. *sales@british-salt.co.uk* Web. *www.british-salt.co.uk Aquasol – Glacia Granulite – Glacia PDV*

British Sanitized Ltd 19 Babelake Street Packington, Ashby De La Zouch LE65 1WD Tel. *01530 415533* Fax. *01530 411180* E-mail. *ian.dring@actifresh.freeserve.co.uk* Web. *www.sanitized.com Actifresh – *Sanitized*

British Thornton E S F Ltd Prospect Works South Street, Keighley BD21 5AA Tel. *01535 683250* Fax. *01535 680226* E-mail. *stuartl@british-thornton.co.uk* Web. *www.british-thornton.co.uk British Thornton*

British Vehicle Rental & Leasing Association River Lodge Badminton Court Church Street, Amersham HP7 0DD Tel. *01494 434747* Fax. *01494 434499* E-mail. *info@bvrla.co.uk* Web. *www.bvrla.co.uk B.V.R.L.A.*

British Vita plc Central Industrial Estate Oldham Road, Middleton, Manchester M24 1QZ Tel. *0161 6431133* Fax. *0161 6535411* E-mail. *info@britishvita.com* Web. *www.britishvita.com Acoustilux – Adormo – Aquafil – Armourcrete – Autothane & Autothane Logo – Barafoam – Beddington – British Vita & Group Symbol – Caligen – Celflex – Celmar – Celvin – Cloud 7 – Cloud 9 – Con Amore – Cortx – Diolpate – Diorez – Diprane – Doeflex – Dolplas – Draka Cel Label (1) – Draka Cel Label (2) – Draka Cel Sterschuim – Draka Polyaether & Logo – Drakacel – Duraloft – Duramould – Durap – Durelast – Dynathane – Enviroflex – Ethafoam – Fabprene – Fibreblok – Filtalux – Filtron – Filtronic – Firmwall – Floor-cel, Floor-Cell, Floorcell – Floorline & Device – Foampac – Foampak – Furnicel – Genefoam – Genelay – Glazepta – Group Symbol – Hilex – Hydraseal – Hydratex – Hypercrete – Hyperkote – Hyperlast – Hyseal – Insulflex – Insulux – Interfoam – Inversale – Kombiflex – Luxalay – Luxan – Luxbond – Luxbond Fibreblok – Luxwol – Macwax – Minipol – Olga – Olga Device – Olga Eurocel – Olga Sanocel – Perfolatex – Perriprene – Poly-Select Logo – Polydol – Polypress – Porcel – Portex – Portex Vilum – Portways – Propyform – Propylex – Pyrosorb – Radium – Reflex – Relaxair, Relax Air – Rotakote – Royalite – Safecrest – Sleepmaster – Solidair – Stowaway – Supersoft Logo – Tercel – Traffideck – Traffigrip – Tramivex – Union Logo – Vari-Warm – Vasco – VC & Group Symbol – Vicel – Vifil – Vita – VITA & Group Symbol – Vita-Lenton – Vita-one – Vitabond – Vitacal – Vitacare – Vitachem – Vitafibre – Vitafil – Vitaflight – Vitafoam – Vitalam – Vitalay – Vitaline – Vitality – Vitaluxan – Vitaluxe – Vitamat – Vitamol – Vitamousse – Vitapad – Vitapedic – Vitaphram – Vitapol – Vitaprene – Vitapruf – Vitaquilt – Vitaseal – Vitasoft – Vitasol – Vitasorb – Vitastretch – Vitatex – Vitathane – Vitatherm – Vitatread – Vitaweb – Vitawrap – Vitec – Vitesta*

British Wax Refining Co. (Office & Works) 62 Holmethorpe Avenue, Redhill RH1 2NL Tel. *01737 761242* Fax. *01737 761472* E-mail. *rob@britishwax.com* Web. *www.britishwax.com Karnabax*

British Wood Preserving & Damp Proofing Association 1 Gleneagles House Vernon Gate, Derby DE1 1UP Tel. *01332 225100* Fax. *01332 225101* E-mail. *enquiry@bpca.org.uk* Web. *www.bwpda.co.uk BPCA*

Bri-Ton Fine Foods Ltd Rowhurst Close, Newcastle ST5 6BE Tel. *01782 561422* Web. *www.bri-ton.co.uk *Fairway*

Britspace Modular Buildings Ltd Unicorn House Broad Lane, Gilberdyke, Brough HU15 2TS Tel. *01430 444400* Fax. *01430 444401* E-mail. *dharris@britspace.com* Web. *www.britspace.com Britspace Modular*

Brittany Ferries Millbay Docks, Plymouth PL1 3EW Tel. *08712 441400* Fax. *0870 9020300* E-mail. *enquiries@brittanyferries.com* Web. *www.brittanyferries.com Brittany Ferries – Truckline*

Britton Decoflex Skerne Road, Hartlepool TS24 0RH Tel. *01429 272102* Fax. *01429 860388* E-mail. *simon.rowe@britton-group.com* Web. *www.decoflex-flexibles.co.uk Cointaner – Merlin – Securiseal – Walrus*

Britton Taco Ltd 20 Road One Winsford Industrial Estate, Winsford CW7 3RD Tel. *01606 593434* Fax. *01606 866436* E-mail. *stephen.goodman@britton-group.com* Web. *www.brittontaco.com Britain Taco – Tacolin*

Brixworth Engineering Creaton Road Brixworth, Northampton NN6 9BW Tel. *01604 880338* Fax. *01604 880252* E-mail. *sales@benco.co.uk* Web. *www.benco.co.uk Benco*

Broadstone Mill Shopping Outlet Broadstone House Broadstone Road, Stockport SK5 7DL Tel. *0161 9534470* Fax. *0161 9534456* E-mail. *sarah@broadstone.co.uk* Web. *www.broadstone-shopping.co.uk Broadstone House Ltd*

Broady Flow Controller Ltd English Street, Hull HU3 2DU Tel. *01482 619600* Fax. *01482 619700* E-mail. *sales@broady.co.uk* Web. *www.broady.co.uk Balflo – Broady Flow Control – F7000 – F8000 – Series 3500/2600*

Broag Ltd Remeha House Molly Millars Lane, Wokingham RG41 2QP Tel. *0118 9783434* Fax. *0118 9786977* E-mail. *brian@broag-remeha.com* Web. *www.uk.remeha.com Broag Remeha*

Broanmain Forge Works Horsham Road, Mid Holmwood, Dorking RH5 4EJ Tel. *01306 885888* Fax. *01306 885889* E-mail. *info@broanmain.co.uk* Web. *www.broanmain.co.uk Lemco – Zoketts*

Brockhouse Modernfold Ltd Kay One 23 The Tything, Worcester WR1 1HD Tel. *01905 330055* Fax. *01905 330234* E-mail. *markdavis@brockhouse.net* Web. *www.brockhouse.net 200 Series – 500 Series – 600 Series – Modernfold 800*

Brockway Carpets Ltd Hoobrook, Kidderminster DY10 1XW Tel. *01562 824737* Fax. *01562 863598* E-mail. *sales@brockway.co.uk* Web. *www.brockway.co.uk Amore – Berber Twist – Craftsman Elite – Craftsman Twist – Lantana – Lycidas – Lysander – MasterCraftsman – PalestrinA – Pegasus – Sundance – Super Lincoln Twist – Woodman Twist*

Broen Valves Ltd Unit 7 Cleton Street Business Park, Tipton DY4 7TR Tel. *0121 5224515* Fax. *0121 5224535* E-mail. *as@broen.com* Web. *www.broen.co.uk Boss Lab –*

STD Boss Lab – Redline – Cleanline – Docmix – Alsident – Uniflex

Broker Ltd Banner Lane, Coventry CV4 9GH Tel. *024 76855200* Fax. *024 76465317* E-mail. *reception@broker.co.uk* Web. *www.broker.co.uk Autoclean*

Bromwich Insurance Brokers 311a Kingstanding Road, Birmingham B44 9TH Tel. *0121 3848499* Fax. *0121 3842114* E-mail. *mikenuttal@btconnect.com* Web. *www.big4insurance.co.uk Q.P. The Quotepanel*

Bronkhorst UK Ltd 1 Willie Snaith Road, Newmarket CB8 7TG Tel. *01223 833222* Fax. *01223 837683* E-mail. *sales@bronkhorst.co.uk* Web. *www.bronkhorst.co.uk CEM – Combi-Flow – Combi-Flow Filters – Cori-Flow – El-Flow Controllers – El-Flow Digital – El-Flow Meters – El-Press – Ex-Flow – Flow Calculations – Fluical Calibrators – In-Flow – In-Line Filters – Liqui-Flow – Low DP Flow – Low-ap-Flow – Mani-Flow – Microflow – Physical Properties – Portable Calibrator – Series E-5700 – Series E-7000 – U-Flow*

H Bronnley & Co. Ltd Bronnley Works Radstone Road, Brackley NN13 5AU Tel. *01280 702291* Fax. *01280 703912* E-mail. *declan.salter@bronnley.co.uk* Web. *www.bronnley.co.uk Bronnley*

Bronx Engineering Ltd Unit 48 Enterprise Trading Estate Pedmore Road, Brierley Hill DY5 1TX Tel. *01384 486648* Fax. *01384 486440* E-mail. *operations@bronx.co.uk* Web. *www.bronx.co.uk Bronx Engineering – Bronx England*

Brook Crompton UK Ltd St Thomas' Road, Huddersfield HD1 3LJ Tel. *01484 557200* Fax. *01484 557201* E-mail. *paul.hopley@brookcrompton.com* Web. *www.brookcrompton.com Argus 55 – Brook Crompton – Fumex – Monsoon – WP*

Brooke Concrete Products Ltd Monksbridge Road Dinnington, Sheffield S25 3QS Tel. *01909 550455* Fax. *01909 568780* E-mail. *claz.smyth@brooke.concrete.co.uk* Web. *www.brookeconcrete.co.uk Durapave*

Brookite Ltd Brightley Mill, Okehampton EX20 1RR Tel. *01837 53315* Fax. *01837 53223* E-mail. *amanda.harrison@brookite.com* Web. *www.brookite.com Brookite*

Brooklands College Heath Road, Weybridge KT13 8TT Tel. *01932 797700* Fax. *01932 797800* E-mail. *info@brooklands.ac.uk* Web. *www.brooklands.ac.uk *Bakery Level 2 – Food Hygiene – National Cert. for personal License Holders – *NVQ Catering & Hospitality – *Sugarcraft Diploma*

Brooksbank Holdings Station Yard Elslack, Skipton BD23 3AS Tel. *01282 444610* Fax. *01282 444611* E-mail. *sales@brooksbank.com* Web. *www.brooksbank.com BK – Combi – *Yamauchi (Japan)*

Brookside Metal Co. Ltd 28 Bilston Lane, Willenhall WV13 2QE Tel. *01902 365500* Fax. *01902 636671* E-mail. *ian.kirk@brooksidemetal.com* Web. *www.brooksidemetal.com Brookside*

Broste Ltd Unit 8 North Lynn Business Village, North Lynn Indl-Est, Kings Lynn PE30 2JG Tel. *01323 640485* Fax. *01553 767319* E-mail. *uk@azelis.co.uk* Web. *www.broste.com Azelis - Pioner Salt - Scansmoke - Sweetmaster – Pioner Salt – Scansmoke – Sweetmaster*

Brother International Europe Ltd 1 Tame Street Audenshaw, Manchester M34 5JE Tel. *0161 3306531* Fax. *0161 9312209* E-mail. *yuji.ishiguro@brother-uk.com* Web. *www.brother.com Brother*

Brotherton Esseco Ltd Calder Vale Road, Wakefield WF1 5PH Tel. *01924 371919* Fax. *01924 290408* E-mail. *russel.etherington@brothertonesseco.com* Web. *www.brothertonesseco.com Armakleen – Armex – Armex - cleaning systems Safegrip - runway de-icer – Safegrip*

Broughton & Co Bristol Ltd (t/a Busicom Business Machines) 4 Axis Hawkfield Way, Hawkfield Business Park, Bristol BS14 0BY Tel. *0117 9641300* Fax. *0117 9641003* E-mail. *broughtons1bristol@btinternet.com* Web. *www.busicom.com *Bistec (Hong Kong) – *Busicom (Taiwan, Hong Kong, Malaysia and Japan)*

Alan Browne Gauges Ltd Blackdown Mill Blackdown, Leamington Spa CV32 6QT Tel. *01926 424278* Fax. *01926 451865* E-mail. *info@alanbrowne.co.uk* Web. *www.alanbrowne.co.uk Alan Browne – DuraGrade*

Brown Knight & Truscott Ltd North Farm Road, Tunbridge Wells TN2 3BW Tel. *01892 511678* Fax. *01892 511343* E-mail. *maureen.burns@bkt.co.uk* Web. *www.bkt.co.uk Brown Knight & Truscott*

Brown & Newirth Ltd Elma House Beaconsfield Close, Hatfield AL10 8YG Tel. *01707 255000* Fax. *01707 255055* E-mail. *sales@brownandnewirth.com* Web. *www.brownandnewirth.com Wedding Ring Company*

Brown's Agricultural Machinery Company Ltd Grovebury Road, Leighton Buzzard LU7 4UX Tel. *01525 375157* Fax. *01525 385222* E-mail. *john.bam@btconnect.com* Web. *www.brownsagricultural.co.uk Buzzard – Chopmaster – Compactor – Consort – Hectavator – Jumbo – Log Chop – Megascrape – Regent – Slitmaster – Squeezer – Super Buzzard – Tipper – Unigrab – Viceroy – Viscount – Woodworker – Yardmaster*

Browns S M S Ltd 23-27 South Molton Street, London W1K 5RD Tel. *020 75140000* Fax. *020 74081281* E-mail. *buyingoffice@brownsfashion.com* Web. *www.brownsfashions.com Browns*

Browns of Wem Ltd Four Lane Ends Wem, Shrewsbury SY4 5UQ Tel. *01939 232382* Fax. *01939 234032* E-mail. *info@brownsofwem.com* Web. *www.brownsofwem.com Aintree – Ambassador – Browns – Browns Buildings – Doncaster – Kempton – Paramount – Supreme*

Bruce Douglas Marketing Ltd (t/a Ultratape) Unit 10-12 Block 22 Kislpindie Road, Dunsinane Industrial Estate, Dundee DD2 3JP Tel. *01382 832999* Fax. *01382 833422* E-mail. *sales@ultratape.com* Web. *www.ultratape.com Ultra Tape*

Bruce & Hyslop Brucast Ltd 1 Well Lane, Bootle L20 3BS Tel. *0151 9222404* Fax. *0151 9225994* E-mail. *mail@bruceandhyslop.com* Web. *www.bruceandhyslop.com B & H – Brucast*

Bruderer UK Ltd Cradock Industrial Estate Cradock Road, Luton LU4 0JF Tel. *01582 560300* Fax. *01582 570611* E-mail. *mail@bruderer.co.uk* Web. *www.bruderer.co.uk Bimax – Blackalloy – Christen – Eubama – Meyer*

Brunner Machine Tools Ltd 6 Colville Road, London W3 8BL Tel. *020 89926011* Fax. *020 89927559* E-mail. *sales@brunnermachine.co.uk* Web. *www.brunnermachine.co.uk *Alesa (Switzerland) – *Armag (Switzerland) – *Bimax (Switzerland) – *Blackalloy (U.S.A.) – *Buchador (Germany) – *Christen (Switzerland) – *Eubama (Germany) – *Hofmann Karl (Germany) – *Kleim & Ungerer (Germany) – *Nann (Germany) – *Rego-Fix (Switzerland) – *Saacke (Germany) – *Sandoz (Switzerland) – *Simonet (Switzerland) – *Thommen (Switzerland) – *Turbo (Switzerland) – *Vidmar (Switzerland)*

Brunswick Tooling Ltd 3 The Sidings Industrial Park Birds Royd Lane, Brighouse HD6 1LQ Tel. *01484 719900* Fax. *01484 404727* E-mail. *pbriggs@brunswicktooling.co.uk* Web. *www.brunswicktooling.co.uk Brunswick Tooling*

Bruntons Propellers Ltd Oakwood Business Park Stephenson Road West, Clacton On Sea CO15 4TL Tel. *01255 420005* Fax. *01255 427775* E-mail. *sales@bruntons-propellers.com* Web. *www.bruntons-propellers.com Autolock – Autoprop – Hydromet – Variprop*

Brush Electrical Machines Ltd Falcoln Works Nottingham Road, Loughborough LE11 1EX Tel. *01509 611511* Fax. *01509 610440* E-mail. *sales@brushtransformers.com* Web. *www.brushtransformers.com Brush*

Bryan & Clark Ltd Unit 2-3 Bowman Trading Estate Westmoreland Road, London NW9 9RL Tel. *020 82062200* Fax. *020 89607430* E-mail. *sales@bryanandclark.co.uk* Web. *www.bryanandclark.co.uk *Casement (Belgium) – *Dekocord (Belgium) – *Dekofelt (Germany) – *Dekosuede (Belgium) – *Fuldapark (Germany)*

Bry-Kol Developments Ltd 10 Newcastle Street Burslem, Stoke On Trent ST6 3QF Tel. *01782 577991* Fax. *01782 577511* E-mail. *lorraine@bry-kol.co.uk* Web. *www.bry-kol.co.uk *Bry-Kol (Spain and S. Korea)*

B S A Guns UK Ltd Armoury Road, Birmingham B11 2PP Tel. *0121 7728543* Fax. *0121 7730845* E-mail. *sales@bsaguns.com* Web. *www.bsaguns.com 240 Magnum – B.S.A. Pylarm – Gold Star – Meteor – Meteor Carbine – R.B.2 Airsporter – R.B.2 Airsporter - SS Carbine – R.B.2 Stutzen – Super Sport – Super Sport Custom – Super Star – Supersport SS Carbine – SuperTEN*

B S A Machine Tools Mackadown Lane, Birmingham B33 0LE Tel. *0121 7834071* Fax. *0121 7899509* E-mail. *sales@bsamachinetools.co.uk* Web. *www.bsamachinetools.co.uk Alfred Herbert – B S A Tools – Batchmatic – Churchill – MOSTANA – Speedturn – Winchester*

B S A Tube Runner Speedwell House West Quay Road, Southampton SO15 1GY Tel. *023 80366410* Fax. *01280 709674* E-mail. *sales@tuberunner.co.uk* Web. *www.tuberunner.co.uk 13000 Series – 15000 Series – 18000 series – Centromat – Cobra – *Delta (Japan) – Honer – *Sumner (U.S.A.) – T.R. 2000 – *Teco (Netherlands)*

BS&B Safety Systems (UK) Ltd Adamson House Tower Business Pk, Wilmslow Rd, Didsbury, Manchester M20 2YY Tel. *0161 9554202* Fax. *0161 9554282* E-mail. *sales@bsb-systems.co.uk* Web. *www.bsb.ie BPRV – BS & B – STA-SAF*

B S Executive Travel Ltd Albany House Hurst Street, Birmingham B5 4BD Tel. *0121 6666336* Fax. *0121 6667620* E-mail. *mike.barnard@bstravel.co.uk* Web. *www.bsexec.co.uk B.S. Executive Travel – Promotivation – Vacation Travel Centre*

B S H Grand Union House Wolverton, Milton Keynes MK12 5PT Tel. *01908 328300* Fax. *01908 328440* E-mail. *admin@neff.co.uk* Web. *www.boschappliances.co.uk *Circotherm (Germany) – *Neff (Germany)*

B S H Industries Ltd Rutland Street Swinton, Manchester M27 6AU Tel. *0161 7935148* Fax. *0161 7944793* E-mail. *bsh@boltblue.com Bi-Fi*

B S K Laminating Ltd Commissioners Road, Rochester ME2 4ED Tel. *01634 292700* Fax. *01634 291029* E-mail. *mike.speller@bsk-laminating.com* Web. *www.bsk-laminating.com Insulex – Rustop – Seekure*

B Sky Cars A 147 Soho Road, Birmingham B21 9ST Tel. *0121 5545555* E-mail. *info@skyradiocars.co.uk* Web. *www.skyradiocars.co.uk Sky Airports Direct – Sky Radio Cars*

B S P International Foundations Ltd Claydon Industrial Park Gipping Road, Claydon, Ipswich IP6 0BZ Tel. *01473 830431* Fax. *01473 832019* E-mail. *jwakeling@bspif.co.uk* Web. *www.bsp-if.com Hydropac – Hydropile – Piling hammers – Ric – Vibro Pile*

B S S (a division of BSS Group) Unit 6-7 Industrial Estate Thomas Road, London E14 7BN Tel. *020 75313900* Fax. *020 75374849* E-mail. *tony-maxwell@bssgroup.com* Web. *www.bssgroup.com B.S.S. Manor*

B S S Pipe Fitting Stockholders Head Office Fleet House Lee Circle, Leicester LE1 3QQ Tel. *0116 2623232* Fax. *0116 2531343* E-mail. *andy.vaughan@bssgroup.com* Web. *www.bssgroup.com Aerco – Angelery – Boss – Boss Green – Boss Minivent – Boss-Flamco – Bossblue – Bossmatic – Bosswhite – Rad-Line*

BST Products Unit 7 Delta Court Sky Business Park, Robin Hood Airport, Doncaster DN9 3GN Tel. *0845 6430950* Fax. *0845 6430960* E-mail. *info@detectable-products.co.uk* Web. *www.detectable-products.co.uk Detectapen*

B T A L Incorporating Kadtal Universal Mills Bradford Road, Keighley BD21 4BW Tel. *01274 668149* Fax. *01535 609998* E-mail. *info@btal.co.uk* Web. *www.btal.co.uk BTAL*

B T M UK Automation Products Unit 6 Stephenson Road, St Ives PE27 3WJ Tel. *01480 497498* Fax. *01480 497479* E-mail. *btmautomation@btconnect.com* Web. *www.btmcorp.com Tog-L-Loc – Tri-Lok*

B T T G Ltd Ring Road West Park, Leeds LS16 6QL Tel. *0113 2591999* Fax. *0113 2780306* E-mail. *sdonnelly@bttg.co.uk* Web. *www.bttg.co.uk BCTC-CAMRASO – BTTG – Shirley Technologies – Wiratec*

B T U Europe Ltd Unit 13 LDL Business Centre Station Road West, Ash Vale, Aldershot GU12 5RT Tel. *01252 549848* Fax. *01252 660011* E-mail. *sales@btu.com* Web. *www.btu.com Transheat*

Bucher Hydraulics Ltd 9 Eastboro Fields Hemdale Business Park, Nuneaton CV11 6GL Tel. *024 76353561* Fax. *024 76353572* E-mail. *info@bucherhydraulics.com* Web. *www.bucherhydraulics.com B.E.M.A - Barmag Hydraulic - Beringer Hydraulic - Bucher Hidroirma - Bucher Hydraulik - HTF Frutigen AG – B.E.M.A. – Barmag Hydraulic – Beringer Hydraulic – Bucher Hidroirma – Bucher Hydraulik – HTF Frutigen AG – Truninger*

Buckhill Ltd 60a Newland Road, Worthing BN11 1JX Tel. *01903 238012* E-mail. *sales@buckhill.co.uk* Web. *www.buckhill.co.uk BCMS – BGMS – Buckhill DRPS*

J E Buckle Engineers Ltd High Street Cromer, Stevenage SG2 7QA Tel. *01438 861257* Fax. *01438 861783* E-mail. *gary.buckle@jebuckle.co.uk* Web. *www.jebuckle.co.uk Dieci Telehandlers – Gregoire Besson*

Buckley Lamb Ltd Eastfield Side, Sutton In Ashfield NG17 4JW Tel. *01623 550350* Fax. *01623 440384* E-mail. *sales@buckleylamb.co.uk* Web. *www.buckleylamb.co.uk Buckley Lamb*

Buckleys Uvral Ltd Range Road Industrial Estate Range Road, Hythe CT21 6HG Tel. *01303 260127* Fax. *01303 262115* E-mail. *sales@buckleys.co.uk* Web. *www.buckleys.co.uk Buckleys – Buckleys (UVRAL) Ltd – U.V.R.A.L.*

Bucon Ltd Braintree House Braintree Road, Ruislip HA4 0EJ Tel. *020 88421440* Fax. *020 88423881* E-mail. *info@bucon.co.uk* Web. *www.bucon.co.uk Allermuir – Albion – Amat – Ares Line – Artifort – Assmann – Bisley – Blaze Design – Boss Design – Connection – Cambridge Park – Corrigo – Clarke Rendall – Cosmetal – Dauphin – Davison Highley – Dyna Mobe – Eborcraft – ECP – Elite – Eurotek – Essepiu – Flexiform – FG Workspace – Fabritec – Free Wall – Frem – Frezza – Fritz Hanson – Fusion10 – Future Glass – GDB – Grisburger – Green SRL – Helmsman – Hands of Wycombe – Herman Miller – Howe – Human Scale – ICF – Inter Stuhl – James Tobias – Kl – Klober – KM – Komac – Kokuyo – Las Mobili – Lee & Plumpton – Maine – OCEE Design – Mobili Office – Office Speciality – Orange Box – Pledge – Protocol – Rack – Renz – Senator – Silverline – Space Oasis – Status Seating – Steelcase – Teknion – Summit – Treston – Triumph – Tula – Uffix – Verco – Vitra – Via-Sit – W J White – Wiesner Hager – Zon*

Budd Shirt Makers Ltd 1a-3 Piccadilly Arcade, London SW1Y 6NH Tel. *020 74930139* Fax. *020 74917524* E-mail. *mail@buddshirts.co.uk* Web. *www.buddshirts.co.uk Budd*

D H Budenburg PO Box 224, Manchester M44 5AY Tel. *08707 877370* Fax. *08707 877369* E-mail. *info@dh-budenberg.co.uk* Web. *www.dh-budenberg.co.uk Budenberg – Budenberg - Desgranges et Huot*

Buffalo Timber Buildings Ipsden, Wallingford OX10 6BS Tel. *01491 837682* Fax. *01491 825418* E-mail. *sales@buffalo-fence.co.uk* Web. *www.buffalo-fence.co.uk Buffalo – Buffalo – Enduro – Marathon*

Buhler Sortex Ltd Sortex Ltd 20 Atlantis Avenue, London E16 2BF Tel. *020 70557777* Fax. *020 70557700*

E-mail. *sales@buhlersortex.com*
Web. *www.buhlergroup.com Sortex*
Buhrs UK Ltd Ashwood Park Ashwood Way, Basingstoke RG22 6NQ Tel. *01256 329191* Fax. *01256 843245*
E-mail. *sale@computermail.co.uk*
Web. *www.computermail.co.uk Compaddress – ITM – Kirk Rudy – Mediacraft – *Muller (Germany) – Zaandam*
Build Centre Earls Road, Grangemouth FK3 8DJ
Tel. *01324 483574* Fax. *01324 665442*
E-mail. *sales@buildcentre.co.uk* Web. *www.wolseley.co.uk Scotcut*
Builder Center Ltd Nunnery Drive, Sheffield S2 1TA
Tel. *0114 2724001* Fax. *0114 2412840*
E-mail. *enquiries@buildercentre.co.uk*
Web. *www.thebuilderscentre.com Wolseley Centres*
Builder Center Ltd 2 London Road Warmley, Bristol BS30 5JB
Tel. *0117 9670702* Fax. *0117 9675719*
E-mail. *tony.belston@wolseley.co.uk*
Web. *www.buildcenter.co.uk Plumb Centres*
Building Additions Ltd Southgate Commerce Park, Frome BA11 2RY Tel. *01373 454577* Fax. *01373 454578*
E-mail. *sales@buildingadditions.co.uk*
Web. *www.buildingadditions.co.uk Bruynzeel Aqualine – Doors & partition manufrs – Marleyfold*
Building Chemical Research Ltd Mount Sion Road Radcliffe, Manchester M26 3SJ Tel. *0161 7232237* Fax. *0161 7247699*
E-mail. *brooksc@buildchem.co.uk*
Web. *www.buildchem.co.uk Brickies Mate*
Building Design Partnership PO Box 85, Manchester M60 3JA Tel. *0161 8282200* Fax. *0161 8324280*
E-mail. *manchester@bdp.com* Web. *www.bdp.com B.D.P.*
Building Product Design North Frith Oasts Ashes Lane, Hadlow, Tonbridge TN11 9QU Tel. *01732 850770*
Fax. *01732 355536* E-mail. *lynnm@willantn.demon.co.uk*
Web. *www.buildingproductdesign.com Glidevale – Kingfisher – Passivent*
Roger Bullivant Ltd Walton Road Drakelow, Burton On Trent DE15 9UA Tel. *01283 511115* Fax. *01283 540826*
E-mail. *marketing@roger-bullivant.co.uk*
Web. *www.roger-bullivant.co.uk R.B.*
Bulroc Ltd Station Lane Old Whittington, Chesterfield S41 9QX Tel. *01246 450608* Fax. *01246 454621*
E-mail. *info@bulroc.com* Web. *www.bulroc.com Bulroc*
Bunce Ashbury Ltd Ashbury, Swindon SN6 8LW
Tel. *01793 710212* Fax. *01793 710437*
E-mail. *philip.bunce@bunce.co.uk* Web. *www.bunce.co.uk Bunce – *Bunce Epoke (Denmark) – Bunce Maxi – *Fresia (Italy) – Noremat – *Sep (Italy) – Vandaele*
Bunzl Catering Supplies Ltd (a division of Bunzl Disposables Europe Ltd) Epsom Chase 1 Hook Road, Epsom KT19 8TY Tel. *01372 736300* Fax. *01372 736301*
E-mail. *reception.epsom@bunzlcatering.co.uk*
Web. *www.bunzlcatering.co.uk ACS Whittaker – Alpha Supplies – Bunzl Disposables – HOPA – KOve Pac*
Bunzl Cleaning & Hygiene Supplies Bone Lane, Newbury RG14 5SH Tel. *01635 528550* Fax. *01635 528822*
E-mail. *newbury@bunzlchs.co.uk* Web. *www.bunzlchs.com Alpha Supplies*
Bunzl Lockhart Catering Equipment Lockhart House Brunel Road, Theale, Reading RG7 4XE Tel. *0118 9303900*
Fax. *0118 9303931* E-mail. *lockhart.marketing@bunzl.co.uk*
Web. *www.bunzlce.com *Eschenbach (Germany) – Lockhart – *Nomar (France) – *Rolex (Belgium) – *Spring (Switzerland)*
Bunzl S W S Unit 2b Abergelly Road, Fforestfach, Swansea SA5 4DY Tel. *01792 355600* Fax. *01792 355700*
E-mail. *sales@bunzlsws.com* Web. *www.bunzlsws.com A.C.S. – Ni-Trax – Pro-Boot – T.U.F. – Talisman – Tuftrax – Zetanite*
Bunzl Vending Services Ltd 19 Aintree Road Perivale, Greenford UB6 7LG Tel. *020 89982828* Fax. *020 89980704*
E-mail. *enquiries@bunzlvend.com*
Web. *www.bunzlvend.com Blue Chip – Canterbury – Kensington – Konditorei – Pembroke – Stirling – Valufare*
Buoyant Upholstery Ltd Hallam Road, Nelson BB9 8AJ
Tel. *01282 691631* Fax. *01282 697298*
E-mail. *maramayo@buoyant-upholstery.co.uk*
Web. *www.buoyant-upholstery.co.uk Buoyant*
B U P A Dale Buildings Cook Street, Coventry CV1 1JH
Tel. *024 76811700* Fax. *024 76227363*
E-mail. *barrya@bupa.com* Web. *www.bupa.co.uk/cashplan BUPA Cash Plan*
Burberry Ltd 21 New Bond Street, London W1S 2RE
Tel. *020 33673000* Fax. *020 78392666*
E-mail. *marketing@burberry.com* Web. *www.burberry.com Burberry – Scotch House *The – Thomas Burberry*
Richard Burbidge Ltd Whittington Road, Oswestry SY11 1HZ
Tel. *01691 655131* Fax. *01691 657694*
E-mail. *info@richardburbidge.co.uk*
Web. *www.richardburbidge.com Richard Burbidge Architectural Mouldings*
Burcas Ltd Park Lane Handsworth, Birmingham B21 8LT
Tel. *0121 5532777* Fax. *0121 5531284*
E-mail. *info@burcas.co.uk* Web. *www.burcas.co.uk Aldridge – Burcas*
Burden Ltd 5 The Cobden Centre Folly Brook Road, Emersons Green, Bristol BS16 7FQ Tel. *08706 006068*
Fax. *0117 3014400* E-mail. *j-burden@burdens.co.uk*
Web. *www.burdens.co.uk Environmental Street Furniture (ESF) – Integrated Ducting Solutions (IDS)*
Bureau Of Analysed Samples Ltd Newham Hall Stokesley Road, Newby, Middlesbrough TS8 9EA Tel. *01642 300500*
Fax. *01642 315209* E-mail. *rpmeeres@basrid.co.uk*
Web. *www.basrid.co.uk British Chemical Standard*
Bureau Veritas 130 Sandringham Avenue Sandringham Avenue, Harlow CM19 5QA Tel. *01279 634000*
Fax. *020 83353056* Web. *www.bureauveritas.co.uk Winton Environmental Management Ltd*
Burgess Architectural Products Ltd PO Box 11, Hinckley LE10 2LL Tel. *01455 618787* Fax. *01455 251061*
E-mail. *info@burgessceilings.co.uk*
Web. *www.burgessceilings.co.uk Nelson Burgess*
Ben Burgess Beeston Dereham Road Beeston, Kings Lynn PE32 2LE Tel. *01328 701347* Fax. *01328 700111*
E-mail. *raymondsumner@benburgess.co.uk*
Web. *www.benburgess.co.uk *Amazone – Grimme – *Irrimec – *John Deere – *Simba*
Burgess C R Commissioning Ltd 19 Mount Ephraim, Tunbridge Wells TN4 8AE Tel. *01892 515169*
Fax. *01892 547716*
E-mail. *burgesscomm@burgessgroup.co.uk*
Web. *www.burgessgroup.co.uk Burgess – International*
Burgess Dorling & Leigh Ltd Middleport Pottery Port Street, Stoke On Trent ST6 3PE Tel. *01782 577866*
Fax. *01782 575529* E-mail. *info@burleigh.co.uk*
Web. *www.burleigh.co.uk Burleigh*
Burgess Furniture Ltd Hanworth Trading Estate Hampton Road West, Feltham TW13 6EH Tel. *020 88949231*
Fax. *020 88942943* E-mail. *sales@burgessfurniture.com*
Web. *www.burgessfurniture.com Burgess – G B – Hireburgess*
Burgon & Ball Ltd La Plata Works Holme Lane, Sheffield S6 4JY Tel. *0114 2338262* Fax. *0114 2852518*
E-mail. *enquiries@burgonandball.com*
Web. *www.burgonandball.com AIX – BBA – BBN – Begornia – Corona – Drummer Boy – Duckfoot – Hindes – Master Shear – Montevideo – Multi-Shear – T.U.S – Tyzack Turner*
Burkard Manufacturing Company Ltd Woodcock Hill Estate, Rickmansworth WD3 1PJ Tel. *01923 773134*
Fax. *01923 774790* E-mail. *sales@burkard.co.uk*
Web. *www.burkard.co.uk Burkard*
Burkert Controlmatics Ltd Fluid Control Centre Brimscombe Port Business Park, Brimscombe, Stroud GL5 2QQ
Tel. *01453 731353* Fax. *01453 731343*
E-mail. *sales.uk@burkert.com* Web. *www.burkert.co.uk Burkert – Burkert Fluid Control Systems*
Burlen Fuel Systems Ltd Spitfire Hous Castle Road, Salisbury SP1 3SA Tel. *01722 412500* Fax. *01722 334221*
E-mail. *info@burlen.co.uk* Web. *www.burlen.co.uk Burlen – Burlen – SU Fuel Systems – SU Fuel Systems – SU-Zenith – Su/Zenith – Zenith – Zenith*
Burlington Engineers Ltd Unit 11 Perival Industrial Park Horsenden Lane South, Perivale, Greenford UB6 7RL
Tel. *020 88107266* Fax. *020 89983517*
E-mail. *info@burlington-engineers.co.uk*
Web. *www.burlington-engineers.co.uk *Alpine Westfalia (Germany/Austria) – *Delmag (Germany) – *Muehlhauser (Germany) – *Normet (Finland) – *Schwing (Germany) – *Stetter (Germany)*
Burlington Slate Ltd (Head Office) Cavendish House, Kirkby In Furness LA17 7UN Tel. *01229 889661*
Fax. *01229 889466* E-mail. *sales@burlingtonstone.co.uk*
Web. *www.burlingtonstone.co.uk Brandy Crag – Brandy Crag Silver/Grey Slate – Broughton Moor – Broughton Moor Green Slate – Broughton Moor Slate – Burlington – Burlington Slate – Bursting Stone – Elterwater – Elterwater Slate – Hodge Close – Kirkby*
Burlodge Ltd Unit 5 Hook Rise South Industrial Park Hook Rise South, Surbiton KT6 7LD Tel. *020 88795700*
Fax. *020 88795701* E-mail. *frontdesk@burlodge.co.uk*
Web. *www.burlodge.co.uk *Burlodge*
The Burmatex Victoria Mills The Green, Ossett WF5 0AN
Tel. *01924 263718* Fax. *01924 264004*
E-mail. *info@burmatex.co.uk* Web. *www.burmatex.co.uk Burmatex 2200 Antistat – Burmatex 4200 Sidewalk – Burmatex 4400 Broadway – Burmatex 5500 Luxury – Burmatex 7700 Grimebuster – Burmatex Academy – Burmatex Equity – Burmatex Sport – Burmatex Tivoli – Burmatex Toreador – Burmatex Tuff Plus – Burmatex Velour*
Burnbright Fuels Berisden Brenchley Road, Horsmonden, Tonbridge TN12 8DN Tel. *01892 836588* Fax. *01892 836589*
E-mail. *enquiries@burnbrightfuels.co.uk*
Web. *www.burnbrightfuels.co.uk Burnbright*
N R Burnett Ltd West Carr Lane, Hull HU7 0AW
Tel. *01482 838800* Fax. *01482 822110*
E-mail. *sales@nrburnett.co.uk* Web. *www.nrburnett.co.uk Burnett*
Burnhill Services Ltd Middleton Business Park Cartwright Street, Cleckheaton BD19 5LY Tel. *01274 872423*
Fax. *01274 861499* E-mail. *info@burnhillequestrian.com*
Web. *www.burnhillequestrian.com County Dogs Feeds – County Game Feeds – County Horse Feeds – Premier Mix*
John Burn & Co Birmingham Ltd 74 Albert Road Stechford, Birmingham B33 9AJ Tel. *0121 5084144* Fax. *0121 5084145*
E-mail. *info@johnburn.co.uk* Web. *www.johnburn.co.uk Burnco – Burnco - John Burn & Co (B'ham) Ltd.*
Burrafirm Ltd Croxstalls Road, Walsall WS3 2XY
Tel. *01922 476836* Fax. *01922 479442*
E-mail. *terryfryer@burrafirm.co.uk*
Web. *www.albert-jagger.co.uk Burrafirm*
Burroughes & Watts Carroway Head Farm Carroway Head, Canwell, Sutton Coldfield B75 5RY Tel. *0121 3232043*
Fax. *0121 3232043* E-mail. *sales@burroughesandwatts.com*
Web. *www.burroughesandwatts.com Burroughs & Watts – Burroughs and Watts – Twister*
Burson Marsteller 24-28 Bloomsbury Way, London WC1A 2PX Tel. *020 78312969* Fax. *020 73401033*
E-mail. *enquiries@bein.com* Web. *www.bm.com Burson-Marsteller*
Burton Mccall Ltd 163 Parker Drive, Leicester LE4 0JP
Tel. *0116 2344600* Fax. *0116 2358031*
E-mail. *sales@burton-mccall.co.uk*
Web. *www.burton-mccall.co.uk Burton McCall*
Burton Safes Ltd Unit 28 Brockholes Industrial Park Brockholes, Holmfirth HD9 7BN Tel. *01484 663388*
Fax. *01484 666338* E-mail. *enquiries@burtonsafes.co.uk*
Web. *www.burtonsafes.co.uk *Arfe – *Burton – *Technomax*
Burvills The Forge Cossins Farm Downside Road, Downside, Cobham KT11 3LZ Tel. *01932 589666* Fax. *01932 589669*
E-mail. *chris.clarkson@burvills.co.uk*
Web. *www.burvills.co.uk Burvill – Lettasafe*
Bury Times Ltd Classified Advertising (a division of Newquest Ltd) PO Box 22, Bolton BL1 1DE
Tel. *01204 522333* Fax. *0161 7973277*
E-mail. *sorrell@lancashire.newsquest.co.uk*
Web. *www.thisisbury.co.uk Bury Times*
Busch UK Ltd Hortonwood 3035, Telford TF1 7YB
Tel. *01952 678700* Fax. *01952 677423*
E-mail. *sales@busch-gvt.co.uk* Web. *www.busch.co.uk *Busch (Germany and Switzerland)*
Bushboard Ltd Rixon Road, Wellingborough NN8 4BA
Tel. *01933 232200* Fax. *01933 232280*
E-mail. *washrooms@bushboard.co.uk*
Web. *www.bushboard.co.uk Aero – Baseline – Bushboard – Continuum – Formica Aura – Nuance – Odyssey – Omega – Omega Complete – Options – Options Complete – Paraline – Profiles – System One – Tuff Stuff*
Business & Decision Ltd Broad Street House 55 Old Broad Street, London EC2M 1RX Tel. *020 79976060*
Fax. *020 79976100* E-mail. *info@businessdecision.co.uk*
Web. *www.businessdecision.co.uk ASIZ – CPTrak – P.M.D.C.*
Business Information Service Ellesmere Port Library Civic Way, Ellesmere Port CH65 0BG Tel. *0151 3374693*
Fax. *0151 3354689*
E-mail. *sue.eddison@cheshiresharedservices.gov.uk*
Web. *www.cheshirewestandchester.gov.uk/bis BIS*
Business Resources Development Ltd Suite 7 Haddons Acre Station Road, Offenham, Evesham WR11 8JJ
Tel. *01386 833535* E-mail. *office@brdee.com*
Web. *www.brdee.com officetalk*
Butchers Pet Care Crick, Northampton NN6 7TZ
Tel. *01788 823711* Fax. *01788 822960*
E-mail. *reception@butcherspetcare.com*
Web. *www.butcherspetcare.com Butchers – Butchers Choice – CLASSIC – OLLI*
Butchers Printed Products Ltd Unit 8 Upper Crossgate Road Park Farm Industrial Estate, Redditch B98 7SR
Tel. *0121 4402612* Fax. *01527 524360*
E-mail. *sales@bppdigital.co.uk* Web. *www.bppdigital.co.uk Specialist screen printers*
Bute Fabrics 4 Barone Road Rothesay, Isle Of Bute PA20 0DP Tel. *01700 503734* Fax. *01700 504545*
E-mail. *sales@butefabrics.com* Web. *www.butefabrics.com Bute Fabrics*
Howard Butler Ltd (t/a Hobut) Crown Works Lincoln Rd, Walsall WS1 2EB Tel. *01922 640003* Fax. *01922 723626*
E-mail. *sales@hobut.co.uk* Web. *www.hobut.co.uk Hobut*
Butterick Co. Ltd 38 New Lane, Havant PO9 2ND
Tel. *023 92486221* Fax. *023 92475383*
E-mail. *sales@butterick-vogue.co.uk*
Web. *www.sewdirect.com *Butterick (U.S.A.) – *Butterick Greetings – *See & Sew (U.S.A.) – *Vogue Patterns (U.S.A.)*
Butterworth & Roberts Ltd (a division of Gama Beta Holdings Ltd) Yewtree Mills Holmbridge, Holmfirth HD9 2NN Tel. *01484 691500* Fax. *01484 681783*
E-mail. *sales@butterworthroberts.co.uk*
Web. *www.butterworthroberts.co.uk Yew Tree Fabric, A*
Butterworths Lenses 85 Peffer Place, Edinburgh EH16 4BB
Tel. *0131 6614555* Fax. *0131 6618555*
Web. *www.butterworthsaccountants.co.uk Butterworths*
M. Buttkereit Ltd Unit 2 Britannia Road Industrial Estate, Sale M33 2AA Tel. *0161 9695418* Fax. *0161 9695419*
E-mail. *martin@buttkereit.co.uk* Web. *www.buttkereit.co.uk Arno Arnold – Eitec – EKD GELENKROHR – Elbaron – Flexa – Gmeinder – Icotek – PH-CLEANTEC – RINGLER – SKC Gleittechnik*
Buttle plc Soothouse Spring, St Albans AL3 6NX
Tel. *01727 834242* Fax. *01727 834248*
E-mail. *peter.buttle@buttle.co.uk* Web. *www.buttle.co.uk Buttle's*
Jason Buttons Ltd Unit 40 Mahatma Gandhi Industrial Estate Milkwood Road, London SE24 0JF Tel. *020 72740724*
Fax. *020 77370022 Ace – Golden Fleece – Jason*

Butyl Products Ltd 11 Radford Crescent, Billericay CM12 0DW Tel. *01277 653281* Fax. *01277 657921* E-mail. *rodney@butylproducts.co.uk* Web. *butylproducts.co.uk Butyl*

B & W Billiards Ltd Unit 3 Sapcote Trading Centre Powke Lane, Cradley Heath B64 5QR Tel. *01384 638191* Fax. *01384 638195* E-mail. *sales@bandwbilliards.co.uk* Web. *www.bandwbilliards.co.uk Burroughes and Watts*

B & W Mechanical Handling Gemini House 1 Bartholemews Walk, Ely CB7 4EA Tel. *01353 665001* Fax. *01353 666734* E-mail. *blythe@bwmech.co.uk* Web. *www.bwmech.co.uk Kleen-Line – Samson – Samson, Stormajor, Shiploader, Kleen-Line, Sterling. – Shiploader – Sterling – Stormajor*

B W T Ltd Suite 3 Unit F Warners Mill Silks Way, Braintree CM7 3GB Tel. *01376 334200* Fax. *01376 334201* E-mail. *enquiries@bwt-uk.co.uk* Web. *www.bwt-uk.co.uk Ceramic – Combi-care Compact Scale Inhibitor – Electron – Hi Tec – Hi Tec Meter – Micro – Prismertec*

B X Plant Ltd 11 Dukes Court Bognor Road, Chichester PO19 8FX Tel. *01243 781970* Fax. *01243 533547* E-mail. *rhodge@bxplant.com* Web. *www.bxplant.com Bel-Mix – Bel-Spray*

By Design plc Unit 6 Mountheath Industrial Park Prestwich, Manchester M25 9WB Tel. *0161 2814400* Fax. *0161 2814481* E-mail. *worldwide@by-design.co.uk* Web. *www.by-design.co.uk By Design*

BYPY Hydraulics & Transmissions Ltd Lingen Road Ludlow Business Park, Ludlow SY8 1XD Tel. *01584 873012* Fax. *01584 876647* E-mail. *sales@bypy.co.uk* Web. *www.bypy.co.uk B Y P Y – Bima (Italy) – *Bondioli and Pavesi (Italy) – *Casappa (Italy) – Fira (Italy) – *HP Hydraulic (Italy) – Ikron (Italy) – *LC Oleodinamica (Italy) – *Oleostar (Italy) – *Walvoil (Italy)*

Bysel Ltd Selby House 27a Batley Road, Heckmondwike WF16 9ND Tel. *01924 403857* Fax. *01924 405368* E-mail. *info@byselcandy.com* Web. *www.byselcandy.com Beehive (United Kingdom) – Derbyshire (United Kingdom) – Selby (United Kingdom) – Selby Pop (United Kingdom)*

Bystronic UK Ltd 6 Wayside Business Park Wilsons Lane, Coventry CV6 6NY Tel. *024 76585100* Fax. *0844 8485851* E-mail. *sales.uk@bystronic.com* Web. *www.bystronic.co.uk AFM – Beyeler – Bystronic*

Bytron Concorde House Kirmington, Ulceby DN39 6YP Tel. *01652 688626* Fax. *01652 680788* E-mail. *info@bytron.com* Web. *www.bryton.com ATCOMS*

C

C2C Services Ltd 2308 Coventry Road Sheldon, Birmingham B26 3JZ Tel. *0121 7226181* E-mail. *post@c2cgroup.co.uk* Web. *www.c2cservices.co.uk C2C*

C 4 Carbides Ltd 9 Nuffield Road, Cambridge CB4 1TF Tel. *01223 225400* Fax. *01223 225405* E-mail. *andrew@c4carbides.com* Web. *www.c4carbides.com C.4 Carbides*

Cab Glazing Services Button End Harston, Cambridge CB22 7GX Tel. *01223 872400* Fax. *01223 872866* E-mail. *sales@cabglazing.co.uk* Web. *www.cabglazing.co.uk Cab Glazing*

Cableduct Ltd 30 Selhurst Road, London SE25 5QF Tel. *020 86831126* Fax. *020 86897896* E-mail. *info@cableductuk.com* Web. *www.cableductuk.com Cableduct*

Cabletime Ltd 64 Greenham Road, Newbury RG14 7HX Tel. *01635 35111* Fax. *01635 35913* E-mail. *info@cabletime.com* Web. *www.cabletime.com MediaStar*

Cablofil Unit 9 Ashville Way Sutton Weaver, Runcorn WA7 3EZ Tel. *01928 754380* Fax. *08451 304629* E-mail. *salesuk@cablofil.com* Web. *www.cablofil.co.uk Greening Cable Support Systems – RF6 Cable Duty – RF7 Cable Tray – RM 25 X Cable Tray – RM 50 X Cable Tray – RM Power Trunking – RMB 30 Basket Tray – RML 100 Cable Ladder – RML 125 Cable Ladder – RML 150 Cable Ladder – RML 60 Cable Ladder – Standard X Cable Tray*

Cabot Plastics Ltd Gate Street, Dukinfield SK16 4RU Tel. *0161 9344500* Fax. *0161 9344502* E-mail. *webmaster@cabot-corp.com* Web. *www.cabot-corp.com Cabelec – Plasblak – Plaswite*

C A C I C A C I House Avonmore Road, London W14 8TS Tel. *020 76056000* Fax. *020 76035862* E-mail. *admin@caci.co.uk* Web. *www.caci.co.uk ACORN – Area Data – CACI – Financial ACORN – InSite – InSite Europe – InSite Fieldforce – Irish ACORN – Lifestyles U.K. – Monica – People U.K. – Scottish ACORN*

Caddie Products Ltd Swan Court Swan Street, Isleworth TW7 6RJ Tel. *020 88474321* Fax. *020 85682100* E-mail. *enquiries@caddieproducts.co.uk* Web. *www.caddie.com *Caddie – *Caddie Valet – *Caddinox – *Multi Caddie*

Cadlogic Ltd 3 Greenhill, Lichfield WS13 6DY Tel. *01543 419886* Fax. *01543 419860* E-mail. *steve.tew@cadlogic.com* Web. *www.cadlogic.com archCAD+ – Architect 2000 – LT Architect – Lt Engineer – LT Structural – ParaCAD+*

Cadogan (A Subsidiary Of A. Oppenheimer & Co. Ltd) 20 Vanguard Way Shoeburyness, Southend On Sea SS3 9RA Tel. *01702 98888* Fax. *01702 294225* E-mail. *cad@oppenheimers.co.uk* Web. *www.oppenheimers.co.uk B.B.B – Comoy – Dr Plumb – G.B.D. – Loewe – Medico – Orlik*

Caffyns plc Meads Road, Eastbourne BN20 7DR Tel. *01323 730201* Fax. *01323 739680* E-mail. *info@caffyns.co.uk* Web. *www.caffyns.co.uk Caffyns Wessex*

C A Grant Ltd Orgreave Crescent, Sheffield S13 9NQ Tel. *0114 2695498* Fax. *0114 2695412* E-mail. *sales@cagrant.co.uk* Web. *www.grantmarking.com GRANT – GRANT*

Robert Cain Brewery (The Robert Cain Brewery) Stanhope Street, Liverpool L8 5XJ Tel. *0151 7098734* Fax. *0151 7088395* E-mail. *info@cains.co.uk* Web. *www.cains.co.uk Cains*

Caiyside Imaging Ltd Suite 2 7 Washington Lane, Edinburgh EH11 2HA Tel. *0131 3379996* Fax. *0870 0517085* E-mail. *info@caiysideimaging.co.uk* Web. *www.caiysideimaging.co.uk Mindray*

Cakes By Ann 6 Carron Court, Hamilton ML3 8TD Tel. *01698 336448* E-mail. *fpeter@blueyonder.co.uk* Web. *www.cakesbyann.co.uk Cakes By Ann*

Calder Ltd Gregorys Bank, Worcester WR3 8AB Tel. *01905 723255* Fax. *01905 723904* E-mail. *peter.elton@calder.co.uk* Web. *www.calder.co.uk Calder – Freelance (United Kingdom) – Hammelmann – MultiJet (United Kingdom)*

Caldervale Forge Co. Ltd Dunrobin Road, Airdrie ML6 8LS Tel. *01236 763388* Fax. *01236 765259* E-mail. *john.ramsay@rockeater.co.uk* Web. *www.rockeatertools.com Rockeater – Scotburster*

Calderys UK Ltd Unit 5-8 Ashfield Way Whitehall Industrial Estate Whitehall Road, Leeds LS12 5JB Tel. *0113 2636268* Fax. *0113 2790539* E-mail. *enquiry@lafarge.co.uk* Web. *www.calderys.com A.C.S. – Intracast – Keral – Keralox – Keram – Kercast – Kerex – Kergun – Kerlite – Kermag – Kermix – Kerplast – Monrox – Phlocast – Phlox – Ram – Refrabloc – Refraciment – Ultracast*

Caldi Castle Hire 2 Ferneycross Caldicot, Caldicot NP26 4QY Tel. *0774 7399541* E-mail. *mrk_cochrane@yahoo.com caldi castle hire*

Caldwell Hardware Ltd Herald Way Binley Industrial Estate, Coventry CV3 2RQ Tel. *024 76437900* Fax. *024 76437969* E-mail. *amacaulay@caldwell.co.uk* Web. *www.caldwell.co.uk Pace – Spiralift – Spirex – Timb-a-tilt – Torso – Ultralift*

Caledonian Cables Ltd 27 Old Gloucester Street, London WC1N 3AX Tel. *020 74195087* Fax. *020 78319489* E-mail. *info@caledonian-cables.co.uk* Web. *www.caledonian-cables.co.uk Caledonian*

Caledonian Industries Ltd 5 Atholl Avenue, Glasgow G52 4UA Tel. *0141 8824691* Fax. *0141 8103402* E-mail. *alan@caledonian-group.co.uk* Web. *www.caledonian-group.co.uk Biosystem – Poron (U.S.A.)*

Cal Gavin Ltd Process Intensification Engineering Station Road, Alcester B49 5ET Tel. *01789 400401* Fax. *01789 400411* E-mail. *info@calgavin.com* Web. *www.calgavin.com hiTran (United Kingdom)*

Calibration Dynamics 7 Regents Court South Way, Andover SP10 5NX Tel. *01264 339030* Fax. *01264 339040* E-mail. *sales@calibrationdynamics.com* Web. *www.calibrationdynamics.com Wlka Calibration Line – Mensor Corporation – Scanivalve Corporation – MB Dynamics*

Calibre Ltd 68 Sir Evelyn Road, Rochester ME1 3LZ Tel. *01256 475588* Fax. *01256 475599* E-mail. *info@rubberbands.co.uk* Web. *www.rubberbands.co.uk Calibre – Censtretch*

Caligraving Brunel Way, Thetford IP24 1HP Tel. *01842 752116* Fax. *01842 755512* E-mail. *info@caligraving.co.uk* Web. *www.caligraving.co.uk Caligraving – Music Process Engravers & Printers*

CAL-Logistics Ltd 16 Sea Winnings Way, South Shields NE33 3NE Tel. *0191 4290770* Fax. *0191 4552604* E-mail. *info@cal-logistics.com* Web. *www.cal-logistics.com GeoManager*

Callsure Business Telephone & Fax Numbers 36 Duncroft, Windsor SL4 4HH Tel. *01753 624121* E-mail. *sales@callsure07050.co.uk* Web. *www.callsure07050.co.uk British Telecom – Cable & Wireless – call navigator – Callsure – Digital Mail – email to fax – fax to email – Puma – redstone – skype – T Mobile – telephone – telephone numbers – vodafone*

Calomax Ltd Calomax House Lupton Avenue, Leeds LS9 7DD Tel. *0113 2496681* Fax. *0113 2350358* E-mail. *sales@calomax.co.uk* Web. *www.calomax.co.uk Calomax*

Calor Gas Ltd Athena Drive Tachbrook Park, Warwick CV34 6RL Tel. *01926 330088* Fax. *01926 420609* E-mail. *srennie@calor.co.uk* Web. *www.calor.co.uk Autogas – Calor – Calor Gas – Calor Natural Gas – Calor Propane – Calor Refrigerants*

Calpack Ltd Tonypandy Enterprise Park Llwynypia Road, Tonypandy CF40 2ET Tel. *01443 431544* Fax. *01443 432447* E-mail. *rahul@calpack.co.uk* Web. *www.calpack.co.uk B. Flute – E. Flute – Jacoflute – Micro Sandwich – Micro Sandwich Display*

Calpeda Ltd 8 Wedgwood Road Industrial Estate, Bicester OX26 4UL Tel. *01869 241441* Fax. *01869 240681* E-mail. *pumps@calpeda.co.uk* Web. *www.calpeda.co.uk A. Series – C. Series – C.A. Series – Centrimat – G.M. Series – Idromat – Jetomat – M.P.C. Series – M.X.H. – M.X.S. – M.X.V. – Minimat – N. Series – N.C.A. Series – N.G. Series – N.G.C. Series – N.M. Series – N.P. Series – N.R. Series – N.T. Series – S.D.-S.D.S. Series – S.P.A. Series – T. Series – Turbomat – V.A.L.-S.C. Series*

Calrec Audio Ltd Nutclough Mill, Hebden Bridge HX7 8EZ Tel. *01422 842159* Fax. *01422 845244* E-mail. *enquiries@calrec.com* Web. *www.calrec.com Calrec Audio*

Camberley Catering Equipment 208 Frimley Road, Camberley GU15 2QJ Tel. *01276 681919* Fax. *01276 686254* E-mail. *sales@silesia.co.uk* Web. *www.silesia.co.uk Silesia – Silex – Velox*

Cambio Ltd The Irwin Centre Scotland Road, Dry Drayton, Cambridge CB23 8AR Tel. *01954 210200* Fax. *01954 210300* E-mail. *support@cambio.co.uk* Web. *www.cambio.co.uk Cambio – Parr – Starfish*

Cambridge Electronic Industries Ltd Pembroke Avenue Waterbeach, Cambridge CB25 9QR Tel. *01223 860041* Fax. *01223 863625* E-mail. *sales@cambridgeconnectors.com* Web. *www.cambridgeconnectors.com Cambridge Connectors*

Cambridge Market Research Ltd Unit H South Cambridge Business Park, Sawston, Cambridge CB22 3JH Tel. *01223 492050* Fax. *01223 492079* E-mail. *accounts@cambridgemr.com* Web. *www.cambridgemr.com Fast Foodfax*

Cambridge Newspapers Ltd Winship Road Milton, Cambridge CB24 6PP Tel. *01223 434434* Fax. *01223 434222* E-mail. *newsdesk@cambridge-news.co.uk* Web. *www.cambridge-news.co.uk Cambridge Evening News – Cambridge Weekly News – Ely Weekly News – Haverhill Weekly News – Huntingdon Weekly News – Newmarket Weekly News – Royston Weekly News – Saffron Walden Weekly News – St. Ives Weekly News – St. Neots Weekly News*

Cambridge Numerical Control 8-9 Royce Court Burrel Road, St Ives PE27 3NE Tel. *01480 468639* Fax. *01480 301577* E-mail. *sales@cnc.uk.com* Web. *www.cnc.uk.com Cambridge Numerical Control*

Cambridgeshire Hydraulics Ltd 97 Mereside Soham, Ely CB7 5EE Tel. *01353 721704* Fax. *01353 720653* E-mail. *sales@cambshydraulics.com* Web. *www.cambshydraulics.com Gates – Vestr*

Cambridge Solar Ltd 152 NUNS WAY, Cambridge CB4 2NS Tel. *01223 361112* E-mail. *o.morgan@cambridge-solar.co.uk* Web. *www.cambridge-solar.co.uk Cambridge Solar*

Cambridge Systems Design 1 Andersons Court Newnham Road, Cambridge CB3 9EZ Tel. *01223 518815* E-mail. *info@cds.co.uk* Web. *www.csd.co.uk EcoTerm*

Cambridge Vacuum Engineering 43 Pembroke Avenue Denny Industrial Estate, Waterbeach, Cambridge CB25 9QX Tel. *01223 863481* Fax. *01223 862812* E-mail. *reception@camvaceng.com* Web. *www.camvaceng.com Dynaweld – Free Form Fabrication – Near Nett Shape – Reduced Pressure Electron Beam Welding – Surfi-Sculpt – Torvac – Torvac Furnaces – Wentgate – Wentgate Dynaweld*

Cambridge Vending Unit 4-6 Crane Industrial Estate Cambridge Road Industrial Estate, Milton, Cambridge CB24 6AZ Tel. *01223 425522* Fax. *01223 425515* E-mail. *info@cambridgevending.co.uk* Web. *www.cambridgevending.co.uk CRANE – NEVA*

Camdata Ltd 23 Royston Road Harston, Cambridge CB22 7NH Tel. *0845 0645555* E-mail. *sales@camdata.co.uk* Web. *www.camdata.co.uk Camdata*

Cameo Bathrooms 5 High Street, Iver SL0 9ND Tel. *01753 655255* Fax. *01753 655322* E-mail. *colin@cameobathrooms.co.uk* Web. *www.cameobathrooms.co.uk *Aqata*

Cameron Forecourt Ltd Platts Common Industrial Estate Hoyland, Barnsley S74 9SE Tel. *01226 742441* Fax. *01226 747441* E-mail. *barryjenner@cameron-forecourt.co.uk* Web. *www.cameron-forecourt.co.uk Cameron 2000*

Cameron Price Ltd 1a Charlotte Road Stirchley, Birmingham B30 2BT Tel. *0121 4592121* Fax. *0121 4512303* E-mail. *info@cameron-price.co.uk* Web. *www.cameron-price.co.uk Easy-Air*

Cameron Robb Ltd 48-52 Lombard Street, Birmingham B12 0QN Tel. *0121 7728311* Fax. *0121 7713562* E-mail. *cathy@cameron-robb.co.uk* Web. *www.cameron-robb.co.uk Camro*

Camlab Ltd Unit 24 Norman Way Industrial Estate Norman Way, Over, Cambridge CB24 5WE Tel. *01954 233100* Fax. *01954 233101* E-mail. *mailbox@camlab.co.uk* Web. *www.camlab.co.uk *Hach (U.S.A.) – *Machery-Nagel (Germany) – *Socorex (Switzerland)*

Camlar Ltd 5 Osborne Road Pilgrims Hatch, Brentwood CM15 9LE Tel. *07970 238215* Fax. *0203 236789* E-mail. *info@camlar.co.uk* Web. *www.camlar.co.uk ECS – Philips – Helvar – iLlght – Polaron*

Camlock Systems Ltd Unit 3 Park View Alder Close, Eastbourne BN23 6QE Tel. *01323 410996*

Fax. *01323 411512* E-mail. *enquiries@camlock.com* Web. *www.camlock.com Camatic – Keyosk – Octagon – Sidlock – Sidlock - Keyosk*

Camloc Motion Control Ltd 15 New Star Road, Leicester LE4 9JD Tel. *0116 2743600* Fax. *0116 2743620* E-mail. *tracy.ayres@camloc.com* Web. *www.camloc.com Swift & Sure – Stop & Stay – Econoloc – Vari-Lift – Blocklift – Click & Lock – Dampers*

Cam Metric Holdings The Pingle 85 Histon Road, Cottenham, Cambridge CB24 8UQ Tel. *01954 250880* Fax. *01954 250853* E-mail. *sales@cammetric.co.uk* Web. *www.cammetric.co.uk Dekohm – Evro – Ohmega – Scalamp*

Camozzi Pneumatics Ltd The Fluid Power Centre Watling Street, Nuneaton CV11 6BQ Tel. *024 76374114* Fax. *024 76347520* E-mail. *sales@camozzi.co.uk* Web. *www.camozzi.com/uk Camozzi Pneumatics*

Campbell International PO Box 57, Tonbridge TN9 2NE Tel. *01732 773364* Fax. *01732 362429* E-mail. *info@campbelluk.co.uk* Web. *www.campbelluk.co.uk Panther – Vellotape – Vellotape, Panther*

Campbell Medical Supplies 2 Victoria Estate Violet Street, Paisley PA1 1PA Tel. *0141 8893500* Fax. *0141 8487139* E-mail. *campbellmedical@ukonline.co.uk Prime-Aid – Primeaid*

Campbell Miller Tools Ltd 20 Jordanvale Avenue, Glasgow G14 0QU Tel. *0141 9549557* Fax. *0141 9549979* E-mail. *sales@cmtl.co.uk* Web. *www.cmtl.co.uk Black and Decker – Bosch – Dearman – Festool – Honda – Makita – Rotabroach – Trend – Wachs*

Camper & Nicholsons Mayfair Ltd Fitzroy House 18-20 Grafton Street, London W1S 4DZ Tel. *020 70091950* Fax. *020 76292068* E-mail. *info@lon.cnyachts.com* Web. *www.camperandnicholsons.com Camper & Nicholsons*

Camtek Ltd (Jetcam International) Camtek House 117 Church Street, Malvern WR14 2AJ Tel. *01684 892290* Fax. *01684 892269* E-mail. *sales@camtek.co.uk* Web. *www.camtek.co.uk Camtek – Pentacut – Peps – Solidcut – Tubecut*

Canary Wharf Holdings Ltd One Canada Square Canary Wharf, London E14 5AB Tel. *020 74182000* Fax. *020 74182222* E-mail. *admin@canarywharf.com* Web. *www.sytnercitybmw.co.uk Canary Wharf*

Canburg Hopton Indl-Est, Devizes SN10 2EU Tel. *01380 729090* Fax. *01380 727771* Web. *www.smallbone.co.uk Smallbone*

Cancer Research Ventures Ltd 10 Cambridge Terrace Regents Park, London NW1 4JL Tel. *020 72241333* Fax. *020 74874310* Web. *www.cancer.org.uk The Canser Research Campaign*

Canford Audio Crowther Road, Washington NE38 0BW Tel. *0191 4181000* Fax. *0191 4160392* E-mail. *info@canford.co.uk* Web. *www.canford.co.uk Canford – Tecpro*

Cannock Chemicals Ltd 99a North Street, Cannock WS11 0AZ Tel. *01543 571762* Fax. *01543 466011* E-mail. *sales@thepolishingshop.co.uk* Web. *www.thepolishingshop.co.uk Atotech – Falconbridge – Kocour*

Cannon Technologies Ltd 13 Queensway Stem Lane Industrial Estate, New Milton BH25 5NU Tel. *01425 638148* Fax. *01425 619276* E-mail. *matt.goulding@cannontech.co.uk* Web. *www.cannontech.co.uk Cannon*

Cannon.Co.Uk 214-224 Barr Street, Birmingham B19 3AG Tel. *0121 5514131* Fax. *0121 5549292* E-mail. *peter.cannon@cannon.co.uk* Web. *www.cannon.co.uk Cannon Silverplated Sports Cups – Enviroplac Helps Save The Forests*

Canongate Technology Ltd 17 Edgefield Road Industrial Estate, Loanhead EH20 9TB Tel. *0131 4480786* Fax. *0131 4401739* E-mail. *sales@canongatetechnology.co.uk* Web. *www.canongatetechnology.co.uk Acumet – Embra – Holledge*

Canon UK Ltd Cockshot Hill, Reigate RH2 8BF Tel. *01737 220000* Fax. *01737 220022* E-mail. *andy@canon.co.uk* Web. *www.canon.co.uk Canon Business Service*

Canterbury Cathedral Shop 25 Burgate, Canterbury CT1 2HA Tel. *01227 865300* Fax. *01227 865333* E-mail. *enquiries@cathedral-enterprises.co.uk* Web. *www.cathedral-enterprises.co.uk Cathedral Shop, The, Canterbury*

Cantilever Bar Systems Ltd The Chapel London Road, Brimscombe, Stroud GL5 2SA Tel. *01453 732040* Fax. *01453 886906* E-mail. *caroline.craven@cantileverbars.com* Web. *www.cantileverbars.com *Barmobility – Calabrese Sink – Cantilever – *Portabar*

Capalex CAP, Cleator Moor CA25 5QB Tel. *01946 811771* Fax. *01946 813681* E-mail. *enquiries@capalex.com* Web. *www.capalex.co.uk Capital Aluminium Extrusions Ltd / Capalex*

Caparo Atlas Fastenings Ltd Heath Road Darlaston, Wednesbury WS10 8XL Tel. *0121 2242000* Fax. *0121 2242001* E-mail. *andy.harland@atlasfastenings.com* Web. *www.atlasfastenings.com Armstrong Atlas*

Caparo Precision Tubes (Walsall Division) PO Box 13, Oldbury B69 4PF Tel. *0121 5435700* Fax. *0121 5435750* E-mail. *sales@caparoprecisiontubes.co.uk* Web. *www.caparosteelproducts.com Barton Conduit – Caparo Tubes (United Kingdom)*

Caparo Tubes Unit 4 Tafarnaubach Industrial Estate Tafarnaubach, Tredegar NP22 3AA Tel. *01495 724333* Fax. *01495 717720* E-mail. *david.porter@caparotubestredegar.co.uk* Web. *www.caparo-tubes.co.uk Caparo Coldform – Caparo Coldform - structural hollow sections*

Capatex Ltd 127 North Gate, Nottingham NG7 7FZ Tel. *0115 9786111* Fax. *01933 664455* E-mail. *sales@capatex.com* Web. *www.capatex.com Agro Textiles*

Capex Office Interiors Robert Denholm House Bletchingley Road, Nutfield, Redhill RH1 4HW Tel. *01737 822122* Fax. *01737 822112* E-mail. *ray.allinson@capexinteriors.com* Web. *www.capexinteriors.com Abak – Aeron Seating – Agio Furniture – Allermuir Furniture – Ambus – Brevis – Chilton – Colebrook Bosson Saunders – Connection Seating – Della Rovere Furniture – DPG – Eurotek Office – Fairway – Flight – Frem – Fulcrum – G64 – Glade – Hag Seating – Harley – Herman Miller – Intrigue – Jigsaw Plus – Joy – Lamb Mackintosh – Lateralfile Storage – Morris Office Furniture – Oblique – Office Electrics – Orangebox – Pledge Seating – Senator – Silverline Storage – Status Seating – Sven – Systemfile Storage – Tangent Furniture – Therapod – Torassen Reactive – Tract Seating – V-Smart – Verco – Wallis Seating – Wings Furniture – X10*

C A P Group Of Companies Head Office The Crescent Hockley, Birmingham B18 5NL Tel. *0121 5549811* Fax. *0121 5543791* E-mail. *veronica@capproductions.co.uk* Web. *www.capproductions.co.uk Capco*

Capita Business Services Ltd Unit 3 Franklin Court Stannard Way Priory Business Park, Bedford MK44 3JZ Tel. *01234 838080* Fax. *01234 838091* E-mail. *info@capita.co.uk* Web. *www.capita.co.uk Capita Education Services*

Capital Equipment & Machinery Ltd Mill Mead, Staines TW18 4UQ Tel. *01784 456151* Fax. *01784 466481* E-mail. *sales@capital-equipment.com* Web. *www.capital-equipment.com *Comet (Taiwan) – *Dufour (France) – *G.E.R. (Spain) – *Jeyma (Spain) – *Kondia Powermill (Spain) – *Praga (India) – *Selter (Spain) – *Servo (U.S.A.) – Servo (USA) – *Volstro (U.S.A.)*

Capital Refrigeration Services Ltd 16 Lea Road, Waltham Abbey EN9 1AS Tel. *01992 788844* Fax. *0870 8501141* E-mail. *info@capitalref.com* Web. *www.capitalref.com *Arex – *Blue Seal – *Foster – *Irinox – *Williams*

Capital Roofing Co. Ltd 193 Westcombe Hill Blackheath, London SE3 7BB Tel. *020 88585123* Fax. *020 83051202* E-mail. *info@capital-roofing.co.uk* Web. *www.capital-roofing.co.uk C.R.*

Capital Safety Group Ltd 7 Christleton Court Manor Park, Runcorn WA7 1ST Tel. *01928 571324* Fax. *01928 571325* E-mail. *csgne@csgne.co.uk* Web. *www.capitalsafety.com Basix – Everest – Ladsaf – Railok – Res-Q-Man – Rescumatic – Saflok – Sala – Sala Group – Sayfglida – Sayfguard – Surefit*

Capital World Travel Ic-Id Northgate The Pavilions, Chester Business Park, Chester CH4 9QJ Tel. *01244 625300* Fax. *01244 682197* E-mail. *sales@capitalworldtravel.co.uk* Web. *www.capitalworldtravel.co.uk Capital Bonds – Capital Experiences – Capital Incentives – Capital World Travel – Incentive Award Card*

Capita Secure Information Solutions Unit 7-8 Prospect West Bumpers Way Bumpers Farm, Chippenham SN14 6FH Tel. *08456 041999* Fax. *07002 929999* E-mail. *info@vivista.sungard.co.uk* Web. *www.capitasecureinformationsolutions.co.uk DS2000 - ICCS Product – DS2000 - ICCS Product: Integrated communications control system.*

Caplugs Ltd Unit 5 Overfield Thorpe Way, Banbury OX16 4XR Tel. *01295 263753* Fax. *01295 263788* E-mail. *support@caplugs.co.uk* Web. *www.caplugs.co.uk CAPLUGS*

Captain Tolley Ltd 69 Valiant House Vicarage Cresent, London SW11 3LX Tel. *020 79242817* Fax. *020 72237025* E-mail. *capt.tolleyltd@btinternet.com* Web. *www.captaintolley.co.uk Captain Tolley's Creeping Crack Cure*

Caradel Brick Ltd Lower Bathville Armadale, Bathgate EH48 2LZ Tel. *01501 730671* Fax. *01501 732991* E-mail. *enquiries@caradale.co.uk* Web. *www.caradel.co.uk Caradale*

Carafax Ltd Rotterdam Road, Hull HU7 0XD Tel. *01482 825941* Fax. *01482 878357* E-mail. *derek.waldren@carafax.co.uk* Web. *www.carafax.co.uk CarAseal*

Carbon Guerrilla Floor 1 No. 4 New Burlington Street Mayfair, London W1S 2JG Tel. *020 79568698* Fax. *020 77121501* E-mail. *Peter@carbonguerrilla.com* Web. *www.carbonguerrilla.com Carbon Guerrilla*

Car Care Plan Ltd 5 Jubilee House Thornbury, Bradford BD3 7AG Tel. *08445 738000* Fax. *08707 527100* E-mail. *info@carcareplan.co.uk* Web. *www.carcareplan.com Auto Trust – Car Care Plan – Elite – National Warranty Bond – Prestige – Replicar – Ride On – Value Guard*

Carclo Technical Plastics 103 Buckingham Avenue, Slough SL1 4PF Tel. *01753 575011* Fax. *01753 811359* E-mail. *optics@carclo-optics.com* Web. *www.carclo-plc.com CTP-C.O.I.L. – Hi-Power*

Alexander Cardew Ltd (Head Office) Unit 27 Chelsea Wharf 15 Lots Road, London SW10 0QJ Tel. *020 72353785* Fax. *020 73524635* E-mail. *sales@cardew.com* Web. *www.cardew.com Durabla (U.S.A.) – Harco (U.S.A.) – Icarus S.N. (Belgium) – Knapp – Maloney (U.S.A.) – Peeco (U.S.A.) – Polly Pig – Polyken (U.S.A.) – Thaxton (U.S.A.) – Wheatley (U.S.A.)*

Cardinal Shopfitting Ltd Systems House Ives Street, Shipley BD17 7DZ Tel. *01274 200900* Fax. *01274 588811* E-mail. *barnardm@cardinal.ltd.uk* Web. *www.cardinal.ltd.uk Cardinal*

Cardinal Health U.K. 232 Ltd PO Box 6,, Chatham ME4 4QY Tel. *01634 893500* Fax. *01634 893600* E-mail. *sales@micromedical.co.uk* Web. *www.micromedical.co.uk DiaryCard – MicroGas – MicroLoop – MicroLoop - DiaryCard - MicroGas - PulseTrace - SmokeCheck - PrinterNOX - Spida - MicroRint - MicroPeak - SpiroUSB. – MicroPeak – MicroRint – PrinterNOX – PulseTrace – SmokeCheck – Spida – SpiroUSB*

Card & Party Store Ltd 574 Manchester Road Blackford Bridge, Bury BL9 9SW Tel. *0161 7967353* Fax. *0161 7667678* E-mail. *info@card-party.co.uk* Web. *www.card-party.co.uk Card & Party Store*

Careers In Recruitment Sheraton House Castle Park, Cambridge CB3 0AX Tel. *01223 370021* Fax. *01223 370002* E-mail. *sales@careersinrecruitment.com* Web. *www.crac.org.uk C.R.A.C.*

Carfax Cards Ltd 76 Glentham Road, London SW13 9JJ Tel. *020 87481122* Fax. *020 87487110* E-mail. *carfax.admin@business-cards.co.uk* Web. *www.carfaxltd.co.uk Carfax*

Cargill Flavor Systems UK Ltd Old Trafford Essence Distillery 416 Chester Road, Manchester M16 9HJ Tel. *0161 8720225* Fax. *0161 8487331* E-mail. *sales_enquiries@cargi.com* Web. *www.cargillflavorsystems.com Blue Seal – Gold Seal – Heart – Heart Brand – Riviera*

Cargotec UK Ltd Powerhouse Silverlink, Wallsend NE28 9ND Tel. *0191 2952180* Fax. *0191 2952188* E-mail. *steven.goodchild@cargotech.com* Web. *www.cargotec.com MacGregor Global Services*

Carillion Plant Maintenance Unit 2 Oakbank Park Way Mid Calder, Livingston EH53 0TH Tel. *01506 449350* Fax. *01506 449351* E-mail. *angela.gray@carillionplc.com* Web. *www.carillionplc.com eaga Insulation*

Carlight Caravans Ltd 28 Carre Street, Sleaford NG34 7TR Tel. *01529 415056* Fax. *01529 415057* E-mail. *mail@carlight.co.uk* Web. *www.carlight.co.uk Commander Model*

Carl Kammerling International Ltd C K House Glanydon Industrial Estate, Pwllheli LL53 5LH Tel. *01758 704704* E-mail. *sales@cki.uk.com* Web. *www.carlkammerling.com *Abus (Germany) – Brass Inter-lock – CeKa – CeKa – CK Tools – Golden CeKa – Suisoplus – Triton*

Carlo Gavazzi UK Ltd 7 Springlakes Industrial Estate Deadbrook Lane, Aldershot GU12 4UH Tel. *01252 339600* Fax. *01252 326799* E-mail. *info@carlogavazzi.com* Web. *www.carlogavazzi.com Carlo Gavazzi (Denmark) – *Electromatic (Denmark) – *Feme (Italy) – *Pantec (Italy)*

Carlyle Parts Ltd Carlyle Business Park Great Bridge Street, Swan Village, West Bromwich B70 0XA Tel. *0121 5241200* Fax. *0121 5241201* E-mail. *neilbottrill@carlyle.com* Web. *www.carlyleplc.co.uk Carlyle Bus & Coach – Carlyle Bus Parks – Carlyle Export – Carlyle Service*

Carl Zeiss Ltd 15 Woodfield Road, Welwyn Garden City AL7 1JQ Tel. *01707 871200* Fax. *01707 330237* E-mail. *info@zeiss.co.uk* Web. *www.zeiss.co.uk *Carl Zeiss (Germany)*

Carlzeiss Vision Unit 9 Holford Way, Holford, Birmingham B6 7AX Tel. *08453 007788* Fax. *0121 3567678* E-mail. *marketing@vision.zeiss.com* Web. *www.vision.zeiss.com Graduate – Sola – Spectralite – U.T.M.C. – X.L.*

Carmichael Support Services Weir Lane, Worcester WR2 4AY Tel. *01905 420044* Fax. *01905 420120* E-mail. *brianw@amdac-carmichael.com* Web. *www.carmichael-int.co.uk Cobra – Viper*

Carnation Designs Ltd Unit 1 Smithies Lane Beehive Business Park, Heckmondwike WF16 0PN Tel. *01924 411211* E-mail. *sales@carnationdesigns.co.uk* Web. *www.carnationdesigns.co.uk Betwixt*

Carnhill Transformers Ltd 4 Edison Road, St Ives PE27 3LT Tel. *01480 462978* Fax. *01480 496196* E-mail. *sales@carnhill.co.uk* Web. *www.carnhill.co.uk Carnhill Transformers*

Car Paint Warehouse Ltd 17 & 18 Bonville Business Centre Bonville Road, Bristol BS4 5QR Tel. *0117 3009058* Fax. *0117 3009681* E-mail. *sales@carpaintwarehouse.co.uk* Web. *www.carpaintwarehouse.co.uk Devilbiss – Felisatti – Gramos – Octoral – Starchem*

Carpenter & Paterson Ltd Crown Works Henfaes Lane, Welshpool SY21 7BE Tel. *01938 552061* Fax. *01938 555306* E-mail. *info@cp-ltd.co.uk* Web. *www.cp-ltd.co.uk Witch*

Carpmaels & Ransford 1 Southampton Row, London WC1B 5HA Tel. *020 72428692* Fax. *020 74054166* E-mail. *email@carpmaels.com* Web. *www.carpmaels.com Carpmaels & Ransford*

Carrier Air Conditioning Unit 4 Carrowreagh Business Park Carrowreagh Road, Dundonald, Belfast BT16 1QQ Tel. *028 90483671* Fax. *028 90466418* E-mail. *billy.miskelly@carrier.utc.com Carrier*

Carrier Refrigeration & Retail Systems Ltd Meridian House Sandy Lane West, Littlemore, Oxford OX4 6LB Tel. *01865 337700* Fax. *01865 337799* E-mail. *tracy.noble@carrier.utc.com* Web. *www.carrier.com Chief UK – Crios Bank – Radford Retail Systems – Westward*

Carrington Career & Work Wear Market Street Adlington, Chorley PR7 4HE Tel. *01257 476850* Fax. *01257 476868* E-mail. *sales@carrington-cww.co.uk* Web. *www.carrington-cww.co.uk Admiral (United Kingdom) – Alba (United Kingdom) – Antistat – *Astacon – Athena (United Kingdom) – Atlas (United Kingdom) – Cooltex (United Kingdom) – Firestat – Flamegard – Flameshield (United Kingdom) – Flamestat (United Kingdom) – Flametuff – Glowtex (United Kingdom) – Multiguard – Permagard – Pique (United Kingdom) – Proban (United Kingdom) – Python (United Kingdom) – Tantara (United Kingdom) – Teredo (United Kingdom) – Tomboy (United Kingdom) – Tootella (United Kingdom) – Trident (United Kingdom) – Troy (United Kingdom) – Ultra (United Kingdom) – Viper (United Kingdom) – *Xtraflex – Weldshield*

Tom Carrington & Co. Ltd Willenhall Lane Bloxwich, Walsall WS3 2XN Tel. *01922 406611* Fax. *01922 493493* E-mail. *info@tomcarrington.co.uk* Web. *www.tomcarrington.co.uk Ega-Kut – Lyndon*

Carroll & Meynell Transformers Ltd 5 Guisley Way Durham Lane Industrial Park, Eaglescliffe, Stockton On Tees TS16 0RF Tel. *01642 617406* Fax. *01642 614178* E-mail. *enquiries@carroll-meynell.com* Web. *www.carroll-meynell.com Teesside Industrial Controls*

Carron Phoenix West Carron Works Stenhouse Road, Carron, Falkirk FK2 8DR Tel. *01324 638321* Fax. *01324 620978* E-mail. *sales@carron.com* Web. *www.carron.com Alpha – Carisma – Coral – Granite – Lavella – Select – Silquartz – Summit*

Carr Reinforcements Gordon Street Mill Gordon Street, Worsthorne, Burnley BB10 3NA Tel. *01282 420924* Fax. *0161 4433388* E-mail. *erictaylor@btconnect.com* Web. *www.carr-reinforcements.com Vitech (United Kingdom)*

Carrs Billington Agriculture Sales Ltd Montgomery Way Rosehill Industrial Estate, Carlisle CA1 2UY Tel. *01228 520212* Fax. *01228 512572* E-mail. *rae.tomlinson@carrs-billington.com* Web. *www.carrs-billington.com Unifarm Fertilizer*

Carrtech Engineering Products (Raffle Court Ltd) Crossfield Road, Birmingham B33 9HP Tel. *0121 6832600* Fax. *0121 6832601* E-mail. *sales@carrtech.com* Web. *www.carrtech.com Carrtech*

Carter Controls UK Ltd 4 The Gateway Place The Gateway Industrial Estate, Parkgate, Rotherham S62 6LL Tel. *01709 525800* Fax. *01709 710717* E-mail. *sales@cartercontrols.fsnet.co.uk Carter*

Carter Retail Equipment Ltd 90 Lea Ford Road, Birmingham B33 9TX Tel. *0121 2501111* Fax. *0121 2501122* E-mail. *info@cre-ltd.co.uk* Web. *www.cre-ltd.co.uk Olympian – Stellar*

Richard Carter Ltd Neiley Works 72 New Mill Road, Honley, Holmfirth HD9 6QQ Tel. *01484 666806* Fax. *01484 666802* E-mail. *richard.carter@richardcarterltd.co.uk* Web. *www.richardcarterltd.co.uk Carters – Shocksafe*

Carter Synergy (Northern Division) 111-115 Marsh Lane, Bootle L20 4JD Tel. *0151 9222342* Fax. *0151 9224004* E-mail. *rob.orbell@cartersynergy.com* Web. *www.crrs.co.uk Designs J.C.*

Carter Thermal Industries Ltd Redhill Road Hay Mills, Yardley, Birmingham B25 8EY Tel. *0121 2501000* Fax. *0121 2501005* E-mail. *reception@cti-ltd.co.uk* Web. *www.cartersyrnergy.co.uk Carter-ADB – Carter-Doucet – Carter-Drycool – Carter-Midac – Carter-Visco*

Carval Computing Ltd Innovation & Technology Transfer Centre Tamar Science Park, Plymouth PL6 8BX Tel. *01752 764290* Fax. *01752 764291* E-mail. *c.sweby@carval.co.uk* Web. *www.carval.co.uk Postillion – Unibacs – Unistaff – Unitend – Uniwage*

Carville Ltd Station Road, Dorking RH4 1HQ Tel. *01306 881681* Fax. *01306 876265* E-mail. *sales@carville.co.uk* Web. *www.carville.co.uk Carville*

Case Communication Norths Estate Old Oxford Road, Piddington, High Wycombe HP14 3BE Tel. *01494 880240* Fax. *01494 833741* E-mail. *sales@casecomms.com* Web. *www.casecomms.com Case Communications Ltd*

Cashmaster International Fairykirk Road Rosyth, Dunfermline KY11 2QQ Tel. *01383 416098* Fax. *01383 414731* E-mail. *info@cashmaster.com* Web. *www.cashmaster.com Cash Master – Super VR*

Cash Register Services 176 Albany Road, Coventry CV5 6NG Tel. *024 76443728* Fax. *024 76443728* E-mail. *simon@crs-coventry.co.uk* Web. *www.cashregisterservices.co.uk Busicom Cash Registers – Casio Cash Registers – Epsom Cash Registers – Fujitsu Cash Registers – Geller Cash Registers – Gold Cash Registers – NCR Cash Registers – Olivetti Cash Registers – Samsung Cash Registers – Sharp Cash Registers – Tec Cash Registers – Uniwell Cash Registers*

Castell Safety International Ltd The Castell Building 217 Kingsbury Road, London NW9 9PQ Tel. *020 82001200* Fax. *020 82050055* E-mail. *sales@castell.com* Web. *www.castell.com Castell – Electrobolt – Isolok – Isolok - Mistura – Martello – Microguard*

Castings Technology International Ltd Advanced Manufacturing Park Brunel Way, Catcliffe, Rotherham S60 5WG Tel. *0114 2541144* Fax. *0114 2730852* E-mail. *m.ashton@castingstechnology.com* Web. *www.castingstechnology.com Contirun – Replicast*

Castle Brook Tools Ltd Unit 7 Shepcote Way, Tinsley Industrial Estate, Sheffield S9 1TH Tel. *0114 2617200* Fax. *0114 2617370* E-mail. *info@castlebrooke.co.uk* Web. *www.castlebrooke.co.uk *Beargrip (Czech Republic) – Castle – *Groz (Czech Republic) – H G I – *Hindusthan (Czech Republic) – *Narex (Czech Republic) – *Poldi (Czech Republic) – *Skoda (Czech Republic) – *Tos (Czech Republic)*

Castle Dataware Ltd 7 Partnership House Withambrook Park Industrial Estate, Grantham NG31 9ST Tel. *01476 592123* Fax. *01476 592992* E-mail. *sales@culmak.co.uk* Web. *www.culmak.co.uk Aetel – Comware*

Castle Group Ltd Salter Road Eastfield, Scarborough YO11 3UZ Tel. *01723 584250* Fax. *01723 583728* E-mail. *enquiries@castlegroup.co.uk* Web. *www.castlegroup.co.uk Castle Group Ltd*

Castle View International Holdings Limited Steuart Road Bridge of Allan, Stirling FK9 4JX Tel. *01786 834060* Fax. *01786 832658* E-mail. *enquiries@castleview.co.uk* Web. *www.castleview.co.uk Trigonfm*

Caston PLC Cornford Road, Blackpool FY4 4QW Tel. *01253 766411* Fax. *01253 691486* E-mail. *paul@casdon.com* Web. *www.casdon.co.uk Casdon*

Castrol UK Ltd Wakefield House Pipers Way, Swindon SN3 1RE Tel. *0151 3553737* Fax. *01793 513506* Web. *www.castrol.com Aircol – Alpha – Alphasyn – Anvol – Castrol LMX – Clearedge – Cresta – Dynadrive – Dynamax – Hysol – Hyspin – Icematic – Ilobroach – Ilocut – Iloform – Ilogrind – Magna – Perfecto HT – Perfecto T – R.X. Super Plus – Rustilo – Solvex – Spheerol – Superedge – Syntilo – Turbomax – Variocut*

Caswick Ltd Sandtoft Road Belton, Doncaster DN9 1PN Tel. *01427 872017* Fax. *01427 873541* E-mail. *info@caswick.com* Web. *www.caswick.com Caswick*

Cater Bake UK Ltd Unit A1 Senator Point South Boundary Road, Knowsley Industrial Park, Liverpool L33 7RR Tel. *0151 5485818* Fax. *0151 5485835* E-mail. *info@cater-bake.co.uk* Web. *www.cater-bake.co.uk *Cater-Bake – *Fage – *IGF – *Velma – *Zanolli*

Catercraft Catering Equipment Sussex House Fishersgate Terrace, Portslade, Brighton BN41 1PH Tel. *01273 411020* Fax. *01273 419106* E-mail. *info@catercraft.com* Web. *www.catercraft.com Blue Seal – Clenaware – Enodis – Mitsubishi – Williams*

Caterham Cars Ltd 32 Station Avenue, Caterham CR3 6LB Tel. *01883 333700* Fax. *01883 333707* E-mail. *andynoble@caterham.co.uk* Web. *www.caterham.co.uk Caterham 21 – Caterham 7*

Caterham Fireplaces Unit 5-6 Trentside Business Park, Stoke On Trent ST4 4EU Tel. *01782 410880* Fax. *01782 410908* E-mail. *trudi@caterhamgranite.com* Web. *www.caterhamfireplaces.com Caterham*

Catering Investments Ltd 1 Taylors Business Park Gravel Lane, Chigwell IG7 6DQ Tel. *020 85015353* Fax. *020 85015454* E-mail. *davcateng@btconnect.com* Web. *www.cateringinvestments.com Inoxyform*

Catering Suppliers PO Box 12976, Birmingham B6 7AP Tel. *0121 3314200* Fax. *0121 3314200* E-mail. *sales@chefset.co.uk* Web. *www.catering-suppliers.com Chef Set*

Catersales Ltd 119B Penshurst Road, Thornton Heath CR7 7EF Tel. *020 86846500* Fax. *020 86846686* E-mail. *sales@catersales.co.uk* Web. *www.catersales.co.uk Marcfi – Univerbar*

Cathelco Ltd 18 Hipper Street South, Chesterfield S40 1SS Tel. *01246 277656* Fax. *01246 206519* E-mail. *sales@cathelco.co.uk* Web. *www.cathelco.co.uk C-Shield – Cathelco*

C A T I C Trading Development UK Ltd Ironbridge House, London NW1 8BD Tel. *020 75863854* Fax. *020 75866799* E-mail. *380icuk@dtclict.com CATIC*

Cattle Information Services Scotsbridge House Scots Hill, Croxley Green, Rickmansworth WD3 3BB Tel. *01923 695319* Fax. *01923 770003* E-mail. *info@thecis.co.uk* Web. *www.thecis.co.uk *1 Stop – *Herd Care – *T H R*

Cattles Ltd Kingston House Centre 27 Business Park Woodhead Road, Birstall, Batley WF17 9TD Tel. *01924 444466* Fax. *01924 442255* E-mail. *info@cattles.co.uk* Web. *www.cattles.co.uk Cattle's*

Cattron Theimeg UK Ltd Riverdene Business Park Molesey Road, Hersham, Walton On Thames KT12 4RG Tel. *01932 247511* Fax. *01932 220937* E-mail. *imartin@cattronuk.com* Web. *www.cattron.com Beamer*

Caunton Access Ltd Arrowmax Buildings Langwith Road, Langwith Junction, Mansfield NG20 9RN Tel. *01636 636662* Fax. *0870 7319109* E-mail. *enquiries@cauntonaccess.com* Web. *www.cauntonaccess.com Genie – Niftylift*

Causeway Steel Products Ltd Five Ash Road, Gravesend DA11 0RF Tel. *01474 567871* Fax. *01474 328993* E-mail. *causewaysteel@causeway-steel.co.uk* Web. *www.causeway-steel.co.uk Causeway*

Cavendish French Ltd 22 Church Road Bookham, Leatherhead KT23 3PW Tel. *01372 459944* Fax. *01372 459384* E-mail. *sales@cavendishfrench.com* Web. *www.cavendishfrench.com Cavendish French Recollections*

Cavendish Tea Coffee Ltd Toad Lane Brampton-En-Le-Morthen, Rotherham S66 9BG Tel. *01709 703417* Fax. *01709 703517 La Spaziate Espresso Machines*

Cavern City Tours Ltd Century Buildings 31 North John Street, Liverpool L2 6RG Tel. *0151 2369091* Fax. *0151 2368081* E-mail. *david@thecavernliverpool.com* Web. *www.mathewstreetfestival.com Cavern City Tours – Cavern Club, The*

Cavers Wall China Ltd Berry Hill Road Berryhill Trading Estate, Stoke On Trent ST4 2PQ Tel. *01782 652800* Fax. *01782 652801* E-mail. *sales@caverswallchina.co.uk* Web. *www.caverswallchina.co.uk Thomas Goode*

Cavity Trays Ltd Boundary Avenue Lufton Trading Estate, Lufton, Yeovil BA22 8HU Tel. *01935 474769* Fax. *01935 428223* E-mail. *enquiries@cavitytrays.co.uk* Web. *www.cavitytrays.com Beterprufe – Bituticton – Cavicloser – Cavilintel – Caviroll – Cavitray – Cavivent – Caviweep – Flashertape – Petheleyne – Radonbar*

C A W Cornwall Ltd Threemilestone Industrial Estate Threemilestone, Truro TR4 9LD Tel. *01872 271491* Fax. *01872 222310* E-mail. *cawcornwall@line1.net* Web. *www.cawcornwall.com C.A.W.*

C B F 67 Hatherley Road, Cheltenham GL51 6EG Tel. *01242 237652* Fax. *01242 236186* E-mail. *info@cbfnet.co.uk* Web. *www.cbfnet.co.uk CBF Group*

C B Frost & Co. Ltd Green Street, Birmingham B12 0NE Tel. *0121 7738494* E-mail. *info@cbfrost-rubber.com* Web. *www.cbfrost-rubber.com Angalok – Bisco cellular silicones – Bisco cellular silicones - BF 1000 HT800 – Fomex*

C B L Ceramics Ltd Marble Hall Road Steynton, Milford Haven SA73 2PP Tel. *01646 697681* Fax. *01646 690053 Beramic*

CBM Logix New City Chambers 36 Wood Street, Wakefield WF1 2HB Tel. *0786 7874857* E-mail. *contact@cbm-logix.com* Web. *www.cbm-logix.com Bradley – Mitsubishi – Omron – PLC's – Siemens – Toshiba*

C C A Group Ltd Eastway Fulwood, Preston PR2 9WS Tel. *01772 662800* Fax. *01772 662987* E-mail. *sales@ccagroup.co.uk* Web. *www.ccagroup.com Bucentaur Gallery – Cherish – Christmas Gold – Christmas Greetings – Confetti – Cool Yule – Giving at Christmas – Signature – Something New – Special Day – Wedding Bells*

C C H Hose & Rubber 24 The Shade Soham, Ely CB7 5DE Tel. *01353 722366* Fax. *01353 723464* E-mail. *cchhose@sales24.fsnet.co.uk* Web. *www.cchhose.co.uk BOC – IVG – Murex*

C C L Labels Decorative Sleeves Unit 6 Pioneer Way, Castleford WF10 5QU Tel. *01977 510030* Fax. *01977 521240* E-mail. *mrayner@cclind.com* Web. *www.ccllabel.co.uk Biocode Sscuri Print – Hide-A-Way – Highlite – Promot-A-Pack – Tactsense – Take-Off – Take-Out – Tamp-A-Seal*

CCV Telecom Unit A 46 Brummell Road, Newbury RG14 1TL Tel. *0800 5677568* Fax. *01635 47123* E-mail. *jonathan@ccvtelecom.co.uk* Web. *www.ccvtelecom.co.uk Avaya – Panasonic, Samsung*

CDS UK 4 Ash Walk Alresford, Southampton SO24 9JP Tel. *07866 781379* Fax. *01962 734228* E-mail. *patrick@cdsuk.biz* Web. *www.cdsuk.biz Cryogenic Deflashing Systems*

C Dugard Ltd Machine Tools 75 Old Shoreham Road, Hove BN3 7BX Tel. *01273 732286* Fax. *01698 300258* E-mail. *sales@dugard.co.uk* Web. *www.dugard.com *Chevalier (Taiwan) – CME – Dugard Eagle – Dugard Eagle – Hedelios – *Hyundai (Korea, Republic of) – Sigma – Takumi – *Tos Varnsdorf (Czech Republic) – *Tos Varnsdrof (Czech Republic) – Yoo J*

Ceag Ltd Unit K Zenith Park Whaley Road, Barnsley S75 1HT Tel. *01226 206842* Fax. *01226 731645* E-mail. *sales@ceag.co.uk* Web. *www.ceag.co.uk Ceag – Lumax*

Ceandess Wolverhampton Ltd Ashford Indl-Est Dixon Street, Wolverhampton WV2 2BX Tel. *01902 872000* Fax. *01902 872019* E-mail. *peter.killey@ceandess.co.uk* Web. *www.ceandess.co.uk Ceandess*

Cebo UK Ltd Badentoy Road Portlethen, Aberdeen AB12 4YA Tel. *01224 782020* Fax. *01224 782340* E-mail. *info@cebo-uk.com* Web. *www.cebo-uk.com Cemoil – Copper State Rubber – Dunlop – Dyckerhoff Black Label – Interswage – Rugby – Todo*

Cecil Instruments Ltd Milton Technical Centre Cambridge Road Industrial Estate, Milton, Cambridge CB24 6AZ Tel. *01223 420821* Fax. *01223 420875* E-mail. *ceciltarbet@cecilinstruments.com* Web. *www.cecilinstruments.com Aquaquest – Aquarius – Series 1000 – Series 1100 – Series 2000 – Series 3000 – Series 9000 – Super Aquarius*

Cecil M Yuill Ltd Cecil House Loyalty Road, Hartlepool TS25 5BD Tel. *01429 266620* Fax. *01429 231359* E-mail. *david.mullins@yuill.co.uk* Web. *www.yuillhomes.co.uk Yuill Homes*

C E D Ltd 728 London Road, Grays RM20 3LU Tel. *01708 867237* Fax. *01708 867230* E-mail. *michaelheap@ced.ltd.uk* Web. *www.ced.ltd.uk Cedec – Permknap – Rougeite*

Cedo Ltd Unit 11 Halesfield 11, Telford TF7 4LZ Tel. *01952 272727* Fax. *01952 274102* E-mail. *info@cedo.com* Web. *www.cedo.com Bunny bags – Cling Film – Drawstring Bags – Food & Freezer Bags – Nappy sacks*

Cee Vee Unit 27 Upper Mills Trading Estate, Stonehouse GL10 2BJ Tel. *01453 821666* Fax. *01453 822298* E-mail. *sales@cee-vee.co.uk* Web. *www.cee-vee.co.uk CV3 – Hogfors – Procol – Schlesurger*

Celcoat Ltd 3 Crown Works Rotherham Road, Beighton, Sheffield S20 1AH Tel. *0114 2690771* Fax. *0114 2540495* E-mail. *celcoatltd@tiscali.co.uk Celcoat*

Celef Audio Ltd 1 Riding Court Riding Road, Buckingham Road Industrial Estate, Brackley NN13 7BH Tel. *01280 700147* Fax. *01280 700148* E-mail. *stewart@proac-loudspeakers.com* Web. *www.proac-loudspeakers.com Celef*

Cellhire plc Park House Clifton Park Avenue, York YO30 5PB Tel. *0800 610610* Fax. *01904 611028* E-mail. *info@fonefix.com* Web. *www.cellhire.co.uk Cellhire*

Celotex Ltd Lady Lane Industrial Estate Hadleigh, Ipswich IP7 6BA Tel. *01473 822093* Fax. *01473 822093* E-mail. *info@celotex.co.uk* Web. *www.celotex.co.uk Double R – Double R CW2000 – Double-R GA2000 – Energy-Lok – Flexcell – Hydroform – Sundeala – Tempchek – Tempchek Deck*

Celtic Sheepskin Company Ltd Unit B Treloggan Industrial Estate, Newquay TR7 2SX Tel. *01637 871605* Fax. *01637 851989* E-mail. *support@celtic-sheepskin.co.uk* Web. *www.celtic-sheepskin.co.uk Celt*

Cemb Hofmann UK Ltd 1 Long Wood Road Trafford Park, Manchester M17 1PZ Tel. *0161 8723122* Fax. *0161 8729247* E-mail. *sales@cembhofmann.co.uk* Web. *www.cembhofmann.co.uk Benrath – CEMB – CEMB - Hofmann - Benrath – Hofmann*

Cembrit Ltd 57 Kellner Road, London SE28 0AX Tel. *020 83018900* Fax. *020 83018909* E-mail. *sales@cembrit.co.uk* Web. *www.cembrit.co.uk Alumnasc Aluminium – Contessa Natural Slate (Spain) – *Dequesa Natural (Spain) – *Elith (France) – Embee (France) – *Glendyne Slate (Canada) – Harmer Products – *Heathfield (Belgium) – Metavent – Rofatop (Germany) – Slatevent II – *Wanit (Germany) – *Wanit Repro (Germany)*

Cementation Skanska Maple Cross House Denham Way, Maple Cross, Rickmansworth WD3 9SW Tel. *01923 423100* Fax. *01302 821111* E-mail. *cementation.foundations@skanska.co.uk* Web. *www.skanska.co.uk Cemcol – Cemcore – Cemfound – Cemloc – Cemset – Cemsolve – Concore – Franki – Kvaerner – Timeset*

Cengar Ltd 70 Lister Lane, Halifax HX1 5DN Tel. *01422 354626* Fax. *01422 349024* E-mail. *enquiries@cengar.com* Web. *www.cengar.com Cengar (United Kingdom)*

Centa Transmissions Thackley Court Thackley Old Road, Shipley BD18 1BW Tel. *01274 531034* Fax. *01274 531159* E-mail. *post@centa-uk.co.uk* Web. *www.centa-uk.co.uk *Beier Variodrive – Carini Spa (Germany) – Centa Servogear – Centaflex (Germany) – Centalink (Germany) – Centaloc (Germany) – Centamax (Germany) – Centastart (Germany) – Centax (Germany) – Cyclo (Germany) – Emde GmnH (Germany) – HBE (Germany) – Hyflex (U.S.A.) – SIBRE (Germany) – Sumer SA (France)*

Centaur Fuel Management 251 Manchester Road Walkden, Worsley, Manchester M28 3HE Tel. *08448 586323* Fax. *08448 248031* E-mail. *da@centauronline.co.uk* Web. *www.centauronline.co.uk Fuelsafe – Watchdog*

Central C N C Machinery Ltd Unit 12b Scar Lane Milnsbridge, Huddersfield HD3 4PE Tel. *01484 641641* Fax. *01484 460101* E-mail. *enquiries@centralcnc.co.uk* Web. *www.centralcnc.co.uk Clico – Delcam – Draper – Elu – Jet – Maggi – Record – Sedgwick – Steff – Swedex – Titman – Trend – Victor – Whitehill – Yorkleen*

Central Plant Hire Holmbush Farm Crawley Road, Faygate, Horsham RH12 4SE Tel. *01293 851320* Fax. *01293 851009* E-mail. *sales@centralplanthire.co.uk* Web. *www.centralplanthire.co.uk Caterpillar – JCB – Kubota – Volvo*

Central Soucre Ltd Harris House Moorbridge Road Bingham, Nottingham NG13 8GG Tel. *01949 836622* Fax. *01949 836662* E-mail. *ken.miller@central-source.co.uk* Web. *www.cs-uk.com Bowley'S Of Bedford – Bowleys*

Centrator UK Ltd Albion Rd Sileby, Loughborough LE12 7RA Tel. *01509 814626* Fax. *01509 814626* E-mail. *centrator@supanet.com* Web. *www.centrator.com Centrator*

Centre For Contemporary British History King's College London Strand, London WC2R 2LS Tel. *020 71016090* Fax. *020 71016099* E-mail. *tm@itma.org.uk* Web. *www.ccbh.ac.uk I.T.M.A.*

Centresoft Ltd 6 Pavilion Drive Holford, Birmingham B6 7BB Tel. *0121 6253388* Fax. *0121 6253236* E-mail. *sales@centresoft.co.uk* Web. *www.centresoft.co.uk Centresoft*

Centre Tank Services 41 Forge Lane Minworth Industrial Park, Minworth, Sutton Coldfield B76 1AH Tel. *0121 3514445* Fax. *0121 3514442* E-mail. *sales@centretank.com* Web. *www.centretank.com Piusi – Sapphire*

Centriforce Products Ltd 14-16 Derby Road Kirkdale, Liverpool L20 8EE Tel. *0151 2078100* Fax. *0151 2981319* E-mail. *sales@centriforce.com* Web. *www.centriforce.com Centriboard – Centritile – Holloplas – Stokbord – Groundmate*

Centronic Ltd Centronic House King Henrys Drive, New Addington, Croydon CR9 0BG Tel. *01689 808000* Fax. *01689 841822* E-mail. *info@centronic.co.uk* Web. *www.centronic.co.uk Centronic*

Centura Foods Ltd Bourne Business Park Dashwood Lang Road, Addlestone KT15 2HJ Tel. *01932 265000* Fax. *01784 437096* Web. *www.charnwood.com Sharwood*

V B S Centurion Blinds Oakdale Trading Estate Ham Lane, Kingswinford DY6 7JH Tel. *01384 276240* Fax. *01384 292354* E-mail. *sales@vbscenturion.co.uk Centurian*

Centurion DIY Conservatories Llp Unit 1 City Business Centre Works Road, Letchworth Garden City SG6 1FH Tel. *0800 3897261* Fax. *01462 489908* E-mail. *info@centuriondiyconservatories.com* Web. *www.centuriondiyconservatories.com Centurion DIY Conservatories*

Centurion Safety Products Ltd 21 Howlett Way, Thetford IP24 1HZ Tel. *01842 754266* Fax. *01842 765590* E-mail. *sales@centurionsafety.co.uk* Web. *www.centurionsafety.co.uk Centurion – Connect – Martindale*

C E P Ceilings Ltd Common Road Industrial Estate Verulam Road, Stafford ST16 3EA Tel. *01785 223435* Fax. *01785 251309* E-mail. *steven.ross@cepgroup.co.uk* Web. *www.cepceilings.com CEP Cumbria – CEP Echostop – CEP Fastrack – CEP Heritage – CEP Solitex 90RH – CEP Solitude – CEP Solitude Cumulus – CEP Solitude Nelson – CEP Solitude Rilled – CEP Tonico*

Ceramic Industry Certification Scheme Ltd Queens Road, Stoke On Trent ST4 7LQ Tel. *0151 7071309* Fax. *01782 764363* E-mail. *info@cicsltd.com* Web. *www.cicsltd.com CERAM – CICS*

Ceramic Tile Distributors Ltd 351 Shields Road, Newcastle Upon Tyne NE6 2UD Tel. *0191 2761506* Fax. *0191 2650663* E-mail. *sales@ctdtiles.co.uk* Web. *www.ctdtiles.co.uk Simone*

Ceramique International Ltd Unit 1 Royds Lane, Leeds LS12 6DU Tel. *0113 2310218* Fax. *0113 2310353* E-mail. *cameron@ceramiqueinternationale.co.uk* Web. *www.tilesandmosaics.co.uk Ceramique Internationale*

Ceratech Electronics Ltd 1 Omega Park, Alton GU34 2QE Tel. *01420 85470* Fax. *01420 83545* E-mail. *sales@ceratech.co.uk* Web. *www.ceratech.co.uk Accuratus (Taiwan)*

Ceratizit UK Ltd Sheffield Airport Business Park Europa Link, Sheffield S9 1XU Tel. *01925 261161* Fax. *01925 267933* E-mail. *info.uk@ceratizit.com* Web. *www.ceratizit.com A.260 Milling Cartridge System – Carbide Wear Parts – Ecocut Drill Turn – Engineering – Goldmaster – H.S.C. – M.S.S. – Maxidrill Short Hole Drills – Maxiflex Universal Tooling System – Maxilock – Maxilock F.X. Parting Tools – Maximill – Maximill – Pokolm – S.M.80 – Starmaster – Tizit*

Certikin International Ltd Witan Park Avenue Two, Witney OX28 4FJ Tel. *01993 778855* Fax. *01993 778620* E-mail. *info@certikin.co.uk* Web. *www.certikin.co.uk Calorex – Certikin – Vycon*

Certis Europe 1b Boscombe Down Business Park Mills Way, Amesbury, Salisbury SP4 7RX Tel. *01980 676500* Fax. *01980 626555* E-mail. *info@certiseurope.co.uk* Web. *www.certiseurope.co.uk Cropsafe – Croptex – Fungex – Weedwiper*

Certus UK Ltd Unit 45 Gravelly Industrial Park, Birmingham B24 8TG Tel. *0121 3275362* Fax. *0121 3282934* E-mail. *info@certuss.demon.co.uk* Web. *www.certus.co.uk Certuss*

Cerulean Rockingham Drive Linford Wood, Milton Keynes MK14 6LY Tel. *01908 233833* Fax. *01908 235333* E-mail. *info@cerulean.com* Web. *www.cerulean.com Fidus – Filtrona*

C E S Hire Ltd Binders Industrial Estate Cryers Hill Road, Cryers Hill, High Wycombe HP15 6LJ Tel. *01494 715472* Fax. *01494 712683* E-mail. *info@ces-hire.com* Web. *www.ces-hire.com Alfix – Baron – Cretange – Daines – Groutation – M-Tec – Metrix – PFT – Powersprays – Putzmeister – Reader – Thomsen – Turbosol*

Cesol Tiles Ltd 11 Bushell Business Park Lester Way, Wallingford OX10 9DD Tel. *01491 833662* Fax. *01491 825147* E-mail. *caroline@cesol.co.uk* Web. *www.cesol.co.uk Castelo – Encaustic – Litoceramika – Moorish*

Ceva Container Logistics Unit A Doranda Way Industrial Park Doranda Way, West Bromwich B71 4LE Tel. *0121 5256060* Fax. *0121 5252442* E-mail. *martin.thornhill@cevalogistics.com* Web. *www.cevalogistics.com Flexsol – Pallecon*

Ceva Network Logistics Ltd Norwich Road Mendlesham, Stowmarket IP14 5NA Tel. *01449 766401* Fax. *01449 767881* E-mail. *darren.williams@cevalogistics.com* Web. *www.cevalogistics.com TNT Network Logistics – TNT Newsfast*

C F S Carpets (Part of Landsdon Group) Arrow Valley Claybrook Drive, Redditch B98 0FY Tel. *01527 511860* Fax. *01527 511861* E-mail. *redditch@carpetandflooring.co.uk* Web. *www.cfscarpets.co.uk Carpet & Flooring Midlands – Carpet & Flooring South West – Contract Flooring Suppliers – Vanguard Carpets – Walkwell Flooring Supplies*

C G I International Ltd International House Millfield Lane, Haydock, St Helens WA11 9GA Tel. *01942 710720* Fax. *01942 710730* E-mail. *info@cgii.co.uk* Web. *www.cgii.co.uk *Fireswiss (Switzerland) – *Guardian (Italy) – *Paraflam (Austria) – Pyroguard Clear – Pyroguard Wired – Pyrosten – Safer Glaze*

C G P Chemicals Ltd The Old Dairy Bladon Paddocks Newton Road, Newton Solney, Burton On Trent DE15 0TQ Tel. *01283 511101* Fax. *01283 511102* E-mail. *sales@cgpchemicals.co.uk* Web. *www.cgpchemicals.co.uk Ajett Anaeorobics – AJett Cyanoacrylates – MDF-Bonder – Service Aid – Wyptex Plus*

C & G Services Ltd Unit 201 Sperry Way, Stonehouse GL10 3UT Tel. *01453 826781* Fax. *01453 792123* E-mail. *bob.oldmeadow@cgserv.com* Web. *www.gettrained.co.uk NRSA Training – NRSWA*

C G Tech Ltd Curtis House 34 Third Avenue, Hove BN3 2PD Tel. *01273 773538* Fax. *01273 721688* E-mail. *info.uk@cgtech.com* Web. *www.cgtech.com Optipath*

Chadtex Limited 1 Edward Street Cambridge Industrial Area, Manchester M7 1FN Tel. *0161 8301919* Fax. *0161 8301909* E-mail. *info@chadtex.co.uk* Web. *www.chadtex.co.uk Chadwick Textiles*

Chadwick International 11th Floor Holborn Tower 137 High Holborn, London WC1V 6PW Tel. *020 72690920* Fax. *020 72690929* E-mail. *chadwick@chadwick-international.com* Web. *www.chadwick-international.com *Chadwick Ebert Hoeveler (Germany) – *Chadwick Ledieu Oger (Paris and UK) – *Chadwick South Africa Pty (South Africa) – Organisational Modelling International*

Chafer Machinery Ltd Upton, Gainsborough DN21 5PB Tel. *01427 838341* Fax. *01427 838507* E-mail. *rob.starkey@cropsprayers.com* Web. *www.cropsprayers.com Chafer 418 Spraypack – Chafer 618 Spraypack – Chafer Guardian – Chafer JCB demount Spraypack – Chafer Multidrive demonnt spraypack – Chafer Sentry – Chafer Unimog Spraypack*

Chaintec Ltd Unit 43 & 38 Westbrook Trading Estate, Trafford Park, Manchester M17 1AY Tel. *0161 8777373* Fax. *0161 8760365* E-mail. *info@chaintec.co.uk* Web. *www.chaintec.co.uk CTUK – ABEKO – AICHI – ALLIS CHALMERS – AMEISE – ARMANNI – ARTISON – ASEA – ATLET – AUDUREAU – AUSA – BAKA – BALKANCAR – BAOLI – BATTIONI PAGANI – BAUMANN – BELET – BOBCAT – BOLZONI – BONSER – BOSS – BRUNILIFT – BT – BULLI KAHL – BV VESTERGAARD – CANGURU – CARER – CARREFFE – CATERPILLAR – CESAB – CHARLATTE – CLARK – COLES – CONVEYANCER – CONVENTRY CLIMAX – CROWN – CTC – CVS FERRARI – DALIAN – DAMBACH – DANTRUCK – DATSUN – DECA – DESTA – DHOLLANDIA – DIECI – DINOLIFT – DONGHUA – ECOLIFT – ELITE – EUROLIFT – FABA – FANTUZZI – FENWICK – FIAT – GENIE – GENKINGER – GROVE – HAKO – HALLA – HANGCHA – HANGZHOU – HARLAN – HAULOTTE – HC – HEDEN-DANTRUCK – HELI – HENLEY – HYSTER – HYUNDAI – ICEM – INCAB – INDOS – IRION – ITALMACHINE – IWIS – JCB – JLG – JUMBO – JUNGHEINRICH – KALMAR – KALMAR-CLIMAX – KALMAR-IRION – KENTRUCK – KINGLIFTER – KOMATSU – KOOI AAP – LAFIS – LANCER BOSS – LANSING BAGNALL – LGM – LIFTER – LIFTRITE – LINDE – LINK-BELT – LOC – LOGITRANS – LUGLI – MAGLINER – MANITU – MATBRO – MATRAL – MBB – MERLO – MIAG – MIC – MITSUBISHI – MOFFETT-KOOI – MONTINI – MORA – NICHIYU-NYK – NIFTYLIFT – NISSAN – NUOVA DETAS – O&K – OM – OMG – PATRIA – PEG-FENWICK – PIMESPO – PRAMAC – PRAT – RANGER – Record – REGINA – RENOLD – REXNORD – ROCLA – SALEV – SAMAG – SAMUK – SAMBRON – SAMSUNG – SANDERSON – SAXBY – SEDIS –*

SICHELSMIDT – SISU – SKYJACK – SMV-KONECRANES – STEINBOCK – STILL – STOCKLIN – SVETRUCK – TAILIFT – TCM – TECNOCAR – TENNANT – TEREX – TOTALLIFTER – TOYOTA – UNITRAC – UPRIGHT – VALMET – WAGNER – WHIPTRUCK – YALE – YANG-YAM-PUMA

Challenge Europe Ltd Shuttleworth Road Elm Farm Industrial Estate, Bedford MK41 0EP Tel. *01234 346242* Fax. *01234 327349* E-mail. *sales@challenge-indfast.co.uk* Web. *www.challenge-indfast.co.uk Challenge*

Challenge Power Transmission Ltd Unit 1-2 Merryhills Enterprise Park Park Lane, Wolverhampton WV10 9TJ Tel. *01902 866116* Fax. *01902 866117* E-mail. *uk@challengept.com* Web. *www.challengept.com Challenge*

Challow Products 7 Old Saw Mills Road, Faringdon SN7 7DS Tel. *01367 240091* Fax. *01367 242516* E-mail. *office@challowproducts.co.uk* Web. *www.challowproducts.co.uk Challow*

Chalmit Lighting 388 Hillington Road Hillington Park, Glasgow G52 4BL Tel. *0141 8825555* Fax. *0141 8833704* E-mail. *info@hubbell-scotland.com* Web. *www.chalmit.com Chalmit*

Chamber Of Commerce East Lancashire Red Rose Court Clayton Le Moors, Accrington BB5 5JR Tel. *01254 356400* Fax. *01254 388900* E-mail. *info@chamberelancs.co.uk* Web. *www.chamberelancs.co.uk Export Sales Training Ltd – Unique*

Chamberlain Plastics Ltd Bury Close Higham Ferrers, Rushden NN10 8HQ Tel. *01933 353875* Fax. *01933 410206* E-mail. *sales@chamberlain-plastics.co.uk* Web. *www.chamberlain-plastics.co.uk Chamcoat – Metalon*

Champion Hire Ltd 323 Abbeydale Road, Sheffield S7 1FS Tel. *08453 456902* Fax. *0114 2494202* E-mail. *info@championhire.com* Web. *www.championhire.com Champion Hire (United Kingdom)*

Champneys Wigginton, Tring HP23 6HY Tel. *01442 291000* Fax. *01442 291001* E-mail. *grant.noble@champneys.co.uk* Web. *www.champneys.co.uk Champneys – Champneys Brussells – Champneys Health Resort*

Champ Telephones Ltd 11-15 Station Street East, Coventry CV6 5FL Tel. *024 76667757* Fax. *024 76682290* E-mail. *lynn-aleca.chambers@champtel.co.uk* Web. *www.champtelephones.co.uk Cellnet – Cellular Phones – One 2 One Mobile Phones – Orange – Vodafone*

Chance Glass Ltd Pickersleigh Avenue, Malvern WR14 2LP Tel. *01684 892353* Fax. *01684 892647* E-mail. *sales@chanceglass.co.uk* Web. *www.chanceglass.co.uk Veridia*

Chance & Hunt Ltd Alexander House Crown Gate, Runcorn WA7 2UP Tel. *01928 793000* Fax. *01928 714351* E-mail. *dave@chance-hunt.com* Web. *www.chance-hunt.com Agma – Maskador – Purisoure – Topanol*

Chancellors 31 High Street, Ascot SL5 7HG Tel. *01344 627101* Fax. *01344 875422* E-mail. *paul.bosanko@chancellors.co.uk* Web. *www.chancellors.co.uk Anscombe & Ringland – Chancellors – Chancellors Associates – Russell Baldwin & Bright*

Chandos Records Chandos House 1 Commerce Park Commerce Way, Colchester CO2 8HX Tel. *01206 225200* Fax. *01206 225201* E-mail. *enquiries@chandos.net* Web. *www.chandos.net Chandos*

Channel Advantage Ltd The Old Dairy Stonor, Henley On Thames RG9 6HF Tel. *01491 639100* Fax. *01491 639166* E-mail. *rlipscombe@channel-advantage.co.uk* Web. *www.channeladvantage.co.uk Channel Events – Channel Games – Channel InStore – Channel Knowledge – Channel Specialists*

Channel Four Television Co. Ltd 124-126 Horseferry Road, London SW1P 2TX Tel. *020 73964444* Fax. *020 73068347* E-mail. *sales@channel4.co.uk* Web. *www.channel4.com 124 Facilities Ltd – Channel Four – Channel Four International – Film Four Ltd*

Channelwood Preservation Ltd Unit 12-13 Coalbrookdale Road, Clayhill Light Industrial Park, Neston CH64 3UG Tel. *0151 3423728* Fax. *0151 3429472* E-mail. *info@channelwood.co.uk* Web. *www.channelwood.co.uk Boracol B10RH – Boracol B20RH – Boracol B8.5RH – Boron Rods – Channelwood Rechargeable System – Condense-A-Cure – Floorbor Systems – Fungicidal, AntiCondensation & Protective Paint Coatings – Samson – Samson Column Repair Kit – Timberlast Frames – Timberlast System – Woodweld*

Chap Construction Aberdeen Ltd Head Office Westhill Industrial Estate Westhill Industrial Estate, Westhill AB32 6TQ Tel. *01224 748500* Fax. *01224 748501* E-mail. *mail@chap.co.uk* Web. *www.chap.co.uk Chap*

Chapelfield Veterinary Surgeons Wellesley Road Tharston, Norwich NR15 2PD Tel. *01508 530686* Fax. *01508 532411* E-mail. *cvp.stratton@virgin.net exel vets*

Chapman Envelopes Ltd Waterside Business Park Johnson Road, Eccleshill, Darwen BB3 3RT Tel. *01254 682387* Fax. *01254 775920* E-mail. *sales@heritage-envelopes.co.uk* Web. *www.chapman-envelopes.co.uk Chapman Envelopes*

N H Chapman & Co. Ltd Siesta House Market Street, Newcastle upon Tyne NE1 6NA Tel. *0191 2327628* Fax. *0191 2327627* E-mail. *enquiries@chapmansfurniture.co.uk* Web. *www.chapmansfurniture.co.uk Siesta*

Charger Bay Solutions 7 Fitton Road St Germans, Kings Lynn PE34 3AU Tel. *07723 391485* Fax. *01553 617619* E-mail. *sales@chargerbaysolutions.co.uk* Web. *www.chargerbaysolutions.co.uk AquaPro, – Trojan – Universal*

Charles Blyth & Company Ltd Carnival Way Castle Donington, Derby DE74 2NJ Tel. *01332 810283* Fax. *01332 855810* E-mail. *nab@charlesblyth-co.co.uk* Web. *www.charlesblyth-co.co.uk Charles Blyth*

Charles Cantrill Ltd Block 2 Unit 3 Wednesbury Trading Estate, Wednesbury WS10 7JN Tel. *0121 5673140* Fax. *0121 5673149* E-mail. *sales@charlescantrill.com* Web. *www.charlescantrill.com Neban*

David Charles Childrens Wear Ltd 1 Thane Works, London N7 7NU Tel. *020 76094797* Fax. *020 76099696* E-mail. *davidcharles19@btconnect.com Blue Moon – David Charles – Fairbanks*

Charlton Networks Canterbury Business Centre Ashchurch Road, Tewkesbury GL20 8BT Tel. *01684 856830* Fax. *01684 856849* E-mail. *enquiries@charltonnetworks.co.uk* Web. *www.charltonnetworks.co.uk Checkpoint – Cisco Systems – Enterasys Networks – HP – Microsoft – Sonicwall*

Charnwood Forest Brick Ltd Old Station Close Shepshed, Loughborough LE12 9NJ Tel. *01509 503203* Fax. *01509 507566* E-mail. *sales@charnwoodforest.com* Web. *www.mbhplc.co.uk Charnwood*

Chartered Institute of Building Englemere Kings Ride, Ascot SL5 7TB Tel. *01344 630700* Fax. *01344 630777* E-mail. *reception@ciob.org.uk* Web. *www.ciob.org.uk Chartered Building Company Scheme – Chartered Institute of Building, The – Englemere Ltd*

Chartered Institute Of Marketing Moor Hall Cookham, Maidenhead SL6 9QH Tel. *01628 427500* Fax. *01628 427499* E-mail. *reception@cim.co.uk* Web. *www.cim.co.uk Chartered Institute of Marketing (CIM)*

Chartered Institute Of Personnel & Development 151 The Broadway, London SW19 1JQ Tel. *020 86126200* Fax. *020 86126201* E-mail. *cipd@cipd.co.uk* Web. *www.cipd.co.uk Institute of Personnel and Development*

Charterhouse Holdings plc Trent Lane Castle Donington, Derby DE74 2PY Tel. *01332 855050* Fax. *01332 858383* E-mail. *head.office@charterhouse-holdings.co.uk* Web. *www.charterhouse-holdings.co.uk Chunky Polo – Colour Cut – Flexcut – Grizzly – Grizzly Activewear – Grizzly Golf Wear – Hunky-T – Nyl-Cut – Xpres*

Chartrite Ltd Unit 2 Wireless Road Biggin Hill, Westerham TN16 3PS Tel. *01959 543680* Fax. *01959 543690* E-mail. *john.davis@chartrite.com* Web. *www.chartrite.com Mitsubishi Video Paper – Sony Paper*

Chase Organics Molesey Road Hersham, Walton On Thames KT12 4RG Tel. *01932 253666* Fax. *01932 252707* E-mail. *enquiries@chaseorganics.co.uk* Web. *www.organicgardeningcatalogue.com Chase Blend 14 – Q.R. – Scaraweb – SM-3*

Chase Protective Coatings Ltd Harbour Road, Rye TN31 7TE Tel. *01797 223561* Fax. *01797 224530* E-mail. *info@chaseprotectivecoatings.com* Web. *www.longproducts.co.uk Longcote – Longseal – Longwrap – Maflowline – Maflowrap – Plasgard – Seaguard – Seaguard*

Chaucer Group Ltd 67 Preston Street, Faversham ME13 8PB Tel. *01795 542500* Fax. *08450 724510* E-mail. *rupert.laslett@chaucerconsulting.com* Web. *www.chaucer.com Interface Toolkit*

Checkmate Industries Ltd Bridge House 12 Bridge Street, Halstead CO9 1HT Tel. *01787 477272* Fax. *01787 476334* E-mail. *checkmatecarpets@btconnect.com Developer (United Kingdom) – Checkstat Two (United Kingdom) – Checkstat Extra (United Kingdom) – Bridge (United Kingdom) – Regulator Loop (United Kingdom) – Regulator Cut (United Kingdom) – Regulator Pattern (United Kingdom) – Iboflor (United Kingdom) – Canasta (United Kingdom) – Masterpiece XL (United Kingdom) – Masterflor+ (United Kingdom) – Threshold T80/20 (United Kingdom) – Checkstar (United Kingdom) – Checkloop NY (United Kingdom) – Checkstat Cut (United Kingdom) – Checkrib Plus (United Kingdom) – Patience (United Kingdom) – Accommodation 2 (United Kingdom) – Grandmaster (United Kingdom) – Twinloop (United Kingdom) – Stylemaster Loop (United Kingdom) – Stylemaster Cut (United Kingdom) – Countdown (United Kingdom) – Monopoly Two (United Kingdom) – Liberator (United Kingdom) – Masterpiece XL (United Kingdom) – Masterflor + (United Kingdom) – Checkrib Plus (United Kingdom) – Pontoon (United Kingdom) – Coral Classic (United Kingdom) – Coral Classic FR (United Kingdom) – Coral Duo (United Kingdom) – Coral Duo FR (United Kingdom) – Coral brush Activ (United Kingdom) – Coral Brush Activ FR (United Kingdom) – Grip EV MD (United Kingdom) – Grip MD (United Kingdom) – Grip EV HD (United Kingdom) – Grip HD (United Kingdom) – Coral Luxe (United Kingdom) – Coral Luxe FR (United Kingdom) – Threshold T32 (United Kingdom) – + Threshold T32/Marine (United Kingdom) – Threshold T80/20 (United Kingdom)*

Chefaro UK Ltd (Subsidiary Of Akzo Nobel) Unit 1 Tower Close, Huntingdon PE29 6SZ Tel. *01480 421800* Fax. *01480 434861* Web. *www.omega-pharma.be Equilon – *Jungle Formula (Netherlands) – *Predictor (Netherlands) – Vitalegs*

Chelmix Concrete Ltd Church Farm Leckhampton, Cheltenham GL53 0QJ Tel. *01242 224763* Fax. *01242 237727* E-mail. *info@traditionallime.co.uk* Web. *www.traditionallime.co.uk Chelmix Concrete – Tradlym*

Chelsea Building Society Thirlestaine Hall Thirlestaine Road, Cheltenham GL53 7AL Tel. *01242 271271* Fax. *01242 571441* E-mail. *peter.ford@thechelsea.co.uk* Web. *www.thechelsea.co.uk Chelsea*

Cheltenham & Gloucester plc Barnett Way Barnwood, Gloucester GL4 3RL Tel. *01452 372372* Fax. *01452 373955* E-mail. *info@chelglos.com* Web. *www.cheltglos.co.uk C&G – Cheltenham & Gloucester P.L.C.*

Chemence Ltd 13 Princewood Road Earlstrees Industrial Estate, Corby NN17 4XD Tel. *01536 402600* Fax. *01536 400266* E-mail. *hugh@chemence.com* Web. *www.chemence.com Anacure – Anacure, Kwik-Fix, Verbatim, Mitre Mate, Anaseal. – Anaseal – Ionacure – KwikFix – Mitre Mate – Uvacure – Verbatim*

Chemical Innovations Ltd 211 Walton Summit Road Walton Summit Centre, Bamber Bridge, Preston PR5 8AQ Tel. *01772 322888* Fax. *01772 315853* E-mail. *sales@polycil.co.uk* Web. *www.polycil.co.uk Cilbond – Cilcast – Cilcoat – Cilrelease – Duothane – Monothane – Por-A-Mold – Tyrfil*

Chemplas Ltd Triskell House Brunswick Industrial Estate, Brunswick Village, Newcastle Upon Tyne NE13 7BA Tel. *0191 2170700* Fax. *0191 2170440* E-mail. *mail@chemplas.co.uk* Web. *www.chemplas.co.uk Triskell*

Chemtech International Ltd 1a High Street Theale, Reading RG7 5AH Tel. *0118 9861222* Fax. *0118 9860028* E-mail. *info@chemtechinternational.com* Web. *www.chemtechinternational.com Chemetator – Chempac – Chempac MK IV – Chemtech – *Newpack (Italy) – *T.M.C.I. Padovan (Italy)*

Chemvac Pumps Ltd Unit Redwood Court Tytherington Business Park, Macclesfield SK10 2XH Tel. *01625 443170* Fax. *01625 443179* E-mail. *chemvacpumpsltd@btconnect.com* Web. *www.chemvacpumps.com Chemvac*

Chemviron Carbon Ltd (Sales Office) 434 London Road, Grays RM20 4DH Tel. *01375 381711* Fax. *01375 389644* E-mail. *info@calgoncarbon.com* Web. *www.chemvironcarbon.com Filtrasorb*

Chep UK Ltd Addlestone Road, Addlestone KT15 2UP Tel. *01932 850085* Fax. *01932 850144* Web. *www.chep.com Chep UK*

Chequer Foods Ltd Halesfield 14, Telford TF7 4QR Tel. *01952 680404* Fax. *01952 684164* E-mail. *cfsales@chequer.co.uk* Web. *www.chequer.co.uk Auto-Cup – Contact PKG – Dispensa – Essonia – Flavorpac – In Cup Vending Machines – James Aimer – Portionpak*

Cherry Blossom Ltd Grange Close Clover Nook Industrial Park, Alfreton DE55 4QT Tel. *01773 521521* Fax. *01773 521262* E-mail. *davew@grangers.co.uk* Web. *www.cherryblossom.co.nz Cherry Blossom – Cherry Blossom Original – Handyshine – Padawax – Readywax – Regimental Gloss – Waterstop*

Cherry Valley Farms Ltd Rothwell, Market Rasen LN7 6BJ Tel. *01472 371271* Fax. *01472 362422* E-mail. *kate.butler@cherryvalley.co.uk* Web. *www.cherryvalley.co.uk Cherry Valley*

Cherwell Laboratories Ltd 7-8 Launton Business Centre Murdock Road, Bicester OX26 4XB Tel. *01869 355500* Fax. *01869 355545* E-mail. *karen.munson@cherwell-labs.co.uk* Web. *www.cherwell-labs.co.uk MINICUB (United Kingdom) – MULTI-SAS (United Kingdom) – REDIPOR (United Kingdom)*

Cherwell Valley Silos Ltd Twyford, Banbury OX17 3AA Tel. *01295 811441* Fax. *01295 811228* E-mail. *roger.wertheimer@cherwellvalleysilos.co.uk* Web. *www.cherwellvalleysilos.co.uk Cherco*

Chesham Chemicals Ltd Cunningham House Westfield Lane, Harrow HA3 9ED Tel. *020 89077779* Fax. *020 89270686* E-mail. *sales@cheshamchemicals.co.uk* Web. *www.chesham-ingredients.com Glucovis*

Cheshire Style Ltd Unit 3 Myrtle Grove Mill Lench Road, Rossendale BB4 7JJ Tel. *01706 229909* Fax. *01706 221144* **Arturo Rossi (Spain) – *Costa Verde (Portugal) – *Orlando (Portugal) – Orlando Rui – Paco Marcos (Spain) – *Paco Molina (Portugal) – *Panache (Spain) – *Skittles (Italy) – *Splitz (Portugal)*

Chesterfield P C Support 9 Rufford Close, Chesterfield S40 2PB Tel. *0800 9556968* E-mail. *info@chesterfieldpcsupport.com* Web. *www.chesterfieldcomputers.com Chesterfield Computer Repair Services*

Chester Jefferies Ltd Buckingham Road, Gillingham SP8 4QE Tel. *01747 822629* Fax. *01747 824092* E-mail. *enquiry@chesterjefferies.co.uk*

Web. *www.chesterjefferies.co.uk Baker Browne – Bathard – Cocksedge & Kither – Sportac*

Chevron 1 Westferry Circus, London E14 4HA Tel. *020 77193000* Web. *www.chevron.com Almag Oil – Aquatex – Aries – Capella Oil – Cepheus Oil – Cleartex Oil – Clingtex – Crater – Doro – Eurotex – Geartex – Glytex – Havoline – Havoline Motor Oil – Hytex – Marfak – Meropa – Molytex – Motak – Motex – Multifak – Novatex Grease – Omnis – Phostex – Quenchtex – Rando Oil – Regal Oil – Seltex – Sultex Oil – Synlube 90 – Taro – Texaco 4 Star – Texaco Low Temp – Texaform – Texamatic Fluid – Texando – Texatherm – Texclad – Texnap – Texpar – Texsol – Transultex – Ursa Oils – Ursa Super L.A. – Ursa Super T.D. – Way Lubricant*

Chieftain Forge Unit 1 Block 4 Whiteside Industrial Estate, Bathgate EH48 2RX Tel. *01506 652354* Fax. *01506 656017* E-mail. *sales@chieftainforge.co.uk* Web. *www.chieftainforge.co.uk Barblues – Chieftain – Chieftain – Chieftain Forestry – *Rudd (U.S.A.)*

Childs Play International Ltd Ashworth Road Bridgemead, Swindon SN5 7YD Tel. *01793 616286* Fax. *01793 512795* E-mail. *office@childs-play.com* Web. *www.childs-play.com Child's Play – Mission*

Childwise Queens House Queens Road, Norwich NR1 3PL Tel. *01603 630054* Fax. *01603 664083* E-mail. *research@childwise.co.uk* Web. *www.childwise.co.uk Childwise – Sportswise – Tradewise*

Chillton Agricultural Equipment Ltd Hyssop Close, Cannock WS11 7XB Tel. *01543 462787* Fax. *01543 462765* E-mail. *anthony.johnson@chilton.com* Web. *www.chillton.com TX*

Chiltern I T Parts Anamax House Oxford Road, Gerrards Cross SL9 7BB Tel. *01753 890088* Fax. *01753 891916* E-mail. *graham@chilternit.com* Web. *www.chilternit.com Shackman*

Chinal Management Services Ltd (Head Office) King Charles House 2 Castle Hill, Dudley DY1 4PS Tel. *01384 234234* Fax. *01384 456183* E-mail. *info@chinal.co.uk* Web. *www.chinal.co.uk Card*

Chinese Channel Teddington Studios Broom Road, Teddington TW11 9NT Tel. *020 86148300* Fax. *020 89430982* E-mail. *lawrence@chinese-channel.co.uk* Web. *www.chinese-channel.co.uk Chinese Channel*

Chiorino UK Ltd Phoenix Avenue Featherstone, Pontefract WF7 6EP Tel. *01977 691880* Fax. *0870 6065061* E-mail. *sales@chiorino.co.uk* Web. *www.chiorino.co.uk Chiorino PVC & PU – Meteor – Miracoil – Miracoil Rino – Pegasus – Transfeed – Transfeed*

Chip-It Unit 28 Chapel Place Dentonholme Trading Estate, Carlisle CA2 5DF Tel. *01228 590033* Fax. *01228 590033* E-mail. *info@chip-it.org.uk* Web. *www.chip-it.org.uk DiamondBite – Gizmo – Speedliner*

Chips Away International Chips Away House Hoo Farm Industrial Estate Worcester Road, Kidderminster DY11 7RA Tel. *0800 0287878* Fax. *01482 864969* E-mail. *info@chipsaway.co.uk* Web. *www.chipsaway.co.uk Chipsaway*

Chivas Bros Holdings Ltd Chivas House 72 Chancellors Road, London W6 9RS Tel. *020 82501000* Fax. *020 82501601* Web. *www.chivas.com Beefeater*

Chi Yip Group Ltd Treasure House Greengate Industrial Estate, Middleton, Manchester M24 1SW Tel. *0161 6553600* Fax. *0161 6553188* E-mail. *info@chiyip.co.uk* Web. *www.chiyip.co.uk Medal Duck – Ocean Treasure – Quality & Quality 6556 – Universal – Yippy Yippy Yum Yum*

C H Jones Walsall Ltd Queen Street Premier Business Park, Walsall WS2 9PB Tel. *01922 704400* Fax. *01922 704440* E-mail. *info@keyfuels.co.uk* Web. *www.chjones.co.uk Aspera – Diesel Direct – Fuel IT – Fuelscope – ICR100 – Keyfuels*

C H L Equipment Ltd (Formerly Verstegen Grabs & Cunnington Handling) 24 Solihull Road Shirley, Solihull B90 3HD Tel. *0121 7338100* Fax. *0121 7332796* E-mail. *sales@chlequipment.com* Web. *www.chlequipment.com MRS*

Chloride Motive Power C M P Batteries Ltd Salford Road, Bolton BL5 1BX Tel. *01204 64111* Fax. *01204 62981* E-mail. *elaine.mcleod@eu.exide.com* Web. *www.exide.com 21 Series – Aquajet – Autofil – Classic – FULMEN - – Trekker*

Choice Hotels International 67-74 Saffron Hill, London EC1N 8QX Tel. *020 70619600* Fax. *020 70619601* E-mail. *infouk@choicehotels.com* Web. *www.choicehotels.eu Friendly Hotels – Premier House*

Choice Properties 5-7 Broadwalk, Crawley RH10 1HJ Tel. *01293 611002* Fax. *01293 565477* E-mail. *choices@choices.co.uk* Web. *www.choices.co.uk Choices*

Choose-Hosting 32 Aldrens Lane, Lancaster LA1 2DU Tel. *0844 8700328* Fax. *0844 8700329* E-mail. *kompass.co.uk@upforit.org* Web. *www.choose-a-domain.com Choose-Hosting*

Chorion plc Aldwych House 81 Aldwych, London WC2B 4HN Tel. *020 70613800* Fax. *020 70613801* E-mail. *reception@chorion.co.uk* Web. *www.chorion.co.uk Beatrix Potter's Country World – Brambly Hedge – British Museum The – Cicely Mary Barker's As In Heaven – Fairyworld – Flower Fairies – Golden Days – Gordon Beningfield – Grandma Moses – House Mouse – Ivory Cats – Little Grey Rabbit – Lucy Cousins - Maisy – Mabel Lucy Atwell – May Gibbs – Mrs Beeton – Orlando the Marmalade Cat – Paddington Bear – Peter Pan – Postman Pat – Spot – The Country Diary of an Edwardian Lady – The Snowman – The Wind in the Willows – The Wombles – The World of Beatrix Potter – The World of Lewis Carroll*

Chorus Panel & Profiles Llandybie, Ammanford SA18 3JG Tel. *01269 850691* Fax. *01269 851081* Web. *www.coruspanelsandprofiles.co.uk Clipfix – Colorcoat HPS200 – Colorfarm – Coolsteel – Curveline – E.P. Signature – Formawall – Insulite FR – Plastisol – Rhino Doors – Stratabord – Trimapanel – Trimawall – Trisomet – Trusstray – Ventair*

C & H Precision Measuring Systems Ltd Unit 15 Gec Business Park Blackburn Road, Clayton le Moors, Accrington BB5 5JW Tel. *01254 301777* Fax. *01254 301777* E-mail. *enquiries@ch-precision.co.uk* Web. *www.ch-precision.co.uk. Heidenhain*

Chr. Hansen (UK) Ltd 2 Tealgate, Hungerford RG17 0YT Tel. *01488 689800* Fax. *01488 685436* E-mail. *techservice-gb@chr-hansen.com* Web. *www.chr-hansen.com Cal-Sol-Calcium – Chy-max – Exact – Hannilase – Nutrish*

Christeyns UK Ltd Rutland Street, Bradford BD4 7EA Tel. *01274 393286* Fax. *01274 309143* E-mail. *headoffice@christeyns.co.uk* Web. *www.christeyns.co.uk Jetstream – O.S.C.O.L. – O.S.C.R.E.T.E.*

Christian Day Ltd The Old Dye House Puxton Lane, Kidderminster DY11 5DF Tel. *01562 515579* Fax. *01299 250335* E-mail. *christiandayltd@aol.com* Web. *www.potsofplanters.co.uk Babylon (United Kingdom) – Penang (United Kingdom) – Petra (United Kingdom) – Vista (U.S.A.)*

Christie & Co. Ltd Whitefriars House 6 Carmelite Street, London EC4Y 0BS Tel. *020 72270700* Fax. *020 72270701* E-mail. *enquiries@christie.com* Web. *www.christie.com Christie – Pinders – Quest for Quality – R.C.C. Business Mortgages – R.C.C. Insurance Brokers – Venners – Venners Computer Systems*

Christie & Grey Ltd Morley Road, Tonbridge TN9 1RA Tel. *01732 371100* Fax. *01732 359666* E-mail. *sales@christiegrey.com* Web. *www.christiegrey.com Coresil*

Christie Hospital N H S Foundation Trust 550 Wilmslow Road, Manchester M20 4BX Tel. *0161 4463000* Fax. *0161 4463352* E-mail. *caroline.shaw@christie.nhs.uk* Web. *www.christie.nhs.uk Centenary*

Christie Intruder Alarms Ltd 212-218 London Road, Waterlooville PO7 7AJ Tel. *023 92265111* Fax. *023 92265112* E-mail. *enquiries@ciaalarms.co.uk* Web. *www.ciaalarms.co.uk Dualcom – Dualcom Plus – Gardtec – RedCare – Redcare GSM*

Chromalox UK Ltd 20-28 Whitehorse Road, Croydon CR0 2JA Tel. *020 86658900* Fax. *020 86890571* E-mail. *uksales@chromalox.com* Web. *www.chromalox.com Bray – Braylec – Chromalox – Tubalox*

Chromebar Neachells Lane, Wolverhampton WV11 3PY Tel. *01902 725011* Fax. *01902 305068* E-mail. *sales@chromebaruk.com Hi Cor*

Chrysalis Entertainments Ltd 13 Bramley Road, London W10 6SP Tel. *020 74656346* Fax. *020 72216455* E-mail. *info@chrysalis.com* Web. *www.cre.co.uk Chrysalis – Music Limited*

Chubb Electronic Security Ltd PO Box 233, Sunbury On Thames TW16 7XY Tel. *01932 738600* Fax. *01932 787989* E-mail. *info@chubb.co.uk* Web. *www.chubb.co.uk Apollo – Chubb Atmosfire – Chubb Controlmaster – Chubb Vigil – Chubb Windsor – Chubb Zonemaster – Red Care*

Chuckleprint Unit 7 Crimchard Business Centre, Chard TA20 1JT Tel. *01460 65145* Fax. *01460 65145* E-mail. *dee.mear@gmail.com Chuckleprint*

Chums Ltd Unity Grove Knowsley Business Park, Prescot L34 9AR Tel. *08719 119999* Fax. *0151 5486829* E-mail. *sales@chums.co.uk* Web. *www.chums.co.uk Crimplene*

Church & Dwight UK Ltd Wearbay Road, Folkestone CT19 6PG Tel. *01303 858700* Fax. *01303 858701* E-mail. *info@carterproducts.co.uk* Web. *www.churchdwight.com Arrid – Carters Pills – Cossack – Discover – First Response – Linco Beer – Nair – Pearl Drops*

Churchill China UK Ltd Marlborough Works High Street, Stoke On Trent ST6 5NZ Tel. *01782 577566* Fax. *01782 847617* E-mail. *adrian.botterell@churchillchina.plc.uk* Web. *www.churchill1795.com *Alchemy Fine China – *Churchill*

J J Churchill Ltd Station Road Market Bosworth, Nuneaton CV13 0PF Tel. *01455 299600* Fax. *01455 292330* E-mail. *kevin.mccormik@jjchurchill.com* Web. *www.jjchurchill.com Churchill Tooling – Empire Tooling – Quattrix – ST System – Twin Tip Tooling*

Churchtown Buildings Ltd Lion Acre House Moss Lane, Banks, Southport PR9 8EE Tel. *01704 227826* Fax. *01704 220247* E-mail. *sales@churchtown.co.uk* Web. *www.churchtown.co.uk Accommodator – Churchtown – Churchtown Europa – Land Cruiser – Officemake – Toastywarm*

Cibo Ristorante 289 Gloucester Road Bishopston, Bristol BS7 8NY Tel. *0117 9429475* Fax. *0117 9429483* E-mail. *dino@cibo.co.uk* Web. *www.ciboristorante.co.uk Fresh Pasta – Pasta Fresca*

Cico Chimney Linings Ltd North End Wood Hinton Road, Darsham, Saxmundham IP17 3QS Tel. *01986 784044* Fax. *01986 784763* E-mail. *cico@chimney-problems.co.uk* Web. *www.chimney-problems.co.uk Cico – Cico chimney linings – Cico Flex*

Cifer Data Systems Ltd 1 Main Street West Wilts Trading Estate, Westbury BA13 4JU Tel. *01373 824128* Fax. *01373 824127* E-mail. *enquiries@cifer.co.uk* Web. *www.cifer.co.uk Cifer*

Cimtech College Lane, Hatfield AL10 9AB Tel. *01707 281060* Fax. *01707 281061* E-mail. *hendleyanthony@cimtech.co.uk* Web. *www.cimtech.co.uk Cimtech*

Cinch Connectors Ltd Shireoaks Road, Worksop S80 3HA Tel. *01909 474131* Fax. *01909 478321* E-mail. *info@cinchuk.com* Web. *www.cinchuk.com Cinapse – Cinch – Cinch Pattern 110 – Cylindrical 26500 – Duracon – Econo-D – Filter D – Greenline – J Connectors – Super D*

Cincom Systems UK Ltd 1 Grenfell Road, Maidenhead SL6 1HN Tel. *01628 542300* Fax. *01625 533223* E-mail. *uking@cincom.com* Web. *www.cincom.com AD/Advantage – Business Control Systems – Cincom Encompass – Intelligent Solutions – Mantis – Supra – Total Framework*

The Cinema & Television Benevolent Fund 22 Golden Square, London W1F 9AD Tel. *020 74376567* Fax. *020 74377186* E-mail. *charity@ctbf.co.uk* Web. *www.ctbf.co.uk CTBF*

Cinetic Landis Ltd Skipton Road Cross Hills, Keighley BD20 7SD Tel. *01535 633211* Fax. *01535 635493* E-mail. *rcoverdale@cinetic-landis.co.uk* Web. *www.cinetic-landis.com Citco – Cranfield Precision – Gardner – Landis – Landis Cincinnati – Landis Gardner – Landis Grinding Systems – Landis Lund*

Cintel International Ltd Watton Road, Ware SG12 0AE Tel. *01920 463939* Fax. *01920 460803* E-mail. *sales@cintel.co.uk* Web. *www.cintel.co.uk C-Reality – Electrum – Rascal*

C I Precision 2 Brunel Road, Salisbury SP2 7PX Tel. *01722 424100* Fax. *01722 323222* E-mail. *adrian.roberts@cielec.com* Web. *www.cielec.com C.I. Systems*

Circuit Engineering Marketing Company Ltd 1-2 Silverthorne Way, Waterlooville PO7 7XB Tel. *023 92262120* Fax. *023 92262089* E-mail. *ken.bishop@cemco.com* Web. *www.cemco.com Quicksilver and Alchemy*

Circulating Pumps Ltd 56 Oldmedow Road, Kings Lynn PE30 4PP Tel. *01553 764821* Fax. *01553 760965* E-mail. *sales@circulatingpumps.co.uk* Web. *www.circulatingpumps.net De-Aerator – Domestic Circulators – Light Commercial Pumps – Shower Pumps*

C I Research Alderley House Alderley Road, Wilmslow SK9 1AT Tel. *01625 628000* Fax. *01625 628001* E-mail. *theteam@ci-research.com* Web. *www.ci-research.com Qualserv*

Cirrus Systems Ltd 136 South Way Southwell Business Park, Portland DT5 2NL Tel. *01305 822659* Fax. *08707 064558* E-mail. *sales@cirrus-systems.co.uk* Web. *www.cirrus-systems.co.uk RemovAll*

Cirteq Ltd Hayfield Colne Road, Glusburn, Keighley BD20 8QP Tel. *01535 633333* Fax. *01535 632966* E-mail. *mail@cirteq.com* Web. *www.cirteq.com Anderton – Ellison*

Citech Energy Recovery Systems UK Ltd Salisbury House Saxon Way, Hessle HU13 9PB Tel. *01482 719746* Fax. *01482 719740* E-mail. *info@citech.co.uk* Web. *www.citech.co.uk CiBAS*

Citilites Ltd 397-399 Hornsey Road, London N19 4DX Tel. *020 72814141* Fax. *020 72810030* E-mail. *danielsimons@citilites.co.uk* Web. *www.citilites.co.uk Citilites*

Citisoft 1 Fredericks Place, London EC2R 8AE Tel. *020 77761111* Fax. *020 77761122* E-mail. *jonathan.clark@citisoft.com* Web. *www.citisoft.com Citisoft*

Citizen Machinery UK Ltd 9a Navigation Drive Hurst Business Park, Brierley Hill DY5 1UT Tel. *01384 489500* Fax. *01384 489501* E-mail. *sales@citizen-miyano.co.uk* Web. *www.citizenmachinery.co.uk *Anger (Austria) – *CMZ (Spain) – Hanwha (Korea, Republic of) – *M.A.S. (Czech Republic) – Miyano Machinery Inc (Japan)*

Citizen Machinery UK Ltd 1 Park Avenue, Bushey WD23 2DA Tel. *01923 691500* Fax. *01923 691599* E-mail. *sales@citizenmachinery.co.uk* Web. *www.citizenmachinery.co.uk Boley (Germany) – Cincom (Japan) – Citizen (Japan)*

City Electrical Factors Ltd 141 Farmer Ward Road, Kenilworth CV8 2SU Tel. *01926 514355* Fax. *01926 514340* E-mail. *headoffice@cef.co.uk* Web. *www.cef.co.uk Brook – Cefco – Centaur – Disano – Fosnova – Heatstore – Metrotest – Proteus – R.P.P. – Tamlex – Tamlite – Tamtec*

City & Guilds Of London Institute 1 Giltspur Street, London EC1A 9DD Tel. *020 72942468* Fax. *020 72942400* E-mail. *info@city-and-guilds.co.uk* Web. *www.city-and-guilds.co.uk NEBS Management*

City Of London Courier Ltd Unit A Digbyland Studios Digby Road, London E9 6HX Tel. *08450 600666* Fax. *08450 600888* E-mail. *info@cityoflondoncourier.co.uk* Web. *www.cityoflondoncourier.co.uk City of London Courier Service – Flashpoint Security*

City Sprint Unit 11c West Craigs Industrial Estate Turnhouse Road, Edinburgh EH12 0BD Tel. *0131 4531800* Fax. *0131 3397942* E-mail. *edinburgh@citysprint.co.uk* Web. *www.citysprint.co.uk Citadel*

City Technology Ltd City Technology Centre Walton Road, Portsmouth PO6 1SZ Tel. *023 92325511* Fax. *023 92386611* E-mail. *antony.cowburn@citytech.com* Web. *www.citytech.com Capteur – CiTicel – CiTipel – DiveceL – IRidium – Medicel – MICROcel – MICROpel*

Citywide Estate Agents 1016 Cathcart Road, Glasgow G42 9XL Tel. *0141 6498899* Fax. *0141 6360045* E-mail. *john@citywide.cc* Web. *www.citywide.cc S E A L*

Civica UK Ltd 1 Sovereign Court South Portway Close, Round Spinney Industrial Estate, Northampton NN3 8RH Tel. *01604 798555* Fax. *01604 798505* E-mail. *info@cavetab.co.uk* Web. *www.cavetab.co.uk CaveTab – CTDI – Datafile – File Tracker – Joca – Pinpoint – Tabquick – Twinfile*

Civil Aviation Authority 45-59 Kingsway, London WC2B 6TE Tel. *020 73797311* Fax. *020 74536028* E-mail. *sales@caa.co.uk* Web. *www.caa.co.uk N.A.T.S.*

Civil and Marine Ltd Brigg Road, Scunthorpe DN16 1AW Tel. *01724 282211* Fax. *01724 280338* E-mail. *webenquiry@applebygroup.co.uk* Web. *www.heidelbergcement.com Frodingham*

Civil Service Motoring Association Britannia House 21 Station Street, Brighton BN1 4DE Tel. *01273 744721* Fax. *01273 744751* E-mail. *info@csma.uk.com* Web. *www.csma.uk.com Britannia Continental*

CJ Associates Training Park View 34 Copperfields, High Wycombe HP12 4AN Tel. *0845 3710953* Fax. *0845 3710954* E-mail. *info@cjgroup.co.uk* Web. *www.cjgroup.co.uk CJ Associates*

C J Enterprises (t/a CJ Enterprises) Infield House Old Hay, Brenchley, Tonbridge TN12 7DG Tel. *01892 838094* Fax. *01892 836182* E-mail. *info@cjenterprises.co.uk* Web. *www.cjenterprises.co.uk Clintex – Mastertex*

C J Plant Ltd 27d Harris Business Park Hanbury Road, Stoke Prior, Bromsgrove B60 4DJ Tel. *01527 870793* Fax. *01527 831310* E-mail. *info@cjplant.com* Web. *www.cjplantmaintenance.com Case Sumitomo – Cat – Daewoo – Fiat – Hitachi – Kawasaki – Kayaba – Kobelco – Komatsu – Linde – Neuson – Samsung – Shibaura – Toshiba – Uchida Rexroth – Volvo*

C J Skilton Aquarist Willow Thatch Stebbing Green, Gt Dunmow, Dunmow CM6 3TE Tel. *01371 856257* Fax. *01245 400585* E-mail. *cjskilton@aquaskil.co.uk* Web. *www.aquaskil.co.uk Aquaskil*

C J W T Solutions Unit 20 Bold Business Centre Bold Lane, St Helens WA9 4TX Tel. *01925 220319* Fax. *08707 065878* E-mail. *craig@cjwtsolutions.co.uk* Web. *www.cjwtsolutions.co.uk CJWT Solutions*

C K Chemicals Unit 16 Lady Lane Industrial Estate Hadleigh, Ipswich IP7 6BQ Tel. *01473 822836* Fax. *01473 824044* E-mail. *sales@ckchemicals.co.uk* Web. *www.ckchemicals.co.uk Chemsolve*

C K Tech Serve Ltd 56 Fallow Field, Stoke On Trent ST3 3EJ Tel. *01782 448556* Fax. *01889 570020* E-mail. *info@cktechserve.co.uk* Web. *www.cktechserve.co.uk Copar – Opsigal*

Claas UK Ltd Saxham Business Park Little Saxham, Bury St Edmunds IP28 6QZ Tel. *01284 763100* Fax. *01284 769839* E-mail. *clive.last@claas.com* Web. *www.claasuk.com *Claas (Germany)*

Clamcleats Ltd Clamcleats Building Watchmead, Welwyn Garden City AL7 1AP Tel. *01707 330101* Fax. *020 88019907* E-mail. *sales@clamcleat.com* Web. *www.clamcleats.com Clamcleat (United Kingdom) – Line-Lok*

Clan Douglas PO Box 13331, Hawick TD9 0WX Tel. *01450 363140* Fax. *01450 363111* E-mail. *sales@clan-douglas.com* Web. *www.clan-douglas.com Clan Douglas*

Clan Marketing Co. 77 Harrington Road Loddington, Kettering NN14 1JZ Tel. *01536 711326* Fax. *01536 711326* E-mail. *admin@clanmarketing.co.uk* Web. *www.litterpicker.co.uk Clan – Sure-Stroke*

Clantex Ltd The Moorings Waterside Industrial Park Waterside Road, Leeds LS10 1DG Tel. *0113 2008200* Fax. *0113 2008202* E-mail. *khoulbrook@clantex.co.uk* Web. *www.clantex.co.uk 4 N 1 Cleaner – Carpet King – Escort Elite – Escort Mediclean – Escort Pro System*

E A Clare & Son Ltd 46-48 St Anne Street, Liverpool L3 3DW Tel. *0151 4822700* Fax. *0151 2981134* E-mail. *thurston@eaclare.co.uk* Web. *www.eaclare.co.uk Drakes Pride – Peradon – Thurston*

Clarehill Plastics Ltd New Building 21 Clarehill Road, Moira, Craigavon BT67 0PB Tel. *028 92611077* Fax. *028 92612672* E-mail. *nicola@clarehill.com* Web. *www.harlequinplastics.co.uk Clarehill – Harlequin*

Claremont & May Unit 11 Claremont Way Lakesview International Business Park, Hersden, Canterbury CT3 4JG Tel. *08707 569999* Fax. *0870 4102550* E-mail. *info@claremontandmay.com* Web. *www.claremontandmay.com Claremont & May Fragrance & Home*

R S Clare & Co. Ltd 8 Stanhope Street, Liverpool L8 5RQ Tel. *0151 7092902* Fax. *0151 7090518* E-mail. *sales@rsclare.com* Web. *www.rsclare.com Bimagrip – Clare – Clare Bechem – Clare Lube – Clare Tech – Plastaline – Plastalux Reflective – Plastarib – Plastaspray – Plastathix*

Clariant UK Ltd Unit C7-C8 Haslemere Industrial Estate Wigan Road, Ashton-in-Makerfield, Wigan WN4 0BZ Tel. *01942 296200* Fax. *01942 494555* E-mail. *kelly.morrisey@clariant.com* Web. *www.clariant.com Extru-Clean – Purgex 2000*

Clarity Copiers Capital House Park House Business Centre Desborough Park Road, High Wycombe HP12 3DJ Tel. *01494 448622* Fax. *01494 464765* E-mail. *terry.h@claritycopiershw.co.uk* Web. *www.claritycopiershw.co.uk Canon Photocopiers – Panasonic Photocopiers – Ricoh Photocopiers – Sharp Photocopiers*

Clarke Instruments Ltd (Head Office and Works) Distloc House Old Sarum Airfield, Old Sarum, Salisbury SP4 6DZ Tel. *01722 323451* Fax. *01722 335154* E-mail. *chris@clarke-inst.com* Web. *www.clarke-inst.com 491 – 661 – 771 – 913,903,966 – 918, 919 – 942, 957, 984 – Gatedrives – Gatelocks – Maglease*

Clark Electric Clutch & Controls Ltd Unit 28 Victory Park Trident Close Medway City Estate, Rochester ME2 4ER Tel. *01634 297408* Fax. *020 86608845* E-mail. *sales@clarkelectric.co.uk* Web. *www.clarkelectric.co.uk Silkstart – Z F Industrial Drives*

Clarke Translift Ltd Bilton Way, Lutterworth LE17 4HJ Tel. *01455 552801* Fax. *01455 554112* E-mail. *sales@clarke-transport.co.uk* Web. *www.clarke-transport.co.uk Clarke Transport*

Claron Hydraulic Seals Ltd Station Road, Cradley Heath B64 6PN Tel. *0121 5599711* Fax. *02155 91036* E-mail. *seals@claron.co.uk* Web. *www.claron.co.uk Polyseal*

Claro Precision Engineering Ltd Unit 4 & 5 Manse Lane Industrial Estate, Knaresborough HG5 8LF Tel. *01423 867413* Fax. *01423 861959* E-mail. *engineering@claro.co.uk* Web. *www.claro.co.uk Claro*

Class Building Services 226 Lythalls Lane, Coventry CV6 6GF Tel. *024 76705498* Fax. *ERROR* E-mail. *classbuilding@btconnect.com* Web. *www.classconstruction.co.uk class conservatories*

Classic Fine Foods Ltd D24-D27 Fruit & Vegetable Market, London SW8 5LL Tel. *020 76279666* Fax. *020 76279696* E-mail. *sales@classicfinefoods.co.uk* Web. *www.grivan.co.uk Cap Fruit – Castelanotti – Castelanotti – Jabugo – Paris – Sanchez Romero Carvajal – Soulard – Terre Bormane – Valrhona*

C L A Tools Ltd 10 Binns Close, Coventry CV4 9TB Tel. *024 76465535* Fax. *024 76694543* E-mail. *info@clatools.co.uk* Web. *www.clatools.co.uk Burraway – Burrqwik – Cladrill – Cogsdill – Shefcut*

Claude Lyons Ltd Brook Road, Waltham Cross EN8 7LR Tel. *01992 768888* Fax. *01992 788000* E-mail. *sales@claudelyons.co.uk* Web. *www.claudelyons.co.uk Claude Lyons – M.S. – M.V.C. – Powerstay – PQM – Pure Power – T.E.C. – T.R.X. – TS*

Claudius Consulting 5 Whin Road, York YO24 1JU Tel. *0845 6585705* Fax. *0870 1272471* E-mail. *mail@claudius-consulting.co.uk* Web. *www.claudius-consulting.co.uk Six Sigma*

John Clayden & Partners Lubysil Ltd 9 Frensham Road Sweet Briar Road Industrial Estate, Norwich NR3 2BT Tel. *01603 789924* Fax. *01603 417335* E-mail. *sales@clayden-lubricants.co.uk* Web. *www.clayden-lubricants.co.uk Lubysil*

Claymore 1b Waterloo Industrial Estate Waterloo Road, Bidford-on-Avon, Alcester B50 4JH Tel. *01789 490177* Fax. *01789 490170* E-mail. *sales@claymoregrass.co.uk* Web. *www.fgmclaymore.co.uk Bolens – Masport – Sabo – Simplicity*

Clayton First Aid Ltd Chiddingstone Causeway, Tonbridge TN11 8JP Tel. *01892 871111* Fax. *01892 871122* E-mail. *info@claytonfirstaid.com* Web. *www.claytonfirstaid.com J.S. Clayton*

Clayton Thermal Products Ltd (a division of Clayton Industries) 5 Boleyn Court Manor Park, Runcorn WA7 1SR Tel. *01928 579009* Fax. *01928 571155* E-mail. *gerry.rooney@claytonindustries.co.uk* Web. *www.claytonindustries.co.uk Clayton (Belgium & USA) – Clayton Boilers – Clayton Industries*

Cleanacres Machinery Ltd Hazleton, Cheltenham GL54 4DX Tel. *01451 860721* Fax. *01451 860139* E-mail. *mark_curtoys@cleanacres.co.uk* Web. *www.cleanacres.co.uk Airtec – Airtec Quality Controller – ASA – Atlas – Cropsaver – Magic Box – Swan*

Cleanaway Ltd Warley Hill Business Park The Drive, Great Warley, Brentwood CM13 3BE Tel. *01277 262002* Fax. *01277 230067* E-mail. *information@cleanaway.com* Web. *www.cleanaway.com Chempac – Cleanapack*

Clean Machine UK Ltd The Works Barway, Ely CB7 5UB Tel. *01353 624888* Fax. *01353 624201* E-mail. *sales@cleanmachine.co.uk* Web. *www.cleanmachine.co.uk ADC – Electrolux – Huebsh – Ipso – Loadstar – Maytag – Miele – Speedqueen – Unimac*

Cleansorb Ltd Unit 1J Merrow Business Centre, Merrow Lane, Guildford GU4 7WA Tel. *01483 300107* Fax. *01483 300109* E-mail. *contact@cleansorb.com* Web. *www.cleansorb.com Acidgen – Acidgen FG – Acidgen HA – Arcasolve – Arcasolve Orca – CS-SAFI*

Clear Channel International Ltd 33 Golden Square, London W1F 9JT Tel. *020 74782200* Fax. *020 72879153* E-mail. *sales@moorgroup.com* Web. *www.clearchannel.co.uk Adshel – More O'Ferrall*

Clear Thinking Software Ltd 73 Hartington Road, Brighton BN2 3LS Tel. *01273 570857* Fax. *01273 670730* E-mail. *info@clearthinkingsoftware.co.uk* Web. *www.clearthinkingsoftware.co.uk Unit Manager*

Clear View Ltd Unit 7 The High Cross Centre, Fountayne Road, London N15 4QN Tel. *020 88010020* Fax. *020 88010021* E-mail. *sales@clearview.ltd.uk* Web. *www.clearview.ltd.uk Clearothene – Mirrolene – Mirropack – Mirrophane – Mirrothene*

Cleenol Group Ltd Neville House Beaumont Road, Banbury OX16 1RB Tel. *01295 251721* Fax. *01295 269561* E-mail. *md@cleenol.co.uk* Web. *www.cleenol.co.uk Cleenol – Combat – Crystal – Crystalbrite – *Dreumex (Netherlands) – Lift – Spraytec – Teepol*

Cleghorn Waring & Co Pumps Ltd Icknield Way, Letchworth Garden City SG6 1EZ Tel. *01462 480380* Fax. *01462 482422* E-mail. *mail@cleghorn.co.uk* Web. *www.cleghorn.co.uk F.P. (Italy) – Jabsco – Jabsco – Jabsco – Oberdorfer (U.S.A.) – Rule – *Wanner (U.S.A.)*

Clement Clarke International Ltd Unit A Cartel Business Estate Edinburgh Way, Harlow CM20 2TT Tel. *01279 414969* Fax. *01279 456339* E-mail. *info@c3headsets.com* Web. *www.clementclarke.com A.C. 2000 – Ablespacer – Air Zone – Econoneb – In-Check – Mini-Wright – Mini-Wright AFS – Sonix 2000 – Turboneb – VM1 Ventilometer – World Traveller*

Clement Windows Ltd Clement House Weydown Road, Haslemere GU27 1HR Tel. *01428 643393* Fax. *01428 644436* E-mail. *info@clementwg.co.uk* Web. *www.clementwg.co.uk Cast Rooflight, The*

Clerical Medical Investment Group Ltd 10 Canons Way, Bristol BS1 5LF Tel. *0117 9290290* Fax. *01275 552667* E-mail. *info@clericalmedical.co.uk* Web. *www.clericalmedical.co.uk Performance Pensions – Saphire, Ruby and Emerald (The Gem Collection)*

Clevedon Fasteners Ltd Unit 11 Reddicap Trading Estate, Sutton Coldfield B75 7BU Tel. *0121 3780619* Fax. *0121 3783186* E-mail. *sales@clevedon-fasteners.co.uk* Web. *www.clevedon-fasteners.co.uk Clevedon*

Clico Sheffield Tooling Ltd 7 Fell Road, Sheffield S9 2AL Tel. *0114 2433007* Fax. *0114 2434158* E-mail. *info@clico.co.uk* Web. *www.clico.co.uk Clico – Clifton*

Cliff Electronic Components Ltd 76 Holmethorpe Avenue, Redhill RH1 2PF Tel. *01737 771375* Fax. *01737 766012* E-mail. *sales@cliffuk.co.uk* Web. *www.cliffuk.co.uk Clarke (U.K) – Cliff – *Comar (Italy) – *Japan Servo (Japan) – Quicktest – *Tsukasa (Japan) – *Waka (Japan)*

Clifford & Snell Tom Cribb Road, London SE28 0BH Tel. *020 88546666* Fax. *020 83172400* E-mail. *david.stelling@sarbe.com* Web. *www.cliffordandsnell.com Clifford & Snell – Keyswitch – Sarbe – Varley – Yodac – Yodalarm – Yodalarm - Yodalex - Yodac - Yodalight - Clifford & Snell - Keyswitch - Sarbe – Yodalex – Yodalight*

Clinical Computing 17-19 Bedford Street, London WC2E 9HP Tel. *020 30067536* Fax. *01473 694761* E-mail. *sales@ccl.com* Web. *www.ccl.com Proton*

Clinical Systems Ltd 63 High Street, Princes Risborough HP27 0AE Tel. *01844 342490* Fax. *01844 342940* E-mail. *support@clinical-systems.co.uk* Web. *www.clinical-systems.co.uk Clinaxys*

Clin-Tech Ltd Unit G Perram Works Merrow Lane, Guildford GU4 7BN Tel. *01483 301902* Fax. *01483 301907* E-mail. *info@clin-tech.co.uk* Web. *www.clin-tech.co.uk Shepard's Stain – Sickle-Test – Speedy-Diff*

Clip Display Church Road Wick, Bristol BS30 5RD Tel. *0117 9372636* Fax. *0117 9373172* E-mail. *info@clipdisplay.com* Web. *www.clipdisplay.com Clip – Elementri – Image – Trimesh*

Clippa Safe Ltd Lanthwaite Road, Nottingham NG11 8LD Tel. *0115 9211899* Fax. *0115 9845554* E-mail. *sales@clippasafe.co.uk* Web. *www.clippasafe.co.uk Clippa-Safe – Cosy-Carrier*

J H Clissold & Son Ltd Old Gate Mill North Wing, Bradford BD3 0DH Tel. *01274 721455* Fax. *01274 370694* E-mail. *sales@clissold.co.uk* Web. *www.clissold.co.uk Clissold*

Clivet UK Unit 4 Kingdom Close Segenworth East, Fareham PO15 5TJ Tel. *01489 572238* Fax. *01489 573033* E-mail. *l.joy@clivet-uk.co.uk* Web. *www.clivet.com Compac – Versatemp*

Cloakroom Solutions Ltd Unit 9, Beehive Business Centre Beehive Lane, Chelmsford CM2 9TE Tel. *01245 490333* Fax. *01245 490111* E-mail. *info@cloakroomsolutions.co.uk* Web. *www.cloakroomsolutions.co.uk CoolLine – Flair – GlasModul – Glassrack – High Tech – Julia – Koncetta – Marathon – Ocean – Pollux – Quadro – Romino – Rondal – StoneTec Plus – Tension – Wedge*

Clorox Car Care Ltd Kershaw House Great West Road, Hounslow TW5 0BU Tel. *020 85385400* Fax. *020 85695611* Web. *www.clorox.com STP*

Clovis Lande Associates Ltd 104 Branbridges Road East Peckham, Tonbridge TN12 5HH Tel. *01622 873900* Fax. *01622 873903* E-mail. *info@clovis.co.uk* Web. *www.clovis.co.uk Highlande – Nicodome – *Nicofence (Netherlands) – Profit Haven – Solar Dome*

CLT Innovations Ltd Tawney Barn Yawney Common, Epping CM16 7PX Tel. *01992 524991* E-mail. *john@gallowayfarms.org* Web. *www.scarem.co.uk Scarem*

Clugston Distribution Services Ltd Brigg Road, Scunthorpe DN16 1BB Tel. *01724 281281* Fax. *01724 270240* E-mail. *andrew.hansed@clugston.co.uk* Web. *www.clugston.co.uk Clugston*

Clustan Ltd 16 Kingsburgh Road, Edinburgh EH12 6DZ Tel. *0131 3371448* E-mail. *sales@clustan.com* Web. *www.clustan.com Clustan*

Clyde Bergmann Ltd 47 Broad Street, Glasgow G40 2QR Tel. *0141 5505400* Fax. *0141 5505402* E-mail. *info@clydebergemann.co.uk* Web. *www.clydebergemann.co.uk Clyde – Clyde Bergenmann – Clyde Forest – Clydspin*

Clyde Energy Solutions Ltd 13-14 Charlwoods Road, East Grinstead RH19 2HU Tel. *01342 305550* Fax. *020 83974598* E-mail. *info@clyde4heat.co.uk* Web. *www.clyde4heat.co.uk *Buderus (Germany) – Clyde Combustions*

C M Beasy Ltd Ashurst Lodge Ashurst, Southampton SO40 7AA Tel. *023 80293223* Fax. *023 80292853* E-mail. *info@beasy.com* Web. *www.beasy.com *Beasy (United Kingdom)*

C M D Ltd (CMD Ltd) Claughton Industrial Estate Brockholes Way, Claughton-On-Brock, Preston PR3 0PZ Tel. *01995 640844* Fax. *01995 640798* E-mail. *enquiries@cmd-ltd.com* Web. *www.powerplan.co.uk Alphatrail (United Kingdom) – Cable Hive (United Kingdom)*

CMI Healthcare Services Ltd 5 Rise Road Sunningdale, Ascot SL5 0BH Tel. *01344 621378* Fax. *01344 872204* E-mail. *sales@cmihealthcare.co.uk* Web. *www.cmihealthcare.co.uk CMI Healthcare Services*

C M Machinery 25 Charlestown Avenue Portadown, Craigavon BT63 5ZF Tel. *028 38333341* Fax. *028 38330915* E-mail. *info@cmmachinery.co.uk* Web. *www.cmmachinery.co.uk Delta – Rewinders – Slitter*

C M P UK Ltd A Division Of British Engines Ltd 36 Nelson Way Nelson Park East, Cramlington NE23 1WH Tel. *0191 2657411* Fax. *0191 2650581* E-mail. *enquiries@cmp-products.com* Web. *www.cmp-products.com Poseidon 2000 – Protex – SOLO – Triton*

C M S Kent Ltd Ledgers Works Queens Street, Paddock Wood, Tonbridge TN12 6NN Tel. *01892 832418* Fax. *01892 836077* E-mail. *sales@hasa.co.uk* Web. *www.hasa.co.uk C M S (Kent) – Hasa (Export)*

C M S Pozament Swainspark Industrial Estate Overseal, Swadlincote DE12 6JT Tel. *01283 554800* Fax. *01283 552923* E-mail. *cmspozament@tarmac.co.uk* Web. *www.tarmac.co.uk/cmspozament St. Pauls Mix*

C M S Vocational Training Ltd 29 Green Street, Huddersfield HD1 5DQ Tel. *01484 434800* Fax. *01484 515268* E-mail. *enquiries@cmsvoc.co.uk* Web. *www.cmsvoc.co.uk CMS Vocational*

C M T Tube Fittings Ltd (Division of CMT Engineering) PO Box 36, Cradley Heath B64 7DQ Tel. *01384 563200* Fax. *01384 563225* E-mail. *sales@cmt-engineering.co.uk* Web. *www.cmt-engineering.co.uk Mildsteel – Syphons – Unicone*

C M Z Machinery Ltd Fullers End Elsenham, Bishops Stortford CM22 6DU Tel. *01279 814491* Fax. *01279 814541* E-mail. *info@cmzweb.co.uk* Web. *www.cmzweb.co.uk CMZ*

Coastal Aluminium D'Oriel House Blackhill Road West, Holton Heath Trading Park, Poole BH16 6LE Tel. *01202 624011* Fax. *01202 622465* E-mail. *sales@coastalwindows.co.uk* Web. *www.coastalaluminium.co.uk Buckingham – Canterbury – Chelsea – Coastal Conservatories – Coastal doors and windows – Coastline – Kensington – Norfolk – Richmond – Sherbourne – Warwick – Westminster – Windsor – Woburn – York*

The Coaster Company Coasters House Spring Lane South, Malvern WR14 1AT Tel. *01684 577177* Fax. *01684 577188* E-mail. *info@coaster.co.uk* Web. *www.coaster.co.uk Table Mats & Coasters*

Coates Engineering International Ltd Millfold Whitworth, Rochdale OL12 8DN Tel. *01706 852122* Fax. *01706 853629* E-mail. *info@bchltd.com* Web. *www.bchltd.com BCH Ltd*

Coats Ltd Lingfield House Lingfield Point, Darlington DL1 1YJ Tel. *08456 030150* Fax. *08702 431855* E-mail. *consumer.services@coats.com* Web. *www.coats.com Anchor – Anchor – Anchor – Beatrix Potter – Coats – Deightons – Flexi-Hoops – James Herriot – Lilliput Lane – Milward – Paddington Bear – Patons*

Coba Plastics Ltd Marlborough Drive Fleckney, Leicester LE8 8UR Tel. *0116 2401000* Fax. *0116 2403871* E-mail. *sales@cobaplastics.com* Web. *www.cobaplastics.com Cobamat – Hygimat*

Cobble Blackburn Ltd Gate Street Works Gate Street, Blackburn BB1 3AH Tel. *01254 55121* Fax. *01254 671125* E-mail. *info@cobble.co.uk* Web. *www.cobble.co.uk Cobble – Crabtree – Crabtree Textile Machines*

Cobham Antenna Systems Fourth Avenue Cobham Centre, Marlow SL7 1TF Tel. *01628 472072* Fax. *01628 482255* E-mail. *info@cobham.com* Web. *www.cobham.com Chelton*

Cobham Antenna Systems, Microwave Antennas Lambda House Cheveley, Newmarket CB8 9RG Tel. *01638 731888* Fax. *01638 731999* E-mail. *antennasystems.ma@cobham.com* Web. *www.european-antennas.co.uk European Antenna*

Cobham Mission Equipment Ltd (F R Hitemp Division) Brook Road, Wimborne BH21 2BJ Tel. *01202 882121* Fax. *01202 880096* E-mail. *communications@cobham.com* Web. *www.cobham.com Clearbore – Hitemp – Metaseal – Minilock – Presslock – Raflex – Screwlock – Suitcon*

Cobra Seats Ltd Units D1-D2 Halesfield 23, Telford TF7 4NY Tel. *01952 684020* Fax. *01952 581772* E-mail. *sales@cobraseats.com* Web. *www.cobraseats.com Cobra Seats*

Cobus Communications 22 Strickland Street, Hull HU3 4AQ Tel. *01482 225666* Fax. *01482 225111* E-mail. *enquiries@cobus.co.uk* Web. *www.cobus.co.uk NEC – Nexan – Panasonic – Samsung*

Cobwebb Communications Ltd 134 High Street, Tonbridge TN9 1BB Tel. *01732 447900* Fax. *01732 365604* E-mail. *sales@cobwebb.com* Web. *www.cobwebb.com CPPD*

Cockett Marine Oil Ltd Carrick House 36 Station Square, Petts Wood, Orpington BR5 1NA Tel. *01689 883400* Fax. *01689 877666* E-mail. *enquiries@cockett.co.uk* Web. *www.cockett.co.uk Cockett Bunker Market Report – Cockett Bunker Price Index – Croeckett Marine Oil Ltd*

Coda Systems Ltd Oak Road Little Maplestead, Halstead CO9 2RT Tel. *01787 478678* Fax. *01376 342266* E-mail. *sales@coda-systems.co.uk* Web. *www.coda-systems.co.uk Coda-Pin*

Codel International Ltd Station Building Station Road, Bakewell DE45 1GE Tel. *01629 814351* Fax. *0870 0566307* E-mail. *david.coe@codel.co.uk* Web. *www.codel.co.uk Gard – Model 3000*

Codnor Horticultural Ltd Cherry Tree Cottage Farm 210 Peasehill, Ripley DE5 3JQ Tel. *01773 742847* Fax. *01773 512120* E-mail. *info@gro-welldirect.co.uk* Web. *www.gro-welldirect.co.uk Gro-Well*

Coe's Derby Ltd Engineers in GRP Thirsk Place, Derby DE24 8JL Tel. *01332 299412* Fax. *01332 340774* E-mail. *info@coesofderby.co.uk* Web. *www.coesofderby.co.uk G.R.P. – Glass Fibre*

The Coffee Machine Company 8 The Woodlands Millbank Road, Darlington DL3 9UB Tel. *01325 461215* E-mail. *sarduno@ntlworld.com* Web. *www.rancilio.it Drury – Rancilio – The Coffee Machine Company London*

Coffeetech 9 Holmethorpe Avenue Holmethorpe Industrial Estate, Redhill RH1 2NB Tel. *08707 702951* Fax. *08707 702954* E-mail. *duncan@coffeetech.co.uk* Web. *www.coffeetech.co.uk Animo – *De Jong Duke – *ECM – Macco – Nuova Simonelli – *Solis*

Coffilta Coffee & Spring Water Services 340 Abbey Lane, Sheffield S8 0BY Tel. *0114 2214642* Fax. *0114 2214642* E-mail. *kdmurray@hotmail.com *Coffilta Coffee – *James Aimer*

Cofit T Shirts Deals 6 Wharfeside Rosemont Road, Wembley HA0 4PE Tel. *020 87955700* Fax. *020 89022566* E-mail. *h.chakardjian@sky.com* Web. *www.tshirtdeals.co.uk Finalist Sportswear*

Cogne UK Ltd (division of Cogne UK Ltd) 19 Don Road, Sheffield S9 2UD Tel. *0114 2212020* Fax. *0114 2213030* E-mail. *peter@cogne.co.uk* Web. *www.cogne.co.uk 20 Plus – 20 Plus HS – 420 Plus – A.L.Z. – Benum – Benum Plus – C.R.P. 01 – K.M.V. – Malloy – One Five One – Pneumo – Special K – Uniformity Steel – X.C.16*

Cognis Performance Chemicals Ltd Hardley Hythe, Southampton SO45 3ZG Tel. *023 80894666* Fax. *023 80243113* Web. *www.cognis.com Bisoflex – Bisolube – Bisomer – Breox*

Cognito Ltd Benham Valence Speen, Newbury RG20 8LU Tel. *01635 508200* Fax. *01635 550783* E-mail. *info@cognitomobile.com* Web. *www.cognito.co.uk Cognito*

Cogsdill Nuneaton Ltd Tenlons Road, Nuneaton CV10 7HR Tel. *024 76383792* Fax. *024 76344433* E-mail. *sales@cogsdill.co.uk* Web. *www.cogsdill.com Westwood*

Cohen & Wilks International Ltd Aquatite House Mabgate, Leeds LS9 7DR Tel. *0113 2450804* Fax. *0113 3917858* E-mail. *reception@cwil.co.uk* Web. *www.cohenandwilks.co.uk Cohen & Wilks International*

Cohn & Wolfe Ltd Lynton House 7-12 Tavistock Square, London WC1H 9LT Tel. *020 73315300* Fax. *020 73319083* E-mail. *helen_jones@uk.cohnwolfe.com* Web. *www.cohnandwolfe.com Inform*

Coinage Limited 91 Mayflower Street, Plymouth PL1 1SB Tel. *0870 1600992* Fax. *0845 0532884* E-mail. *sales@coinage.co.uk* Web. *www.coinage.co.uk Cardvendor – Crown – Soap Shop – Sovereign*

Colas Ltd Wallage Lane Rowfant, Crawley RH10 4NF Tel. *01342 711000* Fax. *01342 711198* E-mail. *info@colas.co.uk* Web. *www.colas.co.uk Bitucrete – Bitukold – Bitumac – Bitutex FP – Cariphalte Primer – Colade Masterbatch – Colade TPF – Colas Blown Bitumen – Colas Filled Bitumen – Colcryl/Colcolour – Fibredec – H.4 – Jointgrip 55 – Leocatic Mix – Leocatic Spray – Leochip VLS – Leoclean – Leopave – Leoseal – Leotak – Lion 40% – Lion 55% – Macadamat – Preformed S.A.M. – Preformed Surface Dressing – Premium 80 – Ralumac – Recycling – Repave – Retread – Spray Grip – Spraygrip – Surfix – Surfix 80 – *Wirtgen (Germany)*

Colchester Lathe Co. Ltd PO Box 20, Heckmondwike WF16 0HN Tel. *01924 415000* Fax. *01924 412604* E-mail. *mail@600uk.com* Web. *www.600uk.com Cambi Lathes – Colchester Lathes – Tornado CNC Lathes*

Cold Rolled Strip Stock Charles Street, Willenhall WV13 1HG Tel. *01902 365434* Fax. *01902 365435* E-mail. *uksales@dscm.co.uk* Web. *www.dscm.co.uk HARDENED & TEMPERED – MILD STEEL STRIP – SPRING STEEL STRIP*

Colefax & Fowler Ltd 19-23 Grosvenor Hill, London W1K 3QD Tel. *020 73186000* Fax. *020 74999910* E-mail. *enq@colefax.co.uk* Web. *www.colefax.co.uk Colefax & Fowler*

Coleford Brick & Tile Hawkwell Green, Cinderford GL14 3JJ Tel. *01594 822160* Fax. *01594 826655* E-mail. *sales@colefordbrick.co.uk* Web. *www.colefordbrick.co.uk Coleford*

Coleman Milne Ltd Wigan Road Westhoughton, Bolton BL5 2EE Tel. *01942 815600* Fax. *01942 815115* E-mail. *paul.thompson@woodall-nicholson.co.uk* Web. *www.woodall-nicholson.co.uk Cardinal – Dorchester – Grosvenor – Minster – Windsor*

Thomas Coleman Engineering Ltd Alfreton Road, Derby DE21 4AL Tel. *01332 345519* Fax. *01332 343436* E-mail. *sales@colemaneng.co.uk* Web. *www.colemaneng.co.uk Arch – Coleman's – Heater/Mixers – PPU – Type L*

Cole Metal Products Ltd 71 Strand Road, Bootle L20 4BB Tel. *0151 9338588* Fax. *0151 9330504* E-mail. *sales@colemetal.co.uk* Web. *www.colemetal.co.uk Cole Metal Products – Cole metal products - thermal lance manufrs*

Coler Supply Solutions Manor Road Industrial Estate, Atherstone CV9 1QY Tel. *01827 712910* Fax. *01827 62776* E-mail. *info@coler.co.uk* Web. *www.coler.co.uk COLER SUPPLY*

Coleshill Plastics Ltd Bodmin Road, Coventry CV2 5DB Tel. *024 76724900* Fax. *024 76724901* E-mail. *martinpilley@coleshillplastics.co.uk* Web. *www.coleshillplastics.co.uk Melamaster – MELAMASTER - High quality melamine giftware and tableware*

Colin Blakey's Fireplace Galleries Ltd 115 Manchester Road, Nelson BB9 7HB Tel. *01282 614941* Fax. *01282 698511* E-mail. *enquiries@fireplaceseastlancashire.com* Web. *www.colinblakeyfireplaces.com Blakey*

Collaborative Solutions Ltd 57 Foulden Road, London N16 7UU Tel. *020 72540770* Fax. *020 79230021 Minerva*

College For International Cooperation & Development Winestead Hall Winestead, Hull HU12 0NP Tel. *01964 631824* Fax. *01964 631695* E-mail. *karenb@cicd-volunteerinafrica.org* Web. *www.cicd-volunteerinafrica.org Door to Door Second Hand Clothes – Door to Door Second Hand Shoes*

W L Coller Ltd Unit 1-4 Holloway Drive Worsley, Manchester M28 2LA Tel. *0161 7995353* Fax. *0161 7037180* E-mail. *caroline.merry@wlcoller.co.uk* Web. *www.wlcoller.co.uk Caxton – Petersgate*

George Colliar Ltd Middle Balado Farm Balado, Kinross KY13 0NH Tel. *01577 863173* Fax. *01577 864768* E-mail. *colliar@harleys.co.uk* Web. *www.georgecollier.com *Deutz-Farr – *Grimme – *Rabi*

W H Collier Ltd Brick Works Church Lane, Marks Tey, Colchester CO6 1LN Tel. *01206 210301* Fax. *01206 212540* E-mail. *maurice@thebrickbusiness.com* Web. *www.whcollier.co.uk Chelwood Brick – W.H. Collier*

Collins & Hayes Furniture Menzies Road Ponswood, St Leonards On Sea TN38 9XF Tel. *01424 720027* Fax. *01424 720270* E-mail. *sales@collinsandhayes.com* Web. *www.collinsandhayes.com Collins and Hayes – Collins and Hayes – Collins and Hayes*

John C Collins Honeysuckle Cottage Worcester Road, Inkberrow, Worcester WR7 4JP Tel. *01386 792591* Fax. *01386 792591 Balemate – Calfmate*

Martin Collins Enterprises Ltd Cuckoo Copse Lambourn Woodlands, Hungerford RG17 7TJ Tel. *01488 71100*

Fax. *01488 73177* E-mail. *martin@mceltd.com* Web. *www.mceltd.com Geltrack – Polytrak – Protrak – Rubbertrack – Waxtrack*

Colloids Ltd Kirkby Bank Road Knowsley Industrial Park, Liverpool L33 7SY Tel. *0151 5469222* Fax. *0151 5490489* E-mail. *sales@colloids.co.uk* Web. *www.colloids.co.uk Ceramtex*

Cologne & Cotton 74 Regent Street, Leamington Spa CV32 4NS Tel. *01926 339880* Fax. *01926 332575* E-mail. *info@cologneandcotton.com* Web. *www.cologneandcotton.com Cologne & Cotton*

Colorlites Ltd Unit 23 Lordswood Industrial Estate Revenge Road, Chatham ME5 8UD Tel. *01634 862839* Fax. *01634 865285* E-mail. *salesdesk@colorlites.com* Web. *www.colouredbottles.co.uk Colorlites*

Color Steels Ltd Blackvein Industrial Estate Cross Keys, Newport NP11 7YD Tel. *01495 279100* Fax. *01495 271456* Web. *www.colorsteels.co.uk Stelvertite*

Colour Anodising Ltd Holland Street Radcliffe, Manchester M26 2RH Tel. *0161 7232637* Fax. *0161 7259252* E-mail. *info@anodising.com* Web. *www.anodising.com Anotec*

Colourcraft C & A Ltd Unit 5 555 Carlisle Street East, Sheffield S4 8DT Tel. *0114 2421431* Fax. *0114 2434844* E-mail. *sales@colourcraft-ltd.com* Web. *www.colourcraftltd.com Aztec Range – Brusho – Dytek*

Colourfast Decorating - French Polish Prospect Terrace Willington, Crook DL15 0DT Tel. *07971 980927* E-mail. *info@colourfastdecorating.co.uk* Web. *www.colourfastdecorating.co.uk/ antique furniture restoration, antique restoration, french polish, french polishers*

Colour-Therm Ltd 92 Burdon Lane, Sutton SM2 7DA Tel. *020 86426506* Fax. *020 86424886* E-mail. *mdunk@colour-therm.co.uk* Web. *www.colour-therm.co.uk Compass – Flexible Lacquers – Thermochromic – Thermochromic Photochromic*

Colson Castors Ltd Bagnall Street Golds Hill, West Bromwich B70 0TS Tel. *0121 5567221* Fax. *0121 5026258* E-mail. *info@colson-castors.co.uk* Web. *www.colson-castors.co.uk Colson*

Colt Car Company Ltd Watermoor, Cirencester GL7 1LF Tel. *01285 655777* Fax. *01285 658026* E-mail. *enquiries@mitsubishi-cars.co.uk* Web. *www.mitsubishi-cars.co.uk *Colt Car Co (Japan) – S.D.S.*

Coltraco Ltd Chewton Fields Farm Ston Easton, Radstock BA3 4BX Tel. *01761 241601* Fax. *01761 241685* E-mail. *ghchunter@coltraco.co.uk* Web. *www.coltraco.co.uk Portagauge – Portalevel – Portamarine – Portascanner*

Columbia Metals Ltd Wingfield Mews Wingfield Street, London SE15 4LH Tel. *020 77321022* Fax. *020 77321029* E-mail. *sales@columbiametals.co.uk* Web. *www.columbiametals.co.uk Amazon 256 Cu – Chromzirc 3 – Chromzirc 328 – Colbronze – Colduplex - CS – Coldur-A – Colfit-DZR – Colphos 90 – Colsibro – Colspeed AB – Columbia 310 – Flowbond Special – Narite 300 – Narite 400 – Nibron Special – SAF 2507 – Sea-Col 760 – Trojan XIV*

Colwick Instruments Ltd PO Box 8268, Nottingham NG3 6AJ Tel. *0115 9622999* Fax. *0115 9614582* E-mail. *enquires@colwickinstruments.co.uk* Web. *www.colwickinstruments.co.uk Anagas*

Colyer London 22-26 Vine Hill, London EC1R 5LJ Tel. *020 78378666* Fax. *020 74044762* E-mail. *t.harding@colyer.co.uk* Web. *www.colyer.co.uk Valachrome*

Comag Tavistock Road, West Drayton UB7 7QE Tel. *01895 433600* Fax. *01895 433602* Web. *www.comag.co.uk Comag*

Comar Instruments 70 Hartington Grove, Cambridge CB1 7UH Tel. *01223 866120* Fax. *01223 410033* E-mail. *mail@comaroptics.com* Web. *www.comaroptics.com Comar*

Comark Ltd Comark House Gunnels Wood Park Gunnels Wood Road, Stevenage SG1 2TA Tel. *01438 367367* Fax. *01438 367400* E-mail. *nigelfearn@comarkltd.com* Web. *www.comarkltd.com Comark – Kane-May*

M Comar & Sons Ltd 37 Broughton Street, Manchester M8 8LZ Tel. *0161 8348049* Fax. *0161 8331798* E-mail. *sales@comars.co.uk* Web. *www.comars.co.uk Billa – Reena*

Combidrive Ltd Unit 6 Parc Menter, Cross Hands, Llanelli SA14 6RA Tel. *01269 834848* Fax. *01269 834850* E-mail. *jason@combidrive.com* Web. *www.combidrive.com Combidrive – Industrial power transmission distributors – Mouse*

Combined Catering Services 73 Brewster Street, Bootle L20 9NG Tel. *0151 9224454* Fax. *0151 9225005* E-mail. *office@combinedcatering.com* Web. *www.combinedcatering.com Coffeaco – Vent King*

Combined Trading Garments Ltd 77-79 Great Eastern Street, London EC2A 3HU Tel. *020 77390551* Fax. *020 77292556 Combined Trading Exports*

E A Combs Ltd Quantum House Station Estate Eastwood Close, London E18 1BY Tel. *020 85304216* Fax. *020 85301310* E-mail. *stuart@eacombs.com* Web. *www.eacombs.com Quantum*

Comcen Computer Supplies Ltd Bruce Road Fforestfach, Swansea SA5 4HS Tel. *01792 515560* Fax. *01792 515575* E-mail. *info@comcen.co.uk* Web. *www.comcen.co.uk Comcen*

Comet Catering Equipment Co. Ltd Comet Works Brimsdown Industrial Estate Lockfield Avenue, Brimsdown, Enfield EN3 7XZ Tel. *020 88044779* Fax. *020 88049470* E-mail. *michael@cometcatering.com* Web. *www.cometcatering.com Comet Catering*

Comfy Quilts Ltd Old Hall Street Middleton, Manchester M24 1AG Tel. *08707 662324* Fax. *0161 6553362* E-mail. *info@comfyquilts.com* Web. *www.comfyquilts.com Igloo – Moonbag – Sleepsafe – Visions*

Comma Oil & Chemicals Ltd Comma Works Dering Way, Gravesend DA12 2QX Tel. *01474 564311* Fax. *01474 333000* E-mail. *enquiries@commaoil.com* Web. *www.commaoil.com Coldstream – Comma Europa – Comma Premium – Comma Super Coldmaster – Comma Xstream – Manista*

Commidea Ltd 100 Eureka Park Upper Pemberton Kennington, Ashford TN25 4AZ Tel. *08444 828200* Fax. *0844 4828210* E-mail. *enquiries@commidea.com* Web. *www.commidea.com *Soft-Eft*

Commsandsound.Com Ltd Unit 1250 Sstore 51 Brampton Road, Eastbourne BN22 9AF Tel. *01273 906696* Fax. *01273 906696* E-mail. *sales@commsandsound.com* Web. *www.commsandsound.com commsandsound*

Commtel 56 Causeway Road Earlstrees Industrial Estate, Corby NN17 4DU Tel. *01536 403943* Fax. *01536 408482* E-mail. *john.cook@commteluk.com* Web. *www.commteluk.com Pullway*

The Co Op PO Box 53, Manchester M60 4ES Tel. *0161 8341212* Web. *www.co-operative.coop Babywise – Goliath – Sheer Silk*

Co-Operative Banking Group (Head Office) 1 Balloon Street, Manchester M60 4EP Tel. *0161 8323456* Fax. *0161 8294475* Web. *www.cfs.co.uk The Co-operative Bank P.L.C.*

Component Moulders (Head Office) Unit 4-5 Teville Industrials Dominion Way, Worthing BN14 8NW Tel. *01903 235765* Fax. *01903 212751* E-mail. *sales@nordell.co.uk* Web. *www.nordell.co.uk Como*

Components Direct Nunn Close Huthwaite, Sutton In Ashfield NG17 2HW Tel. *01623 788400* Fax. *01623 788488* E-mail. *sales@comdir.co.uk* Web. *www.comdir.co.uk Rite Lok*

Compressor Products International Ltd Unit 5 Smitham Bridge Road, Hungerford RG17 0QP Tel. *01488 684585* Fax. *01488 684001* E-mail. *sales@compressor-products.com* Web. *www.compressor-products.com Compressor Products International*

Compsoft plc Delta House 7 Oriel Business Park Omega Park, Alton GU34 2YT Tel. *08453 707274* Fax. *01420 81444* E-mail. *info@compsoft.co.uk* Web. *www.compsoft.co.uk Equinox – Blue Sulphur*

Compton Buildings Station Works Fenny Compton, Southam CV47 2XB Tel. *01295 770111* Fax. *01295 770748* E-mail. *richard.curtis@compton-buildings.co.uk* Web. *www.comptonbuildings.co.uk Alton – Alton – Alton Greenhouses – Compton – Compton – Compton Garages – Greenhouse & garage manufrs – Robinsons – Robinsons Greenhouses – Safeguard Garages*

Computalabel International Ltd PO Box 8867, Leicester LE21 3DA Tel. *0116 2700881* Fax. *0116 2704427* E-mail. *info@computalabel.com* Web. *www.computalabel.com Label Designer – MacBarcoda – MacThermal*

The Computastat Group Ltd Smallmead House Smallmead, Horley RH6 9LW Tel. *01293 773221* Fax. *01293 786747* E-mail. *sales@computastat-group.co.uk* Web. *www.computastat-group.co.uk Instabill*

Computeach International Ltd PO Box 51, Dudley DY3 2AH Tel. *01384 458515* Fax. *01384 455650* E-mail. *customercare@computeach.co.uk* Web. *www.computeach.co.uk Computeach International (C.I.L.) – Software Professionals*

Computer Room Consultants 8 Carbis Way Port Solent, Portsmouth PO6 4TW Tel. *023 92220699* E-mail. *doug.latta@computerroomconsultants.co.uk* Web. *www.computerroomconsultants.co.uk CRC*

Computer Services Consultants UK Ltd Yeadon House New Street, Pudsey LS28 8AQ Tel. *0113 2393000* Fax. *0113 2553917* E-mail. *simon.bellwood@cscworld.com* Web. *www.cscworld.com C S C – C S C CAD – C S C Fasteel – Connections – FabTrol – Fastrak 5950 – Fastrak Multi Storey – Fastrak Portal Frame – Softek Structural Office Suite – TEDDS*

Computer Solutions Ltd 1A New Haw Road, Addlestone KT15 2BZ Tel. *01932 829460* Fax. *01932 840603* E-mail. *sales@computer-solutions.co.uk* Web. *www.computer-solutions.co.uk Cardforth – Chipforth – Comsol*

Computertel Ltd 52 Bath Street, Gravesend DA11 0DF Tel. *01474 561111* Fax. *01474 561122* E-mail. *info@computertel.co.uk* Web. *www.computertel.co.uk Computertel*

Computronic Controls Ltd 41-46 Railway Terrace Nechells, Birmingham B7 5NG Tel. *0121 3278500* Fax. *0121 3278501* E-mail. *sales@computroniccontrols.com* Web. *www.computroniccontrols.com Computronic Controls*

Comyn Ching (Solray) Phoenix Way Gorseinon, Swansea SA4 9WF Tel. *01792 892211* Fax. *01792 898855* E-mail. *sales@solray.co.uk* Web. *www.solray.co.uk Comyn Ching – Solray*

Cona Ltd Unit 3 Island Farm Avenue, West Molesey KT8 2UZ Tel. *020 89419922* Fax. *020 89419955* E-mail. *info@cona.co.uk* Web. *www.cona.co.uk Burshaw – Burshaw - Cona - Conamatic – Cona – Conamatic – Stawell*

Concept Systems Design Ltd 1 Pacific Court Pacific Road Atlantic Street, Broadheath, Altrincham WA14 5BJ Tel. *0161 9297434* Fax. *0161 9290904* E-mail. *sales@csd-epi.com* Web. *www.csd-ltd.co.uk Concept Systems Design – MD Asia*

Concord Marlin Ltd International Sales Office Avis Way, Newhaven BN9 0ED Tel. *01273 515811* Fax. *01273 512688* E-mail. *info@concordmarlin.com* Web. *www.concordmarlin.com Cassini – Kometa – LED 100 – LED 150 – Lytespan 1,2,3 – Lytespan LP – Lytetube 75, 90 – Myriad IV – OutdoorExteriot – TeQ Collection*

Concrete Renovations 152 Park Road, Peterborough PE1 2UB Tel. *01733 560362* E-mail. *sales@concreterenovations.co.uk* Web. *www.concreterenovations.co.uk Sponge Blasting*

Condensate systems Ltd 2 Delta Way Business Centre Longford Road, Cannock WS11 0LJ Tel. *01543 378402* Fax. *01543 578202* E-mail. *sales@oil-water.com* Web. *www.oil-water.com Condensate Cleaners – Sepura*

Condor Cycles Ltd 49-53 Gray's Inn Road, London WC1X 8PP Tel. *020 72696820* Fax. *020 72696821* E-mail. *info@condorcycles.com* Web. *www.condorcycles.com Condor*

Confederate Chemicals Ltd Mochdre Industrial Estate Mochdre, Newtown SY16 4LE Tel. *01686 627158* Fax. *01686 627580* E-mail. *sales@confederatechemicals.co.uk* Web. *www.confederatechemicals.co.uk Catron*

Connectomatic Unit E Bretfield Court, Dewsbury WF12 9BG Tel. *01924 452444* Fax. *01924 430607* E-mail. *sales@connectomatic.co.uk* Web. *www.connectomatic.co.uk *Geka (Germany) – *Huedig (Germany) – *Perrot (Germany)*

Connect Packaging 6-8 Brunel Road Manor Trading Estate, Benfleet SS7 4PS Tel. *01268 565656* Fax. *01268 565980* E-mail. *info@connectpackaging.com* Web. *www.connectpackaging.com Essex*

Connect Two Promotions Ltd Kingswick House Kingswick Drive, Ascot SL5 7BH Tel. *01344 292370* Fax. *01344 626176* E-mail. *info@connecttwo.co.uk* Web. *www.connecttwo.co.uk 3M – prodir – Waterfords – Filofax – Kustom kit*

Connect 2 Technology Ltd Longbeck Road Marske-by-the-sea, Redcar TS11 6HQ Tel. *01642 492220* Fax. *01642 492223* E-mail. *enquiries@connect2t.co.uk* Web. *www.connect2t.co.uk Connect-2 Technology*

Connet UK Ltd. Suite B, Harley street 29, London W1G 9QR Tel. *020 71937316* Fax. *020 71826892* E-mail. *info@uk.company-on.net* Web. *www.companyonnet.co.uk Company on Net*

Conquer Pest Control Ltd Chestnut Farm Chestnut Lane, Barton-In-Fabis, Nottingham NG11 0AE Tel. *0115 9830735* Fax. *0115 9831229* E-mail. *info@conquerpestcontrol.co.uk* Web. *www.conquerpestcontrol.co.uk Killgerm*

Jasper Conran Ltd 1-7 Rostrevor Mews, London SW6 5AZ Tel. *020 73840800* Fax. *020 73840801* E-mail. *info@jasperconran.com* Web. *www.jasperconran.com Jasper Conran*

Conren Ltd Ditton Road, Widnes WA8 0PG Tel. *0151 4223999* Fax. *01246 856348* E-mail. *info@conren.com* Web. *www.conren.com Aquasol – Britseal – Congrip – Conpol 80 Polymer Additive – Conren Joint Filler – CS2 Cure and Seal – Decorscreed – Decorseal – Dustguard – Dustguard Antistat – Elastomeric Joint Sealant – Enamelcoat – F.S. Screed – Flexijoint – Floorplate Non Metallic – Floorplate S – High Strength Grout – Highseal – Highseal F1 – Hydrocide SX – Hydrothane Screed – Lapidolith – Levelay – Levelay Antistat – Levelay H.D.T. – Line Paint – Patchfast – Playon – Roofab Scrim – Rooftex – Rooftex GP Primer – Rooftex Granules – Rooftex Silver Coating – Rooftex Urethane Primer – Solvent Cleaner – Stopslip Aggregate – Truegrip BT – Truegrip TCD – Tufcon 80 Screed – W.D. Membrane and Bonder – W.D. Patching Kits – X.D. 80 Degreaser*

Conrico Service Centre Hanworth Lane, Chertsey KT16 9LA Tel. *01932 581090* Fax. *01932 567032* E-mail. *jwood@conrico.com* Web. *www.conrico.com Conrico International Ltd*

Conservation Resources UK Ltd Unit 2 Ashville Way Cowley, Oxford OX4 6TU Tel. *01865 747755* Fax. *01865 747035* E-mail. *conservarts@aol.com* Web. *www.conservation-resources.co.uk Lig-Free – MicroChamber – Polyweld – Silversafe – Trusteam*

Consilium ltd The Old Stables, Onehouse Hall Lower Road, Onehouse, Stowmarket IP14 3BY Tel. *01449 676435*

Fax. *01449 676436* E-mail. *info@consilium.co.uk* Web. *www.consilium.europa.eu *Exclusive Heritage Venues*

Consolidated Spinners & Manufacturers Ltd 177 Stanley Road Cheadle Hulme, Cheadle SK8 6RF Tel. *0161 4373295* Fax. *0161 4364855* E-mail. *william@hallyarns.fsnet.co.uk* *Consolodated Spinners & Manufacturers Ltd*

Consort Equipment Products Thornton Industrial Estate, Milford Haven SA73 2RT Tel. *01646 692172* Fax. *01646 695195* E-mail. *enquiries@consortepl.com* Web. *www.consortepl.com Claudgen (United Kingdom) – Consort (United Kingdom) – Pure Air (United Kingdom)*

Constant Air Systems Ltd Hillbottom Road Sands Industrial Estate, High Wycombe HP12 4HJ Tel. *01494 469529* Fax. *01494 469549* E-mail. *admin@constantair.co.uk* Web. *www.constantair.co.uk Casaire*

Constellation Luggage Ltd Constellation Works Fernhurst Street, Chadderton, Oldham OL1 2RN Tel. *0161 6204231* Fax. *0161 6270914* E-mail. *constellation@japinda.co.uk* Web. *www.japinda.co.uk Japinda*

Construction Industry Accountancy Ltd Airport House Purley Way, Croydon CR0 0XZ Tel. *020 86515050* Fax. *01342 836798* E-mail. *admin@cisvat.co.uk* Web. *www.theconstructionshop.com Portakabin*

The Consumer Council For Water Northgate House St Augustines Way, Darlington DL1 1XA Tel. *01325 464222* Fax. *01325 369269* E-mail. *yorkshire@ccwater.org.uk* Web. *www.ccwater.org.uk Government Watchdog Service*

Contactum Ltd Victoria Works Edgware Road, London NW2 6LF Tel. *020 84526366* Fax. *020 82083340* E-mail. *sales@contactum.co.uk* Web. *www.contactum.co.uk Contactum*

Contiki Travel UK Ltd Royal National Hotel Bedford Way, London WC1H 0DG Tel. *020 76370802* Fax. *020 76372121* E-mail. *basement.rep1@contiki.co.uk* Web. *www.contiki.com Contiki*

Continental Chef Supplies Ltd 2 Swan Road South West Industrial Estate, Peterlee SR8 2HS Tel. *0191 5188080* Fax. *08081 002777* E-mail. *sales@chefs.net* Web. *www.chefs.net Burgvogel – De Berkel – *Demeyere – *Figgio – Hold-o-mat – Nick Munro – RAK – Studio William*

Continental Disc UK Ltd C The Business Centre Faringdon Avenue, Romford RM3 8EN Tel. *01708 386444* Fax. *01708 386486* E-mail. *sales@contdisc.com* Web. *www.contdisc.com Cal-Vac – M/ntrx – Micro x – Mintrx – Pos-A-Set – Sanitrx – Star x – Ultrx*

Continental Tyre Group Ltd Continental House 191 High Street, Yiewsley, West Drayton UB7 7XW Tel. *01895 425900* Fax. *01895 425982* E-mail. *info@conti.de* Web. *www.conti-online.com *Continental (France, Germany) – *Contitech (Germany, France) – *Semperit (Austria & Eire) – *Uniroyal (UK, France, Germany, Belgium)*

Contour Showers Ltd Siddorn Street, Winsford CW7 2BA Tel. *01606 592586* Fax. *01606 861260* E-mail. *tim.robinson@contour-showers.co.uk* Web. *www.contour-showers.co.uk Carescreen – Showercare*

Contraband Unit 35 Union Mills Tanyard Road, Milnsbridge, Huddersfield HD3 4NB Tel. *08454 601800* Fax. *01484 460171* E-mail. *info@carefromcontraband.com* Web. *www.carefromcontraband.com Sequin Stone Ltd T/A Contraband*

Contract Chemicals Ltd Penrhyn Road Knowsley Business Park, Prescot L34 9HY Tel. *0151 5488840* Fax. *0151 5486548* E-mail. *info@contract-chemicals.com* Web. *www.contract-chemicals.com Contrepel – Controlobe – Controvel – Controwet – Envirolats – Enviroquest – Ferriplex – Ferriplus – Nervanaid – Permafresh – Tardex*

Contract Kitchens Ltd Unit 7 Portland Business Park 130 Richmond Park Road, Sheffield S13 8HS Tel. *0114 2750018* Fax. *0114 2798787* E-mail. *info@contractkitchensltd.com* Web. *www.contractkitchensltd.com Trade Kitchen Appliances*

Control Techniques 4 Stafford Park 4, Telford TF3 3BA Tel. *01952 213700* Fax. *01952 213701* E-mail. *dave.baston@emerson.com* Web. *www.controltechniques.com Commander – Mentor – Smart Start – Vector*

Converteam UK Ltd Boughton Road, Rugby CV21 1BU Tel. *01788 563563* Fax. *01788 560767* E-mail. *sales@converteam.com* Web. *www.converteam.com Alspa 8000 – Alspa GD4000 – Alspa MV1000 – Alspa MV3000 – Alspa MV500*

Conveyors International (CI Logistics) (a division of Portec Rail Products (UK) Ltd) 43 Wenlock Way Troon Industrial Area, Leicester LE4 9HU Tel. *0116 2761691* Fax. *0116 2769836* E-mail. *sales@conveyors.co.uk* Web. *www.conveyors.co.uk C.I. – Conveyors International*

Conveyor Units Ltd Sandy Lane Titton, Stourport On Severn DY13 9PT Tel. *01299 877541* Fax. *01299 877921* E-mail. *conveyorsales@conveyor-units.co.uk* Web. *www.conveyor-units.co.uk Uni-Belt – Uni-Xu 1000 – UNI-XU Series – Uniplus – Unitrac*

Convotherm Ltd Enodis UK Food Service Unit 4 Brook Industrial Estate, Bullsbrook Road, Hayes UB4 0JZ. Tel. *020 88482980* Fax. *020 87561720* E-mail. *info@convotherm.co.uk* Web. *www.catercomm.net *Convotherm*

Conway Trailer Division Skull House Lane Appley Bridge, Wigan WN6 9DW Tel. *01257 254535* Fax. *01257 254547* E-mail. *sales@conwaytrailers.com* Web. *www.conwaytrailers.com Conway – Conway Cardinal – Conway Century – Conway Challenger – Conway Classic – Conway Conquest – Conway Countryman – Conway Cruiser – Conway Crusader – Conway Mirage – Conway Voyager – Glidalong*

Henry Cooch & Son Ltd Unit 2 Platt Industrial Estate Maidstone Road, Platt, Sevenoaks TN15 8JL Tel. *01732 884484* Fax. *01732 882681* E-mail. *t-links@dial.pipex.com* Web. *www.henrycooch.co.uk Cooch – Generator sets diesel-electric – Lighting and floodlighting for motorways – Lighting emergency, illuminated self powered – Lighting equipment portable – Skylite*

Cook Compression Ltd 4 Burnell Road, Ellesmere Port CH65 5EX Tel. *0151 3555937* Fax. *0151 3571098* E-mail. *salesuk@cookcompression.com* Web. *www.cookcompression.com Compressor Valve Engineering*

Cooke Brothers Ltd Northgate Aldridge, Walsall WS9 8TL Tel. *01922 740001* Fax. *01922 456227* E-mail. *customerservices@cookebrothers.co.uk* Web. *www.cookebrothers.co.uk Loadmaster – Phoenix – Slim Line*

Cook Hammond & Kell Ltd Aztec House 397-405 Archway Road, Highgate, London N6 4EY Tel. *020 83473700* Fax. *020 83473701* E-mail. *localgov@chk.co.uk* Web. *www.chk.co.uk/contact/contact.htm Cook, Hammond & Kell – Maps Sales*

Cooks Brushes 52 The Street Costessey, Norwich NR8 5DD Tel. *01603 748339* Fax. *01603 271896* E-mail. *sales@cooks-brushes.co.uk* Web. *www.cooks-brushes.co.uk Diamond – Diamond, excel, greenline, Norwich – Excel – Greenline – Norwich*

Cookson Electronics Ltd Forsyth Road, Woking GU21 5SB Tel. *01483 758400* Fax. *01483 758410* Web. *www.cooksonelectronics.com Actane – Actane 70 – Actane 73 – Actane 85 – Actane 97 – Actane Inhibitor – Actane L 59 – Alumon D – Alumon EN – Artform – Aurobond – Autronex – B.D.T. – Clearlyte – Cromylite – Ebonol C – Ebonol S 34 – Ebonol Z80 – Emprep – Enbond 808 – Enbond HD 162 – Endox 214 – Endox L 76 – Enlyte – Enplate – Enplate 432 – Enplate 473 – Enplate 498 – Enplate Accelerator 860 – Enplate Act. 443 – Enplate Activator 850 – Enplate AD 481 – Enplate AD 485 – Enplate CU 406 – Enplate CU 83 – Enplate Cu 872 – Enplate Initiater 582 – Enplate MB 435 – Enplate MB 436 – Enplate MB 6365 – Enplate MLB 495 – Enplate MLB 497 – Enplate MLB 7268 – Enplate Neutraliser 835 – Enplate NI 414 – Enplate NI 415 – Enplate NI 418 Special – Enplate NI 422 – Enplate NI 426 – Enplate NI 429 – Enplate NI 434 – Enplate PC 451 – Enplate Pre Etch 3489 – Enprep – Enprep – Enprep – Enstrip 165S – Enstrip A – Enstrip NP – Enstrip S – Enstrip TL 107 – Enstrip TL 142 – Enstrip TL Conc – Enstrips – Entek – Entek CU 56 – Entek NR 37 – Entek NR 47 – Entek RSO – Enthobrite CAD 900 – Enthobrite CLZ 938 – Enthone – Enthox 8450 – Enthox 986 – Enthox ZB 992 – Enthox ZB992 – Envizion – Evabrite – Hi-Throw PC 339 – Imastrip 122 – Imastrip Conditioner 144 – Imastrip conditioner 147 – Karatclad – Magnum – Neutronex – Niron – Orima – Palladex – Permapass – Pernix – Photec – Platanex – Pur-a-Gold – Rhodex – Ruthenex – Satylite – Silvrex – Udylite – Ultralite – Zincrolyte – Zinloy*

Cookson Precious Metals Ltd 59-83 Vittoria Street, Birmingham B1 3NZ Tel. *0121 2003232* Fax. *0121 2003222* E-mail. *richard.powers@cooksongold.com* Web. *www.cooksongold.com Star Link Chains*

Cookson & Zinn PTL Ltd Station Road Works Station Road, Hadleigh, Ipswich IP7 5PN Tel. *01473 825200* Fax. *01473 828446* E-mail. *andrew.golding@czltd.com* Web. *www.czltd.com Cookson & Zinn*

Thomas Cook Ltd Unit 15 Coningsby Road, Peterborough PE3 8AB Tel. *08443 357564* E-mail. *enquiries@thomascook.com* Web. *www.thomascook.com Thomas Cook Holidays*

Coolicious Frozen Yogurt Taste Trends Ltd 53-57 High Street, Cobham KT11 3DP Tel. *08453 377017* Fax. *0845 3377307* E-mail. *admin@tastetrends.co.uk* Web. *www.coolicious.com Coolicious Frozen Yoghurt – Coolicious Frozen Yogurt – Coolicious Fruit Smoothie – Coolicious Iced Coffee – Coolicious Shakes*

Coolmation Ltd Unit 7 Millstream Trading Estate Christchurch Road, Ringwood BH24 3SD Tel. *0800 7315466* Fax. *01425 470745* E-mail. *enquiries@coolmation.co.uk* Web. *www.coolmation.co.uk Coolmation – Cresta – Power Cool*

Cooper B Line Ltd Commerce Way, Highbridge TA9 4AQ Tel. *01278 783371* Fax. *01278 789037* E-mail. *sales@cooperbline.co.uk* Web. *www.cooperbline.co.uk Access – E2 – Ultima*

Cooper Controls Ltd 20 Greenhill Crescent, Watford WD18 8JA Tel. *01923 495495* Fax. *01923 800190* E-mail. *charlie.madsen@cooperindustries.com* Web. *www.coopercontrols.co.uk/cortina Nelco*

Cooper Controls Ltd Usk House Lakeside, Llantarnam Industrial Park, Cwmbran NP44 3HD Tel. *01633 838088* Fax. *01633 867880* E-mail. *info@zero88.com* Web. *www.coopercontrols.com Zero 88*

Cooperheat UK Ltd Unit 21-24 Slaidburn Industrial Estate Slaidburn Crescent, Southport PR9 9YF Tel. *01704 215600* Fax. *01695 713501* E-mail. *nigel.bleackley@stork.com* Web. *www.storktechnicalservices.com Cooperheat (United Kingdom)*

Cooper Printing Machinery Ltd 42 Coldharbour Lane, Harpenden AL5 4UN Tel. *01582 764431* Fax. *01582 768608* E-mail. *sales@cooperprint.co.uk* Web. *www.cooperprint.co.uk C. – Cooper Man*

Cooper Roller Bearings Co. Ltd Wisbech Road, Kings Lynn PE30 5JX Tel. *01553 763447* Fax. *01553 761113* E-mail. *jruskin@raydon.com* Web. *www.cooperbearings.com Cooper*

Cooper & Turner Templeborough Works Sheffield Road, Sheffield S9 1RS Tel. *0114 2560057* Fax. *0114 2445529* E-mail. *davide@cooperandturner.co.uk* Web. *www.cooperandturner.co.uk Coronet – Renlok – Renlok*

Co-Optimize Marketing Ltd 31 Fieldhead Drive Barwick In Elmet, Leeds LS15 4EE Tel. *0113 3935116* Fax. *0113 2678720* E-mail. *chris.allcoat@co-optimize.co.uk* Web. *www.co-optimize.co.uk Senator pens*

Copa Ltd Unit 6 Crest Industrial Estate Pattenden Lane, Marden, Tonbridge TN12 9QJ Tel. *01622 833914* Fax. *01622 831466* E-mail. *david.scale@copa.co.uk* Web. *www.copa.co.uk Copa – Copaclarifiers – Copasacs – CSO Screening – Filterbed Distributors – Rotating Biological Contractors (RBC) – SAF – Tank Scrapers*

Cope Engineering Ltd Sion Street Radcliffe, Manchester M26 3SF Tel. *0161 7236500* Fax. *0161 7236501* E-mail. *sales@cope-engineering.co.uk* Web. *www.cope-engineering.co.uk Cerl – Equatherm – Hyperform – Proklens – Prolite*

Copely Developments Ltd 54 Wenlock Way, Leicester LE4 9HU Tel. *0116 2765881* Fax. *0116 2460117* E-mail. *sales@copely.com* Web. *www.copely.com Aqvavend – Codeflat – Codeflex – Coplexel – Eurolon – Safestrip*

Coperion Ltd Victoria House 19-21 Ack Lane East, Bramhall, Stockport SK7 2BE Tel. *0161 9256910* Fax. *0161 9256911* E-mail. *info@coperion.com* Web. *www.coperion.com Buss Kneader (Switzerland) – Mixaco (Germany) – Scheer (Germany) – Waeschle (Germany) – Werner & Pfleiderer (Germany)*

Copiertec Ltd 3 Browells Lane, Feltham TW13 7EQ Tel. *020 88900900* Fax. *020 88900919* E-mail. *sales@copiertec.co.uk* Web. *www.copiertec.co.uk Kyocera – Rex Rotary – Ricoh – Samsung – Utax*

Copley Decor Ltd 1 Leyburn Business Park Harmby Road, Leyburn DL8 5QA Tel. *01969 623410* Fax. *01969 624398* E-mail. *info@copleydecor.co.uk* Web. *www.copleydecor.co.uk Copley Decor Mouldings – Dales Decor Ceiling Roses*

Coppard Plant Hire Ltd Wraysbury Crowborough Hill, Crowborough TN6 2JE Tel. *01892 662777* Fax. *01892 667094* E-mail. *sales@coppard.co.uk* Web. *www.coppard.co.uk Coppard – JCB*

Copper & Automotive Washer Co. Ltd Northgate Aldridge, Walsall WS9 8TW Tel. *01922 743951* Fax. *01922 743830* E-mail. *sales@copwash.co.uk* Web. *www.copwash.co.uk Caw – Cawflo – Cawfold*

Coppernob Portland House 4 Great Portland Street, London W1W 8QJ Tel. *020 74363600* Fax. *020 76373232* E-mail. *gifi@coppernob-fashion.com Coppernob*

Copycare Office Equipment Ltd 9 Dorset Road, Bournemouth BH4 9LB Tel. *01202 761111* Fax. *01202 766101* E-mail. *info@copycareoffice.co.uk* Web. *www.copycareoffice.co.uk Ricom – Infotec*

Copyrite Ltd Unit 15 Riverside Park Station Road, Wimborne BH21 1QU Tel. *01202 848866* Fax. *01202 849567* E-mail. *sales@copyrite.co.uk* Web. *www.copyrite.co.uk Nashuatec*

Coram Family 49 Mecklenburgh Square, London WC1N 2QA Tel. *020 75200300* Fax. *020 75200301* E-mail. *reception@coram.org.uk* Web. *www.coram.org.uk The Coram Family*

Coram Showers Ltd Unit 3 Stanmore Industrial Estate, Bridgnorth WV15 5HP Tel. *01746 766466* Fax. *01746 764140* E-mail. *sales@coram.co.uk* Web. *www.coram.co.uk Aqua – Bonus – Premier – Sealskin*

W Corbett & Co Galvanizing Ltd New Alexandra Works Haldane Halesfield 1, Telford TF7 4QQ Tel. *01952 412777* Fax. *01952 412888* E-mail. *mstatham@wcorbett.co.uk* Web. *www.wcorbett.co.uk Iron-Duke*

Corby Radio Services Ltd Dale Street, Corby NN17 2BQ Tel. *01536 401600* E-mail. *sales@corbyradioservices.com* Web. *www.corbyradioservices.com HYT – ICOM – TAIT – TEAM SIMOCO*

Cordek Ltd (Head Office) Unit 1-3 Spring Copse Business Park Stane Street, Slinfold, Horsham RH13 0SZ Tel. *01403 799600* Fax. *01403 791718* E-mail. *info@cordek.com* Web. *www.cordek.com Amopave – Cellcore – Cellform – Claymaster – Correx – Groudform – Propex – Scottlay – Seekure – Tipform – Ventform*

Cordings Ltd 19-20 Piccadilly, London W1J 0LA Tel. *020 77340830* Fax. *020 74942349* E-mail. *shop@cordings.co.uk* Web. *www.cordings.co.uk Cordings of Piccadilly – Original Cordings, The*

CORDS Duaflex Ltd Mayphil Industrial Estate Goatmill Road, Dowlais, Merthyr Tydfil CF48 3TF Tel. *01685 353240* Fax. *01685 353241* E-mail. *sales@mayphil.co.uk* Web. *www.mayphil.co.uk CORDS Duaflex*

Core 1 663 High Road Leytonstone, London E11 4RD Tel. *020 82799189* E-mail. *info@core1.co.uk* Web. *www.core1.co.uk Core1*

Corero Systems Ltd Mondas House 169 High Street, Rickmansworth WD3 1AY Tel. *01923 897333* Fax. *01923 897323* E-mail. *info@corero.com* Web. *www.corero.com Mondas*

Core Technical Solutions 169 St John's Hill, London SW11 1TQ Tel. *020 77382014* E-mail. *jw@coretechnicalsolutions.co.uk* Web. *www.coretechnicalsolutions.co.uk Appla Macintosh*

Core Technology Systems UK Ltd 1 Alie Street, London E1 8DE Tel. *020 76260516* Fax. *020 79533600* E-mail. *webenquiry@coregb.com* Web. *www.coregb.com Sharepoint – Workflow Analyser*

Cormans Mancor House Bolsover Street, Hucknall, Nottingham NG15 7TZ Tel. *0115 9632268* Fax. *0115 9632062 Corman – Gierre Life Limehaus Gibson*

Cormar Carpets (Cormar Carpets) Brookhouse Mill Holcombe Road, Greenmount, Bury BL8 4HR Tel. *01204 881234* Fax. *01706 827633* E-mail. *info@cormarcarpets.co.uk* Web. *www.cormarcarpets.co.uk 4 Star – 5 Star – Country Cable – Cumberland Premier – Cumberland Twist – Goodley Twist – Harvest – Heritage – Herringbone – Homely Loop – Homestyle – Lonsdale – Milano – Nova Star – Paramount – Seasons – Sunburst – Tentwist – Warwick*

Corndell Furniture Company Ltd 5 Windrush Park Road, Witney OX29 7DZ Tel. *01993 776545* Fax. *01993 774052* E-mail. *enquiries@corndell.co.uk* Web. *www.corndell.co.uk Corndell*

Cornerstone Trading Partners Ltd 26 Salmons Road Edmonton London, London N9 7JT Tel. *020 88070870* Fax. *020 88828995* E-mail. *info@cornerstonedesigns.co.uk* Web. *www.cornerstonedesigns.co.uk Cornerstone Trading Partners Ltd t/a Cornerstone D*

Corney & Barrow Ltd 1 Thomas More Street, London E1W 1YZ Tel. *020 72652400* Fax. *020 72652509* E-mail. *wine@corneyandbarrow.com* Web. *www.corneyandbarrow.com Corney & Barrow Ltd*

Cornish Crabbers LLP Pityme St Minver, Wadebridge PL27 6NT Tel. *01208 862666* Fax. *01208 862375* E-mail. *info@cornishcrabbers.co.uk* Web. *www.cornishcrabbers.co.uk *Coolcat (United Kingdom) – *Cornish Clam (United Kingdom) – *Cornish Coble (United Kingdom) – *Cornish Cormorant (United Kingdom) – *Cornish Crabber 17 (United Kingdom) – *Cornish Crabber 22 (United Kingdom) – *Cornish Crabber 24 (United Kingdom) – *Cornish Shrimper (United Kingdom) – *Pilot Cutter 30 (United Kingdom) – *Piper (United Kingdom)*

Corporate Insignia Ltd 1-5 Duncan Mcintosh Road Wardpark North, Cumbernauld, Glasgow G68 0HH Tel. *01236 738520* Fax. *01236 786149* E-mail. *sales@corporate-insignia.com* Web. *www.corporate-insignia.com C.I. Corporate Insignia – Colour Badging Systems*

J B Corrie & Co. Ltd Frenchmans Road, Petersfield GU32 3AP Tel. *01730 237100* Fax. *01730 264915* E-mail. *admin@jbcorrie.co.uk* Web. *www.jbcorrie.co.uk Corax – Corrie – Corrie Products – Corriewise – Corstag*

Corrugated Plastic Products Ltd 21 Hightown Industrial Estate Crow Arch Lane, Ringwood BH24 1ND Tel. *01425 470249* Fax. *01425 480090* E-mail. *sales@cppltd.com* Web. *www.cppltd.com Alpha File, Cyclopak – Alpha-File – Cyclopak – Hydroflute*

Corsair Engineering Ltd Beaumont Close, Banbury OX16 1SH Tel. *01295 267021* Fax. *01295 270396* E-mail. *sales@corsairengineering.co.uk* Web. *www.corsairengineering.co.uk Corsair – Hotlock Food Conveyors*

Corsehill Packaging Ltd Ailsa Road Irvine Industrial Estate, Irvine KA12 8NG Tel. *01294 275133* Fax. *01294 312300* E-mail. *sales@gmccorsehill.co.uk* Web. *www.gmccorsehill.co.uk Annefield Supplies (Gmc Corsehill Ltd)*

Corston Sinclair Ltd 36 Glenburn Road East Kilbride, Glasgow G74 5BA Tel. *01355 222273* Fax. *01355 263682* E-mail. *sales@corstonsinclair.com* Web. *www.corstonsinclair.com *Hillsider (China) – RFM (United Kingdom)*

Cortex Controllers Ltd Unit 2 The Mount Station Road, Longstanton, Cambridge CB24 3DS Tel. *01954 261435* Fax. *01223 462800* E-mail. *sales@cortexcontrollers.com* Web. *www.cortexcontrollers.com Eagle – Egrat – I.Q. Range – Swift*

Cortland Fibron B X Ltd Unit C R D Park Stephenson Close, Hoddesdon EN11 0BW Tel. *01992 471444* Fax. *01992 471555* E-mail. *nmcadam@cortlandfibron.co.uk* Web. *www.cortlandcompany.com Fibrocom – Fibrodata – Fibrodata – Fibroflex – Fibrohyd – Fibrolife – Fibroline – Fibropower – Fibroptic – Fibrorov – Fibrotow – Fibrovision – Fibroweld*

Corus Colndale Road Colnbrook, Slough SL3 0HL Tel. *01753 683131* Fax. *01753 684372* E-mail. *james.larner@corusgroup.com* Web. *www.corusgroup.com Galvatite – Synzintex – Ten Form – Zalutite*

Corus Walker Industrial Estate Walker Road, Guide, Blackburn BB1 2QE Tel. *01254 55161* Fax. *01254 677505* E-mail. *mike.forster@corusgroup.com* Web. *www.corusgroup.com Corus*

Corus Cogier Hebden Road, Scunthorpe DN15 8DT Tel. *01724 862131* Fax. *01724 295243* E-mail. *pat.marshall@coruscogifer.com* Web. *www.coruscogifer.com Grant Lyon Eagre*

Corus Engineering Steels PO Box 50, Rotherham S60 1DW Tel. *01709 371234* Fax. *01709 826233* E-mail. *christianname.surname@corusgroup.com* Web. *www.corus.com Durehete – Esshete – Jethete – Nimar – Red Fox – Silver Fox – Vanard – XlCut*

Corus U K Ltd Llanwern Works, Newport NP19 4QZ Tel. *01663 290011* Fax. *023 80233096* E-mail. *enquiries@cyrus-engineering.com* Web. *www.corus-servicecentres.com Aludip – Celestia – Colorcoat – Colorcoat Connection – Colorstelve – Confidex – Cor-Ten A – Durazec – Durbar – Galvalloy – Galvatite – HP200 – HPS200 – Hyclad – Lasersure – Ruralclad – Scintilla – Stelvetite – Surebuild – Tenform – Vesteel – Zintec*

Cory Logistics Ltd Room 8-13, Currie House Herbert Walker Avenue, Western Docks, Southampton SO15 1HJ Tel. *023 80227338* Fax. *023 80237479* E-mail. *corysoton@cory.co.uk* Web. *www.cory.co.uk Morrison Sale Purchase – Morrison Shipping – Morrison Tours*

Cosalt Kenmore 1 Liddell Street, North Shields NE30 1HE Tel. *0191 2596644* Fax. *0191 2586363* E-mail. *sales@cosalt.com* Web. *www.cosalt.com Cosalt Premier*

Cosmic Automotives Duke Street, Ipswich IP3 0AF Tel. *07906 967262* Fax. *01473 226263* Web. *www.kingavon.co.uk Clearview – Cosmic – Sideliner*

Cosmo Bingo Club 62 Market Street, Stalybridge SK15 2AB Tel. *0161 3385277* Fax. *0161 3039163 Cosmo Bingo & Social CLub – Metro Movie Centre Ltd – Palace Cinema (Stalybridge) Ltd – Slotworld Ltd*

Cosmopolitan Textile Company Ltd Commercial Street, Hyde SK14 2HP Tel. *0161 3671122* Fax. *0161 3671198* E-mail. *info@abcwax.co.uk* Web. *www.cosmopolitan-textiles.co.uk A.B.C. – Brunnschweiler*

Cost-A-Call Ltd De Montalt WD Summer Lane Combe Down, Bath BA2 7EU Tel. *01225 835799* Fax. *01225 835998* E-mail. *charles@kentel.co.uk* Web. *www.gophones.co.uk Kentel – Used Systems Exchange*

Costain Energy & Process Costain House Styal Road, Manchester M22 5WN Tel. *0161 9103444* Fax. *0161 9103399* E-mail. *info@costain.com* Web. *www.costain.com Costain – Costain Oil, Gas & Process Limited*

Cotels Management Ltd Simply Apartments 500 Avebury Boulevard, Milton Keynes MK9 2BE Tel. *01908 802853* Fax. *01908 802864* E-mail. *info@cotels.co.uk* Web. *www.cotels.co.uk Serviced apartments*

Cotesi UK Ltd Suite 7 Harley House Mill Fold, Sowerby Bridge HX6 4DJ Tel. *01422 821000* Fax. *01422 821007* E-mail. *enquiries@cotesi.co.uk* Web. *www.cotesi.co.uk Corfiplaste (Portugal) – Coriflon (Portugal) – Moreplene – Moreplon – Moreprop – Movline (Portugal) – Movlon (Portugal) – Movsplit (Portugal) – Movspun (Portugal) – Movstar (Portugal) – Redline (Portugal) – Seaflex (Portugal) – Vicrin (Portugal)*

Cotswold Architectural Products Manor Park Industrial Estate Manor Road, Swindon Village, Cheltenham GL51 9SQ Tel. *01242 233993* Fax. *01242 221146* E-mail. *info@cotswold-windows.co.uk* Web. *www.cotswold-windows.co.uk Cotswold*

The Cotswold Casements Cotswold Business Village London Road, Moreton In Marsh GL56 0JQ Tel. *01608 650568* Fax. *01608 651699* E-mail. *info@cotswold-casements.co.uk* Web. *www.cotswold-casements.co.uk Cotswold*

Cotswold Seeds Ltd Cotswold Business Village London Road, Moreton In Marsh GL56 0JQ Tel. *01608 652552* Fax. *01608 652256* E-mail. *info@cotswoldseeds.com* Web. *www.cotswoldseeds.com cotswold seeds ltd*

Cotswold Spring Water Dodington Spring Codrington, Chipping Sodbury, Bristol BS37 6RX Tel. *01454 312403* Fax. *01454 273378* E-mail. *sales@cotswold-spring.co.uk* Web. *www.cotswold-spring.co.uk *Cotswold Spring*

Cotswold Treatment P P Ltd Abadan House Gloucester Road, Thornbury, Bristol BS35 3TU Tel. *01454 417199* Fax. *01454 201252* E-mail. *sales@cotswoldtreatments.co.uk* Web. *www.cotswoldtreatments.co.uk Insiplas – Insitimb*

Cotswold Woollen Weavers Filkins, Lechlade GL7 3JJ Tel. *01367 860660* Fax. *01367 860661* E-mail. *info@naturalbest.co.uk* Web. *www.naturalbest.co.uk Cotswold Woollen Weavers*

Cottam & Preedy Ltd 68 Lower City Road Tividale, Oldbury B69 2HF Tel. *0121 5525281* Fax. *0121 5526895* E-mail. *enquiries@cottamandpreedy.co.uk* Web. *www.cottamandpreedy.co.uk Cottam & Preedy*

Coty UK Ltd St Georges House 5 St Georges Road, London SW19 4DR Tel. *020 89711300* Fax. *020 89714101* E-mail. *sales@coty.com* Web. *www.coty.com Adidas – Coty – Goya – Monsoon*

Coty UK Ltd Bradfield Road Eureka Science Park, Ashford TN25 4AQ Tel. *01233 625076* Fax. *01233 628974* E-mail. *gabrielle_gavin@cotyinc.com* Web. *www.coty.com Cutex – N.P.C. – Rimmel – Rimmel Silks – Sensiq – Sensiq Skin Care*

Coughtrie International Ltd Montrose Avenue Hillington, Glasgow G52 4LZ Tel. *0141 8104516* Fax. *0141 8820191* E-mail. *info@coughtrie.com* Web. *www.coughtrie.com Baltronic – Coughtrie – Emerlux – Entrico – Luxico – Optica – Sentrico – Ultralux*

Coulton Instrumentation Ltd Unit 17 Somerford Business Park Wilverley Road, Christchurch BH23 3RU Tel. *01202 480303* Fax. *01202 480808* E-mail. *admin@coulton.com* Web. *www.coulton.com Ettore Cella – Fuji Electric – Hakko – Solid Applied Technologies – Watson Smith*

Counterline 12 Randles Road Knowsley Business Park, Prescot L34 9HZ Tel. *0151 5482211* Fax. *0151 5466666* E-mail. *admin@counterline.co.uk* Web. *www.counterline.co.uk Counterline*

Countrywear Ltd 1b-1c Robinson Way Telford Way Industrial Estate, Kettering NN16 8PT Tel. *01536 481558* Fax. *01536 485218* E-mail. *info@countrywearuk.com* Web. *www.countrywearuk.com Country Wear*

County Construction Chemicals Ltd Unit 4 Chingford Industrial Centre Hall Lane, London E4 8DJ Tel. *020 85241931* Fax. *020 85290103* E-mail. *info@countyconchem.co.uk* Web. *www.countyconchem.co.uk Adshead Ratcliffe – Aquaseal – Arbo – Brutt Bars – Celltex – Colour Mastic – Colour Sealant – Colour Silicone – Coloured Mastic – Coloured Sealant – Coloured Silicone – Cox – Dow – Dow Corning – Feb MBT – Firetherm – Geocel – Hansil – Ladder Stops – Mapei – Modified Silane – Nullifire – Safeguard – Sika – Siroflex – Sovereign – Target Fixings – Vandex*

County Footware 2270 Kettering Parkway Kettering Venture Park, Kettering NN15 6XR Tel. *01536 527201* Fax. *01536 411085* E-mail. *mark.barron@pattersonmedical.com* Web. *www.countyfootwear.com County Orthopedic Footwear*

Court Catering Equipment Ltd Unit 1-2 Acton Vale Industrial Park Cowley Road, London W3 7XA Tel. *020 85766500* Fax. *020 87461116* E-mail. *info@courtcatering.co.uk* Web. *www.courtcatering.co.uk *Cinders – *Dawson – *Dualit – *E & R Moffat – *Falcon – *Foster – *Garland – *Gram – *Hobart – *IMC – *Instanta – *Lincat – *Merrychef – *Panasonic – *Rational – *Valentine – *Williams – *Winterhalter*

Courtenay Stewart Ltd 3 Hanover Square, London W1S 1HB Tel. *0871 2227616* Fax. *0871 2227626* E-mail. *sales@courtenayhr.com* Web. *www.courtenayhr.co.uk Courtenay*

Courtesy Shoes Ltd Park Road Industrial Estate, Bacup OL13 0BW Tel. *01706 874752* Fax. *01706 874827* E-mail. *brian@courtesy.co.uk* Web. *www.wynsors.com Medina – Wynsors World of Shoes*

Courtiers Investment Services Limited Hart Street, Henley On Thames RG9 2AU Tel. *01491 578368* Fax. *01491 572294* E-mail. *info@courtiers.co.uk* Web. *www.courtiers.co.uk Courtiers Financial Services*

Co-Var Ltd Ellenshaw Works Lockwood Street, Hull HU2 0HN Tel. *01482 328053* Fax. *01482 219266* E-mail. *info@coo-var.co.uk* Web. *www.coo-var.co.uk Coo-Var – Floorcote – Glocote – Hammercote – Suregrip – Teamac – Vandalene*

Covelward Ltd (t/a Road Runner Despatch) 19 South Street, Havant PO9 1BU Tel. *023 92492492* Fax. *023 92492493* E-mail. *rob@roadrunnerdispatch.co.uk* Web. *www.roadrunnerdispatch.co.uk Road Runner Dispatch*

Coventry Toolholders Ltd Unit 7 9 & 11 Paragon Way, Bayton Road Industrial Estate, Coventry CV7 9QS Tel. *024 76645999* Fax. *024 76644081* E-mail. *rgordon@coveng.co.uk* Web. *www.coveng.co.uk Centreline – Easy Change – Superac*

The Coverdale Organisation Ltd Westpoint 4 Redheughs Rigg, Edinburgh EH12 9DQ Tel. *0131 3386126* Fax. *0131 3386700* E-mail. *info@coverdale.co.uk* Web. *www.coverdale.com Coverdale*

Coverite Asphalters Ltd Palace Gates Bridge Road, London N22 7SP Tel. *020 88887821* Fax. *020 88890731* Web. *www.coverite.co.uk Coverite*

Cover Structure Blue Zone Newmarket Approach, Leeds LS9 0RJ Tel. *0113 2350088* Fax. *0113 2350333* E-mail. *info@coverstructure.com* Web. *www.coverstructure.com Cover-Structure*

Coversure Insurance Services Ltd (Reigate) 23 Croydon Road, Reigate RH2 0LY Tel. *0800 3081010* Fax. *08704 585746* E-mail. *markba@coversure.co.uk* Web. *www.coversure.co.uk Coversure Insurance Services*

Cover-Zone Unit E Easting Close, Worthing BN14 8HQ Tel. *01903 201555* Fax. *01903 201559* E-mail. *info@cover-zone.com* Web. *www.cover-zone.com Carrelli – cover-zone*

Cov Rad Heat Transfer Canley Works Sir Henry Parkes Road, Coventry CV5 6BN Tel. *024 76713316* Fax. *024 76713316*

E-mail. *bernard.ronchetti@covrad.co.uk*
Web. *www.covrad.co.uk Covrad Dravo – Covrad Heat Transfer*

Cowens Ltd Ellers Mill Dalston, Carlisle CA5 7QJ Tel. *01228 710205* Fax. *01228 710331* E-mail. *info@cowens.co.uk* Web. *www.cowens.co.uk Cowen Flowline – Cowenester – Oilsorb-Ultra – Orthoban – Orthoban - Orthopaedic Bandage, Oilsorb-Ultra - Oil Absorbents, Wetsorb - high capacity water soaking media. – PortPhoenix – River Phoenix – Sea Phoenix – Ultra-boom*

Cowie Technology Group Ltd Ridgeway Coulby Newham, Middlesbrough TS8 0TQ Tel. *01642 599190* Fax. *01642 596810* E-mail. *enquiries@cowie-tech.com* Web. *www.cowie-tech.com Cowie*

Cox Building Products Ltd Unit 1 Bilport Lane, Wednesbury WS10 0NT Tel. *0121 5304230* Fax. *01902 371810* E-mail. *sales@coxdome.co.uk* Web. *www.coxbp.com 2000 – Cox – Coxdomes – Coxspan – Mark5*

Cox Geo J Ltd 160 Alexandra Road, Wellingborough NN8 1EH Tel. *01933 224181* Fax. *01933 277892* E-mail. *steve@georgecox.co.uk* Web. *www.georgecox.co.uk George Cox – Swordfish*

Cox Wokingham Plastics Ltd Fishponds Road, Wokingham RG41 2QH Tel. *0118 9774861* Fax. *0118 9771708* E-mail. *sales@cwpl.net* Web. *www.cwpl.net Brownridge Plastics – Mouldspeed*

Cozens & Cole Ltd Spring Road Ettingshall, Wolverhampton WV4 6JT Tel. *01902 405971* Fax. *01902 497021* E-mail. *sales@cozensandcole.co.uk* Web. *www.cozensandcole.co.uk Colester – Colink – Coronet – H.A.C.*

C P A Ironworks Bradley Hall Bradley Hall Trading Estate Bradley Lane, Standish, Wigan WN6 0XQ Tel. *0800 0933548* Fax. *05602 048647* E-mail. *info@cpagates.co.uk* Web. *www.cpagates.co.uk BFT, – C.P.A 'combi' Gates – Videx*

C P Cases Ltd Unit 11 Worton Hall Industrial Estate Worton Road, Isleworth TW7 6ER Tel. *020 85681881* Fax. *020 85681141* E-mail. *info@cpcases.com* Web. *www.cpcases.com AluCurve – AluWeld – E-Rack – EMS – Hardigg – Hofbauer – Peli – ProBag – ProCase – ProRack*

C P C Packaging Oldmedow Road King's Lynn, Kings Lynn PE30 4LL Tel. *01553 761481* Fax. *01553 766203* E-mail. *max.eaton@cpcpackaging.co.uk* Web. *www.interglas-technologies.com Allen Davies – Berkshire Gravure – Slade Packaging*

CPC Packaging Ltd Knapp's Lane Fishponds Trading Estate, St. George, Bristol BS5 7UN Tel. *0117 9516751* Fax. *0117 9354038* E-mail. *info@groupecpc.co.uk* Web. *www.groupecpc.com Fixecure*

C P D Distribution Hillsborough Works Langsett Road, Sheffield S6 2LW Tel. *0114 2856300* Fax. *0114 2318031* E-mail. *marketing@cpdplc.co.uk* Web. *www.sigplc.co.uk Category Lighting – Pegasus Partitioning*

C P I William Clowes Ltd Copland Way Ellough, Beccles NR34 7TL Tel. *01502 712884* Fax. *01502 717003* E-mail. *thumphrey@cpibooks.co.uk* Web. *www.cpibooks.co.uk Wm Clowes*

C P Kelco Ltd Cleeve Court Cleeve Road, Leatherhead KT22 7UD Tel. *01372 369400* Fax. *01372 369401* E-mail. *malcolm.laws@cpkelco.com* Web. *www.cpkelco.com Genu – Genu Gum – Genugel – Genulacta – Genutine – Genuvisco – Kelco-Crete – Kelcogel – Keldent – Kelgum – Keltrol – Kelzan – Simplesse – Slendid – Xantural*

C P L Aromas Ltd Barrington Hall Dunmow Road, Hatfield Broad Oak, Bishops Stortford CM22 7LE Tel. *01279 717200* Fax. *01279 718527* E-mail. *chrissy.marshall@cplaromas.com* Web. *www.cplaromas.com Aroma Guard – C.P.L. Fragrances – Copol – D Visor – Rubout*

C P L Distribution Mill Lane Wingerworth, Chesterfield S42 6NG Tel. *01246 277001* Fax. *01246 212212* E-mail. *info@cpldistribution.co.uk* Web. *www.coals2u.co.uk Ancit – Cwm Coke – Homefire – Homefire Ovals – Phurnacite – Taybrite – Union Briketts*

C P M Moulds Solutions Ltd Pattison House Addison Road, Chesham HP5 2BD Tel. *01494 782131* Fax. *01494 778542* E-mail. *precision@chesham-moulds.co.uk* Web. *www.chesham-moulds.co.uk C P M*

C P V Ltd Woodington Mill East Wellow, Romsey SO51 6DQ Tel. *01794 322884* Fax. *01794 322885* E-mail. *sales@cpv.co.uk* Web. *www.cpv.co.uk Chemflo – CPV-Bulk – CPV-df – CPV-Safeflo – CPV-Zurn – Floway – Hiline – Polymatic – Proplene – Suncell*

C Q R Ltd 125 Pasture Road, Wirral CH46 4TH Tel. *0151 6061000* Fax. *0151 6061122* E-mail. *info@cqr.co.uk* Web. *www.cqr.co.uk C.Q.R. – Cequra – Maximal – Phoenix*

Crackdown Drug Testing Unit 11 Boarshurst Business Park Boarshurst Lane, Greenfield, Oldham OL3 7ER Tel. *01457 877988* Fax. *01457 877080* E-mail. *sales@crackdown-drugtesting.com* Web. *www.crackdown-drugtesting.com Armor Forensics – Crackdown*

Craftsman Tools Ltd Side Copse, Otley LS21 1JE Tel. *01943 466788* Fax. *01943 850144* E-mail. *sales@craftsmantools.com* Web. *www.craftsmantools.com Chevin – Crafticubes – Craftitools – Flexichuck – Flexiring*

Robert Craig & Sons Ltd Unit 10 Knock Moore Hill Industrial Estate Ferguson Drive, Lisburn BT28 2EX Tel. *028 92668500* Fax. *028 92668550* E-mail. *info@craigs-products.co.uk* Web. *www.craigs.ie Albany – Blakley – Bosch – Goulds – Grosvenor – Harben – Haverhill – Ingersol-Dresser – Jabsco – Neolith – Partner – Pearpoint – Triefus – Volvo – Walker Magnetic*

Craig & Rose Ltd Unit 8 Halbeath Industrial Estate, Dunfermline KY11 7EG Tel. *01383 740011* Fax. *01383 740010* E-mail. *customerservice@craigandrose.com* Web. *www.craigandrose.com 8888 – Alkaprufe – C. & R. – Caledonian – Claymore – Coatosol – Coatostone – Epicon – Eudec – Eudecryl – Forth Bridge – Imperval – Luxine – Metadure – Permadure – Permalux – Permastic – Rapid Metadure – Regal – Rosalac – Silverite – Superose – Undelac – Unipak*

Cralec Electrical Distributors Ltd Foots Cray High Street, Sidcup DA14 5HL Tel. *020 83000186* Fax. *020 83025859* E-mail. *quotes@cralec.com* Web. *www.cralec.com BILL – MEM*

Crane Business Services & Utilities Ltd (Divisional Head Office) Crane House Epsilon Terrace West Road, Ipswich IP3 9FJ Tel. *01473 277300* Fax. *01473 270301* E-mail. *enquiries@crane-ltd.co.uk* Web. *www.cranefs.com Crane – Crusader – Gem*

John Crane UK Ltd Buckingham House 361-366 Buckingham Avenue, Slough SL1 4LU Tel. *01753 224000* Fax. *01753 224153* E-mail. *libby.thompson@johncrane.co.uk* Web. *www.johncrane.co.uk Mechanical Seals*

Crane Process Flow Technology Ltd Grange Road, Cwmbran NP44 3XX Tel. *01633 486666* Fax. *01633 486777* E-mail. *technical.sales@craneflow.com* Web. *www.saundersvalves.com Center line (U.S.A.) – Depa (Germany) – Duo-Chek – ELRO (Germany) – Flowseal (U.S.A.) – Noz-Chek – Revo (Germany) – Saunders HC4 (United Kingdom) – SAUNDERS IDV*

Cranequip Ltd Cattell Road Cape Industrial Estate, Warwick CV34 4JN Tel. *01926 406900* Fax. *01926 406910* E-mail. *cranequip@uk.gantry.com* Web. *www.cranequip.com Gantrex – Gantrex – Molyneux – S.G.M. – S.G.M.*

Crane Stockham Valve Ltd Alexander Road, Belfast BT6 9HJ Tel. *028 90704222* Fax. *028 90401582* E-mail. *sales@cranebelfast.com* Web. *www.crane-energy.com Centerline – Duo-Chek – Duo-Chek/Flow Seal/Centerline/Noz-Chek – Flow Seal – Noz-Chek*

Craven & Co. Ltd Manse Lane, Knaresborough HG5 8ET Tel. *01423 796200* Fax. *01423 869189* E-mail. *sales@craven-solutions.com* Web. *www.craven-solutions.com Catercart – Craven Aluminium – Firmashelf – Medicare – Wheelameal*

Craven Dunnill & Co. Ltd Stourbridge Road, Bridgnorth WV15 6AS Tel. *01746 761611* Fax. *01746 767007* E-mail. *sales@cravendunnill.co.uk* Web. *www.cravendunnill.co.uk Renaissance – Tileshack*

Cravenmount Ltd Water Lane, Leighton Buzzard LU7 1FA Tel. *01525 378104* Fax. *01525 383630* E-mail. *sales@cravenmount.com* Web. *www.cravenmount.com *Hand in Glove (U.S.A.)*

Crawford Precision Engineering Ltd Unit 5 Cross Court Industrial Estate, Kettering NN16 9BN Tel. *01536 417140* Fax. *01536 524059* E-mail. *cpeng@globalnet.co.uk* Web. *www.crawfordprecision.co.uk Spiro Bearings*

C R Clarke & Co UK Ltd Unit 3 Betws Industrial Park, Ammanford SA18 2LS Tel. *01269 590530* Fax. *01269 590540* E-mail. *laurence@crclarke.co.uk* Web. *www.crclarke.com C R C – C R Clarke*

C R D Records Ltd Trelissa Farmhouse Philleigh Truro Cornwall Philleigh, Truro TR2 5NE Tel. *01872 580000* Fax. *01872 580002* E-mail. *info@crdrecords.com* Web. *www.crdrecords.com C.R.D.*

Creaseys Chartered Accountants 12-16 Lonsdale Gardens, Tunbridge Wells TN1 1PA Tel. *01892 546546* Fax. *01892 511232* E-mail. *partners@creaseys.co.uk* Web. *www.creaseys.co.uk Creaseys*

Creatif Leven Displays Ltd 27 Morelands Trading Estate Bristol Road, Gloucester GL1 5RZ Tel. *01452 417832* Fax. *01452 302811* E-mail. *sales@annequin.co.uk* Web. *www.creatifleven.co.uk Creatif*

Creative Art Products Ltd (t/a Scolaquip) 10 Dalton Way, Middlewich CW10 0HU Tel. *01606 836076* Fax. *01606 841727* E-mail. *orders@scolaquip.co.uk* Web. *www.scolaquip.co.uk Artform – Artstart – Chubbi-Stumps – Chublets – Chunki-Chalks – Multicrom – Plastix – Scolaquip – Scolart – Velvawax*

Creative Logistics Duncan Street, Salford M5 3SQ Tel. *0161 8737101* Fax. *0161 8721447* E-mail. *enquiries@creative-logistics.co.uk* Web. *www.creative-logistics.co.uk Duncan street enterprises*

Creative Web Mall UK 33, Banstead Road, Purley CR8 3EB Tel. *020 71937303* E-mail. *uk@creativewebmall.com* Web. *www.creativewebmall.co.uk Search Engine Optimization*

Credit Card Sentinel UK Ltd Sentinel House Airspeed Road, Portsmouth PO3 5RF Tel. *0800 414717* Fax. *023 92677450* Web. *www.sentinelgold.com Sentinel Card Services*

Crendon Timber Engineering Ltd (Gang-Nail Systems Ltd) Carr Wood Road, Castleford WF10 4PS Tel. *01977 554220* Fax. *01977 513017* E-mail. *sales@crendon.co.uk* Web. *www.crendon.co.uk Ecojoist*

Creoseal Ltd 7-11 Brook Street Sileby, Loughborough LE12 7RF Tel. *01509 812473* Fax. *01509 816970* E-mail. *sales@creoseal.co.uk* Web. *www.creoseal.co.uk Creoseal*

Crescent Lighting Ltd 8 Rivermead Pipers Lane, Thatcham RG19 4EP Tel. *01635 878888* Fax. *01635 873888* E-mail. *sales@crescent.co.uk* Web. *www.crescent.co.uk Agabekov – B'Light – Crescent*

Crewsaver Ltd Clarence Square Mumby Road, Gosport PO12 1AQ Tel. *023 92528621* Fax. *023 92510905* E-mail. *info@crewsaver.co.uk* Web. *www.crewsaver.co.uk Crewfit – Y.A.K.*

Criptic Arvis Ltd 16 Bridge Park Road Thurmaston, Leicester LE4 8BL Tel. *0116 2609700* Fax. *0116 2640147* E-mail. *sales@arvis.co.uk* Web. *www.arvis.co.uk Arvis – Croft – Exalign – Hunt*

M Criscuolo & Co. Ltd Crisco House 169 Godstone Road, Kenley CR8 5BL Tel. *020 86607949* Fax. *020 86685334* E-mail. *sales@crisco.co.uk* Web. *www.crisco.co.uk Crisco*

Cristel Paint Finishers Ltd Dunkirk Mills Dunkirk Street, Halifax HX1 3TB Tel. *01422 300580* Fax. *01422 349686* E-mail. *admin@cristelgraphics.co.uk* Web. *www.cristelpaintfinishers.co.uk Cristel – Cristel Graphics – Cristel Paint Finishers*

Cristie Software New Mill Chestnut Lane, Stroud GL5 3EH Tel. *01453 847000* Fax. *01453 847001* E-mail. *sales@cristie.com* Web. *www.cristie.com Power Tower – Powerchanger – TS 5000*

Criterion Ices Manor Farm Creamery Pakenham Road, Thurston, Bury St Edmunds IP31 3QJ Tel. *01359 230208* Fax. *01359 232838* E-mail. *enquiries@criterion-ices.co.uk* Web. *www.criterion-ices.co.uk Criterion – Myatts – Yodel*

Critical Environment Solutions Ltd (CES) Unit 2276 Dunbeath Road, Elgin Industrial Estate, Swindon SN2 8EA Tel. *01793 512505* Fax. *01793 541884* E-mail. *a.holbrook@cesltd.uk.com* Web. *www.cleanroomdirect.com CES*

Crittall Windows Ltd Unit 4 Francis House Freebournes Road, Witham CM8 3UN Tel. *01376 530800* Fax. *01376 530801* E-mail. *hq@crittall-windows.co.uk* Web. *www.crittall-windows.co.uk Clittall Composite – Corporate 2000 – Corporate W2O – Duralife – Homelight – Kiddicare*

Croboride Engineering Ltd Little Burton West, Burton On Trent DE14 1PP Tel. *01283 511188* Fax. *01283 530845* E-mail. *office@croboride.co.uk* Web. *www.croboride.co.uk Croboride*

Crockett & Jones Ltd Perry Street, Northampton NN1 4HN Tel. *01604 631515* Fax. *01604 230037* E-mail. *info@crockettandjones.com* Web. *www.crockettandjones.com Crockett & Jones*

Croco Worldwide Ltd 107 Power Road, London W4 5PY Tel. *020 87423636* Fax. *020 89951350* E-mail. *sales@crocoworldwide.com* Web. *www.crocoworldwide.com *Croco (Far East)*

Croda Chemicals Europe Ltd Oak Road, Hull HU6 7PH Tel. *01482 443181* Fax. *01482 341792* Web. *www.croda.com Crodacid – Crodaclear – Crodafat – Crodamide – Crodastat – Croderol – Crosterene – Syncroflex – Syncrolube*

Croda Europe Ltd Foundry Lane, Widnes WA8 8UB Tel. *0151 4233441* Fax. *0151 4233441* E-mail. *patrick.quinn@croda.com* Web. *www.croda.com Byco – Calfos – Coltide FP – Crodroit CS – Sodium Heptonate – Spa Gelatin*

Croda International plc Cowick Hall Snaith, Goole DN14 9AA Tel. *01405 860551* Fax. *01405 860205* E-mail. *enquiries@croda.com* Web. *www.croda.com Estasan – Esteram – Estol – Priadit – Pricerine – Prifac – Prifat – Prifrac – Priolene – Priolube – Priplast – Pripol – Prisavon – Prisorine – Pristerene – Supoweis – Unichema – Unislip/Uniwax*

Crofton Engineering Ltd Cambridge Road Linton, Cambridge CB21 4NN Tel. *01223 892138* Fax. *01223 893547* E-mail. *info@crofton-eng.co.uk* Web. *www.crofton-eng.co.uk Crofton Engineering*

Crofton House Associates Crofton House The Moor, Hawkhurst, Cranbrook TN18 4NN Tel. *01580 752919* Fax. *01580 754173* E-mail. *jim@crofton-house.co.uk* Web. *www.crofton-house.co.uk Gregomatic Cleaning Machines (Switzerland) – Saturno Steam Vapour Systems (Italy) – Westech*

Croft & Assinder Ltd 95 Lombard Street, Birmingham B12 0QU Tel. *0121 6221074* Fax. *0121 6225718* E-mail. *general@crofts.co.uk* Web. *www.crofts.co.uk Crofts and Assinder*

Crohn's & Colitis UK 4 Beaumont House Beaumont Works Sutton Road, St Albans AL1 5HH Tel. *01727 830038* Fax. *01727 862550* E-mail. *enquiries@crohnsandcolitis.org.uk* Web. *www.crohnsandcolitis.org.uk N.A.C.C.*

Cromac Smith Ltd 34-40 Warwick Road, Kenilworth CV8 1HE Tel. *01926 865800* Fax. *01926 865808* E-mail. *albatros@cromacsmith.com* Web. *www.cromacsmith.com Albatrose Sea-Air Service – S.A.T. Sea-Air Transport*

Cromer Crab Company 33 Holt Road, Cromer NR27 9EB Tel. *01263 519800* Fax. *01263 514496* Web. *www.theseafoodcompany.co.uk Cromer Crab Co., The*

Cromwell Group Holdings 65 Chartwell Drive, Wigston LE18 2FS Tel. *0116 2888000* Fax. *0116 2885050* E-mail. *hq@cromwell-tools.co.uk* Web. *www.apexindustrial.co.uk Arno – I.B. System – Indexa*

Cronapress Ltd Parkside Works Otley Road, Guiseley, Leeds LS20 8BH Tel. *01943 876600* Fax. *01943 870088* E-mail. *sales@cronapress.co.uk* Web. *www.cronapress.co.uk Cronapress*

Croner Reward Reward House Diamond Way, Stone Business Park, Stone ST15 0SD Tel. *01785 813566* Fax. *01785 817007* E-mail. *enquiries@wolterskluwer.co.uk* Web. *www.croner-reward.co.uk Croner Reward*

James Cropper plc Burneside Mills Burneside, Kendal LA9 6PZ Tel. *01539 722002* Fax. *01539 818239* E-mail. *info@cropper.com* Web. *www.cropper.com Elation – Kendal Cover – Kendal Manilla – Kendal Pressboard – Lorenzo – Mirage – Palazzo – Siena – Sprint*

Crosbie Casco Coating Wood Lane Partington, Manchester M31 4BT Tel. *0161 7753025* Fax. *0161 7779076* E-mail. *sales@crosbie-casco.co.uk* Web. *www.crosbie-casco.co.uk Viternus*

Crosland Cutters Ltd Nimmings Road, Halesowen B62 9JE Tel. *0121 5597915* Fax. *0121 5613064* E-mail. *sales@croslandcuttersltd.co.uk* Web. *www.croslandcutterslтd.co.uk CC*

Crosland Laser Guarding Ltd 4 Lyons Road Trafford Park, Manchester M17 1RN Tel. *0161 8778668* Fax. *0161 8765234* E-mail. *sales@croslandvk.com* Web. *www.croslandvk.com Avoplaten – Crosland – Crosland Platen*

Crosscheck Systems Ltd Office 29 Greenbox Weston Hall Road, Stoke Prior, Bromsgrove B60 4AL Tel. *01527 839010* Fax. *01527 839011* E-mail. *sales@x-check.co.uk* Web. *www.x-check.co.uk Scan-Care – VeriBox*

Cross Electrical Nottingham Ltd Trace Works Debdale Lane, Keyworth, Nottingham NG12 5HN Tel. *0115 9375121* Fax. *0115 9375116* E-mail. *david.rogers@cross-electrical.co.uk* Web. *www.cross-electrical.co.uk Teflon PFA*

John R Crossland Construction Ltd 18-20 New Road Tintwistle, Glossop SK13 1JN Tel. *01457 868642* Fax. *01457 862161* E-mail. *enquiries@crossties.co.uk* Web. *www.connectfree.co.uk Cross-Ties*

Crosslee plc Lightcliffe Factory Hipperholme, Halifax HX3 8DE Tel. *01422 203555* Fax. *01422 206304* E-mail. *general@crosslee.co.uk* Web. *www.crosslee.co.uk Hostess – Odell – Royal Cozyfires – White Knight – White Knight – White knight*

Crossley & Davis The Coach House 7 Mill Road, Sturry, Canterbury CT2 0AJ Tel. *01227 712714* Fax. *01227 712721* E-mail. *finance@crossleydavis.com* Web. *www.crossleydavis.com Crossley & Davis*

M & T Crossley Tordoff Jubilee Way, Pontefract WF8 1DH Tel. *01977 702002* Fax. *01977 600002* E-mail. *info@ctski.co.uk* Web. *www.ctski.co.uk Strika*

Cross & Morse Shady Lane Great Barr, Birmingham B44 9EU Tel. *0121 3600155* Fax. *0121 3251079* E-mail. *sales@crossmorse.com* Web. *www.crossmorse.com Avante – Cross – Crossbore (United Kingdom) – Crossgard (Japan) – Duo-Cam (United Kingdom) – Morflex (U.S.A.) – Morse (United Kingdom) – Safegard – Sealmaster (U.S.A.) – Sheargard (United Kingdom)*

T D Cross Ltd Shady Lane Great Barr, Birmingham B44 9EU Tel. *0121 3600155* Fax. *0121 3251079* E-mail. *accounts@cross-morse.co.uk* Web. *www.crossmorse.com Cross and morse*

Crouzet Ltd 8 Crockford Lane Chineham Business Park, Chineham, Basingstoke RG24 8WD Tel. *01256 318900* Fax. *01256 318901* E-mail. *info@crouzet.co.uk* Web. *www.crouzet.com Automation control manufrs – Crouzet*

Crowcon Detection Instrument Ltd Unit 2 2-6 Blacklands Way, Abingdon OX14 1DY Tel. *01235 557700* Fax. *01235 553062* E-mail. *sales@crowcon.com* Web. *www.crowcon.com Cellarsafe – Checkbox – Cirrus – Detective + – Ditech Range – Eikon – Flamgard Plus – Gas Tec – Gaseeker – Gasflag – Gasman – Gasmaster – Gasmonitor Plus – Laser Methane – Nimbus – Sprint – Spygas – TCgard – Tetra – Tetra 3 – Triple Plus + – TXgard Plus – TXgard-IS+ – Vortex – Xgard*

Crown Catering Equipment Ltd 41 Manasty Road Orton Southgate, Peterborough PE2 6UP Tel. *01733 231666* Fax. *01733 231636* E-mail. *sales@crowncateringequipment.co.uk* Web. *www.crowncateringequipment.co.uk *Blue Seal – *Classic – *Falcon – *Fosters – *Lincat – Parry*

Crown Computing Ltd Tamworth Business Park Amber Close Amington, Tamworth B77 4RP Tel. *01827 309800* Fax. *01827 309810* E-mail. *sales@crowncomputing.co.uk* Web. *www.crowncomputing.co.uk D.C. Connect – D.C. Flex – Factory Monitoring & Control – Open Options*

Crown Lift Trucks Ltd Stirling Road South Marston Industrial Estate, Swindon SN3 4TS Tel. *08458 509270* Fax. *01925 425656* Web. *www.crown.com Hamech – Mitsubishi*

Crown Memorials Ltd Hamilton House 39 Kings Road, Haslemere GU27 2QA Tel. *01428 641941* Fax. *01428 641881* E-mail. *info@crownmemorials.co.uk* Web. *www.crownmemorials.co.uk Crown Memorials*

Crown Packaging Downsview Road, Wantage OX12 9BP Tel. *01235 772929* Fax. *01905 762357* E-mail. *jenny@crowncork.com* Web. *www.crowncork.com Caranaudmetalbox – Crown Cork and Seal Inc*

Crown Speciality Packaging Edgefield Avenue Fawdon, Newcastle upon Tyne NE3 3TS Tel. *0191 2858168* Fax. *0191 2847570* E-mail. *kevin.hall@eur.crowncork.com* Web. *www.eur.crowncork.com Tyneside Printers*

Crowson Fabrics Limited Crowson House Bellbrook Park, Uckfield TN22 1QZ Tel. *01825 761044* Fax. *01825 764283* E-mail. *sales@crowsonfabrics.com* Web. *www.crowsonfabrics.com Crowguard*

J Crowther Royton Ltd (t/a Crowther Marine) Eden Works Belgrave Mill Honeywell Lane, Oldham OL8 2JP Tel. *0161 6524234* Fax. *0161 6274265* E-mail. *crowther.marine@tiscali.co.uk* Web. *www.crowthermarine.co.uk Crowther Marine – Tonks Book Case Strip*

Croylek Ltd 23 Ullswater Crescent, Coulsdon CR5 2UY Tel. *020 86681481* Fax. *020 87630750* E-mail. *sales@croylek.co.uk* Web. *www.croylek.co.uk Periflex (Spain) – *Revitex (Spain)*

Cryoservice Ltd Prescott Drive, Worcester WR4 9RH Tel. *01905 758200* Fax. *01905 754060* E-mail. *info@cryoservice.co.uk* Web. *www.cryoservice.co.uk Carbostore – Cryosafe – Cryosafe, Cryospec, Dial-a-flow, Fix-a-Flow, Ultracert - gas mixtures with UKAS certification – Dial-A-Flow – Fix-a-Flow – Photogen*

Cryotherm Insulation Ltd Hirst Wood Road, Shipley BD18 4BU Tel. *01274 589175* Fax. *01274 593315* E-mail. *enquiries@cryotherm.co.uk* Web. *www.cryotherm.co.uk Cryoclad – Cryosil – Cryostop – Fireplank – Rockliner – Spiralite*

Crypton Ltd Hopton Road Hopton Park Industrial Estate, Devizes SN10 2EU Tel. *01278 436205* Fax. *01278 450567* E-mail. *sales@cryptontechnology.com* Web. *www.cryptontechnology.com Act – Cadet – Checkmate – Cmt – Codes – Comet – Crypton – Cudos – Handy Scan*

Crystal Palace FC Selhurst Park Stadium Holmesdale Road, London SE25 6PU Tel. *020 87686000* Fax. *020 87686106* E-mail. *info@cpfc.co.uk* Web. *www.cpfc.co.uk Crystal Palace FC*

Crystal Structures Ltd Crystal Park 50 Tunbridge Lane, Bottisham, Cambridge CB25 9EA Tel. *01223 811451* Fax. *01223 11451* E-mail. *info@crystalstructures.com* Web. *www.crystalstructures.com Wooster*

C S A Cleaning Equipment Broad Lane Cottenham, Cambridge CB24 8SW Tel. *01954 251573* Fax. *01954 206506* E-mail. *sales@csacleaningstore.co.uk* Web. *www.csacleaningstore.co.uk ALTO – *Butchers (U.S.A.) – C S A – CE – *Centret (Netherlands) – *Clarke (U.S.A.) – *Durasystems (U.S.A.) – Eagle – *KEW (Denmark) – Numatic – Prochem*

C-Scope International Ltd Kingsnorth Technology Estate Wotton Road, Ashford TN23 6LN Tel. *01233 629181* Fax. *01233 645897* E-mail. *info@cscope.co.uk* Web. *www.cscope.co.uk C-Scope – Uscan*

C S M UK Ltd Stadium Road, Wirral CH62 3NU Tel. *0151 3431600* Fax. *0151 3461334* E-mail. *orders@bakemark.co.uk* Web. *www.arkady-craigmillar.co.uk Arkady – Bon Vivant – Caravan Brill – Craigmillar – Diamond – Fix – Forepaste – Pearl – Platinum – Readi-Bake – Sapphire – Satin*

C T C National Cyclists Organisation Parklands Railton Road, Guildford GU2 9JX Tel. *08447 368450* Fax. *01483 426994* E-mail. *kevin.mayne@ctc.org.uk* Web. *www.ctc.org.uk Cyclists Touring Club*

C-Tec Security Ltd Challenge Way Martland Mill Industrial Estate, Wigan WN5 0LD Tel. *01942 322744* Fax. *01942 829867* E-mail. *info@c-tec.co.uk* Web. *www.c-tec.co.uk 800 Series – AFP – Avac – C-call – CFP – CFP Alarmsense – EFP – EP203 – FP – Hush Button – MFP – ML1/K1 – NC951 – PDA – PDA Range – PDA102 – PDA200E – PL1/K1 – Quantec – Quantec Surveyor – Sigtel – XFP*

C T L Components plc Falcon House 19 Deer Park Road, London SW19 3UX Tel. *020 85458700* Fax. *020 85400034* E-mail. *info@ctl-components.com* Web. *www.ctl-components.com C-Shrink (United Kingdom) – Clearcast (United Kingdom)*

C T P Wipac Ltd London Road, Buckingham MK18 1BH Tel. *01280 822800* Fax. *01280 822802* E-mail. *info@wipac.com* Web. *www.wipac.com Dayco – FAE – Purolator – Quadoptic – RX 400D2 – Super Blades*

C T S Corporation Block 6 Fourth Road Blantyre, Glasgow G72 0XA Tel. *01698 505050* Fax. *01698 506050* E-mail. *allan.white@ctscorp.com* Web. *www.ctscorp.com C.T.S. Corporation UK Ltd*

Cube Epos Ltd 2 Montpelier Central Station Road, Montpelier, Bristol BS6 5EE Tel. *0117 9705000* Fax. *0117 9705050* E-mail. *jeff@qube-epos.co.uk* Web. *www.bcgcomputers.co.uk Uniwell*

Cubicle Centre Caldervale Mills 33 Huddersfield Road, Dewsbury WF13 3JL Tel. *08451 701240* Fax. *01924 437600* E-mail. *sales@plumbware.co.uk* Web. *www.plumbware.co.uk Brecon cubicle – Cairngorm cubicles – Grampian cubicles – Malvern cubicles – Pennine cubicles*

Cullen Metcalfe & Co. Ltd Southmill Road, Bishops Stortford CM23 3DH Tel. *01279 505533* Fax. *01279 504697* E-mail. *sales@cullenmetcalfe.com* Web. *www.cullenmetcalfe.com Drizit – Dry-Cargo – Dry-Cargo, Drizit, Hatch Tape. – Hatch Tape*

Culpitt Ltd Jubilee Industrial Estate, Ashington NE63 8UQ Tel. *01670 814545* Fax. *01670 815248* E-mail. *info@culpitt.com* Web. *www.culpitt.com Culpitt*

Cumberland Cathodic Protection 4 Strand View Liverpool Intermodal Freeport Terminal, Bootle L20 1HA Tel. *0151 9223041* Fax. *0151 9224605* E-mail. *sales@cumberlandcp.com* Web. *www.cumberlandcp.com Coralite – Cumberland – Platinite*

Cumberland Europe Ltd Daniels Industrial Estate 104 Bath Road, Stroud GL5 3TJ Tel. *01453 768980* Fax. *01453 768990* E-mail. *europeansales@cumberland-plastics.com* Web. *www.cumberland-plastics.com Cumberland Europe Ltd*

Cumberland Pencil Museum Southey Works Main Street, Keswick CA12 5NG Tel. *01768 773626* Fax. *01768 774679* E-mail. *museum@acco-uk.co.uk* Web. *www.pencils.co.uk Blackedge – British Drawing – Derwent – Five Star – Lakeland*

Cumbria Limoscene 17 Punton Road, Carlisle CA3 9BB Tel. *01228 537058* E-mail. *enquiries@cumbrialimoscene.co.uk* Web. *www.cumbrialimoscene.co.uk Cumbria Limoscene*

Cumbrian Goat Experience Woodhow Farm Wasdale, Seascale CA20 1ET Tel. *01946 726246* E-mail. *info@cumbrian-goat-experience.co.uk* Web. *www.cumbrian-goat-experience.co.uk Cumbrian Goat Experience*

Cummins Power Generation Ltd Manston Park Columbus Avenue, Manston, Ramsgate CT12 5BF Tel. *01843 255000* Fax. *01843 255902* Web. *www.cumminstower.com Generator set manufrs – Powercommand*

Cummins Turbo Technologies Ltd St Andrews Road, Huddersfield HD1 6RA Tel. *01484 422244* Fax. *01484 511680* E-mail. *gillian.murray@cummins.com* Web. *www.cummins.com/turbos Holset*

Robert Cupitt Ltd Joplin Court Crownhill, Milton Keynes MK8 0JP Tel. *01908 563063* Fax. *01908 562910* E-mail. *sales@robertcupitt.co.uk* Web. *www.robertcupitt.co.uk Airheart (U.S.A.) – Distributors for: Tol-O-Matic Inc.,(USA); Hayes Brake LLC.,(USA); Zero-Max Inc.,(USA) – Hayes Brake LLC (U.S.A.) – Tol-O-Matic (U.S.A.) – Zero-Max (U.S.A.)*

Curtis Holt Southampton Ltd Westwood Business Park Nutwood Way, Totton, Southampton SO40 3WW Tel. *023 80861991* Fax. *023 80664555* E-mail. *sales@tallbank.com* Web. *www.tallbank.com Toolbank*

Curtis & Co Oundle Ltd 22 West Street Oundle, Peterborough PE8 4EG Tel. *01832 273515* Fax. *01832 275490* E-mail. *martinleecurtis@btopenworld.com *Bibby Feeds – *Trident Feeds*

Custom Accessories Europe Ltd Unit 10 Minton Distribution Park London Road, Amesbury, Salisbury SP4 7RT Tel. *01980 676400* Fax. *01980 676401* E-mail. *sales@caeurope.co.uk* Web. *www.caeurope.co.uk *Custom Accessories (USA and Asia) – Divers – Gripper*

Custom Brakes & Hydraulics Ltd Prospect House City Road, Sheffield S2 5HH Tel. *0114 2767971* Fax. *0114 2723538* E-mail. *sales@custombrakes.co.uk* Web. *www.custombrakes.co.uk Benford – CancerBoss – CAT – Caterpillar – Clarke – Daewoo – Fantuzzi – Ferodo – JCB – Kalmar – Kessler – Komatsu – Mintex – Nissan – Sanderson – Terex – Thwaites – Twiflex – Volvo*

Custom Chrome Ltd Lomond House Weddington Terrace, Nuneaton CV10 0AG Tel. *024 76387808* Fax. *024 76341660* E-mail. *nigel@custom-chrome.co.uk* Web. *www.customchromeracing.co.uk Cherry Bomb*

Custom Composites Ltd Ensor Mill Queensway, Rochdale OL11 2NU Tel. *01706 526255* Fax. *01706 350187* E-mail. *mail@customcom.co.uk* Web. *www.customcom.co.uk Lectraglas – Lectraglas, Unilam – Unilam*

Custom Control Sensors International Apollo House Calleva Park, Aldermaston, Reading RG7 8TN Tel. *0118 9820702* Fax. *0118 9821825* E-mail. *pswitch@ccsdualsnap.co.uk* Web. *www.ccsdualsnap.com CCS – Dual-Snap (U.S.A.)*

Custom Foams Ltd a division of Kay-Metzeler Ltd 2-17 Deans Road Old Wolverton, Milton Keynes MK12 5NA Tel. *01908 312331* Fax. *01908 220715* E-mail. *vivien.gebbie@vcfuk.com*

Web. *www.customfoams.co.uk Basotect - Basotect - Malamine FoamNovada - Polyurethane foam – Novada*

Custom Hose & Fitting Ltd 194 Queens Road, Watford WD17 2NT Tel. *01923 225534* Fax. *01923 818714* E-mail. *enquiries@customhose.co.uk* Web. *www.customhose.co.uk Custom Hose & Fittings*

Custom Transformers Ltd Unit 23 Whitewalls, Easton Grey, Malmesbury SN16 0RD Tel. *01666 824411* Fax. *01666 824413* E-mail. *kevin.baldwin@custom-transformers.co.uk* Web. *www.custom-transformers.co.uk Custom Transformers*

CUT 8 Smart repairs 85 Mooresfield, Houghton Le Spring DH4 5PG Tel. *0191 5801888* E-mail. *info@cut8.co.uk* Web. *www.cut8.co.uk CUT 8*

Cutlass Fasteners Ltd Penny Lane Old Boston Trading Estate, Haydock, St Helens WA11 9ST Tel. *01942 712387* Fax. *01942 722306* E-mail. *higton@cutlassfst.aol.com* Web. *www.cutlass-studwelding.com Clipper – Cobra – Commander*

Cutwel Ltd Central Offices Central Street, Dewsbury WF13 2LZ Tel. *01924 869610* Fax. *01924 869611* E-mail. *sales@cutwel.net* Web. *www.cutweltools.co.uk KORLOY*

Cuxson Gerrard & Company Ltd 125 Broadwell Road, Oldbury B69 4BF Tel. *0121 5447117* Fax. *0121 5448616* E-mail. *info@cuxsongerrard.com* Web. *www.cuxsongerrard.com Adaptoplast – Carnation – Carnation Professional Paddings – Chirofix – Chiroform Gel With Mineral Oil – Hapla – Protex – Zopla*

C V C Chelmer Valve Co. Ltd Scatterbrook Farm Rectory Lane, Latchingdon, Chelmsford CM3 6HB Tel. *01621 745450* Fax. *01245 241309* E-mail. *sales@chelmervalve.com* Web. *www.chelmervalve.com Chelmer Valve*

Cyberlux 4 Red Brick Cottages Rhode Common, Selling, Faversham ME13 9PU Tel. *01227 752406* Fax. *01227 752406* E-mail. *spike@thelightingworkshop.co.uk Rankin McGregor Ltd*

Cyclops Electronics Ltd Link Business Park Osbaldwick Link Road, York YO10 3JB Tel. *01904 415415* Fax. *01904 424424* E-mail. *sales@cyclops-electronics.com* Web. *www.cyclops-electronics.com 3M – Aavid Thermalloy – Actel – Aerovox – Agilent – Airpax – Alliance – Alpha – Altera – AMD – Amphenol – Analog Devices – Aromat – Artesyn – Astec – AT&T – Atmel – Augat – AVX – BC Components – Belden – Belfuse – Belling Lee – Benchmarq – Bendix – Beyschlag – BHC Aerovox – BI Technologies – BLP Components – Bourns – Brooktree – Bulgin – Burgess – Bussmann – C & K Switches – Cal-Chip – Catalyst – Central Semi – Cherry Semi – Chicago Miniature – Chips & Tech – Cinch – Cirrus Logic – Citizen – Coilcraft – Coiltronics – Conexant – CP Clare – Crydom – Crystal Semi – Cypress – Dallas – Datel – Deutsch – Dialight – Diodes Inc. – Diotec – Eaton – Elco – Epcos – Epson – Ericsson – Etri – Everlight – Evox Rifa – Exar – Exel – Fagor – Fairchild – FCI Framatone – Finder – Fujitsu – Glenair – Grayhill – Hamlin – Harting – Hewlett-Packard – Hirose – Hitachi – Honeywell – Hughes – Hynix – ICT – IDT – IMO – Infineon – Intel – International Rectifier – Intersil – Isocom – ISSI – ITT Cannon – ITW – IXYS – Jamicon – Johanson – JST – Kemet – Kingbright – Knitter – KOA – Lattice – Lemo – Lg Semicon – Linear Technology – Linfinity – Lite-on – Littlefuse – Lsi Logic – Lucent – Lumex – M/A Com – Macronix – Matsuo – Matsushita – Maxim – Meggitt – Methode – Micrel – Microchip – Micronas – Microsemi – Mini-circuits – Mitel – Mitsubishi – Molex – Motorola – Murata – National Semiconductor – NDK – Nec – Nic – Nichicon – Nippon Chemi-con – Novacap Inc – Ohmite – OKI – Omron – Optek – Osram – Panasonic – Panduit – Papst – Performance Semi – Pericom Semiconductor – Philips – Phoenix contact – Phycomp – Piher – Plessey – Potter & Brumfield – Power Innovations – Preci-Dip – Pulse – QTC – Quality Semiconductor – Quality Tech – Radiall – Raychem – Raytheon – Rectron – Redpoint – Renesas – Robinson Nugent – Rockwell – Rohm – Rubycon – Samsung – samtec – Samwha – Sanken – Sanyo – Schaffner – Schurter – Seiko – Semikron – Sharp – Shindengen – Siemens – Siliconix – Sipex – SMC Electronics – Sony – Sprague – ST Microelectronics – Stanley – STM – Supertex – Switchcraft Inc – Syfer Technology – Symbois Logic – Tag Semi – Takamisawa – TDK – Teccor – Telcom Semi – Teledyne – Telefunken – Texas Instruments – Thermalloy – Thermoalloy – Thomas & Betts – Three-five systems – Toko – Toshiba – TRW – Tyco – Umc – United Chemi-con – Unitrode – Vantis – Varitronix – VCH – Via Technologies – Vishay – Vitelec – Vlsi – Waferscale – Welwyn – Western Digital – Wima – Winbond – Xicor – Xilinx – Yageo – Yamaha – Yamaichi – Yuasa – Zetex – Zettler – Zilog – ZMD*

Cytec Engineered Materials Ltd Abenbury Way Wrexham Industrial Estate, Wrexham LL13 9UZ Tel. *01978 665200* Fax. *01978 665222* E-mail. *info@cytec.com* Web. *www.cytec.com AVIMID – BR – COM – CYFORM – DECLAR – FM – Karbon – PRIFORM – SURFACE MASTER*

D

D42 Thermal Ltd 46 Cavendish Street Arnold, Nottingham NG5 7DL Tel. *07581 218299* E-mail. *csmith@dept-42.co.uk* Web. *www.d42thermal.co.uk Thermal Shield*

Daas Organic Beer 35 Brompton Rd Knightsbridge, London SW3 1DE Tel. *020 32865958* E-mail. *enquires@daasbeer.com* Web. *www.daasbeer.com Daas Organic Beer*

Dacrylate Paints Ltd Lime Street Kirkby-In-Ashfield, Nottingham NG17 8AL Tel. *01623 753845* Fax. *01623 757151* E-mail. *sales@dacrylate.co.uk* Web. *www.dacrylate.co.uk Acrylacote – Alkysil – Dac Varnish – Dac-Crete – Dac-Pol 9 – Dac-Pol V.8 – Dac-Roc Smooth – Dacsil – Marclean – Margard – Margard W.B. – Nordac – Vinadac*

D A D UK Unit 12-15 Wotton Trading Estate, Ashford TN23 6LL Tel. *01233 630406* Fax. *01233 630708* E-mail. *info@dadgroup.co.uk* Web. *www.dadgroup.co.uk Decayeux*

Daiglen 27 Stirling Street, Tillicoultry FK13 6EA Tel. *01259 750440* Fax. *01259 752212* E-mail. *daiglen@macall.co.uk* Web. *www.mccalls.co.uk Daiglen of Scotland*

Dainippon Screen UK Ltd Michigan Drive Tongwell, Milton Keynes MK15 8HT Tel. *01908 848500* Fax. *01908 848501* E-mail. *forsdike@screen.co.uk* Web. *www.screeneurope.com *Screen (Japan)*

Dairy Produce Packers Ltd Millburn Road, Coleraine BT52 1QZ Tel. *028 70325500* Fax. *028 70356412* E-mail. *garnette.faulkner@kerry.ie* Web. *www.kerrygroup.com Black Diamond – Coleraine*

Daisy D West Mains Gleneagles, Auchterarder PH3 1PJ Tel. *01764 682202* Fax. *01764 682202* E-mail. *daisyd@farmersweekly.net* Web. *www.daisyd.co.uk Daisy D*

Daiwa Sports Ltd Netherton Industrial Estate, Wishaw ML2 0EY Tel. *01698 355723* Fax. *01698 372505* E-mail. *info@daiwasports.co.uk* Web. *www.daiwasports.co.uk Alltmor – Connoisseur – Cruiser – Crusader – Daiwa Specialist – Emblem – Flipper – Harrier – Infinity – Interline – Jupiter – Moonraker – Osprey – Powerlift – Powermesh – Pro Pike – Pro Specialist – Pro-Carp – Regal – Samurai – Sealine – Sensor – Slidewinder – Strikeforce – Super Shinobi – Supercast – Supersensor – Surfcast – Team Daiwa – Tornado – Tournament – Tri Force – Trio – Trumf – Vulcan – Zoom-Whip*

Dakat Ltd Maple Cottage Beaver Lane, Yateley GU46 6XJ Tel. *01252 872256* Fax. *01252 872256* E-mail. *gellicott@yahoo.com* Web. *www.dakat.co.uk Pulsar Instruments*

Dalau Ltd Ford Road, Clacton On Sea CO15 3DZ Tel. *01255 220220* Fax. *01255 221122* E-mail. *sales@dalau.com* Web. *www.dalau.com Dalau – Dalcon PTFE*

Dalco International Ltd 166 Commercial Road, London E1 2JY Tel. *020 77909319* Fax. *020 77913174* E-mail. *dalcoltd@aol.com *Stamp (Europe and Asia)*

Alan Dale Pumps Ltd 75 Clockhouse Lane, Ashford TW15 2HA Tel. *01784 421114* Fax. *01784 421092* E-mail. *info@alandalepumps.wanadoo.co.uk* Web. *www.alandalepumps.co.uk Alan Dale Pumps – Casuma Pumps – Distrimex Pumps – Judo Water Filters – Pratissoli Pumps – Wepuko Hydraulic Pumps*

Dale Lifting and Handling Equipment Specialists 2 Kelbrook Road, Manchester M11 2QA Tel. *0845 2702919* Fax. *0161 2236767* E-mail. *sales@dale-lifting.co.uk* Web. *www.dale-lifting.co.uk Donati – Genie – Hyprosteps – Morris Material Handling – Pewag – PFAFF – Steerman Load Moving Systems – Tractel – Waldens – Warrior Trucks – Yale Industrial Products*

Dale Mansfield Ltd Rotherham Road New Houghton, Mansfield NG19 8TF Tel. *01623 810659* Fax. *01623 811660* E-mail. *enquiry@dale-mansfield.co.uk* Web. *www.dale-mansfield.co.uk Dale*

Dalen Ltd Garretts Green Trading Estate Valepits Road, Birmingham B33 0TD Tel. *0121 7849399* Fax. *0121 7846348* E-mail. *clive.beardmore@top-tec.co.uk* Web. *www.top-tec.co.uk Dalen – Top Tec*

Dales Of Liverpool Ltd 325 Prescot Road Old Swan, Liverpool L13 3AT Tel. *0151 2204341* Fax. *0151 2542626 Dales – Deep Fjord – Islander – Mrs Dales Garden – Polar Bear – Sea Cove – Seaglow*

Dalesway Print Technology Victoria House Gisburn Road, West Marton, Skipton BD23 3UA Tel. *08452 241204* Fax. *0845 2241205* E-mail. *info@dalesway.co.uk* Web. *www.dalesway.co.uk ID-MARK – Kwikprint – Printa*

Damart Thermal Wear Ltd Bowling Green Mills Lime Street, Bingley BD97 1AD Tel. *01274 568211* Fax. *01274 551024* E-mail. *andrew.hill@damart.com* Web. *www.damart.co.uk *Damart Thermolactyl (France)*

Damixa Ltd Edison Courtyard Brunel Road, Earlstrees Industrial Estate, Corby NN17 4LS Tel. *01536 409222* Fax. *01536 400144* E-mail. *uksales@damixa.com* Web. *www.damixa.com Damixa – NewTeam – Tapmate*

Dampco UK Ltd 21 Lythalls Lane, Coventry CV6 6FN Tel. *024 76687683* Fax. *01536 410944* E-mail. *info@dampco.org* Web. *www.dampco.org Dampco*

Danagri - 3 S Ltd The Livestock & Auction Centre Unit 8 Wenlock Road, Bridgnorth WV16 4QR Tel. *01746 762777* Fax. *01746 764777* E-mail. *info@danagri-3s.com* Web. *www.danagri-3s.com Cimbria*

Danaher Motion UK Company Fishleigh Road Roundswell Business Park, Barnstaple EX31 3UD Tel. *01271 334500* Fax. *01271 334502* E-mail. *information@tiblmail.com* Web. *www.danahermotion.com Thomson*

Danaher Tool Group Kingsway West, Dundee DD2 3XX Tel. *01382 591400* Fax. *01382 591474* E-mail. *sales@dt-europe.com* Web. *www.dtg-europe.com Allen – Holo-Krome – Jacobs*

Danarm Machinery Ltd Unit 1 Gigg Mill Old Bristol Road, Nailsworth, Stroud GL6 0JP Tel. *01453 835577* Fax. *01453 765553* E-mail. *info@danarm.com* Web. *www.danarm.com *Asuka (Japan) – *Danarm (Japan) – *Earthway (U.S.A.) – *Kaaz (Japan)*

Dando Drilling International Old Customs House Wharf Road, Littlehampton BN17 5DD Tel. *01903 731312* Fax. *01903 730305* E-mail. *info@dando.co.uk* Web. *www.dando.co.uk Dando (United Kingdom)*

Dane Colour UK 7 Stanley Street, Stalybridge SK15 1SS Tel. *0161 3044000* Fax. *0161 3382611* E-mail. *sharon.mcdernot@danegroup.co.uk* Web. *www.danecolouR.co.uk Nova-Glo*

Danfoss Ltd Capswood Business Centre Oxford Road, Denham, Uxbridge UB9 4LH Tel. *0870 6080008* Fax. *0870 6080009* E-mail. *henrik.hansen@danfoss.com* Web. *www.danfoss.co.uk ADAP-KOOL – Nessie – VLT*

Danfoss Randall Ampthill Road, Bedford MK42 9ER Tel. *08451 217400* Fax. *08451 217515* E-mail. *gordon_macpherson@danfoss.com* Web. *www.danfoss-randall.co.uk Danfoss Randall*

Daniel Europe Ltd Logie Court Stirling University Innovation Park, Stirling FK9 4NF Tel. *01786 433400* Fax. *01786 433401* E-mail. *mark.dutton@emerson.com* Web. *www.daniel.co.uk Daniel*

Daniels Group Waterside Road Waterside Industrial Park, Leeds LS10 1RW Tel. *0113 2025160* Fax. *0113 2761956* Web. *www.danielsgroup.eu Sun Ripe*

Danielson Ltd 29 Stocklake Industrial Estate Pembroke Road, Aylesbury HP20 1DB Tel. *01296 319000* Fax. *01296 392141* E-mail. *sales@danielson.co.uk* Web. *www.danielsoneurope.com Danielson – K-Box – Quantaflex*

Danline International Ltd Nebo Road, Llanrwst LL26 0SE Tel. *01492 640651* Fax. *01492 641601* E-mail. *sales@danline.co.uk* Web. *www.danline.co.uk Brushmate – Hy-Dan – Scavenger – Towsweep*

Dan Medica South Ltd 28 Downsview Ave Storrington, Pulborough RH20 4PS Tel. *208 1332851* Fax. *208 1962364* E-mail. *info@danmedicasouth.co.uk* Web. *www.danmedicasouth.co.uk Debbonair Dynamics*

Danone Ltd International House 7 High Street, London W5 5DW Tel. *020 87995800* Fax. *020 87995801* Web. *www.danone.co.uk *Badott – *Danone Activ – *Volvic Touch of Fruit*

Danor Engineering Ltd 465 Hornsey Road, London N19 4DR Tel. *020 72810182* Fax. *020 72630154* E-mail. *danor.uk@btinternet.com* Web. *www.danor-engineering.co.uk *C.O.M.E.L (Italy) – Danor – *Ironmaster (Italy)*

Dantec Ltd Tarran Way Tarran Industrial Estate, Wirral CH46 4TL Tel. *0151 6782222* Fax. *0151 6060188* E-mail. *sales@dantec.com* Web. *www.dantec.com Danchem – Danchem - Danoil - Danflex – Danflex – Danflon – FIRESAFE – Danoil*

Dantec Dynamics Ltd UK Garanor Way Portbury, Bristol BS20 7XE Tel. *01275 375333* Fax. *01275 375336* E-mail. *uk@dantecdynamics.com* Web. *www.dantecdynamics.com Disatac – SensorLine*

Dantherm Filtration Ltd Limewood Approach, Leeds LS14 1NG Tel. *0113 2739400* Fax. *0113 2650735* E-mail. *rh@danthermfiltration.com* Web. *www.danthermfiltration.com Airmaster – Airmaster Auto M – Airmaster M J C – Airmaster M J X – BMD-GARANT – Combi Fab – Cyclopax – Cydopac – Duct QF – FK 25 – FMK 25 – NF 2000 – NFK 2000 – Nordfab*

W H Darby Ltd 16 Well Street, Birmingham B19 3BJ Tel. *0121 5549817* Fax. *0121 5233585* E-mail. *info@whdarby.co.uk* Web. *www.whdarby.co.uk T J Skelton*

Darcy Products Ltd 157 Mill Street East Malling, West Malling ME19 6BP Tel. *01732 843131* Fax. *01732 525500* E-mail. *enqs@darcy.co.uk* Web. *www.darcy.co.uk Brickseal – Dammit – Dampcoat – Drainseal – Drizit – Drizit - Serviron - Tracklube - Wetlube - Wirelube - Drainseal - Hydrotemp - Brickseal - Dammit – Envirovalve – Hydrotemp – Serviron – Sumpclean – Tracklube – Xzit GB*

Darent Wax Co. (Proman Coatings) Unit 1 Horton Kirby Trading Estate Station Road, South Darenth, Dartford DA4 9BD Tel. *01322 865892* Fax. *01322 864598* E-mail. *acw@darentwax.com* Web. *www.darentwax.com Alphamin*

Darfen Durafencing Ltd Herons Way Balby, Doncaster DN4 8WA Tel. *01302 360242* Fax. *01302 364359* E-mail. *northern@darfen.co.uk* Web. *www.darfen.co.uk Dura fencing*

Dark Matter Composites Ltd Unit 20 Thrales End Farm, Harpenden AL5 3NS Tel. *01582 469069* Fax. *01582 469069* E-mail. *info@darkmattercomposites.co.uk* Web. *www.darkmattercomposites.co.uk Dark Matter*

Darley Ltd Wellington Road, Burton On Trent DE14 2AD Tel. *01283 564936* Fax. *01283 545688* E-mail. *mailbox@darley.co.uk* Web. *www.darleylimited.co.uk Darley Forms – Darley Labels – Darley Leaflets*

Dasic International Ltd Winchester Hill, Romsey SO51 7YD Tel. *01794 512419* Fax. *01794 522346* E-mail. *info@dasicinter.com* Web. *www.dasicinternational.com Aerokleen – Aerostrip 323 – Fuelguard – Kleenfuel AS – Slickgone*

D A S Legal Expenses Insurance Co. Ltd D A S House Quay Side Temple Back, Bristol BS1 6NH Tel. *0117 9342000* Fax. *0117 9342109* E-mail. *s_skull@das.co.uk* Web. *www.das.co.uk D.A.S.*

Data Card Ltd Forum 3 Parkway, Whiteley, Fareham PO15 7FH Tel. *01489 555600* Fax. *01489 555601* E-mail. *jim_runcie@datacard.com* Web. *www.datacard.co.uk DataCard Ltd*

Data Command Ltd 1 Castle Ditch Lane, Lewes BN7 1YJ Tel. *01273 483548* E-mail. *david.echlin@datacommand.com* Web. *www.datacommand.com Demon – Demon for windows – Infobook*

Data Know How 17 St Annes Court, London W1F 0BQ Tel. *020 77343532* Fax. *020 77341779* E-mail. *info@dataknowhow.co.uk* Web. *www.dataknowhow.co.uk T S M*

Datamonitor plc Guardian House 119 Farringdon Road, London EC1R 3DA Tel. *020 75519000* Fax. *020 76757500* E-mail. *lindsey.roberts@informa.com* Web. *www.datamonitor.com Datamonitor*

Datapro Software Ltd North Street Portslade, Brighton BN41 1DH Tel. *01273 886000* Fax. *01273 886066* E-mail. *info@datapro.co.uk* Web. *swiftdatapro.com FICS – Pharoah – Shortlands*

Data Systems Computers Ltd Unit 21 Wellington Business Park Dukes Ride, Crowthorne RG45 6LS Tel. *01344 755000* Fax. *01344 779256* E-mail. *sales@datasystemsltd.co.uk* Web. *www.datasystemsltd.co.uk Citrix*

Data Track Technology plc 153 Somerford Road, Christchurch BH23 3TY Tel. *01425 270333* Fax. *01425 270433* E-mail. *sales@dtrack.com* Web. *www.datatrackpi.com Eclipse – Eclipse - Tracker – Tracker*

Datatrade Ltd Unit 35 Cornwell Business Park Salthouse Road, Brackmills Industrial Estate, Northampton NN4 7EX Tel. *01604 666666* Fax. *01604 768666* E-mail. *enquiries@datatrade.co.uk* Web. *www.datatrade.co.uk *Datasouth (U.S.A.) – Eltron – Lexmark*

Datum Monitoring Ireland 36 Lurganville Road Moira, Craigavon BT67 0PL Tel. *028 92616800* Fax. *028 92610524* E-mail. *info@lloydacoustics.co.uk* Web. *www.datumireland.com Datum Ireland*

Davan Caravans Ltd Shepherds Way Willow Close, St Georges, Weston Super Mare BS22 7XF Tel. *01934 510606* Fax. *01934 516025* E-mail. *info@davan.co.uk* Web. *www.davan.co.uk Davan – Davan Caravans Limited*

Davenport Burgess 47 Wednesfield Road, Willenhall WV13 1AL Tel. *01902 366448* Fax. *01902 602472* E-mail. *jenny@davenport-burgess.com* Web. *www.davenport-burgess.com Davenport & Burgess*

Davico Industrial Ltd Charles Street, West Bromwich B70 0AZ Tel. *0121 5207101* Fax. *0121 5207775* E-mail. *sales@davico.co.uk* Web. *www.davico.co.uk Euroduct – Eurolok – Krimpit*

David Auld Valves Ltd Finlas Street Cowlairs Industrial Estate, Glasgow G22 5DQ Tel. *0141 5570515* Fax. *0141 5581059* E-mail. *sales@auldvalves.com* Web. *www.auldvalves.com A. 100 – D.A. Series – Quitetite – Standfast – Vigilant*

David Hart Alcester Ltd Berrowhill Lane Feckenham, Redditch B96 6QS Tel. *01527 821197* Fax. *01527 821503* E-mail. *fran@dhart.co.uk* Web. *www.dhartgraphite.co.uk Hart*

Helen David 22 South Grove, London N6 6BB Tel. *020 84407325* Fax. *020 72842530* Web. *www.englisheccentrics.com Helen David English Eccentrics*

Lawrence David Ltd Maxwell Road, Peterborough PE2 7JR Tel. *01733 397600* Fax. *01733 397601* E-mail. *info@lawrencedavid.co.uk* Web. *www.lawrencedavid.co.uk Armoursheet – FastStrap – Kerbsider – Maxcess – Roller Sider – Slidax – Traccess*

David Morbey Timpani & Percussion 55 Braemar Place, Aberdeen AB10 6EQ Tel. *01224 212557* Fax. *01224 212557* E-mail. *david@timpanisticks.com* Web. *www.timpanisticks.com David Morbey Timpani Sticks – Solo Percussion Mallets*

David Ritchie Implements Ltd (David Ritchie (Implements) Ltd) Carseview Road, Forfar DD8 3BT Tel. *01307 462271* Fax. *01307 464081* E-mail. *info@ritchie-uk.com* Web. *www.ritchie-uk.com Cook – Ritchie Agricultural – Ritchie Industrial – Ritchie Water, Ritchie Industrial, Ritchie Agricultural, Cook.*

John Davidson Pipes Ltd Townfoot Longtown, Carlisle CA6 5LY Tel. *01228 791503* Fax. *01228 791682* E-mail. *iain.mcguiness@jdpipes.co.uk* Web. *www.jdpipes.co.uk Davigulli*

Davies & Company 12 Beatrice Road, Kettering NN16 9QS Tel. *01536 513456* Fax. *01536 310080* E-mail. *sales@equimat.co.uk* Web. *www.equimat.co.uk Equimat – *Vibram (Italy)*

Davies Harvey & Murrell 236-237 Record Street, London SE15 1TL Tel. *020 77329988* Fax. *020 77325415* E-mail. *mail@dhmpaper.com* Web. *www.dhmpaper.com Adhoc (Italy) – Attache – Biotop Colour (Austria) – Colorcopy (Austria) – Copytec (Austria) – Forest Offset – Media Print (Sweden) – *Snowhite (France) – *Triple Crown (Spain) – *White Rhino (Netherlands)*

John Davies 2001 Ltd 61 Waterloo Road, Liverpool L3 7BE Tel. *0151 2275728* Fax. *0151 2550652* E-mail. *sales@johndavies.co.uk* Web. *www.johndavies.co.uk Bohler Thyssen (Germany) – Cremont (Italy) – Flexovit – Jangy Engineering (U.S.A.) – Mosa*

Davies Products Liverpool Ltd Alsol House Laburnum Place, Bootle L20 3NE Tel. *0151 9224246* Fax. *0151 9441901* E-mail. *sales@daviesproducts.co.uk* Web. *www.daviesproducts.co.uk Jetsetter*

Davis Decade Ltd 30 Spring Lane, Birmingham B24 9BX Tel. *0121 3776292* Fax. *0121 3776645* E-mail. *enquiries@decade.co.uk* Web. *www.decade.co.uk Decade – Signature Technology*

Davis Derby Ltd Chequers Lane, Derby DE21 6AW Tel. *01332 341671* Fax. *01332 372190* E-mail. *enquiries@davisderby.com* Web. *www.davisderby.com Davis Derby – Minewatch – Trucklog – Unicon*

Davis & Hill 50-60 Pritchett Street Aston, Birmingham B6 4EY Tel. *0121 3594091* Fax. *0121 3333163* E-mail. *sales@davisandhill.co.uk* Web. *www.davisandhill.co.uk Davis and Hill*

Davis Industrial Plastics Ltd 1 Dialog Fleming Way, Crawley RH10 9NQ Tel. *01293 552836* Fax. *01293 553459* E-mail. *carol.davis@davis-plastics.co.uk* Web. *www.davis-plastics.co.uk Durapipe – Effast – George Fischer – Nylatron – Peek – Quadrant – Symalit – Torlon*

Davpack Charlton House Riverside Park, Spondon, Derby DE21 7BF Tel. *01332 821200* Fax. *01332 821209* E-mail. *sales@davpack.co.uk* Web. *www.davpack.co.uk Davenport Packaging (United Kingdom) – Davpack (United Kingdom) – Davpack; Davenport Packaging. – Jiffy – Nomapack – Packaging Directory – Store Pack*

Davstone Holdings Ltd 19-20 Grosvenor Street, London W1K 4QH Tel. *020 74939613* Fax. *020 74910692* Web. *www.regalianplc.com Regalian*

Dawbarn & Sons Ltd Dawbarns Harecroft Road, Wisbech PE13 1RL Tel. *01945 461741* Fax. *01945 585501* E-mail. *victoria.timms@dawbarn-evertaut.co.uk* Web. *www.dawbarn-evertaut.co.uk Dawbarn Evertaut*

D A W Enterprises Ltd (t/a Scalemaster) Unit 6 Emerald Way, Stone Business Park, Stone ST15 0SR Tel. *01785 811636* Fax. *01785 811511* E-mail. *info@scalemaster.co.uk* Web. *www.scalemaster.co.uk Rotobac – Rotocare – Rotoclene – Rotogard – Rotomaid – Rotosan – Rotosoap – Scalemaster – Softline Showers*

Dawes 35 Tameside Drive Castle Vale, Birmingham B35 7AG Tel. *0121 7488050* Fax. *0121 7488060* E-mail. *julie.hayward@dawescycles.com* Web. *www.dawescycles.com Dawes*

Dawson Downie Lamont Ltd (Thom Lamont Ltd) 13 Faraday Road, Glenrothes KY6 2RU Tel. *01592 775577* Fax. *01592 775517* E-mail. *sales@ddl-ltd.com* Web. *www.ddl-ltd.com Dawson & Downie – Thom Lamont*

Dawson Home Group Limited PO Box 60 Deansgate, Manchester M3 2QG Tel. *0844 8003744* Fax. *0161 2514417* E-mail. *info@dorma.co.uk* Web. *www.dorma.co.uk Dorma*

Dawson International plc Burnfoot Industrial Estate, Hawick TD9 8RJ Tel. *01577 867000* Fax. *01577 867010* E-mail. *enquiries@dawson-international.co.uk* Web. *www.dawson-international.co.uk Ballantyne – Barrie – Duofold – Glenmac – J E Morgan – Pringle*

James Dawson & Son Ltd Tritton Road, Lincoln LN6 7AF Tel. *01522 781800* Fax. *01522 510029* E-mail. *sales@james-dawson.com* Web. *www.james-dawson.com Compacta – Cordex – Dawson – Enduraflex – Rollers – Silicone – Silicone Hose – Speedona – Super-Tensile – Superspan*

Dax International Ltd ' Unit E4 Green Lane Business Park Green Lane, Tewkesbury GL20 8SJ Tel. *01684 276688* Fax. *01684 276699* E-mail. *sales@daxinternational.co.uk* Web. *www.daxinternational.co.uk AB Connectors – Aero Electric – Amphenol – Amphenol – Amphenol - Bendix – ARINC 404 – ARINC 600 – C11 – Cinch – Deutsch – Deutsch – Deutsch – Eaton/Cutler Hammer – Electro Adaptor – FIREWALL – Glenair – Hartman – Hi Rel – ITT Cannon – ITT Cannon – J-Tech – JN1003 (Eurofighter/Typhoon) – Kings – Leach/LRE – MIL-C-24308 – MIL-C-26482 (Series 1, Crimp) – MIL-C-26482 (Series 1, Solder) – MIL-C-26482 (Series 2) – MIL-C-26500 – MIL-C-38999 (Series 1) – MIL-C-38999 (Series 2) – MIL-C-38999 (Series 3) – MIL-C-38999 (Series 4) – MIL-C-39012 – MIL-C-39029 – MIL-C-5015 – MIL-C-81511 (Series 1,2,3 & 4) – MIL-C-83723 (Series 3) – MIL-C-83733 – MIL-C-85049 – Miles Royston – Nexon – PAN6432 (602 Series) – PAN6433 – Polamco – Pyle National – Pyle National – Rack and Panel – Radiall – RMS – Sabritec – Sealtron – Souriau – Souriau – Sunbank – Teledyne – Tri-Star – Tri-Star – Tyco – Tyco*

Day Impex Ltd Station Road Earls Colne, Colchester CO6 2ER Tel. *01787 223232* Fax. *01787 224171* E-mail. *info@day-impex.co.uk* Web. *www.day-impex.co.uk Daymaster – Dilvac – Labguard – Procare – Safety Soft – Virkon*

D B Shoes Ltd 19-21 Irchester Road, Rushden NN10 9XF Tel. *01933 359217* Fax. *01933 410218* E-mail. *enquiries@dbshoes.co.uk* Web. *www.dbshoes.co.uk Comfitts – Comfitts Nice "N' Easy – Comfitts Soft 'N' Easy – DB Shoes – Easyb's – Finn*

D D Hire 67 London Road Blackwater, Camberley GU17 0AB Tel. *01276 31132* Fax. *01276 600818* E-mail. *steve@ddhire.co.uk* Web. *www.ddhire.co.uk Berg Mixers – Bosch – Dewalt – Honda Generators and Industrial Engines – Husqvarna – Makita – Paslode – Petzl – Ryobi – Stanley Hand Tools – Stihl – Trend Router Cutters – Viking Mowers*

D D M Agriculture Eastfield Albert Street, Brigg DN20 8HS Tel. *01652 653669* Fax. *01652 653311* E-mail. *tony.dale@ddmagriculture.co.uk* Web. *www.ddmagriculture.co.uk *D D M Agriculture – *Screetons Agriculture*

D Drill Master Drillers Ltd Unit D Shilton Industrial Estate Bulkington Road, Coventry CV7 9QL Tel. *024 76618602* Fax. *024 76604409* E-mail. *admin@d-drill.co.uk* Web. *www.d-drill.co.uk D-Drill*

D D S 3b Church Street, Berwick upon Tweed TD15 1EE Tel. *01289 306921* Fax. *01289 466000* E-mail. *info@dds-uk.co.uk* Web. *www.dds-uk.co.uk DDS Collections – DDS VAT – DDS Fuels*

Deaf Alerter plc Enfield House 303 Burton Road, Derby DE23 6AG Tel. *01332 363981* Fax. *01332 293267* E-mail. *steveh@deaf-alerter.com* Web. *www.deaf-alerter.co.uk Asset Collector – Data Collector – Job Collector – Kegscan – Time Collector*

Deans Blinds & Awnings UK 4 Haslemere Industrial Estate Ravensbury Terrace, London SW18 4SE Tel. *020 89478931* Fax. *020 89478336* E-mail. *info@deansblinds.co.uk* Web. *www.deansblinds.co.uk Compact – Deanlite – Markilux – *President (Germany) – Vehicle*

Dean Smith & Grace Lathes Ltd PO Box 15, Keighley BD21 4PG Tel. *01535 605261* Fax. *01535 680921* E-mail. *robert@deansmithandgrace.co.uk* Web. *www.deansmithandgrace.co.uk Dean – Grace – Smith*

Deanston Electrical Wholesalers Ltd 27 Munro Place, Kilmarnock KA1 2NP Tel. *01563 533921* Fax. *01563 536409* E-mail. *helen@deanston-electrical.co.uk* Web. *www.deanston-electrical.co.uk Deanston*

Dean & Tranter Rockbourne Road Sandleheath, Fordingbridge SP6 1RA Tel. *01425 654011* Fax. *01425 654141* E-mail. *office@deantranter.co.uk* Web. *www.deantranter.co.uk Buxton Instulation – Dacier – Mica Supplys – Vandervelde*

Dearnleys Ltd 120-128 Wrenthorpe Road Wrenthorpe, Wakefield WF2 0JN Tel. *01924 371791* Fax. *01924 386001* E-mail. *info@dearnleys.com* Web. *www.dearnleys.com Astralux – Switchtrack System*

Deben Group Industries Ltd Gore Cross Business Park Corbin Way, Bradpole, Bridport DT6 3UX Tel. *01308 423576* Fax. *01308 425912* E-mail. *johnp@deben.com* Web. *www.deben.com Bird Chain – *Spike 2000 (U.S.A.)*

Deb R & D Ltd Denby Hall Way Denby, Ripley DE5 8JZ Tel. *01773 855300* Fax. *01773 855107* E-mail. *enquiry@debgroup.com* Web. *www.debgroup.com Altrans – Ambisan – Contect Duck Oil – Cutan Alcohol Gel – Cutan Dispenser – Cutan Multi Surface Wipes – Cutan Soaps – Deb 1000 – Deb 2000 – Deb Apple – Deb Green – Deb Lime – Deb Natural – Deb Peach – Deb Printers Hand Wipes – Deb Protect – Deb Pure – Deb Restore – Fastapine – Florafree – Florafresh – Great White – Heiress – Hyfoam – Hyfoam Antibac – Hyfoam Cartridge Dispensers – Hypor – Janitol Original – Janitol Plus – Janitol Rapide – Janitol Sanitiser – Jizer – Jizer Bio – Jizon Marine – Lanimol – Marinol – Maxipor – Powerwash T.F.R.'s – Ready To Use TFR – Rustoff – Sceptre – Stop Quick – Swarfega Plus – Swarfega – Swarfega Orange – Swarfega Power – Swarfega Red Box – Tot – Treetop – Tufanega – Wash & Wax*

Decopierre UK Ltd 68 lyles road Cottenham, cambridge CB24 8QR Tel. *020 81338990* E-mail. *info@decopierre.co.uk* Web. *www.decopierre.co.uk Decopierre*

Dedicated Micros Ltd Unit 1200 Daresbury Park, Daresbury, Warrington WA4 4HS Tel. *01928 706400* Fax. *01928 706350* E-mail. *customerservices@dmicros.com* Web. *www.dedicatedmicros.com D.V.S.T. – Digital Sprite – Sprite – Sprite Lite – System Sprite – Uniplex*

De Dietrich Process Systems Ltd Tollgate Drive Barlaston, Tollgate Industrial Estate, Stafford ST16 3HS

Tel. *01785 609900* Fax. *01785 609899* E-mail. *sales@ddpsltd.co.uk* Web. *www.ddpsltd.co.uk Corwrap – Q.V.F.*

Deepak Fasteners 12-14 Tower Street, Birmingham B19 3RR Tel. *0121 3334610* Fax. *0121 3334525* E-mail. *andesh.gupter@deepakfastners.com* Web. *www.deepakfastners.com DFL – UNBRAKO*

Deepak Sareen Associates Ltd Ambassador House 2 Cavendish Avenue, Harrow HA1 3RW Tel. *020 84238855* Fax. *020 84238992* E-mail. *sales@dsareen.com* Web. *www.dsareen.com *Deepak Sareen Associates (U.S.A.)*

Deep Clean Cleaning Ltd Unit 1 Badger Way, Prenton CH43 3HQ Tel. *0151 6088860* Fax. *0151 6470606* E-mail. *deepcleancleaning@hotmail.com* Web. *www.deepcleancleaning.co.uk Deep Clean Cleaning*

Deep Sea Seals Ltd 4 Marples Way, Havant PO9 1NX Tel. *023 92492123* Fax. *023 92492470* E-mail. *robert.burford@deepseaseals.com* Web. *www.wartsila.com Coastguard – Manebar – Manebrace – Manecraft – Maneguide – Manesafe – Maneseal – Safeguard*

John Deere Ltd Harby Road Langar, Nottingham NG13 9HT Tel. *01949 860491* Fax. *01949 860490* E-mail. *richardjohnson@johndeere.com* Web. *www.johndeere.co.uk John Deere*

Dee Valley Water plc Pentre Bychan, Wrexham LL14 4DS Tel. *01978 846946* Fax. *01978 846888* E-mail. *contact@deevalleygroup.com* Web. *www.deevalleywater.co.uk Dee Valley Water*

Definitive Computing Ltd Haldon House 385 Brettell Lane, Brierley Hill DY5 3LQ Tel. *01384 261727* Fax. *01384 261727* E-mail. *info@dclsoftware.co.uk* Web. *www.dclsoftware.co.uk Buttress*

Dejay Distribution Ltd Unit 1 Rocks Farm Business Centre, Stone Cross, Crowborough TN6 3SJ Tel. *08453 700266* Fax. *0118 9788123* E-mail. *info@dejaydistribution.co.uk* Web. *www.dejaydistribution.co.uk Dejay Distribution*

Dek Printing Machines Ltd 11 Albany Road Granby Industrial Estate, Weymouth DT4 9TH Tel. *01305 760760* Fax. *01305 760123* E-mail. *pdavey@dek.com* Web. *www.dek.com Dek Printing Machines*

Delaval Oak House Pascal Close, St Mellons, Cardiff CF3 0LW Tel. *029 20775800* Fax. *01633 838054* E-mail. *info@delaval.co.uk* Web. *www.delaval.com Alfa Acid Clean – Alfa Blue Plus – Alfa Laval Agri – Alfa Plast – Alfa Red – Alfa Sept Mint – Alfafeed – Alfaklor – Alfinance – Alodine – Alphos – Alpro – Blue Diamond – C6 Extra – Cascade – Cascade – Dipal – Dryflex (U.S.A.) – Duovac 300 – DX2000 – Hamra – Harmony – Hiactive – Hygemics Cleaning Systems – Hygenius Ultra – Hyphos – Jodozyme (U.S.A.) – Microtherm – Pacer – Quartermate – Rinse-Clene – RX 2000 – Shielded Liners – Stop – Superteat – Tanklenz – Thovex – Ultra Brilliant – VMS*

Delavan Ltd Gorsey Lane, Widnes WA8 0RJ Tel. *0151 4246821* Fax. *0151 4951043* E-mail. *dave.percival@goodrich.com* Web. *www.delavan.co.uk Color-Brate – Compactrol – Dela-Fit – Delavan – Fanjet – Floodjet – Mistaire – Raindrop – Stripjet*

Delcam plc Talbot Way, Birmingham B10 0HJ Tel. *0121 7665544* Fax. *0121 7665511* E-mail. *marketing@delcam.com* Web. *www.delcam.com Artcam – Copycad – Powerinspect – Powermill – Powershape*

Delifrance UK Ltd 17 Chartwell Drive, Wigston LE18 2FL Tel. *0116 2571871* Fax. *0116 2571608* E-mail. *info@delifrance.co.uk* Web. *www.delifrance.com Délifrance – Déliquick – *Provencette*

Delkim Ltd PO Box 270, Bedford MK43 7DZ Tel. *01234 721116* Fax. *01234 721116* E-mail. *office@delkim.co.uk* Web. *www.delkim.co.uk Delkim*

Deloro Stellite Ltd Unit 3 Kembrey Street, Elgin Industrial Estate, Swindon SN2 8UY Tel. *01793 498500* Fax. *01793 498501* E-mail. *sales@delorostellite.co.uk* Web. *www.stellite.com Delcrome – Deloro – Nistelle – Starweld – Stellite – Stellundum – Tribaloy*

Delta A G Ltd 10 The Butts, Warwick CV34 4SS Tel. *01926 493017* Fax. *01926 403711* E-mail. *davidj@delta-ag.co.uk* Web. *www.delta-ag.co.uk Delta Activator – Delta DP200 – Delta Graffi-gard – Delta Microblitz – Delta Rapid-strip*

Delta Civil Engineering Group Holdings Ltd Newtown Road, Highbridge TA9 3HX Tel. *01278 764100* Fax. *01278 764111* E-mail. *civils@deltace.com* Web. *www.deltace.com Decon – Delta Civil Engineering – TMS*

Delta Computer Services (Head Office) 4-5 Falmer Court London Road, Uckfield TN22 1HN Tel. *01825 768123* Fax. *01825 769756* E-mail. *sales@deltacomputerservices.co.uk* Web. *www.deltacomputerservices.co.uk EXTOL – RIP – Scuba – Showbis – Snapshot*

Delta Controls Ltd Island Farm Avenue, West Molesey KT8 2UZ Tel. *020 89393500* Fax. *020 87831163* E-mail. *sales@delta-controls.com* Web. *www.delta-controls.com Delta Controls – Deltrol*

Delta Dampacure Fakenham Ltd Heath Barn Norwich Road, Fakenham NR21 8LZ Tel. *01328 863451* Fax. *01328 855050* E-mail. *elderton@deltadampacure.com* Web. *www.deltadampacure.com Delta Dampacure*

Delta Fluid Products Ltd Delta Road, St Helens WA9 2ED Tel. *01744 611811* Fax. *01744 611818* E-mail. *enquiry@deltafluidproducts.co.uk* Web. *www.cranebsu.com Brown Owl – Nabic – Rhodes – Wade*

Delta GB N Ltd 115 Lodgefield Road, Halesowen B62 8AX Tel. *0121 6021221* Fax. *0121 6023222* E-mail. *rogerw@deltagbn.co.uk* Web. *www.deltagbn.co.uk Delta Seal – Delta Tone – Deltacoll – Deltaloc – Deltaloc Nut*

Delta Neu Ltd Newby Road Industrial Estate Newby Road Hazel Grove, Stockport SK7 5DR Tel. *0161 4565511* Fax. *0161 4562460* E-mail. *mail@delta-neu.co.uk* Web. *www.delta-neu.com *Jet Line – Jet Line - reverse jet dust filter.*

Delta T Devices 130 Low Road Burwell, Cambridge CB25 0EJ Tel. *01638 742922* Fax. *01638 743155* E-mail. *lea.dodds@delta-t.co.uk* Web. *www.delta-t.co.uk Delta-T Logger – Theta-Probe – WET Sensor*

Deluxe Chauffeurs of London Deluxe Office Crown House North Circular Road, London NW10 7PN Tel. *020 89078884* E-mail. *info@deluxechauffeurs.com* Web. *www.deluxechauffeurs.com Deluxe Chauffeurs of London*

Deluxe London North Orbital Road Denham, Uxbridge UB9 5HQ Tel. *01895 832323* Fax. *01895 833617* E-mail. *k.biggins@bydeluxe.com* Web. *www.bydeluxe.com Deluxe London*

Demag Cranes & Components Ltd Beaumont Rd, Banbury OX16 1QZ Tel. *01295 676100* Fax. *01295 226106* E-mail. *help@demagcranes.com* Web. *www.demagcranes.com Demag (Germany)*

Demag Hamilton Guarantee Ltd Accent House, Triangle Business Park Wendover Road, Stoke Mandeville, Aylesbury HP22 5BL Tel. *01296 9500* Fax. *01296 739501* E-mail. *salesuk@dpg.com* Web. *www.dpg.com Demag Ergotech*

Deminos 8 Bankside The Watermark, Gateshead NE11 9SY Tel. *0191 4600707* Fax. *0191 4600707* E-mail. *office@deminos.co.uk* Web. *www.deminos.co.uk Deminos HR*

Deminos HR 145 157 St John Street, London EC1V 4PY Tel. *020 78701090* Fax. *020 32921752* E-mail. *neil.atkinson@deminos.co.uk* Web. *www.deminos.co.uk Deminos HR*

Demountable Partitions Ltd Unit 4 Twin Bridges Business Park 232 Selsdon Road, South Croydon CR2 6PL Tel. *020 84103800* Fax. *020 82390083* E-mail. *brian@demountables.co.uk* Web. *www.demountables.co.uk Demountable Partitiions Ltd (United Kingdom)*

B P Dempsey Ltd 8 March Street, Sheffield S9 5DQ Tel. *0114 2421900* Fax. *0114 2432232* E-mail. *info@bpdempsey.com* Web. *www.bpdempsey.com B P D Heating Controls*

Dempson Crooke Ltd Premier Works 134-140 Idle Road, Bradford BD2 4NE Tel. *01274 632911* Fax. *01274 626126* E-mail. *sales@dempson.co.uk* Web. *www.dempson.co.uk Dependable*

Dencon Accessories Ltd Lyden House South Road, Harlow CM20 2BS Tel. *01279 433533* Fax. *01279 433633* E-mail. *info@vernons.co.uk* Web. *www.dencon.co.uk V.F.*

Denford Ltd Armytage House Armytage Road, Brighouse HD6 1QF Tel. *01484 728000* Fax. *01484 722160* E-mail. *info@denford.co.uk* Web. *www.denford.co.uk Cyclone – Micromill – Microturn – Mirac – Novamill – Novaturn – Triac – Triac-fanuc*

Dengie Crops Ltd Hall Road Asheldham, Southminster CM0 7JF Tel. *01621 773883* Fax. *01621 773717* E-mail. *chris.petts@dengie.com* Web. *www.dengie.com Alfa-A – Dengie – Hi=Fi – Medi-Bed*

Denholm Barwil Avonmouth Dock, Bristol BS11 9DN Tel. *0117 9802710* Fax. *0117 9821265* E-mail. *enquiries@denholm-group.co.uk* Web. *www.denholm-group.co.uk Denholm Shipping Services*

Denholme Velvets Ltd Halifax Road Denholme, Bradford BD13 4EZ Tel. *01274 832185* Fax. *01274 832646* E-mail. *sales@denholme-velvets.co.uk* Web. *www.denholmevelvetsltd.co.uk Denholme*

Denison Mayes Group Ltd Unit 14 Enterprise Park Moorhouse Avenue, Leeds LS11 8HA Tel. *0113 2708011* Fax. *0113 2712850* E-mail. *sales@denisonmayesgroup.com* Web. *www.denisonmayesgroup.com Denison Mayes Group*

Denman International Ltd Clandeboye Road, Bangor BT20 3JH Tel. *028 91462141* Fax. *028 91451654* E-mail. *info@denmanpro.com* Web. *www.denmanpro.com Denman*

Dennis Publishing 30 Cleveland Street, London W1T 4JD Tel. *020 79076000* Fax. *020 79076020* E-mail. *reception@dennis.co.uk* Web. *www.dennis.co.uk Audio Visual – Men's Magazine – Music Magazine – P.C. Pro*

Denplan Ltd Denplan Court Victoria Road, Winchester SO23 7RG Tel. *01962 828000* Fax. *01962 840846* E-mail. *denplan@denplan.co.uk* Web. *www.denplan.co.uk Denplan*

Rodney Densem Wines Ltd Regent House Lancaster Fields, Crewe CW1 6FF Tel. *01270 212200* Fax. *01270 212300* E-mail. *sales@rdwines.com* Web. *www.rodneydensemwines.com Accolado – Al Verde – Alenya – Chateau Lamothe de Haux – Domaine Balland – Domaine Chatelus de la Roche – Domaine Juliette Avril – Domaine le Verger – Domaine les Chatelaines – Domaine Loberger – Domaine Masson Blondelet – Domaine Michel Mallard – Domaine Michel Servin – Domaine Prieure – En Colline – Forget Brimont – La Brasserie – La Manda, Nuevo Extremo – Sendas del Rey – Vina Bondad – Wallaby Creek – Wallaby Ridge – Zorzettig*

Denso Marston Ltd Otley Road Baildon, Charlestown, Shipley BD17 7JR Tel. *01274 582266* Fax. *01274 597165* E-mail. *martin.mcnally@uk.fujitsu.com* Web. *www.denso-europe.com Marston*

Dent Instrumentation Ltd Enterprise Way Whitewalls Industrial Estate, Colne BB8 8LY Tel. *01282 862703* Fax. *01282 862037* E-mail. *andrew.dent@dentsensors.com* Web. *www.dentsensors.com Dent – Uster*

Denton Clark Rentals 4 Vicars Lane, Chester CH1 1QU Tel. *01244 624027* Fax. *01244 315954* E-mail. *info@dentonclarkrentals.co.uk* Web. *www.dentonclarkrentals.co.uk Denton Clark*

Denton Pumps Ltd 191 Vale Road, Tonbridge TN9 1ST Tel. *01732 354847* Fax. *01732 770152* E-mail. *martin@dentonpumps.co.uk* Web. *www.dentonpumps.co.uk Ensine Driven Pumps – Espa Pumps – Flygt Pumps – Iwaki Pumps – Jung Pumps – KSB Pumps – Lotus Pond Filters – Lotus Pond Pumps – Mono Pumps – Nocchi Pumps – Otter Pumps – Pedrollo Pumps – Robinson Pumps – Rutax Pumps – Stuart Turner Pond Pumps – Stuart Turner Pumps – Stuart Turner Shower Pumps – TT Pumps – Well Pumps*

Dents (a division of Dewhurst Dent P.L.C.) Warminster Business Park Furnax Lane, Warminster BA12 8PE Tel. *01985 217367* Fax. *01985 216435* E-mail. *customerservice@dents.co.uk* Web. *www.dents.co.uk Dents*

D E P Frith Park Sturts Lane, Walton On The Hill, Tadworth KT20 7NQ Tel. *01737 813517* Fax. *01737 813442* E-mail. *cep@frithpark.com* Web. *www.frithpark.com Astrafoil*

Dependable Springs & Pressings Ltd (Head Office & Factory) Stewart Street, Wolverhampton WV2 4JZ Tel. *01902 420934* Fax. *01902 423453* E-mail. *mail@dependablesprings.co.uk* Web. *www.dependablesprings.co.uk Dependable*

Depuy International (a division of Johnson & Johnson Co.) St Anthonys Road Beeston, Leeds LS11 8DT Tel. *0113 2700461* Fax. *0113 2724101* E-mail. *depuy@dpygb.jnj.com* Web. *www.depuy.com Charnley – Depuy International*

Derbyshire Building Society Duffield Hall St Ronans Avenue, Duffield, Belper DE56 4HG Tel. *08456 004005* Fax. *01332 840350* E-mail. *customerservices@thederbyshire.co.uk* Web. *www.thederbyshire.co.uk Crown – Derbyshire Capital Reserve, The – Derbyshire Deal Check, The – Derbyshire Direct – Derbyshire Harvester, The – Derbyshire Life – Derbyshire Manx Bond – Derbyshire Memberloan, The – Derbyshire Moneylink, The – Derbyshire Mortgagecover – Derbyshire Paymentscover, The – Derbyshire Total Homecover, The – Derbyshire Travelcover – Derbyshire, The – Derbysure – Helping Hands – Liberator – Peak – Silver Link – Summit – Timemaster – Triple Gold*

Derby Telegraph Media Group Northcliffe House Meadow Road, Derby DE1 2BH Tel. *01332 291111* Fax. *01332 253011* E-mail. *newsdesk@derbytelegraph.co.uk* Web. *www.thisisderbyshire.co.uk Belper Express – Derby Evening Telegraph – Derby Express – Ilkeston Express*

Deritend PO Box 36, Wolverhampton WV2 4PB Tel. *01902 426390* Fax. *01922 723128* E-mail. *induction@deritend.co.uk* Web. *www.deritend.co.uk Deritend Induction Services (United Kingdom)*

Dernier & Hamlyn Ltd Unit 5 Jaycee House 214 Purley Way, Croydon CR0 4XG Tel. *020 87600900* Fax. *020 87600955* E-mail. *info@dernier-hamlyn.com* Web. *www.dernier-hamlyn.com Dernier & Hamlyn*

Desch Plantpak Ltd Burnham Road Mundon, Maldon CM9 6NT Tel. *01621 745500* Fax. *01621 745525* E-mail. *sales@desch-plantpak.co.uk* Web. *www.desch-plantpak.co.uk Glenco – Horticultural plastic products & plastic mouldings manufrs – Optipot – Plantpak*

Design & Display Structures Ltd The Studio, Amberley Hempstead Road, Uckfield TN22 1DZ Tel. *0844 7365995* Fax. *0844 7365992* E-mail. *sales@design-and-display.co.uk* Web. *www.design-and-display.co.uk Aquaglide – Aquaglide Interactive (United Kingdom)*

Designed Architectural Lighting Ltd 6 Conqueror Court Spilsby Road, Harold Hill, Romford RM3 8SB Tel. *01708 381999* Fax. *01708 381585* E-mail. *sales@dal-uk.com* Web. *www.dal-uk.com Dal*

Designed For Sound Ltd 61-67 Rectory Road Wivenhoe, Colchester CO7 9ES Tel. *01206 827171* Fax. *01206 826936* E-mail. *info@d4s.co.uk* Web. *www.d4s.co.uk Amber Booth – *Krantz (Germany) – Silvent*

Design Initiative Ltd The Old Granary The Street, Glynde, Lewes BN8 6SX Tel. *01273 858525* Fax. *01273 858531* E-mail. *info@post.eu.com* Web. *www.post.eu.com Postal Initiative*

Designplan Lighting Ltd 6 Wealdstone Road, Sutton SM3 9RW Tel. *020 82542000* Fax. *020 86444253* E-mail. *reception@designplan.co.uk* Web. *www.designplan.co.uk Assembly Hall – Athlon – Aztec – Bastion – Bergen – Brunel – Callisto – Capella – Centaur – Circo – Circo – Concourse Lantern – County II – Cupola – Curso – Demi-Slot – Disc – Forum – Frac – Fric – Gemini – Harrier – Hood – Isis – Milford – Mini Quad – Monitor – Monitor III – Nebular – Pantheon – Parapet – Parsec – Quadrangle – Quadrant – Quadring – Quantum 1 – Quantum 2 – Quay – Rampart – Slot – Sparta – Spartox – Spoke – Squiggle – Stadia – Tic Tac – Tuscan – Vision – Wall Mount Brunel – Zermatt – Zero – Ziggy*

Designs In Aluminium (D I A) Dayton House Bolney Avenue, Peacehaven BN10 8HF Tel. *01273 582241* Fax. *01273 580644* E-mail. *info@designs-in-aluminium.co.uk* Web. *www.designs-in-aluminium.co.uk Mirror Trim – Tempwall*

Destec Systems Ltd 21 Grovelands Avenue, Swindon SN1 4ET Tel. *01793 496217* Fax. *01793 610739* E-mail. *info@destecsystems.co.uk* Web. *www.destec.sagehost.co.uk Safeframe – Sekure Controls*

Deutscha Asset Management Ltd PO Box 135, London EC2A 2HE Tel. *020 75456000* Fax. *020 75457700* Web. *www.deam.co.uk Deutsche Asset Management*

Deutsch UK 4 Stanier Road, St Leonards On Sea TN38 9RF Tel. *01424 852721* Fax. *01424 851532* E-mail. *gcook@deutsch.net* Web. *www.deutsch.net Deutsch*

Devaco International Ltd Riverside House Brymau Three Trading Estate River Lane, Saltney, Chester CH4 8RQ Tel. *01244 671700* Fax. *01244 680655* E-mail. *devaco@mcmail.com* Web. *www.devaco.co.uk Multistar – Probe – Stainless Steel Mesh*

Deva Tap Co Brooklands Mill English Street, Leigh WN7 3EH Tel. *01942 680177* Fax. *01942 680190* E-mail. *nigel.darbyshire@devatap.com* Web. *www.deva.org.uk Attersall & Rothwell & Deva – Windsor*

Development Securities Investments plc Portland House Bressenden Place, London SW1E 5DS Tel. *020 78284777* Fax. *020 78284999* E-mail. *debbie.whetstone@devsecs.co.uk* Web. *www.developmentsecurities.co.uk Development Securities*

Devlin Electronics Ltd Unit D1 Grafton Way, Basingstoke RG22 6HZ Tel. *01256 467367* Fax. *01256 840048* E-mail. *sales@devlin.co.uk* Web. *www.devlin.co.uk Devlin Electronics*

Devol Engineering Ltd 13 Clarence Street, Greenock PA15 1LR Tel. *01475 720934* Fax. *01475 787873* E-mail. *sales@devol.com* Web. *www.devol.com Devol*

Devon Cattle Breeders Society Wisteria Cottage Iddesleigh, Winkleigh EX19 8BG Tel. *01837 810942* Fax. *01837 810942* E-mail. *lane@dcbf.fsbusiness.co.uk* Web. *www.redrubydevon.co.uk red ruby*

Devon Contractors Ltd Clyst Court Hill Barton Business Park, Clyst St Mary, Exeter EX5 1SA Tel. *01395 234280* Fax. *01395 234281* E-mail. *pete.alderson@devoncontractors.co.uk* Web. *www.devoncontractors.com Devon Contractors*

Dewhirst Group Ltd Dewhirst House Westgate, Driffield YO25 6TH Tel. *01377 252561* Fax. *01377 253814* E-mail. *enquiries@dewhurst.co.uk* Web. *www.dewhirst.com Dewhirst – Dewhirst Childrenswear – Dewhirst Ladieswear – Dewhirst Menswear*

Dewhurst plc Inverness Road, Hounslow TW3 3LT Tel. *020 86077300* Fax. *020 85725986* E-mail. *fixtures@dewhurst.co.uk* Web. *www.dewhurst.co.uk Compact – Dupar*

James Dewhurst Ltd Altham Lane Altham, Accrington BB5 5YA Tel. *01282 775311* Fax. *01282 774717* E-mail. *info@jamesdewhurst.com* Web. *www.jamesdewhurst.com Dewtex – Jamette*

Dexam International Holmbush Industrial Estate, Midhurst GU29 9HX Tel. *01730 811864* Fax. *01730 815721* E-mail. *sales@dexam.co.uk* Web. *www.dexam.co.uk *Chasseur (France) – Chichester – *Hackman (Finland) – *Iittala (Finland) – *Invicta (France) – *J.A. Henckles (Germany) – *Kuchenprofi (Germany) – *Lladro (Spain) – *Nao (Spain) – *Skanwood (Scandinavia) – *Spring (Switzerland) – *Vista Alegre (Portugal) – *Zyliss (Switzerland)*

Dexine Rubber Co. Ltd Jape Two Business Centre Dell Road, Rochdale OL12 6BZ Tel. *01706 640011* Fax. *01706 527714* E-mail. *info@dexine.com* Web. *www.dexine.com Dexine – Dexonite – Dexoplas – Duodex – Tridex – Vibradex*

D F Webber & Harrison Ltd Unit 270 Ricardo Way, Lymington SO41 8JU Tel. *01590 689009* Fax. *01590 689006* E-mail. *allanwebber@btconnect.com* Web. *www.webberfurniture.co.uk Croydon Range*

D F Wishart Holdings Ltd PO Box 208 St Clair Street, Edinburgh EH6 8LJ Tel. *0131 5544393* Fax. *0131 5537242* E-mail. *info@wishart.co.uk* Web. *www.wishart.co.uk Picardy*

D G Protective Coatings 12 Banbury Road Ettington, Stratford Upon Avon CV37 7TB Tel. *01789 740286* Fax. *01789 740599* E-mail. *sales@dgprotective.co.uk* Web. *www.dgprotective.co.uk Jenoseel*

D H Industries Ltd Sullivan House Fenton Way, Southfields Business Park, Basildon SS15 6TD Tel. *01268 410666* Fax. *01268 410777* E-mail. *dh@dhi.co.uk* Web. *www.dhi.co.uk 'Jenag' – D H River Conveyors – dh Electrolink*

The Diageo Dundas House 99 Borron Street, Glasgow G4 9XF Tel. *0141 3323323* Fax. *0141 3332121* E-mail. *donald.a.dempsey@diageo.com* Web. *www.diageo.com United Distillers*

Diagnostic Reagents Ltd Wenman Road, Thame OX9 3NY Tel. *01844 212426* Fax. *01844 216162* E-mail. *sales@diagen.co.uk* Web. *www.diagen.co.uk Diagen*

Diagraph Products Unit 9 Brunel Gate West Portway Industrial Estate, Andover SP10 3SL Tel. *01264 357511* Fax. *01264 355964* E-mail. *denewth@loveshaw_europe.co.uk* Web. *www.diagraohproducts.co.uk Diagraph*

Dialog Technivac Ltd Unit 5 Raven Close, Bridgend Industrial Estate, Bridgend CF31 3RF Tel. *01656 645856* Fax. *01656 646541* E-mail. *info@technivac.co.uk* Web. *www.technivac.co.uk Clamflo – Portflo – Smoothcat – Sofflo – Technivac*

Diamond Detectors Element Six House Kings Ride Park, Ascot SL5 8BP Tel. *01344 638200* Fax. *01344 638236* E-mail. *c.hultner@e6.com* Web. *www.e6.com A B N – AMB 90 – AMBORITE – AMBRAZITE – C D A – D B C 50 – D.B.C. 80 – DBA 80 – DBN 45 – De Beers – DSN – E M B – E M B S – Hardcore – M D A – MONODIE – MONODITE – MONODRESS – PDA – Premadia – S D A Plus – SDB – SYNDAX – SYNDAX 3 – SYNDIE – SYNDITE – SYNDRILL*

Diamond Edge Ltd 126 Gloucester Road, Brighton BN1 4BU Tel. *01273 605922* Fax. *01273 625074* E-mail. *diamondedge@btclick.com* Web. *www.diamondedgeltd.com *Aesculup (Germany) – *Bernina (Germany) – Diamond Edge – *Filarmonica (Spain) – Foster Ray – Joewell (Japan) – *Mars (Germany) – Sahara – Supajet – *Thrive (Japan) – *Universal (Germany) – Wren*

The Diamond Stylus Company Ltd Council Street West, Llandudno LL30 1ED Tel. *01492 860880* Fax. *01492 860653* E-mail. *sales@diamondstylus.co.uk* Web. *www.diamondstylus.co.uk Diamond Stylus*

Dibro Ltd Unit 2 Valentines Building Aintree Racecourse Business Park, Aintree Racecourse Retail & Bus Pk, Liverpool L9 5AY Tel. *0151 5250365* Fax. *0151 5250342* E-mail. *tom@dibro.com* Web. *www.dibro.com Dibro*

Dickies Workwear Second Avenue Westfield Trading Estate, Midsomer Norton, Radstock BA3 4BH Tel. *01761 419419* Fax. *01761 414825* E-mail. *eurosales@dickies.com* Web. *www.dickiesworkwear.com Dickies – Dickies 22 – Eisenhower – Grafter – Kodiak – Makita – Redhawk*

Didsbury Engineering Ltd Unit 1b Lower Meadow Road Brooke Park, Handforth, Wilmslow SK9 3LP Tel. *0161 4862200* Fax. *0161 4862211* E-mail. *sales@didsbury.com* Web. *www.didsbury.com Ezi-Lift – Minilift*

Dieselprods Ltd Finlan Road, Widnes WA8 7RZ Tel. *0151 4951945* Fax. *0151 4951908* E-mail. *sales@dieselprods.ltd.uk* Web. *www.dieselprods.ltd.uk Polo Diesel – Superpar*

Dietary Food Ltd Cumberland House Brook Street, Soham, Ely CB7 5BA Tel. *01353 720791* Fax. *01353 721705* E-mail. *graham@dietaryfoods.co.uk* Web. *www.dietaryfoods.co.uk *Sweet n Low*

Diffusion Alloys Ltd 160-162 Great North Road, Hatfield AL9 5JW Tel. *01707 266111* Fax. *01707 276669* E-mail. *enquiries@diffusion-alloys.com* Web. *www.diffusionalloys.co.uk *Interal – *Interchrome – *Siclean*

Diffusion Systems Ltd 43 Rosebank Road, London W7 2EW Tel. *020 85795231* Fax. *020 85661524* E-mail. *sales@diffusion-systems.com* Web. *www.diffusion-systems.com Eel*

Digbits Ltd 1 Towers Business Park Wheelhouse Road, Rugeley WS15 1UZ Tel. *01889 503020* Fax. *01889 503021* E-mail. *karen@digbits.co.uk* Web. *www.digbits.co.uk Bavtrak – Micro Crusher – Trak Crusher*

Digico UK Ltd Unit 10, Chessington KT9 2QL Tel. *01372 845600* Fax. *01372 845656* E-mail. *info@digiconsoles.com* Web. *www.digico.biz DPC II – Jade – Megas II Monitor – Megas II Stage – Sequel II – Solitaire – Solo 8 Live – Solo Live – Solo Logic – Solo Monitor – Topaz – Virtua*

Digital Technology International Ltd 4-6 Crescent Road Warley, Brentwood CM14 5JR Tel. *01277 246000* Fax. *01277 228767* E-mail. *info@dtint.com* Web. *www.dtint.com Digital Technology Intl*

Digitrol Ltd Coronet Way Swansea Enterprise Park, Swansea SA6 8RH Tel. *01792 796000* Fax. *01792 701600* E-mail. *info@digitrol.com* Web. *www.digitrol.com Digitrol*

Dimar Ltd 18 East Street, Farnham GU9 7SD Tel. *01252 719997* Fax. *01252 719998* E-mail. *enquiries@dimar.co.uk* Web. *www.dimar.co.uk Dimar*

Dineshco Textiles Ltd 134-136 Commercial Road, London E1 1NL Tel. *020 74806101* Fax. *020 74805752* E-mail. *dtluk@btinternet.com Catch One – Treblegem*

Dinkum Products Ltd St Clements House St Clements Road, Birmingham B7 5AF Tel. *0121 2451945* Fax. *0121 3281966* E-mail. *admin@dinkum.net* Web. *www.dinkum.net Cappuccino Cool – Fresh Shakes*

Diodes Zetex Semiconductors Ltd Zetex Technology Park Chadderton, Oldham OL9 9LL Tel. *0161 6224400* Fax. *0161 6224446* E-mail. *colin_greene@eu.diodes.com* Web. *www.zetex.com BiMos – E.-Line – Mosfet – Sotfet – Supersot*

Direct Adhesives Ltd Unit 15 Chartmoor Road, Leighton Buzzard LU7 4WG Tel. *01525 381111* Fax. *01525 381115* E-mail. *simon.walker@directsportswear.com* Web. *www.directnationaladhesives.co.uk Direct Adhesive*

Direct Instrument Hire Ltd 16 Swordfish Close Swordfish Business Park, Burscough, Ormskirk L40 8JW Tel. *01704 896966* Fax. *01704 896956* E-mail. *sales@instrument-hire.co.uk* Web. *www.instrument-hire.co.uk Budenberg – Comark – Data Taker – Datataker – Druck – Fluke – GE Druck – Haven – LEM – Lem Heme – Megger – Robin – Unomat*

Directional Data Systems Ltd 5 Dalsholm Avenue, Glasgow G20 0TS Tel. *0141 9454243* Fax. *0141 9454238* E-mail. *ronald.dunbar@directionaldata.co.uk* Web. *www.directionaldata.co.uk Directional Data Systems Ltd*

Direct Line Insurance plc 3 Edridge Road, Croydon CR9 1AG Tel. *020 86863313* Fax. *020 82565202* Web. *www.directline.com Direct Line Accident Management – Direct Line Financial Services – Direct Line Insurance – Direct Line ISA – Direct Line Life – Direct Line Mastercard – Direct Line Pensions – Direct Line Rescue – Direct Line Unit Trust – Privilege Insurance*

Direct Manufacturing Supply Co 19 Anne Road, Smethwick B66 2PJ Tel. *0121 5584591* Fax. *0121 5657513* E-mail. *kevinh@slemcka.co.uk* Web. *www.directo.co.uk Direct Manufacturing Supply Co*

Direct Packaging Solutions Ltd Grove Works Battersea Road, Stockport SK4 3EA Tel. *0161 9755360* Fax. *0161 9755361* E-mail. *sales@dpack.co.uk* Web. *www.dpack.co.uk Direct Packaging Solutions*

Direct Visual Ltd The Gateway Lowfields Close, Lowfields Business Park, Elland HX5 9DX Tel. *08453 575757* Fax. *01422 313473* E-mail. *marketing@direct-visual.com* Web. *www.direct-visual.com Multipoint Connections – Stratus*

Direct Voice & Data Ltd Direct House 16 Commercial Road, Skelmanthorpe, Huddersfield HD8 9DA Tel. *01484 867867* Fax. *01484 867860* E-mail. *info@direct-voiceanddata.com* Web. *www.direct-voiceanddata.com Alcatel – AVAYA – Avaya Communications – Avaya Telephone Systems – Panasonic Telephone Systems*

Disco Drive Kings Lynn Ltd Oldmedow Road, Kings Lynn PE30 4LE Tel. *01553 761331* Fax. *01553 692137* E-mail. *sales@discodrives.co.uk* Web. *www.discodrives.com ABB Industrial Systems – David Brown Radicon – Disco – Electropower – Supaflex*

Discount Leisure UK ltd Carlton House 101 New London Road, Chelmsford CM2 0PP Tel. *01245 477333* Fax. *01245 477888* E-mail. *sales@discount-leisure.com* Web. *www.discountleisure.co.uk BELLE MAISONS – DOUGHBOY POOLS – NATURELOOK WOVEN FLOORING*

Discretely Different 21 Ferndale Drive Ratby, Leicester LE6 0LH Tel. *0116 2386338* E-mail. *info@discretelydifferent.com* Web. *www.underwearfordisabled.co.uk Discretely Different*

Disklabs Ltd Unit 6 & 7 Mercian Park Felspar Road, Tamworth B77 4DP Tel. *01827 50000* Fax. *01827 66666* E-mail. *website@disklabsforensics.co.uk* Web. *www.disklabs.com Disklabs, Disklabs Data Recovery, Disklabs Compute*

Diskshred Unit 2 Mallusk View, Newtownabbey BT36 4FR Tel. *028 90844400* E-mail. *info@amiltd.ie* Web. *www.amiltd.ie DiskShred*

The Disney Store Ltd 3 Queen Caroline Street, London W6 9PE Tel. *020 82221000* Fax. *020 82222795* Web. *www.disney.co.uk *Buena Vista (U.S.A.) – *Buena Vista Home Entertainment (U.S.A.) – *Buena Vista International (U.S.A.) – *Disney Holidays (U.S.A.) – *Disney Land Paris (France) – *Touchstone Movies (U.S.A.) – *Walt Disney Consumer Products (U.S.A.) – *Walt Disney Parks & Resorts (U.S.A.)*

Dispak Ltd Lysander House Bowerhill, Melksham SN12 6SP Tel. *01225 705252* Fax. *01225 706915* E-mail. *sales@dispak.co.uk* Web. *www.dispak.co.uk Hartmann – CDL*

Dispense Technology Services Ltd 19a Watts Road, Studley B80 7PT Tel. *01527 853014* Fax. *01527 853014* E-mail. *j_pickering@btconnect.com* Web. *www.beer-coolers.co.uk DTS LTD*

Display Solutions Ltd Osprey House 1 Osway Court Hinchingbrooke Business Park, Huntingdon PE29 6FN Tel. *01480 411600* Fax. *01480 412266* E-mail. *sales@displaysolutions.co.uk*

Web. *www.displaysolutions.co.uk 3M – Aaeon – Citizen – Data Image – Portwell*

Display Wizard Ltd Unit 5 Avon Building Wallops Wood Farm, Droxford, Southampton SO32 3QY Tel. *01489 878200* Fax. *01489 878201* E-mail. *info@displaywizard.co.uk* Web. *www.displaywizard.co.uk Advance 2 – Airframe – Arena – Barracuda – D4 – D400 – Discovery – Evollution – Expand – FLEX-display – Genie – Imagine – Linear – Media Screen – Nimlok – Octanorm – Orient – Pacific – Plex Display – Quick Fix – Sidewinder – Supremacy – Tiwst – Ultima Display – Vario – Xpress – Xpressions*

Dispo International Express Way Wakefield Europort, Normanton WF6 2TZ Tel. *01924 891462* Fax. *01924 896568* E-mail. *sales@dispo.co.uk* Web. *www.dispo.co.uk *Katerglass*

Distributed Management Systems Ltd Carmel Stockclough Lane, Feniscowles, Blackburn BB2 5JR Tel. *01254 208419* Fax. *01254 208418* E-mail. *marg@casque.co.uk* Web. *www.dms-soft.com Casque*

Diverco Ltd 4 Bank Street, Worcester WR1 2EW Tel. *01905 23383* Fax. *01905 613523* Web. *www.diverco.co.uk Diverco*

Divex Enterprise Drive Westhill Industrial Estate, Westhill AB32 6TQ Tel. *01224 740145* Fax. *01224 740172* E-mail. *info@divexglobal.com* Web. *www.divex.co.uk AquaBeam – DiveDynamics – Divex – Hyfex – Hyox – Kinergetics – Kinergetics - Ultrathermics - Stealth,Bauer Compressors, Aqua Beam, Hyox – Stealth – Ultrathemics*

Dixon Bate Ltd Unit 45 First Avenue Deeside Industrial Park, Deeside CH5 2LG Tel. *01244 288925* Fax. *01244 288462* E-mail. *technical@dixonbate.co.uk* Web. *www.dixonbate.co.uk Grippa – Pinball Wizard*

Dixon Group Europe Ltd Dixon House 350 Walton Summit Centre, Bamber Bridge, Preston PR5 8AS Tel. *01772 323529* Fax. *01772 314664* E-mail. *enquiries@dixoneurope.co.uk* Web. *www.dixoneurope.co.uk Adflex – Adlock – *Bayco (U.S.A.) – *Boss (U.S.A.) – Bradford – Dixon Boss (U.S.A.) – Holedall – Hydrasearch – Hyparflex – Perfecting (U.S.A.) – Sanbrew – Sanflex – Sanfood – Sno-Lock – Suparflex*

J Dixon & Son Ltd 10 Lowther Street, Whitehaven CA28 7AL Tel. *01946 692351* Fax. *01946 66657* E-mail. *wrcs_dixon@hotmail.com* Web. *www.sjdixon.co.uk Dixon*

Dixons Retail Maylands Avenue Hemel Hempstead Industrial Estate, Hemel Hempstead HP2 7TG Tel. *08448 002030* Fax. *01442 233218* E-mail. *john.browett@dsgiplc.com* Web. *www.dixons.co.uk Currys – Dixons – Dixons On-line – Link – Matsui – Miranda – P C World – Saisho*

Dixon Turner Wallcoverings Ltd Henfaes Lane, Welshpool SY21 7BE Tel. *01938 552671* Fax. *020 74360324* E-mail. *enquiries@dixon-turner.co.uk* Web. *www.dixon-turner.co.uk Blenheim – Ethos – Gainsborough – Geneis – Matrix*

D J Az Productions 9 Duffield Drive, Colchester CO4 3YQ Tel. *07990 626729* E-mail. *djazproductions@toucansurf.com* Web. *www.djazproductions.co.cc DJ AZ*

D J B Projects 6 Hobbs Barn Grevatts Lane, Climping, Littlehampton BN17 5RE Tel. *01903 723550* Fax. *01903 724120* E-mail. *info@djbprojects.co.uk* Web. *www.djbprojects.co.uk Brise Soleil*

D & K Europe Ltd Unit 38-39 Crossgate Road, Park Farm Industrial Estate, Redditch B98 7SN Tel. *01527 520073* Fax. *01527 524056* E-mail. *robin@dkeurope.co.uk* Web. *www.dkeurope.co.uk Drytek – Drytek - Accufeed - Accumatic – Meteor – Super N T Meteor – System 32 10*

D K Holdings Ltd Station Approach Staplehurst, Tonbridge TN12 0QN Tel. *01580 891662* Fax. *01580 893675* E-mail. *info@dk-holdings.co.uk* Web. *www.dk-holdings.co.uk Dia-Link – Diagrit – Electroflex – Kendia – Metoid – Scorpion – Tornado*

D L Products Ltd 13 Redhills Road South Woodham Ferrers, Chelmsford CM3 5UL Tel. *01245 426001* Fax. *01245 320040* E-mail. *sales@dlproducts.co.uk* Web. *www.auto-bar.co.uk Auto Bar*

DMC Creative World 13 Leicester Road, Wigston LE18 1NR Tel. *0116 2883133* Fax. *0116 2813592* E-mail. *kim@kimscrafts.co.uk* Web. *www.dmc.com D.M.C. – Gloria & Pat – Margot De Paris – Something Special – Zweigart*

D M G UK Ltd Regus Regus House, Atterbury, Milton Keynes MK10 9RG Tel. *01582 570661* Fax. *01582 593700* E-mail. *richard.watkins@gildemeister.com* Web. *www.gildmeister.com *Deckel (Germany) – Deckel-Maho – Famot – *Gildemeister (Germany and Italy) – Gital – Graziano – *Maho (Germany) – *Max Mueller (Germany) – Microset – Pratt Burnerd America – Saco – Sauer*

D & M Machinery 40 Thornes Lane, Wakefield WF1 5RR Tel. *01924 290206* Fax. *01924 371852* E-mail. *info@dmmachinery.co.uk* Web. *www.dmmachinery.co.uk D&M MACHINERY LTD*

D M S-Diemould 4a Anglo Office Park Lincoln Road Cressex Business Park, High Wycombe HP12 3RH Tel. *01494 523811* Fax. *01494 452898* E-mail. *david.odlin@dms-diemould.co.uk* Web. *www.dms-diemould.co.uk DMS*

D M S Technologies Ltd Belbins Business Park Cupernham Lane, Romsey SO51 7JF Tel. *01794 525400* Fax. *01794 525450* E-mail. *info@dmstech.co.uk* Web. *www.dmstech.co.uk Red Flash – Red Top*

Dnata Unit 8 Radius Park Faggs Road, Feltham TW14 0NG Tel. *020 88906861* Fax. *020 88932543* E-mail. *sales@planehandling.com* Web. *www.dnata.co.uk Plane Handling*

Dobson & Crowther New Berwyn Works Berwyn Road, Llangollen LL20 8AE Tel. *01978 862100* Fax. *01978 860410* E-mail. *sales@dobsonandcrowther.com* Web. *www.dobsonandcrowther.com Smurfit Print UK*

John Dobson Milnthorpe Ltd Bela Mill, Milnthorpe LA7 7QP Tel. *01539 563528* Fax. *01539 562481* E-mail. *sbrown@combs.co.uk* Web. *www.combs.co.uk Duralon – Langdale - Duralon Solace - Shoe laces – Solace*

Docdata Ltd 4th Floor 20 Margaret Street, London W1W8RS Tel. *020 75802880* Fax. *020 75802926* E-mail. *sales@docdatacommerce.co.uk* Web. *www.docdata.co.uk Ablex*

Docklands Light Railway Ltd PO Box 154, London E14 0DX Tel. *020 73639898* Fax. *020 73639708* E-mail. *betty.waight@dlr.tfl.gov.uk* Web. *www.dlr.co.uk Docklands Light Railway*

Doctorcall 121 Harley Street, London W1G 6AX Tel. *08442 570345* Fax. *020 75895862* E-mail. *info@doctorcall.co.uk* Web. *www.doctorcall.co.uk Doctorcall – S.O.S. Medecins*

DocuPrint Ltd 64-65 Eastern Way, Bury St Edmunds IP32 7AB Tel. *01284 748560* Fax. *01284 764033* E-mail. *sales@docuprint.co.uk* Web. *www.docuprint.co.uk Selwyn Thermography*

Dodd's Group Diana House Bonham Drive, Eurolink Commercial Pk, Sittingbourne ME10 3RR Tel. *01795 435000* Fax. *01795 479790* E-mail. *sales@dodds.co.uk* Web. *www.dodds.co.uk Dodd's Group*

Dodson & Horrell Country Store Spencer Street Ringstead, Kettering NN14 4BX Tel. *01933 461539* Fax. *01832 737303* E-mail. *rclark@dodsonandhorrell.com* Web. *www.dodsonandhorrellcountrystore.co.uk Chudleys – Dodson & Horrell Ltd*

Dod's Parliamentry Communications Ltd Westminster Tower 3 Albert Embankment, London SE1 7SP Tel. *020 70917500* Fax. *020 70917505* E-mail. *gerry.murray@dods.co.uk* Web. *www.dods.co.uk Dod's*

Doepke UK Ltd 3 Bentley Way Royal Oak Industrial Estate, Daventry NN11 8QH Tel. *01628 829133* Fax. *01628 829149* E-mail. *sales@doepke.co.uk* Web. *www.doepke.co.uk *Doepke (Germany)*

Doe Sport Ltd Unit 4 Threshelfords Business Park Inworth Road, Feering, Colchester CO5 9SE Tel. *01376 572555* Fax. *01376 572666* E-mail. *sarah.swanick@doesport.co.uk* Web. *www.doesport.co.uk Doe*

Dok Tek Systems Ltd D7d Woodland Way, Bristol BS15 1QH Tel. *0117 9145510* Fax. *0117 9145103* E-mail. *sales.doktek@ukf.net* Web. *www.dok-tek.co.uk RG100*

Dole Fresh UK Ltd Unit 12 Newtons Court Crossways, Crossways Business Park, Dartford DA2 6QL Tel. *01322 293355* Fax. *01322 299700* E-mail. *admin@jpfruit.co.uk* Web. *www.dolefreshuk.com *Jamaican Best (Jamaica) – *Jamaican Pride (Jamaica) – *JP (Costa Rica)*

Dometic UK Ltd Dometic House The Brewery, Blandford Forum DT11 9LS Tel. *01582 494111* Fax. *01582 490197* E-mail. *sales@dometic.co.uk* Web. *www.dometic.co.uk AutoClassic – Classic – DMS – Dometic InSight – HiPro – HiPro Vision – HiPromatic – ProSafe*

Donaldson Filteration GB Ltd Humberstone Lane Thurmaston, Leicester LE4 8HP Tel. *0116 2696161* Fax. *0116 2693028* E-mail. *info@donaldson.com* Web. *www.donaldson.com *Ultrafilter (Germany)*

Donaldson & Mcconnell Ltd Grangemouth Road, Boness EH51 0PU Tel. *01506 828891* Fax. *01506 829070* E-mail. *samantham@donaldsonandmcconnell.co.uk* Web. *www.donaldsonandmcconnell.co.uk Ecojoist*

Donatantonio Lupa House York Way, Borehamwood WD6 1PX Tel. *020 82362222* Fax. *020 82362288* E-mail. *lupa@donatantonio.com* Web. *www.donatantonio.com *Casalinga – *Dececco – *Levoni – *Londina – *Lupa*

Doncasters F B C Ltd PO Box 160, Sheffield S4 7QY Tel. *0114 2431041* Fax. *0114 2431358* E-mail. *pthompson@doncasters.com* Web. *www.doncasters.com Firth – Vikro Steel*

Doncasters Paralloy Ltd Paralloy House Nuffield Road, Cowpen Lane Industrial Estate, Billingham TS23 4DA Tel. *01642 370686* Fax. *01642 564811* E-mail. *paralloysales@doncasters.com* Web. *www.doncasters.com Doncasters Paralloy*

Doncasters Sterling Ltd Colliery Lane Exhall, Coventry CV7 9NW Tel. *024 76645252* Fax. *024 76645312* E-mail. *info@doncasters.com* Web. *www.doncasters.com Sterling*

Doncasters Structures Ltd (Bramah Division) Holbrook Works Station Road, Halfway, Sheffield S20 3GB Tel. *0114 2483981* Fax. *0114 2474105* E-mail. *n.middleton@doncasters.com* Web. *www.doncasters.com Doncasters Bramah*

Don Construction Products Ltd Station Road Churnetside Business Park, Cheddleton, Leek ST13 7RS Tel. *01538 361799* Fax. *01538 361899* E-mail. *info@donconstruction.com* Web. *www.dcp-int.com Betonac – Cemairin 3 – Cempatch L.W. – Cempatch N – Cempatch Primer – Flo-Grout – Flocrete – Keygrout – Keyston and Keyfix – Quickmast – Repcoat – Repelicone – Setcrete – Setseal – Supaflo – Trowelite*

Don & Low Broad Cross Depot 15 St James Road, Forfar DD8 1LE Tel. *01307 452249* Fax. *01307 452201* E-mail. *info@donlow.co.uk* Web. *www.donlow.co.uk Daltex – Daltex Allershield – Daltex Cladshield – Daltex Covershield – Daltex Frameshield – Daltex Gro-Shield – Daltex Roofshield – Daltex Workshield*

Don Springs Sheffield Ltd 340 Coleford Road, Sheffield S9 5PH Tel. *0114 2441545* Fax. *0114 2435291* E-mail. *tony@donsprings.co.uk* Web. *www.donsprings.co.uk Don Springs*

Doorfit Products Ltd Icknield House 90 Heaton Street, Birmingham B18 5BA Tel. *0121 5234171* Fax. *0121 5543859* E-mail. *enquiries@doorfit.co.uk* Web. *www.doorfit.co.uk Doorfit*

Door Loading Services UK Ltd Unit 12 Horton Court Hortonwood 50, Telford TF1 7GY Tel. *01952 676600* Fax. *01952 676100* E-mail. *info@doorloadingservices.co.uk* Web. *www.doorloadingservices.co.uk Compact Door*

Doormen Wennington Road, Southport PR9 7TN Tel. *01704 518000* Fax. *01704 518001* E-mail. *jab@doormen.co.uk* Web. *www.doormen.co.uk ConeLITE – ProFLASH – ProLITE – Rail – Rail – Rail – Rail – SunFLASH – TrafiBEACON – TrafiLAMP E – TrafiLITE – TwinFLASH – TwinLITE – ViLITE*

Doors & Hardware Ltd Taskmaster Works Maybrook Road, Minworth, Sutton Coldfield B76 1AL Tel. *0121 3515276* Fax. *0121 3131228* E-mail. *sales@taskmaster.co* Web. *www.doors-and-hardware.com Taskmaster*

R.J. Doran & Co. Ltd Unit 1 West Kingsdown Industrial Estate London Road, West Kingsdown, Sevenoaks TN15 6EL Tel. *01474 854417* Fax. *01474 853968* E-mail. *customers@primalec.co.uk* Web. *www.primalec.com Autokool – Glo-Leak – Primalec*

Dorcom Ltd 25 Brunswick Road, Shoreham By Sea BN43 5WA Tel. *01273 202851* Fax. *01273 220108* E-mail. *admin@dorcom.co.uk* Web. *www.dorcom.co.uk TADOR – TelePorter*

Dorlux Beds Elizabeth Industrial Estate Shroggs Road, Halifax HX3 5HA Tel. *01422 399250* Fax. *01422 399251* E-mail. *denise.morgan@dorlux.co.uk* Web. *www.dorlux.co.uk Dorlux Beds – Flexiform*

Dorset Lake Shipyard Ltd Lake Drive, Poole BH15 4DT Tel. *01202 674532* Fax. *01202 677518* E-mail. *office@lakeyard.com* Web. *www.bostonwhaler.co.uk *Boston Whaler (U.S.A.)*

Dorset Metal Spinning Services Building 107 Aviation Business Park Hurn, Christchurch BH23 6NW Tel. *01202 593670* Fax. *01202 593670 *Dorset Metal Spinning Services (United Kingdom)*

Dortrend International Ltd Riverside Business Centre Worcester Road, Stourport On Severn DY13 9BZ Tel. *01299 827837* Fax. *01299 827094* E-mail. *sales@dortrend.co.uk* Web. *www.dortrend.co.uk Astral – Clifford Brothers – Sadler Range – Wilden*

Dorvic Engineering Ltd New Street Holbrook Industrial Estate, Holbrook, Sheffield S20 3GH Tel. *0114 2485633* Fax. *0114 2510654* E-mail. *sales@dorvic.com* Web. *www.dorvic.com Dorvic*

Double D Electronics Ltd 6 Robins Wharf Grove Road, Northfleet, Gravesend DA11 9AX Tel. *01474 333456* Fax. *01474 333414* E-mail. *sales@ddelec.co.uk* Web. *www.ddelec.co.uk D.D. – D.D.A. – D.D.S.*

Double Gee Hair Fashions Ltd Unit 12 Trojan Industrial Estate Cobbold Road, London NW10 7ST Tel. *020 84592046* Fax. *020 84590320* E-mail. *doublegee35@aol.com Afco of London Sundries – Afco-Wigs – Affco – Bump Guard Products – Dermo Vedic Products – Gro-Aid Products – Hair Vadic Products – Jambo Products – Kiddie's Gro Aid Products – Kis Cosmetics – Master Curl Products – Oil De Naturelle Products – Perm Kare Products – Pom Pom Braids – Pride of U.S.A. Products*

Double Parking Systems 132 Heathfield Road, Keston BR2 6BA Tel. *01689 856636* Fax. *01689 860429* E-mail. *info@doubleparking.co.uk* Web. *www.doubleparking.co.uk Interpark – Katopark – Klaus Parking System – Maywood – Skyparks – Spacemaker – Stockvis – Traspark – Westfalia*

Double Two Ltd PO Box 1, Wakefield WF1 5RQ Tel. *01924 375651* Fax. *01924 290096* E-mail. *kevin.mellor@wsg.co.uk* Web. *www.wsg.co.uk Bar Harbour – Double Two – Double Two Collections – Mudie*

Douglas Electronic Industries Ltd 55 Eastfield Road, Louth LN11 7AL Tel. *01507 603643* Fax. *01507 600502* E-mail. *sales@douglas-transformers.co.uk* Web. *www.douglas-transformers.co.uk Douglas – Ultravolt*

Douglas Equipment Douglas House Village Road, Cheltenham GL51 0AB Tel. *01242 527921*

Fax. *01242 221198*
E-mail. *reception@douglas-equipment.com*
Web. *www.douglas-equipment.com Douglas Tugmaster – Douglas-Kalmar – Douglas-Kalmar - Douglas Tugmaster – Mu-Meter – *Tugmaster*

Douglas Gill Ltd 429 Tamworth Road Long Eaton, Nottingham NG10 3JT Tel. *0115 9735251* Fax. *0115 9460855* E-mail. *rod@douglasgill.co.uk* Web. *www.douglasgill.co.uk Douglas Gill Ltd*

Oliver Douglas Ltd Amberley Works Chelsea Close, Leeds LS12 4HP Tel. *0113 2797373* Fax. *0113 2791014* E-mail. *admin@oliver-douglas.co.uk* Web. *www.oliverdouglas.com Bullit – Carousel – Hubble Bubble – Panamatic – Rotary Jet – Skipper*

Douglas Press Gaff House Walton Lane, Bosham, Chichester PO18 8QF Tel. *01243 572603* Fax. *01243 572603* E-mail. *info@douglaspress.co.uk* Web. *www.douglaspress.co.uk Tide Tables*

Douwe Egberts UK 225 Bath Road, Slough SL1 3UQ Tel. *08452 711818* Fax. *0845 2711819* E-mail. *info@douwe.com* Web. *www.douwe.com *Cafitesse – *Douwe Egberts – Frappiato – *Piazza D'Oro – *Pickwick – Van Nelle*

Doves Farm Foods Ltd Salisbury Road, Hungerford RG17 0RF Tel. *01488 684880* Fax. *01488 685235* E-mail. *mail@dovesfarm.co.uk* Web. *www.dovesfarm.co.uk Doves Farm*

Dow Corning Ltd Cardiff Road, Barry CF63 2YL Tel. *01446 732350* Fax. *01446 730495* E-mail. *henry.ott@dowcorning.com* Web. *www.dowcorning.com Dow Corning - sealants, Firestop - fire protection sealants, Painters Mate - decorators filler, Plumba - sealants, Trade Mate - sealants, QuickGrip - gap filling adhesive.*

Dow Hyperlast Station Road Birch Vale, High Peak SK22 1BR Tel. *01663 746518* Fax. *01663 746605* E-mail. *info@dow.com* Web. *www.dow.com Autothane – Monothane (United Kingdom) – Diprane – Duramould – Durelast – Dynathane – Hyperkote – Hyperlast – Rotakote – Traffideck*

Down & Francis Industrial Products Ltd (Part of MRX Engineering Services) Ardath Road Kings Norton, Birmingham B38 9PN Tel. *0121 4333300* Fax. *0121 4333325* E-mail. *reception@downandfrancis.co.uk* Web. *www.downandfrancis.co.uk Down & Francis*

Downhole Products plc Badentoy Road Badentoy Industrial Estate, Portlethen, Aberdeen AB12 4YA Tel. *01224 784411* Fax. *01224 785222* E-mail. *ian@downhole.co.uk* Web. *www.downhole.co.uk Spir-o-lizer*

Downland Bedding Co. Ltd 23 Blackstock Street, Liverpool L3 6ER Tel. *0151 2367166* Fax. *0151 2360062* E-mail. *graham@downlandbedding.co.uk* Web. *www.downlandbedding.co.uk Downland – Marchioness – Stardust*

D-Pac Ltd 4 Sketty Close Brackmills Industrial Estate, Northampton NN4 7PL Tel. *01604 705600* Fax. *01604 708100* E-mail. *sales@unipacpet.com* Web. *www.unipacpet.com *Unipac (Denmark)*

D P C Screeding Ltd Brunswick Industrial Estate Brunswick Village, Newcastle Upon Tyne NE13 7BA Tel. *0191 2364226* Fax. *0191 2362242* E-mail. *dpcscreeding@btconnect.com* Web. *www.decorativeplastercompany.com Permascreed – Synthascreed*

D P I Services 33 Moores Lane Standish, Wigan WN6 0JD Tel. *01257 424340* Fax. *01257 424340* E-mail. *ian@dpiservices.co.uk *Corgi*

D P M Electronics Ltd 53 West Bank Drive Anston South Anston, Sheffield S25 5JG Tel. *01909 567105* E-mail. *dave@dpm.org.uk* Web. *www.dpm.org.uk Citrix – Ericom – Microsoft*

D P T S Group Holdings Ltd Unit 2 02 Crayfields Industrial Park Main Road, Orpington BR5 3HP Tel. *01689 824777* Fax. *01689 834550* E-mail. *richard.purves@dpts.co.uk* Web. *www.dpts.co.uk Copy – Demux – Diplomat Tm Multistore – Reformat – Utility – Varscan – Wellman*

D P T Wear Ltd 30 Watchmead, Welwyn Garden City AL7 1LT Tel. *01707 373838* Fax. *01707 332288* E-mail. *info@dptwear.com* Web. *www.dptwear.com Davis and Oliver – Distinctive D – Jaques Estier*

Dragon Ceramex 5 Nomis Park Congresbury, Bristol BS49 5HB Tel. *01934 833409* Fax. *01934 833409 Clay Bulley*

Drainage Center Ltd 116 London Road, Hailsham BN27 3AL Tel. *01323 442333* Fax. *01323 847488* E-mail. *sales@drainagecenter.co.uk* Web. *www.drainagecenter.co.uk Barflo*

Drain-Medic plumbing Gwynfa Chapel Road, Prestatyn LL19 7TH Tel. *0800 2118301* E-mail. *info@drain-medic.com* Web. *www.drain-medic.com Drain-medic*

Dr A J Burch - Harlestone Road Surgery 117 Harlestone Road, Northampton NN5 7AQ Tel. *01604 751832* Fax. *01604 756700* E-mail. *sales@harlestonewoodengates.co.uk* Web. *harlestonewoodengates.co.uk Harlestone Wooden Gates*

Drake Extrusion Ltd Old Mills Moor Top, Drighlington, Bradford BD11 1BY Tel. *0113 2852202* Fax. *0113 2853328* E-mail. *cporteous@drakeuk.com* Web. *www.drakeuk.com Astra – Astra-Star – Gymlene – Gymlene H T*

Drake Medox Nursing 20 Regent Street, London SW1Y 4PH Tel. *0800 1114335* Fax. *020 74951522* E-mail. *reception@drakeintl.co.uk* Web. *www.drakemedoxnursing.co.uk Drake International*

R J Draper & Co. Ltd PO Box 3, Glastonbury BA6 8YA Tel. *01458 831420* Fax. *01458 835355* E-mail. *info@draper-of-glastonbury.com* Web. *www.draper-of-glastonbury.com Buckle My Shoe – Chilkwell – Draper Glastonbury*

Draper Tools Ltd Hursley Road Chandler's Ford, Eastleigh SO53 1YF Tel. *023 80266355* Fax. *023 80260784* E-mail. *sales@drapertools.com* Web. *www.drapertools.com Draper Tools*

Drawmer Electronics Ltd Coleman Street Parkgate, Rotherham S62 6EL Tel. *01709 527574* Fax. *01709 526871* E-mail. *tech@drawmer.com* Web. *www.drawmer.com Drawmer*

Drawn Metal Ltd Anchor Works Swinnow Lane, Leeds LS13 4NE Tel. *0113 2565661* Fax. *0113 2393194* E-mail. *r.copping@drawnmetal.co.uk* Web. *drawnmetal.co.uk Diamond – Drawmet – Drawn Metal*

Drennan International Ltd Bocardo Court Temple Road, Oxford OX4 2EX Tel. *01865 748989* Fax. *01865 748565* E-mail. *sales@drennan.co.uk* Web. *www.drennan.co.uk Acuma – Boilie Bayonet – Buffer Bead – Crystal – Doza – Drenchwear – Drennan – DRX – Extra Sensory Perception – Fidgit – Floozy – Fodder – Ghost – Gripmesh – Loafer – Millennium – Polemaster – Puddle Chucker – Raptor – Red Tails – Silkskin – Spinflex – Squawk – Starpoint – Trollop – UNS*

Drill Service Horley Ltd 23 Albert Road, Horley RH6 7HR Tel. *01293 774911* Fax. *01293 820463* E-mail. *sales@drill-service.co.uk* Web. *www.drill-service.co.uk DIATOOL – Electro-Mechano (U.S.A.) – *Gammons (U.S.A.) – *Holdridge (U.S.A.) – *Najet (U.S.A.) – *Starbide (U.S.A.) – Starlite (U.S.A.)*

Drinkmaster Ltd Plymouth Road, Liskeard PL14 3PG Tel. *01579 342082* Fax. *01579 342591* E-mail. *sales@drinkmaster.co.uk* Web. *www.drinkmaster.co.uk DrinkPac – Mini-Bar – Rotondo – Series 200 – Series 400 – Series 500 – Water point*

Drivall Ltd Narrow Lane, Halesowen B62 9PA Tel. *0121 4231212* Fax. *0121 4229498* E-mail. *ray.hill@drivall.com* Web. *www.drivall.co.uk *Auto-Auger (U.S.A.) – *Drivall (New Zealand) – Drivall – Drivall – Roadall – Shuvholer – *Tru-Test (New Zealand) – *Wirelok (New Zealand)*

Drive2arrive Light Haulage Services Ltd 18 Quinton Close, Solihull B92 9BL Tel. *0121 6840107* E-mail. *sales@drive2arrive.org.uk* Web. *www.drive2arrive.org.uk Drive2arrive*

Dr Oetker 4600 Park Approach Thorpe Park, Leeds LS15 8GB Tel. *0113 8231400* Fax. *0113 8231401* E-mail. *info@oetker.co.uk* Web. *www.oetker.co.uk Supercook*

D R S Data Services Ltd 1 Danbury Court Linford Wood, Milton Keynes MK14 6LR Tel. *01908 666088* Fax. *01908 607668* E-mail. *enquiries@drs.co.uk* Web. *www.drs.co.uk CD 220 – CD 400 – CD 800 Series – CD210 – CD360 – *DRS Infoscan System (U.S.A.) – Edpac – Flips for Windows*

Druces LLP Salisbury House London Wall, London EC2M 5PS Tel. *020 76389271* Fax. *020 76287525* E-mail. *info@druces.com* Web. *www.druces.com Druces & Attlee – Druces International*

Drugasar Service Ltd 2 Deans Trading Estate Deans Road, Swinton, Manchester M27 0JH Tel. *0161 7938700* Fax. *0161 7278057* E-mail. *info@drugasar.co.uk* Web. *www.druservice.co.uk *'G' SERIES (Netherlands) – *Diamond (Italy) – Diamond Art Series – *Diamond Super (Italy) – Diamond Super Style Series – Dik Guerts – *Horizon, (Netherlands) – Kamara – Kamara power flu – Spartherm – Stoves – U.K. Sierra*

Drum Closures Ltd Borwick Rails, Millom LA18 4JT Tel. *01229 772101* Fax. *01229 774972* E-mail. *timc@drum-closures.co.uk* Web. *www.drum-closures.co.uk Drum Closures*

Drum Systems Ltd (Fenner Engineering Ltd) 2 Forge Mills Park Station Road, Coleshill, Birmingham B46 1JH Tel. *01675 467636* Fax. *01675 467582* E-mail. *info@drumsystems.com* Web. *www.drumsystems.com PHARMADRUM*

D R Warehouse Ltd 60-64 Great Hampton Street, Birmingham B18 6EL Tel. *0121 5514920* Fax. *0121 5516504* Web. *www.drwarehouse.co.uk *Discount Radio & Watch Co. Ltd (Hong Kong & Far East)*

Dryer & Hoffman Ltd 4 Lockwood Industrial Park Mill Mead Road, London N17 9QP Tel. *020 83651414* Fax. *020 83651457* E-mail. *info@dryerandhoffmanltd.com* Web. *www.dryerandhoffmanltd.com Manita – Manna*

Drywite Ltd The House of Lee Park Lane, Halesowen B63 2RA Tel. *01384 569556* Fax. *01384 410583* E-mail. *enquiries@drywite.co.uk* Web. *www.drywite.co.uk Drywite – Goldbata – Greenvale – Leezone – Maltflaven*

D S Commodities Ltd Rannoch House 4 Main Street, Queniborough, Leicester LE7 3DA Tel. *0116 2640461* Fax. *0116 2640584* E-mail. *derek@dscommodities.co.uk Briscol*

D S F Refractories & Minerals Ltd Friden Newhaven, Buxton SK17 0DX Tel. *01629 636271* Fax. *01629 636892* E-mail. *info@dsf.co.uk* Web. *www.dsf.co.uk Chemcast – D.S.F. – Dome – Durocast – Durosil – Frisil*

D S G Canusa GmbH & Co. Sales Bergstrand House Parkwood Close, Plymouth PL6 7SG Tel. *01752 209880* Fax. *01752 209850* E-mail. *info-uk@dsgcanusa.com* Web. *www.dsgcanusa.shawcor.com Deray*

DSM UK Ltd Cloister Way Bridges Road, Ellesmere Port CH65 4EL Tel. *0151 3488800* Fax. *01527 590555* E-mail. *sales@dsm.com* Web. *www.dsm.com Atlac – Flomat – Freefix – Freemix – Spectralite – Synolite – Urad – Uradil – Uradur 2P – Uraflex – Uragum – Uralac – Uramex – Uramol – Uranox – Urathix – Uravar – Vracron*

D S Safety 123 St Marychurch Road, Torquay TQ1 3HL Tel. *01803 327543* Fax. *08450 941229* E-mail. *sales@dssafety.co.uk* Web. *www.dssafety.co.uk Beeswift – Caterpillar – Dr Martens – Timberland*

D S Smith Correx 7 Madleaze Trading Estate Madleaze Road, Gloucester GL1 5SG Tel. *01452 316500* Fax. *01452 300436* E-mail. *sales@kayplast.com* Web. *www.dssmithcorrex.com Akylux – Akyplen – Akyver – Combi-Pak – Correx – Correx SM – DucaPlex – Duro-Pallet – HyRack – Sleeve-Pak – Tray-Pak – Uni-Pak*

D S Smith Packaging Ltd Hurdon Road, Launceston PL15 9HN Tel. *01566 772303* Fax. *01566 774489* Web. *www.dssmith-packaging.com Klean Cut – PrestoPac – RegaPaK*

D S Smith Recycling PLC Campbell Road, Stoke On Trent ST4 4RW Tel. *01782 849985* Fax. *01782 412660* E-mail. *enquire@recycleseverns.demon.co.uk* Web. *www.dssmithrecycling.com Trentside Recycling Ltd*

D S Smith Ukraine 4-16 Artillery Row, London SW1P 1RZ Tel. *020 79325000* Fax. *020 72225003* E-mail. *sales@kayplast.com* Web. *www.dssmith.uk.com David S Smith*

D S Technology UK Ltd 43-45 Avenue Close, Birmingham B7 4NU Tel. *0121 3593637* Fax. *0121 3591868* E-mail. *info@dstechnology.co.uk* Web. *www.dstechnology.co.uk Berthiez – Dörries – Droop & Rein – DS Aircraft – Scharmann*

D S T Global Solutions D S T House St Marks Hill, Surbiton KT6 4QD Tel. *020 83905000* Fax. *020 83907000* E-mail. *webmaster@dstintl.com* Web. *www.dstintl.com A.W.D. – Crest Management System – HiPortfolio/2 – Impart/2 – Open Front Office – Open Messenger – Paladign – Uptix*

D T L Broadcast Ltd 5 Johnsons Industrial Estate Silverdale Road, Hayes UB3 3BA Tel. *020 88135200* Fax. *020 88135022* E-mail. *sales@dtl-broadcast.com* Web. *www.dtl-broadcast.com Avey – Routemaster*

Dualit Ltd County Oak Way, Crawley RH11 7ST Tel. *01293 652500* Fax. *01293 652555* E-mail. *info@dualit.com* Web. *www.dualit.com Dualit – Hot Pot – Selectronic*

Dual Pumps Ltd 47 Norman Way, Melton Mowbray LE13 1JE Tel. *01664 567226* Fax. *01664 410127* E-mail. *info@dualpumps.co.uk* Web. *www.dualpumps.co.uk *Banjo (U.S.A.) – *Comet (Spain) – *Flo-Coupling (U.S.A.) – *Flojet (U.S.A.) – *Hypro (U.S.A.) – *Interpump Spa (Italy) – *Pacer (U.S.A.) – *Pratissoli (Italy) – *Precision Fitting (U.S.A.) – *Renson (France) – *Ron-Vik (U.S.A.)*

Dubois Ltd t/a AGI Amaray Arkwright Road Willowbrook North Industrial Estate, Corby NN17 5AE Tel. *01536 274800* Fax. *01536 274902* E-mail. *ian.poore@uk.agimedia.com* Web. *www.amaray.com DuBOIS – Plastic moulding manufrs*

Duco International Ltd 4 Eastbourne Road, Slough SL1 4SF Tel. *01753 522274* Fax. *01753 691952* E-mail. *info@duco.co.uk* Web. *www.duco.co.uk Cow Gum – Cow Proofing – Dunlop Graphic Products*

Ductile Stourbridge Cold Mills Ltd Charles Street, Willenhall WV13 1HG Tel. *01902 365400* Fax. *01902 365444* E-mail. *uksales@dscm.co.uk* Web. *www.dscm.co.uk Ducktile Stourbridge Coldmills*

Ductmate (Europe) Ltd Arrol Road Wesker Gourdie Industrial Estate, Dundee DD2 4TH Tel. *01382 622111* Fax. *01382 621444* E-mail. *enquiries@gallowaygroup.co.uk* Web. *www.ductmate.co.uk Ductmate*

Dudley Factory Doors Ltd G6 Grice Street, West Bromwich B70 7EZ Tel. *0121 5558989* Fax. *0121 5584616* Web. *www.priory-group.com D.F.D.*

Thomas Dudley Ltd 295 Birmingham New Road, Dudley DY1 4SJ Tel. *0121 5575411* Fax. *0121 5575345* E-mail. *info@thomasdudley.co.uk* Web. *www.thomasdudley.co.uk Acclaim – Dauntless – Diplomat – Domino – Dudley – Elite – Japtic – Mirage – Rubberline – Rubberwell – Slimline – Tri-Shell – Turbo*

Dufaylite Developments Ltd 6 Cromwell Road, St Neots PE19 1QW Tel. *01480 215000* Fax. *01480 405526* E-mail. *enquiries@dufaylite.com* Web. *www.dufaylite.com Clayboard – Dualstrip – Dufaylite – Fireblock – Firesleeve – Fittapanel – Interdens – Ultra Board*

M G Duff International Ltd Unit 1 Timberlane Industrial Estate Gravel Lane, Chichester PO19 8PP Tel. *01243 533336*

Fax. *01243 533422* E-mail. *sales@mgduff.co.uk* Web. *www.mgduff.co.uk M.G. Duff*

Dugdale Bros & Co. Ltd 5 Northumberland Street, Huddersfield HD1 1RL Tel. *01484 421772* Fax. *01484 435469* E-mail. *sales@dugdalebros.com* Web. *www.dugdale-bros.com Dugdale*

Dugdale Nutrition Ltd Bellman Mill Salthill, Clitheroe BB7 1QW Tel. *01200 420200* Fax. *01200 428975* E-mail. *info@dugdalenutrition.com* Web. *www.dugdalenutrition.com Home 'N"' Dry – Sweet 'N Dry*

Dulux Ltd Aspect House Manchester Road, West Timperley, Altrincham WA14 5PG Tel. *0161 9736206* Fax. *0161 9629539* Web. *www.dulux.co.uk M.R.*

Dunfermline Building Society Carnegie Avenue, Dunfermline KY11 8PE Tel. *01383 622678* Fax. *01383 627800* E-mail. *comments@dunfermline.com* Web. *www.dunfermline-bs.co.uk Dunfermline Building Society*

Dunfermline Press Pitreavie Business Park Queensferry Road, Dunfermline KY11 8QS Tel. *01383 728201* Fax. *01383 737040* E-mail. *editorial@dunfermlinepress.co.uk* Web. *www.dunfermlinepress.com Alloa Advertiser – Central Fife Times – Dunfermline Press & West of Fife Advertiser – Fife & Kinross Directory – Fife & Kinross Extra – Scottish Curler – Stirling News*

Duni Ltd Chester Road Preston Brook, Runcorn WA7 3FR Tel. *01928 712377* Fax. *01928 754580* E-mail. *info@duni.com* Web. *www.duni.com Duni Banquet Line – Dunilin – Dunisilk – Dunitex*

Dunira Strategy Ltd 33 West Preston Street, Edinburgh EH8 9PY Tel. *08453 708076* Fax. *0845 3708188* E-mail. *info@dunira.com* Web. *www.dunira.com Dunira Strategy*

Dunkelman & Son Ltd Manor House Gold Street, Desborough, Kettering NN14 2PF Tel. *01536 760760* Fax. *020 72870933* E-mail. *sales@dunkelman.com* Web. *www.dunkelman.com Dasco – Dunks – Equitree*

Dunlop Slazenger International Ltd (Golf Division) Unit A Brook Park East, Shirebrook, Mansfield NG20 8RY Tel. *08708 387310* Fax. *0870 8387158* Web. *www.dunlopsports.com 65 – D.D.H. – Dunlop – Dunlop Carry Bags – Dunlop D D H 110 – Dunlop D D H Tour – Dunlop D D H-O C G – Dunlop Insertouch – Dunlop Stand Bag – Dunlop Titanium – Dunlop Vision Putter – Maxfli – Maxfli Australian Blade – Maxfli Briefcase – Maxfli Carryall – Maxfli Deluxe Carry Bag – Maxfli Deluxe Stand 1 – Maxfli Dual Purpose – Maxfli Executive Umbrella – Maxfli Head Covers – Maxfli HT – Maxfli JT Glove – Maxfli Junior Staff – Maxfli Practise Ball Bag – Maxfli Pro Umbrella – Maxfli Revolution – Maxfli Staff Bag – Maxfli Stand Bag – Maxfli Tour Textured – Maxfli Tour Twill Caps – Maxfli Travel Cover – Maxfli Vision – Maxfli XD All Weather – Maxfli XF Maxflex – Maxfli XS Distance – Maxfli XS Tour – Maxfli XS Tour Ltd – Maxfli XS Towel – Maxfli XT All Cabretta – Powermax – Slazenger*

Dunphy Combustion Ltd Queensway, Rochdale OL11 2SL Tel. *01706 649217* Fax. *01706 655512* E-mail. *info@dunphy.co.uk* Web. *www.dunphy.co.uk Dunphy – Ratiotronic TM – Unibloc*

Dunsley Heat Ltd Bridge Mills Holmfirth, Holmfirth HD9 3TW Tel. *01484 682635* Fax. *01484 688428* E-mail. *sales@dunsleyheat.co.uk* Web. *www.dunsleyheat.co.uk Bretton – Dunsley – Enterprise – Firefly – Glo-Flame – Oxypic – Shev 30 – Wentworth*

Duo-Fast Queensway Fforestfach, Swansea SA5 4AD Tel. *01792 563540* Fax. *01792 587649* Web. *www.paslode.com *Duo-Fast (Worldwide)*

Duo GB Ltd 4 Monks Pond Street, Northampton NN1 2LF Tel. *01604 230445* Fax. *01604 231389* E-mail. *sales@duogb.co.uk* Web. *www.leitner.co.uk *Leitner (Germany)*

Duplex Corporate Communications 55 Station Road, Beaconsfield HP9 1QL Tel. *08452 600781* Fax. *08452 600782* E-mail. *sales@duplexcomms.co.uk* Web. *www.ect-av.com BT – GN Netcom – JPL Comms – Plantronics – Sennheiser*

Duplo International Ltd Automated Precision House Hamm Moor Lane, Addlestone KT15 2SD Tel. *01932 263900* Fax. *01372 460252* E-mail. *enquiries@duplointernational.com* Web. *www.duplointernational.com *Duplo (Japan) – Duplo International Ltd*

Duplus Architectural Systems Ltd 370 Melton Road, Leicester LE4 7SL Tel. *0116 2610710* Fax. *0116 2610539* E-mail. *sales@duplus.co.uk* Web. *www.duplus.co.uk Duplus Domes Lightspan – Lightspan*

DuPont Animal Health Solutions (Head Office) Windham Road Chilton Industrial Estate, Sudbury CO10 2XD Tel. *01787 377305* Fax. *01787 310846* E-mail. *biosecurity@gbr.dupont.com* Web. *www.ahs.dupont.com Farm Fluid S – Longlife 2505 – Oocide – Virkon*

Du Pont UK Ltd Wedgewood Way, Stevenage SG1 4QN Tel. *01438 734000* Fax. *01438 734836* Web. *www.dupont.co.uk Ally – Antron – Aracon – Astron – Avitex – Avitone – Bexloy – Butacite – Centari – Clysar – Coolmax – Cordura – Corebond – Corian – Corlar – CorMax – Cromalin – Cronar – Curzate – Cyrel – Dacron – Delrin – Dymel – Elvaloy – Elvamide – Elvanol – Elvax – Fodel – Freon – Harmony Extra – Hypalon – Hytrel – Hyvar – Imron – Kalrez – Kapton – Keldax – Kevlar – Korex – Krytox – Ludox – Lycra – Maranyl – Merpol – Micro-Loft – Minlon – Mylar – Nafion – Nomex – Oxone – Permasep – Pyralin – Pyralux – Quallofil – Riston – Rynite – Selar – Silverstone – Sinbar – Sontara – Stainmaster – Supplex – Surlyn – Suva – Tactel – Tedlar – Teflon – Tefzel – Tepex – Terathane – Terinda – ThermaBlock – Thermolite – Thermoloft – Thermount – Ti-Pure – Tufcote – Tynex – Typar – Tyvek – Tyzor – Vacrel – Vamac – Vazo – Vespel – Viton – Vydate – Zelec – Zemdrain – Zonyl – Zymaxx – Zytel*

Du Pre plc Unit 3-4 The Vo-Tec Centre Hambridge Lane, Newbury RG14 5TN Tel. *01635 555555* Fax. *01635 555533* E-mail. *info@dupre.co.uk* Web. *www.dupre.co.uk du-Pre P.L.C.*

Durable Contracts Ltd Crabtree Manorway South, Belvedere DA17 6AW Tel. *020 83111211* Fax. *020 83107893* E-mail. *sales@durable-online.com* Web. *www.durable-online.com Durable*

Duradec Wales Ltd 30 Ellwood Path St Dials, Cwmbran NP44 4RD Tel. *01633 485309* Fax. *01633 863949 Duradec – Wadec*

Durham Duplex 312 Petre Street, Sheffield S4 8LT Tel. *0114 2432313* Fax. *0114 2444329* E-mail. *sales@durham-duplex.co.uk* Web. *www.durham-duplex.co.uk Durham-Duplex*

Durotan Ltd 20 West Street, Buckingham MK18 1HE Tel. *01280 814048* Fax. *01280 817842* E-mail. *sales@durotan.ltd.uk* Web. *www.durotan.ltd.uk Ecoflex System – Safety Pipe – Spirogal System – Standard System – Starpipe – Steel-in-Steel*

James Durrans & Sons Ltd Phoenix Works Thurlstone, Sheffield S36 9QU Tel. *01226 370000* Fax. *01226 370336* E-mail. *info@durrans.co.uk* Web. *www.durrans.co.uk James Durrans – Phoenix – Pulverbond – Pulverite*

Duscovent Engineering Ltd 86 Wellington Road North, Stockport SK4 1HT Tel. *0161 4804811* Fax. *0161 4806503* E-mail. *sales@duscovent.co.uk* Web. *www.duscovent.co.uk Duscovent – Dusfilt – Dusjet – Dusmatic – Duspray*

Dustraction Ltd 1 Pomeroy Drive Oadby, Leicester LE2 5NE Tel. *0116 2713212* Fax. *0116 2713215* E-mail. *info@dustraction.co.uk* Web. *www.dustraction.co.uk Catinair – Dustrax*

Dutton Forshaw Ltd Bircholt Road, Maidstone ME15 9YN Tel. *01622 699350* Fax. *01622 699204* E-mail. *maidstone.skoda@duttonforshaw.com* Web. *www.bristolaudi.co.uk Dutton Forshaw*

D W B Anglia Ltd Gang-Nail Systems Ltd Mapledean Industrial Estate Maldon Road Maldon Road, Latchingdon, Chelmsford CM3 6LG Tel. *01621 744455* Fax. *01621 744976* E-mail. *trevor.t@dwbgroup.co.uk* Web. *www.dwbgroup.co.uk Ecojoist*

D W Group Ltd Unit 7 Peverel Drive Bletchley, Milton Keynes MK1 1NL Tel. *01908 642323* Fax. *01908 640164* E-mail. *sales@photopages.com* Web. *www.photopages.com Viewbox – Viewpack*

Dycem Ltd Unit 2-4 Ashley Trading Estate Ashley Parade, Bristol BS2 9BB Tel. *0117 9559921* Fax. *0117 9541194* E-mail. *mark.dalziel@dycem.com* Web. *www.dycem.com 3 Step Mat – Clean-Zone – Grip-It-Hold – Jar Opener – Protectamat – *Work Zone (U.S.A.)*

Dyebrick Ripley House Keycol Hill Newington, Sittingbourne ME9 8NE Tel. *01795 871972* Fax. *01795 871077* E-mail. *mail@dyebrick.com* Web. *www.dyebrick.com Dyebrick*

George Dyke Ltd Imperial Works Heath Road, Darlaston WS10 8LP Tel. *0121 5267138* Fax. *0121 5688956* E-mail. *gsmith@george-dyke.co.uk* Web. *www.george-dyke.co.uk George Dyke – Keep It (United Kingdom)*

Dymet Alloys (Division of Corewire Ltd) Station Road West Ash Vale, Aldershot GU12 5LZ Tel. *01252 517651* Fax. *01252 522517* E-mail. *info@corewire.com* Web. *www.corewire.com Dymet*

Dynamic Battery Services Ltd Unit 1 Gillibrands Road, Skelmersdale WN8 9TA Tel. *01695 557575* Fax. *01695 557676* E-mail. *paul.buttrick@dynamicbatteries.co.uk* Web. *www.dynamicbatteries.com Blue Star Battery*

Dynamic Ceramic Ltd Unit 10 Crewe Hall Enterprise Park Weston Road, Crewe CW1 6UA Tel. *01270 501000* Fax. *01270 501423* E-mail. *sales@dynacer.com* Web. *www.dynacer.com Dynallox – Technox*

Dynamic Controls Ltd Union Street Royton, Oldham OL2 5JD Tel. *0161 6333933* Fax. *0161 6334113* E-mail. *sales@dynamiccontrols.co.uk* Web. *www.dynamiccontrols.co.uk Dycon – Dynamic Controls*

Dynamic Drawings Ltd (Head Office) 4 Harbour House Harbour Way, Shoreham By Sea BN43 5HZ Tel. *01273 464417* Fax. *01273 239740* E-mail. *ddl@globalnet.co.uk* Web. *www.hdp.co.uk H.D.P. 105 – H.D.P. Swell – Hydronox – S.P.3*

Dynamometer Services Group Ltd Stock End Station Road, Bransford, Worcester WR6 5JH Tel. *01886 834860* Fax. *01886 834879* E-mail. *sales@dsgroup.uk.com* Web. *www.dsgroup.uk.com APICOM – AVL Zollner – Borghi – Froude Consine – SAJ – Schenck*

Dynashape Ltd 117 Station Rd Old Hill, Cradley Heath B64 6PL Tel. *0121 5595931* Fax. *0121 5592008* E-mail. *sales@dynashape.co.uk* Web. *www.dynashape.co.uk Alloymaster – Alumaster – Beammaster – Dynasaw – Dynashape – Evolution – Encore – Geomevary – Palletsupremo – Pozi-Combi – Pozi-Pitch – Pozi-Rake – Pozi-Tooth – Pozi-Vari – Premflex*

D Y N Metal Ltd 25-29 Chase Road, London NW10 6TA Tel. *020 89610656* Fax. *020 89618820* E-mail. *info@dynmetal.co.uk* Web. *www.dynmetal.co.uk D.Y.N – D.Y.N. Gz 10 – D.Y.N. Gz 14 – D.Y.N. Rm – P.A.N. 7 – P.A.N. Al 7 – P.A.N. Al10 – P.A.N. B – P.A.N. Soms – Thermoject*

Dyno Rod Ltd Zockoll House 143 Maple Road, Surbiton KT6 4BJ Tel. *0800 112112* Fax. *01256 780417* E-mail. *postmaster@dyno.com* Web. *www.dyno.com Dyno-Kil – Dyno-Locks – Dyno-Plumbing – Dyno-Rod – Dyno-Roofing*

D Young & Co. 120 Holborn, London EC1N 2DY Tel. *020 72698550* Fax. *020 72698555* E-mail. *mail@dyoung.co.uk* Web. *www.dyoung.com D. Young*

Dyson Thermal Technologies Baslow Road Totley, Sheffield S17 3BL Tel. *0114 2355300* Fax. *0114 2356010* E-mail. *enq@dysontt.com* Web. *www.dysontt.com Clinoblock – Clinotherm – Zedflo – Zedmark – Zedtec*

E

E 2 V Technologies Ltd 106 Waterhouse Lane, Chelmsford CM1 2QU Tel. *01245 493493* Fax. *01245 492492* E-mail. *keith.attwood@e2vtechnologies.com* Web. *www.e2v.com Argus – E.E.V. – Pevicon – Photon – Super Photon*

Eagle Automation Systems Ltd Newhouse Farm Vicarage Lane, North Weald, Epping CM16 6AP Tel. *01992 524800* Fax. *01992 522208* E-mail. *info@eagleautogate.co.uk* Web. *www.eagleautogate.co.uk BFT – BPT – Came – Facc – Genius – SEA*

Eagleburgmann Industries UK Llp Welton Road, Warwick CV34 5PZ Tel. *01926 417600* Fax. *01926 417617* E-mail. *warwick@uk.eagleburgmann.co.uk* Web. *www.burgmann.com EagleBurgmann – KE-Burgmann – DiamondFaces – TotalSealCare*

Eagle Envelopes Ltd Unit 1 Block 1 Whiteside Industrial Estate, Bathgate EH48 2RX Tel. *01506 634463* Fax. *01506 634366* E-mail. *sales@eagle-envelopes.com* Web. *www.eagle-envelopes.com Autofast – Condor – Eagle – Falcon – Harrier – Hawk – Merlin – Osprey – Peregrine – Treesaver*

Eagle Ottawa UK Ltd Thelwall Lane Latchford, Warrington WA4 1NQ Tel. *01925 650251* Fax. *01925 655547* E-mail. *contact@eagleottawa.com* Web. *www.eagleottawa.com Eagle O'Hawe Warrington*

Eagle Security Solutions Ltd 162 Trafalgar Road, London SE10 9TZ Tel. *020 88530580* Fax. *020 88549701* E-mail. *info@eaglesecuritysolutions.co.uk* Web. *www.eaglesecuritysolutions.co.uk ADT – BPT – DSC – Eagle Security – Redcare – Redcare GSM*

E A O Ltd Albert Drive, Burgess Hill RH15 9TN Tel. *01444 236000* Fax. *01444 236641* E-mail. *susan.jacques@eao.com* Web. *www.eao.co.uk *E.A.O. (Switzerland) – E.B.T. – *EAO Secme (France) – *EAO Swisstac (Germany) – *Grayhill (U.S.A.) – *Sanyo Denki (Japan)*

E A P International Ltd Junction 19 Industrial Park Green Lane, Heywood OL10 1NB Tel. *01706 624422* Fax. *0161 8352619* E-mail. *sales@eapseals.com* Web. *www.eapseals.com *Eriks (Netherlands)*

Earth Anchors Ltd 15 Campbell Road, Croydon CR0 2SQ Tel. *020 86849601* Fax. *020 86842230* E-mail. *enquiries@earth-anchors.com* Web. *www.earth-anchors.com Rootfast*

Easab Cutting Systems Unit 2-3 Crown Way, Andover SP10 5LU Tel. *01264 332233* Fax. *01264 332074* Web. *www.easab.co.uk Combirex CXA – Condor – Ergorex EXA – Falcon – Firebird – Hancommander – Imp – Minigraph – Numorex NXA – Picorex PXC – Star – Suprarex SXE-P – Telerex TXB – Tubocadet – Ultrarex*

Easat Antennas Ltd Goodwin House Leek Road, Stoke On Trent ST1 3NR Tel. *01782 208028* Fax. *01782 208060* E-mail. *rgoodwin@goodwingroup.com* Web. *www.easet.co.uk Easat*

R M Easdale 67 Washington Street, Glasgow G3 8BB Tel. *0141 2212708* Fax. *0141 2043159* E-mail. *robert.easdale@rmeasdale.com* Web. *www.rmeasdale.com Dale – Dale Brand – Leeswood*

Ease Electrical Goods Unit 2 1000 North Circular Road, London NW2 7JP Tel. *020 84521203* Fax. *020 84527819* E-mail. *sales@ease.ltd.uk* Web. *www.ease.ltd.uk ES*

Ease-E-Load Trolleys Ltd Saunders House Moor Lane, Birmingham B6 7HH Tel. *0121 3562228* Fax. *0121 3562220* E-mail. *info@ease-e-load.co.uk* Web. *www.ease-e-load.co.uk Ease-E-Load*

Easifix 7 Oakwood Business Park Stephenson Road West, Clacton On Sea CO15 4TL Tel. *08456 018291* Fax. *01255 436852* E-mail. *info@easifix.co.uk* Web. *www.easifix.co.uk Easi-Glide – Easi-pave – Easifix*

Eastbrook Farm Organic Meat Ltd The Calf House Cues Lane, Bishopstone, Swindon SN6 8PL Tel. *01793 790460* Fax. *01793 791239* E-mail. *info@helenbrowningorganics.co.uk* Web. *www.helenbrowningorganics.co.uk *Eastbrook Farm Organic Meats – *Helen Browning's Totally Organics*

Easterby Trailers Ltd Cottam Grange Cottam, Driffield YO25 3BY Tel. *01377 267415* Fax. *01377 267416* E-mail. *info@easterbytrailers.co.uk* Web. *www.easterbytrailers.co.uk *Easterby Trailers – *Monocoque Trailers*

Eastern Water Treatment Ltd 241 Heigham Street, Norwich NR2 4LN Tel. *01603 877222* Fax. *01603 877223* E-mail. *keith@dolphinspas.co.uk* Web. *www.easternwatertreatment.com Eastern Water Treatment – EWT*

East Lancs Chemical Co. Ltd Edge Lane Droylsden, Manchester M43 6AU Tel. *0161 3715585* Fax. *0161 3011990* E-mail. *info@eastlancschemical.com* Web. *www.eastlancschemical.com Elco – Opal*

Eastman Staples Ltd (Eastman Machine Co. Ltd) Lockwood Road, Huddersfield HD1 3QW Tel. *01484 888888* Fax. *01484 888800* E-mail. *c.werb@eastman.co.uk* Web. *www.eastman.co.uk Blue Streak II – Brute – C.R.A. – Duro – Eastman – Summit*

East Midland Coatings Ltd Barleyfield, Hinckley LE10 1YE Tel. *01455 619176* Fax. *01455 619051* E-mail. *sales@eastmidlandcoatings.co.uk* Web. *www.eastmidlandcoatings.co.uk E-Coat – Emcoat – Emralon – Greblon – Molykote – Nylon – Senotherm – Suncorite – Teflon – Xylan – Xylan - Teflon - Molykote - Suncorite - Greblon - Senotherm - Emralon - Nylon - E-Coat - Emcoat*

East Midland Computers Ltd Downing Road West Meadows Industrial Estate, Derby DE21 6HA Tel. *01332 362481* Fax. *01332 291272* E-mail. *info@emc.cc* Web. *www.emc.cc Emcom Emcom Plus*

East Yorkshire Motor Services Ltd 252 Anlaby Road, Hull HU3 2RS Tel. *01482 327142* Fax. *01482 212040* E-mail. *helpdesk@eyms.co.uk* Web. *www.eyms.co.uk Bus UK – Connor & Graham – Diplomat Holidays – E.Y.M.S. – E.Y.M.S. Group – East Yorkshire – East Yorkshire Buses – East Yorkshire Coaches – East Yorkshire Diplomat – East Yorkshire Investments – East Yorkshire Motor Services – East Yorkshire Properties – East Yorkshire Railways – East Yorkshire Tours – East Yorkshire Travel – Finglands Coachways – Finglands Travel Agency – Hull and District Motor Services – Little Bus – Minster Link – Primrose Valley Coaches – Reddy – Scarborough and District – Scarborough Skippers – Skipper – Sound Travels – Torfirth*

Easygates Ltd Unit 4 Broadcott Industrial Estate, Cradley Heath B64 6NT Tel. *08707 606536* Fax. *0121 5613395* E-mail. *info@easygates.co.uk* Web. *www.easygates.co.uk Liftmaster*

Easymatics Ltd Clock House High Street, Wadhurst TN5 6AA Tel. *08702 416275* Fax. *0870 4580387* E-mail. *terry@easymatics.net* Web. *www.easymatics.net Entivity VLC – Steeplechase VLC – Think & Do – Think & Do Live – Think & Do Studio*

Eaton Aerospace Ltd Abbey Park Southampton Road, Titchfield, Fareham PO14 4QA Tel. *01329 853000* Fax. *01202 880096* Web. *www.cobham.com DTS 2000 – Falconet – M.R.T.T. – RDS 1600*

Eaton Electric Ltd Reddings Lane Tyseley, Birmingham B11 3EZ Tel. *0121 6852100* Fax. *08700 507525* E-mail. *s.parker@mem250.com* Web. *www.mem250.com Delta Electrical Systems – Johnson & Phillips*

Eaton Electric Sales Ltd (a division of Eaton Group) 221 Dover Road, Slough SL1 4RF Tel. *01753 608700* Fax. *01753 608995* E-mail. *razahussain@eaton.com* Web. *www.eaton.com/powerquality *Powerware (U.S.A.) – Powerware Systems*

Eaton Valve Products Limited 32 The Nurseries Eaton Bray, Dunstable LU6 2AX Tel. *01525 229170* Fax. *01525 229425* E-mail. *sales@eaton-valves.co.uk* Web. *www.eaton-valves.co.uk TRP Perar – Curtiss Wright*

W G Eaton Ltd 61-63 Lower Essex Street, Birmingham B5 6SN Tel. *0121 6222611* Fax. *0121 6666367* E-mail. *sales@wgeaton.co.uk* Web. *www.wgeaton.co.uk Fibertherm – Vulcan*

Eaton-Williams Group Ltd Fircroft Way, Edenbridge TN8 6EZ Tel. *01732 866055* Fax. *01732 863461* E-mail. *gerald.stapley@eaton-williams.com* Web. *www.eaton-williams.com B T X & NBTX/CTX (United Kingdom) – Colman – Cubit (United Kingdom) – Eaton-Williams Service (United Kingdom) – Edenaire – Minicentral – Moducel FLEXaire – Qualitair – Vapac – VapaNet – Varivap*

Ebac (Dehumidifier/Industrial Division) St Helen Trading Estate, Bishop Auckland DL14 9AL Tel. *01388 605061* Fax. *01388 609845* E-mail. *info@ebac.com* Web. *www.ebac.co.uk BD & CD – Cool N Easy – E-Max – E.B.A.C. – Easycooler – EBAC – EBAC 2000 Series – Eddy – Hepa-Air-Deluxe – Homedry – PF400*

Ebm-Papst The Barn Sheepdown, East Ilsley, Newbury RG20 7ND Tel. *0870 7665170* Fax. *0870 7665180* E-mail. *gareth.jones@uk.ebmpapst.com* Web. *www.ebmpapst.co.uk B C I – Dc Brushless Motors – *Mechatronic (Germany and USA) – Megafan (Germany) – Multifan (Germany) – *PAMOdrive – *PAMOdyn – *PAMOtronics – *Papst (Germany) – Sintec Bearings – Superquiet – Variodrive – Variofan – Variopro*

Ebor Concrete Ltd PO Box 4, Ripon HG4 1JE Tel. *01765 604351* Fax. *01765 690065* E-mail. *paul.whitham@eborconcrete.co.uk* Web. *www.eborconcrete.co.uk Ebor*

Eborcraft Ltd 11-12 Chessingham Park Common Road Dunnington, York YO19 5SE Tel. *01904 481020* Fax. *01904 481022* E-mail. *sales@eborcraft.co.uk* Web. *www.eborcraft.co.uk Eborcraft*

E B S Safety Netting Bretts Farm Romford Road, Aveley, South Ockendon RM15 4XD Tel. *01708 860341* Fax. *01708 865701* E-mail. *info@safety-netting.net* Web. *www.safety-netting.net E.B.S. – External Building Services Ltd*

E C G D Harbour Exchange Square, London E14 9GE Tel. *020 75127000* Fax. *020 75127649* E-mail. *ian.dykstra@ecgd.gsi.gov.uk* Web. *www.ecgd.gov.uk E.C.G.D.*

E C Group Ltd Europa Park London Road, Grays RM20 4DN Tel. *01375 484555* Fax. *01375 484556* E-mail. *info@ecgroup.co.uk* Web. *www.ecgroup.co.uk E Christian & Company (Holdings) Limited – E Christian & Company Limited – EC Group – EC Logistics*

ECi Software Solutions Limited Building C West CentralRuncorn Road, Lincoln LN6 3QP Tel. *0333 1230333* Fax. *0333 1230313* E-mail. *eu-info@ecisolutions.com* Web. *www.ipuk.com Progress (United Kingdom) – M1 (United Kingdom) – Horizon (United Kingdom) – NGV (United Kingdom) – Vision (United Kingdom) – EasyOrder (United Kingdom) – FMAudit (United Kingdom) – Acsellerate (United Kingdom)*

Eckold Ltd 15 Lifford Way Binley Industrial Estate, Coventry CV3 2RN Tel. *024 76455580* Fax. *024 76302777* E-mail. *sales@eckold.co.uk* Web. *www.eckold.co.uk *Eckold (Germany) – Horning*

Eclipse Blind Systems 10 Fountain Crescent Inchinnan Business Park, Inchinnan, Renfrew PA4 9RE Tel. *0141 8123322* Fax. *0141 8125253* E-mail. *info@eclipse-blinds.co.uk* Web. *www.eclipse-blinds.co.uk Blind System Selection – Elan – Europa – Gazelle – ISO Design Venitian Blind – Isodesign Blind – Mirage – Myotex – Neotex – Panther – Powershade – Shades of Light Roller Blind Fabrics Collection – Shades of Light Venetian Blind Collection – Shades of Light Vertical Blind Collection – Shades of Light Wooden Venetian Blind Collection – Techniflam – Total Solutions Total Eclipse – Unipleat*

Eclipse Magnetics Ltd Atlas Way, Sheffield S4 7QQ Tel. *0114 2250600* Fax. *0114 2250610* E-mail. *sales@eclipse-magnetics.co.uk* Web. *www.eclipse-magnetics.co.uk Applied Magnetic Systems – Eclipse Magnetics – Ultralift – Ultralift Plus*

Eclipse Nursecall Systems Ltd The Mount Mount Gawne Road, Port St Mary, Isle Of Man IM9 5LX Tel. *01624 832821* Fax. *01624 836279* E-mail. *sales@nursecall.co.uk* Web. *www.nursecall.co.uk Linecall 2000 – Linecall 3000*

Eclipse Sprayers Ltd 120 Beakes Road, Smethwick B67 5AB Tel. *0121 4202494* Fax. *0121 4291668* E-mail. *davepennock@btconnect.com* Web. *www.eclipsesprayers.com Eclipse – Finasrain – Haws – Haws watering cans*

ECO Hydraulic Presses Ltd Unit 1 Stanley Business Park Prospect Road, Burntwood WS7 0AL Tel. *01543 671011* Fax. *01543 676266* E-mail. *ehp@edbroemt.co.uk* Web. *www.edbroemt.co.uk Pilot – Edbro – EMT*

Ecolab Duke Avenue Stanley Green Trading Estate, Cheadle SK8 6RB Tel. *0161 4856166* Fax. *0161 4884127* E-mail. *inge.van.der.linden@ecolab.com* Web. *www.ecolab.com Delco*

Ecolec Ltd Sharrocks Street, Wolverhampton WV1 3RP Tel. *01902 457575* Fax. *01902 457797* E-mail. *info@ecolec.co.uk* Web. *www.ecolec.co.uk Ecolec (United Kingdom)*

Econ Engineering Ltd Boroughbridge Road, Ripon HG4 1UE Tel. *01765 605321* Fax. *01765 607487* E-mail. *sales@econ.uk.com* Web. *www.econ.uk.com Hedgemaster – Hot Asphalt – Snow – ZeroC*

Ecopure Waters 9 Alexander House Thame Road, Haddenham, Aylesbury HP17 8BZ Tel. *01844 290088* Fax. *01844 292969* E-mail. *sales@ecopurewaters.com* Web. *www.ecopurewaters.com *Classic Crystal – *Classic Crystal Ireland – Classic Crystal Scotland*

Ecorys UK Albert House 92-93 Edward Street, Birmingham B1 2RA Tel. *0121 2128800* Fax. *0121 6163699* E-mail. *chris.ralph@uk.ecorys.com* Web. *www.uk.ecorys.com Polmark*

E C Smith & Sons Ltd Unit H-J Kingsway Industrial Estate Kingsway, Luton LU1 1LP Tel. *01582 729721* Fax. *01582 458893* E-mail. *enquiries@ecsmith.com* Web. *www.ecsmith.com E.C.S.*

E C U S Endcliffe Holt 343 Fulwood Road, Sheffield S10 3BQ Tel. *0114 2669292* Fax. *0114 2667707* E-mail. *contactus@ecusltd.co.uk* Web. *www.ecusltd.co.uk Environmental Consultancy University of Sheffield*

Edbro plc Nelson Street, Bolton BL3 2JJ Tel. *01204 528888* Fax. *01204 531957* E-mail. *postmaster@edbro.co.uk* Web. *www.edbro.co.uk Edbro hydraulic tipping systems – Edbro steel tipping bodies*

E D C International Ltd Brook House 14 Station Road Pangbourne, Reading RG8 7AN Tel. *0118 9842040* Fax. *0118 9845300* E-mail. *j.major@edcpumps.com* Web. *www.edcpumps.com Drain Pan Pump – Limpet Pump – MasterPump – Pacific Pump – Skyjet High Performance Tank Pump*

Edding UK Ltd Edding House Merlin Centre Acrewood Way, St Albans AL4 0JY Tel. *01727 846688* Fax. *01727 839970* E-mail. *info@edding.co.uk* Web. *www.edding.co.uk Edding – Legamaster*

Edeco Petroleum Services Ltd Bessemer Way, Great Yarmouth NR31 0LX Tel. *01493 653555* Fax. *01493 657428* E-mail. *enquiries@edeco.co.uk* Web. *www.edeco.co.uk Edeco Engineering – Edeco Power Systems – Edeco Pressure Systems – Valve Healthcare Services*

Eden Halls Greenhouses Ltd The Distribution Centre Stoke Road, Stoke Orchard, Cheltenham GL52 7RS Tel. *01242 676625* Fax. *01242 676626* E-mail. *mail@eden-greenhouses.com* Web. *www.edengreenhouses.com Louvamatic – Princess Greenhouses – Ventomatic*

Eden Rose Lifestyle 11 St Mary Street, Chepstow NP16 5EW Tel. *01291 627340* Fax. *01291 431636* E-mail. *info@edenroselifestyle.co.uk* Web. *www.edenroselifestyle.co.uk Eden Rose Lifestyle*

E D F Energy 40 Grosvenor Place, London SW1X 7EN Tel. *020 72429050* Fax. *020 73313455* E-mail. *vincent.derivaz@seeboardenergy.com* Web. *www.edfenergy.com London Electricity (LE)*

Edf Energy 329 Portland Road, Hove BN3 5SU Tel. *01273 422666* Fax. *01273 432883* Web. *www.edfenergy.com Seeboard*

E D F Man Hornby Dock Regent Road, Bootle L20 1EF Tel. *0151 9222803* Fax. *0151 9443919* E-mail. *phil.higgins@edfman.com* Web. *www.edfman.com *Biopro – *Fulcrum – *Molasses – *Regumaize – *Transition Cow*

Edicron Ltd The Rac Building Park Road, Faringdon SN7 7BP Tel. *01367 243030* Fax. *01367 243131* E-mail. *sales@edicron.co.uk* Web. *www.edicron.com Edicron – EEV (United Kingdom) – EI – Eimac (U.S.A.) – Eratron – JJ (Slovakia) – RFT (Germany) – Sovtek (Russian Federation) – Svetlana (Russian Federation) – Tesla (Czech Republic) – Valve Art (China) – Western Electric (U.S.A.)*

E D L Lighting Ltd Redbrook Lane, Rugeley WS15 1QU Tel. *01889 582112* Fax. *01889 584012* E-mail. *sales@edl-lighting.co.uk* Web. *www.edl-lighting.co.uk E.D.L. – *Haloflex (Germany) – Task*

E D M E Ltd Edme House High Street, Mistley, Manningtree CO11 1HG Tel. *01206 393725* Fax. *01206 395471* E-mail. *info@edme.com* Web. *www.edme.com Autumn Sun – Dextramalt – Edme – Extratone – Frumalo – H.D.A. – Malt Cob – Maltone – Roalt – Ryetone – Stickimalt – Wheatone – Zymax*

Edmolift UK Ltd Blois Meadow Business Centre Blois Road, Steeple Bumpstead, Haverhill CB9 7BN Tel. *01440 730640* Fax. *01440 730004* E-mail. *info@edmolift.co.uk* Web. *www.edmolift.co.uk Edmolift*

Edmundson Electrical Ltd Unit 1 Westpoint, Aylesbury HP19 8YZ Tel. *01296 486251* Fax. *01296 423374* E-mail. *aylesbury.218@eel.co.uk* Web. *www.edmundson-electrical.co.uk/ Edmundson Electrical*

Edo M B M Technology Ltd (Head Office) Emblem House Home Farm Business Park, Brighton BN1 9HU Tel. *01273 810500* Fax. *01273 810565* E-mail. *info@itt.com* Web. *www.mbmtech.co.uk Filmwire*

E D T Direct Ion Ltd Unit 5 Waldershare Park, Waldershare, Dover CT15 5DQ Tel. *01304 829960* Fax. *01304 829970* E-mail. *sales@edt.co.uk* Web. *www.edt.co.uk Chromajet – Qualiprobe*

Educational & Municipal Equipment Scotland Ltd Blackaddie Road, Sanquhar DG4 6DE Tel. *01659 50404* Fax. *01659 50107* E-mail. *info@emefurniture.co.uk* Web. *www.emefurniture.co.uk Modulink*

Educational & Scientific Products Ltd Unit A2 Dominion Way Rustington, Littlehampton BN16 3HQ Tel. *01903 773340* Fax. *01903 771108* E-mail. *sales@espmodels.co.uk* Web. *www.espmodels.co.uk E S P – Educational and Scientific Products – Skeletorso – Tube Aid*

Edu-Sci Ltd Unit 4 Teal Farm Way, Washington NE38 8BG Tel. *0191 4174173* Fax. *0191 4972920* E-mail. *sales@edu-sci.com* Web. *www.edu-sci.com Astronaut Food – Astronaut Foods – Astronaut Ice Cream*

Effortec Ltd 13 Station Road Cam, Dursley GL11 5NS Tel. *01453 546011* Fax. *01453 549222* E-mail. *rtn@f4tec.co.uk* Web. *www.f4tec.co.uk Manner (Finland) – Okartek (Finland) – Roll-Flex (Finland) – Sofame*

(France) – Stockmaster (Australia) – Tango (Finland) – Trader (United Kingdom)

Eggbox Graphics Crawley House Shelton Road, Willowbrook East Industrial Estate, Corby NN17 5XH Tel. *01536 260038* Fax. *01536 407927* E-mail. *emailus@eggboxgraphics.co.uk* Web. *www.eggboxgraphics.co.uk Eggbox Graphics*

Egger UK Ltd Anick Grange Road, Hexham NE46 4JS Tel. *01434 602191* Fax. *01434 600122* E-mail. *info@egger.co.uk* Web. *www.egger.co.uk Egger Laminates (Austria) – Eurodekor (United Kingdom) – Eurospan (United Kingdom) – Eurostrand OSB (Germany) – Formline (Austria) – Formline (Germany) – Formline Dekor (Austria) – Formline Dekor (Germany) – Formline DHF (Germany) – The Floorline Collection (Austria) – The Floorline Collection (Germany) – Weyroc HDX (United Kingdom) – Weyroc PCX (United Kingdom) – Weyroc PFB (United Kingdom) – Weyroc U313 (United Kingdom)*

Egginton Bros Ltd 25-31 Allen Street, Sheffield S3 7AW Tel. *0114 2766123* Fax. *0114 2738465* E-mail. *steve@eggintongroup.co.uk* Web. *www.eggintongroup.co.uk Action Knives – Double Sharp – George Wostenholm – I Cut My Way – I.XL – John Clarke – Joseph Rodgers – Resqhook – Star & Cross*

Patrick Eggle 63 Water Street, Birmingham B3 1HN Tel. *0121 2121989* Fax. *0121 2121990* E-mail. *gordon@patrickeggleguitars.com* Web. *www.patrickeggleguitars.com Patrick Eggle Guitars*

Egon Publishers Ltd 618 Leeds Road Outwood, Wakefield WF1 2LT Tel. *01924 871697* Fax. *01924 871697* E-mail. *information@egon.co.uk* Web. *www.omega-cottage.eu Maths Made Easy – Literacy for Life – Sound Activities*

E H Smith 357-363 Haslucks Green Road Shirley, Solihull B90 2NG Tel. *0121 7137100* Fax. *0121 7137101* E-mail. *john.parker@ehsmith.co.uk* Web. *www.ehsmith.co.uk E.H. Smith*

E Jeffries & Sons Ltd Unit 32 New Firms Centre Fairground Way, Walsall WS1 4NU Tel. *01922 642222* Fax. *01922 615043* E-mail. *d.kent@ejeffries.co.uk* Web. *www.ejeffries.co.uk Brady – Eldonian – Falcon – Jeffries – Mountfort – Saddlery World – Wembley*

Eka Ltd Valkyrie House 38 Packhorse Road, Gerrards Cross SL9 8EB Tel. *01753 889818* Fax. *01753 880004* Web. *www.ekalimited.com Compact – Ekalift – S.R.T.E. – Stevedore*

EK Williams Limited 1 Pavilion Square Cricketers Way, Westhoughton, Bolton BL5 3AJ Tel. *01942 811767* Fax. *01942 814636* E-mail. *info@payepeople.co.uk* Web. *www.ekwilliams.co.uk E.K. Williams*

Eland Engineering Company 29 Lyon Road, Walton On Thames KT12 3PU Tel. *01932 252666* Fax. *01932 252583* E-mail. *info@elandeng.co.uk* Web. *www.elandeng.co.uk Compact – Eland – H.D. – H.D.S. – HD Signal – Series 5000*

Elanders Unit B Merlin Way, New York Industrial Park, Newcastle upon Tyne NE27 0QG Tel. *0191 2800400* Fax. *0191 2800401* E-mail. *uk-sales@elanders.com* Web. *www.elanders.com Elanders Hindson Ltd*

Elan Digital Systems Ltd Elan House Little Park Farm Road, Fareham PO15 5SJ Tel. *01489 579799* Fax. *01489 577516* E-mail. *melanie.howard@elandigitalsystems.com* Web. *www.elandigitalsystems.com Elan*

Elan-Dragonair Ltd 162 Southampton Road, Portsmouth PO6 4RY Tel. *023 92376451* Fax. *023 92370411* E-mail. *david@elan-dragonair.co.uk* Web. *www.elandragonair.co.uk Dragonair HLO – Dragonair HNG – Elan-Dragonair*

Elastomer Engineering Ltd Rushgreen Works Carlton Road, Lymm WA13 9RF Tel. *01925 753456* Fax. *01925 755416* E-mail. *sales@elastomer.co.uk* Web. *www.elastomer.co.uk HEX-AIR*

Elcock's Ltd Hospital Fields Road Fulford Industrial Estate, York YO10 4FT Tel. *01904 611100* Fax. *01904 628453* E-mail. *andrew@elcocks.co.uk* Web. *www.elcocks.co.uk Elcock Power*

Elcometer Instruments Ltd Elcometer Edge Lane, Droylsden, Manchester M43 6BU Tel. *0161 3716000* Fax. *0161 3716010* E-mail. *catherine.lund-barker@elcometer.com* Web. *www.elcometer.com Coatest – Dataputer – Datastat Plus – Elcometer*

Elcontrol Ltd 5 Regulus Works 79 Lynch Lane, Weymouth DT4 9DW Tel. *01305 773426* Fax. *01305 760539* E-mail. *sales@elcontrol.co.uk* Web. *www.elcontrol.co.uk Elcontrol*

Eleco Timber Frame Ltd (Eleco PLC) Oaksmere Business Park Eye Airfield Industrial Estate, Yaxley, Eye IP23 8BW Tel. *01379 783465* Fax. *01379 783659* E-mail. *stramit@eleco.com* Web. *www.eleco.com Canberra – Cladding 280 – Concor – SpeedDeck – Stramclad – Stramit – Stramliner – StramTile*

Electrak Holdings Ltd Number One Industrial Estate Medomsley Road, Consett DH8 6SR Tel. *01207 503400* Fax. *01207 501799* E-mail. *sales@electrak.co.uk* Web. *www.electrak.co.uk Electrak – Lightrak – Raak*

Electric Co. 190 Main Street Invergowrie, Dundee DD2 5BD Tel. *0774 0609881* E-mail. *bob@theelectriccompany.co.uk* Web. *www.theelectriccompany.co.uk The Electric Company*

Electric Actuator Co. Ltd Bolling Road, Bradford BD4 7BZ Tel. *01274 732931* Fax. *01274 393674 *Kozako (Canada)*

Electrical Carbon UK Ltd Reg'd Office: 788-790 Finchley Road, London NW11 7TJ Tel. *0114 2316454* Fax. *0114 2385464* E-mail. *sales@ecarbonuk.com* Web. *www.ecarbonuk.com Gerken – Pantrac – E-Carbon – Carbowind*

Electrical Testing & Inspection FWT Ltd 4 The Dairy Crewe Hall Farm Old Park Road, Crewe CW1 5UE Tel. *01270 211587* Fax. *01270 214467* E-mail. *david@joycemontague.co.uk* Web. *www.joycemontague.co.uk Electrical Testing and Inspection FWT Ltd – Joyce Montague Contracts Ltd*

Electricars Ltd (Manufacturing Division) Carlyon Road, Atherstone CV9 1LQ Tel. *01827 716888* Fax. *01827 717841* Web. *www.electricars-group.com Electricar – Electricar*

Electricold Refrigeration 60 Moat Road, East Grinstead RH19 3LH Tel. *020 86604641* Fax. *020 86682358* E-mail. *info@electricold.co.uk* Web. *www.electricold.co.uk Electricold*

Electrium Sales Ltd Lakeside Plaza Walkmill Way, Cannock WS11 0XE Tel. *01543 455000* Fax. *01543 455001* E-mail. *barry.glew@electrium.co.uk* Web. *www.electrium.co.uk Appleby – Britmac – Crabtree – Marbo – Supelec – Volex – Wyle X*

Electro Arc Co. Ltd The Wallows Industrial Estate Fens Pool Avenue, Brierley Hill DY5 1QA Tel. *01384 263426* Fax. *01384 79017* E-mail. *sales@electroarc.co.uk* Web. *www.electroarc.com Ames Precision Hardness Testers (Portable) – Electro Arc*

Electrocomponents plc 8050 Alec Issigonis Way Oxford Business Park North, Oxford OX4 2HW Tel. *01865 204000* Fax. *01865 207400* E-mail. *simon.boddie@electrocomponents.com* Web. *www.electrocomponents.com Clippaplug*

Electro Group Ltd Unit 9 Meadowbrook Park Halfway, Sheffield S20 3PJ Tel. *0114 2764300* Fax. *0114 2486654* E-mail. *sales@electro-group.co.uk* Web. *www.electro-group.co.uk *Acesa (Spain) – *Beha (Germany) – *Bonkote (Japan) – Connel of York – Connell of York – *Denon (Japan) – Filtronic AB (Sweden) – *Irazola (Spain) – *Irega (Spain) – *Larsson (Sweden) – *Regine (Switzerland) – Tiro-Clas (France) – *Vallorbe Usines (Switzerland)*

Electrolube (a division of H.K. Wentworth Ltd) Ashby Park Coalfield Way, Ashby De La Zouch LE65 1JF Tel. *0844 3759700* Fax. *0844 3759799* E-mail. *info@hkw.co.uk* Web. *www.electrolube.com Electrolube*

Electrolux Laundry Systems 99 Oakley Road, Luton LU4 9GE Tel. *01582 578900* Fax. *08700 604113* E-mail. *els.info@electrolux.co.uk* Web. *www.electrolux.co.uk BP – Electrolux Wascator – Macron – PR2001 – PT 5 – PT 6 – PT 7 – PT 9 – PT4 4 – SAF/Apollo – ST – Tip Top – Zeus*

Electro Mechanical Systems (EMS) Ltd (EMS) Eros House Calleva Industrial Pk, Aldermaston, Reading RG7 8LN Tel. *0118 9817391* Fax. *0118 9817613* E-mail. *sgoulding@emsltd.com* Web. *www.ems-limited.co.uk Faulhaber (Germany) – Minimotor (Switzerland) – Precistep (Switzerland) – MPS (Switzerland) – Piezomotor (Sweden) – Nidec (Germany) – Nidec Servo (Japan) – Kahlig (Germany) – SKF (Switzerland) – Mingardi (Italy) – Magnetic AutoControl (Germany)*

Electronic Data Processing plc Beauchief Hall Beauchief, Sheffield S8 7BA Tel. *0114 2621621* Fax. *0114 2621126* Web. *www.edp.co.uk B.M.L Charisma – E D P Merchant – Quantum/V.S. – Univision D B M S – Viaduct*

Electro Refrigeration Unit 5 193 The Garth Road Industrial Centre Garth Road, Morden SM4 4LZ Tel. *020 32771090* Fax. *020 86841899* E-mail. *info@electroref.co.uk* Web. *www.electroref.co.uk PROFI*ICE – proifinox*

Electro Replacement Ltd Unit 1 Moor Park Industrial Centre Tolpits Lane, Watford WD18 9EU Tel. *01923 255344* Fax. *01923 255829* E-mail. *info@apt-erlltd.co.uk* Web. *www.apt-erlltd.co.uk APT – ERL*

Electrosonic Ltd Hawley Mill Hawley Road, Dartford DA2 7SY Tel. *01322 222211* Fax. *01322 282282* E-mail. *information@electrosonic.co.uk* Web. *www.electrosonic.com C-Through – E.S.T.A. – Eslinx – Image Star – Imagemag – Picbloc – Vector*

Electrotec International Ltd Manchester Road, Oldham OL9 7AA Tel. *0161 6881542* E-mail. *lheywood@electrotec-ltd.co.uk* Web. *www.electrical-deals.co.uk Sony – Panasonic – Philips – LG – Samsung*

Electrotex Sales Co. 86d Lillie Road, London SW6 1TL Tel. *020 73850836* Fax. *020 73818776 Electrotex Sales Co.*

Electrovision Group Ltd Lancots Lane, St Helens WA9 3EX Tel. *01744 745000* Fax. *01744 745001* E-mail. *richard@electrovision.co.uk* Web. *www.electrovision.co.uk Altai – Cheetah – Commtel – Eagle – Soundlab*

Electrox Avenue One, Letchworth Garden City SG6 2HB Tel. *01462 472400* Fax. *01462 472444* E-mail. *sales@electrox.com* Web. *www.electrox.com Cobra – Cobra - E-Box - MaxBox - Maxbox Plus - Maxim - Raptor - Razor - Scorpion - Scorpion Rapide - Scriba. – E-Box – MaxBox – MaxBox plus – Maxim – Raptor – Razor – Scorpion – Scorpion Rapide – Scriba*

Elegant Homes Ltd (t/a kilian craft) The Praze, Penryn TR10 8AA Tel. *01326 377113* Fax. *01326 378691* E-mail. *kilian.craft@lineone.net* Web. *www.eleganthomescornwall.co.uk Elegant Homes – Killan Craft*

Ele International Chartmoor Road, Leighton Buzzard LU7 4WG Tel. *01525 249200* Fax. *01525 249249* E-mail. *giovanni.simoni@eleint.co.uk* Web. *www.ele.com A.D.U. – ADR Auto – Cumulus – Dialog 300 – Dialog 900 – Dialog ADU – Dialog EMS – E.L.E. – Flowstream – Gyrotest – M.M.900 – M.M.950 – Paqualab – Rotasift*

Elektron Components Ltd Melville Court Spilsby Road, Harold Hill, Romford RM3 8SB Tel. *01708 343800* Fax. *01708 376544* E-mail. *johnwilson@bulgin.co.uk* Web. *www.elektronplc.com Clarity – Clarity Focus – Control Knobs – Director – Monitor – Presentor – Select – Sifam*

Elephante Service & Maintenance Ltd 2 Goddard Road Astmoor Industrial Estate, Runcorn WA7 1QF Tel. *01928 500005* Fax. *01928 500006* E-mail. *sales@elephante-lifts.com* Web. *www.elephante-lifts.com Elephante*

Elesa (UK) Ltd 26 Moorlands Estate Metheringham, Lincoln LN4 3HX Tel. *01526 322670* Fax. *01526 322669* E-mail. *sales@elesa.co.uk* Web. *www.elesanow.co.uk Elesa – Ergostyle – Elesa-Clayton – Elesa SOFT – Elesa CLEAN – Elesa SAN – Elesa ESD – Elesa Self Extinguish – Ganter*

Elesta PO Box 3418, Slough SL1 0BR Tel. *01628 664441* Fax. *01628 664441* E-mail. *info@elesta.co.uk* Web. *www.elesta.co.uk Controlesta RCO*

Eley Metrology Ltd (Incorporating Crown Windley) Beaufort House Mansfield Road, Derby DE21 4FS Tel. *01332 367475* Fax. *01332 371435* E-mail. *sales@eleymet.com* Web. *www.eleymet.com Crown*

Elfab Ltd Alder Road West Chirton North Industrial Estate, North Shields NE29 8SD Tel. *0191 2931234* Fax. *0191 2931200* E-mail. *sales@elfab.com* Web. *www.elfab.com Bio-Gard (United Kingdom) – Bio-Guard (United Kingdom) – Bio-Tel (United Kingdom) – Burst-Tel (United Kingdom) – Integral Flo-Tel (United Kingdom) – Multi-Guard (United Kingdom) – Omni-Guard (United Kingdom) – Opti-Gard (United Kingdom) – Posi-Guard (United Kingdom) – Safe-Guard (United Kingdom) – System-Loc (United Kingdom) – Uni-Guard (United Kingdom) – Vac-Guard (United Kingdom)*

Elgate Products Ltd Patricia Way 1 Pysons Road Industrial Estate, Pysons Road Industrial Estate, Broadstairs CT10 2LF Tel. *01843 609200* Fax. *01843 866234* E-mail. *sales@elgate.co.uk* Web. *www.elgate.co.uk Chapel Hill – Elliott Bear – House of Valentina, The*

Elisabeth The Chef Ltd 4 Berrington Road, Leamington Spa CV31 1NB Tel. *01926 311531* Fax. *01926 426888* E-mail. *enquiries@elisabeth-the-chef.co.uk* Web. *www.elisabeth-the-chef.co.uk Broadheath*

Elite Bedding Co. Ltd 135 Moffat Street, Glasgow G5 0NG Tel. *0141 4291124* Fax. *0141 4291599* E-mail. *info@simplyelite.co.uk* Web. *www.simplyelite.co.uk Elite – Sleeprite*

Elite Energy - The Specialist Energy Consultancy Unit 1 Mariner Court Durkar, Wakefield WF4 3FL Tel. *0800 0438100* E-mail. *enquiries@eliteenergy.org.uk* Web. *www.eliteenergy.org.uk Elite Energy*

Elite Energy - The Specialist Energy Consultancy 1St Floor Arundel House 42 Arundel Street, Portsmouth PO1 1NL Tel. *023 93660106* E-mail. *portsmouth@eliteenergy.org.uk* Web. *www.eliteenergy.org.uk Elite Energy*

Elite Engineering Ltd 1 Davis Way, Fareham PO14 1JF Tel. *01329 231435* Fax. *01329 822759* E-mail. *johnp@eliteeng.com* Web. *www.elite-eng.co.uk Automatic Pick and Place Machines – Convection – Cropelle – F.P. – Format – Formelle – Formette – K.25 – Multipoint – Pneumatic*

Elite Heating Ltd Henderson Works Henderson Road, Croydon CR0 2QG Tel. *020 86649099* Fax. *020 86648699* E-mail. *shaun@eliteheating.com* Web. *www.eliteheatingservice.co.uk Baxi boilers – Potterton boilers – Glowworm boilers – Worcester boilers*

Elite Papers Ltd Unit 5 Little Row Fenton Industrial Estate, Stoke On Trent ST4 2SQ Tel. *01782 749200* Fax. *01782 749300* E-mail. *sales@elitepapers.com* Web. *www.elitepapers.com Custom Print*

EliteXecutive Travel 78 Tal Y Coed Hendy, Pontarddulais, Swansea SA4 0XR Tel. *01792 886999* E-mail. *enquiries@elitexecutivetravel.co.uk* Web. *www.elitexecutivetravel.co.uk EliteXecutive Travel*

Elizabeth Arden 87-91 Newman Street, London W1T 3EY Tel. *020 75742700* Fax. *020 75742727* E-mail. *david.davies@elizabetharden.com* Web. *www.elizabetharden.com 2 Brush Mascara – Blue Grass – Ceramide – Cheek Colour Naturals – Defining Mascara – Dual Perfection – Eau Fraiche – Exceptional Lipsticks – Fifth Avenue – Flawless Finish – Flawless Finish Mousse Make-Up – Hydrolite – Lip Definer – Lip Gloss – Millenium – Modern Skin Care – Perfect Covering Concealer – Red Door – Skin Illuminating Complex – Smokey Eyes – Smooth Lining Eye Pencil – Sunflowers – Visible Difference*

Elkay Electrical Manufacturing Co. Ltd A Smiths Group Company Unit C Mochdre Industrial Estate, Mochdre, Newtown SY16 4LF Tel. *01686 611500* Fax. *01686 611501* E-mail. *info@cm-products.com* Web. *www.cm-products.com Aqua -Safe, Conclamp, Conta-Op, Ensto, HPM, Multiplug – Aqua-Safe – Conclamp – *Ensto (Finland) – *H.P.M. (Australia)*

Ellesco Ltd 6 Airfield Road, Christchurch BH23 3TG Tel. *01202 499400* Fax. *01202 484202* E-mail. *general@ellesco.co.uk* Web. *www.ellesco.co.uk Autopulit – Cascade System – Ellesco Diamond Paste – Ellesco Diamond Products – Ellesco Machines – Grindingmaster – Kuhlmeyer – Sugino – Timesaver – Vangroenweghe – VG*

J T Ellis & Co. Ltd Crown Works Silver Street, Huddersfield HD5 9BA Tel. *01484 514212* Fax. *01484 456433* E-mail. *sales@ellisfurniture.co.uk* Web. *www.ellisfurniture.co.uk Ellis – Ellis-Hotel Collection – Ellis-Scholar – Ellis-Solo Graduate – Ellis-Vanity Flair*

Ellison Switchgear Mounts Road, Wednesbury WS10 0DU Tel. *0121 5052000* Fax. *0121 5561981* E-mail. *enquiries@ellison.co.uk* Web. *www.ellison.co.uk Bantam – E. – Ellison – Expressway – Lambar – Sentinel*

Ellis Patents Ltd High Street Rillington, Malton YO17 8LA Tel. *01944 758395* Fax. *01944 758808* E-mail. *sales@ellispatents.co.uk* Web. *www.ellispatents.co.uk Apache – Atlas – Atlas (Cable Cleat) Emperor (Cable Cleat) Elite (Cable Cleat) Vulcan (Cable Cleat) Vari-Cleat (Cable Cleat) Apache (Pipe Clamps) – Elite – Emperor – Vari-Cleat – Vulcan*

Ellis Williams Architects Ltd Wellfield Chester Road, Preston Brook, Runcorn WA7 3BA Tel. *01928 752200* Fax. *01928 795953* E-mail. *mailbox@ewa.co.uk* Web. *www.ewa.co.uk *EW (United Kingdom) – *EWA (United Kingdom)*

E L M Construction Blundells Lane Rainhill, Prescot L35 6NB Tel. *0151 4263511* Fax. *0151 4327000* E-mail. *sales@elmsheds.co.uk* Web. *www.elmconstruction.co.uk Conquest Sheds*

Elmcrest Diamond Drilling Ltd 4 Duncrievie Road, London SE13 6TE Tel. *020 83189923* Fax. *020 83181034* E-mail. *office@elmcrest-diamond.co.uk* Web. *www.elmcrest-diamond.co.uk Brokk – Darda*

Elmelin Ltd 1 Betts Mews, London E17 8PQ Tel. *020 85202248* Fax. *020 85212889* E-mail. *info@elmelin.com* Web. *www.elmelin.com Elmelec – Elmelin – Elmflex – Elmtube – Perforelm*

Elmwood Ghyll Royd Guiseley, Leeds LS20 9LT Tel. *01943 870229* Fax. *01943 870191* E-mail. *jonathan.sands@elmwood.co.uk* Web. *www.elmwood.com Elmwood*

Elsan Ltd (Head Office) 15 Brambleside Bellbrook Industrial Estate, Uckfield TN22 1QF Tel. *01825 748200* Fax. *01825 761212* E-mail. *sales@elsan.co.uk* Web. *www.elsan.co.uk Coachkem – Elsan – Hygenus – Lansdowne – Oxford – Pottikem – Sani Safe – Sapovis – Sitekem – Skykem – Trailer Barrow – Visa*

Elsevier Publishers Ltd The Boulevard Langford Lane, Kidlington OX5 1GB Tel. *01865 843000* Fax. *01865 843010* E-mail. *gavin.howe@rbi.co.uk* Web. *www.elsevier.co.uk Compsec*

Elster Kromschroder Ulster Buidling Tollgate Drive, Tollgate Industrial Estate, Stafford ST16 3AF Tel. *01785 275342* Fax. *01527 888821* E-mail. *p.morris@kromschroder.co.uk* Web. *www.jeavonsltd.co.uk Elster Jeavons*

Elsy & Gibbons Amos Ayre Place Simonside Industrial Estate, South Shields NE34 9PE Tel. *0191 4270777* Fax. *0191 4270888* E-mail. *ian.lock@baxigroup.com* Web. *www.elsonhotwater.co.uk Elson*

Elumatec UK Ltd 2 Europa Business Park Maidstone Road, Kingston, Milton Keynes MK10 0BD Tel. *01908 580800* Fax. *01908 580825* E-mail. *sales@elumatec.co.uk* Web. *www.elumatec.com *Elumatec (Germany) – *Striffler (Germany) – *Sturtz (Germany)*

Elvetham Hotel Ltd Elvetham, Hook RG27 8AR Tel. *01252 844871* Fax. *01252 844161* E-mail. *enquiries@elvethamhotel.co.uk* Web. *www.elvethamhotel.co.uk Elvetham Hall*

Elvstrom Sails Ltd Unit 2 Hys, Hamble, Southampton SO31 4NN Tel. *023 80450430* Fax. *023 80452465* E-mail. *sales@sobstad.co.uk* Web. *www.elvstromsails.co.uk Sobstad*

Emak UK Ltd Unit 8 Zone 4, Burntwood Business Park, Burntwood WS7 3XD Tel. *01543 687660* Fax. *01543 670721* E-mail. *nturner@emak.co.uk* Web. *www.emak.co.uk Sawtec*

Emap Ltd Greater London House Hampstead Road, London NW1 7EJ Tel. *020 77285000* Fax. *01733 465353* E-mail. *enquiries@emap.com* Web. *www.emap.com Angling Plus – Angling Times – Angling Times Yearbook – Bird Watching – Boat Angler – Country Walking – Fore – Gold Industry News – Golf Weekly – Golf World – Improve Your Coarse Fishing – Improve Your Sea Angling – Match Bigshots – Match Weekly – Match Yearbook – Sea Angler – Today's Golfer – Today's Runner – Trail – Trout & Salmon – Trout Fisherman – Your Horse*

Embassy Machinery Ltd 104 High Street London Colney, St Albans AL2 1QL Tel. *01727 823461* Fax. *01727 826822* E-mail. *info@embassy-mach.co.uk* Web. *www.embassy-mach.co.uk *Bamatec (Switzerland) – *Graebener (Germany) – *Karl Roll (Germany) – *L. Schuler (Germany) – *M. & M. (Switzerland) – *Roll (Germany) – *S.M.G. (Germany) – *Schleicher (Germany) – *Vitari (Italy)*

E M C Advertising Gifts Ltd Derwent House 1064 High Road, London N20 0YY Tel. *08453 451064* Fax. *08453 451065* E-mail. *simonkay@emcadgifts.co.uk* Web. *www.emcadgifts.co.uk E M C Advertising Gifts*

Emcel Filters Ltd Blatchford Road, Horsham RH13 5RA Tel. *01403 253215* Fax. *01403 259881* E-mail. *filtration@emcelfilters.co.uk* Web. *www.emcelfilters.co.uk Activ-V – Activated Carbon Cells – Chemicarb – Circaframe – Cylindrical Air Intake – Dustrap – Emcel – Emcel-X Replacement Carbon Cells – Emcron – Emflex – Katercarb – Maxicarb – Plipad – Regenacell – Slimline – Sonoxcarb – Tank Breather*

E M Coating Services Enterprise Way Vale Park, Evesham WR11 1GX Tel. *01386 421444* Fax. *01386 765410* E-mail. *emukenquiries@metalimprovement.com* Web. *www.emcoatingsuk.com E.M. Coatings – EVER SLIK – Everlube – Flurene – Flurene - Perma-Slik - Microseal - Lube-Lok - Everlube – Lube-Lok – Microseal – Perma-Slik*

Emcor UK plc 1 Thameside Centre Kew Bridge Road, Brentford TW8 0HF Tel. *020 83806700* Fax. *020 83806701* E-mail. *ukinfo@emcoruk.com* Web. *www.emcoruk.com Delcommerce (Contract Services) Ltd – Drake & Scull Airport Services Ltd – Drake & Scull Engineering – Drake & Scull Engineering (north) Ltd – Drake & Scull International – Drake & Scull Technical Services Ltd*

Emco Wheaton Unit K Channel Road Westwood Industrial Estate, Margate CT9 4JR Tel. *01843 221521* Fax. *01843 295444* E-mail. *gmurphy@emcowheaton.com* Web. *www.emcowheaton.com Emco-Wheaton*

Emergency Planning Solutions 34 Chester Road Dobshill, Deeside CH5 3LZ Tel. *01244 550253* E-mail. *davidashford@epstraining.co.uk* Web. *www.epstraining.co.uk ESSENTIAL TRAINING SOLUTIONS*

Emergi Lite Safety Systems Ltd Bruntcliffe Lane Morley, Leeds LS27 9LL Tel. *0113 2810600* Fax. *0113 2810601* E-mail. *emergi-lite_sales@tnb.com* Web. *www.emergi-lite.co.uk Anatec-Pro – Day-Lite – Energilite – Eurofire – Firetec – Flashpoint Infrared Testing*

Emerson Climate Technologies Ltd Unit 17 Theale Lakes Business Park, Sulhamstead, Reading RG7 4GB Tel. *0118 9838000* Fax. *0118 9838001* E-mail. *uk.sales@emerson.com* Web. *www.emersonclimate.eu *Alco (Germany) – *Copeland (Germany & USA) – D.W.M. Copeland – Prestcold*

Emerson Network Power Embedded Power Astec House Waterfront Business Park, Merry Hill, Dudley DY5 1LX Tel. *0800 0321546* Fax. *01384 843355* E-mail. *sales@emerson.com* Web. *www.powerconversion.com Artesyn – Astec*

Emerson Network Power Ltd Fourth Avenue Globe Park, Marlow SL7 1YG Tel. *01628 403200* Fax. *01628 403203* E-mail. *kevin.harris@emerson.com* Web. *www.emersonnetworkpower.com 7200 Series – 7400 Series – 9000 Series – AP200 Series – AP400 Series – AP4300 Series – Databond – Frame Work – Little Glass House – Powersure – Select – Sitenet Software – UP Station GX*

Emerson Process Management 158 Edinburgh Avenue, Slough SL1 4UE Tel. *01753 756600* Fax. *01753 823589* E-mail. *sales@solartron.com* Web. *www.emersonprocess.co.uk Annubar – Bestobell – K.D.G. – Meterflow – Mobrey – Rotameter – Sparling – Tylor – Tylors*

E M & F Group Ltd 3 Cornhill, Ottery St Mary EX11 1DW Tel. *01404 813762* Fax. *01404 815236* E-mail. *devdor@emfgroup.com* Web. *www.emfgroup.com *E.M. and F. – *Everett Masson and Furby*

Emhart Teknologies (Tucker Fasteners Ltd) 177 Walsall Rd Perry Barr, Birmingham B42 1BP Tel. *0121 3564811* Fax. *0121 3561598* E-mail. *uk.marketing@bdk.com* Web. *www.emhart.com Helicoil – *Jack Nut (U.S.A.) – POP – *Well Nut (U.S.A.)*

Emics Calibration Services 248 Radford Boulevard Radford, Nottingham NG7 5QG Tel. *0115 9424748* Fax. *0115 9424746* E-mail. *garyswift@emics.co.uk* Web. *www.emics.co.uk Mitutoyo*

Emi-Mec Ltd Unit E2 Doulton Trading Estate Doulton Road, Rowley Regis B65 8JQ Tel. *01384 633968* Fax. *01384 633946* E-mail. *sales@emi-mec.eu* Web. *www.emi-mec.eu Auto-Sprint – EMI-MEC – Feeler – Microsprint – Multisprint CNC – Supersprint*

Eminox Ltd North Warren Road, Gainsborough DN21 2TU Tel. *01427 810088* Fax. *01427 810061* E-mail. *enquiries@eminox.com* Web. *www.eminox.com CRT – Eminox – Greencat*

E M J Management Ltd Aspen House Airport Service Road, Portsmouth PO3 5RA Tel. *023 92434650* Fax. *023 92434681* E-mail. *sales@emjltd.com* Web. *www.emjltd.com Times Microwave*

Emko Consumer Products Ltd 19 Neville Court Abbey Road, London NW8 9DD Tel. *020 72893213* Fax. *020 72893213* E-mail. *emehl@uk.co.uk *Bruni Bear (China) – *Bruni Bear (Italy, Portugal & USA)*

Emmark UK Ltd Emmark House 5 Carlisle Drive, Pudsey LS28 8QS Tel. *0113 2552344* Fax. *0113 2393856* E-mail. *mtillotson@emmark.co.uk* Web. *www.emmarkuk.co.uk Emmark*

Emmerich Berlon Ltd Kingsnorth Industrial Estate Wotton Road, Ashford TN23 6JY Tel. *01233 622684* Fax. *01233 645801* E-mail. *enquiries@emir.co.uk* Web. *www.emir.co.uk Emir – Harris Looms*

Emmerson Doors Ltd Unit 1a Enterprise Way Salerburn In Elmet, Sherburn In Elmet, Leeds LS25 6NA Tel. *01977 685566* Fax. *01977 681981* E-mail. *sales@emmerson-doors.co.uk* Web. *www.emmerson-doors.co.uk Chieftain – Commander – Mainstay – Securfold – Steadfast – Supreme – Thermalux – Thermaroll*

Emos-Infineer Ltd Balloo Avenue, Bangor BT19 7QT Tel. *028 91476000* Fax. *028 91476001* E-mail. *phunter@infineer.com* Web. *www.infineer.com ChipNet – Chipnet Quickstart – Infineer Chipcard Systems – Smart Track – SmartPrint Central*

E M P Intelligence Service Springfield House 7 The Avenue, Dallington, Northampton NN5 7AJ Tel. *01604 755005* Fax. *01604 755104* E-mail. *apollard@emp-is.com* Web. *www.emp-is.com EMP Intelligence Service*

Empteezy Ltd 4 Muir Road Houstoun Industrial Estate, Livingston EH54 5DR Tel. *01506 430309* Fax. *01506 441466* E-mail. *sales@empteezy.co.uk* Web. *www.empteezy.co.uk Empteezy*

E M R Ltd Tynedale Works Factory Road, Blaydon On Tyne NE21 5RZ Tel. *0191 4143618* Fax. *0191 4140751* E-mail. *info@emrltd.com* Web. *www.emr.com EMR Company*

Emreco International Ltd 69 Springkell Avenue, Glasgow G41 4NU Tel. *0141 4241914* Fax. *0141 4232997* E-mail. *info@emreco.co.uk* Web. *www.emreco.co.uk Chianti – Emreco – Shiraz*

E M R Sliverthorn Ltd 4 Abercorn Commercial Centre Manor Farm Road, Wembley HA0 1AN Tel. *020 89031390* Fax. *020 89039092* E-mail. *sales@emrsilverthorn.co.uk* Web. *www.emrsilverthorn.co.uk ABB – AEG*

E M S-Chemie UK Ltd Darfin House Priestly Court Gillette Close, Staffordshire Technology Park, Stafford ST18 0LQ Tel. *01785 283739* Fax. *01785 607570* E-mail. *welcome@uk.emsgrivory.com* Web. *www.emschem.com Grilamid (Switzerland) – *Grilamid (Switzerland) – Grilamid TR (Switzerland) – Grilbond (Switzerland) – Grilon (Switzerland) – *Grilon (Switzerland) – Grilon C (Switzerland) – Grilon T (Switzerland) – Grilon TS – *Grilonit (Switzerland) – Grilpet (Switzerland) – Griltex (Switzerland) – *Grivory (Switzerland) – Grivory GV (Switzerland) – Grivory HT*

EMS Physio Ltd Unit 20 Grove Technology Park Downsview Road, Wantage OX12 9FE Tel. *01235 772272* Fax. *01235 763518* E-mail. *sales@emsphysio.co.uk* Web. *www.emsphysio.co.uk E.M.S. – Electro-Medical Supplies (Greenham) Ltd*

Emsworth Yacht Harbour Ltd Thorney Road, Emsworth PO10 8BP Tel. *01243 377727* Fax. *01243 373432* E-mail. *info@emsworth-marina.co.uk* Web. *www.emsworth-marina.co.uk Emsworth Yacht Harbour*

Emusol Products Ltd 7b Trevanth Road, Leicester LE4 9LS Tel. *0116 2741114* Fax. *0116 2741114* E-mail. *sales@emusolproducts.com* Web. *www.emusolproducts.com Beemul – CEPAC – Colaquex – Diamard R – Emuflo – Emupad – Emupol – Emuseal – Kolorcourt – Kolourcourt Porous Acrylic – Latex-ite – Premier Court*

Enable Access 16 Plantagenet Road, Barnet EN5 5JG Tel. *020 82750375* Fax. *020 84490326* E-mail. *sales@enable-access.com* Web. *www.enable-access.com Stairmate (United Kingdom)*

Enalon Ltd PO Box 2, Tonbridge TN9 1TB Tel. *01732 358500* Fax. *01732 770463* E-mail. *sr@enalon.co.uk* Web. *www.enalon.co.uk Enalon*

Encase Ltd Beaumont Road, Banbury OX16 1RE Tel. *01295 752900* Fax. *01295 752910* E-mail. *info@encase.co.uk* Web. *www.encase.co.uk Encase Ltd*

Encoders UK Unit 5a The Courtyard Reddicap Trading Estate, Sutton Coldfield B75 7BU Tel. *0121 3785577* Fax. *0121 3785599* E-mail. *info@encoders-uk.com* Web. *www.encoders-uk.com Absolute – Acu-rite – AMI – Balluff – Baumer – Bosch – British Encoder Company – Dynapar – Eltra – Encoders – Endat – Euchner – Fanuc – Gaebridge – Gaebridge Encoders – Heidenhain – Hengstler – Hohner – Hubner – IMEK Precision – Incremental – Indramat – Industrial Encoders – Leine & Linde – Litton – Newall – Omron – Renco – Resolver – Siemens – Sony – Sumtak – Tacho – Transducer*

Encomech Engineering Developments Ltd Sheffield Airport Business Park Europa Link, Sheffield S9 1XU Tel. *01709 726500* Fax. *0141 2611719* Web. *www.siemens-vai.com Encopanel*

Encyclopaedia Britannica UK Ltd Unity Wharf 13 Mill Street, London SE1 2BH Tel. *020 75007800* Fax. *020 75007878* E-mail. *enquiries@britannica.co.uk* Web. *www.britannica.co.uk Britannica CD – Britannica Online – Encyclopaedia Britannica*

Endeavour International Ltd Unit 13 The Maltings Industrial Estate Brassmill Lane, Bath BA1 3JL Tel. *01225 446770* Fax. *01225 446775* E-mail. *sales@endeavourinternational.co.uk* Web. *www.endeavourinternational.ltd.uk Hydralok – Wells Valves*

Endicott Interconnect UK Ltd Unit 62 Waterhouse Business Centre 2 Cormar Way, Chelmsford CM1 7GB Tel. *01245 392500* Fax. *01245 443193* E-mail. *steve.payne@eitny.com* Web. *endicottinterconnect.com HyperBGA*

Endon Lighting Ltd 1-3 Cross Green Way, Leeds LS9 0SE Tel. *0113 3805700* Fax. *0113 2484519* E-mail. *neil.baldwin@endon.co.uk* Web. *www.endon.co.uk *Endon (Italy and Spain)*

Endress Hauser Ltd Floats Road Roundthorn Industrial Estate, Manchester M23 9NF Tel. *0161 2865000* Fax. *0161 9981841* E-mail. *sales@uk.endress.com* Web. *www.uk.endress.com Cerabar – Deltabar – Dosimag – Liquiphant – Micropilot – Mycom – Promag – Promass – Prosonic – Prowirl – Soliphant – t-mass*

Energas Ltd Haslams Lane, Derby DE22 1EB Tel. *01332 364121* Fax. *01332 291590* E-mail. *derby@engworld.co.uk* Web. *www.energas.co.uk Energas*

Ener-G Combined Power Ener G House Daniel Adamson Road, Salford M50 1DT Tel. *0161 7457450* Fax. *0161 7457457* E-mail. *info@energ.co.uk* Web. *www.energ.co.uk ENER-G – ENERGOS – Petbow Cogeneration – SeaChange – Smartkontrols*

Energy I C T Leeside Works Lawrence Avenue, Stanstead Abbotts, Ware SG12 8DL Tel. *01920 871094* Fax. *01920 871853* E-mail. *info@energyict.com* Web. *www.energyict.com Powerfect – Seltek*

Energy Networks Association Ltd 6th Floor Dean Bradley House 52 Horseferry Road, London SW1P 2AF Tel. *020 77065100* Fax. *020 77065101* E-mail. *info@energynetworks.org* Web. *www.energynetworks.org E.T.A. – E.T.A. Electricity Training Association – Economy 7 – Electricity Association*

Enerpac UK Unit 601 Axcess 10 Business Park Bentley Road South, Wednesbury WS10 8LQ Tel. *0121 5050787* Fax. *01527 585500* E-mail. *james.mitchell@enerpac.com* Web. *www.enerpac.com Enerpac*

Enersys Ltd Stephenson Street, Newport NP19 4XJ Tel. *01633 590310* Fax. *01633 281787* E-mail. *lee.wood@uk.enersysinc.com* Web. *www.enersys.com S.B.S.*

Engelbert Strauss 1 Apollo Rise Southwood Business Park, Farnborough GU14 0GT Tel. *0800 2949000* Fax. *0800 1974444* E-mail. *sales@engelbert-strauss.co.uk* Web. *www.engelbert-strauss.co.uk e.s. motion – e.s. active – e.s. image – 3M – Puma*

Engelmann & Buckham Ltd Access House 16a Lenten Street, Alton GU34 1HG Tel. *01420 824210* Fax. *01420 89193* E-mail. *sales@buckham.co.uk* Web. *www.buckham.co.uk *Actini (France) – *Ceramic Technologies (U.S.A.) – *Comet (Italy) – *Curioni Sun (Italy) – *Curti (Italy) – *Egli (Switzerland) – *Flexotecnica (Italy) – *Hamba (Germany) – *Hassia (Germany) – *Hoerauf (Germany) – *Krantz (Germany) – *Melegari (Italy) – *O.M.S.O. (Italy) – *O.M.V. (Italy) – *Pieper (Germany) – *Rychiger (Switzerland) – *Schaefer & Flottmann (Germany) – Schroder – *Sipa (Italy) – *Sitma (Italy) – *Sluis (Netherlands) – *Sorema (Italy) – *Tirtiaux (Belgium) – *Uviterno (Switzerland) – *Van Pamel (Belgium) – *Vits (Germany)*

Engineering & Welding Supplies Ltd Adam Smith Street, Grimsby DN31 1SJ Tel. *01472 353596* Fax. *01472 241991* E-mail. *sales@engweld.co.uk* Web. *www.engweld.co.uk Energas*

Engis UK Ltd Unit 9 Centenary Business Park Station Road, Henley On Thames RG9 1DS Tel. *01491 411117* Fax. *01491 412252* E-mail. *sales@engis.uk.com* Web. *www.engis.uk.com Diamond – Engis – Hyprez – Microtech*

G English Electronics Ltd Unit 8 Skeffington Street, London SE18 6SR Tel. *020 88550991* Fax. *020 88545563* E-mail. *info@gelec.co.uk* Web. *www.gelec.co.uk *Gelec (Worldwide)*

Enham Charity Shop 13 Newbury Road Enham Alamein, Andover SP11 6HQ Tel. *01264 359391* Fax. *01264 333638* E-mail. *richard.ashdown@enham.co.uk* Web. *www.gordonsfinefoods.com Enham Candles (United Kingdom)*

Enodis Group Enodis UK Food Service Unit 5e Langley Business Centre Station Road, Langley, Slough SL3 8DS Tel. *020 73046000* Fax. *01753 485901* E-mail. *thomas.doerr@manitowoc.com* Web. *www.enodis.com *Frymaster*

Enspire Health 10 Harforde Court John Tate Road, Hertford SG13 7NW Tel. *01992 526300* Fax. *01992 526320* Web. *www.enspirehealth.com Ferraris – Haloscale – Magtrak – Oneflow – Pocketpeak – Watson – Wright – Wright*

Enterpride P.L.C. 1A Chalk Lane Cockfosters, Barnet EN4 9JQ Tel. *020 83700800* Fax. *020 83700888* Web. *www.enterprise.plc.uk Brophy, Thames Water and Metro Rod*

Enterprise Education Trust 1-2 Hatfields, London SE1 9PG Tel. *020 76200735* Fax. *020 79280578* E-mail. *info@enterprise-education.org.uk* Web. *www.enterprise-education.org.uk Understanding Industry*

Envair Ltd York Avenue Haslingden, Rossendale BB4 4HX Tel. *01706 228416* Fax. *01706 242205* E-mail. *info@envair.co.uk* Web. *www.envair.co.uk BIO 2+ – C-Flow – CDC 'C' – Clean rooms – Pharm-assist – RAD*

Envirogard Specialist Hires Ltd Units 5 & 6 Wembdon Farm Bower Road, Smeeth, Ashford TN25 6SZ Tel. *01303 814930* Fax. *01233 720846* E-mail. *accounts@envirogard.co.uk* Web. *www.envirogard.co.uk Envirogard – Ventsafe*

Envirogreen Special Waste Services Ltd Regus House 268 Bath Road, Slough SL1 4DX Tel. *01753 537362* Fax. *01753 537314* E-mail. *info@envirogreen.co.uk* Web. *www.envirogreen.co.uk Envirogreen – Standard Golf U K*

Envirohold Ltd Viking Close Willerby, Hull HU10 6DZ Tel. *01482 651090* Fax. *01482 651002* E-mail. *michael.roberts@envirohold.com* Web. *www.envirohold.com Envirofast – Envirolite – Enviroplast – Enviroshield – Espero – Eurosprint – Flexi-Dock – Flexi-Door – Flexion – Flipflap – Makroswing – Markus – Megalite – Speedfold – Trenomat – Whirlwind*

Environmental Equipments Ltd 12 Queen Eleanor House Kings Clere, Kingsclere, Newbury RG20 4SW Tel. *01635 298502* Fax. *01635 296499* E-mail. *info@e-equipments.com* Web. *www.e-equipment.com *Vibrex (U.S.A.)*

Environmental Technology Entech House London Road, Woolmer Green, Knebworth SG3 6JR Tel. *01438 812812* Fax. *01438 814224* E-mail. *entech.admin@etl-entech.co.uk* Web. *www.etl-entech.co.uk Entech*

Envirotec Ltd Desborough Park Road, High Wycombe HP12 3BX Tel. *01494 525342* Fax. *01494 440889* E-mail. *sales.info@envirotec.co.uk* Web. *www.envirotec.co.uk Envirolator – Enviroscreen*

E P Barrus Granville Way, Bicester OX26 4UR Tel. *01869 363636* Fax. *01869 363660* E-mail. *robert.muir@barrus.co.uk* Web. *www.barrus.co.uk *Cub Cadet (U.S.A.) – Kohler (U.S.A.) – *Lawnflite (U.S.A.) – *Lawnflite (U.S.A.) – *Mariner (U.S.A.) – MTD (U.S.A.) – *Polaris (U.S.A.) – Quicksilver (U.S.A.) – *Shanks (Italy) – Shire (United Kingdom) – Victa (Australia) – Yanmar (Japan) – Yard-Man*

E P C 43 Alexandra Road, Farnborough GU14 6BS Tel. *01252 547939* Fax. *01252 377588 Alber – Invacare – Kuschall – Quickie – RGK*

E P C UK Rough Close Works Carnfield Hill, South Normanton, Alfreton DE55 2BE Tel. *01773 832253* Fax. *01726 828826* Web. *www.exchem-explosives.co.uk Ammonium Nitrate – Delta – Gelamex – Multiblend – Pentaflex*

E P E UK Ltd 16 Manor Industrial Estate, Flint CH6 5UY Tel. *01352 730720* Fax. *01352 730820* E-mail. *a.fairclough@epe-uk.com* Web. *www.epe-uk.com EPE – K & H Eppensterner*

Epicor Software UK Ltd 1 The Arena Downshire Way, Bracknell RG12 1PU Tel. *01344 468468* Fax. *01344 468010* E-mail. *jbrims@epicor.com* Web. *www.epicor.com Avante*

Epilepsy Action New Anstey House Gateway Drive, Yeadon, Leeds LS19 7LY Tel. *0113 2108800* Fax. *0113 3910300* E-mail. *p.lee@epilepsy.org.uk* Web. *www.epilepsy.org.uk BEA Branches – BEA Trading*

Episys Group Ltd Newark Close York Way, Royston SG8 5HL Tel. *01763 248866* Fax. *01763 246000* E-mail. *reception@episys.com* Web. *www.episys.com Chemprint – Epitag 2400 – Epitag Elite – Epitag Elite Lite – Equila – Hiways by Episys – Printell – R.P.A.S. – Rapid – Sign Solutions Software – Super Batch Manager*

E Plan Solutions Ltd Tates Avis Way, Newhaven BN9 0DH Tel. *01273 517711* Fax. *01273 512889* E-mail. *mike@eplansolutions.co.uk* Web. *www.eplansolutions.co.uk E. Plan*

E P S Logistics Technology Ltd 152 Staplehurst Road, Sittingbourne ME10 1XS Tel. *01795 424433* Fax. *01795 426970* E-mail. *sales@epslt.co.uk* Web. *www.epslt.co.uk EPS-Dricase – EPS-Driclad – EPS-Dripak – Humidicare – Storlina*

Epsom Downs Racecourse Entrance Pavillian Epsom Downs, Epsom KT18 5LQ Tel. *01372 726311* Fax. *01372 748253* E-mail. *epsom@thejockeyclub.co.uk* Web. *www.epsomdowns.co.uk Derby – Oaks, The*

Epsom Quality Line Roy Richmond Way, Epsom KT19 9AF Tel. *01372 731703* Fax. *01372 731740* E-mail. *steve.whiteway@epsomcoaches.com* Web. *www.epsomcoaches.com Epsom Buses – Epsom Coaches – Epsom Holidays – Epsom Travel*

Epson 100 The Campus Maylands Avenue, Hemel Hempstead HP2 7TJ Tel. *08702 416900* Fax. *01422 227227* E-mail. *retailpos@epson.co.uk* Web. *www.epson.co.uk Epson*

Equifax plc Capital House 25 Chapel Street, London NW1 5DH Tel. *08443 350550* Fax. *020 77237555* E-mail. *info@equifax.co.uk* Web. *www.equifax.co.uk Equifax (United Kingdom) – Equifax Cheque Solutions – Equifax HPI – Equifax Payment Services – HPI – Transax*

Equipline Ashley House Ashley Road, Uxbridge UB8 2GA Tel. *01895 272236* Fax. *01895 256360* E-mail. *walker@equipline.co.uk* Web. *www.equipline.co.uk *Alto-Shaam – Bertos – Bofi – Escapism – Euro-Grill – Euro-Merchandisers – Euro-Ovens – *Fri-Jado – *Hanson Brass – Intellistream – *Nieco – *Ram – *Roundup – *Wells – Whirlpool Professional*

Equipment For You PO Box 6, Cheltenham GL51 9NJ Tel. *01242 241822* Fax. *01242 222994* E-mail. *sales@3dsports.co.uk* Web. *www.e4u.co.uk Beamstroker – Bench Hone – E1000 – E2000 – E3000 – E3500 – Powerhone – Smart-Hone – Speedhone – Speedhone Ea – Speedhone Em*

Equity Insurance Library House New Road, Brentwood CM14 4GD Tel. *01277 200100* Fax. *01277 206283* E-mail. *info@equitygroup.co.uk* Web. *www.equitygroup.co.uk Boncaster*

Equity Shoes Ltd Catherine House Upper Poppleton, York YO26 6QU Tel. *0844 8440203* Fax. *01904 528791* E-mail. *helpdesk@pavers.co.uk* Web. *www.equityshoes.com Equity*

Eras Ltd Providence Court 104-106 Denmark Street, Diss IP22 4WN Tel. *01379 652171* Fax. *01379 644225* E-mail. *expertise@eras.co.uk* Web. *www.eras.co.uk The Quest Profiler*

Ercol Furniture Ltd Summerleys Road, Princes Risborough HP27 9PX Tel. *01844 271800* Fax. *01844 271888* E-mail. *sales@ercol.com* Web. *www.ercol.com Ercol*

E R F Ltd E R F Way, Middlewich CW10 0TN Tel. *01606 843000* Fax. *01606 843005* E-mail. *tgrove@erf.com* Web. *www.erf.com E.R.F. Ltd – E.R.F. Select – Starteam*

Ergomounts Ltd Unit 10 Pegasus Court North Lane, Aldershot GU12 4QP Tel. *01252 333326* E-mail. *sales@ergomounts.co.uk* Web. *www.ergomounts.co.uk Delta series – VisionPro*

Ergonom Ltd Whittington House 19-30 Alfred Place, London WC1E 7EA Tel. *020 73232325* Fax. *020 73232032* E-mail. *sales@ergonom.com* Web. *www.ergonom.com *Misura (Italy) – *Mood (Italy) – *Programme 3 (Italy) – *Satelliti (Italy) – *Sealed (Italy)*

Eriez Magnetics Europe Ltd Bedwas House Industrial Estate Bedwas, Caerphilly CF83 8YG Tel. *029 20868501* Fax. *029 20851314* E-mail. *info@eriezeurope.co.uk* Web. *www.eriez.com E-Z Tec – Eriez – Metalarm – PRISECTER*

Ernest Bennett & Co Darlington Ltd Aviation Way Durham Tees Valley Airport, Darlington DL2 1NA Tel. *01325 332656* Fax. *01325 333137* E-mail. *david@ernestbennett.co.uk* Web. *www.ernestbennett.co.uk H.P.G. (High Precision Ground) – Jag Hond Made In England*

Ernest B Westman Ltd 43 Lower Street, Merriott TA16 5NL Tel. *01823 321844* Fax. *01823 321876* E-mail. *ebw@dircon.co.uk* Web. *ebwestman.co.uk Wonsover*

Erro Tool Co. Ltd 70 Iddesleigh Road, Bournemouth BH3 7NH Tel. *01202 466447* Fax. *01202 466447* E-mail. *sales@holtwaterloo.com* Web. *www.holtwaterloo.com Ampro – Autosol – Erro – Waterloo*

Ervin Amasteel Ltd George Henry Road, Tipton DY4 7BZ Tel. *0121 5222777* Fax. *0121 5222927* E-mail. *sales@ervinindustries.com* Web. *www.ervinindustries.com Amacast – Amacast, Amasteel, Amacut, Excalibur, Amamix – Amamix – Amasteel – Excalibur – Supergrit*

E S A B Group UK Ltd Hanover House Britannia Road Queens Gate, Waltham Cross EN8 7TF Tel. *01992 768515* Fax. *01992 715803* E-mail. *info@esab.co.uk* Web. *www.esab.co.uk ESAB*

Esa Mcintosh Ltd West Way Hillend Industrial Park, Hillend, Dunfermline KY11 9HE Tel. *01592 656200* Fax. *01592 656299* E-mail. *bill.mccoll@esamcintosh.co.uk* Web. *www.esamcintosh.co.uk E.S.A.*

Escada Systems Ltd Swinton Grange, Malton YO17 6QR Tel. *01653 697378* Fax. *01653 697595* E-mail. *sandra.hinds@escadasystems.com* Web. *www.escadasystems.co.uk Optima (United Kingdom) – Syncro7 (United Kingdom) – Profile (United Kingdom) – Vision (United Kingdom)*

Escol Products Ltd Windover Road, Huntingdon PE29 7EB Tel. *01480 454631* Fax. *01480 411626* E-mail. *info@escolproducts.co.uk* Web. *www.escolproducts.co.uk Escol*

Escor Toys Limited St Stephens Road, Bournemouth BH2 6DY Tel. *01202 451451* Fax. *01202 454690* E-mail. *enquiries@bournemouth.gov.uk* Web. *www.bournemouth.gov.uk Escor*

E S E Direct 150 Northumberland Street, Norwich NR2 4EE Tel. *01603 629956* E-mail. *lee@ese.co.uk* Web. *www.ese.co.uk ESE Direct*

E-Signs Cheshire Ltd Moss Lane Business Centre Moss Lane, Sandbach CW11 3YX Tel. *01270 759171* E-mail. *sales@e-signscheshire.co.uk* Web. *www.inspiredbysigns.co.uk E-Signs*

Eskimo Ice New Covent Garden Market Unit A 45-48 Nine Elms, London SW8 5EE Tel. *020 77204883*

Fax. *020 77202731* E-mail. *mishalle@eskimo-ice.co.uk* Web. *www.eskimo-ice.co.uk Eskimo Ice*

E S K Industrial Roofing Ltd 5 Linton Avenue, Wigan WN6 7PR Tel. *01942 820377* Fax. *01942 244076* E-mail. *esk@blueyonder.co.uk* Web. *www.eskroofing.co.uk KINGSPAN*

Esko-Graphics D S M House Paper Mill Drive, Redditch B98 8QJ Tel. *01527 585805* Fax. *01527 584395* E-mail. *nathan.chapman@esko.com* Web. *www.esko.com ARTIOS – BARCO – CONGSBERG*

Eskro Hydra Mining Divison Rotheham Works Wortley Road, Rotherham S61 1LZ Tel. *01709 857500* Fax. *01709 857501* E-mail. *john@hydramining.com* Web. *www.hydramining.com Jiffee Jet – Jiffee Systems*

Esmerk County House 3rd Floor 17 Friar Street, Reading RG1 1DB Tel. *0118 9565820* Fax. *0118 9565850* E-mail. *response@esmerk.com* Web. *www.esmerk.com Esmerk*

Essential Cuisine Ltd Browning Way Woodford Park Industrial Estate, Winsford CW7 2RH Tel. *01606 541490* Fax. *0870 0501143* E-mail. *alan@essentialcuisine.com* Web. *www.essentialcuisine.com *Essential Cuisine*

Essex Chronicle Media Group Westway, Chelmsford CM1 3BE Tel. *01245 600700* E-mail. *switchboard@essexchronicle.co.uk* Web. *www.thisistotalessex.co.uk Brentwood Gazette, The – Essex Chronicle, The*

Essex Gate Systems High Lodge Boxford Lane, Boxford, Sudbury CO10 5JX Tel. *01787 211779* E-mail. *info@essexgates.com* Web. *www.essexgates.com Came*

Essex Pat Testing Tabor Avenue, Braintree CM7 2SX Tel. *01634 305962* Fax. *01634 308749* E-mail. *info@pat-testing-essex.com* Web. *www.pat-testing-essex.com PAT Testing*

Essex UK Ltd Ellis Ashton Street, Liverpool L36 6BW Tel. *0151 4436000* Fax. *0151 4436025* Web. *www.essexgroup.co.uk Bicobond 180 – Biconester – Biconester – Bicosol – Bicosol – Bicotherm – Bicotherm – Formvar*

Estuary Automation Ltd 40 Shoebury Avenue Shoeburyness, Southend On Sea SS3 9BH Tel. *01702 293901* Fax. *01702 297318* E-mail. *estaut@netscapeonline.co.uk* Web. *www.estuaryautomation.co.uk Automate – Automate Major – Automate Super – Automite – Series 110 – Series 55 – Series 80*

Eswa Ltd 32 Monkton Street, London SE11 4TX Tel. *020 75824300* Fax. *020 77351456* E-mail. *info@eswa.co.uk* Web. *www.eswa.co.uk ESWA – Millimat – Nexans – Up and Under*

E T A Circuit Breakers Ltd Unit 6 Telford Close, Aylesbury HP19 8DG Tel. *01296 420336* Fax. *01296 488497* E-mail. *info@e-t-a.co.uk* Web. *www.e-t-a.com E-T-A*

E T N A Assist UK Unit 30 Calibre Industrial Park Laches Close, Four Ashes, Wolverhampton WV10 7DZ Tel. *01902 798606* Fax. *01902 798686* E-mail. *info@etna-ct.com* Web. *www.etna-ct.com ETNA Mundo – ETNA Vega – *Linea Arte – Linea Gastro – *Linea Piccola*

Ets-Lindgren Ltd 4 Eastman Way, Stevenage SG1 4SZ Tel. *01438 730700* Fax. *01438 730750* E-mail. *info@ets-lindgren.com* Web. *www.ets-lindgren.com Bellinge Lee – Bellinge Lee - Rantec - Ray Proof - Emco - Holday - Euroshield - Lindgren - ETS – Emco – ETS – Euroshield – Holaday – Lindgren – Rantec – Ray Proof*

E Turner & Sons 32 Cathedral Road, Cardiff CF11 9UQ Tel. *029 20221002* Fax. *029 20388206* E-mail. *construction.turner@willmottdixon.co.uk* Web. *www.willmottdixon.co.uk Wilmot Dickson*

E2l Ltd 19 White Swan Court, Monmouth NP25 3NY Tel. *01600 714856* E-mail. *info@e2l.uk.com* Web. *www.e2l.uk.com LANDMARKA – ULTRASCAN*

Euchner UK Ltd Unit 2 Petre Drive, Sheffield S4 7PZ Tel. *0114 2560123* Fax. *0114 2425333* E-mail. *sales@euchner.co.uk* Web. *www.euchner.com Euchner*

Euler Hermes 1 Canada Square, London E14 5DX Tel. *020 7512933* Fax. *020 75129186* E-mail. *creditinfo@eulerhermes.com* Web. *www.eulerhermes.com Euler Hermes Collections UK Ltd – Euler Hermes Risk Services UK Ltd – Euler Hermes UK plc – First Source*

Euro Bond Adhesives Ltd Bonham Drive Eurolink Business Park, Sittingbourne ME10 3RY Tel. *01795 427888* Fax. *01795 479685* E-mail. *sales@eurobond-adhesives.co.uk* Web. *www.eurobond-adhesives.co.uk Cyanolit – Elecolit – Europurge – Panasolve – Penloc – Vitralit*

Eurobond Laminates Ltd Wentloog Corporate Park Wentloog Road, Rumney, Cardiff CF3 2ER Tel. *029 20776677* Fax. *029 20369161* E-mail. *sales@eurobond.co.uk* Web. *www.eurobond.co.uk Eurobond – Europanel – Firemaster – Rockspan*

Euro Car Parks Ltd 31 Byrom Street, Manchester M3 4PF Tel. *0161 8329777* Fax. *0161 8317088* E-mail. *humanresources@eurocarparks.com* Web. *www.eurocarparks.com Euro Car Parks*

Eurocastors Ltd Dalton Road, Glenrothes KY6 2SS Tel. *01592 774770* Fax. *01592 772736* E-mail. *sales@eurocastors.co.uk* Web. *www.eurocastors.co.uk *Eurocastors (Germany)*

Euro Catering Equipment 3 Turnpike Close, Lutterworth LE17 4YB Tel. *01455 559969* Fax. *01455 559979* E-mail. *sales@euro-catering.co.uk* Web. *www.chefsrange.co.uk American Range – *Aristarco – *Arris – *Artic – *Glorik – Inoxtrend – *Olis*

Eurocell Building Plastics Ltd Cheeseboroughclover Nook Road Cotes Park Industrial Estate, Somercotes, Alfreton DE55 4RF Tel. *01773 842300* Fax. *01773 842399* E-mail. *marketing@eurocell.co.uk* Web. *www.eurocell.co.uk Bay-bee – Eurocell – Eurologic – Eurologic ovolo – IQ750 – Marshall Tufflex – Vista*

Eurocoin Ltd Fortune House Moxon Street, Barnet EN5 5TS Tel. *020 82753000* Fax. *020 82753030* E-mail. *reception@eurocoin.co.uk* Web. *www.eurocoin.co.uk Eurocoin*

Eurocraft Trustees Ltd Cinderbank Netherton, Dudley DY2 9AE Tel. *01384 230101* Fax. *01384 256883* E-mail. *sales@eurocraft.co.uk* Web. *www.eurocraft.co.uk Eurocraft*

Eurofix Ltd Doranda Way, West Bromwich B71 4LU Tel. *0121 5535151* Fax. *0121 5005001* E-mail. *sales@reca-uk.com* Web. *www.eurofix.co.uk Profix*

Euro Group UK 7 Coopers Way Temple Farm Business Park, Southend On Sea SS2 5TE Tel. *01702 614444* E-mail. *grahame@essexupholstery.com* Web. *www.euro-group-uk.com Essex Upholstery – Euro Seating UK – My Cinema*

Eurohill Traders Ltd (t/a Associated Packaging) 195 Vale Road, Tonbridge TN9 1SU Tel. *01732 770777* Fax. *01732 770757* E-mail. *sales@apac.co.uk* Web. *www.apac.co.uk Apac*

Euro Label Printers 119-123 Hackford Road, London SW9 0QT Tel. *020 75829579* Fax. *01306 881900* E-mail. *info@eurolabelprinters.com* Web. *www.eurolabelprinters.com Reelstick*

Eurolines UK Ltd 4 Cardiff Road, Luton LU1 1PP Tel. *01582 404311* Fax. *01582 400694* E-mail. *welcome@eurolines.co.uk* Web. *www.eurolines.co.uk Eurolines*

Euroliters Ltd Hornhouse Lane Knowsley Industrial Park, Liverpool L33 7YQ Tel. *0151 5492122* Fax. *0151 5484008* E-mail. *jeff@euroliters.co.uk* Web. *www.euroliters.com Fireglow – Flamefast*

Euro Matic Ltd Clausen House Perivale Industrial Park, Horsenden Lane South, Greenford UB6 7QE Tel. *020 89912211* Fax. *020 89975074* E-mail. *adrian.wilkes@wppg.co.uk* Web. *www.euro-matic.com Bird Balls – Euro-Matic – *Euro-Matic (Denmark) – Euro-Plus – Roll-on Balls*

Euromedica plc 3 Muirfield Crescent, London E14 9SZ Tel. *020 75367950* Fax. *020 75388362* E-mail. *andy.macleod@euromedica.com* Web. *www.euromedica.com Euromedica*

Eurometals UK Ltd 16a Forge Lane Horbury, Wakefield WF4 5EH Tel. *01924 262020* Fax. *01924 266822* E-mail. *eurometals@easynet.co.uk* Web. *www.easynet.co.uk USF*

Euromixers PO Box 94, Stockport SK6 6HP Tel. *0161 4498559* Fax. *0161 4260456* E-mail. *sales@euromixers.co.uk* Web. *www.euromixers.co.uk IBC Mixers*

Europasonic UK Ltd 11 Sherbourne Street, Manchester M3 1JS Tel. *0161 8317879* Fax. *0161 8352125* E-mail. *jill.prendergast@panasonic.co.uk* Web. *www.europasonic.com *Eurosonic (Hong Kong)*

European Colour plc 5 Edwardes Place, London W8 6LR Tel. *020 76037788* Fax. *020 76037667* E-mail. *mail@ecplc.com* Web. *www.ecpigments.com Corbrite – Corfast – Cortone – Eljon – Printel*

European Drives & Motor Repairs 9 Mansion Close Moulton Park Industrial Estate, Northampton NN3 6RU Tel. *01604 499777* Fax. *01604 492777* E-mail. *malcolms@edmr.co.uk* Web. *www.edmr.co.uk ABB – Ansaldo – *ASR Servotron – *Aximaster (U.S.A.) – *Baldor – Baumuller – BOSCH – Boston – *Brush – Bull – C.M.C. – CMC – Contraves – CONTROL TECHNIQUES – *CSR – *E G & G Controls – Electrocraft – *Fanuc – Fuji – *GEC – General Electric – *Gettys – Gettys Fanuc – *Gettys Gould – H K Porter – Indiana General – *Indramat – Infranor – *Inland – Isoflux – Kessler – Kollmorgen – *Lenze – *Leroy Somer – *M.A.S. (Switzerland) – Magnetek – Mannesmann Demag – Mavilor – Mawdsley – Mitsubishi – OEMER – *Pacific Scientific – Parvex – *Peerless/Winsmith – PMI – POWERTEC – S.D.A. – S.D.B. – *SEM – SERVOMAC – Siemens – *Sigma – Slosyn – *Stromag – Thrige-Titan – Tuscan – VASCAT*

European Freeze Dry Roman Way Industrial Estate Longridge Road, Ribbleton, Preston PR2 5BD Tel. *01772 654441* Fax. *01772 655004* E-mail. *sales@europeanfreezedry.com* Web. *www.europeanfreezedry.com Mountain House*

European Lamp Group Knowles Lane, Bradford BD4 9AB Tel. *08449 914400* Fax. *0870 4450001* E-mail. *sales@europeanlampgroup.com* Web. *www.edmundson-electrical.co.uk/ City Lights – Hobbylite – Lampways – Lampways Lamp Shop – Triple-Plus*

European Mezzanine Systems Ltd Berrington Lodge 93 Tettenhall Road, Wolverhampton WV3 9PE Tel. *0845 2609601* Fax. *0845 2609602* E-mail. *info@mezzstore.com* Web. *www.mezzstore.com Mezzstore*

European Music Co. Ltd Unit 5/6, Concorde Business Centre Airport Industrial Estate, Main Road, Biggin Hill, Westerham TN16 3YN Tel. *01959 571600* Fax. *01959 572267* E-mail. *marc@tanglewoodguitars.co.uk* Web. *www.tanglewoodguitars.co.uk *Tanglewood (Korea, Republic of)*

European O G D Ltd Nortonthorpe Mills Wakefield Road, Scissett, Huddersfield HD8 9LA Tel. *01484 865228* Fax. *01484 861887* E-mail. *info@eogd.co.uk* Web. *www.eogd.co.uk BEST DYES – EBEST DYES*

European Squash Federation The Firs Barston Lane, Barston, Solihull B92 0JP Tel. *01675 443922* Fax. *01675 443440* E-mail. *info@europeansquash.com* Web. *www.europeansquash.com World Squash*

European Technical Sales Ltd Chroma House Shire Hill, Saffron Walden CB11 3AQ Tel. *01799 508076* Fax. *01799 508024* E-mail. *etsltd@globalnet.co.uk* Web. *www.eurotechspares.com ABB Preciflex – Ace Shock Absorbers – Aciera – Alfing – Alpha Laval – AMK – Andantex – Angst+Pfister – Arburg – Argus – ARO – Aschenbrenner – Autoblok – Axa – Azo – Baldor Motors – Balluff – bar – Barger Seals – Bauer GB – Baumgartner – Bauromat – Berendsen Pumps – Berger Tools – Bernstein switches – Beru – Binder Magnets – Binzel – Blum – Bobolowski – Bosch – Bostik – Breco – Brinkmann – Brown Pestell – Buhl – Bühler – Bürkle – Bussmann – Cetronic – Chambrelan – Cincinnati – Cone Blanchard – Contitech – Contraves Drives – Contraves Motors – Copas – De-Sta-Co – Delkor – Deltaweld – Demag Cranes – Deutsche Techna – Devlieg – Dina Relays – Dörries Scharmann – Draftex – Draka Welding Cables – Dung – Durbal – E.S.A. – Elan – Elasto Valves – Elektro-Kohl – Elesta – Elge – Elges – Endress & Hauser – Engelmotoren – Erwin Sick – ESA Encoders – Etatron – Euchner – Euchner Connectors – Euchner Electronic Handwheels – Euchner Enabling Switches – Euchner Joystick Switches – Euchner Limit Switch – Euchner Pendant Stations – Euchner Plunger Limit Switch – Euchner Position Switch – Euchner Safety Relay – Euchner Safety Switch – F.H. Jung – Fanuc – Fanuc Boards – Fanuc Control PCBs – Fanuc Drive Cases – Fanuc Drives – Fanuc Encoders – Fanuc Fuses – Fanuc Input Units – Fanuc Linear Motors – Fanuc Machine Tool Controls – Fanuc Membranes – Fanuc Memory – Fanuc Monitors – Fanuc Motors – Fanuc Power Supply – Fanuc Servo Drives – Fanuc Servo Motors – Fanuc Spindle Motors – Fanuc Spindles – Fenner – Festo – Fexmo – Fibro – Fibromanta – Flenco – Flender – Flohr – Fluke – Folliard – Fraba – Freudenberg – Fuchs Lubricants – Fuji – Furmanite – Genorma – Gerb – Gillardon – Gleason – Goldammer – Gossen – GS Industrie – Gutekunst – Harting – Hartmann&Braun – Hasco – Haug – HAWE – Hebor – Heenan – Heinz Mayer Clamps – Heiss – Hellermann Tyton – Hema – Hengstler – Hennig – Hensoldt – Hepco – Heraeus – Herion – Hetak – Hohner – Homag – Honeywell – Hörbiger-Origa – Horiuchi Cylinders – Hottinger – Hübner Tachos – Hurth – Hydraulikring – Hypneumat – I.M.O. – IMO – Indramat Motors – Ingemat – Jaeger Looms – Jahns – Judo Valves – Jumo Instruments – Jumo Poressure Gauges – Jumo Pressure Switches – Jumo Rod Thermostats – Jumop Level Probes – Kabelschlepp – Kastl – Kissling – Kitagawa – Kitz – Klaschka – Kleinknecht – Klippon – Kniel – Knoll Chip Reducers – Knoll Filters – Knoll Pumps – Knoll Pumps & Conveyors – Knoll Separators – KnollExtraction Stations – Kobold Flow Meters – Kolbenseeger – Köllmann – Kollmorgen – Körting – Krautkrämer – Kromschröder – KTR – Kübler – Kuka Welding Equipment – Küma – Labino Lamps – Lamborghini Pumps – Lang Spannwerkzeuge – Lang-Laru – Lapp Cables – Legrand – Lemo – Lenze – Lenze Controls – Lenze Drive PLCs – Lenze Gearboxes – Lenze Geared Motors – Lenze Industrial PCs – Lenze LCU Motor Starters – Lenze Motors – Lenze Servos – Leuze-Mayser – Lineartechnik – LJM – LJU Light Barriers – Lumberg – Lutz – Maedler – Mahle – Makino – Martor – Matech – Mattke – Mayr – MCM – Mecanocaucho – Megatron – MEL – Moklansa – Mondeo – Morgan Rekofa – MSE – Müller Co-Ax – Multiswitch – Murr – Myford – Namco – National Machinery – Naxos – Neff Lineartechnik – Nilos – Nord Gears – Obara – Olimpic – Olma Leduc – Olten – Omron – Omron Counters – Omron Digital Panel Indicators – Omron Electromechanical Relays – Omron Fibre Optic Sensor – Omron Frequency Converrters – Omron Inductive Sensors – Omron Limit Switches – Omron Low Voltage Switch Gear – Omron Machine Interfaces – Omron Measurement Sensor – Omron Monitoring Products – Omron Motion Controllers – Omron Photo Electric Sensors – Omron PLCs – Omron Power Supplies – Omron Programmable Logic Controllers – Omron Pushbutton Switches – Omron Relays – Omron Rotary Encoder – Omron Sensors – Omron Servo Systems – Omron Solenoids – Omron Solid State Relay – Omron Temperature Controller – Omron Timers – Omron Vision*

Sensor – Orbit GmbH – Ormon – Ortlinghaus – Orwak – Ott-Jakob – Otto Holland GmbH – Parker Hannifin – Pee Wee – Peerless Winsmith – Perma – Perske Motors – Pfauter – Phoenix – Piab – Pilz – Pilz Control Relays – Pilz Monitoring Relays – Pilz Operator Display – Pilz Safety Relays – Pilz Sensors – Pilz Switches – Pittler – Pleiger – Poeppelmann – Powergrip – Powertronics – Prima – Prometec – Prominent – Promot – Prudhomme – Räder Vogel – RaJa – Ravitex/Sinterleghe – Reihansl – Rekofa – Remco Motors – Rickmeier – Riedel – Ringflex – Rittal Coolers – Rittal Enclosures – Röhm – Röhm Adaptor Plates – Röhm Compact Vices – Röhm Drill Chucks – Röhm Driven Tools – Röhm Lathe Chucks – Röhm Machine Vices – Röhm Mandrels – Röhm Power Chucks – Röhm Tailstocks – Römheld – Röperwerk – Ross Valves – Rotech – RSF Encoders – Ruez – Ruhle Inductosyn – Sankyo – Savair – SBB – Schaffner – Schaudt Mikrosa – Schell – Schleicher Relays – Schleifring – Schmalenberger – Schmalz – Schmersal – Schmersal Interlock Switches – Schmersal Limit Switches – Schmersal Safety Controllers – Schmersal Safety Interlocks – Schmersal Safety Relays – Schrack – Schultz – Schumacher Filter – Schunk – Secosim – Sedis – Semens Transformers – Semikron – Sick Colour Sensors – Sick Encoders – Sick Industrial Sensor – Sick Motors – Sick Positioning Drives – Sick Proximity Sensors – Sielemann – Siemens – Siemens Dives – Siemens AC Converters – Siemens AC Drives – Siemens AC Motors – Siemens Acoustic Sensors – Siemens DC Drives – Siemens DC Motors – Siemens Drive Systems – Siemens Drives – Siemens Electric Actuators – Siemens Fans – Siemens Filters – Siemens Flamproof Motors – Siemens Flow Indicators – Siemens Flow Sensors – Siemens Flow Switches – Siemens Flow Transducers – Siemens Flowmeters – Siemens Frequency Inverter – Siemens Gear Controller – Siemens Geared Motor – Siemens Generators – Siemens High Efficiency Motors – Siemens High Voltage AC Motors – Siemens High Voltage Drives – Siemens High Voltage Motors – Siemens HV Drives – Siemens HV Motors – Siemens Induction Motors – Siemens Industrial PCs – Siemens Inverter Drives – Siemens Inverters – Siemens Isolation Transformers – Siemens Isolators – Siemens Laser Sensors – Siemens LCD Monitors – Siemens Low Voltage Motors – Siemens LV Motors – Siemens Machine Tool Controls – Siemens Machine Tools – Siemens Master Drives – Siemens Motion Sensors – Siemens Motor Spindle – Siemens Motor Starter – Siemens Motors – Siemens Operator Interface – Siemens Panel Boards – Siemens PLC Boards – Siemens Position Switch – Siemens Power Supplies – Siemens Pressure Gauges – Siemens Proximity Switches – Sigloch&Schrieder – Sihi – Sirai Coils – Sirai Micro Solenoid Valves – Sirai Pressure Switches – Sirai Solenoid Valves – Sirai Valves – Softinger – Sopap – Spectrum – Spieth – Spitznagel – Springfix – Square D – Square D AC Contactors – Square D Circuit Breakers – Square D Coils – Square D Heater Units – Square D Magnetic Starters – Square D Moulded Case Circuit Breakers – Square D Safety Switches – Square D Starters – Square D Transfer Switches – Stanler – Stäubli – Stauff – Stefani – Stegmann Encoders – Steinecker – Sterling – Stic Havroy – Stromberger – Struckmeier – Studer – Stuewe – Suga Switches – T.V.L. – Teigler – Telemecanique – Tesch – Thielmann – Thome – Tönshoff – TOS – Tox-Pressotechnik – Tracoinsa – Trafag – Trafag Pressure Switches – Trafag Pressure Transmitters – Trafag Temperature Transmitter – Trafag Thermostats – Tschan – Tünkers – Turck – TWK Transducers – Ungerer – Unimatic – Vahle – Variohm Transducers – Vishay – Vogel Gearboxes – W. Logan – W. Sahlberg – Wago Connectors – WEG Motors – Weko – Wenglor – Wenzel – Wichita – Will&Hahnenstein – Willi Vogel AG – Winkel – Wippermann – Witamwas – Zasche – ZF – Ziehl Abeg – Ziehl-ABM – Zollern

Europ Assistance Holdings Ltd Sussex House Perrymount Road, Haywards Heath RH16 1DN Tel. *01444 442800* Fax. *01444 459292* E-mail. *david_crapnell@europ-assistance.co.uk* Web. *www.europ-assistance.co.uk Family Continental Motoring – Family Continental Travel Assistance – Personal Travel Insurance – Select – Voyager*

Europrint Promotions Ltd Lancaster House 52 Preston New Road, Blackburn BB2 6AH Tel. *01254 588400* Fax. *01254 588401* E-mail. *alan.rogers@gtech.com* Web. *www.europrint-group.com Bingovision – Cashcade – Cashlines – Golden Goal – Lucky Shirt – Split Level – Wingo*

Euro Stock Springs Ltd PO Box 133, Evesham WR11 1ZJ Tel. *01527 540600* Fax. *01527 540700* E-mail. *rr@eurostock.co.uk* Web. *www.eurostock.co.uk Terry Stock Springs*

Eurosuits Ltd 631-637 Watford Way, London NW7 3JR Tel. *020 89063446* Fax. *020 89061775* E-mail. *p.graham@eurosuits.co.uk* Web. *www.eurosuits.co.uk Eurosuits*

Euroteck Systems UK Ltd Unit 6-7 Kepler, Tamworth B79 7XE Tel. *01827 312455* Fax. *01827 312548* E-mail. *sales@euroteck.co.uk* Web. *www.euroteck.co.uk Bosello – Cegelec – Comet – Cygnus Instruments Ltd – Hamamatsu – Icm – Thales – Tiede – Utex – Vallon*

Evac+Chair International Ltd Paraid House Weston Lane, Birmingham B11 3RS Tel. *0845 2302253* Fax. *0121 7066746* E-mail. *info@evacchair.co.uk* Web. *www.evacchair.co.uk Evac+Chair – Paraid*

Evamix Aggregates (a division of Paull & Co.) Coat Road, Martock TA12 6EX Tel. *01935 825252* Fax. *01935 822721 Evamix*

Evans Concrete Products Ltd Pease Hill Road, Ripley DE5 3HZ Tel. *01773 748026* Fax. *01773 570354* E-mail. *evans@evansconcreteproducts.co.uk* Web. *www.evansconcreteproducts.co.uk Evans*

Evans Cycles Ltd Camino Park James Watt Way, Crawley RH10 9TZ Tel. *01293 574999* E-mail. *info@wizzbike.com* Web. *www.evanscycles.co.uk WiZZBiKE.com*

Evans Textiles Sales Ltd Helmet Street, Manchester M1 2NT Tel. *0161 2744147* Fax. *0161 2744322* E-mail. *peter@kgchristys.co.uk* Web. *www.kgchristys.co.uk Collafix – *Mills & Co (Textiles) (India and The Far East) – O.H. Evans – Texifused*

Evans Vanodine International plc Brierley Road Walton Summit Centre, Bamber Bridge, Preston PR5 8AH Tel. *01772 322200* Fax. *01772 626000* E-mail. *devans@evansvanodine.co.uk* Web. *www.evansvanodine.co.uk 1066 Blocks – Acid Brite – Airfresh – Bac-Det – Barrier Cream – Beaded Gel – Beerline – Bleach – Blusyl – Buffodine – C.L.S. – Cetyl – Citrand – Clean & Shine – Clean Hands – Clear – Crystal – Deep Kleen – Deep Strip – Dish Wash Extra – Dri-Foam – E.-Gel – E.-Phos – E.-Pine – Easikleen – Easy Strip – Easyshine – Enhance – Evans Extraction Cleaner – Evans Spray Polish – Everfresh – F.A.M. 30 – Fabric – FinalTouch – Florazol – Fresh – G.P.C. 8 – Glass Wash – Glaze – H.S.C. – HI-Phos – High Class – Jaspa – Lemon Gel – Lift – Lime – Low Foam Cleaner – Maintenance Cleaner – Masocare – Masodine – Masodip – Metron – Mexapol – Mystrol – Odoron – Ovacryl – Oven Cleaner – Pine Gel – Pink Pearl – Protect – Pynol – Pynolic – Q'Sol – Quillon – Rubicon – Sanitize – Sapphire – Sealant B – Search – Shift – Sirtan – Superseal – Sure Strip – Sustain – T.T.C. – Traffic Soil Remover – Trigon – Tuffa – V. 18 – Vanodox – Vanorinse – Vanosan – Versatile*

Eveden Ltd Rothwell Road Desborough, Kettering NN14 2PG Tel. *01536 760282* Fax. *01536 762149* E-mail. *info@eveden.com* Web. *www.eveden.com Fantasie – Footprints – Rigby & Peller*

E-Vend UK PO Box 104, Newport TF10 0AA Tel. *08700 052633* Fax. *0870 0052644* E-mail. *submissions@e-vend-uk.com* Web. *www.e-vend-uk.com E-Vend UK*

Evenproducts Ltd A46 Evesham Bypass, Evesham WR11 4TU Tel. *01386 760950* Fax. *01386 765404* E-mail. *sales@evenproducts.com* Web. *www.evenproducts.com Evenmist – Evenproducts – Evenshower – Evenstorm – Eventrickle*

Everbright Stainless Brimington Road North, Chesterfield S41 9BE Tel. *01246 451600* Fax. *01246 451611* E-mail. *chris.tyrrell@anixter.com* Web. *www.anixter.com Everbright Stainless*

Everbuild Building Products Ltd 41 Knowsthorpe Way Cross Green Industrial Estate, Leeds LS9 0SW Tel. *0113 2403456* Fax. *0113 2400024* E-mail. *reception@everbuild.co.uk* Web. *www.everbuild.co.uk Black jack – Colourmatch – Everbuild – Everline – Evferflex – Gunanail – Instant Nails – Lumberjack – Microbuild – Stick 2*

Evergreen Office Supplies Evergreen Turnpike Close, Ardleigh, Colchester CO7 7QW Tel. *01206 231111* Fax. *01206 231476* E-mail. *sales@evergreen.co.uk* Web. *www.evergreen.co.uk Evergreen*

Evergreen Tractors Ltd Lynn Road, Kings Lynn PE34 3ES Tel. *01553 617666* Fax. *01553 617673* E-mail. *mail@evergreentractors.co.uk* Web. *www.evergreentractors.co.uk *Kverneland – *Verdestan*

Everlac GB Ltd Moonhall Business Park Helions Bumpstead Road, Haverhill CB9 7AA Tel. *01440 766360* Fax. *01440 768897* E-mail. *admin@everlac.co.uk* Web. *www.everlac.co.uk Everflex – Everseal – Evertex – Exterior Guard – Hi-Build – Impbond – Impsil – Sports Coating – Stormguard – Topcover – Weatherguard*

Eversheds Bridgewater Place Water Lane, Leeds LS11 5DR Tel. *0113 2430391* Fax. *0113 2456188* E-mail. *d-gray@eversheds.com* Web. *www.eversheds.com Eversheds*

Eversheds Kett House 1 Station Road, Cambridge CB1 2JY Tel. *01223 443666* Fax. *01223 443777* E-mail. *ianmather@eversheds.com* Web. *www.eversheds.com Eversheds*

Eversheds Franciscan House 51 Princes Street, Ipswich IP1 1UR Tel. *01473 284428* Fax. *01473 233666* E-mail. *lorrainegouch@eversheds.com* Web. *www.eversheds.com Eversheds*

Evertile Ltd 6 Moresby Road, London E5 9LF Tel. *020 88063167* Fax. *020 88067434* E-mail. *sales@evertile.co.uk* Web. *www.evertile.co.uk Locktile*

Everymans Library Ltd Northburgh House 10 Northburgh Street, London EC1V 0AT Tel. *020 75666350* Fax. *020 74903708* E-mail. *books@everyman.uk.com* Web. *www.randomhouse.com/classics Everyman's Library*

Everyvalve Ltd 19 Station Close, Potters Bar EN6 1TL Tel. *01707 642018* Fax. *01707 646340* E-mail. *sales@everyvalve.com* Web. *www.everyvalve.com Aquamatic (U.S.A.) – Astore (Europe, Western) – Astral (Europe, Western) – ASV (Europe, Western) – B.D. (Europe, Western) – Efast (Europe, Western) – Eve (Europe, Western) – EvE - 85 Mfd Lines - Everyvalve Ltd – FSV (Europe, Western) – Irritec (Italy) – Kraft (Europe, Western) – RIA (Europe, Western) – Safi (Europe, Western) – Tefen (Israel) – TT (Europe, Western) – WV (Europe, Western)*

Eve Trakway Ltd Bramley Vale, Chesterfield S44 5GA Tel. *01246 858600* Fax. *08700 737373* E-mail. *mail@evetrakway.co.uk* Web. *www.evetrakway.co.uk Eve Barriers – Eve Shieldtrack – Eve Trakway*

E V O Instrumentation Ltd 31a Coppice Trading Estate, Kidderminster DY11 7QY Tel. *01562 741212* Fax. *01562 741666* E-mail. *sales@evoinstrumentation.co.uk* Web. *www.evoinstrumentation.co.uk Leiten Berger – Leitenberger – Nuova FIMA*

Evolution Glass Ltd Unit 7 Copthorne Business Park Dowlands Lane, Copthorne, Crawley RH10 3HX Tel. *01342 718668* Fax. *01342 714077* E-mail. *danielfoggerson@evolutionglass.co.uk* Web. *www.evolutionglass.co.uk Evolution Glass Ltd*

E W A B Engineering Ltd 16 Stafford Park, Telford TF3 3BS Tel. *01952 239220* Fax. *01952 239258* E-mail. *glyn.punter@ewab.com* Web. *www.ewab.com Ewab*

Ewart Chain Ltd Colombo Street, Derby DE23 8LX Tel. *01332 345451* Fax. *01332 371753* E-mail. *sales@ewartchain.co.uk* Web. *www.ewartchain.co.uk Ewart – Ewplas*

Ewos Ltd Westfield, Bathgate EH48 3BP Tel. *01506 633966* Fax. *01506 632730* E-mail. *john.christie@ewos.com* Web. *www.ewos.com Ewos – Fish food manufrs*

Exaclair Ltd Oldmedow Road, Kings Lynn PE30 4LW Tel. *01553 696600* Fax. *01553 767235* E-mail. *enquiries@exaclair.co.uk* Web. *www.exaclair.co.uk Bockingford – Chartwell – Duodisc – Europa – Goldline – Goldlone – Greenleaves – Guildhall – Guildhall Spiral Files – Headliner – Lanaquarelle – Tachograph – Technik Art – True Knit*

Excalibur Screwbolts Ltd Gate 3 New Hall Nursery Lower Road, Hockley SS5 5JU Tel. *01702 206962* Fax. *01702 207918* E-mail. *info@screwbolt.com* Web. *www.screwbolt.com Excalibur*

Exmac Gregorys Bank, Worcester WR3 8AB Tel. *01905 721500* Fax. *01905 613024* E-mail. *gjs@exmac.co.uk* Web. *www.exmacautomation.co.uk Excelvayor – Lazer Way*

Excel Machine Tools Ltd Colliery Lane Exhall, Coventry CV7 9NW Tel. *024 76645038* Fax. *024 76366666* E-mail. *sales@excelmachinetools.co.uk* Web. *www.excel-machine-tools.co.uk EXCEL – PINNACLE*

Excel Packaging & Insulation Company Ltd Unit 9 Woodcock Hill Estate Harefield Road, Rickmansworth WD3 1PQ Tel. *01923 770247* Fax. *01923 770248* E-mail. *enquiries@excelpackaging.co.uk* Web. *www.excelpackaging.co.uk Ferribox – Profoil*

Excelsior Textiles Ltd 74 Wentworth Street, London E1 7TF Tel. *020 73779304* Fax. *020 73772743* E-mail. *enquiries@excelsiortextiles.co.uk *Excelsior (Europe and The Far East)*

Excelsior Tours Ltd Central Business Park, Bournemouth BH1 3SJ Tel. *01202 652222* Fax. *01202 652223* E-mail. *info@videostudio.co.uk* Web. *www.excelsior-coaches.com Excelsior Coachways – Excelsior Holidays - Bournemouth*

Exclusive Leisure Ltd 28 Cannock Street, Leicester LE4 9HR Tel. *0116 2332255* Fax. *0116 2461561* E-mail. *info@exclusiveleisure.co.uk* Web. *www.exclusiveleisure.co.uk Tiger T.*

Exclusive Ranges Ltd 1 Sutherland Court Brownfields, Welwyn Garden City AL7 1BJ Tel. *01707 361770* Fax. *01707 361777* E-mail. *sales@exclusiveranges.co.uk* Web. *www.exclusiveranges.co.uk *Ambach – Beech – *Inotech – *Rorgue – Salvis*

The Exe Engineering Company Limited 60-64 Alphington Road St Thomas, Exeter EX2 8HX Tel. *01392 275186* Fax. *01392 260336* E-mail. *sales@exeengineering.co.uk* Web. *www.exeengineering.co.uk Exe*

Exel Composites Fair Oak Lane Whitehouse Industrial Estate, Runcorn WA7 3DU Tel. *01928 701515* Fax. *01928 713572* E-mail. *office.runcorn@exelcomposites.com* Web. *www.exelcomposites.com *Fibreforce (U.S.A.)*

Exhaust Ejector Co. Ltd 11 Wade House Road Shelf, Halifax HX3 7PE Tel. *01274 679524* Fax. *01274 607344* E-mail. *simon.conway@eeco-ltd.co.uk* Web. *www.eeco-ltd.co.uk Cornette – Eeco – Hotline – Stylemaster – Truckmaster – Windmaster*

EXHEAT Ltd Threxton Road Industrial Estate Watton, Thetford IP25 6NG Tel. *01953 886200* Fax. *01953 886222* E-mail. *sales@exheat.com* Web. *www.exheat.com Heatex – M.I.H. – Marine & Industrial Heat*

Exhibitions South West Ltd Glenthorne House Truro Business Park, Threemilestone, Truro TR3 6BW

Tel. *01872 245220* Fax. *01872 572551*
E-mail. *peter.sugden@expowestexhibitions.com*
Web. *www.expowestexhibition.com Expowest Displays – Expowest Exhibitions*

Exitflex UK Ltd 5 Airfield Road, Christchurch BH23 3TG
Tel. *01202 478334* Fax. *01202 488110*
E-mail. *sales@exitflex.co.uk* Web. *www.exitflex.co.uk Blastaway (Switzerland) – Speedy V (Switzerland) – Tri A*

Exopack Advanced Coatings Ltd Ash Road North Wrexham Industrial Estate, Wrexham LL13 9UF Tel. *01978 660241*
Fax. *01978 661452* E-mail. *peter.morris@exopack.com*
Web. *www.exopackadvancedcoatings.com Inspire – Reflex – Rexam - Inspire - StratFX – StratFX*

Ex Or Ltd Haydock Lane Haydock Indl-Est, Haydock, St Helens WA11 9UJ Tel. *01942 719229* Fax. *01942 272767*
E-mail. *marketing@ex-or.com* Web. *www.ex-or.com Exor*

Expamet Building Products Ltd Longhill Industrial Estate North Greatham Street, Hartlepool TS25 1PU
Tel. *01429 866688* Fax. *01429 866633*
E-mail. *sales@expamet.net* Web. *www.expamet.co.uk Bat – Exmet Brickwork Reinforcement – Expamet – HY-Rib Permanent Formwork – Maxicon – Metdeck – Metpost – Redrib*

Experian Q A S George West House 2-3 Clapham Common North Side, London SW4 0QL Tel. *020 74987777*
Fax. *020 74980303* E-mail. *reception@qas.com*
Web. *www.qas.com QAS Systems Ltd, The*

Expert Rule Software Ltd Newlands Road, Leigh WN7 4HN
Tel. *0870 6060870* Fax. *0870 6040156*
E-mail. *info@expertrule.co.uk* Web. *www.expertrule.com Xpertrule*

Expert Tooling & Automation 1 Banner Park Wickmans Drive, Coventry CV4 9XA Tel. *024 76428520*
Fax. *024 76428501* E-mail. *sales@exta.co.uk*
Web. *www.experttooling.co.uk Linkline – Pressflow*

Export Ltd 37 Station Road, Lutterworth LE17 4AP
Tel. *01455 555340* Fax. *01455 555381*
Web. *www.husky-products.com *Husky*

Expo Technologies Ltd Unit 1 Hampton Court Estate Summer Road, Thames Ditton KT7 0RH Tel. *020 83988011*
Fax. *020 83988014* E-mail. *sales@expoworldwide.com*
Web. *www.expoworldwide.com Expo-Telektron Safety Systems Ltd*

The Express & Echo Heron Road Sowton Industrial Estate, Exeter EX2 7NF Tel. *01392 442211* Fax. *01392 442298*
Web. *www.thisisexeter.co.uk Express & Echo – Leader*

Express Instrument Hire Ltd Express House Church Road, Tarleton, Preston PR4 6UP Tel. *01772 815600*
Fax. *01772 815937* E-mail. *sales@expresshire.net*
Web. *www.expresshire.net Flir Systems – Thermacam*

Express Moulds Ltd Jubilee Works 40 Alma Crescent, Birmingham B7 4RH Tel. *0121 3596378* Fax. *0121 3593792*
E-mail. *paul.yeomans@expressmoulds.co.uk*
Web. *www.expressmoulds.co.uk Express Moulds*

Express & Star Queen Street, Wolverhampton WV1 1ES
Tel. *01902 313131* Fax. *01902 319721*
E-mail. *business@expressandstar.co.uk*
Web. *www.expressandstar.co.uk Express & Star*

Extract Technology Bradley Junction Industrial Estate Leeds Road, Huddersfield HD2 1UR Tel. *01484 432727*
Fax. *01484 432659*
E-mail. *awainwright@extract-technology.com*
Web. *www.extract-technology.com Downflow Containment Booths – High Containment Barrier Isolators – Pharma Filters – Process Containment Systems*

Extra Space Industries Unit 27 Hobbs Industrial Estate Newchapel, Lingfield RH7 6HN Tel. *01342 830040*
Fax. *01342 836978* E-mail. *enquiries@extraspace.co.uk*
Web. *www.extraspace.co.uk Armadillo – Armadillo - armoured security units .Extra Cab - Jack Leg Cabin.Extra Mod - modular building systemTranspak - flat pak transportable system.Extraspan - industrial ware house building – Extra Cab – Extra Mad – Extraspan – Transpak (Austria)*

E X X Projects 72 Rivington Street, London EC2A 3AY
Tel. *020 76848200* Fax. *0845 6301282*
E-mail. *exx@plax.co.uk* Web. *www.plax.co.uk Airone – Chemisorb – Safelab*

Eye 2 Eye Gartshore Optical Centre 231 Grange Road, Birkenhead L41 2YX Tel. *0151 6473048* Fax. *0151 6662174*
Web. *www.eye2eyeshop.com EYE 2 EYE*

Eye for Marketing 34 Queen Anne's Road Bootham, YORK YO30 7AA Tel. *01904 625182*
E-mail. *support@eyeformarketing.com*
Web. *www.eyeformarketing.com Eye for Marketing*

F

Fabdec Ltd Grange Road, Ellesmere SY12 9DG
Tel. *01691 622811* Fax. *01691 627222*
E-mail. *reception@fabdec.com* Web. *www.fabdec.com Fabdec Ltd – Heat Transfer Technology*

Faber Blinds UK Ltd Pond Wood Close Moulton Park Industrial Estate, Northampton NN3 6RT Tel. *01604 766251*
Fax. *01604 768802* E-mail. *sales.uk@faber.com*
Web. *www.faberblinds.co.uk Ambassador – Faber 1800 Blackout Blind – Faber 2000 Blackout Blind – Faber Autostop – Faber Charleston – Faber Escalade – Faber Gallery – Faber Illusion – Faber Maximatic – Faber Metalet 16/25/43/61 – Faber Metalet 61AV – Faber Metalet SV35 – Faber Metamatic – Faber Metamatic AV – Faber Midimatic – Faber Minimatic – Faber Multistop – Faber Nizza Awning – Faber Rollotex – Faber Series One Blackout Blind – Faber Softline – Faber Uprite – Faber Vertibay 40 – Faber Vertical 30 – Faber Vertical 40 – MechoShade – Sunfilm – Suntime*

Fabricast Multi Metals Ltd Main Street, Hull HU2 0LF
Tel. *01482 327944* Fax. *01482 216670*
E-mail. *sales@fabricast.co.uk* Web. *www.fabricast.co.uk Fabricast*

Fabric Care Dry Cleaners 280a Brixton Hill, London SW2 1HT
Tel. *020 86747192* Fax. *020 86747835*
E-mail. *kola.taiwo@fabric-care.co.uk*
Web. *www.fabric-care.co.uk Fabric-Care*

Fabris Lane Ltd 1 Lion Park Avenue, Chessington KT9 1ST
Tel. *020 89741642* Fax. *020 89741672*
E-mail. *rod.lane@fabrislane.co.uk* Web. *www.fabrislane.com *Fabris Lane (Italy) – *Mondo (Italy)*

Fabrizio Fashions Ltd 138 Fonthill Road, London N4 3HP
Tel. *020 75610102* Fax. *020 75610103*
E-mail. *barry.greenfield@fabrizio.co.uk*
Web. *www.fabrizio.co.uk Fabrizio – Fun Sport & People*

Facilities Staff Training 7a Glebe Road, Warlingham CR6 9NG Tel. *01883 623839* Fax. *01883 626365*
E-mail. *rlbransby@btconnect.com* Web. *www.fastrain.co.uk Basic Food Hygiene – Health & Hygiene – Healthy Eating – Level 2 Food Safety – Nutrition Training*

Factair Ltd 49 Boss Hall Road, Ipswich IP1 5BN
Tel. *01473 746400* Fax. *01473 747123*
E-mail. *enquiries@factair.co.uk* Web. *www.factair.co.uk Air Purity Analyser (H) – AiroGen – Factair – Safe-Air – Safe-Air Tester – SafeAir Tester*

Facts International Ltd Fact Centre 3 Henwood, Henwood Industrial Estate, Ashford TN24 8FL Tel. *01233 637000*
Fax. *01233 626950* E-mail. *crispin@facts.uk.com*
Web. *www.facts.co.uk F.I.L.*

Facultatieve Technologies Ltd Moor Road, Leeds LS10 2DD
Tel. *0113 2768888* Fax. *0113 2718188*
E-mail. *info@facultatieve-technologies.co.uk*
Web. *www.facultatieve-technologies.co.uk Tabo – Universal – Universal - Dowson & Mason - Evans Universal - Tabo Inex - Evans Tabo Universal - Fours Delot International*

Fagioli Ltd The Ridgeway, Iver SL0 9JE Tel. *01753 659000*
Fax. *01753 655998* E-mail. *info@fagioli.com*
Web. *www.fagioli.com Flat Jacks – Flat Jacks - Towerlift - Strand Jacks – Strand Jacks – Tower Lift*

Failsworth Hats Ltd Crown Street Failsworth, Manchester M35 9BD Tel. *0161 6813131* Fax. *0161 6834754*
E-mail. *sales@failsworth-hats.co.uk*
Web. *www.failsworth-hats.co.uk Failsworth*

Faire Bros & Co. Ltd Elan House Waterloo Road, Llandrindod Wells LD1 6BH Tel. *01597 827800* Fax. *01597 827899*
E-mail. *sales@fairebros.co.uk* Web. *www.fairebros.co.uk Hurculace – St. George*

Fairey Industrial Ceramics Lymedale Cross Lower Milehouse Lane, Newcastle ST5 9BT Tel. *01782 664420*
Fax. *01782 664490* E-mail. *filtersales@faireyceramics.com*
Web. *www.faireyceramics.com Aerox – British Berkefeld – Doulton – Pyrolith*

Fairfax Coffee Ltd 2 Regency Parade Finchley Road, London NW3 5EQ Tel. *020 77227646* Fax. *020 77222333*
E-mail. *info@fairfaxcoffee.com* Web. *www.fairfaxcoffee.com *Briel (Portugal) – *I.P.S. Imperia (Italy) – *Inox Pran (Italy) – *Italexpress (Italy) – *La Pavoni (Italy) – *O.M.G. (Italy)*

Fairless Engineering Webb Road Skippers Lane Industrial Estate, Middlesbrough TS6 6HD Tel. *01642 676070*
Fax. *01642 606401* E-mail. *enquiries@fairless.co.uk*
Web. *www.fairless.co.uk Cable Glands*

Fairline Boats Ltd Nene Valley Business Park Oundle, Peterborough PE8 4HN Tel. *01832 273661*
Fax. *01832 273432* E-mail. *alan.bowers@fairline.com*
Web. *www.fairline.com Fairline – Fairline Phantom – Fairline Squadron – Targa*

Fairway Hydraulics Ltd Unit 96a Blackpole Trading Estate West, Worcester WR3 8TJ Tel. *01905 457519*
Fax. *01905 456054*
E-mail. *enquiries@fairwayhydraulics.co.uk*
Web. *www.fairwayhydraulics.co.uk Aeroquip – Casappa – Hydac International – Ikron – LC-Oledoinamica – Oleostar – Voss – Walvoil*

Faith Footwear Holdings Ltd 42 48 Chase Road, London NW10 6PX Tel. *020 88381759* Fax. *020 89303499*
Web. *www.faith.co.uk Faith Footwear Ltd – Rin Tin Tin*

Faith Products Ltd Faith House James Street, Radcliffe, Manchester M26 1LN Tel. *0161 7244016*
Fax. *0161 7248210* E-mail. *info@faithinnature.co.uk*
Web. *www.faithinnature.co.uk Clearspring – Faith In Nature – Just Essential*

Fakir Halal Doners Unit 2 19-23 Green Lane, Small Heath, Birmingham B9 5BU Tel. *0121 7532226* Fax. *0121 7532228 *Premium Halal Burgers*

Falcon Cycles Ltd PO Box 3, Brigg DN20 8PB
Tel. *01652 656000* Fax. *01652 650040*
E-mail. *info@falconcycles.co.uk*
Web. *www.falconcycles.co.uk Boss – British Eagle – Claud Butler – Falcon – Harrier – Townsend*

Falcon Fire Ltd PO Box 114, Heywood OL10 9AD
Tel. *0800 6123595* Fax. *0844 5678685*
E-mail. *info@falconfire.co.uk* Web. *www.falcon-fire.co.uk Falcon Fire Ltd*

Falcon Panel Products Ltd Clock House Station Approach, Shepperton TW17 8AN Tel. *01932 256580*
Fax. *01932 230268* E-mail. *sales@falconpp.co.uk*
Web. *www.falconpp.co.uk Strebord*

Family Pet Services 88 Victoria Road New Barnet, Barnet EN4 9PB Tel. *020 84418361*
E-mail. *orders@familypetservices.co.uk*
Web. *www.familypetservices.co.uk eagle pack – fromm family*

Fane Valley Feeds Ltd Bankmore Way, Omagh BT79 0NW
Tel. *028 82243221* Fax. *028 82245992*
E-mail. *info@fanevalleyfeeds.com*
Web. *www.scottsfeeds.com Scotts Feeds*

Fantasia Distribution Ltd Unit B The Flyers Way, Westerham TN16 1DE Tel. *01959 564440* Fax. *01959 564829*
E-mail. *info@fantasiaceilingfans.com*
Web. *www.fantasiaceilingfans.com *Fantasia (Taiwan)*

Fantasy Island Watford Road, Wembley HA0 3HG
Tel. *020 89049044* Fax. *020 89049046*
Web. *www.wherekidsplay.co.uk Fantasy Island*

Fargro Toddington Lane Wick, Littlehampton BN17 7QR
Tel. *01903 721591* Fax. *01903 730737*
E-mail. *paul.sopp@fargro.co.uk* Web. *www.fargro.co.uk Clarital – Dyna-Fog – Green Team, The*

Farleygreene (Sieving & Mixing Technology for Powders or Liquids) Unit 8 Alpha Centre Alpha Road, Aldershot GU12 4RG Tel. *01252 322233* Fax. *01252 325111*
E-mail. *info@farleygreene.com* Web. *www.farleygreene.com Alpha-Mix (United Kingdom) – Sievmaster – Sievmaster, Alpha-Mix*

Farm Energy & Control Services Ltd Unit 4 Wyvols Court Farm Basingstoke Road, Swallowfield, Reading RG7 1WY
Tel. *0118 9889093* Fax. *0118 9314432*
E-mail. *hugh@farmex.co.uk* Web. *www.farmex.com Dicam*

Farming & Wildlife Advisory Group Ltd National Agricultural Centre Stoneleigh Park, Kenilworth CV8 2RX
Tel. *024 76696699* Fax. *024 76696760*
E-mail. *ceo@fwag.org.uk* Web. *www.fwag.org.uk FWAG Farming & Wildlife Advisory Group*

Farm Supplies Dorking Ltd Ansell Road, Dorking RH4 1QW
Tel. *01306 880456* Fax. *01306 876869*
E-mail. *sales@fslandservices.co.uk*
Web. *www.fslandservices.co.uk Farm Supplies (Dorking) Ltd*

Farm Tours Devonshire House Devonshire Lane, Loughborough LE11 3DF Tel. *01509 618810*
Fax. *01509 610585* E-mail. *sales@farm-tours.co.uk*
Web. *www.farm-tours.co.uk Ranch Rider – The Independent Traveller*

Farmura Ltd Stone Hill Stone Hill Road, Egerton, Ashford TN27 9DU Tel. *01233 756241* Fax. *01233 756419*
E-mail. *info@farmura.com* Web. *www.farmura.com *Blazon (U.S.A.) – Farmgran – Farmura – *Ferrosol (U.S.A.) – Flo-Gro – Foresight – Inhibiter – *Kelpak (South Africa) – *Kelplant (South Africa) – *Matrix (Germany) – Mebasol – *Turf Iron (Australia)*

Farnham Castle Briefings Ltd Farnham Castle, Farnham GU9 0AG Tel. *01252 721194* Fax. *01252 711283*
E-mail. *info@farnhamcastle.com*
Web. *www.farnhamcastle.com Farnham Castle International Briefing and Conference Centre*

Farrat Isolevel Balmoral Road, Altrincham WA15 8HJ
Tel. *0161 9283654* Fax. *08700 111809*
E-mail. *rjf@farrat.com* Web. *www.farrat.com Cornerfoot/Sidefoot (United Kingdom) – Cornerfoot/Sidefoot - Far-mat - HM Hamamat - Isolevel - Isomat - Isomount - Jackmount - Levalator - Squaregrip - Vidam - Wedgemount – Far-Mat (United Kingdom) – H M Hamamat (United Kingdom) – Isolevel (United Kingdom) – Isomat (United Kingdom) – Isomount (United Kingdom) – Jackmount (United Kingdom) – Levalator (United Kingdom) – Squaregrip (United Kingdom) – Vidam (United Kingdom) – Wedgemount (United Kingdom)*

Farrel Ltd PO Box 27, Rochdale OL11 2PF Tel. *01706 647434*
Fax. *01706 638982* E-mail. *ashaio@farrel.com*
Web. *www.farrel.com Banbury – CP Series II – M.V.X.*

Fashion Spinners 108 Commercial Road, London E1 1NU
Tel. *020 74881133* Fax. *020 74814488*
E-mail. *fashion-spinners@hotmail.com Extractor – Jassino – *Stand By (India & Pakistan) – Trix*

fashy UK Ltd 192 Alma Road, Bournemouth BH9 1AJ
Tel. *01202 515251* Fax. *01202 531409*
E-mail. *alan@fashy.co.uk* Web. *www.fashy.com fashy*

Faspak Containers Ltd 6 Ashville Close Queens Drive Industrial Estate, Nottingham NG2 1LL Tel. *0115 9869391*
Fax. *0115 9868310* E-mail. *diane@faspak.co.uk*
Web. *www.faspak.co.uk Faspak – Instabox*

Fastbolt Distributors UK Ltd Sherbourne Drive Tilbrook, Milton Keynes MK7 8AW Tel. *01908 650100*
Fax. *01908 650101* E-mail. *sales@fastbolt.com*
Web. *www.fastbolt.com Shark They Bite – Tritap*

FastClamp Cradley Business Park Overend Road, Cradley Heath B64 7DW Tel. *01952 632387* Fax. *01952 632384*
E-mail. *info@fastclamp.com* Web. *www.fastclamp.com BeamClamp – BoxBolt – Kee access – Kee anchor – Kee dome – Kee guard – Kee klamp – Kee lite – Kee mark – Kee nect – Kee stainless*

Fastec Engineering Ltd 8 Studlands Business Centre Studlands Park Avenue, Newmarket CB8 7SS Tel. *01638 660186* Fax. *01638 667374* E-mail. *sales@fastecengineering.co.uk* Web. *www.fastecengineering.co.uk Certificated 316 Welding – Certificated Carbon Steel Welding – Certificated Stainless Steel Welding – Fastec Engineering (United Kingdom)*

Fast Engineering Ltd 5 Windmill Court, Antrim BT41 2TX Tel. *028 94428686* Fax. *028 94429929* E-mail. *info@fastank.com* Web. *www.fastank.com Ezeebox – Fastank – Fastasleep*

Fast Fit Nationwide Ltd Unit 3 Buntsford Park Road, Bromsgrove B60 3DX Tel. *01527 575729* Fax. *01527 576175* E-mail. *davefowler@fastfitnationwide.co.uk* Web. *www.fastfitnationwide.co.uk Parrot – RAC Trackstar – Tracker UK*

Fast International Inc 31 Saffron Court Southfields Business Park, Basildon SS15 6SS Tel. *01268 544000* Fax. *01268 544500* E-mail. *gkoether@fastinc.com* Web. *www.fastinc.com *Fast – *Fastimer – *Fastron – *Magnesol*

Fast Lane Training Ltd The Oaks Water Lane Greenham, Thatcham RG19 8SH Tel. *01672 564481* E-mail. *info@fastlanetraining.co.uk* Web. *www.fastlaneresults.co.uk Fast Lane Training*

Fast React Systems Ltd Evolution House Wyvern Business Park, Chaddesden, Derby DE21 6LY Tel. *01332 668942* Fax. *0115 9149873* E-mail. *sales@fastreact.com* Web. *www.fastreact.com Fastreact*

Fast Systems Ltd Dalton House Newtown Road, Henley On Thames RG9 1HG Tel. *01491 419200* Fax. *01384 252160* E-mail. *sales@scalewatcher.co.uk* Web. *www.fastpress.co.uk Blanca Press – Blancapress – Fast Press – Fastpress*

Fata Automation Ltd Elgar House Shrub Hill Road, Worcester WR4 9EE Tel. *01905 613931* Fax. *01905 613913* E-mail. *nicola.cipolletta@madacaserta.com* Web. *www.fataautomation.co.uk Automotor*

Fawcett Christie Hydraulics Ltd Sandycroft Industrial Estate Chester Road, Sandycroft, Deeside CH5 2QP Tel. *01244 535515* Fax. *01244 533002* E-mail. *sales@fch.co.uk* Web. *www.fch.co.uk *Air Blast Cooler (Sweden) – Fawcett Accumulator – Filterpak – Hydracushion*

F B H Associates Ltd Hi Point House Thomas Street, Taunton TA2 6HB Tel. *01823 335292* Fax. *01823 332104* E-mail. *info@fbh.co.uk* Web. *www.fbh.co.uk Phone Data – Viewbase Link*

Fbh-Fichet Ltd (formerly Fichet (UK) Ltd) 7-8 Amor Way, Letchworth Garden City SG6 1UG Tel. *01462 472900* Fax. *01462 472901* E-mail. *sales@fbh-fichet.com* Web. *www.fbh-fichet.com Fichet*

F B S Prestige Unit Blilac Grove Beeston, Nottingham NG9 1PF Tel. *0115 9431111* Fax. *01254 690484* E-mail. *info@fluorocarbon.co.uk* Web. *www.fbsprestige.co.uk Prestige Industrial*

F & C Asset Management 8th Floor Exchange House, London EC2A 2NY Tel. *020 76288000* Fax. *020 76288188* Web. *www.fandc.com Foreign & Colonial*

F C Brown Steel Equipment Ltd 17 Queens Road Bisley, Woking GU24 9BJ Tel. *01483 685600* Fax. *01483 485610* E-mail. *john.irwin@bisley.com* Web. *www.bisley.com Bisley*

F C G Software Solutions Ltd Whitelands Cottage Kington Langley, Chippenham SN15 5PD Tel. *01522 722232* Fax. *01249 750151* E-mail. *software@fcgagric.com* Web. *www.fcgagric.com *Agribudget – *Farmer Counts*

F C Lane Electronics Ltd Slinfold Lodge Stane Street, Slinfold, Horsham RH13 0RN Tel. *01403 790661* Fax. *01403 790849* E-mail. *sales@fclane.com* Web. *www.fclane.com B.A. – BA, D2, LMA, LMF, LMG, LMH, LMHF, LMJ, LMV, SM, SMA, SMC. – D.2. – L.M.A. – L.M.F. – L.M.G. – L.M.H. – L.M.H.F. – L.M.J. – L.M.V. – S.M. – S.M.A. – S.M.C.*

F C M Travel Solutions Farringdon Point 29-35 Farringdon Road, London EC1M 3JF Tel. *020 70254545* Fax. *020 70254546* E-mail. *keith.slater@fcmtravel.co.uk* Web. *www.tq3.co.uk Britannic Travel*

F D B Electrical Ltd Unit 20 Worton Hall Industrial Estate Worton Road, Isleworth TW7 6ER Tel. *020 85684621* Fax. *020 85697899* E-mail. *brianjury@fdb.uk.com* Web. *www.fdb.uk.com Emguard – MSP – Optima – RTD*

F D R Ltd F D R House Christopher Martin Road, Basildon SS14 9AA Tel. *01268 296431* Fax. *01268 296352* Web. *www.firstdatacorp.co.uk First Data Europe*

Febland Group Ltd Flag House Ashworth Road, Blackpool FY4 4UN Tel. *01253 600600* Fax. *01253 792211* E-mail. *info@febland.co.uk* Web. *www.febland.co.uk Marton Forge (United Kingdom) – Marton Weaver – Ray Gold (Asia)*

F E C Services Ltd Stoneleigh Park, Kenilworth CV8 2LS Tel. *024 76696512* Fax. *024 76696360* E-mail. *info@fecservices.co.uk* Web. *www.fecservices.co.uk *Farm Electric – *Grow Electric*

Federal Mogul Friction Products Hayfield Road Chapel-E N-Le-Frith, Chapel-En-Le-Frith, High Peak SK23 0JP Tel. *01298 811200* Fax. *01298 811319* E-mail. *santino.lammond@federalmogul.com* Web. *www.federalmogul.com Ferodo*

Feedback Data Ltd Park Road, Crowborough TN6 2QR Tel. *01892 601400* Fax. *01892 601429* E-mail. *feedback@fdbk.co.uk* Web. *www.feedback-data.com F-Log (United Kingdom) – FKSII (Germany) – Microtrak (United Kingdom)*

Feedwater Ltd Tarran Way West Tarran Industrial Estate, Wirral CH46 4TU Tel. *0151 6060808* Fax. *0151 6785459* E-mail. *info@feedwater.co.uk* Web. *www.feedwater.co.uk Activ-8 – Activ-Ox – Activ-Ox – Amine F,N and X – Amine N & X – Boilertan – Bromgard – Bromgard – Coolguard – Coolplex – Corroban – Corrosperse – Deminpac – FeedFloc – Polyshield – Polytan – Waterguard*

Felcon Ltd Euro Business Park New Road, Newhaven BN9 0DQ Tel. *01273 513434* Fax. *01273 512695* E-mail. *ian.mutton@felcon.co.uk* Web. *www.felcon.co.uk Felcon Ltd*

Feldbinder UK Ltd Tydd Bank Sutton Bridge, Spalding PE12 9XE Tel. *01406 353500* Fax. *01606 832525* E-mail. *i.swann@feldbinder.com* Web. *www.feldbinder.co.uk Feldbinder GmbH (Germany) – Tanker*

Fellows (Pressings & Presswork Products Division) Graiseley Row, Wolverhampton WV2 4HL Tel. *01902 576400* Fax. *01902 576404* E-mail. *sue.shinton@fellowsltd.co.uk* Web. *www.ricalltd.com *Vulcan*

Roger Fell Ltd Northside Industrial Park Whitley Bridge, Goole DN14 0GH Tel. *01977 662211* Fax. *01977 662334* E-mail. *tim.fell@fellscarpets.co.uk* Web. *www.fellscarpets.co.uk Fells carpetss*

Fellside Recordings Ltd PO Box 40, Workington CA14 3GJ Tel. *01900 61556* Fax. *01900 61585* E-mail. *info@fellside.com* Web. *www.fellside.com Fellside Recordings – Fellsongs – Lake Records – Sound Transfer*

C P L Felthams Estover Road, March PE15 8SF Tel. *01354 652545* Fax. *01354 650476* E-mail. *sales@cplfelthams.co.uk* Web. *www.cplfelthams.co.uk Felthams – Transit Wrap*

Fendor Ltd Heworth House William Street, Gateshead NE10 0JP Tel. *0191 4383222* Fax. *0191 4381686* E-mail. *cd@fendorhansen.co.uk* Web. *www.fendor.co.uk Fineline – Pyro-lam – Pyro-lithic – Pyro-rest – Swingline*

Fenland Laundries Ltd Roman Bank, Skegness PE25 1SQ Tel. *01754 767171* Fax. *01754 610344* E-mail. *keith.brown@fenlandlaundries.co.uk* Web. *www.bournegroup.co.uk Fenland*

Fenner Drives Ltd Hudson Road, Leeds LS9 7DF Tel. *0870 7577007* Fax. *0113 2489656* E-mail. *sales@fennerdrives.com* Web. *www.fennerdrives.com Bytel – Cleargo – Hyfen – Nu-T-Link – Quikgo – Redgo – Standard T-link – T.A.B.-link*

Fenner Paper Co. Ltd 15 Orchard Business Centre Vale Road, Tonbridge TN9 1QF Tel. *01732 771100* Fax. *01732 771103* E-mail. *lorna@fennerpaper.co.uk* Web. *www.fennerpaper.co.uk Abstract – Aerographic – Altura Gloss & Satin – Avrolux – Brabazon Art & Matt – Brand X – Celebrations Colours – Clarion Print – Colorset – Concept – Concorde Matte Ivory – Concorde Pure Brilliance – Concorde Pure Silk – Enviro-Tech – Episode 4 – Epsilon – Fabrique – Fiber-Tone – Flockage Litho – *Flora (Italy) – Formation Superfine Offset – Genus Eco-Matt – Jumbo Art and Velvet – Laserprint Premium – Lasertech – Legacy Recycled Art & Matt – Lightning Art & Silk – Lightning Ivory Board – Mandricote – Matrisse – Message – Millenium Text & Cover – Millennium Laser – Millennium Real Art – Millennium Real Silk – Mojo – Neptune Unique – Octane – Octavie – Odyssey Superfine – Offenbach Bible – Omnia – Optimale – Orchard Laid and Wove – Orchard Superfine – Origina Watermarked – Phantom Glossart & Satin – Recovery Text and Cover – Redeem 100% Recycled – Replay Matt – Rhythm – Rib-Tone – Shine – Solstis – Squadron Self Adhesive – STiK – Tallistag – Tectonic – True – Valiant Satin*

Fentex Ltd 3 Brook Farm Thrapston Road, Ellington, Huntingdon PE28 0AE Tel. *01480 890104* Fax. *01480 890105* E-mail. *sales@fentex.co.uk* Web. *www.btinternet.com Spill Pod*

F E P Heat Care Ltd 194 Cumbernauld Road Chryston, Glasgow G69 9NB Tel. *0141 7792215* Fax. *0141 7799191* E-mail. *fepheatcare@hotmail.co.uk* Web. *www.fepheatcare.com Fepcare – Fepheat – Fepstor*

Feralco UK Ltd Ditton Road, Widnes WA8 0PH Tel. *0151 8022930* Fax. *0151 8022999* E-mail. *info.uk@feralco.com* Web. *www.feralco.com Aluminium Sulphate – P.A.S.S.*

Ferelco UK Ltd 6 The Docks, Grangemouth FK3 8UB Tel. *01324 665455* Fax. *01324 474754* Web. *www.feralco.com Bulk Aluminium Sulphate – Bulk Sulphuric Acid – PAC*

Ferex Ltd Unit 22 Cam Centre Wilbury Way, Hitchin SG4 0TW Tel. *01462 420666* Fax. *01462 420779* E-mail. *sales@euraqua.co.uk* Web. *www.euraqua.co.uk Euraqua (UK) – Ferex*

Ferguson Group Ltd Harlaw Drive Harlaw Road Industrial Estate, Inverurie AB51 4SF Tel. *01467 626500* Fax. *01467 626559* E-mail. *info@fergusonmodular.com* Web. *www.fergusonmodular.com Modupack*

Ferguson & Menzies Ltd 312 Broomloan Road, Glasgow G51 2JW Tel. *0141 4453555* Fax. *0141 4251079* E-mail. *joyce.duthie@fergusonmenzies.co.uk* Web. *www.fergusonmenzies.co.uk Fergatac – Ferquatac – *Millennium (U.S.A.) – *Millennium (U.S.A.) – Opus*

Ferguson Polycom Ltd Windsor Mill Hollinwood, Oldham OL8 3RA Tel. *0161 6812206* Fax. *0161 9471326* E-mail. *info@fergusonpolycom.co.uk* Web. *www.fergusonpolycom.co.uk A.O.F. – Polycom – Superide*

Fermod Ltd Unit 2 Northumberland Close Stanwell, Staines TW19 7LN Tel. *01784 248376* Fax. *01784 257285* E-mail. *sales@fermod.co.uk* Web. *www.fermod.com *Fermod – *Fermoflex – *Fermostock – *Fuermatic*

Fernan Trading Ltd 4 Burrowmeadow Road Springkerse Industrial Estate, Stirling FK7 7UW Tel. *01786 450900* Fax. *01786 450049* E-mail. *sales@fernan.com* Web. *www.fernan.com Benjy – Benjywear – Trend to Beauty*

Fernbank Shed Company Ltd Fernbank Shed, Barnoldswick BB18 5UY Tel. *01282 813395* Fax. *01282 813172 Fernbank – Sterco Fabrics*

Fern-Howard Ltd Unit 1 Bordon Trading Estate Old Station Way, Bordon GU35 9HH Tel. *01420 470400* Fax. *01420 489536* E-mail. *peter.scott@fernhoward.com* Web. *www.fernhoward.com Columbus – Columbus Minor – Meridian – Micromax – Minimax – Moonlight – Romax*

Fernite Of Sheffield Ltd Fernite Works Coleford Road, Sheffield S9 5NJ Tel. *0114 2440527* Fax. *0114 2445922* E-mail. *sales@fernite.co.uk* Web. *www.fernite.co.uk Fernite*

Fernox Forsyth Road Sheerwater, Woking GU21 5RZ Tel. *01483 793200* Fax. *0870 6015005* E-mail. *sales@fernox.com* Web. *www.fernox.com Alphi 11 – Fernox – Fry's – Hawk – Lime Scale Preventer – MB-1 – Sterox – Superconcentrate*

Fern Plastic Products Ltd Macrome Road, Wolverhampton WV6 9HD Tel. *01902 758282* Fax. *01902 757500* E-mail. *igraham@fern-plastics.co.uk* Web. *www.fern-plastics.co.uk Fern Plastics*

Ferroalloy Trading Company UK Limited Unit 3, The Business Centre Greys Green Rotherfield Greys, Henley On Thames RG9 4QG Tel. *0118 9864310* Fax. *0118 9864310* E-mail. *ftcuk@ymail.com* Web. *www.ftc-uk.com FTC UK Ltd*

F F Franklin & Co. Ltd Platt Street, Sheffield S3 8BQ Tel. *0114 2721429* Fax. *0114 2727030* E-mail. *sales@franklin-tools.co.uk* Web. *www.franklin-tools.co.uk F.F.F.*

F F P Packaging Solutions Ltd 1-7 Tenter Road Moulton Park Industrial Estate, Northampton NN3 6PZ Tel. *01604 643535* Fax. *01604 492427* E-mail. *info@ffppkg.co.uk* Web. *www.ffppkg.co.uk Esterpeel*

FFS Brands Ltd Unit 1 Headley Park 9 Headley Road East, Woodley, Reading RG5 4SQ Tel. *0118 9441100* Fax. *0118 9441080* E-mail. *sales@fast-food-systems.co.uk* Web. *www.fast-food-systems.co.uk Broaster – SFC Express – Southern Fried Chicken – VIZU*

F G H Controls Ltd Blackhorse Road, Letchworth Garden City SG6 1HN Tel. *01462 686677* Fax. *01462 480633* E-mail. *sales@fgh.co.uk* Web. *www.fgh.co.uk Ezecal – Proteus*

F & G Smart Shopfittings Ltd Unit 16 Tyseley Industrial Estate Seeleys Road, Birmingham B11 2LA Tel. *0121 7725634* Fax. *0121 7668995* E-mail. *sales@smartshopfittings.co.uk* Web. *www.smartshopfittings.co.uk Norlyn Shopfittings*

F H Brundle 24-32 Ferry Lane Industrial Estate Lamson Road, Rainham RM13 9YY Tel. *01708 253545* Fax. *01708 253550* E-mail. *sales@brundle.com* Web. *www.fhbrundle.co.uk Brunmesh – Brunperf – Brunperf - Perforated metals. Brunmesh - Welded & woven mesh. – Pro-Railing*

F H G Guides Ltd Abbey Mill Business Centre Seedhill, Paisley PA1 1TJ Tel. *0141 8870428* Fax. *0141 8897204* E-mail. *admin@fhguides.co.uk* Web. *www.holidayguides.com FHG (United Kingdom)*

Fibercill The Moorings Hurst Business Park, Brierley Hill DY5 1UF Tel. *01384 482221* Fax. *01384 482212* E-mail. *mail@fibercill.com* Web. *www.fibercill.co.uk Fibercill – Fiberskirt – Fibertrave*

Fibet Rubber Bonding UK Ltd Unit 9 Dale Mill Hallam Road, Nelson BB9 8AN Tel. *01282 878200* Fax. *01282 878201* E-mail. *sales@fibet.co.uk* Web. *www.fibet.co.uk ASP – Fibel – Fivistop – Fivilever*

Fibrax Ltd Queensway, Wrexham LL13 8YR Tel. *01978 356744* Fax. *01978 365206* E-mail. *info@fibrax.co.uk* Web. *www.fibrax.co.uk Raincheater*

Fibre Fillings Albion Mill Cawdor Street, Farnworth, Bolton BL4 7JE Tel. *01204 578141* Fax. *01204 793087* E-mail. *info@john-holden.com* Web. *www.john-holden.com Fibre Fillings*

Fibrelite Composites Ltd Unit 2 Snaygill Industrial Estate, Skipton BD23 2QR Tel. *01756 799773* Fax. *01756 799539* E-mail. *ian@fibrelite.com* Web. *www.fibrelite.com Fibrelite*

Fibresand International Ltd Ash House Ransom Wood Business Park Southwell Road, Rainworth, Mansfield NG21 0HJ Tel. *01623 675305* Fax. *01623 675308* E-mail. *enquiries@fibresand.com* Web. *www.fibresand.com Fibresand – Fibreturf*

Fibrestar Drums Ltd Redhouse Lane Disley, Stockport SK12 2NW Tel. *01663 764141* Fax. *01633 762967* E-mail. *antoni.starsiak@fibrestar.co.uk*

Web. *www.fibrestar.co.uk 30li Unitainer – L Ring Drum – Surftech – Universal Drum – XL Drum*

Fibre-Tech Industries LLP Unit 12 Saxon Way Melbourn, Royston SG8 6DN Tel. *01763 269600* Fax. *01763 260632* E-mail. *david.smith@rbfindustries.co.uk* Web. *www.fibre-tech.net Fibre-Tech – SOLAS*

Fiddes Payne 4 Network Eleven Thorpe Way, Banbury OX16 4XS Tel. *01295 253888* Fax. *01295 269166* E-mail. *info@fiddespayne.co.uk* Web. *www.fiddespayne.co.uk Fiddes Payne – Global Gourmet – Grind Fresh – Hidden Valley – Pep N Spice – Shear N Spice – Spice Trader*

Fidgeon Ltd Unit 3 Wingate Grange Industrial Estate, Wingate TS28 5AH Tel. *01429 836655* Fax. *01429 837766* E-mail. *sales@fidgeon.co.uk* Web. *www.fidgeon.com Fuji – Premier Range*

Field Box More Labels Roman Bank, Bourne PE10 9LQ Tel. *01778 426444* Fax. *01778 421862* E-mail. *spencer.johnston@chesapeakecorp.com* Web. *www.fieldboxmore.com Multi-Peel – Tudor Labels*

Fieldway Supplies Ltd Unit 12 Block E Paramount Business Park Wilson Road, Liverpool L36 6AW Tel. *0151 4809909* Fax. *0151 4809902* E-mail. *brian@fieldwaysupplies.com* Web. *www.fieldway.co.uk BLACK & DECKER – Boat Level – BOSCH POWER TOOLS – Chubb – De-walt – Disto – Draper Tools – Eternit – FISCO – Flir (Thermal Imaging) – Fluke – Goretex – Hameg – JSP Pollution Control – JSP Spillage Kits – Leica – Makita – Marshall Town – Monarflex – Pendock Profiles – Scutches – Spear & Jackson – Stabila – Stabilo – Stanley – Supalux – Tektronix – Trench Plate – Trespa – TYVEK – UNILITE – Van Vaults – Wheel Barrows – Wheelie Bins*

Fife Engineering Co. Ltd Longrigg Swalwell, Newcastle upon Tyne NE16 3AW Tel. *0191 4961133* Fax. *0191 4965502* E-mail. *admin@fife-engineering.com* Web. *www.fife-engineering.com Fifelon*

Fife Tidland Ltd Millennium House Progress Way, Denton, Manchester M34 2GP Tel. *0161 3202000* Fax. *0161 3204513* E-mail. *sales_uk@maxcess.eu* Web. *www.tidland.co.uk ESP – InPrint – InSpectra – MSP – SuperVision – Symat – Symat - InPrint - MSP - ESP.*

Fi Glass Developments Ltd Station Road, Edenbridge TN8 6EB Tel. *01732 863465* Fax. *01732 867287* E-mail. *sales@fi-glass.co.uk* Web. *www.fi-glass.co.uk Fi-Glass*

Fike Protection Systems Ltd 4 The Moorfield Centre Moorfield Road, Slyfield Industrial Estate, Guildford GU1 1RA Tel. *01483 457584* Fax. *01483 456235* E-mail. *sales@fike.com* Web. *www.fike.com FE 227 – FE 25 – MICROMIST – PROINERT*

Fike Safety Technology Ltd Unit 31 Springvale Industrial Estate, Cwmbran NP44 5BD Tel. *01633 865558* Fax. *01633 866656* E-mail. *fstinfo@fike.com* Web. *www.fikesafetytechnology.co.uk Multipoint (United Kingdom) – Quadnet – Sita 200 Plus (United Kingdom) – Twinflex (United Kingdom) – Twinflex Plus (United Kingdom)*

Fike UK 4th Floor County House 35 Earl Street, Maidstone ME14 1PF Tel. *01622 677081* Fax. *01622 685737* E-mail. *keithavila@fike.co.uk* Web. *www.fike.co.uk Fike*

Filigree Ltd South Normanton, Alfreton DE55 2EG Tel. *01773 811630* Fax. *01773 862777* E-mail. *tmulligan@filigree.org* Web. *www.filigreeholdings.co.uk Bonfab – Filigree – Filigree Finesse – Stiebel of Nottingham*

Filofax Stationary Suppliers 68 Neal Street, London WC2H 9PF Tel. *020 78361977* Fax. *020 78364736* E-mail. *shop@filofax.co.uk* Web. *www.filofax.co.uk Filofax – Filofax Time Management – Microfile – Yard-O-Led*

Filplastic UK Ltd High Street Eastrington, Goole DN14 7PW Tel. *01430 410450* Fax. *01430 410449* E-mail. *sales@filplastic.com* Web. *www.filplastic.co.uk Filplastic*

Filtermist International Ltd Stourbridge Road Industrial Estate Faraday Drive, Bridgnorth WV15 5BA Tel. *01746 765361* Fax. *01746 766882* E-mail. *sales@filtermist.com* Web. *www.filtermist.com Filter Fog – Filtermist – Filtertramp – Loc-Line – Pneumaster – Vacmaster*

Filter Screen Supply Ltd (Head Office) 2 Paynes Place Farm Cuckfield Road, Burgess Hill RH15 8RG Tel. *01444 244406* Fax. *01444 230303* E-mail. *sales@filterscreensupply.co.uk* Web. *www.filterscreensupply.co.uk P.S. Vibro Screen*

Filtex Filters Ltd Unit 4-7 Union Park Navigation Way, West Bromwich B70 9DF Tel. *0121 5531283* Fax. *0121 5005284* E-mail. *sales@ioi.co.uk* Web. *www.filtex.co.uk Filtex*

Filtrona plc 201-249 Avebury Boulevard, Milton Keynes MK9 1AU Tel. *01908 359100* Fax. *01908 359120* E-mail. *enquiries@filtrona.com* Web. *www.filtrona.com Filtrona*

Financial Times 1 Southwark Bridge, London SE1 9HL Tel. *020 78733000* Fax. *020 74075700* Web. *www.ft.com F.T. Actuaries World Indices – F.T. Analysis Business Information – F.T. Annual Report Service – F.T. Cityline – F.T. Profile Business Information*

Finders International Ltd Orchard House Winchet Hill, Goudhurst, Cranbrook TN17 1JY Tel. *01580 211055* Fax. *01580 212062* E-mail. *info@findershealth.com* Web. *www.findershealth.com D.S.D. – D.S.P. – Dead Sea Magik – Dead Sea Spa Magik – Discovery – Finders – Heloderm – Hydratone – Inchwrap*

Findlay Irvine 42-44 Bog Road, Penicuik EH26 9BU Tel. *01968 671200* Fax. *01968 671237* E-mail. *sales@findlayirvine.com* Web. *www.findlayirvine.com Autoheat – Griptester – Icelert*

Finecard International Ltd (t/a Ninja Corporation) Topaz House Oldgate St Michaels Industrial Estate, Widnes WA8 8TL Tel. *0151 4951677* Fax. *0151 4951675* E-mail. *admin@thepopupco.com* Web. *www.theninjacorporation.co.uk Ninja Corporation, The*

Fine Line The Old Quarry Clevedon Road, Failand, Bristol BS8 3TU Tel. *01275 395000* Fax. *01275 395001* E-mail. *contact@fineline.uk.com* Web. *www.fineline.uk.com Fineline – Fineline Asbestos Solutions*

Fineline Environmental Ltd 1 Lovage Way, Waterlooville PO8 0JG Tel. *01237 441772* Fax. *01237 441851* E-mail. *info@finelineonline.co.uk* Web. *www.finelineonline.co.uk Fineline – Fineline Asbestos Solutions*

Finers Stephens Innocent LLP 179-185 Great Portland Street, London W1W 5LS Tel. *020 73234000* Fax. *020 75807069* E-mail. *marketing@fsilaw.com* Web. *www.fsilaw.com Finers Stephen Innocent*

Finishing Aids & Tools Ltd Little End Road Eaton Socon, St Neots PE19 8GF Tel. *01480 216060* Fax. *01480 405989* E-mail. *sales@finaids.com* Web. *www.finaids.com 3M – Artifex – Ekamant – Finaids – Finweb – Suhner*

James A S Finlay Holdings Ltd 29 Maghaberry Road Moira, Craigavon BT67 0JG Tel. *028 92611300* Fax. *028 92611971* E-mail. *sales@finlayfoods.com* Web. *www.finlayfoods.com Finlay Foods – Finlays – Spice is Nice – Sunflower*

Finlays Ltd Office Suite 1 St Marys Green, Whickham, Newcastle upon Tyne NE16 4DN Tel. *0191 4883144* Fax. *01833 638340* E-mail. *m.raistick@btconnect.com* Web. *www.finlays-newsagents.co.uk Finlays*

Finlex International Ltd 1 Bunkell Road Rackheath Industrial Estate, Rackheath, Norwich NR13 6PU Tel. *08452 410487* Fax. *0845 2412241* E-mail. *kay.partner@finlexuk.com* Web. *www.finlexuk.co.uk FINCLASS – HYUNDAI*

Finning UK Ltd 688-689 Stirling Road, Slough SL1 4ST Tel. *01753 497300* Fax. *01753 497333* E-mail. *mbarnes@finning.co.uk* Web. *www.finning.co.uk Caterpillar*

Fira International (Furniture Industry Research Association) Maxwell Road, Stevenage SG1 2EW Tel. *01438 777700* Fax. *01438 777800* E-mail. *info@fira.co.uk* Web. *www.fira.co.uk F.I.R.A. International*

Fire Fighting Enterprises 9 Hunting Gate, Hitchin SG4 0TJ Tel. *01462 444740* Fax. *0845 4024201* E-mail. *info@ffeuk.com* Web. *www.ffeuk.com F.F.E. – Fireray*

Fireguard safety equipment co ltd 2Nd Floor,145-157 St John Street, London EC1V 4PY Tel. *0845 0751042* Fax. *0845 0751043* E-mail. *info@fireguard-uk.com* Web. *www.fireguard-uk.com Fireguard*

Fireprotect Chester Ltd Factory Road Sandycroft, Deeside CH5 2QJ Tel. *01244 536595* Fax. *01244 533592* E-mail. *info@fireprotect.co.uk* Web. *www.fireprotect.co.uk Protect-a-Pad – Protect-a-Shield – Protect-a-Tape – Protect-a-Wrap*

Fire Protection Services Ltd 19 Brithwen Road Waunarlwydd, Swansea SA5 4QS Tel. *01792 874434* E-mail. *fpsfire@tiscali.co.uk* Web. *fpsfire.co.uk Fire Protection Services Ltd*

Fire Security Sprinkler Installations Ltd Homefield Road, Haverhill CB9 8QP Tel. *01440 705815* Fax. *01440 704352* E-mail. *info@firesecurity.co.uk* Web. *www.firesecurity.co.uk Fire Security*

FireworkGuy.Co.Uk Rear of 92 Grange Lane, Barnsley S71 5QQ Tel. *07940 074044* Fax. *01226 246101* E-mail. *info@fireworkguy.co.uk* Web. *www.fireworkguy.co.uk FireworkGuy*

Firma Chrome Ltd Soho Works Saxon Road, Sheffield S8 0XZ Tel. *0114 2554343* Fax. *0114 2587375* E-mail. *enquiries@firmachrome.co.uk* Web. *www.firmachrome.co.uk Diacrome – Firma-Loy – Firma-Pol – Micro-Lub*

First Assist Group Ltd (Head Office) Marshalls Court Marshalls Road, Sutton SM1 4DU Tel. *0800 0721197* Fax. *020 86617604* E-mail. *corporate.info@firstassit.co.uk* Web. *www.firstassist.co.uk Rescueline*

First Bus Coldborough House Market Street, Bracknell RG12 1JA Tel. *01344 782222* Fax. *01344 868332* E-mail. *simon.goff@firstgroup.com* Web. *www.firstgroup.com First Beeline – Green Line – Londonlink – Rail Air*

First Databank Europe Ltd Swallowtail House Grenadier Road, Exeter Business Park, Exeter EX1 3LH Tel. *01392 440100* Fax. *01392 440192* E-mail. *info@fdbhealth.com* Web. *www.fdbhealth.co.uk *IDDF (U.S.A.) – Lex Browser – Multilex Drug Data Files*

The First Financial Consultancy Ltd 33-34 Cheap Street, Newbury RG14 5DB Tel. *01635 35071* Fax. *01635 529933* E-mail. *tony@thefirstfinancial.co.uk* Web. *www.thefirstfinancial.co.uk First Financial Consultancy*

First Group plc Kirkstall Road, Leeds LS3 1LH Tel. *08456 045460* Fax. *0113 3815097* E-mail. *info@firstleeds.co.uk* Web. *www.firstgroup.com Bradford Traveller – Calder Line – Kingfisher Huddersfield – Leeds City Link – Quickstep Travel – Rider York – Yorkshire Rider*

First Impressions Europe Ltd Cedar House 14 Hurstmead Drive, Stafford ST17 4RX Tel. *01785 623183* Fax. *01785 623184* E-mail. *info@firstimpressionseurope.com* Web. *www.firstimpressionseurope.com Fruit of the Loom – Henbury – Jerzees – Kustom Kit – Mantis – Result – RTY – Screen Stars – Uneek*

First Light London 9 Laker Road Rochester Airport Industrial Estate, Rochester ME1 3QX Tel. *01634 685500* Fax. *01634 685544* E-mail. *info@firstlightlondon.co.uk* Web. *www.mobideque.co.uk Mobi-Deque Discotheques*

First Personnel Group plc 1 Cromwell Road, Grays RM17 5HF Tel. *01375 391111* Fax. *01375 390151* E-mail. *contactus@firstpersonnel.co.uk* Web. *www.firstpersonnel.co.uk First Personnel*

First Point Assessment Ltd 7 Burnbank Business Centre Souter Head Road, Altens Industrial Estate, Aberdeen AB12 3LF Tel. *01224 337500* Fax. *01224 337522* E-mail. *enquiries@fpal.com* Web. *www.fpal.com First Point Assessment*

First Stop Computer Group Ltd 15-18 Progress Business Park Progress Way, Croydon CR0 4XD Tel. *020 86884432* Fax. *020 86881226* E-mail. *sales@firststoptraining.co.uk* Web. *www.firststop.co.uk Microsoft*

Firth Rixson Ltd Firth House Meadowhall Road, Sheffield S9 1JD Tel. *0114 2193000* Fax. *01709 388889* E-mail. *info@firthrixson.com* Web. *www.firthrixson.com Firth Rixon Rings*

Firth Rixson Metals Ltd Meadow Mills Shepley Street, Glossop SK13 9SA Tel. *0114 2193006* Fax. *01457 855529* E-mail. *lbrierley@firthrixson.com* Web. *www.firthrixson.com Supermet*

Firth Steels Ltd Calderbank River Street, Brighouse HD6 1LU Tel. *01484 405940* E-mail. *sales@firth-steels.co.uk* Web. *www.firth-steels.co.uk Norclad*

Firwood Paints Ltd Victoria Works Oakenbottom Road, Bolton BL2 6DP Tel. *01204 525231* Fax. *01204 362522* E-mail. *asmith@firwoodpaints.com* Web. *www.firwood.co.uk Firaqua – Firglo – Firlene – Firlex – Firmatch – Firpavar – Firsyn – Firwood – Mervene*

Fischbein-Saxon 274 Alma Road, Enfield EN3 7RS Tel. *020 88056111* Fax. *020 83446625* E-mail. *sales@fischbein-saxon.co.uk* Web. *www.fischbein-saxon.co.uk Airwash – Dapper – Pulsar – Saxon*

Fischer Fixings UK Ltd Whitely Road, Wallingford OX10 9AT Tel. *01491 827900* Fax. *01491 827953* E-mail. *sales@fischer.co.uk* Web. *www.fischer.co.uk *C box (Germany) – *Fischer Fixings (Germany) – *Fischer Plug (Germany) – *Fischer System (Germany) – *Fischerbolts (Germany) – *Wallbolts (Germany) – *Zykon (Germany)*

George Fischer Sales Ltd Paradise Way, Coventry CV2 2ST Tel. *024 76535535* Fax. *024 76530450* E-mail. *uk.ps@georgfischer.com* Web. *www.georgefischer.co.uk Coolfit – Drawlock – G.F. – Instaflex – Instaflex - Signet - Primofit - GF - Coolfit. – Primofit – Signet – Aquasystem*

Fischer Instrumentation GB Ltd Gordleton Industrial Park Pennington, Lymington SO41 8JD Tel. *01590 684100* Fax. *01590 684110* E-mail. *mail@fischergb.co.uk* Web. *www.fischergb.co.uk Fischerscope – Poroprint*

Fisco Tools Ltd 21 Brook Road, Rayleigh SS6 7XD Tel. *01268 747074* Fax. *01268 772936* E-mail. *info@fisco.co.uk* Web. *www.fisco.co.uk Euromet – Fibar – Fisco – Futura – Measure-Mark – Meteor – Pacer – Prospector – Ranger – Satellite – Tracker – Tri-Lok – Tri-matic – Unimatic – Uniplas – Videoflex*

Fisher Bent Ley Industrial Estate Bent Ley Road, Meltham, Holmfirth HD9 4AP Tel. *01484 854321* Fax. *01484 854244* E-mail. *jeff.monks@fisherplastics.co.uk* Web. *www.fisherplastics.co.uk Fisher Plastics*

Fisher Alvin Ltd Unit 102 Pointon Way, Stonebridge Cross Business Park, Droitwich WR9 0LW Tel. *01905 779944* Fax. *01905 779133* E-mail. *info@fisheralvin.com* Web. *www.fisheralvin.com Alvin*

James Fisher Inspection & Measurement Services Ltd (t/a N D T Radiography) Factory Road Sandycroft, Deeside CH5 2QJ Tel. *01244 520058* Fax. *01244 535440* E-mail. *contact@jfims.co.uk* Web. *www.jfims.co.uk NDT Radiography*

Fisher Offshore North Meadows Oldmeldrum, Inverurie AB51 0GQ Tel. *01651 873932* Fax. *01651 873939* E-mail. *info@fisheroffshore.com* Web. *www.fisher.co.uk Ingersol Rand*

Fisher Scientific UK Ltd Bishop Meadow Road, Loughborough LE11 5RG Tel. *01509 231166* Fax. *01509 231893* E-mail. *info@fisher.co.uk* Web. *www.fisher.co.uk Insight*

Clare Fishers Ltd Hartford House Weston Street, Bolton BL3 2AW Tel. *01204 521631* Fax. *01204 527391* E-mail. *info@clarefishers.co.uk Clare – Rigigrip*

Fiskars Brands UK Ltd Newlands Avenue Brackla Indl-Est, Litchard Indl-Est, Bridgend CF31 2XA Tel. *01656 655595* Fax. *01656 659582* E-mail. *sales@fiskars.com* Web. *www.fiskars.com Kitchen Devils – Wilkinson Sword*

Fistreem International Ltd Monarch Way Belton Park, Loughborough LE11 5XG Tel. *01509 224613* Fax. *01509 260210* E-mail. *sales@fistreem.co.uk* Web. *www.fistreeminternational.com Aquarec – Autobomb – Calypso – Cyclon – FISTREEM*
Fives Fletcher Ltd Brunel Parkway Pride Park, Derby DE24 8HR Tel. *01332 636000* Fax. *01332 636020* E-mail. *alan.mclean@fivesgroup.com* Web. *www.fivesgroup.com Fletcher Smith – Fletcher Smith Ltd*
Fixfirm Ltd Pyke Road, Lincoln LN6 3QS Tel. *01522 500002* Fax. *0870 7773828* E-mail. *sales@fixfirmlincoln.com* Web. *www.fixfirmlincoln.com Bedloc*
Flag Paints Unit 8 Springfield Industrial Estate Springfield Road, Burnham On Crouch CM0 8UA Tel. *01621 785173* Fax. *01621 785393* E-mail. *sales@flagfinishes.co.uk* Web. *www.flagfinishes.co.uk Flag Brand*
Flags & Standards Ltd Evanlode 5 Bramble Bank Frimley Green, Camberley GU16 6PN Tel. *01252 835225* Fax. *020 83633377* E-mail. *sales@flagsandstandards.com* Web. *www.flagsandstandards.co.uk Flags & Standards Ltd*
Flair Electronics Ltd Brittania House 24-26 Boulton Road, Stevenage SG1 4QX Tel. *01438 727391* Fax. *01438 740232* E-mail. *sales@flairelectronics.co.uk* Web. *www.flairelectronics.co.uk *Ejectadip (U.S.A.)*
Flakt Woods Ltd Axial Way, Colchester CO4 5ZD Tel. *01206 222555* Fax. *01206 222777* E-mail. *marketing.uk@flaktwoods.com* Web. *www.flaktwoods.co.uk 2100 Series – Axcent 2 – Axico – Axijet – Centripal EU – Climafan – Climafan Aerofoil – Colchester Range – Compac Climafan – EC – EU – I.L.C. – JM Aerofoil – JM Aerofoil - Series 2100 - Aerofoil Climafan - Colchester Range - Axcent - Airpac - KB Series 28 - Compac Climafan - Varofoil. – Mersea*
Flametec Ltd Newstead Trading Estate Trentham, Stoke On Trent ST4 8HT Tel. *01782 657331* Fax. *01782 644600* E-mail. *tepsolutions@turner-eps.co.uk* Web. *www.flametec.co.uk AIR*
Flanges Ltd PO Box 1, Stockton On Tees TS18 2PL Tel. *01642 672626* Fax. *01642 617574* E-mail. *sales@flanges-ltd.co.uk* Web. *www.flanges-ltd.co.uk Flanges*
Flashpoint England Ltd PO Box 726, London NW11 7XQ Tel. *020 74901444* Fax. *020 72534491* E-mail. *sales@flashpoint.ws* Web. *www.flashpoint.ws Flashpoint – Flashpoint Computer Parts – Flashpoint England – Flashpoint UK & Europe*
Flatau Dick UK Ltd 22 Tally Road, Oxted RH8 0TG Tel. *01883 730707* Fax. *01883 717100* E-mail. *bob@flataudick.co.uk* Web. *www.flataudick.co.uk Flatau Dick – Flatau Dick & Co – Flatau Dick Overseas – Seaking Podmore*
Flatford York Road Elvington, York YO41 4DY Tel. *01904 608383* Fax. *01904 608483* E-mail. *sales@flatford.co.uk Flatford*
Flavour Master Ltd Unit 17d Makerfield Way Ince, Wigan WN2 2PR Tel. *01942 498500* E-mail. *sales@flavourmaster.co.uk* Web. *www.flavourmaster.co.uk B & A*
F L D Chemicals Ltd Oakcroft Road, Chessington KT9 1RH Tel. *020 83912331* Fax. *020 89742850* E-mail. *info@fld.co.uk* Web. *www.fld.co.uk Blazemaster – Ionol – Ionox – Rust-Busters – Santoquin – TempRite – Topanol*
Fleet Line Markers Ltd Spring Lane South, Malvern WR14 1AT Tel. *01684 573535* Fax. *01684 892784* E-mail. *sales@fleetlinemarkers.com* Web. *www.fleetlinemarkers.com Fleet*
Fleetwood Group Holdings Ltd Hall Street Long Melford, Sudbury CO10 9JP Tel. *0870 7740008* Fax. *0870 7740009* E-mail. *fleetwoodcaravans@dial.pipex.com* Web. *www.fleetwoodcaravans.co.uk Colchester – Countryside – Garland – Heritage*
Fleetwood Trawlers Supply Company 1 Denham Way, Fleetwood FY7 6PR Tel. *01253 873476* Fax. *01253 773230* E-mail. *info@ftsgroup.co.uk* Web. *www.ftsgroup.co.uk Allan Dingle – Fleetwood Blacksmith – Fleetwood Industrial Sack – Fleetwood Port Services – Fleetwood Sheet Metal – Fylde Sails – Peter Hall*
C W Fletcher & Sons Ltd Sterling Works Mansfield Road, Wales Bar, Sheffield S26 5PQ Tel. *0114 2942200* Fax. *0114 2942211* E-mail. *pl@cwfletcher.co.uk* Web. *www.cwfletcher.co.uk C.W. Fletcher*
Flexelec UK Ltd Unit 11 Kings Park Industrial Estate Primrose Hill, Kings Langley WD4 8ST Tel. *01923 274477* Fax. *01923 270264* E-mail. *sales@omerin.co.uk* Web. *www.flexelec.com Electrace – Hotrace – Jimi-Heat*
Flexel International Ltd Flemington Road, Glenrothes KY7 5QF Tel. *01592 757313* Fax. *01592 754535* E-mail. *george.graham@flexel.co.uk* Web. *www.flexel.co.uk Flexel*
Flexello Ltd Bagnall Street Hill Top, Golds Hill, West Bromwich B70 0TS Tel. *0121 5061770* Fax. *0121 5022658* E-mail. *info@flexello.co.uk* Web. *www.flexello.co.uk Flexello – Flexello Polynyl – Flexello Superthane – Mallmaster*
Flexible Ducting Ltd Cloberfield Industrial Estate Milngavie, Glasgow G62 7LW Tel. *0141 9564551* Fax. *0141 9564847* E-mail. *sales@flexibleducting.co.uk* Web. *www.flexibleducting.co.uk Flexflyte (United Kingdom) – Flexflyte Super (United Kingdom) – Flextract (United Kingdom) – Flextract - Superflextract - Flexflyte Super - Wyrem - Flexflyte - Kehroflex-S – Kehroflex-S (United Kingdom) – Superflextract (United Kingdom) – Wyrem (United Kingdom)*
Flexible Reinforcements Ltd Bancroft Road, Burnley BB10 2TP Tel. *01282 478222* Fax. *01282 478210* E-mail. *sales@flexr.co.uk* Web. *www.flexr.co.uk Bondwave – Wavelene – Wavelock – Wavespan – Weavetop*
Flexicon Ltd Roman Way Coleshill, Birmingham B46 1HG Tel. *01675 466900* Fax. *01675 466901* E-mail. *sales@flexicon.uk.com* Web. *www.flexicon.uk.com Flexicon*
Flexicon Europe Ltd 89 Lower Herne Road, Herne Bay CT6 7PH Tel. *01227 374710* Fax. *01227 365821* E-mail. *sales@flexicon.co.uk* Web. *www.flexicon.co.uk Flexicon Europe*
Flexiform Business Furniture Ltd (Head Office, Factory and Northern Showroom) The Office Furniture Centre 1392 Leeds Road, Bradford BD3 7AE Tel. *01274 656013* Fax. *01274 665760* E-mail. *info@flexiform.co.uk* Web. *www.flexiform.co.uk Chess – Evolve – Flexiburo – Flexiflair – Flexiform – Flexiglide – Flexilink – Fleximetric – Flexistor – Laser*
Fleximas Ltd Ashtree House Ashbrook Lane, Abbots Bromley, Rugeley WS15 3DW Tel. *01283 841800* Fax. *01283 841801* E-mail. *enquiry@flexibulk.co.uk* Web. *www.flexibulk.co.uk *Beco (Germany) – *Celatom (U.S.A.) – *Diacel (Germany) – Fleximas*
Flexipol Packaging Ltd 14 Bentwood Road Haslingden, Rossendale BB4 5HH Tel. *01706 222792* Fax. *01706 224683* E-mail. *info@flexipol.co.uk* Web. *www.flexipol.co.uk Flexipol – Flexistrong – Ripp 'n' Flow*
Flexitallic Ltd Scandinavia Mills Hunsworth Lane, Cleckheaton BD19 4LN Tel. *01274 851273* Fax. *01274 851386* E-mail. *dmitchell@flexitallic.com* Web. *www.flexitallic.eu Enviroflex – Flexicarb – Flexitallic – Flexite – Flexpro (TM) – SIGMA – Thermiculite*
Flex Seal Couplings Ltd Endeavour Works Newlands Way Valley Park Industrial Estate, Wombwell, Barnsley S73 0UW Tel. *01226 340222* Fax. *01226 340400* E-mail. *sales@flexseal.co.uk* Web. *www.flexseal.co.uk Flex-Seal*
Flickers Ltd Cottage Farm Cobbetts Lane, Blackwater, Camberley GU17 9LW Tel. *01252 860403* Fax. *01252 860404* E-mail. *info@flickers.co.uk* Web. *www.flickers.co.uk *Kerzolin – *Towe Lamps*
Flintshire Chronicle Newspapers Chronicle House Commonhall Street, Chester CH1 2AA Tel. *01244 821911* Fax. *01244 349975* E-mail. *carl.wood@cheshirenews.co.uk* Web. *www.flintshirechronicle.co.uk Chester Chronicle – Chester Mail – Chronicle ,The (Flintshire Editions) – Crewe Chronicle – Crewe Chronicle Sandbach Edition – Crewe Mail – Ellesmere Port Pioneer – Middlewich Chronicle – Nantwich Chronicle – Northwich Chronicle – Northwich Herald & Post – Runcorn and Widnes Herald and Post – Runcorn Weekly News – South Wirral News – Whitchurch Herald – Widnes Weekly News – Winsford Chronicle*
Flir Systems Ltd 2 Kings Hill Avenue Kings Hill, West Malling ME19 4AQ Tel. *01732 220011* Fax. *01732 220014* E-mail. *info@flir.com* Web. *www.flir.com FLIR Systems – thermaCAM*
Flitterman Investments Ltd Michael House Rennie Hogg Road Riverside Business Park, Nottingham NG2 1RX Tel. *0115 9852200* Fax. *0115 9863271* E-mail. *laurence.flitterman@outdoorscene.com* Web. *www.outdoorscene.com *Bodge The Badger (Far East) – *Indra (Far East) – *Jakes (Far East) – *Nitro (Far East) – *Outdoor Scene (Far East)*
Flixborough Wharf Ltd Trent Port House Stather Road, Flixborough, Scunthorpe DN15 8RS Tel. *01724 867691* Fax. *01724 851207* E-mail. *info@flixboroughwharf.co.uk* Web. *www.rms-humber.co.uk Flixborough*
Ian Flockton Developments Ltd Estate Road 1 South Humberside Industrial Estate, Grimsby DN31 2TB Tel. *01472 359634* Fax. *01472 241392* E-mail. *info@ianflockton.co.uk* Web. *www.ianflockton.co.uk Flotanks – Kingflo-Tanks*
Flo Mech Ltd Flo-Mech House Paxton Road, Orton Goldhay, Peterborough PE2 5YA Tel. *01733 233166* Fax. *01733 235200* E-mail. *enquiries@flo-mech.com* Web. *www.flo-mech.com *Flo-Cut – Flo-Filter – *Flo-Therm*
Flomotion Rental Ltd 7 Wilton Close Partridge Green, Horsham RH13 8RX Tel. *01403 711170* Fax. *01403 711059* E-mail. *sales@flomotion.uk.com Flobox – Flofast – Flofast 2 – Flofold – Flopax – Flostax – Flotrip*
Flooring Trade Supplies Oakdene Road, Redhill RH1 6BT Tel. *01737 765075* E-mail. *sales@flooringtradesuppliesuk.com* Web. *www.flooringtradesuppliesredhill.co.uk Mexica*
The Florida Group Dibden Road, Norwich NR3 4RR Tel. *01603 426341* Fax. *01603 424354* E-mail. *mailroom@floridagroup.co.uk* Web. *www.floridagroup.co.uk Brooke – Van-Dal*
Flotronic Pumps Ltd (Head Office) Ricebridge Works Brighton Road, Bolney, Haywards Heath RH17 5NA Tel. *01444 881871* Fax. *01444 881860* E-mail. *sales@flotronicpumps.co.uk* Web. *www.flotronic.co.uk Flotronic – CHEMFLO – One Nut – Slimline*
Flowcrete UK Stud Green Industrial Park Booth Lane, Moston, Sandbach CW11 3QF Tel. *01270 753000* Fax. *01270 753333* E-mail. *mark@flowcrete.com* Web. *www.flowcrete.com Deckshield – Flowcoat SF41 – Flowprime – Flowseal WD – Flowshield – Hydraseal DPM – Mondéco*
Flowdrill UK Ltd Unit 7 105 Hopewell Business Centre Hopewell Drive, Chatham ME5 7DX Tel. *01634 309422* Fax. *01634 303306* E-mail. *flowdrill.uk@virgin.net* Web. *www.flowdrill.com *Flowdrill (Netherlands)*
Geraldine Flower Publications (Trading As Geraldine Flower Publications) 71 Thornton Avenue, London W4 1QF Tel. *020 87478028* Fax. *020 87478054* Web. *www.green-pages.co.uk Blue Pages – Green Pages*
Flowering Plants Ltd Unit 12 Homeground, Buckingham Industrial Estate, Buckingham MK18 1UH Tel. *01280 813764* Fax. *01280 823735* E-mail. *mail@fpl-irrigation.com* Web. *www.fpl-irrigation.com Irrigation Systems*
Flowflex Components Ltd Samuel Blaser Works Tongue Lane Industrial Estate, Buxton SK17 7LR Tel. *01298 77211* Fax. *01298 72362* E-mail. *sales@flowflex.com* Web. *www.flowflex.com Flowflex – Kingley – Lamontite – Securex*
Flowgroup Ltd Bestobell Valves & Conflow President Way, Sheffield S4 7UR Tel. *0114 2240200* Fax. *0114 2784974* E-mail. *lyndab@flowgroup.co.uk* Web. *www.flowgroup.co.uk Bestobell – Bestobell Birflo – Bestobell Valves – Constaflo – Truflo*
Flowline Manufacturing Ltd Elstree Business Centre Elstree Way, Borehamwood WD6 1RX Tel. *020 82076565* Fax. *020 82073082* E-mail. *mark.davis@flowline.co.uk* Web. *www.flowline.co.uk Delta Mag – Delta Mag, Demi Mag, MiniSonic, DigiSonic P/E, Vortex PhD, Flo-Gage, Deltaflow, Multi-Mag, Hydro-Flow, V-Bar,Master Touch, Flo-System, Flo-Tote, Flo-Dar, Flo-Tracer, Flo-Mate, Ultraflux. – Deltaflow – Demi Mag – DigiSonic P/E – Flo-Dar – Flo-Gage – Flo-System – Flo-Tote – Hydro-Flow – Master Touch – MiniSonic – Multi-Mag – V-Bar – Vortex PhD*
Flow Mech Products Ltd Charter Street, Leicester LE1 3UD Tel. *0116 2425425* Fax. *0116 2425555* E-mail. *info@flowmech.co.uk* Web. *www.flowmech.co.uk ABS – Grundfos – Lowara – Watts Valves – WILO Pumps – Zilmet Vessels*
Flowplant Group Ltd (Harben Neolith) Gemini House 3 Brunel Road, Salisbury SP2 7PU Tel. *01722 325424* Fax. *01722 411329* E-mail. *info@flowplant.com* Web. *www.flowplant.co.uk Harben & Neolith – Harben & Neolith - Aqua*
Flowserve Hawton Lane New Balderton, Newark NG24 3BU Tel. *01636 494600* Fax. *01636 705991* E-mail. *newark@flowserve.com* Web. *www.flowserve.com D.-Line – E.-Line – Magline – Multiline – S.-Line*
Flowtech Fluid Handling Ltd 8 Gresham Way Industrial Estate Gresham Way, Tilehurst, Reading RG30 6AW Tel. *0118 9413121* Fax. *0118 9431221* E-mail. *info@flowtechfh.com* Web. *www.flowtech.com Alphacel – Carbon-X – *Cuno Europe (France) – *Cuno Filters (U.S.A.)*
Flowtek H D D Ltd Unit B Sandall Stones Road Kirk Sandall Industrial Estate, Doncaster DN3 1QR Tel. *01302 880582* Fax. *01302 884590* E-mail. *flowtekuk@btconnect.com* Web. *www.flowtekhdduk.co.uk FlowTek HDD (UK) Ltd*
Fluid Pumps Ltd Unit 2 The Grange Rawcliffe Road, Goole DN14 6TY Tel. *01405 780660* Fax. *01482 866472* E-mail. *leebarker@fluidpumps.co.uk* Web. *www.fluidpumps.co.uk Blagdon Pumps – Mono pumps – Sandpiper pumps – Versamatic pumps – Wilden pumps*
Fluorel Ltd Riverside Works Broadmead Road, Woodford Green IG8 8PQ Tel. *020 85049691* Fax. *020 85061792* E-mail. *djones@flourel.co.uk* Web. *www.flourel.co.uk Fluorel*
F M C Chemicals Ltd Lithium Division Commercial Road, Wirral CH62 3NL Tel. *0151 3348085* Fax. *0151 3348501* E-mail. *stephen.lewis@fmc.com* Web. *www.fmclithium.com FMC Lithium*
F M C G Ltd (Personal Care Division) Prospect House Featherstall Road South, Oldham OL9 6HT Tel. *0161 6273061* Fax. *0161 6273134* E-mail. *info@fmcgltd.com* Web. *www.fmcgltd.com 3R Plus – Active – Baby Sense – Cool Feet – Dentiplus – Escenti – Granny's Original – Groovy Glitz – Head Funk – Hygienics – Indulge – Nuage – Purity Plus – Room Scents – Salon Chic – Swirl – Systeme*
F & M Steed Upholstery Ltd Bonsall Street Long Eaton, Nottingham NG10 2AL Tel. *0115 9734166* Fax. *0115 9461845* E-mail. *richard@steedupholstery.com* Web. *www.steedupholstery.com Steed Upholstery*
F M X Ltd Westfield House Bonnetts Lane, Ifield, Crawley RH11 0NY Tel. *01293 560056* Fax. *01293 610500* E-mail. *admin@cafmexplorer.com* Web. *www.cafmexplorer.com Cafm*
Foam Engineers Ltd Dashwood Avenue, High Wycombe HP12 3EA Tel. *01494 448855* Fax. *01494 461841* E-mail. *jwiles@foamengineers.co.uk*

Web. *www.foamengineers.co.uk Durapac – Interlock – Kubic – Petrocel – Rhinohide*
Focal Point Audio Visual Ltd 1-3 Kew Place, Cheltenham GL53 7NQ Tel. *01242 693118* Fax. *01242 693118 Focal Point Audio Visual – Focal Point Audio Visual Slide Sets – Mainmast Books*
FOCUS Eap 1st Floor The Podium Metropolitan House Darkes Lane, Potters Bar EN6 1AG Tel. *01707 661300* Fax. *01707 661242* E-mail. *info@focuseap.co.uk* Web. *www.focuseap.co.uk Critical Incident Service – Employee Counselling – Employees Assistance Programmes – Focus EAP Limited – Mediation & Conciliation*
FOCUS International Ltd 109 Ashley Road, St Albans AL1 5UB Tel. *01727 883555* Fax. *01727 883550* E-mail. *reception@focus-south.net* Web. *www.focusg.co.uk Bear USA – Le Coq Sportif – Lotto – Penn Athletic*
FOCUS International 6 Tonbridge Road, Maidstone ME16 8RP Tel. *01622 351000* Fax. *01622 351001* E-mail. *joanne.northen@focusfo.com* Web. *www.focusfo.com Spectralux 2000 – Spectralux 3000 – Spectralux 3000M – Spectralux 6000 – Spectralux 6000 IP65 – Spectralux 6000 IP68*
Fogarty Filled Products Ltd Havenside Fishtoft Road, Boston PE21 0AH Tel. *01205 361122* Fax. *01205 353202* E-mail. *stuart.macdonald@fogarty.co.uk* Web. *www.fogarty.co.uk Ariel – Fogarty – Haven – Moments*
Foilco Ltd Enterprise Way Lowton, Warrington WA3 2BP Tel. *01942 262622* Fax. *01942 267200* E-mail. *sales@foilco.co.uk* Web. *www.foilco.co.uk Momentim Packaging (United Kingdom)*
Folding Sliding Doors FSD Works Hopbine Avenue West Bowling, Bradford BD5 8ER Tel. *01274 715880* Fax. *0845 6446631* E-mail. *tracey.shearman@foldingslidingdoors.com* Web. *www.foldingslidingdoors.com FSD UK*
Folex Ltd Suite 10 Cranmore Place Cranmore Drive, Shirley, Solihull B90 4RZ Tel. *0121 7333833* Fax. *0121 7333222* E-mail. *sales@folex.co.uk* Web. *www.folex.co.uk Foladraft – Folajet – Folamask – Folaproof – Folarex – Folex A.N. – Folex Digiprint – Folex Fotojet*
The Folio Society 44 Eagle Street, London WC1R 4FS Tel. *020 75733477* Fax. *020 74004242* Web. *www.foliosociety.com The Folio Society*
Fondera Ltd Unit 7a Beadle Trading Estate Hithercroft Road, Wallingford OX10 9EZ Tel. *01491 836222* Fax. *01491 836776* E-mail. *fonderaltd@aol.com* Web. *www.fondera.co.uk Comec (Italy) – Delta (Canada) – Irontite (U.S.A.) – Kwik-Way (U.S.A.) – Martin Wells (U.S.A.) – Peg (Italy) – Robbi (Italy)*
Fontware Ltd 25 Barnes Wallis Road, Fareham PO15 5TT Tel. *01489 505075* Fax. *0870 0515816* E-mail. *kevin@fontware.com* Web. *www.fontware.com Bitstream – Fontware – True Type*
Foodcare Systems Ltd Unit 1 North Lynn Business Village Bergen Way, North Lynn Industrial Estate, Kings Lynn PE30 2JG Tel. *01553 770148* Fax. *01553 770146* E-mail. *sales@foodcaresystems.com* Web. *www.foodcaredirect.com Dinex – Tuxton*
Food & Drink Federation 6 Catherine Street, London WC2B 5JJ Tel. *020 78362460* Fax. *020 73795735* E-mail. *reception@fdf.org.uk* Web. *www.fdf.org.uk Feedback*
Forac Ltd Unit 9 Riverbank Business Centre Old Shoreham Road, Shoreham By Sea BN43 5FL Tel. *01273 467100* Fax. *01273 467101* E-mail. *sales@forac.co.uk* Web. *www.forac.co.uk Forac*
Forbo PO Box 1, Kirkcaldy KY1 2SB Tel. *01592 643111* Fax. *01772 627361* E-mail. *headoffice@forbo.com* Web. *www.forbo.com Artoleum Scala (Netherlands) – *Bulletin Board (Netherlands) – *Colorex A.S. (Switzerland) – *Colorex E.L. (Switzerland) – *Colour-Step (Sweden) – Cushionfloor Classic – Cushionfloor Deluxe – Cushionfloor Elite – Cushionfloor Super Glass – Cushionfloor Super Luxury – Cushionfloor Supreme – Cushionfloor Ultima – *Desktop (Netherlands) – *Marmofloor (Netherlands) – Marmoleum Dual – *Marmoleum Fresco – *Marmoleum Real (Netherlands) – *MultiStep (Sweden) – Nairn 1600 – Nairn 1800 – Nairn 2000 – Nairn 2500 – Nairn Classic 1400 – Nairn Cushionfloor – *SafeStep (Sweden) – *Smaragd (Sweden) – *SureStep (Sweden) – *Walton (Netherlands)*
Forbo Siegling Unit 4 Fifth Avenue, Dukinfield SK16 4PP Tel. *0161 3306521* Fax. *0161 3084385* E-mail. *siegling.uk@forbo.com* Web. *www.forbo-siegling.co.uk Extremultus Miraclo – Prolink – Siegling (Germany) – Transilon*
Forbo Adhesives UK Ltd (a Reichhold Co.) Bridge Street, Chatteris PE16 6RD Tel. *01354 692345* Fax. *01354 696661* Web. *www.forbo.com Compex – Fomebond – Fortum – Gelbond – Polyfree – Polyfree – Swiftak – Swiftbond – Syncol – Velotak*
Force Engineering International Ltd Old Station Close Shepshed, Loughborough LE12 9NJ Tel. *01509 506025* Fax. *01509 505433* E-mail. *stanley.proverbs@kirton.co.uk* Web. *www.force.co.uk Forcepack (United Kingdom)*
Ford Component Manufacturing Ltd Unit 2 Postal Number 3, Hebburn NE31 2JZ Tel. *0191 4286600* Fax. *0191 4286620* E-mail. *mark.podmore@ford-aerospace.com* Web. *www.ford-components.com Easipeel*
Ford Motor Company Ltd Central Office Eagle Way, Great Warley, Brentwood CM13 3BW Tel. *01277 253000* Web. *www.ford.co.uk Ford*
Fords Packaging Systems Ltd Ronald Close Kempston, Bedford MK42 7SH Tel. *01234 846600* Fax. *01234 841820* E-mail. *geoff.brim@fords-packsys.co.uk* Web. *www.fords-packsys.co.uk Fords (United Kingdom)*
Forelink Limited PO Box 484, Northwich CW9 7XN Tel. *01606 44863* E-mail. *david@forelink.co.uk* Web. *www.forelink.co.uk Forelink – CNC Training*
Foremost Electronics Ltd Bluegate Hall Braintree Road, Great Bardfield, Braintree CM7 4PZ Tel. *01371 811171* Fax. *01371 810933* E-mail. *info@4most.co.uk* Web. *www.4most.co.uk Accord – Cherry Switches – Seuffer – Thermodisc*
Forest Of Dean Stone Firms Ltd Cannop Road Parkend, Lydney GL15 4JS Tel. *01594 562304* Fax. *01594 564184* E-mail. *info@fodstone.co.uk* Web. *www.fodstone.co.uk Royal Forest of Dean Blue – Royal Forest of Dean Grey Sandstone*
Forest Garden plc Unit 291 296 Hartlebury Trading Estate, Hartlebury, Kidderminster DY10 4JB Tel. *08701 919800* Fax. *08701 919898* E-mail. *jhalford@forestgarden.co.uk* Web. *www.forestgarden.co.uk Larch-Lap*
Forest Sofa Newbury House Greenwood Street, Salford M6 6PD Tel. *0161 7376918* Fax. *0161 7457830* E-mail. *david.foster@forestsofa.co.uk* Web. *www.forestsofa.co.uk Design for Living*
Forever Scotland IT Consultancy 22 Leishman Place, Hawick TD9 8EZ Tel. *01450 377071* E-mail. *labourparty@foreverscotland.co.uk* Web. *www.foreverscotland.co.uk EPSON – IBM – Microsoft*
Fork Truck Centre Ltd 43 Steward Street, Birmingham B18 7AE Tel. *0121 4547514* Fax. *0121 4561792* E-mail. *rwilliams@wilmat-handling.co.uk* Web. *www.wilmat-handling.co.uk Fork Truck Centre*
Format International Ltd Format House Poole Road, Woking GU21 6DY Tel. *01483 726081* Fax. *01483 722827* E-mail. *just_ask@formatinternational.com* Web. *www.formatinternational.com Global-Mix – Multi-Mix – New Century – Single-Mix – Uni-Mix*
Formscan Limited Park House, Kidwells Park Drive,, Maidenhead SL6 8AQ Tel. *0844 5617276* Fax. *07006 082546* E-mail. *info@formscan.com* Web. *www.formscan.com Anacomp – Laser Printers – X.F.P. – Xidex*
Forrester Ketley & Co. Forrester House 52 Bounds Green Road, London N11 2EY Tel. *020 88896622* Fax. *020 88811088* E-mail. *steven_wake@forresters.co.uk* Web. *www.forresters.co.uk Forrester Ketley*
Forresters Pressure Washer Services Ltd 12 Courtyard Works Newstet Road, Knowsley Industrial Park, Liverpool L33 7TJ Tel. *0151 5492003* Fax. *0151 5464009* E-mail. *peter_forrester@btinternet.com* Web. *www.kellysearch.com/partners/forresterspressurewash.asp American-Lincoln – Clarke*
Forster & Hales Ltd 24 Wadsworth Road Perivale, Greenford UB6 7JD Tel. *020 89989057* Fax. *020 89982922* E-mail. *sales@forsterandhales.com* Web. *www.forsterandhales.com Blue Triangle – Forster & Hales*
R E Forster Ltd Grey Street, Warrington WA1 2PH Tel. *01925 634334* Fax. *01925 235082 R.E. Forsters*
Forsyth Bros Ltd 126 Deansgate, Manchester M3 2GR Tel. *0161 8343281* Fax. *0161 8340630* E-mail. *info@forsyths.co.uk* Web. *www.forsyths.co.uk Music Minus One – Opus – *Pocket Songs (U.S.A.) – Schimmel*
Forteq UK Ltd Tandem Industrial Estate Wakefield Road, Tandem, Huddersfield HD5 0QR Tel. *01484 424384* Fax. *01484 535053* E-mail. *paul.w@forteq-group.com* Web. *www.forteq-group.com Mikron*
Forticrete Ltd Anstone Works Kiveton Park Station, Sheffield S26 6NP Tel. *01909 775000* Fax. *01909 773549* E-mail. *dseekings@forticrete.com* Web. *www.forticrete.co.uk Anstone – Shearstone*
Fortis UK Ltd Fortis House Tollgate, Chandler's Ford, Eastleigh SO53 3YA Tel. *023 80644455* Fax. *023 80641146* Web. *www.fortisinsurance.co.uk Assistance International – Bishopsgate*
Forum Products Ltd Betchworth House 57-65 Station Road, Redhill RH1 1DL Tel. *01737 773711* Fax. *01737 779382* E-mail. *animal.health@forumgroup.co.uk* Web. *www.forum.co.uk *Clampzyme – *Diaproof-K – Kling-on Blue*
Forward Chemicals Ltd PO Box 12, Widnes WA8 0RD Tel. *0151 4221000* Fax. *0151 4221011* E-mail. *salesandservice@forwardchem.com* Web. *www.forwardchem.com 5V 50 – Aluminus – Amphoclens – Aquasolv – Autosheen – Beltlife – Bioclene – Bisandet – Brickleen – Brisol – C-Lube – Carbonex 250 – Chemcoat 90 – Chemexol – Chemseal – Clearguard – Concentrate – Contraqua – Coolcut – Counterbact – CS24 – De-Icer – De-Scale 10 – Degraffit – Deodamate – Deodasan – Deodis – Deodorant Blocks – Dermagel – Dizzolv – Dizzolv Viscous – Drube – Ecoline – Ecosafe – Ecotect – Ecozyme – Elecsols – Envirosol – Envydro – Epoxytect – Exodor – Foamfree – Formcote – Freeit – FS80 – Gearlube – Gleam – Glycair – Graffex – Hand Over Fist – Hands On – HI-Tempreze – Inkoff – Jeldis – Kleen-Screen – Kremtect – Lavette – Lectrotect – Liftcon – Lubesaf – Malkyl – Metsol – Mortadd – Multiclene 100 – Multiclene 200 – Neutrasol – Niclene – Niclube – Ovencut – Phetch – Pinefresh – Powaclene – Powaclene Plus – Powaclene T.F.R. – Powafoam – Powasol 10 – Powasol 20 – Powasteam 200 – Powerdis – Powerfresh – Pressclene – Printex – Pyrakill – Qualdis – Scaffbrite – Scaffeze – Scaffeze Plus – Self-Shine – Showerclene – Silitect – Siltexol – Soak Up – Solstrip – Spillaway – Spraysheen – Spraywash – Supasol – Supasol Hydro – Supathaw – Tapcut – Up-n-Away – Whispex – X-Pol – Zingalv*
Foseco International Limited Drayton Manor Business Park, Tamworth B78 3TL Tel. *01827 289999* Fax. *01827 250806* Web. *www.foseco.co.uk Foseco*
Fospat Industrial Ltd Hints Road Mile Oak, Tamworth B78 3PQ Tel. *01827 288188* Fax. *01827 251444* E-mail. *ha.frend@fospat.com* Web. *www.fospat.com Diamet HF5 – Fospat – Fospat – Fospat*
Foster Enterprises 2 Whingate, Leeds LS12 3BL Tel. *0113 2797075* Fax. *0113 2798493 Device Only – Triangle Sports*
Foster Refrigerator UK Ltd Oldmeadow Road Hardwick Industrial Estate, Kings Lynn PE30 4JU Tel. *01553 691122* Fax. *01553 691447* E-mail. *sales@foster-uk.com* Web. *www.fosterrefrigerator.co.uk Foster*
W H Foster & Sons Ltd Stourdale Road, Cradley Heath B64 7BG Tel. *08453 313491* Fax. *01384 415185* E-mail. *sales@whfoster.co.uk* Web. *www.whfoster.co.uk Formica – Solid Surfaces*
Fotek School Portraits 1b Bramble Road Techno Trading Estate, Swindon SN2 8HZ Tel. *01793 615681* Fax. *01793 512826* E-mail. *roberts@fotekportraits.co.uk* Web. *www.fotekportraits.co.uk Fotek*
Fothergill Crenette Ltd Greenvale Mill Summit, Littleborough OL15 9QP Tel. *01706 371137* Fax. *01706 371821* Web. *www.porcher-ind.com Crenette*
Fothergill Engineered Fabrics Ltd Summit, Littleborough OL15 0LR Tel. *01706 372414* Fax. *01706 376422* E-mail. *sales@fothergill.co.uk* Web. *www.fothergill.co.uk Aramid – Carbon – Glass – Tygashield – Tygasil – Tyglas – Tyglas 1000 C*
Foundocean Ltd Liston Exchange Liston Court High Street, Marlow SL7 1ER Tel. *01628 567000* Fax. *01628 788604* E-mail. *info@foundocean.com* Web. *www.foundocean.com SeaMark Systems*
Foundrax Engineering Products Limited Wessex Park, Somerton TA11 6SB Tel. *01458 274888* Fax. *01458 274880* E-mail. *sales@foundrax.co.uk* Web. *www.foundrax.co.uk Brinscan – Foundrax*
Foundrometers Instrumentation Ltd Unit 17 Enterprise Court Pit Lane, Micklefield, Leeds LS25 4BU Tel. *0113 2874411* Fax. *0113 2874422* E-mail. *p.hargraves@foundrometers.co.uk* Web. *www.foundrometers.co.uk Aric Wardbrooke – Red Point – Revometer (United Kingdom) – Rolux – Rotaro – Rotas*
Four D Rubber Co. Ltd Delves Rd Heanor Gate Industrial Estate, Heanor DE75 7SJ Tel. *01773 763134* Fax. *01773 763136* E-mail. *sales@fourdrubber.com* Web. *www.fourdrubber.com Isodam – Supatex – Supatex – Supatex – Isodam – Tridex*
Four Seasons France Ltd 19 Carr Road Calverley, Pudsey LS28 5NE Tel. *0113 2564373* Fax. *0113 2555923* E-mail. *info@fourseasonsfrance.co.uk* Web. *www.fourseasons.uk.net Four Seasons – Four Seasons France*
Fourth Passenger Ltd 29 Meridian Place, London E14 9FE Tel. *020 71003322* E-mail. *mail@4puk.com* Web. *www.4puk.com Fourth Passenger Film – Fourth passenger Music video*
Fox Brothers & Company Ltd Fox Bros & Co. Tonedale Mill Wardleworth Way, Wellington TA21 0BA Tel. *01823 662271* Fax. *01823 666963* E-mail. *info@foxflannel.com* Web. *www.foxflannel.com Bliss – Fox*
Fox It Ltd 111 Chertsey Road, Woking GU21 5BW Tel. *01483 221200* Fax. *01483 221500* E-mail. *training@foxit.net* Web. *www.foxit.net Helmsman – Open Process – Red Box Change Management – Red Box Configuration Management – Red Box Help Desk & Problem Management – Sceptre – UCMS – Ultracare – Ultraframe Works*
foxstandpipes 9-11 Siddeley Way Royal Oak Industrial Estate, Daventry NN11 8PA Tel. *01327 311011* Fax. *01327 300216* E-mail. *sales@kaver.co.uk* Web. *foxstandpipes.co.uk foxstandpipes*
F P International UK Ltd Boundary Road Buckingham Road Industrial Estate, Brackley NN13 7ES Tel. *01280 703161* Fax. *01280 701915* E-mail. *james.blood@fpintl.com* Web. *www.flo-pak.co.uk Flo-Pak*
Fraikin Ltd Fraikin House Torwood Close, Westwood Business Park, Coventry CV4 8HX Tel. *024 76694494* Fax. *024 76470419* E-mail. *enquiries@vilresins.co.uk* Web. *www.fraikin.co.uk Lex Transfleet*
Framptons Ltd 76 Charlton Road, Shepton Mallet BA4 5PD Tel. *01749 341000* Fax. *01749 344997* E-mail. *enquiries@framptons.ltd.uk* Web. *www.framptons.ltd.uk Easy Eggs – Ovablend*

Franchise Development Services Ltd Franchise House 56 Surrey Street, Norwich NR1 3FD Tel. *01603 620301* Fax. *01603 630174* E-mail. *roy@fdsltd.com* Web. *www.fdsfranchise.com Franchise Development*

Francis and Francis Ltd P.O. Box 3284, South Croydon CR2 1FU Tel. *020 86689792* Fax. *020 86689793* E-mail. *sales@powertransmissions.co.uk* Web. *www.powertransmissions.co.uk AWEK NORD – AWEK NORD – TRIP DOGS & RAILS – FRANCI MECHANICAL POWER TRANSMISSION PRODUCTS – INKOMA 'PK' Offset Couplings – INKOMA 'Lineflex' Couplings – INKOMA 'Inkoturn' Encoder Couplings – CV IN-LINE FLEXIBLE COUPLINGS – CAPTON – EUCHNER – FRANCI – KBK KB – KBK KBE – KBK KBK – LONERTIA – POGGI A2000 – POGGI GDR/GDA – POGGI LOK-FIT – SCHMIDT CONTROL-FLEX – SCHMIDT IZ – SCHMIDT LOEWE – SCHMIDT OFF-SET – SCHMIDT OMNI-FLEX – SCHMIDT SEMI-FLEX – A2000 – GDR/GDA – LOK-FIT – POGGI 'System-P' – POGGI 'System-P' – System-P – System-P – INKOMA 'PK' OFFSET – INKOMA 'LINEFLEX' – INKOMA 'INKOTURN' – INKOMA 'INKOFLEX' – INKOMA 'INKOCROSS' – INKOMA 'KSO' CRUCIFORM – INKOMA 'ELAFLEX' – 'PK' OFFSET – LINEFLEX – INKOTURN – INKOFLEX – INKOCROSS – 'KSO' CRUCIFORM – ELAFLEX – INKOMA – POGGI – KBK – PROXITRON – AWEK – EUCHNER*

Francis Chichester Ltd 9 St James's Place, London SW1A 1PE Tel. *020 74930931* Fax. *020 74091830* E-mail. *sales@francischichester.com* Web. *www.francischichester.co.uk 5-Language Guide to London – Educational Wallcharts – Francis Chichester's Pocket Map & Guide of London – Guide to Good Living in London – London Man – London Woman – Map & Guide to European Cities*

Franke UK Ltd Manchester Int Office Centre Styal Road, Manchester M22 5WB Tel. *0161 4366280* Fax. *0161 4362180* E-mail. *info.uk@franke.com* Web. *www.franke.co.uk *Franke (Switzerland) – *Franke Compact (Switzerland) – Franke Divida – Franke Fragranite – Franke Fraquartz – Franke Rotondo – Franke Sorter – Franke Triflow – Franke Undermounted Bowls*

Franklin Hodge Industries Ltd Jubilee Building Faraday Road, Westfields Trading Estate, Hereford HR4 9NS Tel. *01432 269605* Fax. *01432 277454* E-mail. *sales@franklinhodge.com* Web. *www.franklinhodge.com Firestore – Firetainer – Liquistore – Refurbplus – Tritainer*

Frank Usher Group 66 Grosvenor Street, London W1K 3JL Tel. *020 76299696* Fax. *020 76296886* E-mail. *avril.bell@frankusher.co.uk* Web. *www.frankusher.co.uk Coterie – Dusk – Frank Usher – Oliver James*

Fraser & Ellis 80-100 Gwynne Road, London SW11 3UW Tel. *020 72289999* Fax. *020 72287250* E-mail. *sales@fraserellis.co.uk Beardson – Fraser & Ellis*

Stewart Fraser Ltd Henwood Industrial Estate, Ashford TN24 8DR Tel. *01233 265911* Fax. *01233 633149* E-mail. *cbrimson@stewartfraser.com* Web. *www.stewartfraser.com Lockseam*

Fray Design Ltd Ghyll Way Airedale Business Centre Keighley Road, Skipton BD23 2TZ Tel. *01756 704040* Fax. *01756 704041* E-mail. *sales@fraydesign.co.uk* Web. *www.fraydesign.co.uk Reflex R – Spyda workstations*

Freddy Products Ltd Unit 19 Kempton Road, Pershore WR10 2TA Tel. *01386 561113* Fax. *01386 556401* E-mail. *lisashaw@freddy-products.co.uk* Web. *www.freddy-products.co.uk Coolant Recycling Machines*

Frederick Spring Co. Unit 4a Princes End Industrial Park Nicholls Road, Tipton DY4 9LG Tel. *0121 5574080* Fax. *0121 5576959* E-mail. *sales@reliablespring.co.uk* Web. *www.reliablespring.co.uk Reliable Spring Manufactures*

Freed Of London Ltd 62-64 Well Street, London E9 7PX Tel. *020 85104700* Fax. *020 85104750* E-mail. *info@freedoflondon.com* Web. *www.freedshop.com Freed of London Ltd*

Freedown Food Co. Unit 43 London Stone Business Estate Broughton Street, London SW8 3QR Tel. *020 77204520* Fax. *020 77202166* E-mail. *info@freedownfood.co.uk* Web. *www.freedownfood.co.uk Camdeboo – O'Hagan's Sausage – Southern Game Meat*

Freeman Automotive UK Ltd Upton Valley Way East Pineham, Northampton NN4 9EF Tel. *01604 583344* Fax. *01604 583744* E-mail. *studio@ebcbrakes.com* Web. *www.ebcbrakes.com E.B.C.*

Anna French Ltd 36 Hinton Road, London SE24 0HJ Tel. *020 77376555* Fax. *020 72748193* E-mail. *jonathan@annafrench.co.uk* Web. *www.annafrench.co.uk Anna French*

French Connection Ltd Unit B Dolphin Way, Purfleet RM19 1NZ Tel. *020 70367000* Web. *www.frenchconnection.com French Connection Group Plc*

French & Jupps The Maltings Roydon Road, Stanstead Abbotts, Ware SG12 8HG Tel. *01920 870015* Fax. *01920 871001* E-mail. *david.jupp@frenchandjupps.co.uk* Web. *www.frenchandjupps.co.uk French and Jupp*

Thomas French Ltd James Street, Bury BL9 7EG Tel. *0161 7645356* Fax. *0161 7646416* E-mail. *peter.owen@thomasfrench.com* Web. *www.thomasfrench.com Curtain Styling*

Frenstar Unit 160 Ordnance Business Park Aerodrome Road, Gosport PO13 0FG Tel. *01329 233445* Fax. *01329 233450* E-mail. *info@frenstar.co.uk* Web. *www.frenstar.co.uk El-O-Matic – GK – Intervalve – IV – IVC – IVEX – IVF – IVR – IVTFE – IVTL – LBX*

Freshfield Lane Brickworks Ltd Danehill, Haywards Heath RH17 7HH Tel. *01825 790350* Fax. *01825 790779* E-mail. *sales@mbhplc.co.uk* Web. *www.mbhplc.co.uk F.L.B.*

Fretwell-Downing Hospitality Ltd 1 Hawke Street, Sheffield S9 2SU Tel. *0114 2816060* Fax. *0114 2816061* E-mail. *info@fdhospitality.com* Web. *www.fdhospitality.com MICa – Provision*

Freudenberg Household Products 2 Chichester Street, Rochdale OL16 2AX Tel. *01706 759597* Fax. *01706 350143* E-mail. *peter.gough@fhp-ww.com* Web. *www.vileda.com Vileda*

Freudenberg Simrit LP Simrit Service Centre Lutterworth Unit 7 Wycliffe Industrial Park, Lutterworth LE17 4HG Tel. *01455 204444* Fax. *01455 204455* E-mail. *info@simrit.com* Web. *www.simrit.com C.F.W. – Integral Accumulator – Meillor – Merkel – *N.O.K. (Japan, Singapore and USA) – Pneuko – Sikkufit – Simko – Simmerring – Simmerring – Simrax – Simrit – Simritan – Usit*

Fridays Ltd Swattenden Lane, Cranbrook TN17 3PN Tel. *01580 710200* Fax. *01580 714760* E-mail. *fridays@fridays.co.uk* Web. *www.fridays.co.uk Fridays – Oasters*

Fridge Freezer Direct Company Ltd 41-43 Brookside Burbage, Hinckley LE10 2TG Tel. *08456 800695* Fax. *01454 250434* E-mail. *enquiries@fridgefreezerdirect.co.uk* Web. *www.fridgefreezerdirect.co.uk Beko – Vestfrost – Gamko*

Friendberry Ltd Kingswood Stogumber, Taunton TA4 3TP Tel. *01984 656310* Fax. *01984 656667* E-mail. *karen@friendberry.co.uk* Web. *www.friendberry.co.uk A.D.R. – C.P.C. – L.G.V. – P.C.V.*

Friendly Soap 6 Church Hill Shepherdswell, Dover CT15 7NR Tel. *01304 830522* E-mail. *info@friendlysoap.co.uk* Web. *www.friendlysoap.co.uk Friendly Soap*

Friends Of The Earth 26-28 Underwood Street, London N1 7JQ Tel. *020 74901555* Fax. *020 74900881* E-mail. *info@foe.co.uk* Web. *www.foe.co.uk Friends of the Earth*

Frimatec UK Ltd 5 Townsend Centre Blackburn Road Townsend Industrial Estate, Houghton Regis, Dunstable LU5 5BQ Tel. *01582 471600* Fax. *01582 472050* E-mail. *info@frimatecuk.com* Web. *www.frimatec-isocab.com Isocab*

Frimstone Ltd Ely Road Waterbeach, Cambridge CB25 9PG Tel. *01223 860000* Fax. *01223 440378* E-mail. *reception@frimstone.co.uk* Web. *www.frimstone.co.uk Donarbon – M Dickerson – Princestone*

Frith Flexible Packaging Ltd 1 The Forum Coopers Way, Temple Farm Industrial Estate, Southend On Sea SS2 5TE Tel. *01702 463566* Fax. *01702 616954* E-mail. *davidw@macleansfoils.co.uk* Web. *www.sfw.co.uk Spectro Foil*

Francis Frith Collection Oakley Wylye Road, Dinton, Salisbury SP3 5EU Tel. *01722 716376* Fax. *01722 716881* E-mail. *john_buck@francisfrith.co.uk* Web. *www.francisfrith.com Francis Frith Collection, The*

Frontier Pitts Ltd Crompton House Crompton Way, Crawley RH10 9QZ Tel. *01293 548301* Fax. *01293 560650* E-mail. *sales@frontierpitts.com* Web. *www.frontierpitts.co.uk Dutyman – Garrison – LiteTracker – Lotracker – Qwicket – Roadblocker – Securistile – Traffic Flow Plate – Trojan*

Frost Electroplating Ltd 19-21 Great Hampton Street, Birmingham B18 6AX Tel. *0121 2364135* Fax. *0121 2365823* E-mail. *wsouthall@frost-electroplating.co.uk* Web. *www.frost-electroplating.co.uk Frost Electroplating*

F C Frost Ltd 7 Benfield Way, Braintree CM7 3YS Tel. *01376 329111* Fax. *01376 347002* E-mail. *info@fcfrost.com* Web. *www.fcfrost.com Biomatic – Frost Drainage Products – Secure Mix – Vari-Purpose – Watrous*

Frostholme Furniture Ltd Frostholme Mill Burnley Road, Todmorden OL14 7ED Tel. *01706 815133* Fax. *01706 818701* E-mail. *linda.hooper@sutcliffegroup.co.uk* Web. *www.sutcliffegroup.co.uk Charles Sheraton – Sutcliffe Furniture – White & Newton Furniture*

Froude Hofmann Ltd (part of the F K I Group of Companies) Blackpole Road, Worcester WR3 8YB Tel. *01905 856800* Fax. *01905 856881* E-mail. *bhemstock@froudehofmann.com* Web. *www.froudehofmann.com Bennett Controls – Froude Hofmann – Go Power (U.S.A.) – Texcel (United Kingdom)*

Fruit Of The Loom Ltd Fruit of The Loom House Halesfield 10, Telford TF7 4QP Tel. *01952 587123* Fax. *01952 581898* E-mail. *leonard@ftlte.fruit.com* Web. *www.fruitoftheloom.co.uk Fruit of The Loom – Screen Stars*

Frutarom UK Ltd Zinc Works Road Seaton Carew, Hartlepool TS25 2DT Tel. *01429 863222* Fax. *01429 867567* E-mail. *sales@uk.frutarom.com* Web. *www.frutarom.com Lithene – Oxford Chemicals*

F T L Foundry Equipment Ltd 6-11 Riley Street, Willenhall WV13 1RH Tel. *01902 630222* Fax. *01902 636593* E-mail. *sales@ftl-foundry.co.uk* Web. *www.ftl-foundry.co.uk F.T.L.*

F T M Materials Handling Ltd Unit 1 Ewenny Industrial Estate, Bridgend CF31 3EX Tel. *01656 766200* Fax. *01656 767976* E-mail. *admin@ftmbridgend.co.uk* Web. *www.ftmbridgend.co.uk fantuzzi industrial equipment – manitou industrial handling equipment – toyota industrial equipment,*

F T V Proclad International Ltd Viewfield, Glenrothes KY6 2RD Tel. *01592 772568* Fax. *01592 631252* E-mail. *darbon@ftvproclad.co.uk* Web. *www.procladgroup.com Proclad*

Fuchs Lubricants UK plc New Century Street Hanley, Stoke On Trent ST1 5HU Tel. *01782 203700* Fax. *01782 202072* E-mail. *richard.halhead@fuchs-oil.com* Web. *www.fuchs-oil.com Century – Ecocool – Ecocut – Eskimo – Planto – Renoclean – Renolin – Renolit – Silkair – Silkolene – Sirius – Titan*

Fuel Proof Ltd Middleton Business Park Middleton Road, Middleton, Morecambe LA3 3FH Tel. *01524 850685* Fax. *01524 859681* E-mail. *info@fuelproof.co.uk* Web. *www.fuelproof.co.uk AdBlue*

Fugro Seismic Imaging Ltd Horizon House Azalea Drive, Swanley BR8 8JR Tel. *01322 668011* Fax. *01322 613650* E-mail. *andy.cowlard@fugro-fsi.com* Web. *www.fugro.com Short-Offset 3D – Uniseis*

Fugro Survey Denmore Industrial Estate Denmore Road, Bridge Of Don, Aberdeen AB23 8JW Tel. *01224 257500* Fax. *01224 853919* E-mail. *phil.meaden@fugro.com* Web. *www.fugro.com Fugro Survey Ltd*

Fujichem Sonneborn Ltd Jaxa Works 91-95 Peregrine Road, Ilford IG6 3XH Tel. *020 85000251* Fax. *020 85003696* E-mail. *sales@fcsonneborn.com* Web. *www.fcsonneborn.co.uk Jaxa – Jaxacel – Jaxacryl – Jaxafil – Jaxagard – Jaxakote – Jaxalac – Jaxamel*

Fuji Copian Unit 21a Bailey Drive Gillingham Business Park, Gillingham ME8 0PZ Tel. *01634 371137* Fax. *01634 366560* E-mail. *sales@fujicopian.co.uk* Web. *www.fujicopian.co.uk Instarite Glue – Instarite II – Instarite S*

Fujifilm Sericol Ltd Patricia Way Pysons Road Industrial Estate, Broadstairs CT10 2LE Tel. *01843 866668* Fax. *01843 872184* E-mail. *human.resources@sericol.com* Web. *www.sericol.co.uk Aquacolor QL – Aquaspeed Flute FZ – Aquaspeed Ultra Display AS – Colorjet CO – Colorplus Fluorescent CF – Colorstar CS – Coolstar OT – Corripol CR – Dirasol – Drystick – Flexitex FE – Hystar HY – Mattplat MG – Monotex ML – Nylobag NB – Nylotex NX – Plastijet XG – Plastipure Fluorescent FP – Polydyne YD – Polyplast PY – Polyscreen PS – Prostar OS – Sericard CD – Serifix – Seripol SO – Seriprep – Seristar SX – Seritec TH – Subliscreen Aqua HQ – Texcharge TC – Texopaque OP – Tristar GT – Ultratone TN – Unipol UF – Uvibond UV – Uvipak NG – Uviplast UP2000 – Uvispeed Gloss UX – UVivid CN – UVivid Flexo FL – Uvivid RN*

Fujitsu General UK Co. Ltd 330 Centennial Avenue Centennial Park, Elstree, Borehamwood WD6 3TJ Tel. *020 82387810* Fax. *020 87313469* E-mail. *h.shimanoe@fujitsu-general.com* Web. *www.fujitsu-general.com Fujitsu*

Fulda Tyres 88-98 Wingfoot Way Erdington, Birmingham B24 9HY Tel. *01902 327000* Fax. *01902 327494* E-mail. *fuldainfo-uk@fulda.com* Web. *www.fulda.com Fulda Tyres*

Fullbrook Systems Ltd Unit 4 Bourne End Mills Upper Bourne End Lane, Hemel Hempstead HP1 2UJ Tel. *01442 876777* Fax. *01442 877144* E-mail. *carlton@fullbrook.com* Web. *www.fullbrook.com Brookfield – Chemotronic – Collomix – Dispermat – Kreis Dissolver – Liros – Lithotronic – Torusmill – Turbiscan*

Fulleon Llantarnam Industrial Park, Cwmbran NP44 3AW Tel. *01633 628500* Fax. *01633 866346* E-mail. *info@fulleon.co.uk* Web. *www.fulleon.co.uk Askari (United Kingdom) – Clarifire (United Kingdom) – CX Call Point – Flashni (United Kingdom) – Fulleon (United Kingdom) – Inergi – Roshni (United Kingdom) – Squashni (United Kingdom) – Symphoni (United Kingdom)*

H B Fuller Outram Road, Dukinfield SK16 4XE Tel. *0161 6660666* Fax. *0161 6660667* Web. *www.hbfuller.com Advantra – Datac – Ipacoll – Labelfix – Lunatack – Rakoll – WarmMelt*

Fulton Boiler Works Ltd 210 Broomhill Road, Bristol BS4 4TU Tel. *0117 9772563* Fax. *0117 9723358* E-mail. *paul.richards@fulton.com* Web. *www.fulton.com Cleansteam – Dragon – EFS – Electropack – Europack – JFS – Mini Compack – Pulse Plus – RB – Series E – Series E 440LDC – Series J*

Fulwith Textiles Sunny Bank Mills Farsley, Pudsey LS28 5UJ Tel. *0113 2579811* Fax. *0113 2577064 Decooflair*

Functional Foam Beacons Products Ltd (t/a Functional Foam & Beacons Leisure) Efi Industrial Estate Brecon Road, Merthyr Tydfil CF47 8RB Tel. *01685 350011* Fax. *01685 388396* E-mail. *sales@beaconsproducts.co.uk* Web. *www.beaconsproducts.co.uk Acoustalay – Beacons Leisure – Ecolay – Fitness Pro-mat – Functional Foam – Kumfies – Multimat*

Funke 387 Wellingborough Road, Northampton NN1 4EY Tel. *01604 239716* Fax. *01604 239719* Web. *www.funke.de AD2000 – ASME – ASME U Stamp – PED – TEMA*

Furmanite International Ltd Furman House Shap Road, Kendal LA9 6RU Tel. *01539 729009* Fax. *01642 465692* E-mail. *infouk@furmanite.co.uk* Web. *www.furmanite.co.uk Furmanite – Silk – Trevitest*

Furneaux Riddall & Co. Ltd Alchorne Place, Portsmouth PO3 5PA Tel. *023 92668621* Fax. *023 92690521* E-mail. *sales@furneauxriddall.com* Web. *www.furneauxriddall.com Halo Plus – Halo Plus 2-IS – White Knight*

Furness Building Society 51-55 Duke Street, Barrow In Furness LA14 1RT Tel. *01229 824560* Fax. *01229 837043* E-mail. *avril.willis@furness-bs.co.uk* Web. *www.furnessbs.co.uk Bonus 180 – Tessa – Young savers*

Furness Controls Ltd 4 The Pavilions Amber Close, Tamworth B77 4RP Tel. *01827 59950* Fax. *01827 59540* E-mail. *sales@furness-controls.com* Web. *www.furness-controls.com Furness Controls Ltd*

K & A Furness Ltd Trent Industrial Estate Duchess Street, Shaw, Oldham OL2 7UT Tel. *01706 843411* Fax. *01706 882289* E-mail. *admin@kafurness.co.uk* Web. *www.jet-vac.co.uk Jet-Vac*

Fusion Workshop 200 Brook Drive Green Park, Reading RG2 6UB Tel. *0118 9497557* E-mail. *chris.short@fusionworkshop.com* Web. *www.fusionworkshop.com Immediacy*

Fusion Workshop Quebec House Cowbridge Road East, Cardiff CF11 9AB Tel. *029 20666655* Fax. *029 20666644* E-mail. *chris.short@fusionworkshop.com* Web. *www.fusionworkshop.co.uk Immediacy*

Fussell's Rubber Co. Ltd 2 Brimbleworth Lane St Georges, Weston Super Mare BS22 7XS Tel. *01934 513473* Fax. *01934 521529 Fussells*

Future Publishing Ltd 30 Monmouth Street, Bath BA1 2BW Tel. *01225 442244* Fax. *01225 446019* E-mail. *mark.wood@futurenet.com* Web. *www.futurenet.com .net – 101 PC Games – 3D World – Bang – Classic Rock – Complete Guide Series – Computer Arts – Computer Arts Special – Computer Music – Cre@te Online – Cross Stitch Collection – Cross Stitcher – Cycling Plus – Digital Camera Magazine – Edge – Future Music – Gamesmaster – Glory Glory Man United – Good Woodworking – Guitar Techniques – Guitarist – Hi Fi Choice – Home Entertainment – Internet Advisor – Internet Works – Jane Greenoff's Cross Stitch – Linux Format – MacFormat – Manchester United – Masterclass Series – Max - Playstation 2 Gaming – MBUK – Metal Hammer – Microsoft Windows XP – Needlecraft – NGC Magazine – Official Playstation 2 Special Edition – Official Playstation 2 Tips – Official UK Playstation 2 Magazine – Official UK Playstation Magazine – PC Answers – PC Format – PC Gamer – PC Gamer Presents – PC Plus – PC Software – PSM2 – Quick & Easy Cross Stitch – Redline – Rhythm – SFX – T3 – Total Film – Total Guitar – What guitar? – What Mountain Bike? – Windows XP Answers – Xbox Gamer – Xbox UK*

The Futures Company (Head Office) 6 More London Place, London SE1 2QY Tel. *020 79551800* Fax. *020 79551900* E-mail. *reception@tnsglobal.com* Web. *www.thefuturescompany.com Henley Centre*

F W Mason & Sons Midland Ltd Road 8 Colwick Industrial Estate, Nottingham NG4 2EQ Tel. *0115 9113500* Fax. *0115 9113555* E-mail. *sales@masons-timber.co.uk* Web. *www.masons-timber.co.uk Newaplas*

F X Airport Services Ltd 5 The Pavement Worple Road, London SW19 4DA Tel. *020 88793334* Fax. *020 82416215* E-mail. *info@fxairports.co.uk* Web. *www.fxairports.co.uk FX-Airport Service Ltd*

Fyffes Group Ltd Houndmills Road, Basingstoke RG21 6XL Tel. *01256 383200* Fax. *01256 383259* E-mail. *c.bos@fyffes.com* Web. *www.fyffes.com Fyffes*

G

G 4 S Cash Solutions Sutton Park House 15 Carshalton Road, Sutton SM1 4LD Tel. *020 87707000* Fax. *020 86431059* Web. *www.g4s.co.uk Securicor*

G8 Systems 96 Ropeland Way, Horsham RH12 5NZ Tel. *01403 262611* Fax. *01403 262611* E-mail. *info@g8systems.co.uk* Web. *www.g8systems.co.uk Casali Electric Gates – Genius Electric Gates – Powerdoor Electric Gates – Terraneo Intercoms*

gabicci York House Empire Way, Wembley HA9 0PA Tel. *020 89039037* Fax. *020 89032493* E-mail. *info@gabicci.com* Web. *www.gabicci.com Gabicci*

Gabriel & Co. Ltd 10 Hay Hall Road, Birmingham B11 2AU Tel. *0121 2483333* Fax. *0121 2483330* E-mail. *sales@gabrielco.com* Web. *www.gabrielco.com Abroclamp – Abrotube – G103 – G4 – System 2000*

Gabriel Chemie UK Ltd Transfesa Road Paddock Wood, Tonbridge TN12 6UT Tel. *01892 836566* Fax. *01892 836979* E-mail. *info@gabriel-chemie.com* Web. *www.gabriel-chemie.com Maxithen – Unimax*

Gabriel Contractors Ltd 15 Edison Road Brimsdown Industrial Estate, Enfield EN3 7BY Tel. *020 83444300* Fax. *020 83444343* E-mail. *volkerhighwayscallcentre@volkerhighways.co.uk* Web. *www.volkerhighways.co.uk/bin/ibp.jsp?ibpPage=S3_HomePage Gabriel Contractors*

G A Fixings Ltd Cannon Way Claycliffe Business Park Claycliffe Road, Barugh Green, Barnsley S75 1JU Tel. *01226 380779* Fax. *01226 385558* E-mail. *info@gafixings.com* Web. *www.gafixings.com Windposts*

Gaggenau UK Ltd Grand Union House Old Wolverton Road, Wolverton, Milton Keynes MK12 5PT Tel. *01908 328360* Fax. *01908 328370* E-mail. *info@gaggenau.com* Web. *www.gaggenau.com *Gaggenau (Germany)*

Gailarde Ltd 9 Mill Hill Industrial Estate Flower Lane, London NW7 2HU Tel. *020 87311313* Fax. *020 87311300* E-mail. *office@gailarde.com* Web. *www.gailarde.com Taftex*

Gainsborough Ltd Canal Road, Trowbridge BA14 8RQ Tel. *01225 779132* Fax. *01225 779129* E-mail. *sales@gainsborough-beds.co.uk* Web. *www.gainsborough-beds.co.uk Gainsborough*

Gainsborough Silk Weaving Co. Ltd Gainsborough Silk Ltd Alexandra Road, Sudbury CO10 2XH Tel. *01787 372081* Fax. *01787 881785* E-mail. *sales@gainsborough.co.uk* Web. *www.gainsborough.co.uk Gainsborough*

Galloway Eggs Ltd Kempleton Mill Twynholm, Kirkcudbright DG6 4NJ Tel. *01557 860268* Fax. *01557 860257* E-mail. *info@gallowayglassfibremoulds.co.uk* Web. *www.gallowayglassfibremoulds.co.uk GGF*

Gall Thomson Environmental Ltd Pommers Lane, Great Yarmouth NR30 3PE Tel. *01493 857936* Fax. *01493 850888* E-mail. *mail@gall-thomson.co.uk* Web. *www.gall-thomson.co.uk Camlock Couplings – Gall Thomson - Marine Breakaway Couplings, Camlock Couplings; Klaw Breakaway Couplings, Flip-flap Breakaway Couplings. – Gall Thomson Marine Breakaway Couplings – Welin*

Galpeg Ltd 70 Hampden Road, London N10 2NX Tel. *020 84444455* Fax. *020 84420357* E-mail. *info@galpeg.com* Web. *www.galpeg.com *Bagda (United Kingdom) – *BPMA (United Kingdom) – *P.S.I (Germany)*

James Galt & Co. Ltd Sovereign House Stockport Road, Cheadle SK8 2EA Tel. *0161 4289111* Fax. *0161 4286597* E-mail. *j.bolton@jamesgalt.com* Web. *www.galttoys.com Galt*

Galvoptics Optical Goods Harvey Road, Basildon SS13 1ES Tel. *01268 728077* Fax. *01268 590445* E-mail. *info@galvoptics.fsnet.co.uk* Web. *www.galvoptics.fsnet.co.uk Hoya Filters – Kodak Filters – Kopp Filters – Schott Filters – Schott Filters - Kopp Filters - Kodak Filters - Wratten Filters - Hoya Filters. – Wratten Filters*

Games Workshop Ltd Warhammer World Willow Road, Nottingham NG7 2WS Tel. *0115 9168410* Fax. *0115 9168008* E-mail. *orders@games-workshop.co.uk* Web. *www.games-workshop.com Armageddon – Blood Bowl – Chivalry – Citadel – Codex – Dark Angels – Dark Future – Deathwing – Dungeonquest – Eavy Metal – Eldar – Epic – Flame – Forgeworld – G.W. – Games Workshop – Genestealer – Marauder – Necrons – Space Hulk – Space Marine – Spacefleet – Talisman – Tyranid – Warhammer – Warmaster – White Dwarf*

Gamet Bearings Hythe Station Road, Colchester CO2 8LD Tel. *01206 862121* Fax. *01206 868690* E-mail. *sales@gamet-bearings.co.uk* Web. *www.gamet-bearings.com Gamet*

Gamma Beta Holdings Ltd Briggella Mills, Bradford BD5 0QA Tel. *01274 525508* Fax. *01274 521157* E-mail. *furnishing@hield.co.uk* Web. *www.hield.co.uk *Hield (Europe)*

The Gammidge Kettering Parkway Kettering Venture Park, Kettering NN15 6EZ Tel. *01536 415222* Fax. *01536 532970* E-mail. *mail@gammidge.co.uk* Web. *www.wranglerfootwear.co.uk Beechwood – Kingsway*

Gandlake Computer Services Ltd Gandlake House London Road, Newbury RG14 1LA Tel. *01635 34547* E-mail. *john.gandley@gandlake.com* Web. *www.gandlake.com Gandlake Computer Services*

Gang-Nail Christy Estate Ivy Road, Aldershot GU12 4XG Tel. *01252 334691* Fax. *01252 334562* E-mail. *info@gangnail.co.uk* Web. *www.gangnail.co.uk EcoJoist – Gang Nail – Gang-Nail Systems Limited – GN Roof – GN Truss – M@trix/Matrix*

G A P Group Ltd Carrick House 40 Carrick Street, Glasgow G2 8DA Tel. *0141 2254600* Fax. *0141 2432540* E-mail. *info@gap-group.co.uk* Web. *www.gap-group.co.uk Gap Group*

Garbuiodickinson Moorside Road, Winchester SO23 7SS Tel. *01962 842222* Fax. *01962 840567* E-mail. *sales@garbuiodickinson.eu* Web. *www.garbuiodickinson.eu Admoist – DCC – ITM Dryers – STS – Weycon*

The Garden Buildings Centre Sheffield Road, Chesterfield S41 7LX Tel. *01246 220301* Fax. *08707 460204* E-mail. *nicp@thediyconservatorycentre.co.uk* Web. *www.greenhousesupply.co.uk lidget garages, lidget concrete*

Gardencast Estate House 143 Connaught Avenue, Frinton On Sea CO13 9AB Tel. *01255 679600* Fax. *01255 679825* E-mail. *enquiries@gardencast.co.uk* Web. *www.gardencast.co.uk *Elegant (Philippines) – Fiberstran – Gardencast – Jardine*

Garden Retreat Ltd 14 Poole Road, Wimborne BH21 1QG Tel. *01202 885663* Fax. *01202 881933* E-mail. *jim.parker@garden-retreat.co.uk* Web. *www.garden-retreat.co.uk Forest*

Gardiner Bros & Co. Unit F-G Quedgeley West Business Park Bristol Road, Hardwicke, Gloucester GL2 4PH Tel. *01452 727300* Fax. *01452 307220* E-mail. *sales@gardinerbros.co.uk* Web. *www.gardinerbros.co.uk Cotswold Golf – Footsure Western – Group Five*

Gardiner Of Selkirk Ltd Riverside Mills Dunsdalehaugh, Selkirk TD7 5EF Tel. *01750 20283* Fax. *01750 22525* E-mail. *sales@gardiner.yarns.co.uk Gardiner of Selkirk*

Gardman Ltd High Street Moulton, Spalding PE12 6QD Tel. *01406 372222* Fax. *01406 372233* E-mail. *sales@gardman.co.uk* Web. *www.gardman.co.uk Gardman*

Gardner Denver Ltd Unit 1 Waterbrook Estate, Alton GU34 2UD Tel. *01420 567424* Fax. *01420 544183* E-mail. *info.alton@gardnerdenver.com* Web. *www.gd-alton.co.uk *Werie*

Gardner Denver Ltd Claybrook Drive Washford Industrial Estate, Redditch B98 0DS Tel. *01527 525522* Fax. *01457 838630* E-mail. *sales@compair.com* Web. *www.gardnerdenver.com Hamworthy Belliss and Morcom*

Gardner Denver Nash UK Road One Winsford Industrial Estate, Winsford CW7 3PL Tel. *01606 542400* Fax. *01606 542434* E-mail. *sales@nashpumps.co.uk* Web. *www.gdnash.com Nash Hytor (U.S.A.) – Nash Kinema – nash_elmo (Germany)*

Gardner & Newton Ltd Queens Mill Road Lockwood, Huddersfield HD1 3PG Tel. *01484 517010* Fax. *01484 517050* E-mail. *sales@n-gn.co.uk* Web. *www.glassbending.co.uk Eden Mirror – Glass Bends – Newdome*

Gareth Pugh Steel Framed Buildings Agrimont Depot Station Yard, Abermule, Montgomery SY15 6NH Tel. *01686 630500* Fax. *01686 630441* E-mail. *enquiry@garethpugh.co.uk* Web. *www.garethpugh.co.uk Gareth Pugh Steel Framed Buildings – G M Profiles & Supplies*

Gargsales (UK) Ltd Garg Inox Ltd. 30 DENTON GROVE, Walton On Thames KT12 3HE Tel. *01932 240086* Fax. *01932 254424* E-mail. *j.juneja@gargwire.com* Web. *www.gargwire.com Garg Wire*

Garran Lockers Ltd Garran House Nantgarw Road, Caerphilly CF83 1AQ Tel. *08456 588600* Fax. *08456 588601* E-mail. *info@garran-lockers.co.uk* Web. *www.garran-lockers.co.uk Garran (United Kingdom)*

James Garside & Son Ltd Grantham Works Grantham Road, Halifax HX3 6PL Tel. *01422 347212* Fax. *01422 349465* E-mail. *jamesgarsideltd@hotmail.com* Web. *www.jamesgarsideltd.com Garside*

Mike Garwood Ltd Shelleys Barn Shelleys Lane, East Worldham, Alton GU34 3AQ Tel. *01420 84458* Fax. *01420 88594* E-mail. *m.garwood@mikegarwoodltd.co.uk* Web. *www.mikegarwoodltd.co.uk Bomford – Castel Mowers – Kawasaki – Knight – Kuha – Laverda – McCormick – Stihl*

Gast Group Ltd (incorporating Jun-Air UK Ltd & Gast Manufacturing) Unit 11 The I O Centre Nash Road, Redditch B98 7AS Tel. *01527 504040* Fax. *01527 525262* E-mail. *alee@idexcorp.com* Web. *www.gastmfg.com JUN-AIR*

Gateacre Press Ltd 260 Picton Road Wavertree, Liverpool L15 4LP Tel. *0151 7343038* Fax. *0151 7342860* E-mail. *info@onthebell.co.uk* Web. *www.inattendance.co.uk In Attendance – On the Bell*

Gate Machinery International Ltd Unit B Penfold Works Imperial Way, Watford WD24 4YY Tel. *01923 211000* Fax. *01923 682875* E-mail. *sales@gatemachinery.com* Web. *www.gatemachinery.com Eclipse – Gate Ayce – Gate Delta – Gate Elliot – Gate Giewont – Gate Milko – Gate Nodo – Gate Profitdrill – Gate Profitmill – Gate Proth – Gate Rigidturn – Gate Sovereign – Gate Stefor – Gate Sturditurn – Gate Unimill – Gate Urpe – Genius – IPO – Progress – Tesl – Victoria-Milford Grinders – Victoria-Velox Hacksaw*

Gates Hydraulics Ltd Alpha Drive Eaton Socon, St Neots PE19 8JJ Tel. *01480 402300* Fax. *01480 402350* Web. *www.gates.com Lock On Plus – Megaflex – Megaspiral Hose – Megatuff – Megavac – Powerwash – Tuffcoat – Xtratuff*

GATIC Poulton Close, Dover CT17 0UF Tel. *01304 203545* Fax. *01304 215001* E-mail. *p.burnap@gatic.com* Web. *www.gatic.com Elkington – Elkington Coex – Elkington*

Cubic – Elkington-Gatic – Gatic 2000 – Gatic Hydralift – Gatic Slotdrain

Gawler Tapes & Plastics Ltd Unit 7 Easter Court Woodward Avenue, Yate, Bristol BS37 5YS Tel. *01454 324265* Fax. *01454 315158* E-mail. *phil@gawlertapes.co.uk* Web. *www.gawlertapes.co.uk Lohmann – Nitto – Scapa – Stera-Tape – Tesa – Velcro*

Gaylee Ltd (t/a Brooks Fork Lift Service) Pope Street, Smethwick B66 2JP Tel. *0121 5582027* Fax. *0121 5582029 Brookes Forklift Service*

Gazette Media Company Borough Road, Middlesbrough TS1 3AZ Tel. *01642 245401* Fax. *01642 254915* E-mail. *news@gazettemedia.co.uk* Web. *www.gazettelive.co.uk Evening Gazette – South Durham Herald & Post – Stokesley Town Crier – Teesside Herald & Post*

GB Beverages 3 Drake Avenue, Slough SL3 7JR Tel. *08706 094652* Fax. *01753 584545* Web. *www.gbbeverages.co.uk Rhino*

GB Fuels Ltd Albany Road, Gateshead NE8 3BP Tel. *0191 4904311* Fax. *0191 4779544* Web. *www.gb-lubricants-fuels.co.uk G & B Fuels*

GB Kent & Sons plc London Road, Hemel Hempstead HP3 9SA Tel. *01442 251531* Fax. *01442 231672* E-mail. *info@kentbrushes.com* Web. *www.kentbrushes.com Kent – Kent GB*

G B R Technology Ltd 6 Jupiter House Calleva Park, Aldermaston, Reading RG7 8NN Tel. *0118 9820567* Fax. *0118 9820590* E-mail. *info@gbrtech.co.uk* Web. *www.gbrtech.co.uk Dupont – Krytox – P F P E*

G C Supplies UK Ltd 13-15a Reliance Trading Estate Reliance Street, Manchester M40 3ET Tel. *0161 6818114* Fax. *0161 9470148* E-mail. *gcsuppliesukats@googlemail.com* Web. *www.stainlessvalves.co.uk G.C. Supplies*

G D C Microscopes 1 Weald Way, Reigate RH2 7RG Tel. *01737 240099* E-mail. *cliff@gdcmicroscopes.com* Web. *www.gdcmicroscopes.com Motic – Moticam – Photonic*

G D Rectifiers Ltd Victoria Gardens, Burgess Hill RH15 9NB Tel. *01444 243452* Fax. *01444 870722* E-mail. *enquiries@gdrectifiers.co.uk* Web. *www.gdrectifiers.co.uk Bi-Sonic – Cooper Bussman – Edi – Ferraz Shawmut – Ixys – Semikron – Sirio – Telcon – Westcode*

G & E Automatic Equipment Ltd North Bridge Road, Berkhamsted HP4 1GE Tel. *01442 872323* Fax. *01442 866900* E-mail. *sales@geautomatic.co.uk* Web. *www.geautomatic.co.uk Peko*

G E Baker UK Ltd (t/a Quality Equipment) The Heath Woolpit, Bury St Edmunds IP30 9RN Tel. *01359 240529* Fax. *01359 242086* E-mail. *baker@quality-equipment.co.uk* Web. *www.quality-equipment.co.uk Quality Equipment*

Geemarc Telecom S A 5 Swallow Court, Welwyn Garden City AL7 1SB Tel. *01707 372372* Fax. *01707 372529* E-mail. *sales@geemarc.com* Web. *www.geemarc.com *Ansamac (Far East) – *Dialatron (Far East) – *Geemarc (Far East) – Geemarc Clear Sound – Geemarc Safety Line*

Geerings Of Ashford Ltd Cobbs Wood House Chart Road, Ashford TN23 1EP Tel. *01233 633366* Fax. *01233 663357* E-mail. *info@geerings.co.uk* Web. *www.geerings.co.uk 24Seven-Nero – 24Seven-Spa – *Bouquet Collection – *Caledonian Collection – *Celtic Collection – Croeso – *Ebony Collection – Verdi Collection*

Geesink Norba Ltd Llantrisant Business Park Llantrisant, Pontyclun CF72 8XZ Tel. *01443 222301* Fax. *01443 237192* E-mail. *geoff.rigg@geesinknorba.com* Web. *www.geesinknorbagroup.com Geesink Norba – Kieggen*

Phil Geesin Machinery Ltd 101 Carlisle Street East, Sheffield S4 7QN Tel. *0114 2797619* Fax. *0114 2797620* E-mail. *phil@philgeesinmachinery.co.uk* Web. *www.philgeesinmachinery.co.uk Colchester Student 1800 lathes – Colchester master lathes – Colchester mascot lathes – Colchester mastiff lathes – Colchester magnum lathes – Colchester lathes – Colchester lathes spares – Dean Smith and grace lathes – DSG lathes – Dean Smith & Grace type 13, 1307, 1609, 1709, 2112, 25, 30 – Harrison m250 lathes – Harrison m300 lathes – Harrison m400 lathes – Harrison m500 lathes – Harrison V 350 lathes – Harrison V 390 lathes – Harrison V460 lathes – Harrison V550 lathes – Mostana 165 lathes – Mostana 1m63 centre lathes – Mostana heavy duty lathes – Stanko lathes – Russia Heavy lathes – Crawford Swift lathes – Churchill lathes – Churchill Denham lathes – Denham lathes – XYZ lathes – Model Makers lathe – Binns and Berry lathes – Binns and Berry trident lathes – Gildemeister CNC lathes – Kitchen & Walker radial arm drills – Kitchen & Wade Radial arm Drills – Kitchen & Walker Pillar Drills – Richmond Envoy drilling machines – Qualter & Smith Drilling machines – KRV Turret Mills – KRV 2000 Turret Mills – KRV 3000 Turret Mills – KRV 4000 bed Mills – Huron Milling Machine – Huron MU6 – Huron Mu4 – Huron Nu4 – Webster and Bennett DH type vertical boring machines – Webster and Bennett M type vertical boring machines – Webster and Bennett V type vertical boring machines – Webster and Bennett EV vertical boring machines – Webster and Bennett elevating rail vertical boring machines – Webster and Bennett vertical lathes – Butler Newall boring machines – Kearns Richard boring machines – Jones and Shipman 540 grinder – Jones and Shipman 1400 grinder – Jones and Shipman 1011 grinder – Jones and Shipman 1415 grinder – Jones and Shipman 1300 grinder – Jones and Shipman 1302 grinder – Jones and Shipman 1305 grinder – Jones and Shipman 1307 grinder – Jones and Shipman 1314 grinder – Jones and Shipman 310 tool and cutter – Jones and Shipman 1310 grinder – Jones and Shipman rise & fall grinders – Snow ring Grinders – Snow RT Ring grinder – Snow Danobat Grinder – Snow OS horizontal Grinders – Snow vertical spindle grinders – Kingsland machines – Pearson machines – Addison machines – Kingsland iron workers*

William Gee Ltd William Gee House 520 522 Kingsland Road, London E8 4AH Tel. *020 72542451* Fax. *020 72498116* E-mail. *wmgeetrims@aol.com* Web. *www.williamgee.co.uk Atlas – Coats – Danubia – Donisthorpe – Geepol – *N.B.T. (U.S.A.) – Trowel – Trowelette – Velcro – Wilkinsons – YKK*

Gefran UK 7 Pearson Road Central Park, Telford TF2 9TX Tel. *01952 291361* Fax. *08452 604556* E-mail. *mark@gefran.co.uk* Web. *www.gefran.co.uk CRL Control & Readout*

G E Healthcare Amersham Place, Amersham HP7 9NA Tel. *01494 544000* Fax. *01494 542266* Web. *www.amersham.com Abdoscan – Accupaque – Acoustitag – Acupaque – Amerscan – Amersham – Amersham & Flying A – Amertec – Amipaque – Bariotrast – Bilopaque – Ce Gold – Ceretec – Clariscan – Datscan – Diapaque – Dicopac – Diodrast – Drygen – Ecudex – Ecuscan – Exypaque – Exytrast – Feroxascan – Flexipak – Frixipaque – Giazoid – Hiflo – Hypaque – I-125 Rapid Strund – I-125 Seeds – I.O.C.M. – Image – Imagopaque – Incite – Indiclor – Indomab – Isipaque – Isopaque – Ivepaque – Jecudex – Jesuscan – Lumopaque – Magnapaque – Medi+Physics – Metastron – Mpoptions – Myoview – Neoscan – Nephroflow – Omnigraf – Omnipaque – Omniscan – Omnitone – Omnitrast – Oncopro – Oncoseed – Optipaque – Orascan – Oxascan – Perfuscan – Physiopaque – Prognox – Rapid Strand – Rapidat – Retropaque – Rheopaque – Roxascan – Safepak Device – Scintadren – Scintimab – Sefa – Sehcat – Slogan – Sonazoid – Sproscan – Tagytt-90 – Technemab – Telepaque – Teslapaque – Teslascan – Theracap – Tyropaque – Vesipaque – Viaseed – Visipaque – Visiplant – Visopaque – Vivoseed – Winopaque – Winpac – Zonoson*

G E I Electronic Industries Ltd Linley Lodge Works Westgate, Aldridge, Walsall WS9 8EX Tel. *01922 458020* Fax. *01922 452608* E-mail. *adrian@gei-elec.com* Web. *www.gei-elec.com G.E.I.*

Kurt Geiger Ltd 75 Bermondsey Street, London SE1 3XF Tel. *020 75461888* Fax. *020 75461880* E-mail. *info@kurtgeiger.com* Web. *www.kurtgeiger.com *Adesso (Italy and UK) – *Carvela (Italy and UK) – *Kurt Geiger (Italy and UK)*

Gelpack Excelsior Ltd Westfields Trading Estate, Hereford HR4 9NT Tel. *01432 267391* Fax. *01432 264809* E-mail. *info@gelpack.co.uk* Web. *www.gelpack.co.uk Excelthene*

Gemelli Childcare Vouchers Ltd Gemelli House Shalstone, Buckingham MK18 5DZ Tel. *01280 851113* E-mail. *enquiries@gemelliccv.co.uk* Web. *www.gemellichildcarevouchers.co.uk GEMELLI CHILDCARE VOUCHERS*

Gemini Dispersions Ltd Holt Mill Road, Rossendale BB4 7JB Tel. *01706 214751* Fax. *01706 218152* E-mail. *p.gabriel@geminidispersions.com* Web. *www.geminidispersions.com H-D-Sperse*

The Gemmological Association Of Great Britain 27 Greville Street, London EC1N 8TN Tel. *020 74043334* Fax. *020 74048843* E-mail. *info@gem-a.com* Web. *www.gem-a.com Chelsea – *Dendritics (U.S.A.) – Diamond Tester – Gemmological Text Books – Refractometer Fluid 1.79 – Student Stone Specimens*

Gem Tool Hire & Sales Ltd England House Beaumont Road, Banbury OX16 1TF Tel. *01295 252288* Fax. *01295 272052* E-mail. *office@gemtools.co.uk* Web. *www.gem-tools.co.uk Abus – AEG – Arrow – Bahco – Black & Decker – Bosch – Bostik – Bostitch – Brennenstuhl – Britool – Bulldog – Calor – Cannon – Concept – Defiance – Delonghi – Dewalt – Disston – Draper – Duracell – Dynamik – Earlex – Einhell – Electro – Eski – Estwing – Everbuild – Faithfull – Fakeham – Fisco – Fisher – Footprint – Gorilla – Hanson – Hilka – Hilti – Hitachi – Holts – India – Irwin – Jack – Karcher – Kestrel – Ledco – Lighthouse – Loctite – Maglite – Makita – Marples – Marshaltown – Masterplug – Matabi – Miller – Milwaukee – Monument – Neill – Nobex – Norbar – Olympic – Paslode – PDP – Plano – Power Master – Raghi – Rapesco – Rawlplug – Rehau – Rothenberger – Roxon – Rustins – Ryobi – Silverline – SIP – SMJ – Spear & Jackson – Stabila – Stanley – Sykes-Pikavant – Tanaka – Titan – Trend – Triton – Unibond – Urko – Visegrip – Vitrex – WD-40 – Weldability – Wiss – Wolfcraft*

General Catering Supplies Ltd Tuborg House Mandrell Rd, London SW2 5DL Tel. *020 77337590* Fax. *020 77379201* E-mail. *info@gcsgroup.co.uk* Web. *www.gcsgroup.co.uk *Youngs Talbot*

General Fabrications Ltd 26 Orphanage Road, Birmingham B24 9HT Tel. *0121 3776070* Fax. *0121 3777175* E-mail. *info@genfab.co.uk* Web. *www.genfab.co.uk 3M – Clipper – Nitto – Tesa – Vibac*

General Hoseclips Ltd Royston Road Byfleet, West Byfleet KT14 7NY Tel. *01932 343515* Fax. *01932 351285* E-mail. *info@generalhoseclips.com Gemi*

General Kinematics Ltd Dawley House Dawley Brook Road, Kingswinford DY6 7BB Tel. *01384 273303* Fax. *01384 273404* E-mail. *mail@generalkinematics.com* Web. *www.generalkinematics.com General Kinematics Ltd (United Kingdom)*

The General Packaging Company Ltd Unit 3 Cooksland Indl-Est, Bodmin PL31 2QB Tel. *01208 265870* Fax. *01208 72457* E-mail. *enquiries@generalpackaging.co.uk* Web. *www.generalpackaging.co.uk General Packaging*

General Vacuum Equipment Ltd Pennine Business Park Pilsworth Rd, Heywood OL10 2TL Tel. *01706 622442* Fax. *01706 622772* E-mail. *sales.general@bobst.com* Web. *www.bobst.com K5000 – K4000 – K3000 – Holosec – EHF – Optilab – Opticoat – PECVD*

Generator Associates Ltd Glendale House Lime Tree Drive, Harlow Wood, Mansfield NG18 4UZ Tel. *01623 624005* Fax. *01623 635595* E-mail. *sales@generatorassociates.com* Web. *www.generatorassociates.com SDMO*

Genesis Risk Solutions Ltd 2nd Floor Suite The Maltings Locks Hill, Rochford SS4 1BB Tel. *01702 209520* Fax. *01702 543728* E-mail. *p.gibson@grslimited.co.uk* Web. *www.grslimited.co.uk Contractors Insurance Services – Demolition Insurance Services – Scaffolding & Roofing Insurance Services*

Genesis V Systems Ltd 14 Hawthorne Grove Poynton, Stockport SK12 1TR Tel. *01625 879938* E-mail. *sm@genesisv.com* Web. *www.genesisv.com Genesis*

Genevac Ltd 6 Farthing Road, Ipswich IP1 5AP Tel. *01473 240000* Fax. *01473 461176* E-mail. *info@genevac.com* Web. *www.genevac.com Genevac*

Genlab Ltd Tanhouse Lane, Widnes WA8 0SR Tel. *0151 4245001* Fax. *0151 4952197* E-mail. *enquiries@genlab.co.uk* Web. *www.genlab.co.uk Genlab*

Genpower Ltd Unit 1 Dowty Park Thornton Road, Milford Haven SA73 2RS Tel. *08450 942452* Fax. *0845 0942453* E-mail. *sales@genpoweruk.com* Web. *www.genpoweruk.co.uk Evopower*

Gentech International Ltd 10 Grangestone Industrial Estate Ladywell Avenue, Girvan KA26 9PS Tel. *01465 713581* Fax. *01465 714974* E-mail. *sales@gentechsensors.com* Web. *www.gentechsensors.com Gentech (United Kingdom)*

Genus Group The Microfilm Shop 15 Hammond Close, Nuneaton CV11 6RY Tel. *024 76254955* Fax. *024 76382319* E-mail. *info@genusit.com* Web. *www.genusit.com Archive Imaging – Genneg – Avision – Book2net – SMA – Fujitsu – Ozaphan – Crowley – Genus – JRK Imagingraphics – Hyperware – Real – InoTec – Real, JRK Imagingraphics, Archive Imaging, Genneg, OIT, Genus.*

Genwork Ltd Bromley Street, Stourbridge DY9 8HU Tel. *01384 636588* Fax. *01384 410306* E-mail. *robert@bache-pallets.co.uk* Web. *www.firstmesh.co.uk Expamet – Weldmesh*

Geographers A Z Map Co. Ltd 197 Fairfield Road Borough Green, Sevenoaks TN15 8PP Tel. *01732 781000* Fax. *01732 780677* E-mail. *tradesales@a-zmaps.co.uk* Web. *www.a-zmaps.co.uk A-Z*

Geomatix Ltd Inglenook Cottage Westoby Lane, Barrow Upon Humber DN19 7DJ Tel. *01469 532481* E-mail. *set@geomatix.net* Web. *www.geomatix.net DatumPro – GeoTide – XYit*

Geomem Ltd 1 Ralston Business Centre Newtyle, Blairgowrie PH12 8TL Tel. *01828 650618* Fax. *0845 6446290* E-mail. *james@geomem.co.uk* Web. *www.geomem.co.uk GeoMEM Consultants (United Kingdom)*

Geoplan Spatial Intelligence Ltd Bilton Court Wetherby Road, Harrogate HG3 1GP Tel. *01423 569538* Fax. *01423 819494* E-mail. *sales@geoplan.com* Web. *www.geoplan.com Yellow Marketing Information*

Geoquip Ltd Little Eaton, Derby DE21 5DR Tel. *01629 824891* Fax. *01629 824896* E-mail. *info@geoquip.com* Web. *www.geoquip.com CentrAlert – Defensor – Guardwire – Impactor – Psicon – Rafid*

George Barkers (A Member Of The Epta Group) Highfield Road Highfield Works, Idle, Bradford BD10 8RF Tel. *01274 703200* Fax. *01274 615916* E-mail. *info@georgebarker.co.uk* Web. *www.georgebarker.co.uk Industrial refrigeration distributors – Series 2000 and Series 3000*

George Broughton & Co. Ltd Whitebirk Road, Blackburn BB1 3HZ Tel. *01254 53644* Fax. *01254 690598* E-mail. *sales@geo-broughton.co.uk* Web. *www.geo-broughton.co.uk Gebrol*

George Emmott Pawsons Ltd Wadsworth Mill Oxenhope, Keighley BD22 9NE Tel. *01535 643733* Fax. *01535 642108* E-mail. *mail@emmottsprings.co.uk* Web. *www.emmottsprings.co.uk Emo*

John George & Sons Ltd 2-4 Deacon Way Tilehurst, Reading RG30 6AZ Tel. *0118 9411234* Fax. *0118 9451059*

E-mail. *reading@johngeorge.co.uk*
Web. *www.johngeorge.co.uk John George*

George Kingsbury Ltd Quay Lane Hardway, Gosport PO12 4LB Tel. *023 92580371* Fax. *023 92501741* E-mail. *richard.kingsbury@gkholdings.com* Web. *www.gkholdings.com Geo. Kingsbury Machine Tools Ltd*

Georgia Pacific GB Ltd Stadium House 2 Eastgate Approach, Horwich, Bolton BL6 6SY Tel. *01204 673300* Fax. *01204 673301* E-mail. *lorraine.payne@gapac.com* Web. *www.gp.com Bonus – Dandy – Go-Wipe – Mardi Gras – Nouvelle – Options – Preference – Softone – Ultimate*

Geo Robson & Co Conveyors Ltd Coleford Road, Sheffield S9 5PA Tel. *0114 2444221* Fax. *0114 2433066* E-mail. *info@robson.co.uk* Web. *www.robson.co.uk Airglide – Cleanflo – Romag – Romag - magnetic conveyors; Cleanflo - enclosed belt conveyor, Airglide - enclosed, air supported belt conveyor.*

Geoscience Ltd Unit 2 Falmouth Business Park Bickland Water Road, Falmouth TR11 4SZ Tel. *01326 211070* Fax. *01326 212754* E-mail. *batchelor@geoscience.co.uk* Web. *www.geoscience.co.uk Earth Energy – GeoScience*

Geosynthetic Technology Ltd Nags Corner Wiston Road, Nayland, Colchester CO6 4LT Tel. *01206 262676* Fax. *01206 262998* E-mail. *sales@geosynthetic.co.uk* Web. *www.geosynthetic.co.uk Excelastic – Exceliner – *Somdrain – *Somtube*

Gerflor Ltd Wedgnock House Wedgnock Lane, Warwick CV34 5AP Tel. *01926 622600* Fax. *01926 401647* E-mail. *pbuchon@gerflor.com* Web. *www.gerflor.co.uk Ambiance – Architection – Classic Imperial – Creation – Elegance – Evolution – G.T.I. – Millennium – Nera – Plaza – Robust EL7 – Saga – Taraflex Sport – Taralay Confort – Tarasafe – Technic ELS*

Gericke Ltd Victoria House Cavendish Street, Ashton Under Lyne OL6 7DJ Tel. *0161 3441140* Fax. *0161 3083403* E-mail. *info@gericke.net* Web. *www.gericke.net Microfeeder – Minisender – Multiflux mixer – Nibbler – P.S.F. – PULS-TAKT – Pulse-flow – R.A.-Discharger – Sifter*

Germains Seed Technology Hansa Road, Kings Lynn PE30 4LG Tel. *01553 774012* Fax. *01553 773145* E-mail. *info@germains.com* Web. *www.germains.com Germain's*

G E Sensing Fir Tree Lane Groby, Leicester LE6 0FH Tel. *0116 2317100* Fax. *0116 2317101* E-mail. *tim.povall@ge.com* Web. *www.geinfrastructure.com Druck*

Gesipa Blind Riveting Systems Ltd Dalton Lane, Keighley BD21 4JU Tel. *01535 212200* Fax. *01535 212232* E-mail. *n.anand@gesipa.co.uk* Web. *www.gesipa.co.uk AccuBird – Bulb-Tite – FireBird – Firefly – FireFox – GAV 8000 – GBM – G-Bulb – Gesipa – Mega-Grip – PolyGrip – PowerBird – PowerBird-Solar – SolarGrip – Taurex – Taurus – Tri-Fold*

G E T Key Point 3-17 High Street, Potters Bar EN6 5AJ Tel. *01707 601601* Fax. *01707 601708* E-mail. *sales@getplc.com* Web. *www.getplc.com G.E.T.*

Getaway Executive Travel Ltd 192-198 Vauxhall Bridge Road, London SW1 1DX Tel. *0845 1807820* Fax. *020 79730014* E-mail. *travel@getaway.co.uk Getaway Executive Travel*

Geti Ltd 44 Hockley Street, Birmingham B18 6BH Tel. *0121 5070994* Fax. *0121 5236849* E-mail. *getiuk@aol.com* Web. *www.gegi.cc GETi*

G F Smith Lockwood Street, Hull HU2 0HL Tel. *01482 323503* Fax. *01482 223174* E-mail. *info@gfsmith.com* Web. *www.gfsmith.com Beckett Expression – *Beckett Paper (U.S.A.) – Beckett Ridge – Brilliant – Cambric – Color Plan – Duo Plan – Fiesta – Foxriver Paper – Gainsborough – Grandee – Marlmarque – Marltone – New England – Parch Marque – Pastelle – Phase 2 – *Rising Paper (U.S.A.) – Simpson – *Simpson Paper (U.S.A.) – Smith – Strathmore – Strathmore Element – Strathmore Papers – Strathmore Renewal – Strathmore Writing – Teton – Trans-Marque – Transclear – Writing 90 G.S.N. – Writing Text Cover*

GGB UK Wellington House Starley Way, Birmingham International Park, Birmingham B37 7HB Tel. *0121 7679100* Fax. *0121 7817313* E-mail. *greatbritain@ggbearings.com* Web. *www.ggbearings.com DU – DU B – DP4 – DP10 – DP11 – DP31 – DX – DX 10 with DuraStrong technology – HI-EX – DS – SY – SP – EP – EP12 – EP22 – EP43 – EP44 – EP63 – EP64 – EP73 – EP79 – GLACETAL KA – MULTILUBE – MULTIFIL – DB – GAR-MAX – HSG – DX-B – DP4-B – GAR-FIL – GAR-FIL – MLG – HPF – HPM – MEGALIFE XT – SBC – MLG*

G & G Food Supplements Unit 2 Imberhorne Way, East Grinstead RH19 1RL Tel. *01342 311401* Fax. *01342 315938* E-mail. *sales@gandgvitamins.com* Web. *www.gandgvitamins.com G&G Vitamins.*

G & G Food Supplies Unit H Queens Walk, East Grinstead RH19 4DW Tel. *01342 322795* Fax. *01342 315938* Web. *www.gandgvitamins.com Cal-m – Fizz 'C' – G & G – Pro-Dophilus – Protein Plus – Supavits – Xtra Protection*

G H L Liftrucks Ltd Unit 10 Hewitts Industrial Estate, Elmbridge Road, Cranleigh GU6 8LW Tel. *01483 276101* Fax. *01483 277430* E-mail. *surrey@forktrucks.co.uk* Web. *www.forktrucks.co.uk *Puma (Taiwan)*

G H P Solicitors Greenland Houchen Pomeroy 36 - 40 Prince of Wales Road, Norwich NR1 1HZ Tel. *01603 660744* Fax. *01603 610700* E-mail. *james-knight@ghlaw.co.uk* Web. *www.greenlandhp-solicitors.co.uk Greenland Houchen*

G H Warner Footwear plc Mercury House Lea Road, Waltham Abbey EN9 1AT Tel. *01992 769612* Fax. *01992 701123* E-mail. *admin@mercuryhouse.com* Web. *www.mercurysports.co.uk *Mercury (Far East) – *Pullman (Far East and Europe)*

James Gibbons Format Ltd Unit 214-216 Telsen Industrial Centre 55 Thomas Street, Birmingham B6 4TN Tel. *0121 3335201* Fax. *0121 3599068* E-mail. *info@jgf.co.uk* Web. *www.jgf.co.uk Format*

Gibbs Sandtech Ltd (t/a Tregarne) Station Road Braughing, Ware SG11 2PB Tel. *01920 822404* Fax. *01920 822909* E-mail. *info@gibbsfinishing.com* Web. *www.gibbsfinishing.com Woodwelder*

Gibson Hanson Graphics Ltd 2nd Floor Amp House Dingwall Road, Croydon CR0 2LX Tel. *020 82601200* Fax. *020 82601212* E-mail. *clare.stead@gibsonhanson.co.uk Hanson White – Xpressions Card & Gift Co*

The G I Group 222 Farnborough Road, Farnborough GU14 7JT Tel. *01252 522299* Fax. *01252 375548* E-mail. *farnborough@right4staff.com* Web. *www.right4staff.com Job Spot*

Gilbert & Mellish Ltd 3 Lightning Way, Birmingham B31 3PH Tel. *0121 4751101* Fax. *0121 4780163* E-mail. *sales@gilbert-mellish.co.uk* Web. *www.gilbert-mellish.co.uk George Wright – Orthosport – Orthotrek – Orthowrap – Piedro*

Gilberts Blackpool Ltd Gilair Works Clifton Road, Blackpool FY4 4QT Tel. *01253 766911* Fax. *01253 767941* E-mail. *sales@gilbertsblackpool.com* Web. *www.gilbertsblackpool.com Airgard – Airjet – Ductgard – Fanjet – Firegard – Smokegard*

Gilberts Food Equipment Ltd Gilbert House 1 Warwick Place Warwick Road, Borehamwood WD6 1UA Tel. *020 87313700* Fax. *0845 2300682* E-mail. *sales@topgourmet.co.uk* Web. *www.gilberts-foodequipment.com *Gustav Emil Ern – Kisag – Nemco – Solicut – Swiss Diamond – Top Gourmet – Top Gourmet – Zassenhaus*

Gilbertson & Page Ltd 45-55 Brownfields, Welwyn Garden City AL7 1AN Tel. *01707 367900* Fax. *01707 339221* E-mail. *info@gilpa.co.uk* Web. *www.gilpa.co.uk Gilpa Pup – Junior – Kemmel – Nuggets – Pro-Active – Trinkets – Umami – Valu Mix*

Gilchrist & Soames Unit 1 John Wesley Road, Werrington, Peterborough PE4 6ZL Tel. *01733 384100* Fax. *01733 384101* E-mail. *sales@gilchristsoames.com* Web. *www.gilchristsoames.com Gilchrist & Soames – Potter & Moore*

Gillespie UK Ltd Silvertree Coxbridge Business Park, Farnham GU10 5EH Tel. *01252 747825* Fax. *0871 4298062* E-mail. *pamgarratt@gillespieuk.co.uk* Web. *www.gillespieuk.co.uk Zeroclad – Zerodec – Zerospan*

Gillett & Sibert Ltd Kirktonfield Road Neilston, Glasgow G78 3PL Tel. *0141 8815825* Fax. *0141 8815825* E-mail. *mail@elcomatic.co.uk* Web. *www.elcomatic.co.uk Series 10 – Series 20 – Tropical medicine microscope – XTD-4 – XTL-1*

Gillhams 47 Fleet Street, London EC4Y 1BJ Tel. *020 73532732* Fax. *020 73532733* E-mail. *solicitors@gillhams.com* Web. *www.gillhams.com Gillhams Intellectual Property Lawyers*

P S Gill & Sons 261-277 Rookery Road Handsworth, Birmingham B21 9PT Tel. *0121 5547521* Fax. *0121 5549033* E-mail. *sales@psgill.com* Web. *www.psg.com Electric Label – Laird of Kilkelly, The – Openair by Proudhart – Sky Divers*

Gills Cables Ltd 25 Apollo, Tamworth B79 7TA Tel. *01827 304777* Fax. *01827 314568* E-mail. *petergreensmith@gillscables.com* Web. *www.suprajit.com Gills Cables*

Gilmex International Ltd Unit 40 The I O Centre Armstrong Road, London SE18 6RS Tel. *020 83314130* Fax. *020 84630565* E-mail. *sales@gilmex.com* Web. *www.bindingbazaar.com Bindfast – Fast-Binda – G I Products – Gilmex – Interbook – Interlock – *Koloman Handler (Austria) – Neta Bar – *PAS (Netherlands) – *Planatol (Germany) – Regubinder – Regutapes*

Gina Shoes Ltd 104-106 Brantwood Droad, London N17 0XW Tel. *020 88857500* Fax. *020 72491984* E-mail. *sales@gina.com* Web. *www.gina.com Gina*

Giro Food Ltd Welcome House Glover Street, Birmingham B9 4EP Tel. *0121 7735811* Fax. *0121 2021555* E-mail. *javedsarwar@girofood.com* Web. *www.girofood.com *Winflo Brand*

Girovac Ltd 2 Douglas Bader Close, North Walsham NR28 0TZ Tel. *01692 403008* Fax. *01692 404611* E-mail. *enquiries@girovac.com* Web. *www.girovac.com Kinney (United Kingdom) – MIL'S (France)*

T Giusti Ltd Briggs House Derby Street, Burton On Trent DE14 2LH Tel. *01283 566661* Fax. *01933 272363* E-mail. *sales@tgiusti.briggsplc.co.uk* Web. *www.giusti.co.uk Cosmix – Flochill – G.I.I. Giustimix – G.I.I. Intermix – Giustimix – Impacton – Labomix – Pharmix – Ultimix – Universal – Yorkway*

G & J Greenall Distribution Point, Melbury Park Clayton Road, Birchwood, Warrington WA3 6PH Tel. *01925 286400* Fax. *01925 286485* E-mail. *internet@gjgreenall.com* Web. *www.gjgreenall.com G. & J. Greenall*

G K N Aerospace Ltd Airport Service Road, Portsmouth PO3 5PE Tel. *01983 283000* Fax. *023 92670899* E-mail. *neil.house@gknaerospace.com* Web. *www.gknaerospace.com A.P.F.C. – E.F.S. – Flamatrol – Hycadamp – Hycaflex – Hycalite – Hycalite – Hycatrol – Hycatrol HE-4 – Hycatrol HG. 334 – Hycatrol HP. 257 – Hyclad – Jerribags – Promel*

G K N Aerospace Transparancy Systems Ltd Eckersall Road, Birmingham B38 8SR Tel. *0121 6064100* Fax. *0121 4586880* Web. *www.gknplc.com Chemplex – Hyviz*

G K N Driveline Services Ltd 5 Kingsbury Business Park Kingsbury Road, Minworth, Sutton Coldfield B76 9DL Tel. *0121 3131661* Fax. *0121 3132074* E-mail. *sales@gkn.com* Web. *www.gkndriveline.co.uk ARB – GKN Motorsport – Lobro – Spidan – Uni-Cardan Service*

G K N Driveline Walsall 2, Walsall WS9 8DT Tel. *01922 453371* Fax. *01922 451716* E-mail. *ryan.callaghan@gkndriveline.com* Web. *www.gknplc.com G.K.N.*

GKN Sinter Metals Ltd P.O. Box 3 Trent Valley Road, Lichfield WS136HF Tel. *01543 403000* Fax. *01543 403001* E-mail. *info@gknsintermetals.co.uk* Web. *www.gknsintermetals.co.uk GKN Sinter Metals*

Glamair Supplies Ltd Lewis House Alexandra Docks, Newport NP20 2NP Tel. *01633 221300* Fax. *01633 221600* E-mail. *sales@glamair.co.uk* Web. *www.glamair.co.uk Hoerbiger Origa – Nvmatics – PCL*

Glamox Luxo Lighting Ltd Unit 1 Abbey Industrial Estate 24 Willow Lane, Mitcham CR4 4NA Tel. *020 86873370* Fax. *020 82743501* E-mail. *romana.berzolla@glamoxluxo.com* Web. *www.luxo.co.uk Broens*

Glasdon International Ltd Glasdon Inovation & Export Centre Preston New Road, Blackpool FY4 4UY Tel. *01253 600435* Fax. *01253 600436* E-mail. *sales@glasdon.com* Web. *www.glasdon.com Beaver Spaceliner – Brunel – Centuro – Clifton Bollard – Froggo – Integro – Jubilee Bollard – Litta Pikka – Mini Plaza – Neopolitan Bollard – Neopolitan Plaza – Novo – Retriever 55 – Topsy – Topsy 2000 – Topsy Jubilee*

Glasgow Prestwick Airport Parking Aviation House Glasgow Prestwick Intnl Airport, Prestwick KA9 2PL Tel. *08701 181844* Fax. *01292 511120* E-mail. *sales@upia.co.uk* Web. *www.glasgowprestwick.com Glasgow prestwick bond ltd – Sky travel*

Glasgow Steel Nail Co. Ltd Unit 3 Lancaster Road Bishopbriggs, Glasgow G64 2HX Tel. *0141 7623355* Fax. *0141 7620914* E-mail. *glasgowsteelnail@compuserve.com* Web. *www.glasgowsteelnail.com Blocnail Slimline Clasp – Clyde Rail Spike*

Glassman Europe Ltd 21 Campbell Court Campbell Rd, Bramley, Tadley RG26 5EG Tel. *01256 883007* Fax. *01256 883017* E-mail. *sales@glassmaneurope.co.uk* Web. *www.glassmaneurope.co.uk Caton – Ross Engineering*

Glastonbury Spring Water Co. Park Corner Farm Park Corner, Glastonbury BA6 8JY Tel. *01458 834344* Fax. *01458 833360* E-mail. *sales@glastonburyspringwater.com* Web. *www.glastonburyspringwater.com *Glastonbury Spring Water*

Glazing Vision Ltd 36 Wimbledon Avenue, Brandon IP27 0NZ Tel. *01842 815581* Fax. *01842 815515* E-mail. *david@glazing-vision.co.uk* Web. *www.glazing-vision.co.uk Bespoke Sliding Rooflights – Cosmos & Orion – Flushgaze – Jupiter – P2000 Pyramid – Skyglide – Visionvent*

Glazeparts UK Ltd Wildmere Road Daventry Road Industrial Estate, Banbury OX16 3JU Tel. *01295 264533* Fax. *01295 266699* E-mail. *mark.nelson@glazpart.co.uk* Web. *www.glazpart.co.uk Glazpart – Glazpart over Glaz*

G L Designs Ltd 5 Links View, Cirencester GL7 2NF Tel. *01285 650682* Fax. *01285 644891* E-mail. *graeme@gldesigns.co.uk* Web. *www.gldesigns.co.uk GL Designs Ltd*

Gleave & Co. 111-113 St John Street, London EC1V 4JA Tel. *020 72531345* Fax. *020 72530447* E-mail. *sales@gleaveandco.com* Web. *www.gleaveandco.com Gleave*

Glenair UK 40 Lower Oakham Way, Mansfield NG18 5BY Tel. *01623 638100* Fax. *01623 638111* E-mail. *enquiries@glenair.co.uk* Web. *www.glenair.co.uk D.M.C. – Glenair – Microway – Miles Roystone*

Glen Dimplex UK Ltd Millbrook House Grange Drive, Hedge End, Southampton SO30 2DF Tel. *08456 005111* Fax. *0870 7270109* E-mail. *enquiries@dimplex.co.uk* Web. *www.dimplex.co.uk Dimplex,Glen,Berry,Unidare,EWT,Electricaire – Dimplex, – Duo heat – Electricaire – EWT – Glen – Heatovent – OPTIFLAME – Unidare*

Glen Electric Ltd Greenbank Industrial Estate Rampart Road, Newry BT34 2QU Tel. *028 30264621* Fax. *028 30266122* E-mail. *neil.collins@glendimplex.com*

Web. *www.glendimplex.com Blanella – Burco – Dimplex – Glen – Morphy Richards – Prilect*
Glenfield Valves Ltd Glenfield Works Queens Drive, Kilmarnock KA1 3XF Tel. *01563 521150* Fax. *01563 541013* E-mail. *enquiries@glenfield.co.uk* Web. *www.glenfieldvalves.co.uk Ductile & Grey*
Glenmuir Ltd Delves Road, Lanark ML11 9DX Tel. *01555 662244* Fax. *01555 665734* E-mail. *customerservice@glenmuir.com* Web. *www.glenmuir.com Glenmuir*
Glen Office Supplies Ltd Unit 3 Faverdale Industrial Estate, Darlington DL3 0PP Tel. *01325 382020* Fax. *01325 380988* E-mail. *sales@glenoffice.co.uk* Web. *www.glenofficesupplies.co.uk Printerbox*
Glen Spectra Ltd 2 Dalston Gardens, Stanmore HA7 1BQ Tel. *020 82049517* Fax. *020 82045189* E-mail. *info@glenspectra.co.uk* Web. *www.glenspectra.co.uk LI-COR (U.S.A.) – Omega Optical – Optronic Laboratories (U.S.A.) – Photo Research (U.S.A.)*
Glentree Estates 698 Finchley Road, London NW11 7NE Tel. *020 82091144* Fax. *020 82090307* E-mail. *rentals@glentree.co.uk* Web. *www.glentree.co.uk Glentree Estates*
Glenvale Packaging Unit 3 Edison Close, Park Farm Industrial Estate, Wellingborough NN8 6AH Tel. *01933 673677* Fax. *01933 676728* E-mail. *garrycoleman@glenvale-pkg.co.uk* Web. *www.glenvale-pkg.co.uk Mastermeasure – MultiPharma – Nasserheider – Schaefer Technologies Inc. – Yener – KMA-Process – Wick Machinery*
Glitterati Dresswear Hire 99 King Street, Glasgow G1 5RB Tel. *0141 5523567* Fax. *0141 5523567 Glitterati*
Global Doors Ltd Unit 4 Roundwood Industrial Estate, Ossett WF5 9SQ Tel. *01924 283004* Fax. *01924 264329* E-mail. *dale@globaldoorsltd.co.uk* Web. *www.globaldoorsltd.co.uk Wilro ASSY – Wilro BZS*
Global Fasteners Ltd Unit 19 Delph Industrial Estate Delph Road, Brierley Hill DY5 2UA Tel. *01384 480793* Fax. *01384 482522* E-mail. *sales@global-fasteners.co.uk* Web. *www.global-fasteners.co.uk Cat – Devualt – Dr Martins – Himalayan – Makita – Timberland – Toesavers*
Global Graphics Software Ltd Building 2030 Cambourne Business Park, Cambridge CB23 6DW Tel. *01954 283100* Fax. *01954 283101* Web. *www.globalgraphics.com DataWorks – Dylan Works – Elementory Watson – Freelisp – Harlequin Intelligence – Harlequin Screening Library – Harpoon – Knowledge Works – Liquid Commom Lisp – Lispworks – ML. Works – Panoptica – Powercase – Scriptworks – ScriptWorks MicroRip – Watson – Watson Mapping – Watson Pro*
Global Industries Ltd 8 Leopold Road, London W5 3PB Tel. *020 89928497* Fax. *020 89922917* E-mail. *angela.keshishian@importcarsearch.com* Web. *www.global-ind.com Global*
Global Laser Technology Solutions Cwmtillery Industrial Estate Cwmtillery, Abertillery NP13 1LZ Tel. *01495 212213* Fax. *01495 212004* E-mail. *davidb@globallasertech.com* Web. *www.globallasertech.com Imatronic – Laserlyte – Vector*
Global Parasols Ltd Abbeylands Farm Wineham Lane, Wineham, Henfield BN5 9AQ Tel. *01273 494169* Fax. *01273 495972* E-mail. *sales@globalparasols.com* Web. *www.globalparasols.com Burda World Wide Technologies – Caspar – Severin Quick-Table – Shademakers – Tophoven – Tradewinds Parasol – Tuuci*
Global Radio 30 Leicester Square, London WC2H 7LA Tel. *020 77666001* Fax. *020 77666111* E-mail. *info@thisisglobal.com* Web. *www.thisisglobal.com 1548 A.M. Capital Gold – 95.8 Capital F.M. – Capital Advertising – Capital Radio London – Flying Eye – XFM*
Global Translators UK Ltd 21 Jiniwin Road, Rochester ME1 2DJ Tel. *07854 169165* Fax. *01634 408040* E-mail. *info@globaltranslators.co.uk* Web. *www.globaltranslators.co.uk Translations*
Glo-Marka Beeches Westminster Villas, Ilfracombe EX34 9NX Tel. *01271 865528* Fax. *01271 864664* E-mail. *sales@glo-marka.co.uk* Web. *www.glo-marka.co.uk Glo-Marka*
Gloverall PLC T/A Peter Scotts 11 Buccleuch Street, Hawick TD9 0HJ Tel. *01450 372311* Fax. *01450 374610* E-mail. *sales@peterscott.co.uk* Web. *www.peterscott.co.uk Pesco – Peter Scott*
Stephen Glover & Co. Ltd 2-8 Laporte Way, Luton LU4 8RJ Tel. *01922 611311* Fax. *01922 721824 Glover – Verglo*
Glowbug Ltd (a division of Capricorn Chemicals) Faraday Road Business Park, Littleport, Ely CB6 1PE Tel. *01353 863686* Fax. *01353 863990* E-mail. *sales@capricorn.co.uk* Web. *www.capricorn.co.uk Glowbug*
Glynwed Pipe Systems Ltd (An Aliaxis Co.) St Peter's Road, Huntingdon PE29 7DA Tel. *01480 52121* Fax. *01480 458829* E-mail. *enquiries@gpsuk.com* Web. *www.gpsuk.com Capper P-C – Durapipe – Victaulic – Viking Johnson – Wask-RMF*
G M A C (Head Office) Unit 6.1 Heol Y Gamlas Parc Nantgarw, Nantgarw, Cardiff CF15 7QU Tel. *08448 712222* Fax. *01273 771501* E-mail. *erhard.paulat@gmacfs.com* Web. *www.gmacfs.co.uk Expofin*
G M B Associates Unit 5 Ariane, Tamworth B79 7XF Tel. *01827 57561* Fax. *01827 61832* E-mail. *sales@gmbassociates.co.uk* Web. *www.gmbassociates.co.uk Americardan Universal Joints – Ameridrives International – Ameriflex – Ameriflex Couplings – Amerigear – Amerigear Couplings and Spindles – Boston Gear – Boston Gear Motion Control Products – Centric Clutch – Delroyd Worm Gear – Nuttall Gear – Nuttall Gear Corporation – Nuttall Gear Motors and Drives*
G M C Corsehill Ailsa Road Irvine Industrial Estate, Irvine KA12 8NG Tel. *01294 322807* Fax. *01294 312300* E-mail. *sales@gmccorsehill.co.uk* Web. *www.corsehill.co.uk Annefield Supplies (Gmc Corsehill Ltd)*
G M Instruments Ltd 6 Ashgrove Workshops, Kilwinning KA13 6PU Tel. *01294 554664* Fax. *01294 551154* E-mail. *gminstruments@aol.com* Web. *www.gm-instruments.com Mercury*
G&M Loft Conversions White House Farm, Braintree CM7 4HF Tel. *0800 3287216* E-mail. *enqs@gmloftconversions.com* Web. *www.gmloftconversions.com Velux*
G & M Power Plant Ltd 31 Anson Road Martlesham Heath, Ipswich IP5 3RG Tel. *01473 662777* Fax. *01473 662785* E-mail. *gandm@gmpp.co.uk* Web. *www.gmpp.co.uk Countryman Power – G&M Power - Countryman Power – G&M Power Plant*
G M S Co. 35 Southfields Industrial Park Hornsby Square, Southfields Business Park, Basildon SS15 6SD Tel. *01268 419909* Fax. *01268 544346* E-mail. *office@gamasco.co.uk* Web. *www.gamasco.co.uk Gamasco – Prekev – Thermapad – Thermapad - Gamasco - Prekev*
G M S Music Kinneil House Kirk Entry Boness Road, Polmont, Falkirk FK2 0QS Tel. *01324 711011* Fax. *01324 711533* E-mail. *info@gmsmusic.com* Web. *www.gmsmusic.com G.M.S.*
P & D J Goacher 8 Tovil Green Business Park Burial Ground Lane, Tovil, Maidstone ME15 6TA Tel. *01622 682112* Web. *www.goachers.com *Goachers*
Gobina London Ltd Unit 8-10 Hallmark Trading Estate Fourth Way, Wembley HA9 0LB Tel. *020 89002707* Fax. *020 89039171* Web. *www.gobina.co.uk Babydoll – Cruise Control – G.B. – Gasoline – Pacific Jeans – Radar*
Godiva Ltd Charles Street, Warwick CV34 5LR Tel. *01926 623600* Fax. *01926 623666* E-mail. *godiva@idexcorp.com* Web. *www.godiva.co.uk Cafsmaster Foam Systems – Godiva – Hale Foam Systems – Typhoon*
E J Godwin Peat Industries Ltd St Marys Road Meare, Glastonbury BA6 9SP Tel. *01458 860644* Fax. *01458 860587* E-mail. *ejgodwin@btinternet.com* Web. *www.ejgodwin.biz Godwin Crop Bag*
Godwin Pumps Ltd Quenington, Cirencester GL7 5BX Tel. *01285 750271* Fax. *01285 750352* E-mail. *sales@godwinpumps.co.uk* Web. *www.godwinpumps.co.uk Heidra*
GO Enterprise Po Box 398, Guernsey GY1 3FT Tel. *07781 414844* E-mail. *info@goe.gg* Web. *www.goenterprise.co.uk GOE*
Going Places 22 Town Square, Sale M33 7SN Tel. *08443 357618* Fax. *0161 9764930* Web. *www.goingplaces.co.uk Going Places*
Goldcrest Chemicals Ltd Dodworth Business Park Dodworth, Barnsley S75 3SP Tel. *0370 7800100* Fax. *01506 630087* E-mail. *customerservices@goldcrestchemicals.co.uk* Web. *www.goldcrestchemicals.co.uk Golkem – Polygold*
Goldenberg Real Estate LLP Fifth Floor Linen Hall 162-168 Regent Street, London W1B 5TF Tel. *020 74914101* Fax. *020 74910809* E-mail. *reception@goldenberg.co.uk* Web. *www.goldenberg.co.uk Another Successful Transaction*
Golden Plan Ltd Second Floor Linen Hall 162-168 Regent Street, London W1B 5TB Tel. *020 74342066* Fax. *020 72872329 *Adjustabed (Netherlands) – *Divanette (Netherlands) – *Wentelbed (Netherlands)*
Golden River Traffic Ltd Unit A4 Telford Road, Bicester OX26 4LD Tel. *01869 362800* Fax. *01869 246858* E-mail. *sales@goldenriver.com* Web. *www.goldenriver.com Archer – Fleet Track – Marksman – Microtel – Showman – Target – Weighman – Wimstrip*
Goldring Products Ltd 8 Greyfriars Road, Bury St Edmunds IP32 7DX Tel. *01284 701101* Fax. *01284 750040* E-mail. *sales@goldring.co.uk Goldring*
Goldsmiths Jewellers Ltd 186-190 Bishopsgate, London EC2M 4NL Tel. *020 72836622* Fax. *020 76233696* Web. *www.goldsmiths.co.uk Antiquity Pewter – Brietling – Cartier – Ebel – Endurance Plate – Goldsmiths – Old Father Time – Ringcraft – Rolex – Walker and Hall*
Gold & Wassall Hinges Ltd (U.K. Dept) Castleworks Staffs Moor Industrial Estate Lichfield Road, Tamworth B79 7TH Tel. *01827 63391* Fax. *01827 310819* E-mail. *sales@goldwassallhinges.co.uk* Web. *www.goldwassallhinges.co.uk Castle*
Goliath International Ltd Unit 2 Aston Express Way Industrial Estate 64 Pritchett Street, Birmingham B6 4EX Tel. *0121 3596621* Fax. *0121 3596882* E-mail. *info@goliathinternational.com* Web. *www.goliathinternational.com Goliath*
Gomex Tools Ltd Unit 1 Phoenix Court Everitt Close Denington Industrial Estate, Wellingborough NN8 2QE Tel. *01933 228185* Fax. *01933 229224* E-mail. *info@gomex.co.uk* Web. *www.gomex.co.uk Gomex - T.C.T. – Minibel – Multix*
Goodfellow Cambridge Ltd Units C1-C2 Ermine Business Park Spitfire Close, Ermine Business Park, Huntingdon PE29 6WR Tel. *01480 424800* Fax. *01440 730661* E-mail. *info@goodfellow.com* Web. *www.goodfellow.com Goodfellow Cambridge*
Goodrich Control Systems Stratford Road Shirley, Solihull B90 4LA Tel. *0121 4515975* Fax. *0121 4516111* E-mail. *martin.butler@goodrich.com* Web. *www.goodrich.com Lucas – Lucoi*
Good Thinking 9 Fort End Haddenham, Aylesbury HP17 8EJ Tel. *01844 291803* E-mail. *info@goodthinking.co.uk Freelink*
Good to Go Safety Ltd Waverley Road Mitchelston Industrial Estate, Kirkcaldy KY1 3NH Tel. *01592 655646* Fax. *01592 655330* E-mail. *enquiries@goodtogosafety.co.uk* Web. *www.goodtogosafety.co.uk Good to Go Safety*
Goodwill Trophy Company Ltd Unit 7 Junction 2 Indust Estate Demuth Way, Oldbury B69 4LT Tel. *0121 5443444* Fax. *0121 5441947* E-mail. *sales@goodwill-trophy.co.uk* Web. *www.goodwilltrophy.co.uk Trophies for Tities*
Goodwood Metalcraft Ltd Terminus Industrial Estate, Chichester PO19 8UH Tel. *01243 784626* Fax. *01243 787643* E-mail. *sales@goodwood-metalcraft.co.uk* Web. *www.goodwood-metalcraft.co.uk Chichester – Cryo Products – Tawlite*
Goodyear Dunlop UK Ltd Tyrefort 88-98 Wingfoot Way, Erdington, Birmingham B24 9HY Tel. *0121 3066000* E-mail. *info@dunloptyres.co.uk* Web. *www.dunlop-tires.com Dunlop Tyres – India Tyres*
Gopak Ltd Range Road Industrial Estate Range Road, Hythe CT21 6HG Tel. *01303 265751* Fax. *01303 268282* E-mail. *andrewfieldwick@gopak.co.uk* Web. *www.gopak.co.uk Gopak*
Gordano Ltd Unit 1 Yeo Bank Business Park Kenn Road, Kenn, Clevedon BS21 6UW Tel. *01275 345100* Fax. *01275 345132* E-mail. *sales@gordano.com* Web. *www.gordano.com NTMAIL*
Gordian Strapping Ltd Brunel Road, Basingstoke RG21 6XX Tel. *01256 394400* Fax. *01256 394429* E-mail. *sales@gordianstrapping.com* Web. *www.gordianstrapping.com Hiten – Strapack – Hyplex – Pakord – Tycord – Tytape*
Gordon Equipments Ltd Durite Works Valley Road, Harwich CO12 4RX Tel. *01255 555200* Fax. *01255 555222* E-mail. *sales@durite.co.uk* Web. *www.durite.co.uk Acfil – Durite – Gordon – Nolten*
Gordon & Macphail 58 South Street, Elgin IV30 1JX Tel. *01343 545110* Fax. *01343 540155* E-mail. *info@gordonandmacphail.com* Web. *www.gordonandmacphail.com Ben Alder – Dunkeld Atholl Brose – Glen Avon – Glen Calder – Highland Fusilier – MacPhails – Pride Of Strathspey*
J Gorstige Ltd Unit 10 Carlton Mill Pickering Street, Leeds LS12 2QG Tel. *0113 2795200* Fax. *0113 2795200 Empire – Monarch – Sure*
Gosport Marina Mumby Road, Gosport PO12 1AH Tel. *023 92524811* Fax. *023 92589541* E-mail. *gosport@premiermarinas.com* Web. *www.premiermarinas.com Marina*
Goss & Crested China Ltd 62 Murray Road Horndean, Waterlooville PO8 9JL Tel. *023 92597440* Fax. *023 92591975* E-mail. *info@gosschinaclub.co.uk* Web. *www.gosschinaclub.co.uk Milestone*
Gotec Trading Ltd Boulton Road, Stevenage SG1 4QL Tel. *01438 740400* Fax. *01438 740005* Web. *www.gotectrading.com *Gotec (Germany) – Gotec – *Rench-Rapid (Germany)*
Goulds Pumps a Division of ITT Industries Ltd Millwey Rise Industrial Estate, Axminster EX13 5HU Tel. *01297 639100* Fax. *01297 630476* E-mail. *axminster.sales@itt.com* Web. *www.gouldspumps.com PumpSmart – i-Frame – PPS Plant Performance Services – ProCast – Goulds Pumps*
Goyen Controls Co UK Unit 3b Beechwood Lime Tree Way Chineham Business Park, Chineham, Basingstoke RG24 8WA Tel. *01256 817800* Fax. *01256 843164* E-mail. *asimpson@tyco-environmental.co.uk* Web. *www.cleanairsystems.com *Goyen (Australia)*
G & P Autocare 41 Birkbeck Road, London W3 6BQ Tel. *020 89925031* Fax. *020 89925031 Garage*
G P Burners C I B Ltd 2d Hargreaves Road Groundwell Industrial Estate, Swindon SN25 5AZ Tel. *01793 709050* Fax. *01793 709060* E-mail. *info@gpburners.co.uk* Web. *www.gpburners.co.uk Unigas – Unigas - gas and oil burner.*
G P E Scientific Ltd 5 Greaves Way Industrial Estate Stanbridge Road, Leighton Buzzard LU7 4UB Tel. *01525 382277* Fax. *01525 382263* E-mail. *sales@gpelimited.co.uk* Web. *www.gpelimited.co.uk Meterate – Uni-Form – Uniform*
G P W Recruitment Worsley House Windle Street, St Helens WA10 2BL Tel. *08453 301111* Fax. *0845 3301112* E-mail. *recruitment@gpw.uk.com* Web. *www.gpw.uk.com*

GPW Appointments – GPW Construction – GPW Research & Development – GPW Secretarial – GPW Trade

Grace Construction Ltd 58- Ipswich Road, Slough SL1 4EQ Tel. *01753 790000* Fax. *01753 691623* E-mail. *graham.moorfield@grace.com* Web. *www.gracec-onstruction.co.uk Bituthene – Insupak – Korkpak – Prepufe – Procor – Servidek – Servipak – Servirufe – Serviseal – Servitite – Serviwrap – Vertiseal*

Grace Construction Products Ltd Unit 830 Birchwood Boulevard, Birchwood, Warrington WA3 7QZ Tel. *01925 855330* Fax. *01925 824033* E-mail. *andrew.meakin@grace.com* Web. *www.grace.com Grace*

Gradwood Ltd Lansdown House 85 Buxton Road, Stockport SK2 6LR Tel. *0161 4809629* Fax. *0161 4747433* E-mail. *sales@gradwood.co.uk* Web. *www.gradwood.co.uk Gradwood*

Grafo Products Ltd St Old Good Depot St Johns Road, Saxmundham IP17 1BE Tel. *01986 873127* Fax. *01986 872850* E-mail. *info@grafoproducts.fsnet.co.uk* Web. *www.grafoproducts.co.uk Grafo-therm*

Grafton Recuitment 49 Queens Square, Belfast BT1 3FG Tel. *028 90329032* Fax. *028 90326032* E-mail. *hq@grafton-group.com* Web. *www.graftonrecruitment.com Try and Hire*

Graham & Brown Ltd PO Box 39, Blackburn BB1 3DB Tel. *01254 691321* Fax. *01254 582208* E-mail. *andrew.graham@grahambrown.com* Web. *www.grahambrown.com Fresco – Moonstone – Superfresco*

William S Graham & Sons Dewsbury Ltd Ravens Ing Mills Huddersfield Road, Dewsbury WF13 3JF Tel. *01924 462456* Fax. *01924 457985* E-mail. *info@wsgraham.co.uk* Web. *www.wsgraham.co.uk Airlay*

Grainger Tubolt Ltd Unit A - B Meyrick Owen Way, Pembroke Dock SA72 6WS Tel. *01646 683584* Fax. *01646 621392* E-mail. *jwild@graingertubolt.com* Web. *www.graingertubolt.com Interclamp*

Grampian Motors Musker Street, Liverpool L23 0UB Tel. *0151 9315009* Fax. *0151 9314959* E-mail. *sales@mi-taka.com Mini-Bar*

Gram UK 2 The Technology Centre London Road, Swanley BR8 7AG Tel. *01322 616900* Fax. *01322 616901* E-mail. *glro@gramuk.co.uk* Web. *www.gram-commercial.com *Gram*

Granada Cranes & Handling Parsonage Street, Oldbury B69 4PH Tel. *0121 5524503* Fax. *0121 5111152* E-mail. *info@granada-cranes.co.uk* Web. *www.granada-cranes.co.uk Antifoam 86/013 – Antifoam 96/071 – Antifoam AP – Antifoam AR – Antifoam AR20 – Antifoam AR30 – Antifoam C100 – Antifoam C100F – Antifoam C133 – Antifoam E6 – Antifoam ED5 – Antifoam FD – Antifoam FD20P – Antifoam FD30 – Antifoam FD50 – Antifoam FDP – Antifoam FG10 – Antifoam FG50 – Antifoan C100N – BC 2105 – BC 2153 – BC 2191 – BC 2211 – BC 2231 – BC 2262 – BC 2275 – BC 2335 – BC 2366 – BC 2398 – BC 2421 – BC 2426 – BC 2440 – BC 30EPHV – BC 330/60 – BC 330LV – BC 338 – BC 361 – BC 380E – BC 380S – BC 403 – BC 404 – BC 83/132 – BC 85/76 – BC 88/161 – BC 89/175 – BC 90/080 – BC 91/023 – BC 93/018 – BC 96/004 – BC 96/042 – BC 96/061 – BC 98/073 – BC 99/012 – BC 99/099 – BC Silicone Fluids – BC Volatile Silicone 4 – BC Volatile Silicone 5 – Dimethicone 1000cs – Dimethicone 350cs – Powder Antifoam 2527 – Simethcone Antifoam C100EP – Simethicone – Simethicone Antifoam C100F*

Granada Material Handling Ltd Sherwood Industrial Park Queensway, Rochdale OL11 2NU Tel. *01706 653620* Fax. *01706 523943* E-mail. *info@gmh.co.uk* Web. *www.gmh.co.uk Fezer – SWF*

Granant Precast Concrete Grannant Uchaf St Dogmaels, Cardigan SA43 3LY Tel. *01239 881232* Fax. *01239 881269* E-mail. *granant.precast1@btconnect.com* Web. *www.agregister.co.uk/company-75056746.html *Granant*

Grand Age Engineering Ltd Elm Tree Farm Kirby Misperton, Malton YO17 6XT Tel. *01653 668288* Fax. *01653 668289* E-mail. *sales@grandsweep.com* Web. *www.grandsweep.com Grandage – Grandsweep*

Grange Fencing Ltd Halesfield 21, Telford TF7 4PA Tel. *01952 586460* Fax. *01952 684461* E-mail. *sales@grangefen.co.uk* Web. *www.grangefen.co.uk Grange – Grange Supafence*

Grange Marketing Hillside House Cwmcarvan, Monmouth NP25 4PL Tel. *01600 869079* Fax. *01600 869079* E-mail. *enquiries@gm-uk.com* Web. *www.grange-marketing.co.uk *Grange Marketing*

Grangers International Ltd Grange Close Clover Nook Industrial Park, Somercotes, Alfreton DE55 4QT Tel. *01773 521521* Fax. *01773 521262* E-mail. *neil@grangers.co.uk* Web. *www.grangers.co.uk Granger's 1210 – Granger's Boot 'N' Shoe Glue – Granger's Boot Deodorant – Granger's Cemcol – Granger's Country Sports Range – Granger's Damp Sealer – Granger's Extreme Superpruf – Granger's Fabsil – Granger's Fabsil Gold – Granger's G-Sport – Granger's Gore-Tex Approved Range for Footwear – Granger's Mesowax – Granger's Nubuck Conditioner – Granger's Tent and Awning Cleaner – Granger's Wax – Grangers Extreme Wash-in – Grangers Extreme Wash-In Cleaner*

Grantham Manufacturing Ltd Alma Park Industrial Estate, Grantham NG31 9SW Tel. *01476 566414* Fax. *01476 590225* E-mail. *sales@gmluk.com* Web. *www.gmluk.com Diamond Bonewrap – Diamond Gripkraft – Diamond M.P.I. – Diamond Twistwrap*

Granton Medical Ltd (t/a The Granton Knife Co.) Parkway Close, Sheffield S9 4WJ Tel. *0114 2757290* Fax. *0114 2634833* E-mail. *info@granton.co.uk* Web. *www.granton.co.uk Granton – John Walker – Ragg*

Richard Grant Mouldings Ltd Unit K4 & K5 Cherrycourt Way, Leighton Buzzard LU7 4UH Tel. *01525 853888* Fax. *01525 383229* E-mail. *sales@rgmouldings.com* Web. *www.rearguards.co.uk Richard Grant*

Granwood Flooring Ltd Greenhill Lane Riddings, Alfreton DE55 4AT Tel. *01773 602341* Fax. *01773 540043* E-mail. *sales@granwood.co.uk* Web. *www.granwood.co.uk Granfix – Gransprung – Granwax – Granwood*

Grapevine International 28 Clay Road Caister-on-Sea, Great Yarmouth NR30 5HB Tel. *01622 734619* E-mail. *office@grapevine-int.co.uk* Web. *www.grapevine-int.co.uk *Grapevine International (HK) Ltd – *Grapevine International Ltd – *Grapevine International Services Ltd*

Graphics Arts Equipment Ltd 11 Aintree Road Perivale, Greenford UB6 7LE Tel. *020 89978053* Fax. *020 89977706* E-mail. *brian.godwyn@gae.co.uk* Web. *www.gae.co.uk *Faltex (Switzerland) – *Horizon (Japan) – *Itoh (Japan) – *Shinohara (Japan)*

Graphoidal Developments Broombank Road, Chesterfield S41 9QJ Tel. *01246 266000* Fax. *01246 269269* E-mail. *sales@graphoidal.com* Web. *www.graphoidal.com Autoswabbing – CWM-2000 – Friction Glide – Grad – Gradmatic*

Graphtec GB Ltd Coed Aben Road Wrexham Industrial Estate, Wrexham LL13 9UH Tel. *01978 666700* Fax. *01978 666710* E-mail. *sales@graphtecgb.com* Web. *www.graphtecgb.co.uk Encad – Graphtec Corporation – Showa Strain Gauges – W.D.V.*

Grasam Samson Ltd Unit E1 Doulton Trading Estate Doulton Road, Rowley Regis B65 8JQ Tel. *01384 634162* Fax. *01384 568051* E-mail. *sales@grasamsamson.co.uk Grasam Samson Tools – Samson*

Grass Concrete Ltd Duncan House 142 Thornes Lane, Thornes, Wakefield WF2 7RE Tel. *01924 379443* Fax. *01924 290289* E-mail. *bob@grasscrete.com* Web. *www.grasscrete.com Betoatlas – Betoconcept – Betoflor – Betojard – Betonap – Betotitan – Binwall – Grassblock – Grasscrete – Grasskerb – Grassroad – Leromur – Grassroof*

Grasslin UK Ltd Tower House Vale Rise, Tonbridge TN9 1TB Tel. *01732 359888* Fax. *01732 354445* E-mail. *rjo@tfc.uk.com* Web. *www.grasslin-controls.co.uk Q.E.1 & Q.E.2 – QM1 & QM2 – Tower – Towerstat*

Grass Roots Tring Business Centre Icknield Way Industrial Estate, Tring HP23 4RN Tel. *01442 829400* Fax. *01442 829405* E-mail. *david.evans@grg.com* Web. *www.grg.com Bonusbond – Grass Roots – Grass Roots Travel Services*

Graticule 2 Blenheim Court, Leeds LS2 9AE Tel. *0113 2344000* Fax. *0113 2465071* E-mail. *sales@graticule.com* Web. *www.graticule.com Geosoft – Map Server 4 – Maptools*

Gratnells Ltd 8 Howard Way, Harlow CM20 2SU Tel. *01279 401550* Fax. *01279 419127* E-mail. *nevilleh@gratnells.co.uk* Web. *www.gratnells.co.uk Gratnell*

Grattan plc Anchor House Ingleby Road, Bradford BD99 2XG Tel. *01274 575511* Fax. *01274 625591* E-mail. *sales@grattan.co.uk* Web. *www.grattan.co.uk Grattan*

Gratte Brothers Ltd 2 Regents Wharf All Saints Street, London N1 9RL Tel. *020 78376433* Fax. *020 78376779* E-mail. *info@gratte.com* Web. *www.gratte.com Gratte Brothers (GB)*

Gravity Internet Ltd 17 Fairlawns, Sunbury On Thames TW16 6QR Tel. *08707 651802* Fax. *08707 651803* E-mail. *tema@gravityinternet.net* Web. *www.gravityinternet.net Gravity Internet*

Gravograph Ltd Unit 3 Trojan Business Centre Touch Brooke Park Drive, Warwick CV34 6RH Tel. *01926 884433* Fax. *01926 883879* E-mail. *info@gravograph.co.uk* Web. *www.gravograph.co.uk *Gravograph (France)*

Gray Campling Ltd 91a Southcote Road, Bournemouth BH1 3SN Tel. *01202 291828* Fax. *01202 297304* E-mail. *sales@graycampling.co.uk* Web. *www.graycampling.co.uk *Cold Front (U.S.A.) – *Meyer (Germany) – *Muleskinner (U.S.A.) – *Sicmo-Bendix (Monaco) – *Speeflo (U.S.A.) – *Titan (U.S.A.) – *Titan (U.S.A.)*

Gray Nicolls Station Road, Robertsbridge TN32 5DH Tel. *01580 880357* Fax. *01580 881156* E-mail. *info@gray-nicolls.co.uk* Web. *www.gray-nicolls.co.uk 1823 – Barbarian – Gripsure 8 Panel – Gripsure-All Weather – GXS2000 – League 6 Panel – Match – Murrayfield – Office Match Ball – Official Match Ball – Official World Championship Netball – Official World Cup – Reflex Trainer – Renown – Rugbeian – Triple Crown*

Grays Packaging Ltd PO Box 237, Grays RM17 6WL Tel. *01375 399128* E-mail. *sales@grayspackaging.co.uk* Web. *www.grayspackaging.co.uk Paksol – Topmatic*

Great British Card Company plc Waterwells Drive Quedgeley, Gloucester GL2 2PH Tel. *01452 888999* Fax. *01452 888912* E-mail. *enquiries@paperhouse.co.uk* Web. *www.paperhouse.co.uk Aries Design – Elgin Court – Eric the Penguin – Humour Factory – Paper House – Parnassus Gallery – Royle Publications*

Greater London Fund For Blind 12 Whitehorse Mews 37 Westminster Bridge Road, London SE1 7QD Tel. *020 76202066* Fax. *020 76202016* E-mail. *info@glfb.org.uk* Web. *www.glfb.org.uk G.L.F.*

Great Western Ambulance Sevice N H S Trust Dorman House Malmesbury Road, Chippenham SN15 5LN Tel. *01249 443939* Fax. *01249 443217* E-mail. *exec.office@wiltsambs.nhs.uk* Web. *www.wiltsamb.nhs.uk Medicar*

Great Yarmouth Port Company Ltd Eastport UK House South Beach Parade, Great Yarmouth NR30 3GY Tel. *01493 335500* Fax. *01493 852480* E-mail. *rlewin@eastportuk.co.uk* Web. *www.eastportuk.co.uk Great Yarmouth Port Authority*

Greaves Welsh Slate Co. Ltd Llechwedd Slate Mines, Blaenau Ffestiniog LL41 3NB Tel. *01766 830522* Fax. *01766 830711* E-mail. *llechwedd@aol.com* Web. *www.welsh-slate.com Greaves Portmadoc Slate*

R W Greeff A division of Univar Ltd Tame Park Vanguard, Wilnecote, Tamworth B77 5DY Tel. *01827 255200* Fax. *01827 255255* E-mail. *rwgreeff@univareurope.com* Web. *www.rwgreef.co.uk 3M – Dow Corning – Molykote – Mykal – Vertrel*

Greenbank Technology Ltd Unit 3 Greenbank Business Park, Blackburn BB1 3AB Tel. *01254 690555* Fax. *01254 690666* E-mail. *info@greenbanktechnology.co.uk* Web. *www.greenbanktechnology.co.uk Cleanflo – Jetflo – Papermaster – Truflo – Truflo – Vacflo – Vacflo, The*

The Green Consultancy Unit D Second Avenue Westfield Industrial Estate, Midsomer Norton, Radstock BA3 4BH Tel. *08450 176300* Fax. *0845 0176277* E-mail. *manager@greenconsultancy.com* Web. *www.greenconsultancy.com Forestsaver*

Greencore Frozen Foods Midland Road Hunslet, Leeds LS10 2RJ Tel. *0113 2976000* Fax. *0113 2976001* E-mail. *info@greencore.com* Web. *www.greencore.com *Grandma Batty – *Nordale – *Roberts*

D A Green & Sons Ltd High Road Whaplode, Spalding PE12 6TL Tel. *01406 370585* Fax. *01406 370766* E-mail. *pc@dagreen.co.uk* Web. *www.dagreen.co.uk Green Cladding – Green Structural*

Greene Tweed & Co. Ltd Mere Way Ruddington Fields Business Park, Ruddington, Nottingham NG11 6JS Tel. *0115 9315777* Fax. *0115 9315888* E-mail. *info@greenetweed.com* Web. *www.gtweed.com Altymid – Arlon – Chemraz – Fluoraz – G.T. Rings – G.T.B. Bandseal – G.T.S. Slipseal – MSE – Orthtek – R.S.A. – Rotalip – Slipstrip – WR525*

Greengages Limited 105 Fairfield Road, Buxton SK17 7EZ Tel. *0845 6588984* E-mail. *info@greengages.com* Web. *www.gogreengages.com Greengages Limited*

P W Greenhalgh & Co. Ltd Ogden Mill Milnrow, Rochdale OL16 3TH Tel. *01706 847911* Fax. *01706 881217* E-mail. *information@pwgreenhalgh.com* Web. *www.pwgreenhalgh.com Furnsafe – Pyroban – Pyrodry – Qualicol – Sundown – Sundown - curtain lining, Furnsafe - F.R. back coating upholstery, Pyroban - permanent F.R. for curtain linings, Pyrodry - non-permanent F.R. for curtain linings.*

Greenhouse Supply Ltd The Garden Buildings Centre Sheffield Road, Chesterfield S41 7LX Tel. *01246 220301* Fax. *01246 271110* E-mail. *nicp@conservatorycentre.co.uk* Web. *www.greenhousesupply.co.uk alton greenhouses robinsons greenhouses*

Green Island (UK) Ltd Stirling House 107 Stirling Road, London N22 5BN Tel. *020 88818686* Fax. *020 88818688* E-mail. *info@greenislandrum.com* Web. *www.greenislandrum.com CNS Systems*

Greenjackets Roofing Services Ltd 61 The Waterside Trading Centre Trumpers Way, London W7 2QD Tel. *020 85716555* Fax. *020 85716633* E-mail. *sales@greenjackets.co.uk* Web. *www.greenjackets.co.uk Greenjackets*

Greenshires Group Ltd 160-164 Barkby Road, Leicester LE4 9LF Tel. *0116 2022600* Fax. *0116 2022601* E-mail. *paul.heath@greenshires.com* Web. *www.greenshires.com Greenshires*

Green's Restaurant 36 Duke Street St James, London SW1Y 6DF Tel. *020 79304566* Fax. *020 79302958* E-mail. *lld@greens.org.uk* Web. *www.greens.org.uk Green's*

Greenwich Instruments Limited Meridian House Park Road, Swanley BR8 8AH Tel. *01322 668724* Fax. *01322 660352* E-mail. *sales@greenwichinst.com* Web. *www.greenwichinst.com Data Converters – Fibre Optic Modems – Girbil (United Kingdom) – GPS (United Kingdom) – Greenwich Instruments – Line Drivers – Stepper Motor Drivers*

Greenwood Magnetics Ltd Unit 4c Buckley Road Industrial Estate, Rochdale OL12 9EF Tel. *01706 645824* Fax. *01706 642458* E-mail. *sales@greenwoodmagnetics.com* Web. *www.greenwoodmagnetics.com Greenwood Magnetics*

Greenwood Menswear 2nd Floor Bradford Business Park Kings Gate, Bradford BD1 4SJ Tel. *01274 659650* Fax. *01274 659691* E-mail. *sales@gwmw.com* Web. *www.1860.com Greenwoods*

Greenwood Personal Credit Colonnade Sunbridge Road, Bradford BD1 2LQ Tel. *01274 304044* Fax. *01274 722715* E-mail. *enquiries@providentfinancial.com* Web. *www.greenwoodpersonalcredit.co.uk Provident Financial*

Greggs plc Fernwood House Clayton Road, Newcastle upon Tyne NE2 1TL Tel. *0191 2817721* Fax. *0191 2811444* E-mail. *roym@greggs.co.uk* Web. *www.greggs.co.uk Bakers Oven – Birketts – Greggs – Olivers*

Greif UK Ltd Merseyside Works Oil Sites Road, Ellesmere Port CH65 4EZ Tel. *0151 3732000* Fax. *0151 3732072* E-mail. *info.uk@greif.com* Web. *www.greif.com Quadratainer – Spiralon – Tab-seal – Tri-Sure – Valerex – Valethene*

Grenson Shoes Ltd Queen Street, Rushden NN10 0AB Tel. *01933 358734* Fax. *01933 410106* E-mail. *customerservices@grenson.co.uk* Web. *www.grenson.co.uk Grenson – Grenson Feathermaster – Grenson Footmaster*

Gresolvent Ltd Unit C1a Wem Industrial Estate Soulton Road, Wem, Shrewsbury SY4 5SD Tel. *01939 232326* Fax. *01939 232386* E-mail. *gresolvent@btconnect.com* Web. *www.gresolvent.co.uk Abragel – Abrasol – Boraxo – Gre-Sol Jelly – Gresolvent Paste*

Gresso Ltd Wheatley Business Centre Old London Road, Wheatley, Oxford OX3 1YW Tel. *01865 522889* E-mail. *enquiry@gresso.eu* Web. *www.gresso.eu Gresso*

Greycar Ltd Greycar House 5 Ferns Mead, Farnham GU9 7XP Tel. *01252 821937* Fax. *01252 734071* E-mail. *info@greycar.com* Web. *www.greycar.com Greycar*

Griff Chains Ltd Quarry Road Dudley Wood, Dudley DY2 0ED Tel. *01384 569512* Fax. *01384 410580* E-mail. *sales@griffchains.co.uk* Web. *www.griffchains.co.uk Griff*

Griffith Laboratories Ltd Cotes Park Estate Somercotes, Alfreton DE55 4NN Tel. *01773 837000* Fax. *01773 837001* E-mail. *info@griffithlaboratories.com* Web. *www.griffithlaboratories.com Panko*

Grimme UK Ltd Station Road Swineshead, Boston PE20 3PS Tel. *01205 821182* Fax. *01205 821196* E-mail. *b.white@grimme.co.uk* Web. *www.grimmeuk.com *Rotary Cultivator*

Grimsby Telegraph Telegraph House 80 Cleethorpe Road, Grimsby DN31 3EH Tel. *01472 360360* Fax. *01472 372257* E-mail. *mark.price@gsmg.co.uk* Web. *www.thisisgrimsby.co.uk Axholme Herald, The – Grimsby Evening Telegraph, The – Grimsby Target – Scunthorpe Evening Telegraph, The – Scunthorpe Target, The*

G R Lane Health Products Ltd Sisson Road, Gloucester GL2 0GR Tel. *01452 524012* Fax. *01452 300105* E-mail. *info@laneshealth.com* Web. *www.laneshealth.com Aqua-Ban – Fort-E-Vite – Jakemans Confectioners – Kalms – Lanes – Olbas Oil – Preconceive – Quiet Life – Symingtons*

Grosvenor Gallery 21 Ryder Street, London SW1Y 6PX Tel. *020 74847979* Fax. *020 74847980* E-mail. *art@grosvenorgallery.com* Web. *www.grosvenorgallery.com Grosvenor Gallery*

Grosvenor Pumps Ltd Trevoole Praze, Camborne TR14 0PJ Tel. *01209 831500* Fax. *01209 831939* E-mail. *sales@grosvenorpumps.com* Web. *www.grosvenorpumps.com G.P. – Grosvenor Packaged Systems – Grosvenor Pumps – M-Type – Pygme – Pyxel – S-Type*

Grosvenor Technology Ltd Millars Three Southmill Road, Bishops Stortford CM23 3DH Tel. *01279 838000* Fax. *01279 504776* E-mail. *customerservices@gtl.biz* Web. *www.grosvenortechnology.com Janus (United Kingdom)*

Grosvenor Windows Ltd Lodge Bank Estate Crown Lane, Horwich, Bolton BL6 5HY Tel. *01204 664488* Fax. *01204 664499* E-mail. *sales@grosvenorwindows.co.uk* Web. *www.grosvenorwindows.co.uk Grosvenor*

Groundwork UK Lockside 5 Scotland Street, Birmingham B1 2RR Tel. *0121 2368565* Fax. *0121 2367356* E-mail. *info@groundwork.org.uk* Web. *www.groundwork.org.uk Groundwork*

Groupco Ltd Unit 130 Culley Court, Orton Southgate, Peterborough PE2 6WA Tel. *01733 393330* Fax. *01733 235246* E-mail. *sales@groupcoltd.co.uk* Web. *www.groupcoltd.co.uk *C.E.S. (Germany) – *Fuhr (Germany)*

Group 4 Total Security Ltd Alexandra Way Ashchurch, Tewkesbury GL20 8NB Tel. *08704 117700* Fax. *01684 295574* E-mail. *enquires@group4.com* Web. *www.group4.co.uk Group 4 Total Security*

Group Seb Ltd 11-49 Station Road Langley, Slough SL3 8DR Tel. *01753 713000* Fax. *01753 583938* E-mail. *groupseb@groupseb.co.uk* Web. *www.groupseb.co.uk Tefal (UK)*

James Grove & Sons Properties Ltd Bloomfield Works 136 Stourbridge Road, Halesowen B63 3UW Tel. *0121 5504015* Fax. *0121 5013905* E-mail. *john.brougham@jamesgroveandsons.co.uk* Web. *www.jamesgroveandsons.co.uk Deconite*

Groves Batteries Park Mews Works Lypiatt Street, Cheltenham GL50 2UB Tel. *01242 514940* Fax. *01242 256218* E-mail. *groves.batteries@virgin.net* Web. *www.grovesbatteries.co.uk DURACELL – GENESIS – ODYSSEY – OPTIMA – VARTA – YUASA*

Groz-Beckert UK Groz-Beckert House 139-139a Gloucester Crescent, Wigston LE18 4YL Tel. *0116 2643500* Fax. *0116 2643505* E-mail. *contact@groz-beckert.com* Web. *www.groz-beckert.com *Groz-Beckert (Germany) – *Jomro (Germany) – Kern Liebers – *Schmetz (Germany)*

Grundfos Pumps Ltd Grovebury Road, Leighton Buzzard LU7 4TL Tel. *01525 850000* Fax. *01525 850011* E-mail. *ukindustry@grundfos.com* Web. *www.grundfos.com Grundfos – Selectric – Home Booster – Max-E Boost – CUE – Super Selectric – ALPHA+ – Pump Plan – WasteMate – WasteMate Plus – WaterMate – MAGNA – Comfort – Drainaway – SQFlex – Monopress – Duopress – Monocompact – Tricompact – Quadcompact – Pentacompact – Hexacompact – Byepac – Byepac – Liftaway – Digital Dosing – ALPHA2 – IMpress – ALPHA – Conlift – LiqTec – Euro-HYGIA – Contra – SIPLA*

G S F Promount Unit 9 Gledrid Industrial Park Gledrid, Chirk, Wrexham LL14 5DG Tel. *01691 770303* Fax. *01691 776900* E-mail. *info@gsfslides.com* Web. *www.gsf-promounts.com Ballrace – Chambrelan – GSF – Telerace – Thomas Regout – Waterloo*

G S I Group Ltd Cosford Lane Swift Valley Indl-Est, Rugby CV21 1QN Tel. *01788 570321* Fax. *01788 579824* E-mail. *sales@jklasers.com* Web. *www.gsiglasers.com J.K. 700 – J.K. 700 Series – J.K. Lasers – JK 700 Series – JK Lasers – LaserMark – LuxStar – MultiWave*

G T Factors Ltd GTF 22-22a Hawthorn Rd, Eastbourne BN23 6QA Tel. *01323 728626* Fax. *01323 728890* E-mail. *sales@gtf.co.uk* Web. *www.gtf.co.uk Euroweb – Euroweb - lashing systems*

GTH Photography 3 Birds Road, North Walsham NR28 0WE Tel. *01692 402501* E-mail. *sales@gthphotography.co.uk* Web. *www.gthphotography.co.uk GTH Photography*

G T Lifting Solutions Ltd 14 Cokeham Lane Sompting Sompting, Lancing BN15 9UW Tel. *08456 037180* Fax. *08456 021741* E-mail. *sales@gtplant.co.uk* Web. *www.gtplant.co.uk Merlo – Merlo Telescopic*

G T S Flexible Materials Ltd G T S House 3 Wellington Business Park, Crowthorne RG45 6LS Tel. *01344 762376* Fax. *01344 761615* E-mail. *sales@gts-flexible.co.uk* Web. *www.gts-flexible.co.uk Ultraflex*

Guardall Ltd Lochend Industrial Estate Queen Anne Drive, Newbridge EH28 8PL Tel. *0131 3332900* Fax. *0131 3334919* E-mail. *clive.garlick@guardall.co.uk* Web. *www.guardall.com Apollo – Astra – Beammaster – Excalibur – Jupiter – Windsor*

Middleton Guardian 1 Scott Place, Manchester M3 3RN Tel. *0161 6433615* Fax. *0161 6539968* Web. *www.middletonguardian.co.uk City Life – Guardian Weekly, The – Guardian, The – Manchester Evening News – Manchester Morning Metro – Observer, The*

Guest Medical Ltd Enterprise Way, Edenbridge TN8 6EW Tel. *01732 867466* Fax. *01732 867476* E-mail. *sales@guestmedical.co.uk* Web. *www.guestmedical.com Aquasan – Dispette – Haz-Tab Granules – Haz-Tabs – Mini Haz-Tabs – Neatstain*

Guildford Shades (t/a Guildford Shades) Keens Lane, Guildford GU3 3JS Tel. *01483 232394* Fax. *01483 236420* E-mail. *sales@guildfordshades.co.uk* Web. *www.guildfordshades.co.uk Faber – Louvrelite – Marquees – Modernfold – Monobloc – Sunseeker*

The Guild Of Mastercraftsmen G M C Publications Ltd 166 High Street, Lewes BN7 1XU Tel. *01273 478449* Fax. *01273 478606* E-mail. *johnp@thegmcgroup.com* Web. *www.guildmc.com Guild Of Master Craftsmen, The*

Guilford Europe Ltd Cotes Park Lane Somercotes, Alfreton DE55 4NJ Tel. *01773 547200* Fax. *01773 547315* E-mail. *dturner@eu.gfd.com* Web. *www.guilfordproducts.com Guilford Europe – Guilford International*

Guinness World Records 184-192 Drummond Street, London NW1 3HP Tel. *020 78914567* Fax. *020 78914501* E-mail. *enquiries@guinnessworldrecords.com* Web. *www.guinnessworldrecords.com Guinness*

J P Guivier & Co. Ltd 99 Mortimer Street, London W1W 7SX Tel. *020 75802560* Fax. *020 74361461* E-mail. *sales@guivier.com* Web. *www.guivier.com Astrea*

Gullivers Sports Travel Fiddington Manor Fiddington, Tewkesbury GL20 7BJ Tel. *01684 293175* Fax. *01684 297926* E-mail. *pscholfield@gulliversports.co.uk* Web. *www.gulliverstravel.co.uk Atchison Topeka – Beaver Bureau – Gullivers Sports Travel*

Gul Watersports Ltd Callywith Gate Industrial Estate Launceston Road, Bodmin PL31 2RQ Tel. *01208 262400* Fax. *01208 262474* E-mail. *gul@gul.com* Web. *www.gul.com Gul – Gul – Morey Boogie – Woof Wear*

A & J Gummers Ltd Unit H Redfern Park Way, Birmingham B11 2DN Tel. *0121 7062241* Fax. *0121 7062960* E-mail. *sales@gummers.co.uk* Web. *www.sirrusshowers.co.uk Rothermix – Sirrus – Stuart Reducing Valve*

Gunnebo Entrance Control Ltd Bellbrook Business Park Bellbrook Industrial Estate, Uckfield TN22 1QQ Tel. *01825 746122* Fax. *01825 763835* E-mail. *robert.wheeler@csisec.com* Web. *www.gunneboentrance.com AutoSec – ClearSec – ClubStile – FlapStile – FS – GlasStile – RevoSec – RotaSec – Slimstile Range – SpeedStile – Tristile – TubeSec – Vehicle Control – WingStile*

Gunnebo Industries Ltd Woolaston Road Park Farm North, Redditch B98 7SG Tel. *01527 522560* Fax. *01527 510185* E-mail. *sales@gunneboindustries.co.uk* Web. *www.gunneboindustries.co.uk Gunnebo*

Gunnebo UK Ltd Woden Road, Wolverhampton WV10 0BY Tel. *01902 455111* Fax. *01902 351961* E-mail. *marketing@gunnebo.com* Web. *www.gunnebo.com John Tann Ltd – Rosengrens Tann Ltd*

Gunn J C B Atlantic Street Broadheath, Altrincham WA14 5DN Tel. *0161 9412631* Fax. *0161 9423399* E-mail. *gordon.smith@gunn-jcb.co.uk* Web. *www.gunn-jcb.co.uk Bomag – Gunn JCB – Thwaites*

Gunn & Moore Trent Lane Industrial Estate, Nottingham NG2 4DS Tel. *0115 9853500* Fax. *0115 9853501* E-mail. *peterwright@unicorngroup.com* Web. *www.unicorngroup.com Botra – G.M. – Powerglide*

Gurit UK Ltd St Cross Business Park, Newport PO30 5WU Tel. *01983 828000* Fax. *01983 828100* E-mail. *graham.harvey@gurit.com* Web. *www.gurrit.com Ampreg 20 – Ampreg 22 – Ampreg 26 – Ampreg Pregel – *Core-Cell Foam (Canada) – CR3400 – Eposeal 300 – Handipack – Hibuild 302 – Prime 20 – Protecta – QE XXX – Quadran – RA XXX – RC XXX – RE XXX – S'Fill 400 – S.P. Glass Bubbles – S.P. Micro Balloons – S.P. Microfibres – SA 80 – SE 130 – SE 135 – SE 84 – SE 85 – SE 90 – SP 106 – SP 115 – SP 127 – SP 320 – SP 531 – SP 631 – Spabond 120 – Spabond 125 – Spabond 130 – Spabond 330 – Spabond 335 – Spabond 340 – Spabond 345 – Spabond 720 – Spabond 735 – Spabond 740 – Spabond 765 – Sprint – UAXXX – UCXXX – UEXXX – UFCXXX – UFEXXX – Ultravar 2000 – Unifibre Reinforcement – Unitex Reinforcement – Unix Reinforcement – UTCXXX – XCXXX – XEXXX*

D Gurteen & Sons Ltd PO Box 1, Haverhill CB9 8AZ Tel. *01440 702601* Fax. *01440 703394* E-mail. *sales@gurteen.co.uk* Web. *www.gurteen.co.uk Augusta – Gurteen – Hucklecote – Mode – Ultimo*

Gustair Materials Handling Equipment Ltd Unit 1 Denbigh Road, Tipton DY4 7QF Tel. *0121 5200555* Fax. *0121 5200777* E-mail. *i.hollingworth@gustair.co.uk* Web. *www.gustair.co.uk Aero-motive – Air Logic & Cylinders – Airmachines – Aro – Aro Corporation – Aro Hoists – Aro Pneumatics – Aro Pumps – Aro Tools – Asco-Joucomatic – Atlas-Copco – Avdel – Bosch – C-Matic – Cengar – Columbus McKinnon – Compair air machines – Compair Broomwade – Compare – Consolodated Pneumatic Tools – Crosby – Crouzet – Desoutter – Domnick Hunter – Dynafile – Fiam – Fixtured tools – Gast – Georges Renault – Gesipa – Gustair – Gy-roll – I-R – I-R Aro – Ingersoll-rand – JDN – John Guest – Julilee – Legris – Lobster – M Series Balancer – MLK hoist – Morris – Norbar – NPK – P C T – Palair – PCL – Pneumax – PU & Nylon Tube – Pulse Tools – Rapesco – Red Rooster – Ross – Rud Chains – Self feed drill – Sentronic – Sfu – Sioux Tools – SMC – Stahl Hoist – Super Speed Fit – Yokota*

Guttridge Ltd Wardentree Park Pinchbeck, Spalding PE11 3UU Tel. *01775 765300* Fax. *01775 765301* E-mail. *sales@guttridge.co.uk* Web. *www.guttridge.co.uk Laserfab*

Guyson International Ltd (Hose and Couplings Division) Southview Business Park Ghyll Royd, Guiseley, Leeds LS20 9PR Tel. *01943 870044* Fax. *01943 870066* E-mail. *leeds@guyson.co.uk* Web. *www.guyson.co.uk Hansen – Kaptech*

Guyson International Ltd Snaygill Industrial Estate Keighley Road, Skipton BD23 2QR Tel. *01756 799911* Fax. *01756 790213* E-mail. *info@guyson.co.uk* Web. *www.guyson.co.uk Autotrans – Medsonic HS – Microclean – Microsolve – Neptune – Pulsatron*

G V E Ltd Ashburton House Ashburton Road East, Trafford Park, Manchester M17 1BN Tel. *0161 8729777* Fax. *0161 8729324* E-mail. *info@gvepumps.co.uk* Web. *www.gvepumps.co.uk Blowers (Roots) – Centrifugal Transfer Pumps – Gear Pumps – Sump Pumps – Vacuum Fittings – Vacuum Gauges – Vacuum Pumps*

Gwaza Ltd Ennerdale Road, Shrewsbury SY1 3NR Tel. *01743 461371* Fax. *01743 463732* E-mail. *sales@gwaza.co.uk* Web. *www.gwaza.co.uk *F.P. (Worldwide)*

G Webb Automation Ltd Howsell Road, Malvern WR14 1TF Tel. *01684 892929* Fax. *01684 892880* E-mail. *salesadmin@webbautomation.co.uk* Web. *www.webbautomation.co.uk Digifill – Easifill – Minifill – Rotoplant – Servofill – Weighmaster – Weighmaster - Easifill - Minifill - Servofill - Digifill - Rotoplant*

G W E Business West Unit 22 Midsomer Enterprise Park Radstock Road, Midsomer Norton, Radstock BA3 2BB Tel. *01761 411800* Fax. *01761 411431* E-mail. *info.wansdyke@businesswest.co.uk* Web. *www.businesswest.co.uk Business West*

G W S Engineers Ltd First Avenue Flixborough Industrial Estate, Flixborough, Scunthorpe DN15 8SE Tel. *01724 856665* Fax. *01724 280805* E-mail. *mail@gws-engineers.co.uk* Web. *www.gws-engineers.co.uk G.W.S. Engineers*

Gy-Roll Ltd Caxton Road Great Gransden, Sandy SG19 3AW Tel. *01767 677377* Fax. *01767 677900* E-mail. *info@gy-roll.com* Web. *www.gy-roll.com Gy-Roll*

G & Y Services Stocktakers & Valuers 44 Hazelmere Road, Stevenage SG2 8SF Tel. *01438 355049* Fax. *01438 355049* E-mail. *info@stocktaker.co.uk* Web. *www.stocktaker.co.uk G & Y SERVICES*

H

Habasit Rossi Ltd Habegger House Keighley RoadSilsden, Keighley BD20 0EA Tel. *0844 8359555* Fax. *0844 8359669* E-mail. *sales.uk@habasitrossi.com* Web. *www.habasit.co.uk Charles Walker – Habasit*

Hachette UK Ltd 338 Euston Road, London NW1 3BH Tel. *020 78736000* Fax. *020 78736024* Web. *www.hachette.co.uk Asterix – Coronet Paperbacks – Edward Arnold – Headway – Knight Paperbacks – New English Library – Sceptre – Teach Yourself – Young Headway*

Haddonstone Ltd Forge House Church Lane, East Haddon, Northampton NN6 8DB Tel. *01604 770711* Fax. *01604 770027* E-mail. *simons@haddonstone.co.uk* Web. *www.haddonstone.com Haddon-Tecstone – Haddonstone – Stoneage – Tecstone*

Haesler Machine Tools 19 Whitney Drive, Stevenage SG1 4BE Tel. *01438 350835* Fax. *01438 229482* E-mail. *ben.haesler@ntlworld.com Alpasonic SA (France) – Bechet Productique Cluses SA (France) – Brand & Heinz – Bremor SA (Switzerland) – Edalco SA (Switzerland) – Egaclean (Switzerland) – Emissa (Switzerland) – Fleury SA (Switzerland) – Interfel SA Machines (Switzerland) – M Wolf (Germany) – Manser (Switzerland) – Modern Industrie SA (France) – Monnier & Zahner AG – Mupem SA (Spain) – Novel Industrie SA (France) – *Petit-Jean SA (France) – Petitjean Swarf Processing Plant (France) – Promatec SA (France) – S.A. Florenza (France) – *Swisstool AG (Switzerland) – Tecaro AG (Switzerland) – Willemin-Macodel SA – *Wirth & Gruffat (France) – Witech (Switzerland)*

Hager Engineering Ltd 50 Horton Wood, Telford TF1 7FT Tel. *01952 677899* Fax. *01952 676935* E-mail. *info@hager.co.uk* Web. *www.hager.com Ashley – Hager – Klik – Tehalit*

The Haigh Group Ltd Alton Road, Ross On Wye HR9 5NG Tel. *01989 763131* Fax. *01989 766360* E-mail. *info@haigh.co.uk* Web. *www.haigh.co.uk Ace Package – Ace System – Chumpit – Disposamatic – Incomaster – Macipump – Sanimatic – Sluicemaster*

Hainenko Ltd 284 Chase Road, London N14 6HF Tel. *020 88828734* Fax. *020 88827749* E-mail. *h.laubis@hainenko.com* Web. *www.hainenko.com *Baron Pen (Italy) – *Ciak (Italy) – Corporate – Dataglo – Flamenco – Ikon – Ikon - The Writing Edge – *Korint (Italy) – *Kreta (Italy) – Kwiktip – Micron – Status - Smart Writers – Strategy – *Tethys (Italy) – Totem Glue Stick*

Hainsworth Industrial Textiles Spring Valley Stanningley, Pudsey LS28 6DW Tel. *0113 2570391* Fax. *0113 3955686* E-mail. *sales@hainsworth.co.uk* Web. *www.hainsworth.co.uk A.W. Hainsworth & Sons*

Hako Machines Ltd Eldon Close Crick, Northampton NN6 7SL Tel. *01788 823535* Fax. *01788 823969* E-mail. *sales@hako.co.uk* Web. *www.hako.co.uk City Master – Contract Master – E.B. 450/530 – Hako Hamster 600/700 – Hako Jonas 1450 – Hako-Flipper – Hako-Hamster 1050 – Hako-Hamster 800 – Hako-Jonas 1100 – Hako-Jonas 1700 – Hako-Jonas 950 – Hakomatic 100/130 – Hakomatic 1100B – Hakomatic 1500B – Hakomatic B900*

Halbro Sportswear Ltd Chorley New Road Horwich, Bolton BL6 7JG Tel. *01204 696476* Fax. *01204 699479* E-mail. *info@halbro.com* Web. *www.halbro.com Halbro Sportswear*

Halcrow Group Ltd Arndale House Otley Road Headingley, Leeds LS6 2UL Tel. *0113 2208220* Fax. *0113 2742924* Web. *www.halcrow.com H.G.A.*

Halcyon Building Systems Unit 2f Trimdon Grange Industrial Estate Trimdon Grange, Trimdon Station TS29 6PA Tel. *01429 882555* Fax. *01429 882666* E-mail. *halcyon.bs@ntlworld.com* Web. *www.halcyonbuildingsystems.co.uk Gustafs – Metsec*

Halcyon Solutions Lawday Link, Farnham GU9 0BS Tel. *01252 715765* Fax. *01252 715765* E-mail. *mike.hearsey@btinternet.com* Web. *www.halcyon-solutions.co.uk ANALITE – Casella – CCD – CMOS – Contact Gauge – D1236 – D4140 – D4150 – D7000 – D7140 – D7150 – DIDCOT – DIPMETER – DIPTONE – DIVER – Druck – Duracell – Dynamic Logic (ITT Flygt) – ELPRO – ESP – FURSE – Geothechnical Instruments – HAWK – Hydro-Logic – Impress – Isodaq – M20 – M40 – McVan Instruments Pty Ltd – Multiform Technologies – Munro – OCTAPENT – Opus Software Limited – OTT Hydrometry – Penny & Giles – PULSAR – RIMCO – SERIES FOUR – Snowdon – SPLAYED BASE – STARFLOW – STARLOG – Technolog – Thistle – TINYLOG – Valeport – VARTA – VF1 – Waterline Envirotech – Westermo (Elpro) – YUASA – ZTV Electronics – Zymax*

Haldo Developments Ltd Haldo House Western Way, Bury St Edmunds IP33 3SP Tel. *01284 754043* Fax. *01284 767260* E-mail. *info@haldo.com* Web. *www.haldo.com Baselite – Haldolite – Haldopillar – Haldopost – Haldoset – Halo – Pathlite – Re-Flex – Safelite – Springbak*

Halfen Ltd Unit 2 Humphrys Road Woodside Estate, Dunstable LU5 4TP Tel. *01582 470300* Fax. *08705 316304* E-mail. *info@halfen.co.uk* Web. *www.halfen.co.uk Deha – Frimeda – Halfen – Kwikastrip – Lutz*

Halifax Fan Ltd Mistral Works Unit 11 Brookfoot Business Park, Brookfoot, Brighouse HD6 2SD Tel. *01484 475123* Fax. *01484 475122* E-mail. *sales@halifax-fan.com* Web. *www.halifax-fan.co.uk Beaufort – Chinook – Mistral*

Halifax Numerical Controls Ltd Holmfield Works Shay Lane, Halifax HX3 6RS Tel. *01422 360607* Fax. *01422 360614* E-mail. *mike.d@hnc.ltd.uk* Web. *hncl.co.uk C.B. Ferrari – G E Fanuk – H N C – Heidenhain – N U M – Siemens*

Hallam Polymer Engineering Ltd Traso House Callywhite Lane, Dronfield S18 2XR Tel. *01246 415511* Fax. *01246 414818* E-mail. *martin@hallampolymer.com* Web. *www.hallampolymer.com Betathane – Supol – V-Thane*

Hallamshire Hardmetal Products Ltd 315 Coleford Road, Sheffield S9 5NF Tel. *0114 2441483* Fax. *0114 2442712* E-mail. *sales@halhard.co.uk* Web. *www.halhard.co.uk Camlock – Eastern Carbide*

G & J Hall Ltd Burgess Road, Sheffield S9 3WD Tel. *0114 2440562* Fax. *0114 2449256* E-mail. *info@gjhall.co.uk* Web. *www.gjhall.co.uk Bradrad – Conecut – Hall – Handiburr – Hexibit – Multicut*

H J Hall Coventry Road, Hinckley LE10 0JX Tel. *01455 638800* Fax. *01455 610535* E-mail. *enquiries@hjhall.com* Web. *www.hjhall.com Executive – Softop*

Hallis Hudson Group Ltd Unit B1 Red Scar Business Park, Ribbleton, Preston PR2 5NJ Tel. *01772 909500* Fax. *01772 909599* E-mail. *info@hallishudson.com* Web. *www.hallishudson.co.uk 22o Celsius Blinds – 22o Celsius Fabrifix – Rolls – Rolls Emporium – Rolls Majorglide – Rolls Miniglide – Rolls Retrospectives – Rolls Statements – Rolls Staywite – Rolls Superglide – Rolls-Nylastic*

Hallite Seals International Ltd 130 Oldfield Road, Hampton TW12 2HT Tel. *020 89412244* Fax. *020 87831669* E-mail. *seals@hallite.com* Web. *www.hallite.com Hallite – Hythane*

J & E Hall Ltd Hansard Gate West Meadows Industrial Estate, Derby DE21 6JN Tel. *01332 253400* Fax. *01332 371061* E-mail. *graham.chamberlain@jehall.co.uk* Web. *www.jehall.co.uk H.T.I. – H.T.P. – Hall Thermotank – Hallmark – Hallscrew – Halltherm – J & E Hall – McQuay – Sterne – Sternette – Wesper*

Hallmark Cards Bingley Road, Bradford BD9 6SD Tel. *01274 252000* E-mail. *steven.wright@hallmark.co.uk* Web. *www.hallmarkuk.com Hallmark Cards UK*

Hallmark Cards Dawson Lane, Bradford BD4 6HN Tel. *01274 784200* Fax. *01274 687386* Web. *www.hallmark-uk.com Britannia product ltd*

Hallmark Ip Ltd 1 Pemberton Row, London EC4A 3BG Tel. *020 31029000* Fax. *020 31029001* E-mail. *info@hallmark-ip.com* Web. *www.hallmark-ip.com Tmoa*

Halsall Toys Europe Ltd Eastham House Copse Road, Fleetwood FY7 7NY Tel. *01253 778888* Fax. *01253 878711* E-mail. *general@htigroup.co.uk* Web. *www.htigroup.co.uk Fun Sport – My Toy – Navigator – Water Fun*

Halver Ltd Pearith Farm Long Wittenham, Abingdon OX14 4PS Tel. *01235 511666* Fax. *01235 811566* E-mail. *info@halver.com* Web. *www.halver.com Halver Ltd*

Ham Baker Pipelines Ltd Garner Street Etruria, Stoke On Trent ST4 7BH Tel. *01782 202300* Fax. *01782 203639* E-mail. *sbailie@hambaker.co.uk* Web. *www.hambaker.co.uk Ham Baker Adams*

Hamble Distribution Ltd 15 Ashley Street, Glasgow G3 6DR Tel. *0141 3323232* Fax. *0141 3326335* E-mail. *david@blackspur.com* Web. *www.blackspur.com Blackspur*

Hambledon Studios Unit 1a Parkhill Business Centre Padiham Road, Burnley BB12 6TG Tel. *01282 686000* Fax. *01282 686001* E-mail. *hambledon@aol.com Arnold Barton – Donny Mac – New Image – Reflections*

Hamelin Stationery Ltd River Street, Brighouse HD6 1LU Tel. *01484 385600* Fax. *01484 385602* E-mail. *francis.werner@hamelinstationery.com* Web. *www.hamelinstationery.com Hamelin Stationery – Hamelin Stationery*

Hamer Stevenson Ltd 1 Gateworth Industrial Estate Forrest Way, Warrington WA5 1DF Tel. *0161 6336424* Fax. *0161 6274797* E-mail. *sales@hamer-stevenson.co.uk* Web. *www.hamer-stevenson.co.uk Barco – Flexmaster*

Hamilton Acorn Ltd Halford Road, Attleborough NR17 2HZ Tel. *01953 453201* Fax. *01953 454943* E-mail. *info@hamilton-acorn.co.uk* Web. *www.hamilton-acorn.co.uk Acorn – Hamilton – Perfection*

R Hamilton & Co. Ltd (Hamilton Litestat Group) Quarry Industrial Estate Mere, Warminster BA12 6LA Tel. *01747 860088* Fax. *01747 861032* E-mail. *info@hamilton-litestat.com* Web. *www.hamilton-litestat.com Bloomsbury (United Kingdom) – Cheriton (United Kingdom) – Digital Mercury (United Kingdom) – Hamilton Litestat (United Kingdom) – Hartland (United Kingdom) – Linea (United Kingdom) – Litestat – Mercury Litestat – Sheer (United Kingdom) – Woods (United Kingdom)*

Hamlin Electronics Europe Ltd Broadland Business Park, Norwich NR7 0WG. Tel. *01603 257700* Fax. *01379 649702* E-mail. *sales.uk@hamlin.com* Web. *www.hamlin.com Hamlin – Hamlin - Reed switches, Reed relays, proximity switches, shock sensors*

Hammerite Products Ltd Eltringham Works, Prudhoe NE42 6LP Tel. *01661 830000* Fax. *01661 835760* E-mail. *sales@hammerite.com* Web. *www.hammerite.com Hammerite Garage Door Enamel – Hammerite Metal Finish – Hammerite Radiator Enamel – Hammerite Underbody Seal – Hammerite Waxoyl – Hermetite – Hylamor – Joy – Kidde – Kurust – No1 Rustbeater – Solvol*

Hammond & Co. Ltd Finway Road Hemel Hempstead Industrial Estate, Hemel Hempstead HP2 7PT Tel. *01442 212211* Fax. *01442 252003* E-mail. *sales@hammco.com* Web. *www.hammco.com Coolant Fed Rotating Toolholders – Gun Drills – Gun Reamers – High Pressure Coolant Pumps – Proten Drills – ROK-IT Gauges – Speedfeed – Spraymist Pumps – Valve Guide Reamers – Ventec – Ventec Drills*

Hammond Lubricants & Chemicals Ltd Unit 2-4 Porters Way, Birmingham B9 5RR Tel. *0121 7721375* Fax. *0121 7723530* E-mail. *sales@hammondlubricants.co.uk* Web. *www.hammondlubricants.co.uk Bp – Esso – Mobil – Q8 – Shell – Texaco*

Hampshire Electroplating Co. Ltd 69-75 Empress Road, Southampton SO14 0JW Tel. *023 80225639* Fax. *023 80639874* E-mail. *info@hepcoltd.co.uk* Web. *www.hepcoltd.co.uk Empress*

Hampshire Hose Services Ltd 1 The Crosshouse Centre Crosshouse Road, Southampton SO14 5GZ Tel. *023 80335588* Fax. *023 80631509* E-mail. *sales@hampshirehose.co.uk* Web. *www.hampshirehose.co.uk Norma – Merlett – Alfagamma – Synflex – Goodridge – Metalwork Pneumatic – Watershield*

Hampshire Press Unit 4-5 Dukes Road, Southampton SO14 0SQ Tel. *023 80011911* Fax. *023 80581970* E-mail. *enquiries@hampshirepress.co.uk* Web. *www.hampshirepress.co.uk Hampshire Press*

Hampson Composites Ltd Vale Mill Vale Street, Bolton BL2 6QF Tel. *01204 381626* Fax. *01204 529457* E-mail. *liz@hampson-composites.co.uk* Web. *www.hampson-composites.co.uk Clini-Board*

Hamptons International 11-13 Queen Street, Maidenhead SL6 1NB Tel. *01628 622131* Fax. *01628 785446* E-mail. *maidenhead@hamptons-int.com* Web. *www.hamptons.co.uk Hamptons*

The Hampton Works Ltd Twyning Road Stirchley, Birmingham B30 2XZ Tel. *0121 4582901* Fax. *0121 4333819* E-mail. *sales@hamptonworks.co.uk* Web. *www.hamptonworks.co.uk Atlas – Bulldog – Fort – Samson*

Hamster Baskets Aylhill Aylton, Ledbury HR8 2QJ Tel. *01531 670209* Fax. *01531 670630* E-mail. *richard@hamsterbaskets.co.uk* Web. *www.hamsterbaskets.co.uk Bumf-Lugger – Dog Cages – Free Flow Trays – Hamster Baskets – Hoddle – Milk Tippler – Tray Shifters – Vacu-Rack*

Hamworthy Combustion Engineering Ltd Fleets Corner, Poole BH17 0LA Tel. *01202 662700* Fax. *01202 669875* E-mail. *info@hamworthy-combustion.com* Web. *www.hamworthy-combustion.com Axiflo 6000 (United Kingdom) – D.F.R. (United Kingdom) – Dualscan (United Kingdom) – Enviromix 2000 (United Kingdom) – Flare Seals (United Kingdom) – Flarescan (United Kingdom) – Flarestream (United Kingdom) – Radol (United Kingdom) – Tribolite (United Kingdom) – Unimax (United Kingdom) – Venturi 5000 (United Kingdom) – Walrad (United Kingdom)*

Hamworthy Heating Ltd Fleets Corner, Poole BH17 0HH Tel. *01202 662500* Fax. *01202 662550* E-mail. *sales@hamworthy-heating.com* Web. *www.hamworthy-heating.com Broadstone HE – Dorchester – Flue & Chimney Systems – Forston 200+400 – Lilliput HE – Lulworth – Marshall – Pipework Kits – Portland – Powerstock – Purewell – Shaftesbury H.E. – Tarrant – Warmwell H.E. – Wessex 100m – Wessex HE – Wimborne H.E.*

Hamworthy Waste Water plc Fleets Corner, Poole BH17 0JT Tel. *01202 662600* Fax. *01202 666363* E-mail. *info@hamworthy.com* Web. *www.hamworthy.com Chockfast – Dolphin – Monovec – Super Trident – Svanehoj – V-Line – Vectwin*

Hanbury Autogil Bradley Lane, Newton Abbot TQ12 1LZ Tel. *01626 333366* Fax. *01626 333388*

E-mail. *sales@hanbury-autogil.co.uk*
Web. *www.hanbury-autogil.co.uk Autogil – Autogil*

Hancocks Cash & Carry Ltd 25 Jubilee Drive, Loughborough LE11 5TX Tel. *01509 216644* Fax. *01509 237104* E-mail. *info@hancocks.co.uk* Web. *www.hancocks.co.uk *Kiddies Way – *Kingsway*

Hands Industries Ltd 111 Kimberley Street, Warrington WA5 1PA Tel. *0870 9917182* Fax. *0870 1281665* E-mail. *yvonne@hands-soap.com* Web. *www.hands-soap.com Hands Soap Shop*

John Hanna Ltd Kildrum Dyeworks Kells, Ballymena BT42 3DL Tel. *028 25891206* Fax. *028 25891423* E-mail. *clifford.barr@birdmcnutt.com* Web. *www.bairdmcnutt.com John Hanna Ltd*

Hanovia Ltd 780 Buckingham Avenue, Slough SL1 4LA Tel. *01753 515300* Fax. *01753 534277* E-mail. *sales@hanovia.com* Web. *www.hanovia.com Hanovia*

Hanson Building Products Hanson House 14 Castle Hill, Maidenhead SL6 4JJ Tel. *01628 774100* Fax. *020 72353455* E-mail. *enquiries@hanson.com* Web. *www.hanson.com Hanson*

Hanson Concrete Products plc Hoveringham Works Hoveringham Lane, Hoveringham, Nottingham NG14 7JX Tel. *01636 832000* Fax. *01636 832020* E-mail. *enquiries@hanson.com* Web. *www.hanson.com Jetfloor 300 – Jetfloor Plus – Jetfloor Slab – Jetfloor Standard – Jetfloor Super*

Hantarex International Ltd 34 Salisbury Street, London NW8 8QE Tel. *020 87781414* Fax. *020 86599348* E-mail. *sales@hantarex.com* Web. *www.hantarex.com *Hantarex (Italy)*

Harbro Ltd Markethill Industrial Estate Markethill Road, Turriff AB53 4PA Tel. *01888 545200* Fax. *01888 563939* E-mail. *info@harbro.co.uk* Web. *www.harbro.co.uk *Biosuper – *Clover Sheep – *Grampian Minerals – *Harbro Ruminant – *Highland Game*

Hardall International Ltd Fairway Works Southfields Road, Dunstable LU6 3EP Tel. *01582 500860* Fax. *01582 690975* E-mail. *abishop@hardalluk.com* Web. *www.hardall.co.uk Harcon – Hardall – Hardall Bergmann – Hardall Gannet – Hardall Ise – Hardall Trident – Harpac – Harpac Centaur – Harpac Jenpak – Tripak*

Hardware.com Trafalgar House Kemble Enterprise Park Kemble, Cirencester GL7 6BQ Tel. *01285 771633* Fax. *0870 2429825* E-mail. *info@hardware.com* Web. *www.hardware.com hardware.com*

Hardwood Dimensions Holdings Ltd Trafford Park Road Trafford Park, Manchester M17 1WH Tel. *0161 8725111* Fax. *0161 8737004* E-mail. *sales@hardwooddimensions.ltd.uk* Web. *www.hardwooddimensions.ltd.uk Hardwood Dimensions*

Hardy Amies London Ltd 14 Savile Row, London W1S 3JN Tel. *020 77342436* Fax. *020 74397116* E-mail. *reception@hardyamies.com* Web. *www.hardyamies.com Hardy Amies*

Hardy & Greys Ltd Willowburn Trading Estate, Alnwick NE66 2PF Tel. *01665 602771* Fax. *01665 602389* E-mail. *enquiries@hardygreys.com* Web. *www.hardyfishing.com Hardy Advanced Composites*

Hardy & Hanson Ltd Longlands Road, Dewsbury WF13 4AB Tel. *01924 462353* Fax. *01924 457883* E-mail. *info@hardy-hanson.co.uk* Web. *www.hardy-hanson.co.uk Hardy & Hanson (United Kingdom)*

Hardy Marine Ltd Gaymers Way, North Walsham NR28 0AN Tel. *01692 408700* Fax. *01692 406483* E-mail. *sales@hardymarine.co.uk* Web. *www.hardymarine.co.uk Hardy – Seawings*

James Hare Ltd Monarch House Queen Street, Leeds LS1 1LX Tel. *0113 2431204* Fax. *0113 2347648* E-mail. *sales@james-hare.com* Web. *www.james-hare.com James Hare Silks*

Harford Control Ltd 35 Harford Street, Trowbridge BA14 7HL Tel. *01225 764461* Fax. *01225 769733* E-mail. *clive@harfordcontrol.com* Web. *www.harfordcontrol.com Harford Control*

Hargreaves Promotions Aspen House Airport Service Road, Portsmouth PO3 5RA Tel. *023 92822436* Fax. *023 92822177* E-mail. *sales@hargreavespromotions.co.uk* Web. *www.hargreavespromotions.co.uk Hargreaves*

Harland Machine Systems Ltd 2 Michigan Avenue, Salford M50 2GY Tel. *0161 8484800* Fax. *0161 8484830* E-mail. *enquiries@harland-hms.com* Web. *www.harland-hms.com Comet – Enterprise – Gemini – Harland Europa – Jupiter – Locator B – Neptune – Orion – Orion - Comet - Gemini - Neptune - Proteus - Saturn - Sirius - Jupiter - Pulsar - Titan - Enterprise - Harland Europa - Proteus – Saturn – Sirius – Titan*

Harland Simon plc Bond Avenue Bletchley, Milton Keynes MK1 1TJ Tel. *01908 276700* Fax. *01908 276701* E-mail. *sales@harlandsimon.com* Web. *www.harlandsimon.com Harland Simon*

Harlequin Ladybird House Beeches Road, Loughborough LE11 2HA Tel. *08445 430100* Fax. *0844 5430101* E-mail. *harsales@harlequin.uk.com* Web. *www.harlequin.uk.com Ajanta – Amorini – Antiquity – Archive – Arlington Court – Brushed Plains – Casablanca*

A R Harley & Sons Station Road Crowhurst, Battle TN33 9DB Tel. *01424 830542* Fax. *01424 830532* E-mail. *arharley@harleycustom.com* Web. *www.harleycustom.com A R Harley & Sons Ltd*

Harlow Agricultural Merchants Ltd Latchmore Bank Little Hallingbury, Bishops Stortford CM22 7PJ Tel. *01279 658313* Fax. *01279 755395* E-mail. *ron@harlow-ag.co.uk* Web. *www.harlow-ag.co.uk Black Prince – Ham – Hemcore*

Harlow Brothers Ltd Hathern Road Long Whatton, Loughborough LE12 5DE Tel. *01509 842561* Fax. *01509 843577* E-mail. *sales@harlowbros.co.uk* Web. *www.harlowbros.co.uk Harlow Bros*

Harlow Printing Ltd 7 Maxwell Street, South Shields NE33 4PU Tel. *0191 4554286* Fax. *0191 4270195* E-mail. *sales@harlowprinting.co.uk* Web. *www.harlowprinting.co.uk H. 77*

Harman International Bennett Street Bridgend Industrial Estate, Bridgend CF31 3SH Tel. *01656 645441* Fax. *01656 650327* E-mail. *info@harman.com* Web. *www.harman.com Harman Motive*

Harman Technology Ltd Ilford Way Mobberley, Knutsford WA16 7JL Tel. *01565 650000* Fax. *01565 872734* E-mail. *sales@ilfordphoto.com* Web. *www.ilfordphoto.com Delta 100 – Delta 3200 – Delta 400 – FP4 Plus – Galerie – HP5 Plus – Hypam – Ilfobrom – Ilfochrome – Ilfoclean – Ilfocolor – Ilfofix – Ilfoguard – Ilfojet – Ilfolab – Ilford – Ilford XP2 – Ilfosol – Ilfospeed – Ilfostar – Ilfotec – Ilfotol – Microphen – Multigrade IV – Omnipro – Perceptol – Printasia*

Harmsworth Townley & Co. Ltd The Melting Pot White Hart Fold, Todmorden OL14 7BD Tel. *01706 814931* Fax. *01706 812382* E-mail. *glen@harmsworth-townley.co.uk* Web. *www.highpowersemiconductors.com Westcode, Hind, International Rectifier, IXYS*

Harness Flex Ltd Station Road Industrial Estate Station Road, Coleshill, Birmingham B46 1HT Tel. *01675 468222* Fax. *01675 464930* E-mail. *sales@harnessflex.co.uk* Web. *www.harnessflex.co.uk Harnessflex*

Harpercollins Publishers Ophelia House Elsinore House 77 Fulham Palace Road, London W6 8JB Tel. *020 87417070* Fax. *020 77923176* E-mail. *victoria.barnsley@harpercollins.co.uk* Web. *www.harpercollins.co.uk Bartholomew – Cobuild – Collins – Collins book bus – Collins Educational – Elements – Flamingo – Fontana – Fount – Fourth Estates – Gem – Harper Collins – Marshall Pickering – Thorsons – Times Books – Voyager – Willow – Young Lions*

Harrier Fluid Power Ltd Parys Road Ludlow Business Park, Ludlow SY8 1XY Tel. *01584 876033* Fax. *01584 876044* E-mail. *sales@harrieronline.co.uk* Web. *www.harrieronline.co.uk A.C. Delco – A.P. Precision – A.P.M. – AAACO – ABAC – AC – Advance Machine – AGEMA – AIAG – AICHI – Air Maze – Akerman – Alco – Allen – Allied Systems – Allis Chambe – Allison Trans – Alsa – Alsop – Alsthorn – Alta Brescia – Alup – Amadausa – Ambac – AMC – American Parts – Ametek – Antonio Carra – Aquapure – Arburg – ARGO – Ariens – Army Navy – Ashi Japan – Astra Veic Ind – Ateso – ATHEY – Atlas – Atlas Copco – Atlet – Atos – Austin Western – Aveling Bar – Bafco – Baker – Baldwin – Banner – Barko – Battenfield – Baudouin – Bauser – Bea Filtri – Bebco – Beckarnley – Becker – Behringer – Benati – Bendini – Bendix – BENFORD – Benfra – Betaflow – BIG A – Bitelli – Blaw Knox – Blount – BMW – Boge – Bohl & Kirk – Bomag – Bombardier – Bosch – Bowser Briggs – Boy – Briggs & Strat – British Filters – Broomwade – Bros MFG – Brueninghaus – Buamann – Bucher – Bucyrys-Erie – Buessing – Bullard – Busch – Can flo – Capa – Capitol – Carquest – Casagrande – Casappa – Case – Case Poclain – Caterpillar – Ceccato – Cerraro – Cessna – Champion – Charlynn – Chaseside – CIFA – Cimtek – Cincinnati Mil – Claas – Clark – Clark Michigan – CO-PO – Coles – Commercial – Como – Compare Holman – Conair – Condor – Consler – Continental HY – Coopers – Coventry – Craver – Crosland – Cross – Cummins – Cuno – Cyclone – DAHL – Dairymaster – Danfoss – David Brown – Davies – Davis – Dayton – Delaval – Deltech – Deltrol – Deluxe – Demag – Denco – Denison – Dennis Eagle – Dept of Army – Deutz – Diagnetics – Diexa – Ditchwitch – Dodge – Dolling – Dollinger – Domange – Dominion – Donaldson – Dresser Clar – Drott – Ducati – Dulevo – Dynahoe – Dynamic – Dynapac – Eastern – Eaton – Ecoair – Eder – Edmas – Effer – Elasia – Electromotiv – Elgin – Elox – Enpro – Euromach – Europ Hydro – Excel – F.ILLI DIECI – Facet – Fahr Butcher – FAI – Fairey Arlon – Falk – Farr – Faun/Frisch – Fawcett – FBN – FBO – Fendt – Fenwick – Fiaam – Fiat Allis – Fife – Filmax – Filpro – Filter Produ – Filterdyne – Filtermart – Filterrite – Filters – Filtersoft – Filtratio – Filtre – *Filtrec (Italy) – Filtrex – Filu – Fincantieri – Finn Filter – Fispa – Fleet Guard – Flexider – Flli Dieci – Flow Ezy – Flow-line – Fluidpower – Fluidtech – Fluitek – Fluitron – Foden – Foredil – Fox equip – FPC – Fram – Franklin – Frimocar – Fuchs – Furukawa – G.U.D. – Gardener Denv – Garret – GB Filtri – Gehl – General Electric – General Vacuum – Gesto – Giesse Filtri – Giletta – GM – GMC – Gonker – Gresen – Greyfriars – Grove Coles – Guardian – Guiot – Gulfgate – Gutbrod – Hako – Halla – Haller – Hamm – Hankinson – Hann – Hanomag – Hanta – Harmsco – Harvard – Hastings – Haulotte – Hayporter – Hayruard – HBE – Heil – Hengst – Henschel – Hesston – Hiab Foco – Hifi – Hilco – Hilfex – Hillard – Hinomoto – HITACHI – Hitzmann – Hoes – Hoffman – Hokuetsu – HP Hydrali – HPC – Huber-Warco – Hutchins – Hycon – Hydac – Hydema – Hydramac – Hydraotechni – Hydraumatec – Hydreco – Hydrocraft – Hydrofilt – Hydroflex – Hydromac – Hymac – Hypro – Hyster – Hytrex – Hyundai – IHC – IHI – Ikron – Indufil – Industrial Filter – Ingersoll – Insley – Internor/Sachn – Internormen – Iowa Mold – Iseki – Isotta Franschini – Isuzu – Iveco – Jacobsen – JCB – Jellif Hydrau – Jlfas – John Deere – Joy – Jungheinrich – Kaercher – Kaeser – Kaessbohrer – Kaiser-Kamo – Kalmar – Kamag – Kamokasier – Kato – Kaydon – Keene – Kellog – KHD – Knecht – Kobelco – Koehring – Kohler – Komori Oil – Kooi – Kralinator – Kramer – Kubota – Laltesi – Lansing – LB Filters – LC Oleddinamica – Lebtourneau – Lenz – Leroi – Leybold – Leyland – LHA – Liebherr – Linde – Lister Petter – Lombardini – Long – Luberfiner – M. Filter – Mack – Macomeudon – Mahle Purolator – Makino – Manitou – Mann & Hummel – Marion – Mark – Marlow – Marvel – Marzak – Masey Ferguson – Matbro – Mather & Platt – Maxiflow – Mazak – Mcmastercar – Mecalac – Mectron – Meiller – Mengle – Menzimuck – Mercedes Benz – Merlo – Messer – Michigan – Microfilter – Micropore – Millipore – Mintaurus – Mitsubishi – Moog – Mopar – Morooka – Motorcraft – Motorguard – Motorolla – MP Filtri – MTC – Multiquip – Murphy Broth – Mustang – Nalg – Napa – Nelson Winslow – Nessie – Netstal – Neuson – New Holland – Nikko – Nippon – Nippondenso – Nissan – Norba – Norco – Norman – Norman Filters – Nuclepore – Nugent – Nuovo Pignone – Nupro – O&K – Oleostar – OMC – OMT – Onan – Osmonics – Owatonna – Packfab – Palfinger – Pall – Pall Trinity – Panther – Parker – Pasquali – Paus – PBR – Peco – Peerless – Peljob – Perkins – Perry – Pingon – Pioneer – Plasser – PLM – PMI – Pneumatech – Poclain – Poltpro – Priestman – Prince – Profitlich – PTI Technology – Pulimat – Purflux – Putzmeister – PX Filtration – QUD – Quincy – Racfil – Racinedana – Rammax – Ransomes – Ratfischatlas – Refilco – Regeltechnik – Renault – Rexroth – Rheinstahl – Rietschle – Ripley – Robert Gord – Rocla – Rolba – Rossi Cogeme – Royal – Ruggerini – RX – Ryco – S+L+H – Sakai – Same – SAMSUNG – Sanderson – Sauer – Savara – Scania – Scarab – Schaefer – Schroeder – Schwing – Semier – Sennebogen – Separation Technology – Shibaura – Shinnihon Yuken – Simas Filters – Simplicity – SMC – SMW – Snaptte – Sofima – Sofra – Sofralub – Sofrance – Solberg – Somet – Somos – Soparis – stauff – Steiger – Sternerblomqui – Steyr – Still – Stokes – STP – Submitomo – Sullair – Sunbeam – Sunnen Products – Sunstrand – SWC – Swing – Tadano – Taisei Kogyo – Takeuchi – Tamrock – TCM – Tecnocar – Tecumseh – Tennant – Terex – Texaco – Texax Filtra – Textron – Thermoking – Thomas – Thwaites – Timberjack – Tiocco – TM – Torit Donald – Torite – Toro – Towmotor – Toyota – Triboguard – Tridek – Tuxco – U.S. Army Tank – UCC – UCD – UFI – Unitec – United Engines – Universal Hydr – Vacuhoist – Vag – Valmet – Valveoil – Vanair – Vapormatic – Velcon – Vender – Venieri – Vermeer – Versalite – Vescor – Vessel – Vibromax – Vickers – VME – Voegele – Voith – Vokes – Volvo – Vortox – Wabco – Wacker – Wako – Waterguard – Waterman – Watts – Waukensha – Wayne – Webtec – Weidermann – Weimar – Werie – Western – Westinghouse – WGB – Wilkenson – Winget – Winslow – Wintec – Wirtgen – Wix – Woodgate – Worthington – Yale – Yamashin – Yanmar – Zettelmeyer – ZF – Zinga – Zurn*

Harrington Generators International Ltd Ravenstor Road Wirksworth, Matlock DE4 4FY Tel. *01629 824284* Fax. *01629 824613* E-mail. *enquiries@hgigenerators.com* Web. *www.hgigenerators.com Merlin – Powerfusion – Silent Knight – Spitfire*

Harris & Bailey Ltd 50 Hastings Road, Croydon CR9 6BR Tel. *020 86543181* Fax. *020 86569369* E-mail. *mail@harris-bailey.co.uk* Web. *www.harris-bailey.co.uk Granite Setts – Harbex – Harbex-Ware*

Harris Cleaning Services Hanbury Road Hanbury, Bromsgrove B60 4BU Tel. *01527 575441* Fax. *01953 455905* E-mail. *sales@lgharris.co.uk Aristocat – Ideal Lawn – Kleencoat – Longlife – Norfolk Brushes – Victory*

Harris Hart & Co. Ltd Gregge Street Works Gregge Street, Heywood OL10 2EJ Tel. *01706 625355* Fax. *01706 360570* E-mail. *info@epsom-salts.com* Web. *www.epsom-salts.com Epsom Salt – Epsom Salt Crystals – Magnesium Sulphate Crystals – Magnesium Sulphate Dryed Powder – Magnesium Sulphate Exsiccated Powder*

L G Harris & Co. Ltd Hanbury Road Stoke Prior, Bromsgrove B60 4AE Tel. *01527 575441* Fax. *01527 575366* E-mail. *garyj@lgharris.co.uk* Web. *www.lgharris.co.uk Definition – Delta – EasyClean – Harris – Harris- paint brushes, paint rollers, paint pads, painters tools,decorative brushes and rollers, household & shoe brushes. – No Loss – T-Class – Ultima*

David Harrison & Sons Ltd Canal Mills Hillhouse Lane, Huddersfield HD1 1ED Tel. *01484 533391*

Fax. *01484 434934* E-mail. *sales@dharrisonandsons.co.uk* Web. *www.dharrisonandsons.co.uk David Harrison & Sons*

Harrison Group Enviromental Ltd 12 Kimberley Street, Norwich NR2 2RJ Tel. *01603 613111* Fax. *01603 618120* E-mail. *info@harrisongroupuk.com* Web. *www.harrisongroupuk.com Harrison*

J A Harrison & Co Manchester Ltd Britain Works Sherborne Street, Manchester M8 8HP Tel. *0161 8322282* Fax. *0161 8323263* E-mail. *enquiries@jaharrison.co.uk* Web. *www.jaharrison.co.uk Ivy – Magnet*

Harrison Lubrication Engineering Ltd Lynstock Way Lostock, Bolton BL6 4SA Tel. *01204 691352* Fax. *01204 669200* E-mail. *sales@hle.co.uk* Web. *www.nippleshop.co.uk Interlube – Lincoln – Perma – Vogel*

Harrison Thompson & Co. Ltd Yeoman House Whitehall Industrial Estate Whitehall Road, Leeds LS12 5JB Tel. *0113 2795854* Fax. *0113 2310406* E-mail. *info@yeomanshield.com* Web. *www.yeomanshield.com Vinylac – Yeoman Rainguard – Yeoman Shield – Yeomanshield - Rainguard - Anticlimb - Custom Mouldings - Formula One - Colourcap*

T S Harrison & Sons Ltd Union Works Union Street, Heckmondwike WF16 0HL Tel. *01924 015000* Fax. *01924 415011* E-mail. *mail@600lathes.co.uk* Web. *www.600uk.co Alpha Plus S – Alpha T – Alpha U – Harrison – Harrison - metal turning lathes, Alpha Plus S - the ultimate turning machine.*

Harris Walton Lifting Gear Ltd Two Woods Lane, Brierley Hill DY5 1TR Tel. *01384 74071* Fax. *01384 74070* E-mail. *sales@harriswaltonliftinggear.co.uk* Web. *www.harriswaltonliftinggear.co.uk Harris-Walton Lifting Gear*

Harrod UK Ltd 1-3 Pinbush Road, Lowestoft NR33 7NL Tel. *01502 583515* Fax. *01502 582456* E-mail. *sales@harrod.uk.com* Web. *www.harrod.uk.com Harrod Industrial – Harrod Sport*

Harrow Tool Co. Ltd 853-857 Harrow Road, London NW10 5NH Tel. *020 89698237* Fax. *020 89686121* E-mail. *sales@harrowtool.co.uk* Web. *www.harrowtool.co.uk *Atlas Copco (Germany) – *Bosch (Germany) – *Dewalt (United Kingdom) – *Hitachi (Japan) – *Makita (Japan) – *Ridgid (U.S.A.) – *Ryobi (Japan)*

Harsco Rail Ltd Unit 1 Chewton Street Eastwood, Nottingham NG16 3HB Tel. *01773 539480* Fax. *01773 539481* E-mail. *awardle@harsco.com* Web. *www.harscorail.com Permaquip*

Harsh Ltd The Industrial Estate Full Sutton, York YO41 1HS Tel. *01759 372100* Fax. *01759 371414* E-mail. *grant.faulkner@harshuk.com* Web. *www.harshuk.com Harsh*

Hart Door Systems Redburn Road, Newcastle upon Tyne NE5 1PJ Tel. *0191 2140404* Fax. *0191 2711611* E-mail. *doug@speedor.com* Web. *www.speedor.com Firebrand – Securigrille – Speedor*

Hartest Precision Instruments Ltd 2 Gatton Park Business Centre Wells Place, Merstham, Redhill RH1 3LG Tel. *01737 649300* Fax. *020 85493374* E-mail. *info@h-pi.co.uk* Web. *www.h-pi.co.uk Cogenix – H.W. Wallace – Wallace Instruments*

Harting Ltd Caswell Road Brackmills Industrial Estate, Northampton NN4 7PW Tel. *01604 827500* Fax. *01604 706777* E-mail. *gb@harting.com* Web. *www.harting.co.uk Han – Han HC – Han - Modular – Han - Yellock – Han - Eco – Han - Snap – Han - Port – Han - Q – Han DD – Han E – Han Q 5/0 – Han Q 7/0 – Han Q 4/2 – Han Q 8/0 – Han DD Module – Han Axiel Screw Module – Han - Power – Han - Power S – Han - Power T – Ha - Vis – Ha - Vis RFID – Harting Push Pull RJ45, IP67 – Harting Push Pull LC Duplex, IP67 – Harax – Har-bus – Har-bus HM – har-flex connectors – Advanced TCA – Har-mik – har-link – Harting Integrated Solutions (HIS)*

Hartle I G E Ltd Demesne Drive St Pauls Trading Estate, Stalybridge SK15 2QF Tel. *0161 3037394* Fax. *0161 3031110* E-mail. *info@hartleige.com* Web. *www.hartleige.com Baelz – Hunton – Paramount – Vickery*

Hartley Botanic Ltd Wellington Road Greenfield, Oldham OL3 7AG Tel. *01457 873244* Fax. *01457 821968* E-mail. *info@hartleybotanic.co.uk* Web. *www.hartley-botanic.co.uk Clear Span – Hartley Botanic*

Fred Hartley Estates Ltd The Offices 110 Town Street, Upwell, Wisbech PE14 9DQ Tel. *01945 773789* Fax. *01945 772928* E-mail. *office@fhestates.co.uk* Web. *www.fhestates.com Jolly Roger*

Hartley & Sugden Atlas Works Gibbet Street, Halifax HX1 4DB Tel. *01422 355651* Fax. *01422 359636* E-mail. *paulcooper@ormandyltd.com* Web. *www.hartleyandsugden.co.uk Compact – Compact Gas – Junior SCP – Metrose – S.C.P. – SCPE – Super Colifax*

Hart Materials Ltd Carrier House Carriers Fold Church Road, Wombourne, Wolverhampton WV5 9DH Tel. *01902 895446* Fax. *01902 897469* E-mail. *info@hartmaterials.com* Web. *www.hartmaterials.com Hart Coating Technology – *Novamet (U.S.A.)*

Harton Services Ltd Unit 6 Thistlebrook Industrial Estate Eynsham Drive, London SE2 9RB Tel. *020 83100421* Fax. *020 83106785* E-mail. *info@hartons.co.uk* Web. *www.hartons.co.uk Boosted – Cosybug – H.T. – Harco Pack – Harton Metro – Hartonaut – Hartonstore – Metrotherm – Preform – Thermaline – Vice Roy*

K Hartwall Ltd 4 Park Square Thorncliffe Park Estate Newton Chambers Road, Chapeltown, Sheffield S35 2PH Tel. *0114 2573631* Fax. *0114 2573630* E-mail. *chris.sampson@k-hartwall.com* Web. *www.k-hartwall.com Bekaert*

Hartwell plc Faringdon Road Cumnor, Oxford OX2 9RE Tel. *01865 866000* Fax. *01865 866010* E-mail. *georgina.forbes@hartwell.co.uk* Web. *www.hartwell.co.uk Hartwell*

Harvey Map Services Ltd 12-22 Main Street, Doune FK16 6BJ Tel. *01786 841202* Fax. *01786 841098* E-mail. *sales@harveymaps.co.uk* Web. *www.harveymaps.co.uk Duxbak – Mazzle – Munro Corbett Chart – Superwalker*

Harveys Nursery Glodwick Road, Oldham OL4 1YU Tel. *0161 6249535* Fax. *0161 6272028* E-mail. *sales@harveys.co.uk* Web. *www.harveys.co.uk *Harpoon (United Kingdom)*

Harvey Water Softeners Ltd Hipley Street, Woking GU22 9LQ Tel. *01483 753404* Fax. *01483 726030* E-mail. *info@harvey.co.uk* Web. *www.harveywatersofteners.co.uk Harvey Softeners – Kinetico*

Harvie & Hudson Ltd 96 Jermyn Street, London SW1Y 6JE Tel. *020 78393578* Fax. *020 78397020* E-mail. *matthew@harvieandhudson.com* Web. *www.harvieandhudson.com Harvie & Hudson*

Hasbro UK Ltd 2 Roundwood Avenue Stockley Park, Uxbridge UB11 1AZ Tel. *020 85691234* Fax. *020 85691133* E-mail. *john.harper@hasbro.co.uk* Web. *www.hasbro.co.uk Hasbro – Kenner – M.B. – Parker – Play School – Sindy – Waddingtons*

Haskel Europe Ltd North Hylton Road, Sunderland SR5 3JD Tel. *0191 5491212* Fax. *0191 5490911* E-mail. *sales@haskel.co.uk* Web. *www.haskel.com Butech – Durameter – Haskel*

Hassett Industries Stonehenge Road Durrington, Salisbury SP4 8BN Tel. *01980 654333* Fax. *01980 654326* E-mail. *info@hassettindustries.com* Web. *www.hassettindustries.com Hi-Heat – Hi-Heat*

H A S T A M 10 Sovereign Court 8 Graham Street, Birmingham B1 3JR Tel. *08445 610434* Fax. *01621 851756* E-mail. *info@hastam.co.uk* Web. *www.hastam.co.uk Chase For Windows (United Kingdom)*

Hatfields Machine Tools Ltd 12 Boughton Road, London SE28 0AG Tel. *020 86446661* Fax. *020 86444233* E-mail. *len.martin@hatmac.co.uk* Web. *www.hatmac.com Hatfield Precision – Hatfield-Gasparinl*

Hava Shapiro 1878 Ltd Stratford Workshops Burford Road, London E15 2SP Tel. *020 85559607* E-mail. *info@technicalsupermarket.com* Web. *www.technicalsupermarket.com Hava Shapiro*

Havelock Europa plc Moss Way Hillend Industrial Park, Hillend, Dunfermline KY11 9JS Tel. *01383 820044* Fax. *01383 820064* E-mail. *richard.lowery@havelockeuropa.com* Web. *www.havelockeuropa.com Castle – Duradec – Euroshop – Havelocktagou – Mirrospot*

Haven Automation Ltd Measurement House Kingsway, Fforestfach, Swansea SA5 4EX Tel. *01792 588722* Fax. *01792 582624* E-mail. *sales@haven.co.uk* Web. *www.haven.co.uk Minical Mk III – Minicall – Modeq – Spec-Cal – Tempcal*

Hawco The Wharf Abbey Mill Business Park, Lower Eashing, Godalming GU7 2QN Tel. *01483 869000* Fax. *01204 675010* E-mail. *info@hawco.co.uk* Web. *www.hawco.co.uk Bourns – Cantherm – *Microtherm (Germany) – *Moxie (Canada)*

Hawke International Oxford Street West, Ashton Under Lyne OL7 0NA Tel. *0161 8306698* Fax. *0161 8306648* E-mail. *mconnolly@ehawke.com* Web. *www.ehawke.com Enclosures – Ex Connectors – Fieldbus ROUTE-MASTER – Fire Barrier Transits – RAC Cable Gland – Universal Cable Gland*

Hawkesworth Appliance Testing Guidance House York Road, Thirsk YO7 3BT Tel. *01845 524498* Fax. *01845 526884* E-mail. *t.crowley@hawketest.co.uk* Web. *www.hawktest.co.uk Hawkesworth Appliance Testing*

Hawk Lifting Unit 3 Spring Park Clayburn RoadGrimethorpe, Barnsley S72 7FD Tel. *01226 718830* E-mail. *info@hawklifting.co.uk* Web. *www.hawklifting.co.uk Crosby Group PLC – Yale Industrial products – CAICO (Columbus McKinnon) – Camlock – Tractel*

Hawkridge & Co. 39 Canterbury Street, Gillingham ME7 5TR Tel. *01634 854381* Fax. *01634 280200* E-mail. *enquiries@hawklaw.co.uk* Web. *www.hawklaw.co.uk Hawkridge*

Hawksley & Sons Ltd (Head Office) Marlborough Road, Lancing BN15 8TN Tel. *01903 752815* Fax. *01903 766050* E-mail. *rrobin@hawksley.co.uk* Web. *www.hawksley.co.uk Crista – Hawksley*

Haws Watering Cans 120 Beakes Road, Smethwick B67 5AB Tel. *0121 4202494* Fax. *0121 4291668* E-mail. *davepennock@btconnect.com* Web. *www.haws.co.uk Finasrain – Genuine Haws – Haws – Pot Pouree*

Hawthorn Printmaker Supplies Hawthorn Houseappleton Roebuck, Appleton Roebuck, York YO23 7DA Tel. *01904 744649* Fax. *01904 744649* E-mail. *hpsupplies@tiscali.co.uk* Web. *www.hawthornprintmaker.co.uk handy rollers – Nnonskin Linseed inks – Nonskin Ettching Inks – Stay open*

Haymarket Media Group Teddington Studios Broom Road, Teddington TW11 9BE Tel. *020 82675000* Fax. *020 82675844* E-mail. *ian.burrows@haymarket.com* Web. *www.f1racing.co.uk Motor Sport – Motoring News*

Haynes & Cann Ltd 1-9 Overstone Road, Northampton NN1 3JL Tel. *01604 626143* Fax. *01604 604721* E-mail. *haynes.cann@btconnect.com Haynes & Cann*

Haynes International Ltd Parkhouse Street, Manchester M11 2JX Tel. *0161 2307777* Fax. *0161 2232412* E-mail. *pcrawshaw@haynesintl.com* Web. *www.haynesintl.com Hastelloy (U.S.A.) – Haynes (U.S.A.)*

Hayter Ltd Spellbrook Lane West Spellbrook, Bishops Stortford CM23 4BU Tel. *01279 723444* Fax. *01279 723821* E-mail. *sales@hayter.co.uk* Web. *www.hayter.co.uk Hayter – Hayter Professional and Domestic Range*

Hayward & Green Aviation Ltd (Head Office Dept K) Unit 1 & 2 Terrys Cross Farm Horn Lane Woodmancote, Woodmancote, Henfield BN5 9SA Tel. *01273 492237* Fax. *01273 493898* E-mail. *simon.green@haywardandgreen.com* Web. *www.aviationspares.net Aeropeltor – Clement Clarke – H R Smith – Sennheiser – Thales Acoustics*

Hayward Tyler Ltd 1 Kimpton Road, Luton LU1 3LD Tel. *01582 731144* Fax. *01582 393400* E-mail. *info@haywardtyler.com* Web. *www.haywardtyler.com Hayward Tyler – Varley*

Hayward Tyler Fluid Handling 41-43 Glenburn Road East Kilbride, Glasgow G74 5BJ Tel. *01355 225461* Fax. *01355 263496* E-mail. *pauln@haywardtyler.com* Web. *www.haywardtyler.com H.T.F.H.*

H Breakell Company Ltd Heywood Distribution Park Pilsworth Road, Heywood OL10 2TT Tel. *01706 369272* Fax. *01706 629448* E-mail. *sales@breakell-lifts.co.uk* Web. *www.breakell-lifts.co.uk Breakell Lifts*

H C R Ltd Copenhagen Court 32 New Street, Basingstoke RG21 7DT Tel. *01256 812700* Fax. *01256 333420* E-mail. *info@hcr.co.uk* Web. *www.hcr.co.uk Countrywide Mobility*

H D Sports Ltd Rutland Way, Sheffield S3 8DG Tel. *0114 2725190* Fax. *0114 2729330* E-mail. *customerservice@hdsports.co.uk* Web. *www.theworldsbestblades.com MK – Wilson Blades*

Headen & Quarmby Ltd Sadler Street Middleton, Manchester M24 5UJ Tel. *0161 6432576* Fax. *0161 6530554* E-mail. *ho@headen-quarmby.co.uk* Web. *www.headen-quarmby.co.uk Q'Preme*

Headstock Distribution Unit G1 Steelpark Road, Halesowen B62 8HD Tel. *0121 5086666* Fax. *0121 5086677* E-mail. *sales@headstockdistribution.com* Web. *www.headstockdistribution.com Laney Heatstock*

Headway Music Audio Ltd Headway House Walnut Tree Lane St Thomas Street, Deddington, Banbury OX15 0SY Tel. *01869 338404* Fax. *01869 338395* E-mail. *sales@headwaymusicaudio.com* Web. *www.headwaymusicaudio.com *Headway*

James H Heal & Co. Ltd Richmond Works Lake View, Halifax HX3 6EP Tel. *01422 366355* Fax. *01422 352440* E-mail. *info@james-heal.co.uk* Web. *www.james-heal.co.uk Deltamoist – Elmatear Tautex – Etadry – Gyrowash – Heals Of Halifax – Idealair – Megasol – Movistrob – Nu-Martindale – Pickxi – Rhoburn – SDC – Sigmascope – Titan – Toyburn – Verivide – Wascator – Zetascan*

Heal's The Heal's Building 196 Tottenham Court Road, London W1T 7LQ Tel. *020 76361666* Fax. *020 76375582* E-mail. *enquiries@heals.co.uk* Web. *www.heals.co.uk Heal's*

Health Protection Agency Colindale, London NW9 5DF Tel. *020 82004400* Fax. *020 82008130* E-mail. *maria.zambon@hpa.org.uk* Web. *www.hpa.org.uk P.H.L.S.*

Heartbeat Manufacturing Ltd Arthur Street, Redditch B98 8JY Tel. *01527 522020* Fax. *01527 524919* E-mail. *james.pritchard@heartbeatuk.com* Web. *www.heartbeatuk.com Heartbeat*

Heatcall Group Services Nottingham Road, Belper DE56 1JT Tel. *01773 828100* Fax. *01773 828123* Web. *www.vaillant.co.uk Glow Worm Ulitimate – Glow-Worm Chatsworth And Dovedale – Glow-Worm Complheat – Glow-Worm Energy Saver Combi – Glow-Worm Energysaver – Glow-Worm Fuelsaver – Glow-Worm Hideaway – Glow-Worm Melody – Glow-Worm Miami – Glow-worm Micron – Glow-Worm Opulence – Glow-Worm Opus – Glow-Worm Saxony – Glow-Worm Swift Flow*

Heathcoat Fabrics Ltd Westexe, Tiverton EX16 5LL Tel. *01884 254949* Fax. *01884 252897* E-mail. *cameron@heathcoat.co.uk* Web. *www.heathcoat.co.uk Flare Free & Head Dev – Flare Free Device – Gardtex – H.S.T. 46 – Heathcoat 1808 with Portrait of J.H. – Heathcoat Fabrics – Richard Hayward – Seaspeed – Spacetec*

D G Heath Ltd Unit 3 Tyn Y Bonau Industrial Estate Tyn Y Bonau Road, Pontardulais, Swansea SA4 8SG Tel. *01792 884828* Fax. *01792 884936* E-mail. *info@dgheath.co.uk* Web. *www.dgheath.co.uk Hoebeek – QuickStep – Richard Burbridge*

Heath Filtration Ltd PO Box 1, Stoke On Trent ST6 1BY Tel. *01782 838591* Fax. *01782 835508* E-mail. *info@heathfiltration.com* Web. *www.heathfiltration.com Filtrex*

Samuel Heath & Sons plc Cobden Works Leopold Street, Birmingham B12 0UJ Tel. *0121 7722303* Fax. *0121 7723334* E-mail. *info@samuel-heath.com* Web. *www.samuel-heath.com Antique – Georgian – Jubilee – Langtry – Master-Style*

Heathylee House Farm Hollinsclough, Buxton SK17 0RD Tel. *01298 83659* E-mail. *karen@heathylee.co.uk* Web. *www.heathylee.co.uk Heathylee Guanaco*

Arthur Heaton & Co. Ltd Station Lane, Heckmondwike WF16 0NF Tel. *01924 403731* Fax. *01924 410069 Acme Brand*

Heatrae Sadia 1 Hurricane Way, Norwich NR6 6EA Tel. *01603 420100* Fax. *01603 420219* E-mail. *paul.rivett@baxigroup.com* Web. *www.heatraesadia.com Accolade – Cameo – Carousel – Concept Handwash – Express – F.B.M. – Gold Dot – Handy – Handy Dri – Heatrae – Heatrae Sadia – Heatrae Sadia – Megaflo – Megalife – Sapphire – Sawton – Streamline – Supreme – Sureflow – U.T.C.*

Heber Ltd Belvedere Mill Chalford, Stroud GL6 8NT Tel. *01453 886000* Fax. *01453 885013* E-mail. *les.ashton-smith@heber.co.uk* Web. *www.heber.co.uk Firefly – Pluto*

Heckmondwike FB PO Box 7, Liversedge WF15 7FH Tel. *01924 410544* Fax. *01924 413613* E-mail. *sales@heckmondwike-fb.co.uk* Web. *www.heckmondwike-fb.co.uk Battleship – Broadrib – Cumulus – Diamond – Dragoon – Dreadnought – Gympro – Hippo – Hobnail – Iron Duke – Supacord – SuperDreadnought – Wallcord – Wellington – Zephyr Rib*

Heidelberg Graphic Equipment Ltd 69-76 High Street, Brentford TW8 0AA Tel. *020 84903500* Fax. *020 84903589* E-mail. *info@heidelberg.com* Web. *www.heidelberg.com Fontshop – *Heidelberg (Germany) – *Heidelberg Harris (France) – *Polar (Germany) – *Stahl (Germany)*

HEIDENHAIN GB LTD 200 London Road, Burgess Hill RH15 9RD Tel. *01444 247711* Fax. *01444 870024* E-mail. *sales@heidenhain.co.uk* Web. *www.heidenhain.co.uk Heidenhain – ACU-RITE – Anilam – Etel – Renco – RSF – Numerik Jena – Metronics – Quadra Chek – Gage Chek – TNC – Endat*

Heimbach UK Bradnor Road Sharston Industrial Area, Manchester M22 4TS Tel. *0161 9986911* Fax. *0161 9988095* E-mail. *info@heimbach.com* Web. *www.heimbach-group.com Autovac – Centurion – Duoflo – Durafoil – Duramic – Isoflo – Monoflex – Orthoflo – Quadraflex*

H J Heinz Co. Ltd South Building Hayes Park, Hayes UB4 8AL Tel. *020 85737757* Fax. *020 88482325* E-mail. *enquiries@heinz.co.uk* Web. *www.heinz.co.uk Heinz 57*

Heinzmann UK Ltd Durham Tees Valley Airport, Darlington DL2 1PD Tel. *01325 332805* Fax. *01325 333631* E-mail. *info@heinzmannuk.com* Web. *www.heinzmann.de Heinzmann*

Heldite Ltd 1a Bristow Road, Hounslow TW3 1UP Tel. *020 85779157* Fax. *020 85779057* E-mail. *sales@heldite.com* Web. *www.heldite.com Heldite*

Helical Technology Dock Road, Lytham St Annes FY8 5AQ Tel. *01253 733122* Fax. *01253 794880* E-mail. *sales@helical-technology.co.uk* Web. *www.helical-technology.co.uk Helical – Helical*

Helifix Ltd 21 Warple Way, London W3 0RX Tel. *020 87355200* Fax. *020 87355201* E-mail. *robert.paterson@helifix.co.uk* Web. *www.helifix.co.uk BowTie – CemTie – Crack Bond TE – DryFix – Helibeam System – HeliBond MMZ – InSkew – MorTie – PolyPlus – ResiTie – RetroTie – TimTie – TurboFast – TurboTie*

Helipebs Controls Ltd Premier Works Sisson Road, Gloucester GL2 0RE Tel. *01452 423201* Fax. *01452 307665* E-mail. *sales@helipebs.co.uk* Web. *www.helipebs-controls.co.uk Helipebs*

Helix Trading Ltd PO Box 15, Stourbridge DY9 7AJ Tel. *01384 424441* Fax. *01384 892617* E-mail. *info@helixhq.com* Web. *www.helix.co.uk Achiever – Data Care – Doodle Sticks – Fortress – Guardsman – Helix – Helix Crystal – Helix Images – Helix Lock-Down – Hi-Tech – Locksafe – Oxford – Roundup – Safeflex – Sapona – Sapona – Stronghold – Top Secret – Treasure Chest*

Heller Machine Tools 1 Acanthus Road, Redditch B98 9EX Tel. *0121 2753300* Fax. *0121 2753380* E-mail. *info@heller.co.uk* Web. *www.heller.co.uk Heller Machine Tools Ltd*

Esmond Hellerman Ltd Hellerman House Harris Way, Sunbury On Thames TW16 7EW Tel. *01932 781888* Fax. *01932 789573* E-mail. *sales@hellermans.com* Web. *www.hellermans.com Hellerman*

Hellermann Tyton 1 Robeson Way, Manchester M22 4TY Tel. *0161 9454181* Fax. *0161 9472233* E-mail. *sales@hellermanntyton.co.uk* Web. *www.hellermanntyton.co.uk Arrowtags – Cradle Clip – Flexiform – Fospro – H.I. – Helafos – Helagaine – Helagrip – Helashrink – Helatemp – Helawrap – Helerman – Hellerine – Hellerman – Hellermann – Hellermark – Helsyn – Helvin – Insuloid – Insulok – Insultite – Klambush – Klamklip – Moldanized Shapes – Ovalgrip – ServIdent – Snapper – T.I.P.S. – Triklamp – Twintex – Unicut*

Helman Workwear Egerton Street Farnworth, Bolton BL4 7ER Tel. *01204 709400* Fax. *01204 862460* E-mail. *sales@helmanworkwear.co.uk* Web. *www.helmanworkwear.co.uk 3M – C Plus – C Teq – Carringtons – Du Pont – Firefly – Hasler – Heltex – Mellobase – Melloguard – Proban – Proshield – Reflexite – Scotchlite – Tempro – Tychem – Tyvek Protech – Vizlite*

Helmet Integrated Systems Ltd Unit 3 Focus 4 Fourth Avenue, Letchworth Garden City SG6 2TU Tel. *01462 478000* Fax. *01462 478010* E-mail. *sales@helmets.co.uk* Web. *www.helmets.co.uk *Alpha (United Kingdom) – Cromwell – Pureflo – Purelite Airshield*

Helmsman (W.B. Bawn Ltd) Northern Way, Bury St Edmunds IP32 6NH Tel. *01284 727600* Fax. *01284 727601* E-mail. *sales@helmsman.co.uk* Web. *www.helmsman.co.uk Helmsman*

Helping Hand Co. Unit 9 Bromyard Road Industrial Estate, Ledbury HR8 1NS Tel. *01531 635388* Fax. *01531 638059* E-mail. *sales@helpinghand.co.uk* Web. *www.thehelpinghand.co.uk Alouette – Helping Hand – Litterpicker – Long Handled Sponges – Lowzone – Mouette – Octopus Toilet Arms – Softop Comfort Cover – Soxon – Toe Foot Cleaner*

Hempel UK Ltd Llantarnam Industrial Park, Cwmbran NP44 3XF Tel. *01633 874024* Fax. *01633 489089* E-mail. *sales.uk@hempel.com* Web. *www.hempel.com Galvosil – Hempadur – Hempalin – Hempanyl – Hempatex – Hempathane – Hempatone – Hempinol*

Hemsec Group Stoney Lane Rainhill, Prescot L35 9LL Tel. *0151 4267171* Fax. *0151 4931331* E-mail. *sales@hemsec.com* Web. *www.hemsec.com Hemsec – Supersave – Supersave*

Henderson Group Ltd 9 Hightown Avenue, Newtownabbey BT36 4RT Tel. *028 90342733* Fax. *028 90342484* E-mail. *info@henderson-group.com* Web. *www.henderson-group.com Spar – V.G. – Vivo*

J & K Henderson Enterprises Ltd Unit 45 Great Bank Road, Westhoughton, Bolton BL5 3XU Tel. *01942 845600* Fax. *01942 845601* E-mail. *james@jkhenderson.co.uk* Web. *www.jkhenderson.co.uk *Citron (Far East)*

P C Henderson Ltd Unit 1 Durham Road, Bowburn, Durham DH6 5NG Tel. *0191 3770701* Fax. *0191 3771309* E-mail. *sales@pchenderson.com* Web. *www.pchenderson.com Abbey – Arcade – Ashton – Bergen – Bergen Chevron – Bifold – Buckingham – Caversham – College – Consort – Cornthian – Council – Cumberland – Double Top – Flexirol – Gloucester – Highline – Husky Folding 25 and 40 – Lincoln – Loretto – Majestic – Mansion – Marathon – Marathon Fire Door – Merlin – Minster – Phantom – President – Profile – Regent – Regent Chevron – Senator – Single Top – Slipper – Solstice – Sovereign – Sterling – Straight Sliding 280-307 Top Hung – Tangent – Titan – Ultra – Versa Frame – Warwick*

Hendy Ford Southampton 360-364 Shirley Road, Southampton SO15 3UF Tel. *023 80701700* Fax. *023 80702437* E-mail. *paul@hendy.co.uk* Web. *www.hendy-group.com Hendy Body – Hendy Ford (United Kingdom) – Hendy Hire (United Kingdom) – Hendy Lennox Honda – Hendy Truck (United Kingdom)*

Henkel Ltd Winthorpe Road, Newark NG24 2AL Tel. *01636 646711* Fax. *01636 605187* E-mail. *eric.norman@uk.henkel.com* Web. *www.henkel.com Crodacoat – Crodafix – Crodaglu – Crodagrip – Crodalam – Crodamelt – Crodaseal*

Hennig UK Ltd Unit 5 Challenge Business Park Challenge Close, Coventry CV1 5JG Tel. *024 76555690* Fax. *024 76256591* E-mail. *sales@henniguk.com* Web. *www.henniguk.com Stabiflex*

Henri Picard & Frere 8 Pixham Court Pixham Lane, Dorking RH4 1PG Tel. *020 89493142* Fax. *020 89493142* E-mail. *sales@picard.co.uk* Web. *www.picard.co.uk Bernstein (Germany) – G.E.C. – HIPIC – Hipic Pliers – *Lerloy (U.S.A.) – Picard – Progress – Shockbox – Windles*

Henry Bell & Co Grantham Ltd Dysart Road, Grantham NG31 7DB Tel. *01476 565761* Fax. *01476 566950* E-mail. *tom@henry-bell.co.uk* Web. *www.henrybell-services.com Leeway – Supervite*

Henry's Electronics Ltd 404-406 Edgware Road, London W2 1ED Tel. *020 72581831* Fax. *020 77240322* E-mail. *sales@henrys.co.uk* Web. *www.henrys.co.uk Henry's*

Henry Squire & Sons Ltd Unit 2 Hilton Cross Business Park Featherstone, Wolverhampton WV10 7QZ Tel. *01902 308050* Fax. *01902 308051* E-mail. *info@henry-squire.co.uk* Web. *www.squirelocks.co.uk Defender, The – Defiant, The – Oasis – Paramount – Protector – Squire – Squire Blue Blade – Squire Cablelocks – Squire Clam – Squire Cycle Shacks Locks UBX – Squire Hi-Security Lock-Sets – Squire High Security XL70 – Squire Lock-Set – Squire Miniciam – Squire Motorbike Shackle Locks UBXM – Squire Mystic – Squire Old English – Squire Stonghold - HS4 – Squire Stronglock – Squire Vulcan – Stronglock*

Henry Technologies Ltd Mossland Road Hillington Park, Glasgow G52 4XZ Tel. *0141 8824621* Fax. *0141 8824624* E-mail. *sales@henrytech.co.uk* Web. *www.henrytech.co.uk A.C. & R – Henry*

Henshaw Inflatables Ltd 7 The Tythings Commercial Centre, Wincanton BA9 9RZ Tel. *01963 33237* Fax. *01963 34578* E-mail. *mail@henshaw.co.uk* Web. *www.henshaw.co.uk Air-Lift – Inflatable Collars for Rigid Hull Inflatable Boats – Milltest – Tinker*

Mike Henson Presentations Ltd 18 Portway Drive, High Wycombe HP12 4AU Tel. *01494 438904* Fax. *01494 448154* Web. *www.mikehenson.com Mike Henson Presentations Ltd*

H E Olby & Co. Ltd 299-313 Lewisham High Street PO Box 293, London SE13 6NW Tel. *020 86903401* Fax. *020 86901408* E-mail. *info@heolby.co.uk* Web. *www.vergin.net H.E. Olby*

Hepco Motion Lowermoor Business Park Tiverton Way, Tiverton EX16 6TG Tel. *01884 243400* Fax. *01884 243399* E-mail. *enquiries@hepco.co.uk* Web. *www.hepcomotion.com *A.S.K. Linear Bearings (Japan) – Hepco – Technobi*

Heraeus Noble Light Analytic Ltd 3-4 Nuffield Close, Cambridge CB4 1SS Tel. *01223 424100* Fax. *01223 426338* E-mail. *darren.golding@heraeus.com* Web. *www.heraeus.com Cathodeon*

Herald Plastics Ltd Anglian Industrial Estate Atcost Road, Barking IG11 0EQ Tel. *020 85077900* Fax. *020 85072914* E-mail. *sales@heraldplastics.com* Web. *www.heraldplastics.com Alpha – Km*

Heras Ready Fence Service Unit B1 Eurolink Industrial Estate, Sittingbourne ME10 3RL Tel. *01795 423261* Fax. *01795 426351* E-mail. *tony.wells@readyfence.co.uk* Web. *www.herasreadyfence.co.uk Heras – Heras Readyfence*

Herbert Retail Ltd Rookwood Way, Haverhill CB9 8PD Tel. *01440 711400* Fax. *01440 710469* E-mail. *sales@herbertgroup.com* Web. *www.herbertgroup.com The Herbert Group*

Herbert Tooling Ltd Rosne Sandy Lane, Fillongley, Coventry CV7 8DD Tel. *01676 540040* Fax. *01676 542093* E-mail. *info@herberttooling.com* Web. *www.herberttooling.com Ackworthie – Alfred Herbert – Archer – Coventry Colletts – Hertbert Equipment – Jay Dee*

Hercules Holding Ii Ltd Langley Road Pendelbury, Salford M6 6JU Tel. *0161 7458905* Fax. *0161 7457009* E-mail. *name@herc.com* Web. *www.herc.com Abalyn – Abitol – Adtac – Amine D – Amylotex – AquaCEL – AquaFLO – AquaPAC – Aquapel – *Aquasorb (France) – *Benecel (Belgium) – Blaken piling system – *Blanose (France) – C.M.H.E.C. – *Carboxymethylcellulose (France) – Cellolyn – Crepetrol – *Culminal (Belgium) – Delfloc – Di-Cup – Dresinate – Dresinol – Dymerex – *Ethylcellulose (U.S.A.) – Foral – Foral ester – Galactasol – Genu Pectin – Genuagar – Genugel – Genulacta – Genuvisco – H.P.-007 – Hercat – Hercobond – Hercofloc – Hercolyn – Hercosett – Hercotac – Hercules – Hi-Phase – Hi-Phorm – *Hydroxyethylcellulose (Netherlands) – *Hydroxypropylcellulose (U.S.A.) – *Klucel (U.S.A.) – Kristalex – Kymene – Lewisol – *Natrosol (Netherlands) – *Natrosol Plus (Netherlands) – Neolyn – *Nexton (Netherlands) – *Nitrocellulose (U.S.A.) – Pamak – Pamolyn – Paracol – Pentalyn – Permalyn – Pexalyn – Picco – Piccolastic – Piccolyte – Piccopale – Piccotac – Piccotex – Piccovar – Poly-pale – Polyrad – Pomosin – Regalite – Regalrez – Resin Size 249 – Reten – S.T.-Size – Slendid – Solvenol – Staybelite – Staybelite Ester – T-Size 22 – Tacolyn – Vinsol – Vul-Cup – Yarmor*

Hercules Security Fabrications Ltd Coundon Industrial Estate Coundon, Bishop Auckland DL14 8NR Tel. *01388 458794* Fax. *01388 458806* E-mail. *info@hercules-security.co.uk* Web. *www.hercules-security.co.uk Cacti*

Herga Electric Northern Way, Bury St Edmunds IP32 6NN Tel. *01284 701422* Fax. *01284 753112* E-mail. *info@herga.com* Web. *www.herga.com Herga – Hergair – Hergalite*

Heritage Belt Company Leo House The Business Centre Ross Road, Weedon Road Industrial Estate, Northampton NN5 5AX Tel. *01604 684700* Fax. *01604 684719* E-mail. *info@regentbelt.co.uk* Web. *www.regentbelt.co.uk Braces*

Heritage Cashmere UK Ltd White Rose Mill Holdsworth Road, Halifax HX3 6SN Tel. *01422 247800* Fax. *01422 247544* E-mail. *info@heritage-cashmere.co.uk* Web. *www.heritage-cashmere.co.uk Herritage cashmeer – Walbrad*

Heron Cardiff Properties Ltd 19 Marylebone Road, London NW1 5JP Tel. *020 74864477* Fax. *020 74863349* E-mail. *l.zeltser@heron.co.uk* Web. *www.heron.co.uk Heron International*

Walter Heselwood Ltd Stevenson Road, Sheffield S9 2SG Tel. *0114 2442042* Fax. *0114 2432806* E-mail. *admin@heselwood.com* Web. *www.heselwood.com WH*

H & E Smith Britannic Works Broom Street, Stoke On Trent ST1 2ER Tel. *01782 281617* Fax. *01782 269882* E-mail. *fred@hesmith.co.uk* Web. *www.hesmith.co.uk Firetile – Period Embossed Tiles – Van Delft*

H E S Sales Ltd Prospect Way Royal Oak Industrial Estate, Daventry NN11 8PL Tel. *01327 300322* Fax. *01327 311411* E-mail. *daventry@hes-sales.com* Web. *www.hes-sales.com H.E.S.*

Heuft Ltd Ninian Park Ninian Way Wilnecote, Tamworth B77 5ES Tel. *01827 255800* Fax. *01827 716146* E-mail. *uk@heuft.com* Web. *www.heuft.com Heuft Basic – Heuft Spectrum*

Hewden Hire Centres Ltd 39-40 New Summer Street, Birmingham B19 3QN Tel. *0121 3594282* Fax. *0121 3336866* Web. *www.hewden.co.uk Hewden*

Hewitt & May (Shirtmakers) Ltd Unit G32b Waterfront Studios 1 Dock Road, London E16 1AG Tel. *020 75116829* Fax. *0870 4711421* E-mail. *info@hewittandmay.com* Web. *www.hewittandmay.co.uk Hewitt & May, Classic V1*

Hewi UK Ltd Scimitar Close Gillingham Business Park, Gillingham ME8 0RN Tel. *01634 377688* Fax. *01634 370612* E-mail. *info@hewi.co.uk* Web. *www.hewi.co.uk *HEWI (Germany) – HEWI Nylon*

Hexagon Metrology Hexagon AB Halesfield 13, Telford TF7 4PL Tel. *01952 681300* Fax. *01952 681311* E-mail. *peter.freer@hexagonmetrology.com* Web. *www.hexmet.co.uk Global – PC Dmis*

Hexham Sealants Ltd Station Yard Station Road, Corbridge NE45 5AY Tel. *01434 633344* Fax. *01434 633346* E-mail. *sales@hexaflex.co.uk* Web. *www.hexhamsealants.co.uk Castlebond – Castlecoat – Castleseal – Hexaflex*

John Heyer Paper Ltd 14 Langwood House 63-81 High Street, Rickmansworth WD3 1EQ Tel. *01923 713870* Fax. *0870 2421114* E-mail. *sales@johnheyerpaper.co.uk* Web. *www.johnheyerpaper.co.uk *Recyconomic (Germany) – *Signa Set Plus (Germany) – *Silk FCO (Germany)*

H F C Bank (Head Office) North Street Winkfield, Windsor SL4 4TD Tel. *01344 890000* Fax. *01344 892667* Web. *www.hfcbank.co.uk H.F.C. – H.F.C. Bank*

H Gostelow Terapin Sales 21-22 Francis Street, Hull HU2 8DT Tel. *01482 323459* Fax. *01482 586325* E-mail. *tim@gostelow.karoo.co.uk Terrapin*

H G Stephenson Ltd 161 Buxton Road, Stockport SK2 6EQ Tel. *0161 4836256* Fax. *0161 4832385* E-mail. *robert@hgs.co.uk* Web. *www.stephensons.com Arma Ware – Palatine*

H H B Communications Ltd 73-75 Scrubs Lane, London NW10 6QU Tel. *020 89625000* Fax. *020 89625050* E-mail. *richard.kershaw@hhb.co.uk* Web. *www.hhb.com H.H.B.*

H & H Commercial Truck Services Ltd Sneyd Industrial Estate, Stoke On Trent ST6 2NT Tel. *01782 575522* Fax. *01782 812913* E-mail. *martynhancock@handhcommercials.co.uk* Web. *www.trucksales.me.uk AUTOSAN – BMC – Eurocoaches – King Long*

Hidentity Ltd Unit 3 Victoria Street, Mansfield NG18 5RR Tel. *01623 429090* Fax. *01623 429090* E-mail. *hide@hidentity.co.uk* Web. *www.hidentity.co.uk Hidentity Ltd*

Higgins & Hewins Ltd Titan Works High Street, Amblecote, Stourbridge DY8 4LR Tel. *01384 397700* Fax. *01384 397701* E-mail. *sales@handhltd.co.uk* Web. *handhltd.co.uk Beltafine – Comminutor – *Econabator (U.S.A.) – Jeta – Odorgard – Pista – *Purafil (U.S.A.) – Rotafine – Washpactor – Worcester*

Highlander Snacks Ltd Inchcorse Place Whitehill Industrial Estate, Bathgate EH48 2EE Tel. *01506 630778* Fax. *01506 653781* E-mail. *brian.robertson@highlandersnacks.co.uk* Web. *www.unichips.com Highlander*

Highlands & Islands Enterprise Cowan House Highlander Way, Inverness Business & Retail Park, Inverness IV2 7GF Tel. *01463 234171* Fax. *01463 244469* E-mail. *info@hient.co.uk* Web. *www.hie.co.uk H.I.E.*

Highlead Ltd 5 Cheltenham Street, Salford M6 6WY Tel. *0870 1398869* Fax. *0870 1398869* E-mail. *info@highlead.co.uk* Web. *www.highlead.co.uk Highlead*

High-Point Rendel Ltd 61 Southwark Street, London SE1 1SA Tel. *020 76540400* Fax. *020 72610588* E-mail. *london@hprworld.com* Web. *www.hprworld.com High Point Rendel*

High Society 23 Market Avenue, Ashton Under Lyne OL6 6AL Tel. *0161 3390886 Veba*

High Style Furnishings Saxon Way Melbourn, Royston SG8 6DN Tel. *01763 261837* Fax. *01763 262489* E-mail. *enquiries@highstyle.co.uk* Web. *www.highstyle.co.uk High Style Furnishings – S.J. Clarke*

High Tech Fabrications Ltd Unit 1 & 2 Crown Estate Sudmeadow Road, Gloucester GL2 5HG Tel. *01452 304466* Fax. *01452 306622* E-mail. *sales@hightechfabrications.co.uk* Web. *www.hightechfabrications.co.uk Super Duplex*

Highwood Engineering Ltd Parkfield Road, Birmingham B8 3AZ Tel. *0121 3279212* Fax. *0121 3274329 S & B – Sweeney & Blocksidge*

Hijack Systems Mews Cottage 9 Otley Road, Harrogate HG2 0DJ Tel. *01423 563879* Fax. *01423 520344* E-mail. *enquiries@hijacksystems.com* Web. *www.hijacksystems.com Hijack – Skelton design*

Hilger Crystals Ltd Unit R1 Westwood Industrial Estate Continental Approach, Margate CT9 4JL Tel. *01843 231166* Fax. *01843 290310* E-mail. *sales@hilger-crystals.co.uk* Web. *www.hilger-crystals.co.uk Hilger Crystals*

Hi-Lite Signs Ltd 28 Bolingbroke Road, Louth LN11 0WA Tel. *01507 600500* Fax. *01507 600309* E-mail. *sales@hi-litesigns.com* Web. *www.hi-litesigns.com Fibrelite – Fibreseal – H.L.S. Higlow*

Hillarys Blinds Northern Ltd Private Road No 2 Colwick Business Park, Colwick Industrial Estate, Nottingham NG4 2JR Tel. *0115 9617420* Fax. *0115 9614176* E-mail. *enquiries@hillarys.co.uk* Web. *www.hillarys.co.uk Albany – Hillarys – Wholesale*

Hillbrook Printing Inks Ltd New Street Slaithwaite, Huddersfield HD7 5BB Tel. *01484 843535* Fax. *01484 840031* Web. *www.hillbrook.co.uk Deltapack – Deltasack – Status*

The Hill Brush Company Ltd Woodlands Road Mere, Warminster BA12 6BS Tel. *01747 860494* Fax. *01747 860137* E-mail. *info@hillbrush.com* Web. *www.hillbrush.com Salmon*

Hill Cliffe Garage 48 Catley Road, Sheffield S9 5JF Tel. *0114 2619965* Fax. *0114 2423319* E-mail. *info@hillcliffe.co.uk* Web. *www.hillcliffegarage.co.uk Camlock – *Kopal (France) – Magic – Niagara*

Ernest H Hill Ltd Unit 10-12 Meadowbrook Park, Halfway, Sheffield S20 3PJ Tel. *0114 2484882* Fax. *0114 2489142* E-mail. *info@hillpumps.com* Web. *www.hillpumps.com Hill*

Hill & Smith Ltd Springvale Industrial Park, Bilston WV14 0QL Tel. *01902 499400* Fax. *01902 499419* E-mail. *mark@hill-smith.co.uk* Web. *www.hill-smith.co.uk Berry Systems – Hill & Smith*

Hilltop Products Kirkstead Way Golborne, Warrington WA3 3PJ Tel. *01942 723101* Fax. *01942 273817* E-mail. *sales@hilltop-products.co.uk* Web. *www.hilltop-products.co.uk Hilflex – Hillflex S300*

Walter Hill Plant Ltd Maze Street, Bristol BS5 9TQ Tel. *0117 9555151* Fax. *0117 9413685 Minnimatic – Portamatic*

Hilson Ltd Shentonfield Road Sharston Industrial Area, Manchester M22 4SD Tel. *0161 4917800* Fax. *0161 4281179* E-mail. *vasant@hilson.co.uk* Web. *www.hilson.co.uk Hilson – Hilson*

Hilti GB Ltd (Head Office) 1 Trafford Wharf Road Trafford Park, Manchester M17 1BY Tel. *0800 886100* Fax. *0161 8721240* E-mail. *gbsales@hilti.com* Web. *www.hilti.com D.C.230EX – D.C.M.1 – D.C.M.1.5 – D.C.M.2 – D.D.100 – DC230-S/EX – DD160-E – DD250-E – DD80-E – Eradicate – Eraser – H.S.L.-B(-TZ) – Heavy Duty anchors – Hilti – Hilti Bolt – Hilti Ceiling hanger – Hilti DBZ – Hilti DBZ-X – Hilti DD100 – Hilti DX A40-M/41-M – Hilti DX A40/41 – Hilti DX-E 37/72 – Hilti DX351 – Hilti DX36M – Hilti DX36MX – Hilti DX450 – Hilti DX600N – Hilti DX750 – Hilti DX750MX – Hilti Firestop Range – Hilti HA8 – Hilti HDA – Hilti HEH – Hilti HGN – Hilti HGT – Hilti HHD – Hilti HHD-2 – Hilti Hit Resin Systems – Hilti HKD – Hilti HKD-S – Hilti HLD – Hilti HMDS – Hilti HPF – hilti HPS Hammascrew – Hilti HRD – Hilti HSA – Hilti HSC – Hilti HSL/HSL-TZ – Hilti HST-R – Hilti HT – Hilti HUC-2 – Hilti HUD – Hilti HUS – Hilti HVA – Hilti HVB Shear Connectors – Hilti HVU – Hilti IDMR – Hilti IDP – Hilti IZ – Hilti PD25 – Hilti PHB – Hilti PM10 – Hilti PR20 – Hilti PR60 – Hilti SD45 – Hilti SF100 / 120-A – Hilti ST18 – Hilti SU 25 – Hilti TE 1 – Hilti TE 104 – Hilti TE 15C – Hilti TE 25 – Hilti TE 35 – Hilti TE 5 – Hilti TE 505 – Hilti TE 55 – Hilti TE 6A – Hilti TE 706 – Hilti TE 76-ATC – Hilti TE 805 – Hilti TE 905 – Hilti TE15 – Hilti TKD3000 – Hilti TKD5000 – Hilti TKT2000 – Hilti Transformers – Hilti WFE 150 – Hilti WSC 55 – Hilti WSC 85 – Hilti WSJ 110-ET – Hilti X-IE – Hit RE 500 – Hilti WFO 280 – Hilti TKT 1300 – HSL-G-TZ – HSL-TZ – HSLB – Remedial Wall Ties – Shear Connector System – T.D.A.-VC30/60 – T.E. 804 – T.E.15 – T.E.18-M – T.E.24 – T.E.5 – T.E.504 – T.E.54 – T.E.74 – T.P.400 – T.R.H.1800 – Transformers – W.S. 230 – X.T.K.T. 2000 Single Speed Screwgun*

Hilton Banks Ltd 74 Oldfield Road, Hampton TW12 2HR Tel. *020 89798284* Fax. *020 89798294* E-mail. *hilltonbanks@btinternet.com Hilton's – *Hiltons (Italy)*

Hilton International Eye Wear Ltd 21 Sapcote Trading Centre 374 High Road, London NW10 2DH Tel. *020 84517800* Fax. *020 84516357* E-mail. *sales@hilton-eyewear.com* Web. *www.hilton-eyewear.com Aviator – Bentley – Gucci – Hilton – Le Club – Lenon – Marco Polo – Mayfair Match – Monsieur – Panda – Philip – Princess – Racer – Rider – Safilo – Senator*

Hima Sella Ltd Carrington Field Street, Stockport SK1 3JN Tel. *0161 4294500* Fax. *0161 4763095* E-mail. *reception@hima-sella.co.uk* Web. *www.hima-sella.co.uk HIMA – HIMA-SELLA*

P E Hines & Sons Ltd Whitebridge Lane, Stone ST15 8LU Tel. *01785 814921* Fax. *01785 818808* E-mail. *barry.rowley@iclweb.com* Web. *www.hines.co.uk Crown Polymer – Hi-Den – *Projecem (France) – Shelley F.S.C.S. – Silicate Enriched – Zircozon*

Hinton Perry Davenhill Dreadnought Works, Brierley Hill DY5 4TH Tel. *01384 77405* Fax. *01384 74553* E-mail. *office@drednort.tiles.co.uk* Web. *www.dreadnought-tiles.co.uk Dreadnought*

F W Hipkin Ltd Coppen Road, Dagenham RM8 1NU Tel. *020 89841000* Fax. *020 89840101 Adriatic – Beta – Cerambeta – Whirline*

H Hipkiss & Co. Ltd Park House Clapgate Lane, Birmingham B32 3BL Tel. *0121 4215777* Fax. *0121 4215333* E-mail. *info@hipkiss.co.uk* Web. *www.hipkiss.co.uk Beaver Brand – Hipkiss*

Hi-Power Hydraulics Unit E Bankside Business Park Coronation Street, Stockport SK5 7PG Tel. *0161 4806715* Fax. *0161 4804511* E-mail. *hipower.hydraulics@gmail.com* Web. *www.roquet.co.uk Firestone – Haskel – Roquet – Satair*

Hi-Pro Pressure Products Ltd Unit 10 Bessemer Crescent, Rabans Lane Industrial Area, Aylesbury HP19 8TF Tel. *01296 431804* Fax. *01296 431845* E-mail. *contactus@hi-pro.co.uk* Web. *www.hi-pro.co.uk High pressure optical cells*

The Hira Company Ltd Hira House 1 Elizabeth Street, Manchester M8 8PR Tel. *0161 8342868* Fax. *0161 8324566* E-mail. *reception@hira.co.uk* Web. *www.hira.co.uk Hira – Texet*

Hire It Limited Magnum House Cookham Road, Bracknell RG12 1RB Tel. *01344 456600* Fax. *01344 401344* E-mail. *info@hamilton.co.uk* Web. *www.hamilton.co.uk A.T.S. Technirent*

Hire Technicians Group Ltd Chalk Hill House 8 Chalk Hill, Watford WD19 4BH Tel. *01923 252230* Fax. *01923 238799* E-mail. *sales@hiretech.biz* Web. *www.hiretech.biz Clarke – Floor Team – Hirestar – Hiretech – Hiretech – Steam Team*

Hirsh Diamonds 10 Hatton Garden, London EC1N 8AH Tel. *020 74044392* Fax. *020 74300107* E-mail. *enquiries@hirsh.co.uk* Web. *www.hirsh.co.uk Hirsh*

Hi-Store Station Approach Four Marks, Alton GU34 5HN Tel. *01420 562522* Fax. *01420 564420* E-mail. *info@hi-store.com* Web. *www.hi-store.com Canti Frame – Canti-Clad – Canti-Guide – Canti-lec – Canti-track – Cantilite – Cantilock – Hi Stack – Hi-deck flooring – Hi-frame – Hi-Trolley – Mezzanine – Rigideck*

Hitashi Kokusai Windsor House Britannia Road, Waltham Cross EN8 7NX Tel. *08451 212177* Fax. *08451 212180* E-mail. *p.roache@hitachi-keu.com* Web. *www.hitachi-keu.com Hitachi Denshi*

F L Hitchman Unit 46 Ditton Priors Trading Estate Station Road, Ditton Priors, Bridgnorth WV16 6SS Tel. *01746 712242* Fax. *01746 712055* E-mail. *enquiries@aquaroll.com* Web. *www.aquaroll.com Aquaroll – Wastemaster, The*

Hitex UK Ltd Millburn Hill Road, Coventry CV4 7HS Tel. *024 76692066* Fax. *024 76692131* E-mail. *info@hitex.co.uk* Web. *www.hitex.co.uk DBox – DProbe – HiTOP – JProbe – PressOn – teletest 32*

H J Sock Group Ltd 57 Coventry Road, Hinckley LE10 0JX Tel. *01455 638800* Fax. *01455 610535* E-mail. *enquiries@hjhall.com* Web. *www.hjhall.com Commando – H.J. Countryman – H.J. Executive – H.J. Immaculate – H.J. Indestructible – H.J. Rambler – H.J. Softop*

H K L Gas Power Ltd 260 Windsor Street, Birmingham B7 4DX Tel. *0121 3596131* Fax. *0121 3598580* E-mail. *info@hkl-gaspower.co.uk* Web. *www.hkl-gaspower.co.uk ALGAS SDI – BEAM – BLACKMER – CORKEN – ELY ENERGY – EMMEGAS – HYDRO-VACUUM – IMPCO – REGO – SAM DICK – WVM – ZAVOLI Antom*

H K Technologies Ltd Unit 7 Hadrians Way Glebe Farm Industrial Estate, Rugby CV21 1ST Tel. *01788 577288* Fax. *01788 562808* E-mail. *smitht@hktechnology.com* Web. *www.hktechnologies.com H K Laser Marking Systems – H K Laser Systems – H.K. Technologies*

H L N Supplies 67 Upper Accommodation Road, Leeds LS9 8JP Tel. *0113 2402000* Fax. *0113 2404000* E-mail. *sales@hlnsupplies.co.uk* Web. *www.hlnsupplies.co.uk Pers-pex*

H & M Automotive UK Ltd 70 Fred Dannatt Road Mildenhall, Bury St Edmunds IP28 7RD Tel. *01638 640100* Fax. *01638 781111* E-mail. *sales@hmauto.com* Web. *www.hmauto.com Vauxhall/Opel parts*

H M G Paints Ltd Riverside Works Collyhurst Road, Manchester M40 7RU Tel. *0161 2057631* Fax. *0161 2058823* E-mail. *sales@hmgpaint.com* Web. *www.hmgpaint.com Acrythane – H.M.G. – Slippy Bottom*

H M T Rubbaglas Ltd 2a Newman Road, Bromley BR1 1RJ Tel. *020 84647888* Fax. *020 84647788* E-mail. *info@hmttank.com* Web. *www.hmttank.com Flex-A-Seal – H.M.T. Inc – *Pivot Master (U.S.A.)*

H M V & Waterstones Royal House Princes Gate Buildings Homer Road, Solihull B91 3QQ Tel. *0121 7038000* Fax. *0121 7117478* Web. *www.waterstones.co.uk Waterstones*

Hobart UK 51 The Bourne, London N14 6RT Tel. *08448 887777* Fax. *020 88860450* E-mail. *chris.birch@hobartuk.com* Web. *www.hobartuk.com Hobart*

Hobbs Ltd Milton Gate 60 Chiswell Street, London EC1Y 4AG Tel. *0845 3133130* Fax. *020 34402198* E-mail. *customerservices@hobbs.co.uk* Web. *www.hobbs.co.uk Hobbs*

Hocaps Ltd 7 Eccleston Street, London SW1W 9LX Tel. *020 77308883* Fax. *020 77308885* E-mail. *mail@hocaps.com* Web. *www.hocaps.com *Belgravia International – *HOCAPS International – *MAG.NET – *Simply Chefs*

Hockley International Ltd Hockley House Ashbrook Office Park3 Longstone Road, Manchester M22 5LB Tel. *0161 2097400* Fax. *0161 2097401* E-mail. *mail@hockley.co.uk* Web. *www.hockley.co.uk Alphamost – Deltamost – Hockley – Hockley - Mostyn - Permost - Alphamost - Deltamost – Mostyn – Permost*

Hockway 6 The Trowers Way Centre Trowers Way, Redhill RH1 2LP Tel. *01737 762222* Fax. *01737 236100* E-mail. *enquiries@hockway.com* Web. *www.hockway.com Cpmat – Irod – Polatrak (U.S.A.) – Polatrak - Retropod - Cpmat - Irod. – RetroBouy – Retropod*

Hodge Clemco Ltd Orgreave Drive, Sheffield S13 9NR Tel. *0114 2540600* Fax. *0114 2540250* E-mail. *sales@hodgeclemco.co.uk* Web. *www.hodgeclemco.co.uk Clemco – Clemcote – Clemvac – Crusader – Eductoblast – Eductomatic – Enviraclean – Enviraclean - Clemco - Clemcote - Holloblast. – *Munkebo Beholder-Fabrik Trading A/S (Denmark) – Spinblast and Holloblast*

Hoerbiger Rings & Packings Ltd Edderthorpe Street, Bradford BD3 9RB Tel. *01274 733801* Fax. *01274 736887* E-mail. *mark.woodward@hoerbiger.com* Web. *www.hoerbiger.com Hoerbiger Rings & Packings*

Hoerbiger UK 1649 Pershore Road Stirchley, Kings Norton, Birmingham B30 3DR Tel. *0121 4333636* Fax. *0121 4597794* E-mail. *timothy.haviland@hoerbiger.co.uk* Web. *www.hoerbiger.com Hoerbiger*

Hofbauer (UK) Ltd St Albans Road Empire Way, Gloucester GL2 5FW Tel. *01452 309782* Fax. *01452 309884* E-mail. *cases@hofbauer.co.uk* Web. *www.hofbauer.co.uk Alupro – Citybag – Dimension – Ecobag – Elitebag Astro – Elitebag Enduro – Elitebag Pro – Flitebag – Hofbauer – Maxibag – Megabag – Minibag – Multibag – Polybox – Profiline – Promoline – Servicebag – Serviceline – Softbag – Technobag – Thermodyne – Ultrabag – Unibag – Xtrabag*

Hoggs of Fife Ltd Eden Valley Business Park, Cupar KY15 4RB Tel. *01334 653733* Fax. *01334 653553* E-mail. *sales@hoggs.co.uk* Web. *www.hoggs.co.uk Hoggs of Fife*

Hohner Automation Ltd Unit 14-16 0 Whitegate Road, Wrexham LL13 8UG Tel. *01978 363888* Fax. *01978 364586* E-mail. *info@hohner.com* Web. *www.hohner.com Hohner*

Holborn Direct Mail Capacity House 2-6 Rothsay Street, London SE1 4UD Tel. *020 74076444* Fax. *020 73576065* E-mail. *sales@holborndirectmail.co.uk* Web. *www.holborndirectmail.co.uk Holborn Direct Mail – L.S. Opticians Record System*

Holdens Supaseal Ltd 505 Garretts Green Lane, Birmingham B33 0SG Tel. *0121 7897766* Fax. *0121 7897237* E-mail. *info@holdens-supaseal.co.uk* Web. *www.holdens-supaseal.co.uk Pilkington*

Holden Vintage & Classic Ltd Linton Trading Estate, Bromyard HR7 4QT Tel. *01885 488000* Fax. *01885 488889* E-mail. *sales@holden.co.uk* Web. *www.holden.co.uk Bygone Era*

Holemasters Scotland Unit 2 Block 5 Whiteside Industrial Estate, Bathgate EH48 2RX Tel. *01506 653303* Fax. *01506 652991* E-mail. *jim@holemastersltd.com* Web. *www.dmhall.co.uk Holemasters*

Holger Christiansen UK Ltd Unit 7-8 Glaisdale Business Centre Glaisdale Parkway, Nottingham NG8 4GP Tel. *0115 9280086* Fax. *0115 9280033* Web. *www.hcdk.com *Cargo Auto Electrics (Denmark)*

Holland & Barrett Ltd Samuel Ryder House Townsend Drive, Attleborough Fields Ind Estate, Nuneaton CV11 6XW Tel. *01455 251900* Fax. *024 76320094* E-mail. *rcraddock@hollandandbarrett.co.uk* Web. *www.hollandandbarrett.com Holland and Barrett*

Holland & Holland Holdings Ltd 33 Bruton Street, London W1J 6HH Tel. *020 74994411* Fax. *020 74994544* E-mail. *reception@hollandandholland.com* Web. *www.hollandandholland.com Guncare – Royal – Royal Deluxe – Royal Double Rifle – Royal Over and Under – Sporting Model Over and Under*

Holland Publishing Ltd Unit 18 Bourne Court Unity Trading Estate, Woodford Green IG8 8HD Tel. *020 85517711* Fax. *020 85511266* E-mail. *sales@holland-enterprises.co.uk* Web. *www.holland-publishing.co.uk Arty*

Holland & Sherry PO Box 1, Peebles EH45 8RN Tel. *01721 720101* Fax. *01721 722309* E-mail. *enquiries@hollandandsherry.co.uk* Web. *www.hollandandsherry.co.uk Holland & Sherry*

Holliday Pigments Ltd Morley Street, Hull HU8 8DN Tel. *01482 329875* Fax. *01484 329791* E-mail. *sales@holliday-pigments.com* Web. *www.holliday-pigments.com Premier – Prestige – Seagull*

Hollingsworth & Vose Co UK Ltd Postlip Mills Winchcombe, Cheltenham GL54 5BB Tel. *01242 602227* Fax. *01242 604099* E-mail. *info@hovo.com* Web. *www.hovo.com Hollingsworth & Vose – Postlip Papers*

Holmbury Ltd (Group Head Office) Tower House Vale Rise, Tonbridge TN9 1TB Tel. *01732 378912* Fax. *01732 357666* E-mail. *sales@holmbury.co.uk* Web. *www.holmbury.co.uk Holmbury*

Holmes Catering Equipment Ltd The Industrial Estate Full Sutton, York YO41 1HS Tel. *01759 375500* Fax. *01759 375509* E-mail. *alawson@hce.co.uk* Web. *www.hce.co.uk *Granuldisk – *Wexiodisk*

Graham Holmes Astraseal Ltd Astraseal House Paterson Road, Finedon Road Industrial Estate, Wellingborough NN8 4EX Tel. *01933 227233* Fax. *01933 228951* E-mail. *info@astraseal.com* Web. *www.astraseal.com Astraseal*

Holmes Hose Ltd Moston Road, Sandbach CW11 3HL Tel. *01270 753331* Fax. *01270 753332* E-mail. *info@holmeshose.co.uk* Web. *www.holmeshose.co.uk Alpha – Amiflex – IVG – Petzetakis – Trelleborg*

Holophane Europe Ltd Bond Avenue Bletchley, Milton Keynes MK1 1JG Tel. *01908 649292* Fax. *01908 367618* E-mail. *amcrury@holophane.co.uk* Web. *www.holophane.co.uk 6240 – 7110 – 8224 – Atlanta – Caribe – Denver – H.M.S. – Hydrel – LED Series – Merculume – Metrolux – Module 600 – Panel-Vue – Park Pack – Petxina – Predator – Prismalume – Prismasphere – Prismatron – Prismpack – Prismpackette – Somerset – Terralux – Vantage – Vista – Wallpackette – Wallpackette III – Widerlite*

Holt Lloyd International Ltd (Holt Lloyd International Ltd) Unit 100 Barton Dock Road Stretford, Manchester M32 0YQ Tel. *0161 8664800* Fax. *0161 8664854* E-mail. *info@holtsauto.com* Web. *www.holtsauto.com Holts – Holts/Simoniz*

Holywell Engineering Ltd Station Road Shiremoor, Newcastle Upon Tyne NE27 0AE Tel. *0191 2684365* Fax. *01665 712727* E-mail. *eng@holywell.com* Web. *www.holywel.com Hollywell*

Homelux Nenplas Blenheim Road Airfield Industrial Estate, Ashbourne DE6 1HA Tel. *01335 347300* Fax. *01335 340271* E-mail. *enquiries@homeluxnenplas.co.uk* Web. *www.homelux.co.uk Nenplas – Nenplas - Amerock (die cast handles and knobs)*

Homeserve Emergency Services Unit 7a Orwell Close Fairview Industrial Estate, Marsh Way, Rainham RM13 8UB Tel. *01708 555088* Fax. *01708 554236* E-mail. *phillip.bremner@evander.com* Web. *www.homeserve.com Highway*

Honeycomb Computer Technology 31 Cranleigh Road, Bournemouth BH6 5JT Tel. *01202 432053* Web. *www.worka-b.com Worka-B*

Honeywell 140 Waterside Road Hamilton, Leicester LE5 1TN Tel. *0116 2462000* Fax. *0116 2462300* E-mail. *mark.ayton@gent.co.uk* Web. *www.honeywell.com Gent – S.M.S.*

Honeywell Countess Avenue Cheadle Hulme, Cheadle SK8 6QS Tel. *0161 4863000* Fax. *0161 4861267* Web. *www.honeywell.com Allied Signal Automotive*

Honeywell Aerospace Bunford Lane, Yeovil BA20 2YD Tel. *01935 475181* Fax. *01935 427600* E-mail. *gary.simpson@honeywell.com* Web. *www.honeywell.com Honeywell Normalair-Garrett Ltd – Normalair-Garrett*

Honeywell Analytics Ltd Hatch Pond House 4 Stinsford Road, Poole BH17 0RZ Tel. *01202 645577* Fax. *01202 678011* E-mail. *info@zellweger-analytics.co.uk* Web. *www.honeywellanalytics.com MDA Scientific – Neotronics – Siegar*

Honeywell Control Systems Ltd Honeywell House Anchor Boulevard Crossways, Crossways Business Park, Dartford DA2 6QH Tel. *01322 484800* Fax. *01322 484899* E-mail. *bob.morris@honeywell.com* Web. *honeywell.com Koden*

Hood Sailmakers (Kemp Sail Ltd) Unit 16 Sandford Lane Industrial Estate Sandford Lane, Wareham BH20 4DY Tel. *01929 554308* Fax. *01590 673797* E-mail. *sales@hoodsails.com* Web. *www.hood-sails.com Hood One Design – Hood Sailmakers Ltd*

Hoofmark UK Ltd Suite C Rickleton 2 Lambton Park, Chester le Street DH3 4AN Tel. *0191 3853238* Fax. *0191 5845577* E-mail. *info@hoofmark.co.uk* Web. *www.hoofmark.co.uk D-Rainclean – D-Raintank – Fastlay – Golpla – Mesh Tracks – Naue Fasertechnik*

P D Hook Hatcheries Ltd Cote, Bampton OX18 2EG Tel. *01993 850261* Fax. *01993 851441* E-mail. *sales@pdhook.co.uk* Web. *www.pdhook.co.uk *Cob – *Ross*

H T Z Ltd Vulcan Way New Addington, Croydon CR0 9UG Tel. *01689 843345* Fax. *01689 841792* E-mail. *james.bagshawe@htz.biz* Web. *www.htz.biz Guardian – Magellan – Qasar*

Hooper Engineering Products Ltd Nelson Street, Oldbury B69 4NY Tel. *0121 5522835* Fax. *0121 5523821* E-mail. *hooper.sheetmetal@virgin.net Hoopro*

Hoover Ltd Pentrebach, Merthyr Tydfil CF48 4TU Tel. *01685 721222* Fax. *01685 382946* E-mail. *a.bertali@hoovercandy.com* Web. *www.hoover.co.uk Alpina – *Arianne (Portugal) – *Brush N Wash (U.S.A.) – *Jet N Wash (Germany) – Junior – Maxi 6 – Performa – Performa Eco – PurePower – Quattro – Quattro Easy Logic – Telios – Turbopower – Vortex*

Hopkins Catering Equipment Ltd Valley Mills 151 Kent Road, Pudsey LS28 9NF Tel. *0113 2577934* Fax. *0113 2576759* E-mail. *info@hopkins.biz* Web. *www.hopkins.biz Hopkins*

E C Hopkins Ltd 82 Kettles Wood Drive, Birmingham B32 3DB Tel. *0121 5066090* Fax. *0121 4218286* E-mail. *steve@echopkins-bham.co.uk* Web. *www.echopkins.co.uk Hopflex – Hopflex - Hopgen – Hopgen*

E C Hopkins Ltd Unit 1-3 Barton Industrial Estate Mount Pleasant, Bilston WV14 7LH Tel. *01902 401755* Fax. *01902 495097* E-mail. *enquiries@echopkins.co.uk* Web. *www.echopkins.co.uk E.C. Hopkins (United Kingdom) – Hopflex (United Kingdom)*

F E & J R Hopkinson Ltd 124 Scotland Street, Sheffield S3 7DE Tel. *0114 2727486* Fax. *0114 2750290* E-mail. *info@sheffieldknives.co.uk* Web. *www.sheffieldknives.co.uk Hopkinsons – Nowills*

Thomas Hopkinson & Son Ltd Victor Works Bolton Hall Road, Bradford BD2 1BQ Tel. *01274 582056* Fax. *01274 531328* E-mail. *ian@triple-king.co.uk* Web. *www.triple-king.co.uk Triple King*

Horizon Mechanical Services International Ltd Unit 1 Willment Way, Bristol BS11 8DJ Tel. *0117 9821415* Fax. *0117 9820630* E-mail. *sales@horizon-int.com* Web. *www.horizon-int.co.uk Filto-Bench – Heat-Rad – Heat-Saver – Hippo – Max-Econ – Panda – Smog-Eater – Smog-Mobile – Smog-Rambler – Swing-Boom*

Hörmann (UK) Ltd Gee Road, Coalville LE67 4JW Tel. *01530 513000* Fax. *01530 513051* E-mail. *marketing.lei@hormann.co.uk* Web. *www.hormann.co.uk SPU 40 – DPU – ASP 40 – TAP 40 – ASR 40 – ALR 40 – ALR Vitraplan – ALS 40 – TAR 40 – Duratec – HSS 6530 – V 2715 SE R – V 5015 SE – V 10008 – V 3515 Iso – V 1401 Atex – V 3015 RW – V 2515 Food L – V 3015 Clean – V 3009 Conveyor – H 3530 – Decotherm A/S/E – HR 116 A/S – HR 120 A/S – HR 120 aero – HG-A/-V/-S/-E/-L – ZAK system – Hörmann Dobo system – FSN – FAW – FPU – FMI – Series 2000 – Series 2000 – Decograin – Silkgrain – RollMatic – Ecostar – EKD – SupraMatic – SupraMatic E – SupraMatic P – SupraMatic H – ProMatic – ProMatic P – ProMatic Akku – C-Panel – ETE – EPU – LPU – LTH – Comfort Front Entrance Door – Top Comfort Entrance Door – Top Prestige Entrance Door – Top Prestige Plus Entrance Door – ThermoPro – LineaMatic – RotaMatic – N800*

Hornby Hobbies Ltd H1-H2 Unit Enterprise Road Westwood Industrial Estate, Margate CT9 4JX Tel. *01843 233500* Fax. *01843 233513* E-mail. *frank.martin@hornby.com* Web. *www.hornby.com Hornby – Micro Scalextric – Scalextric*

Horne Engineering Ltd PO Box 7, Johnstone PA5 8BD Tel. *01505 321455* Fax. *01505 336287* E-mail. *sales@horne.co.uk* Web. *www.horne.co.uk Horne*

Hornett Bros & Co. Ltd Ferry Lane, Rainham RM13 9YH Tel. *01708 556041* Fax. *01708 557546* E-mail. *john@hornett-bros.co.uk* Web. *www.hornett.net Epoil – Miscol*

Horsehage Manufacturers Mark Westaway & Son Love Lane Farm Marldon, Paignton TQ3 1SP Tel. *01803 527257* Fax. *01803 528010* E-mail. *sales@horsehage.co.uk* Web. *www.horsehage.co.uk HorseHage – Mollichaff*

Horseley Bridge Garth Works Taffs Well, Cardiff CF15 7YF Tel. *029 20815270* Fax. *029 20815275* E-mail. *dewaters@connect-2.co.uk* Web. *www.horseleybridgetanks.com Horseley Bridge*

John Horsfall & Sons Ltd West Vale Works Greetland, Halifax HX4 8BB Tel. *01422 372237* Fax. *01422 310105* E-mail. *info@johnhorsfall.co.uk* Web. *www.johnhorsfall.co.uk Ashdown – Balmoral – Cuddledoon – Extermisect – Sandringham – Somacel*

Horsleys Ltd PO Box 119, Reading RG7 5NQ Tel. *0118 9713223* Fax. *0118 9713225* E-mail. *info@horsleys.com* Web. *www.horsleys.com *Horsleys (United Kingdom)*

Horstine Farmery 1 Cow Lane Upton, Gainsborough DN21 5PB Tel. *01427 838383* Fax. *01427 838507* E-mail. *c.allen@horstinefarmery.com* Web. *www.horstinefarmery.com Agroband – Cascade – Horstine Farmery – Microband – Microstat – Surefill*

Horstmann Group Ltd Roman Farm Road, Bristol BS4 1UP Tel. *0117 9788700* Fax. *0117 9878701* E-mail. *reception@horstmann.co.uk* Web. *www.horstmann.co.uk Horstmann – Horstmann Timers & Controls*

Horwood Homeware Ltd Avonmouth Way, Bristol BS11 9HX Tel. *0117 9400000* Fax. *0117 9401100* E-mail. *sales@horwood.co.uk* Web. *www.stellarcookware.co.uk Harmony – Horwood – Judge – Stellar*

Hoskins Medical Equipment Ltd Admail 1001, Birmingham B1 1HJ Tel. *0121 7076600* Fax. *0121 6075555*

E-mail. *sales@hoskinsme.co.uk* Web. *www.hoskinsme.co.uk Apollo – Birthday Bed – Prestbury – Princess*

Hosokawa Micron Ltd Rivington Road Whitehouse Industrial Estate, Whitehouse, Runcorn WA7 3DS Tel. *01928 755100* Fax. *01928 714325* E-mail. *info@hmluk.hosokawa.com* Web. *www.hosokawa.co.uk Agglomaster – Alpine – Bepex – Faculty – Hosokawa – Hosokawa bepex – Hosokawa Rietz – Mechanofusion – Micron – Mikro – Nanocular – Nobilta – Schugi – Stott – Vitalair – Vrieco-Nauta*

Hospitality A V Unit 2 Martels High Easter Road, Barnston, Dunmow CM6 1NA Tel. *01371 872288* Fax. *01371 875881* E-mail. *sales@hospitalityav.com* Web. *www.hospitalityav.com *Bic – *Kodak – *NEC – *Nobo – *Sony*

Hospitality & Leisure Manpower 8 Lower Teddington Road, Kingston Upon Thames KT1 4ER Tel. *020 89774419* Fax. *020 89775519* E-mail. *hlm@halm.co.uk* Web. *www.halm.co.uk *Hospitality Skills – *Learning Network*

Hospitality Search International Ltd 8 West Bar Street, Banbury OX16 9RR Tel. *01295 279696* Fax. *01295 279697* E-mail. *sales@hospitalitysearch.co.uk* Web. *www.hospitalitysearch.co.uk H S I*

Hostombe Group Ltd Minalloy House 10-16 Regent Street, Sheffield S1 3NJ Tel. *0114 2724324* Fax. *0114 2729550* E-mail. *roger.hostombe@hostombe.co.uk* Web. *www.hostombe.co.uk DAM (France) – Defesi – Montanal (Germany) – Zschimmer & Schwarz (France)*

Host Von Schrader Ltd Unit 6b Capenhurst Technology Park, Capenhurst, Chester CH1 6EH Tel. *0151 3471900* Fax. *0151 3471901* E-mail. *mikee@hostvs.co.uk* Web. *www.hostvonschrader.co.uk *Cleanmaster (U.S.A.)*

Hot A V Ltd 6 Barnes Wallis Court Wellington Road, Cressex Business Park, High Wycombe HP12 3PS Tel. *08451 306161* Fax. *08451 306262* E-mail. *info@hotav.uk.com* Web. *www.hotav.uk.com D-Tex – HotAV – Pay as you go Projectors*

John D Hotchkiss Ltd Main Road West Kingsdown, Sevenoaks TN15 6ER Tel. *01474 853131* Fax. *01474 853288* E-mail. *william@hotchkiss-engineers.co.uk* Web. *www.hotchkiss-engineers.co.uk Hotchkiss*

Hotchkiss Ltd 7 Marshall Road, Eastbourne BN22 9AX Tel. *01323 501234* Fax. *01323 508752* E-mail. *info@hotchkiss.co.uk* Web. *www.hotchkiss.co.uk Fire Protection – Fire Spray – Hotchkiss Air Supply – Hotchkiss Ductwork – System Hygienics – Triventek*

Hotchkiss Air Supply Heath Mill Road Wombourne, Wolverhampton WV5 8AP Tel. *01902 895161* Fax. *01902 892045* E-mail. *glattimer@hotchkissairsupply.co.uk* Web. *www.hotchkissairsupply.co.uk Colorduct – Hasflex – Metu System – Soundpac – TDB*

Hotel Complimentary Products Mountfield House Mountfield Road, New Romney TN28 8LH Tel. *01797 362895* Fax. *01797 366722* E-mail. *sales@hcp-ltd.com* Web. *www.hcp-ltd.com Balmoral – Elsyl Range – Giovani Milan – Health & Spa – Just for you – Regency Collection – Taylor of London - Natural Range – Taylor of London - Platinum Range – White & Gold Collection*

Hotel Inspector 56 Gloucester Road, London SW7 4UB Tel. *0207 1172760* E-mail. *sales@hotelinspector.us* Web. *www.hotelinspector.org.uk Hotel Inspector*

Hotelscene 17 Portland Square, Bristol BS2 8SJ Tel. *0117 9166300* Fax. *0844 8264423* E-mail. *chris.needham@hotelscene.co.uk* Web. *www.hotelscene.co.uk Hotelscene Conference Plus – Hotelscene Corporate Xtranet*

Hotwork Combustion Technology Bretton Street Savile Town, Dewsbury WF12 9DB Tel. *01924 465272* Fax. *01924 506311* E-mail. *info@hotworkct.com* Web. *www.hotworkct.com Hotwork*

Houlder Group Michaels House 10-12 Alie Street, London E1 8DE Tel. *020 79803800* Fax. *020 79803814* E-mail. *general@houlder.co.uk* Web. *www.houlder.co.uk Leigh*

Hoults Group Heritage house 345 Southbury Road, Enfield EN1 1UP Tel. *0800 515675* Fax. *0191 4916009* E-mail. *houltsremovals@hoults.co.uk* Web. *www.hoults.co.uk Hoults*

House Of Colour Ltd Unit 2 Building 6 Hatters Lane, Watford WD18 8YH Tel. *0800 318526* Fax. *01923 218823* E-mail. *info@houseofcolour.co.uk* Web. *www.houseofcolour.co.uk House of Colour*

House Of Dorchester Unit 10 Alton Business Centre Omega Park, Alton GU34 2YU Tel. *01420 84181* Fax. *01420 543047* E-mail. *info@hodchoc.com* Web. *www.hodchoc.com Spotkleen*

House Of Flags Ltd 1048 Coventry Road Yardley, Birmingham B25 8DP Tel. *0121 7736789* Fax. *0121 7736757* E-mail. *solutions@flags.co.uk* Web. *www.flags.co.uk House of Flags*

Househam Sprayers Ltd The New Forge Leadenham, Lincoln LN5 0PE Tel. *01400 276000* Fax. *01400 273388* E-mail. *info@hosehamsprayers.com* Web. *www.househamsprayers.com AirRide 2000 – AirRide 2500 – AirRide 3000 – AirRide 3600 – AirRide Trailed 3000 – AirRide Trailed 4000 – AR 5000*

House Of Flags River Road Bicton Industrial Park, Kimbolton, Huntingdon PE28 0LQ Tel. *01480 861678* Fax. *01480 861618* E-mail. *solutions@flags.co.uk* Web. *www.flags.co.uk Flame & Fume – House of Flags – River Mill Flags – Simmonds Hobson*

House Of Townend Wyke Way Melton West Business Park East, North Ferriby HU14 3BQ Tel. *01482 638888* Fax. *01482 587042* E-mail. *info@houseoftownend.co.uk* Web. *www.houseoftownend.com Dromana Estate*

House Of York Norham Road, North Shields NE29 7UN Tel. *0191 2570101* Fax. *0191 2586649 Welchs*

Hoval Ltd North Gate, Newark NG24 1JN Tel. *01636 672711* Fax. *01636 673532* E-mail. *dhemington@hoval.co.uk* Web. *www.hoval.co.uk Hoval – Hoval*

Hovis Hovis Court 69 Alma Road, Windsor SL4 3HD Tel. *08707 288888* Fax. *01753 791739* Web. *www.premierfoods.co.uk Hovis – Mothers Pride*

Howard Bros Joinery Ltd Station Approach, Battle TN33 0DE Tel. *01424 773272* Fax. *01424 773836* E-mail. *john@howard-bros-joinery.com* Web. *www.howardbros.com Howard Bros*

The Howard Group (Head Office) 93 Regent Street, Cambridge CB2 1AW Tel. *01223 312910* Fax. *01233 312911* E-mail. *admin@howard-ventures.com* Web. *www.howard-ventures.com Cyclone – Donlite – Jupiter – Longley Systems – Mars – Mercury – Metspeed – Planet – Sellite*

Howardson Ltd Howardson Works Ashbourne Road, Kirk Langley, Ashbourne DE6 4NJ Tel. *01332 824777* Fax. *01332 824525* E-mail. *ian@dennisuk.com* Web. *www.dennisuk.com Dennis*

Howden Electro Heating 10-12 Belgowan Street Bellshill Industrial Estate, Bellshill ML4 3NS Tel. *01698 573100* Fax. *01698 573121* E-mail. *sales@howden-electric.com* Web. *www.howden-electric.com H. D. Howden Ltd – Howden Electro Heating*

Howdon Power Transmission Ltd Paganhill Lane, Stroud GL5 4JT Tel. *01453 750814* Fax. *01453 765320* E-mail. *heath.pinkney@howdon.co.uk* Web. *www.howdon.co.uk Howdon (United Kingdom) – Wedgegard (United Kingdom)*

Howe Cool The Cottage Low Street, Brotherton, Knottingley WF11 9HQ Tel. *01977 677077* Fax. *01977 677077* E-mail. *cliff@howecool.com* Web. *www.howecool.com howecool*

Edward Howell Galvanizers Ltd (Wedge Group Galvanizing) Watery Lane, Willenhall WV13 3SU Tel. *01902 637463* Fax. *01902 630923* E-mail. *edward.howell@wedge-galv.co.uk* Web. *www.wedge-galv.co.uk Wedge Group Galvanizing*

M Howgate Ltd 1 Listerhills Road, Bradford BD7 1HX Tel. *01274 731660* Fax. *01274 394755 Solaro*

Howmet Ltd Kestrel Way Sowton Industrial Estate, Exeter EX2 7LG Tel. *01392 429700* Fax. *01392 429701* E-mail. *lluis.fargasmas@howmet.com* Web. *www.howmet.com Howmet*

Howsafe Ltd 18-20 Challenger Way, Peterborough PE1 5EX Tel. *01733 560669* Fax. *01733 348115* E-mail. *sales@howsafe.co.uk* Web. *www.howsafe.co.uk Portwest – Regatta – Tusker*

H P B Management Ltd 24 Old Station Road, Newmarket CB8 8EH Tel. *01638 660066* Fax. *01638 660213* E-mail. *info@hpb.co.uk* Web. *www.hpb.co.uk Villa Owners Club*

H P P UK Ltd 82 Cliveland Street, Birmingham B19 3SN Tel. *0121 3596465* Fax. *0121 3590746* E-mail. *hppukltd@aol.com* Web. *www.hppuk.com Trojan*

HR4 Ltd Unit 6-7 Ravenswood Court, Rotherwas Industrial Estate, Hereford HR2 6JX Tel. *01432 353555* Fax. *01432 353797* E-mail. *info@hr4.co.uk* Web. *www.hr4.co.uk DST*

H R O D C 122a Bhylls Lane, Wolverhampton WV3 8DZ Tel. *01902 763607* Fax. *01902 569133* E-mail. *sales@hrodc.com* Web. *www.hrod-consultancy.com HRODC Ltd*

H R P Ltd Rougham Industrial Estate Rougham, Bury St Edmunds IP30 9XA Tel. *01359 270888* Fax. *01359 271132* E-mail. *ralph.alliston@hrponline.co.uk* Web. *www.hrponline.co.uk H. R. P.*

H R S Heat Exchanges Ltd HRS House 1012 Caxton Way, Watford WD18 8UA Tel. *01923 232335* Fax. *01923 230266* E-mail. *mail@hrs.co.uk* Web. *www.hrs.co.uk Cetecoil – Cetetherm – Plate Heat Exchanger – Scraped Surface – Spiratube – Spiratube - Unicus - Cetecoil - Spiravap – Unicus*

H S O P Text Processing Services Shortlands Snowdenham Lane, Bramley, Guildford GU5 0AT Tel. *01483 892287 HSOP*

Htec Ltd Unit H George Curl Way, Southampton SO18 2RX Tel. *023 80689200* Fax. *023 80689201* E-mail. *sales@htec.co.uk* Web. *www.htec.co.uk HTEC*

H T G Trading Ltd Hillview Church Road, Otley, Ipswich IP6 9NP Tel. *01473 890522* Fax. *01473 890758* E-mail. *malcolm.paxman@hubbard.co.uk* Web. *www.hubbard.co.uk *Frascold (Italy) – Hubbard Commercial – Hubbard Transport – *L'Unite Hermetique (France) – *Lu-Ve Contardo (Italy)*

H T S Direct Ltd Units 17-18 Emerald Way, Stone Business Park, Stone ST15 0SR Tel. *01785 816747* Fax. *01543 462789* E-mail. *sales@hts-direct.co.uk* Web. *www.hts-direct.co.uk Actek – Eco*

Hubdean Contracting Ltd Unit 3 Wornal Park Menmarsh Road, Worminghall, Aylesbury HP18 9PH Tel. *01844 338833* Fax. *01844 338844* E-mail. *taniasanders@hubdean.co.uk* Web. *www.hubdean.co.uk Agproshield*

Huber+Suhner (UK) Ltd Telford Road, Bicester OX26 4LA Tel. *01869 364100* Fax. *01869 249046* E-mail. *info.uk@hubersuhner.co.uk* Web. *www.hubersuhner.com Antennas – *Data Clear (U.S.A.) – *E.Z. Form Cable Corp (U.S.A.) – *Exar (U.S.A.) – Exar (USA) – Ez-form cable corp (USA) – *Huber & Suhner AG (Switzerland) – Masterline – *Radio coverage (Switzerland) – *Radox (Switzerland) – *Sucofit (Switzerland) – *Sucoflex (Switzerland) – *Sucoform (Switzerland) – Sucoplate – *Sucoplate (Switzerland) – *Sucorad (Switzerland) – Suhner Fiberoptic*

Hubron Speciality Ltd Albion Street Failsworth, Manchester M35 0FP Tel. *0161 6812691* Fax. *0161 6834045* E-mail. *info@hubron.com* Web. *www.hubron.com Black Fibre – Black Silk – Black Tek – Hubron – Hubron*

Huck Nets UK Ltd Gore Cross Business Park Corbin Way, Bradpole, Bridport DT6 3UX Tel. *01308 425100* Fax. *01308 458109* E-mail. *sales@hucknetting.co.uk* Web. *www.hucknetting.co.uk Bird's Nest – Dralo*

Huco Dynatork 5-8 Merchant Drive, Hertford SG13 7BL Tel. *01992 509888* Fax. *01992 509890* E-mail. *sales@huco.com* Web. *www.huco.com Dynatork – *Elliott (U.S.A.) – Huco - Huco-Flex - Huco-Pol - Uni-Lat - Vari-Tork - Oldham - Huco-Teleshaft - Poly-Flex - Placid Industries - Kerk - Inertia Dynamics - Hysteresis - Magnetic Technologies. – Huco Dynatork – Huco-Flex – Huco-Pol – Huco-Teleshaft – *Inertia Dynamics – *Kerk – *Magnetic Technologies – Micro-Beam – Multi-Beam – Oldham – Oldham X-Y – Panamech – *Placid Industries – Step Beam – Uni-Lat – Vari-Tork*

Hudson Of England Ltd Sutherland Works Normacot Road, Stoke On Trent ST3 1PP Tel. *01782 319256* Fax. *01782 343300* E-mail. *sales@hudsonandmiddleton.co.uk* Web. *www.hudsonandmiddleton.co.uk Hudson Middleton*

Hugall Services Ltd Unit 16 250 Milkwood Road, London SE24 0HG Tel. *020 77386104* Fax. *020 77383994* E-mail. *robin@hugallservices.co.uk* Web. *www.hugallservices.co.uk Lincoln – Middleby Marshall*

Kelvin Hughes Ltd (Charts & Maritime Supplies) New North Road Hainault, Ilford IG6 2UR Tel. *020 85026887* Fax. *020 85598535* E-mail. *marketing@kelvinhughes.co.uk* Web. *www.kelvinhughes.com Husun – Nucleus – Nucleus - Huson*

Hughes Pumps Ltd Highfield Works Spring Gardens Washington, Pulborough RH20 3BS Tel. *01903 892358* Fax. *01903 892062* E-mail. *pcranford@hughes-pumps.co.uk* Web. *www.hughes-pumps.co.uk CPE – Dualway – Jetin – Jetin, Dualway, CPE.*

Hughes Safety Showers Ltd Whitefield Road Bredbury, Stockport SK6 2SS Tel. *0161 4306618* Fax. *0161 4307928* E-mail. *info@hughes-safety-showers.co.uk* Web. *www.hughes-safety-showers.co.uk Hughes Safety Showers – Portaflex*

Huhtamaki UK Ltd Grange Road, Gosport PO13 9UP Tel. *023 92584234* Fax. *023 92512330* E-mail. *sales@gb.huhtamaki.com* Web. *www.huhtamaki.com BioWare – Chinet – Huhtamaki*

Human Computer Interface Ltd 17 Signet Court Swann Road, Cambridge CB5 8LA Tel. *01223 314934* Fax. *01223 462562* E-mail. *info@interface.co.uk* Web. *www.interface.co.uk Human Computer Interface*

Humber Fabrications Hull Ltd 99 Wincolmlee, Hull HU2 8AH Tel. *01482 226100* Fax. *01482 215884* E-mail. *sales@humberboats.co.uk* Web. *www.ribworld.co.uk Humber – Humber Fabrications*

Humber Galvanising Ltd J Citadel Trading Park Citadel Way, Hull HU9 1TQ Tel. *01482 322466* Fax. *01482 227201* E-mail. *info@wedge-galv.co.uk* Web. *www.wedge-galv.co.uk Wedge Group Galvanizing*

Humiseal Europe Ltd (Head Office) Albany Park, Camberley GU16 7PH Tel. *01276 691100* Fax. *01276 691227* E-mail. *dgreenman@chasecorp.com* Web. *www.humiseal.com Concoat – Concoat Auto-SIR – Delta 5 – *Humiseal (U.S.A.) – Kace – MAX In-Line – Microdot – Solder Resist – Synergie*

Humphrey & Stretton plc Stretton House 20 Pindar Road, Hoddesdon EN11 0EU Tel. *01992 462965* Fax. *01992 463996* E-mail. *david.humphrey@humphreystretton.com* Web. *www.humphreystretton.com BSH Management*

Hunter Hields Gearcutting Ltd Addison Works Haugh Lane, Blaydon On Tyne NE21 4SB Tel. *01642 782407* Fax. *0191 4140135* E-mail. *kencliffe@gmail.com Hunter Gears*

Hunter Plastics Nathan Way Woolwich, London SE28 0AE Tel. *020 88559851* Fax. *020 83177764* E-mail. *bill.wallace@hunterplastics.co.uk* Web. *www.hunterplastics.co.uk Highflo – Hunter – OGEE –*

Plumbers Bits – Regency Superflo – Surefit – Surefit Squareflo – Surefit Stormflo

Hunters & Frankau Ltd Hurlingham Business Park Sulivan Road, London SW6 3DU Tel. *020 74718400* Fax. *020 73710374* E-mail. *p.hambidge@cigars.co.uk* Web. *www.cigars.co.uk *Agio (Cuba) – *Bolivar (Cuba, Jamaica, Europe and Honduras) – *Cohiba (Cuba, Jamaica, Europe and Honduras) – *Don Ramos (Cuba, Jamaica, Europe and Honduras) – *H. Upmann (Cuba, Jamaica, Europe and Honduras) – *Montecristo (Cuba, Jamaica, Europe and Honduras) – *Partagas (Cuba, Jamaica, Europe and Honduras) – *Punch (Cuba, Jamaica, Europe and Honduras) – *Quintero (Cuba, Jamaica, Europe and Honduras) – *Ramon Allones (Cuba, Jamaica, Europe and Honduras) – *Romeo & Juliet (Cuba, Jamaica, Europe and Honduras) – *Villiger (Cuba, Jamaica, Europe and Honduras)*

Hunter Vehicles Ltd Crown Works Southbury Road, Enfield EN1 1UD Tel. *020 83443900* Fax. *020 88057292* E-mail. *info@huntervehicles.co.uk* Web. *www.huntervehicles.co.uk Huntalloy – Huntaplex – Rolstak*

Hunting Plc 3 Cockspur Street, London SW1Y 5BQ Tel. *020 73210123* Fax. *020 78392072* E-mail. *pr@hunting.plc.uk* Web. *www.huntingplc.com Hunting*

Huntingdon Fusion Techniques Stukeley Meadow Gwscwm Road, Burry Port SA16 0BU Tel. *01554 836836* Fax. *01554 836837* E-mail. *jonlewis@huntingdonfusion.com* Web. *www.huntingdonfusion.com Testweld*

Huntleigh Healthcare Unit 35 Portmanmoor Road Industrial Estate, Cardiff CF24 5HB Tel. *029 20485885* Fax. *029 20492520* E-mail. *sales@huntleigh-diagnostics.co.uk* Web. *www.huntleigh-diagnostics.co.uk Audio Dopplex – Dopplex Assist Range – Dopplex Printa – Fetal Dopplex 11 – Flowpac – Flowtron Plus – Mini Dopplex – Multi Dopplex 11 – Rhos Dopplex – Super Dopplex 11*

H Huntsman & Sons Ltd 11 Savile Row, London W1S 3PS Tel. *020 77347441* Fax. *020 72872937* E-mail. *sales@h-huntsman.com* Web. *www.h-huntsman.com Huntsman*

Hunwick Engineering Ltd Kings Road, Halstead CO9 1HD Tel. *01787 474547* Fax. *01787 475741* E-mail. *sales@plc-hunwick.co.uk* Web. *www.hunwick-engineering.co.uk Ligntinh Crushers*

Hurry Bros Ltd 2117 London Road, Glasgow G32 8XQ Tel. *0141 7785591* Fax. *0141 7782110* E-mail. *enquiries@hurrybros.co.uk* Web. *www.hurrybros.co.uk Alex Borlands*

Husco International Ltd 6 Rivington Road Whitehouse Industrial Estate, Runcorn WA7 3DT Tel. *01928 701888* Fax. *01928 710813* E-mail. *uksales@huscointl.com* Web. *www.huscointl.com Caterpillar – JCB*

Hussmann Refrigeration Ltd Clydeway Skypark 8 Elliot Place, Glasgow G3 8EP Tel. *0141 2858500* Fax. *0141 2272734* Web. *www.hussmann.com Ambassador – VISION 93*

Hutchings & Harding Ltd 163 High Street Sawston, Cambridge CB22 3HN Tel. *01223 832281* Fax. *01223 836401* E-mail. *john@chamois.com* Web. *www.chamois.com Veltex*

Huthwaite International Hoober House Hoober, Rotherham S62 7SA Tel. *01709 710081* Fax. *01709 710065* E-mail. *info@huthwaite.co.uk* Web. *www.huthwaite.co.uk SPIN (United Kingdom)*

Huttenes-Albertus UK Ltd Vision Point Sedgley Road East, Tipton DY4 7UJ Tel. *0121 2700834* Fax. *0121 2700839* E-mail. *info@huttenes-albertus.co.uk* Web. *www.huttenes-albertus.co.uk Premcote Mould Dress – Primfil – Primweld*

H V R International Ltd Bede Trading Estate, Jarrow NE32 3EN Tel. *0191 4897771* Fax. *0191 4839501* E-mail. *sales@hvrint.com* Web. *www.hvrint.com H.V.R.*

H V Sier Ltd Unit 5-6 Meridian Trading Estate Bugsby's Way, London SE7 7SJ Tel. *020 83312070* Fax. *020 83312071* E-mail. *sales@hvsier.co.uk* Web. *www.hvsier.co.uk Crystal Glassine – Economy Cover – *Excelda Ivory Board (Netherlands) – *Fantasy Parchment (Netherlands) – Snowflake Ivory BD's*

H W Cooper 1 Farnham Royal, London SE11 5RQ Tel. *020 75821874* Fax. *020 75822386* E-mail. *hwcooper@hotmail.com Cooper – Fixed Blade – Lisson – Remote Control – Solar*

H West Prees Ltd Lower Heath Prees, Whitchurch SY13 2BT Tel. *01948 840465* Fax. *01948 841055* E-mail. *info@harrywest.co.uk* Web. *www.harrywest.co.uk Harry West – West*

Hycontrol Ltd Larchwood House Orchard Street, Redditch B98 7DP Tel. *01527 406800* Fax. *01527 60046* E-mail. *ballen@hycontrol.com* Web. *www.hycontrol.com Hycontrol*

Hycor Biomedical Ltd Douglas House Pentland Science Park Bush Loan, Penicuik EH26 0PL Tel. *0131 4457111* Fax. *0131 4457112* E-mail. *jweston@hycorbiomedical.com* Web. *www.hycorbiomedical.com Autostat*

Hydac Technology Ltd Woodstock Road Charlbury, Chipping Norton OX7 3ES Tel. *01608 811211* Fax. *01608 811259* E-mail. *george.muscat@hydac.co.uk* Web. *www.hydacuk.com *Hydac (Germany)*

Brian Hyde Ltd Stirling Road Shirley, Solihull B90 4LZ Tel. *0121 7057987* Fax. *0121 7112465* E-mail. *richard@brianhyde.co.uk* Web. *www.brianhyde.co.uk Hyde – Rhodius (Germany) – Stabila*

Hyde Sails Ltd PO Box 441, Southampton SO31 0AA Tel. *0845 5438945* Fax. *0800 3899254* E-mail. *sales@hydesails.co.uk* Web. *www.hydesails.com Hyde Sails*

Hydrachem Ltd (Head Office) Gilmans Industrial Estate, Billingshurst RH14 9EZ Tel. *01403 787700* Fax. *01403 785158* E-mail. *info@hydrachem.co.uk* Web. *www.hydrachem.co.uk BIOSPOT (United Kingdom) – FLUE FREE – HOTSPOT – HYZYME – IMP – OASIS (United Kingdom) – WITCH*

Hydrafeed Ltd Talgarth House Bond Avenue, Bletchley, Milton Keynes MK1 1JD Tel. *01908 376630* Fax. *01908 647843* E-mail. *info@hydrafeed.co.uk* Web. *www.hydrafeed.co.uk Acrogrip – Autofeed – Feedmaster – Hydrafeed – Multifeed – Vanco – X-Tract*

Hydrainer Pumps Ltd Rotherham Close Norwood Industrial Estate, Killamarsh, Sheffield S21 2JU Tel. *0114 2484868* Fax. *0114 2472060* E-mail. *davestock@hydrainer.co.uk* Web. *www.hydrainer.com Hydrainer*

Hydralon Coatings Ltd Britannia Road Northam, Southampton SO14 5RH Tel. *023 80225573* Fax. *023 80332145* E-mail. *info@hydralon.com* Web. *www.hydralon.com HydraGRIP*

Hydrapower Dynamics Ltd St Marks Street, Birmingham B1 2UN Tel. *0121 4565656* Fax. *0121 4565668* E-mail. *pbrowne@hdl.uk.net* Web. *www.hydrapower-dynamics.com Arthur Webb Test Stands – Finnpower – Hosemobile – Synflex*

Hydrasun Ltd Hydrasun House 392 Kings Street, Aberdeen AB24 3BU Tel. *01224 618618* Fax. *01224 618701* E-mail. *info@hydrasun.com* Web. *www.hydrasun.com Action (United Kingdom) – Artifex (United Kingdom) – Autoclave (U.S.A.) – Autoclave, Firegard, I.V.G, Manuli, Offshore 850, Parker Hannifin, Seco, Snaptite, Synflex, Firemaster, Ponsloc. Action, Artifex, Bourdon Sedeme, Gates, ITR SPA, Jaymac, McDonald, Norgren, Oglaend, RSB, Polyflex, Titeflex, Tungum, Wade – Bourdon Sedeme (France) – *Firemaster (Germany) – Gates (Belgium) – *Hydrofit (Italy) – *I.V.G. (Italy) – ITR SPA (Italy) – Jaymac (Germany) – *Manuli (Italy) – McDonald Couplings (United Kingdom) – Norgren (United Kingdom) – Offshore 850 – Oglaend Systems (Norway) – *Parker Hannifin (U.S.A.) – Polyflex (Germany) – *Ponsloc (France) – RSB (Germany) – *Seco (U.S.A.) – Snaptite (U.S.A.) – *Stratoflex (U.S.A.) – *Synflex (U.S.A.) – Titeflex (U.S.A.) – Tungum (United Kingdom) – Wade (United Kingdom)*

Hydra Technologies ltd Unit 5 Europa Way, Fforestfach, Swansea SA5 4AJ Tel. *01792 586800* Fax. *01792 561606* E-mail. *salesdept@hydratech.co.uk* Web. *www.coolflow.co.uk CoolFlow*

Hydratight Morpeth 5 Coopies Field Coopies Lane, Morpeth NE61 6JT Tel. *01670 515432* Fax. *01670 513110* E-mail. *philip.maxted@hydratight.com* Web. *www.hydratight.com Aquajack (United Kingdom) – Hypuremate (United Kingdom) – Informate (United Kingdom)*

Hydratron Ltd Unit A1 Stuart Road, Broadheath, Altrincham WA14 5GJ Tel. *0161 9286221* Fax. *0161 9277085* E-mail. *info@hydratron.co.uk* Web. *www.hydratron.co.uk AZ – Butech – Hydratron – KMT – Rice Hydro*

Hydraulic Component & Systems Ltd Unit 14 Sovereign Park Cleveland Way, Hemel Hempstead Industrial Estate, Hemel Hempstead HP2 7DA Tel. *01442 240202* Fax. *01442 243133* E-mail. *hydcompdrf@hotmail.com* Web. *www.hydrauliccompsyst.co.uk Aron – Dowty – Enerpac – Heypac – Marzocchi – MHS – Norgren – Parker – Rampower – Rexroth – SMC – Vickers*

Hydraulic & Offshore Supplies Ltd Offshore House Southwick Industrial Estate, Sunderland SR5 3TX Tel. *0191 5497335* Fax. *0191 5160004* E-mail. *hos@hos.co.uk* Web. *www.hos.co.uk A B S – A R O – A-LOU – AAF – ABAC – ABB – ABBEY EXTRUSTIONS LTD – ABEX DENISON – ABEX MEAD – ACCUSPRAY – ACE – ACTION-SEALTITE – ADAN – AEROQUIP – AFLEX PTFE HOSE & FITTINGS – AFON – AFTON CHEMICAL LTD – AIGNEP – AIR LOGIC – AIR PINCH – AIR-VAC – AIRFIT – AIRLINES PNEUMATICS – ALBROCO – ALDONA SEALS LTD – ALENCO – ALFA GOMMA – ALLIANCE PLASTICS – ALLISON HYDRAULICS – ALLS – AMCO VEBA – AMEROID – AMIFLEX LARGE BORE HOSE ASSEMBLIES – ANACO – AND LETHEM – ANDERSON HUGHES LTD – ANDREW FRASER – ANGAR – ANGUS HOSE – ANSON LTD – APITECH – APOLLO – ARGO – ARGO ECOTEC – ARGO FILTERS – ARIES ENGINEERING CO. INC 'HYPERCYL' – ARIFLEX FLEXIBLE TUBES LTD – ARLON ATLAS AUTOMATION – ARON – ARON CETOP VALVES – ARTI – ARTI INSTRUMENTS – ASCA – ASCA JOUCOMATIC – ASCO – ASHFIELD SPRINGS LTD – ASTON – ATLAS AUTOMATION – ATLAS COPCO – ATOS – AUBURN GEAR – AUSCO – AUTOSTAR – AV PNEUMATICS – AVALCO – AVELAIR – AXIAL PUMP SPA – B & C VANE PUMPS – B Y P Y – BALDWIN DAVIS – BALLUFF – BALSTON – BAMBI – BAND-IT – BANNER SERVICES – BARNES HYDRAULICS – BAUER – BAUER COUPLINGS – BECK IPC Gmbh – BEKO – BELLE – BELLOFRAM – BERARMA – BERARMA S R L – BETABITE – BICKERS – BILSOM – BLACK DIAMOND – BLACKWATER HYDRAULICS – BLAGO – BLANKE ARMATUREN – BOGE COMPRESSORS – BOLENZ & SCHAFFER – BONFIGLIOLI TRASMITAL – BONOMI – BORELLI – BOSCH – BOSCH REXROTH – BOSTON – BRAND HYDRAULICS – BRAUER – BREVINI – BREVINI FLUID POWER – BREVINI HYDRAULICS – BRITAX – BROOK HYDRAULIC CUTTERS – BRUENINGHAUS – BSO – BUCHER – BUCHER HYDRAULICS – BULLFINCH – BURGAFLEX – BURKETT – BURNETT & HILLMAN – BUSAK & SHAMBAN – BUSCHJOST – C C JENSEN – C-MATIC – C.K.D. CORPORATION – CALZONI – CAM AUTOS – CAMOZZI – CAMOZZI PNEUMATIC – CASAPPA – CASAPPA SPA – CAST COMPRESSION FITTINGS – CASTROL – CASTROL TECHNOLOGY CENTRE – CATERPILLAR – CBF – CENTRE FOR POWER TRANS & MOTION CONTROL – CEWEL – CF – CFR ITALY – CHAR-LYNN – CHEVRON TEXACO TECHNOLOGY – CHICAGO-RAWHIDE – CHOTMERICS – CIOCCA – CIRTEQ UK – CJC – CLARIFIAR – CLARIS – CLARISEP – CLARKE – CLARON – CLAYMORE LUBRICANTS – CLIMAX – CLIPPARD – CM20 – COHLINE – COL.O.RING – COLEX – COLEX INTERNATIONAL – COLEY – COMATROL – COMATROL SRL – COMMAND CONTROL CARTRIDGES – COMMERCIAL – COMPACT – COMPACT CONTROLS – COMPARE HYDROVANE – COMPUMOTOR – CONEPT POWER – CONTI-TECH – CONTINENTAL – CONTROL DEVELOPMENTS – COPELEY – CORELESS – CORTECO – CORUS – COTTAM & PREEDY LTD – COXREELS – CPC – CPOAC – CRANE – CROSLAND FILTERS – CROSS HYDRAULICS – CROUZET – CTS – CULLIGAN – CUSTOM – DAEDAL – DAEWOO – DALLAI – DALMAR – DANFOSS – DANFOSS FLUID POWER – DAVID BROWN HYDRAULICS LTD – DAYCO – DEGUSSA LTD – DELTA FLUID PRODUCTS – DELTA POWER – DELTADYNE – DELTALOG – DELTASENSE – DELTROL PRODUCTS – DENISON HYDRAULICS – DENSION BERI – DESOUTTER – DEUTSCHE STAR – DEUTZ DIESEL ENGINES – DIAMONDSPIR – DICHTOMATIK GMBH – DIESSE – DIGI PLAN – DINAMIC OIL – DINOIL – DIRT-FUSE – DIXON-ADFLOW – DIXON-ADFLOW COUPLINGS – DLI – DNP QUICK RELEASE COUPLINGS – DNV – DOMNICK HUNTER – DONALDSON FILTER COMPONENTS LTD/ULTRAFILTER – DONNOLDSON – DOWMAX – DOWTY – DR BREIT – DRAPER – DRAPER TOOLS – DUNLOP HIFLEX HYDRAULICS FITTINGS – DUNLOP HYDRAULIC HOSE – DUNLOP INDUSTRIAL HOSE – DUPLOMATIC SRL – DURA INDUSTRIAL HOSE – DURAD – DUSTERLOH Gmbh – DYNAMIC VALVES - DYVAL SERVOS – EATON CORPORATION – EATON-AEROQUIP – EBARA – ECKERLE – EDER – EDI SYSTEM – EHRCO – ELWOOD CORPORATION – EM&S – EMB – EMMEGI – EMMERGI – ENDECOTTS – ENERGY PROCESS – ENERPAC – ENERPAC INDUSTRIAL TOOLS – ENERPAC PRODUCTION AUTOMATION – ENERPAC TORQUE WRENCHES – ENIDINE – ENOTS – ENOTTS – ENTERTROLS – EO – EO2 – EPE – EPP-MAGNUS – EURO HI-TEMP – EUROFLARE – EUROFLOW – EUROLOK – EUROPOWER HYDRAULICS – EUROPULSE – EUROSLEEVE – EUROWASH – EXAPORE ELEMENTS – EXCELON – EXITFLEX HOSE/FITTINGS – F.LLI TOGNELLA – FAIRCHILD – FAIREY ARLON – FAIRWAY SEALS – FASTER – FAWCETT CHRISTIE – FAWCETT CHRISTIE HYDRAULICS – FEDERAL MOGUL – FENNER – FENTEX – FER HYDRAULICS – FESTO – FESTO DIDACTC – FIAC – FIAT-HITACHI – FILSEAL – FILTERTECHNIK – FILTREC S R L – FINE TUBES LTD – FINITE – FIT – FLEETFIT – FLEXEQUIP HYDRAULICS LTD – FLEXIQUIP – FLOWEZY – FLOWTECH – FLOWTECHNIK – FLUPAC – FLUTEC – FOREST HYDRAULICS – FORSHEDA – FOSSE LIQUITROL – FREUDENBERG SIMRIT – FRUTIGEN A G – GALTECH – GAPI – GAS – GASK-O-SEAL – GAST – GATE HYDRAULICS – GATES AUTOMOTIVE PRODUCTS – GES – GIRAIR – GLENTHORPE – GLOBE – GLYDRING "T" – GOLDENBLAST – GOOD YEAR – GOODRIDGE – GORDON – GRESEN – GROMELLE – GUARDINN – GUYSON – GUYSON INTERNATIONAL – H P C – H+L HYDRAULIC – H.O.S – HACH ULTRA ANALYTICS – HAGGLUNDS DRIVES – HAGGLUNDS-DENISION – HAINZL – HALDEX AB – HALDEX GMBH – HALDEX LTD – HALLITE SEALS INTERNATIONAL – HAM-LET – HAM-LET ADVANCED CONTROL TECHNOLOGY – HAMWORTHY – HANKISON – HANNIFIN – HANSER HYDRAULIC – HARRIER – HARRIER FILTERS – HARTMANN & LAMMLE – HATTERSLEY – HAUHINCO – HAVIT HYRAULIK – HAWE – HBS – HDYRAULIC NORD – HELIDEBS CONTROL – HELITECH – HERCULES HYDRAULICS – HERION – HESSELMAN – HEYPAC – HI-FORCE – HIAB – HIDROIRMA – HITACHI – HKS GMBH – HMT – HOERBIGER – HOERBIGER ORIGA – HOKE – HOLBURY – HOLDTITE INDUSTRIAL ADHESIVES – HOLMBURY – HOZELOCK – HP HYDRAULICS – HPI – HSP – HUMPHREY – HUSCO INTERNATIONAL LTD – HYCO –*

HYCON – HYDAC – HYDAC-FLUPAC – HYDERCO – HYDRACLAMP – HYDRADYNE – HYDRAFORCE – HYDRAOVANE – HYDRASCAND – HYDRASTORE – HYDRAULIC PROJECTS LTD – HYDRAULIK RING – HYDRAUTO – HYDRO-LINE – HYDROCONTROL – HYDROKRAFT – HYDROLUX – HYDROMATIK – HYDRONIT-EOS – HYDROTECHECNIK – HYDROTECHNIK TEST EQUIPMENT – HYDROVANE – HYDROWA – HYLOK – HYPRO CORPORATION – HYR-APP – HYTAR – HYTEC – HYTHANE – HYTHOS VALVES – HYTOS – HYUPDONG – IKRON – IMI NORGREN – IMO – INDEQUIP – INDRAMAT – INFINEUM PARATAC – INFINEUM SYNACTO – INFINEUM VISTONE – INGERSOLL RAND – INTEGRAL – INTEGRATED HYDRAULICS – INTERLUBE – INTERMOT – INTERNORMEN – IPL – ISC – ISIS FLUID CONTROL – ISOLAST – ITR – IVG – J C B – J S BARNES – JAYMAC – JOHN CRANE – JOHN GUEST – JOHN S BARNES – JOJO – JOUCOMATIC – JSB HESSELMAN – JUBILEE – JUN-AIR – K-FIT – KANTSEAL – KARBERG & HENNEMANN – KATAS – KAVAC – KAVAIR – KAWASAKI – KEELARING – KEELAVITE – KINETROL – KING & CO – KIP – KLEEN-CHANGE – KOHLSWA ESSEM AB – KOMATSU – KONTAK – KR – KR FITTINGS – KRP – KUHNKE – KV – KV AUTOMATION – L-CUP – L.C. OLEODINAMICA – LAMBORGHINI – LANTEC INDUSTRIES – LARGA – LARZEP – LASER FIX – LEGIRS – LEGRIS CONNECTIC – LEIBHERR – LEO ELECTRIC – LHA – LINDE – LINDE HYDRAULICS – LINDOS – LINTRA – LINTRONIC – LITHOPURE – LLOYDS – LOCITE – LOCITITE – LODEMATIC – LOHMANN ISTOLTERFOKT – LOKOMEC – LOMBARDINI – LOMBARDINI ENGINES – LTR – LUBRIZOL INTERNATIONAL LABORATORIES – LUCIFER – LUDECKE – LUEN – LYTEFLEX – MAC – MACDONALD COUPLINGS – MACNAUGHT – MADAN – MAGANESE – MAGNUS – MAHLE – MANNESMANN REXROTH – MANULI – MANULI HAYDRAULICS – MANULI HOSE & FITTINGS – MANULI POWERTEAM – MARSH – MARSH BELLOFRAM – MARSH BELLOFRAM EUROPE – MARSH PRESSURE GAUGES – MARTONAIR – MARZOCCHI – MATARA – MATRIX – MAXAM – MECMAN – MEECH – MEILLOR – MERKEL – MERLETT – MERLETT PLASTICS – METAL WORK – METARIS HYDRAULICS – METRULOK – MF-4000 – MF2000 – MF3000 – MHA – MICRO-FAG – MICROBORE – MICROPAC PUMPS – MIDISTAR – MIDLAND PNEUMATIC – MIKROSPIN – MILLERS – MINI STAR – MINIBOOSTER – MINSUP – MINTOR – MODUL AIR – MODULAR CONTROLS – MOFFET MOUNTY – MOOG – MOOG ATCHLEY – MOOG PEGASUS – MOOG WHITTON – MORAVIA – MORRIS – MORRISON-ITI – MOTOFLOW – MSS SP 44 – MTE – NABIC – NAK – NESSIE WATER HYDRAULICS – NEXIS – NITTO – NO SKIVE – NORD – NORELEM – NORGREN – NORMA – NORSEMAN – NU TOOL – NUGGET – NUMATICS – NYCOIL – O-LOK – OCCO – OCCO COOLERS – ODE – ODESSE – OETIKER – OIL CONTROL – OIL GEAR – OIL GEAR TOWLER – OIL SISTEM – OIL SISTEM SRL – OILTECH – OLAB – OLAER – OLEDINAMICA – OLEO DINAMICA L.C. – OLEODINAMICA REGGIANA – OLEOSTAR – OLEOTECHNICA – OPENRAM – ORIGA – ORIGA SYSTEM PLUS – ORKOT – OTC – P.G. SERIES – P.O.D.S. – PALL – PALLSORB – PALMER CHENARD – PAMARGAN – PARFLEX – PARKER – PARKER ARLON – PARKER CAD – PARKER CYLINDERS – PARKER DAYCO – PARKER FILTRATION – PARKER FLUID CONNECTORS – PARKER HANNIFIN – PARKER HANNIFIN FLUID CONNECTORS – PARKER HANNIFIN INDUSTRIAL – PARKER ILUCIFER – PARKER MAXAM – PARKER MOBILE – PARKER PNEUMATIC – PARKER PNEUMATIC CONNECTORS – PARKER PNEUMATIV FILTRATION DIVISION – PARKER PUMP & VALVE DIVISION – PARKER UCC – PARKERTRONIC – PARKRIMP – PARL – PC9000 – PCL – PCL AIR TECHNOLOGY – PCM – PEDRO – PERMABOND ENGINEERING ADHESIVES – PERMCO – PETROCHEMICAL – PHOENIX HYDRAULIC – PIAB – PIONEER – PIONEER WESTON – PISCO – PISTER KUGLEHAEHNE – PLASFIT – PNEUFIT – PNEUMADYNE – PNEUMAX – PNEUMOTUBE – PNUE-LOK – POCLAIN – POLAR SEALS – POLYFLEX – POLYPAC – PONAR WADOWICE – POWER JACK – POWER TEAM – POWERLOCK – POWRLOCK – PRADIFA – PRATT – PREMIAIR – PRESTOLOK – PRIMARY FLUID POWER – PROCESS – PROFILE – PROSEP – PROXAL – PSI – PSI GLOBAL LTD – PTFE HOSE – PTI TECHNOLOGIES – PTI WATER FILTERS – PULSAFE – PUSH-LOK – QHP – QUADRING – QUAKER CHEMICAL LTD – QUALITY HYDRAULIC POWER LTD – QUICK-FIT – QUIET – QUIETAIRE – R.I. VALVES – RACINE – RACOR – RAJA-LOVEJOY – RAM POWER – RAM REMAN LTD – RAMPARTS – RAPESCO – RAPISARDA HOSE AND FITTINGS – RE PAK ELEMENTS – RECTUS – RED HAT – REDASHE – REEDEX – RELATED FLUID POWER – REOLUBE – REXROTH – REYROLLE – RHL – RIETSCHLE – RIGIMESH – RIMSEAL – RING – RIVA CALZONI – RMF – ROBBOLITE – ROBERT BOSCH – ROCKMASTER – ROLLSTAR AG – RTI APPLICATION DRYER – RUALTEC – RUELCO PRODUCTS – RUSTON – S M C – SAE – SAE FLANGES – SAI – SAINT GOBAIN PPL – SALAMI – SAM HYDRAULIK – SAMSUNG – SANDERSON – SANDVIK MATERIALS TECHNOLOGY – SARUM HYDRAULICS – SCANWILL – SCAPA GROUP – SCHRADER – SCHRADER BELLOWS – SCHROEDER – SCHROEDER FILTRATION – SCHUNK – SCHWER – SEALING PARTS – SEALTITE – SEMI SRL – SEMPAS – SEMPERIT – SEMPRESS – SENSITUBE – SENSOCONTROL – SEPTRA – SERA – SESINO – SHAMBAN – SHEILDMASTER – SHELL GLOBAL SOLUTIONS LTD – SHELL OILS AND LUBRICANTS – SHELL UK OIL PRODUCTS LTD – SIEBE – SIEBE AUTOMOTIVE – SIEMENS – SIGMA – SILCOFAB – SILVENT – SILVERLINE – SIMMERRING – SIMRIZ – SIP – SIRAL – SKEGA – SKF (UK) LTD – SLYDRING – SLYDWAY – SMC PNEUMATICS – SMEL S.R.L. – SMITHS INDUSTRIES – SNAP TITE – SNAP-FIT – SNAP-TITE EUROPE B.V. – SOFIMA – SOFIMA FILTERS – SPEEDFIT – SPEEDI-SLEEVES – SPENCER FRANKLIN – SPENKLIN – SPX – STAFFA – STANDARD POWER – STAR – STARK – STAUBLI UNIMATION – STAUFF – STAUFF CONNECT – STAUFF FILTRATION – STAUFF FLEX – STAUFF FORM – STAUFF LOGISTICS – STAUFF PRESSURE TEST SYSTEMS – STAUFF TYPE – STAUFF TYPE CLAMPS – STECKO – STEERFORTH – STEFA – STEPSEAL – STERLING – STERLING HYDRAULICS – STONE – STRAUB – STUCCHI – SUN CARTRIDGE VALVES – SUN HYDRAULICS LTD – SUPER DUPLEX – SWAGELOK / PARKER EQUIVALENT – SWEP – SYNCHRON – SYNFLEX – TAKEUCHI – TARP – TCH – TECALEMIT – TECHNODRIVE TWIN DISC – TEFEN – TELE MECANIQUE – TELEDYNE – TELEPNEUMATIC – TELL TALE – TEMA – TEMA-UK – TETROSYL – TRANS TECHNOLOGY (GB) LTD – UNICORNM CHEMICALS SPECIALIST SOLUTIONS – VOITH ENGINEERING – VON RUDEN – VOSS – VPS BREVINI – WALPRO – WALTERSCHEID – WALVOIL – WEBTECH – WELLMASTER – WILKA – WILMS – WORTHINGTON – X-TRACOAT – YUATANAI – YUKEN – ZOOMATIC

Hydraulic Pneumatic Services Unit 17 King Street Trading Estate, Middlewich CW10 9LF Tel. *01606 835725* Fax. *01606 737358* E-mail. *capper59@btconnect.com* Web. *www.pressure-pumps.co.uk Beaver – Madan Pumps*

Hydravalve Ltd Unit 4 Noose Lane, Willenhall WV13 3BX Tel. *01902 637263* Fax. *01902 637264* E-mail. *andy@hydravalve.co.uk* Web. *www.hydravalve.co.uk Paint Star*

Hydro Aluminium Extrusion Ltd Pantglas Industrial Estate Bedwas, Caerphilly CF83 8DR Tel. *029 20854600* Fax. *029 20863728* E-mail. *tracey.gifford@hydro.com* Web. *www.hydro.com/extrusion/uk Hydro Aluminium Extrusion*

Hydro Aluminium Extrusion Durham Road Birtley, Chester le Street DH3 2AH Tel. *0191 3011200* Fax. *0191 3011234* E-mail. *sales@hydro.com* Web. *www.hydro.com/extrusion/uk Hydro Aluminium – Hydroluminium Extrusion*

Hydro Static Extrusions Ltd Arran Road North Muirton Industrial Estate, Perth PH1 3DX Tel. *01738 494500* Fax. *01738 633933* E-mail. *sales@hydrostatic.co.uk* Web. *www.hydrostatic.co.uk Cuponal*

Hydrotechnik UK Ltd Unit 10 Easter Park Lenton Lane, Nottingham NG7 2PX Tel. *0115 9003550* Fax. *0115 9705597* E-mail. *info@hydrotechnik.co.uk* Web. *www.hydrotechnik.co.uk Filtration – Flowmeters – Macnaught – Minicheck – Minimess – Minimess - Minicheck Schroeder, Filtration, Macnaught, Flowmeters PC 9000 – PC 9000 – Schroeder*

Hydrotech Systems Ltd Unit 11d Vicarage Lane Hoo, Rochester ME3 9LB Tel. *01634 252265* Fax. *01634 250755* E-mail. *info@hydrotechsystemsltd.co.uk* Web. *www.hydrotechsystems.eu Hydrotech*

Hygiene Warehouse Unit 6 Ashmead Park, Keynsham, Bristol BS31 1SU Tel. *0117 9461960* Fax. *0117 9461959* E-mail. *sales@hygienewarehouse.co.uk* Web. *www.hygienewarehouse.co.uk *Liptons*

Hygiplas Containers Ltd Unit 27 5th Avenue Bluebridge Industrial Estate, Halstead CO9 2SZ Tel. *01787 472308* Fax. *01787 474290* E-mail. *sales@hygiplas.co.uk* Web. *www.hygiplas.co.uk Hygiplas*

Hyma UK Ltd Unit 2-3 Hargreaves Street, Oldham OL9 9ND Tel. *0161 6204137* Fax. *0161 6270713 Hyma*

Hypnos Ltd Longwick Road, Princes Risborough HP27 9RS Tel. *01844 348200* Fax. *01844 275012* E-mail. *info@hypnosbeds.com* Web. *www.hypnosbeds.com Hypnos – Hypnos Contracts*

Hypocell Ltd Unit 4 Longscorner Farm Bethersden, Ashford TN26 3HD Tel. *01233 627209* Fax. *01233 629846* E-mail. *generalenquiries@hypocell.co.uk* Web. *www.hypocell.org Hypocell*

Hypro Eu Ltd Station Road Longstanton, Cambridge CB24 3DS Tel. *01954 260097* Fax. *01954 260245* E-mail. *info@hypro-eu.com* Web. *hypro-eu.com A & R - pumps; Eezifit - range of nozzle holders; Lo-Drift _ drift reducing spray nozzles; Twin Cap - nozzle holders; DriftBETA - drift reducing spray nozzles - Berthoud Knapsacks. – A. & R. – Berthoud – Drift Beta – DriftBETA – Eezifit – Eezispray Valve – Hypro – Lo-Drift – Twin Cap*

Hytec Information Security 9-10 Oasis Park Stanton Harcourt Road, Eynsham, Witney OX29 4TP Tel. *01865 881616* Fax. *01865 887444* E-mail. *alan.hunt@hytec.co.uk* Web. *www.hytec.co.uk Hytecinformation Systems Ltd*

Hytorc Unex Ltd 24a Spencer Court Blyth Riverside Business Park, Blyth NE24 5TW Tel. *01670 363800* Fax. *01670 363803* E-mail. *sales@hytorc.co.uk* Web. *www.hytorc.co.uk AEA – Blitz – Tital*

Hyundai Motor UK Ltd 728 London Road, High Wycombe HP11 1HE Tel. *01494 428600* Fax. *01494 428699* E-mail. *fleet.sales@hyundai-car.co.uk* Web. *www.hyundai-car.co.uk *Hyundai (Korea, Republic of)*

I

I A C Company Ltd Winnall Industrial Estate Moorside Road, Winchester SO23 7RX Tel. *01962 873000* Fax. *01962 873111* E-mail. *info@iacl.co.uk* Web. *www.iacl.co.uk Accu-tone – Acoustack – Clean-Flow – Conic-Flow – Continuline – Metadyne – Moduline – Noise-Foil – Noise-Lock Panel – Noishield Louvre – Noishield Panel – Packless – Quiet-Duct – Quiet-Vent – Trackwall – Varitone – Vision-wall*

I A C Plastics Ltd (Industrial Anti-Corrosives Ltd) Oak Mill Manchester Road, Dunnockshaw, Burnley BB11 5PW Tel. *01706 212225* Fax. *01706 229926* E-mail. *sales@iacplastics.com* Web. *www.iacplastics.com Corromide – Corromide - Cast nylon products and materials, Corroplas - Thermoplastic materials, Corrothene - UHMW polyethylene products and materials. – Corroplas – Corrothene*

I A L Consultants C P House 97-107 Uxbridge Road, London W5 5TL Tel. *020 88327780* Fax. *020 85664931* E-mail. *enquiries@brggroup.com* Web. *www.brg.co.uk I.A.L.*

Ian Leach Plumbing & Heating 1 Walnut Cottage Oil Mill Lane, Clyst St Mary, Exeter EX5 1AH Tel. *07879 066065* E-mail. *ianleach.plumbing@googlemail.com Ian Leach Plumbing & Heating*

I A S Smarts Ltd Clarence Mill Clarence Road, Bollington, Macclesfield SK10 5JZ Tel. *01625 578578* Fax. *01625 578579* E-mail. *info@iasb2b.com* Web. *www.iasb2b.com Brit-Am – I.A.S.*

Iauctionshop Ltd 1 The Coachouse Zan Drive Wheelock, Sandbach CW11 4QQ Tel. *01270 767158* E-mail. *enquiry@iauctionshop.co.uk* Web. *www.iauctionshop.co.uk R & S Collectables*

Iberia Airlines Iberia House 10 Hammersmith Broadway, London W6 7AL Tel. *08706 090500* Fax. *020 82228983* E-mail. *sales@iberiaairlines.co.uk* Web. *www.iberiaairlines.co.uk Iberia Airlines*

Ibex Marina Ropes Cartridge Ropery Brunswick Street, Heywood OL10 1HA Tel. *01706 360363* Fax. *01706 622986* E-mail. *sales@ibexmarina.com* Web. *www.ibexmarina.com Aero-Cord – Storm – Storm*

ibm247 Unit 2 Castle Grove Studios 18 Castle Grove Drive, Leeds LS6 4BR Tel. *0845 3457859* Fax. *0845 3457897* E-mail. *sales@ibm247.co.uk* Web. *www.ibm247.co.uk IBM*

I B M UK Ltd PO Box 41, Portsmouth PO6 3AU Tel. *01962 815000* Fax. *0870 5426329* E-mail. *goldservice@uk.ibm.com* Web. *www.ibm.com ACTIVECM – Telelogic UK*

Ibstock Brick Ltd Swine Lane Nostell, Wakefield WF4 1QH Tel. *01924 866123* Fax. *01924 866101* E-mail. *d.humphrey@ibstock.co.uk* Web. *www.ibstock.co.uk Bretton – Bretton Red – Harewood – Harewood Burgundy Rustic – Harewood Charcoal Grey – Harewood Russet Buff – Harewood Russet Cream – Harewood Russet Orange – Harewood Sunset Multi Red – Harwood Sandal Rustic – Leyburn Blend – Malham – Malham Blend – Melton – Melton Antique Blend – Melton Blend – Red Multi – Royston – Royston Brown – Royston Golden Buff – Royston Red*

Ibstock Building Products Ltd Brickyard Road Aldridge, Walsall WS9 8TB Tel. *01922 741400* Fax. *01922 743086* E-mail. *r.hall@ibstock.co.uk* Web. *www.ibstock.co.uk Shenstone – Staffordshire – Walmey*

Icam Ltd Unit 2 Spring Gardens, Washington, Pulborough RH20 3BS Tel. *01903 892222* Fax. *01903 892277* E-mail. *icam@icam.ltd.uk* Web. *www.icam.ltd.uk Firetracer – Gastracer*

Ice Cool Services Ltd B9 Telford Road, Bicester OX26 4LD Tel. *01869 247947* Fax. *01869 253368* E-mail. *sales@icecoolservices.com* Web. *www.icecoolservices.com *Gem – *Triton – *Wilshire*

Iceni Productions Ltd Advertising/Broadcast/Corporate/Video Production The Studio Bell House Lane, Anslow, Burton on trent DE13 9PA Tel. *01283 567815* Fax. *01283 792993* E-mail. *studio@iceni.tv* Web. *www.iceni-tv.co.uk iceni*

Icework Ltd Lamberhurst Road Horsmonden, Tonbridge TN12 8DP Tel. *01892 722522* Fax. *01892 722578* E-mail. *info@icework.co.uk* Web. *www.icework.co.uk *Alcoluge*

I C International Gower Street Trading Estate St Georges, Telford TF2 9HW Tel. *01952 620206* Fax. *01952 620456* E-mail. *sales@ic-international.com* Web. *www.ic-international.com Bridela (United Kingdom)*

Icn Pharmaceuticals Ltd Cedarwood Crockford Lane Chineham Business Park, Chineham, Basingstoke RG24 8WD Tel. *01256 707744* Fax. *01256 707334*

E-mail. *sales@valeant.com* Web. *www.icnpharm.com I.C.N. Biomedicals – Titertek*

Icore International 220 Bedford Avenue, Slough SL1 4RY Tel. *01753 696549* Fax. *01753 896601* E-mail. *greg.burland@zodiacaerospace.com* Web. *www.icore.co.uk Conflex – Deltaflex – Entra-Lok – Fliteline – Isoflexit – Isoplat – Kafon – Lohal – Optigland – Optimum – Superflexit – System Fifty – System Sixty – Termilock*

I C R Touch LLP 26 Daish Way Dodnor Industrial Estate, Newport PO30 5XB Tel. *08446 931119* Fax. *01983 821682* E-mail. *sales@icrtouch.com* Web. *www.icrtouch.com *Casio – *ICR Touch – *Sharp – *Sure Pos 500 – *Vectis 500*

I C S Birmingham Science Park Aston Faraday Wharf Holt Street, Birmingham B7 4BB Tel. *0121 3267771* Fax. *0121 3274114* E-mail. *info@icstemp.com* Web. *www.icstemp.com Glycool*

I C S Robotics & Automation Ltd Unit 6 Manor Park Industrial Estate Station Road South, Totton, Southampton SO40 9HP Tel. *023 80667661* Fax. *023 80667881* E-mail. *martin.templeman@ics-robotics.co.uk* Web. *www.ics-robotics.co.uk I C S Robotics & Automation Ltd – ICS Robotics & Automation*

I C S Triplex 10-14 Hall Road Heybridge, Maldon CM9 4LA Tel. *01621 854444* Fax. *01621 859221* E-mail. *antonyp@icstriplex.com* Web. *www.icstriplex.com Brisco Engineering – I.C.S. Scotland – Industrial Control Services*

I C T C Ltd 3 Caley Close Sweet Briar Road Industrial Estate, Norwich NR3 2BU Tel. *01603 488019* Fax. *01603 488020* E-mail. *sales@ictc.co.uk* Web. *www.ictc.co.uk *I.C.T.C. (France, Italy and Germany)*

Ideagen Software Ltd Lime Tree Business Park Lime Tree Road, Matlock DE4 3EJ Tel. *01629 761590* Fax. *01629 56060* E-mail. *sales@ideagenplc.com* Web. *www.ideagen.co.uk Ideagen Software Ltd*

Ideal Bean Bags Unit 3 , Savill Road, Lindfield, Haywards Heath RH16 2NY Tel. *01444 482811* E-mail. *info@idealbeanbags.co.uk* Web. *www.idealbeanbags.co.uk Ideal Bean Bags*

Ideal Heating National Avenue, Hull HU5 4JN Tel. *01482 492251* Fax. *01482 448858* E-mail. *enquires@idealboilers.com* Web. *www.idealheating.com Caradon Plumbing Solutions*

Ideal Manufactures Atlas House Burton Road, Finedon, Wellingborough NN9 5HX Tel. *01933 681616* Fax. *01933 681042* E-mail. *enquiries@idealmanufacturing.com* Web. *www.idealmanufacturing.com Ideal Manufacturing*

Ideal Standard Ltd National Avenue, Hull HU5 4HF Tel. *01482 346461* Fax. *01482 445886* E-mail. *webmaster@ideal-standard.co.uk* Web. *www.idealstandard.co.uk ACADEMY – Accent – Airspa – Angle – Ascot – Bari – Birkdale – Cabria – Capolago – Caspian – Ceramix – Chester – Chloe – Class – Cleaners Sink – Cleopatra – Copacabana – Dallas – Dolciano – Domi – Duchess – Empress – Epsom – Europa – Harrow – Ideal-Standard – Isis – Jetline – Kingston – Kyomi – Lido – Linda – Marmara – Meadow – Mitre – Oval – Palladian – Playa – Plaza – Prima – Princess – Quadrant – Ravenna – Reflections – Revue – Rialto – Ropetwist – Sophie – Sottini – Space – Standard – Studio – Tamura – Tangent – Tantofex – Tempo – Traditional – Tratto – Trevi Showers – Tristar – Tulip – Utility Sink – Waterways – Whirpool – Xanto*

Ideal Studios 11 Maritime Street, Edinburgh EH6 6SB Tel. *0131 2026209* E-mail. *info@ideal-studios.co.uk* Web. *www.ideal-studios.co.uk Ideal Studios – ideal Studios Print – Ideal Studios Promotional Merchandise*

Ideasbynet Promotional Items Kings Croft Savage Lane, Sheffield S17 3GW Tel. *08448 117566* Fax. *0114 2621201* E-mail. *sales@ideasbynet.com* Web. *www.ideasbynet.com IDEASBYNET (United Kingdom)*

Ideas Furnace Ltd Tournai Hall Evelyn Woods Road, Aldershot GU11 2LL Tel. *08456 188291* E-mail. *info@ideas-furnace.com* Web. *www.ideas-furnace.com Ideas Furnace*

Idea Showcases Ltd 32 Hallowes Lane, Dronfield S18 1SS Tel. *01246 415535* Fax. *01246 415535* E-mail. *mail@ideashowcases.co.uk* Web. *www.ideashowcases.co.uk Fabframe*

Identilabel Ltd Unit 2a The Gattinetts Hadleigh Road, East Bergholt, Colchester CO7 6QT Tel. *01206 299777* Fax. *01206 299007* E-mail. *sales@identilabel.co.uk* Web. *www.identilabel.co.uk Alexander Collection, The*

Identilam plc John Bostock House Faygate Business Centre Faygate Lane, Faygate, Horsham RH12 4DN Tel. *01293 851711* Fax. *01293 851742* E-mail. *sales@identilam.co.uk* Web. *www.identilam.co.uk B.I.C.S. – Compic – Doppie*

I D Products Ltd West End Ashwell, Baldock SG7 5PL Tel. *01462 742305* Fax. *01462 742171* E-mail. *info@id-products.co.uk* Web. *www.id-products.co.uk Flexolite*

I E C Engineering Ltd Brookside Avenue Rustington, Littlehampton BN16 3LF Tel. *01903 773337* Fax. *01903 786619* E-mail. *info@iecengineering.com* Web. *www.iecengineering.com I.E.C. Engineering*

Ie-Ndt Manufacturer Unit C Heath Farm Swerford, Chipping Norton OX7 4BN Tel. *01608 683985* Fax. *01608 683476* E-mail. *enquiries@ie-ndt.co.uk* Web. *www.ie-ndt.co.uk C-Scan – Fedrex – Iridex – Kowo – Kowolux – Kowomat – *Nuclear (Germany)*

Ig Ltd Ryder Close, Swadlincote DE11 9EU Tel. *01633 486486* Fax. *01633 486492* E-mail. *info@igltd.co.uk* Web. *www.igltd.co.uk I.G. – I.G. Cavity Trays – *Weatherbeater Doors (Canada & USA) – *Weatherbeater Garage Doors (U.S.A.)*

Iggesund Paperboard Ltd (division of The Holmen Group) Siddick, Workington CA14 1JX Tel. *01900 601000* Fax. *01900 605000* E-mail. *info.as@iggesundpaperboard.com* Web. *www.iggesund.com Planet Nod*

Igloo RPO Ltd The Dower House 108 High Street, Berkhamsted HP4 2BL Tel. *0844 3570189* E-mail. *info@igloorpo.com* Web. *www.igloorpo.com Igloo RPO Ltd*

Igranic Control Systems Ltd Murdoch Road, Bedford MK41 7PT Tel. *01234 267242* Fax. *01234 219061* E-mail. *info@igranic.com* Web. *www.igranic.com Igranic*

Igus (UK) Ltd 51A Caswell Road Brackmills Industrial Estate, Northampton NN4 7PW Tel. *01604 677240* Fax. *01604 677242* E-mail. *sales_uk@igus.co.uk* Web. *www.igus.co.uk Chainflex. – Drylin – E-Chains – Energy Chain – Iglidur – Iglidur, Igubal, Drylin, Polysorb, Chainflex, E-Chains, Energy Chain, Readychain, Triflex – Igubal – Polysorb – Readychain – Triflex*

I H S Global Willoughby Road, Bracknell RG12 8FB Tel. *01344 328000* Fax. *01344 424971* E-mail. *customer.support@ihs.com* Web. *www.uk.ihs.com Rapidoc*

Iicorr Ltd 1 Minto Place Altens Industrial Estate, Aberdeen AB12 3SN Tel. *01224 898282* Fax. *01224 898202* E-mail. *info@iicorr.com* Web. *www.iicorr.com FSM – FSM - monitering systems RCP - (Resistor controlled cathodic protection) SenCorr - Multipurpose probe system. – RCP – SenCorr*

Ikegami Electronics Unit E1 Cologne Court Brooklands Close, Sunbury On Thames TW16 7EB Tel. *01932 769700* Fax. *01932 769710* E-mail. *mark@ikegami.co.uk* Web. *www.ikegami.co.uk *Ikegami (Japan)*

I K V Tribology Ltd Bramble Hollow The Narth, Monmouth NP25 4QJ Tel. *01600 869120* Fax. *01600 869101* E-mail. *sales@ikvlubricants.com* Web. *www.ikvlubricants.com Brugarolas – Filmsec – Fluor – Krytox – Zarox*

Illig UK Ltd Stratton Business Park London Road, Biggleswade SG18 8QB Tel. *01767 310555* Fax. *01767 318888* E-mail. *sales@illig.co.uk* Web. *www.illig.co.uk Illig*

Illston & Robson Ltd Herbert Road Small Heath, Birmingham B10 0QQ Tel. *0121 7725674* Fax. *0121 7666452* E-mail. *info@illstonandrobson.com* Web. *www.illstonandrobson.com Clevis Ends – I. & R. Standard – S.A.E. J490*

Imagefarm Ltd 175 Brent Crescent, London NW10 7XR Tel. *020 89631277* Fax. *020 89612404* Web. *www.imagefarm.co.uk Imagefarm*

Imagenta Moulding plc Unit 2 Coach Crescent, Shireoaks, Worksop S81 8AD Tel. *01909 472210* Fax. *01909 472211* E-mail. *sales@imagentaplc.co.uk* Web. *www.imagentaplc.co.uk Impbins.com*

Imagination Technology Canal Wharf, Leeds LS11 5DB Tel. *0113 2429814* Fax. *0113 2426163* E-mail. *info@imgtec.com* Web. *www.imgtec.com Code Scape – Mirage*

Imagine Transfers Teybrook Centre Brook Road, Great Tey, Colchester CO6 1JE Tel. *01206 210221* Fax. *01206 213613* E-mail. *jlmassoc@aol.com* Web. *www.imagine-transfers.co.uk Texiflock – Texipress Impressions – v-trans*

I M C Abbey Road Wrexham Industrial Estate, Wrexham LL13 9RF Tel. *01978 661155* Fax. *01978 729990* E-mail. *mail@imco.co.uk* Web. *www.imco.co.uk Argenta – Barcooler – Barkeller – Bartender – Eurobar – Frostar – I.M.C. – Impactor – Mistral – Nappigon – Pot Boy – Sanistrel – Sys2000*

I M C D UK Ltd Times House Throwley Way, Sutton SM1 4AF Tel. *020 87707090* Fax. *020 87707295* E-mail. *info@imcd.co.uk* Web. *www.imcdgroup.com Acclaim – Arcol – Baygal – BICAT – Brijonate – Brijonol – CAPA – DABCO – Desmodur – Desmophen – Fumyl-o-Gas – Fyrol – Polycat – Scuranate – Sobrom – Stepanpol – Terathane*

Imex Print Services Ltd Unit 1 Ash Court Viking Way Winch Wen, Swansea SA1 7DA Tel. *01792 719756* Fax. *01792 719021* E-mail. *info@imex-group.com* Web. *www.imex-print.co.uk Displays – Giclee – Plex Displays – Poster Clamp – Poster Snap*

I M H Technologies Ltd 8 Roach View Boss Millhead Way, Purdeys Industrial Estate, Rochford SS4 1LB Tel. *01702 545429* Fax. *01702 545428* E-mail. *sales@imh.co.uk* Web. *www.imh.co.uk BTech Inc (U.S.A.) – Dent Instruments (U.S.A.) – Dranetz-BMI (U.S.A.) – DRANETZ-BMI Power Quality Analysers, Electrotek - software, Satec - digital energy meters, Dent Instruments, energy loggers, BTech Inc Battery Validation Systems – Satec (Israel)*

I M I Cornelius UK Ltd Russell Way, Brighouse HD6 4LX Tel. *01484 714584* Fax. *01789 761469* E-mail. *jeremyf@corneliusuk.com* Web. *www.corneliusuk.com Apexx – Cannon – Coldflow – Cornelius – Dalex – Gaskell & Chambers – Jetspray – Polarflow – Remcor – Wilshire*

I M I Scott Ltd Dallimore Road Roundthorn Industrial Estate, Manchester M23 9WJ Tel. *0161 9985533* Fax. *0161 9460538* E-mail. *sales@imiscott.co.uk* Web. *www.imiscott.co.uk Cromaloy – IMI – Kutherm – Scott*

I M I Watson Smith Ltd Cross Chancellor Street, Leeds LS6 2RT Tel. *0113 2457587* Fax. *0113 2465735* E-mail. *aaith@northen.com* Web. *www.watsonsmith.com IMI – Watson Smith*

I M O Electronics Ltd Unit 15 1000 North Circular Road, London NW2 7JP Tel. *020 84526444* Fax. *020 84502274* E-mail. *sales@imopc.com* Web. *www.imopc.com *Benedikt & Jager (Austria) – I.M.O. – Jaguar – N.E.C.*

Impac Infrared Ltd Thompson House Thompson Close, Chesterfield S41 9AZ Tel. *01246 269066* Fax. *01246 269564* E-mail. *info@impac-infrared.com* Web. *www.impac-infrared.com E2T – Impac – Impac, Mikron, Kleiber E2T, Quantum Technology – Kleiber – Mikron – Quantum Technology*

Impacta Ltd Field Street, Bilston WV14 8RW Tel. *01902 496307* Fax. *01902 493937* E-mail. *sales@impacta.co.uk* Web. *www.impacta.co.uk Impacta*

IMPACT JOINERS 20 Ryedale view kirkbymoorside, york YO62 6EH Tel. *01751 431436* E-mail. *impactjoiners@btinternet.com* Web. *www.impactjoiners.co.uk IMPACT JOINERS*

Impalloy Willenhall Lane Industrial Estate Willenhall Lane, Bloxwich, Walsall WS3 2XN Tel. *01922 714400* Fax. *01922 714411* E-mail. *sales@impalloy.com* Web. *www.impalloy.com C-Sentry – C-Guard – C-Gard – Impalloy*

The Imperial Bathroom Company Ltd Empire Industrial Park Brickyard Road, Aldridge, Walsall WS9 8XT Tel. *01922 743074* Fax. *01922 743180* E-mail. *sales@imperial-bathrooms.co.uk* Web. *www.imperial-bathrooms.co.uk Astoria – Classic – Oxford – Westminster – Windsor*

Imperial Catering Equipment Ltd Elite House Castle Business Park, Loughborough LE11 5GW Tel. *01509 260150* Fax. *01664 424955* E-mail. *sales@imperialrange.co.uk* Web. *www.imperialrange.co.uk *Imperial*

Imperial Society Of Teachers Of Dancing Imperial House 22-26 Paul Street, London EC2A 4QE Tel. *020 73771577* Fax. *020 72478979* E-mail. *sales@istd.org* Web. *www.istd.org I.S.T.D.*

Imperial Tobacco Group PLC (Incorporating W.D. & H.O. Wills, John Player & Sons and Ogdens) PO Box 244 Upton Road, Bristol BS99 7UJ Tel. *0117 9636636* Fax. *0117 9667405* E-mail. *itg@uk.imptob.com* Web. *www.imperial-tobacco.com Capstan Full Strength – Capstan Ready Rubbed – Castella Panatella – Classic – Davidoff – Davidoff Gold – Drum – Drum Gold – Embassy Blue – Embassy Filter – Embassy Number 1 – Gold Block – Gold Leaf Concept – Golden Virginia – Hedges L260 – J & H Wilson SP No 1 – J & H Wilson Top Mill No 1 – J & H Wilsons Medicated No 99 – Job – John Player Special King Size – John Player Special White – King Edward Coronets – King Edwards Crowns – Lambert & Butler Gold – Lambert & Butler King Size – Lambert & Butler Menthol – Lambert & Butler White – Panama – Players Navy Cut – Players Navy Cut Flake – Regal Filter – Regal King Size – Richmond King Size – Richmond King Size Menthol – Richmond Smooth King Size – Richmond Superkings – Richmond Superkings Menthol – Richmond Superkings Smooth – Rizla – Rizla King Size – Rizla Regular – Small Classic – Small Classic Filter – St. Bruno Flake – St. Bruno Ready Rubbed – Superkings – Superkings Blue – Superkings Menthol – Superkings White – Three Nuns – Walnut Flake – Whiskey Ready Rubbed – Woodbine*

Imp UK Ltd Harby Road Langar, Nottingham NG13 9HY Tel. *01949 861020* Fax. *01949 861067* E-mail. *enquiries@catensa.co.uk* Web. *www.catensa.co.uk Catflax – Flex-Xel – Porofib – Poroflex – Poroil*

I M S International Marketing Services Ltd Boulton Works 54 College Road, Perry Barr, Birmingham B44 8BS Tel. *0121 3445500* Fax. *0121 3445505/01213445524* E-mail. *djbiggs@ims-ltd.co.uk* Web. *www.ims-ltd.co.uk I.M.S. – I.M.S. Interanational Marketing Services – M F Promotions (United Kingdom)*

Inca Geometric Ltd Bolts Hill Chartham, Canterbury CT4 7JZ Tel. *01227 738565* Fax. *01227 730915* E-mail. *sales@inca-ltd.demon.co.uk* Web. *www.incageometric.com Inca Geometric*

Incair Ltd 62 Garman Road Tottenham, London N17 0UT Tel. *020 88019400* Fax. *020 88019405* E-mail. *info@incair.co.uk* Web. *www.incair.co.uk Eurocare*

Incamesh Filtration Ltd Moss Farm Occupation Lane, Antrobus, Northwich CW9 6JS Tel. *01565 777681* Fax. *01565 777682* E-mail. *sales@incamesh.co.uk* Web. *www.incamesh.co.uk Allgaier – Boulton – Cuccolini –*

Farleygreene – Gough – Incamesh Filtration – Minox – Rotex – Russell Rinex – Sweco

In Case Solutions Nevis House Rush Green, Hertford SG13 7SD Tel. *01920 464333* Fax. *020 84413432* E-mail. *roy@incasesolutions.co.uk* Web. *www.incasesolutions.co.uk In Case Solutions, Custom ProductsAlulite, HiGloss ABS, Full Fight*

The Incentive Works Ltd Shendeck House 13 Harold Road, Braintree CM7 2RU Tel. *01376 550442* E-mail. *sales@theincentiveworks.co.uk* Web. *www.theincentiveworks.co.uk The Incentive Works*

Incinco 113-115 Codicote Road, Welwyn AL6 9TY Tel. *01438 821000* Fax. *01438 820888* E-mail. *enquiries@incinco.com* Web. *www.incinco.com Firestream – Incinco – Securifire*

Inciner8 Ltd Inciner8 House Balmoral Business Centre Balmoral Drive, Southport PR9 8PZ Tel. *01704 506506* Fax. *01704 506666* E-mail. *sales@inciner8.com* Web. *www.inciner8.com Inciner8*

Incon (Inspection Consultants) Ltd Rosscliffe Road Ellesmere Port, South Wirral CH65 3BS Tel. *0151 3565666* Fax. *0151 3574181* E-mail. *mail@incon.co.uk* Web. *www.incon.co.uk Incon – Inspection Consultants – Ultratec*

Incotech Ltd (Spraymation Ltd) 9 Lion Industrial Park Northgate Way, Walsall WS9 8RL Tel. *01922 455299* Fax. *01922 452288* E-mail. *colin@incotech.co.uk* Web. *www.incotech.co.uk Tippkemper - Matrix*

Incotes Ltd The Street Lamas, Norwich NR10 5AF Tel. *01603 279995* Fax. *01603 279928* E-mail. *incotes@btinternet.com Incotes*

Indasa Abrasives UK Ltd Viking Works Greenstead Road, Colchester CO1 2ST Tel. *01206 870366* Fax. *01206 860525* E-mail. *andrew@indasa.co.uk* Web. *www.indasaabrasives.com *Hermes (Germany) – *Indasa (Portugal) – *Linbide (New Zealand) – *Nitto (Japan) – Tex – Tex*

Indentec Hardness Testing Machines Ltd Unit 9-10 Lye Valley Industrial Estate, Stourbridge DY9 8HX Tel. *01384 896949* Fax. *01384 424470* E-mail. *john.piller@indentec.com* Web. *www.indentec.com Indentec*

Independent News & Media (NI) Ltd Independent News & Media (Northern Ireland) 124-144 Royal Avenue, Belfast BT1 1EB Tel. *028 90264000* Fax. *028 90554506* E-mail. *writeback@belfasttelegraph.co.uk* Web. *www.belfasttelegraph.co.uk Ads for Free – Belfast Telegraph – Community Telegraph – Irelands Saturday Night – North West Telegraph – Sunday Life*

Independent Power Systems Canada House 272 Field End Road, Ruislip HA4 9NA Tel. *020 88664400* Fax. *020 88663725* Web. *www.independent-power.co.uk BrainStorm*

Independent Radio News Ltd Mappin House 4 Winsley Street, London W1W 8HF Tel. *020 71828591* Fax. *020 71828594* E-mail. *news@irn.co.uk* Web. *www.irnco.uk I.T.N.*

Independent Tool Consultants Ltd Unit 7 Bamfurlong Industrial Park, Staverton, Cheltenham GL51 6SX Tel. *01452 712519* Fax. *01452 714786* E-mail. *sales@intoco.co.uk* Web. *www.intoco.co.uk Intoco*

Independent Twine Manufacturing Co. Ltd Westbank Road Llay Industrial Estate, Llay, Wrexham LL12 0PZ Tel. *01978 854812* Fax. *01978 854229* E-mail. *robert.macguire@indtwineco.com* Web. *www.indtwineco.com Cotlene – Gala Rope – Gold Strand – Gold wrap – Powerfil – Siltye*

Independent Welding Services Ltd Unit 2 15 Douglas Road Kingswood, Bristol BS15 8NH Tel. *0117 9352540* Fax. *0117 9352627* E-mail. *info@indeweld.com* Web. *www.indeweld.co.uk ArcGen – Cebora – Esab – GenSet – Hyperthern – Migatronic – Miller – Mosa – Murex – Saf – Thermal Dynamics*

Indesit Company UK Ltd Morley Way, Peterborough PE2 9JB Tel. *08452 235858* Fax. *01733 341783* E-mail. *sales@gda.uk.com* Web. *www.indesit.uk Camberley – Cambridge – Caress Royale – Cathedral – Country – Harmony – Lincoln – Manor – Manor B.F. – Manor E.F. – Manor P.F. – Midnight Deluxe – Nisermatic Deluxe – Nouveau – Oxford – Pearl Duo – Portico – Precept Deluxe – Rectory – Salisbury – Strata – Warwick – Winchester*

Indespension Ltd (Head Office) Paragon Business Park Chorley New Road, Horwich, Bolton BL6 6HG Tel. *01204 478500* Fax. *01204 478583* E-mail. *info@indespension.co.uk* Web. *www.indespension.co.uk Big Dipper – Brink – Coaster – Daxara – Dipper – Indespension – Indespension.com – Merit – Regent, Monarque, Emperor – Roller Coaster – Super Roller Coaster – SuperRide – Tow-a-Van – Tow-it – TripleLock – Witter*

Indespension Ltd Ascot Drive, Derby DE24 8ST Tel. *01332 348555* Fax. *01332 294614* E-mail. *sales@indespension.co.uk* Web. *www.indespension.co.uk Challenger – Tow A Van*

Index Unit D The Loddon Centre Wade Road, Basingstoke RG24 8FL Tel. *01256 843844* Fax. *01256 843367* E-mail. *sales@indexplastics.co.uk* Web. *www.indexplastics.co.uk Bilitene – Easy-Slide – Hang up Bags – Hang-Strip – Hang-Ups – Pet-Pick – Rigi-Hooks*

Indisplay Ltd Ventura Park Old Parkbury Lane, Colney Street, St Albans AL2 2DB Tel. *01923 851580* Fax. *01923 854681* E-mail. *sales@jmtindisplay.co.uk* Web. *www.jmtindisplay.co.uk Indisplay*

Inditherm Houndhill Park Bolton Road, Wath-upon-Dearne, Rotherham S63 7LG Tel. *01709 761000* Fax. *01709 761066* E-mail. *info@indithermplc.com* Web. *www.inditherm.com Inditherm*

Induchem Unit 1 Greenfield Farm Indl-Est, Congleton CW12 4TR Tel. *01260 277234* Fax. *01260 277649* E-mail. *sales@induchem.biz* Web. *www.induchem.ie Matryx (U.S.A.) – Naegelen valves (Germany) – Pliaxseal Valves (U.S.A.) – Tuflin Valves (United Kingdom)*

Inductotherm Europe Ltd The Furlong Berry Hill Industrial Estate, Droitwich WR9 9AH Tel. *01905 795100* Fax. *01905 795138* E-mail. *sales@inductotherm.co.uk* Web. *www.inductotherm.co.uk Dual-Melt – Dual-Trak – Duraline – Linemelt – Liquimetrics – Mainline – Powertrak – V.I.P.*

Inductotherm Heating & Welding Technologies Ltd Thermatool House Crockford Lane, Chineham, Basingstoke RG24 8NA Tel. *01256 335533* Fax. *01256 467224* E-mail. *info@inductothermhw.co.uk* Web. *www.thermatool-europe.com Inductoheat Banyard*

Indukey UK Ltd 11 Begbroke Lane Begbroke, Kidlington OX5 1RN Tel. *01865 841882* Fax. *01865 373102* E-mail. *info@indukey.co.uk* Web. *www.indukey.co.uk InduKey UK Ltd – InduMedical – InduProof – InduSteel*

Indusmond Diamond Tools Ltd 9 Dawson Place, London W2 4TD Tel. *020 77067640* Fax. *020 77275268* Web. *www.indusmond.com I.D.T. – Intrabonded*

Industrial Brushware Ltd Ibex House Malt Mill Lane, Halesowen B62 8JJ Tel. *0121 5593862* Fax. *0121 5599404* E-mail. *andrew.biggs@industrialbrushware.co.uk* Web. *www.industrialbrushware.co.uk Ibex*

Industrial Capacitors Wrexham Ltd Miners Road Llay Industrial Estate, Llay, Wrexham LL12 0PJ Tel. *01978 853805* Fax. *01978 853785* E-mail. *sales@icwltd.co.uk* Web. *www.icwltd.co.uk 'Clarity cap'*

Industrial Computers Ltd Unit 3 & 4 New Bury Park Marsh Lane Easthampnett, Chichester PO18 0JW Tel. *01243 380780* Fax. *01243 538035* E-mail. *sales@industrial-computers.com* Web. *www.industrial-computers.com Industrial Computers Ltd*

Industrial Friction Materials Ltd Unit 7 East Moors Business Park East Moors Road, Cardiff CF24 5JX Tel. *029 20499111* Fax. *029 20490011* E-mail. *mail@industrialfriction.com* Web. *www.industrialfriction.com Cordaflex (SMK) – Cordaflex (SMK) - V – Optoflex – Panoflex – Protolon (FL) – Protolon (FL) LWL – Protolon (SMK) – Protolon (SMK) LWL – Rondoflex – Rondoflex (C) - FC – Rondoflex (Chain) – Spreaderflex*

Industrial Hose & Pipe Fittings Ltd Bannerley Road, Birmingham B33 0SR Tel. *0121 7838118* Fax. *0121 7844844* E-mail. *sales@ihp.co.uk* Web. *www.ihp.co.uk Hiplok*

Industrial Power Units Ltd Churchbridge, Oldbury B69 2AS Tel. *0121 5110400* Fax. *0121 5110401* E-mail. *robert.beebee@ipu.co.uk* Web. *www.ipu.co.uk *DORI (France) – *FERRIS (U.S.A.) – *G.A.C. (U.S.A.) – *Hoaf (Netherlands) – I.P.U. – *KOCSIS (U.S.A.) – *Subair (U.S.A.)*

Industrial Batteries UK Ltd Unit 32 Greenlands Business Centre Studley Road, Redditch B98 7HD Tel. *01527 520052* Fax. *01527 520053* E-mail. *sales@ibluk.co.uk* Web. *www.ibluk.co.uk Alcad*

Industrial Services York Ltd Station Estate Station Road, Tadcaster LS24 9SG Tel. *01937 832761* Fax. *01937 833012* E-mail. *info@suremark.ltd.uk* Web. *www.suremark.ltd.uk Alpha-80 – Suremark – Suremark Drywype – Suremark Magnum – Suremark Metal Marker*

Industrial Textiles & Plastics Ltd Easingwold Business Park Oaklands Way, Easingwold, York YO61 3FA Tel. *01347 825200* Fax. *01347 825222* E-mail. *mv@itpltd.com* Web. *www.indtex.co.uk Industrial fabric producers – Powerbase – Powerclad – Powerclad DN – Powerclad FR – Powerclean – Powerclene – Powerfoil – Powerlon – Powerlon BM – Powerlon HP – Powerlon SP – Powerlon VCL – Powermesh – Powermex – Powernet – Powertarp – Powerton HP*

Industrial Trading Co. Ltd PO Box 51, Worcester WR1 1QE Tel. *01905 20373* Fax. *01905 27158 C.B. – I.T.C. – Intra – Laminated Shim Material*

Industrial Waxes Marle Place Marle Place Road, Brenchley, Tonbridge TN12 7HS Tel. *01892 724088* Fax. *01892 724099* E-mail. *sales@marlinchemicals.ltd.uk* Web. *www.marlinchemicals.co.uk *Cerit (Brazil) – Iwox*

I Nemetnejad Ltd 403-405 Edgware Road, London NW2 6LN Tel. *020 88305511* Fax. *020 85305522* E-mail. *info@inemetnejad.com* Web. *www.inemetnejad.com *Nemetnejad (Far East)*

Inenco Ltd Petros House Street Andrews Road North Lytham Street Annes, Lytham St Annes FY8 2NF Tel. *01253 785000* Fax. *01253 785001* E-mail. *marketing@inenco.com* Web. *www.inenco.com System 3000*

INEOS Enterprises Ltd Salt Business Mersey View Road, Weston Point, Runcorn WA7 4HB Tel. *01928 514640* Fax. *01928 572261* E-mail. *salt-enquiries@ineosenterprises.com* Web. *www.INEOS.co.uk Direct Salt – Hydrosoft – Whiterox*

Infield Safety UK Ltd Vanilla House Cambridge Road, Babraham, Cambridge CB22 3GN Tel. *01223 836222* Fax. *01440 705557* E-mail. *info@infield-safety.co.uk* Web. *www.infield-safety.co.uk Terminator*

Infinity Motorcycles Ltd 153 Lynchford Road, Farnborough GU14 6HG Tel. *01252 400400* Fax. *01252 400001* E-mail. *farnborough@infinitymotorcycles.com* Web. *www.infinitymotorcycles.com Motor Cycle City*

Infogenerics Ltd Unit 4 Innovation Centre Warwick Technology Park Gallows Hill, Warwick CV34 6UW Tel. *01926 422911* E-mail. *info@infogenerics.net* Web. *www.infogenerics.net infoGenerics Ltd.*

Information Strategies Key Intangible Value 2 Corve View Culmington, Ludlow SY8 2DD Tel. *0701 7026815* Fax. *07017 026814* E-mail. *iskiv@iskiv.net* Web. *www.iskiv.net/ i-Meta Manager – iSk-Portal – iSkiv – Quest-i*

Information Technology Infrastructure Ltd 12 Pierrepont Street, Bath BA1 1LA Tel. *01225 313549* Fax. *01225 448620* E-mail. *enquiries@itiltd.co.uk* Web. *www.itiltd.co.uk ITI*

Information Transfer LLP Burleigh House 15 Newmarket Road, Cambridge CB5 8EG Tel. *01223 312227* Fax. *01223 310200* E-mail. *info@intran.co.uk* Web. *www.informationtransfer.com Seminar Authoring Tool – Seminar Learning System – Write First Time*

Inform Plastics Ltd Unit 6 Block 2 Woolwich Dockyard Industrial Estate Woolwich Church Street, London SE18 5PQ Tel. *020 83177095* Fax. *020 83166720* E-mail. *info@informplastics.com* Web. *www.informplastics.com Polyprotec*

Infraglo Sheffield Ltd Dannemora Drive, Sheffield S9 5DF Tel. *0114 2495445* Fax. *0114 2495066* E-mail. *ken.crane@infraglo.co.uk* Web. *www.infraglo.co.uk Flamrad – Infraglo*

Infrared Heater UK Unit 2 Torridge Close Telford Way Industrial Estate, Kettering NN16 8PY Tel. *01536 525136* Fax. *01536 481569* E-mail. *infraredheater@rackett.freeserve.co.uk* Web. *www.infrared-heater-radiant-electric-gas-kerosene.co.uk Red Rad, Big Rad, Master Heater, Easiheat*

Ingen Ideas Ltd 111 Gallowgate, Aberdeen AB25 1BU Tel. *01224 619700* Fax. *01224 619749* E-mail. *info@ingen-ideas.com* Web. *www.ingen-ideas.com RAVE*

Inger Rose 5 Royston Park Road Hatch End, Pinner HA5 4AA Tel. *020 84211822* Fax. *020 84213187* E-mail. *info@ingerrose.co.uk* Web. *www.ingerrose.co.uk Inger Rose*

Ingleby Trice 11 Old Jewry, London EC2R 8DU Tel. *020 76067461* Fax. *020 77262578* E-mail. *enquiries@inglebytrice.co.uk* Web. *www.inglebytrice.co.uk Ingleby Trice Kennard*

Ingram Bros Ltd 15 East Lane, Paisley PA1 1QA Tel. *0141 8405870* E-mail. *sales@ingrambrothers.com* Web. *www.ingrambrothers.com Ingram Bros*

In the Hot Seat 36 Heath Road Helpston, Peterborough PE6 7EG Tel. *01733 252642* E-mail. *sue@inthehotseat.co.uk* Web. *www.inthehotseat.co.uk Land that Job – Reinvent Your Career*

inkstinx 744 Bishport Avenue, Bristol BS13 9EJ Tel. *0117 3042396* E-mail. *sales@inkstinx.co.uk* Web. *www.inkstinx.co.uk Inkstinx – Brother, HP, Lexmark, Samsung – Xerox, Epson, Canon, Kyocera*

Inkxperts 13 Yorke Street, Wrexham LL13 8LW Tel. *01978 261368* Fax. *01978 262735* E-mail. *sales@inkxperts.co.uk* Web. *www.inkxperts.co.uk Brother – Canon – Epson – HP – Lexmark*

Inline London Unit 3 Bridge Park Merrow Lane, Guildford GU4 7BF Tel. *08450 770045* Fax. *08450 770046* E-mail. *info@inlinelondon.co.uk* Web. *www.inlinelondon.co.uk Keey Clothing*

Inman & Co Electrical Ltd 2-4 Orgreave Place, Sheffield S13 9LU Tel. *0114 2542400* Fax. *0114 2542410* E-mail. *mlobar@inmanselectrical.co.uk* Web. *www.inmanswebstore.co.uk Emma*

Inmarsat Global Ltd 99 City Road, London EC1Y 1AX Tel. *020 77281000* Fax. *020 77281044* E-mail. *customer_care@inmarsat.com* Web. *www.inmarsat.com Fleetnet – Inmarset – Safetynet*

Innotech Controls UK Ltd 18 Henley Gardens, Yateley GU46 6LG Tel. *01252 669317* Fax. *01252 877644* E-mail. *sales@innotechcontrolsuk.com* Web. *www.innotechcontrolsuk.com Genesis – Innotech – Maxim*

innovations-tech Ltd. 28 Osprey Road, Weymouth DT4 9BU Tel. *020 32862626* E-mail. *info@innovations-tech.com* Web. *innovations-tech.com innovations-tech*

Innovia Films Ltd Station Road, Wigton CA7 9BG Tel. *01697 342281* Fax. *01697 341417*

E-mail. *filmsinfo@innoviafilms.com* Web. *www.innoviafilms.com Cellophane(tm) (United Kingdom) – CelloTherm(tm) (United Kingdom) – NatureFlex(tm) (United Kingdom) – Propafilm(tm) (United Kingdom) – PropaFresh(tm) (United Kingdom) – Propaream(tm) (United Kingdom) – Rayoface(tm) (United Kingdom) – Rayofoil(tm) (United Kingdom) – Rayoweb(tm) (United Kingdom) – StarTwist(tm) (United Kingdom) – Rayoform (tm) (United Kingdom)*

Inoxpa Ltd 15 Ormside Way Holmethorpe Industrial Estate, Redhill RH1 2LW Tel. *01737 378060* Fax. *020 86890245* E-mail. *shutton@inoxpa.com* Web. *www.inoxpa.com Realm – Realm Monarch Valves – Realm RPRII Hygienic Pressure Relief Valves*

In Practice Systems Ltd Bread Factory 1a Broughton Street, London SW8 3QJ Tel. *020 75017000* Fax. *020 75017100* E-mail. *max.brighton@inps.co.uk* Web. *www.inps.co.uk CPL – V.A.M.P. – V.A.M.P. Data – V.A.M.P. Links*

Inrekor Ltd Unit 1c Chalwyd Industrial Estate St Clements Road, Poole BH12 4PE Tel. *01202 721211* E-mail. *fpr@inrekor.co.uk* Web. *www.inrekor.com Inrekor*

Inshore Fisheries Ltd Inshore Fisheries House Tod Point Road, Redcar TS10 5AU Tel. *01642 484125* Fax. *01642 486749* E-mail. *sales@inshore.co.uk* Web. *www.inshore.co.uk Inshore*

Insitive Media 32-34 Broadwick Street, London W1F 8JB Tel. *020 73169000* Fax. *020 73169003* Web. *www.vnunet.com Easy Net – Jobworld – Recruitment Matters – VNU Net*

Inspection Consultant Ltd Unit 1 Terrace Factory Rossfield Road, Ellesmere Port CH65 3BS Tel. *0151 3572212* Fax. *0151 3574181* E-mail. *mail@incon.co.uk* Web. *www.incon.co.uk Incon – Inspection Consultants – Ultratec*

Instem LSS Stanley Hall Edmund Street, Liverpool L3 9NG Tel. *0151 2247700* Fax. *01785 825625* E-mail. *info@instem.com* Web. *www.instem.com Artemis II*

Insteng Process Automation Ltd Unit 3 Moy Road Industrial Estate Taffs Well, Cardiff CF15 7QR Tel. *029 20815000* Fax. *029 20813051* E-mail. *sylviaburris@insteng.co.uk* Web. *www.insteng.co.uk FLIR – IRCON – Raytek – Signatrol*

Institute Of Chartered Accountants Regus House Falcon Drive, Cardiff CF10 4RU Tel. *020 79208100* Fax. *020 79200547* E-mail. *feedback@icaew.co.uk* Web. *www.icaew.com ABG Professional Information – Accountancy Magazine – Accounting and Business Research – Institute of chartered accountants in England & Wales – The Institute of Chartered Accountants in England & Wales*

Institute Of Practitioners In Advertising Ltd 44 Belgrave Square, London SW1X 8QS Tel. *020 72357020* Fax. *020 72459904* E-mail. *info@ipa.co.uk* Web. *www.ipa.co.uk Institute of Practitioners*

Institute Of Spring Technology Henry Street, Sheffield S3 7EQ Tel. *0114 2760771* Fax. *0114 2726344* E-mail. *l.peel@ist.org.uk* Web. *www.ist.org.uk Version 7.50 – version 8*

Institution Of Engineering & Technology 2 Savoy Place, London WC2R 0BL Tel. *020 72401871* Fax. *020 72407735* E-mail. *postmaster@theiet.org* Web. *www.theiet.org I.E.E. – Inspec*

Instron Coronation Road Cressex Business Park, High Wycombe HP12 3SY Tel. *01494 464646* Fax. *01494 456454* E-mail. *adam_baxter@instron.com* Web. *www.instron.com Instron*

Instrument Plastics Ltd 33-37 Kings Grove Industrial Estate Kings Grove, Maidenhead SL6 4DP Tel. *01628 770018* Fax. *01628 773299* E-mail. *tim@instrumentplastics.co.uk* Web. *www.instrumentplastics.co.uk Optolite – *Polaroid (U.S.A.)*

Intacab Ltd Service House West Mayne, Basildon SS15 6RW Tel. *01268 545454* Fax. *01268 886707* E-mail. *mgreenaway@toomey.uk.com* Web. *www.intacabessex.co.uk Intacab – Intercar*

Intech Ltd Link House 273 Crown Lane, Horwich, Bolton BL6 5HY Tel. *01204 675675* Fax. *01204 695172* E-mail. *ian.clough@intech.co.uk* Web. *www.intech.co.uk Dialafile – Intech*

In-Tech Solutions UK Ltd 65 Park Road Hammerwich, Burntwood WS7 0EE Tel. *01543 672774* E-mail. *annette.james@in-techsolutions.co.uk* Web. *www.in-techsolutions.co.uk CHOISE*

Integer Micro Systems Ltd Dugard House Peartree Road, Stanway, Colchester CO3 0UL Tel. *01206 564600* Fax. *01206 369620* E-mail. *sales@ims-integer.com* Web. *www.ims-integer.com FreighterBase – Tankerbase*

Integra I C T Ltd 1 Gateshead Close, Sandy SG19 1RS Tel. *01767 692792* Fax. *01767 692992* E-mail. *info@integra-ict.co.uk* Web. *www.integra-ict.co.uk HICOM – HIPATH – Siemens*

Integra Products High Point Sandy Hill Park Sandy Way, Tamworth B77 4DU Tel. *01543 267100* Fax. *01543 267104* E-mail. *john.martin@integra-products.co.uk* Web. *www.integra-products.co.uk Britannia (United Kingdom) – Cedenza (United Kingdom) – Consort (United Kingdom) – Coronation (United Kingdom) – Coronet (United Kingdom) – Decorail (United Kingdom) – Decorpole (United Kingdom) – Double Duty (United Kingdom) – Golden Glide (United Kingdom) – Handitrack (United Kingdom) – Jubilee (United Kingdom) – Monorail (United Kingdom) – Slimglide (United Kingdom) – Super Twosome (United Kingdom) – Swanglide (United Kingdom) – Threesome (United Kingdom) – Twosome (United Kingdom) – Ultraglide (United Kingdom)*

Integrated Technologies Ltd Ellingham Industrial Centre Ellingham Way, Ashford TN23 6NF Tel. *01233 638383* Fax. *01233 639401* E-mail. *thc@itl.co.uk* Web. *www.itl.co.uk Wilj*

Integrate HR Ltd Bloxham Mill Barford Road, Bloxham, Banbury OX15 4FF Tel. *01295 722833* Fax. *0870 4602968* E-mail. *sales@integratehr.com* Web. *www.integratehr.com Integrate360 – IntegrateOS – IntegrateRecruit*

Integrex Portwood Industrial Estate Church Gresley, Swadlincote DE11 9PT Tel. *01283 550880* Fax. *01283 552028* E-mail. *sales@integrex.co.uk* Web. *www.integrex.co.uk Integrex Colourjet*

Intelesis Ltd Unit 7 First Floor Offices Aizlewood's Mill Business Centre, Nursery Street, Sheffield S3 8GG Tel. *0844 8444555* Fax. *0844 8444567* E-mail. *info@intelesis.co.uk* Web. *www.intelesis.co.uk 0844*

Interactive Data Fitzroy House, London EC2A 4DL Tel. *020 78258000* Fax. *020 72512725* E-mail. *investorrelations@interactivedata.com* Web. *www.interactivedata.com Exbond – Exshare – Financial Times Electronic Publishing – Interactive Data*

Interagro UK Ltd Sworder's Barn North Street, Bishops Stortford CM23 2LD Tel. *01279 501995* Fax. *01279 501996* E-mail. *info@interagro.co.uk* Web. *www.interagro.co.uk Arma – Banka – Interagro – Ryda – Slippa – Stamina – Toil*

Interbrand 85 Strand, London WC2R 0DW Tel. *020 75541000* Fax. *020 75541001* E-mail. *reception@interbrand.com* Web. *www.interbrand.com Interland Newell and Sorrell*

Intercity Telecom Ltd 101-114 Holloway Head, Birmingham B1 1QP Tel. *0121 6437373* Fax. *0121 6436160* E-mail. *sales@intercity-uk.com* Web. *www.intercity-uk.com Unipage*

Interclad Ltd 173 Main Road Biggin Hill, Westerham TN16 3JR Tel. *01959 572447* Fax. *01959 576974* E-mail. *sales@interclad.co.uk* Web. *www.interclad.co.uk Caterclad – Interclad – Interlock Ceiling – Mediclad – Mediclad H D – Waterfield*

Intercover (E Hampson) Ltd Unit B12a, Broadlands Heywood Distribution Park, Pilsworth Road, Heywood OL10 2TS Tel. *01706 623344* Fax. *01706 623345* E-mail. *sales@intercover.co.uk* Web. *www.intercover.co.uk Cabra – Kidrel – Kidrex – Regency*

Intereurope Ltd 21-23 East Street, Fareham PO16 0BZ Tel. *01329 823047* Fax. *01329 822058* Web. *www.intereurope.com Intereurope – Intereurope Regulations*

Interface Europe Ltd Shelf Mills, Halifax HX3 7PA Tel. *08705 304030* Fax. *01274 694095* E-mail. *info@interface.com* Web. *www.interfaceflor.eu 532 Naturelle – 536 Perspectives – 537 Perspectives Prints – 720 Moresque – 725 Phoenix – Aiki – Amber Waves – Bright Ideas – Caribbean – Connections – Dashes – Dots – Dynamics – Factor 4 – Festival – Flor – Frise – Galleria 80/20 – Galleria Antron – Giant Steps – Hawk – Interface, Heuga, Firth, Bentley, Solenium, Intercell, Image, Renovisions. – Interlock – Jakarta – Landscape – Light Show – Moraine – New England – North Exposure – Nylfloor – Olympic 580 – Orthomat – Palette 2000 – Palette 3000 – Palette 4000 Flecks – Palette 4000 Tweeds – Panorama – Phoenix – Prelude – Quantum 530 – Rain Forest – Reflex – Reflex With Accents – Structure – Superflor – Tatami – Ultimum 584 – Universe – World Alpha – World Beta – World Delta – World Epsilon – World Gamma – World Lambda – World Omega – World Sigma*

Interflex Hose & Bellows Ltd Orleton Road Ludlow Business Pk, Ludlow SY8 1XF Tel. *01584 878500* Fax. *01584 878115* E-mail. *enquiries@interflex.co.uk* Web. *www.interflex.co.uk Interflex Hose & Bellows – Mason Safeflex – Mason Superflex – Mercer Rubber Bellows – Dilatoflex – Rubber Bellows – Trelleborg Teguflex – Willbrandt Expansion Joints – Oria Airspring Bellows – Springride Spring Bellows – Torpress Airspring Bellows – Pneuride Airspring Bellows – Powerflex Expansion Joints*

Interfuse Ltd Unit 19 Corringham Road Industrial Estate Corringham Road, Gainsborough DN21 1QB Tel. *01427 810290* Fax. *01427 810405* E-mail. *rogerjones@interfuseblocks.com* Web. *www.interfuseblocks.com Intercrete – Interlyte – Lytag*

Intergrated Electronics Ltd 20 Ferry Lane Wraysbury, Staines TW19 6HG Tel. *01784 483633* Fax. *01784 483918* E-mail. *contact@ielco.com* Web. *www.ielco.com Intelect*

Interior Property Solutions Unit 17 Wrotham Business Park Wrotham Park, Barnet EN5 4SZ Tel. *020 82751095* Fax. *020 84490521* E-mail. *contact@ips-interiors.co.uk* Web. *www.ips-interiors.co.uk Fireplan System – Interplan System – Multiplan System*

Interlevin Refrigeration Ltd Unit 6a West Meadow Rise, Castle Donington, Derby DE74 2HL Tel. *01332 850090* Fax. *01332 810685* E-mail. *trade.sales@interlevin.co.uk* Web. *www.interlevin.co.uk Arcaboa – Criocabin (Italy) – *Elcold (Denmark) – Elstar – *Framec (Italy) – Frigorex (Greece) – Frilixa – Gayc – IARP (Italy) – Levin – Mercatus – *Norcool (Norway) – Nortech (Italy) – *Staycold (South Africa) – Tecfrigo (Italy) – Tefcold*

Interlink Express Parcels Ltd Roebuck Lane, Smethwick B66 1BY Tel. *0121 5002500* E-mail. *marketing@geopostuk.com* Web. *www.interlinkexpress.com Interlink Direct*

Interlube Systems Ltd 85 St Modwen Road, Plymouth PL6 8LH Tel. *01752 676000* Fax. *01752 676001* E-mail. *info@interlubesystems.co.uk* Web. *www.interlubesystems.com E.G.R. – Interlube – Tecreel (United Kingdom)*

Intermedical UK Ltd Unit 6 Mill Hall Business Estate Mill Hall, Aylesford ME20 7JZ Tel. *01732 522444* Fax. *01732 872883* E-mail. *derek.curtis@intermedical.co.uk* Web. *www.intermedical.co.uk Elite Portable Oxygen Systems (United Kingdom) – Medel Nebulisers (Italy) – NDD Pulomary Function Systems (United Kingdom) – Sim Travelair (Italy)*

International Lamps & Components Stadium Way, Harlow CM19 5FG Tel. *01279 442266* Fax. *01279 442222* E-mail. *sales@internationallamps.co.uk* Web. *www.internationallamps.co.uk Luxina – Luxina - The Wholesale Lamp Co Ltd*

International Syalons Newcastle Ltd Stevenson Street Willington Quay, Wallsend NE28 6TT Tel. *0191 2951010* Fax. *0191 2633847* E-mail. *enquiries@syalons.com* Web. *www.syalons.com Si-AL-O-N*

International Labmate Ltd Oak Court Business Centre Sandridge Park Porters Wood, Porters Wood, St Albans AL3 6PH Tel. *01727 855574* Fax. *01727 841694* E-mail. *info@intlabmate.com* Web. *www.labmate-online.com International Environmental Technology – International Labmate – *Lab (South America) – Lab Africa – Lab Asia – *Labmote (UK and Ireland)*

International Packaging Corporation 14 Redbrae, Maybole KA19 7HJ Tel. *01655 882381* Fax. *01655 883789* E-mail. *sales@interpak.co.uk* Web. *www.interpak.co.uk INTERPAK*

International Paint Ltd Stoneygate Lane, Gateshead NE10 0JY Tel. *0191 4696111* Fax. *0191 4012473* E-mail. *john.lockhart@akzonobel.com* Web. *www.akzonobel.com Interbond – Interchlor – Intergard – Interlac – International – Interplate – Interprime – Interthane – Intertuf – Intervinux – Interzinc – Wintercure*

International Paper Equipment Finance LP Inverurie Mills, Inverurie AB51 5NR Tel. *01467 627000* Fax. *01467 627102* E-mail. *bill.conn@ipaper.com* Web. *www.ipaper.com Captain Card – Captain Colours – Captain White Copier – Duolaser – Presentation – Talisman*

International Pheromone Systems Ltd Units 10-15 Meadow Lane Industrial Estate, Ellesmere Port CH65 4TY Tel. *0151 3572655* Fax. *0151 3550299* E-mail. *dave@internationalpheromone.co.uk* Web. *www.internationalpheromone.co.uk Agricon – Capilure – Cue-Lure – Dorsalure*

International Power Presses (Hulbert Engineering Limited) Peartree Lodge Grazebrook Industrial Park Peartree Lane, Dudley DY2 0XW Tel. *01384 457595* Fax. *01384 457280* E-mail. *enq@hulbert-group.co.uk* Web. *www.int-power-presses.co.uk International Power Presses*

International Scientific Supplies Ltd Richmond House, Bradford BD2 1AL Tel. *01274 720070* Fax. *01274 728295* E-mail. *info@intscientific.com* Web. *www.intscientific.com ISS Ltd*

International Training Service Ltd (ITS) 37 Parkfield Road Coleshill, Birmingham B46 3LD Tel. *01675 466466* Fax. *01675 466404* E-mail. *johnh@itsconsult.com* Web. *www.itsconsult.com ITS*

International Waxes Limestones Victoria Road, Milford On Sea, Lymington SO41 0NL Tel. *01590 641542* Fax. *01590 641299* E-mail. *peter@rigidaxuk.com Rigidax*

Interpower International PO Box 70, Pickering YO18 7XU Tel. *01751 474034* Fax. *01751 476103* E-mail. *info@interpower.co.uk* Web. *www.interpower.co.uk Interpower*

Interprint Ltd Lingerfield Business Park Market Flat Lane, Scotton, Knaresborough HG5 9JA Tel. *0800 9757514* Fax. *01423 798470* E-mail. *sbruce@interprint-ltd.co.uk* Web. *www.interprint.co.uk Colour Express – Firecrest Design – Firecrest Photography – Interprint*

Interroll Ltd Brunel Road Earlstrees Industrial Estate, Corby NN17 4UX Tel. *01536 200322* Fax. *01536 748505* E-mail. *c.middleton@interroll.com* Web. *www.interroll.com Modulink*

Interspiro Ltd 7 Hawksworth Road Central Park, Telford TF2 9TU Tel. *01952 200190* Fax. *01952 299805* E-mail. *infouk@interspiro.com* Web. *www.interspiro.com/uk Divator MK11 – Divator MKII – Savox – Spiroline – Spiromatic – Spiromatic 90 – Spiromatic Escape – Spiroscape – Spirotroniq*

Interventus Business Psychologists 12 Church Street, Omagh BT78 1DG Tel. *028 82243100* E-mail. *info@interventus.net* Web. *www.interventus.net Interventus*

Intourist Ltd 7 Wellington Terrace, London W2 4LW Tel. *020 77274100* Fax. *020 77278090*

E-mail. *info@intourist.co.uk* Web. *www.intouristuk.com Intourist – Intourist Travel*

Intra Ltd 27 Wilbury Way, Hitchin SG4 0TS Tel. *01462 424800* Fax. *01462 453667* E-mail. *info@intra-corp.co.uk* Web. *www.intra-corp.co.uk Data Gage – Labmaster – Lad Micrometer – Modular Fixturing – MPACS – Supermicrometer*

Intrad Ltd St Albans Road West, Hatfield AL10 0TF Tel. *01707 266726* Fax. *01707 263614* E-mail. *sales@intrad.co.uk* Web. *www.intrad.co.uk Intrad – Intrad Reflex – Intrad System 545 – Intrad TSM*

Intumescent Seals (a division of Dixon International Group Ltd) Brewery Road Pampisford, Cambridge CB22 3HG Tel. *01223 832758* Fax. *01223 837215* E-mail. *sales@intumescentseals.co.uk* Web. *www.intumescentseals.co.uk Dragon*

Invensys PLC 3rd Floor 40 Grosvenor Place, London SW1X 7AW Tel. *020 31551200* Fax. *020 78343879* E-mail. *reception@invensys.com* Web. *www.invensys.com Brook Hansen – BTR – Hawker – Huyck – Rexnord – Stowe Woodward – Weavexx*

Invertec Ltd Whelford Road, Fairford GL7 4DT Tel. *01285 713550* Fax. *01285 713548* E-mail. *sales@invertec.co.uk* Web. *www.invertec.co.uk Invertec*

Investalist Ltd Dimmings Cottage Chapmore End, Ware SG12 0HG Tel. *0870 9109400* E-mail. *admin@investalist.co.uk* Web. *www.investalist.co.uk Investalist*

Investment Tooling International Ltd 4a Moston Road Middleton, Manchester M24 1SL Tel. *0161 6538066* Fax. *0161 6553095* E-mail. *ray@iti-manchester.co.uk* Web. *www.iti-manchester.co.uk Investment Tooling International*

Invicta Paints 59-61 Sturry Road, Canterbury CT1 1DR Tel. *01227 866146* Fax. *01227 864718* E-mail. *geoff.nickols@invictamotors.com* Web. *www.invictamotors.co.uk Ford – Ford Maindealer – Iveco – Iveco Ford – Transit Specialist Dealer*

Invictas Group Invicta Works Houghton Road, Grantham NG31 6JE Tel. *01476 515500* Fax. *01476 515540* E-mail. *info@invictasgroup.co.uk* Web. *www.sitedumpers.com Taylor Valves Ltd*

Invictus Locks & Security 10c Carnock Road, Dunfermline KY12 9AX Tel. *07726 012000* E-mail. *invictuslocks@tiscali.co.uk* Web. *www.invictuslocks.co.uk key edge*

Inwido UK Ltd Delta House Harris Business Park Stoke Prior, Bromsgrove B60 4DJ Tel. *01527 881060* Fax. *01527 881061* E-mail. *mail@inwido.co.uk* Web. *www.inwido.co.uk *Swedhouse (Sweden)*

Ioma Clothing Co. Ltd Woodend Avenue Speke, Liverpool L24 9WF Tel. *0151 4489000* Fax. *0151 4489009* E-mail. *sales@iomaclothing.co.uk* Web. *www.iomaclothing.co.uk Ioma*

Ion Information Technologies Ltd Buckingham House Desborough Road, High Wycombe HP11 2PR Tel. *01494 512490* Fax. *01494 512491* E-mail. *chander@ionit.co.uk* Web. *www.ionit.com ION Information Technology*

Ion Science Ltd The Way Fowlmere, Royston SG8 7UJ Tel. *01763 208503* Fax. *01763 208814* E-mail. *info@ionscience.com* Web. *www.ionscience.com CalCheck – Gas-Check – GasCheck R – GasCheck SF6 – Hydrosteel – PhoCheck – Photec*

Iot PRC Northern House Moor Knoll Lane, East Ardsley, Wakefield WF3 2EE Tel. *01924 823455* Fax. *01924 820433* E-mail. *enquiries@iotplc.com* Web. *www.iotplc.com Electronic Office*

I P A Systems Ltd The Priory 37 London Road, Cheltenham GL52 6HA Tel. *01242 573344* Fax. *01242 519364* E-mail. *sales@ipasystems.co.uk* Web. *www.ipasystems.co.uk I.P.A.*

I P C Media Ltd Blue Fin Building 110 Southwark Street, London SE1 0SU Tel. *0800 7310616* E-mail. *press_office@ipc.media.com* Web. *www.horseandhound.co.uk 25 Beautiful Homes – 4 X 4 – Aeroplane – allthinshome.co.uk – Amateur Gardening – Amateur Photographer – Anglers Mail – Beautiful kitchens – Cage & Aviary Birds – Caravan – Chat – Chat - It's Fate – Chat Passion – Classic Boat – Country Homes & Interiors – Country Life – Cycle Sport – Cycling Weekly – Decanter – Essentials – European Boatbuilder – Eventing – Golf Monthly – Goodtoknow.co.uk – Guitar & Bass – Hair – Hi-Fi News – Homes & Gardens – Horse – Horse & Hound – housetohome.co.uk – Ideal Home – In Style – International Boat Industry – Land Rover World – Livingetc – Loaded – Look – Marie Claire – MiniWorld – Model Collector – Motor Boat & Yachting – Motor Boats Monthly – Motor Caravan – Mountain Bike Rider – Mousebreaker.com – myholidayideas.co.uk – NME – Now – Nuts – Park Home & Holiday Caravan – Pick Me Up – Practical Boat Owner – Practical Parenting – Prediction – Racecar Engineering – Rugby World – Ships Monthly – Shoot – Shooting Times & Country Magazine – Soaplife – Sporting Gun – Stamp Magazine – SuperBike – Superyacht business – SuperYacht World – T.V. Times – The Field – The Railway Magazine – The Shooting Gazette – TrustedReviews.com – TV & Satellite week – TV easy – Uncut – VolksWorld – VW Golf+ – Wallpaper – Webuser – Wedding – Wedding Flowers – What Digital Camera – Whats on T.V. – Woman – Woman & Home – Womans Own – Womans Weekly – Women & Golf – World Soccer – Yachting Monthly – Yachting World – YBW.com*

I P L Information Processing Ltd Eveleigh House Grove Street, Bath BA1 5LR Tel. *01225 475000* Fax. *01225 444400* E-mail. *sean.davey@ipl.com* Web. *www.ipl.com Adatest – Cantata – Testing Times*

I P P E C Systems Ltd 21 Buntsford Drive, Bromsgrove B60 3AJ Tel. *01527 579705* Fax. *01527 574109* E-mail. *info@ippec.co.uk* Web. *www.ippec.co.uk *Pexapipe (Germany) – *Pexatherm (Germany)*

I P P Mardale Unit 5b Christleton Court Manor Park, Runcorn WA7 1ST Tel. *01928 580555* Fax. *01283 722010* E-mail. *sales@ippgrp.com* Web. *www.ippgrp.com Flowrite*

iPRT Group Ltd Iprt House 37 Swanton Close, Newcastle upon Tyne NE5 4SL Tel. *0871 9007456* Fax. *0871 9007432* E-mail. *amer@iprtgroup.com* Web. *www.iprtgroup.com iProjects – iRegeneration – iTransport Group – iTransport Planning*

I P S Converters Ltd Featherstall Road South, Oldham OL9 6HS Tel. *0161 6261844* Fax. *0161 6275202* E-mail. *info@ipsconverters.co.uk* Web. *www.ipsconverters.co.uk Foldex – Hizorb*

I P S Fencing 65 Toms Lane, Kings Langley WD4 8NJ Tel. *01923 264831* Fax. *01923 261459* E-mail. *emma@ipsfencing.com* Web. *www.ipsfencing.com ISP*

Ipsos Mori Market & Opinion Research International, London SE1 1FY Tel. *020 73473000* Fax. *020 73473800* E-mail. *info@ipsos.com* Web. *www.ipsos.com Focus Group – Research in Focus – Strategy in Focus*

Ip Test Ltd 15 The Pines Trading Estate Broad Street, Guildford GU3 3BH Tel. *01483 567218* Fax. *01483 506054* E-mail. *sales@iptest.com* Web. *www.iptest.com iPtest*

I Q D Frequency Products Ltd Station Road, Crewkerne TA18 8AR Tel. *01460 270200* Fax. *01460 72578* E-mail. *info@cmac.com* Web. *www.cmac.com/mt C-MAC – C-MAC Frequency Products Ltd – C-MAC Quartz Crystals*

iQlink Ltd Abbey House Grenville Place, Bracknell RG12 1BP Tel. *01344 667363* E-mail. *marketing@iqlink.co.uk* Web. *www.iqlink.co.uk Sky Technologies Innerware Solution*

I Q Management Systems Business & Innovation Centre Wearfield, Sunderland Enterprise Park, Sunderland SR5 2TA Tel. *0191 5169191* Fax. *0191 5169194* E-mail. *enquiries@iqms.co.uk* Web. *www.iqms.co.uk iq management systems – qualatis*

Ireland FX Malindi House 14 Lambert Avenue, Slough SL3 7EB Tel. *028 90998578* Fax. *028 90998570* E-mail. *info@irelandfx.com* Web. *www.irelandfx.com Ireland FX*

Iris Group Victoria House 36 Derringham Street, Hull HU3 1EL Tel. *01482 326971* Fax. *01482 228465* E-mail. *richard.bearpark@aim.co.uk* Web. *www.iris.co.uk AIM – Debtco – Didos – Evolution – Retailbase – Retailkey – U-Bond*

Ironsides Lubricants Ltd Shield Street, Stockport SK3 0DS Tel. *0161 4775858* Fax. *0161 4806203* E-mail. *enquiries@ironsideslubricants.co.uk* Web. *www.ironsideslubricants.co.uk Foodshield – Lithoshield – Rolashield – Ropeshield – Shield*

I R S Ltd 59 Turbine Way, Swaffham PE37 7XD Tel. *01760 721399* Fax. *01760 723726* E-mail. *l.forster@irs.uk.com* Web. *www.irs.uk.com Glo-Tape – IRSbar – Norfolk – Scotchlite*

Irvin Brothers Ltd Fishponds Road, Wokingham RG41 2QX Tel. *0118 9781499* Fax. *0118 9771530* E-mail. *paul@padblocks.com* Web. *www.padblocks.com Padblocks*

Irwin Mitchell Solicitors (The Debt Recovery Division of Irwin Mitchell Solicitors) 150 Holborn, London EC1N 2NS Tel. *020 74043600* Fax. *020 74040208* E-mail. *sales@imonline.co.uk* Web. *www.imonline.co.uk Braby & Waller*

Irwins Ltd Low Hall Road Horsforth, Leeds LS18 4EW Tel. *0113 2506811* Fax. *0113 2506933* E-mail. *paul.worcester@irwins.co.uk* Web. *www.irwins.co.uk Irwins*

Iscar Tools Woodgate Business Park Bartley Green, Birmingham B32 3DE Tel. *0121 4228585* Fax. *0121 4218255* E-mail. *sales@iscar.co.uk* Web. *www.iscar.co.uk Chamdrill – Chamgroove – Chammill – Cut-Grip – Do-Grip – Heli Octo – Heli Quad – Heli-Ball – Heli-Face – Heli-Grip – Heli-Mill – Heli-Tang – Heli-Turn – Muti-Master – Penta-Cut – Picco – Self-Grip – Swisscut – Swissturn – Tangmill – Top-Grip*

I S Enterprises International Clement House Commerce Way, Colchester CO2 8HY Tel. *01206 798131* Fax. *01206 791186* E-mail. *jgranger@isenterprises.co.uk* Web. *www.isenterprisesintl.co.uk I.S. Stocklines – Result*

Iskra UK Ltd Unit A6, Redlands, Ullswater Crescent,, Coulsdon CR5 2HT Tel. *020 86687141* Fax. *020 86683108* E-mail. *sales@iskra-agency.co.uk* Web. *www.iskra-ae.com Iskra – Iskra*

Isla Components Ltd Bishops Frome Technology Park Bishops Frome, Worcester WR6 5AY Tel. *01885 485950* Fax. *01885 490472* E-mail. *islasales@lineone.net* Web. *www.islacomponents.co.uk Ace – Casteels – Clearco – Silbak*

Island Getaways Champion House Highwood Lane, Rookley, Ventnor PO38 3NN Tel. *01983 721111* Fax. *08718 710072* Web. *www.islandgetaways.co.uk Timescape*

IsoCool Ltd Urban Hive, 460 Avenue West Skyline 120, Great Notley, Braintree CM77 7AA Tel. *01376 928455* Fax. *01376 328873* E-mail. *info@isocool.ltd.uk* Web. *www.isocool.ltd.uk Energy Efficient – Energy Saving – Frigomeccania – Industrialla spa*

I S O Covers Ltd Trent Valley Trading Estate Station Road, Rugeley WS15 2HQ Tel. *01889 574333* Fax. *01889 574111* E-mail. *sales@isocovers.com* Web. *www.isocovers.com ISO Couers*

Isola Manufacturing Co Wythenshawe Ltd Harper Road Northenden, Sharston Industrial Area, Manchester M22 4SH Tel. *0161 9982294* Fax. *0161 9460390* E-mail. *isola.sales@nu-pax.com* Web. *www.nu-pax.com Isola*

Isothane Ltd Newhouse Road Huncoat Industrial Estate, Accrington BB5 6NT Tel. *01254 872555* Fax. *01254 871522* E-mail. *info@isothane.com* Web. *www.isothane.com Isothane - Agrispray - Foamshield - Technitherm - Duratherm - Bodymould - Ecofil - Reprocell - Armour-Flex - Armour -Lyte - Exoset - Pirthane - Themespray - Thermadek*

Isringhausen GB Ltd Second Avenue Redwither Industrial Complex, Redwither Business Park, Wrexham LL13 9XQ Tel. *01978 666300* Fax. *01978 660192* E-mail. *sales@isrigb.co.uk* Web. *www.isri.de I.S.R.I.*

Ist Ltd Station Road, Alton GU34 2PZ Tel. *01420 541600* Fax. *01420 541700* E-mail. *info@istcourt.com* Web. *www.istimaging.com Industrial C.C.T.V. Systems – Radiation Tolerant TV System*

Isuzu (UK) Ltd Halfords Lane, Smethwick B66 1EL Tel. *0121 5001720* Fax. *0121 5001721* Web. *www.isuzu.co.uk Isuzu*

I S Y S Ltd Churchward House Fire Fly Avenue, Swindon SN2 2EY Tel. *08448 802919* Fax. *01793 715470* E-mail. *info@isys-group.co.uk* Web. *www.isys-group.co.uk Intelligent Time – Intelligent Access – Intelligent HR – Intelligent Job Costing*

Isys Interactive Systems Ltd 45 Brunel Parkway Pride Park, Derby DE24 8HR Tel. *01332 380311* Fax. *01332 342975* E-mail. *richard.bowers@isys-waste.com* Web. *www.isys-waste.com Gatehouse – Mediwaste – Swops*

Itec North East Ltd The Digital Factory Durham Way South, Aycliffe Business Park, Newton Aycliffe DL5 6XP Tel. *01325 320052* Fax. *01325 317530* E-mail. *info@itecne.co.uk* Web. *www.itecne.co.uk NAITeC*

It Job Board 41-44 Great Windmill Street, London W1D 7NB Tel. *020 72923899* Fax. *020 72923898* E-mail. *r.macdonald@theitjobboard.com* Web. *www.theitjobsboard.co.uk IT Jobs for Graduates – IT Jobs in the CIty – The IT Job Board – The SAP Job Board*

Itm Soil Ltd Bell Lane Bellbrook Industrial Estate, Uckfield TN22 1QL Tel. *01825 765044* Fax. *01825 761740* E-mail. *sales@itmsoil.com* Web. *www.itmsoil.com Crackmeter – Extensometers – Inclinometers – Load Cells – Piezometers – Settlement Gauges – Tilt Sensors*

Itochu Europe plc 76 Shoe Lane, London EC4A 3JB Tel. *020 78270822* Fax. *020 75831847* E-mail. *enquiry@itochu.co.uk* Web. *www.itochu.eu.com Itochu*

It's Done 4 New Wave House Humber Road, London NW2 6DW Tel. *08450 605566* Fax. *020 82018594* E-mail. *info@itsdone.info* Web. *www.itsdone.info It s done! Studio*

I T @ Spectrum Ltd 1 Trinity Street, Hull HU3 1JR Tel. *01482 586732* Fax. *01482 211428* E-mail. *smonkman@itatspectrum.co.uk* Web. *www.itatspectrum.co.uk Canon / Invu*

Its Training Services Cliff House Hamilton Gardens, Felixstowe IP11 7EJ Tel. *08456 123344* Fax. *01394 458501* E-mail. *info@itstraining.co.uk* Web. *www.itstraining.co.uk ENROL*

I T T Ltd Viables Industrial Estate Jays Close, Basingstoke RG22 4BA Tel. *01256 311200* Fax. *01256 322356* E-mail. *info@i-t-t.com* Web. *www.ittind.com I.S.C.S. – I.S.N.S. – ITT Cannon – LAN Components – Neptune – Sealflex 2 – Tempus – TNM – Trail – Trident*

ITT Industries Jabsco Pumps Bingley Road, Hoddesdon EN11 0BU Tel. *01992 450145* Fax. *01992 467132* E-mail. *enquiries.emea@itt.com* Web. *www.jabsco.co.uk Flojet – Flojet - Jabsco - Rule - Danforth - Sudbury - Aquameter – Jabsco – Rule*

I T V Wales plc The Television Centre Culverhouse Cross, Cardiff CF5 6XJ Tel. *08448 810100* Fax. *029 20597183* E-mail. *phil.henfrey@itv.com* Web. *www.itv.com H.T.V. Group*

I T W Constructions Productions (ITW Construction Products) Diamond Point Fleming Way, Crawley RH10 9DP Tel. *0800 6529260* Fax. *01293 515186* E-mail. *jwhite@itwcp.co.uk* Web. *www.itwcp.co.uk Buildex – Duofast – Impulse – Impulse Cordless – Paslode – Ramset – Spit*

I T W Devcon Unit 3 Shipton Way Express Business Park, Northampton Road, Rushden NN10 6GL Tel. 0870 4587388 Fax. 0870 4589077 E-mail. info@itwdevcon.eu.com Web. www.itw-devcon.co.uk '2 Ton' Epoxy – '5 Minute' Epoxy – Devweld – Flexane – Plastic Steel – Zip-Patch

I T W Nexus Europe (Division of ITW) Unit 12 Bilton Industrial Estate, Bilton Road, Basingstoke RG24 8NJ Tel. 01256 317663 Fax. 01256 317682 E-mail. mike@itwnexes.co.uk Web. www.itwnexus.com Fix Lock – Nexus

I T Works 51 Water End Road Maulden, Bedford MK45 2BD Tel. 01525 862266 Fax. 01525 862166 E-mail. j.upton@itworks-uk.com Web. www.itworks-uk.com ACT – ACT 2000 – ACT Professional – ACT Professional for workgroups – SAGE – SAGE CRM – SAGE FORECASTING – SAGE INSTANT ACCOUNTS – SAGE INSTANT PAYROLL – SAGE LINE 50 – SAGE PAYROLL – SAGE PERSONEL – SAGE PIID

I T W Plexus (a division of I T W Ltd) Unit 3 Shipton Way Express Business Park, Northampton Road, Rushden NN10 6GL Tel. 0870 4587588 Fax. 0870 4589077 E-mail. sales@itwplexus.co.uk Web. www.itwplexus.co.uk EP202 – EP205 – EP225 – EP250 – MA1020 – MA1021 – MA1023 – MA1025 – MA300 – MA310 – MA320 – MA3940 – MA3940LH – MA403 – MA420 – MA422 – MA425 – MA550 – MA556 – MA557 – MA820 – MA821 – MA822 – MA922 – MA925 – Plexus

I T W Switches & Switch Panel Ltd Norway Road Hilsea, Portsmouth PO3 5HT Tel. 023 92694971 Fax. 023 92656278 E-mail. info@itwswitches.co.uk Web. www.itwswitches.com Licon – Switchpanels

Iveco UK Ltd Road One Winsford Industrial Estate, Winsford CW7 3QP Tel. 01606 541000 Fax. 01606 541126 E-mail. alan.coppin@iveco.com Web. www.iveco.com Iveco Aifo – Iveco Ford Truck Ltd

I V O C M S 9 Trewetha Lane, Port Isaac PL29 3RN Tel. 01208 881056 Fax. 01208 881055 E-mail. ivocms@aol.com Web. www.ivocms.co.uk *I.V.O. (Germany)

Ivory & Ledoux Ltd 201 Haverstock Hill, London NW3 4QG Tel. 020 78870770 Fax. 020 74364877 E-mail. enquiries@ivory-ledoux.co.uk Web. www.ivory-ledoux.co.uk *A la Perruche – *Fontinella – *Ja Ja – *La Tour Polignac – *Moulin

Iwis Drive Systems Unit 8c Bloomfield Park Bloomfield Road, Tipton DY4 9AP Tel. 0121 5213600 Fax. 0121 5200822 E-mail. salesuk@iwis.com Web. www.iwis.com EURO CHAIN – JWIS

J

Jabez Cliff Company Ltd Aldridge Road, Walsall WS4 2JP Tel. 01922 621676 Fax. 01922 722575 E-mail. jennifer@barnsby.com Web. www.barnsby.com Cliff – Cliff-Barnsby

Jacarem Ltd 78 Asheridge Road, Chesham HP5 2PY Tel. 01494 791336 Fax. 01494 792336 E-mail. sales@jacarem.co.uk Web. www.jacarem.co.uk Emulation Technology Inc – Positronic Industries

Jackaman's Park House Mere Street, Diss IP22 4JY Tel. 01379 643555 Fax. 01379 652221 E-mail. james.laband@jackamans.co.uk Web. www.jackamans.co.uk Jackaman, Smith & Mulley

Jack Electrical Ltd 27 High Street Barwell, Leicester LE9 8DQ Tel. 07985 884499 E-mail. chippendalegroup@googlemail.com Web. www.jackltd.com Chippendale Electrical

Jackel International Ltd Dudley Lane, Cramlington NE23 7RH Tel. 0191 2504400 Fax. 0191 2501727 E-mail. mail@jackel.co.uk Web. www.tommeetippee.co.uk Jackel – Jackel International – Sangenic International

Jack Sealey Ltd Kempson Way, Bury St Edmunds IP32 7AR Tel. 01284 757500 Fax. 01284 703534 E-mail. sales@sealey.co.uk Web. www.sealey.co.uk *American Pro (U.S.A.) – *Supermig (Italy) – *Supersnap (Taiwan) – *Viking (Denmark) – *Walldrive (Taiwan)

Douglas Jackson Ltd 23 Lichfield Business Village The Friary, Lichfield WS13 6QG Tel. 08456 209720 Fax. 08456 209721 E-mail. mail@douglas-jackson.com Web. www.douglas-jackson.com Douglas Jackson Limited

Ernest Jackson & Co. Ltd 29 High Street, Crediton EX17 3AP Tel. 01363 636000 Fax. 01363 636063 E-mail. dave.walter@craftfoods.com Web. www.ejackson.co.uk Bassetts – Bassetts soft & Chewey Vitamins – Imps – Kia-ora – Mac – Potter's – Proctors Pinelyptus – Special Recipe – Throaties – Victory V – Zubes

Jacksons Fine Fencing Ltd Stowting Common Stowting, Ashford TN25 6BN Tel. 01233 750393 Fax. 01233 750403 E-mail. info@jacksons-fencing.co.uk Web. www.jacksons-fencing.co.uk Jacksons Fencing – Jacksons Fine Fencing

Jackson Stops & Staff 20 Bridge Street, Northampton NN1 1NR Tel. 01604 632991 Fax. 01604 232613 E-mail. northampton@jackson-stops.co.uk Web. www.jackson-stops.co.uk Jackson-Stops

Thomas Jacks Ltd Unit B2 The Bridge Business Centre, Stratford Enterprise Park, Stratford Upon Avon CV37 9HW Tel. 01789 264100 Fax. 01789 264200 E-mail. sales@thomasjacks.co.uk Web. www.thomasjacks.co.uk Adventure Lights – ASP – Baigish – Cobra Optics – Yukon

Jacobi Carbons Croft Court Unit E12 Moss Industrial Estate, Moss Industrial Estate, Leigh WN7 3PT Tel. 01942 670600 Fax. 01942 670605 E-mail. info@jacobi.net Web. www.jacobi.net AddSorb – Aquaflow – AquaSorb – *ColorSorb – DioxSorb – EcoFlow – EcoSorb – GoldSorb

Jacobs Engineering UK Ltd 95 Bothwell Street, Glasgow G2 7HX Tel. 0141 2438000 Fax. 0141 2263109 E-mail. david.biggott@jacobs.com Web. www.jacobs.com Babtie Group

D Jacobson & Sons Ltd Bacup Road, Rossendale BB4 7PA Tel. 01706 219444 Fax. 01706 214324 E-mail. admin@jacobsongroup.co.uk Web. www.jacobsongroup.co.uk Astro – Balloons – Bumpers – Classique – Cosy Tots – Cosyskin – Depeche – Deva – Dunlop – Earth Wear – Freeman Hardy Willis – Gola – Hot Shots – Image – Infiniti – Lullaby – Manfield – Milano – Mirage – New Image – Odeon – One Step – Outlaw – Outrage – Prelude – Red Rock – Socumfi – Step In – Terrain – Tiffany – Trueform – Zig Zag

Jacobs & Turner Ltd Vermont House 149 Vermont Street, Glasgow G41 1LU Tel. 0141 5688000 Fax. 0141 5688080 E-mail. grahamh@trespass.co.uk Web. www.trespass.co.uk Trespass

Albert Jagger Ltd Centaur Works Green Lane, Walsall WS2 8HG Tel. 01922 471000 Fax. 01922 648021 E-mail. export@albert-jagger.co.uk Web. www.albert-jagger.co.uk Anti-Luce – Aquamaster – Centaflex – Centaur – Centoplas – Jagalok – Jagger

Jaguar Epresso Systems Unit 1 Albury Close, Reading RG30 1BD Tel. 0118 9599204 Fax. 0118 9599205 E-mail. sales@jaguarespresso.co.uk Web. www.jaguarespresso.co.uk *Iberital

J & A International Ltd Vale Road, Spilsby PE23 5HE Tel. 01790 752757 Fax. 01790 754132 E-mail. ja-int@ja-int.co.uk Web. www.ja-int.co.uk Classic Badges – Embroidery Badges – Endura Transfers – FR Trans Transfers – Identa Tape – Multi Mark Heat Seal Machine – Optima Badges – Patch N Match – Prima Plus Tape – Prima Tape – Trademark Transfers – Trimaz Transfers – Ultima heat seal machine

Jakar International Ltd Hillside House 2-6 Friern Park, London N12 9BX Tel. 020 84456376 Fax. 020 84452714 E-mail. info@jakar.co.uk Web. www.jakar.co.uk *Caran D'Ache – *Caran D'Ache (Switzerland) – *Cutting Mats and Knives (Taiwan) – *Jakar (Germany) – *Jakar Erasersharp (Germany) – *Minerva (France) – *Moebius & Rupert (Germany)

Jalite plc 1 Bentalls, Basildon SS14 3BS Tel. 01268 242300 Fax. 01268 274148 E-mail. info@jalite.com Web. www.jalite.com Jalite – Jaltex – Jlume

Jamak Fabrication Europe Ltd Unit 53 Oakhill Trading Estate Devonshire Road, Worsley, Manchester M28 3PT Tel. 01204 794554 Fax. 01204 574521 E-mail. sales@jamak.co.uk Web. www.jamak.com Jamak – SILFAB

James Finlay Limited Swire House 59 Buckingham Gate, London SW1E 6AJ Tel. 020 78023230 Fax. 020 78340587 E-mail. sec@finlays.co.uk Web. www.finlays.net Finlay's

James Latham plc 13 Chartwell Drive, Wigston LE18 2FN Tel. 0116 2889161 Fax. 0116 2813806 E-mail. andrew.craig@lathams.co.uk Web. www.lathamtimber.co.uk Lathamclad

James Walker Rotabolt Ltd Unit F Peartree Industrial Park Crackley Way Peartree Lane, Dudley DY2 0UW Tel. 01384 214442 Fax. 01384 455186 E-mail. sales@rotabolt.co.uk Web. www.rotabolt.co.uk RotaBolt

James Walker Textiles Ltd Station Road, Mirfield WF14 8NA Tel. 01924 492277 Fax. 01924 480263 E-mail. sales@jwalker.co.uk Web. www.jwalker.co.uk Imperial Comfort – Tranquilitie

James Walker Townson Ltd Unit 1B Castlehill Hersfield WayBredbury Park Industrial EstateBredbury, Stockport SK6 2SU Tel. 0161 4063350 Fax. 0161 4307615 E-mail. sales.townson.uk@jameswalker.biz Web. www.jameswalker.biz/townson Comflex

Janspeed Technologies Ltd Castle Works Castle Road, Salisbury SP1 3RX Tel. 01722 321833 Fax. 01722 412308 E-mail. sales@janspeed.com Web. www.janspeed.com Janspeed

Jardin Corrugated Cases Ltd Elean Business Park Sutton, Ely CB6 2QE Tel. 01353 778522 Fax. 01353 777708 E-mail. kevin.hennessy@jccltd.com Web. www.jccltd.com Jardin

Jarroy Importers Ltd (t/a jarroy of london) Unit 8 Heron Industrial Estate Barbers Road, London E15 2PE Tel. 020 85197780 Fax. 020 85197265 E-mail. info@jarroy.com Web. www.jarroy.com FUNNYMAN

Jarshire Ltd (Waste Management Division) 2-4 Bristol Way Stoke Gardens, Slough SL1 3QE Tel. 01753 825122 Fax. 01753 694653 E-mail. sales@jarshire.co.uk Web. www.jarshire.co.uk *Frihopress – *Jarshire

Jarvis Hotels Ltd Castle House 71-75 Desborough Road, High Wycombe HP11 2PR Tel. 01494 473800 Fax. 01494 471666 E-mail. steve.hebborn@jarvis.co.uk Web. www.ramadajarvis.co.uk Embassy Leisure Breaks – Jarvis Breaks – Jarvis Hotels – Sebastian Coe Health Clubs – Summit

Jason's Cradle Unit 6 Ariel Park Uddens Trading Estate, Wimborne BH21 7NL Tel. 01202 874365 Fax. 01202 876296 E-mail. suematthews@jasonscradle.co.uk Web. www.jasonscradle.co.uk Jasons' Cradle – Land & Marine Products Ltd – Scramble Nets

Jay Be Ltd Spen Lane Gomersal, Cleckheaton BD19 4PN Tel. 01924 517820 Fax. 01924 517910 E-mail. sales@jaybe.co.uk Web. www.jay-be.co.uk Jay-Be

Jaybeam Ltd Rutherford Drive Park Farm South, Wellingborough NN8 6AX Tel. 01933 408408 Fax. 01933 408404 E-mail. uk.sales@jaybeamwireless.com Web. www.jaybeam.co.uk CSA Ltd

Jayex Technology Ltd Unit 13 Sovereign Park Coronation Road, London NW10 7QP Tel. 020 88386222 Fax. 020 88383222 E-mail. sales@jayex.com Web. www.jayex.com Jayex

Jaymart Roberts & Plastics Ltd Woodland Trading Estate Eden Fell Road, Westbury BA13 3QS Tel. 01373 864926 Fax. 01373 858454 E-mail. sales@jaymart.net Web. www.jaymart.net Air-Go – Bladerunner – Brush N Dry – Brush-Off – Buffer-Zone – Bullfighter – Caro – Clean-Off – Eurostud System 30 – Ezykleen – Fatigue-Checker – Flexi-Brush – Flextuft – Gatekeeper – Grime Grabber – Grime Stopper – High Street – Interzone – Leg-O-Mat – Limontamoquette – Mainstay – Mandalay – Matkandu – Matlocker – Nero Stop – Plastiflor – Pyramat – Rushtik Chequers – Safe-T-Guard – Safe-T-Zone – Safedeko/Chip – Safedeko/Diamond – Safedeko/Metal – Sarina – Soft-Foot – Street Fighter – Street King – Stronghold – Superguard A.L. – Terra – Topdeck – Treadlock – Zigazaga 2000

J B Broadley Reeds Holme Works Burnley Road, Rawtenstall, Rossendale BB4 8LN Tel. 01706 213661 Fax. 01706 227786 E-mail. sales@jbbroadley.co.uk Web. www.jbbroadley.co.uk Altora – Aztex – Biasyde – Broadley J.B. – Chamette – Chamolux – Flexetta – Kintrella – Laminex – Ny-Bias – Pellafino – Permatex – Plastexa – Querella – Serenella – Soft Line

J B Furnace Engineering Ltd Unit 2a 21-2 Forge Lane Minworth Industrial Park, Minworth, Sutton Coldfield B76 1AH Tel. 0121 3513496 Fax. 0121 3131432 E-mail. sales@jbfurnace.com Web. www.jbfurnace.com J B Furnace Engineering Ltd – L&N Furnace Equipment – Leeds & Northrup

J B H Property Consulting Ltd Broseley House 81 Union Street, Oldham OL1 1PF Tel. 0161 3365068 Fax. 0161 3200512 E-mail. info@jbh-property.co.uk Web. www.jbh-property.co.uk JBH PROPERTY

J B J Techniques Ltd 28 Ormside Way, Redhill RH1 2LW Tel. 01737 767493 Fax. 01737 772041 E-mail. info@jbj.co.uk Web. www.jbj.co.uk Des Case – Dusterloh – Emmegi – Haldex Barnes – Havit – JBJ – JBJ - Marzocchi - Mintor - Raja - Dentex - Spidex - Technodrive - Havit - SIEM - SMEI - Dusterloh - Haldex - Haldex Barnes - NewCool - Lovejoy - JoyTork - DesCase - Tranter - Emmegi - Swep - Scanwill - Emmegi – Marzocchi – Mintor – NewCool – Oleo Tecno – RAJA-Lovejoy – Scanwill – Smei – Swep – Technodrive – Tranter – B & C vane pumps

J B Systems Ltd Unit 13 Bridgegate Business Park Gatehouse Way, Aylesbury HP19 8DB Tel. 01296 489967 Fax. 01296 393515 E-mail. info@jbsystems.co.uk Web. www.jbsystems.co.uk Iris – Legrand ATX/EEXE/EEXD – Rose Eexe

J B Treasure & Co. Ltd 36 Vauxhall Road, Liverpool L3 6DN Tel. 0151 2368314 Fax. 0151 2362804 E-mail. treasurejb@aol.com Web. www.jbtreasure.co.uk Adamant – Bishop's Adamant – Durus – Pyrex

J C Decaux UK Ltd Summit House 27 Sale Place, London W2 1YR Tel. 020 72988000 Fax. 020 72988190 E-mail. sales@jcdecaux.co.uk Web. www.jcdecaux.co.uk AdRail – Citipak – Road

J D Williams Mail Order Group Griffin House 40 Lever Street, Manchester M60 6ES Tel. 0161 2382000 Fax. 0161 2382030 E-mail. info@jdwilliams.co.uk Web. www.nbrown.co.uk Aldrex – Ambrose Wilson – Bury Boot & Shoe – Candid – Classic Combination – Fashion World – Fifty Plus – Hartingdon House – Heather Valley – J.D. Williams – Oxendales – Sander and Kay – Selections – Special Collections – Whifords

Jedtec Finishing Equipment Ann Street, Stockport SK5 7PP Tel. 0161 4808087 Fax. 0161 4299322 E-mail. sales@abraclean.co.uk Web. www.sfeg.co.uk Blast N'Vac (United Kingdom) – BNR – Satblast (United Kingdom)

Jeeves Of Belgravia 94 High St Wimbledon, London SW19 5EG Tel. 020 89460665 Fax. 020 88097833 E-mail. a@jeevesofbelgravia.co.uk Web. www.jeevesofbelgravia.co.uk Jeeves

Jegs Electrical Ltd 20 Progress Road, Leigh On Sea SS9 5PR Tel. 01702 421555 Fax. 01702 420363 E-mail. sales@jegs.co.uk Web. www.jegs.co.uk *Jegs Electrical (Worldwide)

J & E Hall Ltd Questor House 191 Hawley Road, Dartford DA1 1PU Tel. 01322 223456 Fax. 01322 394421 E-mail. helpline@jehall.co.uk Web. www.jehall.co.uk Hall Service – Hall Thermotank – Hallscrew – Halltherm – McQuay Service

Jeld Wen UK Ltd Retford Road Woodhouse Mill, Sheffield S13 9WH Tel. *0114 2542000* Fax. *0114 2542860* E-mail. *martin.crowther@jeld-wen.co.uk* Web. *www.jeld-wen.co.uk Jeld-Wen*

Jena Rotary Technology Ltd Willow Drive Annesley, Nottingham NG15 0DP Tel. *01623 726010* Fax. *01623 726018* E-mail. *sales@jena-tec.co.uk* Web. *www.jena-tec.co.uk Jena-Tec*

Jena UK Ltd Unit 17 Romsey Industrial Estate, Romsey SO51 0HR Tel. *01794 519220* Fax. *01794 519188* E-mail. *sales@jena-uk.com* Web. *www.jena-uk.com JENA*

Jendico Ltd Unit G3 Welland Industrial Estate Valley Way, Market Harborough LE16 7PS Tel. *01858 464888* Fax. *01858 464030* E-mail. *sales@jendico.co.uk* Web. *www.jendico.co.uk Bonaire – Countourail – Harmony – Jendico – Jendiwhirl – Martinique – Oysterette*

Jenex Ltd 5 Shuttleworth Close, Great Yarmouth NR31 0NQ Tel. *01493 602211* Fax. *01493 602221* E-mail. *val@jenex.co.uk* Web. *www.jenexltd.co.uk Canalta – Chandler – Clif Mock – DeWitt – Pulseguard – Shockguard – True-Cut*

Anthony Jenkins Fuel Oil Ltd Oil Storage Depot Canterbury Road West, Cliffsend, Ramsgate CT12 5DU Tel. *01843 596431* Fax. *01843 590946 Jentex Fuel Oils*

Jenks & Cattell Engineering Ltd Neachells Lane, Wolverhampton WV11 3PU Tel. *01902 305530* Fax. *01902 305529* E-mail. *sales@jcel.co.uk* Web. *www.jcel.co.uk Cattell*

Jennings Building & Civil Engineering Ltd Bod Hyfryd Tanygraig Road, Llysfaen, Colwyn Bay LL29 8TH Tel. *01492 514006* Fax. *01492 512820* E-mail. *reception@jenningsbce.co.uk* Web. *www.jennings-construction.co.uk JPS*

Jeol UK Ltd Silver Court Watchmead, Welwyn Garden City AL7 1LT Tel. *01707 377117* Fax. *01707 373254* E-mail. *uk.sales@jeoluk.com* Web. *www.jeoluk.com Jeol*

Jepson & Co. Ltd 44 East Bank Road, Sheffield S2 3QN Tel. *0114 2731151* Fax. *0114 2731156* E-mail. *sales@jepsonandco.com* Web. *www.jepsonandco.com Jepson*

Jepway Associates Ltd Euridge Works Thickwood Lane, Chippenham SN14 8BG Tel. *01225 742301* Fax. *01225 743457* E-mail. *info@jetway.co.uk* Web. *www.jetway.co.uk Berwyn – Berwyn Engineering - Now owned by Jetway.*

Jespro 2000 Ltd Central Mills Raymond Street, Bradford BD5 8DT Tel. *01274 735446* Fax. *01274 394909* E-mail. *sales@jespro.com* Web. *www.jespro.com Jespro*

Jessops plc Jessop House 98 Scudamore Road, Leicester LE3 1TZ Tel. *0116 2326000* Fax. *0116 2320060* E-mail. *ghenson@jessops.com* Web. *www.jessops.co.uk *Centon (Far East) – Econofix – Econoprint – Econostop – Econotol – Econowet – *Flagship (Far East) – *I.Q. Video (Far East) – Jessops – *Portaflash (Far East) – Powerflash*

Jetchem Systems Ltd Cuba Industrial Estate Bolton Road North Ramsbottom, Bury BL0 0NE Tel. *01706 828888* Fax. *01706 828000* E-mail. *kevin@jetchem.com* Web. *www.jetchem.com Superjet*

Jetform Services Ltd Heath Road Ramsden Heath, Billericay CM11 1HU Tel. *01268 711700* Fax. *01268 711600* E-mail. *mail@jetformpools.co.uk* Web. *www.jetformpools.co.uk Blue Ripple*

Jet Press Ltd Nunn Close Huthwaite, Sutton In Ashfield NG17 2HW Tel. *01623 551800* Fax. *01623 551175* E-mail. *sales@jetpress.com* Web. *www.jetpress.com *Jet Nut (Ireland) – Jetloc – Jetpress – *Palnut (U.S.A.) – *Spiderfix (Spain) – Tee-Nuts – Tuflok*

The Jewel Blade Ltd 442 Penistone Road, Sheffield S6 2FU Tel. *0114 2217000* Fax. *0114 2852473* E-mail. *jtaylor@jewelblade.co.uk* Web. *www.jewelblade.com Food Processing Blades – Jewel*

Jewellery World Ltd 5 Chatley Street, Manchester M3 1HU Tel. *0161 8345007* Fax. *0161 8353238* E-mail. *jewelleryworld@btinternet.com* Web. *www.jewellery-world.co.uk *Jewellery World (Worldwide)*

Jewson Ltd Spencer Bridge Road, Northampton NN5 7DR Tel. *01604 581214* Fax. *01604 759658* Web. *www.jewson.co.uk Graham's*

Jeyes Brunel Way, Thetford IP24 1HF Tel. *01842 757575* Fax. *01842 757824* E-mail. *bernard.daymon@jeyes.co.uk* Web. *www.jeyes.co.uk Baby wet ones – Brobat – Ibcol – Izal – Jeyes – Jeyes Bloo – Moists – Parozone – Sanilav – Superblend – Three Hands – Wet ones – Zal – Zal Bath Cleaner*

J Floris Ltd 89 Jermyn Street, London SW1Y 6JH Tel. *020 79302885* Fax. *020 79301402* E-mail. *fragrance@florislondon.com* Web. *www.florislondon.com Floris*

J G Coates Ltd (t/a Cotel Mouldings) Trafalgar Street, Burnley BB11 1TH Tel. *01282 424376* Fax. *01282 456166* E-mail. *sales@cotel.co.uk* Web. *www.cotel.co.uk Cotel*

J G Fenn Ltd West Court Campbell Road, Stoke On Trent ST4 4FB Tel. *01782 315782* Fax. *01782 344060* E-mail. *sales@fenns.co.uk* Web. *www.fenns.co.uk Fenn – Fenn-O – Fenn-O-Furniture*

J Haynes Ltd (t/a Haynes Publishing) High Street Sparkford, Yeovil BA22 7JJ Tel. *01963 440635* Fax. *01963 440001* E-mail. *sales@haynes.co.uk* Web. *www.haynes.co.uk G.T. Foulis – Haynes Owners Workshop Manual – *Motorbooks Int (U.S.A.) – O.P.C. – Oxford Illustrated Press – Patrick Stephens*

J H Richards & Co. 112 Saltley Road, Birmingham B7 4TD Tel. *0121 3592257* Fax. *0121 3597340* E-mail. *info@jhrichards.co.uk* Web. *www.jhrichards.co.uk J H Richards – Richards – Whitemetal*

J Hudson & Co Whistles Ltd 244 Barr Street, Birmingham B19 3AH Tel. *0121 5542124* Fax. *0121 5519293* E-mail. *info@acmewhistles.co.uk* Web. *www.acmewhistles.co.uk Acme – Acme Thunderer – City – Metropolitan – Survival – Tornado*

Jiffy Packaging Company Ltd 9 Road Four Winsford Industrial Estate, Winsford CW7 3QR Tel. *01606 867200* Fax. *01606 592634* E-mail. *sales@jiffy.co.uk* Web. *www.jiffy.co.uk Custom Wrap – Jiffy – Jiffy Bubble – Jiffy Foam – Jiffy Superlite – Jiffy Utility Bags – Jiffycel – Jiffylite – Kushion Kraft – Mail Miser – Vanguard*

Jinlogic Ltd 14 Scrubbitts Square, Radlett WD7 8JR Tel. *01923 855306* E-mail. *enquiries@jinlogic.com* Web. *www.jinlogic.com Jinlogic*

Jiskoot Ltd Jiskoot Technology Centre Longfield Road, Tunbridge Wells TN2 3EY Tel. *01892 518000* Fax. *01892 518100* E-mail. *sales@jiskoot.com* Web. *www.jiskoot.co.uk 007 – 210 – 710 – Byscoop – G5 – Insight 2000 – Insight Controller – Inturbine – Mixmeter – Pr53, 23 & 103 – Puls-O-Rev – Pulstrak*

J J Farm Services Ltd Far Stanley Winchcombe, Cheltenham GL54 5HF Tel. *01242 620631* Fax. *01242 620423* E-mail. *sales@jjfarm.co.uk* Web. *www.jjfarm.co.uk *Fendt – *Massey Ferguson*

J & J W Longbottom (Incorporating Sloan & Davidson Ltd) Bridge Foundries, Holmfirth HD9 7AW Tel. *01484 682141* Fax. *01484 681513 Sloan & Davidson*

J K H Drainage Units Ltd Hampstead Avenue Mildenhall, Bury St Edmunds IP28 7AS Tel. *01638 713795* Fax. *01638 716313* E-mail. *brian@jkhdrainageunits.co.uk* Web. *www.jkhdrainageunits.co.uk J.K.H.*

J L A Meadowcroft Lane Ripponden, Sowerby Bridge HX6 4AJ Tel. *0800 591903* Fax. *01507 611132* E-mail. *info@jla.com* Web. *www.jla.com Circuit – JLA – Laundry F.M. – Wash Angel*

J Lacey Steeplejack Contractors Ltd 50 Bickford Road, Birmingham B6 7EE Tel. *0121 3276376* Fax. *0121 3284692* E-mail. *info@jlacey.com* Web. *www.jlacey.com Helita – Pulsar*

JLG Industries, Inc. Units 4 & 5 Bentley Avenue, Middleton, Manchester M24 2GP Tel. *0870 2007700* Fax. *0870 2007711* E-mail. *jlguk@jlg.com* Web. *www.jlg.com J.L.G. Accessmaster – J.L.G. Boom Lifts – J.L.G. Scissor Lifts*

J L Lord & Son Ltd Wellington Cement Works Ainsworth Road, Bury BL8 2RS Tel. *0161 7644617* Fax. *0161 7631873* E-mail. *enquiries@john-lord.co.uk* Web. *www.john-lord.co.uk Cerunert – Gripcast – Konduct – Protect – R.12 Epoxy Jointing Cement – Rizistal – Rizistalcrete polymer screed – Uragard*

J L M Security 43 Rosebank Terrace, Aberdeen AB11 6LQ Tel. *01224 594200* Fax. *01224 584571* E-mail. *jlmlocks@aol.com* Web. *www.jlmsecurity.com Abloy – Abloy - locks, Chubb - locks, Yale - locks – Chubb – Yale*

J long & Son 10A Upper Cairncastle Road, Larne BT40 2DT Tel. *028 28275980* Fax. *028 28275980* E-mail. *info@jlongandson.com* Web. *www.jlongandson.com delcarmen , slate ni, aluminium and iron*

J M C Q Huston & Son 24a Meeting House Street, Ballymoney BT53 6JN Tel. *028 27662195* Fax. *028 27665056* E-mail. *jmcqhuston@gmail.com Gladiator – Richmond – Somax – Stronghold*

J M E Civils 1 Adelaide House Corby Gate Business Park Priors Haw Road, Corby NN17 5JG Tel. *01536 206688* Fax. *01536 206544* E-mail. *iain@jme3d.co.uk* Web. *www.jmecivils.co.uk JME3D*

J M R Section Benders Ltd Sterling Industrial Estate Rainham Road South, Dagenham RM10 8TX Tel. *020 85937324* Fax. *020 85956139* E-mail. *roger@jmrsectionbenders.co.uk* Web. *www.jmrsectionbenders.co.uk Roll-a-Ring*

Jobs@Pertemps Meriden Hall Main Road, Meriden, Coventry CV7 7PT Tel. *01676 525000* Fax. *01676 525259* E-mail. *press.office@pertemps.co.uk* Web. *www.pertemps.co.uk Pertemps*

Joe Turner Equipment Ltd Mill Ford Cottage Coughton Fields Lane, Coughton, Alcester B49 6BS Tel. *01789 763958* Fax. *01789 400330* E-mail. *sales@joturnerequipment.co.uk* Web. *www.joeturnerequipment.co.uk Bomford – Econ – McConnell – Orsi – Spearhead – Twose – Twyman*

Jofemar UK Unit 39 Britannia Way, Britannia Enterprise Park, Lichfield WS14 9UY Tel. *01543 251253* Fax. *01543 251259* E-mail. *sales@jofemar.com* Web. *www.jofemar.com J2000 (Spain) – STAR (Spain) – T11 (Spain)*

John Brown Publishing 136-142 Bramley Road, London W10 6SR Tel. *020 75653000* Fax. *020 75653050* E-mail. *info@johnbrownmedia.com* Web. *www.johnbrownmedia.com Abbeyview – Bizarre – Classic FM – Debenhams – Fortean Times – Gardens Illustrated – Hot Air – Hotline – SCHWA – Spice – Viz – Waitrosse Food Illustrated – Wisden*

John Deere Credit J D C House Meteor Court Barnett Way, Barnwood, Gloucester GL4 3GG Tel. *01452 372255* Fax. *01452 376066* E-mail. *sales@johndeerecredit.co.uk* Web. *www.johndeerecredit.co.uk John Deere Credit*

John Foster Ltd Black Dyke Mills Brighouse Road, Queensbury, Bradford BD13 1QA Tel. *01274 885800* Fax. *01274 885810* E-mail. *sales@john-foster.co.uk* Web. *www.john-foster.co.uk Beckside Mills (United Kingdom) – Benn's Mohair (United Kingdom) – Butterfield & Frazer (United Kingdom) – Charles Sowden (United Kingdom) – D & R England (United Kingdom) – Darrowdale (United Kingdom) – Duncan Baraclough (United Kingdom) – Dyckoff Shackleton (United Kingdom) – E A Matthews (United Kingdom) – John Foster (United Kingdom) – John Halliday (United Kingdom) – Pepper Lee (United Kingdom) – Preston Mills (United Kingdom) – Priestleys (United Kingdom) – Queensbury Fabrics (United Kingdom) – Queensbury Textiloes (United Kingdom) – Standeven (United Kingdom) – Staveley Fine Worsteds (United Kingdom) – Wallace (United Kingdom) – Wike Mills (United Kingdom) – William Laycock (United Kingdom)*

John Gosnell Ltd (Head Office) 20 Phoenix Place, Lewes BN7 2QJ Tel. *01273 473772* Fax. *01273 472217* E-mail. *chris.warner@johngosnell.com* Web. *www.newscientist.net Famora*

John Guest Horton Road, West Drayton UB7 8JL Tel. *01895 449233* Fax. *01895 420321* E-mail. *info@johnguest.co.uk* Web. *www.johnguest.co.uk J.G. Speedfit – Super Speedfit Centre*

John Hornby Skewes & Co. Ltd Salem House Parkinson Approach, Garforth, Leeds LS25 2HR Tel. *0113 2865381* Fax. *0113 2868515* E-mail. *info@jhs.co.uk* Web. *www.jhs.co.uk *Adamas (U.S.A.) – *Angel (Korea, Republic of) – *Antoni (China and Korea) – *Applause (Korea, Republic of) – *Augustine (U.S.A.) – *Camber (U.S.A.) – *Celebrity (Korea, Republic of) – *D'Aquisto (U.S.A.) – Danelectro (China) – Dunlop – Duracell – *Encore (South Korea, Romania India, Taiwan and Slovenia) – *Fast Fret (U.S.A.) – *Flitz (U.S.A.) – *Fort Bryan (U.S.A.) – Generation – *George Dennis (Czech Republic) – Get Yourself Connected – *Grover (U.S.A.) – *Hannabach (Germany) – *HK Audio (Germany) – Hornby Skewes – J.H.S. – Kinsman (China) – *Kustom (USA and China) – *Kyser (U.S.A.) – *L.R. Baggs (U.S.A.) – *Lark (China) – *Linear Pro (Germany) – *Manuel Rodriguez (Spain) – *MXR (U.S.A.) – *Ovation (U.S.A.) – Palma (China) – Performance Percussion – *Qwik Time (China) – *Qwik Tune (China) – *Rapco (U.S.A.) – *Regal Tip (U.S.A.) – *Reghin (Romania) – *Rhythm-Tech (U.S.A.) – *Rico (U.S.A.) – *Rocktek (China) – Santos Martinez (Romania) – Scanner Cadet, The – *Seiko (Japan) – *Sharkfin (Sweden) – *Shubb (U.S.A.) – *Skylark (China) – Softapads – *String Swing (U.S.A.) – *Target (U.S.A.) – TDK – *Teckpik (U.S.A.) – *The Blues (Korea) – *The Scanner (Taiwan) – Vintage (India) – *Wings (India) – *Wittner (Germany)*

John Hunt Bolton Ltd Alma Works Rasbottom Street, Bolton BL3 5BZ Tel. *01204 521831* Fax. *01204 527306* E-mail. *spencer@johnhuntbolton.co.uk* Web. *www.johnhuntbolton.co.uk Duratax – Little Champion – Medium Champion*

John Leach Spares & Equipment Rowan Cott Everton, Doncaster DN10 5AU Tel. *01777 817708* Fax. *01777 817708 Breakir Centrifugal Disintegrator*

John Moore Tractor Parts Ltd Ladford Covert Seighford, Stafford ST18 9QG Tel. *01785 282705* Fax. *01785 282664* E-mail. *shirley.moore@johnmoore.co.uk* Web. *www.johnmoore.co.uk Caterpillar – Komatsu*

John O'Donnell Ltd Victoria Road, Chelmsford CM1 1NZ Tel. *01245 256112* Fax. *01245 492854* E-mail. *sales@johnodonnell.com* Web. *www.johnodonnell.com JOD – *Joda (Pakistan) – *Jodine (China) – *John O'Donnell (Korea, Republic of) – *Malteser (Germany)*

Johnson Apparel Master Ltd Aldridge Road Perry Barr, Birmingham B42 2EU Tel. *0121 3564512* Fax. *0121 3443520* E-mail. *davidray@johnsonplc.com* Web. *www.apparelmaster.co.uk Apparelmaster – City Service – Johnsons*

Johnson Controls Ltd Royal Pavilion Wellesley Road, Aldershot GU11 1PZ Tel. *01252 346300* Fax. *01252 346301* Web. *www.jci.com Integrated Systems Network (ISN) – ISN Advantage*

Johnson Elevanja Ltd Bath Road, Bridgwater TA6 4YQ Tel. *01278 456411* Fax. *01278 429949* E-mail. *sales@jbrakes.com* Web. *www.elevanja.com Johnson Elevanja*

Johnson Services Group Unit 9 Monks Way, Preston Brook, Runcorn WA7 3GH Tel. *01928 704600* Fax. *01928 704620* E-mail. *enquiries@jsg.com* Web. *www.johnsonplc.com Sketchley*

Johnsons Photopia Ltd Hempstalls Lane, Newcastle ST5 0SW Tel. *01782 753300* Fax. *01782 753399* E-mail. *info@johnsons-photopia.co.uk* Web. *www.johnsons-photopia.co.uk B & W – Cokin – Lexmark – Loersch – Mamiya – Microtek – Ricoh – Schneider – Sekonic – Teleplus*

Johnson & Starley Ltd Rhosili Road Brackmills Industrial Estate, Northampton NN4 7LZ Tel. *01604 762881*

Fax. *01604 767408* E-mail. *info@johnsonandstarleyltd.co.uk* Web. *www.johnsonandstarley.co.uk Cleanflow – Janus – Modairflow – Reznor*

Johnson Tiles Ltd Harewood Street, Stoke On Trent ST6 5JZ Tel. *01782 575575* Fax. *01782 577377* E-mail. *info@johnson-tiles.com* Web. *www.johnson-tiles.com Absolute – Artile – Aspects – Elegance – Elements – Freedom – H & R Johnson - Cristal - Campbell's - Minton Hollins - H & R Johnson International - Prismatics - Prismafit - Sensations - Freedom - Kerastar -Elements - Spirit - Aspects - Artile - Johnson Professional - Norcros Adhesives – Johnson Professional – Johnson Tiles – Kerastar – Minton Hollins – Norcros Adhesives – Origins – Prismafit – Prismatics – Spirit*

W T Johnson & Sons Huddersfield Ltd Bankfield Mills Moldgreen, Huddersfield HD5 9BB Tel. *01484 549965* Fax. *01484 448106* E-mail. *reception@wtjohnson.co.uk* Web. *www.wtjohnson.co.uk Perfectaset – VV*

Johnstone's Paints Ltd 3 Mayfield Trade Centre Acre Road, Reading RG2 0RJ Tel. *0118 9875266* Fax. *0118 9750281* Web. *www.johnstonespaint.com Johnstone/Manders*

Johnstone's Paints Ltd Unit 7 Boucher Cresent, Belfast BT12 6HU Tel. *028 90664772* Fax. *028 90664783* Web. *www.johnstontrade.com Johnstones Paints*

Johnstons Of Mountnorris 48 Lower Lisdrumchor Road Glenanne, Armagh BT60 2HT Tel. *028 37507281* Fax. *028 37507333* E-mail. *jam.johnston@btconnect.com* Web. *www.johnstonspoultry.co.uk Goldline & Nera – Hybro Broilers*

John White & Son Weighing Machines Ltd 6 Back Dykes Auchtermuchty, Cupar KY14 7DW Tel. *01337 827600* Fax. *01337 827600* E-mail. *enquiries@johnwhiteandson.com* Web. *www.johnwhiteandson.com J W & S*

John Wilson Skates and MK Blades 2 Bells Square, Sheffield S1 2FY Tel. *0114 2725190* Fax. *0114 3240189* E-mail. *customerservice@hdsports.co.uk* Web. *www.mkblades.com M.K.*

John Wilson & Sons Industrial Engineer Blacksmith High Road Wisbech St Mary, Wisbech PE13 4RA Tel. *01945 410238* Fax. *01945 410238 Hudson Major – John Wilson*

Jolly Learning Ltd Tailours 59 High Road, Chigwell IG7 6DL Tel. *020 85010405* Fax. *020 85001619* E-mail. *info@jollylearning.co.uk* Web. *www.jollylearning.co.uk Finger Phonics books 1-7 – Jiglets – Jolly Phonics Box – Jolly Phonics Videos 1 And 2 – Jolly Phonics Wall Frieze – Jolly Phonics Workbooks 1-7 – Letter Sounds Games – Phonics Handbook, The – Stencilets – Using Jolly Phonics*

Jolly's L W C Wilson Way Pool, Redruth TR15 3JD Tel. *01209 213504* Fax. *01209 210342* E-mail. *robin.gray@lwc-drinks.co.uk* Web. *www.lwc-drinks.co.uk Jolly's Drinks*

Joloda Hydraroll Ltd 51 Speke Road Garston, Liverpool L19 2NY Tel. *0151 4278954* Fax. *0151 4271393* E-mail. *info@joloda.com* Web. *www.joloda.com Airoll – Cantilever – Joloda – M.D.S. – Moving Floor – Piggyback – Skate & Track*

Jonathan Berney Chartered Surveyors 35 Bruton Street Mayfair, London W1J 6QY Tel. *0871 2183771* Fax. *0704 0900561* E-mail. *headoffice@jonathanberney.co.uk* Web. *www.jonathanberney.co.uk 'Property Matters'*

Jonathan James Ltd Carter Lane Shirebrook, Mansfield NG20 8AH Tel. *01623 746270* Fax. *01623 744304* E-mail. *robert.nightingale@jonathan-james.co.uk* Web. *www.jonathan-james.co.uk Jonathan James*

Jonesco (Preston) Ltd Pittman Way Fulwood, Preston PR2 9ZD Tel. *01772 706809* Fax. *01772 702209* E-mail. *dstark@jonesco-plastics.com* Web. *www.jonesco-plastics.com DrumKart – Highgard – Highguard - High density plastic Sologuard - Mudguard incorporating anti spray – Sologard – XGard*

Jones Cranes Parts 3 Firsland Park Estate Henfield Road, Albourne, Hassocks BN6 9JJ Tel. *01273 494020* Fax. *01273 494294* E-mail. *sales@ironfairycranes.com* Web. *www.ironfairycranes.com Grove – Grove - Jones - NCK – Jones Cranes – NCK – Smith*

Gus Jones 109 High Street, Blackwood NP12 1AD Tel. *01495 223338* Fax. *01495 224220* E-mail. *michael@royalmasonic.herts.sch.uk* Web. *www.gusjonesjewellers.co.uk *Volvo (Switzerland)*

Jones Lang LaSalle (West End Office) 22 Hanover Square, London W1S 1JA Tel. *020 74936040* Fax. *020 74080220* E-mail. *jason.stone@eu.jll.com* Web. *www.joneslanglasalle.com Jones Lang LaSalle*

Jones & Palmer Ltd 95 Carver Street, Birmingham B1 3AR Tel. *0121 2369007* Fax. *0121 2365513* E-mail. *james.houston@jonesandpalmer.co.uk* Web. *www.jonesandpalmer.co.uk Jones & Palmer – P.C. Publishing*

S E Jones & Son 95 Swinton Hall Road Swinton, Manchester M27 4AU Tel. *0161 7943172* Fax. *0161 7943562 Open The Box*

Jones & Shipman Grinding Ltd (a division of Renold Engineering Products Co.) Murrayfield Road, Leicester LE3 1UW Tel. *0116 2013000* Fax. *0116 2013002* E-mail. *michael.duignan@jonesshipman.com* Web. *www.jonesshipman.com 1001 – 1300 – 1300x – 1305 – 1310 – 1400 – 1400e – 1400x – 1415 – 2000 – 524 – 540 – 540e – 540x – Dominator – Easy – Format – Honamat – Honamould – J. & S. – Jones & Shipman – Progrind – Promat – Suprema – Supromat – Techmaster – Techmat – Ultramat*

Jones Steel Ltd PO Box 66, Huddersfield HD1 1YQ Tel. *01484 513888* Fax. *01484 513999* E-mail. *sales@jonessteel.com* Web. *www.jonessteel.com Jones Electrical – Jones Marine – Jones Metals – Jones Steel*

Jones Stroud Insulations Ltd Queen Street Longridge, Preston PR3 3BS Tel. *01772 783011* Fax. *01772 784200* E-mail. *n.currie@jsi.krempel.com* Web. *www.krempel-group.com Hyperfil – Hyperlam – Hyperseal – Hypertape – Hyperten – Hypertex – Hypertherm – Isobond – Novaflex – Novobond – Polymica – Polyrod – Thermoguard – Thermoseal – Vidacord – Vidaflex XGR – Vidaflex XGS – Vidaflex XNF – Vidaseal – Vidatape*

William Jones Packaging Unit B5 South Point Foreshore Road, Cardiff CF10 4SP Tel. *029 20486262* Fax. *029 20481230* E-mail. *sales@wjpackaging.co.uk* Web. *www.wjpackaging.co.uk William Jones Packaging*

Jones & Wilson Ltd Unit 5 Brandon Way Industrial Estate Brandon Way, West Bromwich B70 9PW Tel. *0121 5254973* Fax. *0121 5534013* E-mail. *jonesr383@aol.com* Web. *www.jonesandwilsonltd.com UDAL*

Jordans Ltd 21 St Thomas Street, Bristol BS1 6JS Tel. *0117 9230600* Fax. *0117 9230063* E-mail. *customersupport@jordans.co.uk* Web. *www.jordans.co.uk Jordans*

Joseph Clayton & Sons Ltd Clayton Street, Chesterfield S41 0DU Tel. *01246 232863* Fax. *01246 207807* E-mail. *sales@claytonleather.com* Web. *www.claytonleather.com Cestretan – JeTan – PDFlex – Spa-Tan – Tanflex – Victan*

Joseph & Co The Piper Centre 50 Carnwath Road, London SW6 3JX Tel. *020 77362522* Fax. *020 77361644* E-mail. *andrew.franklin@joseph.co.uk* Web. *www.joseph.co.uk Joseph*

Joseph & Jesse Siddons Ltd Howard Street Hill Top, West Bromwich B70 0TB Tel. *0121 5560218* Fax. *0121 5563843* E-mail. *ian.parker@jjsiddons.co.uk* Web. *www.jjsiddons.co.uk J.J.S.*

Josery Textiles Ltd Unit 2 Benneworth Close, Hucknall, Nottingham NG15 6EL Tel. *0115 9632200* Fax. *0115 9640223* E-mail. *enquiries@josery.co.uk* Web. *www.josery.co.uk Josery – Sportswell – Welbeck*

Joshua Ellis & Co. Grange Valley Road, Batley WF17 6GH Tel. *01924 350070* Fax. *01924 350071* E-mail. *genoffice@joshuaellis.co.uk* Web. *www.joshuaellis.co.uk Ellis*

Jost Great Britain Ltd B7 Broadlands Heywood Distribution Park, Heywood OL10 2TS Tel. *0161 7630200* Fax. *0161 7630234* E-mail. *sales@jostgb.co.uk* Web. *www.jostgb.co.uk Jost*

Jowett & Sowry Ltd Barbondale Mill Lane, Bardsey, Leeds LS17 9AN Tel. *0113 2635317* Fax. *0113 2890429* E-mail. *nick@jowettandsowry.co.uk* Web. *www.jowettandsowryltd.co.uk Jowett & Sowry*

George Jowitt & Sons Ltd Bridgeway Broombank Road, Chesterfield S41 9QJ Tel. *01246 572230* Fax. *01246 572249* E-mail. *sales@jowitt.com* Web. *www.jowitt.com Jowitt Grinding Wheels*

Joy Mining Machinery Ltd Bromyard Road, Worcester WR2 5EG Tel. *08702 521000* Fax. *0870 2521888* E-mail. *mmannion@joy.co.uk* Web. *www.joy.com Joy Mining Machinery*

J P Whitter Ltd Smallbrook Service Station Smallbrook Lane, Leigh WN7 5PZ Tel. *01942 871900* Fax. *01942 896843* E-mail. *sally@waterwell-engineers.co.uk* Web. *www.waterwell-engineers.co.uk CAPRARI – DAB – GOULDS – GRUNDFOS – HAYWARD TYLER – ITT LOWARA*

J R D Rubber Mouldings Ltd 26 Regal Drive Industrial Estate Soham, Ely CB7 5BE Tel. *01353 720480* Fax. *01353 624304* E-mail. *sales@jrd-mouldings.com* Web. *www.jrd-mouldings.com J.R.D. Mouldings (United Kingdom) – J.R.D. Mouldings. and J.R.D. Pressings – J.R.D. Pressings (United Kingdom)*

J R Industries Ltd 1 Sir Alfred Owen Way Pontygwindy Industrial Estate, Caerphilly CF83 3HU Tel. *029 20857630* Fax. *029 20857633* E-mail. *julial@jrindustries.co.uk* Web. *www.jrindustries.co.uk J.R. Industries Ltd – Loadmaker – Robinson – Whiting*

J Roberts Ltd St Peg Lane, Cleckheaton BD19 3SL Tel. *01274 874631* Fax. *01274 851084* E-mail. *bok@jroberts.co.uk* Web. *www.jroberts.co.uk Wieland*

J R Technical Services UK Ltd 17 Bloomsbury Court Kenton, Newcastle Upon Tyne NE3 4LW Tel. *0191 2855977* Fax. *0870 8381245* E-mail. *info@jrts.co.uk* Web. *www.jrts.co.uk Desch – Transtech Sys Inc*

J R Technology 30a Barrington Road Shepreth, Royston SG8 6QE Tel. *01763 260721* Fax. *01763 260809* E-mail. *enquiries@jrtech.co.uk* Web. *www.jrtech.co.uk Delta Fasteners – J.R. Prepreg – J.R. Seal Strip – J.R. Vac Film – Masterblok – None Destructive Test Equipment – Processing Plant – Reinforced Plastics*

J R Webster & Co. Ltd Prince William Avenue Sandycroft, Deeside CH5 2QZ Tel. *01244 520373* Fax. *01244 535866* E-mail. *sales@jrwebster.co.uk* Web. *www.jrwebster.co.uk *Action Discs*

J Salmon Ltd 100-104 London Road, Sevenoaks TN13 1BB Tel. *01732 452381* Fax. *01732 450951* E-mail. *enquiries@jsalmon.co.uk* Web. *www.jsalmon.co.uk Academy – Ambassador – Cameracolour*

J. S. Bradley Ltd Park Farm Close Park Farm Industrial Estate, Folkestone CT19 5ED Tel. *01303 850011* Fax. *01303 244028* E-mail. *info@bradleyfurniture.co.uk* Web. *www.bradleyfurniture.co.uk Bradleys*

J & S Franklin Holdings & Management Services Ltd Franklin House 151 Strand, London WC2R 1HL Tel. *020 78365746* Fax. *020 78362784* E-mail. *defence@franklin.co.uk* Web. *www.franklin.co.uk Franklin*

J S Humidifiers plc Artex Avenue Rustington, Littlehampton BN16 3LN Tel. *01903 850200* Fax. *01903 850345* E-mail. *info@airandwatercentre.com* Web. *www.airandwatercentre.com ElectroVap – HumEvap – HumiPac – Jetspray AHU – Jetspray Direct Air – JS Air Curtains – Neptronic – PureFlo – RV Live Steam*

J & S Lewis Ltd Hope Carr Lane, Leigh WN7 3XA Tel. *01942 682828* Fax. *01942 680101* E-mail. *enquiries@jslewis.co.uk* Web. *www.jslewis.co.uk Bailey – Breviglieri – Deutz Fahr – Grimme – Lamborghini – Lemken – Merlo – Quickie – Vicon – West*

J S R Farming Group Southburn Offices Southburn, Driffield YO25 9ED Tel. *01377 229264* Fax. *01377 229253* E-mail. *info@jsr.co.uk* Web. *www.jsr.co.uk J.S.R. Arable Farms – J.S.R. Healthbred*

J T Inglis & Sons Ltd Riverside Works Carolina Port Stannergate Road, Dundee DD1 3LU Tel. *01382 462131* Fax. *01382 462846* E-mail. *enquiries@jtinglis.com* Web. *www.jtinglis.com Aquakinetic – Diamondback – Regentex – Weathermarque*

J T Price & Co. Holditch Road, Newcastle ST5 9JG Tel. *01782 562311* Fax. *01782 565654* Web. *www.westlygroup.com Sweetmore Engineering Holdings Ltd*

J T Sawyer & Co. Ltd 18 Mottram Street, Stockport SK1 3PA Tel. *0161 4803366* Fax. *0161 4809201* E-mail. *boxes@sawyers.boxes.co.uk* Web. *www.sawyerboxes.co.uk Pamphlox*

Juice Coperation Ltd 16 Bury New Road, Manchester M8 8FR Tel. *0161 8324951* Fax. *0161 8351446* E-mail. *mail@juicecorp.co.uk* Web. *www.juicecorporation.co.uk Joe Bloggs – Junior Bloggs*

Charles H Julian Ltd Lambourne Hall Church Lane, Abridge, Romford RM4 1AH Tel. *01992 814242* Fax. *01992 813536* E-mail. *recption@theparsonage.co.uk* Web. *www.theparsonage.co.uk Carlton – Icy – Royal Award – Royal Club – Tears of Scotland Liquer*

Jumo Instrument Co. Ltd Temple Bank River Way, Harlow CM20 2DY Tel. *01279 635533* Fax. *01279 635262* E-mail. *sales@jumo.co.uk* Web. *www.jumo.co.uk Jumo Instrument Co.*

June Productions Ltd The White House 6 Beechwood Lane, Warlingham CR6 9LT Tel. *01883 622411* Fax. *01883 622081* E-mail. *davidmackay99@gmail.com* Web. *www.mackay99.plus.com June Productions*

Just Diaries 17 Albemarle Road, Bournemouth BH3 7LZ Tel. *01202 248494* E-mail. *paul@justdiaries.co.uk* Web. *www.justdiaries.co.uk Just Diaries*

Justina Of London Ltd 6 Lockwood Industrial Park Mill Mead Road, London N17 9QP Tel. *020 88013663* Fax. *020 88084578* E-mail. *michael@justinaoflondon.biz* Web. *www.justinaoflondon.biz Three's Company*

Just Jamie & the Paulrich Ltd Unit 1 City North, Fonthill Road, London N4 3HN Tel. *020 75614500* Fax. *020 75614501* E-mail. *martin@justjamie.com Just Jamie – Paulrich*

Just Tiles Ltd 88 Headley Road Woodley, Reading RG5 4JE Tel. *0118 9697774* Fax. *0118 9441235* E-mail. *enquiries@justtiles.co.uk* Web. *www.justtiles.co.uk J.T.*

J V C Forex UK Ltd JVC House JVC Business Park, London NW2 7BA Tel. *020 84503282* Fax. *020 82084385* Web. *www.jvc.co.uk *J.V.C. (Worldwide)*

J V Hydraulics Ltd 1 Stroud Enterprise Centre Lightpill, Stroud GL5 3NL Tel. *01453 767729* Fax. *01453 767099* E-mail. *sales@jvhydraulics.co.uk* Web. *www.jvhydraulics.co.uk Larzep – Pneumax – Roemheld – Roquet – Stauff – Watershield – Yuken*

J V M Castings Ltd Borman Lichfield Road Industrial Estate, Tamworth B79 7TA Tel. *01827 64096* Fax. *01827 69497* E-mail. *sales@jvmcastings.com* Web. *www.jvmcastings.com Ali Studs – Master Casters*

J W T 1 Knightsbridge Green, London SW1X 7NW Tel. *020 76567000* Fax. *020 76567010* E-mail. *peter.womersley@jwt.com* Web. *www.jwt.co.uk J. Walter Thompson – J.W.T.*

K

K3 Business Technology Group plc 50 Kansas Avenue, Salford M50 2GL Tel. *0161 8764498* Fax. *01362 691710* E-mail. *info@k3btg.com* Web. *www.k3btg.com Encore – Impact Encore – Syspro*

Kaba Door Systems Halesfield 4, Telford TF7 4AP Tel. *08700 005235* Fax. *01952 682101* E-mail. *marketing@kcb.kaba.com* Web. *www.kaba.co.uk A.N.O. 1000F/1200S – A.N.O. Acmex – Defendor – Delta – Firetex – Hufcor – Insugard – K40 Slideover – Kwikroll – Panoramic – Sapphire – Sidewinder – Speedgard – Visiongard – Windowgard*

Kaba Ltd Head Office Lower Moor Way Tiverton Industrial Estate, Tiverton EX16 6SS Tel. *08700 005625* Fax. *01884 234415* E-mail. *info@kaba.co.uk* Web. *www.kaba.co.uk Elolegic – GCGE Cylinders – Kaba 20 – Kaba Delta – Kaba EXOS8000 – Kaba Legic – Kaba Macs – Kaba Mini S – Kaba Quattro S*

Kaby Engineers Ltd 14-16 Upper Charnwood Street, Leicester LE2 0AU Tel. *0116 2536353* Fax. *0116 2515237* E-mail. *kaby@kaby.co.uk* Web. *www.kaby.co.uk Kaby Engineers*

Kac Alarm Co. Ltd Kac House Thorn Hill Road, Moons Moat North Industrial Estate, Redditch B98 9ND Tel. *01527 406655* Fax. *01527 406677* E-mail. *dwilson@kac.co.uk* Web. *www.kac.co.uk K.A.C.*

Kadant UK Ltd PO Box 6, Bury BL8 1DF Tel. *0161 7649111* Fax. *0161 7971496* E-mail. *ron.chambers@kadant.com* Web. *www.kadant.com AES – Lodding – Vickery*

K & A Fashions 22-24 Russell Square, Leicester LE1 2DS Tel. *0116 2626229* Fax. *0116 2512982* E-mail. *info@ka-fashion.com* Web. *www.ka-fashions.com Mitsy*

Kalamazoo - Reynolds Ltd 1200 Bristol Road South Northfield, Birmingham B31 2RW Tel. *0121 4832000* Fax. *0121 4757566* E-mail. *marketing@kalamazoo.co.uk* Web. *www.kalamazoo.co.uk Answer – Autoscan – Elite – Esprit – KDMS – Recall – Tetra – Virtual Showroom – Worklink*

Kallo Foods Ltd Coopers Place Combe Lane, Wormley, Godalming GU8 5SZ Tel. *01428 685100* Fax. *01428 685800* E-mail. *sales@kallofoods.com* Web. *www.kallofoods.com *Just Bouillon (Germany) – *Kallo (Belgium)*

Kaloric Heater Co. Ltd 31-33 Beethoven Street, London W10 4LJ Tel. *020 89691367* Fax. *020 89688913* E-mail. *admin@kaloricheater.co.uk* Web. *www.kaloricheater.co.uk Kaloric – Mayfair*

Kalsep UK Unit 2f Albany Park Frimley Park, Camberley GU16 7PL Tel. *01276 675675* Fax. *01276 676276* E-mail. *ggregory@kalsep.co.uk* Web. *www.kalsep.co.uk Enviro-X – Fibrotex – Hydro-X – Kalmem LF – WWMPS*

Kappa Paper Recycling Mount Street, Birmingham B7 5RE Tel. *0121 3271381* Fax. *0121 3226300* E-mail. *sales@sskpaper.co.uk* Web. *www.smurfitkappa.com Corruchip – Corruflute – Corruliner – DLiner*

Kardex Systems UK Ltd Kestrel House Falconry Court Bakers Lane, Epping CM16 5LL Tel. *01992 566200* Fax. *0870 2400420* E-mail. *richard.price@kardex.co.uk* Web. *www.kardex-remstar.co.uk ATD – Citadel – Colourdex – Cribmaster – DataStack – Industriever – Kardex – KIS – Lektriever – Shuttle – Times 2*

S Karir & Sons Ltd 2 Brick Lane, London E1 6RF Tel. *020 72477762* Fax. *020 73750980* E-mail. *info@skarir.com Karir – *Skira (Far East) – St. Mark's*

Karpelle Ltd Varley Business Centre Varley Street, Manchester M40 8EE Tel. *0161 2032400* Fax. *0161 2051583* E-mail. *hklepper@karpelleltd.co.uk* Web. *www.karpelle.co.uk Breckmoor – Di-Vita – Karpelle*

Karramandi 111 Kimberley Street, Warrington WA5 1PA Tel. *07807 083502* E-mail. *yvonne@karramandi.com* Web. *www.karramandi.com Karramandi*

Karrimor Ltd 440 - 450 Cob Drive Swan Valley, Northampton NN4 9BB Tel. *0870 8387300* Fax. *01254 893100* E-mail. *info@sports-world.com* Web. *www.karrimor.com Aergo – Aurora – Baltoro – Condor – Jaguar – K.S. 100e – Karrimat – Karrimor – Papoose – *Trangia (Sweden)*

Kort Propulsion Co. Ltd The Boat House Erith High Street, Erith DA8 1QY Tel. *01322 346346* Fax. *01322 347346* E-mail. *info@kortpropulsion.com* Web. *www.kortpropulsion.com Kort Engineering – Kort Engineering - Marine engineering, Kort Propulsion - Marine engineering, Kort Nozzle - Marine engineering, – Kort Propulsion*

K A S Paper Systems Ltd Brewers Hill Road, Dunstable LU6 1AD Tel. *01582 662211* Fax. *01582 664222* E-mail. *mail@kaspapersystems.com* Web. *www.kaspapersystems.com Collator-Matic – Kasfold – Mailmaster – Set-Matic – Spacesaver – Velopost*

Kauser International Trading Ltd PO Box 85, Radlett WD7 7ZN Tel. *01727 874088* Fax. *01727 874088* E-mail. *info@kauserinternational.com* Web. *www.kauserinternational.com Advance Copystands – Capital Exposure Meters – Fujitsu – Itohnar – Kauser – Phenix – Seagull*

Kawasaki Precision Machinery UK Ltd Ernesettle Lane, Plymouth PL5 2SA Tel. *01752 364394* Fax. *01752 364816* E-mail. *sales@kpm-uk.co.uk* Web. *www.kpm-eu.com Staffa*

Kawneer UK Ltd Astmoor Road Astmoor Industrial Estate, Runcorn WA7 1QQ Tel. *01928 502500* Fax. *01928 502501* E-mail. *phil.randles@alcoa.com* Web. *www.kawneer.co.uk 1200 – 1200 – 1200 – 1600 – 190, 350, 1040 – 400 – 451 – 451T – 501 – 502 – 503 – 504 – Alderley – Designer – Econ 40/75 – Econ 75 T.S. – Econ Door – Kingsley – PG 38 & PG 45 – RS-100 – Trusswall*

Kay Dee Engineering Plastics Ltd 2 Jubilee Court Thackley Old Road, Shipley BD18 1QF Tel. *01274 590824* Fax. *01274 531409* E-mail. *info@kaylan.co.uk* Web. *www.kaylan.co.uk Kaylan*

J & A Kay Ltd Cotton Hall Mill Cotton Hall Street, Darwen BB3 0DP Tel. *01254 873535* Fax. *01254 873463* E-mail. *info@jakay.co.uk* Web. *www.jakay.co.uk Sign Systems Centre*

Kaylee Transfers Ltd PO Box 11, Nottingham NG10 2DP Tel. *0115 9735247* Fax. *0115 9460801* E-mail. *sales@kaylee.uk.com* Web. *www.kaylee.uk.com Kaylee Transfers*

Kay-Metzeler Ltd (Polystyrene Division) Brook Street, Chelmsford CM1 1UQ Tel. *01245 342100* Fax. *01245 342123* E-mail. *epssales@vcfuk.com* Web. *www.kay-metzeler.com Kay-Cel*

Kay Optical Servicing 89b London Road, Morden SM4 5HP Tel. *020 86488822* Fax. *020 86872021* E-mail. *info@kayoptical.co.uk* Web. *www.kayoptical.co.uk Kay Optical Servicing*

Kays Ramsbottom Ltd Britannia Works Kenyon Street, Ramsbottom, Bury BL0 0AE Tel. *01706 822216* Fax. *01706 828615* E-mail. *sales@kays-soap.com* Web. *www.kays-soap.com Falcon Carbolic Soap*

K B C Process Technology Ltd 42-50 Hersham Road, Walton On Thames KT12 1RZ Tel. *01932 242424* Fax. *01932 224214* E-mail. *info@kbcat.com* Web. *www.kbcat.com Catop – Cruise – Distop – Petrofine – Profit Improvement Program – Utopia – Vistop*

K B C Process Technology Ltd Unit 4 Cheshire Avenue Lostock Gralam, Northwich CW9 7UA Tel. *01606 815100* Fax. *01606 815151* E-mail. *info@linnhoffmarch.com* Web. *www.kbcat.com Prosteam – Super Target – SuperTarget – Water Pinch – Water Tracker*

K B Import & Export Ltd 43-45 North Street, Manchester M8 8RE Tel. *0161 8348485* Fax. *0161 8328057* E-mail. *sales@kbie.co.uk* Web. *www.plustron.com Conquest – Corrina – Elizabethan – Hey Presto – Hi Tech – Kaytime – Louis Santini – Plustron – Traveller Products – Tree Tops – Undercover – Value Rite*

Kone Cranes Machine Tool Services 1 Farrier Road, Lincoln LN6 3RU Tel. *01522 687878* Fax. *01522 687879* E-mail. *service@kandbmts.com* Web. *www.konecranes.co.uk Brother – EMT – Kawatatec – Midaco – Troyke*

KBOS2 Flat 1 65 Rothbury Terrace, Newcastle Upon Tyne NE6 5XJ Tel. *07724 165507* E-mail. *kbos2hm@yahoo.co.uk* Web. *www.kbos2.co.uk kbos2*

K B Refrigeration Ltd 31-33 Colquhoun Avenue Hillington Park, Glasgow G52 4BN Tel. *0141 8105577* Fax. *01463 713264* E-mail. *enquiries@kb-services.co.uk* Web. *www.kb-services.co.uk K.B. Refrigeration*

K & C Mouldings England Ltd Spa House Church Road, Shelfanger, Diss IP22 2DF Tel. *01379 642660* Fax. *01379 650304* E-mail. *sales@kcmouldings.co.uk* Web. *www.kcmouldings.co.uk Downland*

K Com 2nd & 3rd Floor 4 Crown Place, London EC2A 4BT Tel. *020 74228700* Fax. *0121 7797222* E-mail. *info@kcom.com* Web. *www.kcom.com *Timeplex (U.S.A.)*

Martin Andrew Kearney Fairview Croft-Mitchell, Troon, Camborne TR14 9JH Tel. *01209 831662* Fax. *01209 831662 Sporting-Links*

Kearsley Precision Engineering Unit 8 9 Herons Gate Trading Estate, Basildon SS14 3EU Tel. *01268 289422* Fax. *01268 282318* E-mail. *sales@kearsleyprecision.com* Web. *www.kearsleyprecision.com Stone Platt – Stone Wallwork – Wellman Bibby*

K E B UK Ltd 6 Morris Close Park Farm Industrial Estate, Wellingborough NN8 6XF Tel. *01933 402220* Fax. *01933 400724* E-mail. *info@keb-uk.co.uk* Web. *www.keb-uk.co.uk *Combibox – *Combigear – Combinorm – Combiperm – *Combistop – *Combitron – *Combivert – Combivert - Open loop and closed loop frequency inverters. Combigear - Helical geared motors. Combistop - Spring applied brakes. Combinorm - Electromagnetic clutches and brakes. Combibox - electromagnetic clutch brake units. Combiperm - permanent magnetic brakes. Combitron - Power supply modules.*

Kedek Ltd Heath Place, Bognor Regis PO22 9SL Tel. *01243 861421* Fax. *01243 826108* E-mail. *sales@kedek.co.uk* Web. *www.kedek.co.uk Diamond Facia Cladding (United Kingdom) – Regis Ovens (United Kingdom) – Topper Ovens (United Kingdom)*

Alan Keef Ltd Lea Line Lea, Ross On Wye HR9 7LQ Tel. *01989 750757* Fax. *01989 750780* E-mail. *sales@alankeef.co.uk* Web. *www.alankeef.co.uk Lister – Planet – Ruston Hornsby – Simplex – Simplex - Planet.*

Keeler Ltd Clewer Green Works Clewer Hill Road, Windsor SL4 4AA Tel. *01753 857177* Fax. *01753 830247* E-mail. *info@keeler.co.uk* Web. *www.keeler.co.uk Keeler – Keeler Loupes – Microlase – Multilase – Pulsair*

Keeling & Walker Ltd Whieldon Road, Stoke On Trent ST4 4JA Tel. *01782 744136* Fax. *01782 744126* E-mail. *sales@keelingwalker.co.uk* Web. *www.keelingwalker.co.uk Stanostat – Superlite – Thermox*

Keemlaw Ltd Unit 4 Super Abbey Estate Off Beddow Way, Aylesford ME20 7BH Tel. *01622 717177* Fax. *01622 790348* E-mail. *info@keemlaw.co.uk* Web. *www.keemlaw.co.uk *Churchill – *Falcon – *Graham – *Steelite – *Winterhalter*

Keen World Marketing Ltd 1 Northbrook Street, Newbury RG14 1DJ Tel. *01635 34600* Fax. *01635 33360* E-mail. *info@keen-newport.com* Web. *www.keen-newport.com Aquanol – Glowman – Keen – Keen Superkill – Newport – Newport Mini-Filters – Tox – Zeste*

Keep-it Security Products Imperial Works Heath Road, Darlaston, Wednesbury WS10 8LP Tel. *0870 4442820* Fax. *0870 4442826* E-mail. *sales@keep-it.co.uk* Web. *www.keep-it.co.uk Keep-It*

Kee Systems Ltd 11 Thornsett Road, London SW18 4EW Tel. *020 88746566* Fax. *020 88745726* E-mail. *sales@keesystems.com* Web. *www.keesystems.com Kee Klamps*

Kee Valves Greenacres Road, Oldham OL4 2AB Tel. *01782 523388* Fax. *01782 523399* E-mail. *sales@keevalves.co.uk* Web. *www.keevalves.co.uk Bopp & Reuther – Broby – Check Rite – CMO – CYL – Engelsberg – Glimakra – J.H. Witzel – Naf – Naval – Schroder – Vexve – Von Roll – Westad – World-valve*

K E F Eccleston Road Tovil, Maidstone ME15 6QP Tel. *01622 672261* Fax. *01622 750653* E-mail. *info@kef.com* Web. *www.kef.com KEF – KEF Uni-Q Technology*

Keithley Instruments Ltd 2 Commerce Park Brunel Road, Theale, Reading RG7 4AB Tel. *0118 9297500* Fax. *0118 9297519* E-mail. *info@keithley.co.uk* Web. *www.keithley.com *Keithley (U.S.A.) – *Keithley (U.S.A.)*

Keith Mount Liming Ltd Unit A8 Risby Business Park Newmarket Road, Risby, Bury St Edmunds IP28 6RD Tel. *01284 811729* Fax. *01284 811590* E-mail. *info@mountliming.co.uk* Web. *www.mountliming.co.uk Ferteco – Fibrophos – Limex70*

Kelda Group Western House Western Way, Buttershaw, Bradford BD6 2SZ Tel. *01274 600111* Fax. *01274 608608* E-mail. *kevin.whiteman@keldagroup.com* Web. *www.keldagroup.com Alcontrol – Global Enviromental – White Rose Environmental – Yorkshire Water Projects – Yorkshire Water Services*

Kelgray Products Ltd Kelgray House Spindle Way, Crawley RH10 1TH Tel. *01293 518733* Fax. *01293 518803* E-mail. *chris@kelgray.co.uk* Web. *www.kelgray.co.uk Code Red Distribution – Kelgray Products – Securi-Key Petromatic*

Keller Geo Technique Unit 611 Avenue D Thorp Arch Estate, Wetherby LS23 7FS Tel. *01937 541118* Fax. *01937 541371* E-mail. *info@keller-ge.co.uk* Web. *www.keller-geotechnique.co.uk Colgrout – Colmono – Colplus – KGE*

Kellett Engineering Co. Ltd Jasper Street, Halifax HX1 4NT Tel. *0113 2639041* Fax. *0113 2310717* E-mail. *sales@kellettwindows.co.uk* Web. *www.kellettwindows.co.uk K.L.T. – *Nyliners (Holland and Germany) – *Thomson Industries Inc (U.S.A.)*

Kelvin Diesels British Polar Engines Ltd 133 Helen Street Govan, Glasgow G51 3HD Tel. *0141 4452455* Fax. *0141 4452185* E-mail. *stewart.davis@britishpolarengines.co.uk* Web. *www.BritishPolarEngines.co.uk Polar Bear*

Kelvin Top-Set Ltd 55a Main Road Fairlie, Largs KA29 0AA Tel. *01475 560007* Fax. *01475 569011* E-mail. *sales@kelvin.org* Web. *www.kelvintopset.com Kelvin Top Set – Thought Train – Top Safe – Top Set*

Kelvin Valley Properties 23 Main Street Kilsyth, Glasgow G65 0AH Tel. *01236 826661* Fax. *01236 826661* E-mail. *jrafferty@kelvinvalleyproperties.co.uk* Web. *www.kvps.co.uk Kelvin Valley Properties – Your Local Property Shop*

Kembrey Wiring Systems Ltd 1 Garrards Way, Swindon SN3 3HY Tel. *01793 693361* Fax. *01793 614298* E-mail. *enquiries@kembrey.co.uk* Web. *www.kembrey.co.uk Telecrimp*

Kemco Fabrications Ltd Dane Road Bletchley, Milton Keynes MK1 1JQ Tel. *01908 375451* Fax. *01908 375044* E-mail. *b.sullivan@kemco-aegis.com* Web. *www.kemcoenv.com Aegis Security Enclosures*

Kemdent Kemdent Works Cricklade Road, Purton, Swindon SN5 4HT Tel. *01793 770256* Fax. *01793 772256* E-mail. *sales@kemdent.co.uk* Web. *www.kemdent.co.uk Anutex – Diamond Glass – Godiva – Kemco – Kemdent – Tenacetin – Tenasyle – Tenatex*

Kemet International Ltd Parkwood Trading Estate, Maidstone ME15 9NJ Tel. *01622 755287* Fax. *01622 670915*

E-mail. *sales@kemet.co.uk* Web. *www.kemet.co.uk Abracap – Abradisc – Applikator – Bramet – Gesswein – Helilaps – Kemesonic – Kemet 300*

Kemmel Ltd Unit 6-7 Cradle Hill Industrial Estate, Seaford BN25 3JE Tel. *01323 899010* Fax. *01323 893149* E-mail. *sales@kemmel.co.uk* Web. *www.kemmel.co.uk Sylbert*

Kemp Engineering & Surveying Ltd 8 Barncoose Industrial Estate Barncoose, Redruth TR15 3RQ Tel. *01209 214687* Fax. *01209 215189* E-mail. *office@kempengineering.co.uk* Web. *www.kempengineeringsurvey.co.uk Kemp Engineering – Seeka Utility Surveying*

Kempsafe Ltd Kemps Quay Industrial Park Quayside Road Bitterne Manor, Southampton SO18 1BZ Tel. *023 80227582* Fax. *023 80226002* E-mail. *sales@kempsafe.com* Web. *www.kempsafe.com Kempsafe*

Kemps Publishing Ltd 11 Swan Courtyard Charles Edward Road, Birmingham B26 1BU Tel. *0121 7654144* Fax. *0121 7066210* E-mail. *info@kempspublishing.co.uk* Web. *www.kempspublishing.co.uk Kemps*

Kempston Controls Ltd Shirley Road, Rushden NN10 6BZ Tel. *01933 411411* Fax. *01933 410211* E-mail. *richard.regan@kempstoncontrols.co.uk* Web. *www.kempstoncontrols.co.uk Amaster – Camaster, Safeloc, Redspot, Safe Clip, Microswitch – Microswitch – Redspot – Safe Clip – Safeloc*

Kemwall Engineering Co. 52 Bensham Grove, Thornton Heath CR7 8DA Tel. *020 86537111* Fax. *020 86539669* E-mail. *sales@kemwall.co.uk* Web. *www.kemwall.co.uk Kemwall*

Kemwell Thermal Ltd Roma Road, Birmingham B11 2JH Tel. *0121 7081188* Fax. *0121 7063390* E-mail. *enquiries@kemwellthermal.com* Web. *www.kemwellthermal.co.uk Kemwell*

Kenex Electro Medical Ltd 24 Burnt Mill Industrial Estate Elizabeth Way, Harlow CM20 2HS Tel. *01279 417241* Fax. *01279 443749* E-mail. *ken.hunt@kenex.co.uk* Web. *www.kenex.co.uk Cawo – Kenex – Lytatype – Lytatype, Kenex, Cawo, Rothband, Wardray Premise, PREMAC – PREMAC – Wardray Premise*

Ken Kimble Reactor Vessel Ltd Unit 85 Thomas Way Lakesview International Business Park, Hersden, Canterbury CT3 4NH Tel. *01227 710274* Fax. *01732 885840* E-mail. *general@kenkimble.co.uk* Web. *www.kenkimble.com BUCHI – Huber – Julabo*

Kenlowe Accessories & Co. Ltd Burchetts Green, Maidenhead SL6 6QU Tel. *01628 823303* Fax. *01628 823451* E-mail. *sales@kenlowe.com* Web. *www.kenlowe.com Aircool – Booster Rad – Heatomatic – Hi-Temp – Hotstart – Interiorcooler – Interiorheater – Kenlofan – Kenlowemotor – Oilcooler – Oilheater – Tempostatic – Thermomatic – Thermomatic H.D. – Unifan – Unifan O/E*

Kennametal Lake Road Leeway Industrial Estate, Newport NP19 4SR Tel. *01633 636500* Fax. *01633 636501* E-mail. *newport.info@kennametal.com* Web. *www.kennametal.com Boron Nitride – Non-Oxide – PBN – Sintec – Stabor – Technical Ceramics – Titanium Diboride*

Kennametal Extrude Hone Ltd 1 Sovereign Business Park Joplin Court, Crownhill, Milton Keynes MK8 0JP Tel. *01908 263636* Fax. *01908 262141* E-mail. *sean.trengove@kennametal.com* Web. *www.extrudehone.com AFM – ECM – Extrude Honing – TEM*

Kennametal UK Ltd PO Box 29, Kingswinford DY6 7NP Tel. *01384 401000* Fax. *01384 408015* E-mail. *andy.godwin@kennametal.com* Web. *www.kennametal.co.uk Acramil – Ball Lock – Ball Track – G.A.A. – Grade Application Advisor – K.060 – K.090 – K.1 – K.313 – K.420 – K.68 – K.C.250 – K.C.710 – K.C.720 – K.C.725M – K.C.730 – K.C.740 – K.C.792M – K.C.810 – K.C.850 – K.C.910 – K.C.935 – K.C.950 – K.C.990 – K.C.992M – K.D.050 – K.D.100 – K.D.120 – K.D.200 – K.T.125 – K.T.175 – Kendex – Kengrip – Kenloc – Kyon – Modbore – N.G.D., N.R.D., N.F.D. – R.P.F. – Super Point – T.L.M. – Tenthset – Tool Location Management – Toolpro – Top Notch – V.-Flange – V.-Notch – Wedgelock*

Kennedy Occupational Health The Kinetic Centre Theobald Street, Borehamwood WD6 4PJ Tel. *020 83874050* E-mail. *imp@kennedyoh.co.uk KennedyOH*

Kennedy's Publications Ltd First Floor Offices Stafford House, 16 East Street, Tonbridge TN9 1HG Tel. *01732 371510* Fax. *01732 352438* E-mail. *post@kennedys.co.uk* Web. *www.kennedysconfection.com Kennedys*

Kennett & Lindsell Ltd Crow Lane, Romford RM7 0ES Tel. *01708 749732* Fax. *01708 733328* E-mail. *sales@kennettlindsell.com* Web. *www.kennettlindsell.com K & L Ltd – Kenneform*

Gavin Kenning Engineering Whites Close, Alfreton DE55 7RB Tel. *01773 607505* Fax. *01773 540505* E-mail. *sales@tradersupplies.co.uk* Web. *www.tradersupplies.co.uk Gavin Kenning Engineering*

Archibald Kenrick & Sons Union Street, West Bromwich B70 6DB Tel. *0121 5532741* Fax. *0121 5006332* E-mail. *sales@kenricks.co.uk* Web. *www.kenricks.co.uk Excalibur – Kenrick – Kenrick – Minicastor – Olympi Castor – P.F.S. – Rapier – Readybolt – Sentrilock – Shepherd – Shepherdette – Twin Wheel*

Kentex Jeans & Casuals (Labmen Ltd, A Division of SLK Kentex Fashions Ltd) 33 Hampton Street, Birmingham B19 3LS Tel. *0121 2330203* E-mail. *kentex@btinternet.com* Web. *www.kentex.co.uk Miss Navita – No Logo! – Palvini – Popsy – Shivaru – Slik 7*

Kent Frozen Foods Ltd Priory Park Mills Road, Aylesford ME20 7PP Tel. *01622 612400* Fax. *01622 612401* E-mail. *caroline.harrison@kff.co.uk* Web. *www.kfs.co.uk Excellence – Heavenly Delights – Purple Pineapple*

Kentinental Engineering Ltd Platt Industrial Estate Maidstone Road, Borough Green, Sevenoaks TN15 8JA Tel. *01732 882345* Fax. *01732 885703* E-mail. *sales@keg.co.uk* Web. *www.kentinental.com Demtruk – KE – Kentinental*

Kentmere Ltd Kentmere Mills Staveley, Kendal LA8 9PB Tel. *01539 821365* Fax. *01539 821399* E-mail. *sales@kentmere.sale.co.uk* Web. *www.kentmere.co.uk Kentmere*

Kent Messenger Group Ltd Messenger House New Hythe Lane, Larkfield, Aylesford ME20 6SG Tel. *01622 717880* Fax. *01622 719637* E-mail. *mphippen@thekmgroup.co.uk* Web. *www.kentonline.co.uk Ashford KM Extra – Canterbury KM Extra – Dartford and Swanley Informer Extra – East Kent Mercury – Faversham News – Folkestone & Dover KM Extra – Gravesend KM Extra – Gravesend Messenger – Job Southeast – Kent Business – Kent Messenger – Kent Today – Kentish Express – Kentish Gazette – Maidstone KM Extra – Medway KM Extra – Sheerness Times Guardian – Sittingbourne KM Extra – Thanet KM Extra – Tunbridge Wells & Tonbridge KM Extra – What's On*

Kent Pharmaceuticals Ltd Wotton Road, Ashford TN23 6LL Tel. *01233 638614* Fax. *01233 646899* E-mail. *oneilld@kentpharm.co.uk* Web. *www.kentpharm.co.uk Early Bird*

Kent Regional News & Media Unit 4 Ambley Green Gillingham Business Park, Gillingham ME8 0NJ Tel. *01634 236320* Web. *www.thisiskent.co.uk Crowborough Courier – East Grinstead Courier – East Sussex Courier – Edenbridge Courier – News in Focus – Paddock Wood Courier – Sevenoaks Chronicle – Tonbridge Courier – Tunbridge Wells Courier – Uckfield Courier – Weald Courier*

Kent Regional News & Media (a division of The Trinity Mirror Group) Westcliff House West Cliff Gardens, Folkestone CT20 1SZ Tel. *01303 850999* Fax. *01303 226658* E-mail. *newdesk.heraldexpress@kentregionalnewpaper.co.uk* Web. *www.thisiskent.co.uk Ashford Adscene – Dover Adscene – Dover Express – Folkestone Adscene – Folkestone Herald – Hythe Herald – Romney Marsh Herald*

Kent & Co Twines Ltd Long Lane Walton, Liverpool L9 7DE Tel. *0151 5251601* Fax. *0151 5231410* E-mail. *kenttwines@aol.com Cardoc – Cardoc Three Fishes – Wellington*

Kenure Developments Ltd 2-3 Springlakes Estate Deadbrook Lane, Aldershot GU12 4UH Tel. *01252 338554* Fax. *01252 329105* E-mail. *sales@kenure.co.uk* Web. *www.kenure.co.uk RHOMBOS TECHNOLOGIES*

S W Kenyon PO Box 71, Cranbrook TN18 5ZR Tel. *01580 850770* Fax. *01580 850225* E-mail. *bob.houlden@btinternet.com* Web. *www.swkenyon.com K-Line (United Kingdom)*

Keraflo Ltd Unit 1 Woodley Park Estate 59-69 Reading Road, Woodley, Reading RG5 3AN Tel. *0118 9219920* Fax. *0118 9219921* E-mail. *info@keraflo.co.uk* Web. *www.keraflo.co.uk Aylesbury Float Valves – Aylesbury K type float valve – Aylesbury KAX float valve – Aylesbury KB float valve – Aylesbury KP float valve – Aylesbury Valves – Keraflow – Keraflow Ball Valves*

Kerneos Ltd Dolphin Way, Purfleet RM19 1NZ Tel. *01708 863333* Fax. *01708 861033* E-mail. *a.beardmore@kerneos.com* Web. *www.kerneosinc.com Alag – Calcium Aluminates Cements – Ciment Fondu Lafarge – Secar Cements*

Kerr Multilingual 41-42 Haven Green, London W5 2NX Tel. *020 88107839* Fax. *020 89980388* E-mail. *info@kerr-recruitment.co.uk* Web. *www.kerr-recruitment.co.uk Kerr Bi-Lingual – Kerr Recruitment*

Kerry Foods Ltd (Golden Vale) Godley Hill Road, Hyde SK14 3BR Tel. *0161 3684080* Fax. *0161 3511070* E-mail. *aylesbury.sales@kerry-foodservice.co.uk* Web. *www.kerrygroup.com *Angelito – *Black Diamond – *Golden Vale – *La Scala*

Kesslers International Ltd 11 Rick Roberts Way, London E15 2NF Tel. *020 85223000* Fax. *020 85223129* E-mail. *john.anderson@kesslers.com* Web. *www.kesslers.com Kesslers International*

Kestrel B C E Ltd Billet Lane, Scunthorpe DN15 9YH Tel. *01724 400440* Fax. *01724 280241* E-mail. *enquiries@kbp.co.uk* Web. *www.kestrelbce.co.uk K-Clad – Roofline*

Kestrel Design 32 Loxwood Avenue, Worthing BN14 7RA Tel. *01903 212680* Fax. *01903 239001* E-mail. *d.elliott@kestrel-design.co.uk* Web. *www.kestrel-design.co.uk *Kason Contract Furniture*

Ketchum Pleon 35-41 Folgate Street, London E1 6BX Tel. *020 76113500* Fax. *020 76113501* E-mail. *david.gallagher@ketchum.com* Web. *www.ketchum.com Brodeur A Plus – Brodeur Worldwide*

Keter UK Ltd 12-14 Kettles Wood Drive, Birmingham B32 3DB Tel. *0121 4226633* Fax. *0121 4220808* E-mail. *sales@outstanding-keter.com* Web. *www.keter.com Keter*

Kettler GB Ltd Merse Road Moons Moat North Industrial Estate, Redditch B98 9HL Tel. *01527 591901* Fax. *01527 62423* E-mail. *sales@kettler.co.uk* Web. *www.kettler.co.uk *Kettler (Germany) – Nistac – Royal Garden*

Keyline Builders Merchants Lister Close Newnham Industrial Estate, Plympton, Plymouth PL7 4BA Tel. *01752 335956* Fax. *01752 342895* E-mail. *ply0235@keyline.co.uk* Web. *www.keyline.co.uk Travis perkins*

Keymed Ltd Keymed House Stock Road, Southend On Sea SS2 5QH Tel. *01702 616333* Fax. *01702 465677* E-mail. *keymed@keymed.co.uk* Web. *www.keymed.co.uk KeyMed – Olympus Industrial – Olympus-KeyMed*

Keymer Tiles Ltd Nye Road, Burgess Hill RH15 0LZ Tel. *01444 232931* Fax. *01444 871852* E-mail. *info@keymer.co.uk* Web. *www.keymer.co.uk Keymer*

Key Source Ltd North Heath Lane Industrial Estate, Horsham RH12 5QE Tel. *01403 243333* Fax. *01403 243300* E-mail. *info@keysource.co.uk* Web. *www.keysource.co.uk Sentinel – Sentry*

Keystone Castor Co. Unit 19 Avon Business Park Lodge Causeway, Bristol BS16 3JP Tel. *0117 9657777* Fax. *0117 9652177* E-mail. *bristol@keystonecastors.com* Web. *www.keystonecastors.com Keco – Keystone*

Keystone Castor Co. Unit 1, St Andrews Trading Estate 111 Gt Barr StreetDigbeth, Birmingham B9 4 BB Tel. *0121 7721010* Fax. *0121 7731103* E-mail. *info@keystonecastors.com* Web. *www.keystonecastors.co.uk Keco – Keco - range of castors and wheels.Flexello - range of castors and wheels.Keystone - stockists and distributors of castors and wheels.Revvo - range of castors and wheels.Shepherd castors - range of castors.G-Dok Footmaster range - multifunctional castors. – Keystone*

Keytrak Lock & Safe Company Unit 1 Heron Business Park Tanhouse Lane, Widnes WA8 0SW Tel. *0151 4955740* Fax. *0844 6691293* E-mail. *sales@keytrak.co.uk* Web. *www.keytrak4security.co.uk Crimeshield – Crossguard – Extendor – Grifinguard – Razor Spike – Seceuroguard – Trellidor*

KFS Service Ltd The Avenue, Lightwater GU18 5RF Tel. *01276 479404* Fax. *01276 479504* E-mail. *enquiry@kfsservice.co.uk* Web. *kfsservice.co.uk Kuppersbusch*

Kids Unlimited (t/a Kids Unlimited) 1 Summerfield Village Centre Dean Row Road, Wilmslow SK9 2TA Tel. *01625 540883* Fax. *0845 3652196* E-mail. *summerfield.manager@kidsunlimited.co.uk* Web. *www.kidsunlimited.co.uk Kids of Wilmslow*

Kilburn & Strode Blenheim Gate 22-24 Upper Marlborough Road, St Albans AL1 3AL Tel. *020 75394200* Fax. *020 75394299* E-mail. *ks@kstrode.co.uk* Web. *www.kstrode.co.uk Kilburn & Strode*

Killgerm Group Ltd PO Box 2 Denholme Drive, Ossett WF5 9NA Tel. *01924 268400* Fax. *01924 274385* E-mail. *sales@killgerm.com* Web. *www.killgerm.com Killgerm – PX*

Kilner Vacuumation Co. Ltd Callywhite Lane, Dronfield S18 2XR Tel. *01246 416441* Fax. *01246 290573* E-mail. *sales@kilner-vacuum-lifting.com* Web. *www.kilner-vacuum-lifting.com Kilner Vacuumation*

Kilrock Products Ltd 1b Alma Road Industrial Estate, Chesham HP5 3HB Tel. *01494 793900* Fax. *01494 793400* E-mail. *sales@kilrock.co.uk* Web. *www.kilrock.co.uk Descalene – Gel Kilrock – Kilbrock – Kilrock – Kilrock CHC – Kilrock CHP – Kilrock Moisture Traps – Spirits of Salt*

Kilwaughter Chemical Co. Ltd Kilwaughter Lime Works 9 Starbog Road, Kilwaughter, Larne BT40 2TJ Tel. *028 28260766* Fax. *028 28260136* E-mail. *sales@kilwaughter.com* Web. *www.kilwaughter.com Divis – K-Rend*

Kimber Allen UK Ltd Broomfield Works London Road, Swanley BR8 8DF Tel. *01322 663234* Fax. *01322 668318* E-mail. *ka@kimberallen.freeserve.co.uk* Web. *www.kimberallen.8m.net K.A.*

Kinetico UK Ltd Bridge House Park Gate Business Centre Chandlers Way, Park Gate, Southampton SO31 1FQ Tel. *01489 566970* Fax. *01489 566976* E-mail. *info@kinetico.co.uk* Web. *www.kinetico.co.uk Hypure – Kinetico*

Kinetrol Ltd Farnham Trading Estate, Farnham GU9 9NW Tel. *01252 733838* Fax. *01252 713042* E-mail. *sales@kinetrol.com* Web. *www.kinetrol.com Kinetrol*

King Builders Golders Way, London NW11 8JX Tel. *0800 1182206* Fax. *020 87316678* E-mail. *info@kingbuilders.com* Web. *www.kingbuilders.co.uk Importech Ltd*

C & D King Ltd 15 Havenbury Industrial Estate, Dorking RH4 1ES Tel. *01306 876767* Fax. *01306 887479* E-mail. *kings@lineone.net* Web. *www.moleskins.co.uk Wathen Gardiner – Wisewear*

King Dick Tools Unit 11 Roman Way, Coleshill, Birmingham B46 1HG Tel. *01675 467776* Fax. *01675 464277* E-mail. *info@kingdicktools.co.uk* Web. *www.kingdicktools.co.uk King Dick*

Kingdom Blinds 189 Rannoch Road Balfarg, Glenrothes KY7 6XR Tel. *01592 787715* E-mail. *infokingdomblinds@yahoo.co.uk* Web. *www.kingdomblinds.co.uk Kingdom Blinds*

Kingdom Security Ltd Mill Brow Eccleston, St Helens WA10 4QG Tel. *08450 517700* Fax. *01744 616699* E-mail. *terry@kingdomsecurity.co.uk* Web. *www.kingdomsecurity.co.uk sia*

E W King & Co. Ltd Monks Farm Kelvedon, Colchester CO5 9PG Tel. *01376 570000* Fax. *01376 571189* E-mail. *sales@kingsseeds.com* Web. *www.kingsseeds.com Kings – Suffolk Herbs*

Kingfisher Lubrication 136 Meanwood Road, Leeds LS7 2BT Tel. *0113 2098989* Fax. *0113 2374027* E-mail. *info@kingfisherlub.co.uk* Web. *www.kingfisherlub.co.uk Kingfisher – Kingfisher - hardened steel & stainless steel grease fittings Kinglok - angle grease fittings – Kinglok*

King Lifting Ltd King Road Avenue Avonmouth, Bristol BS11 9HF Tel. *0117 9821121* Fax. *0117 9235762* E-mail. *sales@kinglifting.co.uk* Web. *www.kinglifting.co.uk Versa Lifting*

Kingsdown Mid Kent Business Park Brook Street, Snodland ME6 5BB Tel. *01634 249555* Fax. *01634 249550* E-mail. *sales@kingsdownuk.com* Web. *www.kingsdownuk.com Kingsdown*

Kingsland Engineering Company Ltd Weybourne Road, Sheringham NR26 8HE Tel. *01263 822153* Fax. *01263 825667* E-mail. *peter@kingsland.com* Web. *www.kingsland.com Ironworkers – Kingsland*

Kingsmead Unit 34 Bookham Industrial Estate Bookham, Leatherhead KT23 3EU Tel. *01372 459678* Fax. *01372 454894* E-mail. *graham@kingmead.com* Web. *www.kingsmead.com Kingsmead Publications*

Kingspan Ltd Unit 2-4 Greenfield Business Park 2 Bagillt Road, Greenfield, Holywell CH8 7GJ Tel. *01352 716100* Fax. *01352 710161* E-mail. *tom.mcguinness@kingspan.com* Web. *www.kingspanpanels.co.uk Kingspan – Kingspan Envirodek – Kingspan Lo-Pitch – Kingspan Longspan – Kingspan Optimo – Kingspan Rooftile – Kingspan Thermabrick – Kingspan Thermastone – Kingspan Thermatile – Kingspan Tile Support – Kingspan WoodTherm – KS1000 Kingzip – Optimo*

Kingspan Insulation Ltd Torvale Industrial Estate Pembridge, Leominster HR6 9LA Tel. *08708 508555* Fax. *08708 508666* E-mail. *johntreanor@kingspan.com* Web. *www.insulation.kingspan.com Kingspan Purlcrete Chevron – Kingspan Purlcrete Promenade – Kingspan Styrodur 3035 C.S. – Kingspan Styrodur 3035 N – Kingspan Styrodur 3500 L – Kingspan Styrodur 4000 S – Kingspan Styrodur 5000 S – Kingspan Tapercork – Kingspan Thermafloor T.F.70 – Kingspan Thermafloor T.F.72* – Kingspan Thermafloor T.F.73 – Kingspan Thermaliner T.L.63 – Kingspan ThermalinervT.L.60 – Kingspan Thermapitch T.P.10 – Kingspan Thermaroof T.R.20 – Kingspan Thermaroof T.R.21 – Kingspan Thermaroof T.R.22 – Kingspan Thermaroof T.R.23 – Kingspan Thermaroof T.R.24 – Kingspan Thermaroof T.R.25 – Kingspan Thermaroof T.R.26 – Kingspan Thermaroof T.R.26 F.M. – Kingspan Thermaroof T.R.27 – Kingspan Thermaroof TR27FM – Kingspan Thermaroof TR31 – Kingspan Thermataper T.T.40 – Kingspan Thermataper T.T.42 – Kingspan Thermataper T.T.46 – Kingspan Thermataper TT47 – Kingspan Thermawall T.W.50 – Kingspan Thermawall T.W.51 – Kingspan Thermawall T.W.52 – Kingspan Thermawall T.W.53 – Kingspan Thermawall TW55 – Kooltherm – Kooltherm K1 – Kooltherm K10 – Kooltherm K2 – Kooltherm K3 – Kooltherm K5 – Kooltherm K5 E.W.B. – Kooltherm K7 – Kooltherm K8 – Nilflan – Niluent – Tekhaus*

Kings Road Tyres & Repairs Ltd Pump Lane, Hayes UB3 3NB Tel. *020 85614747* Fax. *020 85614012* E-mail. *accounts@kingsroadtyres.co.uk* Web. *www.kingsroadtyres.co.uk *Kingstone (Hungary)*

Kingston Communications Technology House Hemel Hempstead Industrial Est, Hemel Hempstead HP2 7DS Tel. *01908 442000* Fax. *01442 883315* E-mail. *me@kcom.com* Web. *www.kingstoncommunications.co.uk 3Com (U.S.A.) – Bay Networks (U.S.A.) – Cisco (U.S.A.) – Fully accredited with major manufacturers. – Newbridge (U.S.A.) – Siemens Network Systems – Vendor – Whittaker Xyplex (U.S.A.)*

Kingston Communications Telephone House 37 Carr Lane, Hull HU1 3RE Tel. *0800 9155777* Fax. *01482 320652* E-mail. *bill.halbert@kcom.com* Web. *www.kcom.co.uk Kingston Eclipse – Kingston Messenger*

Kingston Craftsmen Timber Engineering Ltd Cannon Street, Hull HU2 0AB Tel. *01482 225171* Fax. *01482 217032* E-mail. *sales@kingston-craftsmen.co.uk* Web. *www.kingston-craftsmen.co.uk Gluelam*

Kingstonian Paints Ltd Sculcoates Lane, Hull HU5 1DR Tel. *01482 342216* Fax. *01482 493096* E-mail. *info@kpaints.co.uk* Web. *www.kpaints.co.uk Fascinating Finishes – Mayflower*

Kingswood Canvas Ltd Unit 8-9 Douglas Road Industrial Park Douglas Road Kingswood, Bristol BS15 8PD Tel. *0117 9601281* Fax. *0117 9352632* E-mail. *kingswoodcanvas@btconnect.com* Web. *www.kingswoodcanvas.co.uk Chantelle*

Kingtools Norris Way, Rushden NN10 6BP Tel. *01933 410900* Fax. *01933 350471* E-mail. *dennis.dangerfield@kingtools.co.uk* Web. *www.kingtools.co.uk Portasign – Toolsafe*

King Trailers Ltd Riverside, Market Harborough LE16 7PX Tel. *01858 467361* Fax. *01858 467161* E-mail. *sales@kingtrailers.co.uk* Web. *www.kingtrailers.co.uk King – King - King Trailers - Skyking - Traiload - Swingthru - Wumag - GSR - Zwiehoff - Lolode – King Rail – King Trailers – SkyKing Equipment – Swingthru' International – Traiload – Wumag – Zwiehoff-Zagro*

King Vehicle Engineering Ltd Riverside, Market Harborough LE16 7PX Tel. *01858 467361* Fax. *01858 467161* E-mail. *sales@kingtrailers.co.uk* Web. *www.kingtrailers.co.uk GSR – King – King Highway Products – Lolode – SkyKing – Traiload – Wumag*

Kinnersley Engineering Ltd Kerswell Green, Worcester WR5 3PF Tel. *01905 371200* Fax. *01905 371049* Web. *www.kinnersleyengineering.co.uk Rentaweigh*

Kinnerton Confectionery Co. Ltd 53-79 Highgate Road, London NW5 1TL Tel. *020 72849500* Fax. *020 72489501* E-mail. *info@kinnerton.com* Web. *www.kinnerton.com Cheterfields Fine Foods – Kinnerton*

Kipfold Ltd Cheetwood House Cheetwood Road, Manchester M8 8AQ Tel. *0161 7924040* Fax. *0161 7922280* E-mail. *sales@kipfoldgroup.com* Web. *www.kipfoldgroup.com Chantal – Dream Lovers – May Fair – Sleepscene – Snowqueen*

Kirkpatrick Ltd PO Box 17, Walsall WS2 9NF Tel. *01922 620026* Fax. *01922 722525* E-mail. *enquiries@kirkpatrick.co.uk* Web. *www.kirkpatrick.co.uk Antique – Builders – Imak siccar*

Kirton Kayaks Ltd Marsh Lane Lords Meadow Industrial Estate, Crediton EX17 1ES Tel. *01363 773295* Fax. *01363 775908* E-mail. *sales@kirton-kayaks.co.uk* Web. *www.kirton-kayaks.co.uk Kirton – Klepper – Plastex*

Kistler Instruments Ltd Unit 13 Murrell Green Business Park London Road, Hook RG27 9GR Tel. *01256 741550* Fax. *01256 741551* E-mail. *sales.uk@kistler.com* Web. *www.kistler.com Kistler*

Kitchen Worktops London Unit 3 Abbey Industrial Estate 24 Willow Lane, Mitcham CR4 4NA Tel. *020 86851555* Fax. *020 86851777* E-mail. *business@dostone.co.uk* Web. *www.dostone.co.uk Do Stone*

Kitfix Swallow Group Ltd Castle Acre Road, Swaffham PE37 7HU Tel. *01760 721390* Fax. *01760 723717* E-mail. *sales@ksg.co.uk* Web. *www.sequinart.com Artfoil – Artwood Collage – Easi Stitch – Individual Crafts Range – Kitfix – Let's Cast – Masterpiece – Matchmaster – Paper Sculture – Pastiche Art – Pastimes Crafts Range – Pin Yarn – Sequin Art – Spare Moments*

Kittiwake Procal Ltd 5 Maxwell Road, Peterborough PE2 7HU Tel. *01733 232495* Fax. *01733 235255* E-mail. *post@procal.com* Web. *www.procal.com P.U.L.S.I.*

Kitz Corporation Windsor House Cornwall Road, Harrogate HG1 2PW Tel. *01423 875225* Fax. *01423 875226* E-mail. *office@kitzcorporation.com* Web. *www.kitzcorporation.com Kitz*

K K Balers Ltd Victory Park Road, Addlestone KT15 2AX Tel. *01932 852423* Fax. *01932 847170* E-mail. *sales@kkbalers.com* Web. *www.kkbalers.com Brickman – Dixi – K.K. Balers*

Klargester Environmental Ltd College Road North Aston Clinton, Aylesbury HP22 5EW Tel. *01296 633000* Fax. *01296 633001* E-mail. *david.anderson@klargester.com* Web. *www.klargester.com Fullstop*

Kleeneze Sealtech Ltd Ansteys Road Hanham, Bristol BS15 3SS Tel. *0117 9582450* Fax. *0117 9600141* E-mail. *sales@ksl.uk.com* Web. *www.ksltd.com Agriseal – Bumperseal – Escalator Safetystrip – Excel – Kam Conveyor Cleaners – Lift Guard – Rollaseal – Statstrip – Superseal – Tech Brush*

Klinge Chemicals Ltd 1 Bessemer Drive Kelvin Industrial Estate, East Kilbride, Glasgow G75 0QX Tel. *01355 238464* Fax. *01355 264328* E-mail. *enquiries@klinge-chemicals.co.uk* Web. *www.klinge-chemicals.co.uk LoSalt – Low Salt*

Klinger Ltd Klinger Building Wharfedale Road, Euroway Industrial Estate, Bradford BD4 6SG Tel. *01274 688222* Fax. *01274 688962* E-mail. *info@klingeruk.co.uk* Web. *www.klingeruk.co.uk Klingersil – PSM Antistick Graphite – Sealex*

Klingspor Abrasives Ltd 31-33 Retford Road, Worksop S80 2PU Tel. *01909 504400* Fax. *01909 504405* E-mail. *louisa.widderson@klingspor.co.uk* Web. *www.klingspor.co.uk *Kronenflex (Germany) – *R.-Flex (Germany) – *Sandflex (Germany)*

Klockner Pentaplast Ltd Unit 33-34 Fern Close Pen-Y-Fan Industrial Estate, Crumlin, Newport NP11 3EH Tel. *01495 241800* Fax. *01495 241811* E-mail. *g.peacock@kpfilms.com* Web. *www.kpfilms.com Alfoil – Pentaclear – Pentafood – Pentapharm – Pentaprint – Pentaprop*

K M P Crusader Manufacturing Co. Ltd Oldmedow Road, Kings Lynn PE30 4LD Tel. *01553 817200* Fax. *01553 691909* E-mail. *sales@kmp-uk.co.uk* Web. *www.kmp-europe.com *K.M.P. Brand (Germany)*

K M Products Europe Ltd Unit B The Forum, Chertsey KT16 9JX Tel. *01932 571991* Fax. *01932 571994* E-mail. *sales@kmpuk.com* Web. *www.kmpuk.com KMP Brand*

Knauf Drywall Kemsley Fields Business Park Ridham Dock, Iwade, Sittingbourne ME9 8SR Tel. *01795 424499* Fax. *01795 428651* E-mail. *info@knauf.co.uk* Web. *www.knauf.co.uk Fireboard Systems – Steel Building Systems*

Knauf Insulation Ltd PO Box 10, St Helens WA10 3NS Tel. *01744 24022* Fax. *0870 4005797* E-mail. *sales@knaufinsulation.com* Web. *www.knaufinsulation.co.uk Crown – Crown 100 Roll – Crown Dritherm – Crown Factoryclad – Crown Factoryclad S.E. – Crown Floor Slab – Crown Foiltherm – Crown Frametherm Batt – Crown Frametherm Roll U.F. – Crown Frametherm Roll V.B. – Crown Lamella – Crown Navy Board – Crown Pipe Insulation – Crown Rigid Duct Insulation – Crown Slabs – Crown Universal Ductwrap – Crown Wool – Crown Wool Combi-Roll – Icerock Ductwork – Icerock Rolls – Icerock Slabs – Paroc Pipe Insulation – Polyfoam Plus Agriboard 220 – Polyfoam Plus Cavity Closer – Polyfoam Plus Cavityboard – Polyfoam Plus Floorboard – Polyfoam Plus I.D.P. System – Polyfoam Plus Laminating Board – Polyfoam Plus Liner Board – Polyfoam Plus Pitched Roofboard – Polyfoam Plus R.V.B. – Polyfoam Plus Roofboard – Polyfoam Plus Sarking Board – Polyfoam Raft-R-Vent – Quietzone Acoustic Absorbers – Quietzone Acoustic Blanket – Quietzone Acoustic Floor Slab – Quietzone Acoustic Sealant – Quietzone Acoustic Shield – Quietzone Floor Foam – Quietzone Floorlam – Quietzone Liner Board – Quietzone Mufti-Lag – Quietzone Partition Batt – Quietzone Partition Roll – Quietzone Resilient Channel – Quietzone Sonic Liner – Quietzone Sound Deadening Quilt – Quietzone Studio Mattress – Rocksil – Rocksil Fire Protection Slabs – Rocksil Firetech 160 – Rocksil Firetech Ductslab – Rocksil Floor Slab – Rocksil Insulation Mat – Rocksil Lamella – Rocksil Pipe Insulation – Rocksil Roofmax – Rocksil Slabs – Rocksil Smoke and Fire Barrier – Supafil – Supawrap Pinkplus*

The Knife Sharpening Company 5 Henryson Road, London SE4 1HL Tel. *020 86905163* Fax. *020 86905163* E-mail. *info@knifesharpeningcompany.com* Web. *www.knifesharpeningcompany.com Tridentum,Dolomiten,Itaglia,Salvador,Mondini,Victo*

Knife Wizard A2 Murdock Road, Bicester OX26 4PP Tel. *01869 357700* Fax. *01869 357758* E-mail. *enquiries@knifewizard.co.uk* Web. *www.knifewizard.co.uk I.O Shen Mastergrade Triplex Steel Knives – Knife Wizard*

Knighton Tool Supplies 17 Lothair Road, Leicester LE2 7QE Tel. *0116 2834021* Fax. *0116 2440289* E-mail. *sales@knighton-tools.co.uk* Web. *www.knighton-tools.co.uk Aero – Bosch – Caterpillar – Dewalt – Dr Martins – Makita – Milwaukee – Timberland*

Knightsbridge Ltd 191 Thornton Road, Bradford BD1 2JT Tel. *01274 731442* Fax. *01274 736641* E-mail. *mmiller@knightsbridge-furniture.co.uk* Web. *www.knightsbridge-furniture.co.uk Knightsbridge*

Knight Scientific Ltd Unit 15 Wolseley Business Park Wolseley Close, Plymouth PL2 3BY Tel. *01752 565676* Fax. *01752 561672* E-mail. *info@knightscientific.com* Web. *www.knightscientific.com Abel*

Knight Strip Metals Ltd Saltley Business Park Cumbria Way, Saltley, Birmingham B8 1BH Tel. *0121 3228400* Fax. *0121 3228401* E-mail. *alan.woodhouse@knight-group.co.uk* Web. *www.knight-group.co.uk Knufoil*

Knight Strip Metals Ltd Linkside Summit Road Cranborne Road, Potters Bar EN6 3JB Tel. *01707 650251* Fax. *01707 651238* E-mail. *sales@knight-group.co.uk* Web. *www.knight-group.co.uk Knight – Knu Foil*

Knit and Sew (t/a Knitters & Sewers World) 21-22 Park Street, Swansea SA1 3DJ Tel. *0845 0940835* Fax. *01792 644535* E-mail. *sales@knitandsew.co.uk* Web. *www.knitandsew.co.uk Knitters and Sewers World*

Knollands Station Road, Chipping Norton OX7 5HX Tel. *0845 0945603* Fax. *01295 688261* E-mail. *wayne@knollands.co.uk* Web. *www.knollands.co.uk Knollands Septic Tanks & Drainage*

Knott-Avonride Ltd Unit 4 Spelter Site, Caerau, Maesteg CF34 0AQ Tel. *01656 739111* Fax. *01656 737677* E-mail. *rmorgan@knottuk.com* Web. *www.knottuk.com Avonride*

Knowledge Now Limited The Innovation Centre 217 Portobello Sheffield, Sheffield S1 4DP Tel. *0114 2242420* E-mail. *info@k-now.co.uk* Web. *www.k-now.co.uk/ K-Forms – K-Integrate – K-Now – K-Search – K-Store*

Knowledge Software Ltd 62 Fernhill Road, Farnborough GU14 9RZ Tel. *01252 520667* Fax. *01252 377226* Web. *www.knosof.co.uk Poptyser*

Knowledgewire Systems 4 Grosvenor Place, London SW1X 7HJ Tel. *0845 0945669* Fax. *020 78232602* E-mail. *info@knowledgewire.co.uk* Web. *www.KnowledgeWire.co.uk TalkSheet CRM*

R E Knowles Ltd Buxton Road Furness Vale, High Peak SK23 7PJ Tel. *01663 744127* Fax. *01663 741562* E-mail. *fred@hesmith.co.uk G.P.*

Knowsley S K Ltd Centrepoint Marshall Stevens Way, Trafford Park, Manchester M17 1AE Tel. *0161 8727511* Fax. *0161 8488508* E-mail. *sales@knowsleysk.co.uk* Web. *www.knowsleysk.co.uk Dominator – Fyrex – Knowsley – Striker*

Kobo UK Ltd Ketten House Leestone Road Sharston Industrial Area, Manchester M22 4RB Tel. *0161 4919840* Fax. *0161 4281999* E-mail. *info@kobo.co.uk* Web. *www.kobo.co.uk Kobo – Rosta*

Kodak Morley Howley Park Estate Morley, Leeds LS27 0QT Tel. *0113 2537711* Fax. *0113 2830499* E-mail. *hardingm@kpgraphics.com* Web. *www.kodak.com Capricorn – Emerald – Formula 1 – Gemini – Hi Speed Gemini – Hi Tone – Jupiter – Mercury Mark 5 – Monarch – Newstreet – Platestreet – Regal – Rolldamp – Scorpio – ULTRAtherm – ULTRAthin*

Kognitio Ltd 3a Waterside Park Cookham Road, Bracknell RG12 1RB Tel. *01344 300770* Fax. *01344 301424* E-mail. *info@kognitio.com* Web. *www.kognitio.com White Cross Systems*

Kohler Daryl Ltd Alfred Road, Wallasey CH44 7HY Tel. *0151 6065000* Fax. *0151 6380303* E-mail. *karger@daryl-showers.co.uk* Web. *www.daryl-showers.co.uk Daryl*

Kohler Mira Ltd Cromwell Road, Cheltenham GL52 5EP Tel. *08445 715000* Fax. *01242 724721* E-mail. *dave_hill@mirashowers.com* Web. *www.mirashowers.com Alstone – Meynell – Mira – Rada*

Koito Hampton Lovett Industrial Estate Kingswood Road, Hampton Lovett, Droitwich WR9 0QH Tel. *01905 790800* Fax. *01905 798432* E-mail. *david.bevan@koito-europe.co.uk* Web. *www.koito-europe.co.uk Britax Vega*

Kombimatec Machines Ltd Unit 10-11 Kingfisher Trading Estate Camford Way, Luton LU3 3AN Tel. *01582 562218* Fax. *01582 564468* E-mail. *derek.parsons@gtikombi.co.uk* Web. *www.kombimatec.com Kombimatec*

Komet Ltd Unit 4 Clico Business Park Hamel House, Tamworth B77 4DU Tel. *01827 302518* Fax. *01827 300486* E-mail. *info.uk@kometgroup.com* Web. *www.kometgroup.com Centron – Dihart – Duon – Duplon – Jel – Komet – Komtronic – Kub – Quatron – Trigon*

Komfort Workspace plc Unit 1-10 Whittle Way, Crawley RH10 9RT Tel. *01293 592500* Fax. *01293 553271* E-mail. *general@komfort.com* Web. *www.komfort.com 600 Series – Ekom-50 – Impression – K.M.3 – K7 – Kameo 50 – Kameo 75 – Klassic – Komfire 100 – Komfire-75 – Konfigure – Mirage – Polar*

Kompass (UK)Ltd St James's House 150 London Road, East Grinstead RH19 1XA Tel. *0800 0185882* Fax. *01342 327940* E-mail. *sales@kompass.co.uk* Web. *www.kompassinfo.co.uk Easybusiness (United Kingdom)*

Kompress Holdings Ltd Unit 5 Little Tennis Street, Nottingham NG2 4EL Tel. *0115 9581029* Fax. *0115 9584180* E-mail. *sales@kompress.com* Web. *www.kompress.com Kompress*

Kookaburra Reader Ltd Unit 25 The Alders Seven Mile Lane, Mereworth, Maidstone ME18 5JG Tel. *01622 812230* Fax. *01622 814224* E-mail. *sales@alfredreader.co.uk Allround – C. & D. – H.T.B. – Indoor – Sovereign – Tugite – Victa – Windian*

Kooltech Ltd 433-437 Hillington Road Hillington Park, Glasgow G52 4BL Tel. *0141 8830447* Fax. *0141 8835642* E-mail. *murray.sharp@kooltech.co.uk* Web. *www.kooltech.co.uk Kooltech*

Koppen & Lethem Ltd 3 Glenholm Park Brunel Drive, Newark NG24 2EG Tel. *01636 676794* Fax. *01636 671055* E-mail. *helen@koppen-lethem.co.uk* Web. *www.koppen-lethem.co.uk Braden – Frank and Pignard – Gearmatic – H.P.I. – Hawe – Koppen and Lethem – R.M.F.*

Korg UK Ltd 9 Newmarket Court Kingston, Milton Keynes MK10 0AU Tel. *01908 857100* Fax. *01908 857199* E-mail. *john@korg.co.uk* Web. *www.korg.co.uk *Korg UK (Japan)*

KOTHEA Fairfax Road, Teddington TW11 9BX Tel. *08702 854768* E-mail. *info@kothea.com* Web. *www.kothea.com KOTHEA*

Koyo UK Ltd Whitehall Avenue Kingston, Milton Keynes MK10 0AX Tel. *01908 289300* Fax. *01908 289333* E-mail. *info@koyo.co.uk* Web. *www.koyo.co.uk Koyo (UK)*

Kraft Foods UK Ltd St George's House Bayshill Road, Cheltenham GL50 3AE Tel. *01242 236101* Fax. *01242 512084* E-mail. *nbunker@krafteurope.com* Web. *www.krafteurope.com Bird's – Cafe Hag – Kenco – Kraft – Maxwell House – Philadelphia – Suchard*

Kramp UK Ltd Stratton Business Park, Biggleswade SG18 8QB Tel. *01767 602600* Fax. *01767 602620* E-mail. *info.agri.uk@kramp.com* Web. *www.kramp.com Agricultural parts suppliers – Zircon*

Kranzle UK Ltd Unit 6 Cedar Park Stock Road, Southend On Sea SS2 5QA Tel. *01702 603462* Fax. *01702 603488* E-mail. *sales@kranzle.co.uk* Web. *www.kranzle.co.uk Alto – Karcher – Kew – Kranzle – Quadro – Therm*

Kratos Analytical Ltd Trafford Wharf Road Trafford Park, Manchester M17 1GP Tel. *0161 8884400* Fax. *0161 8884401* E-mail. *info@kratos.co.uk* Web. *www.kratos.co.uk Amicus – Axima – Axis – Kompact*

K R L PO Box 5577, Glasgow G77 9BH Tel. *0141 6160900* Fax. *0141 8833686* E-mail. *krl@krl.co.uk* Web. *www.krl.co.uk E.L.M. – I.G.U.S. – Lochshore – Monarch – O.K.*

Krogab Unit 2 Station Road Goostrey, Crewe CW4 8PJ Tel. *01477 544144* Fax. *01477 544456* E-mail. *info@krogab.co.uk* Web. *www.krogab.co.uk *Krogab – *Krogab 100% Coffee – *Krogab Bag In Box Juice System – *Krogab Classic Pure Orange Juice – Krogab Toscane Coffee System*

Kromachem Ltd Unit 10-11 Moor Park Industrial Centre Tolpits Lane, Watford WD18 9ER Tel. *01923 223368* Fax. *01923 239308* E-mail. *info@kromachem.com* Web. *www.kromachem.com Florplast – Florstab – Kromacryl – Microfast – Microtint – Rad-Active – Rad-Color – Rad-Flow – Rad-Matt – Rad-Start – Rad-Wax – Waxpersion*

Kronoplus Ltd Maesgwyn Farm Holyhead Road Chirk, Wrexham LL14 5NT Tel. *01691 773361* Fax. *01691 773292* E-mail. *sales@kronospan.co.uk* Web. *www.kronospan.co.uk Keyboard – Kronofloor – Kronospan*

Kronos Ltd Barons Court Manchester Road, Wilmslow SK9 1BQ Tel. *01625 547200* Fax. *01625 533123* E-mail. *kronos.sales.uk@nli-usa.com* Web. *www.kronosww.com Kronos 1001 – Kronos 1014 – Kronos 1071 – Kronos 1074 – Kronos 1075 – Kronos 1077 – Kronos 1080 – Kronos 1171 – Kronos 2044 – Kronos 2047 – Kronos 2056 – Kronos 2059 – Kronos 2063 – Kronos 20635 – Kronos 2073 – Kronos 2081 – Kronos 2160 – Kronos 2190 – Kronos 2220 – Kronos 2222 – Kronos 2225 – Kronos 2230 – Kronos 2257 – Kronos 2300 – Kronos 2310 – Kronos 2330 – Kronos 2400 – Kronos 3000 – Kronos 3025*

K S B Ltd 2 Cotton Way, Loughborough LE11 5TF Tel. *01509 231872* Fax. *01509 215228* E-mail. *sales@ksb.com* Web. *www.ksb.com Amajet – Duojet – Amarex N – CK Pump Station – Ama Porter – Ama Porter ICS – Amarex KRT – Etanorm – Etabloc – Rio – Riotec – Riotherm – Multitec – Hyamat – Hya Solo – Boa – Boax – Isoria – Danais – Amtronic – Omega – Sewatec – Magnochem – Level Control – Ama Drainer – Boax B – Boostermat – Secochem – Movitec – Swing Amajet – Pump Expert – Pump Drive – Pump Control – CPK-N – Etaline*

K-Tron Great Britain Ltd 4 Acorn Business Centre Acorn Business Park Heaton Lane, Stockport SK4 1AS Tel. *0161 2094810* Fax. *0161 4740292* E-mail. *mplant@ktron.com* Web. *www.ktron.com Hurricane – Machinery manufrs*

KT Technology 5 Percy Street Office 4, London W1T 1BG Tel. *020 71932740* E-mail. *sales@kioskterminals.co.uk* Web. *www.kioskterminals.co.uk T / C / X series*

Kuehne & Nagel UK Ltd (Branch) Unit 0-1 Hazelmere Trading Estate Third Way, Avonmouth, Bristol BS11 9YE Tel. *0117 9827101* Fax. *0117 9824606* E-mail. *robert.jones@kuehne-nagel.com* Web. *www.kuehne-nagel.com Blue Anchor Line*

Kuhrt Leach LLP 81-82 Akeman Street, Tring HP23 6AF Tel. *01442 822880* Fax. *01442 381669* E-mail. *contact@kuhrtleach.com* Web. *www.kuhrtleach.com Kuhrt Leach LLP*

Kumi Solutions Ltd Unit 6 Innovation Centre St Davids Way, Bermuda Park, Nuneaton CV10 7SG Tel. *024 76350360* Fax. *05601 277115* E-mail. *simon@kumi-solutions.com* Web. *www.kumi-solutions.com Arrt International*

Kuoni Travel Ltd Kuoni House Deepdene Avenue, Dorking RH5 4AZ Tel. *01306 740888* Fax. *01306 744288* E-mail. *holidays@kuoni.co.uk* Web. *www.kuoni.co.uk Executive Occasions – Far East Travel Centre (F.E.T.C.) – Kuoni (Trade Fairs) – Kuoni Schools – Kuoni Travel – Perform Europe – Sport Abroad – The Travel Collection – UK Connection*

Kurt J Lesker Company Ltd (European H.Q.) 15-16 Burgess Road, Hastings TN35 4NR Tel. *01424 458100* Fax. *01424 421160* E-mail. *timp@lesker.com* Web. *www.lesker.com Luminos – Octos – Spectros – Torus*

Kurt Salmon Bruce Court 25a Hale Road, Altrincham WA14 2EY Tel. *020 77109500* Fax. *0161 9277135* E-mail. *manchester@kurtsalmon.com* Web. *www.kurtsalmon.com Kurt Salmon Associates*

Kutrite Of Sheffield Ltd 72 Russell Street, Sheffield S3 8RW Tel. *0114 2739977* Fax. *0114 2768876* E-mail. *sales@kutrite-of-sheffield.co.uk* Web. *www.kutrite-of-sheffield.co.uk Horse's Head (United Kingdom) – Kutrite (United Kingdom)*

Kuwait Petroleum GB Ltd Burgan House The Causeway, Staines TW18 3PA Tel. *01784 467788* Fax. *01784 467600* E-mail. *sales@kuwait.com* Web. *www.q8.co.uk Kuwait Fuelcare (Edenbridge) – Kuwait Fuelcare (Midlands) – Kuwait Fuelcare (North & Scotland) – Kuwait Fuelcare (South) – Kuwait Fuelcare (East)*

Kuwait Petroleum International Lubricants UK Ltd Kuwait Petroleum Lubricants Knowsthorpe Gate, Leeds LS9 0NP Tel. *0113 2350555* Fax. *0113 2485026* E-mail. *stuart.drom@kuwaitoils.com* Web. *www.q8oils.com Advanced – Bach – Beethoven – Brahms – Dynobear – Erebus – Gold X – Haydn – Priamus – Q.8 – Schubert – Super Plus*

Kween B Ltd 29 Dalkeith Road, Sutton Coldfield B73 6PW Tel. *0121 3552662* Fax. *0121 3558566* E-mail. *duncan@kweenb.co.uk* Web. *www.kweenb.co.uk P.A.L. (Taiwan)*

Kwik-Fit GB Ltd 216 East Main Street, Broxburn EH52 5AS Tel. *01506 856789* Fax. *01506 855912* E-mail. *info@kfis.co.uk* Web. *www.kwik-fit.com Kwik Fit*

L

L-3 T R L Technology Shannon Way Ashchurch, Tewkesbury GL20 8ND Tel. *01684 278700* Fax. *01684 850406* E-mail. *p_mckee@trltech.co.uk* Web. *www.l-3comm.com T.R.L. Technology*

Labco Brow Works Copyground Lane, High Wycombe HP12 3HE Tel. *01494 459741* Fax. *01494 465101* E-mail. *sales@labco.co.uk* Web. *www.labco.co.uk Cinbins – Exetainer*

Lab Craft Ltd Thunderley Hall Barns Thaxted Road, Wimbish, Saffron Walden CB10 2UT Tel. *01799 513434* Fax. *01799 513437* E-mail. *sales@labcraft.co.uk* Web. *www.labcraft.co.uk Alexa – Contour – Crystalite – Domino – Lab-Craft – Nordic – Pearl – Solitaire – Tempest – Tri-Lite – Twinspot*

Labelsco 29 Moat Way Barwell, Leicester LE9 8EY Tel. *01455 852400* Fax. *01455 841444* E-mail. *sales@labelsco.co.uk* Web. *www.labelsco.co.uk Labelsco*

Lablogic Systems Ltd Paradigm House 3 Melbourne Avenue Broomhill, Sheffield S10 2QJ Tel. *0114 2667267* Fax. *0114 2663944* E-mail. *solutions@lablogic.com* Web. *www.lablogic.com *Ambis – *B.-ram – Bioscan – Debra – G.C.-Ram – Laura – Marie – Sara*

Laboratory Facilities Ltd 24 Britwell Road Burnham, Slough SL1 8AG Tel. *01628 604149* Fax. *01628 667920* E-mail. *ataka@laboratoryfacilities.com* Web. *www.laboratoryfacilities.co.uk Ataka – Nilbite – NuNale Cream – NuNale Sapphire Nail File – Super NuNale Lotion*

Laboratory Sales UK Ltd Unit 20-21 Trans Pennine Trading Estate Gorrells Way, Rochdale OL11 2PX Tel. *01706 356444* Fax. *01706 860885* E-mail. *sales@ls-uk.com* Web. *www.ls-uk.com L.S.L.*

La Cafetiere Coast Road Greenfield Llanerch-Y-Mor, Holywell CH8 9DP Tel. *01352 717555* Fax. *01352 715699* E-mail. *john.jackson@lacafetiere.com* Web. *www.lacafetiere.com Cadnit – Corkscrew Co – Corkscrew Co., The – La Cafetiere – La Cafetiere – La Cafetiere Di Moda – Metropolitan – Rialta*

Lactosan UK Ltd Lacsan House 5 Swinbourne Drive, Braintree CM7 2YP Tel. *01376 342226* Fax. *01376 342132* E-mail. *enquiries@lactosan.co.uk* Web. *www.lactosan.com *Sanovo (Denmark)*

Ladco Sir William Smith Road Kirkton Industrial Estate, Arbroath DD11 3RD Tel. *01241 434444* Fax. *01241 434411* E-mail. *enquiries@macintyre.co.uk* Web. *www.macintyre.co.uk Anderson – Ladco Advanced Engineering – MacIntyre*

Ladder & Fencing Industries Newent Ltd Horse Fair Lane, Newent GL18 1RP Tel. *01531 820541* Fax. *01531 821161* E-mail. *david.walker@lfi-ladders.co.uk* Web. *www.lfi-ladders.co.uk L.F.I. (United Kingdom)*

Ladderfix Ltd Fairholme Avenue, Romford RM2 5UX Tel. *01268 732607* Fax. *01708 475113* E-mail. *sales@ladderfix.co.uk* Web. *www.ladderfix.co.uk Compacy – Extra – Ladderfix – Ladderscaff – Leveliser – Microlite – O.D. Wheels – Safety Base*

Ladybird Books Ltd 80 Strand, London WC2R 0RL Tel. *0845 3134444* Fax. *020 87574099* E-mail. *ladybird@uk.penguingroup.com* Web. *www.ladybird.co.uk Ladybird*

Lady Clare Ltd Oldends Lane Industrial Estate Oldends, Stonehouse GL10 3RQ Tel. *01453 824482* Fax. *01453 827855* E-mail. *info@lady-clare.com* Web. *www.lady-clare.com Lady Clare Ltd*

L A E Valeo Ltd Unit 4 Wissenden Corner Wissenden Lane, Bethersden, Ashford TN26 3EL Tel. *01233 822580* Fax. *01233 820701* E-mail. *sales@laeltd.co.uk* Web. *www.laeltd.co.uk Cibie – Osram – Prestolite – Valeo – Vignal*

La Furnitura, Ltd. Formations House 42, Crosby Road North Crosby, Liverpool L22 4QQ Tel. *020 81237263* Fax. *020 81817869* E-mail. *info@lafurnitura.com* Web. *lafurnitura.com La Furnitura, Ltd.*

Lakeland Alexandra Buildings, Windermere LA23 1BQ Tel. *01539 488200* Fax. *01224 620961* E-mail. *sam.rayner@lakeland.co.uk* Web. *www.lakeland.co.uk Lakeland Limited*

Lakes Bathrooms Ltd Alexandra Way Ashchurch, Tewkesbury GL20 8NB Tel. *01684 853870* Fax. *01684 276979* E-mail. *info@lakesbathrooms.co.uk*

Web. *www.lakesbathrooms.co.uk Italia Range – AllClear© – Lakes Collections – Provex Range*

Laltex & Co. Ltd Leigh Commerce Park Green Fold Way, Leigh WN7 3XH Tel. *01942 687000* Fax. *01942 687070* E-mail. *mail@laltex.com* Web. *www.laltex.com Lloytron*

La Maison des Sorbets Foods Ltd Unit 10 Gateway Industrial Estate Hythe Road, London NW10 6RJ Tel. *020 89680707* Fax. *020 89601332* E-mail. *sales@lmdsfoods.com* Web. *www.lamaisondessorbets.com *La Maison des Sorbets – *Les Glaciers – *Les Pâtissiers*

Lambourne Agricultural Consultants Ltd Grange Barn Birds Lane, Epwell, Banbury OX15 6LQ Tel. *01295 788006* Fax. *01295 788006* E-mail. *enquiry@ruralagriculturalconsultants.co.uk Alasdair Lowe*

Lambs Crener Whiting Sumpter Way Lower Road, Faversham ME13 7NT Tel. *01795 532610* Fax. *01403 784663* E-mail. *sales@lambsbricks.com* Web. *www.lambsbricks.com Cremer Whiting & Co.*

Lambson Fine Chemicals Ltd Cinder Lane, Castleford WF10 1LU Tel. *01977 510511* Fax. *01977 603049* E-mail. *sales@lambson.com* Web. *www.lambson.com Aquadose – Booster – Cutonic – Speedcure*

Lamina Dielectrics Ltd Daux Road, Billingshurst RH14 9SJ Tel. *01403 783131* Fax. *01403 782237* E-mail. *sales@lamina.uk.com* Web. *www.lamina.uk.com Insulotube – Plamar – Plamar - Plamaron - Plamec - Plamide - Plamon - InsulOtube. – Plamaron – Plamec – Plamide – Plamon*

Laminated Supplies Ltd Valletta House Valletta Street, Hull HU9 5NP Tel. *01482 781111* Fax. *01482 701185* E-mail. *info@hallmarkpanels.com* Web. *www.hallmarkpanels.com Specibord*

Lamphouse Ltd Fitzgerald House 9 Avenue Road, Doncaster DN2 4AH Tel. *08456 440100* Fax. *01302 563855* E-mail. *mike@lamphouse.co.uk* Web. *www.lamphouse.co.uk 3D Perception – 3M – Acer – ADI – Advert – Ampro – Anders Kern – Apollo – Apti – Ask – Avio – Barco – Benq – Boxlight – Canon – Casio – Chatanienrich – Christie – Citizen – Clarity – Compaq – CTX – Davis – Dell – Delta – Digital Projection – Dream Vision – Dukane – Eiki – Eizo – Electrohome – Elite Video – Elmo – Elux – Epson – Everest – Faqtor – Faraoudja – Fujitsu – Fujitsu-Siemens – Gateway – GE – Geha – Hewlett Packard – Hitachi – Hughes JVC – IBM – Iiyama – Infocus – IQI – Ixenon – JVC – Kinderman – Knoll – Kodax – Lasergraphics – LG – Liesegang – Lightware – Lumens – Luxeon – Maginin – Maranitz – Mediavision – Medion – Medium – Megapower – Metavision – Mitsubishi – Mix – Multuvision – Mustek – Navitar – NEC – Nobo – NView – OHP – Olympus – Optoma – Panasonic – Philips – Pioneer – Pkus – Planar – Plus – Polaroid – Premier – Projectiondesign – Projectioneurope – Prokia – Proxima – RCA – Reflectra – Reflex – Relisys – Rollei – Runco – Sagem – Sahara – Samsung – Sanyo – Sauerwein – Saville AV – Schneider AG – Scott – Seleco – Sharp – SIM2 – Smartboard – Sony – Studio Experience – Synelec – TA – Taxan – Telex – Thomson – Toshiba – Umax – Utax – Video 7 – Vidikron – Viewsonic – Vision – Vivitar – Xerox – Yamaha – Yokogawa – Zenith*

Lampitt Fire Escapes Lymore Ltd Keepers Road, Sutton Coldfield B74 3AX Tel. *0121 3531522* Fax. *0121 3531917* E-mail. *richard@lymore.com* Web. *www.lymore.com Davy – Firefly – Ingstrom Chute – Ladder-X-it*

Lamplighter Plastic Mouldings Ltd Unit L Mount Pleasant Street, Ashton Under Lyne OL6 9HX Tel. *0161 3431113* Fax. *0161 3395557* E-mail. *mprady@lamplighterproducts.co.uk* Web. *www.lamplighterproducts.co.uk Pyraclean*

Lanarkshire Welding Co. Ltd John Street, Wishaw ML2 7TQ Tel. *01698 264271* Fax. *01698 265711* E-mail. *enquiries@lanarkshirewelding.co.uk* Web. *www.lanarkshirewelding.co.uk Lanarkshire Welding*

Lancashire Glass & Solar Ltd Unit 1 George Business Park Cemetery Road, Southport PR8 5EF Tel. *01704 533888* Fax. *01704 501183* E-mail. *admin@lancsglass.co.uk* Web. *www.lancashire-glass.co.uk Lancashire Glass*

lancashire school of welding Unit 45 Hollins Grove Mill, Darwen, Blackburn BB3 1HG Tel. *07543 958289* E-mail. *welding_lst@live.co.uk* Web. *www.lancashireschoolofwelding.co.uk lancashire school of welding*

Lancashire Sock Manufacturing Co. Britannia Mill New Line, Bacup OL13 9RZ Tel. *01706 873188* Fax. *01706 879007* E-mail. *sales@lancashiresock.com* Web. *www.lancashiresock.com Brycham – Chamex – Eurocham – Luminex – Pearlex – Polycham*

Lancaster & Winter Ltd Brownroyd Street, Bradford BD8 9AE Tel. *01274 546303* Fax. *01274 481143* E-mail. *contact@lancasterwinter.co.uk* Web. *www.lancasterandwinterltd.co.uk Lancaster & Winter*

Lancer Labels Ltd Unit 26a Basepoint Enterprise Centre Stroudley Road, Basingstoke RG24 8UP Tel. *08458 330854* Fax. *028 704586883* E-mail. *info@lancerlabels.co.uk* Web. *www.lancerlabels.co.uk Armor – Datamax – Eltron – TEC – Zebra*

Lancing Linde Creighton Ltd Radial Point Dartmouth Road, Smethwick B66 1BG Tel. *0121 5243300* Fax. *0121 5243399* E-mail. *enquiries@linde-creighton.co.uk* Web. *www.linde-creighton.co.uk Lansing/Linde*

Lancing Marine (Prop: Bellamys (M & A) Ltd) 51 Victoria Road Portslade, Brighton BN41 1XY Tel. *01273 411765* Fax. *01273 430290* E-mail. *data@lancingmarine.com* Web. *www.lancingmarine.com *Barr (U.S.A.) – *Casale (U.S.A.) – *Castoldi (Italy) – Gaines – *Hydrodrive (Italy) – Jabsco – *Lombardini (Italy) – P.R.M. – *Starpower (U.S.A.) – *Sternpower (U.S.A.) – *Super-Trapp (U.S.A.) – *Trimmaster (U.S.A.)*

Landauer Ltd 25 Beaufort Court Admirals Way, London E14 9XL Tel. *020 75385383* Fax. *020 75382007* E-mail. *trading@landauerseafood.com* Web. *www.landauergroup.co.uk Elements of Spice – Tastee Foods*

Landlife Ltd Court Hey Park, Liverpool L16 3NA Tel. *0151 7371819* Fax. *0151 7371820* E-mail. *jpell@landlife.org.uk* Web. *www.landlife.org.uk Landlife*

Landlink Ltd North Bridge Road, Berkhamsted HP4 1EF Tel. *01442 879777* Fax. *01442 877720* E-mail. *info@landlinkltd.co.uk* Web. *www.landlinkltd.co.uk Landlink*

Land Machinery Ltd Redlake Trading Estate, Ivybridge PL21 0EZ Tel. *01752 891336* Fax. *01752 891338* E-mail. *info@pottingeruk.co.uk* Web. *www.landmecpottinger.co.uk Landmec*

Landor Associates Level 7 2 More London Riverside, London SE1 2AP Tel. *020 78808000* Fax. *020 78808001* E-mail. *london.reception@landor.com* Web. *www.landor.com Branding Consultants and Designers Worldwide*

Landowner Liquid Fertilizers Ltd Farley, Much Wenlock TF13 6NX Tel. *01952 727754* Fax. *01952 727755* E-mail. *info@landowner.co.uk* Web. *www.qlf.co.uk Fosfol – Magnifol*

Landsmans Ltd Brampton Road, St Neots PE19 5UJ Tel. *01480 810972* Fax. *01480 810287* E-mail. *landsmans-ltd@btconnect.com* Web. *www.landsmansloos.co.uk Landloo – Light Haulage Contractors – Midgi-Toilet – Mobile Exhibition Units – Mobile Mains Toilets – Mobile Mess Rooms – Recirculating Toilets – Site Offices – Steel Security Containers*

George Lane & Sons Ltd Bannerley Road, Birmingham B33 0SL Tel. *0121 7845525* Fax. *0121 7836988* E-mail. *info@georgelane.co.uk* Web. *www.georgelane.co.uk Min-Stretch Thin – Monogrid*

Lanemark International Ltd Whitacre Road Industrial Estate Whitacre Road, Nuneaton CV11 6BW Tel. *024 76352000* Fax. *024 76341166* E-mail. *info@lanemark.com* Web. *www.lanemark.com Thermimax*

Percy Lane Products Ltd Lichfield Road, Tamworth B79 7TL Tel. *01827 63821* Fax. *01827 310159* E-mail. *main@percy-lane.co.uk* Web. *www.percy-lane.co.uk Beclawat – Overton – Percy Lane – Percy Lane Products – Perry Lane Products – Perryform – Planet*

Lanfranchi Uk 34 Harrier Drive, Blackburn BB1 8LW Tel. *01254 694348* Fax. *01254 290054* E-mail. *alex@lanfranchi.co.uk* Web. *www.lanfranchi.co.uk Lanfranchi*

Langford Electronics UK Ltd Unit B19 Little Heath Industrial Estate Old Church Road, Coventry CV6 7NB Tel. *024 76700320* Fax. *024 76700321* E-mail. *sales@langfordelectronics.com* Web. *www.langfordelectronics.co.uk Sonomatic*

Langley Alloys Ltd The Wharf 504-506 Lowfield Dr, Newcastle ST5 0UU Tel. *01782 610250* Fax. *01782 612219* E-mail. *info@langleyalloys.com* Web. *www.langleyalloys.com Meighs*

Langstane Press Ltd (Head Office & Office Products Division) 1 Links Place, Aberdeen AB11 5DY Tel. *01224 212212* Fax. *01224 210066* E-mail. *sales@langstane.co.uk* Web. *www.langstane.co.uk Langstane Press*

Langtec Ltd Unit 1 Calder Court Altham, Accrington BB5 5YB Tel. *01282 772544* Fax. *01282 772740* E-mail. *info@langtec.co.uk* Web. *www.langtec.co.uk Filamic – Lantex – Spirex*

Lansing Linde Ltd Kingsclere Road, Basingstoke RG21 2XJ Tel. *01256 342000* Fax. *01256 342921* E-mail. *enquiries@linde-mh.co.uk* Web. *www.linde-mh.co.uk Lansing Linde*

Lantor UK 73 St Helens Road, Bolton BL3 3PP Tel. *01204 855000* Fax. *01204 61722* E-mail. *sales@lantor.co.uk* Web. *www.lantor.co.uk Lantor – Lantor C-Knit – Lantor Cube – Lantor Equaliser – Lantor Formflex – Lantor Formflex Duo – Lantor Formflex Natural – Lantor Synthetic*

Lanway Ltd PO Box 3568, Bewdley DY12 1ZU Tel. *01299 861733* Fax. *08717 333899* E-mail. *enquiries@lanway.ltd.uk* Web. *www.lanway.ltd.uk Lanway*

Lanxess Ltd Lichfield Road Branston, Burton On Trent DE14 3WH Tel. *01283 714200* Fax. *01283 714201* E-mail. *kim.oconnor@lanxess.com* Web. *www.lanxess.co.uk Decrotex – Hydrocol – Hydroferrox – Integra – Shadeacrete*

Lapmaster International Ltd North Road Lee Mill Industrial Estate, Ivybridge PL21 9EN Tel. *01752 893191* Fax. *01752 896355* E-mail. *sales@lapmaster.co.uk* Web. *www.lapmaster.co.uk Lapmaster – Lapmaster - lapping and polishing machines.*

La Porcellana Tableware International Ltd 1 Somers Place, London SW2 2AL Tel. *020 86715959* Fax. *020 86715956* E-mail. *info@laporcellana.co.uk* Web. *www.laporcellana.co.uk *Elivero Porcelain – *I V V – *Sambonet – *Schonwald*

Laptop Screen Online Flat 1 Cutberth Court 7 Malvern Grove, Manchester M20 1HT Tel. *0161 4347449* Fax. *0161 8840048* E-mail. *sales@laptopscreenonline.co.uk* Web. *www.laptopscreenonline.com Laptop Screen Online*

La Roche Unit 11-12 Danes Road, Romford RM7 0HL Tel. *01708 730488* Fax. *01708 749358* E-mail. *email@la-roche.co.uk* Web. *www.la-roche.co.uk *Diamond (Japan) – *Enarco (Spain) – *Hambi (Germany) – La Roche – *Laier (Germany) – *Lievers (Netherlands) – Schnell – *Ugarola (Spain)*

Laryngograph Ltd Laryngograph Limited 1 Foundry Mews, Tolmers Square, London NW1 2PR Tel. *020 73877793* Fax. *020 73832039* E-mail. *sales@laryngograph.com* Web. *www.laryngograph.com Laryngographs*

LaserPerformance Station Works Long Buckby, Northampton NN6 7PF Tel. *01327 841600* Fax. *01327 841651* E-mail. *shop.uk@laserperformance.com* Web. *www.lasersailing.com Dart 15 – Dart 16 – Dart 18 – Dart Hawk – Laser – Laser 16 – Laser 2000 – Laser 3000 – Laser 4000 – Laser 5000 – Laser Eps – Laser II Regatta – Laser Pico – Laser Radial*

Laser Trader Ltd Hillhouse Court New Road, Wingerworth, Chesterfield S42 6TD Tel. *01246 238670* Fax. *01246 269381* E-mail. *sales@lasertrader.co.uk* Web. *www.lasertrader.co.uk Amada – BLM-Adige – Bystronic – LaserLab – LVD – Mazak – Messr Greisham – Precitec – Prima – Salvagnini – Trumpf*

Laser Transport International Ltd Lympne Industrial Estate Lympne, Hythe CT21 4LR Tel. *01303 260471* Fax. *01303 264851* E-mail. *office@laserint.co.uk* Web. *www.laserint.co.uk Laser*

Latchways plc Waller Road, Devizes SN10 2JP Tel. *01380 732700* Fax. *01380 732701* E-mail. *info@latchways.com* Web. *www.latchways.com Constant Force (United Kingdom) – LadderLatch (United Kingdom) – Mansafe (United Kingdom) – PushLock (United Kingdom) – RotoLatch (United Kingdom) – Transfastener (United Kingdom)*

LatestSol Website Design & Development 72a Ilford Lane, Ilford IG1 2LA Tel. *020 84785532* E-mail. *info@latestsol.co.uk* Web. *www.latestsol.co.uk website design website development website hosting*

Latty International Ltd (in association with Latty International - France) Westfield Road, Retford DN22 7BT Tel. *01777 708836* Fax. *01777 707474* E-mail. *sales@latty.co.uk* Web. *www.latty.com Latty*

Launa Windows Bradley Mill Bradley Lane, Newton Abbot TQ12 1LZ Tel. *01626 367666* Fax. *01626 367668* E-mail. *info@launa.co.uk* Web. *www.launa.co.uk Launa*

Arnold Laver Call Collect (Gang-Nail Systems Ltd) Oxclose Park Road North Halfway, Sheffield S20 8GN Tel. *0114 2764800* Fax. *0114 2764801* E-mail. *sales@sheffield.timberworld.co.uk* Web. *www.arnoldlavertimberworld.co.uk Ecojoist*

Lawnet 93-95 Bedford Street, Leamington Spa CV32 5BB Tel. *01926 886990* Fax. *01926 886553* E-mail. *admin@lawnet.co.uk* Web. *www.lawnet.co.uk LawNet – LawNet Quality in Law*

Lawrence Industries Ltd Lawrence House Apollo Lichfield Road Industrial Estate, Tamworth B79 7TA Tel. *01827 314151* Fax. *01827 314152* E-mail. *sales@l-i.co.uk* Web. *www.l-i.co.uk 3M Glass Bubbles – A.S.P. – Aerosil – Agitan – Attagel – Attapulgus – Attasurf – Corn Cob – Edaplan – Emcor – Fullers Earth – Halox – Interfibre – Just Fiber – Metamax – Meteor – Metolat – Mica – Micaclad – Orgal – Porocel – Satintone – Sipernat – Solucote – Tafigel – Tamsil – Translink – Trockenperlen – Zeeospheres*

Lawson Consulting Church Gables Wilsthorpe, Stamford PE9 4PE Tel. *01778 429553* Fax. *07092 252676* E-mail. *info@lawsonconsulting.co.uk* Web. *www.lawsonconsulting.co.uk Cost Reduction Associates – Lawson Consulting – PracticeProfit*

Lawsons Fuses Ltd Meadowfield Ponteland, Newcastle upon Tyne NE20 9SW Tel. *01661 823232* Fax. *01661 824213* E-mail. *info@lawson-fuses.co.uk* Web. *www.lawson-fuses.co.uk Botlin – Clipfit – Lawson – Pullcap – Slydlok*

Laystall Engineering Company Ltd Dixon Street, Wolverhampton WV2 2BU Tel. *01902 451789* Fax. *01902 451539* E-mail. *martin.bowers@laystall.co.uk* Web. *www.laystall.co.uk Cromard – Laycarb*

Lazer Systems 36 Lawrence Avenue, New Malden KT3 5LY Tel. *020 84016818* Fax. *020 84016818* E-mail. *lazersystems@blueyonder.co.uk* Web. *www.lazersystems.co.uk Lazer System – SolaRay*

L B B C Technologies Beechwood Street Stanningley, Pudsey LS28 6PT Tel. *0113 2057400* Fax. *0113 2563509* E-mail. *sales@lbbc.co.uk* Web. *www.lbbc.co.uk Boilerclave – Dontlock – Mustlock – Quicklock – Surelock – Thermoclave – Wontlock*

L B Plastics Ltd Firs Works Heage Firs, Nether Heage, Belper DE56 2JJ Tel. *01773 852311* Fax. *01773 857080* E-mail. *info@lbplastics.co.uk* Web. *www.litchfield-group.co.uk Heritage – Hometrim – NuFrame – Nulene – Sheerblend – Sheercell – Sheerclad – Sheeredge – Sheerframe – Sheerframe Curtain Walling System – Sheerframe Louvre System – Sheerframe System 5000 – Sheerframe System 6000 – Sheerglide – Sheerline – Sheervent – Slimline – Timesaver – Twinwall*

L B S Group 6 Sterling Industrial Estate Rainham Road South, Dagenham RM10 8TX Tel. *020 85176655* Fax. *020 89840378* E-mail. *martin.olsen@lbsgroup.co.uk* Web. *www.lbsgroup.co.uk LBS Autodoor Systems – LBS Dagendor – LBS Diamondguard – LBS Doorguard SD & FD – LBS Fastguard – LBS Fenceguard – LBS Fire Curtain – LBS Fireguard – LBS Heatguard – LBS Homeguard 150 – LBS Homeguard 38 – LBS Induguard 75 – LBS Insugard 100 – LBS Insuguard F100 – LBS Permaguard – LBS Polyguard 90 – LBS Secureguard 150 – LBS Secureguard 229 – LBS Secureguard F150 – LBS Secureguard F229 – LBS Shopguard 178 – LBS Shopguard 230 – LBS Shopguard 75 – LBS Specialized Door Services – LBS Viewguard 75*

LBW Machines 7 Millbrook House 24 South Parade, Sutton Coldfield B72 1QY Tel. *0121 4489660* E-mail. *kieran@lineboringandwelding.com* Web. *www.lineboringandwelding.com LBW Machines*

L.C. Automation Ltd Duttons Way Shadsworth Business Park, Blackburn BB1 2QR Tel. *01254 685900* Fax. *01254 685901* E-mail. *sales@lca.co.uk* Web. *www.lcautomation.com L.C. Automation*

L C Designs Ltd London House Larkfield, Aylesford ME20 6SE Tel. *01622 716000* Fax. *01622 791119* E-mail. *raycarr@lc-designs.co.uk* Web. *www.lcdesigns.com Churchill – Dulwich design – Eurastyle – Eurostar – London Clock Co. – Rhythm – Timemaster*

L C H Clearnet Group Ltd Aldgate House 33 Aldgate High Street, London EC3N 1EA Tel. *020 74267000* Fax. *020 74267011* E-mail. *roger.liddell@lchclearnet.com* Web. *www.lchclearnet.com LCH - London Clearing House, The – LCH RepoClear – LCH SwapClear*

L D S Test & Measurment Ltd Jarman Way, Royston SG8 5BQ Tel. *01763 242424* Fax. *01763 249711* E-mail. *sales@lds-group.com* Web. *www.lds-group.com L.D.S. – Ling Dynamic – Ling Dynamic Systems*

Leach Lewis Ltd Victoria House Britannia Road, Waltham Cross EN8 7NU Tel. *01992 704100* Fax. *01992 704170* E-mail. *sales@leachlewis.co.uk* Web. *www.leachlewis.co.uk Leach Lewis Plant Ltd*

Leader Chuck Systems Ltd PO Box 16050, Tamworth B77 9JP Tel. *01827 700000* Fax. *01827 707777* E-mail. *information@leaderchuck.com* Web. *www.leaderchuck.com Hainbuch – Iram – Microcentric – Multichuck and Multivice Leader Gamet – Richard R Leader – Zweifel*

Leadership Development Ltd 495 Fulham Road, London SW6 1HH Tel. *020 73816233* Fax. *020 73816917* E-mail. *learning@ldl.co.uk* Web. *www.ldl.co.uk Leadership Development Ltd*

Lead Precision Machine Tools Ltd Calamine House Calamine Street, Macclesfield SK11 7HU Tel. *01625 434990* Fax. *01625 434996* E-mail. *fiona@leadmachinetools.co.uk* Web. *www.leadmachinetools.co.uk Breton – Hwacheon – Ibarmia – Leadwell – Microcut – Sachman*

Lea Manufacturing Co. Tongue Lane, Buxton SK17 7LN Tel. *01298 25335* Fax. *01298 79945* E-mail. *info@lea.co.uk* Web. *www.lea.co.uk CuB – Decoral – Emslie Fallows – FeB – Grainlock – Lea Compound – Leaflex – Learok Britelea – Learok Classic – Learok Ferrobrite – Learok Tripolea – LeaWeb – Liquabrade Ferrospray – Liquabrade Spraybrite – Liquabrade Tripospray – Liqualube – Lubar – Mastral – Menzerna – Plastibrade – Plastiglue – ProFin – Prosol – Royce – Satinex – Zenith*

Leamington Spa Courier 32 Hamilton Terrace Holly Walk, Leamington Spa CV32 4LY Tel. *01926 457777* Fax. *01926 451690* E-mail. *editorial@leamingtoncourier.co.uk* Web. *www.leamingtoncourier.co.uk Banbury Citizen – Banbury Guardian – Bicester Review – Buckingham Advertiser – Bucks Advertiser – Bucks Herald – Daventry Express – Hemel Hempstead Gazette – Hemel Hempstead Herald Express – Kenilworth Weekly News – Leamington Spa Courier – Leamington Spa Review – Rugby Advertiser – Rugby Review – T.V. Guide (Hemel) – T.V. Guide Aylesbury – Thame Gazette*

Lea Ray Retail Ltd Hertford House 122 St Mary's Road, Faversham ME13 8EG Tel. *01795 535353* Fax. *01795 536991* E-mail. *sales@learay.co.uk* Web. *www.learay.co.uk Plaaya*

Lear Corporation UK Ltd Glaisdale Parkway, Nottingham NG8 4GP Tel. *0115 9012200* Fax. *0115 9289688* Web. *www.lear.com Lear*

Learning & Teaching Scotland (Scottish Council for Educational Technology) 58 Robertson Street, Glasgow G2 8DU Tel. *0141 2825000* Fax. *01382 443645* E-mail. *b.mcleary@ltscotland.org.uk* Web. *www.ltscotland.org.uk Chronicle – Expression – Let's Go With Katy – Lifeskills Smart Spender – Lifeskills Time and Money – SCETNet – SCETPioneer – SCETWorks – Storybook CD-ROM – Writer's Toolkit*

Leaseplan UK Ltd 165 Bath Road, Slough SL1 4AA Tel. *01753 802000* Fax. *01753 802010* E-mail. *david.brennan@leaseplan.co.uk* Web. *www.leaseplan.co.uk Auto Leasing Europa – Barclays Vehicle Management Services – Dial Accident Management – Dial Contracts – Network Vehicles*

Leathams Ltd 227-255 Ilderton Road, London SE15 1NS Tel. *020 76354000* Fax. *020 76354040* E-mail. *customerservice@merchant-gourmet.com* Web. *www.leathams.co.uk Charcuti – Chefs Brigade – Merchants Gourment Chef's – SunBlush*

Leatherhead Food Research Randalls Road, Leatherhead KT22 7RY Tel. *01372 376761* Fax. *01372 386228* E-mail. *enquiries@lfra.co.uk* Web. *www.leatherheadfood.com Foodline*

Lea Valley Packaging Ltd 1 Lords Way, Basildon SS13 1TN Tel. *01268 885858* Fax. *01992 626328* E-mail. *sales@packer-products.co.uk* Web. *www.leapack.com Packer – Packpoint*

Leay Ltd Unit 1-3 Lake Road Quarry Wood, Aylesford ME20 7TQ Tel. *01622 882345* Fax. *01622 882208* E-mail. *enquiries@leay.com* Web. *www.leay.com Leay*

Lechler Ltd 1 Fell Street, Sheffield S9 2TP Tel. *0114 2492020* Fax. *0114 2493600* E-mail. *saraheccles@lechler.com* Web. *www.lechler.co.uk Lechler*

L E C Liverpool Ltd L E C House Picton Road, Wavertree, Liverpool L15 4LH Tel. *0151 7341411* Fax. *0151 7344054* E-mail. *sales@insette.com* Web. *www.insette.com Body Spray – Classix – Classix Hairspray and Mousse – Insett Air Freshner – Insette – Insette Furniture Polish – Insette Smells Nice Toilet Freshener – Insette Spikey – Shaving Foam – Spikey*

Lectros International Ltd Unit 3 Boran Court Network 65 Business Park, Hapton, Burnley BB11 5TH Tel. *0845 4006666* Fax. *0845 4003333* E-mail. *sales@lectros.com* Web. *www.lectros.com Lectros*

Leec Ltd Private Road 7 Colwick Industrial Estate, Nottingham NG4 2AJ Tel. *0115 9616222* Fax. *0115 9616680* E-mail. *general@leec.co.uk* Web. *www.leec.co.uk Duoduct – Leec*

Lee-Dickens Ltd Rushton Rd Desborough, Kettering NN14 2QW Tel. *01536 760156* Fax. *01536 762552* E-mail. *sales@lee-dickens.co.uk* Web. *www.lee-dickens.co.uk Alphabet Blocks – BM SERIES – BD SERIES – AlphaDIN – AlphaMINI – HP400/HP500 Series – ID Series – ID/IDT Series – MicroDin – Noflote – Q.C. Series – Sitewatch – Tektor – Telstor*

Leek United Building Society 50 St Edward Street, Leek ST13 5DL Tel. *01538 384151* Fax. *01538 399179* E-mail. *finance@leekunited.co.uk* Web. *www.leekunited.co.uk Leek United Building Society – Pyramid*

J B & S Lees Trident Steel Works Albion Road, West Bromwich B70 8BH Tel. *0121 5533031* Fax. *0121 5537680* E-mail. *eugene.harkins@jbslees.co.uk* Web. *www.caparo.com Trident*

Lees Newsome Ltd Rule Business Park Grimshaw Lane, Middleton, Manchester M24 2AE Tel. *08450 708005* Fax. *0845 0708006* E-mail. *philip@leesnewsome.co.uk* Web. *www.leesnewsome.co.uk Ashley Mill*

Lee Spring Ltd Latimer Road, Wokingham RG41 2WA Tel. *0118 9781800* Fax. *0118 9774832* E-mail. *sales@leespring.co.uk* Web. *www.leespring.co.uk Lee Spring*

Lees Of Scotland Ltd North Caldeen Road, Coatbridge ML5 4EF Tel. *01236 441600* Fax. *01236 441601* E-mail. *sales@leesofscotland.co.uk* Web. *www.leesofscotland.co.uk Heather Cameron Foods – Lees'*

Legal & General Group P.L.C. (Head Office) (Holding Company) Temple Court 11 Queen Victoria Street, London EC4N 4TP Tel. *020 75286200* Fax. *020 75286222* Web. *www.legalandgeneral.com Legal & General – Legal & General Assurance Society Ltd (United Kingdom)*

Legend Signs Ltd 1 Benham Business Park Ashford Road, Newingreen, Hythe CT21 4JD Tel. *01303 261278* Fax. *01303 261280* E-mail. *info@legendsigns.co.uk* Web. *www.legendsigns.co.uk Kullasigns – Signax*

Lego UK Ltd 33 Bath Road, Slough SL1 3UF Tel. *01753 495000* Fax. *01753 495100* E-mail. *sales@lego.com* Web. *www.lego.com *DUPLO (Denmark) – *LEGO (Denmark) – Lego Mindstorms – *Lego Technic (Denmark) – Z'Nap*

Legrand 20 Great King Street North, Birmingham B19 2LF Tel. *0121 5150515* Fax. *0121 5150516* E-mail. *philip.middlemast@legrand.co.uk* Web. *www.legrand.com Tenby*

Leica Camera Ltd Davy Avenue Knowlhill, Milton Keynes MK5 8LB Tel. *01908 256400* Fax. *01908 609992* E-mail. *dgailliez@leica-camera.co.uk* Web. *www.leica-camera.co.uk *Leica (Germany) – *Minox (Germany)*

Leica Microsystems Davy Avenue Knowlhill, Milton Keynes MK5 8LB Tel. *01908 246246* Fax. *01908 609992* E-mail. *ukinfo@leica-microsystems.com* Web. *www.leica-microsystems.co.uk E.B.P.G. 5000 – Lion – Vectorbeam – ZBA Services*

Leica Microsystems Cambridge Ltd Lothbury House Newmarket Road, Cambridge CB5 8PB Tel. *01223 411411* Fax. *01223 210692* E-mail. *ia-support@lis.leica.co.uk* Web. *www.leica-microsystems.com Leica Microsystems Imaging Solutions*

Leicester Mail Ltd St Georges Street, Leicester LE1 9FQ Tel. *0116 2512512* Fax. *0116 2624687* E-mail. *enquiries@leicestermercury.co.uk* Web. *www.thisisleicestershire.co.uk Leicester Mercury Group Ltd – Mercury Distribution*

Leigh House Facilities Management Ltd Leigh House Varley Street, Stanningley, Pudsey LS28 6AN Tel. *0113 2557979* Fax. *0113 2557970* E-mail. *mail@leighhouse.com* Web. *www.leighhouse.com Leigh House*

Leighs Paints Tower Works Kestor Street, Bolton BL2 2AL Tel. *01204 521771* Fax. *01332 371115* E-mail. *enquiries@leighspaints.com* Web. *www.leighspaints.com Arpax – Biogard – Dox Anode – Envirogard – Epidek – Epigrip – Firetex – Jetrone – Leigh's – Leighs Roadline – Metagard – Metagrip – Nulon – Resistex – Vitaglo*

Leigh Spinners Ltd Park Lane, Leigh WN7 2LB Tel. *01942 673232* Fax. *01942 261694* E-mail. *sales@leighspinners.com* Web. *www.leighspinners.com Leigh Spinners*

Leighton Buzzard Observer & Citizen 17 Bridge Street, Leighton Buzzard LU7 1AH Tel. *01525 858400* Fax. *01525 850043* E-mail. *news@lbobserver.co.uk* Web. *www.leightonbuzzardtoday.co.uk Leighton Buzzard Observer*

Leisuredrive Ltd Unit 4 Fishbrook Industrial Estate, Kearsley, Bolton BL4 8EL Tel. *01204 574498* Fax. *01204 574488* E-mail. *derek.andrews@leisuredrive.co.uk* Web. *www.leisuredrive.co.uk Crusader – Occasion – Renoir – Vivante*

Leitz Tooling UK Ltd Flex Meadow The Pinnacles, Harlow CM19 5TN Tel. *01279 454530* Fax. *01279 454509* E-mail. *salesuk@leitz.org* Web. *www.leitz.org Keil – Leitz – P.C.D. Tooling*

L E K Sales 30 Cumber Lane Whiston, Prescot L35 2XQ Tel. *0151 4307158* Fax. *0151 4269116* E-mail. *info@beka-max.co.uk* Web. *www.beka-max.co.uk Beka-max – Vogel*

Lemon Groundworks Russell Gardens, Wickford SS11 8BH Tel. *01268 571571* Fax. *01268 571555* E-mail. *wickford@lemon-gs.co.uk* Web. *www.lemon-gs.co.uk Cellcore – Clayboard – Claymaster – Eazistrip – Groundform*

Lemo UK Ltd 12-20 North Street, Worthing BN11 1DU Tel. *01903 234543* Fax. *01903 206231* E-mail. *uksales@lemo.com* Web. *www.lemo.co.uk Coelver (Switzerland) – *Lemo (Switzerland) – Redel (Switzerland)*

Lemsford Metal Products 1982 Ltd 24 Hyde Way, Welwyn Garden City AL7 3UQ Tel. *01707 323725* Fax. *01707 373059* E-mail. *sales@lemsford.co.uk* Web. *www.lemsford.co.uk Elwood Clamp (United Kingdom) – Lemsford Cases (United Kingdom)*

Len Beck 443 Endike Lane, Hull HU6 8AG Tel. *01482 852131* Fax. *01482 805850* E-mail. *lenbeck@lenbeck.karoo.co.uk* Web. *www.lenbeck.co.uk Beks*

Lennox Industries Cornwell Business Park Salthouse Road, Brackmills, Northampton NN4 7EX Tel. *01604 669100* Fax. *01604 669150* E-mail. *info.uk@lennoxeurope.com* Web. *www.lennoxuk.com Lennox*

Lenze UK Ltd Lenze Limited Caxton Road Elm Farm, Elm Farm Industrial Estate, Bedford MK41 0HT Tel. *01234 321200* Fax. *01234 261815* E-mail. *sales@lenze.co.uk* Web. *www.lenze.co.uk Baumann (Switzerland) – E.T.P. (Sweden) – Ferri (Italy) – G-Motion (Germany) – HexaFlex (Germany) – Lenze (Germany) – Lovejoy (U.S.A.) – Moditorque (Germany) – Monninghoff (Germany) – Panasonic – Patlite (Japan) – Rexneed – Ruland (U.S.A.) – Servomech (Italy) – Simplabelt (Germany) – Simplabloc (Germany) – Simplaflex (Switzerland) – Simplatroll (Germany) – Simplavolt – SIT (Italy) – Spaggiari (Italy) – Stockline (Italy) – Thalheim (Germany) – Tollok (Italy) – Vogel (Germany)*

Leonardt Ltd New Road Highley, Bridgnorth WV16 6NN Tel. *01746 861203* Fax. *0121 6153352* E-mail. *info@leonardt.com* Web. *www.leonardt.com Leonardt & Co – Berkeley & Co.*

Leoni-Temco Ltd Whimsey Industrial Estate Whimsey, Cinderford GL14 3HZ Tel. *01594 820100* Fax. *01279 816270* E-mail. *general@leonitemco.com* Web. *www.leoni-special-conductors.com Leoni*

Lesney Industries Ltd Norwood House Temple Bank, Harlow CM20 2DY Tel. *01279 260130* Fax. *01279 413100* E-mail. *sales@lesney.co.uk* Web. *www.lesney.co.uk Lesney*

Letchford Supplies Ltd 2 Bourne Enterprise Centre Wrotham Road, Borough Green, Sevenoaks TN15 8DG Tel. *01732 882633* Fax. *01732 884551* E-mail. *lee@letchford-supplies.co.uk* Web. *www.letchford-supplies.co.uk 3M – Devil Biss – Du Pont – Farecla – RM Automotive – Sata – Sealey – Standox – UPOL*

Letchworth self storage limited 1 Works Road Corner of Pixmore Ave, Letchworth Garden City SG6 1FR Tel. *01462 674666* E-mail. *info@thesecure-store.com* Web. *www.thesecure-store.com The Secure-store*

Letraset Ltd Kingsnorth Industrial Estate Wotton Road, Ashford TN23 6FL Tel. *01233 624421* Fax. *01233 658877* E-mail. *enquiries@letraset.com* Web. *www.letraset.com Fontek – Letraline – Letraset – Letratone – Pantone – Pantone Books (U.S.A.) – Phototone – TRIA – Tria Marker*

Lettershop Group Whitehall Park Whitehall Road, Leeds LS12 5XX Tel. *0113 2311113* Fax. *0113 2311444* E-mail. *info@tlg.co.uk* Web. *www.tlg.co.uk Laser Folio – Laser Royal – Laserlope*

Charles Letts Group Ltd Thornybank Industrial Estate, Dalkeith EH22 2NE Tel. *0131 6631971* Fax. *0131 6603225* E-mail. *gpresly@letts.co.uk* Web. *www.letts.co.uk Letts – Letts of London – Letts Year Plan – Quikref – Slim – Timeplan*

James Lever & Sons Ltd Unit 26 Morris Green Business Park Fearnhead Street, Bolton BL3 3PE Tel. *01204 61121* Fax. *01204 658154* E-mail. *james@jameslever.co.uk* Web. *www.jameslever.co.uk Blue Wrapper – Everlasto – Kleenwash – Longlast – Orient – Superbraid – Wyercentor – Wyercentor - Clothes Line, Superbraid - Sash Cord, Orient - Clothes line, Longlast - Clothes Line, Everlasto - Ropes, twines, cord, Blue Wrapper - Sash Cord Waxed*

Levolux A T Ltd Levolux House 24 Eastville Close Eastern Avenue, Gloucester GL4 3SJ Tel. *01452 500007* Fax. *01452 527496* E-mail. *sales@levoluxat.co.uk* Web. *www.levolux.co.uk Levelox Smoke Curtains – Levolux – Levolux – Levolux – Levolux – Levolux – Levolux Easi Hook – Levolux Easi Roller – Levolux External Sunbreaker Fin System – Levolux Fascade – Levolux Markisolette – Levolux Matrix – Levolux Rollscreen – Levolux Skyvane – Levolux Slimgroove – Levolux Solashade – Levolux Ventilation Louvre – Levolux Walk-On Brise Soleil – Levolux Window Curtains*

Levy Gems Ltd Minerva House 26-27 Hatton Garden, London EC1N 8BR Tel. *020 72424547* Fax. *020 78310102* E-mail. *info@levygems.co.uk Levy Gems*

A Lewis & Sons Willenhall Ltd 47 Church Street, Willenhall WV13 1QW Tel. *01902 605428* Fax. *01902 601181* E-mail. *lewislocksltd@aol.com* Web. *www.lewislocksltd.co.uk A. Lewis & Sons*

Chris Lewis Faraday House 38 Poole Road, Bournemouth BH4 9DW Tel. *01202 751599* Fax. *01202 759500* E-mail. *sales@chrislewissecurity.co.uk* Web. *www.chrislewissecurity.co.uk Meggitt Marsh Guardian Systems*

Lewis & Hill Lazarus Court Woodgate, Rothley, Leicester LE7 7NR Tel. *0116 230485* E-mail. *enquiries@lewisandhill.co.uk* Web. *www.lewisandhill.co.uk Lewis&Hill*

R G Lewis Ltd 29 Southampton Row, London WC1B 5HL Tel. *020 72422916* Fax. *020 78314062* E-mail. *sales@rglewis.co.uk* Web. *www.rglewis.co.uk Leica*

Samuel Lewis Ltd PO Box 65, Cradley Heath B64 5PP Tel. *0121 5612157* Fax. *0121 5615273 Lewis Anglo*

Lewis's Medical Supplies Bankside Business Park Coronation Street, Stockport SK5 7PG Tel. *0161 4806797* Fax. *0161 4804787* E-mail. *sales@lewis-plast.co.uk* Web. *www.lewis-plast.co.uk *Lewis-Grip (United Kingdom) – *Lewis-Plast (United Kingdom) – *Lewis-Sauz (United Kingdom)*

Lewmar Ltd South Moore Lane, Havant PO9 1JJ Tel. *023 92471841* Fax. *023 92485770* E-mail. *reception@lewmar.com* Web. *www.lewmar.com Lewmar Marine*

Lexcast Ltd Ashbrow Mills Ashbrow Road, Huddersfield HD2 1DU Tel. *01484 513833* Fax. *01484 534131* E-mail. *malcolm@lexcast.co.uk* Web. *www.lexcast.co.uk Lexcast*

L G C Executive Search 148 Westbury Road Westbury-on-Trym, Bristol BS9 3AL Tel. *0117 9046504* Fax. *0117 9046504* E-mail. *les@lgcexecsearch.com* Web. *www.lgcexecsearch.com LGC Executive Search*

L G S A Marine 67-83 Mariners House Queens Dock Commercial Centre Norfolk S, Liverpool L1 0BG Tel. *0151 7072233* Fax. *0151 7072170* E-mail. *liverpool@lgsamarine.co.uk* Web. *www.lgsamarine.co.uk LGSAmarine (United Kingdom)*

Lhoist UK Hindlow, Buxton SK17 0EL Tel. *01298 768666* Fax. *01298 768667* E-mail. *sales@lhoist.co.uk* Web. *www.lhoist.co.uk Saniblanc D – Neutralac – Proviacal – Sorbacal – Tradical*

L H Safety Ltd Greenbridge Works Fallbarn Road, Rossendale BB4 7NX Tel. *01706 235100* Fax. *01706 235150* E-mail. *enquiries@lhsafety.co.uk* Web. *www.lhsafety.co.uk A.B.S. (Italy) – Capps (China) – Footlites – Globe Trotters (Italy) – Redwood – Redwood (China) – Redwood (Portugal) – Redwood (Vietnam)*

Libran Laminations Ltd The Finishing Factory Unit 4 156 Coles Green Road, London NW2 7HW Tel. *020 84522006* Fax. *020 84524456* E-mail. *info@libranlaminations.co.uk* Web. *www.libranlaminations.co.uk Elephant Planners (United Kingdom) – Libran Laminators (United Kingdom) – Wembley Laminations (United Kingdom)*

Librex Ltd Colwick Road, Nottingham NG2 4BG Tel. *0115 9504664* Fax. *0115 9586683* E-mail. *sales@librex.co.uk* Web. *www.librex.co.uk Librex*

Robert Lickley Refractries Ltd PO Box 24, Dudley DY1 2RL Tel. *01902 880123* Fax. *01902 880019* E-mail. *admin@robertlickley.co.uk* Web. *www.robertlickley.co.uk Arel*

Liebherr-Great Britain Ltd Normandy Lane Stratton Business Park, Biggleswade SG18 8QB Tel. *01767 602100* Fax. *01767 602110* E-mail. *info.lgb@liebherr.com* Web. *www.liebherr.com/lh/ *Liebherr-Great Britain (Germany)*

Lifeline Fire & Safety Systems Ltd Burnsall Road Industrial Estate Burnsall Road, Coventry CV5 6BU Tel. *024 76712999* Fax. *024 76712998* E-mail. *sales@lifeline-fire.co.uk* Web. *www.lifeline-fire.co.uk Lifeline Fire Systems*

Lifeplan Products Ltd Unit 1 Elizabethan Way, Lutterworth LE17 4ND Tel. *01455 556281* Fax. *01455 556261* E-mail. *enquiries@lifeplan.co.uk* Web. *www.lifeplan.co.uk Lifeplan – Mortons*

Lifting Gear Products (Europa Engineering Ltd) Goliath Works 395 Petre Street, Sheffield S4 8LN Tel. *0114 2443456* Fax. *0114 2433373* E-mail. *lgp@liftinggearprod.co.uk* Web. *www.liftinggearprod.co.uk Goliath*

Liftstore Ltd Unit 15 Manor Farm Industrial Estate, Flint CH6 5UY Tel. *01352 793222* Fax. *01352 793255* E-mail. *r.young@liftstore.com* Web. *www.liftstore.com T.V.C.L.*

Lightdome Road Products 4 Fielder Drive, Fareham PO14 1JE Tel. *01329 284780* Fax. *01329 829485* E-mail. *sales@lightdome.co.uk* Web. *www.lightdome.co.uk Cats Eyes*

Light Fantastic 12 Cambridge Street, St Neots PE19 1JL Tel. *01480 407872* Fax. *01480 219343* E-mail. *sales@lightfan.co.uk* Web. *www.lightfan.co.uk Brooklands Brass Lighting – Dar Lighting – David Hunt Lighting – Eglo Lighting – Egoluce – Elstead Lighting – Endon Lighting – Fantasia Ceiling Fans – Firstlight – Franklite Lighting – Ghidine Lighting – Grossmann Lighting – Intalite – Interiors 1900 – Loxton Lighting – Oaks Lighting – Quality Lighting Design – Searchlight Electric – Smithbrook Lighting – Vibia Lighting*

Charles Lightfoot Ltd Orchard House Heywood Road, Brooklands, Sale M33 3WB Tel. *0161 9736565* Fax. *0161 9625335* E-mail. *info@charleslightfoot.co.uk* Web. *www.charleslightfoot.co.uk Deltos*

Lightsource Event Technology Ltd Fox Studio King Street, Much Wenlock TF13 6BL Tel. *01952 727715* Fax. *08704 204316* E-mail. *lights@lightsource.co.uk* Web. *www.lightsource.co.uk Biz Presentation – Light Source Digital Video*

Lignacite Ltd Norfolk House High Street, Brandon IP27 0AX Tel. *01842 810678* Fax. *01842 814602* E-mail. *info@lignacite.co.uk* Web. *www.lignacite.co.uk Apollo – Lignacite*

Lignacite Ltd Meadgate Works Meadgate Road, Nazeing, Waltham Abbey EN9 2PD Tel. *01992 464441* Fax. *01992 445713* E-mail. *alan@lignacite.co.uk* Web. *www.lignacite.co.uk Lignacite – Lignacrete*

Lil-lets UK Ltd PO Box 14568, Solihull B91 9LN Tel. *08456 020061* Fax. *0121 3276172* E-mail. *corporate@lil-lets.com* Web. *www.lil-lets.co.uk Atrixo – Dr Whites – Dr Whites Allnights – Dr Whites Contour – Dr Whites Maxi – Dr Whites Panty Pads – Dr Whites Secrets – Elastoplast – Labello – Lil-lets – Limara – Nivea – Nivea Facials – Simple – Tender Touch*

John Lilley & Gillie Ltd Unit 17 Elm Road, North Shields NE29 8SE Tel. *0191 2572217* Fax. *0191 2571521* E-mail. *sales@lilleyandgillie.co.uk* Web. *www.lilleyandgillie.co.uk Francis – Gillie – Sestrel*

Lillywhites 24-36 Regent Street, London SW1Y 4QF Tel. *08443 325602* Fax. *020 79302330* Web. *www.lillywhites.com Lillywhites*

Limab UK Unit 3I Westpark, Chelston, Wellington TA21 9AD Tel. *01823 668633* E-mail. *john.miller@limab.co.uk* Web. *www.limab.co.uk LIMAB*

Limagrain UK Ltd Camp Road Witham St Hughs, Lincoln LN6 9TW Tel. *01522 861300* Fax. *01522 869703* E-mail. *limagrain@advanta-seeds.co.uk* Web. *www.limagrain.co.uk Alaska – Baroness – Camargue – Compass – Corniche – Derkado – Designer – Elka – Energy – Grafila – Hanna – Kyros – Monarch – Norlin – O.R.B. – Princess – Samson*

Lime Technical Recruitment Lime House 102 High Street, Stevenage SG1 3DW Tel. *01438 362088* E-mail. *info@lime-tr.co.uk* Web. *www.lime-tr.co.uk Lime*

Linacre Plant & Sales Ltd Boundary Road, St Helens WA10 2PZ Tel. *01744 751237* Fax. *01744 20318* E-mail. *sales@linacrehire.co.uk* Web. *www.linacrehire.co.uk Bosch – Makita – Portwest – Tuskers*

Linak UK Actuation House Crystal Drive Sandwell Business Park, Smethwick B66 1RJ Tel. *0121 5442211* Fax. *0121 5442552* E-mail. *louisee@linak.co.uk* Web. *www.linak.co.uk Careline – Desklift – Deskline – Deskpower – Homeline – Jumbo – Jumbo Home – Linak Power – LINAK – Medline – Netline – Techline – Twindrive*

Linatex Ltd Wilkinson House Galway Road Blackbushe Business Park, Yateley GU46 6GE Tel. *01252 743000* Fax. *01252 743030* E-mail. *helen.kenward@linatex.com* Web. *www.linatex.com Enviromat – Flexdek – Linaclad – Linacut – Linadek – Linaflex – Linaflow – Linapump – *Linard (Malaysia) – *Linatex (Malaysia)*

Lincat Ltd Whisby Road, Lincoln LN6 3QZ Tel. *01522 875555* Fax. *01522 875530* E-mail. *sales@lincat.co.uk* Web. *www.lincat.co.uk Lynx – Opus 700 – Opus Combis – Panther – Seal – Silver Link*

Lincoln Cleaning Technology 179, Batley Road,, Wakefield WF2 0AH Tel. *01924 820876* Fax. *01924 826830* E-mail. *info@lincolncleaningtechnology.co.uk* Web. *www.lincolncleaningtechnology.co.uk Lincoln Cleaning Machines*

Lincoln Electric UK Ltd Mansfield Road Aston, Sheffield S26 2BS Tel. *0114 2872401* Fax. *0114 2872582* E-mail. *salesuk@lincolnelectric.eu* Web. *www.lincolnelectric.eu Arosta – Fleetweld – Harris – Idealarc – Innershield – Invertec – Limarosta – Lincolnweld – Magnum – Outershield – Supramig*

Lincolnshire Chamber Of Commerce & Industry Commerce House Outer Circle Road, Lincoln LN2 4HY Tel. *01522 523333* Fax. *01522 546667* E-mail. *enquiries@lincs-chamber.co.uk* Web. *www.lincs-chamber.co.uk Chamber of Commerce (LCCI)*

Lindab Building Systems Evans Business Centre Mitchelston Drive, Mitchelston Industrial Estate, Kirkcaldy KY1 3NB Tel. *01592 652300* Fax. *01592 653135* E-mail. *info@astron.biz* Web. *www.lindabbuildings.com Butlerib – MR-24 – Shadowrib*

Lindapter International Brackenbeck Road, Bradford BD7 2NF Tel. *01274 521444* Fax. *01274 521130* E-mail. *enquiries@lindapter.com* Web. *www.lindapter.com Floorfast – Flush Clamp – Grate-Fast – Hollo-Bolt – Lindapter – Lindibolt – Lindiclip*

Lindchem Ltd 245 Southtown Road, Great Yarmouth NR31 0JJ Tel. *01493 850303* Fax. *01493 332292* E-mail. *paul@abbeychemicals.co.uk* Web. *www.abbey-chemicals.co.uk www.chem-distribution.com*

Linde Heavy Truck Division (Linde Material Handling Division) Linde Industrial Park Pentrebach, Merthyr Tydfil CF48 4LA Tel. *01443 624200* Fax. *01443 624300* E-mail. *info@linde.com* Web. *www.linde-htd.com Lansing Linde (Blackwood) Ltd – Linde Heavy Truck Division Ltd*

Linde Hydraulics Ltd 12-13 Eyston Way, Abingdon OX14 1TR Tel. *01235 522828* Fax. *01235 554036* E-mail. *enquiries@lindehydraulics.co.uk* Web. *www.lindehydraulics.co.uk Linde – Lintronic – Lindos – Synchron*

Linden Textiles Ltd Linden Court House 52 Liverpool Street, Salford M5 4LT Tel. *0161 7459268* Fax. *0161 7376061* E-mail. *accounts@thomasfrederick.co.uk Bang-The-Door – Country Flower – Pall Mall – Silhouette – Sunset – Thomas Frederick – Top Table*

Lindisfarne Hotel Green Lane Holy Island, Berwick Upon Tweed TD15 2SQ Tel. *01289 389273* Fax. *01289 389284* Web. *www.thelindisfarnehotel.co.uk Lindisfarne*

Lindsay Ford 2 Highfield Park, Craigavon BT64 3AF Tel. *028 38342424* Fax. *028 38342440* E-mail. *billy.purvis@lindsay-cars.co.uk* Web. *www.lindsayford.co.uk Irish Road Motors*

Lindy Electronics Ltd Sadler Foster Way Teesside Industrial Estate, Stockton On Tees TS17 9JY Tel. *01642 754000* Fax. *01642 754027* E-mail. *info@lindy.co.uk* Web. *www.lindy.co.uk Lindy Electronics*

Linear Composites Vale Mills Oakworth, Keighley BD22 0EB Tel. *01535 643363* Fax. *01535 643605* E-mail. *sales@linearcomposites.com* Web. *www.linearcomposites.com Parafil – Paralink – Paraloop – Paraweb*

Linear Tools Ltd 1 Clock Tower Road, Isleworth TW7 6DT Tel. *020 84002020* Fax. *020 84002021* E-mail. *sales@lineartools.co.uk* Web. *www.lineartools.co.uk Linear*

Line Markings Ltd New Works Road Low Moor, Bradford BD12 0RU Tel. *01274 606770* Fax. *01274 602802* E-mail. *johnrainey@rommco-uk-ltd.com* Web. *www.linemarkingsltd.com Ribline*

Linens Direct Langston Road, Loughton IG10 3TQ Tel. *020 85080707* Fax. *020 85321352* E-mail. *customerservices@lduk.co.uk* Web. *www.linensdirect.co.uk *Whispers (World Wide)*

Ling Design Ltd 14-20 Eldon Way Paddock Wood, Tonbridge TN12 6BE Tel. *01892 838574* Fax. *01892 838676* E-mail. *enquiries@lingdesign.co.uk* Web. *www.lingdesign.co.uk Ling Design*

Linic Products Ltd Victoria Works Saddington Road, Fleckney, Leicester LE8 8AW Tel. *0116 2403400* Fax. *0116 2403300* E-mail. *sales@linic.co.uk* Web. *www.linic.co.uk Proops*

Link 51 Ltd Link House Halesfield 6, Telford TF7 4LN Tel. *01952 682251* Fax. *01952 682452* E-mail. *services@wagon-storage.com* Web. *www.link51.co.uk Clearstor – Stormor Euroshelving – Stormor Longspan – XL Pallet Racking*

Link-A-Bord Ltd Colliery Industrial Estate Main Road, Morton, Alfreton DE55 6HL Tel. *01773 590566* Fax. *01773 590681* E-mail. *sales@link-a-bord.co.uk* Web. *www.armillatox.co.uk Armillatox – Armillatox - Link-a-bord – Link-a-bord*

Link Hamson Ltd 6 York Way Lancaster Road, Cressex Business Park, High Wycombe HP12 3PY Tel. *01494 439786* Fax. *01494 526222* E-mail. *sales@linkhamson.com* Web. *www.linkhamson.com County – ELVO – epc – iteco – kic – martin – Senju – Sparkle – Superform – techno print*

Link Lockers Link House Halesfield 6, Telford TF7 4LN Tel. *0800 0730300* Fax. *01952 684312* E-mail. *sales@linklockers.co.uk* Web. *www.linklockers.co.uk Ambassador – CFG – Echelon – Envoy – Rhino – Standard Lockers – Triple A*

Linmech Technical Solutions Ltd York Eco Business Centre Amy Johnson Way, Clifton Moor, York YO30 4AG Tel. *01904 479701* Fax. *01347 811138* E-mail. *enquiries@linmech.co.uk* Web. *www.linmech.co.uk Pro Engineer – Solid Edge – Unigraphics*

Linpac Allibert Ltd 17 Ridgeway Quinton Business Park, Quinton, Birmingham B32 1AF Tel. *0121 5060100* Fax. *0121 4221771* E-mail. *linpacallibert-uk@linpac.com* Web. *www.linpacallibert.com Allibin – Geobox – Helix Tanks – Jumbox – Maestro Pallet*

Linton & Co Engineering Ltd Unit 11 Forge Business Centre, Diss IP22 1AP Tel. *01379 651344* Fax. *01379 650970* E-mail. *mail@lintoninst.co.uk* Web. *www.lintoninst.co.uk *Apollo (U.S.A.) – *Axopatch (U.S.A.) – Fleisch – *Mini Logger (U.S.A.) – *Neurostim (Germany) – *Transonic (U.S.A.) – *Wenking (Germany)*

Linton Metalware Linton Works Studley Street, Birmingham B12 8JD Tel. *0121 7724491* Fax. *0121 7667218* E-mail. *action@linton.co.uk* Web. *www.littersolutions.co.uk Linton*

Linton Tweeds Ltd Shaddon Mills Shaddongate, Carlisle CA2 5TZ Tel. *01228 527569* Fax. *01228 512062* E-mail. *info@lintondirect.com* Web. *www.lintondirect.com Linton*

Linvic Engineering Ltd Hickman Avenue, Wolverhampton WV1 2DW Tel. *01902 456333* Fax. *01902 455856* E-mail. *sales@linvic.co.uk* Web. *www.linvic.co.uk Linvic*

Linx Printing Technologies plc Burrel Road, St Ives PE27 3LA Tel. *01480 302100* Fax. *01480 302116* E-mail. *sales@linx.co.uk* Web. *www.linx.co.uk Linx – Xymark*

Lion Industries UK Ltd 9-10 Titan Way Britannia Enterprise Park, Lichfield WS14 9TT Tel. *01543 251560* Fax. *01543 251395* E-mail. *info@lionindustries.co.uk* Web. *www.lionindustries.co.uk *Graco (U.S.A.) – Power Painting – Power Strainer – *Rocket Burner – *Titan (U.S.A.)*

Liquid Control Ltd Stewarts Road Finedon Road Industrial Estate, Wellingborough NN8 4RJ Tel. *01933 277571* Fax. *01933 440273* E-mail. *sales@liquidcontrol.co.uk* Web. *www.liquidcontrol.co.uk Dispensit – Dispenstech – Posifill – Posiflow – Posiload – Posimixer – Posishot – Posivalve – *Techcon (U.S.A.) – Twinflow*

Lismore Instruments Ltd 2 Tristar Business Centre Star Road, Partridge Green, Horsham RH13 8RA Tel. *01403 713121* Fax. *01403 713141* E-mail. *sales@lismore.uk.com* Web. *www.intercall.co.uk Guardian – Intercall*

Lismor Recordings PO Box 7264, Glasgow G46 6AL Tel. *0141 6376010* Fax. *0141 6376010* E-mail. *lismor@lismor.com* Web. *www.allcelticmusic.com Iona – Lismor*

Lister Petter Ltd Long Street, Dursley GL11 4HS Tel. *01453 544141* Fax. *01453 546732* E-mail. *sales@lister-petter.co.uk* Web. *www.lister-petter.co.uk Lister Diesel Gensets – Lister Marine Diesels – Lister Petter – Lister Petter Diesels*

Lite-Tec Unit 5 Hutton Business Park Hangthwaite Road, Adwick-le-Street, Doncaster DN6 7BD Tel. *01302 338210* Fax. *05601 138409* E-mail. *info@litetec.co.uk* Web. *www.litetec.co.uk Fibsta Fibre Optic Panel*

Lithgow Saekaphen Ltd Birksland Street, Bradford BD3 9SU Tel. *01274 721188* Fax. *01274 720088* E-mail. *gary@qgroup.com* Web. *www.qgroup.com Calvinac – *Derakane (Germany) – Isolemail (France) – *Sakaphen (Germany)*

Litre Meter Ltd Hart Hill Barn Granborough Road, North Marston, Buckingham MK18 3RZ Tel. *01296 670200* Fax. *01296 670999* E-mail. *sales@litremeter.com* Web. *www.litremeter.com Euromay (Italy) – Hoffer (U.S.A.) – Kral (Austria) – Litre Meter (United Kingdom) – Sierra (U.S.A.) – Sierra Instruments*

The Little Brown Book Group Unilever House 100 Victoria Embankment, London EC4Y 0DY Tel. *020 79118000* Fax. *020 79118100* E-mail. *info@littlebrown.co.uk* Web. *www.littlebrown.co.uk Abacus – Little Brown – Orbit – Time – Virago – Warner*

Little Giants Ltd Unit 2 30 Broughton Street, Manchester M8 8NN Tel. *0161 8321526* Fax. *0161 8391754* E-mail. *littlegiantsltd@hotmail.com Little Giants – Little Leader*

Littlemore Scientific Gutch Pool Farm, Gillingham SP8 5QP Tel. *01747 835550* Fax. *01747 835552* E-mail. *elsec@elsec.co.uk* Web. *www.elsec.com ELSEC*

Littlewoods Home Shopping Orders & Enquiries Skyways House Speke Road, Speke, Liverpool L70 1AB Tel. *08448 228000* Fax. *0870 2631701* Web. *www.littlewoods.com All Of Us – Brian Mills – Burlington – Index Extra – Janet Frazer – John Moores – Littlewoods – Peter Craig*

Litton Group Ltd 38 Young Street, Lisburn BT27 5EB Tel. *028 92672325* Fax. *028 92607473* E-mail. *graham.green@ukcities.co.uk* Web. *www.litton.co.uk Litton*

Livebookings Ltd 5th Floor Elizabeth House, 39 York Road, London SE1 7NQ Tel. *020 71994300* Fax. *020 71994301* E-mail. *info@livebookings.co.uk* Web. *www.livebookings.com Console*

Liverpool Daily Post & Echo PO Box 48, Liverpool L69 3EB Tel. *0151 2272000* Fax. *0151 2364682* E-mail. *hr@liverpool.com* Web. *www.icliverpool.co.uk Bootle Times – Crosby Herald – Formby Times – Midweek Visiter – Southport Visiter*

Liverpool Football Club Ticket Bookings Anfield Road, Liverpool L4 0TH Tel. *08431 705555* Fax. *0151 2608813* Web. *www.liverpoolfc.tv Liverpool Football Club*

Liverpool Victoria County Gates, Bournemouth BH1 2NF Tel. *01202 292333* Fax. *01202 292253* E-mail. *sales@liverpoolvictoria.co.uk* Web. *www.lv.com Liverpool Victoria Friendly Society*

Living Space Ltd 12a Earlstrees Road Earlstrees Industrial Estate, Corby NN17 4AZ Tel. *01536 446980* Fax. *01536 446981* E-mail. *sales@livingspaceltd.co.uk* Web. *www.livingspaceltd.co.uk CONTOUR LINE CURVED ROOF CANOPIES – HOMESTYLE MULTI PURPOSE CANOPIES – LIVING SPACE GLAZING BARS – WEATHERGUARD CANTILEVER CANOPIES*

Livingston & Doughty Ltd 17 Mandervell Road Oadby, Leicester LE2 5LR Tel. *0116 2714221* Fax. *0116 2716977* E-mail. *paul@flexofil.co.uk* Web. *www.flexofil.co.uk Cellax – Cello – Flexofil – Shoe Findings*

Livingston UK Livingston House 2 Queens Road, Teddington TW11 0LB Tel. *020 89435151* Fax. *020 89776431* E-mail. *info@livingston.co.uk* Web. *www.livingston.co.uk Livingston*

L J Hydleman & Co. Ltd Marton Street, Skipton BD23 1TF Tel. *01756 706700* Fax. *01756 798083* E-mail. *info@hydleman.co.uk* Web. *www.hydleman.co.uk *Bessey (Germany) – *Gedore (Germany)*

Llanrad Distribution plc Unit 26 Bookers Way Dinnington, Sheffield S25 3SH Tel. *01909 550944* Fax. *01909 568403* E-mail. *albert.haugg@llanrad.co.uk* Web. *www.llanrad.co.uk Llanrad*

Llewellyn Ryland Ltd Haden Street, Birmingham B12 9DB Tel. *0121 4402284* Fax. *0121 4400281* E-mail. *sales@llewellyn-ryland.co.uk* Web. *www.llewellyn-ryland.co.uk Duralac – Ryland – Rylands*

Llonsson Ltd 49 Court Farm Road, Warlingham CR6 9BL Tel. *01883 622068* Fax. *01883 623280* E-mail. *sales@llonsson.co.uk* Web. *www.llonsson.co.uk Mez+za+nine – Rigidgrid – Modugrid*

Lloyd Ltd (Head Office) Kingstown Broadway Kingstown Industrial Estate, Carlisle CA3 0EF Tel. *01228 517100* Fax. *01228 531212* E-mail. *derek.marlborough@lloyd.co.uk* Web. *www.lloyd.ltd.uk Lloyd Lawn & Leisure*

Lloyd Instruments Ltd Steyning Way, Bognor Regis PO22 9ST Tel. *01243 833370* Fax. *01243 833401* E-mail. *uk-far.general@ametek.co.uk* Web. *www.lloyd-instruments.co.uk AMETEK – DAVENPORT – LLOYD INSTRUMENTS – *Nexygen*

Lloyd Loom Ltd Foxwood Industrial Park Foxwood Road, Chesterfield S41 9RN Tel. *01246 264600* Fax. *01246 264609* E-mail. *lloyd.loom.nova@dsl.pipex.com Lloyd Loom*

Lloyds & Co Letchworth Ltd Birds Hill, Letchworth Garden City SG6 1JE Tel. *01462 683031* Fax. *01462 481964* E-mail. *sales@lloydsandco.com* Web. *www.lloydsandco.com Leda – Paladin – Pentad Titan*

L & M Ltd L & M Business Park Norman Road, Altrincham WA14 4ES Tel. *0161 9286131* Fax. *0161 9277277* E-mail. *info@landmproducts.co.uk Hunter – Intertype – Linonews – Linotype – Ludlow*

L M C Hadrian Ltd Quartermaster Road West Wilts Trading Estate, Westbury BA13 4JT Tel. *01373 865088* Fax. *01373 865464* E-mail. *ken@lmchadrian.com* Web. *www.hadriancarpanels.com Alfa – Audi – Austin – BMW – Chrysler – Citroen – Daewoo – Daihatsu – Datsun – Ferguson – Fiat – Ford – Honda – Hyundai – Isuzu – Jaguar – Kia – Lada – Lancia – Mazda – Mercedes – MG – Mini – Mitsubishi – Morris – Nissan – Opel – Peugeot – Porsche – Renault – Rover – Saab – Seat – Simca – Skoda – Subaru – Sunbeam – Suzuki – Talbot – Toyota – Triumph – Vauxhall – Volkswagen – Volvo*

L M K Thermosafe Unit 9-10 Moonhall Business Park Helions Bumpstead Road, Haverhill CB9 7AA Tel. *01440 707141* Fax. *01440 713344* E-mail. *sales@drumheating.com* Web. *www.drumheating.com Digiheat – Inteliheat – Thermosafe (United Kingdom) – Tote Heater*

L M L Products Ltd 13 Porte Marsh Road, Calne SN11 9BN Tel. *01249 814271* Fax. *01249 812182* E-mail. *sales@lmlproducts.co.uk* Web. *www.lmlproducts.co.uk Defence Manufacturers Association*

L.N. E-Consulting Ltd Flat 12 16 Carlton Drive, Putney, London SW15 2BDÂ Tel. *07939 325816* E-mail. *info@webservicesconsultancy.com* Web. *www.webservicesconsultancy.com L.N. E-Consulting Ltd*

L N S Turbo UK Ltd Waterside Park Valley Way, Wombwell, Barnsley S73 0BB Tel. *01226 270033* Fax. *01226 270044* E-mail. *sales@lnsturbouk.com* Web. *www.lns-world.com Microfine 2 – Microscraper 500 – Star Micronics (Japan) – Turbo-Jet*

Loadpoint Ltd Unit K Chelworth Industrial Estate Chelworth Road, Cricklade, Swindon SN6 6HE Tel. *01793 751160* Fax. *01793 750155* E-mail. *sales@loadpoint.co.uk* Web. *www.loadpoint.co.uk EMM – Micro Dicing Systems – MicroAce – NanoAce – PicoAce – Tetraform – Videoscope – Washpoint*

Loake Shoemakers Wood Street, Kettering NN16 9SN Tel. *01536 415411* Fax. *01536 410190* E-mail. *mail@loake.co.uk* Web. *www.loake.co.uk Loake Bros Shoemakers*

William Lockie & Co. Ltd 27-28 Drumlanrig Square, Hawick TD9 0AW Tel. *01450 372645* Fax. *01450 373846* E-mail. *info@williamlockie.com* Web. *www.williamlockie.com William Lockie of Hawick*

Lock Inspection Systems Ltd Lock House Neville Street, Chadderton, Oldham OL9 6LF Tel. *0161 6240333* Fax. *0161 6245181* E-mail. *sales@lockinspection.com* Web. *www.lockinspection.com Ferochek – Metalchek – Metalchek, Ferochek & Needlechek manufrs – Needlechek*

Lockmasters Mobile Safes & Locks Keys House Vyne Close, Alton GU34 2EH Tel. *01420 542448* Fax. *01420 542448* E-mail. *enquiries@lock-masters.co.uk* Web. *www.lock-masters.co.uk Lockmaster*

Loddon Engineering Ltd Little Money Road Loddon, Norwich NR14 6JJ Tel. *01508 520744* Fax. *01508 528055* E-mail. *sales@loddon.co.uk* Web. *www.loddon.co.uk Loddon*

Lodge Cottrell Ltd George Street, Birmingham B3 1QQ Tel. *0121 2141300* Fax. *0121 2002555* E-mail. *irf@lodgecottrell.com* Web. *www.lodgecottrell.com FabriClean - Pulse-Jet Fabric and Ceramic Filters - SmartPulse Controller - for optimisation of APC control – Lodge Cottrell*

Lodge Furniture Ltd PO Box 61, Oxford OX33 1WQ Tel. *08452 570254* Fax. *0870 1656856* E-mail. *judithh@lodge.co.uk* Web. *www.lodgefurniture.co.uk Lodge (Furniture) Limited*

M Lodge & Son Failsworth Mill Ashton Road West, Failsworth, Manchester M35 0FR Tel. *0161 9344050* Fax. *0161 6834280* E-mail. *indo@fabric.co.uk M. Lodge & Son*

Philip Lodge Ltd Machine Works New Mill Road, Brockholes, Holmfirth HD9 7AE Tel. *01484 661143* Fax. *01484 661164 Scourmaster – Scourmatic*

Lodge Tyre 25-29 Lord Street, Birmingham B7 4DE Tel. *0121 3803207* Fax. *0121 3590046* E-mail. *martin@lodgetyre.com* Web. *www.lodgetyre.com Lodge Tyre Co – Truetreads*

O W Loeb & Co. Ltd 3 Archie Street, London SE1 3JT Tel. *020 72340385* Fax. *020 73570440* E-mail. *chrisdavey@owloeb.com* Web. *www.owloeb.com *Aschrott'sche Gutsverwaltung (Germany) – *Bertrand et Fils – *C. Von Schubert (Germany) – *Caves des Vinsde Sancerre (France) – *Charles Joguet (France) – *Domaine Abel Garnier (France) – *Domaine Armand Rousseau (France) – *Domaine de Courcel (France) – *Domaine de Montille (France) – *Domaine Dujac (France) – *Domaine Etienne Sauzet (France) – *Domaine Gagnard-Delagrange (France) – *Domaine Henri Gouges (France) – *Domaine Jean Pascal (France) – *Domaine Louis Michel (France) – *Domaine Michel Niellon (France) – *Domaine Ramonet (France) – *Domaine Saier (France) – *Egon Muller (Germany) – *Erben J. Fischer (Germany) – *Friedrich Wilhelm Gymnasium (Germany) – *George Muller Stiftung (Germany) – *Gustav Gessert (Germany) – *H.H. Eser (Germany) – *Hugel Et Fils – *J. Aulanier (France) – *J. Reynaud (France) – *J.J. Preum (Germany) – *Jacques Depagneux (France) – *Jean-Jacques Vincent (France) – *Josef Schmitt (Germany) – *M. Von Othegraven (Germany) – *Marquis d'Angerville (France) – Melnotte & Fils – *Paul Jaboulet Aine – *Ph Foreau (France) – *Rautenstrauch (Germany) – *Renaud-Bossuat (France) – *Staatliche Weinbaudomaene (Germany) – *Von Hoevel (Germany) – *Von Kesselstatt (Germany) – *Willi Haag (Germany)*

Loganair Ltd Glasgow Airport Abbotsinch, Paisley PA3 2TG Tel. *08714 321338* Fax. *0141 8876020* E-mail. *davidharrison@loganair.co.uk* Web. *www.loganair.co.uk Loganair*

Logan Teleflex UK Ltd (a member of Daifuku Group) Sutton Road Kingston Upon Hull, Hull HU7 0DR Tel. *01482 785600* Fax. *01482 785699* E-mail. *marketing@loganteleflex.com* Web. *www.loganteleflex.com Logan Fenamec (UK)*

Logax Ltd PO Box 26, Rickmansworth WD3 3HW Tel. *01923 223660* Fax. *01923 252601* E-mail. *info@logax.com* Web. *www.logax.com Adaptafile – Gamesfax – Logax – Motorfax – Videofax*

The Logic Group Logic House Waterfront Business Park, Fleet GU51 3SB Tel. *01252 776755* Fax. *01252 776758* E-mail. *info@the-logic-group.com* Web. *www.the-logic-group.com Commslogic*

Logic Programming Associates Ltd Studio 30 Royal Victoria Patriotic Building John Archer Way, London SW18 3SX Tel. *020 88712016* Fax. *020 88740449* E-mail. *info@lpa.co.uk* Web. *www.ita.co.uk LPA 386 Prolog for DOS – LPA DataMite – LPA Flex – LPA FLINT – LPA Intelligence Server – LPA MacProlog – LPA Prolog for Windows – LPA Prolog++ – LPA ProWeb Server*

Logma Systems Design Ltd Logic Centre Cunliffe Street, Chorley PR7 2BA Tel. *01257 233123* Fax. *01257 237215* E-mail. *sales@logma.co.uk* Web. *www.logma.co.uk Sage*

Logo Bugs Plus Ltd 9 Airfield Way, Christchurch BH23 3PE Tel. *01202 588500* Fax. *01202 487177* E-mail. *sales@logobugsplus.co.uk* Web. *www.logobugsplus.co.uk Adman – Logo Bugs – LogoBugs – Promotional Bugs*

Loheat Fordbrook Estate Marlborough Road, Pewsey SN9 5NT Tel. *01672 564601* Fax. *01672 564602* E-mail. *sales@loheat.com* Web. *www.loheat.com Loheat – Vecta*

Lohmann GB Ltd Shire Business Park Wainwright Road, Worcester WR4 9FA Tel. *01905 459460* Fax. *01526 352022* E-mail. *j.adams@lohmanngb.co.uk* Web. *www.lohmanngb.co.uk Lohmann GB Limited*

Lojigma International Ltd Block 19 Ridge Way, Hillend, Dunfermline KY11 9JN Tel. *01383 822003* Fax. *01383 822007* E-mail. *admin@lojigma.com* Web. *www.lojigma.com Gore – Lojiclean – Rotecno*

Lola Cars Ltd 12 Glebe Road St Peters Hill, Huntingdon PE29 7DY Tel. *01480 456722* Fax. *01480 482970* E-mail. *lola@lolacars.com* Web. *www.lolacars.com Lola Cars*

Lombard Risk India House 45 Curlew Street, London SE1 2ND Tel. *020 74032188* Fax. *020 74034425* E-mail. *info@stbsystems.com* Web. *www.stbsystems.com STB Detector – STB GlobalView – STB Reporter – STB Super Consolidator – STB TaxMan*

London City Airport Ltd Royal Docks, London E16 2PX Tel. *020 76460000* Fax. *020 75111040* E-mail. *richard.gooding@londoncityairport.com* Web. *www.londoncityairport.com London City Airport*

London City Mission 175 Tower Bridge Road, London SE1 2AH Tel. *020 74077585* Fax. *020 74036711* E-mail. *enquiries@lcm.org.uk* Web. *www.lcm.org.uk Span*

London Electronics Ltd Warren Court Chicksands, Shefford SG17 5QB Tel. *01462 850967* Fax. *01462 850968* E-mail. *support@london-electronics.com* Web. *www.london-electronics.com Ditel – Intuitive – Laureate*

London Emblem Plc "All About Badges" Unit 9 Apex Centre Speedfields Park, Newgate Lane, Fareham PO14 1TP Tel. *01329 822900* Fax. *01329 829000* E-mail. *suem@londonemblem.com* Web. *www.allaboutbadges.com Badgeworx (United Kingdom)*

The London Fan Co. Ltd 75-81 Stirling Road, London W3 8DJ Tel. *020 89926923* Fax. *020 89926928* E-mail. *sales@londonfan.co.uk* Web. *www.londonfan.co.uk Breeza – Breeza - industrial fans Breezax - impellers – Breezax Impellers*

The London Fancy Box Company Ltd Poulton Close Coombe Valley, Dover CT17 0XB Tel. *01304 242001* Fax. *01304 240229* E-mail. *sales@londonfancybox.co.uk* Web. *www.londonfancybox.co.uk Discpac – DVDiscpac*

London Letter File Company Ltd Tenet House 7 Mons Close, Harpenden AL5 1TD Tel. *01582 460547* Fax. *01582 460482* E-mail. *sales@londonletterfile.com* Web. *www.londonletterfile.com Compak – Datox – Pendata – Tenastic – Tenet – Tenet - Tenastic - Compak - Datox - Pendata.*

London Linen Supply Ltd Unit 6-8 Jackson Way, Southall UB2 4SF Tel. *020 85745569* Fax. *020 85712487* E-mail. *roger.oliver@londonlinen.co.uk* Web. *www.londonlinen.co.uk Caterers Linen Supply – London Linen Supply – London Workwear Rental*

London Metals Ltd 10 Graham Street, London N1 8GB Tel. *020 73545450* Fax. *020 73595064* E-mail. *trading@londonmetals.co.uk* Web. *www.londonmetals.co.uk L.M.*

London Name Plate Manufacturing Co. Ltd Zylo Works Sussex St, Brighton BN2 0HH Tel. *01273 607025* Fax. *01273 571214* E-mail. *sales@lnp.co.uk* Web. *www.lnp.co.uk Easy-Cals (United Kingdom) – Plasti-Cals (United Kingdom) – Ready-Cals (United Kingdom)*

London Pressed Hinge Co. Ltd 6 Swinborne Drive Springwood Industrial Estate, Braintree CM7 2YG Tel. *01376 347074* Fax. *01376 340347* E-mail. *sales@lph-uk.co.uk* Web. *www.lph-uk.co.uk Rhinoceros*

London Stock Exchange plc The London Stock Exchange 10 Paternoster Square, London EC4M 7LS Tel. *020 77971000* E-mail. *enquiries@londonstockexchange.com* Web. *www.londonstockexchange.com London Market Information Link – R.N.S. – S.E.A.Q. International – Seaq*

Lonewolf B2b Tele Marketing 31 Southampton Row, London WC1B 5HA Tel. *020 33973559* E-mail. *nigel@lwolf.co.uk* Web. *www.lwolf.co.uk Lone Wolf B2B Telemarketing*

Longcliffe Quarries Ltd Longcliffe Brassington, Matlock DE4 4BZ Tel. *01629 540284* Fax. *01629 540569* E-mail. *sales@longcliffe.co.uk* Web. *www.longcliffe.co.uk Longcliffe*

Longs Ltd Hanworth Lane Business Park, Chertsey KT16 9LZ Tel. *01932 561241* Fax. *01932 567391* E-mail. *sales@longs.co.uk* Web. *www.longs.co.uk Convac – Fluke – Heme – Jensen – Kenwood – Longs – Muller – Panavise – *Quick-Wedge (U.S.A.) – Tektronix – Weller*

Longworth Ltd Leltex House Longley Lane, Manchester M22 4SY Tel. *0161 9451333* Fax. *0161 9460026* E-mail. *info@longworth.co.uk* Web. *www.longworth.co.uk Leltex*

Lonsto Insternational Ltd Lonsto House 276 Chase Road, London N14 6HA Tel. *020 88828575* Fax. *020 88866676* E-mail. *py@lonsto.co.uk* Web. *www.lonsto.co.uk Counterflow – Lonsto – Lonsto Security – Lonsto Systems – Nemo Q – Queue Management Systems*

Lonza Biologics plc 224-230 Bath Road, Slough SL1 4DX Tel. *01753 777000* Fax. *01753 777001* E-mail. *gerard.kennedy@lonza.com* Web. *www.lonza.com CARNICHROME – CARNIPURE 50% IN WATER – CARNIPURE ALC – CARNIPURE CRYSTALLINE – CARNIPURE MO CITRATE – CARNIPURE TARTRATE*

Look Designs Ltd Unit A2-A3 Ropemaker Park Diplocks Way, Hailsham BN27 3GU Tel. *01323 841765* Fax. *01323 444824* E-mail. *lookdesigns@clara.co.uk* Web. *www.lookdesigns.co.uk Look*

Lookers plc 776 Chester Road Stretford, Manchester M32 0QH Tel. *0161 2910043* Fax. *0161 8642363* E-mail. *robingregson@lookers.co.uk* Web. *www.lookers.co.uk Used Direct – Lock & Leave*

Loot Ltd Wembley Point 1 Harrow Road, Wembley HA9 6DA Tel. *0871 2225000* Fax. *020 89004505* E-mail. *marketing@loot.com* Web. *www.loot.com Loot*

Lorien Resourcing Ltd Bankside House 107-112 Leadenhall Street, London EC3A 4AF Tel. *020 76541000* Fax. *020 76541066* E-mail. *info@lorien.co.uk* Web. *www.lorien.co.uk Custom 2000 – Finsys – Hocus – Stradis – Trandos – Transloc – Transpath – Transplan – Transtrip*

Lorlin Electronics Ltd (Halifax Industrial Group) Harwood Industrial Estate Harwood Road, Littlehampton BN17 7AT Tel. *01903 725121* Fax. *01903 723919* E-mail. *admin@lorlin.co.uk* Web. *www.lorlinelectronics.com *Lorlin Electronics (United Kingdom)*

Lothian Buses plc 55 Annandale Street, Edinburgh EH7 4AZ Tel. *0131 5544494* Fax. *0131 5543942* E-mail. *mail@lothianbuses.co.uk* Web. *www.lothianbuses.co.uk L.R.T. Lothian Airlink – L.R.T. Lothian Talisman – Lothian Buses*

Louver-Lite Ashton Road, Hyde SK14 4BG Tel. *0161 8825000* Fax. *0161 8825009* E-mail. *sales@louvolite.com* Web. *www.louvolite.com Louvolite*

Lovato UK Ltd Lovato House Providence Drive Lye, Stourbridge DY9 8HQ Tel. *0845 8110023* Fax. *0845 8110024* E-mail. *sales@lovato.co.uk* Web. *www.lovato.co.uk Lovato*

J M Loveridge 6a Kingsway, Andover SP10 5LQ Tel. *023 80222008* Fax. *023 80222117* E-mail. *admin@jmloveridge.com* Web. *www.jmloveridge.com B.C.K. – Cetriad – Citrazine – Lethobarb – Phenogel*

Lowes Financial Management Ltd Holmwood House Clayton Road, Newcastle upon Tyne NE2 1TL Tel. *0191 2818811* Fax. *0191 2818365* E-mail. *postmaster@lowes.co.uk* Web. *www.lowes.co.uk Lowes Financial Management Limited*

Low Profile B D C House 590-598 Green Lanes, London N8 0RA Tel. *020 88008083* Fax. *020 88090567* E-mail. *mustafa.suleyman@low-profile.com* Web. *www.low-profile.com Low Profile*

Lowther Loudspeaker Systems Ltd 26 Footscary Lane, Sidcup DA14 4NR Tel. *020 83009166* Fax. *020 83080778* E-mail. *diane@lowtherloudspeakers.com* Web. *www.lowtherloudspeakers.com Accolade – Bel Canto – Bicor – E.X.4 – P.M.4 – P.M.6 – Soundranger*

Loxford Equipment Co. Ltd Wood Hall Church Lane, Great Holland, Frinton On Sea CO13 0JS Tel. *01255 851555* Fax. *01255 851051* E-mail. *enquiries@loxford-equipment.co.uk* Web. *www.loxford-equipment.co.uk Loxford*

Loxston Garden Machinery New Road Seavington, Ilminster TA19 0QU Tel. *01460 242562* Fax. *01460 241680* E-mail. *info@loxston.co.uk* Web. *www.loxston.co.uk Aebi – Alko – Gianni Ferrari – John Deere – Stiga*

Loxton Foods Rowan House, Stockport SK5 7LW Tel. *0161 4741444* Fax. *0161 4741222* E-mail. *info@loxtonfoodco.com* Web. *www.loxtonfoodco.com Loxtons Cuisine Sous-Vide – *Loxtons Heat and Serve – Loxtons Ready-t-cook*

L P A Channel Electric Bath Road, Thatcham RG18 3ST Tel. *01635 864866* Fax. *01635 869178* E-mail. *enquiries@lpa-channel.com* Web. *www.lpa-channel.com Rediboard*

L P C Elements Ltd Coundon Industrial Estate Coundon, Bishop Auckland DL14 8NR Tel. *01388 608270* Fax. *01388 450048* E-mail. *enquiries@lpcholdings.co.uk* Web. *www.lpcholdings.co.uk Megnam – Miflex – Mikram*

L P Import Export Supplies Ltd Chartists Way Morley, Leeds LS27 9ET Tel. *0113 2524999* Fax. *0113 2380769* E-mail. *orders@lpssupplies.com* Web. *www.lpssupplies.com L.P. (Import Export) Supplies*

L P M Cleaning Cross Green Way, Leeds LS9 0SE Tel. *0113 2486000* Fax. *01691 654789* E-mail. *info@morrisholdings.co.uk* Web. *www.morrisholdings.co.uk D.S.*

L Robinson Company Gillingham Ltd Gads Hill, Gillingham ME7 2RS Tel. *01634 281200* Fax. *01634 280101* E-mail. *sales@jubileeclips.co.uk* Web. *www.jubileeclips.co.uk Jubilee – Jubilee Clipdriver – Jubilee Flexidriver – Jubilee Wingspade*

L & R Saddles Ltd Clifford House 10-14 Butts Road, Walsall WS4 2AR Tel. *01922 630740* Fax. *01922 721149* E-mail. *landrsaddles@btconnect.com* Web. *www.landrsaddles.com Lovatt & Rickett*

L S Starrett Co. Ltd Oxnam Road, Jedburgh TD8 6LR Tel. *01835 863501* Fax. *01835 863018* E-mail. *ggill@starrett.co.uk* Web. *www.starrett.co.uk Bearcat – Bluestripe – Controlok – Digitape – Green Stripe – Grey-Flex – Red Stripe – Safe Flex – Starrett – Tru-Lok*

L S Systems Ltd 188 Blackgate Lane Tarleton, Preston PR4 6UU Tel. *01772 812484* Fax. *01772 815417* E-mail. *sales@lssystems.co.uk* Web. *www.lssystems.co.uk Benson – Biological Crop Protection Ltd – *Certis Europe – Desch Plantpak – Dosmatic – ELKA Rainwear – Ermaf – Grundfos Pumps – Sinclair Horticulture – *Teku – Titan Tanks*

L T H Electronics Ltd Eltelec Works Chaul End Lane, Luton LU4 8EZ Tel. *01582 593693* Fax. *01582 598036* E-mail. *sales@lth.co.uk* Web. *www.lth.co.uk Aquacal 2000*

L-3 Communications Security & Detection Systems Astro House Brants Bridge, Bracknell RG12 9BG Tel. *01344 477900* Fax. *01344 477901* E-mail. *melanie.dormand@l-3com.com* Web. *www.l-3com.com Linescan (EG & G) – Sentrie – Vivid – Vivid (EG & G)*

Lubeline Lubricating Equipment 4 Collins Yard Mill Lane, Dronfield S18 2XL Tel. *01246 292333* Fax. *01246 292444* E-mail. *sales@lubeline.co.uk* Web. *www.lubeline.co.uk Dualine – GX – Lubeplus – Progressive*

LUCID PRODUCTIONS Hollybush Place, London E2 9QX Tel. *020 77390240* Fax. *020 77390240* E-mail. *info@clubdecor.co.uk* Web. *www.clubdecor.co.uk Clubdecor – Lucid*

Lucite International Speciality Polymers & Resins Ltd Horndale Avenue Aycliffe Industrial Estate, Aycliffe Business Park, Newton Aycliffe DL5 6YE Tel. *01325 300990* Fax. *01325 314925* E-mail. *ann-marie.stannard@lucite.com* Web. *www.luciteinternational.com/resins Colacryl*

Luckins Cherryholt Road, Stamford PE9 2EP Tel. *01780 750500* Fax. *01780 750567* E-mail. *donna.ward@luckins.co.uk* Web. *www.luckins.co.uk Luckins*

Martin Luck Group Ltd Rowdown House Rowdown Close Langage Business Park, Plympton, Plymouth PL7 5EY Tel. *01752 336699* Fax. *01752 330022* E-mail. *sales@martinluck.co.uk* Web. *www.martinluck.co.uk Martin Luck Group*

Lucy Switchgear Howland Road, Thame OX9 3UJ Tel. *01844 267267* Fax. *01844 267223* E-mail. *info@lucyswitchgear.com* Web. *www.lucyswitchgear.com Lucy Lighting – Lucy Oxford – Lucy Switchgear*

Lumatic Ga Ltd Theaklen Drive, St Leonards On Sea TN38 9AZ Tel. *01424 436343* Fax. *01424 429926* E-mail. *terry@lumatic.co.uk* Web. *www.lumatic.co.uk *Abnox (Switzerland) – *Alfa (Italy) – *Beka (Germany) – Ecotechnics (Italy) – Lumatic – Pom Pom – *Synchrolub (France) – *Wanner (Switzerland)*

Lumineri 8 London Road Balderton, Newark NG24 3AJ Tel. *07875 715904* Fax. *0845 0946302* E-mail. *info@lumineri.co.uk* Web. *www.lumineri.co.uk Lumineri*

Lumitron Lighting Services Ltd Unit 31 The Metro Centre Dwight Road, Watford WD18 9UD Tel. *01923 226222* Fax. *01923 211300* E-mail. *sales@lumitron.co.uk* Web. *www.lumitron.co.uk Lumitron*

Lumsden Grinders Ltd Hawks Road, Gateshead NE8 3BT Tel. *0191 4783838* Fax. *0191 4900282* E-mail. *sales@lumsden-grinders.co.uk* Web. *www.lumsden-grinders.co.uk Lumsden*

Lunds New Factory Brookside Avenue, Rustington, Littlehampton BN16 3LF Tel. *01903 784242* Fax. *01903 787126* E-mail. *sales@lunds.co.uk* Web. *www.lunds.co.uk Luncase – Lundesk – Lunrac – Twin Set*

Lunex Ltd 151-153 Cheetham Hill Road, Manchester M8 8LY Tel. *0161 8333435* Fax. *0161 8333332* E-mail. *sales@lunex.co.uk* Web. *www.microcityuk.com Althea – Clip Box – Heidrun – Lunex – Quasar*

Lunn Engineering Co. Ltd Manor Road Industrial Estate, Atherstone CV9 1RB Tel. *01827 713228* Fax. *01827 717624*

E-mail. *info@lunnengineering.co.uk*
Web. *www.lunnengineering.co.uk Keyseater – Lunn Davis*

Lureflash International Chesterton Road Eastwood Trading Estate, Rotherham S65 1SU Tel. *01709 724700* Fax. *01709 724701* E-mail. *sales@lureflash.co.uk* Web. *www.lureflash.co.uk Lureflash – Wickhams*

Lusso Interiors Unit 20 Marsh Lane Industrial Estate Marsh Lane, Easton-In-Gordano, Bristol BS20 0NH Tel. *01275 372293* Fax. *01275 371217* E-mail. *andrewbailey@lussointerior.com* Web. *www.lussointerior.com 3M – Avanti – Avanti Eclipse – Avanti Eclipse Plus – Avanti Elite – Avanti Fireshield – Avanti Glass Doors – Avanti Legno – Avanti Matrix – Avanti Solare – Avanti Unity – Beldon – Broadsword – Excalabur – Forster – Kameo – Komfie – Komfort – London Wall – Mirage – Mistral – Optima – Planet – Polar – Sabre – Scimitar – Screenbase – Solar – Solare – Tenon*

Luton Steels Ltd Wharley Farm College Road, Cranfield, Bedford MK43 0AH Tel. *01234 750003* Fax. *01234 750084* E-mail. *sales@lutonsteels.com* Web. *www.lutonsteels.com Central Steels – Steel World*

Luvata Sales Oy (UK) P.O. Box 640, Brentford TW8 0AB Tel. *01689 825677* Fax. *01926 459149* E-mail. *enquiries@outokumpu.com* Web. *www.luvata.com Nordic Green Plus*

Luwa UK Ltd Wrigley Street, Oldham OL4 1HN Tel. *0161 6248185* Fax. *0161 6264609* E-mail. *sales@luwa.co.uk* Web. *www.luwa.com Luna – Luwa – Pneumablo – TAC – Uniluwa*

Luxaflex Mersey Industrial Estate Battersea Road, Stockport SK4 3EQ Tel. *0161 4325303* Fax. *0161 4315087* E-mail. *info.retail@luxaflex-sunway.co.uk* Web. *www.luxaflex.co.uk Apollo – Filtrasol – Hunter Douglas – Luxaflex – Luxalon – Sunflex – Sunway – Vista*

Luxia Catering Equipment 51 Higher Dunscar Egerton, Bolton BL7 9TF Tel. *01204 591111* Fax. *01204 595858* E-mail. *sales@luxia-nce.co.uk* Web. *www.luxia.co.uk Luxia/NCE*

Luxonic Lighting plc 17 Priestley Road, Basingstoke RG24 9JP Tel. *01256 363090* Fax. *01256 842349* E-mail. *info@luxonic.co.uk* Web. *www.luxonic.co.uk Alterlux – Hi-Lo – Luxonic – Programs – Surelux*

Luxus Ltd Belvoir Way Fairfield Industrial Estate, Louth LN11 0LQ Tel. *01507 604941* Fax. *01507 609154* E-mail. *info@luxus.co.uk* Web. *www.luxus.co.uk Encore*

Luxus Loft Conversions Luxus House 275 Deansgate, Manchester M3 4EL Tel. *0844 8004165* E-mail. *info@luxuslofts.co.uk* Web. *www.luxuslofts.co.uk Luxus*

L V D UK Ltd Unit 3 Wildmere Road, Banbury OX16 3JU Tel. *01295 676800* Fax. *01295 262980* E-mail. *j.goodwin@lvduk.com* Web. *www.lvdgroup.com LVD*

L V H Coatings Ltd Station Road Coleshill, Birmingham B46 1HT Tel. *01675 466888* Fax. *01675 466260* E-mail. *ron@lvh-coatings.co.uk* Web. *www.lvh-coatings.co.uk Clearclad – Lectrapearl – Lectraseal – Lectrobase – Lectrobond – Marban – Photo Resists – Tektor – Uviclad – Zetaclad*

Lyn Plan Upholstery Ltd 43 Imperial Way, Croydon CR9 4LP Tel. *020 86811833* Fax. *020 86805727* E-mail. *sales@lynplan.com* Web. *www.lynplan.com Furnifix – Lynn Wood Designs – Lynplan – Marco Leer*

Lynton Trailers UK Ltd Unit 16 Graphite Way Hadfield, Glossop SK13 1QH Tel. *0161 2238211* Fax. *0161 2230933* E-mail. *darran.reynolds@lyntontrailers.co.uk* Web. *www.lyntontrailers.co.uk Koolman – Load Lugger – Loadmaster – Loadrunner – Lynton Exhibition/Demonstration Trailers – Lynton Hydraulic Tipping Trailers – Lynton Mobile Works Units – Lynton Vending Trailers – Minitran – Ripple Retail Concepts – Showmaster – Showpoint*

Lynwood Products Ltd Ridings Business Park Hopwood Lane, Halifax HX1 3TT Tel. *01422 343257* Fax. *01422 347524* Web. *www.lynwoodproducts.co.uk Lynwood*

Lyons Instruments Brook Road, Waltham Cross EN8 7LR Tel. *01992 768888* Fax. *01992 788000* E-mail. *li@claudelyons.co.uk* Web. *www.claudelyons.co.uk *HTBasic (U.S.A.) – *Lineman (U.S.A.) – *Matchbox (U.S.A.) – *Sinadder (U.S.A.) – *TransEra HT Basic (U.S.A.)*

Lyson Ltd Barton Road Heaton Mersey Ind. Est., Stockport SK4 3EG Tel. *0161 4422111* Fax. *0161 4422001* E-mail. *ukphoto@nazdar.com* Web. *www.lyson.com Printgard*

Lyte Industries Wales Ltd Siemens Way Swansea Enterprise Park, Swansea SA7 9BB Tel. *01792 796666* Fax. *01792 796796* E-mail. *sales@lyteladders.co.uk* Web. *www.lyteladders.co.uk Lyte*

Lyteze Products Ltd 8 Colne Road Brightlingsea, Colchester CO7 0DL Tel. *01206 302699* Fax. *01206 302699* E-mail. *anne@lyteze.com* Web. *www.lyteze.com Lyteze*

M

Mabey Holdings Ltd Floral Mile Twyford, Hare Hatch, Reading RG10 9SQ Tel. *0118 9403921* Fax. *0118 9403941* E-mail. *sales@mabey.co.uk* Web. *www.mabey.co.uk Mabey*

Macandrews & Co. 75 King William Street, London EC4N 7BE Tel. *020 72206100* E-mail. *info@macandrews.com* Web. *www.macandrews.com CMA CGM*

Mcarthur Group Ltd Raglan Street Ashton-On-Ribble, Preston PR2 2AX Tel. *01772 556042* Fax. *0113 2421150* E-mail. *alan.curme@mcarthur-group.com* Web. *www.mcarthur-group.com McArthurs*

Macart Textiles Machinery Ltd The Grange Industrial Park Macart House Farnham Road, Bradford BD7 3JG Tel. *01274 525900* Fax. *01274 525901* E-mail. *sales@macart.com* Web. *www.macart.com Hattersley - Macart – Pegg Whiteley - Macart – Platt UK Ltd - Macart – Repco - Macart*

Mcbean's Orchids Mcbeans Nursery Resting Oak Hill, Cooksbridge, Lewes BN8 4PR Tel. *01273 400228* Fax. *01273 401181* E-mail. *sales@mcbeansorchids.co.uk* Web. *www.mcbeansorchids.co.uk McBean's*

Bernard Mccartney Ltd Unit 2 National Trading Estate Bramhall Moor Lane, Hazel Grove, Stockport SK7 5AA Tel. *0161 4560102* Fax. *0161 4835399* E-mail. *neil@macpactor.co.uk* Web. *www.macpactor.co.uk Macpactor*

Macclesfield Stone Quarries Ltd Bridge Quarry Windmill Lane, Kerridge, Macclesfield SK10 5AZ Tel. *01625 573208* Fax. *01625 573208* E-mail. *datooth@tiscali.co.uk Kerridge – Maccstone – Sandy Stone*

Mccomb Developments Unit 3 Westwood Farm Highcross Road, Southfleet, Gravesend DA13 9PH Tel. *01474 833175* Fax. *01892 752161* E-mail. *info@teleseal.co.uk* Web. *www.teleseal.co.uk Teleseal*

Mccormick Europe Ltd Haddenham Business Park Pegasus Way, Haddenham, Aylesbury HP17 8LB Tel. *01844 292930* Fax. *01844 294294* E-mail. *lawrence.kurzius@mccormick.co.uk* Web. *www.mccormick.com *Schwartz (Worldwide)*

Mccormick John & Co. Ltd 46 Darnley Street, Glasgow G41 2TY Tel. *0141 4294222* Fax. *0141 4296777* E-mail. *david.mccormick@jmccormick.co.uk* Web. *www.jmccormick.co.uk Relionmac*

Mccreath Simpson & Prentice Ltd Ordfield House Tweedside Trading Estate, Tweedmouth, Berwick Upon Tweed TD15 2XZ Tel. *01289 330022* Fax. *01289 333390* E-mail. *nigelforster@mspagriculture.co.uk* Web. *www.simpsonsmalt.co.uk M.S.P Ltd*

Macdermid Autotype Ltd Grove Road, Wantage OX12 7BZ Tel. *01235 771111* Fax. *01235 771196* E-mail. *info@macdermidautotype.com* Web. *www.macdermidautotype.com Autofilm – Autoflex IMD – Automask – Autostat – Autotex – Blue Line – Capillex – Five Star – FootPrint – Omega – Plus Direct Emulsions – SIGMAGraF*

Mace Industries 1-3 Macadam Road Earlstrees Industrial Estate, Corby NN17 4JN Tel. *01536 206600* Fax. *01536 206173* E-mail. *sales@maceindustries.co.uk* Web. *www.maceindustries.co.uk Bumpa Hoddi Boxa*

Macfarlanes 20 Cursitor Street, London EC4A 1LT Tel. *020 78319222* Fax. *020 78319607* E-mail. *bibi.ally@macfarlanes.com* Web. *www.macfarlanes.com Macfarlanes*

Macfarlan Smith Ltd Wheatfield Road, Edinburgh EH11 2QA Tel. *0131 3372434* Fax. *0131 3379813* E-mail. *simon@macsmith.com* Web. *www.macsmith.com Bitrex*

John Mcgavigan Ltd 111 Westerhill Road Bishopbriggs, Glasgow G64 2QR Tel. *0141 3020000* Fax. *0141 3020290* E-mail. *david.taylor@mcgavigan.com* Web. *www.advanceddecorative.com Lumenox*

Mcgeoch Technology Ltd 86 Lower Tower Street, Birmingham B19 3PA Tel. *0121 6875850* Fax. *0121 3333089* E-mail. *info@mcgeoch.co.uk* Web. *www.mcgeoch.co.uk McGeoch*

Machinagraph Ltd Unit 2 Bailey Drive Killamarsh, Sheffield S21 2JF Tel. *0114 2280006* Fax. *0114 2280440* E-mail. *machinagraph@msn.com* Web. *www.machinagraph.co.uk Machinagraph*

Machine Building Systems Ltd Heage Road Industrial Estate, Ripley DE5 3GH Tel. *01773 749330* Fax. *01773 749560* E-mail. *sales@mbsitem.co.uk* Web. *www.mbsitem.co.uk Item (Germany) – MTA (Switzerland)*

Machineco Ltd 181a Burton Road Monk Bretton Barnsley, Barnsley S71 2HG Tel. *01226 321919* Fax. *01226 249328* E-mail. *sales@machineco.co.uk* Web. *www.machineco.co.uk Niika*

Machine Guard Solutions Ltd 86 Leyland Trading Estate, Wellingborough NN8 1RT Tel. *01933 226335* Fax. *01933 276501* E-mail. *mgsolutions@btconnect.com* Web. *www.machineguardsolutions.com Safety Scan – Astro – Hibass – Hibass - Optoscan - Safety Scan - Astro – Optoscan*

Machine Mart 211 Lower Parliament Street, Nottingham NG1 1GN Tel. *0115 9561811* Fax. *08707 707811* E-mail. *sales@machinemart.co.uk* Web. *www.machinemart.co.uk Jack-King – Machine Mart – Tool-King*

Machines Automation Robotic Systems Ltd Stamford Bridge Road Dunnington, York YO19 5LJ Tel. *01904 489888* E-mail. *sales@mars.gb.net* Web. *www.mars.gb.net Kuka Robotics*

Machines4sale Knockalls Farm, Mitcheldean GL17 0DP Tel. *01594 542578* E-mail. *team@machines4sale.com* Web. *www.machines4sale.com machines4sale.co.uk*

Machine Tool Supplies Ltd 302-304 Chorley Old Road, Bolton BL1 4JU Tel. *01204 840111* Fax. *01204 844407* E-mail. *sales@mtsdriventools.co.uk* Web. *www.MTSDRIVENTOOLS.CO.UK Biglia – Daewoo – Diplomatic – Mori Seiki – Nakamura – Okuma – Sauter & Barruffalid Turrets*

Machining Centre Ltd Pembroke Lane Milton, Abingdon OX14 4EA Tel. *01235 831343* Fax. *01235 834708* E-mail. *sales@machiningcentre.co.uk* Web. *www.machiningcentre.co.uk The Machining Centre Ltd*

Macinnes Tooling Ltd Thistle House 29 Adelaide Street, Helensburgh G84 7DL Tel. *01436 676913* Fax. *01436 678877* E-mail. *sales@macinnes.co.uk* Web. *www.macinnes.co.uk *Acculok (Germany) – *Beck (Germany) – *Edalco (Switzerland) – Edalmatic – *Hangsterfer's (U.S.A.) – *Hartner (Germany) – *Kendu Milling Cutters (Spain) – *Modulock (Germany) – *Paradur (Germany) – *Protostar (Germany) – *Prototex (Germany) – *Speedmax (Germany)*

MacIntyre Chocolate Systems Ltd (Incl. Petzholdt Heidenauer) Sir William Smith Rd Kirkton Industrial Estate, Arbroath DD11 3RD Tel. *01241 434444* Fax. *01241 434411* E-mail. *enquiries@macintyre.co.uk* Web. *www.macintyre.co.uk Bake-A-Matic – MacIntyre Chocolate Systems*

Mcivor Plastics Ltd 161-171 Strand Road, Londonderry BT48 7PT Tel. *028 71267535* Fax. *028 71269313* E-mail. *info@mcivor.co.uk* Web. *www.mcivor.co.uk Artguard – Polyrib*

Mackays Ltd James Chalmers Road Kirkton Industrial Estate, Arbroath DD11 3LR Tel. *01241 432500* Fax. *01241 432444* E-mail. *info@mackays.com* Web. *www.mackays.com Mackay's of St Andrews*

McKenzie Martin Ltd Eton Hill Works Eton Hill Road, Radcliffe, Manchester M26 2US Tel. *0161 7232234* Fax. *0161 7259531* E-mail. *general@mckenziemartin.co.uk* Web. *www.mckenziemartin.co.uk Clearfire – Clearlite – Firemac – Kenstack – Mackridge – Macstream – Maximair – Multifire – Thermac – Ventura*

Mackey Bowley International Ltd Norfolk Road Industrial Estate, Gravesend DA12 2PT Tel. *01474 363521* Fax. *01474 334818* E-mail. *g.c.fenton@mackeybowley.co.uk* Web. *www.mackeybowley.co.uk Europress – Europressmen – Fontijne – Italpresse – Parmigiani – Stenhoj – Tiger*

Mackwell Electronics Ltd Vigo Place Aldridge, Walsall WS9 8UG Tel. *01922 458255* Fax. *01922 451263* E-mail. *nick.brangwin@mackwell.com* Web. *www.mackwell.com AutoTest - FastStart - Emergipack - TwinStart - Q Start - Smart Start - UniStart – Mackwell*

Mclaren Packaging Ltd Block 4 Gareloch Road Industrial Estate Gareloch Road, Port Glasgow PA14 5XH Tel. *01475 745246* Fax. *01475 744446* E-mail. *sales@mclarenpackaging.com* Web. *www.mclarenpackaging.com McLaren*

Mclaren Racing Mclaren Technology Centre Chertsey Road, Woking GU21 4YH Tel. *01483 261000* Fax. *01483 261963* E-mail. *webmaster@mclaren.com* Web. *www.mclaren.com McLaren*

Maclean Electrical (t/a Maclean Electrical) Plot 6 Peterseat Park Peterseat Drive Altens Industrial Estate, Altens Industrial Estate, Aberdeen AB12 3HT Tel. *01224 894212* Fax. *01224 894214* E-mail. *aberdeen@maclean.co.uk* Web. *www.maclean.co.uk Maclean Lighting*

Maclean Electricals (t/a Maclean Electrical) 16d Airport Industrial Estate Wick Airport, Wick KW1 4QS Tel. *01955 606611* Fax. *01955 606636* E-mail. *wick@maclean.co.uk* Web. *www.maclean.co.uk McLean Lighting*

Maclellan International Ltd (Integrated Cleaning & Support Services Ltd) 4 Bromells Road, London SW4 0BG Tel. *020 74980220* Fax. *020 74983191 Ramoneur*

Mcminn Hardware Wholesalers Latimer Road, Chesham HP5 1QJ Tel. *01494 786241* Fax. *01494 786864* E-mail. *liam.hyland@decco.co.uk* Web. *www.decco.co.uk Mcminn*

McNealy Brown Ltd Prentis Quay Mill Way, Sittingbourne ME10 2QD Tel. *01795 470592* Fax. *01795 471238* E-mail. *info@mcnealybrown.co.uk* Web. *www.mcnealybrown.com UNIPOD*

Macroberts LLP Capella 60 York Street, Glasgow G2 8JX Tel. *0141 3031100* Fax. *0141 3328886* E-mail. *maildesk@macroberts.com* Web. *www.macroberts.com MacRoberts*

Mactenn Systems Ltd 1 Bull Lane Acton, Sudbury CO10 0BD Tel. *01787 882422* Fax. *01787 882433* E-mail. *sales@mactenn.com* Web. *www.mactenn.com Dosamatic – Inflatek Valve – Maxflo – Maxflo - MaxSandflo - MultiAshflo - Inflatek Valve - SuperMaxflo - Dosamatic – MaxSandflo – MultiAshflo – SuperMaxflo – MiniMaxflo*

John Maden & Sons Ltd Market Street, Bacup OL13 0AU Tel. *01706 873544* Fax. *01706 879130* E-mail. *info@johnmaden.com Maidenese*

Madgecourt Curtains Cockfosters Parade Cockfosters Road, Barnet EN4 0BX Tel. *020 84470220* Fax. *020 84470330*

E-mail. *info@madgecourt.com* Web. *www.madgecourt.com Madgecourt*
Madhouse 369-391 Burnt Oak Broadway, Edgware HA8 5AW Tel. *020 89057664* Fax. *020 89057654* Web. *www.madhouse.co.uk Cromwells Madhouse*
Madison Burnell House 8 Stanmore Hill, Stanmore HA7 3BQ Tel. *020 83853385* Fax. *020 83853444* E-mail. *dominic.langan@madison.co.uk* Web. *www.madison.co.uk Aztec – *Buddy (Taiwan) – *Madison (Far East) – *Nutrak (Taiwan) – *Yakpak (Taiwan)*
Madison Filter Knowsley Road Industrial Estate Haslingden, Rossendale BB4 4EJ Tel. *01706 213421* Fax. *01706 221916* E-mail. *info@madisonfilter.com* Web. *www.madisonfilter.com Amitex – Azurtex – Cerafil – Cerifil – Neotex – Prestex – Primapor – Propex*
The M A D Virtual Assistant 23 Corstorphine Hill Road, Edinburgh EH12 6LQ Tel. *0131 6295117* E-mail. *twmacgregor@yahoo.co.uk* Web. *www.themadvirtualassistant.co.uk The M.A.D. Virtual Assistant*
The Maersk Company UK Ltd Maersk House Brayham Street, London E1 8EP Tel. *020 77125000* Fax. *020 77125120* E-mail. *info@kerr-mcgee.com* Web. *www.maersk.com Maersk – Maersk Line*
Magiboards Ltd Unit F Stafford Park 12, Telford TF3 3BJ Tel. *01952 292111* Fax. *01952 292280* E-mail. *sales@magiboards.com* Web. *www.magiboards.com *Magiboards (United Kingdom)*
Magill Henshaw Ltd Unit 16 Ashtree Enterprise Park Rathfriland Road, Newry BT34 1BY Tel. *028 30261311* Fax. *028 30262930* E-mail. *nuala@magillhenshaw.com* Web. *www.magillhenshaw.com JIMMY JOE*
Magna Colours Ltd 3 Dodworth Business Park Upper Cliffe Road, Dodworth, Barnsley S75 3SP Tel. *01226 731751* Fax. *01226 731752* E-mail. *enquiries@magnacolours.com* Web. *www.magnacolours.com *Evercion (Taiwan) – Magnaprint – *Minerprint (Italy)*
Magna Exteriors & Interiors Ltd Spade Lane Hartlip, Sittingbourne ME9 7TT Tel. *01634 385200* Fax. *01634 269840* Web. *www.magna.com Magna Interior Systems*
Magnaflux (a division of I T W Ltd) Faraday Road Dorcan, Swindon SN3 5HE Tel. *01793 524566* Fax. *01793 619498* E-mail. *sales@magnaflux.co.uk* Web. *www.eu.magnaflux.com Magnaflux – Magnaglo – Penecert – Spotcheck – Zyglo*
Magna Industrials Ltd Rissington Business Park Upper Rissington, Cheltenham GL54 2QB Tel. *01451 821775* Fax. *01451 824159* E-mail. *paul@magna-industrials.com* Web. *www.magna-industrials.com Fired Refractory Shapes – Hydrostatically Pressed Crucible – Magnabond – Magnacote – Magnamal – Mipex*
Magneco Metrel UK Ltd Hackworth Industrial Park, Shildon DL4 1HG Tel. *01388 777484* Fax. *01388 776286* E-mail. *colleen@magneco-metrel.com* Web. *www.magnaco-metrel.com *Met-Pump (U.S.A.)*
Magnesium Elektron PO Box 23, Manchester M27 8DD Tel. *0161 9111000* Fax. *0161 9111010* E-mail. *info@magnesium-elektron.com* Web. *www.magnesium-elektron.com Elektron – Elektron - MEL - Melmag - Zirmax - Melrasal – MEL – Melmag – Melram – Melrasal – Zirmax*
Magnet Applications Ltd North Bridge Road, Berkhamsted HP4 1EH Tel. *01442 875081* Fax. *01442 875009* E-mail. *sales@magnetuk.com* Web. *www.magnetapplications.com *Arelec (France) – Bremag – Compact – Flexam – Flexor – Gemo – Lattam – Placam – Placor – Raly*
Magnetic Rubber Direct Ltd 64 Salisbury Road, Sheffield S10 1WB Tel. *0114 2319840* Fax. *0114 2420081* E-mail. *info@mrd-magnets.com* Web. *www.mrd-magnets.com MRD Magnets*
Magnetrol International UK Ltd 1 Regent Business Centre Jubilee Road, Burgess Hill RH15 9TL Tel. *01444 871313* Fax. *01444 871317* E-mail. *sales@magnetrol.co.uk* Web. *www.magnetrol.co.uk E.Z. – Echotel – Kotron – Modulevel – Tuffy*
Magnet Schultz Ltd 3-4 Capital Park High Street, Old Woking, Woking GU22 9LD Tel. *01483 794700* Fax. *01483 757298* E-mail. *sales@magnetschultz.co.uk* Web. *www.magnetschultz.co.uk Electro Kabuki*
Magnify B 205 Woodseats Road, Sheffield S8 0PL Tel. *0114 2580088* E-mail. *info@magnifyb.co.uk* Web. *www.magnifyb.co.uk MagnifyB*
Magnum Venus Plastech Ltd Chilsworthy Beam, Gunnislake PL18 9AT Tel. *01822 832621* Fax. *01822 833999* E-mail. *rtm@plastech.co.uk* Web. *www.plastech.co.uk Hypaject – Megaject – MIT (Multiple Insert Tooling)*
Magnus Power (Division of Aker Subsea Ltd) 29-30 Brunel Road Churchfields Industrial Estate, St Leonards On Sea TN38 9RT Tel. *01424 853013* Fax. *01424 852268* E-mail. *magnuspower.sales@akersolutions.com* Web. *www.magnuspower.co.uk Magnus Power*
Magstim Co. Ltd Spring Gardens, Whitland SA34 0HR Tel. *01994 240798* Fax. *01994 240061* E-mail. *sales@magstim.com* Web. *www.magstim.com Bistim – Magstim 200 – Magstim 220 – Magstim 250 – Magstim Rapid – Neurosign 100 – Neurosign 800 – QuadroPulse*
Mag-Tech 53 Wordsworth Crescent, Littleborough OL15 0RB Tel. *07952 587246* Fax. *01706 371266* E-mail. *sales@mag-tech.co.uk* Web. *www.mag-tech.co.uk MAG - TECH LIMITED*
Maher Ltd 2 Brightside Way, Sheffield S9 2RQ Tel. *0114 2909200* Fax. *0114 2909290* E-mail. *info@maher.com* Web. *www.maher.com Invar*
Mahle Engine Systems New Street Kirkstyle, Kilmarnock KA1 3NA Tel. *01563 521190* Fax. *01563 539730* Web. *www.mahle.com Exalign – Glacetal*
Mahle Industrial Filteration UK Ltd Navigation Road, Stoke On Trent ST6 3RU Tel. *01782 575611* Fax. *01782 577001* E-mail. *salesuk@amafiltergroup.com* Web. *www.amafiltergroup.com Jord-Rotary Drum Filters*
Maidaid Halcyon The Engine Shed Top Station Road Industrial Estate Top Station Road, Brackley NN13 7UG Tel. *01280 845344* Fax. *01280 845340* E-mail. *sales@maidaid-halcyon.co.uk* Web. *www.maidaid.co.uk *Bezzera – *Cuppone – *Elettrobar – *Elframo – *Maidaid-Halcyon*
Mail News Media Blundells Corner Beverley Road, Hull HU3 1XS Tel. *01482 327111* Fax. *01482 872170* Web. *www.thisishull.co.uk Advertiser Series – Hull Daily Mail – Sports Mail – This Is Motor – This Is Property*
Mail Solutions Ltd Cronin Courtyard Weldon South Industrial Estate, Corby NN18 8AG Tel. *01536 400558* Fax. *01536 400889* E-mail. *print@mailsolutions.com* Web. *www.mailsolutions.com Tradesource*
Maineport Ltd 8 Terrace Factory Rossfield Road, Ellesmere Port CH65 3BS Tel. *0151 3550111* Fax. *0151 3561093* E-mail. *sales@uecnet.co.uk* Web. *www.maineport.com Active – Unitherm*
Mainetti UK Ltd Oxnam Road, Jedburgh TD8 6NN Tel. *01835 865000* Fax. *01835 863879* E-mail. *sales.uk@mainetti.com* Web. *www.mainetti.com Mainetti (UK) Ltd*
Maingate Ltd 6 Manor Way Old Woking, Woking GU22 9JX Tel. *01483 727898* Fax. *0845 2307585* E-mail. *ole@maingate.co.uk* Web. *www.maingate.co.uk Cosmo – Fort – Fort potmover – Ravendo – Siteblazer – Trallnor*
Main Road Sheet Metal Ltd Unit 2 Lancashire Enterprise Business Park, Leyland PR26 6TZ Tel. *01772 424172* Fax. *01772 456245* E-mail. *graham@mainroadsheetmetal.com* Web. *www.mainroadsheetmetal.com Main Road (Sheet Metal) Ltd*
Maisonneuve & Co. 29 Newman Street, London W1T 1PS Tel. *020 76369686* Fax. *020 74360770* E-mail. *enq@maisonneuve.co.uk* Web. *www.maisonneuve.co.uk Maisonneuve*
Majestic Shower Co 1 North Place Edinburgh Way, Harlow CM20 2SL Tel. *01279 443644* Fax. *01279 635074* E-mail. *jean@majesticshowers.com* Web. *www.majesticshowers.com Majestic*
Major International Ltd Higham Business Park Bury Close, Higham Ferrers, Rushden NN10 8HQ Tel. *01933 356012* Fax. *01933 274168* E-mail. *dbryant@majorint.com* Web. *www.majorint.com Major Demi-Glace – Major Mari-Base – Major Stock Base*
The Makaton Charity 46 London Road Blackwater, Camberley GU17 0AA Tel. *01276 606760* Fax. *01276 36725* E-mail. *info@makaton.org* Web. *www.makaton.org Makaton*
Making Computers Easy I.T - Visulizing Unit 38 Abbeyfields, Randlay, Telford TF3 - 2AL Tel. *07765 061174* Fax. *07765 061174* E-mail. *making.computers.easy.it.visual@googlemail.com* Web. *itvisualmakingcomputerseasy.synthasite.com/ Making Computers Easy I.T - Visulizing*
Making the Link 3 Maytree Close Coates, Cirencester GL7 6NQ Tel. *07812 596943* E-mail. *info@makingthelink.co.uk* Web. *www.makingthelink.co.uk Making the link*
Makin Metal Powders UK Ltd Buckley Road, Rochdale OL12 9DT Tel. *01706 717317* Fax. *01706 717303* E-mail. *derek.oldham@makin-metals.com* Web. *www.makin-metals.com Hymod – Powmet*
Makita UK Ltd Vermont Place Michigan Drive, Tongwell, Milton Keynes MK15 8JD Tel. *01908 211678* Fax. *01908 211400* E-mail. *info@makitauk.com* Web. *www.makitauk.com Finder Driver – Makita*
Malakoff Ltd North Ness Lerwick, Shetland ZE1 0LZ Tel. *01595 695544* Fax. *01595 695720* E-mail. *enquiries@malakofflimited.co.uk* Web. *www.malakoff.co.uk Voe*
Malem Medical 10 Willow Holt Lowdham, Nottingham NG14 7EJ Tel. *0115 9664440* Fax. *0115 9664672* E-mail. *malem@enterprise.net* Web. *www.malem.co.uk Malem Alarm – MicroMed*
Mallatite Ltd Hardwick View Road Holmewood, Chesterfield S42 5SA Tel. *01246 593280* Fax. *01246 593281* E-mail. *sales@mallatite.co.uk* Web. *www.mallatite.co.uk Abcite*
M A Lloyd & Son Ltd 47 Princip Street, Birmingham B4 6LW Tel. *0121 3596434* Fax. *0121 3335333* E-mail. *info@malloyd.com* Web. *www.malloyd.com Adsit – Adsit - V.J. Green.*
Maloto Property Consultants Ltd Fernacre Business Park Budds Lane, Romsey SO51 0HA Tel. *01794 324320* Fax. *01794 324330* E-mail. *jo@maloto.com* Web. *www.malotopc.com Maloto Property Consultants Ltd*
Malroy Products Dudley Ltd Shaw Road, Dudley DY2 8TR Tel. *01384 254178* Fax. *01384 230126* E-mail. *mhadley@malroyco.freeserve.co.uk* Web. *www.malroy.co.uk Malroy*
Malvern Instruments Ltd Grovewood Road, Malvern WR14 1XZ Tel. *01684 892456* Fax. *01684 892789* E-mail. *helpdesk@malvern.com* Web. *www.malvern.com Malvern Instruments – MasterSizer – Ultrasizer – Zetasizer*
Mamas & Papas (Stores) Ltd Colne Bridge Road, Huddersfield HD5 0RH Tel. *08452 682000* Fax. *01484 438210* E-mail. *sales@mamasandpapas.co.uk* Web. *www.mamasandpapas.com *Mamas & Papas (Italy)*
Mamelok Holdings Ltd Northern Way, Bury St Edmunds IP32 6NJ Tel. *01284 762291* Fax. *01284 703689* E-mail. *sales@mamelok.com* Web. *www.mamelok.com H & P – MPL – Paper-Masters*
Management Forum 98-100 Maybury Road, Woking GU21 5JL Tel. *01483 730071* Fax. *01483 730008* E-mail. *info@management-forum.co.uk* Web. *www.management-forum.co.uk Management Forum (United Kingdom)*
The Manchester Conference Centre Trading Services Umist, Manchester M60 1QD Tel. *0161 9558000* Fax. *0161 2752223* Web. *www.meeting.co.uk Manchester Conference Centre (United Kingdom)*
Manchester Hosiery A Division Of Aikon Europe Group Ltd Queens Road, Hinckley LE10 1EE Tel. *01455 632161* Fax. *01455 635390* E-mail. *info@palmunderwear.co.uk* Web. *www.palmunderwear.co.uk Kiddee Palm – Palm*
Mandarin Creative Solutions Ltd Carne Main Street, Blidworth, Mansfield NG21 0QH Tel. *0845 8330030* Fax. *0845 8330040* E-mail. *studio@mandarincreates.co.uk* Web. *www.mandarincreates.com Mandarin*
Manderstam International Group Ltd 10 Greycoat Place, London SW1P 1SB Tel. *020 77309224* Fax. *020 78233056* E-mail. *peterlumley@manderstam.com* Web. *www.manderstam.com MIGL*
Manesty Kitling Road Knowsley Business Park, Prescot L34 9JS Tel. *0151 5478000* Fax. *0151 5478001* E-mail. *matthias.meyer@oystar.manesty.com* Web. *www.oystar.manesty.com Manesty*
Mangar International Ltd Presteigne Industrial Estate, Presteigne LD8 2UF Tel. *01544 267674* Fax. *01544 260287* E-mail. *info@mangar.co.uk* Web. *www.mangar.co.uk Mangar Air Flow Compressor – Mangar Bathlift – Mangar Booster – Mangar ELK – Mangar Freestyle and Freestyle Junior – Mangar Handy Pillow Lift – Mangar Leg Lifter/Cotside – Mangar Leg Support – Mangar Lifting Cushion – Mangar Porter – Mangar School Porter – Mangar Situp – Mangar Surf Bather – Mangar Therapy Wedge – Mangaroo*
Manhattan Furniture (t/a Manhattan Furniture) Blenheim Road, Lancing BN15 8UH Tel. *01903 524300* Fax. *01903 750679* E-mail. *jonathanh@manhattan.co.uk* Web. *www.manhattan.co.uk Manhattan Series 5 Bathrooms – Manhattan Series 7 Kitchens*
Manitou Site Lift Ltd Black Moor Road Ebblake Industrial Estate, Verwood BH31 6BB Tel. *01202 825331* Fax. *01202 813027* E-mail. *info@manitou.com* Web. *www.manitou.com Buggie – Buggiscopic – Maniaccess – Manilec – *Maniloader (France) – *Maniscopic (France) – *Manitou (France) – Manitransit – Twisco*
Manitowoc Foodservice UK Limited Enodis UK Food Service Ashbourne House The Guildway, Old Portsmouth Road, Guildford GU3 1LR Tel. *01483 464900* Fax. *01483 464905* E-mail. *fsuk.info@manitowoc.com* Web. *www.enodisuk.com Masterwash*
Manitowoc Food Service UK (A Manitowoc Company) 5 E Langley Business Centre Station Road, Langley, Slough SL3 8DS Tel. *01753 485900* Fax. *01753 485901* E-mail. *john.rourke@manitowoc.com* Web. *www.manitowocssuk.com Advanced Counters and Services – Chefaire – Commodore 2000 – Electroway – Henry Nuttall – Jackson – L.C.F. Bishop – Masterchef – Masterwash – MLine – Moorwood Vulcan – Sadia Refrigeration – Sadia Senator – Sadia Sovereign – Sadia Sterling*
Manor Coating Systems Otley Road Charlestown, Shipley BD17 7DP Tel. *01274 587351* Fax. *01274 531360* E-mail. *sales@manorcoatingsystems.co.uk* Web. *www.manorcoatingsystems.co.uk Manor*
Manrose Manufacturing Ltd 1 Albion Close, Slough SL2 5DT Tel. *01753 691399* Fax. *01753 692294* E-mail. *sales@manrose.co.uk* Web. *www.manrose.co.uk *Manrose (Spain)*
Mansell Construction Services Ltd Roman House, Croydon BR9 6BU Tel. *020 86548191* Fax. *020 86553916* E-mail. *mailbox@mansell.plc.uk* Web. *www.constructingcommunities.com Mansell*
Manse Masterdor Ltd Halfpenny Lane, Knaresborough HG5 0SL Tel. *01423 866868* Fax. *01423 866368* E-mail. *sales@masterdor.co.uk* Web. *www.masterdor.co.uk Masterdor*

Mantair 13 Baker Close Oakwood Business Park Stephenson Road West, Clacton On Sea CO15 4TL Tel. *01255 476376* Fax. *01255 476817* E-mail. *enquiries@mantair.com* Web. *www.mantair.com Mantair*

Mantek Manufacturing Ltd 11 Holder Road, Aldershot GU12 4RH Tel. *01252 343335* Fax. *01252 343570* E-mail. *sales@mantek.co.uk* Web. *www.mantek.co.uk Hirschmann – Hirschmann - Bearings & Axial Shaft Seals.*

Manx Independent Carriers Union Mills, Isle Of Man IM4 4LG Tel. *01624 692100* Fax. *01624 610987* E-mail. *sales@mic.co.im* Web. *www.mic.co.im Manx Independent Carriers*

Mapa Spontex Berkeley Business Park Wainwright Road, Worcester WR4 9ZS Tel. *01905 450300* Fax. *01905 450350* E-mail. *robert.gibbons@spontex.co.uk* Web. *www.spontex.co.uk Dextram – Harpon – Jersetlite – Jersette – Mapa – Neotex – Petrolier – Protective clothing distributors – Super Jersette – Technic – Telsan – Titan – Titanlite – Trionic – Ultranitril – Ultril*

Maple Aggregates UK Ltd 50 Preston Road, Brighton BN1 4QF Tel. *01273 699001* Fax. *01273 670977* E-mail. *enquiries@mapleaggregates.com* Web. *www.mapleaggregates.com *Maplelite Pumice (Greece and Italy) – *Marble Chippings (Greece and Italy)*

Mapra Technik Co. Unit D13 The Seedbed Centre, Loughton IG10 3TQ Tel. *020 85084207* Fax. *020 85025107* E-mail. *info@mapra.co.uk* Web. *www.mapra.co.uk ADI METALPARTS – AUBERT – BAREISS – KAFER – MARCEL AUBERT – NUCAP EUROPE*

Map Trading Ltd 2 Abbey Road, London NW10 7BS Tel. *020 89650193* Fax. *020 89631184* E-mail. *post@whitepearl.co.uk* Web. *www.whitepearl.co.uk *Map (Worldwide)*

Marathon Belting Ltd Healey Mill Whitworth Road, Rochdale OL12 0TF Tel. *01706 657052* Fax. *01706 525143* E-mail. *sales@marathonbelting.co.uk* Web. *www.marathonbelting.co.uk Blue Roller – ColourMesh – Copsil – Gold Roller – Green Roller – Red Roller – Triple A Plus*

M A R C Co GB Ltd Rear of Gardeners Paradise Stodmarsh Road, Canterbury CT3 4AP Tel. *01227 459999* Fax. *01227 459990* E-mail. *info@marcltd.com* Web. *www.marcltd.com M.A.R.C. – Oak Glade*

Marchant Manufacturing Co. Ltd Piperell Way, Haverhill CB9 8QW Tel. *01440 705351* Fax. *01440 762593* E-mail. *philipmarchant@marchant.co.uk* Web. *www.marchant.co.uk Safewrap – Safewrap - Caterpack - Marchant - Big Value*

Marco Beverage Systems Ltd The Shire House Strixton, Wellingborough NN29 7PA Tel. *01933 666488* Fax. *01933 666968* E-mail. *sales@marco-bev.co.uk* Web. *www.marco-bev.co.uk Aquarius – *Autobev – Ciocco – Cup Carousel – *Ezt – Filtro – Filtro Shuttle – Freshcup – Libra – *Maxibrew – *Qwikbrew*

Marcon Diamond Products Ltd Marcon House 131 High Street, Codicote, Hitchin SG4 8UB Tel. *01438 820581* Fax. *01438 821352 Boride – Marcon*

Marcrist International Ltd Marcrist House Sandall Stones Road, Kirk Sandall Industrial Estate, Doncaster DN3 1QR Tel. *01302 890888* Fax. *01302 883864* E-mail. *info@marcrist.com* Web. *www.marcrist.com Hallmarc – Marcrist – Marcrist – Marcrist – Marxo – Powermarc – Trademarc – Turbolite*

Mar Deb 2-4 Pavilion Business Park Speculation Road, Forest Vale Industrial Estate, Cinderford GL14 2YD Tel. *01594 826944* Fax. *01594 826637* E-mail. *info@mardeb.co.uk* Web. *www.mardeb.co.uk Correx – Jiffy – Mastershield – Octabin*

Marden Edwards Ltd 2 Nimrod Way East Dorset Trade Park, Wimborne BH21 7SH Tel. *01202 861200* Fax. *01202 842632* E-mail. *sales@wrapsuk.com* Web. *www.mardenedwards.com Marden Edwards (United Kingdom) – Wraps UK (United Kingdom)*

Marflow Engineering Ltd Britannia House Austin Way, Hampstead Industrial Estate, Birmingham B42 1DU Tel. *0121 3581555* Fax. *0121 3581444* E-mail. *sales@marflow.co.uk* Web. *www.marflow.co.uk Britannia Water Fittings – Compel – Consort – Impel – St. James Collection – Wolf*

Marigold Industrial Ltd B2 Vantage Office Park Old Gloucester Road, Hambrook, Bristol BS16 1GW Tel. *08450 753355* Fax. *0845 0753356* E-mail. *sales@marigold-industrial.com* Web. *www.marigold-industrial.com *Comasec (France) – Comasec Yate*

Marine & General Engineers Ltd (Head Office) PO Box 470, Guernsey GY1 6AT Tel. *01481 243048* Fax. *01481 248765* E-mail. *sales@mge.gg* Web. *www.mge.gg Caterpiller – Volvo Penta – Volvo Penta & Caterpiller*

Mark C Brown Ltd PO Box 69, Hull HU2 8HS Tel. *01482 323464* Fax. *01482 214999* E-mail. *info@markcbrown.co.uk* Web. *www.markcbrown.co.uk Colop – Everink – Permastamp – Porelon – Sprinty – Stamp-Ever (R)*

Markel UK Ltd Riverside West Whitehall Road, Leeds LS1 4AW Tel. *08453 512600* Fax. *0113 2450924* Web. *www.markeluk.com R E Brown underwriting ltd*

Markem-Imaje Ltd Astor Road, Salford M50 1DA Tel. *0161 3338400* Fax. *0161 7075566* E-mail. *kappleton@markem.com* Web. *www.markem-imaje.com Cimjet – SmartDate – Touch Dry*

Market Harborough Building Society 15-17 The Square, Market Harborough LE16 7PD Tel. *01858 412250* Fax. *01858 410169* E-mail. *mrobinson@mhbs.co.uk* Web. *www.mhbs.co.uk Discount – Fixed Rate – Flexible Mortgage – Low Cost*

Marketing Dynamics Ltd 55 Lancaster Grove, London NW3 4HD Tel. *020 74333555* Fax. *020 74333560* E-mail. *info@marketingdynamics.co.uk* Web. *www.marketingdynamics.co.uk Customer Dynamics*

Marketpoint Europe Ltd Unit 6 The Western Centre Western Road, Bracknell RG12 1RW Tel. *01344 350250* Fax. *01344 488045* E-mail. *sales@mktpoint.com* Web. *www.mktpoint.com Marketpoint*

Markforce Emperor House 35 Vine Street, London EC3N 2PX Tel. *020 75541800* Fax. *020 75541801* Web. *www.markforce.com Markforce*

Marks & Clerk LLP 19 Long Acre, London WC2E 9RA Tel. *020 74200000* Fax. *020 78363339* E-mail. *rwaldren@marks-clerk.com* Web. *www.marks-clerk.com Roystons*

Mark's & Clerk LLP 27 Imperial Square, Cheltenham GL50 1RQ Tel. *01242 524520* Fax. *01242 579383* E-mail. *cheltenham@marks-clerk.com* Web. *www.marks-clerk.com A R Davies & Co.*

Mark's & Clerk LLP Alpha Tower Suffolk Street Queensway, Birmingham B1 1TT Tel. *0121 6435881* Fax. *0116 2330192* E-mail. *birmingham@marks-clerk.com* Web. *www.marks-clerk.com Lewis & Taylor*

Mark Simpkin Ltd (Simply Group) Unit F1 Adelphi Mill Grimshaw Lane, Bollington, Macclesfield SK10 5JB Tel. *01625 576527* Fax. *01625 576545* E-mail. *info@simplygroupuk.co.uk* Web. *www.simplygroupuk.co.uk Simply Cubicles – Simply Lockers – Simply Seating – Simply Shelters – Simply Tables and Chairs*

Marlborough Communications Ltd Dovenby Hall Balcombe Road, Horley RH6 9UU Tel. *01293 775071* Fax. *01293 820781* E-mail. *enquiries@marlboroughcomms.com* Web. *www.marlboroughcomms.com Comsecpack*

Marlborough Tiles Elcot Lane, Marlborough SN8 2AY Tel. *01672 512422* Fax. *01672 515791* E-mail. *sales@marlboroughtiles.com* Web. *www.marlboroughtiles.com Marlborough Tiles*

Marley Eternit Ltd Lichfield Road Branston Industrial Estate, Branston, Burton On Trent DE14 3HD Tel. *01283 722222* Fax. *01283 722242* E-mail. *info@marleyeternit.co.uk* Web. *www.marleyeternit.co.uk Decorative Finals – Marley Bold Roll – Marley Cloak Verge System – Marley Dry Ridge and Dry Mono Ridge System – Marley Eaves Ventilation System – Marley Gas Vent Ridge Tiles – Marley Interlocking Dry Verge System – Marley Ludlow Major – Marley Marlden – Marley Marquess – Marley Marvent Roof Ventilating Tiles – Marley Mendip – Marley Modern – Marley Plain – Marley Plain Tile Cloak Verge – Marley Plain Tile Dry Ridge System – Marley Ridge Vent Terminal – Marley Ventilated Dry Ridge System – Marley Ventilating Ridge Tiles – Marley Wessex – Rooftile Clansman – Rooftile Heritage – Rooftile Mock Bond Modern – Rooftile Thaxden – Thermalite Coursing Bricks – Thermalite Floorblock – Thermalite Hi-Strength 10 – Thermalite Hi-Strength 7 – Thermalite Hi-Strength Smooth Face – Thermalite Hi-Strength Trenchblock – Thermalite Large Format Blocks – Thermalite Party Wall – Thermalite Shield 2000 – Thermalite Smooth Face – Thermalite Thin Joint Mortar - Thermalite Trenchblock – Thermalite Turbo*

Marling Leek Ltd Marling Mills Nelson Street, Leek ST13 6BB Tel. *01538 384108* Fax. *01538 387350* E-mail. *sales@marling.co.uk* Web. *www.marling.co.uk Marlin Leek*

Marl International Ltd Morecambe Road, Ulverston LA12 9BN Tel. *01229 582430* Fax. *01229 585155* E-mail. *sales@marl.co.uk* Web. *www.leds.co.uk Marl – Marl Creative Arc – Marl International Limited – Marl Optosource – Optosign*

Marlow Industries Europe Aberdeen House South Road, Haywards Heath RH16 4NG Tel. *01444 443404* Fax. *01444 443334* E-mail. *info@marlow-europe.co.uk* Web. *www.marlow.com Dura TEC*

Marlow Ropes Ltd Rope Maker Park Dipilocks Way, Hailsham BN27 3GU Tel. *01323 444444* Fax. *01323 444455* E-mail. *sales@marlowropes.com* Web. *www.marlowropes.com Hi-Brites – K.T.3 – Marlow Ropes – Marlow Ropes – Marlowbraid – Multiplait – Nelson – Paraline – S.D. 3 – Silver Star – Static L.S.K. – Sturdee*

Marrill Engineering Co. Ltd Waterman Road, Coventry CV6 5TP Tel. *024 76689221* Fax. *024 76668114* E-mail. *sales@marrill.co.uk* Web. *www.marrill.co.uk Alfred Herbert Rebuilding Services – Marrill*

Marsden Weighing Machine Group Anvil House Tuns Lane, Henley On Thames RG9 1SA Tel. *08451 307330* Fax. *08451 307440* E-mail. *sales@marsdengroup.co.uk* Web. *www.marsden-weighing.co.uk *Digi (Japan) – Tanita – Weighcare*

The Marsh Agency Ltd 50 Albemarle Street, London W1S 4BD Tel. *020 74934361* Fax. *020 74958961* E-mail. *paterson@patersonmarsh.co.uk* Web. *www.marsh-agency.co.uk Mark Paterson & Associates – Quentin Books – Sigmund Freud Copyrights*

Marshall Amplifications plc Denbigh Road Bletchley, Milton Keynes MK1 1DQ Tel. *01908 375411* Fax. *01908 376118* E-mail. *contactus@marshallamps.com* Web. *www.marshallamps.com Marshall*

Marshall Arts Unit 7 Elvington Industrial Estate York Road, Elvington, York YO41 4AR Tel. *01904 607055* Fax. *01904 608188* E-mail. *paul@marshall-art.net* Web. *www.marshallarts.co.uk Marshall Arts*

Marshall Cavendish Ltd 5th Floor 32/38 Saffron Hill, London EC1N 8FH Tel. *020 74218120* Fax. *020 74218121* E-mail. *info@marshallcavendish.co.uk* Web. *www.marshallcavendish.co.uk Marshall Cavendish Books – Marshall Cavendish Multimedia*

Marshall Deacon Knitwear Ltd 122 Fairfax Road, Leicester LE4 9EL Tel. *0116 2461260* Fax. *0116 2743528* E-mail. *info@marshalldeacon.com* Web. *marshalldeacon.com M.D.*

E W Marshall Ltd 79 Enid Street, London SE16 3RA Tel. *020 73940900* Fax. *020 73940827* E-mail. *info@ewmarshall.com* Web. *www.ewmarshall.com Bisley – Complete Office Interiors – Giroflex – Harvey – Pentos – President – Senator – Verco*

Marshalls Hard Metals Ltd Windsor Street, Sheffield S4 7WB Tel. *0114 2752282* Fax. *0114 2738499* E-mail. *sales@hardmet.com* Web. *www.hardmet.com H.S.M. – Halco – *T.G.I. (U.S.A.)*

Marston Agricultural Services Ltd Toll Bar Road Marston, Grantham NG32 2HG Tel. *01400 250226* Fax. *01400 250540* E-mail. *sales@marstontrailers.co.uk* Web. *www.marstontrailers.co.uk A.S. Trailers – Collins Trailers (Marston) – Griffiths Trailers – Salop Trailers*

Marstons plc Marstons House Brewery Road, Wolverhampton WV1 4JT Tel. *01902 711811* Fax. *01902 429136* E-mail. *ralph.findlay@wdbbrands.co.uk* Web. *www.marstonsplc.com Elridge, Pope & Co.*

Martec International Ltd 40 High Street, Taunton TA1 3PN Tel. *01823 333469* Fax. *01823 332423* E-mail. *info@martec-international.com* Web. *www.martec-international.com Martec*

Martec Of Whitwell Ltd Unit 12 Midway Business Centre Bridge St Industria Bridge Street, Clay Cross, Chesterfield S45 9NU Tel. *01246 860855* Fax. *01246 860877* E-mail. *sales@martec-conservation.com* Web. *www.martec-conservation.com Marplug – Plugloc*

Martin Co. Ltd (Armac) 160 Dollman Street Duddeston, Birmingham B7 4RS Tel. *0121 3592111* Fax. *0121 3594698* E-mail. *sales@martin.co.uk* Web. *www.martin.co.uk Martin*

Brett Martin Ltd 24 Roughfort Road, Newtownabbey BT36 4RB Tel. *028 90849999* Fax. *028 90836666* E-mail. *mail@brettmartin.com* Web. *www.brettmartin.com Foamalux – Foamalux Ultra – Marcryl – Marlon - Trilite – Marlon CS Longlife – Marlon FSX Longlife – Marlon ST Longlife – Marvec*

Martin Manufacturing UK plc Belvoir Way Fairfield Industrial Estate, Louth LN11 0LQ Tel. *01507 604399* Fax. *01507 601956* E-mail. *info@martin.dk* Web. *www.martin.dk J.E.M. – Martin*

Martin Yale International Ltd Unit C2 Fleming Centre Fleming Way, Crawley RH10 9NN Tel. *01293 441900* Fax. *01293 611155* E-mail. *enquiries@intimus.co.uk* Web. *www.martinyale.com Intimus – Martin Yale – Premier*

Marubeni Komatsu Ltd (Head Office) Padgets Lane, Redditch B98 0RT Tel. *01527 512512* Fax. *01527 502310* E-mail. *info@mkl.co.uk* Web. *www.mkl.co.uk *Furukawa (Japan) – *Kobelco (Japan) – *Komatsu (Japan) – *Moxy (Norway)*

Marwel Conveyors Dudley Road East, Oldbury B69 3EB Tel. *0121 5524418* Fax. *0121 5524018* E-mail. *sales@marwel.com* Web. *www.marwel.uk.com MARWEL – Marwel - conveyors*

Marwood Group Ltd 72 Roding Road London Industrial Park, London E6 6JG Tel. *020 75402500* Fax. *020 75402521* E-mail. *london@marwoodgroup.co.uk* Web. *www.marwoodgroup.co.uk Marwood*

Masco Print Developments Ltd Stags End Cottage Barn Gaddesden Row, Hemel Hempstead HP2 6HN Tel. *01582 791190* Fax. *01582 791199* E-mail. *info@mascoprint.co.uk* Web. *www.mascoprint.co.uk Mascoprint*

Geoffrey Maskell Engineering Ltd Londonderry Works, Seaham SR7 7SL Tel. *0191 5813244* Fax. *0191 5810273* E-mail. *info@maskelleng.co.uk* Web. *www.maskelleng.co.uk Ganntri-Tilt*

Mason Price Fluid Solutions Ltd The Workshops 13 Bath Road, Wootton Bassett, Swindon SN4 7DF Tel. *01793 321020* Fax. *01793 321019* E-mail. *enquiries@masonprice.co.uk* Web. *www.masonprice.co.uk Angus Wellmaster*

Mass Consultants Ltd Enterprise House Great North Road, St Neots PE19 6BN Tel. *01480 222600* Fax. *01480 407366* E-mail. *alane@mass.co.uk* Web. *www.mass.co.uk Atracks – Domain Guard – EW – EWOS – FRES – ISTAR – OFCOM – Sonic – Thurbon – Trap*

Massey Truck Engineering Ltd Station Road Halfway, Sheffield S20 3GX Tel. *0114 2483751* Fax. *0114 2478246* E-mail. *mail@masseytruckengineering.co.uk* Web. *www.masseytruckengineering.co.uk M.T.E.*

Masson Seeley & Co. Ltd Rouses Lane, Downham Market PE38 9AN Tel. *01366 388000* Fax. *01366 385222* E-mail. *admin@masson-seeley.co.uk* Web. *www.masson-seeley.co.uk 9000 System – D.I.S.C. – Masseeley – Module 2000 – Module 60*

Masstock Arable UK Ltd Station Road Andoversford, Cheltenham GL54 4LZ Tel. *0791 7220868* Fax. *01242 820807* Web. *www.masstock.co.uk Cleanacres*

Mastenbroek Ltd Swineshead Road Wyberton Fen, Boston PE21 7JG Tel. *01205 311313* Fax. *01205 310016* E-mail. *info@mastenbroek.com* Web. *www.mastenbroek.com Mastenbroek*

Master Chemical Europe Ltd Unit 33 Maitland Road Lion Barn Industrial Estate Needham Market, Ipswich IP6 8NZ Tel. *01449 726800* Fax. *01449 721719* E-mail. *info@masterchemical.co.uk* Web. *www.masterchemical.com Scrounger – Trim – Unimix – Xybex*

Mastercut Cutting Systems Ltd Unit 9 Upper Mantle Close Bridge Street Industrial Estate, Clay Cross, Chesterfield S45 9NU Tel. *01246 860811* Fax. *01246 866928* E-mail. *info@mastercut.co.uk* Web. *www.mastercut.co.uk B.M.E. – Jaycee – Mastercut*

Master Farm Services GB Ltd Bures Park Colne Road, Bures CO8 5DJ Tel. *01787 228450* Fax. *01787 229146* E-mail. *enquiries@masterfarm.co.uk* Web. *www.masterfarm.co.uk *Funki (Denmark) – Master – Tramspread*

Master Magnets Ltd (Incorporating Metal Detection Ltd) Burnt Meadow Road Moons Moat North Industrial Estate, Redditch B98 9PA Tel. *01527 65858* Fax. *01527 65868* E-mail. *info@mastermagnets.co.uk* Web. *www.mastermagnets.com Master Magnets*

J B Masters Ltd Dorset Avenue, Thornton Cleveleys FY5 2DB Tel. *01253 856096* Fax. *01253 856096* E-mail. *jb@mastersltd.freeserve.co.uk JB Masters Ltd*

The Mast Group Ltd Mast House Derby Road, Bootle L20 1EA Tel. *0151 9337277* Fax. *0151 9441332* E-mail. *sales@mastgrp.com* Web. *www.mastgrp.com Adatab – Bacteruritest – Cryobank – Discmaster – Intralactam – M.I.D.8 Mastring – Mast Assure – Mast ID – Mast Redipac – Mast Rediprep – Mastafluor – Mastascan – Mastascanelite – Mastazyme – Mastring – Mastring S – Multipointelite – Occutest – Selectatab – Selectavial – Sputagest – X.V. Mirror Ring*

Mastiff Electronic Systems Ltd 8 Holder Road, Aldershot GU12 4RH Tel. *01252 342200* Fax. *01252 342400* E-mail. *enquiries@mastiff.co.uk* Web. *www.mastiff.co.uk Mastiff Hands Free – Mastiff Network – Mastiff Viewcard*

M A S T International Group Ltd Hermitage House Bath Road, Taplow, Maidenhead SL6 0AR Tel. *01628 784062* Fax. *01628 773061* E-mail. *earmstrong@mast.co.uk* Web. *www.mast.co.uk Mast*

Matchmakers International Ltd Park View Mills Wibsey Park Avenue, Wibsey, Bradford BD6 3SR Tel. *01274 711011* Fax. *01274 711030* E-mail. *david.brook@matchmakers.co.uk* Web. *www.harryhall.co.uk Cottage Craft – Harry Hall – Masta – Stylo – Stylo Matchmakers*

Matcon Ltd Matcon House London Road, Moreton In Marsh GL56 0HJ Tel. *01608 651666* Fax. *01608 651635* E-mail. *charles.lee@matcon-cone.com* Web. *www.matcon.com Matcon*

Mateline Engineering Ltd 42 Walkers Road Moons Moat North Industrial Estate, Redditch B98 9HD Tel. *01527 63213* Fax. *01527 584530* E-mail. *matelineengineering@tiscali.co.uk* Web. *www.mateline.com Mateline*

Materion Brush Ltd Unit 4 Ely Road Theale Commercial Estate, Theale, Reading RG7 4BQ Tel. *0118 9303733* Fax. *0118 9203635* E-mail. *guy.shapland@materion.com* Web. *www.materion.com Albemet – Alloy 171 – Alloy 174 – Alloy 360 – Alloy 60 – Alloy 60, Alloy 171, Alloy 174, Toughmet, Moldmax, Protherm, Albemet, Alloy 360, Brush 60, Brush 390, Foramet, Moldmax, Toughmet. – Brush 390 – Brush 60 – Formamet – Moldmax – Protherm – Toughmet*

Matki plc Churchward Road Yate, Bristol BS37 5PL Tel. *01454 322888* Fax. *01454 315284* E-mail. *helpline@matki.co.uk* Web. *www.matki.co.uk Classica – Colonade – Continental – Eleganza – Fincline – Finesse – Infold – Matki – Mirage – Quintesse – Radiance – Synthastone – Universal*

Mato Industries Ltd Unit 1 Philips Road Whitebirk Industrial Estate, Blackburn BB1 5PG Tel. *01254 387638* Fax. *01254 238023* E-mail. *info@mato.co.uk* Web. *www.mato.co.uk *Comet – M.R.E. 557 – *Mastabar – Mastabar 'C' Type – Mastascrape*

Matrix Composite Materials Company Ltd Unit E Paintworks, Arnos Vale, Bristol BS4 3EH Tel. *0117 9715145* Fax. *0117 9778388* E-mail. *sales@mcmc-uk.com* Web. *www.mcmc-uk.com Sicomin (France)*

Matrix International Ltd Eastmill Road, Brechin DD9 7EP Tel. *01356 602000* Fax. *01356 602060* E-mail. *info@matrix-international.com* Web. *www.matrix-international.com Airchamp – Matrix – Matrix – Waldron – Waldron*

Mats4U 17 Maybrook Road Minworth, Sutton Coldfield B76 1AL Tel. *0800 1804024* Fax. *0121 3511991* E-mail. *sales@mats4u.co.uk* Web. *www.mats4u.co.uk Waterhog*

Matsuura Machinery Ltd Gee Road, Coalville LE67 4NH Tel. *01530 511400* Fax. *01530 511440* E-mail. *marketing@matsuura.co.uk* Web. *www.matsuura.co.uk M S T – Matsuura – Muratec Murata – Romi – Shin Nippon Koki – Stama*

Mattei Compressors Ltd Admington Lane Admington, Shipston On Stour CV36 4JJ Tel. *01789 450577* Fax. *01789 450698* E-mail. *andy.jones@mattei.co.uk* Web. *www.mattei.co.uk Mattei*

Mattel Vanwall Road, Maidenhead SL6 4UB Tel. *01628 500000* Fax. *01628 500075* Web. *www.mattel.com Fisher Price – Mattel*

Matthew Hebden 54 Blackamoor Road, Sheffield S17 3GJ Tel. *0114 2368122* Fax. *0114 2368127* E-mail. *sales@matthewhebden.co.uk* Web. *www.matthewhebden.co.uk Prestige – T-Pren – Tegola*

E F G Matthews Office Furniture Ltd Reginald Road, St Helens WA9 4JE Tel. *08456 084100* Fax. *01744 819431* E-mail. *craig.howarth@efgoffice.co.uk* Web. *www.efgoffice.co.uk Add-Infinitum – Econ – Hushbox – Matthews – Splice – Teamleader – Teamspirit – Teamtalk – Teamwork – Uniformity – Zest*

Mavitta Division Morson Projects Mavitta Division Unit 8 Furnace Lane Moira, Swadlincote DE12 6AT Tel. *01283 211711* Fax. *01283 226868* E-mail. *info@mavitta.com* Web. *www.mavitta.com Mavitta*

Mawsley Machinery Ltd Brixworth Industrial Estate Brixworth, Northampton NN6 9UA Tel. *01604 880621* Fax. *01604 881746* E-mail. *sales@mawsley.com* Web. *www.mawsley.com Bomag – CompAir – Manitou – Sthil – Thwaites – Volvo*

Maxam 14 Cultins Road, Edinburgh EH11 4DZ Tel. *0131 4424343* Fax. *0131 4772112* E-mail. *info@maxam.co.uk* Web. *www.maxam.co.uk Maxam*

Max Appliances Ltd Unit 16 Wheel Park Farm Industrial Estate Wheel Lane, Westfield, Hastings TN35 4SE Tel. *01424 751666* Fax. *01424 751444* E-mail. *sales@max-appliances.co.uk* Web. *www.max-appliances.co.uk Max Appliances – Max St – Maxmatic – Wastematic*

Maxa Technologies Ltd Atlantic Street Broadheath, Altrincham WA14 5QJ Tel. *0161 9427850* Fax. *0161 9277664* E-mail. *steve.berry@maxatec-europe.com* Web. *www.maxatec-europe.com Cognitive TPG – MCR – Bluebird 'Pidion' – TSC – Sewoo – Catchwell – Xplore – Arbor – Skeye – Zebex*

Max Frank Ltd Whittle Road, Stoke On Trent ST3 7HF Tel. *01782 598041* Fax. *01782 315056* E-mail. *info@maxfrank.co.uk* Web. *www.maxfrank.co.uk *Cresco (Germany) – Creteco – Frank – *Geku (Germany) – Insitex – *Intec (Germany) – Tub-Box – *Zemdrain (Luxembourg)*

MaxMax Ltd Beech Grove Wootton, Eccleshall, Stafford ST21 6HU Tel. *0845 6066853* Fax. *01785 226767* E-mail. *sales@maxmaxltd.com* Web. *www.maxmaxltd.com LinkLite*

Maxon C I C Europe Ltd Maxon House Cleveland Road, Hemel Hempstead Industrial Estate, Hemel Hempstead HP2 7EY Tel. *01442 267777* Fax. *01442 215515* E-mail. *sales@maxoncic.co.uk* Web. *www.maxoncic.co.uk Maxon*

Max Power Sports Co. 126 Edward Road Balsall Heath, Birmingham B12 9LS Tel. *0121 4401841* Fax. *0121 4406279* E-mail. *rkumar@maxpowersports.co.uk* Web. *www.maxpowersports.co.uk Ladymax – Max Power – Max Power Sports – Stich*

Maxview Ltd Common Lane Setchey, Kings Lynn PE33 0AT Tel. *01553 813300* Fax. *01553 813301* E-mail. *info@maxview.ltd.uk* Web. *www.maxview.ltd.uk Omnimax – Selfix 10 – Slate-Mate*

Max Web Solutions Ltd 188 Liscard Road, Wallasey CH44 5TN Tel. *0151 6914939* Fax. *01582* E-mail. *info@maxwebsolutions.co.uk* Web. *www.maxwebsolutions.co.uk EasiRental*

Maybrey Reliance 16-18 Kennet Road, Dartford DA1 4QN Tel. *01322 550724* Fax. *01322 550724* E-mail. *sales@maybrey.co.uk* Web. *www.maybrey.co.uk Maybrey*

Mayday Seals & Bearings Units 3 & 4 The Runnings, Cheltenham GL51 9NJ Tel. *01242 241022* Fax. *01242 253214* E-mail. *info@maydayseals.co.uk* Web. *www.maydayseals.co.uk Busak Shamban – ClaronPolyseal – CR Seals – DLI – GACO – Gates – Hallite – IKO – INA – JW – Merkel – Parker – Pradifa – Seal Jet – Simrit – SKF – Torrington*

Mayflex UK Ltd Junction 6 Industrial Park 66 Electric Avenue, Birmingham B6 7JJ Tel. *0121 3267557* Fax. *0121 3275886* E-mail. *sales@mayflex.com* Web. *www.mayflex.com Mayflex*

Robert S Maynard Ltd PO Box 8, Wilmslow SK9 5ES Tel. *01625 524055* Fax. *01625 524584* E-mail. *robert.s.maynard.ltd@dial.pipex.com* Web. *www.robertsmaynard.com *De Beleyr (Belgium) – *Delpiano (Italy) – *Fibro Sacco (Italy) – *Gilbos (Belgium) – Maynard – *Plastimec (Italy) – *Stüber (Germany) – *Temafa (Germany) – *Valvan Baling Systems (Belgium) – *Van Dommele (Belgium)*

Maypole Ltd 162 Clapgate Lane, Birmingham B32 3DE Tel. *0121 2704301* Fax. *0121 4233020* E-mail. *sales@maypole.ltd.uk* Web. *www.maypole.ltd.uk Maypole*

Maywick Ltd Unit 7 Hawk Hill Battlesbridge, Wickford SS11 7RJ Tel. *01268 573165* Fax. *01268 573085* E-mail. *sales.maywick@btconnect.com* Web. *www.maywick.co.uk Luminous Wall – Rayette – Raymaster*

William May Ltd Cavendish Street, Ashton Under Lyne OL6 7QW Tel. *0161 3303838* Fax. *0161 3391097* E-mail. *info@william-may.com* Web. *www.william-may.com *Accorroni (Italy) – *Lochinvar (Netherlands) – Parflu – Parmet*

M B K Motor Rewinds Ltd 10a Lythalls Lane, Coventry CV6 6FG Tel. *024 76689510* Fax. *024 76662944* E-mail. *sales@mbk-rewinds.co.uk* Web. *www.mbk-rewinds.co.uk BOSCH – NILFISK*

Mcalpine & Company Ltd 45 Kelvin Avenue Hillington Park, Glasgow G52 4LF Tel. *0141 8823213* Fax. *0141 8915065* E-mail. *kennethg.mcalpine@mcalpine.demon.co.uk* Web. *www.mcalpineplumbing.com All-One – McAlpine – Multifit – Silentrap – Surefit – Ventapipe – Wasteflow*

Mccann Erickson Ltd Communications House 125 Redcliff Street, Bristol BS1 6HU Tel. *0117 9211764* Fax. *0117 9493395* E-mail. *info@corixa.co.uk* Web. *www.corixa.co.uk McCann Erickson*

Mccarthy & Stone Ltd 26-32 Oxford Road, Bournemouth BH8 8EZ Tel. *01202 292480* Fax. *01202 557261* E-mail. *info@mccarthyandstone.co.uk* Web. *www.mccarthyandstone.co.uk McCarthy & Stone*

Mccaw Allan Ltd Victoria Street Lurgan, Craigavon BT67 9DU Tel. *028 38341412* Fax. *028 38324867* E-mail. *mail@samuellamont.co.uk* Web. *www.mccaw-allan.com Irish Cabin*

Mcdonald Brown & Facilities Ltd 7 Eastbury Road, London E6 6LP Tel. *020 75118899* Fax. *020 74731133* E-mail. *gdm@mcdonaldbrownltd.co.uk* Web. *www.mcdonaldbrownltd.co.uk Macbro Services*

M C D Virtak Ltd 13 Rabans Close Rabans Lane Industrial Area, Aylesbury HP19 8RS Tel. *01296 484877* Fax. *01296 393122* E-mail. *john.mckenzie@btconnect.com* Web. *www.x-stat.co.uk Aspec – Ionovax – Pro-Co – Pro-Wynd – Proclean – Procostat – Provac – Statbrush – Tempatrol – Vakstat – X-Stat*

Mcerlains Bakery 31 Aughrim Road, Magherafelt BT45 6BB Tel. *028 79632465* Fax. *028 79634207* E-mail. *brian.mcerlain@genesisbreads.com* Web. *www.genesisbreads.com Genesis bread*

Mcewens Of Perth 56 St John Street, Perth PH1 5SN Tel. *01738 623444* Fax. *01738 620564* E-mail. *mail@mcewensofperth.co.uk* Web. *www.mcewensofperth.com McEwens of Perth*

Mcgill Security Harrison Road, Dundee DD2 3SN Tel. *01382 833999* Fax. *01382 828777* E-mail. *info@mcgill.co.uk* Web. *www.mcgill-electrical.co.uk McGill Heating & Plumbing – McGill Security*

M C I Durford Mill, Petersfield GU31 5AZ Tel. *01730 821969* Fax. *0870 4429940* E-mail. *sales@mci-group.com* Web. *www.mci-group.com Status Incentive Travel Programmes – Status Meetings – Status Study Missions*

Mckechnie Brass Middlemore Lane, Walsall WS9 8DN Tel. *01922 742400* Fax. *01922 451566* E-mail. *sales@mckbrass.com* Web. *www.mckbrass.com Boliden Brass*

Mckenna Group Ltd Lawn Road Carlton-in-Lindrick, Worksop S81 9LB Tel. *01909 541414* Fax. *01909 541415* E-mail. *enquiries@mckennagroup.co.uk* Web. *www.mckennagroup.co.uk Award Toolmakers – Finecast Aluminium Division – Orthopaedic solutions*

M C L Group Ltd 77 Mount Ephraim, Tunbridge Wells TN4 8BS Tel. *01892 705600* Fax. *01892 536571* E-mail. *dsisley@mclgroup.co.uk* Web. *www.mclgroup.co.uk Mazda*

M C M Rudgate Thorp Arch Estate, Wetherby LS23 7AT Tel. *01937 844000* Fax. *01937 842524* E-mail. *sales@mcm-moisture.com* Web. *www.mcm-moisture.com Alphadew – Auto-Veri-Si – Dewdicator – Dewluxe – Microview – Push Purge – Si-Gro Scan – Si-Grometer*

M C M Conveyor Systems Crompton Street Chadderton, Oldham OL9 9AA Tel. *0161 2842222* Fax. *0161 6270075* E-mail. *info@amber-industries.ltd.uk* Web. *www.amber-industries.ltd.uk D.P.R. – Hytrac – Sovex Series 200 – Torvale Fisher*

Mcnaughton James Paper Group Ltd Jaymac House Church Manorway, Erith DA8 1DF Tel. *020 83203200* Fax. *020 83114162* E-mail. *igeorge@mcnaughton-paper.com* Web. *www.jmcpaper.com Astralux Card – Astralux Care – Aurocard – Avalon – British Strongart – Carolina – Carton Excel – Carton Silkia – Challenger Art – Challenger Offset –*

Challenger Superbank – Challenger Supertac – Challenger Tinted Offset – Challenger Velvet – Challenger White Postcard – Challenger White Pulpboard – Claymore – Colorit – Command Gloss – Command Matt – Contender Laser Offset – Copimax – Croxley Script – Cyberstar – Cyclus Copy – Cyclus Offset – Cyclus Print – Datacheck CBS 1 – Datacheck CBS 2 – Dry Gummed – Duralin – Envirocote Plus – Esse – Eurobulk – Evenmore Opaque – Evergreen Laid & Wove – Festival Satir – Festival Superart – Gemini C2/S Montrose – Hailer Matt Extra – Hannoart Gloss – Hannoart Matt – Hannoart Silk – Hermicoat – Hi-Form – Highland Antique Linen – Highland Chromo – Highland Laid – Highland Sandgrain – Highland Superwhite – Image 4 Colour copier – Image Executive – Image Leader – Image Office – Image Premium – JAC – Mailer Matt Extra – Matchpoint – Modo Pre-print – Pickwick – Reacto – Regal Tinted Ivory – Regal Ultrawhite – Repeat Laser – Skye PXM Xantia – Skye PXM Xantur – Skye PXM Xenon – Skye Satin – Skye Silk Natural White – Skyegloss Ivory – Skyelux 2000 – Skyesilk – Skyesilk Ivory – Skyewhite Superior – Skygloss – Speckletone – St James Blade – Supercol – Symbio – T2000 – Terreus – Xerox Business

M C P Ltd 1-4 Nielson Road Finedon Road Industrial Estate, Wellingborough NN8 4PE Tel. 01933 225766 Fax. 01933 227814 E-mail. info@mcp-group.co.uk Web. www.mcp-group.co.uk Bismuth metal and Chemicals – Indium – MCP

MCP Group 8 Whitebridge Industrial Estate Whitebridge Lane, Stone ST15 8LQ Tel. 01785 815651 Fax. 01785 812115 E-mail. info@mcp-group.co.uk Web. www.mcp-group.com MCP Metal – Rabit – Sprite – Tafa Arc Spray

M C R Systems Ltd 14 High View Close, Leicester LE4 9LJ Tel. 0116 2997000 Fax. 0116 2997001 E-mail. sales@mcr-systems.co.uk Web. www.mcr-systems.co.uk J2 – Orderman – Symphony – Uniwell

M C S Technical Products Ltd Building 2 Westmead Industrial Estate Westmead, Swindon SN5 7YT Tel. 01793 538308 Fax. 01793 522324 E-mail. sales@mcstechproducts.co.uk Web. www.mcstechproducts.co.uk *Accutemp – *Cooktek – Cooper Atkins

M C T Reman Ltd Winterstoke Road, Weston Super Mare BS24 9AT Tel. 01934 428000 Fax. 01934 428001 E-mail. gearboxes@gearboxes.com Web. www.gearboxes.com Mitchell Cotts Transmissions

M & D Cleaning Supplies Ltd Grove Road Upholland, Skelmersdale WN8 0LH Tel. 01695 632765 Fax. 01695 632760 E-mail. sales@mandd.co.uk Web. www.mandd.co.uk Diversey Lever – Johnson Wax – Kimberley Clark

M & D Drainage Ltd Unit 2 Friths Farm Colchester Road, Stones Green, Harwich CO12 5DF Tel. 01255 870993 Fax. 01255 870393 E-mail. suzanne@mddrainage.co.uk Web. www.mddrainage.co.uk M and D Drainage

M D M Timber Ltd 6 Howard Chase Pipps Hill Industrial Estate, Basildon SS14 3BE Tel. 01268 530550 Fax. 0845 1304696 E-mail. sales@mdmtimber.co.uk Web. www.mdmtimber.co.uk Kronospan – Medite MDF – Smartply OSB

Meadowbank Associates Ltd 42 Welsh Row, Nantwich CW5 5EJ Tel. 01270 629090 Fax. 01270 624541 E-mail. reception@meadowbankassociates.co.uk Web. www.meadowbankassociates.co.uk Meadowbank Associates – Recruitment Consultants

Meadows Bridal Shoes Ltd Cordova Building Starling Road, Norwich NR3 3ED Tel. 01603 219174 Fax. 01603 762690 E-mail. sales@meadowsbridal.co.uk Web. www.meadowsbridal.co.uk Meadows Bridal Shoes Ltd

Meadows & Passmore Ltd 1 Ellen Street Portslade, Brighton BN41 1EU Tel. 01273 421321 Fax. 01273 421322 E-mail. sales@m-p.co.uk Web. www.m-p.co.uk Medmaw

Measom Freer Company 37-41 Chartwell Drive, Wigston LE18 2FL Tel. 0116 2881588 Fax. 0116 2813000 E-mail. sales@measomfreer.co.uk Web. www.measomfreer.co.uk Injectoid – M.F. – Measom Freer

Measurement Technology Ltd 920 Butterfield Great Marlings, Luton LU2 8DL Tel. 01582 723633 Fax. 01582 422283 E-mail. enquiry@mtl-inst.com Web. www.mtl-inst.com MTL100 Series – MTL2000 Series – MTL3000 Series – MTL400 Series – MTL4700 Series – MTL4840 Series – MTL5000 Series – MTL611B – MTL630 Series – MTL643 – MTL644 – MTL645 – MTL650 Series – MTL670 Series – MTL680 Series – MTL700 Series – MTL7000 Series – MTL800 Series – MTL8000 Series – MTL8800L Series – MTL901 System – MTL920 Series – Process I/O

Meatec Unit 7 Charlwood Place Charlwood, Horley RH6 0EB Tel. 01293 863791 Fax. 01293 863298 E-mail. info@meatec.co.uk Web. www.meatec.co.uk Formax (U.S.A.) – Koppens (Netherlands) – Provatech (Switzerland)

MECG Ltd Unit 28 Woodridge Close, Enfield EN2 8HJ Tel. 0845 4744561 Fax. 0871 5288032 E-mail. info@mecg.co.uk Web. www.mecg.co.uk MECG

Mechadyne International Ltd Park Farm Technology Centre Akeman Street, Kirtlington, Kidlington OX5 3JQ Tel. 01869 350903 Fax. 01869 351302 E-mail. info@mechadyne-int.com Web. www.mechadyne-int.com Mechadyne

Mechline Developments Ltd 15 Carters Lane Kiln Farm, Milton Keynes MK11 3ER Tel. 01908 261511 Fax. 01908 261522 E-mail. info@mechline.com Web. www.mechline.com AquaJet – AquaVend Water Hoses – BaSiX – CaterConneX – CaterGuard – CaterTap – CaterZap – *Delabie – *Dormont – GastroTechniX – GreasePaK – *Mechline – Mo-El – Pegler – *QuickLink – SaniFloor

Mecmar Driers 2000 Ltd Council Farm Gunthorpe, Doncaster DN9 1BQ Tel. 01427 728186 E-mail. info@mecmar.co.uk Web. www.mecmar.co.uk *Mecmar

MEC Medical Ltd Ivenhoe Business Centre Blackburn Road, Dunstable LU5 5BQ Tel. 01582 661885 Fax. 01582 602527 E-mail. sales@mecmedical.com Web. www.mecmedical.com PURAIR

Mecwash Systems Ltd 64 Hundred Severn Drive Tewkesbury Business Park, Tewkesbury GL20 8SF Tel. 01684 271600 Fax. 01684 271601 E-mail. enquiries@mecwash.co.uk Web. www.mecwash.co.uk AquaSave – AutoSeal – MecWash

Medbrook Services Ltd 79 Southgate Drive, Crawley RH10 6EP Tel. 01293 420994 Fax. 01293 420995 E-mail. david@medbrook.co.uk Web. www.medbrook.co.uk AMX – Crestron – Life-size – Polycom

Meddings Machine Tools Kingsley Close Lee Mill Industrial Estate, Ivybridge PL21 9LL Tel. 01752 313323 Fax. 01752 313333 E-mail. sales@meddings.co.uk Web. www.meddings.co.uk C S Products (Testing Equipment) – *Imet (Italy) – Meddings – Meddings Flott – Meddings Machine Tools – Meddings Thermalec – Meddings-Ibarmia (Spain) – *Procyon (U.S.A.) – *Quickmill (Canada) – *Serv-o-Dex (Germany) – *Servopress (Germany) – *Square Tap (U.S.A.) – *Style (Netherlands) – *Teplast (Germany) – *Tepro (Germany)

Media & Marketing Services 230 Warwick Road, Kenilworth CV8 1FD Tel. 01926 864834 Fax. 01926 851061 E-mail. info@m-ms.co.uk Web. www.m-ms.co.uk Media & Marketing Services

Medical Air Technology Ltd Gateway Crescent Broadway Business Park, Chadderton, Oldham OL9 9XB Tel. 08448 712100 Fax. 0161 6247547 E-mail. sales@medicalairtechnology.com Web. www.medicalairtechnology.com Aseptic Sweets – Biomat 2 – Isomat – Ultraflow – Unimat

The Medici Galleries 19 - 23 White Lion street Islington, London N1 9PD Tel. 020 77138800 Fax. 020 78377579 E-mail. info@medici.co.uk Web. www.medici.co.uk Cosimo – Ganymed – Lorenzo – Medici – Modern Art Society – Pallas – Pandora – Pavilion

Medicina (UK) Ltd 145-147 St John Street, London EC1V 4PY Tel. 020 82052369 Fax. 020 82052346 E-mail. info@medicina-uk.com Web. www.naturalrussia.com Rapan

Medicom UK Ltd Thames Side House Hurst Road, East Molesey KT8 9EY Tel. 020 84818100 Fax. 020 84818105 E-mail. enquiries@medicomgroup.com Web. www.medicomgroup.com Medicom

Mediplus Ltd Unit 7 The Gateway Centre Coronation Road, Cressex Business Park, High Wycombe HP12 3SU Tel. 01494 551200 Fax. 01494 536333 E-mail. help@mediplus.co.uk Web. www.mediplus.co.uk Mediplus

Medisafe UK Ltd Twyford Road, Bishops Stortford CM23 3LJ Tel. 01279 461641 Fax. 01279 461643 E-mail. info@medisafeinternational.com Web. www.medisafeinternational.com Medisafe

Meditelle Meditelle Product Division Beautelle Manufacturing Centre, Birmingham B6 7HH Tel. 0121 3321850 Fax. 0121 3321851 E-mail. enquiry@meditelle.co.uk Web. www.meditelle.co.uk Meditelle

Medway Galvanising & Powder Coating Ltd 9a-9c Eurolink Industrial Centre Castle Road, Sittingbourne ME10 3RN Tel. 01795 479489 Fax. 01795 477598 E-mail. info@medgalv.co.uk Web. www.medgalv.co.uk Mono

Medway Sling Company Knight Road, Rochester ME2 2AH Tel. 01634 726400 Fax. 01634 726420 E-mail. sales@medwayslingcompany.co.uk Web. www.medwayslingcompany.co.uk Sureweb

Meech Static Eliminators Ltd Unit 2 Network Point Range Road, Witney OX29 0YN Tel. 01993 706700 Fax. 01993 776977 E-mail. sales@meech.com Web. www.meech.com Meech Air Technology – Meech S C T – Meech Static Eliminators

Megator Ltd Hendon Street, Sunderland SR1 2NQ Tel. 0191 5675488 Fax. 0191 5678512 E-mail. info@megator.co.uk Web. www.megator.co.uk Alpha Skimmer – Beta Skimmer – Dolphin Floating Strainers – Megator Sliding – Mini Booms – Oily Water Seperator – Puddlemop – Sigma Skimmer – System 88

Megger Ltd Archcliffe Road, Dover CT17 9EN Tel. 01304 502100 Fax. 01304 241491 E-mail. uksales@megger.com Web. www.megger.com AVO – Avometer - analogue digital multimeters Megger - electrical testing instruments, telecomms testing instruments Foster - high voltage and heavy current test equipment Ducter - low resistance ohmmeters Biddle - high voltage and cable fault location equipmen – Avonmeter – Biddle – DUCTER – Foster – MEGGER – Multi-Amp

Meggitt Avionics 7 Whittle Avenue, Fareham PO15 5SH Tel. 01489 483300 Fax. 01489 564092 E-mail. richard.greaves@meggitt.com Web. www.meggitt-avionics.co.uk Agilite – Baromec – Bryans Aeroquipment – Negretti Aviation – Secondary Flight Display System – Secondary Navigation Display System

Meggitt Control Systems Unit 19 Eyncourt Road, Woodside Estate, Dunstable LU5 4TS Tel. 01582 473600 Fax. 01442 230035 E-mail. alanclark@meggitt.com Web. www.meggit.com Avica Products

Meiko UK Ltd 393 Edinburgh Avenue, Slough SL1 4UF Tel. 01753 215120 Fax. 01753 215159 E-mail. meikouk@meiko-uk.co.uk Web. www.meiko-uk.co.uk *Meiko – Sirocco

M E L Chemicals PO Box 6, Manchester M27 8LS Tel. 0161 9111100 Fax. 0161 9111090 E-mail. joy.walters@melchemicals.com Web. www.zrchem.com M.E.L. – MelCat – Melox – Meloxide – Zircosol – Zirgel – Zirmel

Melcourt Industries Boldridge Brake Long Newnton, Tetbury GL8 8RT Tel. 01666 502711 Fax. 01666 504398 E-mail. mail@melcourt.co.uk Web. www.melcourt.co.uk Adheart – Adventure Bark – Amenity Bark Mulch – Arbor Compost – Bark Nuggets – Biomulch – Decorative Biomulch – Equichip – Equichips – Equifall – Equifibre – Equisand – Garden Bark – Graded Bark Flakes – Growbark – Kushyfall – Landscape Bark – Melcourt – Mini Biomulch – Mulchip – Play Chips – Playbark – Playchip – Rustic Biomulch – Softfall – Specimen Bark – Super Humus – Sylvefibre – Topgrow – Verdigreen – Walkchips – Woodfibre

Thomas Meldrum Ltd Freedom Works John Street, Sheffield S2 4QT Tel. 0114 2725156 Fax. 0114 2726409 E-mail. sales@melco-tools.co.uk Web. www.thomasmeldrumltd.co.uk Melco

Melitta System Service Unit 21 Grove Park Industrial Estate Waltham Road, White Waltham, Maidenhead SL6 3LW Tel. 01628 829888 Fax. 01628 825111 E-mail. paul@mssuk.co.uk Web. www.melittasystemservice.co.uk *Cafina (Switzerland) – *Militta (Germany)

Melitzer Safety Equipment 7 Frimley Road, Camberley GU15 3EN Tel. 01276 65474 Fax. 01276 62880 E-mail. j.angove@tiscali.co.uk Aimont – Caterpillar – Eurotec – Fusion – Grafters – PSF Terrain – Snickers – Target Safety – TK Steel – Trucker – Tuf – Tuffking – Workforce

Mellor Bromley 141 Barkby Road, Leicester LE4 9LW Tel. 0116 2766636 Fax. 0116 2460426 E-mail. mail@mellorbromley.co.uk Web. www.mellorbromley.co.uk Cool-A-Zone

Mells Roofing Ltd Beehive Lane Works Beehive Lane, Chelmsford CM2 9JY Tel. 0800 2983251 Fax. 01245 260060 E-mail. info@mellsroofing.co.uk Web. www.mellsroofing.co.uk Anderson – Callenders – Ruberoid

Melrose Textile Co. Ltd Allerton Mills Allerton Road, Allerton, Bradford BD15 7QX Tel. 01274 491277 Fax. 01274 547231 E-mail. bill@melrose-textile.co.uk Web. www.melrose-textile.co.uk Allerton Mills Collection – Aquastyle – Classic Collection – Colorama Collection – Craft Collection – Decora Collection

Memex Technology Ltd 2 Redwood Court East Kilbride, Glasgow G74 5PF Tel. 01355 233804 Fax. 01355 239676 E-mail. info@memex.com Web. www.memex.com MR-Memex

Mems Power Generation Beechings Way, Gillingham ME8 6PS Tel. 08452 230400 Fax. 01634 263666 E-mail. sales@memsgen.co.uk Web. www.memsgen.co.uk MEMS Power Generation

Mena Engineering UK Ltd Unit 70 Elms Business Park Main Road, Great Haywood, Stafford ST18 0RJ Tel. 01889 883111 Fax. 01889 883222 E-mail. neil@menaengineering.co.uk Web. www.menaengineering.co.uk Wonderwall Water Features

Mentholatum Co. Ltd 1 Redwood Avenue East Kilbride, Glasgow G74 5PE Tel. 01355 848484 Fax. 01355 263387 E-mail. a.tasker@mentholatum.co.uk Web. www.mentholatum.co.uk Cutipen – Deep Heat – Deep Relief – Mentholatum – Snug – Stop'n Grow

John Menzies plc 108 Princes Street, Edinburgh EH2 3AA Tel. 0131 2258555 Fax. 0131 4591150 E-mail. paul.dollman@johnmenziesplc.com Web. www.menziesgroup.com A.M.I. – Concorde Express – Early Learning Centre – John Menzies Wholesale – London Cargo Centre – Menzies Transport Services – Skyport Handling – T.H.E. – T.H.E. Games

Menzolit Perseverance Works Halifax Road, Todmorden OL14 6EG Tel. 01706 814714 Fax. 01706 814717 E-mail. richard.fiddling@menzolit.com Web. www.menzolit-uk.co.uk Flomat – Freemix

Mercedes A M G Morgan Drive Brixworth, Northampton NN6 9GZ Tel. 01604 880100 Fax. 01604 882800 E-mail. reception@mercedes-benz-hpe.com Web. www.mercedes-amg-HPP.com Ilmor

Mercedes Benz UK Ltd Delaware Drive Tongwell, Milton Keynes MK15 8BA Tel. 01908 245000 Fax. 01908 245472

Web. *www.mercedes-benz.co.uk *Mercedes-Benz (Germany) – *Unimog (Germany)*

Mercer 1 Tower Place West, London EC3R 5BU Tel. *020 76266000* Fax. *020 72226140* Web. *www.mercer.com William M. Mercer*

Merchant House Financial Services Alexander House Alexandra Road, Wisbech PE13 1HQ Tel. *01945 585721* Fax. *01945 464712* E-mail. *wisbech@theclarksonhillgroup.com* Web. *www.theclarksonhillgroup.com Barwick Group, The*

Merchants Ltd (Telephone Marketing) 500 Avebury Boulevard, Milton Keynes MK9 2BE Tel. *01908 232323* Fax. *01908 242444* E-mail. *sales@merchants.co.uk* Web. *www.dimensiondata.co.uk The Merchants Group*

Mercia Fine Foods Bromyard Road A44 Crown East, Worcester WR2 5TR Tel. *01905 422245* Fax. *01905 337186* E-mail. *sales@merciafinefoods.com *Bottle Green Drinks – Brecon Water – *Dormen Nuts – *Farmhouse Biscuits – Salty Dog Crisps – *Twinings*

Mercia Flexibles Orleton Road Ludlow Business Park, Ludlow SY8 1XF Tel. *01584 874999* Fax. *01584 874007* E-mail. *enquiries@merciaflexibles.co.uk* Web. *www.merciaflexibles.co.uk DILATOFLEX – KLEDIL*

Mercian Masterplan Ltd Drury Lane Rodington, Shrewsbury SY4 4RG Tel. *01952 770167* Fax. *01952 770965* E-mail. *sales@mercianmasterplan.com* Web. *www.mercianmasterplan.com Mercian Masterplan*

Merck Serono Ltd Bedfont Cross Stanwell Road, Feltham TW14 8NX Tel. *020 88187200* Fax. *01895 420605* E-mail. *serono_uk@serono.com* Web. *www.merckserono.net *Curosurf (Switzerland) – *Geref (Switzerland) – *Metrodin High Purity (Switzerland) – *Pergonal (Switzerland) – *Profasi (Switzerland) – *Refit (Switzerland) – *Saizen (Switzerland) – *Serono GPM (Spain) – *Serophene (Switzerland) – *Ukidan (Switzerland)*

Merc Millipore (Bio Process Division) Unit 31 Number One Industrial Estate, Consett DH8 6SZ Tel. *01207 581555* Fax. *01207 500944* E-mail. *lesley_wallace@millipore.com* Web. *www.millipore.com PROSEP (R)*

Mercuri Urval ltd 35 Portman Square, London W1H 6LR Tel. *020 74673730* Fax. *020 74673738* E-mail. *stephen.finley@mercuriurval.com* Web. *www.mercuriurval.co.uk Mercuri Urval*

Mercury Bearings Ltd 4 Redburn Industrial Estate Woodall Road, Enfield EN3 4LE Tel. *020 88051919* Fax. *020 88059599* E-mail. *enfield@mercuryltd.co.uk* Web. *www.mercuryltd.co.uk Alinabal – Asahi – Baldor – Barden – Benzler – Binder – Blickle – Bonfiglioli – Bowex – Camozzi – Cemp – Cross & Morse – Davall Gears – Dayco – Dodge – Elges – Fafnir – FAG – Fenner – Ferri – Flexello – FYH – Gaco – Hepco – Holdtite – Igus – IKO – INA – Kayden – KEB – Kluber – Kobo – Kopp – Koyo – LAG – Lenze – Megadyne – Morflex – Motovario – Nachi – Nord – NSK – NTN – Optibelt – Posiva – Pujol – Radicon – Regina – Renold – Revvo – Rexnord – Rhombus – RHP – Rollway – Rose – Rossi – Roulunds – Sealmaster – Sedis – SEW – Sigma – Siti – SKF – SNFA – Star – Stieber – STM – Tandler – Tellure Rota – Tolomatic – Tsubaki – Unichain – VEM – Wicke*

Mercury Records 1 Sussex Place, London W6 9EA Tel. *020 89105333* Web. *www.umusic.co.uk Fontana – Mercury – Philips – Rocket – Talkin' Loud – Vertigo*

Merial Animal Health Ltd PO Box 327, Harlow CM19 5TG Tel. *01279 775858* Fax. *01279 775888* Web. *www.merial.com *Eprinex – *Eqvalan – *Ivomec – *Oramec*

Meritor HVS Ltd Rackery Lane Llay, Wrexham LL12 0PB Tel. *01978 852141* Fax. *01978 856173* E-mail. *thomas.hughes@arvinmeritor.com* Web. *www.arvinmeritor.com Flexair – Indair – Levelride*

P W Merkle Ltd 18 Oakhurst Rise, Carshalton SM5 4AG Tel. *020 86425755* Fax. *020 86463000* E-mail. *sales@pw-merkle.co.uk* Web. *www.pw-merkle.co.uk P.W. Merkle*

Merlett Plastics UK Ltd Unit 2 Waverley Road Beeches Industrial Estate, Yate, Bristol BS37 5QT Tel. *01454 329888* Fax. *01454 324499* E-mail. *pvchose@merlett.com* Web. *www.merlett.com America Oil – Ariflex – Arizona Superelastic – Armorvin – Detroit – Florida – Jamaica – Luisiana – Nevada – Oregon – Polido – Ragno – Shark Hose – Spiralina – Stonehose – Superflex – Texoil – Thermaresistant – Vacupress (Food Quality) – Vacupress Oil – Viniflex – Vohran*

Merlin Precision Engineering Ltd Eldon Street, Halifax HX3 6DW Tel. *01422 300420* Fax. *01422 300420* E-mail. *gary@merlin-printing.co.uk* Web. *www.merlin-printing.co.uk Heidelberg – Millar – Mitsubishi – Roland*

Mer Products Ltd 12 Centrus Mead Lane, Hertford SG13 7GX Tel. *01992 512698* Fax. *020 84010003* E-mail. *sales@merproducts.com* Web. *www.merproducts.com A.2000 (Germany)*

Merryhill Envirotec Ltd Merryhill House Budds Lane, Romsey SO51 0HA Tel. *01794 515848* Fax. *01794 525386* E-mail. *paul.fox@merryhill-idm.co.uk* Web. *www.merryhillenvirotec.com Disaster Response Network – International Damage Management – Restart*

Mersen UK South Street Portslade, Brighton BN41 2LX Tel. *01273 415701* Fax. *01273 415673* E-mail. *mike.denyer@carbonelorraine.com* Web. *www.mersen.co.uk Aerolor – Ellor – Graphilor – Papyex – Protistor – Rigilor – Sparkal*

Merseyside Galvanising Ltd (Wedge Group Galvanizing) Unit 10 Weaver Industrial Estate Blackburne Street, Liverpool L19 8JA Tel. *0151 4271449* Fax. *0151 4272690* E-mail. *merseyside@wedge-galv.co.uk* Web. *www.wedge-galv.co.uk Wedge Group Galvanizing*

Merseyside Metal Services 36 Lord Street, Birkenhead CH41 1BJ Tel. *0151 6501600* Fax. *0151 6476157* E-mail. *sales@merseymetals.co.uk* Web. *www.merseymetals.co.uk Celazole – CESTILENE – Delrin – Deltrin AF – ERTA-PC – ERTACETAL – ERTALON – ERTALYTE – FERROTRON – Fluorosint – FLUROSINT – Ketron Peek – Nylatron MC901 – Nylotron – PEEK – PEI – PES – PTFE – PUDF – PVDF – Semitron – TORLON – Turlon – ULTRWEAR*

Merseytravel 24 Hatton Garden, Liverpool L3 2AN Tel. *0151 2275181* Fax. *0151 2362457* Web. *www.merseyferries.co.uk Mersey Ferris – Merseylink – Merseytravel*

M&ES Flexilope Campions Cottage 129 Sheering Road, Harlow CM17 0JP Tel. *01279 454500* Fax. *01279 435400* E-mail. *sales@flexilope.co.uk* Web. *www.flexilope.co.uk Barbour – Basler – Coleman – Extronics – FLEXILOPE – Selco*

Messer Cutting Systems Northumberland Business Park West, Cramlington NE23 7RH Tel. *0191 2504610* Fax. *0191 2501471* E-mail. *alan.cardwell@messer-cw.co.uk* Web. *www.messer-cw.co.uk Hypotherm – Kjellberg – Messer – Messer Greishiem*

Messier Dowty Ltd Cheltenham Road East, Gloucester GL2 9QH Tel. *01452 712424* Fax. *01452 713821* E-mail. *neville.kite@messier-dowty.com* Web. *www.messier-dowty.com Messier-Dowty*

Metabrasive Ltd Ironmasters Way Stillington, Stockton On Tees TS21 1LE Tel. *01740 630212* Fax. *01740 630555* E-mail. *claire-louise.foster@metabrasive.com* Web. *www.metabrasive.com N.E.*

Metafour UK Ltd 2 Berghem Mews Blythe Road, London W14 0HN Tel. *020 79122000* E-mail. *sales@metafour.com* Web. *www.metafour.com Metafour*

Metair Mechanical Services Unit 21d Queensway, Enfield EN3 4SZ Tel. *020 84435777* Fax. *020 84433366* E-mail. *metair@metair.co.uk* Web. *www.metair.co.uk Metair*

Metalbor Ltd 10 Sandiford Road, Sutton SM3 9RS Tel. *020 86417788* Fax. *020 86415511* E-mail. *sales@metalbor.com* Web. *www.metalbor.com Coolbor – Swiftic – Trubor*

Metal Deck Ltd 1a Prestwood Place, Skelmersdale WN8 9QE Tel. *01695 555070* Fax. *01695 555180* E-mail. *sales@metaldeck.ltd.uk* Web. *www.metaldeck.ltd.uk Multideck*

Metal Drum Denebridge Chilton, Ferryhill DL17 0NU Tel. *01388 720391* Fax. *01388 721880* E-mail. *sales@metal-drum.co.uk* Web. *www.metal-drum.co.uk Metal Drum*

Metal Finishing Ltd 16-18 Station Street, Walsall WS2 9JZ Tel. *01922 720720* Fax. *01922 723400* E-mail. *paul.walford@lbparkes.net* Web. *www.lbparkes.net Anolite*

Metal Improvement Co. (Derby Division) (Subsidiary of Curtiss-Wright Corporation) Ascot Drive, Derby DE24 8ST Tel. *01332 756076* Fax. *01332 754392* E-mail. *steve_panther@metalimprovemtn.com* Web. *www.metalimprovement.co.uk C.A.S.E. – Peenflex – PEENSCAN – Peentex*

Metal Improvement Co. (Subsidiary for Curtiss-Wright Corporation) Chester Road Broughton, Chester CH4 0BZ Tel. *01244 534999* Fax. *01244 521500* E-mail. *ray.lopuc@cwst.com* Web. *www.cwst.co.uk C.A.S.E. – Dyescan – Peenflex – PEENSCAN – Peentex*

Metal Improvement Company LLC (a subsidiary of Curtiss-Wright Corporation) European Corporate Office Hambridge Lane, Newbury RG14 5TU Tel. *01635 279621* Fax. *01635 279629* E-mail. *eurosales@metalimprovement.co.uk* Web. *www.metalimprovement.co.uk C.A.S.E. – Peenflex – PEENSCAN – Peentex*

Metalliform Holdings Chambers Road Hoyland, Barnsley S74 0EZ Tel. *01226 350555* Fax. *01226 350112* E-mail. *sales@metalliform.co.uk* Web. *www.metalliform.co.uk Buroflex – Innesenti – Metalliform*

Metallisation Ltd Peartree Lane, Dudley DY2 0XH Tel. *01384 252464* Fax. *01384 237196* E-mail. *sales@metallisation.com* Web. *www.metallisation.com Met-Jet – Purecoat*

Metal Spinners Group Ltd Newburn Industrial Estate Shelley Road, Newcastle Upon Tyne NE15 9RT Tel. *0191 2671011* Fax. *0191 2647137* E-mail. *info@metal-spinners.co.uk* Web. *www.metal-spinners.co.uk Spectrum Wheels*

Metaltex UK Ltd Brunleys Kiln Farm, Milton Keynes MK11 3HR Tel. *01908 262062* Fax. *01908 262162* E-mail. *info@metaltex.co.uk* Web. *www.metaltex.com Metaltex*

Metaltreat Ltd 359 Canal Road, Bradford BD2 1AN Tel. *01274 211555* Fax. *01274 221520* E-mail. *metaltreat@wedge-galv.co.uk* Web. *www.wedge-galv.co.uk Wedge Group Galvanizing*

Metalweb Ltd Unit 20 Newby Road Industrial Estate Newby Road, Hazel Grove, Stockport SK7 5DA Tel. *0161 4839662* Fax. *0161 4839668* E-mail. *info@metalweb.co.uk* Web. *www.metalweb.co.uk Aquarius Metals – Caterbridge – Metalweb – Metalweb Shapes*

Metal Working Lubricants Ltd Braemar House 274 Manchester Road, Woolston, Warrington WA1 4PS Tel. *01925 816666* Fax. *01925 816666* E-mail. *info@mwl-uk.com* Web. *www.mwl-uk.com Koolmax – Koolmax N.F. (United Kingdom)*

Metapraxis Ltd Kingstons House Coombe Road, Kingston upon Thames KT2 7AB Tel. *020 85412700* Fax. *020 85462105* E-mail. *info@metapraxis.com* Web. *www.metapraxis.com Metapraxis Business Control Cycle – Metapraxis EKS (Enterprise Knowledge Server) – Metapraxis Empower*

Metatec Metaflux Ltd Fitzherbert Road, Portsmouth PO6 1RU Tel. *023 92381382* Fax. *023 92380888* E-mail. *metatec.sales@btconnect.com* Web. *www.metatec.co.uk Metatec & Metaflux*

Metax Ltd Unit 77 Capital Business Centre 22 Carlton Road, South Croydon CR2 0BS Tel. *020 89162077* Fax. *01689 889994* E-mail. *info@metax.co.uk* Web. *www.metax.co.uk *C.I. Systems (Israel) – *Instrument Systems (Germany) – *Topcon (Japan)*

Metcalfe Catering Equipment Ltd Haygarth Park, Blaenau Ffestiniog LL41 3PF Tel. *01766 830456* Fax. *01766 831170* E-mail. *info@metcalfecatering.co.uk* Web. *www.metcalfecatering.com Edlund – Hamilton Beach – Metcalfe – Santos – Sunkist*

Meters UK Ltd Whitegate White Lund Industrial Estate, Morecambe LA3 3BT Tel. *01524 555929* Fax. *01524 847009* E-mail. *sales@meters.co.uk* Web. *www.meters.co.uk meters uk HCM4 TOMi & MAXi Water Meters*

Metflex Precision Moulding Ltd 20 Alan Ramsbottom Way, Blackburn BB6 7SE Tel. *01254 884171* Fax. *01254 887753* E-mail. *sales@metflex.co.uk* Web. *www.metflex.co.uk Metflex*

Methodist Insurance plc Brazennose House West Brazennose Street, Manchester M2 5AS Tel. *0161 8339696* Fax. *0161 8331287* E-mail. *enquiries@micmail.com* Web. *www.methodistinsurance.co.uk Methodist*

Metool Products Ltd Mercian Close, Ilkeston DE7 8HG Tel. *0115 9225931* Fax. *0115 9224578* E-mail. *postmaster@metool.com* Web. *www.kabelschlepp.co.uk Bubenzer Bremsen (Germany) – Hannay (U.S.A.) – Kabelschlepp (Germany) – Metool – Nexans Cable (France) – Sturge*

Metra Martech Ltd 7 Chiswick High Road, London W4 2ND Tel. *020 87427888* Fax. *020 87428558* E-mail. *research@metra-martech.com* Web. *www.metra-martech.com Martech – Martech Publications – Martech Software – Metra – Metra Martech*

Metra Non Ferrous Metals Unit N7rd Park Essex Road, Hoddesdon EN11 0FB Tel. *01992 460455* Fax. *01992 451207* E-mail. *enquiries@metra-metals.co.uk* Web. *www.metra-metals.co.uk Metiflash – Metizinc*

Metreel Ltd Cossall Industrial Estate, Ilkeston DE7 5UA Tel. *0115 9327010* Fax. *0115 9306263* E-mail. *admin@metreel.co.uk* Web. *www.metreel.co.uk *Akapp (Netherlands) – Met-Boom – Beam-Rider – Alulift – Crane-In-A-Box – Dangleflex Black – Deco – Fallguard – Safewire – Invisirung – Lugall – Met-Track – Met-Trak – Safetrack – *TER (Italy)*

Metrix Electronics Precision Enterprise House Rankine Road Daneshill West, Basingstoke RG24 8PP Tel. *01256 864150* Fax. *01256 864154* E-mail. *p.rummer@metrix-electronics.com* Web. *www.metrix-electronics.com B&K Precision (U.S.A.) – Muller & Weigert (Germany) – OR-X (Israel) – Sefram (France) – STIX (United Kingdom)*

Metrodent Ltd PO Box B29, Huddersfield HD3 4EP Tel. *01484 461616* Fax. *01484 462700* E-mail. *sales@metrodent.com* Web. *www.metrodent.com *Bego (Germany) – *Intensiv (Switzerland) – Kallodoc – Kindercryl – Metro – Metrocryl – Metrodent – Metrolux – Metrotone – *Pro-Form (U.S.A.) – Replica*

Metrode Products Ltd Hanworth Lane, Chertsey KT16 9LL Tel. *01932 566721* Fax. *01932 565168* E-mail. *info@metrode.com* Web. *www.metrode.com Armet – Chromet – Cobstel – Cormet – Cupromet – Die-Tough – Met-Hard – Met-Max – Metrode – Nimax – Nimrod – Supercore – Supermet – Supermig – Thermet – Tuf-Met – Ultramet – Ultramet B – Vertamet – Work-Hard*

Metromold Ltd Unit 19c Elm Road, North Shields NE29 8SE Tel. *0191 2963303* Fax. *0191 2963303* E-mail. *info@metromold.co.uk* Web. *www.metromold.co.uk Metromold*

Metro Textiles Ltd 35a Walm Lane, London NW2 5SH Tel. *020 84593756* Fax. *020 84514410* Web. *www.metrotextiles.co.uk *Executive (Worldwide) – *Supermet (Worldwide)*

Metso Minerals UK Ltd Parkfield Road, Rugby CV21 1QJ Tel. *01788 532100* Fax. *01788 560442*

E-mail. *sami.tackaluma@metso.com* Web. *www.metso.com Allis Mineral Systems – Barmac – Braham Millar – Demag – Denver Sala – Dragon – Dynapac – Goodwin Barsby – Lindemann – Loro & Parisini – MPSI – NEI – Nordberg – Rammer – Skega – Tidco – Trellex – Weda*

Metway Electrical Industries Ltd Barrie House 18 North Street, Portslade, Brighton BN41 1DG Tel. *01273 439266* Fax. *01273 439288* E-mail. *sales@metway.co.uk* Web. *www.metway.co.uk Metway – Metway – Metway – *Metway (Malaysia) – Mistral By Metway*

M & F Components PO Box 18, Accrington BB5 5BE Tel. *01254 301121* Fax. *01254 391416* E-mail. *sales@mafcobell.co.uk* Web. *www.mafcobell.co.uk Bell Autoparts – J.P.I. Tools – Mafco*

M F Hydraulics Ltd Pony Road Cowley, Oxford OX4 2RD Tel. *01865 715757* Fax. *01865 748140* E-mail. *mike@mfhydraulics.co.uk* Web. *www.mfhydraulics.co.uk Parker Store (Redding)*

MFS Stone Surfaces Ltd Verona House Filwood Road, Fishpond, Bristol BS16 3RY Tel. *0117 9656565* Fax. *0117 9656573* E-mail. *maryford@marbleflooring.co.uk* Web. *www.marbleflooring.co.uk *Agglosimplex (Italy) – *Loc Strip (Australia) – *M.I. Joint (Australia) – *Marghestone (Italy) – *Quartzo 88 (Italy)*

M G C Lamps Unit 1 The Sovereign Centre Farthing Road, Ipswich IP1 5AP Tel. *01473 466300* Fax. *01473 240081* E-mail. *sales@mgc-lamps.com* Web. *www.mgc-lamps.com M.G.C. Lamps*

M G Electric Wyncolls Road Severalls Industrial Park, Colchester CO4 9HX Tel. *01206 842244* Fax. *01206 853889* E-mail. *sales@mgelectric.co.uk* Web. *www.mgeworldwide.com NIVEC (Italy) – S.A.M.*

M & G Group plc Governors House 5 Laurence Pountney Hill, London EC4R 0HH Tel. *020 76264588* Fax. *020 76238615* E-mail. *info@mandg.co.uk* Web. *www.mandg.co.uk M & G – M & G Life*

M G H Interiors 111 Mousehole Lane, Southampton SO18 4TA Tel. *023 80672245* E-mail. *sales@southamptonceilings.co.uk* Web. *www.ceilingsdryliningpartitions.co.uk Suspended Ceilings*

M G M Advantage M G M House Heene Road, Worthing BN11 3AT Tel. *01903 836000* Fax. *01903 836001* E-mail. *customers@mgmadvantage.com* Web. *www.mgmadvantage.com M.G.M. Assurance*

M Gordon & Sons Lawrence House Derby Street, Manchester M8 8AT Tel. *0161 8344528* Fax. *0161 8340111* E-mail. *sales@gordons-manchester.co.uk* Web. *www.gordons-manchester.co.uk Two Ticks*

Michael Clothing Co 1 Amico Works 232-234 Waterloo Street, Bolton BL1 8HU Tel. *01204 524846* Fax. *01204 524846 Michael Leather Clothing*

Michael George Manufacturing Ltd 236 Lockwood Road, Huddersfield HD1 3TG Tel. *01484 533787* Fax. *01484 549147* E-mail. *enquiries@micheal-george.co.uk Flash Connectors*

Michael Lupton Associates Ltd Halifax House Seaton Ross, York YO42 4LU Tel. *01759 318557* Fax. *01759 318947* E-mail. *sales@mlaltd.co.uk* Web. *www.mlaltd.co.uk Belts and Carrying Pouches – Drylon – FURNO – Police, Fire and Ambulance – Waddington*

Michelin Tyre plc Campbell Road, Stoke On Trent ST4 4EY Tel. *01782 402000* Fax. *01782 402253* E-mail. *info@michelin.com* Web. *www.michelin.co.uk Michelin*

Michell Instruments Ltd 48 Lancaster Way Business Park, Ely CB6 3NW Tel. *01353 658000* Fax. *01353 658199* E-mail. *info@michell.com* Web. *www.michell.com CERMAX – CERMET II – CONDUMAX – DEWMET – HG-1 – PROMET – S4000 – TRANSMET*

Microbore Tooling Systems Whitacre Road Industrial Estate Whitacre Road, Nuneaton CV11 6BX Tel. *024 76373355* Fax. *024 76373322* E-mail. *sales@microbore.com* Web. *www.microbore.com Devlieg – Formbore – Microbore – Microset – Tribore – Twinbore*

Micro Clutch Developments Ltd Unit 8-9 Kiln Park Searle Crescent, Weston Super Mare BS23 3XP Tel. *01934 415606* Fax. *01934 636658* E-mail. *info@microclutch.com* Web. *www.microclutch.com *AEG (Spain) – *Bodine (U.S.A.) – *Cemp S.r.l. (Italy) – *Horton (U.S.A.) – *Kop-Flex Inc (U.S.A.) – *Lafert S.r.l. (Italy) – *S.T.M. (Italy) – *Spaggiari (Italy) – *Spaggiari Transmission (Italy)*

Microface Ltd Woodcock Hall Cobbs Brow Lane, Newburgh, Wigan WN8 7NB Tel. *01257 463225* Fax. *01257 463416* E-mail. *sales@microface.com* Web. *www.microface.com Microface*

Microfilm Shop Hammond Close Attleborough Fields Ind Estate, Nuneaton CV11 6RY Tel. *024 76383998* Fax. *024 76382319* E-mail. *paulnegus@microfilm.com* Web. *www.genusit.com Microfilm Shop, The – Real*

Microflow Europe T/A Total Celler Systems Globe Square, Dukinfield SK16 4RF Tel. *0161 3431557* Fax. *0161 3433762* E-mail. *william.johnston@microfloweurope.com* Web. *www.totalcellers.com Microflow*

Micro Focus Ltd The Lawn 22-30 Old Bath Road, Newbury RG14 1QN Tel. *01635 565200* Fax. *0118 9241401* E-mail. *enquiries@microfocus.com* Web. *www.microfocus.com Micro Focus Cobol (United Kingdom)*

Micron Bio-Systems Bath Road, Bridgwater TA6 4NZ Tel. *01278 427272* E-mail. *info@micronbio-systems.co.uk* Web. *www.micronbio-systems.co.uk *Bio-Boost – *Bio-Chlor – *Fermos – *Nutracell*

Micronclean Laundry Roman Bank, Skegness PE25 1SQ Tel. *01754 767377* Fax. *01754 610344* E-mail. *simon.fry@micronclean.co.uk* Web. *www.micronclean.co.uk Micronclean*

Micron Europe Ltd Lavenir Opladen Way, Bracknell RG12 0PH Tel. *01344 383400* Fax. *01344 750710* E-mail. *sgamble@micron.com* Web. *www.micron.com Crucial (U.S.A.)*

Micronizing UK Ltd Off Saxtead Road Framlingham, Woodbridge IP13 9PT Tel. *01728 723435* Fax. *01728 724359* E-mail. *info@micronizing.com* Web. *www.micronizing.com Micronizer*

Micron Sprayers Ltd Bromyard Industrial Estate, Bromyard HR7 4HS Tel. *01885 482397* Fax. *01885 483043* E-mail. *john.clayton@micron.co.uk* Web. *www.micron.co.uk Accudos – Accudos 2/25P – Herbi – Micro-Ulva – Microair – Microfit – Micromax – Micron/X1 – Micron/X15 – Micronair – Micronex – Micropak – Turbair – Ulva – Ulvafan – Ulvamast*

Micron Workholding Ltd Unit 5 Nene Road Kimbolton, Huntingdon PE28 0LF Tel. *01480 861321* Fax. *01480 861515* E-mail. *sales@microloc.com* Web. *www.microloc.com *MicroLoc*

Micro Peripherals Ltd Unit 1 Elmwood Crockford Lane Chineham, Chineham, Basingstoke RG24 8WG Tel. *01256 707070* Fax. *01256 707505* E-mail. *sales@micro-p.com* Web. *www.micro-p.com Cannon – Panasonic*

Micropol Ltd Bayley Street, Stalybridge SK15 1QQ Tel. *0161 3305570* Fax. *0161 3305576* E-mail. *j.hardacre@micropol.co.uk* Web. *www.micropol.co.uk Binisil – Isoplas – Microcene – Microcoat – Microcoat – Microlin – Microlink – Micropol – Microstat*

Micro-Reg Carousels 31 Hawthorn Grove, London SE20 8LS Tel. *020 86599362* E-mail. *bill_folley@tiscali.co.uk MICRO-REGCAROUSELS*

Micross Electronics Ltd Units 4-5 Great Western Court, Ashburton Industrial Estate, Ross On Wye HR9 7XP Tel. *01989 768080* Fax. *01989 768163* E-mail. *sales@micross.co.uk* Web. *www.micross.co.uk *Frames (United Kingdom) – *Miscross Laundry Systems (United Kingdom) – *Tracknet 2000 (United Kingdom) – *Tracknet Pro (United Kingdom)*

Microsystems Technology 12 Paradise Close Moira, Swadlincote DE12 6EE Tel. *01283 225890* E-mail. *pete.shaw@microtechsoftware.com* Web. *www.microtechsoftware.co.uk M.P.M.S. – Microtech – Microtech Software*

Microtech Filters Ltd Alva Lodge Kirkby Lane, Pinxton, Nottingham NG16 6HW Tel. *01773 862345* Fax. *01773 863111* E-mail. *info@microtechfilters.co.uk* Web. *www.microtechfilters.co.uk Brightspark – Elinca – Microtech*

Mid Blue International Ltd Laburnham Cottage Hawley Road, Dartford DA1 1PX Tel. *01322 407000* Fax. *07092 364351* E-mail. *paul.williams@mid-blue.com* Web. *www.mid-blue.com 9406 – AS400 – eserver – i5 – i5os – IBM – IBM computers – iSeries – OS400 – pSeries – xSeries*

Middleby UK Ltd 4 Cranford Court Hardwick Grange Woolston, Woolston, Warrington WA1 4RX Tel. *01925 821280* Fax. *01925 815653* E-mail. *sales@middlebyuk.co.uk* Web. *www.middlebyuk.co.uk Blodgett Convection – Blodgett Conveyor – *Brema – *Magikitch'n – *Moretti Forni – *Pitco Frialator – Southbend – *Toastmaster*

Middlesborough Football Club Riverside Stadium Middlehaven Way, Middlesbrough TS3 6RS Tel. *08444 996789* Fax. *01642 877840* E-mail. *enquiries@mfc.co.uk* Web. *www.mfc.co.uk Middlesbrough Football & Athletic Co. (1986) Ltd*

Middlesex County Cricket Club Lords Cricket Ground St Johns Wood Road, London NW8 8QN Tel. *020 72891300* Fax. *020 72895831* E-mail. *enquiries@middlesexccc.com* Web. *www.middlesexccc.com Middlesex County Cricket Club*

A J Middleton & Co. Ltd 45 York Road, Ilford IG1 3AD Tel. *020 84781501* Fax. *020 84781501* E-mail. *geoff612phillips@googlemail.com Middleton*

Midland Air Tools Ltd Unit 1 Apex Business Park Walsall Road, Norton Canes, Cannock WS11 9PU Tel. *01543 276119* Fax. *01543 276612* E-mail. *sales@midlandairtools.co.uk* Web. *www.midlandairtools.co.uk Atlas Copco – Chicago Pneumatic, CP – Desoutter – George Renault – Rock Air*

Midland Automation Ltd P O Box 395, Huddersfield HD3 4NY Tel. *01484 461133* Fax. *01484 461123* E-mail. *richard_regan@midlandjay.co.uk* Web. *www.midlandjay.co.uk Midland Automation – Tectrite*

Midland Brass Fittings Ltd Wynford Industrial Trading Estate Wynford Road, Birmingham B27 6JT Tel. *0121 7076666* Fax. *0121 7081270* E-mail. *sales@midbras.co.uk Metro Era – Midbras – Mini-Xtra – Mustang – Superails*

Midland Diving Equipment Ltd 57 Sparkenhoe Street, Leicester LE2 0TD Tel. *0116 2124262* Fax. *0116 2124263* E-mail. *sales@midlanddiving.com* Web. *www.midlanddiving.com M.D.E.*

Midland HR Ruddington Hall Loughborough Road, Ruddington, Nottingham NG11 6LL Tel. *0115 9456000* Fax. *0115 9405286* E-mail. *reception@midlandhr.co.uk* Web. *www.midlandhr.co.uk Delphi – Trent-Midland Software Enterprise*

Midland Industrial Glass 51 Downing Street, Smethwick B66 2PP Tel. *0121 5656500* Fax. *0121 5656501* E-mail. *enquire@miglass.com* Web. *www.miglass.com Midland Industrial Glass Ltd – Splintex*

Midland Oil Refinery Ltd Shelah Road, Halesowen B63 3PN Tel. *0121 5856006* Fax. *0121 5855405* E-mail. *admin@midlandoil.co.uk* Web. *www.midlandoil.co.uk Starcut – Stargear – Starlube – Starpress – Starpress - Starlube - Starquench - Starsol – Starquench*

Midland Power Machinery Distributors Reed House Orchard Street, Worcester WR5 3DW Tel. *01905 763027* Fax. *01905 354241* E-mail. *mpmd@midlandpower.co.uk* Web. *www.midlanpower.co.uk *POWER-MEC – *SARP*

Midland Power Press Services Ltd Unit 2 High Street Princes End, Tipton DY4 9JA Tel. *0121 5204320* Fax. *0121 5577395* E-mail. *admin@mpps.co.uk* Web. *www.mpps.co.uk Millenium press metal*

Midland Pump Manufacturing Co. Ltd Unit 19a Tyseley Industrial Estate Seeleys Road, Birmingham B11 2LF Tel. *0121 7738862* Fax. *0121 7714363* E-mail. *alan@midlandpump.co.uk* Web. *www.midlandpump.co.uk Armourface – Spray Inject*

Midland Safe Load Indicators Watling Street Works Watling Street, Brownhills, Walsall WS8 7JT Tel. *01543 453166* Fax. *01543 453167* E-mail. *midlandsafeload@aol.com Weighload Systems Ltd*

Midland Scales Unit 33 Second Avenue, Pensnett Trading Estate, Kingswinford DY6 7UG Tel. *01384 841430* Fax. *01384 841450* E-mail. *sales@midlandscales.com* Web. *www.midlandscales.com Jadever*

Midlands Co Op Food 170 Evington Road, Leicester LE2 1HL Tel. *0116 2736251* Fax. *0116 2734162* E-mail. *jbishop@tomorrows-world.co.uk* Web. *www.co-operative.coop Tomorrows World Travel*

Midland Steel Traders Ltd Shadon Way Birtley, Chester le Street DH3 2SW Tel. *0191 4105311* Fax. *0191 4100482* E-mail. *rw@msttracks.com* Web. *www.msttracks.com Berco – ESCO – Expander – Hensley – MiniMax*

Midland Systems Ltd Charnwood House 21 Fairyfield Ave, Birmingham B43 6AG Tel. *0121 2334242* Fax. *0121 3570350* E-mail. *info@knightkit.co.uk* Web. *www.knightkit.co.uk Knight Kit*

Midland Tube & Fabrications 4 Corngreaves Works Corngreaves Road, Cradley Heath B64 7DA Tel. *01384 566364* Fax. *01384 566365* E-mail. *keithcadman@btconnect.com* Web. *www.midlandtubeandfabrications.co.uk Victaulic – Viking-Johnson*

Mid Sussex Times & Citizen 7-9 South Road, Haywards Heath RH16 4LE Tel. *01444 452201* Fax. *01444 416241* E-mail. *john.hammond@sussexnewspapers.co.uk* Web. *www.midsussextoday.co.uk Mid Sussex Citizen – Mid Sussex Times*

Mid-Ven Doors Ltd The Hayes Trading Estate Folkes Road, Stourbridge DY9 8RG Tel. *01384 424924* Fax. *01384 424929* E-mail. *dav@mid-ven.co.uk* Web. *www.mid-ven.co.uk Corinthian – Mid-Ven – Olympian*

Mid Wales Tourism The Station, Machynlleth SY20 8TG Tel. *01654 702653* Fax. *01654 703235* E-mail. *valerie.hawkins@midwalestourism.co.uk* Web. *www.midwalestourism.co.uk Cwmni Twristiaeth Canolbarth Cymru – Mid Wales Tourism*

Miele Fairacres Marcham Road, Abingdon OX14 1TW Tel. *01235 554455* Fax. *01235 554477* E-mail. *info@miele.co.uk* Web. *www.miele.co.uk Miele*

Mighty 2 Colwick Quays Business Park Private Road 2, Colwick Industrial Estate, Nottingham NG4 2JR Tel. *0115 9402222* Fax. *0115 9402232* E-mail. *mark.murphy@robert-prettie.co.uk* Web. *www.robert-prettie.co.uk Robert Prettie*

M I K O Coffee Ltd Unit 7 Ember Centre Lyon Road, Walton On Thames KT12 3PU Tel. *01932 253787* Fax. *01932 253520* E-mail. *info@miko.co.uk* Web. *www.miko.co.uk Faema Bean to Cup Espresso Machines – Faema Espresso Machines – Fair Trade Coffee – Miko Coffee*

Mila Hardware 1 Brunel Close Drayton Fields Industrial Estate, Daventry NN11 8RB Tel. *01327 872511* Fax. *01327 872575* E-mail. *sales@mila.co.uk* Web. *www.mila.co.uk *Mila (United Kingdom)*

Milbury Systems Ltd Milbury Precast Lydney Industrial Estate, Harbour Road, Lydney GL15 4EJ Tel. *01594 847500* Fax. *01594 847501* E-mail. *sales@milbury.com* Web. *www.milbury.com Syloguard – Syloseal*

Miles Macadam Ltd Malpas Station Hampton Heath Industrial Estate, Hampton, Malpas SY14 8LU Tel. *01948 820489* Fax. *01948 820267* E-mail. *crac@milesmacadam.co.uk* Web. *www.milesmacadam.co.uk Hardicoat – Hardicrete –*

Hardigrip – Hardipave – Milecoat – Mileflex – Milegrip – Mileguard – Milepave – Mileseal – Miletac – Miletex

Miles Waterscapes Ltd School House Farm Norton Road, Great Ashfield, Bury St Edmunds IP31 3HJ Tel. *01359 242356* Fax. *01359 241781* E-mail. *contact@miles-water.com* Web. *www.miles-water.com Water Storage & Engineering*

Mileta Ltd Spen Vale Mills Station Lane, Heckmondwike WF16 0NQ Tel. *01924 409311* Fax. *01924 409839* E-mail. *brianward@tog24.com* Web. *www.tog24.com Mileta – Tog 24*

Charlie Miller Hairdressing 13 Stafford Street, Edinburgh EH3 7BR Tel. *0131 2265551* Fax. *0131 2254949* Web. *www.charliemiller.co.uk Charlie Miller*

Miller Pattison Ltd 9 Albone Way, Biggleswade SG18 8BN Tel. *01767 314444* Fax. *01767 317601* E-mail. *biggleswade@miller-patterson.co.uk* Web. *www.miller-pattison.co.uk Miller Pattison*

Millers Music Centre Ltd 12 Sussex Street, Cambridge CB1 1PW Tel. *01223 354452* Fax. *01223 362480* E-mail. *info@millersmusic.co.uk* Web. *www.millersmusic.co.uk Millers*

Millers Oils Ltd 6 Carlyle Avenue Hillington Park, Glasgow G52 4XX Tel. *0141 8823216* Fax. *01224 248335* E-mail. *info@millersoils.co.uk* Web. *www.millersoils.co.uk Truckmaster – X.H.P.D. Engine Oil*

Millers Oils Ltd Hillside Oil Works Rastrick, Brighouse HD6 3DP Tel. *01484 713201* Fax. *01484 721263* E-mail. *martyn.mann@millersoils.co.uk* Web. *www.millersoils.co.uk Kaystol – Magnafleet SHPD – Maxifleet MP – Milgear EP – Millair – Millers Black Moly – Millers Classic 20W-50 – Millers Classic Mini – Millers Classic Mini Sport – Millers Classic Sport – Millers Dieselclean Plus – Millers Hi-Wax – Millers Injectoclean – Millers Panolin – Millers TRX – Millers XFE – Millers XFS – Millers XSS – Millitex – Millmax AW – Millube – Millway – Multicut Universal – Suprex – Syntran II – Truckmaster XHFE – Truckmaster XHPD*

Milliken Industrials Ltd Beech Hill Plant Gidlow Lane, Wigan WN6 8RN Tel. *01942 826073* Fax. *01942 826570* Web. *www.milliken.com Milliken Carpet – Milliken Carpet - contract carpet tiles.*

Milliken Woollen Speciality Products Lodgemore Mills, Stroud GL5 3EJ Tel. *01453 764456* Fax. *01453 752919* E-mail. *davidwsp.smith@milliken.com* Web. *www.milliken-wsp.co.uk Playnes – Strachan – Strachan - west of England billiards cloth; Playnes - tennis ball melton.*

Millipore UK Ltd Suite 3-5 Building 6 Crossley Green Business Park Hatters Lane, Watford WD18 8YH Tel. *08709 004645* Fax. *0870 9004646* E-mail. *csr_uk@millipore.com* Web. *www.millipore.com Millipore (UK)*

Mills C N C Unit 2-3 Tachbrook Link Tachbrook Park Drive, Warwick CV34 6SN Tel. *01926 736736* Fax. *01926 736737* E-mail. *sales@millscnc.co.uk* Web. *www.millscnc.co.uk Doosan Daewoo – Kuraki CNC – OM CNC*

Mills & Reeve LLP Francis House 112 Hills Road, Cambridge CB2 1PH Tel. *01223 364422* Fax. *01223 355848* E-mail. *guy.hinchley@mills-reeve.com* Web. *www.mills-reeve.com Law-Direct – Legal-Direct – Tax-Direct*

Millward Brown Olympus Avenue Tachbrook Park, Warwick CV34 6RJ Tel. *01926 452233* Fax. *01926 833600* E-mail. *info@uk.millwardbrown.com* Web. *www.millwardbrown.com ATP tm – Brand Dynamics tm – Force tm – Kidspeak tm – Link tm – Millward Brown*

Milton Keynes Citizen (a division of Johnson press) Napier House Auckland Park, Bletchley, Milton Keynes MK1 1BU Tel. *01908 371133* Fax. *01908 371112* E-mail. *john.francis@jpress.co.uk* Web. *www.miltonkeynes.co.uk Leighton Buzzard Citizen*

Milton Pipes Ltd Cooks Lane, Sittingbourne ME10 2QF Tel. *01795 425191* Fax. *01795 420360* E-mail. *sales@miltonprecast.com* Web. *www.miltonprecast.com Milton*

M & I Materials Ltd Stretford, Manchester M32 0ZD Tel. *0161 8645422* Fax. *0161 8752695* E-mail. *kimwhittle@mimaterials.com* Web. *www.mimaterials.com Apiezon (United Kingdom) – Apiezon - Metrosil - Midel - Wolfmet – Metrosil (United Kingdom) – Midel (United Kingdom) – Wolfmet (United Kingdom)*

Minelco Ltd Mica Works Raynesway, Derby DE21 7BE Tel. *01332 673131* Fax. *01332 677590* E-mail. *jane.potts@minelco.com* Web. *www.minelco.com DekorLux – DupreVermiculite – FireCarb – FordaCal – FordaDol – FordaGard – FordaTal – HyperCarb – MagniF – Micafil – MicroBar – MicroCarb – MicroGel – MicroNex – MicroSpar – Muscovite Mica – OxiMag – Phlogopite Mica – UltraCarb*

Minelco Free Wharf Brighton Road, Shoreham By Sea BN43 6RE Tel. *01273 452331* Fax. *01273 464741* E-mail. *bob.bolton@minelco.com* Web. *www.minelco.com Forda Cal – Forda Dol*

Mineral & Chemical Services Ltd 1 Britannia House Britannia Business Park, Wallsend NE28 6HA Tel. *0191 2623311* Fax. *0191 2623344* E-mail. *patrickhegarty@minchemical.co.uk* Web. *www.minchemical.co.uk Budit – FR Cros – Goldflam – IronOr – Zircon*

Mineral Products Association Gillingham House 38-44 Gillingham Street, London SW1V 1HU Tel. *020 79638000* Fax. *020 79638001* E-mail. *info@mineralproducts.org* Web. *www.mineralproducts.org Quarry Products Association*

Minerva Football Company Ltd Unit 10 Metro Centre Ronsons Way, Sandridge, St Albans AL4 9QT Tel. *01727 845550* Fax. *01727 841555* E-mail. *sales@minervafootballs.co.uk* Web. *www.htsports.co.uk Minerva Football Co Ltd*

N Minikin & Sons Ltd Spa House Hookstone Park, Harrogate HG2 7DB Tel. *01423 889845* Fax. *01423 880724* E-mail. *tony.minikin@minikins.co.uk* Web. *www.minikins.co.uk Emflex*

Minimoves Unit 38 Lansdown Industrial Estate, Cheltenham GL51 8PL Tel. *01242 256858* E-mail. *office@minimoves.co.uk* Web. *www.minimoves.co.uk MiniMoves*

Miniplas Ltd 3-5 West Burrowfield, Welwyn Garden City AL7 4TW Tel. *01707 332801* Fax. *01707 371574* E-mail. *info@miniplas.co.uk* Web. *www.miniplas.co.uk Mini-Plas*

MINNI-DIE LIMITED 40 TRENT SOUTH INDUSTRIAL PARK LITTLE TENNIS STREET, NOTTINGHAM NG2 4EQ Tel. *0115 9419009* Fax. *0115 0503921* E-mail. *sales@minni-die.co.uk* Web. *www.minni-die.co.uk Minni-Die*

Minni-Die Ltd Unit 40 Trent South Industrial Park Little Tennis Street, Nottingham NG2 4EQ Tel. *0115 9419009* Fax. *0115 9503921* E-mail. *sales@minni-die.com* Web. *www.parsellminni-die.com Airdromatic – Minni-Die – Parsell – Uni-Cage – Uni-Ram*

Minova Weldgrip Ltd Unit 19 Redbrook Business Park Wilthorpe Road, Barnsley S75 1JN Tel. *01226 280567* Fax. *01226 731563* E-mail. *steve.jackson@minovaint.com* Web. *www.weldgrip.com Fibregrip – Gripforce – Weldgrip*

Minsterstone Ltd Harts Close, Ilminster TA19 9DJ Tel. *01460 52277* Fax. *01460 57865* E-mail. *sales@minsterstone.ltd.uk* Web. *www.minsterstone.ltd.uk Minster Balustrading – Minster Fireplaces – Minster Garden Ornaments – Minster Paving*

Mintel Group Ltd 18-19 Long Lane, London EC1A 9PL Tel. *020 76064533* Fax. *020 76065932* E-mail. *info@mintel.com* Web. *www.mintel.com GNPD – Mintel International – POS+*

Minuteman Press Ltd 15 Nelson Parade, Bristol BS3 4HY Tel. *0117 9665566* Fax. *0117 9665511* E-mail. *info@minutemanbristol.com* Web. *www.minutemanbristol.com Minuteman Press*

Mira Ltd Watling Street, Nuneaton CV10 0TU Tel. *024 76355000* Fax. *024 76358000* E-mail. *graham.townsend@mire.co.uk* Web. *www.mira.co.uk MIRA*

Miracle Mills Ltd Knightsdale Road, Ipswich IP1 4LE Tel. *01473 742325* Fax. *01473 462773* E-mail. *info@cristy-turner.com* Web. *www.miracle-mills.co.uk Miracle*

Miracon Conveyors Ltd Drayton Road Shirley, Solihull B90 4NG Tel. *0121 7058468* Fax. *0121 7112074* E-mail. *sales@miracon.com* Web. *www.miracon.com Miracon*

Mirrorpix 1 Canada Square, London E14 5AP Tel. *020 72933700* Fax. *01923 815015* E-mail. *desk@mirrorpix.com* Web. *www.mirrorpix.com The Mirror – The People – The Sunday Mirror*

Mirror Technology Ltd 4 Redwood House Orchard Industrial Estate, Toddington, Cheltenham GL54 5EB Tel. *01242 621534* Fax. *01242 621529* E-mail. *sales@mirrortechnology.co.uk* Web. *www.mirrortechnology.co.uk Poly-Vu*

M I T Ltd Queenborough Shipyard South Street, Queenborough ME11 5EE Tel. *01795 580808* Fax. *01795 580900* E-mail. *reception@mitgroup.co.uk* Web. *www.mitgroup.co.uk Arneson – Rubber Design – MIT – Quincy – Transfluid – Transfluid - all transmission systemsTwin disc - transmission systemArneson - propulsion systemMIT - Marine Industrial Transmissions Quincy - Air Compressors – Twin disc*

Andrew Mitchell & Co. Ltd 15 Dunivaig Road, Glasgow G33 4TT Tel. *0141 7735454* Fax. *0141 7735455* E-mail. *kmoodie@mitco.co.uk* Web. *www.mitco.co.uk Mitco – Nytarp – Polymit – Protectomuffs – Safex – Uni-Shel*

Mitchell & Cooper Ltd (Head Office) 138-140 Framfield Road, Uckfield TN22 5AU Tel. *01825 765511* Fax. *01825 767173* E-mail. *sales@mitchellcooper.co.uk* Web. *www.mitchellcooper.co.uk Bonzer (United Kingdom) – Hovicon – Matfer-Bourgeat (France) – Peek (U.S.A.) – Pulltex – *Zeroll (U.S.A.) – Kisag (Switzerland)*

Mitchell Grieve 129 Parker Drive, Leicester LE4 0HZ Tel. *0116 2350512* Fax. *0116 2340273* E-mail. *sales@mitchell-grieve.co.uk* Web. *www.mitchell-grieve.co.uk Grieve*

Mitchell Interflex Ltd County Brook Mill County Brook Lane, Foulridge, Colne BB8 7LT Tel. *01282 813221* Fax. *01282 813633* E-mail. *adrian@mitchell-interflex.co.uk* Web. *www.mitchell-interflex.co.uk Hiyasun – Laptair Interlinings*

J & A Mitchell Co. Ltd Springbank Distillery Well Close, Campbeltown PA28 6ET Tel. *01586 552085* Fax. *01586 553215* E-mail. *stuart@jandamitchell.com* Web. *www.springbankwhisky.com *Springbank (United Kingdom)*

The Mitchell Library North Street, Glasgow G3 7DN Tel. *0141 2872999* Fax. *0141 2872815* E-mail. *libraries@glasgowlife.org.uk* Web. *www.glasgowlife.org.uk Business @ The Mitchell*

Mitecon Ltd 28 Cooper Avenue, Carluke ML8 5US Tel. *01555 752352* Fax. *08707 626223* E-mail. *info@mitecon.co.uk* Web. *www.mitecon.co.uk MITECON*

Mitek Mitek House Grazebrook Industrial Park, Dudley DY2 0XW Tel. *01384 451400* Fax. *01384 451411* E-mail. *sgriffiths@mitek.co.uk* Web. *www.mitek.co.uk MiTek*

Mitex Ltd 4 Towers Business Park Carey Way, Wembley HA9 0LQ Tel. *020 89000440* Fax. *020 89001908 Ad Lib*

Mito Construction & Engineering Ltd Adams Wharf 19 Yeoman Street, London SE8 5DT Tel. *020 72310918* Fax. *020 72316307* E-mail. *mitocons@aol.com Stahlschluessel*

Mitre Linen 1 Goat Mill Road Dowlais, Merthyr Tydfil CF48 3TD Tel. *01685 353456* Fax. *01254 614222* E-mail. *sales@mitrehallandletts.com* Web. *www.mitrelinen.com Windsor Castle (United Kingdom)*

Mitre Sports International Ltd Pentland Centre Squires Lane, Finchley, London N3 2QL Tel. *020 83462600* Fax. *020 89702887* E-mail. *enquiries@mitre.com* Web. *www.mitre.com Delta – *Mitre (Worldwide) – Mouldmaster – Multimould – Multiplex*

Mitsubishi Carbide (M M C Hardmetal UK Ltd) 5-7 Galena Close, Tamworth B77 4AS Tel. *01827 312312* Fax. *01827 312314* E-mail. *sales@mitsubishicarbide.co.uk* Web. *www.mitsubishicarbide.com Mitsubishi Carbide*

Mitsubishi Electric Europe BV Power Systems Group (Engineering Division) 7th Floor Stephenson House 2 Cherry Orchard Road, Croydon CR0 6BA Tel. *020 86869551* Fax. *020 86882035* E-mail. *tetsuya.shinohara@crd.meuk.mee.com* Web. *www.mitsubishielectric.co.uk Mitsubishi*

M J Maillis UK Ltd Monarch House Chrysalis Way, Eastwood, Nottingham NG16 3RY Tel. *01773 539000* Fax. *01773 539090* E-mail. *info@mallis.co.uk* Web. *www.maillis.co.uk Hyperlyn – MANCON – Millennium – Monolyn – Pal Rapper – SIAT – Tensolyn – Wulftec*

MJM Data Recovery Ltd The Somerset Barn The Old Redhouse Farm, Stratton-on-the-Fosse, Radstock BA3 4QE Tel. *01761 402686* Fax. *01462 483648* E-mail. *mjm@mjm.co.uk* Web. *www.mjm.co.uk RAID*

M K Electric Ltd Paycocke Road, Basildon SS14 3EA Tel. *01268 563000* Fax. *01268 563563* E-mail. *jeff.stacey@honeywell.com* Web. *www.mkelectric.co.uk Albany plus – Aspect – Chroma plus – Commando – Commando Combi – Duraplug – Edge – Ega Mini – Grid Plus – Grosvenor plus – Logic Plus – Masterseal – Metalclad Plus – Pinnacle – Powerlink – Prestige 2com – Prestige Plus – Prestige Power Poles and Posts – Red Alert – Safetyswitch – Savoy – Sentry*

M L P S 3 Wharf Road, Grantham NG31 6BA Tel. *01476 578654* Fax. *01476 590400* E-mail. *enquiries@mlps.co.uk* Web. *www.printingsystemsuk.com Brother – Casio – Croy – Wasp – Zebra*

M M A Insurance plc 2 Norman Place, Reading RG1 8DA Tel. *0118 9552222* Fax. *0118 9552211* E-mail. *info@mma-insurance.com* Web. *www.mma-insurance.com Bed & Breakfast Insurance – Contractors Combined Insurance – Flagship – Home Gold – Landlords Insurance – M. les Mutuelles du Mans – Master Build Insurance – Multi-trip Insurance – Offices & Surgeries Insurance – *Prime 100 – Profile – Profile Gold – Property Owners Insurance – Shops, Restaurants & Public Houses Insurance – Value 100 – Value Home – Working from Home Insurance*

M M D Mining Machinery Developments Cotes Park Lane Cotes Park Industrial Estate, Somercotes, Alfreton DE55 4NJ Tel. *01773 835533* Fax. *01773 835593* E-mail. *reception@mmdsizers.com* Web. *www.mmdsizers.com M.M.D.*

M M H Recycling Systems Ltd Unit 6 Broomers Hill Park Broomers Hill Lane, Pulborough RH20 2RY Tel. *01798 874440* Fax. *01798 875613* E-mail. *sales@mmhrecsys.com* Web. *www.mmhrecsys.com Bonbiglioli – Elda Scandinavian Recycling – M. & J. – Moros – Rad/Comm Systems Corp*

MML Ltd 30 Fountain Crescent Inchinnan Business Park, Inchinnan, Renfrew PA4 9RE Tel. *0141 8146550* Fax. *0141 8146554* E-mail. *sales@m-m-l.com* Web. *www.mmlmarine.com MML McGeoch Marine*

Mobile Applications Ltd 14 Chemical Lane, Stoke On Trent ST6 4PB Tel. *01782 790824* Fax. *01782 790825* E-mail. *sales@mobileapplicationsltd.co.uk* Web. *www.mobileapplicationsltd.com MA615*

Mobile Expertise Ltd Unit B Wooland Works Water End Road, Potten End, Berkhamsted HP4 2SH Tel. *01442 874604*

Fax. *01442 500577* E-mail. *sales@mobile-expertise.co.uk* Web. *www.mobile-expertise.co.uk me**

Mode Lighting Chelsing House Mead Lane, Hertford SG13 7AW Tel. *01992 554566* Fax. *01992 553644* E-mail. *sales@modelighting.com* Web. *www.modelighting.com C.A.L. – Chelsing*

Mode Lighting UK Ltd The Maltings 63 High Street, Ware SG12 9AD Tel. *01920 462121* Fax. *01920 466882* E-mail. *sales@modelighting.com* Web. *www.modelighting.com Mode Lighting*

Models Direct-National Model Register Men/Women Children Centre King Street, Norwich NR1 1QH Tel. *08705 010101* Fax. *01603 767858* E-mail. *email@modelsdirect.co.uk* Web. *www.modelsdirect.com Models Direct*

Models One Ltd 12 Macklin Street, London WC2B 5SZ Tel. *020 70254910* Fax. *020 70254921* E-mail. *info@models1.co.uk* Web. *www.models1.co.uk Models 1*

Modern Health Systems Glydegate, Bradford BD5 0BQ Tel. *01274 590235* Fax. *01274 590235* E-mail. *sales@modernhealthsystems.com* Web. *www.modernhealthsystems.com Drugalysers; Nicoscreen;Draeger alcohol tests*

Modern Screws Ltd 5 Dartford Road, Bexley DA5 2BH Tel. *01322 553224* Fax. *01322 555093* E-mail. *sales@modern-screws.co.uk* Web. *www.modern-screws.co.uk Modern Screws*

Modrec International Holdings Ltd Bugatti House Norham Road, North Shields NE29 7HA Tel. *0191 2584451* Fax. *0191 2582983* E-mail. *sales@modrec.co.uk* Web. *www.modrecinternational.com Amica – GF2K – Gino Ferrari – Pierre Cardin – UK Licensee for Camel Travel Bags & Luggage*

Moflash Signalling Ltd Unit 18 Klaxon Industrial Estate Warwick Road, Tyseley, Birmingham B11 2HA Tel. *0121 7076681* Fax. *0121 7078305* E-mail. *uksales@moflash.co.uk* Web. *www.moflash.co.uk Klaxet – Rotoflash – Spectrum600*

Molecular Control Systems Ltd Unit 1 Greetby Place, Skelmersdale WN8 9UL Tel. *01695 566700* Fax. *01695 50329* E-mail. *mary.webb@porpoise.co.uk* Web. *www.porpoise.co.uk/service.html P3 – P5 – P7 – Porpoise*

Molecular Properties Ltd Mill End Thaxted, Dunmow CM6 2LT Tel. *01371 830676* Fax. *01371 830998* E-mail. *info@molecularproducts.co.uk* Web. *www.molecularproducts.co.uk Ethysorb – Moleculite – Sofnocarb – Sofnocat – Sofnofil – Sofnolime*

Molins plc Rockingham Drive Lindford Wood East, Linford Wood, Milton Keynes MK14 6LY Tel. *01908 246870* Fax. *01908 234224* E-mail. *molins.ho@molins.com* Web. *www.molins.com Langen – Molins – Sandiacre*

Mollart Engineering 106 Roebuck Road, Chessington KT9 1EU Tel. *020 83912282* Fax. *020 83916626* E-mail. *info@mollart.com* Web. *www.mollart.com Botek – Mollart*

Molten Metal Products Ltd Unit 7 Crucible Business Park Woodbury Lane, Norton, Worcester WR5 2PU Tel. *01905 728200* Fax. *01905 767877* E-mail. *marketing@morganitecrucible.com* Web. *www.morganitecrucible.com Morgan – Morgan Central – Morgan Dual Energy Bale Out Furnace – Morgan Electric – Morgan Electric – Morgan Electric Resistance Bale Out Furnace – Morgan Gas Fired Bale Out Furnace – Morgan HE – Morgan High Efficiency – Morgan Miniature – Regenerative – Salamander Copperstar – Salamander Excel – Salamander Excel E – Salamander Iso-Suprex – Salamander Plumbago – Salamander S.R. – Salamander Super*

Molton Brown Ltd The Terrace Camden Wharf 28 Jamestown Road, London NW1 7AP Tel. *020 74282400* Fax. *020 74282401* E-mail. *info@moltonbrown.com* Web. *www.moltonbrown.co.uk Colourfreedom – Molton Brown*

Molyslip Atlantic Ltd Unit A1 Danebrook Court Langford Lane, Kidlington OX5 1LQ Tel. *01865 370032* Fax. *01865 372030* E-mail. *enquiries@molyslip.co.uk* Web. *www.molyslip.co.uk Combat – Copaslip – Dieslip – Fuelslip – Moly Slip – Molyslip – Radsil – Slip Radsil – Slip Tuneslip – Tuneslip*

Momentive Specialty Chemicals UK Ltd Sully Moors Road Sully, Penarth CF64 5YU Tel. *01446 725500* Fax. *08453 109201* E-mail. *phil.frampton@momentive.com* Web. *www.momentive.com Cellobond*

Monarch Airlines London Luton Airport, Luton LU2 9LX Tel. *01582 424211* Fax. *01582 398323* E-mail. *sales@flymonarch.com* Web. *www.flymonarch.com Crown Class – Monarch*

Monax Glass Ltd 22 Charles Jarvis Court, Cupar KY15 5EJ Tel. *01334 657800* Fax. *01334 657857* E-mail. *monax@sol.co.uk* Web. *www.monaxglass.com Monax*

Monckton Coke & Chemical Co. PO Box 25, Barnsley S71 4BE Tel. *01226 722601* Fax. *01226 700307* E-mail. *iarchibold@hargreavesservices.co.uk* Web. *www.moncktoncoke.com Cosycoke and Sunbrite – Monckton Sunbrite*

Mondial Assistance Ltd Mondial House 102 George Street, Croydon CR9 1AJ Tel. *020 86812525* Fax. *020 86880577* E-mail. *anthony_lancaster@mondial-assistance.co.uk* Web. *www.mondial-assistance.co.uk Mondial Assistance*

Mondi Packaging Limited Pulham St. Mary, Diss IP21 4QH Tel. *01379 676531* Fax. *01379 676275* E-mail. *sales.bux@mondipackaging.com* Web. *www.mondigroup.com Panisco Pack Bux*

Money Controls Ltd Coin House New Coin Street, Royton, Oldham OL2 6JZ Tel. *0161 6780111* Fax. *0161 6267674* E-mail. *slindon@moneycontrols.com* Web. *www.moneycontrols.com Ardac – C400 Series – Coin Controls – Compact Hopper – Condor – DBA – Gamesman – Lumina – Paytrack – S2000 – SR Series – SR3 – SR5 – Stealth Hopper – Universal Hopper – World Acceptor*

Moneyfacts Group plc 66-70 Thorpe Road, Norwich NR1 1BJ Tel. *01603 476476* Fax. *01603 476477* E-mail. *enquiries@moneyfacts.co.uk* Web. *www.moneyfactsgroup.co.uk Moneyfacts*

Monier Ltd Sussex Manor Business Park Gatwick Road, Crawley RH10 9NZ Tel. *01293 618418* Fax. *01293 614548* E-mail. *info@lafarge-roofing.com* Web. *www.monier.com Cambrain – Delta – Dove Tail – Downland – Dry Tech – Farmhouse – Grovebury – QuantMuster – Redland – Redland 49 – Redvent – Regent – Renown – Richmond – Roofscape – Rosemary – Saxon – SpecMaster – Stonewold – Uni-Dry*

Monitor Audio Ltd 2 Brook Road Industrial Estate Brook Road, Brook Road Industrial Estate, Rayleigh SS6 7XL Tel. *01268 740580* Fax. *01268 740589* E-mail. *info@monitoraudio.co.uk* Web. *www.monitoraudio.com Monitor Audio*

Monitor Coatings Ltd Monitor House 2 Elm Road West Chirton Industrial Estate, North Shields NE29 8SE Tel. *0191 2937040* Fax. *0191 2937041* E-mail. *sales@monitorcoatings.co.uk* Web. *www.monitorcoatings.co.uk Monitor*

Monks & Crane Industrial Group Ltd Unit 2 Atlantic Way, Wednesbury WS10 7WW Tel. *0121 5064000* Fax. *01952 684064* E-mail. *twd@mcrane.co.uk* Web. *www.monks-crane.com/branch Atorn*

Mono Pumps Ltd Martin Street Audenshaw, Manchester M34 5JA Tel. *0161 3399000* Fax. *0161 3440727* E-mail. *pnaylon@mono-pumps.com* Web. *www.mono-pumps.com Discreen (United Kingdom) – Flexishaft (United Kingdom) – Mono – Muncher (United Kingdom) – Merlin – Stormscreen – Flexishaft – EZstrip*

Monotype Imaging Ltd Unit 2 Perrywood Business Park Honeycrock Lane, Redhill RH1 5DZ Tel. *01737 765959* Fax. *01737 769243* E-mail. *info@fonts.com* Web. *www.fonts.com Abadi – Bembo – Calisto – Cantoria – Clarion – Footlight – Gill Sans – Joanna – Monotype C.D. 6.0. – Nimrod – Photina – Plantin – Qubic Fonts – Rockwell – Times New Roman – Van Dijck*

Mont Blanc Industry UK Ltd Unit 21 Pages Industrial Park Eden Way, Leighton Buzzard LU7 4TZ Tel. *01525 850800* Fax. *01525 850808* E-mail. *mike.holmes@montblancuk.co.uk* Web. *www.montblancuk.co.uk Paddy Hopkirk*

Montgomery Exhibitions 9 Manchester Square, London W1U 3PL Tel. *020 78863000* Fax. *020 78863001* E-mail. *enquiries@montex.co.uk* Web. *www.montex.co.uk Interbuild*

Montien Spice Co. Ltd 214b Sandycombe Road, Richmond TW9 2EQ Tel. *020 83329888* Fax. *020 82871010* E-mail. *sales@namjai.co.uk* Web. *www.namjai.co.uk *Namjai*

Monument Tools Ltd Restmor Way, Wallington SM6 7AH Tel. *020 82881100* Fax. *020 82881108* E-mail. *jonathan@monument-tools.com* Web. *www.monument-tools.com Monument*

Moog Aircraft Group Wobaston Road, Wolverhampton WV9 5EW Tel. *01902 397700* Fax. *01902 394394* Web. *www.geaviation.com Downel*

Moog Components Unit 30 Suttons Park Avenue Earley, Reading RG6 1AW Tel. *0118 9666044* Fax. *0118 9666524* E-mail. *david.norman@idmelectronics.co.uk* Web. *www.moog.com I.D.M. Electronics*

Moore Large & Co. Ltd Grampian Buildings Sinfin Lane, Derby DE24 9GL Tel. *01332 274200* Fax. *01332 270635* E-mail. *sales@moorelarge.co.uk* Web. *www.moorelarge.co.uk Barracuda (Taiwan) – *Emmelle (Taiwan) – *Freespirit (Taiwan) – Haro (Taiwan) – Sonic (United Kingdom) – Yakari (Italy)*

Moorepay Ltd Palmerston House 111-113 Fleet Road, Fleet GU51 3PD Tel. *0845 1844615* Fax. *0845 2701150* E-mail. *sales@moorepay.co.uk* Web. *www.moorepay.co.uk Moorepay*

Moores Furniture Group Unit 350 Thorp Arch Trading Estate, Thorp Arch Estate, Wetherby LS23 7DD Tel. *01937 842394* Fax. *01937 845396* E-mail. *marketing@moores.co.uk* Web. *www.moores.co.uk Bolero – Cantata – Caprice – Cathedral Oak – Chateau – Concerto – Duette – Elgar – K2R/Project T/Concept – Melody – Minuet – Opus – Palazzo – Prelude – Prelude Plus – Rhapsody – Serenade – Solo and Duo – Sonata – Tempo – Trio – Verdi*

Moore Speed Racing Ltd Unit 12 Cortry Close, Poole BH12 4BQ Tel. *01202 746141* Fax. *01202 739955* E-mail. *colin@moore-international.com* Web. *www.moore-speed-racing.co.uk Power Commander – Simpson*

Moorgate Ltd 2 Cedar Court Taylor Business Park, Risley, Warrington WA3 6BT Tel. *01925 765432* Fax. *01925 765422* E-mail. *sales@moorgate.co.uk* Web. *www.moorgate.co.uk IBM – Lexmark – Printronix – Zebra*

Moorwood Vulcan Enodis UK Food Service 5 E Langley Business Centre Station Road, Langley, Slough SL3 8DS Tel. *01753 485900* Fax. *01753 485901* E-mail. *info@enodis.com* Web. *www.moorwoodvulcan.co.uk *Moorwood Vulcan*

Moplant Riverbridge Bow Street, Langport TA10 9YA Tel. *01458 253300* Fax. *01458 253996* E-mail. *sales@moplant.co.uk* Web. *www.moplant.co.uk MOPLANT*

Moresecure Ltd PO Box 34, Telford TF7 4EH Tel. *01952 683900* Fax. *01952 683982* E-mail. *sales@moresecureint.co.uk* Web. *www.moresecureint.com Moresecure – Moresecure British Standard – Moresecure Clearstor 2 – Moresecure Clip-on Longspan – Moresecure Containers – Moresecure Euro Shelving – Moresecure Palletstor – Moresecure Rolled Edge – Moresecure Square Tube*

Morgan Contract Furniture Ltd Clovelly Road Southbourne, Emsworth PO10 8PQ Tel. *01243 371111* Fax. *01243 378796* E-mail. *info@morganfurniture.co.uk* Web. *www.morganfurniture.co.uk Lockinlyne*

Morganite Upper Fforest Way Swansea Enterprise Park, Swansea SA6 8PP Tel. *01792 763000* Fax. *01792 702399* Web. *www.morgancarbon.com Electro Carbon – Morganite – National*

J P Morgan Ltd 3 Lochside View, Edinburgh EH12 9DH Tel. *0131 2704300* Fax. *0131 2704301* Web. *www.jpmorganchase.com Heaxagon R Save & Prosper*

Morgan Motor Co. Ltd Pickersleigh Road, Malvern WR14 2LL Tel. *01684 573104* Fax. *01684 892295* E-mail. *contacts@morgan-motor.co.uk* Web. *www.morgan-motor.co.uk Four Four – Plus 4 – Plus 8*

Morgans Pomade Company Ltd Tyler Way, Whitstable CT5 2RT Tel. *01227 792761* Fax. *01227 794463* E-mail. *admin@morganspomade.co.uk* Web. *www.morganspomade.co.uk Morgan's – Morgan's Dark Secret – Morgan's Hair Darkening Cream – Morgan's Perfumed Pomade – Morgan's Pomade – Morgan's Revitalising Shampoo*

T Morgan & Sons Ltd 136 Wolverhampton Road, Walsall WS2 8PP Tel. *01922 637022* Fax. *01922 631811* E-mail. *sales@tmorgan.co.uk* Web. *www.tmorgan.co.uk Bulldog*

Morlands Glastonbury 3 Creeches Lane Walton, Street BA16 9RR Tel. *01458 446969* Fax. *01458 840108* E-mail. *morlandsltd@btconnect.com* Web. *www.morlandssheepskin.co.uk Morlands*

Morpho Cards UK Ltd 250 Wharfedale Road Winnersh, Wokingham RG41 5TP Tel. *0118 3776000* Fax. *0118 3776001* E-mail. *info-uk@morpho.com* Web. *www.morpho.com ICT (South Africa)*

Morphy Richards Ltd Talbot Road Swinton, Mexborough S64 8AJ Tel. *01709 582402* Fax. *01709 587510* E-mail. *info@glendimplex.com* Web. *www.morphyrichards.co.uk Morphy Richards*

Morplan PO Box 54, Harlow CM20 2TS Tel. *01279 435333* Fax. *01279 451928* E-mail. *sales@morplan.com* Web. *www.morplan.com Morplan*

W J Morray Engineering Ltd Anglia Way, Braintree CM7 3RG Tel. *01376 322722* Fax. *01376 323277* E-mail. *kevin@morray.com* Web. *www.moray.com Morray – *Morray (Japan) – *Newlong (Japan)*

Morris Bros Ltd Phoenix Works 215 Scotia Road, Stoke On Trent ST6 4HB Tel. *01782 834242* Fax. *01782 575686* E-mail. *sales@morrisbrothers.com* Web. *www.morrisbrothers.com Phoenix*

Morris Lubricants 38 -41 Castle Foregate, Shrewsbury SY1 2EL Tel. *01743 232200* Fax. *01743 353584* E-mail. *info@morris-lubricants.co.uk* Web. *www.morrislubricants.co.uk A.G. Gear Oils – Abgel Hand Cleanser – Airforce Compressor Lubricants Range – Alto Mineral Oils – Ambesta Fuel Additives – Ankor Corrosion Preventives – Arcato – Atonal Heat Transfer Oils – Bearing Oils – Cadence – Calando Pine Disinfectant – Cora Cutting Oils – Croma Chain Saw Oils – Crystal Light/Heavy Liquid Paraffin – Deionised Water – Dorian Soluble Oils – Duplex XC – Groundforce Horticultural Range – K. 968 White Grease – K.15, 16, 60 Open Gear Oils – K.2 EPGX Grease – K.383 Anti Seize Compound – K.4000,400,40,41,42,43, EP Grease – K.48 Grease – K.57 Grease – K.62 Grease – K.84 Grease – Liquimatic 1-8 – Liquimatic 17 37A & 47A – Liquimatic 33G – Liquimatic BVG – Liquimatic C3 – Liquimatic DII – Liquimatic E85 – Liquimatic HY – Liquimatic JDF – Liquisafe 46 – Lodexol – Lodexol SS43 – Lodexol W – Lydian – M.L.R. 2 – M.L.R. 2 Stroke Engine Oils – M.L.R. 30. 40 & 50 – M.L.R. 4 Stroke Engine Oil – M.L.R. Chain Lube – M.L.R. Light/Medium Gear Oil – M.L.R. Motor Cycle Products – M.L.R. Premium 4 – M.L.R. Racing Brake Fluid – M.L.R. Racing Grease – Magnol – Marcia Cutting Oils – Morris Brake Fluid – Morris*

Universal Antifreeze – Multilife – Multivis – Ring Free XHD – Ring Free XHD Plus – Ring-Free – Scyllan Diesel Fuel Additive – Sentinel Crankcase Oil – Servol – Servol EP Gear Oil – Steam Cylinder Oils – Sulto Oils – Super Versitrac – Triad Hydraulic Oils – Unison Soluble Oils

J E Morrison & Sons Ltd Burton Weir Works Warren Street, Sheffield S4 7WT Tel. *0114 2701525* Fax. *0114 2434158* *Pigeon Brand*

Morrison McConnell Ltd (t/a British Van Heusen Co. Ltd) Keys Road, Alfreton DE55 7SQ Tel. *01773 727500* Fax. *01773 727501* Web. *www.m2c2.co.uk British Van Heusen – Peter England – Vyella Rocola*

Morris & Spottiswood Ltd 54 Helen Street, Glasgow G51 3HQ Tel. *0141 4251133* Fax. *0141 4251155* E-mail. *georgem@morrisandspottiswood.co.uk* Web. *www.morrisandspottiswood.co.uk Alrot – Assab – Morspot – Thomas Coulter Building Services – Trowel Trades – TTarr*

Vernon Morris Utility Solutions Ltd Chester Road Bretton, Chester CH4 0DH Tel. *01244 660794* Fax. *01244 661291* E-mail. *sales@vernonmorris.co.uk* Web. *www.vernonmorris.co.uk *Quickfit – V.M. – Vermor*

Morton Mixers & Blenders Ltd Unit 37 Grovewood Business Centre Wren Court, Strathclyde Business Park, Bellshill ML4 3NQ Tel. *08452 770939* Fax. *0845 2770949* E-mail. *info@morton-mixers.co.uk* Web. *www.morton-mixers.co.uk Air Pressure Whisk – Duplex-Z Blades – Gridlap – Morton Ploughshares – Ribbon Blenders – Vertical Mixers*

Morton Young & Borland Ltd Stoneygate Road, Newmilns KA16 9AL Tel. *01560 321210* Fax. *01560 323153* E-mail. *info@mybtextiles.com* Web. *www.mybtextiles.com Morton Youngs Borland Ltd*

Moseley Rubber Company Pty Ltd Europa House Barcroft Street, Bury BL9 5BT Tel. *0161 4478867* Fax. *0161 4478868* E-mail. *info@moseleysrubber.com* Web. *www.moseleyrubber.com G.R.P. – Porta Ramp – Rollcovering*

Mosses & Mitchell Ltd 18 The Street All Cannings, Devizes SN10 3PA Tel. *01380 722993* Fax. *01380 728422* E-mail. *sales@mosses-mitchel.com* Web. *www.mosses-mitchell.com Flexipatch – Mosses & Mitchell*

Moss Express Unit 2a Shepcote Way, Tinsley Industrial Estate, Sheffield S9 1TH Tel. *0114 2446614* Fax. *0114 2446615* E-mail. *sales@mossexpress.co.uk* Web. *www.mossexpress.co.uk Spiral Guard*

Motan Ltd 10 Blacklands Way, Abingdon OX14 1RD Tel. *01235 550011* Fax. *01235 550033* E-mail. *sales.ltd@motan.com* Web. *www.motan.co.uk Regloplas*

Mothercare plc Cherry Tree Road, Watford WD24 6SH Tel. *01923 241000* Fax. *01923 240944* Web. *www.mothercare.com Mothercare*

Motion Drives & Controls Ltd 1a Budbrooke Road Budbrooke Industrial Estate, Warwick CV34 5XH Tel. *01926 411544* Fax. *01926 411541* E-mail. *sales@motion.uk.com* Web. *www.motiondrivesandcontrols.co.uk Boston Gear – Boston Gear - Watt Drive - Magpowr - Nexen Horton - Horton - Sitema - Coil Technology. – Coil Technology – Horton – Magpowr – Nexen Horton – Sitema – Watt Drive*

Motion29 Ltd U29 Woodfieldside Business Park Penmaen Road Pontllanfraith, Blackwood NP12 2DG Tel. *01495 227603* Fax. *08450 942520* E-mail. *sales@motion29.co.uk* Web. *www.motion29.com Bircher Reglomat – Brad Harrison – Jay Electronque – mPm – Patlite*

Motivair Compressors Ltd Crompton Court Attwood Road, Waltham Cross EN8 7NU Tel. *01992 704300* Fax. *01992 704170* E-mail. *enquiries@leachlewis.co.uk* Web. *www.motivair.co.uk Airlink – Broomwade – Hydrovane*

Motivation Traffic Control Ltd Unit 5 Horton Court Hortonwood 50, Telford TF1 7XZ Tel. *01952 670390* Fax. *01952 670379* E-mail. *info@motivation-tc.co.uk* Web. *www.motivation-tc.co.uk Cheetah (United Kingdom) – Panther (United Kingdom) – Puma (United Kingdom) – Tiger (United Kingdom)*

Moto Hospitality Ltd PO Box 218, Dunstable LU5 6QG Tel. *01525 873933* Fax. *01525 878325* E-mail. *tim.moss@moto-way.co.uk* Web. *www.moto-way.com Burger King – Granada Forecourts – Granada Lodge – Granada Shopping – Little Chef*

Moto-Lita Ltd Thruxton, Andover SP11 8PW Tel. *01264 772811* Fax. *01264 773102* E-mail. *info@moto-lita.co.uk* Web. *www.moto-lita.co.uk Moto Lita*

Motoman Robotics UK Ltd Unit 2 Johnson Park Wildmere Road, Banbury OX16 3JU Tel. *01295 272755* Fax. *01295 267127* E-mail. *davewalsh@motoman.co.uk* Web. *www.motoman.co.uk *Motoman (AB) (Sweden)*

Motorola Ltd (Radio Network Solutions Group) Viables Industrial Estate Jays Close, Basingstoke RG22 4PD Tel. *01256 358211* Fax. *01256 469838* E-mail. *graeme.hobbs@mot.com* Web. *www.motorola.com Mobius – Radius*

MotorSport Vision Brands Hatch Circuits Ltd Brands Hatch Road, Fawkham, Longfield DA3 8NG Tel. *01474 872331* Fax. *01474 874766* E-mail. *marketing@motorsportvision.co.uk* Web. *www.motorsportvision.co.uk Earlydrive – Nigel Mansell*

Motor Technology Ltd Unit 1 Motec House Chadkirk Business Centre Vale Road, Romiley, Stockport SK6 3NE Tel. *0161 2177100* Fax. *0161 4271306* E-mail. *sales@motec.co.uk* Web. *www.controlinmotion.com Acroloop – ASB – Axor – CSM – Danaher Motion – Eisele – Euroservo – Eurotherm – Girard – Kollmorgen – Lenord + Bauer – Lenord + Bauer - Ormec - Eurotherm - Seidel - Kollmorgen - R + W - Eisele - Girard - Euroservo - Zebotronics - Papst - CSM - ASB - Acroloop - Axor - Danaher Motion – Ormec – Papst – R + W – Seidel – Zebotronics*

Motovario Ltd Rushock Trading Estate Rushock, Droitwich WR9 0NR Tel. *01299 250859* Fax. *01299 251493* E-mail. *sales@motovario.co.uk* Web. *www.motovario.co.uk *Lafert (Italy) – *Leeson (U.S.A.) – *Motovario (Italy) – *Unimec (Italy) – *Washguard (U.S.A.)*

Mouse Training 7th Floor Crystal Gate 28-30 Worship Street, London EC2A 2AH Tel. *020 79209500* Fax. *020 79209502* E-mail. *info@mousetraining.co.uk* Web. *www.mousetraining.co.uk Mouse Training*

Movevirgo Ltd New Portreath Road, Redruth TR16 4QL Tel. *01209 843484* Fax. *01209 843488* E-mail. *stephen@movevirgo.co.uk* Web. *www.movevirgo.co.uk Softfoam Surfboards – Softfoam Surfboards- Swell – Swell*

Moving Picture Co. Ltd 127 Wardour Street, London W1F 0NL Tel. *020 74343100* Fax. *020 74373951* E-mail. *mailbox@moving-picture.com* Web. *www.moving-picture.com Filmtel – Moving Picture Co.*

Moy Park Ltd Gonerby Hill Foot, Grantham NG31 8HZ Tel. *01476 571015* Fax. *01476 579713* E-mail. *adrian.downs@moypark.com* Web. *www.moypark.com *Chick n Ferno – Chick n Teddies*

M P E Ltd Hammond Road Knowsley Industrial Park, Liverpool L33 7UL Tel. *0151 6329100* Fax. *0151 6329112* E-mail. *sales@mpe.co.uk* Web. *www.mpe.co.uk Ashcroft – Custom Filters – Dubilier – EMP – High Performance Installation Filters – HPM – LEMP – NEMP*

M P N Upvc Windowsdoors & Conservatories 10A EWENNY ROAD, Bridgend CF31 3HL Tel. *01656 648464* Fax. *01639 851287* E-mail. *mpnwindows@aol.com* Web. *www.mpn.com NETWORK VEKA AND FENSA*

M P S I Systems Ltd 19B Osprey Court Hawkfield Business Park, Whitchurch, Bristol BS14 0BB Tel. *0117 9645132* Fax. *0117 9645163* E-mail. *info@mpsisys.co.uk* Web. *www.mpsisys.com M.P.S.I.*

MPW Group Manby Business Park, Louth LN11 8UT Tel. *01507 328031* Fax. *01507 328039* E-mail. *sales@manby.com* Web. *www.mpw-group.net Light-Store – Lumineux – M.P.W.*

Mr Fothergills Seeds Ltd Gazeley Road Kentford, Newmarket CB8 7QB Tel. *01638 751161* Fax. *01638 554083* E-mail. *katherine.watt@mr-fothergills.co.uk* Web. *www.mr-fothergills.co.uk Johnsons Seeds – Mr Fothergill's Seeds – Mr Fothergills*

M R P Trucks & Trolleys 40 Horringer Road, Bury St Edmunds IP33 2DR Tel. *01284 766300* Fax. *01284 766500* E-mail. *michael@mrptruckstrolleys.co.uk* Web. *www.mrptruckstrolleys.co.uk M.R.P. – MRP Trucks & Trolleys*

M S A Britain Ltd Lochard House, Linnet Way,, Strathclyde Business Park,, BELLSHILL ML4 3RA Tel. *01698 573357* Fax. *01698 740141* E-mail. *info@msabritain.co.uk* Web. *www.msabritain.co.uk Affinity – Cobra – Cresta – Explosimeter – Gasgard II – Lamb Air Mover – Linesman – Sound Control – Super-V-Gard – Turbo-Flo*

M S C Gleichmann UK Ltd Shaftesbury Court Ditchling Road, Brighton BN1 4ST Tel. *01273 622446* Fax. *01273 622533* E-mail. *brighton@msc-ge.com* Web. *www.msc-ge.com Alliance Semi – Ampire – APTA – Arm – ASI – Atmel – CAB – Cage – Clover – Diotec – Disglaign – Elec & Eltek – Enhanced Memory – ERG – Everlight – F&S Electronik – Fairchild Semi – Hirose – Hitachi – HMP – HRS – Hydis – Hynix – I-SFT – Intio – Ixys – Kontron – L&G – Lattice – Macronix – Micron – Microtouch – Mintech – MSC Vertriebs GmbH, Gleichmann Electronics – MXIC – NEC – NFREN – Omron – Paradigm – Ramtron – Renesas – Samsung – Sandisk – Sanyo – Scott – Shindengen – ST – Systems Inc – Tokin – Truly – Uniroyal – Weitronic*

M S D Animal Health Breakspear Road South Harefield, Uxbridge UB9 6LS Tel. *0370 0603380* Fax. *01895 672429* E-mail. *spahuk@spcorp.com* Web. *www.intervet.co.uk Afrazine Spray – Clariteyes – Clarityn Allergy – Clarityn Allergy Syrup – Cushion Grip – Lacto Calamine Lotion – Lacto-Calamine – Meggezones – Probase 3 Cream – Probase 3 Lotion – Puritabs – Puritabs Maxi – Rinstead Adult Gel – Rinstead Contact Pastilles – Rinstead Sugar Free Pastilles – Rinstead Teething Gel – Solarcaine – Solarcaine Spay – Teeda Hair Straightener – Tinaderm Cream – Tinaderm Plus Powder Aerosol – Tinderm Plus Powder*

M Squared Instrumentation Unit 36d New Forest Enterprise Centre Chapel Lane, Totton, Southampton SO40 9LA Tel. *023 80868393* Fax. *023 80667720* E-mail. *sales@msquaredinst.co.uk* Web. *www.msquaredinst.co.uk FGH – Raytek*

M S S Clean Technology Castle House 14 Dale Road, Sheriff Hutton, York YO60 6RZ Tel. *01347 878877* Fax. *01347 878878* E-mail. *postbox@mss-ct.co.uk* Web. *www.mss-ct.co.uk Chrysalid – Imago*

M S S Watch Company Labtec Street Pendlebury, Swinton, Manchester M27 8SE Tel. *0161 7947310* Fax. *0161 7947311* E-mail. *soamesclocks@tesco.net* Web. *www.msswatch.co.uk *Howard Miller*

M Suleman & Co. 32-36 Stromness Street, Glasgow G5 8HS Tel. *0141 4293017* Fax. *0141 4293473* E-mail. *margaret@msulemangroup.com* Web. *www.msulemangroup.com Kasco*

M-Tech Printers 7 Maidenhills, Middlewich CW10 9PJ Tel. *01606 837550* Fax. *08721 116386* E-mail. *sales@mtechprinters.co.uk* Web. *www.mtechprinters.co.uk AM Tech – Argox – Kyosha Industries – Mylox Technologies – Trentino Systems*

M T M Ltd Unit 1-9 Waterside Industrial Estate Doulton Road, Rowley Regis B65 8JG Tel. *01384 633321* Fax. *01384 565782* E-mail. *sales@mtm.ltd.uk* Web. *www.mtm.ltd.uk Mawson Triton Mouldings*

Muddy Boots Software Ltd Phocle Green, Ross On Wye HR9 7XU Tel. *01989 780540* Fax. *01989 780436* E-mail. *sales@muddyboots.com* Web. *www.muddyboots.com *CropWalker – *ProCheck*

Andrew Muirhead & Son Ltd Dalmarnock Leather Works 273-289 Dunn Street, Glasgow G40 3EA Tel. *0141 5543724* Fax. *01282 420209* E-mail. *sales@muirhead.co.uk* Web. *www.muirhead.co.uk Lustrana – Lustrol*

Muirhead Aerospace Oakfield Road, London SE20 8EW Tel. *020 86599090* Fax. *020 86599906* E-mail. *sales@muirheadaerospace.com* Web. *www.muirheadaerospace.com Linvar*

Mullett & Company UK Ltd Raven Hill Leys Lane, Frome BA11 2JT Tel. *01373 455665* Fax. *01373 455667* E-mail. *mulletts@mullettand.co.uk* Web. *www.mullettand.co.uk Mulcare – Mulcare & Multex*

Multicom Products Ltd 33 Victoria Street, Bristol BS1 6AS Tel. *0117 9081250* Fax. *0117 9081394* E-mail. *info@multicom.co.uk* Web. *www.multicom.co.uk Kaleidoscope – Multicom*

Multigerm Ltd Sandy Farm Sands Road, The Sands, Farnham GU10 1PX Tel. *01252 783374* Fax. *01252 782567* E-mail. *smith@mgerm.demon.co.uk* Web. *www.mgerm.demon.co.uk Lactosym – Multigerm*

Multi Installations 502 Honeypot Lane, Stanmore HA7 1JR Tel. *020 87311212* Fax. *020 82042888* E-mail. *info@multi1.co.uk* Web. *www.multi1.co.uk Multi Installations Ltd*

Multiload Technology 2 Rosemont Road, London NW3 6NE Tel. *020 77949152* Fax. *020 77949257* E-mail. *mail@multiload.co.uk* Web. *www.multiload.co.uk Lampconserver – Lampmaster – Multiload – Voltmaster*

Multi Marque Production Engineering Ltd Unit 33 Monckton Road Industrial Estate, Wakefield WF2 7AL Tel. *01924 290231* Fax. *01924 382241* E-mail. *enquiries@multi-marque.co.uk* Web. *www.multi-marque.co.uk Liner Major – Liner Mini Handler – Liner Rolpaint – Liner Rough Rider*

Multivac UK Ltd Multivac House Rivermead Drive, Swindon SN5 7UY Tel. *01793 425800* Fax. *01793 616219* E-mail. *sales@multivac.co.uk* Web. *www.multivac.co.uk *Gastrovac (Germany) – *Multivac (Germany)*

Munro & Miller Fittings Ltd 3 Westerton Road East Mains Industrial Estate, Broxburn EH52 5AU Tel. *01506 853531* Fax. *01506 856628* E-mail. *info@munro-miller.co.uk* Web. *www.munro-miller.co.uk Munro & Miller Fittings*

Munster Simms Engineering Ltd Old Belfast Road, Bangor BT19 1LT Tel. *028 91270531* Fax. *028 91466421* E-mail. *info@whalepumps.com* Web. *www.whalepumps.com Gusher – Tiptoe – Titan – Whale – Whale Flipper – Whale Henderson*

Munters Ltd Blackstone Road Stukeley Meadows Industrial Estate, Huntingdon PE29 6EE Tel. *01480 432243* Fax. *01480 458333* E-mail. *alistair.phillips@munters.co.uk* Web. *www.munters.co.uk Biodeck – Glasdek – Mould-Dry – Pool-Dry*

Murco Petroleum Ltd 4 Beaconsfield Road, St Albans AL1 3RH Tel. *01727 892400* Fax. *01727 892544* E-mail. *murco_uk@murphyoilcorp.com* Web. *www.murco.co.uk Murco – Murco Shopstop*

Murder One 71-73 Charing Cross Road, London WC2H 0ND Tel. *020 77343483* Fax. *020 77343429* E-mail. *murderone.mail@virgin.net* Web. *www.murderone.co.uk Murder One*

Murex Welding Products Ltd Hanover House Queensgate, Britania Road, Waltham Cross EN8 7TF Tel. *01992 710000* Fax. *01992 716486* E-mail. *info@murexwelding.co.uk* Web. *www.murexwelding.co.uk Bostrand – Corofil – Ferex – Mig Pak – Nicrex – Sabre Arc – Saffire – Tradesmig – Tradestig – Transarc – Transmig – Transtig – Vodex*

Murley Agricultural Supplies Ltd Nelson Lane, Warwick CV34 5JB Tel. *01926 494336* Fax. *01926 401510* E-mail. *sales@murley-agri.co.uk* Web. *www.murley.co.uk Bomford – *Manitou Telescopic Handlers – *New-Holland Tractors – *Reco Complete Range – *Vaderstad Drills*

Murodigital Oldmixon Crescent, Weston Super Mare BS24 9AY Tel. *01934 636393* Fax. *01934 641194* E-mail. *sales@muro.co.uk* Web. *www.muro.co.uk *Muro (France and The Far East)*

Murphy & Son Alpine Street, Nottingham NG6 0HQ Tel. *0115 9785494* Fax. *0115 9244654* E-mail. *sales@murphyandson.co.uk* Web. *www.murphyandson.co.uk Antiscale – Betazyme – Cellabrite – D.W.B. – Dionic – Esco – Esco – Finings Adjunct – Hypochloros – Isinglass Finings – Kilamic – Metabs – Murphy Yeast Aid – N.D.B.1. – N.D.B.3. – Salicon – Scotchbrite – Trizyme – Yeast Aid*

Paul Murray plc School Lane Chandler's Ford, Eastleigh SO53 4YN Tel. *023 80460600* Fax. *023 80460601* E-mail. *nhayton@paulmurrayplc.co.uk* Web. *www.murrayshealthandbeauty.com Cassandra – Clio – HandyGuard – Head Girl – Junior Macare – Meridiana – Murrays Manicure – Safe & Sound – Sunsetters – Westpoint*

S Murray & Co. Ltd Holborn House High Street, Old Woking, Woking GU22 9LB Tel. *01483 740099* Fax. *01483 755111* E-mail. *sales@smurray.co.uk* Web. *www.smurray.co.uk Samco*

Musks Ltd Goodwin House Goodwin Business Park Willie Snaith Road, Newmarket CB8 7SQ Tel. *01638 662626* Fax. *01638 662424* E-mail. *office@musks.com* Web. *www.musks.com Musks*

Musonic UK Ltd Unit 271b The Wenta Business Centre Colne Way, Watford WD24 7ND Tel. *020 89505151* Fax. *020 89505391* E-mail. *info@musonic.co.uk* Web. *www.musonic.co.uk Musonic*

Mustang Communications Ltd Dunslow Road Eastfield, Scarborough YO11 3UT Tel. *01723 582555* Fax. *01723 581673* E-mail. *info@mustang.com* Web. *www.mustang.co.uk Mustang Communications*

Mustang Tools Ltd 7 Cornish Way, North Walsham NR28 0AW Tel. *01692 404005* Fax. *01692 409943* E-mail. *sales@mustangtools.co.uk* Web. *www.mustangtools.co.uk Mustang Tools*

Musto Ltd Unit 4 Juniper West Fenton Way, Basildon SS15 6SJ Tel. *01268 491555* Fax. *01268 491440* E-mail. *customerservices@musto.co.uk* Web. *www.musto.co.uk Musto Yachting*

Mute A & R 1 Albion Place, London W6 0QT Tel. *020 89642001* Fax. *020 89684977* E-mail. *sales@mute.com* Web. *mutedotcom.wordpress.com Mute Records*

M V Sport & Leisure Ltd 35 Tameside Drive Castle Vale, Birmingham B35 7AG Tel. *0121 7488000* Fax. *0121 7488010* E-mail. *john.bellamy@mvsports.com* Web. *www.mvsports.com Admiral Skates & Accessories – Apolco Skates & Accessories – Mrs Ultra Skates – Seneca Skates & Accessories – Snakeboard*

M W A International Ltd Bridge Street, Wednesbury WS10 0AW Tel. *0121 5566366* Fax. *0121 5565566* E-mail. *sales@mwa-international.com* Web. *www.mwa-international.com Mac-Electrodes – Mac-Trode*

M W Equipment Unit 5 Maybrook Industrial Estate Maybrook Road, Walsall WS8 7DG Tel. *01543 378805* Fax. *0161 4290296 M.W.*

MWP Advanced Manufacturing Ascent B2B, Unit 2 Sugar Brook Court Aston Road, Bromsgrove B60 3EX Tel. *020 79704420* Fax. *020 79704494* E-mail. *mike.excell@centaur.co.uk* Web. *www.advancedmanufacturing.co.uk M W P – mwponline.com*

Myford Ltd Wilmot Lane Chilwell Road, Beeston, Nottingham NG9 1ER Tel. *0115 9254222* Fax. *0115 9431299* E-mail. *sales@myford.com* Web. *www.myford.com Myford*

Mykal Industries Ltd Farnsworth House Morris Close, Park Farm Industrial Estate, Wellingborough NN8 6XF Tel. *01933 402822* Fax. *01933 402488* E-mail. *enquiries@mykal.co.uk* Web. *www.mykal.co.uk Aquasolv – De.Solv.It – Mysolv – Special Blends*

N

N A G Ltd Wilkinson House Jordan Hill Banbury Road, Oxford OX2 8DR Tel. *01865 511245* Fax. *01865 310139* E-mail. *support@nag.co.uk* Web. *www.nag.co.uk N.A.G.*

Naim Audio Ltd Southampton Road, Salisbury SP1 2LN Tel. *01722 426600* Fax. *01722 412034* E-mail. *info@naimaudio.com* Web. *www.naimaudio.com Naim*

Nairda Ltd 1 St Johns Wood Rednal, Birmingham B45 8DL Tel. *0121 4579571* Fax. *0121 4579571* E-mail. *info@nairda.co.uk* Web. *www.nairda.co.uk Machsize – System E*

Naish Felts Ltd Crow Lane Wilton, Salisbury SP2 0HD Tel. *01722 743505* Fax. *01722 743910* E-mail. *sales@naishfelts.co.uk* Web. *www.naishfelts.co.uk Naish Felt – Naish Felts*

Nampak Carton Cockburn Fields Middleton Grove, Leeds LS11 5LX Tel. *0113 2760730* Fax. *0113 2760165* E-mail. *cartons@eu.nampak.com* Web. *www.mypackaging.com Bonnet – Certipak – Convocan – Horauf Pots – Kliklok – Neckline – Toppa – Ultrakan*

Napp Pharmaceutical Group Ltd Science Park Milton Road, Cambridge CB4 0GW Tel. *01223 424444* Fax. *01223 424441* E-mail. *vacancies@napp.co.uk* Web. *www.napp.co.uk Adizem XL – Depocyte – MST Continus – oncology – Oxycontin – Oxycontin - analgesic, Transtec - analgesic, Adizem XL - hypertension and angina, Zanidip - hypertension, MST Continus - analgesic, Depocyte - oncology – Transtec – Zanidip*

Narrow Aisle Ltd Great Western Way Great Bridge, Tipton DY4 7AU Tel. *0121 5576242* Fax. *0121 5208585* E-mail. *info@flexi.co.uk* Web. *www.flexi.co.uk Flexi G4, Flex, Euro – Hi-Racker – Rotareach, Flexi, Easipick, Hi-Racker, Dambach, lexi GAS, Flexi AC, Flexi G3*

National Auto Parts Willow Road, Nottingham NG7 2TA Tel. *0115 9738100* Fax. *0115 9738101* E-mail. *daveh@national-auto.co.uk* Web. *www.national-auto.co.uk National Autoparts*

National Care Association 45-49 Leather Lane, London EC1N 7TJ Tel. *020 78317090* Fax. *020 78317040* E-mail. *claire@nca.gb.com* Web. *www.nationalcareassociation.org.uk N.C.H.A.*

National Car Parks Ltd 21 Bryanston Street, London W1H 7AB Tel. *020 76296702* Fax. *020 74913577* E-mail. *info@ncp.co.uk* Web. *www.ncp.co.uk N.C.P.*

National Clamps PO Box 208, Preston PR1 2AE Tel. *01772 882992* Fax. *01772 882882* E-mail. *sales@national-clamps.com* Web. *www.national-clamps.com National Clamps*

National Counties Building Society 30 Church Street, Epsom KT17 4NL Tel. *01372 742211* Fax. *01372 745607* E-mail. *info@ncbs.co.uk* Web. *www.ncbs.co.uk National Counties*

National Door Co. Pyramid House 52 Guildford Road, Lightwater GU18 5SD Tel. *01276 451555* Fax. *01276 453666* E-mail. *info@nationaldomes.com* Web. *www.nationaldomelightcompany.co.uk Astrofade – Coxdomes – Crittall – Merchandome – Metro Rooflights – NaturaLight Systems – Ritchlight Hartington Conway – Skydome – Stardome – Ubbink – Ventura – Whitesales – Xtralite*

National Extension College The Michael Young Centre Purbeck Road, Cambridge CB2 8HN Tel. *01223 400200* Fax. *01223 400399* E-mail. *gavin.teasdale@nec.ac.uk* Web. *www.nec.ac.uk Conect – FlexiStudy*

National Instrument UK Corp Ltd Measurement House Newbury Business Park London Road, Newbury RG14 2PS Tel. *01635 34189* Fax. *01635 523154* E-mail. *info.uk@ni.com* Web. *www.ni.com LabVIEW – LabWindows/CVI – Lookout – Measurement Studio – TestStand – Virtual Bench*

National Magazine Company Ltd 72 Broadwick Street, London W1F 9EP Tel. *020 74395000* Fax. *020 74376886* Web. *www.natmags.co.uk Company – Cosmopolitan – Country Living – Esquire – Good Housekeeping – Harper's & Queen – House Beautiful – She – Zest*

National Newspaper Safe Home Ordering Protection Scheme 22-24 King Street, Maidenhead SL6 1EF Tel. *01628 641930* Fax. *01628 637112* E-mail. *satkins@shops-uk.org.uk* Web. *www.shops-uk.org.uk MOPS*

National Office Of Animal Health Ltd Crossfield Chambers Gladbeck Way, Enfield EN2 7HF Tel. *020 83673131* Fax. *020 83631155* E-mail. *p.sketchley@noah.co.uk* Web. *www.noah.co.uk COMISA – FEDESA – N.O.A.H.*

National Readership Surveys 40-42 Parker Street Covent Garden, London WC2B 5PQ Tel. *020 72428111* Fax. *020 76322916* E-mail. *info@nrs.co.uk* Web. *www.nrs.co.uk N.R.S.*

National Tyre Service Ltd Regent House Heaton Lane, Stockport SK4 1BS Tel. *0161 4291200* Fax. *0161 4753540* E-mail. *customerservices@national-tyres.co.uk* Web. *www.national.co.uk Continental – Pirelli – Sempra*

National Union Of Rail Maritime & Transport Worker 39 Chalton Street, London NW1 1JD Tel. *020 73874771* Fax. *020 73874123* E-mail. *info@rmt.org.uk* Web. *www.rmt.org.uk R.M.T.*

National Windscreens Ltd Bolehall House Amington Road, Tamworth B77 3PA Tel. *01827 304160* Fax. *01827 304161* E-mail. *info@nationalwindscreens.co.uk* Web. *www.nationalwindscreens.co.uk National Windscreens*

Nationwide Signs Ltd Derry Street, Wolverhampton WV2 1EY Tel. *01902 871116* Fax. *01902 351195* E-mail. *roadframes@aol.com Quick Fit*

Natural Environment Research Council Polaris House North Star Avenue, Swindon SN2 1EU Tel. *01793 411500* Fax. *01793 411501* E-mail. *requests@nerc.ac.uk* Web. *www.nerc.ac.uk N.E.R.C.*

Naturelli Stone The Ronson Building, Outer Ring Road Limewood Approach, Seacroft, Leeds LS14 1NG Tel. *0113 2188887* Fax. *0113 2188966* E-mail. *info@naturelli.com* Web. *www.naturelli.com Naturelli*

Natures Own Ltd Hanley Workshops Hanley Swan, Worcester WR8 0DX Tel. *01684 310022* Fax. *01684 312022* E-mail. *jim@natures-own.co.uk* Web. *www.natures-own.co.uk Cytoplan – Nature's Own – Nature's Own*

Nauticalia Ltd Ferry Lane, Shepperton TW17 9LQ Tel. *01932 244396* Fax. *01753 850721* E-mail. *sales@nauticalia.com* Web. *www.nauticalia.com Nauticalia – Sea Searcher & Retreaver*

Navico UK (Marine Division UK) Navico Premier Way, Romsey SO51 9DH Tel. *01794 510010* Fax. *01794 510006* E-mail. *paul.griffiths@navico.com* Web. *www.navico.com Navico – Robertson – Shipmate – Simrad*

Navimo UK Ltd Hamilton Business Park Botley Road, Hedge End, Southampton SO30 2HE Tel. *01489 778850* Fax. *0870 7511950* E-mail. *stephen.pusey@navimo.co.uk* Web. *www.plastimo.com Canpa – Minnkota Electric Outboards – Old Town Canoe*

Nayler Group Ltd Aero Mill Kershaw Street, Church, Accrington BB5 4JS Tel. *01254 234247* Fax. *01254 383996* E-mail. *alastair.nayler@marineworldmagazine.com* Web. *www.printerslancashire.com Nayprint*

Chris Naylor Research Ltd 14 Castle Gardens, Scarborough YO11 1QU Tel. *01723 354590* E-mail. *chrisnaylor@chrisnaylor.co.uk* Web. *www.chrisnaylor.co.uk Tubes – Xmaster*

Naylor Drainage Ltd Clough Green Cawthorne, Barnsley S75 4AD Tel. *01226 790591* Fax. *01226 790531* E-mail. *sales@naylor.co.uk* Web. *www.naylor.co.uk Band-Seal – Denduct – Denline – Denlok – Denrod – Denseal – Densleeve – L-Strip – Unidrain – Zedstrip*

Naylors Abrasives Unit G7 Newton Business Park Talbot Road, Hyde SK14 4UQ Tel. *0161 3671000* Fax. *0161 3671012* E-mail. *info@naylors-abrasives.co.uk* Web. *www.naylors-abrasives.co.uk *Awuko (Germany) – Jaylon – Magnet – Naylobon – Nayloflex – Naylon – Naylors – Naylorsafe*

Naylor Specialists Plastics Unit 47 Coneygree Industrial Estate, Tipton DY4 8XP Tel. *0121 5220290* Fax. *0121 5220299* E-mail. *specialistplastics@naylor.co.uk* Web. *www.naylor.co.uk ABS – EVA – FLEX-PVC – HDPE – HIPS – LDPE – MDPE – Polypropylene*

Nazeing Glassworks Ltd Nazeing New Road, Broxbourne EN10 6SU Tel. *01992 464485* Fax. *01992 450966* E-mail. *sales@nazeing-glass.com* Web. *www.nazeing-glass.com Craftsman – Wild Rose*

N C C Group Manchester Technology Centre Oxford Road, Manchester M1 7EF Tel. *0161 2095200* Fax. *0161 2095400* E-mail. *info@nccglobal.com* Web. *www.nccgroup.com Centrelink – Filetab – Filetab – Intergrator – N.C.C. – NCC Escrow International – NMAE – NMCE – Observer – Stormer – Vistrain*

N C T Leather Ltd Locher Works Kilbarchan Road, Bridge of Weir PA11 3RL Tel. *01505 612182* Fax. *01505 612123* E-mail. *sales@nctleather.co.uk* Web. *www.nctleather.co.uk N.C.T. Leather*

N D C Infra-Red Engineering Ltd Quayside Industrial Estate, Maldon CM9 5FA Tel. *01621 852244* Fax. *01621 856180* E-mail. *sales@ndcinfrared.co.uk* Web. *www.ndc.com BG710 – CM710 – Gaugetools – Infralab – MM710 – Moistrex MX8000 – PowderVision – PowderVision - for the measurement of materials in enclosed ductingInfralab - for the non contact multicomponent measurement of moisture, nicotine, sugars and temp in tobacco and moisture, and fat protein, oil in foods and bulk powders either in the lab or at lineTM710 - for the non contact on line measurement if nicotine, sugars, temperature and moisture in tobaccoMM710 - for the non contact on line measurement of moisture, fat, oil and protein in foods and bulk materials Gaugetools - statistical analysis package for data gathered by on line or at line gaugesMoistrex MX8000 - for the easy and rapid moisture analysis of paper and board samples either at line or in the lab. – TM710*

N D S L Ltd Unit 2 Oakfield Industrial Estate Eynsham, Witney OX29 4TS Tel. *01865 884288* Fax. *01865 884289* E-mail. *sales@ndsl.co.uk* Web. *www.ndsl.co.uk CELLWATCH*

Neale Dataday Ltd 3 Neale Courtyard Shannon Way, Canvey Island SS8 0PD Tel. *01268 510123* Fax. *01268 510125* E-mail. *stephen.treacy@ndpublishing.co.uk* Web. *www.netcomuk.co.uk Dataday – Leathersmith*

Neal Pestforce Ltd Unit 1 North End Business Park Station Road, Swineshead, Boston PE20 3PW Tel. *01205 822970* Fax. *01205 460886* E-mail. *anninkirton@aol.com Neal Pestforce*

Neat Concepts Ltd F25 Hastingwood Trading Estate 35 Harbet Road, London N18 3HU Tel. *020 88075805* Fax. *020 88844963* E-mail. *info@neatconcepts.com* Web. *www.neatconcepts.com *Neatform (United Kingdom) – Neatmatch – *Neatmould (United Kingdom) – Neatrout – *Neatrust (United Kingdom) – Neatslot*

Nec Europe Ltd N E C House 1 Victoria Road, London W3 6BL Tel. *020 89938111* Fax. *020 89927161* E-mail. *sales@neceurope.com* Web. *www.nec.com MultiSync – N.E.C. – N.E.C. phones – Nefax – Superscript*

Nec Group National Exhibition Centre, Birmingham B40 1NT Tel. *0121 7804141* Fax. *0121 7673815* E-mail. *feedback@necgroup.co.uk* Web. *www.necgroup.co.uk ICC – NEC Arena – NEC Ltd – NIA – Symphony Hall*

Nectar Group Ltd 1 Ashton Gate Ashton Road, Romford RM3 8UF Tel. *01708 386555* Fax. *01708 386665* E-mail. *guy@nectar.co.uk* Web. *www.nectargroup.net *Nectar (Netherlands)*

Nederman Ltd 91 Seedlee Road Walton Summit Centre, Bamber Bridge, Preston PR5 8AE Tel. 08452 743434 Fax. 01772 315273 E-mail. info@nederman.co.uk Web. www.nederman.com Ad-Hyde – Guardian

Roger Needham & Sons Ltd Unit 2a-2b Waymills Industrial Estate Waymills, Whitchurch SY13 1TT Tel. 01948 662629 Fax. 01948 665045 E-mail. sales@needham-group.com Web. www.needham-group.com Britink – Emphasis – R.N. Metal Marker

neighbo 140 Brompton Road, London SW3 1HY Tel. 020 81449196 E-mail. hello@neighbo.com Web. neighbo.com link2home

Nemco Metals International Ltd 5 Pennard Close Brackmills Industrial Estate, Northampton NN4 7BE Tel. 01604 766181 Fax. 01276 61704 E-mail. fred.weyler@nemcometals.co.uk Web. www.nemcometals.com Carl Schlenk – Wieland Werke

Nendle Acoustics Ltd 153 High Street, Aldershot GU11 1TT Tel. 01252 344222 Fax. 01252 333782 E-mail. enquiries@nendle.co.uk Web. www.nendle.co.uk Nendle

Neogene LLP 14 Caxton Way, Watford WD18 8UJ Tel. 01923 213737 Fax. 01923 213617 E-mail. mail@neogenepaints.co.uk Web. www.neogenepaints.co.uk Neogene

The Neoknitting & Trim Ltd Peter Pal House Albion Street, Oadby, Leicester LE2 5DE Tel. 0116 2714923 Fax. 0116 2714422 E-mail. paresh@neotrims.com Web. www.neotrims.com NEO Trims

Neomet Ltd 92 Cross Lane Marple, Stockport SK6 7PZ Tel. 0161 4277741 Fax. 0161 4490080 E-mail. richard.hammersley@sulzer.com Web. www.sulzermetco.com Brazcor – *Metglas (U.S.A.) – Westaim

Neophix Engineering Co. Ltd Devonshire House West Lane, Keighley BD21 2LP Tel. 01535 667382 Fax. 01535 680825 E-mail. info@neophix.co.uk Web. www.neophix.co.uk Neoflex

Nessco Group Ltd Discovery Drive Arnhall Business Park, Westhill AB32 6FG Tel. 01224 428400 Fax. 01224 722707 E-mail. enquiries@nesscogroup.com Web. www.nesscogroup.com Nessco

Ness Furniture Ltd Croxdale, Durham DH6 5HT Tel. 01388 816109 Fax. 01388 812416 E-mail. johnwilliams@nessfurniture.co.uk Web. www.nessfurniture.co.uk Ness Furniture

Nestledown Beds Knight Road, Rochester ME2 2BP Tel. 01634 723557 Fax. 01634 290257 E-mail. k.foulstone@simmonsbeds.co.uk Web. www.nestledown.co.uk Nestledown

Netcargo International UK Ltd 1 Nestles Avenue, Hayes UB3 4UZ Tel. 020 86063602 Fax. 08452 308083 E-mail. sales@netcargouk.com Web. www.netcargo-intl.co.uk Netcargo International

Netvue Kingsdowne Court 10 The Common, London W5 3TT Tel. 020 85672201 E-mail. info@netvue.co.uk Web. www.netvue.co.uk Netvue

Netzsch-Instruments Hayward Industrial Park Vigo Place, Walsall WS9 8UG Tel. 01922 459006 Fax. 01922 453320 E-mail. sales@netzsch-therma1.co.uk Web. www.netzsch-thermal.co.uk DIL 402 C – DSC 204 F1 Phoenix – LFA 427 – STA 449 C Jupiter – TG 209 F1 Iris

Netzsch Mastermix Ltd 23 Lombard Street, Lichfield WS13 6DP Tel. 01543 418938 Fax. 01543 418926 E-mail. nmx@netzsch-mastermix.co.uk Web. www.netzsch-grinding.com De-aerators – Netzsch Mastermix (United Kingdom)

Neuson Ltd Crown Business Park Dukestown, Tredegar NP22 4EF Tel. 01495 723083 Fax. 01495 713941 E-mail. ukoffice@neuson.com Web. www.neusonkramer.com 5 Star – Gopher – Micron – Shifter

Nevica Ltd 8 Scrubs Lane, London NW10 6RB Tel. 020 89682300 Fax. 020 89682330 E-mail. sales@nevicakilly.com Web. www.nevica.com *Killy Sport – *Killy Technical Equipment (Far East) – *Nevica (Far East)

Neville UK plc Viking Way, Erith DA8 1EW Tel. 01322 443143 Fax. 01322 443153 E-mail. sales@nevilleuk.com Web. www.nevilleuk.com *Diablo Chafing Fuel – Genware – *Kahla – *Pardini – *Royal Genware

Newall Measurement Systems Ltd Technology Gateway Cornwall Road, Wigston LE18 4XH Tel. 0116 2642730 Fax. 0116 2642731 E-mail. sales@newall.co.uk Web. www.newall.co.uk A50 – B60 – C Series – E Series – Magnasyn Tape – MHG – MICROSYN – SA100 Linear & Rotary – SHG – SPHEROSYN

Newall UK Ltd 354 Padholme Road East, Peterborough PE1 5XL Tel. 01733 265566 Fax. 01733 843819 E-mail. sales@newall.com Web. www.newall-uk.com Danobat – Estarta – Lealde – Newall – Overbeck

Neway Doors Ltd Lionel Works 8991 Rolfe Street, Smethwick B66 2AY Tel. 0121 5586406 Fax. 0121 5557140 E-mail. sales@priory-group.co.uk Web. www.priory-group.co.uk Autoflex – Interflex – Multiflex – Neway – Powerflex – Stripflex – Superflex

New Brunswick Scientific UK Ltd 17 Alban Park Hatfield Road, St Albans AL4 0JJ Tel. 01727 853855 Fax. 01727 835666 E-mail. sales@nbsuk.co.uk Web. www.nbsuk.co.uk *BioFlo (U.S.A.) – C/Line – *Innova (U.S.A.)

Newburgh Engineering Co. Ltd Newburgh Works Bradwell, Hope Valley S33 9NT Tel. 01709 724260 Fax. 01433 620771 E-mail. sales@newburgh.co.uk Web. www.newburgh.co.uk Newburgh

Newburgh Engineering Co. Ltd (T/A Newgurgh Pelleting Solutions) Centurion Business Park Bessemer Way, Rotherham S60 1FB Tel. 01709 724260 Fax. 01709 839312 E-mail. vincent.middleton@newburgh.co.uk Web. www.newburgh.co.uk British Springs – CQR Security – Hydrar – OSL Seals and Numatics – OSL Stock Holders – Rota Broach – Scandura Seals – Stuma Plastics – Turner chilled Rose

The Newcomen Society Exhibition Road, London SW7 2DD Tel. 020 73714445 Fax. 020 73714445 E-mail. office@newcomen.com Web. www.newcomen.com Newcomen Society, The

Newey & Eyre Yardley Court 11-13 Frederick Rd, Edgbaston, Birmingham B15 1JD Tel. 0800 7836909 Fax. 0121 4551413 E-mail. customer.info@hagemeyer.co.uk Web. www.neweysonline.co.uk Data Networking Division – Newlec – Specialist Cables Division – Specialist Lamps & Lighting Division

New Haden Pumps Ltd New Haden Works Draycott Cross Road, Cheadle, Stoke On Trent ST10 2NW Tel. 01538 757900 Fax. 01538 757999 E-mail. carole.edwards@nhpumps.com Web. www.nhpumps.com New Haden Pumps – Ritz – Ritz Atro

Newhall Publications Ltd Newhall Lane, Wirral CH47 4BQ Tel. 08445 458102 Fax. 08707 453003 E-mail. chris@candis.co.uk Web. www.candis.co.uk Cadis

New Horizon Systems Ltd Unit 8 Thames Road Crayford, Dartford DA1 4QX Tel. 08456 250055 E-mail. info@newhorizon-systems.co.uk Web. www.newhorizon-systems.co.uk Geller Cash Registers – Geller CX-200 – Geller ET-6800 – Geller EX-300 – Geller ML-780 – Geller SX-580 – Geller SX-680 – Geller TS-600 – Geller Vectron Pos Colour Touch – Geller Vectron Pos Mini Colour – Geller Vectron Pos Mobile – Geller Vectron Pos Vario – Till Rolls

New Information Paradigms Ltd Manhattan House 140 High Street, Crowthorne RG45 7AY Tel. 01344 753700 Fax. 01344 772510 E-mail. sales@nipltd.com Web. www.nipltd.com Blockware – Med Info Sys

Newland Engineering Co. Ltd Captain Clarke Road, Hyde SK14 4RF Tel. 0161 3680326 Fax. 0161 3678004 E-mail. info@newland-conveyors.com Web. www.newland-conveyors.com Autoloader – Bulkloader – Carpet Loader – Deescan – Glassveyor – Loadmaster – MTC – Newland – Railcar Loader – Vanloader

New & Lingwood Ltd 118 High Street Eton, Windsor SL4 6AN Tel. 01753 866286 Fax. 01753 861892 E-mail. info@newandlingwood.com Web. www.newandlingwood.com N.L.

Newman Labelling Systems Ltd Newman House Queens Road, Barnet EN5 4DL Tel. 020 84400044 Fax. 020 84492890 E-mail. sales@newman.co.uk Web. www.newman.co.uk Newman

Newmans Footwear Ltd Garden Street, Blackburn BB2 1TZ Tel. 01254 296540 Fax. 01254 296541 E-mail. info@nfw.co.uk Web. www.nfw.co.uk Drive-Ins – Newman's – Newman's Bambinos – Newman's Corkers – Newman's Mama Mia – Royald Herald & Shield Device

Newpark Security Ltd Unit A15 Kilcronagh Business Park, Cookstown BT80 9HJ Tel. 08448 793319 Fax. 028 86769338 E-mail. info@newparksecurity.com Web. www.newparksecurity.com Newpark – NP2000 – NP3000 – NP3000

New Pro Foundries Ltd Unit C Horton Close, West Drayton UB7 8EB Tel. 01895 443194 Fax. 01895 442968 E-mail. info@newpro.co.uk Web. www.newpro.co.uk New Pro Foundries

Newross Impex Ltd (t/a Skopes) New Skopes House 2 Cross Green Garth, Cross Green Industrial Estate, Leeds LS9 0SF Tel. 0113 2402211 Fax. 0113 2489544 E-mail. info@skopes.com Web. www.skopes.com *Deacondale (Worldwide) – *Skopes (Worldwide)

Newsmith Stainless Ltd Fountain Works Child Lane, Liversedge WF15 7PH Tel. 01924 405988 Fax. 01924 403304 E-mail. john.chappell@newsmith.co.uk Web. www.newsmith.co.uk Newsmith

Newson Gale Ltd Omega House Private Road 8, Colwick Industrial Estate, Nottingham NG4 2JX Tel. 0115 9407500 Fax. 0115 9407501 E-mail. groundit@newson-gale.co.uk Web. newson-gale.co.uk Plant & Process Safety

Newsquest Essex Ltd (Newsquest (Essex) Ltd) Newspaper House Chester Hall Lane, Basildon SS14 3BL Tel. 01268 522792 Fax. 01268 532060 E-mail. michael.harper@nqe.com Web. www.echo-news.co.uk Basildon Recorder – Billericay Recorder – Evening Echo – Southend Standard – Thurrock Gazette – Wickford Recorder

Newsquest Group 200 Renfield Street, Glasgow G2 3QB Tel. 0141 3027000 Fax. 0141 3027799 E-mail. tim.blott@glasgow.newsquest.co.uk Web. www.glasgow.newsquest.co.uk Boxing News – Components in Electronics – Great Outdoors, The – Home Show – Independent Community Pharmacist – Independent Electrical Retailer – Scottish Farmer, The

Newton Derby Ltd Grangefield House Richardshaw Road, Pudsey LS28 6QS Tel. 0113 2180717 Fax. 0113 2572206 E-mail. sales@newtonderby.co.uk Web. www.newtonderby.co.uk Newton Derby

Nexor Ltd Bell House Nottingham Science & Technology Park, Nottingham NG7 2RL Tel. 0115 9520500 Fax. 0115 9520519 E-mail. info@nexor.com Web. www.nexor.com Messageware - X400 – NEXOR

Next plc Desford Road Enderby, Leicester LE19 4AT Tel. 08448 448888 Fax. 0116 2848998 Web. www.next.co.uk Next – Next Directory – Next Retail

Nextwave It Ltd Flat 2/2 268 Berryknowes Road, Glasgow G52 2DA Tel. 07806 197987 E-mail. enquiry@nextwaveit.biz Web. www.nextwaveit.biz Nextwaveit

Nexus Nexus House St James Boulevard, Newcastle Upon Tyne NE1 4AX Tel. 0191 2033333 Fax. 0191 2033304 E-mail. customerservices@nexus.org.uk Web. www.nexus.org Metro

N Froy & Son Focal Point Fleming Way, Crawley RH10 9DF Tel. 01293 521764 Fax. 01306 712749 E-mail. sales@froy.co.uk Web. www.explorebathrooms.com Froy

N G K Berylco UK Ltd Houston Park, Salford M50 2RP Tel. 0161 7457162 Fax. 0161 7457520 E-mail. enquiries@ngkberylco.co.uk Web. www.ngkberylco.co.uk Bealon – BERYLCO – BERYLCO 10 – BERYLCO 14 – BERYLCO 165 – BERYLCO 25

N G K Spark Plugs UK Ltd Maylands Avenue Hemel Hempstead Industrial Estate, Hemel Hempstead HP2 4SD Tel. 01442 281000 Fax. 01442 281001 E-mail. enquiries@ngk.co.uk Web. www.ngkntk.co.uk N.G.K. – N.T.K. – NGK – NTK

Niagri Engineering Ltd 1 Station Road Lakenheath, Brandon IP27 9AA Tel. 01842 862500 Fax. 01842 862501 E-mail. info@niagri.co.uk Web. www.niagri.co.uk Dewulf

Nichols plc Laurel House 3 Woodlands Park Ashton Road, Newton Le Willows WA12 0HH Tel. 01925 222222 Fax. 01925 222233 E-mail. reception@nicholsplc.co.uk Web. www.nicholsplc.co.uk Cabana – Freshers – Pin-Hi – Vimto

Nicholson Plastics Ltd Riverside Road Kirkfieldbank, Lanark ML11 9JS Tel. 01555 664316 Fax. 01555 663056 E-mail. info@nicholsonplastics.co.uk Web. www.nicholsonplastics.co.uk Long Life

Nickel Electro Ltd Oldmixon Cresent, Weston Super Mare BS24 9BL Tel. 01934 626691 Fax. 01934 630300 E-mail. adrian@nickel-electro.co.uk Web. www.nickel-electro.co.uk Clifton (United Kingdom)

Nickerson Bros Ltd Binbrook Hill Binbrook, Market Rasen LN8 6BL Tel. 01472 398498 Fax. 01472 398111 E-mail. nickersonbrothersltd@hotmail.co.uk *Almaco (U.S.A.) – Ruberg (Germany) – *Seedburo (U.S.A.)

Nico Manufacturing Co. Ltd 109 Oxford Road, Clacton On Sea CO15 3TJ Tel. 01255 422333 Fax. 01255 432909 E-mail. sales@nico.co.uk Web. www.nico.co.uk Nico

Nicotra-Gebhardt Ltd Unit D Parkgate Business Park Rail Mill Way, Parkgate, Rotherham S62 6JQ Tel. 01709 780760 Fax. 01732 866370 E-mail. info@kiloheat.co.uk Web. www.nicotra-gebhardt.com Kiloheat – Rotaflow – Volumeter

Nidd Valley Medical Ltd Nidd Valley House Unit 22 Claro Court Business Centre Claro Road, Harrogate HG1 4BA Tel. 01423 817920 Fax. 01423 817933 E-mail. sales@niddvalley.co.uk Web. www.niddvalley.co.uk Acupad

David Nieper Nottingham Road, Alfreton DE55 7LE Tel. 01773 833335 Fax. 01773 520246 E-mail. angela.durose@davidnieper.co.uk Web. www.davidnieper.co.uk David Nieper

Nifco UK Ltd Yarm Road, Stockton On Tees TS18 3RX Tel. 01642 672299 Fax. 01642 611004 E-mail. matthewsm@nifcoeu.com Web. www.nifcoeu.com Nifco

Niftylift Ltd Unit 1 Fingle Drive, Stonebridge, Milton Keynes MK13 0ER Tel. 01908 223456 Fax. 01908 312733 E-mail. info@niftylift.com Web. www.niftylift.com Niftylift

Nimlok Ltd Nimlok House 45 Booth Drive, Park Farm Industrial Estate, Wellingborough NN8 6NL Tel. 01933 409409 Fax. 01933 409451 E-mail. info@nimlock.co.uk Web. www.nimlock.co.uk Nimlok

Nine Shipton 1 Frogmore Road Industrial Estate Frogmore Road, Hemel Hempstead HP3 9TG Tel. 01442 345600 Fax. 01442 345612 Web. www.shipton.co.uk DeTeWe Shipton – I.S. 128/400 – I.V.M. 1000 – S.D.X. Index – Toshiba Strata DK Range

Ninja Corporation Ltd Topaz House St Michaels Industrial Estate, Widnes WA8 8TL Tel. 0151 4951677 Fax. 0151 4951675 E-mail. admin@thepopupco.com Web. www.theninjacorporation.co.uk Real Pop Up Company

Nippon Distribution 8c Reddicap Trading Estate, Sutton Coldfield B75 7BU Tel. 0121 3110313 Fax. 0121 3110338 E-mail. nippondis@hotmail.com Web. www.nippon-dis.co.uk Nippon

Nisa Waldo Way, Scunthorpe DN15 9GE Tel. *01724 282028* Fax. *01724 278727* E-mail. *info@nisaretail.com* Web. *www.nisaretail.com Nisa*

Nisbets plc Fourth Way, Bristol BS11 8DW Tel. *08451 405555* Fax. *08451 435555* E-mail. *sales@nisbets.co.uk* Web. *www.nisbets.co.uk Berto's – *Comersa – Dexion – *Fed Pizza Ovens – Haka-woks*

Nissan Technical Centre Europe Ltd Cranfield Technology Park Moulsoe Road, Cranfield, Bedford MK43 0DB Tel. *01234 755555* Fax. *01234 755799* E-mail. *kunio.nakaguro@ntc-europe.co.uk* Web. *www.nissan-europe.com N.E.T.C.*

Nitech Ltd Unit 4-6 Highfield Business Park Sidney Little Road, St Leonards On Sea TN38 9UB Tel. *01424 852788* Fax. *01424 851008* E-mail. *sales@nitech.co.uk* Web. *www.nitech.co.uk X-CELL (United Kingdom)*

Nitto Kohki Europe Co. Ltd Unit 21 Empire Centre Imperial Way, Watford WD24 4TS Tel. *01923 239351* Fax. *01923 248815* E-mail. *info@nitto-europe.com* Web. *www.nitto-europe.com MEDO – Nitto Kohki Europe*

Nixon Flowmeters Ltd Unit 1-3 Badminton Close Leckhampton, Cheltenham GL53 7BX Tel. *01242 243006* Fax. *01242 222487* E-mail. *mail@nixonflowmeters.co.uk* Web. *www.nixonflowmeters.co.uk Streamflo*

N J Bradford Ltd Ashes Road, Oldbury B69 4RA Tel. *0121 5595555* Fax. *0121 5593826* E-mail. *ian.bradford@nj-bradford.co.uk* Web. *www.nj-bradford.co.uk Fortrex*

Nmb-Minebea UK Ltd 2 Sadler Road, Lincoln LN6 3RA Tel. *01522 500933* Fax. *01522 500975* E-mail. *mark.stansfield@nmb-minebea.com* Web. *www.minebea.co.uk Rose – Rosejoint – Unimesh*

Nobel Electronics Ltd Tudor Cottages Footscray High Street, Sidcup DA14 5HN Tel. *020 83090500* Fax. *020 83027901* E-mail. *sales@nobelelectronics.co.uk* Web. *www.nobelelectronics.co.uk Vishay Spectrol – Vishay Sfernice – GE Thermometrics*

Robert Noble March Street, Peebles EH45 8ER Tel. *01721 720146* Fax. *01721 721893* E-mail. *enquiries@robert-noble.co.uk* Web. *www.robert-noble.co.uk Robert Noble – William Brown*

No Climb Products Ltd Eddison House 163 Dixons Hill Road, North Mymms, Hatfield AL9 7JE Tel. *01707 282760* Fax. *01707 282777* E-mail. *m.rossiter@noclimb.com* Web. *www.detectortesters.com No-climb – Solo – Suretest – Trutest*

Nodor International Ltd Nodor House South Road, Bridgend Industrial Estate, Bridgend CF31 3PT Tel. *01656 653553* Fax. *01656 650468* E-mail. *info@nodor-darts.co.uk* Web. *www.reddragon.com Brackla Engineering – Nodor*

Noel Village Steel Founder Ltd Balby Carr Bank, Doncaster DN4 8DE Tel. *01302 768000* Fax. *01302 360665* E-mail. *anv@noelvillage.com* Web. *www.noelvillage.com Vistar – Wheelsets UK – Wheelsets UK - Vistar*

Noirit Ltd Newman & Field Ltd 21 Portland Street, Walsall WS2 8AB Tel. *01922 625471* Fax. *01922 722339* E-mail. *sales@noirit.com* Web. *www.noirit.com Century – Newman & Field – Noirit – Tirion*

Noma Lites Southey House 43 Avro Way Brooklands Business Park, Weybridge KT13 0XQ Tel. *01932 411330* Fax. *01932 411321* E-mail. *sales@noma.co.uk* Web. *www.noma.co.uk *Noma (China) – *Noma Moonrays (Canada)*

Non Standard Socket Screws Ltd 358-364 Farm Street, Birmingham B19 2TZ Tel. *0121 5150100* Fax. *0121 5234440* E-mail. *sales@nssocketscrews.com* Web. *www.nssocketscrews.com NSS*

N O P Research Group Ltd Ludgate House 245 Blackfriars Road, London SE1 9UL Tel. *020 78909000* Fax. *020 78909001* E-mail. *ukinfo@gfk.com* Web. *www.gfknop.com NOP Research Group*

Norbar Torque Tools Ltd Beaumont Road, Banbury OX16 1XJ Tel. *01295 270333* Fax. *01295 753643* E-mail. *enquiry@norbar.com* Web. *www.norbar.com Electrotorque – Norbar – Pneutorque*

Norbord Station Road Cowie, Stirling FK7 7BQ Tel. *01786 812921* Fax. *01786 815622* E-mail. *info@norbord.com* Web. *www.norbord.com Caberboard – Caberfloor – Caberwood – Conti Board – Sterling Board*

Norbord Europe Ltd Hill Village Nadder Lane, South Molton EX36 4HP Tel. *01769 572991* Fax. *01769 574848* E-mail. *sales@norbord.com* Web. *www.norbord.com Caber Decor – Conti*

Norbrook Research Camlough Road, Newry BT35 6JP Tel. *028 30264435* Fax. *028 30251141* E-mail. *enquiries@norbrook.co.uk* Web. *www.norbrook.co.uk Calciject – Intravit 12 – Ketosaid – Levacide – Levafas – Life-Aid – Multivitamin Injection*

Nordair Niche (Northern Office) 6-14 Bean Leach Road Hazel Grove, Stockport SK7 4LD Tel. *0161 4827900* Fax. *0161 4827901* E-mail. *sales@nordair.co.uk* Web. *www.nordairniche.co.uk AHBB – CHV – DF/IDF – DV/DH – LSD – MUA – TTW*

Nordair Niche (Southern Office) Unit 4 Chilford Court Rayne Road, Braintree CM7 2QS Tel. *01376 332200* Fax. *01376 332201* E-mail. *mail@nordairniche.co.uk* Web. *www.nordairniche.co.uk AHBB – CHV – DF/IDF – DV/DH – LSD – MUA – TTW*

Nordic Style Ltd 109 Lots Road, London SW10 0RN Tel. *020 73511755* Fax. *020 73514966* E-mail. *sales@nordicstyle.com* Web. *www.nordicstyle.com Nordic Style*

Nordson UK Ltd Wenman Road, Thame OX9 3SW Tel. *01844 264500* Fax. *01844 215358* E-mail. *salesoxf@uk.nordson.com* Web. *www.nordson.com *FoamMelt (Reg) (U.S.A.) – Nordson – *Nordson (Reg) (U.S.A.)*

Norfine Nets The Broadway Fen Road, Scarning, Dereham NR19 2LH Tel. *01362 690900* Fax. *01362 695912* E-mail. *info@norfinenets.co.uk* Web. *www.norfinenets.co.uk Norfine*

Norfloat International Ltd Unit 3a Woodlands Business Park Burlescombe, Tiverton EX16 7LL Tel. *01823 672772* Fax. *01823 672773* E-mail. *info@norfloat.com* Web. *www.norfloat.com Norfloat*

Norfolk Greenhouses Ltd Chiswick Avenue Mildenhall, Bury St Edmunds IP28 7AZ Tel. *01638 713418* Fax. *01638 714715* E-mail. *info@norfolk-greenhouses.co.uk* Web. *www.norfolk-greenhouses.co.uk Norfolk Greenhouses*

Norfolk Lavender Trading Ltd Caley Mill Lynn Road, Heacham, Kings Lynn PE31 7JE Tel. *01485 570384* Fax. *01485 571176* E-mail. *info@norfolk-lavender.co.uk* Web. *www.norfolk-lavender.co.uk English Lavender, The – Lily of the Valley – Men of England – Night Scented Jasmine – NL Special Treatments – Norfolk Lavender – Rose with English Lavender – The Fragrent Gardener*

Norfran Ltd West Morland Road West Chirton Estate, North Shields NE29 8RF Tel. *0191 2916000* Fax. *0191 2571549* E-mail. *jb@norfran.co.uk* Web. *www.norfran.co.uk Norfran*

Norgine International Ltd (Head Office) Chaplin House Widewater Place Moorhall Road, Harefield, Uxbridge UB9 6NS Tel. *01895 826600* Fax. *01895 825865* E-mail. *enquiries@norgine.com* Web. *www.norgine.com Movicol – Normacol – Posalfilin – Pyralvex – Somnite – Spasmonal – Waxsol*

Norgren Ltd Box 22 Eastern Avenue, Lichfield WS13 6SB Tel. *01543 265000* Fax. *01543 265854* E-mail. *enquiry@norgren.com* Web. *www.norgren.com Buschjost – Enots – Excelon – Fleetfit – Herion – IMI – KIP – Lintra – Martonair – Microfog – Microtrol – Midi Star – Mini Star – Norgren Martonair – Nugget – Olympian – Plasfit – Pneufit C – Quietaire – Ultraire – Watson Smith – Webber – Weldfit*

Norinco UK Ltd The Sharman Law Building 1 Harpur Street, Bedford MK40 1PF Tel. *01234 348219* Fax. *01234 349497* E-mail. *sales@norinco-uk.com* Web. *www.norinco-uk.com Alumatic – Arrol – Avon – Brindley – Brunel – Edison – Eiffel – Ermatic – Forth – Forth Promenade – Gloster – Humber – Hydrocompact – Hydrofilter – Mersey – Pavior – Paxton – Severn – Smeaton – Stephenson – Tamar – Tees – Telford – Watt – Whittle – Wren*

Norit UK Ltd Clydesmill Place Cambuslang Industrial Estate, Clydesmill Industrial Estate, Glasgow G32 8RF Tel. *0141 6418841* Fax. *0141 6418411* E-mail. *sales@norit.com* Web. *www.norit.com Aero Pure – Automotive Emission Control Carbons – Darco – Liquidpure – Norit – Norithene – Sorbonorit*

Norland Burgess Ltd 93-105 St James Boulevard, Newcastle upon Tyne NE1 4BW Tel. *0191 2329722* Fax. *0191 2329722* E-mail. *admin@norlandburgess.co.uk* Web. *www.norlandburgess.co.uk Farb – Harlequin – Heirloom – Lastu – Reliable Brand – Silkanray – Sunstrand – Sunstrand Hose*

Norland Managed Services Ltd City Bridge House 57 Southwark Street, London SE1 1RU Tel. *020 76453750* Fax. *020 78719101* E-mail. *info@norlandmanagedservices.co.uk* Web. *www.norlandmanagedservices.co.uk Norland*

Norman Linton Ltd Linton House 39-51 Highgate Road, London NW5 1RT Tel. *020 74287700* Fax. *020 72670928* E-mail. *brian@normanlinton.co.uk* Web. *www.lintonoffices.co.uk Lyndella – Norman Linton – Norman Linton Petite*

Normans Queen's Road St Helier, Jersey JE2 3GR Tel. *01534 883388* Fax. *01534 883334* E-mail. *sales@normans.je Ecojoist*

Norma UK Ltd Unit 33 New Greenham Park Weber Road Greenham, Thatcham RG19 6HW Tel. *01635 521880* Fax. *01635 57403* E-mail. *mike.lawrence@normagroup.com* Web. *www.normagroup.com Manex – Power Grip – Terry*

Normesh Ltd 18-20 Miles Street, Oldham OL1 3NU Tel. *0161 6289849* Fax. *0161 6275732* E-mail. *sales@normesh.co.uk* Web. *www.normesh.co.uk MiniSIV – Normesh*

Norris Brothers Ltd Ricebridge House Brighton Road Bolney, Haywards Heath RH17 5NA Tel. *01444 881099* Fax. *01444 881631* E-mail. *rodpartlett@mac.com Norris Brothers*

Nortech Control Systems Ltd Brecon House William Brown Close, Llantarnam Industrial Park, Cwmbran NP44 3AB Tel. *01633 485533* Fax. *01633 485666* E-mail. *sales@nortechcontrol.com* Web. *www.nortechcontrol.com Apollo – Hyperx*

Nortel Networks UK Ltd Maidenhead Office Park Westacott Way, Littlewick Green, Maidenhead SL6 3QH Tel. *01628 432000* Fax. *01628 432810* E-mail. *enquiries@nortelnetworks.com* Web. *www.nortel.com A.C.N. – A.P.N.S.S. – A.R.C.S. – Accelar – Alex – B.N.R. – Baystack – BusinessExpress – C.M.T.S. – C.V.X. – Call Pilot – Cellplus – Centillion – Centrex – Cogent – Companion – Contempra – Contivity – Cornerstone – Courier – D.M.S. – D.M.S. Supernode – D.P.N. – D.P.N.S.S. – Dataflo – Datex – Deputy – Elektron – Entrust – Envoy – Executel – F.D.M.X. – Fibrelux – Helios – Hotwire – I.B.D.N. – I.P. Connect – L.C. (LANcity) – Maestro – Magellan – Making Contact – Medley – Meridian – Meridian 1 – Mobex – Multiview – N.T. – Nautica – Netgear – Norstar – Nortel – Nortel A World of Networks – Northern Telecom – Novakey – OPTera – Optivity – P.D.M.X. – Passport – Powercard – Powerdol – Powermod – Preside – Protest – Proximity – Remote Annex – Reunion – S./D.M.S. Accessnode – S./D.M.S. Transportnode – S.D.M.X. – Sabex – Scarab – Scopple – Seistream – Selectronic – ServiceBuilder – Signature – Sleekline – Star-Light – Startalk – Succession – Supernode – Symposium – System 5000 – T.D.M.X. – T.N.-X. – Teladapt – Telecomvision – Termiscan – Unistor – Unity II – Universal Edge – Vector – Versalar – Versarray – Visit*

North Aluminium 31 Argyle Crescent Hillhouse Industrial Estate, Hamilton ML3 9BQ Tel. *01698 284088* Fax. *01698 891825* E-mail. *sales@northaluminium.com* Web. *www.northaluminium.com aluminium curtain walling*

North British Tapes Ltd Unit 5 Locomotion Way Camperdown Industrial Estate, Newcastle Upon Tyne NE12 5US Tel. *0191 2686272* Fax. *0191 2687400* E-mail. *info@nbtapes.co.uk* Web. *www.nbtapes.co.uk 3M – Hookit – Jet Melt – Nomad – Scotch – Scotch-Brite – Scotchcast – Scotchlite – Stera Tape – Stikit – Surface-Walk*

Northcot Brick Station Road Blockley, Moreton In Marsh GL56 9LH Tel. *01386 700551* Fax. *01386 700852* E-mail. *sales@northcotbrick.co.uk* Web. *www.northcotbrick.co.uk Northcot Bricks Ltd*

North Devon Journal 96 High Street, Barnstaple EX31 1HT Tel. *01271 343064* Fax. *01271 323165* E-mail. *advertising@northdevon.journal.co.uk* Web. *www.thisisnorthdevon.co.uk Mid Devon Gazette – North Devon Journal*

North East Observation Ltd 34 Pembridge, Washington NE38 0LQ Tel. *07931 999123* E-mail. *enquiries@pattestingnortheast.co.uk* Web. *www.pattestingnortheast.co.uk www.newcastle-pat-testing.co.uk*

North East Surrey College Of Technology Nescot W52 Reigate Road Ewell, Epsom KT17 3DS Tel. *020 83941731* Fax. *020 83943030* E-mail. *reception@nescot.ac.uk* Web. *www.nescot.ac.uk Nescot College*

Northern Candles 10 Carrickrovaddy Road, Newry BT34 1SN Tel. *028 30821424* Fax. *028 30821735* E-mail. *brendanreavey@hotmail.com Mourn Range*

Northern Crop Driers Ltd Melrose Farm Melbourne, York YO42 4SS Tel. *01759 318396* Fax. *01759 318948* E-mail. *info@northerncropdriers.co.uk* Web. *www.northerncropdriers.co.uk grazeon – megazorb*

Northern Design Ltd 228 Bolton Road, Bradford BD3 0QW Tel. *01274 729533* Fax. *01274 750024* E-mail. *admin@ndmeter.co.uk* Web. *www.ndmeter.co.uk Abacus II – Drive – *EZ-901E (U.S.A.) – M.T.S. 1000 – M.T.S. 3000 – P.M. 303 – P.M.301 – P.M.305 – P.M.390 – Power Rail 323 – Powerminder – R.M.303 – W.M.302 – W.M.305 – X.D.10/19*

Northern Fan Supplies Ltd Unit E1 Longford Trading Estate Thomas Street, Stretford, Manchester M32 0JT Tel. *0161 8641777* Fax. *0161 8642777* E-mail. *jonathan.parry@nfan.co.uk* Web. *www.nfan.co.uk Elta Fans – Flakt Woods – Vent Axia – Vortice*

Northern Ireland Plastics Ltd 39 Shrigley Road Killyleagh, Downpatrick BT30 9SR Tel. *028 44828753* Fax. *028 44828809* E-mail. *sales@nip-ltd.co.uk* Web. *www.niplastics.com Corriboard*

Northern Joinery Daniel Street Whitworth, Rochdale OL12 8DA Tel. *01706 852345* Fax. *01706 853114* E-mail. *office@northernjoinery.co.uk* Web. *www.northernjoinery.co.uk Northern Joinery*

Northern Marine Management Ltd 2 Central Avenue Clydebank Business Park, Clydebank G81 2QR Tel. *0141 8763000* Fax. *0141 9412791* E-mail. *jacqueline.tierney@stena.com* Web. *www.nmm-stena.com Northern Marine*

Northern Tool & Gear Co. Ltd John Street West, Arbroath DD11 1RT Tel. *01241 872626* Fax. *01241 870040* E-mail. *general@ntgear.co.uk* Web. *www.ntgear.co.uk N.T.G.*

Northern Wall & Floor Ltd Bismark House Bower Street, Oldham OL1 3XB Tel. *0161 6263366* Fax. *0161 6273306* E-mail. *sales@thetileshop.co.uk* Web. *www.thetileshop.co.uk Grespania – S.I.M.A.*

Northgate & Arinso 2 Peoplebuilding Estate Maylands Avenue, Hemel Hempstead Industrial Estate, Hemel Hempstead HP2 4NW Tel. *01442 232434* Fax. *01442 256454* E-mail. *solutions@northgate-is.com*

Web. *www.northgate-hrs.com Glovia – Proiv – Reality – Reality Series M6000 – Sequoia Series M9000 – Series 19*

Northgate H R Ltd Thorpe Park, Peterborough PE3 6JY Tel. *01733 555777* Fax. *01733 312347* E-mail. *enquiries@northgatehr.com* Web. *www.northgatearinso.com Opendoor – PS Assessa – PS enterprise – PS Financials – RebusHRonline*

Northgate Managed Services Ltd 61 Church Road The Linen Green, Newtownabbey BT36 7LQ Tel. *028 90859085* Fax. *028 90859086* E-mail. *sales@northgate-is.com* Web. *www.northgate-is.com Service & Systems Solutions*

Northshore Composites Ltd Brockhampton Road, Havant PO9 1JU Tel. *023 92471428* Fax. *023 92452228* E-mail. *lester.abbott@northshore.co.uk* Web. *www.northshore-composites.co.uk G.R.P. – Northshore*

Northshore Yachts Ltd Itchenor, Chichester PO20 7AY Tel. *01243 512611* Fax. *01243 511473* E-mail. *sales@northshore.co.uk* Web. *www.northshore.co.uk Fisher – Freebird – Southerly – Sovereign – Vancouver*

Northvale Korting Ltd 2 Uxbridge Road, Leicester LE4 7ST Tel. *0116 2665911* Fax. *0116 2610050* E-mail. *sales@northvalekorting.co.uk* Web. *www.northvalekorting.co.uk Bossmatic – Conbraco – Korting – Minimatic – Naf-Check – Norval*

North West Dental Equipment 11 St Annes Gardens, Llandudno LL30 1SD Tel. *01492 582404* E-mail. *info@dental-chairs.co.uk* Web. *www.dental-chairs.co.uk Fimet*

North West Development Agency Centre Park Warrington, Warrington WA1 1QN Tel. *01925 400100* Fax. *01925 400400* E-mail. *nigel.dove@nwda.co.uk* Web. *www.nwda.co.uk N.W.*

North Western Lead Company Mill Street Newton Moor Industrial Estate, Hyde SK14 4LJ Tel. *0161 3684491* Fax. *0161 3665103* E-mail. *sales@decraled.co.uk* Web. *www.decraled.co.uk Decra-Led*

North West Sheeting Supplies Unit 23 Bizspace Lomeshaye Business Village Turner Road, Nelson BB9 7DR Tel. *01282 619430* Fax. *01282 619431* E-mail. *sales@steelroofing.co.uk* Web. *www.steelroofing.co.uk FFM non-drip/anti condensation coating – Insulated Composite Panels – Steel 6/metal profile to match Big 6*

Norton Plastics The Old Gasworks Belfield Street, Ilkeston DE7 8DU Tel. *0115 9441245* Fax. *0115 9328975* E-mail. *norton.plastics@vigin.net N.P.L. – Norton*

Norwesco Coffee 12 Powis Road Ashton-on-Ribble, Preston PR2 1AD Tel. *01772 729413* E-mail. *matt@fischealthcare.co.uk *norwesco*

Norwich City Football Club Carrow Road, Norwich NR1 1JE Tel. *01603 760760* Fax. *01603 628373* E-mail. *edward.jones@ncfc-canaries.co.uk* Web. *www.canaries.co.uk Junior Canaries*

Notcutts Ltd Garden Centre 74 Cumberland Street, Woodbridge IP12 4AF Tel. *01394 445400* Fax. *01394 445440* E-mail. *reception@nottcutts.co.uk* Web. *www.notcutts.co.uk Notcutts*

Notedome Ltd 34 Herald Way Binley Industrial Estate, Coventry CV3 2RQ Tel. *024 76635192* Fax. *024 76635509* E-mail. *sales@notedome.co.uk* Web. *www.notedome.co.uk *Millathane 300 (U.S.A.) – *Millathane E-34 (U.S.A.)*

Notice Board Company Po Box 2986, Coventry CV3 6YP Tel. *024 76010076* Fax. *024 76012862* E-mail. *sales@noticeboardcompany.com* Web. *www.noticeboardcompany.com Street Case Notice Boards*

Nottingham Building Society Nottingham House 5-13 Upper Parliament Street, Nottingham NG1 2BX Tel. *0115 9564256* Fax. *0115 9483948* E-mail. *sales-development@thenottingham.com* Web. *www.thenottingham.com N.B.S. – Nottingham Property Services*

Nottingham Evening Post Castle Wharf House, Nottingham NG1 7EU Tel. *0115 9482000* Fax. *0115 9644032* Web. *www.thisisnottingham.co.uk Evening Post Group*

Nottingham Industrial Flooring Ltd Unit 2 Beckside Court Annie Reed Road, Beverley HU17 0LF Tel. *01482 856162* Fax. *01482 856168* E-mail. *paul@nifl.co.uk* Web. *www.nisl.co.uk Altro Resins – Flowcrete – Resdev*

Notts Contractors Ltd Barton Yards Abbotsham, Bideford EX39 5AP Tel. *01237 421066* Fax. *01237 478800* Web. *www.nottscontractorsltd.co.uk Q Plant & Haulage*

Notts Sport Ltd Innovation House Magna Park, Lutterworth LE17 4XH Tel. *01455 883730* Fax. *01455 883755* E-mail. *info@nottssport.com* Web. *www.nottssport.com Notts Sport*

Nova Comex Ltd 51 Blackbird Drive, Bury St Edmunds IP32 7DS Tel. *01284 731018* Fax. *020 71831188* E-mail. *info@novacomex.com* Web. *www.novacomex.com Novax*

Nova Contract Cleaners 12 Smithfield Place, Bournemouth BH9 2QJ Tel. *01202 536770* Fax. *01202 520475* E-mail. *sales@nova-cleaners.co.uk* Web. *www.nova-cleaners.co.uk *Carpet Cleaning – *High Level Cleaning – *Kitchen Cleaning – *Spring Cleaning – *Window Cleaning*

Nova Group Ltd Norman Road, Altrincham WA14 4EN Tel. *0161 6139600* Fax. *0161 9268405* E-mail. *it@novagroup.co.uk* Web. *www.novagroup.co.uk Nova Challenger*

Nova International Newcastle House Albany Court Monarch Road, Newcastle Business Park, Newcastle upon Tyne NE4 7YB Tel. *0191 2727033* Fax. *0191 2727036* E-mail. *eric.wilkins@nova-international.com* Web. *www.greatrun.org View From*

Novelis Foil & Technical Products Stourbridge Road, Bridgnorth WV15 6AW Tel. *01746 713000* Fax. *01746 761860* E-mail. *jane.hyde@novelis.com* Web. *www.novelis.com Lawson Mardon Star*

Novellini UK Ltd Orchard Industrial Estate Toddington, Cheltenham GL54 5EB Tel. *01242 621061* Fax. *01242 622151* E-mail. *info-uk@novellini.com* Web. *www.novellini.com Diamant – Giada – Harmony – Jolly – King – Maldive – Prestige – Rubino – Star – Victory – Whirlpool – Young*

Novinit Ltd 56 Lever Street, Manchester M1 1FJ Tel. *0161 2361223* Fax. *0161 2110090* E-mail. *samsainz@ntlworld.com Bonnie – Jesta – Lina Chirino – Madam's Choice – Non Stop – Sam Sainz*

Novus Sealing Hunsworth Lane, Cleckheaton BD19 4EJ Tel. *01274 878787* Fax. *01274 862588* E-mail. *mailbox@novussealing.com* Web. *www.novussealing.com Ball Valves UK*

Noyna School Aprons 222 Stretford Road Urmston, Manchester M41 9NT Tel. *0161 7482724* Fax. *0161 7478775* E-mail. *info@noyna.com* Web. *www.noyna.com Noyna – Noyna Safety*

N P Aerospace Ltd 473 Foleshill Road, Coventry CV6 5AQ Tel. *024 76702802* Fax. *024 76687313* E-mail. *info@np-aerospace.co.uk* Web. *www.np-aerospace.com NP Aerospace Defence & Composite Products*

N P S Shoes Ltd South Street Wollaston, Wellingborough NN29 7RY Tel. *01933 664207* Fax. *01933 664699* E-mail. *info@nps-solovair.co.uk* Web. *www.nps-solovair.co.uk Solovair*

N R C Plant Ltd Neagron House Stanford Road, Orsett, Grays RM16 3BX Tel. *01375 361616* Fax. *01375 361818* E-mail. *sales@nrcplant.co.uk* Web. *www.nrcplant.co.uk *Allied – *Landers (Germany) – N.R.C. – Wylie*

N R G Group Ltd 4 Rushmills, Northampton NN4 7YB Tel. *01604 732700* Fax. *01752 340173* Web. *www.nrg-group.com *Gestetner (EU & Japan) – *Nashuatec (EU & Japan) – *Rex Rotary (EU & Japan)*

N S D International Ltd Mayfield Industrial Estate, Dalkeith EH22 4AF Tel. *0131 6542800* Fax. *0131 6636185* E-mail. *e.martin@nsdinternational.co.uk* Web. *www.nsdinternational.co.uk Barcode Systems – Digital Labels – Self Adhesive Labels*

N S F Controls Ltd Ingrow Bridge Works Ingrow Lane, Keighley BD21 5EF Tel. *01535 661144* Fax. *01535 661474* E-mail. *info@nsfcontrols.co.uk* Web. *www.nsfcontrols.co.uk Keylite – N.S.F.-Cutler-Hammer – N.S.F.-Rotary wafer – NSF- Slimline - Keylight Keyboard Switches – Slimline*

N S K Europe Northern Road, Newark NG24 2JF Tel. *01636 643000* Fax. *01628 509808* E-mail. *info-uk@nsk.com* Web. *www.eu.nsk.com Centaline – Elektrosafe – NSK – RHP – Self-Lube – Silver-Lube*

N S S L Ltd 6 Gatton Park Business Centre Wells Place, Merstham, Redhill RH1 3DR Tel. *01737 648800* Fax. *01737 648888* E-mail. *customer.centre@satcom-solutions.com* Web. *www.satcom-solutions.com Nera Telecommunications*

N T N Bearings UK Ltd 11 Wellington Crescent Fradley Park Fradley Park, Lichfield WS13 8RZ Tel. *01543 445000* Fax. *01543 445035* E-mail. *lex.browning@ntn-europe.com* Web. *www.ntn-europe.com N.T.N.*

Nuaire Ltd Western Industrial Estate Lon-Y-Llyn, Caerphilly CF83 1NA Tel. *029 20885911* Fax. *029 20887033* E-mail. *info@nuaire.co.uk* Web. *www.nuaire.co.uk Axus – Drimaster – Ductmaster – Flatmaster – Genie – M.S.E. – Microsave – NuAire – Opus – Platemaster – Quietwin – Single Pak – Smoke Clearer – Squaremaster – Squrbo – Terminator*

Nullifire Ltd A Division of Tremco Illbruck Coatings Ltd Torrington Avenue, Coventry CV4 9TJ Tel. *024 76855000* Fax. *024 76469547* E-mail. *protect@nullifire.com* Web. *www.nullifire.com System "M" – System "S" – System B – System J – System W*

Numatic International Millfield Industrial Estate Millfield, Chard TA20 2GB Tel. *01460 68600* Fax. *01460 68458* E-mail. *sales@numatic.co.uk* Web. *www.numatic.co.uk Henry – Numatic*

N U M UK Ltd Unit 5 Fairfield Court Seven Stars Industrial Estate Wheler Road, Coventry CV3 4LJ Tel. *024 76301259* Fax. *08717 504021* E-mail. *sales.uk@num.com* Web. *www.num.com Num – NUN-CNC TELENUMERICS SERVOMAC*

Nursery Window Ltd 83 Walton Street, London SW3 2HP Tel. *020 75813358* Fax. *020 78238839* E-mail. *info@nurserywindow.co.uk* Web. *www.nurserywindow.co.uk Nursery Window, The*

Nursey Of Bungay 12 Upper Olland Street, Bungay NR35 1BQ Tel. *01986 892821* Fax. *01986 892823* E-mail. *sales@nurseysheepskin.co.uk* Web. *www.nurseysheepskin.co.uk Larrykins – Nursey's – Nursey's Lamb & Sheepskin Products*

Nu Swift International Ltd PO Box 10, Elland HX5 9DS Tel. *01422 372852* Fax. *01422 379569* E-mail. *rpollard@nuswift.co.uk* Web. *www.nuswift.co.uk Nu-Swift – Nu-Swift ABC Multy-Purpose*

Nutrel Products Ltd Park Farm Park Farm Road, Kettlethorpe, Lincoln LN1 2LD Tel. *01522 704747* Fax. *01522 704748* E-mail. *sales@nutrelgroup.co.uk* Web. *www.nutrelgroup.co.uk *FASTMIX – *FASTPHITE – *INTRAFOL – *MICROBOOSTERS – *NUTRICHEL*

Nutriculture 3-5 Paddock Road, Skelmersdale WN8 9PL Tel. *01695 554080* Fax. *01695 554081* E-mail. *sales@nutriculture.com* Web. *www.nutriculture.com Gro-Tank – Nutriculture – Power-Gro*

Nutscene Breahead Works, Forfar DD8 2NS Tel. *01307 468589* Fax. *01307 467051* E-mail. *sales@nutscene.com* Web. *www.nutscene.com Accessories – Fillis – Garden Rack – GreenTwist – Polytwist – Tartwist*

Alan Nuttall Ltd Hall Street, Dudley DY2 7DQ Tel. *01384 245100* Fax. *01384 245102* E-mail. *nino.calandra@nuttalls.co.uk* Web. *www.nuttalls.co.uk Nuttall*

Nu-Type Ltd Millwey Rise Industrial Estate, Axminster EX13 5HU Tel. *01297 33114* Fax. *01297 34935* E-mail. *nu-type@telinco.co.uk* Web. *www.nu-type.co.uk Nu-Type*

Nu Way PO Box 1, Droitwich WR9 8NA Tel. *01905 794331* Fax. *01905 794017* E-mail. *info@nu-way.co.uk* Web. *www.nu-way.co.uk Nu-Way*

N V Tools Ltd 28 Wash Road Hutton, Brentwood CM13 1TB Tel. *01277 214455* Fax. *01277 227341* E-mail. *enquiries@nvtools.co.uk* Web. *www.nvtools.co.uk Curastat – Envetron – N.V. Tools – SOSS*

N W Flooring Ltd Unit 9 Lyttleton Road, Pershore WR10 2DF Tel. *0781 3696618* E-mail. *nickwinnall@aol.com* Web. *www.nwflooring.co.uk Amtico – Arden – Boen – Karndean – Laybond – pergo – Quickstep – Tarkett – Uzin*

N & W Global Vending Ltd Dudley Street, Bilston WV14 0LA Tel. *01902 355000* Fax. *01902 402272* E-mail. *david.ward@nwglobalvending.co.uk* Web. *www.nwglobalvending.co.uk *Wittenborg Easy Vend (U.S.A.) – Wittenborg FB50 – Wittenborg FB55 – Wittenborg FM4000 – *Wittenborg Instant 5100 (U.S.A.) – Wittenborg Snack*

Nylacast 200 Hastings Road, Leicester LE5 0HL Tel. *0116 2764048* Fax. *0116 2741954* E-mail. *malvin.fookes@nylacast.com* Web. *www.nylacast.com Aquanyl – Aquanyl Blue – Aquanyl Yellow – Nylacast – Nylacast Bigfoot – Nylacast H.S. Blue – Nylacast Moly – Nylacast Nylube – Nylacast Nylube – Nylacast Oilon*

Nylon Colours Ltd Chamberlain Rd, Aylesbury HP19 8DY Tel. *01296 433754* Fax. *01296 392285* E-mail. *sales@nyloncolours.co.uk Nylon R-AM – Nylon-D – Nylon-RNylon-D – Nylon-R – Rilsan*

Nylon Fasteners Ltd Unit 14 Hazel Road, Alton GU34 5EY Tel. *01256 533088* Fax. *01256 651143* E-mail. *sales@nyfast.co.uk* Web. *www.nyfast.co.uk Nyfast*

Nylon Hosiery 44 Upper Bond Street, Hinckley LE10 1RJ Tel. *01455 631413* Fax. *01455 636345* E-mail. *rob@nylonhosiery.co.uk* Web. *www.webleicester.co.uk Pamela Mann*

Nynas UK Ab East Camperdown Street, Dundee DD1 3LG Tel. *01382 462211* Fax. *01382 456846* E-mail. *steven.lockhart@nynas.com* Web. *www.nynas.com P M Oils*

O

Oakes Bros Ltd Clemsfold Corner Guildford Road, Clemsfold, Horsham RH12 3PW Tel. *01403 790777* Fax. *01403 790086* E-mail. *ccharman@oakesbros.co.uk* Web. *www.oakesbros.co.uk Oakes Bros Ltd*

Oakland Excelsior 6 Mandervell Road Oadby, Leicester LE2 5LL Tel. *0116 2720800* Fax. *0115 9899016* E-mail. *sales@oakland-elevators.co.uk* Web. *www.oakland-elevators.co.uk Oakland*

Oakland Financial Advisors Unit 2 Popi Business Centre South Way, Wembley HA9 0HB Tel. *020 89034054* Fax. *020 89038045* Web. *www.orkin.co.uk Leather Food Cream – Leather Groom – Sprush – Swade Aid – Swade Groom – Swade Guard*

Oakmain Ltd Oak House Kendon Road, Crumlin, Newport NP11 3AP Tel. *01495 248877* Fax. *01495 249854* E-mail. *sales@oakmain.co.uk* Web. *www.oakmain.co.uk Kendon Automotive*

Oasis Art & Craft Products Ltd Goldthorn Road, Kidderminster DY11 7JN Tel. *01562 744522* Fax. *01562 823181* E-mail. *penny.waldron@colart.co.uk* Web. *www.windsornewton.com Acroil – Essdee – Page – Paint By Numbers – Scraperfoil*

Oasis Fashions Limited The Triangle Stanton Harcourt Industrial Estate, Stanton Harcourt, Witney OX29 5UT Tel. *01865 874700* Fax. *01865 734898* E-mail. *help@oasis-stores.co.uk* Web. *www.oasis-stores.com Oasis*

Oasis Systems 31 Quarry Road Kingswood, Bristol BS15 8PA Tel. *0117 9603882* E-mail. *info@oasis-systems.co.uk* Web. *www.oasis-systems.co.uk Geller – Samsung – Vectron*

Obara UK 1 Tomlinson Industrial Estate Alfreton Road, Derby DE21 4ED Tel. *01332 297868* E-mail. *sales@obara.co.uk* Web. *www.obara.co.uk Martin Electric – Obara Europe – Obara Europe - Martin Electric*

Obart Pumps Ltd Obart House Twenty Twenty Industrial Estate, Maidstone ME16 0FZ Tel. *0800 0924423* Fax. *01622 355019* E-mail. *sales@obartpumps.co.uk* Web. *www.obartpumps.co.uk Tsurumi – Honda – Speroni – Alma – Umbra – Tellarinni – Piusi – Matic*

Obelisk Music 32 Ellerdale Road, London NW3 6BB Tel. *020 78132253* Fax. *020 74310621* E-mail. *heinzherschmann@yahoo.co.uk* Web. *www.apollosound.com Obelisk Music*

Oceaneering Asset Integrity 109 Bowesfield Lane, Stockton On Tees TS18 3HF Tel. *01642 604661* Fax. *01642 670300* E-mail. *jwatkinson@oceaneering.com* Web. *www.oceaneering.com Heat treatment – Inspection management – Manpower – Mechanical Testing – N.D.T. – Non destructive testing – Vendor Inspection*

Ocean Express Ltd Station House Station Road, Maldon CM9 4LQ Tel. *01621 878800* Fax. *01621 878888* E-mail. *clive.lewis@vanguardlogistics.co.uk* Web. *www.oceanexpress.co.uk Caribe MarinExpress Lines Salaco Express Line – Salaco Express Line*

Ocean Magic Surf Boards Unit 6c St Columb Industrial Estate, St Columb TR9 6SF Tel. *01637 880421* Fax. *01637 852042* E-mail. *info@nsboards.co.uk* Web. *www.nsboards.co.uk Ocean Magic*

O C S Group Ltd 79 Limpsfield Road Sanderstead, South Croydon CR2 9LB Tel. *020 86513211* Fax. *020 86514832* E-mail. *enquiries@ocs.co.uk* Web. *www.ocs.co.uk Centuryan Security – OCS Support Services*

Oddy Hydraulics Ltd Tristran Centre Brown Lane West, Leeds LS12 6BF Tel. *0113 2448787* Fax. *0113 2449786* E-mail. *sales@oddy-hyds.com* Web. *www.oddy-hyds.com Bosch*

Odin Unit 4 Fullwood Close, Aldermans Green Industrial Estate, Coventry CV2 2SS Tel. *024 76602622* Fax. *024 76602649* Web. *www.odinengineering.co.uk Odin*

Oem - Automatic Ltd Whiteacres Cambridge Road, Whetstone, Leicester LE8 6ZG Tel. *0116 2849900* Fax. *0116 2841721* E-mail. *information@uk.oem.se* Web. *www.oem.co.uk *Codicount (Switzerland) – *Codisplay (Switzerland) – *Multiswitch (Switzerland) – *Proface (Switzerland)*

O E M Group Ltd Pavilion Business Centre 6 Kinetic Crescent, Enfield EN3 7FJ Tel. *020 83448777* Fax. *020 83448778* E-mail. *cameron@secureseal.com* Web. *www.secureseal.com *Accu Trak (U.S.A.) – Nuway – Secureseal – *Siebe (U.S.A.)*

Oetiker UK Ltd (Head Office & Factory) Unit H Foundry Close, Horsham RH13 5TX Tel. *01403 260478* Fax. *01403 240690* E-mail. *sales@uk.oetiker.com* Web. *www.oetiker.com Allert (Germany) – *Band Clip (Worldwide) – *O-Clip (Worldwide) – *Oetiker (Worldwide) – Swing Couplings – Safety Couplings*

Office Depot UK Guilbert House Greenwich Way, Andover SP10 4JZ Tel. *08444 120042* Fax. *08704 114735* E-mail. *john.moore@officedepot.com* Web. *www.officedepot.co.uk 30-45 – 50-60 – Accuwriter – Anglia – Clarafile – Clearcut – Correx – Crystaltype – Durahide – Duralon – Evergreen – Flowball – Giant – Grafylon – Guilbert – Highlighters – Jumbo Markers – Labelprinter – Magnaflow – Miracle Tape – Novatip – Ofrahide – Ofrex – Ofrex Slim – Papersafe – Papersafe Neon Notes – Papersafe Removeable Notes – Popular – Robust – Slimlock – Solid Streak – Storafile – Super Folders – Terylon – Wessex – Zip Clip*

Office Options Sotherby Road, Middlesbrough TS3 8BS Tel. *01642 211100* Fax. *01642 227878* E-mail. *sales@officeoptionsuk.com* Web. *www.officeoptionsuk.com Office Options Interiors*

Office Team Unit 4 500 Purley Way, Croydon CR0 4NZ Tel. *020 87743422* Fax. *020 86402905* E-mail. *info@officeteam.co.uk* Web. *www.officeteam.co.uk Helofile – Oyez – Oyez Copier – Oyez Legal Support Systems – Oyez Multicopier Laser Plus – Oyez Stronghold – Oyez Strongmail – Oyez Supertype – Oyez Trifilm – Oyez Wills – Visitape*

Office Team 7 Spa Road Bermondsey, London SE16 3QQ Tel. *020 75563345* Fax. *020 72319810* E-mail. *angie.deverell@officeteam.co.uk* Web. *www.officeteam.co.uk Envoy – Notary*

Offspring International Unit 8 Castle Court 2 Castlegate Way, Dudley DY1 4RH Tel. *01384 415540* Fax. *01384 415544* E-mail. *david.rowley@offspringinternational.com* Web. *www.offspringinternational.com Quintas & Quintas – Zheng Mao*

Off The Wall Graffiti Solutions Carver Buildings Littles Lane, Wolverhampton WV1 1JY Tel. *01902 426479* Fax. *01902 426574* E-mail. *sales@antigraffiti.co.uk* Web. *www.antigraffiti.co.uk Mathys – Rustoleum*

Ogden Transteel Ltd Stanningley Works Butler Way, Stanningley, Pudsey LS28 6EA Tel. *0113 2578221* Fax. *0113 2362340* E-mail. *ogdensteel@hotmail.co.uk* Web. *www.ogdentransteelleeds.co.uk Ogden (Transteel) Ltd*

Ogle Models & Prototypes Ltd Birds Hill, Letchworth Garden City SG6 1JA Tel. *01462 682661* Fax. *01462 680131* E-mail. *sales@oglemodels.com* Web. *www.oglemodels.com Ogle Design*

Oil Pollution Environmental Control Ltd Martin Street Birstall, Batley WF17 9PJ Tel. *01924 442701* Fax. *01924 471925* E-mail. *info@opec.co.uk* Web. *www.opec.co.uk Coastguard – E. Series – Force 3 – Force 5 – Force 7 – H.V. – H.W. 33 – Harbourguard – Opec - Oil Pollution Environmental Control – R.B. Booms – R.P. 18 – SB Booms – St Tanks*

Oil States Industries UK Ltd Blackness Road Altens Industrial Estate, Aberdeen AB12 3LH Tel. *01224 290000* Fax. *01224 896199* E-mail. *mick.mccafferty@oilstates-uk.com* Web. *www.oilstates.com Alligator – Cheetah – Hihos – Leopard – Lynx – Merlin – Octopus – Swift – Talon*

Oiluk 145-157 St John Street, London EC1V 4PY Tel. *029 20575515* Fax. *029 20575595* E-mail. *info@oiluk.net* Web. *www.oiluk.net Gulf*

O Kay Engineering Services Ltd Eagle Avenue Magnetic Park, Desborough, Kettering NN14 2WD Tel. *01536 765010* Fax. *01536 765011* E-mail. *postbox@okay.co.uk* Web. *www.okay.co.uk O.Kay*

O K W Enclosures Ltd 15 Brunel Way, Fareham PO15 5TX Tel. *01489 583858* Fax. *01489 583836* E-mail. *sales@okw.co.uk* Web. *www.okw.co.uk OKW Enclosures – ROLEC Enclosures – SERPAC Enclosures*

Old Bushmills Distillery Co. Ltd The Distillery, Bushmills BT57 8XH Tel. *028 20731521* Fax. *028 20731339* E-mail. *gordon.donoghue@diageo.com* Web. *www.bushmills.com Black Bush – Bushmills – Bushmills Malt – Coleraine*

Bruce Oldfield Ltd 27 Beauchamp Place, London SW3 1NJ Tel. *020 75841363* Fax. *020 77610351* E-mail. *hq@bruceoldfield.com* Web. *www.bruceoldfield.com Bruce Oldfield*

J Oldham & Co. Ltd Tearne House Hollington, Stoke On Trent ST10 4HR Tel. *01889 507353* Fax. *01889 507212* E-mail. *enquiries@joldham.co.uk* Web. *www.joldham.co.uk Hollington*

Oldham Lighting Projects Ltd Claudgen House Eastwick Road, Bookham, Leatherhead KT23 4DT Tel. *01372 459999* Fax. *01372 459559* E-mail. *sales@oldhamlighting.co.uk* Web. *www.oldhamlighting.co.uk Hi-Slim*

Oldham Trade Plastics Unit 5 Victoria Trading Estate Drury Lane, Chadderton, Oldham OL9 7PJ Tel. *0161 6833250* Fax. *0161 6833259* E-mail. *sales@oldhamtradeplastics.co.uk* Web. *www.oldhamtradeplastics.co.uk Swish*

Old Park Engineering Services 36b Woods Lane, Cradley Heath B64 7AN Tel. *01384 412550* Fax. *01384 410784* E-mail. *info@oldparklpg.co.uk* Web. *www.oldparklpg.co.uk Old Park*

Oldrids Co. Ltd 11 Strait Bargate, Boston PE21 6UF Tel. *01205 361251* Fax. *01205 356402* E-mail. *lesley.mcgarry@oldrids.co.uk* Web. *www.oldrids.co.uk Downtown*

Oleo International Ltd Grovelands Estate Longford Road, Exhall, Coventry CV7 9ND Tel. *024 76645555* Fax. *024 76645777* E-mail. *roy@oleo.co.uk* Web. *www.oleo.co.uk Oleo*

Ollard Westcombe Cameo Works Bridge Street, Downpatrick BT30 6HD Tel. *028 44617557* Fax. *028 44613580* E-mail. *admin@cameoequestrian.co.uk* Web. *www.cameoequestrian.co.uk Cameo*

Olympia Foods Ltd Unit 6 Estover Road, Plymouth PL6 7PF Tel. *01752 201685* Fax. *01752 201769* E-mail. *info@olympiafoods.co.uk* Web. *www.olympiafoods.co.uk Bindi Cakes – Curry Sauce Co. – Discovery Foods – Funnybones – La Pizza Co.*

Olympic Blinds Ltd Unit 11 Bilton Court Bilton Way, Luton LU1 1LX Tel. *01582 737878* Fax. *01582 402182* E-mail. *joew@olympicblinds.co.uk* Web. *www.olympicblinds.co.uk Olympic Blinds Ltd*

Olympus Distribution Ltd Olympus Drive Great Bridge, Tipton DY4 7HY Tel. *0121 5225600* Fax. *0121 5225601* E-mail. *sales@olympusglobal.co.uk* Web. *www.olympusglobal.co.uk Olympus Distribution*

Olympus Technologies Ltd Melbourne Works 8 Firth Street, Huddersfield HD1 3BA Tel. *01484 514513* Fax. *01484 435027* E-mail. *info@olympustechnologies.co.uk* Web. *www.olympustechnologies.co.uk *Dinse (Germany) – *Ess (Germany) – Olympus – Panasonic – *Reis (Germany)*

Omar Park Homes Ltd London Road, Brandon IP27 0NE Tel. *01842 810673* Fax. *01842 814328* E-mail. *info@omar.co.uk* Web. *www.omar.co.uk Brentmere Leisure – Omar – Omar Leisure – Omar UPVC – Woodbury Leisure*

Omdesign London Ltd 4 Montrose Court Finchley Road, London NW11 6AG Tel. *020 87319230* E-mail. *contact@omdesign.co.uk* Web. *www.omdesign.co.uk OMdeSIGN London Partnership*

Omeg Ltd Imberhorne Industrial Estate, East Grinstead RH19 1RJ Tel. *01342 410420* Fax. *01342 316253* E-mail. *sales@omeg.co.uk* Web. *www.omeg.co.uk Omeg – Castelco*

Omega Import Export Ltd 6 Beresford Avenue, Wembley HA0 1SA Tel. *020 89026222* Fax. *020 89035011* E-mail. *enquiry@elftone.com* Web. *www.elftone.com *Elftone – *Omega – Texson*

Omega Resistance Wire Ltd Hadley Works Cranborne Road, Potters Bar EN6 3JL Tel. *01707 620111* Fax. *01707 649225* E-mail. *sales@omega-wire.com* Web. *www.omega-wire.com Hecnum – Regent*

Omex Environmental Ltd Riverside Industrial Estate, Kings Lynn PE30 2HH Tel. *01553 770092* Fax. *01553 776547* E-mail. *alistarr@omex.com* Web. *www.omex.co.uk Ferromex – Magmex – Nutromex – Nutromex, Ferromex, Magmex*

Omnikote Ltd Chamberlain Road, Aylesbury HP19 8DY Tel. *01296 483266* Fax. *01296 392285* E-mail. *sales@omnikote.co.uk* Web. *www.omnikote.co.uk Nylon R-AG – Nylon R-Ag+*

Omniledger Ltd 5 Bridge Gate Centre Martinfield, Welwyn Garden City AL7 1JG Tel. *01707 324201* Fax. *01707 375572* E-mail. *sales@omniledger.co.uk* Web. *www.omniledger.co.uk *Omniledger (U.S.A.)*

Omnitrack Ltd Ball Unit House Station Road Industrial Estate Station Road, Woodchester, Stroud GL5 5EQ Tel. *01453 873345* Fax. *01453 878500* E-mail. *info@omnitrack.co.uk* Web. *www.omnitrack.co.uk Autoset (Production) (United Kingdom) – Autotrack (Birmingham) (United Kingdom) – OMNI-BALL – OMNI-FLOAT – OMNI-GLIDE – OMNI-SLIDE – OMNI-SWEEP – Omniball (United Kingdom) – Omnidirectional (United Kingdom) – Omnimat (United Kingdom) – Omnitrack Ltd (United Kingdom) – Omniwheel (United Kingdom)*

Omya UK Ltd Stephensons Way Wyvern Business Park, Chaddesden, Derby DE21 6LY Tel. *01332 674000* Fax. *01332 544700* E-mail. *suzanne.bunting@omya.com* Web. *www.omya.co.uk Britomya – Calmote – Caloxol – CEPO – Coatex – Dolofil – Elvax – Engage – *Faci (Italy) – Fintalc – Firebrake – Garoflam – Garolite – *Hydragloss (U.S.A.) – Hydrocarb – Hypalon – Maglite – Magnifin – Martinal – Microdol – Millicarb – Minfil – Multibase – Multisperse – Neoprene – Nordel IP – Omya – Paraplex – Plasthall – Plusaqua – Promindsa – Repsol – Snowcal – Snowfort – Tylose – Tyrin – Unicell – Vamac – Viscoatex*

On Demand Technology 5 Eastern Way, Bury St Edmunds IP32 7AB Tel. *01284 749105* Fax. *01284 749074* E-mail. *juliant@ondemandtechnology.co.uk* Web. *www.ondemandtechnology.co.uk On Demand Technology*

Oneida International Ltd 106 Brent Terrace, London NW2 1BZ Tel. *020 84508900* Fax. *020 84509985* E-mail. *james.joseph@oneida.co.uk* Web. *www.oneida.co.uk Viners*

O'Neill Medicalia Ltd 10 Percy Street, Liverpool L8 7LU Tel. *0151 7085268* Fax. *0151 7071314* E-mail. *vincent@medicalia.co.uk* Web. *www.medicali.co.uk Fluthane – Halothane – Iso Fluthane*

One Vision Imaging Herald Way Binley Industrial Estate, Coventry CV3 2NY Tel. *024 76440404* Fax. *024 76444219* E-mail. *info@onevisionimaging.com* Web. *www.onevisionimaging.com Colab*

Online Electrical Wholesalers 9 Welling High Street, Welling DA16 1TR Tel. *020 83038461* Fax. *020 83038681* E-mail. *neil@onlineelctrical.co.uk* Web. *www.onlineelctrical.co.uk plug and grow*

Online Lubricants 20 The I O Centre 59-71 River Road, Barking IG11 0DR Tel. *020 85070123* Fax. *020 85930234* E-mail. *john@online-lubricants.co.uk* Web. *www.online-lubricants.co.uk Elf – Fina*

Onyx Software 6 Tamar House Brants Bridge, Bracknell RG12 9BQ Tel. *01344 322000* Fax. *01344 489035* E-mail. *sales@onyx.com* Web. *www.onyx.com MarketForce*

Opas Southern Limited Enterprise House St. Lawrence Avenue, Worthing BN14 7JH Tel. *01903 239955* Fax. *01903 239966* E-mail. *sales@opas.co.uk* Web. *www.opas.co.uk Beaver – Common Sense – DOT – Durable Dot – Lift the Dot – Tenax – VELCRO*

O P Chocolate Ltd High Street Dowlais, Merthyr Tydfil CF48 3TB Tel. *01685 352560* Fax. *01685 352599* E-mail. *sales@opchocolate.com* Web. *www.opchocolate.com Cantalou – Caxton – Cemoi – Majestic – Mega choc – Private label – Snack manufrs*

Openbet Retail Bishopsgate House Broadford Park, Shalford, Guildford GU4 8ED Tel. *01483 293900* Fax. *01483 533333* E-mail. *solutions@openbet.com* Web. *www.openbetretail.com Alphameric 100 – Alphameric Broadcast Solutions – Alphameric Red Onion – Alphameric Solutions – Alphameric Technologies*

Open Date Equipment Ltd Unit 8 9 Puma Trade Park 145 Morden Road, Mitcham CR4 4DG Tel. *020 86554999* Fax. *020 86554990* E-mail. *francess@opendate.co.uk* Web. *www.opendate.com Open Date*

Open G I Buckholt Drive, Worcester WR4 9SR Tel. *01905 754455* Fax. *01905 754441* E-mail. *stacy.prosser@opengi.co.uk* Web. *www.opengi.co.uk Misys*

Open University Worldwide The Michael Young Building Walton Hall, Milton Keynes MK7 6AA Tel. *01908 858785* Fax. *01908 858787* E-mail. *t.strudwick@open.ac.uk*

Web. *www.ouw.co.uk Open Business School – Open University Press, The – Open Unversity, The – Optel*

Opico Ltd Cherry Holt Road, Bourne PE10 9LA Tel. *01778 421111* Fax. *01778 425080* E-mail. *james.woolway@opico.co.uk* Web. *www.opico.co.uk Opico*

Opperman Mastergear Ltd Hambridge Lane, Newbury RG14 5TS Tel. *01635 811500* Fax. *01635 811501* E-mail. *sales@opperman-mastergear.co.uk* Web. *www.opperman-mastergear.co.uk Dapta-gear – Heligear – Mastergear – Revmaster – Tango – Tempo*

Opsec Security Ltd 2 Penman Way Enderby, Leicester LE19 1ST Tel. *0116 2822000* Fax. *0116 2822100* E-mail. *sales@opsecsecurity.co.uk* Web. *www.appliedopsec.com Aegis – Applied Holographics – Holofilm – Holoflex – ISIS – Multigram – Pass*

Optare Group Ltd Hurricane Way South Sherburn In Elmet, Leeds LS25 6PT Tel. *0113 2645182* Fax. *0113 2606635* E-mail. *info@optare.com* Web. *www.optare.com Alero – Bonito – Excel – Nuvelle – Optare – Optare Coach Sales – Solera – Solo – Sorocco – Spectra – Unitec – Unitec Rotherham*

Optibelt UK Ltd 5 Bishops Court Winwick Quay, Warrington WA2 8QY Tel. *01925 415777* Fax. *01925 573751* E-mail. *info@optibelt.com* Web. *www.optibelt.com Optibelt – Optibelt D.K. – Optibelt DK – Optibelt K.B. – Optibelt KB – Optibelt KR – Optibelt P.K. – Optibelt R.B. – Optibelt RB – Optibelt S.K. – Optibelt SK – Optibelt SVX – Optibelt V.B. – Optibelt V.X. – Optibelt VB – Optibelt Z.R. – Optibelt Z.R.M. – Optibelt ZR – Optiblet ZRM – Optichain – Optiflex – Optimat – Optimax*

Optical Filters Unit 13-14 Thame Park Business Centre Wenman Road, Thame OX9 3XA Tel. *01844 260377* Fax. *01844 260355* E-mail. *information@opticalfilters.co.uk* Web. *www.opticalfilters.co.uk P.S.C. – T-Shield*

Optical Tools For Industry Ltd Brickfield Lane Denbigh Road, Ruthin LL15 2TN Tel. *01824 704991* Fax. *01824 705075* E-mail. *john@optical-tools.co.uk* Web. *www.optical-tools.co.uk OTI*

Optikinetics Ltd 38 Cromwell Road, Luton LU3 1DN Tel. *01582 411413* Fax. *01582 400613* E-mail. *phil@optikinetics.com* Web. *www.optikinetics.com Club Strobeflower – GoBoPro – GoBoShow – K4 – Solar 100C – Solar 250 – Solar System – Terrastrobe – Trilite*

Optima Ltd Mill Road, Radstock BA3 5TX Tel. *01761 433461* Fax. *01761 433919* E-mail. *marketing@optima-group.co.uk* Web. *www.optimasystems.com Optima 117 – Optima 217 – Optima 97 – Optima Bi-Panel – Optima Elements – Optima Spacewall*

Optiquality Holdings Ltd 6a Larch Street, Southport PR8 6DP Tel. *01704 538921* Fax. *01704 544132 *Opti (Worldwide) – *Roberto Rossini (Worldwide)*

Opto Electronic Manufacturing Corporation Ltd (t/a OMC UK Ltd) Candela House Cardrew Industrial Estate, Redruth TR15 1SS Tel. *01209 215424* Fax. *01209 215197* E-mail. *heaths@omc-uk.com* Web. *www.omc-uk.com Fibre-Data – L.E.D. Technology – Ledtech Europe – O.M.C. – O.M.C.- Fibredata*

Opto International Ltd Stamford Mill Bayley Street, Stalybridge SK15 1QQ Tel. *0161 3305577* Fax. *0161 3437332* E-mail. *p.moulder@optoint.co.uk* Web. *www.stamford-products.co.uk Opto*

Opus Consultancy Service (An Organisation for Promoting Understanding of Society) 26 Fernhurst Road, London SW6 7JW Tel. *020 77363844* Fax. *020 77363844* E-mail. *director@opus.org.uk* Web. *www.opus.org.uk Opus Consultancy Services – Opus Education & Research*

Opus Energy Ltd Summerhouse Road Moulton Park Industrial Estate, Northampton NN3 6BJ Tel. *08453 302655* E-mail. *contactus@opusenergy.com* Web. *www.opusenergy.co.uk Opus Business Customers – Opus Corporate Solutions*

Opus Windows 166 Collier Row Lane, Romford RM5 3EA Tel. *01708 723131* Fax. *01708 749994* E-mail. *info@opus-windows.co.uk* Web. *www.opus-windows.co.uk Opus*

Orapi Ltd 15 Spring Road, Smethwick B66 1PT Tel. *0121 5254000* Fax. *01274 822002* E-mail. *info@orapiapplied.com* Web. *www.orapi.com Gramos – TAKrag*

Orbinox UK Ltd Orbinox Group Orbinox House 6-7 Clock Park Shripney Road, Bognor Regis PO22 9NH Tel. *01243 810240* Fax. *08702 407469* E-mail. *uk@orbinox.co.uk* Web. *www.orbinox.co.uk Bettis – El-O-Matic – Penta – Somas*

Orbit Developments Emerson House Heyes Lane, Alderley Edge SK9 7LF Tel. *01625 588400* Fax. *01625 585791* E-mail. *info@emeson.co.uk* Web. *www.orbit-developments.co.uk Orbit Developments*

Orbit Distribution Ltd Unit 2 Lymedale Business Centre Hooters Hall Road, Lymedale Business Park, Newcastle ST5 9QF Tel. *01782 564757* Fax. *01782 561089* E-mail. *info@orbitdistribution.co.uk* Web. *www.orbitdistribution.co.uk Orbit Distribution*

Orby Engineering Ltd 26 Seagoe Industrial Area Portadown, Craigavon BT63 5QD Tel. *028 38339145* Fax. *028 38350540* E-mail. *orbyengineering@btconnect.com* Web. *home.btconnect.com/orby-engineering Orby – Orby Ezi-Fit – Orbyveyor*

Orchard Drawing Boards Union Square, Wakefield WF1 1TT Tel. *01924 291333* Fax. *01924 290909* E-mail. *vicky@thebigorchard.com* Web. *www.thebigorchard.com Orchard – Tecnostyl – Planhorse*

Orchestra Wotton Group Ltd Walk Mills Kingswood, Wotton Under Edge GL12 8JT Tel. *01453 843621* Fax. *01453 845019* E-mail. *enquiries@orchestragroup.co.uk* Web. *www.orchestragroup.co.uk Inchbrook Printing Services Ltd*

Organic Concentrates Ltd Hotley Bottom Hotley Bottom Lane, Prestwood, Great Missenden HP16 9PL Tel. *01494 866768* Fax. *01494 867653* E-mail. *organic6x@btconnect.com* Web. *www.6-x.co.uk 6X – 6X Energy Drink*

Orica UK Ltd 4 Stonecrop North Quarry Business Park, Appley Bridge, Wigan WN6 9DL Tel. *01257 256100* Fax. *01257 256166* E-mail. *enquiries@orica.com* Web. *www.orica.com Anobel – Anopril – Betapril – Carrick – Cordtex – Dynagex – Exel – Penobel – Powergel – Sabrex – Super-Ajax – Superflex – Unigel*

Orien Cards LLP 37 LUNDHOLME HEELANDS, Milton Keynes MK13 7QJ Tel. *0845 3519934* Fax. *0845 3519941* E-mail. *cards@oriengroup.co.uk* Web. *www.oriengroup.co.uk ORIEN CARDS*

Original Addidtions Ventura House Bullsbrook Road, Hayes UB4 0UJ Tel. *020 85739907* Fax. *020 85736824* E-mail. *reception@originaladditions.co.uk* Web. *www.originaladditions.co.uk Elegant Touch – Eylure*

Orion Electric UK Co. Ltd Unit 3 Kenfig Industrial Estate, Margam, Port Talbot SA13 2PE Tel. *01656 742400* Fax. *01656 744700* E-mail. *info@orion-electric.co.uk* Web. *www.orion-electric.co.uk Orion*

Orissor Trust Ltd 14 Craigmore Road Rothesay, Isle Of Bute PA20 9LB Tel. *01700 503540* Fax. *01700 505394* E-mail. *admin@orissor.net* Web. *www.orissor.com Isle of Bute Candles – Isle of Bute Jewellery – Orissor – Orissor Productions*

Ormandy Rycroft (a division of BAXI Heating UK Ltd) Duncombe Road, Bradford BD8 9TB Tel. *01274 490911* Fax. *01274 498580* E-mail. *sales@rycroft.com* Web. *www.rycroft.com Autolec – Dunlow – Megatherm*

Orman Risk Analysts 10 Albert Bridge Road, London SW11 4PY Tel. *020 76228645* Fax. *020 74980346* E-mail. *geraldorman@btconnect.com* Web. *www.contrac-texpert.com Orman Risk Analysts*

Steve Orr Ltd 1 Quillyburn Business Park Banbridge Road, Dromore BT25 1BY Tel. *028 92699020* Fax. *028 92699029* E-mail. *info@steve-orr.com* Web. *www.steve-orr.com Blue Moon – Farmers – Harvest Star – Super Star*

Ortak Jewellery Ltd Hatston Hatston Industrial Estate, Kirkwall KW15 1RH Tel. *01856 872224* Fax. *01856 875165* E-mail. *alistair@ortak.co.uk* Web. *www.ortak.co.uk Ortak*

Ortho Europe Ltd Mill Lane, Alton GU34 2PX Tel. *01420 83294* Fax. *01420 80068* E-mail. *info@ortho-europe.co.uk* Web. *www.ortho-europe.co.uk Quantum System*

Orthos Engineering Ltd 2 The Point, Market Harborough LE16 7QU Tel. *01858 464246* Fax. *01858 434480* E-mail. *sales@orthos.uk.com* Web. *www.orthos.uk.com *Alexanderwerk (Germany) – *Brunitec (Sweden) – Diamondback (U.S.A.) – Drais (Germany) – Eirich (Germany) – *Firefly (Sweden) – *Gustafson (U.S.A.) – Inotec (Germany) – Lindor (Netherlands) – Tyco (U.S.A.) – Ventilex (Netherlands) – Vicentini (Italy)*

Orthos Projects Ltd Fernie Road, Market Harborough LE16 7PH Tel. *01858 462806* Fax. *01858 464403* E-mail. *nick.hall@orthosprojects.com* Web. *www.orthosprojects.com Orthos*

Ortlinghaus UK Ltd Unit 19 Sugarbrook Road, Bromsgrove B60 3DN Tel. *01527 579123* Fax. *01527 579077* E-mail. *sales@ortlinghaus.co.uk* Web. *www.ortlinghaus.co.uk Ortlinghaus – Ortlinghaus - brakes, clutches*

Orvec International Ltd Malmo Road, Hull HU7 0YF Tel. *01482 625333* Fax. *01482 625325* E-mail. *service@orvec.com* Web. *www.orvec.com Cover-Ups – Microgard – Orvec*

Osborne Refrigerators Ltd 148 Rose Green Road, Bognor Regis PO21 3EG Tel. *01243 267711* Fax. *01243 265853* E-mail. *sales@osborne-ref.co.uk* Web. *www.osborne-ref.co.uk Osborne*

Osborn Unipol Ltd Dendix House Lower Church Street, Chepstow NP16 5XT Tel. *01291 634000* Fax. *01291 634098* E-mail. *lpainter@osborn-unipol.co.uk* Web. *www.osborn.de AA Rouge – Carbrax – Coolair – Dialux – Finefin – Hyfin – Limpet – Lipprite – Lipprox – Lippryll – Lustre – Scovax – Stapol – Steelbrite – Vonax*

Oscar Press Ltd Potters Lane Kiln Farm, Milton Keynes MK11 3HQ Tel. *01908 260333* Fax. *01908 560223* E-mail. *sales@oscar.uk.com* Web. *www.oscar.uk.com info carte*

Osprey Ltd Unit 12a Pages Industrial Park Eden Way, Leighton Buzzard LU7 4TZ Tel. *01525 851505* Fax. *01525 851501* E-mail. *denise@osprey.co.uk* Web. *www.osprey-plastics.co.uk N.B. Mouldings*

Osprey Deep Clean Ltd 41 Central Way Cheltenham Trade Park, Cheltenham GL51 8LX Tel. *01242 513123* Fax. *01242 518666* E-mail. *info@ospreydc.com* Web. *www.ospreydc.com *Robby*

Osram Ltd PO Box 17, Slough SL3 6EZ Tel. *01744 812221* Fax. *01753 484222* E-mail. *rune.narki@osram.co.uk* Web. *www.osram.co.uk *BELLALUX (France) – *BELLAPHOT (Germany) – *BIOLUX (Germany) – *COMPACTA (Germany and Italy) – *CONCENTRA (France and Germany) – *DEKOLUX (Germany) – DEOS – *FLUORA (Germany) – GIGANT – *H.M.I. (Germany) – *H.T.I. (Germany) – HALOMET – *HALOSTAR (Germany) – HALOTRONIC – *LIMINESTRA (Germany) – LINESTRA – *LUMILUX (Germany) – METALLOGEN – MINIWATT – OPALINA – *OSRAM DULUX (Germany) – *OSRAM GMBH (Germany) – *POWERSTAR (Germany) – SICCATHERM – SUPERLUX – THERATHERM – ULTRA-VITALUX – ULTRAMED – *VIALUX (Germany and UK) – *XENOPHOT (Germany)*

O S R International Ltd 361-365 Moseley Road, Birmingham B12 9DE Tel. *0121 4403655* Fax. *0121 4464183* E-mail. *info@osrinternational.com* Web. *www.osrinternational.com Babybasics – Blueblur – Clever Cloggs – Kool N Krazy Gang – *Little Aristocrat (Portugal and The Far East)*

Oswald Bailey Group 72-74 Palmerston Road, Bournemouth BH1 4JT Tel. *01202 397273* Fax. *01202 397274* E-mail. *sales@oswaldbailey.co.uk* Web. *www.oswaldbailey.co.uk Ozzie*

Otis Ltd 187 Twyford Abbey Road, London NW10 7DG Tel. *020 89553000* Fax. *020 89553001* E-mail. *lindsay.harvey@otis.com* Web. *www.otis.com Otis – Trav-O-Lator*

Otterburn Mills Ltd Otterburn, Newcastle Upon Tyne NE19 1JT Tel. *01830 520225* Fax. *01830 520032* E-mail. *mailorder@otterburnlife.co.uk* Web. *www.otterburnlife.com Otterburn*

Otter Controls Ltd Hardwick Square South, Buxton SK17 6LA Tel. *01298 762300* Fax. *01298 72664* E-mail. *sales@ottercontrols.com* Web. *www.ottercontrols.com Castlestat – Dualstat – Fanstat – Jugstat – Otter Controls Ltd – Otterguard – Otterstat – Plugstat – Singlestat – Steamstat – Vapourstat – Wiperstat*

Otto Bock Healthcare plc 32 Parsonage Road Englefield Green, Egham TW20 0LD Tel. *01784 744900* Fax. *01784 744901* E-mail. *philip.yates@ottobock.com* Web. *www.ottobock.co.uk *Myobock (Germany) – *Orthocryl (Germany) – *Otto Bock (Germany) – *Pedilan (Germany) – *Pedilen (Germany) – *Pedilin (Germany) – *Pedilon (Germany)*

Ottoman Textiles Ltd 4 Alexandra Trading Estate Alexandra Road, Denton, Manchester M34 3DX Tel. *0161 3207644* Fax. *0161 3203747* E-mail. *info@ottomantextiles.com* Web. *www.ottomantextiles.com Comfortable Options – Easycomfort*

Out Board Unit 4a Church Meadows Haslingfield Road, Barrington, Cambridge CB22 7RG Tel. *01223 871015* Fax. *01223 208190* E-mail. *info@outboard.co.uk* Web. *www.outboard.co.uk O.B.*

Outside In Designs UK Ltd Phoenix House London Road, Corwen LL21 0DR Tel. *01490 413322* Fax. *01490 413336* E-mail. *mail@westmeters.co.uk* Web. *www.westmeters.co.uk West Meters*

Outsource Ireland Ltd 30 Market Street, Omagh BT78 1EH Tel. *07590 367207* E-mail. *sales@outsourceireland.co.uk* Web. *www.outsourceireland.co.uk Outsource Ireland*

Ovako Ltd Unit 2 Yorks Park Blowers Green Road, Dudley DY2 8UL Tel. *01384 213940* E-mail. *graham.butler@ovako.com* Web. *www.ovaka.com *280 Hollow Bar (Sweden) – *Ceax (Sweden) – *E.T.G. (Switzerland)*

Overland Leisure & Caravans 263 Main Street, Larbert FK5 4PX Tel. *01324 554131* Fax. *01324 563165* E-mail. *graeme@overlandcaravans.co.uk* Web. *www.overlandcaravans.co.uk Overland kincardine*

Ovivo UK Ltd Kennicott House Well Lane, Wolverhampton WV11 1XR Tel. *01902 721212* Fax. *01902 721333* E-mail. *info.uk@ovivowater.com* Web. *www.ovivowater.com Aquapac – Conesep – CPP – Hero – R.O – UV*

Owen & Palmer Ltd Unit 12 Llandygai Industrial Estate Llandygai, Bangor LL57 4YH Tel. *01248 353515* Fax. *01248 353736* E-mail. *accounts@owenandpalmer.co.uk* Web. *www.opalcom.co.uk Opal computors*

O W L Electronics Ltd PO Box 1330, Tamworth B77 1AW Tel. *08456 430212* Fax. *01827 60579* E-mail. *info@o-w-l.co.uk* Web. *www.o-w-l.co.uk Back Sounder – BigMouth – BikeMinder – MoveAway – Powersaver – Quevebuster – SalesTalk – Stentor – VendaGuard – Voice-on-Hold*

Owlett Jaton Regus House Victory Way, Crossways Business Park, Dartford DA2 6QD Tel. *01322 277733* Fax. *01322 288043* E-mail. *dartford.sales@owlett-jaton.com* Web. *www.owlett-jaton.com T.Q. – T.Q. Anker-u-fix – T.Q. Ankercoach – T.Q. Ankerdriva-screw – T.Q. Ankerframe – T.Q. Ankerhammer – T.Q. Ankerit – T.Q. Ankermasonry-nail – T.Q. Ankerplasta-Screw – T.Q. Ankerplug – T.Q. Ankerset – T.Q. Ankershield – T.Q. Ankersleeve – T.Q. Ankertog –*

T.Q. Ankerwindow – T.Q. Euroscrew – T.Q. Fastascrew – T.Q. Keypsafe – T.Q. Plusdriv – T.Q. Polypak – T.Q. TwinQwik

Owl House Fruit Farm Mount Pleasant Lamberhurst, Tunbridge Wells TN3 8LY Tel. *01892 890553* Fax. *01892 890370* E-mail. *ccorfield@aol.com* Web. *www.owletfruitjuice.co.uk *Owlet Apple Juice*

Owon Technology Ltd 69 Studfold, Chorley PR7 1UA Tel. *0845 0508168* Fax. *0845 0508169* E-mail. *info@owon.co.uk* Web. *www.owon.co.uk OWON*

Oxbridge Old Fruiterers Yard Osney Mead, Oxford OX2 0ES Tel. *01865 246510* Fax. *01865 794305* E-mail. *oxbridge@btconnect.com Bulldog – Oxbridge*

The Oxford Duplication Centre 29 Banbury Road, Kidlington OX5 1AQ Tel. *01865 457000* E-mail. *info@theduplicationcentre.co.uk* Web. *www.theduplicationcentre.co.uk The Oxford Duplication Centre*

Oxford Innovation Ltd Oxford Centre For Innovation New Road, Oxford OX1 1BY Tel. *01865 261480* Fax. *01865 261401* E-mail. *enquiries@oxin.co.uk* Web. *www.oxin.co.uk Oxford Innovation*

Oxford Instruments Tubney Wood, Abingdon OX13 5QX Tel. *01865 393200* Fax. *01865 393333* E-mail. *plasma.technology@oxinst.co.uk* Web. *www.oxford-instruments.com Ionfab 300 Series – Ionfab 500 Series – Plasma Technology – Plasmalab*

Oxford Lasers Ltd Moorbrook Park, Didcot OX11 7HP Tel. *01235 810088* Fax. *01235 810060* E-mail. *alan.ferguson@oxfordlasers.com* Web. *www.oxfordlasers.com Visisizer*

Oxford Law & Computing Ltd Tatham House Northcourt Lane, Abingdon OX14 1PN Tel. *01235 203690* Fax. *01235 553379* E-mail. *rjb@oxfordlaw.co.uk* Web. *www.oxfordlaw.co.uk Openlaw*

Oxford Neckties Oxford Houseunit 6, Bristol BS15 9GE Tel. *0871 9960323* Fax. *0871 9960502* E-mail. *sales@ehomeshopper.biz* Web. *www.ehomeshopper.biz oxford neckties*

Oxford Software (a division of Applied Systems (Oxford) Ltd) Clockhouse Barn Sugworth Lane, Radley, Abingdon OX14 2HX Tel. *0845 1300332* Fax. *0845 1300334* E-mail. *enquiry@oxfordsoftware.com* Web. *www.oxfordsoftware.com supplied systems*

Oxley Developments Company Ltd Priory Park, Ulverston LA12 9QG Tel. *01229 582621* Fax. *01229 585090* E-mail. *sales@oxleygroup.com* Web. *www.oxleygroup.com Barb conelock – Ceramox – E-Tag – Ezeled – Kinky pin – Microslim – NVG Friendly – Rotox – Smox – Snale – Snaplox – Survivolite*

Oxoid Holdings Ltd Wade Road Kingsland Industrial Park, Basingstoke RG24 8PW Tel. *01256 841144* Fax. *01256 463388* E-mail. *oxoid@oxoid.com* Web. *www.oxoid.com Oxoid – Signal*

Oxon Fastening Systems Ltd Academic House Oakfield Industrial Estate, Eynsham, Witney OX29 4AJ Tel. *01865 884022* Fax. *01865 884033* E-mail. *dave@oxonfasteningsystems.ltd.uk* Web. *www.oxonfasteningsystems.ltd.uk Bosch – Dewalt – Elektrabeckum – Hitachi – Makita – Metabo – Milwalkee – Panasonic – Ryobi*

P

Pacer Components plc Unit 4 Horseshoe Park Pangbourne, Reading RG8 7JW Tel. *0118 9845280* Fax. *0118 9845425* E-mail. *graham_rothon@pacer.co.uk* Web. *www.pacer.co.uk Pacer Components*

Pacet Manufacturing Ltd Wyebridge House Cores End Road, Bourne End SL8 5HH Tel. *01628 526754* Fax. *01628 810080* E-mail. *sales@pacet.co.uk* Web. *www.pacet.co.uk Pacet*

Pacific Solutions International Ltd Bordesley Hall The Holloway, Alvechurch, Birmingham B48 7QA Tel. *08450 589686* Fax. *01252 846333* E-mail. *support@pacsol.co.uk* Web. *www.pacsol.co.uk Coldpoint (United Kingdom) – FileMagic (U.S.A.) – Fortis (U.S.A.) – Fortis ERM (U.S.A.) – PowerWeb (U.S.A.) – Q Flow (United Kingdom) – Viewpoint (United Kingdom) – Webpoint (United Kingdom)*

Package Boiler Services Ltd Back Forshaw Street, Warrington WA2 7HH Tel. *01925 411937* Fax. *01925 418268* E-mail. *boden.j@sky.com Therma-Stak*

Packaged Ice Co. Ltd Dock Avenue, Fleetwood FY7 6NN Tel. *01253 873249* Fax. *01253 777752* E-mail. *frank@party-ice.co.uk* Web. *www.fyldecoldstores.co.uk Party Ice*

Packaging Products Ltd Collyhurst Road, Manchester M40 7RT Tel. *0161 2054181* Fax. *0161 2034678* E-mail. *sales@packagingproducts.co.uk* Web. *www.packagingproducts.co.uk Blond Coat – Blond Union – Kraftex*

Packaging Team Ltd Venture House Arlington Square Downshire Way, Bracknell RG12 1WA Tel. *08450 941791* E-mail. *enquiries@packagingteam.com* Web. *www.packagingteam.com PackagingTeam*

Sydney Packett & Sons Ltd Salts Wharfashley Lane, Shipley BD17 7DB Tel. *01274 206500* Fax. *01274 206506* E-mail. *mail@packetts.com* Web. *www.packetts.com Sydney Packett (Life & Pensions) – Sydney Packett and Sons*

PACK Innovation Ltd Unit 12, Sunfield Business Park New Mill Road, WOKINGHAM RG40 4QT Tel. *05603 449162* Fax. *05603 449163* E-mail. *info@packinnovation.com* Web. *www.packinnovation.com EasySnap*

Paddock Fabrications Ltd Fryers Road, Walsall WS2 7LZ Tel. *01922 711722* Fax. *01922 476021* E-mail. *sales@paddockfabrications.co.uk* Web. *www.paddockfabrications.co.uk Classic – Flapmaster – Glidebolt – Lockmaster – Paddock – Postmaster – Proton – Quantum – Slimaster – Sprint*

Padgett Bros A To Z Ltd Darton Business Park Barnsley Road, Darton, Barnsley S75 5QX Tel. *01226 381188* Fax. *01226 388855* E-mail. *info@padgettatoz.co.uk* Web. *www.padgettatoz.co.uk I Hate School – Skidder*

Padley & Venables Ltd Callywhite Lane, Dronfield S18 2XT Tel. *01246 299100* Fax. *01246 290354* E-mail. *darren.bradwell@padley-venables.com* Web. *www.padley-venables.com P&V (United Kingdom)*

Paella Co. Ltd Lodge Farm Hook Road North Warnborough, Hook RG29 1HA Tel. *01256 702020* Fax. *01256 703086* E-mail. *info@thepaellacompany.co.uk* Web. *www.thepaellacompany.co.uk Garcima Paella Pans*

Pa Finlay & Company Ltd 8 Gemini Business Park Hornet Way, London E6 7FF Tel. *020 75406450* Fax. *020 85347652* E-mail. *hugh.finlay@pa-finlay.co.uk* Web. *www.pa-finlay.co.uk P.A. Finlay & Co.*

P A G Ltd 565 Kingston Road, London SW20 8SA Tel. *020 85433131* Fax. *020 85404797* E-mail. *sales@paguk.com* Web. *www.paguk.com Analyser – Pag ACS – Pag AR Series – Pag Belt – Pag Light – Pag LOK – Pag Pac – Pag RTI*

Page Bros Norwich Ltd Mile Cross Lane, Norwich NR6 6SA Tel. *01603 778800* Fax. *01603 778801* E-mail. *sales@pagebros.co.uk* Web. *www.pagebros.co.uk Microcreation*

Page Systems 2 Corn Hill Conisbrough, Doncaster DN12 2BG Tel. *01709 863384* E-mail. *pagesystems@btinternet.com* Web. *page-systems.co.uk Texecom*

Paineman Waring Easting Close, Worthing BN14 8HQ Tel. *01903 237522* Fax. *01903 236511* E-mail. *robert@painemanwaring.co.uk* Web. *www.painemanwaring.co.uk Paine Manwaring*

Pains Wessex Ltd Chemring House 1500 Parkway, Whiteley, Fareham PO15 7AF Tel. *01489 884130* Fax. *01489 884131* E-mail. *info@chemringmarine.com* Web. *www.pwss.com Buoylite L41 – Buoysmoke – Handsmoke – Lifesmoke – Manoverboard – Miniflare – Pains-Wessex – Para Red – Pinpoint – Schermuly – Speedline*

Painter Bros Ltd Holmer Road, Hereford HR4 9SW Tel. *01432 374400* Fax. *01432 374427* E-mail. *enquiries@painterbrothers.com* Web. *www.painterbrothers.com Callender-Hamilton – P.U. Poles*

Pakawaste Rough Hey Road Grimsargh, Preston PR2 5AR Tel. *01772 654348* Fax. *01772 792474* E-mail. *sales@pakawaste.co.uk* Web. *www.pakawaste.co.uk Powerkube – Powerkube Plus – Powerkube XL*

Pak Nylon Hosiery Co. 31 Broughton Street, Manchester M8 8LZ Tel. *0161 8327371* Fax. *0161 8395134* E-mail. *c_m_afzal_khan@hotmail.co.uk* Web. *www.paknylon.co.uk DG by Dancing Girl – Pretty Polly, Aristoc, Elbeo, Golden Lady, Cindy*

Palace Chemicals Ltd Unit 49 Spindus Road Speke Hall Industrial Estate, Liverpool L24 1YA Tel. *0151 4866101* Fax. *0151 4481982* E-mail. *sales@palacechemicals.co.uk* Web. *www.palacechemicals.co.uk Palace*

Paladon Systems Ltd Ferro Fields Brixworth, Northampton NN6 9UA Tel. *01604 880700* Fax. *01224 772868* E-mail. *matthew.shepherd@paladonsystems.com* Web. *www.paladonsystems.com Bettis (United Kingdom)*

Palagan Ltd Tavistock Street, Dunstable LU6 1NE Tel. *01582 600234* Fax. *01582 601636* E-mail. *sales@palagan.co.uk* Web. *www.palagan.co.uk Palastrong*

Palatine Precision Ltd Airport Industrial Estate 45 Laker Road, Rochester ME1 3QX Tel. *01634 684571* Fax. *01634 200836* E-mail. *sales@palatineprecision.co.uk* Web. *www.palatineprecision.co.uk Hi-Presflex*

Palco Industries Ltd Palco House 11 Beavor Lane, London W6 9AR Tel. *020 87411222* Fax. *020 87419116* Web. *www.palco.co.uk Handibags – Handle-Tie – Slingits – Ultra*

Pal International Ltd Bilton Way, Lutterworth LE17 4JA Tel. *01455 555700* Fax. *01455 555777* E-mail. *info@palinternational.com* Web. *www.palinternational.com La Toque Blanche – Pal*

Palintest Ltd Halma Group Kingsway Team Valley Trading Estate, Gateshead NE11 0NS Tel. *0191 4910808* Fax. *0191 4825372* E-mail. *sales@palintest.com* Web. *www.palintest.com Alkaphot – Alkavis – Colilert – Coppercol – Magnecol – Nitricol – Palintest – Tubetest*

Palletower GB Ltd Dane Road Industrial Estate, Sale M33 7BH Tel. *0161 9052233* Fax. *0161 9720922* E-mail. *info@palletower.com* Web. *www.palletower.co.uk Hypacage – Palletower – Palletruck – Retention Units – Toweracks*

Pall Europe Corporate Services Europa House Havant Street, Portsmouth PO1 3PD Tel. *023 92303303* Fax. *023 92302506* E-mail. *info@pall.com* Web. *www.pall.com Biodyne – Centrisep – Claris – Deltadyne – Deltalog – Deltasense – Dirt-Fuse – Emflon – Epocel – Filseal – Nexis – P.S.S. – Pall – Poly-Fine XLD – Posidyne – Profile – Rigimesh – Rotolok – Sealkleen – Supramesh – Ultipleat – Ultipor*

Palmer Agencies Ltd Unit 1 Beechill Business Park 96 Beechill Road, Belfast BT8 7QN Tel. *028 90647119* Fax. *028 90645655* E-mail. *brent@palmeragencies.com* Web. *www.palmeragencies.com Angel Hair – *Cesar (France) – Crazy String – *Festival (Netherlands) – Fun World – *Papillon (Italy) – Partygear*

Palmer & Harvey Ltd 11 Barnes Wallis Road, Fareham PO15 5TT Tel. *01489 555800* Fax. *01489 555883* E-mail. *graham.barton@palmerharvey.co.uk* Web. *www.palmerharvey.co.uk Palmers – Palmers Industrial Services*

Palram Europe Ltd Unit 2 Doncaster Carr Industrial Estate White Rose Way, Doncaster DN4 5JH Tel. *01302 344121* Fax. *01302 344121* E-mail. *steve.shore@palram.com* Web. *www.palram.com Sun Lite – Pal Sun – Pal Shield – Palight – Pal Gard – Pal Opaque – Pal Door – Sun Tuf – Pal Glas – Sun Top – Sun Opak – Pal Clear – Pal Ruf – Pal Bond*

Pama & Co. Ltd Pama House Stockport Road East, Bredbury, Stockport SK6 2AA Tel. *0161 4944245* Fax. *0161 4944231* E-mail. *i.farshi@pama.co.uk* Web. *www.pama.com PAMA, COBRA, KRUSELL, BLUETOOTH, PLUG N GO*

Pamargan Products Ltd (Pamargan Products Ltd) Unit 47 Mochdre Industrial Estate, Mochdre, Newtown SY16 4LE Tel. *01686 625181* Fax. *01686 627849* E-mail. *sales@pamargan.com* Web. *www.pamargan.com Pamargan Products*

Pamma Rugs 25-29 Northgate, Bradford BD1 3JR Tel. *01274 739505* Fax. *01274 739505* E-mail. *sales@pammarugs.com* Web. *www.pammarugs.com Pamma Rugs*

panache interiors Crowthorns School Lane, Childer Thornton, Ellesmere Port CH66 5PL Tel. *0151 3397134* Fax. *0151 3397134* E-mail. *rachelhunt@iloveinteriordesign.co.uk* Web. *www.iloveinteriordesign.co.uk Panache Interiors*

Panache Lingerie 7 Drake House Crescent Waterthorpe, Sheffield S20 7HT Tel. *0114 2418888* Fax. *0114 2418889* E-mail. *info@panache-lingerie.com* Web. *www.panache-lingerie.com Panache – Panache Atlantis – Panache Special Occasions – Panache Sport – Panache Superbra – Panache Swimwear*

Panaf & Company Unit 5 Swanbridge Industrial Park Black Croft Road, Witham CM8 3YN Tel. *01376 511550* Fax. *01376 515131* E-mail. *info@panaf.co.uk* Web. *www.lrspareparts.com L R spare Parts – P & C*

Panalpina World Transport Ltd Great South West Road, Feltham TW14 8NE Tel. *020 85879000* Fax. *020 85879200* E-mail. *info@panalpina.com* Web. *www.panalpina.com Panalpina*

Panalux Ltd Sunset Business Park Manchester Road, Kearsley, Bolton BL4 8RL Tel. *01204 794000* Fax. *0117 9235745* E-mail. *info@panalux.biz* Web. *www.panalux.biz Lee Lighting*

Panasonic Electric Works Sunrise Parkway Linford Wood, Milton Keynes MK14 6LF Tel. *01908 231555* Fax. *01908 231599* E-mail. *r.thornton@eu.pewg.panasonic.com* Web. *www.panasonic-electric-works.co.uk Aromat – Matsushita – N.A.I.S. – National – S.D.S-Relais*

Panavision Grips Ltd The Metropolitan Centre Bristol Road, Greenford UB6 8UD Tel. *020 88397333* Fax. *020 88397360* E-mail. *enquiries@panavision.co.uk* Web. *www.panavision.co.uk Boomslang – Fraser Dolly – *Giraffe Classic (South Africa) – Grip House – Long-roger Giraffe – Python – *Supertechno (Germany)*

Panaz Ltd Spring Mill 422 Wheatley Lane Road, Fence, Burnley BB12 9HP Tel. *01282 696969* Fax. *01282 611519* E-mail. *admin@panaz.co.uk* Web. *www.panaz.co.uk Panaz*

Pandect Instrument Laboratories Ltd Wellington Road Cressex Business Park, High Wycombe HP12 3PX Tel. *01494 526301* Fax. *01494 464503* E-mail. *rodney.pope@pandect.co.uk* Web. *www.pandect.co.uk Pandect Instrument Laboratories*

Pandet Ltd 1 Premier Drum Works Canal Street, Wigston LE18 4PL Tel. *0116 2772372* Fax. *0116 2772672* E-mail. *sales@kuroma.com* Web. *www.kuroma.com Kuroma*

Panelcraft Access Panels Unit H The Pavilons, Abeles Way, Holly Lane Industrial Estate, Atherstone CV9 2QZ Tel. *01827 720830* Fax. *01827 720860* E-mail. *sales@panelcraftaccesspanels.com* Web. *www.panelcraftaccesspanels.com Discpan (United Kingdom) – Slimpan (United Kingdom) – Tilepan (United Kingdom) – Loftpan (United Kingdom) – Plasticpan (United Kingdom) – Firepan (United Kingdom) – Tradpan (United Kingdom) – Firepan Magna (United Kingdom) – Plastapan (United Kingdom)*

Panel Systems Ltd Unit 3-9 Welland Close, Sheffield S3 9QY Tel. *0114 2752881* Fax. *0114 2768807* E-mail. *sales@panelsystems.co.uk*

Web. *www.panelsystems.co.uk Aluglaze – Decalux – Insuglaze – Meleto – Styroclad – Styrofloor – Styroglaze – Styroliner – Vitraglaze*

Panema Trailer Engineering Ltd Chalk Lane Snetterton, Norwich NR16 2JZ Tel. *01953 887622* Fax. *01953 888515* E-mail. *info@panematrailers.co.uk* Web. *www.panematrailers.co.uk Pan Hire – Panema – Pantrak*

Pangea Ltd 185 Oxford Road Calne, Chippenham SN15 1EN Tel. *01249 462677* Fax. *01249 463841* E-mail. *sales@pangeauk.com* Web. *www.pangeauk.com Pangea Iron Oxides*

The Paper Company Ltd 217 Maclellen Street Kinning Park, Glasgow G41 1RR Tel. *0141 4279900* Fax. *0141 4279911* E-mail. *sales@donaldmurray.co.uk* Web. *www.paperco.co.uk Bunzl Fine Paper – Crusade – Europoint – Harlequin – Rapid Reel*

Paperchase 213-215 Tottenham Court Road, London W1T 7PN Tel. *020 74676200* Fax. *020 76361322* E-mail. *timothy@paperchase.co.uk* Web. *www.paperchase.co.uk Paperchase*

Paperchasers Ltd Logistics House, Birmingham B28 9HL Tel. *08456 344170* Fax. *08456 344170* E-mail. *sales@paperchasers.biz* Web. *www.paperchasers.biz Ethical office recycling*

Paper Flow Ltd Unit 5-6 Meridian Trading Estate Bugsby's Way, London SE7 7SJ Tel. *020 83312000* Fax. *020 83312001* E-mail. *sales@paperflowonline.com* Web. *www.useonesource.com Paperflow*

Papersticks Ltd Govett Avenue, Shepperton TW17 8AB Tel. *01932 228491* Fax. *01932 242828* E-mail. *sales@papersticks.co.uk* Web. *www.papersticks.co.uk Lollipop Safety Stick – Papersticks – Plasticsticks*

Paperun Group Of Companies 1 East Barnet Road, Barnet EN4 8RR Tel. *020 84474141* Fax. *020 84474241* E-mail. *paperun@paper4u.com* Web. *www.paperun.com Art Americaine – Bulkigloss – Diamondstar – Ice Queen – Polar – Printers Choice*

Paragon Group UK Ltd Pallion Trading Estate, Sunderland SR4 6ST Tel. *0191 5140716* Fax. *0191 5671842* E-mail. *ukenquiries@paragonuk.com* Web. *www.paragon-europe.com Notestix – Pressure Seal – Rediform – Speedi-Copies – Speedi-Memos – Speedibook – SpeediForm – Speedilabel – Speedimailer – Speediseal – Speediset – Speediweb*

Paragon Products UK Ltd 8 Newhailes Industrial Estate Newhailes Road, Musselburgh EH21 6SY Tel. *0131 6532222* Fax. *0131 6532272* E-mail. *sales@paragononline.co.uk* Web. *www.paragononline.co.uk Paragon Products, Paragon Hygiene Specialists*

paramelt Cowling Road, Chorley PR6 9DR Tel. *01257 274232* Fax. *01257 275333* E-mail. *info@paramelt.com* Web. *www.paramelt.com Aquaseal – Aquatack – Astor – Cartokote – Dextrol – Dextrolin – Dicera – Dijell – Dynol – Enzieflex – Excelta – Ferumelt – Kartofix – Mycroply – Nowax – Okerin – Paracera – Paracoat – Paradip – Paraflex – Paramelt – Plasticote – Plastoflex – Plastomelt – Properseal – Rheogel – Syncera*

Paramount Knitwear Leicester Ltd Unit 22a Centurion Way Meridian Business Park, Leicester LE19 1WH Tel. *0116 2630044* Fax. *0116 2630101* E-mail. *sales@paramountknitwear.com* Web. *www.paramountknitwear.com Lexy Collection – Paramour*

Parasene Allfor House Hayes Lane, Stourbridge DY9 8QT Tel. *01384 898911* Fax. *01384 899100* E-mail. *jpc@bretshaweltex.com* Web. *www.parasene.com *Bacaware (United Kingdom) – *Bretshaw (United Kingdom) – *Eltex (United Kingdom) – *Rocar (United Kingdom)*

Parcels To Ireland Lawford Road, Rugby CV21 2UY Tel. *01788 542500* Fax. *01788 550896* E-mail. *christopher.putt@parcelstoireland.co.uk* Web. *www.parcelstoireland.co.uk Parcels to Ireland*

Pareto Golf Ltd Unit 25 Aston Cross Business Centre 19 Wainwright Street, Birmingham B6 5TH Tel. *0121 3259100* Fax. *0121 3259220* Web. *www.paretogolf.co.uk Driving force leisure – Epic – Heritage fairway – *Par Aide (Canada) – Pareto (United Kingdom) – Pattisson – Penfold – Sheerwater leisure*

Parex Ltd Abeles Way Holly Lane Industrial Estate, Atherstone CV9 2QZ Tel. *01827 711755* Fax. *01827 711330* E-mail. *enquiries@parex.co.uk* Web. *www.parex.co.uk Davment – Tec Cote – Tec Roc Eprorange – TecEtch – TecFast – TecFix – TecFlor – TecFlow – TecGrip – TecGrout – TecPatch – TecRoc – TecRoc Appleby*

Parexel M M S Europe Ltd Wicker House High Street, Worthing BN11 1DJ Tel. *01903 288000* Fax. *01903 234862* E-mail. *info@parexel-mms.com* Web. *www.parexel-mms.com Parexel MMS*

Parker New Courtwick Lane Wick, Littlehampton BN17 7PD Tel. *01903 737000* Fax. *01903 737100* E-mail. *peter.vos@parker.com* Web. *www.parker.com (Shackleton System Drives) SSD – Eurotherm Drives – Link 2 – Quadraloc*

Parker Dominic Hunter Ltd (Industrial Division) Dukesway Team Valley Trading Estate, Gateshead NE11 0PZ Tel. *0191 4029000* Fax. *0191 4826296* E-mail. *sales@dominichunter.com* Web. *www.dominichunter.com ASYPOR – Bevpor – BIO-X – D.H. Dryfil – D.H. Puredri – Domnick Hunter – FILTERPAC – HIGHFLOW TETPOR – Mist-X – NITROX – NYPOR – OIL-X – PEPLYN – PNEUDRI – TURBOSEP – VALAIR DATA*

Parker & Farr Furniture Ltd 75 Derby Road Bramcote, Nottingham NG9 3GY Tel. *0115 9252131* Fax. *0115 9683129* E-mail. *sales@parkerandfarr.co.uk* Web. *www.parkerandfarr.co.uk Parker & Farr*

Parker Hannifin Ltd 1 Treleigh Industrial Estate Jon Davey Drive, Redruth TR16 4AX Tel. *01209 712712* Fax. *01209 713579* E-mail. *parkerpneumatic@parker.com* Web. *www.parker.com Auximax – Isomax – Maxam – Micromax – Optima – Pneumaid – Polylog – Qube – Technomax*

Parker Hannifin Tachbrook Park Drive, Warwick CV34 6TU Tel. *01926 317878* Fax. *01926 889172* E-mail. *nigel_judd@parker.com* Web. *www.parker.com Hiross – Zander*

Parker Hannifin UK plc (Climate & Industrial Controls Group) Walkmill Lane, Cannock WS11 0LR Tel. *01543 456000* Fax. *01543 456001* E-mail. *parkercicgroup@parker.com* Web. *www.parker.com Byron – Gold Ring – Lucifer – Refrigerating Specialties – Sinclair Collins – Skinner*

Parker Hannisin plc 66 Wakefield Road, Ossett WF5 9JS Tel. *01924 282200* Fax. *01924 282299* E-mail. *info@parker.com* Web. *www.parker.com Abex-Denison – Calzoni – Denison Hydraulics – Dusterloh – Hagglunds-Denison*

Parker International Ltd Globe Works Globe Lane, Dukinfield SK16 4RE Tel. *0161 3307421* Fax. *0161 3392653* E-mail. *info@parkerinternational.co.uk* Web. *www.parkerinternational.co.uk Parker Packaging – Warehousing Storage*

Parker Merchanting Ltd 4 Horton Industrial Park Horton Road, West Drayton UB7 8JD Tel. *01895 444040* Fax. *01895 420036* E-mail. *pparker.nationalsales@parkermerchanting.co.uk* Web. *www.parker-merchanting.com Defiance – eski*

Parker Merchanting Ltd Depot 74 Liverpool Street, Salford M5 4QP Tel. *08451 202454* Fax. *0161 7457152* E-mail. *info.parker@hagemeyer.co.uk* Web. *www.parker-direct.com Defiance – eski*

Parker Merchanting Ltd Chester Street Aston, Birmingham B6 4AE Tel. *0121 5034500* Fax. *0121 5034501* E-mail. *info.parker@hagemeyer.co.uk* Web. *www.parker-merchanting.com Defiance – eski*

Parker Merchanting Ltd John O Gaunts Trading Estate Leeds Road, Rothwell, Leeds LS26 0DU Tel. *08451 202454* Fax. *0121 5034501* E-mail. *pclarney@parker-merchanting.co.uk* Web. *www.parker-merchanting.com Defiance – Eski – Protective & site equipment manufrs*

Parker Merchanting Ltd (Depot) Unit 1-3 Garonor Way Portbury, Bristol BS20 7XE Tel. *08451 202454* Fax. *01275 375050* E-mail. *info.parker@hagemeyer.co.uk Defiance – eski*

Parker Merchanting Ltd J Guild Trading Estate Ribbleton Lane, Preston PR1 5DP Tel. *01772 796939* Fax. *01772 793138* E-mail. *info.parker@hagemeyer.co.uk* Web. *www.parker-merchanting.com Defiance – eski*

Parker Merchanting Ltd Cofton Road Marsh Barton Trading Estate, Exeter EX2 8QW Tel. *01392 288900* Fax. *01392 288901* E-mail. *info.parker@hagemeyer.co.uk* Web. *www.parker-direct.com Defiance – eski*

Parker Merchanting Ltd Larkfield Trading Estate New Hythe Lane, Larkfield, Aylesford ME20 6XQ Tel. *08451 202454* Fax. *01622 719222* E-mail. *info.parker@hagemeyer.co.uk* Web. *www.parker-direct.com Defiance – eski*

Parker Plant Ltd Viaduct Works Canon Street, Leicester LE4 6GH Tel. *0116 2665999* Fax. *0116 2681254* E-mail. *info@parkerplant.com* Web. *www.parkerplant.com Cone Ranger – Crush-Ranger – Hunter – Kubitizer – Kubitranger – Loadascreen – Mass-Sieve – N.C. Conveyor – Q.L. Conveyor – Rapide – Rock-Ranger – Rock-Sledger – Rocksizer – Sandor – Sandowheel – Screenranger – Sledger-Kubit – Spot-Mix – Stonesizer – Super Blackmobile – Superloadascreen – Trackranger – Transmix – Waterscreen*

Park Farm Design 5 Park Farm Main Street, Carlton-On-Trent, Newark NG23 6NW Tel. *01636 822221* E-mail. *info@parkfarmdesign.co.uk* Web. *www.parkfarmdesign.co.uk Sunflex Folding Sliding Doors – Sunflex Sliding Door – Oslo Lift and Slide – Sunflex*

Park Group plc 1 Valley Road, Birkenhead CH41 7ED Tel. *0151 6531700* Fax. *0151 6535416* E-mail. *peter.johnson@parkgroup.co.uk* Web. *www.parkdirect.co.uk Country Hamper – Highstreet Vouchers – Park Hampers*

Parkheath 8a Canfield Gardens, London NW6 3BS Tel. *020 76254567* Fax. *020 73272033* E-mail. *info@parkheath.com* Web. *www.parkheath.com Parkheath Estates*

Park Lane News Ltd Unit 5, Sunderland SR1 3NX Tel. *0191 5676925* Fax. *0191 5673714 Marco (United Kingdom) – Raffletech (United Kingdom)*

Parklines Buildings Ltd Gala House 3 Raglan Road, Birmingham B5 7RA Tel. *0121 4466030* Fax. *0121 4465991* E-mail. *sales@parklines.co.uk* Web. *www.parklines.co.uk Parkline*

Park Street People Ltd 12 Park Street, Windsor SL4 1LU Tel. *01753 830706* Fax. *01753 831298* E-mail. *windsor@parkstreetpeople.com* Web. *www.parkstreetpeople.com World Is Your Oyster, The*

Parkway Marine 202 Sandbanks Road, Poole BH14 8HA Tel. *01202 745568* Fax. *01202 742978* E-mail. *sales@parkwaymarine.co.uk* Web. *www.parkwaymarine.co.uk Parkway*

Parkway Plant Sales Ltd Bredbury Park Way Bredbury Bredbury, Stockport SK6 2SN Tel. *01942 684804* Fax. *0161 4946333* E-mail. *ian.wood@parkway-plant.co.uk* Web. *www.parkwayplantsales.com Kramer Allrad – Lifton Dumpers – Messersi Tracked Carriers – Takeuchi Mini Excavators – Tracker Vehicle Recovery Systems*

Parmeko plc Percy Road, Leicester LE2 8FT Tel. *0116 2440044* Fax. *0116 2440000* E-mail. *info@parmeko.co.uk* Web. *www.parmeko.co.uk Parmeko*

Parmelee Ltd PO Box 9 Middlemore Lane West, Walsall WS9 8DZ Tel. *01922 457421* Fax. *01922 473275* E-mail. *gary@parmelee-safety.com* Web. *www.parmelee-safety.com Arrago – Arriva – Cushionflex – Matrix – Maxfit – Mirada – Parmask – Phoenix – S.A.F.I. – Saf-Twist – Stylsafe*

Parquip Of Somerset Unit 1 Monument View Summerfield Avenue, Chelston Business Park, Wellington TA21 9ND Tel. *01823 669205* Fax. *01823 669205* E-mail. *sales@parquip.co.uk* Web. *www.parquip.co.uk Click Workwear – Indequip – Merlett*

Partech Electronics Ltd Charlestown Road, St Austell PL25 3NN Tel. *01726 879800* Fax. *01726 879801* E-mail. *info@partech.co.uk* Web. *www.partech.co.uk Partech Electronics – Turbi-Tech*

Partex Marking Systems UK Ltd Unit 61-64 0 Station Road Coleshill, Birmingham B46 1JT Tel. *01675 463670* Fax. *01675 463520* E-mail. *sales@partex.co.uk* Web. *www.partex.co.uk M.G.G. Lamps – Partex – Reiku*

R & J Partington Failsworth Mill Ashton Road West, Failsworth, Manchester M35 0FR Tel. *0161 9344040* Fax. *0161 6834280* E-mail. *partington@fabric.co.uk* Web. *www.fabric.co.uk R. & J. Partington*

Partner Tech UK Corp Ltd Unit 11 Berkeley Court, Manor Park, Runcorn WA7 1TQ Tel. *01928 579707* Fax. *01928 571308* E-mail. *sales@partnertech-uk.com* Web. *www.partnertech-uk.com Partner Tech*

Partwell Cutting Technology Ltd Bridge Works 120 Stanley Street, Blackburn BB1 3BW Tel. *01254 671875* Fax. *01254 674823* E-mail. *info@partwell.com* Web. *www.partwell.com Apex – Bohler Cutting Steel – Bohler Steel – Cutting Presses – Frisylen Plastics – W.S.K. Machines – Wieser*

Parvalux Electric Motors Ltd 490-492 Wallisdown Road, Bournemouth BH11 8PU Tel. *01202 512575* Fax. *01202 530885* E-mail. *sales@parvalux.co.uk* Web. *www.parvalux.co.uk Parvalux*

Parweld Ltd Bewdley Business Park Long Bank, Bewdley DY12 2TZ Tel. *01299 266800* Fax. *01299 266900* E-mail. *reception@parweld.co.uk* Web. *www.parweld.com Parweld*

Pascal & Co. Ltd 112 Cherrywood Road, Birmingham B9 4JJ Tel. *0121 7537720* Fax. *0121 7711179* E-mail. *sales@lloydpascal.co.uk* Web. *www.lloydpascal.co.uk Elpec*

Pashley Cycles Ltd Masons Road, Stratford Upon Avon CV37 9NL Tel. *01789 292263* Fax. *01789 414201* E-mail. *hello@pashley.co.uk* Web. *www.pashley.co.uk Ad Bikes – Bicycles – Bicycles – Bicycles – Delivery Bicycles and Tricycles – Ice Cream Tricycles – Tricycles – Tricycles – Tricycles – Tricycles – Unicycles – Vending Tricycles – Workbikes*

Passion Knitwear Ltd Unit 2 Dark Lane, Manchester M12 6FA Tel. *0161 2743786* Fax. *0161 2737499* E-mail. *tiberius66@yahoo.com Passion Knitwear – Signal – Stealaway*

Pasta Foods Ltd Pasteur Road, Great Yarmouth NR31 0DW Tel. *01493 416200* Fax. *01493 653346* E-mail. *enquiries@pastafoods.com* Web. *www.pastafoods.com Marshalls – New Technology Snacks – Pasta Foods – Record Pasta – Santarini – Sitoni – Waveney Mills Semolina*

J Paterson & Sons Bank Square, Dalbeattie DG5 4HZ Tel. *01556 610249* Fax. *01556 611345 *Honda – *Kawasaki – *Kew – *Logic*

P A Testing Ltd Bow House 3 Brookway, Newbury RG14 5RY Tel. *07920 221422* Fax. *01635 48600* E-mail. *info@pa-testing.co.uk* Web. *www.pa-testing.co.uk P A Testing*

Pat Freight Ltd 119 Turnpike Lane, London N8 0DU Tel. *020 83404395* Fax. *020 83488036* E-mail. *enquiries@patfreight.co.uk* Web. *www.patfreight.co.uk Globe Frieght Ltd*

Pathtrace plc 45 Boulton Road, Reading RG2 0NH Tel. *0118 9756084* Fax. *0118 9756143* E-mail. *enquiry@pathtrace.com* Web. *www.pathtrace.com EdgeCAM (United Kingdom) – Pathtrace (United Kingdom)*

Patriarche Wine Agencies 4 Rickett Street, London SW6 1RU Tel. *020 73814016* Fax. *020 73812023* E-mail. *sales@patriarchewines.com* Web. *www.patriarchewines.com Champagne de Castelnau – Cycles Gladiator (California) – Hahn Estates (California) – Heath Wines (Australia) – Las Olas (Argentina) – Mount Riley (New Zealand) – Patriarche (France) – Vina Cantaluna (Chile)*

Patrick Shoes Ltd Broad March Long March Industrial Estate, Daventry NN11 4HE Tel. *01327 703841* Fax. *01327 300209* E-mail. *mark@patrickshoes.co.uk* Web. *www.patrickshoes.co.uk Excelsior – Montecatini – Patrizio – Pyrenees*

Patterson Products Ltd Ford Road, Chertsey KT16 8HG Tel. *01932 570016* Fax. *01932 570084* E-mail. *andrew@patterson.co.uk* Web. *www.golfbuggy.org Relaxator – Spraymar – Trio*

Paula Designs Ltd Unit 1 Hurlingham Business Park, London SW6 3DU Tel. *020 73846200* Fax. *020 73846262* E-mail. *valerie@pauladesigns.co.uk* Web. *www.pauladesigns.co.uk Paula Designs*

Paula Rosa Kitchens Water Lane Storrington, Pulborough RH20 3DS Tel. *01903 746666* Fax. *01903 742140* E-mail. *info@paularosa.com* Web. *www.paularosa.com Paula Rosa*

Pauley Equipment Solutions 625 Shore Road, Newtownabbey BT37 0ST Tel. *028 90865186* Fax. *08712 641552* E-mail. *info@pauleyequipment.co.uk* Web. *www.pauleyequipment.co.uk Christ – Gerhardt – Mettler Toledo – Ohaus – Sigma*

Pavigres UK Ltd Unit E Aerial Business Park Lambourn Woodlands, Hungerford RG17 7RZ Tel. *01488 674500* Fax. *01488 674505* Web. *www.pavigres.com Cerev (Portugal) – Grespor (Portugal) – Pavigres (Portugal) – Pavisolo (Portugal)*

Pavilion Textiles Ltd 17 Gate Lodge Close Round Spinney, Northampton NN3 8RJ Tel. *01604 741111* Fax. *01604 670611* E-mail. *contact@paviliontextiles.com* Web. *www.paviliontextiles.com Pavilion*

Paxton Computers Ltd 15 Kingsway, Bedford MK42 9EZ Tel. *01234 216666* Fax. *01234 212705* E-mail. *info@paxsoft.co.uk* Web. *www.paxsoft.co.uk Business Desk – EMS*

Paybare Paycare House George Street, Wolverhampton WV2 4DX Tel. *01902 371000* Fax. *01902 371030* E-mail. *enquiries@paycare.org* Web. *www.paycare.org Paycare*

Paylor Controls Ltd Unit 7 Waters Meeting Britannia Way, Bolton BL2 2HH Tel. *01204 370067* Fax. *0161 7642745* E-mail. *sales@paylor.co.uk* Web. *www.paylor.co.uk Paylor Controls*

Payne Giltway Giltbrook, Nottingham NG16 2GT Tel. *0115 9759000* Fax. *0115 9759001* E-mail. *nottingham@payne-worldwide.com* Web. *www.payne-worldwide.com Rippatape – Supastrip – Tagax – VakTape*

Payne Security Ltd Wildmere Road, Banbury OX16 3JU Tel. *01295 265601* Fax. *01295 251109* E-mail. *markpalmer@payne-worldwide.com* Web. *www.payne-security.com Morane*

P B K Micron Ltd Unit 6 Kingfield Industrial Estate, Coventry CV1 4DW Tel. *024 76220376* Fax. *024 76607819* E-mail. *sales@pbk-micron.co.uk* Web. *www.pbk-micron.co.uk Wickman*

P B S I Group Ltd Belle Vue Works Boundary Street, Manchester M12 5NG Tel. *0161 2306363* Fax. *0161 2306464* E-mail. *mail@pbsigroup.com* Web. *www.pbsigroup.com Feeder vision – MIRD-G – MIRD-T – MIRI-E – MIRI-ES – MIRI-I – MIRI-IE – MIRP-1 – MIRV-0 – MIRV-NVD – MIRV-U – MIRV-U0 – Motorvision – MPR10 – MPR20 – MPR2000 And MPC2000D – MPR3E5 – MRAR – MRAU – MRAW – MRCS – MRDG – MRDT-T2/T3 – MREF-1/3 – MRFF – MRI-E – MRI-ED – MRI-EX – MRI-I – MRI-ID – MRI-IDS – MRI-IE – MRI-IED – MRI-V – MRMF – MRNS – MROS – MRRP-1/3 – MRTR – MRTS – MRVT – P & B – P & B Engineering – P & B Power Engineering – P & B Technical Services – P & B Weir Electrical*

P B T International Haydon, Wells BA5 3EF Tel. *01749 685685* Fax. *01749 834834* E-mail. *sales@xinia.com* Web. *www.xinia.com P.B.T.I.*

P & B Weir Electrical Unit 1 Leafield Industrial Estate Leafield Way, Corsham SN13 9SW Tel. *01225 811449* Fax. *01225 810909* E-mail. *sales@pbsigroup.com* Web. *www.pbsigroup.com Weir Electrical Instrument*

P C D Maltron Ltd Castle Fields New Port Road, Stafford ST16 1BU Tel. *08452 303265* Fax. *0845 2303266* E-mail. *sales@maltron.com* Web. *www.maltron.com Maltron*

P C F Secure Document Systems Ltd Oak House Langstone Business Park, Langstone, Newport NP18 2LH Tel. *01633 415570* Fax. *01633 415599* E-mail. *info@pcf.co.uk* Web. *www.pcf.co.uk Data Logic – Instapass – Intermec – P F E – T E C – Troy – Zebra*

PCI Membranes Unit H Victory Park Solent Way, Whiteley, Fareham PO15 7FN Tel. *01256 303800* Fax. *01256 303801* E-mail. *pcimembranes@itt.com* Web. *www.pcimembranes.com PCI Membranes*

P C L Machinery 5 Elan Court Norris Way, Rushden NN10 6BP Tel. *01933 410707* Fax. *01933 410807* E-mail. *sales@pclmachinery.co.uk* Web. *www.pclmachinery.co.uk PCL Machinery*

Pcme Clearview Building Edison Road, St Ives PE27 3GH Tel. *01480 468200* Fax. *01480 463400* E-mail. *sales@pcme.com* Web. *www.pcme.co.uk TribeACE*

P C Paramedics 1 Highdown Court, Crawley RH10 6PR Tel. *01293 428882* E-mail. *john@hbird.freeserve.co.uk *Hotel - Minders*

P C P Micro Products Ltd 18 St Peters Terrace, Bath BA2 3BT Tel. *01225 480888* Fax. *01225 483232* E-mail. *info@electrocoin.net* Web. *www.pcpmicro.co.uk P.C.P.*

P D A Ltd Alder House Booths Lane, Lymm WA13 0GH Tel. *01925 759380* Fax. *01925 759320* E-mail. *philipdunbavin@pdaltd.com* Web. *www.pdaltd.com Phillip Dunbaven Acoustics*

P D Edenhall Caldicot Road Rogiet, Caldicot NP26 3TF Tel. *01291 426700* Fax. *01291 425463* E-mail. *steve.kitchen@pd-edenhall.co.uk* Web. *www.pd-edenhall.co.uk Marflex MB – Marflex ML – Marflex QL – Marflex Typex HP – Marlex G.F.*

P D G Helicopters The Heliport Dalcross Industrial Estate, Inverness IV2 7XB Tel. *01667 462740* Fax. *01667 462376* E-mail. *reception@pdghelicopters.com* Web. *www.pdghelicopters.com PDG Helicopters*

P D Interglas Technologies Ltd Westbury, Sherborne DT9 3RB Tel. *01935 813722* Fax. *01935 811800* E-mail. *shane.cherrington@interglas-technologies.com* Web. *www.pd-fibreglass.com Alpha HU-Al – Alpha Maritex – Alpha Temp – Alpha Weld – Double-safe – Weldshield*

P D L Solutions Europe Ltd 1 Tanners Yard Tanners Yard, Hexham NE46 3NY Tel. *01434 609473* Fax. *01434 606292* E-mail. *sales@polymer-distribution.com* Web. *www.polymer-distribution.com RTP Company*

Peak Trailers Ltd Unit 2a Waterloo Industrial Estate Waterloo Road, Bidford-On-Avon, Alcester B50 4JH Tel. *01789 778041* Fax. *01789 490331* E-mail. *sales@peaktrailers.com* Web. *www.peaktrailers.com Peak*

N Peal Victoria Road, Hawick TD9 7AH Tel. *020 74939220* Fax. *01450 377581* E-mail. *d@npeal.co.uk* Web. *www.npeal.co.uk N. Peal & Co.*

Pearl Assurance plc The Pearl Centre Peterborough Business Park, Lynch Wood, Peterborough PE2 6FY Tel. *08458 828121* Fax. *01733 475141* E-mail. *enquiries@pearl.co.uk* Web. *www.pearl.co.uk Pearl*

Pearson Eduction Ltd Edinburgh Gate Edinburgh Way, Harlow CM20 2JE Tel. *01279 623623* Fax. *01279 431059* E-mail. *john.fallon@pearsoned-ema.com* Web. *www.pearsoneducation.co.uk Heinemann – Reed Educational & Professional Publishers*

Pearson Panke Ltd 1-3 Hale Grove Gardens, London NW7 3LR Tel. *020 89593232* Fax. *020 89595613* E-mail. *stephen.panke@pearsonpanke.demon.co.uk* Web. *www.pearsonpanke.co.uk *Andromat (Germany) – *Beche (Germany) – *Felss (Germany) – *Heinrich Wagner Sinto (Germany) – *Mall Herlan (Germany) – Muller Weingarten – *Oberburg (Switzerland) – *PEI (France) – *Roland (Italy) – *Sprimag (Germany) – *Stam (Italy) – *Thyssen Henschel (Germany)*

Richard Pearson Ltd Priory Road Freiston, Boston PE22 0JZ Tel. *01205 760383* Fax. *01205 760822* E-mail. *info@richardpearson.com* Web. *www.richardpearson.com Pearson Challenger – Pearson Enterprise Plus 2000 – Pearson Jumbo – Pearson Maverick – Pearson Megastar – Pearson Mini Jumbo – Pearson Quality Master – Pearson Rapier – Pearson Rotaforma*

Peco Publications & Publicity Ltd Underleys Beer, Seaton EX12 3NA Tel. *01297 20580* Fax. *01297 20229* E-mail. *sales.peco@btconnect.com* Web. *www.peco-uk.com Continental Modeller – Railway Modeller*

Pedley Furniture International Ltd Shire Hill, Saffron Walden CB11 3AL Tel. *01799 522461* Fax. *01799 543403* E-mail. *alan.pedley@pedley.com* Web. *www.pedley.com Kontrakt – Select – Spirotred – Woodgrip*

Pedrollo Distribution 9 Cavendish Lichfield Road Industrial Estate, Tamworth B79 7XH Tel. *01827 313000* Fax. *01827 313008* E-mail. *sales@pedrollo.co.uk* Web. *www.pedrollo.co.uk City Pumps – Faggiolati – Pedrollo*

Pedro Pet Foods Ltd 51a Brocklis Road Sion Mills, Strabane BT82 9LZ Tel. *028 81658808* Fax. *028 81659903* E-mail. *info@pedropetfoods.com* Web. *www.pedropetfoods.com Pedro Gold – Pedro Original*

Peekay National Eyecare Group Ltd Clermont House High Street, Cranbrook TN17 3DN Tel. *01580 713698* Fax. *01580 713178* E-mail. *michael.wheeler@nationaleyecare.co.uk* Web. *www.nationaleyecare.co.uk Vision now*

Peek Traffic Ltd Unit 5 Handley Page Way, Colney Street, St Albans AL2 2DQ Tel. *01923 289300* Fax. *01923 858453* E-mail. *sales@peek-traffic.co.uk* Web. *www.peek-traffic.co.uk Peek Elive – Peek Guardian – Peek Traffic – Sarasota*

Peek Traffic Ltd Hazelwood House Lime Tree Way, Chineham, Basingstoke RG24 8WZ Tel. *01256 891800* Fax. *01256 891871* E-mail. *bryan.east@peek-traffic.co.uk* Web. *www.peek.co.uk Peek Elite (United Kingdom) – Peek Guardian (United Kingdom) – Peek Traffic – Sarasota*

Peek Traffic Ltd Meridian Business Park Centurion Way, Leicester LE19 1WH Tel. *0116 2828500* Fax. *0116 2828528* E-mail. *steve.wright@peek.co.uk* Web. *www.peekglobal.com Peek Elive – Peek Guardian – Peek Traffic – Sarasota*

John Peel & Son Ltd Baildon Mills Northgate, Baildon, Shipley BD17 6JY Tel. *01274 583276* Fax. *01274 598533* E-mail. *robert.askew@peelflock.com* Web. *www.peelflock.com Decofloc*

Peel Jones Copper Products Ltd Maynard Foundry Kilton Lane, Carlin How, Saltburn By The Sea TS13 4EY Tel. *01287 640658* Fax. *01287 642906* E-mail. *ian@peeljonescopper.com* Web. *www.peeljones.sageweb.co.uk Peel Jones*

Peerless Plastics & Coatings 16-20 Howlett Way, Thetford IP24 1HZ Tel. *01842 750333* Fax. *01842 750770* E-mail. *sales@peerless-coatings.co.uk* Web. *www.peerless-coatings.co.uk Peerafilter – Peeraguard – Peeraguard Exterior – Peeramist – Peerashield*

Pektron Alfreton Road, Derby DE21 4AP Tel. *01332 832424* Fax. *01332 833270* E-mail. *info@pektron.co.uk* Web. *www.pektron.co.uk Pektron*

Pelham Leather Goods Ltd 110 Centennial Park Centennial Avenue, Elstree, Borehamwood WD6 3SB Tel. *020 87313500* Fax. *020 87313501* E-mail. *sales@pelhamgroup.co.uk* Web. *www.delsey.com Delsey*

Pelican Healthcare Ltd Quadrant Centre Cardiff Business Park, Cardiff CF14 5WF Tel. *029 20747000* Fax. *029 20747001* E-mail. *mailroom@pelicanhealthcare.co.uk* Web. *www.pelicanhealthcare.co.uk Pelican*

Pelloby Engineering Ltd Halesfield 19, Telford TF7 4QT Tel. *01952 586626* Fax. *01952 587871* E-mail. *sales@pelloby.com* Web. *www.pelloby.com Pelloby*

Pelltech Ltd Station Lane, Witney OX28 4YS Tel. *01993 776451* Fax. *01993 771606* E-mail. *enquiries@pelltech.co.uk* Web. *www.pelltech.co.uk A P L I – Decadry – Linex – Papyrobord – Southworth*

Pembar Ltd (t/a Hatt Kitchens) Unit 111 Hartlebury Trading Estate, Hartlebury, Kidderminster DY10 4JB Tel. *01299 251320* Fax. *01299 251579* E-mail. *sales@hatt.co.uk* Web. *www.hatt.co.uk Hatt Kitchens*

Pendeford Metal Spinnings Ltd Neachells Lane, Willenhall WV13 3SF Tel. *01902 733145* Fax. *01902 721136* E-mail. *info@pendeford.co.uk* Web. *www.pendeford.co.uk *Silver Shield (United Kingdom)*

Pendle Frozen Foods Ltd 40 Churchill Way, Nelson BB9 6RT Tel. *01282 691177* Fax. *01282 690011* E-mail. *aplatt@pendlefrozenfoods.co.uk* Web. *www.pendlefrozenfoods.co.uk *Krunchy Fried Chicken – Pendle Cold Store*

Pendragon Contracts Ltd Sir Frank Whittle Road, Derby DE21 4AZ Tel. *01332 292777* Fax. *01332 364270* E-mail. *neal.francis@pendragon.uk.com* Web. *www.pendragon-contracts.uk.com Pendragon Contracts*

Norman Pendred & Co. Ltd Unit B1 Broomsleigh Business Park Worsley Bridge Road, London SE26 5BN Tel. *020 84611155* Fax. *020 84611166* E-mail. *info@pendred.com* Web. *www.pendred.com Pendred – pentic – Rollerbarker – Rollerprice*

Penguin Books Ltd 80 Strand, London WC2R 0RL Tel. *020 70103000* Fax. *020 70106060* E-mail. *helena.peacock@penguin.co.uk* Web. *www.penguin.com Dorling Kindersley – Frederick Warne – Hamish Hamilton – Ladybird – Michael Joseph – Penguin – Puffin – Rough Guides – Viking*

Penguin Swimming Pools Ltd 5a Thorpe Close, Banbury OX16 4SW Tel. *01295 269091* Fax. *01295 266881* E-mail. *mail@penguinpools.co.uk* Web. *www.penguinpools.co.uk Penguin*

Penlon Ltd Abingdon Science Park Barton Lane, Abingdon OX14 3PH Tel. *01235 547000* Fax. *01235 547021* E-mail. *alison.tarrant@penlon.com* Web. *www.penlon.com Penlon*

Penman Engineering Ltd Heathhall Industrial Estate Heathhall, Dumfries DG1 3NY Tel. *01387 252784* Fax. *01387 267332* E-mail. *info@penman.co.uk* Web. *www.penman.co.uk Hotspur Hussar (United Kingdom)*

Pennine Castings Ltd Pennine Industrial Estate Modder Place, Armley, Leeds LS12 3ES Tel. *0113 2638755* Fax. *0113 2791134* E-mail. *info@penninecastings.co.uk* Web. *www.penninecastings.co.uk Blakey's Boot Protectors – Pennine Castings – Segs*

Pennine Cycles Whitaker & Mapplebeck Ltd 1019 Thornton Road, Bradford BD8 0PA Tel. *01274 881030* Fax. *01274 881030* E-mail. *penninecycles@yahoo.com* Web. *www.penninecycles.com Colnago (Italy) – Pennine Cycles – *Peugeot (France)*

Pennine Instrument Services Ltd 82-86 Upper Allen Street, Sheffield S3 7GW Tel. *0114 2730534* Fax. *0114 2751818* E-mail. *info@pennineinstruments.co.uk* Web. *www.penineinstruments.co.uk Megger*

Pennine Automation Spares Ltd Brookwoods Industrial Estate Burrwood Way, Holywell Green, Halifax HX4 9BH Tel. *01422 310259* Fax. *01422 371338* E-mail. *neil@pennineuk.com* Web. *www.pennineuk.com Pal*

Pennine Optical Group Ltd Pennine House Manchester Road, Stockport SK4 1TX Tel. *0161 4806468* Fax. *0161 4776949* E-mail. *pennine@pog.co.uk* Web. *www.pennineoptical.co.uk Bittner Collection – Cacharel – Cazal – Clipwell Collection – College Collection – Cool Eyed Kids – Diamond Collection – Lanvin – Les Lunettes Essilor – Marvel Comics – Noddy – Palm Beach – Pennine – Royal Collection*

Pennine Products Fold Mill Bradley Lane, Bolton BL2 6RR Tel. *01204 361547* Fax. *01204 380872* E-mail. *info@pennineindustries.com* Web. *www.pennineindustries.com Pennine Industries Ltd*

Pennine Radio Ltd 82 Fitzwilliam Street, Huddersfield HD1 5BE Tel. *01484 538211* Fax. *01484 542004* E-mail. *info@pr1.co.uk* Web. *www.prl.co.uk Pennine*

Penny Hydraulics Ltd Station Road Industrial Estate Station Road, Clowne, Chesterfield S43 4AB Tel. *01246 811475* Fax. *01246 810403* E-mail. *sales@pennyhydraulics.com* Web. *www.pennyhydraulics.com Swinglift cranes*

Pentag Gears & Oil Field Equipment Ltd PO Box 24, Sheffield S2 4QR Tel. *0114 2583473* Fax. *0114 2584264* E-mail. *a.larkin@pentag-gears.com* Web. *www.pentag-gears.com Pentag – Pentag – Pentag Gearbelt – Pentag Hubdriva – Pentag Milldriva – Pentag Mitredriva – Pentag Universal*

Pentagon Fine Chemicals Ltd Lower Road Halebank, Widnes WA8 8NS Tel. *0151 4243671* Fax. *0151 4201301* E-mail. *enquiries@pentagonchemicals.co.uk* Web. *www.pentagonchemicals.co.uk Aduvex – Quantacure*

Pentagon Plastics Ltd Plastic Injection Moulder Unit 4 Blatchford Rd, Horsham RH13 5QR Tel. *0845 4744187* Fax. *01403 267095* E-mail. *websales@pentagonplastics.co.uk* Web. *www.pentagonplastics.co.uk Small Batch Plastics – Jarzon Plastics Ltd*

Pentagon Protection plc Solar House Amersham Road, Chesham HP5 1NG Tel. *01494 793333* Fax. *01494 794123* E-mail. *enquiries@pentagonprotection.com* Web. *www.pentagonprotection.com Doortek – Elite – FT800 – Select*

Pentagram Design 11 Needham Road, London W11 2RP Tel. *020 72293477* Fax. *020 77279932* E-mail. *hyland@pentagram.co.uk* Web. *www.pentragram.com Pentagram Design Ltd*

Pentangle Puzzles & Games PO Box 5, Llanfyllin SY22 5WD Tel. *01691 649123* Fax. *01691 649926* E-mail. *info@pentangle-puzzles.co.uk* Web. *www.pentangle-puzzles.co.uk Paradox – Roly-Poly – Woodchuck*

Pentax UK Ltd Pentax House Heron Drive, Slough SL3 8PN Tel. *01753 792792* Fax. *01753 792794* E-mail. *info@accounts.pentax.co.uk* Web. *www.pentax.co.uk *Cosmicar (Japan) – Efina (Japan) – Espio (Japan) – MZ (Japan) – *Pro-Quartz (Japan) – *Profile (Japan)*

Penthouse Carpets Ltd Buckley Carpet Mill Buckley Road, Rochdale OL12 9DU Tel. *01706 341231* Fax. *01706 860577* E-mail. *alex.dyson@penthousecarpets.co.uk* Web. *www.penthousecarpets.co.uk Dominance – Harmony – Medallion Twist – New Pentwist – New Studio – Penistone – Shepley – Super Penistone – Super Pentwist – Super Woodlands – Supreme – Supreme Deluxe – Tallon – Woodlands*

Pentland Ltd 5 Station Road Ballinderry Upper, Lisburn BT28 2LW Tel. *0844 3578825* Fax. *020 84575021* E-mail. *info@pentland.com* Web. *www.pentlands.com Red or Dead*

Pentland Group plc 8 Manchester Square, London W1U 3PH Tel. *020 75353800* Fax. *020 75353837* E-mail. *sales@pentlandwholesale.co.uk* Web. *www.pentlandwholesale.co.uk Kickers*

Pentland Wholesale Ltd Unit 13 Whitebirk Industrial Estate, Blackburn BB2 3BA Tel. *01254 614444* Fax. *01254 614477* E-mail. *sales@pentlandwholesale.co.uk* Web. *www.pentlandwholesale.co.uk *Blizzard – *Break-Line – *Infrico – *Inomak – *Mondial Elite – *Whirlpool*

P E P Ltd Unit 23-24 Capstan Centre Thurrock Park Way, Tilbury RM18 7HH Tel. *01375 850300* Fax. *01375 851099* E-mail. *sales@pep.ltd.uk* Web. *www.rentdisplayboards.co.uk Plex – Plex, portable display systems - Ultima, portable display systems – Ultima*

Pepe Jeans London 99C Talbot Road, London W11 2AT Tel. *020 73133800* Fax. *020 73133803* E-mail. *nsoneji@pepejeans.co.uk* Web. *www.pepejeans.com Pepe*

Perancea Ltd Unit 36 Silicon Business Centre 28 Wadsworth Road, Perivale, Greenford UB6 7JZ Tel. *020 83652520* Fax. *020 85667217* E-mail. *sales@perancea.com* Web. *www.perancea.com Apra-norm – Apranorm – Clipper Series – Eddystone – Fibox – Hammond – Mimram – Perancea – Sink Box – Tame – West Hyde*

P E R Design UK Ltd Booths Hall Booths Park Chelford Road, Knutsford WA16 8GS Tel. *01565 757810* Fax. *01565 650755* E-mail. *info@perdesignuk.com* Web. *www.perdesignuk.com PER Design*

Perei Group Ltd Sunbury House 4 Christy Estate Ivy Road, Aldershot GU12 4TX Tel. *01252 350833* Fax. *01252 350875* E-mail. *sales@perei.co.uk* Web. *www.perei.co.uk *L.E.P. (United Kingdom)*

Perennis Ltd 807 Staffords Green Corton Denham, Sherborne DT9 4LY Tel. *020 74825920* Fax. *020 74825964* E-mail. *perennisltd@msn.com Perennis*

Perfect Leather Sales Ltd Carmel Works Chapel Street, Porth CF39 0PU Tel. *01443 757150* Fax. *01443 757150* E-mail. *petervalek@petervalek.worldonline.co.uk* Web. *www.leatherwatchstraps.co.uk Perfect*

Peritys Greenhouses Bona Lane Leverington, Wisbech PE13 5JQ Tel. *01945 410471* Fax. *01945 410471* E-mail. *perity@peritys.co.uk* Web. *www.peritys.co.uk Clearspan – Dutch Light*

Perkins Engines Group Ltd Eastfield, Peterborough PE1 5NA Tel. *01733 583000* Fax. *01733 582240* E-mail. *purdy_claire@perkins.com* Web. *www.perkins.com 100 Series – 1000 Series – *1300 Series (U.S.A.) – 2000 Series – 3000 Series – 4000 Series – 700 Series – 900 Series – Condor – Eagle – ElectropaK – HD Power – Perama – Perkins – Sea King*

Permadeck Systems Ltd Unit 12 Westside Indl-Est Jackson Street, St Helens WA9 3AT Tel. *01744 751869* Fax. *01744 22551* E-mail. *enquiries@nlwgroup.com* Web. *www.nlwgroup.com Permadeck – Permagrip*

Permali Gloucester Ltd Bristol Road, Gloucester GL1 5TT Tel. *01452 528282* Fax. *01452 507409* E-mail. *sales@permali.co.uk* Web. *www.permali-gloucester.co.uk Permaglass – Permaglass-X – Plasticell*

Permanoid Ltd 107 Hulme Hall Lane, Manchester M40 8HH Tel. *0161 2056161* Fax. *0161 2059325* E-mail. *sales@permanoid.co.uk* Web. *www.permanoid.co.uk Permanoid*

Permarock Products Ltd Jubilee Drive, Loughborough LE11 5TW Tel. *01509 262924* Fax. *01509 230063* E-mail. *info@permarock.com* Web. *www.permarock.com Disbocrete – Disbon – Permaguard Conductive Coatings – PermaRend – PermaRock*

Permastore Ltd Eye Airfield, Eye IP23 7HS Tel. *01379 870723* Fax. *01379 870530* E-mail. *sales@permastore.com* Web. *www.permastore.com Ecofusion – Fusion – Isofusion – Permastore – Trifusion*

Permatex Protective Coatings UK Ltd The Colchester Centre Hawkins Road, Colchester CO2 8JX Tel. *01206 266867* Fax. *01708 378868* E-mail. *permatexpcltd@hotmail.co.uk* Web. *www.permatexpcukltd.co.uk Asplit – Ault & Wiborg – Betonol – Permacor – Spies Hecker – Standox – Superfleet – Unitherm – Viton*

Permat Machines Ltd Station Road Coleshill, Birmingham B46 1JG Tel. *01675 463351* Fax. *01675 465816* E-mail. *sales@permat.com* Web. *www.permat.com Nagel – Permat – Precidor Bore Finishing Systems*

Perrigo UK Staggers Lane Wrafton, Braunton EX33 2DL Tel. *01271 815815* Fax. *01283 228328* E-mail. *russell.howard@perrigouk.com* Web. *www.perrigouk.com Calcia – Catarrh Eeze – Folic Plus – Gerrardhouse – Healthcrafts – Herbulax – Natracalm – Natrasleep – Red Kooga – Rheumasol – Travelcaps*

Perrite (a division of Vita Thermoplastic Compounds Ltd) 1 Kingsland Grange Woolston, Warrington WA1 4RA Tel. *01925 810608* Fax. *01925 840001* E-mail. *sales@perrite.com* Web. *www.perrite.com Percom – Perflex – Perlac – Perlene – Perlex – Perloy – Pertal – Pyronyl – Syncon*

Perrys Griffin Lane Industrial Estate Griffin Lane, Aylesbury HP19 8BY Tel. *01296 426162* Fax. *01296 745276* E-mail. *normanholmes@perrys.co.uk* Web. *www.perrys.co.uk Perrys*

Perscent Churchill Point Lake Edge Green, Trafford Park, Manchester M17 1BL Tel. *08702 084444* Fax. *08702 085555* E-mail. *accounts@per-scent.co.uk* Web. *www.per-scent.co.uk Calvin Klein – D&G – Paul Smith*

Peshawear UK Ltd Millars 3 Southmill Road, Bishops Stortford CM23 3DH Tel. *01279 306257* Fax. *020 86549524* E-mail. *david@peshawear-bs.com* Web. *www.peshawear.co.uk Happy Hands*

Pestcatcher 27 Iffley Road, Swindon SN2 1DL Tel. *01793 324982* E-mail. *markb@pestcatcher.co.uk* Web. *www.pestcatcher.co.uk Pestcatcher*

Pest Help Ltd Unit 1 Fairfax Industrial Estate Eastern Road, Aldershot GU12 4TU Tel. *023 92178584* Fax. *0114 2766556* E-mail. *sales@pesthelp.co.uk* Web. *www.pesthelp.co.uk Pest Control*

P E S UK Ltd Unit 1 Watling Close, Hinckley LE10 3EZ Tel. *01455 251251* Fax. *01455 251252* E-mail. *sales@pesukltd.com* Web. *www.pesukltd.com P.E.S. (United Kingdom)*

P E Systems Ltd Victoria Street, Leigh WN7 5SE Tel. *01942 260330* Fax. *01942 261835* E-mail. *sales@pe-systems.co.uk* Web. *www.pe-systems.co.uk Westat*

Petal Postforming Ltd Dromore Road Irvinestown, Enniskillen BT94 1ET Tel. *028 68621766* Fax. *028 68621004* E-mail. *sales@petalgroup.com* Web. *www.petalgroup.com Formica*

Peta UK Ltd Marks Hall Marks Hall Lane, Margaret Roding, Dunmow CM6 1QT Tel. *01245 231118* Fax. *01245 231811* E-mail. *peta@peta-uk.com* Web. *www.peta-uk.com Peta Easi-Grip – Peta Fist-Grip – Peta Wide-Grip*

Peter Gillard Company Ltd Alexandra Way Ashchurch, Tewkesbury GL20 8NB Tel. *01684 290243* Fax. *01684 290330* E-mail. *sales@wecut.eu* Web. *www.wecut.eu Accia-Feed – Bench-Cut – Metal-Cut – Neuma-Torq – Servo-Torq – Vac-U-Torq*

Peter Haddock Ltd Pinfold Lane Industrial Estate, Bridlington YO16 6BT Tel. *01262 678121* Fax. *01262 400043* E-mail. *rodney.noon@phpublishing.co.uk* Web. *www.phpublishing.co.uk Big Time Books*

Peter Hird & Sons Ltd English Street, Hull HU3 2BT Tel. *01482 227333* Fax. *01482 587710* E-mail. *peterj@peter-hird.co.uk* Web. *www.peter-hird.co.uk Valla Cranes U.K.*

Peterkin UK Ltd 85 Commercial Square, Leicester LE2 7SR Tel. *0116 2543645* Fax. *0116 2470618* E-mail. *sales@peterkin.co.uk* Web. *www.peterkin.co.uk Peterkin*

Petersen Stainless Rigging Ltd Blaydon Business Centre Cowen Road, Blaydon On Tyne NE21 5TW Tel. *0191 4140156* Fax. *0191 4990041* E-mail. *sales@petersen-stainless.co.uk* Web. *www.petersen-stainless.co.uk Hi-Mod (United Kingdom)*

David Peterson Ltd (David Peterson Clocks Ltd) Jade House 25-27 Farnham Drive Caversham, Reading RG4 6NY Tel. *0118 9471405* Fax. *0118 9471605* E-mail. *sales@dpclocks.co.uk* Web. *www.dpclocks.co.uk David Peterson*

Peterson Spring Europe Ltd Heath Plant Unit 21 Trescott Road, Redditch B98 7AH Tel. *01527 585657* Fax. *01527 58837* E-mail. *sales@pspring.eu.com* Web. *pspring.com Peterson Spring*

Stuart Peters Ltd 184-192 Drummond Street, London NW1 3HP Tel. *020 75548440* Fax. *020 73835425* E-mail. *esspee@speters.co.uk* Web. *www.speters.co.uk Stuart Peters*

Petit Forestier Birch Coppice Industrial Estate Watling Street, Dordon, Tamworth B78 1SZ Tel. *01827 263100* Fax. *01827 289071* E-mail. *enquiries@petitforestier.co.uk* Web. *www.petitforestier.co.uk V.I.A. Contract Hire – V.I.A. Countryside*

Pet Mate Ltd Lyon Road, Walton On Thames KT12 3PU Tel. *01932 700000* Fax. *01932 700002* E-mail. *sales@pet-mate.com* Web. *www.pet-mate.com Cat Mate – Dog Mate – Fish Mate – Pet Mate*

Petrel Ltd Fortnum Close, Birmingham B33 0LB Tel. *0121 7837161* Fax. *0121 7835717* E-mail. *sales@petrel-ex.co.uk* Web. *www.petrel-ex.co.uk Clip-In – Clip-In – Fitter & Poulton – Petrel – Petrel*

Petre Process Plant Ltd Carr Cottage Mill Whalley New Road, Blackburn BB1 9SR Tel. *01254 682030* Fax. *01254 55752* E-mail. *sales@petreprocess.com* Web. *www.petreprocess.com APV – Greaves – Lightnin – Silverson*

Petrie Technologies Ltd Common Bank Industrial Estate Ackhurst Road, Chorley PR7 1NH Tel. *01257 241206* Fax. *01257 267562* E-mail. *sales@petrieltd.com* Web. *www.nisltd.com Fast Thaw – P & M – Petrie & McNaught*

Petrofac Bridge View 1 North Esplanade West, Aberdeen AB11 5QF Tel. *01224 247000* Fax. *01224 247001* E-mail. *eleanor.bentley@petrofac.com* Web. *www.petrofac.com PGS Production Services – PGS Production Services.*

Petroplan 91 Walnut Tree Close, Guildford GU1 4UQ Tel. *01483 881500* Fax. *01483 881501* E-mail. *info@petroplan.com* Web. *www.petroplan.com Petroplan*

Petroplastics & Chemicals Ltd Unit 18 Silicon Business Centre Wadsworth Road, Perivale, Greenford UB6 7JZ Tel. *020 89972300* Fax. *020 89974964* E-mail. *sales@petroplast.co.uk* Web. *www.petroplast.co.uk Petroplast*

Pfaff-Silberblau Ltd 7 Durley Park Close North Cheshire Trading Estate, Prenton CH43 3DZ Tel. *01244 375375* Fax. *0151 6090200* E-mail. *anyone@pfaff-silberblau.co.uk* Web. *www.pfaff-silberblau2.co.uk *Columbus McKinnon (U.S.A.) – *Gis (Switzerland) – *Pfaff Silberblau (Germany)*

P4 Ltd 1 Wymans Way, Fakenham NR21 8NT Tel. *01328 850555* Fax. *01462 851123* E-mail. *info@p4fastel.co.uk* Web. *www.p4fastel.co.uk fastel*

P F T Central Laxton Meadow Farm Southam Road, Prestbury, Cheltenham GL52 3NQ Tel. *01242 236383* Fax. *01242 224794* E-mail. *sales@pftcentral.co.uk* Web. *www.pftcentral.co.uk British Gypsum – K-Rend – KNAUF – M-Tec – Monocouche – MP 75 – PFT*

P G Drive Technology 1 Airspeed Road, Christchurch BH23 4HD Tel. *01425 271444* Fax. *01425 272655* E-mail. *sales@pgdt.com* Web. *www.pgdt.com Access – Egis – OMNI+ – Pilot+ – Solo – Trio – VSI*

P G T Ceewrite Ltd Falcon Business Centre 2-4 Willow Lane, Mitcham CR4 4NA Tel. *020 86489461* Fax. *020 86859638* E-mail. *sales@pgt-uk.co.uk* Web. *www.pgtechnology.co.uk*

620 System – Microdress – Optidress – Poly-Tip – Projectordress – Projectorscope – Tunbo

Phaidon Press Ltd 18 Regents Wharf All Saints Street, London N1 9PA Tel. *020 78431000* Fax. *020 78431010* E-mail. *enquiries@phaidon.com* Web. *www.phaidon.com Phaidon*

Pharmaq Ltd Unit 15 Sandleheath Industrial Estate Old Brickyard Road Sandleheath, Fordingbridge SP6 1PA Tel. *01425 656081* Fax. *01425 655309* E-mail. *ben.north@pharmaq.no* Web. *www.pharmaq.no *Aquatet – *Vetremox – *Vitamax*

Pharmarquip Spectrum Business Estate Bircholt Road, Maidstone ME15 9YP Tel. *01622 686050* E-mail. *leegifford74@hotmail.com* Web. *www.pharmaquipe.co.uk Pharmaquipe*

Pharos Engineering Ltd 228 Lythalls Lane Foleshill, Coventry CV6 6GF Tel. *024 76687235* Fax. *024 76666355* E-mail. *mwinstone@pharosengineering.co.uk* Web. *www.pharosgroupuk.com Hydrogrip Machine Vices – Redco Hydrogip Machine Vices – Redco – Redco Broaches – *Redco LSP (U.S.A.)*

P H I Group Ltd Hadley House Bayshill Road, Cheltenham GL50 3AW Tel. *01242 707600* Fax. *08703 334121* E-mail. *southern@phigroup.co.uk* Web. *www.phigroup.co.uk Anda Crib – Lockstone – Permacrib – Soil Panal*

Philip Cowan Interiors Sutterton Enterprise Park Sutterton, Boston PE20 2JA Tel. *01205 461111* Fax. *01205 461119* E-mail. *enquiries@cowans.co.uk* Web. *www.cowans.co.uk Gardisette – Panaz – Pinewood – Silent Gliss – Zoffany*

Phillips Foils Ltd 1 Olympic Business Centre Paycocke Road, Basildon SS14 3ET Tel. *01268 288955* Fax. *01268 286080* E-mail. *info@pfl.uk.com* Web. *www.pfl.uk.com Phillips Foils*

Maurice Phillips 1 Old Parkbury Lane Colney Street, St Albans AL2 2EB Tel. *01923 289289* Fax. *01923 289200* E-mail. *joannerobbins@mauricephillips.co.uk* Web. *www.maurice-phillips.co.uk A. Forester – Aeresta – Barbican – Doble Dew – Maurice Phillips – Tremain Textiles*

Phillips Plastics Ltd North Bridge Road, Berkhamsted HP4 1EH Tel. *0845 4567007* Fax. *0845 4567706* E-mail. *sales@phillipsplastics.co.uk* Web. *www.phillipsplastics.co.uk Club Class*

Phillips Tuftex Ltd Albion Buildings Attleborough Road, Nuneaton CV11 4JJ Tel. *024 76382100* Fax. *024 76342449* E-mail. *info@phillipstuftex.co.uk* Web. *www.tuftexsports.co.uk Albion – Tuftex*

Phoenix Abrasive Wheel Co. Ltd Shepley Industrial Estate South Audenshaw, Manchester M34 5DW Tel. *0161 3209580* Fax. *0161 3359074* E-mail. *grant.roberts@phoenixabrasives.co.uk* Web. *www.phoenixabrasives.co.uk Phoenix*

Phoenix Air Cargo Unit 11 Ashford Industrial Estate Shield Road, Ashford TW15 1AU Tel. *01784 420114* Fax. *01425 673391* E-mail. *mail@phoenix-cargo.com* Web. *www.phoenix-cargo.com PHOENIX*

Phoenix Utility Services Ltd 44 Windsor Road Denton, Manchester M34 2HD Tel. *0161 3207202* Fax. *0161 3207202* E-mail. *shaun.ellam@pusl.co.uk* Web. *www.pusl.co.uk Grundotug*

Phoenix Weighing Services Ltd Unit 9 Lower Rectory Farm Snarestone RoadAppleby Magna, Swadlincote DE12 7AJ Tel. *07866 772394* E-mail. *info@phoenixweigh.com* Web. *www.phoenixweigh.com e 3 Fibres – ENDURO – Fibercast – Fibermesh – Harbourite – Novocon – Novomesh – Novotex – Stealth – Vertiforce*

Phoenox Textiles Ltd Spring Grove Mills Scissett, Clayton West, Huddersfield HD8 9HH Tel. *01484 863227* Fax. *01484 865352* E-mail. *sales@phoenox.co.uk* Web. *www.phoenox.co.uk Waterfall*

Photogold Web Design 40 Dunvegan Place Polmont, Falkirk FK2 0NX Tel. *01324 883305* E-mail. *sales@photogoldecommerce.com* Web. *www.photogoldecommerce.com Photogold ecommerce solutions*

Photo Me (International) plc Church Road Bookham, Leatherhead KT23 3EU Tel. *01372 453399* Fax. *01372 459064* E-mail. *info@photo-me.co.uk* Web. *www.photo-me.co.uk Photo-Me International Plc*

Photon Power Technology Ltd Suite 8 Brambles Business Centre, Hussar Court, Waterlooville PO7 7SG Tel. *023 92264890* Fax. *0845 8338923* E-mail. *info@photonpower.co.uk* Web. *www.photonpower.co.uk Magic Power Technology Ltd*

P H S Datashred Ltd Rennys Lane, Durham DH1 2RW Tel. *0800 3764422* Fax. *0191 3709850* E-mail. *info@phs.co.uk* Web. *www.shredding.info Securishred*

Phytron UK Ltd 17 Kingsway Caversham, Reading RG4 6RA Tel. *0118 9462132* Fax. *0118 9473059* E-mail. *info@phytron.co.uk* Web. *www.phytron.co.uk Synchrochop*

P I Castings Ltd Davenport Lane Broadheath, Altrincham WA14 5DS Tel. *0161 9285811* Fax. *0161 9277023* E-mail. *admin@pi-castings.co.uk* Web. *www.pi-castings.co.uk Picast – Picastings*

Pickering Electronics Ltd Stephenson Road, Clacton On Sea CO15 4NL Tel. *01255 428141* Fax. *01255 475058* E-mail. *graham.dale@pickeringrelay.com* Web. *www.pickeringrelay.com Microsil – Minisil – Picosil*

Pickfords Ltd Unit 10 Laxcon Close, London NW10 0TG Tel. *020 31882655* Fax. *020 82198516* Web. *www.pickfords.com Allied Pickfords – Pickfords – Pickfords Records Management – Pickfords Vanguard*

Pickhill Engineers Ltd Pickhill, Thirsk YO7 4JU Tel. *01845 567234* Fax. *01845 567690* E-mail. *enquiries@pickhill-engineers.co.uk* Web. *www.pickhill-engineers.co.uk Oxford Welders – Pic Arc Welders*

Pico Technology Ltd James House Marlborough Road, Eaton Socon, St Neots PE19 8YP Tel. *01480 396395* Fax. *01480 396296* E-mail. *post@picotech.com* Web. *www.picotech.com Dr. Daq – Pico Technology*

Pigney H Son Agricultural Engineers Chapel Street, Appleby In Westmorland CA16 6QR Tel. *01768 351240* Fax. *01768 353033* E-mail. *pigney@pigney.co.uk Same Tractors – Suzuki ATV*

Pike Signals Ltd 7-11 Phoenix Business Park Avenue Close, Birmingham B7 4NU Tel. *0121 3594034* Fax. *0121 3333167* E-mail. *enquiries@pikesignals.com* Web. *www.pikesignals.com Micro X – MK10B – Pikes*

Piling Equipment Ltd 1 Camargue Road, Westbury BA13 3GG Tel. *07885 379866* E-mail. *info@piling-equipmnet-ltd.com* Web. *www.piling-equipment-ltd.com Piling*

Pilkington Agr UK Ltd (Automotive) Unit 4 Queenborough Business Park Main Road, Queenborough ME11 5DY Tel. *07802 204589* Fax. *01795 668059* E-mail. *peter.swann@pilkington.com* Web. *www.pilkington.com Triplex*

Pilkington Automotives Triplex House Eckersall Road, Birmingham B38 8SR Tel. *0121 2543000* Fax. *0121 2543188* E-mail. *tim.bayliss@pilkington.com* Web. *www.pilkington.com Pilkington Automotive*

Pilkington Group Ltd Prescot Road, St Helens WA10 3TT Tel. *01744 28882* Fax. *01744 692880* E-mail. *ashtons@pilkington.com* Web. *www.pilkington.com activ – Pilkington*

Pilkingtons Ltd (t/a Weitzer Parket UK) Belgrave Court Caxton Road Fulwood, Preston PR2 9PL Tel. *01772 790990* Fax. *01772 701044* E-mail. *info@pilkingtonsltd.com* Web. *www.pilkingtons.co.uk *Cincla (Italy) – *Derix (Germany) – Durwood – Handles – Impregnawood – *Mallein (France) – Parquet – Rapier Tapes – Shuttles – Sperloplast – Sperlowood – Superwood – Turnings – *Weitzer (Austria)*

Pillar Wedge Ltd Green Lane, Heywood OL10 2DY Tel. *01706 366191* Fax. *01706 625939* E-mail. *pillar-wedge@wedge-galv.co.uk* Web. *www.wedge-galv.co.uk Wedge Group Galvanizing*

Piller UK Ltd Westgate Phoenix Way, Cirencester GL7 1RY Tel. *01285 657721* Fax. *01285 654823* E-mail. *daniel.thomas@piller.com* Web. *www.piller.com A.P.O. – Anton Piller – Piller*

Pindar plc Thornborough Road Eastfield, Scarborough YO11 3UY Tel. *01723 581581* Fax. *01723 583086* E-mail. *enquiries@pindar.com* Web. *www.pindar.co.uk G.A. Pindar & Son Ltd – MacDonald Lindsay Pindar – Pindar P.L.C. – Pindar Systems Inc – Pindar-Routel Ltd – Pinder Set*

William Pinder & Sons Ltd 4 Harling Road Sharston Industrial Estate, Sharston Industrial Area, Manchester M22 4UZ Tel. *0161 9981729* Fax. *0161 9460734* E-mail. *info@pinderblades.com* Web. *www.pinderblades.com Chuch*

Pinelog Ltd Riverside Business Park Buxton Road, Bakewell DE45 1GS Tel. *01629 814481* Fax. *01629 814634* E-mail. *admin@pinelog.co.uk* Web. *www.pinelog.co.uk Chaletpool – Pinelodge – Pinelog*

Pinewood Associates Barton Hall Works Hardy Street Eccles, Manchester M30 7NB Tel. *0161 7077076* Fax. *0161 7076766* E-mail. *sales@pinewoodassociates.com* Web. *www.pinewoodassociates.com Black Diamond – Events – Kepac – Panelflex*

Pinewood Drapilux UK Ltd Albert Street, Leek ST13 8AH Tel. *01538 399153* Fax. *01538 373235* E-mail. *sales@pinewood-fabrics.com* Web. *www.pinewood-fabrics.com Pinewood*

Pinks Syrups 86 Alston Drive Bradwell Abbey, Milton Keynes MK13 9HF Tel. *01908 321516* Fax. *01327 856766* E-mail. *info@pinkssyrups.com* Web. *www.pinkssyrups.com Pinks Syrups*

Pin Mill Textiles Ltd Dreamscene House Park House Bridge Estate, Salford M6 6JQ Tel. *0161 7373300* Fax. *0161 7373100* E-mail. *info@pinmill.com* Web. *www.pinmill.com Ashbourne Collection – Brantwood – Colour Studio – Creative Colours – Dallas Dream – De Ville – Designer Collection – Dreamscene – M. and M. – Premier – Rompa – Tik Tok*

Pinpoint Presentation Green Zone 3b 54 Bayton Road Industrial Estate Bayton Road, Exhall, Coventry CV7 9TH Tel. *024 76646103* Fax. *0121 2756183* E-mail. *sales@pinpointpresentation.co.uk* Web. *www.pinpointpresentation.co.uk Zenith cases*

Pinstructure Ltd Unit 50 Enfield Industrial Estate, Redditch B97 6DE Tel. *01527 67999* Fax. *01527 66557* E-mail. *sales@pinstructure.com* Web. *www.pinstructure.com KALE MAKINA LTD – MIKALOR – TELLAFEDA – TRIDON*

Pioneer Marquees 30 Villiers Rd, Southall UB1 3BS Tel. *020 85741742* E-mail. *sales@pioneermarquees.com* Web. *www.pioneermarquees.com Pioneer Marquees*

Pioneer Weston Amber Way, Halesowen B62 8WG Tel. *01925 853000* Fax. *01925 853030* E-mail. *sales@pioneer.weston.co.uk* Web. *www.pwi-ltd.com Axseal – B.H. – Impax Seals – K.A. Seals – Marathon Seals – Nu-Lip Rings – Pioneer Oil Seals – Pioneer Weston Oil Seals – T.X. Split Seals – Weston Oil Seals*

Pioner Fristads Unit 7 Low Road Hellesdon, Norwich NR6 5AT Tel. *01282 858304* Fax. *01603 414540* E-mail. *sales@fristads-co.com* Web. *www.pionerfristads.co.uk A-code – Fristads – Kansas – Pionér*

Pipeline Engineering & Supply Company Ltd Gatherley Road Industrial Estate Brompton On Swale, Richmond DL10 7JG Tel. *01748 813000* Fax. *01748 818039* E-mail. *sales@pipelineengineering.com* Web. *www.pipelineengineering.com Omnithane*

Pipestoppers Stukeley Meadow, Burry Port SA16 0BU Tel. *01554 836836* Fax. *01554 836837* E-mail. *pipe@pipestoppers.net* Web. *www.pipestoppers.net Argon Sniffer – Argweld – Dissolvo – Multistrike – Oxygen Sniffer – Pipestoppers – Purge Dams – Techweld – Test Weld – Tungsten Intert Gas (TIG) – Water Soluble Dam, Dissolvo – Weld Purge – Weld Purging Dams*

Pipminster Ltd 1 Queens Road, London N11 2QJ Tel. *020 88811888* Fax. *020 88888153* E-mail. *info@pipminster.com* Web. *www.pipminster.com Pip*

Pippin Products 41 Church Street Clifton, Shefford SG17 5ET Tel. *01462 811485* Fax. *01462 851618* E-mail. *janeparry@tiscali.co.uk Pippin Products*

Piquant Ltd Piquant House Willenhall Lane Industrial Estate Willenhall Lane, Bloxwich, Walsall WS3 2XN Tel. *01922 711116* Fax. *01922 473240* E-mail. *salesinfo@piquant.co.uk* Web. *www.piquant.co.uk *Piquant – *Simply Sauces*

Pira Ltd Warwick House 116 Palmerston Road, Buckhurst Hill IG9 5LQ Tel. *01279 508111* Fax. *01279 508550* E-mail. *sales@pira.info* Web. *www.pira.info *Ferlea – *Magis – *Robots – *Segno Lighting*

Piroto Labelling Ltd 9 Pond Wood Close Moulton Park Industrial Estate, Northampton NN3 6RT Tel. *01604 646600* Fax. *01604 492090* E-mail. *l.mann@piroto-labelling.com* Web. *www.piroto-labelling.com Detect-A-Tag – Piroto*

Pisani plc 2a Plane Tree Crescent, Feltham TW13 7AL Tel. *020 89173350* Fax. *020 88473406* E-mail. *sales@pisani.co.uk* Web. *www.pisani.co.uk Pisani*

P I Tape Ltd Dean Court Upper Dean, Huntingdon PE28 0NL Tel. *01234 708882* Fax. *01234 708677* E-mail. *sales@pitape.co.uk* Web. *www.pitape.co.uk Pi Tape*

Pitkin Healey House Dene Road, Andover SP10 2AA Tel. *01264 409200* Fax. *01264 334110* E-mail. *sales@tempus-publishing.com* Web. *www.pitkin-guides.com Pitkin Unichrome Ltd*

Pitney Bowes Software Ltd Minton Place Victoria Street, Windsor SL4 1EG Tel. *01753 848200* Fax. *01753 621140* E-mail. *gary.roberts@mapinfo.com* Web. *www.pb.com Mapinfo*

Pittaway Sempol Ltd 106-114 Flinton Street, Hull HU3 4NA Tel. *01482 329007* Fax. *01482 213053* E-mail. *graeme.pittaway@ilumitex.co.uk* Web. *www.ilumitex.co.uk Ilumitex – Ilumitextra*

Pittsburgh Corning UK Ltd 63 Milford Road, Reading RG1 8LG Tel. *0118 9500655* Fax. *0118 9509019* E-mail. *paul.jones@pcenet.com* Web. *www.foamglass.co.uk *FOAMGLAS (Belgium) – *P.C. Glassblocks (U.S.A.)*

Pixel Power Ltd Unit 5 College Park Coldhams Lane, Cambridge CB1 3HD Tel. *01223 721000* Fax. *01223 721111* E-mail. *info@pixelpower.com* Web. *www.pixelpower.com Pixel Power*

P J P Plant Hire Mill Bank Radcliffe, Manchester M26 1AJ Tel. *0161 9590000* Fax. *0161 9599011* E-mail. *hire@pjpuk.com* Web. *www.pjpuk.com Barford – Benford – Bobcat – Bomag – Case – Hitachi – JCB – Kobelco – Komatsu – New Holland Kobelco – Takeuchi – Terex – Volvo – Yanmar*

Place UK Ltd Church Farm Church Road, Tunstead, Norwich NR12 8RQ Tel. *01692 536225* Fax. *01692 536928* E-mail. *info@placeuk.com* Web. *www.placeuk.com Place UK – R. & J.M. Place*

Plain Sailing Communications Ltd PO Box 335, Sevenoaks TN13 3ZX Tel. *01732 743746* Fax. *01732 743670* E-mail. *info@psworld.co.uk* Web. *www.psworld.co.uk FaxByNet*

Plalite Ltd Unit 9 Styles Close, Sittingbourne ME10 3BF Tel. *01795 476367* Fax. *01795 476369* E-mail. *sales@plalite.com* Web. *www.plalite.com Plalite*

Plandent Summit House Cranborne Road, Potters Bar EN6 3EE Tel. *01707 822400* Fax. *01438 758905* Web. *www.claudiusash.co.uk Casco – Claudius Ash – Cordent – J & S Davis – Mouthcare – *Orthologic (U.S.A.) – *Planmeca (Finland) – Solo*

Planglow Ltd Quorum House Bond Street South, Bristol BS1 3AE Tel. *0117 3178600* Fax. *0117 3178639* E-mail. *contactus@planglow.com* Web. *www.planglow.com *Day Labels – *Label Logic – *Nutri Logic*

Plannja Ltd 69 High Street, Maidenhead SL6 1JX Tel. *01628 637313* Fax. *01628 674940* E-mail. *enquire@plannja.co.uk* Web. *www.plannja.co.uk* **Energi Roof (Sweden) – *Korrugal (Sweden) – *Metallack (Sweden) – Plannja – *Rapide (Sweden) – *Royale (Sweden) – *Scanroof (Sweden) – Standing Semam Roofing (UK)*

Plantation Coffee Ltd xchange House 494 Mid Summer Boulevard, Milton Keynes MK9 2EA Tel. *01908 306008* Fax. *01908 255700* E-mail. *jw@plantationcoffee.co.uk* Web. *www.plantationcoffee.co.uk Plantation Direct*

Plants Of Distinction Abacus House Station Yard, Needham Market, Ipswich IP6 8AS Tel. *01449 721720* Fax. *01449 721722* E-mail. *sales@plantsofdistinction.co.uk* *Plants of Distinction*

Plascoat Farnham Trading Estate, Farnham GU9 9NY Tel. *01252 736800* Fax. *01252 724503* E-mail. *sales@plascoat.com* Web. *www.plascoat.com* *Deconyl – Plascoat*

Plasma Biotal Ltd Unit 3 Meverill Road, Tideswell, Buxton SK17 8PY Tel. *01298 872348* Fax. *01299 873708* E-mail. *info@plasma-group.co.uk* Web. *www.plasma-group.co.uk Biotal – Talograft*

Plasman Laminate Products Ltd Plasman Industrial Centre Marquis Street, Manchester M19 3JH Tel. *0161 2240333* Fax. *0161 2249961* E-mail. *sales@plasman.co.uk* Web. *www.plasman.co.uk Artis – Plasmanite*

Plasmor Ltd PO Box 44, Knottingley WF11 0DN Tel. *01977 673221* Fax. *01977 607071* E-mail. *jslater@plasmor.co.uk* Web. *www.plasmor.co.uk* *Aglite – Fibolite – Plascon – Plaslite – Plasmor Architectural Masonry – Plaspave – Rococo – Stranlite – Stranlite Thermalbond Blocks*

Plasplugs Main Line Industrial Estate Wetmore Road, Burton On Trent DE14 1SD Tel. *0800 8406820* Fax. *01283 531246* E-mail. *neale.turner@plasplugs.com* Web. *www.plasplugs.com MasterSharp – Plasplugs*

Plastestrip Profiles Ltd Unit 1-4 St Austell Enterprise Park Treverbyn Road, Carclaze, St Austell PL25 4EJ Tel. *01726 74771* Fax. *01726 69238* E-mail. *sales@plastestrip.com* Web. *www.plastestrip.com* *Plastestik – Plastestrip (Profiles) – Plasticlad*

Plastic Extruders Ltd Russell Gardens, Wickford SS11 8DN Tel. *01268 571116* Fax. *01268 560027* E-mail. *info@plastex.co.uk* Web. *www.plastex.co.uk* *Crossgrip (United Kingdom) – Ecopet (United Kingdom) – Firmagrip (United Kingdom) – Flexi Mats – Flexigrid (United Kingdom) – Floorline (United Kingdom) – Frontrunner – Frontrunner (United Kingdom) – Heron (United Kingdom) – Heronair – Herongripa – Heronrib – Herontile – Herontred – HVD – Pillomat (United Kingdom) – Plastex (United Kingdom) – Plastex Grid – Sparksafe – Tuff Spun – Tuff Spun Wear – Vynagrip (United Kingdom) – Vynastat – Zed Chex – Zed Land – Zed Tred*

Plastic ID 2 Redhouse Square, Duncan Close Moulton Park, Northampton NN3 6WL Tel. *0844 7361563* Fax. *0844 7362793* E-mail. *sales@plastic-id.com* Web. *www.plastic-id.com Magicard – Datacard – Evolis – Zebra – HID*

Plastic Mouldings Ltd 4 Ailsa Road, Irvine KA12 8LP Tel. *01294 278091* Fax. *01294 311655* E-mail. *info@plasticmouldings.com* Web. *www.plasticmouldings.com Bellows – Bellows - Boots Electrical - Dust Covers - End Caps - Gaiters - Neoprene - P.V.C. - Shrouds. – Boots Electrical – Demco – Dust Covers – End Caps – Gaiters – Neoprene – P.V.C. – Shrouds*

Plastico Ltd 100 Morden Road, Mitcham CR4 4DA Tel. *020 86460456* Fax. *020 86465440* E-mail. *sales@plastico.co.uk* Web. *www.plastico.co.uk Airlite – Airlite - Clarity - Elite - Flexy-Glass - Hilite - Rollor - Shatterproof - Spork - Starlite - Superjet – Bon Appetit – Clarity – Elite – Flexy-Glass – Hilite – Rollor – Shatterproof – Spork – Starlite – Superjet*

Plasticom Ltd Hilton Road, Ashford TN23 1EW Tel. *01233 621601* Fax. *01233 622169* E-mail. *user@plasticomgroup.com* Web. *www.plasticom.softnet.co.uk Ashford Moulding*

Plastiflex UK Ltd Ripley Close Normanton Indl-Est, Normanton WF6 1TB Tel. *01924 783600* Fax. *01924 896715* E-mail. *ian.howe@plastiflex.co.uk* Web. *www.plastiflex.co.uk* *Buflex – Reflex – Spiralectric – Spiralock – Spirapool – Sunflex – Tuflex – Zephlex*

Plastigauge Unit 2 Gaugemaster Way, Ford, Arundel BN18 0RX Tel. *01903 882822* Fax. *01903 884962* E-mail. *sales@plastigauge.co.uk* Web. *www.plastigauge.co.uk Plastigauge (United Kingdom)*

Plastotype Crucible Close Mushet Industrial Park, Coleford GL16 8RE Tel. *01594 837474* Fax. *01594 837312* E-mail. *info@plastotype.com* Web. *www.plastotype.com* **Anderson & Vreeland (U.S.A.) – B.A.S.F. – Cushion Adhesive Backing – *Harley (U.S.A.) – Jet Europe – Jiffy Mounts – Plasto – Plastoshim – Rigilon – Rubber – *Stereoprint (Switzerland) – Tesa – Vam Soli*

Platipus Anchors Ltd Unit Q Kingsfield Business Centre Philanthropic Road, Redhill RH1 4DP Tel. *01737 762300* Fax. *01737 773395* E-mail. *info@platipus-anchors.com* Web. *www.platipus-anchors.com Platipus*

Platt & Hill Ltd Belgrave Mill Fitton Hill Road, Oldham OL8 2LZ Tel. *0161 6214400* Fax. *0161 6214408* E-mail. *sales@phfillings.co.uk* Web. *www.phfillings.com* *Quallafil – Quallofil – Allerban – Thermolite*

Plaut International Heron Mews House 1a Balfour Road, Ilford IG1 4HP Tel. *020 85533471* Fax. *020 84781876* E-mail. *john@plautint.co.uk* Web. *www.plautint.co.uk* *Alcantara – Antique Pine Shelves – Bi-Fold Doors – *Gifu (Japan) – Mouldings – Mujur – Natural Pine Shelves – Pine Doors – Plaut International – Sinora – Solid Timber Doors*

Playdale Playgrounds Ltd Haverthwaite, Ulverston LA12 8AE Tel. *01539 531561* Fax. *01539 531539* E-mail. *enquiries@playdale.co.uk* Web. *www.playdale.co.uk* *Playdale – Playgrounds*

Playtex Ltd Unit D Park Industrial Estate Gareloch Road, Port Glasgow PA14 5XH Tel. *01475 741631* Fax. *01475 743119* E-mail. *dougie.bratt@dbaeu.com* Web. *www.playtex.co.uk* *Playtex*

Pledge Office Chairs Ltd Millstream Works Mill Road, Leighton Buzzard LU7 1BA Tel. *01525 376181* Fax. *01525 382392* E-mail. *sales@pledgechairs.co.uk* Web. *www.pledgechairs.com Aquarius – Arena – Aries – Campus – Contract – Finmere – Gemini – Industrial – Largo – Libra – Melody – Opus – Pro-Activ – Relax – Resta – Sonata – Taurus – Venue – Xpose – Zante*

Plenty Mirrlees Pumps 8 Earl Haig Road Hillington Industrial Estate, Glasgow G52 4JN Tel. *0141 8830314* Fax. *0141 8822752* E-mail. *plentypumps@spx.com* Web. *www.spxft.com CPC – G 2000 – MAGMO – P 2000 – TRIRO – TWINRO – U 2000 – Magmo – Mirrlees – Plenty*

Plescon Security Products Unit 9 Sterling Complex Farthing Road, Ipswich IP1 5AP Tel. *01473 745375* Fax. *01473 747252* E-mail. *info@plescon.co.uk* Web. *www.plescon.co.uk Gogglelox – Kwik-Case – Kwik-Issue*

Plexus Corp UK Ltd Pinnaclehill Industrial Estate, Kelso TD5 8XX Tel. *01573 223601* Fax. *01573 223600* E-mail. *willie.mackinnon@plexus.com* Web. *www.plexus.com Keltek*

Plimto Ltd Thruxton Airport Thruxton, Andover SP11 8PW Tel. *01264 773173* Fax. *01264 772936* E-mail. *sales@plimtosolder.com* Web. *www.plimtosolder.com Amtech Solder Paste (U.S.A.) – Circuit Brand – Cobar Wire, Fluxes & Solder Paste (Netherlands)*

PLM Illumination Ltd 6 Hoo Farm Industrial Estate Arthur Drive, Kidderminster DY11 7RA Tel. *01562 66441* Fax. *01562 829992* E-mail. *kelly@plmgroup.co.uk* Web. *www.plmgroup.co.uk UniLED*

Plowden & Thompson Ltd Dial Glass Work Stewkins, Stourbridge DY8 4YN Tel. *01384 393398* Fax. *01384 376638* E-mail. *sales@plowden-thompson.com* Web. *www.plowden-thompson.com Dial-Glass – Dial-Redrawn*

Plumbs Brookhouse Mill Old Lancaster Lane, Preston PR1 7PZ Tel. *01772 838301* Fax. *01772 838396* E-mail. *geoffrey.plumb@plumbs.ltd.uk* Web. *www.plumbs.co.uk Classic Covers – Plumbs – Plumbs Mail Order*

Plymovent Limited Beaumont House Beaumont Road, Banbury OX16 1RH Tel. *01295 259311* Fax. *01295 271750* E-mail. *info@plymovent.co.uk* Web. *www.plymovent.co.uk* *E.F.O. – Extractor Crane – Flex Max – Junior – M.D.B.*

P M A Group 181 Waterside Road Hamilton, Leicester LE5 1TL Tel. *0116 2461808* Fax. *0116 2761600* E-mail. *mike.westwood@pmagroup.co.uk* Web. *www.pmagroup.co.uk P.M.A. Group*

P M D UK Ltd Broad Lane, Coventry CV5 7AY Tel. *024 76466691* Fax. *024 76473034* E-mail. *sales@pmdgroup.co.uk* Web. *www.pmdgroup.co.uk* *Alchromate – Argonaut – Brasspol – Cirgold 90 – Cirgold 965 – Decramerse – Econoclense – Econopic – Econovate – Emerald – Goldstrike – H.Y.-C – H.Y.-Trac – Hyclad – Hylo – Hyreel – Micro-Em – Nistan – Nistar – No-Tarn – Nustrip 93 – Onyx – P.M.D. 505 – P.M.D. 606 – Phoschromate – Procirc – Procirc 900 – Procirc 9001 – Procirc 9002 – Procirc 9003 – Procirc 901 – Procirc 9010 – Procirc 9020 – Procirc 9021 – Procirc 9022 – Procirc 903 – Procirc 905 – Procirc 909 – Procirc 911 – Procirc 9110 – Procirc 9121 – Procirc 9122 – Procirc 9130 – Procirc 9132 – Procirc 921 – Procirc 9342 – Procirc 9361 – Procirc 9362 – Procirc 9390 – Procirc 9401 – Procirc 9421 – Procirc 9422 – Procirc 945 – Procirc 952(80) – Procirc 961 – Procirc 963 – Procirc 964 – Procirc 965 – Procirc 9691 – Procirc 971M – Procirc 980 – Procirc 981TK – Procirc 985 – Procirc 986 – Procirc 987 – Procirc 9870 – Procirc 9902 – Procirc 9945 – Procirc 9990 – Procirc 9991 – Procirc SP230 – Procirc SP236 – Procirc SP237 – Procirc SP239 – Procirc SP240 – Procirc SP263 – Procirc SP264*

P & M Pumps Unit 1 Sawtry Court Brookside Industrial Estate, Sawtry, Huntingdon PE28 5SB Tel. *01487 830123* Fax. *01487 832888* E-mail. *sales@thesolidsolution.co.uk* Web. *www.pandmpumps.co.uk Discflo – Pioneer Pump – Vaughan*

P M S International Group plc International House Cricketers Way, Basildon SS13 1ST Tel. *01268 505050* Fax. *01268 505000* E-mail. *info@pmsinternational.com* Web. *www.pmsinternational.com Action Force – Aquafun – Blackfoot – Claire dolls – Essential – Essential Auto Accessories – Games 2 Play – Great Oak Lifestyles – Headlines – HomeAid – Mintax – On Top – PataMates – Pooch Pets – Power Makes Sense – Roots and Shoots – Securelock – Snowflake – Splashinator – Sunstoppers – Sydewynder – Tender Moments – Toys 2 Play – Travel Bug – Victor Hugo, Steven Daniels, and Ruffino*

P M S York Ltd 34 Buckingham Street, York YO1 6DW Tel. *01904 636969* Fax. *01904 647724* E-mail. *training@pmsyork.co.uk* Web. *www.pmsyork.co.uk* *Purchasing Management Services*

PNMsoft 38 Clarendon road, Watford WD17 1JJ Tel. *01923 813420* E-mail. *info@pnmsoft.com* Web. *www.pnmsoft.com PNMsoft*

Pobjoy Mint Ltd Millennia House Kingswood Park, Kingswood, Tadworth KT20 6AY Tel. *01737 818181* Fax. *01737 818199* E-mail. *sales@pobjoy.com* Web. *www.pobjoy.com Coinart – Mint – Nicklon – Olympic – Pobjoy Crownfolio – Pobjoy mint – Pobjoy Mint Crownmedal – Pobjoy Mint Jewellery – Pobjoy silverclad – Virenium*

Podmores Engineers Ltd H Great Fenton Business Park Grove Road, Stoke On Trent ST4 4LZ Tel. *01782 747478* Fax. *01782 416606* E-mail. *info@podmores-systems.com* Web. *www.podmores-systems.com Podmores Engineers*

Pod Space Ltd. 1 Camp Hill, Scammonden, Huddersfield HD3 3FR Tel. *01484 841167* E-mail. *info@pod-space.co.uk* Web. *www.pod-space.co.uk Pod Space Limited*

Poeton Gloucester (Coating Technology Worldwide) Southbrook Road Eastern Avenue, Gloucester GL4 3DN Tel. *01452 300500* Fax. *01452 500400* E-mail. *sales@poeton.co.uk* Web. *www.poeton.co.uk* *Apticote – Apticote, Nedox, Tufram – Nedox – Tufram*

Polar Ford York Jockey Lane Huntington, York YO32 9GY Tel. *01904 625371* Fax. *01904 622238* E-mail. *sales@polarmotor.co.uk* Web. *www.polarmotor.co.uk* *Polar*

Polaron Cortina Ltd 20 Greenhill Crescent, Watford WD18 8JA Tel. *01923 495495* Fax. *01923 228796* E-mail. *rkay@polaron.co.uk* Web. *www.coopercontrols.co.uk/cortina E and G – G.Y.R.D. – Gyro Switches – Levelling Switches*

Poli Film UK Ltd 7 Brunel Close Drayton Fields Industrial Estate, Daventry NN11 8RB Tel. *01327 876071* Fax. *01327 300005* E-mail. *sales@poli-film.co.uk* Web. *www.poli-film.de Poli Film Adhesive Products*

Polimeri Europa Ltd Cadland Road Hythe, Southampton SO45 3YY Tel. *023 80894919* Fax. *023 80883306* E-mail. *james.macdonald@polimerieuropa.com* Web. *www.enichem.it Butaclor (France) – Dutral (Italy) – Edistir – Europreme N (Italy) – Europreme SOLT (Italy) – Europreme SOLT (U.S.A.) – *Europrene CIS (Italy) – Europrene Neocis (Italy) – Extir – Intene – Intex – Intol – Koblend – Kostil – Simkral – Tedimom – Tercarol*

Gregory Pollard Ltd Regent Road Countesthorpe, Leicester LE8 5RF Tel. *0116 2773857* Fax. *0116 2784395* E-mail. *david@magicfit.co.uk* Web. *www.magicfit.co.uk* *Magicfit*

Pollards International 83 Sefton Lane Maghull, Liverpool L31 8BU Tel. *0151 5263456* Fax. *0151 5266969* E-mail. *info@pollardsinternational.com* Web. *www.pollardsinternational.com Cool case co uk ltd*

William Pollard & Company Ltd Oak House Falcon Road, Sowton Industrial Estate, Exeter EX2 7NU Tel. *01392 445333* Fax. *01392 276503* E-mail. *info@pollardsprint.co.uk* Web. *www.pollardsprint.co.uk Masterfile – Securiticket*

Pol Roger Ltd 4 Coningsby Street, Hereford HR1 2DY Tel. *01432 262800* Fax. *01432 262806* E-mail. *polroger@polroger.co.uk* Web. *polroger.co.uk* *Andean Wineries (Argentina) – *Cousino Macul (Chile) – *Josmeyer (Alsace) – *Maison Champy (Burgundy) – *Omaka Springs (New Zealand) – *Querciabella (Tuscany) – Rymill Coonawarra (South Australia)*

Polux Ltd Elliott Street, Rochdale OL12 0LH Tel. *01706 358466* Fax. *01706 642841* E-mail. *info@polux.co.uk* Web. *www.polux.co.uk "Polux" – "Polux" – Polutef-PTFE*

Polybags Ltd Lyon Way, Greenford UB6 0AQ Tel. *020 85758200* Fax. *020 85782247* E-mail. *sales@polybags.co.uk* Web. *www.polybags.co.uk* *Polybags*

Polydiam Industries 70-80 Markfield Road, London N15 4QF Tel. *020 84931060* Fax. *020 88855711* E-mail. *sales@rubberstamp.co.uk* Web. *www.polydiam.com* *Alphalets – Jettsetter – Polydiam – Polydiam – Polydiam*

Polyfashions Ltd 27 Whitmore Road Small Heath, Birmingham B10 0NR Tel. *0121 7727754* Fax. *0121 7666744* E-mail. *info@polyfashion.co.uk* Web. *www.polyfashion.co.uk Coot*

Polymeric Labels Ltd 12 Greenacres Road, Oldham OL4 1HA Tel. *0161 6789005* Fax. *0161 6271378* E-mail. *sales@polymeric.co.uk* Web. *www.polymeric.co.uk* *Mericbrand – Primabrand – Unibrand*

Polymer Products UK Ltd Forest of Dean Business Estate 4 Stepbridge Road, Coleford GL16 8PJ Tel. *01594 833100* Fax. *01594 835666* E-mail. *sales@polymerproducts.co.uk* Web. *www.polymerproducts.co.uk Scafpad – Scafpad -*

scaffolding steel & rubber base plates for upright scaffolding tube.

Polypack Packaging Supplies 48 New Broadway Tarring Road, Worthing BN11 4HS Tel. *01903 200984* Fax. *01903 200984* E-mail. *info@thepolyshop.co.uk* Web. *www.thepolyshop.co.uk Polypack*

Polytank Ltd Naze Lane East Freckleton, Preston PR4 1UN Tel. *01772 632850* Fax. *01772 679615* E-mail. *sales@polytank.co.uk* Web. *www.polytank.co.uk Circular Polytanks – Framed Polytanks – Polytank Combination Tanks – Polytank Lofttanks – Polytank Poly A30 – Polytank Slimtanks – Rectangular Polytanks*

Polytech International Long Lane Pott Shrigley, Macclesfield SK10 5SD Tel. *01625 575737* Fax. *01625 575720* E-mail. *sales@mri-polytech.com* Web. *www.mri-polytech.com Polyplay – Polytrak*

Polytec Holden Ltd Porthouse Industrial Estate, Bromyard HR7 4NS Tel. *01885 483000* Fax. *01885 483057* E-mail. *reception@polytec-group.com* Web. *www.polytec-group.com Holden Hydroman*

Polytronics Design Ltd The Old Flour Mill Queen Street, Emsworth PO10 7BT Tel. *01243 372207* Fax. *01243 379383* E-mail. *info@polytronics.co.uk* Web. *www.polytronics.co.uk Midicraft*

Polyurethane Products Ltd Stirling Road West Carr Industrial Estate, Retford DN22 7SN Tel. *01777 712500* Fax. *01777 707001* E-mail. *wynn.crorkin@poly-products.co.uk* Web. *www.poly-products.co.uk Greenthane – Redthane – Transthane*

Polyurethane Progress Ltd Church Street, Wakefield WF1 5QY Tel. *01924 387310* Fax. *01924 382951* E-mail. *office@polyprog.co.uk* Web. *www.polyprog.co.uk Dobi – Dobi Cable Safe*

Pompadour Laboratories Ltd Mount Street New Basford, Nottingham NG7 7HF Tel. *0115 9781383* Fax. *0115 9784598* E-mail. *sales@pompadour.co.uk* Web. *www.pompadour.co.uk Pompadour*

Poole Lighting Ltd Cabot Lane, Poole BH17 7BY Tel. *01202 690945* Fax. *01202 600166* E-mail. *trevor.hodder@poolelighting.com* Web. *www.poolelighting.com Poole lighting*

Pool Installers 18 Easter Bankton, Livingston EH54 9BD Tel. *07772 736120* E-mail. *info@poolinstallers.co.uk* Web. *www.poolinstallers.co.uk Pool Installers*

Pool Vac Ltd 229 London Road, Camberley GU15 3EY Tel. *01276 25252* Fax. *01276 21796* E-mail. *poolvac@web-hq.com Pool-Vac*

Porcher Abrasive Coatings Ltd Nursery Road Industrial Estate, Boston PE21 7TN Tel. *01205 356666* Fax. *01205 351646* E-mail. *info@porcher.co.uk* Web. *www.porcher.co.uk TREADSAFE (United Kingdom)*

Portabello Fabrications 3 Long Acre Close Holbrook Industrial Estate, Holbrook, Sheffield S20 3FR Tel. *0114 2513092* Fax. *0114 2487936* E-mail. *sales@pfl-rmf.co.uk* Web. *www.portobello-fab.co.uk Portobello*

Portakabin Ltd New Lane Huntington, York YO32 9PT Tel. *01904 611655* Fax. *01233 661557* E-mail. *sales@portakabin.com* Web. *www.portakabin.com Duplex – Lilliput – Pacemaker – Porta – Porta-Hire – Porta-Xtra – Portakabin – Pullman – Xporta*

Portastor Ltd New Lane Huntington, York YO32 9PR Tel. *01904 656869* Fax. *01904 687257* E-mail. *action@portastor.com* Web. *www.portastor.com Portacell – Portastor Communications – Smartcell*

Portex Technologies Ltd Merlin House Alness Point Business Park, Alness IV17 0UP Tel. *01349 884060* Fax. *01349 884076* E-mail. *julie.adams@porex.com* Web. *www.porex.com Fluorat – Microporous PTFE Products – Mupor – Mupor Plus – Mupor tm*

Portland Engineering Co. Ltd Wide Street, Portland DT5 2JP Tel. *01305 821273* Fax. *01305 821499* E-mail. *office@portlandengineering.com* Web. *www.portlandengineering.com Tellenco*

Portman Building Society Richmond Hill, Bournemouth BH2 6EP Tel. *08456 090600* Fax. *01202 563800* Web. *www.portman.co.uk Harvest – Harvest Gold – Portman – Regency – Regency & West of England – Ridgeway – Senator – Tree Logo – Triangles*

Portman Travel Ltd (Head Office) Capital Tower Greyfriars Road, Cardiff CF10 3PN Tel. *029 20402600* Fax. *01792 653101* Web. *www.portmantravel.com Cory Freight – Portman Travel*

Portman Travel Ltd 15th Floor Edgbaston House 3 Duchess Place, Birmingham B16 8NH Tel. *0121 4528800* Fax. *0121 4528810* E-mail. *mhumphries@portmantravel.co.uk* Web. *www.portmantravel.com Portman Travel*

Portmeirion Group Ltd London Road, Stoke On Trent ST4 7QQ Tel. *01782 744721* Fax. *01782 744061* E-mail. *splimbley@portmeiriongroup.com* Web. *www.portmeiriongroup.com Royal Worcester*

Portugalia Wines UK 4-7 Whitby Avenue, London NW10 7SF Tel. *020 89658970* Fax. *020 89658971* E-mail. *sales@portugaliawines.co.uk* Web. *www.portugaliawines.co.uk *Delta Cafès*

Portway Press Ltd Timeform House Northgate, Halifax HX1 1XF Tel. *01422 330330* Fax. *01422 398017* E-mail. *peter.bell@timeform.com* Web. *www.timeform.com Timeform Racing Publications*

Port Of Workington Prince of Wales Dock, Workington CA14 2JH Tel. *01900 602301* Fax. *01900 604696* E-mail. *jlihou@portofworkington.co.uk* Web. *www.portofworkington.co.uk Port of Workington*

Porvair plc 7 Regis Place Bergen Way, North Lynn Industrial Estate, Kings Lynn PE30 2JN Tel. *01553 765500* Fax. *01553 765599* E-mail. *sales@porvair-sciences.com* Web. *www.porvair-sciences.com Advanced Materials (U.S.A.) – *Ceramic Foam Filters (U.S.A.) – CZerbide (U.S.A.) – *Dual Stage Filtration Systems (U.S.A.) – Easy Fit Dome – *FE Iron Foundry Filters (U.S.A.) – *HVB Burner Systems (U.S.A.) – HYcarb (U.S.A.) – HYcor (U.S.A.) – *Kiln Furniture (U.S.A.) – Krystal Plate – Krystal Plate- Micromass - Porvent - Spinmaster - Multi-Pore Ceramic Filters - Selee Foam Filters - Sinterflo - Super Dome - Vyon - Easy Fit Dome - Kiln Furniture - HVB Burner Systems - Dual Stage Filtration Systems - Ceramic Foam Filters - FE Iron Foundry Filters - Microlute - Porvair Fuel Cell Technologies - Mictofiltrex - Megga Gaz - Ultravap - Talvic - Hycor - Hycarb - CZerbide - Metpore - Metflome. – Megga Gaz – Metflame (U.S.A.) – Metpore EFCS – Microfiltrex – Microlute – *Micromass (U.S.A.) – *Multi-pore Ceramic Filters (U.S.A.) – Porvent – *Selee Foam Filters (U.S.A.) – Sinterflo – Spinmaster – Super Dome – Talvic (U.S.A.) – Triseal – Ultravap – Vyon*

Porvair Sciences Ltd (a Division of Porvair Filtration Group Ltd) Unit 73 Clywedog Road South, Wrexham Industrial Estate, Wrexham LL13 9XS Tel. *01978 661144* Fax. *01978 664554* E-mail. *enquiries@porvair-sciences.com* Web. *www.porvair-sciences.com Easy Fit Dome – Porvent – Sinterflo – Spinmaster – Super Dome – Vyon*

POS Display Shop 6A Challenger Way Edgerley Drain Road, Peterborough PE1 5EX Tel. *01733 892815* Fax. *01733 558232* E-mail. *info@posdisplayshop.co.uk* Web. *www.posdisplayshop.co.uk Barkers*

Poselco Lighting Ltd Unit 1 The Metropolitan Park Bristol Road, Greenford UB6 8UW Tel. *020 88130101* Fax. *020 88130099* E-mail. *c.tribe@poselco.co.uk* Web. *www.poselco.co.uk Circulux – Fraud Scanner – Guard-Dog – Poselco – Rondelux – Ziggurat*

Possum 8 Farmbrough Close, Aylesbury HP20 1DQ Tel. *01296 461000* Fax. *01296 394349* E-mail. *sales@possum.co.uk* Web. *www.possum.co.uk Palantype – Possum*

Posturite Ltd The Mill Berwick, Polegate BN26 6SZ Tel. *08453 450010* Fax. *08453 450020* E-mail. *support@posturite.co.uk* Web. *www.posturite.co.uk Posturite*

Pot Black UK Bowden Green Clovelly, Bideford EX39 5TH Tel. *01237 478061* Fax. *01237 471044 Childcraft – Pot Black (UK) Ltd*

Potclays Ltd Albion Works Brickkiln Lane, Stoke On Trent ST4 7BP Tel. *01782 219816* Fax. *01782 286506* E-mail. *sales@potclays.co.uk* Web. *www.potclays.co.uk Artisan – Craft Crank – Flecked Stoneware – Industrial Crank – Keuper Red – St Thomas*

Potter Cowan & Co Belfast Ltd Phoenix House 20 Duncrue Cresent, Belfast BT3 9BW Tel. *028 90370050* Fax. *028 90777333* E-mail. *sales@pottercowan.com* Web. *www.pottercowan.com "Now" – "Plan D" – Astracast – Burbury & Scott – Chic – Concept Laminates – *Cuisine Schmidt (France) – Millenimum – P.A.C.E. – Perstorp Axiom – Silkstone & Millenium Acrylic – Tweeny – Vision Work Surface – *Whirlpool "BauKnecht" Ignis (Germany & Italy)*

Potteries Power Transmission Ltd 32 Hartshill Road, Stoke On Trent ST4 7QU Tel. *01782 844144* Fax. *01782 745222* E-mail. *david@ppt-ltd.co.uk* Web. *www.ppt-ltd.co.uk Bauer – Bauer Gearboxes – Bonfiglioli Gearboxes – CMG Electric Motors – Fenner Gearboxes – Leroy Somer Electric Motors – Leroy Somer Gearboxes – Marelli Electric Motors – Motovario Gearboxes – Renold Chains – Renold Conveyor Chains – Renold Geareboxes – Rossi Gearboxes – Schneider Inverters – Telemecanique Inverters – Tsubakimoto Chains – Vacon Drives – Vacon Inverters*

Potters 1 Botanic Court Martland Park, Wigan WN5 0JZ Tel. *01942 219960* Fax. *01942 219966* E-mail. *info@pottersherbals.co.uk* Web. *www.potterspoultry.co.uk Granny-Ann – Kwoffit*

Potts Buckets & Attatchments Ltd 6-9 Longridge Road, Blaydon On Tyne NE21 6JJ Tel. *0191 4144186* Fax. *0191 4142211* E-mail. *sales@potts-buckets.com* Web. *www.potts-buckets.com Potts – Potts Buckets*

Poulten & Graf Ltd 1 Alfreds Way Alfreds Way, Barking IG11 0AS Tel. *020 85944256* Fax. *020 85948419* E-mail. *jason.robson@poulten-graf.com* Web. *www.poulten-graf.com Volac*

Poultry First Ltd The Manor House Greenways Manor Estate, Woodhall Spa LN10 6PY Tel. *01526 352471* Fax. *01526 352022* Web. *www.poultryfirst.co.uk Poulty First – Sterling Farm*

Poundfield Products Ltd Grove Farm Creeting St Peter, Ipswich IP6 8QG Tel. *01449 723150* Fax. *01449 723151* E-mail. *sales@poundfield.com* Web. *www.poundfield.com Alfabloc Walling Systems – Alfabloc – Betabric – Betabric Walling system – Interlocking 1 metre L-bloc – Interlocking 2 metre L-bloc – Interlocking L-bloc – L-bloc – Stilcons*

Poundstretcher Ltd Trident Business Park Leeds Road, Huddersfield HD2 1UA Tel. *01484 431444* Fax. *0113 2549371* E-mail. *customercare@poundstretcher.co.uk* Web. *www.poundstretcher.co.uk Poundstretcher*

Pound World Ltd Unit 27 Oakwell Way Birstall, Batley WF17 9LU Tel. *01924 220511* Fax. *01924 220512* E-mail. *info@poundworld.net* Web. *www.inthepink.fsnet.co.uk Everything A Pound*

Powakaddy International Ltd Unit N1 Eurolink Industrial Centre Castle Road, Sittingbourne ME10 3RN Tel. *01795 473555* Fax. *01795 474586* E-mail. *sales@powakaddy.co.uk* Web. *www.powakaddy.co.uk PowaKaddy (United Kingdom)*

Powel Automation Ltd (Head Office) Powel Buildings Commerce Way, Lancing BN15 8TA Tel. *01903 762700* Fax. *01903 763652* E-mail. *roy@powel.co.uk* Web. *www.powel.co.uk Powel*

Powelectrics Ltd 2 Sandy Hill Park Sandy Way, Tamworth B77 4DU Tel. *01827 310666* Fax. *01827 310999* E-mail. *sales@powelectrics.co.uk* Web. *www.powelectrics.co.uk EGE – FASOP – IN4MA – PROXISTOR*

C B Powell Ltd 10 St Josephs Close, Hove BN3 7ES Tel. *01273 771144* Fax. *01273 726966* E-mail. *cbpowell@btconnect.com* Web. *www.cbpowellengineeringsussex.co.uk Basex*

Powell Marketing Ltd P M House Cromer Industrial Estate Hilton Fold Lane, Middleton, Manchester M24 2LE Tel. *0161 6537770* Fax. *0161 6553795* E-mail. *enq@powellmarketing.com* Web. *www.powellmarketing.com Hi-glo – Message makers*

Power Access Systems Ltd Parish Lane Pease Pottage, Crawley RH10 5NY Tel. *01293 561892* Fax. *01293 561896* E-mail. *mail@poweraccess.co.uk* Web. *www.poweraccess.co.uk P K*

Power Adhesives Ltd 1 Lords Way, Basildon SS13 1TN Tel. *01268 885800* Fax. *01268 885810* E-mail. *s.sweeney@poweradhesives.com* Web. *www.poweradhesives.com Hotfix – Tec – Tecbond*

Powerail Ltd High Road Finchley, London N12 8PT Tel. *020 84460350* Fax. *020 84467054* E-mail. *enquiries@powerailltd.com* Web. *www.powerailltd.com Powerail Vahle*

Power Assemblies Ltd Cooper Street, Wolverhampton WV2 2JL Tel. *01902 456767* Fax. *01902 456761* Web. *www.pump.net Villiers*

Power Blast International 9 Colhook Industrial Park, Petworth GU28 9LP Tel. *01428 707895* Fax. *01428 707894* E-mail. *info@powerblast.co.uk* Web. *www.powerblast.co.uk Powerblast*

Powerbox Group Ltd 4-5 Knights Court Magellan Close, Andover SP10 5NT Tel. *01264 384460* Fax. *01264 334337* E-mail. *patricia.mitter@powerbox.se* Web. *www.powerbox.co.uk Powerbox*

Power Gems Ltd Unit 1 Fairhills Road Irlam, Manchester M44 6BA Tel. *0161 7767030* Fax. *0161 7767039* E-mail. *patrick.mcguane@powergems.com* Web. *www.powergems.com PG Lighting – Power Gem*

Power Jacks Ltd South Harbour Road, Fraserburgh AB43 9BZ Tel. *01346 513131* Fax. *01346 519737* E-mail. *charlesb@powerjacks.co.uk* Web. *www.powerjacks.com Power Jacks (United Kingdom) – Power Jacks (United Kingdom) – Power Jacks (United Kingdom) – Power Jacks - Screw Jacks, Linear Actuators & Gearboxes, Precision Actuation Systems, Neeter Drive Bevel Gearboxes, Spiracon Roller Screws, Rolaram Linear Actuators, Youngs Lifting, Duff-Norton Actuators , Duff-Norton Rotary Unions. – Precision Actuation Systems (PAS) (United Kingdom) – Precision Actuation Systems (PAS) (United Kingdom) – Power Jacks (United Kingdom) – Youngs Lifting (United Kingdom) – Fortune Engineering (United Kingdom) – Precision Actuation Systems (PAS) (United Kingdom) – Neeter Drive (United Kingdom)*

Powerlite Lighting Solutions Ltd Units H34 Gildersome Spur Morley, Leeds LS27 7JZ Tel. *0113 2897832* Fax. *0113 2597917* E-mail. *info@powerlite-lighting.com* Web. *www.powerlite-lighting.com Classic – Crystaline – Decobrik – Decordrum – Decorline – Decorsquare – Decoslim – Decotrim – Ensign – Espha – Espia – Laser – Metaflood – Microlux – Mondolux – Omnilux – Power Flood – Powergem – Powerson – Powerstream – Regency – Starlux – Starmaster*

Powermatic Ltd The Factory Hort Bridge Hort Bridge, Ilminster TA19 9PS Tel. *01460 53535* Fax. *01460 52341* E-mail. *info@powermatic.co.uk* Web. *www.powermatic.co.uk Atriavent – Hopper Window – Open Sky*

Power Plant & Drives Hydepark Industrial Estate McKinney Road, Newtownabbey BT36 4PX Tel. *0845 6256256* Fax. *028 90020424* E-mail. *sales@wpmurray.com* Web. *www.wpmurray.com *A.B.B. (Germany) – *S.E.W. (Germany) – *Siemens (Germany)*

Power Plant Gears 1 Eagle Works Greets Green Road, West Bromwich B70 9EJ Tel. *0121 5576334* Fax. *0121 5200951* E-mail. *uk@davidbrown.com* Web. *www.davidbrown.com P.P.G.*

Power Plastics Station Road, Thirsk YO7 1PZ Tel. *01845 525503* Fax. *01845 525485* E-mail. *info@powerplastics.co.uk* Web. *www.powerplastics.co.uk Fumaplas – Powerlite – Powerplas – Powerplas – Tarpee – Thermacel – Thermaquilt*

Power Products International Ltd Commerce Way, Edenbridge TN8 6ED Tel. *01732 866424* Fax. *01732 866399* E-mail. *sales@ppi-uk.com* Web. *www.ppi-uk.com P.P.I*

Power-Rite UK Ltd The Gate House Claypit Lane, Carlton, Goole DN14 9PR Tel. *0844 8008472* Fax. *01405 869686* E-mail. *shaun@power-rite.co.uk* Web. *www.power-rite.co.uk Atlas Copco*

Powersense Technology (UPS & Generators) Unit 3 Morley Business Centre Morley Road, Tonbridge TN9 1RA Tel. *01732 771818* Fax. *01732 771881* E-mail. *alanbrailsford@talk21.com* Web. *www.powersense.co.uk Advance Galatrek (United Kingdom) – Best Power (United Kingdom) – Powersense (United Kingdom) – Powerware (United Kingdom)*

Powershield Doors Ltd 21 Ferguson Drive Knockmore Hill Industrial Park, Lisburn BT28 2EX Tel. *028 92662200* Fax. *028 92603600* E-mail. *sales@powershield.co.uk* Web. *www.powershield.co.uk Powershield – Pressfold*

Power Sonic Europe 3 Buckingham Square Hurricane Way, Wickford SS11 8YQ Tel. *01268 560686* Fax. *01268 560902* E-mail. *sales@power-sonic.co.uk* Web. *www.power-sonic.co.uk Power-Sonic*

Powersource Projects Ltd Powerpro House Capital Park Combe Lane, Wormley, Godalming GU8 5TJ Tel. *01428 684980* Fax. *01428 667979* E-mail. *sales@power-source-pro.co.uk* Web. *www.power-source-pro.co.uk PowerPro (United Kingdom)*

Power Stax plc Unit B5 Armstrong Mall, Southwood Business Park, Farnborough GU14 0NR Tel. *01252 407800* Fax. *01252 407810* E-mail. *sales@powerstaxplc.com* Web. *www.powerstaxplc.com Technotrend*

Powertron Converters Ltd Glebe Farm Technical Campus Knapwell, Cambridge CB23 4GG Tel. *01954 267726* Fax. *01954 267626* E-mail. *sales@powertron.co.uk* Web. *www.powertron.co.uk Electronic equipment & instruments suppliers – Powertron*

Powerwall Space Frame Systems Ltd 4 Netherton Road, Wishaw ML2 0EQ Tel. *01698 373305* Fax. *01698 374503* E-mail. *sales@powerwall.co.uk* Web. *www.powerwall.co.uk Power Wall*

Powlift Handling Systems Ltd 3a Blackberry Lane, Halesowen B63 4NX Tel. *0121 5504750* Fax. *0121 5855226* E-mail. *sales@powlift.co.uk* Web. *www.powlift.co.uk Powlift*

J F Poynter Ltd (t/a Maxim Lamps Works) Unit 23 More House Farm Business Centre Ditchling Road, Wivelsfield, Haywards Heath RH17 7RE Tel. *01444 471491* Fax. *01444 471777* E-mail. *sales@maximlamps.co.uk* Web. *www.maximlamps.co.uk Maxim Lamps*

PPG Aerospace Darlington Road, Shildon DL4 2QP Tel. *01388 770222* Fax. *01388 770288* Web. *www.ppg.com Desoprime – Desothane – DeSoto – Impactoflex – Permapol – PRC – ProSeal – Semco – Semfreeze – Semfreeze – Semkit – Sempen – Skycryl – Skyflex – Skyshield – Skythane*

P P G Industries UK Ltd PO Box 132, Wigan WN2 4XG Tel. *01942 257161* Fax. *01942 522385* E-mail. *b.pollock@ppg.com* Web. *www.ppg.com P.P.G.*

P P M A Ltd 34 Stafford Road, Wallington SM6 9AA Tel. *020 87738111* Fax. *020 87730022* E-mail. *administration@ppma.co.uk* Web. *www.ppma.co.uk P.P M A Show*

P P S Rotaprint Ltd Unit 720 Tudor Estate Abbey Road, London NW10 7UN Tel. *020 89519500* Fax. *020 89631940* E-mail. *sales@rotaprint.com* Web. *www.wwpps.com Adast Dominant – Hamada – Rotaprint*

Practical Car & Van Rental Practical House 21-23 Little Broom Street, Camp Hill, Birmingham B12 0EU Tel. *0121 7728599* Fax. *0121 7666229* E-mail. *info@practicalburton.co.uk* Web. *www.practical.co.uk Practical*

Practice Net Ltd Cardiff Business Technology Centre 2 Capital Business Park Par, Cardiff CF3 2PX Tel. *029 20837410* Fax. *029 20837427* E-mail. *dalerogers@practicenet.co.uk* Web. *www.practicenet.co.uk Radius Professional Office*

Practicon Ltd The Old School House Chapel Lane, Rode Heath, Stoke On Trent ST7 3SD Tel. *01270 876211* Fax. *01270 878887* E-mail. *sales@practicon.co.uk* Web. *www.practicon.co.uk Practicon*

Prater Ltd Perrywood Business Park Honeycrock Lane, Redhill RH1 5JQ Tel. *01737 772331* Fax. *01737 766021* E-mail. *mail@prater.co.uk* Web. *www.prater.co.uk Prater Roofing*

Praxair Whisby Road North Hykeham, Lincoln LN6 3DL Tel. *01522 878200* Fax. *01522 878250* E-mail. *enquiries@sermatech.com* Web. *www.praxair.com SermAlcote coating – SermaLoy coating series – SermeTel coating series*

Precious Washers Stafford Ltd Unit 24 Wolseley Court, Staffordshire Technology Park, Stafford ST18 0GA Tel. *01785 227722* Fax. *01785 227744* E-mail. *info@preciouswashers.co.uk* Web. *www.preciouswashers.co.uk Alto – Techtron – Wesley Group*

Precise Pro Audio Hire Unit 5 Concept Green Business Park 16 George Street, Eccles, Manchester M30 0RG Tel. *0161 7892246* Fax. *0161 4257651* E-mail. *info@preciseaudiohire.com* Web. *www.preciseaudiohire.com precise pro audio hire*

Precision Ceramics (a division of McGeoch - Technology Ltd) 86 Lower Tower Street, Birmingham B19 3PA Tel. *0121 6875858* Fax. *0121 6875857* E-mail. *info@precision-ceramics.co.uk* Web. *www.precision-ceramics.co.uk Macor – Shapal – Corning – Shapal – AX05 boron nitride – HP boron nitride – M26 boron nitride*

Precision Chains Ltd Clee Road, Dudley DY2 0YG Tel. *01384 455455* Fax. *01384 230751* E-mail. *julia.gorton@precision-chains.com* Web. *www.precision-chains.com Precision Chains England – Precision England*

Precision Components & Equipment Ltd Railway Street Works, Heywood OL10 1LX Tel. *01706 621421* Fax. *01706 621319* E-mail. *mike-pce@johnbradleygroup.co.uk* Web. *www.johnbradleygroup.co.uk Hyde*

Precision Disc Castings Ltd 16 Mannings Heath Road, Poole BH12 4NJ Tel. *01202 715050* Fax. *01202 715068* E-mail. *reception@pdcastings.co.uk* Web. *www.pdcastings.co.uk B.S. 1452/1977 – Carballoy – Discalloy – Various Alloys*

Precision Optical Engineering A Business Centre of MBDA UK Ltd Pb75A Mbda, Six Hills Way, Stevenage SG1 2DA Tel. *01438 754477* Fax. *01438 751198* E-mail. *sales@p-oe.co.uk* Web. *www.p-oe.co.uk INTERFIRE (United Kingdom)*

Precision Polymer Engineering Ltd Greenbank Road, Blackburn BB1 3EA Tel. *01254 295400* Fax. *01254 680182* E-mail. *sales@prepol.com* Web. *www.prepol.com Precision Polymer Engineering*

Precision Technologies International Ltd 22 Mariner, Tamworth B79 7UL Tel. *01827 54371* Fax. *01827 310406* E-mail. *sales@ptiltd.co.uk* Web. *www.ptiltd.co.uk P.T.I. – Precision Technologies International – Spline Masters*

Precision Tools Unit 40 Kingfisher Court, Newbury RG14 5SJ Tel. *01635 31977* Fax. *01635 528865* E-mail. *enquiries@precisiontoolsnewbury.co.uk* Web. *www.precisiontoolsnewbury.co.uk Accu-trak – Arno – Ceratizit – Deb – Emuge – Fampla – Garr Tool – Guhring – Integi – Isenr – Jimmore – Knurlcut – Mitsubishi Carbide – Mitutoyo – Nikken – OSG – Ph Horn Ph – Sandvik – Seco – Stellram – Sumitomo – Titex Plus – Walter – Wohlhaupter*

Precision Waterjet Ltd Unit 1 Uplyme Business Park Uplyme Road, Lyme Regis DT7 3LS Tel. *01297 444456* Fax. *05601 135290* E-mail. *sales@precisionwaterjet.co.uk* Web. *www.precisionwaterjet.co.uk Waterjet*

Preco Ltd 3 Four Seasons Crescent Kimpton Road, Sutton SM3 9QR Tel. *020 86444447* Fax. *020 86440474* E-mail. *info@preco.co.uk* Web. *www.preco.co.uk Preco*

Precolor Sales Ltd (Precolor Tank Division) Newport Road, Market Drayton TF9 2AA Tel. *01630 657281* Fax. *01630 655545* E-mail. *enquiries@precolor.co.uk* Web. *www.precolortankdivision.co.uk Precolor*

Preconomy Orchard Way, Sutton In Ashfield NG17 1JU Tel. *01623 554211* Fax. *01623 514057* E-mail. *ngiles@preconomy.com* Web. *www.preconomy.com Preconomy Ltd*

Pregis Rigid Packaging Ltd 10 Sir Alfred Owen Way Pontygwindy Industrial Estate, Caerphilly CF83 2WL Tel. *029 20858900* Fax. *029 20858909* E-mail. *nbridge@pregis.com* Web. *www.pregis.com Caterware – Eurosalad – Hefty – Hexquisite – Hexware – Mealmaster – Micromax – Onecup – Placesetter – Pressware – Showcase – Smartlock – Uni-hinge Packs*

Preheat Engineering Ltd Unit 1 Adler Industrial Estate Betam Rd, Hayes UB3 1ST Tel. *020 88481912* Fax. *020 88481913* E-mail. *sales@preheat.co.uk* Web. *www.preheat.co.uk Peregrine – Peregrine – Peregrine – Peregrine – Peregrine*

Preisser UK Ltd 37 Dickerage Road, Kingston Upon Thames KT1 3SR Tel. *020 83361290* Fax. *020 83361651* E-mail. *sales@preisser.co.uk* Web. *www.preisser.co.uk DigiMet (Germany)*

Pre Mac International Ltd Unit 5 Morewood Close, Sevenoaks TN13 2HU Tel. *01732 460333* Fax. *01732 460222* E-mail. *office@pre-mac.com* Web. *www.pre-mac.com Travel Well Range*

Premdor Crosby Ltd Gemini House Hargreaves Road, Groundwell Indl-Est, Swindon SN25 5AJ Tel. *01793 708200* Fax. *01793 708254* Web. *www.premdor.co.uk Alpha 20 – Artform – Bijou – Bijou Chameleon – Firemaster – Fireshield – Landscape – Marlborough – Popular – Quickfix 2 – Rectory – Roseberry – Superdeluxe – Wordsworth*

Premier PO Box 2663, Reading RG2 0EG Tel. *0118 9872894* Fax. *0118 9872894* E-mail. *sales@rombouts.co.uk* Web. *www.rombouts.co.uk Rombouts*

Premier Braking Ltd 15-17 Oliver Crescent, Hawick TD9 9BJ Tel. *01450 373333* Fax. *01450 375252* E-mail. *sales@premierbraking.com Premier*

Premierchoice Ltd 3 Algores Way, Wisbech PE13 2TQ Tel. *01945 589558* Fax. *01945 587937* E-mail. *info@premierchoice.co.uk* Web. *www.premierchoice.co.uk *Premier Choice*

Premier Coatings Ltd Marley Farm Headcorn Road, Smarden, Ashford TN27 8PJ Tel. *01233 770663* Fax. *01233 770633* E-mail. *tcapps@denso.net* Web. *www.premiercoatings.com Hi-Proof – Prembond – Premcote – Premseal – Premshield – Premtape – Tilesafe*

Premier Engineering Unit 14 Hoddesdon Industrial Centre Pindar Road, Hoddesdon EN11 0DD Tel. *01992 304300* Fax. *01992 304307* E-mail. *ian.willmot@iwilimited.co.uk* Web. *www.iwilimited.co.uk Centennial (U.S.A.) – Fujisoku (Japan) – Kingmax Taiwan (Taiwan) – Pacific Corp (Taiwan) – Sony (Japan)*

Premiere Products Ltd Oakley Gardens Bouncers Lane, Cheltenham GL52 5JD Tel. *01242 537150* Fax. *01242 528445* E-mail. *custserv@premiereproducts.co.uk* Web. *www.premiereproducts.co.uk Air Freshener – Air Sanitiser – Bactericidal Hand Soap – Bactericidal Springclean – Biological Laundry Powder 100 – Blue Ram Lavatory Cleaner – C.S.8 – Carpet Mousse – Caterclean 50 – Caterclean Spray – Chewing Gum remover – Contact Bleach – Country Fresh – D.E.P.20 – Erasit – Fabric Conditioner – Floor & Wall Cleaning Powder – Floral Disinfectant – Fly & Wasp Killer – Foam Carpet Cleaner – Force – Freshaloo – G.C.10 – G.C.20 – Gel Hand Clean – Graffiti Remover – H.D. Liquid – J.D.2 – Laundry Fresh – Lemon Cream Cleanser – Lemon Disinfectant – Liquid Spray Polish – Loquid Spray Polish – Low Foam – M.P.10 – M.P.9 – Machine Dishwashing Liquid – Machine Dishwashing Powder – Nature's Way – Oleo Resinous Seal – Oven Cleaner – Ovenclean – P.I.C – P.S.5 – Pearlised Liquid Hand Soap – Pine Disinfectant – Plastic Cleaner – Platinum 18 – Platinum 25 – Premac Super – Premiere Antistatic – Premiere Automatic – Premiere Bio Automatic – Premiere Clean & Buff – Premiere Cream Cleanser – Premiere Foam Cleanser – Premiere Safestrip – Premiere Stone Vitrifier – Premisan – Prempol X – Premstrip 90 – Premturps – Promisan – Raftor – Rapid Seal – Raptor – Reflection – Release – Revolution 500 – Rinse Aid – S.B.1 – S.P.66 – S.S.80 – Savona – Screen – Silver Rinse – Spray Polish Cleaner – Stainless Steel Cleaner – Strike – Super Mirage – T.D.10 – T.D.30 – Telephone Sanitiser – W.S.70 – White Disinfectant – Window Spirit – Window Spray*

Premier Filtration 26 St Birinus Flackwell Heath, High Wycombe HP10 9DJ Tel. *01628 527704* Fax. *01628 520502* E-mail. *info@premierfiltration.com* Web. *www.premierfiltration.com Spinclean*

Premier Housewares LLP 55 Jordanvale Avenue, Glasgow G14 0QP Tel. *0141 5792000* Fax. *0141 5792005* E-mail. *info@premierhousewares.co.uk* Web. *www.premierhousewares.co.uk Premier Housewares*

Premier Lift Trucks Ltd Unit 17 Cinnamon Brow Business Park Makerfield Way, Ince, Wigan WN2 2PR Tel. *01942 825757* Fax. *0161 7457779* E-mail. *info@fork-lift.co.uk* Web. *www.fork-lift.co.uk JUNGHEINRICH – Mitsubishi – Nissan – TCM – Toyota – Yale*

Premier Marinas Brighton Western Concourse Brighton Marina Village, Brighton BN2 5UP Tel. *01273 819919* Fax. *01273 675082* E-mail. *philg@premiermarinas.com* Web. *www.premiermarinas.com Brighton Marina – Premier Marina Brighton*

Premier M & D Windows 34 Strawberry Close Tividale, Oldbury B69 1NU Tel. *01384 565787* Fax. *01384 410951* E-mail. *sales@premierglass.co.uk* Web. *www.premierglass.co.uk Premier*

Premier Mobiles 89 High Street Hanham, Bristol BS15 3QG Tel. *0117 9477377* Fax. *0117 9352773* E-mail. *info@premiermobileshop.co.uk* Web. *www.premiermobileshop.co.uk 3 – O2 – Orange – T.Mobile – Vodafone*

Premier Paper Group Midpoint Park Kingsbury Road, Minworth, Sutton Coldfield B76 1AF Tel. *0121 3131115* Fax. *0121 3132390* E-mail. *graham.griffiths@paper.co.uk* Web. *www.paper.co.uk Tuffjack*

Premier Paper Group Ltd Unit 1 Wilks Avenue Questor, Dartford DA1 1JS Tel. *01322 421940* Fax. *01322 227716* E-mail. *graham.caistor@paper.co.uk* Web. *www.paper.co.uk Nimrod Plus Gloss Paper and Board – Nimrod Plus Matt Paper – Nimrod Plus Silk Paper and Board*

Premier Solutions Nottingham Ltd 11 Ascot Industrial Estate Sandiacre, Nottingham NG10 5DL Tel. *0115 9394122* Fax. *0115 9490453* E-mail. *info@premiersolutions.co.uk* Web. *www.premiersolutions.co.uk Datamoon – Electrovision – Logic – Merlin – N.J.D. – Predator – Vortex*

Premier Storage & Office Solutions Ltd Unit 4 Delta Court Sky Business Park, Auckley, Doncaster DN9 3GN Tel. *01302 300200* Fax. *01302 601436* E-mail. *hello@premier-storage.co.uk* Web. *www.premier-storage.co.uk Premier Storage and Office Solutions Ltd*

Premier Supply Co. Perram Works Merrow Lane, Guildford GU4 7BN Tel. *01483 534346* Fax. *01483 303992* E-mail. *info@premiersupply.co.uk* Web. *www.premiersupply.co.uk County*

Premier Welding Services Scotland Ltd Unit 5 28 Queen Elizabeth Avenue, Hillington Park, Glasgow G52 4NQ Tel. *0141 8824514* Fax. *0141 8104659* E-mail. *ronnie@premierwelding.com* Web. *www.premierwelding.co.uk Binzel – Elga – Hilo Gas Equipment – Miller – Speedglass – Weldcraft*

Premier World Trading Ltd Raintex House, Smethwick B66 2AA Tel. *0121 5556479* Fax. *0121 5556532* E-mail. *sales@pwtltd.co.uk* Web. *www.jackorton.com Heraldry – Safetywear*

Presco Components Selborne Street, Walsall WS1 2JN Tel. *01922 620202* Fax. *01922 632695* E-mail. *cparkes@presco.co.uk* Web. *www.presco.co.uk Presco*

President Blinds Ltd 13 Forest Hill Business Centre 2 Clyde Va, London SE23 3JF Tel. *020 86998885* Fax. *020 86998005* E-mail. *info@presidentblinds.com* Web. *www.flyscreens-uk.co.uk *President Screens*

Pressavon Ltd Masons Road Stratford Enterprise Park, Stratford Upon Avon CV37 9NP Tel. *01789 206610* Fax. *01789 415735* E-mail. *sales@pressavon.co.uk* Web. *www.pressavon.co.uk Pressavon – Weatherstrip*

Press & Shear Machinery Ltd Unit 12-14 Ninian Park Ninian Way, Wilnecote, Tamworth B77 5ES Tel. *01827 250000* Fax. *01827 250022* E-mail. *sales@pressandshear.com* Web. *www.pressandshear.com Darley – Elga – Elga-Synchro – Fasti – Finn-Power – Pivatic – Stierli*

Press To Print 6 Beacontree Plaza Gillette Way, Reading RG2 0BS Tel. *0118 9310210* Fax. *0118 9310220* E-mail. *reading@presstoprint.co.uk* Web. *www.presstoprint.co.uk Presto Print*

Pressure Design Hydraulics Ltd Commercial Road Goldthorpe, Rotherham S63 9BL Tel. *01709 897121* Fax. *01709 895305* E-mail. *sales@pressuredesign.co.uk* Web. *www.pressuredesign.co.uk Bosch – Denison – Hydac – Hydrotechnik – MOOG – Rexroth – Sterling – Vickers*

Prestige Industrial Pipework Equipment Unit L10 Telford Road, Bicester OX26 4LD Tel. *01869 324424* Fax. *01869 323273* E-mail. *sales@pipe-ltd.com* Web. *www.pipe-ltd.com E-Z- Fit – Pipe Wizards*

E Preston Electrical Ltd Unit 28 Broadway Globe Lane, Dukinfield SK16 4UU Tel. *0161 3395177* Fax. *0161 3431935* E-mail. *sales@epreston.co.uk* Web. *www.epreston.co.uk ABB/entrelec – Arcolectric Switches PLC – Bulgin – Bussmann – CAL – Chint – CML – Crouzet – Crydom International – Cynergy3 components – E B T Lamps & LED's – E T A Circuit Protection & Control – Eaton – Finder Relays – Honeywell – Kraus & Naimer – Littelfuse – Moeller – Otehall – Pepperl+Fuchs – Saia-Burgess – Schaffner – Schurter – TOK Switches – Tranilamp – Werma – Wieland Electrical Connections*

Preston Plywood Supplies (Nationwide) River Street Off Bow Lane, Preston PR1 8NS Tel. *01772 561656* Fax. *01772 561256* E-mail. *liam@prestonplywood.co.uk* Web. *www.cubiclesanddoors.co.uk Formica – jeldwyn – Mezzdek – Mezzdek p5 – Mezzdek p6 – Premdor – Preston Plywood – Retrowall – Slatwall*

Preston & Thomas Ltd Unit 3 Heron Road Rumney, Cardiff CF3 3JE Tel. *029 20793331* Fax. *029 20779195* E-mail. *davidthomas@prestonandthomas.co.uk* Web. *www.prestonandthomas.co.uk Radi-Heat*

Prestoplan Ltd 366 Four Oaks Road Walton Summit Centre, Bamber Bridge, Preston PR5 8AP Tel. *01772 627373* Fax. *01772 627575* E-mail. *john.bedford@prestoplan.co.uk* Web. *www.prestoplan.co.uk Prestoplan*

Price & Pierce Softwoods Ltd Cavendish House 36-40 Goldsworth Road, Woking GU21 6JT Tel. *01483 221800* Fax. *01483 726203* E-mail. *softwood.woking@price-pierce.co.uk* Web. *www.price-pierce.co.uk *Duraplac (Brazil) – *Duratex (Brazil) – *Eagle (Indonesia) – *Eagle C H G (Malaysia) – *Mademer (Brazil) – *Persada (Indonesia)*

Prices Patent Candles Ltd 16 Hudson Road Elm Farm Industrial Estate, Bedford MK41 0LZ Tel. *01234 264500* Fax. *01234 264561* E-mail. *sales@prices-candles.co.uk* Web. *www.prices-candles.co.uk Calorettes – Chelsea – Old English – Prices – Sentinel – Sherwood – Spirette – Venetian*

Pricewaterhousecoopers LLP 1 Embankment Place, London WC2N 6RH Tel. *020 75835000* Fax. *020 78224652* E-mail. *info@pcwglobal.com* Web. *www.pwc.com Pricewaters Coopers*

Prima Care Unit 26 Heads of The Valley Industrial Estate Rhymney, Tredegar NP22 5RL Tel. *01685 845900* Fax. *01495 718777* E-mail. *info@primacare.co.uk* Web. *www.primacare.co.uk Aberdare – Brecon – Conway – Denbigh – Ellesmere – Ferndale – Harlech*

Prima Dental Group Ltd Statesman House Stephenson Drive Quedgeley, Gloucester GL2 2AG Tel. *01452 307171* Fax. *01452 307187* E-mail. *admin@primadentalgroup.com* Web. *www.sswhite.com A.I.C. – Black Diamond – Casting Wax – Colour Percha – Colour Points – Crown Sticky Wax – Improved True Dentalloy – Inlay Wax – Legend – Legend Restorative – Legend Silver – M.Q. Lubricant – Modelling Wax – Orapol – Oraproph – P.C.A. – Panorex – Precise – Profile – Profile TLC – Profile Universal – Rotaklenz – S.S. White – S.S.W. Black Diamonds – S.S.W. Diamonds – S.S.W. Impression Paste – S.S.W. Impression Tray Adhesive – S.S.W. Instruments – S.S.W. New True Dentalloy N T D A – S.S.W. Steel Burs – S.S.W. TC Burs – S.S.W. Tray Adhesive Solvent – Tenax Wax – Texton – Z.C.I. – Z.O.E.*

Primaflow Ltd Unit 2 Stargate Business Park Cuckoo Road, Birmingham B7 5SE Tel. *0121 3274000* Fax. *01543 571851* E-mail. *sales@muellerprimaflow.com* Web. *www.muellerprimaflow.com Vogue - radiator valves kwik pack prepacked plumbing products*

Primalec Green Farm Cottage Maidstone Road, Nettlestead, Maidstone ME18 5HD Tel. *01622 816955* Fax. *01474 853968* E-mail. *customers@primalec.co.uk* Web. *www.primalec.com Airco (United Kingdom) – AIRCO-LUBE – Airco-Seal Pro – AircoFlush (United Kingdom) – CONCERTINA – Glo-Leak (United Kingdom) – Invictalux (United Kingdom) – Mercury (United Kingdom) – Piranha (United Kingdom) – Primalec (United Kingdom) – USX*

Prime Appointments Ltd Christmas House 98b Newland Street, Witham CM8 1AH Tel. *01376 502999* Fax. *01376 502846* E-mail. *general@prime-appointments.co.uk* Web. *www.prime-appointments.co.uk *Select Golf*

Primesight London Ltd Metropolis House 22 Percy Street, London W1T 2BU Tel. *020 79084300* Fax. *020 78821212* E-mail. *zoew@primesight.co.uk* Web. *www.primesight.co.uk Primelite*

Princess International Sales & Service Ltd Athena Drive Tachbrook Park, Warwick CV34 6RT Tel. *01926 359977* Fax. *01926 461591* E-mail. *sales@princess.co.uk* Web. *www.princess.co.uk Princess International*

Princes Soft Drinks Swaledale House Weaverthorpe Road, Bradford BD4 6SX Tel. *01274 651777* Fax. *01274 651088* E-mail. *enquiries@princes.co.uk* Web. *www.princes.co.uk Barraclough – Gee Bee – Jucee – Princes Soft Drinks – Spata – Vogue*

Princess Yachts International plc Newport Street, Plymouth PL1 3QG Tel. *01752 203888* Fax. *01752 203777* E-mail. *info@princessyachts.com* Web. *www.princessyachts.com Moody Sigma Yachts – Princess Motor Cruisers*

Principal Catering Consultants Ltd 321 Upper Elmers End Road, Beckenham BR3 3QP Tel. *020 86636686* Fax. *020 86630383* E-mail. *catering@pc-fare.co.uk* Web. *www.fare-catering.com Fare Catering*

Principality Building Society PO Box 89, Cardiff CF10 1UA Tel. *08450 450452* Fax. *029 20234427* E-mail. *enquiries@principality.co.uk* Web. *www.principality.co.uk Principality Building Society*

Printmet Ltd Sully Moors Road Sully, Penarth CF64 5RP Tel. *01446 737417* Fax. *01446 748348* E-mail. *printmetlimited@btconnect.com Printmet*

Printpack Enterprises Ltd T/A Printpack Bridge Hall Mills Bridge Hall Lane, Bury BL9 7PA Tel. *0161 7645441* Fax. *0161 7051624* E-mail. *jaustin@printpack.com* Web. *www.printpack.eu.com Barrierflex – Coldflex – Flexotone – Gravure – Holographic – Peelseal – Roll Fed*

Prior Diesel Ltd Gapton Hall Road, Great Yarmouth NR31 0NL Tel. *01493 441383* Fax. *01493 441796* E-mail. *info@priordiesel.com* Web. *www.priordiesel.com Prior Diesel*

Prior Scientific Instruments Ltd Unit 3-4 Fielding Industrial Estate Wilbraham Road, Fulbourn, Cambridge CB21 5ET Tel. *01223 881711* Fax. *01223 881710* E-mail. *stephenling@prior.com* Web. *www.prior.com Conncert – Epimet – Episcan – ErgoScan – OptiScan – Priorlab – PriorLux – PriorSpec – ProScan*

The Priory Castor & Engineering Co. Ltd 160 Aston Hall Road, Birmingham B6 7LA Tel. *0121 3270832* Fax. *0121 3222123* E-mail. *enquiries@priorycastor.co.uk* Web. *www.priorycastor.co.uk Priory Castor*

Priory Publications Ltd The Priory 36 Wappenham Road, Syresham, Brackley NN13 5HH Tel. *01280 850603* Fax. *01280 850576* E-mail. *info@signpost.co.uk* Web. *www.signpost.co.uk Signpost*

Prismtech Ltd Prismtech House Fifth Avenue, Team Valley Trading Estate, Gateshead NE11 0NG Tel. *0191 4979900* Fax. *0191 4979901* E-mail. *phil.wright@prismtechnologies.com* Web. *www.prismtechnologies.com OpenBase*

Pritchard Patent Product Co. Ltd Underleys Beer, Seaton EX12 3NA Tel. *01297 21542* Fax. *01297 20229* Web. *www.peco-uk.com Peco*

Pritchard Tyrite Crockford Lane Chineham, Basingstoke RG24 8NA Tel. *01256 400600* Fax. *01256 400622* E-mail. *sales@pritchard-tyrite.co.uk* Web. *www.pritchard-tyrite.co.uk Hi-Py – Texplus – Texspan*

Pritchitts 21-23 Elmfield Road, Bromley BR1 1LT Tel. *020 82907020* Fax. *020 82907030* E-mail. *info@pritchitts.com* Web. *www.pritchitts.com *Cafe Maid – *Comelle – *Millac – *Millac Gold – Millac Maid – *Roselle Supreme*

Pritex Station Mills, Wellington TA21 8NN Tel. *01823 664271* Fax. *01823 660023* E-mail. *iwilliams@pritex.co.uk* Web. *www.pritex.co.uk Pritex*

Prizeflex Ltd 3 Cygnus Business Centre Dalmeyer Road, London NW10 2XA Tel. *020 84517071* Fax. *020 84598979* E-mail. *nishel@prizeflex.co.uk* Web. *www.prizeflex.co.uk *Daniel Koeman (India) – Lesu (France)*

Proactive Test Solutions Ltd 15a The Old Silk Mill Brook Street, Tring HP23 5ES Tel. *01442 825547* E-mail. *info@proactivetest.com* Web. *www.proactivetest.co.uk Proactive Hire – Proactive Test*

Probiotics International Ltd Lopenhead, South Petherton TA13 5JH Tel. *01460 243230* Fax. *0121 7793110* E-mail. *info@protexin.com* Web. *www.protexin.com Bio-Kult – Bio-Lapis – Denamarin – Fibre-Plex – Pro-Balance – Pro-Fibre – Pro-Kolin – Protexin – Synbiotic DC*

Process & Plant Equipment Ltd Unit 4 Dock Meadow Industrial Estate Lanesfield Drive, Wolverhampton WV4 6UD Tel. *01902 495913* Fax. *01902 498945* E-mail. *sales@pps-awb.co.uk* Web. *www.processandplant.com Proforce*

Process Technology Europe Ltd 18 North Street Whitwick, Coalville LE67 5HA Tel. *01530 810333* Fax. *08717 504327* E-mail. *tony.bolton@process-technology.co.uk* Web. *www.process-technology.co.uk Rapid Shell Dry*

Procon Engineering Ltd Vestry Estate Vestry Road, Sevenoaks TN14 5EL Tel. *01732 781300* Fax. *01732 781311* E-mail. *sales@proconeng.com* Web. *www.proconeng.com *Batch Weighing – *Belt Weighing – *Datum – *Inflo Resometric – *Lintvalve – *Loss of Weight – *Transducer Systems – *Transducers (UK) – *Transducers Data Sense – *Transducers Data Weigh – *Ultramax*

Procter Fencing Isabella Road Garforth, Leeds LS25 2DY Tel. *0113 2872777* Fax. *0113 2422649* E-mail. *enquiries@procterfencing.co.uk* Web. *www.procterfencing.co.uk Procter*

Procter Machinery Guarding Ltd 11 Pantglas Indl-Est Bedwas, Caerphilly CF83 8XD Tel. *029 20882222* Fax. *029 20887005* E-mail. *jeremy.procter@procterbedwas.co.uk* Web. *www.machinesafety.co.uk Angel – Earlybird – Little Nipper – The Little Nipper – The Nipper – The Sentry – Trip-Trap*

A Proctor Group Ltd The Haugh Ashgrove Road, Rattray, Blairgowrie PH10 7ER Tel. *01250 872261* Fax. *01250 872727* E-mail. *sales@proctorgroup.com* Web. *www.proctorgroup.com Cladshield – Frameshield – Probuild – Procelinc – Procheck – Prodeck – Profloor Dynamic – Profoil – Protec – Prowall – Roofshield*

James Proctor Ltd P O Box 19, Burnley BB11 1NN Tel. *01282 453816* Fax. *01282 416178* E-mail. *info@jamesproctor.com* Web. *www.jamesproctor.com Mini Coker – Oldbury Chain Grate – Proctor Ash Crusher – Proctor Screw Elevator – Submerged Ash Conveyor – Wide Ram*

Product Innovation Ltd 39 St Gabriels Road, London NW2 4DT Tel. *020 84523968* Fax. *020 84525665* E-mail. *enquiries@productinnovation.com* Web. *www.productinnovation.com HotSpotter – Megahorn*

Production Techniques Ltd 13 Kings Road, Fleet GU51 3AU Tel. *01252 616575* Fax. *01252 615818* E-mail. *sales@production-techniques.com* Web. *www.production-techniques.com Chemcon*

Profast Ni Ltd 26-30 Rydalmere Street, Belfast BT12 6GF Tel. *028 90243215* Fax. *028 90333301* E-mail. *sales@profast.co.uk* Web. *www.profast.co.uk Kwik Fix*

Professional Cycle Marketing Forge Lane, Cradley Heath B64 5AL Tel. *01384 568521* Fax. *01384 634494* E-mail. *enquires@pcmgroup.co.uk* Web. *www.pcmgroup.co.uk Arden – Bubbles – Hawk – Trakatak*

Professional Fee Protection Ltd Sylvan Way Southfields Business Park, Basildon SS15 6TW Tel. *08453 071177* Fax. *01277 622475* E-mail. *f.pons@pfp.uk.com* Web. *www.pfponline.com Professional Fee Protection*

Professional Fitness & Education 9a Cleasby Road Menston, Ilkley LS29 6JE Tel. *01943 879816* Fax. *01943 870887* E-mail. *christine.north@northernfitness.co.uk* Web. *www.nothernfitness.co.uk Aquafusion*

Professional Technology UK Ltd 375 High Street, Rochester ME1 1DA Tel. *01634 815517* Fax. *01634 829032* E-mail. *info@ptuk.co.uk* Web. *www.ptuk.co.uk Quaestor – Seriatim – Seriatim*

Profusion plc 4 T A H House Aviation Way, Southend Airport, Southend On Sea SS2 6UN Tel. *01702 543500* Fax. *01702 543700* E-mail. *sales@profusionplc.com* Web. *www.profusionplc.com Exicon (United Kingdom)*

Progreen Weed Control Solutions Ltd Kellington House South Fen Business Park South Fen Road, Bourne PE10 0DN Tel. *01778 394052* Fax. *01778 394499* E-mail. *info@progreen.co.uk* Web. *www.progreen.co.uk Progreen*

Progressive Media Group Progressive House 2 Maidstone Road, Sidcup DA14 5HZ Tel. *020 82697700* Fax. *020 82697878* E-mail. *wbp@progressivemediagroup.com* Web. *www.progressivemediagroup.com BTP – Cranes Today – Dairy Industries International – Electrical Equipment – Electronics – Factory Equipment – Hospital Development – Hospital Equipment & Supplies – Medical Laboratory*

World – Modern Power Systems – OEM Design – Office Equipment News – Process Control – Soaps, Perfumery & Cosmetics

Progressive Product Developments Ltd 24 Beacon Bottom Park Gate, Southampton SO31 7GQ Tel. *01489 576787* Fax. *01489 578463* E-mail. *sales@ppd-ltd.com* Web. *www.ppd-ltd.com *Biomass Grease Trap – *Bug Fluid – *Bug Socks – *Grease Bugs – *Kitchen Filtertrap – *Lamina Filtertraps*

Progress Shaving Brush Vulfix Ltd Unit 24 Spring Valley Industrial Estate, Douglas, Isle Of Man IM2 2QR Tel. *01624 676030* Fax. *01624 662056* E-mail. *enquiries@progress-vulfix.com* Web. *www.vulfixoldoriginal.com Burlington – Grosvenor – Hyde Park – Marvel – Mayfair – Piccadilly – Strand – Vulfix – Vulfix Service – Vulfix Travel*

Project Building Company Ltd (t/a Gadmon Industries) Kofo House 57 Glengall Road, London SE15 6NF Tel. *020 72778878* Fax. *020 72779476* E-mail. *leke@gadmon.com* Web. *www.gadmon.com Redways*

Projects Department Ltd 26 Woodlands Road, Camberley GU15 3NA Tel. *01276 681423* Fax. *01276 537170* E-mail. *info@projectsdepartment.com* Web. *www.projectsdepartment.com ARRI – Photon Beard – Strand*

Prolou Ltd Unit 11, Pilgrims Close, Flitwick MK45 1UL Tel. *01525 715786* Fax. *01525 715717* E-mail. *tracey@prolou.co.uk* Web. *www.prolou.com Prolou Ltd*

Pro Machine Tools Ltd 17 Station Road Barnack, Stamford PE9 3DW Tel. *01780 740956* Fax. *01780 740957* E-mail. *promachuk@aol.com* Web. *www.inputmachinetools.co.uk Emco Hobbymachines – Golmatic – Knapp – Wabeco*

Promac Solutions Ltd Unit 5 Youngs Industrial Estate Paices Hill, Aldermaston, Reading RG7 4PW Tel. *0118 9817337* Fax. *0118 9811213* E-mail. *grant.linton@firetecsolutions.com* Web. *www.promac-solutions.co.uk Doosan,Merlo,Sanvik Rammer,Ausa*

Promat UK Ltd Sterling Centre, Bracknell RG12 2TD Tel. *01344 381300* Fax. *01344 381301* E-mail. *salesuk@promat.co.uk* Web. *www.promat.co.uk Cafco 300 – Fendolite M11 – Fire Barrier – Mandolite 550 – Mandolite CP2 – T.D. Board – Vermiculite*

Promo2u Ltd First Floor 4 Kings RoadNorth Chingford, London E4 7 EY Tel. *0203 6407670* E-mail. *sales@promo2u.com* Web. *www.promo2u.com Eco Promo2u – Promo2u*

Promtek Ltd Fisher Street Brindley Ford, Stoke On Trent ST8 7QJ Tel. *01782 375600* Fax. *01782 375605* E-mail. *pwilliams@promtek.com* Web. *www.promtek.com Promtek*

Property Log Book Company Ltd 5 New Mart Place, Edinburgh EH14 1RW Tel. *08456 120205* Fax. *08456 120206* E-mail. *enquiries@propertylogbook.co.uk* Web. *www.propertylogbook.co Interactive Property Log Book – Property Log Book*

Propex Concrete Systems Ltd Synthetic Industries Europe Limited Propex House 9 Royal Court Basil Close, Chesterfield S41 7SL Tel. *01246 564200* Fax. *01246 564201* E-mail. *enquiries@propexinc.co.uk* Web. *www.fibermesh.com e3 Fibres – ENDURO – Fibercast – Fibermesh – Harbourite – Novocon – Novomesh – Novotex – Stealth – Vertiforce*

Proplas International Ltd Lancashire Digital Technology Centre Bancroft Road, Burnley BB10 2TP Tel. *01282 872450* Fax. *01282 872501* E-mail. *info@proplasint.com* Web. *www.proplasint.com ABB – ABB ACS 150 – ABB ACS 350 – ABB ACS 550 – ABB Drives – Altivar – Altivar ATV11 – Altivar ATV31 – Altivar ATV61 – Altivar ATV71 – Aoki – Arburg – B & W – Baldor – Battenfeld – Bekum – Boy – Brook Crompton – BSL – Cincinnati – Cincinnati Milacron – Commander SE – Control Techniques – Crouzet – CT – Danfoss – Demag – Engel – Envirostart – Eurotherm 650 – Eurotherm Drives – Farnell – Ferromatik Milacron – Group Schneider – Guardmaster – Hitachi – Honeywell – IMO – Klockner Moeller – Krauss Maffei – Krupp Kautex – Legrand – Leroy Somer – Magic – Magplastic – MEM – Mitsubishi – Mitsubishi F500 – Mitsubishi S500 – Mitsubishi S500 FR-F700 – Moeller – MTE – Negri Bossi – Netstal – Nissei – NRG – Omron – Pepperl and Fuchs – Pilz – Powerboss – Powerflex 40 – Powerflex 70 – Powerflex 700 – Ralspeed – Rittal – Rockwell – Rockwell Automation – Routeco – RPC – RS Components – Sandretto – Sarel – Siemans – SIG – Silverteam – SSD – Telemecanique – Unidrive – Vacon – Vacon 10 – Vacon NXL – Vacon NXS – Wago – WEG – Wyko – Yashkawa*

Proquis Ltd Building 1050 Cornforth Drive Kent Science Park, Sittingbourne ME9 8PX Tel. *01795 479001* Fax. *01795 479009* E-mail. *info@proquis.com* Web. *www.proquis.com/content/pages/why-proquis allCLEAR the smarter flowcharter – PROQUIS*

Prosaw Ltd Telford Way Telford Way Industrial Estate, Kettering NN16 8UN Tel. *01536 410999* Fax. *01536 410080* E-mail. *sales@prosaw.co.uk* Web. *www.prosaw.co.uk *Bauer (Germany) – *Danobat (Spain) – Maco – *Mega (Taiwan) – *O.M.P. (Italy) – P.H.S. - Material Handling Systems – *Piranha (U.S.A.) – Prosaw – *Reimu (Italy) – *Rusch (Italy) – *Thomas (Italy) – *Tyro (France)*

Prosig Ltd 44a High Street, Fareham PO16 7BQ Tel. *01329 239925* Fax. *01329 239159* E-mail. *chris.mason@prosig.com* Web. *www.prosig.com DATS For Windows – P5600 – Protor*

Prospect 360 Intertec House 1 Tomlins Avenue, Frimley, Camberley GU16 8LJ Tel. *01276 691199* E-mail. *data@prospect360.co.uk* Web. *www.prospect360.co.uk Intertec Data Solutions T/a Prospect 360*

Protag Retail Security Unit 3 Short Way, Thornbury, Bristol BS35 3UT Tel. *01454 418500* Fax. *01454 413708* E-mail. *m.strange@protagsecurity.co.uk* Web. *www.protagsecurity.co.uk Protag*

Protec Fire Detection Lomeshaye Industrial Estate, Nelson BB9 6RT Tel. *01282 717171* Fax. *01282 717273* E-mail. *sales@protec.co.uk* Web. *www.protec.co.uk Protec – Provoice*

Protechnic Unit 1 West End Trading Estate Netherton Wood Lane, Nailsea, Bristol BS48 4DG Tel. *01275 811312* Fax. *01275 835560* E-mail. *sales@protechnic.com* Web. *www.protechnic.com BWH – Peli*

Protective Finishing Group 33 Crossgate Road Park Farm Industrial Estate, Redditch B98 7SN Tel. *01527 524126* Fax. *01527 510361* E-mail. *sales@profingroup.co.uk* Web. *www.profingroup.co.uk Cataphoresis – Dacromet – Deltatone – Ecoat – ELVD – PTFE – Techseal – Xylan – Zintek*

Protective Supplies & Services Ltd Castlecroft Business Centre Tom Johnston Road, Dundee DD4 8XD Tel. *01382 731073* Fax. *01224 890030* E-mail. *sales@protectivesupplies.com* Web. *www.protectivesupplies.com Balon – Dickies – Grainger – McMaster Carr – Skinner*

Protector Alarms UK Ltd 20-22 Gipsy Hill, London SE19 1NL Tel. *020 87613771* Fax. *020 86709441* E-mail. *sales@protectoralarms.com* Web. *www.protectoralarms.com Sav-Wire*

Protekor UK Ltd Powerforce House Hoo Farm Industrial Estate Worcester Road, Kidderminster DY11 7RA Tel. *01562 515200* Fax. *01562 864063* E-mail. *info@protektor.co.uk* Web. *www.protektor.co.uk Cornercare – Protoktor*

Proteus Equipment Ltd P O Box 33, Bury St Edmunds IP33 2RS Tel. *01284 753954* Fax. *01284 701369* E-mail. *info@proteusequipment.com* Web. *www.proteusequipment.com Bituclean – Bitukleen – Bituslip*

Protex Fasteners Ltd Arrow Road, Redditch B98 8PA Tel. *01527 63231* Fax. *01527 66770* E-mail. *sales@protex-fasteners.com* Web. *www.protex.com Junior Prolatch – Protex – Protex BANDCLAMP (TM) – Protex CatchBolt – Protex CATCHBOLT (R) – Protex ProLatch – Protex ProLatch (TM) The*

Protim Solignum (t/a Osmose) Thames Indl-Est Fieldhouse Lane, Marlow SL7 1LS Tel. *01628 486644* Fax. *01628 476757* E-mail. *info@osmose.co.uk* Web. *www.ofmose.co.uk Fentex – Osmose Celbrite – Osmose Lifewood – Osmose Naturewood – Protim Clearchoice – Protim Prevac System – Protim Solignum Architectural – Protim Solignum Timbertone – Protim Wood Preservatives – Solignum*

The Proton Group Ltd Ripley Drive Normanton Industrial Estate, Normanton WF6 1QT Tel. *01924 892834* Fax. *01924 220213* E-mail. *mail@proton-group.co.uk* Web. *www.proton-group.co.uk Hydrodet – Protoplex – Quash – Renovate – Simply Bio – Spraydet*

Provident Financial Colonnade Sunbridge Road, Bradford BD1 2LQ Tel. *01274 351135* Fax. *01274 727300* E-mail. *info@provident.co.uk* Web. *www.providentpersonalcredit.com Provident – Provident Financial*

Provq Ltd Unit 32a Atcham Business Park Atcham, Shrewsbury SY4 4UG Tel. *01743 762055* Fax. *01743 709011* E-mail. *info@provq.com* Web. *www.provq.com ProVQ Limited*

PR Photographer London PO Box 555, South Croydon CR2 7WU Tel. *07721 398747* E-mail. *contact@pr-photographer.com* Web. *www.pr-photographer.com Neale Atkinson*

Pruce Newman Pipework Ltd Ayton Road, Wymondham NR18 0QJ Tel. *01953 605123* Fax. *01953 601115* E-mail. *mail@prucenewman.co.uk* Web. *www.prucenewman.co.uk Ayton Fabrication – Ayton Fabrications*

Pryor Marking Technology Ltd Egerton Street, Sheffield S1 4JX Tel. *0114 2766044* Fax. *0114 2766890* E-mail. *j.tiffiman@pryormarking.com* Web. *www.pryormarking.com EMA – Eurotype – Imperial – Magsi – Marktronic – Modelmark – Modelmark – Pryor – Pryormark*

P S Analytical Ltd 3 Crayfield Industrial Park Main Road, Orpington BR5 3HP Tel. *01689 891211* Fax. *01689 896009* E-mail. *mas@psanalytical.com* Web. *www.psanalytical.com Excalibur – Merlin – Sir Galahad*

P S G Group Ltd Polymex House 49-53 Glengall Road, London SE15 6NF Tel. *020 77409740* Fax. *020 72775654* E-mail. *sales@psggroup.co.uk* Web. *www.psggroup.co.uk Polymex*

P S H A 14 St Cuthberts Street, Bedford MK40 3JU Tel. *0800 3894433* Fax. *01234 218174* E-mail. *secretariat@phsa.org.uk* Web. *www.phsa.org.uk Medicaid – Medicare – Medicover*

P S I Global Ltd Bowburn South Industrial Estate Bowburn, Durham DH6 5AD Tel. *0191 3777000* Fax. *0191 3770769* E-mail. *sales@psiglobal.co.uk* Web. *www.psiglobal.co.uk PSI*

PSI Ltd (Skiweb UK) Llantrisant Road Capel Llanilltern, Cardiff CF5 6JR Tel. *029 20890800* Fax. *029 20890800* E-mail. *info@skiweb.uk.com* Web. *www.skiweb.uk.com Ski Web*

P S S Lyngate Industrial Estate Folgate Road, North Walsham NR28 0AJ Tel. *01692 406017* Fax. *01692 406957* E-mail. *sales@pss.co.uk* Web. *www.pss.co.uk M.H.A.*

P & S Textiles Ltd Hornby Street, Bury BL9 5BL Tel. *0161 7648617* Fax. *0161 7637260* E-mail. *info@pstextiles.co.uk* Web. *www.pstextiles.co.uk Arroboard – Arrodrive – Arrolink – Arromex – Arropak – Arroproof – Arroweb – Porspen – Porweb – Tirrobond – Tirropeen*

P3 Medical Ltd Unit 1 Newbridge Close, Bristol BS4 4AX Tel. *0117 9728888* Fax. *0117 9724863* E-mail. *hallj@p3-medical.com* Web. *www.p3medical.com Clinicol – Comforts – Opedic*

Publicis Chemistry 82 Baker Street, London W1U 6AE Tel. *020 79354426* Fax. *020 74875351* E-mail. *info@publicis-networks.com* Web. *www.publicis.co.uk Publicis (France)*

Puckator Ltd Lowman Works East Tap House, East Taphouse, Liskeard PL14 4NQ Tel. *01579 321550* Fax. *01579 321520* E-mail. *customerservices@puckator.co.uk* Web. *www.puckator.co.uk Puckator*

Pullingers Furnishers Ltd 108-110 Elm Grove, Hayling Island PO11 9EN Tel. *023 92463922* Fax. *023 92461123* E-mail. *sales@pullingers.net* Web. *www.pullingers.net Shepherds International*

Pulp & Paper Machinery Ltd Holman House Station Road, Staplehurst, Tonbridge TN12 0QQ Tel. *01580 893200* Fax. *01580 893229* E-mail. *sales@pandpmachinery.com *Acta (Denmark/Norway) – *Algas (Norway) – *BemaTec (Germany/Switzerland) – *Cellwood Fractionators (Sweden) – *Cyclotech (Sweden) – *Dox (Germany) – *Jud (Liechtenstein) – Kenfil – *Kumera (Finland) – *M.L. Gatewood (U.S.A.) – *Safematic (Finland) – *Spirac (Sweden) – *Tamfelt (Finland) – *Techpap (France) – Toftejorg – *Valmet (Finland) – *VIB (Germany)*

Pulsar Developments Ltd Spracklen House Dukes Place, Marlow SL7 2QH Tel. *01628 474324* Fax. *01628 474325* E-mail. *brian.murphy@pulsardevelopments.com* Web. *www.pulsardev.com *C & D Technologies (U.S.A.) – C.E.I.A. S.p.A – *Celwave RF (U.S.A.) – Crystal – *CTS (Motorola) (U.S.A.) – Elpower – *Johnson Controls (U.S.A.) – *Mascot (Norway) – *Mitralux International (Switzerland) – *Multiplier Industries (U.S.A.) – Phelps Dodge – Power Sonic – *Sa Ronix (U.S.A.) – Technacell*

Pulsar Light Of Cambridge Ltd Unit 3 Coldhams Business Park Norman Way, Cambridge CB1 3LH Tel. *01223 403500* Fax. *01223 403501* E-mail. *sales@pulsarlight.com* Web. *www.pulsarlight.com Pulsar*

Pulsation Dampers At Pulseguard Ltd Unit 1 Greg Street Industrial Centre, Greg Street, Reddish, Stockport SK5 7BS Tel. *0161 4809625* Fax. *0161 4809627* E-mail. *sales@pulsationdampers.co.uk* Web. *www.pulseguard.co.uk CAVGUARD – FLEXO – FLEXOCRAT – FLEXOR – FLEXORBER – FLEXOTEE – FLOATOLATOR – FOODOLATOR – HYDROBELLO – HYDROFLEX – INDACC – JUMBOFLEX – LIQUIBELLO – LIQUIFLEX – MAGDACC – MINITROL – PIPEGUARD – PIPEHUGGER – PISTOFLEX – PISTOFRAM – PISTOLITE – PULSEGUARD – PULSETWIN – PUMPGUARD – SHOCKGUARD – SURGEGUARD – TUBEGUARD – UNOFRAM – WAVEGUARD*

Pulse Home Products Ltd Vine Mill Middleton Road, Royton, Oldham OL2 5LN Tel. *0161 6521211* Fax. *0161 6260391* E-mail. *info@pulse-uk.co.uk* Web. *www.pulse-uk.co.uk *Breville (Hong Kong) – *Breville Pie Magic (Hong Kong) – *Breville Pizza Wizard (Hong Kong)*

Pultrex Ltd 18-20 Riverside Avenue West Lawford, Manningtree CO11 1UN Tel. *01206 395559* Fax. *01206 576554* E-mail. *sales@pultrex.com* Web. *www.pultrex.com Multi-Axis Filament Winding Machinery – Pullwinding Machines – Pultrex – Pultrusion Machines*

Puma UK Trustees Ltd Challenge Court Barnett Wood Lane, Leatherhead KT22 7LW Tel. *01372 360255* Fax. *01372 362081* E-mail. *info-uk@puma.com* Web. *www.puma.com *Puma UK (United Kingdom)*

Pump International Ltd (Head Office) Trevool Praze, Camborne TR14 0PJ Tel. *01209 831937* Fax. *01209 831939*

E-mail. *admin@pumpinternational.com* Web. *www.pumpinternational.com Patay*
Pumps & Gear Boxes Ltd Churwell Vale Shaw Cross Business Park, Dewsbury WF12 7RD Tel. *01924 468683* Fax. *01924 469247* E-mail. *info@pumpsandgearboxes.co.uk* Web. *www.pumpsANDgearboxes.co.uk P. Rayner*
Pump Technical Services Unit 2b Beco Works Kent House Lane, Beckenham BR3 1LA Tel. *020 87784271* Fax. *020 86593576* E-mail. *sales@pts-jung.co.uk* Web. *www.pts-jung.co.uk Jung Baufix – Jung Compli – Jung Hebefix – *Jung Pompen GmbH (Germany) – P.T.S. Foulmaster – P.T.S. Sumo – P.T.S. Trashmaster*
Pumptronics Europe Ltd Folgate Road, North Walsham NR28 0AJ Tel. *01692 500640* Fax. *01692 406710* E-mail. *sales@pumptronics.co.uk* Web. *www.pumptronics.co.uk Pumptronics*
Punjana Ltd 2 Carnforth Street, Belfast BT5 4QA Tel. *028 90450631* Fax. *028 90453261* E-mail. *info@punjana.com* Web. *www.punjana.com Punjana*
Purcon Consultants Ltd Prospect House Repton Place, Amersham HP7 9LP Tel. *01494 737300* Fax. *01494 737333* E-mail. *aenglish@purcon.com* Web. *www.purcon.com Purcon*
Pure Bathrooms Reflections Studio, Grove House 473 Dudley Road, Smethwick, Birmingham B18 4HE Tel. *0121 5653445* Fax. *0121 5557039* E-mail. *esales@purebathrooms.net* Web. *www.purekbb.com Mira Showers, whirlpool baths, Triton Mixer Shower*
Pure Beauty Online PO Box 4880, Lichfield WS14 4DA Tel. *0121 3147039* E-mail. *shop@pure-beauty.co.uk* Web. *www.pure-beauty.co.uk Dermalogica*
Pure Malt Products Ltd Victoria Bridge, Haddington EH41 4BD Tel. *01620 824696* Fax. *01620 822018* E-mail. *bruce.turner@puremalt.com* Web. *www.puremalt.com Pure Malt – Pure Roast*
PureSil Technologies Ltd Process House Acornfield Road Knowsley Industrial Estate, Knowsley Industrial Park, Liverpool L33 7PA Tel. *0151 5484000* Fax. *0151 5488000* E-mail. *sales@puresil.com* Web. *www.puresil.com Ameprene – Amesil – C-Flex Moulded Manifolds – Chemsure – Pureprene – Puresil – Puretrans – Santoprene – Stapure – Techniprene*
Puretech Process Systems Ltd Aztec House Perrywood Business Park, Redhill RH1 5DZ Tel. *01737 378000* Fax. *01737 378055* E-mail. *sales@puretech.uk.com* Web. *www.puretech.uk.com Genesys – OASYS*
Purification Products Ltd Reliance Works Saltaire Road, Shipley BD18 3HL Tel. *01274 530155* Fax. *01274 580453* E-mail. *sales@purification.co.uk* Web. *www.purification.co.uk Garfil – Liquifil – Odasorb*
Purlfrost Ltd Vision Kendal Avenue, London W3 0AF Tel. *020 89924024* Fax. *0871 7334587* E-mail. *info@purlfrost.com* Web. *www.purlfrost.com Purlees – Purlfrost*
Purolite International Ltd (Sales Office) Unit D Llantrisant Business Park, Llantrisant, Pontyclun CF72 8LF Tel. *01443 229334* Fax. *01443 222336* E-mail. *sales@purolite.com* Web. *www.purolite.com Chromalite – Hypersol Macronet – Microlite – Purasorb – Purofine – Purolite – Puropack – Purosep*
PV Crystalox Solar PLC Brook House 174 Milton Park, Abingdon OX14 4SE Tel. *01235 437160* Fax. *01235 770111* E-mail. *info@crystalox.com* Web. *www.crystalox.com Crystalox*
P V L Ltd 9 Lexden Lodge Industrial Estate Crowborough Hill, Crowborough TN6 2NQ Tel. *01892 664499* Fax. *01892 663690* E-mail. *info@pd1.co.uk* Web. *www.pvl.co.uk Elettrotec – Honsberg – RCI – RIKO*
PWM Distribution Wild Cherry saunders lane, awbridge, Romsey SO51 0GP Tel. *01794 830841* Fax. *0844 7790347* E-mail. *enquiries@pwm-distribution.com* Web. *www.pwm-distribution.com Manhole Buddy – Pointmaster – Quikpoint – TV50*
P W S Distributors PO Box 20, Newton Aycliffe DL5 6XJ Tel. *01325 505555* Fax. *01325 505500* E-mail. *mail@pws.co.uk* Web. *www.pws.co.uk P.W.S. Distributors Ltd*
Pyramid Engineering & Manufacturing Co. Ltd 8 Palace Road, East Molesey KT8 9DL Tel. *020 89794814* Fax. *020 89794814 Autograph – Delta – Pyramark*
Pyramid Engineering Services Co. Ltd 25 Hailey Road, Erith DA18 4AA Tel. *020 83209590* Fax. *020 83112567* E-mail. *chris.watkins@pyramideng.com* Web. *www.pyramideng.com Pyramid*
Pyramid Valley Computers 2c Heapriding Business Park Ford Street, Stockport SK3 0BT Tel. *0161 4773880* Fax. *0161 4808741* E-mail. *andrew.mills@pyramidvalley.co.uk* Web. *www.pyramidvalley.co.uk Piramid Valley Computers*
Pyroban Endeavour Works 59 Dolphin Road, Shoreham By Sea BN43 6QG Tel. *01273 466200* Fax. *01629 640247* E-mail. *ian.ratcliff@pyroban.com* Web. *www.pyroban.com Automech 3 – System 4000*
Pyropress Engineering Co. Ltd Bell Close Newnham Industrial Estate, Plympton, Plymouth PL7 4JH Tel. *01752 339866* Fax. *01752 336681* E-mail. *carol@pyropress.com* Web. *www.pyropress.com Pyropress*
Pyrotek Engineering Materials Ltd Garamonde Drive Wymbush, Milton Keynes MK8 8LN Tel. *01908 561155* Fax. *01908 560473* E-mail. *allan.roy@pyrotekeurope.com* Web. *www.pyrotek.info Pyrotek Engineering*
P Z Cussons International Ltd Cussons House Bird Hall Lane, Stockport SK3 0XN Tel. *0161 4918000* Fax. *0161 4918191* E-mail. *anthony.green@pzcussons.com* Web. *www.CUSSONS.COM 1001 – Carex – Imperial Leather – Limelite – Morning Fresh – My Fair Lady – Pearl – Rumours*

Q

Q E D 4 Soar Road Quorn, Loughborough LE12 8BW Tel. *01509 412317* Fax. *01509 416555* E-mail. *sales@qedmotorsport.co.uk* Web. *www.qedmotorsport.co.uk Q.E.D. Quorn Engine Developments*
Q E P Ltd Everest Road Queensway Industrial Estate, Lytham St Annes FY8 3AZ Tel. *01253 789180* Fax. *01253 789182* E-mail. *pboyce@vitrex.co.uk* Web. *www.qep.com Handibit – Hi-access – Versatile – Vitrex*
Q H I Group Ltd 9-10 Allied Business Centre Coldharbour Lane, Harpenden AL5 4UT Tel. *01582 461123* Fax. *01582 461117* E-mail. *info@qhigroup.com* Web. *www.qhigroup.com ExerTherm (United Kingdom) – LubriCurve (United Kingdom)*
Q K Honeycomb Products Ltd Creeting Road, Stowmarket IP14 5AS Tel. *01449 612145* Fax. *01449 677604* E-mail. *sales@qkhoneycomb.co.uk* Web. *www.qkhoneycomb.co.uk Quikaboard – Quikapanels*
Q-Lab Corporation Express Trading Estate Stone Hill Road, Farnworth, Bolton BL4 9TP Tel. *01204 861616* Fax. *01204 861617* E-mail. *info.eu@q-lab.co.uk* Web. *www.q-lab.com MTG – Q-Fog – Q-Lab – Q-Panel – Q-Phos – Q-Sun – Q-Track – QUV*
Q Lawns In The Midlands a division of David P. Fisher Landscapes 41 Grafton Lane Bidford-on-Avon, Alcester B50 4DX Tel. *01789 772626* Fax. *01789 772963* E-mail. *davidpfisher@btconnect.com* Web. *www.qlawnsinthemidlands.co.uk Enviromat*
Q M P Timmis Road, Stourbridge DY9 7BQ Tel. *01384 899800* Fax. *01384 899801* E-mail. *sales@qmp.uk.com* Web. *www.qmp.uk.com Eurobench – Euroslide – Welmade*
Q-Par Angus Ltd Barons Cross Laboratories Barons Cross Road, Barons Cross, Leominster HR6 8RS Tel. *01568 612138* Fax. *01568 616373* E-mail. *sales@q-par.com* Web. *www.q-par.com QPA – SilQdec*
Q P I Ltd Melton Road East Langton, Market Harborough LE16 7TG Tel. *01858 540121* Fax. *01858 540133* E-mail. *sales@qpiltd.co.uk* Web. *www.qpiltd.co.uk C&Y INDUSTRIES*
Quad Electroacoustics Ltd I A G House Sovereign Court, Ermine Business Park, Huntingdon PE29 6XU Tel. *08454 580011* Fax. *01480 431767* E-mail. *anne@quad-hifi.co.uk* Web. *www.quad-hifi.co.uk Quad*
Quadralene Ltd Bateman Street, Derby DE23 8JL Tel. *01332 292500* Fax. *01332 295941* E-mail. *info@quadralene.co.uk* Web. *www.quadralene.co.uk Autoval – Nuval – Quadcare – Quadralene*
Quadrant Security Group Ltd 3a Attenborough Lane Beeston, Nottingham NG9 5JN Tel. *0115 9252521* Fax. *01923 211590* E-mail. *info@qsg.co.uk* Web. *www.qsg.co.uk Quadrant Visual Solutions*
Quadwall Ltd Unit B5 Walter Leigh Way, Moss Industrial Estate, Leigh WN7 3PT Tel. *01942 674012* Fax. *01942 260167* E-mail. *sales@quadwall.co.uk* Web. *www.quadwall.co.uk Octabin – Octobin – Quadwall*
R T Quaife Engineering Ltd Vestry Road Otsford, Sevenoaks TN14 5EL Tel. *01732 741144* E-mail. *info@quaife.co.uk* Web. *www.quaife.co.uk Quaife*
Quality Irrigation Ltd 309 Vale Road Ash Vale, Aldershot GU12 5LN Tel. *01252 328017* Fax. *01252 328017* E-mail. *alanaustin@qualityirrigation.co.uk* Web. *www.qualityirrigation.co.uk Quality Irrigation*
Quality Lift Products Ltd Unit 6 Whaddon Business Park Whaddon, Salisbury SP5 3HF Tel. *01722 711122* Fax. *01722 711041* E-mail. *ingo@qualitylifts.co.uk* Web. *www.orona.co.uk *Quality Lifts (Spain)*
Quality Liquid Feeds Ltd Farley, Much Wenlock TF13 6NX Tel. *01952 727754* Fax. *01952 727755* E-mail. *info@qlf.co.uk* Web. *www.qlf.co.uk Energiser 4:19 – Super 40 – World*
Quality Manufacturing Services Ltd Coteleasowe Heath House Lane Codsall, Wolverhampton WV8 2HW Tel. *01902 842022* Fax. *01902 842022* E-mail. *andy@qmsgb.co.uk* Web. *www.qmsgb.co.uk BF Entron – Ravitex*
Quality Marking Services Ltd 6 Cannon Road Heathfield Industrial Estate, Newton Abbot TQ12 6SG Tel. *01626 836777* Fax. *01626 836774* E-mail. *info@qmarkings.co.uk* Web. *www.qmarkings.co.uk HyperLine*
Quality Monitoring Instruments Q M I 224 Iverson Road Unit 5 Hampstead West, London NW6 2HL Tel. *020 73283121* Fax. *020 73285888* E-mail. *josh@oilmist.com* Web. *www.oilmist.com Duoplex – Q M I Atmospheric Detector – Q M I Engine Detector – Q M I Multiplex – Uniplex*
Qualter Hall & Co. Ltd 16 Johnson Street, Barnsley S75 2BY Tel. *01226 205761* Fax. *01226 286269* E-mail. *admin@qualterhall.co.uk* Web. *www.qualterhall.co.uk I.B.S. – Lofco – Markloc – Qualtermatic – Rhino*
Quantel Ltd 31 Turnpike Road, Newbury RG14 2NX Tel. *01635 48222* Fax. *01635 815815* E-mail. *john.claridge@quantel.com* Web. *www.quantel.com Cachebox – Clipbox – Dominio – Editbox – Graphic Paintbox – Hal – Henry – paintbox – Picturebox – Pictureframe*
Quantum Industries Ltd Diamond Road, Norwich NR6 6AN Tel. *01603 789000* Fax. *01603 405476* E-mail. *enquiries@quantum-ind.co.uk* Web. *www.quantum-ind.co.uk Avancia – Iceni – Iceni Cadet*
Quantum Profile Systems Salmon Fields Royton, Oldham OL2 6JG Tel. *0161 6274222* Fax. *0161 6274333* E-mail. *sales@quantum-ps.co.uk* Web. *www.dacatie.co.uk Dacafix – Dacaform – Dacaproof – Dacatie – Flexi-Tile – Reflex Flexitile – Steps*
Quarry Tours Ltd Llechwedd Slate Caverns, Blaenau Ffestiniog LL41 3NB Tel. *01766 830306* Fax. *01766 831260* E-mail. *bookings@llechwedd.co.uk* Web. *www.llechwedd-slate-caverns.co.uk Llechwedd Slate Caverns – Quarry Tours*
Quatroserve Ltd Bay 11 Central Works Peartree Lane, Dudley DY2 0QU Tel. *01384 480326* Fax. *01384 74119* E-mail. *s.anderson@quatroserve.co.uk* Web. *www.quatroserve.co.uk Quatro brush – Quatro clean – Quatro lift – Quatro Maxi screen – Quatroscreen*
Quay Surface Engineering Metalblast Ltd 11 Cowley Road Nuffield Industrial Estate, Poole BH17 0UJ Tel. *01202 684231* Fax. *01202 675470* E-mail. *metalblast@onetel.com* Web. *www.quaysurface.co.uk Metco (United Kingdom) – Praxair Metallisation (United Kingdom) – Deloro Stellite (United Kingdom)*
Queen Anne Tableware Ltd Classic Works Holyhead Road, Wednesbury WS10 7PD Tel. *0121 5561471* Fax. *0121 5564966* E-mail. *info@queenanneuk.com* Web. *www.queenanneuk.com Queen Anne*
Quelfire Ltd PO Box 35, Altrincham WA14 5QA Tel. *0161 9287308* Fax. *0161 9241340* E-mail. *stephendunbar@quelfire.co.uk* Web. *www.quelfire.co.uk Intufoam – Quelfire*
Quester Assessment Systems Ltd Thanet House Sleapshyde, Smallford, St Albans AL4 0SE Tel. *01727 826183* E-mail. *crawford@quester.uk.com* Web. *www.quester.uk.com Quester*
Quest International UK Ltd Unit 2 Demmings Road Industrial Road Estate, Cheadle SK8 2PP Tel. *0161 4910339* Fax. *01233 644146* E-mail. *linda.harman@givaudan.com* Web. *www.airmanager.com 2-N-Heptyl Cyclopentanone – 9-Decenal – Acetylcedrene FLC – Amberlyn – Anther – Applinal – Aquantraal 50% DPG – Aurantion – Avalone M – Azarbre – Bangalol – Beauvertate – Benzyl Acetate – Benzyl Isoeugenol Forte – Benzyl Propionate – Benzyl Salicylate – Bourgeonal – Calyxol – Cervolide – Chrysanthal – Citral Ex Litsea – Citrathal – Citronellyl Nitrile – Cressanther – Cumin Nitrile – Decyl Acetate Rectified – Dihydroeugenol – Dihydrojasmone – Dihydromyrcenol – Dihydromyrcenol Acetate – Dupical – Elintaal – Elintaal Forte – Empetal – Ethyl Safranate – Eugenol – Felvinone – Fiorivert ABQ7046 – Fleuroxene – Florane – Floranyl AB 256 – Florocyclene – Florosa (Q) – Frescile – Gardamide – Gardocyclene – Gyrane – Herboxane – Hexyl Benzoate – Hexyl Crotonate – Inonyl Acetate – Inonyl Formate Extra – Ionone – Iso-Jasmone Pure – Isobutavan – Isoeugenol – Isolongifolanone – Jasmacyclene – Jasmatone – Jasmopyrane – Jasmopyrane Forte – Jessate – L-Carvone – Ligantraal – Ligustral – Lixetone – Lixetone Coeur – Lyrantion 50% DPG – Maceal – Manzanate – Mefranal – Methyl Ionone – Methyl Ionone Alpha ISO – Methyl Myrisate – Mevantraal – Musk R-1 – Neobergomate Forte – Octyl Acetate – Ortholate – Patchouli Oil Acid Washed – Pelargene – Petiole – Phenoxyethyl Isobutyrate Beta – Phenyl Ehtyl Formate – Phenyl Ethyl Acetate – Pivacyclene – Pivarose – PTBCHA – PTBCHA High-Cis – Rhubafuran – Seringone 50% Benzyl Acetate – Sinodor – Traseolide – Tridecene-2-Nitrile – Ultravanil ABQ7012 – Verdalia A – Verdilyn – Verdinal – Verdoracine – Vertelon – Vetiveryl Acetate Subst. ABX7062 – Viotril ABQ5770 – Yuzuzest ABJ 7091*
Question Mark Computing Ltd 4Th Floor Hill House Highgate Hill, London N19 5NA Tel. *020 72637575* Fax. *020 72637555* E-mail. *info@qmark.co.uk* Web. *www.questionmark.com/uk Question Mark*
Quicks Ltd 7 Gardner Industrial Estate Kent House Lane, Beckenham BR3 1JR Tel. *020 86591931* Fax. *020 86768939* E-mail. *ian@quicks.biz* Web. *www.quicks.biz Bowcourt*
Quicks Archery 18-22 Stakes Hill Road, Waterlooville PO7 7JF Tel. *023 92254114* Fax. *023 92251519* E-mail. *quicks@quicks.com* Web. *www.quicksarchery.co.uk *Egertec (United Kingdom) – *Longshot (United Kingdom) – *Quicks (United Kingdom)*

Quicksilver Automotive 11-15 Stoney Lane Balsall Heath, Birmingham B12 8DL Tel. *0121 7737000* Fax. *0121 7739420* E-mail. *mail@satnavshop.com* Web. *www.bettercarlighting.co.uk Clifford – Limo Darkglass – Quicksilver – Venom*
Quick-Strip Ltd Unit 2 Bridge Industrial Estate, Silfield Road, Wymondham NR18 9AU Tel. *01953 604399* Fax. *01953 602556* E-mail. *sales@quickstrips.co.uk* Web. *www.quickstrips.co.uk Quick-Strip*
Quiligotti Terrazzo Ltd PO Box 4, Manchester M27 8LP Tel. *0161 7271189* Fax. *0161 7931173* E-mail. *sales@pilkingtons.com* Web. *www.quiligotti.co.uk Fusion – Precast*
Quintech Computer Systems Ltd Ashton Road Beckford, Tewkesbury GL20 7AU Tel. *01386 883800* Fax. *01386 883801* E-mail. *info@quintech.co.uk* Web. *www.quintech.co.uk ACER – Fujitsu Siemens – Hewlett Packard – Microsoft – SAGE*
The Quintessa Art Collection 8 Watkin Road, Wembley HA9 0NL Tel. *020 87953620* Fax. *020 87953634* E-mail. *robert@quintessa-art.com* Web. *www.quintessa-art.com Quintessa Art Collection*
Quinton Dental Air Services P.O.Box 6686, Birmingham B63 3LJ Tel. *0845 4722013* E-mail. *quintonair@btinternet.com* Web. *www.quintondentalairservices.co.uk gardener denver*
Quitmann Furniture (t/a Old Mill Oak Furniture Ltd) Unit 1 Avonmouth Way West, Bristol BS11 9EX Tel. *0117 9822004* Fax. *0117 9822009* E-mail. *info@quitmannfurniture.co.uk* Web. *www.quitmannfurniture.co.uk *O. Quitmann (Czech Rep, Slovak Rep and Malaysia)*

R

Ra'Alloy Ramps Ltd Unit B8 Hortonwood 10, Telford TF1 7ES Tel. *01952 677877* Fax. *01952 677883* E-mail. *stuart@raalloy.co.uk* Web. *www.raalloy.co.uk Ra'alloy ramps*
Rabtherm International Ltd Shelco House Northgate, Aldridge, Walsall WS9 8TH Tel. *01922 743273* Fax. *01922 743119* E-mail. *bgas@rabtherm.co.uk* Web. *www.rabtherm.co.uk B-Gas (United Kingdom) – Rabtherm (United Kingdom)*
R A C 1 Forest Road, Feltham TW13 7WB Tel. *08457 414151* Fax. *020 89172525* Web. *www.rac.co.uk British School of Motoring, The*
Race Furniture Ltd Spartacus House Bourton Industrial Park, Bourton-On-The-Water, Cheltenham GL54 2HQ Tel. *01451 821446* Fax. *01451 821686* E-mail. *enquiries@racefurniture.com* Web. *www.racefurniture.com Antelope – B.A.3 – D.B. – H.D.S. – Pedestal – S.C.500 – Stork – Z.S.*
Race Industrial Products Ltd Unit A1 The Wallows Industrial Estate Fens Pool Avenue, Brierley Hill DY5 1QA Tel. *01384 263614* Fax. *01384 261154* E-mail. *sales@raceindustrial.com* Web. *www.raceindustrial.com BP Lubricants – Castrol Lubricants – Dodge Bearings – EDM Fluid – Gates Hose Fittings – Gates Hydraulics – Industrial Automotive Lubricants*
Raceparts Unit 3 Rockfort Industrial Estate, Wallingford OX10 9DA Tel. *01491 822000* Fax. *01491 822009* E-mail. *sales@raceparts.co.uk* Web. *www.raceparts.co.uk Racetech*
Racetech 88 Bushey Road Raynes Park, London SW20 0JH Tel. *020 89473333* Fax. *020 88797354* E-mail. *admin@racetech.co.uk* Web. *www.racetech.co.uk RaceTech*
Rack International UK Ltd Pant Industrial Estate Dowlais, Merthyr Tydfil CF48 2SR Tel. *01685 383133* Fax. *01685 383836* E-mail. *sales@rackinternational.com* Web. *www.rackinternational.com Canti-Triever – Extractor – Glide-Out – Haz-Mat Stak – Heavy Duty Glide-Out – Janmak Ro-Ro – Pyrosilo – Sheetmaster – Stak A.S.R. – Superglide*
Rackline Ltd Oaktree Lane Talke Pits, Stoke On Trent ST7 1RX Tel. *01782 777666* Fax. *01782 777444* E-mail. *lindsay.khan@rackline.com* Web. *www.rackline.co.uk Axcess – Glidetrak – Monotrak – Multitrak – Pirouette – Powertrak – Profile – Proform – Sidetrak*
Rack & Shelf Labels 2809 Sharman Way, Gnosall, Stafford ST20 0LX Tel. *08448 009288* Fax. *08448 009289* E-mail. *info@rackandshelflabels.co.uk* Web. *www.rackandshelflabels.co.uk Rack and Shelf Labels*
Radamec Control Systems Ltd Euro House Abex Road, Newbury RG14 5EY Tel. *01635 40528* Fax. *01635 47453* E-mail. *sales@radamec-controls.co.uk* Web. *www.radamec-controls.co.uk Microshift – Servostep – Teleserv*
Radan Limpley Mill Limpley Stoke, Bath BA2 7FJ Tel. *01225 721330* Fax. *01225 721333* E-mail. *sales@uk.radan.com* Web. *www.radan.com Radprofile – Radpunch*
Radar Signs 12 High View Parade Woodford Avenue, Ilford IG4 5EP Tel. *020 85510216* Fax. *020 85511458* E-mail. *radarsigns@btclick.com Radar*
Alan James Raddon Clifton House Aberarth, Aberaeron SA46 0LW Tel. *01545 570904* E-mail. *alraddon@aol.com AL'S Feet – Alan James Raddon – Shandals*
Radflex Contract Services Ltd Unit 35 Wilks Avenue Questor, Dartford DA1 1JS Tel. *01322 276363* Fax. *01322 270606* E-mail. *grahamh@radflex.co.uk* Web. *www.radflex.co.uk Radcrete – Radflex – Radjoint – Radmat*
Radford Supplies Ltd Unit 2 Little Tennis Street White City Trading Estate, Nottingham NG2 4EL Tel. *0115 9486990* Fax. *0115 9486991* E-mail. *sales@radfordjewellery.com* Web. *www.radfordaccessories.com Radford*
Radiall Ltd Ground Floor 6 The Ground Union Office Park, Uxbridge UB8 2GH Tel. *01895 425000* Fax. *01895 425010* E-mail. *infouk@radiall.com* Web. *www.radiall.com *NK Networks Coaxial & TV Camera Cables (TRIAX) (Germany) – *Radiall (France) – Transradio*
Radio Detection Western Drive, Bristol BS14 0AZ Tel. *0117 9767776* Fax. *0117 9767775* E-mail. *info@radiodetection.spx.com* Web. *www.radiodetection.com ARRM – C A T – C.A.T - Cable Avoiding Tool; RADIODETECTION - Buried Pipe and Cable Locators by Radiodetection; RD PRECISION LOCATORS - Locating Underground Services; RL 200 - High Voltage Cable Identifier; PHASOR - Phase and feeder identification instrument. Gatorcam - Inspection Calleras Duct & Pipe. – Drill Track – Electrolocation – Gatorcam – Genny – LMS – PCM – R.D. – R.D. Precision Locators – Radiodetection – Radiodetection – RD4000 – Riserbond – SCM*
Radio Relay Old Brighton Road, Lewes BN7 3JL Tel. *01273 476456* Fax. *01273 483193* E-mail. *salesteam@radiorelay.co.uk* Web. *www.radiorelay.co.uk Hyt – Icom – Motorola – Standard Horizon – Tom Tom – Vertex Standard*
Radir Ltd Douglas House Simpson Road, Bletchley, Milton Keynes MK1 1BA Tel. *01908 370000* Fax. *01908 370055* E-mail. *ianh@radir.com* Web. *www.radir.com Datatemp – Eurotherm – Fluke – Hart – Hart Scientific – INSIDEIR – Ircon – Linscan – Marathon – Marathon MM – MiniTemp – Power Quality – Pyrometer – Raynger – Raytek – Raytek Corp – Raytek GmbH – Raytek Inc – Smart View – Thermalert – ThermoView*
Radius Solutions Ltd Manor House High Street, Dronfield S18 1PY Tel. *01246 290331* Fax. *01246 412401* E-mail. *david.taylor@radiussolutions.com* Web. *www.radiussolutions.com PECAS*
Radleys 5 The Shires Shire Hill, Saffron Walden CB11 3AZ Tel. *01799 513320* Fax. *01799 513283* E-mail. *sales@radleys.co.uk* Web. *www.radleys.co.uk Benchtidy – BT's – Carousel – Cryovials – Duraseal – Gogglebox – Ice'n'easy – Lollipop – Pro-Mem – Radlab – Rodaviss – Titan – Tough Tags*
Rael Brook Group Ltd Rael Brook House Grosvenor Street, Ashton Under Lyne OL7 0RE Tel. *0161 3445618* Fax. *0161 3085060* E-mail. *b.deas@raelbrookshirts.com* Web. *www.raelbrookshirts.com David Latimer – Folkespeare – Rael Brook – Southern Comfort*
Raflatac Ltd Wareham Road Eastfield, Scarborough YO11 3DX Tel. *01723 583661* Fax. *01723 584896* E-mail. *info@upmraflatac.com* Web. *www.upmraflatac.com Raflatac*
Rahmqvist UK Ltd Crabtree Road Thorpe Industrial Estate, Egham TW20 8RN Tel. *01784 439888* Fax. *01784 471419* E-mail. *tony.cracknell@rahmqvist.com* Web. *www.rahmqvist.com Rahnqvist UK*
Railex Filing Ltd Crossens Way Marine Drive, Southport PR9 9LY Tel. *01704 222100* Fax. *01923 252211* E-mail. *sales@railex.co.uk* Web. *www.railexfiling.co.uk Designline – Doublestore – Duba – Easifile – Essex – Fastashelf – Fichefile – Midlock – Mobilfile – MTM (Made To Measure) – Rotary – Rotascan – Tabula*
Rainbow Recruitment UK Ltd Park Lane House 7 High Street, Welshpool SY21 7JP Tel. *01938 555222* Fax. *01938 555800* E-mail. *jobs@rainbow-recruitment.co.uk* Web. *www.rainbow-recruitment.co.uk Rainbow Recruitment*
Rainbow Woodchips Higher Whitnell Farm Binegar, Radstock BA3 4UJ Tel. *01749 841728* Fax. *01749 841728* E-mail. *enquiries@rainbowwoodchips.com* Web. *www.rainbowwoodchips.com rainbow woodchips, natures colourful compainion*
Raindrop Information Systems Ltd Queens House 55-56 Lincoln's Inn Fields, London WC2A 3LJ Tel. *020 72698500* Fax. *020 72698501* E-mail. *info@raindrop.co.uk* Web. *www.manhattansoftware.co.uk Manhattan II*
Rainer Schneider & Ayres 3 Hereford Close, Buxton SK17 9PH Tel. *01298 79903* Fax. *01298 72124* E-mail. *rsa_bxt@btconnect.com* Web. *www.rainer-schneider-ayres.co.uk Norwe – Thermik Thermal Cutouts – Widia Magnetic Materials – PTC's – Schwarzpunkt – Grau*
Raisin Social 34 Crowhurst Mead, Godstone RH9 8BF Tel. *01883 731173* Fax. *01883 731174* E-mail. *info@raisin-social.com* Web. *www.raisin-social.com *Goiya Kgeisje (South Africa) – *Namaqua (South Africa)*
Raith Rovers Football Club Starks Park Pratt Street, Kirkcaldy KY1 1SA Tel. *01592 263514* Fax. *01592 642833* E-mail. *eric.drysdale@raithroversfc.com* Web. *www.raithroversfc.com R.R.F.C.*
Raja Frozen Foods Ltd Unit A4 Amyco Works Doris Road, Bordesley Green, Birmingham B9 4SJ Tel. *0121 7710039* Fax. *0121 7710030* E-mail. *rajafrozenfoods@btconnect.com* Web. *www.rajafrozenfoods.co.uk *Raja – *Shajah*
Rake 'N' Lift & Co - Nottingham Rakes UK Rakes Specialists (Rake UK Rake Specialists) 33 Firs Road Edwalton, Nottingham NG12 4BY Tel. *07802 857103* Fax. *07802 857103 M.A. Garton-Smith Exclusive Commissions – Prism Projects – Rake 'N' Lift, The Nottingham Rakes*
Rakusens Ltd Rakusen House Clayton Wood Rise, Leeds LS16 6QN Tel. *0113 2784821* Fax. *0113 2784064* E-mail. *reception@rakusens.co.uk* Web. *www.rakusens.co.uk Rakusen's*
Raleigh UK Ltd Church Street Eastwood, Nottingham NG16 3HT Tel. *01773 532600* Fax. *01773 532601* E-mail. *sales@raleigh.co.uk* Web. *www.raleigh.co.uk B.S.A. – Carlton – Diamondback – Hercules – Phillips – Raleigh – Rudge – Rudge Whitworth – Triumph*
Ralspeed Ltd Hurstwood Court Mercer Way Shadsworth Business Park, Shadsworth Business Park, Blackburn BB1 2QU Tel. *01254 582345* Fax. *01254 668414* E-mail. *sales@ralspeed.com* Web. *www.ralspeed.com Torq-Master*
Ramco Tubular Services Ltd Badentoy Road Badentoy Park Badentoy Industrial Estate, Portlethen, Aberdeen AB12 4YA Tel. *01224 782278* Fax. *01224 783001* E-mail. *info@ramco-plc.com* Web. *www.ramcotubular.co.uk Ramco*
Ramon Hygiene Products 380 Thurmaston Boulevard, Leicester LE4 9LE Tel. *0116 2761881* Fax. *0116 2460224* E-mail. *admin@ramonhygiene.co.uk* Web. *www.ramonhygiene.com Bright Wipe – Ramon – Sundown*
Ramostyle Ltd 21 Noel Street, London W1F 8GP Tel. *020 74371127* Fax. *020 72870971 Dominici (Italy) – *Redskins (France)*
Ramsell Naber Ltd Vigo Place Aldridge, Walsall WS9 8YB Tel. *01922 455521* Fax. *01922 455277* E-mail. *info@ramsell-naber.co.uk* Web. *www.ramsell-naber.co.uk Ceramotherm – *Grafit – Labotherm – Liquitherm – Loramatic – *Multitherm – *Nabertherm – *Noltina – *Noltina-Stabil – *Safed – *Syncarb-F*
Randalls Fabrications Ltd Hoyle Mill Road Kinsley, Pontefract WF9 5JB Tel. *01977 615132* Fax. *01977 610059* E-mail. *info@randallsfabrications.co.uk* Web. *www.randallsfabrications.co.uk Simpack – Simpack - Waste Compactors*
R & M Metal Finishing Ltd Unit 8 Old Forge Trading Estate Dudley Road, Stourbridge DY9 8EL Tel. *01384 266022* Fax. *01384 898766* E-mail. *enquiries@rmmetalfinishing.co.uk* Web. *www.rmmetalfinishing.co.uk R & M Metal Finishing*
Rand Rocket Ltd Abcare House Hownsgill Industrial Park Knitsley Lane, Consett DH8 7NU Tel. *01207 591099* Fax. *01207 591098* E-mail. *sales@rand-rocket.co.uk* Web. *www.randrocket.com Abcare*
Range Choice Unit 24-25 Lake Business Centre Tariff Road, London N17 0YX Tel. *020 88085757* Fax. *020 88083232* E-mail. *rangechoice@hotmail.com O.J's*
Rank Brothers Ltd (Dept K) 56 High Street Bottisham, Cambridge CB25 9DA Tel. *01223 811369* Fax. *01223 811441* E-mail. *info@rankbrothers.co.uk* Web. *www.rankbrothers.co.uk PDA2000*
Rankins Glass Company Ltd 24-34 Pearson Street, London E2 8JD Tel. *020 77294200* Fax. *020 77297135* E-mail. *sales@rankinsglass.co.uk* Web. *www.rankinsglass.co.uk CCS1 – Colorclear – Colorline – Pyratak – Pyroballistic – Pyrobel – Pyrobelite – Pyroclear – Rankins – Royale*
Rannoch Smokery Kinloch Rannoch, Pitlochry PH16 5QD Tel. *01796 472194* Fax. *08701 601558* E-mail. *enquiries@rannochsmokery.co.uk* Web. *www.rannochsmokery.co.uk *Rannock Smokery*
Ransomes Jacobsen Ltd West Road Ransomes Industrial Estate, Ipswich IP3 9TT Tel. *01473 270000* Fax. *01473 276300* E-mail. *sales@ransomesjacobsen.com* Web. *www.ransomesjacobsen.com Cushman – E-Z-GO – Iseki – Ransomes*
Rapid Hire Centres Ltd 34 Oxford Road, Wokingham RG41 2XZ Tel. *0118 9776217* Fax. *0118 9776218* E-mail. *kaydmoss@hotmail.com Rapid Hire Centres*
Rapid International Ltd 96 Mullavilly Road Tandragee, Craigavon BT62 2LX Tel. *028 38840671* Fax. *028 38840880* E-mail. *info@rapidinternational.com* Web. *www.rapidinternational.com Rapid*
Rapid Newscommunications Group Unit 2 Chowley Business Centre Chowley Oak Lane Tattenhall, Chester CH3 9GA Tel. *01829 770037* Fax. *01829 770047* E-mail. *info@rapidnews.com* Web. *www.rapidnews.com Time-Compression*
Rapid Rail GB Ltd (Worldwide Installation Specialists) Empire Way, Gloucester GL2 5HY Tel. *01452 383001* Fax. *01452 301301* E-mail. *info@rapidrail.co.uk* Web. *www.rapidrail.co.uk EN795 – Thermic Welding – Thermit Welding*
Rapleys LLP 51 Great Marlborough Street, London W1F 7JT Tel. *08707 776292* Fax. *01480 433070* E-mail. *info@rapleys.co.uk* Web. *www.rapleys.co.uk Rapleys*

M A Rapport & Co. Ltd Ivor House Bridge Street, Cardiff CF10 2TH Tel. *029 20373737* Fax. *029 20220121* E-mail. *info@rapportlondon.com* Web. *www.rapportlondon.com Customer Zone – Matthew Norman – Rapport*

Rare Manor Park Twycross, Atherstone CV9 3QN Tel. *01827 883400* Fax. *01827 883410* Web. *www.rareware.com Battlemaniacs – Battletoads – Ironsword*

R A Rodriguez UK Ltd 28 Campus Five, Letchworth Garden City SG6 2JF Tel. *01462 670044* Fax. *01462 670880* E-mail. *info@raruk.com* Web. *www.rarodriguez.co.uk *A.R.B. (U.S.A.) – Bryant – FK – Greenlign – Greenlign – *I.E.F. Werner (Germany) – IEF Werner – IEF Werner – IEF Werner – IEF Werner – *K.H.K. (Japan) – *Kahr (U.S.A.) – Kaydon – Kaydon – Kaydon – Kaydon, Spirolox, IEF Werner, KHK, Bryant, Schatz, A.R.B., FK, Greenlign, Kahr, MRC, RBC, Unitec, Valve Research, Zetassi. – MRC – RBC – RBC – RBC – *Reali - Slim (U.S.A.) – *Schatz (U.S.A.) – *Spirolox (U.S.A.) – *Telescoper (U.S.A.) – TMT – Ultra-Slim – Unitec – Valve Research – Zetasassi*

Ratcliff Palfinger Bessemer Road, Welwyn Garden City AL7 1ET Tel. *01707 325571* Fax. *01707 327752* E-mail. *reception@ratcliffpalfinger.co.uk* Web. *www.ratcliffpalfinger.co.uk Passenger Lifts – Passenger Step Lifts – Ratcliff Cantilever Lifts – Ratcliff Column Lifts – Ratcliff Light Van Lifts – Ratcliff Tail lifts – Wheelchair Lifts*

Ravensburger Ltd 1 Avonbury Business Park Howes Lane, Bicester OX26 2UB Tel. *01869 363800* Fax. *01869 363815* E-mail. *sales@ravensburger.com* Web. *www.ravensburger.com Ravensburger Ltd*

Raves Clothing Ltd 101-113 Branston Street, Birmingham B18 6BA Tel. *0121 5544142* Fax. *0121 5544452* E-mail. *info@ravesuk.com Emporio – Herbie – Raves – Respect*

Denis Rawlins Ltd Unit 17 Castle Vale Industrial Estate Maybrook Road, Minworth, Sutton Coldfield B76 1AL Tel. *0121 3514444* Fax. *0121 3511991* E-mail. *stephen.rawlins@rawlins.co.uk* Web. *www.rawlins.co.uk Litterbug – Macroclean – Master Vac – Nilco – Simmm – Waterhog*

Rawlplug Ltd Skibo Drive Thornliebank Industrial Estate, Thornliebank, Glasgow G46 8JR Tel. *0141 6387961* Fax. *0141 6387397* E-mail. *sales@rawlplug.co.uk* Web. *www.artexrawlplug.co.uk Blue Flash – Impactor – Interset – Kemfast 2 – Kemfix – Mason Master – Poly-Toggle – Rawlbloc – Rawlbolt – Rawldrill – Rawlnut – Rawlok – Rawlplug – Rawlplug Fibre Plugs – Rawlplug Plastic Plugs – Rawlplug Plastic Wood – Rawlplug Rapid – Rawlplug Self Drill Plasterboard Fixing – Rawlplug Spring Toggles – Rawlplug Throughbolt – Rawlplug Wedge Anchors – Rawltool – Safetyplus*

W E Rawson Ltd Castlebank Mills Portobello Road, Wakefield WF1 5PS Tel. *01924 373421* Fax. *01924 290334* E-mail. *reception@werawson.co.uk* Web. *www.rawsoncarpets.co.uk Bordalok – Bordatex – Flexbond – Flexfelt – Springflex – Springlok – Superfil*

Rayhome Ltd Rayhome House Walshaw Road, Bury BL8 1PY Tel. *0161 7611132* Fax. *0161 7646015* E-mail. *sales@rayshim.co.uk* Web. *www.rayshim.co.uk Raybloc (United Kingdom) – Rayshim (United Kingdom) – Raystoc (United Kingdom)*

Rayleigh Instruments Ltd Raytel House 19 Brook Road, Rayleigh SS6 7XH Tel. *01268 749300* Fax. *01268 749309* E-mail. *sales@rayleigh.co.uk* Web. *www.rayleigh.co.uk Control Master – Minitemp – Raytel*

Guy Raymond Engineering Company Ltd Rollesby Road, Kings Lynn PE30 4LX Tel. *01553 761401* Fax. *01553 767459* E-mail. *cedricdaniels@guy-raymond.co.uk* Web. *www.guy-raymond.co.uk Guy-Raymond*

Rayner Opticians Lowndes House The Bury Church Street, Chesham HP5 1DJ Tel. *01494 797400* Fax. *01494 797419* Web. *www.rayneropticians.co.uk Rayner*

R A Young & Abercairn Of Scotland Ltd 1145 Cathcart Road, Glasgow G42 9HD Tel. *0141 6325950* Fax. *0141 6361656* E-mail. *abercairn@abercairn.co.uk* Web. *www.abercairn.co.uk Cathcart – Karrson from Norway – Maban*

Raytel Security Systems Ltd 19 Brook Road, Rayleigh SS6 7XH Tel. *01268 749310* Fax. *01268 745001* E-mail. *info@raytelsecurity.co.uk* Web. *www.raytelsecurity.co.uk Digitac – *Elvox (Italy) – *Innocard (Malaya) – Raytel - Generic – *Sesam (Germany)*

Raytheon UK Fullerton Road Queensway Industrial Estate, Glenrothes KY7 5PY Tel. *01592 754311* Fax. *01592 759775* E-mail. *jim.trail@raytheon.co.uk* Web. *www.raytheon.co.uk H.M.E.*

R Bance & Co. Ltd Powamate Division 3i Sandall Stones Road Kirk Sandall Industrial Estate, Doncaster DN3 1QR Tel. *01302 887821* Fax. *01302 887823* E-mail. *admin@bance.com* Web. *www.powamate.co.uk Bancelamp – Dynalight*

R B Cranes Ltd 111 Station Road Selston, Nottingham NG16 6FF Tel. *01773 811400* Fax. *01773 580483* E-mail. *info@rbcranes.co.uk* Web. *www.rbcranes.co.uk 'CH' – Grabs Priestman – Priestman Grabs – R-B International – V C Long Reach Excavators*

R B F Healthcare 55 Comet Way, Southend On Sea SS2 6UW Tel. *01702 527401* Fax. *01702 420240* E-mail. *sales@rbf-products.co.uk* Web. *www.rbfhealthcare.co.uk Bath Bubble – Bath Bubble - bath lift – Bath Buddy – Bath Wizard – Burnett – Pillow Perfect – RBF Healthcare – Spa 2000*

R B G Norfolk House Pitmedden Road, Dyce, Aberdeen AB21 0DP Tel. *01224 722888* Fax. *01224 773568* E-mail. *sales@rbgltd.com* Web. *www.rbgltd.com Rigblast*

R B Health & Safety Solutions Ltd Blacklands Business Centre 15 Fearon Road, Hastings TN34 2EP Tel. *08452 571489* E-mail. *admin@rbhealthandsafety.co.uk* Web. *www.rbhealthandsafety.co.uk BAFE – CIEH – HSE – IOSH*

R Bickley & Co. 13 Redcar Road, Romford RM3 9PT Tel. *07768 984720 R. Bickley*

R C Brady & Co. 112 Down Street, West Molesey KT8 2TU Tel. *020 87830760* Fax. *020 87830811* E-mail. *sales@rcbrady.co.uk* Web. *www.rcbrady.co.uk R.C. Brady*

R & D Laboratories Ltd Unit U Enkalon Industrial Estate Randalstown Road, Antrim BT41 4LJ Tel. *028 94465753* Fax. *028 94460754* E-mail. *agnes.mcfarlane@rdlabs.co.uk* Web. *www.mistralni.co.uk R & D Laboratories*

R & D Marketings Ltd 11a Anyards Road, Cobham KT11 2LW Tel. *01932 866600* Fax. *01932 866688* E-mail. *ruth@demista.co.uk* Web. *www.demista.co.uk Cosyfloor – demista – Ecofloor – Ecomat*

R D M Industrial Services Ltd Stakehill Lane Middleton, Manchester M24 2RW Tel. *0161 6439333* Fax. *0161 6553467* E-mail. *sales@rdmengineering.co.uk* Web. *www.rdmengineering.co.uk Drivloc*

Read Management Services Ltd International House 35 St Davids Road South, Lytham St Annes FY8 1TJ Tel. *01253 780000* Fax. *01253 781111* E-mail. *rms@rms-group.com* Web. *www.rms-group.com International Sport*

Readymade Companies Worldwide.com Overseas House 66-68 High Road, Bushey Heath, Bushey WD23 1GG Tel. *020 84217475* Fax. *020 84219883* E-mail. *info@readymadecompaniesworldwide.com* Web. *www.readymadecompaniesworldwide.com Readymade Companies*

Readyspex Ltd Glenfield Park Two Blakewater Road, Blackburn BB1 5QH Tel. *01254 680010* Fax. *01254 680241* Web. *www.readyspex.co.uk *Readyspex (Far East)*

Really Useful Research & Development Balmoral House 9 Balmoral Grange, Prestwich, Manchester M25 0GZ Tel. *0161 7209924* Fax. *0161 7400561* E-mail. *john@reallyusefulresearch.co.uk* Web. *www.reallyusefulconsultency.co.uk Forensic Marketing – John Ardern – John Arderne*

Real Organic Foods Couching House Couching Street, Watlington OX49 5PX Tel. *01491 615280* Fax. *01491 615289* E-mail. *info@realorganic.co.uk* Web. *www.realorganic.co.uk Real Organic*

Realstone Ltd Bolehill Quarry Bolehill, Wingerworth, Chesterfield S42 6RG Tel. *01246 270244* Fax. *01246 220095* E-mail. *info@realstone.co.uk* Web. *www.realstone.co.uk Bolehill Delph – Cove – Dukes – Lazonby – Peak Moor – Realslate – Realstone – Watts Cliff*

R E A Metal Windows Ltd 126-136 Green Lane Stoneycroft, Liverpool L13 7ED Tel. *0151 2286373* Fax. *0151 2541828* E-mail. *all@reametal.co.uk* Web. *www.reametal.co.uk Rea Fireact – Rea Firebreak – Rea Frame – Rea Steel – Rea Therm*

Rea Plasrack Ltd Unit 18e Hartlebury Trading Estate Hartlebury, Kidderminster DY10 4JB Tel. *01299 251960* Fax. *01299 253670* E-mail. *info@plasgroup.co.uk* Web. *www.plasgroup.co.uk Plaspal – REA*

Recital Corporation Ltd Seymour House The Courtyard Denmark Street, Wokingham RG40 2AZ Tel. *0118 9783888* E-mail. *sales@recitalsoftware.com* Web. *www.recitalsoftware.com Recital Corporation*

Reckitt Benckiser plc 103-105 Bath Road, Slough SL1 3UH Tel. *01753 217800* Fax. *01753 217899* E-mail. *sales@rb.com* Web. *www.reckittbenckiser.com Bronalin – Burnaid – Cupanol – Cuprofen – Cystoleve – Dentogen – Dusk – Flurex – Glucolyte – Kao-C – Meltus – Novasil – Regulett – Sooth-Tan – Totavit – Tyrocane – Ulcaid – Vitathone – Waxaid*

Recognition Express Wheatfield Way, Hinckley LE10 1YG Tel. *01455 445555* Fax. *01455 445566* E-mail. *manchester@re-trade.co.uk* Web. *www.re-trade.co.uk Recognition Express*

Reco-Prop UK Ltd Unit 4 New Town Trading Estate Chase Street, Luton LU1 3QZ Tel. *01582 412110* Fax. *01582 480432* E-mail. *info@reco-prop.com* Web. *www.reco-prop.com Power-Line by Reed*

Record Electrical Associates Unit C1 Longford Trading Estate, Thomas Street, Stretford, Manchester M32 0JT Tel. *0845 2571053* Fax. *0845 2571054* E-mail. *sales@reauk.com* Web. *www.reauk.com Circscale – Record – Townson & Mercer*

Rectella Unit 2 Blackmore Road, Stretford, Manchester M32 0QY Tel. *0161 8662610* Fax. *0161 8662620* E-mail. *sales@rectella.co.uk* Web. *www.rectella.co.uk Rectella*

Recticel Corby 83-84 Manton Road Earlstrees Industrial Estate, Corby NN17 4JL Tel. *01536 402345* Fax. *01536 400524* E-mail. *miller.chris@recticel.com* Web. *www.recticel.com Colourful Novelty/Promotional Sponges – Comfortseal – Kingfisher – *Natural Loofah – Selmat – Superseal*

Redcats UK 2 Holdsworth Street, Bradford BD1 4AH Tel. *01274 729544* Fax. *01274 729544* E-mail. *sales@empirestores.co.uk* Web. *www.redcats.com *Empire Bow (Worldwide)*

Reddiplex Ltd The Furlong Berry Hill Industrial Estate, Droitwich WR9 9BG Tel. *01905 795432* Fax. *01905 795757* E-mail. *reception@reddiplex.com* Web. *www.reddiplex.com Reddihinge – Reddilock – Reddipile – Reddiprene – Reddisealant – Redditape*

Reddish Joinery Ltd Lambeth Road, Stockport SK5 6TW Tel. *0161 4327682* Fax. *0161 4310183* E-mail. *reddish.joinery@btconnect.com* Web. *www.reddishjoinery.co.uk Reddish Joinery*

Redditch Anodising 37 Heming Road, Redditch B98 0DP Tel. *01527 526855* Fax. *01527 502856* E-mail. *marysalter@redditchanodising.wanadoo.co.uk* Web. *www.redditchanodising.wanadoo.co.uk Westminster Chemicals*

Red Funnel Ferries Ltd 12 Bugle Street, Southampton SO14 2JY Tel. *08704 448898* Fax. *0844 8442698* E-mail. *post@redfunnel.co.uk* Web. *www.redfunnel.co.uk Red Funnel – Red Funnel Towage*

Redhead Freight Ltd Unit E Zenith Business Park Paycocke Road, Basildon SS14 3DW Tel. *01268 884488* Fax. *01268 884489* E-mail. *ros@redhead-int.com* Web. *www.redhead-int.com M. & M. Redhead*

Redhill Manufacturing Unit 6 Padgets Lane, Redditch B98 0RA Tel. *01527 529002* Fax. *01527 523950* E-mail. *sales@redhillmanufacturing.co.uk* Web. *www.tradercatalogue.co.uk Trader*

Red House Industrial Services Ltd Cromwell Street, Coventry CV6 5EZ Tel. *024 76637700* Fax. *024 76667777* E-mail. *sales@redhouseuk.com* Web. *www.redhouseuk.com Abwood – Adcock & Shipley – Agathon – Airmaster – Alfred Herbert – Archdale – Armstrong – Asquith – Avondale – Bellis & Morcom – Black & Decker – Boremaster – Boxford – Britan – Broom & Wade – Bryant – Burgmaster – Churchill – Cincinnait – Clarke – Clarkson – Colchester – D.C.E. – Denbigh – Eagle – Edgwick – Elliot – Essex – F. Werner – Fuho – Harrison – Heald – Heid – Herbert – Hydrovane – Jones & Shipman – Kearney & Treker – Kendall & Gernt – Lumsden – Makino – Manumold – Manurhin – Marwin – Matrix – Meddings – Milford – Mohawk – Moss – Myford – Newall – Norton – Oelikon – Ormerod – Pfauter – Pittler – Pollard – Progress – Quickwork – Rambaudi – Spencer & Holstead – Startrite – Steelweld – Thiel – Unicrane – Varian – Vickers – Wadkin – Ward – Webster & Bennet – Wolf*

Redirack Ltd Wharf Road Kilnhurst, Mexborough S64 5SU Tel. *01709 584711* Fax. *01709 589821* E-mail. *rob.dargue@redirack.co.uk* Web. *www.redirack.co.uk Redirack*

Rediweld Rubber & Plastics Ltd 6-10 Newman Lane, Alton GU34 2QR Tel. *01420 543007* Fax. *01420 544090* E-mail. *info@rediweld.co.uk* Web. *www.rediweld.co.uk BUSPAD – CARSTOPPERS – Gripchocks – Redipave – Sitecop – SURFACE KERBING – Takpave – Traficop*

Red Lion 49 Ltd (t/a Solid State Logic) Spring Hill Road Begbroke, Oxford OX5 1RU Tel. *01865 842300* Fax. *01865 842118* E-mail. *sales@solidstatelogic.com* Web. *www.solid-state-logic.com Avant – Axiom – Axiom-MT – Aysis Air – OmniMix – S.L.4000 G + Master Studio System – S.L.9000 J – Scenaria – ScreenSound – Total Recall – Ultimation – VisionTrack*

Red Mosquito Ltd 27 Blairtummock Place, Glasgow G33 4EN Tel. *08719 181984* Fax. *0871 9181984* E-mail. *andy@redmosquito.co.uk* Web. *www.redmosquito.co.uk Red Mosquito*

Red Rooster Industrial UK Ltd The Meadows Meldrum Meg Way Oldmeldrum, Inverurie AB51 0EZ Tel. *01651 872101* Fax. *01651 871405* E-mail. *info@rriuk.com* Web. *www.rriuk.com Red Rooster – Toku – Yokota*

Redsky It (Formerly Ramesys Construction Services) Viking House Swallowdale Lane, Hemel Hempstead HP2 7EA Tel. *020 30028600* Fax. *020 30700925* E-mail. *construction.webenquiry@redskyit.com* Web. *www.redskyit.com Assimilate – AXIM – CAESOR – DEMA – ESTEEM – ETCi – MENTOR Enterprise – Proform – Progression AEC – Ramesys CONSTRUCT – Ramesys SUMMIT – Winbuild*

Red Sky I T Ltd Viking House Swallowdale Lane, Hemel Hempstead HP2 7EA Tel. *020 30028600* Fax. *020 30700925* E-mail. *enquiry@redskyit.com* Web. *www.redskyit.com Saturn 95 – Saturn Web – Workmate 95 – Workmate Executive – Workmats PVS*

Red Technology E-Commerce House Oakfield Industrial Estate, Eynsham, Witney OX29 4AG Tel. *01865 880800* Fax. *01865 880865* E-mail. *info@redtechnology.com* Web. *www.redtechnology.com Freecom.Net*

Redwood Stone The Stoneworks West Horrington, Haydon, Wells BA5 3EH Tel. *01749 677777* Fax. *01749 671177*

E-mail. *mail@redwoodstone.com* Web. *www.redwoodstone.com Kingfisher Stone – Redwood Stone – The Granite Collection*

G Reekie Group Ltd Ruthvenfield Road Inveralmond Industrial Estate, Perth PH1 3EE Tel. *01738 622471* Fax. *01738 639613* E-mail. *info@reekiegroup.wannadoo.co.uk* Web. *www.reekie.co.uk Komatsu – Massey-Ferguson – Sambron – Yamaha*

Reekie Machining Ltd (David Reekie & Son) Inchinnan Business Park South Street, Inchinnan, Renfrew PA4 9RL Tel. *0141 8120411* Fax. *0141 8120137* E-mail. *info@reekiemachining.co.uk* Web. *www.reekiemachining.co.uk Reekie*

Reeth Garage Ltd Arkengarthdale Road Reeth, Richmond DL11 6QT Tel. *01748 84243* Fax. *01748 884691* E-mail. *reeth.garage@virgin.net *ATV – *Fraser – *Ifor Williams – *Kuhn – *Twose*

Reeve (Derby) Ltd Pentagon Island Nottingham Road, Derby DE21 6HB Tel. *01332 362661* Fax. *01332 292736* E-mail. *info@pentagon-group.co.uk* Web. *www.pentagon-group.co.uk Pentagon Ltd*

Ann Reeves & Co. Ltd 78 Great Titchfield Street, London W1W 7QS Tel. *020 76377965* Fax. *020 76379272* E-mail. *peter@annreeves.com* Web. *www.annreeves.com Ann Reeves*

Reflecting Roadstuds Ltd 1 Mill Lane, Halifax HX3 6TR Tel. *01422 360208* Fax. *01422 349075* E-mail. *ts@craglands.demon.co.uk* Web. *www.percyshawcatseyes.com Catseye*

Regalead Ltd Columbus House Altrincham Road, Manchester M22 9AF Tel. *0161 9461164* Fax. *0161 9461033* E-mail. *guy.hubble@regalead.co.uk* Web. *www.regalead.co.uk RegaLead*

Regalzone LLP Dukes Valley Windsor Road, Gerrards Cross SL9 8SR Tel. *01753 662666* Fax. *01753 664463* E-mail. *info@regalzone.com* Web. *www.regalzone.com *Isap – *Kristal – *Master Plastics – Selfkep*

Regatta Ltd Risol House Mercury Park Mercury Way, Urmston, Manchester M41 7RR Tel. *0161 7491200* Fax. *0161 7491210* E-mail. *mweisz@regatta.com* Web. *www.regatta.com Kex – Landtrekka – Regatta – Survivor – Union Hardwear*

Regent Engineering Company Darlaston Central Trading Estate Salisbury Street, Wednesbury WS10 8BQ Tel. *0121 5686063* Fax. *0121 5264789* E-mail. *alan@regenteng.com* Web. *www.regenteng.com Regent*

Regina Industries Ltd Brookhouse Road Parkhouse Industrial Estate West, Newcastle ST5 7RU Tel. *01782 565646* Fax. *01782 565610* E-mail. *mbeardmore@regina.co.uk* Web. *www.regina.co.uk Regina*

Regina International Ltd (Sales & Service Centre) Unit 1 Greenbank Business Park Dyneley Road, Blackburn BB1 3AB Tel. *01254 661116* Fax. *01254 59456* E-mail. *sales.uk@reginachain.net* Web. *www.regina.it Flitetop – Flitetop - Matveyor - Ultop – Matveyor – Ultop*

Regus Management Ltd 3000 Hillswood Drive, Chertsey KT16 0RS Tel. *01932 895000* Fax. *01932 895001* E-mail. *enquiries@regus.com* Web. *www.regus.com Regus Office*

Reid Printers 79-109 Glasgow Road Blantyre, Glasgow G72 0LY Tel. *01698 826000* Fax. *01698 824944* E-mail. *sales@reidprinters.com* Web. *www.reid-print-group.co.uk Alwych – Denbeigh – Greenback – Litao*

Reid & Taylor Ltd Williams Street Langholm Woollen Mills, Langholm DG13 0BN Tel. *01387 380311* Fax. *01387 380720* E-mail. *office@reidandtaylor.com* Web. *www.reidandtaylor.co.uk Bantam Weight – Derby Top – Derbystar – Eskbank – Fidenter – Glazy – Gold – Laverock – Perfectum – Recordon – Scotsman*

Reinforced Shuttlecocks Ltd Sandown Road, Sandwich CT13 9NU Tel. *01304 612366* Fax. *01304 615484* E-mail. *sales@maxsports.co.uk* Web. *www.tennisdiscount.co.uk *R.S.L. (China) – *R.S.L. Ace (China) – *R.S.L. Official (China) – *R.S.L. Silver Feather (China) – *R.S.L. Tourney (China)*

Reiss Retail Ltd 114 Kings Road, London SW3 4TX Tel. *020 72254910* Fax. *020 72254901* E-mail. *reception@reiss.co.uk* Web. *www.reiss.co.uk Reiss Retail*

Rekord Sales Manor Road Mancetter, Atherstone CV9 1RJ Tel. *01827 712424* Fax. *01827 715133* E-mail. *terry@universal.co.uk* Web. *www.rekord.com Rekord*

Relats UK Ltd Suflex Estate Risca, Newport NP11 7BH Tel. *01495 271161* Fax. *01633 615975* E-mail. *relatsuk@relats.com* Web. *www.relats.com Periflex – Perisil – Polycryl – Revitex – VAC – Varcon*

Relec Electronics Ltd Sandford Lane, Wareham BH20 4DY Tel. *01929 555700* Fax. *01929 555701* E-mail. *sales@relec.co.uk* Web. *www.relec.co.uk Egston – Elobau – Timonta – Timonta, Egston, Varitronix, Elobau, Electrodynamics. – Varitroix*

Reliance Precision (Reliance Precision Ltd) Rowley Mills Penistone Road Penistone Road, Fenay Bridge, Huddersfield HD8 0LE Tel. *01484 601000* Fax. *01484 601001* E-mail. *sales@reliance.co.uk* Web. *www.reliance.co.uk Flex-Plate – P.R.C. – R.G.T. – R.S.E. – R.S.G. – *Reli A Flex (U.S.A.)*

Reliance Water Controls Ltd Worcester Road, Evesham WR11 4RA Tel. *01386 712400* Fax. *01386 47028* E-mail. *reception@rwc.co.uk* Web. *www.rwc.co.uk Caremix – Filmaster – Floguard – Heatguard – Hoseguard – Promix – Reliance – Reliance Worldwide – Syr*

Reliant Machinery Ltd Unit L Cradock Road, Luton LU4 0JF Tel. *01582 584999* Fax. *01582 581117* E-mail. *sales@reliant-machinery.co.uk* Web. *www.reliant-machinery.com Coolstream – Elite – Nova – Powerbond*

Relyon Ltd Station Mills, Wellington TA21 8NN Tel. *01823 667501* Fax. *01823 666079* E-mail. *enquries@reylon.co.uk* Web. *www.relyon.co.uk Deptich – Relyon*

Rema Tip Top UK Ltd Westland Square, Leeds LS11 5XS Tel. *0113 2770044* Fax. *0113 2772139* E-mail. *info@tip-top.co.uk* Web. *www.rema-tiptop.co.uk Rema Tip Top UK*

Remote Estimating Ltd 2 Cherry Grove Royton, Oldham OL2 5YL Tel. *0780 9158186* E-mail. *info@remoteestimating.co.uk* Web. *remoteestimating.co.uk Remote Estimating Ltd*

Removals In Nottingham 252 Alfreton Road, Nottingham NG7 5LS Tel. *07850 157618* E-mail. *vanmannotts@googlemail.com* Web. *www.bg-removal.co.uk Bg Removals*

Remploy Ltd Manor Mill Lane, Leeds LS11 8DF Tel. *0113 2726900* Fax. *0113 2779170* E-mail. *alan.hill@remploy.co.uk* Web. *www.remploy.co.uk Babe-eze – Flexfit – Myron – Pacesetter – Power Rider – Proshifter – Prosoc – Rembelt – Roller, Access, Stowaway*

Remsdaq Ltd Parkway Deeside Industrial Park, Deeside CH5 2NL Tel. *01244 286495* Fax. *01244 286496* E-mail. *reception@remsdaq.com* Web. *www.remsdaq.com Callisto (United Kingdom) – Resque (United Kingdom) – Sabre (United Kingdom) – Starwatch (United Kingdom)*

Rem Systems Ltd Unit 24-26 Sabre Close Quedgeley, Gloucester GL2 4NZ Tel. *01452 314100* Fax. *01452 314101* E-mail. *jryland@remsystems.co.uk* Web. *www.remsystems.co.uk Certa (Switzerland) – Erowa (Switzerland) – Triag (Switzerland)*

REMTV AGENCY LTd Second Floor 6, LONDON STREET, London W2 1HR Tel. *020 70600859* Fax. *0207 0601409* E-mail. *ibiza@remtv.org* Web. *www.remtv.org MEKANO – REMTV*

Remys Ltd Unit 6 ZK Park 23 Commerce Way, Croydon CR0 4ZS Tel. *020 86802191* Fax. *020 86813514* E-mail. *mail@remys.co.uk* Web. *www.remys.co.uk *Apollo (Far East) – *Cross Country (Far East) – Diva – Gianni Vitorio – *Gym Sports (Far East) – *Heat-Wave (Far East) – Irena – *La-Reine (Far East) – Millennium – Perfume – *Woodland (Far East) – *Worldteam (Far East)*

Renair Ltd 11-15 Chase Road, London NW10 6PT Tel. *020 89653001* Fax. *020 89655773* E-mail. *sales@renair.co.uk* Web. *www.renair.co.uk Bantex*

Renault UK Ltd Rivers Office Park Denham Way, Maple Cross, Rickmansworth WD3 9YS Tel. *01923 895000* Fax. *01923 895101* E-mail. *customer.services@renault.co.uk* Web. *www.renault.co.uk Renault*

Rencol Components Ltd (Ray Engineering Co Ltd) Unit 2 Avonbridge Trading Estate Atlantic Road, Bristol BS11 9QD Tel. *0117 9160090* Fax. *0117 9504550* E-mail. *sales@rencol.com* Web. *www.rencol.com Rencol*

Rendit Ltd One Acre Thorpe In Balne, Doncaster DN6 0DZ Tel. *01302 884385* Fax. *01302 885498* E-mail. *support@rendit.co.uk* Web. *www.rendit.co.uk Rendit*

Renishaw plc New Mills, Wotton Under Edge GL12 8JR Tel. *01453 524524* Fax. *01453 524901* E-mail. *uk@renishaw.com* Web. *www.renishaw.com Renishaw*

Renold Clutches & Couplings Ltd Newlands Road, Cardiff CF3 2EU Tel. *029 20792737* Fax. *029 20791360* E-mail. *martin.slade@renold.com* Web. *www.renold.com Chainflex Coupling – Croftair Clutches – Crofts – Crownpin – Crownpin Coupling – DCB-GS Coupling – Discflex Coupling – DM Series Sprag Clutch – Gearflex – Gearflex DA Coupling – Gearflex HDB Coupling – Hydrastart – Hydrastart Fluid Coupling – MSC Coupling – Pinflex – Pinflex Coupling – REGF Trapped Roller Freewheel – REGLP Trapped Roller Freewheel – REGV Trapped Roller Freewheel – Renoldflex – REUF Trapped Roller Freewheel – REUK – REUKC – REUKCC – REUS Trapped Roller Freewheel – REUSNU Trapped Roller Freewheel – Rigid Coupling – SA Series Sprag Clutch – SB Series Sprag Clutch – SO/SX Series Sprag Clutch – Spider Coupling – Spiderflex – Spiderflex Coupling – Tyreflex – Tyreflex Coupling – VF Coupling*

Renson Fabrications Ltd Fairfax Units 1-2-3 Bircholt Road Parkwood Industrial Estate, Maidstone ME15 9SF Tel. *01622 754123* Fax. *01622 689478* E-mail. *info@rensonuk.net* Web. *www.uk.renson.be/solutions-for-ventilation-and-sun-protection-unite Renson UK Ltd*

Rentokil Initial plc 2 City Place Beehive Ring Road, London Gatwick Airport, Gatwick RH6 0HA Tel. *01293 858000* Fax. *01342 326229* Web. *www.rentokil-initial.com Initial Washroom Management Service*

Renubath Services Ltd Unit 17g Village Farm, Preston, Cirencester GL7 5PR Tel. *01285 656624* Fax. *01285 652446* E-mail. *info@renubath.co.uk* Web. *www.renubath.co.uk Vitrocoat*

Re-Nu Kitchens Ltd 60 Nuffield Road Nuffield Industrial Estate, Poole BH17 0RT Tel. *01202 687642* Fax. *01202 671773* E-mail. *sales@re-nukitchens.co.uk* Web. *www.re-nukitchens.co.uk Re-Nu*

Reo UK Ltd Unit 2-4 Callow Hill Road, Craven Arms SY7 8NT Tel. *01588 676167* Fax. *01588 672718* E-mail. *main@reo.co.uk* Web. *www.reo.co.uk ReoVib – ReoVib - Vareotron - Reotron*

Replin Fabrics March Street Mills March Street, Peebles EH45 8ER Tel. *01721 724310* Fax. *01721 721893* E-mail. *enquiries@replin-fabrics.co.uk* Web. *www.robert-noble.co.uk Replin Fabrics – Robert Noble*

Repro Arts Ltd Monument Road, Great Yarmouth NR30 3PS Tel. *01493 855515* Fax. *01493 851557* E-mail. *marissa@reproart.co.uk* Web. *www.reproart.co.uk Easy Sign – Sale Systems – Tool Store*

Repropoint Ltd 15 Poole Road, Woking GU21 6BB Tel. *01483 596281* Fax. *01483 596292* E-mail. *enquiries@repropoint.com* Web. *www.repropoint.com Repropoint*

Research For Today Ltd 77 Gunnersbury Avenue, London W5 4LP Tel. *020 89924877* Fax. *020 89935818* E-mail. *simalto@researchfortoday.com Simalto Plus*

Research International Group Ltd 6-7 Grosvenor Place, London SW1X 7SH Tel. *020 76565500* Fax. *020 72350202* E-mail. *j.bower@research-int.com* Web. *www.research-int.com Conceptor – Locator – Marplan – Microtest – Publi Test – Research International – S.M.A.R.T. – Sensor*

Resimac Ltd Knaresborough Technology Park Manse Lane, Knaresborough HG5 8LF Tel. *01765 677757* Fax. *01765 677757* E-mail. *info@resimac.co.uk* Web. *www.resimac.co.uk Resimetal*

Resin Bonded Surfacing 51 Ansten Crescent, Doncaster DN4 6EZ Tel. *01302 533562* Fax. *01302 533562* E-mail. *resinsurfacing@aol.com* Web. *www.resinbondedsurfacing.co.uk ADDAGRIP – ADDASET – ADDASTONE – NAPEX – POROUS PAVING – TRUSTMARK*

Resin Building Products Ltd Resbuild House Unit 2, Durham Lane, Doncaster DN3 3FE Tel. *01302 300822* Fax. *01302 300833* E-mail. *carl@resbuild.co.uk* Web. *www.resbuild.co.uk Resbuild (United Kingdom) – TTURA (United Kingdom)*

Resinex UK Ltd 11 Valley Business Centre Gordon Road, High Wycombe HP13 6EQ Tel. *01494 459881* Fax. *01494 795334* E-mail. *info@resinex.co.uk* Web. *www.resinex.co.uk Affinity – Alcryn – Attane – Calibre – Crastin – Cycolac – Cycoloy – Delrin – Dow HDPE – Dow LDPE – Dowlex – Electrafil – Elite – Eltex – Esdash – Hytrel – Isoplast – Ixef – Lexan – Luranyl – Mablex – Mafill – Maflex – Magnum – Megarad – Minlon – Noryl – Nylatron – Nylind PA6, PA66 (Ind. Quality) – Orgalloy – Oroglas – Padmex – Pebax – Pellethane – Plaslube – Polyfast – Polypropylene – Prevail – Primacor – Primef – Pulse – Questra – Rapidpurge – Ravago Off Grades – Ravago Recycled Material – Ravamid – Ravatal – Resinex – Rilsan B PA11 – Rislan A PA12 – Rynite – Scolefin – Sconablend – Sicoflex – Sicoklar – Sicoran – Sicostirolo – Sicotal – Sicoter – Stamylan P – Styron – Styron A-Tech – Taylor Made Compounds – Tector – Teflon – Tefzel – Tyril – Ultem – Ultrason – Valox – Xenoy – Zenite – Zytel*

Resintech Ltd Unit 1-2 Horcott Industrial Estate Horcott Road, Fairford GL7 4BX Tel. *01285 712755* Fax. *01285 712999* E-mail. *info@resintech.co.uk* Web. *www.resintech.co.uk SHIELDFAST*

Resin Technical Systems (a division of R.M.P Plastics Ltd) Fort Brockhurst Industrial Estate Alphage Road, Gosport PO12 4DU Tel. *023 92585899* Fax. *023 92510306* E-mail. *sales@resintek.co.uk* Web. *www.resintek.co.uk Eccobond – RTS Systems – Scotchcast – Stycast*

ReSpace Acoustics Ltd 19 Stansfield Road Brixton, London SW9 9RY Tel. *0844 8844011* Fax. *0844 8844019* E-mail. *yebullen@gmail.com* Web. *www.respace-acoustics.co.uk Ecophon*

The Retail Doctor PO Box 463, Stevenage SO30 2NF Tel. *0845 1162138* E-mail. *enquiries@theretaildoctor.co.uk* Web. *www.theretaildoctor.co.uk The Retail Doctor*

Retail Websites Limited Unit 24 - Business Centre Izatt Avenue, Dunfermline KY11 3BZ Tel. *0845 3134747* E-mail. *sales@retail-websites.com* Web. *www.quicksafe.co.uk Quicksafe.co.uk*

Retell 53 Thames Street, Sunbury On Thames TW16 5QH Tel. *01932 779755* Fax. *01932 780383* E-mail. *steve.cobley@retell.co.uk* Web. *www.retellrecorders.co.uk 121 – 151 – 160 – 701 – 704 – 752 – 902 – 953 – 955*

Retrofit Rubberroofing 44 Townsend Road, Sunderland SR3 4LW Tel. *08450 091975* Fax. *08450 092441* E-mail. *retrofitrubberroofing@ntlworld.com firestone epdm*

Review Display Systems Ltd Horton Place Hortons Way, Westerham TN16 1BT Tel. *01959 563345*

Fax. *01959 564452* E-mail. *info@review-displays.co.uk* Web. *www.review-displays.co.uk 3M – Aaeon – AMT – Dale – Electro Plasma – Futuba – Hampshire – Lumitex, Inc. – NEC – Optrex – Palm – Panasonic – Planar*

Revol Ltd Samson Close, Newcastle upon Tyne NE12 6DZ Tel. *0191 2684555* Fax. *0191 2160004* E-mail. *sales@revol.co.uk* Web. *www.revol.co.uk Revol – Voler*

Rewarding Dogs Alburn Drummond Road, Inverness IV2 4NA Tel. *01463 230757* E-mail. *info@rewardingdogs.com* Web. *www.rewardingdogs.com Rewarding Dogs*

Reward Manufacturing Co. Ltd Sackville Mills Sackville Street, Skipton BD23 2PR Tel. *01756 797755* Fax. *01756 796644* E-mail. *jonathan.hooper@rewardtrolleys.com* Web. *www.rewardtrolleys.com Reward*

Rexam Holding plc Third Floor 4 Millbank, London SW1P 3XR Tel. *020 72274100* Fax. *020 72274109* E-mail. *stuart.bull@rexam.com* Web. *www.rexam.com Ecodrum – Hiway – Leverpak – Liquipak – Omega – Ovenable Board – Pattern 3 – Pay-Off-Pak – Rexam – Surelift – Unicup – Unifoil – Unipak – Weathertop*

Rex Bousfield Ltd 18-20 Fairviews, Oxted RH8 9BD Tel. *01883 717033* Fax. *01883 717890* E-mail. *jeff.thompson@bousfield.com* Web. *www.bousfieldltd.com Antivlam – Arpa – *Fipro (Slovenia) – Firespec – Flamcor – Holdfast – *Melafac – *Melafac Flame (Belgium) – *Novolam Securite (France) – Panoflam – *Trespa (Netherlands)*

Rexnord NV UK Office 32 Imex Business Centre Oxleasow Road, Redditch B98 0RE Tel. *01527 830473* Fax. *01527 830501* E-mail. *robert.sillis@rexnord.com* Web. *www.rexnord.co.uk Rexnord*

Reynolds Boughton Unit 9 Graycar Business Park Barton Turn, Barton under Needwood, Burton On Trent DE13 8EN Tel. *01283 711771* Fax. *01283 711669* E-mail. *ceh@reynoldsboughton.com* Web. *www.reynoldsboughton.com Boughton – Boughton Reynolds – Kwikcova*

Reznor UK Ltd Park Farm Road Park Farm Industrial Estate, Folkestone CT19 5DR Tel. *01303 259141* Fax. *01303 850002* E-mail. *orders@reznor.co.uk* Web. *www.reznor.co.uk Ecco 5000 (Belgium) – Enviropak – Euro C – Euro T – Euro X – LCSA – Novojet – RAR – Reznor. – RHC – RPVE – Smartcom – Thermocool (Belgium) – UCA (Belgium) – UESA – UPA (Belgium) – V3 (Belgium) – Vision*

R F Bright Enterprises Ltd Unit 6 Access 4.20 New Hythe Business Park Bellingham Way, Aylesford ME20 7HP Tel. *01622 717141* Fax. *01622 717163* E-mail. *enquiries@rfbright.co.uk* Web. *www.rfbright.co.uk Chemset – *Portion-aire (U.S.A.) – *Portionator (U.S.A.) – Unipre*

R F D Beaufort Ltd Kingsway Dunmurry, Belfast BT17 9AF Tel. *028 90301531* Fax. *028 90621765* E-mail. *dbaxter@rfdbeaufort.com* Web. *www.rfdbeaufort.com ACR – Aerolite – Aerospace – Ferryman – Heliraft – Heliraft XDS – M.E.S. – Marin Ark – S.A.R. – Seasava Plus – Surviva*

RFDS Consultants 253 Dysart Road, Grantham NG31 7LP Tel. *01476 409929* Fax. *01476 409929* E-mail. *office@quenvhas.co.uk* Web. *www.rfdsconsultants.com Quenvhas*

R F Lifting & Access Ltd Unit 18 Carrock Road Croft Business Park, Bromborough, Wirral CH62 3RA Tel. *0151 3461365* Fax. *0151 3461366* E-mail. *sales@rflifting.co.uk* Web. *www.rflifting.co.uk Columbus McKinnon – Genie – Gis – Houlotte – JLG – NiftyLift – Pfaff – Skyjack*

R F S UK Ltd 9 Haddenham Business Park Thame Road, Haddenham, Aylesbury HP17 8LJ Tel. *01844 294900* Fax. *01844 294944* E-mail. *sales@rfsworld.com* Web. *www.rfsworld.com Cellflex – Flexwell – Radiaflex*

R G Engineering 54 Dunster Street, Northampton NN1 3JY Tel. *01604 639673* Fax. *01604 639673* E-mail. *rgengineering@btopenworld.com R.G. Engineering*

R G I S Inventory Specialists (Head Office) Imperial Court Holly Walk, Leamington Spa CV32 4YB Tel. *01926 888882* Fax. *01926 888883* E-mail. *sales@rgis.com* Web. *www.rgis.com Audit – RGIS*

R G K UK Ltd Champfleurie House, Linlithgow EH49 6NB Tel. *01506 847999* Fax. *01506 847174* E-mail. *sales@rgk.co.uk* Web. *www.rgk.co.uk Amcor – De Longhi – Domena – Dyson – Honeywell – Insectocutor – Karcher – Mediclinics – Numatic – Prodifa – Supermat – Witness*

R G R Fabrications & Welding Services Ltd Unit 23 Pensnett Trading Estate Second Avenue, Pensnett Trading Estate, Kingswinford DY6 7PP Tel. *01384 401055* Fax. *01384 400068* E-mail. *david.yellowley@btconnect.com* Web. *www.rgrltd.com RGR Fabricating*

RhinoCo Technology 3B Vernon Drive, shrewsbury SY1 3TF Tel. *0845 6445421* Fax. *0845 6445431* E-mail. *sales@rhinoco.co.uk* Web. *www.rhinoco.co.uk Watchguard*

Rhinowash Ltd 149a Glasgow Road, Wishaw ML2 7QJ Tel. *08708 600600* Fax. *01698 356697* E-mail. *info@rhinowash.com* Web. *www.rhinowash.com C.X. & C.S. – Centreclean – Centrepoint – H.S. & H.X. – Washpoint*

Joseph Rhodes Ltd Bell Vue Elm Tree Street, Wakefield WF1 5EQ Tel. *01924 371161* Fax. *01924 370928* E-mail. *sales@grouprhodes.co.uk* Web. *www.josephrhodes.co.uk A.H. Presses – Bentley – Cuboid – D.S. 1 – D.S. 2 – Dualform – G.I. Presses – H.D.S. – H.M.E. – Hi-Mech CNC Mechanical Shears – Hydraversal Shears – K.J. Extrusion Press – Q.T.C. – Quartz – R.F. & R.M. Open Presses – R.H. Open Front Presses – R.H.D.S. Double Sided Press – Rhobot – Rhodes – Rhofeed – Rhomint – Rhosort – Stagger Feed Press*

Rhodia Ltd Oak House Reeds Crescent, Watford WD24 4QP Tel. *01923 485868* Fax. *01923 211580* E-mail. *info@rhodia.com* Web. *www.rhodia.com Aliso – Alusec – Cozirc – Kolate – Manalox – Manomet – Manosec – Manosperse – Zircomplex*

Ribble Valley Homes Ltd 21 Manor Road, Clitheroe BB7 2LH Tel. *01200 427966* E-mail. *a.hodgson1@gmail.com* Web. *hogroastlancashire.co.uk RIBBLE VALLEY HOG ROAST*

Richard Alan Engineering Company Ltd Richard Alan House Churwell Vale, Shaw Cross Business Park, Dewsbury WF12 7RD Tel. *01924 467040* Fax. *01924 454377* E-mail. *robertjohnson@richardalan.co.uk* Web. *www.richard-allen.co.uk Ramco CNC Ltd*

Richard Atkinson 10 Nicholson Drive, Newtownabbey BT36 4FD Tel. *028 90843323* Fax. *020 89084850* E-mail. *info@atkinsons-irishpoplin-ties.com* Web. *www.atkinsonsties.com Atkinsons All Silk – Atkinsons All Wool – Atkinsons Polyester – Atkinsons Royal Irish Poplin*

Richard Keenan UK Ltd 6th Street National Agricultural Centre, Stoneleigh Park, Kenilworth CV8 2RL Tel. *024 76698288* Fax. *024 76698273* E-mail. *info@keenansystem.com* Web. *www.keenansystem.com Keenan Klassik Bale Handler – Keenan Refurb*

Richard Newnham Project Management Services 4 Princes Esplanade, Cowes PO31 8LE Tel. *01983 290168* Fax. *01983 281882* E-mail. *ricnewnham@onwhite.net* Web. *www.richardnewnham.co.uk Richard Newnham Project Management Services*

Richards Hose Ltd Unit 7 Roman Way Centre Longridge Road, Preston PR2 5BB Tel. *01772 651550* Fax. *01772 651325* E-mail. *info@richardsfire.co.uk* Web. *www.richardsfire.co.uk Aquaflex – Aquaman – Brigadier – Commando – Reflex (Highviz) – Highlander – Marine – Ribblelite – Sentinel*

Richardson & Co. Ltd Smithfold Lane Worsley, Manchester M28 0GP Tel. *0161 7027002* Fax. *0161 7908263 Steely Products – Vari-flow*

Richardson Ford Ltd Westgate, Driffield YO25 6SY Tel. *01377 252166* Fax. *01377 252887* E-mail. *info@richardson-ford.co.uk* Web. *www.richardson-ford.co.uk Ford Main Dealer*

Richardsons R F P D Ltd 226 Berwick Avenue, Slough SL1 4QT Tel. *01753 733010* Fax. *01753 733012* E-mail. *mevans@richardsonrftd.com* Web. *www.richardsonrfpd.com Amperex – Cetron – Haltron – National Electronics – R.F. Gain*

Richardsons Stalham Ltd The Staithe Stalham, Norwich NR12 9BX Tel. *01692 581081* Fax. *01692 581522* E-mail. *info@richardsonsgroup.net* Web. *www.richardsonsboatingholidays.co.uk Benson Pleasurecraft – Broads Holidays – Diamond Cruisers – Ferryline Cruisers – Hearts Cruisers – Hemsby Holiday Centre – Horizon Craft – Horning Pleasurecraft – Maidline – Mundesley Holiday Centre – Richardsons Stalham – Stalham Pleasure Craft*

Richco International Co. Ltd Richco House Springhead Enterprise Park, Springhead Rd, Gravesend DA11 8HE Tel. *01474 327527* Fax. *01474 327455* E-mail. *sales@richco.co.uk* Web. *www.richco-int.com Cableeater – Hook & Loop – Wrap-it-Ties*

E M Richford Ltd Curzon Road, Sudbury CO10 2XW Tel. *01787 375241* Fax. *01787 310179* E-mail. *andrew@richstamp.co.uk* Web. *www.richstamp.co.uk E.M. Richford*

Richypucci Ltd 10 Rosemary Close, Peacehaven BN10 8BY Tel. *0845 1307438* E-mail. *info@richypucci.com* Web. *www.richypucci.com RICHYPUCCI*

Ricoh UK Ltd Ricoh House 15 Ullswater Crescent, Coulsdon CR5 2HR Tel. *020 87631010* Fax. *020 87631110* Web. *www.ricoh.co.uk Ikon Office Solutions Plc*

Ridge Tool UK - Division Of Emerson Ridge Tool PO Box 893, Crick, Northampton NN6 7TY Tel. *08082 389869* Fax. *0808 2389904* E-mail. *sales.uk@ridgid.com* Web. *www.ridgid.eu Ridgid – Ridgid Kollmann*

Rieter Automotive Great Britain Ltd Flushmill West Gate, Heckmondwike WF16 0EP Tel. *08706 066608* Fax. *01924 236340* E-mail. *roger.lacey@rieterauto.com* Web. *www.riter.com Automotive Floor Systems*

Riggs Autopack Ltd Southfield Street, Nelson BB9 0LD Tel. *01282 440040* Fax. *01282 440041* E-mail. *info@autopack.co.uk* Web. *www.autopack.co.uk Auger Filler 4000 Series – Automatic Liquid Filling Systems – Automatic Rotary Filling Machine 3000 Series – Autopack – Linear Weighing 3000 Series – Tri-Tech*

Right For Staff Draefern House Dunston Court, Dunston Road, Chesterfield S41 8NL Tel. *01246 267021* Fax. *01246 267001* E-mail. *info@right4staff.com* Web. *www.right4staff.com Draefern*

Righton Ltd Righton House Elliott Way, Nexus Point, Holford, Birmingham B6 7AP Tel. *0121 3561141* Fax. *0121 3323829* E-mail. *marketing@righton.co.uk* Web. *www.righton.co.uk D.S.M. Engineering Plastics – Filon – Foamalux (United Kingdom) – Marlon (United Kingdom) – PQ – Righton – Speedal – Ultragrain*

Righton Fasteners Ltd Unit H2 Elliott Way Nexus Point, Holford, Birmingham B6 7AP Tel. *0121 3568181* Fax. *0121 3444028* E-mail. *sales@rightonfasteners.com* Web. *www.righton.co.uk Righton Fasteners*

Rigibore Ltd Guildford Road Industrial Estate, Hayle TR27 4BA Tel. *01736 755355* Fax. *01736 756100* E-mail. *info@rigibore.com* Web. *www.rigibore.com Rigibore – Rigiflex*

Rigidal Systems Ltd Unit 62 Blackpole Trading Estate West, Worcester WR3 8ZJ Tel. *01905 750500* Fax. *01905 750555* E-mail. *sales@rigidal.co.uk* Web. *www.rigidal.co.uk RIGIDAL – Rigidal - Rigidal Thermowall - Rigidal Ziplok - Rigidal Lokroll - Rigidal Deadpan - Rigidal Thermohalter - Rigidal Corogrid. – Rigidal corogrid – Rigidal Deadpan – RIGIDAL LOKROLL – Rigidal MicroMatt – Rigidal Safewire – Rigidal Themohalter – RIGIDAL THERMOWALL – Rigidal ZIPLOK*

Ringflex Drive Systems Ltd 4 Bankside Business Park Coronation Street, Stockport SK5 7PG Tel. *0161 4740464* Fax. *0161 4290272* E-mail. *info@ringflex.co.uk* Web. *www.ringflex.co.uk Reich – Reich Couplings – Ringfeder – TAS Schafer*

Ringspann UK Ltd 3 Napier Road Elm Farm Industrial Estate, Bedford MK41 0QS Tel. *01234 342511* Fax. *01234 217322* E-mail. *info@ringspann.co.uk* Web. *www.ringspann.co.uk Berg (Germany) – Borg Warner (Germany) – Cecon (U.S.A.) – Compomac (Italy) – Conex (Italy) – Marland (U.S.A.) – Mytec (Germany) – Mytec - RCS - Borg Warner - Compomac - Conex - Tollok - Sikumat - Rimostat - Cecon - Marland – *Quadco (U.S.A.) – RCS – RCS Controls (Germany) – Rimostat – Ringspann – *Ringspann (Germany) – Siam (France) – Sikumat – Tollok (Italy)*

Ringway Specialist Services Ltd Winterstoke Road Springfield Road, V, Weston Super Mare BS24 9BQ Tel. *01934 421400* Fax. *01934 421401* E-mail. *info@ringway.co.uk* Web. *www.ringway.co.uk Ringway signs Ltd*

Rinku Group plc 622 Western Avenue, London W3 0TF Tel. *020 88969922* Fax. *020 88969977* E-mail. *mail@rinku.co.uk* Web. *www.rinku.co.uk Bader – Rinku – Tigi Wear – Viz-a-Viz*

Risbridger Ltd 25 Trowers Way, Redhill RH1 2LH Tel. *08456 442323* Fax. *08456 442453* E-mail. *annie@risbridger.com* Web. *www.risbridger.com Risbridger*

The Risc Group Ltd Church Walks, Llandudno LL30 2HL Tel. *08448 420100* Fax. *0870 0503201* E-mail. *information@risc-group.com* Web. *www.clunkclick.net clunk click total backup solutions*

Rita Fancy Goods Ltd 4-6 Gravel Lane, London E1 7AW Tel. *020 72474616* Fax. *020 73776040* E-mail. *ritaltd@btinternet.com* Web. *www.ritadirect.com *Sutus Far East (Hong Kong)*

Ritrama UK Ltd Lynwell Road Lyntown Trading Estate, Eccles, Manchester M30 9QG Tel. *0161 7861700* Fax. *0161 7861701* E-mail. *mark.evans@ritrama.co.uk* Web. *www.ritrama.co.uk Floor Talkers – Floor Talkers - Polytex - RI-Barrier - RI-Mark - RI-Triplex - RI-Cote - RI-Print - RI-Flex. – Polytex – RI-Barrier – RI-Cote – RI-Flex – RI-Mark – RI-Print – RI-Triplex*

The Ritz Hotel 150 Piccadilly, London W1J 9BR Tel. *020 74938181* Fax. *020 74932687* E-mail. *alove@theritzlondon.com* Web. *www.theritzlondon.com Ritz*

R I W Ltd Arc House Terrace Road South, Binfield, Bracknell RG42 4PZ Tel. *01344 397788* Fax. *01344 862010* E-mail. *enquiries@riw.co.uk* Web. *www.riw.co.uk C.T.W. Cement – C.T.W. Screed – Deck Screed – Flexiseal – Furacin – L.A.C. – Orglas – Prodor bond '50' – Prodorbond – Prodorcrete G.T. – Prodorfilm Easy Clean – Prodorflor – Prodorglaze – Prodorguard – Prodorite – Prodorshield – Toughseal*

R J H Finishing Systems Ltd Artillery Street, Heckmondwike WF16 0NR Tel. *01924 402490* Fax. *01924 404635* E-mail. *sales@rjhfinishing.co.uk* Web. *www.rjhfinishing.co.uk Antelope (United Kingdom) – Autofin (United Kingdom) – Bear (United Kingdom) – Biax (Germany) – Bison (United Kingdom) – Boa (United Kingdom) – Buffalo (United Kingdom) – Bull (United Kingdom) – Chamois (United Kingdom) – Cobra (United Kingdom) – Cougar (United Kingdom) – Cub (United Kingdom) – Deer (United Kingdom) – Elk (United Kingdom) – Ferrett (United Kingdom) – Grit (Denmark) – Gryphon (United Kingdom) – Leopard (United Kingdom) – Lion (United Kingdom) – Moose (United Kingdom) – Morrisflex (United Kingdom) – Powerfin (United Kingdom) – Squirrel (United Kingdom) – Stag (United*

Kingdom) – Tiger (United Kingdom) – Unicorn (United Kingdom)

R J Stokes Company Ltd Little London Road, Sheffield S8 0UH Tel. *0114 2589595* Fax. *0114 2509836* E-mail. *sales@rjstokes.co.uk* Web. *www.rjstokes.co.uk Stokes Interiors*

R K International Machine Tools Ltd 7 Europa Trading Estate Fraser Road, Erith DA8 1PW Tel. *01322 447611* Fax. *01322 447618* E-mail. *sales@rk-int.com* Web. *www.rk-int.com Cantaluppi (Italy) – Colchester – Danobat – Europa – Geka – Guyson – Hardinge Bridgeport – Harrison – Hmv – Kingsland – Kitchen and Walker – Meddings – Mega – Morgan – Newall – Prosaw – Rjh tool and equipment – Robbi (Italy) – Startrite – Waltons – Comev – SAHOS – MELCHIORRE – EUROPA – LISTA – SABRE EUROPA JAINNHER – BIGLIA – PERFECT – HARDWEB BRIDGEWEB*

R K Printcoat Abington Road Litlington, Royston SG8 0QZ Tel. *01763 852187* Fax. *01763 852502* E-mail. *sales@rkprint.com* Web. *www.rkprint.com K Bar – K Bar - Meteringbar, Rotary Koater - Pilot Coating Machine. – Meteringbar – Pilot Coating Machine – Rotary Koater*

R & L Enterprises Ltd Swinnow View, Leeds LS13 4NA Tel. *0113 2574208* Fax. *0113 2560876* E-mail. *admin@rexaloy.co.uk* Web. *www.rexaloy.co.uk Rexaloy*

R L M International Ltd Unit 1 Cargo Terminal 4, Beverley Road East Midlands Airport, Castle Donington, Derby DE74 2SA Tel. *01332 853040* Fax. *01332 850404* E-mail. *d.orme@mies.co.uk* Web. *www.rlm-ema.co.uk R. Mould*

R L Polk UK Ltd 26-30 Upper Marlborough Road, St Albans AL1 3UU Tel. *01727 845558* Fax. *01727 734700* E-mail. *info@polk.co.uk* Web. *www.polk.com Mitac Consultancy & Training – Motorplan*

RMD Kwikform Limited Brickyard Rd Aldridge, Walsall WS9 8BW Tel. *01922 743743* Fax. *01922 743400* E-mail. *info@rmdkwikform.com* Web. *www.rmdkwikform.com Airodek – Albeam – Alform – Alsec – Alshor Plus – Autoclimb – GTX – Kwikstage – Maxima – Megashor – MINIMA – R700/H33 – Rapid Bar Tie 15/20mm – Rapidclimb – Rapidshor – Super Slim Soldier/Slimshor – Ascent – Tru-Lift*

R & M Electrical Group Ltd Unit 1 Central Trading Estate Marine Parade, Southampton SO14 5JP Tel. *023 80231800* Fax. *01425 471012* E-mail. *sales@rm-electrical.com* Web. *www.rm-electrical.com Bosch Power Tools – Channel Safety Systems – Klik Lighting – Unistrut Cable Management – Unistrut Channel*

R M J M Ltd 10 Bells Brae, Edinburgh EH4 3BJ Tel. *0131 2252532* Fax. *0131 2265117* E-mail. *edinburgh@rmjm.com* Web. *www.rmjm.com R.M.J.M.*

R M Sealers Ltd Valley Farm Hemel Hempstead Road, Dagnall, Berkhamsted HP4 1QR Tel. *01442 843387* Fax. *01442 843387* E-mail. *rmtool@hotmail.com* Web. *www.rmtool.co.uk BD Range – DoBoy – R M Sealers*

R M S International Ltd 66 Pendlebury Road Swinton, Manchester M27 4GY Tel. *0161 7278182* Fax. *0161 7278191* E-mail. *enquiries@rmsint.com* Web. *www.rmsint.com Grafix – Jade*

Rnid 19-23 Featherstone Street, London EC1Y 8SL Tel. *08088 080123* Fax. *020 72968199* E-mail. *informationline@rnid.org.uk* Web. *www.rnid.org.uk One In Seven*

Roadlink International Ltd Strawberry Lane, Willenhall WV13 3RL Tel. *01902 606210* Fax. *01902 631515* E-mail. *sales@roadlink-international.co.uk* Web. *www.roadlink-international.co.uk Beral – BPW – Brembo – Bryden – ContiTech – Corteco – Hendrickson – Knecht – Koni – Meritor – Perrot – Roadlink – Saf – Stemco – Timken – Zen*

Roband Electronics plc Charlwood Works Lowfield Heath Road, Charlwood, Horley RH6 0BU Tel. *01293 843000* Fax. *01293 843001* E-mail. *postroom@roband.co.uk* Web. *www.roband.co.uk Ro-Mil*

Robant Services Ltd Unit 24 Mersey Street, Stockport SK1 2HX Tel. *0161 4298728* Fax. *0161 4747630* E-mail. *sales@robant.co.uk* Web. *www.robant.co.uk Robant*

C Roberson & Co. Ltd 1a Hercules Street, London N7 6AT Tel. *020 72720567* Fax. *020 72630212* E-mail. *info@robco.co.uk* Web. *www.robco.co.uk Roberson*

Robert Gordon Europe Ltd Kings Hill Business Park Darlaston Road, Wednesbury WS10 7SH Tel. *0121 5067700* Fax. *0121 5067701* E-mail. *uksales@rg-inc.com* Web. *www.rg-inc.com Combat – DualAir*

Robert Half Ltd Oceana House 39-49 Commercial Road, Southampton SO15 1GA Tel. *023 80718900* Fax. *01202 786550* E-mail. *sales@accounttemps.net* Web. *www.roberthalf.co.uk Progress Accountancy*

Roberts & Burling Roofing Supplies Ltd 120 Beddington Lane, Croydon CR0 4YZ Tel. *020 86890481* Fax. *020 86893063* E-mail. *bmcroydon@robertsandburling.co.uk Robert Burling*

Roberts Of Churchgate 47 Church Gate, Leicester LE1 3AL Tel. *0116 2629061* Fax. *0116 2629062* E-mail. *robertsofchurchgates@fsmail.net Roberts of Churchgate*

Derek Roberts Antiques 25 Shipbourne Road, Tonbridge TN10 3DN Tel. *01732 358986* Fax. *01732 771842* E-mail. *drclocks@clara.net* Web. *www.qualityantiqueclocks.com Derek Roberts Antiques*

J E Roberts & Son 47 Moat Road, Oldbury B68 8EB Tel. *0121 5523189* E-mail. *house.doctor@btinternet.com* Web. *www.aatishoo.co.uk A-A-Tishoo*

Patricia Roberts Knitting Ltd 60 Kinnerton Street, London SW1X 8ES Tel. *020 72354742* Fax. *020 72356517* E-mail. *shop@patriciaroberts.co.uk Patricia Roberts*

Roberts Radio Ltd PO Box 130, Mexborough S64 8AJ Tel. *01709 571722* Fax. *01709 571255* E-mail. *information@robertsradio.co.uk* Web. *www.robertsradio.co.uk Roberts Radio*

Robinson Brothers Ltd Phoenix Street, West Bromwich B70 0AH Tel. *0121 5532451* Fax. *0121 5005183* E-mail. *enquiries@robinsonbrothers.co.uk* Web. *www.rbltd.co.uk Robac*

Robinson Engineering Ltd Durham Way North Aycliffe Business Park, Newton Aycliffe DL5 6HP Tel. *01325 304070* Fax. *01325 304088* E-mail. *info@robinson-engineering.com* Web. *www.robinson-engineering.com Robinson Iron Work*

G S Robinson & Co. Ltd Unit 30 West Chirton South Trading Estate, North Shields NE29 7TY Tel. *0191 2575374* Fax. *0191 2961341* E-mail. *david@gsrobinson.co.uk* Web. *www.gsrobinson.co.uk G.S. Robinson*

Robinson Healthcare Ltd Lawn Road Carlton In Lindrick, Carlton-in-Lindrick, Worksop S81 9LB Tel. *01909 735000* Fax. *01246 559929* E-mail. *leigh.thomasson@robinsonhealthcare.com* Web. *www.robinsonhealthcare.com Activ – Animalintex – Big John Drum – Blue Eyetec – Cestra – Cohfast – Cool-X – Cottontails – Easy Breather – Easy Breathers – Equiwrap – Fast-Aid – Feverscan – Flexi-Stretch – Flexocrepe – Flexopads – Flexoplast – Flexus – Fresh-ups – Gamgee Tissue – Inco – Inco Care – Inco Readiwipes – Namelet – Ouchless – Printapot – Readi Bed Pads/Seat Pads – Readibibs – Readibriefs – Readistretch – Readiwash – Readiwipes – *Relief-Xtra (Japan) – Robinson Activate – Robinson Superflex – Rompa – Safegrip – Safehip – Sentinel Major – Sentinel Minor – Sitting Pretty – *Skintact (Japan) – Snoezelen – Soft & Pure – Stayform – Ugly Bug – Ultra Four – Wipedown – Wipedowns*

Robinson & Neal Ltd 129 Sefton Street Toxteth, Liverpool L8 5SN Tel. *0151 7099481* Fax. *0151 7071377* Web. *www.robinson-neal.com Dale*

Robinsons Soft Drinks Ltd Carrow Works Bracondale, Norwich NR1 2DD Tel. *01603 632633* Fax. *01603 724106* Web. *www.britvic.co.uk Robinsons*

Robinson Willey Trinity Park Orrell Lane, Bootle L20 6PB Tel. *0151 5301900* Fax. *0151 2286661* E-mail. *colinpemberton@robinson-willey.com* Web. *www.robinson-willey.co.uk Athena LF – Athena RS – Bantam Compack 2 – Belvedere Electric – Belvedere LF – Belvedere RS – Black Knight 2 Gas – Black Knight Classic Collection – Black Knight Electric – Commodore – Firecharm LF – Firecharm RS – Firegem Visa 2 – Firegem Visa Deluxe Highline – Firegem Visa Highline – Firegem Visa Super Deluxe – Firegem Visa Super Deluxe Highline – Nomad – Optik 1 – Optik 2 – Quartz Auto – Quartz Manual – Rainproof Heater – Riveria RS – Riviera Electric – Riviera LF – Sahara Deluxe – Sahara LF – Sahara RS – Sahara Safeguard – Salisbury 2 LF – Salisbury 2 RS – Salisbury Turbo – Sanburst – Warmplan XX Auto – Warmplan XX Manual*

Robinson Young Ltd Equis House 4 Eastern Way, Bury St Edmunds IP32 7AB Tel. *01284 766261* Fax. *01284 701105* E-mail. *info@ry.tm* Web. *www.robinsonyoung.co.uk Big Value – Party Time – Quality Catorpack – Sincerely Yours – Valupax*

Robnor Resins Ltd Hunts Rise South Marston, Swindon SN3 4TE Tel. *01793 823741* Fax. *01793 827033* E-mail. *drew@robnor.co.uk* Web. *www.robnor.co.uk Emdithene – Jidenco*

Robojet Ltd 49 Gosbrook Road Caversham, Reading RG4 8BT Tel. *0118 9479900* Fax. *0118 9461110* E-mail. *sales@robojet.co.uk* Web. *www.robojet.co.uk robojet*

Robot Coupe UK Ltd 2 Fleming Way, Isleworth TW7 6EU Tel. *020 82321800* Fax. *020 85684966* E-mail. *sales@robotcoupe.co.uk* Web. *www.robotcoupe.co.uk *Chute (U.S.A.) – *Musso (Italy) – *Robot Coupe (France) – *Tellier (France) – *Waring (U.S.A.)*

Kenneth Robson Equipment Ltd 5 Tewkesbury Place Great Barton, Bury St Edmunds IP31 2TP Tel. *01284 787330* Fax. *01284 788002 *Ford – *Hitachi – *Hy Mac – *Komatsu – *Poclain*

N A Robson Ltd 4a Robson Way Industrial Estate Robson Way, Blackpool FY3 7PP Tel. *01253 393406* Fax. *01253 300160* E-mail. *i.robson@robson.uk.com* Web. *www.robson.uk.com Ecostrip*

Roche Diagnostics Ltd Charles Avenue, Burgess Hill RH15 9RY Tel. *01444 256000* Fax. *01993 892241* E-mail. *burgesshill@roche.com* Web. *www.roche.com Amplitaq – Cardiotrol – Cobas – Isomune*

Rock Chemicals Ltd (t/a Rock Oil) 90 Priestley Street, Warrington WA5 1ST Tel. *01925 636191* Fax. *01925 632499* E-mail. *sales@rockoil.co.uk* Web. *www.rockoil.co.uk Viscol*

Rock Fall UK Ltd Major House Wimsey Way Alfreton Trading Estate, Somercotes, Alfreton DE55 4LS Tel. *01773 608616* Fax. *01773 608614* E-mail. *stephen@rockfall.co.uk* Web. *www.rockfall.co.uk Pro-Man – Rock Fall – Tomcat*

Rock-It Cargo Ltd Thorpe Industrial Estate Delta Way, Egham TW20 8RX Tel. *01784 431301* Fax. *01784 471052* E-mail. *chrisw@rock-it.co.uk* Web. *www.rock-itcargo.co.uk Rock-It Cargo*

Rockwell Sheet Sales Ltd Rockwell House Birmingham Road, Millisons Wood, Coventry CV5 9AZ Tel. *01676 522224* Fax. *01676 523630* E-mail. *ann@rockwellsheet.com* Web. *www.rockwellsheet.com Polydekk – Polyu' – Rockwell – Rockwell Twin-Pro*

Rockwood Pigments Birtley, Chester Le Street DH3 1QX Tel. *0191 4102361* Fax. *0191 4106005* E-mail. *info@elementis.com* Web. *www.rockwoodpigments.com Activox C50.C80 – Activox R50/R90 – Celerate – Durham – Durham CA*

Rockwool Rockpanel B V Wern Tarw Rhiwceiliog Pencoed, Bridgend CF35 6NY Tel. *01656 863210* Fax. *01656 863611* E-mail. *info@rockwool.co.uk* Web. *www.rockpanel.co.uk Access Floor Fire Stops – Acoustic Partition Slab – Acoustic Party Wall DPC – Acoustic Partywall DPC – BeamClad Systems – Bevelled Lags – Blown Loft Insulation – C.-Liner and C.-Board – Cavity – Cladding Roll – ColumnClad Systems – Ductwrap and Ductslab – DuoRock Roofing Boards – EnergySaver Blown Cavity Wall Insulation – Fire Barrier Systems – Fire Duct Systems – Fire Tube – Flexible, Semi-Rigid and Flexible Slabs – H. & V. and Process Pipe Sections – H1100 Systems – Hardrock Dual Density Range – High Impact Liner Board – High Performance Partial Fill Cavity Slab – Lamella Mat – Linear and Trapezodal Firestop Systems – Marine Hydrocarbon Firewall Slab – Partial Fill Cavity Slabs – Pipe Section Mat – Pipe Sections – Rainscreen Duo-Slab – Rockclose – Rockfloor – Rocklap – Rockliner – RockShield – Rollbatts – Soffit Lining Solutions – SP Firestop Systems – T.C.B. Cavity Barrier – Wired Mat*

Rococo Style Ltd 80-81 Walsworth Road, Hitchin SG4 9SX Tel. *01462 435393* Fax. *01462 452773* E-mail. *des.rococo@virgin.net* Web. *rococostyleschoolwear.co.uk Rococo – Trax Active – Wild Trax – Zika*

Rocom Unit 6 First Floor Temple Point Finch Drive, Leeds LS15 9JQ Tel. *01937 847777* Fax. *01937 847788* E-mail. *enquiries@rocom.co.uk* Web. *www.rocom.co.uk Teleconcept*

Rocon Foam Products Ltd Unit 14 Shrub Hill Industrial Estate, Worcester WR4 9EL Tel. *01905 26616* Fax. *01905 612319* E-mail. *sales@roconfoam.co.uk* Web. *www.roconfoam.co.uk Rocon Foam Products Ltd*

Rodol Ltd Richmond Row, Liverpool L3 3BP Tel. *0151 2073161* Fax. *0151 2073727* E-mail. *accounts@rodol.co.uk* Web. *www.rodol.co.uk Rodatherm – Rodol – Rodpak*

Rodwell H T B Ltd Bentalls, Basildon SS14 3SD Tel. *01268 286646* Fax. *01268 287799* E-mail. *sales@rodwell-autoclave.com* Web. *www.rodwell-htb.com Robay*

Roe Ltd (Gang-Nail Systems Ltd) Enterprise Road Westwood Industrial Estate, Margate CT9 4JA Tel. *01843 232888* Fax. *01843 232233* E-mail. *info@roeltd.co.uk* Web. *www.roeltd.co.uk Ecojoist*

Roechling Engineering Plastics Ltd Waterwells Drive Waterwells Business Park, Quedgeley, Gloucester GL2 2AA Tel. *01452 727900* Fax. *01452 728056* E-mail. *m.knowles@roechling.co.uk* Web. *www.roechling.co.uk Durostone (Germany) – Lignostone (Germany) – Polystone (Germany)*

Roemheld UK Ltd Rubery House The Avenue Rednal, Birmingham B45 9AL Tel. *0121 4531414* Fax. *0121 4601798* E-mail. *sales@roemheld.co.uk* Web. *www.roemheld.co.uk Bock Workholding (U.S.A.) – *Hilma Romheld (Germany) – *Kostyrka (Germany) – Roemheld (Germany) – Romheld - Hydraulic work holding equipmentF.T.W. - Rotary indexing tablesStark - Zero point mounting systems – Ruckle – Stark – *W.P.R. (Germany)*

Rogers Chapman plc Grantley House 9 Park Lane, Hounslow TW5 9RW Tel. *020 87594141* Fax. *020 87595367* E-mail. *enquiries@rogerschapman.co.uk* Web. *www.rogerschapman.co.uk Rogers Chapman*

Rohan Designs Ltd 30 Maryland Road Tongwell, Milton Keynes MK15 8HN Tel. *01908 517900* Fax. *01908 211209* E-mail. *post@rohan.co.uk* Web. *www.rohan.co.uk Rohan Design*

Rohmann UK Ltd Unit 6 Glenmore Centre Vincients Road, Bumpers Farm, Chippenham SN14 6BB Tel. *01249 659346* Fax. *01249 443097* E-mail. *info@rohmann.co.uk* Web. *www.rohmann.co.uk *Elotest – *Elotip – *Rototest*

Rohm Great Britain Ltd 12 Ashway Centre Elm Crescent, Kingston Upon Thames KT2 6HH Tel. *020 85496647* Fax. *020 85411783* E-mail. *rohm@rohmgb.co.uk* Web. *www.rohm.co.uk Röhm*

Roland Plastics Ltd High Street Wickham Market, Woodbridge IP13 0RF Tel. *01728 747777* Fax. *01728 748222* E-mail. *maggie@rolandplastics.com*

Web. *www.rolandplastics.com Portapath – Portapath - Technotile – Technotile*

Rolawn Ltd at Rolawn Head Office Elvington, York YO41 4XR Tel. *08456 046075* Fax. *01904 608272* E-mail. *info@rolawn.co.uk* Web. *www.rolawn.co.uk Rolawn*

Rolfe Industries 28 Market Field, Steyning BN44 3SU Tel. *08452 303601* Fax. *08452 303605* E-mail. *brolfe@vac.uk.com* Web. *www.vacuumschmelze.com *Beryvac (Germany) – *Clickflex (Germany) – *Crovac (Germany) – *Cryoperm (Germany) – *DAU (Austria) – DAV – *Duratherm (Germany) – *HaKRon (Germany) – *HKR (Germany) – *Isovac (Germany) – *Magnetoflex (Germany) – *Megaperm (Germany) – *Permenorm (Germany) – *STS (Germany) – *Thermalast (Germany) – *Thermoflux (Germany) – *Ultraperm (Germany) – *VAC (Germany) – VAC - Vacuumschmelze - Vacomax - Vacodym - Vitrovac - Ultraperm - Vitroperm - DAU - HKR - Hakron-STS – *Vacodil (Germany) – *Vacodur (Germany) – *Vacodym (Germany) – *Vacoflex (Germany) – *Vacoflux (Germany) – *Vacomax (Germany) – *Vacon – *Vacoperm (Germany) – *Vacuumschmelze (Germany) – Vitropac – *Vitroperm (Germany)*

Rollalong Ltd 309 Old Barn Farm Road Three Legged Cross, Wimborne BH21 6SF Tel. *01202 824541* Fax. *01202 826525* E-mail. *enquiries@rollalong.co.uk* Web. *www.rollalong.co.uk Executive – Instacom – Low Maintenance PB4 – Preplan – Rollajack – Rollaskid – Rollawheel*

Rollem Ltd 3A wentworth Industrial Estate Wentworth WayTankersley, Barnsley ST5 3DH Tel. *01226 745476* Fax. *0114 2465487* E-mail. *info@rollem.com* Web. *www.rollem.co.uk Rollem*

Rollercoaster Records Ltd Rock House St Marys Chalford, Stroud GL6 8PU Tel. *01453 886252* Fax. *01453 885361* E-mail. *john@rollercoasterrecords.com* Web. *www.rollercoasterrecords.com *Bear Family (Germany) – Rollercoaster – Swan – *Zuzazz (Germany)*

Rollform Sections Ltd PO Box 92, Smethwick B66 2PA Tel. *0121 5551310* Fax. *0121 5551311* E-mail. *belinda.fleming@hadleygroup.co.uk* Web. *www.hadleygroup.co.uk Ziptubes*

Rolls-Royce plc 65 Buckingham Gate, London SW1E 6AT Tel. *020 72229020* Fax. *020 72279170* E-mail. *info@nelincs.gov.uk* Web. *www.rolls-royce.com Adour – Allen – Avon – Bergen – Conway – Crossley – Dart – Gem – Gnome – MT 30 – Nimbus – Olympus – Pegasus – Proteous – R.B.211 – Spey – Syncrolift – Tay – Trent – Tyne – Viper – WR-21*

Rolls Royce (Commercial Marine UK) The Nucleus Brunel Way, Dartford DA1 5GA Tel. *01322 312028* Fax. *01322 312054* E-mail. *alan.reid@rolls-royce.com* Web. *www.rollsroyce.com Bergen – Brattvaag – Frydenbo – Kamewa – Rauma – Tenfjord*

Rolls Royce Marine Electrical Systems Ltd Northarbour Road, Portsmouth PO6 3TL Tel. *023 92310000* Fax. *023 92310001* Web. *www.rolls-royce.com Digicon – Dynalec – Hystep*

Rol Trac Automatic Doors Ltd Unit 1 Brookfield Works Quebec Street, Elland HX5 9AP Tel. *08450 042502* Fax. *01422 379076* E-mail. *info@roltrac.com* Web. *www.roltrac.com Rol-Trac*

Romaco Holdings UK Ltd Lake View Court Ermine Business Park, Huntingdon PE29 6WD Tel. *01480 435050* Fax. *01478 0414220* E-mail. *thomas.luken@romaco.com* Web. *www.romaco.com *Argus (Germany) – *Bosspak (Australia) – *Garvens (Germany) – *HAPA (Switzerland) – *Index (U.S.A.) – *Koruma (Germany) – *Lumat (Germany) – *Macofar (Italy) – *Noack (Germany) – *Polyphem (Germany) – *Polyphem III (Germany) – *Promatic (Italy) – *Unipac (Italy) – *Zanchetta (Italy)*

Roma Medical Aids Ltd York Road Bridgend Industrial Estate, Bridgend CF31 3TB Tel. *01656 674488* Fax. *01656 674499* E-mail. *sales@romamedical.co.uk* Web. *www.romamedical.co.uk Roma Medical Aids Ltd (United Kingdom)*

Romax Technology Ltd Rutherford House Nottingham Science & Technology, Nottingham NG7 2PZ Tel. *0115 9518800* Fax. *0115 9518801* E-mail. *sales@romaxtech.com* Web. *www.romaxtech.com RomaxDesigner*

Romco Equipment Ltd Meadow Works Great North Road, Barnet EN5 1AU Tel. *020 84499515* Fax. *020 84496021 Romco*

Ronhill Sports Unit 4 Dawson Street Redfern Industrial Estate, Hyde SK14 1RD Tel. *0161 3665020* Fax. *0161 3669732* E-mail. *info@ronhill.com* Web. *www.ronhill.com Brite-Lite – Lycra – Pertex Windsuits – Ronhill – Tempo – Trackster*

Ronis-Dom Ltd Unit 1 Junction Two Industrial Estate Demuth Way, Oldbury B69 4LT Tel. *0800 9884348* Fax. *0800 9884349* E-mail. *sales@ronis-dom.co.uk* Web. *www.ronis-dom.co.uk Dom-Nemef-Corbin*

Ronseal Ltd Thorncliffe Park Chapeltown, Sheffield S35 2YP Tel. *0114 2467171* Fax. *0114 2455629* E-mail. *enquiries@ronseal.co.uk* Web. *www.ronseal.co.uk Colron – Isoflex – Ronseal – Thompson Damp Seal – Thompsons Drive Seal – Thompsons Patio Seal – Thompsons Roof Seal – Thompsons Water Seal*

Ronson Incorporated Ltd Station Works Station Road Long Buckby, Northampton NN6 7PF Tel. *01327 841500* Fax. *01327 841501* Web. *www.ronson.com Ronson – Yves Saint Laurent*

Roodsafe Ltd Unit 21 Parklane B C, Old Basford, Nottingham NG6 0DU Tel. *0115 9274111* Fax. *0115 9274117* E-mail. *info@roodsafe.com* Web. *www.roodsafe.com Ariana – Kalsafe – Protecta*

Roof Units Ltd (t/a Vent-Axia Incorp Roof Units) Blackbrook Road Narrowboat Way, Dudley DY2 0NB Tel. *01384 418800* Fax. *01384 418831* E-mail. *ru@roofunitsltd.co.uk* Web. *www.vent-axia.com *Euroflow (Sweden) – Euroflow - duct fan - Eurofoil - plate and duct axial fan - Europak - roof extract unit - Europitch - adjustable pitch cased axial fan - Euroseries - plate and duct axial fan - Gemini - twin ventilation - Powerline - duct fan - Slimpack - duct fan - Viking - air handling units – *Eurofoil (Germany) – Europak – Europitch – *Euroseries (Germany) – Gemini – Powerline – Quartz – Slimpack – Viking*

Rooksmere Studios Sywell Road Overstone, Northampton NN6 0AG Tel. *01604 495310* Fax. *01604 643382* E-mail. *info@rooksmerestudios.com* Web. *www.rooksmerestudios.com Rooksmere Recording Studios*

Roquette UK Ltd Sallow Road Weldon North Industrial Estate, Corby NN17 5JX Tel. *01536 273000* Fax. *01536 263873* E-mail. *chris.scarrott@roquette.com* Web. *www.roquette.com Abracadabra – Abracarb – Abrafloc – Abrapro – Abraret – Abrasoft – Abrasorb – Abrastarch – Corracide – Corrakote*

Rose Hill Polymers Ltd Watson Mill Lane, Sowerby Bridge HX6 3BW Tel. *01422 839456* Fax. *01422 316952* E-mail. *sales@rosehillpolymers.com* Web. *www.rosehillpolymers.com Artificial Grass*

Rose & Krieger (a Phoenix Mecano Company) 26 Faraday Road Rabans Lane Industrial Area, Aylesbury HP19 8RY Tel. *01296 611660* Fax. *01296 399339* E-mail. *paul.burnham@phoenix-mecano.com* Web. *www.rk-online.com Blocan – Easy-Link*

J & H Rosenheim & Co. Ltd Lancaster Fields, Crewe CW1 6FF Tel. *01270 585959* Fax. *01270 586611* E-mail. *enquiries@rosenheim.co.uk* Web. *www.rosenheim.co.uk Rosetto*

J Rosenthal & Son Ltd 158 Bury Road Radcliffe, Manchester M26 2JR Tel. *0161 7230404* Fax. *0161 7245358* E-mail. *info@jrosenthal.co.uk* Web. *www.jrosenthal.co.uk Dreams 'N' Drapes – Rosenthal (J. Rosenthal & Son Ltd)*

Roset UK Ltd Overcroft House Badminton Court Church Street, Amersham HP7 0DD Tel. *01494 545910* Fax. *01494 545911* E-mail. *info@ligne-roset.co.uk* Web. *www.ligne-roset.com *Ligne Rose*

Roskel Contracts Ltd Old Bank House 50 St Johns Close, Knowle, Solihull B93 0NN Tel. *01564 732292* Fax. *01564 732296* E-mail. *ian.horton@roskel.co.uk* Web. *www.roskel.co.uk Roskel Contracts Ltd*

Ross Care Community Equipment Centre 2-3 Westfield Road, Wallasey CH44 7HX Tel. *0151 6539988* Fax. *0151 6538543 Ross Care Centres*

Rossendale Group Of Lifting Gear Co. Ltd Portside North, Ellesmere Port CH65 2HQ Tel. *0151 3555091* Fax. *01706 830490* E-mail. *sales@rossendalegroup.co.uk* Web. *www.rossendalegroup.co.uk Safelift*

Ross Farm Machinery Ltd 8-9 Alton Road, Ross On Wye HR9 5NB Tel. *01989 768811* Fax. *01989 768465* E-mail. *postroom@rossfarm.co.uk* Web. *www.rossfarm.co.uk Massey Ferguson*

Rossi Clothing 2 Victoria Park Way Netherfield, Nottingham NG4 2PA Tel. *0115 9870319* Fax. *0115 9873572* E-mail. *margaret@rossi-clothing.co.uk* Web. *www.rossi-clothing.co.uk Rossi*

Thomas Ross Ltd St Marks Road Binfield, Bracknell RG42 4TR Tel. *01344 862686* Fax. *01344 862575* E-mail. *sales@thomasross.co.uk* Web. *www.thomasross.co.uk Thomas Ross*

Rotadex Systems Ltd Systems House Central Business Park, Birmingham B33 0JL Tel. *0121 7837411* Fax. *0121 7831876* E-mail. *sales@rotadex.co.uk* Web. *www.rotadex.co.uk Binelace – Cardmaster – Chipguard – Com.Bine.Lace – Cresta Files – Datafind – Desk Files – Firecrest – Harwell – Hotspur – Mini Card – Rotadex – Rotadisc – Rotanote – S.A.21 – Standafile – Visicard – Visipanel – Westra*

Rotafix Ltd Rotafix House Hennoyadd Road, Abercrave, Swansea SA9 1UR Tel. *01639 730481* Fax. *01639 730858* E-mail. *dave.smedley@rotafix.co.uk* Web. *www.rotafixltd.co.uk Aquachem – Rendacrete – Resi Wood – Rotafix – Timberset – Vinachem*

Rotaflow F V Ltd Rotec House Bingswood Trading Estate, Whaley Bridge, High Peak SK23 7LY Tel. *01663 735003* Fax. *01663 735006* E-mail. *sales@rotaflow.com* Web. *www.rotaflow.com ROTAFLOW (United Kingdom)*

Rotalac Plastics Ltd Southmoor Road Roundhorn Industrial Estate, Roundthorn Industrial Estate, Manchester M23 9DS Tel. *0161 9469460* Fax. *0161 9469461* E-mail. *enq@rotalac.com* Web. *www.rotalac.com Rotashutter*

Rota Precision Ltd 94a High Street Portishead, Bristol BS20 6AJ Tel. *01275 818918* Fax. *01275 818828* E-mail. *sales@rotaprecision.com* Web. *www.rotaprecision.com Aurora – Rodobal – Rodobal, rodoflex, Rodogrip, Aurora. – Rodoflex – Rodogrip*

Rotary Engineering UK Ltd Old Lane Halfway, Sheffield S20 3GZ Tel. *0114 2513134* Fax. *0114 2586066* E-mail. *sales@rotary.co.uk* Web. *www.rotary.co.uk Bull (Smithfield)*

Rotary Power Ltd 11 Glass House Street St Peters, Newcastle Upon Tyne NE6 1BS Tel. *0191 2764444* Fax. *0191 2764462* E-mail. *info@rotarypower.com* Web. *www.rotarypower.com R.H.L. (United Kingdom)*

Rotatools UK Ltd 2a Atherton Road, Liverpool L9 7EL Tel. *0151 5258611* Fax. *0151 5254868* E-mail. *richard_dearn@hotmail.com Chippa – Expanda – Flexpanda – Rotatool – Supasafe*

Rotatrim 8 Caxton Park Caxton Road, Elm Farm Industrial Estate, Bedford MK41 0TY Tel. *01234 224545* Fax. *01234 224540* E-mail. *uksales@rotatrim.co.uk* Web. *www.rotatrim.co.uk Rota Trim – Rota Trim - rotary action cutters for boards, card, paper and film up to 20mm thickness. – Rotatrim*

Rotomarine Boat Equipment Haslar Marina Haslar Road, Gosport PO12 1NU Tel. *023 92583633* Fax. *023 92583634* E-mail. *info@rotostay.co.uk* Web. *www.rotostay.co.uk Rotostay*

Rotor Clip Ltd Meadowbrook Park Halfway, Sheffield S20 3PJ Tel. *0114 2473399* Fax. *0114 2474499* E-mail. *geoff.haigh@rotorclip.com* Web. *www.rotorclip.com Rotor Clip*

Rotork plc Brassmill Lane, Bath BA1 3JQ Tel. *01225 733200* Fax. *01225 333467* E-mail. *information@rotork.com* Web. *www.rotork.com A Range Actuator – AWT Range Actuator – CVA Range Actuator – GH Range Actuator – GP Range Actuator – H Range Actuator – IQ Range Actuator – IQT Range Actuator – NA Range Actuator – CP Range Actuator – Pakscan – Q Range Actuator – S Range Actuator – Skilmatic Range Actuator*

Rotrex Winches Griffon Works Wimsey Way, Somercotes, Alfreton DE55 4LS Tel. *01773 603997* Fax. *01773 540566* E-mail. *sales@rotrexwinches.co.uk* Web. *www.rotrexwinches.co.uk Nim Winches*

Rotronic Distribution Services Unit 1a Crompton Fields Crompton Way, Crawley RH10 9EE Tel. *01293 565556* Fax. *01293 843710* E-mail. *sales@rotronic.co.uk* Web. *www.rotronic.co.uk Roline*

Rough Guides 80 Strand, London WC2R 0RL Tel. *020 70103000* Fax. *020 70106060* E-mail. *mail@roughguides.com* Web. *www.roughguides.com Rough Guides*

Rough Trade Management 66 Golborne Road, London W10 5PS Tel. *020 88755194* Fax. *020 89686715* E-mail. *info@roughtraderecords.com* Web. *www.roughtraderecords.com Blanco Y Negro – Rough Trade – Tugboat*

Roundel Manufacturing Ltd Harton Centre 52 Harton Lane, South Shields NE34 0EE Tel. *0191 4271222* Fax. *0191 4270902* E-mail. *info@roundelkitchens.co.uk* Web. *www.roundelkitchens.co.uk Roundel*

Route V J Horticultural Unit 10 Common Lane North, Beccles NR34 9BN Tel. *01502 716450* Fax. *01502 715006* E-mail. *battzztastic@aol.com *Hayter – *John Deere – *Snapper*

Rowan Precision Ltd 2-4 Poplar Drive Witton, Birmingham B6 7AD Tel. *0121 3569981* Fax. *0121 3569982* E-mail. *martin.barker@rowanprecision.co.uk* Web. *www.rowanprecision.co.uk Bumotec – Mazak – Citizen – Deco – Deco - Tornos deco sliding head automatics. – Tornos Deco*

Rowebb Ltd 33-53 Charles Street, Glasgow G21 2PR Tel. *0141 5486010* Fax. *0141 5531039* E-mail. *rowebbltd@aol.com* Web. *www.rowebb.com Decarock – *Essno (Norway) – Plaidcrete*

Rowland Sandwith Ltd 32 Canford Bottom, Wimborne BH21 2HD Tel. *01202 882323* Fax. *01202 842815* E-mail. *office@rowland-sandwith.co.uk* Web. *www.h-h-hancock.co.uk H.H.Hancocks Clasped Hand – MasterMark*

J C Roxburgh & Co. Ltd 151 Glasgow Road, Clydebank G81 1LQ Tel. *0141 9520371* Fax. *0141 9520255* E-mail. *info@jcroxburgh.co.uk* Web. *www.jcroxburgh.co.uk Roxsure*

Roxspur Measurement & Control Ltd 2 Downgate Drive, Sheffield S4 8BT Tel. *0114 2249200* Fax. *0114 2434838* E-mail. *gswindell@roxspur.com* Web. *www.roxspur.com Amalgams – FI – Flowbits – Furnace Instruments – MTM – Neggretti – Nulectrohms – Platon*

Royal Aeronautical Society 4 Hamilton Place, London W1J 7BQ Tel. *020 76704300* Fax. *020 76704309* E-mail. *sales@raes.org.uk* Web. *www.aerosociety.com Royal Aeronautical Society*

The Royal & Ancient Golf Club Of St Andrews Golf Place, St Andrews KY16 9JD Tel. *01334 460000* Fax. *01334 460001* E-mail. *thesecretary@randagc.org* Web. *www.randa.org R & A – R and A – Royal & Ancient – Royal and Ancient*

Royal Birkdale Golf Club Waterloo Road, Southport PR8 2LX Tel. *01704 552020* Fax. *01704 552021* E-mail. *secretary@royalbirkdale.com* Web. *www.royalbirkdale.com Royal Birkdale*

Royal Brierley Crystal Ltd Tipton Road, Dudley DY1 4SH Tel. *0121 5305607* Fax. *01384 457302* E-mail. *rhixon@dartington.co.uk* Web. *www.royalbrierley.com Royal Brierley – Stevens & Williams*

The Royal Crown Derby Porcelain Company Ltd 194 Osmaston Road, Derby DE23 8JZ Tel. *01332 712800* Fax. *01332 712863* E-mail. *stuart.hughes@royal-crown-derby.co.uk* Web. *www.royal-crown-derby.co.uk Derby Panel Green – Imari – Posie – Royal Antoinette*

Royal Incorporation Of Architects In Scotland 15 Rutland Square, Edinburgh EH1 2BE Tel. *0131 2297545* Fax. *0131 2282188* E-mail. *nbaxter@rias.org.uk* Web. *www.rias.org.uk Royal Incorporation of Architects in Scotland, The*

Royal Liver Assurance Royal Liver Building Pier Head, Liverpool L3 1HT Tel. *0151 2361451* Fax. *0117 9817449* E-mail. *william.connelly@royalliver.com* Web. *www.royalliver.co.uk Royal Liver Assurance*

Royal Selangor Ltd 21 Eastbury Road, London E6 6LP Tel. *020 74745511* Fax. *020 74745522* E-mail. *marketing@royalselangor.co.uk* Web. *www.royalselangor.com *Comyns (Malaysia) – *Crown & Rose (Malaysia) – *Royal Selangor (Malaysia) – *Selmark (Malaysia)*

Royal Society Of Chemistry Thomas Graham House 290 Science Park Milton Road, Cambridge CB4 0WF Tel. *01223 420066* Fax. *01223 423623* E-mail. *sales@rsc.org* Web. *www.rsc.org R.S.C.*

Royal Society For The Prevention Of Accidents Ltd 353 Bristol Road Edgbaston, Birmingham B5 7ST Tel. *0121 2482000* Fax. *0121 2482001* E-mail. *help@rospa.com* Web. *www.mohsg.org.uk R.o.S.P.A. – Tufty*

Royal Tool Control Ltd Unit 1 Amberley Court, Sheffield S9 2LQ Tel. *0114 2441411* Fax. *0114 2432247* E-mail. *royal@royaltool.co.uk* Web. *www.royaltool.co.uk ERGO / MEGA/COMPACT – Royal – Tool boy – Toolmaster – Variset*

Royce Communications Ltd 1 Joule Road, Basingstoke RG21 6XH Tel. *01256 814814* Fax. *01256 810940* E-mail. *info@roycecomms.com* Web. *www.roycecomms.com CableEase*

RPC Containers Ltd Grove Street Raunds, Wellingborough NN9 6ED Tel. *01933 623311* Fax. *01933 622126* E-mail. *sales@rpc-oakham.co.uk* Web. *www.rpc-containers.co.uk Image – Impact – Laser*

R P C Containers Ltd 4 Sallow Road Weldon North Industrial Estate, Corby NN17 5JX Tel. *01536 263488* Fax. *01536 272910* E-mail. *v.dean@rpc-corby.co.uk* Web. *www.rpc-containers.co.uk Alpha – Cabaret – Eclipse – Sapphire – Thermic Ultra*

R P C Containers Ltd Haslingden Road, Blackburn BB1 2PX Tel. *01254 682298* Fax. *01254 583752* E-mail. *a.bloor@rpc-blackburn.co.uk* Web. *www.rpc-containers.co.uk Aztec – R. Range*

R P S Planning & Development Ltd Conrad House Beaufort Square, Chepstow NP16 5EP Tel. *01291 621821* Fax. *01291 627827* E-mail. *cliftona@rpsgroup.com* Web. *www.rpsgroup.com RPS Group Plc*

R P Towing Unit 1d Abercromby Avenue, High Wycombe HP12 3BW Tel. *01494 528233* Fax. *01494 638802* E-mail. *rp.towing@ntlworld.com R.P. Towing*

Rsi 69 Manor Park Road, London NW10 4JX Tel. *020 89652510* Fax. *020 89630662* E-mail. *sales@ariane-int.com* Web. *www.rsi-cycles.com *Ambrosio (Italy) – *Excelto (France) – Hell-Cat – *Nervar (France) – *Parentini (Italy) – *Stelvio (Italy)*

R Taylor & Sons Ltd 12 Cheapside, Spennymoor DL16 6DJ Tel. *01388 815426* Fax. *01388 801477* E-mail. *barriebt@yahoo.co.uk Taylors NewsForce – Top News*

RTD Systems Limited (t/a Octanorm UK) 10 Lyon Road South Wimbledon, London SW19 2RL Tel. *020 85452945* Fax. *020 85452955* E-mail. *solutions@rtdsystems.co.uk* Web. *www.rtdisplay.co.uk Double Form – Mini New Line – Octanorm – Octanorm-Newline – Sofadi – Struktur – Viking*

R T E UK Ltd 101a Hall Farm Road, Benfleet SS7 5JW Tel. *01268 569393* Fax. *01268 751753* E-mail. *rte-uk@lineone.net* Web. *www.rte-timberengineering.co.uk Bolted Trusses – Duodeck – Glulam*

R. Twining & Co. Ltd South Way, Andover SP10 5AQ Tel. *0845 6019612* Fax. *01264 337177* E-mail. *info@twinings.com* Web. *www.twinings.com Twinings Classic*

Rubber Consultants (MRPRA) Brickendonbury Brickendon, Hertford SG13 8NL Tel. *01992 554657* Fax. *01992 504248* E-mail. *general@tarrc.co.uk* Web. *www.tarrc.co.uk Novor 950*

Rubert & Co. Ltd Acru Works Demmings Road, Cheadle SK8 2PG Tel. *0161 4286058* Fax. *0161 4281146* E-mail. *info@rubert.co.uk* Web. *www.rubert.co.uk Acrulite – B. (Ball) Blocks*

Ruda Holiday Park Ltd Croyde Bay Croyde, Braunton EX33 1NY Tel. *01271 890477* Fax. *01271 890656* E-mail. *info@ruda.co.uk* Web. *www.ruda.co.uk Ruda*

Rud Chains Ltd Unit 10-14 John Wilson Business Park Harvey Drive, Chestfield, Whitstable CT5 3QT Tel. *01227 276611* Fax. *01227 276586* E-mail. *sales@rud.co.uk* Web. *www.rud.co.uk Rotogrip (Germany) – Rud Matic Disc (Germany) – Starpoint (Germany)*

Rudford Property Management Church Farm Barn Horsemere Green Lane, Climping, Littlehampton BN17 5QX Tel. *01903 731177* Fax. *01903 726968* E-mail. *rudford@pavilion.co.uk* Web. *www.pavilion.co.uk Rudford Property Management*

Rudge & Co UK Unit E2 Hilton Trading Estate Hilton Road, Lanesfield, Wolverhampton WV4 6DW Tel. *01902 402225* Fax. *01902 404477* E-mail. *sales@rudgeandco.com* Web. *www.rudgeandco.com Gaslight – Highgate – Original – Parasol – Pauraqua – Renown*

Rudrumholdings 33-35 High Street Shirehampton, Bristol BS11 0DX Tel. *0117 9826781* Fax. *0117 9379037* E-mail. *enquiries@rudrumholdings.co.uk* Web. *www.rudrumholdings.co.uk *Chinacite (China) – *Longflame (Columbia) – *Warmacite (South Africa)*

Rugby Football Union Rugby Road, Twickenham TW1 1DZ Tel. *020 88922000* Fax. *020 88929816* E-mail. *sales@rfu.co.uk* Web. *www.rfu.co.uk R.F.U. England*

Rumenco Ltd Derby Road Stretton, Burton On Trent DE13 0DW Tel. *01283 511211* Fax. *01283 546152* E-mail. *info@rumenco.co.uk* Web. *www.rumenco.co.uk Fivex – Forager – Lactomix – Main Ring – Mollasine – Promaize – Promol – Protofish – Rumag – Rumevite – Ruminlix – Rumins – Stay Dry – Supalick – Supercharge*

Rupert Magnus Trading Co. Ltd 160 Dukes Road, London W3 0SL Tel. *020 89932231* Fax. *020 89934445* E-mail. *bernardcrist@ukonline.co.uk* Web. *www.rupertmagnus.co.uk MAGNUS Imprints*

Ruption Bikes (t/a Split Second Imports) Cheddar Business Park Wedmore Road, Cheddar BS27 3EB Tel. *01934 743888* Fax. *01934 743073* E-mail. *sales@ruption.co.uk* Web. *www.rupton.com Ruption*

Rural Energy 21 Burrough Court Burrough On The Hill, Melton Mowbray LE14 2QS Tel. *01664 454989* Fax. *01664 454230* E-mail. *info@ruralenergy.co.uk* Web. *www.ruralenergy.co.uk Herz*

Rushton Ablett Ltd Arthur Street, Northampton NN2 6DX Tel. *01604 715474* Fax. *01604 791069* E-mail. *ianf@rablett.co.uk* Web. *www.jujujellies.co.uk Juju*

Peter Rushton Ltd Albion Street, Willenhall WV13 1NN Tel. *01902 368444* Fax. *01902 601757* E-mail. *sales@peterrushton.co.uk* Web. *www.peterrushton.co.uk Ajax – Bewo – Bridgeport – Colchester – HM – Jones & Shipman – Meddings – Rexon – Semco – Startrite – Stien*

Ruskin Air Management Ltd (Part of Ruskin Air Management Ltd) Joseph Wilson Industrial Estate South Street, Whitstable CT5 3DU Tel. *01227 276100* Fax. *01227 264262* E-mail. *sales@actionair.co.uk* Web. *www.actionair.co.uk Actionair – Ruskin Air Management*

H & L Russell Russel House Hornsby Way, Southfields Business Park, Basildon SS15 6TF Tel. *01268 889000* Fax. *01268 889100* E-mail. *pauls@russel.co.uk* Web. *www.russell.co.uk H. & L. Russel*

Russell & Bromley Ltd 24-54 Farwig Lane, Bromley BR1 3RB Tel. *020 84601122* Fax. *020 84604424* E-mail. *roger.bromley@russellandbromley.co.uk* Web. *www.russellandbromley.co.uk Chiquitta – Drylens – Feet First – Pant Pumps – Toby*

Russell Ductile Castings Ltd Trent Foundary Dawes Lane, Scunthorpe DN15 6UW Tel. *01724 862152* Fax. *01724 280461* E-mail. *general@russellductile.co.uk* Web. *www.ductile.co.uk Russell Castings*

Russell Finex Ltd Russell House Browells Lane, Feltham TW13 7EW Tel. *020 88182000* Fax. *020 88182060* E-mail. *marketing@russellfinex.com* Web. *www.russellfinex.com Russell Finex – Compact Sieve – Finex Separator – Vibrasonics – Blow Thru Sieve – Compact Airlock Sieve – Compact 3in1 Sieve – Compact Airswept Sieve – liquid Solid Separator – Eco Separator – Mini Sifter – Russell Eco Filter*

Russell Hobbs Ltd Bridgnorth Road Wombourne, Wolverhampton WV5 8AQ Tel. *0161 9473000* Fax. *0161 6821708* E-mail. *service@russellhobbs.com* Web. *www.saltoneurope.com Carmen – Pifco – Russell Hobbs – Salton – Tower*

Russell Plastics Progress House 37 Grove Avenue, Harpenden AL5 1EY Tel. *01582 762868* Fax. *01582 461086* E-mail. *sales@russellplastics.co.uk* Web. *www.russellplastics.co.uk Cladding*

Russell Play Ltd Newbridge Industrial Estate, Newbridge EH28 8PJ Tel. *0131 3355400* Fax. *0131 3355401* E-mail. *sales@russell-play.com* Web. *www.russell-play.com Colorado – Kiddie Kabin – Ludo – Metro Active – Metro Play – Metro Sport – Varioplanter – Voyager*

Russell Scientific Instruments Ltd Rashs Green Industrial Estate, Dereham NR19 1JG Tel. *01362 693481* Fax. *01362 698548* E-mail. *sales@russell-scientific.co.uk* Web. *www.russell-scientific.co.uk F Darton & Co – Tetcol – Tolni*

Russell Shutters Ltd (Part of the LBS Group) Unit 6 Sterling Trading Estate Rainham Road South, Dagenham RM10 8TX Tel. *020 85176655* Fax. *020 89840378* E-mail. *sales@lbsgroup.co.uk* Web. *www.lbsgroup.co.uk Olsen Shutters – Ranford Doors – Russell Shutters*

Russums Edward House Tenter Street, Rotherham S60 1LB Tel. *01709 372345* Fax. *01709 829982* E-mail. *info@russums.co.uk* Web. *www.russums.co.uk *De Berkel – *Global – *Le Chef – *Russums – Victorinox*

Rustic Touch Ltd 453 Preston Road Clayton-Le-Woods, Chorley PR6 7JD Tel. *01772 698175* Fax. *01257 220498* E-mail. *sales@rustictouch.co.uk* Web. *www.rustictouch.co.uk www.sleepersdirect.co.uk*

Ruston's Engineering Co. Ltd Brampton Road, Huntingdon PE29 3BS Tel. *01480 455151* Fax. *01480 52116* E-mail. *info@reco.co.uk* Web. *www.reco.co.uk Reco*

Rutherfords Unit 12 Cliffe Industrial Estate South Street, Lewes BN8 6JL Tel. *01273 478860* Fax. *01273 479015* E-mail. *adrianshorter@rutherfords.info* Web. *www.jdrutherford.co.uk *BASF – Baya – *Cyngenta – Dupont – *Monsanto*

Ruxley Manor Garden Centre Maidstone Road, Sidcup DA14 5BQ Tel. *020 83000084* Fax. *020 83023879* E-mail. *kevin@ruxley-manor.co.uk* Web. *www.ruxley-manor.co.uk Alton – Compton – Crane – Malvern – Robinsons*

R V Fire Systems Unit 17 Deanfield Court Link 59 Business Park, Clitheroe BB7 1QS Tel. *01200 428400* Fax. *01200 428004* E-mail. *info@rvfiresystems.co.uk* Web. *www.rvfiresystems.co.uk EDA Radio Fire Alarm Systems – Notifier Fire Alarm Equipment*

R W E Npower (Headquarters) Windmill Hill Business Park Whitehill Way, Swindon SN5 6PB Tel. *01793 877777* Fax. *01905 727100* E-mail. *info@npower.com* Web. *www.rwenpower.com Midlands Electricity – n-power – Powerline*

R W O Marine Equipment Ltd 231 Church Road, Benfleet SS7 4QW Tel. *01268 566666* Fax. *01268 795118* E-mail. *info@rwo-marine.com* Web. *www.rwo-marine.com Omniflex – R.W.O. – Swivelstat*

R W S Group plc Europa House Chiltern Park Chiltern Hill, Chalfont St. Peter, Gerrards Cross SL9 9FG Tel. *01753 480200* Fax. *01753 480280* E-mail. *rwstrans@rws.com* Web. *www.rws.com PatBase – EuroFile – WordFile*

Ryalux Carpets Ltd Mossfield Mill Chesham Fold Road, Bury BL9 6JZ Tel. *0161 7623030* Fax. *01706 716035* E-mail. *sales@ryalux.com* Web. *www.ryalux.com Bedroom Classic – Bedroom Collection – City Style – Crown Velvet – Devonshire Axminster – Devonshire Twist – Drysdale Heather Twist – Drysdale Twist – Easycare Twist – Fine Velvet – Finetwist – Firetwist Heather – Golden Velvet – Kings and Queen Velvet – Natural Harvest – New Ryalux – Ryadream – Ryasax – Ryasilk – Ryatwist Colour Collection – Ryatwist Royale – Ryatwist Tweed – Ryavelvet Royale – Ryaweave Natural Collection – South Seas – Superfine Velvet – V & A Twist*

Rydal Precision Tool Ltd Unit 5 Technology Centre London Road, Swanley BR8 7AG Tel. *01322 614661* Fax. *01322 614760* E-mail. *sales@rydal.co.uk* Web. *www.mjallen.co.uk Rydal Engineering*

Ryder Towing Equipment Alvanley House Alvanley Industrial Estate Stockport Road, Bredbury, Stockport SK6 2DJ Tel. *0161 4301120* Fax. *0161 4308140* E-mail. *d.ryder@rydertowing.co.uk* Web. *www.rydertowing.co.uk Clone – Midwife – Rearguard – Ryder*

Ryebrook Resins Ltd Unit 4 Kelvin Business Centre, Crawley RH10 9SF Tel. *01293 565500* Fax. *01293 565472* E-mail. *sales@ryebrook.co.uk* Web. *www.ryebrook.co.uk Ryecrete*

Ryepac Packaging Unit G30 Rye Industrial Park Rye Harbour Road, Rye TN31 7TE Tel. *01797 222295* Fax. *08717 819208* E-mail. *sales@ryepac.co.uk* Web. *www.ryepac.co.uk Rye-Pac Packaging Supplies*

Rykneld Metals Ltd Derby Road, Burton On Trent DE14 1RS Tel. *01283 562745* Fax. *01283 562745 Rykneld Metals*

Rykneld Tean Ltd Hansard Gate West Meadows Industrial Estate, Derby DE21 6RR Tel. *01332 542700* Fax. *01332 542710* E-mail. *sales@rykneldtean.co.uk* Web. *www.rykneldtean.co.uk Rykneld Tean*

S

Saacke Combustion Services Ltd Marshlands Spur, Portsmouth PO6 1RX Tel. *023 92383111* Fax. *023 92327120* E-mail. *m.cook@saacke.co.uk* Web. *www.saacke.co.uk Saacke – Sentinel*

Saarlander UK Ltd Unit 7 Wickford Enterprise Centre Enterprise Way, Wickford SS11 8DH Tel. *01268 561291* Fax. *01268 561292* E-mail. *sales@saarlander.co.uk* Web. *www.saarlander.co.uk *Saarberg – *Saarlander*

S A Brain & Co. Ltd Crawshay Street, Cardiff CF10 5DS Tel. *029 20402060* Fax. *029 20403344* E-mail. *colin.gin@sabrain.com* Web. *www.sabrain.com Brains Bitter – Brains Dark – Brains S.A.*

Sabreglaze Window Repairs 7 Oakwood Business Park Stephenson Road West, Clacton On Sea CO15 4TL Tel. *01255 436852* Fax. *01255 436852* E-mail. *w.huckle@easifix.co.uk* Web. *www.sabresharp.co.uk Sabreglaze*

Safe Computing Ltd 20 Freeschool Lane, Leicester LE1 4FY Tel. *08445 832134* Fax. *0116 2515535* E-mail. *sandy.scott@safecomputing.co.uk* Web. *www.safecomputing.co.uk Safes XI – SaFeS-VII – SaPHuR – Saphur Tempest*

Safecontractor Brecon House, Caerphilly Business Park, Caerphilly CF83 3GG Tel. *029 20266242* Fax. *029 20808547* E-mail. *sc.contractorsales@safecontractor.com* Web. *www.safecontractor.com Safecontractor Approved*

Safeguard Electronic Systems Ltd (t/a Thermatek) Unit 5A Station Yard Station Road, Hungerford RG17 0DY Tel. *01488 684888* Fax. *01488 682686* E-mail. *sales@thermatek.co.uk* Web. *www.thermatek.co.uk Thermatek – Thermatek, Thermatrad, Thermamod, Thermafoil, Thermaphase.*

Safelab Systems Ltd Unit 29 Lynx Crescent, Weston Super Mare BS24 9DJ Tel. *01934 421340* Fax. *0870 2402274* E-mail. *r.guess@safelab.co.uk* Web. *www.safelab.co.uk Airone – Chemisorb – Safelab*

Safety Assured Ltd Home Farm Fen Lane, North Ockendon, Upminster RM14 3RD Tel. *01708 855777* Fax. *01708 855125* E-mail. *info@safetyassured.com* Web. *www.safetyassured.com Aspivenin – Dorgard – Finger Protector – Slidesafe*

Safety Kleen UK Ltd Profile West 950 Great West Road, Brentford TW8 9ES Tel. *020 84909084* Fax. *020 84903859* E-mail. *sbrain@sk-europe.com* Web. *www.SK-europe.com Safety Kleen*

Safety Letter Box Company Ltd Unit B Milland Road Industrial Estate, Neath SA11 1NJ Tel. *01639 633525* Fax. *01639 646359* E-mail. *sales@safetyletterbox.com* Web. *www.safetyletterbox.com COM 3 – COM1 & SRX1 – COM2 & SRX2 – Eurobox – Guardian 1 & 2 – Mailforce 1 – Mailforce 2 – Mailforce 3*

Safety Signs & Notices Unit C & D Digby Street, Ilkeston DE7 5TG Tel. *0115 7270172* Fax. *0115 7270173* E-mail. *info@safetysignsandnotices.co.uk* Web. *www.safetysignsandnotices.co.uk Safety Signs & Notices*

Safety Systems UK Ltd Sharp Street Worsley, Manchester M28 3NA Tel. *0161 7907741* Fax. *0161 7994335* E-mail. *support@safetysystemsuk.com* Web. *www.safetysystemsuk.com Amal – IMI*

Safety Unlimited Unit 2 40 Comet Way, Southend On Sea SS2 6XW Tel. *01702 420000* Fax. *01702 528128* E-mail. *sales@safetyunlimited.co.uk* Web. *www.safetyunlimited.co.uk Abbey Cross – *Eagle (U.S.A.) – Enpac – *Protectoseal (U.S.A.)*

Safety Works & Solutions Ltd Unit 6 Earith Business Park Meadow Drove, Earith, Huntingdon PE28 3QF Tel. *01487 841400* Fax. *01487 841100* E-mail. *info@safetyworksandsolutions.co.uk* Web. *www.safetyworksandsolutions.co.uk DeMarcit – Easyguard – Fallguard – Fast Clamp – Flexideck – Inter Clamp – Kee Klamp – Mansafe – Uniline – Walksafe*

Safic Alcan UK Ltd 812 Birchwood Boulevard Birchwood, Warrington WA3 7QZ Tel. *01925 838880* Fax. *01925 838883* E-mail. *info@safic-alcan.co.uk* Web. *www.safic-alcan.co.uk A.K.M.*

Safilo UK Ltd Lambert House 108 Station Parade, Harrogate HG1 1HQ Tel. *01423 520303* Fax. *01423 565889* E-mail. *info@safilo.com* Web. *www.saflio.com Carrera – Christian Dior – Sunjet – Terri Brogan – Viennaline*

Sage Zander Ltd Triad House Mountbatten Court Worrall Street, Congleton CW12 1DT Tel. *01260 295264* Fax. *01260 295349* E-mail. *sales@sagezander.com* Web. *www.sagezander.com Tairyfil – Zanderlon*

Sahara Presentation Systems plc Williams House 61 Hailey Road, Erith DA18 4AA Tel. *020 83197700* Fax. *020 83197775* E-mail. *info@saharaplc.com* Web. *www.saharaplc.com Sahara Presentation Systems*

Saia Burgess (Gateshead) Plc Dukesway Team Valley Trading Estate, Gateshead NE11 0UB Tel. *0191 4016100* Fax. *0191 4016305* E-mail. *office@saia-burgess.com* Web. *www.saia-burgess.com BAR – BURGESS – Ledex & Dormeyer – Otehall – SAIA – SAIA - motors BURGESS - switches – th Contact – Werma*

St Andrews Link Trust Pilmour House, St Andrews KY16 9SF Tel. *01334 466666* Fax. *01334 479555* E-mail. *alanmcgregor@standrews.org.uk* Web. *www.standrews.org.uk Badge + (no words) – Badge + Words – Divice – Links and Badge – Old Course St Andrews*

St. Clare Engineering Ltd (Grab-O-Matic) Unit 4 Trinity Industrial Est Millbrook Road West, Southampton SO15 0LA Tel. *023 80510770* Fax. *023 80510772* Web. *www.stclare-engineering.co.uk Grab-O-Matic – TVS*

Saint-Gobain Limited Saint-Gobain House Binley Business Park, Coventry CV3 2TT Tel. *024 76560700* Fax. *024 76560705* E-mail. *info@saint-gobain.co.uk* Web. *www.saint-gobain.co.uk Cotech*

Saint-Gobain Abrasives Ltd Anson Business Park Cheltenham Road East, Gloucester GL2 9QN Tel. *01452 858700* Fax. *01452 858800* E-mail. *sales.gloucester.uk@saint-gobain.com* Web. *www.saint-gobain.com Norton – Winter*

Saint Gobain Industrial Ceramics Ltd Mill Lane Rainford, St Helens WA11 8LP Tel. *01744 882941* Fax. *01744 883514* E-mail. *alun.oxenham@cduk.saint-gobain.com* Web. *www.cduk.saint-gobain.com Advancer Crystar – Alfrax – Carbofrax – Cast Refrax – Cryston – Dry Ram Cements – Durafrax – Mullfrax – Refrax – Rokide – Silit*

Saint Gobain P A M UK PO Box 9, Ilkeston DE7 4QU Tel. *0115 9305000* Fax. *0115 9329513* E-mail. *paul.minchin@saint-gobain-pam.co.uk* Web. *www.saint-gobain-pam.co.uk inea - Selecta PAM UTILITY: Opt-Emax - Tri-Glide - Guardsman - Warrior PAM TELECOM: SHD Briton -Opt-Emax - BT Precinct Cover PAM COMMERCAIL & INDUSTRIAL: Pametic - Bri-Pave - Broadstel - Bristeel ESTATE RANGE: Non-Rock Access Cover - Solid single Seal - Gully Grates PAM INTERNATIONAL: Inter-Ax - Watershed - Autolinea - Siltseal - Warrior SOIL & DRAIN ABOVE GROUND: Ensign - Timesaver - Roof Outlet BELOW GROUND: Ensign - Timesaver - Floor Drainage RAINWATER: Classical - Classical Plus - Classical Express*

Saint-Gobain Weber Ltd Unit 1 Spiersbridge Business Park Spiersbridge Avenue, Thornliebank, Glasgow G46 8NL Tel. *0141 6212510* Fax. *0141 4450122* E-mail. *idris.crumlish@netweber.co.uk* Web. *www.netweber.co.uk Expobrick – Expolath – Expomesh – ExpoTherm – Fibrelite*

St Martin Vintners Ltd Trafalgar Street, Brighton BN1 4FQ Tel. *01273 777788* Fax. *01273 721403* E-mail. *sales@stmartinvintners.co.uk* Web. *www.stmv.co.uk *Cuvee St Martin – *Rolleston Vale Still and Australian*

St Regis Paper Co. Ltd Wansbourh Paper Mills, Watchet TA23 0AY Tel. *01984 631456* Fax. *01984 634123* E-mail. *info@stregis.co.uk* Web. *www.stregis.co.uk Washford*

St Regis Paper Co. Ltd Higher Kings Mill, Cullompton EX15 1QJ Tel. *01884 836300* Fax. *01884 836333* E-mail. *sales@stregis.co.uk* Web. *www.stregis.co.uk Culm Valley – Culmbrite – Ecofile – Kaleidoscope – Kempton – Kingsmill Sugar – Otter Manilla – Otterbrite*

Sal Abrasives Technologies 44-45 Drumhead Road Chorley North Industrial Park, Chorley PR6 7BX Tel. *01257 271914* Fax. *01257 260702* E-mail. *abrasives@salgroup.co.uk* Web. *www.salgroup.co.uk Dynabraid – English Abrasives – GEM – SAL – Universal*

Salco Group plc Salco House 5 Central Road, Harlow CM20 2ST Tel. *01279 439991* Fax. *01279 410984* E-mail. *sales@salcogroup.com* Web. *www.salcogroup.com *Salco (Hong Kong)*

Salesmark Ltd Howard Road Eaton Socon, St Neots PE19 8ET Tel. *01480 212888* Fax. *01480 218585* E-mail. *sales@salesmark.co.uk* Web. *www.salesmark.co.uk New Decade*

Sales Point 75 Wilmslow Road Handforth, Wilmslow SK9 3EN Tel. *01625 525226* Fax. *01625 533307* E-mail. *info@salespoint.co.uk* Web. *www.salespoint.co.uk Newspoint – Salespoint*

Sallis Healthcare Ltd (Healthcare) Waterford Street, Nottingham NG6 0DH Tel. *0115 9787841* Fax. *0115 9422272* E-mail. *info@sallis.co.uk* Web. *www.sallis.co.uk Eesiban – Eesilas – Eesilite – Eesiness – Eesinet*

Sallu Plastics 21 Ferney Hill Avenue, Redditch B97 4RU Tel. *01527 404305* Fax. *01527 908863* E-mail. *sales@sallu.co.uk* Web. *www.sallu.co.uk Cobex – Darvic – Pacton – Salbak – Salbex – VB241 – Velbex – Vybak – Vynalast*

Salon Services Hair & Beauty Supplies Ltd Unit 7 Evanton Drive Thornliebank Industrial Estate, Glasgow G46 8HZ Tel. *0141 6213600* Fax. *0141 6213660* E-mail. *enquiries@salon-services.com* Web. *www.salon-services.com Avec – Bounce – Sassi*

Salts Healthcare Unit 1 Richard Street, Birmingham B7 4AA Tel. *0121 3332000* Fax. *0121 3590830* E-mail. *philipsalt@salts.co.uk* Web. *www.salts.co.uk Salts Healthcare*

Salty Yacht Productions Ltd Unit 44 Enterprise Way, Newport NP20 2AQ Tel. *01633 250652* Fax. *01633 842267* E-mail. *sales@saltyyachts.com* Web. *www.strandek.co.uk Strandek*

Samelco Automation Systems Ltd Unit 5 The Odyssey Centre Corporation Road, Birkenhead CH41 1LB Tel. *0151 6472123* E-mail. *general@samelco.com* Web. *www.samelco.com Samelco Web Technology*

Samoa Ltd Asturias House Barrs Fold Road Wingates Industrial Estate, Westhoughton, Bolton BL5 3XP Tel. *01942 850600* Fax. *01204 812160* E-mail. *sales@samoa.ltd.uk* Web. *www.samoa.ltd.uk Samoa*

Samrex Textiles 24 Church Lane, Wolverhampton WV2 4BU Tel. *01902 427733* Fax. *01902 427765* E-mail. *sam@samrex.com* Web. *www.samrex.com Samrex Textiles*

Samsung Telecom UK Ltd Unit B2 Brookside Business Park Greengate, Middleton, Manchester M24 1GS Tel. *0161 6551100* Fax. *0161 6551166* E-mail. *info@samsungelectronics.co.uk D.C.S – Interconnect 200 – Interconnect 3000 – Rhapsody – Rio*

Samuel Groves Station Road Western Road, Oldbury B69 4LY Tel. *0121 5697900* Fax. *0121 5232924* E-mail. *sales@samuelgroves.co.uk* Web. *www.samuelgroves.co.uk Le Buffet – Longlife – Mermaid*

Sanderson Weatherall Chartered Surveyors 22-24 Grey Street, Newcastle Upon Tyne NE1 6AD Tel. *0191 2612681* Fax. *0191 2614761* E-mail. *tim.catterall@sandersonweatherall.com* Web. *www.sw.co.uk Sanderson Townend & Gilbert*

Sanders Pepper Smith Ltd Unit 14 Cardrew Industrial Estate, Redruth TR15 1SS Tel. *01209 202170* Fax. *01209 310561* E-mail. *enquiries@sanderspeppersmith.com* Web. *www.sanderspeppersmith.com Sanders Pepper Smith RIBA Chartered Practice*

Sanders Polyfilms Ltd Westfields Trading Estate, Hereford HR4 9NS Tel. *01432 277558* Fax. *01432 279898* E-mail. *sales@polyfilms.co.uk* Web. *www.theshrinkfilmcompany.com E.X.L. Shrink – E.X.L. Stretch – Linnex – Tensil Seal*

Sanders & Sanders Ltd Spencer Works Spencer Road, Rushden NN10 6AE Tel. *01933 353066* Fax. *01933 410355* E-mail. *mail@sanders-uk.com* Web. *www.sanders-uk.com Charles Horrell – Diplomat – Regent – Sanders*

Sandfield Engineering Co. Ltd Sandy Lane Industrial Estate, Stourport On Severn DY13 9QB Tel. *01299 823158* Fax. *01299 827011* E-mail. *sales@sandfieldengineering.com* Web. *www.sandfieldengineering.com Sandfield - Sandfield - Sandfield Engineering – Sandfield Engineering*

Sandhurst Instruments Ltd 30 Sudley Road, Bognor Regis PO21 1ER Tel. *01243 820200* Fax. *01243 860111* E-mail. *info@sandhurstinstruments.co.uk* Web. *www.sandhurstinstruments.co.uk Accelerometers – Dytran Instruments – G.P.50 – Validyne*

Sandhurst Plant Ltd Medway City Estate Enterprise Close, Rochester ME2 4JW Tel. *01634 739590* Fax. *0845 1206644* E-mail. *info@sandhurst.co.uk* Web. *www.sandhurst.co.uk Atlas Copco – Daewoo – EGT – SMC – Solmec – Thyssen Krupp*

Sandmaster Ltd Airfield Industrial Estate Hixon, Stafford ST18 0PF Tel. *01889 270695* Fax. *01889 271161* E-mail. *james@sandmaster.com* Web. *www.sandmaster.com Sandmaster*

Sandtoft Holdings Ltd Sandtoft, Doncaster DN8 5SY Tel. *01427 872696* Fax. *01427 871222* E-mail. *info@sandtoft.co.uk* Web. *www.sandtoft.co.uk 20/20 Interlock Clay Plain Tile – Arcadia Pantile – Barrow Bold Roman – Bold Roll – BritLock – BritSlate – Calderdale – County Pantile – Double Pantile – Double Roman – Europa Tile – Flemish Tile – Gaelic – Goxhill handmade clay plain tile – Greenwood pantile – Humber plain tile – Lindum – Old English Pantile – Pennine Slate – Plain Tile – Provincial pantile – Shire Pantile – Standard Pattern*

Sandvik Aghnagar Road Ballygawley, Dungannon BT70 2HW Tel. *028 85567799* Fax. *028 85567007* E-mail. *mobilecs.smcuk@sandvik.com* Web. *www.mc.sandvik.com Finlay BME – Fintec*

Sandvik Ruthvenfield Road Inveralmond Industrial Estate, Perth PH1 3ED Tel. *01738 493300* Fax. *01738 493301* E-mail. *harry.furuberg@kanthal.se* Web. *www.kanthal.com Crusilite – Globar – Kanthal Hot Rod – Silit ED*

Sandvik Bioline Longacre Way Holbrook Industrial Estate, Holbrook, Sheffield S20 3FS Tel. *0114 2633100* Fax. *0114 2633111* E-mail. *stephencowan@sandvik.com* Web. *www.sandvik.com SAF 2507 – Sandvik Bioline Sanmac*

Sandvick Osprey Ltd Milland Road, Neath SA11 1NJ Tel. *01639 634121* Fax. *01639 630100* Web. *www.ospreymetals.co.uk Osprey*

Sangamo Ltd Auchenfoil Road, Port Glasgow PA14 5XG Tel. *01475 745131* Fax. *01475 744567* E-mail. *enquiries@sangamo.co.uk* Web. *www.sangamo.co.uk Flash (United Kingdom) – MZR (United Kingdom) – Powersaver (United Kingdom) – Sangamo (United Kingdom) – SANGAMO - SUNTRACKER - MZR – Suntracker (United Kingdom)*

Sanico Building Services Ltd 17-21 George Street, Croydon CR0 1LA Tel. *07833 118149* Fax. *020 84072032* E-mail. *info@sanico.co.uk* Web. *www.sanico.co.uk Sanico Building Services*

Richard Sankey & Son Ltd Bennerley Road Bulwell, Nottingham NG6 8PE Tel. *0115 9277335* Fax. *0115 9770197* E-mail. *info@rsankey.co.uk* Web. *www.rsankey.co.uk Aquabutt – ConvertaBin – GroMaster – Gropots – GroStart – Plantation – PlantMaster 90 – Terra-Perma – WaterStore*

SANO TOOLS 8 Low Farm Place Moulton Park Industrial Estate, Northampton NN3 6HY Tel. *01604 947179* Fax. *01604 521070* E-mail. *office@sanotools.com* Web. *www.sanotools.com CHILTERN TOOLING – SANO TOOLS*

Sansetsu UK Ltd Bradbourne Drive Tilbrook, Milton Keynes MK7 8AT Tel. *01908 644660* Fax. *01908 367313* E-mail. *info@sansetsu.co.uk* Web. *www.sansetsu.co.uk Sancell*

Santa Pod Raceway Airfield Road Podington, Wellingborough NN29 7XA Tel. *01234 782828* Fax. *01234 782818* E-mail. *info@santapod.com* Web. *www.santapod.co.uk Bug Jam – Santa Pod*

Sanyo Sales & Marketing Europe GmbH Sanyo House 18 Colonial Way, Watford WD24 4PT Tel. *01923 246363* Fax. *01923 477450* E-mail. *b.lakin@sanyo.co.uk* Web. *www.uk.sanyo.com *Sanyo (Japan)*

Sanyo Gallenkamp plc Monarch Way Belton Park, Loughborough LE11 5XG Tel. *01509 265265* Fax. *01509 269770* E-mail. *sales@sanyogallenkamp.com* Web. *www.sanyogallenkamp.com A.F.3 Autoflash – Autobomb – Calypso – Centaur 2 – Climatic Test Chambers – Cyclon – Economy – Fistreem – Fistreem Multipure – Fistreem Puri-Fi – Fitotron – Gallenkamp – Gallenkamp – Gallenkamp 'OMT' – Gallenkamp Climatic Test Chambers – Gallenkamp Pharmaceutical Test Chambers – Gallenkamp Plus – Gallenkamp Prime – Hotbox – M.S.E. Mistral Centrifuges – Melting Point – MSE Harrier – Sanyo – Sanyo – Soniprep*

Sapa Profiles Ltd Unit 1-4 Tibshelf Business Park Sawpit Lane, Tibshelf, Alfreton DE55 5NH Tel. *01773 872761* Fax. *01773 874389* E-mail. *info@sapagroup.com* Web. *www.sapagroup.com S.A.P.A.*

Sapa Profiles UK Ltd Tewkesbury Road, Cheltenham GL51 9DT Tel. *01242 521641* Fax. *01242 513304* E-mail. *kevin.donnelly@sapagroup.com* Web. *www.sapagroup.com/uk/profiles SAPA Profiles (United Kingdom)*

SAP Motor Factors 29-33 Brighton Road, Addlestone KT15 1PG Tel. *01932 857921* E-mail. *inquires@sapmotorparts.com* Web. *www.sapmotorparts.com SAP Motor Factors*

Sapphire Research & Electronics Ltd Amerena House Morris Terrace, Ferndale CF43 4ST Tel. *01443 730782* Fax. *01443 730035* E-mail. *sales@sapphireresearch.com* Web. *www.sapphireresearch.com Sapphire*

Sarah Louise Ltd 10-14 Green Lane, Ormskirk L39 1SL Tel. *01695 576069* Fax. *01695 574805* E-mail. *dgiven@sarah-louise.co.uk* Web. *www.sarah-louise.co.uk Cric and Croc – Dani – Sarah Louise*

Saras Process Ltd Trent Industrial Estate Duchess Street, Shaw, Oldham OL2 7UT Tel. *01706 845960* Fax. *01706 882403* E-mail. *sales@sarasprocess.co.uk* Web. *www.sarasprocess.co.uk Saras Process*

Sarclad Ltd Broombank Park, Chesterfield S41 9RT Tel. *01246 457000* Fax. *01246 457010* E-mail. *sarclad@sarclad.com* Web. *www.sarclad.com Rollscan – Rolltex – Strand Condition Monitor*

Sarco Stopper Ltd 5-7 Brocks Way East Mains Industrial Estate, Broxburn EH52 5NB Tel. *01506 855824* Fax. *01506 855849* E-mail. *mail@sarcostopper.com* Web. *www.sarcostopper.com Drain and Gas Bagstoppers – Pipe Testing Equipment - Sarco Inspectra – Sarco Resistra Gas Bags – Sarco Supra Gas Stoppers – Sarco Ultra Twin Bags – Welding Bags*

Sarena 15 Century House Vickers Business Centre, Basingstoke RG24 9NP Tel. *01634 370887* Fax. *01634 370915* E-mail. *info@sarena.co.uk* Web. *www.sarena.co.uk Benchmark – Sarena – Sarenarap – Techdec*

Sarginsons Industries Sarginsons Precision Components & Advance Tooling Torrington Avenue, Coventry CV4 9AG Tel. *024 76466291* Fax. *024 76468135* E-mail. *reception@sarginsons.co.uk* Web. *www.sarginsons.co.uk Advance Tooling – Sarginsons Precision Components – Sarginsons Precision Components - Advance Tooling.*

Sargrove Automation The Chestnuts 11 Eastern Road, Havant PO9 2JE Tel. *023 92477244* Fax. *023 92471981* E-mail. *sargrove@btinternet.com Countec – Phasitron – Registrac*

Sarum Hydraulics Ltd 7 Centre One Old Sarum Park Lysander Way, Old Sarum, Salisbury SP4 6BU Tel. *01722 328388* Fax. *01722 414307* E-mail. *pumpsales@sarum-hydraulics.co.uk* Web. *www.sarum-hydraulics.co.uk Micropac*

Sasco Sauces Ltd Unit 2 St Michaels Close, Aylesford ME20 7BU Tel. *01622 714940* Fax. *01622 719422* E-mail. *garysauces@aol.com* Web. *www.sascosauces.co.uk *Sasco Real Mayonnaise*

SATCO Tapes (t/a SATCO) 34 Europa Way Martineau Lane, Norwich NR1 2EN Tel. *01603 613434* Fax. *01603 699987* E-mail. *sales@satco.co.uk* Web. *www.satco.co.uk *Orgapack (Switzerland) – Pakprint – Satco – Satcoprint Labels – Tyeband*

Satellite Television Contractors 106 London Road, Hemel Hempstead HP3 9SD Tel. *01442 252051* Fax. *01442 321839* E-mail. *theresa.gee@stcltd.co.uk* Web. *www.stcltd.co.uk *M and M Installations*

SATRA Technology Centre Satra House Rockingham Road, Kettering NN16 9JH Tel. *01536 410000* Fax. *01536 410626* E-mail. *equipsales@satra.co.uk* Web. *www.satra.co.uk Lacsol – Satra Footwear Technology Centre – Satreat*

Saturn Spraying Systems Ltd Unit 3 13 Cobham Road Ferndown Industrial Estate, Wimborne BH21 7PE Tel. *01202 891863* Fax. *01202 871543* E-mail. *sales@saturnspraying.com* Web. *www.saturnspraying.com Discmaster – Discmatic – Portadisc*

Sauer-Danfoss Ltd 130 Faraday Park Faraday Road, Swindon SN3 5JF Tel. *01793 716000* Fax. *01793 716015* Web. *www.sauer-danfoss.com Sauer Sundstrand*

Sauflon Pharmaceuticals Ltd 49-53 York Street, Twickenham TW1 3LP Tel. *020 83224200* Fax. *020 88913001* E-mail. *alanwells@sauflon.co.uk* Web. *www.sauflon.com Sauflon Pharmaceuticals Ltd*

Saunderson House 1 Long Lane, London EC1A 9HF Tel. *020 73156500* Fax. *020 73156550* E-mail. *shl@sanderson-house.co.uk* Web. *www.saunderson-house.co.uk Saunderson House*

Savannah Estates Ltd 61 Bensham Grove Thornton Heath, Thornton Heath CR7 8DD Tel. *020 87712050* Fax. *020 87712051* E-mail. *ed_dublin@hotmail.com* Web. *www.savannahestates.co.uk Intel*

Savant Ltd Dalton Hall Business Centre Dalton Lane, Burton, Carnforth LA6 1BL Tel. *01524 784400* Fax. *0870 4601023* E-mail. *info@savant.co.uk* Web. *www.savant.co.uk Savant – Viewcomp*

Save & Invest Financial Planning 100 West Regent Street, Glasgow G2 2QD Tel. *0141 3328088* Fax. *01738 441315* E-mail. *jdeans@saveandinvest.co.uk* Web. *www.saveandinvest.co.uk Save & Invest*

Saville Heaton Ltd Heaton House Bradford Road, Dewsbury WF13 2EE Tel. *01924 466333* Fax. *01924 456654* E-mail. *sales@saville-heaton.co.uk* Web. *www.saville-heaton.co.uk Beach Club – Cab Co – Club Casuals – Oakman Menswear – Saville Heaton*

S A V UK Ltd Scandia House Armfield Close, West Molesey KT8 2JR Tel. *020 89414153* Fax. *020 87831132* E-mail. *j.hansen@savmodules.com* Web. *www.sav-systems.com *All-Round Patent Band (Norway) – *Cimberio (Italy) – *Cimm (Italy) – *Far-Manifolds/Maddalena (Italy)*

Saw Centre Ltd 650 Eglinton Street, Glasgow G5 9RP Tel. *08707 280222* Fax. *0141 4295609* E-mail. *sales@thesawcentre.co.uk* Web. *www.thesawcentre.co.uk The Saw Centre Ltd*

Saxon Lifts Ltd Grand Union Works Whilton Locks, Whilton, Daventry NN11 2NH Tel. *01327 843355* Fax. *01327 843887* E-mail. *mail@saxonlifts.com* Web. *www.saxonlifts.com Lifting equipment manufrs – Saxon*

S B Electronic Systems Ltd Arden Grove, Harpenden AL5 4SL Tel. *01582 769991* Fax. *01582 461705* E-mail. *sales@telepen.co.uk* Web. *www.telepen.co.uk Telepen*

S B E S Ltd Unit F 47 Blackborough Road, Reigate RH2 7BU Tel. *01737 226622* Fax. *01737 242442* E-mail. *info@sbes.co.uk* Web. *www.sbes.co.uk SBES LifeSaver*

S & B UK Ltd Labtec Street Swinton, Manchester M27 8SE Tel. *0161 7939333* Fax. *0161 7289149* E-mail. *jim_burgess@splusb.co.uk* Web. *www.splusb.co.uk Air Sentry – Powerlab 8 – Smart Fume Cupboard*

Sca Foam Products (Formerly Tuscarora) Cornhill Close Lodge Farm Industrial Estate, Northampton NN5 7UB Tel. *01604 596800* Fax. *01604 759024* E-mail. *jonathan.haddock@sca.com* Web. *www.scafoamproducts.co.uk SCA Tuscarora*

S C A Hygiene Products UK Ltd Southfields Road, Dunstable LU6 3EJ Tel. *01582 677400* Fax. *01582 677502* E-mail. *customers.servicesafh@sca.com* Web. *www.sca-hygiene.co.uk *Tork Classic – Tork Comfort – *Tork Cuisine – *Tork Exclusiv Softline – *Tork Matic*

Scala Agenturen UK Unit 6 Roman Way, Coleshill, Birmingham B46 1HG Tel. *01675 430300* Fax. *01675 430444* E-mail. *scalab46@yahoo.co.uk* Web. *www.scala-nl.com Delta Doc Johnson – Renate Bucone – Scala – Sharon Sloane – Video Vortex*

Scaleaway Tools & Equipment Ltd Station Street West Business Park, Coventry CV6 5BP Tel. *024 76661326* Fax. *024 76688603* E-mail. *sales@scaleaway-tools.co.uk* Web. *www.scaleaway-tools.co.uk Austen Brush Co – Scaleaway Tools & Equipment Ltd*

Scan Coin Dutch House 110 Broadway, Salford M50 2UW Tel. *0161 8730500* Fax. *0161 8730501* E-mail. *dthornber@scancoin.co.uk* Web. *www.scancoin.co.uk *Scan Coin (Sweden)*

Scandinavian Storage Group Sussex Innovation Centre Science Park Square, Brighton BN1 9SB Tel. *01273 704520* Fax. *01273 704499* E-mail. *danielle@ssg.eu* Web. *www.ssg-uk.com Sovella*

Scandura St James Road St James Industrial Estate, Corby NN18 8AW Tel. *01536 267121* Fax. *01536 266392* E-mail. *info@scandura.co.uk* Web. *www.scandura.co.uk Marseline*

SCA Newtec Nutec Mill Eastern Avenue, Lichfield WS13 7SE Tel. *01543 306306* Fax. *01543 306307* E-mail. *enquiries@scanutec.com* Web. *www.scanutec.com/index.html Cerezyme – Neocare – Solvitec*

Scanlift Ltd Causeway End Industrial Estate Station Road, Lawford, Manningtree CO11 2LH Tel. *01206 396111* Fax. *01206 395870* E-mail. *sales@scanlift.co.uk* Web. *www.scanlift.co.uk *Scanlift (Denmark)*

Scanna MSC International House 223 Regent Street, London W1B 2EB Tel. *020 73553555* Fax. *020 73553556* E-mail. *info@scanna-msc.com* Web. *www.scanna-msc.com Scanmail – Scanmax – Scanna – Scantrak*

ScanSense Bekkeveien 163 Queniborough, Leicester LE7 3FP Tel. *0116 2609757* Web. *WWW.SCANSENSE.NO SCANSENSE*

S C A Packaging near Millbrook, Torpoint PL11 3AX Tel. *01752 822551* Fax. *01752 823551* E-mail. *julia.nodder@sca.com* Web. *www.sca.com Rosslite*

Scappa UK Ltd Manchester Road, Ashton Under Lyne OL7 0ED Tel. *01582 478111* Fax. *01582 471085* E-mail. *carole.price@scapatapes.com* Web. *www.scappa.com Cellux – Scapa – Sellotape*

S C C Applied House Birchwood Boulevard, Birchwood, Warrington WA3 7PS Tel. *01925 819939* Fax. *01925 853602* E-mail. *i.smith@scc.com* Web. *www.scc.com Scotbyte supplies*

Sceptre Promotions Ltd 97 Elton Road Stibbington, Peterborough PE8 6JX Tel. *01780 782093* Fax. *01780 783159* E-mail. *grant@sceptre-promotions.freeserve.co.uk* Web. *www.keyboard-cavalcade.co.uk Keyboard Cavalcade – Sceptre Promotions – Sceptre Publishers*

Schaffner Ltd Ashville Way Molly Millers Lane, Wokingham RG41 2PL Tel. *0118 9770070* Fax. *0118 9792969* E-mail. *paul.dixon@schaffner.com* Web. *www.schaffner.com Schaffner*

Schawk St Marks House Shepherdess Walk, London N1 7LH Tel. *020 78617777* Fax. *020 78717777* E-mail. *fred.goff@schawk.com* Web. *www.schawk.com Seven Birmingham – Seven Interactive – Seven London – Seven Manchester – Seven Solutions*

Schenck Ltd Broxell Close, Warwick CV34 5QF Tel. *01926 474090* Fax. *01926 474034* E-mail. *sales@schenck.co.uk* Web. *www.schenck.co.uk Smartbalancer 3 – Distec – Tooldyne – TB SONIO – Pasio – Virio – Ceno – Fluidfill – HGW – Smartbalancer 3 – Pasio – XONDO*

Schenkers Ltd Schenker House Unitair Centre Great South West Road, Feltham TW14 8NT Tel. *020 88908899* Fax. *020 87510141* E-mail. *per.holstnielsen@schenker.co.uk* Web. *www.dbschenker.com Schenker Air Cargo – Schenker Exhibitions – Schenker International – Schenker Logistics – Schenker Seacargo*

Schindler Benwell House Green Street, Sunbury On Thames TW16 6QS Tel. *01932 758100* Fax. *020 88187999* E-mail. *simon.rose@gb.schindler.com* Web. *www.schindler.com Compaveyor – Design S – Dynatron – Miconic – Schindler – Schindler 100 – Schindler 300 (Switzerland)*

Schlegel UK 25 Henlow Industrial Estate, Henlow SG16 6DS Tel. *01462 815500* Fax. *01462 814781* E-mail. *ian.pawson@schlegel.com* Web. *www.schlegel.com Aquamac – Fast Fit – Finseal Pile – Lozaron – Patio Door Rollers – Polyflex – Q-Lon – Retroseal*

Schleifring Systems Ltd Abex Road, Newbury RG14 5EY Tel. *01635 232900* Fax. *01635 38334* E-mail. *dfinnegan@schleifring.co.uk* Web. *www.schleifring.com Franke*

Schloetter Co. Ltd Abbey Works New Road, Pershore WR10 1BY Tel. *01386 552331* Fax. *01386 556864* E-mail. *info@schloetter.co.uk* Web. *www.schloetter.co.uk Culmo – Elfit – Metapas – Slotanit – Slotocoup – Slotolet – Slotoloy – Slotonik – Slotosit – Zincaslot*

Schlumberger Oilfield UK plc Schlumberger House Buckingham Gate, London Gatwick Airport, Gatwick RH6 0NZ Tel. *01293 556655* Fax. *01293 556700* E-mail. *pdroy@slb.com* Web. *www.slb.com Clan – Eclipse – G.R.D. – Grid – P.V.T. – Welltest*

A B Schmidt UK Ltd Southgate Way Orton Southgate, Peterborough PE2 6GP Tel. *01733 363300* Fax. *01733 363333* E-mail. *henk.landeweerd@aebi-schmidt.co.uk* Web. *www.schmidt.co.uk Classic – Moro – SchmidtCare – Swingo*

Schmitt Europe Ltd Unit 4 Sir William Lyons Road University of Warwick Science Park, Coventry CV4 7EZ Tel. *024 76697192* Fax. *024 76412697* E-mail. *jon@schmitt.co.uk* Web. *www.schmitteurope.com Acuity (U.S.A.) – Electrorava (Italy) – Elettrorava (Italy) – Feinmess (Germany) – Hydrokompenser – SBS (U.S.A.) – SBS, SMS, Acuity Research. – Schmitt – SHS – SMS (U.S.A.)*

Schmitz Cargobull UK Ltd North Road, Stanley DH9 8HJ Tel. *01207 282882* Fax. *01207 232479* E-mail. *info@cargobull.com* Web. *www.cargobull.com Schmitz*

Schneider Stafford Park 5, Telford TF3 3BL Tel. *08706 088608* Fax. *0870 6088606* Web. *www.schneider-electric.com Advantage – Advantage - Altistart - Altivar - Axiom SP&N - Canalis - CIDS - Clearstart - Compact NS - Domae - Easergy - Evolis - Factorylink - Fast trans - FIPIO - Form3Fast - Genie - GDV2 - GM set - GM6 - Harmony - IHC - I-Line - Integral - Interpact - Isobar 4c - Isobar 4 SP&N - Isobar 4 TP&N - LoadCentre KQ2 - Magelis - Masterbloc - Masterpact - MC set - MDS - Merlin Gerin - Micro - Micrologic - Minipact - Modbus - Modbus Plus - Modicon - Modicon TSX - Momentum - Multi-Form - Nano - NS Feeder pillar - Nu-Lec - Opus - Osiris -*

Panelmate - Power 2 rack - Power Pact 4 - Power-Style 3 - Power-Style 4 - PowerLogic - Premium - Prisma Evolution - Prisma G - Prisma GK - Prisma GX - Prisma P - Prisma PH - Profibus - Quadbreak - Quantum - Qwikline II - Rectiphase - Rectivar - Reactivar - Ringmaster C - Ringmaster compact - RM6 - Safepact 2 - SAIF feeder pillars - Sarel - Sepam - Shielded feeder pillars - Sinewave - SM6 - Square D - Standard Plus - Startpact - Tego Dial - Tego Power - Telemecanique - Tesys - Transparent building - Transparent factory - Transparent infrastructure - Transparent Ready - Tricast - Trihal - Twinbreak - Twido - Twineline/Lexium - Varlogic - Varplus - Vijeo Look - VIP 300 - YSF6 - Zelio. – Altistart – Altivar – Axiom SP&N – Canalis – CIDS – Clearstart – Compact NS – Domae – Easergy – Evolis – Factorylink – Fast trans – FIPIO – Form3Fast – GDV2 – Genie – GM set – GM6 – Harmony – I-Line – IHC – Integral – Interpact – Isobar 4 SP&N – Isobar TP&N – LoadCentre KQ2 – Magelis – Masterbloc – Masterpact – MC set – MDS – Merlin Gerin – Micro – Micrologic – Minipact – Modbus – Modbus Plus – Modicon – Modicon TSX – Momentum – Multi-Form – Nano – NS Feeder pillar – Nu-Lec – Opus – Osiris – Ospbar 4c – Panelmate – Power 2 rack – Power Pact 4 – Power-Style 3 – Power-Style 4 – PowerLogic – Premium – Prisma Evolution – Prisma G – Prisma GK – Prisma GX – Prisma P – Prisma PH – Profibus – Quadbreak – Quantum – Qwikline II – ReactiVar – Rectiphase – Rectivar – Ringmaster C – Ringmaster compact – RM6 – Safepact 2 – SAIF feeder pillars – Sarel – Sepam – Shielded feeder pillars – Sinewave – SM6 – Square D – Standard Plus – Startpact – Tego dial – Tego Power – Telemecanique – Tesys – Transparent building – Transparent factory – Transparent infrastructure – Transparent Ready – Tricast – Trihal – Twido – Twinbreak – Twineline/Lexium – Varlogic – Varplus – Vijeo Look – VIP 300 – YSF6 – Zelio

Schneider Electric Braywick House East Windsor Road, Maidenhead SL6 1DN Tel. *01628 741050* Fax. *01628 741101* E-mail. *chris.trinder@schneider-electric.com* Web. *www.schneider-electric.com Ali – BAS 2800+ – Climatronic – Climatronic Controllers – I.A. Series Micronet – Invensys Sigma – Keyboard – Micronet – Montage – S E P – SEP – Unifact – Unifact PRO – Zonemaster*

Schneider Electric Ltd 123 Jack Lane, Leeds LS10 1BS Tel. *0113 2903500* Fax. *0113 2903710* E-mail. *chris.gallagher@schneider-electric.com* Web. *www.schneider-electric.com Merlin Gerin – Modicon – Schneider – Square D – Telemecanique*

Schoeller-Bleckmann UK European Business Pk Taylors La, Oldbury B69 2BN Tel. *0121 5521535* Fax. *0121 6279282* E-mail. *sales@schoeller-bleckmann.co.uk* Web. *www.schoeller-bleckmann.co.uk Schoeller-Bleckmann*

Schoeller Bleckmann & Darron Unit 47 Howe Moss Terrace Kirkhill Industrial Estate, Dyce, Aberdeen AB21 0GR Tel. *01224 799600* Fax. *01224 770156* E-mail. *dfindlay@sbdl.co.uk* Web. *www.sbdl.co.uk Oilfield Equipment – Schoeller-Bleckmann*

Schofield & Smith Huddersfield Ltd Unit 26 Upper Mills Slaithwaite, Huddersfield HD7 5HA Tel. *01484 842471* Fax. *01484 842684* E-mail. *sales@schofieldandsmith.co.uk* Web. *www.schofieldandsmith.co.uk *S. & S. (Italy)*

Scholastic School Book Fairs Unit 6 Westfield Road, Southam CV47 0RA Tel. *0800 212281* Fax. *0845 6039092* E-mail. *enquiries@scholastic.co.uk* Web. *www.scholastics.co.uk Art & Craft – Child Education – Cover 2 Cover – Hippo – Infant Projects – Junior Education – Junior Focus – Nursery Projects – Point – Scholastic – Scholatic Press – Teachers Book Club (Red House) – The Red House*

Schottlander Dental Equipment Supplies (t/a Schottlander) Fifth Avenue, Letchworth Garden City SG6 2WD Tel. *01462 480848* Fax. *01462 482802* E-mail. *sales@schottlander.co.uk* Web. *www.schottlander.com Croform – Crystal – Delphic – Doric – Enigma Teeth – Fidelity – Matchmaker – Matchmate – Natura Teeth – Opus P.C.F. – Opus-Silver – Opuscem – Opusfil – Pegasus – Propaque – Starburst – Starlight – Stents – Verone*

Schott UK Ltd Drummond Road, Stafford ST16 3EL Tel. *01785 223166* Fax. *01785 223522* E-mail. *info.uk@schott.com* Web. *www.schott.com/uk *Ceran (Germany) – *Conturan (Germany) – *Duran (Germany) – *Durapack (Germany) – *Irox (Germany) – *Mirogard (Germany) – *Pyran S (Germany) – *Robax (Germany) – *Schott Zwiesel (Germany)*

Schroff UK Ltd Grovelands Business Centre Boundary Way, Hemel Hempstead Indl-Est, Hemel Hempstead HP2 7TE Tel. *01442 240471* Fax. *01442 213508* E-mail. *schroff.uk@pentair.com* Web. *www.schroff.co.uk CompacPRO – Comptec – EuropacPRO – Eurorack – PropacPRO – RatiopacPRO – Novastar – Varistar – MultipacPRO*

Schuh Ltd 1 Neilson Square Deans Industrial Estate, Deans, Livingston EH54 8RQ Tel. *01506 460250* Fax. *01506 460251* E-mail. *colin@schuh.co.uk* Web. *www.schuh.co.uk Horni Monkey – Schuh Clothing for Feet – Slik Cinderella – Surgery Original Footwear Co.*

Schumi Hairdressers 18 Britten Street, London SW3 3TU Tel. *020 73526504* Fax. *020 75813245 Schumi*

Schunk Intec Ltd Unit 10 Cromwell Business Centre Howard Way, Interchange Park, Newport Pagnell MK16 9QS Tel. *01908 611127* Fax. *01908 615525* E-mail. *info@gb.schunk.com* Web. *www.gb.schunk.com Celsio – Fortis – Kontec – Lirax – Plustronic – ROTA – Schunk – SINO-T – Tendo – Tribos – Unilock*

Schurter Ltd 8 Clock Park Shripney Road, Bognor Regis PO22 9NH Tel. *01243 810810* Fax. *01243 810800* E-mail. *sales@schurter.co.uk* Web. *www.schurter.co.uk Linebloc – Minibloc – Quadbloc – Safebloc – Stripbloc – Transpillars – Twinbloc*

Schwarzkopf Ltd Oxford House Oxford Road, Aylesbury HP21 8SZ Tel. *01296 314000* Fax. *01296 398012* Web. *www.schwarzkopf.co.uk *Clynol (Germany and Holland) – *Schwarzkopf (Germany and Holland)*

Sciaky Electric Welding Machines Ltd 212 Bedford Avenue, Slough SL1 4RH Tel. *01753 525551* Fax. *01753 821416* E-mail. *info@sciaky.co.uk* Web. *www.sciaky.co.uk Sciaky electric Welding Machines*

Science Engineering & Manufacturing Technologies 14 Upton Road, Watford WD18 0JT Tel. *01923 238441* Fax. *01923 256086* E-mail. *pwhiteman@semta.org.uk* Web. *www.semta.org.uk ECIS – EMTA – EMTA Awards Ltd*

Scientific Computers Ltd (Head Office) Jubliee House Jubilee Walk, Crawley RH10 1LQ Tel. *01293 403636* Fax. *01293 403641* E-mail. *alan@scl.com* Web. *www.scl.com I.C.S. - *MKS (U.S.A.)*

Scientific Electro Systems Ltd Purdeys Industrial Estate 1 Rose Way, Rochford SS4 1LY Tel. *01702 530174* Fax. *01702 530200* E-mail. *info@sesystems.co.uk* Web. *www.sesystems.co.uk SE Labs*

Scientific Glass Blowing Co. Ltd 163-165 Higginshaw Lane Royton, Oldham OL2 6HQ Tel. *0161 6214700* Fax. *0161 6270493* E-mail. *sales@sciglass.co.uk* Web. *www.sciglass.co.uk Sciglass*

Scientific Instrument Centre Ltd Unit 4 Leylands Park Nobs Crook, Colden Common, Winchester SO21 1TH Tel. *023 80696092* Fax. *023 80695026* E-mail. *sales@sic.uk.com* Web. *www.sic.uk.com *Miele (Germany)*

Scientific Lubricants Ltd Glendene Depot New Hey Road, Huddersfield HD3 3YW Tel. *01422 375401* Fax. *01422 379666* E-mail. *sales@scientificoil.co.uk* Web. *www.scientificoil.co.uk Euro-Lube*

Scientific Optical Ltd Drury Lane Pondswood Industrial Estate, St Leonards On Sea TN38 9YA Tel. *01424 430371* Fax. *01424 441639* E-mail. *sales@scientificoptical.com* Web. *www.scientificoptical.com Scientific Optics Ltd*

Scipac Ltd Unit D7 Broad Oak Enterprise Village, Sittingbourne ME9 8AQ Tel. *01795 423077* Fax. *01795 426942* E-mail. *mail@scipac.com* Web. *www.scipac.com Scigen*

Sciss Ltd 9 Larkstore Park Lodge Road, Staplehurst, Tonbridge TN12 0QY Tel. *01580 890582* Fax. *01580 890583* E-mail. *sales@sciss.co.uk* Web. *www.sciss.co.uk OMAX*

S.C.L Mobile Communications 38 Swinburne Road, Abingdon OX14 2HD Tel. *0800 0856377* Fax. *01235 527003* E-mail. *sclmobilecom@aol.co.uk* Web. *www.sclmobilecommunications.co.uk mobiles*

The Scobie & Junor Group Ltd 1 Singer Road Kelvin Industrial Estate, East Kilbride, Glasgow G75 0XS Tel. *01355 237041* Fax. *01355 263585* E-mail. *info@scobiesdirect.com* Web. *www.scobie-junor.co.uk Henkovac – Scotnet*

Sco-Fro Group Ltd 229 St Vincent Street, Glasgow G2 5QY Tel. *0141 2237707* Fax. *0141 2214701* E-mail. *stewart.macliver@scofro.com* Web. *www.scofro.com *Galloway – *Sco-fro – *Seaspray*

S Collins & Company Ltd Ascot Road, Nottingham NG8 5HD Tel. *0115 9425522* Fax. *0115 9425405* E-mail. *fcollins@proweb.co.uk* Web. *www.collinscashandcarry.co.uk Super C's*

S Com Group Ltd Buckingham House Buckingham Street, Aylesbury HP20 2YD Tel. *01296 311411* Fax. *01296 480688* E-mail. *response@scom.com* Web. *www.scom.com Recruitment agency – Total Recruitment Solutions – Value Management*

Scope Engineers Ltd Unit 4 Beverley Business Centre St. Nicholas Road, Beverley HU17 0QT Tel. *01482 882590* Fax. *01482 867309* E-mail. *info@scopeuk.fsnet.co.uk* Web. *www.scopeuk.co.uk Northern jackson equipment*

Scorpion Power Systems Shenton House Walworth Road, Walworth Business Park, Andover SP10 5LH Tel. *0844 8884445* Fax. *0844 8884446* E-mail. *info@shentongroup.co.uk* Web. *www.shentongroup.co.uk Power House Generators – Powerfirm – Telegen Generators*

Scotcrest Glentana Mill West Stirling Street, Alva FK12 5EN Tel. *01259 761827* Fax. *01259 769445* E-mail. *sales@scotcrest.co.uk* Web. *www.scotcrest.co.uk Scotcrest Uk Ltd*

Scotia Instrumentation Ltd Aberdeen Science & Technology Park Balgownie Road, Bridge of Don, Aberdeen AB22 8GT Tel. *01224 222888* Fax. *01224 826299* E-mail. *info@scotia-computing.com* Web. *www.scotia-instrumentation.com Scotia*

Scot J C B Ltd Millbrook Road Kingstown Industrial Estate, Carlisle CA3 0EU Tel. *01228 536331* Fax. *01228 514698* E-mail. *enquiries@scot-jcb.co.uk* Web. *www.scot-jcb.co.uk Atlas Copco – Benford – J.C.B.*

Scotland Electronics 28 West Road Greshop Industrial Estate, Forres IV36 2GW Tel. *01309 671339* Fax. *01309 678909* E-mail. *diane.middleton@scotlandelectronics.co.uk* Web. *www.scotlandelectronics.co.uk SEIL – SEIL*

Scott & Fyfe Ltd Tayport Works Links Road, Tayport DD6 9EE Tel. *01382 554000* Fax. *01382 552170* E-mail. *solutions@scott-fyfe.com* Web. *www.scott-fyfe.com Bacloc – Polymat 'Hi-Flow' – Scotknit – Scotknit 3D – Scotloop – Scotube – Scotweave – T-RIM – Textron – Textron - Scotweave - Scotube - Polymat - Polymat - "Hi-Flow" - Scotloop - Scotknit - Scotknit 3D - T-TRIM - Bacloc*

Scott International Ltd Pimbo Road, Skelmersdale WN8 9RA Tel. *01695 727171* Fax. *01695 711775* E-mail. *plarge@tycoint.com* Web. *www.scottint.com AIR-PAK FIFTY – Alert – Cenpaq – Chemview – CIVIC Chemi Hood – Contor 300/Contor 500 – Contour – Contour 100 – Control – Data Carrier – Eagle 160 – Easycom – EC10 – EC12 – EC4 – EC8 – EH10 – EH12 – EH4 – EH8 – Elsa – EN397 – EN812 – Envoy – Firstbase+ – Flite – Flite Escape – Focus – G39 – Gemini – Hushair – IRIS – Leak Alert – M98 – Mini SA – Modulair – Panaseal – PAPR - Proflow SC – PAPR-Tornado – Phantom – Phantom – Powerpak – Pro 2000 – Profile 2 – Profile 2tm – Proflow 2/Actoflow – Proflow SC – Proflow SC – Proflow SC Asbestos – Promask – ProPak – Protector – Protector AFU 300 – Protector AFU 600 – Protector Torweld – Protector Vision 2 – Proton – Quadscan – R40 – R60 – RAS Asbestos – Ras/Ras astestic – Revolair – Sabre – Sabre Elsa – Sabrecom – Sari – Scott – Scott M'95 NBC Respirator – Scout – Sentinel 16 – Sentinel II – Sentinel VI 6 – Sigma 2 – Silner – Silner 12, Silner RG, Silner R40/R60 – Spectra VU – Style 300 – Style 600 – T-A-Line – T-Power – Tornado – Tuffmaster – Tuffmaster/Style 600/style 300/First Base – Ventura – Vision*

Scottish Daily Newspaper Society 48 Palmerston Place, Edinburgh EH12 5DE Tel. *0131 2204353* Fax. *0131 2204344* E-mail. *info@spef.org.uk* Web. *www.spef.org.uk Scottish Print Employers Federation*

Scottish Health Innovations 206 St Vincent Street, Glasgow G2 5SG Tel. *0141 2487334* Fax. *0141 2486454* E-mail. *gillian.taylor@shil.co.uk* Web. *www.shil.co.uk OnTrack – Prism Glasses*

Scottish & Newcastle Pub Co. 2-4 Broadway Park South Gyle Broadway, Edinburgh EH12 9JZ Tel. *08459 009074* Fax. *0131 3143273* E-mail. *enquiries@s-npubcompany.co.uk* Web. *www.snpubs.co.uk Beamish Black – Beamish Red – Beck's – Castaway – Courage Best Bitter – Directors Bitter – Foster's Ice – Fosters – Holsten Pils – John Smith's – Kronenbourg 1664 – McEwan's Export – McEwans Larger – Miller Genuine Draft – Miller Pilsner – Newcastle Brown Ale – Theakston Best Bitter – Theakston Old Peculier*

Scottish Quest 49 Castle Gate Uddingston, Glasgow G71 7HU Tel. *01698 816100* Fax. *01698 814846* E-mail. *info@scottishquest.com* Web. *www.scottishquest.com 1745 Trading Company*

Scottish & Southern Energy P.L.C. Energy Sales Inveralmond House 200 Dunkeld Road, Perth PH1 3AQ Tel. *01738 456000* Fax. *01256 304269* E-mail. *marketing.enquiries@sse.com* Web. *www.sse.com Atlantic Electric and Gas – S W A L E C – Scottish Hydro Electric – Southern Electric*

Scottish & Southern Energy plc Inveralmond House 200 Dunkeld Road, Perth PH1 3AQ Tel. *0800 0727282* Fax. *01738 456520* E-mail. *info@scottish-southern.co.uk* Web. *www.sse.com H.E.*

Scottish Youth Hostel 7 Glebe Crescent, Stirling FK8 2JA Tel. *01786 891400* Fax. *01786 891333* E-mail. *syha@syha.org.uk* Web. *www.hostellingscotland.com Scottish Youth Hostels Assoc*

Scott & Newman Ltd 4 Longbow Close, Shrewsbury SY1 3GZ Tel. *01743 452040* Fax. *01743 452044* E-mail. *ro@snpots.co.uk* Web. *www.scottandnewman.co.uk *Plover – *Salopian Gold*

Robert Scott & Sons Oakview Mills Manchester Road, Greenfield, Oldham OL3 7HG Tel. *01457 873931* Fax. *01457 819490* E-mail. *sales@robert-scott.co.uk* Web. *www.robert-scott.co.uk Abbey*

Scotts Co. Ltd Paper Mill Lane Bramford, Ipswich IP8 4BZ Tel. *01473 830492* Web. *www.scottsinternational.com Aquamaster – Greenmaster – Levington TPMC – Osmocote – Sierrablen – Sierrablen – Sportsmaster – Turf chemicals*

Scotwood Interiors Ltd 48 Milton Road East Kilbride, Glasgow G74 5BU Tel. *01355 241727* Fax. *01355 241601* E-mail. *jim@scotwood.com* Web. *www.scotwood.com Armstrong (United Kingdom) – Dexion (United Kingdom) – Dinn (United Kingdom) – Komfort (United Kingdom) – Tenon (United Kingdom)*

Screen Systems Wire Workers Ltd Haydock Lane Industrial Estate Haydock Merseyside, St Helens WA11 9UY Tel. *01942 272895* Fax. *01942 274257*

E-mail. *david.greenall@screensystems.com*
Web. *www.screensystems.com Agatex – Metal Bells – Metal Belts – Screentex – Wedgewire – Woven Wire*

Screwfast Foundations Ltd Unit 7c Smallford Works Smallford Lane, Smallford, St Albans AL4 0SA
Tel. *01727 821282* Fax. *01727 828098*
E-mail. *info@screwfast.com* Web. *www.aardvarksi.com ScrewFast Foundations Ltd (United Kingdom)*

Wilfred Scruton Ltd Providence Foundry Foxholes, Driffield YO25 3QQ Tel. *01262 470221* Fax. *01262 470335*
E-mail. *info@wilfredscruton.co.uk*
Web. *www.wilfredscruton.co.uk Wilfred Scruton*

Sculpture Grain Ltd Warren Court Farm Knockholt Road, Halstead, Sevenoaks TN14 7ER Tel. *01959 534060*
Fax. *01959 522436* E-mail. *mick.sculpturegrinds@virgin.net Sculpture Grain*

S D C Industries Ltd 18 Colvilles Place Kelvin Industrial Estate, East Kilbride, Glasgow G75 0PZ Tel. *01355 265959*
Fax. *01355 265484* E-mail. *info@sdcindustries.co.uk*
Web. *www.sdcindustries.co.uk 3rd Harmonic Filter – Varcap – Varmatic Lightmaster – Varmatic Senator – Varpac*

S D L Atlas PO Box 162, Stockport SK1 3JW
Tel. *0161 4808485* Fax. *0161 4808580*
E-mail. *test@sdlatlas.com* Web. *www.sdlatlas.com Shirley*

S D Plastering 50 Chudleigh Road, Plymouth PL4 7HU
Tel. *07875 460912* E-mail. *sdanplastering@yahoo.co.uk*
Web. *www.plasterersinplymouth.co.uk sd plastering*

S D System Solutions Ltd 129 Devizes Road Hilperton, Trowbridge BA14 7QJ Tel. *01225 751822*
Fax. *01225 764863* E-mail. *info@sdss.co.uk*
Web. *www.sdss.co.uk SDSS*

Seabourne Forwarding Group International Distribution Centre Crabtree Road, Thorpe, Egham TW20 8RS
Tel. *01784 222800* Fax. *01784 222801*
E-mail. *info@seabourne-group.com*
Web. *www.seabourne-group.com Seabourne Express Courier*

Seac Ltd 46 Chesterfield Road, Leicester LE5 5LP
Tel. *0116 2739501* Fax. *0116 2738373*
E-mail. *david.buckley@seac.uk.com* Web. *www.seac.uk.com Lightning Stranglehold – Polytop*

Seafield Logistics Ltd Unit 1 The Point Coach Road, Shireoaks, Worksop S81 8BW Tel. *01909 475561*
Fax. *01909 501043* E-mail. *sales@seafield.co.uk*
Web. *www.seafield.co.uk Seafield*

Seagems Ltd Long Rock Industrial Estate Long Rock, Penzance TR20 8HX Tel. *01736 335840* Fax. *01736 332033*
E-mail. *marcusprice@seagems.co.uk*
Web. *www.seagems.co.uk Sea Gems*

Sea Harris East Tarbert, Isle of Harris HS3 3DB
Tel. *01859 502007* Fax. *07760 216555*
E-mail. *seumas@seaharris.co.uk* Web. *www.seaharris.co.uk Sea Harris*

Seahorse Pools Ltd Le Pavillion De Bel Air La Rue De Bel-Air, St Mary, Jersey JE3 3ED Tel. *01534 484449*
Fax. *01534 484458 Seahorse*

H Seal & Co. Ltd Church Lane Whitwick, Coalville LE67 5DH
Tel. *01530 832351* Fax. *01530 813382*
E-mail. *sales@hseal.co.uk* Web. *www.hseal.co.uk Seal Brand*

Seal UK Ltd Unit 1 Watkins Close Burnt Mill Industrial Estate, Burnt Mills Industrial Estate, Basildon SS13 1TL
Tel. *01268 722400* Fax. *01268 725864*
Web. *www.sealgraphics.com Bienfang – SEAL – Seal*

Seamless Aluminium International Ltd Unit 6b Solihull Building Trade Centre Richmond Road, Solihull B92 7RN
Tel. *0121 7654355* Fax. *0121 7645603*
E-mail. *sales@seaukltd.co.uk*
Web. *www.seamlessaluminium.ie AES – Atral, Daitem – Neowave – SEA – Videx*

A Searle & Co. Ltd Unit 24 Bourne Road Industrial Park Bourne Road, Dartford DA1 4BZ Tel. *01322 529119*
Fax. *01322 528528* E-mail. *info@asearle.co.uk*
Web. *www.asearle.co.uk Water in fuel detection capsules*

Searle Manufacturing 20 Davies Way, Fareham PO14 1AR
Tel. *01329 822222* Fax. *01329 821238*
E-mail. *sales@searle.co.uk* Web. *www.searle.co.uk Searle*

Sears Manufacturing Company Europe Ltd Unit 33 Rassau Industrial Estate Rassau, Ebbw Vale NP23 5SD
Tel. *01495 304518* Fax. *01495 304452*
E-mail. *info@searsseating.co.uk* Web. *www.searsseating.net Fabriform – URS*

Seatem Seatem House 39 Moreland Street, London EC1V 8BB Tel. *020 70148450* Fax. *020 70148451*
E-mail. *commercial@seatem.com*
Web. *www.applausegroups.com BOCS*

Seaton Blinds Unit 10 Hartlepool Enterprise Centre Brougham Terrace, Hartlepool TS24 8EY Tel. *01429 262565*
Fax. *01429 264304* E-mail. *info@seatonblinds.co.uk*
Web. *www.seatonblinds.co.uk Decora, Sunwood*

Seawork UK Ltd 43 Langdon Park Road, london N6 5PT
Tel. *7810447618* Fax. *208 34160555*
E-mail. *john@seawork.biz Seawork*

Sebakmt UK Ltd Unit C Beversbrook Centre Redman Road, Calne SN11 9PR Tel. *01249 816181* Fax. *01249 816186*
E-mail. *sales@sebakmtuk.com* Web. *www.sebakmtuk.com Arm Sangyo – Arrow – CableMate – Chicago Steel Tape CST – Correlux P1 – Ferrolux – Hydrolux – Lasermark – Loop-a-Line – Metrotech Corporation – SebaKMT – Sebalog – Sensistor – Teletech*

Sebo UK Ltd 1 The Merlin Centre Lancaster Road, Cressex Business Park, High Wycombe HP12 3QL
Tel. *01494 465533* Fax. *01494 461044*
E-mail. *info@sebo.co.uk* Web. *www.sebo.co.uk Sebo*

S E C Industrial Battery Co. Ltd Thorney Weir House Thorney Mill Road, Iver SL0 9AQ Tel. *01895 431543*
Fax. *01895 431880* E-mail. *brian.harper@secbattery.com*
Web. *www.secbattery.com *Cellyte (Europe, The Far East and USA) – *Microlyte (The Far East)*

Seckford Wines Dock Lane Melton, Woodbridge IP12 1PE
Tel. *01394 446622* Fax. *01394 446633*
E-mail. *sales@seckfordwines.co.uk*
Web. *www.seckfordwines.co.uk Seckford Wine Agency*

Seco Engineering Co. Ltd 32 Reading Road South, Fleet GU52 7QL Tel. *01252 622333* Fax. *01252 623888*
E-mail. *m.appleton@secoeng.co.uk*
Web. *www.secoeng.co.uk Bandit (United Kingdom) – Beltit (United Kingdom) – Beveller (United Kingdom) – Electro-Wand (United Kingdom)*

Second Nature Ltd 10 Malton Road, London W10 5UP
Tel. *020 89600212* Fax. *020 89608700*
E-mail. *trevor.schragger@secondnature.co.uk*
Web. *www.secondnature.co.uk 3rd Dimension – Second Nature*

Seco Tools UK Ltd 4 Kinwarton Farm Road Kinwarton, Alcester B49 6EL Tel. *01789 764341* Fax. *01789 761170*
E-mail. *uk.sales@secotools.com* Web. *www.secotools.com Bifix – Crownloc – E.P.B. – Jabro – Minimaster – Octomill – Performax – Quattromill – Seco – *Seco-Flex (Sweden) – *Secodex (Sweden) – *Secolor (Sweden) – Secomax – *Seconomy (Sweden) – *Snap-Tap (Sweden)*

Secure A Site UK Ltd 168 Church Lane, London NW9 8SP
Tel. *08455 550999* Fax. *08451 304592*
E-mail. *sales@scaffoldalarms.com*
Web. *www.scaffoldalarms.com Secure A Site*

Securefast PLC Unit 6 Cedars Business Centre Avon Road, Cannock WS11 1QJ Tel. *01543 501600* Fax. *01902 609327*
E-mail. *sales@securefast.co.uk* Web. *www.securefast.co.uk Pinson – Securifast*

Secure Holidays 5 Signet Court Swann Road, Cambridge CB5 8LA Tel. *020 33703810* Fax. *0845 2903381*
E-mail. *bookings@secureholidays.co.uk*
Web. *www.secureholidays.co.uk Chubb – Dudley – Fireking – Rosengrens – Royal – SMP*

The Secure-Store 1 Works Road Corner of Pixmore Avenue, Letchworth Garden City SG6 1FR Tel. *01462 674666*
E-mail. *letchworthstorage@yahoo.co.uk*
Web. *www.thesecure-store.com The Secure-store*

Secure Telecom UK Ltd Unit 7 Poltonhall Industrial Estate, Lasswade EH18 1BW Tel. *08707 776670*
Fax. *0870 7776672* E-mail. *info@securetelecom.co.uk*
Web. *www.securetelecom.co.uk Kingston – Transcend*

Securikey Ltd Unit 5 Springlakes Estate Deadbrook Lane, Aldershot GU12 4UH Tel. *01252 311888* Fax. *01252 343950*
E-mail. *enquiries@securikey.co.uk*
Web. *www.securikey.co.uk Euro Grade – Housesafe – Keybak – Master – Premier – Protector – Safeguard – Securikey – Strongbox*

Securistyle Ltd Kingsmead Industrial Estate, Cheltenham GL51 7RE Tel. *01242 221200* Fax. *01242 520828*
E-mail. *paul_cook@securistyle.co.uk*
Web. *www.securistyle.co.uk Defender – Koncert – President – Senator – Sterling – Vector – Virage – Viscount*

Securitas Mobile Trafalgar Wharf Hamilton Road, Cosham, Portsmouth PO6 4PX Tel. *023 92372502*
Fax. *023 92370054* E-mail. *info@securitas.com*
Web. *www.securitas.com SECURITAS*

Securitas Security Services 203-205 Lower Richmond Road, Richmond TW9 4LN Tel. *020 83926000* Fax. *020 83922088*
E-mail. *jenny.campbell@securitas.uk.com*
Web. *www.securitas.com Securitas Guarding Services*

Securit World Ltd Spectrum House Hillview Gardens, London NW4 2JQ Tel. *020 82663300* Fax. *020 82031027*
E-mail. *ed.heyden@securitworld.com*
Web. *www.securitworld.com Comb Bind – Junior Bind – Seal-It – Securit – *Senior Bind (U.S.A.) – Wire Bind*

Seeability 1a Hook Road, Epsom KT19 8FQ
Tel. *01372 755000* Fax. *01372 755001*
E-mail. *enquiries@seeability.org* Web. *www.seeability.org SeeABILITY*

Seetec 75-77 Main Road, Hockley SS5 4RG
Tel. *01702 201070* Fax. *01702 201224*
E-mail. *info@seetec.co.uk* Web. *www.seetec.co.uk GP Professional – GP Professional - software for general practice*

Sega Europe Ltd 27 Great West Road, Brentford TW8 9BW
Tel. *020 89953399* Fax. *020 89964499*
E-mail. *info@soe.sega.co.uk* Web. *www.sega.com Dreamcast*

Segezha Packaging Priory Road, Rochester ME2 2BD
Tel. *01634 716701* Fax. *01634 717468*
E-mail. *uk@segezha-packaging.com*
Web. *www.segezha-packaging.com Cadisac – Ecosack – Fapsacks – Hypersack*

Sehlbach & Whiting Ltd Exclusive House Oldfield Road, Maidenhead SL6 1TA Tel. *01628 591600*
Fax. *01628 770761* E-mail. *sales@sehlbach.co.uk*
Web. *www.sehlbach.co.uk Exclusive*

Seiki Systems Ltd (a division of Kenard Engineering Group) Olivier House 18 Marine Parade, Brighton BN2 1TL
Tel. *01273 666999* Fax. *01273 602564*
E-mail. *sales@seikisystems.co.uk*
Web. *www.seikisystems.co.uk Direct DNC – NC Program Manager – Networked DNC*

Sekisui Alveo Ag Queens Chambers Eleanors Cross, Dunstable LU6 1SU Tel. *01582 600456* Fax. *01582 600567*
E-mail. *info.gb@sekisuialveo.com*
Web. *www.sekisuialveo.com Alveolen – Alveolit – Alveolux*

Selco Builders Warehouse 1 Charlotte Road Stirchley, Birmingham B30 2BT Tel. *0121 4333355* Fax. *0121 4585996*
Web. *www.selcobw.com Selco*

Selden Mast Ltd Lederle Lane, Gosport PO13 0FZ
Tel. *01329 504000* Fax. *01329 504049*
E-mail. *info@seldenmast.co.uk* Web. *www.seldenmast.com Furlex – Proctor Masts – Selden Mass*

Selden Research Ltd Bradshaws Yard Staden Lane, Buxton SK17 9RZ Tel. *01298 26226* Fax. *01298 26540*
E-mail. *sales@selden.co.uk* Web. *www.selden.co.uk A.C.T. – Selclen Super – Select – Selgiene – Selmex – Selosol – Squad*

Select Cables Ltd Painter Close, Portsmouth PO3 5RS
Tel. *023 92652552* Fax. *023 92655277*
E-mail. *sales@selectcables.com*
Web. *www.selectcables.com CM Srl – Test-um – Times Microwave*

Selections Mail Order Ltd Southover House Tolpuddle, Dorchester DT2 7YG Tel. *01305 848725* Fax. *01305 848516*
E-mail. *sales@selections.com* Web. *www.selections.com selections*

Selective Asia 72b St Georges Road, Brighton BN2 1EF
Tel. *01273 670001* E-mail. *contact@selectiveasia.com*
Web. *www.selectiveasia.com Selective Travel Group*

Selecto Part UK Ltd Top Farm House Shenington, Banbury OX15 6LZ Tel. *01295 670734* Fax. *01295 678170*
E-mail. *info@selecto-part.co.uk*
Web. *www.selecto-part.co.uk Selecto Flash*

Selectronix Ltd Unit 5-6 Minerva House Calleva Park, Aldermaston, Reading RG7 8NE Tel. *0118 9817387*
Fax. *0118 9817608* E-mail. *sales@selectronix.co.uk*
Web. *www.selectronix.co.uk ACPA – Amphenol – Binder – Bogen Electronics – Carlo Gavazzi – Circuit Assembly – DCT – Digisound – EBT – Emistop – Fibox – Foxconn – Greenwich – Hammond – Heito – Honda Connectors – Jaguar – Kingbright – LTW – LTW - Honda Connectors - Methode - Stratos Lightwave - Foxconn - DCT - Woodhead - RJ-Lnxx - Circuit Assembly - SAIA Bugess - Switchcraft - Rectron - ACPA - Greenwich - Heito - Widmaier - Bogen Electronics - Hammond - Fibox - Phoenix Contact - Binder - Omron - Carlo Gavazzi - Otto MEC - Digisound - Kingbright - EBT - Tyco - Weiland - Amphenol - Madison - EMISTOP. – Madison – Methode – Omron – Otto MEC – Phoenix Contact – Rectron – RJ-Lynxx – SAIA Bugess – Stratos Lightwave – Switchcraft – Termacon – Tyco – Weiland – Widmaier – Woodhead – Xtreme*

Selling Sciences 20 High Street, Watlington OX49 5PY
Tel. *01491 614962* Fax. *01491 613367*
E-mail. *sales@sellingsciences.com*
Web. *www.sellingsciences.com Sales Performance*

Selo UK Ltd 3-4 Bankfield Court Commercial Road, Wirral CH62 3NN Tel. *08452 932910* Fax. *0151 6452202*
E-mail. *uk@selo.com* Web. *www.selo.com Crescent Bee – *Daiei Manufacturing (Japan) – *Emsens (France) – Ferrite Inc – *General Machinery Corp (U.S.A.) – *Kobird (Japan) – *Omori Machinery (Japan) – *P.M.C. (U.S.A.) – *Saccardo Arturo (Italy) – SELO – *Stridhs (Sweden) – *Thiessen (Germany) – *Toyo Jidoki (Japan) – *Toyo Machine Manufacturing Co (Japan) – *Wilevco (U.S.A.)*

Selux UK Ltd Titan Business Centre Spartan Close, Warwick CV34 6RR Tel. *01926 833455* Fax. *01926 339844*
E-mail. *enquire@selux.co.uk* Web. *www.selux.co.uk Artec – Artlights – *Citylights (Germany) – Downlights – *Eutrac (Germany) – L.T.S. – Linear – Se'lux – *Shoplights (Germany) – Silhouette – Skylight*

Selwood Ltd Bournemouth Rd Chandlers Ford, Eastleigh SO53 3ZL Tel. *023 80250137* Fax. *023 80271012*
E-mail. *tony.killick@selwoodpumps.com*
Web. *www.selwoodpumps.com SELWOOD SELPRIME – SELWOOD SIMPLITE – SELWOOD SPATE – SELWOOD "PD" RANGE – SELWOOD "D" RANGE – SELWOOD SELTORQUE – SELWOOD "S" RANGE – SELWOOD "HS" RANGE – SELWOOD "H" RANGE – SELWOOD "C" RANGE*

Selwood Pump Company Ltd 188 Robin Hood Lane, Birmingham B28 0LG Tel. *0121 7775631*
Fax. *0121 7022195*
E-mail. *graham.gallen@selwood-pumps.co.uk*
Web. *www.selwood-pumps.com Kral – Seladin – Selite - Seladin - Selpack – Selpack Pumps – Vican*

Sem Ltd Faraday House Faraday Way, Orpington BR5 3QT
Tel. *01689 884700* Fax. *01689 884884*
E-mail. *info@sem.co.uk* Web. *www.sem.co.uk S.E.M.*

Sembcorp Bournemouth Water Ltd George Jessell House Francis Avenue, Bournemouth BH11 8NX
Tel. *01202 591111* Fax. *01202 597022*

E-mail. *itmanager@bwhwater.co.uk* Web. *www.bwhwater.co.uk Airmec (United Kingdom) – Aquaprint (United Kingdom) – Aquatare (United Kingdom)*

Semikron UK Ltd Semikron International GmbH 9 Harforde Court John Tate Road, Hertford SG13 7NW Tel. *01992 584677* Fax. *01992 554942* E-mail. *p.newman@semikron.com* Web. *www.semikron.com Semicell – *Semikron (Germany) – Semipack – Semipont – Semistack – Semitrans – Skiip*

Senator International Ltd Sykeside Drive Altham Business Park, Altham, Accrington BB5 5YE Tel. *01282 725000* Fax. *01282 775039* E-mail. *jsimpson@senator.co.uk* Web. *www.senatorinternational.co.uk Pulse – Sentrix*

Senior Aerospace Bird Bellows Radnor Park Industrial Estate, Congleton CW12 4UQ Tel. *01260 271411* Fax. *01260 270910* E-mail. *apbird@bird-bellows.co.uk* Web. *www.sabird-bellows.co.uk Gimbal – Vibreaker*

Senior Hargreaves Ltd Lord Street, Bury BL9 0RG Tel. *0161 7645082* Fax. *0161 7622333* E-mail. *sales@senior-hargreaves.co.uk* Web. *www.hargreaves-ductwork.co.uk Air-o-leaf – Air-o-seal – Air-o-strip – Air-o-tite – Air-o-turn – Airoduct – Freshair – H.F.D. – Welfold – Welift*

Senlac Stone Ltd Rutherford Business Park Marley Lane, Battle TN33 0TY Tel. *01424 772244* Fax. *01424 772249* E-mail. *senlacstone@aol.com* Web. *www.senlacstone.co.uk Senlac*

Senova Ltd 49 North Road Great Abington, Abington, Cambridge CB21 6AS Tel. *01223 890777* Fax. *01223 890666* E-mail. *info@senova.uk.com* Web. *www.senova.com JB Diego – Mascani – Scout Winter Wheat – Spring Oilseed Rape – Tardis Winter Oat – Triticale*

Sensemaster Ltd Unit 1 Severn Bridge Symondscliffe Way Portskewett, Caldicot NP26 5PW Tel. *01291 422022* Fax. *01291 420022* E-mail. *mail@sensemaster.co.uk* Web. *www.sensemaster.co.uk Sensemaster*

Sensient Oldmedow Road, Kings Lynn PE30 4LA Tel. *01553 669444* Fax. *01553 776409* E-mail. *mark.connolly@eu.sensient-tech.com* Web. *www.sensient-tech.com Ariabel – Arianor – Canacert – Euroblend – Eurocert – Eurocert Instant – Eurocol – Euroglow – Eurogran – Eurolake – Eurosol – Eurovit – Fine Grind Colours – Mastercote – Usacert – Usagran – Usalake*

Sensortek PO Box 222, Bury St Edmunds IP28 6EE Tel. *01284 728150* Fax. *01284 728155* E-mail. *sales@sensortek.co.uk* Web. *www.sensortek.co.uk *Contrinex (Switzerland) – *Disoric (Germany) – *Euchner (Germany) – *Leuzer (Germany) – *NAIS (Japan) – Proxistor – *Seeka (Japan) – *Sensopart (Germany) – *Sunx (Japan) – *Telco (Denmark) – *Visloux (Germany) – *Wenglor (Germany)*

Sercal Electronics Ltd 33 Arksey Lane Bentley, Doncaster DN5 0RX Tel. *01302 739998* Fax. *01302 739739* E-mail. *sales@sercalelectronics.co.uk* Web. *www.sercal-testequipmentsales.co.uk Fluke, Robin, AVO Megger, Chauvin Arnoux, Martindale, Kewtech, KewTechnik, Alphatek, ACT Meters, Seaward.*

Serious P R First Floor Davidson House Glenavy Road Business Park, Moira, Craigavon BT67 0LT Tel. *028 92616840* Fax. *028 90190310* Web. *www.seriouspr.com Serious PR*

Serjeants 25 The Crescent, Leicester LE1 6RX Tel. *0116 2332626* Fax. *0116 2330551* E-mail. *mail@serjeants.co.uk* Web. *www.serjeants.co.uk Serjeants*

Sertronics Ltd 45 Regal Drive Walsall Enterprise Park, Walsall WS2 9HQ Tel. *01922 624412* Fax. *01922 608008* E-mail. *admin@sertronics.org* Web. *www.sertronics.com Toshiba – Sharp – Sanyo – Hitachi*

Servaclean Bar Systems Ltd Gower Street, Bradford BD5 7JF Tel. *01274 390038* Fax. *01274 394840* E-mail. *info@servaclean.co.uk* Web. *www.servaclean.co.uk *Barframe – *Basketshelf – *Glasshelf – *Icechest – *ServaClean*

Server Parts Ltd Unit 3 Castle Grove Studios 20 Castle Grove Drive, Leeds LS6 4BR Tel. *08453 457875* Fax. *0845 3457897* E-mail. *sales@serverparts.co.uk* Web. *www.serverparts.co.uk HP – IBM – Sun Microsystems*

Service Engines Newcastle Ltd Great Lime Road, Newcastle Upon Tyne NE12 6RU Tel. *0191 2681000* Fax. *0191 2160838* E-mail. *admin@serviceengines.co.uk* Web. *www.serviceengines.co.uk Atlas Copco – Benford – Deutz – F.G. Wilson – Kubota – Lister and Petter – Manitou – Poclain Case – Stanley*

Service Partitions Ltd 2nd Floor Freedom House 5 Abbeyfields, Bury St Edmunds IP33 1AQ Tel. *01842 811339* Fax. *01842 812066* E-mail. *sales@servicegroupinteriors.com* Web. *www.servicegroupinteriors.com Alpha – Armstrong – Clips – Deanes – Komfort – Mistral – Pledge*

Service Point UK Ltd 192-198 Vauxhall Bridge Road, London SW1V 1DX Tel. *020 75200200* Fax. *020 78375497* E-mail. *infouk@servicepointuk.com* Web. *www.servicepointuk.com L.D.O. Geodraft – L.D.O. Geofilm – L.D.O. Geomatt – Parque*

Servicom High Tech Ltd Unit 8 The I O Centre Nash Road, Redditch B98 7AS Tel. *01527 510800* Fax. *01527 510975* E-mail. *sales@servicom.co.uk* Web. *www.servicom.co.uk Icom – Motorola – Tait*

Servitir 17c Windmill Way West Ramparts Business Park, Berwick Upon Tweed TD15 1TB Tel. *08453 132212* Fax. *0845 3132213* E-mail. *info@servitir.com* Web. *www.servitir.com SERVITIR*

Servo & Electronic Sales Ltd Conector House Harden Road Lydd, Romney Marsh TN29 9LX Tel. *01797 322500* Fax. *01797 321569* E-mail. *info@servoconnectors.co.uk* Web. *www.servoconnectors.co.uk *Alps (Japan) – Alps Keiki – *C-Y (R.O.C.) (China) – D.D.K. – *Minipa (Hong Kong) – *Sanwa (Japan) – Sesquel*

S E S Glos Ltd Unit 19a Lower Road Trading Estate, Ledbury HR8 2DJ Tel. *01531 637206* Fax. *01531 631152* E-mail. *service@sparcerosion.biz* Web. *www.sparcerosion.biz Glevum – Hurco – Sparcatron*

Sessions Of York Huntington Road, York YO31 9HS Tel. *01904 659224* Fax. *01904 644888* E-mail. *nick.barnes@ppandp.co.uk* Web. *www.sessionsofyork.co.uk Compuprint – Detex – Duropaque – Permaprint – Picturecolour – Useful Labels*

Ses Sterling Ltd Unit 2 Harcourt Business, Telford TF7 4PW Tel. *01952 686196* Fax. *01952 684286* E-mail. *sales@ses-sterling.com* Web. *www.ses-sterling.com Agro – Goliath – Kabex – Pliobord – Pliosil – Pliospire – Tehalit*

Setten Ixl Ltd Waterloo Road, Llandrindod Wells LD1 6BH Tel. *01597 827800* Fax. *01597 827847* E-mail. *admin@ixl.uk.com* Web. *www.ixl.uk.com Bulldog – Premier - HangfileBulldogPremier - Grip – Premier-Grip – Premier-Hangfile*

Sevcon Ltd Kingsway South Team Valley Trading Estate, Gateshead NE11 0QA Tel. *0191 4979000* Fax. *0191 4874223* E-mail. *info@sevcon.com* Web. *www.sevcon.com Micropak – Millipak – Powergauge – Powerpac – Powerpak – Sevcon*

Seven Sea's Ltd Hedon Road, Hull HU9 5NJ Tel. *01482 375234* Fax. *01482 374345* E-mail. *sevenseaspressoffice@virgohealth.com* Web. *www.sseas.com Chamotan – D.X.3 – Epanoil – Fax Canning Oil – Faxfry – Fosol – Mainstay – Seven Seas – Solvitax – Vitapet*

Severn Business Interiors Ltd Unit 4 Kidderminster Road, Ombersley, Droitwich WR9 0JH Tel. *01905 621691* Fax. *01905 621345* E-mail. *sales@shirebusinessinteriors.co.uk* Web. *www.shirebusinessinteriors.co.uk Commercial Furniture Supplies (United Kingdom) – Shire Contract Furniture (United Kingdom) – Shire Design Consultants (United Kingdom)*

Severn Glocon Ltd Olympus Park Quedgeley, Gloucester GL2 4NF Tel. *08452 232040* Fax. *0845 2232041* E-mail. *reception@severnglocon.co.uk* Web. *www.severnglocon.com N. Series – P Series – Series 2000 – Series 3000/4000 – Series 5000 – Series 6000 – Series 7000 – Series 8000 – Series 9000 – W. Series*

Severn Trent Water Customer Relations Po Box 5310, Coventry CV3 9FJ Tel. *0800 7834444* Fax. *0121 7224800* E-mail. *customer.relations@severntrent.co.uk* Web. *www.stwater.co.uk Retrocat – S.T. – Severn Trent Water – Severn Trent Water ST – Spraysafe – Valerie Vole – Waterkey*

Sewaco Ltd 87 Eastgate Deeping St James, Peterborough PE6 8HH Tel. *01778 342202* Fax. *01778 346633* E-mail. *admin@sewaco.co.uk* Web. *www.sewaco.co.uk Hycover – Hyrate Bio Filters – Meterbox Systems*

Seward Ltd Dominion House Eastling Close, Worthing BN14 8HQ Tel. *01903 823077* Fax. *01903 219233* E-mail. *info@seward.co.uk* Web. *www.seward.co.uk Clear-Spin – Cryo sect – Handi-Spin – Stomacher – Stomacher - Clear-Spin - Handi-Spin - Cryo sect*

Sewerin Ltd Walsworth Road, Hitchin SG4 9SP Tel. *01462 634363* E-mail. *info@sewerin.co.uk* Web. *www.sewerin.co.uk Hermann Sewerin GmbH*

S E W Eurodrive Ltd Beckbridge Road Normanton Industrial Estate, Normanton WF6 1QR Tel. *01924 893855* Fax. *01924 893702* E-mail. *info@sew-eurodrive.co.uk* Web. *www.sew-eurodrive.com Movidrive – Movidyn – Movimot – *Moviret (Germany) – Movitrac – Movitron – S.E.W. – SEW - Varimot - Varibloc - Varidisc - Movitrac - Movidrive - Movimot - Movidyn Sales and Service Organisations throughout the world. – *Varibloc (Germany) – *Varidisc (Germany) – *Varimot (Germany)*

Sew Personal Ltd 7 The Dingle Yate, Bristol BS37 7GA Tel. *01454 313166* E-mail. *info@sewpersonal.biz* Web. *www.sewpersonal.co.uk Sew Personal*

Sextons Unit 9 Ferrier Industrial Estate Ferrier Street, London SW18 1SW Tel. *020 88771148* Fax. *020 88707727* E-mail. *sales@sextonslondon.co.uk* Web. *www.sextonslondon.co.uk *Sextons (Worldwide)*

Seymour Manufacturing International Smi Ltd Sutton Hall Farm Sutton Maddock, Shifnal TF11 9NQ Tel. *01952 730630* Fax. *01952 730330* E-mail. *enquiries@seymour-mi.com* Web. *www.seymour-mi.com Tempro – Bio-Gard – Green Door – Cold Stop Curtains – TT33*

Seymour Taylor 57 London Road, High Wycombe HP11 1BS Tel. *01494 552100* Fax. *01494 61157* E-mail. *enquiries@stca.co.uk* Web. *www.stca.co.uk Just Tax*

S F C Wholesale Westminster Chambers Lord Street, Southport PR8 1LF Tel. *01704 548641* Fax. *01704 546412* E-mail. *walter@sfcwholesale.co.uk* Web. *www.sfcwholesale.co.uk *S.F.C. Southern Fried Chicken*

S F M 9 Bancombe Court, Martock TA12 6HB Tel. *01935 822285* Fax. *01935 826199* E-mail. *admin@sfmtechnology.co.uk* Web. *www.sfmtechnology.co.uk SFM Technology Ltd*

S G Magnets Ltd 85 Ferry Lane, Rainham RM13 9YH Tel. *01708 558411* Fax. *01708 554021* E-mail. *sales@sgmagnets.com* Web. *www.sgmagnets.com S.G.M.*

S G System Products Ltd Unit 22 Wharfedale Road, Ipswich IP1 4JP Tel. *01473 240055* Fax. *01473 461616* E-mail. *sales@sgsystems.co.uk* Web. *www.handrails.co.uk AL50 – Citadel – Stargard – Stargard - Stronghold - Strading - Citadel - AL50 – Strading – Stronghold*

S G World Ltd Duchy Road, Crewe CW1 6ND Tel. *01270 500921* Fax. *01270 500220* E-mail. *arnoldhaase@sgworld.com* Web. *www.sgworld.com Safeguard Systems Europe*

Shackell Edwards & Co Corrie Way Bredbury Park Industrial Estate, Bredbury, Stockport SK6 2ST Tel. *0161 4067984* Fax. *0161 4066233* Web. *www.shackelledwards.com 110700 Commodore Black – 118140 Commodore Hi-tone Black – 118185 Intense I.R. Black*

Shades Graphics Ltd Stur Mill Broadstone Hall Road, Stockport SK5 7BY Tel. *0161 4774688* Fax. *0161 4747629* E-mail. *sales@shadesgraphics.co.uk* Web. *www.shadesgraphics.co.uk Shades*

Shading Systems Ltd Unit F5 Innsworth Technology Park Innsworth Lane, Gloucester GL3 1DL Tel. *01452 536000* Fax. *01452 731901* E-mail. *info@shadings.co.uk* Web. *www.shadings.co.uk Crime Guard*

Shakespeare Monofilament UK Ltd Enterprise Way Off Venture Road, Fleetwood FY7 8RY Tel. *01253 858787* Fax. *01253 859595* E-mail. *gary.walsh@jardenuk.co.uk* Web. *www.monofilament.co.uk Shakespeare Monofilament*

Shand Higson & Co. Ltd Lees Road Knowsley Industrial Park, Liverpool L33 7SE Tel. *0151 5492210* Fax. *0151 5491405* E-mail. *info@shandhigson.co.uk* Web. *www.shandhigson.co.uk Scapa Tapes – 3M – tesa – Sekisui – Advance*

Shanks Group plc Astor House Station Road, Bourne End SL8 5YP Tel. *0800 028287* Fax. *01628 524114* E-mail. *customerservices@shanks.co.uk* Web. *www.shanks.co.uk Shanks*

Sharetree Ltd Unit 3 Meadow Mill Eastington Trading Estate Churchend, Eastington, Stonehouse GL10 3RZ Tel. *01453 828642* Fax. *01453 828076* E-mail. *sales@sharetree.co.uk* Web. *www.sharetree.com Cyclone – Rampmaster - hot/cold temperature forcing block - SlimLine – SlimLine – Stress Master – Unizone*

Sharples Stress Engineers Ltd Unit 29 Old Mill Industrial Estate Bamber Bridge, Preston PR5 6SY Tel. *01772 323359* Fax. *01772 316017* E-mail. *sharplesstress@aol.com* Web. *www.sharplesstress.com Senarcom – Sharples – Sharples – Sharples*

Sharp & Nickless Ltd 77 College Street Long Eaton, Nottingham NG10 4NN Tel. *0115 9732169* Fax. *0115 9732169* Web. *www.sharpandnickless.co.uk Sharp & Nickless*

Sharpstuff Event & Business Development Steadman House, High Street East Ilsley, Newbury RG20 7LF Tel. *01635 280654* E-mail. *info@sharpstuff.biz* Web. *www.sharpstuff.co.uk/Contact.asp Sharpstuff*

Shawcity Ltd Unit 91-92 Shrivenham Hundred Business Park Majors Road, Watchfield, Swindon SN6 8TY Tel. *01367 241675* Fax. *01367 242491* E-mail. *info@shawcity.co.uk* Web. *www.shawcity.co.uk AMI – Aplha 3 – *Bacharah Fyrite (U.S.A.) – M.V.I.*

Ena Shaw Ltd Euro Link Lea Green, St Helens WA9 4QF Tel. *01744 851515* Fax. *01744 812412* E-mail. *mark@richardbarrie.co.uk* Web. *www.richardbarrie.co.uk Ena Shaw – Perfect Partners – Richard Barrie*

Frank Shaw Bayonet Ltd Merse Road Moons Moat North Industrial Estate, Redditch B98 9HL Tel. *01527 66241* Fax. *01527 584455* E-mail. *jeremy@frankshaw.co.uk* Web. *www.frankshaw.co.uk Bayonet – Challenge – Solstuds – X.*

Henry Shaw & Sons Ltd Crown Road Bordesley Green, Birmingham B9 4TY Tel. *0121 7725561* Fax. *0121 7666047* E-mail. *sales@henryshaw.co.uk* Web. *www.henryshaw.co.uk H.S.S. – Rifle*

Malcolm W Shaw Church Farm Coughton Fields Lane, Coughton, Alcester B49 6BS Tel. *01789 763453* Fax. *01789 400451* E-mail. *malcomshaw@mwshaw.com* Web. *www.mwshaw.com Hydralogger – Hydrastumper*

Shaw Munster Ltd Winster Grove, Birmingham B44 9EG Tel. *0121 3604279* Fax. *0121 3604265* E-mail. *office@shawmunstergroup.co.uk* Web. *www.shawmunstergroup.co.uk Haskins – R.E.V. Gomm*

Shaws Of Darwen Ltd (a division of Shires Ltd) Higher Waterside Waterside, Darwen BB3 3NX Tel. *01254 775111* Fax. *01254 873462* E-mail. *sales@shawsofdarwen.com* Web. *www.shawsofdarwen.com Faience – Reflectoware – Shaws – Shaws Twintiles – Terracotta*

Shaws Petroleum Ltd Manor Road Farnley Tyas, Huddersfield HD4 6UL Tel. *01484 667744* Fax. *01484 662244* E-mail. *paulsykes@shawspetroleum.co.uk* Web. *www.shawspetroleum.co.uk S.S.S.*

Sheafpower Ltd Wardpower Works Wicker Lane, Sheffield S3 8HQ Tel. *0114 2738855* Fax. *0114 2739780* E-mail. *sales@wardpower.co.uk* Web. *www.wardpower.co.uk Wardpower (United Kingdom)*

Sheardown Engineering Ltd 15 South Road, Harlow CM20 2AP Tel. *01279 421788* Fax. *01279 435642* E-mail. *info@sheardown.co.uk* Web. *www.sheardown.co.uk Admix – Antivac – Aquasaver – Bean – Economix – Founders & finishers – Jacobson – Lotuslyke – Manumix – Mini Seal – Neata Lever – Neata Seal – Neata Spray – Neata Tap – Neata Toggle – Neata Turn – Neataturn – Panelmix – Push Flash – Pushflush – Watasava – Watersaver – Watertimer*

Shearline Precision Engineering Ltd Cambridgeshire Business Park Angel Drove, Ely CB7 4EX Tel. *01353 668668* Fax. *01353 668203* E-mail. *sales@shearline.co.uk* Web. *www.shearline.co.uk Shearline*

Sheen Equipment Greasley Street, Nottingham NG6 8NG Tel. *0115 9272321* Fax. *0115 9770671 Sheen Equipment*

Sheffield United Football Club Ticket Office Bramhall Lane, Sheffield S2 4SU Tel. *08719 951889* Fax. *0870 4428813* E-mail. *boxoffice@sufc.co.uk* Web. *www.sufc.co.uk Sheffield United*

Shelbourne Reynolds Engineering Ltd Shepherds Grove Industrial Estate Stanton, Bury St Edmunds IP31 2AR Tel. *01359 250415* Fax. *01359 250464* E-mail. *info@shelbourne.com* Web. *www.shelbourne.com Shelbourne Reynolds – Shelbourne Reynolds Hectolitre Measure – Shelbourne Reynolds Rape Swather*

Shelectric Control Panel Mnfrs 1 Stone Lane Kinver, Stourbridge DY7 6EQ Tel. *01384 878855* Fax. *01384 878866* E-mail. *frank.shelectric@hotmail.co.uk Shelectric Ltd*

Shelfguard Systems 89 St Leonards Road, Windsor SL4 3BZ Tel. *01753 867257* Fax. *01753 830024* E-mail. *info@shelfguard-systems.co.uk* Web. *www.shelfguard-systems.co.uk *Casio – *Geller – *Hero – *Samsung – *Sharp – *Tec – *Uniwell*

Shelfspan Shelving Systems The Cart Lodge Mayland Hall Farm, Mayland, Chelmsford CM3 6EA Tel. *08450 722385* Fax. *08450 722386* E-mail. *info@shelfspan.co.uk* Web. *www.shelfspan.co.uk *Amco – *Eclipse – *Plate-Mate*

Shelley Thermoformers International Ltd Unit 32 Roman Way Small Business Park London Road, Godmanchester, Huntingdon PE29 2LN Tel. *01480 453651* Fax. *01480 52113* E-mail. *pclarke@cannon-shelley.co.uk* Web. *www.shelley.biz Cannon Shelley – Linearform Thermoformers – Powerform – Shelley – Speedform*

Shell Gas Direct Grand Building 1-3 Strand, London WC2N 5EJ Tel. *020 72573000* Fax. *020 72570101* E-mail. *sgd-enquiries@shell.com* Web. *www.shell.co.uk Quadrant Gas*

Shelters R Us 17-18 Morgan Way Bowthorpe Employment Area, Norwich NR5 9JJ Tel. *01603 743252* Fax. *01603 746927* E-mail. *sales@samsfabrications.co.uk* Web. *www.shelters-r-us.co.uk Shelters r us*

J G Shelton & Co. Ltd The Warren, Ashtead KT21 2SH Tel. *01372 278422* Fax. *01372 279338* E-mail. *tracy.bennett@jg-shelton.co.uk* Web. *www.jg-shelton.co.uk 2000 ES Diamond – Ruby – Sapphire*

Shenu Fashions 3 Western Road, Leicester LE3 0GD Tel. *0116 2543440* Fax. *0116 2470979* E-mail. *info@shenugroup.co.uk* Web. *www.shenugroup.co.uk Angel Kids – Chambo – Little Renown – Natty – Uncle Mick*

Shepherd Engineering Services Ltd Mill Mount, York YO24 1GH Tel. *01904 629151* Fax. *01904 610175* E-mail. *info@ses-ltd.co.uk* Web. *www.ses-ltd.co.uk S.E.S.*

Shepherd Neame Ltd 17 Court Street, Faversham ME13 7AX Tel. *01795 532206* Fax. *01795 538907* E-mail. *company@shepherd-neame.co.uk* Web. *www.shepherd-neame.co.uk Shepherd Neame*

Sheppy Ltd Klondyke Industrial Estate Rushenden Road, Queenborough ME11 5HH Tel. *01795 580181* Fax. *01795 580649* E-mail. *sales@sheppy.ltd.uk* Web. *www.sheppy.ltd.uk Sheppy*

Sherborne Upholstery Ltd Pasture Lane Clayton, Bradford BD14 6LT Tel. *01274 882633* Fax. *01274 815129* E-mail. *sales@sherborne-uph.co.uk* Web. *www.sherborneupholstery.co.uk Comfi-sit Range – Sherborne Occasional Range – Westminster Range*

Shering Weighing Ltd Pitreavie Business Park Queensferry Road, Dunfermline KY11 8UL Tel. *01383 621505* Fax. *01383 620262* E-mail. *sales@shering.com* Web. *www.shering.com Shering*

Sherman Chemicals Ltd Brickfields Business Park, Gillingham SP8 4PX Tel. *01747 823293* Fax. *01747 825383* E-mail. *info@sherchem.co.uk* Web. *www.sherchem.co.uk Thyodene*

Sherwood Agencies Ltd Sherwood House Mutual Mills Aspinall Street, Heywood OL10 4HW Tel. *01706 898100* Fax. *01706 898101* E-mail. *sales@sherwoodagencies.com* Web. *www.sherwoodagencies.com Gino Polli – Grafter – Le Son By Maxim – Maxim – Splash – Suxes – Tamashi*

Sherwood Interiors Ltd The Spire Egypt Road, Nottingham NG7 7GD Tel. *0115 9427870* Fax. *0115 9615505* E-mail. *info@sherwoodinteriors.co.uk* Web. *www.tvedt.co.uk Sherwood Interiors*

Sherwood Systems Ltd Sherwood Systems Ireland Ash Grove Wildflower Way, Belfast BT12 6TA Tel. *028 90668585* Fax. *028 90665547* E-mail. *info@sherwoodsys.com* Web. *www.sherwoodsys.com Parallax*

Shetland Seafish Ltd Symbister Whalsay, Shetland ZE2 9AA Tel. *01595 696949* Fax. *01595 696929* E-mail. *info@shetland-seafish.co.uk* Web. *www.shetlandseafish.co.uk Shetland Seafish*

Shi Cashmere 30 Lowndes Street, London SW1X 9HX Tel. *020 72353829* Fax. *020 72450944* E-mail. *shi@shicashmere.com* Web. *www.shicashmere.com S.H.I. Cashmere*

Shielding Solutions Ltd Braintree Enterprise Centre Springwood Drive, Braintree CM7 2YN Tel. *01376 330033* Fax. *01376 339163* E-mail. *info@shielding-solutions.com* Web. *www.shielding-solutions.com XYShield*

Shilcock Education Advisory Service Ltd (SEAS) 44 Mercury Avenue, WOKINGHAM RG41 3GA Tel. *0118 9629576* Fax. *0118 9629021* E-mail. *jill@seasuk.com* Web. *www.seasuk.com SEAS Limited – Shilcock Education Advisory Service Limited*

Shiloh Computers Ltd Smithfield Centre Whitburn Street, Bridgnorth WV16 4QT Tel. *01746 760780* Fax. *01746 768710* E-mail. *support@shilohcomputers.com* Web. *www.shilohcomputers.com Jentech Computers Ltd*

Shilton plc 90 Peterborough Road, London SW6 3HH Tel. *020 77367771* Fax. *020 77317683* E-mail. *info@janeshilton.co.uk* Web. *www.janeshilton.co.uk *Jane Shilton (China) – *Shilton (China)*

Shindengen Marquis House 68 Great North Road, Hatfield AL9 5ER Tel. *01707 252550* Fax. *01707 252551* E-mail. *info@shindengen.co.uk* Web. *www.shindengen.co.uk Shindengen*

S H L Group Ltd The Pavilion 1 Atwell Place, Thames Ditton KT7 0NE Tel. *020 83358000* Fax. *020 83989544* E-mail. *david.leigh@shl.com* Web. *www.shl.com O.P.Q.*

Shonn Bros Manchester Ltd Emperor House 151 Great Ducie Street, Manchester M3 1FB Tel. *0161 8341394* Fax. *0161 8321875* E-mail. *shonnbros@yahoo.co.uk* Web. *www.shonnbrotherswholesalers.co.uk 151 Brand*

Shoon Trading Ltd Southover, Wells BA5 1UH Tel. *01749 686868* Fax. *01749 686860* E-mail. *info@shoon.com* Web. *www.shoon.com Shoon*

Short Stories of London Ltd 31 The Hale, London N17 9JZ Tel. *020 88014098* Fax. *020 83650012 Short Stories – Telephone Short Stories of London*

Showerlux UK Ltd Stonebridge Trading Estate Sibree Road, Coventry CV3 4FD Tel. *024 76639400* Fax. *024 76305457* E-mail. *reception@showerlux.co.uk* Web. *www.showerlux.co.uk Showerlux*

Showers & Eyebaths Services Ltd Safety House 23c Sandwash Close Rainford, St Helens WA11 8LY Tel. *01744 889677* Fax. *01744 885663* E-mail. *janet@safety-showers.com* Web. *www.safety-showers.com Ponchotech (United Kingdom)*

Showmaster Ltd Taupo House Poundfield Lane, Plaistow, Billingshurst RH14 0NZ Tel. *01403 753633* Fax. *01403 753520* E-mail. *mcardiff@showmaster.co.uk* Web. *www.showmaster.co.uk Cisaplast – Officine Rami – Sovis Saint-Gobain – Vieler*

Shrink Sleeve Ltd Camion House Mill Lane, Sevenoaks TN14 5BX Tel. *01732 462841* Fax. *01732 462851* E-mail. *info@shrinksleeve.com* Web. *www.shrinksleeve.co.uk Canesa*

Shrinktek Polymers International Ltd Herrick Way Staverton, Cheltenham GL51 6TQ Tel. *01452 714900* Fax. *01452 714959* E-mail. *enquiries@shrinktek.co.uk* Web. *www.shrinktek.co.uk Shrinktek*

F W Sibley Ltd 36 Goldcroft, Yeovil BA21 4DH Tel. *01935 423671* Fax. *01935 433407* E-mail. *dillonharris@tiscali.co.uk* Web. *www.fwsibley.com Boss Valves – Crane Valves – Hattersley Valves – Paramo Clay*

Sicame Electrical Developments Ltd 843-855 Leeds Road, Huddersfield HD2 1WA Tel. *01484 681115* Fax. *01484 687352* E-mail. *jim.henderson@sicame.co.uk* Web. *www.sicame.co.uk Erma (United Kingdom) – Hepworth (United Kingdom) – Sicame (France) – Sunbury (United Kingdom)*

Sico-Europe Ltd The Link Park Lympne Industrial Estate, Lympne, Hythe CT21 4LR Tel. *01303 234000* Fax. *01303 234001* E-mail. *sales@sico-europe.com* Web. *www.sico-europe.com Sico*

Sicoma OMG Beach Helm Beach Helm, Arnside, Carnforth LA5 0AX Tel. *01524 762762* E-mail. *info@sicomaomg.co.uk* Web. *www.sicomaomg.co.uk Sicoma OMG*

Siddall & Hilton Holmfield Industrial Estate Holmfield, Halifax HX2 9TN Tel. *01422 233100* Fax. *01422 233111* E-mail. *sales@siddall.com* Web. *siddallandhilton.com Doherty Medical – Ellison*

Siderise Insulation Ltd 15c Oakcroft Road, Chessington KT9 1RH Tel. *020 83913650* Fax. *01656 812509* E-mail. *sales@siderise.com* Web. *www.siderise.co.uk Lamatherm*

Sidetracker Engineering Ltd Station Road Industrial Estate Station Road, Clowne, Chesterfield S43 4AB Tel. *01246 810655* Fax. *01246 812015* E-mail. *info@sidetracker.co.uk* Web. *www.sidetracker.co.uk Sidetracker – Treker*

Sidetrack Solutions Clarence Road, Leighton Buzzard LU7 3EJ Tel. *08453 010363* E-mail. *sales@sidetracksolutions.co.uk* Web. *www.sidetracksolutions.co.uk Sidetrack Webdesign – Sidetrack Hosting – Ezeewebsite.co.uk*

Siebert Head Ltd 35-39 Old Street, London EC1V 9HX Tel. *020 76899090* Fax. *020 76899080* E-mail. *melina.shah@sieberthead.com* Web. *www.sieberthead.com Siebert Head*

Siegrist-Orel Ltd Hornet Close Pysons Road Industrial Estate, Broadstairs CT10 2LQ Tel. *01843 865241* Fax. *01843 867180* E-mail. *info@siegrist-orel.co.uk* Web. *www.siegrist-orel.co.uk Itag*

Siemens plc Loewy House 11 Aviation Park West, Hurn, Christchurch BH23 6EW Tel. *01202 331000* Fax. *01202 581851* E-mail. *sales@vai.co.at* Web. *www.vai.co.at Davy*

Siesta Cork Tile Co. Tait Road Industrial Estate 21 Tait Road, Croydon CR0 2DP Tel. *020 86834055* Fax. *020 86834480* E-mail. *info@siestacorktile.co.uk* Web. *www.siestacorktile.co.uk A.B. Cork (Portugal) – Ambiente (Portugal) – Bathmat (Portugal) – Contract (Portugal) – Cork Master (Portugal) – Cork-A-Bond (Portugal) – Corkboard (Portugal) – Corkwallpaper (Portugal) – Galaxy (Portugal) – Granada (Portugal) – H.D.88 (Portugal) – Kobblecork (Portugal) – Nevada (Portugal) – Pinboard (Portugal) – Pinpanel (Portugal) – Rolcork (Portugal) – Siesta (Portugal)*

Sigma Industries Ltd Unit 25 Dunlop Road Hunt End Industrial Estate, Redditch B97 5XP Tel. *01527 547771* Fax. *01527 547772* E-mail. *sales.sigmaind@btopenworld.com* Web. *www.sigmaind.f9.co.uk B.E.C. – H.M.L. – P.T.E. – R.A.M. – U.N.I.*

Signal Business Systems Ltd Swan Corner, Pewsey SN9 5HL Tel. *01672 563333* Fax. *01672 562391* E-mail. *post@signalbusinesssystems.co.uk* Web. *www.gopher-systems.co.uk Classic Reproductions (Indonesia) – Dyna – Honeycomb – Slide-up Planning*

Signals Ltd Broadgates Market Place, Henley On Thames RG9 2AA Tel. *01491 571812* Fax. *0161 2875511* E-mail. *info@signals.co.uk* Web. *www.signals.co.uk Duplo – Klaxet – Klaxon – Klaxon K Bell – Mono – Syrex – Syrex – Syrex*

Sign A Rama Unit 5 Farnham Business Centre Dogflud Way, Farnham GU9 7UP Tel. *01252 821932* Fax. *01252 734140* E-mail. *farnham@signarama.co.uk* Web. *www.aldershotsigns.co.uk Sign*A*Rama*

Signatime 5 Badbury Close Haydock, St Helens WA11 0FF E-mail. *sales@signatime.co.uk* Web. *www.signatime.co.uk Signatime*

Signconex Ltd Peartree Industrial Estate Bath Road, Langford, Bristol BS40 5DJ Tel. *0161 7649500* Fax. *0161 7649600* E-mail. *info@signconex.co.uk* Web. *www.signconex.co.uk *Innovative displays – *Scroll – *Signco – *Stax – *Varitex*

The Sign Factory Burnbank Road Bainsford, Falkirk FK2 7PE Tel. *01324 501950* Fax. *01324 501950* E-mail. *info@thesignfactory-falkirk.co.uk* Web. *www.thesignfactory-falkirk.co.uk Falkirk Council*

Signscape Systems Ltd Bath Road Langford, Bristol BS40 5DJ Tel. *01934 852888* Fax. *01934 852816* E-mail. *hamish@signscape.co.uk* Web. *www.sign-making-supplies.co.uk Infocurve – Infotex – Iscatex – Lynester – Paneltex – Papyrus – Signcast – Signfix – Tespa – Timbertex – Vitratex – Vydex*

Signs Express Ltd National Headquarters Franchise Headquarters 1-2 The Old Church St Matthews Road, Norwich NR1 1SP Tel. *01603 625925* Fax. *01603 613136* E-mail. *sales@signsexpress.co.uk* Web. *www.signsexpress.co.uk X. Signs Express*

Signum Sign Studio 19 Anglo Business Park Smeaton Close, Aylesbury HP19 8UP Tel. *01296 489099* E-mail. *welcome@signumsign.co.uk* Web. *www.signumsign.co.uk Signum Sign Studio*

Sigta Ltd 26 Abinger Road Portslade, Brighton BN41 1RZ Tel. *01273 416989* Fax. *01273 423982* E-mail. *sales@sigta.co.uk* Web. *www.sigta.co.uk S.I.G.T.A.*

Sika Liquid Plastics Iotech House Miller Street Fishwick Park, Preston PR1 1EA Tel. *01772 259781* Fax. *01772 255670* E-mail. *info@liquidplastics.co.uk* Web. *www.liquidplastics.co.uk Decadex – Decothane – Firecheck – Isoclad – K501 – Monolastex Smooth – Silcabond – Soladex – Steridex – Sterisept – Sterisheen*

Silberline Ltd Unit 2 Banbeath Industrial Estate, Leven KY8 5HD Tel. *01333 424734* Fax. *01333 421369* E-mail. *info@silberline.com* Web. *www.silberline.com Aqua Paste – Aquasil – Aquavex – Aquavex - Aqua Paste - Aquasil - EternaBrite - Sparkle Silver - Silvet - Silcroma - SilBerCotes – Eternabrite – SilberCotes – Silcroma – Silvet – Sparkle Silver – Sparkle Silver Premier*

Silbury Marketing Ltd 2 Trinity Mews Priory Road, Warwick CV34 4NA Tel. *01926 410022* Fax. *01926 476200* E-mail. *adrian@silbury.co.uk* Web. *www.silbury.co.uk *Silbury Boxed Fats*

Silcoms Victoria Mill Piggott Street, Farnworth, Bolton BL4 9QN Tel. *01204 466070* Fax. *01204 861723* E-mail. *keith.harrison@silcoms.co.uk* Web. *www.silcoms.co.uk Silcoms*

Silent Gliss Ltd Pyramid Business Park Poorhole Lane, Broadstairs CT10 2PT Tel. *01843 863571* Fax. *01843 864503* E-mail. *info@silentgliss.co.uk* Web. *www.silentgliss.co.uk Silent Gliss*

Silhouette Beauty Equipment 122-124 Grove Lane Timperley, Altrincham WA15 6PL Tel. *0161 9801080* Fax. *0161 9805040* E-mail. *support@silhouetteinternational.co.uk* Web. *www.silhouettebeauty.com Silhouette – Dermalift – Dermatone – Dermafusion – Interslim – Profile – Bofusion*

Silhouette UK Ltd 2 Bath Road Chiswick, London W4 1LW Tel. *020 89878899* Fax. *020 89872430* E-mail. *office@uk.silhouette.com* Web. *www.silhouette.com *Adidas (Austria) – *Silhouette (Austria)*

Silkmead Tubular Ltd Unit 3 Southfields Road, Dunstable LU6 3EJ Tel. *01582 609988* Fax. *01582 609930* E-mail. *simonb@silkmead.co.uk* Web. *www.silkmead.co.uk Evantech – Silkmead Tubular*

Silkscreen Europe Ltd PO Box 229, Ilkley LS29 1AA Tel. *01943 605650* Fax. *0870 8555550* E-mail. *info@sseworldwide.co.uk* Web. *www.sseworldwide.co.uk SSE*

Sill Lighting UK Ltd 3 Thame Park Business Centre Wenman Road, Thame OX9 3XA Tel. *01844 260006* Fax. *01844 260760* E-mail. *sales@sill-uk.com* Web. *www.sill-uk.com SILL*

Silvaperl Ropery Road Albion Works, Gainsborough DN21 2QB Tel. *01427 610160* Fax. *01427 811838* E-mail. *guy.sinclair@william-sinclair.co.uk* Web. *www.silvaperl.co.uk Hydroleca – Silvalite – Silvalite - expander perliteVermalite - exfoliated vermiculiteHydroleca - expanded claySilverslag - slag coagulare – Silverslag – Vermalite*

Silverson Machines Ltd Waterside, Chesham HP5 1PQ Tel. *01494 786331* Fax. *01494 791452* E-mail. *sales@silverson.co.uk* Web. *www.silverson.com Abramix – Silverson*

Silvertech Safety Consultancy Ltd Holmwood Broadlands Business Campus, Horsham RH12 4PN Tel. *01403 211611* Fax. *01403 211058* E-mail. *sales@silvertech.co.uk* Web. *www.silvertech.co.uk SENTROL 1000 – SENTROL 2000 – SENTROL 3000 – SENTROL 4000 – SENTROL 5000 – SENTROL 6000*

Silverwing UK Ltd Unit 30-31 Cwmdu Industrial Estate Carmarthen Road, Gendros, Swansea SA5 8JF Tel. *01792 585533* Fax. *01792 586044* E-mail. *mfl@silverwinguk.com* Web. *www.silverwinguk.com ATIS – Floormap – Handscan – Pipescan – Scorpion – Scorpion Model SS 360*

Simba International Ltd Unit 11 Woodbridge Road, Sleaford NG34 7EW Tel. *01529 304654* Fax. *01529 413468* E-mail. *info@simba.co.uk* Web. *www.simba.co.uk Mono – Top Tilth*

Simbec Research Ltd Merthyr Industrial Park Pentrebach, Merthyr Tydfil CF48 4DR Tel. *01443 690977* Fax. *01443 692494* E-mail. *alan.woodward@simbec.co.uk* Web. *www.simbecresearch.co.uk Ectquote – Fastintoman*

R W Simon Ltd Hatchmoor Industrial Estate, Torrington EX38 7HP Tel. *01805 623721* Fax. *01805 624578* E-mail. *info@rwsimon.co.uk* Web. *www.rwsimon.co.uk Airstrip – T.T.F. – Ventamatic*

A L Simpkin Co. Ltd 3 Hunter Road, Sheffield S6 4LD Tel. *0114 2348736* Fax. *0114 2325635* E-mail. *karen.simpkin@alsimpkin.com* Web. *www.alsimpkin.com Holex Diabetic Chocolate – JuiCees – Jungle Pops – Old Miners Lozenges*

Simplefit Ltd Marchwood Industrial Estate 4w Normandy Way, Marchwood, Southampton SO40 4PB Tel. *023 80663210* Fax. *023 80663086* E-mail. *ian.macdonald@simplefit.co.uk* Web. *www.simplefit.co.uk Eurocowl*

Simplex Westpile Limited Unit 5 Lidstone Court Uxbridge Road, George Green, Slough SL3 6AG Tel. *01753 215350* Fax. *01753 534653* E-mail. *estimating@westpile.co.uk* Web. *www.simplexwestpile.co.uk Continuous Flight Auger Piles – Cut Off Walls – Embedded Returning Wall – Gas & Leachate Wells – Hardrive – Hardrive Precast Piles – Rotary Bored Piles – Tripod Bored Piles*

Simply Health James Tudor House 90 Victoria Street, Bristol BS1 6DF Tel. *0117 9295529* Fax. *0117 9295539* E-mail. *info@bcwa.co.uk* Web. *www.simplyhealth.co.uk Medisure*

Simply Herbs The Herbary 11 Town Orchard, Southoe, St Neots PE19 5YJ Tel. *01480 472301* E-mail. *handmade@simplyherbs.co.uk* Web. *www.simplyherbs.co.uk Simply Herbs*

Simportex Ltd 452a Finchley Road, London NW11 8DG Tel. *020 84578770* Fax. *020 84577484* E-mail. *sales@simportex.com* Web. *www.simportex.com *Montmere (Worldwide)*

Samuel Simpson & Co. Ltd 30 Broughton Street, Manchester M8 8NN Tel. *0161 8344920* Fax. *0161 8343056* E-mail. *sales@samuelsimpson.com* Web. *www.samuelsimpson.com Symco Linings*

Simpsons In The Strand 100 Strand, London WC2R 0EW Tel. *020 78369112* Fax. *020 78361381* E-mail. *info@simpsonsinthestrand.co.uk* Web. *www.simpsonsinthestrand.co.uk Simpson's-in-the-Strand*

Simpson Strong-Tie International Inc Cardinal Point Winchester Road, Tamworth B78 3HG Tel. *01827 255600* Fax. *01827 255616* E-mail. *info@strongtie.com* Web. *www.strongtie.co.uk Arch Master – Ceejay – Crocodile – Easy Arches – Furfix – Hiload – Panther – Strong-TIE – Tomahawk*

Simtech Simulation Techniques Unit 70 Westcott Venture Park Westcott, Aylesbury HP18 0XB Tel. *01296 655787* Fax. *01296 651729* E-mail. *info@simtech-simulation.com* Web. *www.simtech-simulation.com Autotutor – Sim-L-Bus – Sim-L-Car*

Simulation Solutions Unit 10 Rugby Park Bletchley Road, Stockport SK4 3EJ Tel. *0161 9479113* Fax. *0161 9479099* E-mail. *robbie@simsol.co.uk* Web. *www.simsol.co.uk Amber Vehicle Solutions Ltd*

Sinclair I S Pharma Whitfield Court 30-32 Whitfield Street, London W1T 2RQ Tel. *020 74676920* Fax. *020 74676930* E-mail. *info@sinclairpharma.com* Web. *www.sinclairpharma.com Caprin Tabs – Visclair Tabs*

William Sinclair & Sons Stationers Ltd PO Box 1, Otley LS21 1QF Tel. *01943 461144* Fax. *01943 850017* E-mail. *enquiries@sinclairsproducts.com* Web. *www.silvine.com Silvine*

S I P Industrial Products Ltd Gelders Hall Road Shepshed, Loughborough LE12 9NH Tel. *01509 500500* Fax. *01509 503154* E-mail. *info@sip-group.com* Web. *www.sip-group.com *Airmate (Italy) – *Airstream (Italy) – Alleycat – *Autoplus (Italy) – *Fireball (Italy) – *Ideal (Italy) – Medusa – *Migmate (Italy) – *Omega (China) – *S.I.P. (Italy) – *Sipcut (Italy) – *Spotmatic (Italy) – *Startmaster (Italy) – *Turboweld (Italy) – Workshop*

Sira Test & Certification Ltd Rake Lane Eccleston, Chester CH4 9JN Tel. *01244 670900* Fax. *01244 681330* E-mail. *info@siraservices.com* Web. *www.siraservices.com Fastscan – Image Automation – Ometron – Sira Electro-Optics Limited – SIRA Smart Optics – Sira Technology Centre – Sira Test & Certification Ltd – V.P.I.*

Sirco Controls Ltd Swaines Industrial Estate Ashingdon Road, Rochford SS4 1RQ Tel. *01702 545125* Fax. *01702 546873* E-mail. *info@sirco-controls.co.uk* Web. *www.sirco-controls.co.uk Sirco-Pressure Switches*

Sirdar Spinning Ltd PO Box 31, Wakefield WF2 9ND Tel. *01924 371501* Fax. *01924 290506* E-mail. *enquiries@sirdar.co.uk* Web. *www.sirdar.co.uk 4 ply 100g – 4 PLY 50g – Chenille DK – Country Style 4 Ply – Country Style Aran – Country Style Double Knitting – Country Style Highlands & Islands – Double Knitting 100g – Harlequin Chenille – Highlander Aran – Highlander Chunky – Opium DK – Prize Aran with Wool – Prize Baby DK – Prize Chunky – Prize DK – Pure Cotton Crepe DK – Silky Look DK – Snuggly 2 ply – Snuggly 3 ply 100g – Snuggly 3 ply 50g – Snuggly Aran – Snuggly Double Knitting 50g – Snuggly Lustre 4 ply – Snuggly Lustre DK – Snuggly QK – Supreme Mohair – Wash 'n' Wear 4 Ply – Wash 'n' Wear Aran Crepe – Wash 'n' Wear Double Crepe DK*

Sirius Analytical Instruments Riverside Forest Row Business Park Station Road, Forest Row RH18 5DW Tel. *01342 820720* Fax. *01342 820725* E-mail. *brett.hughes@sirius-analytical.com* Web. *www.sirius-analytical.com GLpKa – SiriusT3*

S I S Chemicals Ltd 22 Whitefield Road Pennington, Lymington SO41 8GN Tel. *01425 621021* Fax. *01425 618191* E-mail. *sales@sischem.co.uk* Web. *www.sischem.co.uk Proswim*

Franke Sissons Ltd Carrwood Road, Chesterfield S41 9QB Tel. *01246 450255* Fax. *01246 451276* E-mail. *ian.king@sissons.co.uk* Web. *www.franke-sissons.co.uk Bradco – Centinel – Citidel – Cromford – Disposapad – Franke WSS – Guardian – Impera – Magnum – Midi – Mini – Nappigon – Quartsan – Sanistrel – Stratos – Xinox*

Sitexorbis plc Beaufort House Cricket Field Road, Uxbridge UB8 1QG Tel. *01895 465500* Fax. *01895 465499* E-mail. *info@sitexorbis.com* Web. *www.sitexorbis.com Orbis*

Sitsmart Ltd Unit 14 Decimus Park Kingstanding Way, Tunbridge Wells TN2 3GP Tel. *01892 510202* Fax. *01892 519834* E-mail. *sales@sitsmart.co.uk* Web. *www.sitsmart.co.uk Bodybuilt – Grahl – Hoganasmobler – KAB – R H Form – Savo – Stokke – Verco*

S J H Row & Son Ltd Unit 6 Riverside Avenue West Lawford, Manningtree CO11 1UN Tel. *01206 396688* Fax. *01206 393392* E-mail. *peter@sjh-row.co.uk* Web. *www.sjh-row.co.uk Econobord – Joshua Row – Row Fabrications – Rowblock – Rowplas*

S & J Roofing Ltd Apex House Kingsfield Lane, Longwell Green, Bristol BS30 6DL Tel. *0117 9604161* Fax. *0117 9352084* E-mail. *enquiries@sjroofing.co.uk* Web. *www.sjroofing.co.uk S.J.*

S J Wharton Ltd Downs Road, Witney OX29 0RF Tel. *01993 779630* Fax. *01993 706602* E-mail. *sales@sjwharton.co.uk* Web. *www.sjwharton.co.uk 3 M – Action Can – Air Products – Ambler – Arrow Staples – Autosol – Bahco – Barrowmix – Belzona – Black & Decker – Bodyguards – Bondhus – Bosch – Bostik – BP Gas – Britool – Caterpillar – Chuck-Eez – Copydex – D E B – Dewalt – Disposable Overalls – Dormer – Dr Marten – Duracell – Eclipse – Einhell – Elora – Esab – Evo-Stik – Facom – Faithfull – Footprint – Gesipa – Handy Gas – Hardman – Harrington – Hitachi – Hylomar – Jack – Jackson – Jubilee – Kamasa – Kimberly-Clarke – Klingspor – Knippex – Laser Tools – Lindapter – Loctite – Lyndon – Makita – Metabin – Metabo – Milwaukee – Morris – Morse – Mouldex – Naylor – Oerlikon – Oetiker – Recoil – Record – Rocol – Ryobi – Sandvik – Sealey – Showa – Squire – Stanley – Starrett – Sykes-Pickavant – Teng – Terry – Tiger Gloves – Timberland – Tool Connection – Trend – Tyrolit – Tyvek – Unbrako – Unior – V-Coil – Vise Grip – Vitrex – WD-40*

Skeldings Ltd 126 Oldbury Road, Smethwick B66 1JE Tel. *0121 5580622* Fax. *0121 5586115 S.L.S.*

H.J. Skelton & Co. Ltd 9 The Broadway, Thatcham RG19 3JA Tel. *01635 865256* Fax. *01635 865710* E-mail. *js@hjskelton.com* Web. *www.hjskelton.co.uk Rawie GmbH and Co. KG (Germany)*

Ski Club Of Great Britain 57-63 Church Road, London SW19 5SB Tel. *020 84102000* Fax. *020 84102001* E-mail. *maggie.colpus@skiclub.co.uk* Web. *www.skiclub.co.uk Freshtracks*

Skills Workshop Ltd 168 Ravensbourne Avenue, Bromley BR2 0AY Tel. *020 84603557* E-mail. *skillsworkshop@hotmail.co.uk* Web. *www.skillsworkshop.net Presentation Skills Workshop*

S K Interiors Ltd 202 Havant Road Drayton, Portsmouth PO6 2EH Tel. *023 92324393* Fax. *023 92377027* E-mail. *info@skinteriors.co.uk* Web. *www.skinteriors.co.uk Armstrong – British Gypsum – Donn – Ecophon – Komfort – Rockfon – Tenon – Troax*

Skipton Building Society plc PO Box 7, Skipton BD23 1AP Tel. *01756 705030* Fax. *01756 705700* Web. *www.skipton.co.uk Skipton*

Skip Units Ltd Block D Industrial Estate Sinfin Lane, Derby DE24 9GL Tel. *01332 761361* Fax. *01332 270013* E-mail. *enquiries@skipunits.co.uk* Web. *www.skipunits.co.uk Simpack – Smoothline*

Skyline Tower Crane Services Ltd 27a Oliver Close, Grays RM20 3EE Tel. *01708 860534* Fax. *01708 861553* E-mail. *info@skylinetcs.com* Web. *www.skylinetcs.com COMEDIL – Raimondi-Tower Cranes – TGM-Tower Cranes*

Skymark Packaging Solutions Ltd Manners Avenue Manners Industrial Estate, Ilkeston DE7 8EF Tel. *0115 9302020* Fax. *0115 9071525* E-mail. *admin@skymark.co.uk* Web. *www.skymark.co.uk McGregor-Rutland*

Skyscan Aerial Photography Oak House Toddington, Cheltenham GL54 5BY Tel. *01242 621357* Fax. *01242 621343* E-mail. *info@skyscan.co.uk* Web. *www.skyscan.co.uk Skyscan (United Kingdom)*

Skytronic Ltd Containerbase Barton Dock Road, Manchester M41 7BQ Tel. *0161 7498180* Fax. *0161 7498181* E-mail. *sales@skytronic.co.uk* Web. *skytroni.en.china.cn Adastra – Skytronic*

Slatebond Ltd Unit 27 Leafield Industrial Estate Leafield Way Neston, Corsham SN13 9RS Tel. *01225 810099* Fax. *01225 811413* E-mail. *sales@slatebond.com* Web. *www.slatebond.com Hy-Bond*

Slater Harrison & Co. Ltd Lowerhouse Mill Bollington, Macclesfield SK10 5HW Tel. *01625 578900* Fax. *01625 578972* E-mail. *c.smallwood@slater-harrison.co.uk* Web. *www.slater-harrison.co.uk Centura Pearl – Colourmount – Day-Glo – Educraft*

Herbert M Slater Ltd 332 Coleford Road, Sheffield S9 5PH Tel. *0114 2612308* Fax. *0114 2612305* E-mail. *info@slaterknives.co.uk* Web. *www.slaterknives.co.uk Venture Brand*

Slaters 165 Howard Street, Glasgow G1 4HF Tel. *0141 5527171* Fax. *0141 5531720* E-mail. *paulslater@slatermenswear.com* Web. *www.slatermenswear.com Slater Menswear*

Slaters Of Abergele Ltd Market Street, Abergele LL22 7AL Tel. *01745 828282* Fax. *01745 825390* E-mail. *action@slaters.com* Web. *www.slaters.com Slaters*

Sleepy Weasel Ltd 125 Newtown Road, Worcester WR5 1HL Tel. *07951 294087* Fax. *01905 764260* E-mail. *swltd@hotmail.co.uk* Web. *www.sleepyweasel.info Pat Says Now*

Slick Willies Ltd 12 Gloucester Road, London SW7 4RB Tel. *020 72250004* Fax. *020 75910918* E-mail. *info@slickwillies.co.uk* Web. *www.slickwillies.co.uk Slick Willies*

Slush Puppie Ltd Coronation Road Cressex Business Park, High Wycombe HP12 3TA Tel. *020 85785785*

Fax. 020 85753611 E-mail. info@slushpuppie.co.uk Web. www.slushpuppie.co.uk Dog Bite – Eskimo Joe – Slush Puppie – Sno Smoothie – Thicko

Smail Engineers Glasgow Ltd 30 Napier Road Hillington Park, Glasgow G52 4DR Tel. 0141 8824882 Fax. 0141 8105460 E-mail. smail@compserve.com *F. Leutert GmbH (Germany) – *H. Maihak A.G. (Germany) – Hi-Force – *SpohrGmbh (Germany) – Stag

Small Engine Services Ltd 5 & 6 Barrow End Centre Chippenham Road, Lyneham, Chippenham SN15 4NY Tel. 01249 892906 Fax. 01249 892911 E-mail. info@small-engine-services.co.uk Web. www.small-engine-services.co.uk Honda – Robin – Victa

Small Products 20 St Andrews Way Bow, London E3 3PA Tel. 020 75374222 Fax. 020 75383957 E-mail. sales@smallproducts.co.uk Web. www.smallproducts.co.uk Aqua Billboard

Smart Stabilizer Systems Ashchurch Business Centre Alexandra Way, Ashchurch, Tewkesbury GL20 8TD Tel. 01684 853860 Fax. 01684 853861 E-mail. dsmith@transnorm.co.uk Web. www.precisiondrilling.com *Transnorm System (Germany)

S M B Bearings Ltd 8 West Oxfordshire Industrial Park Wavers Ground, Brize Norton, Carterton OX18 3YJ Tel. 01993 842555 Fax. 01993 842666 E-mail. sales@smbbearings.com Web. www.smbbearings.com EZO (Japan) – S.M.B. (China)

S M E Ltd Mill Road, Steyning BN44 3GY Tel. 01903 814321 Fax. 01903 814269 E-mail. info@sme.ltd.uk Web. www.sme.ltd.uk S.M.E.

Smeaton Hanscomb & Co. Ltd Lisle Road Hughenden Avenue, High Wycombe HP13 5SQ Tel. 01494 521051 Fax. 01494 461176 E-mail. sales@smeathans.plus.com Web. www.smeathans.plus.com *Holz Her (Germany) – J.K.O. – *JKO Panelmaster (Austria) – *Lamello (Switzerland)

John Smedley Ltd Lea Mills Lea Bridge, Matlock DE4 5AG Tel. 01629 534571 Fax. 01629 534691 E-mail. enquiries@johnsmedley.com Web. www.johnsmedley.com John Smedley

Smet Ltd Unit 19 The Markham Centre Station Road, Theale, Reading RG7 4PE Tel. 0118 9302113 Fax. 0118 9302206 E-mail. info@custompsudesign.com Web. www.custompsudesign.com Handy Mains

S M I 7 Gipping Close, Bedford MK41 7XY Tel. 01234 266255 Fax. 01234 266255 E-mail. grawatts@aol.com Web. www.smi.com.sa Johnson Gears – Saudi National Pump

Smiffy's (R.H. Smith & Sons (Wigmakers) Heapham Road South Caldicott Drive, Heapham Road Industrial Estate, Gainsborough DN21 1FJ Tel. 01427 616831 Fax. 01427 617190 E-mail. sales@smiffys.com Web. www.smiffys.com Smiffys – Smiffys USA – Smiffys, Smiffys USA

Smith & Archibald Ltd 14 Stoneygate Road, Newmilns KA16 9AL Tel. 01560 320240 Fax. 01560 323024 E-mail. enquiries@sandalace.co.uk Web. www.sandalace.co.uk Melova

Smith Bros Quinton Ltd The Wooden Packaging Company Smith Bros Quinton Castle Street, Tipton DY4 8HP Tel. 0121 5570077 Fax. 0121 5570177 E-mail. harveysmith@smith-bros.co.uk Web. www.enviro-materials.co.uk SBQ Flexible

Smith Bros & Webb Ltd 22 Tything Road East Kinwarton, Alcester B49 6EX Tel. 01789 400096 Fax. 01789 400231 E-mail. sales@vehicle-washing-systems.co.uk Web. www.vehicle-washing-systems.co.uk Britannia Jetspray – Britannia Spray – Britannia Streamline – Britannia Strong – Britannia Supreme – Britannia Train Wash

Smith Francis Tools Ltd Priory Works 66 Moseley Street, Birmingham B12 0RT Tel. 0121 6223311 Fax. 0121 6667201 E-mail. sales@smithfrancistools.co.uk Web. www.smithfrancistools.co.uk Priory – Snail – Williams Superslim

Howard Smith Paper Ltd Sovereign House Rhosili Road, Brackmills Industrial Estate, Northampton NN4 7JE Tel. 08456 082370 Fax. 08706 082373 E-mail. marketing@hspg.com Web. www.hspg.com 2800 Laser – 4CC Art – 4CC Reels – 4CC Silk – Arriba! – Artic Extreme – Artic Matt – Artic Silk – Artic Volume – Barbican Lasermatt – Classic Laid – Classic Rib – Classic Superwove – Classic Wove – Concise – Conservation – Consort Complement – Consort Royal Brilliance – Consort Royal Satin – Consort Royal Satin Tint – Consort Royal Silk – Consort Royal Silk Tint – County Copier – DCP – Digi Greeting Card – Digital Zone Gloss – Digital Zone Silk – Distinction Laid & Wove – Folex Digiprint – Freeway Offset – GardaPat 13 Digital – Giroform – Granduer Pure Silk Ivory – Graphiart Card – Graphiart Duo – Greencoat Digital Gloss – Greencoat Digital Velvet – Greeting Cards – Greyboards – HSP Gloss Board – HSP Silk Board – IBM Business Cards – IBM CD Case Labels – IBM CD/DVD Gloss Labels – IBM CD/DVD High Resolution Labels – IBM CD/DVD Labelling Kit – IBM Color Paper – IBM Color Pro – IBM Copy Pro – IBM Digital Photo Inkjet Paper – IBM Document Pro – IBM Gloss Coated Inkjet Paper – IBM Greeting Cards – IBM Inkjet Pro – IBM Inkjet Transparencies – IBM Laser Pro – IBM Matt Coated Inkjet Paper – IBM Multi-Functional Labels – IBM Office Pro – IBM Print Pro – IBM T-shirt Transfer Paper – Indi-cards – IQ Allround – IQ Allround Triotec – IQ Economy – IQ Premium – IQ Selection – Linebacker – Mactac Imagin – Mizar Gloss Digital – Mizar Matt Digital – Modligiani – Multi Digital Gloss – Multi Digital Silk – Munken Lynx – Munken Print – Munken Print Extra Vol 15 – Munken Print Extra Vol 18 – Munken Print Extra Vol 20 – Munken Pure – Nautilus – Neenah Environment – On Business – On Offset – Pacemaker – Pacemaker Laid – Pacesetter Ivory Board – Pacestter Pulp Board – Regency Gloss – Regency Satin – Replica – Replica Digital Reels – Royal Prestige Gloss – Royal Prestige Matt – Royal Prestige Print 500 – Self Adhesive Sheets – Sihl Digital Reels – Sovereign Silk Ivory – Sovereign Gloss – Sovereign Silk – Soveriegn Labels – Superwhite – Tailormade – Trucard – Venicelux Digital – X9 – X9 Digital Reels

Paul Smith Ltd Riverside Building Riverside Way, Nottingham NG2 1DP Tel. 0115 9868877 Fax. 0115 9862649 E-mail. john.morley@paulsmith.co.uk Web. www.paulsmith.co.uk Paul Smith

Smith & Prince Ltd (CPA Electrical) 92 Church Road, Mitcham CR4 3TD Tel. 020 84087200 Fax. 020 86468348 E-mail. sales@smithprince.co.uk Web. www.smithprince.co.uk CPA Electrical

Richard Smith Cash Registers 866 Manchester Road, Bradford BD5 8DJ Tel. 01274 722473 Fax. 01274 732747 E-mail. richard.smith@richardsmithsales.co.uk Web. www.richardsmithsales.co.uk Cash Registers Direct

Smith & Roger Ltd 34 Elliott Street, Glasgow G3 8EA Tel. 0141 2486341 Fax. 0141 2486475 E-mail. i.mcaslan@smithandrodger.co.uk Web. www.frenchpolishes.com Aquacoat SP – Essar – Excellac – Excellose – Solvit – Vitableach – Vitapol

Smiths Coffee Co. Ltd Arabica House Ebberns Road, Hemel Hempstead HP3 9RD Tel. 01442 234257 Fax. 01422 248614 E-mail. sales@smiths-coffee.demon.co.uk Web. www.smithscoffee.co.uk *Crema – *Ozone

Smiths Detection 459 Park Avenue, Bushey WD23 2BW Tel. 01923 658000 Fax. 01923 240285 E-mail. m.maginnis@smithdetection.com Web. www.smithsdetection.com G.D. – Graseby

Smiths Gore Stuart House City Road, Peterborough PE1 1QF Tel. 01733 567231 Fax. 01733 568527 E-mail. shelley.cash@smithsgore.co.uk Web. www.smithsgore.co.uk Smiths Gore

Smiths Medical Boundary Road, Hythe CT21 6JL Tel. 01303 260551 Fax. 01303 266761 E-mail. matt.sassone@smiths-medical.com Web. www.smithsmedical.com Sims Portex

Smiths Medical International Ltd Bramingham Business Park Enterprise Way, Luton LU3 4BU Tel. 01582 430000 Fax. 01582 430001 E-mail. pneupac@smiths-medical.com Web. www.smiths-medical.co.uk Pneupac

Smiths Of Peter Head Buchan Blaes Boddam, Peterhead AB42 3AR Tel. 01779 871400 Fax. 01779 478989 E-mail. marian@smithsofpeterhead.com Web. www.smithsofpeterhead.com Alexander of Scotland – J.C. Rennie & Co. Ltd

S M M T Ltd 71 Great Peter Street, London SW1P 2BN Tel. 020 72357000 Fax. 020 72357112 E-mail. sales@smmt.co.uk Web. www.smmt.co.uk Society of Motor Manufacturers & Traders

Smooth Radio 26-27 Castlereagh Street, London W1H 5DL Tel. 020 77064100 Fax. 020 77239742 E-mail. info@smoothradio.com Web. www.smoothradio.com Jazz Direct – Jazz Enterprises – Jazz FM 100.4 – Jazz FM 102.2 – London Jazz

S M P Playgrounds Ten Acre Lane, Egham TW20 8RJ Tel. 01784 489100 Fax. 01784 431067 E-mail. sales@smp.co.uk Web. www.smp.co.uk 2-2-7 – Action Pack – Aerial Runway – Animal Seats, Benches & Tables – Arena Meeting Point – Arena Sports System – Countryside Range – F.X. Surfacing – Horizon – Multi-Seat Swing – New World

S M P Security Ltd Unit 5-6 Halesfield 24, Telford TF7 4NZ Tel. 01952 585673 Fax. 01952 582816 E-mail. sales@smpsecurity.co.uk Web. www.smpsecurity.co.uk Community Range (United Kingdom)

S M S Mevac UK Ltd Road Four Winsford Industrial Estate, Winsford CW7 3RS Tel. 01606 551421 Fax. 01606 553078 E-mail. mail@sms-mevac.co.uk Web. www.sms-mevac.co.uk Vacmetal

Smudge Ink Tallai House Church Lane, Pyecombe, Brighton BN45 7FE Tel. 01273 841444 Fax. 01273 842442 E-mail. grahamsmudge@talk21.com Smudge

Smurfit Kappa Composites Richmond Works Moresby Road, Hensingham, Whitehaven CA28 8TS Tel. 01946 61671 Fax. 01946 592281 E-mail. marketing@smurfitkappa.co.uk Web. www.smurfitkappa.co.uk Assidoman Packaging UK Limited

Smurfit Kappa Sheetfeeding Fishergate, Norwich NR3 1SJ Tel. 01603 679888 Fax. 01603 679889 E-mail. alex.kelly@smurfitkappa.co.uk Web. www.smurfitsheetfeeding.co.uk Norcor

Smurfit Kappa Townsend Hook Paper Mills Mill Street, Snodland ME6 5AX Tel. 01634 240205 Fax. 01634 243458 E-mail. info@smurfitkappa.co.uk Web. www.smurfitkappa.co.uk Extra – Fab 1,2,3 – Fineblade – Fineblade Satin Webb – Fineblade Smooth – Finechip – Fineflute – Fineliner

S M W Autoblok 8 The Metro Centre, Peterborough PE2 7UH Tel. 01733 394394 Fax. 01733 394395 E-mail. sales@smwautoblok.co.uk Web. www.smwautoblok.co.uk Autoblok – ICMA – Mario Pinto – OML – ONCA – SCA – SMW – SMW-Autoblok

Snappy Snaps Franchises Ltd 12 Glenthorne Mews, London W6 0LJ Tel. 020 87417474 Fax. 020 87483849 E-mail. ann@snappysnaps.co.uk Web. www.snappysnaps.co.uk Snappy Snaps

Snopake Ltd 28 Perivale Park Horsenden Lane South, Perivale, Greenford UB6 7RJ Tel. 020 89911666 Fax. 020 89982000 E-mail. uksales@snopake.com Web. www.snopake.com Classic White – Clipfiles – Docbox – Hangglider Suspension File – Hi Tech – Hide It Roller – PinPoint – Polycase – Polyfile – Polyfile ID – PolyWally – Snappa Clips – Snopake

Snowcard Insurance Services Ltd Long Barn 1st Floor Office Appletree Road, Chipping Warden, Banbury OX17 1LH Tel. 01295 660836 Fax. 01327 263227 E-mail. enquiries@snowcard.co.uk Web. www.snowcard.co.uk Snowcard

S & N Stainless Pipeline Products Ltd Unit B4 Fallons Road, Wardley Road Industrial Estate, Swinton, Manchester M28 2NY Tel. 0161 7281148 Fax. 0161 7281149 E-mail. sales@snstainless.com Web. www.snstainless.com 6% Moly (Uns31254) – Super Duplex (Uns32750) – Super Duplex (Uns32760)

Softbrands The Waterfront 300 Thames Valley Park Drive, Reading RG6 1PT Tel. 08452 236050 Fax. 0118 9358811 E-mail. michael.knight@softbrands.com Web. www.softbrands.com/hospitality Core, Central Reservation System – Emerald f&b – Emerald Golf – Emerald Spa – Epitome PMS – Epitome Res Portal – IGS – Medallion PMS – Medallion, Web Booking Engine – PORTfolio PMS – PORTfolio, Web Booking Engine – Worldwide Support Services

Soft Start UK Unit 14 Brinell Way, Great Yarmouth NR31 0LU Tel. 01493 660510 Fax. 01493 669647 E-mail. sales@silverteam.co.uk Web. www.silverteam.co.uk MV Digistart – Softstart UK

So-Gefi Filtration Ltd Llantrisant Industrial Estate Llantrisant, Pontyclun CF72 8YU Tel. 01443 223000 Fax. 01443 225459 E-mail. gareth.havard@sogefifiltration.com Web. www.sogefifiltration.co.uk *Fiaam (Italy) – Fram – Fram Europe

Soil Fertility Dunns Ltd Carrick Terminal North Harbour, Ayr KA8 8AH Tel. 01292 611622 Fax. 01292 619990 E-mail. rob.cooper@soilfert.co.uk Web. www.soilfert.co.uk G.A.F.S.A. – Moreophos – New Life – New Life 2 – New Life 3 – New Life 4 – New Life 5 – New Life 6 – Phosmin – Phosphate Range

Solaglas Ltd Solaglas Ltd (part of the Saint-Gobain group) Catkin Way Greenfields Industrial Estate, Bishop Auckland DL14 9TF Tel. 01388 603667 Fax. 01388 600594 E-mail. solaglas.gpd@saint-gobain-glass.com Web. www.saint-gobain.com Thermaglass – Thermaglaze – Thermalite – Thermatop

Solaglas Ltd Mill Way, Sittingbourne ME10 2PD Tel. 01795 421534 Fax. 01795 473651 E-mail. solaglas.gpd@saint-gobain-glass.com Web. www.solaglas.sggs.com Solaglas Laminated

Solair Group Architectural Products Smeaton Road, Salisbury SP2 7NQ Tel. 01722 323036 Fax. 01722 337546 E-mail. bill.whitston@solair.co.uk Web. www.solair.co.uk Solair G.R.P. – Solair GRP Dormer Windows

Solar Essence Energy House Fisons Way Industrial Estate 45 St Helens Court, Thetford IP24 1HG Tel. 01842 845845 E-mail. info@solaressence.co.uk Web. www.solaressence.co.uk Solar Essence

Solarfilm Sales Ltd Common Bank Industrial Estate Ackhurst Road, Chorley PR7 1NH Tel. 01257 267418 Fax. 01257 276203 E-mail. info@solarfilm.co.uk Web. www.solarfilm.co.uk Solarfilm – Solartex

Solent Roof Trusses Ltd Gang-Nail Systems Ltd 2 Crompton Way Segensworth West, Fareham PO15 5SS Tel. 01489 578344 Fax. 01489 579485 Web. www.solentrooftrusses.com Ecojoist

Solid Auto UK Ltd Coombswood Way, Halesowen B62 8BH Tel. 0121 5616444 Fax. 0121 5616464 E-mail. uksales@solidautouk.co.uk Web. www.solidautouk.co.uk Solid Auto (UK) Ltd

Solid Contracts Ltd Bristol & West House Post Office Road, Bournemouth BH1 1BL Tel. 01202 314444 E-mail. asorrell@solidcontracts.co.uk Web. www.solidcontracts.co.uk Solid Contracts Ltd

Solid Fuel Association 7 Swanwick Court, Alfreton DE55 7AS Tel. 08456 014406 Fax. 01773 834351 E-mail. martyn@solidfuel.co.uk Web. www.solidfuel.co.uk Solid Fuel Association

Solid Stampings Ltd Porters Field Road, Cradley Heath B64 7BL Tel. *01384 636421* Fax. *01384 639163* E-mail. *aledw@solidswivel.co.uk* Web. *www.solidswivel.co.uk Solswiv*

Solois Thermal Ltd Heathbrook House Heath Mill Road, Wombourne, Wolverhampton WV5 8AP Tel. *01902 324000* E-mail. *stephen.augustine@fivesgroup.com* Web. *www.fivesgroup.com Emix – Idex*

Solmedia Laboratory Supplies 6 The Parade Colchester Road, Romford RM3 0AQ Tel. *01708 343334* Fax. *01708 372785* E-mail. *labsupplies@solmedialtd.com Benchcote – Cellsafe – Cryostat – Dennison – Formaspill – Haemasol – Hycolin – MED E – Microblock – Niftilds – Paraplast – Sharps Bin – supaTag – Terralin – Trident – Trionic – Vials – Virkon*

Solo Sprayers Ltd 4 Brunel Road, Leigh On Sea SS9 5JN Tel. *01702 525740* Fax. *01702 522752* E-mail. *solo.sprayers@fsbdial.co.uk* Web. *www.solosprayers.co.uk Solo*

Solo Timber Frame Ltd Hodore Farm Parrock Lane, Upper Hartfield, Hartfield TN7 4AR Tel. *01892 771354* Fax. *01474 822859* E-mail. *info@solotimberframe.co.uk* Web. *www.12limited.co.uk Twin Frame*

Solutions Four 24 Brunel Drive, Biggleswade SG18 8BH Tel. *01767 687646* Fax. *020 30093444* E-mail. *info@solutionsfour.co.uk* Web. *www.solutionsfour.co.uk/ Solutions Four*

Solvent Solutions Ltd Holmshaw Farm Layhams Road, Keston BR2 6AR Tel. *01332 691579* Fax. *01332 239627* E-mail. *danny@solventsolutions.co.uk* Web. *www.solventsolutions.co.uk Graffsolve*

Solving Ltd Wessex House Oxford Road, Newbury RG14 1PA Tel. *01635 814488* Fax. *01635 814480* E-mail. *sales@solving.co.uk* Web. *www.solving.co.uk Solving*

Somerglaze Windows Ltd 20a Stonewell Drive Congresbury, Bristol BS49 5DW Tel. *01934 830479* Fax. *01934 838557* E-mail. *info@somerglazewindows.co.uk* Web. *www.somerglazewindows.co.uk Fair Trades Member – Fensa Registered Company*

David Somerset Skincare PO Box 8, Henley On Thames RG9 6YZ Tel. *01491 578080* E-mail. *info@somersets.com* Web. *www.somersets.com Handguard (United Kingdom) – Somersets E-Z Shave (United Kingdom) – Somersets Shaving Oil (United Kingdom)*

Somers Forge Ltd Haywood Forge Prospect Road, Halesowen B62 8DZ Tel. *0121 5855959* Fax. *0121 5857154* E-mail. *sales@somersforge.com* Web. *www.somersforge.com Bestem – Electem – Hydie – Hytuf – Somdie – Somers Supamold – Somplas 30 – Thermodie – V.M.C. – V.W.M.C.*

Somers Totalkare Ltd Unit 15 Forge Trading Estate Mucklow Hill, Halesowen B62 8TP Tel. *0121 5852700* Fax. *0121 5011458* E-mail. *sales@somerstotalkare.co.uk* Web. *www.stkare.co.uk Somers Engineering – Somers Vehicle Lifts – Totalkare Prolift*

Somic Textiles New Hall Lane - Alliance Works, Preston PR1 5NY Tel. *01772 790000* Fax. *01772 795677* E-mail. *sales@somic.co.uk* Web. *www.somic.co.uk Panama – Somband – Somcord – Somflex – Somplas – Somtack – Somweave – Somyarn – Stitched Edge – Supersoft*

Sonardyne International Ltd Ocean House Blackbush Business Park, Yateley GU46 6GD Tel. *01252 872288* Fax. *01252 876100* E-mail. *sales@sonardyne.co.uk* Web. *www.sonardyne.com Big Head – BOPNav – CASIUS – Compatt – DORT – HGPS – Homer-Pro – LCU – MicoNav – Mini ROVNav – MRAMS – ORT – PAN – PGT – ROV-Homer – ROV-TRAK – ROVNav – SIPS – SIPS 2 – SIPS Plus – Sub-Mini – Super Sub-Mini – XSRS*

Sonata Ltd 17-20 Parr Street, London N1 7ET Tel. *020 72534221* Fax. *020 72512984* E-mail. *ca@sonata.co.uk* Web. *www.sonata.co.uk Totnoll Promotions*

Sonatest Ltd Head Office Dickens Road, Old Wolverton, Milton Keynes MK12 5QQ Tel. *01908 316345* Fax. *01908 321323* E-mail. *sales@sonatest.com* Web. *www.sonatest.com Alphagage – Masterscan – MicroGage – Microscan – Powerscan – Railscan – Siteplot – Sitescan – Sonacoat – Sonagage – T.-Gage*

Songmaker Ltd Suite 296 2 Lansdowne Row, Mayfair, London W1J 6HL Tel. *0871 7505555* E-mail. *enquiries@songmaker.co.uk* Web. *www.songmaker.co.uk Songmaker Studios*

Sonic Communications International Ltd Starley Way, Birmingham B37 7HB Tel. *0121 7814400* Fax. *0121 7814404* E-mail. *sales@sonic-comms.com* Web. *www.sonic-comms.com Sonic*

Sonic Drilling Supplies Ltd Yew Tree Farm Newcastle Road, Betchton, Sandbach CW11 4TD Tel. *01477 500177* Fax. *01477 500121* E-mail. *info@sonicdrill.co.uk* Web. *www.sonicdrill.co.uk Sonic Drilling*

Sonic Security Services Ltd Unit 3-5 Grange Road Workshops Grange Road, Geddington, Kettering NN14 1AL Tel. *01536 461200* Fax. *01536 461201* E-mail. *delia@sonicsecurity.co.uk* Web. *www.sonicsecurity.co.uk IPSA – NSI NACOSS Gold – SSAIB*

Sonic Windows Ltd Unit 14-15 Beeching Park Industrial Estate Wainwright Road, Bexhill On Sea TN39 3UR Tel. *01424 223864* Fax. *01424 215859* E-mail. *info@sonicwindows.co.uk* Web. *www.sonicwindows.co.uk Sonic – Sonic Clearvox Windows*

Sonique Ltd Burnhill Business Centre 50 Burnhill Road, Beckenham BR3 3LA Tel. *020 82496091* Fax. *020 82496031* E-mail. *info@soniqueltd.com* Web. *www.allmediadirect.co.uk Sonique*

Sony BMG Music Entertainment 9 Derry Street, London W8 5HY Tel. *020 73618000* Fax. *020 73719298* Web. *www.sonymusic.com BMG Classics UK*

Sony Head Office The Heights Brooklands, Weybridge KT13 0XW Tel. *01932 816000* Fax. *01932 817000* Web. *www.eu.sony.com Betacom S.P. – Data Discman – Discman – Hi Black Trinitron – *Sony Corporation (Japan) – Trinitron – Walkman*

Robert Sorby Athol Road, Sheffield S8 0PA Tel. *0114 2250700* Fax. *0114 2250710* E-mail. *sales@robert-sorby.co.uk* Web. *www.robert-sorby.co.uk Robert Sorby*

S O R Europe Ltd (European Headquarters) Farren Court The Street, Cowfold, Horsham RH13 8BP Tel. *01403 864000* Fax. *01403 864040* E-mail. *peter@soreur.co.uk* Web. *www.soreur.co.uk S.O.R.*

Sorex Ltd Oldgate, Widnes WA8 8TJ Tel. *0151 4244328* Fax. *0151 4951163* E-mail. *info@sorexinternational.com* Web. *www.sorex.com Actellic – Brodifacoum – Cesclean – Demand – Demise – Difenacoum – Klerat – Littac – Neokil – Neosorexa – Perkut – Ratak – Renegade – Sorex Super Fly Spray – Sorex Wasp Nest Destroyer – Sorexa – Sorexa CD – Sorgene 5 – Talon – Warfarin*

Sotech Ltd Unit 2 Traynor Way, Whitehouse Business Park, Peterlee SR8 2RU Tel. *0191 5872287* Fax. *0191 5180703* E-mail. *mail@sotech-optima.co.uk* Web. *www.sotech-optima.co.uk Optima*

Sothebys 34-35 New Bond Street, London W1A 2AA Tel. *020 72935000* Fax. *020 72935989* E-mail. *info@sothebys.com* Web. *www.sothebys.com Sotheby's*

Sound Dynamics Ltd Avenue House Sunny Bank Gardens, Belper DE56 1WD Tel. *01773 828486* Fax. *01773 828475* E-mail. *stuartw@sound-dynamics.co.uk* Web. *www.sound-dynamics.co.uk *Instructor System, The – *Powermaster Plus – *Rollerack*

Sound Security Ltd Jasmine Cottage Drury Lane, Ridgewell, Halstead CO9 4SL Tel. *01440 788255* Fax. *01440 788014* E-mail. *info@sound-security.co.uk* Web. *www.sound-security.co.uk Sound Security ITD*

Sound Support PO Box 12, Craigavon BT62 3EG Tel. *028 38330231* Fax. *028 38338721* E-mail. *sales@springco.co.uk Sound Support*

Sourcing Vantage Ltd 4 Lower Knoll Road Diggle, Oldham OL3 5PD Tel. *0845 6026322* E-mail. *david@sourcingvantage.com* Web. *www.sourcingvantage.com StartSource – CompleteSource*

Southco Manufacturing Ltd Farnham Trading Estate, Farnham GU9 9PL Tel. *01252 714422* Fax. *0845 1179445* E-mail. *info@southco.com* Web. *www.southco.com Arrow – Dzus – Dzus Dart – Panex – Pilot – Rapier – Supersonic – Universal*

Southco Manufacturing Co. Shire Business Park Wainwright Road, Worcester WR4 9FA Tel. *01905 751000* Fax. *01905 751090* E-mail. *info@southco.com* Web. *www.southco.com Southco*

South East Galvanizers Ltd Crittall Road, Witham CM8 3DR Tel. *01376 501501* Fax. *01376 513410* E-mail. *south.east@wedge-galv.co.uk* Web. *www.wedge-galv.co.uk Wedge Group Galvanizing*

Southend United Football Club Superstore Roots Hall Victoria Avenue, Southend On Sea SS2 6NQ Tel. *01702 351117* Fax. *01702 330164* E-mail. *info@soughendunited.co.uk* Web. *www.shrimpers-clubshop.co.uk Crevette*

Southern Scientific Scientific House Rectory Farm Road, Sompting, Lancing BN15 0DP Tel. *01903 604000* Fax. *01903 604026* E-mail. *info@ssl.gb.com* Web. *www.ssl.gb.com Knight Imaging – Knight X-Ray*

Southern Springs & Pressings Ltd Stem Lane, New Milton BH25 5NE Tel. *01425 611517* Fax. *01425 638142* E-mail. *enquiries@southernsprings.co.uk* Web. *www.southernsprings.co.uk Southern Spring Technologies*

Southern Valve & Fitting Co. Ltd Units 36 & 37 Innovation Centre Highfield Drive Churchfields, St Leonards On Sea TN38 9UH Tel. *01424 858115* Fax. *01424 858116* E-mail. *sales@southernvalve.co.uk* Web. *www.southernvalve.co.uk Aircomp – Bauer – Bonomi – Bosch Rexroth – Burkert – Burnett Hillman – Camozzi – CDC – Cejn – CKD – Crane – Crouzet – Durapipe – Eaton Walterschied – Enots – Fas – Festo – George Fisher – Ham-let – Herion – Hoke – Ingersoll-Rand – Itap – Jay Mac – John Guest – Joucomatic – Jubilee – KPM – Kuhnke – KV – Legris – M&M – Masterflex – Mead – Merlett – Metal Work – MHA – Nederman – Norgren – Norma – Numatics – Nupro – Nycoil – Oetiker – Omal – Origa – Parker – PCL – Piab – Pneumax – Rectus – Redashe – RuB – SMC – Snap-tite – Starline – Stauff – Swagelock – Tomco – TPC Pneumatics – Univer – Wade – Wikai*

South Lincs Construction Ltd Bars Bridge Bourne Road, West Pinchbeck, Spalding PE11 3NQ Tel. *01775 640555* Fax. *01775 640679* E-mail. *lyn@sldesignandbuild.co.uk* Web. *www.sldesignandbuild.co.uk South Lincs Cladding*

South London Press 2-4 Leigham Court Road, London SW16 2PD Tel. *020 87694444* Fax. *020 86647213* E-mail. *peter.edwards@slp.co.uk* Web. *www.southlondononline.co.uk Bexley Borough Mercury – Greenwich Borough Mercury – Lewisham Borough Mercury – South London Press Friday – South London Press Tuesday – Streatham, Clapham Mercury*

South West Office Supplies Oak Cottage High Street, Combe Martin, Ilfracombe EX34 0HS Tel. *01271 889337* Fax. *01271 828193* E-mail. *sales@swofficesupplies.co.uk* Web. *www.swofficesupplies.co.uk South West Office Supplies*

South West One Ltd Foxhill Herodsfoot, Liskeard PL14 4QX Tel. *01579 321300* Fax. *01579 320586* E-mail. *swonewebsiteenquiries@tauntondeane.gov.uk* Web. *www.southwestone.co.uk South West One*

Southworth Handling Ltd 3 Berkshire Business Centre Berkshire Drive, Thatcham RG19 4EW Tel. *01635 874404* Fax. *01635 874027* E-mail. *sales@southworth.co.uk* Web. *www.southworth.co.uk *Custom Lift (Italy) – *Dandy Lift (Japan) – *Flexlift (Germany) – *GKS Perfekt (Germany) – *LEV Mini-stacker (France) – *Mini-Stacker (Sweden) – *Pal Disc (Australia) – Pal-Lift Stacker (Italy) – Pallet Pal*

Space Labs Healthcare 1-2 Harforde Court John Tate Road, Hertford SG13 7NW Tel. *01992 507700* Fax. *01992 501213* E-mail. *uksales@spacelabs.com* Web. *www.spacelabshealthcare.com 2200 – 6200 – 8200s – Blease – Brompton – Datum – Frontline – Frontline Genius – Frontline Plus – Manley*

Space-Ray UK 4-6 Chapel Lane Claydon, Ipswich IP6 0JL Tel. *01473 830551* Fax. *01473 832055* E-mail. *info@spaceray.co.uk* Web. *www.spaceray.co.uk Space Ray*

Spaceright Europe Ltd 38 Tollpark Road Wardpark East, Cumbernauld, Glasgow G68 0LW Tel. *01236 853120* Fax. *01923 237546* E-mail. *sales@spacerighteurope.com* Web. *www.spacerighteurope.com Unique*

Space Station Self Storage 149 St Paul's Avenue, Slough SL2 5EN Tel. *01753 439022* Fax. *01753 707909* E-mail. *info@space-station.co.uk* Web. *www.space-station.co.uk Space Station*

Space Way Self Premier House The Premier Centre, Romsey SO51 9DG Tel. *01794 835600* Fax. *01794 835601* E-mail. *sales@spaceway.co.uk* Web. *www.spaceway.co.uk Flooritall – Stackitall*

Spafax International Ltd (Head Office) Kingsland Industrial Park Stroudley Road, Basingstoke RG24 8UG Tel. *01256 814400* Fax. *01256 814141* E-mail. *sales@spafaxmirrors.com* Web. *www.spafaxmirrors.com Spafax*

Spalding Pallets Ltd Barr Farm Main Road, Deeping St Nicholas, Spalding PE11 3BW Tel. *01775 630011* Fax. *01775 630073* E-mail. *info@spaldingrecycling.co.uk* Web. *www.spaldingrecycling.co.uk Beast 3860*

Spaldings Ltd 25-35 Sadler Road, Lincoln LN6 3XJ Tel. *01522 500600* Fax. *01522 509300* E-mail. *sales@spaldings.co.uk* Web. *www.spaldings.co.uk Farmguard – Flatlift – *Truecraft (Far East)*

Spandex plc 1600 Park Avenue Almondsbury, Bristol BS32 4UA Tel. *01454 616444* Fax. *01454 616777* E-mail. *info@spandex.com* Web. *www.spandex.co.uk Classica – Dane Board – Galleria – Infopanel – Inline – Miniframe – Monoframe – Sculptura – Signlite – Slatz – Slim Slatz*

Spanset Ltd Telford Way, Middlewich CW10 0HX Tel. *01606 737494* Fax. *01606 737502* E-mail. *customerservices@spanset.co.uk* Web. *www.spanset.co.uk A.B.S. – Ergo – Eurotrucker – Spanset – Stinger – Supra*

Spantech Products Ltd 10 Beech Gardens Crawley Down, South Godstone, Godstone RH9 8HB Tel. *01342 893239* Fax. *01342 892584* E-mail. *spantech@auptag.com* Web. *www.spantech.co.uk Spancan – Spantech*

Sparex International Ltd Exeter Airport Devon, Clyst Honiton, Exeter EX5 2LJ Tel. *01392 368892* Fax. *01392 369904* E-mail. *theunis.stortenbeker@sparex.co.uk* Web. *www.sparex.co.uk Partslift – Sparex – Spenco – Stockshop*

S P Carpentry & Joinery Skipton Street, Batley WF17 6AE Tel. *07988 693188* E-mail. *soybercafe03@hotmail.com S.P CONSTRUCTION*

S & P Coil Products Ltd Evington Valley Road, Leicester LE5 5LU Tel. *0116 2490044* Fax. *0116 2490033* E-mail. *peter.teasdale@spcoils.co.uk* Web. *www.spcoils.co.uk Airdor – Belgravia – Cirrus – Run-Around Coils*

Speakerbus Fourways House Ware Road, Hoddesdon EN11 9RS Tel. *01992 706500* Fax. *01992 706501* E-mail. *info@speakerbus.co.uk* Web. *www.speakerbus.co.uk Softpatch – Spekabox*

Spear & Jackson plc (Neill Tools Ltd) Atlas Way, Sheffield S4 7QQ Tel. *0114 2814242* Fax. *0114 2250810* E-mail. *sales@spear-and-jackson.com* Web. *www.spear-and-jackson.com County – Eclipse - *Eclipse – Eclipse - Spear & Jackson - Elliott Lucas - WHS - Tyzack - Spiralux - Neverbend - Heritage - Razorsharp – Elliott Lucas – Neverbend – Razorsharp – Spear & Jackson – Tyzack – W.H.S.*

Specac Ltd River House 97 Cray Avenue, Orpington BR5 4HE Tel. *01689 873134* Fax. *01689 878527* E-mail. *sales@specac.co.uk* Web. *www.specac.co.uk Graseby Specac*

Specialised Latex Services Ltd 7 Lupton Road, Thame OX9 3SE Tel. *01844 212489* Fax. *01844 212489* E-mail. *sales@specialisedlatex.co.uk* Web. *www.specialisedlatex.co.uk Nitex*

Specialist Computer Centres Ltd Applied House Killingbeck Drive, York Road, Leeds LS14 6UF Tel. *0113 2405250* Fax. *0113 2401093* Web. *www.scc.com Scotbyte*

Specialist Electronics Services Ltd 25 Craven Court Stanhope Road, Camberley GU15 3BS Tel. *01276 63483* Fax. *01276 63327* E-mail. *info@sesltd.com* Web. *www.sesltd.com C3DU – RCD – S3DR – S3DR - Solid State Data Recorder; C3DU - Cockpit Control and Display Unit; RCD - Rugged Computing Device.*

Specialist Tube Supplies Ltd PO Box 6705, Burton On Trent DE15 0ZS Tel. *0870 2406301* Fax. *0870 2406302* E-mail. *info@specialisttubesupplies.co.uk* Web. *www.specialisttubesupplies.co.uk S.T.S*

Specialty Fasteners & Components Ltd Seymour Wharf Steamer Quay Road, Totnes TQ9 5AL Tel. *01803 868677* Fax. *01803 868678* E-mail. *sales@specialty-fasteners.co.uk* Web. *www.specialty-fasteners.co.uk Accuride – Alcoa Fastening Systems – Barry Controls – Barry Controls - Camloc - Hydraflow - Rosan - Pinet - Accuride, - Arvin - Lisi - Stop-choc - Spiralock - Tridair – Camloc – Fairchild – Hydraflow – Rosan – Spiralock – Stop-choc – Tridair*

Specialty Gases Ltd Buiding 940 Kent Science Park, Sittingbourne ME9 8PS Tel. *01795 599099* Fax. *01795 411525* E-mail. *sales@specialty-gases.com* Web. *www.specialty-gases.com gassense – Microcans*

Speck Pumps UK Ltd 11-12 Wycombe Industrial Mall West End Street, High Wycombe HP11 2QY Tel. *01494 523203* Fax. *01494 441542* E-mail. *info@speck.co.uk* Web. *www.speck.co.uk Badu – Buffel – Speck*

Robert Speck Ltd Little Ridge Whittlebury Road, Silverstone, Towcester NN12 8UD Tel. *01327 857307* Fax. *01327 858166* E-mail. *info@robertspeck.com* Web. *www.robertspeck.com *Formdrill (Belgium) – *Microtap (Germany) – *Prototyp (Germany) – Silverstone – *Weeren (Germany)*

Spectro Analytical UK Ltd 2 New Star Road, Leicester LE4 9JD Tel. *0116 2462950* Fax. *0116 2740160* E-mail. *spectro-uk.sales@ametek.com* Web. *www.spectro.com Ciros ICP Systems – ICP-MS Systems – Spectro Xepos – Spectro Xlab 2000 – SPECTROCAST – SPECTROFLAME – SPECTROLAB – SPECTROLUX – SPECTROPORT – Spectrosort – SPECTROTEST – X Test*

Spectron Gas Control Systems Ltd Unit 4 Advanced Technology Unit 1 University of Warwick Science Park, Coventry CV4 7EZ Tel. *024 76416234* Fax. *024 76411987* E-mail. *sales@spectron-gcs.com* Web. *www.spectron-gcs.com Spectrocem – Spectrocom – Spectrolab – Spectron – Spectrotec*

Spectrum Acoustic Consultants Ltd 27-29 High Street, Biggleswade SG18 0JE Tel. *01767 318871* Fax. *01767 317704* E-mail. *enquiries@spectrumacoustic.com* Web. *www.spectrumacoustic.com Pipac – Spectrum*

Spectrum Computer Supplies Ltd PO Box 199, Bradford BD1 5RJ Tel. *01274 308188* Fax. *01274 307264* E-mail. *admin@spectrumltd.co.uk* Web. *www.spectrumltd.co.uk PClab – PCPump*

Spectrum Technologies Ltd Western Avenue Bridgend Industrial Estate, Bridgend CF31 3RT Tel. *01656 655437* Fax. *01656 655920* E-mail. *sales@spectrumtech.com* Web. *www.spectrumtech.com Capris*

Spectus Windows Systems Snape Road, Macclesfield SK10 2NZ Tel. *01625 420400* Fax. *01625 501418* Web. *www.spectussystems.com Spectus Systems*

Speedings Ltd 48 Carrmere Road Leechmere Industrial Estate, Sunderland SR2 9TW Tel. *0191 5239933* Fax. *0191 5239955* E-mail. *mail@speedingsltd.co.uk* Web. *www.speedingsltd.co.uk Reverso*

Speedograph Richfield Ltd 1a Dalton Drive Arnold, Nottingham NG5 7JR Tel. *0115 9264235* Fax. *0115 9209912* E-mail. *info@speedographrichfield.com* Web. *www.speedographrichfield.com Speedograph Richfield*

Speedo International Ltd Ascot Road, Nottingham NG8 5AJ Tel. *0115 9167000* Fax. *0115 9105005* E-mail. *speedoinfo@pentland.com* Web. *www.speedo.com Speedo*

Speed Plastics Ltd Wheatbridge Road, Chesterfield S40 2AB Tel. *01246 276510* Fax. *01246 245400* E-mail. *mikeh@speedplastics.co.uk* Web. *www.speedplastics.co.uk Aquadome – Aquadome; Solar Still; Medimask; Layflat; Supa Support – Layflat – Medimask – Solar Sill – Supa Support*

Spence Bryson Ltd Unit 14a Seagoe Industrial Area Portadown, Craigavon BT63 5QD Tel. *028 38332521* Fax. *028 38351043* E-mail. *sales@spencebryson.co.uk* Web. *www.spencebryson.co.uk Snow Drift*

Spencer Coatings Ltd Froghall Terrace, Aberdeen AB24 3JN Tel. *01224 788400* Fax. *01355 233847* E-mail. *info@spencercoatings.co.uk* Web. *www.spencercoatings.co.uk Floorcote – General Purpose Undercoat – Hammercote – Industrial P.U. Enamel – Kemnay – Liquid High Gloss – Marine H.D. Enamel – Microflex – Premier Vinyl Matt – Premier Vinyl Silk – Speedspray Q.D. Enamel – Spencer Liquid High Gloss – Spencer Marine gloss – Spencers Industrial PU enamel – Stormcote – Stripkwik – Transcote*

Spencer Stuart & Associates Ltd Bain House 16 Connaught Place, London W2 2ED Tel. *020 72983333* Fax. *020 72983388* E-mail. *kwinter@spencerstuart.com* Web. *www.spencerstuart.com Selector Europe (United Kingdom)*

Spendor Audio Systems Ltd Unit G5 Ropemaker Park South Road, Hailsham BN27 3GY Tel. *01323 843474* Fax. *01323 442254* E-mail. *info@spendoraudio.com* Web. *www.spendoraudio.com Spendor*

Sperrin Metal Products Ltd Cahore Road Draperstown, Magherafelt BT45 7AP Tel. *028 79628362* Fax. *028 79628972* E-mail. *info@sperrin-metal.com* Web. *www.sperrin-metal.com Sperrin Metal Products*

Spheric Trafalgar Ltd Wiston Business Park London Road, Ashington, Pulborough RH20 3DJ Tel. *01903 891200* Fax. *01903 891220* E-mail. *sales@ballbiz.com* Web. *www.ballbiz.com Spheric-Trafalgar Ltd – Trafalgar Bearing Co.*

S P H Europe plc Rothwell Mill Rothwell Street, Bolton BL3 6HY Tel. *01204 398400* Fax. *01204 398211* E-mail. *info@sph.co.uk* Web. *www.sph.co.uk Clothescare – Equipcare – Shoecare*

S P I Ltd Morley Carr House Morley Carr Road, Low Moor, Bradford BD12 0RA Tel. *01274 691777* Fax. *01274 693832* E-mail. *info@styrene.biz* Web. *www.styrene.biz Stylite Cavity Wall – Stylite Cavity Wall Stylite Flooring – Stylite Flooring*

Spies Hecker UK Wedgewood Way, Stevenage SG1 4QN Tel. *01438 734705* Fax. *01438 734730* E-mail. *contact-sh-gb@gbr.spieshecker.com* Web. *www.spieshecker.co.uk Aultra 2K – Aultratuff – Gipgloss – *Spies Hecker (Germany)*

Spink & Son Ltd 69 Southampton Row, London WC1B 4ET Tel. *020 75634000* Fax. *020 75634066* E-mail. *info@spink.com* Web. *www.spink-online.com Spink & Son*

Spinlock Ltd 41 Birmingham Road, Cowes PO31 7BH Tel. *01983 295555* Fax. *01983 295542* E-mail. *info@spinlock.co.uk* Web. *www.spinlock.co.uk Power Jammer – Powercleat – Powerclutch – Spinlock*

Spinnaker International Ltd Spinnaker House Saltash Parkway, Saltash PL12 6LF Tel. *01752 850300* Fax. *01752 850301* E-mail. *info@spinnaker.co.uk* Web. *www.spinnakerinternational.com Citadel – Custodian – Genesis – Sentinel*

Spirent plc Swift House Northwood Park Gatwick Road, Crawley RH10 9XN Tel. *01293 767676* Fax. *01293 767677* E-mail. *info@spirent.com* Web. *www.spirent.com Metrohm*

Spire Peugeot Ltd Harpsfield Broadway Comet Way, Hatfield AL10 9TF Tel. *01707 264521* Fax. *01707 251139* E-mail. *peugeot@waters.co.uk* Web. *www.spirepeugeot.co.uk Garden City Coachworks – Vilton Cars*

Spiring Enterprises Ltd Unit 8e Gilmans Industrial Estate, Billingshurst RH14 9EZ Tel. *01403 784033* Fax. *01403 785215* Web. *www.molymod.com Atomod – Molydome – Molymod – Scalink – Scalinks*

Spiroflow Ltd Lincoln Way, Clitheroe BB7 1QG Tel. *01200 422525* Fax. *01200 429165* E-mail. *sales@spiroflow.com* Web. *www.spiroflow.com Spirofil – Spiroflow – Spiroweigh*

Spirol Industries Ltd 17 Princewood Road Earlstrees Industrial Estate, Corby NN17 4ET Tel. *01536 444800* Fax. *01536 203415* E-mail. *info@spirol.com* Web. *www.spirol.com ANACO DISK SPRINGS – SPIROL INSERTS – SPIROL PINS – Spirol Spacers – SPIROL TUBULAR PRODUCTS*

Splendour Snacks 1a Clive Way, Watford WD24 4PX Tel. *01923 253290* Fax. *01923 253290* Web. *www.splendoursnacks.com *Splendour Snacks*

Sponmech Safety Systems Ltd Hayseech Road, Halesowen B63 3PD Tel. *0121 5858730* Fax. *0121 5855128* E-mail. *sales@sponmech.co.uk* Web. *www.sponmech.co.uk Easyguard*

Spooner Industries Ltd Moorland Engineering Works Railway Road, Ilkley LS29 8JB Tel. *01943 609505* Fax. *01943 603190* E-mail. *mbrook@spooner.co.uk* Web. *www.spooner.co.uk Air Turn – ModuleDryer – Spooner – Stairbar*

Sport England Funding Page 3rd Floor Victoria House Bloomsbury Square, London WC1B 4SE Tel. *08458 508508* Fax. *020 73835740* E-mail. *kate.dale@sportengland.org* Web. *www.sportengland.org Sport For All*

Sporting Surface Supplies Ltd Hathersham Lane Smallfield, Horley RH6 9JG Tel. *01342 843663* Fax. *01342 844180* E-mail. *info@sportingsurfacesupplies.com* Web. *www.sportingsurfacesupplies.com Hurstridge*

Sportique Ski Boats Fire Beacon Bridge Fire Beacon Lane, Covenham St Bartholomew, Louth LN11 0PA Tel. *01472 388296* Fax. *01472 388944* E-mail. *info@sportiqueboats.co.uk* Web. *www.sportiqueboats.co.uk Sportique*

Sports Coach UK 114 Cardigan Road, Leeds LS6 3BJ Tel. *0113 2744802* Fax. *0113 2755019* E-mail. *tbyrne@sportscoachuk.org* Web. *www.sportscoachuk.org Champion Coaching – Coachwise*

Sportsmark Group Ltd Unit 4 Clerewater Place Lower Way, Thatcham RG19 3RF Tel. *01635 867537* Fax. *01483 487919* E-mail. *info@sportsmark.net* Web. *www.sportsmark.net Antisocial Stud – Bee Hive Bin – Bee-bump – Bola (United Kingdom) – Bowdry – Cataphos – Centrurion Rugby Training Equipment – Club Concrete (United Kingdom) – Club GRC (United Kingdom) – Club Green – Coloursafe – County Concrete (United Kingdom) – County GRC (United Kingdom) – County Green (United Kingdom) – Dimple Liner – Dimple Marker – Easymark – Flexiline – g m machine – Grid Liner – Groundsman Field Handbook – Guidograph (United Kingdom) – Jubilee – Level-Line – Line Lazer (U.S.A.) – Lobster – Radford Ezy Stumps – Spraymar (United Kingdom) – Verdemat*

Spotlight Casting Directories & Contacts 7 Leicester Place, London WC2H 7RJ Tel. *020 74377631* Fax. *020 74375881* E-mail. *enquiries@spotlight.com* Web. *www.spotlight.com Spotlight CD – Spotlight, The*

S P P Pumps Theale Cross Pincents Kiln, Calcot, Reading RG31 7SP Tel. *0118 9323123* Fax. *0161 9323302* E-mail. *enquiries@spppumps.com* Web. *www.spppumps.com Autoprime – Berkefeld – Halberg – LaBour – Mokveld – Peerless – Service – Sihi – SPP – SPP Projects*

Spraybake Ltd Milner Road Chilton Industrial Estate, Sudbury CO10 2XG Tel. *01787 888650* Fax. *01787 882305* E-mail. *sales@spraybake.co.uk* Web. *www.spraybake.co.uk Bradbury – Peters – Spraybake*

Spraychem Ltd Cardrew Industrial Estate, Redruth TR15 1ST Tel. *01209 312123* Fax. *01209 314333* E-mail. *vernon.holmes@contico.co.uk* Web. *www.spraychem.co.uk Port-A-Cart – Smoothline*

Spraysafe Automatic Sprinklers 6 Westpoint Enterprise Park Clarence Avenue, Trafford Park, Manchester M17 1QS Tel. *0161 8750500* Fax. *0161 8750509* E-mail. *kate.scourfield@centralsprinkler.com* Web. *www.centralsprinkler.com Central Spraysafe*

Springco N I Ltd 21 Carn Road Portadown, Craigavon BT63 5WG Tel. *028 38333482* Fax. *028 38338721* E-mail. *sales@springco.co.uk* Web. *www.springco.co.uk Springco*

Springfast Ltd Southbrook House Southbrook Road, Gloucester GL4 3YY Tel. *01452 416688* Fax. *01452 308723* E-mail. *enquiries@springfast.co.uk* Web. *www.springfast.co.uk Pivi*

Springmasters Ltd 55 Arthur Street, Redditch B98 8LF Tel. *01527 521000* Fax. *01527 528866* E-mail. *sales@springmasters.com* Web. *www.springmasters.com A.B.A.*

Springstop (UK) Ltd 95 Boden Street, Glasgow G40 3QF Tel. *0141 5544424* Fax. *0141 5544423* E-mail. *info@spring-stop.com* Web. *www.spring-stop.com Springstop. Springs custom made to individual specification.*

Springvale E P S Ltd Coach Lane Hazlerigg, Newcastle Upon Tyne NE13 7AP Tel. *0191 2171144* Fax. *0191 2171212* E-mail. *sales@springvale.com* Web. *www.springvale.com Ecowarm Cavity Tag – Ecowarm Fulfil Tag – Ecowarm Warmboard – Ecowarm Warmclad – Ecowarm Warmfloor – Ecowarm Warmlath – Ecowarm Warmroof – Ecowarm Warmsark – Ecowarm Warmsqueez – Microfoam EPS – Springvale Cavity Tag*

Springvale Insulation Ltd 75 Springvale Road Doagh, Ballyclare BT39 0SS Tel. *028 93340203* Fax. *01457 869269* E-mail. *plong@springvale.com* Web. *www.springvale.com Ecowarm Cavity T & G – Ecowarm Flat Roofs – Ecowarm Fulfil T & G – Ecowarm Warmboard – Ecowarm Warmclad – Ecowarm Warmfloor – Ecowarm Warmlath – Ecowarm Warmsark – Ecowarm Warmsqueez – Keps – Microfoam Cavity – Microfoam Flooring*

Sprint Engineering & Lubricant Unit G3 Imperial Business Estate West Mill, Gravesend DA11 0DL Tel. *01474 534251* Fax. *01474 534566* E-mail. *info@sprint-uk.com* Web. *www.sprint-uk.com ABB – Ammeraal Beltech – Baldor – BP – Clean Metals – Cross & Morse – Dayco – Dodge – Elf – Esso – Fag – Falk – Kluber – Magnaloy – Martin Sprocket & Gear – Optimol – Regina – Reliance – Roulunds – Visurgis Optibelt*

S & P Spanarc Ltd Berwick House Dartford Road, Sevenoaks TN13 3TQ Tel. *01732 743456* Fax. *01732 742922* E-mail. *chris.guinane@spanarc.co.uk* Web. *www.spanarc.co.uk *Bematec (Switzerland) – Spairo Shaft – Stephilco – *Swema (Sweden)*

S P S Technologies Ltd Troon Industrial Area 191 Barkby Road, Leicester LE4 9HX Tel. *0116 2768261* Fax. *0116 2740243* Web. *www.sps.com S.P.S. Tech – Unbrako*

S P Technology Ltd Unit3 Camperdown Industrial Park George Buckman Drive, Dundee DD2 3SP Tel. *01382 880088* Fax. *01382 880099* E-mail. *info@sptechnology.co.uk* Web. *www.sptechnology.co.uk Bosch – SP Technology – Staubil*

Spud U Like 9 Central Business Centre Great Central Way, London NW10 0UR Tel. *020 88302424* Fax. *020 88302427* E-mail. *headoffice@spudulike.com* Web. *www.spudulike.com C & G Fast Foods – Spudulike*

S P X Flow Technology 3b Wheatstone Close, Crawley RH10 9UA Tel. *01293 553495* Fax. *01293 524635* E-mail. *peter.robinson@spx.com* Web. *www.johnson-pump.com Combisystem – Fre-Flow – Top Gear – Toplobe – Topwing*

Spyder Cars Ltd Fenland District Industrial Estate Station Road, Whittlesey, Peterborough PE7 2EY Tel. *01733 203986* Fax. *01733 350662* E-mail. *sales@spydercars.co.uk* Web. *www.spydercars.co.uk Spyder Engineering*

Spyra Distribution 112 Beddington Lane, Croydon CR0 4TD Tel. *020 86651155* Fax. *020 86651122* E-mail. *sales@spyradistribution.co.uk* Web. *www.spyradistribution.co.uk Dickies Portwest*

Spysure 109a Digbeth, Birmingham B5 6DT Tel. *08702 004200* E-mail. *info@spysure.com* Web. *www.spysure.com Spysure*

Square Enix Ltd Wimbledon Bridge House 1 Hartfield Road, London SW19 3RU Tel. *020 86363000* Fax. *020 86363001* E-mail. *philr@eidos.co.uk* Web. *www.square-enix.com Championship Manager – Commandos – Death Trap Dungeon – FA Manager – Links 99 – Mel Gibsons Braveheart – Michael Owens World League Soccer – Toom Raider*

Square Two Lubrication Ltd Unit 12 Orleton Road, Ludlow Business Park, Ludlow SY8 1XF Tel. *01584 874220* Fax. *0870 0113324* E-mail. *lube@s2lube.com* Web. *www.s2lube.com Memolub – Whitmore's Lubricants*

S R B Joinery Ltd 232 Mossy Lea Road Wrightington, Wigan WN6 9RL Tel. *01257 424362* Fax. *0845 8674760* E-mail. *sales@srbltd.co.uk* Web. *www.srbltd.co.uk CNC ROUTER – JOINERY*

SRCS Creative 8-9 South Terrace Whitnash, Leamington Spa CV31 2HY Tel. *01926 337440* E-mail. *enquiries@srcscreative.com* Web. *www.srcscreative.com SRCS Creative*

S R L Countertech Ltd Leigh Street, Sheffield S9 2PR Tel. *0114 2560020* Fax. *0114 2560070* E-mail. *paul@srl-countertech.co.uk* Web. *www.srl-countertech.co.uk *PowerSoak – SRL*

S R L Technical Services Ltd Holbrook House Holbrook Hall Park, Little Waldingfield, Sudbury CO10 0TH Tel. *01787 247595* Fax. *01787 248420* E-mail. *eric.knight@soundresearch.co.uk* Web. *www.soundresearch.co.uk S.R.L.*

S R S Product plc 19 Mead Industrial Park Riverway, Harlow CM20 2SE Tel. *01279 635500* Fax. *01279 635282* E-mail. *sales@srs-products.co.uk* Web. *www.srs-products.co.uk Cubic-Casing – Cubic-Casing, Versirak - Sub-frame, Eurorack - Sub-frame - Netcase - Intermas – Eurorack – Intermas – Netcase – Sub-frame – Versirak*

S S A B Swedish Steel Ltd Unit 17 Narrowboat Way Hurst Business Park, Brierley Hill DY5 1UF Tel. *01384 74660* Fax. *01384 77575* E-mail. *paul.cartwright@ssab.com* Web. *www.dobel.co.uk Aluzink (Sweden) – *Dobel (Sweden) – Dobel 200 XT (United Kingdom) – Dobelshield – Petrochem Aluzink (United Kingdom) – *S.S.A.B. Dobel (Sweden)*

S S F Design 44 Botley Gardens, Southampton SO19 0SW Tel. *023 80404818* E-mail. *info@ssfdesign.com* Web. *www.SSFdesign.com SSF Design*

S S I Schaefer Ltd 83-84 Livingstone Road Walworth Industrial Estate, Andover SP10 5QZ Tel. *01264 386600* Fax. *01264 386611* E-mail. *solutions@ssi-schaefer.co.uk* Web. *www.ssi-schaefer.co.uk Auto 3000 – D.R. 20 – F.K. Box – K.S. Containers – P.R. 600 – Regal 3000 System – Regal 4000 System – Regal 7000 – VRS – W.S. & W.S.K.*

S S White Technologies UK Ltd 19 Heathfield Stacey Bushes, Milton Keynes MK12 6HP Tel. *01908 525120* Fax. *01908 319967* E-mail. *insales@sswhite.co.uk* Web. *www.sswhite.co.uk Linkflex – Masterflex – S.S. White Industrial – S.S.W. Automotive – Whiteflex*

Stabilag E S H Ltd Lower Gade Farm Dagnall Road Great Gaddesden, Hemel Hempstead HP1 3BP Tel. *01442 843843* Fax. *0870 9906762* E-mail. *sales@stabilag.com* Web. *www.stabilag.com Raychem – TraceTek*

Stacatruc Unit 12 Stechford Trading Estate Stechford, Birmingham B33 8BU Tel. *0121 2444700* Fax. *0121 2444900* E-mail. *service@stacatruc.co.uk* Web. *www.stacatruc.co.uk Aisle-master – Ariston – Atlet – Balkancar – BKC – Boss – BT Rolatruc – BV Vestergaard – Caterpillar – CE – Cesab – Challenger – Clark – Climax – Crown – CTC – Daewoo – Desta – Electricar – Fiat – Hamech – Harbuilt – Heli – Hubtex – Huyundai – Hystacker – Hyster – Jungheinrich – Kalmar – Kelvin – Komatsu – Lancer Boss – Lansing – Linde – LOLER – M & M – Manitou – Mariotti – Mitsubishi – Nacco – Nexun – Nippon – Nissan – OMG – Pramac – R.I.T.B. – Raymond – Rekord – Roro – ROSPA – Samsung – Samuk – Silverstone – SSP – Stacatruc – Stackatruck – TCM – Toyota – Translift – Tynes – Wells & Edwards – Yale*

Stadco Telford Queensway Hortonwood, Telford TF1 7LL Tel. *01952 222111* Fax. *01952 222050* E-mail. *t_daimon@ogihara.co.uk* Web. *www.stadco.co.uk Ogihara*

Stadium Crayons Ltd Unit 1-5 Muira Off William Street, Southampton SO14 5QH Tel. *023 80226765* Fax. *023 80630304* E-mail. *sales@stadiumcrayons.co.uk* Web. *www.stadiumcrayons.co.uk Stadium – Uncle Bobtail*

Staeng Ltd Unit 1a Goonhavern Industrial Estate, Goonhavern, Truro TR4 9QL Tel. *01872 572071* Fax. *01872 571335* E-mail. *sales@staeng.co.uk* Web. *www.staeng.co.uk Staeng*

Stafforce Reginald Arthur House 2-8 Percy Street, Rotherham S65 1ED Tel. *01709 370000* Fax. *01709 370037* E-mail. *info@stafforce.co.uk* Web. *www.stafforce.co.uk Cra-Cro International Personnel – Cra-Cro Personnel – Nicholas Associates – Stafforce Recruitment*

G H Stafford & Son Ltd 1 Regal Drive Walsall Enterprise Park, Walsall WS2 9HQ Tel. *01922 623993* Fax. *01922 723403* E-mail. *info@ghstafford.com* Web. *www.ghstafford.com *Stafford Leathergoods (China)*

Staffordshire Hydraulic Services Ltd Mount Road Kidsgrove, Stoke On Trent ST7 4AZ Tel. *01782 771225* Fax. *01782 777087* E-mail. *sales@staffshydraulics.co.uk* Web. *www.staffshydraulics.co.uk Dk-Lok – HIP – SC – Spir Star*

Staffordshire Newspapers Ltd The Publishing Centre Derby Street, Stafford ST16 2DT Tel. *01785 257700* Fax. *01785 253287* E-mail. *mike.richardson@staffordshirenewspapers.co.uk* Web. *www.staffordshirenewsletter.co.uk Rugeley Newsletter – South Staffordshire Newsletter – Stafford Newsletter – Staffordshire Life Magazine – Stone Newsletter – Uttoxeter Newsletter*

Stagecoach Ltd Broadacre House 16-20 Lowther Street, Carlisle CA3 8DA Tel. *01228 597222* Fax. *01228 597888* E-mail. *christopher.bowles@stagecoachbus.com* Web. *www.stagecoachbus.com Coachline*

Stagecoach Ltd Railway Terrace, Rugby CV21 3HS Tel. *01788 535555* Fax. *01788 572221* E-mail. *wark.enquiries@stagecoachbus.com* Web. *www.stagecoachbus.com Midland Red*

Stagecoach Ltd Rothersthorpe Avenue Rothersthorpe Avenue Ind Estate, Northampton NN4 8UT Tel. *01604 662266* Fax. *01604 702812* Web. *www.stagecoachbus.com Coachlinks – Stagecoach United Counties – Street Shuttle*

Stagecoach Ltd North Bridge Street, Sunderland SR5 1AQ Tel. *0191 5675251* Fax. *0191 5660202* E-mail. *john.conroy@stagecoachbus.com* Web. *www.stagecoachbus.com Stagecoach Busways*

Stagecoach Ltd Bus Station Sandgate, Ayr KA7 1DD Tel. *01292 613500* Fax. *01292 613501* E-mail. *alan.henry@stagecoachbus.com* Web. *www.stagecoachbus.com A1 Service (pan) – AA Buses – Schoolbuses – Western Buses*

Stagecoach In South Wales 1 St Davids Road, Cwmbran NP44 1PD Tel. *01633 838856* Fax. *01633 865299* E-mail. *angie.williams@stagecoachbus.com* Web. *www.stagecoachbus.com Stagecoach Red & white*

Stage Control Ltd 20 Station Parade Whitchurch Lane, Edgware HA8 6RW Tel. *020 89528982* Fax. *020 89514178* E-mail. *info@stagecontrol.com* Web. *www.stagecontrol.com Starol*

Stage Systems Ltd Stage House Prince William Road, Loughborough LE11 5GU Tel. *01509 611021* Fax. *01509 233146* E-mail. *info@stagesystems.co.uk* Web. *www.stagesystems.co.uk Axess – Crowd Control Barriers – Dance Floor – Dry Dek – Key Stage – Multi-Dek – Q-Build – Q-Plus*

Stags 19 Bampton Street, Tiverton EX16 6AA Tel. *01884 256331* Fax. *01884 258401* E-mail. *tiverton@stags.co.uk* Web. *www.stags.co.uk Stags*

Stainer & Bell Ltd PO Box 110, London N3 1DZ Tel. *020 83433303* Fax. *020 83433024* E-mail. *post@stainer.co.uk* Web. *www.stainer.co.uk Augener – Galliard – Joseph Williams – Weekes*

Stainless Design Services Ltd C The Old Bakery Kiln Lane, Swindon SN2 2NP Tel. *01793 692666* Fax. *01793 487242* E-mail. *barry.nugent@stainlessdesign.co.uk* Web. *www.stainlessdesign.co.uk S.D.S.*

Stainless steel cleaner ltd 17 Treforest Road, Coventry CV3 IFN Tel. *024 76650012* Fax. *024 76650012* E-mail. *sales@stainlesssteelcleaner.co.uk* Web. *www.stainlesssteelcleaner.co.uk The ultimate stainless steel cleaner*

Stainless Tube & Needle Co. Ltd 66 Fazeley Road, Tamworth B78 3JN Tel. *01827 51162* Fax. *01827 65559* E-mail. *robert.gold@stncoltd.co.uk* Web. *www.stncoltd.co.uk Stainless Tube & Needle Co.*

Stakapal Ltd Bettys Lane Norton Canes, Cannock WS11 9NZ Tel. *01543 278123* Fax. *01543 279543* Web. *www.stakapal.co.uk Stakapal*

Stanair Industrial Door Services Ltd Unit 2 Henson Way Telford Way Industrial Estate, Kettering NN16 8PX Tel. *01536 482187* Fax. *01536 411799* E-mail. *info@stanair.co.uk* Web. *www.stanair.co.uk Stanair*

Stanborough Press Ltd Londonthorpe Road, Grantham NG31 9SN Tel. *01476 591700* Fax. *01476 577144* E-mail. *ppodder@stanpress.co.uk* Web. *www.stanboroughpress.co.uk House of natural food Ltd*

Stancold plc (Coldroom Manufacturing). Portview Road, Bristol BS11 9LQ Tel. *0117 3167000* Fax. *0117 3167001* E-mail. *sales@stancold.co.uk* Web. *www.stancold.co.uk Firecold – Stancold*

Standall Tools Ltd Mickley Lane Dronfield Woodhouse, Dronfield S18 8XB Tel. *0114 2620626* Fax. *0114 2620520* E-mail. *jse@standall.com* Web. *www.standall.com Standall Tools*

Standard Industrial Systems Ltd Stanton House Eastham Village Rd, Eastham, Wirral CH62 0DE Tel. *0845 2571985* Fax. *0845 2571986* E-mail. *sales@standardindustrial.co.uk* Web. *www.standardindustrial.co.uk DOWCLENE – Idea Machine – Multimatic*

Standard Life plc Standard Life House 30 Lothian Road, Edinburgh EH1 2DH Tel. *0131 2252552* Fax. *0131 2458390* E-mail. *gerry_grimstone@standardlife.com* Web. *www.standardlife.com Castle – Standard Life – Standard Life Bank – Standard Life Investments – Stanplan*

Standard Motor Products Europe Ltd Unit 5b Little Oak Drive Annesley, Nottingham NG15 0DR Tel. *01623 886400* Fax. *01623 886500* E-mail. *info@smpeurope.com* Web. *www.smpeurope.com Blue Streak Europe – Intermotor – Lemark – Webcon*

Standel Dawman Ltd Pasture Lane Works Pasture Lane, Barrowford, Nelson BB9 6ES Tel. *01282 613175* Fax. *01282 615429* E-mail. *sales@standeldawman.uk.com* Web. *www.standeldawman.net Standel Dawman*

Standen Engineering Ltd Hereward Works 47-49 Station Road, Ely CB7 4BP Tel. *01353 661111* Fax. *01353 662370* E-mail. *info@standen.co.uk* Web. *www.standen.co.uk Rowcrop – Spectrum – Standen Clodmaster – Standen FM Flail Topper – Standen Planter – Standen Spectra – Statesman – Vision*

Stanhope Seta Ltd London Street, Chertsey KT16 8AP Tel. *01932 564391* Fax. *01932 568363* E-mail. *sales@stanhope-seta.co.uk* Web. *www.stanhope-seta.co.uk Seta – Seta-Hot – Setaclean – Setaflash – Setafoam 150 – Setamatic – Setapoint – Setasill – SetaTime – Setavap – Setavis – Stanomatic*

Staniforth Motor Cycles Wholesale Ltd 182 Church Street Ecclesfield, Sheffield S35 9WG Tel. *0114 2462027* Fax. *0114 2454232* E-mail. *peterstaniforth@staniforths.co.uk* Web. *www.staniforth.co.uk *Various Trade Names (Taiwan)*

Stanley Decorating Products 135 Gelderd Road, Leeds LS12 6BE Tel. *0113 2511450* Fax. *0113 2433910* Web. *www.stanleyworks.com Ascot – Comet – Jumbo*

Stanley Gibbons Ltd 399 Strand, London WC2R 0LX Tel. *020 78368444* Fax. *020 78367342* E-mail. *sales@stanleygibbons.co.uk* Web. *www.stanleygibbons.com Collecta – Stanley Gibbons – Urch Harris*

Stanley Handling Ltd 48 Coldharbour Lane, Harpenden AL5 4UR Tel. *01582 767711* Fax. *01582 765994* E-mail. *sales@stanleyhandling.co.uk* Web. *www.stanleyhandling.co.uk Hydratruck – Liftkar – PowerMate – Robur*

Stanley Plastics Ltd Units 4-7 Holmbush Industrial Estate, Midhurst GU29 9HX Tel. *01730 816221* Fax. *01730 812877* E-mail. *maica@stanleyplastics.co.uk* Web. *www.stanleyplastics.co.uk Transpalite*

Stanmatic Precision UK Ltd T/A Axis Group (Axis Group) Unit 5 Lion Centre Hanworth Trading Estate, Feltham TW13 6DS Tel. *020 88938339* Fax. *020 88938439* E-mail. *sales@axis-gb.com* Web. *www.axis-gb.com Sony*

Stannah Management Services Ltd Watt Close East Portway, Andover SP10 3SD Tel. *01264 364311* Fax. *01264 353943* E-mail. *jon_stannah@stannah.co.uk* Web. *www.stannah.co.uk 260 – 300*

Stannah Microlifts Ltd Caxton Close, Andover SP10 3QN Tel. *01264 351922* Fax. *01264 333465* E-mail. *graham_mears@stannah.co.uk* Web. *www.stannah.co.uk *Goodsmaster – *Microlift – *Trolley Lift*

Stanton Bonna Concrete Ltd Littlewell Lane Stanton-by-dale, Ilkeston DE7 4QW Tel. *0115 9441448* Fax. *0115 9441466* E-mail. *b.wilson@stanton-bonna.co.uk* Web. *www.stanton-bonna.co.uk *Moduloval (France) – Vi-King*

StanTronic Instruments 53A High Street Bugbrooke, Northampton NN7 3PG Tel. *01604 832521* Fax. *01604 832521* E-mail. *info@stantronic.co.uk* Web. *www.stantronic.co.uk Acute – GWInstek – Leaptronix – Owon – Ztec*

Stanwell Office Furniture 23 Muswell Avenue, London N10 2EB Tel. *020 88831039* Fax. *020 84443988*

E-mail. *info@stanwellofficefurniture.co.uk* Web. *www.stanwellofficefurniture.co.uk Albion Chairs – Kab Office Chairs – Primeline – Stanwell Office Furniture*

Stapeley Water Gardens Ltd 92 London Road Stapeley, Nantwich CW5 7LH Tel. *01270 611500* Fax. *01270 610616* E-mail. *info@stapeleywg.com* Web. *www.stapeleywg.com Palms Tropical Oasis, The*

Staples Disposables Ltd Hurlingham Business Park Fulbeck Heath, Grantham NG32 3HL Tel. *01400 262800* Fax. *01529 411607* E-mail. *orders@staplesdisposables.com* Web. *www.staplesdisposables.com Handiwype – Mastermask – Uniblue*

Staples Uk Ltd Windover Road, Huntingdon PE29 7EF Tel. *01480 442222* Fax. *01480 442266* E-mail. *sales@staplesbeds.co.uk* Web. *www.staplesbeds.co.uk Horatio Myers & Co – Staples*

Star Automation Uk Ltd 1A Vernon Court Henson Way, Telford Ind Est, Kettering NN16 8PX Tel. *01536 521884* Fax. *01536 512784* E-mail. *sales@amtechuk.com* Web. *star-europe.com Eins – Piovan Star – Star Seiki*

Starchild Shoes Unit 18 The Oak Business Centre 79-93 Ratcliffe Road, Sileby, Loughborough LE12 7PU Tel. *01509 817601* Fax. *01509 817601* E-mail. *info@starchildshoes.co.uk* Web. *www.starchildshoes.co.uk SNUGS – STARCHILD – TRIGGERFISH*

Starcke Abrasives Ltd 2 Alexandra Gate Ffordd Pengam, Cardiff CF24 2SA Tel. *029 20894828* Fax. *029 20487410* E-mail. *info@starckeuk.com* Web. *www.starckeuk.com Ersta – Matador*

H C Starck Ltd Unit 1 Harris Road, Calne SN11 9PT Tel. *01249 822122* Fax. *01249 823800* E-mail. *info@hcstarck.com* Web. *www.hcstarck.com H.C. Starck Ltd*

Starfrost UK Ltd Starfrost House Newcombe Road, Lowestoft NR32 1XA Tel. *01502 562206* Fax. *01502 584104* E-mail. *sales@starfrost.co.uk* Web. *www.starfrost.com Starfrost Helix – Starfrost Turbo – Starlite Helix – Starlite Turbo*

Star Industrial Tools Ltd 42 Westfield Road Kings Heath, Birmingham B14 7ST Tel. *0121 4444354* Fax. *0121 4411838* E-mail. *admin@starindustrialtools.co.uk Diastar – Octacut – Star*

Star Instruments Ltd Barkway, Royston SG8 8EH Tel. *01763 848886* Fax. *01763 848881* E-mail. *sales@star-instruments.co.uk* Web. *www.star-instruments.co.uk Filter Star (United Kingdom) – Lemag (Germany) – Sika (Germany)*

Bruce Starke & Co. Ltd Langton Green, Eye IP23 7HN Tel. *01379 870209* Fax. *01379 871232* E-mail. *info@bruce-starke.com* Web. *www.bruce-starke.com Out and About – Stormsafe – Tropicoir*

Starkstrom Ltd 256 Field End Road Eastcote, Ruislip HA4 9UW Tel. *020 88683732* Fax. *020 88683736* E-mail. *info@starkstrom.com* Web. *www.starkstrom.com *Carel (Italy) – *Circutor (Spain) – *Rex (Germany)*

Starline Hope Road, Bristol BS3 3NZ Tel. *0117 3002213* Fax. *01253 307149* E-mail. *sales@starlinesales.co.uk* Web. *www.starlinesales.co.uk Starline (Sales Ideas)*

Star Micronics GB Ltd Chapel Street Melbourne, Derby DE73 8JF Tel. *01332 864455* Fax. *01332 864005* E-mail. *sales@stargb.com* Web. *www.stargb.com F M B – J B S-Systems GmbH – Partmaker – Star – Swisscam*

Starna Industries Ltd 31-33 Station Road Chadwell Heath, Romford RM6 4BL Tel. *020 85995115* Fax. *020 85990707* E-mail. *info@starnaindustries.co.uk* Web. *www.starna.co.uk Starna*

Starpoint Electrics Ltd Units 1-5 King George's Trading Estate Davis Road, Chessington KT9 1TT Tel. *020 83917700* Fax. *020 83917760* E-mail. *sales@starpoint.uk.com* Web. *www.starpoint.uk.com Starpoint*

Star Refrigeration Ltd Thornliebank Industrial Estate Thornliebank, Glasgow G46 8JW Tel. *0141 6387916* Fax. *0141 6388111* E-mail. *star@star-ref.co.uk* Web. *www.star-ref.co.uk Star Refrigeration*

Star Sportswear Ltd Pro Star PO Box 20, Wakefield WF2 7AJ Tel. *01924 291441* Fax. *01924 384495* E-mail. *sales@prostar.co.uk* Web. *www.prostar.co.uk Delta – Interceptor – Pro Star – Starmax – Starsoft – Super Pro – Terra Firma*

Stately Albion Ltd Unit 20 Darren Drive Prince of Wales Industrial Estate, Abercarn, Newport NP11 5AR Tel. *01495 244472* Fax. *01495 248939* E-mail. *sales@stately-albion.co.uk* Web. *www.stately-albion.co.uk Stately-Albion Ltd*

Statestrong Ltd Boundary Road, Lytham St Annes FY8 5LT Tel. *01253 741806* Fax. *01253 794542* E-mail. *sales@statestrong.com* Web. *www.statestrong.com Flowersharp – Professionaltouch – Shelley – Sportstar*

Static Safe Ltd 6 Timmis Road, Stourbridge DY9 7BQ Tel. *01384 898599* Fax. *01384 898577* E-mail. *sse@static-safe.demon.co.uk* Web. *www.static-safe.co.uk *Freuden berg (Germany) – *West (Switzerland)*

Stat Shop 87 South Road, Faversham ME13 7LY Tel. *01795 425424* Fax. *0870 7777827* E-mail. *admin@statshop.co.uk* Web. *www.statshop.co.uk Sittingbourne Print*

Status Instruments Ltd Green Lane Business Park Green Lane, Tewkesbury GL20 8DE Tel. *01684 296818* Fax. *01684 293746* E-mail. *sales@status.co.uk* Web. *www.status.co.uk Status Instruments*

Status Metrology Solutions Ltd Measurement House Lenton Street, Sandiacre, Nottingham NG10 5DX Tel. *0115 9392228* Fax. *0115 9493355* E-mail. *info@statusmetrology.com* Web. *www.statusmetrology.com Alpha CMMs – Brown & Sharpe – Dell Computers – Etalon – Global CMMs – Lighthouse SPC – PC-DMIS – Renishaw – Swift-Fix – Tessa – Wilcox*

Staubli UK Ltd Lodge Park Hortonwood 30, Telford TF1 7ET Tel. *01952 604984* E-mail. *p.stone@staubli.com* Web. *www.staubli.com *Staubli (France)*

Stauff Anglia Ltd Unit 405 Copper Smith Way, Wymondham NR18 0WY Tel. *01953 857158* Fax. *01953 857159* E-mail. *sales@stauffanglia.co.uk* Web. *www.stauffanglia.co.uk Ciocca Flanges – Stauff Pipe Clamps – Swagelok Tube Fittings*

Stayclean Contract Cleaning Services Ltd Unit 14 Centenary Business Centre Hammond Close, Attleborough Fields Ind Estate, Nuneaton CV11 6RY Tel. *024 76385830* Fax. *024 76385830* E-mail. *info@staycleanltd.co.uk *Cladding Cleaning – *Deep Cleaning – *Factory Cleaning – *High Level Cleaning – *Window Cleaning*

St Bernard Composites Ltd 21 Invincible Road Industrial Estate, Farnborough GU14 7QU Tel. *01252 304000* Fax. *01252 304001* E-mail. *jmerritt@stbernard.co.uk* Web. *www.stbernard.co.uk Sabertube*

Charles F Stead & Co. Ltd Tannery Sheepscar Street North, Leeds LS7 2BY Tel. *0113 2621005* Fax. *0113 2626309* E-mail. *johnt@cfstead.com* Web. *www.cfstead.com Baby Buck – Brontoguard – Cape Butts – Shearguard – Supervelour*

Steatite Batteries Acanthus Road Ravensbank Business Park, Redditch B98 9EX Tel. *01527 512400* Fax. *01527 512419* E-mail. *sales@steatite-batteries.co.uk* Web. *www.steatite-batteries.co.uk Steatite Batteries – Steatite Embedded – Rugged Systems – Wordsworth*

E G Steele & Co. Ltd 25 Dalziel Street, Hamilton ML3 9AU Tel. *01698 283765* Fax. *01698 891550* E-mail. *info@egsteele.com* Web. *www.egsteele.com Locopulsor*

Steelite International plc Orme Street, Stoke On Trent ST6 3RB Tel. *01782 821000* Fax. *01782 819926* E-mail. *sales@steelite.com* Web. *www.steelite.com Albalite – Steelite*

Steel Product Supplies Unit 5 South Leeds Trade Centre Belle Isle Road, Hunslet, Leeds LS10 2DL Tel. *0113 2016677* Fax. *0113 2016688* E-mail. *info@steelproductsupplies.co.uk* Web. *www.steelproductsupplies.co.uk Borg – Locinox – Rolling Center – Weldability – Welka*

Steelway Queensgate Works Bilston Rd, Wolverhampton WV2 2NJ Tel. *01902 451733* Fax. *01902 452256* E-mail. *sales@steelway.co.uk* Web. *www.steelway.co.uk Brickhouse – Fensecure – Steelway (United Kingdom) – Steelway - Fensecure*

Stelrad Group Ltd Stelrad House Marriott Road, Swinton, Mexborough S64 8BN Tel. *01709 578950* Fax. *0870 498058* E-mail. *info@stelrad.com* Web. *www.stelrad.com Accord Compact – Stelrad Elite – Stelrad LST – Stelrad Planar – Stelrad Therma – Stelrad Towel Rail*

Stemcor Special Steels Pottery Lane, Chesterfield S41 9BH Tel. *01246 451666* Fax. *01246 260092* E-mail. *adrian@chesterfieldsteels.co.uk* Web. *www.stemcorspecialsteels.com Chesterfield Steel Services*

Stemmer Imaging The Old Barn Grange Court, Tongham, Farnham GU10 1DW Tel. *01252 780000* Fax. *01252 780001* E-mail. *sales@stemmer-imaging.co.uk* Web. *www.stemmer-imaging.co.uk Allied Vision Technologies – CCS – Computar – Cyberoptics – DALSA – Fujinon – IDS – IPD – JAI – NER – Pentax – Photonfocus – Schneider-Kreuznach – Sill Optics – SONY – STEMMER IMAGING – StockerYale – Tamron – Unibrain – Volpi*

Stenhouse Equipment Safety Co. Ltd Seco Works Cannon Street, Hull HU2 0AE Tel. *01482 329045* Fax. *01482 226774* E-mail. *info@stenhouse-safety.co.uk* Web. *www.stenhouse-safety.co.uk Seco – Stenhouse*

Stentor Music Co. Ltd 44 Albert Road North, Reigate RH2 9EZ Tel. *01737 240226* Fax. *01737 242748* E-mail. *info@stentor-music.com* Web. *www.stentor-music.com *Andreas Zeller (Romania) – *Hokada (Romania) – *Mistral (Taiwan) – *Ozark (S.Korea and Japan) – P & H – Stentor – *Stentor Student (China)*

Stepan UK Ltd Bridge House Bridge Street, Stalybridge SK15 1PH Tel. *0161 3385511* Fax. *0161 3032991* E-mail. *customer.service@stepaneurope.com* Web. *www.stepan.com Manro*

Stephens Gaskets Ltd (Incorporating S J Feasey Ltd) Unit 1-4 Portway Road Industrial Estate Alston Road, Oldbury B69 2PP Tel. *0121 5445808* Fax. *0121 5444188* E-mail. *sales@stephensgaskets.co.uk* Web. *www.stephensgaskets.co.uk Stephens – Stephens Pre-Cut Alignment Shims – Stephens Shim Stock*

Stephens Midlands Ltd Unit 6 Greets Green Industrial Estate Greets Green Road, West Bromwich B70 9EW Tel. *0121 5222221* Fax. *0116 2864957* E-mail. *info@stephenslube.co.uk* Web. *www.stephenslube.co.uk GESPA – *J.W.L. (Denmark) – Lumatic – Metalwork – Stephens – Tecalemit – Wanner*

Stephenson Group Ltd P.O. Box 305 Listerhills Road, Bradford BD7 1HY Tel. *01274 723811* Fax. *01274 370108* E-mail. *newsmakers@stephensongroup.com* Web. *www.stephensongroup.com Alkon*

Stephens Plastics Ltd (Plastics) Hawthorn Works, Corsham SN13 9RD Tel. *01225 810324* Fax. *01225 811390* E-mail. *info@stephens.co.uk* Web. *www.stephens-plastics.co.uk Firestone*

Sterling Fluid Systems UK Ltd Atlantic Street Broadheath, Altrincham WA14 5DH Tel. *0161 9286371* Fax. *0161 9252129* E-mail. *uksales@sterlingfluid.com* Web. *www.sterlingsihi.com Ryax – Ryblock – Rycent – Rycom – Ryend – Ryflex – Ryheat – Ryomatic – Rypos – Rypulp – Ryseal – Ryside – Rytherm – Rytor – Ryvac – Ryval Roll Seal Control Valves – Ryvert – Ryvin – Schabaver – Sterling*

Sterling Springs Ltd Cranborne Industrial Estate Cranborne Road, Potters Bar EN6 3JB Tel. *01707 650191* Fax. *01707 649677* E-mail. *mike.thompson@knight-group.co.uk* Web. *www.sterling-springs.co.uk Springs Sterling*

Sterling Thermal Technology Ltd Brunel Road Rabans Lane Industrial Area, Aylesbury HP19 8TD Tel. *01296 487171* Fax. *01296 436805* E-mail. *mail@sterlingtt.com* Web. *www.sterlingthermaltech.com Thermo – Urquhart*

Steroplast Ltd Alpha Point Bradnor Road, Sharston Industrial Area, Manchester M22 4TE Tel. *0161 9023030* Fax. *0161 9023040* E-mail. *sales@steroplast.co.uk* Web. *www.steroplast.co.uk Family Care – Steroban – Sterochef – Sterocrepe – Steropad – Steroplast – Steroply – Sterowipe*

Stertil UK Ltd Caswell Road Brackmills Industrial Estate, Northampton NN4 7PW Tel. *08707 700471* Fax. *01604 765181* E-mail. *info@stertiluk.com* Web. *www.stertiluk.com *Combilok (Netherlands) – *Condensamax (Netherlands) – Econocast – *Econoflame (Netherlands) – *Economatic (Germany) – Econoplate – *Econorad (Germany) – *Econotwin (Germany) – *Heatpak (Netherlands) – *Insudoor (Sweden) – *Insuroll (Netherlands) – *Rapid Roll (Sweden) – *Rapitech (Sweden) – Roladoor – Stoklift – Strata – Thermadoor – Thermaroll*

Stevenage Knitting Co. Ltd Sish Lane, Stevenage SG1 3LS Tel. *01438 353240* Fax. *01438 748364* E-mail. *stevenageknitting@hotmail.co.uk Whaler*

Stevens Group Ltd Greenback Technology Park, Blackburn BB1 5QB Tel. *01254 685200* Fax. *01254 685202* E-mail. *info@stevensgroupltd.com* Web. *www.stevensgroupltd.com Compupak IV – Data Mail – K.E.G. Checkweighers – Profit Controller – Quality Management Systems – Recipe Formulation – System 290*

Michael Stevens & Partners Ltd Invicta Works Elliott Road, Bromley BR2 9NT Tel. *020 84607299* Fax. *020 84600499* E-mail. *penelope.stevens@michael-stevens.com* Web. *www.michael-stevens.com *Bel – *Chromatec – *Panorama D.T.V. – *Provideo – *Wohler*

Stevenson & Kelly Grampian (Gang-Nail Systems Ltd) Wester Hatton Balmedie, Aberdeen AB23 8YY Tel. *01358 743399* Fax. *01358 743044* E-mail. *t.ralston@btinternet.com Ecojoist*

Roger Stevenson Ltd The Mews House 1b Bradley Street, Southport PR9 9HW Tel. *01704 534000* Fax. *01704 538094 Dooby Duck*

Stevens Scotland Ltd Denburn Way, Brechin DD9 7DW Tel. *01356 625111* Fax. *01356 623755* E-mail. *twalker@stevensscotland.co.uk* Web. *www.stevensscotland.co.uk Chris Craft – Sun Vista*

Stewart-Buchanan Gauges Ltd Burnside Industrial Estate 7 Garrell Road Kilsyth, Glasgow G65 9JX Tel. *01236 821533* Fax. *01236 824090* E-mail. *sales@stewarts-group.com* Web. *www.stewarts-group.com Stewart Buchanan Gauges*

Duncan Stewart Textiles Aztex House Ivy Arch Road, Worthing BN14 8BX Tel. *01903 201251* Fax. *01903 520007* E-mail. *sales@towelsrus.co.uk* Web. *www.towelsrus.co.uk *Aztex*

Stewart Gill Conveyors Ltd (a division of Air-Log Ltd) 1 Brook Business Park Brookhampton Lane, Kineton, Warwick CV35 0JA Tel. *01926 641424* Fax. *01926 641426* E-mail. *info@stewart-gill.co.uk* Web. *www.stewart-gill.co.uk Cleantrack – Closedtrack – Stainless Steel Twin Track – Stortrack – Twin Track*

S T G Ltd Unit 14 Stephenson Court Fraser Road, Bedford MK44 3WJ Tel. *01234 213339* Fax. *01234 212224* E-mail. *info@stgtransport.com* Web. *www.stgtransport.com S T G*

Stieber Clutch Twiflex Building Ampthill Road, Bedford MK42 9RD Tel. *01234 355499* Fax. *01234 214264* E-mail. *graham.whiffin@wichita.co.uk* Web. *www.stieber.de *Freewheels (Germany) – Stieber*

Stiefel Laboratories (UK) Ltd Eurasia Headquarters Concorde Road, Maidenhead SL6 4BY Tel. *01628 612000*

Fax. *01628 810021* E-mail. *general@stiefel.co.uk* Web. *www.stiefel.com Stiefel Laboratories (UK) Ltd*

Stillmuchtooffer Ltd Ysgubor Isa Bontuchel, Ruthin LL15 2BE Tel. *01824 710342* E-mail. *smto@stillmuchtooffer.co.uk* Web. *www.stillmuchtooffer.co.uk Stillmuchtooffer*

Stiona Software Ltd 91-97 Ormeau Road, Belfast BT7 1SH Tel. *028 90322011* E-mail. *info@stiona.com* Web. *www.stiona.com Fusion Accounts*

Stirling Park LLP 24 St Enoch Square, Glasgow G1 4DB Tel. *0141 5655765* Fax. *01463 250921* E-mail. *info@stirlingpark.co.uk* Web. *www.stirlingpark.co.uk Intrum Justitia Ltd*

S T Micro Electronics Ltd 1000 Aztec West Almondsbury, Bristol BS32 4SQ Tel. *01454 616616* Fax. *01454 617910* E-mail. *postmaster@st.com* Web. *www.st.com I.M.S. – O.C.C.A.M. – Transputer*

S T Microelectronics 33 Pinkhill, Edinburgh EH12 7BF Tel. *0131 3366000* Fax. *0131 3366001* E-mail. *steve.east@st.com* Web. *www.st.com ColorMOS*

Stoakes Systems Ltd 1 Banstead Road, Purley CR8 3EB Tel. *020 86607667* Fax. *020 86605707* E-mail. *mailbox@stoakes.co.uk* Web. *www.stoakes.co.uk Astralite – Astraroof – Astrawall*

Stockline Plastics Ltd Grovepark Mills Hopehill Road, Glasgow G20 7NF Tel. *0141 3329077* Fax. *0141 3329079* E-mail. *sales@stockline-plastics.co.uk* Web. *www.stockline-plastics.co.uk Deglas – Paraglas*

Stocksigns Ltd 43 Ormside Way Holmethorpe Industrial Estate, Redhill RH1 2LG Tel. *01737 764764* Fax. *01737 763763* E-mail. *sales@stocksigns.co.uk* Web. *www.stocksigns.co.uk Burnhamsigns – Smartsign – Stocksigns*

Stoddard Manufacturing Co. Ltd Blackhorse Road, Letchworth Garden City SG6 1HB Tel. *01462 686221* Fax. *01462 480711* E-mail. *admin@stoddard.co.uk* Web. *www.stoddard.co.uk Denturax – Letchworth – Rotakit – Rotapol – Stoddard*

Stodec Products Ltd 8 James Way Bletchley, Milton Keynes MK1 1SU Tel. *01908 270011* Fax. *01908 270022* E-mail. *mike@stodec.co.uk* Web. *www.stodec.com Clean Room Installation Services*

Stokvis Tapes UK Ltd Unit 8 Tring Industrial Estate Icknield Way, Tring HP23 4JX Tel. *01442 821700* Fax. *01442 248871* E-mail. *info@stokvistapes.co.uk* Web. *www.stokvistapes.co.uk 3M (United Kingdom) – *Lohmann (Germany) – *Permacel (U.S.A.) – Saint Gobain – SCAPA (United Kingdom)*

Stone Fasteners Ltd 669a Woolwich Road, London SE7 8SL Tel. *020 82935080* Fax. *020 82934935* E-mail. *info@stonefasteners.com* Web. *www.stonefasteners.com Stone Fasteners*

Stone Foundries Ltd 669a Woolwich Road, London SE7 8SL Tel. *020 88534648* Fax. *020 83051934* E-mail. *sales@stonefoundries.com* Web. *www.stonefoundries.com Stone – Stone Fasteners – Stone Foundries*

Stonehouse Paper & Bag Mills Ltd Lower Mills, Stonehouse GL10 2BD Tel. *01453 822173* Fax. *01453 822174* E-mail. *stonehousepaper@aol.com* Web. *www.spbm.com Stonehouse Paper & Bag Mills Ltd*

Stone Marine Propulsion Ltd Dock Road, Birkenhead CH41 1DT Tel. *0151 6522372* Fax. *0151 6522377* E-mail. *sales@smpropulsion.com* Web. *www.smpropulsion.com Meridian – Nikalium – Novoston – Sonoston – Superston*

Stone Technology Limited Link House Sandys Road, Malvern WR14 1JJ Tel. *0844 3578045* Fax. *0844 3576945* E-mail. *sales@redantsoftware.co.uk* Web. *www.redantsoftware.co.uk RedAnt Software*

Stoney Cove Diver Training Centre Ltd Sapcote Road Stoney Stanton, Leicester LE9 4DW Tel. *01455 273089* Fax. *01455 274000* Web. *www.stoneycove.com Hydrotech*

Stontronics Ltd Unit 2-4 Chancery Gate Business Centre Cradock Road, Reading RG2 0AH Tel. *0118 9311199* Fax. *0118 9311145* E-mail. *info@stontronics.co.uk* Web. *www.stontronics.co.uk Bestec – DVE – ERA – Meanwell – Minwa – Sinpro – Univ – Vanson*

Stop Choc Ltd Banbury Avenue, Slough SL1 4LR Tel. *01753 533223* Fax. *01753 693724* E-mail. *sales@stop-choc.co.uk* Web. *www.stop-choc.co.uk Barry Controls – Barrycase – Barryflex – Barrymount – Rigidamp – Seamount – Stabl-Levl-Air*

Storacall Engineering Ltd Swan House 69-71 Windmill Road, Sunbury On Thames TW16 7DT Tel. *01932 710950* Fax. *01932 710811* E-mail. *sales@storacall.co.uk* Web. *www.storacall.co.uk Alertmaster – Announce Manager – Ansamaster – Auditmaster – Conference Manager – Dodgebox – Equate – Intercepta – Intercepta Range – Musicon Range – Phonemaster – Store a call voice systems Ltd – Teleacoustics – Voxmail*

Stora Enso UK Ltd 1 Kingfisher House Crayfields Business Park New Mill Road, Orpington BR5 3QG Tel. *01689 883200* Fax. *01992 788498* E-mail. *james.barr@storaenso.com* Web. *www.storaenso.com Solaris*

Storage City Ltd Export Drive Fulwood I E, Huthwaite, Sutton In Ashfield NG17 6AF Tel. *01623 441440* Fax. *01623 516819* E-mail. *mso@storagecity.co.uk* Web. *www.storagecity.co.uk P.C.S. Superbox*

Storage Direct Garamonde Drive Wymbush, Milton Keynes MK8 8ND Tel. *0800 592963* Fax. *01908 263526* Web. *www.storagedirect.co.uk Apex – Clearview Linbins – Linbin Cabinets – Linbins – Linshelf – Linspace – Linvar*

Store 21 Tureck House Drayton Road Shirley, Solihull B90 4NG Tel. *0121 7058286* Fax. *01273 874433* E-mail. *recruitment@storetwentyone.co.uk* Web. *www.gsgroup.co.uk Q.S.*

J Storey & Co. Ltd (part of Petrofern Inc.) Heron Chemical Works Moor Lane, Lancaster LA1 1QQ Tel. *01524 63252* Fax. *01524 381805* E-mail. *sales@samuelbanner.co.uk* Web. *www.josephstorey.com Storflam*

Storm 5 Jubilee Place, London SW3 3TD Tel. *020 73689900* Fax. *020 73765145* E-mail. *info@stormmodels.com* Web. *www.stormmodels.com Storm*

Stormor Systems Ltd 6 Limbrick Corner Palatine Road, Goring-By-Sea, Worthing BN12 6JJ Tel. *01903 244344* Fax. *01903 700571* E-mail. *info@stormorsystems.co.uk* Web. *www.stormorsystems.co.uk Longspan – Powerdeck – Stormor*

Stortext Ltd Hikenield House Icknield Way, Andover SP10 5AH Tel. *01264 360900* Fax. *01264 360901* E-mail. *richard.butler@stortextfm.com* Web. *www.stortextfm.com ECLIPSE – OMNIDOX*

Stourbridge Lion Ltd Parkbrook House Talbot Street, Lye, Stourbridge DY9 8UH Tel. *01384 891297* Fax. *01384 423940* E-mail. *general@brockway-conveyors.com* Web. *www.stourbridge.co.uk Brockway*

Strachan & Livingston 23-25 Kirk Wynd, Kirkcaldy KY1 1EP Tel. *01592 261451* Fax. *01592 204180* Web. *www.fifetoday.co.uk Cirkcaldy Herald – East Fife Mail – Fife Advertiser, The – Fife Free Press – Fife Herald – Fife Leader – Glenrothes Gazette – St. Andrews Citizen*

Straightpoint UK Ltd Clovelly Road Southbourne, Emsworth PO10 8PE Tel. *01243 378921* Fax. *01243 377745* E-mail. *sales@straightpoint.com* Web. *www.straightpoint.com Jumbo Weigher – Load Link – Mini Weigher*

Straight Talk In 45 Parton Street, Liverpool L6 3AN Tel. *0151 2607345* E-mail. *info@straighttalkin.com* Web. *www.straighttalkin.co.uk credhedz*

StrainSense Ltd The Old Barn Woods Lane, Potterspury, Towcester NN12 7PT Tel. *01908 543038* Fax. *08700 940810* E-mail. *sales@strainsense.co.uk* Web. *www.strainsense.co.uk Data track – ENTRAN – H L Planar – HPI – NMB – Schaevitz – SENSY*

Strainstall 8-10 Mariners Way, Cowes PO31 8PD Tel. *01983 203600* Fax. *01983 291335* E-mail. *enquiries@strainstall.com* Web. *www.strainstallloadcells.com Strain Gauging*

Strangfor Arms Hotel 92 Church Street, Newtownards BT23 4AL Tel. *028 91814141* Fax. *028 91811010* E-mail. *info@strangfordhotel.com* Web. *www.strangfordhotel.co.uk Le winters*

Strap Trap Stanmore Road, London E11 3BU Tel. *020 85303484* E-mail. *info@straptrap.co.uk* Web. *www.straptrap.co.uk StrapTrap*

Strata Color (Coated Steels) Ltd Oxwich Road Reevesland Park Industrial Estate, Reevesland Industrial Estate, Newport NP19 4PU Tel. *01633 276111* Fax. *01633 280044 Strata-Color*

Strata Panels UK Lancaster House Airfield Industrial Estate, Warboys, Huntingdon PE28 2SH Tel. *01487 825040* Fax. *01487 823746* E-mail. *sales@stratapanels.co.uk* Web. *www.stratapanels.co.uk Exelite – Foylite*

Stratech Scientific Ltd. 7 Acorn Business Centre Oaks Drive, Newmarket CB8 7SY Tel. *01638 782600* Fax. *01638 782606* E-mail. *info@stratech.co.uk* Web. *www.stratech.co.uk Stratech Scientific*

Strathvac 65 Old Rome Drive Springhill Meadows, Kilmarnock KA1 2RU Tel. *01563 555881* E-mail. *info@strathvac.co.uk* Web. *www.strathvac.co.uk Eureka – Husky – Smart solutions*

Strayfield Ltd Unit 10-11 Ely Road, Theale, Reading RG7 4BQ Tel. *0118 9327760* Fax. *0118 9305634* E-mail. *info@strayfield.co.uk* Web. *www.strayfield.co.uk Magna – Magnarange – Magnatube*

S T R Designers & Lithographic Printers Vellum Mill 76a Mill Lane, Carshalton SM5 2JR Tel. *020 86479790* Fax. *020 86692140* E-mail. *studio@str.uk.com* Web. *www.str.uk.com STR Design & Print*

Streamlined Propeller Repairs Unit 17 Cavendish Mews, Aldershot GU11 3EH Tel. *01252 316412* Fax. *01252 316412* E-mail. *streamlined@ukgateway.net* Web. *www.streamlinedpropellers.co.uk Turning Point*

Streamline Surgical LLP 84-88 Pinner Road Harrow, London HA1 4HZ Tel. *0800 1577033* Fax. *01243 831655* E-mail. *info@streamline-surgical.com* Web. *www.streamline-surgical.com Streamline Surgical*

Stream Measurement Ltd Unit 5 St Johns Industrial Estate Lees, Oldham OL4 3DZ Tel. *0161 6220777* Fax. *0161 6220777* E-mail. *sales@stream-measurement.com* Web. *www.stream-measurement.com Actaris – Energy – Flowmeters – Fuels – Indicator – Industrial Process – Meters – Schlumberger Neptune – Shoflo – Stream Measurement – Traceable calibration services – Unipulse flowmeter*

Street Crane Ltd Townend Works Chapel-En-Le-Frith, High Peak SK23 0PH Tel. *01298 812456* Fax. *01298 814945* E-mail. *admin@streetcrane.co.uk* Web. *www.streetcrane.co.uk Street – TVX Hoists – ZX - range of overhead cranes, ZX Hoists, TX Hoists, CX Chain Hoists. – ZX Hoists*

Stretch Line UK Ltd Old Silk Mill Sherston, Malmesbury SN16 0NG Tel. *01666 842100* Fax. *01666 840903* E-mail. *philip.allen@stretchline.com* Web. *www.stretchline.com CHICO – CHICO - Hook and loop fastener.*

Stribbons Ltd 99 Sanders Road Finedon Road Industrial Estate, Wellingborough NN8 4NL Tel. *01933 443446* Fax. *01933 443435* E-mail. *sales@stribbons.co.uk* Web. *www.stribbons.co.uk Superior Ribbons – Superior Ribbons - range of decorative ribbons.*

Stripe Consulting Ltd 1 Whiteladies Gate, Bristol BS8 2PH Tel. *0117 9745179* Fax. *01278 457299* E-mail. *mark@stripeconsulting.com* Web. *www.stripeconsulting.com Smith Gamblin Haworth*

Strix UK Ltd Pulford House, Bell Meadow Business Park Park Lane, Pulford, Chester CH4 9EP Tel. *01244 572372* Fax. *01244 571327* E-mail. *uksales@strix.com* Web. *www.strix.com Strix*

Stromag Ltd 29 Wellingborough Road, Rushden NN10 9YE Tel. *01933 350407* Fax. *01933 358692* E-mail. *sales@stromag.com* Web. *www.stromag.ltd.uk Hydrospring – Periflex – SIME*

Stronghold International Ltd Unit A Nicholson Court, Hoddesdon EN11 0NE Tel. *01992 479470* Fax. *01992 479471* E-mail. *sales@stronghold.co.uk* Web. *www.stronghold.co.uk Stronghold*

Strong Recycling Balers Ltd 26 Edenbridge View, Dudley DY1 2JJ Tel. *01384 567773* Fax. *01384 567773* E-mail. *jrwebster2000@yahoo.co.uk* Web. *www.strongrecyclingbalers.co.uk Strong Recycling Baler – Strong Recycling Baler – Strong Recycling Baler – Strong Recycling Baler – Strong Recycling Baler*

Stroud College Of Further Education Stratford Road, Stroud GL5 4AH Tel. *01453 763424* Fax. *01453 753543* E-mail. *berihare@stroudcol.ac.uk* Web. *www.stroud.ac.uk Easy FM*

Stroud Metal Co. Ltd Dudbridge, Stroud GL5 3EZ Tel. *01453 763331* Fax. *01453 753804* E-mail. *enquiries@stroudmetal.co.uk* Web. *www.stroudmetal.co.uk Garland – Sportiseat*

Structured Software Systems Ltd 3sl Suite 2 22a Duke Street, Barrow In Furness LA14 1HH Tel. *01229 838867* Fax. *01229 870096* E-mail. *mark.walker@threesl.com* Web. *www.threefl.com Cradle*

Structured Training Ltd Prospero Barn The Green, Snitterfield, Stratford Upon Avon CV37 0TR Tel. *01789 734300* Fax. *01789 730791* E-mail. *info@structuredtraining.com* Web. *www.structuredtraining.com Structured Training*

Structure Flex Peacock Way, Melton Constable NR24 2AZ Tel. *01263 863100* Fax. *01263 863115* E-mail. *enquiries@structure-flex.co.uk* Web. *www.structure-flex.co.uk Structure-Flex*

Struers Ltd Unit 11 Whittle Way, Catcliffe, Rotherham S60 5BL Tel. *08456 046664* Fax. *0845 6046651* E-mail. *info@struers.co.uk* Web. *www.struers.com EMCO-TEST – Galdabini – Struers*

S T R UK Ltd 10 Portman Road, Reading RG30 1EA Tel. *0118 9398700* Fax. *0118 9398701* E-mail. *enquiries@struk.co.uk* Web. *www.struk.co.uk Adron – Dylachem – Dylan – Lanalux – Perlosol – Permavel – Sirovelle – Topsoft – Y-Tack*

A G Stuart Holdings Ltd Old Rayne, Insch AB52 6RX Tel. *01464 851208* Fax. *01464 851202* E-mail. *sales@slyvanstuart.com* Web. *www.sylvanstuart.com Bonocryl*

D A Stuart Ltd Lincoln Street, Wolverhampton WV10 0DZ Tel. *01902 456111* Fax. *01902 453764* E-mail. *dastuart@dastuart.co.uk* Web. *www.dastuart.co.uk Crowncast – Crowncote – Crowncut – Crowndip – Crowndraw – Crownease – Crownforge – Crownform – Crowngrease – Crownlube – Crownpress – Crownroll – Dasco – Dascolene – Dascool – Drawsol – Rol-Kleen – Solvol – Sturaco – Thermex*

Studweldpro UK Ltd Ollerton Road Tuxford, Newark NG22 0PQ Tel. *01777 874500* Fax. *01777 874555* E-mail. *sales@swpuk.com* Web. *www.swpuk.com Convosection – Convowall*

Stulz UK Ltd Epsom First Quarter Blenheim Road, Epsom KT19 9QN Tel. *01372 749666* Fax. *01372 739444* E-mail. *sales@stulz.co.uk* Web. *www.stulz.co.uk COMPACT CW (Germany) – COMPACT DX (Germany) – COMPACT-AIR (Italy) – CYBERAIR (Germany) – CYBERCOOL (Germany) – FREE-AIR – MINI-AIR (Italy) – MINISPACE (Germany) – SPLIT-AIR (Italy) – TEL-AIR (Italy) – WALL-AIR (Italy) – WIND-AIR (Italy) – X-LINE (Italy)*

Stute Foods Ltd Stute House Sunderland Place, Bristol BS8 1EG Tel. *0117 9238823* Fax. *0117 9466446* E-mail. *laurence.hybs@stute-foods.com*

Web. *www.stute-foods.com Choc-o-Nut – It's Apple – Johnson's Coffee – Red Z*

Stylecraft PO Box 62, Keighley BD21 1PP Tel. *01535 609798* Fax. *01535 669952* E-mail. *info@stylecraftltd.co.uk* Web. *www.stylecraft-yarns.co.uk Aran – Baby Time 3 & 4 Ply – Baby Time D.K. – Baby Time DK Prints – Braemar – Braemar (Space Dyed Shades) – Cherub Baby 3 and 4 ply – Cherub Baby D.K. – Cherub Sparkle D.K. – Chunky – Cotton Look DK – Cotton Lookalike Aran – Cotton Lookalike DK – Craft Cotton – Dalesman Aran – Designer Tweed Chunky – Harvest Aran – Harvest Chunky – Harvest DK – Heath DK – Heather DK – Helter Skelter DK – Luxury Mohair – Naturelle Pure Wool DK – Neptune DK – Palladium Chunky – Reflections DK – Soft Cotton – Star Attraction – Twilight D.K. – Wondersoft Baby D.K.*

Style International Ltd Unit 1 Gregston Industrial Estate Birmingham Road, Oldbury B69 4EX Tel. *0121 6653870* Fax. *0845 0760079* E-mail. *info@naturalrugstore.co.uk* Web. *www.naturalrugstore.co.uk The Natural Rug Store*

Style South Consort House Princes Road, Ferndown BH22 9JG Tel. *01202 874044* Fax. *01202 874844* E-mail. *south@style-partitions.co.uk* Web. *www.style-partitons.co.uk Hufcor – Skyfold*

Style Tech Unit 2 1 Vale Rise, Tonbridge TN9 1TB Tel. *01732 369368* Fax. *01732 352233* E-mail. *info@styletechuk.com* Web. *www.styletechuk.com Styletech – Salto*

Subaru (UK) Ltd I M House South Drive, Coleshill, Birmingham B46 1DF Tel. *0844 6626612* Fax. *0121 7308269* E-mail. *info@subaru.co.uk* Web. *www.subaru.co.uk Subaru UK*

Submarine Manufacturing & Products Ltd Blackpool Road Newton, Preston PR4 3RE Tel. *01772 687775* Fax. *01772 687774* E-mail. *dormsby@smp-ltd.co.uk* Web. *www.smp-ltd.co.uk Aga – Bauer – Beaver – Birns – Broco – Coltrisub – Comex – Desco – Heliox – Ingersoll Rand – Kirby Morgan – Posieden – Qunicy – Siebe Gorman – Stanley*

Sub Sea 7 Ltd Greenwell Base Greenwell Road, East Tullos Industrial Estate, Aberdeen AB12 3AX Tel. *01224 292000* Fax. *01224 879312* E-mail. *jean.cahuzac@subsea7.com* Web. *www.subsea7.com Snap-Lay – Snap-Pipe*

Sub Surface Ltd 3 Peel Street Ashton-On-Ribble, Preston PR2 2QS Tel. *01772 561135* Fax. *01772 204907* E-mail. *preston@subsurface.co.uk* Web. *www.subsurface.co.uk Sub Surface*

Sub Zero Technology Ltd Unit 35 Churchill Way Fleckney, Leicester LE8 8UD Tel. *0116 2402634* Fax. *0116 2404099* E-mail. *sales@subzero.co.uk* Web. *www.subzero.co.uk Cool T – Hi Lo – Sub Zero – Sub Zero Technology*

Sud-Chemie UK Ltd Drake Mews 3 Gadbrook Park Rudheath, Northwich CW9 7XF Tel. *01606 813060* Fax. *01606 813061* E-mail. *info.uk@sud-chemie.com* Web. *www.sud-chemie.com *Bentonil (France) – *Copisil (Germany) – *Laundrosil (Germany) – *Optiflo (Germany) – *Optigel (Germany) – *Tixogel (Germany) – *Tixoton (Germany) – *Tonsil (Germany)*

Sudpack UK Ltd 40 High Park Drive Wolverton Mill, Milton Keynes MK12 5TT Tel. *01908 525720* Fax. *01908 525721* E-mail. *uk@suedpack.com* Web. *www.suedpack.com Sudpack UK Ltd*

Sugg Lighting Ltd Unit 1 A Foundry Lane, Horsham RH13 5PX Tel. *01293 540111* Fax. *01293 540114* E-mail. *sales@sugglighting.co.uk* Web. *www.sugglighting.co.uk Sugg Lighting*

Sumitomo Electric Hardmetal Ltd 50 Summerleys Road, Princes Risborough HP27 9PW Tel. *01844 342081* Fax. *01844 342415* E-mail. *sue-pierce@gr.sei.co.jp* Web. *www.sumitomo-hardmetal.co.uk Ace Coat – Aurora Coat – Multidrill – Sumiboron – Sumidia – UFO – Wavemill – ZX Coat*

Sumo IT 35 Brunswick Street Thurnscoe, Rotherham S63 0HU Tel. *07507 445855* E-mail. *info@sumoit.co.uk* Web. *www.sumoit.co.uk Sumo IT*

Sundridge Holdings Vicarage Lane Hoo, Rochester ME3 9LB Tel. *01634 252104* Fax. *01634 250820* E-mail. *sales@sundridge.co.uk* Web. *www.sundridge.co.uk Sundridge*

Sundwel Solar Ltd Unit 1 Tower Road, Washington NE37 2SH Tel. *0800 9808939* Fax. *0191 4154297* E-mail. *solar@sundwel.com* Web. *www.sundwel.com *Atlas Solar (Switzerland) – Sundwel*

Sungerlitt Ltd Suite A2 Stirling Agriculture Centre, Stirling FK9 4RN Tel. *01786 471586* Fax. *01786 464825* E-mail. *enquiries@sundolitt.com* Web. *www.sundolitt.co.uk Sunpack (Norway)*

Sunlight Plastics Ltd 15-16 Aston Road, Waterlooville PO7 7XG Tel. *023 92259500* Fax. *023 92259400* E-mail. *sales@sunlightplastics.co.uk* Web. *www.sunlightplastics.co.uk Lexan – Makrolon – Marlon – Perspex – Plexiglam – Vivak*

Sun 99 Ltd 365 Euston Road, London NW1 3AR Tel. *020 78746900* Fax. *020 78746919* E-mail. *info@stormwatches.com* Web. *www.stormwatches.com Storm – Time Chain*

Sunseeker Poole Ltd Sunseeker Wharf West Quay Road, Poole BH15 1HW Tel. *01202 666060* Fax. *01202 382222* E-mail. *simon.gennery@sunseekerpoole.com* Web. *www.sunseekerpoole.com Camargue – Excess 2000 – Images – Manhattan – Outlaw – Predator – Superhawk*

Sunspel Menswear Ltd Cavendish House Canal Street, Long Eaton, Nottingham NG10 4HP Tel. *0115 9735292* Fax. *0115 9461378* E-mail. *info@sunspel.com* Web. *www.sunspel.com Sunspel Boxer*

Sunvic Controls Ltd Bellshill Road Uddingston, Glasgow G71 6NP Tel. *01698 812944* Fax. *01698 813637* E-mail. *info@sunvic.co.uk* Web. *www.sunvic.co.uk Clock Box II – D.X./S.L. – Duoflow – Minival – SA – Selects – T.K./R./D. – T.L.X./M. – T.Y.J. – TRV400 – Twin Unival – Unishare – Unival – V.K./L. – WT/WTR/WTN/WTO*

Supac Ltd Unit 3 Goatmill Road Industrial Estate, Merthyr Tydfil CF48 3TD Tel. *01685 729850* Fax. *01685 729855* E-mail. *sales@supac.co.uk* Web. *www.supac.co.uk Celtic – Supac*

Supacat The Airfield, Honiton EX14 4LF Tel. *01404 891777* Fax. *01404 891776* E-mail. *generalenquiries@supacat.com* Web. *www.supacat.com Supacat*

Supadance Ltd 159 Queens Road, Buckhurst Hill IG9 5BA Tel. *020 85058888* Fax. *020 85044536* E-mail. *sales@supadance.com* Web. *www.supadance.com Supadance International*

Superdrug Stores plc 118 Beddington Lane, Croydon CR0 4TB Tel. *020 86847000* Fax. *020 86846102* E-mail. *edith.shih@superdrugs.com* Web. *www.superdrug.com Superdrug*

Superfine Manufacturing Ltd Orchardbank Industrial Estate, Forfar DD8 1TD Tel. *01307 463538* Fax. *01307 468505* E-mail. *sales@superfine.co.uk* Web. *www.superfine.co.uk Highland Piper*

Superform UK Cosgrove Close, Worcester WR3 8UA Tel. *01905 874300* Fax. *01905 874301* E-mail. *reception@superform-aluminium.com* Web. *www.superform-aluminium.com Supral*

Superseal Anglia Ltd 40 Mansell Close, Spalding PE11 1NE Tel. *01775 722116* Fax. *07883 399444* E-mail. *info@supersealanglia.co.uk* Web. *www.supersealanglia.co.uk SuperSeal*

Super Sharp Saw Service 174 London Road, Mitcham CR4 3LD Tel. *020 86482154* Fax. *020 86482154 S.S.S.*

Supersport Leisure Shirts Ltd Hope Silk Mills Macclesfield Road, Leek ST13 8JZ Tel. *01538 386226* Fax. *01538 399692* E-mail. *sales@supersport.co.uk* Web. *www.supersport.co.uk Supersport*

Superspray Lube Unit 2 Salford Indl-Est Salford, Todmorden OL14 7LF Tel. *01706 839911* Fax. *01706 839922* E-mail. *mrscreenwash@aol.com Mr Superspray Lube*

Supplements For Pets Ltd 50 Oakley Road Bromham, Bedford MK43 8HZ Tel. *01234 826584* E-mail. *info@supplementsforpets.co.uk* Web. *www.supplementsforpets.co.uk Calm Down – Coat Boost – Health Boost – Joint Boost – Trim Boost*

Supply Chain Solution Ltd 1-11 Mersey View Brighton-Le-Sands, Liverpool L22 6QA Tel. *0151 2848867* Fax. *0151 2133140* E-mail. *sales@supplychainsolution.co.uk* Web. *www.supplychainsolution.co.uk Aldi – Lidl – Makro – Morrisons – Netto – Sainsburys – Tesco*

Support In Sport Ltd Glasson Industrial Estate, Maryport CA15 8NT Tel. *01900 812796* Fax. *01900 815509* E-mail. *sales@supportinsport.com* Web. *www.supportinsport.com Pal Grass – Palmyco*

Sure Names Internet Solutions Ltd 3 The Quadrant, Coventry CV1 2DY Tel. *024 76675112* Fax. *024 76675161* Web. *www.surenames.co.uk BazaarBuilder.com*

Sureskills Callender House 58-60 Upper Arthur Street, Belfast BT1 4GJ Tel. *028 90935555* Fax. *028 90935566* E-mail. *info@sureskills.com* Web. *www.sureskills.com Sureskills Ltd*

Sureweld UK Ltd Sanders Lodge Industrial Estate, Rushden NN10 6BQ Tel. *01933 357005* Fax. *01933 357606* E-mail. *info@sureweld.co.uk* Web. *www.sureweld.co.uk Autospot – Ezestrand – Ezetrode – Monomig – Sure Air Tools – Suremig*

Surex International Ltd Unit 5 Airport Trading Estate, Biggin Hill, Westerham TN16 3BW Tel. *01959 576000* Fax. *01959 571000* E-mail. *info@surex.co.uk* Web. *www.surex.co.uk Surex 002 Oxysure – Surex Voxsan – Water Wizard*

Surface Technology plc 15-17 Colvilles Place Kelvin Industrial Estate, East Kilbride, Glasgow G75 0PZ Tel. *01355 248223* Fax. *01355 237141* E-mail. *ronnie.ross@surfacetechnology.co.uk* Web. *www.surfacetechnology.co.uk Armourcote – Beetleback*

Surface Technology Products Ltd 244 Heneage Street, Birmingham B7 4LY Tel. *0121 3594322* Fax. *0121 3591817* E-mail. *sales@surtech.co.uk* Web. *www.surtech.co.uk Surtech*

Surfcontrol plc Riverside Mountbatten Way, Congleton CW12 1DY Tel. *01260 296200* Fax. *01260 296201* E-mail. *sales@surfcontrol.com* Web. *www.surfcontrol.com SurfControl E-Mail filter – SurfControl Web Filter*

Surgicraft Ltd 16 The Oaks Clews Road, Redditch B98 7ST Tel. *01527 555888* Fax. *01527 551166* E-mail. *customerservice@surgicraft.co.uk* Web. *www.surgicraft.co.uk A.B.C. – ATLAS – Esop – Hartshill – Medicarb – Mityvac – STALIF – Surgicraft-Copeland – Virex*

Surin Restaurant 30 Harbour Street, Ramsgate CT11 8HA Tel. *01843 592001* Fax. *01843 592001* E-mail. *info@surinrestaurant.co.uk* Web. *www.surinrestaurant.co.uk surin*

Surrey & Berkshire Media Ltd 8 Tessa Road, Reading RG1 8NS Tel. *0118 9183000* Fax. *0118 9503592* E-mail. *editorial@reading-epost.co.uk* Web. *www.getreading.co.uk Bracknell Standard – Evening Post – Property – Property Standard – Reading Standard – Wokingham Times Series*

Surtees Southern Ltd 63 Moorlands Road, Verwood BH31 7PD Tel. *01202 821485* Fax. *0845 6526677* E-mail. *avml@surtees.co.uk* Web. *www.surtees.co.uk ANYCAST HIRE*

Sussex Catering Equipment Services Ltd E Ford Industrial Estate Ford Lane, Ford, Arundel BN18 0DF Tel. *01243 553691* Fax. *01243 554449* E-mail. *sales@sussexcateringequip.co.uk* Web. *www.sussexcateringequip.co.uk *Sussex Classic*

Sutcliffe Farrar & Co. Ltd Banksfield Works Mytholmroyd, Hebden Bridge HX7 5LT Tel. *01422 883363* Fax. *01422 885479* E-mail. *sales@fieldclassics.co.uk* Web. *www.fieldclassics.co.uk Field Classics*

Svitzer Humber Ltd Triton House Immingham Dock, Immingham DN40 2LZ Tel. *01469 571115* Fax. *01469 571616* E-mail. *jacqueline.readman@svitzer.com* Web. *www.svitzer.com Howard Smith*

Swada London High Street, London E15 2PP Tel. *020 85347171* Fax. *020 85192818* E-mail. *info@swada.co.uk* Web. *www.swada.co.uk Fiesta*

Swagelok Scotland Silvertrees Drive Silvertrees Business ParkWesthill, Aberdeen AB32 6BH Tel. *01224 759900* Fax. *01224 729495* E-mail. *info@scotland.swagelok.com* Web. *www.swagelok.com/scotland Fluid System Technoligies (Scotland) Ltd*

R Swain & Sons Ocupation Lane Woodville, Swadlincote DE11 8EU Tel. *01283 217051* Fax. *01283 551334* E-mail. *shaunbaker@rswaingroup.com* Web. *www.rswain.com Ensove Concrete Products*

Swains International plc Eastland House Westgate, Hunstanton PE36 5EW Tel. *01485 536200* Fax. *01485 536211* E-mail. *sales@swains.co.uk* Web. *www.swains.co.uk Clubman – Clubman Accessories – Memory*

Swan Generators Ltd Unit 6 Thorpe Close, Banbury OX16 4SW Tel. *01295 261601* Fax. *01295 271352* E-mail. *standby@swangenerators.co.uk* Web. *www.swangenerators.co.uk Swan*

Swan Mill Paper Co. Ltd Swan Mills Goldsel Road, Swanley BR8 8EU Tel. *01322 665566* Fax. *01322 666460* E-mail. *sales@swantex.com* Web. *www.swantex.com Swansilk – Swansoft – Swantex*

Swansea Industrial Components Ltd 66-70 Morfa Road, Swansea SA1 2EF Tel. *01792 458777* Fax. *01792 456252 Swansea Industrial Components Ltd*

Swarovski UK Ltd Unit 10 Perrywood Business Park Honeycrock Lane, Redhill RH1 5JQ Tel. *01737 856814* Fax. *01737 856856* E-mail. *james.dubois@swarovski.com* Web. *www.swarovski.com Daniel Swarovski – Swarovski Crystal Components – Swarovski Crystal Memories – Swarovski Jewelers Collection – Swarovski Selection – Swarovski Silver Crystal*

Sweatshop 148-150 Market Street, Hyde SK14 1EX Tel. *0161 3669191* E-mail. *hyde@sweatshop.co.uk* Web. *www.sweatshop.co.uk Hilly – Monoskin – Twin-Skin – Twinskin*

Swedish Steel De Salis Court De Salis Drive, Hampton Lovett, Droitwich WR9 0QE Tel. *01905 795794* Fax. *01905 794736* E-mail. *ssabuk@ssab.com* Web. *www.swedishsteel.co.uk Armox – Hardox – Hardox - Weldox - Armox – Weldox*

S W G Process Engineering Ltd Gibson Street, Stoke On Trent ST6 6AQ Tel. *01782 824399* Fax. *01782 834015* E-mail. *richard.shufflebottom@vibrodynamics.co.uk* Web. *www.vibrodynamics.co.uk Vibrodynamics*

Swift Business Solutions Ltd Northgate Aldridge, Walsall WS9 8TH Tel. *01922 743454* Fax. *01922 743134* E-mail. *sales@thinkswift.co.uk* Web. *www.thinkswift.co.uk Swift*

Swift Computing 1 & 2 The Sanctuary Eden Office Park, Pill, Bristol BS20 0DD Tel. *01275 376180* Fax. *01275 376181* E-mail. *info@swift-computing.com* Web. *www.swift-computing.com SwiftContext*

J Alex Swift Ltd Cross Street Hathern, Loughborough LE12 5LB Tel. *01509 842284* Fax. *01509 646106* E-mail. *jgander@uk.estee.com* Web. *www.jalexswift.co.uk Socks by Swift – Swift Maid*

Swift J & R Ltd Parsons Lane, Hinckley LE10 1XT Tel. *01455 238398* Fax. *01455 238866* E-mail. *ask@swiftsuniforms.co.uk* Web. *www.swiftsuniforms.co.uk Fair Lady – Mistral*

Swift-Lite Charcoal Innovation Centre Highfield Drive, St Leonards On Sea TN38 9UH Tel. *01424 870333* Fax. *01424 870527* E-mail. *sales@swift-lite.com* Web. *www.swift-lite.com BBQ – Catering – Excelsior Charcoal – Swift Lite*

Swift Medical Trolleys Ltd 7 Micklesmere Drive, Bury St Edmunds IP31 2UJ Tel. *01359 233248* Fax. *01359 233317* E-mail. *info@swiftmedicaltrolleys.co.uk* Web. *www.swiftmedicaltrolleys.co.uk Opmaster – SIMEON*

W B Swift Ltd Leafland Street, Halifax HX1 4LX Tel. *01422 358073* Fax. *01422 330360* E-mail. *lisa.charlton@wbswift.co.uk* Web. *www.wbswift.co.uk Swiftcut*

The Swimming Pool & Allied Trades Association Ltd 4 Eastgate House 5-7 East Street, Andover SP10 1EP Tel. *01264 356210* Fax. *01264 332628* E-mail. *admin@sparta.co.uk* Web. *www.sparta.co.uk S.P.A.T.A.*

Swindens Patents Ltd Suite 404, Albany House 324 Regent Street, London W1B 3HH Tel. *020 75806491* Fax. *020 75804729* E-mail. *am@swindens-vices.co.uk* Web. *www.swindens-vices.co.uk Swindens – Swindens Revolving Head Vices*

S W Industrial Valves Services Ltd Queensway Swasnsea West Industrial Park, Fforestfach, Swansea SA5 4DH Tel. *01792 580260* Fax. *01792 579685* E-mail. *phil.evans@ivs.co.uk* Web. *www.ivs.co.uk FARRIS*

Swire Oilfield Services Swire House Souter Head Road, Altens Industrial Estate, Aberdeen AB12 3LF Tel. *01224 872707* Fax. *01224 874516* E-mail. *reception@swireos.com* Web. *www.swireos.com Swire Oilfield Services*

Swisstulle UK Ltd P O Box 9955, Nottingham NG4 9DY Tel. *0115 8414370* Fax. *0115 8404370* E-mail. *sales@swisstulle.co.uk* Web. *www.swisstulle.co.uk Bobbinet – Pyramids – Swiss Net*

Switch2 Energy Solutions High Mill Mill Street, Cullingworth, Bradford BD13 5HA Tel. *0871 4234242* Fax. *0871 4236161* E-mail. *sales@switch2.com* Web. *www.switch2.com Clorius – Combimeter – Farameter – *G.W.F. (Switzerland) – Mainmet – *S.V.M. (Switzerland)*

Swizzels Matlow Ltd Carlton House Albion Road, New Mills, High Peak SK22 3HA Tel. *01663 744144* Fax. *01663 742800* E-mail. *info@swizzels-matlow.com* Web. *www.swizzels-matlow.com Matlows (United Kingdom) – Swizzels (United Kingdom) – Swizzels Matlow (United Kingdom)*

Sword Ciboodle India of Inchinnan Greenock Road Inchinnan, Renfrew PA4 9LH Tel. *0141 5334000* Fax. *0141 5334199* E-mail. *info@sword-ciboodle.com* Web. *www.swordciboodle.com GT-X (United Kingdom)*

S W P Welded Products Ltd Old Doncaster Road Wath-upon-Dearne, Rotherham S63 7EU Tel. *01709 761200* Fax. *01709 761201* E-mail. *bobbeaumont.swp@dsl.pipex.com Specialist Welded Products*

Sybase UK Ltd Sybase Court Crown Lane, Maidenhead SL6 8QZ Tel. *01628 597100* Fax. *01628 597000* E-mail. *ukinfo@sybase.com* Web. *www.sybase.com Sybase*

Sydney Beaumont Leeds Ltd Unit 5 Sydenham Road, Leeds LS11 9RU Tel. *0113 2458729* Fax. *0113 2428524* E-mail. *info@sydb.co.uk* Web. *www.sydb.co.uk Beaufix – Beauplas – Beaustik – Beautabs – Beautape*

Syfer Technology Ltd Old Stoke Road Arminghall, Norwich NR14 8SQ Tel. *01603 723300* Fax. *01603 665001* E-mail. *hingleson@syfer.co.uk* Web. *www.syfer.co.uk Flexicap – Syfer*

Sykes Global Service Calder House Pentland Gait 599 Calder Road, Edinburgh EH11 4GA Tel. *0131 4586500* Fax. *0131 4586565* E-mail. *marco.kelly@sykes.com* Web. *www.sykes.com Sykes*

Sykes Marine Hydromaster Ltd B6 Fleet House Trading Estate Motherwell Way, Grays RM20 3XD Tel. *01708 862651* Fax. *01708 867905* E-mail. *info@sykeshydromaster.com* Web. *www.sykeshydromaster.com Harbormaster – Hydromaster*

Symbio Unit 8 Coopers Place Combe Lane, Wormley, Godalming GU8 5SZ Tel. *01428 685762* Fax. *01428 685702* E-mail. *info@symbio.co.uk* Web. *www.symbio.co.uk Eco Solutions – *Procede COR (France) – Symbio – Symbio Biofilter – Symbio BLT – Symbio Drainclean – Symbio Green Circle – Symbio Living Water*

Symbol Technologies Ltd Symbol Place Wharfedale Road, Winnersh, Wokingham RG41 5TP Tel. *0118 9457529* Fax. *0118 9457500* Web. *www.motorola.com Air-Aware – Aironet – Telxon*

Synektics Ltd 60 Alton Road, Fleet GU51 3HW Tel. *01252 815281* Fax. *01252 624433* E-mail. *info@synektics.co.uk* Web. *www.synektics.co.uk Securoglide – Somfy*

Synergiq Unit 6 Franklin Park Patterson Street, Blaydon On Tyne NE21 5TL Tel. *0191 4144838* Fax. *08707 418837 Mamut – Synergiq*

Synergy Food Ingredients Ltd 46 Abingdon Road, Melton Mowbray LE13 0SB Tel. *01664 567169* E-mail. *info@sfi-ltd.com* Web. *www.sfi-ltd.com Adinmix – Ceylamix*

Synergy Healthcare plc Lion Mill Fitton Street Royton, Oldham OL2 5JX Tel. *0161 6245641* Fax. *0161 6270902* Web. *www.synergyhealthplc.com Conti Cotton Soft – Conti Moist – Conti Washcloth – Conti Wipe – Contisure – Contura – Cytox – Donald & Taylor – J. Suits – Mediguard – Primeguard – Primetex – Sahara – Visimask*

Synoptics Ltd Beacon House Nuffield Road, Cambridge CB4 1TF Tel. *01223 727100* Fax. *01223 727101* E-mail. *sales@synoptics.co.uk* Web. *www.synoptics.co.uk Syngene – Synoptics*

Synthite Ltd Alyn Works Denbigh Road, Mold CH7 1BT Tel. *01352 752521* Fax. *01352 700182* E-mail. *sales@synthite.co.uk* Web. *www.synthite.co.uk Alcoform*

Systech Instruments Ltd 17 Thame Business Park, Thame OX9 3XA Tel. *01844 216838* Fax. *01844 217220* E-mail. *b.cummings@systechillinois.com* Web. *www.systechillinois.com Anacon – Permox*

Systemair G M P H (t/a Matthews & Yates) Suite 2 Lodge Lane Langham, Colchester CO4 5NE Tel. *01206 543311* Fax. *01206 760497* E-mail. *sales@matthews-yates.co.uk* Web. *www.systemair.com Brook Roof Units – Cyclone*

System Control Solutions Ltd 7 Barley Way, Lowestoft NR33 7NH Tel. *01502 516864* Fax. *01502 501023* E-mail. *rscales@scslow.co.uk* Web. *www.scslow.co.uk Bourdon Haenni – Gamak Motors – Hitachi*

System Hygienics Ltd 8 Industrial Estate Station Road, Hailsham BN27 2EY Tel. *01323 481170* Fax. *01323 483061* E-mail. *onlineenquiry@systemhygienics.co.uk* Web. *www.systemhygienics.co.uk Icevent – Jetvent*

System Insight PO Box 150, Southampton SO32 2PN Tel. *01329 835500* Fax. *01329 835501* E-mail. *info@systeminsight.co.uk* Web. *www.systeminsight.co.uk Inkmun*

Systems Technology Consultants Ltd PO Box 5, Stoke On Trent ST1 4PZ Tel. *01782 286300* Fax. *01782 280036* E-mail. *sytech@sytech-consultants.com* Web. *www.sytech-consultants.com Systems Technology Consultants*

System Uvex Ltd Unit 3 Summit Centre Summit Road, Potters Bar EN6 3QW Tel. *01707 642358* Fax. *01707 645785* E-mail. *info@systemuvex.co.uk* Web. *www.systemuvex.co.uk Uvex*

T

Tabaq Software Limited Building A Trinity Court, Wokingham Road, Bracknell RG42 1PL Tel. *01344 668400* Fax. *01344 668200* E-mail. *sales@tabaqsoftware.com* Web. *www.tabaqsoftware.com jComply*

Taegutec UK Ltd Wetherby Grange Park Boston Road, Wetherby LS22 5NB Tel. *01937 589828* Fax. *01937 589996* E-mail. *sales@taegutec.co.uk* Web. *www.taegutec.co.uk Artmill – Bull Cutter – Chasefeed – Chasemill – Chasemould – Chaseocto – T-Cap – T-Cast – T-Clamp – T-Drill – Z-Mill*

Ta Instruments Fleming Centre Fleming Way, Crawley RH10 9NB Tel. *01293 658900* Fax. *01293 658901* E-mail. *olivia.gibson@taeurope.co.uk* Web. *www.tainstruments.com AR1000 Rheometer – C.S.L. Rheometer – Dielectric Analyser (D.E.A.) – Differential Scanning Calorimeter (D.S.C.) – Micro-Thermal Analyser (M.T.A.) – Thermo-Mechanical Analyser (T.M.A.) – Thermogravimetric Analyser (T.G.A.)*

Takisawa UK Ltd Meir Road, Redditch B98 7SY Tel. *01527 522211* Fax. *01527 510728* E-mail. *takisawa@btconnect.com* Web. *www.takisawa.com *Estarta (Spain) – *Reform (Germany) – Rockwell – *Takisawa (Japan)*

Talbot Designs Ltd 225 Long Lane Finchley, London N3 2RL Tel. *020 83468515* Fax. *020 83490294* E-mail. *sales@talbotdesigns.co.uk* Web. *www.talbotdesigns.co.uk Teedy*

Talbot Tool Co. Ltd Grip Works Crowhurst Road, Brighton BN1 8AT Tel. *01273 508881* Fax. *01273 540544* E-mail. *info@talbot-tool.co.uk* Web. *www.talbot-tool.co.uk Aerogrip – Grip – Talbot Blue – Talbot White – Zin*

Talentmark Ltd King House 5-11 Westbourne Grove, London W2 4UA Tel. *020 72292266* Fax. *020 72293549* E-mail. *william.neilson@talentmark.com* Web. *www.talentmark.com TalentBank – Talentmark – TalentSearch*

Tallon International Ltd Unit4 Cyan Park, Coventry CV2 4QP Tel. *024 76437000* Fax. *024 76452946* E-mail. *ericquantrill@tallon.co.uk* Web. *www.tallon.co.uk Banker – Colouring Club – Pensense – Tallon*

Tallygenicom Rutherford Road, Basingstoke RG24 8PD Tel. *0870 8722888* E-mail. *sales@tallygenicom.co.uk* Web. *www.tally.co.uk Tally*

Talon Chieftain Close Gillingham Business Park, Gillingham ME8 0PP Tel. *08450 952828* Fax. *0845 0952929* E-mail. *sales@talon.co.uk* Web. *www.talon.co.uk Talon*

Tal Talent Colechurch House London Bridge Walk, London SE1 2SS Tel. *020 73787470* Fax. *020 74036729* E-mail. *info@taltalent.com* Web. *www.taltalent.com TAL – TAL Assessment*

The Tambour Company Ltd Warren Road Green Lane Business Park, Featherstone, Pontefract WF7 6EL Tel. *01977 600026* Fax. *01977 600991* E-mail. *william.wesson@tambour.co.uk* Web. *www.tambour.co.uk Flexi MDF – Flexi Ply – Tambour*

Tamo Ltd Unit 22 Sarum Complex Salisbury Road, Uxbridge UB8 2RZ Tel. *01895 200015* Fax. *01895 859888* E-mail. *info@tamo.co.uk* Web. *www.tamo.co.uk Beta-Probe – *Circle Seal (U.S.A.) – Erecta Switch – *Flexim (Germany) – *Flowdata (Germany) – *Jordan Valve (U.S.A.) – Keller – *Miester (Germany) – *Precision Dynamics (U.S.A.) – *Wasco (U.S.A.) – *Wiess (Germany)*

Tampographic Ltd 1 Elan Court Norris Way, Rushden NN10 6BP Tel. *01933 358326* Fax. *01933 316478* E-mail. *sales@tampographic.co.uk* Web. *www.tampographic.co.uk Logica – Marabu*

Tamura Europe Ltd Clarke Avenue, Calne SN11 9BS Tel. *01380 731700* Fax. *01380 731702* E-mail. *info-uk@tamura-europe.co.uk* Web. *www.tamura-europe.co.uk Tamura Europe – Tamura Hinchley*

Tanda Engineering 98 Henshaw Lane Yeadon, Leeds LS19 7RZ Tel. *0113 2502917* Fax. *0113 2505160* E-mail. *enquiries@tandaengineering.co.uk* Web. *www.tandaengineering.co.uk Tanda*

Tandler Precision Ltd 29 Ross Road Business Centre, Northampton NN5 5AX Tel. *01604 588056* Fax. *01604 588064* E-mail. *sales@tandler.co.uk* Web. *www.tandler.co.uk Tandler Zahnrad Und Getriebefabrik Gmbh – R + W Antriebselemente GmbH (United Kingdom)*

Tangi-Flow Products Limited Automatic House Discovery WayLeofric Business Park, Binley, Coventry CV3 2TD Tel. *024 76421200* Fax. *024 76421459* E-mail. *enquiries@tangi-flow.com* Web. *www.tangi-flow.com Tangi-Flow*

Tangye (All Speeds Group Ltd) Royal Works Atlas Street, Clayton Le Moors, Accrington BB5 5LW Tel. *01254 615100* Fax. *01254 615199* E-mail. *info@allspeeds.co.uk* Web. *www.allspeeds.co.uk Hydraclaw – Hydralite – Hydramite – Hydrapak – Superkub – X.R.*

Tannoy Group Ltd Rosehall Industrial Estate, Coatbridge ML5 4TF Tel. *01236 420199* Fax. *01236 428230* E-mail. *andrzej.sosna@tannoy.co.uk* Web. *www.tannoy.com C.P.A. – Definition Series – Dual Concentric – Mercury Series – Precision Series – Prestige series – Profile Series – Studio Monitors – Superdual P.A. – Tannoy*

Tansley Teak 2 Holly Lane Tansley, Matlock DE4 5FF Tel. *01629 593893* E-mail. *info@tansleyteak.co.uk* Web. *www.tansleyteak.co.uk Tansley Teak*

Tapdie 445 West Green Road South Tottenham, London N15 3PL Tel. *020 88881865* Fax. *020 88884613* E-mail. *sales@tapdie.com* Web. *www.tapdie.com T&D, HQS, ZN, Trubor, Swiftic*

Tapeswitch Ltd 38 Drumhead Road Chorley North Industrial Park, Chorley PR6 7BX Tel. *01257 249777* Fax. *01257 246600* E-mail. *info@tapeswitch.co.uk* Web. *www.tapeswitch.co.uk *Guardscan (U.S.A.)*

Tapley Instrumentation (a division of D. Evans Electrical Ltd) Diamond Road,, Norwich NR6 6AW Tel. *01603 485153* Fax. *01603 418150* E-mail. *info@bowmonk.com* Web. *www.tapley.org.uk Tapley*

Tapmatic Engineers' Merchants 7d Millers Close, Fakenham NR21 8NW Tel. *01328 863676* Fax. *01328 856118* E-mail. *info@tapmatic.co.uk* Web. *www.tapmatic.co.uk Alufluid – Clamprite – Comato – Ferrofluid*

Tappex Thread Inserts Ltd Masons Road, Stratford Upon Avon CV37 9NT Tel. *01789 206600* Fax. *01789 414194* E-mail. *sales@tappex.co.uk* Web. *www.tappex.co.uk Dedsert - Drivesert - Drivesert - Flexiarm - Himould - Malesert - Multisert - Pushert - Foamsert - Microbarb - Sonicert - Suresert - Tappex - Trisert - Vandlgard - Trisert 3 - Dedsert – Flexiarm – Foamsert – Himould – Malesert – Microbarb – Multisert – Shearsert – Sonicsert – Suresert – Tappex – Trisert – Trisert-3 – Vandlgard*

Tarak Manufacturing Co. Ltd 61 Hydepark Street, Glasgow G3 8BW Tel. *0141 5691544* Fax. *0141 5691545* E-mail. *info@kidsclothing.co.uk* Web. *www.kidsclothing.co.uk Quiz*

Target Catering Equipment Unit 1 Ashville Trading Estate, Gloucester GL2 5EU Tel. *01452 410447* Fax. *01452 410471* E-mail. *sales@targetcatering.co.uk* Web. *www.targetcatering.co.uk M-A-M – Pedrette Engineering Ltd – Target Counters – Target Kitchen Ventilation – Target Stainless Fabrications*

Target Fastenings Ltd Unit 5-6 Pinecopse Industrial Estate Nine Mile Ride, Wokingham RG40 3ND Tel. *01344 777189* Fax. *01344 779038* E-mail. *sales@targetfastenings.com* Web. *www.targetfastenings.com Brutt Helical – Heli Pile*

Tarkett Ltd Dickley Lane Lenham, Maidstone ME17 2QX Tel. *01622 854000* Fax. *01622 854500* E-mail. *julie.watson@tarkett.com* Web. *www.tarkett.co.uk Embond – Floorcraft – Marley Conductive – Marley Eclipse PUR – Marley Eclipse SD – Marley Elite PUR – Marley Esteem – Marley Europa – Marley HD Synergy PU – Marley Matrix – Marley Matrix Naturals – Marley Reflections – Marley Vylon Plus – Marleyflex – Marleyflor Plus PU – Marleytred – Premier Collection – Safebond – Safetred Aqua – Safetred Dimension – Safetred Universal*

Tarmac Tunstead Quarry Tunstead, Buxton SK17 8TG Tel. *01298 768555* Fax. *01298 72195* E-mail. *info@tarmac.co.uk* Web. *www.tarmac.co.uk Kalic – Limbase – Limbux – Limebond*

Tarmac Precast Concrete Ltd Tallington Factory Barholm Road, Tallington, Stamford PE9 4RL Tel. *01778 381000* Fax. *01778 348041* E-mail. *nd@tarmacprecast.co.uk*

Web. *www.tarmac.co.uk R.C.C. Retaining Walls – Thermocast*

Tarmac Quarry Products Ltd (Silomate) Croxden Quarry Freehay, Cheadle, Stoke On Trent ST10 1RH Tel. *01538 722393* Fax. *01538 723980* E-mail. *hughmcguigan@tarmac.co.uk* Web. *www.tarmac.co.uk Silomate*

Tarmac Topblock Ltd (Western) Hilton Main Industrial Estate Cannock Road, Featherstone, Wolverhampton WV10 7HP Tel. *01902 305060* Fax. *01902 384543* E-mail. *enquiries@tarmac.co.uk* Web. *www.topblock.co.uk Echomaster – Hemelite – Lignacite – Topcrete – Toplite – Weathered Masonry*

Tarpey-Harris Ltd Flamstead House Denby Hall Business Park Hall Road, Marehay, Ripley DE5 8JX Tel. *01332 883950* Fax. *01332 883951* E-mail. *stevej@tarpey-harris.co.uk* Web. *www.tarpey-harris.co.uk Tarpey-Harris*

Task Masters UK Ltd International House Dover Place, Ashford TN23 1HU Tel. *01233 631300* Fax. *01233 631230* E-mail. *info@taskmasters-uk.com* Web. *www.taskmasters-uk.com Safe Return*

Tate & Lyle Public Ltd Company Sugar Quay Lower Thames Street, London EC3R 6DQ Tel. *020 76266525* Fax. *020 76235213* E-mail. *robert.gibber@tateandlyle.com* Web. *www.tateandlyle.com Fermentose – Isosweet – *Meritena 100 (Netherlands) – Meritena 200 – Meritose – *Mylbond (Belgium) – *Resistamyl (Netherlands)*

Tatem Industrial Automation Ltd Unit 4a Derby Small Business Centre Canal Street, Derby DE1 2RJ Tel. *01332 204850* Fax. *01332 204851* E-mail. *info@tatem.co.uk* Web. *www.tatem.co.uk A T I – Amtru – Proteus – Pushcorp – Robot Accessories – Schunk – T D Industrial Covers*

Tavak Ltd 5 White Cottage Farm Lucas Green Road, West End, Woking GU24 9LZ Tel. *08452 235206* Fax. *0845 2235207* E-mail. *info@tavak.co.uk* Web. *www.tavak.co.uk Tavak*

Tawi UK 4 Phoenix Court Everitt Close, Denington Indl-Est, Wellingborough NN8 2QE Tel. *01933 277260* Fax. *01933 277209* E-mail. *simon.coles@tawi.co.uk* Web. *www.tawi.co.uk Lyftman – Protema – TAWI – Vacueasy*

Austin Taylor Communications Bethesda, Bangor LL57 3BX Tel. *01248 600561* Fax. *01248 601674* E-mail. *phil.griffith@austin-taylor.co.uk* Web. *www.austin-taylor.co.uk Austin Taylor*

Taylor Foodservice Facilities Truthwall Mill Crowlas, Penzance TR20 9BL Tel. *01736 711310* Fax. *01736 711317* E-mail. *tffc_ian_taylor@compuserve.com* Web. *www.taylorfoodservice.com *Dispense-Rite – *Moli International*

Henry Taylor Tools Ltd Unit 5-8 Peacock Trading Estate Livesey Street, Sheffield S6 2BL Tel. *0114 2340282* Fax. *0114 2852015* E-mail. *sales@henrytaylortools.co.uk* Web. *www.henrytaylortools.co.uk Acorn – Diamic in a Diamond*

Taylor Hobson Ltd (Head Office) 2 New Star Road, Leicester LE4 9JD Tel. *0116 2763771* Fax. *0116 2741350* E-mail. *kathy.sena@ametek.com* Web. *www.taylor-hobson.com Form Talysurf – Nanostep – Surtronic – Talyrond – Talyrond - Talysurf - Nanostep - Surtronic - Talyscan - Form Talysurf - Talyvel - Talyscan - Talystep – Talysurf – Talytrac – Talyvel – Taylor-Hobson*

Taylor & Jones Ltd Crosland Road Industrial Estate Netherton, Huddersfield HD4 7DQ Tel. *01484 665321* Fax. *01484 666952* E-mail. *kevin@taylorandjones.co.uk* Web. *www.taylorandjones.co.uk T. & J.*

J & S Taylor Ltd Corporation Mill Corporation Street, Sowerby Bridge HX6 2QQ Tel. *01422 832616* Fax. *01422 833686* E-mail. *jands.taylor@btinternet.com* Web. *www.taylorsdirect.co.uk Jastex*

K H Taylor Ltd Sheffield Road Blyth, Worksop S81 8HF Tel. *01909 590000* Fax. *01909 591713* E-mail. *khtaylor@lineone.net* Web. *www.kh-taylor.co.uk Garden Gold*

Taylor & Lodge (t/a Taylor & Lodge) Rashcliffe Mills Albert Street, Huddersfield HD1 3PE Tel. *01484 423231* Fax. *01484 435313* E-mail. *headoffice@taylorandlodge.co.uk* Web. *www.taylorandlodge.co.uk Taylor & Lodge*

Taylor Precision Plastics Ltd Mile Oak Industrial Estate Maesbury Road, Oswestry SY10 8GA Tel. *01691 679516* Fax. *01691 670538* E-mail. *sales@cvrollers.co.uk* Web. *www.cvrollers.co.uk CVR*

R D Taylor & Co. Ltd 240 Edmiston Drive, Glasgow G51 2YU Tel. *0141 4275103* Fax. *0141 4271881* E-mail. *sales@rdtaylor.co.uk* Web. *www.rdtaylor.co.uk 3.M. (United Kingdom) – AK20 Nobel Aerospace Coatings (United Kingdom) – Bostik (UK) (United Kingdom) – *Dow Corning (Belgium) – Elixair (UK) (United Kingdom) – Loctite (UK) – *Molykote (Germany) – Scapa (United Kingdom) – Sellotape (United Kingdom) – Shell Aviation Products (United Kingdom) – Vantico (United Kingdom)*

Samuel Taylor Ltd Arthur Street Central Lakeside, Redditch B98 8JY Tel. *01527 504910* Fax. *01527 500869* E-mail. *info@samueltaylor.co.uk* Web. *www.samueltaylor.co.uk Contact Rivets – Microprofile – Silver Contacts – Steb – Stebmetal – Stebweld*

Taylor Scotland Ltd 14 Westgarth Place East Kilbride, Glasgow G74 5NT Tel. *01355 236422* Fax. *01355 264790* E-mail. *taylorscotland@inbox.com* Web. *www.taylor-company.co.uk *Flavorburst – *Razzle – *Taylor Freezer – *Whipper*

Taylor Special Steels Ltd Unit 1-2 Pearsall Drive, Oldbury B69 2RA Tel. *0121 5522741* Fax. *0121 5111240* E-mail. *accounts@taylorspecialsteels.co.uk* Web. *www.taylorspecialsteels.co.uk ASP Powder Metallurgy High Speed Tool Steels*

Taylor Wimpey UK Ltd Gate House Turnpike Road, High Wycombe HP12 3NR Tel. *01494 558323* Fax. *01494 885663* E-mail. *russell.brittain@taylorwimpey.com* Web. *www.taylorwimpey.co.uk Wimpey Homes*

Tayside Cash Registers 68 Logie Street, Dundee DD2 2QE Tel. *07711 625274* Fax. *01382 566335 *Casio – *Fujitsu – *Samsung – *Sharp*

T B A Textiles Unit 3 Trans Pennine Trading Estate Gorrells Way, Rochdale OL11 2PX Tel. *01706 647422* Fax. *01706 354295* E-mail. *info@tbatextiles.co.uk* Web. *www.tbatextiles.co.uk Firefly – Fortaglas – Fortamid – Glo-Tex – Pro-Bloc – Weldstop*

T C Richards & Sons Calow Green Calow, Chesterfield S44 5XQ Tel. *01246 275612* Fax. *01246 237202 ford tractors*

T C W Services Controls Ltd 293 New Mill Road Brockholes, Holmfirth HD9 7AL Tel. *01484 662865* Fax. *01484 667574* E-mail. *sales@tcw-services.co.uk* Web. *www.tcw-services.co.uk Fireguard – Firewatch*

Teal & Mackrill Ltd Lockwood Street, Hull HU2 0HN Tel. *01482 320194* Fax. *01482 219266* E-mail. *info@teamac.co.uk* Web. *www.teamac.co.uk Suregrip – Teamac – Teamalak*

Teamco International Ltd 2 Old Bath Road Charvil, Reading RG10 9QR Tel. *0118 9694104* Fax. *0118 9694103* E-mail. *sales@valves.org.uk* Web. *www.valves.org.uk Norriseal – Radix*

Team Corporation UK Ltd European Division 11 Old Ladies Court High Street, Battle TN33 0AH Tel. *01424 777004* Fax. *01424 777005* E-mail. *sales@teamcorporation.co.uk* Web. *www.teamcorporation.co.uk Cube – Mantis – Tensor*

Teamlink Sports Tours Victoria Buildings 138-152 Uttoxeter New Road, Derby DE22 3WZ Tel. *0808 1493787* Fax. *01332 384222* E-mail. *info@teamlink.co.uk* Web. *www.teamlink.co.uk Calellafest*

Team Overseas Ltd Meridan Building Nazeing New Road, Broxbourne EN10 6SX Tel. *01992 464462* Fax. *01992 464643* E-mail. *sales@teamoverseas.com* Web. *www.teamoverseas.com Allis Chalmer – American Hoist – Atlas Copco – Borg Warner – Caterpiller – Cummins – Delco Remy – Detroit Diesel – Deutz – Fag – Fiat Allis – Fleetguard – Grove – Hyster – Ingersoll Rand – John Deere – Kenworth – Landrover – Mack – Perkins – Poclain – Thorn Lighting*

Team Sprayers Ltd Unit 3 Lancaster Way Business Park, Ely CB6 3NW Tel. *01353 661211* Fax. *01353 666642* E-mail. *buyer@team-sprayers.com* Web. *www.team-sprayers.com *Team Sprayers*

Teapigs Unit 1 The Old Pumping Station Pump Alley, Brentford TW8 0AP Tel. *020 85681313* E-mail. *help@teapigs.co.uk* Web. *www.teapigs.co.uk Teapigs*

Tecalemit Garage Equipment Co. Ltd Eagle Road Plympton, Plymouth PL7 5JY Tel. *01752 219111* Fax. *01752 219128* E-mail. *sales@tecalemit.co.uk* Web. *www.tecalemit.co.uk Azur – DE5000 – DE7195 – DE7200 – DE8232 – Elan – Equinoxe – Euro Test Lane – Leviathan – Lubemaster – Millennium – Polaris – Quadra – Reflex – Sentinel – Trackalign – Trojan*

Tech Europe 15 Ballinderry Road Ballinderry Industrial Estate, Lisburn BT28 2SA Tel. *028 92665721* Fax. *028 92601611* E-mail. *hwrightturner@euratyrerepair.com Aromet – Cure C Cure*

Techland Group Ltd Techland House Knaves Beech Business Centre, Loudwater, High Wycombe HP10 9YJ Tel. *01628 852000* Fax. *01628 643800* E-mail. *sales@techland.co.uk* Web. *www.techland.co.uk *Autoview 200 (Ireland) – *Autoview Commander (U.S.A.) – *Brook Trout (U.S.A.) – Comcat – *Commander UXP (U.S.A.) – *Facsys (U.S.A.) – *File Room (U.S.A.) – *Keyview II (U.S.A.) – *Longview (U.S.A.) – *Mail Room (U.S.A.) – *PC Extender Plus (U.S.A.) – *Serveview Plc (U.S.A.) – *Switchview (U.S.A.) – *Ultra Matrix (U.S.A.) – *Ultraview (U.S.A.) – *Vista (U.S.A.) – *X.P. 4000 (U.S.A.)*

Technibond Ltd Millboard Road, Bourne End SL8 5XD Tel. *01628 642800* Fax. *01628 642801* E-mail. *sales@technibond.co.uk* Web. *www.technibond.co.uk Technibond – Techniflex – Techniseal*

Technical Absorbents 1 Moody Lane Great Coates, Grimsby DN31 2SS Tel. *01472 244053* Fax. *01472 244266* E-mail. *sales@techabsorbents.com* Web. *www.techabsorbents.com Oasis SAF*

Technical Direct Ltd York Farm Business Centre Watling Street, Towcester NN12 8EU Tel. *01327 830109* Fax. *01327 830969* E-mail. *admin@technicaldirect.co.uk* Web. *www.technicaldirect.co.uk Manhattan*

Technical Sales Ltd 3 Harding Way, St Ives PE27 3WR Tel. *01480 494747* Fax. *020 79241755* E-mail. *geoffrey.redhead@technicsales.co.uk *Aero-Pro (Germany) – *Ecobra (Germany) – *Micron (Italy) – Stanley Tools – T.-S. – Tech-Style*

Technical Vacuum Services Ltd 69 Langley Drive Langley Green, Crawley RH11 7TF Tel. *01293 400887* Fax. *01293 400887* E-mail. *sales@technicalvacuumservices.co.uk* Web. *www.technicalvacuumservices.co.uk 306 coater – Coolstar – Edwards high vacuum – Penning gauges – Pirani gauges – Spectron – Vapour boosters*

Technifor Tachbrook Park Drive, Warwick CV34 6RH Tel. *01926 884422* Fax. *01926 883105* E-mail. *sales@ltd.technifor.com* Web. *www.technifor.com Pro Pen (France) – Technifor (France)*

Techni Measure Alexandra Buildings 59 Alcester Road, Studley B80 7NJ Tel. *01527 854103* Fax. *01527 853267* E-mail. *sales@techni-measure.co.uk* Web. *www.techni-measure.co.uk HUBA (Switzerland) – Sakae (Japan) – DYTRAN (U.S.A.) – CONAX TECHNOLOGIES (U.S.A.) – MICROSTRAIN (U.S.A.)*

Technocover Whittington Road, Oswestry SY11 1HZ Tel. *01691 653251* Fax. *01691 658222* E-mail. *terry.bratten@technocover.com* Web. *www.jonesofoswestry.com Aqua-Dish – Aqua-Drain – Aqua-Slot – Arbor-Slot – Suprabloc – Supraduct – Supragrid – Suprasteel*

Techsil Ltd 34 Bidavon Industrial Estate Waterloo Road, Bidford-On-Avon, Alcester B50 4JN Tel. *01789 773232* Fax. *01789 774239* E-mail. *sales@techsil.co.uk* Web. *www.techsil.co.uk Adhesive suppliers – Techsil. – Techwax – Vactech – VT*

Techspan Systems Ltd Techspan House Griffin Lane, Aylesbury HP19 8BP Tel. *01296 673000* Fax. *01296 673002* E-mail. *enquiries@techspan.co.uk* Web. *www.techspan.co.uk Jarvis Group*

Techviz 33A Fossgate, York YO1 9TA Tel. *01904 630721* E-mail. *martin@techviz.co.uk* Web. *www.techviz.co.uk Techviz*

Teco Ltd Wellington Road Portslade, Brighton BN41 1DN Tel. *01273 410099* Fax. *01273 410074* E-mail. *info@tecoproducts.co.uk* Web. *www.tecoproducts.co.uk Teco – Trip-L-Grip*

Teconnex Ltd Bronte Warehouse Chesham Street, Keighley BD21 4LG Tel. *01535 691122* Fax. *01535 691133* E-mail. *sales@teconnex.com* Web. *www.teconnex.com Connectors – Smith & Johnson*

Tecstar Electronics Ltd Unit 8 Bramley Road, St Ives PE27 3WS Tel. *01480 399499* Fax. *01480 399503* E-mail. *sales@tecstar.co.uk* Web. *www.starcom1.com Kenwood – Kenwood - Tecstar - Prism – Prism – Starconl – Tecstar*

Tecton Ltd Fishers Court Main Road Fishers Pond, Eastleigh SO50 7HG Tel. *023 80695858* Fax. *023 80695702* E-mail. *chrishall@tecton.co.uk* Web. *www.tecton.co.uk Darlex – DRAX17 – Humbug – Kramplex – Mimiplex – Mosail – Q.4*

Tectonic International Ltd The Old School Merthyr Road, Llwydcoed, Aberdare CF44 0UT Tel. *01685 722225* Fax. *01685 722321* E-mail. *sales@tectonicinternational.com* Web. *www.tectonicinternational.com Jaguar – K1 – Lynx*

Tecvac Ltd (A Wallwork Company) Buckingway Business Park Rowles Way, Swavesey, Cambridge CB24 4UG Tel. *01954 233700* Fax. *01954 233733* E-mail. *reception@tecvac.com* Web. *www.tecvac.com Nimplant – Nitron – Tecvac – Tinite – Tinite, Nitron, Nimplant*

Ted Baker Ltd 6a St Pancras Way, London NW1 0TB Tel. *020 72554800* Fax. *020 73870106* E-mail. *charles.anderson@tedbaker.com* Web. *www.tedbaker.com Ted*

Teddington Appliance Controls Ltd Daniels Lane, St Austell PL25 3HG Tel. *01726 74400* Fax. *01726 67953* E-mail. *info@tedcon.com* Web. *www.tedcon.com Teddington Controls Limited*

Teesside Precision Engineering Ltd Skippers Lane Industrial Estate Skippers Lane, Middlesbrough TS6 6HA Tel. *01642 455295* Fax. *01642 440465* E-mail. *enquiry@tpe-ltd.com* Web. *www.tpe-ltd.com Teesside Precision Engineering*

Tegrel Ltd Tundry Way, Blaydon On Tyne NE21 5TT Tel. *0191 4146111* Fax. *0191 4140660* E-mail. *richard.leech@tegrel.co.uk* Web. *www.tegrel.co.uk Electrical Enclosure Manufacturers*

Teignbridge Propellers International Great Western Way Forde Road, Newton Abbot TQ12 4AW Tel. *01626 333377* Fax. *01626 360783* E-mail. *sales@teignbridge.co.uk* Web. *www.teignbridge.co.uk Propellers Sterngear & Associated Marine Hardwear – Temet 25*

Tek Ltd Unit 14 Seeleys Road, Birmingham B11 2LQ Tel. *0121 7665005* Fax. *0121 7665010* E-mail. *sales@tekltd.co.uk* Web. *www.tekltd.com *Madal (Spain)*

Tekdata Distribution Ltd Technology House Crown Road, Stoke On Trent ST1 5NJ Tel. *01782 274255*

Fax. *01782 665511* E-mail. *info@tekdata.co.uk* Web. *www.tekdata.co.uk 1.4mb Disk Drive Floppy Ide Int Laptop Teac Teac – 2440 Diva Eicon – 3.5 Disk Drive Floppy – 3.5in Disk Drive FDD Floppy OEM OEM – ADSL Balancing Load – Anti Kaspersky Personal Spam – Anti Spam – Anti Spam Filter – Anti Spam Services – Anti Spam Tool – Anti Spam Virus – Anti Virus and Firewall – Anti Virus Protection – Assessment Vunerability – Back DVD Up – Back Up – Backup Data Data Storage – Backup Data Online Storage – Balancing Internet Load – Biometric Fingerprint Reader – Biometrics – Biometrics Fingerprint – Biometrics Hardware – Biometrics Identity Reader – Biometrics Precise – Biometrics Reader – Biometrics Reader UK – Biometrics Recognition – Biometrics Recognition Technology – Biometrics Security – Biometrics System – Biometrics UK – Black Cherry Keyboard – Block Detection Intrusion Ping – Bosanova – Boscom – Broadband Router – Buy Data Storage – Buy Floppy Disk Drive – Call IP Over Voice – Calmark – *Cardlok (U.S.A.) – CD Changer Teac – CD Data Storage – CD Driver Rom Teac – Cherry Cherry Electrical Keyboard Mini ml4100 – Cherry Cherry Electrical Keyboard Mini ml4100 ps2 usb – Cherry Cherry Electrical Keyboard PC Standard – Cherry Keyboard UK – Claro – Combined Smart Card Fingerprint Reader – Computer Data Storage – Computer Distributor – Content Filtering Mail – Cymotion – Data Back Up – Data Device Portable Storage – Data Device Storage – Data Device Storage USB – Data DVD Storage – Data External Storage – Data Optical Storage – Data PC Storage – Data Product Storage – Data Raid Storage – Data Storage – Data Storage Solution – Data Storage Tape – Data Storage USB – Detection Intrusion Managed Service – Detection Intrusion Unit – Disk Drive External Floppy USB – Disk Drive Floppy USB – Distributor DVD – Diva Eicon – Diva Eicon Technology – DVD RW Teac – E-Filtering Mail – e1 – Eicon – Eicon Modem – Epos – Epos Hardware – Equipment IP Over Voice – External Floppy Disk Drive – File Back Up – Filtering Mail – Fingerprint Identification Reader – Fingerprint Reader – Fingerprint Reader Security System – Firewall Intrusion Detection – Floppy Disk Drive – Format FXO – FXO – FXO FXS – FXO FXS Interface – Internet Data Storage – Intrusion Detection – Intrusion Detection Software Firewall – Intrusion Detection System – Intrusion Managed Prevention – Intrusion Prevention – IP IP Over Telephony Voice – IP Over Phone Solution Voice – IP Over Solution Voice – IP Over System Voice – IP Over Telephony – IP Over UK Voice – IP Product Telephony – IP Specialist Telephony – IP Telephony – IP Telephony Solution – IP Telephony System – IP Telephony Voip – It Security – It Security Solution – IT Security Training – Kaspersky anti virus – Lan Rover Shiva – Load Balancing – Network Intrusion Detection – Network Intrusion Detection System – Network Load Balancing – Panasonic – Removable Data Storage – Server Load Balancing – Shiva – Shiva Lanrover – Shiva Site – Smart Card – Smart Card Application – Smart Card Reader – Smart Card Reader Writer – Smart Card Security – Smart Card Solution – Smart Card Technology – SonicWall (U.S.A.) – Supplier Teac UK – Teac – Teac CD Rom Drive – Teac CD RW – Teac DVD – Teac UK – Techdata – Teckdata – Tek Data – Tekdata – Tekdata Defender – UK Distributor – Voice Over IP – Voice Over IP Company – Voice Over IP Gateway – Voice Over IP Phone – Voice Over IP Phone System – Voice Over IP Provider – Voice Over IP Software – Voice Over IP Technology – Voice Over IP Telephony – Voice Over IP Voip – Wireless Broadband Router Distributor*

Tekhniseal Ltd Unit 1 Alibion Business Centre Priestley Road, Worsley, Manchester M28 2LY Tel. *0161 7946063* Fax. *0161 7944773* E-mail. *sales@tekhniseal.com* Web. *www.tekhniseal.com Tekhniseal Ltd (United Kingdom)*

Tekmat Ltd Ryan House Trent Lane, Castle Donington, Derby DE74 2PY Tel. *01332 853443* Fax. *01332 853424* E-mail. *sales@tekmat.co.uk* Web. *www.tekmat.co.uk *Ducarbo (Denmark) – *Imco (U.S.A.) – *Menlo (U.S.A.) – *Superion (U.S.A.)*

Tekni Kleen Computer Services Ltd PO Box 200, Staines TW18 4QE Tel. *01784 469133* Fax. *01784 451277* E-mail. *colin@teknikleen.co.uk* Web. *www.teknikleen.co.uk Tekni Kleen Computer Services*

T E K Seating Ltd 14 Decimus Park Kingstanding Way, Tunbridge Wells TN2 3GP Tel. *01892 515028* Fax. *01892 529751* E-mail. *sales@tekseating.co.uk* Web. *www.tekseating.co.uk Grammer – Isri (Isringhausen) – KAB – Pilot – Recaro – Sears*

Teksol Training & Technology Ltd 17 New Eaton Road Stapleford, Nottingham NG9 7EF Tel. *0115 9490497* E-mail. *lizzie.taylor@teksol-gassafetytraining.com* Web. *www.teksol-gassafetytraining.com Gas Safety Workshop*

Tektura plc Harbour Exchange Square, London E14 9JE Tel. *020 75363300* Fax. *020 75363322* E-mail. *enquiries@tektura.com* Web. *www.tektura.com Anya Larkin – Boltawall – *Colour Palette (U.S.A.) – Elements – Essentials – Evans & Brown – Fast-Track – Koroseal – Mia Romanoff – *Moment (Sweden) – *Natural Palette (Switzerland) – Salinas – Tekfix – Tektura – Tektura-Online – Tri-Guard – Vicrtex – Walltalkers – Worldwide – Zanzibar*

Telcon Ltd (Head Office) D1 Old Brighton Road Lowfield Heath, Crawley RH11 0PR Tel. *01293 528800* Fax. *01293 524466* E-mail. *sales@telcon.co.uk* Web. *www.telcon.co.uk A.C.T. – APEX – Current Transformers – H.E.C.T.*

Teleflex Medical Stirling Road Cressex Business Park, High Wycombe HP12 3ST Tel. *01494 532761* Fax. *01494 524650* E-mail. *dclarke@teleflexmedical.com* Web. *www.teleflexmedical.com Crystal – Jaques – Ostopore – Riplex – Simplastic – Translet – W.S.P. – Warne*

Telegan Protection Ltd 3-5 Holmethorpe Avenue Sealand Centre, Redhill RH1 2LZ Tel. *01737 763800* Fax. *01737 782727* E-mail. *sales@teleganprotection.com* Web. *www.teleganprotection.com *Ansul – *Telsyn*

Telehouse International Coriander Avenue, London E14 2AA Tel. *020 75120550* Fax. *020 75120033* E-mail. *info@uk.telehouse.net* Web. *www.telehouse.net Telehouse*

Teleologic Ltd Lion House Muspole Street, Norwich NR3 1DJ Tel. *01603 765737* E-mail. *info@teleologic.co.uk* Web. *www.teleologic.co.uk Teleologic*

Tele-Products Ltd 11 Glaisdale Road Northminster Business Park Upper Poppleton, York YO26 6QT Tel. *01904 794200* Fax. *01904 780054* E-mail. *sales@firststopsafety.co.uk* Web. *www.tele-products.com Crucible Technologies (United Kingdom) – First Stop Safety – Tele-Products Limited (United Kingdom)*

Telesoft Technologies Ltd Observatory House Stour Park, Blandford St Mary, Blandford Forum DT11 9LQ Tel. *01258 480880* Fax. *01258 486598* E-mail. *sales@telesoft-technologies.com* Web. *www.telesoft-technologies.com Okeford – Hinton – Milborne – MPAC – TDAPI*

Tellabs Abbey Place 24-28 Easton Street, High Wycombe HP11 1NT Tel. *0871 5747000* Fax. *0871 5747151* E-mail. *prnews@tellabs.com* Web. *www.tellabs.com Tellabs*

Telspec plc Lancaster Parker Road, Rochester ME1 3QU Tel. *01634 687133* Fax. *01634 684984* E-mail. *fred.white@telspec.co.uk* Web. *www.telspec.co.uk I.S.D.N – Pair Gain Equipment – Switching Systems*

Tema Machinery Ltd 3 Great Central Way Woodford Halse, Daventry NN11 3PZ Tel. *01327 262600* Fax. *01327 262571* E-mail. *sales@tema.co.uk* Web. *www.tema.co.uk Conturbex – Liwell – Vibratom*

Tempatron Controls 5 Darwin Close, Reading RG2 0TB Tel. *0118 9314062* Fax. *0118 9310175* E-mail. *info@tempatron.co.uk* Web. *www.tempatron.co.uk *Autonics (Korea, Republic of) – *Han Young (Korea, Republic of) – Tempatron*

Temple Wines Ltd (Rajni Kataria & Madhu Kataria) 472 Church Lane, London NW9 8UA Tel. *020 89059484* Fax. *020 82008393* E-mail. *neal.nalin@bt.com Baron Pils – Linden – Lobkowicz – Radegast – Super Trix*

Tenants Bitumen 9 Airport Road West, Belfast BT3 9ED Tel. *028 90455135* Fax. *028 90460077* E-mail. *info@ctni.co.uk* Web. *www.ctni.co.uk Bitumen – Cutback – Penetration – Tencoat – Tenset – Tenspray*

Tenax UK Ltd Unit 12 Ash Road North Wrexham Industrial Estate, Wrexham LL13 9JT Tel. *01978 664667* Fax. *01978 664634* E-mail. *info@tenax.co.uk* Web. *www.tenax.co.uk Tenaz Rapitest*

Tenmat Ltd (Head Office) Ashburton Road West Trafford Park, Manchester M17 1RU Tel. *0161 8722181* Fax. *0161 8727596* E-mail. *info@tenmat.com* Web. *www.tenmat.com Arclex – Ferobestos – Feroform – Feroglide – Nitrasil – Refel – Sindanyo*

Tennant Metallurgical Group Ltd Suite 4 Venture House Venture Way Dunston Technology Park, Chesterfield S41 8NR Tel. *01246 263000* Fax. *01246 263001* E-mail. *ross.convery@tenmet.co.uk* Web. *www.tenmet.co.uk *Hafsil (Norway) – Tenbloc – *Tenmag (Norway) – Tensil*

Tennants Inks & Coating Supplies Ltd Eastern United Site, Cinderford GL14 3AW Tel. *01594 822375* Fax. *01594 826251* E-mail. *brian.beddis@tg-tics.com* Web. *www.tennantsinksandcoatings.co.uk Aquapak – Dispercab – Dispercap – Dispercel – Disperchlor – Dispercryl – Disperkyd – Dispermid – Dispervyn – Evasperse – Magnacryl – Magnakyd – Magnaset – Mitchinol – Runnymede Dispersions – Teller Inks & Coatings*

Tennco Distribution Ltd Unit A1-A2 Forelle Centre 30 Blackmoor Road, Ebblake Industrial Estate, Verwood BH31 6BB Tel. *01202 824433* Fax. *01202 814500* E-mail. *matt@tennconet.com* Web. *www.tennconet.com Ethernet – Steadytec*

Tensid UK Ltd 70a Wheatash Road, Addlestone KT15 2ES Tel. *01932 564133* Fax. *01932 562046* E-mail. *info@tensid.com* Web. *www.tensid.com A.G.S. – *Aquila (Denmark) – Proscco*

Tentec Ltd Plymouth House Guns Lane, West Bromwich B70 9HS Tel. *0121 5241990* Fax. *0121 5251999* E-mail. *sales@tentec.net* Web. *www.tentec.net Choc Roll Clamp – Live Load – Manufacture hydraulic bolt tensioning equipment – Tentec*

Tenza Technologies Ltd Carlton Park Industrial Estate Carlton, Saxmundham IP17 2NL Tel. *01728 602811* Fax. *01728 604108* E-mail. *adrian.smith@tenzatech.com* Web. *www.tenzatech.com API Tenza – Cover Clear – Tenza – Tenzalopes*

Tepco Engineering International 13 Overfield Thorpe Way, Banbury OX16 4XR Tel. *01295 264200* Fax. *01295 264901* E-mail. *sales@tepcoengineering.co.uk* Web. *www.tepcoengineering.co.uk Tepco UK*

Terex (BL Pegson) Mammoth Street, Coalville LE67 3GN Tel. *01530 518600* Fax. *01530 518618* Web. *www.bl-pegson.com 428 Trackpactor – Autocone – Automax – Autosand – Eurotrak – Metrotrak – Premier – Premiertrak*

Terex UK Ltd PO Box 26, Coventry CV6 4BX Tel. *024 76339400* Fax. *024 76339500* E-mail. *sales@terexce.com* Web. *www.terexce.com Benford – Fyne – Liftmate*

Terinex Ltd Hammond Road Elm Farm Industrial Estate, Bedford MK41 0ND Tel. *01234 364411* Fax. *01234 271486* E-mail. *paul@terinex.co.uk* Web. *www.terinex.co.uk AluChef – Bakewell – Clingorap – Look – *Polycling (U.S.A.) – *Reynolds (U.S.A.)*

Termate Leone Works John Street, New Basford, Nottingham NG7 7HL Tel. *0115 9784652* Fax. *0115 9702106* E-mail. *sales@termate.com* Web. *www.termate.com Ter-Mate – Ter-Mate Master Frame*

Termodeck Weston Underwood, Ashbourne DE6 4PH Tel. *01332 868510* Fax. *01332 868511* E-mail. *termodeck@tarmac.co.uk* Web. *www.termodeck.co.uk Termodeck*

Terram Ltd Blackwater Trading Estate The Causeway, Maldon CM9 4GG Tel. *01495 757722* Fax. *01495 762383* E-mail. *kate.miles@terram.co.uk* Web. *www.terram.com Filtram – Melfab – Paragrid – Paralink – Roofstat – *Terram (United Kingdom)*

Terrapin Ltd Bond Avenue Bletchley, Milton Keynes MK1 1JJ Tel. *0115 9072700* Fax. *0115 9722203* E-mail. *a.day@terrapin-ltd.co.uk* Web. *www.terrapin-ltd.co.uk Matrex – Prospex – Uni-Trex – Uni-Trex, Prospex, Matrex*

Terry Johnson Ltd 31 Cranmore Lane Holbeach, Spalding PE12 7HT Tel. *01406 422286* Fax. *01406 426372* E-mail. *accounts@terryjohnsonltd.co.uk* Web. *www.terryjohnsonltd.co.uk Bettinson Wheels – G.S. Wheels – Molfit – Swift Lift – Todd – Whitsed*

Terry Lifts Ltd Longridge Trading Estate, Knutsford WA16 8PR Tel. *08453 655366* Fax. *01565 755062* E-mail. *customerservices@terrylifts.net* Web. *www.terrylifts.co.uk Terry Group Ltd*

Tesa Technology UK Ltd Metrology House Halesfield 13, Telford TF7 4PL Tel. *01952 681349* Fax. *01952 681391* E-mail. *tesa-uk@hexagonmetrology.com* Web. *www.tesabs.co.uk DEA – Etalon (Switzerland) – Interapid (Switzerland) – Mauser (Switzerland) – Mercer (Switzerland) – Precision tools suppliers – Roch – Select Gauges – Standard – *Tesa (Switzerland) – Tesa (Switzerland)*

Tesla Engineering Ltd Water Lane Storrington, Pulborough RH20 3EA Tel. *01903 743941* Fax. *01903 745548* E-mail. *sales@tesla.co.uk* Web. *www.tesla.co.uk Tesla Engineering Ltd*

Testbourne Unit 2 The Hatch Industrial Park Greywell Road, Mapledurwell, Basingstoke RG24 7NG Tel. *01256 467055* Fax. *01256 842929* E-mail. *info@testbourne.com* Web. *www.testbourne.com Testbourne*

Testconsult Ltd Ruby House 40a Hardwick Grange, Woolston, Warrington WA1 4RF Tel. *01925 286880* Fax. *01925 286881* E-mail. *jo@testconsult.co.uk* Web. *www.testconsult.co.uk BGCMAP – SIMBAT – SPTMAN – TDR2 – TECO*

Testemp Ltd Rope Walk, Littlehampton BN17 5DE Tel. *01903 714140* Fax. *01903 717435* E-mail. *sales@testemp.co.uk* Web. *www.testemp.co.uk *Shinko (Japan)*

Test Plugs Ltd 12 Falklands Road, Haverhill CB9 0EA Tel. *01440 704201* Fax. *01440 763121* E-mail. *sales@test-plugs.com* Web. *www.test-plugs.com Selfseal (United Kingdom) – Test Plugs (United Kingdom)*

Testrade Ltd Unit 22 Olds Close, Watford WD18 9RU Tel. *01923 720222* Fax. *01923 720444* E-mail. *sales@testrade.co.uk Testrade*

Tetrad plc Hartford Mill Swan Street, Preston PR1 5PQ Tel. *01772 792936* Fax. *01772 798319* E-mail. *sales@tetrad.co.uk* Web. *www.tetrad.co.uk Tetrad Plc*

Tetra Pak Ltd Bedwell Road Cross Lanes, Wrexham LL13 0UT Tel. *08704 426000* Fax. *08704 426001* E-mail. *info@tetrapak.com* Web. *www.cips.org Tetra Brik – Tetra Classic – Tetra Prisma – Tetra Rex – Tetra Top – Tetra Wedge – Tetratainer*

Tetrosyl (International Division) Bevis Green Works Walmersley, Bury BL9 6RE Tel. *0161 7645981* Fax. *0161 7975899* E-mail. *info@tetrosyl.com* Web. *www.tetrosyl.com Autotint – Car-Plan – Technifil – Tetra – Tetra – Tetrabond – Tetrabond – Tetrafix – Tetragrout – Tetratex – Tetrion*

Tev Ltd Armytage Road, Brighouse HD6 1QF Tel. *01484 405600* Fax. *01484 403620* E-mail. *sales@tevlimited.com* Web. *www.tevlimited.com Airking – C.D. Series – Enreco – IMI – Marstair*

Teversham Motors 5 Church Road Teversham, Cambridge CB1 9AZ Tel. *01223 293041*

E-mail. *info@tevershammotors.co.uk*
Web. *www.tevershammotors.co.uk Teversham Motors*

Texas Instruments Ltd 800 Pavilion Drive Northampton Business Park, Northampton NN4 7YL Tel. *01604 663000* Fax. *01604 663001* E-mail. *m-cowles@ti.com* Web. *www.ti.com MicroLazer – Silent 700 – Tiris – Travel Note – Travelmate*

Texcel Division (a division of Crosslink Business Services Ltd) 8 Avebury Court Mark Road, Hemel Hempstead HP2 7TA Tel. *01442 231700* Fax. *01442 261918* E-mail. *info@texcel.uk.com* Web. *www.texcel.uk.com *Flotect (U.S.A.) – Senseal – Texcel*

Texchem Holmes Mill Holmes Street, Rochdale OL12 6AQ Tel. *01706 711990* Fax. *01706 710985* E-mail. *info@texchem.co.uk* Web. *www.texchem.co.uk Controller – Scourtex – Texassist – Texdye – Texfin – Texsoft*

Texkimp Ltd Swan House New Cheshire Business Park Wincham Lane, Wincham, Northwich CW9 6GG Tel. *01606 338748* Fax. *01606 40366* E-mail. *info@texkimp.co.uk* Web. *www.texkimp.com Texkimp*

Restmor Ltd 226-248 Toddington Road, Luton LU4 9DZ Tel. *01582 807488* Fax. *01582 807489* E-mail. *sales@restmor.co.uk* Web. *www.restmor.co.uk Prelude*

Textiliana Ltd Unit G Braintree Industrial Estate Braintree Road, Ruislip HA4 0EJ Tel. *020 88452323* Fax. *020 88451144* E-mail. *info@textiliana.co.uk* Web. *www.textiliana.co.uk Gipsy – Gloriette*

Textra 8 Station Yard Steventon, Abingdon OX13 6RX Tel. *01235 823100* Fax. *0870 2414950* E-mail. *sales@textra.co.uk* Web. *www.textra.co.uk Textra*

T F C Cable Assemblies Ltd Excelsior Park Netherton Industrial Estate, Wishaw ML2 0ER Tel. *01698 355017* Fax. *01698 350559* E-mail. *info@tfcasm.co.uk* Web. *www.ncmail.com TFC Cable Assemblies Ltd*

T F C Group Tower House Vale Rise, Tonbridge TN9 1TB Tel. *01732 351680* Fax. *01732 354445* E-mail. *info@tfc.uk.com* Web. *www.tfc-group.co.uk Airsep – Tower Domestic – Tower Flue – Tower Motorised – Tower Water – Towerchron*

TF Groundworks 291 Northumberland Ave, reading RG2 7QE Tel. *0118 9874039* E-mail. *info@tfgroundworks.co.uk* Web. *www.tfgroundworks.co.uk TF Groundworks*

T Fleming Homes Ltd Station Road, Duns TD11 3HS Tel. *01361 883785* Fax. *01361 883898* E-mail. *enquiries@fleminghomes.co.uk* Web. *www.fleminghomes.co.uk Flemimg Homes*

T G W Ltd 1 The Point, Market Harborough LE16 7QU Tel. *01858 468855* Fax. *01858 419613* E-mail. *ukenquiries@tgw-group.com* Web. *www.tgw-group.com commissioner – magnus – muli – mustang – natrix – stratus*

Thakeham Tiles Ltd Rock Road Storrington, Pulborough RH20 3AD Tel. *01903 742381* Fax. *01903 746341* E-mail. *richarddavidge@thakeham.co.uk* Web. *www.thakeham.co.uk Block Paving – Calxite – Regency – Splitstone – Sunwall*

Thales Avionics Ltd 88 Bushey Road, London SW20 0JW Tel. *020 89468011* Fax. *020 89463014* Web. *www.thales-avionics.com Satfone*

Thales Missile Electronics Basing View Mountbatten House, Basingstoke RG21 4HJ Tel. *01256 387200* Fax. *01256 387650* Web. *www.thales-group.co.uk Thomson-Thorn Missile Electronics*

Thales Optronics Ltd Dettingen House Dettingen Way, Bury St Edmunds IP33 3TU Tel. *01284 750599* Fax. *01284 750598* E-mail. *andy.coe@uk.thalesgroup.com* Web. *www.thalesgroup-optronics.com Vicon*

Thales Training & Consultancy Sackville House Northwood Park Gatwick Road, Crawley RH10 9XN Tel. *0800 163469* Fax. *01293 563301* E-mail. *traininginfo@thalesgroup.com* Web. *www.thales-trainingconsultancy.com AWARD – IMAGE*

Thame Engineering Co. Ltd Field End Thame Road, Long Crendon, Aylesbury HP18 9EJ Tel. *01844 208050* Fax. *01844 201699* E-mail. *sales@thame-eng.com* Web. *www.thame-eng.com Adjustagrip Hard Jaws – *Alufix (Germany) – Diamond Jaws – *Griptech (Germany) – *Howa (Japan) – Powerpull – *T. de G. (Spain) – TEC – Thame – Trueborer – Vac-Mat – *VACU-Systems (Germany)*

Thameside Electrical Ltd 713 London Road, Grays RM20 3HX Tel. *01708 867191* Fax. *01708 866295* E-mail. *dennis@thamesideelec.co.uk* Web. *www.thamesideelec.co.uk Tenside Electrical Ltd*

Thames Lubricants Ltd Garner Street, Stoke On Trent ST4 7DE Tel. *01782 745678* Fax. *01782 848437* E-mail. *sales@thameslubricants.co.uk* Web. *www.thameslubricants.co.uk Thames Lubricants*

Thames Valley Pressings Ltd (Transteel) Unit 2-3 Leyton Road, Brentford TW8 0QJ Tel. *020 88473636* Fax. *020 87581236* E-mail. *enquiries@tvpressings.co.uk Autosafe*

Thatchers Cider Company Ltd Myrtle Farm Station Road, Sandford, Winscombe BS25 5RA Tel. *01934 822862* Fax. *01934 822313* E-mail. *info@thatcherscider.co.uk* Web. *www.thatcherscider.co.uk Chedder Valley – Thatchers Coxs – Thatchers Gold – Thatchers Heritage – Thatchers Katy*

T H Brown Employment Services Ltd Estate Road 1 South Humberside Industrial Estate, Grimsby DN31 2TB Tel. *01472 240824* Fax. *01472 360112* E-mail. *p.marchant@thbrown.co.uk* Web. *www.thbrown.com T.H. Brown Distribution*

The Alexandra Stone Co. Kirby Muxloe, Leicester LE9 2BR Tel. *0116 2392513* Fax. *0116 2393993* E-mail. *collins@castacrete.co.uk* Web. *www.castacrete.co.uk Alexandra*

The Anglering Company Bloomfield Road, Tipton DY4 9EH Tel. *0121 5577241* Fax. *0121 5224555* E-mail. *sales@anglering.com* Web. *www.anglering.com Angle Ring – T. Morley & Co*

The Ashcroft Clinic Hudson Street Deddington, Banbury OX15 0SW Tel. *01869 338854* Fax. *01869 338854* E-mail. *mail@ashcroftclinic.com* Web. *www.ashcroftclinic.com Celandine*

The Barnsley Chronicle Ltd 47 Church Street, Barnsley S70 2AS Tel. *01226 734734* Fax. *01226 734444* E-mail. *enquiries@barnsley-chronicle.co.uk* Web. *www.barnsley-chronicle.co.uk Barnsley Chronicle – Barnsley Chronicle Newspaper Group, The – Barnsley Independent – Caring UK – Centrestyle – Leisure Business – Northern Hotel & Restaurant – Wharncliffe Publishing – Work Out – Yorkshire Web Offset*

The Bentall Centre Bentalls Shopping Centre Wood Street, Kingston Upon Thames KT1 1TP Tel. *020 85415066* Fax. *020 85415077* E-mail. *bentallsonline@bentalls.co.uk* Web. *www.thebentallcentre-shopping.com Bentalls Express – Bentalls Final Touches – Bentalls Spectator – Bentalls Trail Finder – Desire*

The Bournemouth Daily Echo (Newscom & Media P.L.C.) Richmond Hill, Bournemouth BH2 6HH Tel. *01202 411411* Fax. *01202 292115* E-mail. *advertising@bournemouthecho.co.uk* Web. *www.advertiserseries.co.uk Advertiser Series, The – Bournemouth Daily Echo – Prime Time – Property Advertiser – Swanage & Wareham Advertiser*

The Hunter Fan Company Ltd Castle End Business Park Ruscombe, Reading RG10 9XQ Tel. *0845 0940296* Fax. *0845 0940297* E-mail. *plloyd@hunterfan.co.uk* Web. *www.hunterfan.co.uk Hunter Fans*

The Ideal Cleaning Company Woodcut Cottage Crismill Lane, Thurnham, Maidstone ME14 3LY Tel. *01622 735071* Fax. *01622 735097* E-mail. *info@idealgroupuk.co.uk* Web. *www.idealgroupuk.co.uk Ideal Air Europe – Ideal Response – Ideal Cleaning*

The Lancet 32 Jamestown Road, London NW1 7BY Tel. *020 74244910* Fax. *020 74244912* Web. *www.lancet.com Lancet, The*

The Milliput Co. Unit 8 Marian Mawr Industrial Estate, Dolgellau LL40 1UU Tel. *01341 422562* Fax. *01341 422562* E-mail. *info@milliput.demon.co.uk* Web. *www.milliput.com Milliput*

The Moulton Bicycle Co. Ltd Holt Road, Bradford On Avon BA15 1AH Tel. *01225 865895* Fax. *01225 864742* E-mail. *office@moultonbicycles.co.uk* Web. *www.moultonbicycles.co.uk Moulton*

The National Gallery St Vincent House 30 Orange Street, London WC2H 7HH Tel. *020 77475800* Fax. *020 77475951* E-mail. *admin@nationalgallery.co.uk* Web. *www.nationalgallery.co.uk National Gallery London, The*

Theobald Sewing Machines Ltd 71-73 Wellington Street, Luton LU1 5AA Tel. *01582 724644* Fax. *01582 417867* E-mail. *lunadeplata@onetel.net.uk* Web. *www.theobaldsewingmachines.co.uk Theobald*

Theo Fennell plc 169 Fulham Road, London SW3 6SP Tel. *020 75915000* Fax. *020 75915001* E-mail. *gavin.saunders@theofennell.com* Web. *www.theofennell.com Theo Fennell*

The P R Organisation (Personnel Relations Ltd) Burlington House 64 Chiswick High Road, London W4 1SY Tel. *020 89954343* Fax. *020 89952349* E-mail. *robin@personnelrelations.co.uk* Web. *www.personnelrelations.com Personnel Relations*

Thermacore Ltd Unit 12 Wansbeck Business Park Rotary Parkway, Ashington NE63 8QW Tel. *01670 859500* Fax. *01670 859539* E-mail. *info@thermacore.com* Web. *www.thermacore-europe.com Heatpipes – Isojets – ISOPIPES – Quick-Change*

Therma Group Green Lane Burghfield Bridge, Reading RG30 3XN Tel. *0118 9500606* Fax. *0118 9560039* E-mail. *sales@thermagroup.com* Web. *www.thermagroup.com AMP – AMP - Aspera - Bitzer - Bock - Bristol - Carrier - Chrysler - Copeland - Copelametic - Daikin - Danfoss - Dorin - Dunham Bush - Frigipol - Frascold - Frigidaire - Gelphametic - Grasso - Hall APV - Hitachi - Hubbard - Kobe - L'Unite Hermetique - Maneurop - McQuay - Mitsubishi - Prestcold - Refcomp - Sabroe - Tecumseh - Thermoking - Toshiba - Trane - York – Aspera – Bitzer – Bock – Bristol – Carrier – Chrysler – Copelametic – Copeland – Daikin – Danfoss – Dorin – Dunham Bush – Frascold – Handell – Frigidaire – Frigipol – Fu Sheng – Gelphametic – Grasso – Hall APV – Hitachi – Howden – Hubbard – Kobe – L'Unite Hermetique – Maneurop – McQuay – Mitsubishi – Mycom – Prestcold – Refcomp – Sabroe – Stal – Tecumsch – Thermoking – Toshiba – Trane – York*

Thermal Ceramics UK Ltd Tebay Road, Wirral CH62 3PH Tel. *0151 3344030* Fax. *0151 3341684* E-mail. *jsimons@thermalceramics.com* Web. *www.thermalceramics.co.uk Cerawool – Enfil – Firemaster – JM Insulating Firebricks – Kaowool – Pyro-Bloc – Superwool 607 – Superwool 607 Max – Superwool 612 – Tennaglo – Unifelt – Z Bloc*

Thermal Designs UK Ltd Broadway Market Lavington, Devizes SN10 5RQ Tel. *01380 816079* Fax. *01380 813394* E-mail. *sales@tdiuk.com* Web. *www.tdiuk.com K-Cab – K-Guard*

Thermal Economics Ltd 8 Cardiff Road, Luton LU1 1PP Tel. *01582 450814* Fax. *01582 429305* E-mail. *info@thermal-economics.co.uk* Web. *www.thermal-economics.co.uk Alreflex 2L2 – Coldbreak – Miofol Roofshield 125 – S.B.S. – Sentinel Sound Floor – Spanfloor*

Thermal Engineering Systems Ltd Langlands Business Park Uffculme, Cullompton EX15 3DA Tel. *01884 840216* Fax. *01884 840197* E-mail. *sales@thermal-eng.co.uk* Web. *www.thermal-eng.co.uk Humidcoil – Ice Bank – Jetfan – Packaged Air Blast – Packaged Water Chillers – Pumping Sets – Pure Water Cooling – *Stainless Steel Heat Exchangers (France) – T.E.S. Jetfans – T.K. Chillers*

Thermal Reflections Ltd Unit 1-2 400 Cromwell Road, Grimsby DN31 2BN Tel. *01472 346795* Fax. *01472 346796* E-mail. *sales@thermalreflections.co.uk* Web. *www.thermalreflections.co.uk Kapron – Levante – Marmox – Rollamat*

Thermal Spray Material Services Ltd Brook Street Business Centre Brook Street, Tipton DY4 9DD Tel. *0121 5200720* Fax. *0121 5203002* E-mail. *thermalsprayuk@aol.com* Web. *www.thermalspray.co.uk Chatterfree – Chatterfree - tungsten based alloys*

Thermal Technology Sales Ltd Bridge House Station Road, Westbury BA13 4HR Tel. *01373 865454* Fax. *01373 864425* E-mail. *sales@thermaltechnology.co.uk* Web. *www.thermaltechnology.co.uk Galletti (Italy) – *Hydrohil (France) – *Rewpovent (United Kingdom) – *Shalovent (United Kingdom)*

Thermodiffusion Ltd Hill Place London Road, Southborough, Tunbridge Wells TN4 0PY Tel. *01892 511533* Fax. *01892 515140* E-mail. *enquiries@thermodiffusion.co.uk Thermodiffusion*

Thermo Electrical Ion Path Road Three, Winsford CW7 3BX Tel. *01606 548100* Fax. *01606 552588* Web. *www.thermo.com 919 – 929 – 939 – 939QZ – 9400 – 969 – 969Z – 989 – 989QZ – AT150 – AT188 – AT257 – AT557 – AT757 – Atocan 16 – Atocan 25 – Atocan Advantage – Atocan Advantage AP – Axiom – Genesis – ICAP 61 – ICAP 61e – M5 – M6 – MQZ – Plasma 54 – PlasmaQuad 1 (PQ1) – PlasmaQuad 2 (PQ2) – PlasmaQuad 3 (PQ3) – Plasmatrace 1 – Plasmatrace 2 – PQ Eclipse – PQ Excell – PU7000 – PU701 – PU9000 – PU9200 – SH1000 – SH4000 – SOLAAR – SP190 – SP2900 – SP9 – SP91 – Thermo Jarrel Ash – Tracescan – Unicam AA – VG 9000 – VG Elemental – VG9000*

Thermo Fisher Scientific Scientific Instruments 112 Chadwick Road Astmoor Industrial Estate, Runcorn WA7 1PW Tel. *01928 581000* Fax. *01928 581078* E-mail. *alan.wilshire@thermofisher.com* Web. *www.thermofisher.com BetaBasic – BetaMax – Betasil – BioBasic – DASH – Deltabond – Fluophase – Hypercarb – HyperGEL – HyperREZ – HyperSEP – Hypersil – Hypersil B D S – Hypersil Duet – Hypersil Green – HyPURITY – JAVELIN – KAPPA – Keystone – MultiSEP – PIONEER – PRISM – SLIPFREE – UNIGUARD – UNIPHASE*

Thermo Fisher Scientific 1 St Georges Court Hanover Business Park, Broadheath, Altrincham WA14 5TP Tel. *0161 9423000* Fax. *0161 9423001* E-mail. *sales@thermolabsystems.com* Web. *www.thermofisher.com Atlas – Nautilus – SampleManager – Yukon*

Thermoforce Ltd Wakefield Road, Cockermouth CA13 0HS Tel. *01900 823231* Fax. *01900 825965* E-mail. *sales@thermoforce.co.uk* Web. *www.thermoforce.co.uk Thermoforce*

Thermofrost Cryo plc Robert Fawkes House Rea Street South, Birmingham B5 6LB Tel. *0121 6226325* Fax. *0121 6227268* E-mail. *sales@thermofrostcryo.co.uk* Web. *www.thermofrostcryo.co.uk ACC Electrolux – Blue Star – C.E. Set – Cellartemp – Coprel – Dixell – Dorin – Ebm – Ecoflex (GEA) – Eliwell (Invensys) – Emmevi – Euro Motors – Flash – Flocon (Parker) – General Filter – Gomax – GR – HU seris – IDS – Inoac – J E Hall – Jackes Evans (Parker) – Kuba (GEA) – LG Electronics – Maneurop – Marstair – Microtech (Invensys) – Mueller – Multi-Fit – Necchi (ERC) – Papst (Ebm) – Parker – Quietis – Refrigerating Specialities (Parker) – Saftronic – Saginomiya – SCEM (Parker) – Sunon – Televis – Temprite – Transfer Oil – Trion – United Flexible – Univap – Universal - R – Vibraclamp – Wagner – Ziehl Abegg*

Thermographic Measurements Ltd Riverside Buildings Dock Road, Connah's Quay, Deeside CH5 4DS Tel. *01244 818348* Fax. *01244 818502*

E-mail. *sales@tmchallcrest.com* Web. *www.t-m-c.com Chillchecker – Chromazone – Colotemp – Temp-Rite – Thawalert – Thermax – TLC*

Thermomax Ltd Balloo Industrial Estate Balloo Crescent, Bangor BT19 7UP Tel. *028 91270411* Fax. *028 91270572* E-mail. *sales@thermomax.com* Web. *www.thermomax.com Thermomax*

Thermon Electrical Heating Equipment Seventh Avenue Team Valley Trading Estate, Gateshead NE11 0JW Tel. *0191 4994900* Fax. *0191 4994901* E-mail. *uk@thermon.com* Web. *www.thermon.com Cellex – Thermon*

Thermo Packs Unit 70 Condor Close, Three Legged Cross, Wimborne BH21 6SU Tel. *01202 828277* Fax. *01202 826766* E-mail. *sales@thermopacks.com* Web. *www.thermopacks.com Hotmate – Meditherm – Thermogel*

Thermopol Ltd Woolborough Lane, Crawley RH10 2UW Tel. *01293 543615* Fax. *01293 844721* E-mail. *info@contitech.de* Web. *www.thermopolinternational.com/europe.htm Thermopol*

Thermo Radiometrie Ltd Shepherd Road, Gloucester GL2 5HF Tel. *01452 337800* Fax. *01452 415156* Web. *www.radiometrie.com Radiometrie – X-Ray and Isotope*

Thermo Scientific Grange Lane Beenham, Reading RG7 5PR Tel. *0118 9712121* Fax. *0118 9712835* E-mail. *admin@thermormp.co.uk* Web. *www.thermoscientific.com Loadguard – Microload – Uniload*

Thermoscreens Ltd St Marys Road, Nuneaton CV11 5AU Tel. *024 76384646* Fax. *024 76388578* E-mail. *sales@thermoscreens.com* Web. *www.thermoscreens.com Thermoscreens*

The Seaward Group (a division of Seaward Electronic Ltd) 15-18 Bracken Hill South West Industrial Estate, Peterlee SR8 2SW Tel. *0191 5863511* Fax. *0191 5860227* E-mail. *info@seaward.co.uk* Web. *www.seaward.co.uk Burster (Germany) – Cropico – NORMA – Sefelec (France) – Sefelec - Norma - Burster*

TheSonicNet 11 Nokes Court Commonwealth Drive, Crawley RH10 1AL Tel. *0871 2456699* Fax. *0871 2456698* E-mail. *kym@thesonicnet.com* Web. *www.thesonicnet.com TheSonicNet*

Thessco Ltd Royds Mill Windsor Street, Sheffield S4 7WB Tel. *0114 2720966* Fax. *0114 2752655* E-mail. *sales@thessco.co.uk* Web. *www.thessco.co.uk Thesscote - Thesscote - brazing rods*

The Steeplechase Co Cheltenham Ltd Prestbury Park Prestbury, Cheltenham GL50 4SH Tel. *01242 513014* Fax. *01242 224227* E-mail. *cheltenham@jockeyclubracecourses.com* Web. *www.cheltenham.co.uk Festival*

The Trilite Zone 8 Fryers road, Walsall WS2 7LZ Tel. *01922 713713* Fax. *01922 713717* E-mail. *lew.james@nec-g.com* Web. *trilite-zone.co.uk Trilite, truss, opti, trussing*

The Webb Group (Findell P.L.C.) Queen Street, Burton On Trent DE14 3LP Tel. *01283 566311* Fax. *01283 506301* E-mail. *joe.mcnicholas@thewebbgroup.co.uk* Web. *www.webbivorydm.com Webb Ivory*

The Who Cares Trust Kemp House 152-160 City Road, London EC1V 2NP Tel. *020 72513117* Fax. *020 72513123* E-mail. *mailbox@thewhocarestrust.org.uk* Web. *www.thewhocarestrust.org.uk Who Cares*

The Winnen Furnishing Company 35-39 Selkirk Street, Cheltenham GL52 2HL Tel. *01242 521661* Fax. *01242 222360* E-mail. *info@winnens.co.uk* Web. *www.winnens.co.uk 4Living Furniture – Actona – Actona Furniture – Alki Furniture – Altro – *Amtico – Arden – Armstrong – Armstrongs – Ashley House – Balmoral Furniture – Barcelona Chairs – Bevan Funnell – Bevan Funnell Furniture – Bizzarri – Blendworth Fabric – Bo Concept – Boen Parkett – BPA International – Brian Yates Fabric – Brockway – Bronte – Burmalex – Casamance Fabric – Cat Specialist – Causeway – Cavalier – Celebrity Motion Furniture – Cintique – Cintique Furniture – Contemporary Furniture – Copes & Timmings Pole – Corbusier – Cormar – Dalsouple – Dalsuple – Eames Chairs – Ekornes – Eurostyle – Flame Upholstery – Flos Lighting – Forbo-Nairn – G P & J Baker Fabrics – Gainsborough Sofabeds – Gaskell – Gerflor – Giavelli – H T Collection – Hammell – Hammell Furniture – Harlequin Fabrics – Interface – Jab Fabrics – James Brindley Fabric – James Hare Silks – Jaymart – John E Coyle – John E Coyle Furniture – Kamdeals – Kandola Silks – Karndean – Lano – Lewis & Wood – Lloyd Loom – Malabar – Mancini – Marmoleum – McDonagh Furniture – Modern Classics – Modern Furniture – Nya Nordiska – Oak Furniture – Orinal Art – Plynyl Flooring – Prestigious Textiles – Profiles – Recliner Chairs – Rhinofloor – Robert Lloyd – Romo Fabrics – Sherbourne Upholstery – Silent Gliss – Skopos Fabrics – Stressless – Stuart Jones Headboards – The Windsor Bed Co – Titley & Marr – Wade Upholstery – Warwick Fabric – Westex Carpets – Wilcanders – Wilkinson Furniture – Wilton Royal*

The Zerny Engineering Co. Ltd Unit 13-14 Olds Close, Watford WD18 9RU Tel. *01923 774777* Fax. *01923 774777 Dualok – Tuflex – Zedwedge*

Think Mortgage Solutions Unit 1 Mercer Building 1 New Inn Yard, London EC2A 3EE Tel. *020 77299989* Fax. *020 77294099* E-mail. *info@herbline.co.uk* Web. *www.herbline.com Herbline Ayurvedic Cosmetics*

T H K UK 1 Harrison Close Knowlhill, Milton Keynes MK5 8PA Tel. *01908 303050* Fax. *01908 303070* E-mail. *sales.uk@thk.co.uk* Web. *www.thk.com Caged Ball – LM Guide*

A G Thomas Bradford Ltd Tompion House Heaton Road, Bradford BD8 8RB Tel. *01274 497171* Fax. *01274 547407* E-mail. *info@agthomas.co.uk* Web. *www.agthomas.co.uk A.G.T. Tools & Materials – Balco – Hagerty – *Hechinger (Germany) – Jean Pierre – Rayovac – Tompion*

Thomas Bugden & Co. Ltd Unit 4 Stocklake Industrial Estate Pembroke Road, Aylesbury HP20 1DB Tel. *01296 482030* Fax. *01296 487098* E-mail. *thomasbugden@btconnect.com* Web. *www.thomasbugden.co.uk Denmar*

David Thomas Ltd 1 Gate Lodge Close Round Spinney Industrial Estate, Northampton NN3 8RJ Tel. *01604 646216* Fax. *01604 790366* E-mail. *peterrolfe@davidthomas.com* Web. *www.davidthomas.com Hyperm – Ledasoft*

Thomas Elliot Associates 6 High Street Cwmgwrach, Neath SA11 5SY Tel. *0845 5005682* Fax. *05601 508594* E-mail. *admin@thomaselliotassociates.co.uk* Web. *www.thomaselliotassociates.co.uk The Pay People*

Thomas Frederick & Co. Ltd Linden Court House 52 Liverpool Street, Salford M5 4LT Tel. *0161 7457761* Fax. *0161 7376061* E-mail. *jonathanshasha@tiscali.co.uk Silhouette – Sunset – Thomas Frederick*

Thomas H Loveday Belgrade Centre Denington Road, Denington Industrial Estate, Wellingborough NN8 2QH Tel. *01933 652652* Fax. *01933 650454* E-mail. *phl@loveson.co.uk* Web. *www.loveson.co.uk Loveson*

Thomas Hosking Ltd Unit 4 Dumballs Road, Cardiff CF10 5FE Tel. *029 20480324* Fax. *029 20492075* E-mail. *thomashosking@btconnect.com* Web. *www.thomashosking.com Thomas Hosking & Sons*

Thomas Howse Ltd Cakemore Road, Rowley Regis B65 0RD Tel. *0121 5591451* Fax. *0121 5592722* E-mail. *sales@howsepaints.co.uk* Web. *www.howsepaints.co.uk Bitumak – Bulldog – E.C.O. Paint – Howse's – Howse's Rust Convertor – Powder Prime – Rustkote – Swift – Tak Products – Tectyl Valvoline – Valvoline*

Thomas Plant Birmingham Plumb Bob House Valepits Road, Birmingham B33 0TD Tel. *0121 6046000* Fax. *0121 6042222* E-mail. *info@kitchencraft.co.uk* Web. *www.kitchencraft.co.uk Jury – Kitchencraft – Master Class – Master Grip*

Thomas Sanderson Ltd Tileasy House Waterberry Drive, Waterlooville PO7 7UW Tel. *023 92232600* Fax. *023 92232700* E-mail. *curleyj@thomas-sanderson.co.uk* Web. *www.thomas-sanderson.co.uk Thomas Sanderson*

Thomas Swan & Co. Ltd Rotary Way, Consett DH8 7ND Tel. *01207 505131* Fax. *01207 590467* E-mail. *sales@thomas-swan.co.uk* Web. *www.thomas-swan.co.uk Casabond – Casamid – Casamid – Casamine – Casarez – Casastab – Casathane – Pepton*

Thomas Turton Ltd Callywhite Lane, Dronfield S18 2XT Tel. *01246 290000* Fax. *01246 291144* E-mail. *bradwell@padley-venables.com* Web. *www.thomas-turton.co.uk Crossbow (United Kingdom) – Thomas Turton (United Kingdom) – Turton (United Kingdom)*

Thomas Wright-Thorite Thorite House Laisterdyke, Bradford BD4 8BZ Tel. *01274 663471* Fax. *01274 668296* E-mail. *info@thorite.co.uk* Web. *www.thorite.co.uk Comprite – Thorite*

Thom Engineering Ltd Mohawk Buildings Gorse Street, Blackburn BB1 3EU Tel. *01254 676222* Fax. *01254 672053* E-mail. *bryn@thomengineering.co.uk* Web. *www.thomengineering.co.uk Sampletuft*

Thompson & Capper Ltd 9-11 Hardwick Road Astmoor Industrial Estate, Runcorn WA7 1PH Tel. *01928 573734* Fax. *01928 580694* E-mail. *enquiries@tablets2buy.com* Web. *www.tablets2buy.com Chadpac – Kettle Klear – Kjeltabs – Lactabs*

D C Thomson & Co. Ltd Albert Square, Dundee DD1 9QJ Tel. *01382 223131* Fax. *01382 225778* E-mail. *idouglas@dcthomson.co.uk* Web. *www.dcthomson.co.uk Animals and You – Beano – Beano Superstars – Bunty – Dandy – Dundee Courier – Evening Telegraph – My Weekly – My Weekly Puzzeltime – Peoples Friend – Scots Magazine – Shout – Sporting Post – Sunday Post – Weekly News*

Thomson & Joseph Ltd 119 Plumstead Road, Norwich NR1 4JT Tel. *01603 439511* Fax. *01603 700243* E-mail. *enquiries@tandj.co.uk* Web. *www.tandj.co.uk MAAC (U.S.A.) – MAAC, Metalosate Foliar. – Metalosate Foliar (U.S.A.)*

Thor Hammer Company Ltd Highlands Road Shirley, Solihull B90 4NJ Tel. *0121 7054695* Fax. *0121 7054727* E-mail. *info@thorhammer.com* Web. *www.thorhammer.com Thor – Thorace – Thorex – Thorlite – Thorub*

Thorite Barge Street, Huddersfield HD1 3LN Tel. *01484 534245* Fax. *01484 435023* E-mail. *huddersfield@thorite.co.uk* Web. *www.thorite.co.uk HPC – Hydrovane – Norgren – Thorite Diamond*

Thornbury Surfacing Chippenham Ltd 3 Harris Road, Calne SN11 9PT Tel. *01249 813435* Fax. *01249 813233* E-mail. *iainsaunders@thornburysurfacing.co.uk* Web. *www.thornburysurfacing.co.uk Addastone – Marshalls – Natratex – Rocbinda*

Thorn Lighting Ltd House of Light Butchers Race, Spennymoor DL16 6HL Tel. *01388 420042* Fax. *01388 420156* E-mail. *terry.carmichael@thornlighting.com* Web. *www.thornlighting.co.uk Popular Range – Sensa*

Thornycroft Ltd Thornycroft House 107 Holywell Hill, St Albans AL1 1HQ Tel. *01727 840011* Fax. *01727 855030* E-mail. *info@thornycroft.co.uk* Web. *www.thornycroft.co.uk A2Z – Cleo – Royalle*

Thorpe Park Ski Shop Staines Road, Chertsey KT16 8PN Tel. *0870 4444466* Fax. *01932 566367* E-mail. *admin@thorpepark.com* Web. *www.thorpepark.com Thorpe Park*

Thorpe Trees Thorpe Green Lane Thorpe Underwood, York YO26 9TA Tel. *01423 330977* Fax. *01423 331348* E-mail. *sales@thorpetrees.com* Web. *www.thorpetrees.com *Thorpe Trees*

Thorp Modelmakers Ltd High Street Sunningdale, Ascot SL5 0NG Tel. *01344 876776* Fax. *01344 876583* E-mail. *info@atomltd.com* Web. *www.atomltd.com Thorp Modelmakers*

Three Ways House Hotel Chapel Lane Mickleton, Chipping Campden GL55 6SB Tel. *01386 438429* Fax. *01386 438118* E-mail. *reception@puddingclub.com* Web. *www.threewayshousehotel.com Home of the Pudding Club*

Thrislington Cubicles Ltd Prince William Avnorth Wales Trade Centre Sandycroft, Deeside CH5 2QZ Tel. *01244 520677* Fax. *01244 535670* E-mail. *info@thrislingtoncubicles.com* Web. *www.thrislingtoncubicles.com Thrislington*

Thurston 110 High Street, Edgware HA8 7HF Tel. *020 89522002* Fax. *020 89520222* E-mail. *thurston@eaclare.co.uk* Web. *www.thurstongames.co.uk *International (United Kingdom) – *Standfast (United Kingdom) – *Victorian (United Kingdom)*

Thurston (E A Clare & Son Ltd) 46-48 St Anne Street, Liverpool L3 3DW Tel. *0151 4822700* Fax. *0151 2981134* E-mail. *thurston@eaclare.co.uk* Web. *www.thurston.co.uk International – Jubilee – Standfast – Victorian*

Thwaites Ltd Welsh Road Works, Leamington Spa CV32 7NQ Tel. *01926 422471* Fax. *01926 337155* E-mail. *sales@thwaitesdumpers.co.uk* Web. *www.thwaitesdumpers.co.uk A.D. 4000 Hi-Swivel – Alldrive Dumper – Nimline – Orline – Powershuttle – Powerswivel – Skipstar – Slimline*

Thyssenkrupp Bilstein Woodhead 177 Kirkstall Road, Leeds LS4 2AQ Tel. *0113 2441202* Fax. *0113 2347738* E-mail. *jonathan.sandground@tka-wo.thyssenkrupp.com* Web. *www.thyssenkrupp.com Hoesch Woodhead*

Thyssenkrupp Elevator UK Ltd Traffic Street, Nottingham NG2 1NF Tel. *0115 9868213* Fax. *0115 9861549* E-mail. *brian.marcus@tke-uk-thyssenkrupp.com* Web. *www.thyssen-lifts.co.uk Diplomat – T.C.I. Thyssen Control Integral – Thyssen Escalators – Thyssen Modernization – V.V.V.F. -ISOSTOP 60M*

Thyssenkrupp V D M UK Ltd VDM House 111 Hare Lane, Claygate, Esher KT10 0QY Tel. *01372 467137* Fax. *01372 466388* Web. *www.thyssenkruppvdm.com *Cronifer (Germany) – *Magnifer (Germany) – *Nicorros (Germany) – *Nicrofer (Germany) – *Pernifer (Germany)*

Tibco Software Ltd Braywick Gate Braywick Road, Maidenhead SL6 1DA Tel. *01628 786800* Fax. *01628 786874* E-mail. *bsmith@tibco.com* Web. *www.tibco.com Staffware*

Tickhill Engineering Co. Ltd Cow House Lane Armthorpe, Doncaster DN3 3ED Tel. *01302 831911* Fax. *01302 300173* E-mail. *sales@haith.co.uk* Web. *www.haith.co.uk Haith – Tickhill*

Ticona UK Ltd Grosvenor House Hollinswood Road, Central Park, Telford TF2 9TW Tel. *01952 213400* Fax. *01952 213423* E-mail. *info@ticona.com* Web. *www.ticona.com Celanese nylon 66 P.A. – Celanex – Celstran – Fortron – Hostaform – Hostalen GUR – Impet – Topas – Vandar – Vectra*

Tics International Ltd Unit 7 Derby Road Industrial Estate, Hounslow TW3 3UH Tel. *020 85725599* Fax. *08707 874920* E-mail. *sales@tics.co.uk* Web. *www.tics.co.uk TICS*

Tideford Organic Foods Ltd 5 The Alpha Centre Babbage Road, Totnes TQ9 5JA Tel. *01803 840555* Fax. *01803 840551* E-mail. *tideford@btconnect.com* Web. *www.tidefordorganics.com *Hey Pesto!*

Tie Rack Ltd Capital Interchange Way, Brentford TW8 0EX Tel. *020 82302300* Fax. *01208 2302301* E-mail. *reception@tie-rack.co.uk* Web. *www.tie-rack.co.uk Art of Silk, The – Tie Rack*

Tiflex Ltd (James Walker Group) Tiflex House Treburgie Water, Liskeard PL14 4NB Tel. *01579 320808* Fax. *01579 320802* E-mail. *sales@tiflex.co.uk* Web. *www.tiflex.co.uk @-10-u-8 – Acoustic Barrier – Geoflex – Micromax – NEBAR – Oxbridge Cricket – TICO – Tiflex Performance Polymer Components – Trackelast – Treadmaster – Treadmaster Marine*

Tiger Tim Products Ltd Industrial Estate Rhosesmor, Mold CH7 6PZ Tel. *01352 780861* Fax. *01352 781294* E-mail. *sales@tigertimproducts.co.uk* Web. *www.tigertimproducts.co.uk Blue Flame – Dragon*

Tilda Ltd Coldharbour Lane, Rainham RM13 9YQ Tel. *01708 717777* Fax. *01708 717700* E-mail. *feedback@tilda.com* Web. *www.tilda.com Tilda*

Tildenet Ltd (Agricultural Division) Hartcliffe Way, Bristol BS3 5RJ Tel. *0117 9669684* Fax. *0117 9231251* E-mail. *enquiries@tildenet.co.uk* Web. *www.tildenet.com Tidenet*

Till & Whitehead 2 Lonsdale Road, Bolton BL1 4PW Tel. *01204 493000* Fax. *01204 493888* E-mail. *jalfrey@tillwite.com* Web. *www.tillwite.com Tillwite*

Till & Whitehead (t/a L Birkinshaw) Till & Whitehead Main 37 Ings Road, Leeds LS9 9HG Tel. *0113 2496641* Fax. *0113 2488968* E-mail. *leeds@tillwite.com* Web. *www.tillwite.com Henderson*

Tillwise Cash Registers 10 Mwrog Street, Ruthin LL15 1LF Tel. *01824 707361* Fax. *01824 707461* E-mail. *elfedtillwise@aol.com *Scotman – *Whirlpool*

Tilt Measurement Ltd Horizon House Baldock Industrial Estate London Road, Baldock SG7 6NG Tel. *01462 894566* Fax. *01462 895990* E-mail. *info@tilt-measurement.com* Web. *www.tilt-measurement.com Electrolevel (United Kingdom)*

Timber Packing Cases Barnes & Woodhouseferndale One Commercial St, Middlesbrough TS2 1JT Tel. *01642 224092* Fax. *01642 251272* E-mail. *enquiries@timberpackingcases.com* Web. *www.timberpackingcases.com Barnes & Woodhouse*

Timcal Graphite & Carbon PO Box 269, Congleton CW12 3WP Tel. *01260 276009* Fax. *01260 289057* E-mail. *info@uk.timcal.com* Web. *www.timcal.com ENSACO – ROLLIT – SUPER P – TIMREX – TIMROC*

Timeit Software Distribution Ltd Orion House Unit 72 Riverside 3, Chatham ME5 7PZ Tel. *08450 942908* Fax. *0870 1992627* E-mail. *sales@timeitsoftware.co.uk* Web. *www.timeitgroup.com iAccess – TimeIT – TimeIT Ultra*

Time Out Group Universal House 251 Tottenham Court Road, London W1T 7AB Tel. *020 78133000* Fax. *020 78136001* E-mail. *editorial@timeout.com* Web. *www.timeout.com Time Out*

Timeplan Ltd 1 Capital Park High Street, Old Woking, Woking GU22 9LD Tel. *01483 769766* Fax. *01483 730631* E-mail. *sales@timeplan.ltd.uk* Web. *www.timeplan.ltd.uk Timeplan*

Time Products UK Ltd Alexander House Chartwell Drive, Wigston LE18 2EZ Tel. *0116 2882500* Fax. *0870 8508201* E-mail. *info@timeproducts.co.uk* Web. *www.timeproducts.co.uk Bergeon – Crimploc – Dazor – Elma – Factotum – Flaminaire – Galvanofix – Ideal-Tek – K.W.M. – L. & R. – Magna-Sight – Multifix – Precista – S.W.C.S. – Selva – Soder-Wick – Vigor*

The Times Newspaper Classified 1 Virginia Street, London E98 1XY Tel. *020 77824000* E-mail. *home.news@thetimes.co.uk* Web. *www.timesonline.co.uk Times, The*

Times Review Series Of Newspapers Stoke Mill Woking Road, Guildford GU1 1QA Tel. *01483 508700* Fax. *01483 508851* Web. *www.getsurrey.co.uk Aldershot Courier Series – Aldershot Mail Series – Aldershot News Series – Esher News Series – Surrey & Hants Star – Surrey Advertiser – Surrey and Hants Courier Series – Times Review Series – Woking News & Mail Series*

Timet UK Ltd PO Box 704, Birmingham B6 7UR Tel. *0121 3561155* Fax. *0121 3565413* E-mail. *eurosales@timet.com* Web. *www.timet.com Timet UK Ltd*

Timico Ltd Beaconhill Park Cafferata Way, Newark NG24 2TN Tel. *08448 718100* Fax. *0844 8718117* E-mail. *enquiries@timico.co.uk* Web. *www.timico.co.uk Twang.net Ltd*

Timloc Building Products Rawcliffe Road, Goole DN14 6UQ Tel. *01405 765567* Fax. *01405 720479* E-mail. *sales@timloc.co.uk* Web. *www.timloc.co.uk Acoustray – Active-Guard – Everdry – Home Loc – Insu-Loc – Inter-Loc – Step-a-loft – System 6000 – System 9000 – ThermoLoc – Timloc*

Timsons Ltd Perfecta Works Bath Road, Kettering NN16 8NQ Tel. *01536 411611* Fax. *01536 411666* E-mail. *jeff.ward@timsons.com* Web. *www.timsons.com Timson*

Tiniusolsen Ltd 6 Perrywood Business Park Honeycrock Lane, Redhill RH1 5DZ Tel. *01737 765001* Fax. *01737 764768* E-mail. *info@tiniusolsen.com* Web. *www.hounsfield.com Hounsfied H10ks (T) – Hounsfield 100R/S – Hounsfield 500L – Hounsfield H100kS (T) – Hounsfield H1KS (T) – Hounsfield H25kS (T) – Hounsfield H50KS (T) – Hounsfield H5KS T*

Tipmaster Ltd Rigg Approach Lea Bridge Road, London E10 7QN Tel. *020 85390611* Fax. *020 85399462* E-mail. *sales@tipmaster.co.uk* Web. *www.tipmaster.co.uk Dustmaster – Swiftlift – Tipmaster – Tipnology – Tommylift – Vacmaster*

Tipton & Coseley Building Society 70 Owen Street, Tipton DY4 8HG Tel. *0121 5572551* Fax. *0121 5578570* E-mail. *mail@thetipton.co.uk* Web. *www.thetipton.co.uk T.C.*

Tisserand Aromatherapy (Tisserand) 4 Clarks Industrial Estate Newtown Road, Hove BN3 7BA Tel. *01273 325666* Fax. *01273 208444* E-mail. *info@tisserand.com* Web. *www.tisserand.com Tisserand*

Titan West Portway, Andover SP10 3LF Tel. *01264 357666* Fax. *01264 366446* E-mail. *darren.crane@titanpc.co.uk* Web. *www.titanpc.co.uk Biotec*

Titan Distribution Ukltd North Florida Road Haydock, St Helens WA11 9UB Tel. *01942 715333* Fax. *01942 715111* E-mail. *enquiries@titandistributionuk.com* Web. *www.titaneurope.com Titan Distribution UK Ltd*

Titan Ladders Ltd Mendip Road Yatton, Bristol BS49 4ET Tel. *01934 832161* Fax. *01934 876180* E-mail. *sales@titanladders.co.uk* Web. *www.titanladders.co.uk Titan*

Titon Hardware Ltd (Head Office) International House Peartree Road, Stanway, Colchester CO3 0JL Tel. *01206 713800* Fax. *01206 543126* E-mail. *enquiries@titon.co.uk* Web. *www.titon.co.uk Trimvent*

T K A Body Stampings Ltd Wolverhampton Road, Cannock WS11 1LY Tel. *01543 466664* Fax. *01543 466665* E-mail. *les.lees@tka-bs.thyssenkrupp.com* Web. *www.thyssenkrupp.com A.P.M.*

T M A Engineering Ltd 95-111 Tyburn Road, Birmingham B24 8NQ Tel. *0121 3281908* Fax. *0121 3222017* E-mail. *sales@tmaeng.co.uk* Web. *www.tmaeng.co.uk C.V.A. – COFMO – Taylor & Challen*

T M B International Ltd Platt Industrial Estate Maidstone Road, Platt, Sevenoaks TN15 8TB Tel. *01732 887456* Fax. *01732 886345* E-mail. *cos@tmbmailing.com* Web. *www.tmbmailing.com The Mailing Business – TMB International*

T M Electronics Ltd (Electronic Thermometers and Sensors) Unit 12 Martlets Way Goring-By-Sea, Worthing BN12 4HF Tel. *01903 700651* Fax. *01903 244307* E-mail. *sales@tmelectronics.co.uk* Web. *www.tmelectronics.co.uk MM2000 – MMT000 – Solo – Thermo bar scan*

T M Machinery Sales Ltd 49 Iliffe Avenue Oadby, Leicester LE2 5LH Tel. *0116 2717155* Fax. *0116 2715862* E-mail. *matt@tmservices.co.uk* Web. *www.tmpartnership.co.uk AL-KO – Sandingmaster – Striebig*

T-Mobile UK Building 3 T-Mobile Campus Hatfield Business Park Mosquito Way, Hatfield AL10 9BW Tel. *01707 315988* Fax. *01707 319001* Web. *www.t-mobile.co.uk One 2 One*

T M P Worldwide Ltd 53-64 Chancery Lane Chancery House, London WC2A 1QY Tel. *020 74065000* Fax. *020 74065001* E-mail. *admin@tmpw.co.uk* Web. *www.tmp.com T.M.P Worldwide*

T M Robotics (Europe) Ltd Unit 2 Bridge Gate Centre, Martinfield, Welwyn Garden City AL7 1JG Tel. *01707 290370* Fax. *01707 376662* E-mail. *sales@tmrobotics.co.uk* Web. *www.tmrobotics.co.uk ABOT – Toshiba Machine*

T M S Gainsborough Ltd Track Marshalls Building Corringham Road, Gainsborough DN21 1QH Tel. *01427 612301* Fax. *01427 612672* E-mail. *mail@tmsgainsborough.co.uk Track-Marshall*

T Norton Ltd Tinsley Street, Tipton DY4 7LQ Tel. *0121 5576413* Fax. *0121 5575124* E-mail. *sales@jameswshenton.co.uk* Web. *www.jameswshenton.co.uk Norton Flypresses*

T N T Document Services Unit 3a Festival Way Festival Leisure Park, Basildon SS14 3WB Tel. *01268 247800* Fax. *020 72500602* E-mail. *chris.wright@tnt.co.uk* Web. *www.tnt.co.uk Cendris*

Toa Corporation UK Ltd Unit 2 Hook Rise South Industrial Park, Surbiton KT6 7LD Tel. *08707 740987* Fax. *08707 770839* E-mail. *info@toa.co.uk* Web. *www.toa.eu Vecs*

Tobbletag Ltd 30 Somery Road, Birmingham B29 5RY Tel. *0121 3420791* E-mail. *info@tobbletag.com* Web. *www.tobbletag.co.uk Tobbletag*

Tobermore Concrete Products Ltd 2 Lisnamuck Road Tobermore, Magherafelt BT45 5QF Tel. *028 79642411* Fax. *028 79644145* E-mail. *info@tobermore.co.uk* Web. *www.tobermore.co.uk Tegula – Tolite*

Today Interiors Ltd Unit 5 Orchard Park Isaac Newton Way, Grantham NG31 9RT Tel. *01476 574401* Fax. *01476 590208* E-mail. *info@today-interiors.co.uk* Web. *www.today-interiors.co.uk Brantome – Broderie III – Chelsea Classics – Contemporary Vinyls – Court Weaves – Henley Vinyls – Heritage – Heritage Small Prints – Opus Weaves – Pageantry II – Portfolio – Quartet – Repertoire – Weaves Vol II*

Together Ltd 26-28 Conway Street, London W1T 6BH Tel. *020 72092222* Fax. *020 79162277* E-mail. *hello@together.co.uk* Web. *www.together.co.uk Together*

Tom Barron Isa Ltd Green Road Eye, Peterborough PE6 7YP Tel. *01733 222262* Fax. *01733 223345* E-mail. *josie.arman@isapoultry.com Babcock B 380 Egglayer – Isawarren Brown Egglayer – Shaver 579 Brown Egglayer*

Tomtech UK Ltd Red May Farm 317 Broadgate, Sutton St Edmund, Spalding PE12 0LR Tel. *01945 700553* Fax. *01945 700866* E-mail. *a.thompson@tomtech.co.uk* Web. *www.tomtech.co.uk Tomtech*

Tomy International St Nicholas House St Nicholas Road, Sutton SM1 1EH Tel. *020 87227300* E-mail. *robert.mann@tomy.co.uk* Web. *www.tomy.co.uk *Baby Vision (The Far East) – *Pre-School (The Far East) – *Tomica World (The Far East) – Tomy – *Tomy Games (The Far East)*

Tool & Fastener Solutions Ltd (T/A TF Solutions Ltd) Unit 8 Spectrum Way Cheadle Heath, Stockport SK3 0SA Tel. *0161 4295917* Fax. *0161 4295918* E-mail. *sales@tfsolutions.co.uk* Web. *www.tfsolutions.co.uk Armaflex*

Tooling & Equipment Engineers Ltd 114a Earlsdon Avenue South, Coventry CV5 6DN Tel. *024 76691522* Fax. *024 76691544* E-mail. *info@tandee.co.uk* Web. *www.tandee.co.uk Tandee*

Toolite Co. Building 3 Unit 2 The Mews, Mitcheldean GL17 0SL Tel. *01594 544521* Fax. *01594 542552* E-mail. *sales@toolite.org.uk* Web. *www.toolite.org.uk Toolite*

The Toolpost Unit 7 Hawksworth, Didcot OX11 7HR Tel. *01235 511101* Fax. *01235 811185* E-mail. *peter@toolpost.co.uk* Web. *www.toolpost.co.uk Ashley Iles – BCT – Hollomate – Supercut – Beall – Cam Vac – Chestnut Products – Crown Tools – Cyanotec – Duragrit – Ekamant – Flexcut – GPS Agencies – General Finishes – Gorilla – Holzer – Hamlet Craft Tools – Henry Taylor – Hunter – JSP – Kelton – Kreg – McNaughton – Lansky – Liberon – Lovell – Microclene – M-Power – Oneway – O'Donnell – Proxxon – Jill Piers – Leigh – Grip-A-Disc – Planet Plus – Record Power – Robert Sorby – Saburr – Sjöberg – Silverline – Toolstream – Tormek – Tim Skilton – Titebond – Stobart Davies – Thomas Flinn – Trend – U'Beaut – Veritas – Shellawax – Versatool – Antex – Axminster Power Tools*

Topaz Computer Systems Ltd Chrysalis Way Langley Bridge, Eastwood, Nottingham NG16 3RY Tel. *01773 531551* Fax. *01773 716121* E-mail. *info@topaz.co.uk* Web. *www.topaz.co.uk Accounting Software Package – Employee Management System – K-basic – Kismet – Make to Order Manufacture – Topaz – Topaz Insight*

TopDeck Parking Springvale Business & Industrial Park Bilston, Wolverhampton WV14 0QL Tel. *01902 499400* Fax. *01902 494080* E-mail. *info@topdeckparking.co.uk* Web. *www.topdeckparking.co.uk TopDeck*

Topical Time Ltd 5 Bleeding Heart Yard, London EC1N 8SJ Tel. *020 74052439* Fax. *020 78314254* E-mail. *topicaltime@btconnect.com *Jean Pierre (Switzerland) – Mount Royal*

Top Office Equipment Ltd 14 West Place West Road, Harlow CM20 2GY Tel. *020 85193330* Fax. *020 85195142* E-mail. *sales@hogplc.com* Web. *www.topofficebrochure.co.uk Ballamore – Somerton – Stakker – Top Executive – Top Office – Top Plan – Top Tech – Vantage*

Topper Cases Ltd 16-17 Windover Court Windover Road, Huntingdon PE29 7EA Tel. *01480 457251* Fax. *01480 452107* E-mail. *sales@toppercases.co.uk* Web. *www.toppercases.co.uk Topper*

Topper International Kingsnorth Industrial Estate Wotton Road, Ashford TN23 6LN Tel. *01233 629186* Fax. *01233 645897* E-mail. *martin.fry@toppersailboats.com* Web. *www.toppersailboats.co.uk Blaze – Boss – Breeze – Buzz – Byte – Catapult – Classic – Cruz – Hurricane – Iso – Spice – Sport 14 – Sport 16 – Topaz – Topper*

Tops Security Solutions Unit 17 Star West Westmead Drive Westlea, Swindon SN5 7SW Tel. *01793 616626* E-mail. *sales@tops-security.co.uk* Web. *www.tops-security.co.uk ssaib*

Toptech Europe Ltd PO Box 627, Ipswich IP8 3WZ Tel. *01473 373400* Fax. *0871 2186814* E-mail. *info@toptech.co.uk* Web. *www.toptech.co.uk Toptech*

Top Tier Sugarcraft 10 Meadow Road Balloch, Inverness IV2 7JR Tel. *01463 790456* E-mail. *toptier@btconnect.com* Web. *www.toptiersugarcraft.co.uk Top Tier*

Top Tower Ltd Access House Bromsgrove Road, Halesowen B63 3HJ Tel. *0121 5855858* Fax. *0121 5857989* E-mail. *sales@toptower.co.uk* Web. *www.toptower.co.uk Toptower*

Torch Computers Ltd 50 South Street Comberton, Cambridge CB23 7DZ Tel. *01223 263818* Fax. *01223 264118* E-mail. *sales@torchcomputers.co.uk* Web. *www.torchcomputers.co.uk Torch*

Torclad Ltd Rose Park Lutterworth Road, Blaby, Leicester LE8 4DP Tel. *0116 2779577* Fax. *0116 2779804* E-mail. *adam@torclad.com* Web. *www.torclad.com Shire Range – Torclad*

Tor Coatings Ltd Shadon Way Birtley, Chester le Street DH3 2RE Tel. 0191 4106611 Fax. 0191 4920125 E-mail. enquiries@tor-coatings.com Web. www.tor-coatings.com Aquabrand – Aquagene – Aqualife – Aquatread – Ardenbrite – Duraclean – Duraclean Aseptic – Elastaseal – Fencecoat – Florex – Raincoat – Sterithane – Toflife T.P. – Tor Anti Climb Paint – Tor Anti Graffiti Systems – Tor Specialist Floor Coating Systems – Tor Specialist Hygiene Systems – Tor Specialist Masonry Systems – Tor Wood Preservative Stains – Torclad – Torclean – Torcote – Torcrete – Torcure – Tordeck – Torguard – Torlife WB – Torprufe C.M.F. – Torprufe C.R.C. – Torprufe EMF – Torrex – Torsan A Enamel – Torsan P Gloss Finish – Torshield – Torstone – Torstrip – Tortread – Transcoat – Woodcoat

Torex Retail Holdings Ltd The XN Centre Houghton Hall Park, Houghton Regis, Dunstable LU5 5YG Tel. 01582 869600 Fax. 01582 869601 E-mail. info@torex.com Web. www.torex.com Epos – Omron – Riva

Torgy Atlantic Engineering 3 Llandough Trading Estate Penarth Road, Cardiff CF11 8RR Tel. 029 20708461 Fax. 029 20350437 E-mail. sales@torgy-atlantic.co.uk Web. www.torgy-atlantic.co.uk Atplas

Tormo Ltd 7 Devonshire Business Park Chester Road, Borehamwood WD6 1NA Tel. 020 82075777 Fax. 020 82075888 E-mail. dave.rutter@tormo.co.uk Web. www.tormo.co.uk Tormo

Tornado Construction Products (Supply & Distribution Depot) 28 Donisthorpe Street, Leeds LS10 1PL Tel. 0113 2424342 Fax. 0113 2460272 E-mail. sales@tornado-fixings.co.uk Web. www.tornado-fixings.co.uk Tornado

Tornos Technologies UK Ltd Tornos House Garden Road, Coalville LE67 4JQ Tel. 01530 513100 Fax. 01530 814212 E-mail. sales@tornos.co.uk Web. www.tornos.com Deco – Multideco

Torque Control Ltd 60 Alstone Lane, Cheltenham GL51 8HE Tel. 01242 261233 Fax. 01242 221115 E-mail. torquecontrolltd@btinternet.com Web. www.torquecontrol.ltd.uk Jack Nut

Torque Leader (manufactured by M H H Engineering Co. Ltd) The Tannery Tannery Lane Gosden Common, Bramley, Guildford GU5 0AB Tel. 01483 892772 Fax. 01483 898536 E-mail. d.parsley@torqueleader.co.uk Web. www.torqueleader.com PETA – Quickset – TALS – Torque Safe – Torquebreaker – Torqueleader – Torquemaster – Torquemeter – Torqueslipper

Torquemeters West Haddon Road Ravensthorpe, Northampton NN6 8ET Tel. 01604 770232 Fax. 01604 770778 E-mail. info@torquemeters.com Web. www.torquemeters.com Torquetronic

Torque Solutions Ltd Unit 5 Abbey Way North Anston, Sheffield S25 4JL Tel. 01909 550767 Fax. 01909 550825 E-mail. sales@torque-solutions.co.uk Web. www.torque-solutions.co.uk Titan Hydraulic Wrenches

Torres Engineering & Pumps Ltd 448 Brightside Lane, Sheffield S9 2SP Tel. 0114 2493377 Fax. 0114 2425885 E-mail. ken_torres@torrespumps.co.uk Web. www.torrespumps.co.uk Cobra – Corniche – Dart – Eagle – Gem – Griffin – Mustang – Olympus – Pegasus – Phantom – Spur – Tay – Viper

Total Bitumen (a division of Total UK) Chain Caul Way Preston Riversway, Ashton-on-Ribble, Preston PR2 2TZ Tel. 01772 729302 Fax. 01772 724713 E-mail. info@total.co.uk Web. www.total.co.uk Finaflex – Finaseal – Finatex – Lanchor – Lanmix – Lantex – Novalastic – Surphalt

Total Filtration Ltd Ipswich Road, Cardiff CF23 9AQ Tel. 029 20497612 Fax. 029 20471110 E-mail. sales@totalfiltration.com Web. www.totalfiltration.com Liquid Solutions

Total Polyfilm 9a Cranborne Industrial Estate Cranborne Road, Potters Bar EN6 3JN Tel. 01707 650771 Fax. 01707 646736 E-mail. sales@totalpolyfilm.com Web. www.totalpolyfilm.com Bubbleflex – Polyflex – Powerflex – Silaflex

Total Process Cooling Ltd 94 Heaton Road, Solihull B91 2DZ Tel. 0121 7114014 Fax. 0121 7054012 E-mail. sales@totalprocesscooling.co.uk Web. www.totalprocesscooling.co.uk *Kelvin (Italy)

Total Refrigeration Ltd Unit 2a East Tame Business Park Rexcine Way, Hyde SK14 4GX Tel. 08451 272527 Fax. 0161 3667374 E-mail. sales@totalrefrigeration.co.uk Web. www.totalrefrigeration.co.uk Total Refrigeration

Total wall Midland House 117 Trent Boulevard West Bridgford, Nottingham NG2 5BN Tel. 0115 9820810 Fax. 0115 9820830 E-mail. iwa@totalstone.co.uk Web. www.totalstone.co.uk TotalStone – TotalWall

Totslots 14 The Braes Higham, Rochester ME3 7NA Tel. 0781 0143381 E-mail. enquiries@totslots.co.uk Web. www.totslots.co.uk Cuski

Touch A V Ltd 22 Johns Avenue Lofthouse, Wakefield WF3 3LU Tel. 0845 4572113 Fax. 0870 8362113 E-mail. install@touchav.co.uk Web. www.touchaudiovisual.co.uk Projector – Promethean Activboard – Smartboard

Tower Machine Tools Ltd Mayflower Close Chandler's Ford, Eastleigh SO53 4AR Tel. 023 80260266 Fax. 023 80261012 E-mail. info@towermachinetools.co.uk Web. www.towermachinetools.co.uk Muratec Wiedemann (Japan)

Town End Leeds plc Unit 17 Silver Court Intercity Way, Leeds LS13 4LY Tel. 0113 2564251 Fax. 0113 2393315 E-mail. sales@dyes.co.uk Web. www.dyes.co.uk Acrylene – Azonine – Duracet – Duractive – Duralan – Duramine – Durantine – Durapel – Evron – Fast Chrome

Townscape Products Ltd Fulwood Road South, Sutton In Ashfield NG17 2JZ Tel. 01623 513355 Fax. 01623 440267 E-mail. sales@townscape-products.co.uk Web. www.townscape-products.co.uk Bloc – Townscape

Tox Pressotechnik Unit 21 Stafford Business Village Dyson Way, Staffordshire Technology Park, Stafford ST18 0TW Tel. 01785 887903 Fax. 01785 887027 E-mail. sales@tox-uk.com Web. www.tox-uk.com Bret Technology GmbH – Eco Fine Press GmbH

Toye Kenning Spencer Stadden 77 Warstone Lane, Birmingham B18 6NL Tel. 0121 2363253 Fax. 0121 2367217 E-mail. bryan.toye@toye.com Web. www.toye.co.uk Cornelia James Neckwear (United Kingdom) – London Badge & Button Co. (United Kingdom) – Toye Kenning & Spencer (United Kingdom)

Toyk Design 10 Bleak Street, Bolton BL2 2JP Tel. 01204 388261 E-mail. gary@toykdesign.co.uk Web. www.toykdesign.co.uk slube

Tozer Seeds Ltd Pyports Downside Bridge Road, Cobham KT11 3EH Tel. 01932 862059 Fax. 01932 868973 E-mail. info@tozerseeds.com Web. www.tozerseeds.com *Tozer Seeds

T P L Labels Ltd 18 Singer Road Kelvin Industrial Estate, East Kilbride, Glasgow G75 0XS Tel. 01355 900900 Fax. 01355 900600 E-mail. amt@tpl-labels.com Web. www.tpl-labels.com TWINFO

T P Power Services Ltd Rempstone Road Wymeswold, Loughborough LE12 6UE Tel. 01509 889410 Fax. 01509 889445 E-mail. enquiries@tppowerservices.com Web. www.tppowerservices.com TP POWER SERVICES

T P S Fronius 1 The Omni Business Centre Omega Park, Alton GU34 2QD Tel. 01420 546855 Fax. 01420 546856 E-mail. briand@tps-fronius.co.uk Web. www.tps-fronius.co.uk Fronius – Panther

T P S Fronius Ltd 5 Simonsburn Road, Kilmarnock KA1 5LE Tel. 01563 529435 Fax. 01563 523510 E-mail. tomp@tps-fronius.co.uk Web. www.tps-fronius.co.uk Fronius – Panther

T P S Fronius 108 Highfields Road, Bilston WV14 0LD Tel. 01902 495686 Fax. 01902 496461 E-mail. info@tps-fronius.co.uk Web. www.tps-fronius.co.uk Fronius – Panther

T P S Visual Communications Ltd Unit 39 Jubilee Trade Centre Jubilee Road, Letchworth Garden City SG6 1SP Tel. 01462 682203 Fax. 01462 686862 E-mail. info@tpsvisual.com Web. www.tpsdisplay.com Adlite – Graphics Unlimited – Revolver – Rotorpostor

T P Technology plc 2-4 Copyground Lane, High Wycombe HP12 3HE Tel. 01494 535576 Fax. 01494 464175 E-mail. sales@tarn-pure.com Web. www.tarn-pure.com Tarn-Pure – Water systems manufrs

T Q Education & Training Ltd Garden Court Lockington HallMain Street, Lockington, Derby DE74 2SJ Tel. 01509 678400 Fax. 01509 678401 E-mail. enquiries@tq.com Web. www.tq.com Tecquipment

Trac Office Contracts Thornton House Thornton Road, London SW19 4NG Tel. 020 84056446 Fax. 020 84056448 E-mail. info@trac2000.co.uk Web. www.trac2000.co.uk Profile Partitions

Trac Structural Ltd 23 Belvoir Road, Bristol BS6 5DQ Tel. 0117 9240224 Fax. 0117 9248574 E-mail. info@trac.demon.co.uk Web. www.trac-structural.co.uk Fosroc – Helifix – Rotafix

Tractel UK Ltd Holbrook Industrial Estate Old Lane, Halfway, Sheffield S20 3GA Tel. 0114 2482266 Fax. 0114 2473350 E-mail. martyn.reed@tractel.co.uk Web. www.tractel.com *Dynafor (France) – Maxiflex – *Tirak (Germany) – *Tirfor (France)

Traction Equipment Stafford Ltd Glover Street, Stafford ST16 2NY Tel. 01785 223355 Fax. 01785 211074 E-mail. call@tractionequipment.co.uk Web. www.tractionequipment.co.uk Hagglunds – Hilti – Knaack – Spanset – Supacat

Tractive Power Ltd Unit 1, The Old Saw Mill Abbey Green Road, Leek ST13 8SA Tel. 01538 399000 Fax. 0560 1169921 E-mail. info@tractivepower.com Web. www.tractivepower.com Tractive Power

Trada Technology Chiltern House Stocking Lane, Hughenden Valley, High Wycombe HP14 4ND Tel. 01494 569600 Fax. 01494 565487 E-mail. information@trada.co.uk Web. www.trada.co.uk TRADA

Trade 1st Ltd Field House Upper Raby Road, Neston CH64 7TZ Tel. 08448 004167 E-mail. enquiries@trade1st.co.uk Web. www.trade1st.co.uk Trade 1st

Tradebe Solvent Recycling Ltd Hendon Dock, Sunderland SR1 2EW Tel. 01524 853053 Fax. 0191 5660025

E-mail. smcgown@srm-ltd.com Web. www.tradebe.com Solfuel

Tradelinens Ltd Mile Barn Farm Hemel Hempstead Road, Dagnall, Berkhamsted HP4 1QR Tel. 01442 843769 Fax. 01442 843769 E-mail. sales@tradelinens.co.uk Web. www.tradelinens.co.uk *Atkinsons – *Floringo – *Frette – *King Koil Beds – *Northern Feather – *Peter Reed – *Savoir Bed Company

Trade Link London Ltd 31 Wessex Gardens, London NW11 9RS Tel. 020 89055818 Fax. 020 84552987 E-mail. info@saffrondirect.com Web. www.saffrondirect.com *Crane – *Ellora – *Ruby – *Venus

Trademark Consultants 54 Hillbury Avenue, Harrow HA3 8EW Tel. 020 89076066 Fax. 020 84214050 E-mail. info@trademarkco.co.uk Web. www.trademarkco.co.uk Trade Mark Consultants – Trade Mark Intelligence

Trademark Interiors Ltd 8 March Monte Gate, Hemel Hempstead HP2 7BF Tel. 01442 260022 Fax. 01442 232244 E-mail. barrycollins@tmark.co.uk Web. www.tmark.co.uk *Waiko (Germany)

Trade Mark Protection Society Coopers Building Church Street, Liverpool L1 3AB Tel. 0151 7093961 Fax. 0151 7090162 E-mail. j-maddox@tmps.co.uk Web. www.tmps.co.uk T.M.P.S.

Traders Coffee Ltd 274 Ewell Road, Surbiton KT6 7AG Tel. 020 83900311 Fax. 020 83908280 E-mail. jag@coffeebay.co.uk Web. www.coffeebay.co.uk Aristarco – Astoria – Coffee Bay – Oranfresh

Tradex Instruments Ltd Unit C Davis Road, Chessington KT9 1TY Tel. 020 83910136 Fax. 020 83971924 E-mail. info@tradexinstruments.com Web. www.tradexinstruments.com Tradex Instruments

Traditional Games Co. Matrich House Hatfield Hi-Tech Park Goulton Street, Hull HU3 4DD Tel. 01482 327019 Fax. 01482 210490 E-mail. info@sac-games.com Web. www.sac-games.com Cachet Cachet

Trafalgar Tools 116 Market Street, Newton Le Willows WA12 9BU Tel. 01925 298888 Fax. 01925 298888 E-mail. sales@trafalgar-tools.co.uk Web. www.trafalgar-tools.co.uk Abac – Air Comp – Air PRO – ALLMAN – Alto – Ambersil – Armacoil – Armstrong – Beta Tools – Betabite Hydraulics – Bosch Group – Boss – Brauer – Brown Group – Brownall – Burkert – Burnett & Hillman – Caddy – Caldo – Camozzi – Centreglow – Claymore Tools – Corus – Crane – Crouzet – Domnick Hunter – Draper Tools – Eaton – Elora Tools – Ernest Erbe – ETI – FCH – Festo – Flo-tech – Gates – Girair – Goodridge – Goodyear – Graco – Ham-Let Hattersley – Harris – Honeywell – Hozelock – Hy-Fitt – Hydac – Hydrotechnic – Ingersoll-Rand – Interlube – Itap – JCS – Jubilee – JWL – Karcher – King – King Dick Tools – Kuhnke – Legris – Loctite – Lumeter – MacDonald – Manuli Hydraulics – Masterflex – Micromag – Mikalor – Moravia – Nabic – Nilfisk – Norgren – Norma – Parker Filtration – PCL – Pneumax Valves – Rectus – Redashe – Redring – Rexroth – RHODES – Rustoleum – Scapa – Seetru – Silverline Tools – Sirai – Snap-Tite – Stag – Tema – Terry – Tomco – Unicorn – Voss – Wade – Xpelair

Trafford Rubber Products Greengate Works Broadoak Industrial Estate, Trafford Park, Manchester M17 1RW Tel. 0161 8737172 Fax. 0161 8489762 E-mail. website@traffordrubberproducts.co.uk Web. www.traffordrubber.com Sealgrip

Tranfield Of Cumbria Ltd Vion Foods Liverpool Street, Hull HU3 4HW Tel. 01482 326234 Fax. 01482 210375 E-mail. kelly.wood@vionfood.com *Canterbury Foods – *JL Burgers – *Mawbeef – *Plumtree Farm Foods

Transcendata Europe Ltd 4 Carisbrooke Court Buckingway Business Park, Swavesey, Cambridge CB24 4UQ Tel. 01954 234300 Fax. 01954 234349 E-mail. eusales@transcendata.com Web. www.transcendata.com Cadfix

Transcend Group Ltd Crab Apple Way Vale Park, Evesham WR11 1GP Tel. 01386 764900 Fax. 0870 7052886 E-mail. info@transcend-group.com Web. www.transcend-group.com 5s – BPR – FMEA – JIT – Just in time – KAIZAN – KAIZEN – Lean manufacturing – SEIKETSU – SEIRI – SEISO – SEITON – SHITSUKE – Six Sigma – Tops 8D – tops8d

Transdrive Engineering Ltd Milton Street Royton, Oldham OL2 6QU Tel. 0161 6288497 Fax. 0161 6284366 E-mail. sales@transdrive.co.uk Web. www.transdrive.co.uk Technodrives (Netherlands)

Transformation 413 Bury Old Road Prestwich, Manchester M25 1PS Tel. 0161 7734477 Fax. 0161 7736358 E-mail. info@tranformation.co.uk Web. www.transformationshops.co.uk Transformation

Transformation 4 Life 62 Reedham Drive, Purley CR8 4DS Tel. 07802 436159 Fax. 020 86682215 E-mail. louisdesouza@gmail.com Web. www.weightlossonthego.com 60 Minute Money

The Transformer & Electrical Co. (Engineering) Ltd Honywood Road, Basildon SS14 3DT Tel. 01268 520491 Fax. 01268 530414 E-mail. carcher@teccoltd.com Web. www.teccoltd.com Tec

Transformer Equipment Ltd Crystal Business Centre, Sandwich CT13 9QX Tel. 01304 612551 Fax. 01304 613630

E-mail. *luke@transformer-equipment.co.uk* Web. *www.transformer-equipment.co.uk T E L*

The Translation People Limited Adamson House Towers Business Park Wilmslow Road, Manchester M20 2YY Tel. *0845 6430489* Fax. *0870 7598449* E-mail. *manchester@thetranslationpeople.com* Web. *www.thetranslationpeople.com The Translation People*

Transoft Ltd (Part of the Computer Software P.L.C.) Unit 5j Langley Business Centre Station Road, Langley, Slough SL3 8DS Tel. *01753 778000* Fax. *01753 773050* E-mail. *support@blackboxit.com* Web. *www.transoft.com ADAPT/2000 – AIM (Automated INFOS Migration) – Legacy Liberator – OEO (Open Electronic Office) – U/BL – U/Gi – U/SQL Client Server*

Transym Computer Services Limited Chapel House 1 Chapel Street, Guildford GU1 3UH Tel. *01483 538330* E-mail. *sales@transym.com* Web. *www.transym.com Transym OCR (TOCR)*

Travelcare Uk Ltd 68-70 Henderson Street Bridge of Allan, Stirling FK9 4HS Tel. *01786 833685* Fax. *01786 834340* Web. *www.belltravel.co.uk Bell Travel*

Travers Smith Ltd 10 Snow Hill, London EC1A 2AL Tel. *020 72489133* Fax. *020 72363728* E-mail. *david.thomas@traverssmith.com* Web. *www.traverssmith.com Travers Smith Braithwaite*

Travis Perkins plc Stibb Cross, Torrington EX38 8LJ Tel. *01805 601204* Fax. *01805 601561* E-mail. *torrington@travisperkins.co.uk* Web. *www.travisperkins.co.uk P.H.C. Building Supplies*

Trax Unit 1a Severn Farm Industrial Estate, Welshpool SY21 7DF Tel. *01938 554297* Fax. *01938 554597* E-mail. *n.morrison@traxjh.com* Web. *www.traxjh.com TRAX*

T R C Midlands Ltd Mount Pleasant Street, West Bromwich B70 7DL Tel. *0121 5006181* Fax. *0121 5005075* E-mail. *info@totalroofcontrol.co.uk* Web. *www.totalroofcontrol.co.uk Hydroban*

R C Treatt & Co. Ltd Northern Way, Bury St Edmunds IP32 6NL Tel. *01284 702500* Fax. *01284 703809* E-mail. *marketing@rctreatt.com* Web. *www.treatt.com Citreatt, Treattarome – R.C. Treatt*

Trelawny S P T Ltd 13 Highdown Road, Leamington Spa CV31 1XT Tel. *01926 883781* Fax. *01926 450352* E-mail. *steve.williams@trelawny.co.uk* Web. *www.trelawnyspt.co.uk Flexmaster – Hydra – Hydraflex – Trelawny Surface Preparation Technology – Trident-Neptune*

Trelleborg Applied Technology Halfpenny Lane, Knaresborough HG5 0PP Tel. *01423 862677* Fax. *01423 868340* E-mail. *paul.habberfield@trelleborg.com* Web. *www.trelleborg.com/appliedtechnology Celulon – Spraymaker – Ulon – Unileaf – Unilok – Vulkollan*

Trelleborg Ceiling Solutions Ltd Pegasus House Cranbrook Way, Shirley, Solihull B90 4GT Tel. *0121 7332442* Fax. *0121 7332442* E-mail. *d.brown@trelleborg.com* Web. *www.trelleborg.com AQ Seal – Double Delta – Excluder – Glyd Ring – Glydring – Himod – Isolast – Luytex – Orkot – Slydring – Slydway – Stepseal – Turcite – Turcon – Turcon - Turcite - Zurcon – Varilip – Variseal – Wills Rings – Zurcon*

Trelleborg Forsheda Pipe Seals Vantage House Station Road, Bakewell DE45 1GE Tel. *01629 813835* Fax. *01629 814658* E-mail. *mike.chambers@trelleborg.com* Web. *www.trelleborg.com/pipeseals Forsheda*

Trelleborg Industrial A V S Ltd 1 Hoods Close, Leicester LE4 2BN Tel. *0116 2670300* Fax. *0116 2670301* E-mail. *ron.smith@trelleborg.com* Web. *www.trelleborg.com Cushyfloat – Cushyfoot – Cushylevel – Cushymount – Duolastik – Fanflex – High Thrust – Metacone – Metalastik – Novibra – Rotoflex – Rotofloat – Spheriflex – Spherilastik – Steerflex – TrellExtreme – Ultralastik – Uniflex*

Trelleborg Offshore Ltd Stanley Way Stanley Industrial Estate, Skelmersdale WN8 8EA Tel. *01695 712000* Fax. *01695 712111* E-mail. *offshore@trelleborg.com* Web. *www.trelleborg.com Fillite*

Tremco Illbruck Ltd (Factory) Coupland Road Hindley Green, Wigan WN2 4HT Tel. *01942 251400* Fax. *01942 251410* E-mail. *info@tremco-illbruck.com* Web. *www.tremco-illbruck.com Drylok – Renelite – Tremco 440 Tape – Tremco 900 – Tremco Aluminiser – Tremco Burmastic – Tremco Dymeric – Tremco Fibremat – Tremco Mono – Tremco Penefelt – Tremco Proglaze – Tremco Proshim – Tremco Small Joint Sealant – Tremco SST 800 – Tremco Swiggle Strip – Tremco Tremcoveral – Tremco Tremfil – Tremco Tremflex – Tremco Tremfoam – Tremco Weathermat – Tremfoam – Tremgrip – Tremroof 118 – Tremsil – Tretocrete – Tretodek – Tretoflex – Tretolastex – Tretoplast – Tretoshield – Tylex – Vision Strip*

Trenchex Garden Machinery Dovefields Dovefields Industrial Estate, Uttoxeter ST14 8HU Tel. *01889 565155* Fax. *01889 563140* E-mail. *enquiries@trenchex.com* Web. *www.lawn-king.co.uk Diamant Boart – Target – Trenchex – Wisconsin*

Trend Control Systems Ltd Albery House Springfield Road, Horsham RH12 2PQ Tel. *01403 211888* Fax. *01403 241608* E-mail. *jon.cooper@trendcontrols.com* Web. *www.trendcontrols.com IQ – Trend*

Trend Machinery & Cutting Tools Ltd Unit 6 Odhams Trading Estate St Albans Road, Watford WD24 7TR Tel. *01923 249911* Fax. *01923 236879* E-mail. *sales@trendm.co.uk* Web. *www.trend-uk.com Router Cutters – Trend*

Trendsetter Home Furnishings Ltd Cobra Court 10 Blackmore Road, Trafford Park, Manchester M32 0QY Tel. *0161 8645610* Fax. *0161 8650133* E-mail. *sales@trendsetter.co.uk* Web. *www.the-fine-bedding-company.co.uk Four Seasons – Royale – Stratafil – Trendsetter*

Trent Concrete Ltd Private Road 3 Colwick Industrial Estate, Nottingham NG4 2BG Tel. *0115 9879747* Fax. *0115 9879948* E-mail. *anthony.orange@trentconcrete.co.uk* Web. *www.trentconcrete.co.uk Trent – Trent Cladding – Trent T6*

Trenton Box Co. Ltd Marston Road, St Neots PE19 2HF Tel. *01480 473693* Fax. *01480 406225* E-mail. *sales@trentonbox.co.uk* Web. *www.trentonbox.co.uk Trenton Box Co.*

M G Trevett Ltd (t/a Valley Fabrications & Winterbourne Horsebox Co.) West Street Winterborne Stickland, Blandford Forum DT11 0NT Tel. *01258 880490* Fax. *01258 880470 val fabrications – windowborn horsebox company*

Trevross Hotel 57 Apsley Road, Great Yarmouth NR30 2HG Tel. *01493 842030* Fax. *01493 858053* E-mail. *info@trevross.co.uk* Web. *www.trevross.co.uk The Trevross Hotel*

Trewhella Brothers Ltd Bowyer Street, Birmingham B10 0SA Tel. *0121 7667525* Fax. *0121 7668841* E-mail. *sales@trewhella.co.uk* Web. *www.trewhella.co.uk Monkey – Monkey - Monkey Borer - Monkey Jack - Monkey Winch - Monkey Strainer - Wallaby Winch - Trulift – Monkey Borer – Monkey Jack – Monkey Strainer – Monkey Winch – Trulift – Wallaby Winch*

Triad Group plc Huxley House Weyside Park Catteshall Lane, Godalming GU7 1XE Tel. *01483 860222* Fax. *01483 860198* E-mail. *enquiries@triad.co.uk* Web. *www.triad.co.uk Triad Group plc*

Trianco Heating Products Ltd Thorncliffe Chapeltown, Sheffield S35 2PH Tel. *0114 2572349* Fax. *0114 2571419* E-mail. *info@trianco.co.uk* Web. *www.trianco.co.uk Aztec – Eurostar – Eurostar W.M – T.R.G. Range – T.R.H. Range*

Tricho-Tech Unit 1 Pentwyn Business Centre Wharfedale Road, Cardiff CF23 7HB Tel. *029 20540542* Fax. *029 20735036* E-mail. *info@concateno.com* Web. *www.concateno.com Tricho Tech*

Tricool Thermal Ics House, Stephenson Road Calmore Industrial Estate, Totton, Southampton SO40 3RY Tel. *023 80527300* Fax. *023 80428366* E-mail. *info@icstemp.com* Web. *www.tricool.com Combi – Compac – Consort – Minac – Tec – Tricool – Trim*

Trident Blinds Ltd 199 Milton Road, Southsea PO4 8PH Tel. *023 92756011* Fax. *023 92871296* E-mail. *sales@tridentblinds.com* Web. *www.tridentblinds.co.uk Trident Blinds*

Trident Engineering Ltd 2 King Street Lane Winnersh, Wokingham RG41 5AS Tel. *0118 9786444* Fax. *0118 9776345* E-mail. *n-oldland@tridenteng.co.uk* Web. *www.tridenteng.co.uk Canon (Japan) – *Igarashi (Japan) – Portescap (Switzerland) – Trident – Xinruilian (Japan) – Xinrvilian (Japan)*

Trifast Trifast House Bolton Close, Bellbrook Industrial Estate, Uckfield TN22 1QW Tel. *01825 747200* Fax. *01825 767882* E-mail. *sales@trfastenings.com* Web. *www.trfastenings.com Trifast P.L.C.*

Tri Hospitality Consulting Ltd 88 Baker Street, London W1U 6TQ Tel. *020 74865191* Fax. *020 74861189* E-mail. *info@trihc.com* Web. *www.trihc.com T.R.I. Hospitality Consulting*

Trimat Ltd Narrowboat Way Hurst Business Pk, Brierley Hill DY5 1UF Tel. *01384 473400* Fax. *01384 261010* E-mail. *sales@trimat.co.uk* Web. *www.trimat.co.uk Trimat*

Tri Metals Ltd Sunrise Business Park Higher Shaftesbury Road, Blandford Forum DT11 8ST Tel. *01258 459441* Fax. *01258 480408* E-mail. *sales@trimetals.co.uk* Web. *www.trimetals.co.uk Centurian – Titan*

Trimite Scotland Ltd 38 Welbeck Road, Glasgow G53 7RG Tel. *0141 8819595* Fax. *0141 8819333* E-mail. *sales@tslpaints.com* Web. *www.trimite.co.uk Trimite (Scotland)*

Trimline Valves 6 Dales Park Drive Swinton, Manchester M27 0FP Tel. *0161 7278128* Fax. *0161 7279060* E-mail. *harrycope@trimlinevalveslimited.co.uk* Web. *www.trimlinevalveslimited.co.uk Actreg (Spain) – Cepas (Democratic People's Republic of Korea) – Defontaine (France) – JC (Spain) – Orbinox (Spain) – Pekos (Spain) – Starline (Italy) – Stuckham (United Kingdom) – Valmicro (Brazil) – VYC (Spain) – Warren-Morrison (United Kingdom)*

Trimseal Ltd 3b Courtlands Road, Eastbourne BN22 8TR Tel. *01323 730730* Fax. *01424 733666* E-mail. *info@trimseal.co.uk* Web. *www.trimseal.co.uk Trimseal*

Triogen Ltd 117 Barfillan Drive, Glasgow G52 1BD Tel. *0141 8104861* Fax. *0141 8105561* E-mail. *sales@triogen.com* Web. *www.triogen.com Membrel – Ozat – Spazone – Triogen (United Kingdom) – UVAZONE*

Trion The Division Of Ruskin Air Management Ltd Unit 1a The Cavendish Centre Winnall Close, Winchester SO23 0LB Tel. *01962 840465* Fax. *01962 828619* E-mail. *kbristow@airsysco.com* Web. *www.trion.co.uk Electrion – Executive – Herrmidifer – Profile – Space Saver – Supreme – Triumph*

Tri Pack Supplies Ltd 10b Fitzherbert Spur Farlington, Portsmouth PO6 1TT Tel. *023 92326696* Fax. *023 92214447* E-mail. *sales@tripack.co.uk* Web. *www.tripack.co.uk 3M – Bostitch – Featherpost – ITW – Jiffy – Joseph Kielberg – Manuli – Max – Minpack – Minpack, Signode, Tesa, 3M, Jiffy, ITW, Featherpost, Bostitch, Max, Joseph Kielberg, Manuli, Vibac. – Signode – *Tesa – Vibac*

Triple A International 18 Lawrence Avenue, New Malden KT3 5LY Tel. *020 83353135* Fax. *020 83378297* E-mail. *sales@aaa.co.uk* Web. *www.aaa.co.uk Triple A International*

Trisport Ltd 38 Amber Close Tamworth Business Park, Tamworth B77 4RP Tel. *01827 56544* Fax. *01827 53181* E-mail. *info@trisportgolf.com* Web. *www.trisportgolf.com Fast Twist – Fast Twist Systems – Trisport*

Tritech Computer Services Ltd Suite 4 Hillbrow House Linden Drive, Liss GU33 7RJ Tel. *01730 893789* Fax. *01730 894589* E-mail. *info@tritech.org.uk* Web. *www.tritech.org.uk Tritech*

Triten International Ltd Shawfield Road, Barnsley S71 3HS Tel. *01226 702300* Fax. *01226 702311* E-mail. *sales@triten.co.uk* Web. *www.tritenapg.com P.H.C. – Penhard*

Tritex NDT Ltd Unit 10 Mellstock Business Park Higher Bockhampton, Dorchester DT2 8QJ Tel. *01305 257160* Fax. *01305 259573* E-mail. *sales@tritexndt.com* Web. *www.tritexndt.com Multigauge 3000 – Multigauge 5500 – Multigauge 5600*

Triton Chemical Manufacturing Co. Ltd Unit 5 Lyndean Industrial Estate, London SE2 9SG Tel. *020 83103929* Fax. *020 83120349* E-mail. *ian@triton-chemicals.com* Web. *www.triton-chemicals.com Platon Air Gap Technology*

Triton Showers Triton Road Shepperton Business Park, Nuneaton CV11 4NR Tel. *024 76344441* Fax. *024 76349828* E-mail. *lornafellowes@tritonshowers.co.uk* Web. *www.tritonshowers.co.uk Metlex – Triton*

Triumph Furniture (t/a Triumph Business Systems) The Willows, Merthyr Tydfil CF48 1YH Tel. *01685 384041* Fax. *01685 352202* E-mail. *info@triumphstorage.com* Web. *www.triumphstorage.com Triumph Business systems*

Triumph Needle Co. Ltd 14 Albion Street, Wigston LE18 4SA Tel. *0116 2229222* Fax. *0116 2229200* E-mail. *triumphneedle@btclick.com *Kretzer (Germany) – *Maier-Unitas (Germany) – *Muva (Germany)*

Troax UK Ltd Enterprise House Murdock Road, Dorcan, Swindon SN3 5HY Tel. *01793 542000* Fax. *01793 618784* E-mail. *sales@troax.co.uk* Web. *www.gunnebotroax.sa *Troax UK (Sweden)*

Trolex Ltd Newby Road Hazel Grove, Stockport SK7 5DY Tel. *0161 4831435* Fax. *0161 4835556* E-mail. *sales@trolex.com* Web. *www.trolex.com Trolex*

Tron 80-82 Holywell Road, Sheffield S4 8AS Tel. *0114 2425244* Fax. *0114 2444991 Tron*

Trowell Plant Sales Ltd 111 Station Road Selston, Nottingham NG16 6FF Tel. *01773 580878* Fax. *01773 580881* E-mail. *tpsl@btconnect.com* Web. *www.trowellplant.com ABLI Fire retardant coatings – Allison – Aveling Barford – Benford – Broomwade – Compair – Detroit Diesel – Dorman – Goodwin Barsby – Holman – Lister Petter – NCK – Newage Stamford – Perkins – RB – RJE – Rob Roy – Ruston – Seltorque – Terex – Thwaites – Volvo Penta – Winget*

Trucast Ltd Marlborough Road, Ryde PO33 1AD Tel. *01983 567611* Fax. *01983 567618* E-mail. *dtinker@doncasters.com* Web. *www.doncasters.com Trucast*

Truck-Lite Co. Ltd Waterfall Lane, Cradley Heath B64 6QB Tel. *0121 5617000* Fax. *0121 5611415* E-mail. *jhamilton@uk.truck-lite.com* Web. *www.truck-lite.eu.com Raydyot*

True2Life Ltd Mansfield I-Centre Oakham Business Park, Hamilton Way, Mansfield NG18 5BR Tel. *01623 672083* Fax. *01623 600601* E-mail. *sales@true2life.co.uk* Web. *www.true2life.co.uk True2Life*

Truepart Ltd Decoy Bank, Doncaster DN4 5JD Tel. *01302 342211* Fax. *01302 327191* E-mail. *ib@trupart.co.uk* Web. *www.truepart.co.uk *Trupart (Worldwide)*

Truflo Gas Turbines Ltd (A fluid controls business of IMI plc) Westwood Road, Birmingham B6 7JF Tel. *0121 3274789* Fax. *0121 3274132* E-mail. *robert.bowser@truflo-marine.com* Web. *www.fcx-truflow-marine.com Maxseal – Truflo*

Trumans Business Consulting 5 Rodewell House Well Lane, Kettering NN14 6DQ Tel. *07799 766821* E-mail. *info@trumans-consulting.co.uk* Web. *www.trumans-consulting.co.uk Trumans Business Consulting*

Trumeter Co Ltd Milltown Street Radcliffe, Manchester M26 1NX Tel. *0161 7246311* Fax. *0161 7249455* E-mail. *sales@trumeter.com* Web. *www.trumeter.com Measuremeter – Minimeasuremaxx – Trumeter*

Trumpf Ltd Unit A President Way, Luton LU2 9NL Tel. *08444 820188* Fax. *01582 399250* E-mail. *sales@uk.trumpf.com* Web. *www.uk.trumpf.com Trumatic – Trumatic - CNC punches and profiling machines*
Trutex plc Jubilee Mill Taylor Street, Clitheroe BB7 1NL Tel. *01200 421200* Fax. *01200 421209* E-mail. *sales@trutex.com* Web. *www.trutex.com Trutex*
Truvox International Ltd Third Avenue Millbrook, Southampton SO15 0LE Tel. *023 80702200* Fax. *023 80705001* E-mail. *sales@truvox.com* Web. *www.truvox.com Hi-Pro Range – Hydro-Mist Range – Lindhaus Hepa Range – Multiwash – Orbis Range – Traffic Range – Trophy Range – *Valet Aqua Range – Valet Range*
T R W Ltd Stratford Road Shirley, Solihull B90 4AX Tel. *0121 5065000* Fax. *0121 5065001* E-mail. *enquiries@lucasestateagents.co.uk* Web. *www.trw.com Lucas*
Try & Lilly Ltd 95 Kempston Street, Liverpool L3 8HE Tel. *0151 2072001* Fax. *0151 2074878* E-mail. *sales@tryandlilly.co.uk* Web. *www.tryandlilly.co.uk Argyll Deerstalker – Baker Boy – Brighton – Cheviot – Clansman – Cromarty – Deerstalker – Dorset – Drop Brim Panama – Epsom – Folding Panama – Gazelle – Goodwood – Harris County – Hebridean – Jumburry – Linen Formula 1 – Linen Mesh Trilby – Linney – Montrose – Newbury – Newland – Oban – Peebles – Redford – Regent – Scotsman – Sherlock – Snap Brim Panama – Squire – Uniform – Wax County*
Trylon Ltd Bury Close Higham Ferrers, Rushden NN10 8HQ Tel. *01933 411724* Fax. *01933 350357* E-mail. *info@trylon.co.uk* Web. *www.trylon.co.uk Alger Sanders*
T S M Ltd Sensor House Wrexham Technology Park, Wrexham LL13 7YP Tel. *01978 262255* Fax. *01978 291888* E-mail. *tsm@esi-tec.com* Web. *www.esi-tec.com Loadlink – Sensorlink*
T S R Plastics Ltd Station Road Finedon, Wellingborough NN9 5NX Tel. *01536 722333* Fax. *01536 725174* E-mail. *carlo.tai@tsrplastics.co.uk* Web. *www.b-line.uk.com B.-Line*
T S S I Sytems Rutland House Hargreaves Road Groundwell Industrial Estate, Swindon SN25 5AZ Tel. *01793 747700* Fax. *01793 747701* E-mail. *sales@tssi.co.uk* Web. *www.tssi.co.uk Deed Mark – Eu Vision – Q Mark – Verid – Watermark*
T S Technology 7 Langwood 87 Langley Road, Watford WD17 4PW Tel. *01923 221155* Fax. *01923 218625* E-mail. *sales@tstechnology.co.uk* Web. *www.tstechnology.co.uk Astro, Falcon, Planet, Bantam – NSK Nakanishi*
Tsys Fulford Moor House Fulford Road, York YO10 4EY Tel. *01904 562000* Fax. *020 72447233* E-mail. *sales@tsys.com* Web. *www.tsys.com C.T.L. Card Tech*
T-Tech Tooling Ltd 70 Prince of Wales Lane, Birmingham B14 4JZ Tel. *0121 4742255* Fax. *0121 4742066* E-mail. *sales@t-tech.co.uk* Web. *www.t-tech.co.uk T-Tech*
T T Electronics Welwyn Components Ltd Welwyn Electronics Park, Bedlington NE22 7AA Tel. *01670 822181* Fax. *01670 829465* E-mail. *info@welwyn-tt.com* Web. *www.welwyn-tt.com *I.R.C. (U.S.A.) – Welmegox – Welwyn*
T T UK Ltd 10 Windsor Road, Bedford MK42 9SU Tel. *01234 342566* Fax. *01234 352184* E-mail. *sales@tt-uk.com* Web. *www.tt-uk.com Cobra – Grundair – Grundoburst – Grundocrack – Grundodrill – Grundohit – Grundomat – Grundopile – Grundopit – Grundoram – Grundosleeve – Grundotug*
Tube Development Queenzieburn Industrial Estate Kilsyth, Glasgow G65 9BN Tel. *01236 823551* Fax. *01236 825660* E-mail. *info@tubedev.com* Web. *www.tubedev.com TD – Tube Developments*
Tubex Ltd Aberaman Industrial Estate Aberaman, Aberdare CF44 6DA Tel. *01685 883833* Fax. *01685 888001* E-mail. *simonwhite@tubex.com* Web. *www.tubex.com Tubex*
Paul Tuckwell Ltd Chelmsford Road Industrial Estate Chelmsford Road, Dunmow CM6 1HD Tel. *01371 875751* Fax. *01371 874636* E-mail. *dunmow@tuckwell.co.uk* Web. *www.tuckwell.co.uk Gregoire Besson – Kverneland – Main Agents for John Deere – *McConnel – *Vaderstad – Wooton*
Tudor Journals Ltd 97 Botanic Avenue, Belfast BT7 1JN Tel. *028 90320088* Fax. *028 90323163* E-mail. *sales@tudorjournals.com* Web. *www.tudorjournals.com Days Guides – Golf Days – Visitor Days*
Tudor Tea & Coffee Unit 31-35 Thurrock Commercial Centre Juliet Way, Aveley, South Ockendon RM15 4YD Tel. *01708 866966* Fax. *01708 861709* E-mail. *sales@tudorcoffee.co.uk* Web. *www.tudorcoffee.co.uk *Animo – *Franke – *Masterpiece – *Reneka – *Tudor*
Tufcoat Unit 3 Garden Close Langage Business Park, Plympton, Plymouth PL7 5EU Tel. *01752 227333* Fax. *01752 227333* E-mail. *sales@tufcoat.co.uk* Web. *www.boatcoat.com Boatcoat – Tufcoat*
Tuffnelln Parcels Express Shepcote House Shepcote Lane, Sheffield S9 1UW Tel. *0114 2561111* Fax. *0114 2560459* E-mail. *info@tuffnells.co.uk* Web. *www.expressvalves.co.uk Tuffnells*
Tuftop Unit R2 Bourton Link Bourton Industrial Park, Bourton-on-the-Water, Cheltenham GL54 2HQ Tel. *01451 824132* Fax. *01451 824282* E-mail. *rob@tuftop.co.uk Tuftop*
Tukans Ltd 3 Bramleys Barn The Menagerie Skipwith Road, Escrick, York YO19 6ET Tel. *01904 720617* Fax. *01904 720974* E-mail. *sales@tukans.com* Web. *www.tukans.com Clock Audio – Polycom – Tannoy – TV One – Vaddio*
Tuke & Bell Ltd Patent Drive, Wednesbury WS10 7XD Tel. *0121 5067330* Fax. *0121 5067333* E-mail. *sales@tukeandbell.co.uk* Web. *www.tukeandbell.co.uk Autofreway – Biostat – Blake – Carlton – Electromatic – Freway – Ideal – Lift And Force – Pelican – Robec – Robette – Rolls-Rotary – Vulcan*
Tumi Unit 2 Ashmead Business Park Ashmead Road, Keynsham, Bristol BS31 1SX Tel. *0117 9869216* Fax. *01225 444870* E-mail. *info@tumicrafts.com* Web. *www.tumiwholesale.com Tumi*
Tungum Ltd Unit 1 Ashchurch Parkway, Tewkesbury GL20 8TU Tel. *01684 271290* Fax. *01684 291714* E-mail. *sales@tungum.com* Web. *www.tungum.com P.G. Series – Tungum – Tungum Alloy*
Tunnel Steels Prydwen Road Fforestfach, Swansea SA5 4HN Tel. *01792 561777* Fax. *01792 561444* E-mail. *tunnelsteel@btconnect.com* Web. *www.tunnelsteel.net Pandrol – VIC Tavlic*
Tunstall Healthcare UK Ltd Whitley Lodge Whitley Bridge, Whitley, Goole DN14 0HR Tel. *01977 661234* Fax. *01977 662570* E-mail. *enquiries@tunstall.co.uk* Web. *www.tunstall.co.uk Lifeline*
Turbex Ltd Unit 1 Riverwey Industrial Park Newman Lane, Alton GU34 2QL Tel. *01420 544909* Fax. *01420 542264* E-mail. *sales@turbex.co.uk* Web. *www.turbex.co.uk Finnsonic – Promatic – Turbex*
Turbosound Ltd Unit 1-6 Star Road Industrial Estate Partridge Green, Horsham RH13 8RY Tel. *01403 712748* Fax. *01403 710155* E-mail. *sales@turbosound.com* Web. *www.turbosound.com Flashlight – Floodlight – Turbosound*
Turf N Stuff Ltd Unit 8 Elliot Industrial Estate, Arbroath DD11 2NJ Tel. *01241 870415* E-mail. *info@turfandstuff.com* Web. *www.turfnstuff.com Turfandstuff.com*
Turnaround 360 G1300 Lane S 112 Hawley Lane, Farnborough GU14 8JE Tel. *07973 430950* E-mail. *turnaro360@aol.com* Web. *www.turnaround360.co.uk AdMark audio – DVON Audio – Pacrim Audio*
Turnbull & Asser Ltd 71-72 Jermyn Street, London SW1Y 6PF Tel. *020 78083000* Fax. *020 78083001* E-mail. *info@turnbullandasser.co.uk* Web. *www.turnbullandasser.co.uk Turnbull & Asser*
Turnell & Odell Ltd 61-65 Sanders Road Finedon Road Industrial Estate, Wellingborough NN8 4NL Tel. *01933 222061* Fax. *01933 440073* E-mail. *clive@toengineering.co.uk* Web. *www.toengineering.co.uk Wellin*
Turner Bianca Bell Mill Claremont Street, Oldham OL8 3EJ Tel. *0161 6270045* Fax. *0161 6270660* E-mail. *admin@turner-bianca.co.uk* Web. *www.turner-bianca.co.uk Bianca – Bijou by Bianca – Chateau – Country Cooking – Country Memories – Cricket – Inheritance – Madrigal – Metropolis – Primavera by Bianca – Rascals – Richmond House by Bianca – Royal Crest – Snuggle-Dry by Bianca*
Turner Electronics Turner House 11 Roke Close, Kenley CR8 5NL Tel. *020 86680821* Fax. *020 86682782* E-mail. *aj-turner@turnerelectronics.co.uk* Web. *www.turnerelectronics.co.uk Essemtec – Kirsten – Mikron – Rotocut – Schleuniger – Schnyder*
Turner E P S Ltd Newstead Industrial Trading Estate, Stoke On Trent ST4 8HT Tel. *01782 657331* Fax. *01782 644600* E-mail. *jack.caldwell@turner-eps.co.uk* Web. *www.turner-eps.co.uk M.I.E. Power Generators*
Turner Machine Tools 23 Waterloo Park Bidford-on-Avon, Alcester B50 4JG Tel. *01789 772921* Fax. *01789 778614* E-mail. *info@turner-riveters.co.uk* Web. *www.turner-riviters.co.uk Rivetting Machines*
Stuart Turner Ltd Market Place, Henley On Thames RG9 2AD Tel. *01491 572655* Fax. *01491 573704* E-mail. *pumps@stuart-turner.co.uk* Web. *www.stuart-turner.co.uk Boostamatic – Isis – Monsoon – Showermate – Stuart – Water Nymph*
Turner Tools Ltd 15 Armstrong Close, St Leonards On Sea TN38 9ST Tel. *01424 853055* Fax. *01424 851085* E-mail. *turnertools@turnertools.com* Web. *www.turnertools.com *Arno – Boss – *Castrol – Innotool – Jakob Boss – JBO – *Morris Lubricants – *Seco – Shuttle – *Silmax*
Turney Group P A Turney Ltd Middleton Stoney, Bicester OX25 4AB Tel. *01869 343333* Fax. *01869 343540* E-mail. *nigel.barker@paturney.com* Web. *www.turneygroup.com new holland*
Tushingham Sails Ltd PO Box 1, Harrogate HG3 5BN Tel. *01423 712424* Fax. *01423 712273* E-mail. *windsurfing@tushingham.com* Web. *www.tushingham.com Tushingham*
Tuxford & Tebbutt 46-56 Thorpe End, Melton Mowbray LE13 1RB Tel. *01664 502900* Fax. *01664 502901* E-mail. *stuart.scott@milklink.com* Web. *www.milklink.com Tuxford & Tebbutt*
T V H UK Ltd Unit 17 Paragon Way Bayton Road Industrial Estate, Coventry CV7 9QS Tel. *024 76585000* Fax. *024 76585001* E-mail. *sales@tvh.com* Web. *www.tvh.com Allis Chalmers – Atlet – B.T. – Bobcat – Boss – BV Vestergaard – Caterpillar – Clark – Crown – Datsun – Desta – Fenwick – Fiat-Om – Hyster – Icem – Jungheinrich – Kalmar-Climax – Kalmar-Irion – Kalmar-LMV – Komatsu – Lafis – Lancer Boss – Lansing – Linde – Lugli – Manitou – Matral – MIC – Mitsubishi – Nissan – NYK-Nichiyu – Peg – Pimespo – Prat – Salev – Saxby – Steinbock – Still – SVE Truck – T.C.M. – Toyota – Wagner – Yale – Yang-Yam*
Tweedie Evans Consulting The Old Chapel 35a Southover, Wells BA5 1UH Tel. *01749 677760* Fax. *01749 679345* E-mail. *info@tecon.co.uk* Web. *www.tecon.co.uk Tweedie Evans Consulting*
Tweeny Ltd Wheel Park Farm Wheel Lane, Westfield, Hastings TN35 4SE Tel. *01424 751888* Fax. *01424 751444* E-mail. *sales@tweeny.co.uk* Web. *www.tweeny.co.uk Tweeny*
21st Century Energy Publications Ltd 13 Lineacre Close, Gillingham ME8 9NW Tel. *01634 301418* Fax. *01634 301428* E-mail. *energypublications@gmail.com* Web. *www.21stcenturyenergy.co.uk Hazardous Area Product Review – Health & Safety Product Review – Oil & Gas Product Reveiw*
T W B Finishing Ltd Tewkesbury Road, Cheltenham GL51 9AJ Tel. *01242 268000* Fax. *01242 268001* E-mail. *sales@twbfinishing.co.uk* Web. *www.twbfinishing.co.uk Epobond – Eposeal*
T W I Granta Park Great Abington, Cambridge CB21 6AL Tel. *01223 891162* Fax. *01223 892588* E-mail. *christine.wylde@twi.co.uk* Web. *www.twi.co.uk Barrikade – Clearweld – Comeld – Crackwise – JoinIT – Riskwise – Surfi Sculpt – Vitolane – Welderqual – WeldOffice – Weldspec*
Twiflex Ltd Ampthill Road, Bedford MK42 9RD Tel. *01234 350311* Fax. *01234 350317* E-mail. *info@twiflex.co.uk* Web. *www.twiflex.co.uk Magnum (United Kingdom) – Magnum - tension control disc brake. Mistral - tension control disc brake. Wichita - disc brakes. Metana - hydraulic caliper brake. Modevo - tension control disc brake. – Metana (United Kingdom) – Mistral (United Kingdom) – Modevo (United Kingdom) – Wichita (United Kingdom)*
Twiflex Ltd 9 Briar Road, Twickenham TW2 6RB Tel. *020 88941161* Fax. *020 88946056* E-mail. *sales@twiflex.co.uk* Web. *www.twiflex.com Layrub – Twiflex*
Twin Industries International Ltd 1 Hartley Mews High Street, Hartley Wintney, Hook RG27 8NX Tel. *01252 845521* Fax. *01252 845523* E-mail. *julie.outhwaite@twin-industries.co.uk* Web. *www.twin-industries.co.uk Allen Ygnis Boilers – B&E Boilers – Beel Boilers – Beverley – Bradlee Boilers – Certuss Generators – Clayton Generators – Cleaver Brooks Boilers – Cochran Boilers – Collins Walker Boilers – Controlled Flame Boilers – Cradley Boilers – Danks Boilers – Fulton Boilers – Garioni Boilers – Hoval Boilers – Kewanee Boilers – Loos Boilers – Nebraska Boilers – Pirobloc – Robey Boilers – Stone Boilers – Superior Boilers – Viessmann Boilers – Wanson Generators – Wanson Thermal Oil Heaters – York Shipley Boilers*
Twinmar Ltd Maxted Road Hemel Hempstead Industrial Estate, Hemel Hempstead HP2 7DX Tel. *01442 241431* Fax. *01442 230760* E-mail. *enquiries@twinmar.co.uk* Web. *www.soletrader.co.uk Bormer – Falcon – Falcon Sole Trader – Olys – Sole Sister – Soled Out – Treadmaster*
T W Metals Ltd Nursling Industrial Estate Majestic Road, Nursling, Southampton SO16 0AF Tel. *023 80739333* Fax. *023 80739601* E-mail. *paul.sandcraft@twmetals.co.uk* Web. *www.twmetals.co.uk Philip Cornes & Co Ltd – TW Metals*
Twofold Ltd 77 Milford Road, Reading RG1 8LG Tel. *0118 9519800* Fax. *0118 9519899* E-mail. *info@twofold.co.uk* Web. *www.twofold.co.uk Checkpoint*
Twose of Tiverton Ltd 6 Chinon Court Lower Moor Way, Tiverton EX16 6SS Tel. *01884 253691* Fax. *01884 255189* E-mail. *tcoleridge@twose.com* Web. *www.twose.com Twose*
Tyco Tyco Park Grimshaw Lane, Manchester M40 2WL Tel. *0161 4554400* Fax. *0161 4554541* E-mail. *jandreu@tycoint.com* Web. *www.tycofis.com Ace – Mentor*
Tyco Electronics Ltd Terminal House Merrion Avenue, Stanmore HA7 4RS Tel. *0870 6080208* Fax. *020 89546234* Web. *www.tycoelectronics.com AMP – AMP of Great Britain – Tyco Electronics UK Ltd*
Tyco Electronics UK Ltd Faraday Road, Sutton SM3 5HH Tel. *01793 528171* Fax. *01793 572629* E-mail. *picuk@tycoelectronics.com*

Web. *www.tycoelectronics.com Auto-Trace – H.W.A.T. – Icestop – Polyswitch – Thermofit – Tracetek – Zerohal*

Tyco Fire & Integrated Solutions Tyco House Black Horse House Phoenix Way, Swansea Enterprise Park, Swansea SA7 9EQ Tel. *01792 465006* Fax. *01792 648535* E-mail. *fsteel@tycoint.com* Web. *www.tycofis.co.uk Atlas*

Tyden Brooks Unit 3 Berrow Green Road Martley, Worcester WR6 6PQ Tel. *01886 887820* Fax. *01886 812243* E-mail. *sales@tydenbrooks.eu* Web. *www.tydenbrooks.eu Markitwise*

Tye Mann Limited Customer Services Po Box 411, Manchester M16 0YB Tel. *0845 6521505* Fax. *0845 6521505* E-mail. *enquiries@homme-rock.com* Web. *www.homme-rock.com homme rock*

Tyneside Safety Glass Kingsway North Team Valley Trading Estate, Gateshead NE11 0JX Tel. *0191 4875064* Fax. *0191 4870358* E-mail. *chris@tynesidesafetyglass.co.uk* Web. *www.safetyglass.co.uk Tyneside – Tyneside-System MSR*

Typhoon International Ltd Limerick Road, Redcar TS10 5JU Tel. *01642 486104* Fax. *01642 487204* E-mail. *sales@typhoon-int.co.uk* Web. *www.typhoon-int.co.uk Typhoon International*

Tyre Renewals Ltd Torbay Road, Castle Cary BA7 7DT Tel. *01963 350470* Fax. *01963 350503* E-mail. *michael.rees@tyre-renewals.co.uk* Web. *www.tyre-renewals.co.uk Beacon – Bison – City – Haulmark – Kerbmaster*

Tyrone Textiles Ltd Unit 30-31 Riverwalk Business Park Riverwalk Road, Enfield EN3 7QN Tel. *020 82213300* Fax. *020 82213322* E-mail. *enquiries@tyrone-group.com* Web. *www.tyrone-group.com Sheer Luxury – Tyrone*

U

Ubbink UK Ltd Borough Road Buckingham Road Industrial Estate, Brackley NN13 7TB Tel. *01280 700211* Fax. *01280 705331* E-mail. *sales@ubbink.co.uk* Web. *www.ubbink.co.uk Celeste – Orion – Purilan – Slatesoil – Slatevent – Ubbink – Ubiflo – Ubifresh – Ubigas – Ubisoil – Ubivent*

U C D Ltd Unit 1 Sheerland Farm Pluckley, Ashford TN27 0PN Tel. *01233 840296* Fax. *01233 840113* E-mail. *sales@ucd.uk.com* Web. *www.theancillariesstore.co.uk Belgaarde – Bouchard L'Escaut – Elite Biscuits – Fruiss Iced Tea Syrups – Just -T – Kook Kup – MixTender – Montana Syrups – Papadopoulous – Routin 1883 Syrups – Van Houten*

U C M Magnesia Ltd Hull Road Saltend, Hull HU12 8ED Tel. *01482 899141* Fax. *01482 890196* E-mail. *hull@ucm-magnesia.com* Web. *www.ucm-magnesia.com Electromag – Unitec*

Uddeholm Steel Stockholders European Business Park Taylors Lane, Oldbury B69 2BN Tel. *0121 5525530* Fax. *0121 5443036* E-mail. *sales@uddeholm.co.uk* Web. *www.uddeholm.com A.E.B.-L. – Arne – Calmax – Carmo – Chipper – Corrax – Dievar – Domex 5 – Grane – Holdax – Impax – Longlife – Moldmax – Orvar Supreme – Protherm – Q.R.O. 90 Supreme – Ramax S – Remko – Rigor – Serator – Stavax ESR – Strip-Blade – Sverker 3 & 21 – U.H.B. – U.H.B. 11 – Vanadis 10 – Vanadis 23, 30 & 60 – Vanadis 4*

Udny Edgar & Co. Ltd 314 Balham High Road, London SW17 7AA Tel. *020 87678181* Fax. *020 87677709 *Glamos (Japan) – *Matamic (Japan) – *Vitmos (Italy)*

U F A C UK Ltd Waterwitch House 46 Exeter Road, Newmarket CB8 8RX Tel. *01638 665923* Fax. *01638 667756* E-mail. *mail@ufacuk.com* Web. *www.ufacuk.com *Buta-Cup – *Dryfat – *Seapak – *Tasti-Grans*

UK Accreditation Service Accreditation House 21-47 High Street, Feltham TW13 4UN Tel. *020 89178400* Fax. *020 89178500* E-mail. *sylvia.paice@ukas.com* Web. *www.ukas.com UKAS*

UK Distributors Footwear Ltd Churchill Way Fleckney, Leicester LE8 8UD Tel. *0116 403232* Fax. *0116 2402762* E-mail. *derek@ukdistributors.co.uk* Web. *www.ukdistributors.co.uk Airstep – Ambre – Clarion – Clever Kloggs – Crown Comfort – Dek – Grafters – Gringos – Johnscliffe – Lomer – Marlone – Mod Comfys – Route 21 – Scimitar – Tycoons*

UK Office Direct Unit 5 Blackworth Court Blackworth Industrial Estate, Highworth, Swindon SN6 7NS Tel. *0800 6526060* Fax. *01793 762777* E-mail. *info@ukofficedirect.co.uk* Web. *www.ukofficedirect.co.uk 3L – 3M – 5 Star – AA – Accodata – Acorn – Addis – Adobe – Adroit – Advance Agro – AF – Akura – Alba – Alliance Sterling – Ambassador – Amcor – Andrex – Arianex – Armor – Arnos – Artcare – Artline – Atlanta – Aurora – Avery – Bantex – Barton – Basildon Bond – BDS – Beanstalk – Belkin – Berga – Berol – BIC – Bionaire – Bisley – Black & Decker – Black N'Red – Blick – Bluetooth – Bosch – Bostik – Bretford – Bright Ideas – Brillo – Brita – Britvic – Brother – BT – Burco – Cadbury – Cafe Direct – Cambridge – Canon – Carex – Casio – Challenge – Character – Chartwell – Chubb – Churchill – CIF – Citizen – Clairefontaine – Clearspace – Cleartex – Cleenol – Collins – Combs – Compucessory – Computex – Concord – Conqueror – Corxley Script – Cross – Dahle – Datacopy – Dataline – Deflecto – Delonghi – Derwent – Deskplus – Desktex – Dettox – Dormy – Doro – Drakes – Duck – Dura – Durable – Duracell – Dymo – Dyson – E A Combs – Ease-E-Load – Eastlight – Ecover – Edding – Elba – Elysium – Emgee – Emsa – Epsom – Esselte – Essento – Europa – Evian – Evolve – Evrite – Exacompta – Exponent – Fairy – Fast Paper – Fellowes – Fiesta – Filofax – Finish – Fisher Clark – Flash – Flexocare – Floortex – Fujifilm – Fujitsu – GBC – Genicom – Geographics – GGI – Goldline – Guildhall – Hago – Haier – Hallfield – Han – Haze – Heatrunner – Heinz – Helix – Hilton Banks – Honeywell – HP – HSM – Ibico – ID – Imation – Imporient – Indestructable – Inpace – Intimus – Iomega – Ivy – IXL – IXL Premier Grip – Jazz – Jiffy – Johnsons – Just Shelving – Kenco – Kensington – Kikkers – Kimberley-Clark – Kleenex – Kodak – Konika – Kores – Krafty – Kristal – Kyocera – Labtech – Lauffer – Laurel – Leathercraft – Legamaster – Leitz – Lenor – Letraset – Letts – Lexmark – Linex – Loctite – Logitech – Lotus – Lublue – Lyons – Mag-Lite – Magic – Map Marketing – Mark-It – Marland – Martin Yale – Master Lock – Masters – Maul – Maxell – Maxima – Maxwell House – McVitie's – Merit – Mesa – Micromark – Microsoft – Minolta – Mita – Mobi – Motorola – Mr. Muscle – Mr. Sheen – Multiform – Muratec – Navigator – NEC – Nescafe – Nestle – Neusiedler – Neutralle – Neutrogena – New Guardian – Nobo – Nokia – Nouvelle – Novus – Numatic – Nyrex – Oki – Olivetti – Olympia – Olympus – Open Planners – Orbis – Oxford – Paint Shop – Palm – Panasonic – Pantone – Paper Mate – Parazone – Parker – PAS – Pegasus – Pelltech – Pendaflex – Pentel – Percol – Persil – PG Tips – Phillips – Phoenix – Photo Album Company – Pilot – Plantronics – Pledge – Plus Fabric – Polaroid – Polyfile – Polylope – Popinjay – Post-It – Postair – Postmaster – Postsafe – Pot Noodle – Premier – Pringles – Pritt – Pukka Pads – Qualtec – Quartet – Quo Vadis – Raaco – Rapesco – Rapid – Reiner – Retell – Rexel – Ricoh – Robinson Young – Robinsons – Rocado – Rocket Fuel – Rollins – Rosinco – Rotadex – Rotring – Roxio – Royal Sovereign – Rubbermaid – Sage – Sagem – Salestrend – Salter – Samsung – Sanford – Sanyo – Sasco – Scotch – Scotch-Brite – Scott – Securikey – Sellotape – Sentry – Sharp – Sharpie – Sigma – Signature – SIS – Smead – Smith Corona – Snopake – Sonix – Sony – Spaceworx – Spicer Hallfield – Sqware – Stabilo – Staedtler – Stanley – Star – Start – Steam – Steltube – Stephens – Steppy – Stewart Superior – Stoaway – Storall – Strata – Suchard – Summit – Survivor – Sven – Swordfish – Symantec – Systemtray – Tally – Targus – Tarifold – TDK – Technik – Tecnostyl – Tedeco – Tektronix – Tenza – Texas Instruments – Tipp-ex – Tombow – Topstar – Toshiba – Trendline – Trexus – Trim – Trodat – Twinlock – Tyvek – UHU – Valleda – Vanguard – Vent Air – Versapak – Vestry – Wallace Cameron – Waterman – Wedo – Wordgrove – X Stamper – Xerox – Xyron – Your Stationary*

UK Safety Signs 2318 Dumbarton Road, Glasgow G14 ONL Tel. *0141 9542307* Fax. *0141 9545365* E-mail. *office@doubleimage.co.uk* Web. *www.doubleimage.co.uk/safetysi.html Double Image Design Ltd*

UK Sire Services Ltd Venton Stud Dartington, Totnes TQ9 6DP Tel. *01803 863560* Fax. *01803 863560* E-mail. *geoff.corke@uksireservices.com* Web. *www.uksireservices.com British livestock genetics*

UK Solar Ltd 128 Queensway Coney Hall, West Wickham BR4 9DY Tel. *020 83253724* Fax. *020 83256265* E-mail. *uksolar@uksolar.com* Web. *www.uksolar.com Koolcolt – Solargard*

UK Time Ltd 1000 Great West Road, Brentford TW8 9DW Tel. *020 83266900* Fax. *020 83266999* E-mail. *sales@timex.com* Web. *www.timex.com Timex*

Ulkutay & Co. 90 Long Acre, London WC2E 9RZ Tel. *020 88493000* Fax. *020 78493200* E-mail. *tulin@ulkutay.com* Web. *www.ulkutay.com City Bears – Teddy Club*

Ulster Carpet Mills Ltd Castleisland Factory Garvaghy Road, Portadown, Craigavon BT62 1EE Tel. *028 38334433* Fax. *028 38333142* E-mail. *marketing@ulstercarpets.com* Web. *www.ulstercarpets.com Craigavon – Glenavy – Glenavy Donard – Glenavy Tara – Glendun – Glenmoy figured – Glenshane – Glensheske – Glentone – Sheriden – Ulster Classic Wilton – Ulster Velvet – Wilton 2000*

Ulster Weavers Home Fashions Unit 1-6 St Helens Business Park, Holywood BT18 9HQ Tel. *028 90329494* Fax. *028 90326612* E-mail. *sales@ulsterweavers.com* Web. *www.ulsterweavers.com Ulster Weavers*

Ultraclean Systems UK Ltd 11 Gillies Street, Troon KA10 6QH Tel. *01292 679348* Fax. *01292 679585* E-mail. *sales@ultraclean-systems.com* Web. *www.ultraclean-systems.com Ultraclean Systems, X-treme Blue, X70*

Ultra Electronics Upperfield Road Kingsditch Trading Estate, Cheltenham GL51 9NY Tel. *01242 221166* Fax. *01242 221167* E-mail. *mark.doyle@ultra-electrics.com* Web. *www.ultra-electronics.com Helitune*

Ultra Electronics Ltd (P M E S) Towers Business Park Wheelhouse Road, Rugeley WS15 1UZ Tel. *01889 503300* Fax. *01889 572929* E-mail. *enquiries@pmes.com* Web. *www.ultra-electronics.com Linemaster – Stardrive*

Ultravalve Ltd Diamond Works, Maple Tree Lane Colley Gate, Halesowen B63 2BN Tel. *01384 411888* Fax. *01384 411114* E-mail. *sales@ultravalve.co.uk* Web. *www.ultravalve.co.uk AMRI BUTTERFLY VALVES (United Kingdom) – ARI ARMATUREN COMPLETE RANGE INCLUDING 2 PORT, 3 PORT CONTROL VALVES (United Kingdom) – BRAUKMANN WATER PRODUCTS (United Kingdom) – DANFOSS SOCLA PRODUCTS (United Kingdom) – GEMU VALVES (United Kingdom) – GRESSWELL SAFETY VALVES (United Kingdom) – HONEYWELL PRODUCTS (United Kingdom) – MECA INOX VALVES (United Kingdom) – KSB VALVES (United Kingdom) – ODE SOLENOID VALVES (United Kingdom) – VALPRES, VALBIA RANGE OF PNEUMATIC ELECTRIC, MANUAL OPERATED VALVES (United Kingdom) – ULTRAVALVE FLOATING BALL VALVE/TRUNNION IN CAST STEEL (United Kingdom) – ULTRAVALVE CAST STEEL TRUNNION BALL VALVE (United Kingdom) – ULTRAVALVE FORGED STEEL TRUNNION BALL VALVE (United Kingdom) – CLASS 150-2500 FLOATING BALL VALVE USUALLY CLASS 150-600 1/2.-8. (United Kingdom) – TRUNNION MOUNTED 1/2.-36. CLASS 150-2500 (United Kingdom) – Ultravalve complete range of fire protection products :- UL/FM fire protection valves (United Kingdom) – Ultravalve Fireriser gate valves (United Kingdom) – Ultravalve Fireriser Butterfly Valve (United Kingdom) – Ultravalve Check Valve (United Kingdom) – Ultravalve Y Strainer (United Kingdom) – ULTRAVALVE SPECIAL ALLOY VALVES (United Kingdom)*

Ultra-Violet Products Ltd Unit 1 Trinity Hall Farm Estate Nuffield Road, Cambridge CB4 1TG Tel. *01223 420022* Fax. *01223 420561* E-mail. *uvp@uvp.co.uk* Web. *www.uvp.com *Blak-ray (U.S.A.) – *Chromato-vue (U.S.A.) – *Memorase (U.S.A.) – *Mineralight (U.S.A.) – *Pen-ray (U.S.A.) (U.S.A.)*

Ultra Vision International Ltd Commerce Way, Leighton Buzzard LU7 4RW Tel. *01525 381112* Fax. *01525 370091* E-mail. *info@ultravision.co.uk* Web. *www.ultravisiongroup.com Igel 38 – Igel 58 – Igel 67 – Igel 77 – Igel CD – Igel Delta Toric – Igel Hi-Tints – Igel Kerasoft – Igel Omega - 38 – Igel Omega 56 – Igel Presto – Igel Prima – Igel RX Sphere – Igel Rx Toric – Igel SA Multifocal – Igel Stock Toric – Igel Therapeutic – Igel Therapeutic bandage*

Umbro International Ltd Umbro House 5400 Lakeside, Cheadle SK8 3GQ Tel. *0161 4922000* Fax. *0161 4922001* E-mail. *david_hare@umbro.co.uk* Web. *www.umbro.com Umbro*

U M C International Warrior Close Chandler's Ford, Eastleigh SO53 4TE Tel. *023 80269866* Fax. *023 80253198* E-mail. *alan.trevarthen@umc-int.com* Web. *www.umc.co.uk Pamper – Visa*

Umeco Sinclair Close, Heanor DE75 7SP Tel. *01773 766200* Fax. *01773 530245* E-mail. *structural@umeco.com* Web. *www.advanced-composites.co.uk LTM (United Kingdom) – MTM (United Kingdom) – VTM (United Kingdom) – ZPREG (United Kingdom)*

Unbar Rothon Ltd 2 Radford Crescent, Billericay CM12 0DR Tel. *01277 632211* Fax. *01277 630151* E-mail. *prothon@unbarrothon.co.uk* Web. *www.unbarrothon.co.uk Unbar*

Unibind Systems Ltd 3 Oak Court Betts Way, Crawley RH10 9GG Tel. *01293 530182* Fax. *01293 529272* E-mail. *info@unibindsystems.co.uk* Web. *www.unibindsystems.co.uk Unibind*

Unico Ltd North Main Street Carronshore, Falkirk FK2 8HT Tel. *01324 573410* Fax. *01324 573401* E-mail. *sales@unicodirect.com* Web. *www.unicodirect.com Bactogel – Besto – Duraclean – Kleengel – Kleenglass – Rossapol – Sokleen – Triclean – Uniguard – Uniseal*

Unico Components Ltd Unit 2b Henley Business Park Pirbright Road, Normandy, Guildford GU3 2DX Tel. *01483 237621* Fax. *01483 237081* E-mail. *sales@unico.uk.com* Web. *www.unico.uk.com Unico*

Unicol Engineering Green Road Headington, Oxford OX3 8EU Tel. *01865 767676* Fax. *01865 767677* E-mail. *sales@unicol.com* Web. *www.unicol.com Unicol*

Unicorn Chemicals Ltd Unicorn House 141-151 Mowbray Drive, Blackpool FY3 7UN Tel. *01253 396101* Fax. *01253 302895* E-mail. *tim@unicornchemicals.co.uk* Web. *www.unicornchemicals.com C-Solve*

Unicorn Hygienics 5 Ferguson Drive, Lisburn BT28 2EX Tel. *028 92640827* Fax. *028 92625616* E-mail. *info@unicorn-hygienics.com* Web. *www.unicorn-hygienics.com Sani-Fem – Unicorn Products*

Unicorn Products Ltd South Barn Crockham Park, Crockham Hill, Edenbridge TN8 6UP Tel. *0115 9853500* Fax. *01732 782801* E-mail. *elowy@unicorngroup.com* Web. *www.unicorngroup.com Aliflex – Alitec – All Stars Darts – Barry Twomlow – Bob Anderson – Cavalier – Checkout – Cliff Lanzarenco – Club Special – Clubman – Dartsak – Dynamite – Fiesta – Flair – Golden Match – Golden Unicorn – Gripper – Hi-Score – HiLites – Hustler – Jet Set – Jet Stem – JetLite – Jiffy – John Lowe – Karate – Lift-Off – Lim, Paul – Maestro – Nightstar – Polyflite – Premium – Premium MX – Q. – Q. Flights – Quiksteel – Rainbow – Rotajet – Satin Slims – Satinlux – Scoremaster – Sensation – Silver Comet – Slikstik – Slikstik MX – Slims – Status – Sting – Striker – T.90 – T.95 – Tavern – Tri-Point – Trident – Unicorn – X.L. Shafts*

Unifine Food & Bake Ingredients 4-5 Centurion Court Brick Close, Kiln Farm, Milton Keynes MK11 3JB Tel. *01908 260610* Fax. *01908 263213* E-mail. *sales@unifine.uk.com* Web. *www.unifine-fbi.co.uk* **Fruibel – *Sucrea – *Wyko*

Uniflo Systems Ltd 9 Neptune Industrial Estate Neptune Close, Medway City Estate, Rochester ME2 4LT Tel. *01634 716117* Fax. *01634 290235* E-mail. *winifred.betts@uniflo.co.uk* Web. *www.uniflow.co.uk* *Uniflo*

Uniform Express Ltd Unit 5 Haslemere Way, Banbury OX16 5TY Tel. *01295 709774* Fax. *01295 701724* E-mail. *sales@uniformexpress.co.uk* Web. *www.uniformexpress.co.uk Uniform Express*

Unigraph UK Ltd 287 Pitsmoor Road, Sheffield S3 9AS Tel. *0114 2752801* Fax. *0114 2759769* E-mail. *sales@unigraph.co.uk* Web. *www.unigraph.co.uk* *Lanier – Rex Rotary – Ricoh – *Uchida Yoko (Japan) – Unigraph*

Union Industries (Ralf Ellerker Ltd) Whitehouse Street, Leeds LS10 1AD Tel. *0113 2448393* Fax. *0113 2421307* E-mail. *sales@unionindustries.co.uk* Web. *www.unionindustries.co.uk Autostack – Ethafoam – Liondoor – Matadoor – Ramdoor – Unicube – Unimesh*

Union Special (UK) Limited Newline industrial Estate, Bacup OL13 9RW Tel. *0844 8542968* Fax. *0844 8542969* E-mail. *sales@unionspecial.co.uk* Web. *www.unionspecial.co.uk Union Special*

Uniport Business Systems Ltd Unit 80 Claydon Business Park Great Blakenham, Ipswich IP6 0NL Tel. *01473 281155* Fax. *01473 280943* E-mail. *pfg@uniport.co.uk* Web. *www.uniport.co.uk Uniport*

Uniq plc 1 Chalfont Park, Gerrards Cross SL9 0UN Tel. *01753 276000* Fax. *01753 276071* E-mail. *philip.stockill@abagri.com* Web. *www.uniq.com* *Shape – St. Ivel Gold*

Unique Languages 532a Kingston Road, London SW20 8DT Tel. *020 35660145* E-mail. *info@uniquelanguages.com* Web. *www.uniquelanguages.com Unique Languages*

Unispare Domestic Appliances 11 Melbourn Street, Royston SG8 7BP Tel. *01763 247333* Fax. *01763 245988 Unispare*

Unisto Ltd Postford Mill Mill Lane, Chilworth, Guildford GU4 8RT Tel. *01483 209100* Fax. *01483 209109* E-mail. *sales@unisto.co.uk* Web. *www.unisto.co.uk C2K – Crypta – Manta – Manta - C2K – Seal Trak*

Unisys Ltd Hertford Place Denham Way, Maple Cross, Rickmansworth WD3 9AB Tel. *01895 237137* Fax. *01895 862092* E-mail. *sales@unisys.com* Web. *www.unisys.com Unisys*

United Automation Ltd Southport Business Park Wight Moss Way, Southport PR8 4HQ Tel. *01704 516500* Fax. *01704 516501* E-mail. *chloe@united-automation.com* Web. *www.united-automation.com Mono-Link*

United Business Media Ltd Riverbank House Angel Lane, Tonbridge TN9 1SE Tel. *01732 362666* Fax. *01732 367301* Web. *www.ubm.com Aerospace Europe – Benn's Media Directory – Chemical Industry Europe – Chemist & Druggist Directory – Conference Blue & Green – Directory To The Furniture & Furnishing Industry – Electronics Buyers Guide, The – Gas Industry Directory – International Leather Guide – Kempe's Engineers Year-Book – Knowledge, The – Offshore Oil & Gas Directory – Packaging Industry Directory – Phillips International Paper Directory – Printing Trades Directory – Sell's Products & Services Directory – The Engineering Industry Buyers Guide – Timber Trades Address Book – TTG Directory*

United Paper Merchants Ltd 15 Linfield Industrial Estate Linfield Road, Belfast BT12 5LA Tel. *028 90327303* Fax. *028 90438702* E-mail. *sales@united-paper.com* Web. *www.united-paper.com United Paper*

United Utilities Water plc Lingley Green Avenue Great Sankey, Warrington WA5 3LP Tel. *01925 237000* Fax. *01925 233360* Web. *www.unitedutilities.co.uk United Utilities P.L.C*

Unitemp Ltd 14 Treadaway Business Centre Treadaway Hill, Loudwater, High Wycombe HP10 9RS Tel. *01628 850611* Fax. *01628 850608* E-mail. *info@unitemp.co.uk* Web. *www.unitemp.co.uk ESPEC – ESPEC Corp*

Uniter Group Ltd 3 Radford Way, Billericay CM12 0DX Tel. *08458 112000* Fax. *0845 8112001* E-mail. *jo.klingen@uniter.co.uk* Web. *www.unitergroup.co.uk* **Mufax (Japan)*

Unit Pallets Ltd Bank Street Golborne, Warrington WA3 3RN Tel. *01942 713501* Fax. *01942 722756* E-mail. *sales@unit-pallets.co.uk* Web. *www.unit-pallets.co.uk Unit Pallets*

Unit Products Ltd 2 Mount Road, Feltham TW13 6AR Tel. *020 87554216* Fax. *020 88984711* E-mail. *enquiries@unitproducts.co.uk* Web. *www.unitproducts.co.uk Unitair*

Uni Trunk Ltd 4 Altona Road, Lisburn BT27 5QB Tel. *028 92625100* Fax. *028 92625101* E-mail. *david.morrow@unitrunk.co.uk* Web. *www.unitrunk.co.uk Unitrunk*

Unitrust Protection Services Ltd Unitrust House Heather Park Drive, Wembley HA0 1SS Tel. *020 89038303* Fax. *020 89035526* E-mail. *info@unitrust.co.uk* Web. *www.unitrust.co.uk Unitrust*

Unit Two Systems 25-27 Foster Street, Chorley PR6 0AY Tel. *01257 268628* Fax. *01257 268628* E-mail. *glynnhughes2004@yahoo.co.uk Unit Two Systems*

Universal Air Tool Company Ltd Unit 8 Lane End Industrial Park, Lane End, High Wycombe HP14 3BY Tel. *01494 883300* Fax. *01494 883237* E-mail. *sales@universal.co.uk* Web. *www.universal.co.uk* *Ajax – Colibri – U.T. – Universal Air Tools*

Universal Boltforgers Ltd Unit 28 Dudley Road West Tividale, Oldbury B69 2PJ Tel. *0121 5225950* Fax. *0121 5205333* E-mail. *paul@universal-boltforgers.co.uk* Web. *www.universal-boltforgers.co.uk Universal Boltforgers*

Universal Carbon Fibres Ltd Station Mills Station Road, Wyke, Bradford BD12 8LA Tel. *01274 600600* Fax. *01274 711666* E-mail. *info@ucfltd.co.uk* Web. *www.ucfltd.co.uk Panotex*

Universal Components Universal House Pennywell Road, Bristol BS5 0ER Tel. *0117 9559091* Fax. *0117 9556091* E-mail. *info@universal-aluminium.co.uk* Web. *www.universal-aluminium.co.uk Concept 90 – Direx – Dualcase – Flexcase – Locate – Panacase – Panatrim – Slimline – Tranicase – Unicase – Uniflex – Unilight – Unitrim*

Universal Crop Protection Ltd Park House Maidenhead Road Cookham, Maidenhead SL6 9DS Tel. *01628 526083* Fax. *01628 810457* E-mail. *enquiries@unicrop.com* Web. *www.unicrop.com Sistan – Unicrop*

Universal Cycles Unit 8a Festival Way Festival Leisure Park, Basildon SS14 3WB Tel. *08448 888484* Fax. *01268 247047* E-mail. *sarah.markscheffel@universalcycles.plc.uk* Web. *www.universalcycles.plc.uk Sierra Nevada – Super Tracker – Uni-Sport*

Universal Display Fittings Network Hub 300 Kensal Road, London W10 5BE Tel. *020 82065010* Fax. *020 89694215* E-mail. *info@universaldisplay.co.uk* Web. *www.universaldisplay.co.uk *Christmas Presence (United Kingdom) – *Gemini Mannequins (United Kingdom) – Universal Display (United Kingdom)*

Universal Glazing Ltd Unit 12 Silver Court Intercity Way, Leeds LS13 4LY Tel. *0113 2572021* Fax. *0113 2393317* E-mail. *universal@unit12.fsnet.co.uk Universal Glazing*

Universal Hydraulics Ltd Carrwood Road, Chesterfield S41 9QB Tel. *01246 451711* Fax. *01246 450399* E-mail. *sales@universalhydraulics.co.uk* Web. *www.universalhydraulics.co.uk U.H.L.*

Universal Impex Ltd 2 Albert Place, London N3 1QB Tel. *020 83494666* Fax. *020 83434315* E-mail. *info@unitechouse.com* Web. *www.unitechouse.com* *Universal Impex*

Universal Island Music Ltd 364-366 Kensington High Street, London W14 8NS Tel. *020 74715300* Fax. *020 74715001* E-mail. *contact@umusic.com* Web. *www.umusic.co.uk* *Island Records*

Universal Locks Ltd T/A Universal Security Group 894 Plymouth Road Slough Trading Estate, Slough SL1 4LP Tel. *01753 696630* Fax. *01753 696374* E-mail. *info@universalsecurity.co.uk* Web. *www.universalsecurity.co.uk Universal Locks*

Universal Marking Systems Ltd Unit 7 Mount Road, Feltham TW13 6AR Tel. *020 8984884* Fax. *020 88989891* E-mail. *jeff@ums.co.uk* Web. *www.ums.co.uk Brother P-Touch Electronic labelling – Data Matrix Systems (DMx) – Dot Markers (dot peen) – Hand Stamps – Label Printing – Large Character Inkjet Marking – Laser marking – Metaletch – Metaltech Electrochemical – Paintjet Systems*

Universal Sealents UK Ltd Kingston House 3 Walton Road Pattinson North, Washington NE38 8QA Tel. *0191 4161530* Fax. *0191 4155966* E-mail. *info@ufluk.com* Web. *www.ufluk.com Nufinf*

Universal Towel Company Ltd Unit 5 Foundry Court Foundry Lane, Horsham RH13 5PY Tel. *01403 242101* Fax. *01403 242144* E-mail. *info@u-t-c.co.uk* Web. *www.u-t-c.co.uk Universal Towel*

University Of Leeds (Subsidiary of University of Leeds) Woodhouse Lane, Leeds LS2 9JT Tel. *0113 2431751* Fax. *0113 2443923* E-mail. *m.j.p.arthur@adm.leeds.ac.uk* Web. *www.leeds.ac.uk Applied Enzyme Technology – Bethan – Bioventures – Bloodhound Sensors – Caddetc – Cosecure – Downs Syndrome Screening Service – Express – Gelectrix – Getech – Rock Deformation Research – Sound Alert – U.L.I.S. – Valve Testing Centre*

University Of London Senate House Malet Street, London WC1E 7HU Tel. *020 78628000* Fax. *020 78628032* E-mail. *enquiries@london.ac.uk* Web. *www.london.ac.uk* *University of London*

University Of Manchester Incubator Company Ltd 48 Grafton Street, Manchester M13 9XX Tel. *0161 6067200* Fax. *0161 6067300* E-mail. *yvonne.loughlin@umic.co.uk* Web. *www.umic.co.uk Control Technology Centre Ltd – Flow Science – Manchester Informatics Ltd – Manchester Innovation – ManPharm – Visual Automation*

University Of Sussex Intellectual Property Ltd Sussex House University of Sussex Falmer, Falmer, Brighton BN1 9RH Tel. *01273 678888* Fax. *01273 877456* E-mail. *information@sussex.ac.uk* Web. *www.sussex.ac.uk* *Sussex Innovation Centre – SussexIP – University of Sussex*

Uni Vite Healthcare 50 Aylesbury Road Aston Clinton, Aylesbury HP22 5AH Tel. *01296 630900* Fax. *01296 631074* E-mail. *enquiries@acceleratedlearning.com* Web. *www.acceleratedlearning.com Micro Diet*

Updata plc Updata House Podmore Road, London SW18 1AJ Tel. *020 88744747* Fax. *020 88743931* E-mail. *david@updata.co.uk* Web. *www.updata.co.uk* *Indexia*

Uplec Industries Ltd Oakhurst Hall Oakhurst Road, Oswestry SY10 7BZ Tel. *01691 650422* Fax. *01691 658553* E-mail. *enquiries@uplec.co.uk* Web. *www.uplec.co.uk Uplec Industries*

U P M Kymmene Ltd 2 Victoria Street, Altrincham WA14 1ET Tel. *0870 6000876* Fax. *0870 6060876* Web. *www.upm-kymmene.com U.P.M. Kymmene*

U-Pol Ltd 1 Totteridge Lane, London N20 0EY Tel. *020 84925900* Fax. *020 84925999* E-mail. *sales@u-pol.com* Web. *www.u-pol.com Barcoat – Deepcoat – Fibral – Gravitex – Isopon P38 – Isopon P40 – Upol A – Upol B – Upol C – Upol D – Upol E – Upol Top-Stop*

Urbis Lighting Ltd Unit 1-5 Telford Road, Basingstoke RG21 6YW Tel. *01256 354446* Fax. *01256 841314* E-mail. *sales@urbislighting.com* Web. *www.urbislighting.com* *Urbis*

Urquhart Dykes & Lord Tower North Central Merrion Way, Leeds LS2 8PA Tel. *0113 2452388* Fax. *0113 2430446* E-mail. *email@udl.co.uk* Web. *www.udl.co.uk* *Urquhart-Dykes & Lord*

Usborne Publishing 83-85 Saffron Hill, London EC1N 8RT Tel. *020 74302800* Fax. *020 74301562* E-mail. *mail@usborne.com* Web. *www.usborne.com* *Usborne*

U S F Blastrac PO Box 60, Altrincham WA14 5EP Tel. *0161 9286388* Fax. *0161 9290381* E-mail. *uk-info@wheelabrator.co.uk* Web. *www.wheelabrator.com Blastrac*

U S G UK Ltd 1 Swan Road South West Industrial Estate, Peterlee SR8 2HS Tel. *0191 5188600* Fax. *0191 5860097* E-mail. *pdauwe@usg.com* Web. *www.usg.uk.com* *Acoustone – Auratone – Cadre Quadra – Celebration – Cleanroom – Compasso – Curvatura – Donn – Donn DX Screw Fix – Donn Grid – Novatone – Olympia II – Paraline – Paraline – Radar – Sonatone*

U T C Fire & Security 8 Newmarket Court Kingston, Milton Keynes MK10 0AQ Tel. *01908 281981* Fax. *01908 282554* Web. *www.ziton.com Firebeam – Multiplex – P.C.S./P.A.S. – Smometa*

Utile Engineering Co. Ltd New Street, Irthlingborough NN9 5UG Tel. *01933 650216* Fax. *01933 652738* E-mail. *sales@utileengineering.com* Web. *www.utileengineering.com Utile*

Utilux UK Ltd Hillside Road East, Bungay NR35 1JX Tel. *01986 895611* Fax. *01986 895280* E-mail. *sales@utilux.co.uk* Web. *www.utiluxeurope.com* *Utilux*

U T I Worldwide Ltd Overline House Blechynden Terrace, Southampton SO15 1GW Tel. *023 80228351* Fax. *023 80219089* E-mail. *ianmoran@go2uti.com* Web. *www.go2uti.com UTI*

U T I Worldwide UK Ltd (Head Office) Hyperion Way Rose Kiln Lane, Reading RG2 0JS Tel. *0118 9869595* Fax. *0118 9876074* Web. *www.go2uti.com UCI*

Utopia Records Ltd Utopia Village Chalcot Road, London NW1 8LH Tel. *020 75863434* Fax. *020 75863438 Falling on Your Feet – Utopia*

UVFish Ltd 3 Font Villas West Coker, Yeovil BA22 9BY Tel. *01935 804205* Fax. *0870 4798648* E-mail. *enquiries@uvfish.co.uk* Web. *www.uvfish.co.uk HP – MIcrosoft*

U V O 3 Ltd Unit 25 Stephenson Road, St Ives PE27 3WJ Tel. *01480 355446* Fax. *01480 353487* E-mail. *sales@uvo3.co.uk* Web. *www.uvo3.co.uk R-Can Environmental – Sterilight – UV Techniek – Van Remmen UV Techniek*

V

Vacational Studies Pepys Oak Tydehams, Newbury RG14 6JT Tel. *01635 523333* Fax. *01635 523999* E-mail. *vacstuds@vacstuds.com* Web. *www.vacstuds.com* *V.S.I. Vacational Studies (International) Ltd – Vacational Studies*

Vacherin Ltd 16-18 Hatton Garden, London EC1N 8AT Tel. *020 74042277* Fax. *020 74048833* E-mail. *mark.philpott@vacherin.com* Web. *www.vacherin.com Vacherin Limited*

Vacman Specialist Cleaning Budmhor, Portree IV51 9DJ Tel. *01478 613111* Fax. *01478 613321* E-mail. *info@vacman.co.uk* Web. *www.vacman.co.uk* *Vacman Specialist Cleaning*

Vacu Lug Traction Tyres Ltd Gonerby Road Gonerby Hill Foot, Grantham NG31 8HE Tel. *01476 593095* Fax. *01476 513809* E-mail. *info@vaculug.com* Web. *www.vaculug.com Grumac – Vacu-Lug Traction Tyres Ltd*

MDC Vacuum Products Ltd 3 Horsted Square Bellbrook Industrial Estate, Uckfield TN22 1QG Tel. *01825 280450* Fax. *01825 280440* E-mail. *sales@caburn.co.uk* Web. *www.mdcvacuum.co.uk I.T.L.*

Vacuum Reflex West Road Ransomes Europark, Ipswich IP3 9SX Tel. *01473 725176* Fax. *01473 271941* E-mail. *vacuumreflex@compuserve.com* Web. *www.vacuum-reflex.com Icelander – Lifemaster – Vascutherm*

Vaderstad Ltd Unit 1 Ellesmere Business Park Swingbridge Road, Grantham NG31 7XT Tel. *01476 581900* Fax. *01476 568994* E-mail. *elaine.prince@vaderstad.com* Web. *www.vaderstad.com *Carrier – *Nz – *Rapid – *Rexius – *Rexius Twin – *Rollex – Topdown*

V & A Enterprises Ltd 160 Brompton Road, London SW3 1HW Tel. *020 79422966* Fax. *020 79422967* Web. *www.vandashop.co.uk V. & A.*

Vaillant Ltd Vaillant House Trident Close, Medway City Estate, Rochester ME2 4EZ Tel. *01634 292300* Fax. *0121 7797141* E-mail. *info@vaillant.co.uk* Web. *www.vaillant.co.uk *Ecomax (Germany) – *ThermoCompact (Germany) – *TurboMax (Germany) – *Vantage (Germany)*

Valbruna UK Ltd (Head Office) Oldbury Road, West Bromwich B70 9BT Tel. *0121 5535384* Fax. *0121 5005095* E-mail. *philip.wood@valbruna-uk.com* Web. *www.valbruna-uk.com Valbruna*

Valco Cincinnati Unit 8 Hortonwood 32, Telford TF1 7YN Tel. *01952 677911* Fax. *01952 677945* E-mail. *sales@valco.co.uk* Web. *www.valco.co.uk Econ-O-Matic – *Flexoseal (U.S.A.) – *Microseal (U.S.A.) – *Robond (U.S.A.) – Thermojet*

Valeader Pneumatics Ltd 37 Clifton Road, Cambridge CB1 7ED Tel. *01223 248911* Fax. *01223 248922* E-mail. *info@valeader.co.uk* Web. *www.valeader.co.uk *Flo Control (Italy)*

Vale Brothers Long Street, Walsall WS2 9QG Tel. *01922 624363* Fax. *01922 720994* E-mail. *sales@valebrothers.co.uk* Web. *www.valebrothers.co.uk Equbond (United Kingdom) – Eventa (United Kingdom)*

Valeport Ltd St. Peters Quay, Totnes TQ9 5EW Tel. *01803 869292* Fax. *01803 869293* E-mail. *sales@valeport.co.uk* Web. *www.valeport.co.uk BRAYSTOKE – MIDAS – MINI – MONITOR*

Vallectric Ltd Sweet Street, Leeds LS11 9DB Tel. *0113 2423800* Fax. *0113 2424960* E-mail. *andrew.ball@vallectric.co.uk* Web. *www.vallectric.co.uk Vallectric Ltd*

Valley Spring Co. Ltd Pottery Lane East, Chesterfield S41 9BH Tel. *01246 451981* Fax. *01246 454327* E-mail. *sales@valleyspring.com* Web. *www.valleyspring.com Valley Spring*

Valpar Industrial Ltd 13 Balloo Drive, Bangor BT19 7QY Tel. *028 91454544* Fax. *028 91457512* E-mail. *info@valpar.co.uk* Web. *www.valpar.co.uk Brewmaster – Codemaster – Flexmaster – VALPAR T.C.S.*

Valradio Electronic Ltd 1a Mandeville Road, Isleworth TW7 6AD Tel. *020 85603001* Fax. *020 88470783* E-mail. *info@valradio.co.uk* Web. *www.btinternet.com Valradio – Welpower*

Valspar Powder Coatings Ltd (Global Coatings Division) 95 Aston Church Road Nechells, Birmingham B7 5RQ Tel. *0121 3226900* Fax. *0121 3226901* E-mail. *infoeurope@powderstore.com* Web. *www.valsparglobal.com H.B. Fuller Coatings Ltd – Omega – Synthatec*

Valves Instruments Plus Ltd Chaddock Lane Astley, Tyldesley, Manchester M29 7JT Tel. *01942 885700* Fax. *0161 8328099* E-mail. *sales@vip-ltd.co.uk* Web. *www.vip-ltd.co.uk Ashtons-of-Salford*

Valve Spares Ltd Ravenshill Drive Cleland, Motherwell ML1 5QW Tel. *01698 860738* Fax. *01698 861739* E-mail. *valvesspares@btconnect.com Keystone – Weir Pacific*

Valvestock Pipe Center Shogun House 2 Fielder Drive, Fareham PO14 1JG Tel. *01329 283425* Fax. *01329 822741* E-mail. *enquiries@valvestock.co.uk* Web. *www.valvestock.co.uk Ball Valve Sales – Valvestock*

Valvoline Oil Co. Dock Road, Birkenhead CH41 1DR Tel. *0151 6521551* Fax. *0151 6538900* E-mail. *sales@valvoline.com* Web. *www.valvolineuk.com Tectyl – Valvoline*

Vanasyl 2000 32 Cavendish Road, Sheffield S11 9BH Tel. *0114 2587229* Fax. *0114 2500239* E-mail. *db4ram@vanasyl.com* Web. *www.vanasyl.com Clifton Enterprises*

Van Der Lande Industries 59 Marsh Lane Hampton-in-Arden, Solihull B92 0AJ Tel. *01675 443743* Fax. *01675 443169* E-mail. *grahame.bacon@vanderlande.com* Web. *www.vanderlande.com Crossorter – Distrisorter – Exprexorter – Helixorter – Paxorter – Posi2orter – Shoeboxorter – Truxorter – Vanderlande Industries – Vanderlande Industries - materials handling systems – Variostore – Vertisorter – Viper – Vision – Vision ZPS*

Vanguard Logistics Ltd Station House, Maldon CM9 4LQ Tel. *01621 879200* Fax. *01708 555577* E-mail. *ian.gill@vanguardlogistics.co.uk* Web. *www.vls-global.com Confreight Group – Confreight Group - Sea freight consolidators*

Van Leeuwen Wheeler Ltd Unit 1a Rotunda Business Centre Thorncliffe Road, Chapeltown, Sheffield S35 2PG Tel. *0114 2573800* Fax. *0114 2570639* E-mail. *iwaller@vlwheeler.co.uk* Web. *www.vanleeuwenwheeler.co.uk Van Leeuwen*

Vanriet UK Ltd Riverside Industrial Estate Frazeley, Tamworth B78 3RL Tel. *01827 288871* Fax. *01827 250810* E-mail. *sales@vanriet.co.uk* Web. *www.vanriet.co.uk Flexiloader – Flexiveyor – Power Roller – Power-Belt – Powerflexi – Speedway*

Vanton Pumps Europe Ltd Unit 4 Royle Park, Congleton CW12 1JJ Tel. *01260 277040* Fax. *01260 280605* E-mail. *mail@vantonpump.com* Web. *www.vantonpump.com Chem-Gard – Flex-I-Liner – Sump-Gard*

Vapac Humidity Control Ltd Fircroft Way, Edenbridge TN8 6EZ Tel. *01732 863447* Fax. *01732 865658* E-mail. *gerry.stapley@eaton-williams.com* Web. *www.eaton-williams.com Cubit – Vapac*

The Vapormatic Co. Ltd PO Box 58, Exeter EX2 7NB Tel. *01392 435461* Fax. *01392 438445* E-mail. *peter.brennan@vapormatic.com* Web. *www.vapormatic.co.uk Floline – Powerline – PTO Line – Uniline – Vapormatic*

Vapormatt Ltd Monarch Centre Venture Way, Priorswood Industrial Est, Taunton TA2 8DE Tel. *01823 257976* Fax. *01823 336446* E-mail. *ryan.ashworth@vapormatt.co.uk* Web. *www.vapormatt.com Vapormat – Vapormatt*

Vapor Tek Ltd Fairclough Street, Bolton BL3 2AF Tel. *01204 521795* Fax. *01204 364576* E-mail. *info@vapor-tek.co.uk* Web. *www.vapor-tek.co.uk Aquavap – Cablegard – Steelgard – Vaporol – Vapro-Tek*

Varatio Holdings plc 752-753 Deal Avenue, Slough SL1 4SH Tel. *01753 526655* Fax. *01753 693779* E-mail. *alan.clinch@varatiouk.co.uk* Web. *www.varatio.com Anglgear – Anglgear Industrial Bevel Units – Selecta-Speed – Specials – Strateline – Strateline – V.S. Bevel Units*

Vargus Tooling Ltd Halesfield 4, Telford TF7 4AP Tel. *01952 583222* Fax. *01952 583383* E-mail. *asm@vargustooling.co.uk* Web. *www.vargustooling.co.uk Innotool – Kyocera Fineceramics – Stock – Vardex*

Varian Medical Systems UK Ltd (Registered Office) Gatwick Road, Crawley RH10 9RG Tel. *01293 601200* Fax. *01293 510260* Web. *www.varian.com *Clinac (U.S.A.) – ScanVision – VariSource – VarisVision – Ximatron – XimaVision*

Variety Silk House Ltd 150-152 Ealing Road, Wembley HA0 4PY Tel. *020 89036302* Fax. *020 89002497* E-mail. *variety@mailbox.co.uk* Web. *www.varietysilkhouse.com Rani Collection, The – Xerxes*

Varley & Gulliver Ltd Alfred Street Sparkbrook, Birmingham B12 8JR Tel. *0121 7732441* Fax. *0121 7666875* E-mail. *reception@v-and-g.co.uk* Web. *www.v-and-g.co.uk V & G Anchorage – Vargull*

Varley Pumps Ltd 1 Kimpton Road, Luton LU1 3LD Tel. *01582 731144* Fax. *01582 402563* E-mail. *sales@varleypumps.com* Web. *www.varleypumps.com Varley – Varley - pumps.*

Varta Automotive Batteries Ltd Broadwater Park North Orbital Road Denham, Uxbridge UB9 5HR Tel. *01895 838999* Fax. *01895 838981* E-mail. *info-uk@varta-automotive.com* Web. *www.varta-automotive.com *Varta*

Vastern Timber Co. Ltd Saw Mills Wootton Bassett, Swindon SN4 7PD Tel. *01793 853281* Fax. *01793 855336* E-mail. *enquiries@vastern.co.uk* Web. *www.vastern.co.uk Arbardeck – Fiddes – Granwax – Liberon – Sikabond*

Vaughans Hope Works Ltd Baker House The Hayes, Stourbridge DY9 8RS Tel. *01384 424232* Fax. *01384 893171* E-mail. *sales@anvils.co.uk* Web. *www.anvils.co.uk Alcosa – Baker Horseshoes – Baker Horseshoes (horseshoe manufacturer) - Sterling farriers tools) - Alcosa (forges) - Brooks (anvils) - Vaughans (blacksmiths and foundry hand-tools). – Brooks – Flamefast – Readymade – Sterling – Thoroughbred – Vaughans*

Vaultland Engineering Foundry Lane, Horsham RH13 5PX Tel. *01403 260271* Fax. *01403 263083* E-mail. *mmlmfg@talktalkbusiness.net Digi-Speak – *Flubacher (Switzerland) – *Tesa (Switzerland) – *Zentrofix (Switzerland)*

Vax Ltd Kingswood Road Hampton Lovett, Droitwich WR9 0QH Tel. *01905 795959* Fax. *01905 794804* E-mail. *slawson@vax.oxford.co.uk* Web. *www.vax.co.uk Vax Cleaning Solutions and Dust Bags – Vax Luna 1300 – Vax Luna 1400 – Vax Sahara*

Veale Associates Ltd 16 North Road, Stevenage SG1 4AL Tel. *01438 747666* Fax. *01438 742500* E-mail. *va@vealea.com* Web. *www.vealea.com Audiotek*

Vectair Systems Ltd Unit 3 Trident Centre Armstrong Road, Basingstoke RG24 8NU Tel. *01256 319500* Fax. *01256 319510* E-mail. *info@vectair.co.uk* Web. *www.vectair.co.uk Air Force – Air Line – Airtowel – Airwave – Autosan – Babyrendel – Esprit IV – Pulse II – Safeseat – Sensaflush – Sensatap – Wizard System*

Vectra Group Ltd Europa House 310 Europa Boulevard, Westbrook, Warrington WA5 7YQ Tel. *01925 444648* Fax. *01925 444701* E-mail. *info@vectragroup.co.uk* Web. *www.vectragroup.co.uk Amey Vectra Ltd*

Vee Bee Filtration UK Ltd Old Wharf Road, Stourbridge DY8 4LS Tel. *01384 378884* Fax. *01384 374179* E-mail. *bradleyr@veebee.co.uk* Web. *www.veebee.co.uk VEE BEE*

Veetee Rice Ltd Unit 21 Neptune Industrial Estate Neptune Close, Medway City Estate, Rochester ME2 4LT Tel. *01634 290092* Fax. *01634 297792* E-mail. *mvarma@veetee.com* Web. *www.veetee.com *Veetee Brand*

Veevers Carter Flowers Ltd Unit B3-B4 Trading Estate Galleywall Road, London SE16 3PB Tel. *020 72378800* Fax. *020 72377788* E-mail. *info@veeverscarter.co.uk* Web. *www.veeverscarter.co.uk Veevers Carter*

Vegetarian Society UK Ltd Parkdale Dunham Road, Altrincham WA14 4QG Tel. *0161 9252000* Fax. *0161 9269182* E-mail. *jon@vegsoc.org* Web. *www.vegsoc.org Cordon Vert – V.*

Velox Ltd Units 1-4 Manor Road Farm Barn Manor Road, Wantage OX12 8NE Tel. *01235 770133* Fax. *01235 770122* E-mail. *sales@veloxgrills.com* Web. *www.veloxgrills.com Flourish – Silesia Velox – Velox*

Vencel Resil Ltd Infinity House Anderson Way, Belvedere DA17 6BG Tel. *020 83209100* Fax. *020 83209110* E-mail. *admin@vencel.co.uk* Web. *www.vencel.co.uk Cameo – Covemaster – Fillmaster – Jabclad – Jabcore – Jabcork – Jabdec – Jablina – Jablite – Jablite Cavity – Jablite Flooring – Jablite Fulfil – Jablite Insulink – Jablite Roof Element – Jablite Roof Panel – Jablite Thermacel – Jablite WallLok – Jabperl – Jabroll – Jabsqueeze – Jabsueeze – Jarlite Roof Element – Joblite Roof Panel – Thermodek – VR Claymaster – VR Floatmaster – VR Interiors – VR Voidmaster – VR Warmaline*

Vendo plc 215 East Lane, Wembley HA0 3NG Tel. *020 89081234* Fax. *020 89042698* E-mail. *enquiries@pvcvendo.com* Web. *www.pvcvendo.com P.V.C. Vendo*

Ventcroft Ltd Faraday Road Astmoor Industrial Estate, Runcorn WA7 1PE Tel. *01928 581098* Fax. *01928 581099* E-mail. *sales@ventcroft.co.uk* Web. *www.ventcroft.co.uk Ventcroft*

Vent Engineering Unit 16c Chalwyn Industrial Estate St Clements Road, Poole BH12 4PE Tel. *01202 744958* Fax. *01202 733026* E-mail. *info@vent.co.uk* Web. *www.vent.co.uk Eco – Ventec*

Ventrolla Ltd Crimple Court Ventrolla House Hornbeam Square North, Harrogate HG2 8PB Tel. *01423 859323* Fax. *01423 859321* E-mail. *info@ventrolla.co.uk* Web. *www.ventrolla.co.uk Ventrolla*

Ventura Corporation Unit 1 Chancerygate Business Centre Molly Millars Lane, Wokingham RG41 2RF Tel. *0118 9772032* Fax. *0118 9891490* E-mail. *info@venturacorporation.co.uk* Web. *www.venturacorporation.co.uk Anvil R – Exit R – Inliners R – United Skates R*

Veolia Dock Road South, Wirral CH62 4SQ Tel. *0151 6444300* Fax. *0151 6444301* E-mail. *jenny.alexander@veolia.co.uk* Web. *www.veolia.co.uk P.43 – Sludgebuster*

Veolia Water Solutions & Technologies Whittle Road, Stoke On Trent ST3 7QD Tel. *01782 599000* Fax. *01782 599001* E-mail. *ian.ronson@veoliawater.com* Web. *www.veoliawaterst.co.uk Edwards & Jones – EJ*

Verbatim Ltd Prestige House 23-26 High Street, Egham TW20 9DU Tel. *01784 439781* Fax. *01784 470760* E-mail. *info@verbatim-europe.com* Web. *www.verbatim-europe.com DataLife – DataLifePlus*

Verco Office Furniture Ltd Chapel Lane, High Wycombe HP12 4BG Tel. *01494 448000* Fax. *01494 464216* E-mail. *sales@verco.co.uk* Web. *www.verco.co.uk Verco*

Verde Sports Cricket Ltd Gabbotts Farm Bury Lane, Withnell, Chorley PR6 8SW Tel. *01254 831666* Fax. *01254 831066* E-mail. *sales@verdesports.com* Web. *www.verdesports.com Bolltex (Range) – Mastergreen Indoor – Mastergreen Outdoor – Rinktex – Scanabowl – Scanagrene – Scanagrene/Verde Mat/Verde '95 – Ski – Super Verde Wilton Cricket Grass – Tracktex – Verde Artificial Grass – Verde Golf Driving Mat – Verde Tee Frame – Verde Weave – Verde WinterTee – Verdepitch – Verdeturf*

Verdict Gauge Ltd (a member of the M.J. Allen Group of Companies) Hilton Road, Ashford TN23 1EW Tel. *01233 631554* Fax. *01233 631888* E-mail. *sales@mjallen.co.uk* Web. *www.mjallen.co.uk Diatest – Mitotoyo – Priesser – Verdict – Verdict Gauge Ltd*

Verivide Ltd Quartz Close Enderby, Leicester LE19 4SG Tel. *0116 2847790* Fax. *0116 2847799* E-mail. *p.dakin@verivide.com* Web. *www.verivide.com VeriVide*

Vermeer UK 45-51 Rixon Road, Wellingborough NN8 4BA Tel. *01933 274400* Fax. *01933 274403* E-mail. *sales@vermeeruk.co.uk* Web. *www.vermeeruk.co.uk Vermeer*

Veronalder Ltd Unit 16 Chamberlayne Road Moreton Hall Industrial Estate, Bury St Edmunds IP32 7EY Tel. *01284 769565* Fax. *01284 768102* E-mail. *gill@veronalder.co.uk* Web. *www.veronalder.co.uk Unistrut*

Versaduct Sheet Metal Ltd Hoo Farm Industrial Estate Worcester Road, Kidderminster DY11 7RA Tel. *01562 824913* Fax. *01562 823809* E-mail. *enquiries@versaduct.co.uk* Web. *www.versaduct.co.uk Versaduct*

Versalift Distributors UK Ltd 1 Altendiez Way Burton Latimer, Kettering NN15 5YT Tel. *01536 721010* Fax. *01536 721111* E-mail. *admin@versalift.co.uk* Web. *www.versalift.co.uk Condor – EUROTEL – IAD – MEWP – Skyhigh – Time Export – Time Manufacturing – Versalift*

Versapak International Centurion Way, Erith DA18 4AF Tel. *020 83335353* Fax. *020 83122051* E-mail. *sales@versapak.co.uk* Web. *www.versapak.co.uk Versapak*

Version One Ltd Pentland House Village Way, Wilmslow SK9 2GH Tel. *01625 856500* Fax. *01625 856501* E-mail. *info@versionone.co.uk* Web. *www.versionone.co.uk DbArchive – DbAuthorise – DbCapture – DbChequePrint – DbForm*

vertex barrier systems uk Ltd Wyastone Business Park Wyastone Leys, Monmouth NP25 3SR Tel. *01600 891548* Fax. *01600 891568* E-mail. *info@vbsuk.co.uk* Web. *www.vbsuk.co.uk Seceuroglide Excel – Seceuromesh – Seceuroshield 3801 – Seceuroshield 7501 – Seceurovision 7501*

Verto Ltd Unit 14 Britannia Estate Leagrave Road, Luton LU3 1RJ Tel. *01582 410969* Fax. *01582 482557* E-mail. *paul.verto@virgin.net Verto*

Verto Data 33 Brickhill road, Sandy SG19 1JH Tel. *01767 683925* Fax. *07031 151701* E-mail. *sales@vertodata.net* Web. *www.vertodata.net Verto Data*

V E S Ltd Unit 3 Eagle Close, Chandler's Ford, Eastleigh SO53 4NF Tel. *08448 156060* Fax. *023 80261204* E-mail. *vesltd@ves.co.uk* Web. *www.ves.co.uk Adrecool – Airline – Ecopower – Ecovent – Hushvent – Max – Max-Rapide – Myflo – Rapide – Rex – Sam – Skyline – Tex – Twinimum – Weathermaster*

Vetigraph CAD/CAM Ltd Unit 4 Level 5 South Wing New England House, New England Street, Brighton BN1 4GH Tel. *01273 672400* E-mail. *vetigraph_uk@yahoo.co.uk* Web. *www.vetigraph.com GRAPHCAD – STYLGRAPH – VETIGRAPH*

Vetoquinol Ltd Vetoquinol House Great Slade, Buckingham Industrial Estate, Buckingham MK18 1PA Tel. *01280 814500* Fax. *01280 825462* E-mail. *office@vetoquinol.co.uk* Web. *www.vetoquinol.co.uk *Amoxinsol – *Chlorsol – *Grisol V – *Trimediazine – *Trimediazine B.M.P.*

V F Intimates Ltd Block L Westways Business Park Porterfield Road, Renfrew PA4 8DJ Tel. *0141 8854730* Fax. *0141 8854731* E-mail. *robert_latter@eu.vfblp.com Exquisite Form (Philippines)*

V F Northern Europe Ltd Park Road East Calverton, Nottingham NG14 6GD Tel. *0115 9656565* Fax. *0115 9657742* E-mail. *info@scs.com* Web. *www.vfc.com Wrangler*

V H S Hydraulic Components Ltd Unit 2 Carley Drive Westfield, Sheffield S20 8NQ Tel. *0114 2764430* Fax. *0114 2472526* E-mail. *info@hydraulic-components.net* Web. *www.hydraulic-components.net Casappa – Danfoss – Hydac – Hydrocar – Ikron – Oleostar – Rexroth – Sauer – Walvoil*

Viasat Broadcasting Group Ltd 7 Horton Industrial Park Horton Road, West Drayton UB7 8JD Tel. *01895 433433* Fax. *01895 446606* E-mail. *info@viasat.se* Web. *www.viasat.se Viasat*

Viaton Industries Ltd Brassington, Matlock DE4 4ES Tel. *01629 540373* Fax. *01629 540289* E-mail. *sales@viaton.com* Web. *www.viaton.com Airwhite – Barifine – Barytes – Colorana – Viacem*

Vibratory Stress Relieving Company Shrub Hill Industrial Estate Unit 13a, Worcester WR4 9EL Tel. *01905 731810* Fax. *01905 731811* E-mail. *enquiries@v-s-r.co.uk* Web. *www.v-s-r.co.uk Claxton – V.C.M. 80 – V.C.M. 90 – V.C.M. 905*

Benjamin R Vickers & Sons Ltd Clarence Road, Leeds LS10 1ND Tel. *0113 3867654* Fax. *0113 3867676* E-mail. *inbox@vickers-oil.com* Web. *www.vickers-oil.com Carmene – Carminol – Cirnedol – Conyl – Drawspin – Drycol – Electol – Frescol – Frescolene – Frescotex – Genpol – Gerol – Hydrol – Hydrox – Jenilube – Knitol – Laclube – Lainacomb – Lainasil – Lainaspin – Lainatwist – Mulsine – Neox – Noxol – Spinvol – Splashless – Spotless – Spraycot – Talene – Texturol – Thredol – Throwol – Travol – Travolene – Trinadol – Trinivol – Trixol – Vacrol – Vacspin – Vickerlube – Visconol – Vyklene – Vymol – Vymox – Vystat. P – Warnitol – Waxemul – Wyndol – Yarnemul – Yarnol*

Vickers Laboratories Ltd Grangefield Industrial Estate Richardshaw Road, Pudsey LS28 6QW Tel. *0113 2362811* Fax. *0113 2362703* E-mail. *info@viclabs.co.uk* Web. *www.viclabs.co.uk Optomer – Vickers On-Line*

Vicon Motion Systems Ltd Unit 14 7 West Way, Oxford OX2 0JB Tel. *01865 261800* Fax. *01865 240527* E-mail. *sales@vicon.com* Web. *www.vicon.com Vicon*

Victoria Carpets Ltd Worcester Road, Kidderminster DY10 1JR Tel. *01562 749300* Fax. *01562 749349* E-mail. *sales@victoriacarpets.com* Web. *www.victoriacarpets.com Arcadian – Brocade Filigree Axminster – Brocade Plain Wilton – Chateau Royale – Duchess – Firmtwist Elite – La Premiere Enhanced Graphic Tufted – Super Wyndham – The Natural Look*

Victor Manufacturing Ltd Lonsdale Works Gibson Street, Bradford BD3 9TF Tel. *01274 722125* Fax. *01274 307082* E-mail. *email@victormanufacturing.co.uk* Web. *www.victoronline.co.uk Victor Manufacturing Ltd*

Victor Marine Cosgrove Road, Grays RM20 3EE Tel. *01708 899780* Fax. *01708 890599* E-mail. *info@victormarine.com* Web. *www.victormarine.com Autoclude – Victor Pyrate*

Victor Products Ltd New York Way New York Industrial Park, Newcastle upon Tyne NE27 0QF Tel. *0191 2808000* Fax. *0191 2808080* E-mail. *sales@victor.co.uk* Web. *www.victor.co.uk Victor*

Victory Valve Sales Ltd (Head Office) Unit 12a Chalex Works, Manorhall Road, Southwick, Brighton BN42 4NH Tel. *01273 417398* Fax. *01273 430457* E-mail. *sales@segl.co.uk* Web. *www.segl.co.uk "Victory Flush Valves"*

Videcom International Ltd Newtown Road, Henley On Thames RG9 1HG Tel. *01491 578427* Fax. *01491 579368* E-mail. *info@videcom.com* Web. *www.videcom.com Videcom*

Video Arts Group Ltd Elsinore House 77 Fulham Palace Road, London W6 8JA Tel. *020 74004800* Fax. *020 74004900* E-mail. *maddison@videoarts.co.uk* Web. *www.videoarts.com Video Arts Interactive Learning*

Videonations Ltd Unit 20, Edward Court Altrincham Business Park, Altrincham, Manchester WA14 5GL Tel. *0845 0843010* Fax. *0845 0843020* E-mail. *info@videonations.com* Web. *www.videonations.com Aethra – Hitachi – NEC – Polycom – Sanyo – Sony – Tandberg*

Vidlink International Ltd 27 Maylands Avenue Hemel Hempstead Industrial Estate, Hemel Hempstead HP2 7DE Tel. *01442 431300* Fax. *01494 791127* E-mail. *sales@vislink.com* Web. *www.vidlink.com Continental Microwave – Advent – Gigawave – Link – MRC – PMR – LiveGear*

Viglen Technology Ltd 7 Handley Page Way Colney Street Colney Street, St Albans AL2 2DQ Tel. *01727 201800* Fax. *01727 201888* E-mail. *customercare@viglen.co.uk* Web. *www.viglen.co.uk Vigen Ltd*

Vigortronix Ltd 16 De Havilland Way Windrush Park, Witney OX29 0YG Tel. *01993 777570* Fax. *01993 777580* E-mail. *sales@vigortronix.com* Web. *www.vigortronix.com Vigortronix*

Vikan UK Ltd 1-3 Avro Gate South Marston Park, South Marston Industrial Estate, Swindon SN3 4AG Tel. *01793 716760* Fax. *01793 716761* E-mail. *sales@vikan.co.uk* Web. *www.vikan.co.uk Kleen (Denmark) – *Vikan Hygiene System (Denmark) – Vikan Transport System (Denmark) – Vikan UK (Denmark)*

Viking Johnson 46-48 Wilbury Way, Hitchin SG4 0UD Tel. *01462 443322* Fax. *01462 443311* E-mail. *sales@vikingjohnson.com* Web. *www.vikingjohnson.com Aquafast – AquaGrip – Dismantling Joints – EasiClamp, Tap – EasiCollar – EasiTee – FlexLock – HandiBand – HandiClamp – Juno – MaxiFit – Megafit – QuickFit – Viking Johnson*

Viking Optical Ltd Blyth Road Industrial Estate, Halesworth IP19 8EN Tel. *01986 875315* Fax. *01986 874788* E-mail. *enquiries@vikingoptical.co.uk* Web. *www.vikingoptical.co.uk *Femo (Sweden) – *Suunto (Finland) – Viking*

Vikoma International Ltd Kingston Road, East Cowes PO32 6JS Tel. *01983 200570* Fax. *023 80211644* E-mail. *sales@vikoma.com* Web. *www.vikoma.com Hi Sprint – Kebab T Disc Skimmer – Komara – Mini Vac – octopus pressure washer – Powervac – Sea Devil – Sentinel – Shore Guardian – TC 3 – Unicon Connectors – Vikotank – Vikotanks – Weirboom*

Vilene Interlinings Unit B9 Lowfields Close, Lowfields Business Park, Elland HX5 9DX Tel. *01422 327900* Fax. *01422 327999* E-mail. *per.henriksen@freudenberg-nw.com* Web. *www.freudenberg-nw.com Bondina – Viledon – Vilene – Vilmed*

V I L Resins Ltd Union Road Tonge Moor, Bolton BL2 2DT Tel. *01204 388800* Fax. *01204 362775* E-mail. *enquiries@vilresins.co.uk* Web. *www.vilresins.com V.I.L. – Vilamin – Vilaqua – Vilkyd – Vilosyn*

Vincents Norwich Ltd Priory Works Newton Street Newton St Faith, Norwich NR10 3AD Tel. *01603 891050* Fax. *01603 890689* E-mail. *post@vincents.co.uk* Web. *www.vincents.co.uk Flydor Products – Vincents*

Vinceremos Wines & Spirits Ltd Royal House 28 Sovereign Street, Leeds LS1 4BJ Tel. *0113 2440002* Fax. *0113 2884566* E-mail. *info@vinceremos.co.uk* Web. *www.vinceremos.co.uk *Eden Collection Organic Wines – Fairtrade Organic Wines from Stellar Organics & La Riojana – *La Nature Organic Wines – *Moroccan Wines From Celliers Meknes – *Pinkus Muller Organic German Beers*

Vinci plc Astral House Imperial Way, Watford WD24 4WW Tel. *01923 233433* Fax. *01923 256481* Web. *www.vinci.plc.uk Norwest Holst*

Vindotco UK Ltd 11a Elwes Street, Brigg DN20 8LB Tel. *01652 652444* Fax. *01652 652808* E-mail. *vindotco@compuserve.com* Web. *www.vindotco.co.uk Printer & Pressman – Professional – Really Works*

Vinola Knitwear 191 Ross Walk, Leicester LE4 5HH Tel. *0116 2681461* Fax. *0116 2665280* Web. *www.vinola.co.uk Faint – Miss Sparks – Suntoni*

The Vintners Selection Ltd The Barn Church Street, Corby Glen, Grantham NG33 4NJ Tel. *01476 550476* Fax. *01476 550777* E-mail. *sales@vintners.co.uk* Web. *www.vintners.co.uk *Dalva Ports – *Domaine St. Pierre – *Jerome Delahay – *P.H. Gerbaud*

The Vinyl Corporation Decalcraft Park Awsworth Lane, Cossall, Nottingham NG16 2SA Tel. *0115 9301133* Fax. *0115 9441778* E-mail. *dmtvc.march@btconnect.com* Web. *www.thevinylcorporation.co.uk mac tac avery*

Vinyl Fencing Ltd 16 Downs Walk, Peacehaven BN10 7RH Tel. *01273 587260* E-mail. *info@vinylfence.co.uk* Web. *www.vinylfence.co.uk Vinyl Fencing*

Viomedex Ltd Unit 13 Swan Barn Business Centre Old Swan Lane, Hailsham BN27 2BY Tel. *01323 446130* Fax. *01825 733407* E-mail. *vx@viomedex.com* Web. *www.viomedex.com Viomedex*

V I P Stonham Aspal, Stowmarket IP14 6AX Tel. *01473 890285* Fax. *01473 890764* E-mail. *sales@weatherwriter.co.uk* Web. *www.weatherwriter.com Geopuzzle – Green Card, The – Waterbook, The – Weatherwriter – Zecom*

V I P-polymers 15 Windover Road, Huntingdon PE29 7EB Tel. *01480 411333* Fax. *01480 450430* E-mail. *kim.turner@vip-polymers.com* Web. *www.vip-polymers.com Corrugasket*

Virbac Ltd Unit 16 Woolpit, Bury St Edmunds IP30 9UP Tel. *01359 243243* Fax. *01359 243200* E-mail. *enquiries@virbac.co.uk* Web. *www.virbac.co.uk *Albenil – *Equimax – Virbamec – Virbamec Pour-On – Virbamec Super*

Viresco UK Ltd 50a Market Place, Thirsk YO7 1LH Tel. *01845 525585* Fax. *01845 523133* E-mail. *sales@viresco-uk.com* Web. *www.viresco-uk.com *Humate (U.S.A.) – Squelch – Viresco*

Viridian Group Ltd PO Box 2, Belfast BT9 5HT Tel. *028 90668416* Fax. *028 90689117* E-mail. *harry.mccracken@viridiangroup.co.uk* Web. *www.viridiangroup.co.uk Energia*

Visa Energy GB Ltd 400 Pavilion Drive, Northampton NN4 7PA Tel. *01604 410838* Fax. *0844 8007311* E-mail. *enquiries@visaenergy.com* Web. *www.visaenergy.com VISA ENERGY ELECTRICITY GENERATORS*

Visa Hand Tools Ltd Gibson House Barrowby Lane, Garforth, Leeds LS25 1NG Tel. *0113 2869245* Fax. *0113 2866859* E-mail. *sales@visatools.co.uk* Web. *www.visatools.co.uk Diamond Joe*

Viscose Closures Ltd Unit 1 Royce Road, Crawley RH10 9JY Tel. *01293 519251* Fax. *01293 540005* E-mail. *sales@viscose.co.uk* Web. *www.viscose.co.uk Viskproof – Viskring*

Viscount Catering Ltd Enodis UK Food Service Provincial Park Nether Lane, Ecclesfield, Sheffield S35 9ZX Tel. *0114 2570100* Fax. *0114 2570251* E-mail. *ccommile@viscount-catering.co.uk* Web. *www.viscount-catering.com *Lincoln*

Vishay Ltd Pallion Trading Estate, Sunderland SR4 6SU Tel. *0191 5144155* Fax. *0191 5678662* E-mail. *paul.robson@vishay.com* Web. *www.vishay.com Roederstein Capacitors – Sprague Capacitors – Vitramon*

Visilume Ltd High Street West, Glossop SK13 8ER Tel. *01457 865700* Fax. *01923 211432* E-mail. *sales@visilume.com* Web. *www.visilume.com *L J Star (U.S.A.) – *Lumiglas (Germany) – *Metaglas (Germany) – *Vaihinger (Germany)*

Vision Engineering Ltd Monument Way West Monument House, Woking GU21 5EN Tel. *01483 248300* Fax. *01483 248301* E-mail. *mark.curtis@visioneng.co.uk* Web. *www.visioneng.com Alpha – Beta – Dynascope – Hawk – Isis – Kestrel – Lynx – Mantis – Vision Engineering Ltd*

Vision Express UK Abbeyfield Road Lenton, Nottingham NG7 2SP Tel. *0115 9865225* Fax. *0115 9850974* Web. *www.visionexpress.com Vision Express (UK) Ltd*

Vi Spring Ltd Ernesettle Lane, Plymouth PL5 2TT Tel. *01752 366311* Fax. *01752 355109* E-mail. *sales@vispring.co.uk* Web. *www.vi-spring.co.uk Baronet – Baronet Supreme – Bedstead Mattress – Bedstead Supreme Mattress – Classic – Classic Supreme – Earl – Earl Supreme – Elite – Herald – Herald Supreme – Realm – Realm Supreme – Regal – Regal Supreme – Signatory – Sublime – Tiara – Tiara Supreme*

Visqueen Building Products South Wales Ltd Maerdy Industrial Estate Rhymney, Tredegar NP22 5PY Tel. *01685 840672* Fax. *01685 842580* E-mail. *steveharris@visqueenbuilding.co.uk* Web. *www.visqueenbuilding.co.uk Visqueen – Zedex*

Vita Group Times Place 45 Pall Mall, London SW1Y 5JG Tel. *07740 770424* Fax. *01625 574075* E-mail. *info@thevitagroup.com* Web. *www.kay-metzeler.co.uk Kay-Metzeler*

Vita Liquid Polymers Harling Road Sharston Industrial Area, Manchester M22 4SZ Tel. *0161 9983226* Fax. *0161 9460118* E-mail. *info@vita-liquid.co.uk* Web. *www.vita-liquid.co.uk Diptex – Easifoam – Flooring* *services – Floortex – Prevul – Sealex – Tuftex – Vitachem – Vitaplas*

Vitalograph UK Ltd Vitalograph Business Park Maids Moreton, Buckingham MK18 1SW Tel. *01280 827110* Fax. *01280 823302* E-mail. *sales@vitalograph.co.uk* Web. *www.vitalograph.co.uk Vitalograph*

Vitax Ltd Owen Street, Coalville LE67 3DE Tel. *01530 510060* Fax. *01530 510299* E-mail. *julian.plews@vitax.co.uk* Web. *www.vitax.co.uk Bordeaux Mixture – Casoron G4 – Derris Dust – Fruit Tree Grease – Green Sulphur – Green Up – Green Up Feed & Weed & Moss Killer – Green Up Weedfree – Hormone Rooting Powder – House Plant – Hydrangea Colourant – Medo – Nippon – Py – S.B.K. – Scent-Off – Spray 'N' Save Aerosol – Stay Off – Tenax – Vitafeeds – Vitax – Vitax Blood, Fish and Bone – Vitax Bonemeal – Vitax Claybreaker – Vitax Conifer & Shrub – Vitax Garden Lime – Vitax Growmore – Vitax Irish Moss Peat – Vitax Q4 – Vitax Q4 Multipurpose Compost – Vitax Q4 Rose Food – Woolmoss – Yellow Sulphur*

Vitcas Ltd Refractories 8 Bonville Road, Bristol BS4 5NZ Tel. *0117 9117895* Fax. *0117 9711152* E-mail. *info@vitcas.com* Web. *www.vitcas.com Aciduma – Alcuma – Aluma – F.J.C. – Fixatile – Jetcem – Kos – Mouldable – Purimachos – Pyruma – Refractory Glaze Wash – Siluma – Tiluma – X.L.*

Vitco Ltd Vitco House 58 Derby Street, Manchester M8 8HF Tel. *0161 8343579* Fax. *0161 8340471* E-mail. *admin@vitco.co.uk* Web. *www.vitco.co.uk Joysonic – Unistar – *Vitco (Far East)*

Vitec (British Vita) Oldham Road Middleton, Manchester M24 2DB Tel. *0161 6431133* Fax. *0161 6548942* E-mail. *info@vcfuk.com* Web. *www.vitecuk.com Carbotec – Flexitec – Flexmount – Gausstat – Improcel – Puripore – Pyroflex – Pyrosorb – Revesorb – Sipurtec – Statease – Teslatec – Triohmic – Vitaseal*

Vivalis Ltd 22 Grimrod Place, Skelmersdale WN8 9UU Tel. *01695 727317* Fax. *01932 733401* E-mail. *contactus@vivalis.co.uk* Web. *www.vivalis.co.uk Beauty Without Cruelty – Eye Zone Fade Cream – Fade-Out – Hands & Feet – High Colour Control Cream – Hydrowave 2000 – Pin-Up – Skinicles – Taylor of London*

Vivat Direct Limited ((t/a Reader's Digest) 157 Edgware Road, London W2 2HR Tel. *020 70534500* Fax. *020 77158181* E-mail. *info@readersdigest.co.uk* Web. *www.readersdigest.co.uk Reader's Digest Association Ltd – Readers Digest*

Vivimed Labs Europe Ltd PO Box b3, Huddersfield HD1 6BU Tel. *01484 320500* Fax. *01484 320300* E-mail. *sales@vivimedlabs.com* Web. *www.vivimedlabs.com Jarocol – Reversacol – Reversacol - Jarocol*

Vocalink Ltd Drake House Three Rivers Court Homestead, Rickmansworth WD3 1FX Tel. *08700 100699* Web. *www.vocalink.com Bacsafe – Bacstel*

Vodafone Retail Ltd Vodafone House The Connection, Newbury RG14 2FN Tel. *01635 33251* Fax. *01635 45713* E-mail. *info@vodafone.co.uk* Web. *www.vodafone.co.uk C.D.L.C – Citifone – Comcall – Eurocall – Europage – Keycall – Messenger – Metrocall – Micracall – Microcall – On-Call Receptionist – Premierzone – Selectzone – Tonecall – V.M.A.C.S. – Victor Vodac Device – Voda – Vodabase – Vodabit – Vodabreak – Vodac GSM – Vodac PCN – Vodacall – Vodacard – Vodacare – Vodacarte – Vodacom – Vodaconnect – Vodafax – Vodafone – Vodafone Call Manager – Vodafone Creditcall – Vodafone Creditfone – Vodafone Euro Digital – Vodafone GSM – Vodafone Metro Digital – Vodafone PCN – Vodafone Recall – Vodahire – Vodalert – Vodaline – Vodalink – Vodalux – Vodamap – Vodanational – Vodanet – Vodapage – Vodapage Codecall – Vodapoint – Vodarent – Vodaservice – Vodashop – Vodassure – Vodastream – Vodastream Fax – Vodata – Vodatel – Vodatelcom – Vodawatch*

Voiplex 5 Astwood Mews, London SW7 4DE Tel. *020 71008071* E-mail. *info@voiplex.co.uk* Web. *www.voiplex.co.uk Voiplex*

Volex Group Ltd 10 Eastbourne Terrace, London W2 6LG Tel. *020 33708830* Fax. *01925 830141* E-mail. *wtate@volex-group.com* Web. *www.volex.com Ionix – Pencon – Volex – Volex Group – Volex Powercords – Volex Wiring Systems*

Volkerhighways Ltd Hertford Road, Hoddesdon EN11 9BX Tel. *01992 305000* Fax. *01992 446862* E-mail. *enquiries@volkerfitzpatrick.co.uk* Web. *www.volkerhighways.co.uk Fitzpatrick*

Volkmann UK Ltd Unit 50 Cressex Enterprise Centre Lincoln Road, High Wycombe HP12 3RL Tel. *01494 512228* Fax. *01494 512228* E-mail. *mw@volkmann-vacuum.com* Web. *www.volkmann.info Volkmann*

Vollmer UK Ltd Unit 2 Orchard Park Industrial Estate Sandiacre, Nottingham NG10 5BP Tel. *0115 9491040* Fax. *0115 9490042* E-mail. *admin@vollmer-uk.com* Web. *www.vollmer-group.com Akemat – Akernat – Alligator – Ideal – Loroch – Reform – Rivo – Vollmer – Vollmer Kegel-Sport – Widma*

Volumatic Ltd 1a Taurus House Endemere Road, Coventry CV6 5PY Tel. *024 76684217* Fax. *024 76638155* E-mail. *info@volumatic.com* Web. *www.volumatic.com Check-a-Note – Halo – Omal – Polymirror – Videoguard – Volumatic*

Volvo Penta UK (c/o Volvo Group UK Ltd) Wedgnock Lane, Warwick CV34 5YA Tel. *01926 622500* E-mail. *info.vpuk@volvo.com* Web. *www.volvopenta.co.uk Volvo Penta*

Vortex Hydra UK Ltd Kingmoor Industrial Estate Kingmoor Road, Carlisle CA3 9QJ Tel. *01228 510800* Fax. *01228 510808* E-mail. *matt_mccaffrey@vortexhydra.com* Web. *www.vortexhydra.com Annith – Russell – Uno Systems – Vortex Hydra*

Vortok International 3 Western Wood Way Langage Science Park, Plymouth PL7 5BG Tel. *01752 349200* Fax. *01752 338855* E-mail. *sales@vortok.co.uk* Web. *www.vortok.co.uk Vortok*

Votex Hereford Ltd Redhill Depot Redhill, Hereford HR2 8BH Tel. *01432 274361* Fax. *01432 352743* E-mail. *sales@votex.co.uk* Web. *www.votex.co.uk Votex*

V P plc Central House Beckwith Knowle Otley Road, Beckwithshaw, Harrogate HG3 1UD Tel. *01423 533400* Fax. *01423 565657* E-mail. *enquiries@vpplc.com* Web. *www.vpplc.com Groundforce – Safety Services – Vibroplant – Vibroplant - Compressed Air – Vibroplant - Power Generation – Vibroplant - Powered Access – Vibroplant P.L.C. – Vibroplant- Welding Division – Vibroplant-Recycling Division*

Vredestein UK Ltd Unit D Whittle Close Park Farm Industrial Estate, Wellingborough NN8 6TY Tel. *01933 677770* Fax. *01933 675329* E-mail. *bettsm@vredestein.com* Web. *www.vredestein.com Maloya – Vredestein*

V S M Abrasives Ltd 20-21 Heathfield Stacey Bushes, Milton Keynes MK12 6HP Tel. *01908 310207* Fax. *01908 310208* E-mail. *sales@vsm.co.uk* Web. *www.vsm.co.uk Vitex (Germany) – VSM (Germany)*

Vtech Electronics UK plc Napier Court Barton Lane, Abingdon OX14 3YT Tel. *01235 555545* Fax. *01235 546805* E-mail. *steve_mason@vtech.com* Web. *www.vtechuk.com Alphabet Writing Desk – Baby Bear Phone – Baby Driver – Baby Shapes 'N Things – Capsela Science Toys – Learning Pad – Little Smart Smarty Junior – Magic Letters – Master Video Painter – My First Words – PC Power Pad – Pre Computer Graduate – Pre Computer Notebook II – Pre Computer Prestige – Press N' Play Ball – Press N' Play Block – School Talk – Smart Keys – Smart Start Basic Plus – Smart Start Elite – Smart Start Premier – Talk 'N Smile Farm – Talk 'N Tell Phone – Talk 'N Type – Talking Alphabet Desk – Talking Alphabet Picture Desk – Talking Battleship Command – Talking Driving School – Talking Einstein – Talking First Steps Baby Walker – Talking Number Desk – Talking Phone Pals – Talking Smart Start Scholar – Talking Whiz Kid Animated – Talking Whiz Kid Mouse Pro – Talking Whiz Kid Power Mouse – Telephone Answering Machine – Tiny Touch Camera – Tiny Touch Phone – Touch 'N Turn Book – Wizard & Mini Wizard – World Wizard Traveller*

V3 Technologies Coble Dene Road, North Shields NE29 6DE Tel. *0191 2595544* Fax. *0191 2595544* E-mail. *info@v3technologies.com* Web. *www.v3technologies.com E-Portfolio – Live Lecture – Web conferencing*

V T S Royalite Cliftonhall Road, Newbridge EH28 8PW Tel. *0131 3332819* Fax. *0131 3335161* E-mail. *sales@vtsroyalite.co.uk* Web. *www.vitasheetgroup.com A.B.S. – A.B.S.*

Vuba Industrial Supplies 37 Robin Close, Brough HU15 1RY Tel. *01482 665050* Fax. *01482 424081* E-mail. *info@vuba-group.co.uk* Web. *www.vubasupplies.co.uk Vuba-Coat – Vuba-Patch Repair*

Vulcana Gas Appliances Ltd 30 Bridge Road, Haywards Heath RH16 1TX Tel. *01444 415871* Fax. *01444 441433* E-mail. *vulcanagas@pavilion.co.uk* Web. *www.vulcanagas.com Kestrel – Temcana*

Vulcan Refractories Ltd Brookhouse Industrial Estate Cheadle, Stoke On Trent ST10 1PN Tel. *01538 752238* Fax. *01538 753349* E-mail. *nicholas@vulcan-refractories.co.uk* Web. *www.vulcan-refractories.co.uk Vulcasil – Vulcatherm*

Vulco Spring & Presswork Co. Ltd Evesham Road Astwood Bank, Redditch B96 6DU Tel. *01527 892447* Fax. *01527 892196* E-mail. *sales@vulcosprings.com* Web. *www.vulcosprings.com Vulco Spring*

Vycon Products Ltd 57c Main Street Auchinleck, Cumnock KA18 2AF Tel. *01290 425463* Fax. *01290 420311* E-mail. *sales@vycon.co.uk* Web. *www.vycon.co.uk C M L*

George Vyner Ltd Simplex House Mytholmbridge Mills, Holmfirth HD9 7TZ Tel. *01484 685221* Fax. *01484 688538 Simplex*

Vysionics Unit 3 Fishponds Close, Wokingham RG41 2QA Tel. *0118 9792077* Fax. *0118 9774734* E-mail. *kevin.chevis@vysionics.com* Web. *www.vysionics.com ICS – NRS – Reader – Scanmaster – Smart Junior – Smart Reflow – Smart Truline – TAS – Tracker 2 – Videogauge*

W

Wabco Automotive UK Ltd Grange Valley Road, Batley WF17 6GH Tel. *01924 595400* Fax. *0113 2526162* E-mail. *dave.rickell@wabco-auto.com* Web. *www.wabco-auto.com Clayton Dewandre – WABCO – Wabco UK*

W A Cooke & Sons Ellesmere Works Southern Street, Worsley, Manchester M28 3QN Tel. *01204 574721* Fax. *01204 861778* E-mail. *admin@wacooke.co.uk* Web. *www.wacooke.co.uk Ri-Jac*

Harvey Waddington Murray Road, Orpington BR5 3RA Tel. *01689 877020* Fax. *01689 877027* E-mail. *smoon@teepol.co.uk* Web. *www.teepol.co.uk Tagfresh – Teepol ,Teepol HB7,Teepol Multipurpose,Teepol Gold,Teepol 30%,Teepol GD51,Teepol GD53,Teepol 310,Teepol L*

Wade Building Services Ltd Groveland Road, Tipton DY4 7TN Tel. *0121 5208121* Fax. *0121 5577061* E-mail. *sales@wade-bs.co.uk* Web. *www.wade-bs.co.uk Dorman Long Lintels*

Wade International Ltd Third Avenue, Halstead CO9 2SX Tel. *01787 475151* Fax. *01787 475579* E-mail. *sales@wade.eu* Web. *www.wade.eu Actimatic – E.T.U. – Jubilee – Multi-level – P.P.P. – Streamline – Super Seal – Vari-level – Wade*

WAGO Ltd Triton Park Swift Valley Industrial Estate, Rugby CV21 1SG Tel. *01788 568008* Fax. *01788 568050* E-mail. *uksales@wago.com* Web. *www.wago.com Cage Clamp – ProServe – Protect – Topjob S – Toplon – Winsta – Winsta, Toplon, Protect. – X-Com*

Wahoo Enterprises Limited 9 Laburnum Court, Harrow HA1 4YD Tel. *0844 7403213* E-mail. *info@wahooenterprises.biz* Web. *www.wahooenterprises.biz Wahoo – Tien Ying*

Waiter's Friend Company Ltd Unit 12 Quadrum Park Old Portsmouth Road, Peasmarsh, Guildford GU3 1LU Tel. *01483 560695* Fax. *01483 458080* E-mail. *sales@waitersfriend.com* Web. *www.waitersfriend.com Drop Stop – PresorVac (TM) – SLO FLO – The Tasting Game – The Waiters Friend – Thirst Aid*

Wakefield Brush UK Ltd Unit 8 Newhaven Business Park Lowergate, Milnsbridge, Huddersfield HD3 4HS Tel. *01484 642555* Fax. *01484 642888* E-mail. *sales@wakefieldbrushcompany.co.uk* Web. *www.wakefieldbrushcompany.co.uk Firmflex – Wakefield*

The Wakefield Shirt Company Limited Thornes Lane Wharf, Wakefield WF1 5RL Tel. *01924 375651* Fax. *01924 290096* E-mail. *marketing@wsg.co.uk* Web. *www.wsg.co.uk Double Two – Double Two – Jet – Mudie – Threadneedle – Topflight*

Walcon Marine Ltd Cockerell Close Segensworth West, Fareham PO15 5SR Tel. *01489 579977* Fax. *01489 579988* E-mail. *sales@walconmarine.com* Web. *www.walconmarine.com Walcon Marine*

James Walker Moorflex Ltd John Escritt Road, Bingley BD16 2BS Tel. *01274 562211* Fax. *01274 566623* E-mail. *sales.moorflex.uk@jameswalker.biz* Web. *www.jameswalker.biz Moorside – Metaflex*

Walkers Shortbread Ltd Aberlour House, Aberlour AB38 9LD Tel. *01340 871555* Fax. *01340 871355* E-mail. *enquiries@walkers-shortbread.co.uk* Web. *www.walkersshortbread.co.uk Duchy Original – Walkers*

Walker Timber Ltd Carriden Sawmills, Boness EH51 9SN Tel. *01506 823331* Fax. *01506 822590* E-mail. *jccampbelln@walkertimber.com* Web. *www.walkertimber.com Dundas Building Co. – Heatkeeper Homes – Walker Timber Frame – Walker Windows – Walker Woodstock*

Wallace & Tiernan Ltd (Chemfeed Limited) Priory Works Five Oak Green Road, Tonbridge TN11 0QL Tel. *01732 771777* Fax. *01732 771800* E-mail. *sales@wallace-tiernan.com* Web. *www.siemens.com Chemtube – Depolox – Depotrol – Encore – O.S.E.C. – Polyprep – Stranco – V-Notch – Water Champ (U.S.A.)*

Wall Colmonoy Ltd Alloy Industrial Estate Pontardawe, Swansea SA8 4HL Tel. *01792 862287* Fax. *01792 830124* E-mail. *sales@wallcolmonoy.co.uk* Web. *www.wallcolmonoy.co.uk Colmonoy – Colmonoy, Fusewelder, Nicrobraz, Nicrocoat, Nicrogap, Spraywelder, Stop-Off, Wallex – Fusewelder – Nicrobraz – Nicrocoat – Nicrogap – Spraywelder – Stop-Off – Wallex*

Waller Eurosel 43 Bridgeman Terrace, Wigan WN1 1TT Tel. *01942 234897* Fax. *01942 496276* E-mail. *info@waller-eurosel.co.uk* Web. *www.waller-eurosel.co.uk *Nor Reg norway (Norway)*

Wallgate Crow Lane Wilton, Salisbury SP2 0HB Tel. *01722 744594* Fax. *01722 742096* E-mail. *sales@wallgate.com* Web. *www.wallgate.com Wallgate*

Walling UK Ltd Kirk House Over Kellet, Carnforth LA6 1DX Tel. *01524 732370* Fax. *01524 720113* E-mail. *sales@wallinguk.com* Web. *www.wallinguk.com Fendt – Ford – Massey*

Wallis Office Furniture Ltd 8-18 Fowler Road Hainault Industrial Estate, Ilford IG6 3UT Tel. *020 85009991* Fax. *020 85001949* E-mail. *info@wallisoffice.com* Web. *www.wallisoffice.com Chair People, The – Screen People, The*

Walsall Locks Ltd Leamore Close Leamore Enterprise Park, Walsall WS2 7NL Tel. *01922 494101* Fax. *01922 403772* E-mail. *sales@walsall-locks.co.uk* Web. *www.walsall-locks.co.uk Ace – Walsall – Zeni*

Walsall Pressings Co. Ltd Wednesbury Road, Walsall WS1 4JW Tel. *01922 721152* Fax. *01922 721106* E-mail. *info@walpres.co.uk* Web. *www.walpres.co.uk Walpres*

Walter GB Ltd Unit 1 The Courtyard Buntsford Drive, Bromsgrove B60 3DJ Tel. *01527 839450* Fax. *01527 839499* E-mail. *service.uk@walter-tools.com* Web. *www.walter-tools.com Alpha – Alpha 2 – Alpha 22 – Alpha 4 – Alpha 4 Plus – Alpha 4 Plus Micro – Alpha 4 TFT 8XD – Alpha 44 – Alpha TFT 12XD – Alphajet – Megajet – Megajet Hochleistungbohrer – Sprint – Sprint Gewindebohrer – Titex Plus – UFL*

Walter Machines UK Ltd Represented by K--rber Schleifring UK Unit B13 Holly Farm Business Park Honiley, Kenilworth CV8 1NP Tel. *01926 485047* Fax. *01926 485049* E-mail. *info@walter-machines.com* Web. *www.walter-machines.com CYBER GRINDING – HELICHECK – Helitronic - Helicheck - Helitronic Tool Studio - Cyber Grinding – HELITRONIC TOOL STUDIO – HELTRONIC*

Stephen Walters & Sons Ltd Sudbury Silk Mills, Sudbury CO10 2XB Tel. *01787 372266* Fax. *01787 880126* E-mail. *sales@stephenwalters.co.uk* Web. *www.stephenwalters.co.uk Walters*

Walters & Walters Ltd Unit 16 Orchard Road, Royston SG8 5HA Tel. *01763 245445* Fax. *01763 249810* E-mail. *sales@waltersandwalters.co.uk* Web. *www.industrial-markers.co.uk Flomark – Walters*

Walton Engineering Co. Ltd 61 London Road, St Albans AL1 1LJ Tel. *01727 855616* Fax. *01727 841145* E-mail. *pkemp@waltonengineering.co.uk* Web. *www.waltonengineering.co.uk Walton*

Wam Engineering Unit 13 Alexandra Way, Ashchurch, Tewkesbury GL20 8NB Tel. *01684 299100* Fax. *01684 299104* E-mail. *fabrizio@wameng.com* Web. *www.wamgroup.com WAM*

Wandsworth Group Ltd Albert Drive Sheerwater, Woking GU21 5SE Tel. *01483 740740* Fax. *01483 740384* E-mail. *info@wandsworthgroup.com* Web. *www.wandsworthgroup.com Bunnie – Palace Series 2 – Palace Series 3 – QD – Safeguard – Tele-call – Wandsworth – Water Bunnie*

Warden Plastics Luton Ltd Unit 31 Sundon Business Park Dencora Way, Luton LU3 3HP Tel. *01582 573030* Fax. *01582 508751* E-mail. *admin@wardenplastics.co.uk* Web. *www.wardenplastics.co.uk Amity – Plasticuet*

Wardray Premise Ltd 3 Hampton Court Estate Summer Road, Thames Ditton KT7 0SP Tel. *020 83989911* Fax. *020 83988032* E-mail. *sales@wardray-premise.com* Web. *www.wardray-premise.com Premac – Premadex – Wardray*

Wardsflex Ltd Unit 22 James Carter Road, Mildenhall, Bury St Edmunds IP28 7DE Tel. *01638 778666* Fax. *01638 716863* E-mail. *sales@wardsflex.co.uk* Web. *www.wardsflex.co.uk Nucana – Nuflex – Rotoworm – Steelkane – Wardwinch*

T W Ward CNC Machinery Ltd Savile Street, Sheffield S4 7UD Tel. *0114 2765411* Fax. *0114 2700786* E-mail. *sales@wardcnc.com* Web. *www.wardcnc.com Hankook – Hartford – Soraluce – Taiwan Takaswai – Toshulin – Ward CNC Retrofit*

Warlord Contract Carpets Ltd Stanley Mills, Stonehouse GL10 3HQ Tel. *01453 821800* Fax. *01453 791167* E-mail. *sales@warlordcarpets.co.uk* Web. *www.warlordcarpets.co.uk Alpha – Alpha Cord – Braemar – Camouflage – Delta Cord – Delta Plus – Glencoe – Kinross – Martred – Montrose – Saxon Velours – Traffic Zone – Trident Broadcord – Vulcan – Woodstock – Wychwood*

Warrens Display Ltd 359 Burley Road, Leeds LS4 2PX Tel. *0113 2783614* Fax. *0113 2744300* E-mail. *sales@warrens.co.uk* Web. *www.warrens.co.uk Photolabs*

Warwick & Bailey Engineering Witton Mill Stancliffe Street, Blackburn BB2 2QU Tel. *01254 662211* Fax. *01254 662277* E-mail. *sales@warwick-bailey.com* Web. *www.warwick-bailey.com Fuel Tanks – Hydraulic Tanks*

Warwick Evans Optical Co. Ltd 22 Palace Road, London N11 2PS Tel. *020 88880051* Fax. *020 88889055* E-mail. *sales@keystonevision.com* Web. *www.keystonevision.com *All Optik (Sweden) – *Gern Optik (Switzerland) – *Keystone (U.S.A.) – *Keyvox-Benelux (Netherlands) - *Kir Opas (Norway) – *Telebinocular (U.S.A.)*

Warwick Fraser & Co. Ltd Spring Gate Guildford Road, Loxwood, Billingshurst RH14 0QL Tel. *01403 752469* Fax. *01403 752469* E-mail. *sales@warwickfraser.co.uk* Web. *www.warwickfraser.co.uk LanSolve Racking – Polaris – Rosengrens*

Warwick Machinery Ltd Unit 6 Budbrooke Road Budbrooke Industrial Estate, Warwick CV34 5XH Tel. *01926 497806* Fax. *01926 401039* E-mail. *imcdonald@ywmuk.com* Web. *www.warwickmachinery.co.uk Enshu – Kira – Takamaz*

Warwick Test Supplies 93a Warwick Road, Kenilworth CV8 1HP Tel. *01926 851007* Fax. *01926 851588* E-mail. *steve@warwickts.com* Web. *www.warwickts.com Concord – Ez-Hook – Hirschmann – Meterman – Pomoma – Winslow*

Washington Mills Electro Minerals Ltd Mosley Road Trafford Park, Manchester M17 1NR Tel. *0161 8480271* Fax. *0161 8722974* E-mail. *sales@washingtonmills.co.uk* Web. *www.washingtonmills.co.uk Blastite – Duralum – Duralum - Blastite - Silcaride - Dynamag - Duramul - Durazon. – Duramul – Durazon – Dynamag – Silcaride*

Washtec UK Ltd 14a Oak Industrial Park Chelmsford Road, Dunmow CM6 1XN Tel. *01371 878800* Fax. *01371 878810* E-mail. *sales@washtec-uk.com* Web. *www.washtec-uk.com SOFTECS – Softwash – Softwash - SOFTECS*

W A S P Ltd (Wessex Advanced Switching Products Ltd) Alexandria Park 1 Penner Road, Havant PO9 1QY Tel. *023 92457000* Fax. *023 92473918* E-mail. *sales@wasp-ltd.co.uk* Web. *www.waspswitches.co.uk Wasp*

Waste Tech Environmental Ltd Foggathorpe, Selby YO8 6PX Tel. *01757 288022* E-mail. *info@wte-ltd.co.uk* Web. *www.wte-ltd.co.uk Biorock – Crystal Biodigester – Crystal ECO*

Watco UK Ltd Watco House Filmer Grove, Godalming GU7 3AL Tel. *01483 425000* Fax. *01483 428888* E-mail. *sales@watco.co.uk* Web. *www.watco.co.uk Concrex – Timberex – Watco*

Water Of Ayr Dalmore Stair, Mauchline KA5 5PA Tel. *01292 591204 Dalmore Bluestone – Tam O'Shanter – Water of Ayr*

Waterbird Parakites 27 Blue Chalet Industrial Park West Kingsdown, Sevenoaks TN15 6BQ Tel. *01474 854352* Fax. *01474 854474* E-mail. *info@waterbird.co.uk* Web. *www.waterbird.co.uk Water Bird*

Waterloo Air Products 111 Mills Road Quarry Wood, Aylesford ME20 7NB Tel. *01622 717861* Fax. *01622 718863* E-mail. *sales@waterloo.co.uk* Web. *www.waterloo.co.uk Absolute – Aircell – Automatic 'S' Mat – Climatair – Dedust – North Star – Odo-Vent – Ozocap – Ozoflo – Ozokleen – Ozopleat – Ozotex – Ventex*

Watermota Ltd Cavalier Road Heathfield Industrial Estate, Newton Abbot TQ12 6TQ Tel. *01626 830910* Fax. *01626 830911* E-mail. *info@watermota.co.uk* Web. *www.watermota.co.uk C R M Marine Engines – CT Marine – *Daewoo Marine Engines – Watermota – Westerbeke*

Waters 730-740 Centennial Park Centennial Way, Elstree, Borehamwood WD6 3SZ Tel. *020 82386100* Fax. *020 82077070* E-mail. *uk@waters.com* Web. *www.waters.com AutoSpec (United Kingdom) – GCT (United Kingdom) – LCT (United Kingdom) – M@LDI HT (United Kingdom) – MassLynx 4.0 (United Kingdom) – MassPREP Station (United Kingdom) – ProteinLynx GS 2.0 (United Kingdom) – ProteomeWorks System (United Kingdom) – Q-Tof micro (United Kingdom) – Q-Tof Ultima (United Kingdom) – Quattro micro (United Kingdom) – Quattro Ulitima (United Kingdom)*

Waterspace Developments Limited Unit K5 South Point Clos Marian, Cardiff CF10 4LQ Tel. *07860 734600* E-mail. *steve.evans@floating-offices.co.uk* Web. *www.floating-offices.co.uk H2Office or Floating Offices*

Watford Control Instruments Ltd Godwin Road, Corby NN17 4DS Tel. *01536 401345* Fax. *01536 401164* E-mail. *sales@watfordcontrol.co.uk* Web. *www.watfordcontrol.co.uk Rotavolt – Rotavolt - variable transformers.*

Watkins Hire Ltd 48 Grange Park Road, Manchester M9 7AH Tel. *0161 7958666* Fax. *0161 7958008* E-mail. *mark.whittle@watkinshire.co.uk* Web. *www.watkinshire.co.uk Watkins Hire Ltd*

Watkins Hire Steam Boiler Hire Division Southern United Kingdom New Dunn Business Park Sling, Coleford GL16 8JD Tel. *020 86670088* Fax. *01594 837463* E-mail. *mark.hills@watkinshire.co.uk* Web. *www.watkinshire.co.uk Watkins Boilers*

Watlow Ltd Robey Close Linby, Nottingham NG15 8AA Tel. *0115 9640777* Fax. *0115 9640071* E-mail. *ahalton@watlow.co.uk* Web. *www.watlow.co.uk WATLOW – WATLOW.COM – E-SAFE – DIN-A-MITE – FIREBAR – CAST-X – EASY CABLE – EHG SL10 – EXACTSENSE – EZ-ZONE – FIREROD – FREEFLEX – MINICHEF – MODULE-MOUNT – RAYMAX – RELIALINE – SERV-RITE – STRETCH-TO-LENGTH – THERMASLEEVE – THERMOPOLYMER – THINBAND – ULTRAMIC – W & Design – WATLOW – XACTEMP – XACTPAK*

Watson Diesel Ltd Ronian Works Elm Grove, London SW19 4HE Tel. *020 88793854* Fax. *08704 441386* E-mail. *sales@watsondiesel.com* Web. *www.watsondiesel.com *Bosch (Germany) – *Delphi (U.S.A.) – *Stanadyne (U.S.A.)*

Watson Group Ltd Netherwood Heath Farmhouse Netherwood Lane, Solihull B93 0BB Tel. *01724 898252* Fax. *0121 7111086* E-mail. *enquiries@watson-group.co.uk* Web. *www.watson-group.co.uk Exquisite*

Henry Watson Potteries Ltd Pottery Hill Wattisfield, Diss IP22 1NH Tel. *01359 251239* Fax. *01359 250984* E-mail. *sales@henrywatson.com* Web. *www.henrywatson.com Charlotte Watson's Country Collection – Original Suffolk Collection, The – Suffolk Tableware – Wattisfield Ware*

Watson & Lewis Ltd 5 Cullen Way, London NW10 6JZ Tel. *020 89613000* Fax. *020 89651990* Web. *www.watsonandlewis.co.uk W100 – W200 – W500*

Watson Marlow Pumps Ltd Bickland Water Road, Falmouth TR11 4RU Tel. *01326 370370* Fax. *01326 376009* E-mail. *info@watson-marlow.co.uk* Web. *www.wmpg.co.uk Bioprene – LoadSure – Marprene – Pumpsil – Sci-Q – PureWeld XL – AsepticSU – Bredel – MasoSine – Flexicon*

Watts Group plc 1 Great Tower Street, London EC3R 5AA Tel. *020 72808000* Fax. *020 72808001* E-mail. *london@watts.co.uk* Web. *www.watts.co.uk Watts and Partner Management – Watts and Partners*

Watts Industries UK Ltd Grosvenor Business Centre Enterprise Way, Vale Park, Evesham WR11 1GA Tel. *01386 446997* Fax. *01386 41923* E-mail. *adams@wattsindustries.co.uk* Web. *www.wattsindustries.com Cazzaniga – Eurotherm – Intermes – Ocean – SFR – Wattflow – Watts*

Watts Urethane Products Ltd Church Road, Lydney GL15 5EN Tel. *01594 847150* Fax. *01594 843586* E-mail. *sales@wattspu.co.uk* Web. *www.wattsurethane.com Ultrathane Plus*

W Attwood Ltd (established 1894) Milner Road Chilton Industrial Estate, Sudbury CO10 2XG Tel. *01787 373666* Fax. *01787 312353* E-mail. *w.attwood@biasbinding.co.uk* Web. *www.biasbinding.co.uk Bias Binding – Savoy – Savoy - Bias Binding.*

Wavelength Electronics Ltd Kent Innovation Centre Millennium Way Thanet Reach Business Park, Broadstairs CT10 2QQ Tel. *01843 609380* Fax. *01843 609384* E-mail. *sales@wavelengthelectronics.co.uk* Web. *www.wavelengthelectronics.co.uk *API Delevan – *Clairex – *Cornell Dubilier Electronics – Corning Gilbert – E-Switch – *Eastern Wireless Telecommunications Inc – *Electrodynamic Crystal – *Micro Spire – *MidcomInc – *Piazo Technology Ink – *Q-Tech – *State of the Art – *Texas Spectrum Electronics*

Waverley Brownall Ltd Unit 45 The Vintners Temple Farm Industrial Estate, Southend On Sea SS2 5RZ Tel. *01702 613883* Fax. *01702 613600* E-mail. *sales@waverleybrownall.co.uk* Web. *www.waverleybrownall.co.uk Duoloc – Ringlok – Superloc*

Wave Seven Marine Ltd Montpellier House Montpellier Drive, Cheltenham GL50 1TY Tel. *01242 541983* Fax. *0870 7120506* E-mail. *sales@wseven.com* Web. *www.wseven.com Airberth – Anytec – Ez-Dock – Sublift – Vermeer – Versi-Dredge*

Wavin Ltd Parsonage Way, Chippenham SN15 5PN Tel. *01249 766600* Fax. *01249 443286* E-mail. *andrew.taylor@wavin.co.uk* Web. *www.wavin.co.uk Wavin Apollo - Bi-axial PVC-U – Wavin Ducting - Polyethylene and PVC – Wavin SupaGas - Polyethylene (P.E.100) – Wavin SupaSure - Polyethylene (P.E.100) – WavinCoil - PVC – WavinGas - Polyethylene (P.E.80) – WavinSafe - PVC-U – WavinSure - Polyethylene (P.E.80)*

Wavin UK Hazlehead Docksbridge, Sheffield S30 5HG Tel. *01226 768262* Fax. *01226 764827* E-mail. *tim.thompson@wavin.co.uk* Web. *www.wavinuk.co.uk Osma – Wavindrain – Wavinsewer – Hep20*

W Bateman & Co. Garstang Road Barton, Preston PR3 5AA Tel. *01772 862948* Fax. *01772 861639* E-mail. *sales@bateman-sellarc.co.uk* Web. *www.bateman-sellarc.co.uk Reno – Sellarc*

W B Muddeman & Son Ltd The Scope Complex Wills Road, Totnes TQ9 5XN Tel. *01803 862058* Fax. *01803 866273* E-mail. *su4555@eclipse.co.uk* Web. *www.muddemans.com Brutus – Tamara*

W C F Ltd Craw Hall, Brampton CA8 1TN Tel. *01697 745050* Fax. *01697 745090* E-mail. *lanark@wcfcountrycentres.co.uk* Web. *www.wcf.co.uk W.C.F.*

W & Co Design Solutions Ltd West Yoke Ash, Sevenoaks TN15 7EP Tel. *0845 6253545* Fax. *0870 1608071* E-mail. *adam@w-co.co.uk* Web. *www.w-co.co.uk Lightbox – Lightboxes*

W D S Richardshaw Road Grangefield Industrial Estate, Pudsey LS28 6LE Tel. *0113 2909852* Fax. *08456 011173* E-mail. *sales@wdsltd.co.uk* Web. *www.wdsltd.co.uk J. & S. Small Tools – W.D.S. Production Equipment*

Wealden Tyres Ltd 23 Granary Business Centre Broadfarm North Street, Hellingly, Hailsham BN27 4DU Tel. *01323 845544* Fax. *01323 441501* E-mail. *sales@wealdentyres.co.uk* Web. *www.wealdentyres.co.uk Alliance – Avon – Bridgestone – Budget Tyres – Continental – Dunlop – Firestone – Goodyear – Michelin – Pirelli – Supreme – Uniroyal*

Wearnes Cambion Ltd Mill Bridge Castleton, Hope Valley S33 8WR Tel. *01433 621555* Fax. *01433 621290* E-mail. *sales@cambion.com* Web. *www.cambion.com Cambion*

Wearparts UK Ltd Oaks Industrial Estate Gilmorton Road, Lutterworth LE17 4HA Tel. *01455 553551* Fax. *01455 550907* E-mail. *sales@wearparts.com*

Web. *www.wearparts.com AS5 – CY – EV – Wearhard – Wearparts – WYNITE*

Weather Call Avalon House 57-63 Scrutton Street, London EC2A 4PJ Tel. *020 76136000* Fax. *020 76135005* E-mail. *weathercall@itouch.co.uk* Web. *www.itouch.co.uk Marinecall – Racecall – Teleshare – Weathercall*

Weatherford Edinburgh Petroleum Services Ltd 12 Heriot-Watt Research Park Riccarton, Currie EH14 4AP Tel. *0131 4494536* Fax. *0131 4495123* E-mail. *gary.norton@eu.weatherford.com* Web. *www.e-petroleumservices.com FloSystem – PanSystem*

Weatherford UK Kirkton Drive Pitmedden Industrial Estate Dyce, Dyce, Aberdeen AB21 0BG Tel. *01224 767000* Fax. *01224 767104* E-mail. *gary.fines@eu.weatherford.com* Web. *www.weatherford.com *Stabylia (U.S.A.) – *Weatherford (U.S.A.)*

Webasto Products UK Ltd Webasto House White Rose Way, Doncaster DN4 5JH Tel. *01302 322232* Fax. *01302 322231* E-mail. *p.hankin@webastouk.com* Web. *www.webasto.co.uk *Aerotop (Japan) – Diplomat – *Emerald Spoiler Soft Touch (Netherlands) – *Onyx Spoiler (Netherlands) – *Sapphire (Netherlands) – *Skytop 200 (Italy) – *Skyview (Netherlands) – *Sunmate (Netherlands) – *Topslider Spoiler (Italy) – *TVS Glass (Netherlands)*

Jervis B Webb Co. Ltd (European Headquarters) Cob Drive Swan Valley, Northampton NN4 9BB Tel. *01604 658150* Fax. *01604 656246* E-mail. *info@jerviswebb.com* Web. *www.jerviswebb.com Dog Magic – Stop-N-Flow – Towveyer – Unibilt*

Web Labs Ltd 24 Wandsworth Place, Milton Keynes MK13 8BT Tel. *01525 374859* E-mail. *info@web-labs.co.uk* Web. *www.web-labs.co.uk ContentMaster – FormsMaster – ResourceMaster – SearchMaster – Web-labs*

Webster Drives (A Gardner Denver Product) Folds Road, Bolton BL1 2SE Tel. *01204 382121* Fax. *01204 386100* E-mail. *sales@websterdrives.co.uk* Web. *www.websterdrives.co.uk Webster Drives*

Webster & Horsfall Ltd Fordrough, Birmingham B25 8DW Tel. *0121 7722555* Fax. *0121 7720762* E-mail. *sales@websterandhorsfall.co.uk* Web. *www.websterandhorsfall.co.uk Ancor – Atlantic – Hamil – Horn – Ocean – Reddiwire*

Webster-Wilkinson Ltd Unit A Halesfield 10, Telford TF7 4QP Tel. *01952 585701* Fax. *01952 581901* E-mail. *sales@webster-wilkinson.com* Web. *www.webster-wilkinson.com Compact – Perm-a-fix – Super Compact – Vinoseal*

Webtec Products Nuffield Road, St Ives PE27 3LZ Tel. *01480 397400* Fax. *01480 466555* E-mail. *information@webtec.co.uk* Web. *www.webtec.co.uk Webster Instruments – Webster Instruments - instruments for the measurement of flow pressure & temperature. – Webtec Hydraulics*

W E C S Precision Ltd Blenheim Road, Epsom KT19 9BE Tel. *01372 741633* Fax. *01372 740539* E-mail. *npooles@wecsprecision.com W.E.C.S Tools*

Wedge Galvanizing Group Ltd Stafford Street, Willenhall WV13 1RZ Tel. *01902 630311* Fax. *01902 366353* E-mail. *sales@wedge-galv.co.uk* Web. *www.wedge-galv.co.uk Wedge Group Galvanizing*

Wedgewood Travel Ltd (a division of Waterford Wedgwood P.L.C.) 7 Prescot Street, London E1 8AY Tel. *020 72657000* Fax. *020 72657070* E-mail. *alda@wedgewood.co.uk* Web. *www.wedgewood.co.uk Adams – Black Basalt – Coalport – Franciscan – Jasper – Johnson Brothers – Mason's Ironstone – Queen's Ware – Wedgwood*

Weetabix Ltd (Head Office) PO Box 5, Kettering NN15 5JR Tel. *01536 722181* Fax. *01536 726148* E-mail. *richard.martin@weetabix.co.uk* Web. *www.weetabix.co.uk Advantage – Alpen – Crrunch – Crunchy Bran – Minibix with banana – Minibix with chocolate – Minibix with fruit – Ready Brek – Vibixa – Weetabix – Weetabix - Vibixa - Alpen - Crunchy Bran - Weetos - Ready Brek - Advantage - Minibix - Crrrunch. – Weetos*

Weforma Daempfungstechnik GmbH Innovation Centre Highfield Drive, St Leonards On Sea TN38 9UH Tel. *01424 858170* Fax. *01424 858172* E-mail. *info.uk@weformer.com* Web. *www.weforma.com/index.php?id=1&L=1 Mega Line – Weforma*

Weg Electric Motors UK Ltd Unit 28 29 Walkers Road, Moons Moat North Industrial Estate, Redditch B98 9HE Tel. *01527 596748* Fax. *01527 591133* E-mail. *sales@wegelectricmotors.co.uk* Web. *www.wegelectricmotors.co.uk WEG (Brazil)*

Wehrle Environmental A6 Spinners Court 53 West End, Witney OX28 1NH Tel. *01993 849300* Fax. *01993 849309* E-mail. *info@wehrle-env.co.uk* Web. *www.wehrle-env.co.uk Biomembrat*

Weidmuller Ltd 1 Abbey Wood Road Kings Hill, West Malling ME19 4YT Tel. *01732 877000* Fax. *01732 521368* E-mail. *ian.thorndycraft@weidmuller.co.uk* Web. *www.weidmuller.co.uk C.A. Weidmuller – Cableman – Conexel – Klippon – SigNext*

Weir Group Senior Executives Pension Trust Ltd Clydesdale Bank Exchange Building 20 Waterloo Street, Glasgow G2 6DB Tel. *0141 6377111* Fax. *0141 2219789* E-mail. *pr@weir.co.uk* Web. *www.weir.co.uk 988 – Borehole – Canister Pumps – Duoglide – F H – F T – Hydraulic Drive – Isoglide – K.-Range – Lynavane – Spiroglide – Spiroglide – Swallowglide – Ulectriglide – Uniglide – V.L.I./V.C.I.*

Weir Materials & Foundries Park Works Grimshaw Lane, Newton Heath, Manchester M40 2BA Tel. *0161 2034262* Fax. *0161 9544739* E-mail. *wmlinfo@wml.weir.co.uk* Web. *www.weirclearliquid.com Zeraloy – Zeron – Zeron 100 – Zeron 25*

Weir Valves & Controls Markets Britannia House, Elland HX5 9JR Tel. *01422 282000* Fax. *01422 282100* E-mail. *info@weirgroup.com* Web. *www.weirgroup.com Atwood & Morrill – Batley Valve – Blake borough Controls, Batley Valve, Hopkinsons, MAC Valves – Blakeborough – Gitram – Hopkinsons – MAC Valves – Sarasin RSBD – SEBIM – Tricentric*

Weldability S I F 1 The Orbital Centre Icknield Way, Letchworth Garden City SG6 1ET Tel. *01462 482200* Fax. *01462 482202* E-mail. *reception@weldability-sif.com* Web. *www.wholeweld.co.uk Autobronze – Eurobraze – Hilco – Hilco - Eurobraze - Sifbronze - Sifserrate - Sifredicote - SIFMIG - Super Silicon – S.I.F. Silver Solder – Sifalumin – Sifbronze – Sifcupron – Sifflux – Sifmig – Sifredicote – Sifserrate – Sifsteel – Silsilcopper – Super Silicon*

Weldlogic Europe Ltd (Diamond Ground Products Ltd) Blackstone Road Stukeley Meadows Industrial Estate, Huntingdon PE29 6EF Tel. *01480 437478* Fax. *01480 437479* E-mail. *kevin@weldlogic.co.uk* Web. *www.weldlogic.co.uk Centrator – Diamond – Weldlogic*

Weldspares Ltd 50 Melford Court Hardwick Grange, Woolston, Warrington WA1 4RZ Tel. *01925 813288* Fax. *01925 817223* E-mail. *sales@weldspares.co.uk* Web. *www.weldspares-oki.com Bestwelds – Comfort – Red Ram*

Weldspeed Ltd Unit 1-2 The Orbital Centre Icknield Way, Letchworth Garden City SG6 1ET Tel. *01462 481616* Fax. *01462 482202* E-mail. *info@weldability-sif.com* Web. *www.weldability-sif.com Weldspeed*

Weldtite Products Ltd Unit 9 Harrier Road, Humber Bridge Industrial Estate, Barton Upon Humber DN18 5RP Tel. *01652 660000* Fax. *01652 660066* E-mail. *sales@weldtite.co.uk* Web. *www.weldtite.co.uk Weldtite*

Weleda UK Ltd Heanor Road, Ilkeston DE7 8DR Tel. *0115 9448200* Fax. *0115 9448210* E-mail. *robert.ballard@weleda.co.uk* Web. *www.weleda.co.uk Weleda*

Welin Lambie Britannia House Old Bush Street, Brierley Hill DY5 1UB Tel. *01384 78294* Fax. *01384 265100* E-mail. *admin@welin-lambie.co.uk* Web. *www.welin-lambie.co.uk Welin Davits*

Welland Engineering Ltd 31a Cranmore Lane Holbeach, Spalding PE12 7HT Tel. *01406 490660* Fax. *01406 490444* E-mail. *sales@wellandpower.net* Web. *www.wellandpower.net Welland*

Sam Weller Holdings Ltd Pickwick Mill Huddersfield Road Holmfirth, Thongsbridge, Holmfirth HD9 3JL Tel. *01484 683201* Fax. *01484 689700* E-mail. *info@samwellerltd.co.uk* Web. *www.samwellerltd.co.uk Sam Weller & Son*

Wellhead Electrical Supplies Unit 4d Wellheads Crescent Wellheads Industrial Estate, Aberdeen AB21 7GA Tel. *01224 723606* Fax. *01224 723606* E-mail. *sales@wellheads.co.uk* Web. *www.wellheads.co.uk Bandit – DNH – Elastimond – Elpress – Erico – Hawke – Hellerman – Sigma – Simlex Chalmit – Techner Vantrunk – Technor*

Wellman Booth 2 Kirkfields Industrial Centre Kirk Lane, Yeadon, Leeds LS19 7LX Tel. *0113 3879730* Fax. *0113 2506180* E-mail. *maureen.sharman@wellmanbooth.co.uk* Web. *www.wellmanbooth.co.uk Wellman Booth*

Wellman Thermal Services Ltd (a Wellman Thermal Products Company) Newfield Road, Oldbury B69 3ET Tel. *0121 5430000* Fax. *0121 5430199* E-mail. *info@wellman-thermal.com* Web. *www.wellman-thermal.com Helixchanger*

Wells & Young's Brewing Co. Havelock Street, Bedford MK40 4LU Tel. *01234 272766* Fax. *01234 279000* E-mail. *info@wellsandyoungs.co.uk* Web. *www.wellsandyoungs.co.uk Abington – Bombardier – Bowman – Crest – Dragoon – Eagle – Fargo – Kirin – Red Stripe*

The Welly Shop Ltd Fourth Avenue Centrum One Hundred, Burton On Trent DE14 2WL Tel. *01989 730217* Fax. *01989 730217* E-mail. *sales@thewellyshop.com* Web. *www.thewellyshop.com Muck Boot*

Wel Medical Services Southern House Sebastopol Road, Aldershot GU11 1SG Tel. *01252 344007* Fax. *01252 344004* E-mail. *info@welmedical.com* Web. *www.welmedical.com WEL – Boscarol – Contec – CapRescue – Mindray*

Welsh Slates Penrhyn Quarry Bethesda, Bangor LL57 4YG Tel. *01248 600656* Fax. *01248 601171* E-mail. *enquiries@welshslate.com* Web. *www.welshslate.com Cambrian – Capital Grade – County Grade – Cwt-y-Bugail – Ffestiniog – Fullersite – *Hilltop (U.S.A.) – Penrhyn*

Weltonhurst Ltd Centurion Way Roman Road, Blackburn BB1 2LD Tel. *01254 671177* Fax. *01254 671717* E-mail. *cs@weltonhurst.co.uk* Web. *www.weltonhurst.co.uk Aquapak – Eurotainer – Polypak – Polypin – Rigidpak*

Welwyn Tool Group Ltd 9 Blenheim Court 9 Blenhiem Court, Welwyn Garden City AL7 1AD Tel. *01707 331111* Fax. *01707 372175* E-mail. *info@welwyntoolgroup.co.uk* Web. *www.welwyntoolgroup.co.uk *American Electrical (U.S.A.) – Bend-Eze – CooperTools – *Diamond (Japan) – *Drei-s (Germany) – Erem – *Ewenz (Germany) – *Granit (Germany) – Granit - Leister - Drei-S - Welwyn Hot Knife - Simonds - H.K.Porter - Impacto - Cooper Tools - Zangl - Saltus - Owoco - Herbst - Ewenz - Strack - Diamond - Ripley - Kerry - Weller/Ungar. Sole agents for leading Continental, American and Japanese precisio – *H.K. Porter (U.S.A.) – Herbst – Impacto – Kerry – *Leister (Switzerland) – Lindstrom – Owoko – *Ripley (U.S.A.) – Saltus – *Simonds (U.S.A.) – *Squeeze Eze (U.S.A.) – *Strack (Germany) – WDT – Weller-Ungar – Wire-wrap – Xcelite – Xuron*

Wemoto Ltd World's End Motorcycles Ltd Unit 7 Grange Road Industrial Estate - Albion Street, Southwick, Brighton BN42 4EN Tel. *08450 292929* Fax. *01273 593011* E-mail. *info@wemoto.com* Web. *www.wemoto.com Kyoto – Marving – Simota – WEMOTO – WMD*

Wemyss Weavecraft Ltd Unit 7a Nobel Road, West Gourdie Industrial Estate, Dundee DD2 4UH Tel. *01382 908300* Fax. *01382 908308* E-mail. *wemyss@wemyss-fabrics.co.uk* Web. *www.wemyssfabric.com Wemyss Fabrics*

Wenaas Ltd Hareness Circle Altens Industrial Estate, Aberdeen AB12 3LY Tel. *01224 894000* Fax. *01224 878789* E-mail. *richard.wright@wenaas.co.uk* Web. *www.wenaas.co.uk a-code – echo KLM – fristaad – Kansas – Stanley – Wenaas*

Wenban Smith Ltd 14 Newland Road, Worthing BN11 1JT Tel. *01903 230311* Fax. *01903 821780* E-mail. *sales@wenbans.com* Web. *www.wenbans.com Timberworld – Wenban-Smith Joinery*

Wendage Pollution Control Ltd Rangeways Farm Conford, Liphook GU30 7QP Tel. *01428 751296* Fax. *01428 751541* E-mail. *info@wpc.uk.net* Web. *www.wpc.uk.net ABS – Conder – Ebara – Flygt – Grease Guzzler – KSB – Lowara – TT*

Wensleydale Longwool Sheep Shop Cross Lanes Farm Garriston, Leyburn DL8 5JU Tel. *01969 623840* Fax. *01969 623840* E-mail. *sheepshop@lineone.net* Web. *www.wensleydalelongwoolsheepshop.co.uk Wensleydale Longwool Sheepshop*

Wentworth Club Ltd Wentworth Drive, Virginia Water GU25 4LS Tel. *01344 842201* Fax. *01344 842804* E-mail. *reception@wentworthclub.com* Web. *www.wentworthclub.com Wentworth*

Wenzel UK Ltd 29 Brunel Court Stephensons Court, Quedgeley, Gloucester GL2 2AL Tel. *01452 728298* Fax. *01452 728288* E-mail. *info@uk.wenzel-cmm.com* Web. *www.wenzel-cmm.co.uk Metromec – Wenzel – Wenzel Geartec*

Wereldhave Property Management 39 Sloane Street, London SW1X 9WR Tel. *020 72352080* Fax. *020 72459962* E-mail. *sales@wereldhave.com* Web. *www.wereldhave.com W. Wereldhave*

Robert Werner Ltd Rex Mill Don Street, Middleton, Manchester M24 2GG Tel. *0161 6530000* Fax. *0161 6531000 *Fairtex (Worldwide)*

Wescol PO Box 41, Wolverhampton WV1 2RZ Tel. *01902 351283* Fax. *01902 351475* E-mail. *sales@wescol.com* Web. *www.wescol.com Genweld – Maelor – Wescol*

Wessex & Co. 1 Eghams Court Boston Drive, Bourne End SL8 5YS Tel. *01628 522771* Fax. *01628 523090* E-mail. *hugo@wessex-co.co.uk* Web. *www.wessex-co.co.uk Shellwin Plc*

Wessex Galvanisers Ltd Tower Industrial Estate Tower Lane, Eastleigh SO50 6NZ Tel. *023 80629952* Fax. *023 80650289* E-mail. *wessex@wedge-galv.co.uk* Web. *www.wedge-galv.co.uk Wedge Group Galvanizing*

Wessex Resins & Adhesives Ltd Cupernham Lane, Romsey SO51 7LF Tel. *01794 521111* Fax. *08707 701032* E-mail. *info@wessex-resins.com* Web. *www.wessex-resins.com Cascamite – Cascorez – Cascover – Epophen – Pro-Set – West System*

Wessex Welding & Industrial Supplies Ltd Unit 10 Brunel Court Dean Road, Yate, Bristol BS37 5PD Tel. *01454 311033* Fax. *01454 321871* E-mail. *keith.larkin@boc.com* Web. *www.leengate.com 3M Safety Products – Binzel Torches & Spares – BOC Gases – Bosch – Dewalt – Esab Products – Gas Arc Welding Equipment – Kemppi – Makita – Metrode Welding Consumables – Nexus – Salt Abrasives – Silverline – Speed Glass Welding Products – thermal Dynamis S – Unibar Cutting Machines*

J J Westaby & Partners Cape Farm Sheriff Hutton, York YO60 6RT Tel. *01347 878703* Fax. *01347 878771* E-mail. *jjwestaby@btconnect.com Suire*

Westbridge International Group Ltd Westbridge House Holland Street, Nottingham NG7 5DS Tel. *0115 9782254* Fax. *0115 9420547* E-mail. *sales@wbig.co.uk* Web. *www.wbig.co.uk Body Prints – Fastlane*

West Bromwich Building Society 374 High Street, West Bromwich B70 8LR Tel. *08453 300611* Fax. *0161 2375448* E-mail. *mark.brayford@westbrom.co.uk* Web. *www.westbrom.co.uk Corporate Deopsit Account – The Acorn Account*

West Brook Resources Ltd West Brook House Wreakes Lane, Dronfield S18 1LY Tel. *01246 292292* Fax. *01246 292293* Web. *www.wbrl.co.uk Ferro Alloys – Maximag – Pure Metals*

West Design Products Ltd Stoney Lane Industrial Estate 5-7 Red Sands Road, Kidderminster DY10 2LG Tel. *01303 297888* Fax. *01730 815714* E-mail. *sales@westdesignproducts.co.uk* Web. *www.westdesignproducts.co.uk Centafoam – Faber Cartell – Higgns – LazerSharp – *Maped (France) – U.N.O. Drafting Templates*

E A West Pyewipe, Grimsby DN31 2SW Tel. *01472 232000* Fax. *01472 232020* E-mail. *hmats_uk@huntsman.com* Web. *www.huntsman.com Feripol – Mistrale – S.C.A.*

Western Automobile Co. 116 Colinton Road, Edinburgh EH14 1BY Tel. *0131 4436091* Fax. *0131 4557383* E-mail. *mbreception@easternholdings.co.uk* Web. *www.easternholdings.co.uk Mercedes Benz*

Western House Armstrong Road, Basingstoke RG24 8QE Tel. *01256 462341* Fax. *01256 840585* E-mail. *sales@western-house.com* Web. *www.western-house.com Ashdene (Australia) – *J.G. Durand Cristal (France) – Libby (USA) – *Luigi Bormioli (Italy) – The Village Collectables*

Western Morning News Co. Ltd 17 Brest Road Derriford, Plymouth PL6 5AA Tel. *01752 765500* Fax. *01752 765515* E-mail. *plymouthfrontcounter@westcountrypublications.co.uk* Web. *www.thisisplymouth.co.uk Evening Herald – Home Seeker – Plymouth Extra – Western Morning News*

Western Provident Association Ltd Rivergate House Blackbrook Park Avenue, Taunton TA1 2PE Tel. *01823 625000* Fax. *01823 623050* E-mail. *mcd@wpa.org.uk* Web. *www.wpa.org.uk Cedar – Company Supercover – Elect 17 – Enterprise – Health & Sickness Cash Benefit Plan – Healthwise – Oak – Poplar – Providental Personal Dental Plan – Senior Options*

Richard Western Ltd The Durbans Apsey Green, Framlingham, Woodbridge IP13 9RP Tel. *01728 723224* Fax. *01728 724291* E-mail. *sales@richard-western.co.uk* Web. *www.richard-western.co.uk Richard Western Trailers – Weeks Trailers*

Western Welding & Engineering Co. Ltd Unit 9 Atlantic Trading Estate, Barry CF63 3XA Tel. *01446 733466* Fax. *01446 720993* Web. *www.westernwelding.co.uk Western Welding*

Gea Westfalia Seperator UK Ltd Old Wolverton Road Old Wolverton, Milton Keynes MK12 5PY Tel. *01908 576500* Fax. *08708 305515* E-mail. *barry.dumble@gea-group.com* Web. *www.wsgb.co.uk Eisele – Stelzer – Westfalia*

Westgate Group Ltd Newchurch, Romney Marsh TN29 0DZ Tel. *01303 872277* Fax. *01303 874801* E-mail. *sales@wefi.co.uk* Web. *www.wefi.co.uk Saddlecraft*

The West Group Ltd 29 Aston Road, Waterlooville PO7 7XJ Tel. *023 92266366* Fax. *023 92240323* E-mail. *sales@westgroup.co.uk* Web. *www.westgroup.co.uk *80/20 (U.S.A.) – *Aignep (Italy) – *Air Logic (U.S.A.) – *Air-Vac (U.S.A.) – *AirPinch (U.S.A.) – *Airtrol (U.S.A.) – *Bird Precision (U.S.A.) – *Bosch (Germany) – *Clippard (U.S.A.) – *Control Air (U.S.A.) – *Copor (Italy) – *E&E Engineering (U.S.A.) – *Freelin-Wade – *Matrix (Italy) – *Memco (U.S.A.) – *Pneumadyne (U.S.A.) – *Press:Air:Trol (U.S.A.) – *PressMAir (Italy) – *Rygo (United Kingdom) – *Smart (U.S.A.) – *Teledyne (U.S.A.) – *Turn-Act (U.S.A.) – *Twin-Tec (U.S.A.) – *Vesta (Italy)*

West Instruments The Hyde Lower Bevendean, Brighton BN2 4JU Tel. *01273 606271* Fax. *01273 609990* E-mail. *sales@west-cs.com* Web. *www.west-cs.com 4400 – 6000 Series – 8000 Series – 8010*

Westland Casting Co. Ltd 4-5 Vaux Road Finedon Road Industrial Estate, Wellingborough NN8 4TG Tel. *01933 276718* Fax. *01933 442185* E-mail. *paul@westlandcasting.co.uk* Web. *www.westlandcasting.co.uk Westland Casting*

West Leigh Ltd 11-13 Spa Road, London SE16 3RB Tel. *020 72320030* Fax. *020 72321763* E-mail. *info@west-leigh.co.uk* Web. *www.west-leigh.co.uk K.G. Smoke Dispersal*

Westley Of Cardiff PO Box 84, Port Talbot SA13 2ZU Tel. *01639 875061* Fax. *01639 875064* E-mail. *rod.mirams@westleygroup.co.uk* Web. *www.westleygroup.co.uk Alexoy*

Westley Plastics Ltd PO Box 1, Cradley Heath B64 5QY Tel. *01384 414840* Fax. *01384 414849* E-mail. *sales@plasticsuk.com* Web. *www.plasticsuk.com Westex – Westlon*

Westmac Ltd Redlake Trading Estate, Ivybridge PL21 0EZ Tel. *01752 891299* Fax. *01752 891346* E-mail. *info@westmac.co.uk* Web. *www.westmac.co.uk *Gehl (U.S.A.) – *J.F. (Denmark) – *Jeantil (France) – Rabe (Germany) – *Stoll (Germany)*

Westmid Fans Zephyr House Mucklow Hill, Halesowen B62 8DN Tel. *0121 5500315* Fax. *0121 5855185* E-mail. *info@westmidfans.co.uk* Web. *www.westmidfans.co.uk *Next Day Fans (United Kingdom) – *Roof Units Ltd (United Kingdom) – *Vent Axia Ltd (United Kingdom) – *Woods Air Movement Ltd (United Kingdom)*

West Midlands Foundry Co. Ltd Blakemore Road, West Bromwich B70 8JF Tel. *0121 5531515* Fax. *0121 5005839 Tools & Dies*

Westmore Business Systems Ltd 2 Arrow Court Adams Way Springfield Business Park, Alcester B49 6PU Tel. *08452 306500* Fax. *0845 2306511* E-mail. *sales@westmore.co.uk* Web. *www.westmore.co.uk Frama – Post Excel – Sharp – Sharp Photocopier*

Westomatic Vending Services Ltd Units 7-8 Forde Court Forde Road, Newton Abbot TQ12 4BT Tel. *01626 323100* Fax. *01626 332828* E-mail. *sales@westomatic.com* Web. *www.westomatic.com *Coolcentre (Italy) – Riviera – Riviera Plus – *Snackmart (U.S.A.) – Solo – Sonata – Temprano*

Weston Beamor Ltd 3-8 Vyse Street Hockley, Birmingham B18 6LT Tel. *0121 2363688* Fax. *0121 2368100* E-mail. *info@domino-wb.co.uk* Web. *www.domino-wb.co.uk Domino*

H Weston & Sons Ltd The Bounds Much Marcle, Ledbury HR8 2NQ Tel. *01531 660233* Fax. *01531 660619* E-mail. *enquiries@westons-cider.co.uk* Web. *www.westonscider.co.uk First Quality – 1880 Cider – Bounds Brand Scrumpy, – First Quality Draught – Old Rosie – Organic Cider – Organic Vintage – Range of Oak Conditioned Ciders – Stowford Export – Stowford Press – Stowford Press, Stowford Export, Scrumpy Supreme, Old Rosie, Herefordshire Country Perry, Bounds Brand Scrumpy, First Quality, Traditional Scrumpy. Range of Oak Conditioned Ciders, Organic Cider, Vintage Cider, Organic Vintage Cider. 1880 Cider. – Traditional Scrumpy – Vintage Cider*

J Weston & Partners Ltd East Putford, Holsworthy EX22 7XR Tel. *01237 451838* Fax. *01237 451553* E-mail. *n.j.moulder@btconnect.com Everest*

West Scomac Catering Equipment Ltd Hadston Industrial Estate Hadston, Morpeth NE65 9YG Tel. *01670 760082* Fax. *01670 761404* E-mail. *sales@stellex.co.uk* Web. *www.stellex.co.uk Stellex*

West & Senior Ltd Milltown Street Radcliffe, Manchester M26 1WE Tel. *0161 7247131* Fax. *0161 7249519* E-mail. *info@westsenior.co.uk* Web. *www.westsenior.co.uk Fascol – Fascol - polyester pigments, Fastint - mono pigment tinters, Faspak, Corflow - polyester flocoats, Corgel - isophthalic polyester gelcoats.*

West Village Ltd 48 Broughton Street, Manchester M8 8NN Tel. *0161 8346509* Fax. *0161 8349452* E-mail. *xited@hotmail.co.uk* Web. *www.x-ited.co.uk xited uk ltd*

West Yorkshire Drawing Office Services Ltd Swallow Hill Mills Tong Road, Leeds LS12 4QG Tel. *0113 2205400* Fax. *0113 2310615* E-mail. *stuart@wydos.co.uk* Web. *www.wydos.co.uk Wydos*

Wetherby Engineering Co. Ltd Britannia Mills Portland Street, Bradford BD5 0DW Tel. *01274 783434* Fax. *01274 390527* E-mail. *charles@wetherby-engineering.co.uk* Web. *www.wetherby-engineering.co.uk Broadbent Drives – Noram*

Wexas Travel (t/a Wexas International) 47-49 Brompton Road, London SW3 1DE Tel. *08458 386262* Fax. *020 75898418* E-mail. *travel@wexas.com* Web. *www.wexas.com Wexas*

Weyers Bros Ltd Unit 1 Knight House Lenthall Road, Loughton IG10 3UD Tel. *020 85083886* Fax. *020 85087122* E-mail. *john.weyers@weyersbros.co.uk Weyers*

Weyfringe Labelling Systems Longbeck Road Marske-by-the-Sea, Redcar TS11 6HQ Tel. *01642 490121* Fax. *01642 490385* E-mail. *sales@weyfringe.co.uk* Web. *www.weyfringe.co.uk Apollo R.T. – Easy Label – Flexi Label – Label Master – Laser 1000 – Quattro Compact – Quattro Plus – Series 5000*

W F Electrical 301-311 Rainham Road South, Dagenham RM10 8SX Tel. *020 85967200* Fax. *020 89849400* E-mail. *peter.warsap@hagemeyer.co.uk* Web. *www.wf-online.com Alto – Concord – Hitech – Lytespan – *Marcaddy (Germany) – *Martin & Lunel (France) – *Prisinter (France) – World*

W.G. Photo Sweetbriar Cottage The Street, Oulton, Norwich NR11 6AF Tel. *0844 8002990* Fax. *01903 200528* E-mail. *mike@wgphoto.co.uk* Web. *www.wgphoto.co.uk 3D Graphics*

Whale Tankers Ltd Ravenshaw, Solihull B91 2SU Tel. *0121 7045700* Fax. *0121 7045701* E-mail. *r.turner@whale.co.uk* Web. *www.whale.co.uk Blazer – Gully Whale – Gullywhale – Jetvac – Kilowhale – Kilowhale – Molex – MonoWhale – Rotovac – Whale Tankers – Whalevac*

Wharfedale International Ltd I A G House Ermine Business Park, Huntingdon PE29 6XU Tel. *01480 431737* Fax. *01480 431767* E-mail. *tim@wharfedale.co.uk* Web. *www.columbia-tech.com Wharfedale*

Wheatsheaf Jewellers Tools 35 Spencer Street Hockley, Birmingham B18 6DE Tel. *0844 4778193* E-mail. *sales@wheatsheafproducts.com* Web. *www.wheatsheafonline.co.uk Wheatsheaf*

Wheelabrator Allevard Creative Industries Centre Wolverhampton Science Park, Glaisher Drive, Wolverhampton WV10 9TG Tel. *01902 792610* Fax. *01902 712058* E-mail. *sales@metabrasive.com* Web. *www.wabrasives.com Wheel driven & portable shot blasting equipment suppliers for floor surfaces – Wheelabrator*

Wheelabrator Group 107-109 Whitby Road, Slough SL1 3DR Tel. *01753 572400* Fax. *01753 215662* E-mail. *sales@wheelabratorgroup.co.uk* Web. *www.wheelabratorgroup.com Alumaglass – Blastmaster – Dry Honer – Honermaster – Honermatic – Scalomatic – Vacu-Beads – Vacu-Blast – Vacu-Blaster – Vacu-Brasive – Vacu-Dapt – Vacu-Grit – Vacu-Honer – Vacu-Lox – Vacu-Peener – Vacu-Shot – Vacu-Teach – Vacu-Trol – Vacu-Veyor – Vector – Ventus – Waffle Floor*

Wheel Wash Ltd Pyms Lane, Crewe CW1 3PJ Tel. *01606 592044* Fax. *01606 592045* E-mail. *sales@wheelwash.com* Web. *www.wheelwash.com Wheelwash*

Whessoe Oil & Gas Ltd Whessoe Technology Centre Morton Palms, Darlington DL1 4WB Tel. *01325 390000* Fax. *01325 390001* E-mail. *wilf.mcnaughton@whessoe.co.uk* Web. *www.whessoe.co.uk Whessoe*

Charles N Whillans Partnership Teviotdale Mill Commercial Road, Hawick TD9 7AQ Tel. *01450 373311* Fax. *01450 376082* E-mail. *chasnwhillans@ip3.co.uk Scottish Sweater Store – Sport of Kings*

Whistles Ltd 12 St Christophers Place, London W1U 1NH Tel. *020 74874484* Fax. *020 74862043* E-mail. *info@whistles.co.uk* Web. *www.whistles.co.uk Whistles*

Whitaker & Sawyer Brushes Ltd Unit 17 Midas Business Centre Wantz Road, Dagenham RM10 8PS Tel. *020 85937204* Fax. *020 85957353* E-mail. *info@wsbrushes.co.uk* Web. *www.wsbrushes.co.uk Albion – Buckenier – Clipper – Commodore – Dolphin – Neptune – Viking*

White Formula Ltd 14 Regent Road Brightlingsea, Colchester CO7 0NL Tel. *01206 302724* Fax. *01206 305434* E-mail. *info@whiteformula.com* Web. *www.whiteformula.com Hurricane*

Whitehall Recruitment Ltd 37-41 High Street, Edenbridge TN8 5AD Tel. *01732 864777* Fax. *01732 865777* E-mail. *enquiries@whitehall.uk.com* Web. *www.whitehall.uk.com Crosslink – Flexiperm – Target*

Whitehill Spindle Tools Ltd 2 Bolton Road, Luton LU1 3HR Tel. *01582 736881* Fax. *01582 488987* E-mail. *sales@whitehill-tools.com* Web. *www.whitehill-tools.com Whitehill*

Whitehot Creative Southgate House Southgate, Stevenage SG1 1HG Tel. *0845 2015160* E-mail. *info@whitehot-creative.co.uk* Web. *www.whitehot-creative.co.uk Whitehot Creative*

Whitehouse Machine Tools Ltd 7 Princes Drive Industrial Estate Coventry Road, Kenilworth CV8 2FD Tel. *01926 852725* Fax. *01926 850620* E-mail. *tomh@wmtcnc.com* Web. *www.wmtcnc.com Biglia – Brother – Manurhin – Okk – Takahashi – Yasda*

Whitelegg Machines Ltd 19 Crompton Way Manor Royal, Crawley RH10 9QR Tel. *01293 526230* Fax. *01293 538910* E-mail. *sales@whitelegg.com* Web. *www.whitelegg.com BTC – Whitelegg*

Weidmann Whiteley Ltd Pool In Wharfedale, Otley LS21 1RP Tel. *0113 2842121* Fax. *0113 2842272* E-mail. *paul.hirst@wicor.com* Web. *www.wicor.com Elephantide – Fileguide – Harmony – Hi-Ply – Permaply*

White & Newton Furniture Ltd Frostholme Mill Burnley Road, Todmorden OL14 7ED Tel. *01706 812596* Fax. *01706 818701* E-mail. *info@sutcliffefurniture.co.uk* Web. *www.sutcliffegroup.co.uk *White and Newton Furniture*

Whitford Ltd 10 Christleton Court Manor Park, Runcorn WA7 1ST Tel. *01928 571000* Fax. *01928 571010* E-mail. *salesuk@whitfordww.co.uk* Web. *www.whitfordww.co.uk Dykor – Eclipse – Excalibur – QuanTanium – Quantum2 – Suave – Xylac – Xylan – Xylan - Xylar - Xylac - Quantum2 - QuanTanium - Eclipse - Excalibur - Dykor - Suave (fluoropolymer coatings) – Xylar*

Mike Whitley Leather Goods St Marys Chapel Lane Back Street, Langtoft, Driffield YO25 3TD Tel. *01377 267426* Fax. *01377 267477* E-mail. *casework@langtoft.net* Web. *www.cambraicovers.com Mike Whitley*

Whittingdales Solicitors Chancery House 53-64 Chancery Lane, London WC2A 1QU Tel. *020 78315591* Fax. *020 74300448* E-mail. *m.whittingdale@whittingdales.co.uk* Web. *www.whittingdales.co.uk Whittingdales Solicitors*

Whitworth Holdings Ltd Victoria Mills London Road, Wellingborough NN8 2DT Tel. *01933 443444* Fax. *01933 222523* E-mail. *enquiries@whitworthbros.ltd.uk* Web. *www.whitworthbros.ltd.uk Champion – Whitworth Bros*

W H Mason & Son Ltd The Old Sawmills Wetmore Road, Burton On Trent DE14 1QN Tel. *01283 564651* Fax. *01283 511526* E-mail. *sales@justwood.com* Web. *www.justwood.com Burton Wood Turnery – Just Wood*

Wholebake Ltd Ty'N Llidiart Industrial Estate, Corwen LL21 9RR Tel. *01490 412297* Fax. *01490 412053*

E-mail. *info@wholebake.co.uk* Web. *www.wholebake.co.uk* *9 Bar – *NRG flow*

Wholesale Welding Supplies Ltd 1 The Orbital Centre Icknield Way, Letchworth Garden City SG6 1ET Tel. *01462 482200* Fax. *01462 482202* E-mail. *adrian.hawkins@wholeweld.co.uk* Web. *www.wholeweld.co.uk Awac – Coverclear – Duraplas – Filterlite – Welmex*

W H S Halo Midpoint Park Kingsbury Road Minworth, Sutton Coldfield B76 1AF Tel. *0121 7493000* Fax. *0121 7492511* E-mail. *gemma.handley@bowaterbuildingproducts.com* Web. *www.bowaterbuildingproducts.com System 10*

WH Smith Retail Ltd Greenbridge Road, Swindon SN3 3LD Tel. *08456 046543* Fax. *01793 562616* E-mail. *customer.relations@whsmith.co.uk* Web. *www.whsmith.co.uk W.H. Smith*

W H Tildesley Ltd Clifford Works Bow Street, Willenhall WV13 2AN Tel. *01902 366440* Fax. *01902 366216* E-mail. *sales@whtildesley.com* Web. *www.whtildesley.com W.H.T.*

WHW Plastics Ltd Therm Rd Cleveland St, Hull HU8 7BF Tel. *01482 329154* Fax. *01482 217140* E-mail. *mike@whwplastics.com* Web. *www.whwplastics.com Acrylite – Centrilux*

Whyte & Son Nottingham Ltd Lincoln Street Old Basford, Nottingham NG6 0FT Tel. *0115 9784264 California Miss – Majorca – Rocket – Rosaflex – Rose Shoes – Sportsman*

Wicksteed Leisure Ltd Digby Street, Kettering NN16 8YJ Tel. *01536 517028* Fax. *01536 410633* E-mail. *sales@wicksteed.co.uk* Web. *www.wicksteed.co.uk Wicksteed*

Widney Manufacturing Ltd PO Box 133, Birmingham B6 7SA Tel. *0121 3275500* Fax. *0121 3282466* E-mail. *info@widney.co.uk* Web. *www.widney.co.uk Widney*

Wigan Timber Ltd Unit 21 Swan Meadow Industrial Estate Swan Meadow Road, Wigan WN3 5BE Tel. *01942 235353* Fax. *01942 235363* E-mail. *info@wigantimber.co.uk* Web. *www.wigantimber.co.uk Anglo – Kronospan – Smartply – Velux*

John Wigfull & Co. Ltd First Hangings Blaby Road, Enderby, Leicester LE19 4AQ Tel. *0116 2862287* Fax. *0116 2751232* E-mail. *wigfull@btinternet.com* Web. *www.johnwigfull.co.uk John Wigfull*

Wilcox Commercial Vehicles Ltd Blenheim Way Market Deeping, Peterborough PE6 8LD Tel. *01778 345151* Fax. *01778 347269* E-mail. *cbartlett@tippers.co.uk* Web. *www.wilcox.uk.com Wilcolite – Wilcox*

Thomas C Wild Vulcan Works Tinsley Park Road, Sheffield S9 5DP Tel. *0114 2442471* Fax. *0114 2442052* E-mail. *jhancock@tc-wild.co.uk* Web. *www.tc-wild.co.uk Wild*

Wiles Group Walmgate Road Perivale, Greenford UB6 7LN Tel. *020 7587700* Fax. *020 87587722* E-mail. *peter.duncan@wilesgreenworld.co.uk* Web. *www.wiles.co.uk Wiles Group Ltd*

Wilhelmsen Ship Service Unit 3a Newtons Court Crossways, Crossways Business Park, Dartford DA2 6QL Tel. *01322 282412* Fax. *01322 620660* E-mail. *andy.millar@wilhelmsen.com* Web. *www.wilhelmsen.com Unitor*

J & D Wilkie Ltd Marywell Brae, Kirriemuir DD8 4BJ Tel. *01575 572502* Fax. *01575 574564* E-mail. *sales@jdwilkie.co.uk* Web. *www.jdwilkie.co.uk Texbac – Wiltex*

Wilkinson Hardware Stores Ltd JK House Roebuck Way, Worksop S80 3YY Tel. *01909 505505* Fax. *01909 505777* E-mail. *communications@wilko.co.uk* Web. *www.wilko.co.uk Wilkinson Hardware – Wilko*

Wilkinson Star Shield Drive Wardley Industrial Estate, Worsley, Manchester M28 2WD Tel. *0161 7287900* Fax. *0161 7278297* E-mail. *steve.murray@wilkinsonstar.com* Web. *www.wilkinsonstar.com Fleetarc*

Willan 2 Brooklands Road, Sale M33 3SS Tel. *0161 9736262* Fax. *0161 9052085* E-mail. *peterw@willan.co.uk* Web. *www.willan.co.uk Willan Building Services*

William Bain Fencing Ltd Lochrin Works 7 Limekilns Road, Cumbernauld, Glasgow G67 2RN Tel. *01236 457333* Fax. *01236 451166* E-mail. *ikerr@lochrin-bain.co.uk* Web. *www.lochrin-bain.co.uk Lochrin – Lochrin Classic Rivetless – Lochrin Palisading*

William Blyth Ltd Far Ings Road, Barton Upon Humber DN18 5AZ Tel. *01652 637222* Fax. *01652 660966* E-mail. *g-harrison@williamblyth.co.uk* Web. *www.williamblyth.co.uk Celtic – Lincoln*

William Clark & Sons Ltd 72 Upperlands, Maghera BT46 5RZ Tel. *028 79547200* Fax. *028 79547207* E-mail. *sales@wmclark.co.uk* Web. *www.wmclark.co.uk AS-TEC – BWC Textiles – Collapad – Everbond*

William G Search Ltd Whitehall Road, Leeds LS12 6EP Tel. *0113 2639081* Fax. *0151 5491914* E-mail. *info@wgsearch.co.uk* Web. *www.wgsearch.co.uk Handiloo – Moderncross – Search*

William Hall & Company The Estate Office Hawarden, Deeside CH5 3NX Tel. *01244 531547* Fax. *0161 4364855* E-mail. *enquiries@williamhallandco.com* Web. *www.williamhallandco.com William Hall & Co.*

William Hill PO Box 170, Leeds LS2 8JF Tel. *0113 2912000* Fax. *0113 2912282* E-mail. *humanresources-leeds@williamhill.co.uk* Web. *www.williamhill.co.uk William Hill Organization*

William Kenyon & Sons Ropes & Narrow Fabrics Ltd Chapel Field Works Railway Street, Dukinfield SK16 4PT Tel. *0161 3086000* Fax. *0161 3086046* E-mail. *info@williamkenyon.co.uk* Web. *www.williamkenyon.co.uk Kenbraid – Kennylbond*

Williams Fasteners Unit 4a Shepcote Way, Tinsley Industrial Estate, Sheffield S9 1TH Tel. *0114 2565200* Fax. *0114 2565210* E-mail. *sales@williamsfasteners.com* Web. *www.williamsfasteners.com Williams Brothers of Sheffield*

Williams F1 Williams Grand Prix Engineer Grove, Wantage OX12 0DQ Tel. *01235 777700* Fax. *01235 764705* E-mail. *enquiries@williamsf1.com* Web. *www.williamsf1.com Williams*

T & R Williamson Ltd 36 Stonebridgegate, Ripon HG4 1TP Tel. *01765 607711* Fax. *01765 607908* E-mail. *info@trwilliamson.co.uk* Web. *www.trwilliamson.co.uk Abbesyn – Coverflow – Makaurite – Mastercraft – Spurlac – Spurseel – Too Can – Transpeed – Transpeed*

William Teknix 113 London Road Horndean, Waterlooville PO8 0BJ Tel. *023 92592500* Fax. *023 92594081* E-mail. *ian@teknix.me.uk Data Logic – GPA. – Meto-Fer – Panasonic – Univer*

Willis Toys Ltd Church Lane Widdington, Saffron Walden CB11 3SF Tel. *01799 541850* Fax. *01799 541864* E-mail. *tim@willistoys.co.uk* Web. *www.willistoys.co.uk Masoshistigs*

Willpower Breathing Air Ltd 6 Granby Business Park Granby Avenue, Birmingham B33 0TJ Tel. *0121 6052600* Fax. *0121 6052800* E-mail. *info@willpower-ltd.co.uk* Web. *willpower-ltd.co.uk Niltox – Willpower*

Wilmat Ltd Wilmat House 43 Steward Street, Birmingham B18 7AE Tel. *0121 4547514* Fax. *0121 4561792* E-mail. *sales@wilmat-handling.co.uk* Web. *www.wilmat-handling.co.uk Wilmat*

Wilms Heating Equipment 4 Hill Farm Barns Ashbocking Road, Henley, Ipswich IP6 0SA Tel. *01473 785911* Fax. *01473 785921* E-mail. *sales@wilms.co.uk* Web. *www.wilms.co.uk Dibo – Frank – T.W. Franks – Wilms*

Wilson Company Sharrow Ltd PO Box 32, Sheffield S11 8PL Tel. *0114 2662677* Fax. *0114 2670504* E-mail. *info@sharrowmills.com* Web. *www.sharrowmills.com S P Snuff – Tobacconists*

George Wilson Industries Ltd Barlow Road, Coventry CV2 2TD Tel. *024 76603336* Fax. *024 76603128* E-mail. *gwi@bi-group.com George Wilson Industries*

Wilson Sloane Street Ltd 116-120 Coldharbour Lane Camberwell, London SE5 9PZ Tel. *020 77332500* Fax. *020 77387937* E-mail. *sales@wilsonmeats.com* Web. *www.wilsonmeats.com *Traiteur*

Wilson UK Ltd Forge Road, Willenhall WV12 4HD Tel. *01922 725800* Fax. *01922 649888* E-mail. *uksales@wilsononline.com* Web. *www.wilsononline.com Fisher Controls*

Wimbledon Sewing Machine Co. Ltd 292-312 Balham High Road, London SW17 7AA Tel. *020 87674724* Fax. *020 87674726* E-mail. *wimbledonsewingmachinecoltd@btinternet.com* Web. *www.wimsew.com Rushton*

Wim Hemmink 106 Crawford Street, London W1H 2HY Tel. *020 79351755* Fax. *020 72240573* E-mail. *wimhemmink@btinternet.com Wim Hemmink*

Wimpy Restaurants Group Ltd 64 High Street, Marlow SL7 1AH Tel. *01628 483501* Fax. *01628 474025* E-mail. *info@wimpy.uk.com* Web. *www.wimpy.uk.com Wimpy*

Winbro Group Technologies Whitwick Business Park Stenson Road, Coalville LE67 4JP Tel. *01530 516000* Fax. *01530 516001* E-mail. *reception@winbrogroup.com* Web. *www.winbrogroup.com StemTech Twim Ram ECM (United Kingdom) – Zentech/Xtech/Midirobo Tech/Duotech/Maxirobo Tech (United Kingdom) – Zephur/Alpha/Zeta/Delta/Theta (United Kingdom) – Zepkyr/Hypha/Zeta/Delta/Theta (United Kingdom)*

Wincro Metal Industries Ltd 3 Fife Street, Sheffield S9 1NJ Tel. *0114 2422171* Fax. *0114 2434306* E-mail. *accounts@wincro.com* Web. *www.wincro.com Wincro – Wincro Brickwork Support Systems – Wincro Clip – Wincro Safe Tie – Wincro Stainless Steel Reinforcing Bar – Wincro-Suregrip*

Windes Car Centre Moor Lane, Widnes WA8 7AL Tel. *0151 4202000* Fax. *0151 4951382* E-mail. *gould@widnesnissan.com* Web. *www.windesnissan.com Versa*

Windfall Brands Ltd Northfield House Northfield End, Henley On Thames RG9 2JG Tel. *01491 845620* Fax. *01491 412929* E-mail. *info@windfalldrinks.com* Web. *www.windfalldrinks.com Arizona – Big Tom – Brothers Pear Ciders – Hpnotiq – James White – James White Organic Joices – Pama – Pomegreat – Simply Hibi – Tsingtao – Vitsmart*

Windscreen Repair Service 27 Hazel Grove Welton, Lincoln LN2 3LG Tel. *01673 861314* Fax. *01673 862022* E-mail. *info@gtglass.co.uk* Web. *diamondfast.co.uk Glass Technology*

Windsor Life Assurance Winsdor House Telford Centre, Town Centre, Telford TF3 4NB Tel. *0800 0731777* Fax. *08707 091111* E-mail. *graham.singleton@adminre.co.uk* Web. *www.windsor-life.com Windsor Life*

Wine For Spice Ltd 3 Park Steps St Georges Fields, London W2 2YQ Tel. *020 77244606* Fax. *08701 320055* E-mail. *we@dc3.co.uk* Web. *www.dc3.co.uk Dicercy White – Raga Rose – Rani Gold*

Winged Bull Aviation Ltd 5 Norway House Trafalgar Square, London SW1Y 5BN Tel. *0870 8503395* Fax. *0870 8503396* E-mail. *fly@bullwings.com* Web. *www.bullwings.co.uk bullwings*

Winget Ltd Plodder Lane Farnworth, Bolton BL4 0LR Tel. *01204 854650* Fax. *01204 854663* E-mail. *sales@winget.co.uk* Web. *www.winget.co.uk Croaker – Winget*

Winkworth Machinery Ltd Willow Tree Works Swallowfield Street, Swallowfield, Reading RG7 1QX Tel. *0118 9883551* Fax. *0118 9884031* E-mail. *info@mixer.co.uk* Web. *www.mixer.co.uk Winkworth*

Winn & Coales Denso Ltd Denso House 33-35 Chapel Road, London SE27 0TR Tel. *020 86707511* Fax. *020 87612456* E-mail. *mail@denso.net* Web. *www.denso.net Denso Steelcoat System – Denso Tape – Denso Therm – Densoclad Tapes – Densofil – Densopol – Densyl – Protal – Sylglas – Tokstrip*

Winterbotham Darby & Co. Ltd Granville House 9 Gatton Park Business Centre Wells Place, Merstham, Redhill RH1 3AS Tel. *01737 646646* Fax. *01737 646600* E-mail. *info@windar.co.uk* Web. *www.windar.co.uk *Winterbotham Darby & Co. (Worldwide)*

Graham Winterbottom Ltd Unit 33 Victoria Business Centre Mount Street, Accrington BB5 0PJ Tel. *01254 390700* Fax. *01254 390800* E-mail. *info@graham-winterbottom.co.uk* Web. *www.graham-winterbottom.co.uk Gee-Jay*

Winterthur Technology UK Ltd Unit 2 Oakham Drive, Sheffield S3 9QX Tel. *0114 2754211* Fax. *0114 2754132* E-mail. *ralf.egger@wgmbh.wendtgroup.com* Web. *www.wendtgroup.com Expandia – Wendt*

Winter & Co UK Ltd Stonehill Stukeley Meadows Industrial Estate, Huntingdon PE29 6ED Tel. *01480 377177* Fax. *01480 377166* E-mail. *sales@winter-company.com* Web. *www.winteruk.com *Buckray (Netherlands) – *Ecorel (U.S.A.) – PAPVR – *Skivertex (U.S.A.) – *Suedel Luxe (France) – Wibalin – *Wicotex (Netherlands)*

Winther Browne & Company Ltd 75 Bilton Way, Enfield EN3 7ER Tel. *020 83449050* Fax. *020 83449051* E-mail. *sales@wintherbrowne.co.uk* Web. *www.wintherbrowne.co.uk *Brio (France) – Trubeam – Winther Browne & Co Ltd*

Wiper Supply Services Ltd 41 Sedgewick Road, Luton LU4 9DT Tel. *0844 2092620* Fax. *0844 2092621* E-mail. *sales@wipersupply.com* Web. *www.wipersupply.com Cliniclean (United Kingdom) – Polisoft – Novatex (United Kingdom)*

Wire Belt Co. Ltd Castle Road, Sittingbourne ME10 3RF Tel. *01795 421771* Fax. *01795 428905* E-mail. *sales@wirebelt.co.uk* Web. *www.wirebelt.co.uk Flat-Flex – Flex-Turn – Ladder-Flex*

Wire & Plastic Products Ltd Pennypot Industrial Estate Pennypot, Hythe CT21 6PE Tel. *01303 266061* Fax. *01303 261080* E-mail. *sales@delfinware.co.uk* Web. *www.delfinware.co.uk Delphin Ware*

Wisbech Payroll Services 107 Norwich Road, Wisbech PE13 2BB Tel. *01945 464679* Fax. *01945 464680* E-mail. *sales@wispaypayrollbureau.co.uk* Web. *www.wispaypayrollbureau.co.uk Wispay for Windows TM*

Witcomb Cycles (t/a Witcomb Cycles) 25 Tanners Hill, London SE8 4PJ Tel. *020 86921734* Fax. *020 86921734* E-mail. *joymartin@deloittecompanyuk.com* Web. *www.witcombcycles.com Barern – Barrie Witcomb – Brazing – Enamelling – Velo Sport – Witcomb – Witcomb Cycles*

Witham Oil & Paint Lowestoft Ltd Waveney Works Stanley Road, Lowestoft NR33 9ND Tel. *01502 563434* Fax. *01502 500010* E-mail. *tony.baker@withamgroup.co.uk* Web. *www.withamgroup.co.uk Bitumine – Brillite – Clor-O-Cote – Epidox – Epidox 1 – Epidox 2 – Epidox Metacote – Miodox – Unicryl – Unidox – Unidox – Uniglaze – Uniglow – Uniline – Unimatt – Unisil – Unistuc – Unitas – Visco-Led – Woodcote*

Withers & Rogers LLP Goldings House 2 Hays Lane, London SE1 2HW Tel. *020 76633500* Fax. *020 76633550* E-mail. *ndougan@withersrogers.com* Web. *www.withersrogers.com Withers & Rogers*

C P Witter Ltd Unit 1 Drome Road, Deeside Industrial Park, Deeside CH5 2NY Tel. *01244 284500* Web. *www.wittertowbar.co.uk Witter Towbars*

Witton Chemical Co. Ltd Southgate Avenue Mildenhall, Bury St Edmunds IP28 7AT Tel. *01638 716001* Fax. *01638 717658* E-mail. *ukoffice@witton.com* Web. *www.witton.com Acriflow – Metaplex*

Wizzoo 8 Princess Street Bollington, Macclesfield SK10 5HZ Tel. *0844 5048400* E-mail. *info@wizzoo.com* Web. *www.wizzoo.com WIZZOO Limited*

W J P Engineering Plastics Ltd 2 Albert Avenue, Nottingham NG8 5BE Tel. *0115 9299555* Fax. *0115 9290422* E-mail. *sales@wjpengineeringplastics.co.uk* Web. *www.wjpengineeringplastics.co.uk Teflon*

W J Sutton Ltd St Helens House 23-31 Vittoria Street, Birmingham B1 3ND Tel. *0121 6045446* Fax. *0121 2369866* E-mail. *kenneth.sutton@wjsutton.co.uk* Web. *www.wjsutton.co.uk W.J.S.*

W Mannering London Ltd 7 Bellingham Trading Estate Randlesdown Road, London SE6 3BT Tel. *020 84614400* Fax. *020 86958784* E-mail. *sales@mannering-rubber.co.uk* Web. *www.mannering-rubber.co.uk Butyl – Delrin – EPDM – Evazote – Hypalon – Jubilee – Neoprene – Nitrile – Plastazote – Silicone – Tico Pad – Viton – Zotefoams*

W M F UK Ltd 31 Riverside Way Cowley, Uxbridge UB8 2YF Tel. *01895 816100* Fax. *01895 816105* E-mail. *sales@wmf.uk.com* Web. *www.wmf.uk.com *Alfi – Tafelstern – *WMF*

W Moorcroft Ltd Sandbach Road Burslem, Stoke On Trent ST6 2DQ Tel. *01782 820500* Fax. *01782 820502* E-mail. *enquiries@moorcroft.com* Web. *www.moorcroft.com Moorcroft*

W M Web Design 50 Chelveston Crescent, Solihull B91 3YH Tel. *0121 7056502* E-mail. *info@wmwebdesign.co.uk* Web. *www.wmwebdesign.co.uk WM Web Design*

W Neal Services 29 Purdeys Industrial Estate Purdeys Way, Rochford SS4 1ND Tel. *01702 542554* Fax. *01702 542558* E-mail. *sales@wnealservices.com* Web. *www.wnealservices.com WNS*

Woking Funeral Service 119-121 Goldsworth Road, Woking GU21 6LR Tel. *01483 772266* Fax. *01483 729285* Web. *www.wokingfunerals.co.uk Woking Funeral Service*

Wolds Engineering Services Ltd Unit 1 The Wolds Building Pocklington Industrial Estate, Pocklington, York YO42 1NR Tel. *01759 303877* Fax. *01759 306952* E-mail. *john@woldsengineering.co.uk* Web. *www.woldsengineering.co.uk CHATSWORTH – DICKIES – DODGE – FACOM TOOLS – FAG – IWIS CHAIN – MOLYCOTE – MORRIS LUBRICANTS – OPTIBELT – RENOLD – SEALEY – TENTE – TRANSDEV – UNI CHAINS*

Wolf Safety Lamp Company Ltd Saxon Road, Sheffield S8 0YA Tel. *0114 2551051* Fax. *0114 2557988* E-mail. *info@wolf-safety.co.uk* Web. *www.wolf-safety.co.uk Airturbo – LiteTracker – Penlite – Toplite – Turbolite – Wolf – Wolflite*

Wolseley UK PO Box 21 Boroughbridge Road, Ripon HG4 1SL Tel. *01765 690690* Fax. *01224 637598* Web. *www.draincenter.co.uk Broughton Crangrove – Builder Center – Controls Center – Drainage Center – First Base Timber – High Cool – HRPC – Pipeline Center – Plumb Center – Wash Vac*

Wolstenholme Machine Knifes Ltd 1 Downgate Drive, Sheffield S4 8BT Tel. *0114 2445600* Fax. *0114 2446556* E-mail. *sales@wolstenholme.co.uk* Web. *www.wolstenholme.co.uk Wolstenholme Machine Knives Ltd*

Wolters Kluwer Health 250 Waterloo Road, London SE1 8RD Tel. *020 79810600* Fax. *020 79810601* E-mail. *europe@ovid.com* Web. *www.wolterskluwer.com Silverplatter*

Wolverhampton Electro Plating Ltd Wood Lane, Wolverhampton WV10 8HN Tel. *01902 397333* Fax. *01902 785372* E-mail. *info@anochrome-group.co.uk* Web. *www.anochrome-group.co.uk Dacromet – Xylan*

Wolverhampton Handling Ltd Unit 10 Planetary Indl-Est Planetary Road, Willenhall WV13 3XQ Tel. *01902 726481* Fax. *01902 864744* E-mail. *sales@roller.co.uk* Web. *www.roller.co.uk Wolverhampton Handling*

Wood Auto Supplies Ltd Colne Road, Huddersfield HD1 3ES Tel. *01484 428261* Fax. *01484 434933* E-mail. *sales@woodauto.co.uk* Web. *www.woodauto.com B-Line – O.E.B. – Woodauto*

Wood Bros Furniture Ltd London Road, Ware SG12 9QH Tel. *08451 303303* Fax. *01920 464388* E-mail. *sales@oldcharm.co.uk* Web. *www.oldcharm.co.uk Old Charm*

G K Wood & Sons Ltd (t/a Fulbourn Medical) 5 Station Yard Wilbraham Road, Fulbourn, Cambridge CB21 5ET Tel. *01223 880909* Fax. *01223 880078* E-mail. *info@fulbournmedical.com* Web. *www.fulbournmedical.com Fulbourn Medical*

Woodfield Systems Ltd Tyler Way, Whitstable CT5 2RS Tel. *01227 793351* Fax. *01227 793625* E-mail. *richard.williams@akersolutions.com* Web. *www.akersolutions.com Woodfield Systems*

Wood & Floors Com 6 Yew Tree Drive, Guildford GU1 1PD Tel. *0783 5344146* E-mail. *info@woodandfloors.com* Web. *www.woodandfloors.com Alpine Collection*

Woodforde's Norfolk Ales (t/a Woodforde's Norfolk Ales) Broadland Brewery Woodbastwick, Norwich NR13 6SW Tel. *01603 720353* Fax. *01603 721806* E-mail. *dennis@woodfordes.co.uk* Web. *www.woodfordes.co.uk Great Eastern Ale – Headcracker – Kett's Rebellion – Mardlers Mild – Nelsons Revenge – Norfolk Nog – Norkie – Wherry Best Bitter*

Woodgrow Horticulture Burton Road Findern, Derby DE65 6BE Tel. *01332 517600* Fax. *01332 511481* E-mail. *sales@woodgrow.com* Web. *www.woodgrow.com Eco Compost – Flo-Grow – Horticultural Bark – Vita-Bark*

J Wood & Son Bilsdale Ploughs Ltd Kirby Mills Industrial Estate Kirkbymoorside, York YO62 6QR Tel. *01751 433434* Fax. *01751 433094* E-mail. *info@johnwoods.co.uk* Web. *www.johnwoods.co.uk Greenacres – J. Wood & Son*

Woodleigh Power Equipment Ltd Unit 20 Highcroft Industrial Estate Enterprise Rd, Horndean, Waterlooville PO8 0BT Tel. *023 92571360* Fax. *023 92592056* E-mail. *enquiries@woodleighpower.co.uk* Web. *www.woodleighpower.co.uk Kubota – SISU – Briggs & Sutton*

Woodley Equipment Co. Ltd Unit 7 Locomotive House Chorley New Road, Horwich, Bolton BL6 5UE Tel. *08456 777001* Fax. *08456 777002* E-mail. *sales@woodleyequipment.com* Web. *www.woodleyequipment.com Clinispin Horizon Centrifuges*

Richard Wood Babywear Sherbourne Street, Manchester M8 8HF Tel. *0161 8322734* Fax. *0161 8351547* E-mail. *rwbabywear@btconnect.com* Web. *www.richwoodbabywear.co.uk Richardwood*

Woodstock Leabank Ltd Corrie Way Bredbury, Stockport SK6 2ST Tel. *0161 4945868* Fax. *0161 4944409* E-mail. *j.omalley@woodstockleabank.co.uk* Web. *www.woodstockleabank.co.uk Office Furniture Distributors Ltd – Woodstock Leabank*

Woodstock Neckwear Ltd Telford Road, Glenrothes KY7 4NX Tel. *01592 771777* Fax. *01592 631717* Web. *www.randa.net Pierre Cardin – Woodstock*

Woodward Diesel Systems Hatherley Lane, Cheltenham GL51 0EU Tel. *01242 277000* Fax. *01242 277277* Web. *www.woodward.com Lucas Bryce*

The Woolwich Corporate Headquarters Watling Street, Bexleyheath DA6 7RR Tel. *0870 1660060* Fax. *01322 271117* E-mail. *customer.services@woolwich.co.uk* Web. *www.woolwich.co.uk Banca Woolwich – Banque Woolwich UK – Card Saver – Cashbase – Directions – Ecofile – Ekins – Ekins Homefile – Ekins Professional – Ekins Property Doctor – F P Mortgage No.1 – Fastmove – Firstplus Financial Group – Firstplus Management Services – Firstplus Services – Foxbury – G.H.L. 1 – G.H.L. 2 – G.H.L. Technology – Gateway – Global Home Loans – Gresham – Gresham Insurance – Gresham Insurance Company – Holidaywise – Home Smart – Homefile – I SAVE tax with the Woolwich – Ignition – ISAVE – ISAVE tax – Littlewoods Personal Finance – Loans Direct – Moneywise – Motorbase – NuDelta – NuDelta Company – Open Plan Borrowing – Open Plan Mortgage – Open Plan Private Bank – Open Plan Protecting – Open Plan Saving – Open Plan Services – Open Plan Shop – Pathway – Petguard – Sedgwick Independent Financial Consultants – The Woolwich – Touchbase – Town & Country Homebuilders – Town & Country Property Services (East Anglia) – Town & County – Town & County Homecare – W.ISA – W.T.S. – Winguard – Winguard Insurance – Winguard Insurance Company – With – Without – Woolwich – Woolwich (Isle of Man) – Woolwich Agency Services – Woolwich Asset Management – Woolwich Assured Homes – Woolwich Broking Services – Woolwich Card Save – Woolwich Card Services – Woolwich Consumer Finance – Woolwich Contracts – Woolwich Conveyancing Services – Woolwich Credit Services – Woolwich Developments – Woolwich Direct – Woolwich Easy Step – Woolwich Electronic Shopping – Woolwich Enterprises – Woolwich Estate Agency Services – Woolwich Executors – Woolwich Finance – Woolwich Financial Advisory Services – Woolwich Financial Brokers – Woolwich Financial Services – Woolwich Fund Managers – Woolwich Group – Woolwich Group Funding – Woolwich Guernsey – Woolwich Holdings – Woolwich Home Services – Woolwich Home Shopping – Woolwich Homes – Woolwich Housing – Woolwich Housing Management – Woolwich Ignition – Woolwich Independent Financial Advisory Services – Woolwich Individual Savings Account Managers – Woolwich Insurance Services – Woolwich International Trustees – Woolwich Internet Bank – Woolwich Internet Services – Woolwich Investment Services – Woolwich Life – Woolwich Life Assurance – Woolwich Lifestyle – Woolwich Loan Services – Woolwich Monitor – Woolwich Mortgage Services – Woolwich Motorbase – Woolwich Nominees – Woolwich Open Plan – Woolwich Open Plan Borrowing – Woolwich Open Plan Private Bank – Woolwich Open Plan Protecting – Woolwich Open Plan Saving – Woolwich Open Plan Services – Woolwich Open Plan Shop – Woolwich Pension Fund Trust – Woolwich Pension Services – Woolwich Personal Equity Plan Managers – Woolwich Personal Finance – Woolwich Plan Managers – Woolwich Plan Nominees – Woolwich Property Services – Woolwich Property Shop – Woolwich Sharestore – Woolwich Shop – Woolwich Spa – Woolwich Surveying Services – Woolwich Surveying Services Property Management – Woolwich Switch and Save – Woolwich Unit Trust Managers*

Worcester Bosch Group Ltd (t/a The Bosch Group) Cotsworld Way, Worcester WR4 9SW Tel. *08448 929900* Fax. *01905 754863* E-mail. *carl.arntzen@uk.bosch.com* Web. *www.worcester-bosch.co.uk 15 SBi – 24CDi – 24i – 25 SBi – 26CDi Xtra – 28CDi – 35CDi – Danesmoor – Greenstar – Heatslave – Heatslave - Highflow – W.B. – W.R. 325 – WHS*

Worcester Presses (a division of Jones & Attwood Ltd) Titan Works Old Wharf Road, Amblecote, Stourbridge DY8 4LR Tel. *01384 392266* Fax. *01384 374261* E-mail. *sales@worcesterpresses.co.uk* Web. *www.worcesterpresses.co.uk Chinfong*

Wordcraft International Ltd Park Hill Hilton Road, Egginton, Derby DE65 6GU Tel. *01283 731400* Fax. *01283 731401* E-mail. *sales@wordcraft.com* Web. *www.wordcraft.com C.F.P. – Faxlead – Laserfax – Printscan – Respond – The News – Unimessage Pro*

Workhorse Communications Shedfield Grange Sandy Lane, Shedfield, Southampton SO32 2HQ Tel. *01329 833865* Fax. *01329 832543* E-mail. *markphillimore@btconnect.com Workhorse Communications*

Worksop Galvanising Ltd (Wedge Group Galvanizing) Claylands Avenue, Worksop S81 7BQ Tel. *01909 486384* Fax. *01909 482540* E-mail. *david.leverton@wegge-galv.co.uk* Web. *www.wedge-galv.co.uk Wedge Group Galvanizing*

The World Markets Company Public Limited Company 525 Ferry Road, Edinburgh EH5 2AW Tel. *0131 3155515* Fax. *0131 3152999* E-mail. *wmreuters.sales@wmcompany.com* Web. *www.wmcompany.com W.M.*

World's End Couriers Ltd Unit 6b Farm Lane Trading Estate 101 Farm Lane, London SW6 1QJ Tel. *020 73818991* Fax. *020 73854468* E-mail. *info@worldsendcouriers.co.uk* Web. *www.wecouriers.co.uk BISAZZA – CASA DOLCE – REX – SAINT GOBAIN – SALVATORI – SICIS – VIVA*

World Of Spice Ltd Bebington Close, Billericay CM12 0DT Tel. *01277 633303* Fax. *01277 633036* E-mail. *sales@worldofspice.co.uk* Web. *www.worldofspice.co.uk Unbar*

World Trade Publishing Ltd 36 Crosby Road North, Liverpool L22 4QQ Tel. *0151 9289288* Fax. *0151 9284190* E-mail. *wl@worldtrades.co.uk* Web. *www.worldtrades.co.uk World Footwear – World Leather – World Sports Activewear*

Worldwide Dispensers Unit 17-19 Merton Industrial Park Lee Road, London SW19 3WD Tel. *020 85457500* Fax. *020 85457502* E-mail. *marketing@dsswd.com* Web. *www.worldwidedispensers.com Aeroflow – Drum Major – Drum Tap – Jumbo – Press Tap – Quick Serve – Smooth Flow – Syphon*

Worlifts Ltd Guilds House Sandy Lane, Wildmoor, Bromsgrove B61 0QU Tel. *0121 4601113* Fax. *0121 5251022* E-mail. *info@worlifts.co.uk* Web. *www.worlifts.co.uk *Enerpac (U.S.A.) – *P. Tirfor (France) – TANGYE*

Worms Eye Site Investigation Ltd 52 Bank Parade, Burnley BB11 1TS Tel. *01282 414649* Fax. *01282 721916* E-mail. *info@wormseye.co.uk* Web. *www.wormseye.co.uk Kerbfast – Worms Eye*

Worrall Locks Ltd Unit A2 Erebus Works Albion Road, Willenhall WV13 1NH Tel. *01902 605038* Fax. *01902 633558* E-mail. *dcooper@worrall-locks.co.uk* Web. *www.worrall-locks.co.uk Crescent – Spaceguard*

Worson Die Cushions Ltd 89-91 Rolfe Street, Smethwick B66 2AY Tel. *0121 5580939* Fax. *0121 5580017 Worson*

Wovina Woven Labels 1-3 Omaha Road, Bodmin PL31 1ER Tel. *01208 73484* Fax. *01208 78158* E-mail. *m.flowerdew@wovina.com* Web. *www.wovina.com Wovina*

W P Thompson & Co Coopers Building Church Street, Liverpool L1 3AB Tel. *0151 7093961* Fax. *01482 228366* E-mail. *tlbrand@wpt.co.uk* Web. *www.wpt.co.uk W.P. Thompson*

Wrap Film Systems Ltd Hortonwood 45, Telford TF1 7FA Tel. *01952 678800* Fax. *01494 656801* E-mail. *adrian.brown@wrapfilm.com* Web. *www.wrapfilm.com Caterwrap*

Wrapid Manufacturing Ltd 250 Thornton Road, Bradford BD1 2LB Tel. *01274 220220* Fax. *01274 736195* E-mail. *sales@wrapid.co.uk* Web. *www.wrapid.co.uk Dupont Clysar – *Elsner (U.S.A.) – *Pfankuch (Germany) – *Shanklin (U.S.A.) – *Ulma (Spain)*

Wrekin Frame & Truss (Gang-Nail Systems Ltd) Unit 24 Churchfields Business Park Clensmore Street, Kidderminster DY10 2JY Tel. *01562 747555* Fax. *01562 748555 Ecojoist*

Jonathan Wren & Co. Ltd 34 London Wall, London EC2M 5RU Tel. *020 73093550* Fax. *020 76261242* E-mail. *career@jwren.com* Web. *www.jwren.com Jonathan Wren*

Wrexham Mineral Cables Ltd Plot 4 Wynnstay Technology Park Ruabon, Wrexham LL14 6EN Tel. *01978 810789* Fax. *01978 821502* E-mail. *sales@wrexhammineralcable.com* Web. *www.wrexhammineralcable.com Kontimag – WHC 20 – WIG 20*

Wrightbus Ltd Galgorm Industrial Estate Fenaghy Road, Galgorm, Ballymena BT42 1PY Tel. *028 25641212* Fax. *028 25649703* E-mail. *mnodder@wright-bus.com* Web. *www.wright-bus.com Aluminique*

Denis Wright Ltd 1 Purley Place, London N1 1QA Tel. *020 72262628* Fax. *020 72266890*

E-mail. *john.wright@denis-wright.com* Web. *www.denis-wright.com Event – Event Series – Graeme Lawton*

Wright Dental Group Block 11a Dunsinane Avenue, Dunsinane Industrial Estate, Dundee DD2 3QT Tel. *01382 833866* Fax. *01382 811042* E-mail. *sales@wright-cottrell.co.uk* Web. *www.wright-cottrell.co.uk Acrotone – Eezitray – Kromogel – Sentor*

Wrightflow Technologies Ltd Highfield Industrial Estate Edison Road, Eastbourne BN23 6PT Tel. *01323 509211* Fax. *01323 507306* E-mail. *jinfo@idexcorp.com* Web. *www.johnsonpump.com Albin S.L.P. – Classic – Concept 21/60 – On Line – P.D. – RTP – SQ – Sterilobe*

G R Wright & Sons Ltd Ponders End Mills Wharf Road, Enfield EN3 4TG Tel. *020 83446900* Fax. *020 88040533* E-mail. *sales@wrightsflour.co.uk* Web. *www.wrightsflour.co.uk LionHeart – Scofa*

Wright Machinery Ltd (Head Office) Stonefield Way, Ruislip HA4 0JU Tel. *020 88422244* Fax. *020 88421113* E-mail. *sales@wright.co.uk* Web. *www.wright.co.uk Flowright – Pacwright*

M Wright & Sons Ltd Quorn Mills Leicester Road, Quorn, Loughborough LE12 8FZ Tel. *01509 412365* Fax. *01509 415618* E-mail. *info@mwright.co.uk* Web. *www.mwright.co.uk Quorna*

Wrightrain Environmental Ltd Foxhill Farm Stables Foxhill Road, West Haddon, Northampton NN6 7BG Tel. *01788 510529* Fax. *01788 510728* E-mail. *sales@wrightrain.co.uk* Web. *www.the-wright-group.co.uk Supertouraine & Touraine – *Wright Rain (Italy)*

W R T L Exterior Lighting Ltd Waterside Park Golds Hill Way, Tipton DY4 0PU Tel. *0121 5211234* Fax. *0121 5211250* E-mail. *r.schmit@wrtl.co.uk* Web. *www.wrtle.co.uk Industria*

W R T L I-Tunnel Llys Edmund Prys St Asaph Business Park, St Asaph LL17 0JA Tel. *01745 582918* Fax. *01745 585317* E-mail. *i-tunnel@wrtl.co.uk* Web. *www.wrtl.co.uk Scouts – T.S.S.D.P.S.C. Isolator Range*

W T Lamb Holdings Property Services Nyewood Court Brookers Road, Billingshurst RH14 9RZ Tel. *01403 785141* Fax. *01403 784663* E-mail. *sales@lambsbricks.com* Web. *www.lambsbricks.com Cremer Whiting – Godstone – Lambs Bricks & Arches – Pitsham*

Www.Safetysignsonline.Co.Uk 5 Chelford Road, Macclesfield SK10 3LG Tel. *0800 2889874* Fax. *01625 508261* E-mail. *info@safetysignsonline.co.uk* Web. *www.safetysignsonline.co.uk Crown – Dulux – Ruskins – Rustoleum – Sickens*

www.tap-die.com 445 West Green Road, London N15 3PL Tel. *020 88881865* Fax. *020 88884613* E-mail. *sales@tap-die.com* Web. *www.tap-die.com Swiftic – T&D HQS – Totem – Trubor*

Wyastone Estate Ltd Wyastone Leys Ganarew, Monmouth NP25 3SR Tel. *01600 890007* Fax. *01600 891052* E-mail. *sales@wyastone.co.uk* Web. *www.wyastone.co.uk Nimbus Records*

Wyatt Bros Water Services Ltd Waymills Industrial Estate Waymills, Whitchurch SY13 1TT Tel. *01948 662526* Fax. *01948 667560* E-mail. *info@wyattbros.com* Web. *www.wyattbros.com Dab – Grundfos – Lowara*

Wybone Ltd Mason Way Hoyland, Barnsley S74 9TF Tel. *01226 744010* Fax. *01226 350105* E-mail. *sales@wybone.co.uk* Web. *www.wybone.co.uk Fireguard Sack Holders – Rhino Tough Glass – Wybone*

Wylie Systems Drury Lane, St Leonards On Sea TN38 9BA Tel. *01424 421235* Fax. *01424 433760* E-mail. *georges@raycowylie.com* Web. *www.raycowylie.com Rayco – Weighload – *Wylie*

Wyman Gordon Tower Works Spa Road, Lincoln LN2 5TB Tel. *01522 565000* Fax. *01522 521701* E-mail. *chris.thomas@wyman-uk.com* Web. *www.wyman-gordon.com Wyman-Gordon*

WyseGroup Ltd Lancaster Road Cressex Business Park, High Wycombe HP12 3QP Tel. *01494 560900* Fax. *01494 560889* E-mail. *info@wysepower.com* Web. *www.wysepower.com Wyseplant – Wysepower*

Wyvern Cargo Distribution Ltd (Southern Distribution Centre) Broom Road, Poole BH12 4NR Tel. *01202 307500* Fax. *01202 715066* E-mail. *sales@wyverncargo.com* Web. *www.wyverncargo.com A.N.C. Express – Wyvern Cargo*

Wyvern Scaffolding 37 Wellfield Road, Hatfield AL10 0BY Tel. *01707 251591* Fax. *01707 276879* E-mail. *wyvernscaff@aol.com Wyvern*

X

Xara Ltd Gaddesden Place Great Gaddesden, Hemel Hempstead HP2 6EX Tel. *01442 350000* Fax. *01442 350010* E-mail. *sales@xara.com* Web. *www.xara.com ArtWorks – AudioWorks – Compression – Formulix – GreyHawk – Impression Publiser – Impression Style – MacFS – MidiMax – Publisher Plus – Scanlight – TurboDriver – WordWorks*

Xfurth Ltd Unit 4 Firbank Industrial Estate Dallow Road, Luton LU1 1TW Tel. *01582 436000* Fax. *01582 455955* E-mail. *sales@xfurth.com* Web. *www.xfurth.com Herfurth – Herfurth Laser Technology*

Xixin Ltd Bilton Way, Luton LU1 1UU Tel. *01582 400340* Fax. *01582 481498* E-mail. *sales@xixin.co.uk* Web. *www.xixin.co.uk Xixin*

XN Hotel Systems Ltd The Old Vicarage Market Street, Castle Donington, Derby DE74 2JB Tel. *0845 0942220* Fax. *0845 0942221* E-mail. *sales@xnhotels.com* Web. *www.xnhotels.com E P O S*

Xodus Group Ltd Xodus House 50 Huntly Street, Aberdeen AB10 1RS Tel. *01224 628300* Fax. *01224 628333* E-mail. *info@xodusgroup.com* Web. *www.xodusgroup.com Xodus Group, oil and gas, consultants, subsea, dri*

Xrio Ltd 357 Roundhay Road, Leeds LS8 4BU Tel. *08456 443226* E-mail. *sales@xrio.com* Web. *www.xrio.com ubm – UBMi – Unified Bandwidth Management – VBond*

Xstrahl Ltd Watchmoor Park The Coliseum, Camberley GU15 3YL Tel. *01276 462696* Fax. *01276 684205* E-mail. *support@xstrahl.com* Web. *www.xstrahl.com KRAUT KRAMER – PANTAK – SEIFERT – THERAPAX*

Xtratherm Park Road Holmewood Industrial Park, Holmewood, Chesterfield S42 5UY Tel. *01246 858100* Fax. *01246 857447* E-mail. *info@xtratherm.com* Web. *www.xtratherm.com Xtratherm XTCW – Xtratherm XTPR – Xtratherm XTSP – Xtratherm XTUF*

Xtreme Vortex Chessington Avenue, Bexleyheath DA7 5NP Tel. *07739 560990* E-mail. *mail@xtremevortex.co.uk* Web. *www.xtremevortex.co.uk Xtreme Vortex – Mobile rock climbing wall – Mobile laser tag arena*

Xylem Unit 11 Fulcrum 2 Solent Way, Whiteley, Fareham PO15 7FN Tel. *01489 563470* Fax. *01489 563471* E-mail. *info@totton-pumps.com* Web. *www.itt.com Totton Pumps*

Y

Yachting Instruments Ltd Mappowder, Sturminster Newton DT10 1EH Tel. *01258 817662* E-mail. *office@tidemaster.co.uk* Web. *www.tidemaster.co.uk Dry Gloves – Dry Mitts – Drysocks – Memoquartz – *Seamaster (Japan) – *Stockburger (Germany) – Tidemaster – *Walk & Surf (Italy) – Windmaster*

Yale Flagship House, Fleet GU51 4WD Tel. *01252 770700* Fax. *01252 770791* Web. *www.nmhg.com Yale Fork Lift Trucks – Yale Industrial Trucks – Yale lift trucks*

Yamazaki Machinery UK Ltd Badgeworth Drive Warndon, Worcester WR4 9NF Tel. *01905 755755* Fax. *01905 755001* E-mail. *dcleugh@mazak.co.uk* Web. *www.mazak.eu CAMWARE – Cyber machine monitor – Cyber Scheduler – Cyber tool management – Mazak – Mazak, Mazatrol, CAMWARE, Cyber Tool Management, Cyber Machine Monitor – Mazatrol*

Yara UK It Ltd Fertilizers Immingham Dock, Immingham DN40 2NS Tel. *01469 571136* Fax. *01469 571624* E-mail. *yarauk.info@yara.com* Web. *www.yara.com Classic Royale – Double Season – Extra Grass – Extran – Extran PLan – Flying Start – Hydro Precise – Kristalon – Nitrotop – Nutran – Paddock Royale – PG Mix – Precision Plan – Shepherds – Sulphurcut – Super Sward – Topgro – Turf Royale*

Yarmouth Stores Ltd 117 South Quay, Great Yarmouth NR30 3LD Tel. *01493 842289* Fax. *01493 853416* E-mail. *sales@ybeauty-uniforms.co.uk* Web. *www.yarmo.co.uk Yarmo*

Brian Yates Lansil Way Lansil Industrial Estate, Lancaster LA1 3QY Tel. *01524 35035* Fax. *01524 32232* E-mail. *sales@brian-yates.co.uk* Web. *www.brian-yates.co.uk Belle Isle – Fidelio – Foxfield – Heversham – Leyburn – Lindale – Pepe Penalver – Sharrow Bay – Sheila Coombes – Sheila Coombes 111 – Sheila Coombes Abbey Garden – Sheila Coombes I – Sheila Coombes II – Sheila Coombes Tara – Taco*

Yateson Stainless Osman House Prince Street, Bolton BL1 2NP Tel. *01204 370099* Fax. *01204 392634* E-mail. *info@yateson-stainless.com* Web. *www.yateson-stainless.com *Modentic*

Yoga Model London Limited 1, ajax avenue, london NW9 5EY Tel. *07961 882895* Fax. *020 79790093* E-mail. *sales@yogamodel.co.uk* Web. *www.yogamodel.co.uk Yoga*

Yokota UK Low Common Road Dinnington, Sheffield S25 2RJ Tel. *01909 552471* Fax. *01909 552472* E-mail. *info@duro-diamonds.co.uk* Web. *www.yokota.co.uk Action Sockets – Diamond Tools and Abrasive Solutions – DTAS – EDI – Electrode Dressers Inc – NPK – Red Rooster – Toku – Yokota – Yokota Airtools*

York Archaeological Trust For Excavation & Research Ltd Cuthbert Morrell House 47 Aldwark, York YO1 7BX Tel. *01904 663000* Fax. *01904 663024* E-mail. *pnicholson@yorkarchaeology.co.uk* Web. *www.yorkarchaeoligy.co.uk A.R.C. – Barley Hall – Jorvik Viking Centre*

York Brewery Co. Ltd 12 Toft Green, York YO1 6JT Tel. *01904 621162* Fax. *01904 621216* E-mail. *sales@york-brewery.co.uk* Web. *www.york-brewery.co.uk *Mildly Mad Pub Company*

York House Meat Products Ltd Shannon Place Potton, Sandy SG19 2YH Tel. *01767 260114* Fax. *01767 262165* E-mail. *trm@yorkhousemeatproducts.com* Web. *www.yorkhousefoods.com *York House The Taste Of Excellence*

Yorkon Ltd New Lane Huntington, York YO32 9PT Tel. *01904 610990* Fax. *01904 610880* E-mail. *contact@yorkon.com* Web. *www.yorkon.co.uk Yorkon*

Yorkshire Building Society Yorkshire House Yorkshire Drive, Bradford BD5 8LJ Tel. *01274 740740* Fax. *01274 652134* E-mail. *atgosling@ybs.co.uk* Web. *www.ybs.co.uk Yorkshire Building Society – Yorkshire by Post – Yorkshire Guernsey*

Yorkshire Post Wellington Street, Leeds LS1 1RF Tel. *0113 2432701* Fax. *01274 370165* Web. *www.yorkshireposttoday.co.uk Yorkshire Evening Post, The – Yorkshire Post, The*

Yorkshire Precision Gauges Ltd Cuckoo Lane Hatfield, Doncaster DN7 6QF Tel. *01302 840303* Fax. *01302 843570* E-mail. *gauges@ypg.co.uk* Web. *www.ypg.co.uk Split Mate – YPG*

Yorkshire Refractory Products Ltd Unit 9 Lee Bridge Industrial Estate, Halifax HX3 5HE Tel. *01422 353344* Fax. *01422 353366* E-mail. *sales@yrpl.com* Web. *www.yorkshirerefractoryproducts.com Refrex – Teknilite*

Yorkshire Regional Newspapers Ltd 17-23 Aberdeen Walk, Scarborough YO11 1BB Tel. *01723 363636* Fax. *01723 383825* E-mail. *editorial@scarborougheveningnews.co.uk* Web. *www.scarboroughtoday.co.uk Bridlington Free Press – Driffield Times – Filey & Humamby Mercury – Malton & Pickering Mercury – Pocklington Post – Scarborough Evening News – Scarborough Mercury Series – The Trader – Whitby Gazette*

Yorkshire Rubber Linings Ltd Preistley House Spenborough Industrial Estate Union Road, Liversedge WF15 7JZ Tel. *01924 410414* Fax. *01924 410413* E-mail. *sales@rubberlinings.co.uk* Web. *www.rubberlinings.co.uk YRL 105 (United Kingdom) – YRL 106 (United Kingdom) – YRL 110 (United Kingdom) – YRL 120 (United Kingdom) – YRL 138 (United Kingdom) – YRL 146 (United Kingdom) – YRL 178 (United Kingdom) – YRL 200 (United Kingdom) – YRL121 (United Kingdom) – YRL136 (United Kingdom) – YRL137 (United Kingdom)*

Yorkshire Window Co. Ltd Hellaby Lane Hellaby, Rotherham S66 8HN Tel. *01709 540982* Fax. *01302 366684* E-mail. *info@ywcgroup.co.uk* Web. *www.ywcgroup.co.uk Yorkshire Windows*

Yougovcentaur 50 Poland Street, London W1F 7AX Tel. *020 79704000* Fax. *020 79704398* E-mail. *ian.roberts@centaur.co.uk* Web. *www.centaur.co.uk Lawtel*

J Youle & Co. Ltd Chesterton Road Eastwood Trading Estate, Rotherham S65 1SU Tel. *01709 375349* Fax. *01709 363872* E-mail. *chris@youleandco.co.uk* Web. *www.youleandco.com Youle*

Youngs Seafood Ross House Wickham Road, Grimsby DN31 3SW Tel. *01472 585858* E-mail. *askus@youngsseafood.co.uk* Web. *www.youngsseafood.co.uk Bluecrest – Kingfrost – Ross – Youngs*

Your Key To Spain 83 Baker Street, London W1U 6AG Tel. *0121 3639374* E-mail. *brittney.jackeline@mail.com* Web. *www.yourkeytospain.co.uk Spanish Property*

Your Move Newcastle House Albany Court, Newcastle Business Park, Newcastle upon Tyne NE4 7YB Tel. *0191 2334600* Fax. *0191 2735005* E-mail. *enquiries@your-move.co.uk* Web. *www.your-move.co.uk GA Town & Country – General Accident – General Accident Property Services*

Y S E Ltd Church House Abbey Close, Sherborne DT9 3LQ Tel. *08451 221414* Fax. *0845 1221415* E-mail. *sales@yseski.co.uk* Web. *www.yseski.co.uk France – Ski – Val d'Isère*

A C Yule & Son Ltd Craigshaw Road West Tullos Indl-Est, Aberdeen AB12 3ZG Tel. *01224 230000* Fax. *01224 230011* E-mail. *byule@acyule.com* Web. *www.acyule.co.uk Keepheat – Tempa Glass – Tempaflam – Yuleplus*

Yule Catto & Co plc Central Road, Harlow CM20 2BH Tel. *01279 442791* Fax. *01279 641360* E-mail. *info@yulecatto.com* Web. *www.yulecatto.com Anteco – Autoclenz – Baselock – *Bik Bouwprodkiten (Netherlands) – Brencliffe – Coxdome – Dimex – Envioroclean – Greenhill – *Jet Kunststofftechnik (Germany) – *Kimmenade (Netherlands) – Pyrovent – Revertex – Screenbase – Skyline – Synthomer – Transplastix – Unilock*

Z

Zamo Household Products Ltd 27 White Post Lane, London E9 5EN Tel. *020 85251177* Fax. *020 85334013* E-mail. *zamoproducts@aol.com* Web. *www.zamohouseholdproductsltd.co.uk Zamo*

Zap Controls Ltd Unit 100 Anglesey Business Park Littleworth Road, Hednesford, Cannock WS12 1NR Tel. *01543 879444* Fax. *01543 879333* E-mail. *mail@zap-uk.com* Web. *www.zap-uk.com Access Control – Remote Controls – Zap Controls*

Zeag UK Ltd Zeag House 17 Deer Park Road, London SW19 3XJ Tel. *0800 6524111* Fax. *020 84435344* E-mail. *paul.woods@zeaguk.com* Web. *www.zeaguk.com*

Cantilevered Sliding Gate – Champion – Conqueror – Flexipark – M.K.11 Rising Arm Barrier – Rising Kerb – Tully Perimeter Security

Zeal Clean Supplies Ltd 8 Deer Park Road, London SW19 3UU Tel. *020 82548800* Fax. *020 82540930* E-mail. *enquiries@zealpackaging.com* Web. *www.zealcleansupplies.co.uk G.H. Zeal*

Zeiss Unit 2 Hadrians Way Glebe Farm Industrial Estate, Rugby CV21 1ST Tel. *01788 821770* Fax. *01788 821755* E-mail. *a.thompson@zeiss.co.uk* Web. *www.zeiss.co.uk Calypso – Prismo – Vast – Zeiss*

Zeitlauf Little Balmer Buckingham Industrial Estate, Buckingham MK18 1TF Tel. *01280 824516* Fax. *01280 824517* E-mail. *chris.robinson@zeitlauf.co.uk* Web. *www.zeitlauf.co.uk ZEITLAUF antriebstechnik*

Zella Instrumentation & Control Ltd Unit 2 Cook House Brunel Drive, Newark NG24 2FB Tel. *01636 704370* Fax. *01636 640296* E-mail. *sales@zella-instrumentation.co.uk* Web. *www.zella.co.uk Italvalvole – RQ Motor Range – Setex*

Zeon Chemicals Europe Ltd Sully Moors Road Sully, Penarth CF64 5ZE Tel. *01446 725400* Fax. *01446 747988* E-mail. *debbie.smith@zeon.eu* Web. *www.zeon.eu *Equinox (Far East) – *Ingersoll (Far East) – *Zeon Chich (Far East)*

Zero Clips Ltd 100 Charles Henry Street, Birmingham B12 0SJ Tel. *0121 6223211* Fax. *0121 6222813* E-mail. *sales@zeroclips.com* Web. *www.zeroclips.com JCS – Tridon – Zeroclips – Zeroclips - JCS - Tridon.*

03 Solutions Ltd Centre House 79 Chichester St, Belfast BT1 4JE Tel. *028 90656552* E-mail. *mail@o3solutions.com* Web. *www.o3solutions.com Cig Arrete – germazap – insectazap – oxizone – XLerator*

Zhender Group UK Ltd Unit 4 Watchmoor Point, Camberley GU15 3AD Tel. *01252 515151* Fax. *01276 605801* Web. *www.bisque.co.uk Faral*

Zipex UK Ltd 15 Abbey Gate, Leicester LE4 0AA Tel. *0116 2624988* Fax. *0116 2513745* E-mail. *sales@zipex.co.uk* Web. *www.zipex.co.uk Pex*

Zippo UK Ltd Unit 27 Grand Union Centre West Row, London W10 5AS Tel. *020 89640666* Fax. *020 89680400* E-mail. *sales@zippo-uk.co.uk* Web. *www.zippo.co.uk *Zippo (U.S.A.)*

Z-Laser Uk Sales Office PO Box 55, Merthyr Tydfil NP11 9AB Tel. *07515 574756* E-mail. *rees@z-laser.com* Web. *www.z-laser.co.uk Z-Laser Optoelektronik GmbH*

The Zockoll Group Ltd 143 Maple Road, Surbiton KT6 4BJ Tel. *0800 749927* Fax. *020 84812288* E-mail. *postmaster@dyno.com* Web. *www.dyno.com Dyno Glazing – Dyno Locks – Dyno Plumbing – Dyno Roofing – Dyno-Kil – Dyno-Rod*

Zodiac Screw Gauge Ltd 15-17 Fortnum Close, Birmingham B33 0LG Tel. *0121 7840474* Fax. *0121 7897210 Zodiac*

Zodiac Stainless Products Co. Ltd Selly Oak Industrial Estate Elliott Road, Birmingham B29 6LR Tel. *0121 4727206* Fax. *0121 4715109* E-mail. *sales@zodiacspco.co.uk* Web. *www.zodiacspco.co.uk *Sunnex Products (Hong Kong) – *Tramontina (Brazil) – Zodiac*

Zodion Ltd Zodion House Station Road, Sowerby Bridge HX6 3AF Tel. *01422 317337* Fax. *01422 836717* E-mail. *info@lucyzodion.com* Web. *www.zodionltd.eu.com Cableform Controls (United Kingdom) – ENM (United Kingdom) – H.A. Birch (United Kingdom) – Lighting (United Kingdom) – Lumo (United Kingdom) – Zodion (United Kingdom)*

Zoedale plc Stannard Way Priory Business Park, Bedford MK44 3WG Tel. *01234 832832* Fax. *01234 832800* E-mail. *enquiries@zoedale.co.uk* Web. *www.zoedale.co.uk Bernard (France) – Magnatrol (U.S.A.) – Olab (Italy) – Omal (Italy) – Peter Paul (U.S.A.) – Sirai (Italy) – Valpes (France)*

Zoffany Chalfont House Oxford Road, Denham, Uxbridge UB9 4DX Tel. *08445 434600* Fax. *0844 5434602* E-mail. *enquiries@zoffany.uk.com* Web. *www.zoffany.uk.com Arcadia – Archive Collection – Archive Folio – Archive Prints – Aubusson Prints – Aubusson Wallpaper – Big Weaves – Black Book, The – Blue Book, The – Chenille Book – Compendium – Damask Book – Damask Vol II – Ducato – Fontenay Prints – Fontenay Wallpaper – Fontenay Weaves – French Prints – French Wallpapers – French Weaves – Green Book – Hilliard – Hilliard Wallpaper – Little Book – Oiseaux de Paradis – Parchment Book – Plains Collection – Small Weaves – Small Weaves II – Temple Newsam – Textures – Velvet Book II – Velvets – Vinyl Book 1 – Vinyl Book II – Vinyl Book III – Vinyl Book IV – Vinyl v – Vinyl VI – Window Book – Zofanny Paints – Zoffany Trimmings*

Zoki UK Ltd 44 Alcester Street, Birmingham B12 0PH Tel. *0121 7667888* Fax. *0121 7667962* E-mail. *zokiuk@btconnect.com* Web. *www.zokiuk.co.uk *The White Light Room*

Zones4U Ltd Westfield Industrial Estate Horndean, Waterlooville PO8 9JX Tel. *0870 7122200* Fax. *0870 7122201* E-mail. *sales@mainzone.co.uk* Web. *www.mainzone.co.uk Hewlett-Packard*

Zotefoams plc 675 Mitcham Road, Croydon CR9 3AL Tel. *020 86641600* Fax. *020 86641616* E-mail. *info@zotefoams.com* Web. *www.zotefoams.com Evazote – Plastazote « - Evazote « - Supazote « - Propozote«. - Plastazote – Propozote – Supazote*

Zurich Assurance Bishops Cleeve, Cheltenham GL52 8XX Tel. *01242 221311* Fax. *01242 221554* Web. *www.zurich.com Eagle Star Home Insurance – Eagle Star Motor Insurance – Eagle Star Travel Insurance*

Zycomm Electronics Ltd 51 Nottingham Road, Ripley DE5 3AS Tel. *01773 570123* Fax. *01773 570155* E-mail. *sales@zycomm.co.uk* Web. *www.zycomm.co.uk Zycomm*

Zygology Ltd 2 Barnes Wallis Court Wellington Rd, High Wycombe HP12 3PS Tel. *0845 8121220* Fax. *0845 8121221* E-mail. *sales@zygology.com* Web. *www.zygology.com Arrow – ATLAS – Avdel – Avdelok – Avex – Avibulb – Avinox – Avlug – Avseal – Avsert – Avtainer – Avtronic – Briv – Bulbex – Camtainer – Chobert – Dzus – Earth tab Rivet – Eurosert – Genesis – Grovit – Gesipa – Hartwell – Hemlok – Hexsert – Interlock – Lockwell – Maxlok – Monobolt – Nutsert – Nylatch – Panex – PEM – PEMSERTER – Permabond – Pilot – Quadpanel – R'ANGLE – REELFAST – Rivscrew – SI INSERTS – Southco – Speed Riveting – SPOTFAST – Squaresert – SR Rivet – Stavex – STRICKSCREW – Supersert – T-lok – Textron – TLR – TY-D – VALUE RIVET NUT – Versanut – Zygology*

AGENCIES

This section shows Foreign Companies in alphabetical sequence for whom the
UK company is an agent.

OVERSEAS COMPANY	COUNTRY OF ORIGIN	PRODUCT	UK COMPANY
2K Electronics	New Zealand	Resistance Bridge Calibrators	Lyons Instruments
360 Systems Inc	U.S.A.	Broadcast Audio Prods	Preco Ltd
3M	U.S.A.		Lawrence Industries Ltd
3M (Formerly Polaroid Corporation)	U.S.A.	Polarizing Filters	Comar Instruments
A. Anger GmbH	Austria	High Speed CNC Milling Machines, High Speed CNC Machining Centres	Citizen Machinery UK Ltd
A.B.C. Spax	Germany	Spax 'S' Screws Distributors	Unico Components Ltd
A.C.P.	Spain	Potentiometers	G English Electronics Ltd
A.C. Trading K.F.T.	Hungary	Vacuum Processes	J R Technology
A.R.M.A. B.V.	Netherlands	Vehicle Leasing and Management	Leaseplan UK Ltd
A.R.M.A. N.V.	Belgium	Vehicle Leasing and Management	Leaseplan UK Ltd
A. Rawie	Germany	Friction Buffers	H.J. Skelton & Co. Ltd
A/S Dansk (Funki) Staldindustri	Denmark	Livestock Feeding Systems	Master Farm Services GB Ltd
A.T.	Germany	Pinch Valves	Texcel Division (a division of Crosslink Business Services Ltd)
A.V.C	Netherlands	Impulse Heat Sealers	Lea Valley Packaging Ltd
A.V.C.	Taiwan	Cable Accessories	Elkay Electrical Manufacturing Co. Ltd A Smiths Group Company
A W L	Netherlands	Bending Machines	Embassy Machinery Ltd
A.W.T.	Belgium	Badges, Transfers, Tapes And Heat Seal Machines	J & A International Ltd
Aaronco Inc	U.S.A.	Grooming Equipment Books	Diamond Edge Ltd
AB Morinder	Sweden	Briquette Press	K K Balers Ltd
Abatron	Switzerland	Bdm Deluggers	Computer Solutions Ltd
Abel & Geiger	Germany	Ammenity Lighting-Various	W R T L Exterior Lighting Ltd
Abu Dhabi Oilfield Services	United Arab Emirates	Oilfield Engineering Workshops And Representatives of Manufactures Of Oilfield Equipment	Incotes Ltd
Ace Glass	U.S.A.	Scientific Glassware	Radleys
Ace Products	U.S.A.	Cymbals	John Hornby Skewes & Co. Ltd
Ace S.A.	Spain	Spanners, Sockets and Accessories	Electro Group Ltd
ACRA Control Ltd	Ireland	mail@acracontrol.com	Specialist Electronics Services Ltd
Acta	Denmark	Norba Wood and Waste Crushers	Pulp & Paper Machinery Ltd
Acta	Norway	Norba Wood and Waste Crushers	Pulp & Paper Machinery Ltd
Actreg	Spain	Pneumatic Activator Manufacture	Trimline Valves
ACWa Air	United Kingdom	Air Filtration Systems for Stenters and Dryers	Robert S Maynard Ltd
Adast Dominant	Czech Republic	Printing machines	P P S Rotaprint Ltd
ADC	U.S.A.	Commercial Tumble Dryers	J L A
Adolf Illig Maschinenbau GmbH & Co	Germany	Plastics Thermoforming Machinery	Illig UK Ltd
Advanced Calibration Designs Inc	U.S.A.	Check gas generators	Spantech Products Ltd
AEC	U.S.A.	temperature control for plastics moulding machinery	Demag Hamilton Guarantee Ltd
AEG	Spain	Electric Motors	Micro Clutch Developments Ltd
Aerni-Leuch GmbH	Switzerland	Barrier Film	Klockner Pentaplast Ltd
Aero-Pro	Germany	Airbrushing Equipment	Technical Sales Ltd
Aeroxon	Germany	Pest Control Products	Tiger Tim Products Ltd
Aesculap AG	Germany	Electric Animal Clippers Veterinary Instruments	Diamond Edge Ltd
Afflerbach Boedenpresserei GmbH & Co Kg	Germany	Dished & Flanged Heads, Closures & Special Pressed Parts In Steel, Aluminium & Alloys	Mito Construction & Engineering Ltd
AGFA Type	U.S.A.	Fonts	Monotype Imaging Ltd
AGI	U.S.A.		Armstrong Optical Ltd
Agorespace France S.A.R.L.	France	Recreational multi-sports centres	Playdale Playgrounds Ltd
Air Products	Netherlands	Polyurethane Additives	I M C D UK Ltd
Airflow SA	Switzerland	Automatic Battery Management Conditioner	Haldo Developments Ltd
Airflow SA	Switzerland	Air Chamber In Controlled Environment For Storage	Haldo Developments Ltd
Akapp	Netherlands	Enclosed Conductor Systems	Metreel Ltd
akteLUX	Canada	sales@aktelux.com	Specialist Electronics Services Ltd
Akzo Nobel	Netherlands	Caustic Soda Methylene Chloride	Gelpke & Bate Ltd
Akzo Nobel	Netherlands	Fyrol Flame Retardants	I M C D UK Ltd
Alan Morris Architects	Italy	Steel windows and doors	Crittall Windows Ltd
Albion Advanced Nutrition	U.S.A.	Animal Feed Additives	Thomson & Joseph Ltd
Albrecht Baumer GmbH & Co K.G.	Germany	Foam Converting Machines	Apropa Machinery Ltd
Alcar S.r.l.	Italy	Motor Vehicle Parts	Panaf & Company
Alcatel Kabel Norge	Norway	Heating Cables	Eswa Ltd
Alessandrini	Italy	Menswear	Ramostyle Ltd
Alexandria Trading & Imp Co Ltd	United Arab Emirates		Hawker Electronics Ltd
ALFA Gomma Sud spA	Italy	Industrial Hose Range	Holmes Hose Ltd
Alfachimici	Italy	Inner Layer and P.T.H. Processes	Schloetter Co. Ltd
Algas	Norway	Filters and Thickeners	Pulp & Paper Machinery Ltd
Algodue Electronica	Italy	Test And Measurement Equipment	Energy I C T
All other Countries:Cambridge Vacuum Engineering	Worldwide		Cambridge Vacuum Engineering
Allma	Germany	twisting machinery-service & spare parts	Macart Textiles Machinery Ltd
Almaco	U.S.A.	Manufacturers of Specialized Agricultural Equipment for Drilling.	Nickerson Bros Ltd
Alpex Protection	France	Breathable, Windroof, Waterproof Fabrics	Emko Products Ltd
Alpine Westfalia	Austria	Tunnelling Equipment	Burlington Engineers Ltd
Alpine Westfalia	Germany	Tunnelling Equipment	Burlington Engineers Ltd
Alps Keiki	Japan	Meters	Servo & Electronic Sales Ltd
ALS	Germany	Architectural Lighting	Selux UK Ltd
Alsale	Saudi Arabia	Weighbridge Installation	Shering Weighing Ltd
Aluminium Martigny France	France	Foundry Fluxes	Ramsell Naber Ltd
Aluminium-Verlag Marketing & Kommunication GmbH	Germany	Technical Publications on Aluminium	Mito Construction & Engineering Ltd
Alweco Tuinbouwprojecten B.V.	Netherlands	Glasshouse Structures	Fargro
AM System A.S.	Denmark	Shopfittings	A M System UK Ltd
Amazone	Germany	Grain Drills, Fertilizer Spreaders, Sprayers, Power Harrows	Wilfred Scruton Ltd
Ambiance Lumiere	France	Exterior Lighting	Crescent Lighting Ltd
Amdent	Sweden	Ultra Sonic Scalers	Plandent
American Aerostar	U.S.A.	Quick Tool/Die Clamping Systems	Pharos Engineering Ltd
American Historical Foundation	U.S.A.	Commemorative Knives	Herbert M Slater Ltd
American Hydrotech Inc.	U.S.A.	Hydrotech 625 Monolithic Roofing & Structural Waterproofing	Alumasc Exterior Building Products
American International Assistant Services Inc	U.S.A.	Medical Insurance	Doctorcall
American Roller Bearing Co.	U.S.A.	Roller Bearings	R A Rodriguez UK Ltd
American Tape Co	U.S.A.	Speciality Self Adhesive Tapes	Stokvis Tapes UK Ltd
Ametek	U.S.A.	Valve Boxes	Connectomatic
Ametek Inc	U.S.A.	Air and Noise Monitoring Instruments	Shawcity Ltd

1

OVERSEAS COMPANY	COUNTRY OF ORIGIN	PRODUCT	UK COMPANY
Amorim Isolamentos	Portugal	Korklite, Korklite Taper	Alumasc Exterior Building Products
Amphenol	U.S.A.	Rf Connectors	Richardsons R F P D Ltd
Amsler Tex	Switzerland	yarn and sliver effects	Macart Textiles Machinery Ltd
Amtech	U.S.A.	Solder Paste	Plimto Ltd
Amysa	Switzerland	Induction Heat Equipment	Pearson Panke Ltd
Anacom Systems Corporation	U.S.A.	RF Analogue Fibre Optic Links	Aspen Electronics Ltd
Anacomp	U.S.A.	Microfiche-Roll Readers	Microfilm Shop
Anchor Products Co.	U.S.A.	Surgical Needles	Mediplus Ltd
Andeen-Hagerling Inc	U.S.A.	Capacitance Standards, Precision Capacitance Bridge	Lyons Instruments
Anderson & Vreeland	U.S.A.	Flexographic Printing Products	Plastotype
Andrew Scicom	U.S.A.	Microwave & Communication Receivers Pulse Analysers	Marlborough Communications Ltd
Angus Chemie	Germany	Amines, Ph Stabilisers	Banner Chemicals Ltd
Annovi & Reverberi	Italy	Pumps	Hypro Eu Ltd
Ansell Edmont Europe N.V.	Belgium	Industrial Gloves	Cravenmount Ltd
Anson Ltd	United Kingdom	Hammer Lug Unions	Cebo UK Ltd
AP Burg & Beck	United Kingdom	Automotive spare parts	Kingsdown
AP Lockhead	United Kingdom	Automotive spare parts	Kingsdown
Apache Mills Inc	U.S.A.	carpet mats & anti-fatigue foam	Jaymart Roberts & Plastics Ltd
Apex Laboratories	U.S.A.	Biological Indicators	Cherwell Laboratories Ltd
Apex Microtechnology	U.S.A.	Power Integrated Circuits	Campbell Collins
Apollo Masters Inc	U.S.A.	Broadcast Audio Products	Preco Ltd
Appiani	Italy	Glazed Wall And Floor Tiles	Ceramique International Ltd
Aquaclean	Finland	Spray Washing Machines	Turbex Ltd
Aquametro AG	Switzerland	Oil and Water Meters, Heat MEters	Bayham Ltd
Aquarius (Saudi Arabia) Ltd	Saudi Arabia		Hawker Electronics Ltd
Aquaspersions (M) Sdn Bhd	Malaysia		Aquaspersions Ltd
ARAG S R L (Arag)	Italy	Plastic Fittings	Hypro Eu Ltd
Archo-rigion	United Kingdom	protective linings	Lithgow Saekaphen Ltd
Arcotronics	Italy	Capacitors	Components Bureau
Ares	Italy	Cutting Presses	Partwell Cutting Technology Ltd
Argylene Biochem Aps	Denmark	Flower Preservative	Fargro
Ariki	New Zealand	Paua Shell Jewellery	W B Muddeman & Son Ltd
Arjay	Canada	Level Controls	Texcel Division (a division of Crosslink Business Services Ltd)
Arlumina	Switzerland	Interior Lighting	Crescent Lighting Ltd
Armglass	Germany	Security Bomb-Blast Film for Vehicles and Property	Homeserve Emergency Services
Armo	Italy	Electro Hydraulic Scissor Lift	Southworth Handling Ltd
Arno	Germany	Grooving	Cromwell Group Holdings
Arrow Specialty Co	U.S.A.	Gas Engines	Turner E P S Ltd
ArsEdition	Germany	Advent Calendars	Mamelok Holdings Ltd
Art URPO Ltd	Finland	Publisher	Acumedic Centre Ltd
Arta	Italy	Drawing Office Supplies	Esmond Hellerman Ltd
Arte	Belgium	Wallcoverings and Fabrics	Brian Yates
Artifex Dr. Lohmann & Co. KG	Germany	Abrasives - Elastic-Bonded	Finishing Aids & Tools Ltd
Artronics	Austria	info@artronics.de	Specialist Electronics Services Ltd
Artronics	Germany	info@artronics.de	Specialist Electronics Services Ltd
Artronics	Switzerland	info@artronics.de	Specialist Electronics Services Ltd
Asahi Chemical Industry Co.	Japan	Clean Room Wiping Cloths	Cravenmount Ltd
Asahi Optical Co Ltd	Japan	Pentax Photographic Products, Endoscopic Equipment, Ophthalmic Lenses	Pentax UK Ltd
Asahi Precision Co Ltd	Japan	Surveying Equipment	Pentax UK Ltd
Asahi-Seiki	Japan	transfer presses (high speed)	Joseph Rhodes Ltd
Askel	France	Agricultural Machinery	Ruston's Engineering Co. Ltd
Associated Marines	Canada	Accomodation Modules	H B Rentals Ltd
Astec	U.S.A.	Asphalt Plant	B G Europa UK Ltd
Astra	Italy	Water Meters	Connectomatic
Astra De Famm	Belgium	Sugar Confectionary	Bysel Ltd
Atlantic	Italy	Hose Clamps	Connectomatic
Atlantic	Italy	Hose Clamps- Technical	Connectomatic
Atlantic Microwave Corp	U.S.A.	Microwave Waveguides	Cobham Antenna Systems
ATM	Germany	Metallographic Preparation Equip	Metprep Ltd
Atofina	France	Methyl Bromide	I M C D UK Ltd
Atom Industries	Australia	Drill Attachments	Emak UK Ltd
Atrix	U.S.A.	Toner Vacuum Cleaners and ESD Kits	Longs Ltd
Audio Control Inc	U.S.A.	Broadcast Audio Products	Preco Ltd
Audiopak Inc	U.S.A.	Broadcast Audio Products	Preco Ltd
Aug. Bremicker Und Sohne	Germany	2 Wheel Security Locks	Michael Brandon Ltd
August Koehler A.G.	Germany	Quality Paper and Board	G F Smith
Augustine	U.S.A.	Strings For Classic Guitars	John Hornby Skewes & Co. Ltd
Aurend	Netherlands	System Range Various Shaped Tops And Shaped Legs	E W Marshall Ltd
Auson	Sweden	Pine Tar	J Allcock & Sons Ltd
Austria:Josef Seidl Industrievertretungen	Austria	electron beam welding & vacuum services	Cambridge Vacuum Engineering
Auto Mercantil	Portugal	Vehicle Leasing and Management	Leaseplan UK Ltd
Autoclave Engineers	U.S.A.	Ultra High Pressure Tube, Fittings & Valves	Hydrasun Ltd
Automator Italia	Italy	Metal Marking Machines	Brandone Machine Tool Ltd
Autonics	Korea, Republic of	Controls	Tempatron Controls
Autotrol France SA	France	Water Softening/Filter Valves	Ferex Ltd
AVOCET	U.S.A.	Computer Development Software	Computer Solutions Ltd
AWA Convert GmbH	Germany	High Speed Mailing Envelopes	U O E UK Ltd East Finchley
Awuko	Germany	Coated Abrasive Wide Belts	Naylors Abrasives
Axelgaard Manufacturing Co. Ltd	U.S.A.	Pals Reusable Electrodes	Nidd Valley Medical Ltd
Axelson Inc	U.S.A.	Safety Shut Down Systems	Edeco Petroleum Services Ltd
Axon Instruments	U.S.A.	Neurophysiological Amplifiers	Linton & Co Engineering Ltd
Axter S.A.	France	Bitumous Waterproofing Membrane & External Wall Insulation	Axter Ltd
B.A.S.F.	Germany	Photopolymer Platemaking Materials	Plastotype
B.A.S.F.	Germany	Building Paints and Products	H M G Paints Ltd
B.A.S.F.	Germany	Solvents (Nylosolv)	C K Chemicals
B & C	Belgium	Sweatshirts, Polo and T-Shirts	I S Enterprises International
B.D.	Italy	Plastic Hose Fitting	Everyvalve Ltd
B&K Precision	U.S.A.	Test & Measuring Instruments	Metrix Electronics
B.M.A. Nederland BV	Netherlands	Food Processing Equipment	Flo Mech Ltd
B.M.D. Garant Entsaubungstechnik GmbH	Germany	Air Pollution Control	Dantherm Filtration Ltd
B.S.V	Denmark	Lifting Equipment	Scanlift Ltd
B.V.M. Brunner GmbH Verpackungsmaschinen	Germany	Packaging Machinery	Advanced Dynamics Ltd
B & W	Germany	Photographic Creative Filters	Johnsons Photopia Ltd
Babini Systems Office Furniture	Italy	System Range Various Shaped Tops And Shaped Legs	E W Marshall Ltd
Bacharach Inc	U.S.A.	Gas Detection and Combustion Testing Instruments	Shawcity Ltd
Baden Chemie GmbH	Germany	Sealant	Henry Shaw & Sons Ltd
Badge A MINIT Badge	U.S.A.	Badge making kits	London Emblem Plc "All About Badges"
Bahmuller	Germany	Reamers	Macinnes Tooling Ltd
Baldor	U.S.A.	Electric Motors	Transdrive Engineering Ltd
Ballarini	Italy	Cookware	Thomas Plant Birmingham
Balteau S.A.	Belgium	Industrial X-ray Equipment & systems	Sonatest Ltd
Bamatec	Switzerland	Wire Machine, Spring Making	Embassy Machinery Ltd
Banswara Syntex	India	Synthetic Yarn	A P Y
Barber Ind	Canada	Engine Shutdown Device	Edeco Petroleum Services Ltd

OVERSEAS COMPANY	COUNTRY OF ORIGIN	PRODUCT	UK COMPANY
Barco Automation BV	Belgium	Computer Integrated Manufacturing Systems	B M S Vision Ltd
Barent Mega-Stahl	Germany	Graphic Arts Furniture	Billows Protocol Ltd
Bartells	Germany	Mobile Stair Climbers For The Disabled	Enable Access
BASF	Germany	Extruded Polystyrene Insulation	Kingspan Insulation Ltd
BASF Coatings AG	Germany	Automotive Refinish Paint	B A S S Hydro Coatings Ltd
Basile	Italy	Biological Test Equipment	Linton & Co Engineering Ltd
Batasan	Indonesia	Solid Door Blanks	Price & Pierce Softwoods Ltd
Bates	Denmark	Inflatable Dunnage Bags	Spanset Ltd
Bauer Maschinenbau	Germany	Horizontal Bandsaws	Prosaw Ltd
Baumann	Switzerland	Flexible couplings	Lenze UK Ltd
Bautronic	U.S.A.	Servo Drives & Motors	European Drives & Motor Repairs
Baycomp Ltd	Canada	Carbon Fibre Composites	A Algeo Ltd
Bayer AG	Germany	Iron Oxides (Synthetic)	Lanxess Ltd
Bayer Polyurethane A.G.	Germany	PPG polyols, Isocyanates (MDI, ADI)	I M C D UK Ltd
BBJ & Bigfoot (subsidiary of Aspen Pumps)	United Kingdom	Air conditioning installation accessoriesModular frameworkCondensate pumps	Tool & Fastener Solutions Ltd (T/A TF Solutions Ltd)
BC Lifts	Denmark	Vertical Step Lifts	Enable Access
Bear Family Records	Germany	Music Various	Rollercoaster Records Ltd
Bear Tracks	Germany	Music Various	Rollercoaster Records Ltd
Beargrip	Netherlands	Hex Keys, Riveters and Driver Bits	Castle Brook Tools Ltd
Beche	Germany	Forging Hammers, Presses	Pearson Panke Ltd
Beck	Germany	H.SS and Carbide Reamers	Macinnes Tooling Ltd
Beckett Paper	Germany	Quality Paper and Board	G F Smith
Bego	Germany	Dental Prods	Metrodent Ltd
Beha Electronics GmbH	Germany	Test and Measurement Equipment	Electro Group Ltd
BEI Ideacod	France	Linear encoders & digital readout systems	Newall Measurement Systems Ltd
Bel Art	U.S.A.	Scienceware	Radleys
Belcor	Israel	Air Conditioning	William May Ltd
Bell	U.S.A.	Bicycle helmets	Madison
BeLomo	Belarus	Night Vision, Binoculars, Monoculars And Cameras	Swains International plc
Belotti SpA	Italy	CNC Trimming Machinery	Shelley Thermoformers International Ltd
Bematec	Switzerland	Coating Machines	S & P Spanarc Ltd
BemaTec	Germany	Pulpers and Refiners	Pulp & Paper Machinery Ltd
BemaTec	Switzerland	Pulpers and Refiners	Pulp & Paper Machinery Ltd
Beral	Germany	brake linings & disc brake pads	Roadlink International Ltd
Berg	Germany	Grippers and die clamping tools	Ringspann UK Ltd
Bernath Atomic	Germany	VOC Emission Monitors	Quantitech Ltd
Berthoud	France	Knapsack Sprayers	Hypro Eu Ltd
Bertolaso & Robino & Galandrino	Italy	Capping and Filling Machines	Viscose Closures Ltd
Bessey	Germany	Clamps	L J Hydleman & Co. Ltd
Bestmann	Germany	Coir Erosion Control Range	A G A Group
Betacontrol GmbH	Germany	measurement systems and density measuring equipment	Apropa Machinery Ltd
Betakut	Italy	Shears and Snips	L J Hydleman & Co. Ltd
Betts China	China	Packaging	Albea UK Ltd
Betts India	India	Packaging	Albea UK Ltd
Betts Indonesia	Indonesia	Packaging	Albea UK Ltd
Betts Poland	Poland	Packaging	Albea UK Ltd
Betts USA	U.S.A.	Packaging	Albea UK Ltd
Bezner Maschinen GmbH	Germany	Automatic Sorting Machines For Waste Materials	O Kay Engineering Services Ltd
Bibielle S.r.l.	Italy	Abrasives - Coated	Finishing Aids & Tools Ltd
Bideseimpianti	Italy	Stone Processing Machinery	Pisani plc
BILZ	Germany	Anti-vibration equipment	P E S UK Ltd
Binary Arts	U.S.A.	Brain Teaser Puzzles and Games	Ravensburger Ltd
Binder	Austria	Form Fill And Seal Systems	W J Morray Engineering Ltd
Biopac	U.S.A.	Physiological Data Acquisition Systems	Linton & Co Engineering Ltd
Bioscan	U.S.A.	Radio Isotope Instruments	Lablogic Systems Ltd
Bioventures	U.S.A.	Dna	Cambio Ltd
Bird B Gone Inc	U.S.A.	Spike 2000 Bird Deterrent	Deben Group Industries Ltd
Bird Electronic Co.	U.S.A.	RF Power Meters, Loads And Attenuators	Aspen Electronics Ltd
Biwin	Taiwan	Switches	Components Bureau
Blackburn	U.S.A.	Cycle Accessories	Madison
Blom & Maters N.V.	Netherlands	Jar & Bottle Cleaning Machines	A M J Maters Partnership Ltd
Blue M	U.S.A.	Static Ovens	B T U Europe Ltd
Bob Bryan	U.S.A.	Guitar Straps And Accessories	John Hornby Skewes & Co. Ltd
Bobst Group Inc	U.S.A.	Whirlwind 185 Automatic Stringing Machine	A B Graphics International Ltd
Bock Work Holding	U.S.A.	Machine Vices	Roemheld UK Ltd
Bodet	France	7 Segment electro-mechanical	Oem - Automatic Ltd
Bodine	U.S.A.	Fractional Geared Motors	Micro Clutch Developments Ltd
Bohlender	Germany	Ptfe Labware	Radleys
Bohler Ybbstal Band GmbH	Austria	Special Cutting Steels	Partwell Cutting Technology Ltd
Bohrs Mediacraft	Norway	Press Wholesaler Systems	Buhrs UK Ltd
Bollig & Kemper	Germany	High performance pigment dispersions	Kromachem Ltd
Bolymin	Taiwan	LCD Displays	C T L Components plc
Bonacker GmbH	Germany	Slide Storage Cabinets (Back Illuminated)	D W Group Ltd
Bondioli and Pavesi	Italy	PTO Shafts and Gearboxes	BYPY Hydraulics & Transmissions Ltd
Bonfiglioli s.p.A.	Italy	Scrap Processing Equipment	M M H Recycling Systems Ltd
Bonkote Co. Ltd	Japan	Soldering/Desoldering Equi	Electro Group Ltd
Borbrick Washroom Equipment Inc	Sri Lanka	Stainless Steel Washroom Equipment	W H Foster & Sons Ltd
Bosch	Germany	Power Tools	Banson Tool Hire Ltd
Bosch	United Kingdom	Automotive spare parts	Kingsdown
Boussac Fadini	France		Wemyss Weavecraft Ltd
BPW	Germany	trailer axle and suspension components	Roadlink International Ltd
Brandt	Germany	Chocolate Confectionary	Bysel Ltd
Braswey S.A.	Brazil	Castor Oil Derivatives	Industrial Waxes
Breka	Italy	Command Devices-Push Button	Electrium Sales Ltd
Brembo	Italy	brake discs, calipers & pads	Roadlink International Ltd
Brigon	Germany	Combustion Kits	Anglo Nordic Burner Products Ltd
Broadcast Electronics Inc	U.S.A.	Broadcast Audio Products	Preco Ltd
Broadley James Corp	U.S.A.	Ptt And Redox Sensors	L T H Electronics Ltd
Brochier S.A.	France	High Performance Blind Fabrics	Levolux A T Ltd
Broll Buntpigmente	Germany	Hi-temperature Pigments	Kromachem Ltd
Brooktract Technology Ltd	U.S.A.	Intelligent Fax Pc Boards	Techland Group Ltd
Brugger	Italy	Carpet Weaving Cop Winders	Pilkingtons Ltd (t/a Weitzer Parket UK)
Bruhl	Germany	Seating & Sofas	Ergonom Ltd
Brunswick Corporation	U.S.A.	Mariner, quicksilver	E P Barrus
Bryant	U.S.A.	Conveyor Take-Up Units	R A Rodriguez UK Ltd
BSO	Germany	Solenoids	Hydac Technology Ltd
Bubenzer Bremsen	Germany	Industrial Brakes	Metool Products Ltd
Buchele	Germany	steel doors (security,acoustic,fire)	P E S UK Ltd
Buhrs ITM	Germany	Inserting Machines	Buhrs UK Ltd
Buhrs Zaandam	Netherlands	Mailing Machines	Buhrs UK Ltd
BUIC	Italy	Rotary Cameras	Microfilm Shop
Bullen Ultrasonics	U.S.A.	Ultrasonic Impact Grinders	Aegis Advanced Materials Ltd
Bultmann KG	Germany	Tube Drawbenches	British & Continental Traders Ltd
Bumag	Germany	Rollers & Vibrating Plates & Rammers	Chippindale Plant Ltd (Head Office)
Burford Foam	Australia	Surfboard Blanks	Ocean Magic Surf Boards

3

OVERSEAS COMPANY	COUNTRY OF ORIGIN	PRODUCT	UK COMPANY
Burger Engineering	U.S.A.	modular water distribution manifolds for plastic processing industry	Demag Hamilton Guarantee Ltd
Burle Industries Inc	U.S.A.	Electronic Tubes	Richardsons R F P D Ltd
Burster	Germany	electrical measuring instruments	The Seaward Group (a division of Seaward Electronic Ltd)
Butchers	U.S.A.	Chemicals/Floor Polish	C S A Cleaning Equipment
BWF	Germany	Fixator levelling systems	P E S UK Ltd
Byk Cera	Netherlands	Wax Additives	Banner Chemicals Ltd
C.A. Delius & Sohne	Germany	Furnishing Fabrics	Maisonneuve & Co.
C.A.S. Corp	Korea, Republic of	Industrial Scales	Kelgray Products Ltd
C.E.R.I. Revetements Technique	France	Synthetic Resinous Linings	Lithgow Saekaphen Ltd
C.F.F.	Germany	Cellulose	Fleximas Ltd
C. Grauff	Germany	Upholstery And Bedding Machinery	Apropa Machinery Ltd
C.I. Systems Ltd	Israel	Infrared Instruments	Metax Ltd
C.M.Z. S.A.	Spain	CNC Turning Centres	Citizen Machinery UK Ltd
C.P.I. Eimac Division	U.S.A.	Eimac Varian Typo Electronic Tubes	Richardsons R F P D Ltd
C R M Spa	Italy	marine engines	Watermota Ltd
C.T.E.	U.S.A.	Flow Monitors-Meters	Boiswood LLP
C-Y-Xoo Enterprise	China	Battery Holders	Servo & Electronic Sales Ltd
CAB GmbH	France	Labelling Systems	Weyfringe Labelling Systems
Calato Corp	U.S.A.	Drum Sticks	John Hornby Skewes & Co. Ltd
Camp Scandinavia	Sweden	Orthopaedic Braces	Gilbert & Mellish Ltd
Canon	Japan	Microfilm Reader Printers	Microfilm Shop
Canon Precision	Japan	canon	Trident Engineering Ltd
Canson	France	Fine Art Papers	Exaclair Ltd
Capxon	Taiwan	Capacitors	Components Bureau
Carbonundum	U.S.A.		Lawrence Industries Ltd
Carel S.p.A.	Italy	Temperature Controls	Tempatron Controls
Carl Bechem GmbH	Germany	High Performance Lubricants	R S Clare & Co. Ltd
Carl Nolte Soehne GmbH.	Germany	Crucibles for Metal Melting	Ramsell Naber Ltd
Carl Wezel KG	Germany	Precision Rolling Mills	British & Continental Traders Ltd
Carmel Olefins	Israel	Plastics Raw Materials	Plastribution
Carmex	Israel	Threading	Cromwell Group Holdings
Carre	France	Handmade Wall And Floor Tiles	Ceramique International Ltd
Carryline AB	Sweden	Flexible Conveyor Systems	Silcoms
Casalgrande	Italy	Porcelain Tiles	Ceramique International Ltd
Casappa	Italy	Hydraulic Pumps and Motors	BYPY Hydraulics & Transmissions Ltd
Casappa	Italy	Hydraulic Piston Pumps	Webster Drives (A Gardner Denver Product)
Casappa	Italy	Hydraulic Gear Pumps	Universal Hydraulics Ltd
Case	United Kingdom	Automotive spare parts	Kingsdown
Case New Holland	U.S.A.	Combines and Farm Tractors	Wilfred Scruton Ltd
Casual	Korea, Republic of	Optical Frames	Hilton International Eye Wear Ltd
Catensa	France	All Felt Products	Imp UK Ltd
Catensa	Spain	All Felt Products	Imp UK Ltd
Cattinair	France	Air Pollution Control	Dantherm Filtration Ltd
Cattinair	France	Cyclo Filters	Dustraction Ltd
Cavex Holland B.V.	Netherlands	Dental Consumables	Plandent
CCL Pheonix	Taiwan	Sample looms with electronic	Robert S Maynard Ltd
CCS, INC	U.S.A.	Pressure & Temperature Switches	Custom Control Sensors International
Cebo Holland B.V.	Netherlands	Oilwell Mud Materials	Cebo UK Ltd
Cecoco	Japan	Motorized Single Row Crop Binder for Standing Crops	Nickerson Bros Ltd
Cedatex	France	Laundry Supplies	Universal Towel Company Ltd
Cefar	Sweden	Electrotherapy equipment	Nidd Valley Medical Ltd
Celanese	Germany	Speciality Solvents	Banner Chemicals Ltd
Cellhire USA Inc.	United Kingdom	Global Phone Rental	Cellhire plc
Cellwood Fractionators	Sweden	Fibre Recovery Systems	Pulp & Paper Machinery Ltd
Cemp S.r.l.	Italy	Flameproof Electric Motors	Micro Clutch Developments Ltd
Centa Antriebe Kirschey GmbH	Germany	Flexible Couplings	Centa Transmissions
Center Pig S.r.l.	Italy	Pig Genetics and Breeding	J S R Farming Group
Central	U.S.A.	Discretes	M B Components Ltd
Centret	Netherlands	Sand Blasters	C S A Cleaning Equipment
Centryco Inc	U.S.A.	Spring-Steel Shaft Covers	Beakbane Ltd
Cepi	Italy	Bulk Handling Plant For Food Products	Robinsons
Ceralit S.A.	Brazil	Synthetic/Vegetable Waxes	Industrial Waxes
Cerim	Italy	Glazed Wall And Floor Tiles	Ceramique International Ltd
Certa	Switzerland	Automation Systems	Rem Systems Ltd
Certis Benelux n.v. Stretch Wrapping Machines	United Kingdom		Gordian Strapping Ltd
CertoClav	Austria	Autoclaves	Radleys
Certuss Warmetechnik GmbH	Germany	Steam Generators	Certus UK Ltd
Cevisa	Spain		Wholesale Welding Supplies Ltd
Champion	United Kingdom	Automotive spare parts	Kingsdown
Charbit Sarl	France	Fashion Fabrics	Combined Trading Garments Ltd
Charles Craft	U.S.A.	Embroidery Fabrics	Coats Ltd
Check-All Valve	U.S.A.	Check Valves	Texcel Division (a division of Crosslink Business Services Ltd)
Chef Set Housewares Psty Ltd	India	S/Steel Cookwares	Catering Suppliers
Chelton Inc	U.S.A.	Aircraft Antennas	Cobham Antenna Systems
Chelton S.A.R.L.	France	Aircraft Test Equipment & Antennas	Cobham Antenna Systems
Chemag Metalgesellschaft	Germany	Chemicals	Fleximas Ltd
Chempur	Germany	Inorganics	Fluorochem Ltd
Chemtronics	U.S.A.	Cleaning Fluids	Longs Ltd
Chi Mei Corporation	Taiwan	Plastics Raw Materials	Plastribution
Chicago Case Co.	U.S.A.	Cases	Longs Ltd
Chin Fong Machine Industrial Co. Ltd	Taiwan	Power Presses	Higgins & Hewins Ltd
China International Book Trading Corporation	China	Publisher	Acumedic Centre Ltd
China Nat. Light Ind. Products	China	Skylark Violins, Brass And Woodwind Instruments	John Hornby Skewes & Co. Ltd
China:Canlin International (Xian)Co. Ltd BETC Ltd	China	electron beam welding & vacuum furnaces	Cambridge Vacuum Engineering
Chiplo International	U.S.A.	Casino Chips	Eurocoin Ltd
Chris Allan Aviation Library	Hong Kong	Aviation Photographs	Skyscan Aerial Photography
Chrismar Inc	Canada	Hiking Maps	Harvey Map Services Ltd
christi's	U.S.A.	Medals & stamps	Spink & Son Ltd
Christopher Group	U.S.A.	Vacuum Packaging Machine	Circuit Engineering Marketing Company Ltd
Chrono Expo	France	Drop Banner Stands	T P S Visual Communications Ltd
Chrysler International	United Kingdom	Automatic /Transmissions and 4WD Units	A T P Automatic Transmission Parts UK Ltd
Chuwac Engineering Ltd	Singapore	Propeller Shaft Seals and Bearings	Deep Sea Seals Ltd
Chyo	Japan	Precision Balances	Stevens Group Ltd
Cinch Connectors	China	Connectors	Cinch Connectors Ltd
Cinch Connectors	India	Connectors	Cinch Connectors Ltd
Cincla	Italy	Weaving Loom Accessories	Pilkingtons Ltd (t/a Weitzer Parket UK)
Circle Seal Controls	U.S.A.	Zero Leakage Valves And Regulators	Tamo Ltd
CISA Textil S.A.	Spain	Simucateo Fur	Emko Products Ltd
Citizen	Japan	Thermal Printers	Kelgray Products Ltd
Citterio	Italy	Storage Wall & Partitioning	Ergonom Ltd
City Minigolf	Sweden	Mini Golf Equipment	Bishop Sports & Leisure Ltd
City of London Courier Service	U.S.A.		City Of London Courier Ltd

4

OVERSEAS COMPANY	COUNTRY OF ORIGIN	PRODUCT	UK COMPANY
CJT	U.S.A.	tipped drills and reamers	Drill Service Horley Ltd
Clarke	U.S.A.	Scrubber/Dryers/Sweepers	C S A Cleaning Equipment
CLB	Netherlands	Cytokines/Monoclonal antibodies	The Mast Group Ltd
Cleanmaster Inc	Switzerland	Hot Water Extraction Carpet Cleaning Equipment	Host Von Schrader Ltd
Clearr corporation	U.S.A.	Illuminated 3 Sided Rotating Displats	T P S Visual Communications Ltd
Clockspring	U.S.A.	Composite Reinforcement Sleeve	Edeco Petroleum Services Ltd
Clover Tech	Australia	GALENA: Slope Stability	Geomem Ltd
CMA	Spain	Articulated arm tapping machines	Robert Speck Ltd
CMG	Australia	Electric motors	Beatson Fans & Motors Ltd
CMX Company	U.S.A.	Computer Development Software	Computer Solutions Ltd
Coats	Portugal	Crochet Threads	Coats Ltd
Coats	U.S.A.	Quilting Threads	Coats Ltd
Cobar	Netherlands	Cobar Wire and Fluxes	Plimto Ltd
Coelver S.A.	Switzerland	Coaxial Circular Connectors	Lemo UK Ltd
Coherent Laser Inc	U.S.A.	Fibre Optic Components	Pacer Components plc
Cohline (UK) Ltd	Germany	Automotive Hose And Fittings	Custom Hose & Fitting Ltd
Coin Mech Inc	U.S.A.	Coin Comparitor Security Coin Validator	Eurocoin Ltd
Cokin	France	Photographic Creative Filter	Johnsons Photopia Ltd
Collomut Staltors	Switzerland	Labelling Machines	Sessions Of York
Colorvir	France	Toners and Dyes	Jessops plc
Columbine International Ltd	U.S.A.	Welding Machines	Butyl Products Ltd
Columbus	Denmark	Pneumatic Timers	Elkay Electrical Manufacturing Co. Ltd A Smiths Group Company
Columbus	U.S.A.	Animal Activity Equipment	Linton & Co Engineering Ltd
ComacA	Italy	Notching Machines	Hatfields Machine Tools Ltd
Comar Condensatore	Italy	Capacitors	Cliff Electronic Components Ltd
Coment Industries Inc	U.S.A.	Aircraft Antennas	Cobham Antenna Systems
Comet	Switzerland	Vacuum Capacitors	Richardsons R F P D Ltd
Comex SAS	Italy	Water Pumps	Loheat
Comminutor Services Co. Ltd	Japan	Fine Bar Screens	Higgins & Hewins Ltd
Communication Techniques Inc	U.S.A.	RF & Microwave Oscillators And Synthesisers	Aspen Electronics Ltd
Comnet	Germany	Communication Network Simulation	C A C I
Compac	U.S.A.	Level Switches	Tamo Ltd
Compagnie des Ciments Belges N.V.	Belgium	Oilwell Cements	Cebo UK Ltd
Compton Greaves	India	Electric Motors	Beatson Fans & Motors Ltd
Comtra	France	Window Fittings	Titon Hardware Ltd (Head Office)
Condea	Germany	Solvents	Banner Chemicals Ltd
Conical	U.S.A.	conical end mills	Drill Service Horley Ltd
Connecticut Clean Room Corp	U.S.A.	Clean Room Stationery	Cravenmount Ltd
Connemara Electronics	Ireland	Test and Measurement Equipment	Electro Group Ltd
Consorzio Cavatori	Italy		C E D Ltd
Contec	U.S.A.	Specialist Clean Room Cloths	Cravenmount Ltd
Contemporary Perfumers (India) Ltd	India	Fragrances	C P L Aromas Ltd
Conti Tech	Germany	B.O.P Control Hoses	Hydrasun Ltd
Continental Laboratory Products	U.S.A.	Pipette Tips	Radleys
Continental Microwave	U.S.A.	Microwave Products	Cobham Antenna Systems
ContiTech	Germany	air springs	Roadlink International Ltd
Contracting & Trading Co	Lebanon	International Civil and Mechanical Engineering Contractor	Incotes Ltd
Contraves	U.S.A.	Servo drives & Motors	European Drives & Motor Repairs
Contrinex	Switzerland	Sensors	Sensortek
Convent catering	Ireland		Pandet Ltd
Copertrole	Egypt	Marine Fuels	Cockett Marine Oil Ltd
Copper State Rubber Inc	U.S.A.	Drilling Hoses	Cebo UK Ltd
Copters PDG	Chile	Aircharter-helicopters	P D G Helicopters
Corbin	Italy	cylinders, padlocks, mortise and multi-point locks	Ronis-Dom Ltd
Coreci	France	% Rh Sensors & Transmitters	Gefran UK
Corghi	Italy	Garage Equipment	Apaseal Ltd
Coronet	Germany	Metal Coathangers	H & L Russell
Corteco	Italy	hub oil seal kits	Roadlink International Ltd
Cosmotec	Italy	Water Chillers	Coolmation Ltd
Cosmotecnica	Italy	Solenoid Valves	Valeader Pneumatics Ltd
Cotesi	Portugal	Types Of Rose	Cotesi UK Ltd
Country	Italy	Spectacle Frames	Optiquality Holdings Ltd
Couth	Spain	Marking Machines, Riveting Machines, Screw Running Machines, Assembly Machines	Brandone Machine Tool Ltd
CPL America Latina	Ecuador	Fragrances	C P L Aromas Ltd
CPL Aromas (Far East) Ltd	Hong Kong	Fragrances	C P L Aromas Ltd
CPL Blayn	France	Fragrances	C P L Aromas Ltd
CPL Columbia Ltda	Colombia	Fragrances	C P L Aromas Ltd
Craig Stewart	Australia	Ventsim: Mine Ventilation Simulation	Geomem Ltd
Crane Pumps & Systems	U.S.A.	Pumps	Allpumps Ltd
Creative Distributors Ltd	Hong Kong	Far Eastern Manufactured Fancy Goods	Shonn Bros Manchester Ltd
Criosbanc	Italy	Refrigerated Display Equipment	Blighline Ltd
CROMA	France	CNC EPS Hot wire cutting machines	Apropa Machinery Ltd
Curtis Dyna Products	Netherlands	Fogging Machines	Fargro
Custom Accessories Inc	U.S.A.	Car Accessories	Custom Accessories Europe Ltd
Cybex Computer Products Corp	U.S.A.	Keyboard video house switches	Techland Group Ltd
Cyclo Getriebabau Lorenz GmbH	Germany	Speed Reducers	Centa Transmissions
Cyclotech	Sweden	Hydrocyclones	Pulp & Paper Machinery Ltd
D and C	Belgium	Metering Systems	Energy I C T
D'Aquisto	U.S.A.	Musical Instrument Strings	John Hornby Skewes & Co. Ltd
D. Bunker	U.S.A.	All Products	J R Technology
D. Evans (Wirelok) Ltd	New Zealand	Fence Connectors	Drivall Ltd
D.G.I.	Denmark	Beach Management System	A G A Group
D.J.W. Enterprises Inc	U.S.A.	Oscillating Fan	March May Ltd
D.M.G	Germany	Mini Golf Equipment	Bishop Sports & Leisure Ltd
D. & R. Electronica BV	Netherlands	Recording Studio Prods	Preco Ltd
Dacor Corporation	U.S.A.	Diving Equipment and Accessories	Stoney Cove Diver Training Centre Ltd
Daewoo Heavy Industries & Machinery	Korea, Republic of	marine engines	Watermota Ltd
Dahimmi	Korea, Republic of	Optical Cleaning Cloth	Kauser International Trading Ltd
Dainippon Screen Manufacturing Co	Japan	Printing Machinery	Dainippon Screen UK Ltd
Dakota Ultrasonics	U.S.A.	Thickness Gauges	Sonatest Ltd
Dandy Lift	Japan	Mobile Scissor Lift	Southworth Handling Ltd
Danobat S.Coop Ltds	Spain	Bandsaws	Prosaw Ltd
Dantorque	Denmark	Valve Actuators	Paladon Systems Ltd
Dart Corporation	U.S.A.	Electronic Controllers	Motovario Ltd
Data Proof Inc	U.S.A.	Cell Scanners	Lyons Instruments
Datalogic	Italy	Barcode Readers and Scanners	Kelgray Products Ltd
Datasouth Computer Corporation	U.S.A.	Serial Impact Dot Matrix Printers	Datatrade Ltd
Datavision	Taiwan	Liquid Crystal Displays	E A O Ltd
Datron	U.S.A.	Communications Receivers	Marlborough Communications Ltd
DAU GmbH & Co KG	Austria	heat sinks and heat pipes	Rolfe Industries
Daval	Hong Kong	Role Play	Peterkin UK Ltd
Davey Pumps	Australia	Pumps	Stuart Turner Ltd
Daw SA	France	Prosthetic Socks	Otto Bock Healthcare plc
Dawa Stone	China		C E D Ltd

OVERSEAS COMPANY	COUNTRY OF ORIGIN	PRODUCT	UK COMPANY
De Beleyr	Belgium	Yarn Conditioning	Robert S Maynard Ltd
Debica	Poland	Passenger Tyres	Kings Road Tyres & Repairs Ltd
Decision Technology Inc.	U.S.A.	Decision Analyzer - Computer Software	Associated Knowledge Systems Ltd
Deco Project	Netherlands	Shopfittings	A M System UK Ltd
Decril Sarl	France	Cable Carrier Systems	Beakbane Ltd
Defi	France	Chalk Lines	Fisco Tools Ltd
Defontaine	France	Hygienic Valves Manufacture	Trimline Valves
Deglas	Germany	Extruded Acrylic Sheet	Stockline Plastics Ltd
Degussa AG	Germany	Precious Metal Plating Processes	Schloetter Co. Ltd
Del-tron Precision Inc	U.S.A.	Linear Positioning Slides	Reliance Precision (Reliance Precision Ltd)
Delmag	Germany	Foundation Equipment	Burlington Engineers Ltd
Delmet Srl	Italy	Metal Finishing Equipment	Anopol Ltd
Delpiano	Italy	Semi-Worsted and Worsted Spinning Frames	Robert S Maynard Ltd
Delta	Italy	Oil Pumps	Anglo Nordic Burner Products Ltd
Delta Electronic Manufacturing Corp	U.S.A.	RF & Microwave Coaxial Connectors	Aspen Electronics Ltd
Demag Ergotech	Germany	injection moulding machines	Demag Hamilton Guarantee Ltd
Den Haan	Netherlands	Navigation and Signalling Lights	John Lilley & Gillie Ltd
Denmark:Scandinavian Aerospace & Industry AB	Denmark		Cambridge Vacuum Engineering
Denon Dic Trading	Japan	Desoldering Guns	Electro Group Ltd
Denso Europe B.V.	Japan	Motorcycle and small engine spark plugs	Michael Brandon Ltd
Dentronic	Denmark	Dental Equipment	Plandent
Derbit S.p.A.	Belgium	Derbigum Roofing, Torchlite Roofing, Landa Roofing	Alumasc Exterior Building Products
Derix	Germany	Weaving Loom Accessories	Pilkingtons Ltd (t/a Weitzer Parket UK)
Desco	Germany	Packaging Machinery	Apropa Machinery Ltd
Destaco (UK) Ltd	Germany	Toggle Clamps	Dejay Distribution Ltd
Detroit	Italy	Refrigerated Display Equipment	Blighline Ltd
Deutsche Tecalemit	Germany	Lube Equipment	Tecalemit Garage Equipment Co. Ltd
Devan Chemicals	Australia	Aegis Anti-Microbial	S T R UK Ltd
Devatech	France	humidifiers	J S Humidifiers plc
Dexter Corporation, The	U.S.A.	Shaped Hot Melts and Hand Held Applicators (Europe)	Power Adhesives Ltd
DHL	Netherlands		Tuffnelln Parcels Express
Dial France	France	Vehicle Leasing and Management	Leaseplan UK Ltd
Dial Italy	Italy	Vehicle Leasing and Management	Leaseplan UK Ltd
Dial Spania	Spain	Vehicle Leasing and Management	Leaseplan UK Ltd
Diamant	Germany	Metal repair systems	P E S UK Ltd
Diamond	Japan	Portable Benders and Straighteners	La Roche
Diamond Antenna & Microwave	U.S.A.	ax And Waveguide Rotary Joint	Aspen Electronics Ltd
Diamond General	U.S.A.	Microphysiology Research	Linton & Co Engineering Ltd
Diamond Scientific Industries Inc	U.S.A.	Diamond Lapping Products	Ellesco Ltd
Diato GmbH	Germany	Diamond/CBN honing stones and diamond reamers	Equipment For You
Didion	U.S.A.	Foundry Plant	F T L Foundry Equipment Ltd
Diesel	Italy	Optical Frames & Sunglasses	Hilton International Eye Wear Ltd
Digitizer Technology	U.S.A.	Digitizing Tablet Support	Pitney Bowes Software Ltd
Diimarzio	U.S.A.	Guitar Pickups	Korg UK Ltd
Dijet	Japan	Indexable Inserts, Milling, Drilling, Turning and End Milling	Cromwell Group Holdings
Dimensions	U.S.A.	Needlecraft	Coats Ltd
Dinse GmbH	Germany	Welding Equipment	Olympus Technologies Ltd
Diprofil AB	Sweden	Complete Range of Power Hand Tools	Kemet International Ltd
Diset	Spain	Puzzles And Games	Willis Toys Ltd
Disoric	Germany	Sensors	Sensortek
Diversified Biotech	U.S.A.	Biotech Products	Radleys
Doepke & Co	Germany	R.C.D.'S & M.C.B.'S	Doepke UK Ltd
Dole Food Co. Inc.	U.S.A.	Fresh Produce	Dole Fresh UK Ltd
Dom Ficherheitstechnik	Germany	patented cylinder systems	Ronis-Dom Ltd
Dong-1	Korea, Republic of	Steering Systems	Watermota Ltd
Dong-I	Korea, Republic of	gearboxes	Watermota Ltd
Dori	France	Grass Cutting Equipment	Industrial Power Units Ltd
Dorned B.V.	Netherlands	Dubo Rings	Challenge Europe Ltd
Dosmatic	U.S.A.	Injectors for Horticulture	Access Irrigation Ltd
Dow Chemical Company (Saran)	Netherlands	Wrapping Film	Bemis Swansea
Dow Corning	U.S.A.	Mould Release Agents	J Allcock & Sons Ltd
Dow Corning	U.S.A.	Solvent Applicable Silicone	S T R UK Ltd
Dow Corning	U.S.A.	Electrical Resins, Varnishes and Transformer Fluids	Croylek Ltd
Dox	Germany	Brush Polishers, Spray Dampers and Reel Handling Equipment	Pulp & Paper Machinery Ltd
Dr Renger GmbH & Co. KG	Germany	Lacquer Products	Schloetter Co. Ltd
Dr. Straetmans GmbH	Germany	Protection Agents, Biocides	Ferguson & Menzies Ltd
Dr Weigert GmbH	Germany	Neodiser Detergents & Disinfectants	Scientific Instrument Centre Ltd
Dr Zanperoni GmbH	Germany	Hiking and Treking Boots/Shoes	UK Distributors Footwear Ltd
Draloric	Germany	Ceramic Capacitors	Richardsons R F P D Ltd
Drew	Netherlands	Foam Control Agents	Banner Chemicals Ltd
DRU B.V.	Netherlands	Gas Heaters	Drugasar Service Ltd
Du Crocq Aromatics Internation BV	Netherlands	Fragrances	C P L Aromas Ltd
Du Crocq Aromatics International B.V.	Netherlands	Perfume Compounds, Flavours, Essential Oils and Aromatics	Bruce Starke & Co. Ltd
Du-Pont	U.S.A.	modified acid copolymer powder	Mallatite Ltd
Du Pont d Nemours	Netherlands	Terathane polyols	I M C D UK Ltd
Dubix	France	Finishing Equipment	J L A
Ducros Services Rapides	France	Express Parcels	Tuffnelln Parcels Express
Due Zeta S.r.l.	Italy	Abrasives - Diamond	Finishing Aids & Tools Ltd
Dumangin Champagne	France	Champagne	Yapp Brothers Ltd
Dunlop Industrial Hose Ltd	United Kingdom	Oilfield Hoses	Cebo UK Ltd
Dunlop Manufacturing	U.S.A.	Guitar Accessories And Effects Units	John Hornby Skewes & Co. Ltd
Duofold	U.S.A.	Thermal Base Layers	Ronhill Sports
Duplicaters Metro	France	Duplicating Machines	Unigraph UK Ltd
Duplo	Japan	Office Products, Graphic Arts Machinery	Duplo International Ltd
Duraloc	Canada	Pitched metal tile strips	Alumasc Exterior Building Products
Duratex S.A.	Brazil	Standard And Decorative Hardwood	Price & Pierce Softwoods Ltd
Durholdt	Germany	Pinch Valves	Texcel Division (a division of Crosslink Business Services Ltd)
Dyckerhoff AG	Germany	Oilwell Cements	Cebo UK Ltd
Dymax Corp	U.S.A.	Adhesives	Intertronics
Dynamco	U.S.A.	Solenoid Valves & Miniature Fittings & Tubing	Valeader Pneumatics Ltd
Dynamic	France	beaters and mixers	Mitchell & Cooper Ltd (Head Office)
Dynamics Research Corp	U.S.A.	Encoders	Huco Dynatork
Dynetics	U.S.A.	AFM machines	Winbro Group Technologies
Dytan Instruments Inc	U.S.A.	Accelerometers, Impulse Hammers, Force and Pressure Sensors	Sandhurst Instruments Ltd
E. Begerow GmbH	Germany	Filter sheets, filter cartridges, beverage chemicals	Fleximas Ltd
E.C. Emmerich	Germany	Wooden Planes & Tools	Emmerich Berlon Ltd
E. Dorken AG	Germany	Delta-Magni Products	Delta GB N Ltd
E.M.C.	U.S.A.	Refractory Metals	Tempatron Controls
E.V.R.	Canada	Pinch Valves	Texcel Division (a division of Crosslink Business Services Ltd)
E.W. Bowman Inc	U.S.A.	Annealing and Decorating Lehrs for Glass/Ceramics	Graphoidal Developments
Eagle	United Kingdom	Pressure Washers/Steam Cleaners	C S A Cleaning Equipment
Eagle Picher Industries	U.S.A.	Lead Powders	Fleximas Ltd
Eagle Picher Minerals Inc	U.S.A.	Diatomaceous Earth Filter Paper & Lead Powders	Fleximas Ltd

6

OVERSEAS COMPANY	COUNTRY OF ORIGIN	PRODUCT	UK COMPANY
Earls Performance Products	U.S.A.	Performance Hoses, Fittings And Accessories	Custom Hose & Fitting Ltd
Earthway	U.S.A.	Garden Seeders	Danarm Machinery Ltd
EasiRun Inc	U.S.A.	Legacy Liberator	Transoft Ltd (Part of the Computer Software P.L.C.)
Eastman	U.S.A.	Speciality Solvents	Banner Chemicals Ltd
EBS	U.S.A.	Software & Webs	Computer Solutions Ltd
Eckart Werke	Germany	Bronze & Aluminium Pigments	Kromachem Ltd
Eclatec	France	Road Lighting-Clip 28-34	W R T L Exterior Lighting Ltd
Ecobra	Germany	Drawing Instruments	Technical Sales Ltd
Ecoflex Anger	Germany	Pre-Insulated Plastic Pipes	Durotan Ltd
Ecoform/Multifol	Germany	Coextruded Semi-rigid Polystryene Films	Sudpack UK Ltd
Ecolight	Netherlands	Interior Lighting	Crescent Lighting Ltd
Econet	Italy	Manufacture x-ray equipment	Celtic SMR Ltd
Ecoseal	Australia	RINVERT: Resiitivity modelling and presentation	Geomem Ltd
Ecotrade	Italy	Automatic Assembly Machines For Wood Pallets & Cases	Duo-Fast
Edalco	Switzerland	Tapping Attachments	Macinnes Tooling Ltd
EDC	Denmark	Tasles Rest Room Furniture	E W Marshall Ltd
Edgeter	U.S.A.	CBN Superabrave machining centres	Jones & Shipman Grinding Ltd (a division of Renold Engineering Products Co.)
Edition Kunzelmann	Switzerland	Music Publisher	Obelisk Music
Edlund Inc	U.S.A.	Stainless Steel Can Openers, can crushers, scales, knife sharpener	Metcalfe Catering Equipment Ltd
Edward Orton Foundation	U.S.A.	Pyrametric Cones	Potclays Ltd
Edwards Signalling	U.S.A.	UL Approved Products, Industrial Beacons, Fire Beacons, Obstruction Beacons, ICAO Approved, Marine Beacons, Hazardous Area Beacons	Moflash Signalling Ltd
Edwards Signals	U.S.A.	UL Hardous Area Products	Signals Ltd
Effective Management Systems	U.S.A.	Manufacturing Control Software	Deaf Alerter plc
Effepi	Italy	Valves (Actuated)	Bonomi UK Ltd
Eheim	Germany	Pumps And Filters	John Allan Aquariums Ltd
Eiken Chemical Company Ltd	Japan	LoopAmp Molecular Diagnostic Products	The Mast Group Ltd
EIM	U.S.A.	Valve Actuators	Paladon Systems Ltd
Eindor	Israel	Minisprinklers for Horticulture	Access Irrigation Ltd
Einsa	Spain	Aircraft Ground Support Equipment Military and Civil	Didsbury Engineering Ltd
Eintal	Israel	Minsprinklers for Horticulture	Access Irrigation Ltd
Ekamant Ab	Sweden	Abrasives - Coated	Finishing Aids & Tools Ltd
Electra Vitoria	Spain	Lift packages	Quality Lift Products Ltd
Electro Corporation	U.S.A.	Magnetic Speed Sensors	Almag Components Ltd
Electro Mechano	U.S.A.	drilling machines	Drill Service Horley Ltd
Electro-Tel Corp	U.S.A.	slip rings	Moog Components
Electromagnetic Technologies	U.S.A.	Beamforming Networks And Associated Components	Aspen Electronics Ltd
Electromatic	Denmark	Electronic Components and Data Transmission Equip	Carlo Gavazzi UK Ltd
Elettrotec	Italy	Pressure and Vacuum Switches, Flow Switches, Level Switches	Applications Engineering Ltd
Elf Atochem	France	Solvents	C K Chemicals
Elitfonster	Sweden	Windows & doors	Inwido UK Ltd
Elkron SpA	Italy		C Q R Ltd
Elliott	U.S.A.	Flexible Drive Shafts	Huco Dynatork
Elliptipar	U.S.A.	Interior Lighting	Crescent Lighting Ltd
Elmet Technologies Inc.	U.S.A.	Molybdenum and Tungsten	Ernest B Westman Ltd
Elora	Germany	Sockets and Wrenches	Draper Tools Ltd
Elvo	Switzerland	Solder Stations	Link Hamson Ltd
Emak S.p.A.	Italy	Chainsaws, Brushcutters, Lawnmowers	Emak UK Ltd
Emhart Teknologies	U.S.A.	Jack nut and well nut	Emhart Teknologies (Tucker Fasteners Ltd)
EMS- Chemie AG	Switzerland	Engineering Thermoplastics	E M S-Chemie UK Ltd
EMS-Chemie (Asia) Ltd	Taiwan	Engineering Thermoplastics	E M S-Chemie UK Ltd
EMS Chemie (Deutschland)	Germany	Engineering Thermoplastics	E M S-Chemie UK Ltd
EMS-Chemie (France) SA	France	Engineering Thermoplastics	E M S-Chemie UK Ltd
EMS-Chemie (Japan) Ltd	Japan	Engineering Thermoplastics	E M S-Chemie UK Ltd
Encardio Rite	India	Load Cells and Pressure Transmitters	Sandhurst Instruments Ltd
Enerdis	France	Measuring Transducers	Energy I C T
Enerpac	U.S.A.	Hydraulic Equipment	Custom Hose & Fitting Ltd
Enerpac	U.S.A.	hydralic equipment.	Worlifts Ltd
Engel	Germany	Thermo Cutting Equipment	Kelgray Products Ltd
Engelhard	U.S.A.		Lawrence Industries Ltd
Enolgas	Italy	Ball Valves	Anglo Nordic Burner Products Ltd
Envic	Finland	Test And Measurement Equipment	Energy I C T
Environmental Stress Systems	U.S.A.	Hot & Cold Test Plates & Chambers	Aspen Electronics Ltd
EPC Identification Systems	U.S.A.	Labels	Link Hamson Ltd
Epicentre Technologies	U.S.A.	Molecular Biologicals	Cambio Ltd
EPM	Netherlands	Mercury Vapour Monitor	Quantitech Ltd
Epoke	Denmark	Gritters	Bunce Ashbury Ltd
Epox	Taiwan	Full Range Of Computer Motherboards	Ceratech Electronics Ltd
Ericsson Components	Sweden	Rf And Microwave Transistors	Richardsons R F P D Ltd
Erlau AG	Germany	Grab Rails	Intrad Ltd
Erowa	Switzerland	EDM Tooling Systems	Rem Systems Ltd
Eshed Robotec	Israel	Educational And Industrial Robots, C I M Systems	Brandone Machine Tool Ltd
Ess Schweisstechnik GmbH	Germany	Welding Machines	Olympus Technologies Ltd
Essemtec	Switzerland	Pick & Place Mics	Turner Electronics
ESWA Heizsysteme GmbH	Germany	Heating Foils	Eswa Ltd
Eternit	France	Fibre Cement Slates	Cembrit Ltd
ETP	Sweden	Locking Bushes	Lenze UK Ltd
Eucher	Germany	Sensors	Sensortek
Eurama S.A.	France	Corn Cob Polishing Media	B & D Clays & Chemicals Ltd
Euring	Italy	Section Rolling Machines	Hatfields Machine Tools Ltd
Eurisotop	France	NMR Deuterated Solvents	Fluorochem Ltd
Euro Tech (Far East) Ltd	Hong Kong		Hawker Electronics Ltd
Euromag	Italy	Electromagnetic Flowmeters	Litre Meter Ltd
Europieske	Denmark	Medical Insurance	Doctorcall
Europpalainen	Finland	Medical Insurance	Doctorcall
Eurotherm	United Kingdom	Brushless Motors & Drives	Mclennan Servo Supplies Ltd
Everite	South Africa	Fibre Cement Products	Cembrit Ltd
Everlight Chemical Industrial Corporation	Taiwan	Reactive Dyestuffs	Magna Colours Ltd
Evets Corporation	U.S.A.	Guitar Tuners And Metronomes	John Hornby Skewes & Co. Ltd
Experimetria	Hungary	Biological Research Equipment	Linton & Co Engineering Ltd
Extramet	Switzerland	Tungsten Carbide Rod & Tube	Albe England Ltd
Extrucen	Spain	Polyfin Films	Eurohill Traders Ltd (t/a Associated Packaging)
Exxon	United Kingdom	LDPE, EVA	Arto Chemicals Ltd
Eyquem	France	Spark Plugs	Standard Motor Products Europe Ltd
F H Papenmeier	Germany	Process Observation	Visilume Ltd
F K S	Germany	Graphic Arts Machinery	Duplo International Ltd
F. Leutert	Germany	Engine Indicators	Smail Engineers Glasgow Ltd
F.lli Ferrari	Italy	Industrial Centrifugal	Nicotra-Gebhardt Ltd
F & M	Netherlands	Stone Set Jewellery	W B Muddeman & Son Ltd
F. Thumb GmbH	Germany	President Awning Systems	Deans Blinds & Awnings UK
F. Vanoutryve & Cie	France	Furnishing Fabrics	Maisonneuve & Co.
F.X. Schmid	Germany	Jigsaws and Playing Cards	Childs Play International Ltd
Faber Castell GmbH	Germany	Art stationery & drawing instruments	West Design Products Ltd

7

OVERSEAS COMPANY	COUNTRY OF ORIGIN	PRODUCT	UK COMPANY
FAG	United Kingdom	Automotive spare parts	Kingsdown
Falquet & Cie	France	Ride On Toys	Peterkin UK Ltd
Faltex AG	Switzerland	Folding Machines	Graphics Arts Equipment Ltd
fas LPG EQUIPMENT	Germany		Combined Gas Systems Ltd
Faulhaber Group	United Kingdom		Electro Mechanical Systems (EMS) Ltd (EMS)
Fauretto S.p.A.	Italy	Large Capacity Surface Grinding Machines	Jones & Shipman Grinding Ltd (a division of Renold Engineering Products Co.)
Fayin Enterprise Ltd	China		Hawker Electronics Ltd
FDK Corporation	Japan	Batteries	Kauser International Trading Ltd
Fed	Ukraine	Cameras	Swains International plc
Feeler	Taiwan	CNC Lathes and CNC Machine Centres	Emi-Mec Ltd
Feisa	Spain	Shrink Films	Eurohill Traders Ltd (t/a Associated Packaging)
Felco	Switzerland	Wire Cutters/Garden Secateurs	Burton Mccall Ltd
Feldbinder GmbH	Germany	Tanker Manufrs	Feldbinder UK Ltd
Fella Werke	Germany	Agricultural Machinery	Ruston's Engineering Co. Ltd
Felss	Germany	Swage Forming Machines	Pearson Panke Ltd
Feme	Italy	PCB Relays	Carlo Gavazzi UK Ltd
Fenn - Torin	U.S.A.	Spring Coiling Machines	Bennett Mahler
Ferris	U.S.A.	Grass Cutting Equipment	Industrial Power Units Ltd
Ferrishield	U.S.A.	Ferrites/Emi Suppressors	Optical Filters
Festival	Netherlands	Make Up And Aerosols For Fun	Palmer Agencies Ltd
Fetra Trucks	Germany	Hand Trucks And Trolleys	Central Soucre Ltd
FEV GmbH Spiral Stretch Wrapping Machines	United Kingdom		Gordian Strapping Ltd
Fiberstars	U.S.A.	Fibre Optic Lighting	Crescent Lighting Ltd
Filarcom SL	Spain	Haircutting Scissors	Diamond Edge Ltd
Filclair S.A.	France	Poly Tunnels	Fargro
Fillauer	U.S.A.	Orthopaedic & Prosthetic Components	Gilbert & Mellish Ltd
Filmop	Italy	Litter Bins	Unicorn Hygienics
Filter Pump Industries Inc	U.S.A.	Filter Systems & Vertical Pumps	March May Ltd
Filtrec SRL	Italy	hydraulic filters	Harrier Fluid Power Ltd
Filtres Philippe	France	Pleated Paper Filters & HSGS	Flowtech Fluid Handling Ltd
Filtronic AB	Sweden	Fume Extraction Commitment	Electro Group Ltd
Filzfabrik Fulda GmbH & Co	Germany	Felt Manufacturer	Bryan & Clark Ltd
Finish Line	U.S.A.	Bicycle Lubricants	Madison
Finland:Scandinavian Aerospace & Industry AB	Denmark		Cambridge Vacuum Engineering
Finnsonic Oy	Finland	Ultrasonic Cleaning Machines	Turbex Ltd
Fira	Italy	Oil Coolers	BYPY Hydraulics & Transmissions Ltd
First Data Bank Inc	U.S.A.	Nutritionist Five-Nutrition Information Qmr-Qual MeDical Reference	First Databank Europe Ltd
Fisba Optik	Switzerland		Armstrong Optical Ltd
Fischer Werke	Germany	Fixing Systems, Audio Cassette Storage System	Fischer Fixings UK Ltd
Fishercontols	U.S.A.		Combined Gas Systems Ltd
Fitjitsu General Ltd	Japan	Air Conditioning	Fujitsu General UK Co. Ltd
Fleck Europe	France	Water Softening/Filter Valves	Ferex Ltd
Fleet Services	Ireland	Vehicle Leasing and Management	Leaseplan UK Ltd
Flexim	Germany	Time Of Flight Flowmeter	Tamo Ltd
Flexlift	Germany	Low Profile Scissor Lift	Southworth Handling Ltd
Flojet	U.S.A.	Dispense pumps	Booth Dispencers
Flott	Germany	Drilling & tapping machines	Robert Speck Ltd
Flowdrill B.V.	Netherlands	Flowdrilling Equipment	Flowdrill UK Ltd
Flowmeca	France	Uhp Fittings	Boiswood LLP
Flubacher & Co.	Switzerland	Measuring Eyeglasses	Vaultland Engineering
Flud-Chemie	France	Condensation Oven	Humiseal Europe Ltd (Head Office)
Fluid Components Inc	U.S.A.	Flow, Level & Mass Flow Meters	Allison Engineering Ltd
Flutec	Germany	Control Valves	Hydac Technology Ltd
Fluvo	Germany	Water Features	Certikin International Ltd
Fochs Veilig	Netherlands	Safety Wear	Wholesale Welding Supplies Ltd
Fogautolube	France	Vechile Lifts	Tecalemit Garage Equipment Co. Ltd
Fong Kee Iron Works Co. Ltd	Taiwan	Blow Moulding Machinery (Plastic)	Kween B Ltd
Fontfonts	Germany	Fonts	Monotype Imaging Ltd
Fontijne Holland	Netherlands	hydraulic laboratory presses	Mackey Bowley International Ltd
Formdrill	Belgium	Flowdrilling equipment	Robert Speck Ltd
Forth Inc	U.S.A.	Computer Development Software	Computer Solutions Ltd
Fotima	China	Pouches And Bags For Photographic And Other Uses	Swains International plc
Four Electrique Delemont S.A.	Switzerland	Electric Furnaces	Ramsell Naber Ltd
Four Seasons Flooring	U.S.A.	synthetic brush matting	Jaymart Roberts & Plastics Ltd
Fox Steel Company	U.S.A.	Steel Windows And Doors	Crittall Windows Ltd
FP	Italy	Bronze Centrifugal Pumps	Cleghorn Waring & Co Pumps Ltd
Francom	Italy	Tool Boxes	L J Hydleman & Co. Ltd
Franklin Electric GmbH	Germany	Sumbersidble Electric Pump Motors	Fletcher Moorland Ltd
Franklin Industrial Minerals	U.S.A.		Lawrence Industries Ltd
Frascold	Italy	Refrigeration Compressors	H T G Trading Ltd
Fratelli Pedrotti S.r.l.	Italy	Mobile Grain Driers	Master Farm Services GB Ltd
Freedom Fenders	U.S.A.	Boat fenders	Nicholas Bray & Son Ltd
Fresia	Italy	Snow Blowers	Bunce Ashbury Ltd
Freuden berg	Germany	Flooring	Static Safe Ltd
Freudenburg-Nok	United Kingdom	Transmission Parts	A T P Automatic Transmission Parts UK Ltd
Friedrich Vollmer Feinmessgeratebau GmbH	Germany	Strip Gauging Systems	British & Continental Traders Ltd
Frimar	Italy	Electric Welding Equipment	Sureweld UK Ltd
Frisylen Plastics	Germany	Industrial Cutting Boards	Partwell Cutting Technology Ltd
FritzStuder	Switzerland	Grinding Machines	E C I S Scotland Ltd
Froude Hofmann Prueftechnik	Germany	End of Line Vehicle Test Equipment-Engine & Vehicle Test Equipment	Froude Hofmann Ltd (part of the F K I Group of Companies)
FSB	Germany	Door Lever Handles, Door Pulls, Door and Window Furniture	Allgood
Fuji Heavy Industries	Japan	Engines/Genes/Pumps	Redbreast Industrial Equipment Ltd
Fuji Robin Industries	Japan	Brushcutters/Hedgetrimmer/blower	Redbreast Industrial Equipment Ltd
Fuji Yusoki	Japan	Robot Palletizers	W J Morray Engineering Ltd
Fujirebio	Japan	Immunodiagnostic Tests	The Mast Group Ltd
Furon	U.S.A.	Teflon Pumps, Valves, Fittings And Accessories	Boiswood LLP
Furon	U.S.A.		Stokvis Tapes UK Ltd
G. Dok	Democratic People's Republic of Korea	Footmaster	Keystone Castor Co.
G. Dok	Democratic People's Republic of Korea	Footmaster	Keystone Castor Co.
G.E. Plastics	Netherlands	Lexan-Polycarbonate Sheet	Stockline Plastics Ltd
G.E. Plastics	Austria	Thermoclear-Twinwall Polycarbonate	Stockline Plastics Ltd
G.M.P.	Korea, Republic of	Laminating Systems	Murodigital
G-Man Tools AB	Sweden	Handsaws	Atkinson-Walker Saws Ltd
G.R.J. Cooper	South Africa	Magnetic and Gravity Geophysical Software	Geomem Ltd
G.W.F.	Switzerland	Gas and Water Meters	Switch2 Energy Solutions
Gac	U.S.A.	Engine Governors	Industrial Power Units Ltd
GAEA	Canada	Borehole logging (GAEA-LoG), cross section (WinFence) and soil analysis (WinSieve) software	Geomem Ltd
Gaia Converters	France	DC/DC Converters	Campbell Collins
Gail-Inax	Germany	Dry Pressed And Extruded Tiles	Ceramique International Ltd

8

OVERSEAS COMPANY	COUNTRY OF ORIGIN	PRODUCT	UK COMPANY
Galletti	Italy	Air Conditioning Products	Thermal Technology Sales Ltd
Gallignani	Italy	Agricultural Machinery	Ruston's Engineering Co. Ltd
Gammons	U.S.A.	tape reamers	Drill Service Horley Ltd
Gantry S.A.	Belgium	Rail Fixing Systems	Cranequip Ltd
Gantry S.A.	Belgium	Motorised Lifting Equipment	Cranequip Ltd
Garaventa	Canada	Vertical Lifts For Disabled Public Access	Enable Access
Garbantex S.L.	Spain	Cotton & Linen Mixture Fabrics	Emko Products Ltd
Garmont	Italy	Leather Footwear	Karrimor Ltd
Gaudino	Italy	worsted, woollen and semi-worsted spinning frames	Macart Textiles Machinery Ltd
GDB SA	Belgium	Office Furniture	Trac Office Contracts
Gebhardt Ventilatoren	Germany	Industrial Centrifugal	Nicotra-Gebhardt Ltd
Gebr. Titgemeyer GmbH	Germany	Commercial Vehicle Fittings	Eckold Ltd
Gedore	Austria	Hand Tools	L J Hydleman & Co. Ltd
Gedore	Germany	Hand Tools	L J Hydleman & Co. Ltd
Gehalin	Germany	Filling Equipment	D H Industries Ltd
Gehl	U.S.A.	Livestock Feeding Equipment	Westmac Ltd
Gems Sensors	U.S.A.	Pressure Level and Flow Sensor Manufacturers	Applications Engineering Ltd
Gencor Industries Inc	U.S.A.	Packaged Burners For The Aggregated Drying Industry	Beverley Environmental Ltd (Head Office)
General Kinematics Corporation	U.S.A.	Vibratory Process Equipment	General Kinematics Ltd
General Monitors	U.S.A.	Gas & Flame Detection	Allison Engineering Ltd
General Wire Spring Co.	U.S.A.	Drain Cleaning Equipment	Monument Tools Ltd
Generalsider	Italy	Pipes	Alexander Cardew Ltd (Head Office)
GEO	U.S.A.	Specialist Monomers	Banner Chemicals Ltd
Georg Kramp	Germany	Jacks And Trolleys	Southworth Handling Ltd
Georg Sahm	Germany	Take Up Winding Machines	Texkimp Ltd
George Dennis	Czech Republic	Effects Pedals For Musical Instruments	John Hornby Skewes & Co. Ltd
GER	Spain	Grinders - Cylindrical And Surface	Capital Equipment & Machinery Ltd
Gericke AG	Switzerland	Powder Handling Equipment	Gericke Ltd
Gericke GmbH	Germany	Feeding/Mixing Equipment	Gericke Ltd
Germany:Josef Seidl Industrievertretungen	Germany	electron beam welding & vacuum services	Cambridge Vacuum Engineering
Gewa Rehabteknik Ab	Sweden	Page Turner	Possum
GFL GmbH	Germany	Mixers shakers incubators hybridisation equipment laboratories	Scientific Instrument Centre Ltd
GFS Chemicals	U.S.A.	Organics, Water Test Kits Prechlorates	Fluorochem Ltd
Giaiotti S.p.A.	Italy	Office Furniture	Trac Office Contracts
Gianni Versace	Italy	Optical Frames & Sunglasses	Hilton International Eye Wear Ltd
Giesse SRL	Italy	chenille machinery	Macart Textiles Machinery Ltd
Giesverpak B.V.	Netherlands	Flower Sleeves	Fargro
Gifu	Japan	Timber	Plaut International
Gilbos	Belgium	Winding Machinery	Robert S Maynard Ltd
Giro	U.S.A.	Bicycle Helmets	Madison
Glas Trosch	Switzerland	Fire-Rated Glass	C G I International Ltd
Glen Research Corp	U.S.A.	Products For Dna Systems	Cambio Ltd
Glendyne Inc	Canada	Natural Slate	Cembrit Ltd
Globas Karl Kremmendaul	Germany	Orthopaedic Materials	A Algeo Ltd
GMM SRL	Italy	Stone Processing Machinery	Pisani plc
GO	U.S.A.	Pressure Regulators	Boiswood LLP
Gok	Germany	De-Aerators	Anglo Nordic Burner Products Ltd
Golden Software, Inc	U.S.A.	Digitising (Didger), Graphing (Grapher), Contouring and 3D Surface (Surfer), borehole logging (Strater) and mapping (MapViewer) Software	Geomem Ltd
Golden West Sales	U.S.A.	Food Preparation Equipment	Robot Coupe UK Ltd
Goldlite	New Zealand	Stone Set Jewellery	W B Muddeman & Son Ltd
Gotec	Germany		Gotec Trading Ltd
GP:50 New York	U.S.A.	Pressure Transducers	Sandhurst Instruments Ltd
Graber Incorporated	U.S.A.	Curtain Drapery Hardware	Hallis Hudson Group Ltd
Graco N.V.	Belgium	Airless & HVLP Paint Application Equipment & Accessories	Lion Industries UK Ltd
Graebener	Germany	Presses	Embassy Machinery Ltd
Grafton Recruitment Kpt	Hungary	Recruitment Agency	Grafton Recuitment
Grafton Recruitment S.A. de Chile	Chile	Recruitment Agency	Grafton Recuitment
Grafton Recruitment S.R.O.	Czech Republic	Recruitment Agency	Grafton Recuitment
Grafton Recruitment Sp, Z0.0	Poland	Recruitment Agency	Grafton Recuitment
Gralpe	Portugal		C E D Ltd
Grammar Engines	U.S.A.	Rom Emulators	Computer Solutions Ltd
Grasslin GmbH	Germany		Grasslin UK Ltd
Gratry Lorthiois Industries	France	Woven Furnishing Fabrics	Maisonneuve & Co.
Grau	United Kingdom		Rainer Schneider & Ayres
Great Plains Industries Inc	U.S.A.	Pumps and Flowmeters for Fuel Dispensing	Atkinson Equipment
Greenland Tourist Board	Greenland	Hiking Maps	Harvey Map Services Ltd
Grego AG	Switzerland	gregomatic surface cleaning system	Crofton House Associates
Grespania S.A.	Spain	Ceramic Tile Manufacturers	Northern Wall & Floor Ltd
Gressel AG	Switzerland	Machine Vices	Craftsman Tools Ltd
Grillo	Italy	Grass Cutting Equipment	Industrial Power Units Ltd
Grimm Aerosol Technik	Germany	Dust Monitors	Quantitech Ltd
Grodania A/S	Denmark	Rockwool	Fargro
grosfillex	France	Garden funiture	Roder UK Ltd
Groundwater Services Inc. (GSI)	U.S.A.	RBCA Tool Kit: Contaminant transport modelling, risk assessment and clean up standards for contaminated land.	Geomem Ltd
Group-Arnold	U.S.A.	Magnetic Cores	Almag Components Ltd
Guest Elchrom A.G.	Switzerland	E.S.R. Pipettes	Guest Medical Ltd
Guest Elchrom AG	Switzerland	E.S.R.'s For Vacuum Systems	Guest Medical Ltd
Gujarat Reclaim & Rubber	India	Reclaimed Rubber	J Allcock & Sons Ltd
Guma	Italy	yarn raising machines	Macart Textiles Machinery Ltd
Gunther Hahn	Germany	Gas Springs	Eckold Ltd
Gustav Ullrich GmbH & Co. KG	Germany	Stabila Spirit Levels	Brian Hyde Ltd
H.B. Fuller GmbH	Germany	Waxes/Wax Blends	Industrial Waxes
H.C.K.	Germany	Test Probes And Leads	Northern Design Ltd
H.Cross	U.S.A.	Refractory Metals	Tempatron Controls
H. Maihak	Germany	Bin Level Indicators	Smail Engineers Glasgow Ltd
H. Schmincke & Co.	Germany	Artists Materials	C Roberson & Co. Ltd
H&T	Japan	ADSL Modems	M B Components Ltd
H. Weiser GmbH	Germany	Tagging and Stapling Machines	Piroto Labelling Ltd
Habero	Germany	Striking Tools	L J Hydleman & Co. Ltd
Habich	Austria	Inorganic Pigments	Kromachem Ltd
Haco	Belgium		Kingsland Engineering Company Ltd
Haddonstone (USA) Ltd	U.S.A.	Reconstructed Ornamental And Architectural Stonework	Haddonstone Ltd
Hafrestroms Ab	Sweden	Artic Coated Papers and Boards	Arctic Paper UK Ltd
Hagemann	Germany	Packaging Machinery	Advanced Dynamics Ltd
Hager & Meisinger	Germany	Dental Rotary Instruments/Diamonds	Plandent
Hain	Germany	DNA Hybridisation Strips	The Mast Group Ltd
Hallins	Sweden	Electric Lifters	Southworth Handling Ltd
Halox	U.S.A.		Lawrence Industries Ltd
Hamada	Japan	Printing machines	P P S Rotaprint Ltd
Hambi	Germany	Mesh Benders and Cutters	La Roche
Hamel	Switzerland	two stage twisting elastotwist-service & spare parts	Macart Textiles Machinery Ltd
Hamilton Beach Commercial Inc	U.S.A.	Kitchen And Bar Blenders, drink mixers and juicers	Metcalfe Catering Equipment Ltd
Hammerle	Austria	Textile Machinery - Shearing Machines	Pilkingtons Ltd (t/a Weitzer Parket UK)
Han Young	Korea, Republic of	Controls	Tempatron Controls

OVERSEAS COMPANY	COUNTRY OF ORIGIN	PRODUCT	UK COMPANY
Hanes	U.S.A.	Sweatshirts, Polo and T-Shirts	I S Enterprises International
Hangsterfers	U.S.A.	Coolants and Cutting Fluids	Macinnes Tooling Ltd
Hannabach	Germany	Musical Instrument Strings	John Hornby Skewes & Co. Ltd
Hannay Reels Inc	U.S.A.	Hose And Cable Reels	Metool Products Ltd
Hans Sasserath	Germany	Pressure Reducing Valves	Reliance Water Controls Ltd
Hans Schmidt & Co. GmbH	Germany	Electronic and Mechanical Yarn Tension and Yarn Spining Meters	James H Heal & Co. Ltd
Hansa	Germany	Paint Brushes	Technical Sales Ltd
Hanwha Corp/Machinery	Korea, Republic of	CNC Swiss Type Turning Centres	Citizen Machinery UK Ltd
Hardie Irrigation	Italy	Irrigation Solenoids/Equipment	Connectomatic
Harfang Microtechniques	U.S.A.	Phased Array Testing	Sonatest Ltd
Harley	U.S.A.	Plate Mounting Material	Plastotype
Harper Collins Publishers Inc	U.S.A.	Fiction and Non Fiction Books in Various Interest Areas	Harpercollins Publishers Ophelia House
Harris Welco	U.S.A.	Consumables	Wholesale Welding Supplies Ltd
Harsh International Inc	U.S.A.	Hydraulic Tipping Gears	Harsh Ltd
Hartner	Germany	H.SS and Carbide Drills	Macinnes Tooling Ltd
Harwil	U.S.A.	Flow Switches	Texcel Division (a division of Crosslink Business Services Ltd)
Hauser Products	U.S.A.	Latex Finger Cotts & Gloves	Cravenmount Ltd
Hawk	Australia	Ultrasonic Level Transmitter	Allison Engineering Ltd
Haynes International Inc	U.S.A.	High Performance Nickel Based	Haynes International Ltd
HBC Radiomatic	Germany	Radion Systems	Crane Care Ltd
HDS Inc	U.S.A.	Radio Products	Marlborough Communications Ltd
Hechinger	Germany	Quartz Clock Movements	A G Thomas Bradford Ltd
Heinrich Wagner Sinto	Germany	Mould Making And Casting Lines	Pearson Panke Ltd
Helios	Netherlands	Broadcast Studio Furniture	Preco Ltd
Hellux Leuchten GmbH	Italy	Modern Amenity Lighting	Sugg Lighting Ltd
Hendrickson	U.S.A.	trailer axle and suspension components	Roadlink International Ltd
Herben	Australia	Perforating Arm & Clam For GTO Press	R M Rotary Services Ltd
Herberts Industriglas	Germany	Metaglas	Visilume Ltd
Hercules Industries Inc	U.S.A.	New 4x4 tyres	Tyre Renewals Ltd
Heresite Protection Coatings	U.S.A.	Synthetic Resinous Linings	Lithgow Saekaphen Ltd
Herlag GmbH	Germany	Garden Furniture	Kettler GB Ltd
Hermadix Coatings B.V.	Netherlands	Coatings Glass Maintenance Products	Fargro
Hilarius	Netherlands	Welding Consumables	Weldability S I F
Hilge	Germany	Hygenic Centrifugal Pumps	Robert Craig & Sons Ltd
Hilger u. Kern	Germany	Electronic Motor Control	Stromag Ltd
Hitachi	Japan	Power Tools	Banson Tool Hire Ltd
Hitachi Metals	Japan	Inductors	M B Components Ltd
HITECH	Australia	Computer Development Software	Computer Solutions Ltd
Hiwave	Switzerland	Compilers Simulators	Computer Solutions Ltd
HKR GmbH	Germany	High power, iron powder composite cores & chokes	Rolfe Industries
Hoaf	Netherlands	Infrared Weed Control System	Industrial Power Units Ltd
Hoesch	Germany	Composite panels	Plannja Ltd
Hoesch	Germany	Steel decking	Plannja Ltd
Hoesch	Germany	Liner trays steel	Plannja Ltd
Hoffer	U.S.A.	Turbine Flowmeters	Litre Meter Ltd
Hoke Int Ltd	U.S.A.	Stainless Steel Valves Fittings	Custom Hose & Fitting Ltd
Holland & Sherry Inc	U.S.A.	Cloth	Holland & Sherry
Holland & Sherry Pty Ltd	Australia	Cloth	Holland & Sherry
Holland & Sherry Sarl	France	Cloth	Holland & Sherry
Holland & Sherry Srl	Italy	Cloth	Holland & Sherry
Holz-Her	Germany	Woodworking and Power Tools	Smeaton Hanscomb & Co. Ltd
Homa Pumpenfabrick GmbH	Germany	Submersible Pumps	Armstrong Holden Brooke Pullen Ltd
Honeywell Chadwick	U.S.A.	Helicopter rotor tracking and balancing equipment HUMS	Environmental Equipments Ltd
Horiba	Japan	Combustion Stack Analyser	Quantitech Ltd
Horita	U.S.A.	Time Code Readers, Generators and Insertels	D T L Broadcast Ltd
Horizon International Inc	Japan	Finishing Equipment	Graphics Arts Equipment Ltd
Horizon Surgical Inc	U.S.A.	Ligating Clips/Appliers	Mediplus Ltd
Horst Witte	Germany	Workholding Equipment	Thame Engineering Co. Ltd
Horton	U.S.A.	Air Clutches and Brakes	Micro Clutch Developments Ltd
Hosmer Dorrance	U.S.A.	Artificial Limb Components	Ortho Europe Ltd
Houston Fearless	U.S.A.	Duplicators And Processors	Microfilm Shop
Hovik Lys	Norway	Interior Lighting	Crescent Lighting Ltd
HP Hydraulic	Italy	Variable Displacement Hydraulic Pumps	BYPY Hydraulics & Transmissions Ltd
HP Hydraulic	Italy	Axial Piston Pumps	BYPY Hydraulics & Transmissions Ltd
HP Technik	Germany	Oil pumps	Anglo Nordic Burner Products Ltd
Huesker	Germany	Fortrac	A G A Group
Hugo Sachs Electronik	Germany	Physiology and Pharmacology Research	Linton & Co Engineering Ltd
Huls	Germany	PVC Flooring	Altro
Hultafors AG	Sweden	Folding Rules	Fisco Tools Ltd
Humate International Inc	U.S.A.	Humic Acid Derivatives for Horticulture Use	Viresco UK Ltd
Humiseal	U.S.A.	Conformal Coatings	Humiseal Europe Ltd (Head Office)
Hunter	U.S.A.	Foundry Plant	F T L Foundry Equipment Ltd
Hunter Industries	U.S.A.	Sprinklers and control systems	Evenproducts Ltd
Huntington Environmental Systems Inc	U.S.A.	Air And Gas Catalytic And Regenerative Thermal Oxidlsers	Higgins & Hewins Ltd
Huppe	Germany	External Blind Systems	Levolux A T Ltd
Hush Puppies	U.S.A.	Shoes	Magill Henshaw Ltd
Huwil Werke	Germany	Locks, Handles And Kd Fittings	Unico Components Ltd
Hycon	U.S.A.	Hydraulic Components	Hydac Technology Ltd
Hydac International	Germany	Filters/Accumulators Hydraulic Components	Hydac Technology Ltd
Hydranautics	U.S.A.	Semi-Permeable Membrianes	Ferex Ltd
Hydrite	U.S.A.	Defoamers and process additives	Kromachem Ltd
Hydron Cyklon	Switzerland	Magnetic Scale Control	Aldous & Stamp Ltd
Hydronic	France	Central Station Air Handling Units	Thermal Technology Sales Ltd
Hydrotech Ab	Sweden	Rotary Drum Filters	Higgins & Hewins Ltd
Hyfarm - J.S.K.	Australia	Pig Genetics and Breeding	J S R Farming Group
Hyper Sport Batteries	China		Michael Brandon Ltd
Hypro	U.S.A.	roller vane pumps & centrifugal pumps	Hypro Eu Ltd
Hyros	Germany	Clamping Systems	Hydac Technology Ltd
Hyundai Petrochemical Co.	Korea, Republic of	SBR, NBR & BR	Arto Chemicals Ltd
I E C	Canada	Shaft encoders	W & S Measuring Systems Ltd
I.E.F. Werner	Germany	Linear, Slides, Guideways, Controllers, Dosing And Soldering	R A Rodriguez UK Ltd
I & J Fisnar	U.S.A.	Dispensing Equipment	Intertronics
I.M.C.O. International Ltd	U.S.A.	load measurement equipment	Joseph Rhodes Ltd
I.M.E.A.S. S.r.l.	Italy	Wide Abrasive Belt Satin Finishing Machines	British & Continental Traders Ltd
I.M.S.	Italy	mechanical presses	Joseph Rhodes Ltd
I.M.V. Corporation	France	Vibration test & measurement equipment	L D S Test & Measurment Ltd
I.T.C. Fontek	U.S.A.	Fonts	Monotype Imaging Ltd
I.V.G.	Italy	Industrial Rubber Hose	Hydrasun Ltd
Ibak	Germany	Searchlights and Floodlights	John Lilley & Gillie Ltd
Ibarmia	Spain	Drilling Machines	Meddings Machine Tools
Icarus	Belgium	Exotic Valves	Alexander Cardew Ltd (Head Office)
Idemitsu Petrochemicals	Japan	Plastics Raw Materials	Plastribution
IDS	Canada	Gc/lms Drug & Explosives Detection	Marlborough Communications Ltd
IEM	Germany	Press tool accessories in tie tapping units	Brauer Ltd
Igarashi	Japan	igarashi	Trident Engineering Ltd

10

OVERSEAS COMPANY	COUNTRY OF ORIGIN	PRODUCT	UK COMPANY
IL Photonics Ltd	Israel	Plastic Pipe Fittings	Everyvalve Ltd
ILCO UNICAN	Canada	Mechanical Digital Locks	Abloy UK
Ilip	Italy	Fruit Punnets	Eurohill Traders Ltd (t/a Associated Packaging)
Illbruck (Acoustics)	Germany	Foam acoustic panels	P E S UK Ltd
Illinois Lock	U.S.A.	Mechanical and Electrical Locks	Elektron Components Ltd
ILSA	Italy	Cast Iron Grills, Stainless Steel Coffee Equipment	Fairfax Coffee Ltd
Imaforni	Italy	Biscuit Machine Makers Inc Ovens, Formers ETC	Robinsons
Imago	Germany	Manufacture x-ray equipment	Celtic SMR Ltd
Imatel	France	Badges, Transfers, Tapes And Heat Seal Machines	J & A International Ltd
IMC GmbH	Germany	Data Acquisition & Analysis Software	J J Systems Ltd
IMD	Germany	Manufacture x-ray equipment	Celtic SMR Ltd
Imet	Italy	Sawing Machines	Meddings Machine Tools
Immix Technologies	U.S.A.	Fluoroelastomer Compounding Materials	J Allcock & Sons Ltd
Imptech	South Africa	Metallographic Preparation Equip	Metprep Ltd
Inaltera of France	France	Fabrics and Wallpaper	Today Interiors Ltd
Inamet	Spain	Heating Replacement Thermocouples	Anglo Nordic Burner Products Ltd
Incab	Italy	Powered Stacker	Southworth Handling Ltd
India:KRS Machining Technologies PVT Ltd	India	electron beam welding & vacuum furnaces	Cambridge Vacuum Engineering
Indikon Co.	U.S.A.	Proximity Transducers	Sandhurst Instruments Ltd
Industria Gomma Affini	Italy	Walk and Surf Shoes	Yachting Instruments Ltd
Industria Technische Verlichting B.V.	Netherlands	Propagation Lighting	Fargro
Industrial Tectonics Inc	U.S.A.	Precision Balls	Dejay Distribution Ltd
Ineco	Italy	Gas Appliance Control Systems	Anglo Nordic Burner Products Ltd
Inertia Dynamics	U.S.A.	Electro magnetic clutches and brakes	Huco Dynatork
Infratek AG	Switzerland	Power Transducers	Energy I C T
Ing, Fritz Kubler Zahlerfabrik GmbH	Germany	Electro-Mechanical Counters	Trumeter Co Ltd
Ingeniofirmast	Denmark	Electric Fence Controllers	Gwaza Ltd
Ingersoll Rand Fluid Products	U.S.A.	Transfer Pumps	Liquid Control Ltd
Innovations	U.S.A.	Bicycle powered inflation	Madison
Innovations Ltd	South Africa	interlocking vinyl flooring	Jaymart Roberts & Plastics Ltd
Inspection Solutions	United Kingdom	Automated and Manual Scanning Systems	Sonatest Ltd
Instrument Systems Gmbh	Germany	Instrument Spectral Measurements	Metax Ltd
Instrumentation Devices	Italy	info@instrumentation.it	Specialist Electronics Services Ltd
Instruments for industry	U.S.A.	high power radio amplifiers	Dowding & Mills Engineering Services Ltd
Insuza Industrias Zumarraga S.A.	Spain	Hand and Power Swaging Machines, Lockformers, Flangers and Bending Rolls	C M Z Machinery Ltd
Integrated Microwave	U.S.A.	RF & Microwave Filters	Aspen Electronics Ltd
Intensiv	Switzerland	Dental Diamonds	Metrodent Ltd
Inter Business Src	Italy	Curative	J Allcock & Sons Ltd
Intermec	Sweden	Barcode Printers	Kelgray Products Ltd
International Cellulose Corporation	U.S.A.	Manufacturers of SonaSpray and Celbar acoustic & thermal treatment	Oscar Engineering Ltd
International PBI	Italy	Microbiological Equipment	Cherwell Laboratories Ltd
International Software Products	Canada	ASI2	Business & Decision Ltd
Interpump Spa	Italy	Piston Pumps	Dual Pumps Ltd
Intertech	Germany	Bavarian Compasses/Dividers	Blundell Harling Ltd (Incorporating Magpie Furniture)
Inus	U.S.A.	Radio Isotope Instruments	Lablogic Systems Ltd
Invesys Sensors	U.S.A.	Opto Sensors	C T L Components plc
IPSO	Belgium	Commercial Washing Machines	J L A
Irathane	United Kingdom	protective linings	Lithgow Saekaphen Ltd
Irazola S.A.	Spain	Screwdrivers	Electro Group Ltd
IRC	U.S.A.	Resistors	T T Electronics Welwyn Components Ltd
Ircon	U.S.A.	Infra red non contact pyrometers & thermal imaging	Insteng Process Automation Ltd
Irega S.A.	Spain	Adjustable Wrenches	Electro Group Ltd
Iris Inspection Systems	U.S.A.	Ultrasonic Tube Inspection System	Sonatest Ltd
Irritec	Italy	B.S.P. Plastic Fittings	Everyvalve Ltd
Irritrol Products	Italy	Irrigation Products	Connectomatic
Isabey	France	Fine Art Paint Brushes	Exaclair Ltd
ISCO Technic B.V.	Netherlands		Livingston & Doughty Ltd
ISK Magnetics	U.S.A.	Magnetic and high purity iron oxides	Kromachem Ltd
ISO Lyon Limitada	Chile		E C U S
Isola A/S	Norway	Cavity Drainage Membrane	Triton Chemical Manufacturing Co. Ltd
Isola A.S.	Norway	Capillary Matting	Fargro
Isorex	France	O.S.B.	N R Burnett Ltd
Ispo	Germany	External wall insulation	Alumasc Exterior Building Products
Italcardano S.r.l.	Italy	Motor Vehicle Parts	Panaf & Company
Italkero	Italy	Gas Heaters	Drugasar Service Ltd
Italpresse S.p.A.	Italy	hydraulic presses	Mackey Bowley International Ltd
Italtubetti	Italy	plastic-paper cones and tubes	Macart Textiles Machinery Ltd
Italy:Dr Nicola Reinach	Italy	electron beam welding & vacuum furnaces	Cambridge Vacuum Engineering
Iteco	Italy	Component Preformers	Link Hamson Ltd
Item	Switzerland	Pick And Place Components	Machine Building Systems Ltd
Item	Germany	Aluminium Machine Construction Systems	Machine Building Systems Ltd
ITK Envifront	Sweden	Central Vacuum Units	Duscovent Engineering Ltd
Itohnar Co. Ltd	Japan	Photo/Video Accessories	Kauser International Trading Ltd
Itotec	Japan	Guillotines	Graphics Arts Equipment Ltd
ITR SPA	Italy	Air Hose	Hydrasun Ltd
Iveco	United Kingdom	Truck spare parts	Kingsdown
IVG Colbachini spA	Italy	Industrial Hose Range	Holmes Hose Ltd
IVO GmbH	Germany	Counters, Hair Meters, Absolute & Incremental Encoders	C T L Components plc
IWM	Germany	Milling Cutters And Hand Tools For Foam	Apropa Machinery Ltd
J B Trading CC	South Africa	Cosmetics	A P Y
J.H.B. International	U.S.A.	Buttons	Shaw Munster Ltd
J M P	Korea, Republic of	flex impeller pumps	Watermota Ltd
J.M.R. Instruments	France		Hawker Electronics Ltd
J.S.R. Espana S.L.	Spain	Pig Genetics and Breeding	J S R Farming Group
J.S.R. Europe	Netherlands	Pig Genetics and Breeding	J S R Farming Group
J.S.R. Genetica Sunicola	Brazil	Pig Genetics and Breeding	J S R Farming Group
J.S.R. Hybrid GmbH	Germany	Pig Genetics and Breeding	J S R Farming Group
J. Willi	Switzerland	Packaging Machinery	Advanced Dynamics Ltd
Jackami Ltd	Hong Kong	General Merchandise	A P Y
Jackson	U.S.A.	Safety Wear	Wholesale Welding Supplies Ltd
Jacuzzi	Canada	Above Ground Pools and Spa Equipment	Certikin International Ltd
James Gilbert	New Zealand		Gray Nicolls
James Gilbert	Australia		Gray Nicolls
James Gilbert	South Africa		Gray Nicolls
James Gilbert	France		Gray Nicolls
Jamicon	Taiwan	Capacitors	Components Bureau
Japan Aviation Electronics Ltd	Japan	Connectors & Switches for Electronic Equipment	Albacom
Japan Marine Technologies Ltd	Japan	Propeller Shaft Seals and Bearings	Deep Sea Seals Ltd
Japan Servo Ltd	Japan	Stepping/Dc Motors	Cliff Electronic Components Ltd
Japan:UK Dodwell	Japan		Cambridge Vacuum Engineering
Jardin	Hong Kong	Steel Windows And Doors	Crittall Windows Ltd
Jayant Oil Mills	India	Castor Oil Derivatives	Industrial Waxes
JC	Spain	Ball Valve Manufacture	Trimline Valves
JC Hansen	Denmark	cast iron gate valves	S A V UK Ltd

11

OVERSEAS COMPANY	COUNTRY OF ORIGIN	PRODUCT	UK COMPANY
JCA Technology Inc	U.S.A.	RF & Microwave Amplifiers	Aspen Electronics Ltd
Jean-Louise Chave	France	Wine	Yapp Brothers Ltd
Jeanne Blanchin	France	Synthetic Sportwear Fabrics	Emko Products Ltd
Jeantil	France	Livestock Feeding and Bedding Equipment	Westmac Ltd
Jenaer Glaswerk GmbH	Germany	Household Glassware	Schott UK Ltd
Jenoptic	Germany		Armstrong Optical Ltd
Jenrite Industries	New Zealand	Roll Laminators	Murodigital
Jensen	U.S.A.	Toolkits	Longs Ltd
Jeol Ltd	Japan	Electron Microscopes and Spectrometers	Jeol UK Ltd
Jergens	Germany	Hoist rings, lifting products & kwik-lok pins	Brauer Ltd
Jofemar SA	Spain	Vending Equipment	Jofemar UK
John Crane Marine	U.S.A.	Propeller Shaft Seals and Bearings	Deep Sea Seals Ltd
John Crane Marine-Lips	Netherlands	Propeller Shaft Seals and Bearings	Deep Sea Seals Ltd
Johnford	Taiwan	Machining Centres & CNC Lathes	Advanced Technology Machines Ltd
Johnson Pump International AB	Sweden	Pumps	S P X Flow Technology
Jokey Plastics	Germany	Make buckets	Taylor Davis Ltd
Jolly Crane	Italy	Vehicle Cranes	Crane Care Ltd
Jordan Valve	U.S.A.	Pressure And Temperature Regulating And Control ValVes	Tamo Ltd
Jost	Germany	Vibratory Equipment	F T L Foundry Equipment Ltd
Jost Werke	Germany	Ball Bearing Turntables, Fifth Wheel Couplings, Trailer King Pins, Trailer Landing Gear and Hubdometers	Jost Great Britain Ltd
JPS Elastormerics	U.S.A.	Stevens EP single ply membrane	Alumasc Exterior Building Products
Jtelec	Belgium	jtelec@jtelec.fr	Specialist Electronics Services Ltd
Jtelec	Luxembourg	jtelec@jtelec.fr	Specialist Electronics Services Ltd
Jtelec	France	jtelec@jtelec.fr	Specialist Electronics Services Ltd
Jud	Liechtenstein	Felt and Wire Guides and Tensioners	Pulp & Paper Machinery Ltd
Jud Binders	France	Hot Melt Binders	Duplo International Ltd
Judson Technologies	U.S.A.	Infrared Detectors	Pacer Components plc
Julius Maschinenbau GmbH	Germany	Strip Edge Trimming Machines	British & Continental Traders Ltd
Jung Pompen	Germany	Submersible Pumps	Pump Technical Services
Junita Knitwear Ltd	India	Knitwear	Bhardwaj Insolvency Practitioners
Jupiter	Taiwan	Brass and Woodwind	Korg UK Ltd
K.B. Electronic	U.S.A.	D.C. Controllers	Micro Clutch Developments Ltd
K.D.S.	U.S.A.	Syringe Pumps	Linton & Co Engineering Ltd
K.H.K.	Japan	Stock And Custom Gears	R A Rodriguez UK Ltd
K.R.B. M/C Co	U.S.A.	Shearlines Link Benders	La Roche
K.S. Terminals	Taiwan	Terminals	Davico Industrial Ltd
K.V.P. Systems Inc	U.S.A.	Plastic Modular Belting	Ammeraal Beltech Ltd
Kaba Holding A.G.	Switzerland	Security LOck Systems	Kaba Ltd Head Office
Kabelschlepp	Germany	Plastic And Steel Cable Carriers	Metool Products Ltd
Kahlig Antriebstechnik GmbH Dc Motors, Gearheads	United Kingdom		Electro Mechanical Systems (EMS) Ltd (EMS)
Kahr Bearing	U.S.A.	Aerospace Journals Spherical Bearings And Rod-End BEarings	R A Rodriguez UK Ltd
Kaiser	Switzerland	Cutting Tools	E C I S Scotland Ltd
Kalimanis	Indonesia	Decorative Plywood	N R Burnett Ltd
Kalimar	China	Cameras	Swains International plc
Kallfass	Germany	Packaging Machinery	Marden Edwards Ltd
Kalwall Corporation	U.S.A.	translucent panel systems	Stoakes Systems Ltd
Kaman Corporation	U.S.A.	Roundback Guitars	John Hornby Skewes & Co. Ltd
Kamer	Barbados	Sweeping brushers.	Harris Cleaning Services
Karasto	Germany	Quick Couplers	Connectomatic
Karges Hammer	Germany	Can-Making Machinery	Pearson Panke Ltd
Karjeni Pty Ltd	Australia	GAS: Geochemical; Analysis System	Geomem Ltd
Karl Limbach, GmbH	Germany	Special Fasteners	Alrose Products British Gas Springs Ltd (British Gas Springs)
Karl Roll	Germany	Ultrasonic Cleaning Plant	Embassy Machinery Ltd
Karzan	Russia	Binoculars, Monoculars And Telescopes	Swains International plc
Kaydon Corporation	U.S.A.	Thin-Section Bearings And Turntable Bearings	R A Rodriguez UK Ltd
Kecskemet Aluminium Rt	Hungary	Cast Aluminium Products	Gardencast
KEF Motor A.S.	Denmark	Backstand And Pedestal Belt/Brush Machines	Ellesco Ltd
Kelvin	Italy	A refrigeration unit.	Total Process Cooling Ltd
Kendu	Spain	Milling Cutters	Macinnes Tooling Ltd
Kerb-Konus-Gesellschaft	Germany	Grooved Pins and Rivets	Tappex Thread Inserts Ltd
Kerb-Konus Vertriebs	Germany	ENSAT range of self-tapping fasteners for metal and plastic applications	Tappex Thread Inserts Ltd
Kerk Motion Products	U.S.A.	Leadscrews	Huco Dynatork
Kessel	Germany	Drainage System Specialist	Armstrong Holden Brooke Pullen Ltd
Keter Plastics Ltd	Israel	Plastic Garden Furniture and Housewares	Keter UK Ltd
Kettler GmbH	Germany	Garden Furniture, Bicycles & Wheeld Toys	Kettler GB Ltd
Kevlin Corp	U.S.A.	Rotary Joints	Cobham Antenna Systems
Keytronic	U.S.A.	Full Range Of Keyboards	Ceratech Electronics Ltd
Kibby-Modra Automation	Australia	Carpet Sampling Machines	Robert S Maynard Ltd
KIC Thermal Profiling	U.S.A.	Thermal Profilers	Link Hamson Ltd
Kiichi	Japan	Pipe Cutting Machine	B S A Tube Runner
Kilgour French Stanbury	United Kingdom	Tailors	Holland & Sherry
Kimo Industrielle	France	Liquid Manometers	Black Teknigas & Electro Controls Ltd
Kinetico Inc	U.S.A.		Harvey Water Softeners Ltd
Kinetico Incorporated	U.S.A.	Kinetico Non-Electric Control Water Softeners	Kinetico UK Ltd
King Metal BV	Netherlands	Piggy Back Fork Lift Trucks	Joloda Hydraroll Ltd
Kingbright	Taiwan	LEDS	Components Bureau
Kingstone	Korea, Republic of	Inner Tubes	Kings Road Tyres & Repairs Ltd
Kipp	Germany	Clamping levers and machine accessories	Brauer Ltd
Kirby Refrigeration	Australia	Hermetic Condensing Units and Compressors for Refrigeration	Kooltech Ltd
Kirk Rudy	U.S.A.	Mailing Machines	Buhrs UK Ltd
Kirsten	Switzerland	Crimping And Solering Machines	Turner Electronics
Kistlet Instruments AG	Switzerland	Piezo Instrumentation	Kistler Instruments Ltd
Klauke Tertron	Germany	Compress Terminals, Lugs, Femiles, Insulated Connectors, Crimping Tools, Hand, Hydraulic & Battery,	C T L Components plc
Klepper	Germany	Kayaks	Kirton Kayaks Ltd
Klett	Germany	Chocolate Confectionary	Bysel Ltd
Klockner Pentaplast GmbH	Germany	Plastic Sheet and Film	Klockner Pentaplast Ltd
Knape & Vogt	U.S.A.	Drawer Slides (Office)	Unico Components Ltd
Knapp	U.S.A.	Foam Polly Pig, Launcher/Receiver	Alexander Cardew Ltd (Head Office)
Knecht	Germany	filters	Roadlink International Ltd
Knipex	Germany	Pliers and Cutters	Draper Tools Ltd
Koch Technik	Germany	material conveying, drying and colouring equipment	Demag Hamilton Guarantee Ltd
Kodak	U.S.A.	Full Microfilm Product Range	Microfilm Shop
Kodenshi	Japan	Optoelectronic Components and Assemblies	Pacer Components plc
Koenig KG	Germany	Book Binding Tape S/A	Gilmex International Ltd
Kohler	U.S.A.	Petrol Engines	E P Barrus
Koll Morgen	U.S.A.	Servo Drives & Motors	European Drives & Motor Repairs
Koloman Handler	Austria	Loose Leaf Metal Mechanisms	Gilmex International Ltd
Kommerling	Germany	Silicone Rubber	Kromachem Ltd
Kondia	Spain	Turret Mills	Capital Equipment & Machinery Ltd
Koni	Netherlands	shock absorbers & bush kits	Roadlink International Ltd
Kop-Flex Inc	U.S.A.	Gear Couplings	Micro Clutch Developments Ltd
Kopal	France	Countersinks And Clamps	Hill Cliffe Garage

12

OVERSEAS COMPANY	COUNTRY OF ORIGIN	PRODUCT	UK COMPANY
Kora Packmat	Germany	Packaging Machinery	Advanced Dynamics Ltd
Korea Engineering Plastics	Korea, Republic of	Polyacetal	Arto Chemicals Ltd
Korea:COMESYS	Korea, Republic of	electron beam welding	Cambridge Vacuum Engineering
Kostrzyn paper Mill	Poland	Uncoated Woodfree Papers	Arctic Paper UK Ltd
Kostyrka GmbH	Germany	Clamping Sleeves, Hydraulic Cylinders	Roemheld UK Ltd
Kowa	Japan	Electro Medical Diagnostic Equipment	Keeler Ltd
Koyo	United Kingdom	Automotive spare parts	Kingsdown
Koyo Seiko Co. Ltd	Japan	Ball and Roller Bearings	Koyo UK Ltd
Kracht GmbH	Germany	Pumps & Flowmeters	K T Hydraulic Ltd
Kraft	Germany	Aluminium Valves	Everyvalve Ltd
Kral	Austria	Positive Displacement Meters	Litre Meter Ltd
Krantz	Germany	Diffusers	Designed For Sound Ltd
Kreinik	U.S.A.	Metallic Threads	Coats Ltd
Kretzer Joh.	Germany	Scissors-hairdressing, industrial	Triumph Needle Co. Ltd
Krohn-Hite Corp.	U.S.A.	Electronic Calibrators & Active/Passive Filters	Lyons Instruments
Krupp Widia	Germany	Magnets	Rainer Schneider & Ayres
Kryptonite	U.S.A.	Bicycle locks	Madison
Kubo B.V.	Netherlands	Glasshouse And Equipment	Fargro
Kuhlmeyer Maschinenbau GmbH	Germany	Semi And Automatic Weld Dressing	Ellesco Ltd
Kuhn	France	Power Harrows, Grass Machines	Wilfred Scruton Ltd
Kuk Do Chemical Industry Co Ltd	Democratic People's Republic of Korea	Epoxy Resins	Thomas Swan & Co. Ltd
Kumag AG	Switzerland	Precision Assembly Equipment	Samuel Taylor Ltd
Kumera	Finland	Geared Motors and Worm and Helical Gearboxes	Pulp & Paper Machinery Ltd
Kumho	Korea, Republic of	Car, Van, 4x4, Truck, Tyres	Kings Road Tyres & Repairs Ltd
Kuraray Europe	Japan	Dental Filling And Adhesion	Plandent
Kuroda Precision Industries Ltd	Japan	Pneumatic Control Equipment	Parker Hannifin Ltd
L.C. Oleodinamica	Italy	Hydraulic Valves	Universal Hydraulics Ltd
L.F.A.	France	Drill Chucks	Castle Brook Tools Ltd
L. Giffard S.A.	France	Disposable Respirators	Alpha Solway Ltd
L'Oblique	France	Files	Flexiform Business Furniture Ltd (Head Office, Factory and Northern Showroom)
L.R. Baggs	U.S.A.	Pick-Ups For Musical Instruments	John Hornby Skewes & Co. Ltd
L.R.O.	Italy	Carbide Cutting/Abrasives	Tech Europe
L & R Ultrasonics	U.S.A.	Ultrasonic Cleaners	Plandent
L S P Industries Inc.	U.S.A.	Airless Lubrications Systems	Pharos Engineering Ltd
L Schuler	Germany	Presses	Embassy Machinery Ltd
L.T.S.	Germany	Architectural Lighting	Selux UK Ltd
L'Unité Hermétique	France	Hermetic Compressors and Condensing Units	H T G Trading Ltd
Laaser	Germany	Flow Switches	Delta Controls Ltd
Label Plastic Holders	Sweden	Scanner Rail Shelf Edge Ticket System	Alplus
Labo Moderne	France	Stillquick Method for Parasite Demonstration	Clin-Tech Ltd
Lafarge Refrataires Monolithiques	France	Cement Castables	Calderys UK Ltd
Lafert S.r.l.	Italy	Electric Motors	Micro Clutch Developments Ltd
Lafert SRL	Italy	A.C. Electric Motors	Motovario Ltd
Laier GmbH	Germany	Vibration Equipment	La Roche
Lamberti	Italy	Photoinitiators	Kromachem Ltd
Lamit	Germany	Laminating machines for foam etc.	Apropa Machinery Ltd
Landers GmbH	Germany	Grabs	N R C Plant Ltd
Lannet	Germany	Local Area Network	C A C I
Lansdale Semiconductors	U.S.A.	Semiconductors	Campbell Collins
Lantec Products Inc	U.S.A.	Tower Packings	Begg Cousland & Co. Ltd
Lares Research	U.S.A.	Dental Handpieces	Plandent
Latour	France	Wire Tube and Strip Bending Machines	Bennett Mahler
Latour-Marliac SA	France	Water Gardens	Stapeley Water Gardens Ltd
Lava S.A.	Greece	Pomice Minerals	Maple Aggregates UK Ltd
Lavato (Italy)	Italy	Electronic control gear manufacturers	Lovato UK Ltd
LC Oleodinamica	Italy	Cetop Hydraulic Valves	BYPY Hydraulics & Transmissions Ltd
Le Granits Sodigranit	France		C E D Ltd
Le Guellec SA	France	Tubes & Tubular Components-Stainless Steel, Nickel & Nickel Alloys, Special Alloys	W L Mets Ltd
Lee Yuan	Taiwan	Printers For Plastic Film	Kween B Ltd
Leeson Corp.	U.S.A.	Motor Manufacturers	Motovario Ltd
Leica	Germany	Microscopes	Metprep Ltd
Leica Camera AG	Germany	Cameras, Binoculars and Projectors	Leica Camera Ltd
Leine & Linde	Sweden	Increment and Absolute Encoders	Mclennan Servo Supplies Ltd
Leister Elektro-Geratebau	Switzerland	Hot Air Tools/Plastic Welding Tools	Welwyn Tool Group Ltd
LEMO S A	Switzerland	Self-Latching Circular Connectors	Lemo UK Ltd
Lengpac AB	Sweden	Pallet Stretch Wrappers	A M J Maters Partnership Ltd
Lenze GmbH	Germany	Power Transmission Equipment	Lenze UK Ltd
Lenzing AG	Austria	Paper Mill	Premier Paper Group
Lestoprex AG	Switzerland	Tramp Oil Separator	Filtermist International Ltd
Letica	Spain	Biological Research Equipment	Linton & Co Engineering Ltd
Leuzer	Germany	Sensors	Sensortek
Lexmark	Japan	Ink Jet Printers	Episys Group Ltd
Lexmark	U.S.A.	Colour Inkjet Printers	Johnsons Photopia Ltd
Liebherr-France SA	France	Hydraulic Excavators	Liebherr-Great Britain Ltd
Liebherr-Hydraulikbagger GmbH	Germany	Hydraulic Excavator	Liebherr-Great Britain Ltd
Liebherr Mining Truck Inc	U.S.A.	Rigid Dump Trucks	Liebherr-Great Britain Ltd
Liebherr-Mischtechnik GmbH	Germany	Concrete Mixing/Batching Equipment	Liebherr-Great Britain Ltd
Liebherr-Werk Biberach GmbH	Germany	Tower Cranes	Liebherr-Great Britain Ltd
Liebherr-Werk Bischofshofen GmbH	Austria	Wheeled Loaders	Liebherr-Great Britain Ltd
Liebherr-Werk Ehingen GmbH	Germany	Mobile Cranes	Liebherr-Great Britain Ltd
Liebherr-Werk Telfs GmbH	Austria	Tracked Loaders and Bulldozers	Liebherr-Great Britain Ltd
Lievers B.V.	Netherlands	Vibration Equipment	La Roche
Limonta Spl	Italy	vinyl floorcoverings	Jaymart Roberts & Plastics Ltd
Linde Materials Handling	Germany	Fork Lift Trucks	Linde Heavy Truck Division (Linde Material Handling Division)
Linden GmbH	Germany	Pneumatic Cylinders	Valeader Pneumatics Ltd
Linder S.A.	France	Furnishing Fabrics	Maisonneuve & Co.
Lineager S.r.l.	Italy	Office Furniture	Trac Office Contracts
Linhardt GmbH	Germany	Collapsible Tubes	The Adelphi Group Adelphi Group of Companies
Link-Belt	U.S.A.	Crawler Cranes and Hydraulic Cranes	N R C Plant Ltd
Link Computer Graphics	U.S.A.	Device Programmers	Computer Solutions Ltd
Linseis	Germany	Thermal Analysis Systems	Linton & Co Engineering Ltd
Lippert GmbH	Germany	Brushes and Rollers for Printed Circuit Boards	Osborn Unipol Ltd
Litton Electron Tubes	U.S.A.	Magnetrons	Richardsons R F P D Ltd
LM Instruments	Finland	Dental Hand Instruments	Plandent
Lockwood Products Inc	U.S.A.	Loc-Line Coolant Hose	Filtermist International Ltd
Loepfe	Switzerland	Yarn Clearers	B M S Vision Ltd
Loersch	Germany	Slide Mounting Systems And Accessories	Johnsons Photopia Ltd
Lomo	Russia	Microscopes And Accessories, Cameras And Telescopes	Swains International plc
Loramend: S.A.	Spain	moulding and core making machines	Ramsell Naber Ltd
Lorch	Germany	Feather And Fibre Filling Machines	Apropa Machinery Ltd
Lovejoy	U.S.A.	Flexible shaft couplings	Lenze UK Ltd

13

OVERSEAS COMPANY	COUNTRY OF ORIGIN	PRODUCT	UK COMPANY
Lowara	Italy	Industrial Pumps	Robert Craig & Sons Ltd
Lu Ve Contardo	Italy	Coolers, Evaporators and Condensers	H T G Trading Ltd
Luitpold Schutt	Germany	Hose Couplings	Action Sealtite
LUK	United Kingdom	Automotive spare parts	Kingsdown
Lundahl	Sweden	Audio Transformers	Canford Audio
Lyondell Chemical Products Europe Inc	U.S.A.	Isocyanates(TDI)	I M C D UK Ltd
Lzos	Russia	Telescopes, Microscopes, Opera Glasses, Fibre OpticS, Night Vision And Monoculars	Swains International plc
M.A.S. Kovosvit	Czech Republic	Automatic Lathes	Citizen Machinery UK Ltd
M.D.M.	U.S.A.	Pumps	Allpumps Ltd
M.L. Gatewood Co	U.S.A.	Needle Jet Nozzles	Pulp & Paper Machinery Ltd
M & M	Switzerland	Spinning Machines	Embassy Machinery Ltd
M.P.D. Inc	U.S.A.	Ge Electron Tubes And Avionic Products	Richardsons R F P D Ltd
M.P. Filtri S.p.A.	Italy	Hydraulic Filtration	M P Filtri UK Ltd
M.R. Etikettiertechnik GmbH & Co K.G.	Germany	Labelling Machine	Multivac UK Ltd
M.S. Kennedy	U.S.A.	Amplifiers, Regulators & Motor Controls	Campbell Collins
M.T.E.	U.S.A.	Harmonic Analyser	Northern Design Ltd
M.W.H. GmbH	Germany	Garden Furniture	Kettler GB Ltd
Maatschappij Bronneberg	Netherlands	Scrap Processing Equipment	M M H Recycling Systems Ltd
Mabeg	Germany	Signage & Information Systems	Ergonom Ltd
Mac 3	Italy	Flow And Level Switches	Texcel Division (a division of Crosslink Business Services Ltd)
Machinery & Electrical Products Inc	U.S.A.	Mechanical Post Hole Borer	Drivall Ltd
Maco	Austria	Window Fittings	Titon Hardware Ltd (Head Office)
Macsoft	France	Wire Tube and Strip Bending Machines	Bennett Mahler
Madal	Spain		Tek Ltd
Maddalena	Italy	watermeters	S A V UK Ltd
Madison	U.S.A.	Level Switches	Texcel Division (a division of Crosslink Business Services Ltd)
Madler GmbH	Germany	Stock gears	Huco Dynatork
MAE	Italy	Stepper and Servo Motors	Mclennan Servo Supplies Ltd
Maersk Line	Denmark	Shipping	The Maersk Company UK Ltd
Maglite	U.S.A.	Torches	Burton Mccall Ltd
Magnetic Autocontrol GmbH Traffic barriers &	United Kingdom	access control	Electro Mechanical Systems (EMS) Ltd (EMS)
Magnetic Technologies Ltd	U.S.A.	Permanent magnet brakes	Huco Dynatork
Mair-Unitas	Germany	Parts, knife grinding machines	Triumph Needle Co. Ltd
Makita	Japan	Power Tools	Banson Tool Hire Ltd
Mall Herlan	Germany	Collapsible Tube Machinery	Pearson Panke Ltd
Mallein	France	Textile Beams And Cloth Rolls	Pilkingtons Ltd (t/a Weitzer Parket UK)
Mallory	U.S.A.	Audibles	E A O Ltd
Maloney	U.S.A.	Pigs, Spheres, Cups, Discs, Pig Detectors, Casing SEals & Insulators	Alexander Cardew Ltd (Head Office)
Mamiya	Japan	Medium Format Cameras	Johnsons Photopia Ltd
MAN Truck & Bus N.V.	Belgium	Oil & Gas Burners for Central Heating	Lion Industries UK Ltd
Mandals Reberbane Christiansen & Co A/S	Norway	Layflat Hoses - Flexitex, Ultraman, Aquaman, GuardmAn, Flowtex	Merlett Plastics UK Ltd
Manford Machines	Taiwan	Machine tool manufacturers	Super-Tec Machine Tools Ltd
Manix Manufacturing Inc	U.S.A.	Component Performing	Elite Engineering Ltd
Manntech Gmbh	Germany	Window cleaning cadles	Cento Engineering Co. Ltd
Manuel Rodriguez S.A.	Spain	Guitars	John Hornby Skewes & Co. Ltd
Manuel Romero S.A.	Spain	Furnishing Fabrics	Maisonneuve & Co.
Manuvit	France	Adjustable Width Stackers	Southworth Handling Ltd
Maped S.A.	France	Drawing instruments, cutting systems & metal rules	West Design Products Ltd
Mapex	Taiwan	Drums	Korg UK Ltd
Marabu	Germany	Craft And Hobby Paints	Edding UK Ltd
Marazzi	Italy	Glazed Wall And Floor Tiles	Ceramique International Ltd
March Manufacturing Inc	U.S.A.	Magnetic Drive Pumps	March May Ltd
Marinflop	Sweden	Build water cleaning systems	Quality Monitoring Instruments Q M I
Markator	Germany	Marking Machines	Brandone Machine Tool Ltd
Marlin	U.S.A.	Plugs And Sockets	West Instruments
Marlux International	Japan	Compact Disc Packaging Products	Cravenmount Ltd
Marmo Meccanica SPA	Italy	Stone Processing Machinery	Pisani plc
Marmoelettromeccanica SRL	Italy	Stone Processing Machinery	Pisani plc
Marquinaria Para el Pulido Automatico S.A.	Spain	Bright Polishing Machines Automatic And Robotic	Ellesco Ltd
Martin	Germany	PCB Rework Equipment	Link Hamson Ltd
Maschinenfabrik Gehring GmbH & Co.	Germany	Honing Tools	Equipment For You
Maschinenfabrik Gustav Eirich	Germany	Intensive Mixers	Orthos Projects Ltd
Maschinenfabrik Herkules GmbH	Germany	Roll Lathes And Grinding Machines	British & Continental Traders Ltd
Maschio	Italy	Agricultural Machinery	Ruston's Engineering Co. Ltd
Mascot International	Denmark	work wear	Murray Uniforms
Mask-Off Company	U.S.A.	Speciality Self Adhesive Tapes	Stokvis Tapes UK Ltd
Massey Ferguson	United Kingdom	Tractor/Agricultural Spare Parts	Kingsdown
Master International Ltd	New Zealand	Vacuum/Blow Guns	Filtermist International Ltd
Matador	Slovakia	Truck Tyres	Kings Road Tyres & Repairs Ltd
Matfer-Bourgeat	France	utensils, cooking and pastry and baking	Mitchell & Cooper Ltd (Head Office)
Matreya	U.S.A.	Lipids And Biochemicals	Radleys
Matsuo	Japan	Thermostats (Precision)	Hawco
Mavil Limited	France	Fast Action Industrial Doors	B I S Door Systems Ltd
Max	Japan	Signmaking System	Murodigital
Max	Japan	Time Recorders	Cristel Paint Finishers Ltd
Mayco	U.S.A.	Glazes & Colours	Potclays Ltd
Mayco Union Broach	U.S.A.	Dental instruments	Plandent
Maytag	U.S.A.	Commercial Washing Machines and Tumble Dryers	J L A
Mazda	Japan	Cars	M C L Group Ltd
Mazzei Injector Corporation	U.S.A.	Venturi Injectors	Ferex Ltd
Mazzuchelli Spa	Italy	Plastics raw materials	Plastribution
MC-S	Belgium	sales@mcs-nederland.com	Specialist Electronics Services Ltd
MC-S	Netherlands	sales@mcs-nederland.com	Specialist Electronics Services Ltd
McKees Rocks	U.S.A.	Forged Crane Wheels	Cranequip Ltd
MDM	U.S.A.	Pumps	Torres Engineering & Pumps Ltd
Meaden Screw Products Inc	U.S.A.	Punches, Dies, Crimps, Wheels	R M Rotary Services Ltd
Measurements International	Canada	Electrical Metrology	Lyons Instruments
Mecagrav	France	Metal Marking Mechanism	Brandone Machine Tool Ltd
Mectec	Sweden	Print and Apply Labelling Systems	Kelgray Products Ltd
MEDA	U.S.A.	Vector Fluxgate Magnetometer	Lyons Instruments
Media & Editorial Projects Ltd	Trinidad & Tobago	BWIA Inflight Magazine	Geraldine Flower Publications (Trading As Geraldine Flower Publications)
Medica GmbH	Germany	Glassblowing Components	Schott UK Ltd
Mefar	Italy	Compressor And Vacuum Pumps	Anglo Nordic Burner Products Ltd
Mega	Italy		Universal Hydraulics Ltd
Mega Manufacturing Co	U.S.A.	Universal Ironworkers	Prosaw Ltd
Mega Stahl	Germany	Graphic Arts Equipment	Billows Protocol Ltd
MEI	Italy	Woven And Printed Label Machines	Pilkingtons Ltd (t/a Weitzer Parket UK)
Mei Long Medical Manufacturer	China	Acupuncture and Medical Equipment	Acumedic Centre Ltd
Meiko Meier Ag	Switzerland	Garment Handling Conveyors	Conveyors International (CI Logistics) (a division of Portec Rail Products (UK) Ltd)
Mekel	U.S.A.	Microfilm Scanners	Microfilm Shop
Melag Apparate	Germany	Autoclave Steriliser	Plandent

OVERSEAS COMPANY	COUNTRY OF ORIGIN	PRODUCT	UK COMPANY
Melcher Carl	Germany	Veterinary Instruments Animal Grooming Tools	Diamond Edge Ltd
Mengele	Germany	Agricultural Machinery	Ruston's Engineering Co. Ltd
Mennes GmbH	Germany	Toughened Glass	N J Bradford Ltd
Mentor GmbH	Germany	Opto Components, LED, Bargraph Arrays, Light Pipes, Handles For Enclosures, Switches, Knobs	C T L Components plc
Meret Optical Communications Inc.	U.S.A.	Direct Digital Sythesisers	Lyons Instruments
Merford	Netherlands	Acoustic rooms and enclosures	P E S UK Ltd
Merit Abrasives Inc	U.S.A.	Abrasive Tools	D F Wishart Holdings Ltd
Mermet	France	High Performance Blind Fabrics	Levolux A T Ltd
Mes Aerospace Systems	Japan	Impedance Ndt Testing	J R Technology
Mesa Laboratories	U.S.A.	DataTrace Data Loggers	Cherwell Laboratories Ltd
Metalset	France	Street Furniture	Townscape Products Ltd
Metalwerk Plansee GmbH	Austria	Powder Metalurgical Products	Ceratizit UK Ltd
Metasys	Austria	Dental Cleaning Solutions	Plandent
Metco Inc	U.S.A.	Sintered Metal Components	Aegis Advanced Materials Ltd
Meteor Corp	U.S.A.	Meteorburst Radios	Marlborough Communications Ltd
Metglas Products	U.S.A.	Amorphous Brazing Foils	Neomet Ltd
Methanor	Netherlands	Methanol	Gelpke & Bate Ltd
Methode	U.S.A.	Connectors	Components Bureau
Metra	France	Injection Mould And Smc Tools; Rapid Prototyping	Pearson Panke Ltd
Metro	Italy	Chocolate Plant	Robinsons
Metrosonics Inc	U.S.A.	Industrial Hygiene Instruments	Shawcity Ltd
Mewaf	Belgium	Office Furniture	Trademark Interiors Ltd
Meyer	Germany	Industrial Lighting	Gray Campling Ltd
Mez	Czech Republic	Electric Motors and Pumps	Beatson Fans & Motors Ltd
Miatech Inc.	U.S.A.	Humidification Equipment	Norman Pendred & Co. Ltd
Michel Van de Wiele	Belgium	Wilton Carpet and Velvet Weaving Machines	Robert S Maynard Ltd
Michelman Inc	U.S.A.	Coatings for corrugated board	Darent Wax Co. (Proman Coatings)
Micro Digital	U.S.A.	Real Time Executives	Computer Solutions Ltd
Micromega S.A.	France	Dental Handpieces And Endodontics	Plandent
Micromotion	Germany	Archiving/Image Analysis	Metprep Ltd
Micron	Italy	Anodyzed Aluminium Straight Edges, Tee Squares and Set Squares	Technical Sales Ltd
Micron Insts	U.S.A.	Pressure Transducers	Sandhurst Instruments Ltd
Micron Tech	U.S.A.	Memory Semiconductors	Micron Europe Ltd
Micropowders Inc.	U.S.A.	Micronised Waxes	Kromachem Ltd
Micropower (Pty) Ltd	South Africa	Shaft Encoders	W & S Measuring Systems Ltd
Microtap	Germany	Bench top tapping machines	Robert Speck Ltd
Microtek	Taiwan	Flatbed And Film Scanners	Johnsons Photopia Ltd
Microtherm GmbH	Germany	Thermal Cutouts And Thermistors	Hawco
MicroVue Products	Israel	Motorised Microfilm Readers	Microfilm Shop
Mietzsch	Germany	Industrial Centrifugal	Nicotra-Gebhardt Ltd
Millennium Speciality Chemicals	U.S.A.	Pine Oil, Terpenes, Solvents, Cleaner	Ferguson & Menzies Ltd
Miller Weldmaster Corporation	U.S.A.	Welding Machines	Butyl Products Ltd
Millers Forge	U.S.A.	Grooming Tools	Diamond Edge Ltd
Milliken & Co.	U.S.A.	Clean Room Wiping Cloths	Cravenmount Ltd
Millutensil	Italy	Coil Feed Line Equipment; Strip Lubricants; ConveyoRs	Pearson Panke Ltd
Milwaukee Cylinders	U.S.A.	Hydraulic Cylinders	Webtec Products
Minerva	Italy	Pigment Printing Products	Magna Colours Ltd
Minicut	Canada	Endmills	Cromwell Group Holdings
Minimotor S.A. Dc Micromotors, Gearheads, Tachogen	Eritrea	ators, EncoderS	Electro Mechanical Systems (EMS) Ltd (EMS)
Minipa	Hong Kong	Meters	Servo & Electronic Sales Ltd
Minox GmbH	Germany	Cameras And Binoculars	Leica Camera Ltd
Mitee-Bite	U.S.A.	Clamps	Hill Cliffe Garage
Mitodaw	Denmark	Hose Couplings	Action Sealtite
Mitre Software	Canada	GTILT: Inclinometer data reduction and presentation	Geomem Ltd
Mitsubishi Electric	United Kingdom	Laser Diodes	Pacer Components plc
Mitsubishi Engineering Polymers	Japan	Plastics Raw Materials	Plastribution
Miyano M/Cy Inc.	Japan	CNC Barworking Lathes, Turning Centres & Drill/Tape Centres	Citizen Machinery UK Ltd
MMO	U.S.A.	Classical backing CD's	Forsyth Bros Ltd
Mo Bio	U.S.A.	Plasmid And Dna Purification	Cambio Ltd
Modco	U.S.A.	Closures	Alexander Cardew Ltd (Head Office)
Modra Technology	Australia	Digital End-Out Detectors for Gripper Axminster Looms, Electronic Card for Jaquard Conversion	Robert S Maynard Ltd
Modsim	Germany	Simulation Language (Object)	C A C I
Modular	U.S.A.	Concealed K.D. System	Unico Components Ltd
Mogami	Japan	Premium Quality Audio And Video Cable	Mosses & Mitchell Ltd
Molecular Analytics	U.S.A.	ION Mobility Speedometer	Quantitech Ltd
Molteni	Italy	Mixing Equipment	D H Industries Ltd
Mona Industries	U.S.A.	Mona Products	Stepan UK Ltd
Monarch	U.S.A.	Oil Burner Nozzles	Anglo Nordic Burner Products Ltd
Mondo	Italy	Rubber Flooring	Altro
Monninghoff	Germany	Tooth Clutches, Flexible Couplings	Lenze UK Ltd
Monomer Polymer & Dajal Labs	U.S.A.	Monomers & Polymers	Fluorochem Ltd
Moore Products Company	U.S.A.	Dimensional gauging and statistical process control	Intra Ltd
Morgan Matroc	United Kingdom	Unilator Capacitors	Richardsons R F P D Ltd
Moros	Spain	Scrap Processing Equipment	M M H Recycling Systems Ltd
Morrow Innovations	Australia	Badges, Transfers, Tapes And Heat Seal Machines	J & A International Ltd
Morsettitalia	Italy	Pcb Terminals/DIN Rail Terminals	Elkay Electrical Manufacturing Co. Ltd A Smiths Group Company
Motomann Ab	Sweden	Motoman	Motoman Robotics UK Ltd
Motorola	U.S.A.	Rf and microware transistor	Richardsons R F P D Ltd
Motortech	Germany	Gas Ignition Systems	Industrial Power Units Ltd
Motovario	Italy	Gear Units and Geared Motor Unit Manufacturers	Motovario Ltd
Motovario SPA	Italy	Fixed and Variable Speed Gear Units	Motovario Ltd
Motraxx	China	geared stepper motors	Trident Engineering Ltd
Mottrax	Japan	stepper motors	Trident Engineering Ltd
Moucour	France		Teignbridge Propellers International
MPS Magnet Physik Steingroever	United Kingdom		Rainer Schneider & Ayres
MPSI Systems Inc	U.S.A.	Computer Software & Information Services	M P S I Systems Ltd
MRL Diagnostics	U.S.A.	Microbiology Diagnostic Kits	The Binding Site Ltd
MTD	U.S.A.	Mtd, Cub Cadet, Yardman	E P Barrus
MTS	Germany	Level Transmitters	Allison Engineering Ltd
Muehlhauser	Germany	Pumps and Tunnelling Equipment	Burlington Engineers Ltd
Muhlmann	Germany	Hydro-Extractors	Robert S Maynard Ltd
Muller	Germany	Guillotines	Buhrs UK Ltd
Muller & Weigert	Germany	Panel Meters & Accessories	Metrix Electronics
Muller Weingarten	Germany	Forging Equipment	Pearson Panke Ltd
Munkedals Ab	Sweden	Munken Uncoated Papers	Arctic Paper UK Ltd
Munzing Chemie	Germany		Lawrence Industries Ltd
Muppet Meeting Films	U.S.A.	Meeting breaks videos (Jim Henson Productions Inc), distributed by Video Arts	Video Arts Group Ltd
Murakami	Japan	Precision Balances	Stevens Group Ltd
Murata Machinery	Japan	CNC Turret Punch Presses & Laser Combination Machines	Tower Machine Tools Ltd
Musso S.r.l.	Italy	Food Preparation Equipment	Robot Coupe UK Ltd
Muva	Germany	Sewing machine needles	Triumph Needle Co. Ltd
N.M.B.	Japan	Rodend & Spherical Bearings	Raceparts

OVERSEAS COMPANY	COUNTRY OF ORIGIN	PRODUCT	UK COMPANY
N.S.K.	Japan	Power Hand Tools	Kemet International Ltd
N.T.P.	Czech Republic	Broadcast Audio Products	Preco Ltd
N.T. Tool	Japan	Titelock Milling Chucks	Cromwell Group Holdings
Nabertherm	Germany	Electric Furnaces for Metal Melting and Heat Treatment	Ramsell Naber Ltd
Nachi	Japan	Endmilling and Slot Drilling	Cromwell Group Holdings
NAF Ab Linkopping	Sweden	Backflow preventers	Northvale Korting Ltd
Nais	Japan	Sensors	Sensortek
Najet	U.S.A.	micro drilling machines	Drill Service Horley Ltd
Nanyo Boeki	Japan	Effects Units For Musical Instruments	John Hornby Skewes & Co. Ltd
Narco	U.S.A.	Physiological Equipment	Linton & Co Engineering Ltd
Nasco	U.S.A.	Sampling	Radleys
Nathan/Tyler Videos	U.S.A.	In Search of Excellence and other award winning video case studies - distributed by Video Arts	Video Arts Group Ltd
National Arnold Magnetics	U.S.A.	Tape Cores	Almag Components Ltd
National Bedford Thread	U.S.A.	Furriers Sewing Thread	William Gee Ltd
NEC Tokin	Japan	EMC Products	Components Bureau
Nelson Irrigation Corp	U.S.A.	Irrigation Rain Guns	Wrightrain Environmental Ltd
Nemef B.V.	Netherlands	mortise locks	Ronis-Dom Ltd
Nemo Q	Sweden	Queue Management Systems	Lonsto Insternational Ltd
NeoMedia Technologies	U.S.A.	Adapt/2000	Transoft Ltd (Part of the Computer Software P.L.C.)
Nerostep OY	Finland	vinyl duckboard matting	Jaymart Roberts & Plastics Ltd
Nester	Germany	automatic nesting software for fabric, foam and wood industries	Apropa Machinery Ltd
Network II	Germany	Computer Communication	C A C I
Netzsch Condux	Germany	Dry Grinding, Recycling, Granulators, Classifiers,Crushers	Netzsch Mastermix Ltd
Netzsch Feinmahltechnik GmbH	Germany	Continuos Wet Grinding Mills, Horizontal and Vertical, Basket Mills	Netzsch Mastermix Ltd
Neu	France	Jumbo Hank and Continuous Belt Dryers	Robert S Maynard Ltd
New Holland	United Kingdom	Agricultural spare parts	Kingsdown
Newall Electronics Inc	U.S.A.	Linear encoders & digital readout systems	Newall Measurement Systems Ltd
Newall Germany	Germany	Linear encoders & digital readout systems	Newall Measurement Systems Ltd
Newlong	Japan	Bagging And Sealing Systems	W J Morray Engineering Ltd
Newmar	U.S.A.	Marine Electrical	Aquapac International Ltd
Nexans	France	Industrial Cables	Metool Products Ltd
NGT	Japan	Thermal Cutouts And Thermistors	Hawco
Nichicon	Japan	Capacitors	Components Bureau
Nicolon	Netherlands	Geolon And Nicotarp	A G A Group
NIDEC Motor & Acuators DC Motors & geared motors	United Kingdom		Electro Mechanical Systems (EMS) Ltd (EMS)
NIDEC Servo Stepper Motors, brushless DC,fans	United Kingdom		Electro Mechanical Systems (EMS) Ltd (EMS)
Nippi Inc	Japan	Sausage Casing	Bemis Swansea
Nippon Automation	Japan	Liquid Level Switches	Applications Engineering Ltd
Niro Ceramic S.A.	Switzerland	Unglazed Ceramic Tiles	A Elder Reed & Co. Ltd (t/a Reed Harris)
Nisshinbo	Japan	Reel-bored Continuous Laser Printers	Episys Group Ltd
Nistac GmbH	Germany	Home Office Desks	Kettler GB Ltd
Nitai	Taiwan	Capacitors	Components Bureau
Nitrom Dental	Denmark	Autoclave	Plandent
Nitto Kohki	Japan	Quick Release Coupling, Air Compressor and Vacuum Pumps	Nitto Kohki Europe Co. Ltd
Nivell AG	Switzerland	Anti-Vibration Mounts and Machine Levelling Wedges	Beakbane Ltd
NK Networks GmbH	Germany	Coaxial And Camera Cables	Radiall Ltd
Nohken Inc	Japan	Level Sensors	Magnetrol International UK Ltd
Nor Reg	Norway	Wrap around packaging machinary.	Waller Eurosel
Norbou	Netherlands	Preformed Cavity Trays	Cavity Trays Ltd
Nordfab A.S.	Denmark	Cassette Filters	Duscovent Engineering Ltd
Nordfab Denmark A.S.	Denmark	Air Pollution Control	Dantherm Filtration Ltd
Nordisk	Denmark	Column Boards	A V M Ltd
Nordiska	Sweden	Dental Consumables	Plandent
Norma	Austria	wattmeters & power analysers	The Seaward Group (a division of Seaward Electronic Ltd)
Normet	Finland	Tunnelling Equipment	Burlington Engineers Ltd
North Coast Medical	Indonesia	Physiotherapy Products	Posturite Ltd
Northern Airborne Technolgy	Canada	Intercoms & Radios	Cobham Antenna Systems
Norway:Scandinavian Aerospace & Industry AB	Norway		Cambridge Vacuum Engineering
Norwe	Germany	Transformer Bobbins	Rainer Schneider & Ayres
Norwegian Handling and Safety	Norway	Accomodation Modules	H B Rentals Ltd
Notz.CTU	Switzerland	Cast Acrylic Sheet	Peerless Plastics & Coatings
Nova Dryers International	U.S.A.	warm air dryers	Vectair Systems Ltd
Nova Systems Inc	U.S.A.	PC Compatible Plug In Cards, Time Base, Connectors Synchronise, Encodes & Decodes	D T L Broadcast Ltd
Nova World Ltd	Hong Kong	Fashion Fabrics	Combined Trading Garments Ltd
Novakust	Germany	Stentering, Steaming, Shrinking, Pressing for Knitted Fabrics; Pleating Machines	Robert S Maynard Ltd
Novamet Specialty Products Corporation	U.S.A.	Metallic Particulate Products	Hart Materials Ltd
Novellini Diffusion S.r.l.	Italy	Bathroom Products	Novellini UK Ltd
Numatic	United Kingdom	Floor Machines/Vacuum Cleaners	C S A Cleaning Equipment
O'Brien	U.S.A.	Trace Heating Bundles	Boiswood LLP
O.H.K.A. Europe Ltd	Netherlands	Photopolymer Platemaking Materials	Plastotype
O.M.P.	Italy	Coldsaws	Prosaw Ltd
O. Malmkvist Ab	Sweden	Spray Washing Machines	Turbex Ltd
Oak Technical Inc	U.S.A.	Clean Room Vinyl Gloves	Cravenmount Ltd
Oberburg	Switzerland	Bottle Cap Making Machines, Thread Rolling, TrimminG And Beading Machines	Pearson Panke Ltd
Oberland GLAS	Germany	Solaris Glassblocks	H W Cooper
OBO	Taiwan	Sounders/Buzzers	Components Bureau
OCM	Japan	industrial chain	F B Chain Ltd
Ocular Instruments Inc	U.S.A.	Diagnostic Contact Lenses	Keeler Ltd
Oerlemans Plastics B.V.	Netherlands	Polythene Film	Fargro
Oetiker	Switzerland	Pipe Clips & Couplings	E C I S Scotland Ltd
Oglaend Systems	Norway	Cable Tray & Clamping Systems	Hydrasun Ltd
Ognibene	Italy	Hydraulic Tyre Removal Tools	Universal Hydraulics Ltd
Ohio	U.S.A.	special drills	Drill Service Horley Ltd
OJ Elektroniks A.S.	Denmark	Electronic Thermostats and Controls	Eswa Ltd
OK Hungarian Gloves KV	Hungary	Leather Gloves	Chester Jefferies Ltd
Okabe	Japan	Lock roll staples	J & H Rosenheim & Co. Ltd
OKI	U.S.A.	Micro-Air Dispensing Systems	Liquid Control Ltd
Oleodinenica Marchesini	Italy		Universal Hydraulics Ltd
Oleostar	Italy	Hydraulic Circuit Valves	BYPY Hydraulics & Transmissions Ltd
Olstyn	Poland	Agricultural Tyres	Kings Road Tyres & Repairs Ltd
Olympic Kilns	U.S.A.	Electric Gas Fired Kilns	Potclays Ltd
OMC	Italy	Torque limiters	Lenze UK Ltd
Omega	U.S.A.	Contact Strips	Optical Filters
Omega Electronics Int.	China	Consumer Electronics Goods, Radios, In-Car Entertainment, CD Players, Clock Radios, Radio Cassette Players/Recorders, Speakers, Clock Radio Cassettes etc	Omega Import Export Ltd
Omexco	Belgium	Textile Wallcoverings	Brian Yates
Omge	Italy	Drawer Slides (Kitchens)	Unico Components Ltd

OVERSEAS COMPANY	COUNTRY OF ORIGIN	PRODUCT	UK COMPANY
OMP Bodega	Italy	winding machines and vigoureux printing	Macart Textiles Machinery Ltd
Ompi	Italy	Pneumatic Brakes & Clutches	Stromag Ltd
OMS S.p.A Pallet Shrink Hooding Machines	United Kingdom		Gordian Strapping Ltd
OMS S.p.A Pallet Strapping Machines	United Kingdom		Gordian Strapping Ltd
OMS S.p.A Pallet Stretch Hooding Machines	United Kingdom		Gordian Strapping Ltd
OMS S.p.A Pallet Stretch Wrapping Machines	United Kingdom		Gordian Strapping Ltd
On-Line	Australia	Keyboard Mechanisms	Unico Components Ltd
Onsrud Cutter Manufacturing	U.S.A.	Router Cutters for CNC Machines	ATA Engineering Processes
Optek Technology	U.S.A.	Optoelectronic Components and Assemblies	Pacer Components plc
Optia Mangel	Germany	Slide Storage Cabinet	A V M Ltd
Opto Electronics Textron	U.S.A.	Infrared Detectors	Metax Ltd
Optus Software Inc	U.S.A.	Facsys - Network Fax Software	Techland Group Ltd
OR-X	Israel	Test & Measuring Instruments	Metrix Electronics
Oralla	Spain	Stainless Bar Mills	Amodil Supplies
Orbinox	Spain	Knife Gate Valves Manufacture	Trimline Valves
Orbis	Spain	Timers	Electro Replacement Ltd
Orbit Controls AG.	Switzerland	Calibration Equipment (Electrical)	Lyons Instruments
Orbital	U.S.A.	Equipment Biologicals	Cambio Ltd
Oregon	Belgium	Sweatshirts, Polo and T-Shirts	I S Enterprises International
Orelude Corpn	U.S.A.	Boelube Metalworking Lubricants	ATA Engineering Processes
Orient	Japan	Thermal Fuses (Surface Mount)	Hawco
ORT	Italy	Machine tool manufacturers	Super-Tec Machine Tools Ltd
Oskar Schwenk GmbH & Co KG	Germany	Bore gauges	Yorkshire Precision Gauges Ltd
Ostberg	Sweden	Industrial Centrifugal	Nicotra-Gebhardt Ltd
Otto Suhner AG	Switzerland	Portable Power Tools Flexible Shaft Machines	Finishing Aids & Tools Ltd
Outils Regine	Switzerland	Tweezers	Electro Group Ltd
Oxford	Korea, Republic of	Optical Frames	Hilton International Eye Wear Ltd
Oxford Instruments	United Kingdom	Positive Materials Idnetification Analyzers	Sonatest Ltd
Ozotech	U.S.A.	Ozone Generators	Ferex Ltd
P E L Industries	New Zealand	Electric Fencing	Drivall Ltd
P.H. Gesswein & Co.	U.S.A.	Abrasive Stones & Mounted Points	Kemet International Ltd
P.P.P. Inc	U.S.A.	Water Hammer Arrestors	Wade International Ltd
P.T. Kayu Permata	Indonesia	Solid Hardwood Doors	Price & Pierce Softwoods Ltd
Pacific	U.S.A.	Linear/ rotary plain bearings	Hepco Motion
Pacific Instruments Inc	U.S.A.	Data Acquisition	J J Systems Ltd
Pacific Scientific	U.S.A.	Servo Drives & Motors	European Drives & Motor Repairs
PACS Handelgesellschaft Backhaus GmbH	Germany	Steel & Alloy Tube, Pipe & Fittings	Mito Construction & Engineering Ltd
Padovani	Italy	Rotary Cutters/Moulders Moulding Machines	Robinsons
Pagel	Germany	Cement based groots	P E S UK Ltd
Palsys	Netherlands	Palletising Systems	A M J Maters Partnership Ltd
Pamasol Willi Maeder	Switzerland	Pharmaceutical, Aersol Fillers	D H Industries Ltd
Pamtech	U.S.A.	RF & Microwave Circulators and Isolators	Aspen Electronics Ltd
Pan Overseas	Taiwan	Varistors	Components Bureau
Panasonic	Japan	Small Geared Motors, Servo Drives	Lenze UK Ltd
Panasonic Consumer Electronics UK Ltd	United Kingdom	Air conditioning equipment	Tool & Fastener Solutions Ltd (T/A TF Solutions Ltd)
Pangaea	Canada	Range of Geological Software	Geomem Ltd
Panhandler Inc.	Brazil	Oven Gloves	Ingram Bros Ltd
Pantec	Italy	Test & Measuring Instruments	Carlo Gavazzi UK Ltd
Papillon	Italy	Domino Masks	Palmer Agencies Ltd
Paradyme	U.S.A.	Rs232 Debue Software	Computer Solutions Ltd
Paraglas	Austria	Cast Acrylic Sheet	Stockline Plastics Ltd
Park Tool Co.	U.S.A.	Bicycle Tools	Madison
Parker	U.S.A.	Guitars	Korg UK Ltd
Parker Symetrics	U.S.A.	Dry Break Fluid Couplings	Raceparts
Parmigiani	Italy	hydraulic dishing presses	Mackey Bowley International Ltd
Paroc Oy A.B. Panel Systems	Finland	Fire Proof Panels	Hemsec Group
PAS BY	Netherlands	Modular Filing System	Gilmex International Ltd
Patlite	Japan	signal towers & beacons	Lenze UK Ltd
PCA (Pty) Ltd	Australia	Shaft Encoders	W & S Measuring Systems Ltd
PCF Chimie	France	Metal salts and bismuth compounds	Thomson & Joseph Ltd
Peder Nielsen	Denmark	Window Fittings	Titon Hardware Ltd (Head Office)
Peeco	U.S.A.	Flow Activated Electr Switches	Alexander Cardew Ltd (Head Office)
Pei-Point S.N.C.	Italy	Resistance Welding Machines	Sureweld UK Ltd
Pekos	Spain	Ball Valve Manufacture	Trimline Valves
Peleng	Belarus	Lenses, Magnifiers And Monoculars	Swains International plc
Pelikan & Co.	Germany	Art and Craft Materials	C Roberson & Co. Ltd
Pentax Vision Corporation	Japan	Ophthalmic Equipment	Pentax UK Ltd
Perkin Elmer Optoelectronics (formerly E.G. & G)	Canada	Leds, Laser and Photosiddes	Pacer Components plc
Perkin Elmer Optoelectronics (formerly E.G. & G.)	U.S.A.	Optoelectronic Components and Assemblies	Pacer Components plc
Perrot	Germany	braking components	Roadlink International Ltd
Perrot Regnerbau	Germany	Irrigation Pipes/Fittings	Connectomatic
Persta	Germany	Pipe lining	Radlett Valve & Engineering Co. Ltd
Pertici Spa	Italy	Non-Ferrous Saws	Prosaw Ltd
Peta Brushes	Cyprus	Paint Brushes/Rollers	Hilton Banks Ltd
Peter Electronic GmbH	Germany	Soft Starters (Ministart, Duostart) & DC Injection Brake Units	Ralspeed Ltd
Peter Hoar Engineering Ltd	United Kingdom	Special laminating and cutting machines for PE	Apropa Machinery Ltd
Peters S.A.	France	Cardiac Structures	Mediplus Ltd
Petroferm	U.S.A.	Specialist Cleaning Products	Banner Chemicals Ltd
Phenix	China	Cameras	Kauser International Trading Ltd
Phifer Wire Products Inc	U.S.A.	Insect and Sunscreening	Vincents Norwich Ltd
Pi Tape	U.S.A.	Diameter Measuring Tape	P I Tape Ltd
Piab	Sweden	Load monitoring products	Crane Care Ltd
Pibal	Spain	Natural Slate	Cembrit Ltd
Pie	Netherlands	Dianostic Equipment	Pie Data UK Ltd
Pielnova Textil S.A.	Spain	Simulateo Fur	Emko Products Ltd
Pigs Unlimited	U.S.A.	Pigs, Cups, Discs, Pig Detectors	Alexander Cardew Ltd (Head Office)
Piller Gmbh	Germany		Piller UK Ltd
Pipeline Cleaners	U.S.A.	Metal Bodies Pigs & Spheres	Alexander Cardew Ltd (Head Office)
Pipeline Inspection	U.S.A.	Pig Tracking Equipment Electrodes	Alexander Cardew Ltd (Head Office)
Pixotec	U.S.A.	SlicerDicer: Graphical visualisation software - 3D+	Geomem Ltd
Placid Industries Inc	U.S.A.	Brakes	Huco Dynatork
Planatol GmbH	Germany	Binding Adhesives	Gilmex International Ltd
Planmeca Oy	Finland	Dental Equipment/Xray	Plandent
Plas Alliance Ltd	Taiwan	Plastic Bag Making Machinery	Kween B Ltd
Plasite	U.S.A.	Synthetic Resinous Linings	Lithgow Saekaphen Ltd
Plastimar Marine Equipment	Italy	Life Rafts and Inflatable Boats	Adec Marine Ltd
Platemate B.V.	Netherlands	Platestackers	Craven & Co. Ltd
Players Guide	U.S.A.	Casting Directory	Spotlight Casting Directories & Contacts
Po-Le Optik	Italy	Metal Spectacle Frames	Look Designs Ltd
Po-Ne-Mah	U.S.A.	Biological Data Acquisition	Linton & Co Engineering Ltd
Pocket Songs	U.S.A.	Singalong Tapes	Forsyth Bros Ltd
Poland:Technika Spawalnicza Sp. z.o.o.	Poland		Cambridge Vacuum Engineering
Polaris	U.S.A.	Atv, Personal Watercraft	E P Barrus

OVERSEAS COMPANY	COUNTRY OF ORIGIN	PRODUCT	UK COMPANY
Polaroid	U.S.A.	Polarizing Filters	Optical Filters
Polidoro	Italy	Atmospheric Gas Burners	Black Teknigas & Electro Controls Ltd
Poligal	Spain	Polypropylene Films	Eurohill Traders Ltd (t/a Associated Packaging)
Polo Ralph Loren	Italy	Optical Frames & Sunglasses	Hilton International Eye Wear Ltd
Poltrona Frau	Italy	Leather Seating & Sofas	Ergonom Ltd
Poly San Company	U.S.A.	Portable Toilets	William G Search Ltd
Polycast	U.S.A.	Specialist and Aircraft Acrylics	Stockline Plastics Ltd
Polyflex	Germany	High Pressure Thermoplastic Hose	Hydrasun Ltd
Polyken	U.S.A.	Pipe & Rapping Tapes	Alexander Cardew Ltd (Head Office)
Polytex	Germany	Badges, Transfers, Tapes And Heat Seal Machines	J & A International Ltd
Pompetrauaini SpA	Italy	Liquid Ring Vacuum Pumps, Centrifugal Process Pumps, Gear Pumps	Chemvac Pumps Ltd
Poolquip	Netherlands	Roldeck Automotic Pool Covers	Certikin International Ltd
Pop-A-Tents	China	Childrens & Adults Tents	Finecard International Ltd (t/a Ninja Corporation)
Pop-A-Tents	China	Childrens and Adults Tents	Ninja Corporation Ltd
Porocel	U.S.A.		Lawrence Industries Ltd
Portescap	Switzerland	dc gearheads	Trident Engineering Ltd
Portugal:Kanthal Sandvik Espanola	Portugal		Cambridge Vacuum Engineering
Positrol Inc	U.S.A.	M/C Tool Accessories, and collet pads	Dejay Distribution Ltd
Power Plastics S.A.	South Africa	Container Liners and Pool Covers	Power Plastics
Powis Parker	U.S.A.	Fastback Binding System	Murodigital
PPG Industries Inc	U.S.A.	Chlorinated Solvents	Banner Chemicals Ltd
Praga	India	Grinders - Surface	Capital Equipment & Machinery Ltd
Praher	Austria	Valves	C P V Ltd
Precision Dynamics	U.S.A.	Laboratory Consumables	Radleys
Precision Dynamics	U.S.A.	Solenoid Valves	Tamo Ltd
Precision Dynamics Inc	U.S.A.	Identification Bracelets	P3 Medical Ltd
Precistep Stepper Motors	United Kingdom		Electro Mechanical Systems (EMS) Ltd (EMS)
Prefer	Netherlands	Professional Audio Products	Preco Ltd
Press Metal	Italy	Coffee Pots	Thomas Plant Birmingham
Pressure Devices Inc	U.S.A.	Pressure and Vacuum Switches	Applications Engineering Ltd
Prestige Air Technology	United Kingdom	Gas Free Building On Contaminated Land	A G A Group
Prima Industrie	Italy	laser cutting machines	Joseph Rhodes Ltd
Princeton Tec	U.S.A.	Torches and Accessories	Stoney Cove Diver Training Centre Ltd
Pro Form	U.S.A.	Vacuum Forming Mats	Metrodent Ltd
Pro Scientific	U.S.A.	Laboratory Homogenisers	Radleys
Prochem	U.S.A.	Carpet Cleaning Machines	C S A Cleaning Equipment
Procoat UK Ltd	United Kingdom	coatings for mineral fibre and metal suspended ceilings	Crofton House Associates
Procyon	U.S.A.	Tapping Machines	Meddings Machine Tools
Prodont Holliger	France	Dental Models And Laboratory Equipment	Plandent
Profile Design	U.S.A.	Bicycle Accessories	Madison
Promach Ltd	Taiwan	Bandsaws	Prosaw Ltd
Promet	Israel	Steel Windows And Doors	Crittall Windows Ltd
Promis	Turkey		Hawker Electronics Ltd
Proteval	France	Prosthetic Knee Components	Gilbert & Mellish Ltd
Prototyp	Germany	Taps and Milling Cutters	Macinnes Tooling Ltd
Prototyp	Germany	Taps for cutting internal threads	Robert Speck Ltd
Provex SRL	Italy	Shower Cubicles and Doors	Lakes Bathrooms Ltd
Pruflex	Germany	Electronic ignition transformers	Anglo Nordic Burner Products Ltd
Pucci	Italy	Fork Lift Truck	Fork Truck Centre Ltd
Pump House Pumps	United Kingdom	Condensate PumpsAir conditioning installation accessories	Tool & Fastener Solutions Ltd (T/A TF Solutions Ltd)
Purafil Inc	U.S.A.	Air And Gas Dry Scrubbers	Higgins & Hewins Ltd
Q.M.S.	U.S.A.	Colour Laser Printers	Episys Group Ltd
Q.V.C.	U.S.A.	European Product	Perennis Ltd
QED Japan	Japan	Historic Lotus Race Engine Parts	Q E D
QMI	U.S.A.	Air Coupled Ultrasonics	Sonatest Ltd
Quadco	U.S.A.	Control Levers	Ringspann UK Ltd
Quality Carbide Tool	U.S.A.	Cutting Tools	Dejay Distribution Ltd
Quartztek Inc	U.S.A.	RF Crystals & Crystal Filters	Aspen Electronics Ltd
Quickmill	Canada	Gantry Milling Machine	Meddings Machine Tools
R.A.E. Systems	U.S.A.	Minirae Hand Held VOC Monitor, Toxirae Personal VOC Monitor, Ultrarae Benzene Specific Monitor	Shawcity Ltd
R.G.M. Co.	Indonesia	Plywood	Price & Pierce Softwoods Ltd
R.P.C. industries	U.S.A.	E.B. curling	Greenbank Technology Ltd
R & S Stanztechnik GmbH	Germany	Interior Trim Tools For Automotive Industry	Silcoms
Raab Karcher	Denmark	Flow and Energy Meters	Switch2 Energy Solutions
Radio Energie	France	Tacho Generators	Transdrive Engineering Ltd
Radio Flyer	U.S.A.	Childrens Pull Along Wagons	Finecard International Ltd (t/a Ninja Corporation)
Radio Flyer	U.S.A.	Childrens Pull Along Wagons	Ninja Corporation Ltd
Radiometric	Germany	Non-Contact Gauges	Thermo Radiometrie Ltd
Rahn AG	Switzerland	Radcure Raw Materials	Pentagon Fine Chemicals Ltd
Rahsol	Germany	Torque Tools	L J Hydleman & Co. Ltd
Raja Garude Mas	Indonesia	Plywood	Price & Pierce Softwoods Ltd
Raja Industries P.V.T.	Pakistan	Mens And Lathes Leather Shoes With P.V.	Cheshire Style Ltd
Ram	U.S.A.	Acrylic Mirrors	Stockline Plastics Ltd
Ramaw Seliger	Germany	Hose couplings	Action Sealtite
Ramco	U.S.A.	Safety Shields Flanges	Allison Engineering Ltd
Randek Maskin Ab	Sweden	Automatic Production Machinery For Manufacturing Timber Frame Building	Duo-Fast
Rapco Corp	U.S.A.	Instrument Cables	John Hornby Skewes & Co. Ltd
Rappold	Austria	Make the gringing wheels	Swift Abrasive Wheels Ltd (t/a Swift & Whitmore Limited)
Raven Laboratories	U.S.A.	Biological Indicators	Cherwell Laboratories Ltd
Ravensburger	Germany	Puzzles and Games	Ravensburger Ltd
Rayan S.A.	France	Aircraft Antennas	Cobham Antenna Systems
Rayco	Canada		Wylie Systems
RBB	Italy	Ball Valves	Bonomi UK Ltd
Rea SNC	Italy	saturno steam vapour system	Crofton House Associates
Realtoy International	Hong Kong	Die Cast	Peterkin UK Ltd
Rebell	Germany	Tapping	Cromwell Group Holdings
Redel Kft	Hungary	Connectors (Various)	Lemo UK Ltd
Redel S.A.	Switzerland	Plastic Self-latching Connectors	Lemo UK Ltd
Redskins	France	Garments	Ramostyle Ltd
Rega	Germany	Travelling Irrigators	Connectomatic
Regus Offices	U.S.A.	Furnished and Serviced Offices	Regus Management Ltd
Reich	Germany	Truck Mounted And Stationery Concrete Pumps And Placement Booms	Hymix Ltd
Reimu	Italy	Friction Bandsaws	Prosaw Ltd
Reis	Germany	Robots-Welding, Robots-Mechanical Handling	Olympus Technologies Ltd
Relats S.A. Ltd	Spain	Electrical Insulating & Thermal Sleevings	Croylek Ltd
Rembar	U.S.A.	Refractory Metals	Tempatron Controls
Rembrandt Packaging B.V.	Netherlands	Case & Case Loaders	A M J Maters Partnership Ltd
Remei AG	Germany	Concrete Additives	Lanxess Ltd
Rench Rapid	Germany		Gotec Trading Ltd
Renus Armaturen	Germany	Quick Couplers	Connectomatic

OVERSEAS COMPANY	COUNTRY OF ORIGIN	PRODUCT	UK COMPANY
Resco	U.S.A.	Grooming Tools	Diamond Edge Ltd
Resnet Microwave Inc	U.S.A.	RF & Microwave Resistors	Aspen Electronics Ltd
Resol GmbH	Germany	Electronic Solar Regulators	Sundwel Solar Ltd
Rexnord	Germany	Metal disc couplings	Lenze UK Ltd
Reynolds Leteron	U.S.A.	Signmaking System	Murodigital
RF Products Inc	U.S.A.	Rf And Microwave Transistors And Amplifiers	Richardsons R F P D Ltd
Rheonik	Germany	Liquid Flow	Allison Engineering Ltd
Rhizopon B.V.	Netherlands	Rooting Hormone	Fargro
Rhode Gear	U.S.A.	car racks and childseats	Madison
Rhoss	Italy	Water Chillers and air conditioning equipment	Coolmation Ltd
Rhythm-Tech Corp	U.S.A.	Tambourines	John Hornby Skewes & Co. Ltd
Riccetti	Italy	Ceramic Tiles	Just Tiles Ltd
Richards	U.S.A.	miniature cutters	Drill Service Horley Ltd
Ricoh	Japan	35mm Camera And Digital Cameras	Johnsons Photopia Ltd
Ricoh Co Ltd	Japan	Photographic Printers And Facsimilies	N R G Group Ltd
Rigert	Switzerland	Curved Stair Platform Lifts For Disabled	Enable Access
Riko Co. Ltd	Japan	Liquid Level Switches	Applications Engineering Ltd
Ringspann	Germany	Workholding & Power Transmission Product	Ringspann UK Ltd
Rioned	Netherlands	Drain Cleaning, Jetting, Spring Cable	Wardsflex Ltd
Rising Paper	Germany	Quality Paper and Board	G F Smith
robe	Germany	Tillage Equipment	Westmac Ltd
Robert Bosch	Germany	Hydraulic Equipment	Oddy Hydraulics Ltd
Robert Bosch	Germany	Industrial Power Tools	Robert Craig & Sons Ltd
Robert Bosch GmbH	Germany	Motor Vehicle Parts	Panaf & Company
Robot Coupe S.A.	France	Food Preparation Equipment	Robot Coupe UK Ltd
Roche	Germany	Beta Carolene	Sensient
Rockshox	U.S.A.	Bicycle suspension	Madison
Rockware, Inc	U.S.A.	Geological Utility Software	Geomem Ltd
Rodaviss	France	Glass Joints	Radleys
Roditer & Philadephia S.r.l.	Italy	Polishing Machinery And Mops	British & Continental Traders Ltd
Rogers	U.S.A.	carbide cutters	Drill Service Horley Ltd
Rohm	Japan	Laser Diddes	Pacer Components plc
Rohm & Haas UK Ltd	France	Resin	Ferex Ltd
Roland	Germany	Sheet Thickness Measurment; Double Sheet And Weld DEtectors	Pearson Panke Ltd
Roll	Germany	Cleaning Degreasing Plants	Embassy Machinery Ltd
Romag Röhren und Maschinen AG	Switzerland	Storm Overflow Screens	Higgins & Hewins Ltd
Romeca	Belgium	Glass Handling Castors	Keystone Castor Co.
Romeca	Belgium	Glass Handling Castors	Keystone Castor Co.
Romheld GmbH	Germany	Hydraulic Clamping Equipment	Roemheld UK Ltd
Ronstan Pty	Australia	Deck Hardware	Bainbridge Aqua-Marine
Roper-Whitney	U.S.A.	Hand and Bench Punches	Hartle I G E Ltd
Rose Electronics	U.S.A.	Keyboard video house switches	Techland Group Ltd
Rossi	Italy	Gearboxes	Transdrive Engineering Ltd
Rossignul	France	Litter Bins/Medical Cabinets	Unicorn Hygienics
Rotecno	Switzerland	Medical Fabric	Lojigma International Ltd
Rotho	Germany	Desk System Drawers Distributors	Unico Components Ltd
Roto	India	Pumps	Allpumps Ltd
Roto	India	Pumps	Torres Engineering & Pumps Ltd
Rotor Tool GMBH	Switzerland	Live Centres	Dejay Distribution Ltd
Roty E Fils Constructor	France	Abrasive Cut Off Machines Friction Saws Ferrous/Non-Ferrous Plate Saws	Prosaw Ltd
Rotzler GmbH & Co	Germany	Winches	Eka Ltd
Roxan GmbH	Germany	Furniture Film	Klockner Pentaplast Ltd
Royal Paris	France	Needlecraft	Coats Ltd
Royal Products	U.S.A.	Air Operated Pumps	Filtermist International Ltd
RSB	Germany	Tube Clamps	Hydrasun Ltd
RSW	U.S.A.	Esoft	Scientific Computers Ltd (Head Office)
Rualtec	Switzerland	Oil/Air Coolers	Hydac Technology Ltd
Ruberg GmbH	Germany	Grain Cleaning and Handling Equipment with capacity from 40-300 t.p.h.	Nickerson Bros Ltd
Rubig	Germany	Carbide Drills and End Mills, H.S.S. and Carbide Counterbores and Countersinks	Macinnes Tooling Ltd
Rubycon	Japan	Capacitors	Components Bureau
Rudd Co Inc	U.S.A.	Forestry/Timber Marking Paint	Chieftain Forge
Ruland	U.S.A.	Flexible couplings	Lenze UK Ltd
Rumpus Corporation	U.S.A.	Plush	Peterkin UK Ltd
Rustoleum Corporation	Netherlands	Protective Coatings	Andrews Coatings Ltd
Ruud Lighting	U.S.A.	Flood & Area Exterior Lighting	Poselco Lighting Ltd
Ruwido	Austria	Full Range Of IR Remote Controls	Ceratech Electronics Ltd
S.A.M.	Switzerland	Packaging Machinery	Advanced Dynamics Ltd
S.A. Mart	Korea, Republic of	steering systems	Watermota Ltd
S.A. Renson N.V.	Belgium	Ventilation Manufacturers Grilles Registers	Renson Fabrications Ltd
S.E.F.	France	Dainel	B N International
S.E.P.	Italy	Two Wheeled Tractors	Bunce Ashbury Ltd
S.F.C.E.	France	Worklift-Filing Software, Saw-Law-Operating Softw are	Delta Computer Services (Head Office)
S.G.M. S.p.A.	Italy	Lifting Magnets	Cranequip Ltd
S.G.M. spA	Italy	Separation units	Cranequip Ltd
S.G.S.-Thomson	U.S.A.	Rf Microwave Transistors And Modules	Richardsons R F P D Ltd
S.I.M.A. S.A.	Spain	Ceramic Cutting Machine Manufacturers	Northern Wall & Floor Ltd
S.M.T. Machine Ab	Sweden	CNC Lathes	Advanced Technology Machines Ltd
S One	Korea, Republic of	multiflex pipe consumers	Watermota Ltd
S.T.M.	Italy	Geared Motors	Micro Clutch Developments Ltd
S.V.M.	Sweden	Energy Meters	Switch2 Energy Solutions
Saargummiwerk GmbH	Germany	rubber floorings & accessories	Jaymart Roberts & Plastics Ltd
Saati	Italy	Screen Printing and Industrial Fabrics	Fujifilm Sericol Ltd
Saci	Spain	Instruments	P B S I Group Ltd
Saf	Germany	trailer axle and suspension components	Roadlink International Ltd
Safelab Systems Deutschland	Germany		Safelab Systems Ltd
Safematic	Finland	Lubrication Systems and Mechanical Seals	Pulp & Paper Machinery Ltd
Safetech	Australia	Low Profile Turntable	Southworth Handling Ltd
Safilo S.p.A.	Italy	Optical Frames And Sunglasses	Hilton International Eye Wear Ltd
Sait	Belgium	Marine Radio Equipment	N S S L Ltd
Sakaphen GmbH	Germany	Synthetic Resinous Linings	Lithgow Saekaphen Ltd
Salavat	Russia	Binoculars And Monoculars	Swains International plc
Sampo	Finland	Medical Insurance	Doctorcall
Samsonite	Belgium	Cases	Topper Cases Ltd
San Jamar Inc	U.S.A.	dispensers	Mitchell & Cooper Ltd (Head Office)
Sandingmaster/Grindingmaster B.V.	Netherlands	Wide Abrasive Belt And Brushing Machines	Ellesco Ltd
Sandoz & Fils	Switzerland	Precision Balls	Dejay Distribution Ltd
Sandpiper	U.S.A.	Air Powered Diaphragm Pumps	Robert Craig & Sons Ltd
Sanitas	Spain	Private Health Care	Bupa
Sanitized AG	Switzerland	Antimicrobal Compositions	British Sanitized Ltd
Sanwa Instrument Co	Japan	Testing Instruments	Servo & Electronic Sales Ltd
Saphire	Korea, Republic of	Optical Frames	Hilton International Eye Wear Ltd
Sapporo Precision	Japan	Miniature, Thin Section and Corrosion Resistant Radial and Axial Ball Bearings-Stainless Steel Bearings	S M B Bearings Ltd
Saunders Group Inc	Indonesia	Back Pain Accessories	Posturite Ltd
Saunier Duval Eau Chaude Chauffage S.A.	France		Heatcall Group Services

OVERSEAS COMPANY	COUNTRY OF ORIGIN	PRODUCT	UK COMPANY
Sauro	Italy	Pcb Terminals	Elkay Electrical Manufacturing Co. Ltd A Smiths Group Company
Savino Barbera	Italy	Vertical Suspended Centrifugal Pumps	March May Ltd
Scaldex	Belgium	Preformed Cavity Trays	Cavity Trays Ltd
Scan Tech Instruments	U.S.A.	Scannings systems ultrasonic/eddycurrent	Sonatest Ltd
Scandura Inc	U.S.A.	Duraline Conveyor Belting	P & S Textiles Ltd
Scantech Pty	Australia	On Line Analysers for CVAL Quality	Procon Engineering Ltd
Schatz Bearing Corporation	U.S.A.	Aircraft Control Bearings	R A Rodriguez UK Ltd
Schaublin S.A.	Switzerland	Rod ends and spherical bearings	Huco Dynatork
Schauman	Finland	Chipboard, Plywood, Hardboard	N R Burnett Ltd
Schenker International AG	Germany	Deep Sea & Air Freight Worldwide	Schenkers Ltd
Schenker International Inc	U.S.A.	Deep Sea & Air Freight Worldwide	Schenkers Ltd
Schimmel	Germany	Piano	Forsyth Bros Ltd
Schleicher	Germany	Coilfeeding And Profiling	Embassy Machinery Ltd
Schleuniger	Switzerland	Cutting Leads And Cable Processing	Turner Electronics
Schmitz-Werke	Germany	Markilux Systems	Deans Blinds & Awnings UK
Schneider	Germany	Large Format Camera Taking Lenses And Enlarging LenSes	Johnsons Photopia Ltd
Schnydcr	Switzerland	Gear Hobs	Turner Electronics
Schober GmbH	Germany	New Generation Punches & Dies	R M Rotary Services Ltd
Schoeller Bleckman Edelstahl ROHR (SBER)	Austria	Seamless Stainless	Schoeller-Bleckmann UK
Scholastic Australia Pty Ltd	Australia		Scholastic School Book Fairs
Scholastic Canada Ltd	Canada		Scholastic School Book Fairs
Scholastic Inc	U.S.A.		Scholastic School Book Fairs
Scholastic Ltd	New Zealand		Scholastic School Book Fairs
Schott Amphabel	Belgium	Glass Vials (Tubular)	The Adelphi Group Adelphi Group of Companies
Schott Auer GmbH	Germany	Special Glass Products	Schott UK Ltd
Schott Glaskontor	Germany	Glass Vials (Tubular)	The Adelphi Group Adelphi Group of Companies
Schott Glaswerke	Germany	Special Glass Products	Schott UK Ltd
Schott Parenta Systems	Germany	Syringes Prefill Glass	The Adelphi Group Adelphi Group of Companies
Schott-Rohrglas GmbH	Germany	Glass Tubing And Rod	Schott UK Ltd
Schott SFAM	France	Glass Ampoule And Phials	The Adelphi Group Adelphi Group of Companies
Schott Verrerie Medicale	France	Glass Ampoules	The Adelphi Group Adelphi Group of Companies
Schroeder	Germany	Screwdrivers	Draper Tools Ltd
SCHWA Corporation	U.S.A.	T-Shirts, Stickers, Cards & Books	John Brown Publishing
Schwing	Germany	Concrete Pumps	Burlington Engineers Ltd
Scortegagna Snc	Italy	Bandsaws Hacksaws	Prosaw Ltd
Screenscan	U.S.A.	Microfilm Scanners	Microfilm Shop
SDI	Italy		Tuffnelln Parcels Express
Se'Lux	Germany	Architectural Lighting	Selux UK Ltd
Sea Inc	U.S.A.	Marine Radio Equipment	N S S L Ltd
Sea Rider	Italy	Stren drive	Watermota Ltd
Seaform	U.S.A.	Buoyancy Compensators & Aids	Stoney Cove Diver Training Centre Ltd
Seaman Corp	U.S.A.	High Strength Geomembranes	A G A Group
Seedburo Equipment Co	U.S.A.	Suppliers of Testing and Handling Equipment for the Grain, Feed and Seed Industries	Nickerson Bros Ltd
Seeka	Japan	Sensors	Sensortek
Seepex	Germany	Progressive Cavity Pumps	Robert Craig & Sons Ltd
Sefelec S.A.	France	Electrical safety testing equipment	The Seaward Group (a division of Seaward Electronic Ltd)
Sefram	France	Recorders & Instruments	Metrix Electronics
SEG	France	Needlecraft	Coats Ltd
Sehempp-Hirth	Germany	Manufacture Gliders	Southern Sailplanes
Seki Technotron Corp	Japan	defense-sys@sekitech.co.jp	Specialist Electronics Services Ltd
Sekonic	Japan	Exposure Meters	Johnsons Photopia Ltd
Sekurit	Germany	Vehicle Glass	Homeserve Emergency Services
Selas	U.S.A.		Nordsea Ltd
Selter	Spain	Magnetic Workholding Equipment	Capital Equipment & Machinery Ltd
Senet	Russia	Night Vision	Swains International plc
Senju Metal Ind.	Japan	Solder	Link Hamson Ltd
Sennelier	France	Fine Art Water Colours, Pastels, Fabric Paints And Dyes	Exaclair Ltd
Sensidyne	U.S.A.	Personal Air Sampling Pumps	Quantitech Ltd
Sensopart	Germany	Sensors	Sensortek
Sentry	U.S.A.	Fire Resistant Cash Boxes And Safes	Helix Trading Ltd
Seoul Nassau Korea	Korea, Republic of	Range balls	Pareto Golf Ltd
Sera	Germany	Foods And Treatments For Fish	John Allan Aquariums Ltd
Serion	Germany	Virology Diagnostic Kits	The Binding Site Ltd
Service Society of the Italian Chemical Society, The	Italy	Books	Royal Society Of Chemistry
Servo	U.S.A.	Drilling Machines - Micro Pressure And Power Feeds	Capital Equipment & Machinery Ltd
Servo	Netherlands	Coating Additives	Banner Chemicals Ltd
Servo Repairs Int Inc	U.S.A.	Servo Drives & Motors	European Drives & Motor Repairs
Servomac	Italy	Servo Drives & Motors	European Drives & Motor Repairs
Servomech	Italy	Linear actuators & screwjacks	Lenze UK Ltd
Servopress	Germany	Indexing Tables	Meddings Machine Tools
Setra	U.S.A.	Pressure Transducers	Boiswood LLP
Shafer	U.S.A.	Pipeline Valve Actuators	Paladon Systems Ltd
Shanghai Seagull	China	Cameras	Kauser International Trading Ltd
Sharkfin	Sweden	Guitar Plectra	John Hornby Skewes & Co. Ltd
Shepherd Chemicals Inc	U.S.A.	Polyurethane additives	I M C D UK Ltd
Shicoh	Japan	Minature Fans	Key Electronic Components
Shield	Korea, Republic of	Optical Frames	Hilton International Eye Wear Ltd
Shimano	Japan	Bicycle components, shoes and clothing	Madison
Shimpo	Japan	Potters Wheel & Pugmill	Potclays Ltd
Shinano Kenshi Co. Ltd	Japan	Small Precision Electric Motors	Astrosyn International Technolgy Ltd
Shinetsu	Japan	Vinyl Resins	Gelpke & Bate Ltd
Shinko	Japan	Electronic Temperature Controllers	Testemp Ltd
Shinohara-Shoji KK	Japan	Ofsett Presses	Graphics Arts Equipment Ltd
Shoda Trading	Japan	Scoring & Bevelling Machines	Circuit Engineering Marketing Company Ltd
Shurtape Technologies	U.S.A.	Adhesive Tapes	Anixter Industrial Ltd
Sibola	Denmark	Wrapping Tables	Herbert Retail Ltd
Siccom	France	Liquid level & switches	Applications Engineering Ltd
Sicmo-Bendix	Monaco	HVLP Spray Equipment	Gray Campling Ltd
Siemans-Furnas Controls	U.S.A.	Pressure Switches For Pumps And Compressors	Tamo Ltd
Sierra Instruments	U.S.A.	Thermal Mass Gas Flowmeters	Litre Meter Ltd
Signature Technologies Inc	U.S.A.	Press Curve Monitoring	Davis Decade Ltd
Signpatterns	U.S.A.		Armstrong Optical Ltd
Sigtek Inc	U.S.A.	Board Level Dsp/Spread Spectrum Radios	Marlborough Communications Ltd
Sihl	Switzerland	Quality Paper and Board	G F Smith
Silar Labs	U.S.A.	Silanes & silicones	Fluorochem Ltd
SILC	Italy	Finishing Equipment	J L A
SILLEM S.p.A.	Italy	Polishing Machinery	British & Continental Traders Ltd

OVERSEAS COMPANY	COUNTRY OF ORIGIN	PRODUCT	UK COMPANY
Simco	Netherlands	Static Control Equipment	Advanced Dynamics Ltd
Simel	Italy	Burner Motors	Anglo Nordic Burner Products Ltd
Simmonds	France	nuts for aerospace industries	S P S Technologies Ltd
Simona	Germany	PVC, PVC Foam and Polypropylene	Stockline Plastics Ltd
Simplex	U.S.A.	Time Recorders	Cristel Paint Finishers Ltd
Simplex-Rapid S.r.l.	Italy	Spring Coiling Machines	Bennett Mahler
Simplify Inc	Ireland	Mailroom fileroom document management	Techland Group Ltd
Simport Plastics	Canada	Laboratory Plastics	Radleys
Simpson Paper	Germany	Quality Paper and Board	G F Smith
Simscript	Germany	Process Orientated Simulation Language	C A C I
Singatron	Taiwan	Connectors	G English Electronics Ltd
Singer Data Products Inc	France	Labelling Systems	Weyfringe Labelling Systems
Sipex	U.S.A.	Integrated Crts	M B Components Ltd
Sirotex	Italy	Irrigation Equipment	Connectomatic
Siso	Denmark	Danish K.D. Fittings	Unico Components Ltd
SIT	Italy	Flexible couplings	Lenze UK Ltd
Skanti A.S.	Denmark	Marine Radio Equipment	N S S L Ltd
SKF	United Kingdom	Automotive spare parts	Kingsdown
SKF Actuation Systems Electric Linear Actuators	United Kingdom		Electro Mechanical Systems (EMS) Ltd (EMS)
SKG	Germany	Botz Glazes & Colours	Potclays Ltd
SMG	Germany	Presses	Embassy Machinery Ltd
Smith & Brighty	Portugal	Trimmings	Gainsborough Silk Weaving Co. Ltd
Smrecina	Slovakia	Soft Board	Price & Pierce Softwoods Ltd
Snaptite Europe	U.S.A.	Quick Release Couplings	Hydrasun Ltd
Snow Lutus Press	U.S.A.	Publishers	Acumedic Centre Ltd
Sobinco	Belgium	Window Fittings	Titon Hardware Ltd (Head Office)
Socatri S.A.	France	Hard Crome, Heavy Nickel, Electroless Nickel	Firma Chrome Ltd
Societe Avebene Aquitaine	France	Lignosulphonates	Sud-Chemie UK Ltd
Socomef	Belgium	Oil pot burners and draft stabilisers	Anglo Nordic Burner Products Ltd
Sodes	France	Synthetic Alochol	Gelpke & Bate Ltd
Softaid	U.S.A.	In Curcuit Emulators	Computer Solutions Ltd
Softkit	Canada	Aquadyn: Surface Water flow modelling	Geomem Ltd
Sogreah	France	Sea Defence Formwork	Heskin Fabrications Ltd
Sola Measuring Tools	Austria	Spirit Levels	Fisco Tools Ltd
Solberg & Anderson A.S.	Norway	Electronic Components	Eswa Ltd
Soler & Palau	Spain	Fans	Beatson Fans & Motors Ltd
Solvay	Belgium	CAPA Polyols	I M C D UK Ltd
Sonaepan	Portugal	M.D.F./Decorative Mfc	N R Burnett Ltd
Sonatech Inc	U.S.A.	High Temperature Consumables	Sonatest Ltd
Sony Precision Technology Inc	Japan	Precision Measuring Equipment	Stanmatic Precision UK Ltd T/A Axis Group (Axis Group)
Southco Europe Ltd	Spain		Southco Manufacturing Co.
Southco GmbH	Germany		Southco Manufacturing Co.
Southco SARL	France		Southco Manufacturing Co.
Southco SRL	Italy		Southco Manufacturing Co.
Spaggiari	Italy	Geared motors	Micro Clutch Developments Ltd
Spaggiari	Italy	Geared motors	Lenze UK Ltd
Spain:Sandvik Espanola S.A. Kanthal Division	Spain	electron beam welding & vacuum furnaces	Cambridge Vacuum Engineering
Sparterie De La Gironde	France	entrance mattings	Jaymart Roberts & Plastics Ltd
SpecNum	Canada	Glazes	Potclays Ltd
Spectra Mat	U.S.A.	Tungsten And Molybdenum Alloys	Ernest B Westman Ltd
Specwell Corporation	Japan	Prismatic Monoculars For Low Vision Use	Carclo Technical Plastics
Speeflo Manufacturing Corp	U.S.A.	Paint Spray Equipment	Gray Campling Ltd
Spies Hecker	Germany	Vehicle Refinish Paint	Spies Hecker UK
Spirac	Sweden	Conveyors, Classifiers, Dewatering Equipment and Compactors	Pulp & Paper Machinery Ltd
Spirec	France	Stainless Steel Heat Exchangers	Thermal Engineering Systems Ltd
Spirolox Div, Kaydon Corporation	U.S.A.	Spiral Wound Retaining Rings	R A Rodriguez UK Ltd
Spohr	Germany	Water Level Recorders	Smail Engineers Glasgow Ltd
Spolek Pro Chemickou	Czech Republic	Epoxy Resin	J Allcock & Sons Ltd
Sprimag	Germany	Industrial Spraying Equipment	Pearson Panke Ltd
Springlite	U.S.A.	Prosthetic Feet	Gilbert & Mellish Ltd
Sproti H.F.	Iceland	Icy Vodka	Charles H Julian Ltd
SSeikosha	Japan	Time Recorders	Cristel Paint Finishers Ltd
St Gayan	France	Wine	Yapp Brothers Ltd
Stager GmbH	Switzerland	PET Plastic Sheet	Klockner Pentaplast Ltd
Stam	Italy	Coil Lines	Pearson Panke Ltd
Standard Motor Products	U.S.A.	Engine Management Components	Standard Motor Products Europe Ltd
Standard Tape Labs Inc	U.S.A.	Broadcast Audio Products	Preco Ltd
Standardbox AB	Sweden	Insulated Trolleys & Boxes	Craven & Co. Ltd
Standardgraph	Germany	Lettering Guides	Blundell Harling Ltd (Incorporating Magpie Furniture)
Starline	Italy	Ball Valve Manufacture	Trimline Valves
Starlite	U.S.A.	grinders, burrs, carbide tools	Drill Service Horley Ltd
Starpide	Denmark	Pre-Insulated Steel Pipes	Durotan Ltd
Stearns	U.S.A.	Clutches and Brakes	Bibby Transmissions Ltd
Steinbeis Temming GmbH	Germany	Recycled, Offset and Copier	John Heyer Paper Ltd
Steinco	Germany	Wheels and Castors	Eurocastors Ltd
Steiner - Lamello	Switzerland	Jointing Systems	Smeaton Hanscomb & Co. Ltd
Steinert GmbH	Germany	Magnetic seperators	Magnetic Separations Ltd
Steinhardt	Germany	Constant Flow Regulators And Non Powered CSO Screens And Hydro Switch & Hydrostyx	Copa Ltd
Stemco	U.S.A.	hub oil seals, hub caps & hubodometers	Roadlink International Ltd
Stenhoj Hydraulik A.S.	Denmark	hydraulic workshop presses	Mackey Bowley International Ltd
Stepan	U.S.A.	(Stepanpol) polyester polyols	I M C D UK Ltd
Stereoprint	Switzerland	Matrix Board	Plastotype
Stetter	Germany	Concrete Mixing Plant	Burlington Engineers Ltd
Stil	France		Armstrong Optical Ltd
Stilolinea	Italy	Baron Pen, Korint, Kreta, Ciak, Tethys	Hainenko Ltd
Stimin	Italy	Ultrasonic Cleaning Of Weaving Accessories-Frames/HEddles/Drop Wires/Reeds	Pilkingtons Ltd (t/a Weitzer Parket UK)
Stinec SA	France	Antennas	Cobham Antenna Systems
Stinger	U.S.A.	Vehicle Arresting Device	Spanset Ltd
Stipo	Sweden	Packing Tables	Lea Valley Packaging Ltd
Stockburger Instruments GmbH	Germany	Clocks, Barometers, Hydrometers, Thermometers and Anometers	Yachting Instruments Ltd
Stoll	Germany	Hay Equipment	Westmac Ltd
Stolle	Germany	Work holding equipment	P E S UK Ltd
Stone Instruments	China		Hawker Electronics Ltd
Stoneland	Germany	Ornamental Stone	Redwood Stone
Stoney Creek	U.S.A.	Needlecraft Clubs and Pubs	Coats Ltd
Storti	Italy	Agricultural Machinery	Ruston's Engineering Co. Ltd
Storz	Germany	Hose couplings	Dixon Group Europe Ltd
STR	Germany	Door Entry Systems	Electro Replacement Ltd
Strack	Germany	Injection Moulding Plates & Acc	Welwyn Tool Group Ltd
Strapack Corp.	Japan	Strapping Machines	Gordian Strapping Ltd
Strathmore Paper	Germany	Quality Paper and Board	G F Smith

OVERSEAS COMPANY	COUNTRY OF ORIGIN	PRODUCT	UK COMPANY
Streeter Store Fixtures	U.S.A.	Modular Metal Shelving System	Cardinal Shopfitting Ltd
String Swing	U.S.A.	Hangers For Musical Instruments	John Hornby Skewes & Co. Ltd
Structural	Belgium	Filtration	Certikin International Ltd
Structural Europe	Belgium	Pressure Vessels	Ferex Ltd
STS GmbH & Co	Germany	Custom designed medium & high frequency transformers and chokes	Rolfe Industries
Stuber	Germany	Electronic Non-Contact Stop Motion Switches	Robert S Maynard Ltd
Studer Digitec S.A.	France	Broadcast Audio Products	Preco Ltd
Stuhl Regelsysteme GmbH	Germany	Heating, Ventilation and Humidity Controls	Eswa Ltd
Style	Netherlands	Cnc Co-Ordinate Tables	Meddings Machine Tools
Subair	U.S.A.	Turf Aeration System	Industrial Power Units Ltd
Sud Chemie AG	Germany	Catalysts, Bleaching Earths, Bentonite Clays, Rheological Additives	Sud-Chemie UK Ltd
Suedpack Verpackungen GmbH	Germany	Laminated/Co-Extruded, Barrier Films	Sudpack UK Ltd
Suedpark Export AG	Switzerland	Coextruded Semi-Rigid Polystyrene/Pe Films	Sudpack UK Ltd
Sugino	U.S.A.	High Pressure Waterjet Deburring	Ellesco Ltd
Sugino	Japan	Roller Burnishing Tools	Dejay Distribution Ltd
Sulky	France	Agricultural Machinery	Ruston's Engineering Co. Ltd
Sumitomo S H I	Japan	Hydraulic Crawler Cranes	N R C Plant Ltd
Sumner	U.S.A.	Pipe Fit-Up Tools	B S A Tube Runner
Sunkist	U.S.A.	fruit juicers and sectionizers	Metcalfe Catering Equipment Ltd
Sunonwealth	Taiwan	Fans	G English Electronics Ltd
Sunset	U.S.A.	Needlecraft	Coats Ltd
Sunx	Japan	Sensors	Sensortek
Superba	France	relaxing and heat setting/space dyeing	Macart Textiles Machinery Ltd
Superwinch	U.S.A.	Winches	Crane Care Ltd
Surfrigo	Italy	Refrigerated Display Equipment	Blighline Ltd
Surtatreat Inc	U.S.A.	Hydrogen Sulphide Dry Scrubbers	Higgins & Hewins Ltd
Suunto Oy	Finland	Compasses & surveying ins	Viking Optical Ltd
Suzuki	Japan	automatic sectional warping	Macart Textiles Machinery Ltd
Svenska Klimatsystem	Sweden	Hygien Humidifiers	Mellor Bromley
Swaroski	Austria	Optical Frames	Hilton International Eye Wear Ltd
Sweden:Scandinavian Aerospace & Industry AB	Sweden		Cambridge Vacuum Engineering
Swema	Sweden	Temperature Measuring Instruments	S & P Spanarc Ltd
Swiss Net	Switzerland	Industrial Netting and Curtain Net	Swisstulle UK Ltd
Swiss Optik	Switzerland		Armstrong Optical Ltd
Switzerland:Josef Seidl Industrievertretungen	Switzerland		Cambridge Vacuum Engineering
Sydney College Publications	Australia	Publishers	Acumedic Centre Ltd
Sydor	U.S.A.		Armstrong Optical Ltd
Sylko	Portugal	Sewing Thread	Coats Ltd
Synergy Inc	U.S.A.	Kaleidagraph: Graphing And Statistical Software	Geomem Ltd
Synergystex International Inc	France	Labelling	Weyfringe Labelling Systems
Synprodo Hortiproducts B.V.	Netherlands	Pots And Trays	Fargro
System GmbH	Germany	In Curcuit Emulations	Computer Solutions Ltd
Systematic Designs	South Africa	info@systematic.co.za	Specialist Electronics Services Ltd
T.B.A.	Austria	Paper Making Instruments and Trouble Shooting	S & P Spanarc Ltd
T.B.A. Techniques et Biochemie Appliquèes	France	Applied Biotechnology	Symbio
T.E.C.	Japan	Systems Thermal Printers	Kelgray Products Ltd
T & G	Italy	Thermostats, Thermomanometers	Anglo Nordic Burner Products Ltd
T. Rapp	U.S.A.	Microphone	Audio Ltd
T S C - Pyroferric	U.S.A.	Iron Powder Cores	Almag Components Ltd
T S System Filter	Germany	Dust Filtration Equipment	Gericke Ltd
Tab Sales Corporation	U.S.A.	Colour Coded filing System & Storage	Civica UK Ltd
Tacchella s.p.A.	Italy	Large Capacity Cylindrical Grinder	Jones & Shipman Grinding Ltd (a division of Renold Engineering Products Co.)
Taco	France	Fabric Collections	Brian Yates
Tae-Ha Machinery	Korea, Republic of	Pulse Valves	Hilson Ltd
Taisan	Japan	Solenoid Pumps	Anglo Nordic Burner Products Ltd
Taiwan Chuan Yng Tech Dev Co.	Taiwan	Cutting Mats	Blundell Harling Ltd (Incorporating Magpie Furniture)
Taiwan Synthetic Rubber	Taiwan	Synthetic Rubber	Arto Chemicals Ltd
Takamine	Japan	Guitars	Korg UK Ltd
Taktronix	U.S.A.		Episys Group Ltd
Takumi	Taiwan	Verticle Machine Centres	Meddings Machine Tools
Tamaris Delachaux S.A.	France	Crane Wheels And Rails	British & Continental Traders Ltd
Tamfelt	Finland	Filter Fabrics, Filter Bags, Deckers and Carrier Ropes	Pulp & Paper Machinery Ltd
Tara	Germany	Polyethelene And Polystyrene	Apropa Machinery Ltd
Tasa	U.S.A.	Earth Science teaching multi-media CDs	Geomem Ltd
TCI BR Communications	U.S.A.	Hf Radios. Frequency Management	Marlborough Communications Ltd
Tec	Japan	Thermal Transfer Printers	Episys Group Ltd
Tecasa	Spain	Thermal Cutouts	Hawco
Tech Spray Inc	U.S.A.	Chemicals	Intertronics
Techni-Tool	U.S.A.	Hand Tools	Longs Ltd
Technical Concepts LP	United Kingdom	neutralle air sanitising & dosing systems	Vectair Systems Ltd
Technomaster	U.S.A.	Pumps	Torres Engineering & Pumps Ltd
Technomaster	U.S.A.	Pumps	Allpumps Ltd
Techpap	France	Formation and Other Sensors	Pulp & Paper Machinery Ltd
Tecnomeccanica Biellese	Italy	automatic fibre blending systems	Macart Textiles Machinery Ltd
Teco	Netherlands	Tube Expanders	B S A Tube Runner
Tecora	Italy	Isokinetic Stack Sampling	Shawcity Ltd
Tecumseh do Brazil	Brazil	Refrigeration Hermetic Compressors	Kooltech Ltd
Tecumseh Products Int	U.S.A.	Refrigeration and Air Conditioning Hermetic compressors	Kooltech Ltd
Tefen	Israel	Plastic Pipe Fittings	Everyvalve Ltd
Tegometall	Germany	Europes No 1 Modular Steel Shelving System	F & G Smart Shopfittings Ltd
Teignbridge Propellers	Australia		Teignbridge Propellers International
Teignbridge Propellers	Netherlands		Teignbridge Propellers International
Teignbridge Propellers	Dubai		Teignbridge Propellers International
Teignbridge Propellers Inc	U.S.A.		Teignbridge Propellers International
Teknion Furniture Systems Inc	Canada	Office Furniture	Trac Office Contracts
Tel-Tru Manufacturing Co	U.S.A.	Bi-Metal Dial Thermometers	Zeal Clean Supplies Ltd
Telco	Denmark	Sensors	Sensortek
Tele Abrasivi Flessibili	Italy	Abrasives - Coated	Finishing Aids & Tools Ltd
Teledyne Sprague	U.S.A.	Pumps	Torres Engineering & Pumps Ltd
Teledyne Sprague	U.S.A.	Pumps	Allpumps Ltd
Teleplus	Japan	Lens Convertors	Johnsons Photopia Ltd
Tellier	France	Food Preparation Equipment	Robot Coupe UK Ltd
Telwin	Italy	Welding Machines	Wholesale Welding Supplies Ltd
Temafa	Germany	Fibre Opening and Blending Equipment for Spinning and Nonwoven Production	Robert S Maynard Ltd
Temet Instruments	Finland	FT/IR Gas Analysers	Quantitech Ltd
Temp-co electric heating corperation	U.S.A.	Industrial heating elements.	Pneu-Therm Ltd
Tentel Corp	U.S.A.	Tape and Video Recorders Test Equipment	Preco Ltd
Teplast	Germany	Oil, Windows & Plugs	Meddings Machine Tools
TER	Italy	Electrical Control Equipment	Metreel Ltd
Teraoka Seiko Co Ltd	Japan	Electronic Scales/Printer/Wrappers	Herbert Retail Ltd
Termo Electro	Norway	Infra Red Dryers	Greenbank Technology Ltd
Ternes	U.S.A.	Plate Clamps	Billows Protocol Ltd
Ternes Burton	U.S.A.	Stepping Boards	Billows Protocol Ltd

OVERSEAS COMPANY	COUNTRY OF ORIGIN	PRODUCT	UK COMPANY
Terry	U.S.A.	Bicycle accessories	Madison
Test S.r.l.	Italy	Ignition Systems	J B Systems Ltd
Tetra Pak International AB	Sweden	Liquid Food Processing, Packaging And Distribution Systems	Tetra Pak Ltd
Texas Advanced Opoelectronics	U.S.A.	Photodetectors	Pacer Components plc
Texas Industrial Remcor Inc	U.S.A.	Electrical Controls and Valves	Hypro Eu Ltd
Texas Opto	U.S.A.	Opto Electronics	M B Components Ltd
Textechno Herbert Stein GmbH & Co KG	Germany	Fibre and Yarn Testing Instruments	James H Heal & Co. Ltd
Textile Transport	Germany	Textile Beam Handling And Storage Devices	Pilkingtons Ltd (t/a Weitzer Parket UK)
Tharo Systems Inc	France	Labelling Systems	Weyfringe Labelling Systems
The Virkler Company	U.S.A.	Textile Process Chemicals	S T R UK Ltd
Themac Inc	U.S.A.	Tool Post Grinders	Aegis Advanced Materials Ltd
Thermik Thermal Cutouts	Germany	Cutouts	Rainer Schneider & Ayres
Thermolyne	U.S.A.	Mixers And Stirrers	Radleys
Thomas S.p.A.	Italy	Coldsaws Bandsaws	Prosaw Ltd
Thornes	France	Electrical Components	Riverdale Mahoney
Thyregod	Denmark	Beet Harvesters	Standen Engineering Ltd
Thyssen Henschel	Germany	Andromat Maniculators	Pearson Panke Ltd
Tiger S.r.l.	Italy	hydraulic presses	Mackey Bowley International Ltd
Tigra Sciences	Japan	Scientific instruments, manufacturer	Applied Photophysics Ltd
Timken	U.S.A.	wheel bearings	Roadlink International Ltd
Timken	United Kingdom	Automotive spare parts	Kingsdown
Tioxide	Italy	Tio2 Food Grade	Sensient
Tiro-Clas	France	Production Workstations for Industry	Electro Group Ltd
Titan Kogyo Kabushiki Kaisha	Japan	Nano TiO2	Kromachem Ltd
Titan Tool Inc	U.S.A.	Airless & HVLP Paint Application Equipment & Accessories.	Lion Industries UK Ltd
Titan Tool Ind	U.S.A.	Paint Spray Equipment	Gray Campling Ltd
TLG SA	Abu Dhabi	Computer and Laser Bureau, Mailing Services	Lettershop Group
Tobro	Germany	Filing Systems	Anson Systems Ltd (a division of G M Business Print & Systems Ltd)
Todo Ab	Sweden	Drybreak Couplings	Cebo UK Ltd
Tokuyama	Japan	Fumed Silica & Matting Silicas	Kromachem Ltd
Tokyo Kasei Kogyo Co. Ltd	Japan	General Organic Compounds	Fluorochem Ltd
Tollok	Italy	Locking Assemblies	Lenze UK Ltd
Tolsa S.A.	Spain	Absorbent Clay	B & D Clays & Chemicals Ltd
Tomah	U.S.A.		Lawrence Industries Ltd
Tommygate Co.	U.S.A.	Tailgate Loaders	Tipmaster Ltd
Topcon	Japan	Opto Electronic Instruments	Metax Ltd
Tornado GmbH	Germany	Tornado Cartridge Hammers	Tornado Construction Products (Supply & Distribution Depot)
Toschi	Italy	Paper Making Machinery	S & P Spanarc Ltd
Tosh S.R.L.	Italy	Logica Pad Printers	Tampographic Ltd
Total Fina	France	Hydrocarbons	Gelpke & Bate Ltd
Toyo Pumps	Japan	Submersible Sand/Gravel Pumps	Abird Ltd
Trackmobile Inc	Germany	Road/Rail Shunters	E G Steele & Co. Ltd
Tractel	France		Rope & Marine Services Ltd
Tranemo	Sweden	work wear	Murray Uniforms
Trangia	Sweden	Lightweight Cooking Stoves	Karrimor Ltd
Transera Corporation Inc	U.S.A.	Computer Software	Lyons Instruments
Transerra SA	Spain		Tuffnelln Parcels Express
Transfluid	Italy	Fluid Couplings	Bibby Transmissions Ltd
Transnorm System	Malaysia		Smart Stabilizer Systems
Transnorm System B.V.	Netherlands		Smart Stabilizer Systems
Transnorm System Inc	U.S.A.		Smart Stabilizer Systems
Transnorn System GmbH	Germany		Smart Stabilizer Systems
Transworld Chemicals	U.S.A.	General Organic Compounds	Fluorochem Ltd
Travallon	France	Wine	Yapp Brothers Ltd
Trax GmBH	Germany	Mediterranean Fountains and Statuary	Redwood Stone
Trayal	Yugoslavia	Industrial Tyres	Kings Road Tyres & Repairs Ltd
Trefil Arbed-Bissen	Luxembourg	Wire Fencing Products	Arce Lormittal
Tresmer	Norway	Plastic Coathangers	H & L Russell
Trevigen	U.S.A.	Molecular Biolicals	Cambio Ltd
Triag	Switzerland	Clamps	Hill Cliffe Garage
Triag	Switzerland	Workholding Systems	Rem Systems Ltd
Tribal Inc	U.S.A.	In Circuit Emulations	Computer Solutions Ltd
Tricoflex	France	Hoses-Professional	Connectomatic
Trioptics	Germany		Armstrong Optical Ltd
Triton Service Inc	U.S.A.	Electronic Tubes	Richardsons R F P D Ltd
Triton Technology	U.S.A.	Sonomicrometers and Doppler Flowmeters	Linton & Co Engineering Ltd
Tsukasa Ltd	Japan	Dc Gear Motor	Cliff Electronic Components Ltd
Tubest	France	Stainless steel convoluted flexible hose couplings	Dixon Group Europe Ltd
Turessons	Sweden	Fantasy Coathangers	H & L Russell
Turmix	Switzerland	Humidifiers and Air Purifiers	Air & Water Centre
U.P.M. Kymmene Corp Oy	Finland	Forestry products	U P M Kymmene Ltd
U.T.P.M. S.A.	France	Cold Store Pallet Converters	Palletower GB Ltd
Uchida Yoko	Japan	Duplicating Machines	Unigraph UK Ltd
Ugarola	Spain	Rod Straightening Cutting	La Roche
Uni-KTC	Germany	Gummed Paper Tape	Lea Valley Packaging Ltd
Uni-Work	Italy	Work Boots	Amber Safetywear Ltd
Unichema International	Netherlands	Esters And Fatty Acids	Hornett Bros & Co. Ltd
Unicontainer S.r.l.	Italy	Wire Formed Cage Pallets	Palletower GB Ltd
Uniflair	Italy	Raised access floors	Quiligotti Terrazzo Ltd
Unifor	Italy	Executive and Systems Furniture	Ergonom Ltd
Unimec	Italy	Screwjack and Gear Unit Manufacturers	Motovario Ltd
Union	Germany	Wooden Coathangers	H & L Russell
Unipre GmbH	Germany	Polyurethane Processing Equipment	R F Bright Enterprises Ltd
Unipress	U.S.A.	Laundry Equipment	B M M Weston Ltd
United Barcode Industries	Sweden	Printers	Herbert Retail Ltd
United Minerals	Germany	Perlite Filter Powders	Fleximas Ltd
United Receptacles	U.S.A.	Bullet Bins/Prestigious Bins	Unicorn Hygienics
Universal Assistance	Argentina	Medical Assistance	Doctorcall
Universal Document Management Systems Inc	U.S.A.	Step 2000 - computer software	Associated Knowledge Systems Ltd
US Ultratek	U.S.A.	PC Cards for NDT	Sonatest Ltd
USA:Cambridge Vacuum Engineering Inc.	U.S.A.		Cambridge Vacuum Engineering
Usines Metallurgiques De Vallorbe	Switzerland	Files	Electro Group Ltd
USTC	U.S.A.	Specialist Plastic Blast Media	Wheelabrator Group
V.I.B.	Germany	Spraydampers, Steamboxes, Steam and Condensate Systems	Pulp & Paper Machinery Ltd
VACOHUB Transportanlagen	Germany	Vacuum Lifting Beams And Stackers	British & Continental Traders Ltd
Vacuumschmelze GmbH & Co KG	Germany	Alloys, Parts & Components with special Magnetic, Electrical & Physical properties	Rolfe Industries
Vaihinger	Germany	Pressure Vessel Clamps	Visilume Ltd
Valbia	Italy	Pneumatic Actuators	Bonomi UK Ltd
Valco	United Kingdom	Automotive spare parts	Kingsdown
Valmet	Finland	Electricity Meters	Switch2 Energy Solutions
Valmet - Tampella	Finland	Stock Preparation Equipment, Pulpers and Pressure Screens	Pulp & Paper Machinery Ltd
Valmicro	Brazil	Ball Valve Manufacture	Trimline Valves

OVERSEAS COMPANY	COUNTRY OF ORIGIN	PRODUCT	UK COMPANY
Valpres	Italy	Industrial Ball Valves	Bonomi UK Ltd
Valvan	Belgium	Hydraulic Baling Presses	Robert S Maynard Ltd
Van Dorn Demag	U.S.A.	injection moulding machines	Demag Hamilton Guarantee Ltd
Van Hool N.V.	Belgium	Coach & Bus Body Builders	Carlyle Parts Ltd
Vanderrijn	Belgium	Manufacture lead	British Lead
Vantage	U.S.A.	Non-Slip Rug Underlays	Dycem Ltd
Vantage Non Slip Products	U.S.A.	Non Slip Underlay	Hilton Banks Ltd
VAO Intourist	Russia	Transport, Accommodation, Tours And Guide/InterpretEr Services	Intourist Ltd
Vapac	United Kingdom	Live Steam Apparatus and Co	Eaton-Williams Group Ltd
Varem	Italy	Expansion Vessels	Reliance Water Controls Ltd
Varta	Germany	Batteries	Components Bureau
VDB	France	Carbon Fibre Microphone Boom Poles	Audio Ltd
Vectron International	U.S.A.	Crystal Oscillators Frequency control products including crystal oscillators	Aspen Electronics Ltd
Vega Industries Ltd	New Zealand	PEL Sector Lights	A B Pharos Marine Ltd
Venco	Australia	Deairing Pugmill	Potclays Ltd
Venture Tape	U.S.A.	Plate Mounting Tape	Plastotype
Verlag Stahlschluessel Wegst GmbH	Germany	Technical Publication - Stahlschluessel	Mito Construction & Engineering Ltd
Verona Marble Co.	U.S.A.	Marghestone And Agglosimplex	MFS Stone Surfaces Ltd
Versadyne Inc	U.S.A.	Broadcast Audio Products	Preco Ltd
Versitron	U.S.A.	Copper to fibre communications (fibre optic)	Dowding & Mills Engineering Services Ltd
Vestjydsk Symaskine Service	Denmark	Fish Net Mounting Sewing Machines	Theobald Sewing Machines Ltd
Victa	Australia	Professional Lawnmowers	E P Barrus
Victorinox	Switzerland	Knives	Burton Mccall Ltd
Video Production House Inc	U.S.A.	Training programmjes featuring Tom Peters and Ken Blanchard	Video Arts Group Ltd
Vidrepur	Spain	Glass Mosaic	Ceramique International Ltd
Vigor Veiktygs Ab	Sweden	Pliers and Cutters For Electronics	Electro Group Ltd
Vischer and Bolli	Switzerland	Milling	Cromwell Group Holdings
Vision Communications Inc	U.S.A.	LED Lenses and Accessories	Paylor Controls Ltd
Viskase France SA	France	Plastic Casings	Bemis Swansea
Viskase France SA	France	Sausage Casings	Bemis Swansea
Visloux	Antigua & Barbuda	Sensors	Sensortek
Vistalite	U.S.A.	Bicycle Lighting	Madison
Vitari	Italy	Straightening And Cutting To Lengths, Barbed Wire, Chain Forming And Welding Machines, Chain Link FencE Machines	Embassy Machinery Ltd
Vitlab	Germany	Ptfe Labware	Radleys
Vitra	Germany	Seaming	E W Marshall Ltd
Vitrifrigo	Italy	Marine/Domestic Refrigeration	Aquapac International Ltd
Vogel GmbH	Germany	Gearboxes	Lenze UK Ltd
Voice Technologies	U.S.A.	Microphone	Audio Ltd
Volk	U.S.A.	Lenses	Keeler Ltd
Volvo	France	Mini Excavators & Dumpers	Chippindale Plant Ltd (Head Office)
Volvo	Sweden	Diesel Engines And Parts	Robert Craig & Sons Ltd
Von Schrader Co.	Switzerland	Dry Foam Carpet and Upholstery Cleaning Equipment	Host Von Schrader Ltd
Vortec	U.S.A.	Compressed Air Operarted Products	Advanced Dynamics Ltd
VP-TE	Germany	Mastic Sausage Filler	D H Industries Ltd
VS	Italy	System furniture & seating	Ergonom Ltd
Vulcain	France	Fire Retardent, Mositure Resistant Chip Board	Rex Bousfield Ltd
VYC	Spain	Relief/Control/Check Valves Manufacture	Trimline Valves
W.E. Anderson	U.S.A.	Flow And Level Switches	Texcel Division (a division of Crosslink Business Services Ltd)
W.E.G.	Brazil	Electric Motors	Micro Clutch Developments Ltd
W.F.	Germany	Spinning Machines	Pearson Panke Ltd
W G Rathmann	Germany	Sight Ports & Lights	Visilume Ltd
W + S GmbH	Germany	Shaft Encoders	W & S Measuring Systems Ltd
WACA	Germany	Melamine products	S J H Row & Son Ltd
Wagner	Germany	Pumps	Torres Engineering & Pumps Ltd
Wagner	Germany	Pumps	Allpumps Ltd
Wala	Germany	Natural Medicines	Weleda UK Ltd
Waldron	U.S.A.	Gear Couplings	Micro Clutch Developments Ltd
Walther	Germany	Printers and Printhead	Weyfringe Labelling Systems
Walvoil	Italy	Hydraulic Valves	Universal Hydraulics Ltd
Walvoil	Italy	Hydraulic Valves	BYPY Hydraulics & Transmissions Ltd
Wand Macher GmbH	Germany	Coated Abrasives	Naylors Abrasives
Wanit Universal	Germany	Fibre Cement Slate	Cembrit Ltd
Wapora	Germany	Special Machines For Foam	Apropa Machinery Ltd
Waring Commercial Products	U.S.A.	Food Preparation Equipment	Robot Coupe UK Ltd
Warner Electric	U.S.A.	Clutches & Brakes	Transdrive Engineering Ltd
Warren-Morrison	United Kingdom	Pinch Valves Manufacture	Trimline Valves
Wasco	U.S.A.	Miniature Pressure Switches	Tamo Ltd
Waterloo Hydrogeologic	Canada	Full range of geo-environmental software	Geomem Ltd
Watkins Johnson	U.S.A.	Rf And Microwave Solid State Components	Richardsons R F P D Ltd
Waukesha Engine Division	U.S.A.	Gas Engines	Turner E P S Ltd
Weathertec	U.S.A.	Irrigation Sprinklers	Connectomatic
Weeren	Germany	Facing & centering machines	Robert Speck Ltd
Weidmann International Corporation	Switzerland	Electrical Insulating Presspapers And Pressboards, Stationery Manillas, Abrasive Base Paper And Electrical Insulating Laminates	Weidmann Whiteley Ltd
Weitzer	Austria	Parquet Wood Flooring	Pilkingtons Ltd (t/a Weitzer Parket UK)
Weldaid	U.S.A.	Chemicals	Wholesale Welding Supplies Ltd
Wemo	Netherlands	Automatic Punching And Bending Wire	Embassy Machinery Ltd
Wenglor	Germany	Sensors	Sensortek
Werner Rietschle GmbH & Co. K9	Germany	Vacuum Pumps, Compressors and Blowers	Gardner Denver Ltd
Wesley Allen	U.S.A.	Metal bedsteads	Vi Spring Ltd
West	Switzerland	Conductive Boxes	Static Safe Ltd
Westek Inc.	U.S.A.	Aqueaous In-Line Cleaners	Humiseal Europe Ltd (Head Office)
Westerbeke Corp	U.S.A.	marine generators and air conditioning	Watermota Ltd
Wieser GmbH	Germany	Punches - Design Tools	Partwell Cutting Technology Ltd
Wiess	Germany	Indicating Pressure Switches	Tamo Ltd
Wilkhann	Germany	Seaming/Conference Furniture	E W Marshall Ltd
Will & Hahnenstein GmbH	Germany	Drum Heating Cabinets	British & Continental Traders Ltd
Willi Wader GmbH	Germany	Blast Furnace Tapping Equipment And Tooling	British & Continental Traders Ltd
Willibald GmbH	Germany	Compost Shredding Equipment	M M H Recycling Systems Ltd
Wilmad Glass	U.S.A.	NMR Tubes & Accessories	Fluorochem Ltd
Win Industry	Taiwan	Rubber Keymats	G English Electronics Ltd
Winkel	Germany	High load radial/ axial combined bearings	Hepco Motion
Winterthur	Switzerland	Grinding Wheels	E C I S Scotland Ltd
Wira Lanao	Indonesia	Solid Timber Doors	Price & Pierce Softwoods Ltd
Wirus	Germany	Decorative M.F.C.	N R Burnett Ltd
Wisconsin Protective Coatings	U.S.A.	Synthetic Resinous Linings	Lithgow Saekaphen Ltd
Wolf Bakns (Reinhart Schmidt) GmbH	Germany	Commercial Paper Envelopes	Versapak International
Wolf Garten Eurogreen Div	Germany	Sports ground renovating contractors	Farmura Ltd
World Assistance	Spain	Medical Assistance	Doctorcall
Worner	Germany	quick mould change systems for injection moulding machines	Demag Hamilton Guarantee Ltd
WPR System	Germany	Lateral Location Studs	Roemheld UK Ltd
Xcelite/Cooper Tools	U.S.A.	Tools and Toolkits	Longs Ltd
XGP Inc	U.S.A.	Copy Control Systems	N R G Group Ltd
Xinruilian	Japan	dc/ac axial fans	Trident Engineering Ltd

24

OVERSEAS COMPANY	COUNTRY OF ORIGIN	PRODUCT	UK COMPANY
XL Microwave	U.S.A.	RF & Microwave Counters	Aspen Electronics Ltd
Yaadim	Israel	Machinery	Tickhill Engineering Co. Ltd
Yaesu Trading Co. Ltd	Japan	Motor Vehicle Parts	Panaf & Company
Yageo	Taiwan	Resistors	G English Electronics Ltd
Yanmar	Japan	Yanmar	E P Barrus
Yaskawa Corp	Japan	Motoman	Motoman Robotics UK Ltd
Yellow Tec	Germany	Voice Processing Equipment	Preco Ltd
Yokogowa Denshikiki	Japan	Gyro-Compasses and Autopilots	John Lilley & Gillie Ltd
York Instrument Ltdch	China	york@public.intercom.com.cn	Specialist Electronics Services Ltd
Ystral GmbH	Germany	Homogenisers for Laboratories	Scientific Instrument Centre Ltd
Yuasa Corporation	Hong Kong		Yuasa Battery UK Ltd
Yunpen Ltd	Taiwan	Emi Filter	Cliff Electronic Components Ltd
Z-Technology	U.S.A.	Field Strength Meters	Aspen Electronics Ltd
Zacmi srl	Italy	Filling Systems For Cans And Glass Jars	Flo Mech Ltd
Zagorsk	Russia	Binoculars, Monoculars, Magnifers, Ophthalmic EquipMent And Night Vision	Swains International plc
Zaniboni	Italy	Electro Chemical Marking Machines	Brandone Machine Tool Ltd
Zawawi Trading Co. L.L.C.	Oman		Hawker Electronics Ltd
Zebra	U.S.A.	Thermal Transfer Printers	Episys Group Ltd
Zeelan	U.S.A.		Lawrence Industries Ltd
Zemex	U.S.A.		Lawrence Industries Ltd
Zen	Italy	brake drums, discs, hubs and flywheels	Roadlink International Ltd
Zenit	Russia	Cameras, Lenses, Night Vision And Magnifiers	Swains International plc
Zenith	France	Counters and Diecastings	Kelgray Products Ltd
Zerbo	Italy	hank reeling and winding	Macart Textiles Machinery Ltd
Zeroll	U.S.A.	Ice Cream Scoops	Mitchell & Cooper Ltd (Head Office)
Zetec	U.S.A.	Eddycurrent equipment and systems - eddycurrent	Sonatest Ltd
ZF Industrial Drives	Germany	Hysteresis Clutches & Brakes	Clark Electric Clutch & Controls Ltd
Ziehl Abegg	Germany	Axial and Centrifugal Motors	Roof Units Ltd (t/a Vent-Axia Incorp Roof Units)
Zimm	Austria	Screw Jacks	Hepco Motion
Zimmer	Germany	Harmonic Analysers	Northern Design Ltd
Zimmer Inc	U.S.A.	Perforation, Cutting, Slitting Rules & Blades	R M Rotary Services Ltd
Zinco GmbH	Germany	Green Roof Systems	Alumasc Exterior Building Products
Zippo Manufacturing Co	U.S.A.	Lighters, Pens and Knives	Zippo UK Ltd
Zuzazz	Germany	Music Various	Rollercoaster Records Ltd